S0-AIQ-357

ENCYCLOPAEDIA JUDAICA

ENCYCLOPAEDIA JUDAICA

SECOND EDITION

VOLUME 15
Nat–Per

Fred Skolnik, *Editor in Chief*
Michael Berenbaum, *Executive Editor*

MACMILLAN REFERENCE USA
An imprint of Thomson Gale, a part of The Thomson Corporation

IN ASSOCIATION WITH
KETER PUBLISHING HOUSE LTD., JERUSALEM

Detroit • New York • San Francisco • New Haven, Conn. • Waterville, Maine • London

ENCYCLOPAEDIA JUDAICA, Second Edition

Fred Skolnik, *Editor in Chief*
Michael Berenbaum, *Executive Editor*
Shlomo S. (Yosh) Gafni, *Editorial Project Manager*
Rachel Gilon, *Editorial Project Planning and Control*

Thomson Gale
Gordon Macomber, *President*
Frank Menchaca, *Senior Vice President and Publisher*
Jay Flynn, *Publisher*
Hélène Potter, *Publishing Director*

Keter Publishing House
Yiphtach Dekel, *Chief Executive Officer*
Peter Tomkins, *Executive Project Director*

Complete staff listings appear in Volume 1

For more information, contact
Macmillan Reference USA
An imprint of Thomson Gale
27500 Drake Rd.
Farmington Hills, MI 48331-3535
Or you can visit our internet site at
http://www.gale.com

LIBRARY OF CONGRESS CATALOGING-IN-PUBLICATION DATA

Encyclopaedia Judaica / Fred Skolnik, editor-in-chief ; Michael Berenbaum, executive editor. -- 2nd ed.
v. cm.
Includes bibliographical references and index.
Contents: v.1. Aa-Alp.
ISBN 0-02-865928-7 (set hardcover : alk. paper) -- ISBN 0-02-865929-5 (vol. 1 hardcover : alk. paper) -- ISBN 0-02-865930-9 (vol. 2 hardcover : alk. paper) -- ISBN 0-02-865931-7 (vol. 3 hardcover : alk. paper) -- ISBN 0-02-865932-5 (vol. 4 hardcover : alk. paper) -- ISBN 0-02-865933-3 (vol. 5 hardcover : alk. paper) -- ISBN 0-02-865934-1 (vol. 6 hardcover : alk. paper) -- ISBN 0-02-865935-X (vol. 7 hardcover : alk. paper) -- ISBN 0-02-865936-8 (vol. 8 hardcover : alk. paper) -- ISBN 0-02-865937-6 (vol. 9 hardcover : alk. paper) -- ISBN 0-02-865938-4 (vol. 10 hardcover : alk. paper) -- ISBN 0-02-865939-2 (vol. 11 hardcover : alk. paper) -- ISBN 0-02-865940-6 (vol. 12 hardcover : alk. paper) -- ISBN 0-02-865941-4 (vol. 13 hardcover : alk. paper) -- ISBN 0-02-865942-2 (vol. 14 hardcover : alk. paper) -- ISBN 0-02-865943-0 (vol. 15: alk. paper) -- ISBN 0-02-865944-9 (vol. 16: alk. paper) -- ISBN 0-02-865945-7 (vol. 17: alk. paper) -- ISBN 0-02-865946-5 (vol. 18: alk. paper) -- ISBN 0-02-865947-3 (vol. 19: alk. paper) -- ISBN 0-02-865948-1 (vol. 20: alk. paper) -- ISBN 0-02-865949-X (vol. 21: alk. paper) -- ISBN 0-02-865950-3 (vol. 22: alk. paper)
1. Jews -- Encyclopedias. I. Skolnik, Fred. II. Berenbaum, Michael, 1945-
DS102.8.E496 2007
909'.04924 -- dc22

2006020426

ISBN-13:

978-0-02-865928-2 (set)
978-0-02-865929-9 (vol. 1)
978-0-02-865930-5 (vol. 2)
978-0-02-865931-2 (vol. 3)
978-0-02-865932-9 (vol. 4)
978-0-02-865933-6 (vol. 5)
978-0-02-865934-3 (vol. 6)
978-0-02-865935-0 (vol. 7)
978-0-02-865936-7 (vol. 8)
978-0-02-865937-4 (vol. 9)
978-0-02-865938-1 (vol. 10)
978-0-02-865939-8 (vol. 11)
978-0-02-865940-4 (vol. 12)
978-0-02-865941-1 (vol. 13)
978-0-02-865942-8 (vol. 14)
978-0-02-865943-5 (vol. 15)
978-0-02-865944-2 (vol. 16)
978-0-02-865945-9 (vol. 17)
978-0-02-865946-6 (vol. 18)
978-0-02-865947-3 (vol. 19)
978-0-02-865948-0 (vol. 20)
978-0-02-865949-7 (vol. 21)
978-0-02-865950-3 (vol. 22)

This title is also available as an e-book
ISBN-10: 0-02-866097-8
ISBN-13: 978-0-02-866097-4
Contact your Thomson Gale representative for ordering information.
Printed in the United States of America

10 9 8 7 6 5 4 3 2

TABLE OF CONTENTS

The letter "N," a part of the illuminated word In (diebus Assueri) *at the beginning of the Book of Esther in a 12th-century Latin Bible. On the right of King Ahasuerus, Haman is being hanged. The "I" frames the figure of Esther. Rheims. Bibliothèque Municipale, Ms. 159, fol. 5v.*

NAT-NY

NATANSON, LUDWIK (1822–1896), physician and communal worker. A member of the Jewish intellectual and assimilationist circle of Warsaw, Natanson was the son of the banker and industrialist Wolf Zelig Natanson (1795–1879). In 1847 he founded the periodical *Tygodnik Lekarski*, one of the first modern medical publications in Polish, which he edited and financed until 1872. Natanson was also one of the public health pioneers in Poland, and was active in the campaign against the cholera epidemic in Warsaw (1848–52). In 1863 he was elected to the presidency of the Polish medical society. In 1871 he became chairman of the executive of the Jewish community of Warsaw, a position he held until his death. As chairman, Natanson successfully reorganized and considerably extended the public and administrative services of the community, managing also to balance its budget. He encouraged productivity among the Jewish poverty-stricken classes and was the initiator and founder of vocational schools and a community workshop center. He supported (1878–88) the secondary school which had 1,400 Jewish pupils. On his initiative, a new school building was erected, and community organizations and the cemeteries were renovated. He was the initiator of a project to erect a modern Jewish hospital in the Czyste district, and it was also during his term of office that the magnificent synagogue of Tłomacka Street was built. In 1874 Natanson obtained authorization to establish a Jewish seminary for teachers. He was supported in his public activities by bourgeois circles and the assimilationist Jewish intelligentsia. The energy which he showed during the pogrom in Warsaw in December 1881 was of great assistance in maintaining the morale of the Jewish community.

BIBLIOGRAPHY: J. Shatzky, *Geshikhte fun Yidn in Varshe*, 2–3 (1948–53), indexes; H. Nussbaum, *Teki weterana warszawskiej gminy Starozakonnych* (1880), 46–50; W. Konie, in: *Głos gminy żydowskiej* nos. 4–5 (1937); S. LŁastik, *Z dziejów oświecenia żydowskiego* (1961), index; *Lu'aḥ Aḥi'asaf*, 5 (1897).

[Arthur Cygielman]

NATANSON, MARK (1849–1919), Russian revolutionary. Born in Svenziany, the son of a wealthy Jewish businessman, Natanson graduated from a Kovno secondary school. He was the leading figure of the "Chaikovski circle," which played a great part in molding the opposition spirit against the Czarist regime among the Russian university youth in the 1870s, and was prominent in the Populist movement ("narodniki"). A brilliant organizer, and possessed of considerable business abilities, he was responsible for many daring revolutionary undertakings. Together with his first wife, Olga – a highly intelligent person and a passionate believer in radical ideas – he masterminded Prince Peter Kropotkin's escape from prison. He was a close friend of Georgi Plekhanov, who later became "the father of Russian Marxism." He managed to continue his revolutionary activities even during the many years he spent as a convict in Siberia. In 1917, he joined the left wing of the Russian Social Revolutionary Party and helped Lenin to disband the Constituent Assembly. He later became disillusioned with the Communist regime, left the Soviet Union, and died a lonely man in Switzerland. From the time that he joined the Russian revolutionary movement, he completely identified himself with Russian life, taking no interest in Jewish affairs.

[Schneier Zalman Levenberg]

NATHAN (Heb. נָתָן), prophet in the days of David and Solomon). Nathan, together with Zadok the priest, anointed Solomon as king after encouraging and activating the people of the royal court to proclaim him king. Two of his prophecies are known: one about the postponement of the building of the Temple from David's time to the time of his son (II Sam. 7; I Chron. 17) and the election of David's dynasty; the second is the prophecy of rebuke to David about Bath-Sheba and the killing of Uriah (II Sam. 12: 1–15). From his involvement in the life of the court and the clear connection of his prophecy to the king and the monarchy, Nathan, like the prophet Gad, may be designated as a court prophet. From the contents of his prophecies, however – not only his sharp rebuke in connection with Bath-Sheba but also his advice regarding the Temple, which was not in any way subject to the king's approval or control – there is justification for placing Nathan in the category of prophets who rebuke and advise, such as Elijah and Elisha (see *Prophets and Prophecy).

In his prophecy about the postponement of the building of the Temple to the time of Solomon, Nathan promises the House of David unconditionally that his dynasty will endure forever, and that the relationship between the Lord and each of David's successors will be like that between father and son. The reason for the postponement of the building of the Temple is not clarified. (The explanation of bloodshed in I Chron. 22:7–10 seems to have been inserted later.) On the basis of the wanderings in the wilderness, where God was present in the Tent and the Tabernacle, it would appear, however, that the monarchy was not yet firmly established and that the time had not yet come for removing the symbols of tribal tradition – the Tent and the Tabernacle and replacing them with a permanent house (temple) of the Lord, similar to the house (palace) of the king. The view of the monarchy in Nathan's prophecy – in which it is seen as granted to David by an act of divine grace (no reference is made to the monarchy of Saul) and as a complete and unbroken continuation of the Lord's providence and governance from the time of the Exodus from Egypt to the time of the judges – differs essentially from that of I Samuel 8–12, according to which Samuel opposed monarchy as such. The antiquity of the prophecy attributed to Nathan is attested by the description of the monarchy as a calm and secure period of respite, without any intimation of the division of the kingdom. The punishment of a king's son who transgresses will be a rebuke only "with the rod of men, and with the stripes of human beings" (II Sam. 7:14). In the rebuke over the affair of Bath-Sheba, Nathan, by means of the parable of the poor man's lamb, traps David (even with his privilege as king) into passing judgment upon himself. This prophecy contains a harsh vision of the future of the house of David: "the sword shall never depart from your house" (II Sam. 12:10). This prediction, which is not recalled in this way in any other passage in the Bible, and which probably does not allude to any actual event such as the division of the kingdom, stamps the rebuke with the seal of authenticity. Nathan appears not only as warning against evil and demanding expiation for murder but also as commanding the king to establish law and justice, which is his duty as judge and is embodied in the monarchy itself, as explicitly stated in the chronicles of David's reign (II Sam. 8:15; see *David, *Solomon). The "book of Nathan the prophet," which relates the histories of David and Solomon, is mentioned in Chronicles (I Chron. 29:9; II Chron. 9:29), in keeping with the theory of the author of Chronicles who also represents other prophets as chroniclers of the events of their days.

BIBLIOGRAPHY: J.A. Montgomery, *The Book of Kings* (ICC, 1951), 67–79; G. Widengren, *Sakrales Koenigtum im Alten Testament* (1955), 59–61; K.H. Bernhardt, in: VT Supplement, 8 (1961), 161–3; H.W. Hertzberg, *Samuel* (1964), 282–7, 312–5.

[Samuel Abramsky]

NATHAN, English family, distinguished in public service. The first member of the family to settle in England was MEYER (Michael) NATHAN who came from Dessau about 1790. His grandson, Jonah, married twice. SIR NATHANIEL (1843–1916), the son of Jonah's first marriage, a barrister practicing in Birmingham from 1873 to 1888, became attorney general, judge of the Supreme Court, and from 1901 to 1903 acting chief justice of Trinidad. His half brother, SIR FREDERIC LEWIS (1861–1933), explosives expert and soldier, joined the Royal Artillery in 1879 and organized explosives manufacture before and during World War I. Later, he specialized in fuel problems and was president of the Institution of Chemical Engineers from 1925 to 1927. From 1905 to 1926 he was commandant of the Jewish Lads' Brigade. Frederic's brother SIR MATTHEW (1862–1939) joined the Royal Engineers in 1880 and served in Sudan and India. The first Jew to be a colonial governor, he was governor of the Gold Coast (1900–03), Hong Kong (1904–07), and Natal (1907–09). Secretary to the General Post Office and the Board of Inland Revenue, he was appointed undersecretary to the Lord Lieutenant of Ireland in 1914 and was in sole charge of Dublin Castle when the Easter Rising occurred in 1916. An inquiry criticized his failure to warn the British government of the danger. After serving as secretary of the Ministry of Pensions he became governor of Queensland (1920–26) and retired to Somerset where he took part in local government and wrote a monumental local history. In Jewish life, he represented the New West End Synagogue on the United Synagogue Council. The fourth brother, SIR ROBERT (1866–1921), served in the Indian civil service from 1888 to 1915 and was appointed chief secretary to the governor of Eastern Bengal and Assam in 1910. In World War I he did important work in counterespionage.

BIBLIOGRAPHY: P.H. Emden, *Jews of Britain* (1943), index; Roth, Mag Bibl. index; DNB, s.v. **ADD. BIBLIOGRAPHY:** ODNB online for Sir Matthew Nathan; A.B. Haydon, *Sir Matthew Nathan, British Colonial Governor and Civil Servant* (1972).

[Vivian David Lipman]

NATHAN, U.S. family. SIMON NATHAN (1746–1822), who was born in England, went to the colonies in 1773 by way of Havana. During the Revolution, he supported the revolutionary cause and helped ship supplies to the colonists from Jamaica where he then resided. After leaving the island, he proceeded to New Orleans and from there went to Williamsburg, Virginia, in 1779. He loaned large sums of money to the Virginia state government for which he received the thanks of the then governor, Thomas Jefferson. When these loans were not repaid he suffered great financial loss, and was involved in protracted litigation with Virginia for many years. Possibly as a consequence of this litigation, he went to Philadelphia and enlisted in the militia. There, in 1780, he met and married Grace Mendes Seixas (1752–1831), the daughter of Isaac Mendes *Seixas. Nathan became a Mason the following year, a trustee of the Congregation Mikveh Israel in 1782, and president of

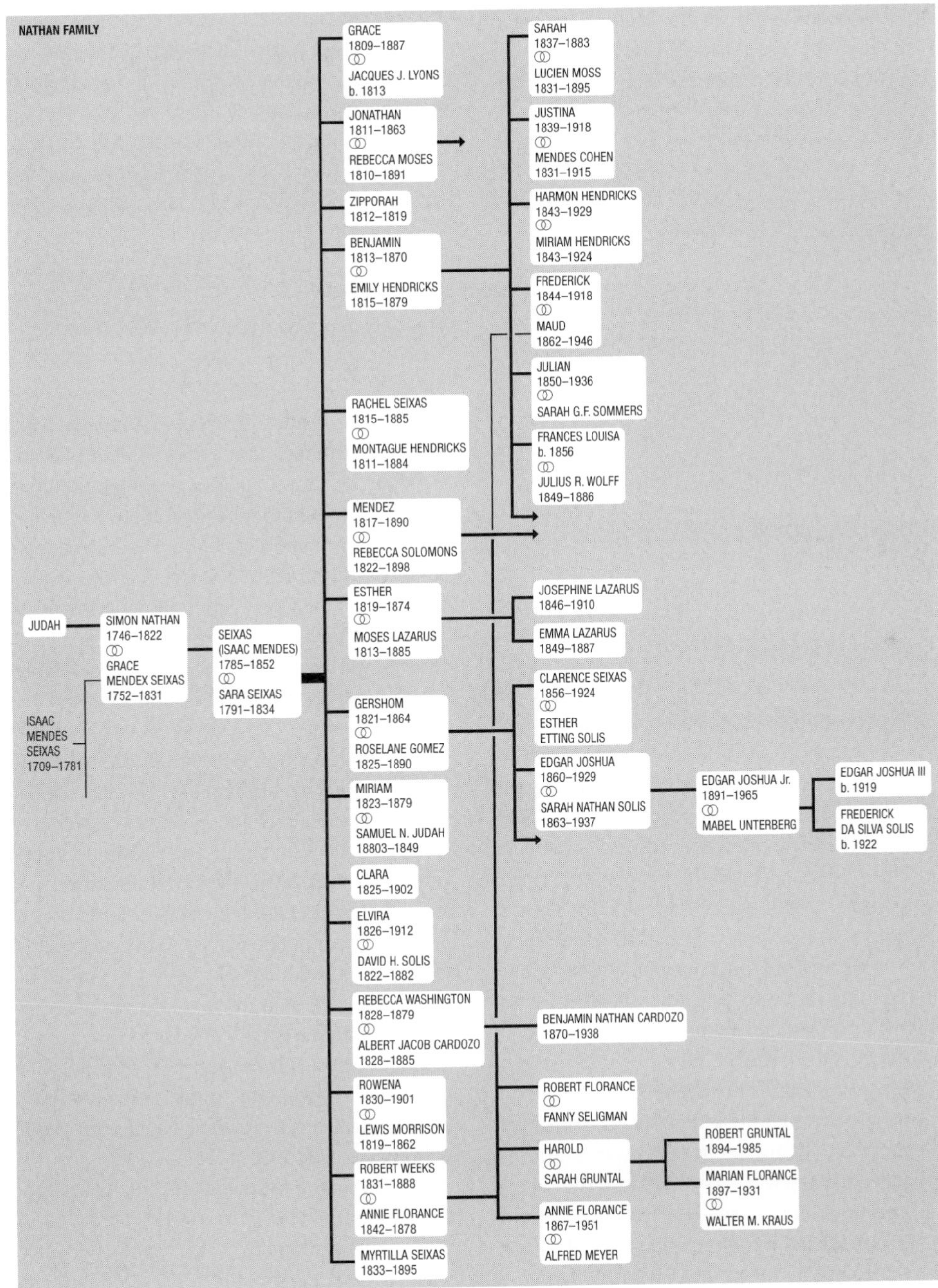

the congregation in the years 1782 and 1783. Soon afterward, he moved to New York, where he served as president of the Congregation Shearith Israel in 1785, 1786, 1794, and 1796. He opened a successful dry goods business with Aaron Pimental, enabling him to contribute sums of money to the synagogue.

Their son SEIXAS (Isaac Mendes) NATHAN (1785–1852) married his cousin Sara Seixas (1791–1834), daughter of Benjamin Mendes Seixas (1746–1817). They had 15 children. They and their children married into the Lazarus, Lyons, Cardozo, Gomez, and Hendricks families among others. Some of Simon Nathan's descendants include: the noted poetess EMMA *LAZARUS; her sister JOSEPHINE (1846–1910), a noted essayist; the novelist ROBERT *NATHAN; ANNIE NATHAN *MEYER, founder of Barnard College; MAUD NATHAN (1862–1946), suffragette and president of the Consumers' League for 20 years; and BENJAMIN N. *CARDOZO, member of the United States Supreme Court.

BIBLIOGRAPHY: D. de S. Pool, *Portraits Etched in Stone* (1952).

[Leo Hershkowitz]

NATHAN, ABRAHAM (d. 1745), founder of the London Ashkenazi community, also known as Reb Aberle, Aberle London, and Abraham [of] Hamburg. The son of R. Moses Nathan (Norden) of Hamburg, he was a wealthy diamond merchant and a rabbinical scholar of considerable attainment. It was through him that Ẓevi *Ashkenazi was induced to go to London in 1705 to arbitrate in the dispute then dividing the Sephardi community regarding the orthodoxy of the opinions of the haham David *Nieto. In 1704 Nathan was prevented by the Court of Aldermen from erecting a separate synagogue with a yeshivah attached. Later, however, he took the lead in vindictive fashion in the divorce dispute which resulted in the setting up of the Hambro' Synagogue by his rival Marcus Moses. He ultimately returned to Hamburg in reduced circumstances.

BIBLIOGRAPHY: C. Roth, *History of the Great Synagogue* (1950), 35–45.

[Cecil Roth]

NATHAN, DAVID (1816–1886), pioneer New Zealand businessman and communal leader. Nathan arrived in Kororareka from London in 1840, trading as storekeeper. In 1841 he married Rosetta Aarons in New Zealand's first Jewish marriage. He opened a store in Auckland when it became the capital and bought 2,500 acres of land in the adjoining Manurewa. Nathan served on the Auckland City Council and on many local bodies. He went into auctioneering and established New Zealand's oldest and most diversified wholesale business. Sabbath and holiday services were held at his warehouse for over a decade. He served four terms as president of the Auckland Hebrew Congregation. Through his leadership and example he unified and conciliated all groups in the congregation. A strong force in the town's financial affairs, Nathan showed particular interest in working class welfare. His two sons L.D. and N.A. Nathan successively led the congregation after his death for almost half a century.

BIBLIOGRAPHY: L.M. Goldman, *History of the Jews in New Zealand* (1958), index. **ADD. BIBLIOGRAPHY:** J.C. Mogford, "David Nathan," in: *The Dictionary of New Zealand Biography;* L.D. Nathan, *As Old as Auckland: A History of L.D. Nathan & Co., Ltd., and of the David Nathan Family* (1984), index.

[Maurice S. Pitt]

NATHAN, ERNESTO (1845–1921), Italian statesman and the first Jewish mayor of Rome. Born in England, he came into contact with the Italian patriot Guiseppe Mazzini who was exiled to London for his radical views. Nathan was taken to Italy by his mother in 1859 and settled in Rome in 1871 soon after Rome became part of the Kingdom of Italy. He became manager of Mazzini's newspaper *Roma del Popolo* and was a passionate republican and an advocate of the secular state. Nathan became an Italian citizen in 1889 and was twice grand master of the Italian Masons. He was elected mayor of Rome in 1907 and held office until 1913. Following the Italian entry into World War I in 1915, Nathan enlisted in the army and although over 70 served at the front as a lieutenant.

ADD. BIBLIOGRAPHY: M.I. Macioti, *Ernesto Nathan: un sindaco che non ha fatto scuola* (1983); P.D. Mandelli, "Ernesto Nathan cittadino pesarese," in: *La presenza ebraica nelle Marche: Secoli XIII–XX* (1993), 355–62; A.M. Isastia, *Ernesto Nathan: un "mazziniano inglese" tra i democratici pesaresi* (1994); R. Ugolini, *Ernesto Nathan tra idealità e pragmatismo* (2003).

NATHAN, GEORGE JEAN (1882–1958), U.S. drama critic and editor. Born in Fort Wayne, Indiana, Nathan became the foremost American critic of his time, and took the lead in freeing the American theater of the stagy and melodramatic trappings of the *Belasco period. He was in journalism for more than 50 years, mostly linked with the world of Broadway as critic for *The Bohemian Magazine* (1906–08), *Harper's Weekly* (1908–10), *The Smart Set* (1908–23), and *The American Mercury*, which he founded with H.L. Mencken in 1924. He was also a founder – with Theodore Dreiser, Eugene O'Neill, and others – of *The American Spectator* (1932–39).

A detached, sophisticated, and cynical figure, Nathan was something of a boulevardier, not only in his personal habits but also in his writings. Nevertheless, he was a man of learning, critical insight, and courage, who paved the way for Eugene O'Neill and his type of dramatic writing. Nathan labored consistently to educate American taste to accept writers such as Sean O'Casey, Jean Giraudoux, and Ludwig Thoma. He wrote several books with Mencken, including the satirical play *Heliogabalus* (1920).

His own books, over 30 in number, include: *Mr. George Jean Nathan Presents* (1917); *The Theater, the Drama, the Girls* (1921); *Materia Critica* (1924); *Testament of a Critic* (1931); *The Theater of the Moment* (1936); *Morning After the First Night* (1938); an *Encyclopaedia of the Theater* (1940); and *The Theater of the Fifties* (1953).

BIBLIOGRAPHY: I. Goldberg, *Theatre of George Jean Nathan* (1926); C. Angoff (ed.), *World of George Jean Nathan* (1952); S.J. Kunitz, *Twentieth Century Authors*, first suppl. (1955), incl. bibl.; *New York Times* (April 8, 1958), 1; (April 9, 1958), 36.

[Charles Angoff]

NATHAN, HARRY LOUIS, BARON (1889–1963), English lawyer and politician. Born in London, the son of a fine arts publisher, Nathan was educated at St. Paul's school before becoming a solicitor. He fought in Gallipoli, Egypt, and France during World War I. In the 1920s he became legal advisor to the British Zionist Organization and to many Jewish bodies in Palestine. From 1929 to 1934 he was a Liberal member of Parliament and then switched and was a Labour member of Parliament from 1934 to 1935 and from 1937 to 1940. Following the outbreak of World War II Nathan became chairman of the National Defense Public Interest Committee. He was elevated to the House of Lords in 1940 as Baron Nathan and from 1946 to 1948 was minister of civil aviation in the postwar Labour government. Later he was departmental chairman of the governmental committee on the law of customs and excise and chairman of the governmental committee to investigate the law and practice of charitable trusts, which led to a new act. Lord Nathan was an active figure in Jewish communal affairs as a member of the Board of Deputies of British Jews, and president of the European Committee of the third, fourth, fifth, and sixth *Maccabiah. He was also prominent in national civic affairs as chairman of the Royal Geographical Society and of the Royal Society of Arts. Lord Nathan wrote *Medical Negligence* (1957) and *The Charities Act, 1960* (1962). His wife, ELEANOR (Stettauer; 1892–1972), was the second female chairperson of the London County Council in 1947–48.

BIBLIOGRAPHY: H.M. Hyde, *Strong for Service: The Life of Lord Nathan of Churt* (1968). **ADD. BIBLIOGRAPHY:** ODNB online.

NATHAN, HENRY (1842–1914), Canadian politician. Nathan was born and educated in London, England, and as a young man of 20 moved to Victoria, British Columbia. In Victoria he established himself as an importer and wholesale merchant, also taking an active interest in public affairs. In 1865 he was elected master of the local Masonic lodge. With the support of prominent politicians, in 1870 Nathan ran successfully for a seat in British Columbia's last legislative assembly before the colony entered the Confederation of Canada. He was strongly in favor of the union of British Columbia with Canada and urged such measures as increased representation, responsible government, and greater nonsectarian education. In November of 1871, shortly after B.C. became part of Canada, Nathan was elected one of the new province's first six members of Parliament, becoming the first Jew to sit in the Canadian House of Commons. As an MP, he was a staunch supporter of Prime Minister John A. MacDonald's government, using his position as the representative of Victoria's business interests to urge that the terminus of the Trans-Canada Railway be built as close as possible to the provincial capital. Nathan was re-elected in 1872 and served until 1874, when he retired from politics. Although the national railway was never extended to Victoria, Nathan is widely credited as being a prime mover in bringing British Columbia into the Dominion of Canada.

[Barbara Schober (2nd ed.)]

NATHAN, ISAAC (1790?–1864), composer, singer, and writer. Nathan was born in Canterbury, England, and his father was probably the local *ḥazzan*. He studied with Solomon Lyon at Cambridge to enter the rabbinate, but in about 1810 he went to London and began a career as singer, composer, and music teacher. From Domenico Corri he learned the classical tradition of Italian vocal culture, stemming from Corri's master, Porpora; Nathan's *Musurgia Vocalis* (1836^2) is one of the few remaining written documentations of this method. In London he became friendly with Lord *Byron, whose *Hebrew Melodies* were written at Nathan's request and set by him to music. In the first editions of this work (from 1815 onward), which achieved great popularity, the name of John *Braham was featured on the title page as composer, in addition to that of Nathan, but Braham contributed nothing to the work except his prestige. After a financial setback, caused mainly by debts incurred while on a secret mission on behalf of King William IV, Nathan immigrated to Australia in 1841 and settled in Sydney as Australia's first resident professional composer. There he organized musical performances, published a magazine entitled *The Southern Euphrosyne*, and composed the first opera written and produced in Australia, *Don Juan of Austria* (1847). Nathan died in Sydney from injuries received while stepping off (or being run over by) a tram. His great-granddaughter Catherine Mackerras wrote his most informed biography, and her son was the conductor Charles Mackerras. His great-nephew was the pianist Harold Samuel.

Nathan's works include various operas and songs. Several traditional Jewish melodies are found in his *Musurgia Vocalis*. For some of the *Hebrew Melodies* he also used some traditional tunes, but, except for *Ma'oz Ẓur (set to Byron's "On Jordan's Banks"), they are quite transformed by his superficial compositional initiative. In certain of the songs published in Australia, he reworked aboriginal melodies. His grandson, Harry Alfred Nathan, has been proposed as the composer of the popular Australian song "Waltzing Matilda," but the claim is a matter of dispute.

BIBLIOGRAPHY: E. Foreman, *The Porpora Tradition* (1968); C. Mackerras, *Hebrew Melodist: A Life of Isaac Nathan* (1963); O.S. Phillips, *Isaac Nathan, Friend of Byron* (1940); C.H. Bertie, *Isaac Nathan, Australia's First Composer* (1922); R. Covell, *Australia's Music* (1967), 13–15, 59, 68–69; E.R. Dibdin, in: *Music and Letters*, 22 (1941), 85.

[Bathja Bayer]

NATHAN, JOSEPH EDWARD (1835–1912), New Zealand businessman and communal leader. Born in London, Nathan prospected unsuccessfully in the Australian goldfields before arriving in Wellington in 1857. There he went into partnership with Jacob Joseph and built up the flourishing wholesale import-export business which later became Joseph Nathan and Company. He held office on the Wellington Harbor Board, the Chamber of Commerce, the Gas Company, and other enterprises, and was chief promoter and chairman of the Wellington-Manawatu railway. Glaxo Laboratories, which later became important in the manufacture of pharmaceutical products in England, developed from his cooperative farming ventures. (The pharmaceutical giant Glaxo Wellcome, developed in part from his firm, became one of the largest drug manufacturers in the world. Nathan's son Alexander registered the name "Glaxo" for his dried milk powder in London in 1906.) In 1887 Nathan retired to London after having been one of the leaders of the Wellington Jewish community for over 40 years and president of its first synagogue (1870). His family remained prominent in New Zealand life.

BIBLIOGRAPHY: L.M. Goldman, *History of the Jews in New Zealand* (1958), 148, 150, 219. **ADD. BIBLIOGRAPHY:** J. Millen, "Joseph Edward Nathan," in: *Dictionary of New Zealand Biography.*

[Maurice S. Pitt]

NATHAN, MANFRED (1875–1945), South African lawyer, author, and communal leader. Born in Hanover (South Africa), the son of a German pioneer in the Cape, Nathan practiced at the Johannesburg Bar. He served for a time on the Natal Bench and became president of the South African Special Income Tax court in 1931. An assiduous writer on legal and constitutional subjects, Nathan was the author of a four-volume work, *The Common Law of South Africa* (1904–09) and the studies *The South African Commonwealth* (1919) and *Empire Government* (1928). Among his many other writings were a life of President Paul Kruger, an autobiography, *Not Heaven Itself* (1944), and several works on South African history. Nathan was active in Jewish communal life. He was a founding member of the Transvaal Jewish Board of Deputies (1903) and was president in 1905 and 1907. He was on the first executive of the South African Board of Deputies (1912) and vice president of the South African Zionist Federation (1904–1907).

Nathan was also active in politics and was elected to municipal and provincial legislative bodies in the Transvaal, and served on the boards of educational institutions and hospitals.

BIBLIOGRAPHY: G. Saron and L. Hotz (eds.), *The Jews in South Africa – a History* (1955), index.

[Louis Hotz]

NATHAN, MAUD (1862–1946), U.S. activist, suffragist, and president of the Consumer's League. The second of four children born to Annie Florance and Robert Weeks Nathan, Nathan descended from a line of Sephardi Jews in America that included Gershom *Seixas, the first *ḥazzan* in the New York Jewish community, poet Emma *Lazurus, and Benjamin *Cardozo, a United States Supreme Court Justice. Her sister, Annie Nathan *Meyer, founded Barnard College. Maud Nathan married wealthy financier Fredrick Nathan, a first cousin 19 years her senior, in 1879; their only child, Annette, died in 1895 at the age of nine. The loss of her daughter and a desire to become more involved in society led Nathan to join the board of directors of New York's Mount Sinai Hospital. She also volunteered as a teacher of English to immigrants at the Hebrew Free School Association and served as her synagogue's first sisterhood president. Expansion of her involvement outside the Jewish community soon followed as the Board of Exchange for Women's Work offered an opportunity to engage in politics. Nathan successfully lobbied the sponsors of a bill placing a high tariff on imported beads, arguing that it would increase the economic pressures already placed upon women doing needlework in their homes. Nathan was then contacted by Josephine Shaw Lowell, founder of the Consumer's League, who asked for her assistance in investigating the conditions under which women worked in retail stores, including bad sanitation and meager earnings. As president of the Consumer's League from 1897 to 1927, Nathan investigated the bad conditions experienced by women working in retail and encouraged consumers to patronize shops which provided decent environments and salaries for their workers. Nathan then became active in the women's suffrage movement, serving as president of the Fifteenth Assembly District of New York's Women's Suffrage Party (WSP). While her husband strongly supported her involvement, other family members, including her three siblings, disagreed with the suffrage platform. Undeterred, Nathan specifically targeted Jewish women, including recent East European immigrants, for involvement in WSP activities. Her efforts within Jewish and non-Jewish circles on behalf of women's rights won her the admiration of individuals such as Carrie Chapman Catt, founder of the League of Women Voters, who wrote the foreword to Maud's autobiography, *Once Upon a Time and Today* (1933). Nathan was also the author of *Story of an Epoch-Making Movement* (1926), about the Consumers League.

BIBLIOGRAPHY: A. Kaufman. "Nathan, Maud," in: P.E. Hyman and D. Dash Moore, *Jewish Women in America*, 2 (1997), 967–68; L. Gordon Kuzmack. *Woman's Cause: The Jewish Woman's Movement in England and the United States, 1881–1933* (1990), 144–45.

[Shira Kohn (2nd ed.)]

NATHAN, MORDECAI (15th cent.), French physician of Avignon, the teacher of Joseph b. Solomon *Colon. Nathan was mentioned among three "Jews and doctors of medicine" together with three "Christian doctors of medicine in Avignon" in a manuscript entitled "Thoroughly Tested Prescription for Pestilential Disease" (Bibliothèque Nationale, Ms. Français 630, fol. 54). It appears that he was also identified with M. Nadi, the mathematician (Wolf, Bibliotheca, 4 (1733), 904).

He is known by his work *Me'ir Nativ*, also called *Ya'ir Nativ* (Venice, 1523), the first Hebrew concordance of the Bible, compiled between 1437 and 1448. Nathan was familiar with Christian scholarly circles, and more than once engaged in theological polemics with them. He became convinced from these polemics of the need to prepare a Hebrew concordance of the Bible to make it easier for Hebrew-speaking Jews to reply to Christians. He arranged the books of the Bible in the order of the Vulgate (Latin translation). He explained the roots of the words in the most concise language. Verbs and nouns, however, appear in disorder, and he omitted prepositions and formative letters. He also omitted proper nouns and the Aramaic words in the Bible. Christian scholars engaged in the study of Hebrew attached great importance to the work. Mario de Calascio published the concordance a second time (Rome, 1621) together with a Latin translation, in which the defects of the Hebrew edition were remedied. Differences of opinion have arisen about the identity of the author of *Me'ir Nativ*. The inner title page gives Mordecai Nathan as the name of the author, whereas the introduction is signed by Isaac Nathan. Johannes Buxtorf concluded, therefore, that Mordecai Nathan was also known as Isaac Nathan. I.S. *Reggio concluded that the author was Isaac Nathan and that the name Mordecai on the title page was an error. A. Tauber thought that the author was Mordecai Nathan, while the Isaac, who wrote the introduction, was apparently his relative.

BIBLIOGRAPHY: I.S. Reggio, *Iggerot Yashar*, 1 (1834), 70–76; Gross, Gal Jud, 10; Gross, in: MGWJ, 29 (1880), 518–523; S. Mandelkern, *Heikhal ha-Kodesh* (1896), introd., 9–11; A. Tauber, in: KS, 2 (1925), 141–4; Renan, Rabbins, 533; E. Wickersheimer, *Dictionnaire biographique des médicins en France au Moyen-Age* (1936), 537; E.R. Malachi, *Oẓar ha-Leksikografyah ha-Ivrit* (an appendix to *Heikhal ha-Kodesh* of S. Mandelkern, 1955), 12f., 27f., 30.

[Isidore Simon and Abraham David]

NATHAN, MULLA IBRAHIM (1816–1868), British intelligence agent born in *Meshed, Persia. In about 1837 he and his brother Musa left their homeland and entered British service. They traveled throughout Afghanistan, Turkestan, and Bukhara and were connected with all the major British expeditions in Central Asia. During the first Anglo-Afghan War (1839–42), they supplied funds for British officers on remote missions, gathered intelligence and information for the military authorities, and rescued and assisted British prisoners in *Afghanistan after the disaster to the British army at Kabul. They left Afghanistan in 1842, and settled in Bombay in 1844. In recognition of their services, the British government in India granted them compensation for their losses as well as a life pension. Mulla Ibrahim was offered diplomatic employment in Meshed, but refused to return to the city in which the Jews had recently been forced to adopt Islam. In Bombay Mulla Ibrahim took an active part in the Baghdadi-Jewish community. Jacob *Saphir states that he was appointed as a customs official, but was exempted from duty on the Sabbath and Jewish holidays.

BIBLIOGRAPHY: Fischel, in: HUCA, 29 (1958), 331–75.

[Walter Joseph Fischel]

NATHAN, PAUL (1857–1927), German politician, Jewish leader, and philanthropist. A protégé of Ludwig *Bamberger and Theodor Barth, he was associated with the Berlin liberal publication *Die Nation*, serving as its editor until 1907. Because of his influence in political circles and as founder in 1901 of the *Hilfsverein der deutschen Juden, Nathan was often regarded as the spokesman of German Jewry apart from the Zionists. He was active in almost all international Jewish conferences on emigration and relief for Jewish victims of pogroms and wars, helping to shape international political and relief campaigns to aid them. Nathan was convinced that the Jewish problem in Russia was part of the general Russian problem, to be solved only by change of regime – if necessary by revolution. He advocated economic pressure on Russia by the West, primarily through refusals to grant loans. Under Nathan's influence the Hilfsverein der deutschen Juden aided liberal and even revolutionary movements in Russia, and he was also instrumental in influencing Lucien *Wolf in England and Jacob H. *Schiff in the United States to accept its policies toward Russia. The Hilfsverein published the *Russische Korrespondenz*, which informed the press, political leaders, and other personalities of the true situation in Russia, and similar bulletins in England and Paris.

During the *Beilis trial of 1913 Nathan, with the help of Lucien Wolf in London, organized the defense of Beilis outside Russia. In Germany Nathan obtained a large number of signatures of non-Jewish personalities in favor of Beilis and expert opinions by scientists. At the same time Nathan published the book *Der Fall Justschinski*, an account of the German pro-Beilis campaign. He was among the founders of the Comite zur Abwehr Anti-semitischer Angriffe in Berlin. In 1896 he published *Die Kriminalitaet der Juden* and *Die Juden als Soldaten* and *Uber das juedische rituelle Schaechtverfahren*.

Nathan was basically a sincere assimilationist who saw only in complete assimilation with the non-Jewish population the possiblity of full emancipation in every country. Thus he strongly opposed the Zionist movement. During World War I, while German Zionists demanded autonomous rights for Jews in countries occupied by the German armed forces, Nathan gave constant help to the assimilationists of Poland. When the war broke out he helped to gain the sympathy of Jews in neutral countries for the cause of the Central Powers, his main argument being that a war against Russia, the country of barbaric pogroms, should be supported by Jews. At the beginning of the Weimar Republic Nathan officially joined the Socialist Party (SPD). The German government asked him to accept the post of its ambassador to Vienna, but Nathan declined the offer because of his close association with the major Jewish organizations at a time when antisemitism was strong in Austria. Through his many friends abroad he tried to gain sympathy for Germany, constantly warning that the harsh conditions of the Versailles Treaty would help bring back a totalitarian and reactionary regime in Germany from which both that nation and others would suffer. Nathan's enthusiasm for Jewish colonization in Soviet Russia led to his publishing a pamphlet in 1926 in which he favored the concentration of Soviet Jews in the far-eastern part of that country.

BIBLIOGRAPHY: E. Feder, *Paul Nathan, ein Lebensbild* (1929); Szajkowski, in: JSOS 19 (1957), 47–50; 29 (1967), 3–26, 75–91; idem, in: PAAJR, 31 (1963), 197–218; idem, in: YLBI, 9 (1964), 131–58; idem, in: YLBI, 3 (1958), 60–80; idem, in: HJ, 14 (1952), 24–37.

NATHAN, ROBERT ROY (1908–2001), U.S. economist. Born in Dayton, Ohio, Nathan joined the Department of Commerce in 1933 and became prominent in President Roosevelt's reconstruction programs. During World War II he was deputy director of the War Production Board and the Office of

War Mobilization and Reconversion. After the war, in 1946, he opened his own consulting firm, Robert R. Nathan Associates, which was active in counseling postwar rehabilitation work and economic development in many countries, such as France, Burma, Indonesia, Korea, Afghanistan, Ghana, Colombia, and El Salvador. During the late 1940s and the early 1950s he devoted much of his time and effort to guiding various Israeli government authorities in their first official contacts with the United States government. His main professional interest was developmental economics; his vision was of a free-enterprise democratic system that benefited all of society. To that end, his economic consulting firm advised business, industry, labor unions; and state, local, national, and foreign governments, applying tested economic principles. The firm became a leader in developing master plans for economic growth, sometimes spending decades in a country. A natural humanitarian, Nathan championed social causes, including civil rights, welfare legislation, and minimum wage, and he was the director of a foundation that contributed to low-income housing and equal opportunity programs. By the time Nathan turned the presidency of his company over to John Beyer in 1978, the firm had provided economic consulting services in most sectors of the U.S. economy.

Nathan Associates Inc. established the Robert R. Nathan Memorial Foundation, which endows a fellowship in applied economics at Nathan's alma mater, the Wharton School of the University of Pennsylvania.

Nathan's major publications include *Mobilizing for Abundance* (1944) and *Palestine – Problem and Promise* (with O. Gass and D. Craemer, 1946).

[Joachim O. Ronall / Ruth Beloff (2nd ed.)]

NATHAN, VENGUESSONE, major landowner and moneylender in 15th-century Provence. In a survey of 1424 Nathan is listed as the largest Jewish landowner in Arles, with property including a house, vineyard, and shop where she sold drapery and crockery. She also owned books in Hebrew and Latin. At her death, she was owed money from debts, claims, and pledges. In her will, notarized in 1436, Venguessone's largest bequests went to her grandsons. (Her son, Isaac, had a great deal of money of his own.) Her unmarried granddaughters received money for their dowries (probably in addition to what their father would contribute) and her married granddaughters received 25 florins for clothing for their first birthing. Venguessone left several charitable legacies, including money for the cemetery, a light for the synagogue, ten florins for the crown of the Torah scroll, and money for dowries for poor brides.

Venguessone's mother, Esther de Caylar, granddaughter of Bonjues Nathan, the patriarch of a prominent Arles family, is known to have represented the Nathan family as a delegate, with one other woman, Regina, at an assembly for the reorganization of a free school for the Arles Jewish community, held from November 8–December 23, 1407.

BIBLIOGRAPHY: P. Hildenfinger, "Documents relatifs aux Juifs d'Arles," in: *Revue des études juives* 42 (1900), 87; D. Iancu-Agou, "Une vente de livres hébreux à Arles en 1434: Tableau de l'élite juive Arlesienne au mileu du XVe siècle," in: *Revue des études juives* 146 (1987), 5–62; L. Stouff, "Isaac Nathan et les siens. Une famille juive d'Arles des XIVe et XVe siècles," in: *Provence Historique* 37:150 (1987), 499–12; E. Taitz, S. Henry, and C. Tallan, "Nathan, Venguessone," in: *The JPS Guide to Jewish Women, 600 B.C.E.–1900 C.E.* (2003), 82; idem, "Esther de Caylar," *ibid.*, 79.

[Cheryl Tallan (2nd ed.)]

NATHAN BEN ABRAHAM I (d. c. 1053), *av bet din* of the academy of Ereẓ Israel in Jerusalem. Nathan was a scion of one of the families whose members held respected positions in the academy. Around 1011 he traveled to Kairouan to settle the estate of his father, who had died there. He remained there for a number of years, studying under R. *Ḥushi'el. After the death of his maternal uncle, Rav ben Yoḥai, *av bet din* of the academy of Ereẓ Israel, Nathan claimed the position – although according to accepted custom it belonged to Tobiah, who ranked third in the academy – at the same time attempting to oust R. Solomon b. *Judah as *gaon* of the academy. In the struggle, Nathan was sponsored by Diaspora scholars, while Solomon b. Judah was supported by the local community and also favored by the Fatimid governor of *Ramleh. Nathan lived in Ramleh, attempting to assume the functions of *gaon* there, while Solomon still held his position in Jerusalem and issued a ban against Nathan. In 1042 both parties agreed that Nathan should succeed Solomon as *gaon* of the academy after the latter's death. However, when this occurred (before 1051) the office of *gaon* passed to Daniel b. *Azariah. Nothing is known of Nathan's teachings. In one of his letters of 1042 he mentions his son Abraham, whose son Nathan *II was later *av bet din* of the academy.

BIBLIOGRAPHY: J. Mann, in: HUCA, 3 (1926), 273–6; R. Gottheil and W.H. Worrell, *Fragments from the Cairo Genizah in the Freer Collection* (1927), 197–201; S. Assaf, in: *Zion*, 2 (1927), 115f.; Mann, Texts, 1 (1931), 323–45; S. Assaf and L.A. Mayer, *Sefer ha-Yishuv*, 2 (1944), index; Shapira, in: *Yerushalayim*, 4 (1953), 118–22; Hirschberg, Afrikah, 1 (1965), 240–3; Goitein, in: *Tarbiz*, 36 (1967), 62f.

[Abraham David]

NATHAN BEN ABRAHAM II (d. before 1102), *av bet din* of the academy of Ereẓ Israel. Nathan was a grandson of Nathan b. Abraham *I. Few biographical details are known of him. He was appointed *av bet din* of the academy of Ereẓ Israel during the gaonate of *Abiathar in 1095, in succession to Zadok b. Josiah. Nathan compiled a short Arabic commentary to the six Orders of the Mishnah, in which he incorporated explanations of many specific words. A Yemenite scholar who lived in the 12th century copied his commentary, and added some commentaries of other scholars to it. In the opinion of some scholars, however, Nathan is himself responsible for some of the additions from the commentaries of his predecessors. It is not clear which literary sources were already used by Nathan himself and which were added by the Yemenite scholar. The scholars quoted in the commentary, except for two contemporaries, Nathan b. Jehiel of Rome and Isaac Alfasi, lived before him. Nathan, or the Yemenite scholar, frequently quotes the later *geonim*, particularly Saadiah Gaon, Samuel b. Ḥophni

Gaon, Sherira Gaon, and Hai Gaon. There are few quotations from the earlier *geonim*. In general the commentary gives the meaning of words and concepts, a more extensive commentary being found only for a few tractates: *Berakhot, Shevu'ot*, and *Avot*. A few tractates are preceded by a short introduction explaining general concepts and essential matters necessary for an understanding of the whole tractate. R. Nathan, or the Yemenite scholar, gives a short survey of the development of the oral law down to his time in his introduction to the work. He discusses the relationship of the Tosefta to the Mishnah, taking the view that the Tosefta explains obscurities of the Mishnah. He also discusses the principles laid down by talmudic scholars for deciding *halakhah* where there are opposing opinions. The chapter divisions of the tractates in the commentary differ from the accepted form. The commentary seeems to have been widely known and it was already used by Baruch Samuel of *Aleppo.

A number of extracts were published in the original with a Hebrew translation by S. Assaf and by M.L. Sachs. The whole commentary in the Hebrew translation of J. *Kafaḥ was published by El ha-Mekorot (Jerusalem, 1955–58) together with the Mishnah text and other commentaries.

BIBLIOGRAPHY: Mann, Egypt, 1 (1920), 151, 193f.; 2 (1922), 229–32; S. Assaf, in: KS, 10 (1933/34), 381–8, 525–45 (= Assaf, Ge'onim, 294–332); M.L. Sachs, in: *Sinai*, 17 (1945), 167–75; S. Abramson, *Rav Nissim Ga'on* (1965), index.

[Abraham David]

NATHAN BEN ISAAC HA-KOHEN HA-BAVLI (i.e., the Babylonian; tenth century), chronicler who probably lived in *Baghdad. The fragments of his work that have been preserved appear to be part of his book on the Jews of Baghdad, *Akhbār Baghdād*. These fragments are an important source for the study of the history of Babylonian Jewry in the tenth century. In the first fragment Nathan gives a description of the office of the exilarch, the method by which he was appointed, his duties, and his functions. The fragment also contains details of two great controversies that raged in Babylonian Jewry in the tenth century. In one, the adversaries were the exilarch *Ukba and the *Gaon* of Pumbedita, Kohen *Ẓedek; it lasted from 909 to 916. In the other controversy, the adversaries were the exilarch David b. *Zakkai and Saadiah *Gaon, in about 930. From the contents of the fragment it appears that Nathan was in Babylonia at the time that the latter controversy took place. His vivid account of the ceremonial observed at the installation of an exilarch is of exceptional interest (see *Exilarch). This fragment was published (in Hebrew) in Samuel Shulam's edition of Abraham *Zacuto's *Sefer Yuḥasin* (Constantinople, 1566), and again in A. Neubauer's *Medieval Jewish Chronicles* 2 (1895), 77–88. A second fragment describes the rise of *Natira and his sons at the court of the Abbasid caliph at the end of the ninth and the beginning of the tenth century. It was published, in Arabic and in a Hebrew translation, by A.E. Harkavy (see bibliography). A third fragment, also dealing with the Ukba-Kohen Ẓedek quarrel, was published, in the original and in English translation, by I. Friedlander (see bibliography). The fragments lead to the assumption that Nathan ha-Bavli was closely associated with the circles surrounding the exilarchs and the academy heads, and that he may have been a student at one of the academies, apparently Sura. His writings contain inaccuracies and glaring omissions, e.g., he errs in the names of the *geonim* and in the chronological data. Nevertheless, he made an honest and unbiased effort to report events as he saw them happen or as they were reported to him. Some of the information contained in the fragments has been confirmed by other sources.

BIBLIOGRAPHY: A. Harkavy, in: *Festschrift... A. Berliner* (1903), 34–43 (Heb. part); I. Friedlander, in: JQR, 17 (1904/05), 747–61; A. Epstein, in: *Festschrift... A. Harkavy* (1908), 169–72 (Heb. part); J.R. Marcus, *The Jew in the Medieval World* (1938), 287–92; L. Ginzberg, *Geonica*, 1 (1909), 22–37, 55–66; A. Kahana, *Sifrut ha-Historyah ha-Yisre'elit*, 1 (1922), 57–72; A. Marx, in: *Livre d'Hommage... Poznański* (1927), 76–81 (Ger.); J. Mann, in: *Tarbiz*, 5 (1933/34), 148ff.; Baron, Social^2, 6 (1958), 213–4; A.N.Z. Roth, in KS: 30 (1954/55), 255–6.

[Abraham David]

NATHAN BEN JEHIEL OF ROME (1035–c. 1110), Italian lexicographer, also called **Ba'al he-Arukh** ("the author of the *Arukh*") after the title of his lexicon. Few biographical details are known of him. Some state that he belonged to the De *Pomis or Delli Mansi family, but the view is widespread that he actually belonged to the famous *Anau (Anav) family. He was taught in his youth by his father, a *paytan* and the head of the yeshivah of Rome, and may as a young man have studied in Sicily under Maẓli'aḥ b. Elijah ibn *al-Bazak, a pupil of Hai Gaon. However, there is reason to believe that the scanty references to Maẓli'aḥ's name in Nathan's work are the addenda of an earlier copyist named Mevorakh, some of whose marginal notes, in which he also mentions that he was al-Bazak's pupil, were later incorporated in the text of the *Arukh*. Nathan also studied under Moses ha-Darshan of Narbonne, as well as, in the view of some scholars, under Moses Kalfo of Bari and Moses of Pavia. When his father died immediately after Nathan's return to Rome about 1070, he and his two brothers Daniel and Abraham succeeded him as the heads of the yeshivah of Rome. With them he wrote responsa to halakhic questions addressed to him by various scholars, among whom was a Solomon Yiẓḥaki, identified by some as Rashi. Noted for his charitable acts, Nathan built a magnificent synagogue and a ritual bathhouse for his community. It was while serving as head of the Rome yeshivah that he wrote his classic work (which he completed in 1101), the *Arukh*, a lexicon of the Talmud and the Midrashim, containing all the talmudic terms in need of explanation; in the course of time various additions were made to it (see below). At the end of the *Arukh* there is a poem written in particularly difficult language and therefore of somewhat obscure meaning; in it the poet, lamenting his bitter lot, tells of the death of four out of his five sons during his lifetime.

In the *Arukh* Nathan gives not only the meaning but also the etymology of the words of the Talmud, including some of Aramaic, Latin, Greek, Arabic, and Persian origin. Nathan quotes many geonic interpretations and an earlier lexicon by a Ẓemaḥ of uncertain identity, as well as the comments of earlier and contemporary rabbis – among them works otherwise unknown – and halakhic decisions, although apparently irrelevant to the object of the work. He describes Jewish customs, such as that of the Babylonian Jews, who in celebrating Purim burned Haman's effigy, singing around and leaping over a bonfire (s.v. *shavvar*). The *Arukh* is important for the study of the **Midrash Yelammedenu*. Of the other Midrashim he cites, particular note should be taken of the *Midrash Hashkem* of which only quotations have survived, and many of his citations from the Midrashim are not to be found in the extant editions. He also quotes the Palestine Targum to the Pentateuch. Words were still treated by Nathan as though they belonged to uniliteral or biliteral consonantal roots, even though the work of Judah ibn Ḥayyuj, showing that the Hebrew verb has a triliteral root, had already appeared.

The main importance of the *Arukh* lies in the extensive collection of explanations of words and subjects in the Talmud and in the profusion of the author's excellent readings, all drawn from the three chief Torah centers of that time: the teaching of the Babylonian *geonim*; the commentaries of Hananel b. *Ḥushi'el of Kairouan, which he uses extensively but in the main without acknowledgment; and the "Mainz commentaries" mentioned by him under different names ("scholars of Mainz," "pious ones of Mainz," "Mainz commentary," etc.). These explanations occur in the extant commentaries of Rabbenu Gershom without mentioning Nathan's name. Apart from these three sources he also had before him not a few of the early commentaries of Provence. Nathan frequently explains words and subjects according to the reading of Hananel b. Ḥushi'el without indicating that his explanation is based thereon. At times he goes beyond the explanation of the word and explains the whole theme. It has now been established that these explanations are also from Hananel, given by him in other contexts. In the printed editions of the Talmud, Rashi mentions him once (Shab. 13b). The whole passage, however, is missing in some manuscripts, and it is clear that Rashi made no use of the *Arukh*. The many anonymous parallels that exist between the two works have their source in the common use made by the two scholars of "the teaching of Mainz" and of the other common exegetical traditions.

The *Arukh* achieved exceptionally wide circulation. It was apparently first published in Rome in 1469–72?, an edition that is a better version than that found in later ones printed from a different manuscript. Because of the great importance attached to the work, many supplements to and emendations of it were written. Among them is the *Agur* of Samuel b. Jacob ibn *Jama (12th century), consisting of addenda to the *Arukh* derived from the language found in geonic writings, which was published by S. Buber in *Jubelschrift…. H. Graetz* (1887). Menahem de *Lonzano wrote addenda, emendations, and explanations to the *Arukh* under the title of *Ha-Ma'arikh*, published in his work *Shetei Yadot* (Venice, 1618). The physician and philologist Benjamin *Mussafia, in his *Musaf he-Arukh*, which was printed in the *Arukh* (Amsterdam, 1655), corrected the Greek and Latin words. Isaiah *Berlin (18th century) wrote *Hafla'ah she-ba-Arakhin*, addenda and notes to the *Arukh* up to the letter *kaf* in the Lemberg 1857 edition of the *Arukh*. A scholarly edition, based on seven manuscripts, was published by Alexander Kohut under the title of *Arukh ha-Shalem* or *Aruch Completum* (1878–92), to which a supplement and addenda were issued by S. Krauss in his *Tosefot he-Arukh ha-Shalem* (1937). A condensed version, entitled *He-Arukh ha-Kaẓar*, by an anonymous epitomist, was first published in Constantinople.

BIBLIOGRAPHY: S.J.L. Rapoport, in: *Bikkurei ha-Ittim* (1830), 2nd pagination, 7–79; Kohut, Arukh, 1 (1926²), introd.; Vogelstein-Rieger, 1 (1896), index; S. Krauss, *Griechische und lateinische Lehnwoerter im Talmud, Midrasch und Targum* (1898), introd. xxiv–xxxix; D.S. Blondheim, in: *Festschrift fuer A. Freimann* (1935), 24–30; idem, *Notes on the Italian Words in the Arukh Completum* (1933); S. Lieberman, in: KS, 14 (1937/38), 218–28; H.Z. Toibes, in: *Scritti in Memoria de Sally Mayer* (1956), Heb. pt. 126–41; H.J. Zimmels, in: Roth, Dark Ages, 182–4; Zunz-Albeck, Derashot, index; S. Abramson, *Rav Nissim Ga'on* (1965), index; S. Speier, in: *Leshonenu*, 31 (1967), 23–32, 189–98; 34 (1967/70), 172–9.

[Abraham David]

NATHAN DE-ẒUẒITA RESH GALUTA, Babylonian exilarch. According to a statement in the Talmud (Shab. 56b), he is identical with Ukban b. Nehemiah (320–340), but in the *Seder Olam Zuta* two different exilarchs are mentioned called both Ukban and Ẓuẓita: one, called Nathan Ukban (Nathan de-Ẓuẓita), lived in the third century, and the other, Mar Ukban de Ẓuẓita, a near contemporary of R. Joseph, in the fourth. Nathan seems originally to have lived a sinful life, but he later repented. The *amora* Joseph expressed the view that he must be regarded as one of the most celebrated of penitents of all time, and that he was much beloved in heaven. According to an old *aggadah* cited by Rashi (Sanh. 31b), Nathan (Masukba) was consumed by passion for a married woman and unfulfilled desire made him ill. On one occasion, in need of money, she paid him a visit of her own free will. Although he could now have had his desire, he restrained himself, and she departed untouched. From that moment his passion subsided, and a ray of light was seen to shine over his head. It is to this that the name Ẓuẓita (ray of light) refers. According to the *geonim* Ẓemaḥ and Sa'adiah, however, the name derives from the fact that in his youth Nathan used to dress and curl the fringes (*ẓiẓiot*) of his hair (B.M. Lewin, *Oẓar ha-Ge'onim* (Shab.; 1930), pt. 2 24). Rashi identified him in that passage with Mar *Ukba the *av bet din*, a contemporary of Samuel (cf. also R. Aḥai Gaon. *She'iltot*, Va-Era 42; ed. by S.K. Mirsky, 3 (1963), 43). In the manuscripts of the *She'iltot*, however, the passage, "and his name is Nathan b. Ẓuẓita" does not occur. See also *Ḥibbur Yafeh min ha-Yeshu'ah* of Nissim Gaon (ed. by H.Z. Hirschberg (1954), 73–76), from which it appears that he lived in the tannaitic period.

BIBLIOGRAPHY: Hyman, Toledot, 956f.; J.N. Epstein, in: MGWJ, 63 (1919), 259–68; S. Abramson, *Rav Nissim Ga'on* (1965), 422f.

[David Joseph Bornstein]

NATHAN HA-BAVLI ("the Babylonian"; middle of the second century C.E.), *tanna*. It is said of Rabbi *Judah ha-Nasi and Rabbi Nathan that they constituted "the conclusion of the Mishnah" (BM 86a), i.e., that they were the outstanding scholars of the close of the tannaitic period. Like other prominent figures of the last generations of *tannaim*, Nathan's statements are rarely quoted in the Mishnah – only twice, and even those two passages are additions which do not appear in the manuscripts. In one passage he interpreted Psalms 119:126 to mean: "They have made void the law because it was a time to work for the Lord" (Ber. 9:5). The other passage lays it down that "The surplus of money collected for burial … is used to build a monument over the grave" (Shek. 2:5). On the other hand, he is quoted by name over 60 times in the Tosefta, and over 100 times in tannaitic midrashim, mostly in midrashim of the school of R. Ishmael. It was reported that he had a Mishnah collection of his own (Tem. 16a). Nathan's appellation "ha-Bavli" ("the Babylonian") is only mentioned in one tannaitic source, and even then only in the Vienna manuscript of the Tosefta (Tosef. Shab. 15:8) in the talmudic parallels of this tradition (Shab. 134a, Ḥul. 47b; cf TJ Ket. 4:11, 29a). According to a geonic tradition (see *Arukh* s.v. *kamra*), he was the *exilarch. He transmitted traditions in the names of *Ishmael (Tosef. Shab. 1:13), *Eliezer b. Hyrcanus (Tosef. Pes. 3:8), *Tarfon (Tosef. Zev. 10:13), and *Yose ha-Gelili (Men. 38b). When the Hadrianic persecutions broke out he fled to his native Babylon. He is reported to have traveled overseas to a number of countries, including Cappadocia (Ḥul. 47b). When *Hananiah the nephew of Joshua b. Hananiah fixed the calendar in Babylon, Nathan was one of the two scholars who were sent to remonstrate with him and succeeded in persuading him to desist (TJ, Ned. 6:13 40a; Sanh. 1:2, 19a). He is cited as the one who transmitted the important halakhic rule that if A owes B money and B owes C, then C may claim from A (Ket. 19a; see **Shi'buda de-Rabbi Nathan*). In later tradition he was considered to be the author of **Avot de-Rabbi Nathan* and of the 49 *hermeneutical rules of Rabbi Nathan. He was regarded as an authority on civil law because of his experience as a *dayyan* (BK 39a; BM 117b). According to the *aggadah* (Git. 70a), the prophet Elijah appeared to him and taught him. Among the aggadic sayings ascribed to him are: "One may modify a statement in the interest of peace" (Yev. 65b); "Do not taunt your neighbor with your own blemish" (BM 59b); and "There is no greater love than love of the Torah; there is no wisdom like the wisdom of Ereẓ Israel, and there is no beauty like the beauty of Jerusalem" (ARN, 28, 85).

According to an *aggadah* in the Babylonian Talmud Nathan was *av bet din* under the *nasi* *Simeon b. Gamaliel, at the time R. Meir was the *ḥakham* (Hor. 13b). According to this tradition Simeon b. Gamaliel took steps to strengthen the status and honor of his office at the expense of these other two sages, which Meir and Nathan took as a personal affront. Nathan and Meir engaged in a conspiracy to discredit Simeon b. Gamaliel and to remove him from office. Their plan was foiled and Simeon in turn attempted, unsuccessfully, to have them removed from the *bet ha-midrash*. Nevertheless, as a punishment for their opposition to the *nasi*, it was decreed that all subsequent statements made by Meir and Nathan should be introduced anonymously, the former being quoted merely as "others say" and the latter as "some say" (Hor. 13b–14a). While some scholars have held that this story accurately reflects the forms of communal leadership practiced during the late tannaitic period, and have also accepted it as evidence for a power struggle between these well-known historical figures, Goodblatt has shown quite convincingly that this story is in fact a late Babylonian elaboration and embellishment of certain earlier Palestinian traditions (cf. TJ MK 3:1, 81c), and has little or no historical value.

BIBLIOGRAPHY: Hyman, Toledot, 949–53; J. Bruell, *Mevo ha-Mishnah*, 1 (1876), 218–23; Frankel, Mishnah, 198–201; Bacher, Tann, 2 (1890), 437–53; Halevy, Dorot, 1 pt. 5 (1923), 3–23; A. Buechler, *Studies in Jewish History* (1956), 160–78; Neusner, Babylonia, 1 (1965), index; M. Baer, *Rashut ha-Golah be-Bavel* (1970), 29 f.; A. Epstein, *Mi-Kadmoniyyot ha-Yehudim-Ketavim*, 2 (1957), 415–7. **ADD. BIBLIOGRAPHY:** D. Goodblatt, in: *Zion*, 49 (1984), 349–74 (Heb.); S. Wald, *BT Pesaḥim III* (2000), 231–33.

[David Joseph Bornstein / Stephen G. Wald (2nd ed.)]

NATHAN OF GAZA (1643/4–1680), one of the central figures of the *Shabbatean movement. His full name was Abraham Nathan b. Elisha Ḥayyim Ashkenazi, but he became famous as Nathan the Prophet of Gaza, and after 1665 his admirers generally called him "the holy lamp" (*buẓina kaddisha*), the honorific given to R. Simeon b. *Yoḥai in the Zohar. His father, Elisha Ḥayyim b. Jacob *Ashkenazi, who had come from Poland or Germany, settled in Jerusalem and for many years served as an emissary of its community, visiting Poland, Germany, Italy, and (frequently) Morocco. He was a respected rabbinical scholar with kabbalistic leanings. Nathan was born in *Jerusalem, probably about 1643/44. His main teacher was the famous talmudist Jacob *Ḥagiz and he seems to have been a brilliant student, quick to understand and of considerable intellectual power. Before he left Jerusalem in 1663, having married the daughter of a wealthy merchant of Gaza, Samuel Lissabonna, and settled in the latter's home town, he must have seen Shabbetai *Ẓevi, then twice his age, in the Jewish quarter of Jerusalem, where Shabbetai lived for almost the whole of 1663. It is also clear that he must have heard a great deal of talk about this strange personality and his tribulations. Strongly attracted by an ascetic way of life, Nathan took up the study of Kabbalah in 1664. The combination of great intellectual and imaginative power which was his main characteristic resulted in his having visions of angels and deceased souls after a short time. He delved deeply into Lurianic Kabbalah, following the ascetic rules laid down by Isaac *Luria. Shortly before or after Purim 1665 he had a significant ecstatic experience accompanied by a prolonged vision (he speaks of 24 hours) of the divine world revealing how its different stages were connected, a vision that differed in many significant details from the Lurianic scheme. Through this revelation he became convinced of the messianic mission of Shabbetai Ẓevi, whose figure he saw engraved on the divine throne. (For his further intensive activities during the following year, see the article on Shabbetai *Ẓevi). When the latter returned from his mission to Egypt and came to see him in Gaza, Nathan finally convinced him of his messianic destiny by producing a pseudepigraphic vision, attributed to a medieval saint, Abraham Ḥasid, who as it were foretold the birth and early history of Shabbetai Ẓevi and confirmed his superior rank.

In his ecstasy Nathan had heard a voice announcing in the name of God that Shabbetai Ẓevi was the Messiah; he therefore became the prophet of the "son of David," the mission that the biblical prophet Nathan had fulfilled for King David. As he had been vouchsafed charismatic gifts since his ecstatic awakening, many people made pilgrimages to him from Palestine, Syria, and Egypt. He showed "the roots of their souls," revealed their secret sins, and prescribed ways to penance. Since his prophetic powers were widely acknowledged as genuine, his endorsement of Shabbetai Ẓevi's messianic claim gave the decisive impetus to the mass movement which swept the Jewish people everywhere. Remaining in Gaza after Shabbetai Ẓevi left for Jerusalem and Smyrna (Izmir), he wrote letters to the Diaspora confirming that redemption was at hand and laying down elaborate kabbalistic rules of penance (*tikkunim*) to be followed by those who wished to usher in the new age. These were widely copied, and the exoteric portions of the ritual were printed in many editions during 1666. It is not known why the rabbis of Jerusalem, the majority of whom (including Jacob Ḥagiz) took a stand against the messianic claims of Shabbetai Ẓevi, did nothing to interfere with Nathan's activities. The fact that the small community of Gaza, including their rabbi, Jacob *Najara, were among his followers, is insufficient explanation. In the summer of 1666, during Shabbetai's confinement in Gallipoli, Nathan composed several kabbalistic tracts of which the *Derush ha-Tanninim* has survived (published in G. Scholem, *Be-Ikkevot Mashi'aḥ*, 1944), glorifying Shabbetai's mystical state since the beginning of creation. His correspondence with Shabbetai Ẓevi during this time, however, is lost.

After receiving the news of Shabbetai's apostasy, he left Gaza early in November 1666, accompanied by a large group of supporters, including his father-in-law and his family. On Nov. 20, 1666, he wrote to Shabbetai Ẓevi from Damascus announcing that he was on his way to see him, apparently on the latter's invitation. By this time he had already begun to sign himself Nathan Benjamin, the new name Shabbetai had given him in Gaza when he appointed 12 scholars to represent the 12 tribes of Israel. Nathan's faith in his messiah never wavered, and from the beginning he hinted at mystical reasons which justified the apostasy. Originally he planned to travel by sea via Alexandretta (Iskenderun) but he changed his route and went with his entourage by land, avoiding the larger Jewish communities which had been warned against him by the rabbis of Constantinople. By the end of January 1667 he arrived at Bursa (Brusa), where he was threatened with a ban unless he stayed out of the town and "kept quiet." Dispersing his group he continued with only six associates, including Samuel Gandoor, a scholar from Egypt, who became his constant companion until his death. Before leaving Bursa, he wrote a letter to Shabbetai's brothers in Smyrna, opening a long series of letters, tracts, and other pronouncements defending the apostasy and Shabbetai's continued messianic mission on kabbalistic grounds. Many of these have been preserved. On March 3, 1667, he arrived at a small village near Smyrna, then stayed until April 30 in Smyrna itself; there he met with some of the believers but kept largely to himself. He became very reserved toward all outsiders and even repelled the delegation of three northern Italian communities who were on their way to Shabbetai Ẓevi and had been waiting to hear Nathan's explanations. The Dutch clergyman Th. Coenen has left a description of his meeting with Nathan on April 25. Nathan tried to reach Adrianople, where he would see his messiah, but he was held up in the nearby small community of Ipsala and met by a delegation from Adrianople and Constantinople. After being interrogated he was forced to sign a document (dated May 31, 1667) promising not to approach Adrianople, not to correspond with "that man" in Adrianople, and not to convene public meetings, but to keep to himself; finally he admitted that all his words would be given the lie unless the messiah appeared before September 14, a date he had fixed earlier on the strength of an additional vision. Later Nathan repudiated all these obligations, claiming that he had acted under duress. He went to see Shabbetai Ẓevi secretly, then wandered with Gandoor through Thrace and Greece where sympathy with the movement was still very strong.

Early in 1668 he traveled from Janina to Corfu, where he held secret conclaves with his adherents. On the initiative of Shabbetai Ẓevi himself he then undertook a journey to Italy, with the intention of carrying out a mystic ritual at the seat of the pope in Rome. His arrival in Venice around March 20 caused considerable excitement and apprehension. Under pressure from someone in the government, he was allowed to enter the ghetto where he spent approximately two weeks, being closely questioned by the rabbis but also beleaguered by a host of admirers and followers. The events of Ipsala were repeated; the rabbis published the results of their examination in a broadsheet, including a declaration in which Nathan admitted his errors; later Nathan repudiated this in statements to the believers. From Venice he and Gandoor traveled to Bologna, Florence, and Leghorn, where he stayed for some weeks strengthening the hopes of the remaining believers. He and a wealthy Italian believer, Moses Cafsuto, then proceeded to Rome, perhaps disguised as gentiles. He stayed a few days only (end of May or beginning of June) performing some secret rituals patterned on those outlined at an earlier time by Solomon *Molcho. He returned to Leghorn or, according to another source, went straight to Ancona, where he was recognized and met the rabbi, Mahalalel *Halleluyah (Alleluyah), a fervent believer, who has left a detailed account of their meeting. By that time Nathan had written an account of his mission to Rome, couched in elusive Aramaic filled with kabbalistic and apocalyptic metaphors. This was widely distributed to the groups of believers. On his return to Turkey via Ragusa and Durazzo, Nathan went to stay for some time with Shabbetai Ẓevi in Adrianople. After this he spent six months in Salonika, where a considerable group of scholars flocked to him to receive his new version of the Kabbalah according to Shabbatean principles. For the next ten years he remained in Macedonia and Bulgaria – apart from secret pilgrimages to Shabbetai Ẓevi after the latter's banishment to Dulcigno in Albania (1673 – staying mainly in Sofia, Adrianople, and Kastoria, and paying occasional visits to Salonika. He maintained close contacts with many other leaders of the movement, who continued to consider him as a charismatic figure of the highest rank. Although Shabbetai Ẓevi never asked him to follow him into Islam, he staunchly defended not only the necessity of the messiah's apostasy but also those "elect ones" who emulated him on his command. Many of the rabbis of the Macedonian communities stood by him, paying no heed to the excommunications and warnings emanating from Constantinople and Adrianople.

Nathan's letters reveal him as a strong personality, although the few that have been preserved from his intense correspondence with Shabbetai Ẓevi are couched in adoring and submissive terms. They contrast curiously with his obvious moral and intellectual superiority over his master. In spite of all this, there were periods of tension between the two. After Shabbetai's death Nathan withdrew even more from public contact, although he continued to preach in the synagogues of Sofia on some occasions. Refusing to admit defeat, he upheld the theory that Shabbetai Ẓevi had only "disappeared" or gone into hiding in some higher sphere, whence he would return in God's own time. Israel Ḥazzan of Kastoria, who served as his secretary for about three years, took down many of his teachings and sayings after Shabbetai's death. Nathan continued to lead an ascetic life and, feeling that his end was near, left Sofia and went to Skoplje (èskśb), where he died on Jan. 11, 1680. His grave was revered as that of a saint, and over the generations many Shabbateans made pilgrimages there. His tombstone, whose inscription has been preserved, was destroyed during World War II. The many legends spread about Nathan during his lifetime increased after his death. He had two sons, of whose fate nothing is known. A sketch of Nathan drawn by a ship's mate who saw him in Gaza in the summer of 1665, which was reproduced in several contemporary broadsheets, may be authentic.

Between 1665 and 1679 Nathan embarked on a manifold literary activity. Some of his many letters are in fact theological treatises. At first, he composed kabbalistic rules and meditations for a fast of six consecutive days, *Seder Hafsakah Gedolah shel Shishah Yamim ve-Shishah Leilot*, partly printed anonymously under the title *Sefer le-Hafsakah Gedolah* (Smyrna, 1732). These were accompanied by *Tikkunei Teshuvah*, both treatises being preserved in several manuscripts. The printed edition omits all mention of Shabbetai Ẓevi's name. At about the same time he began the explanation of his new vision of the process of creation, sending several tracts on this to Raphael Joseph in Cairo. Of these only the *Derush ha-Tanninim* has been preserved. After Shabbetai's apostasy he developed his ideas in a more radical way. The most elaborate presentation of his kabbalistic system, containing constant references to the function of the Messiah and his paradoxical actions, is found in the *Sefer ha-Beri'ah*, written in 1670, in two parts. It was also known under the title *Raza de-Uvda de-Bereshit*, and in some manuscripts was accompanied by a lengthy preface which may have been conceived as a separate literary entity. The work is extant, complete or in parts, in approximately 30 manuscripts and must have enjoyed a wide distribution in Shabbatean circles up to the middle of the 18th century. A short synopsis of its ideas, from Ms. Oxford, Neubauer Cat. (Bod.) no. 2394, is included in Scholem's *Be-Ikkevot Mashi'aḥ*. During the same period Nathan composed the book *Zemir Ariẓim* which, as well as other kabbalistic matters, contains long disquisitions on the state of the Torah in the messianic era and a justification of Shabbetai Ẓevi's antinomian actions (complete in British Museum Or. 4536, Margoliouth, Cat, no. 856 and elsewhere). In some manuscripts it was called *Derush ha-Menorah* and was partly included in the collection *Be-Ikkevot Mashi'aḥ*. These books were widely quoted by secret Shabbateans, sometimes even in printed works. Of his many pastoral letters, special mention must be made of the long apology for Shabbetai Ẓevi, published in *Koveẓ al Yad*, 6 (1966), 419–56, apparently written about 1673–74. Fragments of other writings are dispersed through several manuscripts and Shabbatean notebooks. Collections dealing with his special customs and behavior were made by his pupils in Salonika (who saw him as a reincarnation of Luria) and were distributed in Turkey and Italy. These are extant in several versions. An abridgment of Nathan's system was incorporated as the first part of the *Sha'arei Gan Eden* by Jacob Koppel b. Moses of *Mezhirech and was published as an authoritative kabbalistic text (Korets, 1803) without its heretical character being recognized.

BIBLIOGRAPHY: G. Scholem, Shabbetai Ẓevi, passim, esp. chs. 3, 7–8; idem, *Be-Ikkevot Mashi'aḥ* (1944), a collection of Nathan's writings; idem, in: *Alei Ayin, Minḥat Devarim le-S.Z. Schocken* (1948–52), 157–211; idem, in: *H.A. Wolfson Jubilee Volume* (1965), 225–41 (Heb. sect.); C. Wirszubski, in: *Keneset, Divrei Soferim le-Zekher Ḥ.N. Bialik*, 8 (1943–44), 2nd pagination 210–46; idem, in: *Koveẓ Hoẓa'at Schocken le-Divrei Sifrut* (1941), 180–92; I. Tishby, in: *Tarbiz*, 15 (1943/44), 161–80; idem, in: KS, 21 (1945), 12–17; idem, in: *Sefunot*, 1 (1956), 80–117; idem, *Netivei Emunah ve-Minut* (1964), 30–80, 204–26, 280–95, 331–43.

[Gershom Scholem]

NATHANS, DANIEL (1928–1999), U.S. Nobel laureate in medicine (1978). Nathans was born in Wilmington, Delaware, of Orthodox Jewish immigrants from Latvia and graduated in chemistry from the University of Delaware (1950) and in medicine from Washington University, St Louis, in 1954. His career in medical research began at the Rockefeller Institute in 1959 with work on protein synthesis before he switched to animal viruses, specifically the DNA virus SV40. During a 1969 sabbatical at the Weizmann Institute with Leo *Sachs and Ernest Winocour, Nathans realized the relevance of the newly discovered restriction enzymes to viral research. These enzymes cut DNA at specific sites, providing DNA fragments whose genetic function can be precisely mapped. Daniel's mapping of the SV40 gene pioneered the application of restriction enzyme techniques to genetics and was an essential step in the development of molecular cloning and recombinant technology. He was awarded the Nobel Prize for this work, jointly with Werner Arber and Hamilton Smith. His later interest in the genetic regulation of cell growth led him to study the response of cellular genes to growth factors. He moved to Johns Hopkins University in 1962, where he served as chairman of the Department of Microbiology and university president and was revered for his teaching and organizational skills. His honors included election to the U.S. National Academy of Sciences and the National Medal of Science.

[Michael Denman (2nd ed.)]

NATHANSEN, HENRI (1868–1944), Danish playwright and novelist. Born in Hjørring, Jutland, Nathansen practiced law before becoming a writer. He published some 20 works, nearly half of them plays, and in 1909 became stage director of Copenhagen's Royal Theater. Many of his plays dealt with contemporary Jewish problems. The drama *Daniel Hertz* (1908) was followed in 1912 by *Indenfor murene* ("Within the Walls") considered to be one of the finest plays in the Danish language. Nathansen here analyzes the position of the Jew in a non-Jewish environment and, in portraying the conflicts engendered by a Copenhagen Jewess' wish to marry a gentile, succeeds in airing the whole question of Jewish-Christian relations in a free society. Jewish themes also dominate Nathansen's comedy *Affaeren* (1913), the semi-autobiographical novel *Af Hugo Davids liv* (4 vols., 1917), and the last work published in his lifetime, the novel *Mendel Philipsen og Sön* (1932). His other outstanding publications include a biography of Georg *Brandes (1929) and *Portraetstudier* (1930), studies of eminent Scandinavian writers. In 1919 Nathansen issued a protest against the persecution of Polish Jewry, and in 1930 called for solidarity in the Copenhagen Jewish community to counteract the dangers of Nazi antisemitism. Together with the majority of Danish Jews, he fled to Sweden in October 1943. There, in a fit of depression, he took his own life.

BIBLIOGRAPHY: *Dansk Biografisk Leksikon*, 16 (1939); *Dansk Skönlitteraert Forfatterleksikon*, 3 (1964).

[Torben Meyer]

NATHANSON, BERNHARD (Dov Baer; 1832–1916), Hebrew writer, biographer, and lexicographer. Born in Satanov, Podolia, Nathanson was a contributor to *Ha-Maggid* and *Ha-Meliẓ*. After the death of I.B. *Levinsohn in 1860 he was commissioned to prepare Levinsohn's manuscripts for publication, a task to which he devoted most of his literary career. He wrote a popular biography of Levinsohn, *Sefer ha-Zikhronot* (1876). Nathanson also compiled *Ma'arekhet Sifrei Kodesh* (1870), a Jewish historical lexicon, and *Sefer ha-Millim* (1880), a dictionary of foreign words.

BIBLIOGRAPHY: N. Sokolow (ed.), *Sefer Zikkaron* (1889), 73f.; Frenk, in: *Ha-Ẓefirah* (1916), no. 45–47; Kressel, Leksikon, 2 (1967), 466.

[Yehuda Slutsky]

NATHANSON, JOSEPH SAUL (1810–1875), **posek*. Nathanson was born in Berezhany, the son of Aryeh Leibush Nathanson of Brody, a wealthy businessman who was also a profound talmudist. In 1825 he married Sarah Idel, the daughter of Isaac Aaron Ettinger, who was also a great scholar and a wealthy man. Nathanson, as was customary in those days, was maintained in his father-in-law's home. When his father-in-law died shortly after his marriage, his mother-in-law administered the business and took care that he would be able to live and study without financial cares, and when she died in 1841, his wife took over the responsibility. In his father-in-law's house Nathanson found a colleague in his brother-in-law, Mordecai Ze'ev *Ettinger. They studied together for several years and compiled a series of halakhic works, but they separated as a result of a difference of opinion which came to a head on the question of the permissibility of machine-baked *matzah*. The two brothers-in-law were rival candidates for the rabbinate of Lemberg to which Nathanson was appointed in 1857. The same year his wife died, but in 1858 he married a wealthy woman and did not accept a salary.

Nathanson was the outstanding *posek* and writer of responsa of his generation. Problems reached him from all parts of the world and he corresponded with all the great contemporary scholars. In his works he is revealed principally as an instructor in practical *halakhah*. He regarded himself as responsible for the condition of *halakhah* in his time, in succession to such scholars as Akiva *Eger and Moses *Sofer. He was opposed to the method of **pilpul* for its own sake, regarding it as suitable only for youths (*Divrei Sha'ul*, *Aggadot*, 29b) but not for those destined to be religious teachers. He did not necessarily base his decisions "upon the statements of *aḥaronim*" (*Sho'el u-Meshiv*, 2 pt. 3, no. 108), but based his rulings mainly upon the Talmud and the *rishonim*.

He tended to leniency in his rulings, and took contemporary circumstances into consideration. He was one of those who permitted machine-baked *matzah* in opposition to the view of Solomon *Kluger. Although Kluger decided that **etrogim* from Corfu were invalid because of the fear that they were hybrids, Nathanson permitted them (*Yosef Da'at*, *Kilei Begadim*, no. 302). He also regarded the birds called "kibbitzer" hens as permitted according to the dietary laws although other authorities forbade them (*Sho'el u-Meshiv*, 3 pt. 2, no. 121). Although known for his permissive approach, he sometimes declared things forbidden simply as a precaution (*Yosef Da'at*, *Terefot*, 64–65). It was this which prompted

Dov Berush *Meisels, rabbi of Warsaw, to say of him: "I know him of old as one who adopts a stringent and not a lenient line" (end of the pamphlet *Moda'ah le-Veit Yisrael*). Despite his leniency in halakhic ruling, he fought with all his power against the progressives in his community who wanted to introduce reforms into education. When the government sought to compel the Jews of Galicia to send their children to government schools and to bar them from the *ḥeder* until they had passed four classes of the secular schools, as well as to make the teachers pass an examination in German and pedagogy, Nathanson took the initiative in uniting the great talmudic scholars to obtain the repeal of the edict (see S. Kluger's letter of 1867 in *Toledot Shelomo* (1956), 113ff.).

On the other hand he was resolutely opposed to schism, and when Zalman Spitzer, the son-in-law of Moses Sofer, published a proclamation calling on 400 rabbis to sign a ban against the payment of taxes to communities whose leaders were progressives, he declined to sign because it would lead to discord. He also maintained harmonious relations with the preachers of the "temple" (i.e., Reform synagogue), Dr. Simeon Schwabacher and Bernhard Loewenstein.

Nathanson was completely opposed to the ḥasidic movement and its new customs. As such he upheld the Ashkenazi *minhag* opposing the custom of reciting *Hallel in the synagogues on Passover eve (*Sho'el u-Meshiv*, 2 pt. 4, no. 135) and the custom of not donning *tefillin* during the intermediate days of the festivals (*ibid.*, 2 pt. 3, no. 87). Despite his opposition to Ḥasidism, however, he respected their leaders if they were great scholars and quoted them in his works. While still a youth in the house of his grandfather in Berezhany, he made the acquaintance of the ḥasidic rabbi Abraham David of Buczacz and wrote a commendation for his *Da'at Kedoshim* (1880). In his own works he quotes Levi Isaac of Berdichev (*Divrei Sha'ul* on the Pentateuch, passim), and among the other ḥasidic leaders he had great respect for Isaac Meir Alter, author of the *Ḥiddushei ha-Rim*, and was on friendly terms with Ḥayyim Halberstamm, the author of the *Divrei Ḥayyim*.

Although mainly occupied with *halakhah*, Nathanson devoted part of his time to biblical study, and wrote *Divrei Sha'ul*, on the Pentateuch and the Five *Scrolls. He applied himself to the study of Kabbalah, but like the other great *posekim* of his generation refrained from quoting it in support of the *halakhah (Sho'el u-Meshiv*, 2 pt. 3, no. 87). He was also versed in the scientific works of the Middle Ages and applied modern methods in practical halakhic rulings, such as ordering a chemical analysis to determine the presence of an admixture of forbidden matter in food (*ibid.*, 3 pt. 1, no. 377). He lectured to his students twice daily (*ibid.*, 2 pt. 3, no. 101). He did not prepare his lesson in advance, but involved his pupils in the discussions, and his lesson became a workshop for his novellae. Among his distinguished pupils were Ze'ev Wolf Salat, the publisher of his responsa, and Ẓevi Hirsch Ornstein. He supported talmudic scholars and authors, and Solomon Buber testified of him that "without exaggeration there are extant 300 commendations by him," so that he was designated *Sar ha-Maskim* ("chief approver," a pun on Gen. 40:9).

Besides the works he compiled with his brother-in-law Moses Ze'ev Ettinger, Nathanson wrote a series of works in *halakhah* and *aggadah*. His classic work in *halakhah* is his responsa *Sho'el u-Meshiv* (1865–90), in six volumes comprising 15 parts. He was also the author of *Divrei Sha'ul veha-Sefer Yosef Da'at* (1878–79) on the Shulḥan Arukh, *Yoreh De'ah*, in two parts; *Yad Yosef ve-Yad Sha'ul* (1851); *Hilkhot Nedarim*; Shulḥan Arukh (YD 203–35), *Beit Sha'ul*, on the Mishnah (in the Romm Vilna edition); *Divrei Sha'ul* (1877), on the *aggadot* of the Talmud; *Divrei Sha'ul* (1875), on the Pentateuch and the five scrolls, in two parts; *Divrei Sha'ul ve-hu Sefer Ḥelek le-Shivah* (1879), on the *Naḥalat Shivah* of Samuel b. David ha-Levi; *Torat Moshe*, on the *Torat Ḥattat* of Moses Isserles (in: *Ḥamishah Sefarim Niftaḥim* (1859)); novellae glosses on the four parts of the Shulḥan Arukh; *Melekh be-Yofyo* (1866), a sermon calling to contribute to the Austrian war effort; *Avodat ha-Leviyyim* on the *Torat ha-Adam; Divrei Sha'ul ve-hu Sefer Edut bi-Yhosef* on the topics of Maimonides' *Mishneh Torah* and part of the Shulḥan Arukh; and *Ẓiyyon vi-Yrushalayim*, on the Jerusalem Talmud (in the Zhitomir edition). Many works and articles have remained unpublished.

BIBLIOGRAPHY: *Der Israelit*, 16 (1875), 258; Fuenn, Keneset, 483f.; S. Buber, in: *Ha-Maggid*, 19 (1875), 83; *Anshei Shem* (1895), 97–99; S.M. Chones, *Toledot ha-Posekim* (1910), 277f.; A. Stern, *Meliẓei Esh al Ḥodshei Adar* (1938), 69b no. 336; M. Leiter, in: *Hadorom*, 29 (1969), 146–70; 31 (1970), 171–202; A. Bromberg, *Ha-Ga'on Rabbi Yosef Sha'ul Nathanson mi-Levov* (1960); EG, 4 (1956), 417f.; D. Halachmi, *Ḥakhmei Yisrael* (1957), 318f.; N. Herskovicz, in: *Or ha-Mizraḥ*, 20 (1970/71), 63–72.

[Shillem Warhaftig]

NATHANSON, MENDEL LEVIN (1780–1868), Danish merchant and editor. Born in Altona, Nathanson went to Copenhagen at the age of 12 to join relatives. In 1798 he settled down as a wholesale draper and until 1831 was a prosperous businessman. Later on he wrote works on economics and in 1838 became editor of the *Berlingske Tidende*, making it the leading newspaper in Denmark. Nathanson was a tireless exponent of the emancipation of Danish Jews. Through his initiative the Jewish Free School for boys was founded in Copenhagen in 1805 and five years later a similar school for girls. He organized the administration of the Jewish community, favoring the religious Reform movement, and had a large share in the Danish government's edict of March 29, 1814 which gave the Jews equal rights. His writings on economics are still studied, especially his historical and statistical presentation of Denmark's administration of public revenues up to 1836. Of special Jewish interest is his history of the Jews in Denmark, *Historisk Fremstilling af Jødernes Forhold og Stilling i Danmark* (1860). Nathanson's children all converted to Christianity.

BIBLIOGRAPHY: G. Siesby, *Mendel Levin Nathanson: En biographisk Skizze* (1845); I. Luplan Janssen, *Mendel Levin Nathanson og hans Slaegt* (1960).

[Julius Margolinsky]

NATIONAL CONFERENCE ON SOVIET JEWRY. At the initiative of Rabbi Abraham Joshua *Heschel, a leading Jewish religious figure active in the American civil rights movement, and of Jewish political leaders, the Jewish community had begun to explore strategies to address the plight of Soviet Jews as early as 1963. In April 1964, with Rabbi Heschel's encouragement, and the guidance of Senators Jacob *Javits and Abraham *Ribicoff, as well as Associate Justice Arthur J. *Goldberg, Jewish organizational leaders gathered at the historic Willard Hotel in the nation's capital. Their mission was to articulate the Jewish community's concerns for Soviet Jews, and to engage fellow Americans in their defense.

The convening of an American Jewish Conference on Soviet Jewry (AJCSJ) concluded with a decision to create a continuing but ad hoc arrangement to mobilize the organized Jewish community. Many voices were opposed to the creation of a free-standing advocacy effort, including the leadership of the Conference of Presidents of Major American Jewish Organizations and the National Jewish Community Relations Advisory Council, who were reluctant to see a new, independent organization that might diminish their own central roles in the Jewish community. Some personalities, such as Nahum *Goldmann, feared that aggressive activities would be seen as anti-Soviet and lead to the worsening of the situation for Soviet Jews.

The Israelis, acting under the aegis of the office known as the *Lishkat ha-Kesher* (Contact Office), responsible to the prime minister, were virtually the architects of the new coalition. The rescue of Soviet Jewry was an important task that the Israeli government thought that the people of Israel could not undertake directly and certainly not on their own.

At about the same time other organizations emerged that argued against the seemingly more orderly "establishment" approach of the AJCSJ, or even its more activist successor, the National Conference on Soviet Jewry. This included the Union of Councils for Soviet Jewry, a loose coalition of local activist groups from across the country, and the Student Struggle for Soviet Jewry, launched several weeks after the initial AJCSJ meeting.

Joining such personalities in trying to energize the Jewish world was the eminent author Elie *Wiesel whose visit to the Soviet Union led to his forceful book *The Jews of Silence*. Then only emerging as a voice of conscience, Wiesel linked this effort of rescue with the failure to rescue one generation earlier. He also appealed for the silent Jews in the free West, who had a free choice, to become engaged on behalf of their coreligionists.

In the face of mounting harassment against Soviet Jews, and with the prodding of Israeli officials, the Council of Jewish Federations, the National Jewish Community Relations Advisory Council, and other leading Jewish organizations agreed to fashion the National Conference on Soviet Jewry out of the older AJCSJ.

The newly minted NCSJ began to function in June 1971 and eventually encompassed a massive network of over 50 national Jewish organizations and several hundred local Jewish federations and community relations councils. This extensive coalition would spearhead the advocacy campaign for Soviet Jews for the next 20 years, until the collapse of the Soviet Union and the easing of anti-Jewish restrictions.

The NCSJ created an ever-expanding network of support groups to engage a broad range of citizens, including non-Jews. This included doctors, Congressional Wives (later Congressional Spouses) for Soviet Jews, and a special legal team for Soviet Jewish Prisoners of Conscience.

Concluding that public attention must be focused, NCSJ became more aggressive in its efforts with the national media, the power brokers in Washington, Congress and the administration, and stimulated "grass roots" activism through its member groups. It accelerated local community and synagogue activities as part of a year-round program. To help safeguard individuals in the Soviet Union, and focus attention on the specifics of their cases, the NCSJ created links to Jewish activists in the Soviet Union through visits, telephone calls, and letter writing. Such activities also helped personalize the movement for people thousands of miles away.

Using the expanding concept of politicizing the campaign, the NCSJ fostered meetings with and programs of letter writing to government officials in Moscow and Washington, and organized conferences, public meetings and demonstrations targeting the Soviet Union so that it would loosen anti-Jewish restrictions. It also maintained constant contact with U.S. officials to reinforce their involvement with Soviet officials.

As a result the NCSJ came to be recognized by the White House as acting on behalf of the organized Jewish community in regard to the Soviet treatment of its Jewish citizens. With its broad reach the NCSJ could organize nationwide appeals and petitions, such as the delivery of over one million names to the White House prior to President Richard Nixon's visit to Moscow to meet Soviet leader Leonid Brezhnev.

A major crisis developed following the May 1972 summit meeting between Nixon and Brezhnev, when the Soviet government announced a special tax on would-be emigrants, labeled a "ransom tax." The exorbitant fees embarrassed an administration seeking détente with Moscow, and led to strong reactions. In the United States members of Congress, under the leadership of Senator Henry "Scoop" Jackson and Congressman Charles Vanik, joined with the NCSJ to create legislation linking trade benefits to emigration practices, an effort supported by the UCSJ and the SSSJ.

Despite powerful opposition from the Nixon Administration, a successful two-year campaign served as an effective means of popularizing the issues as well as inflicting additional pressure on Moscow. It also demonstrated how far the Jewish community had come in honing its political skills and resisting high-level political pressure by standing firm on principles.

The Jewish world was again threatened by a divisive issue that erupted over the destination point for Jews finally allowed to leave the Soviet Union. The NCSJ took no formal position. Rather, it attempted to focus on the issues of the right to leave, an end to antisemitism, and the right to recreate Jewish life. But it did support the decision of Jewish refuseniks in the Soviet Union and of Israeli authorities to support direct flights to Israel. This position was based on invitations from Israel, which helped secure the permits to emigrate, and the Zionist orientation of the refuseniks. The UCSJ and others rejected the Israeli plan and pressed for a so-called "freedom of choice" solution. That decision antagonized many of the Zionist organizations in the NCSJ as well as the government of Israel and the Jewish Agency, the instrument for easing emigration to Israel.

Putting aside the controversy over destination, the campaign reached its zenith in the 1980s with a defining moment. On December 6, 1987, on the eve of President Ronald Reagan's first summit meeting in the United States with General Secretary of the Communist Party Mikhail S. Gorbachev, 250,000 people marched in the nation's capital. Christian dignitaries and members of Congress joined Jews from every state as well as leaders of different ethnic groups, students and labor leaders. It was the largest national event ever held in Washington for any Jewish cause.

Organized under the aegis of a special task force created by the NCSJ, the Student Struggle for Soviet Jewry and the Union of Councils for Soviet Jews had been invited to cooperate and help create a wall-to-wall effort. While they could not bring a mass of people needed to give form to the broad scope of the movement, a demonstration of unity was critical.

The march and the broad media coverage did in fact signal to Gorbachev that the Soviet Union would not be considered part of the family of modern, industrial nations until its persecution of Jews and other minorities halted. Within a few years over one million Jews had been allowed to leave for Israel and elsewhere, while Jewish cultural and religious life was allowed to reorganize.

The struggle for Soviet Jews had encouraged the Jewish community in the United States to develop a strategy that encompassed strong national as well as localized efforts, with a strong political overlay. Jews had entered the political mainstream in an aggressive manner. As a result of the experience the community was better prepared in the future to utilize the political process to protect Jews wherever they were threatened. It was a powerful lesson not to be lost.

The Soviet Jewry movement brought together survivors of the Holocaust, their children and their grandchildren. It energized Zionists and non-Zionists as well as secular and religious Jews. Rabbis spoke from the pulpits of synagogues and came down from them; they were joined by Christian clergy of many denominations.

It mobilized activists from the American civil rights movement, who transferred their zeal and their experiences to this new campaign. It enlisted human rights advocates.

Within two decades after the Holocaust, the Jewish community had developed a sense of confidence lacking in earlier years. With this increasing self-confidence it learned how to identify the levers of power, and how to use them. The campaign was an exemplary use of "soft weapons" to achieve Jewish and human rights objectives, rather than call for or rely upon hard or military weapons.

[Jerry Goodman (2nd ed.)]

NATIONAL COUNCIL OF JEWISH WOMEN (NCJW), U.S. national organization, was founded by Hannah Greenebaum *Solomon in 1893, when she and other Jewish women from across the country gathered to participate in the World Parliament of Religions at the Chicago World Exposition. The National Council of Jewish Women undertook a wide range of religious, philanthropic, and educational activities, from organizing vocational training for Jewish women and girls, to managing settlement houses and offering free baths to poor urban dwellers. Starting with the belief that those in need required skills instead of alms, "friendly visitors" acted as pioneer social workers and family aides. Council sections sponsored free libraries, employment bureaus, kindergartens, day nurseries, and projects providing summer outings for children. They also established Sabbath schools in communities without synagogues.

When Jewish immigrants began to arrive in the United States in great numbers at the turn of the century, the council met and cared for incoming women and girls, creating a permanent immigration-aid station at Ellis Island in 1904. Representatives in 250 American cities and in European ports assisted the girls with immigration problems and protected them from white slavery. NCJW also promoted English classes and job-skills training, and guided girls to employment and lodging. The National Council of Jewish Women combined social action with local service, assisting with programs to help poor children with free milk, penny lunches, and health programs in school. In 1909 the council participated in President Taft's White House Conference on Child Welfare, and in 1911 it set forth its first complete program for social legislation, including regulation of child labor, low-income housing, civil rights, public-health programs, and food and drug regulations. After World War I, the council helped thousands of refugees stranded in internment camps as the U.S. tightened its immigration laws. Out of the rescue work came the International Council of Jewish Women, which is today a network of Jewish women in 47 countries. During the 1920s the council sponsored classes for unemployed workers and brought health care to Jewish people in isolated rural communities.

When Nazism brought a new wave of refugees, the council participated in the formation of the National Coordinating Committee for Aid to Refugees and Emigrants Coming from Germany, which became the National Refugee Service. In the post–World War II period, it established homes for unattached girls in Paris and Athens to help victims of the European Holocaust. To help rebuild Jewish welfare and educational institutions, it brought educators and welfare workers from Israel and Jewish communities abroad to the U.S.

for advanced training, with the stipulation that they return home to use their new skills. Toys and educational supplies were sent to children's institutions in Europe, and to Israel, Morocco, and Tunisia. In Israel the council began to assist the Hebrew University's teacher education program, helping to establish its John Dewey School of Education and building a campus for the Hebrew University High School in 1959. In 1968, it established the Research Institute for Innovation in Education, to educate Israeli children who are socially at risk, at the Hebrew University in Jerusalem. In the 1960s the National Council of Jewish Women had more than 100,000 members in communities throughout the U.S. Council women were pioneers of the Head Start pre-school program and the Golden Age Clubs (the first nationwide network providing recreation for seniors). The council has participated in interfaith efforts to assist low-income women, and adopted a major national program to promote day-care facilities in communities across the country.

BIBLIOGRAPHY: H.G. Solomon, *Fabric of My Life* (1946). **ADD. BIBLIOGRAPHY:** F. Rogow, *Gone to Another Meeting: The National Council of Jewish Women, 1893–1993* (1993).

[Hannah Stein]

NATIONAL FEDERATION OF TEMPLE SISTERHOODS (**Women of Reform Judaism**), national organization of synagogue women's organizations dedicated to promoting Reform Judaism, founded in 1913. This organization, renamed the Women of Reform Judaism in 1993, counted 75,000 members in 500 local affiliates in the United States, Canada, and 12 other countries in 2005. Founding President Carrie Obendorfer Simon did not want NFTS to duplicate the work of existing Jewish women's organizations, especially that of the *National Council of Jewish Women, which in 1913 focused especially on immigrant aid. Instead, Simon saw NFTS carrying the banner of religious spirit forward in Jewish congregational life. Although she initially invited women from synagogue sisterhoods of all denominations to join NFTS, within a decade sisterhood women in both Conservative and Orthodox synagogues would create their own national associations.

At its inception NFTS declared that it would use the forum of a broad, public organization to further Jewish women's responsibilities to Reform Judaism, its synagogues, religious schools, seminary, and the wider Jewish community. NFTS encouraged its members to attend services weekly, to beautify their synagogues, and to be involved with their synagogue religious schools and the education their children received there. Reform Jewish women extended their mandate for youth work to rabbis-in-training, funding scholarships and building a dormitory at Hebrew Union College in 1925. After World War II, its leaders helped create the North American Federation of Temple Youth (NFTY) for Reform Jewish high school students.

For decades, the guiding light behind NFTS was executive director Jane Evans. Joining NFTS in 1933 at the height of the Great Depression, Evans pushed Reform Jewish women to look beyond the confines of the synagogue and to engage the great issues of the day. Subsequently, its members took stances on access to birth control, civil rights, fair employment practices, and a host of other issues important to American women. In 1963, NFTS voted overwhelmingly in favor of their movement's considering women's ordination. A decade later they endorsed the Equal Rights Amendment.

Through NFTS, sisterhood women exercised a collective voice. Although they shared the public spaces of their synagogues and Reform Judaism's national institutions with their husbands and sons, NFTS nationally and through its local chapters allowed women a venue for the creation of a female Reform Jewish culture. Through its programs and shifting interests, the NFTS helped change the expectations of American Jewish women's proper behavior within the portals of their Reform synagogues and ultimately prepared them to enlarge their roles there and in the world.

BIBLIOGRAPHY: P.S. Nadell and R.J. Simon, "Ladies of the Sisterhood: Women in the American Reform Synagogue, 1900–1930," in: M. Sacks, *Active Voices: Women in Jewish Culture* (1995), 63–75; P.S. Nadell. "National Federation of Temple Sisterhoods," in: P.E. Hyman and D. Dash Moore, *Jewish Women in America: An Historical Encyclopedia*, 2 (1997), 979–82; *Proceedings of the National Federation of Temple Sisterhoods* (1913–).

[Pamela S. Nadell (2nd ed.)]

NATIONAL FOUNDATION FOR JEWISH CULTURE (NFJC), U.S. organization that supports Jewish artistic creativity, academic scholarship, and cultural preservation in America. The NFJC was established in 1960 by the Council of Jewish Federations and Welfare Funds (now the United Jewish Communities), following a ground-breaking study on National Jewish Cultural Services in America, chaired by Sidney Vincent of Cleveland, Ohio. The study recommended creating a central organization to respond to the cultural needs of the American Jewish community in the post-war era, particularly in the areas of Jewish Studies, scholarly publication, archives, and libraries. The NFJC's mission expanded in the 1980s to include new creativity in the arts as well as the dissemination of contemporary Jewish culture through national programming and publications.

NFJC provides grants and awards to writers, filmmakers, visual artists, composers, choreographers, playwrights, and scholars. Its national and international conferences, networks of cultural institutions, publications, and partnerships with local communities are intended to help define, interpret, and advance the contours of American Jewish culture for both the Jewish community and the broader American public.

Since its inception, the National Foundation for Jewish Culture has awarded over $2.5 million in Doctoral Dissertations Fellowships to more than 400 graduate students pursuing careers in Jewish Studies. This program, along with the Foundation's early support for the Association of Jewish Studies, and its special grants for publication and research projects, helped fuel the development of the field of Jewish Studies in America in the later decades of the 20th century.

Over a 30-year period, the NFJC allocated almost $10 million to major archival, scholarly, and Yiddish culture organizations through the Joint Cultural Appeal, comprised of allocations from the Jewish Federations of North America. Since 2000, the NFJC has awarded more than $1.2 million on a competitive grants basis through the Fund for Jewish Cultural Preservation to libraries and archives for the preservation of historically important books, archives, manuscripts, periodicals, ritual objects, art and artifacts, photographs, recordings, and films.

In addition, the NFJC was instrumental in establishing and administering both the Council of American Jewish Museums (CAJM) and the Council of Archives and Research Libraries in Jewish Studies (CARLJS) as professional associations to support the cultural infrastructure of American Jewish life.

In the area of the arts, the National Foundation for Jewish Culture encourages and supports new creative expression in a wide variety of disciplines – film, theater, literature, music, dance, and visual arts.

The Fund for Jewish Documentary Filmmaking was created in 1996 with a challenge grant from Steven Spielberg's Righteous Persons Foundation and a matching grant from the Charles H. Revson Foundation. It has awarded 49 grants totaling more than $1.25 million toward the production of documentary films which explore the variety of the Jewish experience. The NFJC has also initiated the Conference of American Jewish Film Festivals which provides a forum for film festival directors, staffs, and volunteers to network and address field-wide concerns.

The New Play Commissions in Jewish Theater has supported the initial development of 69 new plays presented by both mainstream and Jewish theaters. An anthology of *Nine Contemporary Jewish Plays*, selected from these commissions, was published by the University of Texas Press in November 2005. The NFJC also maintains an on-line database of *Plays of Jewish Interest*.

Other grants in the arts include the Goldberg Prize, which recognizes the work of young, emerging Jewish writers, and the Heyman Prize, which recognizes the work of emerging visual artists.

The NFJC also presents the premier annual Jewish recognition awards in the arts and humanities, which include the Jewish Cultural Achievement Awards in Scholarship and Arts, the Jewish Image Awards in Film and Television, the Patron of the Arts Award, and the Alan King Award in American Jewish Humor.

Over the years, the National Foundation for Jewish Culture, with support from the U.S. government's National Endowments for the Arts and Humanities, Jewish foundations, and local Federations, has sponsored a number of seminal conferences and special programmatic initiatives across the country. These have included North American and international conferences in Jewish theater, ethnic music, dance, and literature; artist retreats in the performing arts, visual arts, and music; community-based and institution-based artist-in-residence programs; and public lecture series, film programs, and exhibitions.

The NFJC was instrumental in creating "Celebrate 350," the organizing committee for the celebration of the 350th anniversary of Jewish life in America. Its own 350th programs included the commissioning of "Klezmerbluegrass," a new work by the Paul Taylor Dance Company; the production of "Passover Dreams," a radio special distributed by PRI to over 150 stations nationwide; and a series of national conversations – both live in local communities and virtually over the Internet – on "American Jewish Icons."

The NFJC publishes the semi-annual *Jewish Culture News*, reaching over 20,000 households, which provides context and perspective to the contemporary Jewish experience, and the annual *Jewish Literary Supplement*, with a distribution of over 250,000, as a resource for readers, book groups, and schools. It also has an Internet presence through www.jewishculture.org, with on-line resources, information on Jewish culture, interactive discussions, and links to other Jewish and general culture sites.

[Richard Siegel (2nd ed.)

NATIONAL HAVURAH COMMITTEE (NHC). The National Havurah Committee was founded in 1980 to facilitate the activities of fellowships known as havurot and to spread havurah values and enthusiasm to the larger Jewish community, thereby serving as a model for revitalizing Jewish living and learning in North America. The NHC was organized following a successful conference at Rutgers University in July 1979 that brought together different groups that shared the name "havurah." These included independent havurot that were formed as part of the counterculture of the 1960s, synagogue havurot that were created within Reform and Conservative synagogues, and Reconstructionist congregations that considered themselves havurot. Though differently organized, havurot, now as then, share the mission of creating small communities in which all members participate in creating authentic and meaningful Jewish experiences. Independent havurot also tend to be non-denominational, egalitarian, and inclusive. Havurah leadership is generally shared by the members; havurot typically do not have professional rabbinic or spiritual leaders.

The first NHC Summer Institute (at the University of Hartford in July 1980) was organized to help provide and empower havurah members with the knowledge to grow Jewishly and the skills to enable them to create and sustain such communities. (The first institute was organized and co-chaired by Joseph G. Rosenstein and Michael Strassfeld who, with Elaine S. Cohen, coordinated the 1979 conference; they were the first three chairs of the NHC.) Annual week-long summer institutes have been conducted by the NHC each year since 1980 and have attracted an average of 250 adults (plus many children) of varying Jewish backgrounds and observance. Courses at the institute address the variety of Jewish texts, arts, culture, spirituality, issues, and practice from many different perspectives. Institute teachers are expected to attend as well as to offer courses. The NHC has inclusively recruited teachers from many backgrounds and women instructors when that was considered radical, and served as a prominent forum for discussing feminist perspectives of Judaism in the 1980s. The NHC model of summer programs for lay adults has been adapted by other organizations. Both the longevity of the institute and the replication of the model attest to its success.

Since 1996, an important feature of the summer institute is the participation of the Everett Fellows, a cohort of future leaders of the Jewish community who participate, often for the first time, in a heterogeneous community that manifests both excitement and commitment about Judaism and that embraces diverse ways of living Jewishly. (This program is funded by the Everett Foundation, established by Edith and the late Henry Everett.) Another unique annual feature (since 1995) is the celebratory completion (or *siyyum*) of a volume of the *Encyclopaedia Judaica* by study groups who have read a page a day (*daf yomi*) since the last institute.

The NHC also sponsors regional weekend retreats, including an annual New England retreat (since 1986) and an annual Canadian-American retreat (since 1993), publishes newsletters, and maintains on its website (www.havurah.org) a list of havurot. In the 1990s it published in a number of newspapers a weekly D'var Torah column that were written by a diverse group of writers representing all branches of Judaism, and that served as a prototype for subsequent D'var Torah columns; it also published three issues of a journal with the appropriately oxymoronic title of "New Traditions."

Although havurot and individuals participate in the NHC, it has not functioned as a membership organization; its programs have been organized by a volunteer board with modest staff assistance. The NHC has created and sustained programs and promoted values – such as inclusiveness, lay leadership and teaching, involvement, egalitarianism, fellowship – that have had an impact on the wider Jewish community.

[Joseph G. Rosenstein (2nd ed.)]

NATIONAL JEWISH CENTER FOR IMMUNOLOGY AND RESPIRATORY MEDICINE, non-sectarian hospital and research facility in Denver, Colorado, for respiratory, immune and allergic disorders. As early as the 1860s, hundreds and later thousands of men and women flocked to Colorado to "chase the cure" and seek a remedy for tuberculosis, the most dreaded disease of the era and the leading cause of death in 19th-century America. There was no single accepted treatment standard for tuberculosis or consumption as it was commonly called in the early years, but by 1880 medical opinion emphasized fresh air and high altitude for respiratory ailments, and Colorado, with its dry and sunny climate, drew tuberculosis victims like a magnet. By 1896 Colorado was being flatteringly referred to as "the World's Sanatorium." Yet, consumptives who flocked to Denver in the hope of finding a cure were often unable to secure simple lodging, let alone medical care. Since no publicly supported institutions for tuberculosis existed at the time, the challenge of adequate care was left to private institutions. In Denver, the Jewish community was the first to come to their aid with the founding of National Jewish Hospital for Consumptives.

Frances Wisebart *Jacobs, nicknamed Denver's "Mother of Charities," was the impetus behind the founding of National Jewish Hospital. Launching a relentless campaign on behalf of the sick and indigent, she enlisted the assistance of the new rabbi at Temple Emanuel, Rabbi William Friedman, and they worked together with other community members for many years to make her dream a reality. The Jewish community, which numbered about 500 at the time, was composed primarily of acculturated German Reform Jews from Central Europe, and National Jewish Hospital was finally opened in 1899, with the financial assistance of the International Order of B'nai B'rith, the first sanatorium in Denver for tuberculosis patients. The hospital was formally non-sectarian and treated all patients free of charge; however, the vast majority of patients in the early years were East European Jews, and in addition to medical treatment the hospital taught classes in English, civics, and skills for new trades in an effort to Americanize the new immigrants and help make them financially self-sufficient. Like most early TB sanatoria, treatment emphasized enforced rest, fresh air and sunlight, and a diet rich in milk, eggs, and meat.

With the advent of antibiotic treatment, over the years the threat of tuberculosis was brought under control, and National Jewish Hospital evolved with the times. In 1978, National Jewish merged with the National Asthma Center, which grew out of the original Jewish Sheltering Home for Jewish Children (later the famed Children's Asthma Research Institute and Hospital (CARIH)), founded to assist the children of parents who were tuberculosis victims, and in 1986 the two institutions became known as the National Jewish Center for Immunology and Respiratory Medicine. The passing of time brought yet another change, and today the institution is called the National Jewish Medical and Research Center and continues to treat patients from throughout the country with cutting-edge medicine and research. It is known worldwide for treatment of patients with respiratory, immune and allergic disorders, the only facility in the world dedicated exclusively to these illnesses. Since 1998 National Jewish has been ranked by *U.S. News & World Report*'s "America's Best Hospitals" as number one in the nation for excellence in treating respiratory diseases. In 1999 National Jewish marked its centennial and a legacy of one hundred years of healing. Today, it continues as a non-sectarian, independent, not-for-profit clinical and medical research center whose mission is to develop and provide innovative programs for treating patients of all ages and to discover knowledge to educate health care professionals and provide them with the tools for treatment and prevention.

[Jeanne Abrams (2nd ed.)]

NATIONAL JEWISH DEMOCRATIC COUNCIL (NJDC). Jews may be the Democratic Party's second most reliable constituency (after African Americans), but by the mid-1980s Jewish Democrats were beginning to feel insecure as Republican outreach to their community intensified and as the Democrats drifted further away from support for Israel. There was a palpable fear that such a potent combination could portend a Jewish exodus from the Democratic Party. To quell Jewish alienation from the Democratic Party, a group of concerned activists led by Morton Mandel of Cleveland decided to organize a Jewish voice *within* the party, and the NJDC was founded in 1990. Mandel became founding chairman; other initial organizers include Sheldon Cohen of Washington, D.C., Monte Friedkin of Florida, and David Steiner of New Jersey.

Ronald Reagan's early presidency brought a new wave of Jews into the Republican Party; dubbed neo-conservatives, many had been followers of Democratic senators Henry "Scoop" Jackson of Washington and Daniel Patrick Moynihan of New York. Neo-conservatives were ardently pro-Israel and hawkish on Cold War issues but were also domestic liberals, who nonetheless saw their party moving too far to the left and increasingly critical of Israel's hardline Likud-led government.

The Democrats' problem was compounded by the growing influence of the two-time Democratic presidential nominee Rev. Jesse Jackson, an African American civil rights activist. Jackson's hostility toward Jews – he privately referred to them as "hymies" and New York as "hymietown" – his open sympathies for Yasser Arafat and the Palestinian cause, and his avid courtship of Arab-American support were sources of great concern for the Jewish community.

The Republican Party exploited rifts within the Democratic party, as well as new pro-Israel voices within it to draw Jewish defectors. What became known as the Republican Jewish Coalition (RJC) was founded in 1985 to build support for the Republican party and its candidates in the Jewish community. However, Republican outreach to the Jewish community had little impact on Jewish voting habits, despite growing Republican support for Israel during the Reagan years and again under President George W. Bush, whose hostility toward Palestinian leader Yasser Arafat and sympathy for Prime Minister Ariel Sharon won praise from some hardline pro-Israel groups.

In the closing years of the 20th century and the early 21st both Democratic and Republican administrations were pro-Israel, and the majority of Jews (est. 70 percent) voted Democratic because of the conservative domestic agenda of the GOP, and particularly the enormous influence of the party's right-wing evangelical Christian base, widely seen as the Jewish community's most powerful adversaries on church-state issues. Both partisan groups seek to build Jewish support for their party. The RJC focuses overwhelmingly on Israel-related issues, including the war on terror, while the NJDC stresses a much broader agenda, particularly emphasizing the deep differences between the parties on domestic issues, such as civil liberties, reproductive freedom, the environment, gun control, and privacy rights.

The NJDC has always been very open about its ties to the Democratic party, while its rival group was apparently reluctant to advertise its partisan identity. In an apparent appeal for Jewish support and to appear neutral to Democratic voters, the RJC initially simply called itself the National Jewish Coalition.

NJDC is aligned with the Democratic Party and its agenda, but it is not formally linked to the party itself. Legally, it (like RJC) is independent. NJDC, with Democrats' larger and less fragile Jewish voter base, is more likely than its counterpart group to criticize members of its own party who are seen as acting hostile to Israel or the Jewish community's interests. NJDC coaches candidates and politicians on how to deal substantively as well as politically with the Jewish community, and it trains grass roots advocates to work and organize at the local level. A special emphasis has been on developing a new generation of Jewish Democratic leaders around the country. NJDC also stages "get out the vote" efforts for each election and organizes debates among competing candidates or Jewish spokesmen for the two parties. NJDC also works with the Congress and the Jewish and national media in support of its agenda. It sponsors trips to Israel for leading political figures to better educate them on the views and concerns of Jewish voters back home.

[Douglas M. Bloomfield (2nd ed.)]

NATIONAL MUSEUM OF AMERICAN JEWISH HISTORY. The National Museum of American Jewish History opened its doors on July 4, 1976 on Independence Mall in Philadelphia.

At the beginning of the 21st century, the National Museum of American Jewish History announced plans for a new museum in Philadelphia's historic district, at the corner of 5th and Market streets, adjacent to the Liberty Bell, one of the most heavily traversed intersections in the city.

The NMAJH plans to build a landmark museum on Independence Mall dedicated to the history and contributions of Jews in America with dramatic interactive galleries and exhibition halls, a state-of-the-art resource center and a theater for films, lectures and performances. The lead architect is James Polshek, design principal of the Polshek Partnership in New York. The award-winning firm has designed many top museums, including the American Museum of Natural History's Rose Center for Earth and Space, the Smithsonian Institution's National Museum of the American Indian, and the Clinton Presidential Center.

The new location is a half block from the museum's current site, but the new location will put it across the street from the Liberty Bell and a block away from Independence Hall. As Museum board member George Ross said, "Right now we are on the fifty yard line on Independence Mall. With our new location, we will be in the owner's box."

The new location has many advantages over the current one, such as the site's larger footprint offers a more effective layout of exhibition space and the opportunity to build and operate a more efficient museum; visitation will be enhanced by being across the street from Independence Hall and the Liberty Bell Center: the latter attracts more than 2 million tourists annually; the new site's corner is also the location of a subway station, making it easily accessible for public transit riders.

In recent years, both the Liberty Bell Center and the National Constitution Center opened in Independence National Historical Park on Independence Mall as part of the largest urban revitalization project in the nation. Spurred by the new construction, park visitation surged by 35 percent and now has four million visitors annually.

Mary A. Bomar, director of the Northeast Region for the National Park Service, noted that

> The Museum's presence on the mall is fitting because the story of the Jewish community in America is a story of freedom and what can be achieved when a group finds freedom. Visitors from around the world will now have another way to experience this vital American value during visits to Independence National Historical Park.

The museum will connect Jews more closely to their heritage and will inspire in people of all backgrounds a greater appreciation for the diversity of the American experience and the freedoms to which Americans aspire. The museum will collect historical materials and present experiences and educational programs that preserve, explore and celebrate the history of Jews in America. Situated next to Independence Hall and the Liberty Bell, the new museum will cooperate with all parts of the American Jewish community and will provide a symbolic location in the United States that is representative of all American Jews.

Congregation Mikveh Israel, which shares its location with the museum, will remain at the current site.

Among the significant exhibitions the Museum has presented since its opening are "A Worthy Use of Summer: Jewish Summer Camping in America" and "Bridges and Boundaries: Two Peoples Face to Face," a collaborative exhibitions project with the Afro-American Historical and Cultural Museum (now the African American Museum in Philadelphia.) Both museums were awarded the Ione Dugger Multicultural Award from Temple University and the Philadelphia Commission on Human Relations' Human Rights Award in recognition of the project.

The museum's most recent core exhibition (as of 2005), "Creating American Jews," won an Award of Merit for Institutional Achievement from the Pennsylvania Federation of Museums and Historical Organizations.

The museum has also been in the forefront of the Jewish crafts movement. Its first "Contemporary Artifacts" exhibition, in 1981, provided a showcase for Jewish ritual art and help spur the expression of traditional Jewish heritage in an American context.

The museum also innovated an annual family program held each December 25, "Being Jewish at Christmas." The program attracts approximately 1,000 people and provides an opportunity for families to explore their Jewish heritage through performances and other entertainment, crafts projects, and special children's activities.

[Josh Perelman (2nd ed.)]

NATIONAL PARKS IN ISRAEL. The National Parks Authority was established by law in 1963 to take over the functions carried out from 1956 (with the same staff) by the Department for Landscaping and the Preservation of Historic Sites in the prime minister's office. These functions are: the preparation, laying out, and maintenance of park areas for the general public; the restoration, landscaping, and preservation of historical and archaeological sites; the construction of access roads and amenities for recreation and leisure; and, in the case of ancient sites, the provision of explanatory notice boards and pamphlets. The Authority has also established museums at several historic sites.

Israel is rich in biblical sites and the remains of post-biblical Jewish, Roman, Byzantine, Muslim, and Crusader settlements, often in surroundings of beauty, and most of the national parks have been linked with these sites. Many had suffered from centuries of neglect, since they were of little interest to the successive occupying authorities. The Authority had to clear overgrowth and thick layers of debris, undertake restoration programs where possible, and provide amenities and access for visitors, both local and from overseas. Some parks were laid out without any connection with a historic site, in order to preserve rural areas from the encroachment of urban development. Occasionally, archaeological sites were taken over for preservation and maintenance by the Authority, where the excavations had been particularly dramatic, as at *Masada; or where scholars had made spectacular finds of wide public interest, as at *Hazor, the *Bet She'arim necropolis, the ancient synagogues at *Bet Alfa, *Baram, and *Hammath (Tiberias), the Roman theater at *Caesarea, and the excavations at *Bet Yeraḥ and *Ramat Raḥel. At some sites the National Parks Authority was responsible for the excavations, undertaken by specially commissioned archaeologists, as well as for their restoration and current maintenance. Examples are: the Crusader city of Caesarea, complete with moat, walls, gates, and towers; the crypt, tunnels, and some of the walls of Crusader *Acre; the castles of *Yehi'am and *Belvoir; the Roman theater at *Beth-Shean; the Nabatean-Byzantine city of *Avedat, with its citadel, acropolis, and two churches; and the Nabatean cities of *Shivta and *Kurnub. At Masada, much of the restoration work was carried out at the same time as the excavations.

The Authority is also responsible for sites designated as national parks. Those already open to the public, in addition to the ones already mentioned, are: Ḥurshat Tal in Upper Galilee, with its streams, pond, lawns, and woods; the spring, bathing pool, and woodland slopes of Ma'ayan Ḥarod in the

Valley of Jezreel; the three natural pools and landscaped banks of Gan ha-Sheloshah, also in Jezreel; the seashore park and antiquities of *Ashkelon; the natural pools of Ein Avedat in the northern Negev; the 25,000-acre parkland and forest of Carmel; and the Crusader remains at Aqua Bella (Ein Ḥemed) near Jerusalem. The Authority has also renovated some of the medieval synagogues of Safed, and improved the amenities at the tomb of Maimonides in Tiberias. It has carried out site-improvement work at Mount Zion in Jerusalem and at the tomb of R. *Simeon b. Yoḥai at *Meron. The Authority was one of the initiators in setting up the park at *Yad Mordekhai, which contains a reconstruction of the Egyptian attack on the kibbutz in 1948 and a small museum devoted to the defense of the southern kibbutzim during the War of Independence. Among the new parks for which plans have already been completed by the Authority is the Jerusalem national park – a green belt circling the Old City walls and covering 500 acres. The number of visitors to the national parks in 1968 exceeded 2,000,000.

In 1998 the National Parks Authority was united with the Nature Reserves Authority as the Israel Nature and Park Authority. The new Authority's goal is to preserve Israel's green areas in the face of rapid urban development, increasing transportation needs, and the steep growth of Israel's population. The Authority's tasks are to locate sites for the establishment of nature reserves and national parks; to establish, maintain, and manage existing reserves and parks; to oversee natural resources; to initiate educational activities; and to conduct research on nature preservation. The Authority is responsible for 380 nature reserves spread over 2,350 sq. mi. (6,130 sq. km.) and 115 national parks spread over 140 sq. mi. (370 sq. km.). Fifty-eight nature reserves and national parks are open to the public, with over 10 million visitors in 2003.

WEBSITE: www.parks.org.il.

[Yaacov Yannai / Shaked Gilboa (2nd ed.)]

NATIONALRAT (Ger. "[Jewish] National Council"), committee of Zionist roof organization in Austria. It was formed at the time of the collapse of Austria-Hungary in November 1918, in Vienna, to advance the claims of the Jewish people as a national entity in still unsettled postwar Austria and was active until the end of 1920. Initially it consisted of 50 members, representing a number of Jewish organizations. The Zionist Robert *Stricker was its most active chairman and its outstanding leader. The other chairmen were Adolf Boehm, Isidor Margulies, Bruno Pollack Parnau, and Saul Sokal. Its secretary was Robert Weltsch. Due to the segmentation of the Jewish population of old Austria, the sphere of influence of the Nationalrat was limited to the Jews of German-speaking Austria, who were too weak to demand extended minority rights. The Nationalrat was not based on elections and represented only part of the Jewish population. Its claims were opposed by the non-Zionist Jews who were satisfied with the existing legal autonomy of the Jewish religious community, and by the Social-Democratic Party, and were not accepted. Similar organizations were later established in other postwar Central European countries. The Nationalrat organized a legal department, a social welfare department for former soldiers, and an employment exchange. Its department for social welfare was directed by Anitta Mueller-Cohen. The Nationalrat was instrumental in promoting modern Hebrew education by initiating the Hebrew Teachers' College (Hebraeisches Paedagogium), founded in 1917, and by establishing the Jewish Realgymnasium in 1919, a secondary school with the language of instruction partially in Hebrew, directed by Viktor Kellner. The program of the Nationalrat was later taken over by the *Juedische Volkspartei ("Jewish People's Party").

BIBLIOGRAPHY: J. Kreppel, *Juden und Judentum von Heute* (1925), 618, 630–2; R. Weltsch, in: *Der Jude*, 3 (1918/19), 350–8; J. Fraenkel, *Robert Stricker* (Eng., 1950), 78–79; A. Boehm, *Die Zionistische Bewegung*, 2 (1937[2]), 685. **ADD. BIBLIOGRAPHY:** R. Weltsch, in: *Michael. On the History of the Jews in the Diaspora*, 2 (1973), 204–15; D. Rechter, *The Jews of Vienna and the First World War* (2001).

[Hugo Knoepfmacher / E. Adunka (2nd ed.)]

NATIONAL RELIGIOUS PARTY (NRP), Israeli party known in Hebrew as **Hamafdal** (acronym for Ha-Miflagah ha-Datit ha-Le'ummit). The NRP was founded in June 1956 through the merger of two national religious Zionist parties, *Mizrachi and *Ha-Po'el ha-Mizrachi, and additional religious circles. In the elections to the Third to Twelfth Knessets it ran in elections under the name Ha-Ḥazit ha-Datit ha-Le'ummit (the National Religious Front). It constitutes a part of the World Federation of Hamizrachi-Hapo'el Hamizrachi. Unlike the *ḥaredi* religious party, the NRP always considered itself an integral part of the State of Israel, and despite its adherence to *halakhah*, has accepted the supremacy of the secular laws of Israel on most issues. Its basic position was that the secular laws and halakhic laws can exist side by side with each other. Though rabbis have played an important spiritual role in the NRP, and their influence has grown in recent years, the party is run on democratic lines, and it is the members, not the rabbis, who decide the party's line. Like the other Orthodox religious groups in Israel, it opposes recognition of Conservative and Reform Judaism.

Until the Six-Day War the NRP followed a moderate political line, and concentrated its activities on preserving the Jewish character of the state in various spheres, including the provision of religious services, the preservation of the religious *status quo* on such issues as *kashrut*, respect for the Sabbath, nurturing of the national religious education system, the religious kibbutz movement, and social welfare. It advocated full military service for men, together with religious studies within the framework of *yeshivot hesder*, and nonmilitary national service for women.

Until 1976 it maintained a political alliance with *Mapai, and then the *Israel Labor Party, commonly known as "the historical coalition," and was a member of all the Mapai- and Labor-led governments, except for a brief period in 1974, soon after Yitzhak *Rabin formed his first government. However, after the Six-Day War, and even more so after the

Yom Kippur War, a shift to the right began in its political positions, especially with regard to the future of those parts of Ereẓ Israel occupied in the course of the Six-Day War, and in religious terms it shifted to a more messianic brand of Judaism.

In 1968 the NRP convention adopted the following policy decisions: "The National Religious Party views the political and security accomplishments that have been achieved by this generation in Ereẓ Israel, as the beginning of realization of the will of Divine Providence and of the processes directed toward complete salvation of the Jewish people in the land of its forefathers; the State of Israel must pursue all means at her disposal to lay the foundation for peace between itself and the neighboring states, and to negotiate peace treaties; in the negotiations for peace treaties, the State of Israel must be guided by three basic principles: the aspiration toward enduring peace; the historic religious rights over the Promised Land; and assuring secure borders for the state."

The NRP was at first an active actor within the *Gush Emunim settlement movement that was founded in 1974, though quite rapidly Gush Emunim started to develop independently of it. This shift in positions was both the result of the new political circumstances, and the growing influence of the younger generation in the party, headed by Zevulun *Hammer. The formal breach between the NRP and the Labor Party occurred in 1976, after its ministers abstained in a vote in the *Knesset on a motion of no confidence in the government, over the issue of the alleged official breach of the Sabbath as a result of a ceremony held in an air force base on a Friday afternoon.

The NRP joined the government that Menaḥem *Begin formed in 1977 and joined all subsequent governments, except for that formed by Yitzhak Rabin in 1992. In November 2004 it left the government of Ariel *Sharon over his Gaza disengagement plan.

In 1981 the Moroccan-born MK Aharon Abuhazeira left the NRP, claiming that the party had not stood by him during a corruption trial, due to his ethnic origin, and established his own party called Tami, which entered the Tenth Knesset. In 1988 a group of moderate members, who objected to the NRP's religious and nationalist radicalization, left the party and established a moderate religious party called Meimad. However, Meimad remained weak, and entered representatives into the Fifteenth and Sixteenth Knessets only because it ran in a single list with the Labor Party.

The NRP was adamantly opposed to the Oslo process initiated by the Rabin government, and voted against all the various interim agreements signed with the Palestinians, starting with the DoP in September 1993. The assassination of Rabin in November 1995 by a young man, Yigal Amir, who had studied in the religious Bar-Ilan University, resulted in serious soul-searching within the NRP, but this did not stop a further shift to the right thereafter. Prior to the elections to the Sixteenth Knesset, Effie Eitam, a former brigadier general, who was born on a secular kibbutz but gradually adopted radical religious right-wing views, was elected as the leader of the NRP. The NRP was the only religious party that joined the government formed by Ariel Sharon after the elections to the Sixteenth Knesset but soon found itself in opposition to Sharon's disengagement plan. Nevertheless, the majority of the party continued to support a pragmatic line, while Eitam favored taking the NRP into the right-wing National Union Party. This resulted in his being removed from the leadership of the party, and his leaving the party together with MK Yitzhak Levy in June 2004, to form their own parliamentary group called Religious Zionism. The NRP remained in the government for another five months, but finally left the government in November 2004.

The NRP's political leaders since its establishment have been Ḥayyim Moshe *Shapira (1956–70), Dr. Yosef *Burg (1970–86); Zevulun Hammer (1986–98); Yitzhak Levy (1998–2003), Effie Eitam (2003–04), and Zevulun Orlev (2005–).

From the Third to Ninth Knessets the NRP had 10–12 Knesset seats; in the Tenth Knesset it went down to 6, losing seats to the Teḥiya and Tami, and until the Sixteenth Knesset received only 4–6 seats, except for a brief revival in the Fourteenth Knesset when it went up again to 9, as it did in the Seventeenth (2006).

Until 1977 the NRP usually held the ministries of Postal Services, Welfare, Religious Affairs, and the Interior. After 1977 the Ministry of Education and Culture was held by the NRP in numerous governments, and as of the 1990s also Transportation, Construction, and Housing and National Infrastructures.

The party publishes a daily called *Haẓofeh*. From 1957 to 1969 it published an ideological journal called *Gevilin*, which started to appear again in 1990.

BIBLIOGRAPHY: *Ve'idat ha-Yissud shel ha-Miflagah ha-Datit Le'ummit ha-Mizraḥi–Ha-Po'el ha-Mizraḥi* (1957); Y. Cohen, *Esrim Shanah Rishonot li-Medinat Yisrael be-Ḥayyei ha-Yahadut ha-Datit ha-Me'urgenet* (1968); Y. Azri'eli, *Dor ha-Kippot ha-Serugot: ha-Mahapekhah ha-Politit shel ha-Ẓe'irim ba-Mafdal* (1990); A. Cohen and Y. Harel (eds.), *Ha-Ẓiyyonut ha-Datit – Iddan ha-Temurot: Asufat Meḥkarim le-Zekher Zevulun Hammer* (2004).

[Susan Hattis Rolef (2nd ed.)]

NATIONAL SOCIALISM (for short, **Nazism**), a movement in Germany patterned after fascism, which grew under Adolf *Hitler's leadership and ruled Germany from 1933 to 1945. The Deutsche Arbeiterpartei, founded on Jan. 5, 1919, changed its name in the summer of 1920 to Nationalsozialistische Deutsche Arbeiterpartei (NSDAP) and Hitler, who had been the seventh member of the original party, soon became its undisputed leader (*Fuehrer*). From then on, the history of National Socialism became virtually identical with Hitler's career.

As an ideology, National Socialism was a mixture of extreme nationalist, racialist ideas and a trend of populist radicalism which never formed a coherent unity. Among its major tenets were biological racialism, social Darwinism – the survival of the fittest – unrestrained antisemitism, anti-Bolshevism, and the quest for *Lebensraum* – German conquest of living space to the East. It preached a folkish antisemitism, pan-Germanism and the *Dolchstosslegende* – stab in the back myth – that Germany would have won World War I if it had not been attacked at home by Jews and others. It built itself on the myth of blood and soil and on the notion of Germans as the master race and Germany dominating Europe.

Prior to 1923 the Nazi Party was active mainly in Bavaria, where in November it attempted to overthrow the Weimar Republic in what became known as the Munich Beer Hall Putsch, or Hitler's Putsch. The coup was crushed and Hitler was imprisoned for a surprisingly short period of time; and it was there in Landsberg that he wrote *Mein Kampf*. The book became the bible of the movement, the platform of the party. Prior to 1928 it was a marginal party of virtually no significance, receiving less than 3% of the vote in 1928. Yet in the interim it organized, attracting more moderate elements along with folkish groups and a core of militant followers that it knew how and when to deploy effectively. The worldwide economic depression of 1929 and 1930 which hit Germany hard added to the dissatisfaction with the Weimar Republic and to the attraction of extremist parties. In September 1930 the Nazi seat total rose to 107 in the 608-seat Reichstag, winning some 6.4 million (18%) of the vote. They improved their performance in the elections of July 31, 1932, when they received 37.3 percent of the vote, which translated into 230 of 608 seats. Yet in the elections of November 6, 1932, the last free elections before Hitler's rise to power, the Nazis received only 33.1 percent of the vote and won 196 seats. Hitler came to power as the head of a coalition government, with conservative elements believing that once in power he would moderate his views due to the responsibilities of office and that he and his followers could be controlled.

Once in power, Hitler moved swiftly against external opposition, establishing concentration camps to house political opponents of the regime, using the pretext of the Reichstag Fire of February 27, 1933, to establish rule by decree, and suspending existing guarantees, and then eliminating the remaining non-Nazi parties. By July 1933 the Nazi Party was the only party in Germany.

In 1934 Hitler decided to act against his opponents within the party, eliminating SA chief Ernst Rohm and other rivals – perceived or real. On August 2, President Von Hindenburg died and Hitler was named head of state as well. After the pressures of 1933–34, the Nazis consolidated power and achieved successes at home and abroad. Unemployment was lowered and Germany was no longer isolated. Hitler's achievements in the realm of foreign policy were indeed impressive to the German people. He had reversed the shame of Versailles, returning Germany to the world stage and rearming its military. From the Nazi perspective the annexation of Austria and the entrance into the Sudentenland were triumphant.

From 1938 onward Nazism became increasingly unrestrained. **Kristallnacht* was the eruption of violence against Jews, the letting loose of controlled mob violence. Wartime was the best time to solve certain problems that could not be addressed at other times. Thus, the "*Euthanasia Program," an extreme expression of Social Darwinism and of applied biology, was approved in an order backdated to September 1, 1939, to give it the appearance of a wartime measure. The conquest of territories, the incorporation of lands, and the appeal to ethnic Germans living in other countries, were all expressions of Nazi ideology. Above all, so was the "Final Solution to the Jewish Question," which wanted to eliminate all Jewish blood from the face of the earth and therefore remake the human species.

BIBLIOGRAPHY: M. Broszat, *German National Socialism 1919–1945* (1966), incl. bibl. **ADD. BIBLIOGRAPHY:** K.D. Bracher, *The German Dictatorship: The Origins, Structure and Effects of National Socialism* (1970); G.L. Mosse, *The Crisis of German Ideology* (1964); idem, *Nazism: A Historical and Comparative Analysis of National Socialism* (1978, 2006[2]).

[Jozeph Michman (Melkman) / Michael Berenbaum (2nd ed.)]

NATIONAL YIDDISH BOOK CENTER, cultural institution dedicated to collecting and distributing endangered Yiddish books and, through programs and education, opening up their contents to new readers. Located in Amherst, Massachusetts, the Center safeguards a collection of 1.5 million Yiddish books rescued from individuals and institutions worldwide. The collection contains original Yiddish novels, plays, poetry, nonfiction, periodicals, and sheet music, most in duplicate copies. The majority were published between the late 19th- and mid-20th century, mainly in Eastern Europe, the United States, and South America. The books fell into disuse as spoken Yiddish was gradually replaced by English and other languages after World War II. All the Center's volumes are available for sale at nominal cost to individuals, libraries, schools, and colleges and universities.

Because of the physical deterioration of many volumes, the Center created the Steven Spielberg Digital Yiddish Library in 1998, making reprints of every title available for purchase as brand-new, hardcover, acid-free editions. The Spielberg Digital Yiddish Library is believed to be the only project ever to digitize an entire modern literature, preserving it permanently for future generations of readers, students, and scholars.

History

The Yiddish Book Center is a nonprofit institution, and its programs are funded by contributions from over 30,000 (as of 2005) members, and gifts and grants. Founded in 1980 by Aaron Lansky, the Center was one of the first organizations in America dedicated to the preservation of Yiddish literature and culture. As a young graduate student, Lansky saw the need to save endangered books that were being discarded by the children and grandchildren of elderly Jewish immigrants. His call to save Yiddish books from destruction led to a massive, ongoing rescue operation by a worldwide network of *zamlers* (volunteers). Lansky won the John D. and Catherine T. MacArthur Foundation's so-called "genius" award in recognition of his extraordinary work.

In the early years of collection, most books, the personal property of Eastern European Jewish immigrants, came from locations within the United States. The mid-1990s saw a shift in origin, with volumes shipped from South Africa, Argentina, Mexico, and Brazil – sites of once-large Yiddish-speaking immigrant communities. All books coming into the Center are sorted by hand and new titles are catalogued according to library standards. As of 2005, 25 years after its founding, the Center still receives an average of 500 Yiddish books each week.

Programs

In 1997 the Yiddish Book Center moved into permanent headquarters in Amherst. The building, designed by architect Allen Moore, recalls the dramatic lines of the lost wooden synagogues of Eastern Europe. It is open to the public six days per week and houses library-style stacks of Yiddish books as well as exhibits, a theater, bookstore, and offices. Approximately 10,000 visitors come to the Center each year to view exhibits on modern Yiddish literature and culture and to attend programs ranging from week-long conferences to concerts, performances, readings, lectures, films, and family-oriented events.

The Book Center publishes an English-language magazine, *Pakn Treger*, which features essays, fiction, new translations, cultural reporting, photographs, and art connecting contemporary Jewish life to its roots in Yiddish culture. The Center's "Jewish Short Stories from Eastern Europe and Beyond," a 13-part audio series produced for National Public Radio in 1995, introduced hundreds of thousands of listeners to the riches of Yiddish and other modern Jewish literature, in English.

In 1989 the Center invited college students to take part in an internship program that provided Yiddish language instruction in combination with hands-on work sorting and shelves incoming Yiddish volumes. The popular program grew into the Steiner Summer Internship Program and now offers dozens of students an opportunity to study Yiddish language and literature in intensive accredited courses and to take part in the ongoing work of the Center for eight weeks each year. Many alumni of the program have gone on to enter the field of Jewish and Yiddish studies as educators, writers, and community leaders.

In 2002 the Center joined with the Fund for the Translation of Modern Jewish Literature and Yale University Press to create the New Yiddish Library, an initiative producing new translations of modern Yiddish literature. New Yiddish Library titles include works by Shalom Aleichem, Itzik Manger, and Lamed Shapiro. The Center also produced the Rohr Library of Recorded Yiddish, which preserved as CD compilations more than two dozen full-length works of modern Yiddish literature read by native Yiddish speakers, in partnership with the Jewish Library of Montreal.

BIBLIOGRAPHY: A. Lansky, *Outwitting History* (2004).

[Nancy Sherman (2nd ed.)]

NATIONS, THE SEVENTY, a conception based on the list of the descendants of Noah given in Genesis 10, usually called "The Table of Nations." According to the table, all the nations of the earth may be classified as descended from one or another of Noah's three sons, Shem, Ham, and Japheth. The principle behind the classification is generally geographic proximity rather than ethnic or linguistic connections. Those nations descended from Japheth are *Gomer (Cimmerians), Madai (Medes), Javan (Ionians), *Ashkenaz (Scythians), *Elisha and *Kittim (Cypriots), and others (10:2–4). The lands occupied by the Japhethites bordered the Fertile Crescent in the north and penetrated the maritime regions in the west. The principal subdivisions of the descendants of Ham are Cush (the peoples of the southern shore of the Red Sea), Miẓraim (Egypt), Put (location uncertain, probably Cyrene), and Canaan (10:6–20). The descendants of Cush are listed in 10:7 as Seba, *Havilah, Sabtah, Raamah, and Sabtecha. According to 10:8, Cush had another son, *Nimrod, whose rule extended over all Mesopotamia. That a Mesopotamian ruler is here linked to the peoples adjacent to the Red Sea stems from the confusion caused by the fact that there were two nations known by the name Cush, one in the Nile region ("Nubia, Ethiopia") and another in Mesopotamia (the Kassites; Akk. *Kaššû*). The Bible often telescopes the two. The inclusion of the Philistines and the Cretans (Caphtorim) in the list of the descendants of the Egyptians (Miẓraim; verses 13–14) is another problem, as there is clearly no ethnic or linguistic connection between these peoples. The reason for including the Philistines in the list must, therefore, have been geographic; Crete was included because it was the original home of the Philistines. The inclusion of the Ludim, if this refers to the Lydians, in this list is also a problem. It is possible that this refers to the invasion of Egypt by the Sea Peoples. Another Lud is also mentioned as a descendant of Shem (verse 22). The classifying of Canaan in the Hamite branch of nations is again perplexing, there being no ethnic or linguistic connections between the Canaanites and the Egyptians (verse 6). The subdivision of the Canaanites is problematic too: the inclusion of Phoenicia (Sidon) among the subdivisions of the Canaanites is appropriate, since the Phoenicians referred to their country as Canaan, and the Phoenician language is close to Hebrew. However, it cannot be on ethnolinguistic grounds that the Jebusites, Hittites, Hivites, and others are listed as Canaanites (10:15–18). It seems that once again the principle behind the classification is geographic proximity. The territory of the Hamites extended from Phoenicia, through western Palestine, to northeastern Africa. The Shemites included all the "children of Eber," the eponym of the Hebrews (10:21), and hence were therefore given prominence. The Assyrians, Arameans, and numerous tribes of Arabians were classified as Shemites. It is not clear why the Elamites, whose center was southwest Persia, were considered Shemites (10:22). Perhaps they were listed with Ashur (Assyria) because they were the nearest neighbor to the east of Mesopotamia. Arpachshad, listed as the grandfather of Eber, is otherwise unknown; the name appears to be non-Semitic.

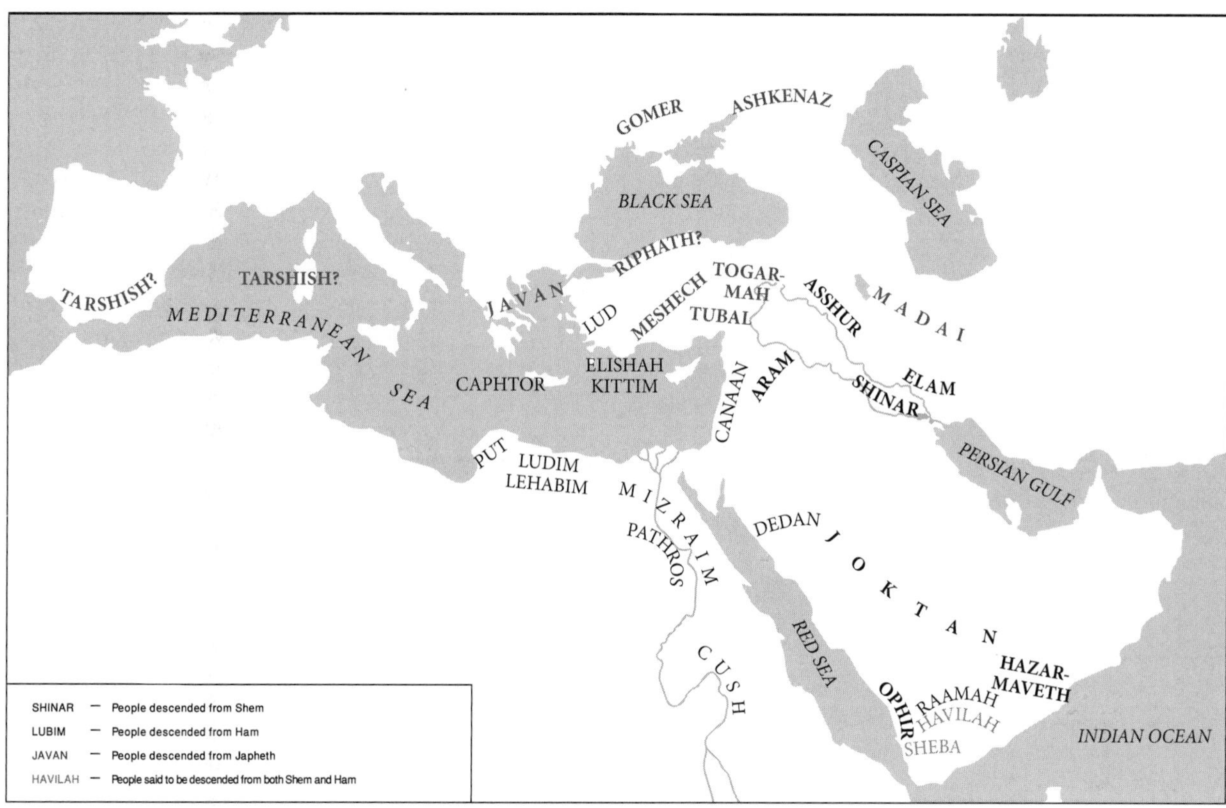

The Hebrew Table of the Nations (from Genesis 10 and related sources). After the Westminster Historical Atlas to the Bible, 1945.

That the table does not aim at completeness is suggested by verse 5a, "From these [sons of Japheth] the maritime nations branched out" – here unnamed. Moab and Ammon, the descendants of Nahor and Keturah, the Ishmaelite tribes and Edom, and Israel itself are intentionally omitted, for they find their place at later stages of the narrative. Unexplained is the omission of Babylon. The earliest dating of the table is determined by the presence of the Cimmerians and the Scythians, who appeared in Asia Minor only in the eighth century. In general, the horizon of the table agrees remarkably (with the exception of Babylon) with that of Jeremiah (e.g., 46:9; 51:27–28) and Ezekiel (27:1 ff.; 38:2 ff.; 39:1), and it is likely that the table in its present form was known to these prophets. Heterogeneous and inconsistent (cf. the discrepancy between verse 7 and verses 28–29 regarding Havilah and Sheba), the table is assumed to be a combination of various sources. The material is conventionally allocated between J (verses 8–19, 25–30) and P (all the rest). Together with the story of the Tower of Babel, the table marks the end of the primeval history of mankind and the transition to the patriarchal history, which is played out against a background of a world filled with nations. Like the genealogies of 11:10–30; 25:12–18; and 36:1 ff., it enables the narrative to maintain its focus on the main line of Israel's descent by summarily disposing of all collateral lines. At the same time, it shows the fulfillment of God's blessing of Noah and his sons with fertility (9:1, 7), and locates the ancestors of Israel in relation to the rest of mankind. The Jewish tradition that mankind is made up of 70 nations is based on the count in the table – although a sum is not stated in the text (cf. the itemization in *Pesikta Zutreta*, *No'aḥ*) and seems to underlie Deuteronomy 32:8, which speaks of God's "dividing mankind… in accord with the number of the sons of Israel" (namely, 70; Gen. 46:27). On the other hand, the Septuagint and the 4Q Deuteronomy fragment that read "the sons of God" (i.e., angels) instead of "the sons of Israel" reflect the notion, dated as early as the Persian period (Dan. 10:20) and possibly earlier (Ps. 82:7) that every nation has a divine patron – again, 70, in accord with Jewish tradition (Charles, Apocrypha, 2 (1913), 363 (late Hebrew Test. Patr., Naph. 9), *Pesikta Zutreta*, *ibid.*).

The Table of Nations served as the basis of later Jewish ethnography; for representative attempts to embrace contemporary ethnogeography under its rubrics compare Jubilees, chapters 8–9; Josephus, *Antiquities*, 1:122–147; Targum Jonathan to Genesis 10; *Genesis Rabbah*, 37; and for the late Middle Ages, Abrabanel, at the end of his commentary to Genesis 10.

In the Midrash

In early Christian sources 72 nations and tongues were assumed (e.g., Hippolytus, 10:26; Clement of Alexandria, *Stromata* 1:26), perhaps following the Septuagint version of Genesis 10. This chapter was considered a scientific account of the division of mankind into three races – Semitic, Hamitic and

Japhethic – distributed in three separate zones (Jub. 7:10 ff.). There are, however, varying opinions as to how many nations belonged to each "race." The commonest system (Mid. Ps. to 9:7; et al.) ascribes to Japheth 14 nations, Ham 30, and Shem 26 (total 70), while the *Yalkut Shimoni*, Genesis 61 gives a reckoning of Japheth 15, Ham 32, and Shem 27. From this total of 74, however, subtract Shem, Arpachshad, Shelah, and Eber, who were righteous, and thus again there is a total of 70.

There is, moreover, another tradition of 60 nations, based on an exegesis of the Song of Songs 6:8 (Mid. Hag. to Gen. 10:1). *Numbers Rabbah* 14:10 speaks of 70 nations and 60 kingdoms, giving a total of 130 (cf. Num. 7:13). The tradition of 72, which is found in A. Zacuto's *Yuḥasin* (ed. Cracow (1580–81), 135) is also echoed in *Midrash Haggadah* to Genesis 10:32. It has been suggested that the 72 nations are the 70 "Noahite" nations plus Israel and Edom. However, Abrabanel (on Gen. 10:2) states that a straightforward reading of chapter 10 suggests 73 nations; thus 72 may have been reached by excluding the Philistines, who in Genesis 10:14 are designated as a mixed race. Just as there were 70 nations, so there were 70 languages (cf. Targ. Jon., Gen. 11:7 and Deut. 32:8). Thus the law engraved on the tablets on Mt. Ebal (Deut. 27:2 ff.) was written in 70 languages (Sot. 7:5), so that all nations might read it. For the same reason, the divine voice that made itself heard at Sinai divided itself into 70 tongues (Shab. 88b et al.). However, according to *Aggadat Bereshit* 14 there are 71 languages. Perhaps the Philistines were included in that reckoning. The motif of the 70 nations is widely used in rabbinic literature (as is its derivative, the 70 tongues, e.g., *Sefer ha-Yashar*, Mi-Keẓ). Thus the 70 sacrifices offered on Tabernacles are said to atone for the 70 nations (Suk. 55b). The silver bowls, which the princes of the 12 tribes offered to the Tabernacle (Num. 7:13) weighed 70 shekels; so too did 70 nations spring from Noah (Num. R. 14:12). The 70 members of the Sanhedrin were likewise thought to correspond to the 70 nations of the world (Targ. Yer., Gen. 28:3).

BIBLIOGRAPHY: S. Krauss, in: *Jewish Studies in Memory of G.A. Kohut* (1935), 379 ff.; J. Simons, in: OTS, 10 (1954), 182–4; E.A. Speiser, in: IDB, 3 (1962), 235 ff. (incl. bibl.); For the 4Q Deut. fragment see P. Skehan, in: BASOR, 136 (1954), 12–15; See also commentaries to Genesis. In the Midrash: Ginzberg, Legends, 5 (1925), 194 f.; 7 (1938), 429; Guttmann, Mafte'aḥ, 2 (1917), 73 ff.; M. Steinschneider, in: ZDMG, 4 (1850), 150 ff.; 57 (1903), 476 f.; S. Krauss, in: ZAW, 19 (1899), 1–14; 20 (1900), 38–43; S. Poznański, *ibid.*, 24 (1904), 301–8.

[Daniel Sperber]

NATONEK, JOSEPH (1813–1892), rabbi, pioneer of Zionism in Hungary, and Hebrew grammarian. Born in Komlo, Hungary, Natonek, as a merchant, supplied the Hungarian revolutionary army in 1848 until its collapse. He became the principal of the Jewish school in Surany (south Slovakia), and subsequently (1861–67) rabbi in Jaszbereny and in Szekesfehervar (Stuhlweissenburg). In 1867, Natonek negotiated with the Turkish government in Constantinople to obtain a charter for the reclamation of Palestinian soil for Jewish settlement. When his endeavors proved fruitless, he returned to Budapest, where he published the magazine *Das einige Israel* ("The United Israel," 1872), in which he propagated the Zionist idea. He also produced a booklet in Hungarian, *Messiás, avagy értekezés a zsidó emancipatióról* ("The Messiah – or On the Emancipation of the Jews," 1861), in which he opposed the idea of ameliorating the Jewish situation by cultural emancipation, advocating in its place national emancipation in the spirit of Moses *Hess and modern Zionism.

Natonek's other works include the unpublished Hebrew manuscript, "On the Divine Revelation to Moses"; *Wissenschaft-Religion* (1876); and an edition of the Song of Songs (1871), published with German translation and commentary by L. Hollaender, with some additional comments of his own. He also began to prepare a dictionary of five languages, *Pentaglotte* (1861) in collaboration with Bishop Feuer of Szekesfehervar.

BIBLIOGRAPHY: S. Weingarten, *Ha-Rav Yosef Natonek* (1942); D.B. Frenkel, *Reshit ha-Ẓiyyonut ha-Medinit ha-Modernit* (1956); Kadar, in: *Sinai*, 45 (1959), 243–52; I.Z. Zahavi, *Me-ha-Ḥatam Sofer ve-ad Herzl* (1966), 196–215.

[Menahem Zevi Kaddari]

NATRA, SERGIU (**Nadler, Serge**; 1924–), Israeli composer. Born in Bucharest, Romania, he studied at the Musical Academy there under Leo Klepper, won the Georges Enesco Prize (1945) for his March and Chorale (which was performed by the Palestine PO in 1947, 14 years prior to his immigration to Israel) and the Romanian State Prize (1951). In 1961, he immigrated to Israel and settled in Tel Aviv and from 1975 to 1985 he taught at the Rubin Academy of Music, Tel Aviv. His Israeli honors include the Milo (1965), Engel (1970), and Prime Minister's (1984) prizes for composers. Natra's early works show the influence of Stravinsky, Prokofiev, and Hindemith. However, after he immigrated to Israel, his works were influenced by the new landscape, the Hebrew language, and biblical themes. In the 1970s he also composed in free atonality. Among his works are *Symphony for Strings* (1960); *Music for Violin and Harp* (1960); *Toccata for Orchestra* (1963); *Music for Harpsichord and Six Instruments* (1964); *Sonatina for Harp* (1965); *Song of Deborah*, for mezzo-soprano and chamber orchestra (1967), *Sonatinas for Trumpet, Oboe, and Trombone with Piano* (1969); *Interlude for Harp and Prayer for Harp* (1970); *Dedication for Mezzo-soprano and Orchestra* (1972); *Trio for Piano, Violin and Cello* (1971); *Divertimento for harp* (1976); *Ness-Amim Cantata* (1984); and *Sonata for harp and string quartet* (1997).

ADD. BIBLIOGRAPHY: Grove online.

[Uri (Erich) Toeplitz / Yohanan Boehm / Israela Stein (2nd ed.)]

NATRONAI BAR HILAI (ninth cent.), *gaon* of Sura from 853 to 858. Natronai's father Hilai, who died in 797, was also *gaon* of Sura. One of the most prolific writers of responsa among the *geonim* of the ninth century, Natronai always replied in the language in which he was addressed, whether Hebrew, Aramaic, or Arabic. He is said to have been the first to use Arabic for scholarly correspondence. He had strong ties with all parts of the Diaspora, especially Spain, and in particular Lucena, of whose Jews he was especially demanding, "since there is no non-Jew among you." His responsa deal largely with matters pertaining to liturgy, and his responsum to a query from the Lucena community as to how to fulfill the rabbinic dictum to recite 100 benedictions daily, constitutes the nucleus of the Jewish prayer book. He gave a historical explanation of Rav's statement (Shab. 24a) that it is necessary to recite the **haftarah* after the reading of the Pentateuch portion at the Sabbath afternoon service. According to him the Persians objected to this custom. This practice was abolished and never reinstated. He is the author of the earliest responsum regarding the geonic ordinance that debts may be collected from movable property. In another responsum, he stresses the importance of the study of the Babylonian Talmud for the unlearned since it includes both Bible and Mishnah.

Natronai did not insist that his questioners act in accordance with the customs prevailing in the two Babylonian academies. Only where he suspected Karaite influence, did his tone become authoritarian, and he declared that he who omitted the midrashic sections in the Passover *Haggadah* should be considered a heretic and liable to excommunication. Natronai once even denounced a Palestinian law which differed from the Babylonian, maintaining, "They err and have gone astray." Natronai insisted on regular congregational recitation of the Aramaic Targum, a decision which was incorporated in R. *Amram's prayer book. He prohibited recitation from vocalized scrolls in the synagogue, a practice encouraged by the Karaites. Natronai also included in his responsa commentaries to various tractates of the Talmud. A collection of *halakhot* similar to the **Ḥalakhot Keẓuvot* which has been ascribed to him is probably a condensation from his responsa, and some of the responsa attributed to Natronai bar Hilai are probably those of Natronai bar Nehemiah, *Gaon* of Pumbedita.

Natronai was also stated to practice mysticism, through the agency of which he caused himself to be transported to Spain, where he taught the people and, just as mysteriously, to have transported himself back to Babylon. Hai Gaon denied this, suggesting that some adventurer may have impersonated Natronai in Spain. Natronai became a legendary personality and many fictitious and fanciful decisions were attributed to him, particularly in Yemenite Midrashim.

BIBLIOGRAPHY: L. Ginzberg, *Geonica*, 2 (1909), 415; S. Assaf, *Teshuvot ha-Ge'onim* (1928), 267; A.L. Frumkin (ed.), *Seder R. Amram*, 1 (1912), 25a–b; Lewin, Oẓar, 2 pt. 2 (1930), 110; 4 pt. 2 (1931), 20; H. Tykocinski, *Takkanot ha-Ge'onim* (1959), passim; M. Havazelet, *Ha-Rambam ve-ha-Ge'onim* (1967), 35 n. 25; S. Liebermann, *Midreshei Teiman* (1940), 39; Baron, Social^2, 3 (1958), index.

[Meir Havazelet]

NATRONAI BAR NEHEMIAH (also known as **Rav Yenuka**), *gaon* of *Pumbedita, 719–730. Natronai married into the family of the exilarch. According to *Sherira Gaon he was said to have dealt so severely with the students of the academy that some of them left and went to the academy at Sura, returning only after his death. Natronai was lenient to the repentant followers of the false messiah Severus (*Serenus), though they had rejected certain talmudic ordinances, permitting them to return to the communal fold. In one responsum however, he opposed the acceptance into the community of children of certain heretical Jews, who had renounced both biblical and talmudic Judaism. Virtually nothing is known of his halakhic decisions.

BIBLIOGRAPHY: Baron, Social^2, 5 (1957), 190, 193f., 207; B.M. Lewin (ed.), *Iggeret R. Sherira Ga'on* (1921), 102f.; *Sha'arei Ẓedek*, responsa (1966^2), 54–55.

[Meir Havazelet]

NATRONAI BEN ḤAVIVAI (**Zavinai**; second half of eighth century), exilarch in Babylonia and pupil of R. *Yehudai Gaon. R. *Sherira relates in his epistle (*Iggeret Rav Sherira Ga'on*, ed. Lewin (1921), 104) that in the year 1082 of the Seleucid era (771) a conflict over the exilarchate broke out between Natronai and Zakkai b. Aḥunai, who had already occupied this position for a number of years. R. Malkha b. R. Aḥa, the *Gaon* of Pumbedita, supported Natronai, but both yeshivot supported Zakkai b. Aḥunai. When R. Malkha died, Natronai was compelled to leave Babylonia. He then traveled to the Maghreb (or Spain). According to Spanish tradition, Natronai prepared from memory a copy of the Babylonian Talmud for the Spanish Jews. It is possible that Natronai was the grandfather of Natronai, the exilarch in Babylonia after 857.

BIBLIOGRAPHY: L. Ginzberg, *Geonica*, 1 (1909), 17–20; B.M. Lewin, *Oẓar ha-Ge'onim*, 1 (1928), 20; S. Abrahamson (ed.), *Massekhet Avodah Zarah; Ketav Yad Beit ha-Midrash le-Rabbanim be-New York* (1957), introd. 13.

[Avraham David]

NATURE. Though the Bible is full of the awareness and appreciation of nature from the creation narrative up to the Psalmist's declaration, "The heavens declare the glory of God…" (Ps. 19:2), it does not profess a comprehensive doctrine of nature in relation to man and God. Nature is a testimony to the work of the Creator (Isa. 40:26; Amos 5:8; Job 38–41), not a subject for speculation. As opposed to the pagan world-view which endowed natural objects with divinity, the Bible makes it quite clear that the natural world was produced by, and totally subject to, God – not in any way part of Him. This, in sum, is its doctrine of nature.

In Rabbinic Literature

A similar lack of speculative interest in nature is apparent in rabbinic literature, though to a lesser degree. Contemplation of the majesty of the heavens or the myriad creatures on earth served the rabbis as a reminder of the wondrous ways of the Creator rather than as the starting point of physical speculation. Thus when R. Akiva considered the manner in which land and sea animals were confined to, and dependent on, their respective elements he would say, "How mighty are Thy works O Lord" (Ps. 104:24; Ḥul. 127a). On the other hand, the purely aesthetic appreciation of nature was played down in preference to the more centrally religious values. This is apparent in the (generally misunderstood) passage, "He who walks by the way studying, and interrupts his studying by saying 'How pleasant is this tree, how pleasant this plowed field'... it is as if he were deserving of death" (Avot 3:8).

The nearest to a conceptual discussion of nature comes in rabbinic consideration of cosmogony and of miracles. The ideas that God looked into the Torah and using it as a blueprint created the natural world (Gen. R. 1:1), and that miracles were built into the natural order at the creation (Avot 5:5; Gen. R. 5:5) would seem to reflect Stoic doctrine (see *Creation and Cosmogony; *Miracles).

The teleological argument, from design in nature to the existence of a Designer, is found in rabbinic literature, albeit in a philosophically naive form. Thus it is said of Abraham that he first came to know God by pondering on the comparison between the world and a palace. Just as a palace which is illuminated must have an owner so too must the world (Gen. R. 39: 1; cf. *Midrash Temurah* 5).

In Hellenistic and Medieval Jewish Philosophy

In their philosophy of nature, as in other branches of philosophy, Hellenistic and medieval Jewish thinkers were influenced greatly by the current general philosophical doctrines. Thus, for the most part, they adopted the view that the universe is governed by immutable laws; that all objects in the sublunar world are formed out of combinations of four basic elements – earth, air, fire, and water; that the celestial world consists of a fifth element; and that substances in the universe can be classified hierarchically as inanimate, vegetative, animate, and rational. However, the philosophical view of nature posed problems for the traditional Jewish view as expressed in the Bible and Talmud. For traditional Judaism the universe did not run according to set immutable laws. Rather God directly regulated the workings of the universe that He had created, ensuring that events would lead to the specific goal He had in mind. The medieval Jewish philosopher, unable to give up this view of nature completely, sought in his philosophies of nature to reconcile the biblical and talmudic concepts of *creation and *miracles with the theories of secular philosophy. For some of them, the design and order that they observed in nature constituted the evidence for the existence of a Creator – the teleological argument.

*Philo held that the world was governed by laws which were instituted by God at the time of creation. He maintained that all objects in the universe were composed of combinations of the four elements, interpreting the wings of the seraphim in Isaiah's vision (Isa. 6) as the four elements, one pair representing earth and water, and the second pair, fire and air. The third pair he interpreted as the forces of love and opposition which initiate movement in the other four elements (*De Deo*, 9–10).

*Saadiah, too, held that all objects are composed of four basic elements (*Emunot ve-De'ot*, 10:17; 1:3; 2:2), and that the world is governed by set laws. As a follower of the *Kalam, which accepted creation and advanced proofs for it, Saadiah had no difficulty with the doctrine of creation. Among the proofs which Saadiah advanced for creation was one based on the order existing in nature, a proof that he adopted from the Kalam. Saadiah argued that since all composite objects must be fashioned from their component parts by an intelligent being, so the world, which is itself a composite of many composites, must have been created (*ibid.*, treatise 1). *Baḥya ibn Paquda employs a similar argument in his *Ḥovot ha-Levavot* (1:6).

NEOPLATONISM. Adopting the neoplatonic conception of the universe as a series of descending spheres, Jewish neoplatonists sought to combine the theory of emanation with the biblical concept of creation. In attempting to do so, Isaac *Israeli, somewhat arbitrarily, maintained that the intellect, which next to God is the highest being in the world, was created by God, and that all other objects emanate from the intellect (S. Fried (ed.), *Sefer ha-Yesodot* (1900), 69). Aristotelian influences are evident in Israeli's doctrine of the elements.

Joseph ibn *Ẓaddik, although generally a neoplatonist, adopted Aristotle's philosophy of nature. However, he deviated from it in his definition of matter and form, assigning to matter the position of the one real substance and to form a status similar to that of accidents (*Sefer Olam Katan*, 1:2).

*Judah Halevi, who was generally critical of Aristotelian philosophy, criticized the Aristotelian doctrine of the four elements on the ground that it has no basis in experience, for while we do perceive the qualities of heat, cold, wetness, and dryness, we do not perceive them in their pure form as primary elements (*Kuzari*, 5:14).

ARISTOTELIANISM. Abraham *Ibn Daud, the first of the Jewish Aristotelians, in his *Emunah Ramah*, adopted the Aristotelian concepts of form and matter, substance and accident, and the categories, finding allusions to the categories in the 139th Psalm. Unable to accept the Aristotelian doctrine of the eternity of matter insofar as it conflicted with the biblical concept of creation, Ibn Daud posited the existence of a formless prime matter which was the first stage in the process of creation.

*Maimonides, while he totally accepted Aristotelian physics, differed with the Aristotelian view that the world is eternal. Maintaining that neither eternity nor creation could be proved, he chose to accept creation as the theory advanced in the Bible. He held that miracles were predetermined at the time of creation, and that they were not abrogations of natural laws, but occurred through the exertion of one natural force upon another.

*Levi b. Gershom disagreed with the Aristotelian notion that time and motion are infinite (*Milḥamot Adonai*, pt. 6, 1:10–12). Levi proved that the world was created from the teleological character of nature. Just as every particular object in nature moves toward the realization of its own particular goal, so the universe, the sum total of all the things that exist within it, moves toward an ultimate end. He is unique among Jewish philosophers in that he rejects the idea of creation *ex nihilo*, maintaining that there existed an eternal absolutely formless matter out of which God at a particular point in time created the universe (*ibid.*, 1:17–28). He interprets the biblical story of creation to coincide with this theory.

*Crescas criticized Aristotelian physics, especially his doctrine of space, maintaining that, in opposition to Aristotle, a vacuum was possible (*Or Adonai*, bk. 1, pt. 2, ch. 3). Crescas believed that it was inconsequential whether or not the world was eternal; what is important is that God created the world *ex nihilo*, but not necessarily at a specific moment in time.

[Alfred L. Ivry]

Modern Period

Scientific philosophy entered a new phase with the doctrine of Kant that the natural world was phenomenal, being the manifestation, through the categories, of the noumenal world – the unknowable *ding an sich*. The development of this doctrine in Fichte, Hegel, and Schelling and the bifurcation of spirit and nature influenced Jewish philosophers of the school of idealism.

Solomon *Formstecher gave Schelling's doctrine of the nonconscious world soul a theistic interpretation. The world soul is the essence of the natural world though separate from and independent of it. Nature, in turn, is totally dependent on the world soul, being but one aspect of its manifestation. Formstecher makes a distinction between the religion of nature – in which the world soul is merely the highest principle of nature, and the religion of the spirit – in which the world soul is independent of nature and is the essence of ethics. The former is paganism, the latter Judaic religion.

In the philosophy of Samuel *Hirsch the central problem is more anthropocentric, namely, the relationship of man to nature, and the framework of his solution is Hegelian. Hirsch relates man and nature to God by regarding Him as the ideal to which man strives in asserting his freedom against nature. For in such ethical striving man is supporting spirit against nature, and spirit is the common element between man and God. Hirsch too distinguishes between the ethical religion of the spirit (Judaism), and nature religion.

Nachman *Krochmal does not, like Formstecher and Hirsch, start from the assumption of a split between spirit and nature. For him nature is merely an end point on the scale of spiritual development, which rises in degrees from primitive religion up to the Jewish world view. This leads him near to a pantheistic position in that he claims that all existence is immanent in the Absolute Spirit, God.

In the early system of Hermann *Cohen, which while accepting Kantianism rejects the unknowable *ding an sich*, the idea of God plays the role of a bridge between ethics and the natural world. It is the guarantee that ethical fulfillment is possible in nature. Since, however, God is ideal rather than real, Judaism is in essence ethics as religion. His later philosophy, however, represents a complete volte-face. There it is God who has prime ontological status, and the natural world is the vehicle of God's manifestation with no independent being of its own.

A.I. *Kook, whose philosophy has been summarized by Hugo Bergman as "mystic pantheism," believed all reality to be a manifestation of God in a myriad of individual forms which in turn have no reality without Him. The plurality of the natural world is unified in God, the source and ground of its being. Adapting a kabbalistic notion, Kook believes that holy sparks are everywhere in nature, for it is shot through with a harmonious divine force. This "life force" of nature is not, like Bergson's *élan vital*, blind, but rather purposive. Evolution of nature is interpreted to mean that all creation, striving to be reunited with God, moves toward the Divinity. Judaism is thus, for Kook, the preeminent attempt to see nature in its total harmony and to sanctify, rather than reject, the material world.

A similarly positive approach to nature is apparent in the ideology of the early Labor Zionist Movement, especially in the work of A.D. *Gordon. Here however, there are clearer heterodox tendencies toward pantheism. Life's ideal, for Gordon, is a form of cosmic harmony of the human and material worlds. This harmony has been interrupted by the unnatural urban life of the Jew in the Diaspora, and in order to reestablish it he has to return to the soil to be as near to nature as possible. Gordon's ideal of unity with nature is not simply an ethical goal but is based on the metaphysical belief that man is organically united to the cosmos, and that it is the unbalanced emphasis on the intellect rather than on man's intuition which is at the root of human alienation.

In the dialogic writings of Martin *Buber, particularly in *I and Thou*, there is an echo of the belief in the existence of "sparks" in all things. It is possible, according to Buber, to enter into an I-Thou relationship even with inanimate objects, and this relationship need not be simply passive but may be one of full mutuality. In answer to criticisms of how one can enter into what seems an essentially personal relationship with non-personal nature, Buber remarks that in such a relationship the natural object reveals its being. There is a reciprocity of being between the person who addresses the object as "Thou" and the object so addressed, for the world is potentially a revelation of the divine (*I and Thou*, postscript, rev. ed. 1958).

BIBLIOGRAPHY: Guttmann, Philosophies, index s.v. *nature; law, natural*; and *science, natural*; Husik, Philosophy, index; I. Efros, *Philosophical Terms in the Moreh Nebukhim* (1924), 50, 134–5; H. Malter, in: *Festschrift… Hermann Cohen* (1912), 253–6 (Eng.); Zunz, Poesie, 634; S.H. Bergman, *Faith and Reason* (1963), 27–54, 81–97, 98–120; I. Epstein, *Judaism* (1954), index; N. Rotenstreich, *Jewish Philosophy in Modern Times* (1968), 52ff.

NATURE RESERVES IN ISRAEL. Despite its limited area, Israel has an extraordinarily varied landscape and a rich array of flora and fauna. There are some 2,800 different species of wild plants (150 of them indigenous) – an extremely high number in relation to the area – in its three geobotanical regions: Mediterranean, Saharo-Sindi, and Irano-Turani, as well as enclaves of tropical and European flora, the most northern and southern known. About 250 of the plants are endemic. The fauna is also varied, though it is only a remnant of the wild life of biblical times; at least 15 large mammalian species have become extinct. There are more than 20 varieties of freshwater fish, several species of amphibians and eight of reptiles, and 380 varieties of birds (150 of which nest in Israel, the remainder being migratory or winter visitors). Israel hosts over 150 million migratory birds each year during the spring and fall seasons. In addition, there are about 70 species of mammals, mostly small rodents and bats. Gazelle, wild boar, ibex, hyena, wolf, jackal, hyrax, caracal, and lynx are still to be found.

The dynamic development of modern Israel has inevitably affected plant and animal ecology. Some 500 new villages and a score of new towns, as well as the rapid expansion of existing ones, have encroached on areas of hitherto undisturbed wild life and natural vegetation. The quadrupling of the population, the rise in the standard of living, and the vast expansion of tourism, have brought large numbers of hikers and trippers to the countryside.

To protect the flora and fauna, a Nature Reserves Authority was established by the government in 1963. Some 380 areas have been selected as nature reserves in which landscape, flora, and fauna are protected in their natural condition. Some are large reserves, in which the flora and fauna maintain an equilibrium, for instance on Mt. Meron (about 70,000 dunams: 17,500 acres). There are also the smaller areas maintained for specific scientific reasons, e.g., winter pools to preserve lower crustacea and amphibians, a ridge of sandstone with its typical flora, islands on which common tern nest, and sites such as Ḥorshat Tal and Circassia as reminders of the landscape that once existed. While most of the reserves are open to the public, some are closed to preserve their scientific value. Facilities for visitors have been provided at Tel Dan, the "Tannur" near Metullah, the cave of "Pa'ar," the "Masrek" near Jerusalem, En-Gedi, etc., and the work is being extended to other places throughout the country. The Nature Reserves Authority has also undertaken to reintroduce species that have become extinct in Israel. At the *Ḥai-Bar* (wildlife) Biblical Game Reserve at Yotvata (34,500 dunams; 8,650 acres), attempts were begun in 1966 to breed some of these extinct species, with the approval of the World Wildlife Fund. Another *Hai-Bar* is located on Mt. Carmel (6,000 dunams; 1,500 acres) and includes species that used to live on the mountain. In 1998 the Nature Reserves Authority became part of the Israel Nature and Park Authority, a combined authority responsible for all the natural and archeological reserves and parks in Israel.

BIBLIOGRAPHY: M. Zohary, *Geobotanikah* (Heb., 1955); Rashut Shemurot ha-Teva, *Pirsumim* (1965–); **WEBSITES:** www.mfa.gov.il; www.parks.org.il.

[Abraham Yoffe / Shaked Gilboa (2nd ed.)]

NATZWEILER-STRUTHOF, Nazi concentration camp in Alsace, southwest of Strasbourg, that operated from May 1941 to Aug. 31, 1944. The site was mainly chosen because of its proximity to vast quarries where prison labor could be exploited. The camp became known as Natzweiler-Struthof because until the Natzweiler camp was completed, prisoners were housed in the nearby former Hotel Struthof. The camp was in the third or harshest category of concentration camps, and served as a concentration and redistribution center for political prisoners. Beginning in the summer of 1943, it was used to intern "Night and Fog" (*Nacht und Nebel*) prisoners from France and southwest Germany. In 1944, the camp was used to produce arms and to construct underground manufacturing facilities. The commandants were Hans Huettig, Egon Zill, Josef Kramer (the "Beast of Belsen," who served at Bergen Belsen), and Fritz Hartjenstein, who was in charge from April 1944 until the camp inmates and staff were evacuated and sent to *Dachau with the approach of the Allies. Natzweiler-Struthof provided the Reich University at Strasbourg with inmates to be used for various pseudo-medical (including lethal) experiments. The scientists at Strasbourg experimented with combat gases and infectious diseases (hepatitis and others), with Roma (gypsies) being the primary victims. In August 1943, a gas chamber was constructed. Kramer gassed about 100 Jewish prisoners specially brought from *Auschwitz to supply August Hirt at the Reich University with specimens for his anthropological and racial skeleton collection in the anatomical institute. Among those especially brought for execution at Natzweiller were female agents of the French Resistance. Altogether, it is estimated that 25,000 prisoners died in the camp.

BIBLIOGRAPHY: Bibliothèque du Centre de Documentation Juive Contemporaine. For further reference see Catalogue no. 1, *La France de l'Affaire Dreyfus à nos jours* (1964), 77–78; Catalogue no. 2 (1968) 40. **ADD. BIBLIOGRAPHY:** United States Holocaust Memorial Museum website, article 10005337.

[Yehuda Reshef / David Weinberg (2nd ed.)]

NAUHEIM (Bad Nauheim), town in Hesse, Germany. Jews may have lived in Nauheim as early as 1303; during the *Black Death persecutions (1348) they were expelled from the duchy of *Hanau. In 1464 three Jewish households are noted in the city; in a document of the same year they appear as imperial *Kammerknechte* ("serfs of the chamber"; see *servi camerae *regis*) whose tax payments form part of a transaction between the margrave of Brandenburg and the count of Hanau. Jews are again attested as taxpayers in Nauheim in the 16th century. They were expelled once more in 1539. From the middle of the 16th century onward some **Schutzjuden* lived in Nauheim, but their number was small. Nauheim Jews began worshiping in a rented prayer room in 1830. In 1861 there were 34 Jews in Nauheim. A Jewish cemetery was consecrated in 1866, and a new one in the first years of the 20th century. The first synagogue dates from 1867; a second larger one was built in 1928. At that time, the community had a religious school and a *ḥevra kaddisha*. In 1933 the Jewish population numbered 300. The synagogue survived the Nazi period and was used once more by a reestablished congregation that totaled 124 persons in 1970. The Jewish community numbered 84 in 1989 and 341 in 2005. The increase is explained by the immigration of Jews from the former Soviet Union.

BIBLIOGRAPHY: R. Stahl, *Geschichte der Nauheimer Juden* (1929); FJW, 395; Germ Jud, 2 (1968), 570. **ADD BIBLIOGRAPHY:** P. Arnsberg, *Die juedischen Gemeinden in Hessen.* Bilder, Dokumente, vol. 3 (1973) 153–54; *op cit.*, Anfang, Untergang, Neubeginn, vol. 1; *op. cit.*, vol 2, 103–11; S. Kolb, *Die Geschichte der Bad Nauheimer Juden. Eine gescheiterte Assimilation* (1987); *Germania Judaica*, vol. 3, 1350–1514 (1987), 927–28.

[Larissa Daemmig (2nd ed)]

NAUMBOURG, SAMUEL (1815–1880), *ḥazzan*, composer, and writer. Born in Dennelohe, near Ansbach (Bavaria), the descendant of almost ten generations of south German *ḥazzanim*, Naumbourg received his musical education at Munich and sang there in Maier *Kohn's synagogue choir. After an engagement as choirmaster in Strasbourg, he came to Paris in 1843. In 1845 he was appointed first *ḥazzan* at the synagogue in the Rue Notre-Dame-de-Nazareth, under the sponsorship of Jacques Fromental *Halévy and with the government authorization to carry out his plans for a thorough reform of liturgic music (which had lapsed into disorder after the death of Israel *Lovy in 1832). In 1847 he published the first two volumes of his *Zemirot Yisrael* (vol. 1 for the Sabbath, vol. 2 for the High Holidays), with vol. 3 *Hymnes et Psaumes* added when the work was reissued in 1864 (repr. 1874, 1954). In 1874 he brought out a collection of traditional synagogue melodies, *Aguddat Shirim*, which also included some western Sephardi material, and a long preface on the history of Jewish religious music. In 1877 Naumbourg published the first modern edition of Salamone de *Rossi's *Ha-Shirim Asher li-Shelomo* (30 out of 33 pieces) and a selection of his madrigals, with the collaboration of Vincent d'Indy, under the name of *Cantiques de Salamon Rossi*; the historical importance of the undertaking is in no way diminished by its many editorial failings and liberties. Naumbourg's *Zemirot Yisrael* achieved an influence comparable to the works of his senior Solomon *Sulzer and his junior Louis *Lewandowsky. The pieces are set for *ḥazzan* and 2- to 4-part choir, with some organ accompaniments and, apart from Naumbourg's own compositions and arrangements, include some melodies by Lovy and two works by Halévy and *Meyerbeer. About half of the pieces are based on traditional material, mainly south German. The others reflect the various styles then current in the Parisian grand opera, which "gave to Naumbourg's work some international features and helped it to become widely known, and much liked and used" (Idelsohn).

BIBLIOGRAPHY: Sendrey, Music, index; Idelsohn, Music, 262–6 and index.

[Bathja Bayer]

NAUMBURG, U.S. family of bankers and philanthropists. The founder, ELKAN NAUMBURG (1834–1924), was born in Germany, and went to the U.S. in 1850. He subsequently became a partner in the clothing firm of Naumburg, Kraus, Lauer & Company. After the firm was dissolved in 1893, Naumburg founded the banking house of E. Naumburg and Co., which specialized in advancing loans to business enterprises. A lover of music, he established and endowed the free summer concert programs at New York City's Central Park in 1905, and contributed the funds for the park's band shell. He also gave liberally to other philanthropies.

His eldest son WALTER WEHLE NAUMBURG (1867–1959), who was born in New York, entered his father's clothing business and then entered the newly established family banking business. He and his younger brother George Washington dissolved the firm in 1931 in order to devote themselves to charity. Besides continuing the Central Park concerts instituted by their father, Walter Naumburg founded the Walter W. Naumburg Musical Foundation (1926) which sponsored the debuts of talented musicians and the Musicians Foundation to care for needy musicians. He was a trustee of Mt. Sinai Hospital and a member of the Salvation Army's board.

His wife, ELSIE MARGARET BINGER NAUMBURG (1880–1953), was a well-known ornithologist who served on the staff of the American Museum of Natural History. Her monograph, *The Birds of Matto Grosso, Brazil* (1930), dealt with the ornithological finds of Theodore Roosevelt's expedition to Brazil. She established the Dr. Frank Chapman Memorial Fund to support ornithological research.

GEORGE WASHINGTON NAUMBURG (1876–1970). George Washington Naumburg was born in New York City, and entered the family banking business after graduating from Harvard in 1898. During World War I, he served as assistant chief of the cotton section of the War Industries Board. In 1933, two years after his bank's dissolution, he was appointed president of the New York Guaranteed Protection Corporation. A vigorous advocate of government economy, Naumburg was treasurer of the National Economy League in the 1930s and a director and vice president of the Citizens Budget Commission. As a philanthropist, Naumburg's principal interest lay in the area of child welfare. He was active in the National Child Welfare Association, and supported psychiatric treatment programs for children. Also active in Jewish affairs, Naumburg was a director of the Joint Distribution Committee, head of the Federation of Jewish Philanthropies finance committee, trustee of the Jewish Board of Guardians, and president of the Baron de Hirsch Fund (1932–70).

ROBERT ELKAN NAUMBURG (1892–1953). Robert Elkan Naumburg was born in New York, and graduated from the Massachusetts Institute of Technology. A mechanical engineer and inventor, Naumburg constructed the visigraph, a machine allowing the blind to "read" electrically-embossed characters on paper. After World War II, Naumburg donated the invention to the federal government for use by sightless veterans.

NAUMBURG, MARGARET (1890–1983), U.S. psychoanalyst, art therapist, and educator. Born in New York, Naumburg graduated from Barnard College, Columbia University. She then studied speech therapy with F. Matthias Alexander at the London School of Economics and child education with Maria Montessori in Rome. Influenced by Freud's theories, Naumburg maintained that the child was an individual with his own inner life and needs and that education should serve the child, and not the child education. In 1913, she founded and conducted the first Montessori class in New York City at the Henry Street Settlement. A year later she launched her own school, the Walden School, based on the importance of the personal relationship between pupils and teachers. She was a pioneer in art education and in the use of art for therapeutic purposes. From 1930 on, she concerned herself primarily with developing art therapy technique and moved away from progressive education. She devoted much of her life to the establishment of art therapy as a discipline. Naumburg taught at New York University into her eighties. She initiated art therapy instruction there at the undergraduate level. A graduate program for art therapy was instituted in 1969.

Naumburg's methods were disseminated by exhibitions at meetings of the American Psychiatric Association and at international psychiatric congresses. Naumburg's books include *The Child and the World* (1928); *Studies of the "Free" Art Expression of Behavior Problem Children and Adolescents as a Means of Diagnosis and Therapy* (1947); *Schizophrenic Art: Its Meaning in Psychotherapy* (1950); *Psychoneurotic Art: Its Function in Psychotherapy* (1953); and *Dynamically Oriented Art Therapy* (1966).

BIBLIOGRAPHY: Walden School, *The Walden Story* (1954); Walden School, *Walden School on Its 50th Anniversary* (1964).

[Ernest Schwarcz / Ruth Beloff (2nd ed.)]

NAUPAKTOS (Lepanto, Inebahti), town in W. central Greece. Benjamin of Tudela, the 12th-century traveler, reported 100 Jews in the town. The Venetians ruled there from 1408 to 1499. Documentation from 1430 shows the existence of large-scale commercial dealings by Jewish bankers between the ports of Lepanto and Patras. There was a *Romaniot community in Naupaktos and after 1492 refugees opened two synagogues, one according to the Spanish rite and the other according to the Sicilian. Jewish merchants used to send to Budapest and Turkey *lulavim* and *etrogim* which they grew in the vicinity of Naupaktos. A special "Purim of Lepanto" was celebrated on the 11th of Tevet in memory of the community's miraculous preservation following the Turkish conquest of the city (1571). In the 16th century R. Joseph Pirmon attempted to unite the three communities but was opposed by the Romaniot minority who were supported by Samuel *Medina. At the beginning of the 17th century, the local Jews suffered greatly from efforts of the local governor to extort large sums of money from them. In the 1720s and 1730s, two local Jewish partners served Ottoman ministers. In 1746, a group of 16 Jews left the city to settle in Ereẓ Israel but were captured at sea and taken to the Island of Mykinos, being released after enduring much hardship. In 1806, the Jewish community numbered 30 families, or 150 people. In the wake of the Greek uprisings against the Turks in 1821-22, the Jewish community was destroyed.

BIBLIOGRAPHY: Rosanes, Togarmah, vols. 1 and 3, passim; S. Krauss, *Studien zur byzantinisch-juedischen Geschichte* (1914), 79. **ADD. BIBLIOGRAPHY:** L. Bornstein-Makovetski, "Naupaktas," in: *Pinkas Kehillot Yavan* (1999), 183–88; S.B. Bowman, *The Jews Of Byzantium 1204–1453* (1985), 88, 307–8.

[Simon Marcus / Yitzchak Kerem (2nd ed.)]

NAVARRO, Portuguese family, prominent in the 14th and 15th centuries.

MOSES NAVARRO of Santarem (d. c. 1370), personal physician to King Pedro I and his chief tax collector, served for nearly 30 years as chief rabbi (**arraby moor*) of Portugal. The king granted Moses and his wife, Salva, the right to adopt the family name Navarro and to bequeath it to his descendants. His son, JUDAH, inherited the posts of personal physician and chief tax collector under Pedro I and continued in the latter capacity under John I. He and Solomon Negro agreed to pay some 200,000 livres annually for five years for the privilege of farming taxes. He is also known to have given the king a rich estate in Alvito, Alemtejo. Moses' grandson (or son according to Amador de los Rios), also called MOSES (d. c. 1410), was likewise chief rabbi and personal physician to the king, in this case John I. All three Navarros used their offices to benefit their fellow-Jews. Particularly noteworthy are the efforts of the younger Moses Navarro at the time of the large-scale massacres of the Spanish Jews in 1391. In that year he presented the Portuguese king with the bull decreed on July 2, 1389, by Pope Boniface IX (based on a bull of Pope *Clement VI), forbidding Christians to harm the Jews, desecrate their cemeteries, or attempt to baptize them by force. On July 17, 1392, the king ordered the promulgation of this bull throughout Portugal, reinforcing it with legislation of his own. Moses was also instrumental in acquiring the king's protection for Jewish refugees from Spain.

BIBLIOGRAPHY: J. Amador de los Rios, *Historia social, politica y religiosa de los judíos de España y Portugal*, 2 (1876), 266ff., 271, 278, 456ff.; M. Kayserling, *Geschichte der Juden in Portugal* (1867), 25, 38ff.; J. Mendes dos Remedios, *Os Judeus em Portugal*, 1 (1895), 157f., 163.

[Martin A. Cohen]

NAVARRO, ABRAHAM (d. c. 1692), envoy in China and India. Navarro, a London Sephardi who may have earlier lived in Jamaica, was commissioned in 1682 by the East India Company to accompany the ship *Delight* to China as interpreter and linguist. In 1683 it reached Amoy, where Navarro began negotiations for opening trade relations. When these failed, Navarro returned to India, and engaged in trade. In 1689 Navarro was sent to the court of the powerful Moghul ruler Aurangzeb to negotiate a peace treaty. After a personal audience with the emperor, a firman for the British trade was obtained.

BIBLIOGRAPHY: Fischel, in: PAAJR, 25 (1956), 39–62; 26 (1957), 25–39.

[Walter Joseph Fischel]

NAVEH (Heb. נָוֶה), city in Bashan, possibly mentioned in the lists of cities conquered by Thutmosis III (no. 75) and Ramses II (no. 13). *Zeno visited it during his travels in 259 B.C.E. In talmudic times, it was a well-known Jewish center with its own territory (Tosef., Shev. 4:8); the *nesi'im* had extensive possessions there. Naveh and the neighboring city of Ḥalamish were at odds (Lam. R. 1:17, no. 52). Eusebius calls it a Jewish town (Onom. 136:3). The Jewish community persisted until the time of the Crusades, and the city was the home town of many scholars. In Byzantine times it was part of Provincia Arabia and had a bishop. It is the present-day Arab village of Nawā, in which the legendary tomb of *Shem and the tomb of Joseph b. Saadiah (1062) are located. Jewish remains include many fragments of a synagogue built by Bar Yudan and Levi.

BIBLIOGRAPHY: G. Schumacher, *Across the Jordan* (1866), 167ff.; Dalman, in: PJB, 8 (1913), 59–60; Mayer and Reifemberg, in: BJPES, 4 (1936), 1ff.; Braslavski, *ibid.*, 8ff.; Klein, *ibid.*, 76ff.; Amiran, in: IEJ, 6 (1956), 243–4; Avi-Yonah, Geog., 155; Press Ereẓ, 3 (1952[2]), 624.

[Michael Avi-Yonah]

NAVON, BENJAMIN MORDECAI BEN EPHRAIM (1788–1851), kabbalist and halakhist, one of the outstanding Jerusalem sages of his time, son of Ephraim b. Jonah Navon. Navon was called Jilibin (Çelebi, a Turkish title of honor). He was head of the kabbalists of the "Midrash Ḥasidim Kehillah Kedoshah Bet El" and head of a *bet din*. He devoted himself to a great extent to communal affairs, and assisted Israel Bak in establishing his pioneer printing press in Jerusalem in 1841. Navon wrote many responsa, some of which were published under the title *Benei Binyamin* (1876) by Jacob Saul *Elyashar, his stepson and disciple, who also included many of his sermons in his *Ish Emunim* (1885).

BIBLIOGRAPHY: Frumkin-Rivlin, 3 (1929), 292f.; M.D. Gaon, *Yehudei ha-Mizraḥ be-Ereẓ Yisrael*, 2 (1937), 450f.; Benayahu, in: *Sinai*, 24 (1948/49), 205–14; idem, *Rabbi Ḥayyim Joseph David Azulai* (1959), 275.

[Abraham David]

NAVON, DAVID (1943–), Israeli psychologist. Born in Tel Aviv, he studied at the Hebrew University of Jerusalem and received his doctorate in psychology from San Diego University in California. He taught at Haifa University where he became a professor in 1984 and was dean of the Faculty of Psychology. He was a leading researcher in cognitive psychology. Among his areas of interest were attention and perception. He is known mainly for a widely used experimental model and for a number of influential theoretical papers. In all, his papers have been cited around 2,400 times. In 1992 he became a member of the Israel Academy of Sciences and Humanities and received the Israel Prize for social sciences.

[Shaked Gilboa (2nd ed.)]

NAVON, EPHRAIM BEN AARON (1677–1735), rabbi and halakhist. Navon was born in Constantinople, and emigrated to Jerusalem about 1700, together with his father-in-law, Judah Ergas. He returned to Turkey in 1721 as an emissary of Jerusalem. On the termination of his mission there in 1723, he was appointed a *dayyan* in the *bet din* of Judah *Rosanes in Constantinople, and later received the appointment of rabbi. While in Constantinople, he continued to concern himself with the amelioration of the material conditions of the Jewish community of Jerusalem. In 1738 his *Maḥaneh Efrayim* appeared in Constantinople, containing responsa and novellae on the Talmud and the works of early halakhic authorities. ARYEH JUDAH NAVON (1707–1761), his son, was the teacher of Yom Tov *Algazi.

BIBLIOGRAPHY: Frumkin-Rivlin, 2 (1928), 157; Rosanes, Togarmah, 4 (1935), 207; M.D. Gaon, *Yehudei ha-Mizraḥ be-Ereẓ Yisrael*, 2 (1937), 449; Yaari, Sheluḥei, 116, 130, 361–2.

[Avraham David]

NAVON, ISAAC ELIYAHU (1859–1952), Israeli composer and poet. Born in Adrianople (Edirne), Turkey, he taught in a Hebrew school established by his father in Constantinople and wrote for Jewish newspapers. He also helped to reorganize the Maftirim fraternity of Adrianople (most of whose members had immigrated to Constantinople), and to publish their songbook *Shirei Yisrael be-Ereẓ ha-Kedem* (1921), which contained a number of his own poems and a foreword by *Bialik. In 1929 Navon settled in Jerusalem, later in Tel Aviv, and devoted himself to spreading the Sephardi musical tradition. Some of the songs he collected or composed entered into the Israeli folksong tradition, notably "*Niẓẓanei Shalom,*" "*Ḥaddesh ke-Kedem Yameinu,*" and "*Gizratekh Tavnit Nogah.*" He published further poems of his own in 1932.

BIBLIOGRAPHY: M.D. Gaon, in: I.E. Navon, *Yinnon* (1932), introd.; I. Levy (ed.), *Yonah Homiyyah, Mi-Shirei Yiẓḥak Eliyahu Navon* (1950), includes music; Barkai, in: *Hallel*, 1 (1930), 45–47; L. Saminsky, *Music of the Ghetto and the Bible* (1934), 159, 161; Bayer, in: *Taẓlil*, 7 (1967), 149; Tidhar, 2 (1947), 728–9.

[Bathja Bayer]

NAVON, JONAH BEN HANUN (1713?–1760), rabbi and author. Navon was born in Jerusalem where his father was a rabbi. He studied in the *bet ha-midrash* Bet Ya'akov Pereira under Israel Meir Mizraḥi. In 1746 he headed the *bet ha-midrash* Keneset Yisrael, founded by Ḥayyim ibn *Attar, and when the yeshivah Gedulat Mordekhai was established Navon was appointed to head it, and was at the same time one of the heads of the Yefa'er Anavim yeshivah. Among his pupils was Ḥ.J.D. *Azulai, who was the son of his brother-in-law. He traveled as an emissary of Jerusalem to North Africa in 1737, and again to Turkey and Greece during 1746–48. He was the author of responsa *Neḥpah ba-Kesef* (2 parts, Constantinople, 1748; Jerusalem, 1843), to which was added his supercommentary on Elijah *Mizraḥi's commentary to the *Sefer Mitzvot Gadol* (*Semag*) of Moses of *Coucy; *Get Mekushar* (Leghorn, 1785), novellae and comments on the *Get Pashut* of Moses ibn *Ḥabib. His other works have remained in manuscript. His sons were Ephraim, Benjamin, and Mordecai.

BIBLIOGRAPHY: Frumkin-Rivlin, 3 (1929), 20–22; Yaari, Sheluḥei, 306–7; M. Benayahu, *Ha-Ḥida* (1959), 333–5.

[Abraham David]

NAVON, JONAH MOSES BEN BENJAMIN (d. 1841), rabbi and Jerusalem emissary. Navon, together with his cousin, Joseph Saadiah Navon, was sent to Gibraltar and to various Moroccan communities by the rabbis of Jerusalem in 1802–03 in order to mobilize financial aid for the Jerusalem community. He went on a second mission in 1804, and on his return was appointed a member of the *bet din* of Solomon Moses Suzin, whom he succeeded at the end of 1836 as *Rishon le-Zion*, a position he held until his death. Navon used his great authority to assist the Ashkenazi community of Jerusalem in acquiring the "Ḥurvah Synagogue" of Judah he-Ḥasid from the Arabs and in erecting a synagogue on the site. Navon added novellae and glosses to the *Neḥpah ba-Kesef*, vol. 2 (Jerusalem, 1843) of his grandfather, Jonah b. Hanun *Navon, and some of his own responsa appear in the *Ḥukkei Ḥayyim (ibid.*, 1843) of Ḥayyim *Gagin.

BIBLIOGRAPHY: Frumkin-Rivlin, 3 (1929), 274–5; M.D. Gaon, *Yehudei ha-Mizraḥ be-Ereẓ Yisrael*, 2 (1937), 453; Benayahu, in: *Sinai*, 24 (1948/49), 25–14; Yaari, *ibid.*, 25 (1949), 320–30; Yaari, Sheluḥei, 566–7.

[Abraham David]

NAVON, JOSEPH (1858–1934), pioneer of Ereẓ Israel development. Navon was born into a prominent Sephardi family in *Jerusalem. His father, Eliahu Navon, was the Jewish representative in the Jerusalem regional council. Joseph was educated in France, and on his return became a merchant and banker. He and his uncle Ḥayyim *Amzalak helped the settlers in Petaḥ Tikvah and Rishon le-Zion enter their lands in the land registry. With his banking partner Frontiger he pioneered in popular housing schemes in Jerusalem (including the Beit Yosef and Battei Navon quarters). He had ambitious schemes for the development of Ereẓ Israel, including railway development, the building of a port in *Jaffa, and providing irrigation facilities for the citrus groves of the coastal plain. After lengthy negotiations in Constantinople, he received a concession in 1888 to construct a railway from Jaffa to Jerusalem, which he, in turn, transferred to the Société Ottomane de Chemin de Fer de Jaffa à Jerusalem et Prolongements founded by him in France in consideration of one million francs. After the opening of the line, he received the title *bey* from the Ottoman government in recognition of his services in developing Ereẓ Israel. After he lost his capital, he moved to Paris in 1894. Here he met *Herzl and tried to interest him in his plans for developing Ereẓ Israel. He died in Paris.

BIBLIOGRAPHY: K. Grunwald, in: K.H. Manegold (ed.), *Festschrift W. Treue* (1969), 240–54 (Eng.); M.D. Gaon, *Yehudei ha-Mizraḥ be-Ereẓ Yisrael*, 2 (1937), 454–6; Tidhar, 1 (1947), 70–71.

[Yehuda Slutsky]

NAVON, YITZHAK (1921–), Israeli politician, writer, and the fifth president of the state of Israel; member of the Sixth to Twelfth Knessets. Navon was born in Jerusalem to an old Sephardi family of well-known rabbis that had settled in Ereẓ Israel in the 17th century. He received religious schooling until the end of primary school, and then attended the Beit ha-Kerem high school. After graduating from the Hebrew University, where he studied Literature, Arabic, Islamic Culture and Education, he became a teacher. In 1946–48 he headed the Haganah Arab Department in Jerusalem. After serving in the Israeli embassy in Argentina and Uruguay in 1949–50, he was appointed political secretary to Minister for Foreign Affairs Moshe *Sharett in 1951, and director of the prime minister's office, serving under both David *Ben-Gurion and Sharett in 1952–63. In 1963–65 he was director of the cultural section in the Ministry of Education and Culture. Navon joined the *Rafi party in 1965 and that year was elected to the Sixth Knesset in which he served as one of its deputy speakers. Within the framework of Rafi he joined the *Israel Labor Party when it was formed in 1968. In 1972 he was elected chairman of the Zionist General Council, in which capacity he served until 1977. In the Eighth Knesset Navon served as chairman of the Knesset Foreign Affairs and Security Committee. In 1977 Navon headed the public committee established to determine the method for determining tuition in universities. In 1978, even though the Likud was in power, Navon was elected by the Knesset as Israel's fifth president. In October 1980 he paid the first-ever official state visit to Egypt by an Israeli president. Navon decided not to run for a second term as president, resigning in 1983 in order to run for the leadership of the Labor Party, being encouraged to do so by Uzi *Baram. He finally decided not to run opposite Shimon *Peres but ran in the elections to the Eleventh Knesset. In the National Unity governments that served from 1984 to 1988 Navon was appointed deputy prime minister and minister of education and culture, continuing to serve as minister of education and culture until March 1990, when Labor left Yitzhak *Shamir's government. As minister of education he paid special attention to education for democracy, the battle against racism, and the inculcation of Jewish and universal values. After leaving the government Navon served as chairman of the public council that prepared the events in commemoration of the 500th anniversary of the expulsion of the Jews from Spain that was to take place in 1994. Navon did not run in the elections to the Thirteenth Knesset, and declined a proposal to run in the 1993 elections for mayor of Jerusalem. Had he run he might well have defeated the Likud candidate Ehud *Olmert. In 1996 he served as chairman of the public committee appointed to investigate the scandal of the destruction of blood donated by Ethiopian immigrants. He served as president of the National Authority for *Ladino which acts for the preservation of the Ladino language and culture.

Navon wrote the text for two popular musical plays based on Sephardi folklore, *Sephardic Romancero* (1968) and *Bustan Sephardi* ("Spanish Garden," 1970). Among his writings are

Sheshet ha-Yamim ve-Shivat ha-She'arim ("The Six Days and The Seven Gates," 1976).

[Susan Hattis Rolef (2nd ed.)]

NAWI, rabbinical and philanthropic family in Iraq. REUBEN BEN DAVID (end of 18th century–1821) was a prominent disciple of outstanding *ḥakhamim* in *Baghdad. His main teacher, the *ḥakham* Moses b. Ḥayyim, nominated him during his lifetime (1810) as his successor as *av bet din* in Baghdad, but he died prior to his master. Nawi's teachings are extant in the works of his disciples, the *dayyanim* R. Abdullah Somekh, Jacob b. Joseph b. Jawb ha-Rofe, and others. Many legends concerning his life are current among Baghdad Jews. At the end of the 19th and in the first quarter of the 20th centuries SOLOMON REUBEN and MANASSEH SOLOMON took an active part in the affairs of the Baghdad community, and improving the health conditions of Baghdad Jewry.

BIBLIOGRAPHY: A. Ben-Yaacov, *Yehudei Bavel* (1965), index; D.S. Sassoon, *History of the Jews in Baghdad* (1949), 136–7.

[Eliyahu Hirschberg]

NAZARETH (Heb. נָצְרַת), town in Galilee, mentioned several times in the New Testament as the home to which Mary and Joseph, her husband, returned with the child from Egypt and where *Jesus was brought up (Matt. 2:23; Luke 2:39, 51). Archaeological evidence has shown that the area was settled as early as the Middle Bronze Age, and tombs have been found dating from the Iron Age to Hasmonean times. According to the New Testament, Joseph and Mary lived in Nazareth before Jesus' birth, which was announced there to Mary by the angel Gabriel (Luke 1:26; 2:4). When Jesus tried to preach to the people of the town, he was attacked, his assailants attempting to throw him headlong from a cliff, identified by tradition as the Jebel Qafza, a hill 350 m. above sea level. Although he left Nazareth, possibly as a result of the incident (Luke 4:16–30; Matt. 4:13), the name Jesus of Nazareth nevertheless remained in common use both in his lifetime and among his followers, especially the apostle Peter. Members of Jesus' family continued to live in Nazareth at least into the second century. The term "Nazarene" was a derogatory name utilized by one's enemies during the first century (Matt. 21:11), and the Hebrew and Arabic terms for Christians (*Noẓeri, Nasrāni*) are derived from the town's name. Nazareth is not mentioned in non-Christian sources until the third or fourth century, when it was recorded in an inscription found at Caesarea listing the priestly courses and their seats in Galilee. According to this list (which is reproduced in the seventh-century liturgical poems of Kallir and others), the family of Happizzez (I Chron. 24:15) settled in Nazareth, a name derived in this source from the root *nṣr* (to guard). It is described by Jerome as a very small village in Galilee (Onom. 141:3). Constantine may have included it in the territory of Helenopolis, a city which he founded, but the town remained purely Jewish in the fourth century.

Excavations conducted by B. Bagatti from 1955 to 1968 on the site of the Church of the Annunciation revealed the remains of a church with a mosaic pavement dating to about 450. Below the church and nearby were the remains of a Jewish town from the Roman period in which were pear-shaped silos, vaulted cellars, cisterns, ritual immersion pools (*mikva'to*), and olive presses. Among the remains were about 80 partly-stuccoed and inscribed stones, as well as column bases. The excavators view these finds as the remnants of a Judeo-Christian synagogue or a Constantinian church built for Jews. The first mention of a church in Nazareth was made in 570 by Antoninus Placentinus, who describes it as a converted synagogue.

In 614 the Jews in the mountains of Nazareth joined the Persians in their war against the Byzantines. Shortly before the Crusader conquest, the town was destroyed by Muslim Arabs. Tancred captured Nazareth, and the Crusaders built a church, whose finely sculptured capitals (now in the Franciscan Museum) exhibit French workmanship of the 12th century. The archbishopric of Beth-Shean was transferred to Nazareth during the Crusades. After winning the decisive battle against the crusader forces on July 4, 1187, Saladin captured the town; its crusader forces and European clergy were forced to retreat to the coast. At that time, according to an eyewitness account, the townspeople were either massacred or imprisoned while the Basilica was profaned. The city was again in Christian hands in 1240 and 1250, and in 1252 St. Louis of France visited there. In 1263 Baybars ordered a pogrom against the Christians and destruction of churches of the land which included the Basilica at Nazareth, which remained in ruins for 400 years. The Franciscans returned to the town in 1620 by permission of the emir Fakhr al-Dīn. A new church was built under Ẓāhir al-ʿAmir in 1730. In 1955 the present Basilica was commissioned by Franciscans, and the building was consecrated in 1969 based upon a three-level design incorporating the remains from a Roman Period pubic building and the Byzantine and Crusader Basilicas in the lower church.

[Michael Avi-Yonah / Stephen Phann (2nd ed.)]

Modern Nazareth and Naẓerat Illit

In April 1799 *Napoleon's troops occupied Nazareth, but with his retreat it was recaptured by Aḥmad Jazzār Pasha. In 1890 the German scholar G. Schumacher estimated Nazareth's population at 7,500. Shortly before the outbreak of World War I, the German military command established its Palestinian headquarters there. The town was taken by the British in 1918; at that time there were 8,000 inhabitants, two-thirds of whom were Christian, and the rest Muslim. In the 1920s Nazareth's economy was still based largely on agriculture, as its inhabitants owned lands in the Jezreel Valley. The town remained surrounded with olive groves, which supplied it with raw materials for the manufacture of oil and soap. The Muslim element in Nazareth was strengthened when villagers from the vicinity were absorbed there. Nazareth became a market center for a wide agricultural region and a pilgrimage and tourist center, developing handicrafts, while inhabitants also found work in the Haifa industrial zone.

In July 1948, during the War of Independence, the Israel army took Nazareth from Kaukji's forces in "Operation Dekel." Its population remained and was augmented by Arabs who had abandoned other locations in Israel. It thus increased from 9,000 inhabitants in 1947 to 25,100 in 1961 and 32,900 in 1969, Muslims attaining a slight majority over Christians. In 2002 the population of Nazareth was 61,700, with a municipal area of 6.4 sq. mi. (16.5 sq. km.). It included 67% Muslims and 33% Christians. Unemployment reached 14%, including 80% among women, and income was about half the national average. Tensions between Muslims and Christians, increasing as the Muslims gained hegemony, reached a peak when Muslim residents sought to build a mosque near the Church of the Annunciation.

Nazareth became the largest Arab center in the State of Israel (in its pre-1967 borders) and, with a number of private and public secondary schools, an important center of Arab education and culture. It has a hinterland of Arab villages both in Galilee to the north and in the southern Jezreel Valley and the Iron Hills to the south, constituting a highway junction connected with Haifa, Tiberias, Afulah, and Shefar'am. In 1970 Nazareth had 24 churches and convents of different Christian denominations, the newest being the Catholic Basilica of the Annunciation – the largest church in the Middle East – constructed between 1955 and 1968 over the Grotto of the Annunciation and the foundations of the original Byzantine church. Tourism and pilgrimages have been important sources of Nazareth's economy. Other branches of its economy comprise small industries and workshops and administrative services. An increasing number of laborers have been employed in Naẓerat Illit.

In 2000, Nazareth was declared a high-priority tourist site, and the Nazareth 2000 Project initiated large-scale roadwork and rehabilitation of the Old City, together with the construction of new hotels and museums.

In 1957 the ground was laid for the neighboring Jewish development town of Naẓerat Illit. Israel-born settlers formed the nucleus of its population, which was augmented by immigrants mainly from Europe. It received city status in 1974. Its population increased from 1,000 in 1957 to 13,200 in 1969, and reached 35,200 by the mid-1990s and 44,290 in 2002, including 91% Jews, 2% Muslims, and the rest Christians. In these latter years the city absorbed 25,000 new immigrants, which led to construction of new neighborhoods. The municipal area extends over 11.5 sq. mi. (29.7 sq. km.). The city has broad avenues tracing the hill contours, with large apartment buildings occupying the western and central sections and industrial structures on the eastern one. The economy of Naẓerat Illit was based on relatively large enterprises. In the early 2000s, its industrial areas included approximately 100 factories in various industries, such as food, textiles, electronics, steel, etc.

[Shlomo Hasson / Shaked Gilboa (2nd ed.)

BIBLIOGRAPHY: C. Kopp, *Holy Places of the Gospels* (1963), 49ff.; idem, in: JPOS, 18 (1938), 181ff.; 20 (1946), 29ff.; M.J. Stiassny, *Nazareth* (Eng., 1967); Prawer, Ẓalbanim, index; M. Barash, in: *Eretz-Israel*, 7 (1964), 125–34 (Heb. section); A. Olivari, in: *La Terre Sainte* (Aug.–Sept. 1961), 201–6; M. Benvenisti, *Crusaders in the Holy Land* (1970), index; W.E. Pax, *In the Footsteps of Jesus* (1970), index. **ADD. BIBLIOGRAPHY:** B. Bagatti, *Excavations in Nazareth*, vol. 1, *From the Beginning till the XII Century*, tr. from Italian by E. Hoade (1969); B. Bagatti and E. Alliata, *Excavations in Nazareth*, vol 2, *From the 12th Century until Today*, tr. from Italian by R. Bonanno (2002). Websites: www.nazareth.muni.il; www.nazareth-illit.muni.il.

NAZI-DEUTSCH, specific use of the German language by the National Socialists. The use of language as a tool of psychological warfare against the "enemies" of the regime occupies a special place among the instruments of persecution and extermination. Nazi-Deutsch concealed the real intentions of the governing authorities from the potential victims and lulled them into submissiveness. Unprecedented crimes were masked by the use of "innocent words." It was, in the words of Raul Hilberg, a tool of concealment, not only from the victims but also – at least psychologically – from the perpetrators as well. Aware that words of long-standing usage acquire frightening meanings, the National Socialists dubbed the deportation to the death camps from Central Europe "evacuation to the East" (*Evakuierung*), from the Netherlands "recruitment for labor in the East" (*Arbeitseinsatz*), from Eastern Europe "resettlement" (*Umsiedlung*). The word "shower" was used to lead the unsuspecting victims to the gas chambers. New secret words were coined with *prima facie* innocent appearance to smooth over ominous meanings. The mass destruction of the Jewish people in Europe was called the "Final Solution" (*Endloesung*), a neologism. The word "final" was altogether apt; the proposed murder of all Jews was conceived to solve the Jewish problem forever. The actual process of physical destruction was mostly referred to as "Special Treatment" (*Sonderbehandlung*). The underground gas chambers were special cellars, the surface chambers were bath houses for special actions. In the daily reports at *Auschwitz, the statistics showing the number gassed refer to numbers of "SB" (*Sonderbehandelte*, "specially treated"). The expression SB was taboo even in interoffice correspondence on the highest level. While no objection was raised by Himmler against the use of the word "Final Solution" by the inspector of statistics, Richard Korherr (author of a November 1943 top secret statistical report on the "progress of the Final Solution"), Himmler ordered the word "special treatment" to be replaced by "transporting." The Ministry of Information gave daily instructions to the press and strictly enforced the proper "use of language" (*Sprachregelung*). Dictionaries of this language exist.

BIBLIOGRAPHY: Blumenthal, in: *Yad Vashem Studies*, 1 (1957), 49–66; 4 (1960), 57–96; 6 (1967), 69–82; Esh, *ibid.*, 5 (1963), 133–67, incl. bibl.; J. Robinson and P. Friedman, *Guide to Jewish History under Nazi Impact* (1960), 97; C. Berning, *Vom Abstammungsnachweis zum Zuchtwart* (1964). **ADD. BIBLIOGRAPHY:** R. Hilberg, *The Destruction of the European Jews*, vol. 3 (2003^3), 1028–33.

[Jacob Robinson / Michael Berenbaum (2nd ed.)]

NAZI MEDICAL EXPERIMENTS. During the Nazi regime a series of medical experiments were carried out, some even before the war, to advance German medicine without the consent of the patients upon whom the experiments were conducted and with total disregard for their suffering or even their survival.

Some experiments had legitimate scientific purposes, though the methods that were used violated the canons of medical ethics. Others were racial in nature, designed to advance Nazi racial theories. Most were simply bad science.

The experiments fall into three categories.

1. Racial experiments
2. War-injury related experiments
3. Pharmaceutical testing of drugs and experimental treatment.

The Law for the Prevention of Offspring with Hereditary Diseases was promulgated on July 14, 1933. It led to the sterilization of more than 200,000 Germans and to a great interest on the part of German physicians in sterilization. If successful, sterilization could rid the master race of those within it who were less than masterful and, if perfected, it could have enabled Germany to utilize the populations in the territories it occupied without fearing their reproduction with its consequences for the master race.

Two modes of sterilization were the subject of experimentation: X-rays and injections.

Air force physician Dr. Horst Schumann ran experiments at Auschwitz. Two to three times a week, groups of 30 prisoners – male and female – were brought in to have their testicles or ovaries irradiated with X-rays. Schumann varied the dosage. As a rule, prisoners subjected to these experiments were sent back to work, even though they suffered from serious burns and swelling. The results of sterilization experiments by means of X-ray irradiation proved disappointing. Surgical castration was more dependable and time-efficient. Nevertheless Schumann continued his experiments.

The most infamous experiments at Auschwitz were conducted by Dr. Josef *Mengele, who became the chief physician of Birkenau in 1943. Mengele wanted to "prove" the superiority of the Nordic race. His first experiments were performed on gypsy children supplied to him from the so-called kindergarten. Before long he broadened his interest to twins, dwarfs, and people with abnormalities. The tests he carried out were painful, exhausting, and traumatic for the frightened and hungry children who made up the bulk his subjects. The twins and the crippled people designated as subjects of experiments were photographed, their jaws and teeth were cast in plaster molds, and prints were taken from hands and feet. On Mengele's instructions, an inmate painter made comparative drawings of the shapes of heads, auricles, noses, mouths, hands, and feet of the twins. When the research was completed some subjects were killed by phenol injection and their organs were autopsied and analyzed so that more information could be obtained. Scientifically interesting anatomical specimens were preserved and shipped out to the institute in Berlin-Dahlem for further research.

On the day Mengele left Auschwitz, January 17, 1945, he took with him the documentation of his experiments. He still imagined that they would bring him scientific honor. According to his son, he took them with him to South America even when he was fleeing for his life.

There were several forms of war injury-related experiments. At Dachau, a series of experiments were conducted to ascertain how German military personnel might survive conditions of combat. Civilian physicians Siegfried Rugg and Hans Romberg of the German experimental Institute of Aviation joined Air Force physician Sigmund Rasher in high-altitude experiments carried out to see how long people could withstand the loss of air pressure. Prisoners were put into pressure chambers to replicate what might happen at high altitudes. Some died; many suffered. Presumably, this was meant to ascertain at what altitude Air Force personnel could bail out of an airplane.

Freezing experiments were conducted to find a treatment for hypothermia. Victims were put into tanks of ice water for an hour or more and various methods of warming up their bodies were tried. No painkillers were used. Others were placed in the snow for hours. Physicians also experimented with prisoners who were forced to drink sea water.

At other concentration camps such as Sachsenhausen, Dachau, Natzweiler, Buchenwald, and Neuengamme, pharmaceutical compounds were tested to fight contagious diseases such as malaria, typhus, tuberculosis, typhoid fever, yellow fever, and infectious hepatitis. Sulfa drugs, only recently discovered, were tested at the Ravensbrueck camp. Elsewhere, prisoners were subjected to gas poisoning to test antidotes. In Ravensbrueck new methods were explored to deal with fractures and war wounds. Prisoners' legs were broken or amputated; transplants were attempted.

The physicians enjoyed complete freedom to act without regard to basic medical ethics, without any consideration for the health of the patient.

There were some 70 such "medical-research" programs at Nazi concentration camps involving some 7,000 prisoners and some 200 physicians, who worked directly in the concentration camps, but they were not alone. They maintained close professional and research contacts with leading medical institutions and universities and an ongoing relationship with research laboratories. Indeed, the German medical establishment was involved in this work.

Medical experimentation on human subjects has long been practiced. This experimentation was different. It was left to the Physicians Trials, begun on October 25, 1946, at Nuremberg, which were the forerunner of the subsequent trials, to determine precisely how different.

Twenty-three men stood in the docket. Seven were sentenced to death; nine to long prison terms and seven were acquitted. Two physicians, Mengele and Schumann, had disappeared, and Clauberg was tried in the Soviet Union.

More important than the judgment were the principles articulated by the Court. They form the foundation for contemporary medical practice and define what was wrong with the Nazi practice.

The judges found that certain basic principles must be observed in order to satisfy moral, ethical, and legal concepts:

1. The voluntary consent of the human subject is absolutely essential.

The duty and responsibility for ascertaining the quality of the consent rests upon each individual who initiates, directs, or engages in the experiment. It is a personal duty and responsibility which may not be delegated to another with impunity.

2. The experiment should be such as to yield fruitful results for the good of society, unprocurable by other methods or means of study, and not random and unnecessary in nature.

3. The experiment should be so designed and based on the results of animal experimentation and knowledge of the natural history of the disease or other problem under study that the anticipated results will justify the performance of the experiment.

4. The experiment should be so conducted to avoid all unnecessary physical and mental suffering and injury.

5. No experiment should be conducted where there is an *a priori* reason to believe that death or disabling injury will occur, except, perhaps, in those experiments where the experimental physicians also serve as subjects.

6. The degree of risk to be taken should never exceed that determined by the humanitarian importance of the problem to be solved by the experiment.

7. Proper preparations should be made and adequate facilities provided to protect the experimental subject against even remote possibilities of injury, disability, or death.

8. The experiment should be conducted only by scientifically qualified persons. The highest degree of skill and care should be required through all stages of the experiment of those who conduct or engage in the experiment.

9. During the course of the experiment the human subject should be at liberty to bring the experiment to an end, if he has reached the physical or mental state where continuation of the experiment seems to him to be impossible.

10. During the course of the experiment the scientist in charge must be prepared to terminate the experiment at any stage, if he has probable cause to believe, in the exercise of the good faith, superior skill, and careful judgment required of him, that a continuation of the experiment is likely to result in injury, disability, or death to the experimental subject.

BIBLIOGRAPHY: A. Gotz, *Cleansing the Fatherland: Nazi Medicine and Racial Hygiene* (1994); R.J. Lifton, *Nazi Doctors: Medical Killing the Psychology of Genocide* (1986); R. Proctor, *Racial Hygiene: Medicine under the Nazis* (1988); P. Weindling, *Nazi Medicine and the Nuremberg Trials: From Medical War Crimes to Informed Consent* (2004).

[Michael Berenbaum (2nd ed.)]

NAZIMOVA, ALLA (1879–1945), Russian-U.S. actress. Born in Yalta, Nazimova went to New York with a Russian company in 1905, making her debut in the play *The Chosen People*. She stayed in the United States, became a success on the U.S. stage, and had her first screen role in *War Brides* (1916). One of the earliest film stars, she played in *Heart of a Child* (1920), *Madonna of the Streets* (1924), *Since You Went Away* (1944), and *In our Time* (1944). She also appeared in the anti-Nazi film *Escape* (1940).

NAZIR (Heb. נָזִיר; "Nazirite"), fourth tractate in the order *Nashim*, in the Mishnah, Tosefta, and the Babylonian and Jerusalem Talmuds. It deals, as its name indicates, with the laws of the *Nazirite (Num. 6:1–21), and its position after the tractate *Nedarim ("Vows") is determined by the fact that the assumption of Naziriteship was by vow. In the Babylonian Talmud it comes before *Sotah* ("The Unfaithful Wife") – although in the Bible it follows it – because "whosoever sees the degradation of an unfaithful wife will forbid himself the use of wine as leading to such behavior" (2a).

The tractate consists of nine chapters. Chapter 1 deals with the various verbal formulas used in undertaking the vow and their implications, and the duration of the three forms – the ordinary, the Samson, and the lifelong Naziriteship. Chapter 2 continues the same theme and discusses whether it is possible to limit Naziriteship to only part of its obligations. Chapter 3 deals with multiple Naziriteships, the procedure of polling the head at the end of the Naziriteship, and the intervening of ritual uncleanness terminating the Naziriteship. In Mishnah 6 of this chapter, there is the story of Queen *Helena of Adiabene who fulfilled a vow that if her son returned safely from war, she would take a Nazirite vow for seven years; this incident confirms the statement of Josephus (Wars, 2:313) that it was the custom for someone in trouble or danger to undertake a Nazirite vow. Chapter 4 deals with Naziriteship made dependent upon that of another, a stranger, husband, or wife; the consequences of annulling a Naziriteship; the father's power to impose Naziriteship upon his son; and the son's right to utilize his deceased father's Nazirite money. Chapter 5 discusses vows made in error and the situation which arose when the destruction of the Temple made the adoption of the complete Nazirite vow impossible. Chapter 6 discusses the duties of a Nazirite in greater detail, as well as the sacrifices to be brought either when the Naziriteship is interrupted by uncleanness or when it is completed in cleanness. Chapter 7 discusses on which occasions the Nazirite may defile himself for the dead, and which sources of uncleanness interrupt the Naziriteship. Chapter 8 deals with uncertain breaches of the vow. Chapter 9 discusses the fact that gentiles cannot, but women and slaves can, become Nazirites and whether the prophet Samuel was a Nazirite.

It can be demonstrated that several *mishnayot* of *Nazir* belong to the Second Temple period. Among them are 1:1, which predates the schools of Shammai and Hillel (Tosef., Naz. 1:1 and 2:1), and *mishnayot* 7:2–3, the laws of which were disputed by the *zekenim ha-rishonim* ("the first elders," who lived during the Second Temple period; Tosef., 5:1 and Naz. 53a). The remainder of the Mishnah of *Nazir* derives from the *Mishnayot* of Akiva's disciples, Meir, Yose, and, especially, Judah and Eleazar (Epstein, Tannaim, 386). The six chapters in the Tosefta to *Nazir* follow a different order from that of the Mishnah. Many *mishnayot* have no corresponding Tosefta and vice versa. The Tosefta includes some aggadic material. Noteworthy is the story of the high priest Simeon the Just who, though in principle opposed to people taking Nazirite vows, made an exception for a handsome youth from the south. When Simeon asked him why he had decided to cut off his flowing hair, he replied that on beholding his reflection in a pool he had become vain of his beauty and had taken a vow to "shear these locks to the glory of Heaven" (4:7).

The Babylonian Talmud to *Nazir* differs from the rest of the Talmud in language and is similar to that of the Jerusalem Talmud (cf. Pseudo-Rashi on Nazir 32a, s.v. *amar mar*). Epstein claims that it was compiled in Maḥoza and Pumbedita, where a special Aramaic dialect was used (Amoraim, 72–83), and that the anonymous discussions in the Jerusalem Talmud were taken from Rava's discussion in the Babylonian Talmud. A. Weiss, however, maintains that there is an essential difference in style, content, and the names of the rabbis quoted, and attributes the differences to the fact that the study of *Nazir* was neglected, and therefore lacks the post-amoraic embellishments given to the other tractates. The Babylonian Talmud has an important passage (23a) dealing with the importance of motive in action. It also contains the dictum (23b): "A man should always occupy himself with the Torah and its precepts even though it be for some ulterior motive, for the result will be that he will eventually do it without ulterior motive."

The rabbinic attitude to *asceticism can be seen in the dictum of Eleazar ha-Kappar (19a); that the Nazirite is called "a sinner by reason of the soul" (Num. 6:11) because he denied himself wine: "If then one who denies himself wine only is termed a sinner, how much so then one who is an ascetic in all things!" Support for this point of view is also found in the Jerusalem Talmud (Kid. 4:12, 66d): Man is destined to be called to account for everything (permitted) he saw (and desired) but did not partake of. After the destruction of the Temple, since it was impossible to complete Naziriteship by offering the sacrifices on its conclusion, the practice fell into disuse. Tractate *Nazir* was not studied in the academies of the *geonim*, nor were there any *halakhot* on it in the *Halakhot Pesukot, Hilkhot Re'u*, or *Halakhot Gedolot* (B.M. Lewin, *Oẓar ha-Ge'onim*, 11 (1942), 8, and Epstein, Tannaim, p. 72). The commentary to *Nazir* attributed to Rashi was apparently written by his son-in-law Meir b. Samuel, who recorded the commentaries of Isaac b. Eleazar ha-Levi, Rashi's teacher. According to Epstein the *tosafot* to *Nazir* were written by the disciples of Perez of Corbeil. The talmudic tractate in the Soncino edition was translated into English by B.D. Klien (1936).

BIBLIOGRAPHY: Halevy, Dorot, 3 (1923), 48ff.; A. Weiss, *Hithavvut ha-Talmud bi-Shelemuto* (1943), 128–57; Epstein, Tanna'im, 383–93; Epstein, Amora'im, 72–83; Ḥ. Albeck, *Shishah Sidrei Mishnah, Seder Nashim* (1954), 189–93; Z.W. Rabinowitz, *Sha'arei Torat Bavel* (1961), 299ff.; D. Halivni, *Mekorot u-Masorot* (1968), 353–433.

NAZIR, MOSES HA-LEVI (second half of 17th century), rabbinic author and Hebron emissary. Moses was the son-in-law of Abraham b. Hananiah, a Jerusalem scholar. He was called Nazir because of his acceptance of the ascetic practices enjoined on the *Nazirite. At the beginning of each year he would undertake the observance of such practices for that year, and the text of one of these resolutions has survived. In 1668–71 he traveled in Syria and Turkey as an emissary of Hebron and a copy of the account book of this mission is extant. It contains the names of the communities he visited, the amount received in each of them, his traveling expenses, how much was stolen during the journey, etc. While on his mission he wrote several responsa to Ḥasdai b. Samuel ha-Kohen Peraḥyah, *av bet din* of Salonika, and these too reveal Moses' fine character. He also wrote halakhic novellae on the laws of the festivals, which were published by his son Joseph, and the *Yedei Moshe* on *Ḥoshen Mishpat*, which is still in manuscript.

Moses' son JOSEPH (d. 1713) was born in Jerusalem, studied under Hezekiah b. David da Silva, then settled in Hebron with his father, and was apparently a Hebron emissary to Europe in 1689. From Hebron, Joseph went to Egypt and served as *av bet din* in Cairo. His responsa and novellae were published after his death by his son-in-law Joshua Zein, according to the order of the *Arba'ah Turim*, under the title *Matteh Yosef* (2 pts., Constantinople, 1717–26); the numerical value of *matteh* is 54, which is the number of responsa. In them he discussed halakhic problems with contemporary scholars, especially with Abraham Blom, rabbi of Egypt.

BIBLIOGRAPHY: Frumkin-Rivlin, 2 (1928), 98f.; J.M. Toledano, *Sarid u-Falit* (n.d.), 39ff.; Yaari, Sheluḥei, 468–70, 480.

[Avraham Yaari]

NAZIRITE, person who vows for a specific period to abstain from partaking of grapes or any of its products whether intoxicating or not, cutting his hair, and touching a corpse (6:3–9). Such a person is called a Nazirite (Heb. *nazir*, נָזִיר) from the root *nzr* (נזר), meaning to separate or dedicate oneself (e.g., *nifal*, Lev. 22:2; *hifil*, Lev. 15:31; Num. 6:2, 5, 12). The subject is dealt with in the Priestly Code (Num. 6:1–21) and the purpose of the law is to prescribe the proper ritual if the Nazirite period is aborted by corpse contamination (Num. 6:9–12) or if it is successfully completed (6:13–21).

In the person of the Nazirite, the layman is given a status resembling that of the priest, as he now is "holy to the Lord" (Lev. 21:6; Num. 6:8; cf. Philo, I LA, 249). Actually, in his taboos, he approximates more the higher sanctity of the high priest in that (1) He may not contaminate himself with the dead of his immediate family (Lev. 21:11; Num. 6:7; cf. the ordinary priest, Lev. 21:1–4); (2) For him, as for the high priest, the head is the focus of sanctity (Ex. 29:7; Num. 6:11b. Note the same motive clauses, Lev. 21:12b; Num. 6:7b and compare the dedication of the ordinary priest, Ex. 29:21); (3) He abstains from intoxicants during his term (Num. 6:4) – a more stringent requirement than that of the high priest, whose abstinence, like that of his fellow priests, is limited to the time he is in the Sanctuary (Lev. 10:9).

A more instructive parallel to the Nazirite is the case of the dedication of land to the Sanctuary (Lev. 27:16 ff.). Both result from a votive dedication (Lev. 27:16; Num. 6:2), and both dedications are for limited periods, the land reverting to its owner on the Jubilee if not redeemed earlier (implied by Lev. 27:21; Num. 6:13). In both cases the period of dedication can be terminated earlier – the Nazirite's by contamination (Num. 6:9–12), the land's by redemption (Lev. 27:16–19). In the case of premature desanctification, a penalty is exacted: the Nazirite pays a reparation offering (*ʾasham*) to the Sanctuary, and the owner of the land pays an additional one-fifth of the redemption price to the Sanctuary. If the dedication period is completed, no desanctification penalty is incurred. True, the Nazirite offers up an array of sacrifices together with his hair (Num. 6:13–20), but the sacrifices are mainly for thanksgiving, and the hair, which may not be desanctified, is consumed on the altar. Similarly, dedicated land (so the text of Lev. 27:22–24 implies) reverts to its original owner on the Jubilee without cost. In the case when the Nazirite period is interrupted by contamination, the following ritual is observed: the Nazirite must undergo sprinkling with purificatory waters on the third and seventh day (inferred from Num. 19:14 ff.); he shaves his hair on the seventh day; and on the following day three rituals are prescribed: he is purified of his contamination by a purification offering, his hair is reconsecrated and his Nazirite period begins anew, and a reparation offering is brought to expiate his desecration.

The uncut hair of the Nazirite is his distinction. (In this respect the priest differs; though forbidden to shave his hair, he is compelled to trim it; cf. Ezek. 44:20.) Its importance is indicated by the root of the term Nazirite, נזר, which refers at times to the hair (Num. 6:6, 7, 12, 18; Jer. 7:29. Note the parallelism in Gen. 49:26; Deut 33:16). Since hair continues to grow throughout life (and apparently for a time after death), it was considered by the ancients to be the seat of man's vitality and life-force, and in ritual it often served as his substitute. A ninth-century B.C.E. bowl found in a Cypriot temple contains an inscription on its outside surface indicating that it contained the hair of the donor. It was placed there, if the reconstructed text is correct, as "a memorial" to Astarte (cf. Ex. 28:12, 29; 30:16; Num. 10:10; Zech. 6:14), i.e., as a permanent reminder to the goddess of the donor's devotion. The offering of hair is also attested in later times in Babylonia (Pritchard, Texts, 339–40), Syria (Lucian, *De dea Syra*, 55, 60), Greece (K. Meuli), and Arabia (W.R. Smith).

The narrative and prophetic literature corroborate the existence of Nazirites in Israel. Samson and Samuel were lifelong Nazirites (Judg. 13:7; I Sam. 1:21 (4Q Samç), 28). Indeed, they resembled the prophets in that their dedication began not at birth but at conception (Isa. 49:1, 5; Jer. 1:5; cf. Amos 2:11). The taboos prescribed in the Torah are verified in their lives. Neither polled his hair (Judg. 13:5; 16:17; I Sam. 1:11) nor drank any wine (to judge by the prohibition to Samson's mother during her pregnancy; Judg. 13:4, 7, 14). However, the law forbidding corpse contamination was not observed (Judg. 14:9, 19; 15:8, 15; I Sam. 15:33). This divergence from the Priestly Code is implicitly reinforced by the rule set down by the angel to Samson's mother (Judg. 13:14), i.e., that she must eschew forbidden food; nothing, however, is said about contracting impurity from the dead which, according to the Priestly Code, would have automatically defiled her embryo.

[Jacob Milgrom]

In Talmud

The Mishnah and the Talmud distinguish between a lifelong Nazirite and a "Samson Nazirite" since Samson, unlike the lifelong Nazirite, was never allowed to thin his hair even when it became burdensome (Naz. 1:2). On the other hand, Samson was permitted to defile himself through contact with the dead, since the angel did not enjoin him from such defilement when delineating the laws of his abstinence (Naz. 4b).

When the period of the vow was not specified, it was understood to be 30 days (Naz. 1:3). In addition to being subsumed under the general regulations governing vows, many specific formulas were developed for Nazirite commitments. "If a man says 'Let my hand be a Nazirite' or 'Let my foot be a Nazirite,' his words are of no effect. However, if he says, 'Let my head be a Nazirite' or 'Let my liver be a Nazirite' [or some other vital organ], he becomes a Nazirite" (Naz. 21b). It was customary for the wealthy to aid poor Nazirites in the purchase of their offerings (Naz. 2:5, 6), since it was felt that the most meritorious aspect of abstinence was the chance to bring a sin-offering at its conclusion (Ned. 10a). It is related that at the time of *Simeon b. Shetaḥ, 300 Nazirites came to Jerusalem. He absolved half of them of their vow, and not revealing the fact to the king Alexander Yannai, persuaded him to give what purported to be half the sacrifices needed, he "offering" to provide the other half (TJ, Ber. 7:2, 11b). The Nazirite laws applied only to Ereẓ Israel. It is related that *Helena of Adiabene took Nazirite vows for seven years. After this period she went to Ereẓ Israel, where Bet Hillel ruled that she must continue for a further seven years (Naz. 3:6).

There were different reasons for taking the Nazirite vow. Some did it for the fulfillment of a wish, such as for the birth of a child (Naz. 2:7–10). One who saw the conduct of an unfaithful wife was advised to abstain completely from wine by becoming a Nazirite (Ber. 63a). Thus the passages on the wife suspected of adultery and the laws of the Nazirite are juxtaposed in the Bible (Num. 5:11–31, 6:1–21). The pious simply made a freewill vow of abstinence to afford them an opportunity to bring a sin-offering at its conclusion (Ned. 10a). The Nazirite vow was severely discouraged by the rabbis, since *asceticism was against the spirit of Judaism (Ned. 77b; Naz. 19a; Ta'an. 11a). Their discouragement of the practice was almost certainly in protest against the excessive mourning after the destruction of the Second Temple, when large numbers of Jews became ascetics, vowing not to eat meat or to drink wine (BB 60b). The rabbis even designated the Nazirites as sinners in accordance with the verse: "And [the priest] shall make atonement for him, for that he sinned against a soul" (Num. 6:11; Ned. 10a). The high priest Simeon the Just only once in his life ate of the trespass-offering brought by a defiled Nazirite. This was when a young, handsome shepherd possessing beautiful, thick locks of hair undertook to become a Nazirite and thus had to cut his hair in order to avoid sinful thoughts (Ned. 9b; cf. the Narcissus legend in Greek mythology). The observance of the Nazirite vow may have continued for many centuries. However, it ultimately disappeared, and there is no reference to Nazirites in the Middle Ages. In modern times Nazirite practices have been observed in Jerusalem by David Cohen, a disciple of Chief Rabbi A.I. Kook.

[Aaron Rothkoff]

BIBLIOGRAPHY: W.R. Smith, *Lectures on the Religion of the Semites* (1927³), 323–36; K. Meuli, in: *Phyllobolia fuer Peter von der Muehl* (1946), 204–11; de Vaux, Anc Isr, 465–7; M. Haran, in: EM, 5 (1968), 795–9 (incl. bibl.); Pederson, Israel, 3–4 (1940), 263–6. IN TALMUD: M. Jastrow, in: JBL, 33 (1914), 266–85; H. Gevaryahu, in: *Iyyunim be-Sefer Shofetim* (1966), 522–46; Z. Weisman, in: *Tarbiz*, 36 (1967), 207–20; E.E. Urbach, *Ḥazal; Pirkei Emmunot ve-De'ot* (1969), index s.v. *nazir*; G. Scholem, *Ursprung und Anfaenge der Kabbala* (1962), 202f.

NEANDER, AUGUST (originally **David Mendel**; 1789–1850), Church historian and convert. His Orthodox father abandoned the family, complaining that his liberally educated wife was corrupting the children (four of five were eventually baptized). Though poor and sickly, David was an immediate success at the Johanneum Gymnasium in Hamburg. His honorary public address presented in Latin on the conclusion of his studies in 1805, demanding equality for the Jews in all respects but advocating the abrogation of some rites, aroused wide interest. The speech was inspired by his rationalist benefactor, who was also principal of the school. David soon fell under the varied influences of Plato, *Schleiermacher, and romanticism, and embraced Christianity at the age of 17. Neander (Gr. "new man") rapidly attained prominence in the field of Church history and became a professor at the age of 24. During the *Damascus affair (1840) he publicized his opinion that the whole ritual murder charge was a falsehood. In 1847 he opposed the admission of Jews to Berlin University, identifying them with the anti-Christian movement of the left-wing Hegelians.

BIBLIOGRAPHY: H. Huettmann, *August Neander* (Ger., 1936); L. Schultze, *August Neander* (Ger., 1890); H. Liebeschuetz, *Das Judentum im deutschen Geschichtsbild von Hegel bis Max Weber* (1967), index.

NEBAIOTH (Heb. נְבָיוֹת, נְבָיֹת), a tribe or a group of tribes of nomads in the border deserts of Israel, identified with the Nabaiāte mentioned in the Assyrian documents from the time of Ashurbanipal. The Nebaioth are not to be connected with the *Nabateans, as some classical authors mistakenly did (cf. Jos., Ant. 1:221; 12:335, et al.; Jerome in his commentary to Gen. 25:13–18). According to Genesis 25:13 and I Chronicles 1:29, Nebaioth was the firstborn of Ishmael and according to Genesis 36:3 he was also the brother of Esau's wife Basemath, daughter of Ishmael. In Isaiah 60:6–7 Nebaioth is mentioned with Kedar, another son of Ishmael (Gen. 25:13), among the nomadic tribes on the border of Israel.

BIBLIOGRAPHY: EM, 5 (1968), 744–6 (incl. bibl.).

NEBENZAHL, ITZHAK ERNST (1907–1992), Israeli state comptroller. Nebenzahl was born in Frankfurt on the Main, Germany, and studied at the universities of Frankfurt, Berlin, and Freiburg. He was appointed lecturer in civil law at Frankfurt in 1932. A strictly observant Jew, Nebenzahl was president of the Ezra religious youth movement in Germany in 1929–30. Following Hitler's rise to power in 1933 he immigrated to Ereẓ Israel. A partner in the world-wide Hollander concern, and chairman of the Board of Directors from 1947 to 1961, he has served on most of the important economic bodies of Israel, including the Jerusalem Economic Corporation, the Israel Post Office Bank, and the Bank of Israel, where he was chairman of the advisory committee and council (1957–62). In 1961 Nebenzahl was elected state comptroller of Israel for a five-year period, and was re-elected in 1966, 1971, and 1976, retiring at the end of 1981. In 1976 he also became ex-officio commissioner for complaints from the public (Ombudsman) of the State of Israel.

NEBO (Heb. נְבוֹ).

(1) High mountain E. of the Jordan River, opposite Jericho. It forms part of the heights of Abarim bordering the Moab plateau, where the Israelites encamped on the last stage of their journey (Deut. 32:49). The mountain is identified with Jebel Shayhān that has two peaks: Ra's al-Nibā', 2,739 ft. (835 m.), and Ra's Siyāgha, 2,329 ft. (710 m.). In the Bible the peak of Mt. Nebo is called Pisgah; from there Moses beheld the Promised Land before dying. Although Ra's al-Nibā' has retained the biblical name, scholars regard the second peak as the more likely site of Pisgah, because of the magnificent view from there. Moses died on the mountain and was buried in a valley "and no one knows his burial place to this day" (Deut. 34:6). According to an apocryphal source, Jeremiah buried the Ark of the Covenant and various other objects from the Holy of Holies on the mountain (II Macc. 2:5ff.). In Byzantine times the tomb of Moses was "rediscovered" by a shepherd (Petrus Iberus, 88) and a memorial church was erected together with a monastery on Ra's Siyāgha. The church consists of a basilica with a trefoil apse, a baptistery (dated 597), and a chapel, all paved with mosaics. Eusebius locates "Phasgo" (= Pisgah) on the way from Livias to Heshbon (Onom. 18:3).

(2) Reubenite town (Num. 32:3, 38) near Mt. Nebo, belonging to the family of Bela (I Chron. 5:8). It remained an Israelite possession till the revolt of the Moabite king Mesha

against the house of Omri. On his stele (lines 14ff.) Mesha describes his conquest of the town, the destruction of the sanctuary of the God of Israel before the Moabite god Chemosh and the sacrifice of 7,000 men, boys, women, girls, and maidservants (see Mesha *Stele). The prophets Isaiah (15:2) and Jeremiah (48:1, 22) mention Nebo among the cities of Moab in their descriptions of the "burdens" on that land. Eusebius refers to it as a ruined town, 6 (or 8) mi. (c. 11 or 14 km.) west of Heshbon (Onom. 136:6–13).

Scholars identify Nebo either with Khirbat al-Muḥayyit southeast of Ra's Siyāgha or with Khirbat ʿUyūn Mūsā ("Springs of Moses") northeast of the mountain, beside a spring of the same name. Iron Age fortresses have been discovered at both sites.

(3) Town in Judah whose inhabitants were among those who returned from Babylonian Exile (Ezra 2:29; 10:43; Neh. 7:33). The place may be identical with Nob.

BIBLIOGRAPHY: Abel, Géog, 1 (1933), 379ff.; 2 (1938), 397–8; N. Glueck, in: AASOR, 15 (1935), 109ff.; S.J. Saller, *The Memorial of Moses on Mount Nebo* (1941); S.J. Saller and B. Bagatti, *The Town of Nebo* (1949); Aharoni, Land, index; EM, 5 (1968), 685–90 (incl. bibl.).

[Michael Avi-Yonah]

NEBRASKA, state on the Great Plains located near the geographical center of continental United States. Its population in 2005 was 1,729,000 of whom approximately 7,200 are Jews, a decline of some 10% in three decades. Most live in Omaha, the home of four synagogues, a Jewish community center, and a *mikveh*; the majority of the other Jews in the state live in Lincoln, the home of the state university and two synagogues.

Nebraska was organized as a territory in 1854, and within a year the stream of Jewish settlement had begun. The first Jewish settlers are believed to have been two brothers, Lewis and Henry Wessel, who went to Nebraska City from St. Louis in 1855. The next few decades brought a steady trickle of Jews who were predominantly of Central European origin (Alsace-Lorraine, Germany, Bohemia). Many had settled briefly in cities on the eastern seaboard before moving to the west, where, especially after the Civil War, the Homestead Act and railroad construction attracted new settlement. The early Jews in Nebraska were mainly merchants, such as Aaron Cahn and Meyer Hellman, who established a clothing business in Omaha to supply pioneers striking out on the Oregon Trail, and Carl Ernest Louis Golding, who was an Indian trader in Plattsmouth.

One of the most colorful figures in early Jewish life in Nebraska was Julius Meyer, who settled in Omaha in 1866 and became a successful Indian trader. He mastered at least six tribal dialects, was adopted into the Pawnee tribe, and was given the name "curly-headed-white-chief-with-one-tongue." He later became a government interpreter for the Indians and accompanied a party of them to the Paris Exposition. Another early Indian merchant, Harris L. Levi, was less fortunate. In 1869 he joined a surveying party, all of whom were massa-

Jewish communities in Nebraska and dates of establishment. Population figures for 2001.

cred by the Indians in retaliation for the slaying of two Indian youths by the surveyors.

The most important early Jewish settler was Edward *Rosewater, who went to Omaha in 1863 as manager of the Western Union, and then became active as a journalist, founding the *Omaha Evening Bee News* (1871). Rosewater was a leading and controversial figure in Republican Party affairs in the state, served as National Republican Committeeman from Nebraska, and was twice defeated for the U.S. Senate.

After 1881 Russian Jews began to arrive in large numbers, many of whom were systematically sent out west by the Industrial Removal Aid Society of New York. Some abortive attempts were made to settle the newcomers on the soil, and the Jewish Agricultural Society tried to found a colony in Cherry County in 1908, but by 1916 the experiment was abandoned.

With the exception of a handful of ranchers, the Jewish population of Nebraska, by 1970, was almost entirely concentrated in business and the professions. Scattered groups of Jews live in some of the smaller Nebraska towns (Grand Island, Norfolk, Scottsbluff, Beatrice), but only *Omaha and Lincoln sustain organized community life. Lincoln has two congregations, one Conservative and one Reform, and a Jewish Welfare Federation. The Esther K. Newman Camp, between the two cities, serves the Jewish youth of the state during the summer.

Jews have served in a wide variety of public offices in the state since its inception. Many have been mayors of their municipalities, and as early as 1863 Aaron Cahn served in the legislature. Henry *Monsky of Omaha gained national importance in the B'nai B'rith. Ben Greenberg of York was chairman of the Board of Regents of the University of Nebraska. Edward Zorinksy was a United States Senator (1976–87) after serving as mayor of Omaha and defeating long-time incumbent Roman Hruska.

BIBLIOGRAPHY: B. Postal and L. Koppman, *Jewish Tourists' Guide to the U.S.* (1954), 289–92.

[Sanford Ragins / Renee Corcoran (2nd ed.)]

NEBUCHADNEZZAR (**Nebuchadrezzar**; Heb. נְבוּכַדְרֶאצַּר, נְבוּכַדְנֶצַּר; Akk. **Nabû-kudurri-uṣur**, "O, Nabû, guard my border!"), son of Nabopolassar the Chaldean, ruler of Babylon (605–562 B.C.E.). Nebuchadnezzar succeeded to his father's throne at the time when the struggle between Babylon and Egypt for the territories that had been part of the Assyrian empire was at its height. According to the *Babylonian Chronicle*, Nebuchadnezzar waged his first war against Egypt in the region of the Euphrates, in the last year of his father's reign (605). In that year he defeated the Egyptian armies in a battle fought at *Carchemish on the Euphrates (cf. Jer. 46:2), thereby frustrating Pharaoh-Neco's attempt to gain control of Syria and Palestine, and at the same time paving the way for the rise of Babylon as a world power. In his pursuit of the Egyptian forces, Nebuchadnezzar reached the region of Hamath in central Syria but was obliged to return to Babylon in consequence of his father's death. In the same year he returned to the land of Ḫatti, i.e., Greater Syria, and according to the *Babylonian Chronicle*, "He marched unopposed through the Ḫatti-land; in the month of Šabāṭu (Shevat) he took the heavy tribute of the Ḫatti-territory to Babylon." It would seem that Nebuchadnezzar reached Palestine and subjected Judah to his rule one or two years later. At the end of 604 he conducted a military campaign against Palestine, besieging and capturing the city of Ashkelon. In the words of the *Babylonian Chronicle*, "All the kings of the Ḫatti-land came before him and he received their heavy tribute." One of these kings was apparently *Jehoiakim of Judah.

After consolidating his rule in Palestine and Syria, Nebuchadnezzar attempted the conquest of Egypt (end of 601). The stubbornly fought encounter between the Babylonian and Egyptian armies was indecisive. Nebuchadnezzar's failure to obtain a clear-cut victory over the Egyptians may have encouraged various states in Syria and Palestine, including Judah, to revolt against Babylon. In Kislev (December) 598 Nebuchadnezzar entered Palestine, and, according to the *Babylonian Chronicle*, "he encamped against the city of Judah [i.e., Jerusalem] and on the second day of the month of Adar [i.e., March 16, 597] he seized the city and captured the king [i.e., Jehoiachin]. He appointed there a king of his own choice [i.e., Zedekiah], received its heavy tribute and sent it to Babylon" (see *Zedekiah). In the following years the Babylonian king was occupied with wars against the Elamites to the east of the Tigris, and was also obliged to suppress a revolt in the country of Akkad (695/94). His absence from Syria, and the events in Babylon and Elam, apparently encouraged the kings of Syria and Palestine to plot a further revolt against their overlord. The Egyptian rulers no doubt lent their support to uprisings against Babylon, and Zedekiah's open revolt enjoyed their active aid (Jer. 37:5ff.). In 588 the siege of Jerusalem began, and in the summer of 586 Nebuchadnezzar captured the city, laid the Temple waste, carried off a large part of the population of Judah into captivity, and put Zedekiah and other Judean nobles to death. The land of Judah was turned into a province (see *Gedaliah son of Ahikam).

Some information about the fate of the exiles in Babylon in Nebuchadnezzar's day is found in Babylonian administrative documents, in which King Jehoiachin and his sons are mentioned as receiving a regular allowance of oil from the royal treasury. On the other hand, it is hard to draw any conclusions from the Book of Daniel about this subject because of the legendary character of the stories related there. Some scholars are of the opinion that the name Nebuchadnezzar in these stories is an error for Nabonidus, since in an Aramaic text from Qumran there is a story about Nabonidus which resembles the story about Nebuchadnezzar in Daniel. Of similarly doubtful authenticity is the mention of Nebuchadnezzar in the Book of *Judith. In the years following the capture of Jerusalem, Nebuchadnezzar waged a war in Phoenicia against Tyre, most probably in 585, which, according to Josephus, lasted for 13 years (Ezek. 29:18; cf. Jos., Ant., 10:220–2; Jos., Apion, 1:154–60). Three years later (582/81) he conducted a campaign against Ammon and Moab (Jos., Ant., 10:181–2), in the course of which he also took captives from Judah (Jer. 52:30). Nebuchadnezzar must have been aware of Egypt's part in inciting the vassal states to revolt against Babylon and of its desire to establish its own power in Palestine and Syria. He therefore attacked Egypt too, but the source material dealing with this war is fragmentary and unreliable.

Despite his many foreign wars, Nebuchadnezzar did not neglect Babylon itself. From various inscriptions and archaeological finds he emerges as a dynamic and able monarch in the administrative and architectural no less than in the military field. He adorned and fortified his capital city, Babylon, with the booty and tribute that poured in from all over the Near East. He restored and renovated ancient temples in the cities of Babylonia in order to gain the support of the Babylonian priests. He also made provision for the regular irrigation of the lands of Babylonia by means of a whole network of canals connected with the Euphrates. In his reign the neo-Babylonian empire attained the pinnacle of its greatness.

[Bustanay Oded]

In the Aggadah

The description of Nebuchadnezzar in the *aggadah* seems largely to be a veiled reference to Titus. He is frequently referred to as "the wicked one" (Ber. 57b; Shab. 149b; et al.) as well as "a wicked slave," and "hater and adversary" of God (Lam. R., Proem 23); Titus is depicted in similar terms (Git. 56b). The "wicked slave" charge may be connected with the notoriously humble origin of the Flavian dynasty (Suetonius, *Vespasian*, 1:1; 3:1).

Despite the relatively favorable attitude to Nebuchadnezzar in Jeremiah, Ezekiel, and Daniel, the rabbis, for the most part, depict him as a cruel, merciless conqueror who, among other things, tore the flesh off a hare and ate it while it was still alive (Ned. 65a; Lam. R. 2: 10, no. 14), and forced his client kings to enter into homosexual relations with him (Shab. 149b). Several Roman emperors, including Titus (cf. Suetonius, *Divus Titus* 7:1), were said to have indulged in pederasty. Nebuchadnezzar was also reported to have cast Jehoiakim's body to the dogs (Lev. R. 19:6) and to have killed large numbers of Judean exiles in Babylonia (Sanh. 92b; PdRE 33). Likewise, he is frequently accused of having made himself into a god (Gen. R. 9:5; Ex. R. 8:2) – a transparent criticism of the Roman emperors who claimed divine honors.

Nebuchadnezzar's treatment of Zedekiah was at first favorable, and he even placed five kings under his rule; but when it seemed that they were prepared to plot against Nebuchadnezzar, Zedekiah reviled him in their presence, whereupon they betrayed Zedekiah to his suzerain (Lam. R. 2: 10, no. 14). Although ostensibly based on Jeremiah 27:3, the story is remarkably similar to Josephus' account of the congress of five kings held by Agrippa I at Tiberias and rudely dispersed by the Roman governor of Syria (Ant., 19:338–41). There, too, it seems that some anti-Roman plot was being hatched, with the result that henceforth the Roman authorities became hostile to Agrippa.

Nebuchadnezzar charged the Sanhedrin with absolving Zedekiah from his vow of loyalty, and he had them punished by having their hair tied to tails of horses and being made to run from Jerusalem to Lydda (Lam. R. 2: 10, no. 14). Since, according to II Kings 25: 18–21, 72 leading citizens of Jerusalem – a number almost equivalent to the traditional great Sanhedrin – were executed at Riblah in Syria, the punishment mentioned in the Midrash undoubtedly alludes to some incident in the Roman period, probably to the execution of Jewish rebels at Lydda by order of Ummidius *Quadratus, governor of Syria; the dispatch from Lydda of a number of Jewish leaders to Rome where their fate was to be decided; and the subsequent beheading of a Roman tribune after being dragged round Jerusalem (Jos., Ant., 20: 130–6; Jos., Wars, 2:242–6).

According to the Midrash, Nebuchadnezzar hesitated to attack Jerusalem and destroy the Temple (Lam. R. Proems 23, 30) – which is precisely what Vespasian did in 68–69 C.E., though his motives were political, not religious. Interpreting Ezekiel 21: 26, the rabbis depict Nebuchadnezzar as practicing belomancy and studying various auguries before deciding whether to proceed against Jerusalem (*ibid.* 23). The same is reported in the Talmud concerning Nero (Git. 56a).

Since Nebuchadnezzar left the task of subduing Jerusalem and burning the Temple to Nebuzaradan, he is assailed mainly for trying to force image worship on the Jewish exiles. Interpreting Daniel 3: 16, the Midrash depicts Shadrach, Meshach, and Abed-Nego as saying to Nebuchadnezzar, "You are our king only as regards taxes, *annonae*, fines, and poll taxes; but in this matter of which you speak to us you are just Nebuchadnezzar … You and a dog are alike to us. O Nebuchadnezzar, bark like a dog, swell like a pitcher, chirp like a cricket" – a curse which was duly fulfilled (Lev. R. 33:6). The Roman taxes enumerated indicate an allusion to the Roman period, probably to Caligula who insisted that his statue be placed in the Temple and who was a madman just like Nebuchadnezzar (Jos., Ant., 18:261ff.; Jos., Wars, 21:184ff.; Tacitus, *Historiae*, 5:9; Philo, *In Flaccum*, 31).

Occasionally, however, Nebuchadnezzar is viewed in a more favorable light, mainly in later rabbinic sources composed at a time when hostility to the Romans had subsided. Thus, he is said to have taken pity on the Jews after the exile of Jehoiachin, and, indeed, on Jehoiachin himself, whom he provided with a wife during his long imprisonment (Lev. R. 19:6; PR 26:129). Nebuchadnezzar was one of the five persons saved from the army of Sennacherib, and from that time he was inspired by the fear of God (Sanh. 95b). He was the scribe of Merodach Baladan and corrected him for writing the name of Hezekiah before that of God (Sanh. 96a). For this act he was rewarded by ruling over the whole world (Song R. 3:4, no. 2), including the world of animals, and by sitting on Solomon's throne (Est. R. 1:12).

A historically significant Midrash reports that when the "exiles of Zedekiah" were brought to Babylonia by Nebuchadnezzar, they were met by the earlier deportees (of 597 B.C.E.), wearing "black underneath but white outside" and hailing Nebuchadnezzar as "conqueror of the barbarians" (Lam. R., Proem 23). This story evidently alludes to the Jews of the Hellenistic and Roman Diaspora, as well as to individuals such as Josephus and Agrippa II, who had to conceal their mourning for Jerusalem and proclaim their loyalty to the Roman conquerors.

[Moses Aberbach]

In Islam

In the *Koran (Sura 17:4–7) it is related that the people of Israel sinned twice and were therefore punished twice. The description of these events in the Koran is very vague, and the traditional Muslim commentators therefore found it difficult to present a clear and crystallized explanation of these verses. According to them, the two sins were the murder of *Isaiah or the imprisonment of *Jeremiah or the murder of *Zechariah son of Iddo; and the murder of John the Baptist. However, some elements from the *aggadah* on the murder of Zechariah have also been introduced into this story (cf. Targum Lam. 2:20). In any case, the Koran clearly hints at two destructions of the Temple.

According to Muslim legend, the punishment was meted out either by *Goliath, Sennacherib, Nebuchadnezzar (Bukhtanaṣar), one of the Nabatean kings, or Persian invaders. Among the intermediaries whom Allah used to punish the people of Israel, the figure of Bukhtanaṣar stands out; folklorists make frequent references to him, even adding a beautiful story about his youth to his biography. According to them, one of the people of Israel dreamed that a poor, orphaned youth would destroy the Temple and exterminate the people. He set out in search of this youth, traveled as far as Babylonia, and almost gave up the hope of finding him. Some people finally pointed out a poor orphan who carried a bundle of twigs on his head. The Israelite gave him three dirhams with which to buy meat, bread, and wine. He repeated this act the next day and for several more days. When his time came to leave, the youth was saddened by the fact that he was unable to repay the generosity of his Israelite benefactor. The latter told the youth that his reward would be the youth's written promise that when he ascended the throne he would spare his life and the lives of all those with him. The youth answered that his benefactor and friend was mocking him. Upon the entreaties of his mother he finally granted the request of the Israelite and gave him the written promise; a sign was even convened upon by which Bukhtanaṣar would recognize the Israelite among the great crowd. The story of Yaḥya ibn Zakariyyā (i.e., John the Baptist) has been added to some versions of this story. The continuation of the story relates that Nebuchadnezzar destroyed the Temple as a punishment for the murder of John the Baptist and that he ordered the bodies of those who had been killed to be thrown among the ruins. Everyone who obeyed his command was exempted from the payment of the *jizya* (poll tax) for that year. The Israelite, the benefactor of Nebuchadnezzar, was not in Jerusalem on that day and was therefore unable to make use of the written promise which he had received years ago; thus, no one was saved by it. As usual, there are several versions of this story. It does not appear to have any Jewish origin, except for a weak echo of the story of the encounter between Rabban Johanan b. Zakkai and Vespasian, when Rabban Johanan announced to Vespasian that he would become king and destroy Jerusalem (Git. 56a–b).

[Haïm Z'ew Hirschberg]

In the Arts

Although few of the literary, artistic, or musical works associated with Nebuchadnezzar are of the first rank, they are rather numerous; and the Babylonian king also figures in works dealing with the notable Jews who have contact with him in the Bible. Two of the earliest literary treatments were an old English play, *Nebuchadnezzar's Fierie Furnace* (re-edited by M. Roesler, 1936), and an Italian miracle play in verse, *La Rapresentatione di Nabucdonosor Re di Babillonia* (c. 1530; Florence, 1558^2). A second English play on the theme is known to have been staged in London in 1596. Nebuchadnezzar's treatment of Zedekiah and the royal house of Judah forms the subject of *Sédécie, ou les Juives* (1583), one of the most important works of the French dramatist Robert Garnier. Later, the German playwright Christian Weise added *Nebukadnezar* (1684) to his series of biblical dramas. In the 18th century, Christian Friedrich Hunold wrote a *"Singspiel," Der gestuerzte und wieder erhoehte Nebucadnezar, Koenig zu Babylon, unter dem grossen Propheten Daniel*, which was staged at Hamburg in 1728; and the Russian writer and publisher Nikolai Ivanovich Novikov published a *Komediya Navukhodonosor* (1791; in *Drevnyaya Rossiyskaya Biblioteka*, Moscow, 1788–91). Works on the subject that appeared in the 19th century include *Nabucco* (1819), a five-act verse tragedy by the Italian writer Giovanni Battista Niccolini; *Nabuco in Gerusalemme* (1829), an Italian *azione sacra* in verse; and *Nebuchodonoser* (1836), a four-act French drama by Auguste Anicet-Bourgeois written in collaboration with Francis Cornu and staged in Paris. The tragic end of the Judean monarchy also inspired Ludwig *Philippson's German dramas *Jojachin* (1858) and *Die Entthronten* (1868). On the whole, 20th-century writers have avoided the subject, an exception being the German author Heinz Welten, whose novel *Nebukadnezar: der Koenig der Koenige* appeared in 1924.

In art, the main subjects treated are the king's dreams and visions and their eventual realization. There are several works illustrating Nebuchadnezzar's dream of the metal statue with feet of clay (Dan. 2:31–35). The stone hewn without hands which topples the statue was thought by the Church Fathers and later Christian symbolists to represent the Virgin Birth (i.e., Jesus conceived without human agency). The dream is depicted in medieval manuscripts and in carvings from the Gothic cathedrals of Amiens and Laon. Nebuchadnezzar's vision of the tree (Dan. 4) appears in medieval illuminated manuscripts and on the front of Laon Cathedral, as well as in stained glass and paintings of the Middle Ages. The pitiful figure of the king reduced to grazing with the beasts (Dan. 4:32) appealed particularly to the artistic imagination of the Romanesque period (11th–12th centuries) with its feeling for the awesome and the grotesque. This scene appeared in illuminated manuscripts of the commentary on the New Testament Book of Revelations by the eighth-century Spanish monk Beatus and on the capitals of French Romanesque churches. A more recent treatment of the episode is the English visionary poet and artist William *Blake's striking depiction of the shaggy, wild-eyed monarch walking on all fours (1795). The image also occurs in Blake's prophetic work *The Marriage of Heaven and Hell* (1790) with the caption "One Law for the Lion and the Ox is Oppression." Nebuchadnezzar occasionally figures in medieval manuscript illustrations of the Three Hebrews in the Fiery Furnace (Dan. 3). In the early 15th-century *Très Riches Heures* of the Duc de Berry (Musée Condé, Chantilly), he is shown complacently stoking the furnace which encloses Shadrach, Meshach, and Abed-Nego.

Musical compositions involving Nebuchadnezzar largely deal with episodes drawn from the Book of Daniel, notably that of the Three Hebrews. They include an opera by Caldara (1731), Darius *Milhaud's *Les Miracles de la Foi* (1951), and Benjamin Britten's *The Burning Fiery Furnace* (1966). To mark the coronation of the Austrian emperor Ferdinand I as king of Lombardy and Venice, a ballet entitled *Nabucodonoser* was performed at La Scala, Milan, on September 6, 1838. The Italian composer Giuseppe Verdi was in Milan at the time and subsequently found inspiring reading in T. Solera's libretto *Nabucodnosor*, which described the Babylonian king's enslavement of the Jews and the plight of the latter in their distant exile. *Va, pensiero...*, the chorus of the Hebrew captives in Solera's text, fired Verdi's dormant patriotism and the opera which he wrote, *Nabucco*, had its premiere at La Scala in 1842. Its performance created widespread enthusiasm in Italy, where the Hebrew captives' prayer for deliverance was seen as a comment on the country's state of subjugation to Austria, or as the lament of exiled Italian patriots. When *Nabucco* was staged at Her Majesty's Theater, London, in 1846, it was retitled *Nino* and the biblical characters renamed, since the stage performance of biblical subjects was then still taboo in England. *Nabucco*, translated into Hebrew by Aharon *Ashman, has often been performed by the Israel Opera since its foundation in 1958.

BIBLIOGRAPHY: Pritchard, Texts, 307–8; D.J. Wiseman, *Chronicles of Chaldaean Kings* (626–556 B.C.)... (1956); Freedman, in: BASOR, 145 (1951), 31–32; A. Malamat, in: IEJ, 18 (1968), 137–55; idem, in: J. Abiram (ed.), *Yerushalayim le-Doroteha* (1969), 27–48 (Eng. section, 59). IN THE AGGADAH: Ginzberg, Legends, index. IN ISLAM: Ṭabarī, 15 (1328 A.H.), 17, 22, 23; Ṭabarī, *Ta'rīkh*, 1 (1357 A.H.), 385 (according to the Bible); C. Shwarzbaum, *Adam-Noah Memorial Volume for A.N. Braun* (1960), 239–63. IN THE ARTS: L. Réau, *Iconographie de l'art chrétien*, 2 (1956), 406–9; *Metropolitan Opera News* (Dec. 3, 1960); G. Martin, *Verdi, his Music, Life and Times* (1963), 97–120.

NEBUZARADAN (Heb. נְבוּזַרְאֲדָן; Akk. **Nabu-zēr-iddina**; "Nabu has given offspring"), commander of *Nebuchadnezzar's guard who was in charge of the destruction of the Temple and the deportation of the people of Judah. Acting on orders, Nebuzaradan set fire to the city of Jerusalem and leveled its walls (II Kings 25:9ff.). Certain of the ecclesiastical, military, and civil officers and leading citizens who were supporters of *Zedekiah were brought before Nebuchadnezzar at Riblah and executed (25:20), and *Gedaliah son of Ahikam was placed in charge of the remaining population. Five years later, Nebuzaradan deported another 745 people (Jer. 52:30).

The official title of Nebuzaradan is given as *sar ha-ṭabbaḥim*, although such a designation of a court official is unknown in Mesopotamian literature. The Septuagint translates the term as "chief cook or butcher." In an inscription from the time of Nebuchadnezzar II, the chief court officer is referred to as Nabû-zēr-iddina, whose official Babylonian title is *rab nuḥatimmê* (cf., talmudic Heb. *naḥtom*, "baker"). Scholars have thus identified this officer with Nebuzaradan, and assume that the biblical title is a translation of the Babylonian one. The Aramaic translations render the term as "chief butcher" or "slaughterer," and it is probable that this official belonged to the king's guards whose duty was the infliction of capital punishment.

In the Aggadah

Nebuzaradan's loyalty to his king is praised. He attached Nebuchadnezzar's portrait to his chariot, so that he might always feel that he stood in his presence. For the same reason he accepted the assignment to conquer Jerusalem, even though he had personally witnessed Sennacherib's defeat there (Sanh. 95a–96b). His success was due to divine aid. According to one Midrash, after three and a half years he was about to abandon the task but was advised by God to measure the city walls. As soon as he did so they began to sink into the ground and ultimately disappeared (Lam. R., introd. 30). According to another account, he was on the point of returning home after all the axes but the one at his disposal had been broken in the attack on Jerusalem. At that moment a voice cried out: "The time has come for the Sanctuary to be destroyed and the Temple burnt," and with his last remaining ax he destroyed one of the city gates (Sanh. 96b).

When he led the exiles into captivity he commanded his soldiers not to touch married women captives, lest they provoke God's wrath (Lam. R. 5:11). He forbade the captives to pray, putting to death those who did so. When, however, they had crossed the Euphrates, he desisted since they were now beyond the territory under the dominion of Israel's God (*ibid.* 5:5). Nebuzaradan is identified with Arioch (Dan. 2: 14), since he roared like a lion (*ari*) at his captives. When he saw the blood of the murdered Zechariah boiling (of. II Chron. 24:22), he put to death in revenge the scholars, young priests, and 14,000 of the people, but still the blood did not rest. In despair he exclaimed: "I have destroyed the flower of them. Do you wish me to massacre them all?" The blood immediately subsided, but so stricken was Nebuzaradan with grief that he exclaimed: "If they who killed only one person have been so severely punished, what will be my fate?" He thereupon became a righteous proselyte (Sanh. 96b).

BIBLIOGRAPHY: J. Montgomery, *Kings* (ICC, 1951), 562; Bright, Hist, 309; EM, 5 (1968), 732. IN THE AGGADAH: Ginzberg, Legends, index: I. Ḥasida, *Ishei ha-Tanakh* (1964), 321–2.

NECO (or **Necoh**; **Wehemibre Neko** II; c. 609–593 B.C.E.), Twenty-fifth Dynasty king of Egypt, who played a major role in the fall of Judah. Marching to aid the Assyrians after the fall of Nineveh in 612, Neco found his passage blocked at Megiddo by King *Josiah (II Kings 23:29ff.; II Chron. 35:20–24). The defeat and death of Josiah there allowed Neco to consolidate and control Syria and Palestine as far as the Euphrates. He deposed *Jehoahaz, Josiah's successor, after a three-month reign and exiled him to Egypt (II Kings 23:31–35 and Jer. 22:10–12), replacing him with *Jehoiakim as an Egyptian puppet. The Babylonian conquerors of Assyria were quick to react. In 605 *Nebuchadnezzar, the son of Nabopolassar, "crossed the river to go against the Egyptian army … He accomplished their defeat and beat them into non-existence" (*Babylonia Chronicle*, ed. Wiseman, 25, 67–68), and "the king of Egypt did not come again out of his land, for the king of Babylon had taken all that belonged to the king of Egypt from the brook of Egypt to the river Euphrates" (II Kings 24:7). Judah and the other Egyptian vassals gained a brief respite, for the death of Nabopolassar compelled Nebuchadnezzar to abandon his victorious advance and hasten back to Babylon to secure the throne. The respite was short, and by the end of 604 the Babylonians were in Philistia. An Aramaic letter, found in Egypt, begging the Egyptian pharaoh for aid against the Babylonian invader, probably came from Ashkelon. Jehoiakim, willingly or not, defected to the Babylonians (II Kings 24:1), but rebelled after Nebuchadnezzar was checked by Neco at the Egyptian frontier in 601. Two years later he died (was perhaps assassinated) and was replaced by his son, *Jehoiachin. Within three months Jerusalem fell, and the royal family was exiled to Babylon (II Kings 24:10–17). In 593 Neco died, but his son Psammetichus II continued to incite Zedekiah, the new ruler of Judah, against Babylon. Egypt provided no assistance, however, when Jerusalem finally fell in 587.

BIBLIOGRAPHY: P.G. Elgood, *The Later Dynasties of Egypt* (1951); Bright, Hist, index; A.H. Gardiner, *Egypt of the Pharaohs* (1961); D.J. Wiseman, *Chronicles of the Chaldean Kings* (1956).

[Alan Richard Schulman]

NEDARIM (Heb. נְדָרִים; "Vows"), third tractate of the order *Nashim*, though in some editions the order varies. It is based upon Numbers 30 and deals mainly with the binding quality of the spoken vow by means of which a person may forbid the use of things to himself and his own property to others. The inclusion of this topic in the order dealing with family law arises, in part, from the right of the father to annul the vows of his daughter during her minority and the right of a husband to annul most or all of his wife's vows. The Mishnah consists of 11 chapters. Chapter 1 deals with the formulas which constitute binding vows and Chapter 2 with formulas that are not binding. Chapter 3 deals with vows not binding because of lack of serious intent, constraint, and the like, as well as the interpretation of certain vow formulas; there is an incidental digression on the importance of circumcision. Chapter 4 discusses the consequences of forbidding benefit to, or being forbidden benefit from, another person. Chapter 5 continues this subject in connection with the property of partners and of members of a community or people. Chapter 6 lays down guidelines for determining what is to be included in, and what excluded from, vows appertaining to produce. Chapter 7 continues this topic in connection with places and periods of time. Chapter 8 deals with the extension in time to be given to expressions connected with recurring events, and vows made in general language arising from some specific event. Chapter 9 deals with the absolution of vows, and the grounds on which such absolution may be granted.

It includes the following moving account (Mishnah 10): It once happened that a man vowed to have nothing to do with his niece (i.e., not to marry her because of her uncomely appearance). R. Ishmael took her into his household and had her treated cosmetically ("beautified her"). He then said to the uncle: "Was it against this woman that you took the vow?" He answered in the negative, and R. Ishmael released him from his vow. Whereupon R. Ishmael wept and said: "the daughters of Israel are comely, but poverty destroys their comeliness!" When R. Ishmael died the women of Israel lamented: "Ye women of Israel, weep for R. Ishmael."

Chapter 10 deals with revocation by both father and fiancé of the vows of an affianced maiden; women whose vows cannot be revoked; the impossibility of revoking vows in advance; and the period allowed for such revocation. Chapter 11 treats of the type of vow that a husband can revoke: those which affect their relations or involve self-denial; vows of women not requiring revocation; and of women whose vows are not subject to revocation. *Nedarim* is a rich source for linguistic and syntactical usages in mishnaic Hebrew and is so used by the *Gemara*. The oldest stratum of this tractate including 1:3; 2:4; 3:4; 5:5 dates from the Second Temple period. *Mishnayot* 1:1; 7:1; 9:5–6; 11:4 are apparently derived from the *mishnayot* of Akiva while the rest of Mishnah *Nedarim* originated in the *mishnayot* of his disciples, Meir, Judah, and Yose. Chapter 4 belongs to Meir; 1:1; 3:6–10; 6:1; 7:5; 8:5–7; 9:1–8 belong to R. Judah, and the passages 3:1–5, 11; chapters 5; 1:1–7 belong to Yose who actually states that Elijah the Prophet taught him the section on *Nedarim* (Songs Zuta, ed. Schachter, 44; Buber 39; Epstein, Tanna'im 140–1). *Mishnah* 11:8 to the end of the tractate consists of supplements and glosses on the laws concerning vows. *Mishnah* 1:2 mentions several terms for vows about which the *amoraim* debate whether they were borrowed from foreign languages or were coined by the rabbis (10a). One of these terms, "*konam*," was found in the Punic inscription of Ashmanezer, king of Sidon (4:20), meaning "curse" or "vow," but it is not certain whether this Phoenician word is connected with the mishnaic term (S. Lieberman, *Greek in Jewish Palestine* (1942), 129 n. 106). Many of the laws in *Nedarim* should be seen in light of the Hellenistic practices of that period (*ibid.*, 115–43).

The Tosefta consists of only seven chapters and many of the *mishnayot* of *Nedarim* have no corresponding comments in the Tosefta, nor does the order of the laws in this Tosefta always follow that of the Mishnah. On the other hand, the Tosefta gives several laws not included in the Mishnah.

There is a *Gemara* to *Nedarim* in both the Babylonian and the Jerusalem Talmuds. The Babylonian *Gemara*, as is the case with regard to the tractate *Nazir*, is written in a peculiar dialect and various theories have been propounded to explain it. Epstein is of the opinion that it originates in the academy of Maḥoza, and since very little of the Talmud of Maḥoza reached Sura or Pumbedita, the *geonim* overlooked this tractate. In fact, during the whole of the geonic period the study of *Nedarim* was neglected in the Babylonian academies (Yehudai Gaon; B.M. Lewin, *Oẓar ha-Ge'onim*, 11 (1942), 23; cf. Adler Ms. no. 2639. See A. Marmorstein, in MGWJ, 67 (1923), 134ff.). A. Weiss maintains that the differences are due solely to its neglect in the academies in later ages, and that it therefore lacked the benefits of final polishing given to the other tractates in the post-amoraic period, though he adds that it contains a certain amount of post-amoraic material, and regards the first two discussions as entirely savoraic. The Babylonian Talmud is usually printed with the commentary of Nissim Gerondi (the Ran) in addition to one attributed to Rashi, and with *tosafot* and the commentary of Jacob b. Asher. The text is not in very good condition and the commentaries contain many variant readings.

Aggadic Material

Both Talmuds, especially the Babylonian, are rich in aggadic material as exemplified by the following sayings: "The ancestors of the arrogant never stood on Mount Sinai" (20a); "If the people of Israel had not sinned, they would have been given only the Pentateuch and the Book of Joshua" (22b); "Why have scholars very often no learned children? In order that knowledge may not be thought transmissible by inheritance and that scholars may not pride themselves on an aristocracy of mind" (81a). Biblical scholars find interest in the Talmud's remarks on the masoretic division of the Bible into verses and on the *keri* and *ketiv* which do not entirely coincide with the existing masoretic text (37b–38a). The Jerusalem Talmud tells of letters which Judah ha-Nasi addressed to Hananiah, the nephew of Joshua b. Hananiah, to dissuade him from decreeing leap years abroad. The discussion that followed ends with the saying that "a small group in Ereẓ Israel is more precious to me than a Great Sanhedrin in the Diaspora" (6:13, 40a).

The talmudic tractate was translated into English in the Soncino edition by H. Freedman (1936).

BIBLIOGRAPHY: Ḥ. Albeck, *Shishah Sidrei Mishnah, Seder Nashim* (1954), 137–46; idem, *Mavo la-Mishnah* (1959), 266; S. Lieberman, *Greek in Jewish Palestine* (1942), 115–43; Epstein, Tanna'im, 376–82; Epstein, Amora'im, 54–71; Halevy, Dorot, 3 (1923), 48f.; A. Weiss, *Al ha-Mishnah* (1969), 155–68; idem, *Hithavvut ha-Talmud bi-Shelemuto* (1943), 57–128; D. Halivni, *Mekorot u-Masorot* (1968), 263–352; Z.W. Rabinowitz, *Sha'arei Torat Bavel* (1961), 299ff.

NE'EMAN, YEHOSHUA LEIB (1899–1979), Israeli **ḥazzan*, writer, and teacher. Born in Jerusalem, Ne'eman sang as a *meshorer* with A.Z. Idelsohn and other *ḥazzanim* and studied liturgical music and singing with Solomon Rosowsky. His lyric tenor voice and emphasis on correct pronunciation and accentuation of the prayers made him a popular *ḥazzan* in many of Jerusalem's synagogues. He was often accompanied by his choir, Shir Ẓiyyon. From 1948 Ne'eman was lecturer in biblical cantillation at the Academy of Music in Jerusalem, and from 1958 to 1965 was director of the school for *ḥazzanim* for the Israel Institute for Sacred Music. He wrote extensively on biblical cantillation including *Ẓelilei ha-Mikra* (1955), and also published *Nusaḥ la-Ḥazzan* (1963, with demonstration records). Rosowsky based his *The Cantillation of Bible* (1957) on Ne'eman's renderings which he accepted as the pure representation of the Ashkenazi tradition.

NE'EMAN, YUVAL (1925–2006), Israeli physicist, defense expert, engineer, and political activist. Born in Tel Aviv, he graduated from high school at the age of 15 and studied at the Technion (1941–45), graduating in mechanical engineering and applying it at the family's pump factory. He had joined the Haganah in 1940 and fought in 1948 defending the Jerusalem road, then on the Egyptian Front (Givati Brigade operations officer), staying on in the IDF until 1960. On the General Staff, serving as director of planning (1952–55), he is credited with the elaboration of the IDF's fundamental strategic and organizational doctrine, followed until after the Six-Day War. From 1955 to 1957 he served as deputy director of the Defense Intelligence Division (with the rank of colonel), where he contributed to the introduction of advanced information technologies and was, in addition, responsible for the operational secret link with France at the time of the Sinai Campaign. In 1958 he was appointed defense attaché to the UK and the Scandinavian countries. At that time he embarked upon a new career, studying physics at London's Imperial College under Nobel laureate A. Salam. Since J.J. Thomson's discovery of the electron in 1897 and E. Rutherford's discovery of the proton (1911), nearly 100 particles had been discovered, forming a confusing jumble for which Ne'eman proposed in 1960–61 a classification scheme based on a mathematical symmetry (the "SU(3)-octet" model, popularly known as the "Eightfold Way") which was experimentally confirmed in 1964. The same scheme was suggested simultaneously and independently by M. *Gell-Mann and is often regarded as an analog of D. Mendeleev's Periodic Chart of the chemical elements or C.V. Linne's classification of the living and plant species. In 1962, Ne'eman also conceived the sub-structure that would create such an order, an idea further developed by M. Gell-Mann and independently by G. *Zweig, now known as the "quark model." During 1961–63, Ne'eman served as scientific director of the Israel Atomic Energy Commission's Soreq Research Establishment.

Appointed professor of physics, he founded the Department of Physics and Astronomy of Tel Aviv University and chaired it from 1965 to 1972. In mathematical physics, from 1974 to 1979, he made important contributions to the new areas of Lie "superalgebras" and to "supergeometry" and "superconnections," including new physical predictions which will be experimentally tested at CERN in Geneva when the construction of a new accelerator will be completed in 2007. He also developed with A. Kantorovich a new approach to evolutionary epistemology.

Ne'eman introduced astronomy in Israel with the inauguration of the Wise Observatory (40" telescope) in the Negev in 1971. At Tel Aviv University he also created the School of Engineering and the Jaffe Institute for Strategic Studies and was elected to succeed George Wise as Tel Aviv University president in 1971. He resigned in 1975, joining the Ministry of Defense as senior advisor to the minister, having served in the same capacity on a part-time basis in 1972 and 1974. At Tel Aviv University he was also director of the Mortimer and Raymond Institute of Advanced Studies from 1979 to 1997. In the Defense Ministry, he resigned as senior advisor in protest over the surrender of the Sinai (Abu Rudeis) oilfields in the Interim Agreement with Egypt, having advocated since the Six-Day War the annexation of Judea, Samaria, the Golan Heights, and parts of Sinai in order to establish secure borders, calling for a massive Jewish settlement in the occupied areas and supporting the Gush Emunim settlement movement. He also served as president of the Israel Bureau of Standards (1972–76) and chief defense scientist (1975–76), chairman of the National Research Council (1982–84), and president of the Israel Association of Engineers, Architects and Academics in the Technological Disciplines (1997–2002).

In the political arena, in the beginning of 1979, around the time when MKs Ge'ula *Cohen and Moshe *Shamir left the Likud and established an independent parliamentary group against the background of the Egyptian-Israeli Peace Treaty, Ne'eman called for all the opponents of the agreement with Egypt to join forces. In October the Teḥiyyah party was formed, and he became its chairman. He was elected to the Tenth Knesset in 1981 on the Teḥiyyah list and served as minister of science and development from 1981 to 1984, simultaneously serving as deputy chairman of the joint Settlement Committee of the government and the World Zionist Organization. In 1983 he founded the Israel Space Agency, chairing it into the 21st century. He was reelected to the Eleventh and

Twelfth Knesset, but in January 1990 resigned from the Knesset to enable the next in line on the Teḥiyyah list – Eliakim Haetzni – to enter the Knesset in his place. In the government formed by Yitzhak *Shamir in June 1990, after the fall of the National Unity Government, Ne'eman was appointed minister of Energy and Infrastructure, without being a member of the Knesset. In this capacity he was the first Israeli minister to meet Soviet President Mikhail Gorbachev, not long before the collapse of the Soviet Union. He resigned from the government in February 1992, against the background of the Madrid Conference and the Washington talks. Following the failure of Teḥiyyah to enter the Thirteenth Knesset, and Cohen's decision to rejoin the Likud, Ne'eman left active political life, and returned to Tel Aviv University. During these years he was also in the forefront of the struggle to get Jewish scientists out of the Soviet Union.

Altogether, he published some 400 research articles and some 20 books in the physics of particles and fields, cosmology, and the history and philosophy of science. Ne'eman received the Israel Prize in 1969 and the EMET Prize in 2003 as well as the Albert Einstein Medal in 1969 and other international awards.

NEGA'IM (Heb. נְגָעִים; "Plagues"), third tractate of the order *Tohorot* in the Mishnah and Tosefta. It deals with ritual uncleanness resulting from the plague referred to in Leviticus 13 and 14, which is usually translated as "leprosy." *Nega'im* consists of 14 chapters. Chapter 1 defines the colors and shades of the various symptoms of human leprosy. Chapter 2 discusses the time these symptoms may be inspected, the posture of the sufferer when being examined, and the person qualified to make the examination. Chapter 3 details when the examination can be postponed, the procedure when the examination is made by a non-priest, and the symptoms of the plague in persons, houses, and garments. Chapter 4 contrasts the various symptoms indicating uncleanness, and the consequence of different leprous signs appearing simultaneously or in succession. Chapter 5 deals with doubtful signs of leprosy and symptoms that disappear and reappear in the same or in changed form. Chapter 6 discusses the minimum sizes of leprous signs and the parts of the body in which the appearance of the symptoms do not give rise to uncleanness. Chapter 7 deals with spots that are clean and natural or induced changes during or after the inspection. Chapter 8 discusses when the symptom covers the whole body and chapter 9 the symptoms of the plagues termed "boil" and "burning" and their relationship to one another. Chapter 10 deals with scales, chapter 11 with the leprosy of garments, and chapter 12 with the uncleanness of houses. Chapter 13 continues with the uncleanness of houses and how they and a leper pass on uncleanness. Chapter 14 deals with the procedure at the leper's cleansing and at his offering of sacrifices.

The Tosefta to *Nega'im* has only nine chapters and contains details not found in the Mishnah, as well as several independent groups of laws. Two groups are found in this Tosefta, the first characterized by the legal formula, "One does not" (1:11–13), and the second group by its opening word "*netek*" (i.e., a bald spot on the head or beard, 4:2–6). *Tosefta* 6:1 cites an anonymous opinion stating that the laws concerning a house defiled by leprosy have only theoretical validity because such houses never existed and never will; other rabbis, however, cite cases of such houses. *Tosefta* 6:7 claims that leprosy is a punishment for the sins of gossip and haughtiness. The laws of *Nega'im* and *Oholot* were regarded as extremely complicated and difficult, and consequently the rabbis referred to them as prototypes of deep halakhic learning. For example, the Talmud relates that Eleazar b. Azariah told Akiva: "Why do you deal with *aggadah*? Occupy yourself with *Nega'im* and *Oholot*" (Ḥag. 14a). The *aggadah* also claims that King David pleaded that his Psalms, the most spiritualized form of worship, be considered before God as *Nega'im* and *Oholot* (Mid. Ps. 1:8). English translations of the Mishnah were published by H. Danby (1939), in the Soncino Talmud by I.W. Slotki (1948), by P. Blackman (1955), and by J. Neusner (1991), who also translated the Tosefta (2002).

BIBLIOGRAPHY: Ḥ. Albeck, *Untersuchungen ueber die Redaktion der Mischna* (1923), 49f.; idem (ed.), *Shishah Sidrei Mishnah, Seder Tohorot* (1959), 195–8. **ADD. BIBLIOGRAPHY:** Epstein, *The Gaonic Commentary on the Order Toharot* (Hebr.) (1982); S. Lieberman, *Tosefet Rishonim*, vol. 3 (1939); J. Neusner, *A History of the Mishnaic Laws of Purities* (1974–77), vol. 6–8; idem, *From Mishnah to Scripture* (1984), 53–58; idem, *The Mishnah Before 70* (1987), 103–40; idem, *The Philosophical Mishnah 3* (1989), 21–33; idem, *Purity in Rabbinic Judaism* (1994), 60–63.

[David Joseph Bornstein]

NEGBAH (Heb. נֶגְבָּה; "toward the Negev"), kibbutz in southern Israel, 6 mi. (10 km.) E. of Ashkelon, affiliated with Kibbutz Arẓi Ha-Shomer ha-Ẓa'ir. Negbah was founded by pioneers from Poland as a *stockade and watchtower settlement in the last month of the Arab riots (July 1939) and constituted the country's southernmost Jewish village at the time. As the kibbutz' name indicates, its establishment was the first of a systematic effort to gain footholds in the south and Negev. Isolated among strong Arab villages, Negbah had to repulse attacks in the first days of its existence. In the Israeli *War of Independence (1948) the Egyptian army made all-out efforts to take the kibbutz. The settlers held out for six months in their entrenchments under continuous shelling, air bombardment, and tank attacks, after Egyptian forces occupied the nearby dominating Iraq Suweidān police fortress. The kibbutz was completely destroyed aboveground. The Egyptians, in violation of the local cease-fire agreement, interfered with the passage of Israeli convoys from Negbah to the Negev settlements and this led to the "Ten Plagues" Operation of the Israeli army (Oct. 15, 1948); a strong Egyptian pocket continued to hold Negbah under fire until the police fortress fell on Nov. 9. The kibbutz preserved its ruined water tower in memory of the battles, and erected a monument to the defenders in its cemetery. After 1948 Negbah developed a flourishing farming economy based on intensive field crops, citrus and other fruit orchards, and dairy cattle. It also established a sewing factory and a metal workshop. Its population in 1968 was 404. In the mid-1990s the population was approximately 665, dropping to 407 in 2002.

[Efraim Orni]

NEGEV (Heb. נֶגֶב; from the root נגב, "dry," "parched"), an area comprising those southern parts of the Land of Israel which are characterized by a totally arid desert climate, contrasting with the semiarid Mediterranean climate of the country's center and north.

Geography

On the map describing an inverted triangle, with an apex directed to Eilat in the south, the Negev covers an area exceeding 4,600 sq. mi. (12,000 sq. km.), i.e., about 62% of Israel's area. Compared with other regions (Sinai excepted), distances in the Negev are considerable, exceeding 150 mi. (250 km.) from north to south, and 80 mi. (125 km.) from west to east. Whereas the Negev's northern border is a climatic one, roughly following the line of 12 in. (300 mm.) annual rainfall, the eastern border is a topographical one, sharply delineated by the Edom scarps emerging from the Arabah Valley, while in the west and southwest there is a gradual transition into Sinai. Structurally, the main partition of Cisjordan – into the Coastal Plain, the hills and the rift – continues into the Negev, with the following subregions recognizable:

(1) the Negev Coastal Plain, linking up in the east with the Beersheba Basin;

(2) the Negev Hills, composed of the northern and central hill regions, the Paran Plateau, and the Eilat Mountains;

(3) the Arabah Valley.

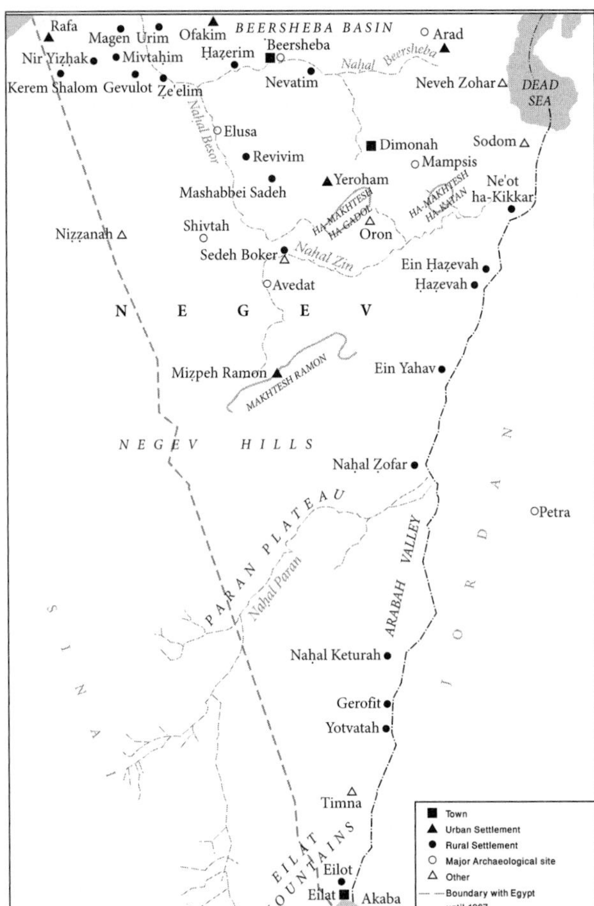

The Negev, ancient sites and modern settlements.

Geologically, most of the Negev hills resemble the hills of central and northern Israel, where folding constitutes the principal tectonic element, and hard limestones and dolomites, or softer chalks with flint intercalations, are the predominant surface rock strata. Desert weathering, however, has imposed on these rocks dissimilar landscape features, which are mostly sharp and angular. The only exception is the Eilat Mountains, which, with their crystalline rocks and Nubian sandstones, form a continuation of the geological province of southern and southeastern Sinai. With the exception of the Beersheba Basin, arable soil is absent from practically all of the Negev, and wide expanses are covered with sharp flint or limestone gravel.

The Negev lies within the global subtropical desert belt of the northern hemisphere. Its climate is of the "continental" type and has two outstanding characteristics – sharp temperature differences between day and night, and summer and winter, and extremely limited amounts of precipitation, which diminish from an annual 10 in. (250 mm.) on the region's northwestern fringe to 2–4 in. (50–100 mm.) in most of its parts, and 1–2 in. (25–50 mm.) or less in the Arabah Valley and the Eilat area. Solar radiation and evaporation are strong during all seasons, and relative humidity and cloudiness remain low. Whereas the tempering influence of the Mediterranean Sea reaches inland for a score of miles at best, the Red Sea and the Eilat Gulf do not exert any such influence on the adjoining land.

The Negev's vegetation cover is universally sparse, and practically absent over large expanses. Most of the Beersheba Basin, together with the highest reaches of the central Negev Hills, falls within the Irano-Turanian semidesert zone, while the rest of the Negev belongs to the Arabian Zone, which has full desert characteristics. Similarly, the Negev has a desert fauna, including a number of indigenous species; its animal kingdom has somewhat increased in numbers due to nature-preservation measures in force since the 1950s. In the Beersheba Basin, which gradually rises eastward from 350 ft. (less than 100 m.) to 1,650 ft. (500 m.) above sea level, a thick cover of yellowish-brown loess, in sections of the west overlaid by coarse dune sands (the Ḥaluẓah, Shunrah, and Agur dunes), determines both landscape features and farming possibilities. In restricted areas, gullying by flashfloods resulted in a broken badland topography, which, however, has since the 1950s largely disappeared thanks to leveling in the framework of the soil reclamation program. Almost the entire Beersheba region belongs to the drainage basin of Naḥal Besor, which crosses it from southeast to northwest and receives three important tributaries from the east and northeast – Naḥal Be'er Sheva, Naḥal Ḥevron, and Naḥal Gerar. The width of their beds bears no relation to the minute annual quantities of water running through them, which, at least during the last millennia, have been limited to occasional, short-lived winter floods.

In the central Negev Hills, whose folds attain heights of 3,000–3,400 ft. (900–1,035 m.) above sea level (Mt. Ramon, Mt. Sagi, Mt. Loẓ, Mt. Arif, and others), the most striking landscape feature is represented by the three huge erosional cirques (Makhtesh Ramon, Ha-Makhtesh ha-Gadol, Ha-Makhtesh ha-Katan). The wild Zin Canyon divides the hills into a northern and central section. The Paran Plateau, whose topography is more monotonous, is inclined from the southwest to the northeast, descending from 2,000 ft. (600 m.) to 330 ft. (100 m.). Naḥal Paran, the longest and most spectacular of Israel's desert wadis, runs through the plateau. Although the peaks of the Eilat Mountains attain heights of only 3,000 ft. (800–900 m.), the landscape of this area is truly mountainous and of infinite variety, with rock towers, indented and crenellated crests, between which narrow clefts cut in various directions. There is a wide range of igneous rocks (granites, diorites, quartz-porphyry, diabase, gneiss, quartzite, etc.), as well as vividly colored (ocher, yellow, rose, red, white, black and so on) Nubian sandstones, but also strongly contorted limestones and other marine sediments.

The Arabah Valley, that section of the rift extending from the Dead Sea to the Gulf of Eilat for 105 mi. (over 170 km.), is hemmed in by the continuous rock wall of Edom in the east and by the Negev Hills, of lesser height and uniformity, in the west. Its bottom ascends from 1,150 ft. (350 m.) below sea level in the Sedom salt flats over a relatively prominent step to 690 ft. (210 m.) below sea level near Ḥaẓevah, and thence continues to rise more gently to 755 ft. (230 m.), above sea level near the Sheluḥat Noẓah ridge, which protrudes into the valley 48 mi. (75 km.) north of Eilat; from that point southward, it gradually descends to the Eilat shore. The Arabah bears a cover of alluvium (sand, gravel, etc.) which obscures its rock foundations. Alluvial fans, mostly spreading in front of the Edom Mountains, obstruct the drainage of the southern Arabah and are the cause of the formation of playas (saline marshes), e.g., those of Eilat, Avronah, Yotvatah, and Sa'īdiyin. The central and northern Arabah are drained by Naḥal ha-Aravah, which is the lower section of Naḥal Paran. Springs in the Arabah are mostly weak and brackish on the western, but stronger and sweeter on the eastern, rim. Deep well drillings in the 1960s yielded water in previously unsuspected quantities.

History

In the Bible, Negev refers to southern and southeastern Judah, an area split up between various groups, each of which is connected with a Negev of its own: Negev of Judah, around Beer-Sheba; Negev of Caleb, north of it; Negev of the Cherethites (Philistines), to the northwest; Negev of the Kenites, to the east; Negev of the Jerahmeelites, to the southeast. Today the name is applied to the whole southern region of Israel, extending from Beersheba to Eilat. In prehistoric times, the Negev was a well-watered and settled region, till the desiccation which accompanied the Mesolithic period. In the Chalcolithic period, a new culture developed along the dry river beds around Beer-Sheba, with pasture-bred animals, underground dwellings, and the beginning of exploitation of the Arabah copper mines for a metallurgic industry. A chain of short-lived settlements of a seminomadic, pastoral populace again appeared in various parts of the Negev in the intermediate period between the Early and Middle Bronze Ages (c. 2000 B.C.E.). The suggestion that these were situated along the main routes in the time of Abraham is refuted by most scholars. At the time of the Exodus, the Amalekites roamed in the southern part of the Negev, while the Canaanites of Arad held strongly to the north. Attempts by the Israelites to pass through the Negev on the direct route to Canaan ended in failure. The northern region is included within the boundaries of the land of Israel (Num. 34:4; Josh. 15:3). After Joshua's conquest, Simeon had a weak hold on the northern Negev centering on Beer-Sheba. Saul and David fended off the Amalekites, and Solomon and his successors set up fortresses to guard the routes to Elath and Egypt. Uzziah made the greatest effort to develop the Negev in the Israelite period, keeping up his communications with Elath through this region, and, apart from extending agriculture (II Chron. 26:10), building large fortresses at Kadesh, Arad, Ḥorvat 'Uza, and other sites.

After the return from Babylonian exile, Jewish connections with the Negev in the post-biblical period are tenuous. The northern part was held by Alexander Yannai (Jannaeus). It came under the control of the *Nabateans, who used its highway (the so-called "spice and incense" route) primarily for conveying caravans of goods (such as frankincense and myrrh) from their capital Petra and from their port Aila (Elath) to Gaza and the shores of the Mediterranean. Sites discovered include way stations, forts and towers, and regional roads. It was once thought the *Nabateans were the first to develop terraced agriculture in the Negev, but although they were undoubtedly masters in sophisticated water-gathering systems, which were especially important for the caravans of camels and men passing through the region, there is no evidence that they practiced wide-scale cultivation in the area, except perhaps in a very limited fashion. Toward the end of Nabatean rule in the Negev, settlements flourished along the trade route, as is now known from remains uncovered at Avedat, Mampsis, and Elusa, with inscriptions, temples, caravanserai, and other structures. After the annexation of Nabatea by Rome in 106 C.E., the importance of the region declined; it revived toward the middle of the third century C.E. and entered its most prosperous era in antiquity during the Byzantine and Umayyad periods. Impressive towns from these periods existed at Elusa (Heb. Halutza), Subeita/Sobata (Arab. Isbeita; Heb. Shivta), Nessana (Arab. Auja al-Hafir; Heb. Nitzana), Oboda (Arab. Abda; Heb. 'Avedat), Rehovot-in-the-Negev (Arab. Ruheibe), and Mampsis (Arab. Kurnub; Heb. Mamshit). Impressive churches are known at many of these sites. An important archive of manuscripts was uncovered at Nessana. It has been estimated that by the Late Byzantine/Umayyad periods 40,000 dunams (10,000 acres) of the Negev highlands were under cultivation; this was mainly achieved by the careful terrace and dam building and the efficient diversion and distribution of rainwater by channels. Numerous agricultural settlements have been investigated. The Negev settlements began declining in the Abbasid period.

[Michael Avi-Yonah / Shimon Gibson (2nd ed.)]

At the earliest stages of the modern Jewish return to the land, the Negev was visualized as a possible area of settlement by men like Z.D. *Levontin, who aimed at founding a settlement south of Gaza (1881–2). Like other Jews at the beginning of the 20th century, however, they had to abandon attempts at purchasing holdings, mainly because Bedouin vendors could not produce title deeds entered in the land registry for the tracts they offered. Attention was again directed to the Negev when Theodor *Herzl took up Davis *Trietsch's proposal of the *El-Arish Project (1903), and a daring plan for a Jewish-Bedouin alliance was also put forward. After World War I, veterans of the Jewish *Legion tried to settle on state land offered by the British authorities near the tell of Arad, but they despaired when no water was found. After the end of the 1930s, the Jewish National *Fund took over, securing and enlarging scattered holdings in the Negev which had been acquired beforehand by Jewish individuals. Thus the three "observation villages" – Gevulot, Beit Eshel, and Revivim – were set up in 1943, followed by 11 more villages established on the night of Oct. 6, 1946 and four more – preceding the outbreak of the War of Independence – in December 1947. All outposts were modestly supplied with water from two pipelines drawn from the Nir Am and Gevar'am wells in the southern Coastal Plain. In the 1949 Armistice Agreements with Egypt and Jordan, Israel's hold of the entire Negev was endorsed, with the single exception of the Gaza Strip. Whereas the Negev Bedouin population, of which about 15,000 remained in the Negev after 1948, increased to about 27,000 in 1969, Jewish settlement was the principal factor causing population density in the Beersheba subdistrict (whose borders are nearly identical with those of the Negev) to rise from 2.85 per sq. mi. (1.1 per sq. km.) in 1948 to 36.5 per sq. mi. (14.1 per sq. km.) in 1969; in the latter year, 180,400 inhabitants were counted, of whom 153,300 were Jews and 27,100 were Arabs. By 2003 the population had increased to 534,700 (107 per sq. mi.; 41.3 per sq. km.), including 366,900 Jews and 135,400 Arabs living in 167 settlements. The Negev's population comprises about 7% of the country's total.

Rural settlement quickly progressed as great efforts were invested in bringing mounting quantities of water to the Negev, first through the reconstituted pipelines from the Nir Am area in the 1950s, from the Yarkon springs ("Yarkon-Negev line"), and in the 1960s via the National Water Carrier. In the pattern of settlement comprising over 70 villages, three groups can be discerned:

(1) the bulk of villages, mostly moshavim, concentrated in the northwestern Negev and arranged in regional projects (Benei Shim'on, Merḥavim, Eshkol regions);

(2) security settlements, preponderantly kibbutzim, along the border of the Gaza Strip;

(3) outpost settlements, of the kibbutz and moshav types (mostly in the Arabah Valley), which combine the task of border defense with pioneering new methods in desert and oasis farming. Agricultural initiative has brought citrus groves to the northwestern Negev and developed out-of-season vegetable and flower cultivation both in the western Negev (Eshkol region) and the Arabah Valley, while cotton, fodder crops, sugar beet (all irrigated), wheat, and other grain crops (the latter grown unirrigated or with auxiliary irrigation) are characteristic of the interior part of the northwestern Negev. However, present-day irrigation is no longer based only on the National Water Carrier; it also utilizes purified sewage water and wells. A number of kibbutzim have also developed industrial enterprises.

Among urban settlements, the city of Beersheba has surpassed all other centers in growth and contains nearly 34% of the Negev's total population; second is Dimona on the Negev Hills; and third is Eilat. Other urban settlements were established, in the northwest (Netivot, Ofakim) to serve as regional centers for agricultural areas and elsewhere to promote mining and industrial development (Arad, Yeroḥam, Miẓpeh Ramon). During the 1990s the region absorbed many immigrants from the former Soviet Union, a process that augmented mainly the urban settlements of the Negev, which include 82% of the Negev's population. However, by the beginning of the 21st century the Negev had not yet realized its full potential for settlement and development.

The Dead Sea minerals, as well as phosphates, copper, clay minerals, glass sand, and methane gas constitute the principal foundation for the Negev's industrial-development projects, whose important centers are the towns of Beersheba, Dimona, and Arad, the Oron and Ẓefa-Efeh phosphate mines, the factories near the latter site. The Sodom Dead Sea industrial zone has no resident population. However, high-tech industries have also begun to find a home in the Negev, mainly in Beersheba's industrial zones. Another economic branch, which developed mainly since the peace agreements with Egypt and Jordan, is tourism. The Negev offers many natural wonders, walking routes, and tourist attractions, among them Ben-Gurion's cabin, which became a museum located at kibbutz *Sedeh Boker.

The communications network of the Negev is of great importance in the framework of Israel's economic infrastructure. Among highways, the Sodom-Eilat road is particularly busy. Second, comes the Beersheba-Dimona-Miẓpeh Ramon-Eilat highway. The northern and western Negev has a well-developed road network. Railways link Beersheba with Kiryat Gat and Lydda in the north and with Dimona and the Oron and Ẓefa-Efeh mines in the south. Another important economic asset is the Eilat-Ashkelon oil pipeline. Finally, the

Eilat port and oilport are Israel's marine outlets to the south and east.

BIBLIOGRAPHY: C.L. Woolley and T.E. Lawrence, *The Wilderness of Zin* (1915); Y. Aharoni, in: IEJ, 8 (1958), 26ff.; 17 (1967), 1ff.; N. Glueck, *Rivers in the Desert* (1959); A. Negev, in: IEJ, 17 (1967), 46ff.; J. Braslavi (Braslavski), *Ha-Yadata et ha-Areẓ*, 2 (1947); idem, *El Eilat ve-el Yam Suf* (1952); D.H. Kallner-Amiran, in: IEJ, 1 (1950/51), 107–20; L. Picard, in: BRCI, 1 no. 1–2 (1951); 5–32: E. Loehnberg, *Ha-Negev ha-Raḥok* (1954): E. Orni and E. Efrat, *Geography of Israel* (1971³), ch. 2; Y. Morris, *Masters of the Desert (6000 Years in the Negev)* (1961). **ADD. BIBLIOGRAPHY:** M. Evenari, L. Shanan, and N. Tadmor, *The Negev: The Challenge of a Desert* (1971); G. Barkay and E. Schiller (eds.), *With One's Face Towards the Negev.* Parts 1–2 (Heb., 2002); R. Rosenthal-Heginbottom (ed.), *The Nabateans in the Negev* (2003). **WEBSITES:** www.boker.org.il/meida/negev; www.negev-net.org.il.

[Efraim Orni]

NEḤALIM (Heb. נְחָלִים; "streams"), moshav in central Israel, near Lydda (Lod) airport, affiliated with Ha-Po'el ha-Mizrachi moshavim association. Originally founded by veteran farm laborers in 1943 in the Ḥuleh Valley (where its name, referring to the Jordan River headstreams, was chosen), the moshav was largely destroyed in the Israeli War of Independence and the settlers were transferred to the present site on the land of the former German colony, Wilhelma (August 1948). There, the group was joined by settlers from moshav Neveh Ya'akov, north of Jerusalem, which had to be given up in May 1948. Later, new immigrants from Hungary and Poland joined the moshav. The village economy was based on intensive and fully irrigated farming. Neḥalim had 710 inhabitants in 1969, part of them staff and pupils of a yeshivah which was opened in 1958. In the mid-1990s, its population was 1,520, growing further to 1,920 residents in 2002.

[Efraim Orni]

NEHAMA, JOSEPH (ca. 1880–1971), Greek educator and historian. Nehama was born in Salonika, the son of the reformist rabbi Judah Nehama, and studied at the Ecole Normale Orientale, the teacher training school of the Alliance Israélite Universelle in Paris. In his capacity as teacher and school principal of the local Alliance Israélite Universelle, Nehama devoted his life to educating several generations of Salonikan youth.

For a number of periods, Nehama was a member of the Committee of the Jewish Community of Salonika representing the non-Zionist general stream of the Jewish community. As a historian he made a major pioneering effort in tracing the Salonikan Jewish community's roots in his seven-volume work, *Histoire des Israélites de Salonique.* Another noteworthy work was *La Ville Convaitée* under the pen name P. Risal.

As a writer Nehama's literary ability was demonstrated in the dozens of essays he contributed to such French literary publications as *Mercure de France.* He wrote numerous studies and articles in Judeo-Spanish on Jewish history, health codes, and commerce which appeared in the press of Salonika and Paris. Nehama made a great contribution to the propagation and research of the Judeo-Spanish language by writing a comprehensive Judeo-Spanish-French dictionary. The work, entitled *Dictionnaire du Judéo-Espagnol*, was published in 1977 several years after his death.

Nehama was a prominent banker in his capacity as president of the Banque Union. During the Holocaust, Nehama managed to escape the Germans in Salonika by fleeing to Athens. However he was caught by the Nazis and deported on March 25, 1944, to Bergen-Belsen. He was liberated by the American army in the last days of the war.

The Holocaust not only was a personal tragedy for Nehama, but a changing point in his attitude toward Zionism. Previously he had little belief in the potential of political Zionism and its ability to create a viable and prosperous homeland for the Jews. He had been one of the key community leaders in the 1930s who encouraged Jews to stay in Salonika and not immigrate to Palestine. After the Holocaust Nehama was greatly saddened that the prosperous Diaspora center of Salonika had come to an end and regretted his earlier stand against emigration. He was joint author (with Michael Molho) of *The Destruction of Greek Jewry 1941–1944* (Hebrew, 1965). In 1973, the Jewish community of Salonika put out a French version of the book.

[Yitzchak Kerem (2nd ed.)]

NEHARDEA, town in Babylon, situated on the Euphrates at its junction with the Malka River, which was an important Jewish center and seat of a famous academy. Nehardea was surrounded by walls and by the Euphrates River, preventing its penetration by enemies (Jos., Ant., 18:311). The Jewish settlement of Nehardea was an early one. The first settlers were, according to tradition, those exiled in the time of Jehoiachin, king of Judah in the sixth century B.C.E. These exiles erected there a synagogue which they built with stones and earth brought from the site of the Temple. The synagogue was called Shaf ve-Yativ, i.e., "[the Divine Presence has] removed [from the Temple] and settled [in this place]" (*Iggeret Rav Sherira Ga'on*, ed. by B.M. Lewin (1921), 72 and appendices). The existence of its Jewish settlement in the century before the destruction of the Temple is attested by the fact that the Jews of Babylon concentrated in it the half-shekel offering and their donations and offerings for the Temple and dispatched them from there to Jerusalem (Jos., *ibid.*). Josephus also relates the exploits of *Anilaus and Asinaus who were natives of Nehardea. At the beginning of the second century C.E., Akiva visited Nehardea and there intercalated the year, thus testifying to the importance of the local Jewish settlements (Yev. 15:7). Nehardea was also the seat of the exilarch and his *bet din.* The town attained the zenith of its influence in the first half of the third century in the days of *Samuel, who headed its academy, and its influence was widespread (Ket. 54a). Of the scholars active there at the beginning of the amoraic period, Karna, Shila, and Abba b. Abba (Samuel's father) were noteworthy. The academy of Nehardea was destroyed in 259 by Papa b. Neẓer and its scholars moved to *Pumbedita. When spiritual activity was renewed there, many important scholars were active in it, including Dimi and Amemar.

[Yitzhak Dov Gilat]

The Arab Period

There is no extant information on a Jewish settlement in Nehardea during the Arab period. Even after the town was rebuilt, the academy did not return there. Its memory was preserved in Pumbedita, however, by the fact that a group of sages who sat in one of the first three rows of the academy was referred to as "the row of Nehardea." In his responsum to R. Moses b. Meshullam of Mainz, *Elijah b. Solomon ha-Kohen refers to the academy of Sura by the name of Nehardea. In connection with a question on the custom of saying the prayer of *Ve-Hassi'enu* on Rosh Ha-Shanah and the Day of Atonement, the *gaon* replied: "Heaven forbid that there be a difference over this matter, because it is our custom in the two *metivta* (academies) in Ereẓ Israel and Nehardea, that *Ve-Hassi'enu* is said on Rosh Ha-Shanah and the Day of Atonement." B.M. Lewin has pointed out that the reference was to Sura, where this custom prevailed, in contrast to Pumbedita, where it did not. On the other hand, for Sherira, Nehardea was synonymous with the academy of Pumbedita because it was the continuation of Nehardea. In connection with the customs of prayer he writes: "the custom is according to the established *battei midrash* of Nehardea and Sura" (B.M. Lewin (ed.), *Ginzei Kedem*, 1 (1922), 5–6). Benjamin of Tudela, who visited *Iraq during the 1170s, also identifies Pumbedita with Nehardea.

[Eliezer Bashan (Sternberg)]

BIBLIOGRAPHY: M.D. Judelevicz, *Ḥayyei ha-Yehudim bi-Zeman ha-Talmud, Sefer Nehardea* (1905); Funk, in: *Festschrift… D. Hoffmann* (1914), 97–104; J. Obermeyer, *Die Landschaft Babylonien…* (1929), 353 (index), s.v.; Neusner, Babylonia, indices. THE ARAB PERIOD: B.M. Lewin (ed.), *Iggeret R. Sherira Ga'on* (1921), 72–73, 100–1; Abramson, Merkazim, 44, 156; Assaf, Ge'onim, 45, 51; R.S. Weinberg, in: *Sinai*, 65 (1969), 71; Benjamin of Tudela, *Massa'ot…* ed. by M.N. Adler (1907, 1960), 46; Levin, Oẓar, 1 (1928), 34, 125; 3 (1931), 28; A. Epstein, in: MGWJ, 47 (1903), 344; Mann, Texts, 1 (1931), 89–90, 103–4; J. Mann, in: JQR, 11 (1920/21), 437.

NEHAR PEKOD, according to earlier scholars a town in the district of Nehardea (Babylonia), and according to more recent research, between Sura and Nippur. Nehar Pekod gained note after the *tanna* R. Hananiah, the nephew of the *tanna* R. Joshua b. Hananiah, settled there following the suppression of the Bar Kokhba revolt in Ereẓ Israel (Sanh. 32b). The town seems to have rapidly developed into a major center of Jewish life. R. Hananiah tried to establish a *bet midrash* and a Sanhedrin with the authority to continue the practice of intercalating years and fixing months, an authority which was a privilege of Ereẓ Israel (see Ber. 63a–b; Sanh. 32b; TJ, Sanh. 1:1, 19a). The reactivated leadership in Ereẓ Israel immediately intervened and quashed this separatist move. It is reported that R. Hananiah died and was buried in Nehar Pekod. Further testimony about the town and its Sages stems from the geonic period.

BIBLIOGRAPHY: A. Berliner, *Beitraege zur Geographie und Ethnographie Babyloniens im Talmud und Midrasch*, in: *Jahres-Bericht des Rabbiner-Seminars zu Berlin pro 5643 (1882–1883)*, 52; J. Obermeyer, *Die Landschaft Babylonien im Zeitalter des Talmuds und des Gaonats* (1929), 270–6; Neusner, History, 1–2 (1965–66), index. **ADD. BIBLIOGRAPHY:** B. Eshel, *Jewish Settlements in Babylonia during Talmudic Times* (1979), 157–58.

[Eliyahu Hirschberg]

NEHĀVAND (also pronounced **Nahāvand**), a city situated in west central Iran about 75 km south of *Hamadan. It was an important city during the Sasanian period. Its conquest by the invading Arabs (642 C.E.) is considered the beginning of the end of the Iranian empire. It is mentioned in the Babylonian Talmud as a *golah* (Diaspora) which may allude to the existence of a Jewish community in Nehāvand (Kid. 72a). *Benjamin of Tudela (1167) mentioned a city by the name "NHR-VNT" where 4,000 Jews lived. It is possible that he meant the city of Nehāvand.

During the medieval period an important *Karaite community lived there. Prominent in it was R. Binyamin ben Mosheh Nehāvandi (mid-9th century). We possess some fragments of his *Sefer ha-Mitzvot* and *Sefer ha-Dinim*. R. David d'Beth Hillel visited the city around the year 1827 and according to him 20 Jewish families lived there, all of whom were poor. He estimated the number of the Muslim population at 3,000 families. Ephraim Neumark (1884), who did not visit the city, heard that 30 Jewish families lived in it.

According to *ʿĀlam-e Yahud* (1945), a Jewish Persian monthly published in *Teheran, 115 Jewish families lived in Nehāvand, of whom 15, among them some physicians and land owners, were considered rich, 50 ranked as middle class, and the rest were poor. There were two synagogues in the city and one elementary school administered by Alliance Israélite Universelle, where 137 pupils (98 boys and 39 girls) studied up to the sixth grade. The sanitary conditions were reported as unsatisfactory (1945). After the 1979 Islamic Revolution many left for Teheran, Israel, and the U.S., so that no Jewish family was reported as living in Nehāvand by the end of the 20th century.

BIBLIOGRAPHY: M.D. Adler (ed.), *The Itinerary of Benjamin of Tudela* (1907); *ʿĀlam-e Yahud*, a Jewish monthly in Persian published in Teheran, 13 (October 1945), 236; David d`Beth Hillel, *Unknown Jews in Unknown Lands (1824–1832)*, ed. by W.J. Fischel (1973); L. Nemoy, *Karaite Anthology* (1952); E. Neumark, *Massa be-Ereẓ ha-Kedem*, edited by A. Ya'ari (1947).

[Amnon Netzer (2nd ed.)]

NEHEMIAH (Heb. נְחֶמְיָה; "YHWH has comforted": fifth century B.C.E.), cupbearer of *Artaxerxes I and later governor of Judah. Nothing is known of the parentage of Nehemiah except that he was the son of Hacaliah. Two other persons of that name are mentioned in the Bible: one returned with Zerubbabel (Ezra 2:2; Neh. 7:7), and the other, a son of Azbuk, was the chief of half the district of Beth-Zur and helped in rebuilding the wall of Jerusalem (Neh. 3:16). Nehemiah the son of Hacaliah was a high official at the Persian court of Artaxerxes I, perhaps a eunuch (cf. LXXć, Neh. 1:11, *eunochos* for *oinochoos* of LXXḃ). Origen considers Nehemiah, the king's cupbearer, and his eunuch as one person. E. Weidner (see bibl.) has pointed out the importance of the cupbearer at the Assyrian court which, according to Herodotus (3:34), continued at the Persian court.

Being a trusted Jew, though a layman, Nehemiah was, at his own request, placed in charge of a very important and delicate mission – that of the governorship of Judah, which involved rebuilding the walls of Jerusalem and reorganizing the Judean province. He was thus invested with great authority which he wielded with distinction and propriety. The first tasks to which he set himself with great zeal were providing protection for Judah by restoring the walls of the capital, and erecting houses for its population so that all aspects of the community could function more smoothly. Though he suffered almost continuous interference from the governor of Samaria, and perhaps from those of Ammon, Arabia, and Ashdod (6:1–9), he was sufficiently astute to avoid serious conflict, probably because he used his authority wisely and gained the confidence of his fellow Jews. Having achieved his primary objective, he next devoted himself to establishing order and justice in the community (7:1–3). Conscious of his position as a layman (and perhaps, eunuch), he submitted to the religious regulations of his time but was himself a profoundly religious man as is evident from his concern for the levites (13:10–14), his conception of the sanctity of the Temple as shown in the Tobiah affair (13:4–9), his appreciation of the Sabbath (10:32; 13:15–21), and his provision for offerings (10:33–40). It is of interest that he had drawn up his memoirs, which were doubtless placed in the Temple precincts as an inscription of his deeds and works.

Nehemiah is praised by Ben Sira (49:12b–13) and in II Maccabees 1:18, 20–36. Josephus (Ant. 11:159–74) embellished the story of Nehemiah, but the Talmud and the Church Fathers were not so complimentary. The date of Nehemiah's first period of service (5:14) extended from the 20th to the 32nd year of Artaxerxes I (i.e., c. 445–433 B.C.E.). The length of his second period (13:6–7) is not stated.

See also *Exile, Babylonian; *Ezra and Nehemia; *History.

[Jacob M. Myers]

In the Aggadah

Nehemiah is identified with *Zerubbabel, the latter name being considered as indicative of his Babylonian birth (Heb. זְרוּעַ בָּבֶל, "conceived in Babylon"; Sanh. 38a). He was called Tirshatha (Neh. 8:9) because the authorities absolved him (*hittir*) from the prohibition against gentile wine, permitting him, as cupbearer to the king, to drink (*shatah*) with him (TJ, Kid. 4:1, 65b). The strict rabbinic enactment prohibiting the handling of most vessels or utensils on the Sabbath was attributed to Nehemiah as a means of counteracting the laxity in Sabbath observance during his period (Shab. 123b; Neh. 13:15). The sages did not call the Book of Nehemiah by his name and referred to it as the second part of Ezra because Nehemiah utilized a seemingly vain expression (Neh. 5:19) and also spoke disparagingly of his predecessors, who included Daniel (Neh. 5:15; Sanh. 93b). Nehemiah completed the Book of Chronicles which was started by Ezra (BB 15a).

[Aaron Rothkoff]

BIBLIOGRAPHY: F. James, *Personalities of the Old Testament* (1943), 443–61; E. Weider, in: AFO, 17 (1956), 264–5; F.L. Moriarty, *Introducing the Old Testament* (1960), 189–201; S. Mowinckel, *Studien zu dem Buche Ezra-Nehemia*, 2 (1964), 76–83; J.M. Meyers (ed.), *Ezra-Nehemiah* (1965), 53–56, 74–77. IN THE AGGADAH: Ginzberg, Legends, 4 (19475), 352; 6 (19463), 438–9.

NEHEMIAH (middle of second century C.E.), *tanna*. Nehemiah was considered one of Akiva's outstanding disciples and is mentioned in all the talmudic traditions that described the reestablishment of the center of learning in Galilee after the Bar Kokhba revolt. Thus it is reported that on the easing of the Hadrianic persecution he took part in the activity for the renewal of the teaching of the Torah (Gen. R. 61:3; Eccles. R. 11:6). Similarly, Nehemiah was listed as one of the five ordained by *Judah b. Bava at the cost of his life (Sanh. 14a), and also among the scholars who gathered at Usha to reconstruct the religious life of the people (Song R. 2:5, no. 3). He was also described as having been active at Bet Rimmon when the renewed calendar arrangements were made (TJ, Ḥag. 3:1), and as having taken part in the convention of Jabneh (Ber. 63b). Though these traditions have been viewed by some as representing distinct historical events, they should more properly be viewed as a family of related traditions with definite lines of literary dependence between them, as has been recently argued convincingly (Oppenheimer, 78–79).

The Talmud (Sanh. 86a) ascribes to R. Johanan the statement that סְתָם תּוֹסֶפְתָּא ר' נְחֶמְיָה (*setam tosefta Rabbi Neḥemyah*), apparently ascribing to Nehemiah the authorship of all anonymous statements in the Tosefta. Both the authenticity and the exact intent of this statement are unclear (see: *Tosefta), and in any case it is clear that R. Nehemiah is neither the author of our Tosefta (nor of any earlier version of the Tosefta which may have once existed), nor do his traditions take up any considerable percentage of this work. His name is mentioned 20 times in the Mishnah and about 60 times in the Tosefta, and given the fact that the Tosefta is between three to four times longer than the Mishnah, the two figures correspond almost exactly. Nehemiah is also mentioned about 60 times in the *midrashei halakhah* and is well represented in both tannaitic *halakhah* and *aggadah*.

The Talmud attributes to him the grammatical rule that the suffix ה to a noun is equivalent to the prefix ל (Yev. 13b). According to the printed edition of the Talmud, Nehemiah's name is associated with the study of Merkabah mysticism (Shab. 80b), but in the manuscript readings of this passage (Oxford, Vatican 108, Munich 95) Nehemiah is not mentioned. Similarly, the Talmud ascribes to him a statement on the creation, transmitted in the name of his father (Pes. 54a). A tannaitic source ascribes to him the following aggadic saying:

"Beloved is suffering. For just as sacrifices bring atonement so does suffering" (Sif. Deut. 32). In a much later aggadic saying he is reported to have said: "A single individual is as important as the whole of creation" (ARN[1] 31, p. 46). According to the Jerusalem Talmud (Ta'an. 4:2, 88a) he was descended from the biblical Nehemiah. He lived in great poverty and on one occasion shared his pottage of lentils with a poor man, who died from eating such scant fare (Ket. 67b). He worked as a potter (TJ, BM 6:8, 11a).

BIBLIOGRAPHY: J. Bruell, *Mevo ha-Mishnah*, 1 (1876), 198–200; Frankel, Mishnah (1923[2]), 185f., 222 n. 5, 324; Bacher, Tann; Hyman, Toledot, 924–6; Ḥ. Albeck, *Meḥkarim ba-Beraita ve-Tosefta* (1944), 63–65, 183; Epstein, Tanna'im, 241f.; A. Oppenheimer, in: Z. Baras, S. Safrai, M. Stern. Y. Tsafrir (eds.), *Eretz Israel from the Destruction of the Second Temple to the Moslem Conquest* (Heb.) (1982).

[Stephen G. Wald (2nd ed.)]

NEHEMIAH BAR KOHEN ẒEDEK (tenth century), *gaon* of the Pumbedita academy from 960 to 968; son of R. Kohen *Zedek, who also held this post. His brother R. Hophni was the father of R. Samuel b. *Hophni. R. *Sherira Gaon tells of the controversy between R. Nehemiah and *Aaron b. Joseph ha-Kohen Sarjado which arose several years after R. Aaron Sarjado had been appointed *gaon* of Pumbedita (943); it appears that the original cause of the controversy was R. *Mubashshir b. R. Kimoi's appointment of R. Aaron as president of his *bet din*, an appointment which Kohen Ẓedek viewed with disfavor. The struggle between Nehemiah and Aaron Sarjado broke out after the death of R. Amram, president of R. Aaron's *bet din*; Aaron wished to appoint R. *Sherira in Amram's place, while Nehemiah contended that the position was properly his. Failing to achieve his aim, Nehemiah set himself up as *gaon* in rivalry with R. Aaron. In 960, when Aaron Sarjado died, Nehemiah officially succeeded him as *gaon* of Pumbedita, and his brother Hophni was the president of his *bet din*. Sherira Gaon refused to recognize Nehemiah's appointment as *gaon*, although he did not suggest himself as *gaon* in his stead. Apparently he did not want to undermine the foundations of the gaonate. After the death of R. Hophni in 962, however, the two men agreed that Sherira Gaon would serve as Nehemiah's *av bet din*, and after the latter's death in 968, Sherira Gaon succeeded him as the *gaon* of Pumbedita. Nothing remains of Nehemiah's teachings or responsa; only a number of letters survive.

BIBLIOGRAPHY: B.M. Lewin (ed.), *Iggeret R. Sherira Ga'on* (1921), 121, 132–4; Cowley, in: JQR, 19 (1906/07), 104–6; J. Mann, *ibid.*, 8 (1917/18), 341–7; Mann, Texts, 1 (1931), 75–83; idem, in: *Tarbiz*, 5 (1933/34), 174–6.

[Abraham David]

NEHEMIAH HA-KOHEN (17th century), Polish kabbalist, apparently born in Lvov. His personality remains obscure, though certain details emerge from the sometimes contradictory sources. Late in the month of Av, 1666, he arrived at the fortress in Gallipoli, Turkey, where *Shabbetai Ẓevi was imprisoned, and visited him there early in the month of Elul. In his memoirs Loeb b. Ozer quotes information that he heard from Nehemiah concerning his disputation with Shabbetai Ẓevi, indicating that Nehemiah rejected the latter's messianic pretensions. According to Christian sources, however, Nehemiah claimed that he himself was Messiah ben Joseph and remonstrated with Shabbetai Ẓevi for announcing himself as Messiah ben David before Messiah ben Joseph had started out on his journey of tribulations. Hence for the first time Shabbetai Ẓevi found himself on the defensive before a man who, unlike all his other visitors, was not overwhelmed by him. I. Sonne questions the truth of the story about the disputation, considering it improbable that in an atmosphere of messianic tension anyone should, in the presence of the Messiah, cast doubts on the very fact of his being Messiah. After three days Nehemiah despaired of Shabbetai Ẓevi, and notified the authorities of the fortress of his own intention of converting to Islam. From there he repaired to Adrianople, where he complained to the civil authorities that Shabbetai was an impostor. Shabbetai was then brought before the sultan, in whose presence he too was converted to Islam. Having passed on his information to the Turkish authorities, Nehemiah returned at once to Lvov and to the religion of his fathers. His activities caused an uproar throughout Poland: some vindicated them, since their sole intention was to bring an end to the specious doings of Shabbetai Ẓevi, while others disapproved, since Nehemiah's activities had terminated the great messianic awakening. Nehemiah, however, was obliged to wander from place to place, ultimately leaving Poland in about 1675, excommunicated and outcast. He even changed his name to Jacob in an attempt to obscure his identity. His persecution presumably stemmed from the bitterness of the Jews of Poland and Germany, and their disillusionment with the messianic movement.

BIBLIOGRAPHY: G. Scholem, in: *Beit Yisrael be-Polin*, 2 (1953), 44–45: idem, *Shabbetai Ẓevi*, 2 (1952), 554–64, 566–7; I. Sonne, in: *Sefunot*, 3–4 (1960), 62–66.

[Abraham David]

NEHER, ANDRÉ (1914–1988), scholar and philosopher; born in Obernai (Alsace). After having taught German in a high school before and some years after World War II, Neher spent the war years together with his father Albert Neher, his elder brother, Judge Richard Neher, and the rest of his family, dedicating his time to intensive Jewish studies. After the liberation of France, Neher emerged as a highly original and captivating thinker, and quickly became one of the spiritual leaders of the young intellectuals of the French-speaking world, preaching ideals of reasoned belief and of respect for tradition. After being appointed to the chair of Jewish Studies at the University of Strasbourg, he contributed to the development among the local Jewish community of deep feelings of responsibility toward the Jewish people in the world and toward the State of Israel in particular. Algerian Jews who came to Strasbourg found a warm welcome there, as a result of Neher's interest in them. Respected in all quarters, Neher was able to convince the local Catholic and Protestant leaders of the legitimacy of Jewish aspirations, including Zionism, and this had its repercussions at various national and international conventions.

Neher took part in various initiatives on behalf of Israel in the Diaspora. He established himself in Jerusalem, dividing his time between the University of Strasbourg and academic activity in Israel (mostly at Tel Aviv University). He was a consulting editor to the *Encyclopaedia Judaica*. The moving force of his philosophy is the "alliance" of God with Man, and in particular with the People of Israel. Neher found in the teachings of Judah Loew b. Bezalel (Maharal) a guide and inspiration.

His principal works include: *Transcendance et immanence* (1946; with Richard Neher); *Amos, contribution à l'étude du prophétisme* (1950); *Notes sur Qohélét* (1951); *L'Essence du prophétisme* (1955); *Moïse et la vocation juive* (1956); *Jerémie* (1960); *Histoire biblique du peuple d'Israël* (2 vols., 1962; with Renée Neher-Bernheim); *L'Existence juive* (1962), a collection of articles; *Le Puits de l'exil – la théologie dialectique du Maharal de Prague* (1966): *De l'hébreu au français* (1969); *Etincelles, textes rabbiniques traduits et commentés* (1970; with Abraham Epstein and Emile Sebban); *L'Exil de la Parole, du silence biblique au silence d'Auschwitz* (1970, English trans., 1980); *Dans tes Portes Jerusalem* (1972); *David Gans, disciple du Maharal de Prague, assistant de Tycho Brahe et de Jean Kepler* (1974); *Clefs pour le Judaisme* (1977); *Oubekhol zot* ("Nevertheless," in Hebrew, 1977); *Le dur bonheur d'être Juif* (1978); *Ils ont refait Leur Ame* (1979); *Jérusalem, vécu juif et message* (1984); *Jewish Thought and the Scientific Revolution of the Sixteenth Century* (1986); *Faust et le Maharal de Prague, le mythe et le réel* (1986); and *Korot Am Israel be-Or ha-Mikra* (an adaptation in Hebrew of his *Histoire Biblique du Peuple d'Israël*, in collaboration with his wife Renée Neher-Bernheim; 1986). In 1980 there appeared the second edition of his *Jeremiah* (1960). On the occasion of his 60th birthday Neher was presented with *Melanges André Neher*, containing a bibliography of his articles, listing 336 items. In addition, in 1983 appeared the third edition in French and the Italian and Japanese translations of his *L'Exile de la Parole*, the Japanese translation of his *Moïse et la vocation juive*, while in 1984 there appeared a selection of his writings in Russian, *The Philosophy of André Neher*. He received the 1977 Remembrance Award for Holocaust Literature established by the World Federation of the Bergen-Belsen Associations.

His wife, RENÉE NEHER-BERNHEIM (1922–), a historian, was born in Paris. In 1972 she was appointed lecturer in Jewish History at the School for Overseas Students of the Hebrew University, Jerusalem. She wrote *Le Judaïsme dans le monde romain* (1959), *La Déclaration Balfour* (1969), and in 1974 completed the publication of her *Histoire Juive – faits et documents – de la Renaissance à nos jours* (1963–65, 1974). In 1977 she published *Documents inédits sur l'entrée des Juifs dans la société française (1750–1850)*, 2 volumes and in 1983, *Feu Vert à Israël, l'époque décisive de la Déclaration Balfour*. She later wrote *Jérusalem, trois millénaires de histoire* (1997), *La vie juive en terre sainte sous les Turcs ottomans (1517–1918)* (2001), and *Histoire juive de la Révolution à l'Etat d'Israël* (2002).

[Moshe Catane]

BIBLIOGRAPHY: M. Blanchot, *L'entretien infini* (1968), 180–192; A. Lacocque and B. Keller, *Foi et Vie* (1968), 1–2, 19–23; J. Nedava, in: *Moshe* (1974), 6–15; A. Hazan, *Mélanges Andre Neher* (1975), Postface, 443–446.

NEHORAH (Heb. נְהוֹרָה; "light"), rural center in southern Israel established in 1956 in the framework of the *Lachish regional development project, to service a bloc of moshavim comprising Nogah, Zohar, Oẓem, Shaḥar, and Nir Ḥen. Nehorah had 131 inhabitants in 1970. By 2002 its population was 1,020.

[Efraim Orni]

NEHORAI (end of second century C.E.), *tanna*. Nehorai is referred to three times in the Mishnah, once in *Nazir* 9:5, mentioning that Samuel was a Nazirite; once in *Avot* 4:14, where he says, "Exile thyself to a place of Torah; and say not it will come after thee or that thy companions will assist thee to maintain it; and lean not upon thine own understanding"; and lastly in *Kiddushin* 4:14, where he states, "I would disregard all other crafts and teach my son only Torah. For man enjoys its reward in this world, while its principal remains to him for the world to come." In *Nazir* he engages in discussion with R. Jose; the Mishnah at the end of *Kiddushin* is a late addition from Tosefta *Kiddushin* 8:16, where his words appear between those of Rabbi and of R. Simeon ben Eleazar. Similarly, in *Avot* 4:14 his statement is placed in the context of 4th and 5th generation *tannaim*. On the other hand he is quoted as transmitting traditions in the name of R. Joshua (*Seder Olam* 22, Nazir 5a). The reference to Nehorai in Tosef. RH 1:16 has been identified with the *tanna* Nehorai ben Shinai mentioned in Tosefta Ma'asrot 1:1 (see Lieberman, *Tosefet Rishonim*, 4, 194). If these two figures are one and the same, then the notion that Nehorai dealt almost exclusively with *aggadah* would have to be modified somewhat.

The Talmud asserts (Shab. 147b) that his name was not Nehorai at all, and that he is actually to be identified with the far better known *tanna* R. *Nehemiah, or perhaps even with the famous figure *Eleazar b. Arakh, and he was called Nehorai ("light") because he enlightened the eyes of his colleagues in knowledge of *halakhah*. This assertion, however, should be understood in the light of the general tendency of the Talmud, both when retelling biblical stories and when elaborating the biographies of early talmudic sages, to identify obscure and little known figures with more famous and well known figures. The further statement (Er. 13b) that Meir is the same as Nehorai is little more than a play on words (both names being derived from words denoting "light"), and cannot be taken as reflecting a serious historical tradition, since Nehorai is found together with Meir in *Avot* 4:10 and in *Kiddushin* 4:14 they are both mentioned in the same Mishnah.

BIBLIOGRAPHY: Hyman, Toledot, 918f.; Bacher, Tann, 2 (1890), 377–83.

[David Joseph Bornstein / Stephen G. Wald (2nd ed.)]

NEḤUNYA BEN HA-KANAH (dates uncertain), *tanna*. Mishnah Ber. 4:2 relates two prayers which he would recite when entering and leaving the study hall. An aggadic statement is transmitted in his name in Avot 3:5, and two *halakhot* are transmitted in his name in Tosefta Ket. 3:5. One of these *halakhot* is brought in Tosefta BK 7:18, apparently responding to the words of R. Meir. Similarly his statement in Avot follows the statements of R. Simeon and Haninah b. Hakinai, which would place him in the fourth generation of *tannaim*, in the middle to end of the second century. On the other hand, the Babylonian Talmud asserts that *Ishmael received from Neḥunya his practice of interpreting the Torah with the hermeneutical rule of *kelal u-ferat* ("general propositions and particulars," see **Midrashei Halakhah*, Distinct Exegetical Methods), which would place him in the second generation of *tannaim*. This tradition may, however, be a later expansion and elaboration of the relatively early tradition according to which Akiva learned the principle of *ribbui u-mi'ut* ("extension and limitation") from *Naḥum of Gimzo (Shevu. 26a). Similarly, the Talmud relates a discussion between Neḥunya and Johanan b. Zakkai (see BB 10b), but this is a relatively late aggadic traditon whose historical authenticity cannot be confirmed. So also the *Tanḥuma* (Deut. to 26:13) cites a halakhic discussion between him and Joshua b. Ḥananiah, referring to him as Neḥunya b. ha-Kanah of Emmaus. He is named in the TB as disputing with R. Eliezer and R. Joshua (Ḥullin 129b), but in *Eduyot* 6:3 and 4 it is clear that the *tanna* originally mentioned in this tradition was Neḥunya b. Elinathan of Kefar ha-Bavli.

He dictum in Avot was: "He who takes upon himself the yoke of Torah will have the yoke of worldly care removed from him; but he who casts off the yoke of Torah will have placed upon him the yoke of the kingdom and the yoke of worldly care" (Avot 3:5). The talmudic tradition transmits the text of the prayers which he spoke when entering and leaving the house of study as follows: "On entering what did he say? 'May it be Thy will, Oh Lord, that I become not impatient with my fellows and that they become not impatient with me, that we declare not the clean unclean nor the unclean clean… so that I be not put to shame both in this world and in the world to come.' On his departure what did he say? 'I give thanks to Thee, O Lord, that thou hast set my portion with those who sit in houses of study and in synagogues and not with those who sit in theaters and circuses. For I toil and they toil. I am industrious and they are industrious. I toil to possess the Garden of Eden and they toil for the pit of destruction'" (TJ, Ber. 4:2, 7d: cf. Ber. 28b for another tradition). The TB relates that when Neḥunya's pupils asked him by what virtue he had attained old age, he replied: "Never in my life have I sought honor through the degradation of my fellow, nor has the curse of my fellow gone up with me upon my bed [i.e., he forgave all who had vexed him before retiring to sleep], and I have been generous with my money" (Meg. 28a). The medieval Kabbalists attributed to him the mystical work *Sefer ha-Bahir*. The prayer *Anna be-Kho'aḥ (based upon the Divine Name of 42 letters) is also ascribed to him.

BIBLIOGRAPHY: Hyman, Toledot, 923; Frankel, Mishnah, 105; Bacher, Tann, 1 (1903[2]), index; J. Bruell, *Mevo ha-Mishnah*, 1 (1876), 94.

[Yitzhak Dov Gilat / Stephen G. Wald (2nd ed.)]

NEHUSHTAN (Heb. נְחֻשְׁתָּן), the name of the *copper serpent which King Hezekiah broke into pieces (II Kings 18:4). The name suggests both its serpentine shape (*naḥash*) as well as the material (*neḥoshet*) of which it was made. Since the smashing of the copper serpent parallels the shattering of the pillars and the cutting down of the Asherah (*ibid.*), it was probably located in the Temple court in Jerusalem. It was thus one of the cultic symbols of the people who assembled in the Temple courts. Like the local shrines (*bamot*), however, and like the two other objects named in the verse, it was illegitimate in the Deuteronomic view, in accordance with which Hezekiah abolished the former and destroyed the latter (*ibid.*). The Nehushtan probably stood in the Temple court, and the people believed that it had the power of curing sicknesses. Serpents are also associated with fertility. In this respect the copper serpent differed from the *cherubim, whose location was in the innermost sanctum of the Temple, hidden from human sight. Some scholars hold that the copper serpent in Jerusalem was set near "the stone of Zoheleth ("the crawler's [i.e., serpent's] stone"), which is beside En-Rogel" (I Kings 1:9), that is, outside the Temple enclosure. However, there are no grounds for connecting the copper serpent with the stone of Zoheleth. At the latter, sheep and oxen were sacrificed (*ibid.*), whereas only meal-offerings were offered to the copper serpent.

The account in Numbers 21:6–9 states that its form was that of a *saraf*, traditionally, a "fiery serpent." It probably had wings, for so *serafim* are described in the Bible (cf. Isa. 14:29; 30:6). Herodotus (2:75; 3:109) also states that in his day people told of the existence of flying serpents in the Arabian desert.

Some scholars assume that the copper serpent entered the Israelite cult as a Canaanite heritage and only popular belief ascribed it to Moses, but this is to assume that we know more about "popular" vs. "official" religion in ancient Israel than we do. (For the problem of "official" vs. "popular," see Berlinerblau.) M. Noth contends that this tradition is somewhat later than the others associated with the Exodus from Egypt, since it can only have arisen after David had captured Jerusalem. H. Gressmann suggested that Moses adopted the copper serpent from the Midianites, but this has been rejected by other scholars. Ackerman believes that Asherah was connected with serpents so that the destruction of Asherah and the serpent would likewise be connected. Note that Nehushta, a name similar to that of the serpent, was borne by the mother of King Jehoiakin (II Kings 24:8). For serpent iconography and the Bible, see Williams-Forte.

BIBLIOGRAPHY: T. Noeldeke, in: ZDMG, 12 (1888), 482; H. Gressmann, *Mose und seine Zeit* (1913), 284–5; W.F. Albright, in: AJSLL, 36 (1920), 258–94; S.A. Cook, *The Religion of Ancient Palestine in the Light of Archaeology* (1930), 98ff., 117–20; M. Noth, *Überlieferungsgeschichte des Pentateuch* (1948), 133–4; M. Haran, in: VT, 10 (1960), 117–8. **ADD BIBLIOGRAPHY:** E. Williams-Forte, in: E.

Williams-Forte and L. Gorelick (eds.), *Ancient Seals and the Bible* (with illustrations; 1983), 18–43; M. Cogan and H. Tadmor, *II Kings* (AB; 1988), 217; S. Ackerman, in: JBL, 112 (1993), 385–401; J. Berlinerblau: in, R. Chazan et al (eds., *Ki Baruch Hu ... Studies B.A. Levine* (1999), 153–70

[Menahem Haran / S. David Sperling (2nd ed.)]

NEḤUTEI (Aram. נָחוֹתָאֵי, נְחוּתָאֵי, *Nahutei*, sing. נְחוּתָא *Neḥuta*; "one who goes down"), rabbis who went from Ereẓ Israel academies to those of Babylonia, or vice-versa. The name was first applied to *Ulla, a native of Ereẓ Israel in the third century C.E. (TJ, Kil. 9:4, 32c). He was given this epithet because from time to time he "went down" from Ereẓ Israel to Babylonia and had discussions in Babylonia with the heads of its academies and its scholars. Rav *Ḥisda referred to Ulla as "our teacher who came down from Ereẓ Israel" (Ber. 38b: see *Dikdukei Soferim*). When he came to Babylonia, Ulla brought with him the halakhic and aggadic sayings of Johanan and Eleazar, the heads of the academy of Tiberias at that time. He also described the customs and ways of the Jews of Israel, and evoked historical memories and popular sayings current among them. He used to compare the customs current among the Jews of Babylonia with those current in Ereẓ Israel. Generally he gave preference to the customs of Ereẓ Israel, and more than once he uttered caustic comments about the Jews and scholars of Babylonia (Ta'an. 9b). In the first half of the fourth century the name *neḥutei* was given to a few scholars, born apparently in Babylonia, who traveled to the academies of Ereẓ Israel and brought back with them the teachings of its scholars. The best known of them were *Dimi, Samuel b. Judah, Rabin, and *Isaac b. Joseph. The purpose of their activity was to transmit the teachings of Ereẓ Israel to Babylonia, and vice versa. Through their activity, the texts of the Mishnah and the *beraitot* and their exact meaning were established, and the halakhic and aggadic sayings of the first *amoraim* of Ereẓ Israel, such as *Ḥanina, *Johanan, *Eleazar, and *Simeon b. Lakish in Tiberias and *Abbahu in Caesarea, and of the first *amoraim* of Babylonia, such as *Rav and *Samuel, *Huna and *Ḥisda, and others, were elucidated.

By their activities the *neḥutei* contributed to the cross-fertilization of the academies of Ereẓ Israel and Babylonia. Their words were tested in the academies and compared with parallel traditions, and in this way they attempted to arrive at the precise implication of the statements, their truth, and their reliability. In this manner the *neḥutei* made their contribution to the formation and elucidation of many topics in the Babylonian Talmud. As a result of the connections established by the *neḥutei* between the academies of Ereẓ Israel and Babylonia the mutual knowledge of the two large Jewish communities was increased, and so the Oral Law was prevented from developing separately with the two communities becoming two nations, alien one to another. The scholars mentioned were especially active in two academies – in Tiberias in Ereẓ Israel and in Pumbedita in Babylonia. References are found at times to the *neḥutei* informing Babylonia of various *halakhot* by means of letters (Git. 9b). These scholars were active until the middle of the fourth century C.E. In the opinion of *Sherira Gaon (*Iggeret…*, ed. B. Lewin, p. 61) their mission ceased because of the increase of restrictive edicts in Ereẓ Israel and the decrease of Torah there. The reference is apparently to the restrictive edicts of Constantius (377–361) in the 340s and 350s and the revolt by a section of the Jews of Ereẓ Israel against Gallus in 351.

BIBLIOGRAPHY: Halevy, Dorot, 2 (1923), 467ff.; A. Steinsaltz, in: *Talpioth*, 9 (1964), 294–306.

[Moshe Beer]

NE'ILAH (Heb. נְעִילָה), a worship service deriving from the ritual of the Second Temple, but subsequently recited only on the Day of Atonement as its concluding rite (see Ta'an. 4:1; Ta'an. 26b and TJ, Ta'an. 4:167c; TJ, Ber. 4:1, 7b–c; Yoma 87b and TJ, Yoma 8:8, 45c). It was originally recited on all public fast days, in addition to the Day of Atonement. It also concluded the daily **Ma'amadot*, where laymen from provincial communities prayed with their priestly delegates in Jerusalem. The full name of the service is *Ne'ilat She'arim* ("Closing of the Gates"), referring to the daily closing of the Temple gates. On the Day of Atonement this literal closing (*ne'ilat sha'arei heikhal*) was associated with the symbolic closing of the heavenly gates, which remained open to prayer until sunset (*ne'ilat sha'arei shamayim*). Throughout the year, according to the Talmud, *Ne'ilah* was recited one hour before sunset, when the Temple Gates were closed; on the Day of Atonement, because of its length, *Ne'ilah* did not begin until close to sunset. Once *Ne'ilah* was limited to the Day of Atonement, it began before twilight and ended at nightfall.

By the third century *Ne'ilah* consisted of an **Amidah* of seven benedictions, parallel to the other statutory services of the day. It likewise featured confession of sins. *Attah yode'a razei olam* ("Thou knowest the secrets of the world"), however, and **Al Ḥet* were replaced by two prayers unique to the confession in the *Ne'ilah* service: *Attah noten yad le-foshe'im* ("Thou stretchest forth Thy hand [in forgiveness] to sinners") and *Attah hivdalta enosh* ("Thou has distinguished man [from the beast]"). These recapitulate the biblical-talmudic doctrine that God eagerly forgives the truly penitent. In accordance with the rabbinic idea that the divine judgment, inscribed on *Rosh Ha-Shanah, is not sealed until the Day of Atonement ends, the word to "inscribe" (כתב, *ktv*) (in the Book of Life) is amended to "seal" (חתם, *ḥtm*). To set it off from the preceding *Minḥah* service, *Ne'ilah* is prefaced by *Ashrei* (Ps. 145) and *U-Va le-Ẓiyyon Go'el*, which ordinarily introduce *Minḥah*.

Ne'ilah was eventually embellished with sacred poetry, especially *Seliḥot*. Impressive melodies heightened the emotional impact of *Ne'ilah*. The central motif is exhortation to make a final effort to seek forgiveness before the heavenly gates close at sunset. Yet the overall tone is one of confidence, especially in the final litany. The service proper concludes with **Avinu Malkenu* and **Kaddish*. The entire ritual culminates in responsive proclamations of **Shema*, followed by *Barukh* *shem kevod malkhuto*, and "The Lord, He is God" (I Kings 18:39). A single *shofar* blast announces the end of the "Sabbath of Sabbaths."

BIBLIOGRAPHY: M. Arzt, *Justice and Mercy* (1963), 271–86; L. Ginzberg, *Perushim ve-Ḥiddushim ba-Yerushalmi*, 3 (1941), 67–108; Morgenstern, in: HUCA, 6 (1929), 12–37; E. Munk, *World of Prayer*, 2 (1963), 262–7.

[Herman Kieval]

NEILSON, JULIA (1868–1957), English romantic actress. Born in London, Julia was the daughter of Alexander Ritchie Neilson, a silversmith and jeweler, and Emily Davis, and was a cousin of three other well-known actresses of the Davis family, Lily Hanbury, Hilda Jacobson, and Nora Kerin. She made her first appearance(1888) in W.S. Gilbert's *Pygmalion and Galatea*, toured with Beerbohm Tree in 1889, and acted with him at the Theatre Royal, Haymarket, for five years. In 1890 she married Fred Terry, brother of the celebrated Ellen Terry. Julia became famous for her acting in such plays as *A Woman of No Importance, The Prisoner of Zenda, Sweet Nell of Old Drury*, and *The Scarlet Pimpernel*. Her greatest success was as Rosalind in *As You Like It* (1896). She visited the U.S. in 1895 and again in 1910. In 1900, she and her husband went into management and for the next 30 years played and toured with their own company. Both their children, Dennis (1895–1932) and Phyllis (1892–1977), acted under the name of Neilson-Terry. Neilson's memoirs, *This for Remembrance*, were published in 1940.

ADD. BIBLIOGRAPHY: ODNB online.

NEIMAN, YEHUDAH (1931–), Israeli painter. Neiman was born in Warsaw. After immigrating to Ereẓ Israel in 1940, he studied painting in Tel Aviv and created stage designs for theaters but settled in Paris in 1954. From 1955 to 1965 he painted lyrical abstract paintings, concerning himself mainly with colors, by means of which he constructed his compositions of line, space, and light. At that time he was known as the leading "Luminist painter" because of his lyrical synthesis of space and light. In 1966, he made his first mechanical works using photographs which were printed on sheets of canvas or painted aluminum. This "photoméchanique," in which he was a master-artist, enabled him to multiply one photograph form and thus create a symmetrical composition. His art portrayed an erotic spirit, using different parts of the human body as subject matter and creating erotic suggestions in the composition. He applied this "photoméchanique" method to silkscreen and sculpture. Neiman held many exhibitions in Europe and Israel, and was represented at the "Erotic Art" exhibition in Sweden (1968), the "Mec-Art" exhibition in the Apollinaire Gallery, Milan (1969), and the Erotic Art exhibition in the Museum of Modern Art, Stockholm, in the same year.

BIBLIOGRAPHY: J.L. Swiners, in: *Terre d'image* 33 (1966); Y. Fischer, in: *Kav*, 7 (1967); J. Kultermann, *The New Sculpture* (1969).

[Judith Spitzer]

NEIPRIS, JOSEPH (1918–1991), Israeli social worker. Neipris was born in Malden, Massachusetts. He served as a psychiatric social worker, and in 1950 settled in Israel, where in 1952 he became administrative director of the Lasker Mental Hygiene and Child Guidance Clinic. In 1968, he was appointed deputy director of the School of Social Work at the Hebrew University of Jerusalem. Neipris was co-author of *The Individual and the Group* (1953) and the author of *Social Welfare and Social Services in Israel* (1981). He was the *Encyclopaedia Judaica* departmental editor for Jews in social welfare.

NEISSER, HANS PHILIPP (1895–1975), economist. Born into a distinguished professional family in Breslau, Germany, Neisser obtained a doctorate in jurisprudence from the University of Breslau. He served on various government economic commissions, was economic adviser to the Weimar government, and edited one of Germany's leading economic weekly magazines, *Wirtschaft* (1922 to 1927). In 1927 he began to teach at the University of Kiel and was at the same time director of the Institute for World Economy. Emigrating to the U.S. in 1933, he was professor of monetary theory at the University of Pennsylvania from 1933 to 1943, the first Jew to attain a position at that university. During the last two years of this period he headed the division of research at the U.S. Office of Price Administration in Washington. He was also research principal at the Institute of World Affairs (1943–51). From 1943 to 1965 he was professor of economics in the graduate faculty of the New School for Social Research in New York City, where he also served in a leadership capacity, including tenure as chairman of the department of economics, until his retirement. He then became professor emeritus (1965–75). Under his guidance, the New School became the first teaching institution in the metropolitan area to establish a training center for econometric study. Described as one of the most brilliant economic minds of his generation, Neisser focused mainly on general economic theory, international economics, and monetary and banking developments.

His publications include *Der Tauschwert des Geldes* (1928); *Some International Aspects of the Business Cycle* (1936); *National Incomes and International Trade* (with F. Modigliani, 1953); and *On the Sociology of Knowledge, an Essay* (1965).

[Joachim O. Ronall / Ruth Beloff (2nd ed.)]

NEIZVESTNY, ERNST (1926–), Russian sculptor and draughtsman. Neizvestny was one of the few living Russian artists whose work became known and admired in the West. This was largely the result of the admiration and advocacy of the English art critic John Berger, in whose opinion "Neizvestny is principally the first visual artist of genius to have emerged in the Soviet Union since the twenties." He came into prominence during the regime of Nikita Khrushchev. On a famous occasion Neizvestny argued with the Russian leader at the opening of an exhibition of advanced art he had organized in Moscow. Neizvestny's art is best when dealing with the human figure. He cast his bronzes personally in a small furnace, since access to a state foundry was denied him. Both his drawings and sculptures have a heroic quality, even willfully abstract. After Khruschev's deposition, a close friendship developed between the two and the headstone over Khrushchev's tomb in the Novodevichi cemetery in Moscow was carved by Neizvestny, in accordance with a wish expressed by Khrushchev before his death.

Neizvestny later immigrated to the United States after leaving the Soviet Union for Switzerland in 1976. He held exhibitions in many countries including Scandinavia, Italy, and Switzerland. His essays on art, literature, and philosophy, collected in *Space, Time and Synthesis in Art*, appeared in English in 1990. After the breakup of the Soviet Union he was commissioned to erect three Gulag memorials.

ADD. BIBLIOGRAPHY: E. England, *Ernest Neizvestny, Life and Work* (1984); A. Leong, *The Life and Art of Ernst Neizvestny* (2002).

[Charles Samuel Spencer]

°**NEKLYUDOV, NICOLAI ADRIANOVICH** (1840–1896), Russian criminologist, counselor to the Ministry of Justice. From 1877 Neklyudov served as member of the committee for the advancement of the economic status of the Jews. In 1880 he, together with V.D. Karpov (an official of the Ministry of Interior), submitted a memorandum to the committee refuting the charge that the Jews were engaged in unproductive activities and exploited the non-Jewish population. Neklyudov stood for the emancipation of the Jews, advocating the dissolution of the *Pale of Settlement. Such a step, he averred, would be advantageous to the non-Jewish population through the development of trade and commerce in the interior of Russia. At the same time he argued that "Reason does not justify placing a population of several millions in the same category as criminals." No action was taken on his proposal, as the committee was soon dismissed.

NELSON, BENJAMIN (1911–1977), U.S. sociologist. Born in New York, Nelson graduated in medieval history from Columbia University. He taught at the universities of Chicago and Minnesota and the State University of New York before taking the position of professor of sociology and history in the graduate faculty of the New School for Social Research in 1966. Nelson's chief interest was in the sociological approaches to history and in the sociology of psychoanalysis and the arts. He opposed theoretical and practical "uniformitarianism" in favor of studying varied cultural histories. For Nelson, history comprised not only all the great civilizations described in the historical record but also their interconnections and evolutions since the beginning of civilization itself. His later work emphasized the study of civilizational complexes and encounters, particularly comparisons between China and the West.

Nelson helped found the Society for the Scientific Study of Religion and served as its vice president from 1976. He also was president of the International Society for the Comparative Study of Civilizations from 1971 until his death.

Among his numerous publications are "The Legend of the Divine Surety and the Jewish Money Lender" (1939); *The Idea of Usury: From Tribal Brotherhood to Universal Otherhood* (1949); and *On the Roads to Modernity* (1981). He also edited *Freud and the Twentieth Century* (1958).

ADD. BIBLIOGRAPHY: E.V. Walter (ed.), *Civilizations East and West: A Memorial Volume for Benjamin Nelson* (1985).

[Werner J. Cahnman / Ruth Beloff (2nd ed.)]

NELSON, LEONHARD (1882–1927), German philosopher, a descendant of Moses Mendelssohn. Born in Berlin, he was baptized while a child. He became lecturer in philosophy in the faculty of natural sciences at Goettingen in 1909 and professor in 1919. He founded the "New Fries School," which, following J.F. Fries (1793–1873) and using psychological method, wanted to renew Kant's teaching, but on a basis entirely different from that of the Neo-Kantians. To provide a forum for this school, Nelson founded the "Discussion groups of the Fries School" (1904–08), and published many articles, the most famous of which is "*Die Unmoeglichkleit der Erkenntnistheorie*"; the English version of which appeared in the collection of his articles *Socratic Method and Critical Philosophy* (1949). His main interest was in ethics, and his own ethics are close to those of Kant but without sharing their severe pendantry. Nelson developed his ethics in *Vorlesungen ueber die Grundlagen der Ethik*, 3 vols. (1917–32). Volume 1 dealt with the bases of ethics, volume 2 with pedagogy, and volume 3 is devoted to the philosophy of law and politics. In politics Nelson was close to moderate Socialism, similar to that of Franz *Oppenheimer. The principles of society's existence cannot be surrendered to majority decisions, since this would abandon them to arbitrariness and chance, for one cannot be certain that the majority even knows what is best for it. His students issued some of his unpublished lectures, among them the great work *Fortschritte und Rueckschritte der Philosophie; von Hume und Kant bis Hegel und Fries* (1962), edited by Julius Kraft. A list of his works is to be found in *L. Nelson zum Gedaechtnis* (1953).

BIBLIOGRAPHY: H. Falkenfeld, *Kantstudien* (1928), 247–55; *Encyclopedia of Philosophy*, 5(1967), 463–7; B. Selchow, *L. Nelson, ein Bild seines Lebens* (1938).

[Samuel Hugo Bergman]

NELSON, LOUIS (1895–1969), U.S. labor leader. Born in Kharkov, Russia, Nelson immigrated to the United States with his family as a young child. He left school at the age of 12 to work in the needle trade, joining the Raincoat Makers' Union and then the Amalgamated Clothing Workers as a tailor. A member of the Young People's Socialist League and affiliated with the left wing of the Socialist movement, he was active in opposition to the Amalgamated leadership. He was expelled from Amalgamated in the early 1920s, became a dressmaker in a dress shop and worked with the dual, Communist-controlled union, the Needle Trades Industrial Union. Later he reappraised his own position and came to believe that the small shop, which he had supported, permitted employers to avoid enforcing union conditions and that the installation of machines had in fact preserved jobs in those shops where they were installed. Nelson rejoined the International Ladies' Garment Workers' Union in 1931 and took an active part in the successful dressmakers' strike of 1933. In the following year he became manager of Local 155, the Knit Goods Workers' Union, an industrial local with a membership of under 1,000. As manager of this union for 35 years, Nelson built it up to one of the strongest and most responsible of the ILGWU locals and by 1969 it had a membership of about 14,000. In 1952 he was elected a vice president of the ILGWU and served in that post until his death.

Long interested in Yiddish culture and education, Nelson supported the Folksbine theater and the work of YIVO. By the 1960s the membership of Local 155 was no longer primarily Jewish but Nelson continued to arrange the appearance of Jewish artists and singers before the local's members. He was prime mover in the establishment of the Jewish Labor Committee. A non-Zionist, he supported the Bund position in regard to a Jewish state.

NEMEROV, HOWARD (1920–1991), U.S. poet and novelist. Nemerov was born in New York. His sister was Diane *Arbus, the photographer. He was educated at Harvard and served as a pilot in World War II. He was awarded the Pulitzer Prize (1978) and was the Poet Laureate from 1988 to 1990. His poetry is marked by a brooding, illuminating intelligence as well as comic irony and wit: for example, in "A Memory of My Friend," a "Jewish atheist stubborn as Freud" says to a departing guest, "… instead of 'Good night,' 'Go with God.'" His Judaism was secular though he did focus on themes drawn from Hebrew Scripture and Jewish history, as, for example, in "To the Babylonians" and "False Solomon's Seal," and in the poetic dramas, "Endor" and "Cain." He also brought Hebrew Scripture into the narrative allusiveness of the poem, as in "Small Moment," with its epigraphic reference to Isaiah 54:7, and in "The First Day." He wrote three novels: *The Melodramatists* (1949); *Federigo; or, The Power of Love* (1954); and *The Homecoming Game: A Novel* (1992). His *Collected Poems* were published in 1977; *A Howard Nemerov Reader*, in 1991.

BIBLIOGRAPHY: R. Labrie, *Howard Nemerov* (1980); W. Mills, *The Stillness in Moving Things: The World of Howard Nemerov* (1975); D. Potts, *Howard Nemerov and Objective Idealism: The Influence of Owen Barfield* (1994).

[Lewis Fried (2nd ed.)]

NÉMETH, ANDOR (1891–1953), Hungarian and French author and critic. From 1938 Németh lived in France, where he published *Kafka ou le mystère juif* (1947). His other works include a study of the empress Maria Theresa (1938). From 1947 until his death as a paralytic, Németh edited the Hungarian literary periodical, *Csillag*, also translating many works from English and French.

NEMETZ, NATHAN THEODORE (1913–1997), Canadian lawyer, judge, and community leader. Born in Winnipeg, Manitoba, Nathan Nemetz moved to Vancouver, British Columbia in 1923. He completed a history degree at the University of British Columbia (UBC) in 1934 and was called to the bar in 1937. Moved by the problem of high unemployment, Nemetz entered the field of labor law, eventually representing both the provincial government and numerous workers' associations as one of BC's top mediators. His strong social conscience also led Nemetz to an active pursuit of anti-discrimination work and inter-ethnic relations. During the 1950s he was a founding member of the Vancouver section of the Canadian Civil Liberties Union and a board member of the Vancouver Civic Unity Association, which successfully lobbied the provincial government to pass legislation making it illegal to discriminate in public places based on racial grounds. Nemetz was also active in the Jewish community. In addition to serving as president of the local chapter of B'nai B'rith and guiding much of the community relations work of the Pacific Region of the Canadian Jewish Congress, Nemetz was for many years the co-chairman of the Canadian Council of Christians and Jews. He was appointed to the BC Supreme Court in 1963 and was named chief justice in 1973. Between 1978 and 1988 he served in the province's top judicial position as chief justice of the BC Court of Appeal, doing much work to modernize the appeal process. Nemetz maintained a long association with the University of British Columbia, serving a term as chancellor from 1972 to 1975. Nemetz was named to the Order of British Columbia and was made a Companion of the Order of Canada, the nation's highest civilian award. Following his 1997 death, the Nathan T. Nemetz Chair in Legal History at the UBC Faculty of Law was endowed in his honor.

[Barbara Schober (2nd ed.)]

NEMIROV (Pol. **Niemirów**), town in Vinnitsa district, Ukraine. It was annexed by Russia after the second partition of Poland (1793), and was incorporated in the district of Podolia until the Russian Revolution. Under Polish rule it was a fortified city of considerable importance. A Jewish settlement in Nemirov is first mentioned in 1603. In the 1630s, Yom Tov Lipmann *Heller held rabbinical office there for a while. During the *Chmielnicki persecutions of 1648 thousands of Jews from other localities sought refuge in Nemirov; however, the city fell to the Cossacks, who massacred 6,000 Jews. The slaughter at Nemirov, one of the worst of that period, created a profound impression, becoming a symbol of all the terrible massacres the Jews suffered at the hands of cruel rioters. Reports and legends spread about the heroic acts of the Jews of Nemirov who chose martyrdom (see **Kiddush ha-Shem*) and rabbis and *paytanim* composed special *kinot* and *seliḥot* on the destruction of the community. At a meeting of the *Council of the Lands held in 1650, the anniversary of the massacre (20th of Sivan – 20 of June) was proclaimed a day of mourning and public fasting. Reports and legends spread about the heroic acts of the Jews of Nemirov who chose martyrdom (see **Kid-*

dush ha-Shem). Jews started to resettle there when the town was retaken by the Poles, and their situation was especially satisfactory under the Turkish rule over Podolia (1672–99). In the 18th and 19th centuries Jews owned a large distillery, dyeing factory, and hide-processing facilities. At the beginning of the 18th century the Great Synagogue was erected. Early in the 19th century, Nemirov became a center for the Ḥasidim of *Naḥman of Bratslav. In 1765, 602 Jewish poll-tax payers were registered; the Jewish population increased from 4,386 in 1847 to 5,287 (59.3% of the total population) in 1897. In 1917 a democratic community headed by the Zionists was established, but with the consolidation of the Soviet régime it was liquidated. During the Russian Civil War, the Jews also suffered, but they created an armed self-defense unit with their Christian neighbors and succeeded in averting a pogrom on January 19, 1918. There were 4,176 Jews (57.2% of the population) living in Nemirov in 1926, dropping to 3,001 (36.7% of the total population) in 1939. Between the wars a Yiddish school and orphanage operated in the town. Most of the Jews worked in artisans' cooperatives and dozen of families in a Jewish kolkhoz. The Germans took Nemirov on July 21, 1941, and created a ghetto. In November 1941 2,000 Jews were murdered, and 1,500 were executed on June 26, 1942. About 1,000 Jews who had been expelled to Nemirov from Transnistria were also murdered. The last group of skilled laborers was executed in April–August 1943.

BIBLIOGRAPHY: N.N. Hannover, *Yeven Meẓulah* (1966), 37–40; H.J. Gurland, *Le-Korot ha-Gezerot al Yisrael*, 1–6 (1887–89); M.N. Litinsky, *Sefer Korot Podolya ve-Kadmoniyyot ha-Yehudim Sham* (1895), 43, 45–49; Y.P. Pograbinski, in: *Reshumot*, 3 (1923), 195–214; idem, in: *Arim ve-Immahot be-Yisrael*, 2 (1948), 270–83.

[Yehuda Slutsky]

NÉMIROVSKY, IRÈNE (1903–1942), French author. Born in Kiev to a well-to-do assimilated family, Némirovsky received an aristocratic education, speaking French at an early age. Her early years were marked by tragic experiences during the civil war in Russia (including a pogrom). Her father was a banker and the revolutionaries set a price on his head. The family hid in a Moscow apartment, until they could escape to Finland. They lived a year in Sweden and eventually settled in Paris, where the father gradually rebuilt his fortune. These experiences found their way, at least indirectly, into Némirovsky's novels. When she married and became a mother, she hoped to live in peace and happiness, but the Nazi occupation shattered all. She sought refuge with her family, in rural central France. She was denounced, arrested by the French police in 1942, and deported to Auschwitz, where she died, apparently of typhus.

Her first and best-known novel, *David Golder* (1930) won wide acclaim. The hero, a Russian Jewish banker, is a ruthless character, ready to sacrifice all in order to strengthen his financial empire. Having destroyed all human relationships, he faces ruin in utter loneliness. His one remaining shred of humanity, manifest in his devotion to an unworthy daughter, gives the elder Golder the strength to rebuild his fortune for her sake and die a grandiose, moving, solitary death.

This was followed by *Le Bal* (1930), a short novel and literary gem. *Les mouches d'automne* (1931) and *L'Affaire Courilof* (1933) illustrate the author's Russian vein. *Le vin de solitude* (1935) her most overtly autobiographical novel, describes her tragic childhood experiences and painful relations with her mother, a strange woman who rejected her daughter in her obsession to preserve her beauty, youth and glowing womanhood. The mother's obsession also forms the subject of *Jezabel* (1936).

As Nazi threats loomed Némirovsky wrote a true "Jewish novel," *Les chiens et les loups* (1939), which opens with a pogrom viewed through the eyes of two ghetto children, Ada and her cousin Ben. The two reach the beautiful and peaceful quarters of their rich cousins, where young Harry lives like a prince, heir to the banking empire of his uncles. As the story unfolds in a French setting, Harry, the wealthy assimilated immigrant, and Ben, the struggling refugee, ever wandering in anguish, realize that they are, in spite of all, identical Jewish brothers with distant roots set in a "peculiar way of loving, of desiring" some unattainable truth set in every Jewish heart. Ada, a painter, expresses the same yearning in the lonely pursuit of artistic creation.

While in hiding Némirovsky wrote *Les Feux de l'automne, La Vie de Tchekhov,* and *Les Biens de ce monde* (posthumously published after the war). She used an original narrative technique: the story builds itself, in the absence of any narrator. The events unfold according to their own implacable logic, leaving no place for the creator's narrative design, ideas, or appeals to pity.

[Marthe Robert]

NEMON, OSCAR (1906–1985), British sculptor. Nemon was born in Croatia, the son of a pharmaceutical manufacturer. He spent his early years training in Vienna, where he knew and modeled a bust of Sigmund Freud, and then studied art in Brussels. Nemon emigrated to Britain in 1939 and was naturalized in 1948. He lived most of the rest of his life in London. He became one of the best known sculptors of important political figures and other notables, and was especially famed for his monumental effigy of Winston Churchill. He also produced busts of Eisenhower, Montgomery, the British Royal family, and Margaret *Thatcher, among others.

BIBLIOGRAPHY: ODNB online.

[William D. Rubinstein (2nd ed.)]

NEMOY, LEON (1901–1997), scholar and librarian. Born in Balta, Russia, Nemoy studied classical and Slavic languages at the University of Odessa. After moving to the U.S. in 1923, he studied Semitic languages at Yale University (1924–29), where he received his Ph.D. He served as a librarian at the Society for the Propagation of Knowledge, Odessa, Russia (1914–21), the Academic Library of Odessa (1919–21), and the University Library of Lvov, Poland (1922–23) before assuming his duties at Yale in 1923. Rising to the post of curator of Hebrew and Arabic literature at Yale's Sterling Memorial Library, he became the university's first Judaica and Arabic curator. During his tenure, Yale received the Alexander Kohut Memorial Collection of Judaica (1915 and 1935) and the Sholem Asch Collection (1946). The acquisition of these significant collections was instrumental in making Yale a center for the study of Jewish literature, history, and culture. Under Nemoy's direction, important Arabic manuscripts were acquired as well. Upon his retirement, Nemoy became scholar-in-residence at Dropsie University, Philadelphia, where he was editor of the *Jewish Quarterly Review.*

Nemoy's scholarly activities were mainly devoted to research on the history of the *Karaites. His major work is his edition of the Arabic text of al-*Kirkisānī's *Kitāb al-Anwār wa-al Maraqib* (5 vols., 1939–43). He also translated a valuable collection of Karaite texts into English from Arabic, Hebrew, and Aramaic (*Karaite Anthology*, 1952), with introduction and annotations. He also compiled *Arabic Manuscripts in the Yale University Library* (1956). Nemoy contributed numerous articles on Arabic philology, Karaite subjects, and the history of Jewish and Arabic medicine to various scholarly journals. He also published a catalog of the Hebrew and Yiddish books donated by Sholem *Asch to Yale (*Catalogue of Hebrew and Yiddish Manuscripts and Books from the Library of Sholem Asch*, 1945). Nemoy was one of the editors of the *Yale Judaica Series* and departmental editor for the *Encyclopaedia Judaica* on the Karaites.

ADD. BIBLIOGRAPHY: S. Brunswick (ed.), *Studies in Judaica, Karaitica and Islamica: Presented to Leon Nemoy on his Eightieth Birthday* (1982).

[Menahem Schmelzer / Ruth Beloff (2nd ed.)]

NEMŢEANU, BARBU (originally **Benjamin Deutsch**; 1887–1919), Romanian poet. Born in Galatz, Nemţeanu was the son of a teacher at the local Jewish elementary school. From 1907 onward his own verse, as well as translations of foreign poetry, appeared in Bucharest literary journals such as *Viaţa Nouă* and *Flacă+ra*, and the Jewish periodicals *Mántuirea* and *Lumea evree*. His collection of verses, *Stropi de soare* ("Drops of Sunshine", 1915) was warmly received by leading critics. Not a profound poet, he wrote lyrical verse about love and everyday life which was touched with light humor. He is better known for his translations from Victor Hugo, Baudelaire, Oscar Wilde, *Lessing, and, above all, *Heine, whose *Hebrew Melodies* appeared posthumously in his Romanian translation in 1919. He also translated Yiddish works by Eliezer *Steinberg and Jacob *Groper. Nemţeanu died of tuberculosis at the age of 32.

BIBLIOGRAPHY: E. Lovinescu, *Istoria Literaturii Române Contemporane*, 3 (1927), 223–5; G. Călinescu, *Istoria Literaturii Romîne…* (1941), 630–1.

[Abraham Feller]

NEO-ARAMAIC, general name for the various branches of spoken Aramaic, both western and eastern. Three groups of dialects are known. The first includes the dialects of Maʿlūla, a continuation of the western branch of Middle Aramaic, spoken by Christians and Muslims in three villages about 60 km. (38 mi.) north of Damascus. The second comprises the dialects spoken by Christians in the Ṭūr ʿAbdīn area in the Mardin region of southern Turkey. These dialects occupy an intermediate position between the first group and the third, the Aramaic dialects that are the continuation of the eastern branch of Middle Aramaic and are used in Kurdistan in the area on the common border of Iraq, Persia, and Turkey. Christians and Jews speak these dialects. Most of the Jews have immigrated to Israel; the Christians have spread out through the United States, Europe, and elsewhere. The recently discovered spoken dialect of the Mandeans in Persia has a special position in the third group.

The Jewish dialects can be divided into three groups:

(1) The dialects spoken in northwest Iraq (Iraqi Kurdistan). Important settlements are Nerwa, ʿAmadiya, Zāxō, and Dehōk, to which Jezira and Čalla (Çukurca) in Turkey should be added. The dialects of this group are particularly important for historical-linguistic study, since they clearly resemble Ancient Aramaic, in pronunciation, forms, and vocabulary.

(2) (Persian) Azerbaijan. Important settlements are Salmas (Shahpur), Urmia (Rizaiyah), Naǵada (Solduz), Ushnuiyeh (Šinno), to which Bašqala in Turkey should be added.

(3) Persian Kurdistan. Important settlements are Sablaǵ (Mahabad), Saqqiz, Bokan, Bana, and Senna, and the Iraqi towns of Rawanduz, Irbil, Sulaymaniya (before Iraq was established as an independent political entity after World War I, it was part of the Ottoman Empire). The southernmost Aramaic-speaking settlement is Kerend.

From the Middle Ages Jews are known to have spoken Aramaic in Kurdistan. Some scholars hold that Aramaic was not the original language of some of these Jews, but that they adopted it after their emigration (from Persia?) to the Aramaic-speaking areas. Perhaps not all the Jews from this area spoke Aramaic. The census takers did not distinguish between Jews who spoke Aramaic and those who spoke other languages. It appears that in the cities where Arabic (or Turkish) rule was strong the Jews adopted the language of their surroundings, after a period of bilingualism. Jews from places where, according to travelers, Aramaic was still spoken in the 19th century, did not bring this language with them to Israel. Immigrants from Irbil exemplify this process: both Arabic and Aramaic are the everyday language of the older generation.

When the State of Israel was established the total number of Aramaic-speaking Jews was estimated at 20,000; most of them are now in Israel, grouped largely according to their provenance. The Jews (especially from Persia and Turkey) have called their language the "language of the Targum." Other names are "the language of the Jews," "our language," and "Jabali." In Israel this language is commonly called Kurdi, even though this is the scientific name for the Iranian language of the Muslim Kurds. It seems that rabbinic scholars on rare occasions called this language Aramaic, as can be seen in two manuscripts, one from the beginning of the 18th century, the other from the beginning of the 20th. The scientific name given this language is "Northeastern Neo-Aramaic" or "modern Syriac" (the latter suitable to the Christian dialects). The Christians who use this language consider Syriac the language from which their language evolved, but there is no linguistic proof for this contention.

From the historical-linguistic point of view it is assumed that the eastern dialects of Neo-Aramaic developed from a language similar to Babylonian talmudic Aramaic and Mandaic, but there are no documents extant in this language since it was not used as a literary vehicle. Similarly, the exact connection between eastern Neo-Aramaic and the Aramaic of the Babylonian Jews before they began speaking Arabic is unknown.

An idea may be obtained of some of the major features of these dialects by a description of the dialect as spoken in Zāxō, which is of particular importance for historical-linguistic study.

Phonology

The glottal stop, ʾ, parallels three consonants of Ancient Aramaic, א, ע, גֿ. ʾ from ע (or גֿ) is always retained, while the ʾ from א is liable to disappear in certain situations: *ʾurxa* ("road"), *burxa* ("on the road") as against *ʾisra* ("ten") and *bʾisra* ("by ten"). This is important in determining the etymological origin of a particular ʾ. ח is pronounced as *x* (= כֿ).

The phonemes of *b, g, d, k, p, t* which in Ancient Aramaic, as in Hebrew, had two variants each, have attained phonemic status in the modern dialects for each of their variants. The spirantized and *dageš* forms appear in all environments and are not conditioned by the accepted rules of Ancient Aramaic, for example, the ת of שתי, יתב is always given the hard pronunciation, even though it was spirantized in Ancient Aramaic under certain conditions.

The following is the transposition of *b, g, d, k, t* in Neo-Aramaic: בֿ = *w*; גֿ (through ע) = ך; כֿ = *x*; דֿ = *z*; תֿ = *s*. The different pronunciations of דֿ and תֿ in the various dialects serve as a criterion for differentiating them.

As in Eastern Syriac, the phoneme פ is always pronounced *p*. In all the Jewish dialects, however, *f* is found only in loanwords, while in most of the Christian dialects *f* is replaced by *p*.

Neo-Aramaic dialects

Anc. Aram.	Zāxō	Dehōk	ʿAmadiya	Urmia	Irbil
ידֿא "hand"	ʾīza	ʾīḏa	ʾīda	īda	īla
ביתֿא "house"	bēsa	bēṯa	bēṯa	bēla	bēla

In loanwords the phonemes ʾ, ḥ, ʿ, ġ, č, j, are also found. The diphthongs in Ancient Aramaic have become monophthongized: *ay* > *ē* (בַּיְתָא > *bēsa*), *aw* > ō (יַוְמָא > *yōma*). The same is true for diphthongs originating in Neo-Aramaic as a result of the בֿ > w shift: חַבְֿלָא *xōla*. The doubling of consonants has largely been eliminated and replaced by the lengthening of the preceding vowel, as יַמָּא > *jāma*.

Morphology

The new status constructus is formed by adding the suffix *it* to the noun base: *baxta* ("a woman"); *baxtit axōna* ("the brother's wife"). In the plural there is no differentiation of gender in adjectives, pronouns, or the verb, as: *gōra sqīla* ("A handsome man"), *baxta sqīlta* ("a beautiful woman"); *gūrē sqīlē* ("handsome men"), *baxtāsa sqīlē* ("beautiful women"). There is only one set of possessive pronouns suffixed to the nouns (both the singular and the plural).

The verb differs radically from Ancient Aramaic both in form and in content. Whereas in Ancient Aramaic the tense system has two parts (past and future), in Neo-Aramaic it is tripartite: past, present, and future. The prefixed and suffixed forms which in Ancient Aramaic were perfect and imperfect have been replaced by other forms. The form *šāqïl* (שָׁקֵל in Ancient Aramaic = active participle) is a subjunctive. It is conjugated by adding the enclitic pronouns. *Šāqil* refers to the actor and the recipient of the act is indicated by-*l*- plus pronominal suffixes, e.g., *šāqïllē* ("that he will take"). The present is formed by prefixing *g/k* to *šāqïl* (*gzamir,* "he plays"); the future by prefixing *b/p* to this form (*bzāmïr,* "he will play").

Šqīl (= שְׁקִיל, the passive participle) is the basis of the past and the recipient of the action. The actor is indicated by-*l*- plus personal suffixes: *šqilē* ("he took"), *šqilālē* ("he took her"), *šqililē* ("he took them").

Neo-Aramaic has also introduced compound tenses which indicate different aspects (continuous action and perfect). The infinitive *šqāla* (*bi* usually precedes the infinitive of the first conjugation) plus the copula produce the continuous present: *bïšqāla lē* ("he is taking"). The form *šqīla*, conjugated according to gender and number, with the copula, forms the present perfect: *šqīlā lē* ("he has taken"), *šqïltā lā* ("she has taken"), *šqīlē lū* ("they have taken"). By adding the suffix *wa* every tense can be cast one degree into the past: *gšaqïlwa* ("he used to take"), *šqïlwālē* ("he had taken").

There are only three conjugations which parallel *qal, pael,* and *afel*. The reflexive conjugations that were used in Ancient Aramaic to express the passive are not found in Neo-Aramaic where the passive is formed with the passive participle plus an auxiliary verb.

Especially noteworthy is the syntax of the copula. In a sentence whose predicate is not a verb, the predicate is formed through the addition of the copula, as: *baxta sqïlta* ("a beautiful woman"), *baxta sqïlta lā* ("the woman is beautiful").

Neo-Aramaic was greatly influenced by the neighboring languages. The impact of Kurdish seems to have been especially strong in the early stages of the language and there are those who attribute the changes in the verb to it. As in all Jewish languages there are many words from Hebrew, especially in the sphere of tradition, which were absorbed in Jewish Aramaic: סעודה (!), ברכה, גזירה, מצוה, נשמה, etc.

Writing

The Jews use the Hebrew alphabet in writing their language and they add certain diacritical signs to represent the missing consonants. In the earliest known manuscripts (17th century, north Iraq) the long vowels are indicated by *matres lectionis*: א = *ā*; ‘י= *ī* or *ē* (final *ē* by ‘ or ה/יה); *waw* for short and long *u* and *o*. In later manuscripts the system was not consistently maintained, vocalization also being used for this purpose.

The use of Neo-Aramaic as a written language was limited to certain literary types intended to be read in the synagogue both during prayers and apart from it: *tafsirs* (elaborated translations) of *haftarot* and *piyyutim*; Midrashim for some of the *parashiyyot*; the midrashic Targum of Song of Songs, etc. Hebrew is used for secular purposes. It seems that the epic poems on biblical themes and the Targum in different dialects were first transcribed in Israel through the efforts of Joseph Joel *Rivlin.

BIBLIOGRAPHY: F. Rosenthal, *Die aramaistische Forschung seit Th. Noeldeke's Veroeffentlichungen* (1939); idem (ed.), *Aramaic Handbook* (1967); R. Macuch, *Handbook of Classical and Modern Mandaic* (1965); R. Duval, *Dialectes neo-araméens de Salamas* (1883); A.J. Maclean, *Grammar of the Dialects of Vernacular Syriac* (1901); idem, *Dictionary of the Dialects of Vernacular Syriac* (1901); J.B. Segal, in: JNES, 14 (1955), 251–70; Polotzky, in: JSS, 6 (1961), 1–32; I. Garbel, *The Jewish Neo-Aramaic Dialect of Persian Azerbaijan* (1965). **ADD. BIBLIOGRAPHY:** W. Arnold, *Das Neuwestaramäische*, 5 vols. (1989–); S.E. Fox, in: JAOS, 114 (1994), 154–61; idem, *The Neo-Aramaic Dialect of Jilu* (1997); W. Heinrichs (ed.), *Studies in Neo-Aramaic* (1990); R.D. Hoberman, in: JAOS, 108 (1988), 557–74; idem, *The Syntax and Semantics of Verb Morphology in Modern Aramaic* (1989); S. Hopkins, in: JSS 34 (1989), 413–32; H. Jacob, *Grammatik des Thumischen Neuaramäisch* (1973); O. Jastrow, *Laut- und Formenlehre des neuaramäischen Dialekts von Mīdin im Ṭur ʿAbdin* (1985³); idem, *Der neuaramäische Dialekt von Hertevin* (1988); idem, *Der neuaramäische Dialekt von Mlaḥsō* (1994); idem, "The Neo-Aramaic Languages," in: R. Hetzron (ed.), *The Semitic Languages* (1997), 334–77; G. Khan, *A Grammar of Neo-Aramaic: The Dialect of the Jews of Arbel* (1999); idem, *The Neo-Aramaic Dialect of Qaraqosh* (2002); idem, *The Jewish Neo-Aramaic Dialect of Sulemaniyya and Ḥalabja* (2004); G. Krotkoff, *A Neo-Aramaic Dialect of Kurdistan* (1982); R. Macuch, *Neumandäische Chrestomathie* (1989); idem, *Neumandäische Texte im Dialekt von Ahwāz* (1993); H. Mutzafi, *The Jewish Neo-Aramaic Dialect of Koy Sanjaq* (2004); T. Nöldeke, *Grammatik der neusyrischen Sprache am Urmia-See und in Kurdistan* (1868); E.Y. Odisho, *The Sound System of Modern Assyrian (Neo-Aramaic)* (1988); H. Ritter, *Ṭuroyo: Die Volkssprache der syrischen Christen des Ṭur ʿAbdīn* (1967–90); Y. Sabar, *Homilies in the Neo-Aramaic of the Kurdistani Jews on the Parashot Wayhi, Beshallah and Yitro* (1984); idem, *The Books of Genesis-Deuteronomy in Neo-Aramaic in the Dialect of the Jewish Community of Zakho* (1983–94); idem, *Targum De-Targum: An Old Neo-Aramaic Version of the Targum on Song of Songs* (1991); idem, *A Jewish Neo-Aramaic Dictionary* (2002); J. Sinha, *Der neuostaramäische Dialekt von Beṣpən* (2000); Y. Younansardaroud, *Der neuostaramäische Dialekt von Särdärïd* (2001).

[David Cohen]

NEO-FASCISM. Neo-Fascism lends itself to an exact definition even less than *Fascism, its ideological progenitor. In the postwar world all radical right-wing movements, irrespective of their doctrinal contents and differences – except those explicitly aiming at the restoration of an antisemitic, racialist, Nazi-type dictatorship (see *Neo-Nazism) – are commonly referred to as "neo-Fascist." They share an attitude of extreme, militant nationalism; a belief in authoritarian rather than democratic government; and a total rejection of socialist, particularly Marxist, dogma with its underlying universalist and egalitarian ethos. Inhabiting the social periphery between the middle and the working class, Neo-Fascism appeals mostly to those deprived of their former independent status (as artisans, white-collar workers, small-holders, craftsmen, etc.) by the growth of an urban, industrialized society and driven to xenophobia and hostility toward minority groups, which they believe to have either caused their social and economic decline or contributed to it. Hatreds vary according to demographic conditions. In the United States and Britain, Neo-Fascist movements have a strong anti-color bias, whereas similar French groups in the 1950s and early 1960s were anti-Algerian, and in Switzerland these prejudices inspired agitation against alien workers. Antisemitism is almost always implicit in such attitudes and it can easily become, as in the case of the Argentinian Tacuara or the Swedish Nordiska Rikspartiet (Nordic Realm Party), an ideological focal point. In the West, the shock of the Nazi Holocaust militated after World War II against the spread of Neo-Fascist movements, particularly obsessively antisemitic ones; however, the Israel-Arab *Six-Day War (1967) modified this trend. Formerly disreputable antisemitic prejudices relabeled "anti-Zionism" became respectable again when disseminated by the Communist establishment, the *New Left, and Black Power activists. Arab anti-Israel propaganda agencies, until 1967 associated with the extreme right, have since – and without breaking their Neo-Fascist links – been courted and supported by the radical left as well.

Neo-Fascism survived best in Italy. The Movimento Sociale Italiano (MSI) obtained close to 1,500,000 votes (5.2% of the total poll) in the 1970 provincial elections, sending 32 deputies to the regional councils. However, neither occasional swastika-daubing forays into Rome's old ghetto (1958, 1960) nor parliamentary representation dating back to the early 1950s elevated the MSI to a significant position. Further to the right, the minuscule Ondine Nuovo (New Order), formed by activist dissidents from the MSI, is a terrorist, but otherwise negligible, force, cultivating links with like-minded European "New Order" movements. Prince Valerio Borghese, a former honorary MSI president, founded the militant National Front which made an abortive attempt to overthrow the government (December, 1970). In France the horrors of Nazi occupation inhibited the revival of overtly Fascist movements. Efforts by the Sidos brothers to channel resentments brought about by the loss of empire (Indochina, North Africa) into the Neo-Fascist Jeune Nation failed, while the less clearly defined anti-establishment campaign of Pierre Poujade won 60 parliamentary seats (1956). Both his party and the anti-Gaullist extremists of the Algérie-Française OAS had Fascist and antisemitic overtones, but neither survived the nationalist appeal of de Gaulle's presidency. In the post–de Gaulle era, Ordre Nouveau, the successor organization to the Occident (banned 1968), gained some notoriety for militancy and street-fighting.

Neo-Fascism also failed to prosper in postwar England. Sir Oswald Mosley's once-powerful British Union Fascists, renamed British Union, had dwindled into irrelevance. A number of extremist organizations like the Empire Loyalists, the British National Party, and the Racial Preservation Society (whose street-fighting propensities gained them brief notoriety in the early 1960s), combined in 1967 to form the National Front, without, however, making any impact on national politics. In the 1970 general election the Front put up ten candidates, none of whom polled more than 1,600 votes. In the United States old-style primitive antisemitism flourished among such movements as the Ku Klux Klan and the Christian Crusader, while the more sophisticated John Birch Society vented their anti-Jewish resentments on the "liberal establishment" represented as being predominantly Jewish. The Klans, Crusaders, and Birchists were typically U.S. phenomena; lacking any party organization able to attain power, they cannot be regarded as true neo-Fascists.

BIBLIOGRAPHY: D. Eisenberg, *The Re-emergence of Fascism* (1967).

[Ernest Hearst]

NEOLOGY (Neologism), unofficial name of the communities in Hungary belonging to the *Reform movement. On the basis of the decisions of the General Jewish Congress (1868–69; see *Hungary), they constituted the majority and therefore called themselves the Congressionals. Reform tendencies had already appeared in the community organizations of Hungary from the beginning of the 19th century. Some were expressed in programs like that of Rabbi A.L. Rappoch (from the town of Veszprem, 1826) which called for centralization and supervision in the choice of rabbis, teachers, and communal officials. At about the same time Aaron *Chorin urged the convention of a synod of rabbis and laymen. From 1850 the Austrian government sought to assure the supervision of Jewish schools in Hungary. At that time a commission was set up to draft a constitution of 285 articles encompassing every aspect of Jewish communal life. One of the demands was for the establishment of a rabbinical seminary, which became one of the main questions of reform that led to the disputes between the communities of *Nagykanizsa, *Papa, Gyöngyős, and others.

The organizational activities of the advocates of Reform aroused the energetic but disunited opposition of *Orthodoxy, expressed particularly in the decisions of the *Michalovce Orthodox convention (1865). After the attainment of full civil rights (1867), the leaders of Pest, the most powerful Neologist community, took the initiative of preparing a memorandum on the organization of Hungarian Jewry which they submitted to the Minister of Public Instruction and Religious Affairs, Baron J. *Eőtvős. They suggested that a convention of the delegates of Hungarian Jewry be held without the participation of the rabbis, in order to prevent a debate on theological questions and because the latter were liable to intervene beyond the scope of their function. This approach, which aroused the objections not only of the Orthodox but also of the Neologist Leopold *Loew, became one of the fundamental platforms in the organization of Neologist communities. Differences of opinion were already apparent at the congress's preliminary meeting, to which Orthodox delegates were not invited. In their discussions with Eőtvős, the Orthodox requested permission to convene a separate congress, but Eőtvős rejected any move which was liable to imply that there were two sects within Judaism. Subsequently, however, it was decided that rabbis would also be invited to the congress. The elections, which were held after extensive propaganda and not always by valid processes, assured a Neologist majority with 57.5% of the vote (the Orthodox gained 42.5%). At the end of 1868 Minister Eőtvős opened the congress, whose principal theme was the organizational structure of the communities. Violent disputes broke out at once over the determination of the objectives of debates. While the Neologists tried to define the community as "a society providing for religious needs," the Orthodox insisted on the declaration that "the Jewish community of Hungary and Transylvania consists of the followers of the Mosaic-rabbinic faith and commands as they are codified in the Shulḥan Arukh." The question of the rabbinical seminary, which was to be financed by the "school fund" granted by Francis Joseph I from the fine paid by the Jews of Hungary after the 1848 Revolution, was also a much disputed one. In the end, 48 of the 83 Orthodox delegates walked out and the decisions of the congress were ratified. The Orthodox, however, succeeded in organizing themselves, obtaining the authorization of the emperor. On several occasions the Neologists endeavored without success to convene another congress. Finally a meeting was held in 1935 (at which only the Neologists were represented). In 1950, on the instructions of the Communist government, a decision on the unification of Hungarian communities was passed.

The attempts of the Neologists to amalgamate with the Orthodox were to no avail. The hope of establishing this union caused the Neologists not only to refrain from introducing drastic reforms in the prayers and religious services (with the exception of the question of the organ and the pulpit, which was removed from the center of most synagogues) but also to adopt a distinctly conservative orientation, particularly in the district synagogues of the capital. There is no doubt that this preserved the unity of Hungarian Jewry in spite of the ideological split. The hoped-for ideological consolidation of the Neologist camp did not materialize either and many differences remained. As early as 1848 a circle of the younger members and even some important personalities of the Pest community sought to establish a Reform synagogue, but the community, which had already alienated itself from Orthodoxy, wished to prevent a complete split; it therefore obtained from the authorities a liquidation order against the small Reform organization (1852). In 1884 a number of individuals once more attempted to establish a Reform community. However, the national office of the Neologists intervened to deny them this right. Some stood for a liberal orientation, and for the adoption of the conservative ideology (1943). The ideological consolidation was hindered by the special organization of the communities. These contradictions were particularly evident after World War I, when the community became the sole focal point for the social activities of those who had been estranged from Judaism over a lengthy period and were attracted by communal life only because they were excluded from general society. These extreme assimilationists prevented Zionism from penetrating the communities.

During the period of Hungarian Jewry's utter isolation from the social and economic life of the country (1938–44), there was a great awakening within the Neologist communities. Their educational and charitable activities were extended until they were among the most developed in the sphere of widespread mutual assistance (where they also collaborated with the Orthodox). When the communities were reorganized after World War II, they were imbued with Zionism and a readiness to maintain relations with world Jewry, but this evolution was halted with the official prohibition of Zionist and foreign relations activities in 1949.

BIBLIOGRAPHY: J.J.(L.) Greenwald (Grunwald), *Korot ha-Torah ve-ha-Emunah be-Ungarya* (1921); idem, *Le-Toledot ha-Reformazyah ha-Datit be-Germanyah u-ve-Ungarya* (1948); L. Loew, *Der Juedische Kongress* (1869); N. Katzburg, in: *Hungarian Jewish Studies*, 2 (1969), 1–33; idem, in: *Bar-Ilan Sefer ha-Shanah*, 2 (1964), 163–77; Weisz, in: *Libanon*, 7 (Hung., 1943), 67–72.

[Baruch Yaron]

NEO-NAZISM, a general term for the related fascist, nationalist, white supremacist, antisemitic beliefs and political tendencies of the numerous groups that emerged after World War II seeking to restore the Nazi order or to establish a new order based on doctrines similar to those underlying Nazi Germany. Some of these groups closely adhered to the ideas propounded in Hitler's *Mein Kampf*; others espoused related beliefs deriving from older Catholic, nationalist, or other local traditions. Some openly embraced the structure and aspirations of the Third Reich by displaying swastika flags and glorifying Nazi achievements, while others sought to mask their ideology and agenda. Neo-Nazi activity has surged and declined in unpredictable waves in Germany, France, England, Russia, the Scandinavian countries, the United States, Canada, South Africa, and elsewhere. In April 1993, after a series of incidents, the Italian government passed an emergency measure aimed at punishing racial, ethnic, and religious discrimination. The Mancino Law (Law No. 205) permits prosecution of individuals who incite violence using a broad range of methods, including displaying symbols of hate, such as swastikas. Hundreds of youths have since been convicted under the law. In February 2005, European Union ministers agreed to continue a long-term debate over the regulation of racism and xenophobia. Among the proposals under consideration is making it punishable by law to deny the Holocaust or other crimes against humanity.

Why do people become neo-Nazis? In the 1980s, social scientists began to move beyond notions of deviance and psychopathology to theories of social mobilization that see people who join any social movement – even neo-Nazis – as motivated by shared grievances shaped by social circumstances, recruited by face-to-face interaction, and focused on goals that seem practical and reachable.

Major factors in the global neo-Nazi upsurge included unstable economic, political, and social conditions, with their many causes – including, in the 1970s, simultaneous inflation and recession caused in great part by dependence on Arab oil; the disruptions of globalization and the collapse of the Soviet empire; waves of nonwhite immigration into Europe (from places formerly ruled or dominated by Europeans) and the United States; the constant threat of war, especially in the Middle East and the Persian Gulf; and the continued sense among white men that they were losing power and prestige in areas ranging from world affairs to their living rooms to their relations with women. In the United States, racial issues, not resolved in the 1960s, took the form of conflict over school desegregation, affirmative action, social welfare provision, and government social spending in general. Moreover, the failure of the Vietnam War, based on untenable Cold War premises, produced an atmosphere of political and cultural resentment on the right that became increasingly strong over time.

Leaders of neo-Nazi groups skillfully exploited the anxieties caused by these and other factors. The worldview of neo-Nazis is shaped by the way leaders frame issues and use narrative stories. While most neo-Nazi frames and narratives are based on myths, demonization, and scapegoating, this does not make them less effective in building a functional identity for individuals, even if they come from dysfunctional families. This process allowed neo-Nazis to adapt to changing historic conditions and expand their targets beyond Jews and black people.

Neo-Nazis were among the earliest users of online computerized networks in the 1980s, and surged onto the Internet with hundreds of websites allowing for the mass distribution of hate material, including claims that America was controlled by "ZOG," the Zionist Occupation Government, in Washington, D.C. As the gay rights movement grew, so did neo-Nazi attacks on gay men and lesbians. In response to the feminist movement, neo-Nazis crafted new roles and avenues for participation by women, while preserving a dominant role for men. Women were still placed on a pedestal with one arm around their children protecting hearth and home, but now they were expected to use the other arm to cradle an automatic weapon. Three other significant ideological innovations among neo-Nazi groups are "Third Position" neo-Nazism, Skinhead neo-Nazism, and neo-Nazi theologies built around hybrids of religion such as Protestantism and Paganism.

One group of neo-Nazis which denounces both capitalism and communism occupies what it calls the Third Position. This merges the early Nazi Party left wing's National Socialism with "revolutionary" white supremacy and opposes both globalization and multiculturalism. It calls for local economic cooperatives, support for the working class, and ecologically sound policy using populist "voelkisch" rhetoric. Third Position National Socialist parties have been organized in Japan, Iran, Scotland, Russia, Lithuania, and the United States, among other countries.

Nonracist Skinheads originated in the late 1960s as a multiracial working class youth subculture in Britain built around black music imported by immigrants from former Caribbean colonies. The neo-Nazi National Front helped convert the skinhead movement into a vehicle of white rage built around racism and violence. In the mid-1980s the movement jumped to continental Europe and the United States through the music of racist bands such as Skrewdriver; skinheads in the U.S.A. then split into racist and anti-racist factions.

A hybrid of Protestant Christianity with neo-Nazi racialism produced the Christian Identity movement in the United States, discussed below. A more widespread phenomenon was the rise of pagan neo-Nazis in the 1990s, built around racist forms of Norse religious traditions: Odinism, Ásatrú, and Wotanism. This drew on Nazi fascination with Aryanism and esoteric religions. These groups appealed primarily to youth.

Bridges to the Mainstream

Starting in the 1970s, a trend of conservative, right-wing populist, ethnonationalist, and neofascist challenges to sitting centrist or social democratic governments allowed right-wing groups a degree of legitimacy they did not possess in the immediate post-World War II era. In response neo-Nazi groups have developed a variety of ways to build bridges to more mainstream political and social movements. Some neo-Nazis repackage their beliefs as forms of "White Nationalism" or "White Separatism," hiding behind broader racist movements for "White Rights," with alliances spanning Europe and North America. At the same time, Europe, North America, the Middle East, and South Asia saw the development of numerous right-wing populist political parties and reactionary fundamentalist religious movements that served to bridge the extreme right to the mainstream.

In several countries neo-Nazis (sometimes in alliance with quasifascist or xenophobic right-wing populist allies) became more involved in electoral politics, stressing anti-immigrant and sometimes antisemitic themes. Rather than simply staging street demonstrations, they ran for office, with surprisingly good results in some instances. According to the political scientist Cas Mudde, between 1980 and 1999 over 50 European extreme-right political parties ran candidates in Austria, Belgium, Denmark, France, Germany, Greece, Italy, Luxembourg, Netherlands, Norway, Portugal, Spain, Sweden, Switzerland, and the United Kingdom.

This interaction has created a dynamic in which antisemitic ideas and conspiracy theories once circulated almost exclusively by German Nazis and their neo-Nazi offspring entered popular culture, mainstream political debate, and even broadcast television series, especially in Islamic and Arab countries in the Middle East. These even included a revival of the false allegations from *The Protocols of the Elders of Zion*. These conspiracy allegations moved into more mainstream circles through bridging mechanisms that often mask the original overtly anti-Jewish claims by using coded rhetoric about "secret elites" or "Zionist cabals." The international organization run by Lyndon LaRouche is a major source of such masked antisemitic theories globally. In the U.S. the LaRouchites spread these conspiracy theories in an alliance with aides to Minister Louis Farrakhan of the Nation of Islam. A series of LaRouchite pamphlets calls the neoconservative movement the "Children of Satan," which links Jewish neoconservatives to the historic rhetoric of the blood libel. In a twisted irony, the pamphlets imply the neoconservatives are the real neo-Nazis.

Another way neo-Nazis launder antisemitic conspiracy theories is through *Holocaust denial, the attempt to "prove" that the Holocaust was a fiction and that the Nazis never used gas chambers to exterminate Jews. The international clearinghouse for this movement is the California-based Institute for Historical Review (IHR), founded in 1979, which held its first conference on "Historical Revisionism" that same year. IHR, publisher of the *Journal of Historical Revisionism*, was established by Willis Carto, founder of the Liberty Lobby and a figure long associated with organizing and propagandizing projects involving neo-Nazi, pro-Hitler, antisemitic and extreme-right alliances. Carto later lost control of IHR in a lawsuit, but started a new denial publication, the *Barnes Review*, edited by former IHR staff members. Holocaust denial also persists in France, where a scandal in the late 1970s was caused by the claims of Professor Robert Faurisson. In Britain, author David Irving sued American historian Deborah Lipstadt in the late 1990s for calling him a Holocaust denier. In 2000 Irving lost the case (see *Irving v. Lipstadt), which gained international headlines. Irving had previously appeared at an IHR conference, and Faurisson and other IHR advisors testified along with Irving on behalf of Canadian Holocaust denier Ernst Zundel.

Neo-Nazis often use Holocaust denial material along with anti-Jewish conspiracy theories, sometimes coming up with grotesque slogans. Neo-Nazis not only blamed the 1973–74 oil crisis on a Jewish conspiracy, but in the U.S. they distributed literature that proclaimed "burn Jews, not oil!" This approach was repeated during the 1990 Gulf War, which saw the extension of a rhetorical device in which Jews, Zionism, Israel, and Israeli government policies were conflated into a conspiracist stew serving up the Israeli spy agency Mossad as the secret power behind world affairs. Thus echoes from the *Protocols* moved from neo-Nazis into wider circles, including some pro-Palestinian organizers and left-wing antiwar activists. After the terror attacks in New York and Washington on September 11, 2001, some neo-Nazi groups praised the terrorists for striking a blow against this global conspiracy.

[Jack Nusan Porter and Chip Berlet (2nd ed.)]

Post–World War II, 1945–1970

Neo-Nazism in Germany came to be identified with antisemitic, ultranationalist, extreme right-wing movements, whether made up of old or new Nazis. In Germany, incitement to race hatred, as well as any attempt to resuscitate the Nazi Party, were and are explicitly outlawed by the constitution and the criminal laws of the German Federal Republic (as they were by the German Democratic Republic); no party overtly attempting to revive Nazism can legally exist there. Without seriously threatening the still fragile West German democracy (in East Germany such political tendencies were severely repressed), a number of such movements gained some short-lived popularity and notoriety. The first to draw ex-Nazis into a political party, if somewhat unwittingly, was Alfred Loritz, a confused demagogue with an anti-Nazi record. His Bavarian Economic Reconstruction Association, founded in 1945 with U.S. consent, denounced Allied policies and articulated the widespread economic discontent of the pre-"economic-miracle" era. The "blonde Hitler," as he was sometimes called, frightened the young republic and the world at large when he gained 14.4 percent of the vote in his native Bavaria, winning 12 seats in the Bundestag, in the first West German general election in 1949. The lack of positive policies, however, coupled with internal dissension, rent the party asunder long before the following general election of 1953, in which it failed to gain a single seat.

Similarly spectacular and ominous was Fritz Dorls' deliberate attempt to revive Nazism through the Socialist Reich Party (SRP). Its leadership was made up entirely of old Nazis, the most prominent of whom was the deputy chairman, Otto-Ernst Remer, the Wehrmacht officer who successfully thwarted the July 20, 1944, plot against Hitler. Apart from distributing antisemitic election leaflets reminiscent of *Der Stuermer*, the SRP even boasted a gang organized on storm-troop lines, the so-called Reichsfront. In 1951 when the SRP gained 11 percent of the Lower Saxony vote, an alarmed federal government contested the party's legality before the Constitutional Court. Declared illegal as an attempt to reestablish the proscribed Nazi Party, this particular specter of resurgent Nazism disappeared. It reappeared a year later when the British arrested Dr. Naumann, one of Goebbels' top-ranking officials, whose plot to subvert the respectable Free Democratic Party by infiltrating ex-Nazis into key positions was well on the way to succeeding.

In the 1960s the spectacular and unexpected success of the NPD (National Democratic Party of Germany) aroused worldwide fears of a Nazi revival. Founded in 1965 by Adolf von Thadden to unite the hitherto splintered and ineffectual "nationalist opposition," the party shocked German and world opinion when in the 1966–67 *Land* (state) elections it gained admission to a number of *Land* parliaments (*Landstagen*) by substantially exceeding the required 5 percent of the vote. Careful not to fall afoul of the Constitutional Court, the NPD, run largely by ex-Nazis, appealed to exactly the same prejudices and national self-assertion to which Germans responded so overwhelmingly in the Hitler era. Jews were not openly denigrated, but the state of Israel and its policies were viciously attacked. The "domination by alien big powers," reminiscent of the Nazi fiction of a "Judeo-Marxist world conspiracy," was denounced, as were references to Nazi crimes. The party manifesto demanded "an end to the lie of Germany's exclusive guilt which serves to extort continuously thousands of millions from our people," apparently a reference to restitution and compensation payments to Israel and individual Jews. Beset like its predecessors by internecine leadership struggles and lacking forward-looking policies, the NPD failed to gain the qualifying 5 percent in the 1969 general election. This failure led to a crisis of confidence, which resulted in the party's losing its seats in the various *Landstagen* after the 1970 elections. At that time it was doubtful whether neo-Nazism still commanded a politically meaningful potential, although the phenomenon still lingered on in violently "anti-Israel" weeklies like the *Deutsche National Zeitung* and in the publications of ex-Reich press chief Suedermann's Druffel Verlag and similar publishing houses.

In Austria, neo-Nazism lacked the organizational framework or a sufficiently numerous following to qualify as a politically relevant force. Among the minuscule groupings more or less openly committed to propagating Nazi ideas and extolling Nazi achievements, Theodor Soucek's Sozialorganische Bewegung Europas (SOBRE) was perhaps the most noteworthy in the early 1950s. It tried to coordinate efforts of Nazi collaborators and sympathizers in the former occupied territories to revitalize the Hitlerian "new order" in the context of the then emerging Europe. SOBRE enjoyed the support of Konrad Windisch, one of the founders of the Bund Heimattreuer Jugend (BHJ, Federation of Homeland-Faithful Youth), whose initials HJ, recalling the Hitler Jugend (Hitler Youth), proclaimed its ideological lineage and identification. Despite the insignificance of these movements, residual antisemitism and subliminal Nazi sympathies seemed to be more widespread in Austria than in Germany; thus the marked reluctance of Austrian authorities to prosecute and of juries to convict such war criminals and Eichmann aides as Murer, Novak, or Raiakovic, and the parsimoniousness of Austrian restitution.

Argentina figured prominently in the Nazis' plans to save the movement and themselves after defeat. This tied in well with President Juan Peron's dreams of Argentinean hegemony based on a modernized army and an independent armaments industry, which the Nazi experts were to develop. Nazis headed nuclear research institutes, while World War II air aces like Rudel and Galland advised the Argentinean air force and Professor Tank, a German jet designer, started an Argentinean aircraft industry. Eichmann and others prominent in the Final Solution (Klingenfuss, Rademacher, and Mengele) found sanctuary, while Johannes von Leers, head of an anti-Jewish department in Goebbels' Propaganda Ministry, became an adviser to Peron. Moreover, the Nazi gospel continued to be preached in German in *Der Weg* (Buenos Aires) and other Duerer Verlag publications. After Peron's fall

(1955), some of these fugitives moved to Egypt (a Nazi sanctuary since 1945), where military needs and anti-Israel, antisemitic resentments offered them scope. Years later the efforts of ex-Nazis to develop Egyptian jet engines, supersonic fighters, and rockets (the Messerschmidt, Brandner, and Pilz teams) caused greater international consternation than the activities of von Leers and SS General Bender in the Egyptian Ministry of National Guidance or of the former Gestapo chief Sellman as a police adviser on "anti-Jewish action."

[Ernest Hearst]

Into the Present, 1970–2006

The interaction among right-wing populist movements, quasi-fascist political parties and organizations, and outright neo-Nazi groups blurred boundaries and created controversy over where specific groups fell on the political spectrum.

The European National Front was a network of right-wing Christian nationalist groups. Members and affiliates included groups in the Czech Republic (Narodni Sjednoceni (National Unity)); France (Renouveau Français (French Renewal)); Greece (Patriotike Summachia (Patriotic Alliance)); Italy (Forza Nuova (New Force)); Latvia (Nacionala Speka Savieniba (National Power Unity)); Netherlands (Nationale Alliantie (National Alliance)); Poland (Narodowe Odrodzenie Polski (National Rebirth of Poland)); Portugal (Partido Nacional Renovador (Party of National Renewal)); Serbia (Otacastveni Pokret Obraz (Dignity Fatherland Movement)); and Slovakia (Slovenska Narodna Jednota (Slovak National Unity)), Jednota Slovenskej Mladeze (Association of Slovak Youth). Delegations attending meetings included those from Hyrsi Avgi (Golden Dawn), Greece; Nationale Alliantie, Netherlands; and Noua Dreapta (New Right), Romania. Supporters included Alternativa Espanola (Spanish Alternative) and La Falange (the Phalanx, the former ruling party under the Franco dictatorship), Spain; Garde Franque, France; and English First, United Kingdom.

Other nationalist far-right parties and groups operated in Australia (National Action, Patriotic Youth League); Austria (Freiheitliche Partei Österreichs (Freedom Party)); Austria and Slovenia (Kärntner Heimatdienst (Carinthian Homeland Service)); Belgium (Vlaams Belang (Flemish Interest), formerly Vlaams Blok); Canada (Heritage Front, Reform Party); Denmark (Dansk Folkeparti (Danish People's Party), Nationalpartiet Danmark (Danish National Party), Fremskridtpartiet (Progress Party)); Estonia (Eesti Rahvuslaste Keskliit (Estonian National League), Eesti Kodanik (Estonian Civic Union), Eesti Paremäärmuslik Organisatsioon (Estonian Extreme Rightist Organization)); France (Front National (National Front), Mouvement National Républicain (National Republican Movement)); Germany (Republikanische Partei (Republican Party), Deutsche Volksunion (German People's Union), Nationaldemokratische Partei Deutschlands (National Democratic Party of Germany)); Greece (Ellinoko Metopo (Hellenic Front)); India (Bharatiya Janata (Indian People's Party)); Italy (Lega Nord (Northern League), Alleanza Nazionale (National Alliance), Movimento Sociale Fiamma Tricolore (Tricolor Flame Social Movement)); Latvia (Nacionala Speka Savieniba (National Power Unity)); Malta (Imperium Europa); Netherlands (Centrumdemocraten (Democratic Center), Nederlandse Volks-Unie (Netherlands People's Union), Nieuwe Nationale Partij (New National Party), Nederlands Blok, Nationale Alliantie, Nieuw Rechts (New Right), Pim Fortuyn's List, Liveable Netherlands, Centrum Partij 86 (banned in 1998)); New Zealand (National Front, New Zealand First); Norway (Progress Party); Portugal (Popular Party); Switzerland (Swiss People's Party); Russia (National Unity, Liberal Democratic Party); and United Kingdom (British National Party, Scottish National Party).

Most of these right-wing nationalist political parties denied any connection to fascism or neo-Nazism, yet they echoed many of the same xenophobic (and sometimes antisemitic and racist) themes, and provided a recruitment pool for neo-Nazi organizers.

Conversely, right-wing politicians in several countries often tried to capture those voters who might be inclined toward neo-Nazism, without offending those segments of the electorate that would be alienated if the appeal were too apparent and the link too explicit.

They walked a political tightrope, especially when it seemed as if they had the opportunity to be acceptable to a mainstream public. Their political parties were described as "extreme right" or "radical right-wing populist" by academics, while their political critics called them quasi-fascist or outright neo-Nazi, with their actual ideologies ranging along a continuum. In some countries, the right-wing electoral parties were built around ethnoreligious forms of nationalism, as was the case with numerous militant Islamic political parties, some sectors of the Israeli right, some Christian Right political groups, and the Hindu nationalist Bharatiya Janata Party (BJP) in India. Another common form, and more easily recognized, were the right-wing ethnonationalist parties that featured xenophobia and populist rhetoric.

In Austria, where an explicit appeal would shut down other forms of political support, the candidacy of Jörg Haider was a prime example of these phenomena. Haider took over the Austrian Freedom Party (Freiheitliche Partei Österreichs (FPO)) in 1986 and moved it further to the political right. By 1999 the FPO was gaining more than 25 percent of the vote, and the next year joined with the conservative People's Party to form a ruling coalition government. The FPO stumbled, however, and in 2002 only attracted some 10 percent of votes.

The French National Front (Front National [FN]) was founded in 1972 by Jean-Marie Le Pen, but only began attracting significant voter support in the mid-1980s. Since then the party and Le Pen have become major players on the French political scene, pulling 10–15 percent of voters. In 2002 Le Pen stunned observers with more than 17 percent of the vote, placing him in the second round of the French presidential election. To the right of the FN is a splinter group, the Mouvement National Républicain, led by Bruno Mégret.

The German Republican Party (Die Republikanische Partei (REP)) was founded by a former member of the Waffen SS in 1983, and began running candidates, whose fortunes varied over time. In 1989 some candidates attracted around 7 percent of votes in a West Berlin election, but then vote totals dropped. In 1992 the party staged a comeback with vote tallies in the 8–10 percent range in some elections. To the right of the REP was the German People's Union (Deutsche Volksunion) and the National Democratic Party (Nationaldemokratische Partei Deutschlands).

Flemish Interest (Vlaams Belang), formerly called the Vlaams Blok, was one of several ethnonationalist regional political parties around the world that called for more autonomy or outright secession, and often were highly critical of immigrants and immigration. The Northern League in Italy was another example.

In Italy, Forza Italia, led by Silvio Berlusconi, forged a fractious parliamentary alliance with the more obviously right-wing Northern League (Lega Nord) and National Alliance (Alleanza Nazionale (AN)), coming to power briefly in 1994, and again in 2001. Further to the right was the Movimento Sociale Fiamma Tricolore. In the late 1980s and early 1990s the Italian Social Movement/National Right (Movimento Sociale Italiano/Destra Nazionale (MSI/DN)) fielded candidates including Alessandra Mussolini (Il Duce's granddaughter). These candidates gained as much as 45 percent of the votes cast in local elections. When the MSI/DN split in 1995, Alessandra Mussolini joined the faction that created the National Alliance (AN), and sat in the national Chamber of Deputies. She left the AN in 2002 after its leader denounced fascism while in Israel. She then founded Liberta d'Azione and won a seat in the European Parliament.

In the United States Pat Buchanan pulled significant vote totals when running as a Republican Presidential candidate in 33 state primaries in 1992, attracting three million votes. His similar campaign in 1996 generally attracted 15–25 percent of Republican primary votes in the states where he was on the ballot. Buchanan's support plummeted, however, when he ran as the Reform Party candidate in 2000. The rhetoric of Buchanan's speeches included specific phrases that seemed innocuous but had special meaning for militant sectors of the Christian Right and the armed militia movement. Critics charged that Buchanan flirted with antisemitism and racism. Notorious antisemite Lyndon LaRouche, who shifted from left to right yet ran as a Democrat, has appeared on the presidential primary ballot for decades, attracting tens of thousands of votes in some states. The Constitution Party led by Howard Phillips and the America First Party (a splinter from the Reform Party) also fielded candidates for office.

Russian variants included several groups that more openly engaged in neo-Nazi and antisemitic rhetoric. These groups frequently complained about a gigantic Jewish or Zionist conspiracy. One of the largest of over 100 nationalist groups in Russia is the Russian National Unity Party, founded in 1990 and led by Aleksandr Barkashov. The founder of the ultranationalist Liberal Democratic Party is Vladimir Zhirinovsky. In 2001 he caused a scandal when, as a member and deputy speaker of the lower house of parliament, the Duma, he refused to stand for a minute of silence in remembrance of the victims of the Nazi genocide. He later expressed regret for his actions, which he claimed did not reflect antisemitism. In 1998, however, Zhirinovsky blamed Jews for starting World War II and provoking the Holocaust.

As extreme-right political parties gained election victories across Europe, the language used to describe them became more moderate, raising fears that the situation was not being openly confronted. As the Belgian political scientist Jérôme Jamin explained:

> Can one still apply the term fascist to a xenophobic party like the Lega Nord now that it has been in power… for many years? Can one view France's Front National as a mere relic of Pétainism when it made it into the second round of the presidential election… and when cities such as Toulon, Orange, Marignane and Vitrolles have had mayors from the FN? In what terms is it possible to stigmatize the Vlaams Blok in northern Belgium – a direct offshoot of pro-Nazi collaboration during World War II – when this party is one of the most powerful in Flanders? It is very hard to use the old words to characterize those parties in power today. It was a lot easier yesterday when they were small and noisy racist parties instead of the big powerful actors they have now become.

While neo-Nazis interacted with right-wing and mainstream political parties, they remained tiny marginal movements compared to national populations, although they were capable of brutal acts of violence. Much of their energy, however, was devoted to organizing within their own subculture.

Some neo-Nazis studied the ideological writings of Julius Evola, who promoted high-culture intellectual fascism, and Corneliu Codreanu, advocate of a mystical-spiritual form exemplified by the Romanian Iron Guard. Others remained disciples of Hitler, or supported the pre-regime national socialism of the Nazi Party's left wing, associated with the Strasser brothers. Many overt neo-Nazis were networked internationally through Blood and Honour, which emerged from the racist skinhead scene. Based in the United Kingdom, in 2006 Blood and Honour claimed active branches in Australia, Canada, Croatia, Cyprus, Denmark, Finland, Flanders (Belgium), France, Germany, Greece, Italy, Netherlands, Portugal, Slovenia, Spain, Ukraine, and the United States. Blood and Honour recruited primarily through white supremacist music. Not all racist skinheads engaged in violence, but violence was a hallmark of the movement. In Canada, for example, neo-Nazi skinheads desecrated Jewish synagogues and cemeteries. In 2005, a report for the International Bureau of Human Rights estimated that there were more than 120,000 neo-Nazi skinheads worldwide. A true count was, of course, difficult because neo-Nazi organizations were rarely registered with any official agency, and they hid their true numbers.

United States

Postwar neo-Nazism in the United States began in earnest

when George Lincoln Rockwell organized the American Nazi Party in 1959, gaining much publicity but negligible support. The group was later renamed the National Socialist White Peoples Party. After Rockwell's assassination by a former party member in 1967, several splinter groups emerged, including the National Socialist Party of America led by Frank Collin, who garnered international headlines in the mid-1970s by threatening to lead a march through the Chicago suburb of Skokie, Illinois, home to many Holocaust survivors. Instead, after winning a legal battle over the free speech issue, Collin led his uniformed brownshirts in several demonstrations in other Chicago suburbs and neighborhoods and a downtown plaza.

The next few years saw a great many neo-Nazis run for office, winning several primaries and one state legislative post. This trend began in 1975–76, when a neo-Nazi named Arthur Jones ran for mayor of Milwaukee, Wisconsin. Jones, campaigning vigorously on radio and in newspapers, gained 5,000 votes and lost decisively against incumbent Mayor Henry Maier, a popular and strongly pro-Israel politician. In November 1976, Richard Johanson, a 31-year-old neo-Nazi, ran for the San Francisco Board of Education and received 9,000 votes. Other neo-Nazi candidates ran and lost in Houston (for mayor), in Chicago (for alderman), and Georgia (for governor and lieutenant governor). The notorious white supremacist J.B. Stoner of Georgia ran for several offices in the 1970s and later on a platform calling for the "eradication" of Jews and blacks. His best finish was in the governor's race in 1978, when he received 71,000 votes and came in fourth out of ten candidates. (In 1980 he was convicted for a church bombing in 1958.)

In August 1980, Tom Metzger, a Ku Klux Klan leader and Nazi sympathizer, surprised political analysts by winning the Democratic primary in the 43rd Congressional District in Southern California, the most populous district in the U.S., although he had fewer than 50 volunteers on his staff and less than $10,000 in campaign contributions. As the Democratic Party nominee in the November general election, however, he received only 35,000 votes (14 percent of the total) and was defeated by the Republican incumbent.

In Detroit, Gerald Carlson, a former member of the Ku Klux Klan, the John Birch Society, and the American Nazi Party, who ran a campaign based on a single issue – white "superiority" over blacks and Jews – defeated the official party candidate in the Republican primary in Michigan's 15th Congressional District to face the Democratic incumbent in the fall of 1980. The Michigan Republican Party was so embarrassed by the victory that it asked voters to vote for his Democratic opponent. Carlson went on to gain 53,000 votes (about 32 percent) in the November general election.

On May 6, 1980, Harold Covington, one of the major leaders of the American Nazi Party, ran in the North Carolina Republican primary election for state attorney general, and although campaigning with virtually no money and no neutral media coverage, received 56,000 votes, 42.88 percent of the total, losing by a narrow margin.

The most successful electoral drive was by David Duke, who spent years moving through various neo-Nazi, Ku Klux Klan, and racist groups. The photogenic Duke attempted to sanitize his views, establishing in 1979 the National Association for the Advancement of White People. In 1989 Duke was elected to the Louisiana House of Representatives as a Republican. He lost his campaign for governor in 1991, but pulled 55 percent of white votes.

NEW FORMS. In the United States, Christian Identity became a significant variant of neo-Nazism in the 1970s by merging a racialized version of Protestantism called British Israelism with theories of racial superiority. By claiming that a tribe of Jews migrated to the British Isles and then to the United States, Identity adherents asserted that White Christian Protestants in the U.S. were the true descendants of the biblical Hebrews, the chosen people of God's Covenant. Contemporary Jews were dismissed as fakes. Adherents of Christian Identity, which had been condemned by Catholic and Protestant leaders, usually blended their theology with race hate and antisemitism. Throughout the 1980s, Richard G. Butler's Aryan Nations compound in Idaho served as the most visible racist Identity institution; however, most practitioners worshipped in small halls and private homes in the absence of an organized national religious structure.

Christian Identity theology foresaw an apocalyptic race war between white Christians and inferior Jews and blacks, seen as doing the bidding of Satan, in the End Times prophesied in the New Testament Book of Revelation. This confrontational stance led to violence, such as the 1999 attack by Buford O'Neal Furrow, Jr., who wounded several children and their teachers at a Jewish community center near Los Angeles, and then killed a Filipino-American postal worker. When arrested, Furrow proclaimed his act was a "wake-up call to America to kill Jews".

The murder in Texas in 1998 of James Byrd, Jr., a black man, was in part motivated by the Christian Identity beliefs shared by some of the white attackers who dragged Byrd to death on a chain attached to a pickup truck. Christian Identity beliefs were often acquired through neo-Nazi prison gangs, as in this incident, especially through the Aryan Brotherhood, which operated inside and outside of prisons. Two California brothers with views similar to Christian Identity's carried out 1999 arson attacks on three synagogues and a reproductive services clinic, and murdered a gay couple.

The National Alliance was founded in the mid-1970s by William Pierce, a former supporter of Rockwell and the National Socialist White People's Party. Pierce used a pseudonym to pen two books that became staples of neo-Nazi libraries, *The Turner Diaries* and *Hunter*. The books celebrated the murder of Jews, blacks, and homosexuals as part of a white revolution against what became known in neo-Nazi circles as the "Zionist Occupation Government" (ZOG) in Washington, D.C.

In the 1990s, the National Alliance was the largest and most active neo-Nazi group in the United States. Pierce paid some $250,000 in 1999 to purchase Resistance Records, a race-hate music company that produced and sold CDs and White Power paraphernalia to a mostly young audience. Within a few years the Alliance was collecting over $1 million in annual sales and had more than a dozen full-time staff, as well as active members in over a score of states. The organization saw bitter feuds and near-collapse after Pierce's death in 2002.

White Aryan Resistance (WAR), founded by former California Klan leader Tom Metzger, brought the Third Position form of neo-Nazism to the United States, where it became popular in the late 1980s. The group collapsed after Metzger lost a civil lawsuit stemming from a murderous racial attack by several of his followers. Third Positionist groups such as National Vanguard and Volksfront continued to operate.

Ben Klassen invented the Creativity religion (originally World Church of the Creator) in 1973, and after his death, the organization eventually ended up in the hands of Matt Hale, later jailed for soliciting the assassination of federal judge. A follower of Creativity, Benjamin Nathaniel Smith went on a 1999 shooting spree across Illinois and Indiana. He was an equal-opportunity racist, wounding six Orthodox Jews on their way home from synagogue on a Friday evening, and a man of Taiwanese descent, and killing an African American and an Asian American.

VIOLENT UNDERGROUND. On November 3, 1979, a confrontation between the National Socialist Party of America (NSPA) and the Ku Klux Klan on the one hand, and the Maoist Communist Workers Party on the other, in Greensboro, North Carolina, led to the shooting death of five communists, one of them a Jew, and the wounding of ten others. Fourteen neo-Nazis and KKK members were arrested and charged with five counts of first-degree murder and conspiracy to commit murder, but they were subsequently acquitted.

Following this incident, a number of neo-Nazis and members of right-wing "Patriot" groups began to move underground, while others began to set up armed survivalist and "militia" units. A 1983 shootout involving law enforcement agents and Gordon Kahl, an organizer for the Posse Comitatus wing of this underground movement, prompted neo-Nazi leader Louis Beam to call for "leaderless resistance" against the government. Kahl later died in a stand-off with authorities. Members of one Oklahoma Christian Identity group, Covenant, Sword, and Arm of the Lord (CSA, not coincidentally the initials of the Confederate States of America), began planning and staging attacks, including the 1984 murder by Richard Wayne Snell of a black Arkansas state police officer.

During this period eight persons affiliated with Aryan Nations, the National Alliance, and the KKK formed an underground terror cell called the Order, known internally as the "Bruder Schweigen" (Silent Brotherhood). The Order staged armed robberies, and was responsible for the June 1984 assassination in Denver of Alan Berg, an outspoken Jewish radio talk-show host. The government responded with arrest warrants, rounding up the cell and killing Order founder Robert J. Matthews in a December 1984 shootout. In 1985 the government raided the CSA headquarters. A second Order cell formed in 1986 and used arson attacks to target human rights advocates, before being rounded up by authorities.

The federal government issued conspiracy indictments in 1987 naming several neo-Nazi and Patriot movement leaders. A jury acquitted the defendants, but the incident only added to growing anti-government anger. This increased after two raids were mishandled by government authorities. In August 1992 a raid on the Weaver family, Christian Identity survivalists, at Ruby Ridge, Idaho left the mother and teenage son dead, along with a federal marshal. In April 1993 a standoff at the Branch Davidian compound in Waco, Texas led to a shootout and conflagration in which 74 men, women, and children in the group died. Four federal agents died during the course of the standoff.

On April 19, 1995, the anniversary both of the first battle of the American Revolution and the raid on the Branch Davidian compound, and the day CSA member Snell was executed for murdering a state trooper, Timothy McVeigh carried out the bombing that destroyed the Oklahoma City Federal Building, killing 168 people. McVeigh, a U.S. Army veteran of the 1991 Gulf War, had drifted into neo-Nazi circles, and sold copies of the *Turner Diaries*. Another group, the Aryan Republican Army, staged 22 bank robberies and bombings between 1992 and 1996. The *Turner Diaries* was required reading for members.

Germany

Both states of the divided Germany were effective in combating neo-Nazism. In Communist East Germany, all neo-Nazi parties were banned, while West Germany was quite stringent in its reaction to right- and left-wing terrorism and successful in containing neo-Nazism. However, a terrorist bomb that exploded during Oktoberfest in Munich in 1980, injuring several people, was attributed to a neo-Nazi group. After the reunification of the country a number of neo-Nazi youth gangs arose, especially in the former East Germany, exploiting economic turmoil and racism toward nonwhite immigrant "guest workers" (many of whom had resided in Germany for decades, or had been born there, and were prevented from becoming citizens by restrictive ethnicity-based naturalization laws).

An American neo-Nazi, Gary R. ("Gerhard") Lauck of Lincoln, Nebraska, was a major publisher of neo-Nazi publications and in the late 1970s began to smuggle them into Germany, which had banned them. Lauck was deported from Germany several times for distributing Nazi material; arrested in Denmark in 1995, he was extradited to Germany where he was convicted and jailed for inciting hatred and distributing banned materials.

Before reunification, there were approximately 18,000 members of extreme right-wing groups in West Germany, members of the National Democratic Party (NDP), Neo-Nazi

(NSDAP) and National Freedom groups, and others. After reunification in 1990, especially in the former East, thousands of young adults joined openly neo-Nazi groups. There followed a wave of violent attacks on refugees, immigrants, "guest workers," and Jews. In 1992 and 1993 two attacks left eight Turkish women and girls dead and a number of other family members and friends seriously injured. During this period German officials banned 17 neo-Nazi organizations, but the groups continued to thrive underground. Small groups called freie Kameradschaften (free fellowships) were set up to operate on a regional level. In 2002 a young man, Marinus Schoeberl, was tortured and murdered by neo-Nazi youth north of Berlin in the village of Potzlow. The attackers thought he "looked like a Jew." More than 100 murders by neo-Nazis and their allies occurred between reunification and the year 2006, with some 150 like-minded groups being monitored by government authorities; the number of adherents was estimated to be in the 10,000–25,000 range. At the same time, there were huge demonstrations in Germany against the rise of neo-Nazism and xenophobic attacks, and the number of neo-Nazis was tiny compared to the size of the population.

France

France's collaborationist and antisemitic legacy during World War II was exploited by neo-Nazi groups to gain legitimacy in France in the late 1970s, as was the strong pro-Arab and anti-Israel position concerning the Middle East. Later, the increase in immigrants from Arab and Muslim countries became a major factor.

In 1980 there were several attacks against individuals in the Jewish quarter of Paris in July and August, and a bomb exploded on October 4 in front of the Rue Copernic synagogue, a few minutes walk from the Arc de Triomphe, killing four passers-by, two of them non-Jews and one of them an Israeli woman, and injuring over 20. A telephone caller claimed responsibility on behalf of the European Nationalist Fascists, a neo-Nazi group led by Marc Fredriksen. Two other synagogues, two Jewish schools, and a Jewish war memorial were machine-gunned.

The bombing had political ramifications since it was alleged that 10–20 percent of the 150 members of the European Nationalist Fascists (FNE) were members of the police, and the government was criticized for its failure to stop the perpetrators. Massive demonstrations took place after the bombing.

Sporadic neo-Nazi activity and violence continued over the next twenty years, built around anti-Jewish, anti-Arab, and anti-Muslim bigotry. In addition, antipathy toward Jews from Muslim immigrants also increased, and it was clear that antisemitic conspiracy theories were shared by a range of anti-Jewish groups, not just in France, but across Europe.

In the mid-1990s the Front National de la Jeunesse (National Front for Youth), claiming 12,000 members, pursued a revolutionary nationalist agenda. This tendency was supported by its parent group, the National Front, led by Jean-Marie Le Pen. The racist skinhead movement in France remained small throughout the 1990s, but its list of targets was familiar, including not just blacks, Arabs, and Jews, but also communists and drug addicts. The Charlemagne Hammerskins, however, claimed 1,500 members in the late 1990s. They blended neo-Nazi lore with pagan satanism and distributed printed and online materials promoting race hate, antisemitism, Holocaust denial, and Hitler.

In 2005 France sought to ban all neo-Nazi groups after violent incidents increased from 27 in 2003 to 65 in 2004. French government agencies estimated that such groups had 3,500 members.

United Kingdom

John Tyndall was a major figure in organizing British neofascist groups. He left the League of Empire Loyalists and in 1960 joined elements from the White Defence League to create the British National Party (BNP). Tyndall became a national BNP organizer, and also worked with a paramilitary group established by Colin Jordan. In the 1960s, neo-Nazis in London carried out 34 arson attacks on Jewish institutions. In 1967, the National Front was formed through a merger of the BNP and the League of Empire Loyalists. Tyndall became chairman of the group, which gained consideration as a serious political movement, garnering electoral support in some districts.

There was a significant increase in racial tensions in England during the 1970s, due to the increased waves of African, Caribbean, Indian, Pakistani, and other "Third World" immigrants. Previously, Jews had been more or less secondary targets but this began to change. The NF made a considerable appeal to the British masses as a result of its constant emphasis on racism, on Britain's loss of power and prestige, and the "grand conspiracy" theory that Jews or pro-Zionist non-Jews dominate the world with their liberal and radical policies, and their assertion that "white races" will become extinct through the "mongrelization" and integration policies espoused by black leaders and their Jewish/Zionist allies.

Tyndall left NF in a dispute to form the New National Front, which reclaimed the name British National Party in 1982. When the NF itself went through further splits, the reformed BNP emerged as the leading far-right electoral party in Britain.

The original skinhead subculture emerged in Britain in the 1970s, but was converted into a racist movement in the 1980s by organizers from the British National Front, including "Ian Stuart" (Ian Stuart Donaldson), who was lead singer in the white power band Skrewdriver. Beginning in 1992 a militant neo-Nazi group named Combat 18, established to provide security for the BNP, was responsible for a wave of street-fighting violence. In April 1999, bombings targeted the black community of Brixton, the Asian community of Brick Lane, and a gay bar in Soho where three died. In all 139 people were injured. David Copeland, active with the neo-Nazi British National Socialist Movement, told police he had acted alone, but had tried blaming the bombings on Combat 18, which he described as a "bunch of yobs." Another neo-Nazi group, the White Wolves, had also been suspected of the bombings. Copeland apparently learned how to make the bombs from Internet instructions. Nick Griffin, educated at Cambridge and trained as a leader of the National Front, took over the British National Party from Tyndall in 1999. In recent years the BNP has combined racism with anti-European Union sentiment to gain a small but significant degree of public support.

Russia

Russian nationalists and neo-Nazis began to emerge and intersect after the collapse of the Soviet Union. Pamyat (Memory) was formed from a number of smaller groups around 1980. It split up in 1985. The National Patriotic Front/Pamyat was formed in 1987 but became inactive in the late 1990s. The Russian National Union, founded by Konstantin Kasimovsky with Aleksei Vdovin in a leadership role, split off from Pamyat in the early 1990s. The group became the Russian National Socialist Party in 1998. A similar group, also split off from Pamyat and the most popular such organization, is Russian National Unity, led by Aleksandr Barkashov. Some followers have used violence, and took credit for the 1998 bomb that exploded outside a synagogue in Moscow, injuring three. The organization began splitting in 2005 as new leaders started to emerge and followers chose sides. The National Front Party, led by Ilya Lazarenko, is more open in celebrating the Nazi heritage, as is the tiny Werewolf Legion, known for terrorist attacks.

In January of 2006, Russian President Vladimir Putin acknowledged that antisemitism and the growth of neo-Nazism in Russia were problems when he attended ceremonies marking the sixtieth anniversary of the liberation of Auschwitz. Also in 2006, Moscow's police chief promised to deploy officers to protect synagogues after a 20-year-old man was arrested for charging into the city's Chabad Bronnaya Synagogue with a knife, shouting "I will kill Jews." He managed to stab at least eight people. Russian newspapers noted that the young man had been reading a book about the Jews betraying Russia.

In a 2005 report for the International Bureau of Human Rights, Semyon Charny estimated that there were more than 50,000 neo-Nazi skinheads in Russia and more than a dozen neo-Nazi organizations there.

Scandinavia

In Scandinavia a number of groups emerged that oscillated between national socialist electoral activity and neo-Nazi activism: in Denmark, Danmarks Nationalsocialistiske Bevegelse (National Socialist Movement of Denmark); in Finland, Blood and Honour; in Norway, Norges Nasjonalsosialistiske Bevegelse (National Socialist Movement of Norway), Blood and Honour, and Vigrid (a branch of the National Alliance); in Sweden, Nationalsocialistisk Front (National Socialist Front), Svenska Motståndsrörelsen (Swedish Resistance Movement), Vitt Ariskt Motstånd (White Aryan Resistance), Riksfronten (Reich Front), Ariska Brödraskapet (Aryan Brotherhood), and a branch of the U.S.-based Creativity Movement.

In Sweden, the number of active neo-Nazis has fluctuated between 100 and 1,000, with at least ten times as many supporters. There were violent acts, such as the murder of John Hron in 1995 by neo-Nazi skinheads. In Norway, a small national socialist skinhead movement has flourished.

The Future

It appears that neo-Nazism has become a permanent fixture on the global political scene. Limiting the growth of neo-Nazi movements in the West is the historical memory of Hitler and his SS, who spread war and genocide across Europe. The main forms of postwar neo-Nazism are xenophobic nationalism and National Socialism, but increasingly there are hybrids similar to the interwar clerical fascism. These theocratic forms of fascism have already produced several neo-Nazi movements. It is possible that if militant religious fundamentalism, especially within Islam, continues to expand, there will more intersections with fascist and Nazi ideas, a process that is already producing lethal threats to societies around the world. Whether these could ever approach or surpass the destruction of Hitler's Nazi movement cannot be predicted.

[Chip Berlet and Jack Nusan Porter (2nd ed.)]

ADD. BIBLIOGRAPHY: M. Barkun, *Religion and the Racist Right* (1997); C. Berlet and M.N. Lyons, *Right-Wing Populism in America* (2000); C. Berlet, in *Home-Grown Hate* (2004), 19–47; H.G. Betz, *Radical Right-Wing Populism in Western Europe* Immerfall (eds.), *The New Politics of the Right*; K.M. Blee, *Inside Organized Racism* (2002); A. Braun and S. Scheinberg (eds.), *The Extreme Right* (1997); D. Burghart (ed.), *Soundtracks to the White Revolution* (1999); S. Diamond, *The Nazi Movement in the United States, 1924–1941* (1974); S. Epstein, "Extreme Right Electoral Upsurges in Western Europe," in *Analysis of Current Trends In Antisemitism*, No. 8 (1996); R.S. Ezekiel, *The Racist Mind* (1995); N. Goodrick-Clarke, *Black Sun* (2002); M.S. Hamm, *American Skinheads* (1994); J. Jamin, "The Extreme Right in Europe: Fascist or Mainstream?" in *Public Eye*, 19:1 (2005); J. Kaplan, *Radical Religion in America* (1997); J. Kaplan and L. Weinberg, *The Emergence of a Euro-American Radical Right* (1998); J. Kaplan and T. Bjørgo (eds.), *Nation and Race* (1998); W. Laqueur, *Fascism* (1996); D. Levitas, *The Terrorist Next Door* (2002); G.E. McCuen (ed.), *The Racist Reader* (1974); H. Meyer, "Worries of Anti-Semitism Spread in Russia" ("Rising Neo-Nazism in Russia"), Associated Press, January 13, 2006; R. Miles and A. Phizacklea (eds.), *Racism and Political Action in Britain* (1979); C. Mudde, *The Ideology of the Extreme Right* (2000); J.N. Porter, in *The Sociology of American Jews* (1980), 175–182; J.N. Porter, *The Genocidal Mind* (2006); W.H. Schmaltz, *Hate* (1999); See also online news archives: *New York Times; Los Angeles Times; Chicago Sun-Times*, *BBC News*, *Reuters*, *Guardian* (London), *Sunday Telegraph* (London), CNN. Online organizational archives: Anne Frank Stichting, Leiden University; Anti-Defamation League; Antisemitism and Xenophobia Today, Institute for Jewish Policy Research; Nizkor Project; Searchlight; Simon Wiesenthal Center; Southern Poverty Law Center; Stephen Roth Institute for the Study of Contemporary Antisemitism and Racism, Tel Aviv University.

NEO-ORTHODOXY, name of the modernistic faction of German *Orthodoxy, first employed in a derogatory sense by its adversaries. Its forerunners were to be found among the more conservative disciples of Moses *Mendelssohn and N.H.

*Wessely, like Solomon *Pappenheim and Naḥman b. Simḥah Barash. At the time of the controversy over the *Hamburg Temple (1818), the participants in the campaign against the reformers included some rabbis who adopted a stance similar to that later advocated by the Neo-Orthodox; for example those of Amsterdam, Hanau, Rawicz, and other communities, who produced the polemic, *Elleh Divrei ha-Berit* (1819). Other forerunners were the new Orthodox preacher of Hamburg, Isaac *Bernays; Jeremiah *Heinemann (1788–1855) of Berlin, the editor of *Jedidja* (1817–31); and Solomon Plessner (1797–1883) of Breslau, the author of various apologetic works.

However, the ideology of Neo-Orthodoxy crystallized later and its institutions were only established during the second half of the 19th century. In essence, the movement is connected with Samson Raphael *Hirsch and his doctrine of *Torah im derekh ereẓ* ("Torah together with the conduct of life," meaning in this context secular culture), which he expressed in his major writings. In 1851 he became rabbi of the Orthodox separatist community of Frankfurt and was able to realize his ideas and plans in a suitable environment. During the second half of the 19th century, the rabbinical leadership had already suffered defeat in the campaign against reformers and assimilationists. The small groups which remained faithful to tradition referred to themselves as "remnants." At the same time, the rising tide of the Reform movement was curbed. The process of Jewish integration into general society was well advanced and was no longer conditional on their "religious" reform. Moreover, the radical line adopted by such Reform leaders as Abraham *Geiger and Samuel *Holdheim during those years had alienated important elements among the non-Orthodox (Leopold *Zunz, Zacharias *Frankel, and others).

The development of a trend combining features from both *Reform and *Orthodoxy thus became feasible. From the Reform movement it adopted the aim of integration within modern society, not only on utilitarian grounds but also through the acceptance of its scale of values, aiming at creating a symbiosis between traditional Orthodoxy and modern German-European culture; both in theory and in practice this meant the abandonment of Torah study for its own sake (as in the classical yeshivah) and adopting instead an increased concentration on practical *halakhah*. Other Reform features were the replacement of Hebrew by German as the language of Jewish culture; the acceptance of the Haskalah program in educational matters; the struggle for emancipation and the positive appreciation of the Exile; the exchange of the material idea of "Return to Zion" for that of the "Universal Mission"; German patriotism; the renouncement of a particular Jewish appearance (involving readiness to cut off the beard and the side-locks, to uncover the head when not at worship, etc.); the education of women, including their participation in religious life and their political emancipation; the abolition of the coercive powers of the community; and the acceptance of the liberal concept of freedom of conscience. From Orthodoxy the faction took: dogmatism (*emunat ḥakhamim*, "faith in the rabbis"); reservation toward the preoccupations of the Wissenschaft des Judentums and opposition to the principle of freedom of research; the acceptance of the authority of the Shulḥan Arukh and the traditions and customs of the late 18th-century German communities; acceptance of the Orthodox position on laws which came into being as a result of its campaign against the reformers, such as those against the demands for changes in synagogue usage; excessive strictness in the observation of the precepts and customs; and acquiescence in the disruption of the Jewish community and the sectarian nature of those remaining true to Orthodoxy. The second most important leader of this trend was Azriel (Israel) *Hildesheimer, who founded a rabbinical seminary (1873) and broke the monopoly of the non-Orthodox in Jewish studies. He thus made possible the integration of the intelligentsia into the neo-Orthodox circle, in contrast to Hirsch, whose system was tailored to the requirements of the ordinary community members, the so-called *ba'alei batim*. Hildesheimer was more attached to ancient rabbinic Judaism than Hirsch and his attitude to Jewish affairs in general was more positive, while his approach to general culture was less enthusiastic. As a result of this, the role Hildesheimer played in world Jewish affairs led to the creation of contacts between the German Neo-Orthodoxy, East European Jewry, and the *Ḥibbat Zion movement. In 1876 a law (the *Austrittsgesetz*) was passed which enabled an individual to secede from a church or community without changing his religious affiliation. This facilitated the secession (*Austritt*) of Orthodox minorities from communities where they considered that coexistence with the reformist leadership was impossible. In many places this situation induced the reformers to make far-reaching concessions to the Orthodox minority. German Orthodoxy thus became split over the question of whether the new law should be exploited in order that they might secede from all communities administered by reformers. To Hirsch, the *Austritt* concept became a supreme religious principle, while Seligmann Baer (or Dov Baer) *Bamberger, his Orthodox opponent, showed reserve toward both the modernism and the extremist separatism of Hirsch, and preferred to preserve the unity of the community. After some time, German Orthodoxy was again divided on another issue: the attitude toward *Zionism. One section joined the *Agudat Israel movement, while the other showed a preference for the *Mizrachi and *Ha-Po'el ha-Mizrachi and later for the *Po'alei Agudat Israel.

BIBLIOGRAPHY: (Note: there is no critical work on the subject.) J. Wohlgemuth, in: *Festschrift… David Hoffmann* (1914), 435–58 (Ger. section); L. Ginzburg, *Students, Scholars and Saints* (1928), 252–62; M. Wiener, *Juedische Religion im Zeitalter der Emanzipation* (1933); O. Wolfsberg, in: *Sinai*, 4 (1939), 164–82; 14 (1944), 65–81; idem, in: Y.L. Fishman (ed), *Sefer ha-Mizrachi* (1946), 150–68 (second pagination); S. Gronemann, *Zikhronotav shel Yekke* (1946); S. Japhet, in: HJ, 10 (1948), 99–122; J. Rosenheim, *ibid.*, 135–46; H. Schwab, *History of Orthodox Jewry in Germany* (1950); I. Heinemann, *Ta'amei ha-Mitzvot be-Sifrut Yisrael*, 2 (1956), 91ff.; idem, in: HJ, 10 (1948), 123–34; 13 (1951), 29–54; J. Immanuel (ed.), *Ha-Rav Shimshon Rafa'el Hirsch, Mishnato ve-Shitato* (1962); B. Kurzweil, in: *Haaretz* (Sept. 26, 1965).

[Moshe Shraga Samet]

NEOPLATONISM, the system elaborated by Plotinus and his pupil Porphyry on the basis of antecedent Middle Platonic and neo-Pythagorean developments. The system was modified by their successors, the main post-Plotinian currents and schools of late antiquity being (according to K. Praechter): the Syrian school founded by Iamblichus; the school of Pergamum (Sallust, Julian); the school of Athens (Plutarch, Syrianus, Proclus, Damascius); the school of Alexandria (Hierocles, Hermias, Ammonius and his followers: the pagans, Asclepius and Olympiodorus, and the Christians, Philoponus, Elias, David, and Stephanus); and the Neoplatonists of the West (Macrobius, Chalcidius, Boethius). In the Middle Ages Neoplatonism survived in the Latin West (Johannes Scotus Erigena) and the Byzantine East (Michael Psellus) and within the Arabo-Hebraic cultural sphere, and it underwent a revival during the Renaissance (Gemistos Plethon in the Byzantine East; Marsilio Ficino, *Pico della Mirandola, and Giordano Bruno in the West).

Neoplatonism postulates the derivation by a process of emanation of a hierarchically ordered series of spheres of being, leading from an ineffable and unqualified first principle (the One) to the material world. The "descent" is associated with increasing determination and multiplicity (imperfection). Although matter at the lowest rank in the scale of being is the principle of evil, the material world, as a reflection of the intelligible, possesses goodness and beauty (cf. *Gnosticism), and by contemplation of it the human soul ascends to the spiritual world. The human soul, being spiritual and self-subsistent, is independent of the body and having descended from the supernal world, reverts to its source by means of ethical and intellectual purification (or by theurgy; e.g., Iamblichus). The stages of ascent were commonly designated (after Proclus) the *via purgativa* (purification), *via illuminativa* (illumination), and *via unitiva* (union), the highest stage, a kind of *unio mystica* (mystical union) and apotheosis, being the sole means by which the One is apprehended. Individuation and investiture of the soul with a body is devalorized; release from the fetters of the body in ecstasy or in death is equivalent to salvation, this philosophical soteriology tending toward combination with a doctrine of metempsychosis.

Neoplatonism is thus seen to be a religious movement and a doctrine of salvation as well as a philosophical system. As such, it was potentially an antagonist and an ally of the monotheistic faiths. Ancient Neoplatonism (excluding the school of Alexandria) was hostile to Christianity: Porphyry and Julian wrote refutations of Christianity; Iamblichus, Proclus, and Damascius were implacable opponents of Christianity. Indeed, Neoplatonism as a philosophical interpretation of pagan mythology (e.g., Iablichus and Proclus) represents the dying gasp of ancient paganism. The fundamental postulates of Neoplatonism conflict with those of the monotheistic faiths: an impersonal first principle, rejection of creation and revelation, the conception of man as essentially soul, and the attendant soteriology-eschatology (including metempsychosis) involving submergence of the individual soul in the universal soul. Nevertheless, for monotheistic philosophers the contradictions were not insurmountable. In fact, the method of figurative interpretation cultivated by ancient Neoplatonists (after the Pythagoreans and Stoics) in order to identify pagan mythological themes with philosophical ideas (Proclus, for example, identified the henads of his system with the traditional gods) was employed by monotheistic philosophers in order to read their neoplatonic doctrines into the text of Scripture. The ladder of Jacob's dream was thus interpreted as a symbol of the soul's ascent (e.g., by Ibn Gabirol; see A. Altman, *Studies in Religious Philosophy and Mysticism* (1969), 54–55; and A. Nygren, *Agape and Eros* (1953^2), 230, 375, 441). Creation became a metaphor for eternal procession. Revelation and prophecy were discussed in terms reminiscent of the *unio mystica*. This identification was not without some basis in ancient Neoplatonism either, if one considers the aspect of grace or divine initiative implicit in *Enneads* 5:3, 17 and 5:5, 8, or the use of the Chaldean Oracles and Orphic Hymns by Porphyry and Iamblichus. Assimilation to the divine, the goal of philosophy according to the neoplatonic introductions to Aristotle of the Alexandria school, resonated with similar ideals of the monotheistic traditions. The deep spirituality of Neoplatonism promoted the kind of synthesis with religious feeling that finds moving expression in Ibn Gabirol's poem, *Keter Malkhut*.

In order to grasp the character of Neoplatonism as it was transmitted to the medieval world of Judaism and Islam, it is necessary to understand that it was closely bound with much of the religious and pseudo-scientific heritage of late antiquity (alchemy), Hermetism (see *Hermetic Writings), magic, theurgy. Also, Neoplatonism was not simply an amplification of *Plato. Plotinus admitted into his system those aspects of Aristotelianism (also Pythagoreanism and *Stoicism) which met its requirements. Porphyry went even further and initiated the reception of *Aristotle's lecture courses into the Neoplatonic curriculum. The school of Alexandria devoted much of its labors to commentaries upon Aristotle. The thesis that the views of Plato and Aristotle coincided, if properly understood, a theme traceable to Ammonius Saccas, the teacher of Plotinus, was embraced by Porphyry and influenced the course of Neoplatonism and its absorption within the Arabo-Hebraic milieu (cf. al-*Fārābī's *On the Harmony of the Opinions of the Two Sages, the Divine Plato and Aristotle*).

While reception of Neoplatonism in the medieval Latin West was mainly confined to Proclus and Pseudo-Dionysius, the Arabo-Hebraic milieu was saturated by numerous currents. Plotinus was conveyed in the guise of the *Theology of Aristotle* (a paraphrase of parts of Books 4–6 of the *Enneads*), through other paraphrases ascribed to "the Greek Sage," and a work entitled *The Divine Science* (J. van Ess, in bibl., 334ff.). The *Theology of Aristotle* is extant in a shorter (vulgate) and longer version, the latter preserved in an Arabic manuscript in Hebrew characters (in Leningrad). This longer version was translated (on the basis of a Damascus manuscript) into Hebrew and Italian by a Cypriot Jewish physician, Moses Arovas, who was also instrumental in having it rendered into Latin (S.M. Stern, in bibl., 59 n. 4, 79 n. 1).

Underlying the longer version of the *Theology of Aristotle* is another Aristotle pseudograph discovered by S.M. Stern and called by him "Ibn Ḥasdāy's Neoplatonist" (it was incorporated by *Ibn Ḥasdai in his *Ben ha-Melekh ve-ha-Nazir; see Altmann and Stern, in bibl., 95ff.; Stern, in bibl.). (On knowledge of Porphyry's work in the medieval world of Islam, see J. van Ess, in bibl., 338; R. Walzer in *Encyclopaedia of Islam*, 2 (1965), 948–50.) Proclus' *Elements of Theology* was transmitted in the guise of the Arabic *Kitāb al-ḥayr al-maḥḍ* ("Book of the Pure Good"), known in the West as *Liber de causis* and generally understood to be a work by Aristotle, and three propositions of the *Elements of Theology* have been recovered in Arabic. Proclus' work *On the Eternity of the Universe* was also known. (For the transmission of works by Proclus, see J. van Ess, in bibl., 339ff.; H.D. Saffrey, in *Miscellanea Mediaevalia*, 2 (1963), 267ff.; and R. Walzer in *Encyclopaedia of Islam*, 1 (1960), 1340.) Another pseudo-Aristotelian work of neoplatonic character was the *Liber de pomo*, which was extremely popular and available in Arabic, Persian, and Hebrew (see J. Kraemer, in *Studi orentalistici in onore di Giorgio Levi della Vida*, 1 (1956), 484–506). Neoplatonic ideas are also associated with pre-Socratics (particularly Pythagoras and Empedocles) in Arabic doxographic and gnomological collections (e.g., Ṣāʿid al-Andalusi's *Ṭabaqāt al-umam* and *al-Shahrastānī's al-Milal wa al-niḥal*). *Empedocles in neoplatonic dress is also preserved in *The Book of Five Substances*, of which a Hebrew translation from Arabic is extant (D. Kaufmann, *Studien ueber Salomon ibn Gabirol* (1899), 16ff.). Teachings of the school of Alexandria were transmitted mainly by Syriac-speaking Christians. The accommodation of Christian beliefs in that school (e.g., by Ammonius; see Westerink, in bibl. xii–xxv) may have served as a model for adjustment to religious belief on the part of Islamic and Jewish philosophers.

Medieval Islamic and Jewish Neoplatonism is not confined to philosophers. In both Judaism and Islam Neoplatonism entered the mystical stream. One finds such influence, for example, in the later Sufi works of al-*Ghazāli (the end of his *Mishkāt al-anwār*); it permeated Jewish kabbalistic circles in Spain and Provence, transforming an earlier gnostic tradition, and had an impact upon the German pietists (Scholem, Mysticism, 117). Israeli's *Chapter on the Elements* ("The Mantua Text"), largely based upon "Ibn Ḥasdāy's Neoplatonist," was studied by the Gerona kabbalists, attracted by the similarity between its emanationist scheme and their own system of *Sefirot*, and it was commented upon by *Azriel of Gerona (*Perush ha-Aggadot*; see Altman and Stern, in bibl., 130–2; Stern in bibl., 61).

Isaac *Israeli is the fountainhead of Jewish Neoplatonism. He defines philosophy, following the neoplatonic introductions to Aristotle, as assimilation to God according to human capacity (from Plato's *Theatetus* 176b; see Altmann and Stern, in bibl., 28ff., 197). Ascent of the human soul to the divine is described according to Proclus' three stages (*ibid.*, 185ff.), the ultimate stage depicted as becoming angelic or divine, an experience to which he applies the term *devekut*, thus anticipating its employment by later Jewish philosophers and mystics (Altmann and Stern, in bibl., 190). The famous Plotinus passage on his own ecstatic union with the One (*Enneads*, 4:8, 1) may have inspired Israeli; quoted in the *Theology of Aristotle* and in the *Rasāʾil Ikhwān al-Safāʾ* ("Epistles of the *Brethren of Sincerity"), it is also referred to by Moses *Ibn Ezra, Ibn *Gabirol, and Shem Tov ibn *Falaquera (Altmann and Stern, in bibl., 191–2). The neoplatonic doctrine concerning the unknowability of the first principle is expressed in Israeli's thesis that only God's existence (or quoddity: *anniyya, ḥaliyya*) is knowable, and not his essence (quiddity: *mahiyya*), a distinction perpetuated by *Baḥya ibn Paquda, *Joseph ben Ẓaddik, *Judah Halevi, and Abraham *Ibn Daud (Altmann and Stern, in bibl., 21–23).

The transplantation of Jewish thought to Andalusia is marked by an initial neoplatonic direction inaugurated by Ibn Gabirol. His *Mekor Ḥayyim* is unique in that it sets forth a philosophical system of neoplatonic tincture without any admixture of Jewish teaching. Significantly, the only authority named is Plato. Characteristically, the goal of human existence is the conjunction (*ittiṣāl, applicatio*) of the human soul with the supernal world through knowledge and action, i.e., intellectual and ethical purification (1:2; Arabic fragments published by S. Pines in *Tarbiz*, 27 (1958), 225–6). The fruit of the study of philosophy is said to be liberation from death and conjunction with the source of life (5:43). In the neoplatonic manner, knowledge of the First Essence is precluded because it transcends everything and is incommensurable with the intellect (1:5; Pines, *ibid.*, 224–5). Like Plotinus, Ibn Gabirol tends to rely upon concrete imagery from the world of senses in order to explain suprasensous phenomena. But the insertion of will (*irāda, voluntas*) after the First Essence and his universal hylomorphism set his system apart from that of Plotinus.

Though the impact of the *Mekor Ḥayyim* was greater upon Christian scholastic philosophy than it was in the Jewish philosophical tradition, it did exert some influence in Jewish circles. Moses ibn Ezra quoted it in his *Arugat ha-Bosem* and a Hebrew epitome was made by Falaquera. Also, Ibn Gabirol's views are quoted by Abraham *Ibn Ezra in his commentaries, from which it can be seen how Ibn Gabirol bridged between his Neoplatonism and Judaism through figurative biblical interpretation.

Ibn Gabirol's successors do not evince his depth or originality. Baḥya ibn Paquda combines commonplace neoplatonic themes (e.g., God's absolute unity as distinct from the relative unity of this world) with his mystical pietism. The anonymous (Pseudo-*Baḥya) *Kitāb Maʿānī al-Nafs* treats its main theme of psychology in a neoplatonic manner. The soul is a spiritual substance whose home is the supernal world. In its descent it assimilates impressions from the celestial spheres and the zones of the elements (a gnostic-Hermetic notion), and it reascends by means of ethical and intellectual purification, whereas evil souls may be confined to the region beneath the heavens (cf. Altmann and Stern, in bibl., 114). There are also neoplatonic elements in *Abraham b. Ḥiyya's writings (his theory of emanation and doctrine of metempsychosis), and Joseph ibn Ẓaddik makes a common neoplatonic motif – that man is a microcosm – the theme of his work (*Ha-Olam ha-Katan*); but no one, aside from Ibn Gabirol, is as deeply committed to a neoplatonic world view as is Abraham ibn Ezra, even as regards such sensitive subjects as creation and prophecy. Also to be considered is Judah Halevi, whose notion of "the divine influence" (*al-Amr al-Ilāhi/ha-inyan ha-Elohi*) may be of neoplatonic origin and whose idea of the God of Abraham is said to have been "conceived metaphysically in terms of the neoplatonic idea of God" (Guttmann, Philosophies, 133).

The Aristotelian reaction in the Islamic world (*Averroes) is paralleled on the Jewish side, where in the middle of the 12th century Aristotelianism begins to displace Neoplatonism as the regnant system. However, despite Ibn Daud's strictures against Ibn Gabirol and the authoritative opinion of *Maimonides in his disesteem for Israeli, neglect of Ibn Gabirol, and contempt for popular neoplatonic works, Neoplatonism did not entirely lose its appeal for Jewish thinkers. In fact, Ibn Ḥasdai respected Israeli, as did Falaquera. Furthermore, Aristotelianism was itself thoroughly suffused with neoplatonic themes. Maimonides was far from untouched by neoplatonic influence. Words for emanation occur approximately 90 times in the first two parts of the *Guide* (D.H. Haneth, in *Tarbiz*, 23 (1952), 178). Neoplatonic traces are also discernible in his description of knowledge in terms of light and lightning metaphors (from *Avicenna or *Avempace: Pines, *Guide of the Perplexed*, civ–cv), his insistence upon denying positive attributes of God, his placing limitations upon human knowledge, and perhaps the idea of assimilation to the divine at the end of the *Guide* (3:54).

The last work in the tradition of Jewish Neoplatonism is Judah *Abrabanel's *Dialoghi di amore*, written in the atmosphere of the Renaissance revival of Neoplatonism in the manner of contemporary discussions of the *Symposium* and love treatises (see J.C. Nelson, *Renaissance Theory of Love* (1958), passim). Love is a universal unifying force. The neoplatonic One and the theory of emanation are ascribed to Plato. Divine intellect (wisdom) emanates from God as light emanates from the sun, and this intellect is the creator of the world (cf. *Enneads*, 5:9, 3), containing all essences or forms in a simple and unified way (S. Caramella (ed.), *Dialoghi d'amore* (1929), 348). Judah Abrabanel was clearly influenced by Ibn Gabirol, whom he mentions by name along with his work (*ibid.*, 246).

BIBLIOGRAPHY: Guttmann, Philosophies, index; Husik, Philosophy, index; A. Altmann and S.M. Stern, *Isaac Israeli* (1958); J. van Ess, in: K. Flasch (ed.), *Parusia* (1965); P. Merlan, *Monopsychism, Mysticism and Metaconsciousness* (1963); idem, *From Platonism to Neoplatonism* (1960^2); R. Klibansky, *The Continuity of the Platonic Tradition* (1953^2); L.G. Westerink, *Anonymous Prolegomena to Platonic Philosophy* (1962); A. Altmann, in: *Tarbiz*, 27 (1958), 501–7; S.M. Stern, in: *Oriens*, 13–14 (1961), 58–120; A.H. Armstrong, *The Cambridge History of Later Greek and Early Medieval Philosophy* (1967); G. Scholem, in: *Eranos-Jahrbuch 1964*, 33 (1965), 9–50; K. Praechter, *Richtungen und Schulen im Neuplatonismus* (1910); J. Schlanger, *La philosophie de Salomon ibn Gabirol* (1968).

[Joel Kraemer]

NE'OT MORDEKHAI (Heb. נְאוֹת מָרְדְּכַי; "Pastures of Mordecai"), kibbutz in northern Israel, 5 mi. (8 km.) S.E. of *Kiryat Shemonah. When the village was founded in 1946, Arabs launched an attack and two of the volunteers who were helping set up the first huts were killed. The founding members were from Czechoslovakia, Austria, and Germany. In 1970 the kibbutz had 625 inhabitants, dropping to 489 in 2002. Originally affiliated with Ha-Kibbutz ha-Me'uḥad, Ne'ot Mordekhai decided, after the 1951 split in the movement, to remain outside any kibbutz federation, thus becoming the only unaffiliated kibbutz in the country. Kibbutz farming included field crops, fruit orchards, turkeys, and beehives; it also operated the Naot shoe factory, Naot Toys, and Palrig, manufacturing, marketing, and exporting polyethylene and polypropylene. The kibbutz is named after the Argentinian Zionist Mordecai Rozovsky.

[Efraim Orni / Shaked Gilboa (2nd ed.)]

NEPHILIM (Heb. נְפִילִים), a race of giants said to have dwelt in pre-Israelite Canaan (Num. 13:33). Genesis 6:1–2 relates that the "sons of gods," i.e., divine or angelic beings, took mortal wives; verse 4 continues, "It was then, and later too, that the Nephilim appeared [lit., were] on earth – when the divine beings cohabited with the daughters of men, who bore them offspring. They were the heroes [Heb. *gibborim*] of old, the men of renown." This could mean that the Nephilim were contemporaneous, but not identical, with the offspring of divine beings and earthly women, who were called *gibborim* (so, e.g., Morgenstern, in HUCA 14 (1939), 85ff.). The above translation, however, follows an ancient tradition in equating the Nephilim and the *gibborim* as offspring of the union of *angels and mortals.

In apocryphal writings of the Second Temple period this fragmentary narrative was elaborated and reinterpreted. The angels were then depicted as rebels against God: lured by the charms of women, they "fell" (Heb, *nfl.* נפל), defiled their heavenly purity, and introduced all manner of sinfulness to earth. Their giant offspring were wicked and violent; the Flood was occasioned by their sinfulness. (None of these ideas is in the biblical text.) Because of their evil nature, God decreed that the Nephilim should massacre one another, although according to another view most of them perished in the Flood. One version asserts that the evil spirits originally issued from the bodies of the slain giants. These giants, or their offspring, are identified as Nephilim (See I En. 6–10, 15–16; Jub. 7:21ff.). As this dualistic myth does not appear in the apocalypses of Baruch and Esdras nor in the *aggadah* of the talmudic period, it was apparently rejected as incompatible with Jewish monotheism. The "sons of God" are explained in the Targum to Genesis

6:4 and the Midrash (Gen. R. 26:5) as young aristocrats who married the daughters of commoners. The Targum renders both *gibborim* and Nephilim by *gibbaraya*; the Midrash (Gen. R. 26:7) lists seven names applied to giants. The Babylonian Talmud mentions the names of Shamhazzai, Uzza, and Uzziel, the leaders of the fallen *angels in Enoch, but does not say that they were angels: *Yoma* 67b alludes to the sins of Uzza and Uzziel; *Niddah* 61a states that Sihon and Og were descendants of Shamhazzai. In Deuteronomy 3:11 *Og is described as a giant, and this theme was developed to a large degree in aggadic legend. In post-talmudic literature (cf. Rashi, Yoma 67b) the long-suppressed myth came to the surface again. The Palestinian Targum gives the orthodox rendering of Genesis 6:1, but translates verse 4 as: "Shamhazzai and Uzziel fell from heaven and were on earth in those days" – identifying the Nephilim as the fallen angels rather than their children. The same identification is found in a late Midrash, which calls the fallen angels Uzza and Uzziel; another passage in the same document says the Nephilim were descendants of Cain (*Aggadat Bereshit*, ed. S. Buber, introd., p. 38). The Zohar (1:58a) also identifies the Nephilim with the fallen angels. The standard medieval Bible commentators generally followed the classical *aggadah* in rejecting the mythological interpretation and asserting that the marriages in Genesis 6 were human. Some variant opinions about the "sons of God" are offered – e.g., that their distinction was not only social, but physical and even moral, and that the offspring were called Nephilim because they "fell short" of their fathers in these respects (Naḥmanides, Abrabanel).

BIBLIOGRAPHY: U. Cassuto, in: *Sefer ha-Yovel… J.H. Hertz* (1943), 35–44; B.J. Bamberger, *Fallen Angels* (1952), 3–59; H.L. Ginsberg, in: EM, 5 (1968), 896–7 (incl. bibl.).

[Bernard J. Bamberger]

NEPPI, HANANEL (Grazziadio; 1759–1863), Italian rabbi and physician. Neppi was born in Ferrara and studied under Jacob Moses *Ayash and Solomon Lampronti. He was a rabbi in Ferrara, and represented his community at the *Assembly of Jewish Notables called by Napoleon in Paris (1806). In 1822 he settled in Cento, where he was rabbi until his death. (The inscription on his tombstone was engraved on a wall of the Cento synagogue.)

His works include *Zekher Ẓaddikim li-Verakhah*, a biographical and bibliographical lexicon of earlier Jewish scholars, modeled on the *Shem ha-Gedolim* of Ḥ.J.D. *Azulai and printed together with the *Toledot Gedolei Yisrael* of Mordecai Samuel *Ghirondi (1853); *Livyat Ḥen*, a collection of responsa in six volumes, in manuscripts, some of which were printed by Yare (1908); sermons (in Mss.). An ardent student of Kabbalah, Hananel was styled "*ḥakham ḥen*" by his contemporaries. A catalog of his library was published at Lemberg in 1873.

BIBLIOGRAPHY: Ghirondi-Neppi, 115–6; Mortara, Indice; Y. Jare, in: *Festschrift… A. Harkavy* (1908), 470.

[Shlomo Simonsohn]

NERGAL-SHAREZER (Heb. נֵרְגַל שַׂר־אֶצֶר, נֵרְגַל שׂ(שׂ)רְאֶצֶר Akk. *dNergal šar-uṣur* ("Nergal protect the king!"), classical: Neriglissar), high-ranking official (*Rab Mag*) of Nebuchadnezzar (Jer. 39:3, 13). Nergal-Sharezer took part in the siege and conquest of Jerusalem in 587 B.C.E. He is probably identical with Neriglissar, a son-in-law of Nebuchadnezzar, the circumstances of whose succession to Evil-Merodach as king of Babylon are unknown, and who reigned from 560 to 556 B.C.E.

BIBLIOGRAPHY: B.H. Langdon, *Die neubabylonischen Koenigsinschriften* (1912), 208–19; D.J. Wiseman, *Chronicles of the Chaldaean Kings* (1956), 37ff.; I. Ephal, in: EM, 5 (1968), 926–7.

NERIAH (Menkin), MOSHE ẒEVI (1913–1995), Israeli rabbi and *rosh yeshivah*. Neriah was born in Lodz, Poland. His father, R. Petahiah Menkin, later served as rabbi in various towns in Belorussia. At the age of 13, Neriah studied at the clandestine yeshivah in Minsk, and later in Shklov. In 1930 he immigrated to Ereẓ Israel to study in the Merkaz Ha-Rav Yeshivah established by Rabbi A.I. Kook, and while still there took a prominent part in the *Bnei Akiva movement, formulating its educational program and editing its monthly *Zera'im*. He received *semikhah* from Rabbi J.M. *Ḥarlap. Neriah was a youth delegate to the 20th and 21st Zionist Congresses. In 1940, he founded the Bnei Akiva Yeshivah in Kefar ha-Ro'eh, where he introduced many original educational principles which opened a new chapter in Torah education in Israel, including youth camps attached to the yeshivah. From this yeshivah there developed a network of some 20 Bnei Akiva yeshivot.

Neriah was particularly active in spreading Torah education, conducting study courses in Talmud over the radio, and lecturing extensively. A prolific writer, he devoted himself to halakhic problems connected with the emergence of the State, contributing articles to *Dat u-Medinah* and publishing *inter alia Milḥemet Shabbat* on the right to wage war on the Sabbath; *Kehal Gerim* on conversion; *Mishmeret Yiḥudenu* on the "Who is a Jew?" question; and *Ki Sheshet Yamim Asah Ha-Shem* on the theological aspects of the Six-Day War. Following the reorganization of the educational system, he was elected to the Seventh Knesset in 1969, where he devoted himself particularly to questions of education, but was not a candidate for the Eighth Knesset.

In 1973 he published his *Massekhet Nazir*, a biography presenting the system of thought of R. David *Cohen, and was awarded the Tel Aviv Municipality Prize for education.

Rabbi Neriah received the Israel Prize for special contribution to Israeli society in 1978.

[Itzhak Goldshlag]

°**NERO**, Roman emperor, 54–68 C.E. Nero reigned during a critical period in the relations between the Jews of Judea and imperial Rome. His reign saw the decline of the authority of the procurators in Judea and the outbreak of the Jewish War. He seems to have had no personal enmity against the Jews. Indeed, he supported Jewish vassal rulers and extended the borders of the kingdom of *Agrippa II to include Tiberias and a number of other towns (Jos., Ant., 20:159; Jos., Wars, 2:252). He also bestowed Armenia Minor upon Aristobulus, son of the Jewish king of Chalcis (Ant., 20:158). In a dispute that broke out between the leaders of the high priesthood and the Jerusalem populace on the one side, and Agrippa and the procurator *Festus on the other, over the wall that had been erected to prevent Agrippa's palace from overlooking the Temple court, he decided in favor of the former (Ant., 20:195). His wife *Poppaea Sabina, who had a certain sympathy for the Jews, had a hand in this decision. Nero's persecutions after the fire in Rome affected only the Christians but not the Jews. However, a number of factors combined to damage relations between the Jews of Ereẓ Israel and the Roman government. The excesses and extravagances of the court were reflected in monetary extortion in the provinces, including Judea. Moreover, the rise of hellenizing elements in the administration benefited the non-Jewish inhabitants of the country while damaging the interests of the Jews. The procurators of Judea in Nero's time apart from Festus (60–62 C E.) were *Felix (52–60 C.E.), who had already been appointed by *Claudius, *Albinus (62–64 C.E.), and Gessius *Florus (64–66 C.E.). They were the worst in the history of the Roman government of the country, and their rule saw the collapse of law and order in Judea. This was particularly so during the procuratorship of Florus, a Greek from Asia Minor, whose oppressive rule showed nothing but hatred toward the Jewish population. The situation was particularly bad in Caesarea, where, in a municipal dispute between the Jews and the Syrians, Nero decided against the Jews, annulling their privileges. Florus' conduct also caused the outbreak of disturbances in Jerusalem, which led up to the great revolt of 66. Nero, determined to crush the rebels, sent *Vespasian at the head of a large army to the country. Galilee was speedily reconquered by the Roman forces, but Jerusalem continued to hold out. According to talmudic tradition Nero became a proselyte (Git. 56a).

BIBLIOGRAPHY: Schuerer, Hist, index; M. Radin, *The Jews Among the Greeks and Romans* (1915), 285–6, 294–8, 315–9; H. Dessau, *Geschichte der roemischen Kaiserzeit*, 2 pt. 2 (1930), 800–16; A. Momigliano, in: CAH, 10 (1934), 854–61.

[Menahem Stern]

NER TAMID (Heb. נֵר תָּמִיד; "eternal lamp"), a light which burns perpetually in front of the *ark in synagogues. It is usually placed in a receptacle suspended from the ceiling. The *ner tamid* consisted of a wick burning in olive oil and it was considered a meritorious deed and an honor to give donations for the upkeep of the *ner tamid*. Indeed, people who do so are specially mentioned in the **Mi she-Berakh* prayer recited after the Torah reading in the synagogue on Sabbath mornings. In modern times, however, the *ner tamid* is an electrical bulb. The receptacle and the chains of the *ner tamid* are usually made of precious metal.

The institution of the *ner tamid* in the synagogue is a symbolic reminder of the **menorah* which burned continually in the Temple (see Ex. 27:20; Lev. 24:2), as the synagogue is considered a spiritual replica of the Temple ("small sanctuary," Meg. 29a). Originally, therefore, the *ner tamid* was placed into a niche in the western wall of the synagogue in remembrance of the position of the *menorah* in the Temple. Later, however, it was suspended in front of the Ark. In many East European synagogues which were built of wood, the *ner tamid* was placed in special vaulted stone niches because of the possible danger of fire. The *ner tamid* has also been interpreted as being symbolic of God's presence amid Israel (Shab. 22b) or as the spiritual light which emanated from the Temple (Ex. R. 36:1).

BIBLIOGRAPHY: Eisenstein, Dinim, 273–4; L. Yarden, *Tree of Light* (1971), index, s.v. *Eternal Light*.

°**NERVA (M. Cocceius Nerva)**, Roman emperor, 96–98 C.E. He mounted the throne at the tumultuous time following the death of *Domitian and succeeded in reconciling the interests of the traditionalist senate with those of the forces of spiritual revolution, Jews, Judeophile, or Christian. He had a generous social and economic policy which attempted to alleviate the fiscal excesses and increasing pauperism in the empire. He abolished the extortionist procedure of the *Fiscus Judaicus that had given rise to abuse under Domitian. In commemoration of this he issued coins with the inscription *Fisci Judaici Calumnia Sublata*. He exempted adherents of the Christian faith from the obligation to pay the *Fiscus Judaicus*, thus officially recognizing Christianity as a new religion and not merely a sect.

BIBLIOGRAPHY: Stein, in: Pauly-Wissowa, 7 (1900), 133–54; R. Syme, in: *Journal of Roman Studies*, 20 (1930), 55–70; E.M. Smallwood, *Documents Illustrating the Principles of Nerva. Trajan and Hadrian* (1966); M.A. Levi, *L'impero romano*, 1 (1967); H.J. Leon, *The Jews of Ancient Rome* (1960), 36, 252; Baron, Social^2, 2 (1952), 83, 106.

[Alfredo Mordechai Rabello]

NESHAMAH YETERAH (Heb. נְשָׁמָה יְתֵרָה, "additional soul"), a popular belief that every Jew is given an additional soul from the entrance of each Sabbath until its termination. This belief originated with the story in the Talmud (Beẓah 16a): "Resh Lakish said, 'On the eve of the Sabbath, God gives man an additional (or enlarged) soul, and at the close of the Sabbath He withdraws it from him, for it says; "He ceased from work and rested," i.e., *va-yinnafash* (Ex. 31:17): once it (the Sabbath) ceased, the additional soul is lost.'" (וַיִּנָּפַשׁ – play on the word which could be read – וַי(לְ)נֶּפֶשׁ *vai* (*lenefesh* "woe to the soul"). The notion of *neshamah yeterah* was richly expanded in kabbalistic literature, especially in the Zohar. One explanation for the use of spices at the *Havdalah service is that with the departure of the *neshamah yeterah* at the end of the Sabbath, it is necessary to strengthen the faint remaining soul (Tur, OḤ 297:1).

NESHER (Heb. נֶשֶׁר), urban community with municipal council status in northern Israel, 4 mi. (6 km.) S.E. of Haifa. Nesher was founded in 1925 as a workers' quarter for employees of the Nesher Cement Works. Until 1948 it consisted mainly of small wooden huts. In the *War of Independence (1948), two nearby Arab villages whose inhabitants had participated in the massacre of Jewish employees from the oil refinery were captured by Jewish forces and abandoned by their inhabitants. The villages were later taken over by new immigrants and renamed Tel Ḥanan. They were finally included in the municipal area of Nesher. Nesher's population increased from 1,500 in 1948 to 9,450 by 1968. In the mid-1990s the population was approximately 16,000, and at the end of 2002 it was 20,900. The growth of Nesher's population was mainly due to its proximity to Haifa, with many young families who work in Haifa moving there, especially to its new neighborhoods. In 1995 Nesher received city status, its municipal area running to 5 sq. mi. (13 sq. km.).

[Efraim Orni / Shaked Gilboa (2nd ed.)]

NESVIZH (Pol. **Nieśwież**), town in Baranovichi district, Belarus; formerly in Poland. Jews are mentioned in Nesvizh in the early 16th century. In 1589 the Radziwill family, who owned the town, granted the Jews certain rights, and they were subject to the jurisdiction of the prince. The Lithuanian Council of 1623 (see *Councils of the Lands) assigned Nesvizh to the Brest-Litovsk province but in 1634 it was made capital of its own province. Nesvizh was a center for fairs, and *dayyanim* were sent there from all Lithuanian communities. The community wielded considerable influence in the Lithuanian Council, which convened there in 1761. According to a council decision of 1634, the Nesvizh representative was one of the five men who determined the amount of funds required "to wreak vengeance for murder," referring to a blood libel against the Jews. Of the 60,000 zlotys demanded as poll tax from the whole of Lithuanian Jewry in 1721, the council fixed the share of Nesvizh and the neighboring town of Sverzhen at 1,000 zlotys, as against 1,100 zlotys imposed on Vilna. In 1811 there were 716 Jews in Nesvizh; 153 of them were craftsmen, including 91 needleworkers, 21 tanners, and 13 barbers. The community numbered 5,053 (72.7% of the total population) in 1878; 4,678 (55.4%) in 1897; 5,344 (53%) in 1914; 3,346 (48.9%) in 1921, and 3,364 (out of a total population of 7,586) in 1931. Besides commerce and crafts the Jews of Nesvizh engaged in horticulture and market gardening, including marketing of agricultural products. It had a textile factory, a sawmill, and a cooperative Jewish bank.

Nesvizh was known for its talmudic scholars. Among the well-known rabbis who officiated in the community at various periods were Isaac Elhanan *Spektor and Samuel Avigdor "Tosfa'ah." The last rabbi was Yitzhak Isaac Rabinovitch. Joseph Baer *Soloveichik and Pinḥas *Rozovski were natives of Nesvizh. The community had a yeshivah, a Hebrew school and kindergarten, and a Yiddish school. A branch of *Ḥovevei Zion was founded in 1871 and revived in 1888. There was considerable Zionist activity and in the 1930s *Ha-Shomer ha-Ẓa'ir maintained a training farm in Nesvizh. An association of Jewish craftsmen originally known as Po'alei Ẓedek was founded in 1908, and there was also a branch of the *Bund and Jewish members of the Communist Party.

Among the outstanding personalities who originated from Nesvizh were the philosopher Solomon *Maimon; Eliezer Dillon, who was one of two "deputies of Jewish people" sent to St. Petersburg; Moses Eleazar *Eisenstadt, the **kazyonny ravvin* in St. Petersburg; the authors and educators Nisan *Touroff and Falk Halperin; the authors Jacob Zalman Reizin and Mordecai Ze'ev Reizin; and Nahum Meyer Shaikevich (*Shomer), the Yiddish author.

[Dov Rabin]

Holocaust Period

During the period of Soviet rule (1939–41), the community institutions were liquidated and the activity of the political parties was forbidden. Zionist youth movements, however, maintained their frameworks underground. Large economic concerns were nationalized, small-scale trade almost came to a complete stop, and artisans were organized in cooperatives. The city was captured by the Germans on June 27, 1941. Looting and anti-Jewish incidents began. On October 19 a fine of 500,000 rubles and 2.5 kg. of gold was imposed. On October 29, 1941, all the Jews were ordered to gather in the market square and a "selection" was carried out. From among those gathered, 585 artisans were picked out and the others, about 4,000 in number, were executed near the city. The remnant of the community was concentrated in a ghetto that was surrounded by a wire fence.

At the end of December 1941, an underground organization was founded in the ghetto. It began with the acquisition of arms and the preparation of other means of self-defense. In July 1942 news of the destruction of nearby communities reached the ghetto and the underground prepared to fight. The chairman of the Judenrat, Magalif, a lawyer from Warsaw, cooperated with the underground. On July 17 the Germans surrounded the ghetto to carry out a selection. When the Germans broke through the gate, the Jews set their houses afire and defended themselves, with the few weapons they had and with knives, hatchets, and sticks. About 40 Germans were hit, but the Germans and their Lithuanian collaborators overcame the inhabitants of the ghetto. About 25 fighters fled into the forests. Some organized into a partisan unit and were integrated into the Chkalov battalion of partisans that was active in the forests of Volozhin. With the liberation of the city by the Soviets, Jewish life was not reconstituted. The survivors went to Poland, and from there some went to Ereẓ Israel and others migrated overseas.

[Aharon Weiss]

BIBLIOGRAPHY: S. Dubnow (ed.), *Pinkas… Medinot Lita* (1925), index; H. Alexandrov, in: Vaysrusishe Visnshaft-Akademie, *Tsaytshrift*, 4 (1930), 67–73; Lita, 3 (1967); *Sefer ha-Partizanim ha-Yehudim*, 1 (1958), 545–55; *Sefer Milḥamot ha-Getta'ot* (1954), 478–80, 607.

NES ẒIYYONAH (Heb. נֵס צִיּוֹנָה; "Banner toward Zion"), semiurban settlement with municipal council status in central

Israel, between Rishon le-Zion and Reḥovot. Nes Ẓiyyonah was founded in 1883 in the Arab hamlet Wadi Ḥanīn on the initiative of a single Jewish immigrant from Russia, Reuben Lehrer. A few more Jewish families joined the founder in the first years. The moshavah was given its present name in the 1890s when, for the first time in the country, the blue and white Jewish flag was raised at its anniversary celebration. In the first decade of the 20th century, citrus groves became prominent there and attracted both immigrants of the Second *Aliyah and, in even greater numbers, Arab workers, some of whom settled there. Nes Ẓiyyonah thus became the principal stage in the struggle for the "conquest of labor." Until 1948 Nes Ẓiyyonah was the only village in the country with a mixed Arab-Jewish population – the two communities living on opposite sides of the main road and, on the whole, coexisting peacefully. In the *War of Independence (1948), the Arabs abandoned the village, which had by then 1,800 Jewish inhabitants. After 1948 Nes Ẓiyyonah quickly expanded and reached 9,500 inhabitants in 1953; its rate of growth, however, slowed down subsequently. There were 11,900 inhabitants in 1968, in a municipal area extending over 6 sq. mi. (16 sq. km.), of which nearly two-thirds were cultivated for farming. Aside from the citrus branch, Nes Ẓiyyonah was a beekeeping center, producing an annual average of 330,000 lb. (150,000 kg.) of honey. Industry was a prime factor in the local economy, employing workers in factories for building materials, electric appliances, fiberglass, rubber, metal, and foodstuffs. The Institute for Biological Research, a top-secret defense establishment employing 350 people, was also located there. By the mid-1990s the population had nearly doubled to 21,800, and in 2002 it was 25,800. In 1992 Nes Ziyyonah received city status.

WEBSITE: www.ness-ziona.muni.il.

[Efraim Orni / Shaked Gilboa (2nd ed.)]

NES ẒIYYONAH, a clandestine Zionist society founded in 1885 by students of the yeshivah in Volozhin. The purpose of Nes Ẓiyyonah was to organize a group of people (rabbis, preachers, and writers) to propagate the idea of the settlement of Ereẓ Israel. The members of the society were sworn to secrecy and took it upon themselves to promote their cause orally and in print and to establish new Ḥovevei Zion societies (see *Ḥibbat Zion). The central committee of Nes Ẓiyyonah distributed circulars among its members and, when it acquired a duplicating machine, also published a *Mikhtav Itti u-Khelali* ("General Periodical") in Hebrew. It also initiated a collection of essays and asked rabbis to submit their views on the idea of settlement in Ereẓ Israel. Replies received from several outstanding rabbis served as a kind of positive "responsa" to the Ḥovevei Zion ideology. Some of the replies were published in the Hebrew press, but the book itself never came out because at the end of 1891 the police discovered the existence of the society, confiscated the duplicating machine and the archives, and put an end to Nes Ẓiyyonah's activities. Some of the rabbis' letters were included in *Shivat Ẓiyyon* (1891), a collection edited by A.J. *Slutzky. A group of former members of Nes Ẓiyyonah then founded another society with similar aims, called Neẓaḥ Israel. Among the founders was Ḥayyim Naḥman *Bialik, who was asked to formulate the aims of the new society. An article by Bialik – his first effort to appear in print – was published in **Ha-Meliẓ* 31, No. 80 (1891). The stated purpose of the society was "the settlement of our holy land in the spirit of holiness and Judaism." The society planned the establishment of a rural settlement in Ereẓ Israel with a majority of members from Nes Ẓiyyonah, which would serve as an example to all the other settlements, especially in matters of education. In 1890 societies by the name of Nes Ẓiyyonah were founded in Aleksot near Kovno and in Suwalki for the purpose of establishing a settlement in Ereẓ Israel based on religious-national ideals. Eventually the two societies merged into one and, augmented by additional members from Mariampol, laid the foundations of Ḥaderah. When the Volozhin yeshivah was closed by Russian authorities, the activities of Neẓaḥ Israel came to an end. It was reestablished at Minsk by I. Nissenbaum and was finally disbanded in 1894.

[Israel Klausner]

NETA'IM (Heb. נְטָעִים; "Plantations"), moshav in central Israel S.W. of Rishon le-Zion affiliated with Tenu'at ha-Moshavim, founded in 1932 by veteran farm laborers of the Second *Aliyah in the framework of the Thousand Families Settlement Scheme. Citrus groves were among its intensive farming branches. In 1968 its population was 212 and in the mid-1990s approximately 265, jumping to 456 in 2002 after expansion.

[Efraim Orni]

NETANYAH (Heb. נְתַנְיָה), city in central Israel, on the Sharon coast. Netanyah is named after the U.S. Jewish philanthropist Nathan *Straus. It was founded in 1929 as a moshavah based on farming by 40 young people of the *Benei Binyamin association, led by Oved *Ben-Ami, whose parents were veteran settlers in moshavot. The village soon served as a nucleus for the settlement of the central Sharon where no Jewish villages had existed before, particularly as its founding coincided with the purchase of the *Ḥefer Plain by the *Jewish National Fund. Because it was situated between Tel Aviv and Haifa, Netanyah was able to develop as a market town for its quickly expanding rural hinterland. In the initial period citrus groves constituted Netanyah's principal economy, employing a considerable number of hired workers and thus causing an increase in population. A further growth factor was Netanyah's location at a communications center. In 1948 the population was 8,500. Later Netanyah was given city status and by 1951 its population had already risen to 30,000, then to 60,100 by 1968 as large numbers of new immigrants were absorbed. By the mid-1990s the population had again more then doubled to 142,700 and in 2002 it was 164,800, making Netanyah the ninth largest city in Israel. Its area was 11 sq. mi. (28.5 sq. km.), with accelerated expansion continuing in the first years of the new century as new neighborhoods burgeoned.

The city's economy was based mainly on tourism and industry. Netanyah is one of Israel's foremost seaside resorts with dozens of hotels and pensions. The foremost industrial branch was diamond polishing, of which Netanyah became the Israeli center in the 1940s, when the industry was transferred from Nazi-dominated Belgium to Palestine – although subsequently the center moved to the Tel Aviv area and over the years most of the diamond-polishing workshops were closed. The city's industry is now concentrated in two industrial areas and includes hi-tech industries, steel, pharmaceuticals, food, beer, textiles, rubber, furniture, electronics, etc. In addition, Netanyah become a regional commercial center, including the first and only branch of the IKEA Corp. Public institutions located at Netanyah included the Ohel Shem Culture Hall, the Malben Old Age Home, the Wingate Sports Center, and Ulpan Akiva. The Netanyah Academic College has an enrollment of 3,500 students. During the al-Aqsa Intifada the city came under a number of terrorist attacks, most notably a suicide bombing at the Park Hotel in 2002, killing 22 and wounding 140 at a Passover *seder.*

WEBSITE: www.netanya.muni.il.

[Shlomo Hasson / Shaked Gilboa (2nd ed.)]

NETANYAHU, BENZION (1910–), scholar and Zionist. Born in Warsaw, Netanyahu moved with his family to Tel Aviv in 1920. There he became active in the Zionist-Revisionist Party and its successor, the New Zionist Organization. From 1932 to 1935 he served on its executive committee and in 1934–35 as editor-in-chief of its daily paper *Ha-Yarden*. In 1940 he went to the United States as a member of the delegation, headed by Jabotinsky, of the World New Zionist Organization, and in the following year was appointed executive director of the New Zionist Organization of America; until 1948 he headed its press campaign and diplomatic action in the United States. From 1946 to 1948 he was a member of the American Zionist Emergency Council, under the leadership of Abba Hillel Silver.

After the establishment of the State of Israel, Netanyahu turned to his numerous scholarly interests in the field of Judaica. He became the editor-in-chief of the *Encyclopedia Hebraica* (1948–62); general editor of *The World History of the Jewish People* (1954–64); editor-in-chief of the *Encyclopaedia Judaica* (1961–63); co-editor of the *Jewish Quarterly Review* (1959–60); and editor of the works of Herzl, Nordau, and Pinsker. He was a professor at Dropsie College from 1957 to 1968, serving as chairman of its Department of Hebrew Language and Literature from 1962 to 1968. From 1968 he was professor of Hebraic studies at the University of Denver and in 1971 was appointed professor of Judaic studies and chairman of the Department of Semitic Languages at Cornell University. Upon his retirement, he became professor emeritus of Jewish studies at Cornell and a scholar at Princeton University.

Netanyahu published numerous original studies in various fields of Jewish history and literature, including *Don Isaac Abravanel* (1953), 1968^2), *The Marranos of Spain* (1966), and *The Origins of the Inquisition in Fifteenth Century Spain* (1995).

He is the father of Binyamin *Netanyahu, prime minister of Israel in 1996–99.

[Martin A. Cohen]

NETANYAHU, BINYAMIN (**Bibi**; 1949–), Israeli politician, prime minister in the years 1996–99. Netanyahu was born in Israel, to a Revisionist family, son of historian Benzion *Netanyahu. He was raised in Jerusalem, and in Philadelphia where his family lived in 1956–58 and 1963–67. Netanyahu returned to Israel in 1967 to do his military service, reaching the rank of captain in the elite *Sayyeret Matkal* unit. He finished his military service in 1972, and then returned to the U.S., where he attended the Massachusetts Institute of Technology, receiving a bachelor's degree in architecture. While studying at MIT he returned to Israel to participate in the Yom Kippur War. He then went back to complete a master's degree in business administration, and considered doing a doctorate in political science. While in the U.S. Netanyahu changed his name to Benjamin Nitai and started working in the international consulting firm the Boston Consulting Group. In these years he was active in presenting information about Israel. After his brother Jonathan (Yonni) was killed in the course of the *Entebbe operation in July 1976, Netanyahu returned to Israel in 1978, and started advocating international action against terrorism. In 1980 he set up and headed the Jonathan Institute for the Study of Terror, which was named for his brother. He also started working as marketing manager for the Jerusalem-based furniture manufacturer Rim. Netanyahu's speaking skills and fluent English brought him to the attention of Israel's ambassador in Washington, Moshe *Arens, who supported his appointment as minister plenipotentiary in the Israel Embassy in Washington, where he served from 1982 to 1984. In 1984–88 he served as Israel's ambassador to the United Nations. Inter alia, he got the UN archive to open its files on Nazi war criminals, and frequently appeared in the American media to explain Israel's positions. Netanyahu returned to Israel in time to run in the elections to the Twelfth Knesset on the Likud list. In the National Unity government he was appointed deputy minister for foreign affairs under Arens. After David *Levy succeeded Arens, Netanyahu was appointed deputy minister in the prime minister's office. During the first Gulf War he was one of Israel's leading spokesmen, and played a similar role in the Madrid Conference of October–November 1991. He was one of the staunch supporters of the direct election of the prime minister. After the Likud's electoral defeat in the elections to the Thirteenth Knesset in 1992, and Yitzhak *Shamir's resignation from the Likud leadership, Netanyahu was elected chairman of the Likud in March 1993, despite a well-publicized scandal over an affair he had had. In the Thirteenth Knesset he served on the Knesset Foreign Affairs and Defense Committee, and headed the opposition to the Oslo process led by Prime Minister Yitzhak *Rabin. Nevertheless, he supported the peace treaty with Jordan. Netanyahu was accused by the left of having participated in the incitement against Rabin that led up to his assassination in November 1995. However, after convincing David Levy's Gesher party and Raphael *Eitan's Tzomet to run together in a joint list with the Likud in the elections to the Fourteenth Knesset in 1996, Netanyahu beat Shimon *Peres in the first direct election for prime minister, thus becoming Israel's first prime minister to be born after the establishment of the state. Netanyahu established a right of center–religious government, and soon after its establishment traveled to Washington, Cairo, and Amman, proclaiming that while Israel was committed to the peace process and the Oslo Accords, he would insist on the Palestinians' implementing all their undertakings, including the cancelation of the articles in the Palestine National Covenant that rejected Israel's right to exist, and putting an end to Palestinian terror against Israel. Netanyahu met with Palestinian leader Yasser *Arafat in September 1996, signed the Hebron Memorandum in January 1997, and the Wye River Memorandum in November 1998. He offered Syria negotiations based on the concept "Lebanon first," and an Israeli withdrawal from the security zone in southern Lebanon as a prelude to talks on other issues. However, Syrian President Hafez el-Asad rejected the initiative.

Netanyahu's government was characterized by a succession of scandals, some connected with his own political style, and others with various controversial decisions that he took, such as his choice of candidates for minister of justice and attorney general. Growing dissatisfaction with his leadership within the Likud led to several prominent members' leaving the party, while the partnership with Gesher and Tzomet fell apart. Finally, a slowdown in the economy and difficulties in getting the 1999 budget approved by the Knesset led Netanyahu to call for early elections to the Fifteenth Knesset.

In the direct election for the prime minister held in May 1999, Netanyahu lost by a large margin to Labor's Ehud *Barak. Rather than continue to lead the Likud in opposition, he decided to leave politics temporarily and engage in business and lecturing. Prior to the elections to the Sixteenth Knesset in January 2003 he returned to active politics and was reelected to the Knesset on the Likud list. In the government formed by Ariel *Sharon in 2003 he was appointed minister of finance, in which task he was forced to confront a deep economic recession. Pursuing an extreme neoliberal economic policy, Netanyahu managed to improve the performance of the economy, though at the cost of severe cuts in Israel's social welfare system and growing gaps between rich and poor.

Netanyahu opposed Sharon's policy of disengagement from the Gaza Strip, and the dismantlement of settlements, but on October 26, 2004, failed in an effort to vote down the policy in the Knesset. He then threatened to resign from the government unless a referendum were held on the disengagement, but he finally lifted his threat due to pressure that he remain in the Ministry of Finance to see the 2005 budget through. Netanyahu finally resigned from the government on August 9, one week before the beginning of the evacuation of the settlements in *Gush Katif and northern Samaria, before the 2006 budget was brought to the Knesset. His intention was to contend for the Likud leadership before the elections to the Seventeenth Knesset, a post he won in December 2005 after Sharon bolted the party to form Kadimah.

He wrote *Don Isaac Abravanel, Statesman and Philosopher* (1982); *Fighting Terrorism: How Democracies Can Defeat Domestic and International Terrorists* (1995); and *A Durable Peace: Israel and Its Place among the Nations* (2000); he edited *Terrorism: How the West Can Win* (1986); and *A Place Among the Nations: Israel and the World* (1993).

BIBLIOGRAPHY: B. Kaspit, *Netanyahu: The Road to Power* (1998); N. Lochery, *The Difficult Road to Peace: Netanyahu, Israel and the Middle East Peace Process* (1999); R. Vardi, *Bibi: Mi Atta Adoni Rosh ha-Memshalah?* (1997); R. Gelbard, *Shinui Emdot Manhigim be-Sikhsukh Kiyyumi u-Murkav: Binyamin Netanyahu* (2003).

[Susan Hattis Rolef (2nd ed.)]

NETHANEL BEN AL-FAYYUMI (d. about 1165), Yemenite scholar and philosopher. Nethanel appears to have been the father of Jacob b. Nethanel to whom *Maimonides addressed his *Iggeret Teiman*, ("Epistle to Yemen").

Nethanel wrote the Judeo-Arabic *Bustān al-ʿUqūl* ("Garden of Intellects"), a compendium of theology published by R. Gottheil, in: *Festschrift… Steinschneider* (1896), 144–7; text edited and translated into English by D. Levine, 1908; translated into Hebrew under the title *Gan ha-Sekhalim* by Y. Kafaḥ, 1954. The seven chapters of the work deal with (1) divine unity, (2) man as a microcosm, (3) obedience to God, (4) repentance, (5) reliance upon God and providence, (6) the nature of the Messiah with a discussion of the Islamic concepts of the abrogation of the Torah and the prophethood of Muhammad, and (7) the future life. In his discussion of the abrogation of the Torah, Nethanel denied that the Torah would be superseded, but, at the same time, maintained that there is a certain validity in the legislation of other religions. His tolerance is evident from his contention that God sent different prophets to the various nations of the world with legislations suited to the particular temperament of each individual nation.

The *Bustān al-ʿUqūl*, a popular work, contains numerous citations from *aggadah* and from Arabic legendary and anecdotal materials. In addition to drawing upon Jewish sources, such as *Saadiah's *Book of Beliefs and Opinions* and *Baḥya's *Duties of the Heart*, Nethanel borrowed heavily from Islamic philosophy, from the Epistles of the *Brethren of Sincerity, and, as S. Pines points out, from the writings of the Ismāʿīllya, in particular of the Fatimid branch. The Ismailian influence is particularly prominent in Nethanel's discussion of the nature of God, and the primary emanations. Pines considers the *Bustān al-ʿUqūl* an Ismailian treatise that was inspired by the theology of the Fatimids, in the same way that a work like Saadiah's *Beliefs and Opinions* was inspired by the Mutazilite *Kalām. Some identify the author of *Bustān* with Nethanel b. Moses ha-Levi the Gaon of Fostat or with the son of Fayyūmī b. Saadiah who sent an epistle to Maimonides.

BIBLIOGRAPHY: EJ, 2 (1925), 260ff.; A.S. Halkin (ed.), *Iggeret Teiman (Moses Maimonides' Epistle to Yemen)* (1952), viiff.; M. Steinschneider, in: JQR, 10 (1897/98), 522–3; idem, Arab Lit, 182; Neubauer, Cat, 2 (1906), 380; Mann, Egypt, 1 (1920), 244; 2 (1922), 315–6; S. Pines, in: *Revue de l'histoire juive en Egypte*, 1 (1947), 5–22.

[Frank Talmage]

NETHANEL BEN ISAIAH (14th century), Yemenite scholar. Nethanel's fame rests upon his extensive midrashic anthology, *Nur al-Ẓalam* ("Light in the Darkness"). The book is a typical Yemenite Midrash: it is based upon the standard Midrashim, though with stylistic changes and adaptations, and the influence of Maimonides, with whom the author shows great familiarity, is conspicuous. Philosophical ideas from other schools as well as kabbalistic sayings are also woven into the work.

Nur al-Ẓalam contains few of the peculiarities of the other Yemenite Midrashim and is of a much higher literary standard, being comparable in this respect to the *Midrash ha-Gadol. It was utilized by authors of later Yemenite Midrashim, among them Manẓur Aldamari, in his *Sarag al-Ekol*, and Shalom *Shabazi. The Midrash was published in its entirety with a Hebrew translation accompanying the Arabic original, by Y. Kafaḥ (1957). Nethanel also wrote a commentary on Maimonides' *Mishneh Torah* which was extant until recently and subsequently lost.

BIBLIOGRAPHY: Nathanel b. Isaiah, *Me'or ha-Afelah*, ed. by Y. Kafaḥ (1957), introd.; A. Kohut, *"Light of Shade and Lamp of Wisdom"*... composed by Nethanel ibn Yeshâya (= *Studies in Yemen-Hebrew Literature*, pt. 2), (bound with proceedings of the fourth Biennial Convention of the Jewish Theological Seminary Association, 1894).

[Israel Moses Ta-Shma]

NETHANEL BEN MESHULLAM HA-LEVI (1660/1665–1735?), Italian kabbalist. Nethanel was born in Modena and was ordained rabbi around 1685. His first rabbinical post appears to have been in his native town, during the lifetime of his father, Meshullam b. Benzion ha-Levi, a kabbalist, who was a member of the Modena rabbinate. From 1693 Nethanel was also rabbi in Lugo, Pesaro, Padua, and Cento. In 1728 he returned to Modena, apparently succeeding Ephraim Kohen of Ostrog as chief rabbi, serving in that position until his death. Some of his responsa were published in the works of his contemporaries, such as the *Paḥad Yiẓḥak* of Isaac *Lampronti and the *Shemesh Ẓedakah* (Venice, 1743) of Samson *Morpurgo. Of great importance is his responsum written in Pesaro (in *Shemesh Ẓedakah*, ḤM, no. 33), in which he discusses communal taxation and intercommunity responsibility, and protests against rabbis who pass judgment on matters concerning other communities without the consent of their local rabbis. In the sphere of Kabbalah his work exhibits affinity with the thought of Moses Ḥayyim *Luzzatto. He was close to the Kabbalah circle of Abraham *Rovigo and Mordecai *Ashkenazi. His son, ẒEVI HA-LEVI, an emissary of the Holy Land, was one of the scholars of the yeshivah of Ḥayyim ibn *Attar in Jerusalem.

BIBLIOGRAPHY: Wilensky, in: KS, 23 (1946/47), 131–9; 24 (1947/48), 160.

[Abraham David]

NETHANEL BEN MOSES HA-LEVI (12th century), *gaon* and *rosh yeshivah* in *Cairo. Nethanel inherited his position from his father Moses and according to documents of the Cairo **Genizah*, he held this position from 1160 to 1170. At that time, the role and the authority of the Cairo *rosh yeshivah* increased to a considerable extent because, after the death of *Samuel b. Hananiah, the position of the **nagid* was weakened as a result of the activities of *Zuta. Nethanel appointed judges and other religious officials in all the communities of Egypt and he headed the great *bet din*. He received a letter of ordination from R. *Daniel b. Ḥasdai, the exilarch in *Baghdad, who thus sought to impose his authority on Egyptian Jewry; on the other hand, *Samuel b. Eli, the head of the *yeshivah* of Baghdad, supported the *geonim* of *Damascus. *Benjamin of Tudela, the 12th-century traveler, relates that Nethanel was in royal service. In 1171 Nethanel was succeeded by *Maimonides as head of the Jews. For some unknown reason Maimonides was compelled to give way to *Sar Shalom ha-Levi, the brother of Nethanel.

BIBLIOGRAPHY: Mann, Egypt, 1 (1920), 234–5, 237; 2 (1922), 292ff.; Mann, Texts, 1 (1931), 230–1, 257–62; Assaf, in: *Tarbiz*, 1:3 (1929/30), 68; idem, *Be-Oholei Ya'akov* (1943), 91; Goitein, in: *Tarbiz*, 33 (1963/64), 184.

[Eliyahu Ashtor]

NETHANEL OF CHINON, French tosafist of the first half of the 13th century. Nethanel is mentioned several times in the standard *tosafot* (e.g., Beẓah 3a) and is probably identical with the Nethanel and the Nethanel ha-Kadosh ("the saint" – so called because of his piety and not because of his having died a martyr's death) mentioned in *Shitah Mekubbeẓet* (BK 18a; Men. 7a). *Jehiel of Paris approached Nethanel with a problem and was directed by him to Isaac b. Todros, his older contemporary (Resp. Maharik 102). *Samuel of Evreux turned to him with halakhic problems (*Mordekhai, Ḥul.* 681). Nethanel's fellow townsman *Samson of Coucy made abundant use of his teaching in his *Sefer ha-Keritut* (Constantinople, 1516). Nethanel b. Joseph of Chinon, younger brother of Eliezer of Chinon, the author of several *piyyutim*, was probably a grandson of this Nethanel.

BIBLIOGRAPHY: A.M. Habermann, *Shirei ha-Yiḥud ve-ha-Kavod* (1948), 73–85; Urbach, Tosafot, index s.v. *Nethanel mi-Kinon*.

[Israel Moses Ta-Shma']

NETHERLANDS, THE (Holland), kingdom in N.W. Europe.

The Middle Ages

It is not known when exactly the Jews settled in the area which is now called The Netherlands. As early as the 11th century one can find some indications of Jewish settlers in what was then called the Lowlands, an area which included the Southern Netherlands.

Main Jewish communities of the Netherlands in 1941 and 1960. Bold face type indicates places of Jewish settlement in the 17th century.

Early sources from the 11th and 12th centuries mention official debates or *Disputationes* between Christians and Jews, in which attempts were made to convince the Jews of the truth of Christianity and to try to convert them. It is not certain whether the Jews were residents in the area or whether they were just passing through.

However, as of the 13th century, there are sources which indicate that Jews were living in the areas of Brabant and Limburg, mainly in cities such as Brussels, Leuven, Tienen, and Maastricht. Sources from the 14th century also mention Jewish residents in the cities of Antwerp and Mechelen and in the northern region of Geldern.

Between 1347 and 1351, the entire area covering Europe was hit by the plague or Black Death and this led to a new theme in medieval antisemitic rhetoric. The Jews were held responsible for the epidemic and for the way it was rapidly spreading, because presumably they were the ones who had poisoned the water of the springs used by the Christians. Various medieval chronicles mention this, e.g., those of Radalphus de Rivo (c. 1403) of Tongeren, who wrote about how the Jews were murdered in the Brabant region and in the city of Zwolle because they were accused of spreading the Black Death. This accusation was added to the other traditional accusations against the Jews, such as piercing the Host used for communion and using Christian children as an offering during Passover. For this reason local Jewish communities were often murdered in part or entirely or exiled. Thus, in May 1370, six Jews were burned at the stake in Brussels because they were accused of theft and of desecrating the Holy Sacrament. In addition to these drastic measures, traces can also be found of abusing and insulting Jews, e.g., in the cities of Zutphen, Deventer, and Utrecht, for allegedly desecrating the Host.

From the 15th century, Jews also resided in the Northern Netherlands. Their most important occupation was moneylending, making them dependent on the economies of the cities. In this way, Nijmegen became an important financial marketplace where a great many of Jewish families came to settle. Nonetheless, Jews continued to choose the large cities in the Southern Netherlands as for their home base. In the 16th century the city of Antwerp came to be a very important location for Jewish tradesmen and moneylenders because of its flourishing economy. This also turned it into a refuge for a number of Marranos who had been expelled from Spain and Portugal after 1492. Jewish bankers usually settled there using a Christian pseudonym. Francisco Mendes, born into a distinguished family of bankers, opened a branch in Antwerp that was one of the largest banks in Europe. After his death in 1536 it was run by his wife Gracia *Nasi. The flourishing Jewish trade in Antwerp ended, however, when The Netherlands were divided during the reign of king Philip II and many Jews took refuge in the Northern Netherlands, especially in *Amsterdam.

[Monika Saelemaekers (2nd ed.)]

Sephardim and Ashkenazim until 1795

The independent Dutch Republic was a popular emigration destination because of its economic prosperity and relative tolerance. Many job-seeking Germans, Huguenot Frenchmen, and dissenting scholars tried their luck in this strange country where, instead of a sovereign, the bourgeoisie were the rulers. Also Jews found their way to the Republic.

Among the Portuguese merchants in the Netherlands in the 17th century many were Marranos. It is known of one of them, Marcus Perez, became a Calvinist and played an important role in the Netherlands' revolt against Spain. Without doubt there were many Marranos among the 20,000 merchants, industrialists, and scholars who left Antwerp in 1585 for the Republic of the United Provinces. Around 1590 the first indications of a Marrano community are to be found in Amsterdam, but its members did not openly declare themselves as Jews. The Beth Jaäcob community was founded around 1600. It was discovered in 1603 and the Ashkenazi rabbi Moses Uri b. Joseph ha-Levi, who had come from Emden the previous year, was arrested. Religious liberty was not yet granted in Amsterdam and therefore the Marranos who had returned to Judaism, along with newly arrived Jews from Portugal, Italy, and Turkey, tried to obtain a foothold somewhere else. In 1604 they were granted a charter in Alkmaar, and in 1605 in Haarlem and Rotterdam. Not only were they accorded privileges regarding military service and the Sabbath but they were also permitted to build a synagogue and open a cemetery as soon as their numbers reached 50, and to print Hebrew books. Nevertheless, only a few availed themselves of these privileges, and in spite of the difficulties most Jews settled in Amsterdam; among them was the representative of the sultan of Morocco, Don Samuel *Palache.

In 1608 a second community, Neveh Shalom, was founded by Isaac Franco and in the same year the first Sephardi rabbi, Joseph *Pardo, was appointed. As the legal status of the Jews was not clearly defined, the authorities were asked by various bodies to clarify their attitude: the two lawyers, Hugo *Grotius and Adriaan Pauw, were asked to draw up special regulations for the Jews. However, in a resolution of Dec. 13, 1619, the provinces of Holland and West Friesland decided to allow each city to adopt its own policy toward the Jews. The other provinces followed this example, and this situation remained in force until 1795. For this reason the status of the Jews differed greatly in the various towns. In Amsterdam there were no restrictions on Jewish settlement, but Jews could not become burghers and were excluded from most trades; however, no such disabilities existed in several other towns. A large number of Portuguese Jews, in search of greater economic opportunities, took part in the expedition to *Brazil and in 1634 Joan Maurits van Nassau-Siegen granted the charter they had requested. When the Netherlands was compelled to cede Brazil to Portugal (1654) many Jews returned to Amsterdam. The Dutch Republic, however, demanded that its Jews be recognized as full citizens abroad and that no restrictive measure be imposed on them if they visited a foreign country, especially Spain (1657). The Ashkenazim also enjoyed the rights which the Portuguese Jews had obtained in the larger towns.

In the first half of the 18th century in the eastern part of the country also, in the area bordering Germany, small communities could be founded with complete religious liberty. Following on the activities of some Jewish robbers, however, several cities enacted measures against Jewish settlement: Groningen (1710), Utrecht (1713), Gouda, the province of Friesland (1712), and the province of Overijssel (1724). Amersfoort protested against one such regulation in the province of Gelderland (1726), and it was decided to introduce a certificate of good behavior, which subsequently became a requirement in most cities. Because this certificate was issued by the *parnasim*, who also had to guarantee the good behavior of the applicant, they acquired considerable power over the newcomers. Until the Emancipation the legal position of the Jews remained unclear since it was wholly dependent on local or provincial authorities. In legal cases the Jews were subject to the laws of the land and were judged in the government courts. As they could not take the usual – Christian – oath, a special formula was introduced by the different provinces (the last in Overijssel in 1746), but this had no derogatory content. Sometimes Jews even sought the decision of Christian scholars in religious affairs. The municipal authorities intervened in the communities in the case of serious internal conflicts, as in Amsterdam in 1673 where the Polish *kehillah* was ordered to join the German one (see below) and when the authorities had to approve the regulations of the *kehillah*.

Economic Expansion

In spite of the restrictive regulations to which they were subject (which included among other things exclusion from the existing guilds), the Sephardi Jews were able to acquire some economic importance. Thanks to their knowledge of languages, administrative experience, and international relationships, they played an important part in the expanding economy of the young Republic of the Netherlands, especially from 1610 onward when Amsterdam became an established center of world trade. After 1640 there was an increase in the number of current account customers and the size of their accounts at the discount bank (Wisselbank). In the second half of the 17th century the Sephardim also occupied an important place among the shareholders of the East India Company, the most powerful Netherlands enterprise. Portuguese Jews also acquired some prominence in industry, especially in sugar refineries, and the silk, tobacco, and diamond industries; although the latter had been initiated by Christian polishers, in the course of time it became an exclusively Jewish industry. However they became most celebrated for book printing; in 1626 a large number of works were produced at a high standard of printing for the day. Among the richest Portuguese Jews, who were purveyors to the army and made loans to the court, were Antonia Alvarez *Machado, the Pereira family, Joseph de Medina and his sons, and the baron Antonio Lopez *Suasso. These and other Portuguese Jews traded in stocks and shares from the second half of the 17th century and probably constituted the majority of traders in this field (see *Stock Exchange). Such activity was centered in Amsterdam; the only other important settlements were in The *Hague, because of the proximity of the royal court, and Maarssen, a village near Utrecht (which itself did not admit Jews) which was the center of the country houses of the rich Portuguese families. From Amsterdam the Portuguese Jews took part in the economic exploration and exploitation of old and new regions, mainly in the Western hemisphere: Brazil, New Amsterdam, *Surinam, and Curaçao.

During the course of the 18th century trade declined and economic activity concentrated to a growing extent on stockjobbing. Daring speculations and successive crises led to the downfall of important families, such as the De *Pintos. The situation worsened after the economic crisis of 1772/73 and became grave during the French occupation (from 1794) when trade in goods practically came to a standstill. Government monetary measures struck especially at the rentiers, and by the end of the 18th century the once wealthy community of Amsterdam included a large number of paupers: 54% of the members had to be given financial support.

Cultural Activities of the Portuguese Community

The 17th century, the "Golden Age" of the Republic of the Netherlands, was also a time of cultural expansion for the Portuguese community. The medical profession was the most popular, and there were often several physicians in one family, as in the case of the Pharar family (Abraham "el viejo," David, and Abraham), and the *Bueno family (no less than eight, the most famous being Joseph, who in 1625 was called to the sickbed of Prince Maurits of Nassau, and whose son, Ephraim *Bueno, was painted by Rembrandt), and the De Meza, *Aboab, and De Rocamora families. The most celebrated physicians were *Zacutus Lusitanus and Isaac *Orobio de Castro. From 1655 onward there were physicians who had completed their studies in Holland, especially in Leiden and Utrecht. They were free to practice their profession among non-Jews also, but they were required to take a special oath. In Amsterdam, where the surgeons and pharmacists (who needed no academic training) were organized into guilds, Jews could not be officially admitted to these professions (according to the regulation of 1632). Nevertheless they set up in practice, with the result that in 1667 they were forbidden to sell medicine to non-Jews. This regulation was ignored, and so when a new

The Maastricht synagogue, built in 1841. Courtesy Maastricht Municipality.

regulation was issued in 1711 the restrictive clause was not included. Many Portuguese Jews were artists (notably the illuminator Shalom *Italia and engraver Jacob Gadella) and writers, mainly of poems and plays in Spanish and Portuguese; there were even two special clubs where Spanish poetry was studied. The best-known poet was Daniel Levi (Miguel) de *Barrios, the first historian of the Marrano settlement in the Netherlands.

More interesting, however, was the high level of study of Judaism and its literature from the early days of the settlement, and this in spite of the fact that large numbers of the newcomers had returned to Judaism at an advanced age. In order to teach the younger generation about Judaism the two *kehillot* in Amsterdam, Beth Jaäcob and Neveh Shalom, founded in 1616 the Talmud Torah or Ets Haim yeshivah. Through the efforts of teachers from the Sephardi Diaspora, such as Saul Levi *Morteira and Isaac *Aboab da Fonseca, the yeshivah became renowned. Among the later teachers were, *Manasseh ben Israel, Moses Raphael de *Aguilar and Jacob *Sasportas. The facilities for printing books (see above) contributed to the high level of scholarship, and the independent production of scientific, theological, and literary works in Hebrew also developed. The most important writers were Moses *Zacuto, Solomon de *Oliveyra, Joseph *Penso de la Vega, and in the 18th century David *Franco-Mendes.

The return of the Marranos to Judaism was accompanied by conflicts about the nature of their religion. In 1618 a group of strictly Orthodox Jews left Beth Jaäcob and founded the Beth Jisrael community because they did not accept the liberal leadership of the *parnas* David Pharar. Soon after, Uriel da *Costa's attack on Orthodox Judaism caused an upheaval throughout the whole *Marrano Diaspora. The most famous case was that of Baruch *Spinoza, who was banned from the *kehillah* for his heretical opinions. At this period – as among Sephardim elsewhere – Lurianic *Kabbalah had many followers in Amsterdam, which explains the enthusiasm for *Shabbetai Zevi that prevailed in the community in 1666. The Shabbateans maintained a strong influence for a long period and, during the chief rabbinate of Solomon *Ayllon, there was a serious conflict in which the Ashkenazi chief rabbi of Amsterdam Zevi Hirsch *Ashkenazi (Ḥakham Ẓevi) was involved (1713). The failure of the Shabbatean movement on the one hand and the power and wealth of the *kehillah* (all three congregations united in 1639) on the other led to an ever-increasing isolation from the rest of the Jewish world and to a rapprochement with Dutch society. The turning point was the founding of the famous Esnoga (synagogue), inaugurated in 1675, which subsequently dominated Sephardi community life.

The Ashkenazim

Unlike the Sephardim, the Ashkenazim spread throughout the whole Republic of the Netherlands, although their main center was also in Amsterdam. The first Ashkenazim arrived in Amsterdam around 1620, establishing their first congregation in 1635. The first emigration was from Germany but in the second half of the 17th century many Jews also came from Poland and Lithuania: they founded a separate community (1660), but in 1673, after disputes between the two, the municipal authorities ordered it to amalgamate with the German one. The community grew rapidly, outnumbering the Portuguese in the 17th century though remaining in a subservient position until the end of the 18th century. During the 17th century, the most important communities outside Amsterdam were in Rotterdam and The Hague. At that time Jews also settled in several towns in the provinces bordering Germany: Groningen, Friesland, Overijssel, and Gelderland. In spite of restrictive measures, their number increased in the 18th century, and they extended to a large number of smaller towns. There were a few very rich Ashkenazi families, such as the *Boas' (The Hague), the Gomperts (Nijmegen and Amersfoort), and the Cohens (Amersfoort), but the overwhelming majority earned a meager living as peddlers, butchers, and cattle dealers. In Amsterdam the economic difficulties of the Ashkenazi Jews were even more acute and the poverty among them even greater. Apart from the diamond and book printing industries, very few trades were open to them and the majority engaged in trading in second-hand goods and foodstuffs. Foreign trade, mainly in money and shares, was concentrated in Germany and Poland. Culturally the Ashkenazi *yishuv* depended on Germany and Eastern Europe, from where most of their rabbis came. The colloquial language was Yiddish, increasingly mixed with Dutch words. Contact with the non-Jewish population was superficial, except among the very small upper class which arose in the second half of the 18th century.

[Jozeph Michman]

Political Emancipation and National Integration, 1795–1870

EMANCIPATION PERIOD, 1795–1815. *Politics.* The Batavian Revolution of 1795, inspired by the French Revolution of 1789, brought an end to the Dutch Republic and the presence of the House of Orange in it. The Oranges left for England and in the local and national authorities the Orangist establishment was replaced by the enlightened party of the Patriots. The French army and French diplomats played a significant role in the political transformation of the country. Gradually the Batavian Republic, as it was called, replaced the old federalist system by a centralist structure. Several coups of more radical groups destabilized the political system. In 1806 the Kingdom of Holland replaced the Batavian Republic, providing the country a more direct link with the French Empire through the appointment of Louis Napoleon as king. He acted, however, too independently of his brother, resulting in his forced abdication and the annexation of the Kingdom of Holland to the Napoleonic Empire (1810). The discontent with the French grew in this period, because of the impoverishment of the country and the forced recruitment of Dutch boys for Napoleon's army. After the fatal Russian campaign, the French left the Netherlands in 1813. William of Orange returned to the country and after the Congress of Vienna in 1815 became the first king of the United Netherlands, which included the Southern Netherlands.

Demography. There was a gradual drop of the number of newcomers, owing to the difficult economic situation and the Napoleonic wars. At the beginning of the Batavian period some influential families left with the stadtholder's family to England, including a part of the important Cohen family. Migration from Germany and Eastern Europe dropped in these years. Most Jews lived in Amsterdam, with significant communities in the other large cities: Rotterdam and The Hague. In 1810 there were 49,973 Ashkenazim and 5,000 Sephardim in the Netherlands.

Economy. The Continental System, introduced by Napoleon to prevent economic relations with his arch-enemy, England, had a devastating impact on Dutch economy. Not only the ties with British companies had to be ended, also the seaways to the colonies were henceforth closed to Dutch traders. The British empire took all Dutch colonies, including the East Indies, Ceylon, and Surinam. Many rich Sephardi families had put their money in the East and West Indies Companies, which were dissolved. This had a great impact on the Sephardi community, resulting in increasing impoverishment. Also the Ashkenazi community was hit by the economic measures. In the cities the proletariat grew, while in the countryside many Jews tried to earn a living as itinerant merchants, peddlers, and beggars.

Political position. The Batavian Revolution resulted in a new republic in which enlightened ideas became policy. On the demand of the predominantly Jewish *Felix Libertate society the national parliament discussed the granting of citizenship to the Jews. On September 2, 1796, the government published the Emancipation Decree, granting civil rights to the Dutch Jews. From now on, Jews could vote and be elected to all political representative functions (including the courts). Jews were also allowed to settle anywhere in the Republic, thus opening cities like Utrecht to Jewish settlement. The ban on Jews in certain economic fields, via exclusion from the guilds, was lifted as well. After a few years the guilds were even abolished.

This political emancipation resulted in the first two Jewish parliamentarians. In 1798 H.L. Bromet and H. de H. Lemon were elected and were active in the radical enlightened faction within parliament. Jews were also elected to the municipal councils of Amsterdam, The Hague, and Rotterdam.

Organization. The Emancipation Decree also meant the abolition of the semi-autonomous "Jewish Nation." The chief rabbis and *parnassim* of the communities no longer had the legal right to rule to community as before and to enforce obedience to the *halakhah* in the private lives of its members. The authority of the *bet din* to settle all internal conflicts according to the *halakhah* was severely diminished and reduced to the strictly religious domain. Because from now on the Jewish community was no longer a corporation within the state but an association of free and independent citizens, the *parnassim* no longer had the right to collect taxes for the community. Although the legal situation changed, in practice many Jewish communities continued operating as before. In Amsterdam, the small group of enlightened Ashkenazi Jews tried to change things from within but failed and founded their own congregation, *Adat Yesurun*. Only under severe pressure of King Louis Napoleon was this community reunited with the older and larger one several years later.

One of the most enduring changes in this period was the centralization of the Jewish community. Just like the other religious groups within the Republic, the Dutch Reformed Church and the Evangelical Lutheran Church, the Jewish community was subsumed under a national organization, uniting all local communities that had enjoyed independence before. Modeled after the French consistorial system, the Opperconsistorie (1808–10) had to unite, control, and reorganize the Dutch Jewish community. The Sephardim were allowed to remain outside this organization. The Opperconsistorie functioned as part of the Department of Religious Affairs and was headed by Jonas Daniel *Meyer. Carel *Asser also played a decisive role in this organization. The Netherlands were divided into 11 provinces, headed by a consistorial synagogue controlling the *kehillot* in its vicinity. Through its rigorous emancipation policy it soon faced considerable opposition from the old establishment of *parnassim* and rabbis. It advocated the translation of the Bible into Dutch, promoted the erection of a special Jewish Corps in the army, and tried to ban Yiddish from synagogue.

After the annexation of the Kingdom of Holland into the French Napoleonic Empire in 1810, the Opperconsistorie was replaced by four regional consistories. These consistories operated under the aegis of the Consistoire Central in Paris, just like other consistories within the Empire. Because of the political developments, however, the new regional consistories had hardly any time to start their activities. In 1813 the French left the Netherlands and the consistories stopped their activities.

CENTRALIZATION AND NATIONALIZATION, 1815–1870.

Politics. The Kingdom of the Netherlands united once again Northern and Southern Netherlands. Both Amsterdam and Brussels acted as its capitals, but The Hague remained the actual administrative city, with the permanent residence of the king and his family. In 1830 a revolt broke out in the Southern Netherlands against William I's enlightened centralistic policies, including use of the Dutch language policy and control over the Catholic Church. This resulted in the establishment of Belgium, a fact accepted at last by William I in 1839. After he abdicated he was succeeded by his son, William II. Growing dissatisfaction with the autocratic style of leadership of the Oranges resulted in a growing Liberal movement. Fearing the wave of liberal revolutions that swept over Europe in 1848, William II agreed to adopt a constitution. The new constitution transferred much of the king's power to parliament. Also the election system was reorganized, resulting in the political participation of a larger part of the population.

Demography. The Jewish community remained stable in this period. As a result of the economic situation, many Jews left the cities and sought to earn their livelihoods in the countryside (called the *mediene* in Dutch Yiddish). Regional cities which had banned Jews in the Dutch Republic were now open to them. Jews settled in even the smallest villages. This resulted in a growing regional differentiation among Dutch Jewry, because regional relations determined the fate of the Jewish families in the countryside. They married among themselves, started communal life, erected synagogues, and buried their dead in new Jewish cemeteries. Also economically the *mediene* Jews cooperated intensively. This is the only period in which the relatively dominant position of Amsterdam within the Jewish community declined.

Economy. The political emancipation of 1796 did not imply socio-economic emancipation. Although political barriers were lifted and the guilds no longer existed, the position of the Jews on the labor market remained one-sided and problematic. Most Jews did not break away from the traditional patterns of employment, because of family traditions and the non-Jewish fear of new competitors. Only in the course of the century did the Jewish poor learn crafts in order to broaden the economic base of the Jewish community. In the first half of the century, however, the situation remained precarious. In the cities no less than half the Jewish population were paupers. In the countryside Jews eked out a living as butchers, peddlers, and petty merchants.

Only a small but nevertheless growing part of the community succeeded in entering new domains. The Jewish newspapers proudly mentioned Dutch Jews who obtained important jobs in the government, juridical system, or army. A number of Jewish lawyers enjoyed authority, such as Jonas Daniel *Meyer, who was a member of the constitutional committee in 1815. The *Asser and De *Pinto families produced a number of renowned lawyers, while M.H. *Godefroi became the first Jewish minister of justice. In the countryside there was a small Jewish elite, such as the families Hartogensius in Brabant, Duparc in Frisia, and Schaap in Amersfoort and Groningen.

Organization. After the collapse of the consistorial system, in the wake of Napoleon's defeat, a number of *kehillot* advocated a return to the old model, in which they enjoyed independence. The Dutch government, however, created a new central organization, the Hoofdcommissie tot de zaken der Israëliten (Supreme Committee on Israelite Affairs). This committee, being a part of the Department for Religious Affairs, functioned as an intermediary body between the government and the Jewish community. In it, the Sephardim and the Ashkenazim were brought together in one national organization. On the one hand, it enforced government laws within the community, which was structured hierarchally with the Hoofdcommissie at the top. On the other hand, the Hoofdcommissie brought complaints of the Jewish community to the attention of the government. In this way, antisemitic local authorities were dealt with by the national government. The Hoofdcommissie, functioning from 1814 to 1870, had two equally important goals: the centralization and the nationalization of the Dutch Jewish community.

In the first half of the 19th century the entire Jewish community was restructured. Local Jewish communities were brought together under the jurisdiction of the largest provincial community, called the Supreme Synagogue. Also the Southern Netherlands, until 1830, and the colonies became part of this structure. For the rabbis a similar structure was created, with the chief rabbis responsible for the jurisdiction of their Supreme Synagogue. But also Jewish education, poor relief, and the *mohalim* were reorganized in order to make it easier to be controlled by the Hoofdcommissie and the national government.

Nationalization. The centralization of the community served the second objective of the Hoofdcommissie, namely its nationalization. The Emancipation Decree reduced Jewish identity to a religious one only. All national Jewish characteristics had to be eradicated and replaced by a Dutch identity. Therefore, Yiddish was combated and Dutch promoted. This language policy was successful in the end. The implementation of the policy was gradual. In order to have the new generation raised with Dutch as its mother tongue, much attention was paid to the Jewish schools. At first new Dutch textbooks were written to replace older Yiddish methods. Besides the Dutch language and Dutch history, also geography and mathematics were introduced into the school curriculum. As most of the teachers were only able to teach in Yiddish – because they were recent immigrants from Poland – they were tolerated for a while, until the new generation of Dutch schoolteachers was ready. Thereafter things went quickly and Yiddish was completely banned from the Jewish schools. The national inspector, Dr. Samuel Israel *Mulder, reported to the Hoofdcommissie on the language situation in the schools. If Yiddish was still in use somewhere, the government subsidy was withdrawn. After the new school law of 1857, which ended government subsidies for religious schools, the Jewish schools were closed and the children started attending public schools. Jewish religious instruction was given after regular school and on Sundays.

No less important was the shunting aside of Yiddish in the religious domain. This began with a prohibition against making announcements in Yiddish. These now had to be in Dutch. The second step was the promotion of Dutch sermons, replacing the Yiddish (and Portuguese) *derashot*. A prize was established for the best Jewish sermon in Dutch. Because many rabbis were from Poland and Germany and were not able to preach in Dutch, they were allowed to give their addresses in German. In the meanwhile the Dutch Israelite Seminary was reorganized in order to produce a new generation of

Dutch-speaking rabbis. After the installation of Joseph Hirsch *Duenner as rector of the Seminary in 1862, his pupils gradually took over the rabbinical positions in the Netherlands. From that moment on, Yiddish vanished from the pulpits and only Dutch was used to address the communities.

This language policy was accompanied by a series of measures to Protestantize synagogal liturgy. The Jewish elite that staffed the Hoofdcommissie and the boards of *parnassim* of the local *kehillot* promoted decorum and order in the synagogue. They forbade speaking during the service, banned traditional *Homenkloppen* on Purim, and tried to introduce the ceremony of confirmation in addition to the bar mitzvah.

Religion. However, these innovations did not result in the founding of Reform communities in the Netherlands. Although there were some attempts to introduce Reform Judaism in the Netherlands, especially in Amsterdam and the Eastern Provinces, they failed. Because the Jewish community, via the Hoofdcommissie, was controlled by the government, there was no chance for Reform Judaism. The government did not want any arguments within the community. The ruling Jewish elite had adopted the same policy as the Dutch patricians: a constant search for the middle way and avoidance of extremes. In order to keep the whole community together, only minor innovations were introduced, and all the religious ones had to be approved by the chief rabbis. The boundaries of the *halakhah* determined the space of policymakers in the Netherlands. On the whole, the Sephardi model, in which social integration and religious halakhic observance were combined, was popular among both Ashkenazi and Sephardi elites.

[Bart Wallet (2nd ed.)]

1870–1940: Rapid Growth and the Emergence of a Dutch-Jewish Sub-Culture

WHY 1870–1940? The year 1870 has been widely accepted in Dutch and Dutch-Jewish historiography as the beginning of a new period. Generally, industrialization and economic expansion improved the economic situation of all sectors of society, but also caused growing social awareness and the creation of trade unions; the democratization process caused the masses to get involved in politics, thus promoting political parties. Yet, this was accompanied in The Netherlands by a segmentation of society into several subgroups (the Protestant "pillar" with its subcurrents; the Catholic one; the Liberal or "neutral" one; and the leftist one, which included Socialists and various Communist factions). These developments affected all Jews very much – but especially those in Amsterdam, which was the capital and a major harbor – and Jewish society was deeply involved in all of them. Additionally, the countrywide community structure (with its two traditional wings: the Ashkenazi Nederlandsch-Israëlitisch Kerkgenootschap and the Sephardic Portugeesch-Israëlitisch Kerkgenootschap), which had started to evolve during the "French period" at the beginning of the 19th century, received its renewed structure in 1870, as a (delayed) result of the introduction of the constitutional principle of separation of church and state some 30 years before.

As the Netherlands did not participate in World War I, it affected Dutch Jewry only partially and indirectly and did not constitute a major turning point in its history, as was the case in most other European countries. Therefore, the period starting in 1870 can be seen as ending only in 1940, with the Nazi German occupation of the country.

DEMOGRAPHY AND OCCUPATIONS. The Jewish population grew during this period from 68,003 in 1869 (1.90% of the general population) to 97,324 in 1889 (2.15%), 106,409 in 1909 (1.81%), and 115,223 in 1920 (1.68). Afterwards a certain decline began: the registered number of Jews (who declared themselves as such) in 1930 was 111,917 (1.41%), a decline that can be attributed to lower birth dates and a growing percentage of intermarriages (in Amsterdam this grew between 1901 and 1934 from 6 to 17 percent, which was still low as compared to other West European countries). However, in the 1930s, mainly due to the emigration of many thousands of Jewish refugees from Nazi Germany and Austria, of whom about 16,000 remained in the country, the number grew again (for the census carried out in 1941 under the German occupation, see the Holocaust section below). The Jews anticipated general demographical trends in the Netherlands, both regarding the rapid growth during the second half of the 19th century and the declining birth and death rates, which point to their earlier and faster modernization. This included urbanization (in 1930, 80% lived in seven major cities: Rotterdam and the Hague, each with more than 10,000 Jews, and Groningen, Apeldoorn, Arnhem, and Utrecht with 2,500 to 10,000; Amsterdam towered over all other communities and became the main Jewish city, with 44% of all Jews in the country in 1869, amounting to 30,000, about 60%, or 68,758, in 1920 and almost 57% in 1941, or 80,000) and an improvement in their socio-economic position. The developments from the beginning of the 20th century also caused the rapid aging of the community.

As a result of the processes of modernization in general and of industrialization in particular, the occupations of Jews diversified. Jews were overrepresented in commerce, but quite underrepresented in the agrarian sector. They constituted a major part of the diamond trade and industry, and had also a considerable share in the textile industry. The poverty among the Amsterdam Jews declined somewhat from the end of the 1860s as a result of the development of the diamond industry. However, this branch had its ups and downs, affecting a great part of the Jewish population in the city, particularly in the 1930s. Thus, in spite of a general improvement, the Jewish proletariat remained large. Some Jewish families became extremely successful (and wealthy) in some economic sectors: textile (Salomonson, Menko, Spanjaard, Van Gelderen, etc.), retail chains (Cohen, Gerzon, Goudsmit, Isaac), food (Van den Bergh, whose enterprise later developed into the multinational Unilever), Zwanenberg, whose meat factory later evolved into the pharmaceutical giant Organon, and some in banking (Lissa en Kann, Van Nierop, Rosenthal, Teixeira de Mattos, Wertheim, Mannheimer). Jews were also overrepresented in the educated classes and the professions (higher percentages with academic titles, dentists, economists, physicians, and lawyers), even though the general numbers were relatively low.

RELIGIOUS DEVELOPMENTS AND SECULARIZATION. The secularization of the Jewish community intensified during this period, and this also eased the accompanying process of acculturation. Indeed, this process was more marked in the big cities, but as a result of the urbanization process its impact was decisive. Nevertheless, most of the Jews remained formally attached to the official orthodox community organizations, especially in the communities in the countryside. Together with the relatively low intermarriage rate, a Dutch-Jewish sub-culture thus crystallized. With the relative improvement in the economic situation of many Jews and the emergence of a Jewish bourgeoisie, many communities decided during this period to build new synagogues or renovate them. Some were designed by well-known architects (for instance, in Groningen).

The secularization process affected the tiny Portuguese (Sephardi) community immensely, and it was hence characterized by ongoing stagnation; only the splendor of the past kept the descendants attached to it. However, in the Ashkenazi community, which was also affected by the same developments, some noteworthy facts should be mentioned. First, it succeeded in keeping wealthy secular figures involved in leading positions in the community, on the condition that they would not interfere in religious issues. An illuminating example of this "pact," which would characterize all the communities in the country for decades, was the banker and politician A.C. *Wertheim, who served as vice chairman of the Amsterdam Jewish community between 1878 and 1886, and afterwards, until his death in 1897, as chairman. In the religious sphere, the coming of the Cracow-born and Bonn University graduate Rabbi Joseph Zwi (Hirsch) *Duenner in 1862 was of major importance. He first was appointed as rector of the Nederlandsch-Israëlitisch Seminarium (rabbinical seminary). In this function, where he served until his death in 1911, he reformed the curriculum by introducing an academic approach to talmudic studies. He thus trained and shaped several generations of Dutch rabbis who served throughout the country. After a decade of success in the seminary, he was appointed chief rabbi of Amsterdam and the province of North Holland in 1874. In this position, and because of his religious and general scholarly capacity, he became the unparalleled spokesman of Dutch orthodoxy and Jewry in general. And as there was no official chief rabbi of the country, he was in effect regarded as such. Duenner had been a proto-Zionist since the 1860s, corresponding with such persons as Moses *Hess and R. Zacharias *Frankel in Germany. Upon the establishment of the Zionist movement by Theodor *Herzl in 1897, he welcomed and supported it. His Zionist views legitimized the movement in the Netherlands but were not accepted by most of his students at the seminary. However, a minority of his students became active in *Mizrachi, and played a significant role in it. Most of his children and descendants also became fervent Mizrachists and made *aliyah* before the Holocaust.

As there was no chief rabbinate for the entire country, the chief rabbis of the different provinces decided at the turn of the century to try to coordinate their views on major issues from time to time. This was done through the unofficial body named Vergadering van Opperrabbijnen, which existed until the deportations of the Jews from the Netherlands in the Holocaust (in 1942).

Reform Judaism, so strongly developing in Central Europe, Britain, and the United States from the mid-19th century, did not find a real echo in the Netherlands until 1930. At the end of the 1920s Lily *Montagu of England, chairperson of the World Union for Progressive Judaism (WUPJ), first approached the industrialist Zwanenberg, and through him contacted several wealthy persons in the Hague. After several speeches on Reform Judaism by visiting leading Reform personalities, a tiny community was established in that city at the end of 1930, headed by Rabbi Meir Lasker, who was chosen and sent by the WUPJ. About a year later a Liberal-Religious Church Organization (i.e., countrywide roof organization) was institutionalized, followed by the establishment of a second community, established in Amsterdam, in January 1932. The appearance of Reform/Liberal Judaism on the Dutch Jewish scene caused much debate, even though the number of adherents of the new stream was at that time actually insignificant. One interesting point was the fact that among the first Reform Judaism activists there were many Zionists. With the influx of German-Jewish refugees from 1933, the movement became rooted, albeit with a clearly German character causing tensions within the movement between the "Dutch" and "Germans". Among the German refugees joining this movement was the Otto *Frank family, whose daughter Anne would become famous for the diary she wrote during the Holocaust.

Jews in politics and Jewish politics: between Socialism and Zionism. While this period witnessed both the emergence of modern antisemitism and vehement outbursts of traditional Jew-hatred in other parts of Europe, the Netherlands was never plagued with these phenomena. Religious anti-Judaism existed, however, as it was part and parcel of Christian thought. It was expressed in some of the literature and also in politics, mostly by the founder of the Anti-Revolutionary (i.e., right-wing Protestant) party, Abraham Kuyper, in the last decades of the 19th century. Fascist and racist antisemitism made its appearance only in the 1930s, and remained marginal. No party proposed the abolition of the emancipation. Nevertheless, the marked segmentation of Dutch society and its relative conservatism perpetuated reservations about the Jews. Consequently, until 1940 no Jews were appointed to national or key representative positions, such as mayors, commissioners of the king, governors of colonies, ambassadors, or consuls. Many other functions also remained closed to Jews. But Jews were members of political parties – from the Liberals to the Social Democrats to the Communists; they were especially strongly represented in the Social Democratic Workers Party (SDAP). The attraction of Jews to socialism had started already in the 1860s, with the Jewish diamond cutters being the first to organize in a general labor union (ANDB). This union served as a cornerstone from which the larger labor union and afterward the SDAP emerged. Henri *Polak (1868–1943) played a major role in these developments; he succeeded in leading large parts of the Jewish proletariat in Amsterdam to socialism. He was for several years chairman of the party, and afterwards its representative in the Dutch senate (Eerste Kamer). A number of other Jews also filled leading positions in the movement. The radical left wing David *Wijnkoop (1876–1941), son of a rabbi, was the most prominent figure. He was one of the founders of the Communist Party, and represented the party in the House of Commons (Tweede Kamer) and in the Amsterdam municipal council for most of the interwar period.

During the first half of the 19th century, Dutch Jewry had developed some strong ties to Palestine. In the beginning of the century the European-wide fundraising organization *Va'ad ha-Pekidim ve-Amarkalim was established by Zwi Hirsch *Lehren, and his sons continued his initiative, playing a major role in the life of the old *yishuv*. A group of Dutch Jews immigrated to Palestine and established Kolel HoD (Holland-Deutschland). But the influence of the Lehrens gradually declined, both in Palestine and in the Netherlands, from the beginning of the second half of the century. The Ḥovevei Zion movement, whose emergence was strongly linked to the difficult situation of the Jews in czarist Russia, did not win much support in the Netherlands.

But the political Zionist movement, established by Herzl, attracted two high-profile figures: the banker Jacobus *Kann, who attended the first Zionist Congress in Basel in 1879, and Rabbi Duenner, who openly and avidly supported the new movement from its inception and thus made possible its introduction into Dutch Jewish society. The Dutch Zionist Union (NZB) was established in 1899. In the beginning it attempted to attract the Jewish proletariat, but this effort failed almost entirely. In middle-class and certain religious circles success was higher, thus creating an active nucleus. Some of the first- and second-generation of Dutch Zionists played an important role in the world movement and in the new *yishuv* in Palestine in the first decades of the 20th century, such as Jacobus Kann, Eliezer Siegfried *Hoofien, Nehemia *de Lieme, and later Fritz (Perez) *Bernstein. The convening of the 1907 Zionist Congress in the Hague, contributed to the growth of the Union. It nevertheless met resistance from many circles. During World War I, a considerable number of East European Jews from Antwerp fled to the country, mainly to Scheveningen. As many among them were Zionists, their presence had an impact on the spread of Zionism in the Netherlands, especially among youngsters. It was in the wake of this and of the Balfour Declaration, which demonstrated the political success of Zionism, that the training of *halutzim* (first from abroad) at Dutch farms started, and a roof organization for all Zionist youth movements in the country – the Joodse Jeugdfederatie (JJF – Jewish Youth Federation) – was established. The Balfour Declaration also contributed to securing for the NZB an important place in Dutch Jewish organizational life. In the 1930s, in the face of the rise of antisemitism in general and the rise of the Nazis to power in particular, the movement continued to grow. Among its youngsters radicalism grew stronger, and calls for "dissimilation" from identification with the Netherlands and Dutch culture were voiced.

Social care, education, and culture. With modernization and acculturation proceeding, the traditional Jewish local organizations for social care ("Chevres") were transformed into a network of modern philanthropic organizations, many of them countrywide. They included organizations such as the Dutch-Jewish Organization for the Poor (Nederlandsch-Israëlitisch Armbestuur) and homes for the aged; health care institutions, such as the Joodsche Invalide and the Nederlandsch Israëlitisch Ziekenhuis (hospital); institutions for the mentally ill, such as the Apeldoornsche Bosch, etc. In the 1920s a (pro-Zionist) Union of Jewish Women (Joodsche Vrouwenraad) was established, which focused on welfare activities. Many organizations dealt especially with youth. Most of these institutions were supported by wealthy assimilated Jews.

The Jewish school system had deteriorated towards the middle of the 19th century. But the Elementary Education Act of 1857 changed the situation dramatically. The Jewish schools for the poor were abolished, and the children were integrated in the general school system (schools with 50% Jewish students would close on the Jewish Sabbath). Almost all children attending middle-class schools were also integrated in the general schools. Only in Amsterdam did several Jewish schools continue to exist, with a reduced numbers of students. The norm for Jewish children became to attend a local public school and have supplementary Jewish lessons on Sundays. In several communities additional lessons in Judaism were given at other times. The impact of this collapse of Jewish education was a rapid decline in Jewish knowledge among Dutch Jews. In order to counter this development a school network – Jewish Special Education – was established in Amsterdam in 1905. As a result of social awareness, teachers of Jewish studies at elementary and high schools organized in a union called Achawa in 1894.

With the growing number of Jews – secular as well as religious – getting academic training, together with a renewed search for Jewish identity, interest in Jewish studies and especially in Dutch Jewish history developed. An association for Jewish studies was established, and many publications, usually with an emancipatory approach, were published and read by a broad audience. In the second half of the 1920s the weekly *De Vrijdagavond* served as a spokesman for this trend. One of the outstanding historians of Dutch Jewish history was Sigmund *Seeligmann, who had emigrated from Germany.

The Jewish press played an important role in daily life and in promoting Jewish identity. The major general weeklies were the Amsterdam *Nieuw Israëlitisch Weekblad* (NIW), established in 1865, which became the leading Jewish newspaper of the country (existing into the 21st century); the *Centraal Blad voor Israëliten in Nederland* and the *Israëlitische Letterbode.* Beside these there were many organizational weeklies, such as the Zionist *Joodsche Wachter*, or cultural ones, such as *De Vrijdagavond.*

This period is also characterized by the emergence of many Jews active in the fields of literature, theater, cabaret, and the arts. The best-known authors were: the dramatist Herman *Heijermans (1864–1924), who depicted Jewish life in Amsterdam; the poet Jacob Israel de *Haan (1881–1924), a Zionist who emigrated to Palestine and became an ultra-Orthodox anti-Zionist and was murdered by an activist of the Haganah; his sister, the prose writer Carry van *Bruggen (1881–1932), who became one of the most influential writers in the Netherlands in the first decades of the 20th century; and the novelist Israel *Querido (1872–1932). There were many performing musicians among the Jews, but the only composer of importance was Sem Dresden (1881–1957). Many more Jews were active in the theater: Esther de Boer van Rijk (1853–1937), Louis de Vries (1971–1940), and the noted cabaret performer Louis Davids (1883–1939). The most famous painter was Jozef *Israëls (1824–1911); others were his son Isaac Israëls (1865–1934) and Martin Monnickendam (1874–1941). The most important sculptor was Joseph Mendes *da Costa (1863–1939), and the best-known architect was Michel *de Klerk (1884–1923), founder of the "Amsterdam School."

Refugees from Nazi Germany and the threat of the 1930s. The rise of Nazism in Germany caused the emigration and flight of tens of thousands of Jews from there. Neighboring Netherlands, with its language close to German, became an important country for the (temporary) stay and for the transit of fleeing German Jews. A total of about 34,000 Jewish refugees arrived in the Netherlands; around 24,000 stayed for more than two weeks, and after the German occupation in 1940 there were still 15,000–16,000 in the country. The rise of Hitler to power and the first anti-Jewish measures prompted the establishment of a Comité voor Bijzondere Joodsche Belangen (CBJB – Committee for Special Jewish Interests) in March 1933, consisting of a number of prestigious figures in the Dutch Jewish community and headed by Abraham *Asscher. The influx of refugees caused the CBJB to establish a subcommittee for Jewish Refugees (JVC), headed by Prof. David *Cohen. The combined CBJB-JVC turned into the most powerful organization in Dutch Jewry on the eve of the Holocaust, which dealt with the Dutch authorities and with international organizations and maintained contact with Jews and non-Jews of all parts of society, monitored political developments, and commanded a large budget. Its leaders and infrastructure became the basis for the Joodsche Raad (Jewish Council) during the Nazi occupation.

On the Eve of the Holocaust. All in all, on the eve of the German invasion in May 1940, Dutch Jewry had generally adapted itself to the Dutch mentality and way of life and saw themselves as full Dutch citizens. However, the percentage of mixed marriages, although growing, was still low as compared with other West European democratic countries; and within the segmented Dutch society Jews had developed a marked subculture. With the influx of Jewish refugees, which were assisted by the Dutch Jewish community, the perception by Gentiles of "the Jews" as a different entity was reemphasized. From the Jewish side, the infusion of Dutch Jewry with new energy linked to general worldwide Jewish crosscurrents and organizations – such as Zionism, which became an important force in the 1920s and 1930s, and Reform Judaism, which emerged in the 1930s – pointed to possible new directions of development.

1940–1945: The Holocaust

The historiography of the Holocaust in the Netherlands has been relatively intensive and comprehensive as compared to almost all countries (except for Germany) and started immediately after the end of World War II. A first comprehensive history (authored by Hans Wielek/Kweksilber) appeared as early as 1947, and another five were written in the following six decades (by Abel Herberg, Jacques Presser, Louis de Jong, Jozeph Michman/Hartog Beem/Dan Michman, and Bob Moore). In addition, many partial studies have been made. The reason for the intensity in research is to be found in the urge to find answers to the puzzling fact that about 102,600 of the 140,000 "full" Jews (according to the German definition) living in the Netherlands at the beginning of the German occupation perished due to the persecutions, i.e., 74%. This is, in relative terms, the highest death toll in any West European Jewish community, including Germany itself. Among the additional 20,000 "half" and "quarter" Jews, most survived.

GERMAN INTENTIONS. Whereas the German attitude towards France in the wake of the occupation of Western Europe starting in May 1940 was relatively conciliatory, and whereas policies regarding Belgium were for a long time undecided, the intentions towards the Netherlands were clear from the start. The Dutch were perceived as a German tribe which had taken a separate course for several centuries, but should now be reintegrated into the commonwealth of Germanic tribes. Consequently, Arthur *Seyss-Inquart, an Austrian Nazi, was appointed Reichskommissar for the occupied country, Reichskommissar being in the Nazi vocabulary a title assigned to persons appointed to carry out a special ideological mission. He articulated his fanatic adherence to his mission in a public speech in Amsterdam on March 12, 1941, which was translated into Dutch and disseminated among the population. Also resulting from this was the fact that the position of the SS in the Netherlands was from the beginning much stronger than in other West European countries. The "final solution" of the Jewish question in the Netherlands was implemented by the German authorities – whose heads consisted of Nazi radicals, among whom were several other Austrians in addition to Seyss-Inquart – with much fervor from shortly after the occupation. Before the Nazi decision in the matter of a

European-wide Final Solution (in the second half of 1941), this meant segregation and impoverishment; afterwards – from 1942 – it meant the nearly total removal of the Jews through well-organized arrests and deportations. Dutch Jewry was not a tabula rasa for the occupiers: the Jewish Department of the *Sicherheitsdient* of the SS had already produced a report in March 1939 on "The Jews in Holland," which outlined the basic structure of Dutch Jewry and included the names of many of its leading figures.

ANTI-JEWISH MEASURES BEFORE THE DEPORTATION PERIOD (1940–1942). The first months following the capitulation of the country (May 14, 1940) passed relatively quietly, although some minor anti-Jewish actions were taken (such as the removal of Jews from anti-aircraft defense units or the first registration of Jews in the province of Zeeland); some Dutch organizations fired Jews on their own initiative. In September 1940 the German authorities, under the direction of Generalkommissar Fritz Schmidt, started the planning of systematic anti-Jewish measures. All Jewish newspapers were closed down. Then, in October–November, all people serving in the civil service (governmental, provincial, municipal, judicial, schools and universities) were ordered to sign an "Aryan declaration" (a statement of not having Jewish parents or grandparents) for themselves and their spouses; Jews were consequently fired (November 4). Both the secretaries-general (the Dutch heads of ministries who had stayed in the country after the flight of the government) and the majority of the Supreme Court decided to accede to this order, which consequently affected even the Jewish president of the Supreme Court, Judge Lodewijk E. *Visser. Protests were limited, and voiced mainly at some universities. At the same time, Jews were ordered to register their enterprises (October 22), making possible "Aryanization" (20,690 enterprises, most of them small, were listed). On this occasion the term "Jew" was legally defined (as in Germany).

On January 10, 1941, registration of all Jews was ordered. Only a small number of Jews did not show up. With the introduction of identification cards, IDs for Jews were stamped with a "J." On March 12, the first of four expropriation and Aryanization decrees was promulgated. The most fateful among them, conceived by the economic mastermind *Generalkommissar* Hans Fischboeck, was the one enacted in August; it ordered the concentration of all bank accounts of Jews in a special branch of the Jewish Lippmann-Rosenthal ("Liro") bank, which was under German control. The possibility to use the accounts was restricted, and on January 1, 1943, all individual accounts were concentrated in one joint account. From the opening of the bank, the Jewish accounts were used by the German authorities to finance, and thus supervise, the activities of the Joodsche Raad (see below). In addition, *Einsatzstab* Rosenberg confiscated Jewish private and public libraries, works of art, and later also furniture. From the summer of 1941 Jews were prohibited from visiting parks and other public places, and a daily curfew from 8 P.M. to 6 A.M. was imposed on them; they were allowed to buy in shops only between 3 and 5 P.M. Jews were also removed from all general organizations and societies. In August *Generalkommissar* Friedrich Wimmer ordered the removal of all Jewish children from the general school system; a Jewish school system was opened under the auspices of the Joodsche Raad.

All these (and more) legal measures were accompanied from time to time by brutal roundups ("razzias") and arrests. On Saturday February 22, in the wake of a violent incident in a Jewish café, in which a *Sicherheitpolizei* unit was involved, the old Jewish quarter in the center of Amsterdam was closed and around 390 Jewish youngsters were brutally arrested and beaten – all upon the orders of *Generalkommissar* Hanns Albin Rauter. They were deported shortly afterwards; 50 died in the Buchenwald concentration camp and only one survived, around 340 were sent to the Mauthausen concentration camp, and died there in horrific conditions. In June another 300 were rounded up in Amsterdam, in mid-September more than a 100 in several cities in the provinces, and in November several dozen in other cities in the east of the country. All were sent to Mauthausen and worked to death. As "death notices" were sent from Mauthausen to the families, "Mauthausen" became the most feared symbol of Nazi terror for Jews in the country (it was replaced by "Auschwitz" only after 1945). During this whole period, from time to time Dutch Nazis acted with violence towards Jews and Jewish institutions, such as synagogues. Such clashes with Jews, in the second week of February 1941, which ended with the death of one Dutch Nazi, served as the background for the establishment of the Joodsche Raad.

JOODSCHE RAAD VOOR AMSTERDAM (JR; JEWISH COUNCIL). The JR, established on February 12, 1941, on the verbal order of Senator Dr. Hans Böhmcker, Seyss-Inquart's personal representative in charge of the city of Amsterdam and of anti-Jewish measures, became a pivotal institution in Jewish life under the German occupation. Its creation was apparently an improvised reaction to the above-mentioned clashes between proletarian Jews and Dutch Nazis several days before. In spite of the abundance of documentary material on the activities of the JR from German, Jewish, and Dutch sources, there is no document from before its establishment regarding any intentions to do so. Its establishment can be seen better in the broader context of the establishment of *Judenraete* on the initiative of SS officials throughout Europe, as a step in controlling the Jewish community as a collective entity. The authority of the JR was first limited to Amsterdam only, but, during 1941, with the involvement and sanction of the German authorities, it gradually extended to the entire country (through a network of "representatives"); this status was finalized at the end of October with the dissolution of the Jewish Coordination Committee (see below). It was headed by Abraham Asscher and Prof. David Cohen, who had chaired the Committee for Special Jewish Affairs and the Jewish Refugee Committee in the 1930s (see above), and were also active in general and Jewish politics. The JR was supervised by the Zentralstelle fuer juedische Auswanderung, established in April 1941. Through the JR the Germans incrementally segregated the Jewish population and created an administrative and mental ghetto. All announcements concerning Jews were disseminated through its weekly, *Het Joodsche Weekblad*. Social care, first of the former refugees from Germany and afterwards of the increasingly impoverished Dutch Jews, was transferred to the JR and made many dependent on its services. It had to organize the segregated Jewish education system from September 1941. When industrialist Bernard van Leer was allowed to leave the country in September 1941, he left behind an enormous fund which enabled the JR to sponsor cultural institutions and activities (orchestras, theaters, cabaret, lectures, sports). For its financial needs the JR first solicited contributions (those who did not contribute money could received no services from the JR), but afterwards it obtained its money from Jewish funds administered by the Germans. Its bureaucracy grew constantly and peaked at the end of 1942 to more than 17,000 people. Although not intended in the beginning to be exploited for deportations, this institution became vital to their success in 1942–43. Through its administration deportation orders were disseminated, and deportees were cared for while those remaining behind were provided with food, health care, and welfare services.

FORCED LABOR, CONCENTRATION OF JEWS IN AMSTERDAM, DEPORTATIONS. Among the later measures of the pre-deportation period was the recruitment of Jews for forced labor. This was imposed on about 7,500 Jewish males from 85 towns (about 2,500 were later released) from the beginning of 1942, through the JR; they were sent to 42 camps, all over the Netherlands. These people were ready victims at the start of the deportations (the so-called "labor recruitment" – *Arbeiteinsatz*) "to the east."

Non-Dutch Jews had to leave the coastal region shortly after the occupation. At the end of 1941 Jews from the coastal region could move only to Amsterdam. Later the Jews in other parts of the country were forced to resettle in Amsterdam. Finally, the Jews were forbidden to live in eight of the eleven provinces. The remaining three provinces were restricted on April 13, 1943, leaving Amsterdam the only city for Jews to live in.

The cleansing of the Netherlands from its Jews as part of the Final Solution was planned by Adolf *Eichmann and his staff as part of the joint cleansing of Western European. Planning commenced in April 1942. On April 29 the JR was ordered to distribute a yellow "Jewish Star" to all Jews in the country; this was carried out within a few days in the beginning of May. Deportation orders were sent out, through the JR, in the beginning of July, and a first roundup was carried out on July 14. From then until September 29, 1943, more than 100,000 Jews were deported in about 100 transports, mainly to Auschwitz (60,000) and Sobibor (34,000, all in 1943); only a handful survived. They were sent via the *Westerbork *Polizeiliches durchgangslager* (Police (Jewish) transit camp), a camp originally established in 1939 by the Dutch government for German Jewish refugees. In the camp certain cultural and religious activities were allowed. Tuesdays, the weekly day on which deportations trains left the camp, were the fearful "judgment days." A tiny group of *Prominenten* was transported to Theresienstadt (about 5,000). In 1943–44 about 4,000 Jews with "Palestine papers" were sent to the Bergen Belsen "exchange camp" (*Austauschlager*) for a possible exchange for Germans from abroad. 222 were indeed exchanged in the summer of 1944 for Templars from Palestine; 136 entered Switzerland; 25% of the Bergen Belsen Jews survived. In addition to Westerbork there was *KL Herzogenbusch*, next to the city of *Vught, a camp built in 1943. It served as a place for forced labor and later also for the concentration of Jews. From June 1943 to June 1944 all 12,000 inmates of Vught were sent to Westerbork.

JEWISH LIFE AND RESPONSES; FLIGHT AND HIDING. At the beginning of the occupation Jews tried to maintain their prewar life. The community organizations continued their existence until the end of the deportations, but from 1941 lost their importance. As pressure on the Jews grew in the fall of 1940, a Joodsche Coordinatie Commissie (Jewish Coordination Committee, JCC), initiated by Zionists, backed by the community organizations, and headed by Lodewijk Visser, was established in December 1940. Its major aims were to advise the Jews politically in the new situation, help those who were in economic distress, and develop cultural activities. It was first helped by the organizational infrastructure of the Committee for Special Jewish Affairs and the Jewish Refugee Committee, headed by David Cohen. With the establishment of the JR less than two months later, the ways of the two organizations parted and later clashed; the JCC was finally dissolved in October 1941. With the growing expropriations, removal from jobs, and other segregation measures, the economic situation of most Jews rapidly deteriorated. Religious life was allowed by the Germans until the end of the deportations. However, ritual slaughter was prohibited, except for poultry. For Sukkot (Feast of Tabernacles) in 1940 and 1941 *etrogim* could be imported from Italy and *matzot* were openly baked by the Hollandia *matzah* factory.

Dutch Jews have been called "naïve" in their reaction to the deportations; this would account in part of the high percentage of deportees. It is, however, clear that the emancipatory background which caused Dutch Jews not to be rebellious vis-à-vis authorities, the late emergence of a significant Dutch resistance (only in 1943), and lack of knowledge about what was happening in "the East" together shaped the pattern of response of many Jews. Additionally, the enormous concentration of Jews in Amsterdam made it hard for many to find hiding places; in other parts of the country the chances of survival were generally higher. As for knowledge about the murders, it is typical that the JR team in charge of gathering information on the fate of the deportees still reported in January 1943 that apparently many of those sent to Auschwitz were alive and living in family units! Nevertheless, after the first weeks of arrests in the summer of 1942, the percentage of Jews ignoring deportation orders grew enormously. According to a recent study by Marnix Croes and Peter Tammes (2004), about 28,000 Jews went into hiding, finding shelter with non-Jews. But only about 16,000 of these "divers" survived, as many were apprehended. Apparently, many more Jews looked for hiding places. Others tried to escape through Belgium and France to Switzerland and Spain, and some succeeded in doing so. Among them was a considerable number of members of the Halutz underground organization, headed by Joachim (Shushu) Simon, succeeding thanks to the organization and support of Joop *Westerweel and some aides. Some Jews, especially from the political left, albeit not too many, participated in general resistance groups

ATTITUDE OF NON-JEWS: PROTESTS, RESCUE, INDIFFERENCE, AND COLLABORATION. In spite of the high percentage of Dutch Jews who perished, the view of the Dutch as having helped the Jews is widespread. Like any historical generalization this perception is a distortion and quite exaggerated – yet not entirely erroneous. With the removal of Jews from the civil service in October 1940, Leiden University law professor R.P. Cleveringa openly delivered a protest lecture, and was later arrested. On February 25–26 a general strike, initiated by the Communist movement but spontaneously supported by many thousands of citizens, was held in Amsterdam and surroundings. The strike was sparked by many weeks of anti-Jewish actions by Dutch Nazis, and by the brutal roundup of February 22. The strike, unparalleled in Europe under the Nazi regime, was suppressed. It became a much-praised symbol, but had no long-term effect on the persecutions. With the beginning of the deportations in July 1942, an unprecedented initiative was undertaken by all Dutch churches to jointly protest against the persecutions during Sunday prayer services. Under the pressure of the occupier the Protestant churches retreated; the Catholics, under the leadership of Archbishop J. de Jong, did not give in and read out the declaration of protest. In reprisal, all Jews converted to Catholicism were arrested and almost all of them sent with the first deportees to Auschwitz. Among them was Edith *Stein (1891–1942). As mentioned, about 28,000 Jews went into hiding, finding shelter with non-Jews – the majority of them Catholics in the southern provinces and *Gereformeerde* Protestants in Friesland and elsewhere. As hiding could be maintained only with a circle of support, this number signifies that a considerable number of ordinary Dutchmen extended help. On the other hand, about 12,000 "divers" were apprehended, many of them through denunciators. Moreover, it can fairly be said that the efficiency and general disciplined obedience of the Dutch bureaucracy served the Germans in the persecution and deportation operations. For instance, the registration of the Jews in 1941 was carried out with the utmost punctuality. And as recent study has shown, during the Final Solution some sectors, such as the police command and especially the Amsterdam police, collaborated to a considerable extent. The overall picture is therefore varied.

[Dan Michman (2nd ed.)]

Postwar and Contemporary Period

RESTORATION. The reintegration of surviving Jews into Dutch society after the devastation of World War II was not without serious problems. Jews who returned from the concentration camps or emerged from their hiding-places were faced with neglect and sometimes outright hostility. In addition, Jews suffered from a trend, supported by the former Resistance movements, to remold them as soon as possible into full Dutchmen without the slightest reference to their Jewishness. This attitude led to the suppression of Jewish identity and also placed Jews in a disadvantageous position, since their situation was the same as that of other Dutchmen. They had lost most of their relatives and all of their possessions and the supportive infrastructure of the Jewish community no longer existed. The Jews received support from international Jewish organizations, such as the American Jewish *Joint Distribution Committee, the *Jewish Agency, and the *Jewish Brigade. In the summer of 1945 the central Jewish weekly, the *Nieuw Israelietisch Weekblad*, resumed publication. Other institutions slowly followed.

Prewar Jewish rights were not automatically restored; for example, a bitter struggle developed over Jewish war orphans who had been in hiding with non-Jewish families. These children were not handed over to the Jewish community as a matter of course. The authorities established a committee with a Christian majority of former rescuers and a minority of Jews. The central issue was not whether it was better for some of these children to remain with their foster families or to return to a Jewish family or orphanage. The main question was who was to decide their fate: the Jewish community – as would have been the case with Jewish orphans in prewar circumstances – or the Christian rescuers. Some 358 children remained in non-Jewish homes, just over a quarter of the cases the committee had to decide upon.

Restitution of buildings and other fixed assets proceeded at a slow pace and while most had been returned to the Jewish community by around 1950, other forms of compensation and restitution came only in stages and over a much longer period of time. The possessions of murdered Jews, who had no heirs, initially were considered Dutch and not specifically Jewish. Insurance companies, banks, and the government itself, after much pressure, made these final restitutions to the Jewish community only around the year 2000.

DEMOGRAPHY. In 1945 the surviving number of Jews in the Netherlands was estimated at between 28,000 and 35,000, of whom about 8,000 had survived because they were married to non-Jews. In addition to this group there were another 20,000 "people of Jewish descent," persons with one Jewish parent or one Jewish grandparent, who also had had a much better chance to survive. Some of them rejoined the community. The fact that many survivors were married to non-Jews or were children of mixed marriages transformed the community into a far more assimilated one when compared with the prewar situation. A second major change was of a socio-economic nature: the proletariat of Amsterdam had been wiped out completely. The postwar community was a typically middle-class one. A third feature was the fact that more Jews who originated in Eastern Europe were among the survivors: being more suspicious than the average Dutch Jew, they had quickly understood the seriousness of their situation and had taken measures at an earlier stage during the occupation. In the immediate postwar years some 5,000 Jews left the country, mainly for the U.S. Some 1,500 Zionists among these emigrants, who were very active in the postwar leadership of the community, went to Israel before 1950.

According to demographic studies in 2000 the total Jewish population in the Netherlands remained at 43,000; 70% had a Jewish mother, and fewer than 25% were affiliated with the official community. In Amsterdam 56% of the Jews still had two Jewish parents, in the Randstad (western part of the Netherlands) 44%, and in the rest of the country 33%. Some 20% of the Jews in the Netherlands come from Israel, and there are several hundreds refugees from Iraq and Iran and the former Soviet Union who were admitted on humanitarian grounds. The community has a low birth rate (1.5) and a disproportionately large number of elderly people, but despite all these factors, the Jewish community of the Netherlands has not declined in absolute numbers since 1945. However, the total population in the Netherlands grew quite dramatically from 9 million in 1945 to over 16 million in 2005.

Ark of the Law and bimah in the Liberal synagogue built in Amsterdam after World War II. Photo M. Ninio, Jerusalem.

INTEGRATION. In general, Jews became well integrated in public life after the war. The relationship between Jews and the Dutch government improved greatly from 1955 on. The 1960s are generally characterized by goodwill, both toward the Jewish community and the state of Israel. A major problem came to the fore in 1972 when the government intended to set free three German war criminals with direct responsibility for the deportation of the Jews. A by-product of the successful protests of the Jewish community was the familiarization of the wider Dutch public with the collective Jewish war trauma and the difficulties some of them had, as a result, even to earn a decent living. A special law came into being, guaranteeing a monthly income to victims of persecution.

In spite of their small numbers, Jews were members of Parliament and several became ministers of government. While before the war Jews did not serve as mayors, after the war several towns, like Amersfoort and Groningen, had Jewish mayors. Amsterdam had four in succession. Jews played an important role as university professors, journalists, artists, and so on. Abel Herzberg, a renowned lawyer and chairman of the Dutch Zionist movement, was a highly respected publicist in non-Jewish circles as well. Henriette *Boas was a prolific writer of articles and letters on the subject of Dutch Jewry and everything connected with Israel. Jaap Meijer was a leading voice in the postwar period castigating the bogus sentiments and pseudo-romanticism in the historical reconstruction of Dutch Judaism. In the literary works of Judith Herzberg, Gerhard Durlacher, Leon de Winter, Marga Minco, and Arnon Grunberg, the Holocaust is often a painful source of inspiration.

Two major changes had an impact on the relationship of the Jews with Dutch society since the 1970s. Firstly, the Netherlands moved from a clear pro-Israel stand to a political position that fell into line with the more critical European one. A second major change was the growth of a considerable Muslim community in the Netherlands. Jews no longer are the only non-Christian minority group. In spite of often opposed views of the Middle East conflict, the Jewish and the Muslim communities actively seek to build a positive mutual relationship. Christian denominations which had shown much interest in their Jewish roots and in the land of Israel in the first decades after World War II, became more critical, but at the same time lost much of their relevance as a result of secularization. Jewish-Christian dialogue, the Protestant-oriented Counsel of Jews and Christians and the Catholic Counsel for Church and Israel, have contributed to a better understanding of Judaism.

INTERNAL ORGANIZATION. The Jewish community has undergone many changes. In 1950 the dominant Ashkenazi Orthodox Nederlands Israelietisch Kerkgenootschap (NIK) had actively registered some 19,500 persons. Many of those were only included since the NIK still claimed to represent "the Jewish Nation" in the Netherlands. The majority of these registered Jews – about 10,000 – lived in Amsterdam, but the real active membership in Amsterdam comprised only some 5,200 Jews in 1951. Other Jews mostly lived in the *Randstad*-area, including The Hague and Rotterdam, where communities of several hundred Jews were reestablished. Smaller numbers of Jews live in towns like Groningen, Enschede, and Amersfoort, where they succeeded in reviving their congregations. Amsterdam is the only place with Jewish day schools. The presence of a considerable number of Israelis – about 8,000 in the whole country around 1995 – contributed to the operation of these schools.

Between 1945 and 2000, the membership of the Ashkenazi Orthodox community dwindled to fewer than 5,000 Jews in the whole country and the NIK lost its dominant position. Until the 1970s the character of Orthodox Judaism under the leadership of Chief Rabbi Aron Schuster hardly changed. Schuster was supported by Rabbi Vorst in Rotterdam and Rabbi Berlinger in Utrecht. Eli Berlinger was rabbi for most of the provinces and caused many Jews from smaller places to move to Israel. Since the 1970s, rabbis from abroad, such as Rabbi Meir Just from Hungary, and the Lubavitch movement had a significant impact on the community. All were more rigorous in their interpretation of the *halakhah* and changed local traditions. This led to a partial estrangement of the original Dutch membership. In 2005, this tendency resulted in the establishment of the first Conservative congregation, which – in Weesp and Almere together – started off with some 80 members. The Portuguese community is also still in existence but its numbers are very small: in 1945 there were about 800 Portuguese Jews left; in 2005 some 450 members were counted.

The only growing community after the war was the Union of Liberal Religious Jews in the Netherlands, established in 1931, and a member of the World Union for Progressive Judaism. Only in Amsterdam did a small community of some 130 Liberal Jews – mainly German refugees – survive the war. During its first 10 years the congregation in danger of disappearing, until Dutch-born Rabbi Jacob *Soetendorp was named to lead it in 1954. Under his leadership, together with Dr. Maurits *Goudeket and Robert *Levisson, the community added dozens of families to its ranks every year. New congregations were established in The Hague, Rotterdam, and Arnhem. Around 1970 a younger generation, represented by David Lilienthal and Awraham Soetendorp, took over as rabbis of Amsterdam, The Hague, and Rotterdam, followed by Rabbi Edward van Voolen in Arnhem in 1978. The Progressive community continued to grow and in 2000 it had a membership of well over 3,000, distributed in nine congregations throughout the country. The community has its own rabbinical seminary.

Outside the religious community – comprising only 20% of the total Jewish population – Joods Maatschappelijk Werk (Jewish Social Work, JMW), undertook much activity. JMW was established in 1946 and all Jewish organizations are represented in it. With its neutral and non-religious character, JMW was able to reach Jews who had lost formal contact with the community. JMW also cared of the elderly and many people who suffered from war trauma. In the days of the establishment of the State of Israel Zionism was very strong: the Dutch Zionist Union (NZB) had a membership of 3,232 in 1948, and nearly all other Jews supported Zionism without formal membership. The NZB reestablished its journal *De Joodse Wachter* ("The Jewish Guardian"). Po'alei Zion was its largest faction, but when most members left for Israel the group declined. During the 1980s ARZA, the new Zionist faction of the Movement for Progressive Judaism, dominated the NZB as part of a worldwide struggle for equal rights for Progressive Jews in Israel. Later on the NZB was reorganized in order to achieve greater efficiency and was renamed the Federation of Netherlands Zionists (FNZ), but the organization barely continued to exist. The need to deal with growing anti-Israel sentiments in the Dutch media and public opinion since the early 1970s led to the establishment of CIDI, the Center for Information and Documentation on Israel. On the board of this organization all streams of Judaism are represented, and CIDI developed into a professional public relations office working on behalf of the organized Jewish community. WIZO is the oldest functioning network for Jewish women in the Netherlands and although both the Orthodox and the Progressive Jewish community developed their own women's networks, WIZO remained very popular. One of its strongest features is that it is open to both religious and non-religious women alike.

Although on an administrative and public relations level the Orthodox and Liberal Jewish communities worked well together, the establishment of an umbrella organization comparable to the Board of Deputies in England or the CRIF in France did not materialize for a long time in the Netherlands. The Orthodox continued to claim that they were the only representative body of the Jews. In the end, however, numerical developments in the religious community shaped a new reality. In 1997, the CJO (or CJOEB: Central Committee of Jewish Organizations – External Affairs) was founded in which the religious, social, and political organizations of the community cooperate.

IDENTITY. Most Jews are not connected with the traditional community. For those who still feel a need for Jewish contacts, informal frameworks came into being, like social cafés and meeting groups. Israelis also have their own social activities. Loneliness is a large problem in the community, since most people still feel the absence of relatives and normal family life as a result of the Holocaust. Visits to the Jewish Historical Museum in Amsterdam and the annual *Yom Havoetbal* (Jewish Soccer Day) are the most popular expressions of identification. The Holocaust plays a major role in both Jewish and national consciousness: the central Jewish memorial sites are the Hollandse Schouwburg in Amsterdam, the Westerbork transit camp, and the Vught camp. Many cities and villages have dedicated local monuments in memory of their own deported Jews.

In the first decades after the war synagogues were sold and turned into churches, shops, garages, and laundries. Hartog Beem, who knew the prewar communities from his own vivid experiences, was for some time the only individual who wrote extensively on earlier Jewish life in provincial towns and villages. He also documented the use of Yiddish in the Dutch language. During the late 1970s and early 1980s the tendency to close synagogues was reversed by a growing interest among Jews and non-Jews in the visible history of their local Jewish communities. New studies were published with detailed descriptions and efforts were made to restore Jewish cemeteries and synagogues. Restored synagogues became museums or were given other useful purposes in memory of the destroyed communities. In several cases synagogues returned to their previous use and became houses of prayer again, mostly for Progressive Jewish congregations. This happened in The Hague with the ancient Portuguese synagogue and also with the Ashkenazi synagogues of Tilburg and Haaksbergen. The synagogue of Weesp is in use by the first Conservative congregation in the Netherlands.

In academic and archival institutions the growing interest in the communities aside from Amsterdam resulted in some large-scale projects, such as in the province of Groningen, where the histories of all communities were written up and all tombstones were photographed and described. The richest center of Jewish studies in the Netherlands is no doubt Amsterdam, but a newly established independent institute of Jewish education is Crescas, which organizes courses in all parts of the Netherlands in an effort to strengthen Jewish identity also outside of Amsterdam.

[Wout J. van Bekkum and Chaya Brasz (2nd ed.)]

Relations with Israel

A long-standing history of cooperation links the Jewish people to the Dutch, from the period of the "Golden Age" of Dutch Jewry after the expulsion of the Jews from Spain and Portugal until the demonstrations of support and acts of rescue during the Nazi occupation of the Netherlands. On Nov. 29, 1947, the Netherlands voted in favor of the UN plan to partition Palestine, and thus for the establishment of a Jewish state, and soon afterward officially recognized the new State of Israel. Formal diplomatic relations were established on the ambassadorial level, with Holland being the first country to set up its diplomatic representation in Jerusalem. The Netherlands supported Israel in the United Nations as well as in other international frameworks on a number of occasions; supported Israel against the Arab boycott and Arab aggression; and played a role in the struggle for persecuted Jews, especially Jews in the Soviet Union and the Arab countries. It was also Israel's major aid in its efforts to establish ties with the European Economic Community. When the Soviet Union severed diplomatic relations with Israel in 1953, the Netherlands represented Israel's interests in the U.S.S.R. and contributed to the resumption of diplomatic ties between the two states. It again assumed this role when the U.S.S.R. and other Communist states broke diplomatic relations with Israel after the Six-Day War (1967); subsequently Israel's interests in the U.S.S.R. and Poland were represented by Holland.

Trade relations between the two countries reached $75,000,000 in 1966 and rose to $84,000,000 by 1968, with Dutch exports to Israel somewhat larger than Israel exports to Holland. Tourism from Holland to Israel also rose, with 7,983 tourists in 1966, 9,308 in 1967, and 14,047 in 1968. The high points in cultural exchanges were the arrangement of a Dutch art exhibit in Israel and an exhibit from the Land of the Bible and appearances of the Israel Philharmonic Orchestra in Holland. Every year an Israel delegation participated in the popular march in Nijmegen, and a Dutch delegation took part in the yearly marches that take place in Israel, which are modeled on the Dutch ones. Prime ministers, foreign ministers, and other members of the government and of parliament of the two countries carried out mutual visits.

[Yohanan Meroz]

Netherlands governments in various coalitions continued to support Israel in the immediate post–Six-Day War period. On several occasions the Netherlands succeeded in having a UN anti-Israel draft resolution toned down. In the UN General Assembly Dec. 4, 1985, it was one of 16 countries voting against a resolution demanding unconditional withdrawal by Israel from all Palestinian and other Arab territories occupied since 1967. It was also among the 22 countries voting against a resolution calling the Israel decision of Dec. 1981 to introduce Israel laws and jurisdiction and Israeli administration into the Golan Heights an act of aggression and demanding a military, economic, diplomatic, and cultural boycott of Israel. On the other hand, it voted in favor of a resolution calling the incorporation by Israel of Jerusalem unlawful. The Dutch government criticized Israel for its bombardment of PLO headquarters in Tunisia.

The Netherlands withheld diplomatic recognition of the PLO and continued to limit the status of the Palestinian office in The Hague, which was opened in July 1983, to that of an Information Office.

In July 1983 the government, with the full approval of Parliament, decided to withdraw the Dutch Unifil battalion from South Lebanon as from October 19, 1983, as it could no longer play a useful role there.

The Netherlands continued to represent Israel's interests in Moscow and to mediate in the applications for visas to Israel by Soviet Jews until Israel was able to open its own consulate in Moscow.

In the Gulf War the Netherlands fully supported the American stand against Iraq and participated in the Allied forces, be it in a modest way.

At the end of January 1991 the entire Second Chamber of Parliament, with the exception of a few members of the

Green Left party, approved the government decision to lend eight Patriot systems to Israel, with 70 instructors and maintenance personnel. By the time they arrived in Israel the Iraqi Scud attacks had ceased, so that they never went into action. At the same time the government, in addition to the F 3,000,000 it had donated already for food for the Palestinians in the Administered Areas, gave another F 2,000,000 for this purpose, plus 10,000 gas masks. The news media had repeatedly pointed to the absence of gas masks for the Palestinians.

The first Intifada, from its start, received very great attention in the Dutch news media. The emphasis was often on the "cruelty" of the Israeli soldiers firing at young children who merely threw stones. Among the organizations showing great sympathy for the Palestinians was the Netherlands Council of Churches (mainly Protestant) and the Dutch branch of the Roman Catholic "Pax Christi."

Two small extreme left-wing parties, the PRP (Political Radical Party) and the PSP (Pacifist Socialist Party), often publicly criticized Israel. In 1987, together with the small Communist Party (CPN), they merged into the Green Left which often criticized Israel, as did some members of the Labor left wing.

On the second anniversary of the outbreak of the *intifada* the PLO representative in The Hague, Afif Safieh, organized a large-scale meeting, to which he invited representatives of all the major parties as speakers, but all declined. Nor was any official representative of the Foreign Ministry present. The meeting was addressed by the chairman of the Netherlands Council of Churches, Prof. Dirk C. Mulder.

The Israel-Palestine peace talks in Madrid had originally been scheduled to take place in The Hague, but Syria had objected for a number of reasons. The Hague was thus dropped, much to the relief of the Dutch authorities, in view of the vast organizational and security problems it would have caused.

No Palestinian terrorist attacks against Jewish persons or property took place throughout the decade under review.

On January 19–21, 1986, Israeli Prime Minister Shimon Peres paid an official visit to Holland, where he also met Spanish premier, Felipe Gonzalez.

The ICN or Israel Committee Netherlands, which consists of orthodox Protestants, is fully pro-Israel and every year from 1980 sent tens of thousand of flower bulbs to Israel to adorn its public gardens.

The Collective Israel Actie (United Israel Appeal) in 1992 raised some F 9,240,000, of which F 6,260,000 came from the campaign itself and some F 3,000,000 from bequests. This was a reduction of F 2,500,000 against 1991, but F 2,500,000 more than in 1989. In contrast to the situation in the 1950s and 1960s, many Israeli institutions now freely solicit funds in Holland.

The disaster of the El Al Boeing 747 cargo aircraft which crashed into two tall apartment buildings in the Bijlmer district of southeastern Amsterdam on Oct. 4, 1992, made a deep impression. In addition to the three Israeli crew members and one Israeli woman passenger, 43 local residents were killed and four seriously wounded, nearly all of them recent immigrants from Third World countries. In all, 80 apartments were destroyed and 160 others were no longer safe for habitation. The ultimate blame for the disaster was eventually placed upon the Boeing company.

On the whole, beginning in the 1970s, the Netherlands has come closer to the more critical attitude of the European community toward Israel, but it still remains a very friendly nation. In 2004, exports to the Netherlands totaled $1.23 billion while imports reached $1.48 billion.

[Henriette Boas]

For the musical tradition of Jews in the Netherlands see *Amsterdam.

BIBLIOGRAPHY: GENERAL AND HISTORICAL: Brugmans-Frank; M.H. Gans, *Memorboeck* (1971); ESN; Graetz, Hist, index; J. Michman (ed.), *Dutch Jewish History* (1982–), 3 vols. (as of 2006); S. Seeligman, *De Emancipatie der Joden in Nederland* (1918); S. van Praag, *De West-Joden en hun letterkunde* (1926); H. Poppers, *De Joden in Overijssel* (1926); E. Boekman, *Demografie van de Joden in Nederland* (1936); H.I. Bloom, *Economic Activities of the Jews of Amsterdam in the Seventeenth and Eighteenth Centuries* (1937, repr. 1969); H. Beem, *De verdwenen mediene* (1950); J. Stengers, *Les juifs dans les Pays-Bas au moyen âge* (1950); J. Melkman, *David Franco Mendes* (1951); D. Cohen, *Zwervend en dolend* (1955); M.E. Bolle, *De opheffing van de autonomie der kehilloth (Joodse gemeenten) in Nederland, 1796* (1960); L. Finkelstein (ed.), *The Jews*, 2 vols. (1960[3]), index; J. Meijer, *Het Jonas Daniël Meijerplein* (1961); idem, *Erfenis der emancipatie: het Nederlandse Jodendom in de eerste helft van de 19e eeuw* (1963); idem, *Zij lieten hun sporen achter* (1964); I. Lipschits, *Honderd jaar het Nieuw Israëlietisch Weekblad, 1865–1965* (1966); C. Reijnders, *Van "Joodsche natiën? tot Joodse Nederlanders* (1969); Shunami, Bibl, index. HOLOCAUST PERIOD: W. Warmbrunn, *The Dutch under German Occupation 1940–1945* (1963); R. Hilberg, *Destruction of the European Jews* (1961), 365–81; J. Presser, *Destruction of the Dutch Jews* (1969); idem, *Ondergang*, 2 vols. (1965); A.J. Herzberg, *Kroniek der Jodenvervolging* (1949–54); De Jong, in: *Yad Vashem Studies*, 7 (1968), 39–55; P. Mechanicus, *In Depot, Dagboek uit Westerbork* (1964); H.G. Adler, *Theresienstadt* (Ger., 1960); E. Kolb, *Bergen-Belsen* (Ger., 1962). CONTEMPORARY PERIOD: JJSO, 3 (1961), 195–242; 4 (1962), 47–71; H. Boas, *ibid.*, 5 (1963), 55–83; J. Melkman, *Geliefde vijand* (1964); M. Snijders, *Joden van Amsterdam* (1958); S. Wijnberg, *De Joden in Amsterdam* (1967); A. Vedder et al., *De Joden in Nederland na de tweede wereldoorlog* (1960). **ADD. BIBLIOGRAPHY:** *Studia Rosenthaliana*, 1–76 (1967–2005); M.H. Gans, *Memorbook* (1977); J. Michman (ed.), *Dutch Jewish History*, vols. 1–3 (1984–93); B. Moore, *Victims and Survivors* (1997); J. Michman, H. Beem, and D. Michman, *Pinkas. Geschiedenis van de joodse gemeenschap in Nederland* (1999); Y. Kaplan and C. Brasz, *Dutch Jews as Perceived by Themselves and Others* (2001); J.Ch Blom, R.G. Fuks-Mansfeld, and I. Schöffer (eds.), *The History of the Jews in The Netherlands* (2002); J. Michman and B.J. Flam, *Encyclopedia of the Righteous Among the Nations: The Netherlands*, 2 vols. (2004).

NETHERWORLD, the abode of the dead. The peoples of the Ancient Near East had elaborate doctrines concerning the dead and their abode. The Egyptians were very optimistic concerning the afterlife. They believed that ceremonies of mummification, rituals and spells, and declarations of guiltlessness would ensure them a happy afterlife almost identical to the life they led in this world. In the afterlife they would plow, harvest, eat, and drink; in short, do all they did while they were alive (*The Book of the Dead*, 110).

For the Babylonians, on the other hand, the realm of the dead was a place to be dreaded. It was a well-organized kingdom with Ereshkigal and *Nergal as its queen and king, respectively. To enter it one had to pass through seven gates and remove one's garments. The netherworld is depicted as "… the land of no return … the dark house … the house which none leave who have entered it … the road from which there is no way back … the house wherein the entrants are bereft of light, where dust is their fare and clay their food, [where] they see no light, residing in darkness, [where] they are clothed like birds, with wings for garments, [and where] over door and bolt is spread dust" (*Descent of Ishtar to the Netherworld*, 1–11, in Pritchard, Texts, 107; cf. *Epic of Gilgamesh*, 7, 3:33–39, in Pritchard, Texts, 87). The plight of the dead could be worsened or alleviated depending on whether they were properly buried, and whether or not food and drink were brought to them. Such practices and speculations are not entirely wanting in the Bible. Deuteronomy 26:12, 14 implies that only food that has been consecrated as tithe may not be left as a gift for the dead, the practice of feeding the dead as such being permitted, while Isaiah 14:14–19 and Ezekiel 38:18ff., reflect a belief that those who are slain by the sword (and not decently buried), as also such as die uncircumcised, are assigned the lowest – and no doubt the least desirable – level of the netherworld (see Ginsberg in bibl.). On the other hand, the practice of occult arts including necromancy was abhorred by the Bible (Deut. 18:11; Isa. 8:19), and there was no sacrifice to the dead (Ps. 106:28). Sacrifice to the dead means sacrifice to no-gods, such as Baal-Peor; cf. Numbers 25:2–3.

Apart from the Isaiah and Ezekiel passages referred to above, the numerous biblical references to the netherworld are vague and inspired by Ancient Near Eastern folklore. Several names are given to the abode of the dead, the most common being *She'ol* – always feminine and without the definite article – a sign of proper nouns. The term does not occur in other Semitic languages, except as a loan word from the Hebrew *She'ol*, and its etymology is obscure. Other common designations of the netherworld are: *ʾereẓ*, "earth" or "underworld" (e.g., I Sam. 28:13; Jonah 2:7; Job 10:21–22); *qever*, "grave" (Ps. 88:12); *ʿafar*, "dust" (Isa. 26:5, 19; cf. Gen. 3:19); *bor*, "pit" (e.g., Isa. 14:15; 38:18; Prov. 28:17); *shaḥat*, "pit" (Ps. 7:16); *ʾavaddon*, "Abaddon" (e.g., Job. 28:22); *dumah* (apparently = "the place of abiding"; Ps. 94:17; 115:17); *naḥale beliyyaʿal* ["the torrents of *Belial"; II Sam. 22:5); "the nether parts of the earth" (Ezek. 31:14); "the depths of the pit" (Lam. 3:55); "the land of darkness" (Job 10:21). The netherworld is located somewhere under the earth (cf. Num. 16:30ff.), or at the bottoms of the mountains (Jonah 2:7), or under the waters – the cosmic ocean (Job 26:5). It is sometimes personified as a voracious monster with a wide-open mouth (e.g., Isa. 5:14; Hab. 2:5; Prov. 1:12). Kings and commoners, nobles and paupers, masters and slaves are equal in Sheol (Job 3:13–19; Ezek. 32:18–32). For Israel's neighbors, the rule of the universe was divided among various deities, and the netherworld was the dominion of a pair of infernal gods. For Israel, however, the Lord rules over the whole universe, His sovereignty extends from heaven to Sheol (Ps. 139; Job 26:6; cf. Ps. 90:2; 102:26–28). However, there is no communication between the dead and the Lord (Ps. 88:6); no praise to the Lord comes from the netherworld (Isa. 38:18; Ps. 30:10; 88:12–13).

[Laurentino Jose Afonso]

In the Aggadah

In the *aggadah*, the name Gehenna takes the place of the biblical Sheol as the abode of the dead. The name is derived from *Gei Ben Hinnom* (Valley of the son of Hinnom, Josh. 15:8; 18:16; et al.), a valley south of Jerusalem where children were made to pass through fire to the god *Moloch (see *Gehinnom). Jeremiah prophesied that it would become "a valley of slaughter" and a place of burial (Jer. 7:32). In the course of time, the name of this accursed valley, designated for suffering, became identified with the place of retribution for the wicked after their death.

No suggestion of this later notion of Gehenna is to be found in Scripture, but in the Talmud and Midrash "Gehenna" is so used. Joshua b. Levi refers to it by seven names (Er. 19a), all of which are synonyms for the netherworld of Scripture. Later, these seven names were given to the seven divisions of Gehenna (Mid. Ps. to 11:6, Sot. 10b). Descriptions of Gehenna include foreign elements which were widespread in the Hellenistic world (through Orphic and Pythagorean sources). The punishment of "the wicked one whose tongue hangs out to lap the water of the river but is unable to reach it" (TJ, Ḥag 2:2 77d) is reminiscent of the punishment of Tantalus in Hades (Odyssey, 11:582–5). The source of this description is probably Greek, passing to Judaism, and thence to Christianity (Luke 16:24) and Islam. Most accounts of Gehenna, however, draw chiefly on the scriptural descriptions of the land of the dead. There is discernible in the *aggadot* on Gehenna a tendency to mitigate the application of strict justice, by limiting the categories of its victims (Ber. 10a; Er. 41b; et al.), and by detailing the many possibilities whereby the Jew might be delivered from its punishment (Pes. 118a; Git. 7a; et al.).

The *aggadot* about Gehenna in the Talmud and Midrash speak of its site, size, entrances, gates, divisions, and princes. A variety of motifs and partial descriptions from the Bible (sometimes self-contradictory) are combined. The *aggadah*, basing itself on verses which describe the site of the land of the dead, variously, as beneath the earth (Gen. 37:35; Deut. 32:22; et al.) and beneath the sea (Jonah 2:3–4; Job 26:5), states that Gehenna has entrances in the sea and on dry land (Er. 19a). In the school of Johanan b. Zakkai it was stated that one of its entrances is in the valley of Hinnom, near Jerusalem. There are also traditions, however, that Gehenna is in the sky (Tam. 32b), and that it is "beyond the dark mountains" (*ibid.*).

As against *aggadot* which, in the main, speak of the fire of Gehenna (Pes. 54a; BM 85a; BB 74a; et al.), there are those which describe the darkness reigning there (I Enoch, 10:4; et al.). According to Josephus, the Essenes described it as a cold and dark cave (Wars, 2:155). There are also sources combining both ideas, speaking of a fire found in Gehenna which gives no light – "fire causing darkness," or "the darkness of eternal fire." Descriptions of rivers of fire (Ḥag. 13b) in Gehenna appear also to be combinations of descriptions of its fire and of a river flowing in or near it (TJ, Ḥag. 2:2, 77d; Shab. 39a) with descriptions of the hot springs of Tiberias, whose heat is conceived as deriving from their passing the entrance to Gehenna. Extravagant accounts are given of the size of Gehenna and the power of its fire. "The world is one sixtieth of the Garden, the Garden one sixtieth of Eden, Eden one sixtieth of Gehenna – hence the world to Gehenna is as the lid to the pot. Others say Gehenna is immeasurable" (Ta'an. 10a). The account of the gates of Gehenna is followed by descriptions of the gatekeepers (Ḥag. 15b; Mid. Gan Eden, in: A. Jellinek (ed.), *Beit ha-Midrasch*, 5 (1938), 42–51) and these gatekeepers are identified with its princes (Shab. 104a).

The descriptions of the sufferings of the wicked in Gehenna are faithful reflections of the judicial procedures during the era of their composition. The concept of "measure for measure" lies at the root of these punishments. "The suffering commences from the limb that began the transgression" (Sif. Num. 18; Tosef., Sot. 3:2). The cruel torments of Gehenna, such as hanging by different limbs of the body (TJ, Ḥag. 2:2, 77d; Mid. Gan Eden, *ibid.*; Mid. *Ke-Tappu'aḥ*), roasting by fire (excerpt from "*Ḥazon Eliyahu*" quoted by Lieberman, in *Louis Ginzberg Jubilee Volume* (1946), 249–70 (Hebrew Section)) and suffocating by smoke (Mid. Gan Eden, *ibid.*), are also found in Christian books of the second, third, and fourth centuries which describe the divisions of Gehenna and the suffering of the wicked therein (e.g., "The Vision of Peter," "The Acts of Thomas," and "The Vision of Paul," the influence of the Jewish *aggadah* being easily recognizable). Undoubtedly, the cruel torments used by the Roman government in its system of punishments played their part in the envisioning of Gehenna. The punishment of the wicked in Gehenna was conceived of as parallel to the procedures for punishment in this world. Just as the lower court does not inflict punishment on the Sabbath, so in Gehenna: "During weekdays they suffer, but on the Sabbath they are given rest" (Gen. R. 11:5).

Some are characterized by severe contrast. The wicked are cast into fire, then into snow, and the process repeated (TJ, Sanh. 10:3, 29b; PDRK, 97). There is a difference of opinion between Bet Shammai and Bet Hillel as to the duration of the punishment in Gehenna (RH 16b–17a); according to the former, the thoroughly wicked remain there for everlasting disgrace; the intermediate ones (between the wicked and the good) descend to Gehenna to be purged, and ascend after purification. According to the latter, the intermediate ones do not go there at all (ARN[1] 41:15), and whereas transgressors (both Jewish and gentile) are punished in Gehenna for only 12 months, only special categories of sinners – informers, those who deny the resurrection of the dead and those who lead the masses into sin – are punished there for all time (RH *ibid.*). Rabbinic literature incorporates legends of visits to Eden and Gehenna of a type similar to that found among other peoples. Some of these are solitary visits in a dream (TJ, Ḥag. 2:2, 177d), and some escorted visits, in a dream at night. At times the visit takes place in a vision ascribed to one of the scriptural personalities, such as Moses (Mid. *Ke-Tappu'aḥ*), Isaiah (Mid. Gan Eden, *ibid.*), Daniel, Enoch, and Baruch (Apocrypha). Similar visits are attributed to *tannaim* and *amoraim* (Joshua b. Levi in Ket. 77b), of whom many *aggadot* are extant.

[Batya Kedar]

BIBLIOGRAPHY: M. Jastrow, in: AJSLL, 14 (1897), 165–70; A. Lods, *La croyance a la vie future et le culte des morts dans l'antiquité israélite* (1906); P. Dhorme, in: RB, 4 (1908), 59–78; E. Ebeling, *Tod und Leben nach den Vorstellungen der Babylonier* (1931); K. Tallquist, *Sumerisch-akkadische Namen der Totenwelt* (1934); T.H. Gaster, *Thespis* (1950); H.L. Ginsberg, in: JAOS, 88 (1968), 51–52, n. 27. IN THE AGGADAH: Ginzberg, Legends, index; Neubauer, Géogr, 36–37; P. Volz, *Die Eschatologie der juedischen Gemeinde im neutestamentlichen Zeitalter…* (1934), 328–9; Lieberman, in: *Harry Austryn Wolfson Jubilee Volume* (1965), 495–532 (Eng. section) = *Texts and Studies* (1974), 29–56.

NETILAT YADAYIM (Heb. נְטִילַת יָדַיִם; lit. "raising the hands"), rabbinic term for the obligatory washing of the hands. The rabbis made this ritual mandatory in the following instances:

(1) upon rising from sleep (Ber. 60b; Sh. Ar., OḤ 4:1)
(2) after the excretion of bodily wastes
(3) after the paring of nails
(4) after the removal of shoes
(5) after the combing of hair or touching parts of the body that are usually covered
(6) after leaving a cemetery or participating in a funeral
(7) after sexual intercourse (Sh. Ar., OḤ 4:18)
(8) before prayer and the recitation of the *Shema (Ber. 15a; Sh. Ar., OḤ 92:4)
(9) before eating bread (Ḥul. 105a; Sh. Ar., OḤ 158:1)
(10) before reciting Grace (Ḥul. 105a; Sh. Ar., OḤ 181:1)
(11) before eating the parsley at the Passover *seder (Pes. 115a–6; Sh. Ar., OḤ 473:6)
(12) the levites wash the hands of the kohanim before the *Priestly Blessing (Sh. Ar., OḤ 128:6)

In all these instances the hands must be washed at least up to the third joint of the fingers, i.e., the junction of the phalanges and the metacarpus. Nevertheless, the rabbis considered it preferable to wash up to the wrist (Sh. Ar., OḤ 161:4). However, when washing before Grace, it is sufficient to wash only up to the second joint of the fingers (Sh. Ar., OḤ 181:4). A minimum of ¼ *log* (approx. ½ pint) of water is poured over the hands from a utensil with a wide mouth, the lip of which must be undamaged (Sh. Ar., OḤ 159:1, 3; 160:13). The hands must be clean without anything adhering to them prior to the ritual washing, and no foreign object such as a ring may intervene between them and the water (Sh. Ar., OḤ 161:1–3). Upon rising from sleep, each hand must be washed three times (Sh. Ar., OḤ

4:2), but before partaking of bread, it is sufficient if they are washed once (Sh. Ar., OḤ 162:2). It is customary to hold the cup in the left hand and wash the right one first, and then to reverse the procedure (Mishnah Berurah to Sh. Ar., OḤ 158:1 n. 4). A benediction is only recited after washing the hands upon rising and before eating bread. Its text reads "… and commanded us concerning the washing of the hands." After rising, it is today recited as part of the preliminary **Shaharit* service, while before the meal it is recited prior to the drying of the hands (Sh. Ar., OḤ 158:11–12).

BIBLIOGRAPHY: Krauss, Tal Arch, 1 (1910), 210f., 667f.; J. Preuss, *Biblisch-talmudische Medizin* (1923[3]), 146ff.; M. Perlman, *Midrash ha-Refu'ah*, 1 (1926), 42.

NETIRA (d. 916), businessman in *Baghdad. Netira wielded considerable influence in the court of the caliphs and the Jewish society of Babylonia. He was at first connected with the business of his father-in-law *Joseph b. Phinehas and his partner Aaron b. Amram. With the appointment of Caliph al-Muʿtaḍid in 892, he became the principal figure of Babylonian Jewry and much authority was accorded him. He held this position until his death. During the reign of Caliph al-Muʿtaḍiḍ, Netira succeeded in frustrating the design of one of the caliph's ministers, Ibn-Abi al-Bagl, who planned to put many Jews to death. Between 909 and 916, when the controversy between the *rosh yeshivah* of *Pumbedita and the *exilarch *Ukva broke out, he and his father-in-law Joseph b. Phinehas supported the *gaon*. As a result of their intervention, the exilarch Ukva was twice banished from the country. According to Nathan b. Isaac ha-Bavli, the *gaon* in question was R. *Kohen Zedek, but J. Mann has proved, on the basis of *Iggeret Rav Sherira Ga'on*, that it was R. Judah b. Samuel, the grandfather of R. *Sherira Gaon. His sons Sahl and Isaac followed their father's example and they also held important positions in Jewish society. When the dispute between the exilarch *David b. Zakkai and R. *Saadiah Gaon broke out in 930, they supported Saadiah, who was also the teacher of Sahl. It seems that his third son was Joseph b. Netira, who was one of the heads of the Fostat community in the second half of the 10th century. Apparently the sons of Netira lost their influence during the rule of Caliph al-Qāhir (932–934).

BIBLIOGRAPHY: Neubauer, Chronicles, 2 (1895), 78–80, 83; A.E. Harkavy, in: *Birkat Avraham (Festschrift… A. Berliner*, 1903), 34–43 (Heb.); S. Fraenkel, in: JQR, 17 (1905), 386–8; I. Friedlander, *ibid.*, 747–61; L. Ginzberg, *Geonica*, 2 (1909), 87–88; Fischel, Islam, 34, 36f., 40–44; J. Mann, in: *Tarbiz*, 5 (1934), 148–65; S.D. Goitein, in: *Eretz-Israel*, 7 (1964), 83–84; A. Scheiber, in: *Zion*, 30 (1965), 123–7. **ADD. BIBLIOGRAPHY:** M. Gil, *Be-Malkhut Ishmael*, 1, 650–56; M. Ben-Sasson, in: *Tarbut ve-Ḥevrah be-Toledot Yisrael bi-Ymei ha-Benayim* (1989), 182.

[Abraham David]

NETIV HA-LAMED-HE (Heb. נְתִיב הַל"ה), kibbutz in the Elah Valley, central Israel, affiliated with Ha-Kibbutz ha-Me'uḥad. It was founded by a group of Israeli youth in 1949, later joined by immigrants from various countries. In the initial years Netiv ha-Lamed-He was an isolated outpost, but it progressed after the *Adullam Region development project was launched in the mid-1950s. Its farming included field crops, fruit plantations, poultry, and dairy cattle. In addition, the kibbutz manufactured water filters and ran a guest house. In 2002 its population was 420. The name of the kibbutz, "Pathway of the Thirty-Five," commemorates the *Haganah unit of 35 men who were killed by Arabs while trying to reach the besieged Eẓyon Bloc in the Israeli *War of Independence (1948; see *Kefar Eẓyon). A memorial has been erected near the kibbutz.

WEBSITE: www.netiv.org.il.

[Efraim Orni / Shaked Gilboa (2nd ed.)]

NETIVOT (Heb. נְתִיבוֹת; "Roads," from Prov. 3:17), Israel development town in N.W. Negev, 9 mi. (15 km.) S.E. of Gaza. Netivot was founded in 1956 in the framework of Israel's regional settlement and population dispersion policy. It was initially named Azzatah ("Toward Gaza"). Although placed in the center of a quickly expanding agricultural region, Netivot's progress was handicapped by the proximity of two other development towns, *Sederot and *Ofakim, and by its inability to attract educated veteran citizens in addition to new immigrants. Netivot's growth was slow, its population rising from 1,231 in 1957 to 4,830 in 1968; 95% of the immigrants came from Tunisia and Morocco. One of Morocco's most renowned rabbis, Yisrael Abuhatzeira (the Baba Sali), settled there as well. After his death in 1984 his tomb became a major pilgrimage site, attracting hundreds of thousands of people every year. In the mid-1990s the population was approximately 13,600, rising further to 21,800 in 2002. The increase was due to the arrival of many new immigrants; 43% of the residents were below the age of 14. In 2000, Netivot received city status. The municipal area was 2.3 sq. mi (6 sq. km.). Most residents worked in local commerce and industry, with others commuting to the bigger cities of the region: Beersheba, Ashkelon, and Kiryat Gat. Income was about half the national average.

[Efraim Orni / Shaked Gilboa (2nd ed.)]

NETOPHAH (Heb. נְטֹפָה), Judean village, evidently near Bethlehem (I Chron. 2:54). It was the hometown of two of David's heroes (II Sam. 23:28, 29) and of a captain of Gedaliah (II Kings 25:23; Jer. 40:8). It appears after Bethlehem in the list of those returning from Babylonian exile (Ezra 2:22; Neh. 7:26). In Byzantine times, it is placed in the vicinity of Tekoa (*Life of Cyriacus*, in: PG, vol. 115, p. 929); the same source mentions a "desert of Netopha." The usual identification is with Khirbat Badd Falūḥ, about 3.4 mi. (5½ km.) south of Bethlehem, where Iron Age to Byzantine pottery was found. It has also been located at Ramat Raḥel, which, however, is identified with Beth-Cherem by its excavator.

BIBLIOGRAPHY: Abel, Geog, 2 (1938), 399; Aharoni, Land, index; EM, 5 (1968), 829–30 (incl. bibl.).

[Michael Avi-Yonah]

NETTER, CHARLES (Yiẓḥak; 1826–1882), leader of the *Alliance Israélite Universelle and founder of the *Mikveh Israel Agricultural School. Born in Strasbourg, Netter went into business, first in Lille and then in Moscow and London. He moved to Paris in about 1851 and began a life-long career of public activities, establishing a Jewish vocational school in 1865, a society for safeguarding the rights of workers, and a hostel for poor artisans in 1880. A founder of the Alliance Israélite Universelle (1860), he was elected its treasurer. Various proposals submitted to the Alliance to extend its activities to Ereẓ Israel met with a favorable response on Netter's part, and the Alliance board, although opposed to the encouragement of emigration to Ereẓ Israel, was ready to help Jews already there. In 1867 Netter submitted a proposal to the Alliance to assist Jews from Persia and other Eastern countries to emigrate to Ereẓ Israel and to found agricultural settlements for them. The following year he visited Ereẓ Israel on behalf of the Alliance, and upon his return he recommended the creation of an agricultural school, to be followed by the founding of settlements for the school graduates. In his report Netter noted that Ereẓ Israel would provide a shelter for Jews fleeing from hostile surroundings and enable them, in the course of time, to occupy and settle the Holy Land. When his proposal was approved, he left for Constantinople in 1869, where he received the approval of the grand vizier of the Imperial State Council for the establishment of the school and the authorization of Rashid Pasha, governor of Syria, for the acquisition of 650 acres (2,600 dunams) of land for the annual rental of 1,800 francs, with a right of renewal for 25 years. A *firman* of 1870 confirmed the arrangement, whereupon he returned to Ereẓ Israel and founded the school, naming it Mikveh Israel. After a stay of four years, he fell ill and had to return to Paris, revisiting Ereẓ Israel for six months in 1873. He resumed his political activities on behalf of Jewish causes and in propaganda for the school. In 1877 he again went to Constantinople on behalf of the Alliance, and on the basis of this visit he submitted a report to the Great Powers on the situation of the Jews, especially in Romania and Serbia. In the following year he attended the Congress of Berlin. In 1880 he was at Madrid, where an international conference was deliberating the status of Morocco, and intervened on behalf of the Jews of that country. He was disappointed with the lack of success recorded by Mikveh Israel and the general unsuitability of Ereẓ Israel for the absorption of large numbers of Jews. As a result, he opposed the *aliyah* of Russian and Romanian Jews in the 1880s, when events in those countries created strong pressure for emigration and a movement developed to resettle Ereẓ Israel. At the end of 1881 he visited Brody, remaining there for some months, during which he arranged for the emigration of 1,200 Russian Jewish refugees to America and of a group of 28 children to Mikveh Israel. In March 1882 he even came out with a statement in the press opposing immigration to Ereẓ Israel. Similarly, a conference of Jewish organizations in Berlin, in which Netter participated, decided to support emigration to the United States and to look for other countries where Jews could find refuge, but failed to consider settlement in Ereẓ Israel. Probably under the influence of Baron Edmond de *Rothschild, who believed that an attempt should be made to turn Ereẓ Israel into a center for Jewish immigration, Netter revised his views, and in August 1882 he revisited the country. There he met Russian Jews who had settled in Rishon le-Zion and members of the *Bilu movement and offered them his help. He developed many plans for agricultural activities and the development of crafts in Ereẓ Israel, but died a month after his arrival.

BIBLIOGRAPHY: Z. Szajkowski, in: JSOS, 4 (1942), 291–310; N. Sokolow, *Ḥibbath Zion* (Eng. 1935), 20, 30–34; S. Jawnieli, *Sefer ha-Ẓiyyonut*, 2 pt. 2 (1944), 16–23, 34–37; A. Druyanow, *Ketavim le-Toledot Ḥibbat Ẓiyyon ve-Yishuv Ereẓ Yisrael* (1919), index; I. Klausner, *Ḥibbat Ẓiyyon be-Rumanyah* (1958), index; idem, *Be-Hitorer Am* (1962), index; B. Dinaburg, *Mefallesei Derekh* (1946), 69–89; J. Shapiro, *Sefer Mikveh Yisrael* (1970); G. Weill, in: *Nouveaux Cahiers*, 21 (1970), 2–36; 11 (1967), 11–16; S. Hillels, *Mikveh Yisrael* (1931).

[Israel Klausner]

NETTL, PAUL (1889–1972), musicologist. Born in Hohenelbe, Bohemia, Nettl was lecturer in musicology in Prague from 1919 until 1939, when he immigrated to the United States. He taught in Chicago, and at Indiana University (1946–60). His works include: *Alte juedische Spielleute und Musiker* (1923); *The Story of Dance Music* (1947); *The Book of Musical Documents* (1948); *The Other Casanova* (1950) concerning Lorenzo da Ponte; *Forgotten Musicians* (1951); *Beethoven Encyclopedia* (1956); and *Mozart and Masonry* (1957). His son BRUNO was an ethnomusicologist, specializing in the study of American Indian music.

NETUREI KARTA, group of ultra-religious extremists, mainly in Jerusalem, who regard the establishment of a secular Jewish state in Ereẓ Israel as a sin and a denial of God, and therefore do not recognize the State of Israel. Their name, which is Aramaic for "guardians of the City," derives from a passage in the Jerusalem Talmud (Ḥag. 76:3) stating that religious scholars are the guardians and defenders of the city. Most of them come from the old *yishuv*, but they have been joined by some immigrants from Hungary, disciples of R. Joel *Teitelbaum of Satmar.

Neturei Karta broke away from *Agudat Israel in 1935, when the latter attempted to restrain extremist demands for an independent ultra-Orthodox Jerusalem community completely separate from the rest of the "Zionist" community. The group first adopted the name Ḥevrat ha-Ḥayyim, after R. Joseph Ḥayyim *Sonnenfeld. It aimed at creating "a circle free from the influence of the contemporary spirit and its fallacious opinions," and a condition of membership was "the education of sons and daughters in the traditional Jewish manner, without any change (girls' schools which teach Hebrew do not provide education in the traditional Jewish manner)." The last phrase alluded to Agudat Israel's Bet Ya'akov girls' schools, where the language of instruction is Hebrew. The name Neturei Karta was first used in 1938 by a group of youths, including members of Ḥevrat ha-Ḥayyim, who violently opposed the Jewish community's levying of the voluntary defense tax, *kofer ha-yishuv*.

During World War II, Neturei Karta came out in opposition to Agudat Israel, when it cooperated more closely with the Jewish community and the *Jewish Agency, and attacked it in *Ha-Ḥomah*, a newspaper which began to appear in 1944. In 1945, at the elections to the Orthodox Community Committee (*Va'ad ha-Edah ha-Ḥaredit*), Neturei Karta and its sympathizers gained control; one of their first acts was to exclude from membership anyone educating his daughters at a Bet Ya'akov school. During the War of Independence, Neturei Karta opposed the creation of a Jewish state and Israel's control of Jerusalem, and tried to bring about the internationalization of the city.

The most consistent members refuse to accept an Israel identity card, to recognize the competence of Israel courts, and to vote in municipal or general elections. Although they consist of only a few dozen families – concentrated in the Me'ah She'arim quarter of Jerusalem and in Bene Berak – they gained some support in wider Orthodox circles by creating periodic religious controversies, such as their demonstrations against Sabbath violation and mixed bathing. In 1966 Neturei Karta split, following the marriage of their leader R. Amram *Blau to a convert, Ruth Ben-David. Members of Neturei Karta derive their livelihood mostly from small trade and contributions from abroad, notably from disciples of the Satmar rabbi in the United States. The Neturei Karta continued its spirited anti-Israel activities into the 21st century, demonstrating against Zionist organizations at every opportunity and agitating for the return of the Land of Israel to the Palestinians.

BIBLIOGRAPHY: Ha-Edah ha-Ḥaredit, *Keẓ ha-Ma'arakhah* (1964); Agudat Israel, *Mi Sam Keẓ la-Ma'arakhah* (1964). **WEBSITE:** www.netureikarta.org.

[Menachem Friedman]

NEUBAUER, ADOLF (Abraham; 1831–1907), scholar, author, librarian, and bibliographer. Born in Nagybanya, Hungary, Neubauer studied in Prague with S.J.L. *Rapaport and at the universities of Prague and Munich. In 1857 he went to Paris, where he pursued research at the Bibliothèque Nationale, and in 1864 to Jerusalem as a member of the staff of the Austro-Hungarian consulate. There, too, he sought out rare Hebrew books and manuscripts, discovering in the Karaite synagogue a manuscript of extracts from the lexicon of *David b. Abraham of Fez (15th century) which he published in the *Journal Asiatique* in 1861–62. Returning to Paris, he was befriended by the Orientalists S. *Munk, J. *Derenbourg, and E. *Renan. Invited to St. Petersburg in 1864 to examine the *Firkovich collection of Karaite manuscripts, Neubauer wrote a report for the French Ministry of Education (*Rapports...* (1865) with S. Munk) and published *Aus der Petersburger Bibliothek, Beitraege und Dokumente zur Geschichte des Karaeerthums und der karaeischen Literatur* (1866). He presented his prize-winning essay *La Géographie du Talmud* (1868) to the Academie des Inscriptions et Belles Lettres which in spite of some criticism (J. Morgenstern, *Die franzoesische Akademie und die "Géographie des Talmuds,"* 1870²) has remained an important reference book. His *Notice sur la lexicographie hebraïque...* (1863), foreshadowing his edition of Jonah *Ibn Janaḥ's *Sefer ha-Dikduk* (1875, 1968²), with additions and corrections by W. Bacher, and *Melekhet ha-Shir* (1865), a collection of extracts from manuscripts concerning Hebrew poetry, belong to the same period.

In 1865 Neubauer settled in England, becoming librarian at the Bodleian Library, Oxford (1868), which he enriched by judicious purchases, particularly from the Cairo *Genizah*; in 1884 he was appointed reader in rabbinic Hebrew at the university. There he produced some of his finest work, cut short in 1899 by failing eyesight. His works there include *Catalogue of the Hebrew Manuscripts in the Bodleian Library* (3 vols., 1886–1906; the second was finished by A.E. Cowley), with over 2,500 entries (some items consisting of 20–50 works); the third volume contains 40 facsimiles that illustrate Hebrew paleography of different countries and periods. He also prepared a *Catalogue of the Hebrew Manuscripts in the Jews' College* (1886).

His *The Fifty-Third Chapter of Isaiah According to the Jewish Interpreters* (vol. 1, texts, 1876; vol. 2, translations with S.R. Driver, 1877; repr. 1969) provided biblical scholarship with an anthology of Jewish reactions to christological interpretations. He was the first to publish original Hebrew portions of *Ben Sira as they were found in the Cairo *Genizah*, together with the text of early versions, quotations of Ben Sira in rabbinical literature, and an English translation (with A.E. Cowley, 1897). His two volumes of *Medieval Jewish Chronicles* (*Seder ha-Ḥakhamim ve-Korot ha-Yamim*, preface and notes in English, 1887–95, repr. 1967) collected texts of a number of talmudic, geonic, and medieval historiographical writings. The fruits of Neubauer's collaboration with Renan were two remarkable works of literary history: *Les rabbins français du commencement du quatorzième siècle* (1877) and *Les écrivains juifs français du XIVe siècle* (1893). Other editions of his include *Vocabulaire hebraïco-français* (in: *Romanische Studien*, 2 (1875)), and *Petite Grammaire hebraique provenant de Yemen* (Arabic, 1891) as well as *Talmudical and Rabbinical Literature* (in: *Transaction of the Philological Society*, 1875–76). Neubauer also contributed a stream of articles, notes, and book reviews to most of the learned Jewish (and many non-Jewish) periodicals of his time. In 1901 he moved to Vienna to live with his nephew A. *Buechler, and when the latter became principal of Jews' College, London, in 1906, he returned to London where he died shortly afterward.

BIBLIOGRAPHY: E. Adler, in: *Studies in Jewish Bibliography... in Memory of A.S. Freidus* (1929), 31–54 (bibliography); B. Cohen, in: KS, 10 (1933/34), 365–71 (supplementary bibliography); H.M.J. Loewe, *Adolf Neubauer 1831–1931* (1931); A. Ben-Reshef, in: S. Federbush (ed.), *Ḥokhmat Yisrael be-Eiropah* (1965), 242–5. **ADD. BIBLIOGRAPHY:** ODNB online.

NEUBAUER, JACOB (Jekuthiel; 1895–1945), halakhist and law historian; born in Leipzig. In 1917 Neubauer published

Bibelwissenschaftliche Irrungen and in 1918 his important dissertation *Beitraege zur Geschichte des biblisch-talmudischen Eheschliessungsrechts*. When he was appointed lecturer at the Wuerzburg teachers' training school, his home became a center of Jewish intellectual life for students of all faculties. In 1933 he was chief lecturer at the rabbinical seminary in Amsterdam. Neubauer was an outstanding scholar in the history of Jewish law and in the exposition of the development of individual laws. He died in Bergen-Belsen. His *Ha-Rambam al Divrei Soferim* was published in Jerusalem in 1957.

BIBLIOGRAPHY: B. de Vries, in: *J.J. Neubauer, Ha-Rambam al Divrei Soferim* (1957), 3–7; I. Grunfeld, *Three Generations* (1958), 65–67.

[Frederik Jacob Hirsch]

NEUBERG, GUSTAV EMBDEN CARL (1877–1956), German biochemist. Born in Hanover, Neuberg joined the Pathological Institute of the University of Berlin, becoming professor in 1919, and from 1920 directed the Kaiser Wilhelm Institute of Biochemistry, Berlin-Dahlem. The Nazis dismissed him in 1938, and he went to Amsterdam. In 1939–40 he was professor of biochemistry at the Hebrew University of Jerusalem. In 1941 he went to America, was professor at New York University until 1950, and then for a time visiting professor at Brooklyn Polytechnic. Neuberg's field of research was principally in sugars, albumen, fermentation processes, the biochemical action of light, and glycerin substitutes. He was an honorary member of ten national academies of science, the recipient of many honorary doctorates, prizes, and medals.

BIBLIOGRAPHY: *Experimental Medicine and Surgery*, 5 (1947), 100–6, incl. bibl.; A. Auhagen, in: *Zeitschrift fuer Naturforschung*, 4 pt. B (1949), 245; *Chemical and Engineering News*, 25 (1947), 3358.

[Samuel Aaron Miller]

NEUBERGER, ALBERT (1908–1996), British biochemist. Neuberger, born in Hassfurt, Bavaria, qualified as a doctor of medicine in Wuerzburg. He then settled in England, where he undertook research first at London University and then (1939–42) at Cambridge. In 1943 he joined the Medical Research Council. After war service in India he returned to work at the University of London until 1947, when he became head of the biochemistry division of the National Institute for Medical Research. In 1955 he was appointed professor of chemical pathology at St. Mary's Hospital Medical School in London. Neuberger's main research was in the metabolism of proteins and amino acids. He was a fellow of the Royal Society, chairman of the Biochemical Society, and a governor of the Hebrew University of Jerusalem.

[Samuel Aaron Miller]

NEUBERGER, RICHARD LEWIS (1912–1960), U.S. senator, journalist, and author. Neuberger, born near Portland, Oregon, graduated from the University of Oregon (1935), where he edited the student newspaper. He began writing in 1928, and in 1933 *The Nation* published an article of his that realistically described the Nazi persecution of Jews and the preparation for war, which he had witnessed on a visit through Germany. From 1939 to 1954 he was the *New York Times'* Northwest correspondent. Neuberger served in the Oregon House of Representatives from 1941 to 1942, when he entered the U.S. Army. An aide-de-camp to General James O'Connor during the construction of the Alaska Military Highway, he left the army a captain in 1945.

In 1948 Neuberger was elected to the State Senate, and in 1955 he became the first Democratic U.S. senator from Oregon in 40 years. An affable liberal, Neuberger was active on behalf of natural conservation, civil rights, cancer research (he was himself afflicted), housing measures, Congressional reform, and Alaska statehood. He was chairman of the Subcommittee on Indian Affairs and a member of the Interior and Public Works committees, which dealt with conservation.

His books, which generally discuss politics and conservation in the northern U.S., include *An Army of the Aged* (with Kelley Loe, 1936), *Integrity – The Life of George W. Norris* (with S.B. Kahn, 1937), *Our Promised Land* (1938), *The Lewis and Clark Expedition* (1951), *Royal Canadian Mounted Police* (1953), and *Adventures in Politics* (1954).

His wife, H. MAURINE (BROWN) NEUBERGER (1907–2000) – who was not Jewish – served in the State House of Representatives from 1951 to 1955. The couple gained notice as the first married couple in U.S. history to serve together in a legislature – he in the Oregon Senate and she in the House. She worked closely with her husband, completing his Senate term after his death. In 1960 she was elected to the Senate, serving until 1967. She was the third woman elected to the U.S. Senate and the only woman from Oregon to serve in the legislative body.

BIBLIOGRAPHY: *New York Times* (March 10, Nov. 10, 1960); U.S. Congress, 86th Congress 2nd Session, *Richard Lewis Neuberger* (1960). **ADD. BIBLIOGRAPHY:** S. Neal (ed.), *They Never Go Back to Pocatello: The Selected Essays of Richard Neuberger* (2000); *Memorial Services: Held in the Senate and House of Representatives of the United States, Together With Remarks Presented in Eulogy of Richard Lewis Neuberger* (1960).

NEUBURGER, MAX (1868–1955), Austrian medical historian. Born in Vienna, Neuburger worked at the Rudolfspital and the Allegemeines Krankhaus and in 1898 went to teach at the University of Vienna. There he devoted himself more and more to medical history and was appointed professor of the history of medicine in 1904. He developed the department into a proper institute for the study of medical history and built up its library and museum (later described by A. Levinson, see bibl.). From 1901 to 1913 he collaborated with J. Pagel on a revised and enlarged edition of the history of medicine by his mentor, Theodor Puschmann. It appeared in three volumes, under the title *Handbuch der Geschichte der Medizin* (1902–05), a comprehensive and authoritative account of medical history. At the same time he wrote *Geschichte* *der Medizin* (vol. 1, 1906; vol. 2, 1911; Eng. trans. by E. Playfair 1910–25) which served at the time as the most authoritative textbook on medical history of the ancient and medieval period, and aroused much interest in its treatment of Arabic and Jewish medicine. In 1928 on the occasion of his 60th birthday, he was presented with a Festschrift by his colleagues, friends, and disciples, *Festschrift zur Feier seines 60. Geburtstages… Max Neuburger.*

He showed an interest in Jewish aspects of medicine, writing *Die ersten an der Wiener medizinischen Fakultaet promovierten Aerzte juedischen Stammes* (1918), and in 1936 he read a paper on Jewish doctors at the international congress for history of medicine in Jerusalem, published as *Die Stellung der juedischen Aerzte in der Geschichte der medizinischen Wissenschaften* (1936). Neuburger fled from the Nazis in 1938, settling in England, where he worked in The Wellcome Historical Medical Museum (1938–48). While in Britain he continued his research, writing *British Medicine and the Vienna School* (1943), in which he showed the reciprocal influence of both countries in medicine in the 18th and 19th centuries, and *British and German Psychiatry in the Second Half of the Early Nineteenth Century* (1945).

On his retirement in 1948 he was presented with *Festschrift zum 80. Geburtstag Max Neuburgers* in his honor (containing a bibliography). He then went to live in the U.S. until 1952, when he moved to Vienna, where he died. His other works include *Die Medizin im Flavius Josephus* (1919); *Hermann Nothnagel; Leben und Wirken* (1922); *Die Lehre von der Heilkraft der Natur im Wandel der Zeiten* (1926); and *Gomez Pereira, ein spanischer Arzt des 16. Jahrhunderts* (1936).

BIBLIOGRAPHY: *The Times* (March 17, 1955), 8e; JC (March 25, 1955), 35; A. Levinson, *Professor Neuburger and his Institute for the History of Medicine* (1924); E. Berghoff, *Max Neuburger, Werken und Wirken* (1948), incl. bibl.

NEUCHÂTEL, canton and its capital city in W. Switzerland. The earliest records of Jews in the canton date from 1288, when they were accused of a blood libel and a number were put to death. During the Black Death excesses in 1348 the Jews of Neuchâtel were burned. After 1476 there are no further references to Jews living in the canton until 1767, when a few who had come from Alsace were expelled. In 1772 they arrived in the towns of *La Chaux-de-Fonds and Le Locle, but were refused permanent residence rights. By the 1780s the Jews were considered useful to the canton as they played an important part in the export of watches, though this did not prevent their expulsion in 1790. They began to return in 1812 and obtained residence rights in 1830. The Jewish population of the canton in 1844 was 144. They thrived economically during the 19th century and in 1900 numbered 1,020, declining, however, to 266 by 2000.

BIBLIOGRAPHY: A. Nordman, *Les Juifs dans le pays de Neuchâtel* (1923); A. Weldler-Steinberg, *Geschichte der Juden in der Schweiz* (1966), 56–57, 103. **ADD. BIBLIOGRAPHY:** Musée Historique de Lausanne and A. Kamis-Müller, *Vie Juive en Suisse* (1992), index; L. Leitenberg, "Evolution et perspectives des communautés en Suisse romande," in: Schweiz. Isr. Gemeindebund (ed.), *Jued. Lebenswelt Schweiz* (2004); *100 Jahre Schweiz. Isr. Gemeindebund*, 153–66.

NEUDA, ABRAHAM (1812–1854), rabbi in *Lostice (Loschitz), one of the first in Moravia to have a secular education. His father, Aaron Moses, was also a rabbi in Lostice from 1812 to 1831. When his father became ill, Abraham, a favorite pupil of the *Landesrabbiner* Nahum *Trebitsch of *Mikulov (Nikolsburg), substituted for him on the authorization of his teacher. After the death of Aaron Moses in 1831 the community elected Abraham rabbi, but this time Trebitsch refused his authorization because Abraham had not only preached in German but also had acquired too much secular education (albeit clandestinely) at the yeshivah. A six-year-long conflict was finally brought before the provincial authorities, who requested the advice of Loeb *Schwab on the matter. Abraham was supported by Isaac Noah *Mannheimer. The authorities compelled Trebitsch to examine Neuda before a committee of two other rabbis and a Catholic priest. In the end Trebitsch was forced to acknowledge Neuda as rabbi of Lostice. Neuda published a collection of his sermons under the title, *Massa Devar Adonai*, in 1845. In his works, he attempted to reconcile the traditional **derash* with the modern sermon. Parts of his historical account of the Jews of Moravia were published posthumously by Gerson *Wolf in **Neuzeit* (1863).

A year after Neuda's death, his wife, FANNY (1819–1894), sister of the Vienna rabbi Abraham Adolf *Schmiedl, published in his memory a prayer book in German for women, entitled, *Stunden der Andacht, ein Gebet-und Erbauungsbuch fuer Israels Frauen und Jungfrauen*, which attained great popularity among Jewish women in central Europe. It was the first prayer book of its kind to be written by a woman and took into account, besides the divine services, all the occasions in the life of a woman. Until the 1920s, 28 editions of the prayer book had been sold. In 1936 Martha Wertheimer published a revised version for the special conditions of Nazi Germany. An English translation by M. Maier, *Hours of Devotion*, was published in New York.

BIBLIOGRAPHY: L. Loew, *Gesammelte Schriften*, 2 (1890), 203–11; B. Wachstein, in: H. Gold (ed.), *Juden und Judengemeinden Maehrens…* (1929), 319, includes bibliography; I.H. Weiss, *Zikhronotai* (1895), 47–49; S.W. Rosenfeld, *Stunden der Andacht* (1857), introd.

[Meir Lamed]

NEUFELD, DANIEL (1814–1874), Polish writer and educator. His name is connected with the Jewish weekly in Polish, *Jutrzenka* (*Ayyelet ha-Shaḥar*). Published in Warsaw from 1861 to 1863, the paper expressed Polish-Jewish solidarity during the 1863 revolution. Its goals were threefold; the diffusion of learning and culture; the promulgation of the idea of Jewish responsibility toward the Polish state; and the defense of Jews against antisemitism. It published serious works of scholarship on Polish Jewry and emphasized Jewish integration into the life and affairs of the general community. Such well-known personalities as Ḥayyim Zelig *Slonimski, editor of *Ha-Ẓefirah*, the historian Alexander Krausshar, and Mattias *Bersohn wrote for the journal. Publication ceased when its editor was exiled to Siberia in 1863.

Neufeld believed in a synthesis of Jewish and Polish cultures which would combine Polish patriotism and the Jewish religion. He was conservative in religious matters and progressive in his social concerns. Positively disposed toward Hebrew language and literature, Neufeld opposed Yiddish as obstructive of Jewish progress. He favored a scientific study of Jewish culture as a way of bridging past and present. Opposed to the *maskilim* of Galicia, he considered *Ḥasidism a positive force, hoping that it would encourage Polonization of the Jews. At the same time he opposed extreme assimilationist tendencies, regarding them as a break with talmudic tradition, which he saw as a nationalistic and political synthesis successful in preserving Jewish spiritual values. Presenting his ideas on education to Marquis Wielopolski, Neufeld called for the compulsory study of religion, along with Hebrew language, Jewish history, and the geography of Ereẓ Israel. Neufeld was editor of the Jewish department of a general encyclopedia published by his friend Orgelbrand. He wrote a scholarly study of Napoleon's *Sanhedrin and a pamphlet on the establishment of a *consistory in Poland. Although he began the important task of translating the Bible into Polish, he had difficulty in obtaining permission to publish his work, the Catholic censors preferring that Jews should have to study the Bible in a Christian translation. Permission was finally granted on condition that the title page carry the notice that the translation was intended for Polish Jews. The Book of Genesis with both the Hebrew text and a Polish translation appeared in 1863, under the title *Piécioksiąg Mojźesza dla Żydów-Polaków.*

BIBLIOGRAPHY: J. Shatzky, *Geshikhte fun Yidn in Varshe*, 1–3 (1947–53), indices; A. Levinson, *Toledot Yehudei Varsha* (1953), 168–9; EG, 1 (1953), 245–6, 507–9.

[Moshe Landau]

NEUFELD, HENRY (1923–1986), Israeli cardiologist. Neufeld was born in Lvov, Poland. He received his M.D. degree at the University of Vienna in 1948 and completed his residency training there in 1951. He emigrated to Israel in 1951 and, from 1951 to 1959 he served as a cardiologist at the Chaim Sheba Medical Center in Tel Aviv. After spending two years at the Mayo Clinic in Rochester, Minnesota, he returned to Israel and became director of the institute of cardiology at Tel Ha-Shomer, introducing cardiac intensive care into Israel for the first time. Neufeld became professor of medicine at the Hebrew University of Jerusalem in 1965. From 1962 he served for eight years as the chief scientist of the Ministry of Health and professor of medicine and cardiology at Tel Aviv University Medical School, where he developed the department of cardiology. He was elected president of the International Cardiological Federation in 1978 and was president of the Israel Heart Association. He was elected in 1984 to the Israel Academy of Sciences and Humanities, and in 1985 he received the Israel Prize for medicine. Neufeld was a man of great academic and personal distinction; he was an excellent clinician and an outstanding humanitarian and leader. He was a member of numerous committees of the World Health Organization, including the WHO Task Force against Heart Disease and the WHO Task Force on Cardiovascular Emergencies. Neufeld received worldwide recognition for his work. He was an honorary member of cardiac associations in Mexico, Portugal, Australia and New Zealand, Germany, and Britain. He was an honorary fellow of the Council of Clinical Cardiology, American Heart Association, and held that society's Honorary Citation for International Achievement. He published over 400 articles in major cardiology journals, 10 books, and 22 book chapters.

[Bracha Rager (2nd ed.)]

NEUGARTEN, BERNICE (1916–2001), U.S. psychologist and leader in the fields of human development and aging. Neugarten was born in Norfolk, Nebraska, to Lithuania-born David Levin and his wife, Sadie. She spent her educational and academic careers at the University of Chicago, obtaining her B.A. (English and French) and M.A. (Educational Psychology), before receiving the first doctorate from the innovative interdisciplinary program, the Committee on Human Development, in 1943. She became chair of the Committee in 1969. In 1980 she started a doctoral program in Human Development and Social Policy at Northwestern University but returned to the University of Chicago in 1988 as Rothschild Distinguished Scholar at the Center on Aging, Health, and Society, retiring in 1994. She and her husband, Fritz, had two children. Neugarten was the author or co-author of eight books and numerous articles, book chapters, addresses, and reports; these include *Vita Humane* (later titled *Human Development*) and a collection of essays, *The Meanings of Age: Selected Papers of Bernice L. Neugarten* (1996), edited by her daughter, Dr. Dail A. Neugarten. Neugarten's research disproved stereotypes about aging and the aged as well as misconceptions about development over the lifespan. Her coinages, including "the social clock," referring to the way individuals judge whether developments in their life are "on-time" or "off-time," "age-integrated society," "fluid life cycle," etc., have become mainstays of development studies; and her ideas greatly influenced social and governmental policies. For example, prior to her research, it was thought that personality was set early on. In contrast, she and her co-author David Gutmann found that personality develops and changes throughout life (1958). Similarly, while a vast body of medical and biological literature focused on the climacteric, her research revealed that middle-aged women did not view menopause as a significant event in their lives (1963). Her recognition that people age differently, based on their health and economic status, as well as chronological age, led her to cluster 55–74-year-olds as what she dubbed "young-old," and those over 75 as "old-old." In 1969–70 Neugarten chaired a faculty study on the status and opportunities open to women faculty and students at the University of Chicago, which made a series of recommendations for improving their experiences and adding to their numbers. She was president of the Gerontological Society of America (1969) and served a term on the United States Federal Council on Aging in the early 1980s.

BIBLIOGRAPHY: N.K. Schlossberg and L.E. Troll, "Bernice L. Neugarten (1916–)," in: A.N. O'Connell and N.F. Russo (eds.), *Women in Psychology: A Bio-Bibliographic Sourcebook* (1990), 256–65.

[Phyllis Holman Weisbard (2nd ed.)]

NEUGEBAUER, OTTO (1899–1990), scientific historian and mathematician. Neugebauer was born in Innsbruck, Austria, and studied mathematics at the University of Gottingen where he later became a staff member. The Nazis forced him to leave in 1933, first to Copenhagen and in 1939 for Brown University in the United States, where he immediately became a citizen. Neugebauer started his career as a mathematician and later became the foremost authority on Babylonian mathematics and mathematical astronomy throughout the ancient world, in Islamic countries, and in medieval and Renaissance Europe. His Jewish interest included a study on Maimonides and astronomy and the Jewish calendar, which he showed to be the source of the Islamic calendar. His polymath knowledge made him a preeminent historian of the exact sciences and Brown became the leading institution in this field. From 1950 he was a member of the Institute for Advanced Studies, Princeton. His many awards included election to the U.S. National Academy of Sciences (1977) and his publications include the definitive history of mathematical astronomy.

[Michael Denman (2nd ed.)]

NEUGEBOREN, JAY (Michael; 1938–), U.S. writer. He graduated from Columbia University, Phi Beta Kappa, in 1959. Originally and primarily a fiction writer, Neugeboren makes sense of the world by imposing narratives on it. In both his fiction and his later nonfiction, he fixes on a narrative thread running through events, following it even as it twists in unexpected and multiple directions. In whichever genre he chooses, Neugeboren is, in short, a teller of tales.

Early in his career, he told tales about invented characters, but with nonfiction he draws increasingly on his own experience. In *Open Heart: A Patient's Story of Life-Saving Medicine and Life-Giving Friendship* (2003), he describes the technology and compassion that saved his life as a quintuple-bypass patient. Without formal training in psychiatry, he questions in *Transforming Madness: New Lives for People Living with Mental Illness* (1999) the puzzling, asystematic system with which America cares for its mental patients. For over 50 years, Neugeboren has been caring for his brother Robert, who has been sporadically institutionalized for a mental illness that has been hard to diagnose and harder to treat. Abandoning polemics to argue for kinder, more inventive, more progressive, and just plain better treatment for the mentally ill, Neugeboren simply tells the stories of the colorful, often strikingly intense mental-health advocates and patients he met while trying to move his brother from one institution to another (and, finally, out of institutions entirely). Though filled with therapeutic and pharmacological detail, *Transforming Madness* is mainly narrated through the stories of these afflicted and driven souls. It is a passionate indictment told by a gifted raconteur.

Neugeboren tells his brother's story somewhat more intimately in his award-winning memoir, *Imagining Robert: My Brother, Madness, and Survival* (1997), and somewhat more obliquely in his fiction: in the powerfully inventive multilayered masterpiece *The Stolen Jew* (1981), one of whose plots concerns a writer's troubled relationship with his deranged brother, the characters are deeply connected and painfully estranged, often both at once. The recurring story of the two brothers, one quite mad, the other brainily rational, may serve as a synecdoche for Neugeboren's overarching interest in closeness and apartness.

The Diaspora is also omnipresent in his work, as a historical theme, as an ongoing development, and as a metaphor. Perhaps the most moving tale in *News from the American Diaspora* (2005) emerges in the preface, where Neugeboren describes his recent first meeting with an elderly cousin, separated from Neugeboren's family for nearly 60 years following the Holocaust. Those early postwar years were covered quite differently in his first collection of stories, *Corky's Brother* (1967), whose themes Neugeboren distinguishes from those in his second collection, *Don't Worry about the Kids* (1997): his early stories, he explains, concerned young people coming of age, "pastoral versions of growing up in Brooklyn, but these new stories are much more demanding of my reader…. If the *Corky's Brother* stories were pretty paintings, maybe you could think of these as woodcuts. The [1997] stories are more challenging, they're about grownups instead of teenagers, and their subject is mainly family life and things that threaten it, though the voices of the stories – and the settings – are more varied than my earlier work. Some … are ghost stories, of a sort, more like Cheever's urban fantasies than like Singer's." Moving beyond the appealing first-person narration employed throughout *Corky's Brother*, particularly in the title story, he noted one technical shift: "I'm able to be a little more expansive in third person, use more far-ranging images and metaphors."

Neugeboren's linguistic playfulness, using puns, stories within stories, jokes, dreams, and fantasy, has increasingly touched on the borders of traditional fiction. As prolific as he has been in other genres – he has written prize-winning screenplays such as *The Hollow Boy* (1991), children's literature such as *Poli: A Mexican Boy in Early Texas* (1989), and personal memoirs such as *Parentheses: An Autobiographical Journal* (1970), and has edited and introduced his brother's *The Hillside Diaries and Other Writings* (2004) and *The Story of* Story *Magazine by Martha Foley* (1980) – Neugeboren is a novelist at heart. In a 20-year period, he wrote six novels, varying widely and inventively in their descriptions of the life of the mind and the life of the body: *Big Man* (1966), *Listen*

Ruben Fontanez (1968), *Sam's Legacy* (1974), *An Orphan's Tale* (1976), *The Stolen Jew* (1981), and *Before My Life Began* (1985); and he continued to write fiction in his retirement from academic life. From 1971 through 2001, Neugeboren served at the University of Massachusetts, Amherst, as writer-in-residence and professor.

[Steven Goldleaf (2nd ed.)]

NEUGROESCHEL, MENDEL (1903–1965), Yiddish poet, essayist, and editor. Born in Nowy Sacz, Galicia, Neugroeschel practiced law in Vienna until the *Anschluss*. He was sent to the Dachau and Buchenwald concentration camps but was released in March 1939 and immigrated to Brazil. Two years later he settled in New York. In his Vienna period he was influenced by Rainer Maria Rilke and *Mani-Leib, as is evident from his first three lyric collections: *In Shvartsn Malkhes* ("In the Dark Realm," 1924), *Getseltn* ("Tents," 1930), and *Kaylikhdige Teg* ("Circular Days," 1935). In 1936 he published *Kleyne Antologye fun der Yidisher Lirik in Galitsye 1897–1935* ("A Brief Anthology of Yiddish Poetry in Galicia"). In New York he felt himself a stranger and wrote sad, nostalgic lyrics about the Jewish world of his youth. His prose study, "Di Moderne Yidishe Literatur in Galitsie" ("Modern Yiddish Literature in Galicia," in: *Fun Noentn Over*, 1 (1955), 267–398), affords rich insight into the Galician neo-romantic group which was influential between 1904 and 1918.

BIBLIOGRAPHY: LNYL, 6 (1965), 212f.; Rejzen, Leksikon, 2 (1927), 552; J. Leftwich, *The Golden Peacock* (1961).

[Melech Ravitch]

NEULANDER, ARTHUR H. (1896– 1988), U.S. Conservative rabbi, author. Neulander was born in Hungary and immigrated to the United States in 1903. He received his M.A. from New York University in 1918 and was ordained at the *Jewish Theological Seminary in 1921. Neulander spent his entire career as a congregational rabbi on the East Coast of the United States, serving Temple Gates of Prayer, Flushing, N.Y. (1922–25); Society for the Advancement of Judaism, New York City (1925–26); Temple Beth-El, Camden, N.J. (1926–27); Temple Beth Israel, Richmond Hill, N.Y. (1928–53); and Bayswater Jewish Center, Far Rockaway, N.Y. (1953–68). Neulander's contributions to the workings of the *Rabbinical Assembly, meanwhile, were instrumental in shaping Conservative Judaism. As a member and later chairman (1954–59) of the RA's Committee on Jewish Law and Standards, he wrote and influenced key responsa that modernized **halakhah*: permitting the use of electricity on Shabbat "in consonance with the spirit of the Sabbath"; permitting *aliyyot* (to the Torah) for women; and reopening the study of the **agunah* problem.

Neulander also served for many years on the RA's executive committee and edited the *Proceedings of the Rabbinical Assembly* (1941–44). In addition, he chaired the Committee on Textbook Publications for the United Synagogue Commission on Jewish Education (1946–47). On behalf of the U.S. government and world Jewry, Neulander traveled to Hungary in the wake of that country's 1956 revolt against Communist oppression to escort 20,000 fleeing Jewish refugees to the United States. As a regional officer of the Zionist Organization of America, he spearheaded fundraising efforts that enabled the purchase of the land now belonging to Neveh Ilan, a moshav in the Jerusalem Corridor settled by many American *olim*.

[Bezalel Gordon (2nd ed.)]

NEUMAN, ABRAHAM AARON (1890–1970), U.S. rabbi, historian, and educator. Neuman was born in Brezan, Austria, and immigrated to the United States in 1898. He studied at the Rabbi Isaac Elhanan Yeshivah, Columbia University, and the Jewish Theological Seminary, where he was ordained in 1912. Before his ordination, he taught at the Teachers Institute of the Seminary, but the year after, he joined the faculty of *Dropsie College in Philadelphia, where he taught history until 1940. Neuman held rabbinical posts in Philadelphia at the B'nai Jeshurun congregation (1919–27) and the Sephardi congregation Mikveh Israel (1927–40). After Cyrus Adler's death in 1940 Neuman became president of Dropsie College, a post he held until his retirement in 1966. During his incumbency the college expanded its curriculum, adding departments in Middle Eastern studies, education, and philosophy. Active in the development of the Zionist movement in the United States and renowned as an orator, he was much sought after as a public speaker. He also participated actively in the work of the United Synagogue of America.

Neuman produced a number of works of high scholarly merit, chief among them being *The Jews in Spain* (2 vols., 1942). Based primarily on the responsa of Solomon ibn *Adret (RaShBA), the work has served as a model of research in this type of Jewish source material. *Cyrus Adler, a Biography* (1942) is the evaluation of the life of an exemplary public servant during the period when American Jewry was assuming worldwide responsibilities. Neuman contributed to many scholarly periodicals, and a number of these studies appeared in *Landmarks and Goals* (1953). From 1940 to 1966 he collaborated with Solomon Zeitlin in editing the *Jewish Quarterly Review*.

BIBLIOGRAPHY: Zeitlin, in: *Studies and Essays in Honor of A.A. Neuman* (1962), vii–xiii.

[Solomon Grayzel]

NEUMANN, ALFRED (1895–1952), German novelist. Born in Lautenburg, West Prussia, Neumann studied in Munich. For several years he was literary adviser to the Munich publishing house of Georg Mueller. In 1938 he settled in Nice and from there emigrated to the U.S. in 1941. Neumann moved from Los Angeles to Florence in 1949 and died in Switzerland. Together with Heinrich Mann, Max *Brod, Alfred *Doeblin and Lion *Feuchtwanger, Neumann was responsible for the revival of the German historical novel.

His first great work, *Der Patriot* (1925), dramatized in English as *Such Men are Dangerous*, dealt with the assassination of Czar Paul of Russia. *Der Teufel* (1926) was set during the reign of Louis XVI of France. *Rebellen* (1927) and *Guerra* (1929) were concerned with the uprising of the Carbonari and the Risorgimento movement in 19th-century Italy. His other historical novels include *Koenig Haber* (1926), in which the central character recalls the rise and fall of Joseph Suess *Oppenheimer ("Jew Suess"); *Koenigin Christine von Schweden* (1936); *Neuer Caesar* (1934); *Kaiserreich* (1936); and *Die Volksfreunde* (1941), concerning the government of Napoleon III, the occupation of Paris in 1870, and the uprising of the commune in 1871. In his *Es waren ihre sechs* (1949) he was inspired by the resistance movement of the White Rose (*Weisse Rose*) among Munich students opposing National Socialism.

In 1950, an editon of his collected works (*Gesammelte Werke*) was published in two volumes. A selection of his work (*Eine Auswahl aus seinem Werk*) in one volume was edited by G. Stern in 1979. In 1977 Neumann's Correspondence with Thomas *Mann appeared (ed. P. de Mendelssohn).

BIBLIOGRAPHY: F. Lennartz, *Deutsche Dichter und Schriftsteller unserer Zeit* (1959[8]), 552–5. **ADD. BIBLIOGRAPHY:** K. Umlauf, *Exil, Terror, Illegalität. Die aesthetische Verarbeitung politischer Erfahrungen in ausgewaehlten Romanen aus dem Exil 1933–1945* (1982); G. Stern, "Alfred Neumann," in: G. Stern, *Literatur im Exil* (1989), 249–81; G.F. Probst, "Alfred Neumann's and Erwin Piscator's Dramatization of Tolstoy's 'War and Peace' and the Role of Theatre as a Contribution to America's War Efforts," in: *Exile and Enlightenment* (1987), 265–72; G. Stern, "The Image of America in Exile Literature: Alfred Neumann's Unpublished Film Script 'Commencement Day'," in: H.D. Osterle (ed), *Amerika* (1989), 19–28.

[Rudolf Kayser / Kurt Feilchenfeld (2nd ed.)]

NEUMANN, EMANUEL (1893–1980), U.S. Zionist leader. Neumann was born in Libau (Liepaja), Latvia, and was brought to the United States by his parents shortly after his birth. He received a B.A. in modern languages and a doctorate of laws from Columbia University; he practiced law in New York City for many years while dedicating much of his life to the establishment and development of the state of Israel.

Active in American Zionist affairs from his youth, Neumann edited the *Young Judean* in 1914–15, and served as education director of the Zionist Organization of America (ZOA) in 1918–20. Neumann was later elected president of the ZOA in 1947–49, and again in 1956–58.

As a co-founder of the *Keren Hayesod in the U.S. in 1921, Neumann served as its director from 1921 to 1925 and was chairman of the executive committee of the United Palestine Appeal from 1925–28. He was also president of the Jewish National Fund in the U.S. from 1929 to 1930, and from 1931 to 1941 he was a member of the Jewish Agency in Jerusalem. Returning to the U.S., he was political representative of the Jewish Agency in Washington during the 1940s and instrumental in winning influential political figures to Zionism.

In 1943 Neumann organized and directed the work of the Commission on Palestine Surveys that presented an investment proposal of approximately $200 million in irrigation facilities and hydroelectric power development in the Jordan Valley.

A close collaborator of Abba Hillel *Silver in influencing the Jewish community and American public opinion to the post–World War II Zionist program, Neumann served with Silver as vice chairman of the American Zionist Emergency Council.

In 1947 he was a member of the Jewish Agency panel in its unsuccessful negotiations with England and a member of the agency's delegation to the UN Special Committee on Palestine which recommended that Palestine be partitioned. Although Neumann had opposed partition, he accepted the committee's recommendation as the best that the Jews would be able to obtain. After Israel's establishment, Neumann devoted himself to obtaining military and economic aid, and political sympathy for the country.

From 1951 to 1953 he headed the Jewish Agency's economic department and its information and public relations department. He was appointed chairman of the United States section of the World Zionist Organization-Jewish Agency in 1956, a position he held until 1972. Neumann also founded the Herzl Foundation in 1954 and the Tarbuth Foundation for the Advancement of Hebrew Culture in 1961, and served as inaugural president for both organizations.

In 1958, he led a majority of the World Conference of General Zionists into a new organization of the same name, remaining as president until 1963 when he was elected president of the World Union of General Zionists. While in these positions, Neumann voiced the belief that while Jews in the United States owed political allegiance only to the United States, their spiritual allegiance belonged to their Jewish heritage. In 1976, he published *In The Arena: An Autobiographical Memoir.* He died in Tel Aviv.

BIBLIOGRAPHY: Alfred E. Clark, Obituary, *New York Times* (Oct. 27, 1980).

[Jonathan Freund (2nd ed.)]

NEUMANN, ERICH (1905–1960), Israeli psychologist and psychoanalyst. Neumann, who was born in Berlin, studied analytical psychology under Carl Jung in Zurich. In 1934 he immigrated to Palestine, where he resumed his career as a psychoanalyst and therapist of the Jungian school. Later he was a frequent lecturer at the Eranos congresses in Ascona.

Neumann dealt with the inner crisis of modern man in two works, *Tiefenpsychologie und neue Ethik* (1949; *Depth Psychology and a New Ethic*, 1966) and *Krise und Erneuerung* (1961). Another major work, *Ursprungsgeschichte des Bewusstseins* (1949), first created a systematization of the human consciousness. The principal themes of his research into depth psychology were the world of archetypes, the psychology of creative man, the psychology of the female, and the archetypal in art. Other major publications were *Umkreisung der Mitte*, 3 vols. (1953–54); *Die Grosse Mutter* (1956; *The Great Mother*, 1955); *Der schoepferische Mensch…* (1959); *Die archetypische Welt Henry Moores* (1961; *The Archetypal World of Henry Moore*, 1959); *Das Kind* (1963); and essays in the *Eranos-Jahrbuch*, and psychological journals.

NEUMANN, HENRY (1882–1966), U.S. Ethical Culture leader. Neumann, who was born in New York, became leader of the newly formed Brooklyn Society for Ethical Culture in 1911, serving until his retirement in 1961. He also taught ethics in New York's Ethical Culture schools. In 1922, with his wife Julie, he founded the Brooklyn Ethical Culture School. Neumann's work reflects a combination of classic wit, moral rigor, and ethical humanism. Chief among his seven books is *Education for Moral Growth* (1923). Key figure in the American Ethical Union (Federation of Ethical Culture Societies), he was editor of *The Standard* (later the *Ethical Outlook*) and chairman of the Fraternity of Ethical Leaders (1952–61).

[Howard B. Radest]

NEUMANN, JOHANN (Johnny) LUDWIG VON (1903–1957), U.S. mathematician. Von Neumann was born in Budapest and showed outstanding mathematical ability at an early age. He accepted a chair at Princeton University in 1931. Two years later he was appointed the first professor of mathematical physics at the newly formed Institute for Advanced Study at Princeton. In 1954 his health began to deteriorate, and he died after a prolonged and painful illness.

Von Neumann's thought processes were rapid and his associates often found it difficult to keep up with his vast flow of ideas. He was also a linguist and could converse in seven European languages. He preferred general to special problems, and rarely worried about mathematical elegance. In connection with a long-winded but straightforward proof he is quoted as saying that he "didn't have the time to make the subject difficult." Von Neumann's interest in quantum mechanics was aroused by his stay in Goettingen in 1926. He aimed at developing the subject as a vigorous mathematical discipline in *Mathematische Grundlagen der Quantenmechanik* (1932). This investigation led him to research in Hilbert space and the initiation of continuous geometry. In addition, Von Neumann made important contributions to measure theory, ergodic theory, continuous groups, topology, classical mechanics, hydrodynamic turbulence, and shock waves. He opened up a new branch of mathematics with his paper "Zur Theorie der Gesellschaftsspiele," (in *Mathematische Annalen*, 100 (1928), 295–320) and the book *Theory of Games and Economic Behavior* (1944, 1953[3]) written in collaboration with O. Morgenstern.

Von Neumann's work in the war effort convinced him of the need for high-speed computers. He was instrumental in the development of MANIAC (the mathematical analyzer, numerical integrator, and computer) and was a member of the U.S. Atomic Energy Commission from 1955 until his death. His *Von Neumann Collected Works* were published in six volumes from 1961 to 1963.

BIBLIOGRAPHY: *Current Biography Yearbook* 1955 (1956), 624–7; Bochner, in: National Academy of Sciences, *Biographical Memoirs*, 32 (1958), 438–57; *Bulletin of the American Mathematical Society*, 64:3, pt. 2 (May 1958), special issue dedicated to J. von Neumann, incl. bibl.; F. Smithies, in: *Journal of the London Mathematical Society*, 34 (1959), 373–84; S. Thomas, *Men of Space*, 1 (1960), 181–203 (incl. bibl.).

[Barry Spain]

NEUMANN, ROBERT (1897–1975), novelist and satirist. Born in Vienna, the son of a mathematician and bank director, Neumann studied chemistry and literature and got his Ph.D. with a thesis on Heinrich Heine. After losing his money in the inflation of the 1920s, he went to sea. His two early verse collections *Gedichte* (1919) and *Zwanzig Gedichte* (1923) attracted little attention, but *Mit fremden Federn* (1927), a volume of parodies, brought him fame. Of the works that followed, the anti-Nazi novels *Sintflut* (1929) and *Die Macht* (1932; Eng. tr. *Mammon*, 1933), and *Unter falscher Flagge* (1932), another book of parodies, were particularly successful. In February 1934, less than a year after the public burning of his books by the Nazis, he moved to England. Other works of his pre-World War II period were the novels *Karriere* (1931; *On the Make*, 1932); *Sir Basil Zaharoff, der Koenig der Waffen* (1934; *Zaharoff, the Armaments King*, 1935); *Struensee* (1935; *The Queen's Doctor*, 1936); and *An den Wassern von Babylon* (written 1937–38, Ger. orig. publ. 1945; *By the Waters of Babylon*, 1939).

Neumann also began to write in English, later novels including *The Inquest* (1944; *Bibiana Santis* (Ger.), 1950); *Children of Vienna* (1946; *Kinder von Wien*, 1948); and *Blind Man's Buff* (1949). A witty and ironical writer and a gifted political and social satirist, he had a fondness for the erotic and a genius for parodying modern poets. After the war, when he settled in Switzerland, he wrote an autobiography, *Mein altes Haus in Kent* (1957), and then turned to somber themes relating to the Holocaust. Works of this kind are the documentaries, *Ausfluechte unseres Gewissens* (1960), on Hitler's "Final Solution"; *Hitler, Aufstieg und Untergang des Dritten Reiches* (1961); *The Pictorial History of the Third Reich* (1962); and *Der Tatbestand oder Der gute Glaube der Deutschen* (1965). Neumann also wrote plays for radio and television and another autobiography, *Vielleicht das Heitere*, was published in 1968. Selected editions of his parodies appeared as *Typisch Robert Neumann* (with a preface by R.W. Leonhardt) in 1975 and *Meisterparodien* (ed. by J. Jessen) in 1988.

BIBLIOGRAPHY: *Robert Neumann: Stimmen der Freunde… Zum 60. Geburtstag…* (1957), incl. bibl.; H. Zohn, *Wiener Juden in der deutschen Literatur* (1964), 89–94. **ADD. BIBLIOGRAPHY:** U. Scheck, *Die Prosa Robert Neumanns: mit einem bibliographischen Anhang* (1985); F. Fuerbeth, "'Iwrí anochí. Ich bin Hebraeer'. Juedische Identitaet bei Friedrich Torberg und Robert Neumann in der Literaturkritik; nur ein Formproblem?" in: I. Wintermeyer (ed.), *Kleine Lauben, Arcadien und Schnabelewopski* (1995), 148–162; R. Dove, "'Ein Experte des Überlebens'. Robert Neumann in British Exile 1933–45," in: *Aliens – Uneingebuergerte* (1994), 159–173; T. Hilsheimer, "Das Scheitern der Wirtschaftsmacht an den politischen Umstaenden. Robert Neumanns Exilerzaehlung 'Sephardi'," in: C.D. Krohn (ed.), *Exil und Avantgarden*, (1998), 127–141; R. Dove, *Journey of No Return. Five German-Speaking Literary Exiles in Britain, 1933–1945*, (2000); idem, *"Fremd ist die Stadt und leer…". Fünf deutsche und oesterreichische Schriftsteller im Londoner Exil 1933–1945* (2004).

[Sol Liptzin]

NEUMANN, YEḤESKEL MOSHE (1893–1956), Yiddish poet, satirist, journalist, editor. Born in Zhichlin, Poland, he was educated in Lodz. He wrote for the *Lodzher Morgnblat*, edited booklets on literature and art, and was a founder of the Lodz writers' group "Yung Yiddish"; he later wrote film and theater reviews for the Warsaw daily *Haynt*, whose literary editor he became in 1933. In addition to contributing to various Yiddish periodicals, he was among the pioneers of Yiddish film, co-writing the scripts for *"Al Ḥet"* ("For the Sin," 1936) and *"Tkias Kaf"* ("Handshake," 1937). During World War II he fled to Russia, before immigrating to Palestine (1940) and joining the editorial board of the daily *Davar*. He wrote about problems of the Yiddish and Hebrew theater, published articles in the Yiddish journal *Di Goldene Keyt*, and wrote about Jewish artists and architects. He also composed the dramatic poem *"Don Kishot in Shotn fun der Palme"* ["Don Quixote in the Shadow of the Palm Tree," in: *Di Goldene Keyt* (1951)] and *"A Khasene in Yerusholayim"* ("A Wedding in Jerusalem," *ibid.*, 1953).

BIBLIOGRAPHY: Rejzen, Leksikon, 2 (1927), 561–4; LNYL, 6 (1965), 222–6. **ADD. BIBLIOGRAPHY:** Sh. Lubetkin, *Publitsistn* (1937), 57–64; M. Ravitch, *Mayn Leksikon*, 1 (1945), 144–46.

[Israel Ch. Biletzky]

NEUMARK, DAVID (1866–1924), scholar and philosopher of Reform Judaism. Born in Galicia, Neumark was ordained as rabbi at the Lehranstalt fuer die Wissenschaft des Judenthums in 1897. He served as rabbi in Rakonitz (Rakovnik), Bohemia, from 1897 to 1904, and as editor in chief of the division of philosophy and *halakhah* of the proposed Hebrew encyclopedia *Oẓar ha-Yahadut* from 1904 to 1907, whose specimen volume on the principle and philosophy of Judaism he edited in 1906. He was professor of Jewish philosophy at the Veitel-Heine-Ephraimschen Lehranstalt in Berlin in 1907 and professor of philosophy at the Hebrew Union College in Cincinnati from 1907 to 1924. In 1919 Neumark founded *The Journal of Jewish Lore and Philosophy*, which became *The Hebrew Union College Annual* in 1921.

Neumark's philosophy of Judaism is representative of the Reform Jewish position of his time, and includes the following points: Judaism is an evolving religion which has undergone change in the past and will continue to do so in the future; the vital continuing element in Judaism is ethical monotheism, which Jewish philosophy must defend, explicate, and refine; the Bible was written by men, and while it is a source of inspiration and instruction, it is not binding and may be disagreed with. Neumark was unusual among the Reformists of his day in that he was an ardent Zionist. However, on the basis of his philosophy of Judaism, he insisted that Zionism must have a religious base, which for him was the only *raison d'être* for any significant Jewish enterprise.

Neumark's scholarship reflected his concept of Judaism. He attempted in his many works to show that throughout the evolution of Judaism the basic commitment of the Jew was to religion, and that the Jews remained true to Judaism through the ages only because their concepts of God and morality differed from and were superior to all other religions and philosophies of their time. Neumark's magnum opus, *Geschichte der juedischen Philosophie des Mittelalters* (1907–10; translated into Hebrew under the title *Toledot ha-Filosofyah be-Yisrael*, vol 1, 1922, vol. 2, 1929), combines considerable acumen and occasional penetrating insights with a lack of critical method and an excess of imagination. His *Essays in Jewish Philosophy* (1929) contains a bibliography of his writings, which also included "The Philosophy of Judaism" (HUCA 1925), *The Philosophy of the Bible* (1918), and *Toledot ha-Ikkarim be-Yisrael* (Odessa, 2 vols., 1912–19).

[Alvin J. Reines]

NEUMARK, EPHRAIM (1860–?), traveler and writer. Born in Eastern Europe, Neumark was taken by his parents to Ereẓ Israel. At the age of 23 he left *Tiberias on a three-year journey through the Jewish communities in *Syria, Kurdistan, Mesopotamia, *Persia, *Afghanistan, and Central Asia. The account of his travels, *Massa' be-Ereẓ ha-Kedem*, is distinguished by critical observation and scholarly approach. He gives a detailed picture of every aspect of the Jewish communities in the Orient, their geographical diffusion, occupations, religious life, practices, and customs.

BIBLIOGRAPHY: KS, 24 (1947–48), 28–29; E. Neumark, *Massa' be-Ereẓ ha-Kedem*, ed. by A. Yaari (1967), with introd. and notes; idem, in: *Ha-Asif*, 5 (1889), 39–75.

[Walter Joseph Fischel]

NEUMEYER, ALFRED (1867–1944), lawyer, chairman of the Jewish Community of Munich (Israelitische Kultusgemeinde Muenchen); founder and chairman of the Association of Jewish Communities in Bavaria (Verband Bayerischer Israelitischer Gemeinden). Born in Munich, Neumeyer completed the renowned Maximilians-Gymnasium and studied law in Munich and Berlin. He worked as a judge in several Bavarian cities until he was appointed to the Higher State Court (*Oberlandesgericht*) in Munich in 1918. In 1929 he was appointed to the Bavarian Highest State Court (*Oberstes Bayerisches Landesgericht*) in Munich. In June 1933 he was forced to retire. Neumeyer led the Jewish community in Munich until his immigration to Colonia Avigdor (Argentina) in January 1941. His brother, Karl *Neumeyer, committed suicide in July 1941.

BIBLIOGRAPHY: Alfred Neumeyer, *Erinnerungen* (Manuscript, Leo Baeck Institute New York; copy of manuscript at Bavarian State Library Munich); A. Neumeyer, "Alfred Neumeyer (1867–1944). Richter und Vorsitzender des Verbandes Israelitischer Kultusgemeinden in Bayern bis 1941," in: *Geschichte und Kultur der Juden in Bayern* (1988), 235–41.

[Andreas Heusler (2nd ed.)]

NEUMEYER, KARL (1869–1941), German international lawyer. Born in Munich, Neumeyer completed the renowned Maximilians-Gymnasium. After studying law in Munich, Berlin, and Geneva, he became a lecturer at the University of Munich in 1910. He was a member of the Institut de Droit

International in The Hague and represented Germany at the sixth Hague conference on private international law in 1928. In 1929 he was made professor of international law at Munich University and in 1931 became dean of the faculty of law. Though removed from all his posts in 1933 following the Nazi rise to power, Neumeyer refused to leave Germany and continued his research under most difficult conditions. After the Nazis confiscated Neumeyer's private library and it became obvious that the couple would be forced to leave their residence at Koeniginstrasse, Karl Neumeyer and his wife, Anna, committed suicide in July 1941. His brother Alfred *Neumeyer immigrated to Argentina in January 1941.

Neumeyer was the author of several important works on international law, including *Die gemeinrechtliche Entwicklung des internationalen Privat-und Strafrechts bis Bartolus* (2 vols., 1901–16), a history of international law; *Internationales Privatrecht* (1923), a detailed analysis of the sources of international law; and *Internationales Verwaltungsrecht* (4 vols., 1910–36), in which he set out his system of international administrative law.

BIBLIOGRAPHY: *American Journal of International Law*, 35 (1941), 672. **ADD. BIBLIOGRAPHY:** K. Vogel, "Karl Neumeyer (1869–1941). Ein Lebenswerk: das "Internationale Verwaltungsrecht," In: H. Heinrichs, H.Franzki, K. Schmalz, and M. Stolleis (eds.), *Deutsche Juristen Juedischer Herkunft* (1993), 531–41; A. Neumeyer, *Lichter und Schatten. Eine Jugend in Deutschland* (1967).

[Andreas Heusler (2nd ed.)]

NEUSNER, JACOB (1932–), leading figure in the American academic study of religion. He has achieved this prominence and influence in three ways. First, he revolutionized the study of Judaism and brought it into the field of religion. Second, he built intellectual bridges between Judaism and other religions and thereby laid the groundwork for durable understanding and respect among religions. Third, through his teaching and his publication programs, he advanced the academic careers of younger scholars and teachers, both within and outside the study of Judaism. Neusner's influence on the study of Judaism and religion is broad, powerful, distinctive, and enduring.

Judaism and the Study of Religion

Educated at Harvard, Jewish Theological Seminary, Oxford, and Columbia, Neusner began his career in the early 1960s, when religion was a minor field in American universities, largely limited to biblical studies and Christian (mostly Protestant) theology. Judaism was studied parochially, confined primarily to Jewish institutions. Neusner changed this. He understood that the power of the study of religion is its capacity to generalize, to discern common structures across religions, and, through them, to understand the similarities and differences among diverse traditions. Neusner also knew, as did no other student of Judaism, that scholars cannot generalize about religions that are closed to them.

Neusner addressed these problems in two ways. First, he established a career agenda to bring critical questions to the study of Judaism. His staggering success transformed not only the study of Judaism; it also affected the study of religion. Neusner was the first to see that the sources of classical Judaism were not constructed to answer standard historical questions. He invented the documentary study of Judaism, through which he showed, relentlessly and incontrovertibly, that each document of the rabbinic canon has a discrete focus and agenda, and that the history of ancient Judaism has to be told in terms of its texts rather than personalities or events. His *Judaism: The Evidence of the Mishnah* (Chicago, 1981, translated into Hebrew and Italian) is the classic statement of his work and the first of many comparable volumes on the other documents of the rabbinic canon.

Neusner's discovery of the centrality of documents led to his even more decisive perception of Judaism as a system: an integrated network of beliefs, practices, and values that yield a coherent worldview and picture of reality for its adherents. This approach generated a series of very important studies on the way Judaism creates categories of understanding and how those categories relate to one another, even as they emerge diversely in discrete rabbinic documents. Neusner's work shows, for instance, how deeply Judaism is integrated with the system of the Pentateuch, how such categories as "merit" and "purity" work in Judaism, and how classical Judaism absorbed and transcended the destruction of the Jerusalem Temple in 70 C.E. His work depicts Rabbinic Judaism as the result of human labor in response to what its adherents believe is God's call and demonstrates its persistent vitality and imagination.

Second, in the process of producing his scholarship, Neusner translated, analyzed, and explained virtually the entire rabbinic canon – a massive compendium of texts – in English. The Mishnah, the Tosefta, the Jerusalem Talmud, the Babylonian Talmud, and nearly every work of rabbinic Bible interpretation are available to scholars of all backgrounds because of Neusner's scholarship. In the study of Judaism, no one in history can match Neusner's work.

In all of this, Neusner made Judaism and its study available to scholars and laypeople of every background and persuasion. That Judaism is now a mainstream component of the American study of religion is due almost entirely to Jacob Neusner's scholarship.

Bridges of Intellect and Understanding

Neusner's work did not stop with his exposition – in translation, description, and interpretation – of Judaism alone. To the contrary, unlike any other scholar of his generation, Neusner deliberately built outward from Judaism to other religions. He sponsored a number of very important conferences and collaborative projects that drew different religions into conversation on common themes and problems. Among other topics, Neusner's efforts have produced conferences and books on the problems of religion and society, religion and material culture, religion and economics, religion and altruism, and religion and tolerance. These collaborations build on Neusner's intellectual vision, his notion of a religion as a system, and would not have been possible otherwise. By working towards general questions from the perspective of a discrete religion, Neusner produced results of durable consequence for understanding other religions as well.

In addition to these efforts, Neusner has written a number of works exploring the relationship of Judaism to other religions around difficult issues of understanding and misunderstanding. For instance, his *A Rabbi Talks with Jesus* (Philadelphia, 1993, translated into German, Italian, and Swedish; second edition Montreal and Kingston, Ithaca, 2004) establishes a religiously sound framework for Judaic-Christian interchange and earned the praise of Pope Benedict XVI. He also has collaborated with other scholars to produce comparisons of Judaism and Christianity, for instance, *The Bible and Us: A Priest and A Rabbi Read Scripture Together* (New York, 1990, translated into Spanish and Portuguese; second edition *Common Ground: A Priest and A Rabbi Read Scripture Together* (Eugene, 2005). He has done the same with scholars of Islam on Judaism and Islam. Neusner conceived the very effective textbook *World Religions in America: An Introduction* (third edition, Nashville, 2004), which explored how diverse religions have developed in the distinctive American context. It has had a strong impact in both colleges and secondary schools. He also has composed numerous college and school textbooks and general trade books on Judaism. The two best known examples are *The Way of Torah: An Introduction to Judaism* (seventh edition, Belmont, 2003) and *Judaism. An Introduction* (London and New York, 2002, translated into Portugese and Japanese). No American scholar of any religion replicates Neusner's intellectual outreach.

Advancing the Careers of Others

Throughout his career, Neusner has established publication programs and series with various academic publishers. Each of these he has opened to the widest range of scholars and scholarship. Through these series, through numerous reference works that he conceived and edited, and through the conferences he has sponsored, Neusner has advanced the careers of literally dozens of younger scholars from across the globe. By fostering scholarship, he has stimulated the research of others and helped many younger scholars from around the world realize their potential. There is no one else in the American study of religion who has had this kind of impact on students of such a broad range of approaches and interests.

Conclusion

Jacob Neusner is often celebrated as the most published scholar in history. He has written or edited more than 900 books. He has taught at Columbia University, University of Wisconsin-Milwaukee, Brandeis University, Dartmouth College, Brown University, the University of South Florida, and Bard College. He is a member of the Institute of Advanced Study, Princeton, NJ, and a life member of Clare Hall, Cambridge University. In addition, he is the only scholar to serve on both the National Endowment for the Humanities and the National Endowment for the Arts. He also has received scores of academic awards, honorific and otherwise.

The real measure of Jacob Neusner's contribution to the study of religion emerges from the originality, excellence, and scope of his learning. He founded a field of scholarship: the academic study of Judaism. He built out of that field to influence a larger subject: the academic study of religion. He created durable networks and pathways of interreligious communication and understanding. And he cared for the careers of others. Ever generous with his intellectual gifts, Neusner is one of America's greatest humanists. In all aspects of his career, he exemplifies the meaning of American learning. In all he has done, Jacob Neusner fulfills the distinctive promise of the academic study of religion in an open and pluralistic society that values religion as a fundamental expression of freedom.

For a discussion of Neusner as a Talmud scholar see *Mishnah.

[Wm. Scott Green (2nd ed.)]

NEUTRA, RICHARD JOSEPH (1892–1970), U.S. architect. Born in Vienna, after World War I Neutra worked in Switzerland as a nurseryman and landscape gardener, an experience which helped to develop his remarkable talent for his buildings fitting into the landscape. In 1922 he joined Erich *Mendelsohn in Berlin, and the following year they were awarded first prize for their joint design for a business center for Haifa, Palestine. Neutra emigrated to the U.S. in 1923 and studied under Frank Lloyd Wright at his architectural center at Taliesin, Wisconsin. In 1926 he settled in Los Angeles, where he entered the office of the Vienna-born architect, Rudolph Schindler. The buildings they designed and erected were among the first creations of the international style in America. Neutra was at this period concerned with town planning and architectural technology. This aspect of his work is seen in his "Rush City Reformed" (1923–30), a plan for an ideal city, in his designs for prefabricated housing units, and in his Channel Heights Housing Project, San Pedro, California (1942–44). It was for his private homes, however, that Neutra was best known. "Lovell House" (1927–29), a rambling construction in the then-modern style, established his reputation. The houses he built after World War II are often regarded as his greatest achievement. They are usually luxurious residences in which glass is extensively used to give a feeling of space; the effect of the glass is often enhanced by the use of reflecting pools of water. Neutra wrote several books, including *Survival Through Design* (1954).

BIBLIOGRAPHY: E. Mc-Coy, *Richard Neutra* (Eng., 1960), includes bibliography; W. Boesiger (ed.), *Richard Neutra, Buildings and Projects* (1951, 1959, 1966); A. Forsee, *Men of Modern Architecture* (1966), 131–60.

NEUWIRTH, BEBE (1958–), U.S. actress. Born in Newark and raised in Princeton, N.J., Neuwirth majored in dance at the Juilliard School in New York. She made her Broadway debut in *A Chorus Line* in 1980 but she achieved fame as Dr. Lilith Sternin-Crane, a dour psychiatrist married to a psychiatrist, in the long-running hit television series *Cheers* and its spin-off *Frasier.* A singer and dancer, she featured in the

Broadway musicals *Damn Yankees, Sweet Charity,* and *Chicago* and won two Tony awards. In 2005 she starred in the crime drama series *Law & Order: Trial by Jury.* She appeared in more than 25 movies.

[Stewart Kampel (2nd ed.)]

NEUZEIT, DIE ("Modern Times"), liberal Austrian Jewish weekly in German language "for political, religious and cultural interests" (*Wochenschrift fuer politische, religioese und Kultur-Interessen*), published in Vienna from 30 August 1861 to 25 December 1903 (43 volumes). Modeled after the **Allgemeine Zeitung des Judenthums* (1837–1922) in Germany, *Die Neuzeit* marked the actual beginning of the Jewish press in Austria in the second half of the 19th century and became the main organ for Jewish emancipation until 1867. Before 1850, the Hebrew year books **Bikkurei ha-Ittim* (1820–45), **Kerem Hemed* (1833–56) and *Kokhevei Yiẓḥak* (1845–73), I. *Busch's German *Kalender und Jahrbuch fuer Israeliten* (1842–47), and his weekly **Oesterreichisches Central-Organ* (1848) had appeared in Vienna, besides a few other short-lived periodicals in 1848. From 1849 to 1852, M. *Letteris continued to publish two far from successful papers, followed by his *Wiener Mitteilungen* (1854–69), Joseph *Wertheimer's *Jahrbuch für Israeliten* (1854–67), and *Das Morgenland* (1855) of Jacob *Goldenthal.

Die Neuzeit was founded by the Bohemian writer Leopold *Kompert (1822–1886) and the Hungarian rabbi and educator Simon *Szántó (1819–1882). In a way, both embodied the continuity of the German-Jewish press in Austria since 1842, taking over Wertheimer's *Jahrbuch*, which had succeeded Busch's annual and the *Central-Organ*. While *Die Neuzeit* was edited by Szántó till his death, Kompert withdrew after the first volume, still contributing articles from time to time. In 1882, the paper was carried on by the Vienna preacher and scholar Adolf *Jellinek (1821–1893), and in 1893, by his colleague D. Loewy (died 1902).

In their first editorial (*"An unsere Leser!"*) of August 30, 1861, Kompert and Szántó were aware of filling a gap in the daily press, especially for Austrian Jewry, at the same time also hoping for non-Jewish readers. Judaism, as they saw it, should serve as a mirror for general society in a modern age, reflecting any progress or disruption in their time. *Die Neuzeit* sought to take the position of a peaceful yet determined mediator, ready to fight if necessary. By spreading information on a scientific basis, the paper was to serve an outward function as an organ for emancipation and apologetics, and an inward function by mediating between East and West, religious stagnation and radical reform.

Szántó, however, who wrote the majority of articles, assumed a rather liberal stance, both politically and religiously. While his paper reflected most religious controversies of the time, he distanced himself from the more conservative Ludwig *Philippson and the *Breslau *Juedisch-Theologisches Seminar* of Zacharias *Frankel, strongly opposing *Neo-Orthodoxy both in Germany and Hungary, which was led by Samson Raphael *Hirsch and Azriel *Hildesheimer. Instead, Szántó favored the reform efforts of Abraham *Geiger and participated in the *synods of Leipzig (1869) and Augsburg (1871), presided over by Moritz *Lazarus. In 1871/72, together with Ignaz *Kuranda, he strongly supported the supposed reforms of Adolf *Jellinek in Vienna against the leader of Austrian Orthodox Jewry, Reb Zalman *Spitzer. In stressing the universalistic and ethical aspects of Judaism and its historic world mission against undue emphasis on ceremonial law, Szántó's *Neuzeit* was largely in keeping with the views of Jellinek, who had been called to Vienna in 1858, contributed to the paper from time to time, and finally became its editor in 1882. Politically, *Die Neuzeit* hailed the new era of Austrian liberalism that began in 1860/61, when a liberal constitution was restored and the situation for Austrian Jewry gradually improved. At the same time, much attention was also given to the newly founded *Alliance Israélite Universelle (1860). Although Szántó's paper promoted the concept of a Jewish *Stamm* as some kind of ethnic unity, it always stressed its loyal liberal German-Austrian position, opposing Polish *Hasidism and East European emigrants, who were unwilling to integrate into Austrian society. While rejecting both secular Jewish nationalism and *Zionism, it called for a common Jewish consciousness and solidarity against *antisemitism.

Like most Jewish weeklies, *Die Neuzeit* appeared on Fridays, and was designed for reading on the Sabbath. Due to a large concession it quickly spread throughout the German-speaking parts of the country and beyond, providing information on all of Austria-Hungary. Besides subscription fees *Die Neuzeit* was financed by a separate advertising section, and it served for some time as the official organ of several Jewish organizations. Its variety of contents also contributed to the paper's success. As stated in its first issue, *Die Neuzeit* was to offer editorials on politics and religion, relevant news from all parts of the country, popular rather than scholarly essays on science and literature, articles on Jewish communal affairs and the educational system in Austria-Hungary, a *feuilleton* section for pleasure and edification, and local news on weddings, births, and funerals in Vienna and beyond.

Szántó's death in 1882 in a way marked the end of the liberal era in Austria, in which *Die Neuzeit* had had its share for more than two decades. The rise of antisemitism in Austria and Hungary from the early 1880s brought about a profound change among the Jewish papers in Vienna – as to both their contents and their staff. Several new periodicals were founded, the most prominent being Dr. Joseph S. *Bloch's *Oesterreichische Wochenschrift* (1884–1920). *Die Neuzeit* was taken over by Jellinek, who considerably changed its style and substance. The paper turned toward the plight of East European Jewry and the question of emigration in a less polemic way, though still rejecting the *Hibbat Zion movement. At the same time, it actively fought antisemitic attacks, especially those of August *Rohling and Georg von *Schoenerer. In 1884, however, Bloch's *Wochenschrift* came to the fore – in opposition to the old liberal German-Jewish attitude of Jellinek's *Neuzeit.* From 1893, when Jellinek was succeeded by D. Loewy, *Die Neuzeit* gradually lost in importance. In 1899, Loewy was joined by Siegfried Fleischer, later secretary-general of the *Oestereichisch-Israelitische Union, to counterbalance Loewy's sympathies with Theodor *Herzl's new movement of *Zionism. *Die Neuzeit* ceased publication at the end of 1903. It has been reproduced on microfilm from the collection of the Leo Baeck Institute New York.

BIBLIOGRAPHY: *Die Neuzeit* 1–43 (1861–1903); M. Rosenmann, *Dr. Adolph Jellinek...* (1931). **ADD. BIBLIOGRAPHY:** J. Toury, *Die Juedische Presse im Oesterreichischen Kaiserreich* (1983), 39–51, 69–74, index; R.S. Wistrich, *The Jews of Vienna...* (1990), index; M.L. Rozenblit, in: LBIYB 35 (1990), 103–131; J. Neumann, "Identitaet und Ort..." (diss. Potsdam University; 2006).

[Hugo Knoepfmacher / Johannes Valentin Schwarz (2nd ed.)]

NEVADA, state located in western U.S.; Jews numbered approximately 82,100 out of a population of 2,019,00 in 2005, which is a dramatic increase from the 2,380 out of a total of 440,000 in 1969 and more than four times the total of 1990. The two principal Jewish communities were in Las Vegas, which in 2005 was the fastest growing Jewish community in the United States, and the Reno-Carson City area which numbers some 2,100 Jews. There are Reform synagogues in Stateline and Summerlin. Reno still has three synagogues – Reform, Conservative, and Chabad – as well as a *mikveh.* More than 600 Jewish families are estimated to move to Las Vegas each month, and in 2005 it had some 80,000 Jewish residents. Las Vegas boasts 18 congregations, three day schools, and a Holocaust memorial and resource library. Chabad operates four centers employing seven full-time rabbis. Orthodox residents and visitors can avail themselves of three *mikva'ot* (ritual baths), six kosher restaurants, a Glatt Kosher market, and two kosher stores embedded in local supermarkets. Three major casinos, meanwhile, maintain full-service kosher kitchens. Community affairs are chronicled in two community newspapers, *The Jewish Reporter* and *The Israelite*, and a monthly periodical, *Life & Style: The Las Vegas Jewish Magazine.* A Hillel Union at the University of Nevada, Las Vegas, tends to the needs of Jewish students on campus.

Jews first went to Nevada from California in 1859 with the discovery of gold on the Comstock Lode and the silver rush around Virginia City in 1862. The gold and silver strikes brought a flood of emigrants from all corners of the country, including Jewish engineers, storekeepers, traders, lawyers, journalists, doctors, and fortune hunters. Nevada's first directory in 1862 listed 200 Jews in Virginia City, Gold Hill, Silver City, Austin, Dayton, Eureka, and Carson City. All but the latter were ghost towns by the 1960s. A congregation and B'nai B'rith lodge were organized in Virginia City in 1862. In the same year a burial society was organized there and in Eureka. Worship services were first held in Carson City in 1869. When the U.S. went on the gold standard and silver deposits gave out, Nevada's population shrank and the Jewish communities in the mining towns faded away. Carson City still has a

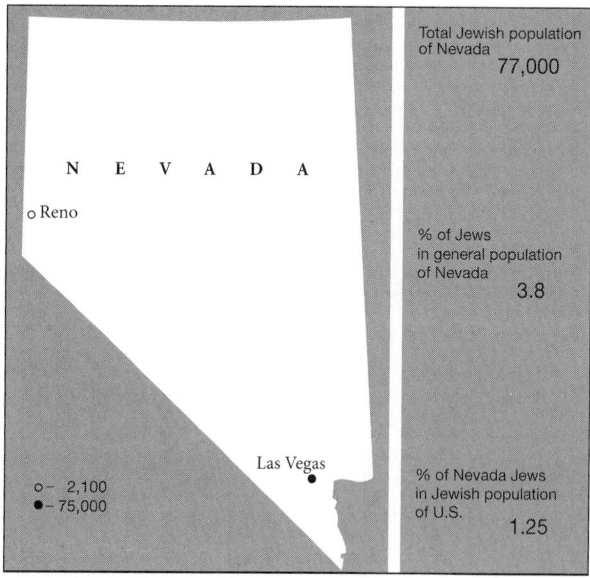

Jewish communities in Nevada. Population figures for 2001.

historic Jewish cemetery known as the Bonanza Days Jewish Cemetary. A short-lived community grew up at Goldfield at the turn of the century when new gold and silver discoveries were made there. In 1969 the oldest permanent Jewish community was in Reno, which became the state's principal city after the mining towns were abandoned in the 1870s.

Among the pioneer Jews was Herman Bien, a rabbi, who opened the first Jewish school at Virginia City in 1861, and served in the first territorial legislature. He was one of four Jewish members of the convention that drafted the state's first constitution in 1864. Adolph *Sutro, later mayor of San Francisco, who arrived in 1860, built the Sutro tunnel that greatly aided mining operations. Albert *Michelson, the United States' first Nobel Prize winner, spent his boyhood in Virginia City, where his father was a storekeeper. Joseph Goodman was coowner of *The Territorial Enterprise*, the first printed newspaper in Nevada, which employed Samuel Clemens (Mark Twain) as a reporter. Samuel Platt, whose father came to Carson City in 1864, served as speaker of the state legislature and U.S. attorney for Nevada, and was three times Republican candidate for the U.S. Senate. Col. David Mannheim commanded troops in the Indian wars of the 1860s, and Mark Strouse was the first sheriff of Carson City. Milton Badt was chief justice of the Nevada Supreme Court from 1947 to 1966, and David Zenoff was appointed to the court in 1965. The mayor of Las Vegas from 1999 was Oscar Goodman (1939–). Brian Greenspun, the scion of newspaper magnate, land developer and arms smuggler to pre-state Israel, Herman "Hank" Milton Greenspun (1909–1989), was the editor of the *Las Vegas Sun* and active in real estate and casino management. Casino mogul Steve *Wynn (1941–), who built the opulent Bellagio and Wynn Las Vegas hotels, is credited with the Las Vegas Strip's successful marketing, during the 1990s, as a family friendly environment. Rival Sheldon Adelson (1933–), who built the

Venetian Hotel, established Las Vegas as a major convention and trade show venue. Democratic Congresswoman Shelley *Berkley (1951–) was elected to the House of Representatives in 1998 and won her fourth term in 2004. Jacob "Chic" Hecht (1928–) served in the Nevada State Senate from 1967 to 1975, as a Republican in the U.S. Senate from 1983 to 1989, and as U.S. Ambassador to the Bahamas (1989–94).

Many Jews serve the casino industry; others are retirees, many more are professionals, physicians, lawyers and accountants, meeting the needs of a booming economy and a growing population. While attention is concentrated on the Las Vegas strip, family life thrives in the suburbs around Las Vegas in Summerlin, Desert Shores, Seven Hills and Green Valley, and Henderson.

BIBLIOGRAPHY: B. Postal and L. Koppman, *A Jewish Tourist's Guide to the U.S.* (1954), 293–8; R.E. and M.F. Stewart, *Adolph Sutro; A Biography* (1962), 41–58; AJA, 8 (1956), 103–5. **ADD. BIBLIOGRAPHY:** O. Osraelowitz, *United States Jewish Travel Guide* (2003).

[Bernard Postal / Sheldon Teitelbaum (2nd ed.)]

NEVAKHOVICH, JUDAH LEIB (1776–1831), one of the earliest *maskilim* in Russia. Born in Polonnoye (today Khmelnitskii district), Ukraine, Nevakhovich was a teacher and a companion of Abraham *Peretz, son-in-law of the wealthy Joshua *Zeitlin of Shklov. Together with the Peretz family, Nevakhovich settled in St. Petersburg at the end of the 18th century. Having mastered German and Russian, he was employed by the Russian government as a translator of Hebrew documents, including those connected with the imprisonment of R. *Shneur Zalman of Lyady.

During the debate over legislation concerning the Jews of Russia at the beginning of the 19th century, Nevakhovich took an active part in the deliberations and wrote the pamphlet *Vopl Dushcheri iudeyskoy* (St. Petersburg, 1803; repr. in *Budushchnost*, Vol. 3, 1902). The purpose of this pamphlet was to combat anti-Jewish hatred. Such hatred, Nevakhovich believed, was the cause of all the decrees and persecutions endured by his coreligionists. He called on his Russian countrymen to treat the Jews with sympathy and tolerance. He pointed out that there was no foundation to the accusations – including blood libels – brought against the Jews, and that Judaism, furthermore, was not opposed to the laws of Russia. Nevakhovich rejected the demands of Christians that the Jews be converted. Within a year of its publication, Nevakhovich's pamphlet also appeared with various changes and additions in Hebrew, under the title *Kol Shavat Bat Yehudah* ("The Cry of the Daughter of Judah" (Shklov, 1804); repr. in *He-Avar*, vol. 2, 1918). The Hebrew version also includes a short history of Russia, followed by an essay on "the hatred of religions, truth and peace," which is in the form of a discussion between "truth" and religious hatred, with words of praise for Alexander I who convened a committee for "the reform of the situation of the Jews to their benefit and that of the country." The pamphlet, in both its Hebrew and Russian versions, marks the beginning of Haskalah literature among Russian Jewry, but it also signifies the end of Nevakhovich's literary activity on behalf of the Jews.

In 1809 his name is present on the list of signatories to *Ha-Me'assef*, and it was about this time that Nevakhovich converted to Lutheranism. He was employed as a government official in Poland and later engaged in commerce. He also wrote dramas which were presented in St. Petersburg's theaters and translated German literature into Russian. The conversion of Nevakhovich and his companion, A. Peretz, turned many Jews away from the Haskalah movement, even in its most moderate forms. Although Nevakhovich's works appear episodic and without continuity in the literature (both Hebrew and Russian) of the Haskalah, they did, nevertheless, herald the arrival of a new period in the spiritual life of Russian Jewry. The scientist Elie *Metchnikoff was the grandson of Nevakhovich, through his daughter.

BIBLIOGRAPHY: B. Katz, in: *Ha-Zeman*, 3 (1904), 11–15; idem, in: *He-Avar*, 2 (1958), 197–201; Klausner, Sifrut, 3 (1953), 20–24; Yu. Hessen (Gessen), *Yevrei v Rossii* (1906), 78–98, 136–9.

[Yehuda Slutsky]

NEVATIM (Heb. נְבָטִים; "Sprouts"), moshav in southern Israel, 5 mi. (9 km.) E. of Beersheba, affiliated with Tenu'at ha-Moshavim. It was the easternmost moshav of the 11 settlements erected in the night of Oct. 6, 1946, in the south and Negev. The founding group originated from various European countries, but immigrants from Cochin (South India) took their place after 1948. Nevatim's farming was of the oasis type, based on greenhouses and poultry. Some residents were employed outside the moshav, in the nearby factories. In 1968 Nevatim's population was 426, increasing to 540 in the mid-1990s and 753 in 2002 after expansion.

[Efraim Orni / Shaked Gilboa (2nd ed.)]

NEVEH EITAN (Heb. נְוֵה אֵיתָן; "Habitation of the Strong"), kibbutz in central Israel in the Beth-Shean Valley, affiliated with Iḥud ha-Kevuẓot ve-ha-Kibbutzim. It was founded in 1938 as a tower and stockade settlement, after the group, which had originated from Poland, had participated in setting up neighboring *Ma'oz Ḥayyim and had lived there for several months. Farming at Neveh Eitan was intensive and irrigated, comprising field crops (e.g., cotton), dairy cattle, and carp ponds. The kibbutz also operated a plastics factory and guest rooms. The name is based on a passage in Jeremiah 49:19. In 1968 its population was 250, dropping to 172 in 2002.

[Efram Orni / Shaked Gilboa (2nd ed.)]

NEVEH YAM (Heb. נְוֵה יָם; "Sea Dwelling"), kibbutz in northern Israel, on the Carmel Coast near Athlit, affiliated with Iḥud ha-Kevuẓot ve-ha-Kibbutzim. Neveh Yam was founded in 1939 by a pioneer group, Ma'pilim-Gordonia, from Poland, which had received training in seafaring in the Polish port of Gdynia; they were joined by immigrants from Austria and Czechoslovakia. The kibbutz sought to develop sea fishing and aid "*illegal" immigration. Farming was at first only a sideline, but after 1948 became the mainstay of the kibbutz's economy, in addition to a guest house and a fish-canning factory. Fishing, however, was discontinued. In 1968 Neveh Yam had 130 inhabitants. In 2002 its population was 178. In the 1990s the kibbutz underwent a severe economic crisis. Its sources of livelihood in the early 2000s were a holiday village, field crops, and a fishery.

At the end of 2002 the population of Neveh Yam was 188 residents.

[Efram Orni / Shaked Gilboa (2nd ed.)]

°**NÈVEJEAN, YVONNE** (1900–1987), head of Belgium's Children's National Care Authority (Oeuvre Nationale de l'Enfance, also known as ONE) and Righteous Among the Nations. During the years of the German occupation in 1940–44, she agreed to shelter in ONE establishments (homes, summer camps, and rehabilitation centers) Jewish children trying to avoid deportation to concentration camps. In this major undertaking she worked closely with the Jewish Defense Committee (Comité de Défense des Juifs – CDJ), a clandestine organization created by Jewish activists to help people find hiding places and provide them with false papers. Yvonne Jospa, in charge of the CDJ's children department, coordinated the rescue effort with Nèvejean. Various religious and lay organizations in the country also lent a hand to save the children. The work involved finding suitable addresses with organizational or private homes for the fleeing children, then assigning people to check on the care and living conditions of the children as well providing them with clothing and defraying the additional costs of their hosts. Nèvejean was also successful in freeing a group of children of the Wezembeek Jewish Children's Home, arrested by the Germans on October 30, 1942, by appealing directly to Queen Elisabeth, who in turn intervened with the German authorities to have the children released. It is estimated that up to a thousand children, and perhaps a bit more, benefited from the care provided by ONE. Local financial institutions, such as the Société Générale Bank, helped defray the costs of Nèvejean's large-scale rescue operation with monthly allowances. The Belgian government-in-exile in London also underwrote some of the debts incurred by ONE. As the Allied armies advanced toward Belgium in August 1944, Nèvejean learned that the Germans planned to pick up the remaining Jewish children, until then permitted to stay in several Jewish children homes, and in one sweep take them away for deportation. She immediately recruited her staff to take emergency measures, to fetch the children in time and remove them to temporary safe havens – an undertaking which proved successful. In 1965, Yad Vashem awarded her the title of Righteous Among the Nations.

BIBLIOGRAPHY: Yad Vashem Archives M31–99; L. Steinberg, *Le Comité de Défense des Juifs en Belgique, 1942–1944* (1973); B. Garfinkels, *Les Belges Face a la Persécution Raciale* (1965).

[Mordecai Paldiel (2d ed.)]

NEVELAH (Heb. נְבֵלָה; "carcass"), descriptive noun for any animal, bird, or creature which has died as a result of any process other than valid ritual slaughter (**sheḥitah*).

The Pentateuch forbids the consumption of such meat, which can be given to a resident alien, or sold to a non-Jew (Deut. 14:21; see also Pes. 21b). Punishment for eating *nevelah* applies only to "clean" animals (Meil. 16a; Maim. Yad, Ma'akhalot Asurot, 4:17) and is not added to the normal punishment for eating "unclean" animals. The *nevelah* is also one of the principal categories of ritual impurity (*tumah*), and touching or carrying it causes ritual impurity (Lev. 11:39–40; Maim. Yad, She'ar Avot ha-Tumah, 1–3).

See *Dietary Laws; *Purity and Impurity, Ritual; Animals.

BIBLIOGRAPHY: Eisenstein, Dinim, 254.

NEVELSON, LOUISE (1900–1988), U.S. sculptor and printmaker. Arriving in the United States in 1905, Nevelson grew up in Rockland, Maine. Her father owned a lumberyard, an important influence on her mature sculpture when Nevelson adopted wood as her most significant material. She took her husband's surname after her marriage in 1920, the same year that the couple moved to New York. Her artistic apprenticeship spanned several years, including private painting and drawing lessons with William *Meyerowitz and Theresa *Bernstein, followed by studies at the Art Students League (1928–31, 1933). Nevelson's drawings and canvases from this period are figurative and expressionistic in nature. In 1931, she studied in Munich with Hans Hoffman, where she became familiar with Cubism. In 1932, Nevelson, along with Ben *Shahn, assisted Diego Rivera with his Rockefeller Center mural.

Nevelson made her first sculpture in 1934, at which time she took a class at the Educational Alliance with Chaim *Gross. Working in terracotta, bronze, and plaster, Nevelson executed blocky, figurative sculptures. Under the auspices of the Works Progress Administration, she taught sculpture at the Educational Alliance in 1937. She exhibited paintings and sculpture influenced by Cubism and Surrealism at her first solo show, held at New York's Nierendorf Gallery in 1941. In the 1940s she began to make sculptural environments around themes, such as *The Circus – The Clown Is the Center of His World* at the Norlyst Gallery in New York (1943). Her sculptures grew increasingly abstract through the 1940s, influenced in part by non-Western art. In 1947 she also started making etchings, drypoints, and aquatints.

Around 1954, Nevelson began designing large wood, Cubist-inspired abstract constructions. In 1956, Nevelson made her first wall sculptures. The dramatic *Moon Garden + One* (1958) established Nevelson's reputation. Open-faced, stacked wood boxes filled with disparate found objects such as furniture legs, broom handles, spindles, and other wooden abstract shapes, covered the walls of the Grand Central Moderns Gallery. The installation, which included the enormous *Sky Cathedral* (Museum of Modern Art, New York), was painted a uniform black in an effort to occlude the original identity of the objects and to unite them.

Subsequent reliefs retained a monochrome appearance, painted entirely in either black, white, or gold. The all-white installation *Dawn's Wedding Feast* appeared in 1959 at the Museum of Modern Art's "Sixteen Americans" exhibition, and gold sculptures showed at *The Royal Tides* exhibition at the Martha Jackson Gallery (1961).

Nevelson expanded her materials in the second half of the 1960s, creating sculptures out of aluminum, Plexiglas, and Cor-ten steel. In 1964 Nevelson made the Holocaust memorial *Homage to 6000000* (private collection) using her iconic stacked boxes filled with wood collage elements. The first version was painted in black, but a second version, installed at the Israel Museum in Jerusalem in 1965, was painted white. In the early 1970s Nevelson received several commissions, including sculptures for Temple Beth-El, Great Neck, New York (1970); Temple Israel, Boston (1973); and seven metal sculptures for the Louise Nevelson Plaza in Lower Manhattan (1979).

BIBLIOGRAPHY: A.B. Glimcher, *Louise Nevelson* (1976); L. Nevelson, *Dawns and Dusks: Taped Conversations with Diana Mackown* (1976); *Louise Nevelson: Atmospheres and Environments* (1980); J. Lipman, *Nevelson's World* (1983); L. Lisle, *Louise Nevelson: A Passionate Life* (1990).

[Samantha Baskind (2nd ed.)]

NEVERS, capital of the Nièvre department, central France. In 1208 Pope Innocent III protested vehemently to Hervé, count of Nevers, against the excessively advantageous conditions which he had granted the Jews of his town and county. This situation changed rapidly: in 1210 Hervé personally signed a promise that he would not retain any of the royal Jews fleeing to his lands from the king's demesne. Countess Mahaut ratified *Louis VIII's restrictive ordinance on the Jews immediately after its publication in 1224. Finally, Count Robert expelled the Jews from his county in 1294.

BIBLIOGRAPHY: Gross, Gal Jud (1897), 387–8; R. de Lespinasse, *Le Nivernais et les Comtes de Nevers*, 2 (1911), 31f., 44, 116, 373; S. Grayzel, *The Church and the Jews in the XIIIth Century* (1966), index.

[Bernhard Blumenkranz]

NEVINS, SHEILA (1939–), U.S. television executive. Born in New York, Nevins earned a bachelor of arts degree from Barnard College and a master of fine arts from the Yale University School of Drama. She began her career with the United States Information Service, which produced and distributed documentaries about American life. After producing children's shows and documentaries for television, she joined Home Box Office, a pay television cable network, in 1979 as director of documentary programming and was named executive vice president, original programming, for HBO and Cinemax, a related company, in 1999. In that role, Nevins oversaw production of nearly 200 documentaries. They earned nine Oscars, 13 Primetime Emmy awards, 22 news and documentary Emmys, and 14 George Foster Peabody awards for HBO and one personal Peabody award. She was inducted into the Broadcasting and Cable Hall of Fame in 2000. Among the notable documentaries she was involved in were *The Times of Harvey Milk* (1984), the story of a gay political activist in San Francisco who was murdered along with the city's mayor; *One Day in September*, the recounting of the events at the 1972 Summer Olympics in Munich, where 11 Israeli athletes were killed; and *Protocols of Zion* (2005), a film that traces the history of the notorious fake antisemitic book. She has had an impressive record of awards with Holocaust-related documentaries based on survivor testimonies. Among her most memorable were *One Survivor Remembers: The Gerda Weissmann Klein Story* and *Into the Arms of Strangers*, a film on the *Kindertransport*.

[Stewart Kampel (2nd ed.)]

NEVU'AT HA-YELED (Heb. נְבוּאַת הַיֶּלֶד; "The Prophecy of the Child"), a medieval Hebrew short story. The body of the tale is followed by a number of occult prophecies in Aramaic. First printed at the end of *Sefer Nagid u-Meẓavveh* by Jacob *Ẓemaḥ (Constantinople, 1726) and published many times since, it was known already as early as the end of the 15th century and the beginning of the 16th when some kabbalists, among them R. *Abraham b. Eliezer ha-Levi, wrote commentaries on the prophecies in *Nevu'at ha-Yeled*. The story tells of a wonder child, Naḥman, born in the fifth century to a kabbalist; the child died very young, but immediately upon birth began to tell his mother secrets of the heavenly worlds. His father cautioned him not to reveal mysteries forbidden to man, and from then the child spoke only obscurely and enigmatically.

Modern scholars have attempted to date the story and the prophecies therein by tracing known historical events hinted at, and relating them to the text. The obscurity of the text makes this very difficult, but it seems probable that historical events in the 15th century, especially in the East, are referred to in the prophecies. However, the purpose of the story and its prophecies was to anticipate the coming of the Messiah and to describe the major political and historical events and catastrophes bringing about his final revelation. The kabbalists interpreted the prophecies as hinting at the coming of the Messiah in the early 16th century.

In literary genre, there is a great similarity between the prophecies of the Jewish child and comparable phenomena in non-Jewish literature, e.g., the cryptic prophecies of the wizard Merlin (according to legend, told when he was a boy) which many medieval Christian scholars interpreted as foretelling future events. A parody on *Nevu'at ha-Yeled* was written by R. Joseph *Delmedigo in his *Maẓrefle-Ḥokhmah* (Basel, 1629) about a child in Poland whose duplicity was revealed.

BIBLIOGRAPHY: A.Z. Aešcoly, *Ha-Tenu'ot ha-Meshiḥiyyot be-Yisrael*, 1 (1956), 283–6; Scholem, in: KS, 2 (1925/26), 115–9:13. **ADD. BIBLIOGRAPHY:** Avraham ben Eli'ezer ha-Levi, *Sheloshah Ma'amre Ge'ulah: Nevu'at ha-Yeled... Mashra Ḳaṭrin... Igeret Sod ha-Ge'ulah...* A. Gros (ed.) (2000); D. Tsadik, in: *Iranian Studies*, 37:1 (2004), 5–15.

[Joseph Dan]

NEVZLIN, LEONID BORISOVICH (1959–), Russian tycoon. Nevzlin was born in Moscow and graduated from the Gubkin Institute of Oil and Gas in 1981, specializing in automation and computers. Subsequently he graduated from the G.V. Plekhanov Economic Academy, specializing in management and marketing. In 1981–87 Nevzlin worked as a programming engineer at the Zarubezhgeologia foreign trade firm. In 1987 he was appointed manager of the contract department of the Center for Scientific and Technical Creativity for Youth (MENATEP), attached to the district Komsomol committee. There he began his long-time association with Mikhail Khodorkovsky, who would become Russia's richest man. In 1989–91 Nevzlin was the president of the Commercial Investment Bank for Scientific and Technical Progress.

In the privatization period Komsomol money was an important source of private business formation. Nevzlin enjoyed rapid advancement in the MENATEP bank and in 1993–96 was first vice chairman of its board of directors and the head of the public relations department (1994–96). In 1996 he became first vice chairman of the board of directors and vice chairman of the executive committee of the ROSPROM financial and industrial group. In 1996 he was appointed vice president of the YUKOS joint-stock oil company and made a member of the board of directors. In 1996 he was named among the 50 most influential businessmen in Russia. He was the chairman of the Russian Investors Union, a director of the TEPKO bank, and a member of the editorial board of *Ekho Planety* magazine. In 1997 Nevzlin became first vice chairman of the joint board of directors of the ROSPROM-YUKOS group. In 1997–98 he was first deputy to the general director of the Russian ITAR-TASS information agency in charge of economic affairs. He worked out the gradual transformation of the agency into a joint-stock company. In 1998 he became first vice chairman of the board of directors of the YUKOS-Moscow company.

Nevzlin was active in Jewish communal life. In 2000 he became chairman of the coordinating council of the Congress of Jewish Religious Communities and Organizations. In 2001 he was nominated acting president of the Russian Jewish Congress. He resigned at the end of year when he was appointed representative of the Mordovian Republic in the Federation Council, the upper chamber of the Russian parliament. The political activity of Nevzlin was greatly appreciated by President Yeltsin. During the Putin presidency, however, relations between the authorities and the business community changed. With Khodorkovsky's arrest and prosecution and later accusations of economic crimes against the heads of MENATEP and YUKOS, Nevzlin came under fire. In 2003 he resigned from the Federation Council and left Russia, becoming an Israeli citizen. In June 2003 the Leonid Nevzlin Center for the Study of Russian and Eastern European Jewry was opened at the Hebrew University of Jerusalem. His net worth has been estimated at $2 billion.

[Naftali Prat (2nd ed.)]

NEW BEDFORD, a city in southeastern Massachusetts; estimated total population of 95,000, in 2005, Jewish population of greater New Bedford (including Dartmouth and Fairhaven) numbers approximately 3,000. Because of its proximity to Newport, the port of New Bedford in colonial days was of importance to two Jewish-Portuguese merchants, Aaron Lopez and Jacob Rodrigues Rivera, who settled in Newport. They came to New Bedford to learn the art of candlemaking at the Rodman Candleworks which was important in the whaling industry at the time. In the middle of the 19th century, a group of German Jews settled in the city and were later joined by new arrivals. The B'nai Israel Society, established in 1857, purchased a cemetery plot for these German-Jewish immigrants in the Peckham West Cemetery in the city.

The New Bedford Directory for 1869 contains Jewish names such as Adolphus Levi; Leon Levy, dry goods and variety store; Louis Henry, cigar maker; and Julius Simon, dry goods, fancy and retail. After 1877, Eastern European Jews went to New Bedford in large numbers. Ahavath Achim Synagogue began in 1893 with the purchase of a plot of land upon which the synagogue was built and incorporated in 1899 in the South End on Howland Street, and in the 1940s moved west to County Street. In 2005 the rabbi was Barry Hartman. Congregation Chesed Shel Emes was incorporated in 1898, and a synagogue was built in 1904 on Kenyon Street in the north end of the city. This synagogue was destroyed in the late 1950s to make room for the highway through the city. The Conservative Congregation Tifereth Israel Synagogue was dedicated in 1924, and its rabbi in 2005 was Raphael Kanter. Other Jewish organizations and branches of fraternal orders also existed. A communal Talmud Torah existed until 1935. The establishment of various industrial enterprises in the 1930s, and the establishment of the JCC (Jewish Community Center) from 1947 to 1972 added to the Jewish activity in the city. Since 1973, the Jewish Federation of Greater New Bedford has absorbed the programs of the JCC and continues to provide for the activities of the Jewish community through Jewish social service programs, under the leadership of executive director, Wil Herrup, and a board of directors.

[Rudolf Glanz / Mel and Cindy Yoken (2nd ed.)]

NEW BRUNSWICK, U.S. industrial city on the Raritan River, in New Jersey, approximately 30 miles S.W. of New York City. It is the home of Rutgers University, the State University of New Jersey. It is estimated that the Jewish population of Middlesex County is 45,000 but given the nature of suburban Jewish life in northeastern New Jersey, it is also part of the larger community of more than 400,000 Jews in the area. Rutgers University has approximately 4,500 students.

New Brunswick's earliest Jewish settler seems to have been Daniel Nunez, who was a justice of the peace in 1722, about 40 years after the founding of the town (1679–80). Nunez was in business in Piscataway, a small village just outside the New Brunswick city limits. Hannah Lonzoda, a widow, lived in New Brunswick from 1750 on. In 1850 some

Bohemian and German Jews settled in the town, and by 1852 about 20 to 25 Jews were living there. The Jewish population grew from 90 in 1865 to 280 in 1897, slightly more than 1% of the general population. In 1888 an influx of Eastern European Jews began, and from the turn of the century on, the Jewish population of the greater New Brunswick area continued. In 1969, two Reform, five Conservative, and five Orthodox synagogues were serving the area. The oldest synagogue in New Brunswick, now Anshe Emeth Memorial Temple (Reform), was founded in 1859, probably as an Orthodox congregation; it became a Reform temple about 1890. Congregation Ahavas Achim (Orthodox) was founded in 1889. The Highland Park Conservative Temple was founded in 1930.

The Jewish Federation of Raritan Valley, launched in 1948, coordinates fund raising, social service, welfare, educational, and communal activities "calculated to enhance Jewish communal life." In 1969, 28 religious, social, and educational organizations were affiliated with the federation. A YM-YWHA was organized in 1911.

Before 1900, most New Brunswick Jews were peddlers and small shopkeepers. A few were professionals, including some Jewish teachers in the public schools in 1893, one of whom served as school principal. From 1900 to the 1930s, most of the Jewish population worked as tradesmen and artisans. In the 1960s many Jews were practicing the professions of law, medicine, accountancy, and teaching; many were engaged in business and industry. A number were serving as elected officials in municipal government. Samuel D. Hoffman (1900–1957), attorney and first president of the Jewish Federation, served as a city commissioner of New Brunswick in 1935. Harry S. Feller (1885–1954), second president of the federation and one of the organizers of the Ad Hoc Committee for United Jewish Appeal, taught in New Brunswick High School (1908–16) and served as first principal of the evening school (1912).

The Allen and Joan Bildner Center for the Study of Jewish Life at Rutgers

The Allen and Joan Bildner Center for the Study of Jewish Life at Rutgers, the State University of New Jersey, is committed to the pursuit of academic excellence, fostering faculty research, and sponsoring a variety of community outreach programs. The Bildner Center promotes scholarly exchange on an international scale by bringing visiting scholars to Rutgers to teach special courses and to contribute to the intellectual life of the University community. The center works closely with the department of Jewish Studies offering a wide range of extracurricular programs for students and seminars for faculty. The center's active agenda of community outreach includes: public lectures and symposia, Jewish communal initiatives, the Rutgers New Jersey Jewish Film Festival, and the activities of the Herbert and Leonard Littman Families Holocaust Resource Center.

The department of Jewish Studies offers an interdisciplinary approach to the academic study of all aspects of the Jewish experience. Courses offered by the department, which are open to all students, address the historical, social, cultural, religious and political life of the Jewish people from ancient times to the present. Drawing on faculty from 12 departments, as well as on visiting fellows sponsored by the Bildner Center, the Jewish Studies curriculum offers over 60 interdisciplinary courses. Students pursuing a B.A. degree may major or minor in Jewish Studies. The department and the Bildner Center work together to promote Jewish Studies at Rutgers.

Hillel

Hillel partners with student leadership in planning and implementing religious, social, and cultural events for Rutgers/New Brunswick's 4,500 Jewish students. While Hillel is physically located on the Rutgers College/College Avenue campus, events are run on all five New Brunswick campuses. Pluralistic events include learning sessions, Birthright Israel, weekly Shabbat services and free dinners, *tikkun olam*/social action program, holiday and cultural commemorations, and programs for graduate students.

At Rutgers University is an active and extremely vibrant Hillel. Its mission is to enrich the lives of Jewish undergraduate and graduate students so that they may enrich the Jewish people and the world. Hillel student leaders, professionals, and lay leaders are dedicated to creating a pluralistic, welcoming, and inclusive environment for Jewish college students, where they are encouraged to grow intellectually, spiritually, and socially. Hillel helps students find a balance in being distinctively Jewish and universally human by encouraging them to pursue *ẓedek* (social justice), *tikkun olam* (repairing the world), and Jewish learning, and to support Israel and global Jewish peoplehood. Hillel is committed to excellence, innovation, accountability, and results.

Chabad House-Lubavitch, founded in 1978, nurtured and supported by concerned members of communities throughout New Jersey, is dedicated to the re-establishment and strengthening of our Judaic faith, principles, identity, commitment, and pride.

The Les Turchin Chabad House, a unique and vibrant center, provides a "home away from home" for college students at Rutgers, the State University of New Jersey. Chabad House operates over 20 community service programs. The new Chabad House is proud to serve as the largest Jewish Center on any university campus in the U.S. The new complex is located in the heart of Rutgers University. Serving as headquarters for all Jewish activities, the building features: housing for students, peer counseling and drug prevention centers, student activity offices, a 300-seat synagogue, a publications center, library, kosher dining hall, student lounges and a computer area. Some of its programs include: hospital and prison visitations; holiday rallies and festivals; counseling and Social Services; and Kosher Meals on Wheels. Rabbi Carlebach, the executive director of Chabad House-Lubavitch, is also the rabbi of Congregation Sons of Israel-Chabad in Wayside.

The Jewish News

The *Jewish News* has been an influential voice in the New Jersey Jewish community since its founding in 1946. Coverage includes local, national and world events; explorations of the world of Jewish culture and the arts; supplements on Israel, the holidays and other topics of interest; and a wide array of feature stories. Beginning as *The Jewish News*, the paper merged in 1947 with the Newark-based *Jewish Times*, keeping *The Jewish News* name. In 1988, reflecting the demographic changes in a community that was moving west to the suburbs, the paper was renamed *MetroWest Jewish News*. In 1997, *MetroWest Jewish News* acquired a second newspaper – *The Jewish Horizon* – of Union and Somerset counties; a new name, *New Jersey Jewish News*; and a new focus on Jewish issues statewide.

In the early 21st century *NJJN* published four editions, reaching more than 50,000 households. The MetroWest edition continued to serve Essex, Morris, Sussex, and part of Union county and was mailed directly to the homes of 24,500 subscribers. In 1998, *Jewish News* further strengthened its position in the state when it acquired the *Jewish Reporter* and started publishing a third edition in the Princeton Mercer Bucks region. That edition covers the area from the Route 1 corridor to the greater Princeton area, to Yardley, Pa., and more.

In November 2000 the *Jewish News* began publishing a greater Middlesex County edition. With its newly acquired 14,500 subscribers, the Middlesex edition gives the paper contiguous coverage from Montclair to Princeton and from Morristown to Newark.

With its growth, the *Jewish News* has become the second largest Jewish newspaper in America, and the largest-circulation weekly newspaper in the state. The *Jewish News*' role is to be a strong, statewide voice representing the interests of all Jews as well as a weekly chronicle of the ways individuals are expressing their Jewishness both within and beyond the institutional Jewish world.

[Abraham Halperin / Allie Rimer (2nd ed.)]

NEWCASTLE-UPON-TYNE, port in Northumberland, N.E. England. Its small medieval Jewish group was expelled in 1234 at the request of the townspeople. Although there were individual Jews in the city by 1775, the organized community dates from 1831 – a year after a cemetery had been acquired –by which time there were about 100 Jewish residents. A synagogue was built in 1838, but by 1868 it had become too small for the growing population and a second congregation was formed. In 1873 the two groups amalgamated and a new synagogue was opened in 1880. The community increased during the mass immigration from Eastern Europe (1881–1914) and by 1900 numbered about 2,000. The small but very Orthodox community of *Gateshead is on the opposite bank of the River Tyne from Newcastle. Newcastle itself has an Orthodox and a Reform congregation. In addition there is the normal structure of communal institutions which is headed by a Representative Council of North-East Jewry. The estimated Jewish population for Tyneside (Newcastle, Gateshead, etc.) was 3,500 (0.38% of the total population) in 1969. In the mid-1990s, the Jewish population of Newcastle numbered approximately 1,230. The 2001 British census found 960 Jews by religion in Newcastle, with another 1,564 in Gateshead.

BIBLIOGRAPHY: C. Roth, *Rise of Provincial Jewry* (1950), 84–85; Roth, England, index. **ADD. BIBLIOGRAPHY:** L. Olsover, *The Jewish Communities of North-East England, 1755–1980* (1980).

[Vivian David Lipman]

NEW CHRISTIANS, a term applied specifically to three groups of Jewish converts to Christianity and their descendants in the Iberian Peninsula. The first group converted in the wake of the massacres in Spain in 1391 and the proselytizing fervor of the subsequent decades. The second, also in Spain, were baptized following the decree of Ferdinand and *Isabella in 1492 expelling all Jews who refused to accept Christianity. The third group, in Portugal, was converted by force and royal fiat in 1497. Like the word *Conversos, but unlike *Marranos, the term New Christian carried no intrinsic pejorative connotation, but with the increasing power of the *Inquisition and the growth of the concept of limpieza de *sangre, the name signaled the disabilities inevitably heaped on those who bore it. In Portugal, the Marquis de Pombal officially abolished all legal distinctions between Old and New Christians in May 1773. Comparable measures were not enacted in Spain until 1860, by which time much of the distinction had been eroded by assimilation and inquisitorial repression. However, pockets of social discrimination against New Christians still continued, as, for example, against the *chuetas of the Balearic Isles.

[Martin A. Cohen]

In Halakhic Literature

The New Christians who continued secretly to observe the precepts of Judaism as much as possible after their conversion were not regarded as voluntary apostates. The basis of this decision was the statement of *Maimonides (Yad, Yesodei ha-Torah 5:3–4) that although one should allow oneself to be put to death rather than abandon one's faith in times of persecution, "nevertheless, if he transgressed and did not choose the death of a martyr, even though he has annulled the positive precept of sanctifying the Name and transgressed the injunction not to desecrate the Name, since he transgressed under duress and could not escape, he is exempted from punishment." In accordance with this, Isaac b. *Sheshet ruled that those New Christians who remained in their countries because they were unable to escape and flee, if they conduct themselves in accordance with the precepts of Judaism, even if only privately, are like full Jews, their *sheḥitah* may be relied upon, their testimony in law cases is accepted, and their wine is not forbidden by touch as that of non-Jews (Resp. Ribash, no. 4). However, some authorities ruled that if the Marranos of a certain locality succeeded in fleeing to a country where they could return to Judaism, while others remained there in order to retain their material possessions, the latter were no longer presumed to have the privilege of being regarded as Jews (Ribash, *ibid.*) nor are they regarded as valid witnesses (*Tashbeẓ*, 3:47; Resp. Redakh, no. 24). Others, however, expressed more lenient views and held that no one is to be deprived of his rights as a Jew as long as he is not seen to transgress the precepts of Judaism even when there is no danger involved (*Tashbeẓ*, 1:23). Moses Isserles, too, rules that even those Marranos who are able to flee but delay because of material considerations and transgress Judaism publicly out of compulsion while remaining observant privately do not make wine forbidden by their touch (Sh. Ar., YD 124:9, and see *ibid.* 119:12).

The problem of the Marranos in *halakhah* became increasingly complex as the length of their stay and that of their descendants in their native lands wore on. Jewish religious tradition was gradually forgotten by the descendants of the Marranos in Spain and Portugal, and many of them assimilated and intermarried with the gentiles. Since for several centuries individuals and groups of descendants of Marranos continued to escape to other countries where they were absorbed in the Jewish community, doubts and differences of opinion related to the laws of marriage and personal status arose among the great talmudists about the Marranos returning to Judaism. Isaac b. Sheshet, Simeon b. Solomon Duran in Algiers, and Elijah Mizraḥi in Constantinople ruled that the children of Marranos counted as Jews in matters of marriage, divorce, levirate marriage, and *ḥaliẓah even after several generations (*Yakhin u-Vo'az*, pt. 2, no. 38; *Mayim Amukkim*, no. 31; Maharik, Resp. no. 85 in the name of Rashi). On the other hand, some ruled that the children of Marranos born after their parents had converted and succeeding generations were to be regarded in all ways as non-Jews; their betrothal to a Jewish woman was invalid, levirate marriage did not apply to them, and even if a Marrano begot a child by a woman forbidden under penalty of *karet the offspring does not rank as *mamzer, and should he become a proselyte would be permitted to marry a Jew. The Marranos who had lived among gentiles for more than a century came to regard those things forbidden by the Torah as permitted and married non-Jewish women, with the result that their children were presumed to be non-Jewish unless it could be proved that their mothers were Jewish (*Keneset ha-Gedolah*, EH 4; Resp. Maharit, vol. 2, EH no. 18).

A Marrano who could have fled but did not was penalized, in that he did not inherit the property of his Jewish relatives, while every Marrano heir who hastened to return to Judaism canceled the rights of the other Marrano heirs (Resp. Reshakh, pt. 1, no. 137). According to some authorities, the customs of dowry and marriage allowance applying to Marranos while they lived as gentiles remain in force (Resp. Maharashdam, ḤM no. 327), but according to others the agreements made by Marranos at the time of their marriages in accordance with gentile usages had no binding force (Joseph Caro, in *Avkat Rokhel*). A testamentary disposition or the gift of a dying person made by a Marrano not in accordance with Torah law was not binding (Joseph ibn Lev in *Edut be-Ya'akov*, no. 71, 195b; *Keneset ha-Gedolah*, ḤM 161; *Torat ha-Minhagot*, no. 51).

The scholars of Safed headed by Jacob Berab imposed flagellation upon Marranos who returned to Judaism as a punishment for transgressing the prohibitions which rendered them liable to *karet* in their previous condition (*Kunteres ha-Semikhah* at the end of Resp. Maharalbaḥ); and since flagellation can be imposed only by ordained *dayyanim*, Jacob Berab and his colleagues wanted to enforce punishment when ordination was renewed (see *Semikhah). A Marrano who escaped from his native land but was not circumcised through neglect was prevented from participating in the sacred service in the synagogue until he was circumcised (*Mayim Rabbim* of Raphael Meldola, YD nos. 51 and 52).

[Moshe Nahum Zobel]

BIBLIOGRAPHY: Roth, Marranos, index; Baer, Spain, 2 (1966), passim; A.J. Saraiva, *Inquisição e Critãos-Novos* (1969). IN HALAKHIC LITERATURE: H.J. Zimmels, *Die Marranen in der rabbinischen Literatur* (1932); S. Assaf, *Be-Oholei Ya'akov* (1943), 145–80.

NEWFIELD, MORRIS (1869–1940), U.S. Reform rabbi and social worker. Newfield was born in Hungary, where he earned a B.D. from the Jewish Theological Seminary in Budapest in 1889. In 1891, he abandoned his studies at the medical college of the University of Budapest to immigrate to the United States and attend Hebrew Union College and the University of Cincinnati concurrently. While at HUC, Newfield taught a course in Talmud and was superintendent of the John Street Temple Sunday School. In 1889, he received his B.A. from the University of Cincinnati and was ordained at HUC, which also awarded him an honorary D.D. in 1939, added to his honorary Doctor of Literature degree from the University of Alabama. Immediately after ordination, Newfield was appointed rabbi of Temple Emanu-El in Birmingham, Alabama, a position he retained throughout his life. He also joined the faculty of Howard College, where he taught Hebrew and Semitics.

In Birmingham, Newfield established himself as a civic and interfaith leader and fighter for social justice in the conservative South; a proponent of social gospel theology, his efforts were motivated by the classical Reform belief that the Jews' mission is to establish a Kingdom of God on earth. Accordingly, he founded the city's first free kindergarten and was an organizer and director of the Associated Charities (precursor of the Community Chest) and of the Citizens Relief Committee. He was particularly active in the fight against tuberculosis, as a founder of the Anti-Tuberculosis Society and of the Alabama Anti-Tubercular League. He also challenged prohibition and Sunday blue laws; despite this latter conflict with local Christian clergy, together they founded a chapter of the National Conference of Christians and Jews. As president of the Alabama Sociological College, he was a driving force behind ending child labor abuses, joining the Alabama Child Labor Committee and helping to establish a juvenile court, the Department of Child Welfare, and the Alabama Children's Aid Society. He also served as chairman of the Red Cross Advisory Case Committee and was responsible for assisting caseworkers in solving difficult problems.

During World War I, despite his misgivings as an advocate of peace, Newfield served as a part-time chaplain at Alabama's Camp McClellan, partly to show the Christian community that Jews were patriotic. After the war, he served as chairman of the Home Services Committee of the local Civilian Relief Committee, assisting returning veterans.

His involvement in the causes of the wider community notwithstanding, Newfield founded the local Federation of Jewish Charities, later renamed the United Jewish Fund. He was also instrumental in organizing the Alabama Jewish Religious School Teachers Association, serving as its president for two years. He brought his passion for social activism to the national stage via the *Central Conference of American Rabbis, which adopted an official position against child labor in 1910.

Newfield went on to serve as secretary of the CCAR and was ultimately elected to its highest office in 1931. During his two-year term as CCAR president, Newfield steered a non-Zionist course; within a few years, however, in response to the rise of Nazism, he had become a staunch Zionist. He spent the final years of his life championing the cause of the Jewish homeland in Palestine.

[Bezalel Gordon (2nd ed.)]

NEW HAMPSHIRE, one of the New England states, located in northeastern United States. One of the original thirteen colonies which broke from England in 1776, in 2005 it ranked 46th in area of the 50 states and 41st in population. While no accurate demographics are available, the best estimate is that 12,000 to 14,000 Jews lived within this small state (9,351 square miles, 1,299,500 inhabitants in 2005). The Jewish population is concentrated in the more urban south and southeast section (Manchester, Concord, Nashua, Portsmouth, and the seacoast).

The state was not always hospitable to its Jewish citizens (or Roman Catholics, for that matter) for the first state constitution in 1784 limited office-holding to Protestants. That requirement was in force until 1877 when the document was amended to remove religious qualifications. However, the number of Jewish inhabitants was small. Early records name William Abrams and Aaron Moses as having moved from New Castle on the coast to Sanbornton in 1693. A list of grants to settlers in 1770 included Joseph Levy, a settler near the present Ossipee. In 1862, the *American Israelite* reported that a *minyan* had gathered in Manchester to observe the holidays, but no further report followed. In 1880, a J. Wolf was the first recorded permanent Jewish resident. Ten years later the first congregation in the State, Adath Yeshurun, was organized.

A second Manchester synagogue, Anshei Sfard (now Temple Israel) followed in 1897 as a dissident breakaway from the Adath Yeshurun group. The first building erected as a synagogue anywhere in New Hampshire was built in 1911 to house the older *shul* and soon thereafter (1917) Anshei Sfard also built its own place of worship. Meanwhile, both congregations had purchased cemetery land, adjacent to each other but separated by a fence. The fence stood until 1946 when elders from the two congregations decided to build a memorial chapel on the dividing line and removed the fence as part of the project.

The early Jewish settlers (particularly from the influx escaping the problems of eastern Europe) came as small merchants and trades people. Few, if any, worked in Manchester's huge Amoskeag textile mills. The first peddlers became merchants, and the downtown areas of Manchester, Nashua, Dover, Portsmouth. Keene, and Claremont soon had numbers of Jewish entrepreneurs. Professional people, lawyers, physicians, dentists, teachers began to appear, often from the first generation of native born Americans. At the same time, economic and political influence grew. No Jews served on the state's bench until Harry Lichman was appointed a probate judge in Keene and Bernard Snierson a municipal court judge in Laconia in the mid-1940s. No Jewish judge served on the Superior Court bench until Philip Hollman in 1987, and no federal judge until Norman Stahl was appointed to the Federal District Court in 1990 (in 2005 he was a senior judge for the U.S. Court of Appeals on the First Circuit). Jews joined bank boards in the late 1940s, Saul Greenspan and Milton Machinist, both in Manchester, being the first, and Jews became members of boards of trustees of the Manchester Historic Association, the Currier Gallery (now Museum) of Art, and the NH Historical Society.

The Jewish community also established its own non-synagogue groups. A YM-YWHA was founded in Manchester in 1906. Over time, the organization metamorphosed into a Jewish Community Center with a community Hebrew school, and later, in the 1970s, into the Jewish Federation. In 2005 the Jewish Federation of Greater Manchester became the Jewish Federation of New Hampshire as the only Jewish social agency

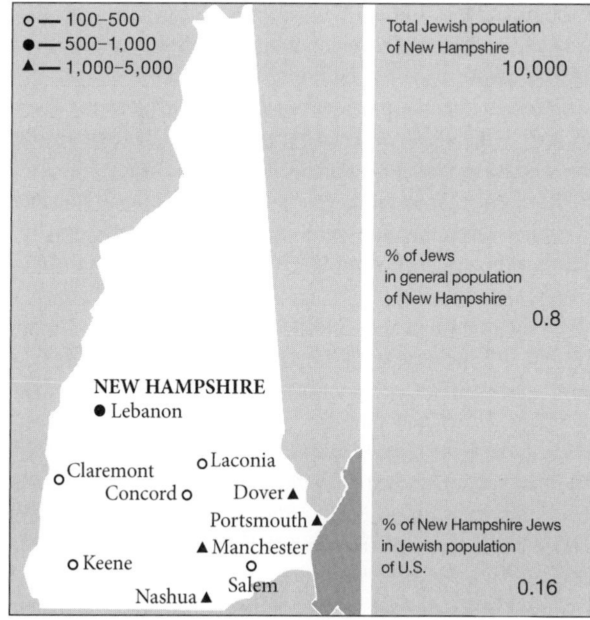

Jewish communities in New Hampshire. Population figures for 2001.

in the State. The Federation produces a monthly newspaper mailed to every identified Jewish household in NH. The mailing list totals 3,100.

New Hampshire's role in national elections from the beginnings of the preferential primary in 1954 grew and Jewish citizens, always alert to the political scene, have been involved at many levels in the national campaigns. Gerald Carmen, Republican activist and state chairman in the first Ronald Reagan campaign, went on to serve as General Services Administrator in Washington and in a State Department role at the League of Nations in Geneva, Switzerland. Jewish voters tended to be Democrats, but many were Republicans. Several have served in the 400-member New Hampshire General Court and a number in the State Senate as well. Saul Feldman of Manchester was probably the first Jewish General Court member in the late 1950s. Manchester lawyer Samuel Green served in the New Hampshire Senate and as its president from 1961 to 1963. During a period of Governor Wesley Powell's illness, Green stepped in as acting governor. In 2005, Debora Pignatelli of Nashua, former legislator, was a member of the five-person Governor's Council. Warren *Rudman, a Republican and former attorney general (an appointive post) served as United States Senator from 1980 to 1993 when he declined to seek re-election.

While there were remnants of discrimination ("No Jews" signs were found in White Mountain resort areas until the 1940s), many barriers dropped after World War II. The state's two largest institutions of higher education (Dartmouth College in Hanover and the University of New Hampshire in Durham) certainly were not friendly to Jewish faculty until after World War II. Dartmouth had only two Jewish faculty members in the early 1940s, and UNH one (in the engineering school) until 1954 when historian Hans Heilbronner was hired in the College of Liberal Arts. Since then Dartmouth has had two Jewish presidents (John Kemeny, 1970–81, and James O. Freedman, a Manchester native, from 1989 to 1998); UNH has had one, Evelyn Handler (1980–83) who left to become president of Brandeis University. Dartmouth, which has the smallest percentage of Jews among its student body of all the Ivy League Colleges, has long had a distinguished Judaic Studies program. Jacob *Neusner, Arthur *Hertzberg, Steven *Katz, Marshall *Meyer and the current incumbent Susannah Heschel have all served on its faculty.

The demise of the Amoskeag Manufacturing Company in 1936 left the largest NH city with a vast surplus of industrial space and a large pool of skilled workers. A concerted effort to attract new employers brought numbers of Jewish manufacturers to New Hampshire. The Blums and Sidores brought Pandora Industries to the city, the Greenspans Waumbec Mills, the Cohens BeeBee Shoe, Boston's Gordon brothers, JS and BD, opened Hampshire Designers and MKM, both textile manufacturers. Until the migration of garment work overseas in the 1980s, there was a thriving Jewish presence in soft goods manufacturing. At the same time, growth in high tech industry with many Jewish participants replaced some of the old industrial base and the number of Jewish professional men and women grew enormously.

As the Jewish population increased, new synagogues have been established in towns like Amherst and Derry, home to few Jews two generations ago. In 2005 there were fifteen synagogues or temples about the state, and most had full-time rabbis. The immigrant community was hardly distinguishable from the general community.

[David G. Stahl (2nd ed.)]

NEW HAVEN, U.S. port city in Connecticut. New Haven has a Jewish population of 24,300 (2001) out of a general population of about 124,000. It was settled in 1638 by Puritans who envisioned it as a Wilderness Zion based on biblical law. It was 120 years later, in 1758, that the first Jews, the brothers Jacob and Solomon *Pinto, arrived. They were soon integrally involved in the city's life. With the outbreak of the Revolutionary War, the three sons of Jacob Pinto – Solomon, Abraham, and William – took up arms in the Continental army. In 1783, Jacob Pinto was a signer of the petition to Connecticut's General Assembly which brought about the incorporation of New Haven as a town.

President Ezra *Stiles of Yale College recorded in his diary the arrival of an unnamed Venetian Jewish family in the summer of 1772 who observed the Sabbath in traditional Jewish manner, "worshiping by themselves in a room in which were lights and a suspended lamp." He noted that this was purely private Jewish worship, since the Venetians were too few to constitute a synagogue quorum, "so that if thereafter there should be a synagogue in New Haven, it must not be dated from this."

A slow influx of Jewish settlers began about 1840. Families from Bavaria, their friends and kinsmen soon constituted a *minyan* which became Congregation Mishkan Israel. A burial ground was acquired in 1843. Mishkan Israel was New England's second congregation and the 14th Jewish congregation established in the United States. Soon after its founding, divergences in religious approach arose, one in the direction of Orthodoxy, the other toward Reform. In 1846 a first break occurred: a Reform group broke away, for several years conducting its own congregational service.

Until 1854 the pioneer New Haven congregation met for prayers in a variety of local halls. In 1854, Mishkan Israel Congregation, along with other U.S. congregations, received a $5,000 bequest from the estate of the philanthropist Judah *Touro. With this sum it purchased and refurbished a church as its first synagogue. By then the Reform segment of the congregation had become the majority and in 1855 the Orthodox members seceded permanently and established B'nai Sholom Congregation, which continued as a small congregation until it went out of existence in the late 1930s. Only the cemetery of this early German Orthodox congregation remains.

Mishkan Israel prospered over the decades, led by German-Jewish rabbis who maintained close ties with Rabbi Isaac

M. *Wise and the growing Reform movement. In 1897 the congregation built a large synagogue in Byzantine style, in keeping with its growing affluence; the sermons, previously in German, and much of the service as well, were now in English.

The first Jewish refugees arrived from Russia in February 1882, and were followed by a steady influx of Russian-Jewish families. By 1887 the Jewish population had grown to about 3,200. In the next decade it grew to about 8,000 and the increase was greatly accelerated in the wake of the Kishinev pogrom of 1903. By the beginning of World War I, New Haven Jewry numbered about 20,000.

The first congregation organized by the immigrants from East Europe was B'nai Jacob Congregation (1882), which grew into New Haven's largest Conservative congregation. Of the 11 Orthodox congregations organized during the height of the immigration period, four remained in 1968. Several new ones have been established as a response to the new religiosity of the last decades of the 20th century.

The first organized charity by the Jews of New Haven was undertaken in 1881. The pioneer German Jews established the Hebrew Benevolent Society to assist the Russian-Jewish immigrants, and the latter established the Hebrew Charity Society in 1885. In 1910 the sisterhood of Mishkan Israel began to devote itself to charitable enterprise, opening a special office for the purpose. In 1919 the three charitable undertakings were formally organized into the United Jewish Charities. The Jewish Family Service, professionally staffed, came into existence in 1939.

By the mid-1920s there were in New Haven over 60 Jewish religious, charitable, fraternal, and Zionist organizations, and in addition the Young Men's and Young Women's Hebrew Association, the Jewish Home for Children, and the Jewish Home for the Aged. Community leaders, recognizing the need for coordination, in 1928 created the New Haven Jewish Community Council, to which member organizations regularly elected delegates. Out of the council's efforts there emerged the Jewish Welfare Fund and, subsequently, the Bureau of Jewish Education.

Jewish education of children has improved since the 1950s with the growth of synagogue schools, the Lubavitcher-sponsored Hebrew Day School, and the Conservative-sponsored Ezra Academy. These schools are coordinated by the Bureau of Jewish Education. A community-sponsored Hebrew High School is maintained under the bureau's supervision. The first memorial to the Holocaust built on public land was erected in New Haven and the first project to video-tape Holocaust Survivors was begun in New Haven by local survivors, psychologist Dore Laub, and media specialist Laurel Vlock. It evolved over time into the Fortunoff Archive housed at Yale University Sterling Library. There are seven synagogues in New Haven itself. Neighboring Orange has three synagogues, Reform, Conservative, and Chabad, and also is the home of the New Haven Hebrew Day School, an Orthodox K-8 school. Woodbridge, which is now the center of Jewish activity, has a major Conservative synagogue, Congegation B'nai Jacob, which moved from the city along with the Jewish Community Center that moved from downtown New Haven to the suburbs and Ezra Academy, a Solomon Schechter Day School affiliated with the United Synagogue of Conservative Judaism. The Jewish Community Center is housed in a 106,000 square foot building containing an Olympic-size shallow depth lap pool, two full-court gymnasiums, racquetball courts, health spa, fitness center, personal training, Judaic gift shop, Claire's kosher vegetarian restaurant, a library, auditorium and more, all on 53 acres. Hamden has two synagogues, one Reform and the other Conservative.

The Jewish Family Service has served the community since 1881.

Yale University is a major center of Jewish life. After generations in which there was a quota on Jews, in the early 21st century Yale has a large Jewish student body, a Jewish president, Richard *Levin, a distinguished Jewish Studies Department with scholars such as Paula *Hyman, Steven Fraude, and Ivan Marcus and a large Hillel building near the Center of campus, the Slifka Center. The Hillel Children's School at Yale which helps children aged 7 to 13 discover positive Jewish identities. Jewish life is a presence on campus and Jewish faculty participate in the community. Judaic scholars are a resource for New Haven Jews. There is an active Chabad presence at Yale.

The most famous Jewish citizen of New Haven is Joseph I. *Lieberman, the United States senator and an observant, self-described Orthodox Jew who was the Democratic nominee for vice president in 2000. He credits the rabbi of the Young Israel of New Haven with mentoring him on how to unite a staunch commitment to Jewish observance with his responsibilities as a United States senator. Marvin Lender, a New Haven based philanthropist whose family began Lender Bagels, is credited as national chairman of the United Jewish Appeal with convening a group of Mega donors to coordinate their own private philanthropy with the ongoing needs of the Jewish community.

[Arthur Chiel / Michael Berenbaum (2nd ed.)]

NEWHOUSE, SAMUEL IRVING (Solomon Neuhaus; 1895–1979), U.S. publisher. Born in New York City, Newhouse was the first of eight children of poor immigrant parents. Newhouse's initial venture came when, as a 16-year-old office boy in a law office, he was told by his employer to take charge of the *Bayonne* (N.J.) *Times*. He made the paper such a success that by age 21 he was earning $30,000 a year. In 1922 he acquired the floundering *Staten Island* (N.Y.) *Advance* for $98,000. Six years later he turned down an offer of $1,000,000 for it. His formula for success was to cut operating costs, stimulate advertising and circulation, and allow local editors complete autonomy. During the Depression of the 1930s he bought five newspapers, and continued adding others, including the *Portland Oregonian* and the St. Louis *Globe-Democrat*. In 1955, in what was described as the biggest transaction in American newspaper history, he paid $18,642,000 for a package that included the *Birmingham* (Alabama) *News*, the *Huntsville* (Alabama) *Times*, and four radio and television stations. In 1959, to diversify his holdings, Newhouse bought controlling interests in two important magazine publishing firms – Condé Nast (*Vogue, Glamour, House and Garden*) and Street and Smith (*Mademoiselle* and five other periodicals). He owned 15 daily newspapers, 12 national magazines, and nine radio and television stations. In 1960 he gave two million dollars to Syracuse University to establish the Newhouse Communications Center, intended to be the world's largest educational and research institute for the study of the mass media, and he made provision for its future maintenance. In the 1960s Newhouse purchased the *Oregon Journal*; the *New Orleans Times-Picayune* newspaper group; three Springfield (Massachusetts) newspapers – *News*, *Republican*, and *Union; the Mobile Register, Mobile Press* and *Mississippi Press-Register;* and the *Cleveland Plain Dealer.* In 1976 he gained total ownership of the eight Booth newspapers and *Parade* Magazine.

ADD. BIBLIOGRAPHY: R. Meeker, *Newspaperman: S.I. Newhouse and the Business of News* (1983)

[Irving Rosenthal / Ruth Beloff (2nd ed.)]

NEW ISRAEL (Rus. **Novy Izrail**), Jewish religious sect initiated in Odessa during the 1880s. At the beginning of 1882 Jacob Priluker, a teacher at the government Jewish school of Odessa, published an article in the *Odesskiy Listok* in which he proclaimed the 15 principles of a sect to be known as New Israel, whose objective was to introduce reforms in the Jewish religion which would reconcile it with Christianity. These principles recognized the Mosaic law only, and articulated "an attitude of contempt" toward the Talmud. The day of rest was transferred from Saturday to Sunday, while circumcision and the dietary laws were abolished. The members of the sect were required to consider Russian as their national language and to observe the laws of the state. The Russian government was requested to grant civic rights to the members of the sect, to authorize them to spread their doctrine among the Jews, and to permit them to wear a special sign which would distinguish them from other Jews. Their platform was to be a breakthrough for Russian Jewry after the tribulations it had suffered through the riots and increased antisemitism which followed the assassination of Czar Alexander II in 1881. However, even those *maskilim* who strove for reforms within Judaism regarded Priluker's proposals with reserve. They pointed to the utilitarian nature of his reforms, which suggested that part of the Jewish heritage be abandoned in exchange for civic rights. On the other hand, Priluker was encouraged by the Russian authorities. During the same year, his book *Reform Jews* (published under the pseudonym of E. Ben-Sion) was published in St. Petersburg with government assistance. It contained a violent attack on the Talmud and traditional Judaism, thus supplying material for antisemitic propaganda. In 1887 Priluker traveled to Western Europe at the government's expense to establish contacts with missionaries. However, his preaching to the Jewish masses of southern Russia met with no success and the Russian government's sympathy for him declined. Indeed, his appeals for support in the publication of a Jewish newspaper which would propagate his ideas were rejected by the government. In 1891 Priluker apostatized to Protestantism and immigrated to England, and this marked the end of the attempt to establish the New Israel sect.

BIBLIOGRAPHY: N.N. (I.L. Gordon), in: *Voskhod*, 8 pt. 2 (1882), 1–29; S. Ginsburg, *Meshumodim in Tsarishn Rusland* (1946), 90–115.

[Yehuda Slutsky]

NEW ISRAEL FUND, THE. Founded in 1979, the New Israel Fund was designed to expand the work that the United Jewish Appeal was then doing. It sought to protect Israel's strength by protecting democracy, human rights, justice, and equality for all Israelis – Jews and Arabs. An international partnership of Israelis, Americans, Canadians, and Europeans, NIF pioneered the funding of Israel's social change organizations and advocacy groups, and is widely credited as the founder of much of Israeli civil society. NIF has funded more than 750 Non-Government Organizations with approximately $200 million in 26 years.

From minority rights to religious pluralism, NIF is widely recognized to be on the "Dovish," "leftist" spectrum of Israeli and American Jewish politics. It perceives itself and structures itself in the vanguard of fighting for social change in Israel. NIF grantees work in three core areas: (1) civil and human rights: Flagship NIF grantees such as B'Tselem and the Association for Civil Rights in Israel have won court battles on issues ranging from the prohibition of torture in civilian interrogations to changes in the route of the separation fence to respect humanitarian concerns. Other grantees work on issues ranging from evenhanded urban planning and land sales to women's and minority rights; (2) social and economic justice: As a nation with many disadvantaged minority groups, from citizen Arabs to Ethiopians to Oriental Jews, Israel has a special responsibility to observe its founders' vision and values of "freedom, justice, and peace as envisaged by the prophets of Israel." Racism, injustice, and fanaticism defile Jewish values and threaten Israel's long-term security. NIF grantees organize communities, advocate for equitable government policies, and empower disadvantaged Israelis to help their communities and themselves; (3) religious pluralism and tolerance: NIF has long been a principal supporter of a pluralistic and tolerant Israeli culture that includes diverse approaches to Judaism and Jewish identity. NIF grantees are in the forefront of the struggle for civil marriage and other life-cycle events, recognition of non-Orthodox conversions, and the equal and unbiased allocation of government resources.

Through Shatil, the Empowerment and Training Center for Social Change Organizations, NIF provides grantees and other social change organizations hands-on assistance and training in the basics of nonprofit management. Widely regarded as one of the world's most successful capacity-building organizations, Shatil regularly originates and discovers best practices for Israel's growing NGO sector and disseminates them.

The New Israel Fund also partners with other philanthropists in joint initiatives, including a multiyear program funded by the Ford Foundation to promote peace and social justice in Israel. Another joint program, the Green Environment Fund, is the first funding collaboration in Israel to protect and preserve the environment. NIF is also partnering with another U.S. foundation and with the Joint Distribution Committee to advance infrastructure development for the Negev Bedouin.

The NIF is headquartered in Washington, D.C., and employs people in the United States, Canada, and the U.K., as well as in four Israeli offices – in Jerusalem, Haifa, Beersheba, and Lod.

WEBSITE: www.nif.org.

[Naomi Paiss (2nd ed.)]

NEW JERSEY, one of the original 13 states of the United States, total population 8,429,000, Jewish population 485,000 (2001 est.). Jews have lived throughout the state from the northern border with New York State to the southern border with Delaware and Pennsylvania, on the eastern coast as well as within the suburban New York communities. The largest concentration of Jews is in Bergen County (83,700), Essex County (76,200), Monmouth County (65,000), Middlesex County (45,000), Cherry Hill and southern New Jersey (49,000), Ocean County in the Northeast (29,000), Union County (30,000), and Atlantic and Cape May counties (15,800). While cities such as Newark, Paterson, and Camden were once the scene of thriving Jewish communities, Jews in New Jersey tend to be suburban and to a lesser extent exurban. New Jersey granted religious tolerance to its citizens as early as 1665, and the state constitution of 1844 abolished all religious qualifications for voting and holding public office.

Although the first organized Jewish communities in New Jersey were not established until the middle of the 19th century, Jewish merchants from Philadelphia and New York conducted business in the state as early as the 17th century. Among the first Jewish settlers were Aaron and Jacob Lozada, who owned a grocery and hardware store in Bound Brook as early as 1718. Daniel Nunez appears in a 1722 court record as town clerk and tax collector for Piscataway Township and justice of the peace for *Middlesex County. Perth Amboy, on the *Trenton-Philadelphia road, was a center for Jewish and other merchants from the time it became the capital of East Jersey in 1685. Among the early prominent settlers in the state was David *Naar, who was active at the state constitutional convention in 1844, became mayor of Elizabeth in 1849, and purchased the Trenton *True American* newspaper in 1853. Naar was instrumental in developing the first public school and public library in Trenton.

German Jews settled in *Trenton, the state capital, in the 1840s, the most prominent among them being Simon Kahnweiler, a merchant and manufacturer. The Mt. Sinai Cemetery Association was incorporated in the town in 1857 and Har Sinai Congregation held its first service in 1858. The first organized Jewish community in New Jersey was in Newark (see *Essex County), where Congregation B'nai Jeshurun was incorporated in 1848. Other early communities with organized congregations included: Paterson (1847), New Brunswick (1861), Jersey City (1864), Bayonne (1878), Elizabeth (1881), *Vineland (1882), *Passaic (1899), Perth Amboy (1890), *Atlantic City (1890), Woodbine (1891), *Camden (1894), and Englewood (1896; see *Bergen County).

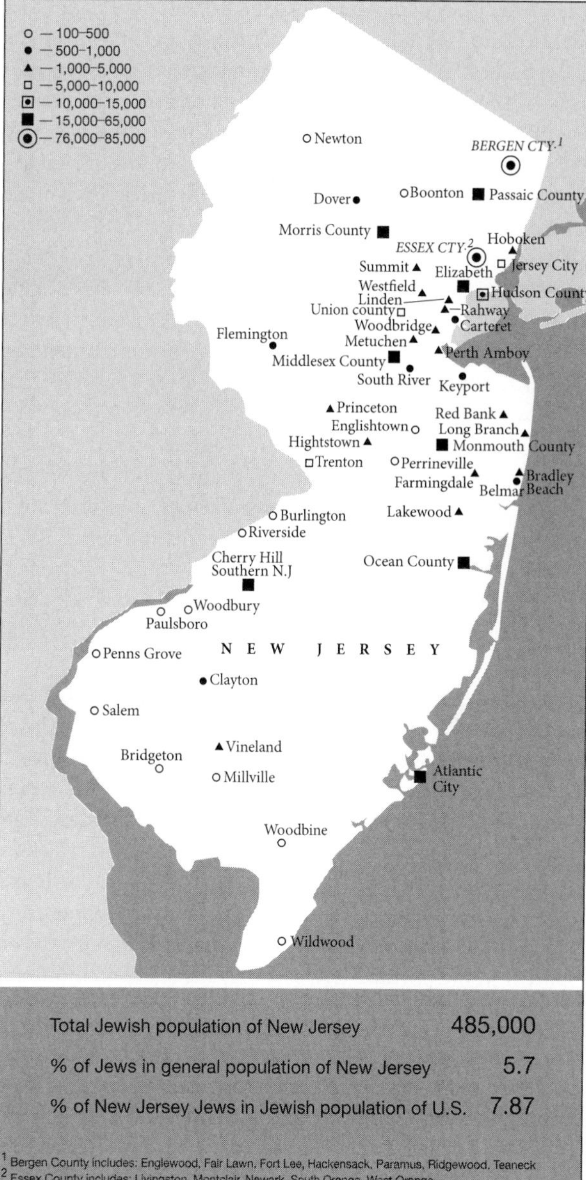

Jewish communities in New Jersey. Population figures for 2001.

Newark once boasted a vibrant community of 80,000 Jews, immigrants from Eastern Europe. They started out destitute and within a generation had achieved a prosperity that fueled a second mass migration, to the suburbs of Essex County and beyond. Newark's demise as a center of Jewish life, and death – at one time there were nearly 100 cemeteries – has been traced to the riots and looting of 1967. The riots wiped out much of the merchant class when stores were pillaged in a burst of rage. Actually, Jews began to leave earlier, lured by the charms of suburbia, the alternative to cramped urban living. The postwar building boom, generous loans to returning GIs, and the affordable automobile sent Jews out of Newark and to Livingston, Millburn, and the Oranges. Philip Roth immortalized the Weequahic section of Newark where he grew up in several novels, particularly *Portnoy's Complaint* and *The Plot Against America*. Weequahic, on the south side of Newark, was a destination place for recently arrived Jews who lived in cold-water flats and then moved up to the middle class. That neighborhood faded away, along with the Riviera, a fancy hotel where Roth's mother and father spent their wedding night. It is now the shabby Divine Hotel Riviera, named after Father Divine, a religious leader who founded a sect in the early part of the 20th century. By 2004, B'nai Jeshurun, Newark's first synagogue, had become the Hopewell Baptist Church on Muhammad Ali Boulevard.

Demographically (1970), New Jersey was divided into two major areas of settlement – northeastern New Jersey, from Bergen County to Middlesex County, which included nearly 300,000 Jews, and the Camden area, near Philadelphia, which included about 18,000 Jews – as well as the northeastern shore area (Long Branch and Asbury Park), the southeastern shore (Atlantic City, 10,000 Jews), the Trenton area (10,000 Jews), and other smaller communities. The Jewish population of New Jersey, which was dependent upon the economic development in the northeastern sector of the state, both for employment and market outlets in nearby New York City, grew from an estimated 5,600 in 1880, to 25,000 in 1900, 40,000 in 1905, 70,000 in 1907, 258,306 in 1927, and leveled off to 259,970 in 1937. By 1969 there were 387,000 Jews in the state. Whereas a third of the state's Jewish population resided in Newark in 1937, by the late 1960s the overwhelming majority of the Jews in the northeastern area (as was also true of the general population) lived in the suburban areas of Bergen, Essex, *Hudson, Passaic, and *Union Counties.

The economic life of New Jersey during the last half of the 19th century was largely dominated by the German Jewish community, which was small in number and engaged in small businesses and merchandising. By the end of the 1920s the waves of East European immigrants from Russia and Poland had changed the demographic nature of the northeastern part of the state. The silk industry of Paterson – largely in the hands of Polish Jews who had worked in the textile industry in Lodz and Bialystok – and the garment industry in Jersey City and Newark, as well as the woolen and worsted mills of Passaic, drew heavily upon the East European and Slavic population of the area. Sephardic families from the Mediterranean and the Balkans settled in New Brunswick and Atlantic City. Between 1912 and 1924 the Sephardim constituted about one third of the Jewish community of 2,500 in New Brunswick. Many worked at Johnson & Johnson, U.S. Rubber, and Michelin Tire. Michelin was a French company, and because many of the Sephardim spoke French, it was an attraction as a workplace. The original members of the Atlantic City community came from many areas of the Middle East, and some worked for or ran auction houses or galleries on the Boardwalk. In the 1970s a large group moved from a Syrian enclave in Brooklyn (their ancestors were from Aleppo and Damascus) to Monmouth County, particularly Deal, Bradley Beach, and Elberon near the Atlantic Ocean. Strictly observant, the community flourished through the early years of the 21st century.

The Jewish colonies of Vineland, Carmel, Woodbine, Rosenhayn, and others, which were started in the late 19th century in southern New Jersey, were helped initially by the Alliance Israélite Universelle and the Baron de Hirsch Fund. Some of the communities, such as Carmel and Woodbine, found the soil generally poor and inadequate for agricultural uses, but Vineland, which had an estimated Jewish population of 2,450 in 1970, established a thriving poultry industry. Jews also played a significant role in the tourist industry of the shore areas of Lakewood, Long Branch, Asbury Park, and Atlantic City.

Jewish community life, which until World War II was largely distinguished by local congregations, Hebrew schools, Jewish centers, fraternal groups, and local philanthropic organizations of an Old World character, quickly changed in the 1950s and 1960s with the mass migration to the suburbs. Center city congregations merged and area-wide organizations like the Community Council of Passaic-Clifton, which administers the United Jewish Appeal, and the Passaic-Clifton Board of Rabbis, which supervises kashrut in the community, served a far-flung community. The Jews of Bergen and Essex counties, with more than 75,000 Jews each, were scattered among 100 communities – 70 separate municipalities in Bergen County alone. More than 100 Jewish organizations operated within Bergen County.

In recent years, younger Jews have moved from New York City to more affordable communities in New Jersey like Fort Lee, Jersey City and the gentrified Hoboken. Their influx was accelerated by an improvement in rail and bus service, which made Essex and adjacent counties a relatively easy commute into Manhattan.

Various community newspapers have appeared in the state since the beginning of the 20th century. In 1910 Mordechai Mansky began publication of the *Newarker Wochenblat*, a Yiddish weekly which appeared until 1914. Among the early Anglo-Jewish newspapers published were the *Jewish Chronicle* of Newark (founded in 1921), *The Jewish Post* of Paterson, and the *Jewish Review* of Jersey City. In 1947 the *Jewish News*, a weekly, was founded, and by 1969 it had a circulation of over 25,000, the largest of any community newspaper in New Jersey.

[Yehuda Ben-Dror / James Marshall (2nd ed.)]

The *Jewish News* has been an influential voice in the New Jersey Jewish community for nearly 60 years. It publishes four editions, reaching more than 50,000 households. With its growth and mergers, the *Jewish News*, or NJJN, has become the second largest Jewish newspaper in America, and the largest-circulation weekly newspaper in the state.

[Abraham Halperin (2nd ed.)]

Several New Jersey universities have thriving programs in Judaic Studies, and Richard Stockton University in the Atlantic City area offers a Master's Program in Holocaust teaching.

U.S. Senator Frank R. *Lautenberg remains the most prominent Jewish political leader in the state and one of its most important philanthropists. He was born, raised, and established his company in New Jersey (A.B. Data). For many years, he was the junior senator to Bill Bradley and then briefly its senior senator before retiring. Recalled into politics following a political scandal, he ran in 2004 and won again.

A New Jersey native, Michael *Chertoff, the Jewish day school-educated son of a rabbi, was President George W. Bush's second secretary of homeland security.

[David Twersky (2nd ed.)]

NEW LEFT, the wave of left-wing radicalism, which attracted many students and other young people in the U.S. and in Western Europe especially in the late 1960s. It had no consistent doctrine and embraced various ideologies, from the Maoist interpretation of Marxism to outright anarchism. The Jewish aspect of the movement was twofold: a disproportionate participation of Jews in the leadership and sometimes also in the ranks, and the issue of Israel and Arab anti-Israel terrorism after the Six-Day War.

In the United States

As mentioned, the New Left counted a disproportionate number of Jews among its leaders and rank-and-file activists. In organizations such as the Students for a Democratic Society (SDS), the Congress of Racial Equality, the Student Non-Violent Coordinating Committee, as well as in the Free Speech and anti-Vietnam war movements, American Jews pressed for a social reform agenda that valued "participatory democracy" and rejected institutionalized power.

By the late 1960s, Jewish New Leftists clashed with their non-Jewish counterparts. The rise of the Black Power movement alienated Jewish civil rights workers while the anti-Cold War ethos of the New Left turned against the Jewish State, deemed an "imperialist aggressor" after its decisive 1967 victory in the Six-Day War. While some Jewish New Leftists remained active in secular political causes, others translated the tactics and strategies of direct-action protests to particularist Jewish causes.

Sociologist C. Wright Mills first coined the phrase in his 1960 "Letter to the New Left." Mills sought to distance himself from the labor-centered leftist political ideologies of the 1930s, which were subsequently labeled the "Old Left." During the era of the Great Depression and Franklin D. Roosevelt's New Deal, most progressive political activism centered on unionization issues and the rights of workers. Members of the Old Left embraced strategies that sought to realign the United States government's relationship to labor.

At the 1962 SDS conference, Tom Hayden issued the founding document and constitution of the New Left movement, the Port Huron Statement. Named for the town that hosted the SDS meeting, the Port Huron Statement joined Old Left Marxism with contemporary liberal beliefs and the hopeful optimism of a post-war American middle class. It called for "participatory democracy" and pressed for direct action protests against injustices. "We are a people of this generation, bred in at least modest comfort, housed now in universities," Hayden and his SDS colleagues lamented, "looking uncomfortably to the world we inherit."

New Leftists opened a broad-ranged movement intended to challenge organizational authority and effect new systems of power and governance. They joined the emerging civil rights movement, engaging in direct-action protests they hoped would focus the world's attention on the injustices of southern racism.

In 1964, New Leftists claimed victory at the University of California, Berkeley, where the Free Speech Movement galvanized students, mobilized faculty support, and helped launch a national student-centered political movement. With Congressional passage of the Civil Rights Act of 1964 and the Voting Rights Act of 1965, New Leftists turned their attention away from domestic issues and focused on United States foreign policy in Southeast Asia. They spearheaded the anti-Vietnam war protest movement, rejecting the Cold War assumptions of mainstream liberal America in favor of an anti-imperialist critique that blamed the United States for much of the world's economic inequality.

In the late 1960s and early 1970s, the New Left fractured beyond repair. Those on the liberal-leaning side of the movement celebrated the successful conclusion of the civil rights movement and the U.S. withdrawal from Vietnam by stepping away from political activism. From the other extreme, New Left radical groups such as the Weather Underground Organization pressed for more confrontational strategies that included violent resistance, alienating their one-time political allies.

Though neither Tom Hayden nor most of the earliest New Left founders claimed Jewish ancestry, the movement grew to include a disproportionate number of Jews, including Mark Rudd, Jerry Rubin, and Abby Hoffman. Scholars estimate that Jews constituted between one-third and one-half of the New Left activists on college campuses across the country.

At a time when Jews represented just three percent of the American population and ten percent of those attending college, they constituted a majority of the New Left's most active members. Numerous social scientific studies pointed to strong Jewish influences in the nation's leading New Left groups. At the University of California, Berkeley, Jewish students lit candles during a sit-in protest that coincided with the holiday of Hanukkah. The Oscar-nominated documentary film *Berkeley In The '60s* features Jewish student protesters leading Israeli folk dancing during a demonstration inside Sproul Hall, the university's main administration building.

During the civil rights movement, American Jews joined a number of local and national organizations including SNCC and CORE. When northern college students ventured south during the 1964 Mississippi summer, between one-third and one-half were Jewish. Jews remained throughout this period the most liberal white ethnic group in the United States, lending their time, money, and political influence to combating Jim Crow.

With Israel's dramatic victory in the 1967 Six Day War, Jewish progressives faced their greatest challenge. The New Left, splintering along racial and ideological lines, grew critical of the Jewish State, equating its occupation of the West Bank and Gaza Strip to the evil imperialist impulses of the United States in the Cold War. Many in the New Left rejected Zionism, labeling it a chauvinistic, even racist, manifestation of nationalism.

At the 1967 Conference for a New Politics held in Chicago, for example, African American delegates pressed for passage of a resolution that characterized the June 1967 conflict as an "imperialist Zionist war." As Black Power leader Stokely Carmichael said at a 1968 convention of the Organization of American Students, "We have begun to see the evil of Zionism and we will fight to wipe it out wherever it exists, be it in the Ghetto of the United States or in the Middle East."

Jewish New Leftists in Berkeley responded by creating the Committee for a Progressive Middle East in March, 1969. The Committee intended to strike a balance between the strident anti-Zionist influences growing with the New Left and the much less critical Zionist voices of Hillel and other Jewish groups. Radical Jewish Zionists, despite their attempts to locate progressive Zionism within the boundaries of the New Left, failed to re-unite Jewish leftists with an ever more radical, and anti-Zionist, movement.

The rise of Black Power also alienated Jews from the New Left, which had, by the mid-1960s, come to locate black militancy in its movement's vanguard. The rise of ethnic nationalism ended the inter-racial civil rights movement of the Martin Luther King, Jr., years. Jews, once valued as liberal America's most committed social reform advocates, faced a Black Power-inspired critique that labeled them white oppressors.

When Jewish New Leftists sought a strategic alliance with Oakland's Black Panther Party, for example, they were rebuffed. As one Jewish New Leftist explained, "Even if I were a superaltruistic liberal and campaigned among the Jews to support the Panthers' program, I would justifiably be tarred and feathered for giving aid and comfort to enemies of the Jews. I would rather it were not this way, but it was you who disowned us, not we who betrayed you." The end of the civil rights movement at home combined with Jewish concerns over the New Left's critique of Israel when, in 1969, Eldridge Cleaver told a *New York Times* reporter that "the Black Panther Party in the United States fully supports Arab Guerillas in the Middle East."

By the early 1970s, the New Left lost most of its earlier Jewish influence. Jews, weary of anti-Zionism, occasional antisemitism, and the rise of ethnic and racial consciousness, turned inward, applying many of the New Left's political strategies to Jewish communal concerns.

The Soviet Jewry movement, nascent since its founding in the 1950s, enjoyed rapid growth in the years after 1964 when Jewish civil rights workers turned their attention to the plight of their co-religionists in the Eastern Bloc. In San Francisco, Jewish radicals staged a "pray in," emulating the Free Speech Movement's "sit in," to force that city's Jewish Federation Council to increase its support of Jewish education. Other groups such as Jews for Urban Justice and Breira – which counteracted the slogan in Israeli politics *ein breira* [there is no choice] – emerged as well, focusing attention on progressive political issues within the Jewish community.

In the final analysis, the New Left offered Jewish radicals a powerful legacy of both ethnic and religious identity. What began as a univeralist movement for participatory democracy and inter-racial cooperation ended with an impressive campaign for progressive Zionism, stronger Jewish education, and greater focus on Jewish ethnic and religious continuity.

[Marc Dollinger (2nd ed.)]

In Western Europe

The West European New Left of the late 1960s differed in two respects from its U.S. counterpart. It lacked the reservoir of supporters among both the black masses and sections of the white population opposed to the war in Vietnam and it was opposed by the entrenched Socialist and Communist parties. The appeal of the European New Left thus tended to be restricted to amorphous groups on the periphery of society. However, the French students' revolt of May 1968 and similar, though less violent, demonstrations in Germany and throughout Europe, proved that under favorable conditions the New Left could act as an ideological catalyst and set into motion events of considerable consequence. Its total rejection of prevailing standards and social structures was echoed in the inarticulate, though widespread, misgivings about the values and workings of the "affluent society" and the "deadness of its culture." This applies to the well-publicized and opinion-forming sector of the New Left. There were, however, particularly in Great Britain, other, near-clandestine groupings that concentrated on disruptive industrial action, as, for example, Tariq Ali's Trotskyist International Marxist Group or the Socialist Labor League, which aimed at the subversion of the trade union and have been more disruptive than the 1968 student demonstrations at the London School of Economics and other British universities.

Whereas the protagonists of the European New Left were young, its ideologues were elderly scholars, such as the French writer-philosopher Jean-Paul Sartre and Herbert *Marcuse, a German-Jewish émigré and a cofounder of the Frankfurt Institute of Sociology. In his attempt to harmonize the teachings of Freud with those of Marx, Marcuse totally rejected the basic assumptions and ultimate objectives of the prevailing industrial society. Alienation in work and the repression of basic human drives could be overcome, Marcuse maintained, in a truly democratic and participatory society so organized as to serve essential human needs rather than the requirements of the socio-industrial complex. Since the service of the latter has corrupted mankind, the only hope for its future lies in the classes still untouched by the exigencies of the productive processes, which have become an obsession both under capitalism and Communism. These classes are the students of the industrialized nations and the masses of the developing Third World. From these assumptions it follows that New Left thinking on the Arab-Israel confrontation tends to sympathize with the Arabs as representatives of the oppressed Third World, while regarding the Westernized, technology-oriented Israelis with instinctive hostility. The Marxist rationalization of these feelings runs along arguments well known to Old Left Communists, that Israel and Zionism in general are only the "lackey of American imperialism," etc. Marcuse, however, disassociated himself from this attitude while on a visit to West Berlin shortly after the Six-Day War (1967).

In the Federal Republic of Germany, the New Left's most important protagonist, the SDS (Sozialistischer Deutscher Studentenbund) in 1969 repeatedly disrupted public meetings at which the Israel ambassador was to appear. Later that year New Left terrorists tried to blow up West Berlin's Jewish community hall during a service commemorating the 1938 Nazi pogroms. The revulsion aroused by these activities was criticized by their perpetrators, who, in leaflets, under the headline "Shalom and Napalm," deplored the guilt feelings of the German Left toward the Jews as "neurotic, backward-looking anti-Fascism" disregarding the "non-justifiability of the state of Israel." German New Left leaders, such as Ulrike Meinhof of the left-wing weekly *Konkret* and Dieter Kunzelmann of West Berlin's Kommune I, joined the Palestinian *fedayeen* in Amman and inveighed against "bourgeois Germany's *Judenkomplex*." Except in the universities, the German New Left remained a negligible factor and failed to gain working-class support. Similar tendencies were at work in Italy, where such New Left organizations as Lotta Continua were militantly "anti-Zionist."

In France, in May 1968, the New Left students' revolt led to nationwide strikes, a grave government crisis, and contributed to the eventual resignation of President de Gaulle (June 1969). Among the student leaders were many Jews, such as Alain Krivine, Marc Kravetz, Alain Geismar, and Daniel Cohn-Bendit, who, as "Red Danny," became the figurehead of the uprising. Although their Jewishness did not induce them to follow an independent line on the Arab-Israel conflict, it sufficed to revive antisemitic resentments on either side of the political spectrum. Attacks against the German-Jew Cohn-Bendit and slogans like "France for the French" were once countered by students chanting "We are all German Jews." The French New Left succeeded temporarily in involving the workers in its struggle, but the subsequent leftist (old and new) defeat at the polls ended its role as a significant political factor. Characteristically it was the non-Jew Sartre who opposed the New Left anti-Israel slogans. It is absurd to pretend, he maintained, that "Israel is an imperialist state and that the Arabs are socialists, including their feudal states."

[Ernest Hearst]

In Israel

In Israel, the New Left remained a fringe phenomenon and those groups which actively identified with the New Left received little support, even in student circles. Maẓpen ("Compass"), which broke away from the Ha-Olam ha-Zeh group in the early 1960s, was especially vocal after the Six-Day War in calling for withdrawal from territories occupied in the war. It never had more than a handful of members and in 1970 these split into three groups.

The Semol Yisra'eli Ḥadash ("Israel New Left," known as Si'aḥ) was founded in 1969. Consisting mainly of students and members of Ha-Shomer ha-Ẓa'ir kibbutzim, it called for a more resolute peace policy on the part of the Israeli government. Si'aḥ was not crystallized as a political party but stressed its nonidentification with the policies of the Rakaḥ Communist Party (see *Communism: Israel).

BIBLIOGRAPHY: M.S. Chertoff (ed.), *The New Left and the Jews* (1971); N. Glazer, in: JJSO, 11 (1969), 121–32; N. Glazer and L. Fein, in: *Midstream*, 17:1 (1971), 32–46; Lipset, in: *Encounter*, 33 (1969), 24–35; P. Seale and M. Mc-Conville, *French Revolution 1968* (1968); W. Laqueur, in: *Commentary*, 47:6 (1969), 33–41; H. Marcuse, *Protest, Demonstration, Revolt* (1968; translation of his: *Das Ende der Utopie*). **ADD. BIBLIOGRAPHY:** V. Gosse, *The Movements of the New Left, 1950–1975: A Brief History with Documents* (2004); M. Isserman, *If I Had A Hammer... The Death of the Old Left and the Birth of the New Left* (1987); S. Rothman and S.R. Lichter, *Roots of Radicalism: Jews, Christians, and the Left* (1996); M. Staub, *The Jewish 1960s: An American Source Book* (2004); idem, *Torn at the Roots: The Crisis of Jewish Liberalism in Postwar America* (2002); J. McMillian and P. Buhle (eds.), *The New Left Revisited* (2003).

°**NEWLINSKI, PHILIPP MICHAEL** (1841–1899), *Herzl's diplomatic agent in Constantinople and the Balkan countries. The son of a Polish aristocratic family, Newlinski took up journalism. He was appointed to the staff of the Austro-Hungarian embassy in Constantinople where he became familiar with the situation in Turkey and the Balkan States, established contacts with the royal houses, and gained influence with the sultan. In 1880 he resumed his profession as a journalist, first in Paris and from 1887 in Vienna, where he founded his own newspaper, *Correspondance de l'Est*. He also published booklets on political themes. Herzl established contact with Newlinski in 1896 and persuaded him to work for the realization of Zionist aims. At first Newlinski was paid for his efforts, but under Herzl's influence he became a zealous supporter of the movement and served as Herzl's trusted adviser. He accompanied Herzl on his first visit to Constantinople and tried to arrange an audience with the sultan, but succeeded only in attaining a decoration for Herzl as a sign of the sultan's esteem. Newlinski did arrange a meeting between Herzl and Crown Prince Ferdinand of Bulgaria, and himself met with the king of Serbia, obtaining the latter's support for the Zionist cause. He tried to gain the sympathy of Bismarck and the Vatican and in general was instrumental in recruiting many prominent personalities in support of Herzl's vision. Illness prevented him from attending the First Zionist Congress, but he was present at the Second Congress. His newspaper devoted a special column to Zionist affairs. In 1899 Herzl sent him to Constantinople, where he was received by the sultan. On his return from this mission Newlinski died.

BIBLIOGRAPHY: T. Herzl, *Complete Diaries*, ed. by R. Patai, 5 (1960), index; N.M. Gelber, in: *Herzl Year Book*, 2 (1959), 113–52.

[Israel Klausner]

NEW LONDON, city in S.E. Connecticut; population (2000) approx. 26,000; Jewish population of New London and its environs, approx. 3,900. The first recorded Jewish presence in New London dates from March 1685 when a Dutch Jew brought the brigantine Prosperous to the port of New London. Due to the official Christian charter of the Connecticut colonial government, which restricted Jewish and Catholic settlement in Connecticut, Jews did not establish a recognized community in Connecticut until 1843. The first Jews to make their home in New London were Joseph Jacob Schwartz, his wife, Esther, and son, David in 1860. The initial Jewish community was entirely German Jews, who came from communities in Central Europe that were not orthodox.

In 1878 the first congregation, Achim Shalom, was organized through the efforts of Joseph Michael, and a burial society was formed and purchased a section of the city's Cedar Grove Cemetery.

The German Jewish community did not grow, and in 1885, Samuel Cott of Lithuania, the first of a wave of refugees from Eastern Europe and Russia arrived in New London and transformed the community. These more orthodox Jews established regular services in 1892 and formed the Sick Benefit Society of Ahavath Chesed in July 1892. They also purchased land for a Jewish cemetery. In 1894 Kalef Soltz and his son Joseph opened the first kosher meat market, which remained open and active under Soltz ownership until 1995.

In 1895 the Ukrainian Jews organized their own congregation but rejoined the Lithuanian-dominated Ahavath Chesed in 1905 when that congregation moved into a new synagogue. In 1911 many of the Ukrainians reestablished their congregation, the Ohave Sholom Sick Benefit Society, and built their own building in 1919.

New London became a vacation destination for Jews from Hartford, CT., and Springfield, MA., and in 1925 a third Orthodox synagogue, Temple Israel was opened near the Neptune Park section of New London to cater to summer residents.

Conservative services began in 1924, with the congregation, Beth El, formally organizing in 1932. Rabbi Samuel Ruderman of Boston was the first rabbi, and services were held at a Community House on Blackhall Street, with *oneg Shabbat* and *kiddush* held at the home of Benjamin Kaplan. The congregation bought land in downtown New London near a major Protestant church but decided to build on Ocean Avenue closer to the beach and to new residences that were being purchased by younger Jewish families. The land in downtown New London was sold to the Greek Orthodox community. In 1951 a permanent home for Beth El was constructed on Ocean Avenue.

In 1960 a Reform congregation, Temple Emanu-El, was organized, meeting first at the Mohican Hotel in New London, then at a church in Groton, before building a permanent home in Waterford, CT.

Just to the north of New London a Jewish farming community was established in the 1890s with the help of the Baron de Hirsch Fund. This community built a synagogue, The New England Hebrew Farmers of the Emanuel Society. The community did not survive, but many of their members moved to New London, two of them, the Gruskins and Schneiders, opening hardware stores that joined a growing collection of Jewish merchants who helped create a vibrant downtown shopping district.

In 1899–1900 the *American Jewish Year Book* records a chapter of Chovevei Zion in New London, and in 1913 Morris Mallove, a jeweler in downtown New London established the Sons of Zion. Mallove became an active Zionist leader in Connecticut and helped raise funds to purchase land in the Jezreel valley of Palestine, near Afulah. He traveled to Israel in 1950 as part of a delegation from Connecticut to show support for the new state of Israel and continued to be active as a leader of Israel Bonds for many years.

The community organized a United Palestine Appeal in 1925, and worked hard after WWII to raise funds and to collect material for the Haganah. As a Navy town (Sub Base New London) there were a lot of surplus supplies that were collected and shipped to Palestine.

New London was one of the first cities, and Connecticut one of the first states, to observe the national Days of Remembrance of the Holocaust, a program supported by the U.S. Holocaust Memorial Council, and organized by New London businessman and Holocaust survivor Sigmund Strochlitz. He succeeded in having all 50 states of the Union officially observe a Holocaust Memorial Day. For two decades New London was represented in Congress by Sam Gejdenson, the child of Holocaust survivors who had settled in nearby Bozarah.

The Jewish community organized a Jewish Federation in 1975, and the Federation began to arrange for social welfare programs for seniors and others in need of help. It became a federally recognized refugee resettlement agency, and resettled over 350 Jews for the former Soviet Union. It was called upon by the state to be the relocation agency for victims of Hurricane Katrina who arrived in southeastern Connecticut.

In 2005 the Jewish community of New London was part of a greater Jewish community in eastern Connecticut. The community supported: a senior center and kosher hot lunch program; a Solomon Schechter school; a bi-weekly paper, the *Jewish Leader*; a full-time Orthodox congregation, Ahavath Chesed; a conservative congregation, Beth El; a summer congregation, Temple Israel: a Reform congregation, Temple Emanu-El (in Waterford); a Chabad House; a Hillel for Connecticut College, the Coast Guard Academy, and Mitchell College; and a Jewish Literacy Project for the public schools, as well as several commemorative and cultural programs that are open to the entire community.

BIBLIOGRAPHY: J.E. Fischer, "From Generation to Generation: A History of the Jews of New London," in: C.C. Kanzler (ed.), *New London – A History of Its People* (1996); D.L. Kline, "To Begin Again: The Russian Jewish Migration to America with Special Emphasis on Chesterfield, Connecticut" (M.A. Thesis, Department of History, Connecticut College, 1976); J. Lesser and J. Florence, *The Jews of New London, A Community in a Community* (1996); J.R. Marcus, "Light on Early Connecticut Jewry," in: J.R. Marcus (ed.), *Critical Studies in American Jewish History*, vol. 1 (1971); E. Sullman, *A Goodly Heritage* (1957).

[Jerome E. Fischer (2nd ed.)]

NEWMAN, ALFRED (1901–1970), U.S. film composer, conductor, pianist. Newman was born in New Haven, Conn., to produce dealer Michael Newman and cantor's daughter Luba Koskoff, both Russian immigrants. As a music lover, his mother took an active role in her son's music career. His first public performance as a piano prodigy was at the age of eight. After winning a scholarship to Sigismond Stojowksi's Von Ende School of Music in New York, Newman's debut recital came on November 5, 1916. However, financial problems at home forced Newman to become a vaudeville musician, working on *Hitchy-Koo* from 1917 to 1918. The show's music director encouraged Newman to study conducting, and by 1919 he was conducting musical comedies. A recommendation from George Gershwin landed him the position as music director for the 1920 Broadway show *Scandals*. In 1930 Newman went to Hollywood at the invitation of United Artists. After working on the musical *Whoopee!* (1930), he became the studio's music director. During almost nine years with UA, Newman composed music for such films as *The Count of Monte Cristo* (1930), *The Prisoner of Zenda* (1937), and *Wuthering Heights* (1939). In 1940, he signed with Darryl F. Zanuck as general music director of Twentieth Century Fox, where he wrote music for such films as *How Green Was My Valley* (1941), *All About Eve* (1950), and *The Robe* (1953). With Martha Montgomery, whom he married in 1947, he had five children in addition to two from previous marriages. The 1960s found Newman working as a freelancer for projects like *How the West Was Won* (1962), *The Greatest Story Ever Told* (1965), *Flower Drum Song* (1967), and *Camelot* (1967). Newman received 45 Oscar nominations during his career and won nine, and was posthumously nominated for his final score, *Airport* (1970).

[Adam Wills (2nd ed.)]

NEWMAN, ARNOLD (1918–), U.S. photographer. Born in New York, Newman studied art at the University of Miami (1936–38) but did not complete his studies due to financial difficulties, and became a photographer's apprentice in Philadelphia. In 1945 he moved to New York, where he did freelance photojournalism for such publications as *Life*, *Look*, *Newsweek*, *The New Yorker*, *Esquire*, and *Fortune*. He specialized in portraiture, developing a style that did not necessarily flatter the subject but revealed his personality. Implementing an approach known as "environmental portraiture," he used as background associations and symbols connected with the life and work of the person he was photographing. Igor Stravinsky, for example, was shown seated at the extreme left of the picture, the lid of his grand piano serving to emphasize the character of the composer. Brooks Atkinson, the critic, was photographed sitting in an empty theater, where the seats created a pattern of forms and highlights. Prime Minister David Ben-Gurion was shown with the 1948 Declaration of Independence of the State of Israel. Over the decades, Newman photographed most of the major celebrities and public figures of the 20th century. His photographs are exhibited in many of the world's major art museums.

Newman's published works include *One Mind's Eye* (1974), *Arnold Newman: Five Decades* (1986), *Tropical Rainforest* (1990), *Arnold Newman's Americans* (1992), and *Arnold Newman* (with P. Brookman, 2000).

[Peter Pollack / Ruth Beloff (2nd ed.)]

NEWMAN, AUBREY (1927–), British historian. Educated at Glasgow and Oxford Universities, Newman was professor of history at Leicester University. He has published widely in two different fields, the 18th-century British aristocracy and Anglo-Jewish history. His work on *The Stanhopes of Chevening* (1970) is well known, as are his works on Anglo-Jewish history such as *The United Synagogue, 1870–1970* (1970). Newman was twice president of the Jewish Historical Society of England and was a founder of the Stanley Burton Centre for Holocaust Studies at Leicester University.

[William D. Rubinstein (2nd ed.)]

NEWMAN, BARNETT (1905–1970), U.S. painter. Newman was born in New York, to immigrant parents who were interested in music, literature, and art. He began to make drawings as soon as he could hold a pencil. At high school he was introduced to the Metropolitan Museum of Art, after which he regularly studied American painting. Deciding to become a professional artist, Newman persuaded his parents to allow him to enroll in the Art Students League, where he spent considerable time learning to draw from casts. He also studied at the City College of New York. At the Art Students League, he met Adolph *Gottlieb, two years his senior, who became one of his closest friends. When Newman graduated in 1927, his father insisted on his joining the family clothing business, which he virtually took over after the 1929 crash. From 1931 to 1939 Newman worked as a substitute art teacher in high schools.

Although he drew and painted throughout this period, it was not until the late 1940s that he emerged as a major artist, alongside a brilliant group of young Americans, including Pollock, de Kooning, Gorky, *Rothko, Gottlieb, and David Smith, now identified as the Abstract-Expressionists. They reacted to the Ecole de Paris in a moralistic, puritanical manner, against art as luxury. Newman in particular, well-educated and articulate, was the intellectual codifier of the movement. His work became abstract and symbolic, with some influence from Surrealism. Gradually he moved toward a single band or stripe, which allied to titles like "Adam," "The Beginning," "The Word," "The Command" indicates their Jewish mystical origin. He held his first one-man exhibition in January/February 1950, at Betty Parsons Gallery, New York; this and similar early displays of his work met with public hostility. Ten years later, Newman and his fellow Abstract-Expressionists were recognized as the first indigenous modern American school of painting. He once wrote: "Instead of working with the remnants of space, I work with the whole space." It is this concept of "wholeness" which has been exploited by the younger generation of American painters.

[Charles Samuel Spencer]

NEWMAN, ISIDORE (1837–1909), U.S. banker and philanthropist. Newman, who was born in Germany, went to the U.S. in 1851. During the Civil War, he founded a bank in New Orleans. He subsequently bought and ran the Carrolton Railroad, before selling it to become main owner of New Orleans' Maison Blanche department store. Active in New Orleans' Jewish affairs, Newman was a founder of that city's B'nai B'rith lodge and a generous patron of the Jewish Children's Home (renamed for him in 1913).

NEWMAN, JON O. (1932–), U.S. Court of Appeals judge. Born in New York City, Newman graduated magna cum laude from Princeton University in 1953 and earned his law degree from Yale Law School in 1956. He was admitted to the bar in Connecticut and in the District of Columbia in 1957, and he served as senior law clerk to Chief Justice Earl Warren in 1957 and 1958. Newman was partner in the law firm of Ritter, Satter and Newman in Hartford, Connecticut, from 1958 to 1960.

In 1959 Newman served as counsel to the majority in the Connecticut General Assembly, then from 1959 to 1961 he was special counsel to the governor of Connecticut. In 1961 and 1962 Newman served as executive assistant to the U.S. Secretary of Health, Education and Welfare, Abraham Ribicoff. From 1963 to 1964 he was administrative assistant to Ribicoff when he was elected to the U.S. Senate from Connecticut. Following that, he served as a U.S. attorney in Connecticut until 1969, when he entered private practice.

In 1972 Newman was appointed a judge on the U.S. Court of Appeals for the District of Connecticut. He served as circuit judge until 1993, then as chief judge until 1997, when he became a senior judge. He made significant contributions to copyright law, issues of federal jurisdiction, and the application of international law by U.S. courts. Within the judiciary, Newman served as a member of the U.S. Judicial Conference, as chairman of its Committee on Federal Rules of Appellate Procedure, and as a member of committees on Appellate Judge Education, Codes of Conduct, and Cameras in the Courtroom.

Newman was a member of the International Society for the Reform of Criminal Law and the American Law Institute, serving as an adviser for its Restatement of the Law of Unfair Competition. He was a fellow of the American Bar Foundation and a member of its Action Commission on Tort Liability, and he is a fellow of the Connecticut Bar Foundation. Judge Newman lectured at the University of Connecticut Law School, and he served as chair of the Board of Regents of the University of Hartford. The author of many articles for law reviews, he has also coauthored a high-school textbook, *Politics: The American Way.*

[Dorothy Bauhoff (2nd ed.)]

NEWMAN, LOUIS ISRAEL (1893–1972), U.S. Reform rabbi and author. Newman was born in Providence, R.I., and received his B.A. from Brown University in 1913 and a Ph.D. from Columbia University in 1924. He became an assistant to Rabbi Stephen *Wise at the Free Synagogue in 1917 and was ordained by Wise and Martin *Meyer in 1918, whereupon he assumed the pulpit of the Bronx Free Synagogue (1918–21). In 1921, he became rabbi of Temple Israel in New York City and was appointed to the faculty of the Jewish Institute of Religion (JIR) when it was founded the following year. He also served as president of the Intercollegiate Menorah Association. In 1924, Newman succeeded Meyer at Temple Emanu-El in San Francisco, returning in 1930 to New York City to become rabbi of Temple Rodeph Sholom, where he was to remain until his retirement. He rejoined the JIR faculty and became active in the Zionist Revisionist movement, championing Zionism as primarily a political movement and the necessity of the creation of a Jewish state in Palestine. He was the chairman of the Palestine Mandate Defense Fund and honorary chairman of both the Revisionist Tel Hai Fund and the American Friends of a Jewish Palestine. He also served on the American advisory committee for the *Hebrew University and as a vice president of the *American Jewish Congress.

His books include *Jewish Influence on Christian Reform Movements* (1924) and *Jewish People, Faith and Life* (1957). He also compiled and translated the classic work *The Hasidic Anthology, Tales and Teachings of the Hasidim: The parables, folk-tales, fables, aphorisms, epigrams, sayings, anecdotes, proverbs, and exegetical interpretations of the Hasidic masters and disciples; their lore and wisdom* (1934, 1968, 1972), which has become a standard textbook for courses in Jewish studies.

BIBLIOGRAPHY: The Louis I. Newman Papers and the American Jewish Archives, Cincinnati.

[Bezalel Gordon (2nd ed.)]

NEWMAN, PAUL (1925–), U.S. actor. Born in Cleveland, Ohio, Newman was the son of an Irish-Catholic mother and a German-Jewish father who owned a successful sporting goods store. After high school he served in the navy until 1946. After graduating from Kenyon College, Newman spent a year at the Yale Drama School and then went to New York, where he attended the Actors Studio.

Newman first appeared on Broadway in *Picnic* (1953) and won a Theater World Award. His first film was *The Silver Chalice* (1954). His performance in the biblical costume epic proved to be such an embarrassment to him that he placed a full-page ad in *Variety*, apologizing for his appearance in the film. His career improved immeasurably after his impressive performance in *Somebody Up There Likes Me* (1956).

Among Newman's many notable films are *The Long, Hot Summer* (1958), *Cat on a Hot Tin Roof* (Oscar nomination for Best Actor, 1958), *Exodus* (1960), *From the Terrace* (1960), *Sweet Bird of Youth* (1962), *The Hustler* (Oscar nomination for Best Actor, 1961), *Hud* (Oscar nomination for Best Actor, 1963), *The Prize* (1963), *Torn Curtain* (1966), *Hombre* (1967), *Cool Hand Luke* (Oscar nomination for Best Actor, 1967), *Rachel, Rachel* (director, 1968), *Winning* (1969), *Butch Cassidy and the Sundance Kid* (1969), *Sometimes a Great Notion* (and director, 1971), *The Effect of Gamma Rays on Man-in-the-Moon Marigolds* (director, 1972), *The Life and Times of Judge Roy Bean* (1972), *The Mackintosh Man* (1973), *The Sting* (1973), *The Towering Inferno* (1974), *The Drowning Pool* (1975), *Fort Apache, the Bronx* (1981), *Absence of Malice* (Oscar nomination for Best Actor, 1981), *The Verdict* (Oscar nomination for Best Actor, 1982), *The Color of Money* (Academy Award for Best Actor, 1986), *The Glass Menagerie* (director, 1987), *The Hudsucker Proxy* (1994), *Nobody's Fool* (Oscar nomination for Best Actor, 1994), *Message in a Bottle* (1999), *Twilight* (1998), *Where the Money Is* (2000), and *Road to Perdition* (Oscar nomination for Best Supporting Actor, 2002).

On the Broadway stage, Newman appeared in *The Desperate Hours* (1955), *Sweet Bird of Youth* (1959), *Baby Want a Kiss* (1964), and *Our Town* (Tony nomination for Best Actor, 2003).

In 1994 Newman was awarded the Jean Hersholt Humanitarian Award, and in 1986 he was given an Honorary Academy Award "in recognition of his many and memorable and compelling screen performances and for his personal integrity and dedication to his craft."

In 1990 he was named by *People* magazine as one of the 50 Most Beautiful People in the World.

In 1982 he founded Newman's Own, a successful line of food products (salad dressing, spaghetti sauce, microwave popcorn, etc.) that has earned in excess of $150 million, all of which he donates to charity and education.

Newman has been married to actress Joanne Woodward since 1958.

Books written by Newman include *Speed: Indy Car Racing* (with C. Jezierski, 1985), *Newman's Own Cookbook* (with A.E. Hotchner, 1999), and *Shameless Exploitation in Pursuit of the Common Good* (with A.E. Hotchner, 2003).

ADD. BIBLIOGRAPHY: L. Quirk, *Paul Newman* (1996); E. Oumano, *Paul Newman* (1990); J. Morella and E. Epstein, *Paul and Joanne* (1988); E. Lax, *Paul Newman: A Biography* (1996).

[Jonathan Licht / Ruth Beloff (2nd ed.)]

NEWMAN, PAULINE (1889–1986), U.S. labor activist and advocate for workers rights. Newman was the first woman organizer for the International Ladies Garment Workers Union (ILGWU). She worked for that organization most of her adult life, also serving the union as a journalist, educator, and government liaison. Born in Kovno, Lithuania, to a traditional Jewish family, Newman was literate in Hebrew and learned Talmud from her father. Her discomfort at a young age with gender segregation in worship was a source of her commitment to fighting sex discrimination in her adult life. Newman emigrated to the United States in 1901 with her mother and two sisters after her father's sudden death, joining her brother, who had already settled in New York City. Newman, who began to work in a hairbrush factory at age nine, taught herself English. By age 16 she was writing commentaries for the *Jewish Daily Forward* about bad conditions for factory workers. In 1907 she organized a rent strike in lower Manhattan; although unsuccessful in its immediate goals, the strike galvanized the tenant movement.

Newman's activism gained the attention of labor leaders. From 1909 to 1913 she traveled around the United States organizing garment worker strikes in Philadelphia, Cleveland, and Boston. She spoke out for women's suffrage and supported electoral efforts of the Socialist Party. From 1913 to 1917 Newman served the New York State Board of Sanitary Control as a factory inspector and lobbyist for safety legislation for women workers. In 1917 she became an organizer for the Women's Trade Union League (WTUL), an organization that brought together upper-class and working-class women in support of the workers' movement, creating a chapter in Philadelphia. It was there that Newman met Frieda Miller, a research assistant in the Economics Department at Bryn Mawr College. Miller and Newman began a relationship that lasted until Miller's death in 1974. The women shared an apartment in Greenwich Village beginning in 1923 and raised a daughter together. Although lesbian relationships were not generally public at that time, Newman's relationship with Miller was known and accepted by her Jewish socialist union organizer colleagues.

From 1923 to 1983, Newman served as the educational director for the ILGWU's Health Center. She was relied upon as an expert consultant by the New York State Legislature, the U.S. Public Health Service, and the United Nations, and was part of the circle of women who advised Eleanor Roosevelt on worker rights. After World War II, Newman and Miller were sent by the Departments of State and Labor to investigate factory conditions in Germany. When the women's movement was revitalized in the 1970s, Newman was recognized by feminist historians as an important figure in the struggle for women's rights in the earlier part of the century. She died in 1986 at the home of her daughter, Elisabeth Burger Owen. Her papers are in the Schlesinger Library, Radcliffe College, Cambridge, Massachusetts.

BIBLIOGRAPHY: A. Kessler-Harris. "Organizing the Unorganizable: Three Jewish Women and Their Union," in: *Labor History* (Winter 1976), 5–23; A. Orleck, *Common Sense and a Little Fire: Women and Working Class Politics, 1900–1965* (1995); R. Alpert, *Like Bread on the Seder Plate: Jewish Lesbians and the Transformation of Tradition* (1997).

[Rebecca Alpert (2nd ed.)]

NEWMAN, PETER CHARLES (1929–), Canadian journalist, author, biographer. Newman was born into a prosperous Jewish family in Vienna, Austria. In 1940 he and his family escaped Nazi Europe when his father, a wealthy Czech factory owner, obtained a rare Canadian visa by promising to buy a farm through the Canadian Pacific Railway. Their ship to Canada, a converted cruise ship, was twice attacked by German U-boats before landing at Halifax's Pier 21. Newman later wrote about Pier 21, the "place where we became Canadians," describing the depth of feeling and expectation of refugees like himself arriving in the "new world." A refugee child, in 1944 Newman was enrolled at Toronto's elite private Upper Canada College. He went on to study at the University of Toronto and to a career in journalism and as an author of Canadian biography and history. While he continued to see himself as something of an outsider, he came to know many in the Canadian political and financial establishment. Newman interviewed every prime minister of Canada since Louis St. Laurent. He also served as editor-in-chief of one of Canada's most important newspapers, the *Toronto Star*, and editor of Canada's foremost news magazine, *Maclean's*.

A fellow writer described Newman as the "chronicler and conscience of a country often confused by its identity and perhaps the most influential journalist Canada has ever known." He remained widely respected for his intimate understanding of Canadian business and politics and of those who wield power in Canadian society. He wrote numerous articles and more than 20 books, mostly biography and history, including a biography of the prominent Canadian Jewish *Bronfman family, *The Bronfman Dynasty: The Rothschilds of the New World* (1978).

In 1978 Newman was named an Officer of the Order of Canada and in 1990 a Companion of the Order of Canada. His autobiography, *Here Be Dragons: Telling Tales of People, Passion and Power*, was published in 2004.

[Mindy Avrich-Skapinker (2nd ed.)]

NEWMAN, RANDY (1943–), U.S. singer-songwriter. He was born Randall Stuart Newman to internist Irving George Newman and secretary Adele (née Fox) in New Orleans, Louisiana. His parents were assimilated Jews, and his father considered himself an atheist. He was a nephew of *Alfred, Emil, and Lionel Newman and a cousin of David and Thomas Newman, all film composers. In 1948, Irving Newman moved his family to Los Angeles. Newman began playing the piano at the age of six. He developed an appreciation for the blues when he visited with his mother's Jewish family in New Orleans, but was also affected by the racism and antisemitism of the South. At 16, he worked as a songwriter for Metric Music, and then studied music composition at UCLA. In 1967, he went on to work as a session arranger at Warner Bros. Newman's first two albums were commercial flops, despite positive reviews for his second album, *12 Songs*. Over the years his hits included *Sail Away* (1972), which contained "You Can Leave Your Hat On"; *Little Criminals* (1977), which featured his breakout hit "Short People"; and *Trouble in Paradise* (1983), which launched his commercial anthem, "I Love L.A." Newman then turned to the family business: composing songs for feature films. His first score was for *Ragtime* (1981), followed by such films as *The Natural* (1984), *Awakenings* (1990), and *Toy Story* (1995). In 1995, he released a musical version of *Faust*, which again received critical acclaim but did not meet with any commercial success. Nominated for 14 Academy Awards, Newman won the Oscar for the *Monsters, Inc.* song "If I Didn't Have You" in 2001.

[Adam Wills (2nd ed.)]

NEWMARK, Los Angeles family. JOSEPH NEWMARK (1799–1881), who was born in Neumark, West Prussia, moved to New York in 1823; he helped to found Congregation B'nai Jeshurun in that city in 1825. He lived in St. Louis from 1840 to 1845, serving there as president of the fledgling congregation. Returning to New York in 1846, Newmark helped to organize yet another congregation before he moved to the village of Los Angeles with his wife and six children in 1854. He was the first spiritual leader of the Jewish community, conducting religious services, weddings, and funerals voluntarily until a professional rabbi was engaged. He founded the Hebrew Benevolent Society in 1855 and was the founding president of Congregation B'nai Brith (today's Wilshire Boulevard Temple) in 1862. During Newmark's lifetime the congregation remained Orthodox out of respect for him.

His nephew HARRIS NEWMARK (1834–1916) went to Los Angeles in 1853 and engaged in a variety of mercantile endeavors, ultimately establishing a wholesale grocery. For more than 60 years he was intimately involved in the civic, economic, and Jewish life of the community. He was a member of the committee that brought the first railroad connection to Los Angeles and was an organizer of the Agriculture Society of the 6th district, the public library, Board of Trade, and Chamber of Commerce. He engaged in real-estate activities and was one of the developers of the town of Newmark, now Montebello.

Toward the end of his life, Newmark wrote his memoirs of early Los Angeles; published as *Sixty Years in Southern California* (1916^1, 1926^2, 1930^3), this work stands as the classic autobiographic history of southern California.

Harris's son MARCO ROSS NEWMARK (1878–1959), like his father a businessman and civic figure, served as president of the Los Angeles Produce Exchange and as vice president of the National Wholesale Grocers Association. He was ardently interested in the early history of Los Angeles and with his brother Maurice Harris (1859–1929) co-edited his father's memoirs. The two brothers also edited and published *Census of the City and County of Los Angeles, California, for the Year 1850*. His numerous articles on general and Jewish history were gathered in *Jottings in Southern California History* (1955). Newmark was a president of the Historical Society of Southern California. One of the leaders in the Jewish community, he served as president of the Federation of the Jewish Welfare Organizations, the Los Angeles Lodge of B'nai B'rith, and of the Los Angeles District of the Zionist Organization of America.

BIBLIOGRAPHY: H. Newmark, *Sixty Years in Southern California, 1853–1913* (1916); M. Vorspan and L.P. Gartner, *History of the Jews of Los Angeles* (1970).

[Max Vorspan]

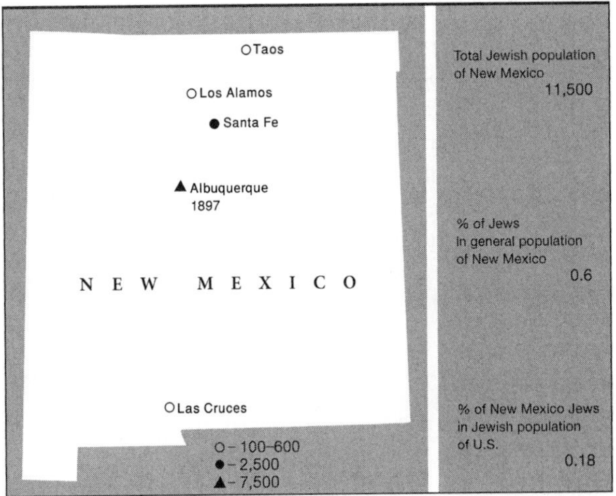

Jewish communities in New Mexico and dates of establishment. Population figures for 2001.

NEW MEXICO, a southwestern state of the U.S. with a minimally estimated Jewish population of 11,500 in the year 2001. Albuquerque, the largest city in the state, held about 7,500 in that year. In 2005, other significant Jewish numbers resided in Santa Fe, Las Cruces, Los Alamos, and Taos. Smaller groups dwelt in a number of towns. In 2005 Albuquerque had organized religious communities of Reform, Conservative, Renewal, Chabad, and Chavurah expression. Santa Fe had several Reform, Orthodox, Renewal, and Chabad communities. Las Cruces had a Reform congregation. Smaller communities such as Carlsbad, Los Alamos, Rio Rancho, Roswell, and Taos had less well-defined groups. Several regional groups existed in Gallup, New Mexico, and in Durango and Trinidad, Colorado, that included parts of New Mexico.

New Mexico became a settled part of New Spain with the expedition northward from Mexico of Juan de Onate in 1598. Recent research suggests the presence of crypto-Jews among the early settlers, following a period of active investigation and trials by the Holy Office of the Inquisition in Mexico City against the well-placed Carvajal family in Nuevo Leon in the mid-1590s. The existence of descendents of crypto-Jews re-emerged in the latter decades of the 20th century with open declarations of their past and, for some, their continuing of reawakened adherence to Judaism.

The takeover of the southwest by the United States from the mid-1840s allowed the influx of Americans (Anglos), among them Jewish traders who had accompanied the American military expeditions into the area. The earliest Jewish settlers, mostly from Germanic states, established a pattern of inviting family members or acquaintances to join them after they established themselves as merchants. Many of their enterprises proved highly successful, producing some of the wealthiest Anglo families in the Territory until the coming of the railroads in 1879–1880. They engaged in retail enterprises along with wholesale operations that linked local farmers with supplying army forts and Indian reservations. They lived mainly in Santa Fe, the capital, Las Vegas, and Las Cruces. Among the best known were the Spiegelbergs and Staabs of Santa Fe, the Ilfelds in Las Vegas, and the Freudenthal-Lesinskys in Las Cruces. In 1880, there were probably some 180 Jews in the whole Territory.

Religious and social institutions developed very slowly. The scarcity of Jewish women and the slow development of family life probably contributed to that condition. It was only after the railroad reached New Mexico that the first formal institutions appeared. B'nai B'rith led the way in Albuquerque in 1883 followed by the first congregation, Congregation Montefiore, in Las Vegas in 1884. Albuquerque's Jews organized Congregation Albert in 1897, today the oldest extant religious community in the state. Both congregations followed the practice of Reform Judaism. In 1920 Congregation B'nai Israel was formed in Albuquerque, which adopted the practice of Conservative Judaism.

Santa Fe suffered a sharp economic decline in the 1880s as a result of the main line of the railroads bypassing the town, and it recovered only in the second decade of the 20th century. Its Jewish population had dwindled as the town's economic condition worsened. No formal Jewish organization existed until the creation of a B'nai B'rith chapter in the mid-1930s.

After the railroad's arrival, the old-style enterprises largely disappeared to be replaced by more modest mercantile operations and some expansion into ranching and mining in the more easterly plains and southwestern mountains where newer towns such as Roswell, Clayton, and Silver City flourished. Where Jews lived in some 16 places in 1880 they lived in no less than 35 towns in 1900. One of the more unusual events arising out of the close contacts of isolated Jews with local populations was the marriage of Solomon Bibo to Juana Valle, a member of the Acoma Indian pueblo. He was appointed its governor in 1888 and served in that post a number of times.

New Mexico's Jews participated heavily in the political life of the territory and state. They served as both appointed and elected officials in local communities and countries across the Territory. Nathan Jaffa of Roswell became secretary of the Territory after 1907. The first mayor of Albuquerque after its incorporation in 1885 was Henry N. Jaffa, who later was a stalwart member of Congregation Albert. In 1890, Mike Mandell was also elected to the post of mayor. In 1930 Arthur Seligman of Santa Fe attained the governorship of the state and died while in office, although his adherence to Judaism has been questioned.

World War II and the half-century since brought great and rapid changes to New Mexico and its Jewish population. Its open spaces, clear weather, and isolation persuaded the federal government to build a number of air force facilities and locate the site for the Manhattan project to create the atomic bomb in Los Alamos. The Cold War that followed World War II witnessed expansion of what had begun during the war years. The half million population of the state in 1940 had more than tripled by the year 2000. Albuquerque grew from 35,000 in 1940 to 200,000 in 1960 to nearly a half-million in 2000.

The Jewish population stood at somewhat over 1,100 in 1940. By the year 2001, it had grown to at least 11,500, outpacing the growth of the general population. Increased numbers also altered the economic makeup of the Jewish community. Where in 1940 merchants had formed an overwhelming proportion of the Jews' economic activity, the changing economy fostered by the federal government's goals brought in a professional population of scientists, engineers, professors, and doctors. The growth of Los Alamos, a new town, exemplifies some of the change. Population growth and the GI Bill offering college education to veterans of the war swelled the numbers in state universities. The University of New Mexico established medical and law schools adding considerable numbers of Jewish professors to the general faculty as well as to the professional school faculties. Growing recognition of New Mexico as a place to retire led to the creation of such towns as Rio Rancho, which drew Jews from the northeast in the 1960s and 1970s. The new population, by the nature of its employment, outdistanced its older mercantile appearance that had existed before World War II.

The problems created by the war, for the Jews, such as a large refugee population in Europe and the establishment of Israel, gave impetus to a rapid expansion of Jewish organization – both secular and religious. Increasing numbers allowed the formation of formal congregations where there had been none before the war and growth in those institutions that did exist. The desire to collect funds for aid and relocation of refugees and support for the new and endangered state of Israel led to the formation of the Albuquerque Jewish Welfare Fund, which translated itself into the Jewish Community Council of Albuquerque and into a broader Jewish Federation of Greater Albuquerque. In 1971 the community created a monthly newspaper, the *New Mexico Jewish Link*, which contains the most concentrated source of information concerning Jewish activity in the state.

Jews continued to make their mark in the economic and political affairs of the state. More specialized than in the past, large businesses made a new appearance or grew greatly in the post-war economy. Among the most successful were those in furniture sales (American Furniture), home building (Sam Hoffman), and building supplies (Duke City Lumber), especially in the early decades after the war. Jews also moved into new areas of visibility, as they became police chiefs, conductors of the symphony, and leading architects. Well-known artists, such as Judy *Chicago, moved to the state. In the late 1980s a Jew and a Republican, Steve Schiff, was elected to the national House of Representatives where he remained for five terms until his death in 1998.

While New Mexico was heavily Catholic historically, the rapid growth of a diverse religious population led to an atmosphere of toleration and interreligious toleration and cooperation in the post-World War II period. Following Vatican II, in 1965, Jews and Catholics established formal dialogues. Jews became far more active in social causes such as civil rights and the rights of women than was the case before World War II. At the turn of the 20th century that expansive mood still existed.

BIBLIOGRAPHY: H. J. Tobias, *A History of the Jews in New Mexico* (1990); F.S. Fierman, *Guts and Ruts: The Jewish Pioneer on the Trail in the American Southwest* (1985); W.J. Parish, *The Charles Ilfeld Company: The Rise and Decline of Mercantile Capitalism in New Mexico* (1961); S. Hordes, *To the End of the Earth: A History of the Crypto-Jews of New Mexico* (2005).

[Henry J. Tobias (2nd ed.)]

NEW MOON (Heb. ראשׁ חֹדֶשׁ, *Rosh Ḥodesh*; "head of the month"), the first day or beginning of the month. The Torah placed its celebration on a par with the observance of the festivals, declaring "Also in the day of your gladness, and in your appointed seasons, and in your new moons, ye shall blow with the trumpets over your burnt-offerings…" (Num. 10:10). A special *Musaf* sacrifice was ordained for the day (Num. 28:11–15). The Bible mentions various practices observed on it, including festive meals (I Sam. 20:18, and Rashi ad loc.), abstention from business transactions (Amos 8:5), and the practice of visiting the prophet (II Kings 4:23). When foretelling the chastisements that will come upon the Jewish people, Hosea says that the joys of the New Moon will cease (Hos. 2:13). The redemption is viewed as a time when "from one new moon to another, and from one Sabbath to another, shall all flesh come to worship before Me saith the Lord" (Isa. 66:23).

Originally, the New Moon was not fixed by astronomical calculations but was solemnly proclaimed after witnesses had testified to the reappearance of the crescent of the moon. On the 30th of each month, the members of the High Court assembled in a courtyard in Jerusalem, named Beit Ya'azek, where they waited to receive the testimony of two reliable witnesses; they then sanctified the New Moon. If the moon's crescent was not seen on the 30th day, the New Moon was automatically celebrated on the 31st day. To inform the population of the beginning of the month, beacons were kindled on the Mount of Olives and thence over the entire land and in parts of the Diaspora. Later, however, the Samaritans began to light misleading beacons, and the High Court dispatched messengers to far-removed communities. Those Jews who lived great distances from Jerusalem always celebrated the 30th day of the month as the New Moon. On those occasions when they were informed of its postponement to the 31st, they also observed this second consecutive day as the New Moon (RH 1:3–2:7). By the middle of the fourth century, the sages had established a permanent *calendar and the public proclamation of the New Moon was discontinued. A relic of the original practice is, however, retained in the synagogue custom of announcing the *New Moon on the Sabbath preceding its celebration.

Work is permitted on the New Moon (Shab. 24a; Ḥag. 18a; Ar. 10b), although it was customary for women to abstain from it (TJ, Ta'an. 1:6, 64c). They were allowed to observe this additional semi-festival as a reward for not having surrendered their jewelry for the creation of the golden calf (Tos. to RH 23a, s.v. *Mishum*). It later became customary for them to refrain from difficult labor, such as weaving, but to do light work such as sewing (Simon b. Ẓemaḥ Duran, *Tashbez*, pt. 3no. 244; cf. Rema, OḤ 417).

The biblical commandment of joy, so basic to festivals, (Deut. 16:14) is not explicitly prescribed in relation to the New Moon. Nevertheless, the rabbis inferred its applicability from the fact that the Bible equated the New Moon with the festivals (Num. 10:10) and from the duty to recite on it "This is the day which the Lord hath made; We will rejoice and be glad in it" (Ps. 118:24; ADPB, 770; Tur, YD, 401). It is therefore forbidden to fast on the New Moon (Ta'an. 2:10), and any funeral service is abbreviated (MK 3:9 and Sh. Ar., OḤ 420). Conversely, it is meritorious to partake of a festive repast (Sh. Ar., OḤ 419:1).

The recitation of the half-**Hallel* on the New Moon goes back to talmudic times (Ta'an. 28b). Parts of the *Hallel* were omitted, since the day was not biblically sanctified by the prohibition of labor (Ar. 10b). There is a difference of opinion among the codifiers as to whether the usual blessing that "who has hallowed us by Thy commandments and has commanded us to read the *Hallel*" (ADPB, 756) should be recited on Rosh Ḥodesh. In most communities, the blessing is recited (Isserles and Sh. Ar., OḤ 422:2), but Shneur Zalman, the founder of Ḥabad Ḥasidism, ruled that only the cantor is to say the blessing, while the congregation merely responds "Amen."

On the New Moon the special prayer **Ya'aleh ve-Yavo* is inserted in the *Amidah* and in the Grace after Meals (Shab. 24a), and *Taḥanun is not recited. The Torah reading designated for the day describes the New Moon sacrifices (Num. 28:1–15; Meg. 21b–22a). *Musaf* is also recited, since an additional sacrifice was brought on this day; it begins with the words: "The beginnings of the months Thou didst assign unto Thy people for a season of atonement throughout their generations" (ADPB, 778).

The day before the New Moon has achieved importance among kabbalists, who observe it as a day of fast and repentance. It is called *Yom Kippur Katan, a minor day of atonement.

[Aaron Rothkoff]

Contemporary Observance by Women

Female Rosh Ḥodesh groups first appeared in New York City in 1972, created and fostered by women seeking a uniquely female communal religious rite with ancient and medieval antecedents. Building on a teaching of the Tosafists (Tos. to RH 23a) which describes Rosh Ḥodesh as a reward for Israelite women's righteousness and an anticipation of the messianic restoration of the moon to the size of the sun, women gathered together to celebrate the new month, to express gratitude to God for being created female and to acknowledge the accomplishments and wisdom of Jewish women over the generations.

Rosh Ḥodesh groups have typically met outside of synagogue and community structures and have no standard form. Activities may include Torah study or other learning, singing, festive eating, story telling, performance of rituals expressing aspects of women's experiences, and prayer. As part of a larger Jewish feminist movement that has encouraged study of Jewish women's history, creation of new Midrash about women, and liturgical innovation, Rosh Ḥodesh groups have produced rituals and prayers subsequently used in other settings. These include the *Kos Miryam* (Cup of Miriam), a ritual vessel of water signifying Miriam's sustaining leadership in Egypt and the wilderness, which has become a part of many American Passover *seders*. As women's Rosh Ḥodesh groups grew in popularity throughout North America and Israel, they also became part of the regular programming of community centers, women's organizations, college Hillel programs, and synagogues from many religious streams.

[Jody Myers (2nd ed.)]

BIBLIOGRAPHY: Elbogen, Gottesdienst, 122–6; S.J. Zevin, *Ha-Mo'adim ba-Halakhah* (196310), 142–8; W. Nowack, *Lehrbuch der hebraeischen Archaeologie*, 2 (1894), 138–44. **ADD. BIBLIOGRAPHY:** P. Adelman. *Miriam's Well: Rituals for Jewish Women Around the Year* (1996); C. Diament, *Moonbeams: A Hadassah Rosh Hodesh Guide* (2000).

NEW MOON, ANNOUNCEMENT OF. The Sabbath before the *New Moon, following the reading of the *haftarah*, the reader leads the congregation in announcing and blessing the coming month. This custom was introduced by the *geonim*, and its main purpose was to make a public pronouncement of the exact day(s) on which the New Moon will fall (*Maḥzor Vitry*, ed. by. S. Hurwitz (1923^2), 173; Abudarham, *Seder Rosh Ḥodesh*, ed. Jerusalem (1959), 193). It is possible that this practice was based upon the statement of R. *Yose, that he did not pray the *Musaf* service (on the Sabbath before the New Moon) until he knew exactly when the New Moon was to occur (TJ,

Sanh. 5:3, 22d; *Arukh ha-Shulḥan*, OḤ 417:8). The announcement is made after a special prayer for the house of Israel, and in the Ashkenazi rite begins: "He Who wrought miracles for our fathers, and redeemed them from slavery into freedom, may He speedily redeem us and gather our exiles from the four corners of the earth, even all Israel united in fellowship; and let us say, Amen." The exact time of the *molad* (see *Calendar) is then announced and the reader proclaims the day(s) of the week on which the first day of the coming month falls; and the blessing concludes with the prayer that the New Moon be for life, peace, gladness, salvation, and consolation for the house of Israel (Hertz, Prayer, 510). Prior to the proclamation of the New Moon, the Ashkenazi ritual contains an introductory prayer, *Yehi Raẓon*, which is substantially the private petition recited daily by Rav upon the completion of the *Amidah* (Ber. 16b). In order to adjust this prayer to the occasion, the sentence "to renew unto us this coming month for good and for blessing" was inserted (Hertz, Prayer, 508). This introductory prayer was first recited in the Polish ritual during the first part of the 18th century. It then gradually spread to all Ashkenazi rituals. In some rites the words "*bi-zekhut tefillat Rav*" ("by the merit of the prayer of Rav") appear at the end of the prayer. It has been suggested that this is a mistake for a marginal note which originally read *berakhot, tefillat Rav* ("blessing [see Tractate *Berakhot*] the prayer of Rav") to indicate the source and authorship of the prayer. These words were later erroneously incorporated in the liturgy, *berakhot* being changed to *bi-zekhut*. A further mistake in some rites changed *Rav* to *rabbim* making it end "by the merit of congregational prayer" (E. Munk, *The World of Prayer*, 2:49). Many Sephardi and Oriental rituals contain introductory prayers for the ingathering of the exiles and the well-being of the rabbis (cf. Abudarham, loc. cit.). It became customary to recite the announcement of the New Moon while standing, in remembrance of the original sanctification of the New Moon by the *bet din* in Jerusalem, which was done when standing (*Magen Avraham* to Sh. Ar., OḤ 417:1). It is also customary for the reader to hold the Torah scroll while reciting this prayer. The Sabbath on which the New Moon is announced is popularly known as *Shabbat Mevarekhim* ("the Sabbath of the Blessing"), or the Sabbath which contains "*Rosh Ḥodesh bentshn.*" A special sermon in honor of the event is preached in some communities. The New Moon of *Tishri is not blessed in advance since it is also Rosh Ha-Shanah and everyone knows when it will occur (*Mishnah Berurah, Sha'ar ha-Ẓiyyun*, 417:1, no. 2).

BIBLIOGRAPHY: Abrahams, Companion, clxi; Elbogen, Gottesdienst, 123 f.; Idelsohn, Liturgy, 141; E. Levy, *Yesodot ha-Tefillah* (1952^2), 206.

[H. Elchanan Blumenthal]

NEWMYER, ARTHUR GROVER (1885–1955), U.S. newspaper publisher. Newmyer, born in Washington, became advertising manager of *The Washington Times* (1906), and national advertising manager of the *Munsey* newspapers (1909). Going to New Orleans as business manager of *The New Orleans Item* (1912), he became its publisher in 1927. After a year with Hearst newspapers, he returned to Washington in 1939 as associate publisher and general manager of *The Times-Herald*.

NEW ORLEANS, U.S. port and commercial center near the mouth of the Misxsissippi River in the State of *Louisiana. Before Hurricane Katrina struck the city on August 29, 2005, had an estimated population of approximately 1,200,000, of which about 12,000 were Jewish. As of January 2006, the future of the city, and its Jewish population remained uncertain. All but one of its major synagogues had been reopened, but the flood damage had wiped out large residential areas.

New Orleans was founded in 1718 by the French, who, six years later enacted *The Code Noir*, or Black Code, which regulated the slave population, but also contained a clause expelling Jews from the territory. There are no records of transient Jewish traders until the arrival of Isaac Rodrigues Monsanto in 1757. He and his family were Dutch Sephardic Jews who had settled in Curaçao until they braved the Code Noir to settle in New Orleans. The French, in their usual lax fashion, ignored the laws and allowed them to prosper, until the cession of Louisiana to Spain following the French and Indian War. In 1769, the Spanish governor Don Alejandro O'Reilly expelled the Monsanto family because they were Jewish, and confiscated their money and property. They fled to Pensacola, then an English territory, but soon were allowed to return minus their possessions.

After the Louisiana Purchase in 1803, and the dissolution of the *Code Noir*, New Orleans became more attractive to Jewish pioneers.

Judah *Touro, later a wealthy merchant and philanthropist, arrived in 1802, and Ezekiel Salomon, son of the American Revolution patriot Haym *Salomon, was a governor of the United States Bank in New Orleans from 1816 to 1821. Two more Jews who later achieved high position settled in the city in 1828: Judah P. *Benjamin, later Secretary of State of the Confederacy, and his cousin, Henry M. Hyams, later lieutenant governor of Louisiana. In the 1830s Gershom Kursheedt, who became the first communal leader, arrived in New Orleans; his nephew, Edwin Isaac Kursheedt, was a colonel in the Washington Artillery, the historic New Orleans regiment.

Shaarei Chessed, the first synagogue, was chartered in 1828. In 1848 James C. Gutheim of Cincinnati was invited to serve as rabbi. The Portuguese Congregation, Nefutzoth Yehudah, was founded in 1845. Temple Sinai, the first Reform congregation, founded in 1870, recalled Rabbi Gutheim to New Orleans from Temple Emanu-El in New York, to be its first rabbi. The first two congregations merged in 1881 to become what later was called Touro synagogue, which was reformed by 1892. Congregation Gates of Prayer, organized in 1850, was Reform by the turn of the century. The Reform congregations have the largest number of members, followed by Shir Chadash, New Orleans's only Conservative congregation, which resulted from the merger of Tikvat Shalom and Chevra Tehillim. Congregation Beth Israel (1904), and Agudas Achim Anshe Sfard (1896) remain the only Orthodox synagogues.

Beth Israel's Synagogue, located near Lake Pontchartrain, was inundated with over ten feet of water during Hurricane Katrina.

The Hebrew Benevolent Association, which funded many Jewish organizations, was founded in 1844. Touro Infirmary, still serving New Orleans, was founded by Judah Touro in 1852. The Jewish Widows and Orphans Home, later the Jewish Orphans and now Jewish Regional Services, was founded in 1856, and the Young Mens' Hebrew Association was founded in 1891. In 1913, 18 separate Jewish welfare and charity organizations merged to form the forerunner of the Jewish Welfare Federation.

Architects of the mid-19th century New Orleans were businessmen like Isidore Newman, Leon Godchaux, and Julius Weis, who led by example in creating and supporting Jewish institutions.

Among some of the prominent Jews of New Orleans in the late 19th and 20th centuries were the attorney Monte M. Lemann; Isaac Delgado, who gave the city its art museum; Samuel *Zemurray, president of the United Fruit Company; Captain Neville Levy, chairman of the Mississippi River Bridge Commission; Percival Stern, benefactor of Tulane and Loyola universities, Newman School, and the Touro Infirmary; Mr. and Mrs. Edgar B. Stern, who supported many institutions and schools as did Malcolm Woldenberg, Steven Goldring, and Sydney J. Besthoff III, whose extensive sculpture collection now graces the New Orleans Museum of Art. Jews have served as presidents and board members of practically all cultural, civic, and social-welfare agencies. Originally, because of its unhealthy climate and poor economy, New Orleans received little of the Eastern European Jewish immigration to America, although a small but vibrant group of Eastern European Jews settled in the Dryades Street neighborhood, with its own kosher markets, Orthodox synagogues, and small shopkeepers. In 2005 that neighborhood had, like the lower east side of New York, completely lost its Jewish flavor, and, like most of America, New Orleans Jews have bonded into a single community, forgetting their origins. In the aftermath of Hurricane Katrina they faced a challenge which exceeded even the Civil War and Reconstruction difficulties, as they sought to return to their city, their jobs, their flooded homes, and their synagogues.

BIBLIOGRAPHY: The Jewish Historical Publishing Company of Louisiana, *History of the Jews of Louisiana* (1905); B.W. Korn, *Early Jews of New Orleans* (1969); L. Huehner, *Life of Judah Touro* (1946); Greater New Orleans Archivist, *Jews of New Orleans, an Archival Guide*, I. Lachoff and C.C. Kahn, *The Jewish Community of New Orleans* (2005).

[Catherine Kahn and Irwin Lachoff (2nd ed.)]

NEWPORT, city in Rhode Island located at the southern tip of Aquidneck Island in Narragansett Bay. Newport was founded in 1639 by religious dissenters from Massachusetts Bay Colony. Roger Williams, also an outcast from the Puritans' dominion, had founded Providence, at the head of Narragansett Bay, three years earlier. Newport became the first of five rotating capitals in a state still known officially as Rhode Island and Providence Plantations.

In 1658, approximately 15 Jews from Barbados settled in Newport. The Jewish cemetery, consecrated in 1677, was the subject of Henry Wadsworth Longfellow's poem published in 1854. Jews Street was identified in John Mumford's map drawn in 1712.

Newport's Jewish community was reestablished during the 1740s, when settlers arrived primarily from New York City. Several Jewish merchants flourished through trade with American ports, the West Indies, England, and West Africa. By far the most successful was Aaron Lopez, who emigrated from Portugal in 1752. He gained renown as a merchant, shipper, and manufacturer.

Congregation Yeshuat Yisrael (Salvation of Israel) was established in 1756, and land for a synagogue was purchased three years later. Peter Harrison, a Newporter and one of the colonies' most distinguished architects, designed an exquisite two-story brick building with a central *bimah* based on prototypes in Amsterdam and London. It accommodated approximately 30 Jewish households or 200 people, less than two percent of the town's population. Ezra Stiles, the Congregational minister who became president of Yale College, documented the synagogue's dedication in 1763 as well as other aspects of Jewish communal life. In 1773, Ḥayyim Caregal, a rabbi from Hebron in the Holy Land, preached in Newport. When it appeared in the *Newport Mercury*, his was the first Jewish sermon published in North America.

During the Revolution, Newport's Jews were loyalists and patriots. Most fled the lengthy British occupation.

In 1781, President George Washington visited the synagogue when it housed Rhode Island's General Assembly and Supreme Court. When he returned to Newport on August 17, 1790, Washington received a congratulatory letter from the Hebrew congregation, written by *ḥazzan* Moses Seixas, a fellow Mason. Washington's reply, perhaps America's most important expression of religious liberty, proclaimed "For happily, the government of the United States, which gives to bigotry no sanction, to persecution no assistance, requires only that they who live under its protection should discern themselves as good citizens, in giving it on all occasions their effectual support." The statement reflected the language of the invitation to Washington, but it help set the tone for religious liberty in the United States.

As Newport's economy continued to decline, however, Jews sought opportunities elsewhere. In 1822, Moses Lopez, the last Jew, departed for New York City.

The first reference to Touro synagogue occurred in 1824, when the nearby street, originally known as Griffin, was renamed Touro. Two years earlier, Abraham Touro provided funds to maintain the synagogue in memory of his father, Isaac, who had been the congregation's first *ḥazzan*. In 1854, the magnanimous bequest by Abraham's unmarried brother

Judah, of New Orleans, provided for the perpetual care of the synagogue and cemetery. Keith Stokes, a business leader and historian currently living in Newport, is a sixth-generation descendant of Judah Touro and his free African-American mistress, Ellen Wilson.

Although the synagogue reopened for summer visitors, it was not reconsecrated until 1883, when Rabbi Abraham Mendes arrived. Its ownership, retained by the founding families, was transferred to New York City's Shearith Israel in 1894. Though there were fewer than 100 Jewish families in Newport, two groups vied for Touro's use. An agreement reached in 1903 permitted Shearith Israel to lease the building to an Orthodox congregation of its choice and participate in the selection of a rabbi. The congregation's longest-serving clergy, beginning in the 1940s, were Cantor Ely Katz and Rabbi Theodore Lewis.

A second Orthodox congregation, Ahavas Achim, which existed from 1915 until 1981, participated in a United Hebrew School. In 1919 a YMHA was established, and in 1926 a historic house was moved to a site opposite Touro for use as a community center.

In 1946, largely through the efforts of Arthur Sulzberger, publisher of the *New York Times*, the synagogue was one of the first buildings designated a National Historic Site by the Interior Department. Though it was America's oldest surviving synagogue, Touro's recognition derived from the building's association with George Washington and its design by Peter Harrison. In 1982, Washington's 250th birthday was commemorated with a postage stamp showing Touro and quoting the "to bigotry no sanction" passage from his letter.

Touro's Society of Friends, which restored and helps maintain the building, has emphasized the synagogue's importance as a symbol of religious liberty. The reading of the Seixas and Washington letters has become an annual tradition. Numerous dignitaries have participated, including President Dwight D. Eisenhower and Justice Ruth Bader Ginsburg. Patriots' Park was built adjacent to the synagogue, and a visitors' center is planned.

Newport has been home to two of America's most successful summer music series. The Jazz Festival began in 1954, and the Folk Festival followed five years later. Both have featured numerous Jewish performers, and both have been produced by George Wein, a Jewish impresario.

In 2002, the Jewish population of Newport County was about 1,000. Rabbi Marc Jagolinzer was the long-time leader of Temple Shalom, a Conservative congregation in Middletown, which built its synagogue in 1978.

BIBLIOGRAPHY: S.F. Chyet, *Lopez of Newport: Colonial American Merchant Prince* (1970); G.M. Goodwin and E. Smith (eds.), *The Jews of Rhode Island* (2004).

[George M. Goodwin (2nd ed.)]

NEWSPAPERS, HEBREW.

This article is arranged according to the following outline:

The term "Hebrew press" has undergone a basic metamorphosis since its early days. Originally, the term covered periodicals of varying frequency (yearbooks, monthlies, and irregular publications), the majority of which were literary and scientific in character, while only a small percentage were devoted to current affairs. News sections were almost nonexistent, and indeed would have been impractical in periodicals appearing infrequently. The first Hebrew newspaper worthy of the name, according to the concept of the time, began to appear in the mid-19th century, giving news of the Jewish and general world and containing literary, scientific, and social columns. Articles on public and current affairs, which were rare in the Hebrew periodicals of the previous 100 years, became increasingly popular in some journals. Thus a differentiation was created between the newspaper and other types of periodicals. The periodicals, too, began to modify their form and gradually devoted more attention to current affairs.

All types of periodicals, therefore, must be included within the term "Hebrew press" in its first century (1750–1856). Following this period, a gradual differentiation set in between scholarly and literary periodicals and purely news media. This development was particularly noticeable in Ereẓ Israel where Hebrew became a living language, and periodicals began to appear, covering every field – literature, art, science, technology – while the daily newspaper grew to resemble its counterpart in European journalism.

THE SPREAD OF THE HEBREW PRESS

The Hebrew press began in Western Europe, mainly in Germany, in the second half of the 18th century. It gradually spread to Austria, and Galicia, and, a century after its initiation, appeared in czarist Russia, where there were more Hebrew readers. As the press began to flourish there, it declined in Western Europe. About the same time, a Hebrew press of an essentially Eastern European nature began to appear in Ereẓ Israel. The waves of Jewish emigration to the United States in the second half of the 19th century brought about the establishment of a Hebrew press in that country too (from the 1870s). Smaller centers of the Hebrew press were also established in England, South Africa, and, in later periods, in Latin America. Two factors determined the expansion or decline of the Hebrew press in the Diaspora: the degree of attachment to Hebrew of the Jews of a particular country, and the extent to which they acquired its native tongue. By the late 1930s the Hebrew press had almost disappeared in Eastern Europe. In Soviet Russia its decline had been deliberately encouraged, while in Poland it was brought about by competition from Polish and Yiddish. By contrast, the Hebrew press flourished in Ereẓ Israel: from modest beginnings in Jerusalem in 1863, it gradually and confidently expanded, becoming the focal point of the Hebrew press after World War I, with its center in Tel Aviv-Jaffa. Since World War II, the Hebrew press in Eastern Europe has ceased to exist; outside Israel, several periodicals are still published with varying frequency, mainly in the United States. A real Hebrew press, encompassing daily papers and periodicals covering a range of subjects, now exists only in Israel.

While, in its early years, the Hebrew press constituted only a small percentage of the total Jewish press in all languages, by the outbreak of World War II it held fourth place in the Jewish press (after English, German, and Yiddish). Today, as a result of the expansion of the Hebrew press in Israel, it holds second place (after English), and, quantitatively, accounts for more than one-quarter of the total Jewish press in all languages.

MAIN STAGES OF DEVELOPMENT

In Europe through the Early 1880s

One of the earliest consequences of the Haskalah movement in Germany was the creation of Hebrew periodicals, such as those published in Germany and devoted to literature, philosophy, and social problems. This initial stage, which lasted almost a century (approximately 1750–1856), was inaugurated by the periodical **Kohelet Musar*, edited by Moses *Mendelssohn. The differing intervals at which the variety of periodicals at this time were published was a decisive factor in determining the contents of those periodicals: much space was given over to belles lettres, translations, world literature, and various aspects of Judaic studies while very little was devoted to news matters. In this early period Hebrew began to adapt itself to modern expression, gradually discarding its cloak of sanctity and adopting neologisms and new literary forms. During the second stage (1856–86), current affairs were gradually introduced, at first by simply citing belatedly news items from other papers. Gradually, however, the traditions of the modern press developed, ranging from reports by regular correspondents to lead articles and political commentary, simultaneously continuing the traditions of the earlier Hebrew periodicals, by devoting considerable space to all subjects. The periodical press also continued to develop as before, improving its standards and its form. The interrelation between these two areas of the press is reflected in the fact that the same writers contributed to both. The Russian censorship constituted a great hindrance to the development of journalism on public affairs, and editors consequently became adept at disguising statements in phraseology whose hidden meaning was clear to their own readers. Hebrew papers appearing outside Russia were also compelled to restrain their political commentaries, since most of their readers lived in Russia, where the papers might be banned. This accounts for the remarkable panegyrics on the czarist regime, which should not be taken at face value.

IDEOLOGY OF THE EARLY PRESS. Up to the early 1880s, the main trend was the dissemination of the Haskalah and its program for attaining equal rights. This ideology resulted in several by-products: the appeal for the creation of a productive Jewish economy by means of agricultural settlement in Russia or by engaging in crafts, and for the improvement of Jewish education by replacing the old-fashioned methods of the *ḥeder* with the teaching of secular subjects and vocational skills. After the anti-Jewish pogroms in southern Russia in the early 1880s, however, Haskalah ideology changed, and almost all the newspapers and periodicals now supported the *Ḥibbat Zion movement. Only **Ha-Maggid* had anticipated this new ideology by 20 years. Attitudes to the movement ranged from hostility (*Ivri Anokhi*) or hesitant support (**Ha-Ẓefirah*) to complete identification (*Ha-Maggid* and later **Ha-Meliẓ*).

Throughout this period, the press gradually progressed technically, nurturing several generations of writers of all types. Indeed, there is hardly a Hebrew writer who did not take his first literary steps in one of the newspapers. Some outstanding writers, such as J.L. *Gordon, also served as editors, acting as patrons to many others.

Two events, however, disturbed the peace of the press. The first, in the late 1860s and early 1870s, was the controversy regarding religious reform, sparked by its two chief advocates, Moses Leib *Lilienblum and J.L. Gordon, mainly in *Ha-Meliẓ*, and taken up by the extreme and moderate Orthodox elements in **Ha-Levanon*. The second event, less significant at the time as regards public reaction and support, but important historically, was the appearance of the socialist organs, *Ha-Emet* and **Asefat Ḥakhamim*, edited by A.S. *Liebermann, Morris *Vinchevsky, and others. These journals attracted a considerable number of writers and contributors and served as a platform for those discontented with the czarist regime on the one hand, and with the traditional Jewish way of life on the other.

In Europe until World War I

The third stage in the Hebrew press was inaugurated by the establishment of the first Hebrew daily **Ha-Yom* edited by J.L. *Kantor (St. Petersburg) – a revolutionary event, the novelty of which is now hard to appreciate. For the first time the Hebrew press and the Hebrew language were faced with the challenge of dealing, journalistically and linguistically, with day-to-day events. *Ha-Yom* introduced many innovations and experiments. Despite the gradual disappearance of florid and involved phraseology (*meliẓah*) in all types of literature, it was still used in Hebrew journalistic writing. The new paper gradually eradicated its last traces. To meet the competition, *Ha-Ẓefirah* and *Ha-Meliẓ* also became dailies in the same year (1886). All at once, a tradition of modern Hebrew journalism developed. Although almost all the Hebrew papers now shared the ideology of Ḥibbat Zion, they varied both in their local color – *Ha-Ẓefirah* being Polish and *Ha-Meliẓ* Russian – and in their particular stands within the Ḥibbat Zion movement.

The Hebrew press of Eastern Europe had now reached a peak which it was to sustain until World War I. A modern press in the true sense of the word, it attracted the best Hebrew writers of almost three generations, and Hebrew literature, in turn, flourished, as it spread to the many and varied literary publications of the day. Both *Aḥad Ha-Am and *Bialik, key figures of Hebrew literature, were nurtured by this press. Though the first Russian Revolution (1905) temporarily halted this development, it resumed shortly afterward, ending only with World War I. There was a brief but glorious and unparalleled era in the history of the Hebrew press and periodicals in Russia after the fall of the czarist regime in 1917. However, the Soviet regime soon declared the Hebrew language counterrevolutionary and suppressed all Hebrew publication.

In Europe between the Wars

The former heights were never regained in Poland between the wars. In the 1930s, after a long struggle for survival, the only daily Hebrew paper ceased publication. It was replaced by the weekly *Ba-Derekh*, and there were years when only the pioneer youth movements maintained Hebrew newspapers in Poland. Some Hebrew journals survived within the framework of the underground movements in Nazi-occupied Poland, but ceased to exist after World War II. Through the efforts of determined individuals, the Hebrew press in other countries, such as England, survived, and appeared regularly for years (cf. Suwalski's *Ha-Yehudi*). But most of the papers and journals published outside Central Europe were short-lived, since their sole support came from emigrants from the East. As these readers acquired the language of their new country, circulation dropped, and the periodicals ceased publication. Apart from Ereẓ Israel, only in North America is there an uninterrupted tradition of Hebrew periodicals.

The one characteristic common to most Hebrew papers and periodicals over the years and throughout the world (with the exception of the extreme Orthodox and left-wing) is their strong attachment to Ḥibbat Zion, Zionism, and the State of Israel. There is an organic fusing of language and Israel content, overlapping their Jewish content. In this they are unique.

THE DURATION OF THE HEBREW PERIODICALS

Only a very small percentage of Hebrew newspapers and periodicals enjoyed longevity. The record until 1970 was held by the weekly **Ha-Po'el ha-Ẓa'ir* (63 years), the dailies **Haaretz* (57) and **Davar* (45) – all in Israel – and the weekly *Hadoar* (49) in the United States. In earlier periods the record was held by *Ha-Maggid* (47 years), *Ha-Ẓefirah* (almost 50, with short intervals), and *Ha-Meliẓ* (43). The latter two began as weeklies and later became dailies. The periodical **Ha-Shilo'aḥ* appeared in 46 volumes. Longevity is not always, however, an indication of the importance of the paper. Some short-lived papers, like the daily **Ha-Ẓofeh* at the turn of the 20th century, were of vital importance. There were also papers which appeared for decades under different names so as to evade censorship or because of licensing problems as was the case with *Ben-Yehuda's papers in Jerusalem.

THE LEADING PERIODICALS AND NEWSPAPERS IN EUROPE

The First Period: Yearbooks and Periodicals

Kohelet Musar, published by Mendelssohn (about 1750), was the first attempt at translating traditional ethical concepts into a modern idiom.

IN GERMANY. Although the initial experiment was short-lived, it was revived in 1783 by a group of Mendelssohn's disciples who published *Ha-Me'assef*, the first modern Hebrew periodical. Appearing sporadically in several German towns between 1783 and 1811, it had considerable influence on the general evolvement of Hebrew Haskalah literature and, in particular, on that of the Hebrew press, both in style (as "purely" biblical as possible) and content (e.g., original and translated belles lettres, and studies of various aspects of Judaism). *Ha-Me'assef* dealt extensively with current affairs, but its main goal – the attainment of the Haskalah – was achieved at a more rapid rate than the editors and participants had ever anticipated. German Jewry, accultured to its society, no longer needed a Hebrew journal. As a result, from the first third of the 19th century, the focal point of the Hebrew Haskalah began to shift to Austria, relying mainly upon readers in Galicia, Moravia, and Italy.

IN AUSTRO-HUNGARY. The new periodical press in Austro-Hungary, which both culturally (i.e., Jewish culture) and geographically lay on the border between West and East, was inaugurated by the yearbooks **Bikkurei ha-Ittim*, **Kerem Ḥemed*, *Kokhevei Yiẓḥak*, *Oẓar Neḥmad*, *Bikkurim* – which appeared for over 40 years (1821–65), mainly in Vienna, but also in Prague and Berlin. Varied in content, they attracted the best of the Haskalah writers. At the same time, periodicals and literary collections began to appear at regular intervals in various parts of Galicia, serving as a nursery for modern Hebrew literature by creating the science of Judaic studies and by adapting the Hebrew language to modern belles lettres. The pioneers of Hebrew periodicals in Germany and Austria were closely attached to the German language, as is evidenced by German sections (printed in Hebrew characters) in the first volumes of *Bikkurei ha-Ittim*, and by the many translations from that language. In contrast to the above-mentioned periodicals, which allotted little or no space to current events, *Zion*, edited by I.M. *Jost and M. *Creizenach, prevailed on East European writers to participate in discussions on contemporary affairs.

An examination of the language and style of these periodicals reveals how the Hebrew language developed in liveliness and suppleness from one issue to the next. Recent studies (particularly those by Dov *Sadan) of the florid *meliẓah* style of the early *maskilim* have demonstrated that this style did not, as was formerly believed, contain biblical elements exclusively, but rather drew from the linguistic and cultural traditions of centuries of Hebrew language and literature. As a result of the intimate acquaintance which the writers of this period had with the Bible and its study over the generations, their biblical commentaries are full of valuable insights. Since, in general, the periodical press was imbued with the spirit of the moderate Haskalah, elements from all movements could contribute to it, and it managed to remain as neutral as possible, apart from sharp polemics against extreme Reform Judaism as practiced by *Geiger. This tradition of neutrality was maintained in the Hebrew press outside Ereẓ Israel as a rule, although there were periodicals that expressed more extreme views, e.g., the extreme Orthodox *Shomer Ẓiyyon ha-Ne'eman*, and the radical **He-Ḥalutz*.

The Second Period: Early Newspapers

These periodicals constituted a 100-year-long preparation for a regular journal with the form and content of a newspaper. Such a newspaper, *Ha-Maggid*, which appeared in 1856 in Lyck, eastern Prussia, on the Russian border, thus inaugurating the second period of the Hebrew press, was meant for Russian Jewry. The only periodical which Russian Jewry had hitherto produced, *Pirkei Ẓafon*, enjoyed only two issues (1841 and 1844) before it ceased publication. With *Ha-Maggid* A.L. Silbermann, the editor, created not only a new organ for Russian Jewry but also the first Hebrew newspaper that devoted considerable space to reportage and editorial comment on the news. As such, the new paper required different tools from those employed in earlier periodicals. It also introduced other innovations, e.g., a section containing translations of news items from the general press which are to be found in almost every issue; other periodicals followed suit. The Hebrew language gradually evolved into a living language, even though it retained a considerable amount of *meliẓah*. *Ha-Maggid* was also the pioneer in two other aspects: in the early 1860s it began to advocate Ḥibbat Zion and the settlement of Ereẓ Israel, while all the other newspapers remained attached to the Haskalah ideology till the early 1880s; for many years it was the only paper of general Jewish character that reflected events in all the Jewish communities, including the United States and Australia. Immediately after its establishment, four other newspapers sprang up (1860–62), which dealt primarily with events in their own geographical area: *Ha-Meliẓ* (Odessa-St. Petersburg) for Russian Jewry; **Ha-Karmel* (Vilna) for Lithuanian Jewry; *Ha-Mevasser* (LVOV) for the Jews of Galicia; and *Ha-Ẓefirah* (Warsaw and, for a short period, Berlin) for Polish Jews. (Originally devoted to science, *Ha-Ẓefirah's* later concern, under the editorship of *Sokolow, was primarily news.) All these newspapers covered current events, but likewise continued their traditions by devoting special columns to belles lettres, science, and criticism, so that even today it is difficult to envisage a Hebrew paper without such columns. These papers still constitute a rich source for Jewish scholarship; only the lack of indexes prevents their being utilized properly. The papers also stimulated additional literary forms, for which there had not been room in periodicals, and developed reportage from provincial towns and, later, from overseas. Although this reportage may contain trivia, it also constitutes an extremely rich source of information on Jewish communities throughout the world.

LINGUISTIC AND IDEOLOGICAL DEVELOPMENT. A superficial comparison of a newspaper of 1856 with one of 1886 is sufficient proof of the radical development of the Hebrew press in this second stage. A new language had been created which differed greatly from that of *Ha-Me'assef* or even *Ha-Maggid* in their first years. There was also a change in the ideological content. Reality, and particularly the pogroms in southern Russia in the early 1880s, made Jews aware of the failure of the Haskalah's proposed solutions to the Jewish problem. There was, therefore, a gradual transition from the old ideals of the Haskalah and the Emancipation to the new ones of settlement of Ereẓ Israel, Zionism and, finally, political Zionism.

The distinction between the periodical press and newspapers was still obscure, since current affairs began to play a more important role in the former. Such was the case with *Smolenskin's monthly **Ha-Shaḥar*, in which an attempt was made, particularly by the editor himself, to clarify Jewish problems, both past and future, and which first arrived at the ideology of "the people of the spirit." It then took up nationalism and Zionism, strongly criticizing the Haskalah and its methods. The same is true of its rival, *Ha-Boker Or*, edited by A.B. *Gottlober, which defended Mendelssohn's school of thought. The articles on Judaica in these publications became more popular and readable as a result of the growing flexibility of the language, while their scientific basis was not impaired.

Hebrew Dailies

In the meantime, the editors were obliged to enlarge the format of their papers and to produce them at greater frequency than the original weeklies. In 1886, exactly 30 years after the publication of the first issue of *Ha-Maggid*, J.L. Kantor published *Ha-Yom*, the first Hebrew daily. To meet the competition, *Ha-Meliẓ* and *Ha-Ẓefirah* also began to be published as dailies. The letters of J.L. Gordon (then editor of *Ha-Meliẓ*), who frowned upon this new development, show the difficulties that faced Hebrew editors. Conditions, however, forced them to accept the new burden. In the daily press it was essential to eliminate florid Hebrew, since the need for rapid translations of news dispatches left no time for complicated phraseology.

From 1886, the feuilleton which had existed before the development of the daily press became an integral part of the dailies, particularly of *Ha-Yom*, to which D. Frischmann and J.L. *Katzenelson (known as Buki ben Yogli) contributed. *Ha-Meliẓ* and *Ha-Ẓefirah* continued, of necessity, to appear as dailies even after *Ha-Yom* ceased publication (1888). The oldest of the papers, *Ha-Maggid*, remained a weekly, until discontinued in 1903.

In the mid-1880s, Sokolow – a man whose grasp of the spirit of the times was almost unique in his generation of Hebrew journalism – radically changed the periodical press. In 1884 he began to publish *Ha-Asif*, weighty annuals encompassing almost all the literary forms. Enjoying unprecedented circulation, their success spurred others to issue similar annuals (e.g., *Keneset Yisrael* by S.P. *Rabinowitz, 1886). It was a new development for Hebrew periodicals to reach thousands of readers, all of them subscribers. The publication of *Ha-Asif* is therefore frequently regarded as the first literary event which created a mass Hebrew readership. Innumerable periodicals, almost all of them short-lived, appeared in the last third of the 19th century in various places in Eastern Europe, and, occasionally in the West (mainly on Judaica or as appendixes to the German Jewish press). An important contribution to the rapid adaptation of Hebrew to everyday life was made by the numerous translations in the press, periodicals, and separate books, some of which were to become classics (particularly in the field of poetry). In the early 1880s even the Orthodox *Ha-Levanon* ceased its ideological polemics with the other papers and, because of its editor, J. *Brill, joined in preaching the settlement of Ereẓ Israel and Ḥibbat Zion. Simultaneously, an Orthodox anti-Zionist press arose, e.g., *Ha-Peles, Ha-Modi'a, Ha-Kol*, which copied the modern style of the pro-Zionist press. In the 1870s the first two Hebrew socialist journals appeared, *Ha-Emet*, and *Asefat Ḥakhamim*, edited by A.S. Liebermann, M. Vinchevsky, and others. These journals, which were short-lived because of the attitude of the East and West European authorities, created a new Hebrew by introducing terms taken from socialism and communism, and by translations.

At the beginning of the present century, the two veteran papers, *Ha-Maggid* and *Ha-Meliẓ*, closed down. As if to symbolize the rise of a new and younger generation in literature and in the press, two new dailies were established in Poland and Russia: *Ha-Ẓofeh*, in Warsaw, and *Ha-Zeman*, first in St. Petersburg, later in Vilna. A new generation of writers and journalists was nurtured by these papers. *Ha-Ẓofeh* was the first paper to hold a literary competition (1903). In that competition Y.D. *Berkowitz was discovered. At the same time, *Ha-Ẓefirah* reappeared after a lengthy interval. In 1904 the weekly **Ha-Mizpeh*, edited by S.M. Lazar, began to appear in Cracow, in place of *Ha-Maggid*, and encouraged many new writers (including S.Y. *Agnon, A. *Hameiri, U.Ẓ. *Greenberg, and Z. *Diesendruck). In none of these papers was there a clear distinction between the literary and journalistic realms. The best of the Hebrew writers of the period contributed to them (e.g., *Fichmann, *Bershadsky, *Shneour, Berkowitz).

The End of the Hebrew Press in Eastern Europe and Russia

The most outstanding of these literary periodicals was the monthly, *Ha-Shilo'aḥ*, edited by Aḥad Ha-Am and, later, by J. Klausner; others included *Ha-Dor*, edited by Frischmann, *Ha-Zeman*, the annuals *Lu'aḥ Aḥi'asaf* and Sokolow's *Sefer ha-Shanah*. **Ha-Olam*, the official Hebrew organ of the Zionist Organization, for decades provided opportunities for Hebrew writers. It would be hard to envisage the development of the young Hebrew literature that flourished at this time – starting with Bialik – without the periodicals of the early 20th century. Although this vital period came to an abrupt end with the outbreak of World War I, its influence could be felt almost until the 1960s. The Hebrew press in Eastern Europe never recovered its former glory after World War I but gradually flickered out. In Russia, after the downfall of czarism, Hebrew literary activity flourished briefly with the appearance of the literary journals **Ha-Tekufah, Massu'ot, He-Avar, Ha-Mishpat ha-Ivri, Ereẓ*, and others, and the establishment of literary projects of formerly unknown scope (e.g., Stybel publishing house). The weekly *Ha-Am*, which later became a daily, also began to appear in this period. Soviet Russia's silencing of the Hebrew language, however, put an end to all this, a circumstance which has persisted, apart from certain isolated periodicals published in Russia, or published abroad by Russian Hebrew writers. The departure from Russia of the great majority of Hebrew writers, beginning with Bialik, marks the end of Hebrew literature and journalism in that country, and the gradual shift of its focal point to Palestine, via Berlin.

The papers and literary journals set up in Western Europe from the turn of the century till the 1930s and 1940s were a natural continuation of the Eastern European tradition. With one notable exception – *Ha-Yehudi*, edited in London from 1897 to 1913 by I. Suwalski – they were all short-lived. Another London-based journal, whose effect was in inverse ratio to its duration, was J.Ḥ. *Brenner's *Ha-Me'orer (1906–07).

While the extreme Orthodox circles, having adopted methods of the secular press, attacked Zionism, the press of the Orthodox *Mizrachi Zionist Organization, which opposed the secular movement, fought anti-Zionist Orthodox elements. It established the monthly *Ha-Mizraḥ* (1903) as well as the weeklies *Ha-Ivri* (first in Berlin and later in New York) and *Ha-Mizraḥi* in Poland after World War I.

Toward the end of the 19th century the Hebrew press in Eastern Europe began to produce more specialized journals. An educational press which lasted for decades was developed in Russia and Poland; magazines for children and youth began to appear, some of them of extremely high standard, such as *Olam Katan*, edited by S.L. *Gordon. I.H. Tawiow even put out a daily for children (*He-Ḥaver*; see *Children's Literature). Poland became the major Hebrew center in Eastern Europe between the wars after that language had been silenced in Soviet Russia. Its one Hebrew daily, however, *Ha-Ẓefirah*, could not survive in the face of the growing competition from Yiddish, on the one hand, and Polish, on the other. *Ha-Ẓefirah* closed down, was revived under another name (*Ha-Yom*), revived again under its old name, and finally discontinued in the early 1930s. For several years, it was replaced by the weekly, *Ba-Derekh*, the last Hebrew paper in Poland, which later also closed down.

A unique phenomenon, particularly in Poland between the wars, was the press of the *He-Ḥalutz and the pioneering youth movements, especially that of Ha-Shomer *ha-Ẓa'ir. At a time when Hebrew was abandoned in Poland even by the official Zionist Organization (the press of which was mainly in Yiddish and Polish), and Hebrew readers could no longer support the burden of maintaining a Hebrew paper, the youth movements safeguarded Hebrew expression (and speech) with unbounded loyalty and material sacrifice. For these young people, the Hebrew language and pioneer training were stepping stones to Zionist self-realization. Thus He-Ḥalutz issued the paper *He-Atid*, and Ha-Shomer ha-Ẓair, its organ, bearing that movement's name; other youth movements followed suit. This press was noted for its ties with Ereẓ Israel and its constant contact with the labor press there.

[Getzel Kressel]

THE HEBREW PRESS IN NORTH AMERICA

Unlike the Anglo-Jewish, German-Jewish, and Yiddish presses in the United States, all of which have served large bodies of readers who often were literate in their native tongue alone, the Hebrew press was restricted from the outset to a relatively small coterie of subscribers. Nevertheless, a Hebrew periodical press has existed practically uninterrupted in the United States since the last decades of the 19th century.

The first Hebrew periodical in the United States, Zvi Hirsch *Bernstein's newsletter *Ha-Ẓofeh ba-Areẓ ha-Ḥadashah* ("The Observer in a New Land") appeared in 1871, a year after the first two Yiddish journals in America, one of which was Bernstein's New York *Juedische Post*. In their early years, in fact, the two presses frequently had intertwined fates: the same publishers, editors, and writers played active roles in both. *Ha-Ẓofeh ba-Areẓ ha-Ḥadashah* appeared irregularly until 1876. Hebrew was also one of four languages to appear in Bernstein's *Hebrew News*, an unusual polyglot venture published for several months in 1871.

A number of Hebrew periodicals appeared briefly in New York in the 1880s and 1890s, many of them largely one-man productions. Among them were the Ḥovevei Zion organ *Ha-Le'ummi* ("The Nationalist," 1888–89), the *maskil* Ezekiel Enowitz's *Ha-Emet* ("The Truth," 1894–95) and *Eẓ ha-Da'at* ("The Tree of Knowledge," 1896), Michael *Rodkinson's *Ha-Sanegor* ("The Defender," 1890) and *Tekhunat Ru'aḥ ha-Yisre'eli* ("The Spirit of the Israelite," 1899), and Abraham *Rosenberg's *Ner ha-Ma'aravi* ("The Western Light," 1895–97). Somewhat longer lived were Zeev Wolf *Schur's *Ha-Pisgah* ("The Summit"), published irregularly in New York, Baltimore, and Chicago from 1891 to 1899, and *Ha-Ivri* ("The Hebrew," 1892–98, 1901–02), which was founded by the Yiddish publisher Kasriel *Sarasohn and edited by Gershon Rosenzweig.

The first attempt to publish a Hebrew daily in the U.S. took place in New York in 1909 with the appearance of *Ha-Yom* ("The Day") under the editorship of Moses Hacohen *Goldman, but the paper failed within a brief time, as did an effort to revive it in 1913. The latter year also witnessed the launching of the literary monthly *Ha-Toren* ("The Mast," weekly from 1916 to 1921), which in quality of contents and regularity of appearance far surpassed any of its predecessors. Edited originally by a staff composed of such eminent Hebraists as Max *Lipson, Daniel *Persky, Abraham *Goldberg, Y.D. Berkowitz, and Benjamin *Silkiner, *Ha-Toren* was managed from 1919 until its demise in 1925 by the author Reuben *Brainin. Contemporary with it was the literary and political Mizrachi weekly *Ha-Ivri* ("The Hebrew," New York, 1916–21), edited by Meir *Berlin, who had previously managed the same journal in Germany.

The most successful and permanent of all Hebrew periodicals in the United States, however, was the weekly *Hadoar* ("The Post"). Started as a daily in 1921 by a staff directed by Lipson and including Persky, Hirsch Leib *Gordon, Abraham Orlans, and Menachem *Ribalow, *Hadoar* was briefly discontinued in the summer of 1922 and then resumed publication as a weekly under the auspices of the *Histadruth Ivrith of America. In 1925 Menachem Ribalow became sole editor, a position he held for nearly 30 years. During this period, except for a brief hiatus in 1925, *Hadoar* appeared every week in spite of continual financial straits, publishing Hebrew authors of note from all over the world and especially numbering among its steady contributors such U.S. Hebrew writers as Hillel *Bavli, Moshe *Feinstein, Reuven *Grossman, Simon *Halkin, Ephraim *Lisitzky, Daniel Persky, Gabriel *Preil, Abraham *Regelson, Zvi *Scharfstein, Eisig *Silberschlag, Yochanan *Twersky, Meyer *Waxman, and Reuven *Wallenrod. From 1934, *Hadoar* issued a biweekly youth supplement titled *Ha-Musaf la-Kore ha-Ẓa'ir*. Ribalow was succeeded as editor in 1953 by Moses *Maisels, who was in turn followed in 1959 by Moshe Yinon. *Hadoar's* circulation in 1970 was about 5,000. It attempted to reconstitute as a quality journal but was unsuccessful. It ceased publication in the early 21st century.

In addition to *Hadoar*, the literary monthly *Bitzaron* was published in New York from 1939 until 1992. Though the establishment of the State of Israel led to a broadening of interest in Hebrew among the U.S. Jewish public, the local Hebrew press has not grown as a result; the reasons are many. Air transportation has allowed the quick distribution of Israeli publications in the United States. Additionally, American Hebraists preferred to write for the much larger Israeli audience and also to read the best of Hebrew literature in Israeli publications. The introduction of the Internet made some Hebrew language publications in the United States superfluous. Some Hebrew newspapers are published in the United States, primarily in New York and Los Angeles, for the Israeli community living the United States. Printed locally, they most often contain reprints of articles that have appeared in Israeli newspapers and advertisements aimed at the local American-Israeli community.

For Hebrew newspapers in Ereẓ Israel and the State of Israel, see *Israel, State of: Cultural Life (Press).

BIBLIOGRAPHY: F.M. Brody, *AJHSP*, 33 (1934), 127–70; M.G. Brown, *AJHSQ*, 59 (1969), 139–78; D. Persky, *Sefer ha-Yovel shel Hadoar* (1952); H.M. Rotblatt, *The Chicago Pinkas* (1952); E.R. Malachi, *Hadoar*, 12 (1931–32), 515, 533, 548; 13 (1932–33), 44, 76, 140.

[Hillel Halkin / Michael Berenbaum (2nd ed.)]

LIST OF HEBREW NEWSPAPERS AND PERIODICALS

Since the 1920s the Hebrew press, particularly in Ereẓ Israel, has greatly and rapidly developed. From the point of view of quantity it exceeds, several fold, all the Hebrew press from its beginning until that time. Consequently, the following list is, of necessity, very selective and only the outstanding Hebrew newspapers and periodicals in all the countries and periods have been included. One of the aims of the list has been to provide a representative sampling of the vast professional and light literature press in the State of Israel, a sampling which is likewise very selective.

Jubilee and memorial volumes, periodicals of all types of educational institutions (from primary school to university), newspapers issued by individual settlements in Israel (of which there are hundreds), house organs of institutions, organizations, factories, and social and political movements, etc. have not been included. There is however a small sampling of Israel governmental publications: for the rest see *Reshimat Pirsumei ha-Memshalah* ("List of Government Publications") which appears quarterly.

The dates of the newspapers listed present a special problem in that it has not always been possible to transalte the Hebrew date accurately because the Hebrew year starts with Rosh Ha-Shanah (which usually falls in September) whereas the secular year starts on January 1. Another problem has been that of the continuity of many of the publications; some newspapers and periodicals did (or do) not actually appear with the regularity claimed and thus many items are described as "irregular." A large number of newspapers are unavailable and have not been litsted; for others of this kind, which have been listed, no exact statistics have been recorded.

Notwithstanding the above factors, however, the list does reflect the scope and nature of the Hebrew press of the last 300 years.

Abbreviations used are:

A. = Annual
B-M. = Bimonthly
B-W. = Biweekly
D. = Daily
F. = Fortnightly
Irr. = Irregular
Jer. = Jerusalem
Lit. = Literary
M. = Monthly
N.S. = New Series
N.Y. = New York
Q. = Quarterly
S-A. = Semiannual
T.A. = Tel Aviv
W. = Weekly

1901–1940 indicates that the item appeared from 1901 until 1904; 1901, 1904 indicates that the item appeared in each of these two years only.

Title	Freq.	Place of Publication	Year(s) of Appearance	Main Characteristics
A.B.	F.	Holon	1969	the first Samaritan newspaper
Adrikhalut	Q.		1966	architecture, city planning, engineering, interior design, and construction arts
Aḥdut – see also: Ha-Aḥdut Le-Aḥdut ha-Avodah				
Aḥdut ha-Avodah	1	Jaffa	1919	the first organ of the Aḥdut ha-Avodah party
Aḥdut ha-Avodah	M.	T.A.	1930–1932	lit., Mapai
Aḥdut ha-Avodah	1–4	T.A.	1943–1946	collections of issues related to Mapai
Aḥi'asaf – see: Lu'aḥ Aḥi'asaf				
Akhsanyah	1	T.A.	1955	lit.
Akhshav	Irr.	Jer.	1957	lit.
Akrav	W.	T.A.	1946–1947	humor and satire
Al Admat Bessarabyah	Irr.	T.A.	1959–1963	history of Bessarabian Jewry, 3 vols.
Alef	1	Lvov, Galicia	1937	lit.
Alef	Irr.	T.A.	1938	organ of the Ha-Ivrim movement (Canaanities)
Aleh	M.	T.A.	1959	youth organ of the Iḥud ha-Kevuẓot ve-ha-Kibbutzim; continuation of Nivim, 1951–59
Alei Hadas	1–4	Odessa, Russia	1865	lit.
Alei Mishmeret	Q.	T.A.	1958	organ of the National Religious Party Youth
Alei Si'aḥ	1–3	T.A.	1966–1967	literary circles of the Iḥud ha-Kevuẓot ve-ha-Kibbutzim
Al ha-Ḥomah	M.	T.A.	1938	organ of Ha-Shomer ha-Ẓa'ir; appeared under various other titles
Al ha-Mishmar	W.	Jer.	1922–1923	nonpartisan
Al ha-Mishmar	D.	T.A.	1943–2005	originally Mishmar, organ of Ha-Kibbutz ha-Arẓi Ha-Shomer ha-Ẓa'ir; from 1948 Al ha-Mishmar, Ḥotam organ of Mapam; from 1970 also weekly magazine
Al ha-Saf	1	Jer.	1918	the last organ of Po'alei Zion in Ereẓ Israel before it merged with Aḥdut ha-Avodah
Al Ḥuk ha-Mikra	1–4	T.A.	1947–1954	biblical research
Alil	1–2	N.Y.	1946–1947	lit.
Alim	1	Kiev, Ukraine	1912	lit.
Alim	Irr.	Jer.	1939–1956	Youth Aliyah; ceased publication in 1956 and renewed in 1970
Alim	Irr.	T.A.	1951–1963	theoretical organ of the Ha-No'ar ha-Ẓiyyoni movement.

Title	Freq.	Place of Publication	Year(s) of Appearance	Main Characteristics
Alim le Bibliografyah u-le-Safranut	B-M.	T.A.	1947–1948	bibliography and librarianship; first volume published under the names Yad la-Safran and Ha-Safran
Alim le Bibliografyah ve-Korot Yisrael	Irr.	Vienna	1934–1937	bibliography and Jewish history
Aliyah	Irr.	Jer.	1934–1937 1969	published by the Aliyah Department of the Jewish Agency
Almanakh ha-Ishah	A.	T.A.	1961–1965	women's almanac
Almanakh Mizpeh	1	T.A.	1930	literary almanac of the Mizpeh Publishing House
Alonekh	M.	T.A.	1950–1963	women's publication
Alon ha-Congress	Q.	T.A.	1967	published by the Israel branch of the World Jewish Congress
Alon ha-Dayyagim	Q.	Haifa	1951–1962	bulletin on fisheries; superseded by Dayig u-Midgeh
Alon ha-Ḥevrah ha-Numismatit	Q.	T.A.	1966	numismatics
Alon ha-Note'a	M.	T.A.	1945	cultivating fruit trees
Alon ha-Palmaḥ	Irr.	T.A.	1942–1950	illegal organ of the Palmaḥ; without a masthead and no mention of an address
Alon ha-Shofetim	Irr.	T.A.	1963	bulletin of soccer referees
Alon ha-Shomerim	Irr.	T.A.	1935–1957	organ of the Association of Guards
Alon ha-Tenu'ah ha-Bein-le'ummit le-Sarevanei Milḥamah mi-Ta'amei Mazpun	Irr.	T.A.	1949–1959 1963–1964	bulletin of the international movement of conscientious objectors
Alonim (Kibbutz Dati) – see: Ammudim				
Alon Kibbutzei ha-Shomer ha-Ẓa'ir	M.	T.A.	1965	economic problems of the settlements organized in Ha-Kibbutz ha-Arẓi ha-Shomer ha-Ẓa'ir
Alon Mishkei ha-Iḥud	Irr.	T.A.	1963	economic problems of the settlements organized in Iḥud ha-Kevuẓot ve-ha-Kibbutzim
Alon Mishkei ha-Kibbutz ha-Me'uḥad	Irr.	T.A.	1961	economic problems of the settlements organized in ha-Kibbutz ha-Me'uḥad
Al Penei Kaddur ha-Areẓ	1	T.A.	1943	view of the world during World War II
Al Saf ha-Maḥar	1	T.A.	1945	problems of the post-World War II period
Alummah	1	Jer.	1936	research in Judaic studies
Almmanah	1	Jer.	1939	research in Judaic studies
Almmanah	A.	Jer.	1956–1957	Torah culture
Ammot	B-M	T.A.	1962–1965	lit. and Jewish problems
Ammud ha-Yirah	Irr.	Jer.	1879–1880	ultra-Orthodox organ devoted to propaganda for the settlement of Ereẓ Israel; previously published in Hungary
Ammudim	W.	T.A.	1944–1947	new Aliyah
Ammudim	Irr.	T.A.	1955	organ of Kibbutz Dati
Am u-Medinah	W.	Jer.	1950–1951	general affairs
Am va-Sefer	Irr.	Jer.-T.A.	1936	Hebrew culture in Ereẓ Israel and the Diaspora; published by Brit Ivrit Olamit; continuation of Berit Am
Am ve-Admato	Q.	Jer.	1963	problems of land settlement; organ of the Jewish National Fund; continuation of Karnenu
Anakh	1	T.A.	1954	lit.
Appiryon	M.	N.Y.	1923–1927	rabbinics; printed in Hungary
Arakhim	1	Warsaw	1919	lit.
Arakhim	Irr.	T.A.	1968–1969	collections for holidays and festivals published by the Religious Department of the Histadrut
Arakhim	Irr.	T.A.	1969	ideological organ of the New Communist Party (Rakaḥ)
Areshet	1	Jer.	1944	lit. organ of religious writers
Aresheth	A.	Jer.	1958	bibliography and Hebrew booklore
Ari'el	W.	Jer.	1874–1877	newspaper published by former members of the editorial board of Ḥavaẓẓelet
Arkhitekturah – see: Adrikhalut				
Asefat Ḥakhamim	M.	Koenigsberg, E. Prussia	1877–1878	the second socialist periodical in Hebrew (after Ha-Emet); officially a supplement to Ha-Kol
Aspaklaryah	M.	N.Y.	1904	lit.
Aspaklaryah	W.	Jer.	1922–1923	lit. and general affairs
Aspaklaryah	M.	T.A.	1938–1947	digest of Hebrew and non-Hebrew newspapers in Ereẓ Israel and abroad
Aspaklaryah shel ha-Sport	W.	T.A.	1946–1948	sports

Title	Freq.	Place of Publication	Year(s) of Appearance	Main Characteristics
Asuppot	Irr.	T.A.	1945	history of Ereẓ Israel and Jewish labor movement
At	M.	T.A.	1967	women's magazine
Atidenu	M.	Berlin	1924	culture and education
Atidenu	M.	Buenos Aires	1926–1927	lit. and current affairs
Atidot	Irr.	T.A.	1944–1959	lit. for youth; frequency of publication changed several times
Attikot	Irr.	Jer.	1946	archaeology
Avaryanut ve-Ḥevrah	A.	Jer.	1966	delinquency; first year semiannually
Avodah u-Vittu'aḥ Le'ummmi	M.	Jer.	1949	labor and national insurance
Ayin	W.	T.A.	1951–1952	lit.
Ayin be-Ayin	W.	Jer.	1958–1959	religious illustrated magazine; superseded by Panim el Panim
Ba-Avodah	1	Jaffa	1918	first publication edited by Berl Katznelson general affairs
Ba-Derekh	F.	Vienna	1920–1921	general affairs
Ba-Derekh	W.	Warsaw	1935–1937	the last Hebrew newspaper in Poland
Ba-Derekh	A.	Givat Ḥavivah-Merḥavyah	1967	Jewish labor movement in Israel and abroad
Ba-Derekh (communist) – see: Zo ha-Derekh				
Ba-Histadrut	M.	T.A.	1943–1970	weekly review of all Histadrut activities; called Pinkas li-Fe'ilei ha-Histadrut during first year of publication; ceased publication in 1960 and renewed in 1962; ceased publication in 1970
Ba-Kefar	M.	T.A.	1947–1952	organ of agricultural workers
Ba-Kibbutz	W.	T.A.	1950	information weekly of Ha-Kibbutz ha-Me'uḥad
Ba-Kibbutz ha-Arẓi – see: Ha-Shavu'a ba-Kibbutz ha-Arẓi				
Ba-Kur	F.	T.A.	1931	organ of Ha-No'ar ha-Oved; seven issues published 1927–30
Ba-Ma'arakhah	W.	Jer.	1931–1934	extreme anti-Mandatory publication
Ba-Ma'arakhah	Irr.	Jer.	1948, 1961–	problems of Sephardi Jews (see also: Shevet va-Am)
Ba-Ma'avar	1–4	Warsaw	1925	published by Hitaḥadut in Poland
Bamah	B-M.	Jer.	1933–1948 1959	theatrical review
Ba-Maḥaneh	W.	T.A.	1948	published by Israel Defense Forces; formerly published underground in mimeographed form
Bamat ha-Ishah	Q.	T.A.	1960	published by WIZO
Ba-Mesillah	M.	T.A.	1946–1947	published by Mizrachi
Ba-Midgeh	M.	Nir David	1948	fisheries; continuation of Alon li-Megaddelei Dagim
Ba-Mifal	M.	Haifa	1942–1950	industrial Histadrut
Ba-Mifneh	F.	T.A.	1935–1940	published by Left Po'alei Zion; formerly collections published for special occasions under this title
Ba-Mishor	W.	Jer.	1940–1946	lit., religious
Ba-Mivḥan	M.	T.A.	1943	published by Maḥanot ha-Olim, Deror, Tenu'at ha-No'ar ha-Ḥalutzi; appeared irregularly from the 1930s to the 1940s
Ba-Nativ	M.	Jer.	1951–1955	aviation club publication
Ba-Nekhar	1	Alexandria, Egypt	1918	published by Palestinian refugees in Egypt during World War I
Ba-Rekhev	M.	T.A.	1955	transportation
Bar-Ilan	A.	Ramat Gan	1963	Judaica and humanities
Barkai	Irr.	Vienna	1886	lit.
Barkai	W.	Odessa, Russia	1919	lit.
Barkai	F.	Johannesburg	1933	lit.; a few first numbers called Ba-Sad
Ba-Sa'ar	1	T.A.	1943	lit.; Hebrew writers for Jewish soldiers
Ba-Sha'ar	F.	T.A.	1947–1952	Youth Movement of Mapam
Ba-Sha'ar	M. & B-M.	T.A.	1958	ideological organ of Mapam
Ba-Telem	Irr.	T.A.	1954–1960	published for moshavim of new immigrants
Bat Kol	D., W.	Cracow-Lvov, Galicia	1911–1914	lit., religious
Be'ad ve-Neged	B-M.	Jer.	1963	social and political problems

Title	Freq.	Place of Publication	Year(s) of Appearance	Main Characteristics
Be'ayot	M.	Jer.	1944–1949	Jewish-Arab cooperation; continuation of Be'ayot ha-Yom
Be'ayot Beinle'ummiyyot	Q.	T.A.	1963	international affairs, underdeveloped countries
Be'ayot ha-Ḥinnukh ha-Meshuttaf	Q.	T.A.	1937	pedagogical organ of Ha-Kibbutz ha-Arẓi Ha-Shomer ha-Ẓa'ir
Be'ayot ha-Yom				Jewish-Arab cooperation, superseded by Be'ayot
Be-Ḥakla'ut u-va-Meshek	M.	T.A.	1960–1995	labor and output
Beḥinot	1–11	Jer.	1952–1955	literary criticism
Beḥinot	Irr.	T.A.	1970	studies of Russian and East European Jews
Beinetayim	1	Jer.	1913	lit.
Bein ha-Meẓarim	1–2	Jer.	1915	organ of Po'alei Zion during World War I
Bein ha-Zemannim	1	Safed	1916	organ of Po'alei Zion during World War I
Bein ha-Zemannim	1–2	Kharkov, Ukraine	1918–1919	lit.
Bein Milḥamah ve-Shalom	1	T.A.	1945	post World War II political problems
Beitar	M.	Jer.	1933–1934	lit.; Revisionist
Beit Eked	1	Berdichev, Ukraine	1892	lit.
Beit ha-Keneset	1	Jer.	1955	studies of synagogues
Beit ha-Midrash	M.	Vienna	1865	Judaic studies
Beit ha-Midrash	1	Cracow, Poland	1888	rabbinics and Judaic studies
Beit ha-Midrash he-Ḥadash	M.	Grajewo, Poland	1928–1931	Judaic studies
Beit Mikra	Q.	Jer.	1956	Bible studies
Beit Oẓar ha-Sifrut – see: Oẓar ha-Sifrut				
Beit Talmud	1–5	Vienna	1881–1889	studies of rabbinic literature
Beit Va'ad la-Ḥakhamim	M.	Grosswardein (Oradea), Transylvania	1875	Judaic studies
Beit Va'ad la-Ḥakhamim	M.	London-Leeds	1902–1904	rabbinics and Judaic studies
Beit Va'ad la-Ḥakhamim	M.	N.Y.	1903	rabbinics
Beit Va'ad la-Ḥakhamim		Satu Mare (Szatmar), Transylvania	1922–1939	rabbinics
Beit Ya'akov	M.	Jer.	1959	education and lit., religious
Beit Yiẓhak	A.	N.Y.	1952–1961	
Beivar	Q.	T.A.	1959	zoo
Be-Maḥaneh Gadna	M.	T.A.	1949	organ of the *Gadna
Be-Maḥaneh Naḥal	M.	T.A.	1949	organ of the *Naḥal
Be-Misholei ha-Ḥinnukh	Irr.	Kaunas (Kovno), Lithuania	1936–1940	pedagogy
Ben Ammi	M.	St. Petersburg	1887	lit.
Bereshit	1	Moscow-Leningrad	1926	lit.; printed in Berlin
Beri'ut	F.	T.A.	1933–1935	health
Beri'ut ha-Am	Q.	Jer.	1926–1927	health
Beri'ut ha-Oved	Irr.	T.A.	1924–1929	workers' health
Beri'ut ha-Ẓibbur	Q.	Jer.	1958	health
Be-Sha'ah Zu	1–3	Jaffa	1916	organ of Ha-Po'el ha-Ẓa'ir during World War I
Be-Sherut ha-Ezaḥ	Q.	T.A.	1957	Magen David Adom in Israel
Be-Sherut ha-Ta'asukah	B-M.	Ramat Gan	1959	problems of employment
Be-Terem	M., F., Q.	T.A.	1942–1960	semilegal organ of the Haganah; originally called Milḥamtenu and also known by other titles until the establishment of the State of Israel
Betiḥut	M.	T.A.	1957	safety and hygiene at work
Be-Ẓok ha-Ittim	1	Safed	1919	lit.
Bikkoret ha-Ittim	Irr.	Leipzig, Germany	1864–1865	the first humor and satire periodical in Hebrew

Title	Freq.	Place of Publication	Year(s) of Appearance	Main Characteristics
Bikkoret u-Farshanut	Irr.	Ramat Gan	1970	literary criticism
Bikkurei ha-Ittim	A.	Vienna	1821–1831	lit. and Judaic studies: first few volumes partly in German
Bikkurei ha-Ittim	1	Vienna	1844	lit. and Judaic studies
Bikkurei ha-Ittim ha-Ḥadashim	1	Vienna	1845	lit. and Judaic studies
Bikkurei ha-Shanah	A.	Amsterdam	1843	Hebrew and Dutch almanac
Bikkurei To'elet	A.	Amsterdam	1820	almanac
Bikkurim	A.	Vienna	1864–1865	lit.
Billui Na'im	F.	Jer.	1969	humor, crossword puzzles, etc.
Bimat ha-Ḥovevim	Irr.	T.A.	1959	amateur theater organ
Binyan va-Ḥaroshet	M.	T.A.	1927–1928	organ of the Engineers' Union; continuation of Yedi'ot
Bi-Sedeh Ḥemed		T.A.	1957	Pedagogical organ of religious teachers
Bi-Sedeh ha-Beniyyah	M.	Haifa	1953	engineering
Bi-Sedeh ha-Tekhnikah	Irr.		1941–1946	Technology; name changed from Bi-Shevilei ha-Tekhnikah to Be-Darkhei ha-Tekhnikah to Bi-Netivei ha-Tekhnikah
Bi-Tefuẓot ha-Golah	A.	Jer.	1958	World Jewry, published by the Zionist Organization
Bittaḥon ve-Higyenah ba-Avodah	Q.	Jer.	1949–1956	safety and hygiene at work
Bitta'on	M.	Chicago	1934–1938	pedagogy, originally mimeographed
Bitte'on Ḥabad	Irr.	T.A.	1953	published by Ḥabad Ḥasidim
Bitte'on Ḥeil ha-Avir – see: Ḥeil ha-Avir				
Bittu'aḥ	Q.	T.A.	1967	insurance
Bitzaron	M.	N.Y.	1939–1992	lit. and Judaic studies
Bul	W.	T.A.	1965	gossip and sex
Bulim – see also: Ha-Bulai	M.	T.A.	1957–1963	stamps; superseded by Ha-Yarḥon ha-Yisre'eli le-Vula'ut
Bulletin shel ha-Makhon le Ḥeker ha-Kalkalah		T.A.	1937–1948	economics
Bustanai – see also: Mi-Yamim	W.	Reḥovot	1929–1939	organ of the Hitaḥadut ha-Ikkarim (Farmers' Association): youth supplement Bustanai la-No'ar, 1934–37
Daf	Irr.	T.A.	1950	information bulletin of the Hebrew Writers Association
Daf ha-Tenu'ah	W.	T.A.	1960	organ of Ha-No'ar ha-Ẓiyyoni
Dagesh	F., M.	T.A.	1950–1954	digest of the Hebrew press abroad
Dappei Aliyah	Irr.	Jer	1949	aliyah problems
Dappim	Q.	Jer.	1948	Youth Aliyah
Dappim	M.	Johannesburg	1950–1953	lit.
Dappim	Irr.	Jerusalem	1950–1955 1964	pedagogical and special problems
Dappim le-Fiyyut u-le Vikkoret	1	Jer.	1916	poetry and criticism
Dappim le-Ḥeker ha-Sho'ah		T.A.	1951	Holocaust research by Isaac Katznelson House, N.S. 1970
Dappim le-Limmud Ta'amei ha-Mikra	Irr.	T.A.	1959	biblical accents
Dappim li-Tezunah	M.	Jer.	1950	nutrition; formerly Yarḥon ha-Tezunah
Dappim li-Ydi'ot ha-Sefer ve-ha-Safranut	Irr.	Jer.	1942–1943	booklore and librarianship
Dappim Refu'iyyim	B-M.	T.A.	1935	medical organ of Kuppat Ḥolim
Darkenu	1	Odessa, Russia	1917	Hebrew culture and education
Darkhei ha-Kalkalah	B-M.	T.A.	1939–1940	economics
Darkhei ha-No'ar	1	Jer.	1938	problems of youth in the Zionist framework
Darom	M.	Buenos Aires	1938	lit.; see also Zohar
Dat u-Medinah	1	T.A.	1949	published by religious members of the Histradut
Davar	D.	T.A.	1925–1994	Histradrut daily; the first daily newspaper of Jewish workers in Ereẓ Israel
Davar la-Golah	W.	T.A.	1939–1940	Davar aimed at a readership abroad
Dayig u-Midgeh	Q.	Haifa	1963	fisheries
Degel ha-rabbanim	Irr.	Lodz, Poland	1926–1929	rabbinics
Degel ha-Torah	M.	Warsaw	1921–1922	rabbinics
De'ot	Irr.	Jer.	1957	published for religious students
Derekh – see also: Ha-Derekh				
Derekh ha-Po'el	M.	T.A.	1934–1946	Left Po'alei Zion

Title	Freq.	Place of Publication	Year(s) of Appearance	Main Characteristics
Devarenu	M.	Vienna	1930–1931	lit.
Devar ha-Moreh	Irr.	Warsaw	1930–1939	pedagogy
Devar ha-Moreh	Irr.	N.Y.	1945	pedagogy
Devar ha-Po'elet	M.	T.A.	1934	women's magazine of the Histadrut
Devar ha-Shavu'a	W.	T.A.	1946	illustrated magazine; became the weekly supplement of Davar
Devar ha-Shilton ha-Mekomi – see: Ha-Shilton ha-Mekomi				
Devir	Q.	Berlin	1923	Judaic studies
Diglenu	M.	Warsaw	1920–1930	Ẓe'irei Agudat Israel
Diglenu	M.	T.A.	1939	Ẓe'irei Agudat Israel in Ereẓ Israel; irregular
Dinei Yisrael	A.	Jer.	1970	Jewish law and family law in Israel; partly in English
Divrei ha-Akademyah le-Madda'im	A.	Jer.	1966	transactions of the Academy
Divrei ha-Keneset		Jer.	1949	deliberations of the Knesset; preceded by deliberations of the Provisional State Council, 1948–49
Divrei Ḥakhamim	1	Metz, Lorraine	1849	collection of edited Hebrew manuscripts from the Middle Ages
Divrei ha-Yamim	1–4	Jer.	1950–1955	ancient and medieval history of the Jews in the form of a modern newspaper
Divrei Soferim	1	T.A.	1944	lit.
Diyyunim	Irr.	Ẓofit (Bet Berl)	1970	discussions of current problems
Do'ar – see also: Ha- Do'ar	Q.	Jer.	1952	published by the Ministry of Posts
Do'ar ha-Yom	D.	Jer.	1919–1936	newspaper published by native-born Palestinian Jews and supported by farming circles and older settlers; for some time edited by V. Jabotinsky and supported by the Revisionist movement
Dorenu	M.	Chicago	1934–1935	lit.
Dorot	F.	T.A.	1949–1950	lit.
Dukhan	A.	Jer.	1960–1966	music and religion
Edot	Q.	Jer.	1945–1948	folklore and ethnology
Edut le-Yisrael	Q.	N.Y.-Lvov	1888–1898	missionary newspaper
Egel ha-Zahav	W.	T.A.	1939	humor and satire
Egoz	A.	Jer.	1968–1969	lit.
Ein ha-Kore	Q.	Berlin	1923	lit. and bibliography
Ein ha-Moreh	Irr.	Sedeh Boker	1969	pedagogy
Ein ha-Sefer	Irr.	T.A.	1945–1947	bibliography
Eitanim – see also: Ha-Eitanim	M.	T.A.	1948	health and hygiene; for a number of years included a youth supplement, Eitanim li-Yladeinu
Eked	Q.	T.A.	1960	poetry
Emunim	1	Jer.	1955	collections of poems by religious poets
Ereẓ	1	Odessa, Russia	1919	lit.
Ereẓ Yisrael		Jer.	1923	the first morning daily in Ereẓ Israel
Eretz Yisrael	A.	Jer.	1951–1969	archaeology and history of the yishuv; each volume is dedicated to a scholar
Eshkolot	Irr.	Kishinev, Moldavia	1927–1929	lit.
Eshkolot	A.	Jer.	1954	the classical world
Eshnav	Irr.	T.A.	1941–1947	illegal organ of the Haganah; 157 issues printed
Etgar	Irr.	T.A.	1960–1967	organ of the "Semitic movement"
Foto-Roman	M.	T.A.	1970	picture stories
Gadish	1	T.A.	1930	lit.
Gallim	F.	Vilna	1929–1930	lit.
Gammad	M.	T.A.	1957	humor
Gan ha-Yerek	M.	Jaffa	1917–1918	vegetable growing; published Berl Katzenelson's articles on vegetables

Title	Freq.	Place of Publication	Year(s) of Appearance	Main Characteristics
Gannenu	Irr.	Jer.	1919–1925	kindergarten
Gan Peraḥim	1–3	Vilna	1882–1893	lit.
Gan va-Nof	M.	T.A.	1945	gardening and planting
Gazit	M.	T.A.	1932	lit. and art; first published in Jerusalem
Genazim – see also: Yedi'ot Genazim	A.	T.A.	1961	collection of documents of modern Hebrew literature
Ge'on ha-Areẓ	A.	Warsaw	1893–1894	lit.
Gerizim	F.	Ḥolon	1970	the second Samaritan newspaper
Gesher	Q.	Jer.	1954	problems of Jews and Judaism
Gevillin	Q.	T.A.	1957	published by the National Religious Party
Gevulot	Irr.	Vienna	1918–1920	lit.
Gilyonenu	Irr.	N.Y.	1946–1954	religious education of American Mizrachi
Gilyonot	M.	T.A.	1933–1954	lit.
Ginzei Kedem	Irr.	Jer.	1922–1944	collections of research on the geonic period
Ginzei Nistarot	Irr.	Bamberg, Germany	1868–1878	Judaic studies
Ginzei Schechter	Irr.	N.Y.	1928–1929	genizah studies
Gittit	M.	T.A.	1964	music
Gordonyah	Irr.	Warsaw	1926–1933	published by World Center of the Gordonia movement
Goren Kiddon	M.	T.A.	1948–1951	sports: published by Hapoel
Ha-Adamah	M.	T.A.	1920, 1923	lit.; final issues appeared after its editor, J.H. Brenner, was killed
Ha-Aḥdut – see also: Aḥdut	W.	Jer.	1910–1915	first Hebrew organ of Po'alei Zion in Ereẓ Israel; a monthly in 1910
Ha-Aḥot be-Yisrael	Q.	T.A.	1948	nursing; copies of Ha-Aḥot came out in Jerusalem during the 1930s and 1940s
Ha-Am	W.	Moscow	1916–1918	lit.
Ha-Am	D.	Moscow	1917–1918	the last Hebrew daily in Russia; closed by the Bolsheviks
Ha-Am	W.	N.Y.	1916	lit.
Ha-Am		Jer.	1931	Revisionist; superseded by Ḥazit ha-Am
Haaretz		Jer.-T.A.	1919	until Dec. 2, 1919 called Ḥadshot ha-Areẓ; in Jerusalem until 1923 and from then in Tel Aviv; many supplements for youth and others; weekly magazine supplement issued since the beginning of 1963
Ha-Areẓ	Irr.	Jer.	1891	lit.
Ha-Areẓ ve-ha-Avodah	Q.	Jaffa	1918–1919	organ of Ha-Po'el ha-Ẓa'ir
Ha-Ari'el – see: Ari'el				
Ha-Asif	A.	London-Leipzig	1847, 1849	Judaic studies
Ha-Asif	A.	Warsaw	1884–1893	lit.
Ha-Be'er	Q.	Zamosc, Poland	1923–1938	rabbinics
Ha-Bimah ha-Ivrit	M.	Buenos Aires	1921–1928	lit.
Ha-Binyan	Irr.	T.A.	1934–1938	architecture; known under other names
Ha-Boker	D.	Warsaw	1909	
Ha-Boker	D.	T.A.	1935–1965	General Zionists (B), Liberals; many supplements
Ha-Boker Or	M.	Lvov-Warsaw	1876–1886	lit.
Ha-Boneh ha-Ḥofshi	B-M.	T.A.	1933	freemasonry; began as a quarterly for a number of years
Ha-Bulai ha-Ivri	Irr.	T.A.	1950–1957	stamps; during the last year of publication known as Ha-Bulai
Ḥadashot	W. & D.	T.A.	1937–1940	general affairs
Ḥadashot Aḥaronot	D.	Jer.	1936–1937	general affairs
Ḥadashot Arkheologiyyot	Q.	Jer.	1962	archaeology
Ḥadashot me-ha-Areẓ ha-Kedoshah	W.	Jer.-Cairo	1918–1919	newspaper of the British occupation authorities; the first newspaper to appear in Palestine after the British conquest; its continuation was Ḥadashot ha-Areẓ the first incarnation of Haaretz
Ha-Dayig ha-Yisre'eli	M.	T.A.	1950–1961	fisheries
Ha-Degel – see: Ha-Yehudi				
Ha-Derekh	M.	Frankfurt Zurich-Vienna	1913–1914 1919–1924	central organ of Agudat Israel

Title	Freq.	Place of Publication	Year(s) of Appearance	Main Characteristics
Ha-Derekh	Irr.	Warsaw	1928	World Union of Jewish Youth
Ha-Derekh	W.	T.A.	1942–1947	Agudat Israel
Ha-Derekh	Irr.	T.A.	1951–1965	theoretical organ of the Israel Communist Party; superseded by Zu ha-Derekh of the New Communist List (Rakaḥ)
Ha-Deror	W.	N.Y.	1911	lit.
Ha-Devir	M.	Jer.	1919–1923	Judaic studies and rabbinics
Ha-Devorah	M.	N.Y	1911–1912	lit. and satire
Hadoar	D.	N.Y.	1921–1923	255 issues
Hadoar	W.	N.Y.	1923	lit.
Ha-Dor	W.	Cracow Poland	1901, 1904	lit.
Ha-Dor	D.	T.A.	1948–1955	Mapai afternoon paper
Hadorom	S-A.	N.Y.	1957	rabbinics and Judaic studies
Ḥadshot ha-Erev	D.	T.A.	1946–1947	afternoon paper of Mapai
Ḥadshot ha-Kalkalah ha-Ereẓ Yisre'elit	M.	Jer.	1945–1948	economics
Ḥadshot ha-Neft	M.	T.A.	1965	published by the Israel Oil Institute
Ḥadshot ha-Sport	D.	T.A.	1954	sports
Ḥadshot ha-Taḥburah	F.	Ramat Gan	1970	air, land, and sea transportation
Ḥadshot ha-Yom	D.	Jer.	1943	a government newspaper in Hebrew that was published when all Hebrew newspapers were confiscated on the eve of the siege and search of Ramat ha-Kovesh by the British; eight issues published in November 1943
Ḥadshot N.C.R.	Q.	T.A.	1964	N.C.R. news
Ḥadshot Pensyah u-Vittu'aḥ Soẓyali	M.	T.A.	1968	pension and social security
Ḥadshot Sport ve-Toto	W.	T.A.	1970	sports and Toto (football pools)
Ha-Edah	Q.	Jer.	1966	ultra-Orthodox community in Jerusalem
Ha-Eitanim	M.	Drohobycz, Galicia	1897–1898	the first pedagogical periodical in Hebrew; only three issues published
Ha-Emet	M.	Vienna	1877	the first Socialist periodical in Hebrew; only three issues published; two reprints
Ha-Em ve-ha-Yeled	A.	T.A.	1934–1936	child care; also under the names Sefer ha-Shanah ha-Em ve-ha-Yeled or Lu'aḥ ha-Em-ve-ha-Yeled
Ha-Esh	M.	T.A.	1955–1962	published by the Fire Department; isolated pamphlets under this title came out in 1930 and 1940
Ha-Eshkol	A.	Cracow, Poland	1898–1913	Judaic studies (1–7)
Ha-Ezraḥ	M.	Jaffa	1919	lit.
Ha-Galgal	F. & W.	Jer.	1943–1948	lit. and radio; continuation of Radio Yerushalayim; official paper of the Mandatory government
Ha-Galill	1	Tiberias-Safed	1919	lit.
Ha-Gan	1	St. Petersburg	1899	lit.
Ha-Gat	1	St. Petersburg	1897	lit.
Ha-Gedud	Irr.	T.A.	1923–1929	published by the "Defenders of the Hebrew language"
Ha-Gesher	Q.	Chicago	1939–1940	pedagogy
Ha-Ginnah	Irr.	Odessa-Jer.	1917–1925	nursery school problems
Ha-Goren	A.	Berdichev-Berlin	1897–1928	Judaic studies
Ha-Goren	1	St. Petersburg	1898	lit.
Ha-Ḥarsa – see: Ha-Shemesh				
Ha-Ḥayyal ha-Ivri	F. & D.		1941–1946	originally mimeographed in the North African desert and later in various places in Europe; a daily under the name La-Ḥayyal, 1944–1946
Ha-Ḥayyal ha-Meshuḥrar	Irr.	T.A.	1946	began to appear as Ha-Ḥayyal ha-Ivri, the newspaper of the demobilized soldiers, and later under other names until it became the organ of disabled veterans of Israel wars; currently Ha-Loḥem
Ha-Ḥayyim	W.	Vilna	1920	lit.
Ha-Ḥayyim	W.	Jer.	1922	illus. lit.; one of the first illustrated weeklies
Ha-Ḥayyim Hallalu	W.	T.A.	1935	illus.
Ha-Ḥazit	Irr.	T.A.	1943–1948	organ of Leḥi; mostly mimeographed organ
Ha-Ḥazit	M.	T.A.	1966	organ of the extreme nationalists (formerly Leḥi) and after the Six-Day War supporting the territorial integrity of Ereẓ Israel

Title	Freq.	Place of Publication	Year(s) of Appearance	Main Characteristics
Ha-Hed	M.	Jer.	1926–1952	lit., religious; unofficial organ of the Department of Religion of the JNF
Ha-Ḥerut – see also: Ḥerut	F. & D.	Jer.	1909–1917	a daily from 1912; the only newspaper to appear in Jerusalem during World War 1
Ha-Ḥerut	D.	Jer.	1932	Sephardi organ
Ha-Ḥevrah	Irr.	T.A.	1940–1946	pro-Revisionist
Ha-Ḥevrah	Irr.	T.A.	1959–1964 1969	pro-Mapai academicians; now under the name Adademot
Ha-Ḥinnukh	M., B-M.Q. Q.	Jer. T.A.	1910	the oldest pedagogical periodical still appearing
Ha-Ḥinnukh ha-Gufani	B-M.	T.A. Netanyah	1944	originally published by the Va'ad Le'ummi and now published by the Wingate Institute; publication periodically interrupted
Ha-Ḥinnukh ha-Ivri	Q.	N.Y.	1938–1939	pedagogy
Ha-Ḥinnukh ha-Meshuttaf – see: Be'ayot ha-Hinnukh				
Ha-Ḥinnukh ha-Musikali	Irr.	Jer.	1950	music education
Ha-Ḥoker	Irr.	Cracow-Vienna	1891–1893	Judaic studies
Ha-Ḥomah	Irr.	Jer.	1944	published by the Neturei Karta under various names, including Ḥomatenu, Mishmeret Ha-Ḥomah, etc.
Ha-Ḥozeh	W.	Berlin-Hamburg	1881–1882	lit.
Ha-Ikkar	Irr.	Jer.	1893–1895	first agricultural periodical in Hebrew – first two issues are partly in Yiddish
Ha-Ishah	M.	Jer.	1926–1929	women's magazine
Ha-Ishah ba-Medinah	M.	T.A.	1949–1953	women's magazine
Ha-Ishah be-Yisrael	Irr.	T.A.	1948–1949	WIZO organ; first issued entitled WIZO bi-Medinat Yisrael
Ha-Itton ha-Demokrati	Irr.	T.A.	1945	the "Third [Trotskyite] Force Movement"
Ha-Itton ha-Rasmi	F.	Jer.	1921–1948	official gazette of the British in Palestine; also in Arabic and English
Ha-Itton ha-Yehudi	Irr.	Jer.-T.A.	1963	organ of the World Union of Jewish Journalists; partly in Yiddish, three in English; first 17 issues entitled Korot
Haivri – see also: Ivri	W.	N.Y.	1892–1898 1901–1902	lit.; with short interruptions
Ha-Ivri	W.	Berlin-N.Y.	1910–1921	Mizrachi; from 1916 in New York
Ha-Ivri	Irr.	T.A.	1935–1936	vocalized, for new immigrants
Ha-Ivri he-Ḥadash	1	Warsaw	1912	lit.
Ha-Kabbai ha-Mitnaddev	B-M.	T.A.	1938–1945	volunteer firemen
Ha-Kabbelan ve-ha-Boneh	M.	T.A.	1952	Building Contractors' Association
Ha-Kalban	M.	Jer.	1944–1947	dog owners and trainers
Ha-Kalkalah ha-Ereẓ Yisre'elit	M.	T.A.	1935–1938	economy of Palestine
Ha-Karmel	W. & M.	Vilna	1860–1879	the first Hebrew weekly of Lithuanian Jews; a weekly until the beginning of 1871
Ha-Karmel	D.	Haifa	1938	afternoon daily
Ha-Kaspan	M.	Jer.	1932–1934	financial and economic affairs
Ha-Kedem	Q.	St. Petersburg	1907–1909	Judaic studies
Ha-Kenes ha-Madda'i ha-Meyuḥad	Irr.	Jer.	1956	published by the Association for the Advancement of Science in Israel
Ha-Kerem	1	Warsaw	1887	Judaic studies, lit.
Ha-Kerem	1	Vilna	1906	lit.
Ha-Kerem	1	Berdichev, Ukraine	1897	lit.
Ha-Kerem	B-M.	Boston, Mass.	1915	pedagogy
Ha-Keshet – see also: Keshet	M.	Berlin	1903	lit. and art; the first art periodical in Hebrew
Ha-Khimai be-Yisrael	Irr.	Haifa	1968	organ of the Israel Chemistry Society
Ha-Kinnus ha-Arẓi le-Torah she-be-Al Peh	A.	Jer.	1959	halakhic transactions
Ha-Kinnus ha-Olami le-Madda'ei ha-Yahadut	Irr.	Jer.	1952, 1967–1968	papers of the First and Fourth World Congress of Jewish studies; partly in other languages

Title	Freq.	Place of Publication	Year(s) of Appearance	Main Characteristics
Ḥakla'ut be-Yisrael		T.A.	1956	agriculture
Ha-Kokhavim	1	Vilna	1865	lit.
Ha-Kokhavim be-Ḥodsham	M.	Jer.	1954	astronomy
Ha-Kol – see also: Kol	F. & W.	Koenigsberg, E. Prussia	1876–1880	the second Hebrew Socialist newspaper, Asefat Ḥakhamim, was published under the auspices of this paper
Ha-Kol	W. & F.	N.Y.	1889	a continuation of the previous entry
Ha-Kol	W.	Warsaw	1907	ultra-Orthodox
Ha-Kol	D.	Jer.	1949–1967	Po'alei Agudat Israel
Ha-Le'om	M. & W.	N.Y.	1901–1908	during the first years partly in Yiddish
Ha-Le'ummi	W.	N.Y.	1888–1889	lit.
Ha-Levanon	M., F. & W.	Jer., Paris-Mainz-London	1863–1886	the first newspaper published in Jerusalem (1863–64); afterward in Europe with interruptions
Halikhot – see also: Shanah be-Shanah	Q.	T.A.	1958	religious publication
Hallel	M.	Jer.	1930	music and song
Ha-Loḥem – see: Ha-Ḥayyal ha-Meshuḥar				
Ha-Ma'arav	F. & W.	T.A.	1950–1952	
Ha-Ma'as	Irr.	T.A.	1944–1950	organ of Leḥi during the British Mandate
Ha-Mabbit	W.	Vienna	1878	lit.; some issues under the title Ha-Mabbit le-Yisrael
Ha-Madda ve-ha-Tekhnikah – Ha-Tekhnai ha-Ẓa'ir – see: Ha-Tekhnai ha-Ẓa'ir				
Ha-Maggid	W.	Lyck-Berlin-Cracow	1856–1903	the first modern newspaper in Hebrew; from the 1890s the name varies: Ha-Maggid he-Ḥadash, Ha-Maggid le-Yisrael, Ha-Shavu'a
Ha-Maḥar	Irr.	T.A.	1927–1931 1940	a nonconformist publication by A. Hameiri
Ha-Makkabbi	Q.	Odessa, Russia	1918	Maccabi Russia
Ha-Makkabbi	Irr.	Jer.-Jaffa-T.A.	1913–1938	various pamphlets and organs by this name were published irregularly by the Maccabi Organization
Ḥammamot u-Feraḥim	Irr.	T.A.	1968	flower growing
Ḥamishah ha-Kunteresim	1	Vienna	1864	collection of edited ancient manuscripts
Ha-Ma'or	M.	N.Y.	1946	rabbinics
Ha-Mashkif	D.	T.A.	1938–1948	Revisionist organ; superseded by Herut
Ha-Matos	M.	T.A.	1954	aviation
Ha-Mattarah	W.	T.A.	1933	published by the Grossman faction, which split from the Revisionist movement in the same year
Ha-Ma'yan	M. & Q.	Jer.	1952	halakhic and Judaic studies
Ha-Mazkir	Irr.	Lvov, Galicia	1881–1886	Hebrew supplement to the Polish-Jewish Assimilations paper Ojczyzna
Ha-Me'ammer	Irr.	Jer.	1905–1920	collections of Palestinography
Ha-Me'assef – see also: Me'assef	Irr.	Koenigsberg-Berlin-Breslau-Altona-Dessau	1783–1811	inaugurated the Haskalah period of modern Jewish literature
Ha-Me'assef	1	Breslau, Germany	1829	lit.; partly in German
Ha-Me'assef	1	Vienna	1862	new edition of the first volume of Ha-Me'assef with many additions
Ha-Me'assef	1	Koenigsberg, Prussia	1879	lit. supplement to Ha-Kol
Ha-Me'assef	M.	Jer.	1896–1915	rabbinics
Ha-Me'assef ba-Arez ha-Ḥadashah	1	N.Y.	1881	organ of the first Society of Lovers of Hebrew in the United States
Ha-Me'assef li-Shenat ha-Sheloshim shel ha-Ẓefirah	1	Warsaw	1903	in honor of the 30th anniversary of Ha-Ẓefirah
Ha-Medinah	D.	T.A.	1948	a political newspaper

Title	Freq.	Place of Publication	Year(s) of Appearance	Main Characteristics
Ha-Me'ir	M.	Jaffa	1912	Palestinography
Ha-Melakhah	Irr.	Jer.	1943–1950 1958	published for craftsmen
Ha-Meliẓ	W. & B-W.	Odessa-St. Petersburg	1860–1903	St. Petersburg from 1871; a daily from 1886
Ha-Melonai	Q.	T.A.	1967	published by the Hotel Association in Israel
Ha-Melona'ut	Irr.	T.A.	1949	published by the Union of Hotel Employees in Israel
Ha-Me'orer	M.	London	1906–1907	lit.
Ha-Me'orer	Irr.	T.A.	1953–1958	organ for Sephardim and members of Oriental communities
Ha-Meshek ha-Ḥakla'i	M.	T.A.	1940	continuation of Ha-Ḥakla'i ha-Ẓa'ir; early volumes entitled Ha-Meshek ha-Ẓa'ir, first volume in German
Ha-Meshek ha-Shittufi	F.	T.A.	1932	cooperative economics; ceased publication in 1948 and reissued in 1953
Ha-Meshek ha-Ẓa'ir – see: Ha-Meshek ha-Ḥakla'i		.		
Ha-Messilah	M.	N.Y.	1936–1943	rabbinics; partly in Yiddish
Ha-Messilah	Irr.	Jer.	1956–1964	organ of yeshivah students and immigrants from Yemen
Ha-Mevakker ha-Penimi	Q.	T.A.-Jer.	1963	published by the Association of Internal Auditors
Ha-Mevasser	W.	Lvov, Galicia	1861–1866	the first Hebrew newspaper in Galicia; its literary supplement was called Ha-Nesher
Ha-Mevasser	W.	Constantinople	1910–1911	a Zionist paper published after the revolution of the Young Turks
Ha-Mevasser	D. & W.	Jer.	1948–1952	Agudat Israel; originally an afternoon daily, later a weekly
Ha-Mevatte'aḥ ha-Yisre'eli	Irr.	T.A.	1941–1960	insurance; two issues appeared in 1932 under the title Ha-Mevatte'aḥ
Ha-Mifal	M.	T.A.	1953	output and export
Ha-Minhal	Q.	T.A.	1950–1959	management
Hamisderonah	M.	Jer.	1886–1887	rabbinics and Judaic studies; the first issues were printed in Frankfurt
Ha-Misḥar	W., F. & M.	T.A.-Jaffa	1933–1940 1945–1956	trade
Ha-Misḥar ba-Ammim u-ve-Yisrael	1	T.A.	1941	trade
Ha-Mishpat – see also: Mishpat	M.	Jer.-T.A.	1927–1934	law
Ha-Mishpat ha-Ivri	1	Odessa, Russia	1918	Jewish law
Ha-Mishpat ha-Ivri	A.	T.A.	1926–1939	Jewish law
Ha-Miẓpeh	M.	St. Petersburg	1886	lit.
Ha-Miẓpeh	W.	Cracow, Poland	1904–1914 1917–1921	S.Y. Agnon published his first literary endeavors in this paper
Ha-Miẓpeh	M.	N.Y.	1910–1911	rabbinics and Judaic studies
Ha-Miẓpeh	Irr.	Warsaw	1926–1936	publication of Ha-Shomer ha-Ẓa'ir in Poland
Ha-Miẓpeh	Irr.	T.A.	1945–1949	publication of Ha-Shomer ha-Ẓa'ir in Israel
Ha-Miẓpeh	S-A.	Jer.	1961–1968	organ of the National Religious Party
Ha-Mizraḥ	M.	Cracow, Poland	1903	first organ of Mizrachi
Ha-Mizraḥ	W.	T.A.	1938	affairs of the Yemenite community
Ha-Mizraḥ he-Ḥadash	Q.	Jer.	1949	published by the Israel Oriental Society
Ha-Mizraḥi	W.	Warsaw	1919–1922	organ of Mizrachi in Poland
Ha-Modi'a	W.	Poltava, Ukraine	1910–1914	ultra-Orthodox
Ha-Modi'a	D.	Jer.	1950	Agudat Israel; supplement for children, 1952–59
Ha-Modi'a le-Ḥodahsim	M.	N.Y.	1900–1901	lit.
Ha-Moreh	M.	N.Y.	1894	lit.
Ha-Moreh	1	N.Y.	1924	pedagogy
Ha-Moriyyah – see also: Moriyyah	F.	Jer.	1892	Informative material from Ereẓ Israel
Ha-Musakh	M.	T.A.	1954	automobile repairs
Handasah ve-Adrikhalut	B-M.	T.A.	1931	engineering; in the first year appeared irregularly under various names
Ha-Ne'eman	Irr.	T.A.	1945	organ of yeshivah students

Title	Freq.	Place of Publication	Year(s) of Appearance	Main Characteristics
Ha-Nesher	M.	Pressburg (Bratislava), Czechoslovakia	1933–1940	rabbinics; for Ha-Nesher of Lvov, see Ha-Mevasser
Ha-Nir	1	Jer.	1909	lit. religious
Ha-No'ar ha-Musikali	M.	T.A.	1957–1961	music education
Ha-No'ar ve-ha-Areẓ	B-M.	T.A.	1926–1927	for older youth
Ha-Noked	Irr.	Merḥ avyah Haifa	1940	published by the Association of Shepherds
Ha-Of	M.	T.A.	1939	poultry raising; superseded by Ha-Meshek ha-Ẓa'ir and Ha-Meshek ha-Ḥakla'i
Ha-Ofek	Irr.	Jer.	1952–1959	published by the "Le-Ma'an ha-Tenu'ah el ha-Makor" faction of Ha-Po'el ha-Mizraḥi
Ha-Ohel	Q.	Jer.	1955	rabbinics
Ha-Ohelah	Irr.	Jer.	1925–1926	Ha-Po'el ha-Mizraḥi
Haolam – see also: Olam	W.	Cologne-Vilna-Odessa-London-Berlin-Berlin	1907–1914 1919–1950	organ of the World Zionist Organization
Ha-Olam ha-Zeh	W.	Jer.-T.A	1937	organ of Ha-Olam ha-Zeh–Ko'aḥ Ḥadash; founded as Tesha ba-Erev; name changed to Ha-Olam ha-Zeh in 1947; came under new direction in 1950; first Hebrew magazine to introduce sex
Ha-Omer	Irr.		1907–1908	lit.; S.Y. Agnon's works first appeared here under the name Agnon
Ha-Or	M.	Lvov, Galicia	1882–1883	lit.
Ha-Or – see: Ha-Ẓevi				
Ha-Or	W. & F.	T.A.	1925 1930–-1939	Communist (Trotskyite)
Ha-Or	M.	Jer.	1956–1958	organ of the Karaite community; mimeographed
Ha-Oved	Irr.	Warsaw	1921–1922	organ of the Ẓ.S. in Poland
Ha-Oved ha-Dati	Irr.	T.A.	1947–1967	Ha-Oved ha-Dati of the Histadrut
Ha-Oved ha-Le'ummi	M.	T.A.	1943–1959	central organ of the Histadrut ha-Ovedim ha-Le'ummit
Ha-Oved ha-Ẓiyyoni	M.	T.A.	1936–1955	organ of Ha-Oved ha-Ẓiyyoni
Ha-Pardes	M.	Several places in Poland & in the U.S.	1913	rabbinics
Ha-Pardes – see also: Pardes	W. & B-W.	Jer.	1909	general affairs
Ha-Pedogog	M.	Cracow, Poland	1903–1904	the first modern educational periodical
Ha-Peles	M.	Poltava-Berlin	1900–1904	ultra-Orthodox, anti-Zionist
Ha-Peraḥ	W.	Calcutta, India	1878–1889	in Hebrew and Arabic
Ha-Peraklit	Q.	T.A.	1943	published by Israel Bar Association
Ha-Pisgah	W.	N.Y.-Baltimore-Boston-St. Louis-Chicago	1888–1900	with interruptions; from the sixth volume known as Ha-Teḥiyyah; Saul Tchernichowsky's first poem was published therein in 1892
Ha-Pisgah	A.	Vilna	1895–1902	rabbinics; 9 vols.: in the second volume were printed articles by Rabbi Y.L. Fishman-Maimon
Ha-Po'el ha-Mizrachi	M.	Jer.	1923–1926	organ of Ha-Po'el ha-Mizraḥi
Ha-Po'el ha-Vatik	Irr.	T.A.	1938	organ of the older workers organized in the Histadrut; changes in title; from 1959 Shelabbim
Ha-Po'el ha-Ẓa'ir	F. & W.	Jaffa-T.A.	1907–1970	organ of Ha-Po'el ha-Ẓa'ir, Mapai, and Ha-Avodah; mimeographed two issues in 1907; from 1912 W.; publication interrupted from 1916 to 1918
Ha-Posek	M.	T.A.	1940–1953	rabbinics
Ha-Problemai	M.	Kabri-Givat Brenner	1954–1969	chess; originally Problemai
Ha-Rashut ha-Mekomit	M.	T.A.	1954–1969	municipality problems
Harefuah – see also: Refuah	Irr.-F.	Jer.-T.A.	1920	newsletter of the Medical Association, 1921–22; known as Harefuah from 1924

Title	Freq.	Place of Publication	Year(s) of Appearance	Main Characteristics
Ha-Ro'eh	Irr.	Lvov-Ofen (Budapest)	1837, 1839	pungent criticism
Ha-Rofe ba-Histadrut	Irr.	T.A.	1953–1956	problems of the physician in the Histadrut
Ha-Rofe ba-Mosad	Irr.	T.A.	1946–1968	organ of the Kuppat Ḥolim physician
Harofe Haivri	Irr., S-A.	N.Y.	1928–1965	medicine and the history of Jewish medicine, special editions for Ereẓ Israel; irregularly from 1928 to 1933; twice annually from 1937; published partly in English
Ha-Roke'aḥ ha-Ivri	Irr., B-M.	T.A.	1940	published by the Pharmaceutical Association; called Ha-Roke'aḥ, 1940–1946
Ḥaroshet u-Melakhah	M.	T.A.	1965	innovations in production in Israel industry and crafts
Ha-Sedeh	M.	T.A.	1920	agriculture; the only publication of its kind to reach its 50th anniversary (1970)
Ha-Sedeh la-No'ar	B-M.	T.A.	1948–1958	agriculture publication for youth; superseded by Teva va-Areẓ
Ha-Sedeh le Gan va-Nof – see: Gan va-Nof				
Ha-Safah	Irr.	St. Petersburg	1912	Hebrew language studies
Ha-Safran – see: Alim le-Bibliografyah u-le-Safranut				
Ha-Sanegor	Irr.	N.Y.	1890	lit.
Ha-Sefer	Irr.	Jer.	1954–1961	bibliography; superseded by Kunteres ha-sefer ha-Torani
Ha-Sefer b-Yisrael	M.	T.A.	1959	organ of publishers in Israel; continuation of Olam ha-Sefer
Ha-Sefer ha-Ivri – see: Jewish Book Annual				
Ha-Segullah	Irr.	Jer.	1934–1940	editions of manuscripts
Ha-Sha'ar	D.	T.A.	1964	management and the stock market
Ha-Shaḥar	M.	Vienna	1868–1884	lit; the leading periodical of this period
Ha-Shaḥmat – see: Shaḥmat				
Ha-Sharon	1	Cracow, Poland	1893	lit.
Ha-Sharon	F.	Lvov, Galicia	1895	lit.
Ha-Shavu'a – see: Ha-Maggid				
Ha-Shavu'a ba-Kibbutz ha-Arẓi	W.	Merḥ avyah-T.A.	1950	appeared from 1930 as under various titles organ of the kibbutzim of Ha-Shomer ha-Ẓa'ir
Ha-Shavu'a la-Mishpaḥah	W.	T.A.	1932	entertainment
Ha-Shemesh	W.	T.A. Sighet, Transylvania–Kolomea, Galicia	1878–1892	lit.
Ha-Shilo'aḥ	M.	Cracow-Warsaw-Odessa-Jer.	1896–1926	lit.; the leading literary journal in Russia until World War I
Ha-Shilton ha-Mekomi be-Yisrael	M. & B-M.	T.A.	1950	municipal problems
Hashkafah – see: Ha-Ẓevi				
Ha-Shofar	Irr.	Haifa	1914, 1923	Jewish-Arab problems; originally as supplement to an Arab newspaper
Ha-Shomer ha-Ẓa'ir	F.	Warsaw	1927–1931	organ of Ha-Shomer ha-Ẓa'ir
Ha-Shomer ha-Ẓa'ir	F.	T.A.	1931–1943	organ of Ha-Shomer ha-Ẓa'ir Ha-Kibbutz ha-Arẓi from 1934; superseded by Mishmar
Ha-Sifrut	Q.	T.A.	1968	science of literature
Ha-Soker		Budapest		Judaic studies
Ha-Solel	M.	Lvov, Galicia	1933–1934	lit.
Ha-Sport – see also: Sport	Irr.	T.A.	1932, 1940–1941	sport
Ha-Sport ha-Le'ummi	W.	T.A.	1949–1950	sport; Betar
Ha-Ta'asiyyah – see also: Ta'asiyyah	M.	T.A.	1937–1938, 1941	published by the Manufacturers' Association
Ha-Tarbut ha-Yisre'elit	1	Jaffa	1913	lit.
Ha-Tashbeẓ – see: Tashbeẓ				

Title	Freq.	Place of Publication	Year(s) of Appearance	Main Characteristics
Ha-Teḥiyyah – see: Ha-Pisgah				
Ha-Teḥiyyah	Irr.	Berlin	1850, 1857	Judaic studies
Ha-Tekhnai be-Yisrael	Q.	T.A.	1963–1967	published by the Technicians' Organization
Ha-Tekhnai ha-Ẓa'ir	M.	Kiryat Shemonah	1945	technical problems for youth; later changed name to Ha-Madda ve-ha-Tekhnikah
Ha-Tekhnion	A.	Haifa	1966	organ of the Technion, Haifa
Ha-Tekufah	Q. & A.	Moscow-Warsaw-Berlin T.A. – N.Y.	1918–1950	lit.
Ha-Tenu'ah le-Aḥdut ha-Avodah – see: Le-Aḥdut ha-Avodah				
Ha-Tenu'ah le-Yahadut shel Torah	A.	Jer.	1966, 1968	published by the Yahadut and Torah movement
Ha-Te'ufah	Irr., M.	T.A.	1947–1956	aeronautics
Ha-Teva ve-ha-Areẓ	M.	T.A.	1932–1940 1947–1954 1959	natural sciences, nature and geography of Israel
Ha-Tikvah	W.	N.Y.	1901	lit.; the first publication in the United States to introduce a vocalized supplement for children
Ha-Tor	M.	Sighet, Transylvania-Kolomea, Galicia-Cracow, Poland	1874–1876 1880–1882	lit.
Ha-Tor	W.	Jer.	1920–1935	organ of Mizrachi in Ereẓ Israel
Ha-Torah ve-ha-Medinah	A.	T.A.	1949–1960	religion in Israel
Ha-Toren	M.W.	N.Y.	1913–1926	lit.; weekly, 1916–19
Ha-Ummah	W.	N.Y.	1915	lit.; merged in 1916 with Ha-Toren ha-Shevu'I
Ha-Ummah	Q.	Jer.	1962	lit.
Ḥavaẓẓelet	W.	Jer.	1863–1864 1870–1911	the second newspaper in Ereẓ Israel
Ha-Ya'ar	Irr.	Jer.-Netanyah	1947–1955	problems of afforestation
Ha-Yahadut	F.	Lvov, Galicia	1885	lit.
Ha-Yahalom	Irr.	T.A.	1943–1944 1947	professional and managerial problems in the diamond industry
Ha-Yahalom	Irr.	T.A.	1967	problems in the diamond industry
Ha-Yam	Irr. M.	T.A.	1938–1963	seamanship
Ha-Yamai ha-Yisre'eli	M.	Haifa	1951	published by the National Union of Seamen
Ha-Yarden	Irr.	Stanislavaov, Galicia	1906	lit.
Ha-Yarden	M.	Zurich-N.Y.	1919–1925	lit.
Ha-Yarden	D. & W.	Jer.-T.A.	1934–1941	Revisionist publication
Ha-Yare'aḥ	Irr.	Koenigsberg, Prussia	1871–1872	lit.
Ha-Yare'aḥ	1	Jer.	1896	lit.
Ha-Yarhon – see also: Yarḥon ha-Yisre'eli le Vula'ut	M.	T.A.	1966	stamps; continuation of Bulim
Ha-Yehudi	W.	Pressburg (Bratislava), Czechoslovakia	1875–1878	lit.; the first Hebrew newspaper in Hungary
Ha-Yehudi	W.	London	1897–1913	lit.; the only Hebrew newspaper in England that enjoyed a long career
Ha-Yehudi	M.	N.Y.	1936–1938	lit.; religious
Ha-Yehudi ha-Niẓḥi	Irr.	Lvov, Galicia	1866	Judaic studies
Ha-Yekev	1	St. Petersburg	1894	lit.
Ha-Yesod	W.	T.A.	1932–1948	religious apolitical

Title	Freq.	Place of Publication	Year(s) of Appearance	Main Characteristics
Ha-Yishuv	W.	T.A.	1924–1927	lit. and general affairs
Ha-Yisre'eli	W.	N.Y.	1903	lit.
Ha-Yom	D.	St. Petersburg	1886–1888	the first Hebrew daily (Feb. 12 1886–March 12, 1888)
Ha-Yom	D.	Warsaw	1906–1907	
Ha-Yom	D.	N.Y.	1909	the first Hebrew daily in the United States (90 days); exact data on the second attempt before World War I unavailable
Ha-Yom	D.	Warsaw	1925–1926	
Ha-Yom	D.	Jer.	1948–1949	originally called Itton ha-Yom; began to appear in Jerusalem during the siege of the War of Independence
Ha-Yom	D.	T.A.	1966–1969	published by Gaḥal; result of merger of two papers, Ha-Boker and Ḥerut
Ha-Yonah	1	Berlin	1851	Judaic studies
Ha-Yonah	1	Odessa, Russia	1907	rabbinics and Judaica; the first editorial endeavors of Y.L. Maimon (Fishman)
Ḥayyei Olam	1	Paris	1878	collection of edited ancient manuscripts
Ḥayyei Sha'ah	W.	T.A.	1953–1958	entertainment
Ha-Ẓafon	W.	Haifa	1926–1927	lit. and general affairs
Ha-Ẓa'ir	Irr.	Zloczow (Zolochev), Ukraine	1910	lit.
Ha-Ẓa'ir	1	Jer.	1916	lit.
Ha-Ẓefirah	1	Zolkiew (Zholkva), Galicia	1823	lit.
Ha-Ẓefirah	W. & D.	Warsaw (Berlin)	1862 1874–1906 1910–1921 1926–1928 1931	the first Hebrew newspaper in Warsaw; during the first years devoted mainly to science; 1874–75 in Berlin; from 1886 a daily and 1917–19 a weekly
Ha-Zeman	W.	N.Y.	1895–1896	lit.
Ha-Zeman	F.	Cracow, Poland	1890–1891	lit.
Ha-Zeman	1	Warsaw	1896	lit.
Ha-Zeman	Q.	St. Petersburg	1903	lit.; published Bialik's famous poem "Be-Ir-ha-Haregah"
Ha-Zeman	M.	Vilna	1905	lit.
Ha-Zeman	B-W., D.	St. Petersburg-Vilna	1903–1915	first 92 issues biweekly; from 1905 in Vilna; know as Hed ha-Zeman, 1907–11
Ha-Zeman	D.	T.A.	1930	general
Ha-Zeman	D.	T.A.	1941–1944	a nonconformist paper edited by B. Katz, editor of Ha-Zeman in Vilna
Ha-Ẓevi	W. & D.	Jer.	1884–1915	a daily from 1908; sometimes called Ha-Or, Hashkafah; the pioneer of modern journalism in Ereẓ Israel; several interruptions in publication
Ha-Zibbul	Q.	Jaffa-T.A.	1924	problems of agricultural fertilization
Ha-Ẓillum	M.	T.A.	1965	originally appeared in 1947 under the title Ẓillum; from 1971 published by the Association of Amateur Photographers
Ha-Ẓir	Irr.	Jaffa	1919	Mizrachi
Ḥazit ha-Am	B-W., W.	Jer.	1932–1934	Revisionist publication
Ḥazit ha-Oved	M.	T.A.	1958	organ of Ha-Oved ha-Le'ummi in the Histadrut
Ha-Ẓiyyoni ha-Kelali	W.	Jer.	1932–1935	General Zionists (B)
Ha-Ẓiyyoni ha-Vatik	Irr.	T.A.	1940–1941	organ of the old-time Zionists; appeared under various titles
Ha-Ẓiyyonut	A.	T.A.	1970	studies in the history of the Zionist movement and of the Jews in Ereẓ Israel
Ha-Ẓofeh	Irr.	Lvov, Galicia	1878	lit.
Ha-Ẓofeh	D.	Warsaw	1903–1905	general; the first to introduce literary contests; the first prize was won by Y.D. Berkowitz
Ha-Ẓofeh	D.	Jer.-T.A.	1937	organ of Mizrachi – National Religious Party; the first issues were published in Jerusalem
Ha-Ẓofeh	Irr.	Jer.	1935–1946	scouting

Title	Freq.	Place of Publication	Year(s) of Appearance	Main Characteristics
Ha-Ẓofeh ba-Areẓ ha-Ḥadashah	W.	N.Y.	1871–1876	the first Hebrew newspaper in the United States
Ha-Ẓofeh le-Ḥokhmat Yisrael	M.	Budapest	1911–1915, 1921–1931	Judaic studies; originally called Ha-Ẓofeh me-Ereẓ Hagar
Ha-Ẓofeh le-Veit Yisrael	Irr.	London	1887	lit.
Ha-Ẓofeh le-Veit Yisrael	M.	Cracow, Poland	1890	lit.
Ḥazon	Irr.	T.A.	1943–1955	Mizrachi youth
Ḥazut	A.	Jer.	1953–1960	discussions on questions of Zionism, the Jewish People, and the State of Israel
He-Atid	Irr.	Berlin	1908–1926	six collections on matters concerning Jews and Judaism
He-Atid	F.	Warsaw	1925–1934	organ of the He-Ḥalutz World Center
He-Atid	Irr.	T.A.	1939–1941	organ of Po'alei Agudat Israel
He-Atid	Q.	T.A.	1966	published by the West German embassy, Tel Aviv
He-Avar	Q.	Petrograd	1918	history of the Jews
He-Avar (Heawar)	Q. & A.	T.A.	1952	history of the Jews in Russia
Hed ha-Am – see also: Ha-Hed	W.	Jer.	1924–1926	religious publication
Hed ha-Defus	Irr.	T.A.	1937–1961	published by the Organization of Printing Workers; the name differs on various editions
Hed ha-Gan	B-M. & M. & Q.	T.A.	1934	published by the Association of Nursery School Teachers
Hed ha-Ḥinnukh	F. & W.	Jer.-T.A.	1926	published by the Teachers' Association; a weekly from 1949
Hed ha-Karmel	D.	Haifa	1940	general affairs; one of the attempts to establish a daily newspaper in Haifa
Hed ha-Kevuẓah	Irr.	Detroit, Mich.	1941–1961	lit.
Hed ha-Mizraḥ	F. & W.	Jer.	1942–1951	Oriental communities in the past; first issues called Ha-Mizraḥ
Hed ha-Moreh	M.	N.Y.	1915	the first Hebrew pedagogical periodical in the U.S.
Hed ha-Sport	W.	T.A.	1965–1966	sports
Hed ha-Zeman – see: Ha-Zeman				
Hed ha-Ẓiyyoni ha-Vatik – see: Ha-Ẓiyyoni ha-Vatik				
Hedim	B-M.	T.A.	1922–1928	the leading literary journal in the 1920s
Hedim li-She'elot ha-Ḥevrah ha-Kibbutzit	Irr. & Q.	Merḥ avyah	1934	organ of Ha-Kibbutz ha-Arẓi Ha-Shomer ha-Ẓa'ir
Hed Lita	F.	Kaunas (Kovno), Lithuania	1924–1925	lit.
Hed Yerushalayim	W.	Jer.	1939–1946	general affairs; during the final year of publication called Ha-Shavu'on ha-Ereẓ Yisre'eli ve-Hed Yerushalayim
Hegeh	D.	T.A.	1940–1947	vocalized daily
Hegeh	W.	T.A.	1939–1940	afternoon paper of Davar
Hegeh	W.	T.A.	1947–1949	Saturday evening paper
He-Hadar	M.	T.A.	1928–1940	citrus
He-Ḥalutz	Irr.	Lvov-Breslau-Prague-Frankfurt-Vienna	1852–1889	Judaic studies
He-Ḥalutz ha-Ẓa'ir	Irr.	Warsaw	1926–1939	published by He-Ḥalutz ha-Ẓa'ir; partly in Yiddish
He-Ḥaver	Irr.	Berne-Berlin	1912, 1914	organ of the student Zionist organization He-Ḥaver
Heikhal ha-Ivri	W.	Chicago	1877–1879	the first Hebrew paper in Chicago
Ḥeil ha-Avir	S-A.	T.A.	1948	air force organ
Ḥeil ha-Yam – see: Ma'arekhot Yam				
Ḥemdah Genuzah	A.	Koenigsberg, E. Prussia	1856	collection of edited ancient manuscripts
Ḥermon	A.	Lvov, Galicia	1902–1903	lit.

Title	Freq.	Place of Publication	Year(s) of Appearance	Main Characteristics
Ḥerut	D.	T.A.	1948–1966	organ of the Ḥerut Party; a number of editions were published earlier in Jerusalem as a weekly
Ḥeshbona'ut u-Missim	Irr.	T.A.-Ramat Gan	1962–1967	published by the Union of Accountants and Tax Consultants
Heyeh Nakhon	Q.	Jer.-T.A.	1946	scouting
Higyenah Ruḥanit	M.	Jer.	1944–1951	hygiene in the schools
Higyenah u-Veri'ut	Q.	Jer.	1940–1948	health and hygiene
Ḥikrei Avodah	Q.	T.A.	1947–1954	labor studies and social security
Ḥinnukh	Q.	N.Y.	1935–1939	education
Ḥok u-Mishpat	F.	Jer.-T.A.	1954	law
Ḥol va-Ru'aḥ	1	Holon	1964	lit., Hebrew and Yiddish
Horeb	S-A.	N.Y.	1934–1960	Judaica studies
Ḥotam	F.	T.A.	1964	Mapam; from 1970 weekly magazine of Al ha-Mishmar
Iddan Ḥadash	M.	T.A.	1968	organ of Ha-Merkaz ha-Ḥofshi
Iggeret la-Ḥaverim	W.	T.A.	1951	organ of Iḥud ha-Kevuẓot ve-ha-Kibbutzim; continuation of Iggeret; organ of Ḥever ha-Kevuẓot
Iggeret le-Ḥinnukh	Q.	T.A.-Tel Yosef	1952	educational organ of Iḥud ha-Kevuẓot ve-ha-Kibbutzim
Iggeret li-Meḥannekhim	B-M.	T.A.	1964	educational organ of Ha-Kibbutz ha-Me'uḥad
Ikkarei Yisrael	A.	T.A.	1954–1962	annual of the Farmers' Association
Ikkarei Yisrael	M.	T.A.	1962	organ of the Farmers' Association
Ittim	W.	T.A.	1946–1948	lit.
Itton ha-Bonim	M.	T.A.	1937–1939 1946–1949	organ of the Association of Landlords and Property Owners
Itton le-Misḥar	Irr.	T.A.	1936–1939	trade
Itton Meyuḥad	W.	T.A.-Jer.	1933–1951	pioneer of sensational reportage
Ivri Anokhi	W.	Brody-Galicia	1865–1890	indirect continuation of Ha-Mevasser, sometimes: Ha-Ivri
Iyyim	1	London	1928	lit.
Iyyun	Q.	T.A.-Jer.	1945	philosophy
Iyyunim Beinle'ummiyyim	Irr.	Ramat Gan	1951–1964	international affairs – superseded by International Outlook
Iyyunim bi-Ve'ayot Ḥevrah	A.	T.A.	1969	social, educational and cultural problems
Iyyunim le-Vikkoret ha-Medinah	Q.	Jer.	1960	Bulletin of the State Comptroller's Office
Jewish Book Annual	Q.	N.Y.	1942	Hebrew-English-Yiddish, bibliography
Kadimah	M.	N.Y.	1899	lit.
Kadimah	1	Kiev, Ukraine	1920	philosophy and science of religion
Kalkelan	W., M.	Jer	1952	finance and economy
Kammah	A.	Jer.	1948–1952	Keren Kayemeth
Karmelit	A.	Haifa	1954	lit.
Karmi	M.	Pressburg (Bratislava), Czechoslovakia	1881–1882	general, Hebrew and Ladino
Karmi Shelli	Irr.	Vienna	1891	general, Hebrew and Ladino
Karnenu	Q.	Jer.	1924–1963	Keren Kayemeth, superseded by Am ve-Admato
Katif	A.	Petaḥ Tikvah	1954	
Kav	Q.	Jer.	1965	lit.
Kavveret	1	Odessa, Russia	1890	lit.; Ḥibbat Zion
Kaẓir	M.	T.A.	1945–1946	digest of books
Kaẓir	1.	T.A.	1964	history of Zionism in Russia
Kedem	Irr.	Jer.	1942, 1945	archaeology of Palestine
Kedmah	M.	T.A.	1963–1964	organ of Betar
Kehilliyyatenu	1	T.A.-Haifa	1922	the first organ of Ha-Shomer ha-Ẓa'ir in Ereẓ Israel, new reprint
Keneset	1	Odessa, Russia	1917	lit.
Keneset	1	T.A.	1928	lit.
Keneset	A.	T.A.	1936–1946 1960	lit.; Bialik and Judaic studies
Keneset ha-Gedolah	Irr.	Warsaw	1890–1891	lit.
Keneset Yisrael	A.	Warsaw	1886–1889	lit.
Keneset Yisrael	M.	Vilna	1930–1934	rabbinics

Title	Freq.	Place of Publication	Year(s) of Appearance	Main Characteristics
Kerem Ḥemed	A.	Vienna-Berlin	1833–1856	lit. and Judaic studies, 9 vols.
Keren Or	M.	Chicago	1889	lit.; only 2 issues
Kesafim u-Mishar	D.	T.A.	1966–1967	finance and economy
Kesher ve-Elektronikah	M.	T.A.	1967	electronics, Israel Defense Forces
Keshet	Q.	T.A.	1958	lit.
Ketavim	Q.	Reḥovot-Bet Dagon	1951	Agricultural Research Station
Ketuvim	W.	T.A.	1926–1933	lit.; organ of the young Avantgardists
Kevuẓat Ḥakhamim	1	Vienna	1861	Judaic studies
Kikyon Yonah	1	Paris	1860	Judaic studies
Kirjath Sepher	Q.	Jer.	1924	bibliography of the Jewish National and University Library Jer.; the first regular scientific publication of the Hebrew University
Kitvei ha-Universitah	1	Jer.	1924	Judaic studies, mathematics and physics; printed in Leipzig
Ko'aḥ Ḥadash	Irr.	T.A.	1966–1967	organ of Ha-Olam ha-Zeh – Ko'aḥ Ḥadash
Kohelet	1	St. Petersburg	1881	lit.
Kohelet Musar	Irr.	Berlin	1750	the first literary-moralistic periodical in Hebrew; 2 issues, 2 reprints
Kokhevei Yiẓḥak	A.	Vienna	1845–1869 1873	lit.; central organ of the Hebrew Haskalah movement; 37 vols.
Kol – see: Ha-Kol				
Kol ha-Am	D., W.	T.A.	1947	Communist; from the 1920s in various forms; underground newspaper; 1970 – weekly
Kol ha-No'ar	Irr.	T.A.	1940–1966	Communist youth
Kol ha-Shabbat	M.	Jer.	1957	Sabbath observance
Kol Nekhei Milḥamah	M.	T.A	1949	war invalids
Kolno'a	F.	T.A.	1931–1935	cinema; the first of its kind
Kolot	M.	Warsaw	1923–1924	lit.
Kol Sinai	M.	Jer.	1962	religious
Kol Torah	M.	Jer.	1929, 1932	rabbinics
Kol Ya'akov	W.	Jer.	1922–1928 1933–1934	religious
Kol Yisrael	W.	Jer.	1921–1929	Agudat Israel
Komemiyyut	A.	T.A.	1951–1954	lit.; appeared each year on Independence Day
Ko'operaẓyah	F.	T.A.	1930–1939	cooperative affairs
Korot – see also: Ha-Ittonai ha-Ivri	Q.	T.A.	1952	history of medicine and science
Korot	M.	T.A	1970	history of the yishuv and Zionism
Koveẓ al Yad (Kobez al jad)	Irr.	Berlin-Jer.	1885	editions of ancient manuscripts; vols. 1–10 Berlin, N.S. Jer. 1937–
Koveẓ ha-Ḥevrah la-Ḥakirat Ereẓ Yisrael	Irr.	Jer.	1921–1945	archaeology of Palestine and history of the yishuv; 4 vols; in several parts
Koveẓ Harẓa'ot ha-Ḥevrah ha-Historit	Irr.	Jer.	1964–1966	lectures on history from the annual seminar of the society
Koveẓ Harẓa'ot shel ha-Iggud ha-Yisre'eli le Ibbud informaẓyah	A.	Jer.	1965	information processing – partly in English
Koveẓ ha-Tammim	Irr.	Warsaw	1935–1937	Ḥasidei Ḥabad, Ḥasidei Lubavitch
Koveẓ li-Ve'ayot ha-Ḥinnukh ha-Gufani	B-M.	T.A.	1962–1965	Wingate Institute, physical education
Koveẓ Ma'amarim le-Divrei Yemei ha-Ittonut ha-Ivrit be-Ereẓ Yisrael	A.	T.A.	1935–1936	history of the Hebrew press in Ereẓ Israel
Koveẓ Schocken le-Divrei Sifrut	1	T.A.	1941	lit.; superseded by Lu'ah ha-Areẓ
Koveẓ Sifruti	A.	Jer.	1914	lit.; ed. by Po'alei Zion
Kunteres	W.	T.A.	1919–1929 1940–1944	organ of Aḥdut ha-Avodah; in the 1940s of Mapai
Kunteres	Irr.	Riga-Warsaw	1929–1937	Ḥasidei Lubavitch
Kunteres Bibliografi	M.	T.A.	1950–1970	bibliography
Kunteres ha-Sefer ha-Torani – see: Ha-Sefer				
Kunteresim	Irr.	Jer.	1937–1942	Hebrew language studies; new ed. 1964
Lada'at	M.	Jer.	1970	popular science
La-Gever	M.	T.A.	1963–1969	entertainment

Title	Freq.	Place of Publication	Year(s) of Appearance	Main Characteristics
La-Ḥayyal – see: Ha-Ḥayyal				
La-Ishah	W.	T.A.	1947	women's magazine
La-Kore ha-Ẓa'ir	M.	T.A.	1950–1954	bibliography
La-Matḥil	W.	Jer.	1955	easy Hebrew; for some years did not appear in order
La-Merḥav	D.	T.A.	1954–1971	organ of Aḥdut ha-Avodah, the first months as F. and W.; merged with Davar
La-Mishpaḥah	M.	N.Y.	1963	general
La-Mo'ed	Irr.	Jer.	1945–1947	collections for festivals; 7 appeared
La-Ya'aran	Q.	Netanyah	1950	forestry
La-Yehudim	A.	Jer.	1909–1912 1921–1925	humor, the first humorist periodical in Ereẓ Israel
La-Yogev	A.	T.A.	1945–1949	cultivation problems
Le-Aḥdut ha-Avodah	W.	T.A.	1944–1948	organ of Le-Aḥdut ha-Avodah party, from its split with Mapai until its amalgamation with Mapam
Lefi Sha'ah	Irr.	Jer.	1915–1917	8 issues during World War I
Leket Amarim	1	St. Petersburg	1889	lit.
Le-Ma'an ha-Yeled ve-ha-No'ar	F.	Jer.	1942–1949	Szold Institute for children and youth
Le-Shabbat	W.	Jer.	1922	general
Leshonenu	Q.	Jer.	1928	Hebrew language studies
Leshonenu la-am	M.	Jer.	1945	Hebrew language studies in popular form
Lev Ḥadash	Irr.	T.A.-Jer.	1922–1928	critical-radical
Le Yad ha-Hegeh	Irr.	T.A.	1952–1959	taxi drivers' bulletin
Li-Kerat	Irr.	T.A.	1952–1953	Hebrew young writers
Likkud	M.	T.A.	1946–1947	leftist
Livyat Ḥen	1	Warsaw	1887	lit.
Lu'aḥ Aḥi'asaf	A.	Warsaw	1893–1904, 1923	lit.; 13 vols.
Lu'aḥ Aḥi'ever	A.	N.Y.	1918, 1921	lit.; 2 vols.
Lu'aḥ Ereẓ Yisrael	A.	Jer.	1895–1915	Palestinography and lit.; 21 vols.
Lu'aḥ ha-Areẓ	A.	T.A.	1941–1954	lit.; almanac of Haaretz
Lu'aḥ ha-Em-ve-ha-Yeled – see: Ha-Em-ve-ha-Yeled				
Lu'aḥ ha-Me'orer	1	T.A.	1935	Ereẓ Israel labor movement
Lu'aḥ Keren Kayemet – see: Moladti				
Lu'aḥ Ko'operativi	A.	T.A.	1931	cooperative types; now; Lu'aḥ ha-Ko'operaẓyah
Lu'aḥ Sha'ashu'im	1	Cracow, Poland	1902	lit.
Lu'aḥ Yerushalayim	A.	Jer.	1940–1951	history of Jerusalem and the yishuv; 12 vols.
Ma'anit	A.	Jer.	1926	lit.; Hebrew writers for Keren Kayemeth
Ma'anit	B-M.	T.A.	1939–1954	youth of Tenu'at ha-Moshavim
Ma'anit	Irr.	T.A.	1946–1958	moshavim of Ha-Po'el ha-Mizrachi
Ma'arakhot	M., Q.	T.A.	1939	military journal of the Haganah and the Israel Defense Forces
Ma'arekhot Ḥimmush	Q.	T.A.	1961	ammunition problems, ordinance corps
Ma'arekhot Yam	Q.	T.A.	1948	naval organ
Ma'ariv	D.	T.A.	1948	independent; the first issues – Yedi'ot Ma'ariv
Ma'avak	Irr.	T.A.	1947	organ of the Kena'anim
Ma'avak	W.	T.A.	1952–1954	party organ which separated from Mapam until its amalgamation with Mapai
Ma'abarot	M.	T.A.-Jaffa	1919–1921	literary organ of Ha-Po'el ha-Ẓa'ir
Mabbat Ḥadash	W.	T.A.	1965–1968	organ of Rafi
Mabbu'a	Q.	N.Y.	1952–1954	lit.
Mabbu'a	A.	Jer.	1963	religious literature
Madda	B-M.	Jer	1956	popular science
Madda'ei ha-Yahadut	A.	Jer.	1926–1927	Judaic studies of the Hebrew University, Jer.; continuation of Yedi'ot ha-Makhon le-Madda'ei ha-Yahadut
Madrikh li-Mekomot Avodah Me'urganim	A.	T.A.	1956–1965	list of work places where work is organized by the Histadrut

Title	Freq.	Place of Publication	Year(s) of Appearance	Main Characteristics
Maggid Mishneh	W.	Lyck, E. Prussia	1879–1881	lit.
Maḥanayim	Irr.	T.A.	1948	collections for the festivals and specific subjects by the army chaplaincy; the first 18 booklets called Yalkut ha-Rabbanut ha-Ẓeva'it
Maḥanot	M.	T.A.	1942–1947	organ of the camp workers
Maḥazikei ha-Dat	W.	Lvov, Galicia	1879–1913	extreme Orthodox, sometimes Kol Maḥazikei ha-Dat
Maḥazikei ha-Dat	W., B-M.	Jer.	1919–1924	extreme Orthodox, partly in Yiddish
Maḥbarot le-Marxizm	Irr.	Givat Ḥavivah	1950–1951	studies on Marxism
Maḥbarot le-Sifrut	B-M.	T.A.	1940–1954	lit.
Maḥbarot le-Sozyologyah	B-M.	T.A.	1943–1945	sociology
Maḥberet	Q.	Jer.	1952–1967	lit. organ of Alliance Israélite Universelle, partly in French
Makkabbi – see: Ha-Makkabbi				
Marot ha-Kalkalah be-Yisrael	M.	Jer.	1955–1966	economics
Masakh	Irr.	T.A.	1954–1955	lit., theater and art
Maslul	W.	T.A.	1951–1952	for Yemenite and Eastern immigrants
Massa	F.	T.A.	1951–1954	lit., from 1954 literary supplement of La-Merḥav and from 1971 of Davar
Massad	A.	N.Y.	1933, 1936	lit.
Massad	Irr.	T.A.	1951, 1967	No'ar Dati Oved
Massekhet	1	T.A.	1951	lit.
Massu'ot	1	Odessa, Russia	1919	lit.
Mattekhet	Q.	Haifa	1958–1967 1971	Israel metal industry in the Technion
Ma'yan ha-Ḥasidut – see also: Ha-Ma'yan	A.	Jer.	1964	ḥasidic affairs
Ma'yanot	A.	Jer.	1952–1968	religious
Maẓpen	Irr.	T.A.	1943–1944	pro-Revisionist
Maẓpen	W.	T.A.	1954–1955	general
Maẓpen	Irr.	T.A.-Jer.	1963	leftist
Me'assef – see also: Ha-Me'assef	1	St. Petersburg	1902	lit.
Me'assef	A.	Jer.-T.A.	1960–1968	lit.; 8 vols.
Me'assefim Madda'iyyim shel ha-Tekhniyyon	Irr.	Haifa	1944–1955	science; 6 vols.
Me'assef Soferei Ereẓ Yisrael	1	T.A.	1940	lit.
Me'assef Soferei Ereẓ Yisrael	1	T.A.	1942	lit.; 2 vols
Me'at me-Harbeh	1	T.A.	1947	lit.
Me-Et le-Et	1	N.Y.	1900	lit.
Me-Et le-Et	M.	Vilna	1918	lit.
Megammot	Q.	Jer.	1949	child problems by Szold Institute
Meged Geresh Yeraḥim	M.	Vienna	1848	lit.; supplement to the weekly Centralorgan fuer juedische interessen
Meged Yeraḥim	M.	Lvov, Galicia	1855–1856	lit.; 4 issues
Megillot	M.	Jer.	1950–1953	Hebrew culture and education
Me-Ḥag le-Ḥag	Irr.	N.Y.-Baltimore	1915, 1918	lit.; 2 issues
Mehallekhim	Irr.	Jer.	1969	organ of the Torah Judaism movement
Me-Havvayot ha-Zeman	M., Irr.	T.A.	1944–1946 1952	contemporary affairs
Meḥkarim be-Geografyah shel Ereẓ Yisrael	A.	Jer.	1960	Palestinography
Me'ir Einayim	A.	Bene-Berak	1968–1969	bibliography
Mekhes ve-Ta'avurah	Irr.	T.A.	1949–1956	organ of the Association of Customs Agents
Mekhon ha-Tekanim	Q.	T.A.	1968	Israel Standards Institute
Melilah	A.	Manchester, England	1944–1955	Judaic studies; 5 vols. (double 3/4)
Meliẓ Eḥad Minni Elef	1	St. Petersburg	1884	lit.; in honor of the 100th copy of Ha-Meliẓ
Menorah	F.	Lodz, Poland	1930	Judaic studies
Meshek ha-Bakar ve-ha-Ḥalav	Q.	T.A.	1952	dairy farming

Title	Freq.	Place of Publication	Year(s) of Appearance	Main Characteristics
Meshek ha-Ofot	M.	T.A.-Tel Yosef	1949	poultry farming
Mesibbah	1	T.A.	1926	lit.; the first editing work in Ereẓ Israel by E. Steinman
Mesillot	M.	Warsaw	1935–1937	education and Hebrew culture
Meteorologyah be-Yisrael	Q.	Bet Dagon	1963	meteorology
Mevasseret Ẓiyyon	M.	Jer.	1884	the first periodical edited by E. Ben-Yehuda; 4 issues
Mevo'ot	M.	T.A.	1953–1956	lit.
Meẓudah	Irr.	London	1943–1954	lit. and Judaic studies; 5 vols. (2 doubles)
Mi-Bayit	1	T.A.	1946	lit.; from Ereẓ Israel authors for the remnants of the Holocaust
Mi-Bifenim	Irr., Q.	En-Harod-T.A.	1923	organ of Ha-Kibbutz ha-Me'uḥad; new reprint of the first 28 issues
Mifgash	Irr.	T.A.	1964	lit.; first of its kind in Hebrew; Hebrew and Arabic literature; Hebrew and Arabic on parallel pages
Mi-Keren Zavit	1	Detroit, Mich.-Baltimore, Md.	1921	lit.
Mikhtav Ḥozer – see: Ha-Refu'ah				
Mikkun Ḥakla'i	Q.	T.A.	1956	farm mechanization
Miklat	M.	N.Y.	1919–1920	lit.
Milḥamtenu – see also: Be-Terem				
Mi-Mizraḥ u-mi-Ma'arav	M., Irr.	Vienna-Berlin	1894–1899	lit. and Judaic studies
Minḥah	1	T.A.	1930	lit.
Min ha-Yesod	F.	T.A.	1962–1965	organ of Min ha-Yesod faction; two collections were issued with the name in 1962–63
Misḥar ha-Makkolet	M.	T.A.	1940–1951	grocery business; previously issued under Soḥer ha-Makkolet
Misḥar ve-Ta'asiyyah	F.	T.A.	1923–1933	trade, factories, and agriculture
Mishmar – see: Al ha-Mishmar				
Mishpat ha-Shalom ha-Ivri	1	T.A.	1925	magistrates' court problems during the Mandate
Mishpat ve-Khalkalah	M.	T.A.	1955–1959	law and economics
Mi-Teiman	1	T.A.	1938	history of the Yemenite Jews' immigration to Israel
Mi-Tekufat ha-Even	A.	Jer.	1960	prehistoric studies in Israel
Mivrak	D.	T.A.	1947–1948	afternoon paper; organ of Leḥi
Mi-Yamim Rishonim	M.	T.A.	1934–1935	history of Zionism and the yishuv
Mi-Yerushalayim	Irr.	Warsaw	1892	lit.; Ereẓ Israel topics; 2 issues
Mi-Ẓiyyon	1	Warsaw	1895	lit.
Miẓpeh – see also: Ha-Miẓpeh	1	T.A.	1953	lit.; Ha-Ẓofeh annual
Mizraḥ u-Ma'arav	M.	Jer.	1919–1932	Judaic studies, in particular on Spanish and Sephardi Jewry
Mo'adon Mekhoniyyot ve-Sayyarut be-Yisrael	M.	T.A.	1966	automobile and touring club
Molad	M., B-M.	T.A.-Jer.	1948	lit.; N.S. 1967-the last years B-M.
Moladti	A.	Jer.	1936–1938	most years on behalf of Keren ha-Kayemeth
Moriyyah	W. & D.	Jer.	1910–1915	Orthodox; from 1913, daily
Moznayim	W.	T.A.	1929–1933	lit.; organ of the Hebrew Writers' Association
Moznayim	M.	T.A.	1933–1947 1955	lit.; organ of the Hebrew Writers' Association
Moznayim	F.	T.A.	1948	lit.; organ of the Hebrew Writers' Association
Muze'on ha-Areẓ	A.	T.A.	1959	on all museums in the Tel Aviv vicinity
Naḥali'el	Irr.	Jer.	1965	religious
Nativ	Irr.	T.A.	1934–1935	a nonconformist periodical by A.L. Yaffe, "the father of the moshavim"
Ner	F., Irr.	Jer.	1950	Jewish-Arab relations
Ner ha-Ma'aravi	M.	N.Y.	1895, 1897	lit.
Ner Ma'aravi	A.	N.Y.	1922, 1925	rabbinics and Judaica

Title	Freq.	Place of Publication	Year(s) of Appearance	Main Characteristics
Nerot Shabbat	Irr.	Jer.	1943–1952	Sabbath observance
Netivah	F., Irr.	Jer.	1926–1938, 1943	Ha-Po'el ha-Mizraḥi
Netivei Irgun	M., B-M.	Jer.	1954	organization and administration; from 1969 B-M.
Netivot	1	Warsaw	1913	lit.
Netivot	A.	Jer.	1953–1968	religious education for Diaspora Jews
Nimim	1	N.Y.	1923	lit.; printed in Berlin
Nir – see also: Ha-Nir	A.	N.Y.	1952	education and lit.; continuation of Ha-Nir 1930–38
Nir	M.	T.A.	1948–1959	education through J.N.F.
Nisan	1	Warsaw	1930	lit.
Nisan	1	T.A.	1942	lit.
Niv	Irr.	N.Y.	1936–1966	lit.; organ of the Young Hebrew Writers in U.S.
Niv ha-Kevuẓah	Irr., Q.	T.A.	1930	organ of Ḥever ha-Kevuẓot and from 1952 of Iḥud ha-Kevuzot ve-ha-Kibbutzim; some interruptions
Niv ha-Midrashiyyah	A.	T.A.	1963	lit. rabbinics, religious education
Niv ha-Moreh	M.	T.A.	1958	teachers of Agudat Israel
Niv ha-Rofe	Q.& S-A.	T.A.	1951	organ of the Histadrut doctors
Niẓoẓ	Irr.	Kaunas (Kovno)-Dachau-Munich	1940–1948	at the beginning in Kovno ghetto and Dachau camp, then in Munich, the only permanent Hebrew newspaper of the remnants from the Holocaust
No'am	A.	Jer.	1958	clarification of contemporary halakhic problems
Nogah ha-Yare'aḥ	M.	Lvov- Tarnopol, Galicia	1872–1873 1880	Judaic studies, lit.
Ofakim	Irr.	Warsaw	1932–1934	education
Ofakim	Irr.	T.A.	1943–1961	education by Ha-Shomer ha-Ẓa'ir
Ofek	1	T.A.	1970	lit.
Ohel – see also: Ha-Ohel	1	T.A.	1921	lit.
Ohel Mo'ed	Irr.	Cracow, Poland	1898–1900	rabbinics
Ohel Mo'ed	Irr.	Warsaw	1926–1935	rabbinics
Ohel Torah	M. Irr.	Jer.	1926–1927 1929	rabbinics
Oholei Gadna	M.	T.A.	1952–1960	vocalized, for Gadna
Olamenu	1	Odessa Petrograd, Moscow	1917	lit.
Olam ha-Defus	M, Q.	T.A.	1956	typography
Olam ha-Elektronikah	M.	Jer.	1962–1965	electronics, continuation of Radio ve-Elektronikah
Olam ha-Ishah	F.	T.A.	1940–1963	women's magazine
Olam ha-Kolno'a	W.	T.A.	1951	cinema
Olam ha-Mistorin	Q.	T.A.	1968	parapsychology
Olam ha-Sefer	Irr.	T.A.	1954–1958	organ of publishers; superseded by Ha-Sefer be-Yisrael
Olam ha-Ẓillum	M.	T.A.	1966–1967	photography
Olamot Aḥerim	Irr.	T.A.	1970	parapsychology
Omer – see also: Ha-Omer	1	T.A.	1927	lit.
Omer	W., Irr.	T.A.	1936–1942	weekly 1936–39; from then on monthly sometimes in place of the banned Davar
Omer	D.	T.A.	1951–1979	daily; vocalized (with Davar)
Omer	A.	T.A.	1955–1960	rabbinics
Ommanut	Q.	Jer.	1940–1942	art
Ommanut ha-Kolno'a	Irr.	T.A.	1957–1963	cinema
Or ha-Mizraḥ	Q.	N.Y.	1954	rabbinics, Judaic studies
Orlogin	Irr.	T.A.	1950–1957	lit.; 13 issues
Orot	Irr.	T.A.	1950–1955	cultural work of the Histadrut; 3 vols.
Orot	B-M. Q.	Jer.	1950–1966 1968	lit. and Hebrew culture; N.S. from 1968 Q.; partly in English

Title	Freq.	Place of Publication	Year(s) of Appearance	Main Characteristics
Or Torah	Irr.	Lvov, Galicia-Frankfurt, Germany	1874	lit.; 4 issues
Or Torah	Q.	Jer.	1897–1901	rabbinics
Oshyot	Irr.	T.A.	1947–1957	educational problems before school
Ot	Irr., W.	T.A.	1966–1968 1971	organ of the Israel Labor Party
Ovnayim	A.	Bet Berl	1961–1966	collection – Bet Berl affairs
Oẓar Genazim	1	Jer.	1960	printed manuscript letters on history of Ereẓ Israel
Oẓar ha-Ḥayyim	Irr.	De a-Seini, Romania	1924–1938	Judaic studies
Oẓar ha-Ḥokhmah ve-ha-Madda	Irr.	N.Y.	1894	lit.; 2 issues
Oẓar ha-Sifrut	A.		1887–1896 1902	lit.; 5 vols.+1
Oẓar Ḥokhmah	Irr.	Lvov, Galicia	1859–1865	lit.; 3 issues
Oẓar Neḥmad	Irr.	Vienna-Pressburg (Bratislava), Czechoslovakia	1858–1863	Judaic studies; 4 vols.
Oẓar Tov	Irr.	Berlin	1878–1886	mainly editions of Hebrew manuscripts
Oẓar Yehudei Sefarad	A.	Jer.	1959	research on Spanish Jewry past and present
Palmaḥ – see: Alon ha-Palmaḥ				
Pamalyah	1	T.A.	1953	lit. collection dedicated to young authors
Panim el Panim	W.	T.A.-Jer.	1954–1956 1959	religious illustrated magazine, during the interruption appeared as Ayin be-Ayin – see there.
Pardes – see also: Ha-Pardes	Irr.	Odessa, Russia	1892–1896	lit. 3 vols; in the first volume Bialik's first poem was published
Pargod	Irr.	Jer.	1963, 1966	theater, 2 issues
Perakim (Peraqim)	Irr.	N.Y.	1955–1966	Judaic studies 4 vols.; organ of Hebrew Academy in N.Y.
Perakim	F.	Haifa	1958–1965	lit. continuation of the journal of the same name in Buenos Aires
Peri Eẓ Ḥayyim	Irr.	Amsterdam	1691–1807	the first rabbinical periodical
Peri To'elet	1	Amsterdam	1825	lit.
Perozedor	Irr.	T.A.	1962–1965 1968	problems of religion
Pesi'ot	Irr.	Jer.	1926–1935	educational problems in the low grades
Petaḥ	A.	Bet-Berl	1959–1968	studies on various problems
Petaḥim	B-M.	Jer.	1967	modern approach to religion
Pinkas Histadrut ha-Ovedim	Irr.	T.A.	1922–1925	the first periodical of the Histadrut; superseded by Davar
Pinkas Histadrut ha-Ovedim	M.	T.A.	1936–1938	new series in another form
Pinkas le-Inyenei ha-Pekidim – see: Shurot				
Pirḥei Ẓafon	A.	Vilna	1841, 1844	lit.; the first Hebrew periodical in Russia
Pirkei Bessarabyah	Irr.	T.A.	1952, 1958	history of the Bessarabian Jewry; 2 vols.
Pirsumei ha-Iggud ha-Yisre'eli le-Ibbud Informaẓyah	A.	T.A.	1968	information processing
Praxis	Irr.	T.A.	1968	leftist
Problemai – see: Ha-Problemai				
Problemot	M., Irr.	T.A.	1962	nonconformist-anarchist; party in Yiddish
Qadmoniot	Q.	Jer.	1968	archaeology of Palestine and biblical lands
Radio	W.	Jer.	1960–1962	Kol Israel newspaper
Radio ve-Elektronikah	M.	Jer.	1957–1961	radio and electronics
Radio Yerushalayim	W.	Jer.	1938–1942	radio newspaper of the Mandate; superseded by Ha-Galgal; in the times of Ha-Galgal, supplement for few years; partly in English

Title	Freq.	Place of Publication	Year(s) of Appearance	Main Characteristics
Ramah	M.	N.Y.	1937–1939	lit.
Ramzor	M.	Jer.-T.A.	1961–1962 1965	in the beginning, organ of the Mapai student cell in Jerusalem; from 1965, Mapai youth in Tel Aviv
Refu'ah Veterinarit	Irr., M.	T.A.-Bet Dagon	1939	in the beginning irregular; organ of veterinary surgeons
Refu'ah ha-Shinnayim	B-M.	T.A.	1944	organ of dentists
Reshafim	W.	Warsaw	1909	lit.; 50 issues
Reshimat Ma'amarim be-Madda'ei ha-Yahadut	A.	Jer.	1967	index of articles on Jewish studies
Reshimat Pirsumei ha-Memshalah	Q.	Jer.	1956	list of government publications
Reshit	Q.	Warsaw	1933–1934	lit.
Reshummot	Irr.	Odessa-Berlin-T.A.	1918–1930	folklore, first issued in Odessa; 6 vols.
Reshumot	A.	T.A.	1945–1953	folklore; 5 vols.
Revivim	Irr.	Lvov-Jer.-Jaffa	1908–1919	lit.; 6 vols.
Rihut ve-Dekorazyah	Q.	T.A.	1961	furnishing and decoration
Rimmon	Irr.	Berlin	1922–1924	lit. and art
Rimmon	W.	T.A.	1956–1957	ill. weekly
Rimmon	Irr.	Buenos Aires	1966–1968	lit.
Rivon ha-Aguddah ha-Zo'otekhnit	Q.	Rehovot	1969	Association of Zootechnics
Rivon Handasat Betihut	Q.	T.A.	1968	security engineering
Rivon Katan	Q.	N.Y.	1944	lit.; 2 issues
Rivon le-Banka'ut	Q.	T.A.	1961	banking
Rivon le-Inyenei Missim	Q.	Jer.	1965	taxes
Rivon le-Khalkalah	Q.	T.A.	1953	economics
Rivon le-Matematikah	Q.	Jer.	1946	mathematics
Rivon Merkaz ha-Beniyyah ha-Yisre'eli	Q,	T.A.	1970	building
Rivon Mishteret Yisrael	Q.	T.A.	1956–1965	police
Ro'eh ha-Heshbon	Irr., B-M.	T.A.	1939–1946 1950	accounting
Rotary Yisrael	Q.	Ramat Gan	1960	Rotary
Sa'ad	B-M.	Jer.	1957	social welfare
Saddan	Irr.	T.A.-Jer.	1924–1926	lit.; organ of U.Z. Greenberg
Sadot	Irr.	T.A.	1938–1945	under various names – Ha-No'ar ha-Lomed
Sarid u-Falit	1	T.A.	1945	Judaic studies (mainly editions of manuscripts)
Sedarim	1	T.A.	1942	lit.; 4 vols.
Sedemot	Irr.	T.A.	1949–1954	Ha-No'ar ha-Lomed
Sedemot	Q.	T.A.	1960	previously Ihud ha-Kevuzot ve-ha-Kibbutzim, later youths from all various collective settlements
Sefatenu	Irr.	Odessa-Berlin	1917, 1923	Hebrew language studies
Sefatenu	1	T.A.	1927	league of defenders of the Hebrew language
Sefer ha-Mishar	Q.	T.A.	1964–1967	commerce
Sefer ha-Shanah – see also: Shenaton	A.	Warsaw	1900–1906	lit.; 5 vols
Sefer ha-Shanah	A.	Chicago	1935–1959	lit.; College of Jewish Studies
Sefer ha-Shanah	A.	N.Y.-T.A.	1964	history of Polish Jewry; first English, Hebrew, and Yiddish, 2–3 Yiddish and Hebrew
Sefer ha-Shanah be-Amerikah shel Histadrut Benei Erez Yisrael	A.	N.Y.	1931–1947	lit.; superseded by Yisrael
Sefer ha-Shanah le Bibliografyah Yehudit be-Polanyah	A.	Warsaw	1934	Jewish bibliography in Poland; 1 vol.
Sefer ha-Shanah ha-Em ve-ha-Yeled – see: Ha-Em ve-ha-Yeled				
Sefer ha-Shanah le-Anaf ha-Beniyyah	A.	T.A.	1966, 1969	building trade; in 1935 building annual issued
Sefer ha-Shanah li-Kehillot ve-Irgunim	A.	Jer.	1970	world Jewish communities and organizations annual
Sefer ha-Shanah li-Melekhet ha-Defus	A.	T.A.	1938	typography and printing; 1 vol.
Sefer ha-Shanah li-Yhudei Amerikah	A.	N.Y.	1931–1949	lit.; 11 vols. (2 doubles)
Sefer ha-Shanah li-Yhudei Polanyah	A.	Cracow, Poland	1938	Polish Jewry; 1 vol.

Title	Freq.	Place of Publication	Year(s) of Appearance	Main Characteristics
Sefer ha-Shanah shel Ereẓ Yisrael	A.	T.A.	1923–1926 1934–1935	lit.
Sefer ha-Shanah shel ha-Ittona'im	A.	T.A.	1942	journalists and journalism
Sefunot	A.	Jer.	1956–1966	research on the Jewish communities in the East
Sekirah Ḥodshit	M.	T.A.	1954	monthly review and for the Israel Defense Forces
Semol	Irr.	T.A.	1953–1954	Moshe Sneh's organ, between his leaving Mapam and joining Maki
Seneh	M.	Warsaw	1929	lit.
Senuit	M.	Lvov, Galicia	1910–1912	lit.
Sha'arei Beri'ut	M.	T.A.	1931–1932	health and hygiene
Sha'arei Halakhot	A.	Jer.	1966	rabbinics
Sha'arei Torah	M.	Warsaw	1907–1927	rabbinics
Sha'arei Ẓiyyon	W.	Jer.	1876–1884	in the first year partly in Yiddish; the first Yiddish newspaper in Ereẓ Israel
Sha'ar la-Kore he-Ḥadash	W.	Jer.	1961	easy Hebrew, vocalized
Sha'ar Ẓiyyon	B-M.	London	1946	religious, Judaic studies; partly in English
Shaḥarit	M.	Odessa-Warsaw	1913	lit.
Shaḥmat	Irr.	T.A.-Haifa-Jer.	1923, 1932 1936–1937 1946, 1960	chess – various newspapers under this name or Ha-Shaḥmat
Shai	1	Jer.	1925	lit.; Hebrew writers for J.N.F.
Shallekhet	1	Lvov, Galicia	1910	lit.
Shalom	Irr.	T.A.	1953–1956	organ of the Peace Movement
Shanah be-Shanah	A.	Jer.	1960	religious, lit.; annual of Hechal Shlomo in Jer.; the first volume called: Halikhot
She'arim	W., D.	T.A.	1945–1981	Po'alei Agudat Israel from 1939; W. from 1949, daily from 1951
Sheḥakim	Irr.	Kefar Ḥabad	1969	organ of Aircraft Industries
She'ifoteinu	Irr., M.	Jer.	1927–1933	organ of Bet Shalom (Jewish-Arab cooperation)
Shelabbim – see: Ha-Po'el ha-Vatik				
Sheluḥot	M.	Jer.	1945–1962	religious youth department of the Jewish Agency, continuation of Iggeret la-Golah
Sheluḥot	F.	T.A.	1950–1955	department of Yemenites belonging to Mapai
Shelumei Emunei Yisrael	A.	Odessa, Russia	1898–1902	lit.; 4 vols.
Shema'atin	Q.	Bene Berak	1963	organ of teachers of religious subjects in religious secondary schools
Shemoneh ba-Erev	W.	T.A.	1968	radio and T.V.
Shenaton – see also: Sefer ha-Shabat Agudat Yisrael-Amerikah	A.	T.A.	1951, 1953	Agudat Israel-America
Shenaton ha-Aguddah ha-Yisre'lit le-Shikkum	A.	T.A.	1964	rehabilitation of invalids and soldiers
Shenaton ha-Histadrut	A.	T.A.	1963	sketches of Histadrut activities
Shenaton ha-Hitaḥadut le-Khadduregei	A.	T.A.	1959 1964/65	football
Shenaton ha-Memshalah	A.	Jer.	1949	activities of the government; appears also in English as Government Yearbook
Shenation ha-Po'el	A.	T.A.	1968	sport
Shenation ha-Sefer – see: Jewish Book Annual				
Shenaton ha-Student	A.	Jer.	1965–1966 1968	students in Israel
Shenaton ha-Televizyah	A.	Haifa	1969	T.V.
Shenaton Ḥerut	A.	T.A.	1953–1954	activities of Ḥerut movement
Shenaton Hidrologi	A.	Jer.	1950	hydrology
Shenaton le-Mishpat Ivri	A.	Jer.	1970	Jewish law
Shenaton Massadah	A.	Ramat Gan	1968	1967 events
Shenaton Statisti le-Yisrael	A.	Jer.	1950	statistical summary
Shenaton Yedi'ot Aḥaronot	A.	T.A.	1966	newspaper annual; also called Yedi'on

Title	Freq.	Place of Publication	Year(s) of Appearance	Main Characteristics
Shenaton Yisrael le-Ommanut ha-Ẓillum	A.	T.A.	1963	photography
Shenayim Plus	M.	T.A.	1970	ill. entertainment magazine
Shevet va-Am	A.	Jer.	1954–1960 1970	Sephardi Jews past and present
Shevilei ha-Ḥinnukh	F., Q.	N.Y.	1925–1930 1940	education
Shevilim	Irr.	T.A.	1955–1958	organ of Ha-No'ar ha-Ẓiyyoni
Shevilin	S-A., A.	T.A.	1962	organ of rabbis in Mizrachi and Ha-Po'el ha-Mizrachi movement
Shevut Teiman	1	T.A.	1945	history of Yemenite Jews; various booklets with this name concerning Yemenites issued in years 1940–44
Shibbolim	F.	N.Y.	1909	lit.; the first modern lit. journal in U.S.; 7 issues
Shittuf	M., B-M.	T.A.	1948	organ of the central cooperative of the Histadrut
Shivat Ẓiyyon	A.	Jer.	1950–1956	history of Zionism and the yishuv; 3 vols. (one double)
Shomer Ẓiyyon ha-Ne'eman	Irr.	Altona	1846–1856	rabbinics, Orthodox; 222 issues, new reprint
Shorashim	Irr.	Jer.	1936–1953	teachers' platform for Keren ha-Kayemeth
Shoval	Q.	T.A.	1962–1967	20 issues; public council for culture and art
Shulamit	F.	Jer.	1935	women's magazine
Shurot	Irr.	Beltsy, Bessarabia	1935–1937	lit.
Shurot	Irr. M.	T.A.	1938	organ of clerks-office workers
Si'aḥ	Irr.	T.A.	1969	New Left in Israel
Sifrei Sha'ashu'im	Irr.	Cracow-Buczacz, Galicia	1896–1899	lit.
Sifrut – see also: Ha-Sifrut	Irr.	Warsaw	1908–1909	lit.; 4 issues
Sifrut Ẓe'irah	W.	Jer.	1939	lit.; organ of young writers
Signon	B-M.	T.A.	1970	architecture and interior design
Sikkot	W.	T.A.	1940–1945	humor
Sinai	A.	Bucharest	1928–1933	Judaic studies; 5 vols
Sinai	M.	Jer.	1937	Judaic studies, rabbinics
Sport ba-Olam – see also: Ha-Sport	M.	T.A.	1964–1965	sport
Sport ha-Am	B-M.	T.A.	1947–1959	sport; from 1951 W., from 1959 included in Davar
Sport ha-Boker	W.	T.A.	1936	sport; separate sport edition of Ha-Boker, afterward included in Ha-Boker
Sport ha-Shavu'a	W.	T.A.	1947–1948	sport
Sport Kadduregel	W.	T.A.	1965–1966	soccer
Sport ve-Toto	W.	T.A.	1968–1969	sport and Toto (lottery)
Sport Yisrael	W.	T.A.	1949–1954	sport
Sugyot	1	Givat Ḥavivah	1956	collection of studies from the Ha-Shomer ha-Za'ir on Jewish and general problems
Sullam	M.	Jer.	1949–1964	theoretical organ of Leḥi members and their adherents in Ereẓ Israel
Sura	A.	Jer.	1954–1964	Judaic studies; 4 vols.
Ta'asiyyah u-Misḥar	M.	Jer.	1959	industry and trade
Ta'asiyyah ve-Khalkalah	M.	Jer.	1937–1941	industry and economics
Tafrit	M.	T.A.	1949–1953	entertainment – army
Tagim	1	Bene-Berak	1969	bibliography
Taḥbiv	M.	T.A.	1962–1963, 1970	hobbies
Taḥburah ve-Tayyarut	M.	T.A.	1962	transport and tourism
Taḥkemoni	Irr.	Berne-Berlin-Jer.	1910–1911	Judaic studies; 2 issues
Talpioth	Q.	N.Y.	1943–1963	rabbinics and Judaic studies

Title	Freq.	Place of Publication	Year(s) of Appearance	Main Characteristics
Talpiyyot	1	Berdichev, Ukraine	1895	lit.; largest collection of its kind issued in those days
Talpiyyot	W.	Jassy (Iasi), Romania	1898	lit.; Zionist
Tambir	Q.	T.A.	1960	costing and business economics
TaRAV(Tav Resh-Ayin-Vav)	1	Jer.	1916	Ereẓ Israel and Jerusalem in World War I
Tarbiz	Q.	Jer.	1930	Judaic studies; in the first years also humanities
Tarbut	M.	N.Y.	1919–1920	education
Tarbut	M.	Warsaw	1922–1924	Hebrew culture and education
Tarbut	B-M.	London	1944–1968	lit.; from 1940 under various names
Tashbeẓ	F., Irr.	T.A.-Nahariyyah-Ramat Gan	1954	crossword
Tav-Shin	A.	T.A.	1943–1956	lit.; almanacs of Davar, some under different names
Taẓlil	A.	Haifa	1960	music research and bibliography
Te'atron	M.	T.A.	1953–1954	theater
Te'atron	B-M.	Haifa	1962–1966	theater
Te'atron ve-Ommanut	M.	T.A.-Jer.	1925–1928	theater and art
Tefuẓot Yisrael	B-M.	Jer.	1962	Jewish life in the Diaspora
Teḥiyyah – see also: Ha-Teḥiyyah	M.	N.Y.	1913	lit.
Teḥumim	Q.	Warsaw	1937–1938	lit.
Tekhnikah u-Madda	M.	T.A.	1937–1954	popular science
Tekhunat ha-Ru'aḥ ha-Yisre'eli	1	N.Y.	1889	lit.
Tekufatenu	Q.	London	1932–1933	lit.
Tekumah	Irr.	N.Y.	1938–1939	education and J.N.F.
Telamim	Irr., Q.	T.A.	1933	organ of the moshav movement
Telegramot Aḥaronot	D.	T.A.	1941	independent afternoon paper
Tel-Talpiyyot	F., Irr.	Vac, Hungary	1892–1938	rabbinics; interruption during years 1921–22
Temurot	M.	T.A.	1938	General Zionist Labor movement, afterward Liberal
Teraklin	M.	T.A.	1949–1965	lit. and entertainment
Terapyah Shimmushit	M.	Petaḥ Tikvah	1965	physiotherapy
Terumah	1	T.A.	1925	lit.; Hebrew writers for J.N.F.
Tesha ba-Erev – see: Ha-Olam ha-Zeh				
Tesha Tesha Tesha	Irr.	T.A.	1953–1957	police (named after the tel. no 999)
Te'urah	Q.	Chicago	1944–1946	education
Tevai	Q.	T.A.	1965	architecture, town planning, plastic art
Teva u-Veri'ut	Q.	Petaḥ Tikvah	1956	organ of vegetarians and naturalists
Teva va-Areẓ – see: Ha-teva ve-ha-Areẓ				
Tevunah	Irr.	Memel-Koenigsberg, E. Prussia	1861	rabbinics; organ of the Musar movement
Tevunah	Irr.	Kovno, Lithuania	1922–1924 1928	rabbinics
Tevunah	W., F.	Jer.	1932–1933 1941–1958	religious
Torah mi-Ẓiyyon	Irr.	Jer.	1886–1906	rabbinics
Torat Ereẓ Yisrael	M.	Jer.	1930–1955	rabbinics; some interruptions
Torat ha-Areẓ	Irr.	Petaḥ Tikvah	1935–1938	rabbinics
Turim	W.	T.A.	1933–1934 1938–1939	lit.
Udim	Irr.	Beltsy, Bessarabia	1939	lit.
Urim	Irr. M.	T.A.	1935–1966	education organ of Ha-Merkaz le-Ḥinnukh of the Histadrut; M. from 1953
Urim le-Horim	Irr. & M.	T.A.	1946	education problems for parents; M. from 1954

Title	Freq.	Place of Publication	Year(s) of Appearance	Main Characteristics
Uvdot u-Misparim	M.	Jer.	1947–1969	facts and figures of the Keren Hayesod and the U.J.A.
Uzzenu	A.	T.A.	1949–1948	sport annual of Hapoel
Uzzenu	F. & M.	T.A.	1933–1935	sport organ of Hapoel
Va'ad Ḥakhamim	M.	Jer.	1923–1924	rabbinics
Va-Yelakket Yosef	F.	Bonyhad-Munkacs, Hungary	1899–1918	rabbinics
WIZO… – see Ha-Ishah be-Yisrael				
Ya'ad	Irr.	T.A.	1962	organ of Ha-No'ar ha-Oved ha-Le'ummi
Yadan Ma'ariv	A.	T.A.	1956	Ma'ariv annual
Yad la-Koré	B-M.	T.A.	1943–1944	bibliography and librarianship
Yad la-Koré	Q.	T.A.-Jer.	1946	bibliography and librarianship
Yad la-Safran – see: Alim le-Bibliografyah u-le-Safranut				
Yad Vashem – see also: Yedi'ot Yad Vashem	A.	Jer.	1957	research on the Holocaust and Resistance
Yagdil Torah	Irr.	Odessa, Russia	1879–1885	rabbinics
Yagdil Torah	Irr.	Berlin	1890–1893	rabbinics
Yagdil Torah	W. & M. B-M. & Irr.	Slutsk, Belorussia	1908–1928	rabbinics; with interruptions; the last rabbinical periodical in Russia
Yagdil Torah	Irr.	London	1949–1959	rabbinics
Yagdil Torah	Irr.	T.A.	1962–1965	history of Polish Jewry; Hebrew and Yiddish; 2 issues
Yaḥdav	M. & Irr.	T.A.	1953	Ha-Kibbutz ha-Me'uḥad brigade
Yalkut ha-Mikhvarot	Irr.	T.A.	1949–1966	bee breeding
Yalkut ha-Mizraḥ ha-Tikhon	M.	Jer.	1935–1951	Middle East affairs
Yalkut ha-Re'im	Irr.	T.A.	1942–1946	lit.; organ of young writers; 4 issues
Yalkut Ma'aravi	A.	N.Y.	1904	lit.
Yalkut Magen	Irr.	T.A.	1956	organ of the Association to Help Soviet Russian Jewry
Yalkut Moreshet	S-A. & A.	T.A.	1963	research on the Holocaust; organ of the M. Anielewicz Institute for Research on the Holocaust at Yad Mordekha
Yalkut Tekhni	B-M.	T.A.	1955–1960	institute for work productivity and production
Yalkut Vohlin	Irr.	T.A.	1945	history of Volhynian Jews
Yarhon ha-Avodah – see also: Ha-Yarḥon	M.	T.A.	1949–1958	labor and social security (National Insurance)
Yarḥon ha-Ḥazzanim	M.	Czestochowa, Poland	1896	song, music, ḥazzanut; the first of its kind in Hebrew; 4 issues
Yarḥon ha-No'ar ha-Musikali be-Yisrael	M.	T.A.	1957–1961	music for youth
Yarḥon ha-Sport	M.	T.A.	1960–1961	sport
Yarḥon Statisti la-Shetaḥim ha-Muḥzakim	M.	T.A.	1971	statistics figures on the occupied territories
Yarḥon Statisti le-Yisrael	M. & Q.	T.A.-Jer.	1949	statistical figures on all walks of life in Israel; some appendices
Yavneh	M.	Lvov, Galicia	1929–1931	Judaic studies and lit.
Yavneh	A.	Jer.	1939–1942	Judaic studies; 3 vols.
Yavneh	Irr.	Jer.	1946–1949	organ of religious academicians
Yeda Am	Irr.	T.A.	1948	folklore
Yedi'on – see: Shenaton Yedi'ot Aḥaronot				
Yedi'on ha-Aguddah le-Gerontologyah	Irr.	T.A.	1945	gerontology
Yedi'ot	A.	Jer.	1959–1966	religious music; 8 vols.
Yedi'ot Aḥaronot	D.	T.A.	1939	independent

Title	Freq.	Place of Publication	Year(s) of Appearance	Main Characteristics
Yedi'ot Arkhiyyon u-Muze'on ha-Avodah	Irr.	T.A.	1933–1951	history of the labor movement in Ereẓ Israel
Yedi'ot Beit Loḥamei ha-Getta'ot	Irr.	Haifa	1951–1960	Holocaust research; organ of the Isaac Katznelson Institute for research on the Holocaust at kibbutz Loḥamei ha-getta'ot
Yedi'ot Ereẓ ve-Emunah	Irr.	T.A.	1954	religious J.N.F.
Yedi'ot Genazim	Irr.	T.A.	1962	documentation material on the history of Hebrew literature by the Genazim Institute
Yedi'ot ha-Ḥevrah le-Ḥakirat Ereẓ Yisrael va-Attikoteha	Q.	Jer.	1933–1967	archaeology of Palestine and Bible lands; superseded by Kadmoniyyot
Yedi'ot ha-Makhon le-Ḥeker ha-Shirah ha-Ivrit	Irr.	Berlin-Jer.	1933–1958	research on Hebrew poetry during the Middle Ages; from 4 vols.; in Jer. 7 vols.
Yedi'ot ha-Makhon le-Madda'ei ha-Yahadut	Q.	Jer.	1925	the first publication of the Judaic Institute of the Hebrew University; 2 issues; superseded by Madda'ei ha-Yahadut
Yedi'ot ha-Mazkirut	Irr.	T.A.	1947	Ha-Kibbutz ha-Me'uḥad secretariat; appeared under various names
Yedi'ot ha-Tenu'ah le-Aḥdut ha-Avodah – see: Aḥdut ha-Avodah				
Yedi'ot Taḥanat ha-Nissayon	Q.	Reḥovot-T.A.	1926–1931 1936–1938	agricultural research station of the Zionist movement; 4 vols.
Yedi'ot Yad Vashem	Q. & Irr.	Jer.	1954	Holocaust research; Yad Vashem, Jer.
Yehudah vi-Yerushalayim	Irr.	Jer.	1877–1878	newspaper interrupted by the editors on occasion of the founding of Petaḥ Tikvah; motif of settling Ereẓ Israel; new ed. 1955
Yerushalayim	A.	Zolkiew-Lvov	1844–1845	lit.
Yerushalayim	A. & Irr.	Vienna-Jer.	1882–1919	Palestinography and history of Ereẓ Israel; 13 vols.; the first of its kind in Hebrew
Yerushalayim	B-M.	Cracow, Poland	1900–1901	bibliography
Yerushalayim	1	Jer.	1913	lit.; dedicated to Jerusalem
Yerushalayim	Q.	Jer.	1947–1955	history of Ereẓ Israel and Jerusalem
Yerushalayim	A.	Jer.	1965	lit.; the collection which was issued in 1968 was called Ve-li-Yrushalayim; a gift to those who fought in the Six-Day War
Yeshurun (Jeschurun)	A.	Lvov-Breslau-Bamberg	1856–1878	Judaic studies; 9 vols.; partly in German
Yeshurun	M.	Bucharest	1920–1923	lit. and Judaic studies
Yokhani	Irr.	T.A.	1961–1967	lit.; 7 issues
Yosef Da'at	F.	Andianople, Turkey	1888–1889	Judaic studies; partly in Ladino
Yuval	1	Jer.	1968	studies in Jewish music
Ẓarekhanut Shittufit	M.	T.A.	1959–1969	economics and cooperatives; afterward incorporated into Davar
Ẓelilim	M.	Jer.	1940–1941	music and art; 6 issues
Ẓelil va-Omer	Q.	Haifa	1957–1962	music for youth; 21 issues
Zemannim	D.	Jer.	1953–1955	Progressives newspaper
Zera'im	M.	Jer.-T.A.	1936	organ of Bnei Akiva, Mizrachi youth, the first two years irregular
Zeramim	W.	Vilna	1931–1932	lit.
Ẓeror Mikhtavim	Irr.	T.A.	1933–1951	organ of Ha-Kibbutz ha-Me'uḥad; continuation of Iggerot mi-Bifenim 1929–1934
Ẓeror Mikhtavim li-She'elot ha-Ḥinnukh ha-Meshuttaf	Irr.	T.A.	1938	pedagogical organ of Ha-Kibbutz ha-Me'uḥad; change of names
Zikhoronot Devrim shel ha-Aguddah ha-Mediẓinit ha-Ivrit	Irr.	Jaffa	1912–1914	the first medical journal in Hebrew; 5 issues (one double)
Zikhronot ha-Akademyah la-Lashon ha-Ivrit	A.	Jer.	1949	Hebrew language studies; until 1954; memoirs of Va'ad ha-Lashon
Ẓiklon	M.	T.A.	1953–1963	included later in Ma'arekhet; world newspaper translations for soldiers
Ẓillum – see: Ha-Ẓillum				
Ẓilẓelei Shama	1	Kharkov, Ukraine	1923	lit.; the only literary publication in Hebrew printed and edited in U.S.S.R.

Title	Freq.	Place of Publication	Year(s) of Appearance	Main Characteristics
Zimrat ha-Areẓ	Q.	Jassy (Iasi), Romania	1872	lit.
Zion	Q.	Jer.	1936	history of Jews
Zion, Me'assef	A.	Jer.	1926–1934	history and ethnography of Jews; 6 vols.
Zion, Yedi'ot	M.	Jer.	1929–1931	folklore and ethnography of Jews; 11 issues
Ẓippor ha-Nefesh	W.	T.A.	1964–1965	humor and satire
Ẓiyyon	Irr. & M.	Drohobycz, Galicia	1885, 1888 1896–1897	lit.
Ẓiyyon	A.	Frankfurt	1841–1842	lit.; 2 vols.
Ẓiyyon he-Ḥadash	1	Leipzig	1845	lit.
Zo ha-Derekh	W.	T.A.–	1965	organ of Rakaḥ
Zohar	M.	Buenos Aires	1961–1964	lit.; joined later with Darom
Zot ha-Areẓ		T.A.	1968	organ of the Greater Israel Movement

[Getzel Kressel]

NEW SQUARE, an incorporated village in Rockland County, southeastern New York. It has close to 6,000 residents. All its inhabitants are Skvera ḥasidim, followers of the Grand Rabbi (Rebbe) of Skvira, David Twersky (1940–). The group has its roots in the Ukrainian town of Skvera (*Skvira). New Square is an anglicized version of New Skvira.

The village was built on property purchased by the Zemach David Corporation, representing the then Skvera Rebbe and father of David, Rabbi Jacob Joseph Twersky (1900–1968), in 1954. Twersky was the third Skvera *rebbe*, whose predecessors were descended from the Chernobyl dynasty. Immediately upon his arrival in America in 1948, the *rebbe* began to lay plans to establish an all-ḥasidic village, outside the New York City area, in order to better maintain their traditional lifestyle and beliefs. Ḥasidism in the United States had taken a decidedly urban character and this was an attempt to build a ḥasidic community apart from the urban environment and its temptations. After two years which the group spent in Boro Park and seven in the Williamsburg sections of Brooklyn, the first four families moved to New Square in December 1956.

The settlement was confronted with a mixed reaction from the local community and the village's early years were plagued with controversy centering on the Ramapo Township's claims that New Square's sewer and drainage facilities and road patterns were not in keeping with required standards. Defenders of the village, including local government leaders as well as rabbis representing all Jewish denominations, saw in these criticisms a veiled desire to prevent the ultra-Orthodox from settling in large numbers.

A solution was sought by New Square leaders via incorporating the community which would free it from much of the Town Board's control. This move was contested in the courts by Ramapo. After a protracted struggle, ending in New York State Supreme Court, the New Squarers emerged triumphant and the village was incorporated in 1961.

New Square has seen rapid growth during its 50 years of existence, with families usually having ten or more children. The village is constantly expanding and was on the verge of having built on all its available space in the early 2000s. Attempts were made to locate another property where the *rebbe*'s followers would found a satellite community. In addition, the movement has a network of affiliated synagogues and schools in Brooklyn's Jewish centers and in major ḥasidic communities worldwide, including Montreal, London, Antwerp, Jerusalem, and Bene-Berak.

The New Square community has strict standards geared to restricting the influences of the modern world, such as the banning of television, maintenance of rigorous separation of the sexes, and requirements that all children be educated in the village schools. In addition, the community requires that its citizens adhere to the customs of the Skvera tradition and follow the *rebbe*'s rulings. These demands upon those choosing to live in the village are accompanied by a welcoming openness to visitors and guests featuring extensive hospitality. New Square also operates a host of charitable services which service people throughout the metropolitan area.

The *rebbe* often travels to Jewish communities around the world and many of his followers make pilgrimages to New Square to seek his counsel.

In 1997 four New Squarers were sentenced to prison terms ranging from two to six years on charges of having allegedly misused federal Pell Grant monies. On January 20, 2005, on his last day in office, President Clinton significantly reduced these sentences, after he was visited several weeks before by the Skvera *rebbe*, who interceded on the men's behalf. Defenders of Clinton's decision claimed that the original sentences were not in keeping with other similar cases of individuals who had channeled federal funding into non-profit institutions.

BIBLIOGRAPHY: S.C.Y. Gruber and Y.Y. Rosenblum, *Bi-Kedushah shel Ma'alah* (2002); Z. Holczler, "Di Ershta Chasidishe Shtat" (unpublished ms.).

NEW TESTAMENT (Gr. ἡ καινὴ διαθήκη), the Christian Holy Scriptures (other than the Hebrew Bible and the Apocrypha).

Content

"The New Testament" (NT) is the usual name for a collection of 27 ancient Greek books concerning Jesus of Nazareth and his earliest followers. It forms the second part of Christian Bibles following "the Old Testament," which in Protestant Bibles contains the same books as Jewish Bibles but in a different order. Catholic and Orthodox Christian Bibles have their own orders of "the Old Testament" in which other ancient books are interspersed. Such additional books are sometimes found in Protestant Bibles in a separate section titled "Apocrypha" and placed between the two "Testaments." Thus, whereas the extra books are authoritative for Catholics and Orthodox, for Protestants they have the lower status of informative and edifying material that bridges between the "Old" and the "New."

The NT begins with the Gospels of Matthew, Mark, Luke and John, four accounts of the activities of Jesus. The authors do not write under those names; the ascriptions come from early Christian traditions. Thus the fourth gospel's anonymous writer claims to be recording the testimony of a source figure identified only as "the beloved disciple" of Jesus. In broad terms, these gospels present similar versions of Jesus' arrest, condemnation, death, and resurrection, but the Gospel of John has a markedly different account of earlier events and of the content of Jesus' teaching. Consequently, the first three are commonly termed the "Synoptic Gospels" because of the ease with which they can be printed in parallel columns as a "synopsis." Matthew and Luke contain versions of the virgin birth of Jesus to Mary (Matthew: shortly before the death of Herod, i.e., 4 B.C.E.) and Luke includes his visit to Jerusalem at age 12; otherwise only the last period of his adult life is featured (Luke: from age "about 30" on).

Next comes the Acts of the Apostles, which introduces itself as the continuation of the third gospel. In it, "apostles" mostly refers strictly to 12 early close disciples of Jesus. Acts begins with the last instructions of Jesus to his followers (after his resurrection), his ascent to heaven from the Mount of Olives, and their subsequent reception of the Holy Spirit. Their attempts to win over other Jews lead to clashes with the authorities and to the dispersal of most of them elsewhere. But then the appearance of Jesus himself in a vision to a certain Saul, who was their chief persecutor, turns Saul into an ardent follower. The latter, now called Paul, makes a series of journeys to the Jewish Diaspora, where his preaching about Jesus causes divisions among Jews but has remarkable success among non-Jews, especially those previously close to Judaism. He eventually returns to Jerusalem, where the followers of Jesus are again living peacefully among other Jews, but his eager style creates new clashes and leads to his arrest. After years of detention by the Romans in Caesarea, he is sent to Rome for two more years, awaiting trial, where the book ends rather abruptly (c. 60 C.E.).

The next 21 books are epistles of various early Christians. Nine epistles to Christian communities and four to individuals announce themselves as from Paul. A 14th, the Epistle to the Hebrews, lacks that announcement, but its concluding statement is in Pauline style. Others come from "James" (1), "Peter" (2), and "Jude" (1), who calls himself "brother of James." Traditionally, Peter is identified with the initial leader of the followers of Jesus in Jerusalem, and James, as "brother of Jesus," with their subsequent leader after Peter set out on his own missionary journeys. The other three epistles are traditionally ascribed to "John," who is identified with the source figure of the fourth gospel and with the author of the last book of the NT, Revelation, in which a certain John records a series of heavenly visions. These include messages to seven Christian communities and prophecies about coming persecutions (mostly Roman) and the eventual end of history, in which a new Jerusalem descends from heaven to inaugurate the universal rule of Jesus with God.

Language and Style

It is frequently, but wrongly, said that the NT books are written in popular Hellenistic Greek as opposed to the literary Attic Greek of the period. In fact, Hellenistic Greek was the language not merely of the populace but of learned scholars and officials in the Greek-speaking world created by the conquests of Alexander of Macedon. This scholarly language modified Attic by replacing its more idiosyncratic features with forms and words current in the wider world. The attempts of purists to impose the exact dialect of ancient Athens began around 200 B.C.E., gained ground slowly, and triumphed completely only in the later second century C.E.

There is indeed great variation in the language of the NT, reflecting the origins and genres of the various books. Thus in Matthew and Luke (to a lesser extent in Mark) and in the early chapters of Acts, much of the language has affinities to the "translation Greek" characteristic of the Septuagint as well as containing Hebraisms recognizable from rabbinic literature. By contrast, the introductions to Luke and Acts, the later chapters of Acts, and the Epistle to the Hebrews consist of elegant Hellenistic prose. Paul's writings addressed to communities are composed in a brilliant epistolary style that evoked the admiration of Wilamowitz, the leading 20th-century authority on Greek literature. Only one book, Revelation, contains plain grammatical errors. The anonymous writer of the Gospel of John, however, writes in a Hellenistic Greek that is both very simple and very correct.

Origins, Acceptance, and Canonization

There is little firm evidence on which to date the precise composition of the NT books, except that the few Christian writings surviving from the early second century indicate knowledge of those four gospels and of collections of Pauline epistles. The NT books give almost no clear dates for Jesus himself (Matthew and Luke, as above). Thus their dating mostly reflects scholarly fashion. Whereas earlier fashion dated many of them to the period 100–140 C.E., current fashion puts almost all of them within 50–100 C.E. One leading scholar, John A.T. Robinson, dated them all before 70 C.E., above all because it is difficult to identify any NT author who is clearly aware of the Jewish catastrophe of that year.

At the beginning of the second century, only the Hebrew Bible or the Septuagint counted as inspired Scripture for Christians. By the end of that century, almost all the 27 books had widely acquired that status and Christian writers were speaking of Scripture as "the writings of the Old Covenant and of the New Covenant." The contrast is derived from the expression "new covenant" (*berit ḥadashah*) of Jeremiah 31:31 (30), which receives various interpretations (as *kainê diathêkê*) in the NT books. The English names "Old Testament" and "New Testament" reflect the translation of that expression (as *novum testamentum*) in Latin versions of the NT.

The final list, the "canon," was established only through the convocation of bishops from all over the Christian world in Ecumenical Councils, beginning in the fourth century. Only in some cases can a doctrinal reason be identified for the exclusion of what are called "New Testament Apocrypha," such as other gospels and the acts of apostles not recorded in the canonical Acts. An interesting case is an ancient account of the childhood of Mary the mother of Jesus, currently called "the Protevangelium of James." Although never canonized, it provides the source for many Christian holy sites in Israel and its story features in well-known traditional icons.

History of Scholarship

Scholarly studies of the NT fall into two main areas: edition of the text and analysis of the content. The widely used early edition of Erasmus (1517) was based on a handful of later manuscripts, among other defects. Later editors have employed hundreds of Greek manuscripts as well as translations into other ancient languages and quotations in early Christian writers. Today's critical texts follow the lead of Westcott and Hort (1882), as updated in the many editions of Eberhard Nestlé and Kurt Aland.

Through his long residence in the Netherlands (1628–49), the philosopher Descartes provoked probably the earliest harsh questioning of the content of the Bible. The "Cartesian method" prescribes that in order to find secure foundations for science, one must first reject any statement about which the slightest doubt can be raised. Descartes himself explicitly excluded theology from such questioning, but his ardent Dutch disciples had fewer scruples. Especially the writings of Baruch *Spinoza and Balthasar Bekker provoked a massive controversy and scores of polemical publications in Dutch. Only the Latin works of Spinoza, however, had a major impact on the broader European public.

In the early 19th century, the Cartesian approach gained ground in classical philology in Germany. Under the influence of Friedrich August Wolf (1759–1824) especially, it became fashionable to question the authenticity of works ascribed to ancient authors merely on the basis of inconsistencies in the alleged author's style and viewpoint. For example, major dialogues of Plato and a dozen speeches of Cicero (including the four against Catilina) were declared unauthentic. The Iliad and Odyssey, following Wolf, were seen as loose collections of poems by multiple authors; "Homer" was a fiction.

This skeptical paradigm of research was at its peak in the middle decades of the century, when German scholars began to apply the methods of classical philology to biblical studies. Ready targets were the differences of style and emphasis in the Pauline writings and the very existence of four different gospels, which contain evident minor discrepancies in parallel passages as well as the broader differences noted above. In particular, the studies of David Friedrich Strauss (1808–1874) and Ferdinand Christian Baur (1792–1860) provoked first furious rejection, then cautious imitation. Both of them employed various arguments to undermine the testimony of the NT authors; then they employed Hegelian dialectics to build up reconstructed versions of the life of Jesus, the history of the first Christian communities, and the process whereby the NT books emerged.

By the early 20th century, classical philology had largely retreated from this kind of skepticism. Plato recovered his dialogues and Cicero his speeches. Both the Iliad and the Odyssey were now seen as brilliantly integrated compositions of a poetic genius; the remaining question was whether there was one Homer or two. In NT studies, by contrast, skepticism spread further, such that today its practitioners and classicists have difficulty in finding a basis for a shared discussion. Anything from four to 13 epistles are ascribed to Paul by different scholars, but using arguments of the kind that classicists today treat with great caution.

The result is that NT scholars have amassed an impressive quantity of information about the background of the NT but are deeply divided over questions of the origins and content of the books. As with Strauss and Baur, skepticism creates room for ingenious speculations rather than firm results. Concomitantly, a host of methods borrowed from elsewhere, be it "form criticism" and "redaction criticism" or methods of analysis of modern literature, are employed to find lasting significance in these theologically authoritative texts. An example is the commonly maintained view that the Gospel of Mark is the oldest and that it was used in the composition of Matthew and Luke in various combinations with a lost document designated as "Q." During the later 20th century the main arguments in favor of this view were undermined by criticism. Yet it continues to be taught, less out of conviction than because its critics failed to gain acceptance for any of the proposed alternatives.

Relationships with Judaism

A Jewish reader will readily note in the NT books such resemblances to Jewish tradition as are evidence that they were written by Jews or in a Jewish milieu. A massive commentary on the NT from rabbinic sources was compiled by Paul Billerbeck (1922–28). Yet the significance of such relationships has often been minimized in skeptical scholarship. Many NT scholars have refused to take rabbinic literature into account because its earliest written source, the Mishnah (early third century), is "too late" for any reliable comparison. For classical scholars, of course, the mere "lateness" of a source is irrelevant; thus the main witness to Parmenides is Simplicius, who wrote a thousand years later.

Since no writing by Jesus himself is known, many scholars have advocated a "criterion of double dissimilarity" in order to ascertain the nature of his teaching. Take all his many sayings in the gospels one by one, they say, and set aside any that have parallels in Jewish tradition or later Christian writings, since the authors of the gospels may have projected the latter back upon Jesus. Whatever little is left may stem from him. Overlooked in this Cartesian approach is that it equates our knowledge with our ignorance. For if a new Dead Sea scroll or a lost early Christian work is discovered, it may well contain parallels with whatever the criterion has not yet excluded. Built into the criterion, therefore, is the assumption that ultimately nothing can be known about what Jesus taught, but that whatever he did teach was antipathetic to Judaism.

Particular violence was done to the interpretation of Paul in attempts to distance him from Judaism. To this end, early 20th century scholars invented a parody of rabbinic Judaism as a religion that sought salvation in an obsessive preoccupation with the minute details of Torah observance. Paul was proclaimed as the liberator from all that. More recent studies, fortunately, have demonstrated the falsity of that image of Judaism. Also, Paul expected Jews to remain faithful to Torah and rather sought to reformulate Judaism's demands upon faithful non-Jews.

Dissent from the dominance of skepticism has come from two directions. On the one hand, there are NT scholars whose original training was in classics. On the other, the renewal of Jewish existence in the Land of Israel created new realities. Besides Israeli scholars who brought their familiarity with land, language, and tradition, there are Christian scholars who acquired similar familiarities by living in this Jewish society. A pioneer among the latter was the Anglican scholar Herbert Danby, whose translation of the Mishnah into English (1933) remains a standard. A pioneer among the former was Joseph *Klausner with his studies of Jesus (1929) and Paul (1946). His major important insight was to see that most characteristic of Jesus is less individual sayings, which have other Jewish parallels, than the ethical vision that suffuses them as a whole.

More recently, the decades-long cooperation at the Hebrew University between David *Flusser and Shmuel Safrai promoted a generation of younger Jewish and Christian scholars whose shared familiarity with both traditions transcends denominational affiliations. One of Flusser's personal contributions was his pioneering use of the Dead Sea scrolls to illuminate a layer of thought that underlies various NT epistles. Another was the realization that the normal language of the teaching of Jesus, and especially of his parables, was not Aramaic but Hebrew, enabling a reconstruction of parts of that teaching through careful comparisons of the text of Luke and Matthew with Jewish sources. Flusser also found a novel solution to the paradox of the Gospel of Matthew, which is in some regards the most Judaic of the four, yet it contains the most severe attacks upon the Jewish people. The attacks occur precisely in passages that are less Hebraic, or lack parallels in Luke and Mark, or give an unusual twist to parallels there. This Greek gospel is an adaptation of a Hebrew original by a sect of non-Jews who (like today's "black Hebrews" in Dimona) felt that the Torah should belong to them because they were observing the Torah far more faithfully than the Jews.

BIBLIOGRAPHY: The literature on the NT is too vast to be surveyed here. Since 1956 it has been recorded systematically in *New Testament Abstracts*. Besides book reviews, this journal summarizes articles from many periodicals both under general categories and by NT book, chapter, and verse. The standard *Greek-English Lexicon of the New Testament* is by F.W. Danker (2000³), continuing the work of Walter Bauer. For the main textual issues, see the various books of Bruce M. Metzger. The relevant work of John A.T. Robinson is *Redating the New Testament* (1976). On the paradigms of scholarship and their history, see Malcolm F. Lowe, "The Critical and the Skeptical Methods in New Testament Research," in: *Gregorianum* 81 (2000), 693–721. The problematic attitude of early 20th-century scholarship to Judaism was exemplified in Emil Schuerer's *The History of the Jewish People in the Age of Jesus Christ*; the thoroughly revised edition by G. Vermes, F. Millar, and M. Goodman (1973–87) eliminated Schuerer's biases and provides excellent background information for the NT. The Flusser-Safrai approach can be seen in the series *Compendia Rerum Iudaicarum ad Novum Testamentum* (many authors). See also the revised version of Flusser's *Jesus* (1997) and his articles collected as *Judaism and the Origins of Christianity* (1988), edited by his pupils Steve Notley and Brad Young, respectively. The reevaluation of Paul and his relationship to Judaism is due to W.D. Davies, E.P. Sanders, Krister Stendah and John Gager among others.

[Malcolm F. Lowe (2nd ed.)]

NEWTON (Neustaedter), HELMUT (1921–2004), fashion photographer. Born in Berlin to a well-to-do German-Jewish family, Newton became a widely imitated fashion photographer after his provocative, erotically charged photographs became a mainstay of *Vogue* and other publications. He was guided by a passion for the strength and allure of the female form and his unquenchable taste for sexual imagery, including the bizarre and scandalous, earning the nickname the King of Kink. Newton got his start in Berlin as an apprentice to the fashion photographer Else Simon. At 18 he fled Nazi Germany and moved to Singapore, then to Melbourne. After serving in the Australian army during World War II, he opened a studio of his own and his photographs appeared in Australian *Vogue*.

In 1961 he moved to Paris with his wife, June (known as the photographer Alice Springs), and made his name with French *Vogue* as well as *Queen, Nova, Marie Claire*, French *Elle, Stern* and *Vanity Fair.* He brought stylized cruelty to mainstream fashion. His images, often in stark black and white, were calculated to shock, and featured tall, blonde, sometimes naked women in heels, perhaps illuminated by headlights or trapped in a dark alley. "Fashion for me," Newton once said, "is not an illustration but an idea around which to create a scene." The scenes were often based on familiar pornographic depictions. Bondage, sadomasochism, voyeurism, murder, pornography, and prostitution were exploited and explored. Models were dressed and used in unexpected ways:

in orthopedic corsets, or in wheelchairs, or on all fours wearing a dog collar. His work was closely associated with leading fashion designers like Yves Saint Laurent, who favored tight, wide-shouldered suits and long-legged models, which Newton embraced. His work was also associated with photographers like Guy Bourdin and Deborah Turbeville, and sometimes drew the ire of groups that felt his depictions of women could be demeaning and exploitive. Newton and his wife frequently photographed themselves and each other naked: at rest, exercising, posing, joking, bathing.

In a 1996 interview, Newton suggested that his German upbringing and his experiences with the Nazis played a large part in his artistic philosophy. "The point of my photography," he said, "has always been to challenge myself. To go a little further than my Germanic discipline and Teutonic nature would permit me to." After working as a freelancer in the 1940s, he moved to France in the late 1950s. He kept a home in Monte Carlo, which was often a setting for his photographs, and from 1981 to his death he wintered at the Chateau Marmont hotel in Hollywood.

Newton published ten books during his lifetime, including an erotic photo album in 1976 called *White Women* and in 2003 *Autobiography*, a memoir of his adventures through life, women and high-fashion photography. Shortly before his death he created the Helmut Newton Foundation in Berlin. He also picked a symbolic home for the foundation, a former Prussian army officers' club that stands beside the railroad station where, as a teenager, he boarded a train and fled Hitler's Germany. He and his wife made an initial permanent loan of 1,000 prints of their work to the foundation. They stipulated that, after their deaths, their negatives and archives as well as all rights, royalties and income from sales of prints will go to the foundation. "It is my wish that the Helmut Newton Foundation be a viable and living institution, not a dead museum, that will financially exploit these archives," he said. Berlin's cultural establishment embraced the foundation with enthusiasm, not only for its artistic merit but also for the message implicit in a Berlin Jew's decision to return home.

Newton was fatally injured when he lost control of his car and crashed into a wall outside the Chateau Marmont. The city of Berlin offered him an honorary grave. On June 2, 2004, two days before the foundation's inauguration, Newton's ashes were laid to rest in the Friedenau cemetery in Berlin.

[Stewart Kampel (2nd ed.)]

NEWTON-JOHN, OLIVIA (1948–), U.K.-born, Australia-raised singer and actress who scored numerous top-10 pop and country hits in the 1970s and 1980s, including, "Physical" and "Have You Never Been Mellow." Newton-John is the granddaughter of German Nobel Prize-winning physicist Max *Born, who was a friend of Albert *Einstein. In a 2004 TV interview, Newton-John said: "My mother tells me … that there used to be music in the house and Einstein used to come and play music with my grandfather." She has never been publicly identified as being Jewish. Newton-John moved to Australia with her family at age five, but was back in the U.K. at age 16 to pursue a singing career. She joined the cast of U.K. singer Cliff Richard's TV show in 1972, and began releasing record albums. Her first British hit was a version of Bob *Dylan's "If Not for You." She topped the U.S. record charts for the first of five times in 1974 with "I Honestly Love You." Other No. 1 titles include: "Have You Never Been Mellow" (1975), "You're the One that I Want" (1978, a duet with John Travolta from the film *Grease*, in which she co-starred), and "Magic" (1980, from the film *Xanadu*). Her 1981 pop-disco song "Physical" spent 10 weeks at No. 1. She has not charted since 1985, but sang at the opening ceremony of the 2000 Sydney Olympics. She recuperated from breast cancer in 1992, and afterward became a spokeswoman for breast cancer awareness. Newton-John was recipient of the OBE (Order of the British Empire) from Queen Elizabeth in 1979.

[Alan D. Abbey (2nd ed.)]

NEW YEAR. The Mishnah (RH 1:1) enumerates four separate days of the year, each of which is regarded as a New Year (Heb. *Rosh Ha-Shanah, lit. "head of the year"). The fixing of those dates was essential, not only for civil and political purposes, but for the regulations concerning the procedure regarding the religious injunctions connected with agricultural produce. Since, for example, the tithe had to be given of animal produce, the fruit from the first three years of a tree's growth (*orlah*) was forbidden, and the beginning and end of the *Sabbatical year had to be determined, it was necessary to lay down when the year began for those various calculations. With one exception (and that only according to *Bet Hillel), all the New Years begin on the first of the month.

(1) The first of Nisan is the New Year for (Jewish) kings and for the religious calendar (for festivals). Thus if a king ascended the throne during Adar, the next month would constitute the second year of his reign, and Passover is the first festival of the year. The Talmud (RH 7a) adds that it is also the New Year for the purchase of congregational sacrifices with the *shekalim collected in Adar, and for the renting of houses.

(2) The first of Elul is the New Year for the tithing of cattle (but see the first of Tishri), i.e., tithes had to be given for all cattle born between the first of Elul and the 30th of Av.

(3) The first of Tishri is the New Year for the civil calendar (including the counting of the reigns of foreign kings; see RH 3a–b and cf. Git. 8:5) for the Sabbatical and Jubilee years (plowing and planting being forbidden from that date), and for the year of planting of fruit and vegetables. The establishment of the first of Tishri as the religious New Year (see *Rosh Ha-Shanah) depends upon the statement that on that day "all the world is judged" (RH 1:2). According to R. Simeon and R. Eleazar the first of Tishri is also the New Year for the tithing of cattle and therefore there are only three New Years.

(4) The first of Shevat is the New Year for trees, according to Bet Shammai, but Bet Hillel fixed the date as the 15th of Shevat, and since the *halakhah* is established accordingly, it is this date which is celebrated today (see *Tu bi-Shevat). The

reason given in the Talmud (RH 14a) is that on that date the greater part of the year's rain has fallen.

Only Rosh Ha-Shanah is fully celebrated, though in recent times a minor celebration has developed, especially in Israel, for Tu bi-Shevat. The others, as stated, are merely for calendrical computations.

NEW YEAR'S CARDS. The widespread custom of sending Jewish New Year's cards dates to the Middle Ages, thus predating by centuries Christian New Year's cards, popular in Europe and the United States only since the 19th century. The custom is first mentioned in the Book of Customs of Rabbi Jacob, son of Moses *Moellin (1360–1427), the spiritual leader of German Jewry in the 14th century (*Minhagei Maharil*, first ed. Sabionetta, 1556). Based on the familiar talmudic dictum in tractate Rosh ha-Shanah 16b concerning the "setting down" of one's fate in one of the three Heavenly books that are opened on the Jewish New Year, the Maharil and other German rabbis recommended that letters sent during the month of Elul should open with the blessing "May you be inscribed and sealed for a good year." Outside of Germany and Austria, other Jewish communities, such as the Sephardi and Oriental Jews, only adopted this custom in recent generations.

The German-Jewish custom reached widespread popularity with the invention – in Vienna, 1869 – of the postal card. The peak period of the illustrated postcard, called in the literature "The Postal Card Craze" (1898–1918), also marks the flourishing of the Jewish New Year's card, produced in three major centers: Germany, Poland, and the U.S. (chiefly in New York). The German cards are frequently illustrated with biblical themes. The makers of Jewish cards in Warsaw, on the other hand, preferred to depict the religious life of East European Jewry in a nostalgic manner. Though the images on their cards were often theatrically staged in a studio with amateur actors, they preserve views and customs lost in the Holocaust. The mass immigration of the Jews from Eastern Europe to the United States in the first decades of the 20th century gave a new boost to the production of the cards. Some depicted America as the new homeland, opening her arms to the new immigrants, others emphasized Zionist ideology and depicted contemporary views of Ereẓ Israel.

The Jews of 19th c. Ereẓ Israel ("the old *yishuv*"), even prior to the invention of the postal card, sent tablets of varying sizes with wishes and images for the New Year, often sent abroad for fundraising purposes. These tablets depicted the "Four Holy Cities" as well as holy sites in and around Jerusalem. A popular biblical motif was the Binding of Isaac, often taking place against the background of the Temple Mount and accompanied by the appropriate prayer for Rosh ha-Shanah. Also common were views of the yeshivot or buildings of the organizations which produced these tablets.

In the 1920s and 1930s the cards highlighted the acquisition of the land and the toil on it as well as "secular" views of the proud new pioneers. Not only did this basically religious custom continue and become more popular, but the new cards attest to a burst of creativity and originality on the subject matter as well as in design and the selection of accompanying text. Over the years, since the establishment of the State of Israel, the custom has continued to flourish, with the scenes and wishes on the cards developing as social needs and situations changed. The last two decades of the 20th century have seen a decline in the mailing of New Year's cards in Israel, superseded by phone calls or internet messages. In other countries, especially the U.S., cards with traditional symbols are still commonly sent by mail, more elaborately designed than in the past. Thus, the simple and naïve New Year's card vividly reflects the dramatic changes in the life of the Jewish people over the last generations.

BIBLIOGRAPHY: R. Arbel (ed.), *Blue and White in Color: Visual Images of Zionism, 1897–1947* (1997); J. Branska, *'Na Dobry Rok badzcie zapisani': Zydowskie karty noworoczne firmy Jehudia* (1997); P. Goodman, "Rosh Hashanah Greeting Cards," in: P. Goodman (ed.), *The Rosh Hashanah Anthology* (1970), 274–79, 356; S. Mintz and S. Sabar, *Past Perfect: The Jewish Experience in Early 20th Century Postcards* (1998); idem, "Between Poland and Germany: Jewish Religious Practices in Illustrated Postcards of the Early Twentieth Century," in: *Polin: Studies in Polish Jewry*, 16 (2003), 137–66; idem, "The Custom of Sending Jewish New Year Cards: Its History and Artistic Development," in: *Jerusalem Studies in Jewish Folklore*, 19–20 (1997/98), 85–110 (Heb.); E. Smith, "Greetings From Faith: Early 20th c. American Jewish New Year Postcards," in: D. Morgan and S.M. Promey (eds.), *The Visual Culture of American Religions* (2001), 229–48, 350–56; D. Tartakover, *Shanah Tovah: 101 Kartisei Berakhah la-Shanah ha-Ḥadashah* (Heb., 1978); M. Tzur (ed.), *Ba-Shanah ha-Ba'ah: Shanot Tovot min ha-Kibbutz* (2001).

[Shalom Sabar (2nd ed.)]

NEW YORK CITY, foremost city of the Western Hemisphere and largest urban Jewish community in history; pop. 7,771,730 (1970), est. Jewish pop. 1,836,000 (1968); metropolitan area 11,448,480 (1970), metropolitan area Jewish (1968), 2,381,000 (including Nassau, Suffolk, Rockland, and Westchester counties). (For later population figures, see below: 1970–2006.)

This article is arranged according to the following outline:

1654–1870

DUTCH COLONIAL PERIOD. The arrival of some 23 *Sephardi and Ashkenazi Jews on the French privateer *St. Catherine* early in September 1654 marked the end of a tortuous journey that began earlier in the year when they left Recife, Brazil, after helping in the unsuccessful defense of the Dutch possession from Portuguese attack, rather than stay and face the Inquisition. The director general of New Netherland, Peter Stuyvesant, and the dominie Johannes Megapolensis tried to refuse haven to the penniless and tired refugees. They protested to the Dutch West India Company against the possible settlement of a "deceitful race" who professed an "abominable religion" and whose worship at the "feet of Mammon" would threaten and limit the profit of loyal subjects of the company. While Stuyvesant's plea was under consideration, other Jews including David de Ferrara and Abraham de *Lucena arrived in the spring of 1655. The population as a whole accepted the group. Instructions from the Dutch West India Company followed letters written by the Jews to their coreligionists in the company, which directed that newcomers be permitted to live, trade, and travel in New Netherland, and, in effect, to have the same privileges enjoyed in the Netherlands. Probably in deference to Stuyvesant, and because of the small size of the Jewish colony, the Jews, although permitted a burial ground, were not allowed to build a synagogue.

Despite the orders of the company, the newcomers faced other obstacles. The right to trade with some areas, including Albany, was denied as were rights to serve in the militia in lieu of paying a special tax, to own land, and to engage in retail trades like baking. These restrictions were all put forth by Stuyvesant. The Jews' response was twofold. The first took the form of a series of petitions drawn by Abraham de Lucena, Salvador d'Andrada, and Jacob Cohen Henriques addressed to the company in 1655 and 1656. The answers were affirmative. Burgher right, the right to conduct retail and wholesale trade in New Amsterdam, was extended to Jews in 1657, and the right to hold property was also upheld. Some Jews fought Stuyvesant on his own ground. Asser *Levy and Jacob *Barsimon (who had arrived with Solomon Pietersen in August 1654, prior to the main body of settlers) began a successful court action in November 1655 to permit Jews to serve in the militia in lieu of the payment of a special derogatory tax. Thus the Jews gained primary civil rights within a few years of settlement.

Having secured a foothold, the first Jews began the task of sustaining themselves. While economic opportunity was quite limited compared with those in the more stable, secure, and richer markets of Europe and the Caribbean, the average Jew managed well. In 1655 Jewish taxpayers paid 8% of the cost of the Palisade or "Waal," later the site of Wall Street, while they made up only about 2% of the assessed population. Asser Levy became the most prominent and successful merchant. He built a prosperous real estate business, had a kosher butcher shop, and won the right to participate in the citizens' guard. Another member of the founding group, Levy, a butcher and tanner by trade, carried on his business just outside the city's wall. He expanded his interests to real estate and trade within the city, as well as in communities along the Hudson River. Levy was one of the few pioneer Jews who remained and died in the province and whose descendants could be traced to 18th-century New York.

ENGLISH COLONIAL PERIOD. The surrender of New Amsterdam to the British in 1664 brought a number of changes to the Jewish settlement. Generally, civil and religious rights were widened. Jews were permitted to hold and be elected to public office and restrictions on the building of a synagogue were lifted. While there is some evidence that a synagogue existed as early as 1695, it was undoubtedly a private home used for this purpose by the Jewish community. Shearith Israel, the first congregation in New York, was probably organized in about 1706. Between 1729 and 1730 the congregation erected the first synagogue, a small building on Mill Lane – known also as Mud Lane – the site of present South William Street. This event occurred some 75 years after the original settlement and was an indication of its permanence as well as of the acceptance by English authority of the Jewish economic and social position. Interestingly, the London and Curaçao communities, which were also founded in 1654, had built synagogues within a few years of their founding. The hesitancy of New York Jews was probably due to the smallness of their numbers, as well as to the transient nature of their status and to governmental opposition.

The roots of the colony depended upon its economic viability. Jewish merchants took a major interest in overseas trade, partly because ocean traffic negated somewhat onerous local control and requirements and partly because it provided a measure of freedom that allowed them to use their special skills. Movement from place to place was its own protection: investments were widespread and thus less vulnerable. The transient, wandering Jew was an answer to the ghetto and enclosing walls, for he was more difficult to tax and to ghettoize. He carried his wealth with him, and he had knowledge of languages – Hebrew, Yiddish, German, Spanish, Portuguese, Dutch. In the correspondence of Nathan Simson, there are letters written in three and sometimes four languages. Simson had knowledge of the international market, and his kinsmen were in the Caribbean, Italy, Spain, the Near East, and India. This provided an opportunity not usually afforded the restricted Catholic or Protestant. Certain markets were specialties. When in 1699 Governor Bellomont wanted a bag of jewels that had been seized from an accused pirate appraised, he "ordered a Jew in town to be present, he understanding Jewells well."

Jews concentrated on such commodities as conditions required. They were among the first to introduce cocoa and chocolate to England and were heavily engaged in the coral, textile, and slave trades, and at times had virtual monopolies in the ginger trade. They are also said to have introduced whale-oil spermaceti candles to the colonies. In 1701 Jewish merchants accounted for 12% of those engaged in overseas trade, though they represented only about 2% of the general population. In 1776 they were less than 1% of the population and less than 1% of the overseas merchants. The decline of the overseas trade indicated not only that New York Jews had become rooted but also that they had found other means of earning a living. The colonial transience gave way to permanence.

During this process Jews struggled to obtain full citizenship, especially as it applied to trade. The Jew who wished to engage in overseas or wholesale trade had to face the question of his status, whether he was a citizen or an alien. As a citizen, except for some ambiguity with respect to his right to vote or hold office, he was allowed most rights including the right to trade. Since the English accepted Dutch citizenship equally with English, Jews who were burghers of New Amsterdam, as well as native-born colonists, continued to be citizens under British rule. The problems facing aliens, the status of the majority of Jews, were clearly set forth in the Trade and Navigation Acts passed between 1650 and 1663. This central body of British law applying to the colonies was intended not only to foster mercantilism but also to prevent the encroachment upon trade by "Jews, French and other foreigners." Under these acts aliens could not engage in British commerce without severe penalty.

The necessity for some form of citizenship became obvious by the Rabba Couty affair. In November 1671 Couty's ship *Trial* was condemned by the Jamaica Vice-Admiralty Court on the ground that Couty, a Jew, was by definition a foreigner. In appealing the decision in England to the Council of Trade and Plantations, Couty obtained certificates from Governor Lovelace of New York indicating that he had been a free burgher of New York for several years. On this evidence and the fact that the ship and crew were English, the council held the sentence illegal. Those Jews, therefore, who could prove native birth did not need to bother with naturalization proceedings, but the alien Jew had to become a citizen if he was to engage in foreign trade. In general, however, the Jews in New York found that the procurement of naturalization, the right to trade and hold property, and the right of inheritance were not too difficult to obtain. Merchants in England were rarely naturalized; mostly they were endenizened – i.e., they could trade, but not hold real estate. In New York, on the other hand, 46 Jews were naturalized but only six endenizened. Freemanship, the right to engage in retail trade, was also relatively easy to obtain, despite instances of prohibition. Forty-seven Jews were made freemen between 1688 and 1770.

The decline of the overseas trade brought a corresponding increase in the numbers of Jews who were local retailers and craftsmen. They sold a wide range of goods, such as guns (especially during war), rum, wine, ironware, glass, furs, and foodstuff. Such merchants as Jacob Franks, Rodrigo *Pacheco, Judah *Hays, and Sampson *Simson often advertised their wares in newspapers. They were frequently in partnership with non-Jews, including members of the Livingston, Cuyler, and Alexander families. In some instances such partnerships developed into long friendships, as was the case of Rodrigo Pacheco with James Alexander. Myer *Myers, made freeman in 1746, became a noted silversmith and goldsmith whose work was much in demand and is displayed today in many museums. Benjamin *Etting, also a goldsmith, was made a freeman in 1769; Michael Solomon *Hays in 1769 was a watchmaker; and Abraham Isaacs in 1770, a tailor. These occupations were not found in the period of initial settlement, and there were few Jews in the professions during this period. Dr. Elias Woolin was in the city in 1744, but there were no Jewish members of the bar, though Jews represented about 10% of the litigants in the various courts. In addition, some Jews were not successful financially. A number, including Isaac Levy, Moses Hart, and Michael Jacobs, became insolvent debtors. Some were jailed and others, like Aaron Machado and Abraham Myers Cohen, were written off as bad debts.

During the period of British control Jewish merchants were able to hold many positions of responsibility. Jacob *Franks and his son David were provision agents for the Crown during the French and Indian War. Sampson Simson was a member of the group that received the charter for the Chamber of Commerce in 1770. Perhaps the highest position held by a Jew in colonial New York was that of colonial agent representing the colony's interests in Parliament. This post was given to Rodrigo Pacheco in 1731. Daniel and Mordecai Gomez served as Spanish interpreters to the Supreme Court in New York. A number of Jews were elected to office, generally as constables or assessors. Members of the Hays family made the constabulary something of a tradition. For Jewish citizens, Christian oaths necessary for office, voting, and naturalization were often modified or eliminated. It was quite unusual for Jews to hold office in the other colonies, and the fact that they did in New York was an indication of the cosmopolitan nature of the colony and its general acceptance of the Jewish community. There was no ghetto and little overt anti-Jewish feeling. Most of the Jewish population lived in the area below Wall Street, generally in the Dock and South wards facing the East

River, mixed among their Christian neighbors. Jacob Franks lived off Coenties Slip and Asser Levy on Stone Street, as did Jacob Acosta. The burial ground off present-day Chatham Square was also on the East Side, at the end of Pearl Street, the main road through that part of town. In 1748 the Swedish naturalist Peter Kalm, then residing in the colony, wrote that Jews "enjoyed all the privileges common to the other inhabitants of the town or the province."

Precise census figures are not generally available, but for most of the 17th and 18th centuries Jews represented 1% to 2% of the total New York City population. In 1700 there were 17 households listed in the assessment rolls; estimating this at six per family, there were about 100 individuals, or 2% of the general population of 4,500. In 1722, 20 households are named, or about 1½%. A peak of 31 families was recorded in 1728, about 2.3% of the general population of 8,000. This was followed by a gradual decline to 19 families in 1734, or 1.2%. In that year Jews paid 1.9% of the city's taxes; in 1722 they had paid 2%. As a group they were seemingly slightly more affluent than their neighbors. After 1734 there are no extant assessment lists for New York City, so population figures are questionable, but it is fairly safe to rely on the 1% figure for the remaining period, although it may have been more.

Congregation Shearith Israel provided a cohesive force. Not the least of its functions was to provide a secular education, for there were no public schools. Religious subjects, as well as arithmetic and English, were taught by itinerant teachers. Moses Fonseca, for example, was brought in from Curaçao to be a *ḥazzan* as well as teacher. There were strong pressures for intermarriage. The limited number of Jews and hostility between Sephardim and Ashkenazim, plus a basic tolerance, created an atmosphere conducive for intermarriage. In 1742 Phila Franks, daughter of Jacob and Abigail Franks, one of the most noted Jewish families, married Oliver Delancey, an aristocrat and an Episcopalian. A few months later her brother David married Margaret Evans of Philadelphia; their children were baptized. By the eve of the American Revolution the pioneer Jewish citizens – the Pinheiros, De Mesquitas, Asser Levys, and their descendants – had all but disappeared from the New York scene.

REVOLUTIONARY PERIOD. The advent of the American Revolution found the Jewish community divided. In the past Jews had expressed their fealty to the Crown by word and deed. Numbers of Jews served in the colonial wars. Samuel Myers Cohen, Jacob Franks, and others were in the militia during the King George War, Abraham Solomon died in service during the French and Indian War, and others had served aboard privateers. Some, like members of the Franks family, were commissary agents for the British government. New York Jews, however, along with many others, sensed the emancipatory action of the Revolution and the possibility of full civil and political rights. Between 1768 and 1770 some 11 Jewish merchants, including Samuel *Judah, Hayman *Levy, and Jonas *Phillips, signed Non-Importation Articles that sought repeal of the Townshend Acts, which placed duties on the importation of tea, paper, lead and paint among other articles. The conquest of the city by the British in 1776 caused many Jews to flee to unoccupied places, such as Philadelphia and several locations in Connecticut. One supporter of the American cause was Haym *Solomon, who for a time was imprisoned by the British as a spy. *Ḥazzan* Gershom Mendes *Seixas fled to Philadelphia and helped found Congregation Mikveh Israel there. Others, confident of British justice, chose to stay, and the congregation carried on services during the occupation. Among the Loyalists was Abraham Wagg, who left for England in 1779 and attempted reconciliation between the contending factions. Uriah *Hendricks, a noted merchant, remained loyal. David Franks was accused by Congress of being a Loyalist and relieved of his commissary rights with the American government. He held a similar post under the British. He also left for England, but returned after the war for a time. The majority of Jews preferred a neutral position in the conflict, partly in fear of the consequences of a wrong guess. Jews sympathetic with the British cause knew what to expect from England but did not know what their status would be under the new government. Patriotic Jews, on the other hand, looked forward to a new freedom.

EARLY AMERICAN PERIOD. The end of the Revolution brought many distinct changes. Civil liberties, often a matter of governmental whim under the English, became part of the New York State constitution. Opportunities were expanded and new fields opened. Within a decade after the Revolution, Judah Zuntz and Solomon *Simson were admitted to the bar. In 1792 Benjamin *Seixas and Ephraim *Hart were among the founders of the New York Stock Exchange. Gershom Mendes Seixas served as a trustee of Columbia College from 1784 to 1814, and was one of 14 ministers who participated at George *Washington's first inaugural in April 1789, and Col. David M. Franks was one of the marshals in charge of the processional at the inaugural. Among the first Jewish graduates of Columbia College was Sampson Simson in 1800. Walter Judah, admitted to the college in 1795, also attended the medical school. He died while treating the sick during the yellow fever epidemic of 1798. In 1818 Governor De Witt Clinton attended the opening of Shearith Israel when the congregation rebuilt the synagogue on the Mill Street site. No colonial governor is known to have ever shown such deference to the community.

The Revolution reduced the Jewish population to less than 1% of the population. It remained at that level until the 1830s and 1840s, when an influx of German and Polish Jews caused a sudden rise to perhaps 15,000 in 1847 and to some 40,000, or approximately 4%, on the eve of the Civil War. Replacing the old and for the most part extinct pioneer generation were mostly German Jews, such as Harmon *Hendricks, son of Uriah, a mid-18th-century immigrant, who established possibly the first copper-rolling mill in the country in 1813. One of the distinctive changes in postwar New York was Jewish involvement in the political life of the community, perhaps best seen in the career of Mordecai Manuel *Noah. Born in Philadelphia in 1785, he entered public service as consul to Tunis in 1813. He became a member of the Democratic Party and was elected high sheriff of New York in 1821, surveyor of the port from 1829 to 1833, and judge of the Court of Sessions in 1841. In 1825 he started the unsuccessful Jewish settlement of Ararat on the Niagara River. As editor of the newspaper *The Evening Star* during the 1830s, he broke with Andrew Jackson and became a founder of the Whig and Nativist parties. His espousal of Jewish causes and his involvement with politics reflected a distinct example of the interests of the community. His funeral in 1851 was attended with the most elaborate ceremony by the Jewish settlement. The publishers Naphtali *Phillips and Naphtali *Judah were powers in the Tammany Society in the first two decades of the 19th century. Mordecai *Myers was elected to the state assembly in 1829 and 1831, while Emanuel B. *Hart was elected to the House of Representatives in 1851. He also held the posts of surveyor of the port and president of the Board of Aldermen. Greater social mobility of the Jews after the Revolution could be seen in their movement uptown from the area below Wall Street into other parts of the city. Sampson *Isaacs and Naphtali and Benjamin Judah lived in the Third Ward, the present-day Greenwich Village. The residences of Jacob B. *Seixas and Asher Marx were located on the newly burgeoning East Side. The lower midtown area was the residence of Henry Hyman, Isaac *Moses, and Hayman *Seixas. The wealthiest Jews and non-Jews resided a little below and a little above Wall Street. Harmon Hendricks, probably the richest Jew of early 19th-century New York, lived at 61 Greenwich Street. Near him, on this "quality lane," resided the almost equally wealthy Solomon J. *Isaacs, Lewis Marks, and Mrs. Isaac Moses.

The changing character of the community was also evident in the changing religious organization. In 1825 a group of Ashkenazi Jews, led by Barrow E. Cohen and Isaac B. *Kursheedt, complaining of its formality and control, broke away from the parent body, Shearith Israel, and formed the Bnai Jeshurun Congregation. In 1828 another dissenting group of Dutch, German, and Polish Jews broke from Bnai Jeshurun and formed the Congregation Anshe Chesed. In 1839, Polish members of these two groups formed Congregation Shaarey Zedek. Other German Jews formed Shaarey Hashamayim in 1839, Rodeph Shalom in 1842, and Temple Emanu-El in 1845. Dutch Jews established Bnai Israel in 1847 and French, Shaarey Brocho in 1851. The proliferation of congregational organizations and divisions of the Jewish community were due partly to the new freedom resulting from the Revolution. At first, these new congregations used a number of privately owned buildings before erecting their own synagogue buildings in what became a period of synagogue construction. The old Mill Street synagogue was sold by Shearith Israel in 1833 and a new building was erected on Crosby Street. In addition, there were five major synagogue structures in New York by 1860: Bnai Jeshurun on Greene Street, Shaarey Tefilah on Wooster, Anshe Chesed on Norfolk Street, Temple Beth El on 33rd Street, and Rodeph Shalom on Clinton Street. In the 1850s Anshe Chesed was the largest congregation in the United States. By the Civil War, Temple Emanu-El and Shearith Israel were the wealthiest and most influential of the congregations.

Religious organizations produced a number of distinguished leaders. Samuel M. *Isaacs, an English Jew who arrived in New York in 1839, was *ḥazzan* and possibly the first regular preacher in New York City. He was engaged as *ḥazzan* by Bnai Jeshurun and Shaarey Tefilah. From 1859 he edited the *Jewish Messenger*, one of the most influential Jewish periodicals. Jacques Judah *Lyons, the *ḥazzan* of Shearith Israel in the 1840s, compiled material for a proposed history of Jews in America, a task he did not complete. The first ordained rabbis arrived in the 1840s from Europe. Among them was Leo Merzbacher who ministered to Anshe Chesed and Rodeph Shalom and helped in establishing the Reform Temple Emanu-El, where he delivered sermons, attended official functions, and assisted in the education of the children. Others included Dr. Max *Lilienthal, considered the most capable preacher in German, and Dr. Morris J. *Raphall, who had a distinguished career with generally German congregations. *Ḥazzanim* with excellent singing voices who enhanced the synagogue services included Leon Sternberger of Warsaw and Ignatius Ritterman of Cracow.

The period after the Revolutionary War also saw the start of mutual-aid societies and *landsmanshaften*, which generally began as burial societies (*ḥevra kaddisha*). The Hebrah Gemilut Hasadim, organized at Shearith Israel in 1786, disbanded in 1790. As a successor, Rabbi Gershom Mendes Seixas founded Hebrah Hesed Vaemet in 1802, an organization still in existence. In 1826 Bnai Jeshurun formed the Hebrah Gemilut Hesed, known as the Hebrew Mutual Benefit Society, the forerunner of many such societies. The first president of this important group was Isaac B. Kursheedt. Anshe Chesed helped organize several societies, including the Montefiore Society in 1841.

Numerous fraternal orders began, the most important being the Independent Order *B'nai B'rith, founded in 1843 by 12 men, including Henry Jones, Isaac Rosenberg, and R.M. Roadacher. It combined mutual aid and fraternal features in an effort to bring harmony and peace among Jews. The groups spread rapidly with lodges and memberships throughout the country. Another such society was the Hebrew Benevolent Society, established in 1822 with Daniel Jackson as its first president. He was succeeded by John I. Hart and Roland M. Mitchell. (These names are an indication of the difficulty of identifying Jews during this period.) In 1820 women of Shearith Israel had organized a Female Hebrew Benevolent Society. In 1844 the German Hebrew Benevolent Society, a more narrowly based *Landsleute* group, was formed. These groups worked so well that by the eve of the Civil War few, if any, Jews had to apply to city institutions for aid. The Hebrew Benevolent Society and German Hebrew Benevolent Society united just prior to the Civil War, but other groups continued to maintain independence. Under the urging of Rev. Samuel

Isaacs in the *Jewish Messenger* and Dr. Samuel *Adler of Temple Emanu-El, the Hebrew and German societies formed the Hebrew Orphan Asylum in 1859.

For years after the Revolution there were demands for a Jewish hospital. It was not until 1852, however, that Sampson Simson, with the assistance of Shearith Israel and Shaarey Tefilah and a group of native and English Jews, founded "Jews' Hospital in the City of New York." This became known as Mount Sinai in 1866. Contributions from Judah *Touro of New Orleans and N.K. Rosenfeld of Temple Emanu-El, among others, helped in the construction of the building in 1853. Poor patients were given free treatment. The staff, as well as patients, were Jewish and non-Jewish.

Young men's Jewish groups also became part of the social scene of 19th-century New York and reflected a universal interest in education and its dissemination, so much a part of Jacksonian America. In 1852 a Hebrew Young Men's Literary Society was founded. A splinter group formed the Philodocean Society, and in 1854 another group formed the Touro Literary Institute. Other groups included the Montefiore Literary Association and the Washington Social Club. In 1858 the Young Men's and Touro groups merged to form the Hebrew Young Men's Literary Society. Jews also organized military organizations that had strong social overtones. These included Troop K, Empire Hussars, and the Young Men's Lafayette Association. Most of these social organizations, which included the Cultur Verein and Sange Verein, were formed as *landsmanshaften*, i.e., Young Men of Germany, Polish Young Men, etc. The Harmonie Club of German Jews is still in existence. Various members of these socially and culturally conscious organizations joined B'nai Brith before the Civil War and in 1850 also founded the Maimonides Library Association. This was a large library, housed on Orchard Street, and it was open to the public. Elaborate balls, dinners, and charity concerts did much to enliven New York Jewish society. The annual ball of the Young Men's Hebrew Benevolent Society was first held in 1842, and the annual dinners of the Hebrew and German Hebrew Benevolent Societies were highlights of the social season.

The flourishing of New York Jewish society found expression in the rise not only of community organizations but also of the press. The late 18th-century bookseller and publisher Benjamin Gomez was joined in his profession by Naphtali Phillips, publisher of the *National Advocate*, and Solomon Jackson, publisher of the first Jewish periodical in the United States, a monthly entitled *The Jew* (issued from 1823 to 1825). The first successful Jewish periodical was Robert Lyon's *The Asmonean* (1848–58), which published the debates between Jewish leaders over the necessity of a union of American Jews. In 1857 Rabbi Samuel Isaacs' *Jewish Messenger* became the voice of Orthodox Judaism and called for a union of Jewish charities, while championing a Jewish free school. There were printers skilled in German type, including Henry Franks, who printed a holiday prayer book, *Maḥzor mi-Kol ha-Shanah*, among other items. Isaac Bondi, rabbi of Anshe Chesed, edited the *Hebrew Leader* from 1859 to 1874. Among the works of Jewish authors published during this period were Mordecai Noah's imaginative *Book of Yashar* and Rev. Raphall's *Post-Biblical History of the Jews*. Despite an interest in literature and the arts, few scholarly works were produced by Jews during this time. Highly skilled Jewish artisans in the tradition of Myer Myers were few, an exception being Jacob R. *Lazarus, a painter and student of Henry Inman, whose works are today in the Metropolitan Museum of Art.

Jewish education varied little from the 18th century, except that free public schools, which were Protestant in tone, were available from 1805. These schools were extensively used by the Jewish population, especially after they came under governmental control in 1842, slowly gave up sectarianism, and greatly expanded, thus lessening the demand for synagogal day schools. In 1842 Rabbi Samuel Isaacs of Bnai Jeshurun converted an afternoon school to the New York Talmud Torah and Hebrew Institute. It lasted until 1847. Other congregations such as Anshe Chesed and Rodeph Shalom also started short-lived Hebrew and English schools. Jews generally objected to the teaching of Christian ethics and the use of Christian textbooks in public schools. Such objections helped trigger the expansion of Hebrew schools in the 1850s. Bnai Jeshurun, Temple Emanu-El, Shaarey Zedek, and Shearith Israel all started parochial day schools combining secular and religious education. By 1854 there were seven such schools but there was great debate over their necessity. As in the colonial period, the education of Jewish girls was not considered too important; they were either sent to public schools or taught by private tutors. A few unsuccessful attempts were made to establish institutions of higher education. Sampson Simson organized the Jewish Theological Seminary and Scientific Institution, but there was little else. Jews of New York did not support Isaac Wise's Zion Collegiate Institute in Cincinnati and little was done for Samuel M. Isaacs' Hebrew high school founded in the 1850s.

Several world events stirred the community. The *Mortara case in Italy in 1859, in which a Jewish boy was converted to Christianity despite family objections, led S.M. Isaacs to form the *Board of Delegates of the American Israelites; it was intended to protect and secure civil and religious rights of Jews in the U.S. and abroad. An earlier episode, the *Damascus Affair (an accusation of ritual murder against the Jews of Damascus), led to several mass meetings in 1840 calling for President Van Buren to protest this accusation.

There was tremendous diversity to Jewish business interests during this period. Generally, however, the latter centered on small retail shops and small handicraft businesses. Some Jews held posts in civil service, generally of a minor nature, an exception being Albert *Cardozo, justice of the Supreme Court of New York. There were a few men of prominence in business. Hayman *Levy, one of the largest fur traders in the colonies, employed John Jacob Astor in his business after the Revolution. Another was Eli Hart, who was in the wheat and flour business. Daniel Jackson was a noted broker and banker.

Bernhard *Hart was honorary secretary of the New York Stock Exchange from 1831 to 1853. August *Belmont represented Rothschild interests in New York after he replaced Joseph L. and J. Josephs in 1836.

CIVIL WAR. The Civil War found the Jewish community, like the rest of the country, divided over slavery. New York City in many ways resembled a Southern city. Though slavery was prohibited after 1827, schools and theaters were segregated. Many Jews, including members of the Manumission Society of New York City, had freed their slaves, others retained them until forced to set them free. Mordecai M. Noah supported the pro-slavery position, as did Dr. Morris J. Raphall, who observed that the Ten Commandments condoned slavery. This position was attacked by Michael *Heilprin, writing in the *Tribune*, and he was joined by Rev. Samuel M. Isaacs as well as many others. With the start of the war the Jewish response was overwhelmingly in favor of the Union. On April 20, 1861, Joseph *Seligman was vice president of a Union meeting held at Union Square. His firm, J. and J. Seligman & Co., sold federal bonds in the astonishing sum of $200,000,000. Although Jews enlisted quickly, there was strong anti-Jewish bias in the army. At first Jewish chaplains were not permitted to serve, but Samuel M. Isaacs and his son Myer were among the leaders of the successful struggle to change the restrictive terms of the law. Jewish soldiers were dispersed throughout the army, and there were few Jewish enclaves, except for Company D of the 8th, New York, National Guard.

Jews also supported the war effort by aiding the United States Sanitary Commission, and held numerous Purim balls or Feasts of Esther to help the sick and wounded. Shearith Israel, Anshe Chesed, and Temple Emanu-El were in the forefront of the effort to raise money for the war effort. The 1864 Sanitary Fair in New York, the largest held during the war, found Benjamin Nathan and Moses Lazarus on the executive committee and Moses Schloss and Lewis May on the general committee. The Jews Hospital opened its wards to the wounded and between 1862 and 1865 treated hundreds of soldiers of all faiths. Judge Albert Cardozo and Col. E.B. Hart were on the Advisory Committee of the New York State Soldiers Committee. By the end of the war the Jewish community was numerous, well-represented, and established. It had prepared the ground for future, more massive immigration. Newcomers after 1865 found a community with a history and a background of accomplishment that proved receptive to them.

[Leo Hershkowitz]

1870–1920

MIGRATION AND POPULATION GROWTH. Beginning in the 1870s and continuing for half a century, the great migration from Eastern Europe radically altered the demography, social structure, cultural life, and communal order of New York Jewry. During this period more than a million Jews settled in the city. They were overwhelmingly Yiddish-speaking and impoverished, the products of intensive, insular Jewish life and wretched economic conditions. Meeting the harsh problems of economic survival, social integration, and the maintenance of the ethnic heritage required vast physical, emotional, and intellectual efforts.

On their arrival in the city the East European Jews (commonly called Russian Jews) found a Jewish settlement dominated by a group strikingly different in cultural background, social standing, and communal outlook. By the 1870s this older settlement had become, with some important exceptions, middle class in outlook, mercantile in its economic base, and Reform Jewish in group identity. Successfully integrated in the economic life of the city and well advanced in its acculturation to the larger society, the established community drew its leadership from a socially homogenous elite of bankers, merchant princes, brokers, and manufacturers. The two groups – the prosperous and Americanized "uptown Jews" and the alien and plebeian "downtown Jews" – confronted and interacted with each other, a process that significantly shaped the course of community development.

Two-thirds of the city's Jews in 1870 were German born or children of German-born parents. Together with the smaller subgroups – descendants of the 18th-century community, clusters of English, Dutch, and Bohemian Jews, and a growing contingent of Polish Jews (who formed a distinctive subcommunity) – the Jewish population numbered 60,000, or 4% of the inhabitants of the larger city (Manhattan and Brooklyn). By 1920, New York (all five boroughs) contained approximately 1,640,000 Jews (29% of the total population), and they made up the largest ethnic group in the city. (The Italians, the second most numerous, formed 14% of the population. Their arrival in the city paralleled the Russian Jewish migration, and their initial areas of settlement adjoined the Jewish immigrant quarters.) By 1920, 45% of the Jewish population of the United States lived in New York.

As the main port of entry for immigrants, New York served as a transit point and temporary domicile. The city also attracted a portion of those who entered the country through other ports, particularly Philadelphia and Baltimore, or who came to the city after having lived inland for a time. Of all immigrant groups, Jews ranked first in their preference for New York. According to S. Joseph, 1,372,189 Jews passed through the port of New York between 1881 and 1911, of whom 73% settled in the city. The Table: Population Growth-NYC and Jews indicates the population growth of New York and of its Jewish community. (The statistical data for New York City and Brooklyn are combined for the period prior to 1898 to permit comparison with the later period. New York City in 1870 was restricted to Manhattan Island. In 1874 it annexed three western townships in the Bronx and in 1895 annexed the eastern towns. Brooklyn remained a separate city until 1898 when it consolidated with Manhattan, the Bronx, Queens, and Richmond (Staten Island) to form the present-day city. Before 1900 only scattered Jews lived in the areas that later became the boroughs of Queens and Richmond.)

New York City Population Growth and Jewish Population Growth: 1870–1920

Year	Total Population of Greater New York	Estimated Jewish Population	Percentage of Jews to Total Population
1870	1,363,213	60,000	4%
1880	1,912,698	80,000	4%
1890	2,507,414	225,000	9%
1900	3,437,202	580,000	11%
1910	4,766,883	1,100,000	23%
1920	5,620,048	1,643,000	29%

Population dispersion within the city accompanied this growth (See Table: New York - Population Growth). In 1870 nearly two-thirds of the inhabitants of Greater New York resided in Manhattan. Fifty years later Manhattan's population had grown two and a half times, but it contained only two-fifths of the city's inhabitants. During this period Brooklyn's population multiplied fourfold, the Bronx's fifteenfold, Queens' ninefold, and Richmond's threefold. Queens and Richmond, still the most thinly inhabited areas of the city, had a density per acre of 6.1 and 3.2 persons, respectively, compared with 27.6 for the Bronx, 39.5 for Brooklyn, and 160 for Manhattan. On Manhattan's Lower East Side – bounded by Catherine Street, the Bowery, Third Avenue, 14th Street, and the East River – the population numbered 415,000 in 1920, a decline from a peak of 540,000 in 1910. At the height of its congestion, one-fourth of Manhattan's residents occupied one-twentieth of the island's space, an area of 1.5 sq. mi. For most of 50 years these East Side blocks, already overcrowded in 1870, were the reception center for the flood of Russian Jewish immigration. Only after 1900, when the immigrants themselves established new neighborhoods in areas like Harlem and Brownsville in Brooklyn, did some newcomers go directly there, bypassing the Lower East Side.

New York by Borough: Population Growth by Boroughs, 1880–1920, and Jewish Population by Boroughs in 1920

	1880	1910	1920	Jewish Population 1920 (est.)	Percentage of Jews to Pop. 1920
Manhattan	1,164,673	2,331,542	2,284,103	657,101	28.8
The Bronx	51,980	430,980	732,016	278,169	38.0
Brooklyn	599,495	1,643,351	2,018,356	604,380	29.9
Queens	56,559	284,041	469,042	86,194	18.4
Richmond	38,991	85,969	116,531	17,168	14.7
Total	1,912,698	4,766,883	5,620,048	1,643,012	29.2

The Jews constituted the most conspicuous element in this dual phenomenon of rising congestion and rapid dispersion. In 1870 the less affluent, and those whose occupations required it, lived in the southern wards of the Lower East Side along the axis of East Broadway. Germans, Irish, and native Americans constituted a majority of the district's population. The northern tier of wards, stretching from Rivington to 14th streets, were heavily populated by Germans. Two-story frame houses were the prevailing type of residence, though many of these had already been converted to multiple-family use. By 1890, with Russian Jews pouring in, the great majority of the earlier inhabitants, including the German Jews, left the 80 square blocks of the southern wards. Ten years later they were in the process of abandoning the entire region below 14th Street to the rising tide of Jewish immigrants. The characteristic type of residency in the enlarged Jewish quarter was now the double-decker or "dumbbell" tenement. (The dumbbell shape met an 1879 municipal regulation requiring an airshaft between contiguously built tenements.) These tenements were five to eight stories in height, they occupied 75 to 90% of a plot 25 feet wide and 100 feet deep, and each floor contained four apartments – a total of 14 rooms, of which only one in each apartment received air and light from the street or from a cramped backyard. The most congested area was the tenth ward, the heart of the Jewish East Side. In the 46 blocks between Division, Clinton, Rivington, and Chrystie Streets that made up the ward (an area of 106 acres), there were 1,196 tenements in 1893. The population was 74,401, a density of 701.9 persons an acre.

The German Jews who left the Lower East Side in this population displacement joined their more prosperous brethren, who had moved halfway up the east side of Manhattan in the years following the Civil War. They settled between 50th and 90th Streets, a region that included the beginnings of Yorkville with its heavy concentration of Germans. Smaller contingents settled farther north in the upper-class neighborhood of Harlem, north of Central Park, and scattered numbers reached the zone of well-situated brownstone homes west of Central Park.

The relocation of synagogues and the establishment of other Jewish institutions underscored this process of removal and social differentiation: the geographical division, in short, of the Jewish populace into "uptown" and "downtown." As early as 1860 the venerable Shearith Israel moved from Crosby Street, in a rapidly declining downtown area, to 19th Street near Fifth Avenue. In 1897 it moved to Central Park West and 70th Street, its present site. (Shaarey Tefillah, the first congregation on the Upper West Side, erected its synagogue on West 82nd Street four years earlier.) Temple Emanu-El, the leading Reform congregation in the city, moved from East 12th Street to Fifth Avenue and 43rd Street, where the congregation in 1868 consecrated an impressive Moorish-style edifice. In 1872 Ahavath Chesed occupied its fourth site in its 26-year existence when it moved to Lexington Avenue and 55th Street (known as the Central Synagogue, this is the oldest building in continuous use as a synagogue in New York). A year later Anshe Chesed left downtown Norfolk Street for Lexington Avenue and 63rd Street. Soon after, it consolidated with Adas Jeshurun to form Temple Beth El, which in 1891 moved to Fifth Avenue and 76th Street. Though Bnai Jeshurun, the oldest Ashkenazi congregation in the city, eventually moved to the West Side, it, too, belonged to the mainstream migration to the mid-East Side. In 1865 it occupied a newly completed house of worship, its third, on 34th Street and Broadway. It migrated further uptown to Madison Avenue and 65th Street in 1884. In 1918 the congregation moved to its present synagogue on West 88th Street near West End Avenue.

Also located in the mid-East Side area were a number of private clubs that catered to the social needs of the wealthier Jewish businessmen: Criterion, Fidelio, Freundschaft, Lotus, Progress, and the prestigious Harmonie, the club of the German-Jewish elite. Harmonie occupied its own building on 42nd Street west of Fifth Avenue from 1867 to 1912, when it moved to 4 East 60th Street. In 1872 uptown Jews transferred one of their most esteemed philanthropic institutions, Mount Sinai Hospital, to 67th Street and Lexington Avenue. By the turn of the century additional institutions supported by the older community were operating in the area. The Baron de Hirsch Trade School on East 64th Street, the Clara de Hirsch Home for Working Girls on East 63rd Street, and the Young Men's Hebrew Association (YMHA) at Lexington and 92nd Street were the most prominent. Fourteen synagogues served the growing Yorkville settlement, half of them Reform or Conservative. They occupied spacious buildings – Beth El seated 2,400 and Emanu-El 1,600 – and congregants had average annual incomes that ranged from Bnai Jeshurun's $20,000 to Emanu-El's $46,000. The Orthodox congregations mainly served a Central European group, though affluent East European Jews were moving into the area and joining them. Zichron Ephraim, organized in 1889 and located on 67th Street near Lexington Avenue, was the wealthiest. Its rabbi was New York-born and had received his university and rabbinical training in Germany and the U.S.

The Jewish settlement in Harlem developed along broadly parallel lines, though with some differences. It grew more slowly at the start. Less accessible to the center of the city – hence beyond the reach of most middle-class families – Harlem became a residential suburb for the wealthy. In 1874, when Temple Israel was established, it was the sole congregation in Harlem. Fourteen years later, when it dedicated its new synagogue on Fifth Avenue and 125th Street, three other small congregations were serving the community as well. By 1900 the number of permanent synagogues had grown to 13. Significantly, four of these had been founded by East European Jews, a sign that the movement of Russian Jews from the Lower East Side to Harlem was already well under way.

The immigrant influx inspired the poet Emma Lazarus in 1883 to compose *The New Colossus*, a paean to the future Americans. The famous sonnet echoes many of the conflicting identities and ideals swirling around the new arrivals. The compassion of the lines "huddled masses yearning to breathe free" welcomes the tired immigrants, but the following image of the "wretched refuse of your teaming shore" hints at the condescension these refugees were to suffer. These tensions, between ancient and modern, Jew and American, freedom and oppression, give Lazarus' work meaning and power. The sonnet was engraved on a plaque and placed in the pedestal of the Statue of Liberty in 1903, 16 years after her death.

The completion of the first elevated railway in the late 1870s inaugurated a new age of transit, opening cheap, semi-rural land to intensive urban development. Along a network of expanding elevated and subway routes, Russian Jewish immigrants moved out of the downtown quarter in two great streams: north to Harlem and then to the Bronx, and southeast across the East River to Brooklyn's Williamsburg and Brownsville. By the 1880s three elevated lines were running the length of Manhattan. In 1904 the first subway was completed. One route extended to the tip of Manhattan and opened the West Side and Washington Heights to mass settlement. A branch ran through Harlem and even before its completion brought a wave of construction to peripheral areas. The subway placed sections of the Bronx within the reach of families of modest means. In like manner the transit net spread to Brooklyn. The barrier of the East River was first breached in 1883 with the completion of the Brooklyn Bridge. The Williamsburg Bridge (1903) and the Manhattan Bridge (1909) and subway tunnels under the river vastly improved interborough transportation. A construction boom in multi-family dwellings marked the years 1904–07. In 1914 and 1915 twice as many apartment units were built in Brooklyn as in Manhattan, a ratio that held into the 1920s, when additional subway facilities were completed.

Though transportation and moderate rents were essential for geographic mobility, rising expectations and economic progress were no less significant. The physical conditions the new immigrant encountered were tolerable while he made his initial adjustment and saved to bring the family that was left behind. With this achieved, the Jewish immigrant family looked beyond the immigrant quarter. Improved housing and environmental conditions, particularly as they might affect the young, were the predominant motives in a family's calculations (new neighborhood housing was superior because of the more stringent municipal regulations under which it was built). For the working class, moreover, the Lower East Side was losing its "walk to work" advantage. By 1910 the main immigrant area of employment – the clothing industry – was moving to the West Side between 14th and 23rd Streets (during the 1920s its center reached the Pennsylvania Station district). This development reflected the decreasing role of the sweatshop. Once the tenement-flat sweatshop, based as it was on cheap labor drawn from the neighborhood, was restricted or eliminated, a major feature that had attracted newly arrived Jewish immigrants to the Lower East Side disappeared. The gradual elimination of the sweatshop belonged to a general improvement in labor conditions beginning after 1900, when municipal housing regulations began having some effect over the worst abuses in the tenement sweatshops, and was especially marked in the 1910s, owing to the new militancy and effectiveness of the labor unions (see below). A shorter work week and higher wages created the margin in time and money needed to leave downtown for more congenial surroundings. In many cases the move became possible, or was hastened, when children became old enough to add to family earnings. A study of pensioned clothing workers shows that 88% of the Russian Jews left the Lower East Side after residing in the area, on the average, for 15 years. In all likelihood those who became entrepreneurs lived on the Lower East Side for a briefer time. Indeed, between 1910 and 1915 the population of the Lower East Side declined by 14% and between 1915 and 1920 by a further 11%.

The most graphic instance of the growth of a new area of settlement is the case of the Brownsville-New Lots district of Brooklyn. A small group of Jews of German origin had settled in the village of New Lots. Only in 1885, however, did they establish a synagogue, Bikur Cholim (Temple Sinai). In 1886 real-estate promoters began dividing the farmland into lots for sale, and between 1890 and 1900 the Jewish population increased from less than 3,000 to more than 15,000. Five years later it had passed 49,000, and by 1916 the Brownsville-New Lots population had reached 225,490. It was served by 72 synagogues, all Orthodox.

In 1920, the primary immigrant quarter, the Lower East Side, was continuing to lose population at a rapid pace. Other areas of settlement, some of which had assumed features of the immigrant quarter, were beginning to lose population as well. Harlem was the outstanding instance. Around 1920 it passed its peak and began a steep decline as a large and culturally important Jewish neighborhood as its Jewish residents moved to the East Bronx and Washington Heights. In the Bronx, the direction was from the East Bronx and south-central region to the upper reaches of the Grand Concourse and the Tremont-Fordham areas. A similar trend occurred in Brooklyn. Though Brownsville and New Lots were still growing in 1920, the more affluent Jews were moving to leafy Eastern Parkway, Boro Park, Coney Island, and Flatbush. They were being replaced, at least in part, by a less affluent exodus from Williamsburg. By 1920 a socioeconomic hierarchy of Jewish neighborhoods had come into being.

The dispersion of Jewish population and the diversification of neighborhoods were indicators and facets of the process of acculturation.

ECONOMY. In a number of fields the Jews of New York loomed large in the economy of the city. One group of German-Jewish families played an outstanding role in revolutionizing retailing. In the decade after the Civil War, fathers and sons entered the dry goods business and transformed their establishments into great department stores, which still bear their names. Bavarian-born Benjamin *Bloomingdale and his sons Lyman and Joseph, both born in New York City, opened a dry goods store in 1872. By 1888, under the sons' direction, Bloomingdale's employed 1,000 people in its East Side emporium. On the West Side, the department store founded by Benjamin *Altman and his brother Morris expanded to the point where it required 1,600 employees. The giant in the field was R.H. Macy, which Isidore and Nathan *Straus joined in 1874, becoming the sole owners in 1887 (Oscar, a third brother, had an interest in the business as well). Lazarus Straus and his three sons had migrated to New York from Georgia in 1865 and opened a pottery and glassware house that became the springboard to their association with Macy's. Stern's, Gimbel's, and the Brooklyn firm of Abraham and Straus (A&S) were also established during this time.

A significant number of German Jews entered investment banking. Closely knit by ethnic, social, and family bonds, they formed a recognizable group within the business community. Membership in the same temples and clubs, common philanthropic endeavors, and frequent marriages within the social set welded the group together, a fact that was important in their business dealings and led to frequent collaboration. Possessing excellent financial ties with banking interests in Europe – and especially in Germany – they were able to tap these sources for the U.S. market. Kuhn, Loeb & Company, under the leadership of Jacob H. *Schiff, was the leading house. But other firms achieved considerable standing in the financial world, including J. and J. Seligman & Co., James Speyer and Company; Goldman, Sachs & Company; Hallgarten and Company; and J.S. Bache and Company. Henry Lehman, an immigrant from Germany, had opened a small shop in Montgomery, Ala., in 1844. Two brothers joined him six years later. But the Civil War disrupted their business. When hostilities ended, the brothers moved to New York, where they helped found the Cotton Exchange. During the vigorous economic expansion of the second half of the 19th century, Lehman Brothers broadened its expertise beyond commodities brokerage to merchant banking. Building a securities trading business, they became members of the New York Stock Exchange in 1887. At the turn of the century, Lehman Brothers was a founding financier of emerging retailers like Sears, Roebuck & Company, F.W. Woolworth Company, May Department Stores, Gimbel Brothers, and R.H. Macy.

German Jews played a central role as entrepreneurs in the city's growing ready-made clothing industry. In 1888, of 241 such clothing manufacturers, 234 were owned by Jews and accounted for an annual product of $55,000,000. The needle trade was fast becoming New York's most important industry. In 1870 the city's factories and shops produced men's clothes worth $34,456,884. In 1900 the value of goods they produced reached $103,220,201, and during the same period their work force rose from 17,084 to 30,272. The growth of the women's clothing branch of the industry was more spectacular. The value of goods produced rose from $3,824,882 in 1870 to $102,711,604 in 1900. Where 3,663 workers were employed in 1870, 44,450 were employed in 1900. In 1913 the clothing industry as a whole numbered 16,552 factories and 312,245 employees.

East European Jews began streaming into the industry in the 1880s and by 1890 were the dominant element. They nearly completely displaced the German, Irish, and English craftsmen, as well as the German-Jewish manufacturers. One estimate, made in 1912, calculated that approximately 85% of the employees in the needle trades were Jewish.

Jewish Craftsmen in New York, 1890

Tailors (General) 9,595	Tailors (Women's Coats) 2,084	Tailors (Wholesale) 1,043	Cigarette Manufacturers 976
Haberdashers 715	Painters 458	Carpenters 443	Tinsmiths 417
Butchers 413	Gold + Silver Smiths 287	Bakers 270	Glaziers 148
Typesetters 145	Machinists 143	Shoemakers 83	Musicians 67

The immigrant Jews entered the apparel trade in such numbers because it was close at hand, required little training, and allowed the congeniality of working with one's kind. The contracting system, which became widespread in the industry by 1890, was responsible in large measure for these conditions. Contractors, acting as middlemen, received cut goods from the merchant or manufacturer, rented shop space (or used their own tenement flat), bought or hired sewing machines, and recruited a labor force. Generally, about ten people worked in these "outside shops" (in contrast to the larger "inside shops," where the manufacturer directly employed the work force and where working conditions were better). The minute division of labor that prevailed permitted the employment of relatively unskilled labor. In the intensely competitive conditions of the time – compounded by the seasonal nature of the industry – hard-pressed contractors recurrently raised the required "task" of garments for payment. Under these circumstances the notorious sweatshops developed with their cramped quarters and long hours of work. In 1890 the journalist and social reformer Jacob Riis wrote:

> The homes of the Hebrew quarter are its workshops also… You are made fully aware of [economic conditions] before you have traveled the length of a single block in any of these East Side streets, by the whir of a thousand sewing-machines, worked at high pressure from earliest dawn till mind and muscle give out altogether. Every member of the family, from the youngest to the oldest, bears a hand, shut in the qualmy rooms, where meals are cooked and clothing washed and dried besides, the livelong day. It is not unusual to find a dozen persons – men, women, and children – at work in a single small room.

Until the turn of the century, a 70-hour work week was not uncommon.

Despite notorious abuses, the system of small shops on the Lower East Side had advantages for the new arrival. Old Country ties often played a role in the system and softened harsh conditions with an element of familiarity. Manufacturers set up fellow townsmen, *landsleit*, as contractors; contractors hired *landsleit*. Bosses who were practicing Orthodox Jews made allowances for the religious requirements of their workers. The smaller shops of the contractors, in particular, were closed on the Sabbath. Reuben Sadowsky, a large cloak manufacturer, not only closed on the Sabbath but encouraged weekday services in his factory. The production system with its extreme specialization also had its advantages. The new immigrant could master a subspecialty commensurate with his experience – or lack of it – and his physical stamina, and do so quickly. Finally, the very competitiveness and instability of the industry provided opportunities and hope. The ascent from worker to contractor to small manufacturer, categories not far removed from one another, beckoned to the enterprising and ambitious.

Although the needle trade was the largest single employer of East European Jews, Jewish immigrants found employment in other industries as well. Approximately 20% of the cigar makers in the city in the early 1900s were Russian Jews. The building boom attracted Russian Jewish builders, who opened the way for their countrymen to enter the field as craftsmen. At first, because of limited capital and the discriminatory practices of the craft unions, Jewish building activity was limited primarily to renovating old tenements. But in 1914, for example, when the Jewish painters were finally accepted into the Brotherhood of Painters and Paperhangers, 5,000 joined the union. An Inside Iron and Bronze Workers Union, organized in 1913 under the auspices of the United Hebrew Trades, had a membership of 2,000 in 1918. Branches of the food-processing industry – like baking and the slaughtering and dressing of meat – were "Jewish industries" because of the ritual requirements of *kashrut*. One of the oldest labor unions in the Jewish quarter represented the bakers. It had 2,500 members by 1918.

The compact Jewish settlements had a broad working-class base. A survey of the most heavily populated Jewish wards of the Lower East Side conducted by the Baron de Hirsch Fund in 1890 showed that 60% of those gainfully employed were shopworkers in the needle trades, 6.9% were shopworkers in other industries, 8.2% were artisans (mainly painters, carpenters, and tinsmiths), and 23.5% were tradesmen, nearly half of these being peddlers. Except for Hebrew teachers and musicians, no other profession was listed, and the latter group accounted for but 1.4%.

By 1920, however, the occupational and class structure had changed considerably. The change was expressed in a decrease in the number of blue-collar workers, an increase in the number of college students, the rise of a professional group of notable size, the growth in the magnitude and income of the mercantile class, and the consolidation of a wealthy stratum composed primarily of clothing manufacturers and real estate entrepreneurs. Jacob Lestchinsky, the sociologist and economist, suggested that in 1916 nearly 40% of all gainfully employed Jews in New York City were garment workers, while the total employed in all manual work was more than 50%. By the turn of the century, a majority of the students at tuition-free City College was Jewish, and in 1918 the proportion of Jewish students was 78.7% of total enrollment. In the College of Dental and Oral Surgery, the comparable figure was 80.9%, while at the city's college for women, Hunter, the proportion was 38.7%. In 1907, 200 physicians, 115 pharmacists, and 175 dentists served downtown's Jews (the number of Jewish physicians in the borough of Manhattan rose from 450 in 1897 to 1,000 in 1907). To this group of professionals, add the growing number of lawyers. Evening law school – generally a two-year course of study – enabled a younger generation to prepare for a professional career while being self-supporting. The careers of Morris *Hillquit and Meyer *London, labor lawyers and socialist leaders; Leo Sanders and Aaron J. Levy, active in Tammany politics; and Isaac A. Allen and Benjamin Koeningsberg, who were involved in Orthodox Jewish causes, indicate some of the avenues open to the young lawyers. Especially striking was the observation of Isaac M. *Rubinow, physician, economist, and statistician. Writing in 1905 he noted the growth of "Russian Jewish fortunes in New York," many of which ranged between $25,000 and $200,000. "Almost every newly arrived Russian-Jewish laborer comes into contact with a Russian-Jewish employer," he wrote, and "almost every Russian-Jewish tenement dweller must pay his exorbitant rent to a Russian-Jewish landlord." He was alluding to such wealthy clothing manufacturers as Joseph H. Cohen, Louis Borgenicht, William Fischman, and Israel Unterberg, and to real-estate developers like Harry Fischel and Nathan Lamport. It was within this context of a "Jewish economy" that the Jewish labor movement in New York developed and made its impact. Organizing the Jewish clothing workers – the primary sphere of trade-union activity – entailed dealing with a constituency that considered its occupation temporary and was conservative in temper to a large degree. It meant negotiating with a multitude of bosses and a host of elusive contractors. However, the fact that the trade-union struggle took place in New York and in the garment industry also made it a Jewish communal affair. This had its mitigating consequences. Clothing manufacturers like Joseph Cohen and William Fischman were also leaders of the community. Downtown social workers like Henry *Moskowitz and Lillian *Wald and their uptown sponsors, Jacob Schiff and Louis *Marshall, were no less concerned with the good name of the community and the social integration of the newcomers. In the 1910s this led to a stabilization of the unions, vastly improved working conditions, and a pioneering formula of labor-industry relations. For the 20 years until the great strikes of 1909–16 the Jewish trade unions were weak and dispirited, despite occasional victories. The 1890 strike of the cloakmakers led by Joseph *Barondess was one such instance. The early success of the United Hebrew Trades was another. But ideological factionalism and seasonal apathy sapped the strength of the unions. From 1901 to 1909, the groundwork was laid, however, for the emergence of an aggressive, responsible, and socially progressive Jewish labor movement. The rising curve of immigration was drawing members and adherents of the *Bund, who were deeply committed to trade-union work. The socialist *Forward* was developing into the most widely read Yiddish daily and becoming a major educational medium for the Jewish working class. The Jewish socialist fraternal order, the Arbeiter Ring (*Workmen's Circle), was gaining strength. The "uprising of the twenty thousand" – a strike of the waistmakers, mostly young women – in the fall of 1909 was followed by the "great revolt" of the cloakmakers a half year later. These strikes increased the numbers and the stability of the *International Ladies Garment Workers Union (ILGWU).

One tragic event in 1911, however – a fire at the Triangle Shirtwaist Company factory in lower Manhattan, in which 146 young women perished – led to sweeping changes in safety laws and gave a powerful impetus to the fledgling labor movement. The fire broke out near the end of a six-day, 52-hour workweek on the top three floors of a 10-story building. About 500 women, mostly Jewish and Italian immigrants, worked there behind locked doors making blouses. Within 15 minutes after the fire broke out, nearly 30% of the workers were killed. Firetruck ladders could reach only to the seventh floor. Firefighters held nets below, but so many women were jumping at the same time that the nets tore and did not hold them. Some rushed to the elevator shaft, hoping to escape by sliding down the cables, only to lose their grip. The owners of the business were acquitted of responsibility for the deaths, but in 1914, civil suits brought by relatives of 23 victims ended with payments of $75 to each of the families. The fire became the most vivid symbol of the struggle for workplace safety. As outrage mounted after the fire, the ILGWU intensified its demands for safer working conditions. New York established a Bureau of Fire Investigation and over the next three years enacted 36 safety laws.

In the summer of 1912, the furriers fought their battle for recognition. From January to March 1913 nearly 150,000 struck different branches of the apparel trades, but in particular the men's clothing industry. The strike led to the founding of the Amalgamated Clothing Workers of America (ACWA). The strikes had much in common. High emotion and a deep sense of dedication marked them all. The scene of workers pouring into the streets from their shops at the appointed hour reminded the chairman of the cloakmakers' strike of the Jews leaving Egypt. Characteristic, too, was the climate of opinion: the Jewish labor movement succeeded in mobilizing broad material and moral support for the strikers both from its own ranks and from reform circles. In all instances, moreover, prominent Jewish communal leaders intervened and mediated between Russian Jewish labor leaders and Russian Jewish manufacturers. In the best-known case, the 1910 strike, Louis *Brandeis, Louis Marshall, A. Lincoln *Filene, Henry Moskowitz, Jacob Schiff, and Meyer Bloomfield became involved at one point or another in mediating the dispute. In the furriers' strike, Judah L. *Magnes, former rabbi of Temple Emanu-El and chairman of the New York Kehillah, was instrumental in ending the dispute. He became permanent chairman of the conference committee of the fur industry and later chairman of the council of moderators of the men's clothing industry. Finally, in all cases, negotiations ended with some form of recognition for the union, a preferential or union shop, a smaller work week (generally 50 hours), a rise in wages, and arrangements for the continual arbitration of grievances. The latter provision led to the creation of joint sanitation, grievance, and arbitration committees under the chairmanship of "impartial chairmen" aided by professional staffs, which supervised the enforcement of the decisions. This groundbreaking innovation in labor relations reflected a particular ethnic-economic reality and a particular Jewish group response.

COMMUNAL LIFE. In 1870 the New York Jewish community appeared to be well on its way to achieving homogeneity in form and content, directed by its Americanized element of German origin. For this group, Jewish communal life expressed itself in membership in a Reform temple, and sponsorship of Jewish welfare institutions. Lay leaders of the established community found in the institutional forms a way to maintain their Jewish identity in a manner they considered compatible with American practice. Though they drew upon Jewish communal traditions, these leaders were profoundly affected by the model of American liberal Protestantism with its emphasis on denominationalism, voluntarism, and morals rather than ritual.

By 1900 there were 14 Reform synagogues in the city: nine in Manhattan, one in the Bronx, and four in Brooklyn. In 1918 there were 16 Reform and 32 Conservative synagogues. These synagogues held services on weekends, sponsored one-day-a-week religious schools, and engaged university-trained rabbis. Their weekly sermons were reported by the leading newspapers as part of the notable sermons in the city's houses of worship.

Among the distinguished Reform rabbis who served in New York between 1870 and 1920 were Gustave Gottheil, Joseph Silverman, Judah L. Magnes, and Hyman G. Enelow at Emanu-El, David Einhorn, Kaufmann Kohler, and Samuel Schulman at Beth El (later amalgamated with Emanu-El), Aaron Wise, and Rudolph Grossman at Rodeph Shalom, Adolf Huebsch, Alexander Kohut, and Isaac S. Moses at Ahavath Chesed (later the Central Synagogue), and Maurice H. Harris at Temple Israel of Harlem (later on the West Side). The establishment of the Free Synagogue in 1907 as a pulpit for Stephen S. *Wise was a novel religious development, for its services were conducted on Sunday mornings at Carnegie Hall, and it also embarked upon a wide-ranging program of social service. Wise, who came to New York in 1907, and Magnes, who arrived in 1904, represented a new type of Jewish minister. American-bred and American-trained, they were young, excellent orators, and forceful – even daring – in espousing their causes and attracting large followings. Wise became best known for his attacks on municipal corruption and industrial conditions, while Magnes' main efforts were directed toward cultural and social improvements within the Jewish community.

During the last third of the 19th century, the established community built a number of large and progressive philanthropic institutions: general relief agencies, hospitals, old-age homes, orphan asylums, vocational training schools, and neighborhood centers. The outlook of these institutions reflected the receptivity of uptown's Jewish leaders to the social thought and patrician practices of the time. The emergence of scientific philanthropy, with its insistence on thorough investigation of the needy applicant, emphasis on economic and vocational rehabilitation, and espousal of the professionalization of welfare services, guided the policies of the older Jewish charities. So did the related sociological view of poverty that emphasized environmental factors, uplift, and "preventive work."

The United Hebrew Charities (UHC; formed in 1874 by six philanthropic societies) was illustrative of this development. In addition to poor relief, UHC operated an employment bureau and a vocational training school, granted loans to aid families launching small businesses, and maintained a work room where women were paid while they learned one of the garment trades. Its medical department employed a physician, visiting nurses, and social workers who handled home births and consumption cases. In 1911 UHC opened a bureau to meet the problems of family desertion. The agency's expenditures rose from $46,000 in 1880, to $153,000 in 1900, to $344,000 in 1917. In 1886, 2,500 applied for assistance, and in 1900, 23,264 asked for aid. Beginning in 1901, the number of families receiving material aid decreased steadily from 8,125 to 6,014 in 1916. The vast majority were by then Russian Jewish immigrants. (As late as 1885 the largest single group of applicants were of non-East European stock.) An excerpt from a Yiddish article published in 1884 suggests the gulf that existed between the "professional methods" employed in the uptown-sponsored institutions, and the immigrant clients:

> In the philanthropic institutions of our aristocratic German Jews you see beautiful offices, desks, all decorated, but strict and angry faces. Every poor man is questioned like a criminal, is looked down upon; every unfortunate suffers self-degradation and shivers like a leaf, just as if he were standing before a Russian official.

Child care was a priority. Two of the leading institutions in the city were the Hebrew Orphan Asylum at Amsterdam Avenue and 136th Street, which in 1917 had a capacity of 1,250 children and an annual budget of $407,130, and the Hebrew Sheltering Guardian Society. The latter moved to Pleasantville, New York in 1912, where it introduced the "cottage plan," a model program. The uptown Jews were the sponsors of Mount Sinai Hospital. In 1904 it moved to its present site, Fifth Avenue and 100th Street. By 1916 the hospital had reached a capacity of 523 beds; its dispensary treated 243,161 patients.

These institutions were served by a distinguished group of lay and professional leaders. Lee K. Frankel and Morris D. Waldman of the United Hebrew Charities, Ludwig B. Bernstein of the Hebrew Sheltering Guardian Orphan Asylum, Solomon Lowenstein of the Hebrew Orphan Asylum, and Dr. Sigismund S. Goldwater of Mount Sinai belonged to the first rank of administrators. Philanthropists like Jacob H. Schiff, Irving Lehman, Isidore Straus, and George Blumenthal were intimately connected with the routine management as well as with the financing of the Montefiore Home, the

92nd Street Young Men's Hebrew Association (YMHA), the Educational Alliance, and Mount Sinai Hospital, respectively.

The notion that philanthropic institutions should be nonsectarian clashed with a second approach, which stressed the encouragement of Jewish cultural and religious activity. Supporters of the latter position debated such fundamental issues as the meaning of Americanization, the legitimacy of preserving the Old World heritage and its secular offsprings, and the nature of inter-group relationships within the New York Jewish community. These issues found their clearest institutional expression in the work of the Educational Alliance, the largest and most influential community center on the Lower East Side. In 1889 a number of uptown societies sponsoring Jewish cultural activities on the Lower East Side amalgamated and formed the Hebrew Institute. Four years later, reorganization led to a change in name, emphasizing its nonsectarian stand by replacing Hebrew Institute with Educational Alliance. Its official scope was "of an Americanizing, educational, social, and humanizing character." In 1897 the agency's president, Isidore Straus, explained that "our work may seem sectarian… [because] we have reached chiefly Jews, but this is due to the fact that the neighborhood is inhabited principally by Jews." Nevertheless, the Alliance did recognize the background of its constituents. The library and reading room were well stocked with Yiddish, Hebrew, and Russian books and periodicals. A synagogue and a religious school were established as well. The Alliance followed on the heels of the founding of the Henry Street Settlement on the Lower East Side by Lillian D. Wald in 1893. Wald, who became one of the most influential and respected social reformers of the 20th century, began teaching health and hygiene to immigrant women. Within a decade the Settlement included a team of 20 nurses and was offering an array of innovative and effective social, recreation, and educational services. In the early 1900s, the Alliance softened its attitude toward Yiddish and Yiddish culture. Zvi H. *Masliansky's discourses became a weekly event that drew large crowds, as did guest appearances by such Yiddish literary figures as Shalom Aleichem. Orthodox Jewish leaders, however, still viewed the Alliance as a bastion of Reform Judaism located in the very heart of their quarter, while to the radical intelligentsia it represented the "uptown's" use of charity and Americanization to silence social protest. Despite the opposition, Jews took advantage of the opportunities the institution opened for them. There were English-language classes and naturalization courses for adults, preschool instruction for newly arrived immigrant children, literary and civic clubs, music classes, and a children's orchestra, drama circles, and art exhibits. The Breadwinner's College, inspired by Thomas Davidson, a physical education program, and the Aguilar Free Library added to the appeal. During the first decade of the 20th century, as many as 37,000 people went weekly to the main building and to the two branch centers. Some of those who served as key members of the staff were David Blaustein, Henry Leipziger, Paul Abelson, and Belle Moskowitz. Similar agencies of smaller scope were the Jewish Settlement House and the Temple Emanu-El Brotherhood.

Important as uptown's welfare agencies were in aiding the immigrants, they at best complemented the communal order being created by the East European Jews. Transplanted religious institutions – synagogues, *talmud torahs*, and traditional charities – constituted a major part of that order. Mutual aid associations, fraternal orders, and benevolent societies provided other avenues of group endeavor. Finally, secular institutions spun a network of facilities, adding to the heterogeneity of Jewish life and enriching it intellectually.

In organizing their synagogues, the first and most typical communal undertaking, the immigrants mostly established congregations of *landsleit*, deriving their synagogues' names mostly from the congregants' town of origin. *Landsleit* congregations proliferated. In 1887 Moses Weinberger estimated there were 130 Orthodox congregations in New York City, by far the largest number on the Lower East Side. By 1902 the number of synagogues there had reached 254, and by 1917, 418. A 1917 study estimated that 40% of 365 congregations located in the older sections of the Lower East Side possessed traditional adult study groups, 45% free loan associations, 33% sick benefit societies, and 91% cemetery plots. Their average seating capacity was about 180. In addition, 50 to 70 "temporary" synagogues operated for the High Holidays on the East Side alone. In 1917 only 20% of the permanent congregations owned their synagogue building.

A few older synagogues gained stature as central institutions in the downtown community. They transcended the localism of *landsmanshaft*, though they still retained a regional identity. These included the Beth Hamidrash Hagadol on Norfolk Street, the Kalvarier Sons of Israel on Pike Street, the First Hungarian Congregation Ohab Zedek on Norfolk Street, and the First Roumanian Congregation Shaarei Shomayim on Rivington Street. (The Beth Hamidrash Hagadol is still located in the Norfolk Street building it acquired in 1888.) These larger synagogues were also among the minority of congregations able to support rabbis. In 1887 there were three or four East European rabbis in New York, and in 1917 the number may not have reached more than 50. Among the most prominent were Philip H. Klein of Ohab Zedek, Moses Z. Margolis of Kehillath Jeshurun of Yorkville, Shlomo E. Jaffe of Beth Hamidrash Hagadol, Simon J. Finkelstein of Oheb Shalom in Brownsville, and Gabriel Z. Margolis of Adath Israel, an East Side mutual aid and burial society. In 1917 the number of congregations in the newer centers of Russian Jewish population was: the Bronx, 35; Williamsburg, 49; and Brownsville and East New York, 70. All of New York City contained 784 permanent and 343 temporary synagogues. In 90% of them, Yiddish was the language of the sermon and of public announcements.

The plethora of small synagogues, the localism that produced them, and their constant precarious financial condition impeded their efficient operation and growth. Rivalries and vested interests compounded the situation and dogged all efforts at community collaboration. There were two signal attempts at unity. In 1887 a number of Orthodox congregations federated for the purpose of creating a central religious authority to be headed by a chief rabbi. A renowned European scholar, Rabbi Jacob Joseph of Vilna, was installed as chief rabbi in 1888. The attempt failed, chiefly because of the inability of the chief rabbi and his supporting organization to establish communal regulation of *kashrut* and in the refusal of other rabbis to accept the chief rabbi's leadership. In 1902 Rabbi Joseph died in poverty. Under the auspices of the New York Kehillah (see below), a renewed effort was made from 1910 on to create an authoritative board of rabbis and to federate all Orthodox institutions in its support. Once again the supervision of *kashrut* was considered the key to its success. By bringing *kashrut* supervision directly under the purview of the board it was hoped that an assured income would be realized from the fees of supervision, which would then be used for financing neighborhood rabbinical courts, placing rabbis and other religious functionaries on the community's budget, and providing for Jewish religious education and other Orthodox needs. After early progress, the undertaking foundered. The community was too fragmentized; the struggle for a livelihood too consuming; and the Old World rabbis ill equipped to provide the kind of leadership required in the complex new conditions of the U.S.

Orthodox religious education suffered as a consequence. In 1909 the first systematic study of Jewish education, by Mordecai M. Kaplan, found that three-quarters of the Jewish children of school age received no religious education at all. Of those who did, 27% supplemented their public school sessions with attendance in 468 or more improvised, ungraded, one-room private schools, the *ḥadarim*. The level of instruction on the whole was poor; the *ḥadarim* were beyond the reach of any form of communal supervision. About 20% of those receiving Jewish instruction attended the city's 24 *talmud torahs*. Since these institutions were supported by independent associations and accepted children who could not pay the tuition fee, they were in effect communal schools, supported by small contributions from over 6,000 people. The eight largest schools averaged 881 students, and were generally superior to the *ḥadarim*. The most auspicious endeavor to upgrade the *talmud torahs* – by means of modern textbooks, a graded curriculum, modern pedagogical methods, improved preparation and remuneration of teachers – was sponsored by the Bureau of Education of the Kehillah beginning in 1910. Dr. Samson Benderly directed the bureau and Jacob H. Schiff and his family were its chief financial supporters. Benderly encountered considerable opposition from Orthodox circles who feared the bureau's interference with the independence of the *talmud torahs* and mistrusted it because of the religious views of its lay supporters and staff. Nevertheless, in its first seven years, the bureau achieved notable results. It recruited and trained a group of young educators, popularized the notion of communal responsibility for Jewish education, established model schools, and conducted educational research. The bureau survived the demise of the Kehillah.

The year 1912 saw the beginning of the Young Israel movement. Immigrants' sons, concerned with what they viewed as the erosion of Orthodoxy, sought to combat radicalism, Reform Judaism, and indifference to the tradition by making the Orthodox service more appealing to younger worshipers. In 1915 Yeshivat Etz Chaim and the Rabbi Isaac Elchanan Theological Seminary united, and the institution began to offer a general high school education as well as yeshivah studies.

The comradeship of *landsleit* and the wish for protection in case of disability or death produced a vast network of mutual benefit societies, benevolent associations, and fraternal orders. Originally part of the congregations, they increasingly developed into separate organizations, offering some form of insurance, sick benefits, and interest-free loans, as well as cemetery rights. In 1917 there were about 1,000 such independent societies in New York with an aggregate membership of over 100,000, many of which found it financially advantageous to affiliate with a fraternal order. The largest order in New York City was the Independent Order Brith Abraham, which in 1917 had 90,000 members in 354 lodges. Various ideological movements recognized the attractiveness of the fraternal order and organized their own. The Arbeiter Ring (Workmen's Circle), appealing to workingmen in the name of socialism and insurance benefits, had 25,000 members in the city, and Zionists and Labor Zionists each had their own fraternal order.

Landsmanshaft societies too began to form federations. The Galician Jews were the first, in 1903. The Polish *landsmanshaftn* united in 1908, while the Romanian Jews were split into two federations. In 1911 the Federation of Oriental Jews was established, reflecting the increasing numbers coming from the Ottoman Empire. These were loose groupings. The unifying factor was some joint effort at overseas aid and some major philanthropic undertaking. The Galicians supported the Har Moriah Hospital, the Polish Jews Beth David Hospital, and the Bessarabians the Hebrew National Orphan Home.

This concern for self-help and for one's own welfare agency also produced central institutions that came to be identified with the city's East European Jewish subcommunity as a whole, of which the Hebrew Sheltering and Immigrant Aid Society (HIAS) was perhaps the most prominent. Beginning in 1909, when two older organizations merged to create it, HIAS expanded rapidly and succeeded in winning broad support in the immigrant community. Beth Israel Hospital, organized in 1890, was an instance of a downtown welfare facility whose standing became comparable to the older community institutions. It was founded in 1890 to provide services like kosher food and places for physicians of East European origin, neither of which were available at Mount Sinai Hospital. By 1917 it had 130 beds and a budget of $155,000. One of the most respected community-wide bodies was the Hebrew Free Loan Society, established in 1892. By 1916 it had branches in the Bronx and in Brooklyn, and had granted 24,330 loans, aggregating $711,940.

During the first decade of the century, influential leaders became increasingly aware of the social costs of institutional parochialism, profusion, and confusion. The sharp rise in immigration following 1903 underscored the need for more rational use of the resources and communal wealth. Uptown Jews, marginally identified with the total Jewish community, sought better ways to stem the social disorganization they sensed in the Jewish quarter and to expedite the integration of the immigrants. Some downtown leaders recognized the ineffectualness of their own institutions. In both sectors of the community some viewed with alarm the alienation of the younger generation from Judaism and Jewish life.

These concerns had led to two seminal events. The first was the short-lived New York Kehillah, an attempt to create a united community structure. The immediate catalyst was the accusation of police commissioner Theodore A. Bingham in 1908 that 50% of the criminals in the city were Jews. (Though the figure was exaggerated, crime in the Jewish quarter was a vexing problem.) Led by Judah *Magnes, a coalition of representative leaders in 1909 established the Kehillah as a federation of Jewish organizations. Magnes served as chairman until its demise in 1922. The Kehillah created a number of bureaus, for education, social morals (dealing with crime), industry (concerned with labor relations), and philanthropy. In addition, it organized a rabbinical board and a school for training communal workers. The Kehillah's productive years, however, were brief. By 1916 it had encountered financial problems, which led to the separation of its bureaus. Ties to the elitist American Jewish Committee drew it into controversies over the establishment of an American Jewish congress. During World War I interest was diverted to overseas relief and international Jewish affairs, while Magnes' pacifist activity crippled his effectiveness as chairman and adversely affected the Kehillah. These factors made it impossible to overcome the fragmented state of organized Jewish life. Though a number of the activities the Kehillah initiated proved to be of lasting significance, its failure pointed to the impediments that lay on the path of community organization. No similar attempt would be made again.

The establishment in 1917 of the Federation for the Support of Jewish Philanthropies, far more limited in scope than the Kehillah, proved more lasting. The federation movement to coordinate fund raising and encourage communal planning came late to New York, and from the early 1900s it encountered the opposition of the older philanthropic institutions sponsored by the German Jews, who feared it might impinge upon their independence. Some, moreover, objected to a federation of Jewish charities since such a grouping cast the pall of sectarianism upon their welfare agencies. However, the proliferation of East European institutions, the failure of the Kehillah as a device of social control, and the consequent threat to their own hegemony softened their opposition to federation.

As in other cities, the New York federation encompassed the larger welfare bodies and was therefore overwhelmingly a federation of the German-Jewish philanthropies primarily interested in nonsectarian social welfare work. Of the original trustees of the federation only three were East European; of 54 constituent societies, four belonged to the East European community. A smaller Brooklyn Federation of Jewish Charities was established in 1909. Its 1917 budget was $174,000 compared to the New York federation's budget of $2,117,410.

There were signs, however, that the New York federation might develop into more than a central fund-raising agency. Soon after its establishment, under the pressure of the group that had supported the Kehillah, the federation accepted five *talmud torahs* and the Kehillah's Bureau of Jewish Education as beneficiary agencies. This implied that the federation would concern itself not only with the relief of distress but with the support of Jewish cultural endeavor. Jewish education was to become a responsibility of the Jewish community's exchequer. The federation also indicated in its first year that it expected to become the spokesman of the entire community. But the statements proved little more than declarations of intention.

After 1900 Zionism and Socialism played, with varying success, many-sided roles in the organizational and cultural life of the New York Jewish community. In institutional terms, the Zionist achievements were minimal. The Federation of American Zionists, the Order Sons of Zion, Mizrachi, Po'alei Zion, the Jewish National Workers Alliance, Hadassah, and the Intercollegiate Zionist Association in 1917 numbered about 8,500 members who belonged to 95 loosely organized chapters. The influence of Zionism, however, went beyond membership figures. Much of the interest in Hebrew culture, Jewish education, and community planning stemmed from Zionist circles. Up to World War I the cultural Zionists who emphasized the need to revitalize Jewish cultural life in the Diaspora predominated. Judah Magnes, Israel Friedlaender, Henrietta Szold, and Mordecai Kaplan gave vigorous expression to this position from the lecture podium, in the press, and as professional and lay leaders of Jewish institutions. The socialist Po'alei Zion was similarly short on numbers and organizational success but strong on ideology and polemics. It constituted an intellectual force of significance at a time when the leadership of the Jewish labor movement was largely cosmopolitan and assimilationist in outlook. Following the outbreak of World War I, Zionists of all shades vastly increased their influence in the community through the Jewish congress movement. In June 1917, 125,000 participated in the election of delegates from New York City. The 100 delegates elected to represent New York's Jews were overwhelmingly of East European origin, the majority sympathizers of Zionism.

The Socialists, through the Workmen's Circle (Arbeiter Ring), possessed a stronger organizational framework than the Zionists. The order's 240 New York lodges and 25,000 members made it in 1917 the second-largest fraternal order in the city. Though the Workmen's Circle drew its membership from the Yiddish-speaking immigrants, it did not consciously identify itself with the Jewish community as a whole until World War I. During the war years Jewish Socialists began participating in Jewish communal affairs. The Workmen's Circle, Jewish labor unions, and the Jewish Socialist Federation (12 branches in New York) were active in the local fund-raising campaigns for overseas relief. They also joined the American Jewish congress movement, and the Workmen's Circle in a principal policy change that undertook direct support of Jewish cultural activity like Yiddish schools.

CULTURAL LIFE. The Yiddish-speaking masses who settled in New York created a rich and varied cultural life. No less than the community's institutional structure, this life aided the newcomers in their adjustment to the great metropolis. The very size of the immigrant community, its compactness and heterogeneity, and the impact of the new condition of freedom encouraged a multiplicity of cultural undertakings. Between 1872 and 1917, for example, about 150 journals in Yiddish appeared. Ideologues, literati, artists, and entrepreneurs competed in offering guidance, information, entertainment, and psychic relief for a generation in the throes of accommodation to a strange civilization.

The Yiddish-language daily press in particular served these ends (see *Press, Jewish, in U.S.A.). By the early 1900s, four stable dailies had evolved: the Orthodox and Zionist *Tageblat*; the **Jewish Morning Journal*, Orthodox, conservative on social issues, and anti-Zionist; the radical and nationalistic *Warheit*; and the socialist **Forward*. In 1914 the **Tog*, pro-Zionist and liberal, was established; it absorbed the *Warheit* in 1919. The estimated daily circulation for New York City in 1916 was: *Forward* (149,170), *Jewish Morning Journal* (81,375), *Warheit Tageblat* (41,335). It was estimated in 1917 that nearly 600,000 people in New York City read the Yiddish newspapers daily. Besides the staple of general and Jewish news the papers contained serialized novels, literary criticism, political essays, and a woman's page. The *Forward* created the *Bintl Brief* column of personal woe and editorial advice. It was so successful that it inspired imitators in other papers. Editorials were slashing and polemical, frequently dealing with municipal problems and local Jewish affairs. The considerable advertising included notices of theaters, cantorial performances, books published, medicine and health aids, and, in the *Jewish Morning Journal*, want-ads. The *Forward*, in particular, sponsored communal undertakings like theater benefits and other fund-raisers.

The functions of the Yiddish press made its publishers and editors major communal leaders. Jacob Saphirstein of the *Jewish Morning Journal* was deeply involved in rabbinical politics. Leon Kamaiky, a proprietor of the *Tageblat*, was a vice president of the Hebrew Sheltering and Immigrant Aid Society and a member of the American Jewish Committee and the executive committee of the Kehillah. *Forward* editor Abraham Cahan's position in the Jewish labor movement was less formal but more powerful. Indeed, the preeminent place of the Yiddish press and its editors was recognized uptown. In 1902 Louis Marshall established the *Yiddishe Velt* in an effort to assert his group's influence. The initiative that led to the establishment of the *Tog* in 1914 came from the same circles and for the same reasons.

The role of the Yiddish press found its fullest expression in the *Forward*. Cahan was the great innovator and his paper the pacemaker of Yiddish journalism. His apprenticeship as a reporter for the New York *Commercial Advertiser* under Lincoln Steffens served him well in turning the *Forward* into the leading Yiddish daily. The simple, direct style of the paper, its humanistic, undogmatic brand of socialism and its eschewal of the Orthodox-baiting of earlier socialist journals won it great popularity. Cahan appealed to highbrow no less than lowbrow tastes, and side by side with the *Bintl Brief* he published virtually every Yiddish author of note. From 1912 the *Forward* occupied its own ten-story building on East Broadway, close to the Educational Alliance. The United Hebrew Trades, the Jewish Socialist Federation, and the Arbeiter Ring (Workmen's Circle) had their offices in the building. The *Forward* was the focal center of the Jewish labor movement, a powerful cultural factor in the community, and thus had become a force for Jewish group continuity. Yiddish was so ubiquitous that when Shalom Aleichem, the great storyteller, died in 1916, his funeral was one of the largest public events in New York history.

Weeklies and monthlies filled out the broad range of ideas, movements, and professional interests of the New York community. Some, like the *Amerikaner* and the *Idishe Gazetten*, were weekly family supplements of existing newspapers. The anarchist *Freie Arbeiter Stimme*, the Zionist *Idishe Folk*, and the socialist *Zukunft* were representative of the literary and political journals sponsored by the various ideological camps. More local in their interests were journals published by the trade unions: the *Fortschritt* of the Amalgamated Clothing Workers of America and *Naye Post* of the Joint Board of the Cloak and Skirt Makers Union. Catering to small audiences were the Hebrew journals *Ha-Ivri* and *Ha-Toren*, and the Ladino *La America* (see Hebrew *Newspapers, N. America). The Yiddish journals and dailies drew to New York and sustained a significant colony of intellectuals, writers, poets, and critics whose work was read in the press and discussed in the lecture halls and coffeehouses of the East Side.

The Yiddish theater reinforced the press. It was, Moses Rischin wrote, "educator, dreammaker, chief agent of charity, social center, and recreation hub for the family." Melodrama and romantic musicals depicted historical and topical events drawn from the classic Jewish past, the "old home," immigrant life in the New World, and current American affairs. Nearly all weekday performances were benefits raising funds for some charity, strike fund, or literary journal. About 1900, three theaters were devoted exclusively to Yiddish drama. Together with other houses giving occasional performances, they drew about 25,000 patrons a week. By 1917 the number of houses presenting Yiddish theater reached seven, including one in Harlem and one in Brownsville.

Jewish immigrant life in New York inspired some of the earliest belles-lettres by Jews in English, notably Cahan's *Yekl* (1896) and *The Rise of David Levinsky* (1917). For most second-generation American Jews, Yiddish literature was a closed book, and Jewish themes in the language of the land were of peripheral interest. The Anglo-Jewish weekly *The American Hebrew* supplied the older settlement with a resume of Jewish news and social happenings. Its circulation was less than 10,000.

POLITICS AND CIVIC AFFAIRS. For Jews, as for all minority groups, election to public office meant social recognition and acceptance into the body politic of the city. Before the 1900s the number of Jewish officeholders was small, their posts for the most part minor, their ethnic identity an insignificant factor, and their political careers brief. Three Jewish congressmen were elected in New York City between 1870 and 1899, and all served but one term; the most prominent was Isidore Straus. Considerably more served in the state legislature. Among them was Joseph Blumenthal, who was a member of the Committee of Seventy, which played a role in the downfall of the Tweed Ring. Joseph Seligman and Simon Sterne were other members of that reform group. Blumenthal was a trustee and president of Shearith Israel and from 1886 to 1901 president of the board of trustees of the Jewish Theological Seminary. In municipal government Adolph L. Sanger, elected in 1885 as an anti-Tammany Democrat, served as president of the Board of Aldermen for one term. He, too, was active in Jewish communal affairs, serving at different times as president of the Board of Delegates of American Israelites and vice president of the Union of American Hebrew Congregations. In the 1890s Edward Lauterbach, a specialist in railway law and a director of a number of street railways, served for three years as chairman of the Republican County Committee. Lauterbach was a director of the Hebrew Benevolent and Orphan Asylum and the Hebrew Technical Institute. Jews held minor judgeships prior to 1900, and only one, Albert Cardozo, served on the state Supreme Court. In 1871, in the wake of the Tweed scandals, Cardozo resigned to avoid impeachment (his son was Benjamin Nathan *Cardozo, on the Court of Appeals from 1914 until his elevation to the U.S. Supreme Court in 1932).

In the years following 1900 the densely populated Jewish neighborhoods and the rising political awareness of the immigrants carried increasing political weight. That a number of assembly districts and several congressional districts had Jewish majorities or pluralities was reflected in the ethnic origin of the candidates, the particular issues raised, and the language of the campaigns. The number of Jewish voters was large enough to influence the outcome of city-wide elections. Though uptown Jews denied it, a "Jewish vote" existed. It was not prone to act en bloc, but nevertheless responded to group interests and ethnic pride and was unafraid to demand its political due.

Jews came of age as a political force during the domination of the Tammany Hall political machine. Led by astute and, if need be, ruthless politicians, Tammany offered a host of services in return for votes, and some of its leaders were attuned to the moods and needs of their Jewish constituents. Although a lag existed between Jewish numbers and numbers of Jewish officeholders, Tammany was sensitive to ethnic ambitions. In 1900 Henry M. Goldfogle went to Congress as representative of the Lower East Side, serving until 1921 with the exception of two terms. By 1910 Aaron J. Levy and Moritz Graubard were entrenched as East Side assemblymen, and Jews received 5 to 8% of the mayor's top appointments.

Support of Tammany was not, however, monolithic, particularly in mayoral and presidential campaigns. Anti-Tammany forces recognized this, and when mounting major reform campaigns, paid particular attention to the Jewish immigrant neighborhoods. In 1901, for example, the Fusion ticket flooded the Jewish districts with Yiddish circulars. Seth Low and William Travers Jerome were elected mayor and attorney general, respectively. Jacob A. Cantor, who had fought for tenement house reform as an assemblyman in the 1880s, was elected borough president of Manhattan as a Reform Democrat. The publisher William Randolph Hearst, in his effort to defeat the Tammany candidate for mayor in 1905, carried the Jewish East Side. His *New York American* had featured stories of Russian barbarism and solicited funds for the relief of pogrom victims. Hearst even launched a Yiddish newspaper for a time. John P. Mitchel, elected mayor in 1913 on a Fusion anti-Tammany ticket, won broad support in the Jewish districts. Henry Moskowitz, head of the Madison House Settlement and a native downtown reformer, became Mitchel's commissioner of Civil Service. The downtown voters exhibited similar independence in presidential elections. From 1888 to 1912 no party carried the Eighth Assembly District, heart of the Jewish quarter, twice in succession. However, Theodore Roosevelt, a Republican, was a particular favorite.

Among the uptown Jews a group of patrician "good government" reformers emerged who helped finance these repeated efforts to dislodge Tammany. Among them were men like Nathan and Oscar *Straus, who belonged to the Grover Cleveland wing of the Democratic Party, and liberal Republicans like Jacob Schiff, Isaac N. *Seligman, and Adolph *Lewisohn. They assumed a particular responsibility for wooing their downtown brethren away from the "twin evils" of Tammany and socialism by supporting the reform candidates in their East Side campaigns.

Socialism indeed had a significant political following in the Jewish immigrant districts. On the Lower East Side the Socialists could count on a straight party vote of about 15%, and in some Jewish election districts in Brooklyn and the Bronx it may have been even higher. However, only when the party offered a candidate able and willing to appeal to the particular interest and ethnic sentiment of the East European Jew did it win at election time. In 1914 it sent Meyer London to Congress, the first socialist elected to the House of Representatives and the first elected socialist for any office from New York City. London, a lawyer for a score of Jewish labor unions, lived in the Jewish quarter, and thus spoke the language of the immigrant. He eschewed party dogma. Reelected in 1916, he won a third term in 1920 despite the fact that his party was then in complete disarray. Of special interest were the elections of 1917. Morris Hillquit, the outstanding figure in the Socialist Party, showed remarkable strength in his bid for the mayoralty. He won 22% of the vote – twice that of the Republican candidate. Ten socialist assemblymen went to Albany, seven aldermen to City Hall, and one socialist, Jacob Panken, was elected municipal court judge. The vote reflected the strong anti-war sentiment among the East European Jews as much as it did socialist sentiment.

The war years expedited the social processes that molded a variegated and fragmented Jewish public into a more homogeneous ethnic community. The same processes integrated that community into the larger polity. War brought prosperity, which enabled families to leave overcrowded immigrant districts for a better, more "American" environment and so accelerated the process of acculturation. The war also confronted all Americans with the problem of their group identity, Americanized Jews of German origin no less than recently arrived East European Jews. Though it brought to the surface sharp tensions, the Jews of New York by 1920 could see themselves as a major group at home in the city.

[Arthur Aryeh Goren]

1920–1970

DEMOGRAPHY. Following World War I the Jewish population of New York City grew moderately to 1,765,000 in 1927 and to 2,035,000 in 1937. It tapered off around 2,100,000 in 1950, and slowly decreased as Jews moved to the suburbs of Long Island, Westchester, and New Jersey from the 1950s. By 1960 the Jewish population of the city had declined to 1,936,000, while that of the metropolitan area increased to 2,401,600, owing to the large growth in the suburban counties (see *New York State). The city's Jewish population, which fell further to 1,836,000 by 1968, was aging as younger families moved out. The move by Jews and other middle-class whites in search of more comfortable residences and greener neighborhoods was intensified from the mid-1950s by negative developments, primarily an increase in crime and racial tensions, a loss of confidence in the public schools, a perceived inadequacy of middle-class housing, and a decline of municipal services.

No less than during immigrant years, New York Jews preferred to dwell near one another. Thus, 676,000 of Brooklyn's 857,000 Jews in 1940 resided in areas where Jews formed 40% or more of the total population; and later, in 1958, 388,000 of the Bronx's 493,000 Jews were similarly concentrated. Anti-Jewish discrimination in the sale and rental of housing had been effectively quashed before 1950, except for isolated instances in opulent areas of Manhattan.

Within the city's five boroughs, Jewish population centers shifted as Jews abandoned highly congested Jewish areas and moved to more widely dispersed areas farther from the older, more centrally located neighborhoods. In 1918, 696,000 Jews (46% of the city's total Jewish population), lived in Manhattan. Most of them were on the Lower East Side and uptown in Harlem. Masses of Jews left the Lower East Side as their economic circumstances improved, mainly before the Depression of 1929. While 314,200 Jews lived on the Lower East Side in 1923, by 1940 only 73,700 remained. By 1960 about 70,000 Jews lived there, mainly in cooperative housing projects sponsored by Jewish-dominated trade unions, and made up 34% of the general population compared with 40% in 1930. West and East Harlem, for a time the home of wealthier immigrant Jews, had about 177,000 Jews in 1923. Immediately thereafter Harlem became a black neighborhood; fewer than 5,000 Jews remained in 1930 and in 1940, only 2,000.

Many Jews from Manhattan and other areas moved north to the more recently settled Bronx, where in 1918 they totaled about 211,000. By 1927 about 420,000 Jews lived there, primarily in its south and south-central districts, where they made up 40% and 70%, respectively, of the general population in 1925. By 1937 the Bronx Jewish population rose above 592,000, making that borough 44% Jewish. As new subway lines and apartment buildings were built, Jews moved increasingly to more northerly and less populous regions of the Bronx. The number of Jews in the South Bronx fell from 34,200 in 1923 to less than 15,000 in 1960. Tremont, in the west-central Bronx, which had 121,000 Jews (96% of its total population) in 1925, dropped to about 44,000 before the 1960s, most of whom also left the area during the decade that followed. However, nearby Fordham rose from 13,600 Jews in 1923 to 83,350 in 1930 and 103,000 in 1960, about 48% of the general population. The middle-class West Bronx Jewish population increased from 26,000 in 1923 to 142,886 in 1940. It declined to 121,000 in 1960, when it was still 65% of the general population, and this downward trend continued. The Jewish population of Pelham Parkway, in the northeast Bronx, rose from 3,000 in 1923 to 65,000 by 1960, or 48% of the general population, and continued to rise. Following the general trend toward the suburbs, Jews began leaving the Bronx in the 1950s, so that by 1968 only 395,000 Jews remained, with new concentrations in the outlying Van Cortlandt and Riverdale areas.

From the 1920s Brooklyn became the borough most heavily populated by Jews as the number rose from 568,000 in 1918 to 797,000 in 1927. In contrast to Manhattan and the Bronx, Brooklyn tended to be a borough of well-defined neighborhood communities. Jewish religious life in Brooklyn apparently was more active than in other boroughs. While the older Jewish neighborhoods in the northern and western regions of Brooklyn began to lose their large Jewish populations by the 1930s, Jews were moving outward to form vast new communities in the central, southern, and eastern sectors. Thus, Williamsburg, across the East River from Manhattan, a community in which Jews numbered 140,000 in 1923, had only 33,400 Jews in 1957, though even as its population declined, it attained some celebrity as the home of a large Hasidic colony of post-World War II immigrants from Hungary and Eastern Europe. Bedford-Stuyvesant's 70,000 Jews in 1923 declined below 30,000 in 1957 and fell further in the 1960s as the area became a low-income African-American neighborhood. In 1925 about 250,000 Jews, or 82% of the population of the area, lived in East New York-New Lots-Brownsville. However, only 96,000 remained in 1957, and most of those left during the 1960s as Brownsville became predominantly black. On the other hand, in central Brooklyn the number of Jews in Boro Park increased from 46,000 in 1923 to 67,000 by 1950, in Bensonhurst from 45,000 in 1923 to 85,000 by 1950, and in Flatbush from 16,400 in 1923 to 123,000 by 1950. Sheepshead Bay in southern Brooklyn had 7,100 Jews in 1923 but 48,000, or 62% of the population, by 1950. Residential, middle-income Midwood-Marine Park grew from 3,200 Jews in 1923 to 64,000 by 1957. Jews settled early in the southern Coney Island-Manhattan Beach area, which was nearly 70% Jewish in 1940 when 53,400 Jews resided there. From the 1930s Jews also began to settle the eastern Flatlands-Canarsie area, whose Jewish population rose from 4,400 in 1923 to 28,000, or 60% of the population, in 1957.

Altogether, the Jewish population of Brooklyn began to decrease, dropping from its heights of 975,000 in 1937 and 950,000 in 1950 to 760,000 in 1968. Thus Crown Heights, close to Bedford-Stuyvesant, dropped from over 75,000 in 1950 to 58,400 by 1957, and similar drops occurred after World War II in Bensonhurst and Coney Island. The heavily Jewish East New York-New Lots area, in which 106,000 Jews lived in 1923, decreased to 74,000 Jews in 1950; it rose again, however, to 90,000 by 1957 with the construction of new housing on unoccupied land. Boro Park, long a center of Orthodox Judaism, became strongly Ḥasidic with an influx of Williamsburg Ḥasidim.

The borough of Queens saw a sustained increase in its middle-to upper-middle class Jewish population, owing to its newness, relative remoteness from the center of the city, and the rapid building of large apartment-house complexes like Lefrak City and other red-brick edifices constructed by Samuel J. LeFrak and his organization. While only 23,000 Jews lived there in 1918, the Jewish population grew to 200,000 by 1950 and 420,000 by 1968. Over 200,000 Jews moved there during the 1950s and large Jewish concentrations developed in Forest Hills-Rego Park, which had over 73,000 Jews, or 66% of the general population, by 1957; the Whitestone area, which had 24,000 Jews in 1957; Central Queens, in which 51,000 Jews lived in 1957; and Douglaston-Little Neck-Bellrose, which had 31,500 Jews in 1957. About 18,200 Jews lived in the Rockaways on the shore in 1923, and nearly 30,000 lived there by 1957.

About 5,000 Jews called the little-settled, isolated borough of Richmond (Staten Island) home in 1918, and that number increased moderately. In 1950 about 8,000 Jews lived there, but by 1968, after the construction of the Verrazano-Narrows Bridge between the borough and Brooklyn, their number reached about 11,000.

The Jewish population of Manhattan declined from the 1920s. In 1937 there were 351,000 Jews on the island, while only 250,000 remained in 1968. Nevertheless, several neighborhoods increased. The number of Jews in well-to-do cosmopolitan sections of the West Side rose from 21,300 in 1923 to 71,000, or 29% of the general population, by 1957. Washington Heights, the uptown residential area, had 31,500 Jews in 1923 but nearly 70,000 by 1957. It was the center for German Jewish refugees of the 1930s. Nearly all Manhattan Jewish neighborhoods experienced declines in the 1960s, however, except the expensive, rebuilt Upper East Side, where Jews increased from 22,000 in 1940 to 42,000 in 1958.

The movement to the suburbs raised the Jewish population of rapidly built Nassau County, across the city boundary, from unknown but small numbers before 1940 to 329,000 in 1957 and 372,000 in 1963. Many families achieved the American dream of owning their own home by obtaining low interest loans offered to veterans of World War II and by buying the low-price, mass-produced homes of William and Alfred Levitt, who created a vast Levittown (17,311 nearly identical homes built between 1947 and 1951) in Long Island. Following already established city patterns, Jews tended to dwell together in suburban centers like Great Neck and Roslyn on the North Shore of Long Island and Woodmere, Cedarhurst, Lawrence, three of the Five Towns, and Baldwin and Hempstead on the South Shore. Beyond Nassau lay Suffolk County, in which the previously negligible Jewish population reached 12,000 in 1957 and 42,000 in 1963, with significant increases thereafter.

ECONOMIC ACTIVITIES. New York Jewry formed so large a proportion of the city's population that Jewish economic habits and aptitudes broadly influenced the city's economy. Jewish labor in the garment industry, the city's foremost industry, reached its peak at about 1920. In 1921, production of men's apparel in New York City was valued at $326,832,000, and of women's, $759,628,000. The value of allied industries like knit goods, was put at $83,490,000. Perhaps 200,000 Jews belonged to the trade unions of the garment industry. From this point, the proportion of Jewish workers in the clothing industry steadily declined, until in the men's clothing branch it reached 39% in 1937; the new working group was largely composed of Italian women and, later, Puerto Ricans. The same process operated in the ladies' garment industry. One large local of the ILGWU was about three-quarters Jewish in the 1940s but declined to 44% in 1958. Jews remained in the garment industry in upper levels of skill as cutters and sample makers, and also as entrepreneurs and salesmen. The city, whose Garment Center epitomized the apparel business, provided the setting for the emergence of Ralph Lauren, Calvin Klein, Anne Klein, Arnold Scaasi (Isaacs backwards), Liz Claiborne, and Donna Karan, among others, in the design and marketing of men's and women's clothing. One woman, Helena Rubinstein, virtually created the cosmetics industry. After World War I, she opened beauty salons around the country, selling pots of face creams and other products. She trained sales people to teach women skin care and devised a diet plan for beauty. An ardent supporter of Israel, she created the Helena Rubinstein Pavilion of Contemporary Art in Tel Aviv, and her foundation, created in 1953, provided funds to organizations concerned with health, medical research, and rehabilitation.

The Jewish labor movement in New York, after its heroic era of strike victories during the 1910s, was firmly established by 1920. The unions turned back attempts between 1920 and 1922 to reestablish the open shop. However, they were beset during the 1920s by violent factional quarrels with Communists. The latter derived support not only because of their tactical and propagandistic skill but also from post-World War I Jewish immigrants who entered the industry and felt somewhat excluded by the established union leadership and ideology. Communists secured control of the New York Joint Board and led it into a series of disastrous strikes culminating in 1926. The union was left in ruins and did not reestablish itself until the New Deal period. The Amalgamated was more fortunate, however, in maintaining its unity and power. A third garment union, the International Fur Workers' Union, succeeded in its trade-union objectives under Communist leadership, while the United Hat, Cap and Millinery Workers did likewise under liberal leaders.

During the 1920s the New York Jewish unions entered areas of activity never previously known to U.S. trade unions. They conducted large-scale adult education, ran health clinics, owned a bank and summer resorts, built model urban housing, and generously subsidized struggling trade unions in such other industries as steel, coal, and textiles. Except for their Communist wing, they became pioneers of liberal political action, thus preparing a place for themselves in New Deal political and legislative affairs.

The Jewish immigrant generation was heavily represented as workers – 23% "operatives and kindred" and 16% "craftsmen, foremen, and kindred" as late as 1950. The 32% who were "managers, officials, and proprietors" included a mass of shopkeepers and small businessmen. Jewish retailers were especially heavily represented in such areas as candy and stationery stores, grocery stores, hardware stores, haberdashery stores, tailor shops, and delicatessens and small restaurants. An incomplete estimate placed Jewish trade-union membership about 1928 at 134,000 of a total of 392,000 concentrated, in addition to needle and leather trades, in amusement and food preparation and distribution.

The immigrants' children, however, shifted towards sales and clerical occupations and independent business; in 1950, 55% of immigrants' sons were in these groups, and only 22% remained in traditional working-class occupations. One important channel of ascent was New York's excellent public school and college system. Jews constituted 51% of enrollment in the city's academic high schools in 1931, and 49.6% of the city's college and university students in 1935. As early as 1915 they were 85% of the student body in the city's unique free municipal college system, a percentage that probably did not decrease before 1960; others attended college outside the city. This higher education launched thousands of young Jews from poor or very modest circumstances into independent business and the professions. During the 1950s about 17% of New York Jews, including the older, immigrant group, were professionally employed.

Areas of Jewish economic activity often were clearly demarcated. Thus, the port of New York, shipping and other transportation, large banks and insurance companies, and heavy industry hardly employed any Jews. Even after the removal of discriminatory employment policies in 1945, there were few Jews in these industries. Small, independent businesses, the garment trade and light industry employed masses of Jews, and Jewish entrepreneurs could be found in those fields as well as in real estate, building, and investment banking. By the 1930s, over half the city's doctors, lawyers, dentists, and public school teachers were Jews, notwithstanding sharp anti-Jewish discrimination in certain universities and schools. After World War II, Jews became strong components of the city's mercantile and professional class, heavily represented in academic, scientific, and civil service organizations. Reflecting their occupational changes, they formed a large part of the membership and most of the leadership in unions of teachers and other public employees.

POLITICAL AND CIVIC LIFE. As the largest single ethnic group, Jews were a highly important factor in the political life of the city. Jews, who were about 27% of the city's population, were outnumbered only by the Irish-dominated Catholics, who were just over half. In no other city could Jews as a group weigh so heavily in politics, or were real or alleged Jewish political interests reckoned with so carefully. Until the 1930s the city was governed through the Manhattan organization of the Democratic Party, known as Tammany Hall, which held the support of most immigrants, including Jews. Jewish Republicans, conspicuous by their low numbers, pursued interests in civic reform, like Stanley M. Isaacs and Nathan Straus Jr., and the party's New York County leader, Samuel S. Koenig. In addition, Jews in East Harlem during the 1920s supported that district's dynamic U.S. Congressman, Fiorello H. *La Guardia, a rebel Republican. On the far left, Jews dominated the Socialists and Communists. Jews generally followed the Democratic Party, and some received the rewards of party loyalty – personal and business favors, municipal appointments, and judgeships.

The period from 1928 to 1945 witnessed far-reaching change. Jews had heavily supported Alfred E. Smith, a liberal Tammany reformer of Irish stock, in his successful campaigns for the governorship of the state and unsuccessful attempt for the presidency in 1928. The onset of the Great Depression in 1929 brought New York Jewry overwhelmingly behind the New Deal and the Democratic Party. Support for Franklin D. *Roosevelt during his presidential campaigns of 1932, 1936, 1940, and 1944 ran from 80% to 90%, higher than among any other group in the city. The urban liberalism of the New Deal had many of its seeds in the Jewish trade unions, East Side settlement houses, and among Jewish philanthropists and social workers. New York Jews were enthusiastic for the New Deal Democrat, Herbert H. *Lehman, elected to the governorship in 1932, 1934, 1936, and 1938, and the German immigrant New Deal Senator, Robert F. Wagner. La Guardia, a Republican, gained the mayoralty of New York in 1933 by the votes of Italians, Jews, mostly of middle-class reform sympathies, and upper-class good-government supporters. Of Italian stock but partially Jewish in descent, and fluent in Yiddish, La Guardia's mastery of ethnic politics succeeded by 1937 in attracting the Jewish working class and left wing for his municipal version of the New Deal. During La Guardia's incumbency, from 1934 to 1946, Jews figured more prominently as city officials and political leaders. As fervent supporters simultaneously of the Protestant aristocrat Roosevelt, the Jewish banker Lehman, and the Italian commoner La Guardia, New York Jews preferred liberal, reform-minded candidates and avoided Republicans unless they significantly differed from the generally conservative habits of that party. The American Labor Party (founded in 1936) and the Liberal Party (organized in 1944), served their intended purpose of drawing voters of the left, especially Jews, to liberal or left-liberal candidates.

Following La Guardia's tenure, the major parties adopted a policy of "ethnic balance." They regarded it as necessary to nominate a Jew, Irishman, and Italian for the three city-wide electoral offices. Under the non-Jewish Democratic mayoralties from 1945 to 1966, Jews remained firmly and prominently Democratic. During most of this period, Jews were elected city-wide comptrollers (Lazarus Joseph, Abraham D. *Beame), presidents of various boroughs (Abe Stark), and to the powerful position of county surrogates as well as other local judgeships. In 1965, the reigning Democrats for the first time nominated a Jew, Beame, for the mayoralty, but largely owing to a considerable Jewish defection to John V. Lindsay, the Republican reformer, Beame lost. As the number of blacks and Puerto Ricans in the city increased, Jewish and other white influence began to decline. But Jews, well-established, assimilated, and with money to finance political campaigns, continued to be major players.

Jews and other minorities suffered widespread discrimination by the hiring practices of banks, insurance companies, large corporations, law firms, and department stores, some of which were even owned by Jews. Several private universities and professional schools also imposed stringent admissions quotas against Jews and others, but the professional schools at the city's Catholic colleges enrolled a high proportion of Jews. Social discrimination against Jews, on the other hand, was so firmly fixed that even the most notable Jews could not belong to many of the city's leading business and social clubs, some of which their grandparents in fact had helped to found. Long-continued pressure, primarily from New York City and led by Jews, resulted in the passage of the state's Fair Employment Practice Act in 1945 prohibiting discrimination in employment. It was the first such law in the U.S.

After World War II, as the Cold War gripped the nation, Jews in New York figured prominently in the signature event of that period. Julius and Ethel Rosenberg, husband and wife, and members of the Communist Party, went on trial in 1951 for conspiracy to commit espionage, specifically for transmitting nuclear weapons secrets to Russian agents. Largely based on testimony by David Greenglass, Ethel Rosenberg's brother, the couple were convicted and sentenced to death by Federal Judge Irving Kaufman. The assistant United States attorney prosecuting the case, Roy Cohn, stated in his autobiography that he had influenced the selection of the judge and had pressed him to impose the death penalty on both defendants. Kaufman held the Rosenbergs responsible not only for espionage but also for deaths in the Korean War. The case became the center of controversy over communism in the United States, with supporters steadfastly maintaining that the convictions were an egregious example of persecution typical of the hysteria of those times. Some likened it to the witch hunts in Salem, a comparison that provided the inspiration for Arthur Miller's critically acclaimed play, *The Crucible*. Despite appeals on humanitarian grounds from Pope Pius XII and others, the Rosenbergs were executed in the electric chair in 1953, both steadfastly maintaining their innocence. The case lingered in the public consciousness for decades, but in 1995, when decrypted Soviet communications became publicly available, the evidence indicated that Julius Rosenberg was actively involved in espionage, but there was no evidence that he was involved in the specific charges against him or that his wife was involved at all.

Antisemitic organizations existed spasmodically in New York City. The Ku Klux Klan barely appeared during the 1920s. The pro-Nazi Friends of New Germany and its successor, the German-American Bund, were active from 1934 to 1941 against fierce Jewish and pro-democratic opposition. The same held true of the contemporary "Christian Front," led by Joseph E. McWilliams and Father Edward Lodge Curran, a leading propagandist, which was close to Father Charles E. Coughlin's antisemitic movement. It conducted antisemitic street meetings and fostered petty hooliganism. These groups collapsed during World War II, following which organized antisemitism was virtually unknown for some 20 years. From about 1965 black militants, on the outer fringe of the civil rights movement, fostering and feeding upon black-Jewish frictions, helped stimulate the renewal of antisemitism. A climax was reached during the New York City teachers' strike of 1968, when some blacks made openly antisemitic remarks about the union and its leadership. The inclusion of antisemitic material at the same time in an exhibit on Harlem at the Metropolitan Museum of Art also proved highly provocative. Anti-Zionist statements from black militants and members of the New Left that emerged in the 1960s became difficult to distinguish from antisemitism. At the same time Jewish militants led by Rabbi Meir *Kahane organized the Jewish Defense League, a vigilante "self-defense" group. Ironically, two young New York Jews, Andrew Goodman and Michael Schwerner, seeking to registers black voters in Mississippi, were killed in one of the watershed events of the civil rights struggle. It took decades for their killers to be brought to justice. Significantly, New York Jews were in the forefront in raising funds for civil rights causes across the country (see *Black-Jewish Relations in the United States).

Between 1940 and 1965, New York's black population tripled as a great wave of migrants poured in from the South. Older black neighborhoods like Harlem and Bedford-Stuyvesant could not accommodate the newcomers, and blacks moved into adjoining areas like Ocean Hill-Brownsville, from which whites, including large numbers of Jews, promptly fled. In 1963 and 1964, at the height of the movement to integrate New York's public schools, Jews in Brooklyn and Queens joined with white Catholics to form Parents and Taxpayers, a militant antibusing organization that eventually had half a million members. The group, known as PAT, staged massive demonstrations and even established a separate private academy. Its efforts were instrumental in the defeat of integration initiatives in the public school system. In response, black leaders sought to control their neighborhood schools. In 1967, the Board of Education began an experiment in community control of schools in the predominantly black Ocean Hill-Brownsville area, where residents elected a local board to run their schools. The local board soon clashed with the United Federation of Teachers over the extent of its personnel powers. The local board claimed the power to hire and fire teachers and administrators; the union argued that only the central board could do so.

In 1968 a junior high school science teacher, Fred Nauman, who was a chapter chairman of the 90%-white, majority Jewish, union, was fired. The action resulted in three citywide teacher strikes aimed at reinstating Nauman and nine co-unionists, who were also fired. The strikes lasted two months in all, affecting almost two million children, and they would be the most bitter in the city's modern history, full of charges of racism, union-busting, and antisemitism. The strikes pitted the city's white middle class, which backed the union, against the city's black poor and supporters of the community control idea. Mostly, the issues pitted blacks against whites, specifically blacks against Jews. The conflict exposed hidden fissures between the races. The strikes ended in mid-November 1968, substantially on the union's terms: the teachers were reinstated and the community control experiment was discontinued. But the controversy went beyond that. It helped to redefine the politics and culture of the city for decades. Outer-borough Jewish voters shifted to the right, moving closer to their white Catholic neighbors. The patrician mayor, John V. Lindsay, lost support in the wake of Ocean Hill-Brownsville, losing almost 60% of the Jewish vote, previously his strength. The city's next mayoral election, in 1973, produced its first Jewish mayor, Abraham D. Beame, elected with strong Jewish and Catholic votes.

The great growth of New York and its suburbs would not have been possible without Robert Moses, the master builder of the 20th century. Although he never held elective office, Moses was probably the most powerful person in New York City government from the 1930s to the 1950s. He changed shorelines, built roadways, and transformed neighborhoods. His decisions favoring highways over public transport helped develop Brooklyn, Queens, and the suburbs of Long Island. Moses rose to power under Al Smith after catching the eye of the governor's top assistant, Belle Moskowitz. In several assigned tasks, Moses excelled, particularly the development of Atlantic Ocean beaches, pools, and parks at Long Island's Jones Beach, a recreation area without peer that accommodated thousands year after year. After Franklin D. Roosevelt became president, Moses anticipated the availability of New Deal dollars and secured funding for a host of projects. At one point, one quarter of federal construction dollars was being spent in New York, and Moses had 80,000 people working under him. He built hundreds of parks and recreation facilities, but just one pool in Harlem. His highway projects on Long Island followed a circuitous path so as not to cross the properties of wealthy land owners, all the while he demolished numerous middle-class neighborhoods throughout New York City. During the Depression, Moses and La Guardia were responsible for the construction in the city of 10 large swimming pools; they could accommodate 66,000 swimmers. At one point Moses held 12 separate city and state titles. For the city he was parks commissioner, and for the state he was chairman of the Long Island Parks Commission and Secretary of State as well as chairman of the New York State Power Commission, responsible for building hydroelectric dams. By doling out contracts and making deals, Moses built support from construction firms, insurance companies, labor unions, and real-estate developers. He used his influence to put projects on fast tracks, a tactic later repaid by legislators with funds for other projects. Moses controlled most public housing construction projects, but exercised vast power as chairman of the Triborough Bridge Authority. The bridge connects the Bronx, Manhattan, and Queens and the income earned from tolls helped Moses finance projects like the Brooklyn Battery Tunnel, a vehicle link to Manhattan. After La Guardia's retirement, a series of mayors agreed to almost all of Moses' proposals. From the 1930s to the 1960s, Moses was responsible for the building of the Throgs Neck, Bronx-Whitestone, the Henry Hudson and the Verrazano Narrows bridges. His other projects included the Staten Island Expressway, the Cross-Bronx Expressway, the Belt Parkway, the Laurelton Parkway, and many more. In the 1960s, he was the mover behind Shea Stadium, home of the New York Mets baseball team, and Lincoln Center for the Performing Arts. After a series of questionable decisions involving the 1964-65 World's Fair, Moses' power began to wane. His high-handedness and arrogance, depicted in Robert Caro's biography, *The Power Broker: Robert Moses and the Fall of New York* (1974), which won the Pulitzer Prize, presented Moses with a different face.

COMMUNAL, RELIGIOUS, CULTURAL, AND EDUCATIONAL AFFAIRS. In the years after World War I, New York retained its unchallenged position as the center of U.S. Jewish life. After World War II, the city became the capital of the entire Diaspora, as Zionist and other Jewish movements established their main offices in New York. The organizations sponsored rallies and mass meetings on behalf of overseas Jewry, sometimes attracting more than 100,000 people.

Jacob H. Schiff's death in 1920, Judah L. Magnes' withdrawal about 1918, and his removal to Palestine in 1922 left as the most representative New York figures Louis Marshall (d. 1929), Felix M. Warburg (d. 1937), and Stephen S. Wise (d. 1949). The former two were distinctly "uptown" leaders, Marshall a lawyer and Warburg a banker-philanthropist. Wise, a Zionist and Reform rabbi, was closely linked with liberal political and religious movements and drew much of his strength as an urban populist spokesman for the mass of working and lower middle-class Jews. His personal stature and influence was the source of much of the influence of the *American Jewish Congress, which he reestablished and headed from 1930 as a politically liberal, activist, pro-Zionist counterweight to the "uptown" bodies, the *American Jewish Committee in particular. Much of the Congress' importance was lost with Wise's death and the softening of social and ideological differences after 1945. Moreover, the Committee eventually broadened its communal base and retracted the anti-Zionism it had adopted during the preceding decade. The ambitious attempt to coordinate communal life in the Kehillah ended by 1920, and by then New York Jewry had acculturated with much rapidity and formed a proportion of the city's ethnically and religiously diverse population.

Virtually every Jewish organization had chapters and members in the city, including *landsmanshaftn* and benefit societies, lodges, cultural bodies, charitable groups, political causes, Zionists, and synagogues, so that the total number of Jewish organizations probably exceeded 4,000 before the 1940s; with the disappearance of many lodges, benefit societies, and small immigrant synagogues there was probably a decrease thereafter. Altogether the city's Jews constituted an agglomeration of social classes, ideologies, clustered interests, and institutions, possessing Jewish identification in varying degrees of intensity.

Alongside vigorous local activity on behalf of such national or worldwide causes as Zionism, there were fairly distinct although overlapping spheres of interest. The Federation of Jewish Philanthropies served the poor and dependent. All of the federation-affiliated hospitals and many other institutions associated with it were nonsectarian. The federation's original 54 affiliates numbered 130 by 1968, and included: hospitals, institutions for the aged and chronically ill, casework agencies, summer camps, Young Men's and Women's Hebrew Associations and neighborhood centers, and the Jewish Education Committee. Affiliates also received funds from patient and client fees, the Greater New York Fund, government assistance, and direct contributions and endowments. Service to the increasing number of aged and to troubled families (through the Jewish Family Service, successor to the United Hebrew Charities), and recreation and informal education for middle-class youth and adults slowly replaced the earlier relief services. The Jewish hospitals, some of which were rated among the world's finest, totaled about 7,000 beds in 1968. They included Mount Sinai, Montefiore, Joint Diseases (orthopedic), Brooklyn Jewish, Long Island Jewish, Jewish Hospital for Chronic Diseases, Beth El (renamed Brookdale), Beth Israel, Maimonides, Bronx-Lebanon, Hillside, and Jewish Memorial. In addition, Jacobi Hospital, a municipal hospital, was attached to Yeshiva University's Albert Einstein Medical School, and Mount Sinai Hospital opened a medical school in 1968 as a unit of the City University of New York.

Life centered on Yiddish institutions typified by the daily *Forward*, the Workmen's Circle, Yiddish cultural societies and schools, the *Jewish Labor Committee after 1934, and the scholarly institution, *YIVO, held on, tenuously. Perhaps the foremost writer in Yiddish of that period was Isaac Bashevis Singer, who emigrated from his native Poland to New York in 1935 and who continued to write in the mother tongue for *The Forward* before achieving widespread recognition in English translation (and the Nobel Prize in literature in 1978). The early associations with Jewish trade unionism lessened as Yiddish secularism became a cultural and fraternal middle-class movement. Hebraists, centered in the *Histadrut Ivrith and the weekly *Hadoar*, and closely tied to Zionist and educational affairs, had a smaller group of adherents. Composed largely of writers, Hebrew teachers, and rabbis, the Hebrew group shrank as the reality of Hebrew in Israel took hold.

Religion played a major role in daily life, especially for the Orthodox. In several neighborhoods, particularly Boro Park, Crown Heights, Williamsburg, and sections of Flatbush in Brooklyn, as well as the Lower East Side even in its decline, Sabbaths and Jewish holidays provided an opportunity for Jews to assert their identity. Orthodox synagogues were full, stores in heavily Orthodox areas were shut, even those owned by non-Jews, and sectors of the garment and diamond industries regularly closed. The commerce and industry of the city came near a standstill on Rosh Ha-Shanah and Yom Kippur. Beginning in the 1960s the public schools closed on those days because Jews, who formed a majority of the teaching staff, absented themselves.

In 1967 there were 539 Orthodox, 184 Conservative, 93 Reform, and five unclassified synagogues known in Greater New York; all but 163 of the total were within the city's boundaries. Actual synagogue affiliation tended to be low, however. A study of Brooklyn suggested that merely one-quarter of its Jews belonged to synagogues in 1945–46, a proportion that probably differed little in other boroughs.

The Reform movement, using a good deal of English in the prayer book, liberal in social outlook, and generally wealthier than the immigrant community, attracted regular worshipers to its major temples, some of which were monumental or historic. Temple Emanu-El continued to be foremost because of its size, wealth, and prestige, and occupied a splendid edifice at Fifth Avenue and 65th Street from 1929. Other major congregations included the Central Synagogue (whose building at Lexington Avenue and 55th Street dated to 1870), the Free Synagogue, Rodeph Shalom, Shaarey Tefilah (West End Synagogue until its transfer from the West Side to the East Side of Manhattan in 1959), Union Temple and Beth Elohim in Brooklyn, and Central Synagogue in Rockville Centre (Nassau County). The older congregations did not share much in the movement within Reform toward more traditional worship. But many Reform Jews became active philanthropists. From the 1950s there was a gradual shift in the Reform movement toward liberal social and political action as a major goal, but there were objections and Temple Emanu-El left the Union of American Hebrew Congregations in protest at this direction. The foremost Reform rabbi was Stephen S. Wise, who in 1922 founded the Hebraic and Zionist-oriented Jewish Institute of Religion (JIR), which opened in 1925. Although the JIR intended to train rabbis for all denominations, most of its graduates went to Reform congregations. The notable early faculty included Salo W. Baron, R. Marcus, H. Slonimsky, S. Spiegel, C. Tchernowitz, and others, but the school declined after its first decade. Other New York Reform rabbinic notables included Samuel Schulman, Jonah B. Wise, Louis I. Newman, Bernard J. Bamberger, Samuel H. Goldenson, Julius Mark, Charles E. Shulman, and Edward E. Klein.

By the 1940s Orthodoxy in New York lost its intimate association with immigrant life, and tended to be divided internally between modernists oriented to the problems of Orthodox Judaism in a secular, scientific, urban society, and others indifferent or hostile to such concerns. The latter stressed piety, study, and aloofness from non-Orthodox Judaism. The modernist trend included such congregations as Kehillath Jeshurun, The Jewish Center, Fifth Avenue Synagogue, Riverdale Jewish Center, and such rabbis as Leo Jung, Emanuel Rackman, Joseph H. Lookstein, Simon G. Kramer, Walter S. Wurzberger, and Irving Greenberg. The "pietist" group was led mainly from yeshivot and was augmented by Ḥasidic immigration from the 1940s. Special Orthodox segments were the S.R. Hirsch school of German Orthodoxy, transplanted in 1938–40 to upper Manhattan under the leadership of Rabbi Joseph Breuer, and Sephardi congregations, largely in Brooklyn, composed of contemporary immigrants from Turkey, Greece, Syria, and Iraq. The venerable Shearith Israel continued under the ministry of H.P. Mendes, D. de Sola Pool, and L.C. Gerstein. The common institutional effort of Orthodox Jewry was the promotion of yeshivot, whose enrollment multiplied from below 2,000 in 1920 to approximately 5,000 in 1935, 8,000 in 1945, and 45,000 in 1968. Yeshiva College became Yeshiva University in 1943 under the leadership of Samuel Belkin, and expanded to include several high schools, the college, graduate and professional schools, and a medical school. Its yeshivah brought notable rabbinic scholars from Europe to serve as principal *rashei yeshivah*, the first two being Rabbis S.H. Polacheck and Moses Soloveichik; Joseph B. Soloveichik later succeeded his father. Other notable Orthodox yeshivah scholars and talmudists were Rabbis Joseph E. Henkin, Moses Feinstein, Jacob Kamenetsky, Moses A. Shatzkes, and Aaron Kotler.

The city's Conservative congregations leaned close to Orthodoxy, in which most of their members had been raised. The Jewish Theological Seminary was the focal institution of the Conservatives, and exercised broad spiritual influence. Partly owing to the influence of Mordecai M. Kaplan, Conservative synagogues also served as community centers, offering social, cultural, and recreational activities. The Jewish Center and the West Side Institutional Synagogue in Manhattan, both Orthodox although founded by Kaplan, began the trend. The Society for the Advancement of Judaism (Reconstructionist), B'nai Jeshurun, and Park Avenue Synagogue in Manhattan and the Brooklyn Jewish Center, Flatbush Jewish Center, and East Midwood Jewish Center in Brooklyn replicated this approach, which was continued in many large newer synagogues in Queens and the suburbs. The Conservative growth was greatest in Queens and the new suburban towns, where 145 of their 184 synagogues were situated in 1967. Rabbinic leaders, besides Kaplan, included Israel Goldstein, Max Drob, Israel H. Levinthal, Harry Halpern (d. 1981), Robert Gordis, Ben Zion Bokser, Milton Steinberg, William Berkowitz, and Judah Nadich.

The Jewish Division of the New York Public Library and the library of the Jewish Theological Seminary (damaged by fire in 1966) were two of the six or seven leading Jewish libraries in the world. No other city of the Diaspora offered such an abundance of Jewish scholars, books and manuscripts, and varied opportunities for study in a communal milieu that was profoundly Jewish.

The city was home to one of the greatest educational achievements of modern times, and it had a lasting effect on the individuals, the city, and the nation. Four colleges, City College and Hunter in Manhattan and Brooklyn and Queens Colleges, offered free tuition to qualified students. In the years when top-flight private schools were restricted to the children of the Protestant Establishment, thousands of indigent but brilliant Jewish New Yorkers attended the colleges. For struggling immigrants and their offspring, this proved an unparalleled opportunity to gain a first-rank education, prepare for life's challenges, and to broaden skills. Building on the accomplishments of earlier graduates like Bernard Baruch in finance and Felix Frankfurter in law, the colleges prepared students in the sciences, government, economics, education, political science, and the law. Beginning with Julius Axelrod, of the class of 1933, City College nurtured nine Nobel Prize winners, all of them Jewish, in economics, chemistry, physics and medicine, a figure unmatched by any public institution in the United States. All nine obtained their undergraduate degrees between 1933 and 1950. Across a wide path, the colleges educated such nationally recognized figures as Daniel Bell in sociology, Nathan Glazer and Irving Kristol in politics, Ira Gershwin, the lyricist, Bernard Malamud, the writer, Stanley Kaplan, founder of Kaplan Educational Services, the actors Edward G. Robinson, Judd Hirsch, Zero Mostel, Eli Wallach and Richard Schiff, and business and technology giants like Andrew Grove of Intel. Graduates of the city colleges rose to prominent positions on Wall Street as teachers, administrators, union officials, journalists, accountants, etc., becoming the backbone of the educational system, the economy, and society in general, all for the cost of subway fare. During the

1930s and through the 1950s, the colleges were bastions of free debate, with roiling political discussions over hot topics like communism vs. socialism and Trotskyites vs. Bolsheviks dominating campus activities. In the last years of the 1930s, as fascism threatened to dominate Spain, a contingent of New Yorkers (many of them leftist Jews recruited from the college campuses) made up the Abraham Lincoln Brigade and set off for Spain to "save" the country from Generalissimo Francisco Franco. These idealists, whose cause was dominated by Communists and other left-wingers, proved unsuccessful. In the late 1960s, black and Puerto Rican activists and their white allies demanded that the City University colleges implement an aggressive affirmative action program. The administration came up with an open-admissions plan under which any graduate of a New York City high school could matriculate at one of the 20 colleges in the system. But that program came at a high cost, as the colleges' academic standing declined (along with the number of Jews, now more affluent and able to afford private, out-of-town schools).

Still another important achievement in higher education involved the founding of the University in Exile at the New School for Social Research. From 1933 until the end of World War II, the University in Exile served as a base for scholars who had been dismissed from teaching and government positions by totalitarian regimes in Europe. The university later became the New School's Graduate Faculty of Political and Social Sciences, providing an academic base for notable scholars like the psychologists Max Wertheimer and Aron Gurwitsch and the political philosophers Hannah Arendt and Leo Straus.

New York provided the launching pad for the nation's feminist movement, beginning with the publication of Betty Friedan's *Feminine Mystique* in 1963. At the time a suburban New York housewife, Friedan analyzed "the problem that has no name," as she called it, based on interviews with women unhappy with their lot as housewives, babysitters, cooks and laundresses, and with limited career prospects. The book struck a nerve, providing the intellectual basis for the feminist movement. It permanently transformed the social fabric and consciousness of American society. Friedan was joined by more than two dozen women, including Gloria Steinem, in founding the National Organization for Women, and was its first president, serving from 1966 to 1970. The two Jewish women became the best-known figures in the feminist movement in the United States. Friedan's death in 2006 reminded generations of women of the debt they owed to the founding mother of feminism, who campaigned tirelessly for equal treatment of women in the workplace and in all areas of public and private life.

CULTURE. The half-century following the end of World War I witnessed the entry of Jews in large numbers into every corner of New York artistic and cultural life. Since this period also marked the growing domination by New York City of U.S. cultural life in general, and in some areas, such as theater, music, and publishing, its virtual monopolization, New York Jews prominent in these fields found themselves automatically at the center of national attention. The role of New York Jews as consumers of the arts also grew immensely. From the 1920s on, Jews formed a disproportionately high percentage of New York's theatergoers, music listeners, book purchasers, and art collectors. (One rough estimate placed Jews at 70% of the city's concert and theater audience during the 1950s.) Similarly, Jews also emerged in these years as major patrons of the arts. After World War II, particularly, they played a prominent part in endowing and supporting local cultural and artistic institutions.

In literature many Jewish writers of the 1920s and especially of the Depression years of the 1930s drew on their backgrounds in the immigrant communities to write memorable novels, essays, poetry, and short stories in the realms of social realism and "proletarian fiction." Left-wing Jewish intellectuals like Sidney Hook, Irving Howe, Alfred Kazin, Philip Rahv, and Michael Gold wrote for *The Nation, The New Masses, The New Leader,* and *Partisan Review.* Some of the best descriptions ever written of New York life in the early and mid-20th century, especially of its immigrant neighborhoods, can be found in books like: Samuel Ornitz' *Haunch, Paunch and Jowl* (1925), Henry Roth's *Call It Sleep* (1934), Michael Gold's *Jews Without Money* (1930), Alfred Kazin's *On Native Grounds* (1942) and *A Walker in the City* (1951), Bernard Malamud's *The Assistant* (1957), Paul Goodman's *The Empire City* (1959), and the novels of Joseph Heller and Wallace Markfield (see *United States Literature, Jews in).

The poetry of Louis Zukofsky was suffused with the atmosphere of New York life, while Kenneth Koch was a leader of the school of "New York poets" in the 1960s. In the years after World War II, the 92nd St. YMHA served as a center for readings of modern American poetry and for the introduction to a wide public of a number of young contemporary poets. Perhaps no poet commanded the attention of the general public as did Allen Ginsberg (d. 1997), who created a storm with his first published work, *Howl* (1956), a long poem about consumer society's negative human values. "I saw the best minds of my generation destroyed by madness" was the opening line, and Ginsberg, a homosexual and leader of the Beat generation, drew on Walt Whitman and others for inspiration. He famously wrote about his relationship with his mentally disturbed mother in *Kaddish for Naomi Ginsberg* (1961).

The Broadway musical theater and the world of popular music from the late 1920s through the 1960s were dominated by Jewish composers and librettists: Irving Berlin, George Gershwin, Jerome Kern, Harold Arlen, Frank Loesser, E.Y. (Yip) Harburg, and the teams of Rodgers and Hart, Rodgers and Hammerstein, and Lerner and Loewe. Many entertainers got their start in vaudeville, including Al Jolson, Eddie Cantor, the Marx Brothers, George Jessel, Fanny Brice and Sophie Tucker, and then transferred their talents to radio, the movies and television. Brooklyn-born Barbra Streisand attained fame on Broadway as a singer and actress before becoming a Hollywood star and director. The leading Broadway playwrights of the 1930s and 1940s, Lillian Hellman, Clifford Odets, and Elmer Rice, achieved renown with their searing, realistic dramas, while George S. Kaufman, Abe Burrows, and Moss Hart, among others, lightened the stage with bon mots and witty comedies. Arthur Miller's *Death of a Salesman* (1949) won recognition as the best drama produced on the American stage in the second half of the 20th century. A series of popular comedies by Neil Simon, beginning with *The Odd Couple* (1968), achieved critical and popular success. In 1931, Lee Strasberg co-founded the Group Theater, a company that spawned such theatrical legends as John Garfield and Stella Adler, and in 1949 Strasberg started the Actor's Studio, where Paul Newman, Dustin Hoffman, and Eli Wallach trained. During this period, all the major Broadway theaters were owned and controlled by members and descendants of the Shubert family, which earned fees for the use of the theaters and sometimes became involved in producing the shows. Although others owned some Broadway theaters, the Shubert organization, by the 1970s, owned half of all the houses. Beginning in the mid-1960s Joseph Papp promoted the idea of offering free performances of Shakespeare in the parks of New York. His long campaign led to the founding of the Public Theater, supported by commercial Broadway productions like *A Chorus Line*. The Shakespeare performances continued well into the 21st century with major actors taking on classic roles in Central Park. David Merrick dominated the Broadway stage, producing successful musicals and straight plays for more than 20 years. Sol Hurok, who began his career organizing local Jewish productions in Brooklyn's Brownsville, developed into the leading musical impresario in the U.S. The avant-garde Off Broadway theater came into its own in the 1960s and provided venues for talented writers and actors. The Living Theater of Julian Beck and Judith Malina and the Open Theater of Joseph Chaikin staged a variety of provocative productions.

Indicative of the impact of Jewish audiences on the New York theater was the fact that a number of Broadway hits of the 1950s and 1960s were on Jewish themes, the most successful of all being the musical *Fiddler on the Roof*. Set in the fictional *shtetl* of Anatevka, the musical drew on the short stories of Shalom Aleichem about Tevye the dairyman. Zero Mostel's over-the-top portrayal of the central character became the talk of the town. The musical, written by Joseph Stein, and the music, by Sheldon Harnick and Jerry Bock, dominated the airwaves and graced stages around the world as it offered a universal message about family life in troubled times. A young Stephen Sondheim began his career as a composer by writing the lyrics for the smash *West Side Story* (1957), which had a book by Arthur Laurents, music by Leonard Bernstein, and was produced, choreographed, and directed by Jerome Robbins. The plot borrowed liberally from Shakespeare's *Romeo and Juliet* and became a staple of the musical repertory. After the 1920s, the Yiddish theater in New York lost much of its vitality. In 1928 there were at least 11 Yiddish theaters, giving hundreds of performances a month, but the number dwindled to a mere handful and only occasional productions by the 1960s.

The New York musical world, both classical and popular, served as a showcase for a host of Jewish talent. Jews, who made up 70% of the membership of the musicians' union, Local 801 from the 1930s on, held most of the important instrumentalist chairs of the New York Philharmonic Orchestra, the Metropolitan Opera Orchestra, and the National Broadcasting Company Symphony Orchestra, which was led by Arturo Toscanini during its heyday. The leading musical performers included the conductors Artur Rodzinski, Bruno Walter, Lukas Foss, and Leonard Bernstein; the opera singers Richard Tucker, Robert Merrill, Jan Peerce, Roberta Peters, Beverly Sills, and Friedrich Schorr; the pianist Vladimir Horowitz and the violinist Isaac Stern. In the 1960s, with the assistance of Jacqueline Kennedy Onassis, Stern led a successful drive to save Carnegie Hall, one of the greatest musical venues in the world. Their effort preserved the New York landmark, which had one of the clarion sounds in the world of music. Although Benny Goodman, one of the most important jazz clarinetists, was born in Chicago, it was in New York that he came to prominence. In 1938, Goodman and his group of swing musicians were booked to play in Carnegie Hall, then a citadel of upper-crust society and "high-class" music. Carnegie Hall had a seating capacity of 2,760 and Goodman's concert had been sold out for weeks. The concert started off on a polite, though tepid note. But when the group tore into *Sing Sing Sing*, an energetic, rhythmic and bouncy tune, the audience responded with deafening applause. That concert came to be regarded as the most significant in jazz history, proving that jazz could be accepted by mainstream audiences. Goodman was also responsible for a significant step in racial integration in the United States. In the early 1930s, black and white jazz musicians could not play together in most clubs or concerts. In the Southern states, racial segregation was enforced by Jim Crow laws. Goodman broke with tradition by hiring Teddy Wilson to play with him and the drummer Gene Krupa in the Benny Goodman Trio. In 1936 he added the black Lionel Hampton on vibes to form the Benny Goodman Quartet.

The financier Otto Kahn was a leading financial backer of the Metropolitan Opera in the 1920s and 1930s, while Morton Baum helped found the City Center for Music and Dance and was instrumental in the establishment of Lincoln Center for the Performing Arts. One of the premier American classical composers, Aaron Copland, got his start in Brooklyn. Lincoln Kirstein paired with the genius of George Balanchine, a non-Jew, to shape 20th-century dance. Kirstein thought of the idea of the New York City Ballet, which became one of the foremost dance companies in the world. It was solely responsible for training its own artists and creating its own works. The company had 90 dancers, making it the largest dance organization in the United States and into the 21st century had an active repertory of more than 150 works, many choreographed by Jerome Robbins, who created serious dance works as well as choreography for the Broadway theater.

In the early 1960s, a young singer-songwriter from Hibbing, Minn., drifted into Greenwich Village and changed the nature of popular music. Originally Robert Zimmerman, he took the name Bob Dylan and performed his own compositions of story songs that quickly gained notice for their fierce political nature and their poetry. His "Blowin' in the Wind," about the changes looming on the American landscape, became one of the anthems of the civil rights movement as well as for the anti-Establishment postcollege generation in the wake of opposition to the war in Vietnam. Dylan's whining delivery of his protest songs, and his adoption of acoustic techniques, also influenced generations of musicians. In the late 1960s, following Dylan's success, the team of Simon and Garfunkel, songwriters and performers from Queens, achieved enduring popularity after their music ("Mrs. Robinson," "The Sound of Silence") was featured in the movie *The Graduate*, directed by Mike Nichols.

In painting, the Soyer brothers – Raphael, Moses, and Isaac – and Chaim Gross were prominent in the social-realistic art movement that flourished in Greenwich Village in the 1920s. Ben Shahn and Jack Levine were among the many Jewish artists whose early careers were associated with the art programs of the Works Projects Administration during the Depression years. The Nazi persecution brought to New York a number of German expressionist painters, including Max Weber. Prominent in the "New York School" of abstract expressionists and other movements that developed after World War II were Franz Klein, Larry Rivers, Louise Nevelson and Mark Rothko. In the 1960s, the Jewish Museum diverged from its tradition of exhibiting Jewish art only to sponsor a number of important avant-garde shows of sculpture and art. The far-flung and diverse Guggenheim family played a major role as patrons. Peggy Guggenheim moved her gallery from Europe to New York during the war years and her uncle, Solomon Guggenheim, endowed a new building for the Guggenheim Museum of Modern Art on upper Fifth Avenue. The only building in New York designed by Frank Lloyd Wright, it opened in 1960 and quickly became one of the architectural landmarks of the city, if not the nation. In 1969 Robert Lehman's world-renowned collection of impressionist and post-impressionist painting was willed to the Metropolitan Museum of Art. New York was the home, and the canvas, for a slew of important photographers: Richard Avedon (fashion), Helen Levitt (street life), Weegee (crime), and Diane Arbus (people on the fringes of society). Richard Meier, Paul Rudolph, Robert A.M. Stern, Gordon Bunshaft, Marcel Breuer, and Frank Gehry cut their architectural teeth in New York during this period.

In WEVD, established by the *Jewish Daily Forward* in 1931 and named with the initials of the socialist Eugene V. Debs, New York boasted the world's only full-time Yiddish radio station, though by 1970 much of its programming had gone over to English. Gertrude Berg, Fanny Brice, Morey Amsterdam, Walter Winchell, and Barry Gray, New York radio personalities, became household names. Berg wrote and starred in *The Goldbergs*, a series about Jewish life in the Bronx. From the show's opening – "Yoo hoo, Mrs. Goldberg!" – listeners got a brace of Jewish New York, complete with mannerisms and Yiddish. The series transferred successfully to television. An entire school of television comedy, often deriving from the comic routines of the "Borscht Belt" (see *New York State), gave professional life to performers like Sam Levenson, Sid Caesar, and Jerry Lewis. But it was Milton Berle, with his Tuesday night variety show, who almost single-handedly changed the nation's evening habits. Television was in its infancy when Berle, broadcasting from New York, wowed audiences week after week, interrupting acts, dressing in drag and participating in skit after skit. Audiences found him outrageously amusing and flocked to buy their own television sets, millions of them in the postwar years. Berle, or Uncle Miltie as he called himself, was known as Mr. Television. The National Broadcasting Company signed him to a 30-year contract, and Berle, who started in show business at the age of 4, continued to perform into his 90s.

Thanks to television, a "new breed" of comedian found favor with more sophisticated audiences. They were social commentators and satirists of common situations. Their styles varied widely, from the comedy sparring of the team of Nichols and May to the storytelling of Alan King to the obscenity spewing Lenny Bruce to the kvetching of the stage milquetoast Woody Allen to the angst of Shelley Berman. Jewish humor, in cabarets, nightclubs, on television, and in the movies, found a broad American audience.

At that time, the three major commercial television networks, the Columbia Broadcasting System (William Paley), the National Broadcasting Company (David and Robert Sarnoff), and the American Broadcasting Company (Leonard Goldenson), were run by Jews.

From the 1920s on, Jews played a prominent role in the New York publishing business, among them Horace Liveright of Liveright & Boni. B.W. Huebsch and Harold Guinzberg of Viking Press, Henry Simon and M. Lincoln Schuster of Simon & Schuster, Alfred Knopf of Alfred A. Knopf, Bennett Cerf of Random House, Roger Straus of Farrar, Straus & Giroux, and Jason Epstein of Anchor Books. The German-Jewish house of Schocken Books moved to New York City in 1946. Bloch Publishing Co., Thomas Yoseloff, and Abelard & Schumann put out a largely or wholly Jewish line. Brooklyn was the launching pad for the literary career of Norman Mailer, who wrote the signature book of World War II, *The Naked and the Dead*. Irwin Shaw, a prolific writer of short stories, got his start in Brooklyn as well. And beginning in 1955, New York was home to Elie Wiesel, the memoirist of the Holocaust and campaigner for human rights, who settled in the city after his liberation from Buchenwald. Wiesel wrote most of his more than 40 published works in the city.

In journalism, the unparalleled international coverage and national reporting of *The New York Times*, under the patronage of the Ochs and Sulzberger families, won widespread respect, proven in 90 Pulitzer Prizes and other recognized awards. Its publisher throughout the 1940s and 1950s, Arthur Hays Sulzberger, was a staunch anti-Zionist who opposed the creation of the State of Israel. He saw Judaism as a religion only and he had a series of disputes with the leading American Jewish organizations over the newspaper's coverage. Particularly galling, in retrospect, was *The Times'* coverage of the Holocaust and Hitler's campaign against the Jews, which received limited space in the "paper of record." After the 1956 war in the Middle East, the newspaper's coverage of Israel got serious attention and its reports competed for space with all other news developments. *The New York Post* during the 1940s and into the 1960s, under the ownership of Dorothy Schiff, a descendant of Jacob Schiff, and the editorship of James Wechsler, gave voice to liberal and underdog causes while walking a financial tightrope. Numerous reporters came to prominence during World War II, the Korean War, and the war in Vietnam, including David Halberstam, Meyer Berger (*About New York*), Bernard Kalb and his brother Marvin Kalb, A.M. Rosenthal (*There Is No News From Auschwitz*, he famously wrote in *The Times* in 1958), Joseph Lelyveld, the son of a rabbi, and Max Frankel, a Holocaust survivor. The Yiddish press flourished despite declining circulations in the 1920s and 1930s, but lost ground steadily in the years after World War II. Three New York periodicals with nation-wide audiences were also under Jewish ownership or editorship: *The New Yorker, The Village Voice*, and the *New York Review of Books*. **Commentary* and *Midstream*, published under the auspices of Jewish organizations, had influential readerships (see *Press, Jewish, in U.S.A.). The Newhouse family played a major role in publishing as owners of newspapers and a plethora of national magazines, based in New York.

After World War I, Jews took a greater interest in popular sports, both as spectators and as performers. Hank Greenberg, a product of the Bronx, achieved renown as a home-run slugger (58 in one season) at a time when there were few Jews in major league baseball. Sandy Koufax, one of baseball's greatest pitchers, pointedly refused to pitch a World Series game on Yom Kippur. Although he was not observant, Koufax said he felt he had to be a role model. Among other well-known New York athletes were the boxers Benny Leonard and Barney Ross, the baseball players Harry Danning, Sid Gordon, and Cal Abrams, the football quarterback Sid Luckman, and the basketball star and coach Nat Holman. One of the signature events in sports occurred during Holman's tenure at City College, which fielded a basketball team assembled from the regular student body, not players recruited for their athletic ability. In the 1950–51 season, City College, known as the "Cinderella team," won the two most important basketball titles of the time, the National Invitational Tournament and the National Collegiate Athletic Association championship. But the celebrations were short-lived when it was disclosed that certain players on the team had "shaved" points, or played to reduce their margin of victory, at the behest of gamblers. It was a watershed moment in basketball, in the lives of the players, Jewish and non-Jewish, some of whom went to prison, and the college, which was forced to de-emphasize basketball.

(For biographies of the figures mentioned above, see individual entries.)

Jewish involvement in New York cultural life in the middle decades of the 20th century was so complete that it had an impact on local speech, gestures, food, humor, and attitudes. It is doubtful if anywhere else in the history of the Diaspora such a large Jewish community existed in so harmonious a symbiosis with a great metropolis, without either isolating itself from its surroundings or losing its own distinct sense of character and identity. If the Jews gave to New York unstintingly of their experience, energies, and talents, they received in return an education in urbanity and a degree of cosmopolitan sophistication unknown to any other Jewish community of similar size in the past. When 20th-century New York Jews thought of the city they lived in, they did not simply consider it a great capital of civilization that had generously taken them in; rather, they thought of themselves as joint builders of this greatness and one of its main continuing supports. Such a relationship marks a unique moment in Jewish history, and one that, given current cultural and demographic trends in the United States and the world at large, is not likely to recur again.

[Lloyd P. Gartner, Hillel Halkin, Edward L. Greenstein, and Yehuda Ben-Dror / James Marshall (2nd ed.)]

1970–2006

DEMOGRAPHY. At the center of international finance, politics, entertainment, and culture, with a nearly unrivaled collection of museums, galleries, performance venues, media outlets, international corporations, and financial markets, New York, the Big Apple, has long attracted large numbers of immigrants, as well as people from all over the United States. They settled in the city because of its culture, energy, cosmopolitanism, and economic opportunity. Perhaps the most compelling reality of the eight-county New York area Jewish community (the five counties of New York City and Westchester County, Nassau County and Suffolk County) at the tail end of the 20th century was its sheer size. The New York area was home to the largest Jewish community in the world outside of Israel: 643,000 Jewish households; 1,412,000 adults who consider themselves Jewish and children being raised as Jews; and 1,667,000 people living in Jewish households, including non-Jews (typically spouses who are not Jewish or children not being raised as Jews).

Kings County (Brooklyn) with 456,000 Jews led the way in a 2002 survey by Jewish Community Studies of New York, followed by Manhattan with 243,000, Nassau with 221,000, Queens with 186,000, and Westchester with 129,000. Suffolk with 90,000, the Bronx with 45,000, and Staten Island with 42,000 Jews had the smallest Jewish populations. One out of eight individuals in the eight-county New York area was Jewish. In the United States as a whole (including New York), nearly one person in 50 was Jewish. Of all the Jewish communities in the United States, only Los Angeles was home to more Jews than the borough of Brooklyn. Manhattan and Nassau County each had more Jews than either the Boston or Philadelphia areas. During the 1990s, the population remained essentially stable: the number of Jewish households increased by less than 1% and the number of Jewish people decreased by less than 1%. But the number of people in Jewish households increased by 7%, from 1,554,000 in 1991 to 1,667,000 in 2002.

The city, despite a 5% decrease in population, towered as the geographic hub of the Jewish community, providing leadership and guidance in social, recreational, health, cultural, and educational programs, as well as delivering major philanthropic support from virtually all fields of endeavor. Unlike other Eastern and Midwestern Jewish communities, where suburbanization changed the geography of Jewish life, most Jewish households – 70% – were found in the city proper.

During the 1990s, however, there were substantial geographic shifts: greener, more affluent, car-friendly Westchester County recorded a 41% increase in the number of Jews from 1991 to 2002. Both Brooklyn, where large-family Ḥasidim and Russian immigrants flourished, and once-remote Staten Island experienced significant increases, 23% and 27%, respectively. The Bronx, despite a stable – and vibrant – Jewish community in Riverdale, showed a 45% decline, continuing a decades-long trend. Smaller declines occurred in Queens (20%) and Manhattan (21%).

During the 1990s, there were substantial changes in the composition of the population. In 1991, children made up 22% of the community while seniors aged 65+ made up 16%. In 2002, the community included about the same percentage of children younger than 18 but seniors were 20%. In addition, reflecting greater longevity because of advances in health care, those 75 or older more than doubled after 1991, from 5% to 11%. One organization, the Jewish Association for Services to the Aged, beginning in 1968, became a prime social-service agency in the city and suburbs, with assistance on home, housing, and legal services on a nonsectarian basis, to help sustain the elderly in their homes and communities and to offer opportunities for a better quality of life.

Unlike Jewish communities in other parts of the United States, New York's was a mix of different kinds of households. Over 378,000 lived in Orthodox homes (240,000 in Brooklyn, many in the distinct Ḥasidic garb). Over 220,000 lived in Russian-speaking households, about 94% of them in the five boroughs. In 1991, 13% of all Jewish adults said they had been born outside the United States. By 2002, this percentage had increased to 27%. Adults born in the former Soviet Union accounted for 43% of all foreign-born adults in 2002, compared with 26% in 1991.

The New York area, with 55,000 people, also had by far the largest number of survivors of the Holocaust in the United States, although it was aging significantly. Singles accounted for 35% of the Jewish households in Manhattan, which was home to one of the greatest concentrations of Jewish singles in the United States, 55,000, according to the 2002 survey. These singles participated in a broad range of social and cultural activities tied to a variety of Jewish institutions. Many singles successfully trolled popular Internet sites like JDate.com in an effort to meet their lifetime mates.

One of the most contentious and troublesome issues in Jewish life was intermarriage. In 2002, according to the survey, the New York rate, 22%, was approximately half the national average, probably because of the large Ḥasidic population, where arranged marriages were not uncommon, and the insular Russian groups, who often selected Russian-speaking mates. While still low by national standards, intermarriage rates in the eight-county area increased significantly (36% of marriages) in the 1998–2002 period.

Jewish children aged 6 to 17 had relatively high levels of Jewish education. About 45% were enrolled in a full-time Jewish day school. Only 13% had not received any formal Jewish education.

While there was substantial affluence within the community, there was also substantial poverty. As 17% of New York Jewish households reported an income of more than $150,000 a year, 31% said they had an annual income of less than $35,000. There were more poor Jews in New York than there were Jews in all but the largest Jewish communities in the United States. Poverty increased significantly in New York City after 1991 during a period when overall poverty rates in the city declined. From 1991 to 2002, the number of people estimated to be living in Jewish households under the poverty level in New York City rose from 167,500 to 226,000, an increase of 35%.

The poorest by far in the survey were in Russian-speaking households with seniors age 65 or older. Eighty-five percent of people who were both older and Russian-speaking reported significant poverty-level incomes, reflecting limited American work histories and therefore lack of qualification for traditional Social Security and private pensions. This group seemed to reflect the immigrant period of struggle and adjustment on the road to absorption in the American community.

Many people have defined New York by its ever-changing and ever-renewing neighborhoods, from the densely populated Lower East Side around the turn of the 20th century to the apartment-house-dominated Bronx and Queens at the middle and end of that century. Jewish New York in the 21st century was a continuation of that phenomenon, of living with like-minded and economically equal neighbors. About 84% of the Jews in the area lived in 26 specific areas. One out of four lived in five areas: Flatbush/Midwood/Kensington (107,800); Boro Park (82,600); the Upper East Side (73,300); the Upper West Side (71,800); and Central/Southeastern Westchester (64,300), a relatively easy commute to Manhattan.

In Brooklyn neighborhoods like Boro Park, Flatbush, Kings Bay/Madison and Coney Island/Brighton and in Nassau County's Five Towns, on the city's border, over 40% of the residents were Jewish. By contrast, areas like the Northeast Bronx, Western Suffolk, Southwestern Westchester, and Central Suffolk had Jewish populations of only 10%.

[Jacob B. Ukeles (2nd ed.)]

POLITICAL AND CIVIC LIFE. In the last quarter of the 20th century and into the 21st, Jews operated at the center of New York political life and power, partly because of numbers and partly because of the high percentage of voter turnout, even in off-year elections. Following in the long tradition of activism and participation in democratic government, Jews took strong roles in city affairs, neighborhood disputes, and grassroots activities. Political-minded individuals often sought change through the ballot box or by becoming candidates themselves. As of 2006, three of the previous five mayors (and none before them) were Jewish: Abraham D. *Beame, elected in 1973, Edward I. *Koch, who served three four-year terms, and Michael R. *Bloomberg, who won re-election in 2005 with a whopping 59% of the vote. The candidates had taken different roads to the top, reflecting the complexity, diversity, and realities of political life in the city. Beame came up through the ranks of the Brooklyn Democratic organization, using his skills as an accountant to eventually win election as city comptroller, guardian of the finances. He followed the flashy tenure of John Lindsay, who led the city into a financial crisis. Beame's financial skills were not deft enough to save the city from near ruin, but eventually the city emerged with the help of some key power brokers (who happened to be Jewish): Felix Rohatyn, a Wall Street figure, and Victor Gotbaum, a labor leader, who put together a plan to save the city with new bonds and commitments from the well-financed union-city pension funds. Koch became active in his local reform Democratic organization in Greenwich Village, fighting to maintain its special neighborhood characteristics. After defeating a longtime "boss" in his home district, Koch secured the nomination to represent the area in the House of Representatives. He won the seat and served until he gained the mayoralty nomination and then triumphed in the citywide election. Bloomberg, a Democrat who ran as a Republican, was given little chance in the heavily Democratic city. But the multibillionaire businessman spent lavishly and campaigned hard and defeated a little-known candidate. When he ran for re-election, the formerly shy Bloomberg, who was not known for his religious observance, had no hesitancy about reaching out to Jewish audiences, and he campaigned in the Catskills, a favorite summertime retreat for New York Jews. Privately, he was one of the most philanthropic individuals in the world. He contributed regularly to at least a dozen Jewish organizations or institutions, and he and his sister endowed a fund in their mother's name to send teenagers to a kosher camp that is part of Young Judaea, a Zionist youth movement. And just before the election, ultra-Orthodox leaders in Williamsburg, Brooklyn, held what was by far the largest rally of Bloomberg's campaign. With searchlights flashing across the sky and klezmer music blaring from loudspeakers hoisted on cranes, thousands of Ḥasidim cheered the mayor from rooftops and blocks upon blocks of bleachers. One barely mentioned controversy involved the city's Health Department drive, as a preventive measure, to ban an ancient form of ritual circumcision practiced by some Ḥasidic *mohelim* that had been linked to three cases of neonatal herpes in late 2004, one of them fatal. And as an indication of the sensitivity and power of the Jewish electorate, a candidate for a fringe party, Lenora Fulani, who had said that Jews "had to sell their souls to acquire Israel" and had to "function as mass murderers of people of color," was removed from a leadership position after her party concluded that her inflammatory comments about Jews were "outrageous and distasteful."

During that period, prominent Jewish officeholders showed their ambitions by making runs for nomination or election but fell short. They included Ruth Messinger, then borough president of Manhattan and later president of the American Jewish World Service; Harrison J. (Jay) Goldin, the city's comptroller during the Beame years and president of the American Jewish Congress' Metropolitan Region; Albert Blumenthal, who was majority leader of the New York State Assembly; Richard Ravitch, former head of the Metropolitan Transit Authority who also served as head of the Jewish Community Relations Council and the Charter Revision Commission; Ronald Lauder, the cosmetics heir and former head of the Conference of Presidents of Major Jewish Organizations and former Ambassador to Austria, and Representative Anthony D. Weiner, a former congressional aide to Charles *Schumer, later U.S. Senator Schumer.

It was not unusual in New York City to see politicians strolling the streets or ambling in the parks, chatting with constituents. Although their surnames easily identified them as Jews, they did not campaign or serve as Jewish office holders, particularly in a vast, multicultural environment. One regular was Henry J. Stern, who served as Parks Commissioner for more than a dozen years under six mayors. Another popular political figure, Robert Morgenthau, son of Franklin D. Roosevelt's Treasury secretary, Henry *Morgenthau, Jr., won election as Manhattan district attorney in 1974 and kept getting elected, even at the age of 86, serving more than 32 years, a record. From his safe Lower East Side district, Sheldon Silver, Orthodox and observant, exercised considerable power in Albany for many years as a leader of the state assembly, a position he attained through seniority and political dexterity. In Congress, no one fought harder for equal rights for women than Bella S. Abzug, who represented a Manhattan district in Congress. Abzug, who was active in several feminist groups, including NOW, pressed for an Equal Rights Amendment, but the measure failed to gain approval in enough state legislatures to be adopted.

A number of Jews tried to use their political and financial base in New York City as a springboard for national or statewide office. These included three attorney generals: Louis *Lefkowitz, a popular Republican who campaigned as Looie, and two Democrats, Robert *Abrams and Elliot *Spitzer; and the comptrollers Alan Hevesi and Arthur Levitt, Sr., who served for six terms until 1979 and whose son, Arthur Levitt, Jr. was chairman of the Securities and Exchange Commission. During the last quarter of the 20th century, all the governors of New York were gentiles. By the second half of the 20th century, realizing that they had to appeal to a broad and more sophisticated electorate, Jewish candidates were barely mentioning their religious affiliation.

One crowning achievement, the appointment of Ruth Bader Ginsberg of New York to the United States Supreme Court in 1993, pointed to the importance of both Jews and women in politics.

In the last quarter of the 20th century, no citywide candidate could be elected without Jewish votes and no statewide candidate could ignore the sizable downstate Jewish vote in the city, on Long Island and in Westchester. Either because of firmly held opinions or because of political considerations, non-Jewish candidates for citywide and statewide office often took strong pro-Israel stances. Famously, Mayor Rudolph Giuliani turned down a donation for the victims of 9/11 from a Saudi Prince who had tied the 9/11 attacks to U.S. policy in favor of Israel. Senator Alfonse D'Amato, who served 18 years in the Senate, was an ardent champion of Israel. Senator Daniel Patrick Moynihan was beloved in the Jewish community because of his support for Israel during his tenure as U.S. ambassador to the United Nations. In 1975, when the U.N. passed a resolution declaring "Zionism is a form of racism and racial discrimination," basically an endorsement of antisemitism, Moynihan said: "This is a lie." And when Idi Amin, the tyrant who ruled Uganda, went before the world body and demanded the "extinction of Israel as a state," Moynihan called him a "racist murderer." Moynihan, who had never visited the Middle East, took his political direction from the State Department, he said, but on Zionism, Jewish history, antisemitism, and related topics, he relied on the advice of Norman Podhoretz, editor of *Commentary* magazine, and by that time a neoconservative, as was Moynihan. The senator was also a vigorous supporter of the rights of Soviet Jewry. Moynihan spoke out publicly and worked tirelessly with Jewish groups to get the Soviet Union to relax its grip on the dissidents and other Jews who sought to leave the Communist state. More recently, Hillary Clinton, who while First Lady committed the faux pas of embracing Suha Arafat, the wife of Yasser Arafat, became one of the most avid supporters of Israel in the U.S. Senate.

New York was the most important source of political fund-raising in the United States. Four of the top five zip codes in the nation for contributions were in Manhattan. The top zip code, 10021, on the Upper East Side, where many wealthy Jews resided, generated the most money for the 2000 presidential campaigns of both George W. Bush and Al Gore.

No event touched the soul of New York more than the attacks on the World Trade Center towers on the morning of Sept. 11, 2001. There were Jewish victims among the almost 3,000 dead, of course, but they had not been singled out as Jews. Indeed, the diversity of the victims was one of the hallmarks of the event, a tragedy that cut across all ethnic and religious lines, but the Moslem extremists who perpetrated the attack had identified Jews with New York City and with American capitalism. One rumor in the Moslem world that circulated shortly after the attacks was that Jews working in the World Trade Center had received phone calls from Israel warning them not to go to work on Sept. 11. The rumor was patently false.

A few years later, after the dust had settled, literally and figuratively, Larry Silverstein, the owner of the property, sought to rebuild after receiving insurance payments for both buildings. He enlisted the architect Daniel Liebeskind to design new towers and a memorial to the victims, but the project became bogged down in disputes among the city, state, families of the victims, commercial interests and others. Liebeskind's design was eventually abandoned and the timetable for construction was delayed.

[Neil Goldstein (2nd ed.)]

BUSINESS AND ECONOMICS. As the city emerged from its financial nightmare of the early 1970s ("Ford to City: Drop Dead," was the headline in *The Daily News* when its plea for aid was turned down by the White House) and became re-energized, it became clear that the economy and the engines that ran it were ready to reassert New York's primary position in the world of finance. On Wall Street, in banking, in fashion and merchandising, in department stores and in diamonds, among other areas, many Jewish New Yorkers were in the front ranks of movers and shakers. The old German-Jewish families that had established beachheads even before the wave of immigrants arrived toward the end of the 19th century, the Schiffs, Warburgs, Lehmans, Morgenthaus, Oppenheims, and Guggenheims, to name a few, remained in the top tier at the giant financial brokerages like Kuhn Loeb, Goldman Sachs, Lazard Frères, and their successors. But the firms were so large that by the 21st century management was in the hands of a multitude of partners and officers, many of whom were Jewish and many of whom were not. Some individuals earned reputations on Wall Street, like Abby Joseph Cohen, a lead financial analyst for Merrill, Lynch, and Felix Rohatyn, who headed Lazard Frères, with time out for service as Ambassador to France, and Saul Steinberg, who rode a tiger to great wealth and renown in the insurance industry, only to suffer a letdown. Henry Kravis and Peter Kalikow won fame in a series of leveraged buyouts and Gerald Levin wound up as chief executive of the merged Time Warner AOL empire. Carl Icahn earned his stripes as a feared corporate raider and Ivan Boesky won riches and then shame dealing in junk bonds and other enterprises. Peter Cohen headed American Express for a time. The Greenberg clan, father Maurice and two sons, were powers in the insurance business, heading major companies until a scandal in 2005. Mortimer Zuckerman, who made a fortune in real estate in Boston and New York, bought and was publisher of *The Daily News,* once the newspaper with the largest daily circulation in the United States. Robert E. Rubin, who was born in New York, rose from the risk arbitrage department at Goldman Sachs to become its vice chairman and co-chief operating officer until he was plucked by President Clinton to serve in his administration. Rubin became the 70th United States Secretary of the Treasury, spanning both Clinton terms. And with New York as his base, George Soros, an immigrant from Hungary, formed private hedge funds and became the wealthiest man in the world – until he decided to start giving away much of his fortune to charitable endeavors. In the same vein, Michael Bloomberg started on Wall Street and established a financial information service that became a "must have" for financial institutions large and small. Bloomberg, removing himself from his far-flung business empire, which included computerized data and radio and television stations stressing financial news, twice won election as Mayor of New York. In banking, Sanford G. Weill rose to become chairman of Citigroup, one of the largest institutions in the United States, encompassing banking, credit cards, mortgages, home equity loans, the brokerage Smith Barney and other consumer financial services. In the unpublicized and lightly regulated field of money management, investors like Michael Steinhardt accumulated fortunes. Steinhardt used some of the funds to become the driving force behind Birthright Israel, a project aimed at strengthening the connection between young Jews and Israel.

Estee Lauder, who was born in Queens, transformed beauty into big business. In the 21st century, her company controlled 45% of the cosmetics market in U.S. department stores. Its products were sold in 118 countries. Even after 40 years in business, she attended the launch of every new cosmetics counter or shop. Her sons Ronald and Leonard were important figures in New York business, culture and philanthropy. Well-known names in the fashion industry like Ralph Lauren, Calvin Klein, Isaac Mizrachi, Liz Claiborne, and Marc Jacobs found exposure in the great department and clothing stores of New York, like Jewish-founded Barney's (once a store for hard-to-fit youth but later a fashion emporium), Bloomingdale's, B. Altman, Gimbel's, Saks, and Macy's. But in the face of competition and changing tastes, the family-started stores found it difficult to continue. Some closed and some were bought out. One venture, Alexander's, the best-known clothing store in the Bronx, was owned by the Farkas family. When it expanded to Manhattan and opened a vast store near Bloomingdale's, Alexander's failed, and the family eventually closed its stores. The tale of Stern's, once a magnet for class-conscious German immigrants early in the century, later a destination for the aspiring middle class after World War II, provided a case in point. Four sons of an impoverished German Jewish immigrant founded Stern's in 1867. Buoyed by their initial success, the Stern brothers led a retail migration to Ladies' Mile in 1878 with the opening of a seven-story building on 23d Street between Fifth and Sixth Avenues. It was the largest department store in New York until 1910. In 1913 the store moved to 42nd Street and Fifth Avenue and catered to show business people because of its proximity to Broadway. The store stocked other merchandise in an attempt to feed the aspirations of less wealthy shoppers. It thrived in this middle-market niche for decades but in 1951 Stern's was bought by Allied Stores and a new era began. In the competitive postwar retail landscape, Stern's began marketing itself to the masses. But ultimately, Stern's lost out to big box stores and to the fact that, during the 1980s, customers of all incomes became bargain hunters. Stern's is now gone. And Bloomingdale's and Macy's became part of Federated Department Stores. Another family-owned concern rose up out of Brooklyn to succeed, on a smaller scale, on Long Island, in Manhattan, and in suburban New Jersey and Westchester. In the Brownsville-East New York section of Brooklyn in the 1920s, under an elevated subway line, Max and Clara Fortunoff sold dishes, linens, and other dry goods at low prices. As they watched the neighborhood decline in the late 1960s, the Fortunoff offspring sensed that their customers were moving to Long Island, so Fortunoff branched out to Long Island with housewares, furniture, luggage, and luxury goods like fine china and jewelry. In Manhattan, Fortunoff opened a jewelry store on Fifth Avenue.

Throughout this period, and stretching back to before World War II, 47th Street between Fifth and Sixth Avenues flourished as the diamond capital of the United States. It was a tightly-knit industry and was controlled by Jews, just as it had been for centuries, from the mines in South Africa to the skilled cutting and polishing craftsmen in Antwerp and other world capitals. As in the diamond exchange in Tel Aviv, deals on 47th Street were consummated by handshake and Yiddish confirmations. Trust ruled the transactions. Dozens of sales people, many in Ḥasidic garb, dominated the streets, which had the highest concentration of police protection in the city to thwart temptation. Secrecy and discretion were unspoken bywords, and in the 21st century the diamond district remained almost totally in Jewish hands.

REAL ESTATE AND HOUSING. The real-estate business in the city was a dynastic enterprise, the great fortunes being passed down from one generation to another, and Jewish families were front-and-center in acquiring land, building homes and commercial structures, and running vast enterprises. The practice bore little relationship to the modern world of the corporation. While the elders and parents of a generation made deals and brokered arrangements, their children went to school and summer camp with one another, cementing relationships for the future. The families, Rose, Tishman, Rudin, Milstein, Tish, LeFrak, to cite a few, occupied the top tiers of the business. These oligarchies were only a few generations old, tracing their roots and business involvement to the immigrant arrivals and pushcarts that flooded New York in the previous century. Some concentrated in Manhattan, shrewdly accumulating property slowly and rarely selling. Others tried to be prudent, rarely taking risks. Others built massively in the outer boroughs like Brooklyn and Queens, where lower prices prevailed. In addition to shaping the landscape of New York City, the families were the backbone of philanthropy. Not only did they give extensively to Jewish charities, but they were identified with hospitals and educational institutions. And many found the time to serve in high positions in government and civic life. Lewis Rudin, for example, was the founder of a group called the Association for a Better New York, which promoted the city's reputation and performed good works. Seymour Milstein and his brothers, on the other hand, used their fortune to buy other companies, and at one time owned United Brands, the Starett Housing Corporation, and Emigrant Savings Bank. Although they gave their word to city officials that they would protect the famed gilded clock and Palm Court lounge of the Biltmore Hotel, they demolished both in 1981. The family, once extraordinarily close, later split, and filed so many suits against one another that they almost destroyed themselves. When Seymour Milstein died in 2001, his nephew issued a statement that read in its entirety: "We will always cherish the happy times we shared and our many years together."

If the real estate interests were bound by common interests, so were the social strivers who sought the best living arrangements. While the state banned discrimination in the sale and rental of housing, Jews in New York sometimes experienced more subtle stumbling blocks. Many of the grand old buildings lining Central Park West and Fifth and Park Avenues in Manhattan were cooperatives, and prospective tenants had to be screened and approved by the respective boards before being allowed to make their purchase. A number of high-profile, wealthy Jews, like Barbra Streisand, the singer; Mike Wallace, the television reporter; Ron Perelman, the financier; and Steve Wynn, the casino entrepreneur, were rejected, usually without reason. The co-ops functioned as private clubs and could determine if the applicant possessed the "right" connections or ethnicity or earned their living in an "approved" manner. Sometimes Jews were admitted one week and not the next, after some quota was reached. Whereas religion was once a key unspoken factor, by the early years of the 21st century rejection on economic grounds was much more common as old prejudices lost much of their sting.

CULTURE. Following the success of Stephen Birmingham's *Our Crowd: The Great Jewish Families of New York*, published in 1967, Irving Howe weighed in with *World of Our Fathers* in 1973. Historically, the exhaustively researched tale of Jewish immigrant life on the Lower East Side provided a cultural anthropology spanning the Old Country to the settlement houses and synagogues, the matchmakers, dance halls, and the culture of Yiddish, from poets, novelists, and intellectuals to theatrical figures and popular entertainers. Although he was a scholar and an intellectual, Howe in *World of Our Fathers* taught a new generation about the notion of egalitarian socialism and how it emerged from the struggle for social justice, according to Morris Dickstein, writing two decades after the publication of the surprise best-seller. The book, written with the assistance of Kenneth Libo, made its way into virtually every Jewish home, and its readers, many of them second-generation Jews who had moved to the suburbs, were able to reconnect to a world of struggle and idealism.

Although Bernard Malamud, who died in 1986, set many of his stories in New York, sometimes a geographical New York, sometimes a metaphysical one, and used Jewish characters extensively, he was not considered a "Jewish" writer, but rather an American writer. To the writer and critic Jonathan Rosen, Malamud's city was a place of surprises, of trials, and of ultimate meaning. In his best fiction, New York haunted his imagination, and his prose told the story of struggling tailors, shoemakers, matchmakers, light-bulb peddlers, and immigrants. His work, critics said, showed a regard for tradition and the plight of ordinary men, and was imbued with the theme of moral wisdom gained through suffering. His death was followed five years later by that of Isaac Bashevis Singer, who won the Nobel Prize in literature in 1978. Singer wrote largely in Yiddish, although he had lived in New York since before World War II. His 1970 novel, *Enemies: A Love Story*, set in 1949 in New York, dealt with survivors of the Holocaust who felt guilty about having survived. It became a successful film in 1989.

The immigrant experience provided the background for E.L. Doctorow's *Ragtime*, first as a novel in 1975 and then as a musical on Broadway in 1998. Doctorow, a New Yorker, had earlier won acclaim for *The Book of Daniel*, a fictionalized story of the executed atomic spies, the Rosenbergs, in 1971.

On the stage, through the end of the 20th century, Arthur Miller continued to churn out drama, although none achieved the commercial or critical success of his earlier works, which included *All My Sons* and *After the Fall*, a fictionalized version of his life with Marilyn Monroe, who converted to Judaism for their marriage.

The Broadway stage proved the perfect vehicle for Wendy Wasserstein (d. 2006), a Brooklyn-born playwright of wry, smart, and often highly comical plays. In 1989 she won both the Tony and Pulitzer Prizes for her play *The Heidi Chronicles*, and explored topics ranging from feminism to family to pop culture in such works as *The Sisters Rosensweig*, *Isn't It Romantic* and *An American Daughter*. Like Miller, who often mixed his art and politics, Tony Kushner, who was born in New York and educated there, made a splash with *Angels in America*, a two-play exploration of the state of the nation in terms of sexual, racial, religious, political, and social issues that confronted the nation during the Ronald Reagan years as the AIDS epidemic spread. *Angels* is really two full-length plays. Part I: *Millenium Approaches*, won the Pulitzer Prize for drama in 1993. Part II: *Perestroika*, won the Tony award. Four characters represented Jews, Christians and agnostics; homosexuals and heterosexuals; blacks and whites; and men and women caregivers and patients – an American mix. The prolific Kushner's masterpiece was directed for television in 2004 by Mike Nichols, proving its durability, and won numerous awards. AIDS, the great affliction of the 1980s in New York, found its chief stage and real-life opponent in Larry Kramer, a dramatist, author and gay rights activist. Beginning in 1981, Kramer published a series of articles on the growing AIDS epidemic, urging immediate government and private action. He was a founder of Gay Men's Health Crisis, a New York-based advocacy group, which remains the world's largest provider of services to gay men with AIDS. In 1987, increasingly discontented with the response to AIDS by both the U.S. government and the gay male community, Kramer founded the AIDS advocacy and protest organization, ACT-UP, which engaged in civil disobedience. His 1985 play about the early years of AIDS, *The Normal Heart*, was one of the most important cultural responses in the 1980s to the devastation of AIDS. It had more than 600 productions all over the world.

By contrast, Mel Brooks, the comedian and comedy writer, adapted his 1968 movie, *The Producers*, into a Broadway musical, with Thomas Meehan. The outrageous work was the smash hit of the 2000-2001 season, winning 12 Tony Awards, the most for one show. Brooks wrote the satiric – and some said offensive – *Springtime for Hitler*, a number that carried the story line, about a down and out producer who raises money for the world's worst show, a musical based on the life of Hitler. The humor took political incorrectness to a new level, which Brooks defended by saying that he had "to bring Hitler down with ridicule. It's been one of my life-long jobs – to make the world laugh at Adolf Hitler."

On television, one of the most popular programs of the 1990s was *Seinfeld*, a comedy about "nothing." Set in New York, the program had four main characters: Jerry Seinfeld, a comedian; George Costanza, played by Jason *Alexander and based on the life of the show's co-creator, Larry David; Elaine Benes, played by Julia *Louis-Dreyfus; and the lovable but loopy Kramer, portrayed by Michael Richards, based on a real New Yorker named Kramer. Many scenes were shot in a reproduction of a Manhattan diner and explored familiar problems among singles in the city.

In 2004 the Jewish Museum celebrated its 100th birthday, having achieved the status of one of the city's major art museums. The museum began as a repository of Jewish culture but became a significant force in the art world, unafraid to mount exhibitions with provocative themes that challenged and sometimes angered visitors. Before World War II, it bought important Judaica and became an important home to objects from a lost civilization. It expanded in 1983, adding exhibition space and a kosher café. Membership reached 11,250 and visitors reached more than 200,000 a year by around 2005. The museum was not the only repository of Jewish heritage. In 2003 a Center for Jewish History opened in four buildings in the Chelsea neighborhood of Manhattan. The center's members include: the American Jewish Historical Society, the American Sephardi Federation, the Leo Baeck Institute, the Yeshiva University Museum, and the YIVO Institute for Jewish Research. At the end of the 20th century, the Museum of Jewish Heritage opened at the foot of Manhattan as a living memorial to the Holocaust. The museum honored those who died by celebrating their lives. Its core exhibition of photographs, personal objects, and original films illustrated the story of Jewish heritage in the 20th century.

Perhaps the best-known cultural center in New York was the 92nd Street Y, a multifaceted institution and cultural center founded in 1874 by German-Jewish professionals. It grew from an organization guided by Jewish principles but serving people of all races and faiths. In 2006, it was serving over 300,000 people annually in 200 programs a day. Its programming encompassed Jewish education and culture, concerts featuring classical, jazz, and popular music, humanities classes, dance performances, film screenings, a nursery school, etc.

RACE RELATIONS. The most densely populated major city in North America, New York became known as "the melting pot" because of its hordes of immigrants from diverse places in Europe. But that sobriquet took on new meaning in the 1960s and later in a changing city as advocates for civil rights stepped up pressure for equal treatment in schools, housing, and employment. In 1984, the Rev. Jesse Jackson became the second black American to mount a nationwide campaign for President of the United States, running as a Democrat. A major controversy erupted early in the campaigns when Jackson, speaking to reporters, referred to Jews as "hymies" and to New York City as "Hymietown." Later he made a perfunctory apology. While Jews, themselves victims of discrimination, had lived side-by-side with blacks for decades, and had been prominent in leadership and financial support for civil rights causes, they, and the city, were living in a new time. Crime was high on the list of concerns in the late 1960s and 1970s, drugs appeared to be easy to come by and many whites and blacks were eyeing each other warily. In 1991, in what came to be an iconic moment in the relationship between Jews and blacks in the city, a car in the motorcade of the Lubavitch grand rabbi, Menachem M. Schneerson, swerved onto a sidewalk, killing a 7-year-old black boy, Gavin Cato. The accident, combined with simmering tensions between Orthodox Jews and black residents, created a cauldron of ethnic suspicions. Three hours later, a group of black youths, incited by cries of "go get a Jew," attacked Yankel Rosenbaum, an Australian Lubavitch student, apparently in retaliation. Four days of rioting and violence engulfed Crown Heights, headquarters of the Lubavitch, and a prosecutor called the crimes "emblematic of the worst kind of violence and religious hatred this city has every seen." Fueling the violence was a deep-rooted belief among many blacks in Crown Heights that Jews received preferential treatment, not only from the police but also in city services. (In fact, studies after the disturbances showed that black organizations in Crown Heights received more city and state money than many Ḥasidic organizations.) Before his death, Rosenbaum identified Lemrick Nelson Jr., then 16, as his assailant. A bloody knife was found in Nelson's possession, and Nelson confessed the murder to the police. But a jury of six blacks, four Hispanics and two whites acquitted him. A day later, the jury members joined Nelson and his lawyer in a New York restaurant to celebrate the verdict. In a second trial, in 2003, Nelson was found guilty of violating Rosenbaum's civil rights, but the jury found that he had not directly caused Rosenbaum's death. The hate-crime killing seemed to have symbolized much of what had gone wrong in the special relationship between blacks and Jews in the city and was tirelessly debated on the streets, in the media, and in the courts. It took years for the case to be settled, and passions aroused by the incident were slow to cool. For David N. Dinkins, the city's first black mayor, Crown

Heights became a crushing political weight, and he was defeated when he sought re-election. Because the case took so many years in the courts, many youths in Crown Heights interviewed in the early years of the 21st century were barely aware of the circumstances of the deaths.

While relations between blacks and Jews were sometimes fragile in New York, Jews in the early 21st century were thrust into the debate over events in Israel, particularly on college campuses, as professors and students took a hostile approach to developments in the Middle East. On the campuses of Columbia University and Barnard, for instance, pro-Israel students said they had been intimidated by professors of Middle Eastern studies both in and out of the classroom. Symbolically, the incident pointed to a mood on American campuses skeptical of Israeli activities and sympathetic to Palestinian complaints, views originally espoused and pursued by the New Left of the 1960s and 1990s.

UJA-FEDERATION AND ITS ROLE IN THE COMMUNITY. As the largest avenue of philanthropy in New York and North America, UJA-Federation consistently ranked in the top tier of *The Chronicle of Philanthropy's* listing of U.S. charities that raised the most in donations from individuals, foundations, and corporations. The only institutions that raised more funds made national appeals (American Red Cross) or used funds primarily for endowment and plant rather than programs (universities, hospitals, and museums), making UJA-Federation of New York the largest broadly-based local philanthropy in the United States. In 2005, its campaign year closed at a record-breaking $231,347,113, including $140 million from its annual campaign, $71.9 million in planned giving and endowments, and $15.9 million raised through capital gifts and special initiatives. An additional $3.3 million was contributed to an emergency relief fund. The total combined budget of UJA-Federation's local network of agencies exceeded $1 billion.

In 1973, at the outbreak of the Yom Kippur War, community leaders combined the Federation campaign with a special United Jewish Appeal Drive called the Israel Emergency Fund. After raising a record $100 million, the UJA-Federation Joint Campaign was created in July 1974 and Israel became the primary Jewish concern of the bulk of New York Jews. To meet both local and overseas needs, the joint effort raised an average of $100 million annually, reaching $110 million by 1983.

In 1999, UJA-Federation of New York became the first federation in the country to see the division of "domestic" and "overseas" as anachronistic and to instead organize its planning and allocations around types of services like health and human services, Jewish education and identity building, and Jewish peoplehood (rescue, resettlement, and fostering connections between Jewish communities in New York, Israel, and around the world).

As political, social, and technological changes fostered this increasingly global focus, other economic, social, and tax law changes forced changes in how the federation raised its funds. The primary vehicle for fundraising remained the Annual Campaign. At the time, 80 to 90 percent of the funds came from just 10 to 20 percent of the donors. While efforts continued to be made to broaden the base, through direct marketing (mail and phone) and the Internet, the majority of the organization's fundraising efforts were targeted at higher-end donors through one-on-one relationships and to mid-level donors at more than 700 fundraising events each year targeting specific trades and professions, synagogues, communities, women, and families. UJA-Federation also opened full-service offices in Westchester (1988) and Long Island (1989), where affluent Jewish populations resided. The Annual Campaign reached over $120 million per year from over 75,000 donors in the first years of the 21st century. At the same time, the donor base was shrinking (as recently as 1996, there had been over 91,000 donors), cuts in government spending for social services placed significant pressure on the agencies, and the modest increases in the campaign were counterbalanced by the effects of inflation.

By the end of the 20th century, needs had further shifted. The majority of Jews in New York were now long-time Americans who no longer needed help with the most basic needs and with integration into American society. The enormous wave of immigration from the former Soviet Union slowed down by the mid-1990s, and immigration was not anticipated ever to reach such heights again. In the 21st century, UJA-Federation's mission was revised to place equal emphasis on caring for those in need, rescuing those in harm's way, and renewing and strengthening the Jewish people in New York, Israel, and around the world. The share of local unrestricted grants for community centers, human-service agencies, and Jewish education increased by 11 percent between 1995 and 2003, while the share of grants to hospitals and geriatric centers decreased by 98 percent and 9 percent, respectively.

For the human-service agenda, the need to provide services to the most vulnerable continued. Despite the upward mobility of much of the community, significant pockets of poverty existed, particularly in Brooklyn and Queens. Publication in 1971 of "The Invisible Jewish Poor," by Anne Wolfe, revealed widespread poverty among Jews, with particular emphasis on senior citizens. The Metropolitan Council on Jewish Poverty was created in 1972 to provide clothing, food, housing, and job-placement services to Jewish New Yorkers in poverty. As poverty continued and some populations experienced difficulty accessing public services, the New York Legal Assistance Group was organized in 1990 to provide free legal help to at-risk and low-income individuals. In 2005, UJA-Federation developed a comprehensive system for individuals and families coping with terminal illness, helping them access medical, social, psychological, and spiritual care through three regional care centers, and opened the first and only state-certified residential hospice under Jewish auspices in New York State.

[Jennifer Rosenberg (2nd ed.)]

RUSSIAN JEWS. Mention "Russian Jews in New York" and what immediately comes to mind for most New Yorkers is

Brighton Beach – a garish, boisterous strip of Russian restaurants, nightclubs, and specialty food stores hunkered under the rumbling elevated subway line. A block or two away is the nearby boardwalk, one of New York's great people-watching locations in the summer, where svelte "New Russians" enjoy caviar and *blini* at a string of outdoor cafes, while babushkas with golden teeth sit on nearby benches watching their grandchildren play, and knots of men sit at tables playing chess and backgammon.

Yet Brighton is only the tip of the iceberg of Russian-speaking New York – a sprawling human archipelago of 350,000 people, 70 to 80% of whom are Jewish. According to a 2003 population survey conducted by UJA-Federation, 19% of the Jews in the five boroughs of New York were Russian-speakers. The survey found that 62% lived in Brooklyn (124,000), 19% in Queens (39,000); 5% in Staten Island (11,000), 5% in Nassau County (10,000), and 4% in Manhattan (9,000). Russians made up 27% of Brooklyn's Jewish community, 21% of Queens Jewry, and 26% of Staten Island's. It was believed that there were as many as 50,000 Russian-speaking Jews in the suburbs of northern New Jersey.

The Russian-speaking community got its start in southern Brooklyn during the mid-1970s but spread far beyond that neighborhood east to the more upscale marine communities of Manhattan Beach and Sheepshead Bay, and west to scruffy Coney Island, where it abutted African-American and Hispanic communities. The Russians then spread north to Bensonhurst, which they shared with Italian-Americans, Ocean Parkway, which had a large Syrian Jewish population, and Midwood, where they intersected with Pakistanis and Arab-Americans.

Away from Brighton Beach and Brooklyn, a second huge enclave of Russian speakers, the exotic Bukharan Jewish community of Persian-speaking Jews from *Uzbekistan, *Tadjikistan, Kyrgyzstan, Kazakhstan and Turkmenistan, all part of the former Soviet Union, set up home and culture in the Central Queens communities of Rego Park, Forest Hills, and Kew Gardens. There, 50,000 Bukharan Jews lived in streets filled with Bukharan yeshivot, synagogues, and restaurants/nightclubs, from which the sound of sinuous but exuberant Bukharan music exploded into the night. Although Bukhara is a city in Uzbekistan, the term Bukharan refers to all Central Asian Jews who speak Bukhari, a Jewish dialect of Persian. Bukharans celebrate and commemorate in big ways. Nightly, the community turned out for events: weddings, bar mitzvahs, birthdays, cultural presentations or memorials. Whereas most of their homes in Europe faced inner courtyards, in Queens they lived in cramped apartments, so restaurants became their courtyards. The neighborhood, along Queens Boulevard, from Rego Park to Forest Hills to Kew Gardens to Briarwood, featured small businesses runs by Bukharans and ethnic specialties like fried fish, dried fruits, and Samarkand raisins. Kosher bakeries with tandor ovens dispensed crusty round breads called non, topped with black sesame seeds, baked on the clay walls. Noni toki, a domed matzolike bread, was also a favorite, as were samosi, a pastry filled with a nut mixture, and lavz, a mixture of nuts and spices compressed into a flat bar. Most community events involved live music, whether the classical tradition of the shash maqam, a repertory of vocal and instrumental sounds, folk songs, or Russian pop. The Bukharan Jewish National Theater performed regularly, sometimes using its other name, Vozrozhdenie (Russian for renaissance). Twenty synagogues served the community; their prayer books featured Hebrew on one side and a Russian transliteration on the other.

In that area, too, were the smaller but still substantial Oriental communities of Georgian and Mountain Jews, who hailed from *Azerbaijan and the northern *Caucasus. Some lived in Washington Heights at the uppermost tip of Manhattan, an area that attracted a community of so-called Russian intelligentsia – artists, writers, and bohemians. Over the years, many Russian families moving into the middle class left the gritty streets of Brooklyn for semi-suburban Staten Island, while others moved on to the commuter towns of northern and central New Jersey, as well as communities in Long Island, Westchester and southern Connecticut.

The origin of the emigration goes back to the period directly after the Six-Day War of 1967, when Soviet Jews giddy with the smashing military victory of the Israel Defense Forces against the armed forces of Egypt and Syria, armed to the hilt by the Soviet government, began to shake off their fear of the Soviet regime and demanded to be allowed to repatriate to Israel.

By the early 1970s, the Soviet government, seeking détente with the West, began to allow some Soviet Jews to leave for Israel on humanitarian grounds, for family reunification. It was during this period that many Soviet Jews who received invitations ("*vysov*") from real or supposed relatives in Israel managed to get out of the Soviet Union, "dropped out" along the way to Israel in Vienna, and instead applied to emigrate to the United States as political refugees. Though the Israeli government objected strongly to the dropout phenomenon and chastised those who decided to go West, the U.S. Jewish community leadership upheld the principle of freedom of choice and by the late 1970s as many or more Soviet Jews were coming to the U.S. as to Israel. Soviet Jewish immigration to the U.S. started en masse.

Close to half of all Soviet Jews headed for New York City and a significant number of families and individuals who were brought to smaller communities across the U.S. under the auspices of local Jewish communities also eventually headed for New York, the only city where it soon became possible to lose oneself in a largely Russian environment.

About a third of the Russian-speaking Jewish population in New York at the beginning of the 21st century arrived during the 1970s. The New York Association of New Americans (NYANA) provided them with housing, language training, and help in finding jobs, began routing many Russian families to southern Brooklyn, a strongly Jewish area with excellent low-rent housing stock that had become increasingly down at the heels as American-born Jewish families left. The rollicking environment of crass mercantilism and *joie de vivre* for which Brighton Beach became known had much in common with the spirit of Odessa on the Black Sea, but even many Jews from very different environments like Moscow and Leningrad initially moved to Brighton so they could live in a Russian linguistic and cultural environment.

By the late 1970s, restaurants and businesses catering to the Russian community began to spring up, helping to bring renewed economic vigor and stabilizing real estate values.

As a result of 35 to 40 years of immigration, 700,000 Soviet-born Jews were living in the U.S., about half of them, or 350,000, chose New York and its vicinity as their permanent home. By any account, the number exceeded those of Russia and Ukraine combined, making New York the world's most populous Russian-Jewish city. The 1990s arrivals differed from their predecessors in many respects. The refugees of the 1970s tended to be ideologically deeply anti-Communist and anti-Soviet, ready to risk everything, including a term in prison, for a chance to get to the West. The refugees of the 1990s came at a time of virtually free emigration after Communism had collapsed, and were more inclined to be pursuers of a better life.

Since education was always a primary social value, Russian Jewish immigrants came with a high level of educational attainment. Their striving for education continued in America, where they made up the best-educated group in U.S. immigration history. Virtually all younger Russian Jews went to college, and New York city, state, and private colleges were full of the Russian-speakers. In 2005, two Russian-Jewish students, Lev Sviridov from the City College and Eugene Shenderov from Brooklyn College, won highly competitive and prestigious Rhodes scholarship for graduate education in Oxford.

[Sam Kliger and Walter Ruby (2nd ed.)]

NEIGHBORHOODS. One of the defining characteristics of New York are the neighborhoods, especially for Jews, who tended to live among fellow religionists for a variety of reasons, including proximity to local synagogues, friends, and familiar foods. Indeed, the history of New York Jewry is intertwined with the history of the neighborhoods: some with accommodating welcome mats, some achieving smashing successes, some declining over the years, some being reborn.

Following are snapshots of four local areas that have a distinctive Jewish flavor and history:

Boro Park. With the largest ultra-Orthodox Jewish enclave in the world outside Jerusalem, Boro Park combined the atmosphere and strictures of a 19th-century European religious-based village with many of the trappings of a 21st-century American consumer-oriented society. As home to several Ḥasidic sects, including the Bobover, Belz, Satmar, Stolin Vizhnitz, Munkacz, Sprinka, Klausenberg, Gerer, and Pupa, Boro Park was a center of Jewish learning and devotion, with hundreds of synagogues and yeshivas, and a Yiddish-speaking community where the rich, poor, and working class could shop in high-priced and low-priced stores and buy kosher specialties from well-stocked supermarket shelves.

Boro Park, also spelled Borough Park, was a mainly rural part of south-central Brooklyn in the last years of the 19th century. One of the original settlers, Electus B. Litchfield, built a subdivision in 1887 and called it Blythebourne. In 1898 State Senator William H. Reynolds bought a tract of land abutting the east side of New Utrecht Avenue, extending from 43rd to 60th Streets. He called it Borough Park, and it eventually swallowed Blythebourne. All that remained of that name by the 21st century was Blythebourne Station, the local post office.

The first synagogue in the area was built in 1904 as Russian Jews, living in the teeming and overcrowded Lower East Side of Manhattan, trickled in to join Italian and Irish families in single-family attached houses. During the Brooklyn real-estate boom of the 1920s, the area thrived in a confluence of democratic trends.

After World War II, the Italian and Irish families began moving out, and Jews who practiced a modern Orthodox faith spread to neighboring Flatbush and Midwood. For the Jewish community, it was the heyday of assimilation, when most were intent upon being inconspicuous. The Ḥasidim, practicing an 18th century form of ecstatic Judaism rich with ceremony and prayer, were different. Wearing beards and side curls, black hats and 19th-century suits and speaking Yiddish, the men stood out. The conservatively garbed women, in wigs and often pushing baby carriages, kept to themselves and their tight-knit families and friends. Many mainstream Jews found Ḥasidim, at first a tiny minority in New York, self-righteous, almost embarrassing, unsettling reminders of what these secular co-religionists once were. Tentatively, the Ḥasidic survivors clustered anew around the few rabbis who had survived the war.

One of the first Ḥasidic groups to move to Boro Park were the Skverer, who trace their roots to Chernobyl, Ukraine. Like other Ḥasidim, who practice an ecstatic brand of Judaism, each sect centers on a charismatic spiritual leader, often called a tzaddik, or righteous one, and on an individual's direct relationship with God. In 1922 Rabbi David Twersky was born in Kishinev, Russia, in a long line of distinguished rabbis. When he was 2, the family moved to the Lower East Side, where his father, Yitzchok, established a synagogue. Yitzchok later moved the synagogue to Williamsburg in Brooklyn and finally to 47th Street in Boro Park. David was 19 when his father died, and he took over the Skverer's leadership. Rabbi Twersky, who raised his sons as though they were in an East European shtetl, aided many victims of the Holocaust in their efforts to emigrate to the United States. He also established a network of yeshivas, separately serving boys, girls, and married men, planting the Old World in the New World of Boro Park.

Rabbi Shlomo Halberstam, a Holocaust survivor, nurtured the postwar rebirth of the Bobover sect, a group based in southeastern Poland that was nearly exterminated by the Nazis. He arrived in New York in the late 1940s, with only his oldest son. Much of his family had been killed. During this period, according to Samuel Heilman, a professor of Jewish studies and sociology at Queens College, the rabbi apparently had a crisis of faith, shaved his beard, and lost his desire to be a rabbi. But he soon recovered, and his change of heart proved inspirational to many Orthodox Jews coping with poverty and psychological distress in the wake of the war. His success in recruiting Jews in America to the Bobov sect was attributed to the fact that he was both nonconfrontational and charismatic. Under about 50 years of his conciliatory leadership, the Bobover became the leading Ḥasidic group in Boro Park, perhaps a third of all the Ḥasidim. The Bobovers tended to look to their grand rabbi more than most sects for advice on business, marriage, and family. Unlike the Satmars and Lubavitch, the Bobovers flourished with little public infighting. The main Bobov synagogue, on 48th Street between 15th and 16th Avenues, was known as Bobover Promenade. The Bobover, who like other Ḥasidism did not recognize the State of Israel, were conspicuously absent from Satmar-inspired anti-Israel rallies at the United Nations, and the Bobover developed good relations with the more ambiguously Zionistic Klausenbergers and Belzers. Those two groups accepted educational stipends from the Israeli government.

As Boro Park became more Ḥasidic, the community's boundaries were considered to be between 12th and 18th Avenues and between 40th and 60th Streets. Its commercial center was 13th Avenue, with its aromatic bakeries, kosher pizzerias, and Judaica shops. But there were no video stores or national retail or food chains on the main shopping streets. The community flourished with the growth of Ḥasidism worldwide. Families grew, not only to follow the Biblical commandment to be fruitful and multiply but to replenish the post-Holocaust Jewish population. The fertility rate in Boro Park was double that of the city as a whole. Families with many children were common, and some had as many as 18 or 19. To accommodate the burgeoning population, homes expanded forward, backward, upward and even downward. In 1992 the city created a special zoning district in Boro Park so homeowners could legally build on 65% of their lot, and the footage for setbacks and rear yards was halved. From 1990 to 1998, the city's Building Department issued more permits, 822, for private construction projects of new homes and additions than in any other residential neighborhood of Brooklyn. Every other family was adding wings or floors just to keep pace with its growing brood. Sometimes wealthy families bought adjacent lots, razed row houses and built imposing single-family edifices from scratch. Others lived in a near-chronic state of renovation.

About 80% of the roughly 100,000 people were Jewish, according to estimates by Community Board 12 and local residents, early in the 21st century. Pockets of Moslems, Italian, and Irish as well as Mexicans, Chinese, Pakistanis, Russians, and Poles also lived in Boro Park, which in the early years of the 21st century also encompassed parts of Bensonhurst, Kensington and Flatbush. The boundaries were determined to be 8th Avenue to 20th Avenue, and 37th to 62d Streets and Dahill Road.

Life in Boro Park was decidedly different from other parts of New York. At 8 A.M. every morning, an armada of yellow buses lined up to transport girls in long skirts and boys in curly earlocks to the 65 religious schools in the neighborhood. Many blocks had several synagogues, from hole-in-the-wall shtiebels to vast tiered synagogues, with a ceiling that reached three stories above long wood tables where clusters of boys and men pored over Hebrew texts late into the night. One synagogue, Shomre Shabos, was called the local minyan factory. From dawn until 1:30 A.M., quorums of 10 men shuffled in and about, arranging themselves in parallel lines, swaying back and forth in prayer.

Rich, poor, and working class lived side by side, praying together and sending their children to the same schools. The wealthy paid tuitions that supported the neighborhood's many religious schools and cobbled together a kind of private social service system, complete with group homes and a volunteer ambulance corps. There were perhaps 150 interest-free loan associations to help the needy. Every night, young men in worn black coats and hats knocked on the back doors of the larger homes seeking charity. Every Thursday afternoon, in a converted transit way station, dozens of students and volunteers packed hundreds of Sabbath charity boxes with eggs, milk, noodles, chickens, and kosher wine. By evening, 65 young men packed the boxes into cars and vans to drop on the doorsteps of the poor families.

From sundown Friday to sundown Saturday, all the shops – perhaps 400 – were closed (while the synagogues were full). A car that traversed the neighborhood on the Sabbath was looked on unkindly, and occasionally was stoned. After Shabbat and on Sunday, most residents shopped, strolled, and frequented kosher food shops like Mendel's 18th Avenue Pizza near 50th Street, where falafel, pirogies, or blintzes could be munched, Amnon's Kosher Pizza on 13th Avenue, the Donut Shop on 13th Avenue and 47th Street, where omelets and pancakes were also on the menu, and China Glatt, on 13th Avenue at 45th Street, one of the few nondairy restaurants. There were no bars on 13th Avenue and there were no parks in Boro Park.

[Stewart Kampel (2nd ed.)]

Upper West Side. Running diagonally across Manhattan, from the lower tip of Manhattan to the island's upper reaches, Broadway on the Upper West Side serves as the areas backbone and heart. Originally a Native American trail and built as Bloomingdale Road in 1703, Broadway, the widest street in the neighborhood, is a well-worn pathway to synagogues, famous food stores, Jewish cultural sites, and schools. With its parklike island, Broadway is also the communal front stoop, the place of serious and friendly networking, or schmoozing, among friends, neighbors, local politicians, and community leaders. The Upper West Side stretches from 59th to 110th Street, from Central Park West to Riverside Drive, and is sandwiched between two large city parks, Central Park and Riverside Park.

According to the Jewish Community Study of 2002, the Jewish population of the Upper West Side is 59,400 (the number of Jewish households is 37,100, with 71,800 people living in those households). Thirty percent of the households belong to a synagogue, with 14% affiliating with Orthodox, 25% with Conservative, and 28% with Reform; 16% identify as non-denominational and 13% as secular. One segment of the community is heavily committed to Jewish life, with 47% of neighborhood children having some day school education, and 64% having visited Israel. On the other hand, the intermarriage rate of 35% is slightly higher than the overall rate for Manhattan.

Although the Upper West Side does not have the largest Jewish population in Manhattan – there are more Jews living on the Upper East Side – the Upper West Side has much more of the distinctive feel of a Jewish neighborhood. Its streets are lined with kosher restaurants and food stores, supermarkets with kosher sections, Jewish bookstores and Judaica shops, schools – from Chabad to the first Reform day school in the country – and cultural institutions like Makor, a division of the 92nd St Y and the Jewish Community Council of Manhattan. Posters hung on street lamps and storefronts announce Jewish speakers and concerts. Its many synagogues range from grand to humble, with rich history behind them. Early mornings, it is not unusual to see people rushing off to shuls for the daily minyan (women too, as there are daily egalitarian services) and to the recently-built JCC for daily meditation.

But it is on Shabbat and holidays that the Jewish character of the neighborhood is most visible. Many families and individuals, dressed up to varying degrees, walk comfortably to the synagogues. An *eruv* strung around the neighborhood enables observant Jews to carry items on Shabbat and push baby carriages, activities otherwise not permitted.

The history of the neighborhood as a Jewish area is closely tied to the history of its synagogues. The neighborhood began to develop as a residential area after 1904, when the subway was constructed, connecting the West Side to midtown and Lower Manhattan. As the area became populated, several synagogues moved uptown, both following and leading their congregants, who moved from Lower Manhattan and points in between. Congregation Shearith Israel, the Spanish-Portuguese Synagogue – the oldest synagogue in New York, founded in 1654 – moved to its striking neoclassical building on Central Park West and 70th Street in 1897. Congregation B'nai Jeshurun – the first Ashkenazi synagogue in New York and the second oldest congregation, having broken from Shearith Israel in 1825 – moved to its Moorish Revival structure, on 88th Street between Broadway and West End, in 1918.

The Reform Rodeph Shalom, founded on the Lower East Side in 1842, moved to its Romanesque building on 83rd Street off Central Park West in 1930, from an intermediary building in the East 60s. In celebration of the synagogue's 150th anniversary in 1991, Rabbi Robert Levine and 75 congregants retraced the six-mile journey on foot, from Clinton Street, the site of its first building, to West 83rd Street.

Other synagogues in the area, like the Institutional Synagogue (now called the West Side Institutional Synagogue), on 76th Street off Columbus, and Ohab Zedek, on 95th Street off Columbus, moved to the area from Harlem.

The Jewish Center, a modern-Orthodox synagogue on West 86th Street, had its roots on the Upper West Side. Led by Rabbi Mordechai Kaplan, it was the first synagogue-center, founded in 1918 on the philosophy that cultural, recreational and religious activities be incorporated in one institution. When Rabbi Kaplan had disputes with the synagogue, he went on to found the Society for the Advancement of Judaism, one block east on 86th Street in 1922, which would become the first Reconstructionist synagogue.

All the synagogues were functioning in 2006.

In the years before and after World War II, many European immigrants moved to the neighborhood, including refugees and Holocaust survivors. Clusters of Jews from Austria, Czechoslovakia, and also Iraq settled in the area, and brought a foreign flavor and accent to the restaurants and cafes. Many who came from European cities felt at home in the stately prewar apartment buildings along Broadway and West End Avenue, built in the similar styles to those they had left behind.

In the 1950s and 60s, new Jewish residents trickled in, while many Jews left the neighborhood for the suburbs and other places in the city. But in the late 1960s and 1970s, younger Jews began moving to the area; the *Havurah* movement, embracing small groups that met for study, prayer, and to observe life cycles, established a strong base on the West Side as progressive Jews, many influenced by the counterculture movement, sought to create alternative, traditional communities based on egalitarianism. Members of groups like the New York *Havurah* sought new ways to reinvigorate ritual with meaning, much in the spirit of the highly successful *Jewish Catalog*, a best-selling book that found an audience among the baby-boom generation. Rejecting existing religious institutions, they favored participatory prayer in intimate settings, often meeting in members' homes. Many leaders of the *Havurah* community would go on to take leadership roles in the New York Jewish community decades later.

One such group began meeting at Ansche Chesed, a once thriving synagogue and community center with a substantial congregation at 100th Street and West End Avenue whose membership had dwindled, and helped bolster and revitalize that congregation. The synagogue and its community center were saved from planned destruction by a community effort that saw Montessori and another locally based, parent-run day-care center rent space in the complex. Since then, many Jewish and non-Jewish organizations and projects co-habitated and revitalized the "plant." That synagogue became a new model: a congregation made up of several lay-led services, going on simultaneously on Shabbat. Rabbi Michael Strassfeld, a co-editor of *The Jewish Catalog* (before he was ordained), was the first rabbinic leader of the reconstituted Ansche Chesed (and later would go on to lead the Society for the Advancement of Judaism).

At the same time as *Havurah* movement was getting under way, another significant development in Jewish life was unfolding about thirty blocks south. Under the leadership of Rabbi Shlomo Riskin, Lincoln Square Synagogue, a modern-Orthodox institution, was founded in 1964; its members first met in the Lincoln Towers complex before erecting their own building in 1970, with an unusual sanctuary-in-the-round. Rabbi Riskin drew young, professional and single people to the new synagogue, delivering weeknight talks on popular topics like relationships, with Torah underpinnings, to overflow audiences. The synagogue became a meeting spot for Jewish singles, many of whom stayed in the area after marrying. In 1983, Rabbi Riskin and his family, along with several Lincoln Square families, moved to Israel and settled in Efrat, where he served as chief rabbi and headed several educational institutions.

In subsequent years, the Lincoln Square population aged, and the center of young Orthodox Jewish single life moved north, to several synagogues in the West 80s and 90s.

Rabbi Sally Priesand, American's first female rabbi, who served the Stephen Wise Free Synagogue for several years beginning in 1972, and Rabbi Marshall Meyer, who died in 1993, made significant contributions to Jewish life in the area. Rabbi Meyer, after spending 25 years in Buenos Aires and founding Jewish institutions there, returned to New York in 1985 and spearheaded the revival of B'nai Jeshurun. Its Friday night services, filled with music, singing, and spirited prayer, attracted more than a thousand individuals, including many young people. The synagogue was nondenominational, having broken with the Conservative movement over the issue of gay ordination. Committed to social action, B'nai Jeshurun became a sought-after model for synagogues around the country.

In 1991, after its roof collapsed, the congregation of B'nai Jeshurun was invited by its neighbors on West 86th Street, the Church of St. Paul and St. Andrew, to hold services in their sanctuary. Together, congregants of the two institutions created a large banner, with the words of Psalm 133: "How good it is when brothers and sisters dwell together in harmony." It hangs at the front of the church. Even after the synagogue roof was repaired, the congregation continued to use the church on Shabbat mornings and holidays, having outgrown the synagogue space.

Rabbi Shlomo Carlebach, the descendent of a German rabbinical family, was known internationally for his neo-Ḥasidic musical style, deep and joyful spirituality and extensive outreach. In his final years, he was based on the Upper West Side, at the Carlebach Shul on West 79th Street. He died in 1994, and the Orthodox congregation continued his tradition of welcoming people from all backgrounds.

Although Lincoln Square Synagogue was the last Upper West Side synagogue to construct a new building, several new congregations were founded without buildings and used the facilities of schools and community centers. These minyan groups stressed community and took prayer seriously; their services were traditional and experimental, not necessarily defined by denominational boundaries.

Along with synagogues of every denomination, there were "beginner's services" in various synagogues as well as smaller congregations known as shtiblach, usually named for the rabbi who led them, and located in brownstones on the side streets. The area also had a Chabad and other Ḥasidic presence: it was not uncommon to see men walking on Shabbat in traditional shtreimels and bekeshes, long black tailored coats.

There was fluidity among the congregations, with some people belonging to several institutions at once, others who attended services in different places, and people who moved from synagogue to synagogue. In the years before 9/11, when there were fewer security concerns, synagogues jointly held outdoor Simchat Torah celebrations, with dancing in the streets, and some returned to the practice as tensions eased. The synagogues and minyan groups convened together for Yom HaShoah commemorations. On the first day of Rosh Hashanah, the Jewish community is out in force. It gathers on the walkway above the banks of the Hudson River for the ceremony of *Tashlikh*, casting breadcrumbs into the water and reciting verses from Scripture relating to repentance. It is one of the more colorful scenes of city life, with fashionably dressed women, men in new suits, and some in more casual clothing exchanging greetings of the new year.

Some of the synagogues featured soup kitchens and operated shelters for the homeless. Some housed nursery and afternoon schools.

A neighborhood landmark that drew shoppers as well as tourists, Zabar's was a long-running family business on Broadway, featuring traditional Jewish specialties along with other food, fancy and plain. Barney Greengrass, an appetizing store and café on Amsterdam Avenue, was famous for its smoked fish, and Murray's, on Broadway, was a neighborhood favorite for similar fare. The dairy restaurants of decades ago, where neighborhood habitués like Isaac Bashevis Singer – the Nobel laureate who had a section of West 86th Street named in his honor – are no more. They gave way to kosher steak houses, sushi bars, pizza shops, and places that served Moroccan, Yemenite, and other ethnic food.

On any given evening on the Upper West Side, it was possible to hear Jewish music, attend a kosher cooking class, or study Jewish texts, listen to a Jewish author read from a new work, participate in a healing service, or sit in on a panel discussion on Jewish issues of the day. That tradition was likely to continue.

[Sandee Brawarsky (2nd ed.)]

Washington Heights. With its hills and parks overlooking the Hudson and Harlem Rivers, Washington Heights at the northern end of Manhattan proved especially attractive to European immigrants. The Heights was one of the last parts of the island to be settled. Before World War I, the areas east of Broadway and south of 181st Street became an urban neighborhood, but the more affluent areas to the north and west were settled mainly in the 1920s and 1930s. Virtually all the neighborhood housing consisted of five- and six-story brick apartment houses.

The first Jews in Washington Heights were mainly immigrants from Eastern Europe and their children who moved to the Heights from the Lower East Side or from neighboring Harlem, especially in the 1920s and 1930s. A number of institutions that were founded in Harlem moved north with their followers and constituents. Although located in Manhattan, Washington Heights resembled Jewish areas of second settlement in the Bronx and Brooklyn more than other parts of its own borough. Jews never made up a majority of the population, though they were probably between 35 and 40% of the total. Other ethnic groups included persons of Irish, Greek, and Armenian background. Washington Heights was considered a prestigious middle-class area, and in 1928 Yeshiva University relocated to Amsterdam Avenue in Washington Heights precisely because of the prestige of the address. The Moorish building of the university's main building became the nucleus of a campus that sprawled over a number of blocks on the eastern end of the neighborhood between 184th and 187th Street.

In the late 1930s the Jewish community was reinforced by a large influx of German-speaking Jews fleeing the Nazis. In all, 20,000 to 25,000 German-speaking Jews settled in, constituting about 40% of the Jewish population. Although Washington Heights was the home of the largest concentration of German Jewish escapees from Nazi Germany, its residents were not typical of the overall wave of German Jewish immigrants of the 1930s. Those in Washington Heights were atypical in their greater religious traditionalism, their overwhelmingly South German and often rural background, and their relatively modest socioeconomic and education levels. Though more "bourgeois" than most immigrants to the United States, the German Jews of Washington Heights bore little resemblance to the famous "intellectual immigrants" of the 1930s.

Most of the newcomers arrived between 1938 and 1940. Some moved to Washington Heights immediately. Others joined them. In the late 1930s, the newcomers began to build a network of institutions and give the neighborhood a German Jewish atmosphere. Social clubs and places of entertainment played an important role in the life of the community until about 1950, although many German Jews also found culture and entertainment outside of Washington Heights. After World War II German Jewish institutional life in the neighborhood was concentrated in the numerous immigrant synagogues founded between 1935 and 1949. Besides a dozen congregations organized by the immigrants themselves, there were several pre-existing synagogues in which they gained a majority and heavily influenced the congregational atmosphere. The synagogues influenced by German Jews in Washington Heights stretched across a broad spectrum, from the Reform Hebrew Tabernacle to right-wing Orthodox congregations.

Most of the synagogues followed Orthodox forms, though in some of them strictly observant Jews were in the minority. The largest German Jewish congregation in Washington Heights was K'hal Adath Jeshurun, founded in 1938 by former members of the separatist Orthodox community of Frankfurt, which had once been headed by Samson Raphael *Hirsch. The congregation was called Breuer's, after its first rabbi, Joseph *Breuer (1882–1980), Samson Raphael Hirsch's grandson. The Breuer community established an all-encompassing European-style communal structure highly unusual for the United States. Besides its large synagogue, social hall, and burial society, it had its own *kashrut* supervision, *mikveh*, school system from nursery school through postgraduate yeshivah, synagogue newspaper (*Mitteilungen*), and charitable and women's groups. Most of the other German synagogues in the neighborhood were also large and formal, often with several cantors, a choir, and an involved institutional structure.

Although German Jews were far from a majority of the population of Washington Heights, the German Jewish character of the neighborhood was evident in many subtle ways. Many of the immigrants spoke German at home and on the street, even after they learned some English, although the German language was almost never used in shop signs or public notices. German was also used in synagogue sermons and bulletins well into the 1960s. From the mid-1950s to the early 1970s, there was a slow transition to English after which German disappeared from every official capacity in synagogue life, though individual congregants sometimes continued conversing in German.

German Jewish culture was also evident in the conservative styles of dress and formalism in interpersonal behavior. German immigrants could often be seen sitting on benches in the park or standing in groups on the sidewalk conversing quietly in German. Some sat for hours over a cup of coffee in local restaurants talking about the olden days. As a sophisticated and educated group, many German Jews brought their libraries of German literature with them and attended classical concerts in other parts of the city. Even synagogue social events sometimes included classical music. These interests in high culture were not nearly as common among the many rural Jews who settled in Washington Heights. In general the immigrants who came to Washington Heights had a far stronger Jewish identity and more intense Jewish religious practice than German Jews who settled in other neighborhoods. Most severed their sense of connection to Germany after World War II. Though some residents of Washington Heights made occasional visits to Germany, to visit the graves of their relatives, see their hometowns, or do business, a larger number visited Israel, with which they had a far closer emotional tie.

Like most other immigrants, the great majority of the German Jews of Washington Heights sent their children to public schools, where they rapidly became acculturated to the English language as well as American political and cultural values. Most gave their children some supplemental Jewish education in synagogue Hebrew schools, though a growing proportion of the Orthodox minority sent their children to Jewish day schools. The American-born generation had little identification with the German culture of their parents, rarely learned German, and almost never spoke it to one another. They also rejected many of the cultural values of their parents, especially what they considered the older generation's formality and rigidity. Members of the second generation saw themselves as American Jews whose German background was only a small part of their identities.

The children of the immigrants generally did well economically and educationally. Unlike most of their parents, they went on to higher education and entered the professions. Probably more than half married outside the German Jewish community (but generally not outside the Jewish community). As they grew up and succeeded, most of the children of the immigrants moved away from Washington Heights to the suburbs or more prestigious neighborhoods in New York. Some of the more successful of the immigrants also moved away.

The overall ethnic makeup of Washington Heights underwent a slow but thoroughgoing change. In the late 1940s and the 1950s, blacks and Hispanics began moving in large numbers into the southern sections of Washington Heights, which soon became merely a part of Harlem. In the 1960s and 1970s people of color slowly became the majority of the population of all of Washington Heights, except a small section of northwest Washington Heights near Fort Tryon Park. Most of the white residents moved away, though German Jewish outmigration may have been a bit slower than the "flight" of other white groups. Washington Heights became a primarily Hispanic neighborhood populated mostly by people from the Dominican Republic. The shops and institutions catered mainly to the new population, with many signs in the Spanish language. The social prestige of the neighborhood declined as crime and drug trafficking increased.

As they became more and more of a minority in the neighborhood, the remaining Jews organized to defend their stake in the area. They ran candidates for the local school board, organized a safety patrol, settled recently arrived Soviet Jews in the neighborhood, and created a Jewish neighborhood council. This council was dominated by the Breuer community, whose role among Jews became ever greater. Unlike other congregations, the Breuer was able to retain a considerable portion of its American-born generations within the neighborhood.

By the late 1980s, the German Jews of Washington Heights were an aging and shrinking community mainly huddled in one part of western Washington Heights. Most of their synagogues closed, moved, or merged, many German Jewish stores and food shops closed, and the German Jewishness of the community became less and less apparent. Besides the remnant of the German Jewish immigrant community, the main Jewish elements that remained were the campus of Yeshiva University and the Russian-speaking recent arrivals, neither of whom interacted very much with the German Jews.

The "decline" of Washington Heights began to be reversed in the late 1990s and thereafter. Two groups of young people began to move into the neighborhood. The first consisted mainly of Orthodox Jewish singles and young couples, often studying at, or recently graduated from, Yeshiva University. They tended to live near the campus in the eastern part of the neighborhood or on Bennett Avenue near the Breuer synagogue. Few of them were of German-Jewish background and most stayed in the area only a few years, but they did give a boost to the German Jews who had remained. The second group consisted of upwardly mobile young professionals attracted by the area's closeness to midtown Manhattan and its picturesque views of the Hudson River. Some of these newcomers were Jews but they rarely showed much interest for the Jewish culture of the neighborhood. They tended to live in co-ops or condominiums on the streets bordering the Hudson River south of Fort Tryon Park, an area that real estate agents began to call "Hudson Heights" to distinguish it from the rest of the neighborhood. This new population brought with it many of the features of gentrification of poor neighborhoods, including finer restaurants and cultural events. By the beginning of the 21st century, real estate values in the area began to skyrocket. The remaining German Jews, in the early 21st century, who had come to America as children or adolescents, were now mostly in their 80s or even older. Whether the Jews ever return in large numbers remains to be seen.

[Steven Lowenstein (2nd ed.)]

Williamsburg. Three bridges unite the boroughs of Manhattan with Brooklyn – the Brooklyn Bridge, the Manhattan Bridge, and the Williamsburg Bridge. After it opened in 1903, the Williamsburg was nicknamed Jews' Highway because it drew immigrants from the teeming Lower East Side to the south Brooklyn neighborhood adjoining the East River. Served by trolley cars and an elevated subway line, Williamsburg became one of New York's major Jewish communities in the early part of the 20th century.

Williamsburgh (the h was later dropped) was first incorporated as a village in 1827, but its history goes back to 1638, when the Dutch West India Company purchased the land from Canarsie Indians. A period of squatting by farmers of various nationalities followed. It did not become a major residential area until 1803, when a real-estate investor, Richard Woodhull, purchased 13 acres of land, to be surveyed by his friend, Jonathan Williams, a grandnephew of Benjamin Franklin who planned and built most of the forts in New York Harbor. Williamsburg would later be named in Williams' honor.

Woodhull and Williams intended the area to be a residential alternative to Manhattan, accessible by ferry. Williamsburg became a city in 1827, with new docks, shipyards, and other businesses that profited from proximity to New York's port. The New York Navy Yard, colloquially known as the Brooklyn Navy Yard, was opened in 1801 and employed 6,000 men by the start of the Civil War. By the 1850s, Williamsburg had grown into a suburban-style city, with 31,000 people, and it was home to resorts, farms, distilleries, and breweries. It later became part of the city of Brooklyn, which joined New York City in 1898. The availability of jobs drew immigrants from Ireland, Italy, Germany, and England.

The character of Williamsburg would change dramatically, though, when the Williamsburg Bridge, built to relieve traffic on the Brooklyn Bridge, caused the displacement of almost 20,000 people and the destruction of their property. With Williamsburg linked to the Lower East Side, farms, resorts and mansions gave way to multiple-unit dwellings to accommodate the waves of immigrants. By the 1920s, the population exceeded 250,000, and the area was one of the most densely populated regions of the country.

In 1938, the growing need for public housing led to the first federal housing project in the nation, the Williamsburg Houses. The project, which cost about $12 million, accommodated 1,622 low-income families in 20 four-story apartment houses. These buildings were the forerunner of a series of low-income and middle-income subsidized housing in the borough and the city. Completed near the end of the Depression, the projects, as they were known, provided clean and fresh apartments for civil servants, small-business owners and others, regardless of religion, and were an oasis of greenery in an area of small, largely dilapidated wood-frame housing. Almost 70 years later, in the 21st century, the projects continued to provide low-rent accommodations to a changing population. The working class influx also fueled an industrial boom, and Williamsburg became a center of manufacturing until a decline in the 1950s.

After World War II, the area was host to the renaissance of the Satmar Ḥasidic sect, which was nearly obliterated by the Nazis, and a majority of Jews living in the neighborhood today are Ḥasidim. The New York Jewish Population Survey of 2002 estimated that 57,600 Jews lived in Williamsburg, 40,000 of them Ḥasidic. In 2006, the Satmar, the men distinctive by their long black coats and *shtreimels*, or fur hats, and the women by their conservative dress and wigs and turbans as head coverings, was believed to be the world's largest Ḥasidic sect with 100,000 adherents. The name Satmar comes from the Romanian Satu Mare, or large village. Members of the Pupa, Wien, and Klausenberger sects, named for the areas of Europe from which they emigrated, also had a presence in Williamsburg.

The explosion of Williamsburg Ḥasidic life began in 1946 with the arrival of the Satmar Grand Rebbe, Joel Teitelbaum, who escaped from Nazi-occupied Hungary and the Bergen-Belsen concentration camp. The community thrived, founding an extensive network of synagogues and yeshivas and organizations like Bikur Cholim, providing help and support for the sick and needy. Overcrowding led followers to establish a satellite community, Kiryas Joel, in Orange County, NY. During the 1950s and subsequent decades Williamsburg's Jews ran the gamut of religious observance and affiliation, but the non-Ḥasidic population gradually declined. When Rabbi Teitelbaum died in 1979, his nephew, Rabbi Moshe Teitelbaum, formerly known as the Sigeter Rebbe, succeeded him. Since 1999, the sect has been engulfed in conflict after Rabbi Teitelbaum named his younger son, Zalman, to lead the central Satmar synagogue, Yetev Lev Bikur Cholim, bypassing his eldest son, Aaron, whose followers were mostly in Kiryas Joel. Factions supporting both brothers battled for years in court, and occasionally on the streets, where their clashes prompted a police response.

Bedford Avenue, with historic brownstones in tip-top condition, was one of the leafier enclaves of Jewish Williamsburg, and was along the route of the annual New York City Marathon. Although they rarely ventured out of their life of study and religious practice, it was not unusual to see the Ḥasidim cheering on the runners and providing refreshments during the race. On one particularly hot day, the Ḥasidim sprayed runners with seltzer, adding to the color of the race. The shopping strip on Lee Avenue had a distinctive Jewish flavor, with decades-old businesses flourishing under signs in Yiddish and English, and restaurants and take-out stores filling the air with the scent of kosher food. Children were everywhere, an average of about eight to a family. By the early years of the century, new grand synagogues were being built by the Satmar, while a few modern Orthodox congregations, like Beth Jacob Ohev Sholom on Rodney Street, persisted.

Beneath the surface of the bustling and thriving community, however, was the reality that Williamsburg harbored one of the poorest Jewish communities in the United States, with an estimated 59 percent living below the poverty line and eligible for government services like food stamps and subsidized housing. Many large families lived in cramped apartments, and it was not uncommon to find bathtubs doubling as beds. Some of the members of the sect supported their families by working in the diamond district in Manhattan, but more commonly the men studied or worked in yeshivahs as teachers, which for many was a calling. Some also earned a kollel, or stipend, for learning. The community itself also provided free food for Shabbat.

Jews were not the only large ethnic group in the neighborhood. Spanish-speaking Latinos or Puerto Ricans had congregated in the area following the end of World War II and the need for affordable housing caused stress between the groups. This conflict required regular intervention and mediation by public officials. In 1997, during the administration of Mayor Rudolph Giuliani, the groups agreed to place proceeds from the sale of city-owned property into a housing fund that would benefit both communities. Amid the conflict, Jews and Hispanics found much common ground, fighting the closing of fire stations and opposing possible environmental hazards like a proposed incinerator on the site of the Brooklyn Navy Yard (since defeated) and hazardous lead paint falling from the Williamsburg Bridge. The area had one of the highest incidences of asthma in the city. Jews and Hispanics joined to address the influx of artists and others fleeing the exorbitant rents of Manhattan studios and apartments. They were drawn to old commercial lofts that the city rezoned for residential use in 1985. Their presence led to the opening of galleries, museums, live-music night clubs, cafes and restaurants and an avant-garde branch of the Museum of Modern Art. The Hasidim, who shun secular culture, called on members of their community to avoid renting to the artists. Both groups feared that they would be priced out of their own neighborhood if developers catered to the newcomers and that the rezoning they fought for to create affordable housing would be exploited for profit. The newcomers, however, helped to stabilize and revive the over-all neighborhood.

In the early 1950s, low-income Williamsburg was the scene of a sweeping transformation when the city planner Robert Moses designed the Brooklyn-Queens Expressway to pass through the neighborhood, cutting it in half and leaving the western segment between the highway and the East River, a destination for poor immigrants, in decline. Some 5,000 people were displaced, and numerous homes and businesses were condemned by eminent domain to clear space for the project. Many later attributed the area's high asthma rate to exhaust from the heavy expressway traffic. The Brooklyn Navy Yard was decommissioned in 1966, although it was sold to New York City and later became a major industrial park, with over 200 business tenants and 3,500 employees.

In addition to rabbinic councils and charities, the area's Jewish community was served by the United Jewish Organizations, an umbrella group affiliated with the Metropolitan Council on Jewish Poverty and the Jewish Community Relations Council of New York. Led for many years by Rabbi David Niederman, the organization lobbied for and administered government funding and acted as liaison with public officials. Jewish leaders played a significant role in charting the future of the neighborhood.

In May, 2005, Mayor Michael Bloomberg and the City Council approved a plan to rezone the North Side of Williamsburg and Greenpoint for residence and a waterfront park as well as luxury high-rises. The population of the area could increase by 40,000. The plan also aimed to attract top-name retailers. Critics lamented that the plan did nothing to return the thousands of lost manufacturing jobs to the neighborhood, which dropped from a peak of 93,000 in 1961 to fewer than 12,000 in 2006. They also feared that the city would not be able to improve transportation and safety in the area, and that it would make Williamsburg more like Manhattan.

[Adam Dickter (2nd ed.)]

BIBLIOGRAPHY: 1654–1870; D. and T. de Sola Pool, *An Old Faith in the New World* (1955); D. de Sola Pool, *Portraits Etched in Stone* (1953); L. Hershkowitz, *Wills of Early New York Jews 1704–1799* (1967); L. Hershkowitz and I.S. Meyer, *Lee Max Friedman Collection of American Jewish Colonial Correspondence: Letters of the Franks Family 1733–1748* (1968); H.B. Grinstein, *Rise of the Jewish Community of New York 1654–1860* (1945); idem, in: HUCA, 18 (1944), 321–52; idem, in: *Jewish Review*, 2 (1944/45), 41–58, 187–203; A.M. Dushkin, *Jewish Education in New York City* (1917); R. Ernst, *Immigrant Life in New York City 1825–1863* (1949); I.J. Benjamin, *Three Years in America 1859–1862*, 1 (1956), 50–85 (trans. from the German). 1870–1920: M. Rischin, *The Promised City: New York's Jews 1870–1914* (1962), incl. bibl.; A.A. Goren, *New York Jews and the Quest for Community: The Kehillah Experiment, 1908–1922* (1970), incl. bibl.; H. Hapgood, *The Spirit of the Ghetto: Studies of the Jewish Quarter of New York* (1902); A. Cahan, *Bleter fun Mayn Lebn*, 5 vols. (1926–31; partial trans. by L. Stein, Eng., 1970); R. Sanders, *The Downtown Jews: Portraits of an Immigrant Generation* (1969); R. Lubove, *The Progressives and the Slums: Tenement House Reform in New York City* (1962); S. Birmingham, *"Our Crowd": The Great Jewish Families of New York* (1967); idem, *The Grandees* (1971); I. Markens, *The Hebrew in America* (1888); *The Jewish Communal Register of New York City, 1917–1918* (1918); J.S. Hertz, *Di Yidishe Sotsyalistishe Bavegung in Amerike* (1954); B.E. Supple, in: *Business History Review*, 31 (Summer, 1957), 143–77; L.P. Gartner, in: AJHSQ, 53 (1964), 264–81; G. Osofsky, *Harlem: The Making of a Ghetto* (1966); M. Rosenstock, *Louis Marshall: Defender of Jewish Rights* (1965); M. Dubofsky, *When Workers Organize: New York City in the Progressive Era* (1968); G. Klaperman, *The Story of Yeshiva University* (1969); N.H. Winter, *Jewish Education in a Pluralistic Society: Samson Benderly and Jewish Education in the United States* (1966); H. Berman, in: Joseph L. Blau et al. (eds.), *Essays on Jewish Life and Thought Presented in Honor of Salo Wittmayer Baron* (1959); M. Berman, in: AJHSQ, 54 (1964), 53–81; T. Levitan, *Islands of Compassion: A History of the Jewish Hospitals of New York* (1964); A. Schoener (ed.), *Portal to America: The Lower East Side 1879–1925* (1967); R. Glanz, *Studies in Judaica Americana* (1970); idem, *Jews and Italians* (1970); C. Reznikoff (ed.), *Louis Marshall: Champion of Liberty; selected papers and addresses*, 2 vols. (1957); M. Weinberger, *Ha-Yehudim ve-ha-Yahadut be-New York* (1886–87); E. Tcherikower et al., *Geshikhte fun der Yidisher Arbeter Bavegung in der Fareynikte Shtatn*, 2 vols. (1943), abbr. trans. rev. ed. A. Antonovsky, *The Early Jewish Labor Movement in the United States* (1961); L.S. Dawidowicz, in: JSOS, 25 (1963), 102–32; idem, in: *For Max Weinreich on his 70th Birthday* (1964), 31–43; Z. Szajkowszki, in: JSOS, 32 (1970), 286–306; A. Gorenstein, in: AJHSQ, 50 (1960/61), 202–38; M. Rischin, *ibid.*, 43 (1953/54), 10–36. 1920–1970: A. Mann, *La Guardia: A Fighter Against His Times, 1882–1933* (1959); idem, *La Guardia Comes to Power, 1933* (1965); T.J. Lowi, *At the Pleasure of the Mayor; Patronage and Power in New York City, 1898–1958* (1964); N. Glazer and D.P. Moynihan, *Beyond the Melting Pot* (1963); Federation of Jewish Philanthropies of New York, *The Golden Heritage* (1969); A. Nevins, *Herbert H. Lehman and His Era* (1963); A.F. Landesman, *Brownsville: The Birth, Development, and Passing of a Jewish Community in New York* (1969); S.S. Wise, *Challenging Years: The Autobiography of Stephen S. Wise* (1949); P.S. Foner, *The Fur and Leather Workers Union: A Story of Dramatic Struggles and Achievements* (1950); B.Z. Hoffman, *Fufzig Yor Klok-Makher Union* (1936); C.S. Liebman, in: AJYB, 66 (1965), 21–97; O.I. Janowsky (ed.), *The American Jew: A Reappraisal* (1964); J.L. Teller, *Strangers and Natives* (1968); S. Poll, *The Ḥasidic Community of Williamsburg; A Study of Sociology of Religion* (1962); AJYB, 31 (1929–30), 203–4; 39 (1937–38), 72; AJYB, 71 (1970), 217–28; W. Herberg, in: AJYB, 53 (1952), 3–74; M.M. Fagen, in: JSS, 1 (Jan., 1939), 73–104; J. Loft, in: JSS, 2 (Jan., 1940), 67–78; D.M. Liberson, in: JSDS, 18 no. 2 (1956), 83–117; B. Lazerwitz, in: JJSO, 3 no. 2 (1961), 254–60; S.P. Abelow, *History of Brooklyn Jewry* (1937); E.J. Lipman and A. Vorspan, *A Tale of Ten Cities* (1962); Federation of Jewish Philanthropies of New York: Demographic Study Committee (C.M. Horowitz and L.J. Kaplan), *Jewish Population of New York Area, 1900–1957* (1959). **ADD. BIBLIOGRAPHY:** Y. Ro'i, *The Struggle for Soviet Jewish Immigration* (1991); Y. Ro'i (ed.), *Jews and Jewish Life in Russia and the Soviet Union* (1995); *Election 2000: Russian Jews as Voters in New York City*, Study Conducted for The American Jewish Committee by Research Institute for New Americans (RINA), The American Jewish Committee (Dec. 2001); N. Foner (ed.), *New Immigrants in New York* (1987); N. Lewin-Epstein, Y. Roi, and P. Ritterband (eds.) *Russian Jews on Three Continents. Migration and Resettlement* (1997); *Presidential Election 2004: Russian Voters*, The American Jewish Committee, Research Institute for New

Americans, Report 2004; *Russian Jewish Immigrants in New York City. Status, Identity, and Integration*, Study Conducted for the American Jewish Committee by Research Institute for New Americans (RINA), The American Jewish Committee (Apr. 2000); N. Strizhevskaya and A. Knopp, *Bukharians in New York. A Review of the Community's Unique Jewish Life and Infrastructure*, Commission on Jewish Identity and Renewal, UJA Federation of New York (Sept. 2, 2004); UJA Federation of New York, *The Jewish Community Study of New York 2002: Highlights*, idem, *The Jewish Community Study of New York: 2002 Geographic Profile*; P. Beck, J.B. Ukeles, and Ron Miller, *The National Jewish Population Survey 2000–2001. Strength, Challenge, and Diversity in the American Jewish Population*, A United Jewish Communities Report in Cooperation with The Mandell L. Berman Institute – North American Jewish Data Bank (Sept. 2003); Z. Gitelman, M. Glants, and M.I. Goldman, M.I. (eds.), *Jewish Life after the U.S.S.R.* (March 2003); R. Pomerance, *Russian Jews: From Clients to Partners*, UJA Federation of New York (Apr. 2004), Homepage http://www.ujafedny.org/site/News2?page=NewsArticle&id=7127; W. Ruby, "Russian Community Melds with American Jewry," in: *The Jewish Week* (Mar. 28, 2003), Homepage http://www.ujafedny.org/site/News2?page=NewsArticle&id=6116; V. Zaslavsky and R.J. Brym, *Soviet Jewish Emigration and Soviet Nationality Policy* (1983); R.O. Freedman (ed.) "*Soviet Jewry in the 1980s: The Politics of Anti-Semitism and Emigration and the Dynamics of Resettlement*" (1989); J. Gorin, "New York's Russian Jews," in: *Insight on the News*, vol. 12 (Oct. 21, 1996); J. Lefkowitz, "The Election and the Jewish Vote," in: *Commentary*, vol. 119 (Feb. 2005); R.J. Brym and R. Ryvkina, *The Jews of Moscow, Kiev, and Minsk: Identity, Antisemitism, and Emigration* (1994); S.J. Gold, "Soviet Jews in the United States, " in: *American Jewish Yearbook 94* (1994); F. Markowitz, *A Community in spite of Itself: Soviet Jewish Émigrés in New York* (1993); B. Kosmin, *The Class of 1979: The "Acculturation" of Jewish Immigrants from the Soviet Union* (1990); W. Ruby, "Russian Jews in America," in: *Jewish World* (Apr. 2–8, 1993); D. Harris, "A Note on the Problem of the 'Noshrim,'" in: *Soviet Jewish Affairs*, 6:2 (1976); idem, *In the Trenches* (2000); S. Kliger, "The Religion of New York Jews from the Former Soviet Union," in T. Carnes and A. Karpathakis (eds.), *New York Glory. Religions in the City* (2001); M. Salz, "The Russians Among us: Their Trials, Triumphs and Struggles to become Jewish Americans," in: *Jewish Exponent* (Apr. 1995); S. Ain, "Ex-Soviet Jews Now Largest Group Settling in City," in: *The Jewish Week* (July–Aug. 1993); R.I. Friedman, "Brighton Beach Goodfellas," in: *Vanity Fair* (Jan. 1993); P.A. Bialor, "Don't Call Us Russians," in: *The New York Times* (Aug. 1994); R. Rosenblatt, "From Russia, with Hope and Fear," in: *The New York Times Magazine* (Nov. 1994); W. Ruby, "Lost in America: The Abandonment of Soviet Jewry," in: *Moment* (Apr. 1995); J. Gorin, "New York's Russian Jews: Streetwise, Conservative," in: *Insight* (Oct. 1996); R. Donadio, "Russian Immigrants Come of Age in 'Little Odessa' Council Race," in: *Forward* (Feb. 2001); S. Brawarsky, "Central Asian Jews Create 'Queensistan,'" in: *The New York Times* (Nov. 2001); P. Kasinitz, A. Zelter-Zubida, and Z. Simakhodskaya, *The Next Generation: Russian Jewish Young Adults in Contemporary New York* (2001); W. Ruby, "To Be Young, Gifted and Pro-Israel," in: *The Jewish Week* (Apr. 2003); idem, "Big Undercount In New Survey, Russians Claim," in: *The Jewish Week* (July 2003); *Jewish Emigration from the former Soviet Union to Israel and the United States*, Statistics, The National Conference on Soviet Jewry (2003); M. Galperin, "Redeeming the Captive: Twenty-Five Years of Successful Resettlement and Acculturation of New Americans," in: *Journal of Jewish Communal Service*, 72:4 (Summer 1996); J. Goldman, "Russians Move from Isolation to Activism in U.S. Jewish Life," in: JTA *Daily News Bulletin* (Sept. 1998); A. Orleck, *The Soviet Jewish Americans* (1999).

NEW YORK STATE, an eastern state of the U.S., bounded on the north and west by the St. Lawrence Seaway, Lake Ontario, and Lake Erie, and at the southern tip, by the Atlantic Ocean. Of its 18,990,000 inhabitants (as reported in 2001), about 1,657,000 are Jews (down from 2,522,000 Jews in 1969).

In 1654, 23 Spanish Portuguese Jews, refugees from the Inquisition, arrived in New Amsterdam (*New York after 1664) from Recife, Brazil, and founded the first permanent Jewish settlement in North America. They stayed in part because they had no choice: they were without resources. When Peter Stuyvesant asked the Dutch West Indies Company what to do with the refugees, Jews who were part of the company in Amsterdam were influential enough to provide for them to stay. While the tiny community did not thrive at first, one of its leaders, Asser *Levy, by 1658 had real-estate holdings as far north as Albany, and in 1678 Jacob de Lucena was trading in Kingston, up the Hudson River. Successful merchants, Luis Gomez and his sons built a trading post on the Hudson near Newburgh in 1717, and in 1732 the *Hays family settled near New Rochelle in Westchester. During the French and Indian War, Hayman *Levy, a Hanoverian, conducted a large fur trade around Lake Champlain in the north, and Lyon and Manuel *Josephson supplied goods to northern British forts. In the 1760s, some Jews settled on Long Island and in Westchester. Until the 19th century, most Jews who settled in the area that became New York State in 1788 were of Spanish-Portuguese origin.

Following the War of 1812, improvements in maritime technology and transportation, particularly the use of steam and the opening of the Erie Canal, combined to intensify Jewish settlement. Aaron *Levy, for example, visited the Lake George region from 1805 to 1834. Significant Jewish communities developed in Albany, Syracuse, Rochester, and Buffalo between 1820 and the Civil War. During the substantial German Jewish immigration that began during the 1830s, many immigrants settled along the upper transportation routes to the Middle West: Newburgh (1848), Poughkeepsie (1848), Kingston (1853), Hudson (1867), *Albany (1838), Schenectady (1840s), Troy (1850s), Amsterdam (1874), Gloversville (1850s), *Utica (1848), Syracuse (1839), *Rochester (1848), and *Buffalo (1847) on the Hudson-Mohawk River route. Other settlements were founded in Binghamton (1885), Elmira (1850), and Olean (1882) along the southern Susquehanna River, Plattsburgh (1861) on Lake Champlain, and Ogdensburg (1865) on the St. Lawrence River. Isaac M. Wise, the principal architect of Reform Judaism in the United States, served briefly in Albany beginning in 1846. There he established the custom of mixed seating in American synagogues. By 1860 there were 20 congregations in the state and 53 by 1877. These Jews were predominantly merchants and peddlers, while some were farmers. By 1909 there were seven Jewish farmers' organizations in the state, and the first Jewish farmers' credit union was formed in 1911.

An estimated 60,000–80,000 Jews lived in the state in 1880. East European immigration increased that number to

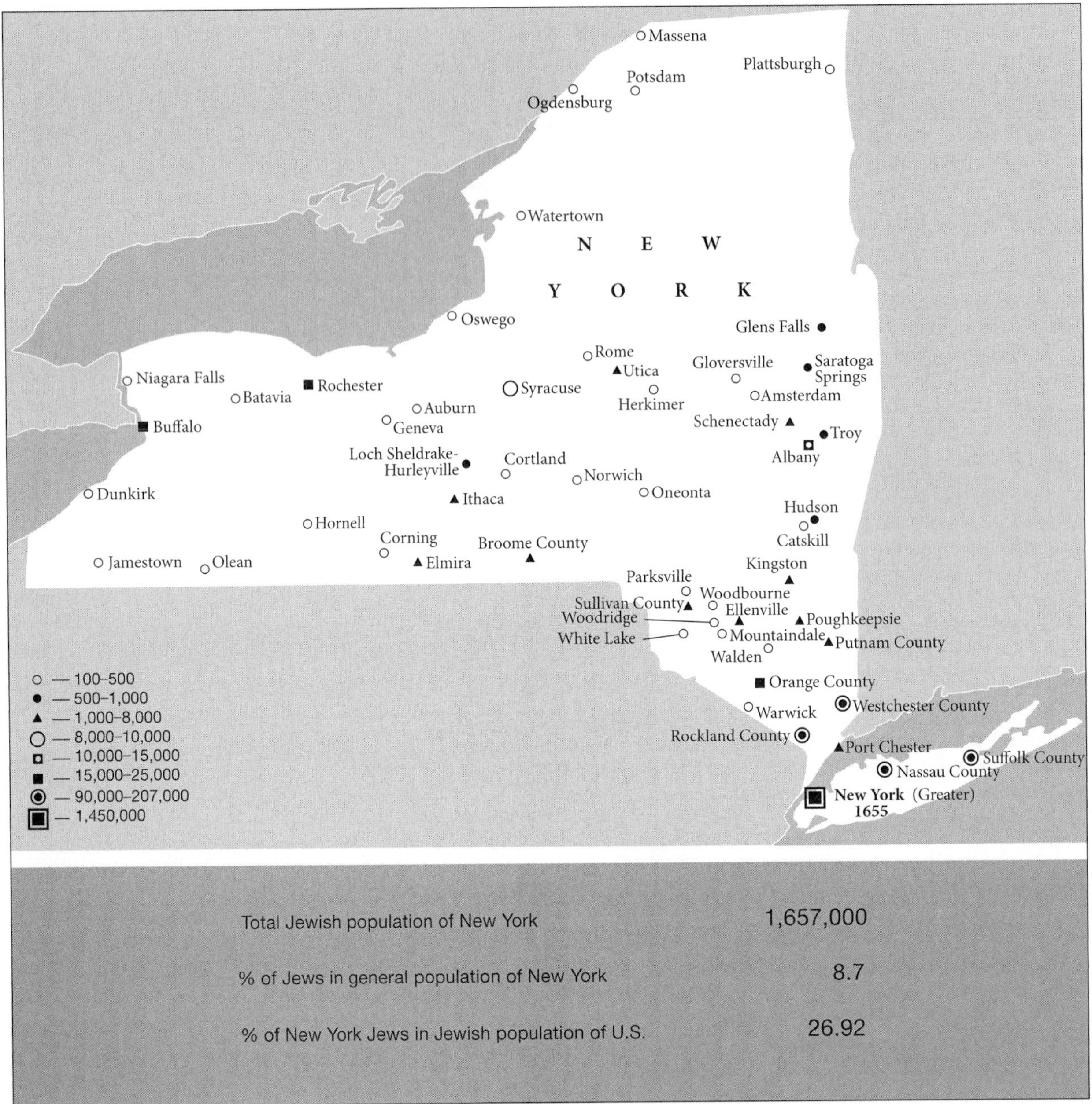

Jewish communities in New York. Population figures for 2001.

900,000 by 1910. By 1928 the number reached 1,835,500. Although most of the East Europeans settled in New York City, others, encouraged to alleviate congestion, went to towns in the north, such as Haverstraw (1896), Ossining (1891), Peekskill (1894), New Rochelle (1880s), Lake Placid (1903), Liberty (1880s), Spring Valley (1901), Yonkers (1860s), Mamaroneck (1890), Massena (1897), Suffern (1880s), and Tarrytown (1887), as well as Ithaca (1891) in the central part of the state. In 1940, 90% of the state's 2,206,328 (1937 figure) Jews resided in the city. However, the next two decades saw a flow to the suburbs. In 1940 fewer than 100,000 Jews lived in all the New York City suburbs, but Nassau, fueled by returning GIs owning their own homes, had 329,000 Jews by 1956 and 372,000 in 1968; Suffolk, 20,000 by 1956 and 42,000 in 1968 and 90,000 at the turn of the 21st century; and Westchester, 116,900 by 1956 and 131,000 in 1968 (the number has been stable since).

In 1902, Jewish organizations established summer camps for urban Jewish youth, beginning with the Educational Alliance's Surprise Lake Camp, in Cold Spring. And Jews made themselves felt on rural Long Island, too. In 1909, a Jewish dentist, Dr. Henry W. Walden, invented and flew the first American monoplane from Mineola Airport. One Long Island company, the Elberson Rubber Factory in Setauket, had so many Jews on its payroll that it had to close for the High

Holidays, even though the owners weren't Jewish. The Baron de Hirsh Jewish Agricultural Society operated a training farm in Kings Park and farm communities in Center Moriches, Riverhead, Calverton, East Islip, and Farmingdale. Turn-of-the-century Centerport was the home of a camp for boys and young men operated by the 92nd Street Y. It advertised "the finest in kosher cuisine."

Relief from summer heat, sweatshops, and squalor led to the development of the "Borscht Belt" in Sullivan, Ulster, and Orange counties. Some left the Lower East Side and bought small farms. But farming was not their forte, and soon the farms became boarding houses, then inns and bungalow colonies for visitors from the city. The guests insisted on entertainment, and by the 1920s that became a major undertaking. Waiters and busboys doubled as comics and entertainers, or tummlers, while the social directors became impresarios. Among the social directors were Moss *Hart, the future playwright, and Don Hartman, who became head of Paramount Pictures. The tummlers included David Daniel Kaminsky, Aaron Chwatt, Jacob Pincus Perelmuth, Morris Miller, Eugene Klass, Joseph Levitch, Milton Berlinger, Joseph Gottlieb and Murray Janofsky, later to become well-known as Danny Kaye, Red Buttons, Jan Peerce, Robert Merrill, Gene Barry, Jerry Lewis, Milton Berle, Joey Bishop, and Jan Murray.

The queen of the mountains was Jennie Grossinger, who became the region's best-known hostess, and her namesake hotel the most imitated. One of the imitators was Arthur Winarick, the bald manufacturer of Jeris hair tonic and the owner of the Concord Hotel, who constantly tried to one-up Grossinger's. In later years, television, jet travel, and increased competition proved serious threats to the region, and Grossinger's was sold in 1985 for conversion to condominiums and ski houses. Dozens of hotels closed or became retreats for religious cultists.

For 100 years, beginning at the end of the 19th century, Jewish life had a presence in the area. Synagogues were constructed in almost every hamlet. By 1999, 15 remained. Seven of them were listed on the National Register of Historic Places. They were: Agudas Achim, Livingston Manor; B'nai Israel, Woodbourne; Anshei Glen Wild, Glen Wild; Bikur Cholim B'nai Yisroel, Swan Lake; Chevra Ahavath Zion, Monticello; Tifereth Israel Anshei, Parksville; and the Jewish Community Center of White Sulphur Springs. Sharon Springs developed as a high-end Jewish refuge. After World War II, Sharon Springs got a second wind from the West German government, which paid medical care reparations to Holocaust survivors, holding that therapeutic spa vacations were a legitimate part of the medical package. Many hotel guests had tattoos on their arms.

Politically, the roster of New York Jews who served in Congress began in the 19th century and included Edwin Einstein (1879–81); Joseph Pulitzer (1883–85); Isidor Straus (1894–95); Israel Frederick Fischer (1894–95); Lucius N. Littauer (1897–1907); Mitchell May (1899–1901); and Jefferson M. Levy (1899–1901; 1911–15). In the 20th century, Herbert Tenzer (1965–69) was the first Orthodox Jew in Congress; Allard K. Lowenstein (1869–71), a leader of the anti-war movement, won election from Long Island, and Gary L. Ackerman (1983–), representing Queens and Long Island, was host in his office to *minḥah* prayers each afternoon at the Capitol.

Herbert H. *Lehman was governor from 1933 to 1942, and U.S. senator from 1949 to 1957. Jacob K. *Javits served as U.S. senator from 1957 to 1981. Charles *Schumer first served as a congressman and later as a senator beginning in 1998. Benjamin N. *Cardozo (1927–32), Irving Lehman (1940–45), and Stanley H. Fuld (1966-73) were chief justices of the Court of Appeals, the state's highest bench. Pressure from Jewish members of the State Legislature led to the passage of the Fair Employment Practice Act in 1945, the first in the U.S. to prohibit discrimination in employment practices.

Jewish newspapers were published in Buffalo (since 1918), Rochester (1924), Westchester (1942), Long Island (1944), and Schenectady (1965).

[Edward L. Greenstein]

The 1,657,000 Jews of New York State represented around 9% of the total population of the state. New York City, long the most populous and influential of the American Jewish communities, had fewer than 1,000,000, with the Bronx being virtually without Jews except for Riverdale (45,000), Manhattan having 243,500 Jews, Brooklyn 456,000, Queens 186,000, and Staten Island 42,700. The metropolitan area, which included the suburbs as well as those in New Jersey and lower Connecticut, was the most predominant Jewish community outside of Israel, containing some 40% of all American Jews. Excluding New York City, there are more than 513 synagogues in New York State and some 50 *mikvehs*. Other population centers include: Nassau County (221,000), Suffolk County (90,000), Westchester (129,000), Rockland County (90,000), Rochester (22,500), Orange County (including Monroe and Newburgh, 19,000), Buffalo (18,500), Albany (12,000), and Syracuse (9,000).

BIBLIOGRAPHY: AJYB, (1938–39, 1970); C.M. Horowitz and L.J. Kaplan, *The Estimated Jewish Population of the New York Area, 1900–1975*; J.R. Marcus, *Early American Jewry*, 1 (1961), 24–101; U.Z. Engleman, in: JSOS, 9 (April 1947), 127–74. **ADD. BIBLIOGRAPHY:** L.S. Maisel and I.N. Forman, *Jews in American Politics* (2001).

NEW ZEALAND, independent country and member of the Commonwealth, situated in the South Pacific. In 1829, some 60 years after the rediscovery of New Zealand, the Sydney firm of Cooper and Levy established itself in the South Island at Port Cooper (Lyttleton) and Port Levy, a little to the north. Solomon Levy, the Jewish partner, later became a benefactor of both Jewish and Christian educational and charitable institutions. During the next decade, other Jewish traders began to arrive. In 1830 Joseph Barrow Montefiore (a member of the English *Montefiore family) from Sydney established Montefiore Brothers, dealing largely in flax and whale oil. In 1831 Joel Samuel *Polack, author of two books on New Zealand, came first to Hokianga to trade and deal in land. He shortly

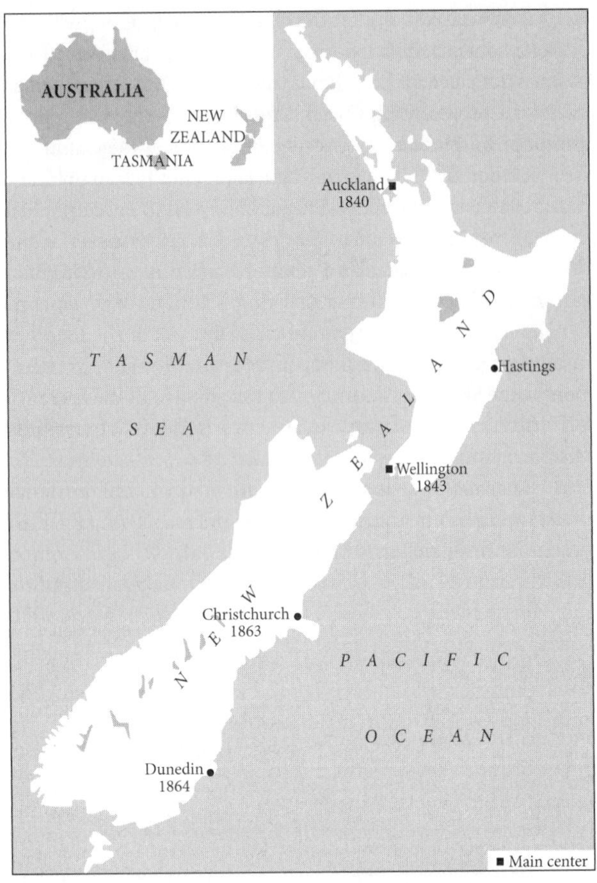

Jewish communities in New Zealand with dates of establishment.

transferred to Kororareka, Bay of Islands, where a cousin of J.B. Montefiore had established a trading post in 1831. Four other Jews were resident at Kororareka in 1838, but along with David *Nathan who had arrived in 1839 they moved to Auckland after it was made the capital in 1840. With a handful of other Jewish storekeepers and traders, David Nathan founded the Auckland Jewish community. Members of the congregation read the services and conducted religious functions – a pattern to be followed elsewhere in New Zealand. The first ordained minister (J.E. Myers of Auckland) was appointed to a New Zealand congregation in 1859.

In Wellington the first Jewish arrival appears to have been Abraham Hort, Jr. who came in 1840 with two carpenter brothers, Solomon and Benjamin Levy. These were followed in 1843 by Abraham *Hort, Sr. (1799–1869), a London Jewish communal leader who went to New Zealand with the intention of founding a community and promoting planned immigration to relieve Jewish poverty in England, through the New Zealand Company which in 1840 had begun colonizing parts of the country. Although successful in founding the Wellington community, he failed to achieve his immigration plans. The discovery of gold in Otago and Westland in the 1860s led directly or indirectly to the establishment of the communities of *Dunedin and *Christchurch and to the temporary founding of those in Hokitika, Timaru, and Nelson; the Timaru synagogue still stands without a congregation. David Isaacs, formerly of the Wellington and Dunedin congregations, was appointed shortly after 1863 to Nelson, and I. Zachariah of the gold-mining town of Hokitika was appointed in 1870 to the Christchurch congregation. Most of the ordained ministers came from Jews' College, England, including Herman Van Staveren (Wellington, 1877–1930) and Alexander Astor (Dunedin and Auckland, 1926–71). Chananiah Pitkowsky (Wellington, 1905–30) and the brothers N. Salas (Auckland and Christchurch, 1929–58) and M. Salas (Auckland, 1934–55) came from Ereẓ Israel.

New Zealand's links with Ereẓ Israel date from the time of the Crimean War, when money was being collected in Auckland and Wellington for starving Jews in Ereẓ Israel. In 1862 Jacob *Saphir of Jerusalem visited Dunedin on a similar mission. Before New Zealand became a British colony in 1840, the Jewish population numbered less than 30. By 1861 it had risen to 326 (0.3% of the total), and six years later to 1,262 (0.6%). The gold rushes brought hundreds of Jews there, but by the 1870s their number had fallen to approximately 0.2%, above which it has never risen. The Jewish population numbered 1,611 in 1901, 2,380 in 1921, 3,470 in 1945, 4,006 (out of 2,750,000) in 1961, and just over 4,000 in 1968. In the 1980s significant numbers of Jews settled in New Zealand from the former U.S.S.R. and especially from South Africa. The number of Jews by religion reported in the 1991 New Zealand Census was 3,126. Most observers regard the actual number as significantly higher, in the range of 4,500–5,000. The vast majority of Jews are distributed between New Zealand's largest city, Auckland, and the country's capital, Wellington. For much of the country's history these two centers have had comparable numbers of Jews. However, from about the mid-1980s as Auckland's growth continued to outpace that of the rest of the country, so too the numbers of Jews in Auckland began to significantly outnumber the numbers in Wellington. Apart from the city's position as New Zealand's economic capital – with roughly one in four New Zealanders residing there – the imbalance between the two communities has also been the result of larger numbers of South African Jews choosing to migrate there.

For much of New Zealand's history there have been highly restrictive government policies on immigration, with migrants from Great Britain receiving preference. Only a minuscule number of Jews seeking to flee from Europe during the years of Nazi rule were able to gain entry to New Zealand. Similarly, after the war only a small number of homeless Jewish refugees were admitted to the country. Those fleeing persecution in Russia and Eastern Europe during the Cold War also faced strong obstacles if they sought haven in New Zealand.

Those European Jews who did manage to go to New Zealand generally did so through family or communal ties to New Zealand Jews. Jewish leaders also made strenuous efforts to assist Jews trying to go to New Zealand, lobbying parliamentarians and cabinet ministers. Communal organizations were established to provide aid to Jewish immigrants to what was, for nearly all of them, a vastly different country from the one they left.

The Jews arriving in the 1930s had an impact on the New Zealand community, as some of them brought with them styles of worship and observance distinct from the largely ex-British Jewry of the country's congregations. Subsequent groups of migrants – including Jews fleeing the Hungarian uprising in 1956, former Soviet Jews during the 1980s and 1990s, and Jews leaving South Africa during the 1990s – have each had an impact on Jewish communities through participation in various communal organizations.

Assimilation into New Zealand society by the country's Jews reflects their being comfortable with the country's predominantly secular outlook and the overall absence of overt antisemitism. The growth of the Jewish population has been small not only because of assimilation and intermarriage, but because there has been substantial emigration from New Zealand over the years, particularly to Australia, by all New Zealanders, Jews among them. Emigration to Israel – *aliyah* – has been a further factor affecting communal growth and vitality, not only in absolute numbers but because many of those emigrating to Israel, identifying with the country and seeking a stronger Jewish lifestyle, have been those who, had they remained, would have been expected to be among the leaders of their communities.

Today, though complemented by various Zionist, social, and educational organizations, the synagogues remain the hub of the communities in Auckland and Wellington, where there are Orthodox ministers under the authority of the chief rabbi in London. Progressive congregations exist in Auckland (1959) and Wellington (1960). Smaller communal groups are also to be found elsewhere, in Christchurch, Dunedin, and Hamilton. Jewish youth groups continue to exist in Auckland and Wellington, with small numbers of Jews going annually on various programs to Israel – for some, the beginning of a process culminating in eventual *aliyah*.

From the turn of the century, Jewish social and welfare organizations have developed. Internationally affiliated *B'nai B'rith lodges were established in Wellington (1960) and Auckland (1961). The first national monthly Jewish journal, the *New Zealand Jewish Times*, was started in the 1920s. In 1971, there was one monthly newspaper, the *New Zealand Jewish Chronicle*.

Interest in Zionism was rather academic until the *Balfour Declaration and the return after World War I of units from the Palestine campaign. After 1918 Louis Phillips of Auckland, who had been New Zealand's first delegate to the International Zionist Conference, led the Zionist movement. A number of young New Zealanders settled in Israel after 1948.

Free from any discriminatory disabilities, the Jews in New Zealand have made valuable contributions to the country's development and progress. Sir Julius *Vogel, twice premier (1873–75 and 1876), has been called New Zealand's most far-sighted statesman, while Sir Arthur *Myers was minister of munitions in World War I. Almost every major city in New Zealand has honored a Jew as its chief magistrate. There have been five Jewish mayors of New Zealand's largest city, Auckland; these were Philip A. Philips (1869–74) and Henry Isaacs in the 1870s, Sir Arthur Myers (1905–08), Sir Ernest David (1935–41), and Sir Dove-Myer Robinson (1959–65 and 1968–80). Sir Michael *Myers of Wellington was Chief Justice from 1929 to 1946 and acted as administrator during the absence of the governor. Some noteworthy Jewish names in New Zealand journalism have been Julius Vogel, Benjamin *Farjeon the poet and novelist, Fred Pirani, Mark Cohen, and Phineas Selig, and in medicine Sir Louis Barnett (surgery), Alfred Bernstein (chest diseases), and Bernard Myers (medical services). Wolf Heinemann, the philologist of Dunedin, was the first Jew to be appointed professor in a New Zealand university (Otago, 1895). Jews have pioneered in both business and farming. The oldest business in New Zealand is that of L.D. Nathan and Company. Joseph Nathan (Wellington) developed the Glaxo pharmaceutical company, a worldwide concern now operating chiefly from England, while the establishment of New Zealand's steel mills owes much to the industrialist Sir Woolf Fisher. Jews were instrumental in developing New Zealand's brewing and hotel industries, and in the wholesale and retail clothing industries they formed early national groups. Among Jewish farmers and agriculturalists was Coleman Phillips, who formed the first cooperative dairy farm in either Australia or New Zealand. In other aspects of New Zealand life, particularly sporting, cultural, and artistic, Jews have also played their full part.

The number of Jews in New Zealand was estimated at around 5,000 in 1980, most of whom lived in Auckland and Wellington, in roughly equal numbers. There was still considerable assimilation, with a high proportion of Jews marrying non-Jewish partners, some of whom chose to convert to Judaism.

In October 1980, Colin King, an Orthodox Jew, was elected mayor of Auckland succeeding Sir Dove Myer Robinson, also Jewish, who had served as mayor for 12 years. Two Jewish day schools exist in New Zealand – Kadimah College in Auckland, opened in the late 1970s, and Moriah College in Wellington, opened in 1987. There are also Jewish preschool facilities.

In 1981 the fresh supply of kosher meat for the Wellington Jewish community was organized by the Wellington Hebrew Congregation's board of management as a cooperative which functions at the local Jewish community center.

The New Zealand Jewish Council was established in 1981 as an umbrella organization authorized to represent the New Zealand Jewish community, and Wally Hirsch of Wellington was chosen to be the first chairman of the council. The council subsequently relocated in Auckland. Regional councils were also established, with leadership of the New Jewish Council alternating between community leaders in Auckland and Wellington.

Relations between the Jewish community and the New Zealand government soured considerably under the Labor government led by David Lange (1984–90), which constantly criticized Israeli policy on the West Bank and opened a dialogue with the PLO. Left-wing unions in New Zealand, powerful under the Labor government, tended to be dominated by hard anti-American elements who are also anti-Zionist. Relations improved following the return of the more conservative, pro-American National Party government in 1990.

A number of books have appeared over the last few years on New Zealand Jewish life, including Ann Beaglehole's *A Small Price to Pay: Refugees from Hitler in New Zealand, 1936–46* (1988), on the very restrictive government policy toward Nazi-era refugees, as well as her *Facing the Past: Looking Back at Refugee Childhood in New Zealand, 1940s-1960s* (1990), which contains accounts of 20th-century Jewish migration to (and adaptation in) New Zealand; Odeda Rosenthal's *Not Strictly Kosher: Pioneer Jews in New Zealand* (1988); and Ann Gluckman's two volumes on the Auckland community, *Identity and Involvement: Auckland Jewry Past and Present* (1990, 1993). Stephen Levine's commemorative volume on the Wellington Jewish community, *A Standard for the People: The 150th Anniversary of the Wellington Hebrew Congregation 1843–1993* (1995) describes the community groups, leaders, rabbis, and families of the Wellington congregation. His book *The New Zealand Jewish Community* (1999) is an analysis of New Zealand's Jewish organizations, part of a worldwide study of Jewish community groups sponsored by the Jerusalem Center for Public Affairs. In 2005 the New Zealand government's Ministry for Culture and Heritage launched its online Encyclopedia of New Zealand, including a chapter (with text and illustrations) on the country's Jews: see Stephen Levine, "Jews [of New Zealand]," in *Te Ara: the Encyclopedia of New Zealand*, New Zealand government, Ministry for Culture and Heritage, 2005 (online): *http://www.teara.govt.nz/NewZealanders/NewZealandPeoples/Jews/en.htm*

Other publications of note include Livia K. Wittmann, *Interactive Identities: Jewish Women in New Zealand* (1998) and Lotte Weiss, *My Two Lives* (2003) – the latter a biography by a Holocaust survivor who subsequently went to Wellington.

A conference was held in Auckland in 1994 under the heading "Beyond 2000 – Jewish Continuity in New Zealand," which provided a forum for frank analysis. The community, still numbering about 5,000, struggles with problems of resources stemming from a lack of involvement and persistently high rates of emigration, both by young and old alike.

During the 1990s the Jewish day schools in Auckland and Wellington continued to maintain high academic standards and substantial enrollments. In both cases, however, there were generally as many non-Jewish students as Jewish, somewhat defeating the purpose of establishing Jewish day schools. Other positive developments during this period included immigration from South Africa and the former Soviet Union; the maintenance of synagogues in Auckland and Wellington (for both Orthodox and Progressive congregations); and the continued distribution of the national Jewish newspaper, the *New Zealand Jewish Chronicle*. An important means of communication is also the various congregational newsletters distributed to the membership.

Expressions of anti-Jewish prejudice were sporadic, although declining support for Israel worldwide and an increasingly antagonistic news media made possible often virulent anti-Jewish and anti-Israel correspondence in the country's newspapers. While the influence of organized religion in New Zealand continued to decline, there was an increase in interfaith activity by the Council of Christians and Jews. The campaign of the Anglican Church to remove references to "Zion" from the Psalms was reversed (see below). Where appropriate, Jewish community leaders involved themselves in lobbying with the government, although the presence of an Israeli ambassador in Wellington made intervention by Jewish leaders seem less necessary than during the pre-1975 period. The New Zealand government joined with other countries in co-sponsoring the successful United Nations resolution reversing the "Zionism is Racism" resolution.

New Zealand's Jewish community in 2005 remained focused around the congregations of Auckland and Wellington. Unlike the colonial period, when the country was being established, or the era during which New Zealand's primary businesses were being developed, Jews were less conspicuous as leading figures within New Zealand society. Although several members of Parliament had Jewish ancestry, there were no members of Parliament identifying themselves as Jews. The communities in Auckland and Wellington were the focal point of much Jewish spiritual and cultural activity, and the leadership of these communities in turn continued to focus on the usual problems of small communities, reflecting limited human and financial resources. As has been the case for some time, rabbinical leadership has been available from non-Commonwealth sources – the United States and Israel – as well as from the United Kingdom and Australia.

The community's concerns about security and survival were augmented by a number of factors during the post-1996 era, a period that coincides with New Zealand's introduction of a new electoral system (based on proportional representation) giving greater political strength to smaller groups that previously were unable to gain much if any representation in Parliament or government. One of the smaller parties, the Greens, has been more hostile to the United States, even opposing a parliamentary resolution of support in the aftermath of September 11, 2001. Another party, New Zealand First, has had much of its support based on its hostility to immigration, a stance that, for some, lends legitimacy to feelings of hostility to immigrants, law-abiding or otherwise. The opportunity for more politically marginal groups to gain a voice, and influence, has coincided with an increased antipathy toward Israel on the part of the news media and the government, particularly with the election of a Labor coalition in 1999. Even when the U.S. government signaled its loss of confidence in Yasser Arafat, the New Zealand government continued its contacts with him, extending to a visit and a handshake in Ramallah from New Zealand's minister of foreign affairs.

The attacks on Jewish cemeteries in Wellington (see below), as well as an attack at a small Jewish memorial in the provincial city of Wanganui, provoked considerable alarm and distress, particularly among remaining Holocaust survivors – migrants from Europe who had been in New Zealand for decades – and their descendants. Their sensitivities have been affected as well by elements of "Holocaust denial" in New Zealand, including controversies at several New Zealand universities. Victoria University introduced a course on the Holocaust in its History program in 2001, making a permanent staff appointment in this subject in 2003. Intermittent (though well-publicized) attempts by a British Holocaust denier, David *Irving, to go to New Zealand have also attracted considerable attention, with editorial writers, talk-back radio participants, and newspaper letter-writers divided over questions about the Holocaust, freedom of expression, and other issues. In 2004 the New Zealand government denied permission for him to go to New Zealand based on a conviction in another jurisdiction.

New Zealand's Jews thus faced the future with some of their institutions intact (but lacking strong numbers); with congregations in place in Auckland and Wellington (but facing decisions about resources and about possible relocation, particularly in Auckland); and with some concern about the reputation of Israel, and the image of Jews (and Judaism), in the news media (both New Zealand-based and from overseas) and more widely.

Antisemitism

Antisemitism (often influenced from abroad) has appeared at times over the years, particularly in periods of economic hardship, but its manifestations have been limited.

In 1989 the Anglican Church in New Zealand changed its Prayer Book to omit any references to "Zion," substituting phrases like "God's Holy City." According to Jewish sources, this was made in part through anti-Zionist pressures, although this has been officially denied by the Anglican Church. On the other hand, Councils of Christians and Jews have been established in Auckland and Wellington.

There was a small but often noisy extreme right-wing movement in New Zealand associated with the Australian League of Rights, as well as antisemitic Christian fundamentalist groups, but levels of antisemitism continued to be low, with few reports of anti-Jewish vandalism or violence. In 1990, there was a serious knife attack on school children at Kadimah College by a deranged non-Jewish woman who was placed under psychiatric care.

However, in 2004 unprecedented events occurred that led to a renewed focus on the dangers of anti-Jewish sentiments in New Zealand. Following a strong public statement from New Zealand's prime minister, Labor leader Helen Clark, downgrading relations with Israel in the wake of an attempt by an alleged Israeli intelligence agent to obtain a New Zealand passport, the historic Jewish cemetery in the capital, containing the graves of early Jewish settlers, was vandalized. Despite an outcry, no arrests were made. Only several weeks later a second Jewish cemetery, currently in use, was also attacked, and the Jewish prayer house at the site was set ablaze. Once again the police were unable to apprehend anyone. In response to this second desecration – each event found New Zealand gaining unwelcome international publicity – the New Zealand Parliament passed a unanimous resolution deploring antisemitism, with many members of the Jewish community watching from the public gallery. The resolution, introduced and passed on August 17, 2004, was moved by Acting Prime Minister Michael Cullen, who opened the debate, saying: "It is a sad day for this nation when it comes to the point that it is necessary to move a motion of this sort in Parliament."

The resolution, unprecedented for New Zealand, stated: "That this House deplores recent attacks on Jewish graves and a Jewish chapel in Wellington; recalls the terrible history of antisemitism stretching over many centuries, culminating in the Holocaust under Nazi rule; and expresses its unequivocal condemnation of antisemitism, violence directed against Jews and Jewish religious and cultural institutions and all forms of racial and ethnic hatred, persecution and discrimination."

Following speeches by each of New Zealand's party leaders, the speaker of the New Zealand House of Representatives rose and, unusually, made his own personal statement, describing the events this way: "In all the 37-and-a-half years I have been in Parliament, this, for me, has been one of the most shocking incidents I have ever noted in this country." He then announced that he was sending the text of the resolution, and all of the speeches made with respect to it, to the speaker of the Knesset, Israel's parliament. Subsequently the speaker of the Knesset expressed his appreciation for the resolution and the action taken by New Zealand's speaker.

Relations with Israel

Friendly ties between the two countries go back to the relations established between the *yishuv* and New Zealand soldiers who served in Palestine and the Middle East during the two world wars. Israel honored the Australian and New Zealand soldiers (ANZAC) by erecting a memorial near Be'eri in southern Israel. New Zealand voted for the partition of Palestine in 1947 and accorded Israel recognition early in 1949. In the early postwar period New Zealand still maintained only a very small foreign service, with embassies located only in a handful of overseas capitals. However, even following subsequent growth in its international representation, New Zealand chose not to be directly represented in Israel, opting instead for one of its ambassadors elsewhere (for many years its ambassador in the Hague) to be accredited to Israel. Israel's ambassador to Australia was accredited to New Zealand until 1975 when the first resident ambassador arrived in Wellington. This asymmetry continued until 2003 when the Israeli government chose to close the Wellington embassy (and consulates in other countries) in a move described by Israel's

Ministry of Foreign Affairs as being taken for financial reasons. As a result, Israel's representation in New Zealand was provided from this point on by an honorary consul; the first such appointee was David Zwartz, who was also head of the New Zealand Jewish Council (and, for one term, a member of the Wellington City Council).

During the early years following Israel's reestablishment as an independent state, New Zealand gave the country its support at the United Nations. New Zealand does not recognize Jerusalem as Israel's capital and, accordingly, the country's news media, and particularly publicly owned broadcast services, refrain from describing the city as part of Israel. New Zealand's reliance on oil imports, as well as its at times highly profitable trade with Arab countries, contributed to a desire on the part of the government (under both National and Labor administrations) to maintain a more distant relationship with Israel. Following the Yom Kippur War in October 1973 the New Zealand government tended to adopt a more pro-Arab stance, but popular support for Israel's achievements continued.

BIBLIOGRAPHY: *Journal and Proceedings of the Australian Jewish Historical Society*, 1 (1939–40), 53–55, 154–9, 293–5; 3 (1949–53), 142–51, 334–50; Hertz, in: JHSET, 10 (1921–23), 162–5; L.M. Goldman, *The History of the Jews in New Zealand* (1960).

[Stephen Levine (2nd ed.)]

NEYRAC, PIERRE, pen name of **Naphtali Cohen** (1898–1960), novelist. A fourth-generation Palestinian, Neyrac immigrated to France in 1927 and practiced as a physician. He expressed nostalgia for his homeland in three novels, *L'indifférence perdue* (1933), *La mort de Frida* (1934), and *La jeunesse d'Elias* (1956).

NEẒER SERENI (Heb. נֵצֶר סִירֶנִי), kibbutz in central Israel, between Nes Ẓiyyonah and Ramleh, founded on June 20, 1948, during a short cease-fire of the Israel *War of Independence, by "Kibbutz Buchenwald," composed of young survivors of the Holocaust who, while still in a displaced persons' camp, had formed a pioneering group for settlement in Palestine. The site, a German farm from the beginning of the century, was temporarily used during World War I as Gen. *Allenby's headquarters. After the 1951–52 split in *Ha-Kibbutz ha-Me'uḥad a large minority group from *Givat Brenner decided to join Kibbutz Neẓer which was affiliated with Iḥud ha-Kevuẓot veha-Kibbutzim. In 1968 the kibbutz numbered 510 inhabitants, in 2002 it was 499. The kibbutz engaged in intensive farming and started up three industrial plants, for foodstuffs, metal, and wood products. The name "Neẓer" ("Young Shoot") refers to Kibbutz Buchenwald's origins. After the members of Givat Brenner joined, the kibbutz was named Neẓer Sereni to commemorate the Haganah parachutist Enzo *Sereni, who had been a member of Givat Brenner.

[Efraim Orni]

NEZHIN, city in Chernigov district, Ukraine. Jews first settled in Nezhin in the early 17th century, but the community was destroyed during the Khmelnitski uprising. They resettled there in the early 18th century. The *ẓaddik* Dov Ber of *Lubavich, the son of *Shneur Zalman of Lyady, the "middle rabbi" of Chabad Ḥasidism, died and was interred in Nezhin in 1827. The town became a center for the Chabad Ḥasidim of the Ukraine. It was especially well known while Israel Noah *Schneersohn lived there from 1867 to 1882. In 1847, 1,299 Jews were registered in the community; in 1897 there were 7,631 Jews (24% of the total population). The waves of pogroms which overtook Russian Jewry on July 20–22, 1881, and in 1905 also affected the Jews of Nezhin. On September 2, 1919, Nezhin's Jews were attacked by soldiers of the "volunteer army" of *Denikin, 100 Jews were killed, many women raped, and much property pillaged. The dead included Menahem Mendel Ḥen, rabbi of Nezhin. The Yiddish poet *Mani-Leib (Mani-Leib Brahinski) was born there. In 1926, there were 6,131 Jews in Nezhin (16.1% of the population), their number dropping in 1939 to 2,725 (7% of the total population). The Germans occupied the town on September 13, 1941. Most of the Jews succeeded in escaping. The few dozens who remained were killed by October 1941. In 1959 there were 1,400 Jews (3% of the total population) in Nezhin.

BIBLIOGRAPHY: S.M. Dubnow and G.I. Krasny-Agman (eds.), *Materialy dlya istorii antiyevreyskikh pogromov v Rossii*, 2 (1923), 153–4, 348–57; *Die Judenpogrome in Russland*, 2 (1909), 287–94; I.B. Shekhtman, *Pogromy Dobrovolcheskoy Armii na Ukrainie* (1932), 323–6.

[Yehuda Slutsky]

NEZIKIN (Heb. נְזִיקִין; "torts"), fourth order of the Mishnah according to the order given by Simeon b. Lakish (Shab. 31a), although according to another tradition (Tanḥuma in Num. R. 13:15), it is the sixth. Originally *Nezikin* was the name of the first tractate only (see below). Because of Simeon b. Lakish's homily applying to it the word *yeshu'ot* ("salvation") in Isaiah 33:6, it is so called in many rabbinic sources, including the Tosefta. *Nezikin* is devoted to civil law (except for matrimonial law, dealt with in the order *Nashim*), and the administration of justice and legal procedure, as well as penal law insofar as the subject does not appertain to some other part of the Mishnah. The tractate **Eduyyot* was included in *Nezikin* because it contains "testimonies" most of which were given before the Sanhedrin of *Jabneh after the destruction of the Temple, and is consequently connected with the tractate **Sanhedrin*. **Avodah Zarah* was placed in *Nezikin* because it deals with the *halakhot* of idolatry, some of which are given in *Sanhedrin-Makkot*, and also because it opens with prohibitions against trade with idolators, thus connecting it with the tractate *Nezikin* (**Bava Kamma*, **Bava Meẓia*, and **Bava Batra*), which gives the laws of trade in general. The inclusion of the aggadic tractate *Avot*, which deals with moral maxims, is due to the fact that it contains an exceptional number of instructions to **dayyanim*, dealt with in *Sanhedrin*.

Nezikin contains ten tractates, although at first there were only seven, the first three originally forming one tractate now divided into *Bava Kamma, Bava Meẓia*, and *Bava*

Batra (see Av. Zar. in Mishnah Kaufmann and Cambridge, etc.). The name of the first tractate was then applied to the whole order. *Sanhedrin* and **Makkot* were also originally one tractate (and are so in the Kaufmann and Parma Mishnah, in *genizah* fragments, and elsewhere), which contained 14 chapters; they were divided into two tractates, also apparently in Babylon, for reasons that are not yet sufficiently clear. Thus in the order *Nezikin*, too, the tractates were originally arranged according to the number of chapters in descending order. *Nezikin* has the following separate tractates: *Bava Kamma*, with 10 chapters; *Bava Meẓia*, 10; *Bava Batra*, 10; *Sanhedrin*, 11; *Makkot*, 3; **Shevu'ot*, 8; *Eduyyot*, 8; *Avodah Zarah*, 5; *Avot*, 5; and **Horayot*, 3.

In the Tosefta of *Nezikin* each of the three *Bavot* has 11 chapters; *Sanhedrin*, 14; *Makkot*, 4 (or 5); *Shevu'ot*, 6; *Eduyyot*, 3; *Avodah Zarah*, 9 (or 8); and *Horayot*, 2 chapters; there is no Tosefta to *Avot*. *Eduyyot* and *Avot* have no *Gemara* in either the Jerusalem or the Babylonian Talmud. The importance of nearly all the tractates in the sphere of practical *halakhah* led to an abundant development of these spheres in rabbinic literature. Especially comprehensive is the literature on the first three tractates and on *Shevu'ot*, about which innumerable studies and commentaries have been written, which have material discussed in the responsa of all periods, and which (together with **Ketubbot* in the order *Nashim*) encompass the whole of Jewish civil law.

English translations of the Mishnah: Danby (1933); Neusner (1988); English translation of the Tosefta: Neusner (2002); English translations of the TJ: Neusner (1984); English translations of the TB: Soncino (1935); Neusner (1984, 1990, 1992); a students' edition of part of TB *Bava Meẓia*, vocalized, with translation, commentary, and notes in English, appeared as part of the Talmud El-Am.

ADD. BIBLIOGRAPHY: A. Geiger, *Ha-Mikra ve-Targumav* (1949), 124–26; S. Lieberman, in *Tarbiz*, 2 (1931), Suppl. 4; idem, *Tosefta: Seder Nezikin* (1988); idem, *Tosefta ki-Feshutah*, parts 9–10 (1988); Ch. Albeck, *Shishah Sidrei Mishnah*, 4 (1959), 57–63, 111–16, 163–68, 211–18, 461–67; L. Jacobs, *Studies in Talmudic Logic and Methodology* (1961), 132–35; Epstein, *Tanna'im*, 417–21; Epstein, Amoraim, 187–270, 279–87, 417; A. Weiss, *Diyyunim u-Verurim be-Vava Kamma* (1966), 10–16; *Yerushalmi Nezikin*, ed. E.S. Rosenthal (1983); Y. Sussmann, in: *Meḥkerei Talmud*, vol. 1 (1990), 55–133; *Talmud Yerushalmi*, with an introduction by Y. Sussmann (2001); S. Friedman, *Talmud Arukh*: BT *Bava Mezi'a VI*, 2 vols. (1990, 1996); C. Hezser, *Form, Function, and Historical Significance of the Rabbinic Story in Yerushalmi Nezikin* (1993), 362–77; D. Halivni, *Mekorot u-Mesorot: Bava Kamma* (1993); idem, *Mekorot u-Mesorot: Bava Meẓia* (2003); *Synopse zum Talmud Yerushalmi*, vol. 4, ed. P. Schäfer and H.J. Becker (1995); Mordekhai Sabato, *Ketav-Yad Temani le-Massekhet Sanhedrin (Bavli) u-Mekomo bi-Masoret ha-Nusaḥ* (1998).

[David Joseph Bornstein / Stephen G. Wald (2nd ed.)]

°**NICANOR**, one of the Syrian officers sent by *Lysias to fight against Judah Maccabee. He is mentioned at length in I and II Maccabees, both passages giving an account of the battle of Emmaus in which Nicanor and Gorgias were defeated by Judah. There is also mention of a Syrian commander called Nicanor who played an important role in the war against Judah in the time of Demetrius. He attempted to approach Judah peacefully or, as another version has it, to capture him by deceit. At all events he was unsuccessful. Enraged that Judah had eluded him once and later defeated him in a battle near Kefar Shalem, he threatened to wreak his vengeance on the Temple and its priests. With the arrival of reinforcements from Syria, Nicanor was once more in a position to confront Judah. In 161 B.C.E. a decisive battle was fought at Bet Horon, but Judah once again triumphed and Nicanor was slain. This was Judah's last military victory. It is uncertain whether the Nicanor who took part in the battle of Emmaus is to be identified with the Nicanor sent by Demetrius against Judah Maccabee, but it is probable that they were two separate persons. The downfall of Nicanor, who had reviled and insulted the Temple, brought joy to the people and the day of triumph, the 13th of Adar, was established as an annual festival.

BIBLIOGRAPHY: Meg. Ta'an. 346; I Macc. 3:38; 7:27–50; II Macc. 8:9ff., 14–15; Jos., Ant., 12:402–5; Polybius, 31:14, 4; Derenbourg, Hist, 63f.; Schuerer, Hist, 31, 40ff.; F.M. Abel, *Les Livres des Maccabées* (1949), 488.

[Uriel Rappaport]

NICANOR'S GATE, one of the gates leading to the Temple courtyard during the period of the Second Temple. According to the Mishnah, "There were seven gates in the Temple courtyard.... In the east there was the gate of Nicanor, which had two rooms attached, one on its right and one on its left, one the room of Phinehas the dresser and one the room of the griddle cake makers" (Mid. 1:4). This gate was one of the best known of the gifts made to the Temple and "miracles were performed in connection with the gate of Nicanor and his memory was praised" (Yoma 3:10). Of these miracles the Talmud states: "What miracles were performed by his doors? When Nicanor went to Alexandria in Egypt to bring them, on his return a huge wave threatened to engulf him. Thereupon they took one of the doors and cast it into the sea but still the sea continued to rage. When they prepared to cast the other one into the sea, Nicanor rose and clung to it, saying 'cast me in with it.'" The sea immediately became calm. He was, however, deeply grieved about the other door. As they reached the harbor of Acre it broke the surface and appeared from under the sides of the boat. Others say a sea monster swallowed it and ejected it out onto dry land. Subsequently all the gates of the Sanctuary were changed for golden ones, but the Nicanor gates, which were said to be of bronze, were left because of the miracles wrought with them. But some say that they were retained because the bronze of which they were made had a special golden hue. R. Eliezer b. Jacob said, "It was Corinthian copper which shone like gold" (Yoma 38a). Corinthian gold was the name given to a family of copper alloys with gold and silver which were depletion-gilded to give them a golden or silver luster (see Jacobson). An important production center for Corinthian gold was in Egypt, where, according to tradition, alchemy had its origins.

Scholars disagree over where the gates stood. Some claim that they were on the western side of the Court of Women which was to the east of the Court of Israelites; others maintain that they were on the eastern side of the Court of Women. The basis of this conflict is in the interpretation of a passage in Josephus (Wars, 5:204). Schalit's discussion of the problem concludes that the words of Josephus are to be explained as meaning that the gates of Nicanor were "beyond" the entrance to the Sanctuary and facing "the gate that was larger," i.e., that it was on the eastern side of the Court of Women. The gates were undoubtedly made after the time of Herod (the most reasonable date being about the middle of the first century, a generation before the destruction) and were the work of an Alexandrian craftsman. Nicanor is also recorded in a first century C.E. inscription on an ossuary found in October 1902 in a cave on Mt. Scopus in Jerusalem ("the Cave of Nicanor"). The Greek inscription reads: "the remains of the children of Nicanor of Alexandria who made the doors." Nicanor's name also appears in a Hebrew inscription as well. Nicanor's gift was so well known that no additional explanation was necessary. Nicanor was an Alexandrian, though he may have gone to live in Jerusalem. It seems more likely, however, that his remains were brought from Alexandria to Jerusalem, where he had a family tomb. The ossuary mentioning Nicanor is now in the collections of the British Museum. Klein (1920; see also Tal 2002) expressed certainty that the Nicanor of the ossuary was the same as the Nicanor who made the set of gates of the Temple according to rabbinic sources; Schwartz (1991), however, has expressed some doubts about this.

BIBLIOGRAPHY: H. Graetz, in: MGWJ, 25 (1876), 434f.; A. Buechler, in: JQR, 11 (1898/99), 46–63; W. Dittenberger, *Orientis Graeci Inscriptiones Selectae*, 2 (1905), 295f., no. 519; E. Schuerer, in: ZNW, 7 (1906), 54ff.; O. Holtzmann, *ibid.*, 9 (1908), 71–74; idem (ed.), *Die Mischna Middot* (1913); H. Vincent and F.M. Abel, *Jérusalem*, 2 (1914), 45ff.; S. Klein, *Juedisch-palaestinisches Corpus Inscriptionum* (1920), 17f., no. 9; *Supplementum Epigraphicum Graecum*, 8 (1937), 30, no. 200; Frey, Corpus, 2 (1952), 261f., no. 1256; M. Avi-Yonah, *Sefer Yerushalayim*, 1 (1956), 412; E. Wiesenberg, in: JJS, 3 (1952), 14–29; E. Bammel, *ibid.*, 7 (1956), 77–78; A. Schalit, *Koenig Herodes*, 1 (1969), 389ff. **ADD. BIBLIOGRAPHY:** G. Dickson, "The Tomb of Nicanor of Alexandria," in: PEFQSt (1903), 326–31; C. Clermont-Ganneau, "The 'Gate of Nicanor' in the Temple of Jerusalem," in: PEFQSt (1903), 125–31; R.A.S. Macalister, "Further Observations on the Ossuary of Nicanor of Alexandria, in: PEFQSt (1905), 253–57; R.D. Barnett, *Illustrations of Old Testament History* (1977), 93–94; J. Schwartz, "Once More on the Nicanor Gate," in: HUCA, 62 (1991), 245–83; T. Ilan, *Lexicon of Jewish names in Late Antiquity. Part 1: Palestine 330 B.C.E.–200 C.E.* (2002), 297–98; D.M. Jacobson, "Corinthian Bronze and the Gold of the Alchemists," in: *Gold Bulletin*, 33 (2) (2000), 60–66.

[Uriel Rappaport / Shimon Gibson (2nd ed.)]

NICARAGUA, Central American republic. Although some Jews settled in Nicaragua in the 19th century, a new community was founded by Jews who arrived from Eastern Europe after 1929. They established the Congregación Israelita de Nicaragua, the most important Jewish association in the country. The majority of the Jews lived in Managua and engaged in commerce, industry, and agriculture; the few who lived in the interior also engaged in agriculture and commercial representation. The congregation maintained close ties with Jewish institutions abroad. All the women in the community belonged to *WIZO, which had been active in the country since 1941. Since 1935 the congregation had its own cemetery and, since 1964, its own synagogue in Managua. Services were held on the Sabbath and on all festivals, and rabbis from abroad were invited to officiate.

[Leonardo Hellemberg]

The community peaked in 1972 with 250 Jews, most living in the capital Managua, but after the disastrous earthquake of December 1972 many Jews emigrated. In 1978, the synagogue in Managua was attacked by five Sandinistas guerrilla fighters. The Sandinista government, which ruled from 1979 to 1990, took different measures against the small Jewish community, which culminated in the virtual expulsion of the few Jewish families that remained in Nicaragua and the implementation of antisemitic propaganda. The government sequestered the synagogue and other Jewish property and imprisoned the community leader Abraham Gorn (at age 70), who however managed to escape. Until 1979 there was a central Jewish organization, but in the early 21st century only a few Jews lived in the country.

Relations with Israel

Nicaragua voted in 1947 for the UN Resolution on the partition of Palestine, and from the establishment of the State of Israel very cordial relations existed between the two countries. Israel was represented in Managua by a nonresident ambassador residing in Costa Rica, and Nicaragua was represented in Israel by a nonresident ambassador residing in Rome. Israel enjoyed Nicaragua's wholehearted support in the international arena, and Nicaragua repeatedly took steps to counteract anti-Israel moves in the United Nations. Israel developed a ramified program in the area of technical aid. Nicaraguan trainees participated in courses in Israel, mainly in the fields of agriculture and community organization. Israel experts were active in Nicaragua in the field of agricultural settlement and conducted a mobile course in agricultural cooperation. In 1969 the scope of trade reached $100,000 in Israeli exports to Nicaragua, mainly in synthetic fibers. In the 1970s Nicaragua became an anti-Israel stronghold, in Latin America and on the international front, particularly following the take-over of power by the Sandinista Junta in July 1979. In 1982 the Sandinista government severed diplomatic relations with Israel, but with the ousting of the Sandinista regime in 1990, ties with Israel were restored.

[Moses Aberbach / Efraim Zadoff (2nd ed.)]

BIBLIOGRAPHY: J. Beller, *Jews in Latin America* (1969).

°**NICARCHUS** (date unknown), author of a book on the Jews in which he says that Moses was called Alpha because of the many leprous spots (*alphous*; cf. a similar canard in *Manetho) which he had on his body. (Alpha was an honorific title for senior members of the museum in Alexandria, and was regarded as synonymous with excellence.)

NICE (Heb. ניצה), capital of the Alpes-Maritimes department, on the Mediterranean coast of France. The first specific mention of Jews can be found in the Statutes of Nice, enacted in 1342 while the town belonged to Provence, which compelled the Jews to wear a distinguishing *badge. By 1406, when Nice belonged to Savoy, the community had a bailiff. In 1408 it owned a cemetery, and from at least 1428, a synagogue. An edict issued by the duke of Savoy in 1430, which was also intended for the Jews of Turin, protected the Jews from forced baptism, while imposing a series of prohibitions (on moneylending, on interest, etc.) and obligations (confining Jewish residence to a separate quarter, the *Giudaria*, etc.). In 1449, a Jew was authorized to settle there and charge a rate of 20% interest. In 1499, Jews expelled from the island of Rhodes were permitted to settle in Nice. From 1551, the Jews were placed under the jurisdiction of a *Conservator* (except in cases of crimes and offenses committed against the Catholic religion) and were allowed to engage freely in moneylending. In the same period, Jews in Nice also engaged in commerce and could practice medicine freely. Beginning in 1648, many newcomers of "Portuguese" origin (*Marranos) from Italy and Holland, attracted by the free port edict, which expressly favored the Jews with numerous privileges, joined the "old Nissards." Twenty years later, many Jews began arriving from Oran (Algeria), often bringing with them their slaves. The newcomers, who settled outside the ghetto, were accorded full rights in the existing community institutions without having to contribute toward its upkeep. The Jewish community of Nice, which had been affiliated to that of Turin, became separated from it from the beginning of the 17th century. The fusion of the diverse groups of Jews was achieved slowly. At the same time, the authorities allowed the legal differences, which had benefited some groups and disadvantaged others, to become obsolete. In particular, beginning in 1732, every Jew was obliged to live in the Jewish quarter, the Rue Giudaria (the present Rue Benoît Brunice). The community, known as *Università*, was led by *massari-parnassim*, deputies, councillors, and a treasurer. The Jews of Nice conversed in Judéo-Niçois, a mixture of the local dialect and Hebrew. The temporary reunion of Nice with France from 1792 to 1814 brought emancipation to the Jews, but they lost their rights after the restoration of Sardinian administration. In 1828, for example, they were ordered to return to the ghetto, and it was only in 1848 that emancipation was finally guaranteed. The annexation of Nice by France in 1860 did not result in further changes in the social and economic situation of the Jews. The number of Jews did not grow substantially during the 19th century. In 1808, the population was approximately 300. In 1909, there were 500 out of a total population of 95,000, and the number did not substantially change up to World War II.

[Bernhard Blumenkranz / David Weinberg (2nd ed.)]

Holocaust and Contemporary Period

During World War II Nice came under Italian control, which was far less severe than the German occupation. As a result, thousands of Jews took refuge there. For a while, the city became an important center for various Jewish organizations, especially after the landing of the Allies in North Africa (November 1942). When the Italians signed the armistice with the Allies, however, German troops invaded the former Italian zone (Sept. 8, 1943) and initiated brutal raids. Alois Brunner, the SS official for Jewish affairs, was placed at the head of units formed to search out Jews. Within five months, 5,000 Jews were caught and deported from Nice and surrounding areas. A great number of others were martyred in the city itself. The courage displayed by the resistance and Jewish youth movements, however, along with the sympathy of the vast majority of the population and clergy, helped save thousands who were either hidden or were helped to escape.

After the liberation several hundred Jews, including original inhabitants of Nice and refugees, reestablished the community. With the influx of Jews from North Africa in the 1960s, the Jewish population in Nice and the vicinity increased from 2,000 to 20,000 by 1969. An estimate of the number of Jews in 1987 in Nice suggested that the population had not changed appreciably since then. The community has two main synagogues (Ashkenazi and Sephardi) and boasts a variety of Jewish institutions, including restaurants, butchers, and a *mikveh*. The Musée Marc Chagall, containing the painter's major works on biblical themes, is situated in Nice.

[Georges Levitte / David Weinberg (2nd ed.)]

BIBLIOGRAPHY: Gross, Gal Jud, 393f.; H. Meiss, *A travers le ghetto… Nice* (1923); Gallois-Montbrun, in: *Annales de la Societé de Lettres des Alpes-Maritimes*, 3 (1875), 242ff.; Giordan, *ibid.*, 46 (1955), 103ff.; Scialtiel, in: REJ, 67 (1914), 118ff.; Bauer, *ibid.*, 63 (1912), 269ff.; V. Emmanuel, *Les Juifs à Nice* (1902); J. Decourcelle, *La Condition des Juifs de Nice…* (1923), includes bibliography; L. Poliakov, *The Jews under the Italian Occupation* (1955), passim; Z. Szajkowski, *Analytical Franco-Jewish Gazetteer 1939–1945* (1966), 156. **ADD. BIBLIOGRAPHY:** *Guide du judaïsme français* (1987), 39; *Jewish Travel Guide* (2002), 73.

°**NICHOLAS**, name of five popes.

NICHOLAS III (Giovanni Gaetano Orsini), pope 1277–80. During his brief reign Nicholas displayed a considerable zeal for the conversion of the Jews. His bull *Vineam sorce* encouraged conversion through "sermons and other means." Copies of the document were sent (1278–79) to the *Franciscans and provincial priors of the *Dominicans in various provinces. Concurrently, however, he renewed the decisions of his predecessors forbidding the forcible baptism of Jews and protecting them from attacks by Christians. Nevertheless, several *Church councils and synods legislated against the free intercourse of Jews and Christians. It is not clear whether it was the supposed hostility of Nicholas or his mildness toward the Jews which prompted Abraham b. Samuel *Abulafia to announce his intention of visiting the pope to demand the release of captive Jews. (When he arrived, however, the pope was already on his deathbed.)

NICHOLAS IV (Girolamo Masci), pope 1288–92. Like many medieval popes, Nicholas IV displayed a mixed attitude toward the Jews. On the one hand, he issued various instructions (1288) to the inquisitors to proceed against *Conversos and he renewed earlier legislation concerning the Jews in Portugal, compelling them to wear a *badge. On the other hand, he specifically protected the Jews of Rome from being molested by Christians (January 1291). He wrote to Emperor *Rudolph (Aug. 29, 1288) requesting the release of *Meir b. Baruch of Rothenburg from prison. There is a belief that he enlisted the services of the Jewish physician and scholar Isaac b. Mordecai Maestro Gaio, who also attended Boniface VIII and who was the first of the Italian Jewish papal physicians.

NICHOLAS V (Tommaso Parentucelli), pope 1447–55. The attitude toward the Jews of this otherwise enlightened pontiff might be characterized as cruelty tempered by a certain moderation. Soon after his election, under the malign influence of John of *Capistrano, he revived the persecutory legislation of his predecessor, *Eugenius IV. Originally framed for Castile and Leon, this legislation was applied en bloc to Italy. Several subsequent edicts, based generally on those of Eugenius, imposed very severe restrictions on Jewish life. Nevertheless, while urging strong measures against Crypto-Jews, Nicholas insisted on the complete equality of New and Old Christians. After a protest by Emperor Frederick III, Nicholas reversed anti-Jewish legislation adopted by various German synods, and he also granted Borso, duke of *Ferrara, complete freedom to allow Jews to reside in his states and operate banks (1451).

BIBLIOGRAPHY: E.A. Synan, *Popes and Jews in the Middle Ages* (1965), 119ff., 122f., 138f.; I. Loeb, in: REJ, 1 (1880), 115ff.; U. Robert, *ibid.*, 3 (1881), 219f.; 4 (1882), 94f.; D. Kaufmann, *ibid.*, 20 (1890), 35f., 48ff.; S. Grayzel, *The Church and the Jews in the* XIII*th* *Century* (1966), index.

[Nicholas de Lange]

°**NICHOLAS**, name of two Russian czars.

NICHOLAS I, czar of Russia from 1825 to 1855. His reign was marked by a general reaction, the persecution of liberal elements in the country, and the oppression of religious and national minorities. Nicholas I regarded the Jews as a harmful alien group whose unity should be destroyed so that it would become completely assimilated within the Russian people. To achieve this, he adopted many measures. The first, which left its imprint on the whole of his Jewish policy, was the introduction of compulsory military service for the Jews (1827). This was accompanied by the seizure of Jewish children, who were to be educated in the schools for soldiers' children in the spirit of the Christian religion (see *Cantonists). The area of the Pale of *Settlement was reduced and the Jews were expelled from *Kiev, *Sevastopol, and *Nikolayev. There was also a suggestion that they be expelled from within 50 versts of the border. On the other hand, the government encouraged renewed agricultural settlement of the Jews in southern Russia and around their townlets, exempting the settlers from military service. The government of Nicholas I supported the *maskilim* in their struggle against Orthodoxy. Under the influence of the *maskilim*, a severe censorship was imposed on Jewish books, their publication being authorized at two presses only, in *Vilna and *Zhitomir. During the 1840s the government set out to develop the network of Jewish government schools, particularly the rabbinical seminaries of Vilna and Zhitomir, which offered a general education in addition to a Jewish education in the spirit of the *Haskalah. At the end of the 1840s, the Jews were forbidden to wear their traditional garb.

Toward the close of Nicholas' reign the "classification" (*razbor*) of the Jews into "useful" (merchants, craftsmen, agricultural workers) and "non-useful" persons was proposed. Severe repressive measures were to be adopted against the "non-useful" – principally the intensification of conscription. This project was interrupted by the death of Nicholas I, which also resulted in the abolition of the special conscription of Jews and in other alleviations. Of the hundreds of anti-Jewish laws which were passed during his reign, the most important for the Jews were the Jewish statutes of 1835 and 1844 (which officially abolished the Jewish communities and introduced the status of **kazyonny ravvin*). In the memory of the Jewish people, the reign of Nicholas I is regarded, especially because of the Cantonists decree, as one of the darkest periods in the history of the Jews in czarist Russia.

NICHOLAS II, Russian czar from 1894 to 1917. His reign was marked by a violent struggle against the revolutionary movement, the war against Japan (1904), which was followed by the first Russian Revolution (1905–06), and Russia's participation (1914–17) in World War I, which culminated in the Revolution of the spring of 1917 and the removal of Nicholas II from the throne. At the outset of his reign the Jews, like other Russian circles, hoped that the new czar would change the extreme reactionary and antisemitic policy of his father *Alexander III. This hope was, however, soon disappointed. The czar, whose education at the hands of Constantine *Pobedonostsev had made him an indubitable Jew-hater, regarded the Jews as the principal factor in the Russian revolutionary movement. He favored antisemitic statesmen, rejected any attempt to change the anti-Jewish laws in spite of the advice of some of the leading statesmen of his court (such as S. *Witte and P. Stolypin), and took under his aegis the violent antisemitic movement, "*Union of Russian People" (popularly known as the "Black Hundreds"), and other organizations formed in reaction to the liberal and revolutionary organizations. The pogroms against the Jews, which were at first due to the free hand given to anti-Jewish incitement and the rioters, were later directly perpetrated by the police and the army, as part of the campaign against the revolution. The *Beilis blood libel trial at Kiev, which was designed to set off renewed persecutions of the Jews, was inspired by the czar. Although no new anti-Jewish laws were passed during the reign of Nicholas II, the administrative pressure which accompanied the pogroms encouraged hundreds of thousands of Jews to emigrate to the U.S. and elsewhere.

BIBLIOGRAPHY: NICHOLAS I: Dubnow, Divrei, 9 (1958[2]), 95–118, 208–11; Dubnow, Hist Russ, index; R. Mahler, *Divrei Yemei Yisrael, Dorot Aḥaronim*, 2 bk 1 (1970), 13–240. NICHOLAS II: Dubnow, Divrei, 10 (1958*), 102–8, 189–207, 218–24, 262–4; Dubnow, Hist Russ, index; Elbogen, Century, 371–404, 453–7; I. Ma'or, *She'elat ha-Yehudim ba-Tenu'ah ha-Liberalit ve-ha-Mahpekhanit be-Rusyah* (1964); *Die Judenpogrome in Russland* (1909); S.W. Baron, *Russian Jews under Tsars and Soviets* (1964).

[Yehuda Slutsky]

°**NICHOLAS, EDWARD**, author of a famous 17th-century plea in favor of the resettlement of the Jews in England. Entitled *An Apology for the Honourable Nation of the Jews, and all the Sons of Israel*, and published in London in 1648, it was translated into Spanish, perhaps by *Manasseh Ben Israel, and made a profound impression. However, since the author is otherwise unknown, there is reason to believe that the publication was inspired or even written by a Jew. Its theme was that England should make amends for her former maltreatment of the Jews by readmitting them to the country. Some scholars believe that its actual author was Rev. Henry Jessey (1601–1663), a philo-semitic Nonconformist minister. Little is known about Edward Nicholas himself beyond the fact that he was apparently a young man reading for the bar in 1648. He is sometimes confused with Sir Edward Nicholas (1593–1669), a government official who was in exile with Charles II in 1648, but this man was 55 when *An Apology* appeared.

BIBLIOGRAPHY: Roth, England, 153, 286; Roth, in: V.D. Lipman (ed.), *The Centuries of Anglo-Jewish History* (1961), 3. **ADD. BIBLIOGRAPHY:** E. Samuel, "Oliver Cromwell and the Re-admission of the Jews to England in 1656," in: idem., *At the Ends of the Earth: Essays on the History of the Jews in England and Portugal* (2004), 180.

[Vivian David Lipman / William D. Rubinstein (2nd ed.)]

°**NICHOLAS DE LYRE** (incorrectly **Lyra**; c. 1270–(not before)1349), Bible commentator and theologian. A 15th-century allegation of his Jewish extraction lacks all basis. Born in Lyre, near Evreux, Normandy, Nicholas joined the Franciscan Order at Verneuil (c. 1291) and subsequently studied in Paris. He held the position of professor of theology at the Sorbonne until he was appointed Franciscan provincial of Burgundy in 1325. He wrote controversial studies against Judaism (e.g., *De Messia ... ad Judaei argumenta, De diversis contra Judaeos ...*) and produced a commentary on Peter Lombard's *Sentences*, which, together with the Bible, constituted the basis of Western theological studies. His importance, however, lies in *Postillae Perpetuae*, which he composed from 1322 to 1330 (published in Rome, 1471–72).

These works form a continuous commentary on the entire Bible, with priority accorded to the literal meaning, while other senses ("*moralitates*") are relegated to 35 substantial appendixes. The *Postillae* constitute the first Christian Bible commentary to be printed. The literalist approach led Nicholas to *Rashi, whom he often cites by name (Salomo). In this he had been anticipated by the Victorine scholars, especially by *Andrew of Saint Victor whom he quotes (G. Calandra, *De... Andreae Victorini... in Ecclesiasten* (1948), 83–85). However, Nicholas, who records his perusal of a controversial tract *hebraice scriptus* ("written in Hebrew"; see Hailperin in bibl., p. 140), used Rashi directly as well. In addition he read some rabbinic material in Raymond *Martini's *Pugio Fidei*. Soon after his death, Nicholas' *Postillae* were available in virtually every library in western Christendom. Nicholas had abiding influence (Hailperin, p. 282f.). Wycliffe acknowledged his indebtedness to Nicholas in his (later) English version of the Bible (c. 1388). *Luther was particularly dependent on him, especially on Genesis. In his commentary to Daniel, Abrabanel controverts Nicholas' christological exegesis.

BIBLIOGRAPHY: L. Wadding, *Scriptores Ordinis Minorum* (1967), 178–9; R. Bellarmin, *De Scriptoribus Ecclesiasticis* (1613), 213 (list of works); *Catholic Encylopedia*, 11 (1913), 63 (incl. bibl.); JE, 8 (1904), 231; EJ, 10 (1934), 1263; B. Smalley, *The Study of the Bible in the Middle Ages* (1952[2]), 185, 355; G.W.H. Lampe (ed.), *The History of the Bible in the West*, 2 (1969), 219; H. Hailperin, *Rashi and the Christian Scholars* (1963), passim.

[Raphael Loewe]

°**NICHOLAS OF DAMASCUS** (b. c. 64 B.C.E.), Greek historian, peripatetic philosopher, orator, dramatist, and statesman. Nicholas came from a distinguished family in *Damascus, where his father, Antipater, occupied a prominent position and was proud of his origin. For a time he was in the service of Antony and Cleopatra, acting as their children's instructor. Later he joined the court of *Herod whose confidant he became, instructing him also in philosophy and rhetoric. It was at Herod's instigation that he wrote his Universal History (see below). Nicholas' fame as a writer and an intellectual, his outstanding talents as an orator, and his connections with leading Romans equipped him to undertake delicate diplomatic tasks. He acted as Herod's representative to Marcus *Agrippa in 14 B.C.E., when the Jews of Asia Minor submitted their complaints against the inhabitants of the Greek cities (Jos., Ant., 16:29–58). He also interceded with *Augustus on behalf of Herod when the latter had lost favor in Rome due to his aggressive action against the Arabs in 8 B.C.E. (*ibid.*, 16:335–55). Nicholas exercised great influence on Herod's internal policy. According to his own testimony, he was a consistent opponent of *Antipater, Herod's eldest son, and helped to get rid of him (*ibid.*, 17:106–21). Even after Herod's death, Nicholas remained loyal to him: he traveled to Rome in 4 B.C.E., with *Archelaus, Herod's son, to obtain Augustus' confirmation of Herod's will and to defend the name of the dead king and the interests of Archelaus against the charges brought by representatives of the Jewish nation (*ibid.*, 240–8). At the same time Nicholas persuaded Archelaus not to oppose the granting of independence to the Hellenistic cities on the borders of Herod's former kingdom. On this occasion, too, Nicholas' efforts were successful, and Augustus confirmed Herod's will in broad outline. This was Nicholas' last active intervention in the affairs of Judea. He apparently stayed on in Rome.

The most famous of Nicholas' many writings was his *His-*

toria Universalis in 144 books, in which events are described in greater detail the nearer they approach the days of the author. Those in which he was personally involved are given special treatment. Nicholas' intervention on behalf of the Jews of Asia Minor is described in books 123 and 124 (Jos., Ant., 12:126–7). He also wrote an autobiography, the contents of which correspond to some extent to the last books of the history, as well as a biography of Augustus. Nicholas used to provide Augustus with a choice variety of dates from his estate, which Augustus called after him (Athenaeus 14:652). They are possibly the dates referred to in rabbinical literature (Av. Zar. 14b; Num. R. 3:1) as "Nikolaos." Nicholas' history is no longer extant, except for lengthy excerpts, particularly those dealing with most ancient times, preserved in the compilations of Constantine Porphyrogenitus, the 10th-century Byzantine emperor. Shorter extracts have been preserved in the works of Josephus, Athenaeus, Stephanus of Byzantium, and others.

Nicholas' connections with Herod, his acquaintance with the Jews, and his defense of them on several occasions precluded him from adopting a contemptuous attitude toward the ancient Jewish tradition, as did most Greek and Roman writers. Thus he reveals a tendency to combine the Damascene-Syrian with the biblical-Jewish traditions. In the fourth book of his history he deals sympathetically with the personality of Abraham (Jos., Ant., 1:159), whom he depicts as a foreigner who came at the head of an army from the land of the Chaldees to Damascus, where he reigned as king and from which he later migrated with his people to the land of Canaan. The name of Abram, says Nicholas, is still honored in the region of Damascus. In the same book of his history he refers to the biblical account of the wars between Israel and Aram in the days of David as well as after the division of the kingdom (*ibid.*, 7:101–3). Among pre-Christian Greek writers, Nicholas is the only one to mention David. He recalls the biblical tradition when referring, in the 96th book of his history, to the Flood, and mentions that "Moses, the Jewish legislator, wrote" (*ibid.*, 1:95). To judge from these fragments, Nicholas' interest in Jewish history is due chiefly to Jewish connections with his native city, Damascus; it seems unlikely that he was a major source for the early books of Josephus' *Antiquities* which parallel the Bible.

In regard to Jewish history in the period of the Second Temple, he describes the actions of *Antiochus Epiphanes against the Jews (Jos., Apion, 2:83–84) and is quoted by Josephus a number of times verbatim. Josephus was perhaps naturally attracted to the work of a man who, like himself, had written an autobiography defending himself against charges of time-serving. Nicholas' *Universal History* provided the basis of Josephus' description of Herod's kingdom in *The Jewish War* (book 1) and *Antiquities* (books 15–17). As is to be expected from a courtier and collaborator in the policy of the king, Nicholas' books about Herod are a panegyric upon him. Marked by their dramatic tension and replete with pathetic descriptions, these books are written in a spirit of open hostility toward Antipater, the son of Herod and Nicholas' mortal enemy. These characteristics are also notable in Josephus' account, except that in the *Antiquities* Josephus makes a conscious effort to free himself from the panegyrical approach of Nicholas. Josephus' dependence on Nicholas is further shown by a comparison between his account and the excerpts preserved in Nicholas' autobiography, and by the fact that for the period no longer covered by Nicholas' work (after 4 B.C.E.) Josephus' narrative is meager. The description, too, of the Hasmonean kingdom in Josephus' two works is chiefly derived from Nicholas' history, a conclusion that necessarily follows from the non-Jewish viewpoint that generally characterizes this description.

BIBLIOGRAPHY: G. Hoelscher, *Die Quellen des Josephus...* (1904), 17ff.; Schuerer, Hist, index; F. Jacoby (ed.), *Die Fragmente der griechischen Historiker,* 2B Texts (1926), 324–430; 2A Commentary (1926), 29–91; R.J.H. Shutt, *Studies in Josephus* (1961), 79–92; B.Z. Wacholder, *Nicholas of Damascus* (1962).

[Menahem Stern]

NICHOLS, JACK (1921–), Canadian painter, draftsman, printmaker, educator. Born in Montreal, Nichols is one of the best-known official Canadian World War II artists. Unable to afford traditional schooling, he was mainly self-taught. However, he occasionally worked with the Montreal artists Louis Muhlstock and Frederick Varley, and considered the former his mentor. After he enlisted in the Merchant Navy in the fall of 1943, the National Gallery of Canada commissioned him to produce drawings during his service on Caribbean-bound ships. In 1944, he was appointed an official war artist with the rank of lieutenant in the Royal Canadian Naval Reserve. Nichols witnessed the D-Day landing, and traveled on a number of warships, including the HMCS *Iroquois*, which together with British warships destroyed a German convoy as it attempted to evacuate the town of Brest in 1944. Nichols depicted this event in at least two compositions: the drawing *Men on H.M.C.S.* Iroquois *at Action Stations* represents a crowd of Canadian soldiers and their varying reactions to the violence at sea. *Action Aboard His Majesty's Canadian Ship* Iroquois again represents a dense mass of soldiers, three of whose massively muscled arms seem to press against the picture plane, while other sailors ready weapons in the background. Nichols' characteristically dark palette and his attention to facial expressions conveying fear, anguish, and suffering draw the viewer's attention to the vulnerability of his subjects as they face their mortality. One of Nichols' most famous paintings, the expressionistically rendered *Drowning Sailor*, depicts the screaming anguish of a seaman desperately trying to extricate himself from the maelstrom of water encircling him. Many of Nichols' compositions have Christian overtones. For example, *Ammunition Passer* is reminiscent of traditional depictions of Christ carrying the Cross. The oil painting *Taking Survivors on Board* portrays a prone man supported by another figure in a position which recalls a Pietà. At the time he left the navy in 1946, Nichols had created 20 works on paper and nine oil paintings. In 1947, Nichols won a Guggenheim fellowship which enabled him to paint and study printmaking in different parts of the United States. He taught at the Vancouver School of Art in 1948. In 1952, he garnered a prize at the Second International Exhibition of Drawing and Engraving in Lugano, Switzerland. Six years later, his lithographs were displayed at the Venice Biennale. Nichols lived and worked in Toronto. The artist had exhibitions at the Ellen Gallery at Concordia University, the McCord Museum, Montreal, the MacKenzie Art Gallery, Saskatchewan, and the Vancouver Art Gallery, among other venues. His work is owned by the Canadian War Museum, Ottawa and the Canadian War Records Collection.

BIBLIOGRAPHY: L. Brandon, "Emotion as Document: Death and Dying in the Second World War Art of Jack Nichols," in: *Material History Review*, 48 (Fall 1998), 123–30; D.F. Oliver, *Canvas of War: Painting the Canadian Experience, 1914 to 1945* (2000).

[Nancy Buchwald (2nd ed.)]

NICHOLS, MIKE (Michael Igor Peschkowsky; 1931–), U.S. comedian and director. Born in Berlin, Nichols and his family fled Germany in 1939. Educated at the University of Chicago, he studied for a time with Lee Strasberg in New York. Nichols was one of the founders of The Compass, an off-campus theater group, later forming the Second City Improvisational company in Chicago. He toured in cabaret with Elaine May (see *Theater) from 1954, and in 1960 they presented *An Evening with Mike Nichols and Elaine May* on Broadway, for which they won a Grammy for Best Comedy Performance (1961).

In 1961 Nichols turned to acting on his own, and then directed a series of successful plays on Broadway. Among them were *Barefoot in the Park* (Tony Award, 1963), *The Knack* (1964), *Luv* (Tony Award, 1964), *The Odd Couple* (Tony Award, 1965), *The Apple Tree* (1966), *The Little Foxes* (1967), *Plaza Suite* (Tony Award, 1968), *The Prisoner of Second Avenue* (Tony Award, 1971), *Uncle Vanya* (1973), *Streamers* (1976), *Comedians* (1976), *Annie* (producer, Tony Award, 1977), *The Gin Game* (1977), *The Real Thing* (two Tony Awards, 1984), *Hurlyburly* (1984), and *Spamalot* (Tony Award, 2005). Turning to movies, he directed the film version of *Who's Afraid of Virginia Woolf?* (Oscar nomination for Best Director, 1966); *The Graduate* (Academy Award for Best Director, 1967); *Catch-22* (1969); *The Day of the Dolphin* (1973); *The Fortune* (1975); *Gilda Live* (1980); *Silkwood* (Oscar nomination for Best Director, 1983); *Heartburn* (1986); *Biloxi Blues* (1988); *Working Girl* (Oscar nomination for Best Director, 1988); *Postcards from the Edge* (1990); *Regarding Henry* (1991); *Wolf* (1994); *The Birdcage* (plus screenplay, 1995); *Primary Colors* (1998); *What Planet Are You From?* (2000); the Emmy award-winning TV movie *Wit* (2001); the Emmy award-winning TV miniseries *Angels in America* (2003); and *Closer* (2004).

Nichols is one of a handful of celebrities to have garnered the coveted quartet of an Oscar, an Emmy, a Tony, and a Grammy.

In 2003 he was one of the recipients of the Kennedy Center Honors. He is chairman emeritus of the non-profit organization Friends in Deed, founded in 1991 to provide support to those affected by life-threatening illness.

After three divorces, Nichols has been married to news personality Diane Sawyer since 1988.

Nichols wrote the books *Life and Other Ways to Kill Time* (1988); *Real Men Belch Downwind* (1993); and *Women Are from Pluto, Men Are from Uranus* (1996).

ADD. BIBLIOGRAPHY: H. Schuth, *Mike Nichols* (1977).

[Lee Healey and Jonathan Licht / Ruth Beloff (2nd ed.)]

NIDDAH (Heb. נִדָּה "menstruating woman"; literally, "one who is excluded" or "expelled"). According to Jewish law, a man is forbidden to maintain sexual relations with his wife during and for some time both before and after (see below) her menses. Marital intimacy may resume only after the wife has undergone ritual immersion (see *Mikveh*; *Ablution) at the appropriate time. These strictures of separation and ritual cleansing, which apply only to married Jewish women, are intended to preserve men from the ritual pollution that would follow from any contact with their ritually impure wives. Procedures for calculating the intervals of time when spousal contact is forbidden rely heavily on a woman's knowledge of the stages of her cycle. Fidelity to the rules of marital separation, self-examination, and expedient immersion comprise one of the three areas of ritual obligations specifically incumbent on women (together with *ḥallah*, separating a part of the dough used to make Sabbath loaves, and *hadlakah*, kindling Sabbath lights (see *Candles)). Jewish girls were traditionally taught to comply strictly and promptly with *hilkhot niddah*, the regulations pertaining to the menstruating woman.

The laws relating to the *niddah* comprise some of the most fundamental principles of the halakhic system. They also constitute one of the few remnants of biblical regulations pertaining to ritual impurities that survived in Jewish life following the destruction of the Second Temple. Among the most difficult and intricate in the entire range of the *halakhah*, these laws are elucidated in a lengthy and detailed tractate of the same name devoted to the subject (see *Niddah*, tractate). The historical development of the relevant *halakhot* through the centuries is likewise extremely complicated. To decide a law relating to a *niddah* demands, besides a profound knowledge of the *halakhah*, experience in various medical matters, and at times also the ability to assume the grave responsibility of disqualifying a woman from pursuing a normal married life and of – at times – separating her forever from her husband. In every generation and in every place there have generally been men, referred to in the Talmud simply as "sages," who specialized in the subject, as did eminent *tannaim* and *amoraim*, to whom particularly difficult questions were sent, even from remote places, together with specimens of blood (Nid. 20b). In brief, the *halakhah* as at present codified is that sexual intercourse (and any other intimacies which may lead to it) is forbidden from the time the woman expects her menses until seven "clean" or "white" days (i.e., days on which no blood whatsoever is seen) have elapsed. For this purpose a minimum of five days is fixed for the menses themselves. Thus the minimum period of abstention from marital intimacies is 12 days. On the evening of the seventh day without sign of blood the woman immerses herself in a **mikveh* and normal marital relations are resumed until the next menses are expected. Any bleeding in ensuing days is considered as menstrual and requires a waiting period of seven "white" days (see below). The laws of *niddah* are codified in the *Shulhan Arukh, Yoreh De'ah*, 183–200.

In the Bible

A detailed discussion is devoted to the *niddah* as part of the general "law of him that hath an issue" (Lev. 15:19–32), within the framework of the many laws of ritual purity and impurity whose main purpose was to preserve the purity of the sanctuary and its precincts. To this aspect the Bible adds a further prohibition against sexual intercourse with a menstruating woman, the punishment for which is *karet* for both the man and the woman (*ibid.* 20:18). While this prohibition at present constitutes the main feature of the *niddah*, in the Bible it is the former context that is the decisive factor. According to the literal meaning of the biblical passages, most of which are, however, unclear, the law is thus: A woman who discerns blood within and up to a period of seven days is ritually "impure" (*teme'ah*) for those seven days from the time the blood first appears. On the eighth day – if she sees no further blood – she is "pure" (*tehorah*). Whoever touches her or anything she sits or lies on during the week of her "uncleanness" is "unclean until the evening" and must bathe himself in water and wash his clothes. One who has sexual intercourse with a menstruant is unclean for seven days, since she transfers her condition of ritual impurity to him ("and her impurity is upon him"). If, however, a woman sees blood for more than seven days, she becomes a *zavah* ("one who has a discharge") and is in a state of ritual impurity until her discharge of blood ceases. All the laws previously mentioned apply to her. Unlike the *niddah*, however, the *zavah* does not revert to her state of ritual purity immediately after her discharge of blood stops but has to wait a further seven "clean" days, reckoned from the day she has ceased to see blood. At the conclusion of this period she brings "two turtle-doves, or two young pigeons" as a sacrifice. Although not specifically mentioned in the Bible, the purification of the *niddah* of both the first and second types was undoubtedly associated with immersion in a ritual bath, since this is clearly stated in the Bible with respect to others rendered levitically impure by reason of a discharge. The Bible does not lay down the normal length of time between one menses and another.

In the Talmud

On the basis of the tradition of the Oral Law, the sages gave the biblical passages a different interpretation. Their basic assumption is that there is a fixed cycle of 18 days, comprising seven days of *niddut* (the state of being a *niddah*) and 11 days between one menses and another, this being, in the view of the sages, the "allotted" interval. This cycle of 18 days is counted consecutively from the appearance for the first time of blood in a female at the age of puberty and in rare instances even earlier. A woman who sees blood on one or all of the seven days is ritually impure for these seven days and becomes ritually pure again on the eighth day on condition that she immerses herself in a *mikveh* ("ritual bath"; see also Ablution) and that no further blood has appeared before her immersion. If blood reappears on the eighth day, she is ritually impure on that day, immerses herself on the following morning, and waits until the evening. If no more blood is seen she is ritually pure; if it is seen, she has to adopt the same procedure on the next day. If after the conclusion of the seventh day blood is discerned on three consecutive or non-consecutive days during the 11 days between one menses and another, the woman becomes a *zavah* and has to count seven "clean" or "white" days, as stated above. If, however, she passes the 11 or at least nine of the days between one menses and another in a state of ritual purity, she reverts to the beginning of a new cycle and any blood that she may see during the subsequent seven days does not necessitate seven "white" days. These 11 days are a traditional law ascribed to Moses (*"Halakhah le-Moshe mi-Sinai"*). Any blood appearing during the interval between one menses and another – on the conclusion of the above-mentioned cycle of 7+11 days – is due to a discharge that requires seven "white" days. This cycle commences from the day blood appeared for the first time and no longer depends on the appearance or nonappearance of blood: the seven days are "appropriate" for blood of menstruation, the 11 days for blood of a discharge, and only childbirth interrupts this automatic reckoning (see below). Such is the basic law; however, as early as the end of the tannaitic period, Jewish women were accustomed to observe seven "white" days for any spot of blood they observed that was as large as a mustard seed (see below).

The problem that arises if a woman does not examine herself during the days when she is in a state of ritual purity and suddenly sees blood is dependent on the tannaitic controversy over whether the laws of fixed menses are of biblical or rabbinical authority. In the former instance, the woman automatically reverts to her state of ritual impurity retrospectively from the beginning of her fixed menses unless she has examined herself and found no blood, whereas in the latter case she is ritually pure until she physically feels the movement of, or sees, blood. In any event it is halakhically of great importance that a woman knows the dates of her menses, since she has to refrain from sexual intercourse near their onset, so that they should not come on during sexual intercourse. In the tractate *Niddah* the various types of menses, the way in which they are fixed, and their halakhic significance form the subject of extensive talmudic discussion.

The sages distinguished among several types of blood, some ritually pure, others ritually impure, that issue from a woman, the distinction being based on the different sources of the blood in the womb. However, since modern knowledge of a woman's anatomy and physiology does not accord with the sages' assumptions, their statements are not clear. Various scholars have unsuccessfully tried to harmonize the statements of the sages on this subject with existing anatomical knowledge. But although the sages have given indications for distinguishing between one type of blood and another, either by its appearance or by various examinations made in a woman's body, already in talmudic times a thorough knowledge of the subject was limited to experts. In consequence, the *halakhah* states that, since we are not adept in the matter, all blood renders a woman ritually impure. A very difficult and painful question concerns instances of a discharge of blood which is due to an external cause, as for example, an internal wound, but cannot definitely be identified as such. This problem was particularly formidable so long as its solution depended on halakhic discussions among the sages and not on a clear, objective medical examination. A more general distinction is made between a woman's blood and her other discharges which are not blood and hence do not render her ritually impure. In this instance, too, the sages have given several indications, based mainly on the intensity of the reddishness of the discharge. Here it has similarly been laid down that we no longer possess the knowledge requisite to make a precise distinction and hence any discharge, unless it is white or green (in their various shades), causes ritual impurity. Whereas nowadays doubt can be easily and definitely resolved, previously this problem, like the former one, was often one of paramount human significance and an obstacle to married life for not a few couples. Accordingly, the works of the codifiers in all periods contain hundreds of responsa dealing with the subject out of a manifest desire to alleviate this hardship, though with a very scant possibility of doing so.

Another problem in this category, much rarer but devoid of any practical solution, concerns a woman who bleeds during the act of sexual intercourse. This blood is assumed to be menstrual blood, and its regular appearance at such a time prevents any possibility, according to the *halakhah*, of a married life between the couple, since after several recurrences it is considered a permanent feature, and hence intercourse is prohibited from the outset. In this case the couple have to be divorced, particularly if the husband has not yet fulfilled the *mitzvah* of procreation. Virginal blood forms a special halakhic subject, being in principle ritually pure, for, since its source is an external one, it is in every respect identical with blood that has issued from a wound. This was the earlier *halakhah*. Later a stricter view was taken in the matter, particularly in Babylonia, for fear that such blood might be mingled with menstrual blood discharged due to sexual excitement, and hence the couple had to keep apart from each other immediately after the first coition. In Ereẓ Israel this stricter view was not common practice. In geonic times this restriction received, in Babylonia, the force of absolute law, but from the many questions addressed to the *geonim*, it is evident that in fact the prohibition did not extend throughout that country. The subject was still included as a section in *Sefer ha-Hillukim she-Bein Benei Bavel u-Venei Erez Yisrael*, compiled in the middle of the geonic period. With the spread of the influence of the Babylonian Talmud this prohibition was generally observed among almost all Jewish communities and was laid down as a *halakhah* in the Shulhan Arukh (EH, 193).

An essential change in the entire laws of the *niddah*, which since talmudic times became the accepted law throughout Jewry, relates to the addition of the seven "clean" or "white" days. This change took place due to a twofold difficulty arising from the earlier procedure: first, the lack of a reasonable and practical possibility of keeping a methodical, precise, and consecutive count of the days of menstruation and of discharge, as described above, from the first day of the appearance of blood until the end of the period of the menses; and secondly, the recognition that there is no real possibility of distinguishing with any certainty between clean and unclean blood, thus making the actual counting impracticable. In the days of Judah ha-Nasi the first regulations in this connection were issued, and in the middle of the amoraic period it was already accepted as axiomatic that seven "white" days were to be counted for any blood seen (Nid. 66a; et al.). The essence of the regulation was that the days of menstruation were henceforth equated with those of any other discharge. To this regulation a further restriction was added, according to which a single spot of blood is treated as a regular flow also with regard to the necessity of counting seven "white" days. It is evident from the sources that originally only sexual intercourse was prohibited during the seven "white" days, as against the prohibition of all physical contact during the actual days of menstruation (see below). In the course of time, however, this latter prohibition was extended to cover the "white" days as well, which thus became further days of ritual impurity (Shab. 13a).

Although trangressing the prohibition with regard to a *niddah* is punishable with *karet*, a marriage with a woman who is menstruating is binding, and her offspring is entirely legitimate, fit even for the priesthood and suffering only from a "taint" which is unattended by any halakhic consequences. The marriage ceremony of a bride who has begun menstruating shortly before is not postponed, even though, generally speaking, a marriage should be capable of immediate consummation. Nevertheless, many restrictions and minutiae with regard to the prohibition relating to the *niddah* came to be observed. In ancient times a *niddah* was completely segregated, particularly in Ereẓ Israel where the laws of purity were still in vogue from the time when the Temple existed. Excluded from her home, the *niddah* stayed in a special house known as "a house for uncleanness" (Nid. 7:4), she was called *galmudah* ("segregated," RH 26a), and was not allowed to adorn herself until R. Akiva permitted her to do so, that she might not be repulsive to her husband (*Sifra, Meẓora*, 9:12). No food was eaten with a *niddah* (Tosef., Shab. 1:14) nor did she attend to her household duties, until the stage was reached in which "during all the days of her menstruation she is to be segregated" (*ARN* A 1, 4). The origin of this segregation lies in the custom, prevalent in Erez Israel long after the destruction of the Second Temple, of eating ordinary meals prepared according to the levitical rules originally prescribed for sacred food. This custom did not obtain prevalence in Babylonia where there was neither any reason for, nor any halakhic possibility of, observing absolute purity, and where accordingly all these expressions of the *niddah*'s segregation were not practiced. Thus, in Babylonia, she attended to all the needs of her household, with the exception of filling her husband's cup of wine, making his bed, and washing him (Ket. 61a). In the latter half of the geonic period the *geonim* of Babylonia, adopting an increasingly stricter view with regard to the ritual impurity of the *niddah*, accepted the restrictions of the earlier scholars of Erez Israel. Related to the spread of the Muslim religion which was particularly strict in matters associated with "cleanness and uncleanness," this process reflects the strong desire of the *geonim* not to be inferior in their practices to their neighbors. Nevertheless, Maimonides at a later stage maintained that the restriction imposed on the *niddah* to refrain from cooking, touching a garment, and so on, was devoid of any significance and might even savor of Karaism. These restrictions were generally not adopted in Europe where the two factors that led to their introduction in Erez Israel and Babylonia were lacking, as well as because of the high status enjoyed there by the Jewish woman in managing the affairs of her household.

Yet it was mainly in Europe that new limitations and prohibitions were imposed on the *niddah* and on the members of her family. These measures are all contained in a small work entitled *Baraita de-Niddah* (1890), which is so strange that some scholars contended that it originated in a heretical Jewish sect. Where and when it was written has, up to the present, not been determined, although it has generally been assigned to the end of the geonic period. The special limitations mentioned in the work include the following: The *niddah* is prohibited from entering synagogue, as is also her husband if he has been rendered impure by her in any way (by her spittle, the dust under her feet, and so on). She is likewise prohibited from kindling the Sabbath lights. One is not allowed to enquire after her welfare or to recite a benediction in her presence. A priest whose wife, mother, or daughter is a *niddah* may not recite the priestly benediction in synagogue. No benefit may be derived from the work of a *niddah*, whose very utterances defile. From the beginning of the Rabbanite period the influence of this work on codifiers has been particularly marked, and although it is generally admitted that its statements have no halakhic validity, they adopted its stringent measures. This is especially notable with regard to prohibiting a *niddah* from entering a synagogue, which gave rise to a not insignificant literature among the early scholars of Germany.

This phenomenon is best understood against the background of the various superstitions current among the Jews, some of which derived from the non-Jewish environment. These superstitions held that the breath of a *niddah*'s mouth causes harm, that her glance "is disreputable and creates a bad impression," that a menstruant's blood proves fatal to anyone drinking it, and if mingled with the bloodstream produces pustules and boils in the newly born child. If a *niddah* looks for a long time in a mirror, red drops resembling blood appear on it. She pollutes the air in her proximity, is regarded as sick and even as afflicted with plague, despite the fact that menstruation is natural to a woman (Nahmanides, *Gen.* 31:35; *Lev.* 12:4, 18:19). A menstruant at the beginning of her menses who passes between two men causes one of them to be killed; she produces strife between them if she is at the end of her period (Pes. 111a).

A Woman after Childbirth

The law relating to the woman who has given birth to a child is stated in Leviticus 12:1–8. According to the literal meaning of the passage, her discharge of blood is in the same category as menstrual blood and hence she is in a state of ritual impurity, like a *niddah*. This extends for seven days if she bears a boy and for 14 days if she has a girl. In addition to this, a further period of 33 days in the former instance and 66 in the latter is laid down, these being "the days of her purification," and the blood seen during that time is called "the blood of purification." During this period she is sexually permitted to her husband but may not enter the sanctuary until the days of her purification have ended. On their conclusion she had to bring the prescribed sacrifices. The law of the post-partum woman was preserved in this form by the sages, who, however, added that any blood seen during the days of her purification renders her ritually impure, requiring immediate ritual immersion before further sexual contact with her husband. In the view of the sages, childbirth and the counting of the days associated therewith annuls that of the above-mentioned 11 days and a new cycle of menses begins. In the geonic period the regulation in respect of the "white" days, previously referred to, was extended to include "the days of her purification," and consequently the custom obtained in Babylonia, Ereẓ Israel, Spain, and North African countries that a woman who had given birth to a child observed seven "white" days for any spot of blood seen during the days of her purification. This extended regulation, which is wholly incompatible with the essential character of "the days of purification," in that they are not subject to the ritual impurity that accompanies menstruation, was not accepted in France and Germany, where sexual intercourse was permitted after a discharge of "blood of purification" (see *Yad, Issurei Bi'ah*, 11:6–7). The *baraita* in tractate *Niddah*, quoted above, mentions a yet more stringent custom according to which a woman is prohibited to her husband as a *niddah* for all the 40 and 80 days after the birth of a son and a daughter respectively, even though she has seen no blood during the entire period of her purification. This custom was regarded by Maimonides (Yad, *ibid.*, 11:15) as "the way of heretics," and is indeed practiced by the *Karaites (Anan, *Sefer ha-Mitzvot*, 19) – as also by *Beta Israel.

Non-Jewish Women

A non-Jewish menstruating woman does not impart ritual impurity (*Sifra, Tazri'a*), but there are scholars who hold that in ancient times this was not so – a state of affairs which explains Bet Hillel's statement in the Mishnah (Nid. 4:3). Furthermore, it is held that it was precisely this ancient *halakhah* that led to the decree that gentiles, in general, were ritually impure as a result of having intercourse with their menstruating wives. Most scholars, however, hold the opposite view, contending that Bet Hillel's statement refers merely to the ritual impurity conveyed by a *niddah*'s blood, and that it did not refer to the actual menstruating woman herself. It was rather the Hasmonean *bet din* which first "decreed that a Jew who had intercourse with a heathen woman is liable on account of her being a *niddah*" (Av. Zar. 36b), and that this decree was a general restriction intended to deter Jewish men from sexual relationships with gentile women.

[Israel Moses Ta-Shma / Judith R. Baskin (2nd ed.)]

Aggadic Traditions

Rabbinic aggadah stresses the seriousness of *niddah* regulations and encourages their observance; they are considered *gufei Torah* ("essential laws"; Avot 3:18). According to the Talmud, when the Romans issued decrees intended to undermine Judaism, they ordered Jews to have intercourse with women in a state of *niddah* (Me'il. 17a). Midrashic homilies praise notable women of Israel who scrupulously prevented themselves and their husbands from transgressing this prohibition; these include Sarah (Gen R. 48:15) and Esther (Meg. 13b). The sages also stressed the psychological importance of the enforced separations required by *hilkhot niddah* in sustaining romance in a married couple's sexual relations (Nid. 31b). Genesis Rabbah 17:8, on the other hand, is among a number of midrashic sources that connects women's three ritual obligations, including *hilkhot niddah*, with women's supposed culpability in bringing death into the world. In several aggadic texts, menstruation and *niddah* regulations are described as atonements or eternal punishments brought upon women to remind them of Eve's responsibility in the death of Adam, and therefore in all human mortality. *Avot de-Rabbi Nathan* B 9 states that the commandments of *niddah* were given to women because "Adam was the blood of the Holy One, blessed be He, and Eve came and spilled it." According to Shabbat 2:6, women who disregard any of these three commandments may die in childbirth (also ARN B 9). Such dire pronouncements may be part of a rabbinic polemic against non-compliance with *hilkhot niddah*.

The rabbinic extension by a week of the length of time a wife and husband were to abstain from physical contact following a woman's menses indicates how seriously later formulators of rabbinic literature and Jewish social practice took the prospect of even accidental contact with a *niddah*. Evidence that this separation was resented by some as onerous is evident in the statement criticizing men who are unable to wait until their wives' purification: it was said that "the law concerning young trees (whose fruit is forbidden for the first three years – Lev. 19:23) cuts off the feet of those who have sexual intercourse with menstruating women" (that is, should teach them patience). Such men were regarded by the sages as the worst type of transgressor. The *Midrash on Psalms*, 146:4, says that although nothing is more strongly forbidden than intercourse with a *niddah*, "In the time-to-come, God will permit such intercourse," based on Zech.13:2. While this minority view is immediately countered with the ascetic statement that it is sexual intercourse itself which will be forbidden in the messianic era, it has been suggested that this midrash may be read as one "voice of protest raised against the legal strictures on sexuality" (D. Biale).

Contemporary Practice

Reform Judaism has consistently held that the observance of the laws of *niddah* is not necessary in modern times. In the first half of the 20th century, observance of these laws appears to have declined significantly, even among nominally traditional families. This was despite Orthodox exhortation in sermons and written tracts on the spiritual and medical benefits of **taharat ha-mishpahah* (family purity regulations), as these laws came to be called. Many Jewish feminist writers of the late 20th century condemned *niddah* regulations as archaic expressions of male anxieties about the biological processes of the female body and argued that they reinforced the predominant construction, in rabbinic Judaism, of women as other and lesser than men.

However, the 1980s and 1990s saw a resurgence in the numbers of Orthodox Jews and a new sympathy for various previously discarded practices of traditional Judaism in Reform, Conservative, and Reconstructionist Judaisms. In this period, positive new interpretations of observance of *hilkhot niddah* emerged, praising the ways in which they enhanced the sanctity of marriage and human sexuality. Some writers maintained that traditional Judaism recognized and valued the fluctuating rhythms of human relationships by mandating a monthly separation between husband and wife when spousal communication and empathy must be enhanced in non-physical ways (Frankiel). Supporters commended the elevating value of fulfilling a demanding divinely ordained mandate and also praised the consciousness of the body and its rhythms that these rules impose on women, as well as the feeling of personal renewal and rebirth following each ritual immersion (Adler).

Reflections on Hilkhot Niddah

In a religious system like rabbinic Judaism, which likens ritual impurity to a state of spiritual death, periodic female flows of blood were central to male characterizations of women as sources of potential pollution and as portents of physical extinction. Such fears were deeply rooted in the cultures of the ancient Near East, and similar taboos are found in cultures worldwide. While separation from the *niddah* is often presented as a matter which is of concern only to husband and wife, both biblical and rabbinic sources connect contact with any menstruating woman to defilement and even to danger (eg: Ezek. 7:19–20; Lam. 1:17; Ezra 9:11; II Chron. 29:5). Shabbat 9:1 quotes Isaiah 30:22 in equating the desecration conveyed by carrying a *niddah* to that acquired by carrying an idol.

S.J.D. Cohen has pointed out that such attitudes, more expressive of folk piety than legal formulation, confirm "the marginality of all women, menstruating or not, in the organized, public expressions of Jewish piety." That *niddah* regulations are essentially androcentric is evident in the fact that menstruating women constitute no danger to themselves or to other women, nor were they halakhically prohibited from taking part in rituals or in study. Ber. 2:12 is quite clear that "Men who have experienced an abnormal genital discharge and women who have experienced an abnormal genital discharge, as well as menstruating women and women who have recently given birth, are permitted to chant Torah, Prophets, and Writings out of a scroll and to chant from memory *mishnah*, *midrash*, *halakhot*, and *aggadot* …" Significantly, however, the Talmud at Ber. 22a omits any mention of the licit participation of women, whether *niddah* or not, in such activities, and takes for granted that these acts of worship and study are exclusively male prerogatives. Since Berakhot 22a affirms that words of Torah are not susceptible to ritual impurity, it seems clear that the exclusion of women from these activities is not based on any apprehension that they might defile the divine word. Rather, it appears to originate in a rabbinic concern that women might defile the men with whom they would come into contact if their presence was encouraged in sites of worship and learning. (Although, as M. Gruber has noted, many Jewish men have been content to let women believe that the reason for their exclusion from study of Torah was because of their susceptibility to menstrual impurity.) *Hilkhot niddah* demonstrate that the rabbis inscribed male piety on female bodies: in order to construct fences to protect male ritual sanctity from the *niddah*, all women had to be eliminated from places of holiness. Moreover, the *halakhah* also subordinated women in the most intimate areas of their lives. As C.E. Fonrobert has observed, in rabbinic writings women appear as ciphers in legal discussions of their bodily discharges or as speakers in narratives fashioned by men. To study tractate *Niddah*, she has argued, is to witness men insisting upon their authority to interpret women's bodies.

[Judith R. Baskin (2nd ed.)]

See also *Purity and Impurity, Ritual; **Taharat ha-Mishpaḥah*.

BIBLIOGRAPHY: C.M. Horowitz (ed.), *Tosefta Attikata*, pts. 4–5 (1890); J. Preuss, *Biblisch-talmudische Medizin* (1923³), 128–46; S. Baumberg, *Golden Chain* (1929); M. Margulies, *Ha-Hillukim she-Bein Anshei Mizrah u-Venei Erez Yisrael* (1938), 99–102, 114–8; S. Lieberman, *Sheki'in* (1939), 22; idem, in: B.M. Levin (ed.), *Metivot* (1934), 115–8; M. Rabinowitz (ed.), *Daughter of Israel* (Eng. and Yid., 1949); Alon, Mehkarim, 1 (1957), 121–31, 135–6, 171–2; N. Lamm, *Hedge of Roses* (1966). **ADD. BIBLIOGRAPHY:** R. Adler, "'In Your Blood, Live': Re-Visions of a Theology of Purity," in: D. Orenstein and J.R. Litman (eds.), *Lifecycles* (1997), 2:197–206; J.R. Baskin, *Midrashic Women* (2002); idem, "Women and Ritual Immersion in Medieval Ashkenaz," in: L. Fine (ed.), *Judaism in Practice* (2001); R. Biale, *Women and Jewish Law* (1984); D. Biale, *Eros and the Jews* (1992); S.J.D. Cohen, "Menstruants and the Sacred in Judaism and Christianity," in: S.B. Pomeroy (ed.), *Women's History and Ancient History* (1991), 273–99; Y. Dinari, "The Customs of Menstrual Impurity," in: *Tarbiz*, 49 (1979–80):302–24 (Heb.); C.E. Fonrobert, *Menstrual Purity* (2000); T. Frankiel, *The Voice of Sarah: Feminine Spirituality and Traditional Judaism* (1990); M. Gruber, "The Status of Women in Ancient Judaism," in: J. Neusner and A.J. Avery-Peck (eds.), *Where We Stand* (1999), 151–76; R. Wasserfall (ed.), *Women and Water: Menstruation in Jewish Life and Law* (1999); A. Zuria (dir.), *Purity (Tehora)* (2002); E. Marienberg, *Niddah: Lorsque les juifs conceptualisent la menstruation* (2003).

NIDDAH (Heb. נִדָּה; "menstruous woman"), seventh tractate of the order *Tohorot* in the Mishnah and in the Babylonian Talmud – the only tractate of the order with *Gemara*. The tractate deals with the ritual uncleanness of a woman which is caused by menstruation or other fluxes, and is based chiefly upon Leviticus chapters 12 and 15:19ff.

The Mishnah consists of ten chapters. Chapter 1 discusses the determining of the onset and duration of menstruation in those with regular and irregular menses. Chapter 2 continues that topic and deals with the source and colors of the blood causing uncleanness. Chapter 3 discusses the uncleanness of a woman following miscarriage, abortion, and childbirth. Chapter 4 deals with the untrustworthiness of Samaritans and Sadducees with regard to menstruation; menstruation in the case of heathens and after childbirth; difficult confinements; and menstrual regularity. Chapter 5 deals with caesarean births; the moment that uncleanness commences; and the different ages and stages in the development of a male and female child. Chapter 6 continues this theme; deals incidentally with a list of cases in which the presence of one factor presupposes another although the reverse is not true; and deals with doubts about the source of bloodstains. Chapter 7 discusses the uncleanness of the blood itself; cases where its origin is uncertain; sources of uncleanness that have dried out; and, once again, with the untrustworthiness of Samaritans in regard to uncleanness. Chapters 8 and 9 continue the subject of doubtful stains or flows of blood. Chapter 10 continues this theme and deals with the duration of menstruation and borderline cases.

It is possible to discern several strata in the Mishnah. Thus 2:6 may predate the schools of Shammai and Hillel, and Akavya b. Mahalalel. Moreover, several earlier *mishnayot* are interpreted in later *mishnayot*: Thus Mishnah 1:1 is explained in 1:2, 1:3 in 1:4–6, and 2:2 in 2:3. *Mishnayot* 5:3–6 form a distinct group, which gives the various ages, from one day to 20 years, at which laws become applicable for males and females. These laws are irrelevant to the subjects of *Niddah* and were incorporated because the first Mishnah states that a female child has the potential of becoming a *niddah* from the age of one day. Similarly *mishnayot* 6:2–10 consist of various laws which have as their common theme that wherever A occurs B will be found, but not the reverse. These follow 6:1, where the formula occurs with regard to the *niddah*. A. Weiss claims that most of these grouped *mishnayot* are of ancient origin, and that the editor collected and condensed most of them from older mishnaic sources (*Al ha-Mishnah* (1969), 31). The end of *Niddah* contains supplements to various *mishnayot* in the tractate; for example, *mishnayot* 9:8–10 are supplements to 1:2; *mishnayot* 9:1 and 10:1 supplement 1:7; and *mishnayot*

10:2–3 supplement 4:7 (see further Ḥ. Albeck, *Shishah Sidrei Mishnah, Seder Tohorot* (1959), 377f.).

In the Tosefta, *Niddah*, containing nine chapters, is the fifth tractate in the order *Tohorot*. It includes original legal and aggadic passages, such as a section on birth control which is debated in 2:6. Another passage sounds like a version of the Jonah story and tells about a ship that was caught in a storm; the passengers prayed to their own gods, but a little boy reproached them: "How long will you delude yourselves? Pray to the Creator of the ocean," i.e., to the God of Israel (5:17). Another group of *beraitot* tells of several reforms of existing customs, some of which were instituted for the dignity of the poor and women (9:16–18), such as the decision to give the same simple burial to both rich and poor alike. Only three chapters (and a fragment of a fourth) of the Jerusalem Talmud to *Niddah* are extant. It is placed after *Nezikin* and contains very little aggadic material. In the Babylonian Talmud there is *Gemara* on the whole tractate. Because of its practical importance the tractate is much studied and much space is devoted to it both in the various codes and in the responsa literature. It contains aggadic material, one noteworthy view being (16b) that while a man's physical qualities are preordained, his moral character and spiritual outlook are left to his free choice. There is also a vivid description of the wonderful life of learning and joy that the embryo enjoys in his mother's womb. Before birth he is made to take the oath: "Be righteous and not wicked, and if all the world tells you 'you are righteous' consider yourself wicked" (30b). Another passage reports 12 questions and answers on law and *aggadah* that the Alexandrians asked Joshua b. Hananiah (69b–71a). The Mishnah was translated into English by H. Danby (*The Mishnah*, 1933), and J. Neusner published a translation of both the Mishnah (1991) and the Tosefta (2002). The Babylonian Talmud was translated into English in the Soncino edition by I.W. Slotki (1948), and the Jerusalem Talmud by J. Neusner (*The Talmud of the Land of Israel;* vol. 34 – *Horayot & Niddah*, 1982).

BIBLIOGRAPHY: Ḥ. Albeck, *Shishah Sidrei Mishnah, Seder Tohorot* (1959), 375–8; A. Weiss, *Al ha-Mishnah* (1969), 31, 57. **ADD. BIBLIOGRAPHY:** Epstein, *The Gaonic Commentary on the Order Toharot* (Hebrew) (1982); S. Lieberman, *Tosefet Rishonim*, vol. 3 (1939); J. Neusner, *A History of the Mishnaic Laws of Purities* (1974–77), vol. 15–16; idem, *From Mishnah to Scripture* (1984), 81–88; idem, *The Mishnah Before 70* (1987), 197–214; idem, *The Philosophical Mishnah* 3 (1989), 35–46; idem, *Purity in Rabbinic Judaism* (1994), 67–68; T. Meacham, *A Critical Edition of Mishnah Niddah with Introduction, Notes on Text, Interpretation and Redaction, and Studies in Legal History and Realia* (Hebrew) (Ph.D. Dissertation, Hebrew University, 1989); idem, in: *Introducing Tosefta* (1999), 181–220.

NIEBUHR, CARSTEN (1733–1815), German traveler. In 1760 he was proposed to join the expedition sent out by Frederick V of Denmark on the initiation of J.D. Michaelis, the renowned German biblical scholar, for the scientific exploration of *Egypt, *Arabia, *Syria, and *Persia (1761–67), visiting *Jerusalem in 1766. He was assigned the position of surveyor and geographer. All the members of the expedition died during the trip, except Niebuhr, who saved his life and restored his health by adopting native habits in dress and food. Niebuhr's account of his travels, *Reisebeschreibung nach Arabien und andern umliegenden Laendern* (2 vols., 1774–78), are considered classics on the geography, the people, the antiquities, and the archaeology of much of the district of Arabia which he traversed and were accepted with enthusiasm by Western scholars. A third volume, *Reisen durch Syrien und Palaestina*, was published by J. Olshausen in 1837. His books were translated into Dutch, French, and English. Two recent Arabic books sum up his travel to *Yemen and to *Iraq. His travels and publications are an important landmark for modern Oriental studies in the West in general and especially for the Jews of Yemen.

BIBLIOGRAPHY: J. Wiesehöfer and S. Conermann (eds.), *Carsten Niebuhr (1733–1815) und seine Zeit* (2002); A. Klein-Franke, in: *Pe'amim*, 18 (1984), 80–101.

[Yosef Tobi (2nd ed.)]

°**NIEBUHR, REINHOLD** (1892–1971), U.S. Protestant theologian who spent most of his teaching career at New York's Union Theological Seminary. Niebuhr brought to this position a social conscience formed during a pastorate in Detroit, Michigan, in the 1920s. Active in many public causes, gifted as a journalist, he fashioned his ethical approach in countless articles and a number of books, the most famous being the Gifford Lectures, *The Nature and Destiny of Man* (1941–43). Niebuhr frequently acknowledged that his social passion had been born at the side of activist Jews, even as his prophetic realism was nurtured by a reading of the Hebrew prophets. His own preaching reproduces something of their cadences and much of their concern for justice. "I have as a Christian theologian sought to strengthen the Hebraic-prophetic content of the Christian tradition." His conception of Judaism and blatant opposition to Christian missionary activity among Jews are expressed in Chapter 7 of his book *Pious and Secular America* (1958; publ. in England under the title: *The Godly and the Ungodly* (1958)). By 1941 Niebuhr had begun publicly to advocate a Jewish homeland, particularly for European refugees, though he also wanted to welcome refugees to America. Though consistently arguing that Palestine should be that homeland, he had a reputation for fair-mindedness in Middle Eastern affairs and was not identified with ideological Zionism. He was awarded an honorary doctorate by the Hebrew University of Jerusalem in 1967.

BIBLIOGRAPHY: S.C. Guthrie, *The Theological Character of Reinhold Niebuhr's Social Ethic* (1959); G. Harland, *The Thought of Reinhold Niebuhr* (1960), includes bibliography; N.A. Scott, *Reinhold Niebuhr* (Eng., 1963), includes bibliography.

[Martin E. Marty]

NIEDERSTETTEN, city in Wuerttemberg, Germany. Jews were mentioned there as victims of the *Rindfleisch massacre of 1298. There is no further trace of them in the city throughout the Middle Ages until their settlement in 1675. By 1714 the community had acquired a prayer room; in 1737 a cemetery was consecrated in which Jews from Archshofen, Creglingen, Gerabronn, and Mulfingen were also buried. In that same period a *ḥevra kaddisha* was also founded. The Jews earned their livelihood mainly from trade in livestock, wine, and wool. By 1744 a synagogue was built, and by 1807 the community numbered 138 Jews. The number rose to 171 in 1824, and in 1832 the community was included in the rabbinate of *Mergentheim. A religious school was also founded in the 1830s. The community numbered 215 in 1854, decreased to 163 in 1900, and to 81 in 1933. In the 20th century, Jews were active as wholesale merchants in leather and wine, and as shopkeepers. They also engaged in textile manufacturing and banking. They were active in the political and cultural life of the town, and one Jew was a member of the municipal council during the Weimar Republic. In 1933 Jewish merchants were subject to the Nazi *boycott, and some leaders of the community were physically assaulted. This resulted in large-scale Jewish emigration. During the general destruction on *Kristallnacht* in 1938, the synagogue itself was preserved, but eight Jewish men were sent to concentration camps. Between 1941 and 1942, 42 Jews were deported to extermination camps, never to return. In early 1945 the synagogue was destroyed as a result of the war. The ritual objects of the community were saved, however, and turned over to a U.S. Army chaplain when the war ended. All that was left of a once active community in Niederstetten was the Jewish cemetery. A plaque has been mounted to commemorate the former synagogue.

BIBLIOGRAPHY: P. Sauer, *Die juedischen Gemeinden in Wuerttemberg und Hohenzollern* (1966), 134–6, incl. bibl. **ADD BIBLIOGRAPHY:** H. Behr, "Gedenket unser. Zur Geschichte der juedischen Gemeinde von Niederstetten," in: W. Krueger (ed.), *650 Jahre Stadt Niederstetten* (Veroeffentlichungen zur Ortsgeschichte und Heimatkunde in Wuerttembergisch Franken, vol. 4 (1991)), 317–31; E. Hahn, "Juedischer Alltag in Niederstetten," in: *ibid.*, 332–35; E. Kraiss and M. Reuter, *Bet Hachajim–Haus des Lebens. Juedische Friedhoefe in Wuerttembergisch Franken* (2003). **WEBSITE:** www.alemannia-judaica.de.

[Alexander Shapiro]

NIEGO, JOSEPH (1863–1945), teacher and social worker. Niego was born in Adrianople into a rabbinical family. In about 1891 he was appointed director of the *Mikveh Israel Agricultural School (near Tel Aviv). He served in this post for 18 years, and during that time he went to Kurdistan on behalf of the *Alliance Israélite Universelle. On his return he presented an interesting report about the Kurdish Jews which was published in French and in a Hebrew translation. Later he was nominated as inspector of the Jewish Colonization Association agricultural settlements in Oriental and European countries, including its colonies in Palestine (Gederah, Be'er-Toviyyah, Sejera, Ḥaderah, etc.). He remained at this post for 20 years. His headquarters were in Istanbul, but he was also very active in agricultural research in Anatolia. In 1923 he became the manager of a loan association in Istanbul which was established by the American Jewish Joint Distribution Committee. Niego took part in the social life of the Jews in the city and was president of the B'nai B'rith Grand Orient Lodge. A jubilee book was published on his 70th birthday that was dedicated to his activities and includes some of his lectures and articles (see bibl.).

BIBLIOGRAPHY: *Cinquante Années de Travail dans les Oeuvres Juives… Bulletin Publié à l'Occasion du sixante-dixième Anniversaire… J. Niego* (1933); M.D. Gaon, *Yehudei ha-Mizraḥ be-Ereẓ Yisrael*, 2 (1938), 468f.; M. Benayahu, *Massa Bavel* (1955), 43.

[Eliyahu Hirschberg]

NIEMIROWER, JACOB ISAAC (1872–1939), chief rabbi of Romania. Niemirower was born in Lemberg. In 1897 he was appointed rabbi of Jassy and in 1911 rabbi of the Sephardi community of Bucharest. In 1921 he was appointed rabbi of the main synagogue of Bucharest and shortly after, chief rabbi of Romania. He succeeded in uniting the Jewish communities of Romania under his leadership. As chief rabbi he was elected in 1926 to the Romanian senate – the first Jew to receive such an appointment – and was recognized by the government as the representative of all Romanian Jewry. He fought against the humiliating wording of the Romanian oath, *more judaico*, and succeeded in having it annulled. By force of his intellect and personality he became the chief figure in the religious as well as in the general communal life of Romanian Jewry. Although his election was largely due to the progressive element which dominated Jewish communal life there, Niemirower's authority was accepted by all circles, including the Orthodox, and his influence was decisive. He did much in the sphere of Jewish education – founding Jewish schools and establishing a theological seminary, a society for Jewish education called Sharon, a society for Jewish studies, etc. He was president of the order of B'nai B'rith in Romania. He was an active Zionist and took part in the First Zionist Congress. In 1936 a Romanian nationalist made an attempt on his life and Niemirower was slightly wounded. He published many works in Romanian, German, and French on various Jewish topics. Between 1918 and 1932 his complete works were issued entitled *Scrieri Complete* (4 vols.). The fourth and fifth volumes of the journal *Sinai* (1932–33) were dedicated to him in honor of his 60th birthday.

BIBLIOGRAPHY: Wininger, Biog, 4 (n.d.), 530f.; S.K. Mirsky (ed.), *Ishim u-Demuyyot be-Ḥokhmat Yisrael be-Eiropah ha-Mizraḥit Lifnei Sheki'atah* (1959), 393–403; A. Shraga (ed.), *Al Yehudei Romanyah – be-Ereẓ Galutam u-va-Moledet* (n.d.), 21, 43f.; *Ha-Rav Dr. Niemirower* (1970).

[Itzhak Alfassi]

NIERMAN, LEONARDO (1932–), Mexican artist. Nierman sought a relationship between abstract art and cosmic phenomena. In 1956 he painted a mural at the Mexico University School of Commerce. In 1965 he executed a mural for the Golden West Savings Bank in San Francisco, California, and in 1966 made the stained glass windows at the Jewish Cultural Center of Mexico City. Collected all over the world, Nierman is considered by many to be Latin America's greatest abstract artist. In 2002 the mayor of Chicago proclaimed a Leonardo Nierman Day, and in 2003 he received the Gloria Award from the International Latino Cultural Center of Chicago. "Painting," he wrote, "is to me the aperture through which it is possible to enter a certain world; in it the viewer may find an endless number of magic images, objects, remembrances, associations, fears, joys, hopes and dreams.... It is my non-verbal world surrounded by combat, stress and sights; joy, sensuality and death. Dreams, moments of ecstasy in the creation of images. Piercing the darkness, radiant smoke and dust, a world of volcanic vapors, lava, storms, prehistoric vegetation, bottoms of oceans, enchanted caves filled with stars, precious stones and cosmic winds ascending into the silence of infinity."

NIEROP, VAN, family of Dutch jurists and bankers. NIEROP, AHASVARUS SALOMON, VAN (1813–1878), jurist, politician, and communal leader. Born at Hoorn, Holland, Van Nierop became a prominent attorney in Amsterdam. He published numerous articles on commercial law in the law journals *Themis* and the *Weekblad voor het Recht*, and sat in the Second Chamber of Parliament from 1851 to 1853 and from 1864 to 1866. Van Nierop was the first Jewish MP in the Netherlands He also became a member of the Communal Council of Amsterdam and of the First Chamber of Parliament. Van Nierop played an important part in the reorganization of Jewish communal bodies which led to the establishment of the Nederlands Israelitisch Kerkgenootschap of which he was chairman of the executive (1870–71). His son FREDERIK SALOMON VAN NIEROP (1844–1924), banker, was born in Amsterdam and graduated in law at the University of Leiden. For some years he practiced law in Amsterdam. In 1871 he became the founder of the Amsterdamsche Bank. As one of its directors Van Nierop played an important part in expanding its operations. A progressive liberal, he was a member of the Amsterdam Municipal Council (1879–1905), of the North Holland Provincial Council (1883–99), and of the First Chamber of Parliament (1899–1922). Though an assimilated Jew and religiously indifferent, he became president of the Nederlands Israelitisch Kerkgenootschap and president of the Consistory of the Amsterdam Kehillah (1876–99). A principled liberal, he favored the emancipation of Jews as Dutch citizens, and opposed private Jewish education and the Zionist movement. His son HENDRIK ABRAHAM VAN NIEROP (1881–1976), banker, succeeded him as a director of the Amsterdamsche Bank in 1916, but played no part in the community.

ADD. BIBLIOGRAPHY: A.S. Rijxman, in: W.J. Wieringa a.o. (eds.), *Bedrijf en samenleving: economisch-historische studies over Nederland in de negentiende en twintigste eeuw, aangeboden aan prof. dr. I.J. Brugmans bij zijn aftreden als hoogleraar aan de Universiteit van Amsterdam* (1967), 137–55; M.A. van Nierop, *Familiegeschiedenis/ family history Van Nierop 1813–2000: Nieuwe Niedorp, Hoorn, Amsterdam: volgend op een gedeelte van de familiegeschiedenis/ and a part of the family history Ephraim 1646–1813* (2000).

[Henriette Boas / H.F.K. van Nierop (2nd ed.)]

NIETO, DAVID (1654–1728), philosopher and haham of the Spanish and Portuguese Synagogue in London (1701–28). Having studied medicine at the University of Padua, Nieto functioned as *dayyan*, preacher, and physician in Leghorn before going to London. He was proficient in languages and an astronomer of some repute. His calendar (1717) served the London community until the 19th century as a guide for the Sabbath and festivals. His works indicate that he was fully aware of the religious currents and crosscurrents of his time, including *Spinozism, Deism (see conceptions of *God), and Shabbateanism. *Matteh Dan* (1714), his *magnum opus*, devoted to a defense of the Oral Law against the attacks of ex-Marranos to whom the rabbinic tradition was both novel and unacceptable, has frequently been reprinted as a defense of rabbinic Judaism (last edition: Jerusalem, 1958). *Esh Dat* (1715) was directed against the Shabbatean heresiarch, Nehemiah Ḥiyya Ḥayon. Previously, Nieto had published *Pascalogia* (1702), dealing with the date of the Christian Easter in relation to that of the Jewish Passover, and *De La Divina Providencia* (1704). The latter was an elaboration of a sermon Nieto had delivered to combat the deistic notion of a "Nature" apart from God. Nieto identified Nature with God; and, although he made it clear that he had *natura naturans*, and not *natura naturata* (see *Spinoza) in mind, he was accused of Spinozistic leanings. Nevertheless, "Ḥakham Ẓevi" Ashkenazi (cf. his responsum no. 18) ruled in his favor. Nieto's *Reply to the Archbishop of Cranganor*, published posthumously in 1729, controverts the christological interpretation of the Bible. In his writings, Nieto gives evidence of wide reading in science and the humanities. He argues for the compatibility of Judaism and scientific investigations. Nieto is also one of the very few Jewish theologians who used the argument *de consensu gentium* to establish the dogmas of God's existence and of retribution.

BIBLIOGRAPHY: I. Solomons, *David Nieto and Some of his Contemporaries* (1931); A.M. Hyamson, *Sephardim of England* (1950), index; J.J. Petuchowski, *Theology of Haham David Nieto* (1954; 1970²); D. Nieto, *Ha-Kuzari ha-Sheni* (1958), introd. by J.L. Maimon, 5–20, biography by C. Roth, 261–75.

[Jakob J. Petuchowski]

NIETO, ISAAC (1687–1773), English rabbi. Born in Leghorn, Nieto was taken to London when his father David *Nieto became haham in 1701. He was appointed to succeed him in 1732, after an interregnum of four years. Nieto seems to have had a difficult character however, and held office only until 1741, when he went abroad. Returning to England, he was admitted as a public notary and built up a considerable practice. On the death of Moses Gomes de *Mesquita (1688–1751), who had been haham since 1744, Nieto was appointed *av bet din* (in effect, acting rabbi) of the community, but resigned in 1757 in protest against the appointment to the *bet din* of Moses Cohen *d'Azevedo (1720–1784, haham from 1761). During the controversy over ritual slaughter in London, which began in 1761 through the captious criticisms of Jacob Kimḥi, Nieto attacked the *bet din* so vigorously that the *Mahamad ordered that his decisions in matters of Jewish law should thereafter be disregarded. Nieto published a number of sermons in Spanish and Portuguese, of which one appeared also in English (London, 1756) on the occasion of the earthquake of 1756; this was the first Jewish sermon to be published in English. His translations into Spanish of the liturgy for Rosh Ha-Shanah and the Day of Atonement (*ibid.*, 1740) and of the daily prayers (*ibid.*, 1771) were highly regarded for their style. Following his father's example, he also published a series of calendars.

His son PHINEHAS NIETO (1739–1812) carried on the family tradition by publishing a "New Calendar" (London, 1791), and his remoter descendant ABRAHAM ḤAYYIM NIETO published "Nieto's Jewish Almanac for One Hundred Years 5663 – 1902 to 5763 – 2002" (1902).

BIBLIOGRAPHY: I. Solomons, in: JHSET, 12 (1931), 78–83; E.R. Samuel, *ibid.*, 17 (1953), 123–5; Roth, Mag Bibl, index.

[Cecil Roth]

°**NIETZSCHE, FRIEDRICH WILHELM** (1844–1900), German philosopher, one of the key influences on modern thinking. The perception of Nietzsche's philosophy is to a considerable extent – more than is the case with other philosophers – marked by the transforming impact of its reception after he himself lapsed into silence (1887–89) due to mental illness. His highly enigmatic philosophy was subsequently adopted by circles which later had a powerful influence on Fascism, Nazism, and related movements. Using barely understood slogans from his works like "the Will to Power," "the Superman," and "Transvaluation of Values," they gave their own racist and antisemitic twist to the philosopher's conceptions. The Nazis hailed Nietzsche as one of the spiritual progenitors of Nazism, along with H.S. *Chamberlain and R. *Wagner. His letters and writings do indeed contain antisemitic remarks, and his nihilistic critique of liberalism, democracy, and modern culture contributed to the rise of irrational political movements. The claim that he was antisemitic was reinforced by Nietzsche's sister Elizabeth (the wife of Bernhard Foerster, a rabid professional antisemite), his literary executor; she forged, emended, and selectively edited his writings to bring them into line with her ideology.

In the course of his friendship with Richard Wagner, Nietzsche himself voiced some anti-Jewish opinions; after his break with the composer, however, he condemned antisemitism in the strongest terms. His attitude toward Judaism is usually described as ambivalent; yet this description blurs the intentions of his statements. His main reproach against Judaism was that it had given birth to Christianity, the religion of humility, weakness, and an inverted and unnatural "slave morality" that had caused immeasurable harm to the Western world. Thus he was attacking ancient, post-exilic Judaism, particularly its priests, who drew the ire of his anticlerical convictions. According to Nietzsche, the "priests" (and Pharisees) of the Second Temple period, or rather the proto-Christian priests, developed a morality according to which the weak hate and negate the strong (his "slave morality," *Sklavenmoral*). Nietzsche saw this development as a total re-evaluation of morality and as a revolutionary success, and it is against this *ressentiment* (that they have in common with his contemporary antisemites) that Nietzsche battled against ardently. Biblical and Diaspora Judaism, by contrast, earned his admiration for their august strength (even in times of persecution) and creativity. Accordingly, he considered contemporary Jewry as a possible source of ferment for his ideal, "dionysian," atheistic world.

His first acclaim came from Georg *Brandes, the Danish literary historian and critic. Oscar Levy was the first to translate Nietzsche into English, further helping to spread his ideas. Nietzsche also exerted a considerable influence on modern Hebrew writers, namely M.J. *Berdyczewski, J.Ḥ. *Brenner, Uri Zevi *Greenberg, and S. *Tchernichowsky. He also influenced certain activist elements within the nascent Zionist movement, an influence severely criticized by *Aḥad Ha-Am.

ADD. BIBLIOGRAPHY: J. Golomb (ed.), *Nietzsche and Jewish Culture* (1997); S. Mandel, *Nietzsche and the Jews* (1994); W. Stegmaier and D. Krochmalnik (eds.), *Juedischer Nietzscheanismus* (1997); Y. Yovel, *Dark Riddle* (1998); S. Broemsel, in: *Nietzsche-Handbuch* (2000), 184–85 and 260–62.

[Henry Wasserman / Marcus Pyka (2nd ed.)]

NIFOCI (Nafusi), ISAAC (late 14th century), physician-astronomer and scholar of *Majorca. In 1359 King Pedro IV of Aragon invited Nifoci to Barcelona to construct clocks and astrolabes. Three years later, he was appointed palace astronomer (*maestre astralabre de casa del senyor rey*) and also received the sinecure of ritual slaughterer and inspector (*shoḥet u-vodek*) of the community of Majorca, an office he was empowered to pass on to his son Joseph. In 1380 he entered the service of the infante John as manufacturer of astrolabes (*maestre de fer stralaus*). During the persecutions of 1391 he was forcibly converted to Christianity. However, shortly afterward he took refuge in Bugia (Bougie), North Africa, where he returned to Judaism, then emigrated to Ereẓ Israel. From Bugia, Nifoci addressed a question to Simon b. Ẓemaḥ *Duran and *Isaac b. Sheshet, on whether it was permissible "to set out on a caravan journey to Palestine, on a Friday" (cf. Duran's responsa, vol. 1, no. 21).

BIBLIOGRAPHY: Baer, Spain, index, s.v. *Isaac Nifoci*; Pons, in: *Hispania*, 16 (1956), 249–51; A.L. Isaacs, *Jews of Majorca* (1936), 93–95; I. Epstein, *Responsa of Rabbi Simon B. Zemah Duran* (1930), 101.

NIGER, SHMUEL (pseudonym of **Shmuel Tsharny**; 1883–1955), Yiddish literary critic. Niger was born in 1883 in Dukor, a village near Minsk. His father was a fervent follower of Chabad Ḥasidim who died when Shmuel was six years old. Among his siblings were BORUCH TSHARNY VLADECK (1886–1935), managing editor at the Yiddish *Forverts* and founding president of the Jewish Labor Committee in New York, and DANIEL TSHARNY (1888–1958), one of the foremost Yiddish poets, journalists, and memoirists of his time. When

Niger attended yeshivah in Minsk, he came in contact with the Zionist ideas of *Aḥad Ha-Am and the socialist doctrines of Russian revolutionists, soon joining the newly founded Vozrozhdenye Party, and helping to found the *Zionist-Socialist Workers Party and participating in its often illegal propaganda activities. Though repeatedly arrested and tortured in Russian prisons, he continued to write revolutionary proclamations and articles, in particular for *Der Nayer Veg*. His 1906 essay, "*Vos iz der Yidisher arbeter*" ("What Is the Jewish Worker"), was his first work with wide distribution. His initial literary efforts were in Russian and Hebrew, but after the onset of the 1905 Revolution he wrote mainly in Yiddish. A major essay on Sholem *Asch, "*Vegn der Tragedye fun Goles*" ("On the Tragedy of Exile," 1907), was his initial attempt to place himself at the forefront of the new Yiddish literary culture as well as to introduce the still relatively unknown Asch to a much broader audience. The following year, together with the Bundist dramatist A. Vayter and the Zionist essayist S. *Gorelik, he founded the short-lived journal *Literarishe Monatshriftn* in Vilna, which is widely credited with having launched the Yiddish literary renaissance. Niger's reputation soon equaled, and later eclipsed that of *Ba'al-Makhshoves, the founder of Yiddish literary criticism. In 1909 Niger left for Berlin and soon after for the University of Berne, Switzerland, in order to extend his knowledge of philosophy, world literature, and European literary criticism. In 1912 he returned to Vilna to edit a new monthly, *Di Yidishe Velt*, which rapidly became the authoritative organ of Yiddish *belles lettres*. That same year he published a collection of his early essays, *Vegn Yidishe Shrayber: Kritishe Artiklen* ("On Yiddish Writers: Critical Articles"). Assisted by Ber *Borochov, he edited *Der Pinkes* (1913), the first Yiddish scholarly volume devoted to the study of Yiddish literature, language, folklore, criticism, and bibliography. He also edited Zalmen *Rejzen's *Leksikon fun der Yidisher Literatur un Prese* ("Lexicon of Yiddish Literature and Press," 1914). The best of his essays from this period were later collected in a volume entitled *Shmuesn vegn Bikher* ("Conversations on Books," 1922). After the 1917 Revolution he edited the Moscow weekly *Kultur un Bildung* (1918), and the Vilna monthly *Di Naye Velt* (1919). In April 1919, Polish legionnaires stormed Vilna, broke into an apartment Niger was sharing with A. Vayter and Leib *Jaffe, shot Vayter, and arrested the others. After his release from prison, Niger left for the U.S. In 1920, he joined the staff of the New York daily *Der Tog* and for 35 years wrote weekly reviews of books and articles on literary trends, becoming the most revered and feared Yiddish critic of his generation. His praise or censure often made or destroyed reputations. His participation in the literary monthly *Di Tsukunft*, which he co-edited from 1941 to 1947, helped to maintain its high quality and enduring influence. Niger was a pillar of the *YIVO Institute for Jewish Research from its very beginning, contributing studies to its important publications. He was also active in CYCO (Central Yiddish Culture Organization), editing its complete edition of the works of I.L. *Peretz, on whom he wrote a definitive study (1952). Niger was the chief adviser of the Louis La-Med Foundation for the Advancement of Hebrew and Yiddish Literature and, under its auspices, published his study *Di Tsveyshprakhikayt fun Undzer Literatur* ("The Bilingualism of our Literature," 1941). In this study, he emphasized that bilingualism had been a Jewish tradition since biblical days and that in the modern era both Hebrew and Yiddish were necessary pillars sustaining Jewish culture. In 1948, Niger helped to found the *Congress for Jewish Culture. In 1954, he undertook to co-edit its *Leksikon fun der Nayer Yidisher Literatur* ("Lexicon of the New Yiddish Literature"). He died while the first volume was in press. A number of his works were published posthumously: *Yidishe Shrayber in Soviet-Rusland* ("Yiddish Writers in Soviet Russia," 1958); *Bleter Geshikhte fun der Yidisher Literatur* ("Page from the History of Yiddish Literature," 1959); *Kritik un Kritiker* ("Criticism and Critics," 1959); *Sholem Asch* (1960).

BIBLIOGRAPHY: Rejzen, *Leksikon*, 2 (1927), 539–51; LNYL, 6 (1965), 190–210; Sh. Bickel and L. Lehrer, *Shmuel Niger-Bukh* (1958); Sh. Bickel, *Shrayber fun Mayn Dor* (1958), 256–93; S.D. Singer, *Dikhter un Prozaiker* (1959), 263–78; J. Glatstein, *Mit Mayne Fartogbikher* (1963), 466–85; H. Leyvik, *Eseyn un Redes* (1963), 174–87; S. Liptzin, *Maturing of Yiddish Literature* (1970), 77–81. **ADD. BIBLIOGRAPHY:** LNYL, 6, 190–210; S. Niger, *Fun Mayn Togbukh* (1973).

[Sol Liptzin / Barry Trachtenberg (2nd ed.)]

NIGER OF PEREA (d. 68 C.E.), patriot leader of Perea, Transjordan. After distinguishing himself in the attack on Cestius at the outset of the revolt against the Romans in the autumn of 66, Niger apparently took charge of operations against them in Idumea, in due course becoming for a short time deputy governor of this province. Later in the same year he was placed in command of the disastrous expedition against *Ashkelon, together with *John the Essene and Silas the Babylonian. He was the only one of the three to survive, leading another attack later on with no greater success from his base in Idumea. During the reign of terror in *Jerusalem after the triumph of the Zealot extremists, he was among the moderates who were executed, apparently on suspicion of wishing to come to terms with the Romans (Jos., Wars, 2:520, 566; 3:11–27; 4:359–63).

BIBLIOGRAPHY: Graetz, Hist, 2 (1893), 264, 296.

[Cecil Roth]

NIGHTINGALE (Heb. זָמִיר (mod.), *zamir*), a name applied to singing birds of the genus *Luscinia*, of which three species are found in Israel. The most outstanding for its song is the *Luscinia megarhynchos* which hatches its eggs in the thickets of the Jordan. It is a small brown bird, common in Western Europe. The Hebrew word is mentioned only once in the Bible in a description of spring in Ereẓ Israel: "The time of the *zamir* is come, and the voice of the turtledove is heard in our land" (Song 2:12). The parallelism between *zamir* and turtledove indicates that the reference here is to a bird and, according to the meaning of the Hebrew root, to a singing one. Apparently the nightingale is not specifically meant but rather all singing birds that in spring and during the breeding season fill the air with their melodious song. Some, however, maintain that *zamir* is derived from the root signifying "fruit-picking," since in the *Gezer Calendar there occurs the expression *yarḥo zamor* denoting the fruit-picking months in summer. But as the Song of Songs speaks of spring, this interpretation is improbable.

BIBLIOGRAPHY: N.H. Tur-Sinai, *Ha-Lashon ve-ha-Sefer*, 1 (1954[2]), 51; J. Feliks, *Animal World of the Bible* (1962), 87.

[Jehuda Feliks]

NIGHT PRAYER (Heb. קְרִיאַת שְׁמַע עַל הַמִּטָּה, *Keri'at Shema al ha-Mittah*; "the reading of the *Shema on retiring," lit. "on the bed"), a prayer recited before retiring for the night. The custom to pray before going to sleep reflects man's need for protection in a state of suspended consciousness and vulnerability, especially since sleep was held in ancient times to be similar to death. Possibly practiced earlier, the Night Prayer in which one commends one's soul to God for the night became obligatory only in mishnaic times. It was incorporated into the prayer book of nearly all Jewish communities in an almost identical form (but see below): When *Arvit became established as a community prayer to be recited in the early evening, the Night Prayer became the individual concluding prayer of the day. The name *Keri'at Shema al ha-Mittah* refers to the central part of the prayer which is the first paragraph of the *Shema*. The Talmud states that he who wishes to go to sleep should say the *Shema* until the words *Ve-hayah im shamo'a* and recite the prayer *Ha-Mappil* to God "Who causes the bands of sleep to fall upon my eyes…" (Ber. 60b). Some codifiers demand the recitation of the first two sections of the *Shema* (see R. Asher to Ber. 9 no. 23); the majority, however, require the first one only (Maim. Yad, Tefillah, 7:1–2; Tur and Sh. Ar., OḤ 239:1), to be preceded by *Ha-Mappil* (Maim. loc. cit., but see Tur and Sh. Ar., loc. cit.). The order of these two portions of the Night Prayer is widely accepted and is probably derived from the talmudic view that "man ought to recite the *Shema* and repeat it until sleep overcomes him" (TJ, Ber. 1:1, 2d). The rabbinic concept of sleep being a state of minor death is in consonance with this outlook; just as one is obliged in the last hour of life to recite the *Shema* and bless the unity of God, so one should recite the *Shema* at night and commend one's spirit to God before succumbing to sleep. The reversed order, in which the *Shema* is recited first and is followed by *Ha-Mappil*, is given by *Amram Gaon, but is less common. In Amram's order, the *Shema* is prefaced by blessing "the Lord Who has sanctified us with His commandments and commanded us to recite the *Shema*," and concludes (as in the Italian rite) with blessing "the Lord Who guards His people Israel forever." The *Ha-Mappil* benediction underwent a number of changes and considerable curtailment compared with the original talmudic version (see Yad, Tefillah 7:1, R. Asher to Ber. 9 no. 23; Tur, OḤ 239).

The significance of the Night Prayer is prophylactic: the *Shema* and *Ha-Mappil* are invocations of divine protection against the various dangers that might befall man at night and during sleep, and especially against sin. The latter idea derives from Psalm 4:51: "Tremble, and sin not, commune with your heart upon your bed, and be still." Consequently, some scholars held (Ber. 5a–b) that for a man whose sole occupation was the study of the Torah no Night Prayer was necessary or one short supplicatory text was sufficient, e.g., "I commend my spirit into Thine hand" (Ps. 31:6). According to the Mishnah (Ber. 2:5), a bridegroom on the night of his wedding was exempted from the obligation of reciting the *Shema* at night because, excited over his nuptials, he would not be able to muster the necessary concentration (Ber. 16a–b; Maim. Yad, Keri'at Shema, 4:1). In later times, however, this exemption was abolished since proper spiritual concentration at prayer was rare anyway (Tur, OḤ 70).

Subsequently more prayers and scriptural texts were added to the Night Prayer by the talmudists and later authorities: e.g., Psalm 91 (also known as *Shir shel Pegga'im*; "Song against Untoward Happenings"), Psalm 3, and certain sections from *Arvit* (e.g., *Hashkivenu* and *Barukh Adonai ba-Yom*). Further additions were made under kabbalistic influence, the latter strengthening earlier angelological elements (e.g., Gen. 48:16) in the Night Prayer.

It is customary not to recite these additional prayers and texts on the first night of Passover; as this is a "night of watching unto the Lord" (Ex. 12:42) God Himself guards the Jews from the dangers of this night (Sh. Ar., OḤ 481:2).

BIBLIOGRAPHY: Idelsohn, Liturgy, 126–7; Abrahams, Companion, ccxiii–ccxv; E. Levi, *Yesodot ha-Tefillah* (1952[2]), 205–8; E. Munk, *The World of Prayer*, 1 (1961) 223–8.

[H. Elchanan Blumenthal]

NIGRI (Niger), PETRUS (Peter Schwarz; 1434–1483), Hebraist and polemist. Born in Bohemia, Nigri entered the Dominican Order and studied Hebrew, perfecting his knowledge in Spain, where he apparently acquired or compiled anti-Jewish polemical material subsequently exploited in his writings. On his return to Germany, he launched a conversionist campaign in several Jewish communities and ingratiated himself with the antisemitic bishop of Regensburg by arranging a week-long religious disputation there in 1474. In the following year, Nigri published his *Tractatus contra perfidos Judaeos de conditionibus veri Messiae…* (Esslingen, 1475), the first incunabulum to contain printed Hebrew characters, which was later consulted by Conrad *Pellicanus. It was followed by a treatise in German, *Der Stern Maschiach* (Esslingen, 1477), another early document of the Christian Kabbalah. Both works contained appended guides to the study of Hebrew and were venomously anti-Jewish and anti-talmudic. Their author characteristically identified the Trinity in the second word of the Hebrew Bible, *bara* ("created"), being said to represent the initials of *Ben* ("Son"), *Ru'aḥ* ("Spirit"), and *Av* ("Father"). Nigri, who also wrote a commentary on the Psalms, is said by Yom Tov Lipmann Heller (*Sefer Nizzaḥon*, 1644, p. 191) to have been a Jewish apostate.

BIBLIOGRAPHY: B. Walde, *Christliche Hebraisten Deutschlands am Ausgang des Mittelalters* (1916), 70–152; F. Secret, *Les Kabbalistes Chrétiens de la Renaissance* (1964), 18; ADB, 33 (1891), 247f.; L.M. Friedman, in: HUCA, 23, 2 (1950–51), 443–46; P. Bowe, *Judenmission im Mittelalter und die Paepste* (1942), index.

NIKEL, LEA (1918–2005), Israeli painter. Nikel was born in Zhitomir, Ukraine, the daughter of Bat Sheva and Haim Nikelshperg, who immigrated to Ereẓ Israel two years after she was born because of the pogroms. Although she lived in many cities during her lifetime, she identified with Tel Aviv. Nikel can be seen as a self-taught artist. She studied for a short while with the artist Haim Gliksberg and spent some time in the famous studios of Yehezkiel *Streichman and Avigdor *Stematzky. In these studios Nikel was exposed through books and reproductions to the world of modern art, and her decision to travel to Paris matured. Nikel remained in Paris 11 years (1950–61). She was fascinated by the artistic atmosphere there, enjoying the possibility of visiting art museums housing European collections and of considering herself an artist. Nikel's first steps in the abstract style took place in this period. The attraction of the art world and the need to become part of it influenced her mode of wandering from place to place. From the 1970s Nikel lived close to open spaces, near nature, in Moshav Kidron. In 1995 she won the Israel Prize.

Nikel was an independent artist committed to her own style. Despite criticism, she continued to work on her abstract, colorful, and optimistic paintings. Nikel's courage in coping with abstraction was unique in Israel's art world. Art critics labeled her style Lyric Abstraction, a term that came from the New Horizons art group. But Nikel's works took abstraction one step further since she examined formal questions of the abstract without linkage to local places as the other members of the group did.

The main artistic tool in Nikel's paintings is color. She used a wide variety of colorful compositions. They move from figurative dark painting to abstract colorful works during the 1960s in Paris. From geometric compositions with contour lines and muddy color (*View from the Window of My Chambre de Bonne: Paris*, 1950, Tel Aviv Museum of Art) she turned to a spontaneous turbulent style (*Untitled*, 1969, Israel Museum, Jerusalem).

In the 1990s her style was still vivid and optimistic, and she was invited to exhibit in very stylish new galleries. Her perception of art as emotional creativity produced nuanced changes and renewal in her painting. Occasionally a new image would appear in some of her paintings and then disappear (*Black Butterfly*, 1994, Private Collection).

Nikel passed away ten years after a retrospective exhibition of her art was shown at the Tel Aviv Museum of Art. During this last decade, being quite elderly and ill, she continued to create in a fresh and vivid style.

BIBLIOGRAPHY: M. Segan-Cohen (ed.), *Lea Nikel* (1995); Y. Fisher (ed.), *Lea Nikel – Book* (1982).

[Ronit Steinberg (2nd ed.)]

NIKITIN, VICTOR (1839–1908), writer and scholar. Nikitin's special field was the history of Jewish agricultural settlement in Russia. At the age of nine, he was kidnapped and sent to the *Cantonist regiment in Nizhni Novgorod. There he was forced to convert to Christianity, and his Jewish name (not known) was changed. Because of his excellent handwriting he was assigned to office work in the army. While in the army, he studied on his own, and after completing his military service (1869), he served as a high official in the Ministry of Agriculture. Nikitin described the life of kidnapped children and the Jewish Cantonists in "*Vek perezhit – ne pole pereyti*" (in *Yevreyskaya Biblioteka*, 4 (1876), 164–213), and in *Mnogostradalnye* ("Those who Suffer"). The latter was banned by the censors but later appeared in two editions (1872, 1896). There is a great deal of material of historical importance in his *Yevrei Zemledeltsy* ("Jewish Tillers of the Soil"), published in *Voskhod* (1881–86) and later in 1887 as a separate work, and in *Yevreyskiye poseleniya severnykh i yugo-zapadnykh guberniy* ("Jewish Settlements in Northern and Southwestern Provinces," 1894), which was written on the basis of archival material.

BIBLIOGRAPHY: S. Ginzburg, in: *Forwards* (N.Y., Nov. 3, 1935); V.E. Rudakov, in: *Istoricheskiy Vestnik*, 5 (1908), 587–98.

[Yehuda Slutsky]

NIKOLAYEV, port on the Black Sea coast, Nikolayev district, Ukraine. The town was founded in 1789 and Jews settled there from its earliest days, engaging in commerce and crafts. Many of them moved there from Galicia. In 1830, among the inhabitants of the town were 24 Jewish families of merchants, 691 families of townsmen, and 424 individual Jews. In 1829 a government order prohibited the residence of Jews (with the exception of those serving in the army) in Nikolayev and *Sevastopol, using the existence of naval bases in the two towns as a pretext. The Jews were allowed two years to arrange their departure. The local authorities opposed the decree, arguing that the expulsion of the Jews would harm the development of the town; the expulsion was therefore postponed until 1834. At the beginning of the reign of Alexander II the right of residence in the town was granted to Jewish merchants and industrialists (1857), and later also to craftsmen (1861). Many Jews lived in the villages and estates in the vicinity of Nikolayev, where they conducted their commerce. In 1866 all restrictions were lifted and the Jewish community of Nikolayev developed rapidly. In 1880 there were 8,325 Jews in Nikolayev, and in 1897 the number rose to 20,109 (21.8% of the total population). A native of the town, Moshe Katz, described Nikolayev in the early 20th century in his memoirs, *A Dor Vos Hot Farloren di Moyre* (1956). Jews suffered in the pogroms of May 1881 and April 1899. The pogrom of 1905 was averted by Jewish self-defense units. In the early 20th century the community supported 15 schools. During the Civil War (1919–20) the Jews of neighboring towns suffered severely. In 1926 there were 21,786 Jews (about 20.8% of the total population) in Nikolayev. A court held its sessions in Yiddish in the 1920s, and 5 elementary schools, a vocational school and a high school existed in Nikolayev between the wars. Many Jews worked in factories, including the steel plant, and in the shipyard. There were 25,280 Jews in 1939 in the city (15.2% of the total population). The Germans occupied the city on August 17, 1941. On September 21–23, 1941, the Germans murdered 7,000 Jews in the vicinity of the city. With the liberation of Nikolayev (March 1944), Jews began to return to the city. According to the 1959 census, there were 15,800 Jews (7% of the population) in Nikolayev, but the actual number was probably closer to 20,000. The last synagogue was closed down by the authorities in 1962. In 1970 there were 17,978 Jews in the Nikolayev district, but later in the 1990s many emigrated to Israel.

[Yehuda Slutsky]

NIKOPOL (Nicopolis), small city in the Plevna district of Bulgaria. A Byzantine Jewish community existed in Nikopol during the tenth century. Jewish refugees arrived in Nikopol after their expulsion from Hungary in 1376 and also from Bavaria after expulsion in 1470. Jews expelled from Spain also sought refuge there. During the 16th century there were six synagogues in Nikopol – a Romanian, Hungarian, Wallachian, and Ashkenazi synagogue and two Sephardi synagogues. From 1523 to 1536 R. Joseph *Caro lived in Nikopol where he founded a famous yeshivah and continued the writing of his *Beit Yosef.* The synagogue that bears his name, Maran Beit Yosef, was destroyed several times and rebuilt in 1895. Some of the Jews expelled from Italy in 1569 by decree of Pope Pius V went to Nikopol. Those Jews who did not succeed in escaping at the approach of Michael the Brave of Wallachia, during the Turkish-Wallachian wars from 1595 to 1599, were taken to Wallachia and executed. After the wars R. Isaac *Beja (d. before 1630), author of *Bayit Ne'eman*, was the rabbi of the city. In 1688 the Jewish population increased with the arrival of war refugees from Smederevo (Semendria; Serbia) following the German invasion.

During the Russian-Turkish War of 1877 the Jews of Nikopol fled to Plevna (Pleven), and Adrianople, returning after the peace treaty of 1878. The economic situation, which deteriorated after the war, induced many Jews to settle in other Bulgarian towns. In 1904 there were still 210 Jews in Nikopol, but in 1926 only 12 Jewish families remained. During World War II the city received refugees from Germany and other European countries. The Nazis converted Maran Beit Yosef synagogue into a warehouse and stable. In 2004, after a process of migration process, only a few Jewish families lived in Nikopol.

BIBLIOGRAPHY: Rosanes, Togarmah, 1 (1930²), 7–8, 206, 213–4, 221, 252, and passim; idem, in *Yevreyska Tribuna*, 1 (1926), 28–37, 172–80; *Bulletin de l'Alliance Israélite Universelle*, 29 (1904), 170; S. Markus, in: *Ha-Ẓofeh* (Dec. 10, 1948).

[Simon Marcus / Emil Kalo (2nd ed.)]

NIKOVA, RINA (1898–1972), Israeli dancer and choreographer, who originated a style for the interpretation of biblical subjects in dance. Born in Russia, trained in Moscow, Nikova made her first appearance in Berlin. In 1925 she joined the opera company of Mordecai *Golinkin in Tel Aviv as prima ballerina. In 1931 she formed the Palestine Singing Ballet, a Yemenite group. She established Jerusalem Biblical Ballet, 1949.

NILE, river in N.E. Africa. The Nile is the lifestream of the civilizations flourishing in the valley bordering it. If the river is too high or too low in one year, disaster and famine follow in the next. Indeed, the ancient Egyptians saw in the yearly inundation the annual renewal of the first act of creation, the rising of the primeval mound out of the primordial ocean. From the correct observation of this yearly flooding, which enriched the fields of the lower Nile Valley with the fertile black alluvial soil, developed much of the later civilization of the pharaohs, and particularly the 365-day calendar. Unquestionably, the Egypt of the pharaohs was "the gift of the Nile." The Hebrew word for the Nile, יְאֹר, is a loan word from the Egyptian *ʾitrw* ("river") which by the period of the Middle Kingdom came to designate the Nile as the river par excellence.

Although the name Nile is not explicitly mentioned in the Bible, it is alluded to as "the river" (Gen. 41:1; Ex. 2:3), the "river of Egypt" (Gen. 15:8), the "flood of Egypt" (Amos 8:8), Shihor (Josh. 13:3), brook of Egypt (according to some, but see *Egypt, Brook of), river of Cush, and many more. The Nile plays a prominent part in the early stories of the Exodus (Moses, Ex. 2:3; the ten plagues, 7:15, 20; et al.), and is used by the prophets as the symbol of Egypt (Amos 8:8; 9:5; Jer. 46:8).

[Alan Richard Schulman]

NILES (Neyhus), DAVID K. (1890–1952), U.S. presidential aide. Born in Boston to immigrant Russian parents, Niles went to work in a local department store. He regularly frequented Ford Hall's Sunday forum of public lectures and discussions, and caught the eye of the forum's director, George W. Coleman, who eventually made him his assistant. During World War I, when Coleman went to Washington as an official in the Labor Department, Niles accompanied him as an aide. After the war he continued his association with Ford Hall, of which he was appointed associate director in 1924. Through his work there he became acquainted with numerous political figures, as a result of which he took part in La Follette's 1924 presidential campaign on the Progressive ticket. In subsequent elections, he was active in the Democratic Party, working for Smith in 1928 and Roosevelt in 1932. In 1935 he returned to Washington as labor assistant to Harry Hopkins, director of the Works Progress Administration and an intimate of President Roosevelt. He remained with Hopkins when the latter was made secretary of commerce in 1938. By then a member of the White House's inner circle, Niles helped to engineer the third-term "draft" of President Roosevelt in 1940 and was appointed assistant to the president in 1942. In this capacity, he performed the functions of a political trouble-shooter, an unofficial dispenser of patronage, and a liaison man with organized labor and various racial and religious minority groups. He remained in the post when President *Truman took office in 1945 and is said to have been instrumental in helping to shape Truman's ultimately positive stand on the partition of Palestine, which led to swift U.S. recognition of the State of Israel in May 1948. With his characteristic aversion to publicity, however, which often caused him to be labeled by the press as a political "mystery man," Niles publicly referred to his interest in Israel only once in the course of his career. That was in his letter of resignation from office in 1951, in which he gave his desire to visit Israel as a private citizen as one of the reasons for his retirement.

BIBLIOGRAPHY: Steinberg, in: *Saturday Evening Post* (Dec. 24, 1949), 24, 69–70; *New York Times* (May 22, 1951), 20.

[Bernard Sternsher]

NILI, secret pro-British spying organization, that operated under Turkish rule in Syria and Palestine during World War I, from 1915 to 1917, under the leadership of Aaron *Aaronsohn, Avshalom *Feinberg, Sarah *Aaronsohn, and Yosef *Lishansky. Its name consists of the initial letters of the Hebrew verse "*Nezaḥ Yisrael Lo Yeshakker*" נֵצַח יִשְׂרָאֵל לֹא יְשַׁקֵּר – "the Strength of Israel will not lie" (I Sam. 15:29), which served as its password. In British official documents it is named the "A. Organization." Nili was founded by a number of Jews in the moshavot (Jewish agricultural villages), most of whom were born in the country. Their disappointment with the Turkish authorities' treatment of the Jewish population and fear of a fate similar to that of the Armenians led them to the conclusion that the future of the Jews depended on Palestine being taken over by Britain. In January 1915, Avshalom Feinberg, who worked in Aaronsohn's agricultural experimental station at Athlit, was arrested with a group of young men in Ḥaderah who were falsely accused of having contact with British boats off the coast. After his release, Feinberg presented to his teacher and friend, Aaronsohn, a plan for a Jewish revolt with the aid of the British army stationed in Egypt. Aaronsohn, who held an important position in locust control under the Turkish authorities, rejected the plan as impractical, but accepted Feinberg's basic assumption that the British army should be aided by espionage.

Establishing contact with the British headquarters in Egypt was quite difficult. The first messenger, Aaronsohn's brother Alexander, met with the disapproval of the British Arab Bureau in Cairo and went to the United States, where he conducted propaganda against Turkey and Germany. The second, Feinberg, was promised in August that contact with the group would be maintained, but the British did not keep their word; he was caught by the Turks and released only after strenuous efforts by Aaronsohn. Feinberg's trip to Turkey in February 1916, with a view to contacting British agents in neutral Romania, did not bear fruit either. In the meantime the group was joined by Sarah Aaronsohn, Aaron's sister; Yosef Lishansky, head of a watchmen organization in the southern villages; and others, most of them from Zikhron Ya'akov, Ḥaderah, and Rishon le-Zion. Some of the recruits were enlisted in Aaronsohn's locust control staff, thus being able to move all over the country and enter military camps. Military, political, and economic information was collected in the experimental station in Athlit, but there was no way of transmitting it to the British.

To contact the British, Aaronsohn went on a fictional Turkish mission to Germany, in the summer of 1916; then to neutral Denmark, where he contacted British agents; and finally to London. There he met statesmen and soldiers, and, having gained their confidence, was sent to Cairo, where he served as intelligence adviser and helped in the planning of the British offensive against Palestine. In January 1917 Feinberg and Lishansky, disguised as Bedouin, tried to get to Egypt by land to renew contact with Aaronsohn. They were attacked by Bedouin and Feinberg was killed near the British front in Sinai. Lishansky was wounded but found his way to the British lines and joined Aaronsohn. In February 1917 contact was first established between the espionage center at Athlit and British intelligence in Egypt through Lishansky, who was brought to the coast by a British boat. The connections were maintained by sea for several months and the British received useful information collected by the group, supplemented by Aaronsohn's extensive knowledge of the geographical conditions and the personnel of the Turkish command.

The group also sought to help the Jewish population, many of whom were expelled from Jaffa and Tel Aviv by the Turks during the spring of 1917. Aaronsohn devoted much publicity to this persecution, which was later stopped. Other members helped transfer financial support to the *yishuv*, a difficult task after the United States broke off relations with Turkey in April 1917. Aaronsohn founded an assistance committee corresponding to the one in Egypt, which was set up by exiles from Palestine at the beginning of the war. Sarah Aaronsohn and Lishansky went to see Aaronsohn in Egypt and brought back £2,000 in gold coins, which they handed over to the political committee of the *yishuv*. This helped change the attitude of the Jewish population and its leaders, who were afraid of the consequences if Nili's activities were discovered by the Turks. The group was asked to arrange for two representatives of the *yishuv* to meet Aaronsohn and Zionist leaders abroad, to show that the latter approved of Nili's operations. Aaronsohn met Chaim *Weizmann and his colleagues in London in September 1917 and succeeded in convincing them of the importance of Nili's work as part of the political and military work of the section of the Zionist movement that had called for an alliance with Britain from the beginning of the war. It seemed that Nili was trying to become a political factor in Palestine and the Zionist movement; it made approaches to *Ha-Shomer and other groups.

In September 1917 the Turks caught a carrier pigeon sent from Athlit to Egypt that provided clear proof of espionage within the Jewish population, and the leadership again dissociated itself from Nili's actions. Internal conflicts weakened the organization, and there were grave suspicions over the circumstances of Feinberg's death. One of the group, Na'aman Belkind, was captured by the Turks while trying to get to Egypt and gave his interrogators information on the organization and its operations. On Oct. 1, 1917, Turkish soldiers surrounded Zikhron Ya'akov and arrested numerous people, including Sarah Aaronsohn, who committed suicide after four days' interrogation and torture. Lishansky managed to escape. The authorities hunted after suspects in other villages as well. The prisoners were taken to the Khan al-Pasha prison in Damascus. Zikhron Ya'akov was given an ultimatum: if Lishansky was not handed over, the village would be destroyed. The Jewish leaders decided to hand over the suspects and wash their hands of responsibility for them.

Lishansky took shelter among his former friends in Ha-Shomer and was taken from one village to another. As it was impossible to go on like that for a long period, the Ha-Shomer committee decided that he must die in case he fell into the hands of the Turks and brought disaster to the whole *yishuv*. Emissaries of Ha-Shomer set out to assassinate Lishansky, but succeeded only in wounding him, and he managed to escape. On his way to Egypt he was caught by Bedouin near Rishon le-Zion and handed over to the Turks. Following his interrogation in Damascus, more people were arrested. Due to the intensive endeavors of Jewish leaders and the secret intervention of German representatives, most of the prisoners were released, but 12 were sentenced to periods of one to three years in prison and 30 were conscripted into the army. Lishansky and Belkind were sentenced to death and were executed on Dec. 16, 1917. The remaining members of the organization went on with their spying activities. Aaronsohn, who was sent by Weizmann on a political and propaganda mission to the U.S., returned to Palestine in the spring of 1918 with the Zionist Commission. With his death in an air accident on May 15, 1919, the group finally broke up.

From a sociological and historical point of view, Nili was an attempt by young people born in the moshavot, under Aaronsohn's leadership, to form an independent political movement that would win the support of the entire *yishuv*. However, it was unable to appeal to a broad social stratum; hence its rapid dissolution after its leader's death. Its aid in the conquest of Palestine by the British, which was well appreciated, was part of the efforts of the pro-British section of the Zionist movement that was active in 1914–18 and determined policies in the subsequent 20 years.

BIBLIOGRAPHY: E. Livneh (ed.), *Nili, Toledoteha shel He'azah Medinit* (1961); idem, *Aaron Aaronsohn, ha-Ish u-Zemanno* (1969); Dinur, Haganah, 1, pt. 1 (1954), 353–68; *Yoman Aaron Aaronsohn 1916–1919* (1970); A. Engle, *Nili Spies* (1959, 1972).

[Yehuda Slutsky]

NÎMES, capital of Gard department, S. France. Although a number of Jews took part in the revolt led by Hilderic, governor of Nîmes, against the Visigothic king Wamba in 673, there is no direct evidence that Jews were then living in the town itself. However, a community was established during the second half of the tenth century at the latest, and from 1009 there is documentary evidence of the existence of a synagogue. From the middle of the 11th century, the name Poium Judaicum was used to designate one of the seven hills enclosed within the wall of Nîmes (later Puech Juzieu, etc.; in 1970 the promenade of Mont-Duplan); the Jewish cemetery was situated there. Toward the close of the 11th century, an entire quarter of the town was known as Burgus Judaicus (later Bourg-Jézieu). At the beginning of the 13th century, the community appears to have consisted of about 100 families. Although a church synod held in Nîmes in about 1284 decreed severe measures against the Jews, the bishop of Nîmes, who had authority over the Jews of the town, was nevertheless able to protect them, even from King *Philip IV the Fair who had ordered the imprisonment of several Jews. But the bishop could not prevail against the royal expulsion order of 1306 which, in Nîmes as elsewhere, was accompanied by the confiscation of all their belongings. When the Jews returned to France in 1359, the Nîmes municipal council allocated them the Rue de Corrégerie Vieille (the modern Rue de l'Etoile). After being harassed by the Christians there, they obtained a new quarter in the Rue Caguensol (part of the Rue Guizot) and the Rue de la Jésutarie or Juiverie (Rue Fresque). Shortly afterward they moved yet again, to the Garrigues quarter. There the 1367 census recorded the only three houses in the town (out of a total of 1,400) that were owned by Jews. This community ceased to exist in 1394, after the general expulsion of the Jews from France.

In a letter to *Abraham b. David of Posquières – who lived in Nîmes long enough to be sometimes named after that town – Moses b. Judah of Béziers stressed the superiority of the yeshivah of Nîmes over all the others in southern France, comparing it to "the interior of the Temple, the seat of the Sanhedrin, from where knowledge goes forth to Israel." Other than Abraham b. David, the only scholar of the town who is known is his uncle, Judah b. Abraham. The municipal library of Nîmes possesses a rich collection of medieval Hebrew manuscripts, several of French origin, in the French provinces; all these volumes were obtained from the Carthusians of Villeneuve-lès-Avignon.

From the 17th century, some Jews of *Comtat Venaissin went to trade in Nîmes and a few of them attempted to settle there; the *parlement* of *Toulouse ordered them to leave in 1653 and again in 1679. From the end of the 17th century, the Jews obtained the right to buy and sell in Nîmes for three weeks or a month in every season. Even though this concession was abolished in 1745 and 1754, some Jews succeeded in settling in the town during the second half of the 18th century. The community of 30–40 families appointed a rabbi, Elie Espir from *Carpentras, and set up a small synagogue in a private house. After a split in the community in 1794, a new synagogue (which has been in use ever since) was built in the Rue Roussy, completed in 1796. During the Reign of Terror, three Jews of Nîmes were imprisoned; one of them was subsequently executed. In 1808, when the *consistories were established, the community was affiliated to the consistory of *Marseilles, and there were then 371 Jews in the town, with the surprising number of eight rabbis. Among the rabbis of Nîmes was Solomon Kahn (1854–1931), historian of the Jews of southern France. Other notable personalities who originated from there include Adolph *Crémieux and Bernard *Lazare. From the close of the 19th century, the community diminished steadily in number. Although 40 families were recorded in 1941, some of these were refugees from the interior of France. In 1970 the community of 1,200 persons, mainly of North African origin, possessed a synagogue and a community center.

BIBLIOGRAPHY: Gross, Gal Jud, 395–9; J. Simon, in: REJ, 3 (1881), 225–37; idem, in: *Nemausa*, 2 (1884/85), 97–124; S. Kahn, *Notice sur les Israélites de Nîmes* (1901); idem, in: REJ, 67 (1914), 225–61; J. Vieilleville, *Nîmes…* (1941); H. Noël, in: *Revue du Midi*, 11 (1897), 182–91; B. Blumenkranz, *Juifs et chrétiens…* (1960), index; Z. Szajkowski, *Analytical Franco-Jewish Gazetteer* (1966), 190.

[Bernhard Blumenkranz]

NIMOY, LEONARD (1931–), U.S. actor and director. Born to Russian immigrant parents in Boston, Massachusetts, Nimoy starred as Hansel as an eight-year-old in a production of *Hansel and Gretel*. He studied drama at Boston College and Antioch University, and then moved to Southern California, where he studied at the Pasadena Playhouse with Jeff Corey. He took roles in low-budget films, like *Zombies of the Stratosphere* (1951) and *Them!* (1954). After an 18-month stint in the U.S. Army Reserve, Nimoy was discharged as a sergeant in 1956. Back in Hollywood, he turned to television roles, appearing on such shows as *Sea Hunt*, *Twilight Zone*, and *Bonanza*. In 1966, Nimoy helped create his Emmy-nominated role of Mr. Spock in the series *Star Trek* (1966–69). Drawing on his Jewish heritage for inspiration, he used a priestly (kohen) blessing as a Vulcan greeting in the series. After *Star Trek* ended, Nimoy went on to play the spy, Paris, in *Mission: Impossible* from 1969 to 1971, and narrated the documentary series *In Search Of…* (1976–82). His frustration at being typecast as Mr. Spock led him to write the autobiography *I Am Not Spock* (1977). Although Nimoy refused to play Spock for a new TV series, he agreed to star in *Star Trek: The Motion Picture* (1978). In 1982, he received an Emmy nod for his supporting role in *A Woman Called Golda*. After directing *Star Trek III: The Search for Spock* (1984) and *Star Trek IV: The Voyage Home* (1986), Nimoy continued to direct such films as *Three Men and a Baby* (1987) and *Funny About Love* (1990). In 1991, Nimoy produced and acted in the made-for-television film *Never Forget*. He released his second autobiography, *I Am Spock*, in 1995. An avid poet and black-and-white photographer, Nimoy also published his Jewish-themed photo collection *Shekhina* in 2002. The annual Nimoy Concert Series at Temple Israel of Hollywood is sponsored by the Nimoys.

[Adam Wills (2nd ed.)]

NIMROD (Heb. נִמְרוֹד, נִמְרֹד), son of *Cush and grandson of *Ham son of *Noah (Gen. 10:8–12; I Chron. 1:10). He is described in the Table of Nations as "a mighty hunter by the grace of the Lord" (Gen. 10:9) whose exploits as a hero of the chase became proverbial. He was also "the first man of might on earth" (Gen. 10:8), i.e., the first to found a great empire after the *flood. He is said to have ruled over the famous capitals of southern Mesopotamia, Babylon, Uruk (Erech), and Akkad as well as, apparently, over the great cities of Calah and Nineveh in the land of Assyria. The term "land of Nimrod" appears as a synonymous variant of Assyria in Micah 5:5. The etymology of the name is uncertain as is also the identification of Nimrod with an historical personality. E.A. Speiser connects him with Tukulti-Ninurta I (13th century B.C.E.), who was the first Mesopotamian ruler effectively to have combined Babylon and Assyria under a single authority. However, the association of Nimrod with Cush son of Ham presents a difficulty if Cush refers to the area south of Egypt. Another possibility is to connect it with the Kassites who conquered Babylon in the second millennium (cf. Gen. 2:13), in which case a confusion of genealogical traditions is to be presumed. The extraordinary notice about Nimrod in the Table of Nations indicates the existence of a well-known and widespread narrative about him. U. Cassuto has postulated that the five verses in Genesis 10 derive from an ancient epic devoted to his heroic exploits.

[Nahum M. Sarna]

In the Aggadah

Nimrod is the prototype of rebellion against the Almighty (Ḥag. 13a), his name being interpreted as "he who made all the people rebel against God" (Pes. 94b). As the first hunter, he was the first to eat meat and to make war on other peoples (Mid. Ag. to Gen. 10:8), and he eventually became a king (PdRE 24). His physical prowess came from his coats of skin, which God had made for Adam and Eve (Gen. 3:21) and which Noah had preserved in the Ark. When the animals saw Nimrod wearing these coats, they knelt before him. He became the first man to rule the whole world and he appointed Terah, Abraham's father, his minister (PdRE 24). Elated by his glory, he became an idolator (*Sefer ha-Yashar*, Noah 9a, 1870). He built the Tower of Babel (which is called by the rabbis, "the house of Nimrod") for idol worship (Av. Zar. 53b) and he had the whole world pay divine homage to him (Mid. Hag to Gen. 11:28). When informed of Abraham's birth, Nimrod ordered all male children to be killed (*Ma'aseh Avraham*, in: A. Jellinek, *Beit ha-Midrash*, 2 (1938²), 118f.) and he later had Abraham cast into a fiery furnace because he refused to worship fire (Gen. R. 38:13).

Nimrod (identified with *Amraphel) became a vassal of his rebellious general Chedorlaomer, and was later defeated by Abraham (see Gen. 14; *Sefer ha-Yashar*, loc. cit.). He was slain by Esau who was jealous of his success as a hunter and who coveted his magic garments (PdRE 24). In messianic times Nimrod will testify before the whole world that Abraham never worshiped idols (Av. Zar. 3a).

In Islam

Namrūd (Namrūdh) b. Kūsh (Cush), or b. Kanʿān (Canaan), is not mentioned by name in the *Koran. The commentators are justified, however, in their contention that Suras 21:69; 29:23; and 37:95, in which it is said that the courtiers and the people of *Abraham suggested that he be thrown into the fiery furnace, refer to Namrūd. In the discussion between the ruler of the land and Abraham (Sura 2:260), another allusion is made to Namrūd. The allusions to the Jewish *aggadot* about Abraham in the fiery furnace are sufficiently evident. At a later period Nimrod b. Cush (Gen. 10:9), or b. Canaan, is mentioned by name. The theme of Abraham, who worships God and is persecuted by the ruler, recurs in various popular literary works. In a fragment of the *qaṣīda* (poem) attributed to Samawʾal al-Quarẓī, found in the Cairo **Genizah*, the following stanza appears: "It was only in the case of one man [among our ancestors] that the fire which encircled him was changed into fragrant and bowing garden plants." The influence of Muslim legend is most clearly evident in late Jewish legend. These same descriptions are again to be found in the writings of later commentators on the Koran: Zamakhsharī (p. 888; 12th century) and Bayḍāwī (vol. 1, p. 620; 13th century).

[Haïm Z'ew Hirschberg]

BIBLIOGRAPHY: A. Falkenstein, in: ZA, 45 (1939), 36; E. Dhorme, *Les Religions de Babylonie et d'Assyrie* (1945), 102, 128–31; E.A. Speiser, in: Eretz Israel, 5 (1958), 32–36; U. Cassuto, *A Commentary on the Book of Genesis* (1964), 200ff.; D.O. Edzard, in: H.W. Haussig (ed.), *Woerterbuch der Mythologie*, 1 (1965), 114–5; E. Lipinski, in: RB, 73 (1966), 77, 93. IN THE AGGADAH: Ginzberg, Legends, 1 (1909), 175–9, and index. IN ISLAM: Ṭabarī, *Taʾrīkh*, 1 (1357 A.H.), 142, 201; Thaʿlabī, *Qiṣaṣ* (1356 A.H.), 80–81; J.W. Hirschberg (ed.), *Der Diwan des as-Samauʾal ibn Adijā…* (1931), 33, 63–64. **ADD BIBLIOGRAPHY:** EIS², 7 (1993), 952–3 (includes bibliography).

NIMRODI, family of Israeli press moguls. The family's financial empire ranges from the media to real estate and tourism. YAACOV NIMRODI (1926–) was born in Baghdad. After the family immigrated to Palestine, Nimrodi and his nine siblings grew up in poverty, Nimrodi working as a gardener and warehouseman. In 1948 he joined the Palmaḥ as an intelligence officer and subsequently worked in the Mossad. In 1956 he was appointed IDF military attaché and Israel Defense Ministry representative at the Israel Embassy in Teheran, in which role he was involved in large-scale arms sales to the Shah of Iran in the 1960s. After he left the IDF, he returned with his family to Teheran where he acted as a middleman in arms sales, including involvement in the so-called Irangate affair. Following the fall of the Shah he returned to Israel to pursue his business interests. In 1988, Nimrodi, worth an estimated $48 million, purchased the Israel Land Development Corporation (Hakhsharat ha-Yishuv) from the Jewish National Fund and Bank Leumi. Established in 1909 as the Palestine Land Development Company, the public corporation purchased and developed land for urban and agricultural settlement. The package which Nimrodi received for $26 million, included properties in prime areas like Jerusalem, Tel Aviv, Jaffa, Rishon le-Zion, and Beersheva, and hotels, private dwellings, and industrial holdings. Yaacov had one son, and three daughters. His son, OFER (1957–), born in Teheran and a law graduate from Tel Aviv University, studied business management at Harvard University and in 1989 was appointed the company's managing director. Over the years, the company increased its profitability and moved into such other areas as the media and tourism. Yaacov's three daughters and their husbands filled various positions in the business empire.

In 1992 Yaacov Nimrodi purchased the shares of the **Maariv* newspaper which had been owned by Robert *Maxwell until his death. Nimrodi subsequently sold 50 per cent of the shares, half to *Haaretz* publisher Amos *Schocken, and the other half to an Australian-Israeli consortium. Appointed by Yaacov the financially ailing newspaper's editor-in-chief, Ofer Nimrodi set for himself the goal of winning the circulation war with the highly successful **Yedioth Aharonoth*. Ofer succeeded in reducing the circulation gap, partly by going downmarket in editorial content and layout, but *Maariv* still lagged behind, with 23% of Israelis read the paper daily and 28% on weekends according to a 2005 Teleseker survey. IDLC earnings enabled Ofer Nimrodi to invest in the paper by purchasing new technologies and employing leading journalists. In the 1990s he established local newspapers in key cities – supplements added to *Maariv*'s Friday weekend issue – tapping local advertising potential. The competition between *Maariv* and *Yedioth Aharonoth* reached a climax in the mid-1990s in the so-called wiretapping scandal, as a result of which Nimrodi was imprisoned in 1999 for tapping the phone of *Yedioth Aharonoth* publisher Arnon *Mozes as well as of Dov *Yudkovsky, who had been *Maariv*'s editor under Maxwell. A *Maariv* investigative reporter, Amnon Abramovitch, resigned after discovering that his phone had also been tapped. In 1999 Ofer Nimrodi sold 25% of *Maariv*'s stock to Vladimir *Gusinsky, a Russian businessman, for $85 million; majority control in the newspaper remained in Nimrodi's hands.

Nimrodi's other media-related interests included: magazines geared to youth; a TV guide (*Ratings*); shares in the Tel-Ad subsidiary of Channel 2 television (including studios), which Nimrodi subsequently sold; *Maariv*'s publishing house (Sifriat Poalim); the Hed-Artzi music company; and interests in the cellular phone business. In 2004 he established the NRG Internet news website.

[Yoel Cohen (2nd ed.)]

NIMZOVITCH, AARON (1886–1935), chess master. Nimzovitch, who was born in Riga, won important tournaments in the 1920s but was particularly important as a theoretician. He was responsible, together with Tartakover, Réti, and Alekhine, for the general departure from the dogmatism of *Tarrasch's "strong center" theory. Two of his openings, the Nimzovitch Defense and the Nimzo-Indian, which remained popular long after their inventor's death, carried "hypermodern" theory into practice. His book, *Mein System* (1925; Eng. tr., 1930), a collection of important aperçus on points of technique, is still of great value.

[Gerald Abrahams]

NINE DAYS, period of mourning from the first of *Av until noon after the fast of the Ninth of *Av commemorating the destruction of the *Temple. The period is also called *Bein ha-Meẓarim* ("In Stress") and actually starts previously with the fast of *Tammuz (see *Three Weeks, The). However, from the first of Av onward, the mourning becomes more severe, and strictly observant Jews, especially in the Ashkenazi rite: (1) abstain from meat and wine except on the Sabbath; (2) recite special dirges of lamentation (*kinot*), as well as Psalm 137 ("By the rivers of Babylon") and Psalm 79 (also recited during *Tikkun Ḥaẓot) every noon and midnight; and (3) refrain from wearing new or festive clothing. Even on the Sabbath some wear ordinary weekday clothes. Others, especially Sephardim, observe these rules of mourning only during the week in which the Ninth of Av falls (See: Maim. Yad, Ta'an. 5:6). This is in accordance with the Mishnah which ordains that during that week one should not cut one's hair or wash clothes (except on the Thursday in honor of the coming Sabbath; Ta'an. 4:7).

BIBLIOGRAPHY: Sh. Ar, OḤ 551:1–18; 552:1–12; J.T. Lewinski (ed.), *Sefer ha-Mo'adim*, 7 (1957), 268–361; Eisenstein, Dinim, 1, 38–39.

NINEVEH (Heb. נִינְוֵה; Akk. Ninua, Ninâ; in Mari Ninuwa; Ar. Ninawa), the capital of the Assyrian empire from Sennacherib's time on, situated about 1 mi. (about 1½ km.) E. of the Tigris, opposite modern Mosul. Since the cuneiform for Nineveh (*Ninâ*) is a fish within a house, it has been suggested that the name of the city was derived from that of a goddess associated with fish, but it seems that it is of Hurrian origin. From the Akkadian period on, the city was dedicated to the "Ishtar of Nineveh."

The ancient citadel of Nineveh was situated on a hill known today as Quyunjiq ("Little Lamb") and located near the center of the western region of the city. On the hill there were also the Assyrian royal palaces and the temples. South of this citadel is a smaller tell, called Nebi Yūnis ("the Prophet Jonah"), where, according to Islamic tradition, the prophet Jonah is buried, and on which is a large mosque. The city, however, extended over a much larger area.

Archaeological excavations were conducted in the city for about a century, mainly by the British (beginning in 1842). The excavations of 1932 (by M.E.L. Mallowan) laid the foundations for the study of the prehistory of northern Mesopotamia, the city thus becoming a key site for a knowledge and understanding of the prehistoric period.

History

The investigation made during the 1932 excavations of Quyunjiq down to its virgin soil uncovered the tell's earliest stratum, which contains remnants of the Hassuna culture and has been assigned to about 5000–4500 B.C.E.

One of the earliest pieces of written evidence is an inscription of Narâm-Sin of the Akkadian dynasty (2291–2255 B.C.E.). Hammurapi king of Babylonia mentions the city in the introduction to his code of laws as the site of a temple of Ishtar. At the beginning of the 14th century B.C.E. Nineveh belonged to Mitanni. Tushratta king of Mitanni sent the image of "Ishtar of Nineveh" (identified with the Hurrian goddess Šauška) twice to Egypt to heal Amenophis III, his ally and in-law. Subsequently, Nineveh reverted to Assyrian rule, since the Assyrian king Ashur-uballiṭ (1364–1329 B.C.E.) stated that he rebuilt the temple of Ishtar which, according to indications, was renovated a number of times between the 13th and ninth centuries B.C.E. Individual bricks, inscribed with the builders' names and with dedicatory inscriptions that have been brought to light, attest to the existence of several palaces built during these centuries. The earliest palace of which actual remains have been uncovered is that of Ashurnaṣirpal II (883–859 B.C.E.).

The city reached its zenith toward the end of the eighth century B.C.E., when it was in effect reconstructed during the reign of Sennacherib (705–681 B.C.E.) and became the capital of the Assyrian empire. Near the city – and in fact within its limits – Sennacherib planted a botanical garden with trees from all parts of the empire, among them vines and fruit-bearing trees. Magnificent spacious palaces were erected in the city. In the southwestern corner of the site, Sennacherib built a new palace to replace the earlier smaller one that had been there, and called it "the palace which has no equal." Today it is known as "the southwestern palace." On most of the walls of the halls, reliefs have been found depicting scenes from the building of the palace as well as war scenes, including the siege of *Lachish (found in Hall XXXVI). In the disorders that broke out upon the death of Sennacherib, part of his palace was apparently burned down and left in ruins for about 40 years. On the smaller tell (Nebi Yūnis), Esarhaddon (681–669 B.C.E.) built himself a palace. Ashurbanipal (668–627 B.C.E.) reestablished his residence on the main tell (Quyunjiq). Not content with merely renovating and embellishing the palace of Sennacherib, his grandfather, he built his own palace at the extremity of the tell. It was explored in the course of the excavation of Quyunjik, 1853–54, and reliefs portraying scenes from various battles and representing Assyrian art at its zenith were uncovered. Ashurbanipal's greatest achievement was the establishment of a vast royal library in the city, containing several thousand cuneiform documents in the fields of literature and ritual, science and mythology, lexicography, astronomy, and history, as well as economic documents, letters, and state contracts.

At the end of Ashurbanipal's reign, the royal residence was apparently transferred from Nineveh and established, according to one view, in Harran. Nineveh was captured, plundered, and destroyed in the summer of 612 B.C.E. by the forces of the Median and Babylonian empires, and became a desolate heap. The site itself was later occupied again until the Mongol invasion of the 14th century.

In the Bible

According to the Table of the Nations, Nineveh was established – together with other principal centers in Mesopotamia – in the days of *Nimrod (Gen. 10:10–12). In the Book of Jonah (3:3) it is referred to as "an exceedingly great city, three days' journey" (from one end to the other). A subsequent verse (4:11) tells that its infant population alone numbered "more than a hundred and twenty thousand persons." Even if this is somewhat exaggerated, it is probable that the number of Nineveh's inhabitants at the pinnacle of its greatness in the seventh century B C.E. was indeed extremely large (see *Jonah).

In II Kings 19:36–37 (and in the parallel passage in Isa. 37:37–38), Nineveh is mentioned as the city to which Sennacherib returned after his failure to capture Jerusalem, and in which he was murdered by his sons.

Two contemporary prophets, *Zephaniah (2:13ff.) and *Nahum, prophesied the destruction of Nineveh.

[Yuval Kamrat]

In the Aggadah

Nineveh was a huge city, covering 40 square parasangs and containing a million and a half persons. The "six score thousand persons" alluded to in Jonah 4:11 refer to the population of only one of the 12 districts into which the city was divided. The voice of the prophet Jonah was so stentorian that it reached every corner of the city and all who heard his words resolved to turn aside from their ungodly ways (Mid. Jonah, 99–100, in A. Jellinek, *Beit ha-Midrash*, 1 (1938[2])). Under the leadership of their king, the people of Nineveh justly compelled God's mercy to descend upon them. The king of Nineveh was the pharaoh of the Exodus, who had been installed by the angel Gabriel. Seized with fear and terror he covered himself with sackcloth and ashes and with his own mouth made proclamation and published this decree through Nineveh: "Let neither man nor beast, herd nor flock taste anything, let them not feed nor drink water, for know that there is no God beside Him in all the world; all His words are truth, and all His judgments are true and faithful" (Yal. Ex. 176). The repentance of the people of Nineveh was sincere. They held their infants heavenward, crying, "For the sake of these innocent babes hear our prayers." They separated the young of their cattle from their dams and both began to bellow. Then the Ninevites cried, "If Thou wilt not have mercy on us, we will not have mercy upon these beasts" (Ta'an. 16a; Mid. Jonah 100–2). The penitence of the people of Nineveh manifested itself not only in fasting and praying, but also in deeds. If a man had usurped another's property, he would return it, even at the cost of leveling his castle in order to restore a stolen beam to its owner (Ta'an. 16a). Others publicly confessed their secret sins and declared themselves willing to submit to their punishment. According to the Palestinian *amoraim*, however, the repentance of the Ninevites was not sincere (TJ, Ta'an. 2:1, 65b). After 40 days they departed again from the path of piety and became more sinful than ever. Then the punishment foretold by Jonah overtook them and they were swallowed by the earth (PdRE 43). The attitude of the Palestinian aggadists in their evaluation of the repentance of the Ninevites may have been a reaction to Christian criticism of the Jews for their stubbornness in not following the example set by the people of Nineveh.

BIBLIOGRAPHY: A.H. Layard, *Nineveh and its Remains* (1849); idem, *Nineveh and Babylon* (1967); H. Rassam, *Ashur and the Land of Nimrod* (1897); R. Buka, *Die Topographie Ninewes* (1915); Luckenbill, Records, 2 (1926), 417–22; R.C. Thompson and R.W. Hutchinson, *A Century of Excavation at Nineveh* (1929); R. Dhorme, in: RHR, 110 (1934), 140–56; C.J. Gadd, *The Stones of Assyria* (1936); A. Parrot, *Nineveh et l'Ancien Testament* (1955); R.W. Ehrich, *Chronologies in Old World Archaeology* (1965), index. IN THE AGGADAH: Ginzberg, Legends, 4 (1913), 250–3;6 (1928), 350–2; E. Urbach, in: *Tarbiz*, 20 (1950), 118–22.

NINGPO, city in Chekiang province, E. China. The presence of Jewish settlers there in 1461 is recorded on the *Kaifeng stele inscriptions, which state that when the Kaifeng synagogue was destroyed by floods in that year and the sacred scriptures were lost, the Jews of Ningpo presented emissaries of the Kaifeng community with a Torah scroll. No other evidence recording the presence of Jews in Ningpo has been preserved.

BIBLIOGRAPHY: W.C. White, *Chinese Jews*, pt. 2 (1966[2]), 13, 27, 98.

[Rudolf Loewenthal]

NINGSIA, a province in N.W. of China, (now **Yinchwan**), city formerly in the predominantly Muslim Kansu province of N.W. China. Members of the Jewish Chin family from *Kaifeng community came to settle there but remained in touch with the religious life of the Kaifeng Jewish community. Their donations and active participation are recorded in the Kaifeng stele inscriptions of 1489 and 1512.

BIBLIOGRAPHY: W.C. White, *Chinese Jews*, pt. 2 (1966[2]), index.

[Rudolf Loewenthal]

NINI, ACHINOAM (1969–), Israeli pop, jazz, blues singer; Israel's most successful performing artist on the international scene. Of Yemenite background, Achinoam Nini or, as she is know abroad, Noa, grew up in New York and returned to Israel at the age of 17. After completing her army service, she enrolled at the Rimon School of Music in Tel Aviv, where she met guitarist Gil Dor, who was on the school's teaching staff, and the two began to perform together. Their first concert, at the Jazz, Blues & Videotape Festival in Tel Aviv, was enthusiastically received. Nini's debut album, *Achinoam Nini and Gil Dor Live*, was recorded live in Tel Aviv and released in 1991. It included songs in Hebrew and reworkings of numbers by the Beatles and Madonna. The material was accessible to audiences both inside and outside Israel and Nini soon began to play at festivals and major venues – such as New York's Carnegie Hall and the White House. In 1993 Nini released an album entitled *Achinoam Nini and Gil Dor* with songs based on the work of two of Israel's most eminent poets – *Raḥel and Leah *Goldberg. This followed a highly successful appearance at that year's Israel Festival and the album sold well in Israel and abroad.

Nini's global profile rose significantly after she released *Noa* in 1994, her first foreign recording. The album, which was produced by acclaimed jazz guitarist Pat Metheny, included a rendition of Bach's "Ave Maria," with new words written by Nini. Following this she became the first Israeli artist to perform in the Vatican when she sang the song in St. Peter's Square, in the presence of Pope *John Paul II. In 1997 Nini performed a program of specially arranged numbers with the Israeli Philharmonic Orchestra, including some of her best-known songs and works by Leonard *Bernstein and by leading Israeli composer Sasha *Argov, as well as a traditional Yemenite song called "Yuma." The concert was recorded and released the following year as *Achinoam Nini & the Israel Philharmonic Orchestra.*

Nini has maintained a very active career, both in Israel and around the globe, and was invited to perform "Ave Maria" for the state Italian television network after the death of Pope John Paul II.

[Barry Davis (2nd ed.)]

NINTH FORT, Nazi killing site four miles from the center of Kovno (Kaunas), Lithuania, which served as the execution and burial site for Jews from Kovno and for German, Austrian, and Czech Jews shipped to Kovno during the Holocaust. Originally built as a military fortress, during German occupation it became a site of torture and mass executions. Abraham Tory reports in his ghetto diary that "single and mass arrests as well as 'actions' in the ghetto almost always ended with a death march to the Ninth Fort, which in a way completed the ghetto area and became an integral part of it."

The road from the ghetto to the Fort was called the "Way to Heaven." Detainees were held in underground cells in conditions of dampness and darkness and above all fear. Jews were forced into pits inside the Fort, which served as mass graves.

In July 1943 the digging of mass graves ceased and in August 1943 under Aktion 1005 the digging up of bodies began. Jewish prisoners of war, ghetto Jews, and four non-Jews made up the squad of 60 men and four women who had to dig up the bodies, extract the gold teeth, and search for valuables in the garments of the dead before they were cremated.

Sixty-four prisoners escaped from the Ninth Fort on December 24, 1943. Some reached the Kovno ghetto; others escaped into the forest. Each escapee brought word of what had happened. Thus this killing field was known even before the war's end.

Some 45,000–50,000 Jews were killed in the Ninth Fort.

BIBLIOGRAPHY: A. Tory, *Surviving the Holocaust: The Kovno Ghetto Diary* (1990); A. Faitelson, *The Truth and Nothing but the Truth: Jewish Resistance in Lithuania (1941–1944)* (2006).

[Michael Berenbaum (2nd ed.)]

NIR AM (Heb. נִיר עָם; "The People's Plowed Field"), kibbutz in southern Israel, 6 mi. (10 km.) N.E. of *Gaza, affiliated with Iḥud ha-Kevuẓot ve-ha-Kibbutzim. Its founding in 1943 by immigrants from Central and Eastern Europe, most of them *Youth Aliyah graduates, constituted a step in the expansion of Jewish settlement toward the Negev. Abundant groundwater reserves were discovered soon after, and in 1947 the first pipeline leading to the Negev outposts was laid from the Nir Am – *Gevar'am area. In the Israeli *War of Independence (1948), the kibbutz became the headquarters, hospital, and supply center for the settlements in the south and Negev, cut off for several months from the rest of Israel. The kibbutz economy was based on intensive field crops, citrus groves, and dairy cattle, as well as a factory for fine cutlery. In addition, the kibbutz developed a tourist industry, including a resort, water museum, paintball, an environmental activities site, and catering. In 2002 its population was 301.

WEBSITE: www.nir-am.co.il.

[Efram Orni / Shaked Gilboa (2nd ed.)]

NIR DAVID (Heb. נִיר דָּוִד; *nir* – "Plowed Field"), kibbutz in central Israel, at the foot of Mt. Gilboa, affiliated with Kibbutz Arẓi ha-Shomer ha-Ẓa'ir, founded in 1936 as the first *stockade and watchtower outpost in the Beth-Shean Valley. The settlers, Israel-born youth and pioneers from Poland, set up camp on the site a year earlier but after the outbreak of the Arab riots had to live temporarily at neighboring *Bet Alfa while continuing to cultivate their land. Nir David repelled Arab attacks and soon became a model farming community, pioneering in carp breeding in ponds and in growing crops adapted to its hot climate. Kibbutz farming also included field crops, plantations, and poultry. In addition, it opened factories for farm equipment and plastic tubes. Later it began to develop tourism, opening 26 guest rooms and an Australian zoo with animals such as kangaroos and koalas. Nir David also had a local museum. In 2002 the population was 534. The name commemorates the Zionist leader David *Wolffsohn.

WEBSITE: www.nir-david.org.il.

[Efraim Orni / Shaked Gilboa (2nd ed.)]

NIRENBERG, MARSHALL WARREN (1927–), U.S. biochemist and Nobel Prize winner. Nirenberg was born in New York City and educated in Orlando, Florida. He received his B.Sc. (1948) and M.Sc. (1952) in zoology from the University of Florida at Gainesville and earned his Ph.D. in biochemistry from the University of Michigan at Ann Arbor, guided by Dr. James Hogg. He joined the staff of the National Institutes of Health, Bethesda, in 1957 where he was appointed chief of biochemical genetics at the National Heart Institute and where he has remained for the rest of his career. Nirenberg and his co-workers showed that genes control protein synthesis through DNA sequences transmitted by RNA. They elucidated the "language" dictating the synthesis of a single amino acid as the first step in understanding what is now termed the "genetic code." He was awarded the 1968 Nobel Prize for physiology or medicine jointly with Robert Holley and Har

Gobind Khorana. Subsequently Nirenberg and his colleagues completed the task of unraveling the full code. He remained an active research worker investigating the conserved genes that control development called "homeoboxes" and the genes and factors that regulate the growth of cell lines derived from the nerve cell tumor, neuroblastoma. His many honors include election to the U.S. National Academy of Sciences (1967), the American Academy of Arts and Sciences, and the American Philosophical Society (2001). His awards include the U.S. National Medal of Science (1966), the Gairdner Award (1967), the Lasker Award in Basic Medical Science (1968), the U.S. National Medal of Honor (1968), and the Joseph Priestley Award (1968). Nirenberg showed great and often controversial interest in the social responsibilities of geneticists and was actively involved in action against world poverty and nuclear proliferation. He often protested against the political repression of fellow scientists including the Soviet refusal to allow Mikhail Stern to immigrate to Israel. He married the biochemist Perola Zaltzman in 1968.

[Michael Denman (2nd ed.)]

NIR EẒYON (Heb. נִיר עֶצְיוֹן), moshav shittufi in N. Israel, on Mt. Carmel, affiliated with Ha-Po'el ha-Mizrachi Moshavim Association. It was founded in 1950, initially as a kibbutz, by the surviving defenders of *Kefar Eẓyon in the Israeli *War of Independence (1948), who were joined by other members of their movement. The economy was based on intensive farming (field crops, orchards, flowers, poultry, and dairy cattle). The moshav opened a resort run on strictly Orthodox Jewish principles and operated a catering service as well. Nir Eẓyon includes the *Youth Aliyah village Yemin Orde, which is named for Orde Charles *Wingate. Its total population in 1970 was 450, rising to 800 in 2002.

[Efraim Orni / Shaked Gilboa (2nd ed.)]

NIRIM (Heb. נִירִים; "Plowed Fields"), kibbutz in southern Israel, in the "Eshkol Region" of the western Negev, affiliated with Kibbutz Arẓi Ha-Shomer ha-Ẓa'ir. Originally established as one of the 11 villages founded in the Negev on the night of Oct. 6, 1946, it was, until 1948, the westernmost Jewish settlement in the country and the closest to Egyptian-held Sinai. The founders, Israel-born youth, were joined by pioneers from Hungary and Romania. In the Israeli *War of Independence Nirim was the first Jewish village exposed to a concentrated attack of the invading Egyptian army (May 1948). Although the kibbutz was entirely leveled, Nirim's members held their ground, compelling the enemy to change tactics and advance exclusively through Arab-inhabited terrain while leaving most of the Jewish settlements to the rear intact. After the cessation of hostilities in April 1949, the kibbutz was transferred to a site further northwest on the Gaza Strip border, while the former site was taken over by Nir Yiẓḥak, another kibbutz of Ha-Shomer ha-Ẓa'ir. Besides partly intensive farming (field crops, avocado plantations, flowers, poultry, and dairy cattle), the kibbutz also developed organic farming. An electronics factory mainly for farming aids was later closed. The kibbutz is co-owner of Nirlat, a paint factory located at nearby Kibbutz Nir Oz. In the mid-1990s the population was approximately 445, dropping to 365 in 2002. A beautiful mosaic synagogue floor, dating from the Byzantine period, was unearthed in the Nirim fields.

[Efram Orni / Shaked Gilboa (2nd ed.)]

NIR-RAFALKES, NAHUM (1884–1968). Israeli labor politician, second speaker of the *Knesset, and member of the First and Third to Fifth Knessets. Born in Warsaw, Nir-Rafalkes studied in a *ḥeder* and then in a gymnasium. He studied natural sciences at the universities of Warsaw and Zurich and law at the University of St. Petersburg, receiving a doctorate in law in 1908. In 1903 he joined the Zionist students' organization Kadimah, and joined *Po'alei Zion in 1905, representing it as a delegate in the Sixth and Seventh Zionist Congresses. In 1906 he was imprisoned for four months for his political activities. In 1917 he represented Po'alei Zion in the All-Russian Soviet of Workers' and Soldiers' Deputies during the revolution. In 1919 he moved back to Warsaw and was elected to its city council. He participated in the Po'alei Zion Conference in Stockholm in 1919, and after the movement split the following year, he joined Left Po'alei Zion, becoming its secretary, and held negotiations for its entry into Comintern. He remained secretary of Po'alei Zion until 1935. In 1925 he settled in Palestine, where he practiced law and represented his party in the *Histadrut and the Va'ad Le'ummi. After Left Po'alei Zion merged with *Aḥdut ha-Avodah and, with it, joined *Mapam, he became a member of the pre-state People's Council and its deputy chairman. He was elected to the First Knesset on the Mapam list, and from the Third Knesset on the Aḥdut ha-Avodah-Po'alei Zion list. Already in the First Knesset he was chosen as one of the deputies to the speaker, and upon the death of Joseph *Sprinzak in 1959, was elected by an *ad hoc* coalition of all the parties in the plenum except *Mapai as speaker, serving in that capacity until after the elections to the Fourth Knesset. He then returned to serve as deputy speaker until leaving the Knesset in 1965. In the First Knesset he served as chairman of the Constitution, Law, and Justice Committee, and in the Fourth and Fifth Knesset as chairman of the Public Services Committee. He wrote many articles in Russian, Yiddish, and Hebrew and published a number of books. Among his writings are *Wirtschaft un Politik in Eretz Yisrael* (Yiddish, 1930); *Leningrad* (Yiddish, 1942); *Pirkei Ḥayyim – Ba-Ma'agal ha-Dor ve-ha-Tenu'ah 1884–1918* (1958); *Vanderungen* (Yiddish, 1966).

[Susan Hattis Rolef (2nd ed.)]

NIŠ (Lat. **Naissus**), town and important communications center in Serbia. Jews lived in Niš apparently from Roman times but there are no documents to confirm their presence before the 17th century. The disappearance of Jacob, a wool trader, was noted in 1651. Visits by *shadarim* (emissaries from Palestine) are on record for the second half of the 18th century.

The rabbis who served in Niš were Levi Jitzhak Yerushalmi, Jacob de Mayo, Rahamim Naftali Gedalya, Moshe Shaban, and Abraham Daniti. In 1900 the town's Jewish population numbered 800, their number gradually diminishing through emigration. A Zionist group called Zion joined the world movement in 1902.

The Jews were engaged mainly in the textile trade and in moneychanging; some were artisans, while a few were manual laborers. A prayer house was built in 1695 and a synagogue in 1909. Local spiritual leaders consulted the rabbis of Belgrade on halakhic matters. The Jews of Niš participated in Serbia's wars and suffered casualties in them. In 1921 there were 547 Jews in the town. In the 1930s there was a good deal of communal activity, including a choir and Zionist youth groups like Ha-Shomer ha-Tza'ir and, later, also Betar.

In 1939 Yugoslav Prime Minister Cvetkovic, a native of the town, offered to arrange exit visas to Turkey for the Jews of Niš, but the Jews chose to remain despite the danger signs. In 1940 they numbered 430, increasing to 970 in 1941 with the arrival of refugees from Germany, Austria, and Poland. The Germans arrived in April 1941. In October 1941 the Jewish men were imprisoned in the "Red Cross" camp at Bubanj. In February 1942 several inmates escaped from the camp after attacking the guards, and in retaliation several prisoners, most of them Jews, were shot. Two days later, more Jews were shot. In the spring of 1942 all women and children were arrested and after a few days in the "Red Cross" camp they were sent to the Sajmiste (Semlin Judenlager) death camp. In 1952 there were 25 Jews in the city. The community was not renewed. The synagogue was used as a concert hall.

BIBLIOGRAPHY: *Bulletin de l'Alliance Israélite Universelle*, 28 (1963), 147–8; *Zločini fašističkih okupatora … u Jugoslaviji* (1952), 38–40. **ADD. BIBLIOGRAPHY:** Z. Loker (ed.), *Pinkas ha-Kehillot – Yugoslavia* (1988); Ž. Lebl, *Do "konačnog rešenja" – Jevreji u Srbiji*, Belgrade, 2003, 65–119; *Dva stoljeća židovske povijesti i kulture u Zagrebu i Hrvatskoj* (1998), issued by Zagreb Jewish community.

[Simon Marcus / Zvi Loker (2nd ed.)]

NISAN (Heb. ניסן), the post-Exilic name of the first month of the Jewish year. Its pentateuchal name is *ḥodesh ha-aviv* (lit. "month of spring," Ex. 13:4 and parallels) and it is also referred to as the month of the ripening ears of barley (*ibid.* 9:31). The post-Exilic name, occurring in the biblical and apocryphal records (Esth. 3:7, Neh. 2:1; I Esd. 5:6, Add. Esth. 1:1) and frequently in Josephus and rabbinic literature (e.g., *Megillat Ta'anit), is linked with the Babylonian first month, Nisannu (derived from *nesa*, Heb., *nasa* "to start"). The Mishnah calls the first of Nisan the "new year for kings and festivals" (RH 1:1). Reigns of monarchs in biblical times were reckoned from that time, but later it was made the seventh month of the civil year (RH loc. cit.). The zodiacal sign of this month is *Aries*. In the present fixed Jewish calendar it invariably consists of 30 days, and the 1st of Nisan never falls on a Monday, Wednesday, or Friday (see *Calendar). In the 20th century Nisan, in its earliest occurrence, extended from March 13 to April 11, and in its latest from April 11 to May 10. According to R. Joshua, this is the month during which the world was created and the Patriarchs were born (RH 11a). It was in Nisan that God spoke to Moses from the burning bush. In this month redemption will occur in the time to come (*ibid.*). The tabernacle was erected in Nisan (Ex. 40:17), and the princes brought their offerings then (Num. 7:1–2). Because the 12 princes offered their gifts to the tabernacle every day beginning with the first of Nisan, each day was considered a festival. All public mourning is prohibited in Nisan. **Taḥanun* and **Ẓidduk ha-Din* are not recited, nor are eulogies allowed (Sh. Ar., OḤ 429:2). As "the greater part of the month was thus sanctified, the entire month is deemed holy" (*ibid.*, comm. of *Magen Avraham*, 3).

Memorable days of Nisan include the Passover period: the 14th of Nisan, the eve of the biblical feast of *Passover when all leaven is cleared from Jewish households, and in Temple times, the *Paschal lamb was sacrificed (Ex. 12 and parallels); and the festival of Passover from the 15th to the 21st (in the Diaspora, the 22nd) of Nisan. The 15th and 21st of Nisan (in the Diaspora 15th–16th and 21st–22nd), the first and last days of Passover, respectively, are full holidays; 16th–20th of Nisan (in the Diaspora 17th–20th) are the intervening days of the festival, **ḥol ha-mo'ed*. The 16th of Nisan is the controversial "morrow of the Sabbath" (see Lev. 23:11, 15, 16) when an *omer* of barley was offered in the Temple and marked the commencement of the counting of the *omer*. Other traditional dates in this month are 1st–7th of Nisan, the defeat by the Pharisees of the Sadducees' claim that the *tamid* (Ex. 29:38–42, Num. 28:1–8) was to be defrayed by private donations (Meg. Ta'an. 1); 8th–21st of Nisan, a Pharisaic victory over the Sadducees in a dispute concerning "the morrow of the Sabbath" and the day of the month on which Shavuot falls (Meg. Ta'an. 1); 1st (or 8th), 10th, and 26th of Nisan, the respective anniversaries of the death of *Nadab and Abihu, of *Miriam, and of *Joshua, once observed as fasts (Meg. Ta'an. 13).

BIBLIOGRAPHY: Eisenstein, Dinim, 267, s.v.

[Ephraim Jehudah Wiesenberg]

NISHAPUR, town in Khurasan, N.E. *Persia. Jewish settlement here allegedly dates from the time of the early Diaspora. According to the 12th-century Jewish traveler *Benjamin of Tudela, the district of Nishapur was inhabited by descendants of the Jewish tribes Dan, Zebulun, Naphtali, and Asher. They were united under a Jewish prince named R. Joseph Amarkala ha-Levi, and were engaged in agriculture and warfare in alliance with the "infidel Turks." There were some scholars among them. In 11th-century fragments from the Cairo **Genizah*, mention is made of an Isaac Nishapuri, an Egyptian silk merchant who settled in *Alexandria.

BIBLIOGRAPHY: A. Asher (ed. and tr.), *Itinerary of R. Benjamin of Tudela* (1840), 83, 85. **ADD. BIBLIOGRAPHY:** EIS^{2} 8 (1995), 62–64.

[Walter Joseph Fischel]

NISHMAT KOL ḤAI (Heb. נִשְׁמַת כָּל חַי; "The soul of every living being"), the initial words and name of a prayer recited at Sabbath and festival morning services at the conclusion of the *Pesukei de-Zimra introductory biblical hymns. This prayer expresses the gratitude men owe to God for His mercies in sustaining them. In talmudic literature it is called *Birkat ha-Shir* ("Benediction of the Song," Pes. 10:7, and 117b–118a). Based upon the opinion of R. Johanan, *Nishmat* also became part of the Passover **Haggadah*.

Nishmat consists of three main sections. The first contains an avowal of God's unity: "Besides Thee we have no King. Deliverer, Savior, Redeemer… We have no King but Thee." Some scholars believed that this passage was composed by the apostle Peter as a protest against concepts foreign to pure monotheism (A. Jellinek, *Beit ha-Midrash*, 6 (1938²), 12; *Maḥzor Vitry*, ed. by S. Hurwitz (1923²), 282; Hertz, 416). The second section starting with the words: "If our mouths were full of song as the sea… " originated in the tannaitic period. It is similar to the formula of thanksgiving for abundant rain recited in that period. The passage: "If our eyes were shining like the sun and the moon… we could not thank God for the… myriads of benefits He has wrought for us" especially, is thought to substantiate this ascription to the tannaitic period since it reflects the opinion of Rav Judah that God has to be praised for each drop of rain (Ber. 59b; Ta'an. 6b; Maim. Yad, Berakhot, 10:5). The third section, starting with the words: "From Egypt Thou hast redeemed us," is believed to have originated in the geonic period (c. tenth century C.E.). There is considerable disagreement among scholars about the original version of the *Nishmat*. There is, however, a general consensus that there existed an ancient but shorter version, called *Birkat ha-Shir*, which was later amplified and enlarged. This view is supported by the fact that the *Nishmat* in the Ashkenazi and in the Sephardi ritual, respectively, differ only in the wording of two or three sentences (compare *Seder R. *Amram Ga'on*, 27b and *Maḥzor Vitry* (1923), 148–54). In most prayer books the words *ha-Melekh, Shokhen ad* and *ha-El* are printed in large type, since the *ḥazzan* starts the central part of the morning service at these places, on High Holy Days, Sabbath, and festivals respectively. In the section *Be-fi yesharim* ("By the mouth of the upright") some prayer books mark an acrostic of the names Isaac and Rebekah, which was not customary in Jewish liturgical poetry prior to the Middle Ages. Some scholars consider it a later addition, but it could be also coincidental.

BIBLIOGRAPHY: Eisenstein, Dinim, s.v.; Elbogen, Gottesdienst, 113–4; Davidson, Oẓar, 3 (1930), 231–2; E. Levy, *Yesodot ha-Tefillah* (1952²), 134–5, 228; E.D. Goldschmidt, *Haggadah shel Pesaḥ, Mekoroteha ve-Toledoteha* (1960), 66–68, 107–8; E. Munk, *The World of Prayer*, 2 (1963), 29–32; J. Heinemann, *Ha-Tefillah bi-Tekufat ha-Tanna'im ve-ha-Amora'im* (1966²), 41–45, 152; idem, in: *Tarbiz*, 30 (1960/61), 409–10.

NISIBIS (Neşibin, Nezibin), the modern townlet Nesib in S. Anatolia. Over a long period (under the Roman rule, until 363; and under the rule of Persia and the Arabs) Nisibis was a flourishing trading station on the commercial route from the Far East to the western countries. During the 13th century, as a result of the *Mongol conquests, the town was destroyed; the Maghrebian traveler Ibn Baṭṭūṭa, who visited it during the first half of the 14th century, relates that most of the town was in ruins.

The first evidence of a Jewish settlement in the town was related by Josephus during the first century C.E.; he says that in Nisibis and *Nehardea the Jews of Babylonia consecrated their half shekels and their vows and donations to the Temple in Jerusalem; they traveled from Nisibis to the Holy City. The community appears to have been well founded because it also absorbed the Jews of Seleucia and Ctesipon who fled the vengeance of their neighbors as a result of the acts of *Anilaeus and Asinaeus (see *Nehardea). The town is known to have been a Torah center during the second century, when Judah b. Bathyra II attracted students from as far away as Palestine. During the third century, as a result of the rising influence of the Christians, which surpassed that of their Jewish neighbors, there was a cooling down of Nisibis' relations with Palestine and its scholars.

During the period of Islamic rule the Jewish settlement in the town prospered. At the time of the great emigration of the Jews of Babylonia to the lands which bordered on the Mediterranean Sea during the tenth century, however, Jews also left Nisibis. In a document of 989, for example, Netira b. Tobiah ha-Kohen of Nisibis is mentioned as an inhabitant of the town *Damietta in Egypt. During the second half of the 12th century the traveler *Benjamin of Tudela nevertheless found about 1,000 Jews there; his contemporary Pethahiah of Regensburg mentions a large community, the synagogue of the *tanna* R. Judah b. Bathyra II, and two synagogues which were built, according to tradition, by Ezra the Scribe. After the campaigns of the Mongols the Jewish settlement of the town was also impoverished. R. Moses Basola, who visited the Oriental countries between 1521 and 1523, met a Jew in Beirut from the environs of Nisibis who told him of the pillar of cloud which appears on the 18th of Sivan and at Pentecost over the tomb of the *tanna* Ben Bathyra in Nisibis and also that pilgrimages to his tomb took place from the surrounding areas. Under Ottoman rule the decline of the community continued and its members even turned to the Jews of Cochin with requests for support (D.S. Sassoon, *Ohel David*, 2 (1931), 995). At the close of the 19th century, according to Obermayer, there were approximately 200 miserable clay houses in the town, half of which belonged to Jews. Apparently no Jews resided in Nisibis at the outset of the 21st century.

BIBLIOGRAPHY: Neubauer, Géogr, 350; Jos., Ant., 18:312; J. Obermayer, *Landschaft Babylonien…* (1929), 128–30; J.B. Segal, in: J.M. Grintz and J. Liver (eds.), *Sefer… M.H. Segal* (1964), 38–39; Neusner, Babylonia, 3 (1968), index.

[Eliyahu Ashtor and Moshe Beer]

NISSAN (Katznelson), AVRAHAM (1888–1956), labor politician in Palestine and Israel diplomat, brother of Reuben *Katznelson. Born in Bobruisk, Belorussia, he was a medical officer in the Russian army during World War I. In 1917, between the two revolutions, he headed the Organization of Jewish Soldiers in the Russian army on the Caucasus front (10,000 men) and was attracted to Joseph *Trumpeldor's plan to set up Jewish battalions of 200,000 soldiers and volunteers and transport them to the front in Palestine to fight together with the British army for the liberation of Ereẓ Israel from the Turks. In 1919–20 he was the head of the Palestine Office of the Zionist Executive in Constantinople. In 1921–23 Nissan was active at the central office of Hitaḥdut (the union of *Ha-Po'el ha-Ẓa'ir and *Ẓe'irei Zion) in Vienna and Berlin. He settled in Palestine in 1924, served as the director of the health department of the Zionist Executive and as a member of the Va'ad Le'ummi (1931–48). He was also a member of the central committee of the Ha-Po'el ha-Ẓa'ir Party and of Mapai. From 1950 until his death, he was Israel's minister to the Scandinavian countries in Stockholm.

[Abraham Aharoni]

NISSELOVICH, LEOPOLD (Eliezer; 1856–1914), delegate to the Third *Duma in Russia. He was born in Bauska district of Courland, Latvia. After graduating from the law faculty of the University of St. Petersburg (1880), he was employed in the Ministry of Finance. In connection with his work he wrote several studies on economic legislation and on the economic and financial institutions of Russia. In 1882 he left his government post to practice law. In the elections to the Third Duma (1907), he was chosen as representative for Courland province. He joined the Cadet Party (the Russian liberals) on the explicit condition that he would not have to follow the party line in matters concerning Jews. Together with his colleague, N. Friedmann, he represented the Russian Jews at this Duma, and both were frequently the target of attacks by rightist members. Nisselovich was responsible for the bill proposing the abolition of the *Pale of Settlement, presented to the Duma on May 31, 1910, with the signatures of 166 members. The bill was transferred for consideration to the Duma commission on personal freedom but did not reach the full session for debate and vote. His activities in the Duma, and fights against antisemitism, severely undermined his health, and he did not offer his candidacy for the 4th Duma. Nisselovich died in Geneva.

BIBLIOGRAPHY: Y. Maor, in: *He-Avar*, 7 (1960), 65–84.

[Yehuda Slutsky]

NISSENBAUM, ISAAC (1868–1942), rabbi, Hebrew writer, and religious Zionist in Poland. Born in Bobruisk, Belorussia, Nissenbaum was ordained as a rabbi. He settled in Minsk, where he began his Zionist activity. When the yeshivah of *Volozhin was closed in 1892, he became head of the secret nationalistic association of that yeshivah, Neẓaḥ Israel, an office which he held until 1894, when he moved to Bialystok. There he became Samuel *Mohilever's secretary. From then on he was a central figure in the Zionist movement, particularly among the Orthodox Jews. After Mohilever's death, Nissenbaum served as a Zionist preacher, traversing towns and townlets in Russia, Poland, Latvia, and Lithuania. He used midrashic elements in his Zionist preachings and had a considerable influence on Orthodox Jews. In 1900 he settled in Warsaw and became a regular preacher in synagogues and other places. He was an active member of Mizrachi from its beginning, a member of the executive of the Polish Zionist Organization, and one of the heads of the Jewish National Fund.

Beginning in 1889, Nissenbaum wrote many essays on current events, Zionism, and religious Zionism, as well as personal memories and several exegetical books. He was one of the editors of *Ha-Ẓefirah*, and after World War I, editor of Mizrachi's weekly in Poland. He edited a series of republished classical books in Jewish studies. The first explanatory pamphlet concerning the Jewish National Fund was written by him (1902). During World War II he remained in the Warsaw ghetto and was murdered there.

Among his homilies are *Derushim ve-Ḥomer li-Derush* (1903), *Derashot le-Khol Shabbatot ha-Shanah ve-ha-Mo'adim* (1908, 1923²), *Hagut Lev* (1911, 1925²), and *Imrei Derush* (1926). In the field of religious Zionism he wrote *Ha-Dat ve-ha-Teḥiyyah ha-Le'ummit* (1920), *Ha-Yahadut ha-Le'ummit* (1920), and a monograph on Samuel Mohilever (1930). He also published an autobiography entitled *Alei Ḥeldi* (1929, 1969²). In 1948 a selection of his writings was published in Israel under the editorship of E.M. Genichovsky, and in 1956 a selection of his letters was edited and published by I. Shapira.

BIBLIOGRAPHY: I. Shapira, *Ha-Rav Yiẓḥak Nissenbaum* (1951).

[Getzel Kressel]

NISSENSON, AARON (1898–1964), Yiddish poet, journalist, and essayist. Born in Chepeli, Belorussia, he immigrated to the U.S. at the age of 13. He graduated as a pharmacist but preferred a literary and journalistic career. In 1918 he co-edited the literary monthly *Der Onheyb*. He was business manager of the New York daily, *Morgn Zhurnal*, for 30 years, while he published his works in the major Yiddish publications of the day, including *Tsukunft*, *Der Yidisher Kemfer*, and *Fraye Arbeter Shtime*. In his later years he was press representative of the *American Jewish Joint Distribution Committee. His first volume of poems, *Hundert Lider* ("Hundred Songs," 1920) was followed by six other books of lyric and dramatic poems. The central hero of his dramatic poem *Der Veg tsum Mentsh* ("The Road to Man," 1934) was the American socialist leader Eugene V. Debs, for him a symbol of a pure-hearted man. In the dramatic poem *Dos Tsugezogte Land* ("The Promised Land," 1937), Nissenson portrayed the struggle between good and evil as embodied in opposing personalities, beginning with Moses and Pharaoh and continuing throughout history. He expressed faith in science as the ultimate redeemer, leading man ever closer to moral perfection. This faith remained with him during World War II, when he composed the poems of *Dos Lebn Zingt Afile in Toyt* ("Life Sings Even in Death," 1943). In his last poems, *In Tsadiks Trit* ("In the Footsteps of the Righteous," 1950), he continued to sing of compassionate, just human beings who would evolve from imperfect contemporary man. Shortly before his death, Nissenson published an English novel, *Song of Man* (1964), whose central character was again Eugene V. Debs.

BIBLIOGRAPHY: Rejzen, Leksikon, 2 (1927), 571ff.; LNYL, 6 (1965), 242–5; Y. Bronshteyn, *Ineynem un Bazunder* (1960), 54–7.

[Sol Liptzin]

NISSENSON, HUGH (1933–), U.S. novelist, short story writer, and essayist. Although born in Brooklyn, Nissenson often turned to a broader time and place for subjects. His novel *The Tree of Life* (1985) depicts a settler's life in early 19th century Ohio. His *Notes from the Frontier* (1968) reflect his impressions of Israel and the 1967 War. *My Own Ground* (1976) takes place in the Lower East Side of New York. *The Song of the Earth* (2001) is set in the future. *The Days of Awe* (2005) intertwines personal and family catastrophe, the events of 9/11, and the act of faith itself. *A Pile of Stones* (1965) and *In the Reign of Peace* (1972), collections of stories, are at home in settings as diverse as Israel, Poland, and America. Much of the strength of his writing resides in his depiction of modern, secular Jewish culture and the faith of the religious. His work captures the dissonance – and eloquence – amongst those Jews who are secular and those who are faithful, both groups searching for values and certainties that comport with their circumstances.

In 1988, Nissenson's *The Elephant and My Jewish Problem: Selected Stories and Journals, 1957–1987* was published.

BIBLIOGRAPHY: *Gale Literary Databases.*

[Lewis Fried (2nd ed.)]

NISSI (Nissim) BEN BERECHIAH AL-NAHRAWANI (late ninth–early tenth century), head of the **kallah* and poet in Babylon. Nissi appears to have come from Nahrawan in Persia. *Nathan ha-Bavli relates (Neubauer, Chronicles 2 (1895), 29–80) that when the Exilarch David b. *Zakkai was embroiled with the head of the Pumbedita Academy Rav *Kohen Ẓedek – in fact, the person involved was Mubashir b. Rav Kimoi *ha-Kohen and not Rav Kohen Ẓedek – it was Nissi, *Resh Kallah* in the Sura Academy, who succeeded in 922 in making peace between the disputants. Nathan ha-Bavli relates there that Nissi was *noda be-nissim* (i.e., a doer of miraculous deeds). In 928 when the question of appointing a *gaon* in the Sura Academy came up, this post was offered to him by *David b. Zakkai, but he refused it because of his blindness. Zemaḥ ibn Shahin and Saadiah b. Josef *Alfayumi competed for this post and despite the recommendation of Nissi that Ẓemaḥ ibn Shahin be appointed, the Exilarch appointed Saadiah to the gaonate. Nissi was one of the most important and fruitful of the *paytanim* of his country. In the Cairo *Genizah*, and also in other sources, poems and *piyyutim* by him were preserved, of which only a few have been published. Well known is his confession for the Day of Atonement, beginning: "Lord of the Universe, before all else, I have no mouth to answer," which has been adopted into many rites and republished hundreds of times. However, only with the discovery of the *Genizah* did the true identity of its author become clear.

BIBLIOGRAPHY: B. Halper, in: *Ha-Tekufah*, 20 (1923), 272–4; Davidson, Oẓar, 4 (1933), 452; J. Mann, in: *Tarbiz*, 5 (1934), 154f., 160; S. Bernstein, in: *Bitzaron*, 36 (1957), 156–64; J. Schirmann, *Shirim Ḥadashim min ha-Genizah* (1965), 23–28; A.M. Habermann, *Toledot ha-Piyyut ve-ha-Shirah* (1920), 100–4.

[Abraham David]

NISSI (Nissim) BEN NOAH (11th century), Karaite writer who lived in Persia. Nissi was formerly thought to be a contemporary of *Anan b. David (c. 800), but on the basis of his use of David *Alfasi's Hebrew dictionary and Judah *Hadassi's apparent knowledge of him, Harkavy placed him in the 11th century. Nissi advocated that Karaites should study rabbinic literature and the Talmud. Two works have been attributed to him, *Sefer Aseret ha-Devarim* (Firkovich Ms. 610), a commentary on the Ten Commandments, and *Bitan ha-Maskilim* (now lost), a treatise on the precepts of Jewish Law.

BIBLIOGRAPHY: S. Poznánski, in: JQR, 11 (1920/21), 249–50; Graetz, Gesch, 5 (1895), 199–201, 443–5; Mann, Texts, 2 (1935), 1350; Z. Ankori, *Karaites in Byzantium* (1959), 241; L. Nemoy, *Karaite Anthology* (1952), 250, 381.

NISSIM, ABRAHAM ḤAYYIM (1878–1952), Iraqi government official and member of Parliament; born in Baghdad. Nissim served as an employee in the administration of the sultan's estates; he later became a senior officer of the German railways in Iraq. After the British conquest he was appointed assistant to the Hilla District political officer and in the 1920s held a senior post in the Ministry of Finance. From 1930 to 1948 he represented Baghdad Jewry in the House of Representatives. During most of this period he was a member of the budget committee, serving as its draftsman. He settled in Israel in 1951 and died in Ramat Gan.

[Haim J. Cohen]

NISSIM, ISAAC (1896–1981), chief rabbi of Israel and *rishon le-Zion*. Nissim was born in Baghdad. His father was a merchant and also a scholar. Nissim early attained a reputation as a scholar and, although he occupied no rabbinic office, his opinion was sought in religious matters. His method of study approximated closely to that of the Lithuanian rabbis and he engaged in halakhic discussion with them and with heads of yeshivot. He had ties with eminent rabbis of Ereẓ Israel as well as with scholars of Germany and Poland. In 1925 he settled in Jerusalem, where he was closely associated with Solomon Eliezer *Alfandari whose lectures he attended. In 1926 he published *Ẓedakah u-Mishpat*, the responsa of Ẓedakah *Ḥozin, an 18th-century Baghdad scholar, together with an introduction and notes from a manuscript in Iris large library. Nissim wrote responsa on a variety of halakhic topics, some of them being published in his *Yein ha-Tov* (1947). In 1955 he was elected to the office of *rishon le-Zion* and chief rabbi of Israel.

He displayed his independence in various fields of activity and strove for understanding and the creation of amicable relations between all sectors of the population, visiting for example, left-wing kibbutzim, which were regarded as closed to rabbis. He took a strong stand in the halakhic recognition of the Bene Israel of India and refused to meet Pope Paul VI when the latter visited Israel in January 1964. After the 1967 Six-Day War he transferred the supreme *bet din* to a building opposite the southern Wall of the Temple near the site of the Chamber of Hewn Stone, which was the ancient seat of the Sanhedrin.

BIBLIOGRAPHY: Shin, in: *Ha-Ẓofeh*, (March 27, 1964), 3; D. Lazar, *Rashim be-Yisrael*, 2 (1955), 114–8.

[Itzhak Goldshlag]

NISSIM, MOSHE (1935–). Israeli politician and lawyer, and member of the Fourth, and then Seventh to Thirteenth Knessets. Born in Jerusalem, Nissim was the son of Rabbi Isaac *Nissim, who served as Sephardi chief rabbi from 1955 to 1973. Nissim went to the Magen David primary school and the Ma'aleh High School in Jerusalem, and received an M.A. in law from the Hebrew University of Jerusalem in 1964. He served in the IDF as a law officer. He was first elected to the Knesset on the list of the *General Zionists in 1959, at the age of 24, and was thus the youngest person ever elected to the Knesset. He was a delegate to numerous Zionist Congresses on behalf of the World Association of the General Zionists. In 1977 he was elected chairman of the*Israel Liberal Party executive, and was a member of its presidium. In 1978 he was elected chairman of the *Likud executive.

Until the Ninth Knesset, Nissim served on various Knesset committees. From January 1978 until August 1980 he served as minister without portfolio, and from August 1980 to April 1986 as minister of justice. Together with Labor's Moshe *Shahal, Nissim drafted the coalition agreement for the National Unity government established in 1984, on the basis of parity and rotation in the premiership. In 1986 he replaced Yitzhak *Modai in the Ministry of Finance, and continued the policy of economic stabilization introduced by him, in addition to reducing both income tax and corporate taxes. As minister of finance he also successfully refinanced the government debt to the U.S., through the Wall Street capital markets. In the National Unity government formed after the elections to the Twelfth Knesset in 1988 he was appointed minister without portfolio, and in March 1990 minister of industry and trade, replacing Ariel *Sharon, who had resigned from the government over the plan to hold elections in the West Bank and Gaza Strip. In the government formed by Yitzhak *Shamir in June 1990, he was appointed deputy prime minister as well. After the elections to the Thirteenth Knesset, which the Likud lost, Nissim served on the Knesset Foreign Affairs and Security Committee. As a politician Nissim was known for his mild manner. After retiring from politics in 1996 Nissim returned to practicing law, serving as arbitrator and mediator in commercial disputes. He served as chairman of the Public Commission on the Immunity of Knesset Members and of the Public Commission on the Reclassification of Public Lands, and he was a member of the Public Commission on the Status and Authority of the Attorney General.

[Susan Hattis Rolef (2nd ed.)]

NISSIM BEN JACOB BEN NISSIM IBN SHAHIN (c. 990–1062), together with *Hananel b. Ḥushi'el, the outstanding leader and talmudist of North Africa. His father headed a *bet ha-midrash* in Kairouan and was the representative of the academies of *Sura and *Pumbedita for the whole of North Africa. Little is known of Nissim's personal history. It is known that he, too, was head of an academy in Kairouan and maintained close ties with the academy of Pumbedita. After the death or Hananel, he was appointed by the Babylonian academies *Rosh bei-Rabbanan* ("Head of the College") in his stead. There were close ties between Nissim and *Samuel ha-Nagid. Samuel supported Nissim financially and Nissim served as the principal channel for Samuel's knowledge of Babylonian teachings, particularly those of Hai Gaon. When one of Nissim's sons died in childhood, Samuel composed a poem in consolation for the bereaved father. Nissim's daughter married Joseph *ha-Nagid, Samuel's son, and on that occasion Nissim visited Granada and taught there. According to Abraham *Ibn Daud, Solomon ibn *Gabirol was among those who heard his lectures. Nissim's teachers were his father, *Ḥushi'el, and possibly also the latter's son Hananel, whose teachings reveal a close affinity with that of Nissim. Nissim obtained a great part of his halakhic tradition from Hai Gaon, with whom he corresponded. Noteworthy among his pupils is Ibn Gasom, the author of a book on the laws of prayer (see Assaf. bibl.).

Nissim was a prolific and versatile writer. Five works of great length and value are known to have been written by him:

(1) *Sefer Mafte'aḥ Manulei ha-Talmud* (Vienna, 1847) on the tractates *Berakhot, Shabbat*, and *Eruvin* was first published from an early Hebrew translation and then included in the Romm (Vilna) editions of the Talmud. Subsequently, many fragments of the Arabic original were published. It is a reference book for quotations encountered in the course of talmudic study. It also gives the sources of the *beraitot* and *mishnayot* quoted in the Talmud as well as parallels in the Talmud and Midrashim and includes extensive commentaries on many talmudic themes. Only the sections on the orders *Zera'im* (*Berakhot*), *Mo'ed*, and *Nashim* are extant but it is probable that the original scope of the work was greater.

(2) Commentaries on a few tractates of the Talmud, apparently written in Hebrew. Only a few fragments from several tractates are extant.

(3) Halakhic rulings. A few fragments of what was evidently a comprehensive work are extant.

(4) *Megillat Setarim* (completed in 1051 at the latest). This work was very well known among the **rishonim*, Sephardim as well as Ashkenazim. It was written for the most part in scholarly terms. The book contains many variegated, unrelated top-

ics on all subjects coming within the range of interest of the scholars of the generation – beliefs and opinions, scriptural exegesis, religious polemics, explanations of passages in the Talmud and Midrashim in *halakhah* and *aggadah*, responsa on various subjects, customs and their sources, and other matters. This characteristic aspect of the book, as well as its bilingual construction (Hebrew and Arabic), which resulted in its division into two works even during the author's lifetime, led copyists in different places to arrange it in different orders according to their needs and interest, and in consequence to vary the numeration of its passages. Various compilations were made of the work, which were occasionally drawn upon by other authors such as Jacob *Tam whose *Sefer ha-Yashar* includes a number of rulings from it. The halakhic compendium *Sefer ha-Pardes* (written by *Rashi's school) may also have drawn upon it. Although the work is no longer extant, the discovery in the **Genizah* of a subject index contained in the indexer's copy (published by S. Assaf, *Tarbiz*, 11 (1940), 229–59) has made knowledge of its contents far more precise. The book exercised a great influence upon the major halakhists of subsequent generations, including Isaac *Alfasi, *Maimonides, *Nathan b. Jehiel of Rome, *Abraham b. Nathan ha-Yarḥi, and *Isaac b. Abba Mari.

(5) *Ḥibbur me-haYeshu'ah* (Ferrara, 1557), Nissim's best-known work, is a collection of Hebrew stories and folktales taken from early sources. It is designed to strengthen belief, faith, and morality among the people and to raise their spirit. This work, possibly the first prose storybook in medieval Hebrew literature, paved the way for Hebrew belletristic literature as a literary genre. Tradition has it that Nissim dedicated the book to his father-in-law, Dunash, who is otherwise unknown, to console him in his mourning. The first printed edition was published from an early Hebrew translation, and the Arabic text was published by J. Obermann (see bibl.). The Hebrew version has been frequently republished, not always according to the same translation. A new Hebrew translation, together with critical annotations by H.Z. Hirschberg, was published in 1954. Additional Arabic texts have been published by S. Abramson (see bibl.). The work circulated widely even before its first printing, and had a great influence on similar story collections. *Ma'asiyyot she-ba-Talmud* (Constantinople, 1519) was based upon it, and the *Ḥibbur ha-Ma'asiyyot (ibid.*, 1519) is an anthology of its stories. Many of the stories included by Gaster in his *The Exempla of the Rabbis* (1924; 1968^2) were taken from it.

Although some other works have been ascribed to Nissim on the basis of various quotations, it may be assumed that all these are from the works already referred to. This may not apply to his many responsa, which are recorded in the works of *rishonim*, though these too may have been included in his *Megillat Setarim*. Most of Nissim's works found in the *genizah* are undergoing the process of identification and publication. S. Abramson devoted the labors of a lifetime to the collection of Nissim's work from the *genizah*, from manuscripts, and from printed works, and published a monumental work.

BIBLIOGRAPHY: Rapoport, in: *Bikkurei ha-Ittim*, 12 (1831), 56–83; S. Poznański, in: *Festschrift... A. Harkavy* (1908), 211–8 (Heb. sect.); Mann, Texts, index; J. Obermann (ed.), *The Arabic Original of Ibn Shahin's Book of Comfort* (1933); A. Aptowitzer, in: *Sinai*, 12 (1943), 118f.; Zunz-Albeck, Derashot, index; S. Lieberman (ed.), *Hilkhot ha-Yerushalmi le-Rabbi Moshe b. Maimon* (1947), 14f.; Assaf, in: KS, 28 (1952/53), 101ff.; S. Abramson, *Rav Nissim Ga'on* (1965); idem, in: KS, 41 (1965/66), 529–32; idem, in: *Sinai*, 60 (1967), 12–16.

[Israel Moses Ta-Shma]

NISSIM BEN MOSES OF MARSEILLES (14th century), radical philosophical exegete. The dates of Nissim's birth and death are unknown. He was the author of a commentary on the Torah, titled, variously, *Ma'aseh Nissim*, *Sefer ha-Nissim*, and *Ikkarei ha-Dat*. The commentary was edited by H. Kreisel (Mekizei Nirdamim, Jerusalem, 2000). This work reflects a single-minded commitment on the part of its author to provide a naturalistic explanation for all seemingly supernatural elements of the Torah, whether it be the story of creation, the longevity of the ancients, the miracles in Egypt, the parting of the Sea of Reeds, the Revelation at Sinai, the rewards and punishments mentioned in the Torah, or the commandments that appear to have no rational reason or appear to involve supernatural intervention (such as the ceremony involving the woman accused of adultery by her husband). In the 14-chapter introduction to the commentary, Nissim deals with such topics as political theology, divine reward, principles of the faith, prophecy (including Mosaic prophecy), providence, and miracles. Most miracles actually occurred in his view, but they were the product of the superior knowledge of the prophet and his divinatory ability. Other miracles did not happen at all but appeared in a vision of prophecy or are to be understood metaphorically. The rewards and punishments mentioned in the Torah are treated by Nissim as the natural consequences of the individual's or nation's behavior. In his commentary he drew heavily from *Maimonides, Abraham *Ibn Ezra, Samuel ibn *Tibbon and his son Moses, as well as other Provençal Jewish thinkers such as *Levi ben Avraham. Nissim was exceptionally well versed in rabbinic literature, which he cites extensively in his commentary. Internal evidence suggests that Nissim composed his treatise sometime after 1315. One of the manuscripts of *Ma'aseh Nissim* contains a philosophical allegorical commentary on Ruth (edited by H. Kreisel in: *Jerusalem Studies in Jewish Thought*, 14 (1998), 158–80), which M. Schorr believes was also written by Nissim. His authorship of this work, however, is questionable.

BIBLIOGRAPHY: M. Schorr, in: *He-Ḥalutz*, 7 (1865), 88–144; C. Sirat, in: *Jerusalem Studies in Jewish Thought*, 9 (1990), 53–76; H. Kreisel, introduction to *Ma'aseh Nissim*, 1–52.

[Howard Kreisel (2nd ed.)]

°**NISSIM BEN REUBEN GERONDI** (known from the acronym of Rabbenu Nissim as the **RaN**; ?1310–?1375), one of the most important Spanish talmudists. Nissim's family originated in Cordova and settled first in Gerona, where he is thought to have been born, and then in Barcelona, which became his permanent place of residence. Few biographical details are known of him. He never held any official rabbinical post, even though in fact he fulfilled all the functions of a rabbi and *dayyan* in his community. Furthermore, many *takkanot* enacted in Spain originated with him, and his reputation as an authoritative *posek* was such that he received queries from as far as Ereẓ Israel and Syria. He is also known to have served as a physician in the royal palace. Because of a calumny, the date and causes of which are not certain, he was imprisoned for some time. It is also known that in 1336 he wrote a *Sefer Torah* for his own use, which became well known and served as a model. This *Sefer Torah* was moved from place to place until it reached Tiberias, where it was preserved until recently. Nissim's main teacher, apart from his father, was Perez ha-Kohen, with whom he was in close correspondence; Nissim even assisted him to become accepted as rabbi of Barcelona (after 1349). It seems that Nissim's main activity in his community was as head of the Barcelona yeshivah. Among his chief pupils were Isaac b. Sheshet *Perfet, who frequently quotes him, mostly anonymously, Ḥasdai *Crescas, Joseph *Ḥabiba, and Abraham *Tamakh.

Nissim's renown rests chiefly on his halakhic works. His method and system were solidly founded in accordance with the tradition of learning acquired from the school of Naḥmanides, Solomon b. Abraham Adret, Aaron ha-Levi of Barcelona, and their contemporaries, and though his works contain many sayings of these scholars without naming them, he adapted their words, crystallized them, and added much of his own so that his works are among the best produced by this school of learning. One of his main works is a commentary on the *halakhot* of Isaac *Alfasi to the Talmud. It seems that all the parts of this work have been preserved, and all have been published on the margin of Alfasi's commentary beginning with its first printed editions down to the present day.

This commentary comprises the tractates *Shabbat*, *Pesaḥim*, *Beẓah*, *Rosh Ha-Shanah*, *Yoma*, *Ta'anit*, *Megillah*, *Sukkah*, *Ketubbot*, *Gittin*, *Kiddushin*, *Shevu'ot*, *Avodah Zarah*, *Ḥullin*, and *Niddah*. He also wrote novellae to the Talmud, of which up to the present the following have been published: *Gittin* (Constantinople, 1711), *Niddah* (Venice, 1741), *Ḥullin* to the end of chapter 8 (in: *Ḥamishah Shitot*, Sulzbach, 1762), *Bava Meẓia* (Dyhrenfurth, 1823), *Shevu'ot* (Venice, 1608, at the end of the responsa of Moses *Galante), *Rosh Ha-Shanah* (1871), *Avodah Zarah* (1888), *Mo'ed Katan* (1937), *Bava Batra* (1963), *Eruvin* (1969), and *Pesaḥim* (1970).

His commentary to the tractate *Nedarim*, which is his best-known work, is published in all the usual editions of the Talmud and serves as the standard commentary to this tractate instead of that of Rashi. Some of his novellae to the Talmud still remain in manuscript, but most of them have been repeatedly republished, since they are among the works most acceptable to scholars of all countries and times. His commentaries to Alfasi differ from those to the Talmud in that they aim at giving the halakhic ruling, and in fact they have no real literary connection with Alfasi, with whom he frequently disagrees. The novellae to tractates *Megillah*, *Shabbat*, *Ketubbot*, and *Sanhedrin* published under Nissim's name are not by him. They represent one of the most difficult problems connected with the study of Nissim's works and teachings, as it is definite that a generation and more before him there lived in Barcelona another scholar with the same acronym – RaN (whose personal name is not certain), and whose works to several talmudic tractates have been recently published. Only 77 of Nissim's responsa are extant (Rome, 1545; Constantinople, 1548[2] from a different manuscript; and thereafter in many editions); also a book of 12 sermons (Constantinople 1533[1] and frequently thereafter), of a decidedly anti-philosophical character, though written in the style of philosophical literature; and a commentary on the Pentateuch of which the section on Genesis has been published (1968). The publication of the commentary to the Pentateuch has removed the few doubts that remained among some scholars as to whether Nissim is the RaN of the book of sermons ascribed to him or whether they were perhaps written by the other scholar of the same name. Discernible in both these works is Nissim's strong desire to prove the superiority of prophecy and Bible over philosophy, and thereby to strengthen the people's faith and their spiritual ability to bear up during the difficult periods of persecution and polemics of those times. He also wrote *piyyutim* and poems, some of which have been preserved and published.

BIBLIOGRAPHY: S. Assaf, *Mekorot u-Meḥkarim be-Toledot Yisrael* (1950), 173–81; A.M. Hershman, *Rabbi Isaac ben Sheshet Perfet and his Times* (1943), 192–6 and index; Baer, Spain, 2 (1966), index; S.H. Kook, *Iyyunim u-Meḥkarim*, 2 (1963), 321–4; L.A. Feldman (ed.), *Shitah la-Ra-N… al Massekhet Ketubbot* (1966) introd.; idem, in: *Koveẓ al Yad*, 7 (17; 1968), 125–60; idem (ed.), in: Nissim b. Reuven Gerondi, *Perush al ha-Torah* (1968), introd.; E. Hurwitz, in: *Hadorom*, 24 (1967), 39–87.

[Leon A. Feldman]

NITRA (Hung. **Nyitra**; Ger. **Neutra**). Slovak historians believe that Nitra is the location of the oldest Slovakian Jewish community. In 896 Hungarian tribes invaded the Panonian plain; in 906 they destroyed the Slavonic kingdom of Moravia and probably captured Nitra as well. One of these tribes may have been the *Khazars of Jewish faith, which settled in the vicinity of Nitra. In a 1248 description of Nitra, "castrum iudeorum" can be interpreted as a Jewish settlement, in the vicinity of the neighboring village of Parovce. For centuries Parovce served as the Jewish extension of Nitra, where Jews were not admitted. In 1840, when the Budapest parliament allowed Jews to settle anywhere, the Jews of Parovce moved to Nitra. Many poor Jews who could not afford to move to Nitra stayed in Parovce. In 1989, with the collapse of Communism in Czechoslovakia, Parovce was inhabited by gypsies.

The anti-Jewish legislation of Emperor Charles VI (1711–1740) encouraged the migration of Moravian and Bohemian Jews to upper Hungary, where those laws did not apply. Nitra and its environs were included in this migration. The 1840 legislation of the Hungarian Parliament permitted Jews to live wherever they chose, which increased the Jewish population of Nitra dramatically.

The Jewish community was established in 1750, numbering 21 families. They had a small synagogue and a rabbi. In 1778 there were 132 people. The royal census of 1785/87 recorded 449 Jews. In 1840 the number rose to 1,654. A Jewish school was established in 1855, with German as the language of instruction. Subsequently, a *talmud torah* was opened. Rabbi Ezekiel ben Jacob Peneth (1773–1864) headed the local yeshivah, which at its peak had 200 students from many countries. In 1880 there were 3,541 Jews (22.4% of the entire population). The 1921 Czechoslovak census records the Jewish population as 3,901; the 1930 census records 3,809. In 1940, on the eve of the deportations, there were 4,358 Jews

After the 1868 Hungarian Jewish Congress, the Nitra congregation remained Orthodox. However, in 1907 a split occurred and a *Neolog congregation was established. Each congregation had a synagogue and a cemetery. The monumental Neolog synagogue was erected in 1914. There was a Jewish hospital in the city, a *mikveh*, an orphanage, a home for the elderly, and a public kosher kitchen. *Machzike Hadas*, the official organ of Slovak Orthodoxy, was published every two weeks.

Nitra was not involved in the riots and vandalism of 1918 and 1919 which spread over Slovakia because the National Guard, manned by Social Democrats and Jews, guarded the town. In 1930 the Catholic Church and the Slovak Nationalist Party, headed by Father Dr. Josef *Tiso, the future president of the wartime Slovak state, instigated against the Jews. Tiso proposed their expulsion. But the Jews had a strong representation in the Social-Democratic Party, and in 1931 Dr. Vojtech Szilagy (Schlesinger) was elected deputy mayor of Nitra. The Zionist movement prospered in Nitra in the early 1900s, but it faced determined Orthodox competition. Rabbi Samuel David *Unger, the leading figure of Slovak Orthodoxy, moved to Nitra from Trnava in 1931 and brought along the Trnava yeshivah. There was long-standing hostility between the two communities. While the Jewish community was generally affluent, there were many impoverished people among them.

On March 14, 1939, the Slovak state was established under the aegis of the Third Reich. The state persecuted Slovak Jewry, peaking in 1942 when the Jews were deported to Poland. Some 4,400 of Nitra's Jews were sent to extermination camps. By the end of August 1944, German troops, accompanied by the local Slovak garrison, entered Nitra and sent the remaining Jews to Auschwitz.

In 1947 there were 784 Jews in Nitra. The returnees established a single congregation, with Rabbi Eliahu Katz serving as its spiritual leader. The synagogue and *mikveh* were re-established, and the cemeteries were cleaned up. In 1948–49, most of the community emigrated; in 1950 there were 150 Jews. In 1957 a kosher restaurant was opened, and a ritual butcher (*shoḥet*) attended to religious needs. In 1963, the authorities destroyed all Jewish public buildings except the Neolog synagogue. After 1989, the cemeteries were again desecrated and besmirched with swastikas. Local authorities claimed that the Jews were responsible, preparing a provocation.

In 1990 there were 65 Jews in Nitra. A *minyan* continued to convene almost regularly in the early 21st century.

BIBLIOGRAPHY: R. Iltis (ed.), *Die aussaeen unter Traenen…* (1959), 169–78; PK Germanyah. E. Bàrkàny and L. Dojč, *Židovské náboženské obce na Slovensku* (1991), 185–88.

[Yeshayahu Jelinek (2nd ed.)]

NITTAI OF ARBELA (= *Arbel in Lower Galilee; second half of second century B.C.E.), one of the **zugot*; a colleague of *Joshua b. Peraḥyah. He was a pupil of *Yose b. Joezer of Zeradah and *Yose b. Johanan of Jerusalem, the first of the *zugot*, whom he and Joshua succeeded with Nittai serving as *av bet din* (Ḥag. 2:2; Avot 1:6). All that is known of his teaching is that he took part in the only halakhic dispute of his time: whether the placing of the hands upon a sacrifice (*semikhah*) during a festival is permitted. Nittai held that it was permitted, in contrast to Joshua b. Peraḥyah who forbade it (Ḥag. 2:2). His saying preserved in Avot is, "Keep at a distance from an evil neighbor; do not make yourself an associate of a wicked man; do not abandon faith in [divine] retribution" (Avot 1:7).

BIBLIOGRAPHY: Hyman, Toledot, s.v.

[David Joseph Bornstein]

°**NIXON, RICHARD MILHAUS** (1913–1994), 37th president of the United States. After his discharge from the U.S. Navy in 1946 with the rank of lieutenant commander, Nixon entered politics and was elected to the 80th Congress in 1946. In his first term, Nixon quickly established himself as a staunch conservative on domestic issues, with a preoccupation with internal security, and a firm supporter of the new global role then being assumed by the Truman administration. By 1950 his slashing political style had earned him the lasting enmity of liberal intellectuals and many Jewish voters committed to its civil libertarian tradition. His opportunity to run for the presidency came in 1960, but pitted against John F. Kennedy, he suffered his first political setback. This was followed two years later by a second political setback when he lost the race for the California governorship, and it seemed that his political career was at an end.

In fact, in June 1963 Nixon left his political base in California to join a Wall Street law firm. During the next six years, however, he traveled extensively, becoming a familiar figure at local Republican Party gatherings and earning political credits everywhere. Soon his name was being mentioned once again as a possibility to head the Republican ticket in 1968. The Vietnam and civil rights issues had created serious schisms in the Democratic Party and not even the sacrifice of Lyndon Johnson seemed able to heal them. His hairbreadth victory over Hubert Humphrey resulted in one of the most remarkable political comebacks in American history.

In a geopolitical sense, Nixon was anxious to restore American influence in the Arab world, so that his primary purpose, the containment of Communist influence, might be served. It was not unexpected therefore that the preinaugural fact-finding mission of William Scranton to the Middle East was accompanied by much talk of a new "evenhanded" policy in the area. The words had an ominous ring for Jews since Nixon could easily impose a settlement from on high without too much fear of domestic repercussions. Some American Zionists sorely regretted the absence of a closer connection to the Republican Party.

By February 1969 the Nixon administration appeared ready to impose such a peace on the basis of the Rogers plan. It called for an overall guarantee of security to all the nations in the area and freedom of navigation along the Suez Canal and Straits of Tiran, in return for which Israel would, with minor modifications, revert to the pre-1967 boundaries. Negotiations were begun with the Russians and a cease-fire was arranged. Arms shipments to the area, including promised Phantom jets, were held up.

Then three events reversed the administration's policy: the Russian rejection of the Rogers plan, the Egyptian deployment of SAM missiles in the cease-fire area, with Russian connivance, and the Jordanian civil war. This last event in particular brought Nixon and the Jewish community closer together. Fearing that Syrian intervention would lead to a direct confrontation with the Soviet Union, Nixon made arrangements in secret talks with Yiẓḥak Rabin, the Israeli ambassador, to prevent such a possibility. Israel would, if necessary, stop the Syrian tank column from reaching Amman, while a reinforced Sixth Fleet would protect Israel's rear against Egyptian action. With such an agreement in hand, Nixon was easily able to face down the Soviet Union in his own version of the Cuban missile crisis. For Jews these events put Nixon in a new light. Even if Nixon had no special attachment to Israel, he could be depended upon in a crisis to act in Israel's interests, motivated by the *realpolitik* of the Middle East situation. Nixon was re-elected in 1972. The aid which he extended to Israel during the Yom Kippur War, in 1973, particularly the airlift which supplied much needed arms, showed him as a supporter of Israel.

His resignation in 1974, as a result of the Watergate affair, brought his political career to an end.

BIBLIOGRAPHY: R. Nixon, *Six Crises* (1962); G. Wills, *Nixon Agonistes, The Crisis of the Self-Made Man* (1969); R. Evans, Jr., and R.D. Novak, *Nixon in the White House, The Frustration of Power* (1971); K. Phillips, *The Emerging Republican Majority* (1969).

[Henry L. Feingold (2nd ed.)]

NIZER, LOUIS (1902–1994), U.S. lawyer and author. Nizer, who was born in London, England, was taken to the United States in 1903. He graduated from the Columbia School of Law in 1924. He was an expert on contract, libel, divorce, and antitrust law. His expertise in the areas of law related to the arts, including copyright and plagiarism, attracted clients from the theatrical and motion picture fields. He rapidly gained the confidence of the movie industry, and in 1928 was appointed attorney and executive secretary of the industry's trade association. He became well known as a magnetic courtroom lawyer, and a play about his career, *A Case of Libel*, written by Henry Denker, was produced in New York in 1963. Reputed to be a spellbinding speaker both in and out of the courtroom, Nizer represented such celebrities as Charlie Chaplin, Mae West, Salvador Dali, and Johnny Carson.

Nizer was active in the United Jewish Appeal and the Federation of Jewish Philanthropies.

His books include *New Courts of Industry* (1935); *Thinking on Your Feet: Adventures in Speaking* (1940); *What to Do with Germany* (1944), in which he advocated war crimes trials for Nazis, reversion of Nazi-appropriated property to the owners, a new educational system for Germany, and the temporary loss of German sovereignty; two widely read autobiographical volumes, *My Life in Court* (1961);*The Jury Returns* (1966); *Between You and Me* (1964); *The Implosion Conspiracy*, which examined the Rosenberg trial and execution (1973); *Reflections without Mirrors: An Autobiography of the Mind* (1978); *The Uncensored John Henry Faulk* (with J.H. Faulk, 1985); and *Catspaw: One Man's Ordeal by Trials* (1992).

The Carnegie Council on Ethics and International Affairs established the Nizer Lectures on Public Policy in 1994.

[Ruth Beloff (2nd ed.)]

NIẒẒANAH (Heb. **נִצָּנָה**; Gr. **Nessana**), a ruined town in the Negev identified with ʿAwjā al-Ḥafīr on the Ismailiya road, 50 mi. (80 km.) S.W. of Beersheba. Nessana was the ancient name of the site as revealed in the papyri found there. It was founded in the second or first century B.C.E. by the Nabateans, who built a small fort with round towers (two of which were found in the excavations there) on a small hill dominating the wide and fertile Wadi Ḥafīr. Hasmonean coins found there indicate that the place had commercial relations with Judea. The site was abandoned after the Roman occupation of Petra, the Nabatean capital, in 106 C.E., but was rebuilt as a frontier post by the emperor Theodosius I (379–95). The soldiers of the garrison received plots of land in the valley, and a town was built beneath the fortress (now called Hospice of St. George). Niẓẓanah was connected by a road with Elusa, the capital of the Byzantine Negev, with Elath and with Sinai. The Byzantine town included two churches with mosaic floors (one dated 435) and a large cemetery with tombstones (dated 430–64). It prospered during this period, serving merchants bound for Egypt, pilgrims traveling to Mt. Sinai, and anchorites living in the desert. The town survived the Persian and Arab conquests; papyri discovered by the Colt Expedition in 1936 show that a mixed Arab-Greek administration persisted until approximately 750 C.E. The settlement declined and was eventually abandoned until its reoccupation by the Turks as a police post in 1908. Under the British Mandate a central headquarters for the border police was located there. In May 1948, during the Israel *War of Independence, the Egyptian invasion started from this point. Israel forces took the area in December, and it was declared a demilitarized zone in the Israel-Egypt Armistice Agreement. It was also the site for the Israel-Egyptian Mixed *Armistice Commission meetings until 1967.

[Michael Avi-Yonah]

The site was discovered by U.J. Seetzen in 1807, with the first proper investigations at the site conducted by E.H. Palmer and C.F. Tyrwhitt-Drake in 1870. A. Musil made a detailed plan of the site in 1902, followed by the investigations of C.L. Woolley and T.E. Lawrence in 1913/14. Important excavations were conducted at the site in 1935–37 by H.D. Colt, with the discovery of an important archive of papyri. In 1987 excavations were resumed at the site under the direction of D. Urman and J. Shereshevski on behalf of Ben-Gurion University. Further parts of the flight of steps connecting the town with the acropolis were uncovered. Two building complexes were unearthed close to the Southern Church, and the excavators suggest that they were used by the priests as their living quarters. Further work was done on the acropolis, and a new area of excavations was opened up next to the bank of the wadi which extends between the lower and upper towns, revealing a large living quarter dating to the Late Byzantine period built above *Nabatean settlement remains. A previously unknown church with a martyrium and baptistery was uncovered in the lower town, and an unknown monastery was found on the north edge of the northern hill of the upper town. Numerous ostraca were uncovered inscribed in Greek, Latin, Syriac, Arabic, and Coptic.

[Shimon Gibson (2nd ed.)]

In 1987 the *Jewish Agency for Israel decided to establish an education center in Niẓẓanah. The main aim was to educate Israeli and Diaspora youth about the settlement potential of the desert. The village served as an absorption center and *ulpan for young immigrants. In addition, it offered various educational programs for Diaspora youth. Niẓẓanah was also a research center for environmental studies attached to the Hebrew University of Jerusalem. It had a guest house with 50 rooms for visitors to the region. At the end of 2002 the educational community numbered 230 residents.

[Shaked Gilboa (2nd ed.)]

BIBLIOGRAPHY: H.D. Colt et el., *Excavations at Nessana*, 3 vols. (1958). **ADD. BIBLIOGRAPHY:** D. Urman (ed.), *Nessana: Excavations and Studies*, vol. 1 (2004). Website: www.nitzana.org.il.

NIẒẒANIM (Heb. נִצָּנִים; "sprouts"), kibbutz and youth village in southern Israel, 5 mi. (8 km.) N. of Ashkelon, affiliated with Ha-No'ar ha-Ẓiyyoni. Niẓẓanim was founded in 1943 by pioneers from Romania, when efforts were made to expand Jewish settlement in the south and Negev. In the early stages of the Israel *War of Independence (1948), Niẓẓanim was subjected to concentrated attack by the advancing Egyptian army and suffered utter destruction. After five days of resistance, Niẓẓanim was given up on June 8, 1948, and most of its surviving defenders fell prisoner. The site was recovered in October 1948, and the kibbutz was rebuilt by the remnants of the group about 2 mi. (3 km.) further south. In 1949 a farming school, belonging to *Youth Aliyah, was opened on the original site by Niẓẓanim. In 1969 the combined population of the kibbutz and youth village was 594. In the mid-1990s the population dropped to approximately 365, maintaining its size at 375 residents in 2002. Niẓẓanim's economy was based on citrus groves, field crops, and dairy cattle as well as the Paltechnica plant for chairs and seating components.

[Efram Orni / Shaked Gilboa (2nd ed.)]

NOACHIDE LAWS, the seven laws considered by rabbinic tradition as the minimal moral duties enjoined by the Bible on all men (Sanh. 56–60; Yad, Melakhim, 8:10, 10:12). Jews are obligated to observe the whole Torah, while every non-Jew is a "son of the covenant of Noah" (see Gen. 9), and he who accepts its obligations is a *ger-toshav* ("resident-stranger" or even "semi-convert"; see Av. Zar. 64b; Maim. Yad, Melakhim 8:10). Maimonides equates the "righteous man (*ḥasid*) of the [gentile] nations" who has a share in the world to come even without becoming a Jew with the gentile who keeps these laws. Such a man is entitled to full material support from the Jewish community (see ET, 6 (1954), col. 289 s.v. *ger toshav*) and to the highest earthly honors (*Sefer Ḥasidim* (1957), 358). The seven Noachide laws as traditionally enumerated are: the prohibitions of idolatry, blasphemy, bloodshed, sexual sins, theft, and eating from a living animal, as well as the injunction to establish a legal system (Tosef., Av. Zar. 8:4; Sanh. 56a). Except for the last, all are negative, and the last itself is usually interpreted as commanding the enforcement of the others (Maim. Yad, Melakhim, 9:1). They are derived exegetically from divine demands addressed to Adam (Gen. 2:16) and Noah (see Gen. R. 34; Sanh. 59b), i.e., the progenitors of all mankind, and are thus regarded as universal. The prohibition of idolatry provides that, to ensure social stability and personal salvation, the non-Jew does not have to "know God" but must abjure false gods (Meg. 13a; Kid. 40a; Maim. Yad, Melakhim, 10:2ff.). This law refers only to actual idolatrous acts, and not to theoretical principles and, unlike Jews, Noachides are not required to suffer martyrdom rather than break this law (Sanh. 74a; TJ, Shev. 4:2). They are, however, required to choose martyrdom rather than shed human blood (Pes. 25b and Rashi). In view of the strict monotheism of Islam, Muslims were considered as Noachides (cf. ET, loc. cit., col. 291, n. 17), whereas the status of Christians was a matter of debate. Since the later Middle Ages, however, Christianity too has come to be regarded as Noachide, on the ground that *shittuf* ("associationism" – this was the Jewish interpretation of Trinitarianism) is not forbidden to non-Jews (see YD 151). Under the prohibitions of blasphemy, murder, and theft Noachides are subject to greater legal restrictions than Jews because non-Jewish society is held to be more prone to these sins (Rashi to Sanh. 57a). The prohibition of theft covers many types of acts, e.g., military conquest (*ibid.*, 59a) and dishonesty in economic life (*ibid.*, 57a; Yad, Melakhim, 9:9). A number of other Noachide prescriptions are listed in the sources (see Sanh. 57b; Mid. Ps. 21; Yad, Melakhim, 10:6), e.g., prohibitions of sorcery, castration, mixed seeds, blemished sacrifices, injunctions to practice charity, procreate, and to honor the Torah (Ḥul. 92a). These are best understood as subheadings of "the seven laws." Noachides may also freely choose to practice certain other Jewish commandments (Yad, Melakhim, 10:9–10). Jews are obligated to try to establish the Noachide Code wherever they can (*ibid.*, 8:10). Maimonides held that Noachides must not only accept "the seven laws" on their own merit, but they must accept them as divinely revealed. This follows from the thesis that all ethics are not ultimately "natural," but require a theological framework (see Schwarzschild, in: JQR, 52 (1962), 302; Fauer, in: *Tarbiz*, 38 (1968), 43–53). The Noachide covenant plays an important part in both Jewish history and historiography. Modern Jewish thinkers like Moses *Mendelssohn and Hermann *Cohen emphasized the Noachide conception as the common rational, ethical ground of Israel and mankind (see H. Cohen, *Religion der Vernunft* (1929), 135–48, 381–8), and see Noah as the symbol of the unity and perpetuity of mankind (*ibid.*, 293). Views differ as to whether the ultimate stage of humanity will comprise both Judaism and Noachidism, or whether Noachidism is only the penultimate level before the universalization of all of the Torah (see TJ, Av. Zar. 2:1). Aimé *Pallière, at the suggestion of his teacher Rabbi E. *Benamozegh, adopted the Noachide Laws and never formally converted to Judaism.

[Steven S. Schwarzschild]

In Jewish Law

While in the amoraic period the above-mentioned list of seven precepts is clearly accepted as the framework of the Noachide Laws, a variety of tannaitic sources indicate lack of complete agreement as to the number of such laws, as well as to the specific norms to be included. The Tosefta (Av. Zar. 8:6) records four possible additional prohibitions against: (1) drinking the blood of a living animal; (2) emasculation; (3) sorcery; and (4) all magical practices listed in Deuteronomy 18:10–11.

The Talmud records a position which would add prohibitions against crossbreeding of animals of different species, and grafting trees of different kinds (Sanh. 56b). Nonrabbinic sources of the tannaitic period indicate even greater divergence. The Book of Jubilees (7:20ff.) records a substantially different list of six commandments given by Noah to his sons: (1) to observe righteousness; (2) to cover the shame of their flesh; (3) to bless their creator; (4) to honor parents; (5) to love their neighbor; and (6) to guard against fornication, uncleanness, and all iniquity (see L. Finkelstein, bibl.).

Acts (15:20) refers to four commandments addressed to non-Jews, "...that they abstain from pollutions of idols, from fornication, from things strangled, and from blood." This latter list is the only one that bears any systematic relationship to the set of religious laws which the Pentateuch makes obligatory upon resident aliens (the *ger ha-gar* and *ezraḥ*).

NATURE AND PURPOSE. There are indications that even during the talmudic period itself there was divergence of opinion as to whether the Noachide Laws constituted a formulation of natural law or were intended solely to govern the behavior of the non-Jewish resident living under Jewish jurisdiction. The natural law position is expressed most clearly by the assertion, as to five of the seven laws, that they would have been made mandatory even had they not been revealed (Yoma 67b; Sifra *Aḥarei Mot*, 13:10). Similarly, the rabbinic insistence that six of the seven Noachide Laws were actually revealed to Adam partakes of a clearly universalistic thrust (Gen. R. 16:6, 24:5). The seventh law, against the eating of flesh torn from a living animal, could have been revealed at the earliest to Noah, since prior to the flood the eating of flesh was prohibited altogether. The very fact that these laws were denominated as the "seven laws of the sons of Noah" constitutes further indication of this trend since the term "sons of Noah" is, in rabbinic usage, a technical term including all human beings except those whom Jewish law defines as being Jews. Nor was there a lack of technical terminology available specifically to describe the resident alien. On the other hand, the entire context of the talmudic discussion of the Noachide Laws is that of actual enforcement by rabbinic courts. To that end, not only is the punishment for each crime enumerated, but standards of procedure and evidence are discussed as well (Sanh. 56a–59a). This presumption of the jurisdiction of Jewish courts is most comprehensible if the laws themselves are intended to apply to non-Jews resident in areas of Jewish sovereignty. Of a similar nature is the position of Yose that the parameters of the proscription against magical practices by Noachides is the verse in Deuteronomy (18:10) which begins, "There shall not be found among you..." (Sanh. 56b). The attempt of Finkelstein (op. cit.) to date the formulation of the seven Noachide commandments during the Hasmonean era would also suggest a rabbinic concern with the actual legal status of the non-Jew in a sovereign Jewish state. It might even be the case that the substitution by the *tanna* of the school of Manasseh of emasculation and forbidden mixtures of plants for the establishment of a judicial system and blasphemy (Sanh. 56b) itself reflects a concern with the regulation of the life of the resident alien already under the jurisdiction of Jewish courts. Of course, the seven commandments themselves are subject to either interpretation; e.g., the establishment of courts of justice can mean either an independent non-Jewish judiciary and legal system or can simply bring the non-Jew under the rubric of Jewish civil law and its judicial system.

THE BASIS OF AUTHORITY. A question related to the above is that of the basis of authority of these laws over the non-Jew. Talmudic texts seem constantly to alternate between two terms, reflecting contradictory assumptions as to the basis of authority, namely seven precepts "which were commanded" (*she-niẓtavvu*) to the Noachides, and seven precepts "which the Noachides accepted upon themselves" (*she-kibbelu aleihem*; BK 38a; TJ, Av. Zar. 2:1; Ḥul. 92ab; Hor. 8b; Sanh. 56b). This disparity between authority based on revelation as opposed to consent reaches a climax when Maimonides asserts that the only proper basis for acceptance of the Noachide laws by a non-Jew is divine authority and revelation to Moses, and that "...if he observed them due to intellectual conviction [i.e., consent] such a one is not a resident alien, nor of the righteous of the nations of the world, nor of their wise men" (Yad, Melakhim 8:11; the possibility that the final "*ve-lo*" ("nor") is a scribal error for "*ella*" ("but rather") while very appealing, is not borne out by any manuscript evidence). Of course, this same conflict between revelation and consent as basis of authority appears with regard to the binding authority of Torah over the Jew, in the form of "we will do and obey" (Ex. 24:7) as opposed to "He (God) suspended the mountain upon them like a cask, and said to them, 'If ye accept the Torah, 'tis well; if not, there shall be your burial'" (Shab. 88a).

NOACHIDE LAWS AND PRE-SINAITIC LAWS. The *amoraim*, having received a clear tradition of seven Noachide Laws, had difficulty in explaining why other pre-Sinaitic laws were not included, such as procreation, circumcision, and the law of the sinew. They propounded two somewhat strained principles to explain the anomalies. The absence of circumcision and the sinew is explained through the assertion that any pre-Sinaitic law which was not repeated at Sinai was thenceforth applicable solely to Israelites (Sanh. 59a), whence procreation, while indeed obligatory on non-Jews according to Johanan (Yev. 62a) would nevertheless not to be listed (cf. Tos. to Yev. 62a s.v. *benei*; Tos. to Ḥag. 2b s.v. *lo*).

LIABILITY FOR VIOLATION OF THE LAWS. While committed to the principle that "There is nothing permitted to an Israelite yet forbidden to a heathen" (Sanh. 59a), the seven Noachide Laws were not as extensive as the parallel prohibitions applicable to Jews, and there are indeed situations in which a non-Jew would be liable for committing an act for which a Jew would not be liable. As to the latter point, as a general rule, the Noachide is criminally liable for violation of any of his seven laws even though technical definitional limitations would prevent liability by a Jew performing the same act. Thus a non-Jew is liable for blasphemy – even if only with one of the divine attributes; murder – even of a *foetus; robbery – even of less than a *perutah*; and the eating of flesh torn from a living animal – even of a quantity less than the size of an olive. In all these cases a Jew would not be liable (Sanh. 56a–59b; Yad, Melakhim, ch. 9, 10). One additional element of greater severity is that violation of any one of the seven laws subjects the Noachide to capital punishment by decapitation (Sanh. 57a).

[Saul Berman]

Noachide Laws as Tools for the Interpretation and Development of Jewish Law

THE LIMITS OF THE RULE "DINA DE-MALKHUTA DINA." Noachide laws, which are seen as reflecting universal law, include the general precept of establishing a legal system (*dinim*). This in turn leads to the delimitation of boundaries governing the interaction between the Jewish and other legal systems, within the framework of the principle "*dina de-malkhuta dina*" (see *Dina de-Malkhuta Dina*). According to Naḥmanides (in his Torah Commentary, at Gen. 34:13), the precept of *dinim* is not limited to the establishment of courts, but includes an entire system of fundamental laws regulating commerce and social order. "In my opinion... He also commanded them to observe the laws of theft, fraud, oppression, wages, the laws of bailees, rape, seduction, the laws of tort, damages, borrowing and lending, commerce and so forth, similarly to the laws commanded to the Israelites. And they are liable to capital punishment for theft, oppression, rape, seduction, arson, battery and so forth...." To be sure, this list does not include laws of betrothal and divorce. The Talmud (Gittin 9a–b) brings a *baraita* stating that Jewish law recognizes all documents made in non-Jewish courts with the exception of writs of *divorce. According to Rashi (ad loc.), the general recognition of documents is based on the "*dina de-malkhuta dina*," which affords competence to non-Jewish legal systems on the assumption that they represent universal legal values. But Jewish marital law is not included in universal law, since there are no Noachide laws pertaining to betrothal and divorce. Therefore, "*dina de-malkhuta dina*" cannot be applied to Jewish marital law, not even with respect to its evidentiary aspects. According to this approach, the rule of "*dina de-malkhuta dina*" is identical with the universal law that existed in ancient Hebrew society before the Torah had been given, and which received expression in the seven Noachide laws. Other authorities have taken a rather different approach, stating that the Noachide laws cannot bind the Jewish people, which was separated from the other nations and received its own set of laws (the Torah). For example, the Jewish laws of evidence are not governed by *dina de-malkhuta dina*, since the laws of evidence originate from the ancient Noachide law: "One – one of the seven precepts of Noachide law is to establish a legal system, and their law is administered by a single judge and one witness. But we, the descendents of Abraham, are no longer included amongst them and we are sanctified by this (our laws), and we require two witnesses for all legal matters. As this is according to their ancient laws – Heaven forbid that we should follow them on the basis of "*dina de-malkhuta dina*," since they are [only] Noachide laws" (*Responsa Ḥakhmei Provence*, Sofer Publications, p. 421)

THE SUBSTANCE AND SCOPE OF THE KING'S LAW. The king's Law constitutes a system of law, supplementary to the laws of the Torah, to adjudicate and punish in cases where it would not be possible in accordance with settled *halakhah* (See *Punishment for extensive discussion). Halakhic authorities of the last century noted the similarity between Noachide law and king's law (R. Meir Dan Poltzki, *Hemdat Israel*, *Ner Mizvah* 288, 19th century, Poland); R. Meir Simḥah of Dvinsk, *Or Same'aḥ*, Melakhim 3:10). The king's law resembles Noachide law in that it reflects "natural conduct" as opposed to the Torah law, unique to the Jews, which reflects "Divine conduct." According to the king's law one is permitted to judge on the evidence of a single witness, as in Noachide law, but the scope of the latter is limited to the seven Noachide precepts. The exclusive laws for Jews, which were added to the seven Noachide laws, must be adjudicated only according to the laws of evidence of the Torah – i.e., on the testimony of two witnesses and forewarning (see *Evidence).

Capital Punishment for Violating Noachide Laws – Maximal, Not Mandatory

Even though the Talmud and Maimonides (Sanh. 47a; Yad, Melakhim 9.14) stipulate that a non-Jew who violated the Noachide laws was liable to capital punishment, authorities in recent generations have expressed the view that this is only the maximal punishment. According to this view, there is a difference in this respect between Noachide law and the *halakhah*. According to the *halakhah*, where a Jew was liable for capital punishment, it was a mandatory punishment, provided that all conditions had been met, whereas in Noachide law death is the maximal punishment, to be enforced only in exceptional cases such as when the need arises to fight against the proliferation of crime (viz. *Or Same'aḥ, ibid.*). This is the similarity between Noachide law and the king's law, as stated above. According to some opinions, this approach, in which a differentiation is made between various levels of severity in crimes and sentencing policy in Noachide law, may be corroborated from the works of Maimonides (viz. Bibliography, Enker).

[Menachem Elon (2nd ed.)]

BIBLIOGRAPHY: S. Krauss, in: REJ, 47 (1903), 32–40; L. Finkelstein, in: JBL, 49 (1930), 21–25; L. Blau, in: *Abhandlungen… Chajes* (1933), 6–21; P.L. Biberfeld, *Das noachidische Urrecht* (1937); ET, 3 (1951), 348–62; R. Loewe, in: *Studies in Memory of Leon Roth* (1966), 125–31, 136–44. **ADD. BIBLIOGRAPHY:** M. Elon, *Ha-Mishpat ha-Ivri* (1988), 1:61, 96, 122, 174f., 208; 3:1562; idem, *Jewish Law* (1994), 1:67, 108, 138, 194, 234; 4:1853; EA 3/2/84 *Naiman v. Chairman Central Elections Committee*, 39 (2) PD 293, 298–302; N. Rakover, *The Law and the Noachides, Jewish Law and Legal Theory* (1993); J.D. Bleich, "Capital Punishment in the Noachide Code," in: *Jubilee Volume in Honor of Rav Soloveitchik*, 1 (1984), 193–208; A. Enker, "*Onesh Mavet be-Sheva Miẓvot Benei No'aḥ*," in: *Iyyunim be-Mishpat Ivri u-ve-Halakhah* (1998), 85–128; A. Kirshenbaum, "*Ha-Kellal Ein Adam Mesim Aẓmo Rasha be-Hilkhot Benei No'aḥ*," in: *Dinei Yisrael*, 2 (1971), 71–82.

NOAH (Heb. נֹחַ), son of Lamech, father of Shem, Ham, and Japheth (Gen. 5:28–29; 6:10; I Chron. 1:4). Noah is described as a righteous and blameless man who walked with God (Gen. 6:9) and whom God decided to save from a universal *Flood to become the progenitor of a new human race. He was given instructions to build an *ark, to provision it, and to take aboard members of his family and representatives of the animal and bird kingdoms. After surviving the Flood, Noah disembarked and offered sacrifices to God, who, in turn, blessed Noah and his sons and made a covenant with them. He also laid upon them certain injunctions relative to the eating of fish and the taking of life (6:9–9:17).

In the genealogical lists of the biblical Patriarchs given in Genesis 5 and 11, Noah occupies a position midway between Adam and Abraham. He is also tenth in the line of antediluvian Patriarchs. This tradition is doubtless dependent upon a Mesopotamian source. It is especially reminiscent of a notation in the writings of Berossus (third century B.C.E.) according to which the hero of the great flood was Babylonia's tenth antediluvian king. In the biblical material dealing with the Patriarchs there is an extension of the use of the number ten, or numbers based on ten, not found in the cognate Mesopotamian notices. For instance, ten generations separate Noah from Abraham, and Noah's age is reckoned by tens and multiples of ten. Noah had reached the age of 500 at the birth of his three sons (5:32) and another period of 100 years elapsed before the onset of the deluge (7:11). However, the biblical treatment differs importantly from its Mesopotamian antecedents, for in the latter, the reigns of the antediluvian kings range from 18,600 to nearly 65,000 years. There is no denying that the lifespans of the corresponding biblical personages, including Noah's 950 years (9:28), have been considerably compressed and fall far short of the briefest reign mentioned in the related Mesopotamian texts.

Another discrepancy between the biblical and Mesopotamian traditions lies in the name of the hero. The earliest Mesopotamian flood account, written in the Sumerian language, calls the deluge hero Ziusudra, which is thought to carry the connotation "he who laid hold on life of distant days." The Sumerian name obviously has in view the immortality granted the hero after the Flood. It is this name which is reflected in the later version set down in writing by Berossus. In the ancient Babylonian versions there is likewise clearly an indebtedness to the prior Sumerian account (see *Flood). In one of these versions the hero bears the name Atra(m)ḫasis, meaning "the exceedingly wise." This name apparently is in the nature of an epithet. Woven into the famous Epic of Gilgamesh is another version, in which the man who survived the flood is known as Utnapishtim, signifying "he saw life." This is patently a loose rendering of the Sumerian Ziusudra, which symbolizes the status attained by the hero. The name Noah, by contrast, cannot be related to any of these on the basis of present knowledge.

The foregoing factors strongly suggest that in the transmission of the Babylonian antediluvian lists to biblical chroniclers an intermediate agent was active. The people most likely to have fulfilled this role are the Hurrians, whose territory included the city of Haran, where the Patriarch Abraham had his roots. The Hurrians inherited the Flood story from Babylonia. Unfortunately, their version exists in an extremely fragmentary condition, so that nothing positive can be said one way or the other on the matter. There is preserved, however, a personal name which invites comparison with the name of Noah. It is spelled syllabically: *Na-aḫ-ma-su-le-el*. It is possible, but by no means certain, that Noah is a shortened form of this name.

The Bible itself attempts to interpret the name: "This one will provide us relief from our work and from the toil of our hands" (5:29). This explanation links Noah with the Hebrew *niḥam*, "to comfort," but this is popular etymologizing and not based on linguistic principles. The true significance of the name was probably unknown to those speakers of Hebrew who inherited the Flood narrative. The interpretation of the name seems to refer to Noah's invention of wine. It is possible, however, that it reflects a lost tradition connecting Noah with the invention of the plow. The biblical statement that Noah was the first to plant a vineyard (9:20–21) seems to reflect an ancient attitude that grape culture and the making of wine were essential to civilization. The account also takes for granted that grapes were properly utilized by turning the juice into a fermented drink. Furthermore, Noah's drunkenness is presented in a matter-of-fact manner and not as reprehensible behavior. It is clear that intoxication is not at issue here, but rather that Noah's venture into viticulture provides the setting for the castigation of Israel's Canaanite neighbors. It is related that *Ham, to whom the descent of the Canaanites is traced, committed an offense when he entered the tent and viewed his father's nakedness. The offender is specifically identified as the father of *Canaan (9:22), and Noah's curse, uttered upon his awakening, is strangely aimed at Canaan rather than the disrespectful Ham. In any event, the inspiration for the scene is clearly not Mesopotamian in origin, as is the case with the greater part of the material in the first 11 chapters of Genesis.

Noah as a personality is again mentioned in the Bible only by the prophet Ezekiel (14:14, 20) who refers to him as one of three righteous men of antiquity, although Isaiah (54:9) does describe the Flood as "the waters of Noah."

[Dwight Young]

In the Aggadah

Although the Bible says of Noah that he was (Gen. 6:9) "in his generations a man righteous and wholehearted," and hence was saved, not a single action is mentioned there to illustrate his righteousness. Philo, too, asks (LA 3:77): "why did he [Moses] say 'Noah found grace in the eyes of the Lord' (Gen. 6:8), when previously he had, as far as our information goes, done nothing good?" Filling in details lacking in the Bible, the *aggadah* tells of Noah's righteousness before and during the building of the ark and while he was in it. Noah's first good deed was to "introduce plows, sickles, axes, and all kinds of tools to his contemporaries," thus freeing them from doing everything with their hands (Tanḥ. Gen. 11). He was what the Greeks would call εὐεργέτης, one whose inventions benefit mankind and cause him to be particularly beloved of the gods. Noah's uprightness and love of his fellowmen are further exemplified in what he did to save his contemporaries. Instead of hurrying to build the ark, he delayed it for many years waiting until the cedars which he had planted for it had grown (Tanḥ. No'aḥ 5). Finding it difficult to disregard God's command, yet dreading the destruction of the human species, he waited for 120 years in the hope that his contemporaries would depart from their evil ways.

Noah also admonished and warned his contemporaries, and called upon them to repent. A similar motif is found also in Josephus (Ant. 1:74) and the Apostolic Fathers (Clement, 1, 7, 6). Noah's reproof of the men of his generation is derived from a reference to him as a righteous man (Gen. 6:9); the *aggadah*, states that "wherever it says 'a righteous man' – the reference is to one who forewarns others" (Gen. R. 30:7), only such a one being worthy of the designation "righteous." In the Bible, Noah figures as a man wholeheartedly righteous and reticent; in the *aggadah*, a prophet, a truthful man, a monitor of his generation, a herald persecuted for his rebukes and honesty.

Noah's righteousness was also shown in his devoted attention to the animals in the ark. Because of the great care taken by Noah and his sons to provide each animal with its usual diet at its usual mealtime, they slept neither by day nor by night (Sanh. 108b; Tanḥ B. 58:2). Noah regarded himself as responsible for the preservation of all the animal species. Philo, too, stresses the fact that when God brought a flood on earth, He wished that all the species He had created should be preserved (Mos. 2:61). Plato, in one of his myths (*Protagoras*, 321), attributes a similar desire to the gods. In spite of these testimonials to Noah's high-mindedness, R. Johanan interpreted the biblical statement, "thee have I seen righteous before Me in this generation" (Gen. 7:1) as indicating Noah's righteousness only in relation to his own generation and not in relation to others (Sanh. 108a). Philo (Abr. 36) concurred, stating that Noah would not have been regarded as upright in relation to the Patriarchs: he affirmed his greatness in opposing the tendencies of his generation (*ibid.* 38).

[Elimelech Epstein Halevy]

In Christianity

In Christian symbolism Noah is one of the most important typological figures. The New Testament describes him as a symbol of the just (II Pet. 2:5), and as an example, in a sinful world, of faith in and submission to God (Heb. 11:7; Luke 17:26–27; I Pet. 3:20). As a type and prefiguration of Jesus, Noah exhorts to repentance and announces the inevitable judgment. Being spared from the universal catastrophe, he appears as a redeemer through whom humanity is saved from complete destruction and is reconciled with God.

The Flood, the ark, and the dove also serve as Christian prefigurations. Just as Noah triumphs over drowning to death in the waters of the flood, so Jesus and the Christians vanquish Satan and death through the water of baptism which initiates them into a new world (I Pet. 3:18–21). In later Christian tradition Noah's ark symbolizes the Church outside of which no salvation is possible. The dove sent out by Noah prefigures the Holy Spirit moving upon the baptismal waters, symbolizing divine reconciliation.

In Islam

Nūḥ (Noah) is one of *Muhammad's favorite biblical characters. He devotes a complete sura to Noah (71) considering Noah's life as a prototype of his own. Noah is the reprover who attempts to make his people repent (7:57–61), but the elders scorn and do not heed him. Following the *aggadah* (Sanh. 108a and other Midrashim) Noah relates that it has been revealed to him that he must build the ark (11:29, 34,

38–39). When Noah and the members of his family entered the ark on Allah's command, one son stood at the side of the Ark and was drowned in the waters of the *Flood because he refused to enter when Noah called (11:43). According to some commentators, this son was *Canaan; hence, the belief that Noah had four sons, and not three as recorded in the Bible. Noah's wife may also have been among those who drowned in the Flood (see Tabarī, below), because as the wife of *Lot, she was not a believer (66:10–11). The Ark settled on Mount Jūdī (11:46). The poets al-Nābigha, al-Aʿshā, ʿAdī b. Zayd, and especially, Umayya ibn Abī al-Ṣalt, who were contemporaries of Muhammad, describe the ark, its construction, and the salvation of Noah. As usual, the commentators on the *Koran add many legendary details and embellishments and are familiar with the names of the sons of Noah (see below). The number of those who were saved varies. One source mentions 80 survivors: Noah, his three sons, their wives, and 73 believers, the descendants of *Seth (Shīth; Tabarī 129). According to others, only eight survived: Noah and his wife (!), his three sons, and their wives.

The three sons of Noah are not mentioned by name in the Koran. Tabarī (vol. 1, pp. 132–3) presents a list stating how the land was partitioned among them, and later (pp. 140–9) includes the genealogies of all the nations which existed in his time. Sām (Shem) was the progenitor of the Arabs, the Persians, and the Rūm (Byzantines) who are considered good nations. Yāfath (Japheth) was the ancestor of the Turks and the Slavs, Yājūj and Mājūj (*Gog and Magog), all of whom possess no good qualities (p. 145), and are not noble. Hām (Ham) gave birth to the Copts, the "Blacks," and the Berbers. His sins were having carnal relations with his wife in the Ark and acting disrespectfully toward his father.

[Haïm Z'ew Hirschberg]

In the Arts

The dramatic aspects of the biblical story of the Flood have ensured Noah's continued popularity as a subject for treatment by writers and artists. During the Middle Ages, Noah was seen as a prefiguration of Jesus (see above) and christological interpretations were also placed on his drunkenness, which was believed to foreshadow the bitter drink of the Passion. At the same time, however, some of the English mystery plays showed Noah and his wife in a comic light, their ribald dialogue appealing to unsophisticated audiences. The English medieval cycles, which used a prefabricated stage setting of the ark, include those of Chester ("The Deluge"), Coventry ("Noah's Flood"), Towneley, and York ("The Building of the Ark" and "Noah and his Wife"). Some of these plays were presented by trade guilds, such as the Newcastle shipwrights (*Noah's Ark, or the Shipwrights' Ancient Play or Dirge*). The theme inspired the Norman poet Olivier Basselin's *"Eloge de Noé"* – a drinking song with the refrain *"O le bon vin!"* Toward the end of the 15th century, the Italian Annius of Viterbo published a book of spurious *Antiquities* (Rome, 1498) containing the "Pseudo-Berosus," a legendary account of Noah and his descendants which especially linked the Japhethites with some of the European nations. The 16th-century epic treatment of the Deluge theme was written by the Polish poet Jan Kochanowski (1558). The subject still retained some popular appeal in 17th-century England, with "Noah's Flood," a musical presentation licensed in 1662; a Bartholomew Fair "droll" entitled *The Creation of the World*; and Edward Ecclestone's opera, *Noah's Flood; or The Destruction of the World* (1679). The Dutch Catholic Joost van den Vondel's five-act drama, *Noah, of ondergang der eerste weerelt* (1667), was on a higher level than all of these.

The only major writer of the 18th century to show interest in the theme was the Swiss poet and dramatist Johann Jacob Bodmer, who devoted two separate epics to the Bible story: *Noah ein Heldengedicht* (1750, 1752²; published as *Die Noachide*, 1765) and *Die Synd-Flut* (1751, 1753²). Twentieth-century interpretations have included *Die Suendflut* (1924), a drama by the German anti-Nazi author and artist Ernst Barlach; a poem by the U.S. writer Robert *Nathan (in "A Cedar Box," 1929); *Noé* (1931; *Noah*, 1935), one of the great successes of the French dramatist André Obey; and *Noah and the Waters* (1936), a poem by the Anglo-Irish author Cecil Day Lewis. Two treatments of the post-World War II period were *The Flowering Peach* (1954) by the U.S. playwright Clifford *Odets, who transferred the Noah story to a modern setting; and Hugo Loetscher's *Noah* (1970), a satire on the affluent society, which used the biblical theme to point a contemporary moral.

In art, the main subjects treated are the Flood (Gen. 7, 8) and the drunkenness of Noah (Gen. 9). The subject matter of catacomb art is often drawn from the prayers of the *Commendatio Animae*. Like Isaac and Daniel, Noah is a popular subject in the art of the catacombs because he figures in the prayers as a symbol of the redeemed soul. Notable representations are those in the second-century murals from the catacomb of Priscilla and the fourth-century murals from that of Domitillus. In early Christian Art, the ark is represented as a small floating cask in which Noah stands alone, his arms upraised in an attitude of supplication. Later it became a floating house or three-tiered basilica, differing from a ship in that it had no oars or sails. A representation of Noah's ark is found on a mosaic from the ancient synagogue in Gerasa, Jordan, and scenes from the story of Noah are depicted in the 12th-century mosaics of Palermo and Monreale, and in the 13th-century mosaics from St. Mark's Cathedral, Venice. The theme also occurs in sculpture, frescoes, manuscript illuminations, and stained glass. There are carvings of the subject in the Gothic cathedrals of Bourges, Wells, and Salisbury, and in 12th-century wall paintings from St. Savin, France. It is illustrated in the sixth-century *Vienna Genesis* (National Library, Vienna), the seventh-century *Ashburnham Pentateuch* (Bibliothèque Nationale, Paris), the 13th-century *St. Louis Psalter*, and in a number of Hebrew manuscripts, including the French 13th-century *British Museum Miscellany* (Add. 11:639) and the 14th-century *Sarajevo Haggadah*. In the 13th-century Hispano-Provençal

Farḥi Bible (formerly in the Sassoon Collection, Letchworth) there is a plan of the ark.

During the Renaissance, Lorenzo Ghiberti executed a bas-relief of the story of Noah after the Flood on his bronze gates to the Florence Baptistery, and Paolo Uccello painted a fresco of the Deluge in the Church of Santa Maria Novella in Florence. One of the most dramatic representations of the Flood is that by Michelangelo (Sistine Chapel, Vatican), who also depicted the sacrifice and the drunkenness of Noah, and Shem and Japheth covering his nakedness. In this, as in other Renaissance paintings of the subject, the sons are themselves oddly depicted in the nude. The story of Noah also figures in the Raphael frescoes in the Vatican. There are paintings of Noah entering and leaving the Ark by Jacopo Bassano in the Prado, and a painting of Noah leaving the ark by Hieronymos Bosch is in the Bojmans Museum, Rotterdam. In the 17th century, Nicolas Poussin painted the Flood as an image of winter in a series of four paintings representing the four seasons (Louvre). Poussin's painting of the sacrifice of Noah is in the Prado. Among modern artists, Lesser *Ury painted the Flood, and a painting of Noah's Ark by Marc *Chagall is in the Louvre.

In music, there were two 19th-century oratorios on the theme of the Flood, one by Johann Christian Friedrich Schmerder (1823); and *Le Déluge* (1876; première at Boston, U.S., 1880) by Camille Saint-Saëns. In 1970 *Two by Two*, a musical on the theme based on Clifford Odets' above-mentioned play and with Danny Kaye in the star role, was staged on Broadway.

BIBLIOGRAPHY: A. Heidel, *The Gilgamesh Epic and Old Testament Parallels* (1946); S.N. Kramer, *History Begins at Sumer* (1959), 214–9; E.A. Speiser, in: J.J. Finkelstein and M. Greenberg (eds.), *Oriental and Biblical Studies* (1967), 244–69; N.M. Sarna, *Understanding Genesis* (1967), 37–62. IN THE AGGADAH: Ginzberg, Legends, index. IN CHRISTIANITY: J. Daniélou, *Sacramentum futuri* (1950), 60ff. IN ISLAM: Tabarī, *Ta'rīkh*, 1 (1357, A.H.), 122–33, 139–49; Tha'labī, *Qiṣaṣ* (1356, A.H.), 45–51; Kisā'ī, *Qiṣaṣ* (1356, A.H.), 85–103; J.W. Hirschberg, *Juedische und christliche Lehren im vor-und fruehislamischen Arabien* (1939), 53–58, 114–22; H. Speyer, *Die biblischen Erzaehlungen im Qoran* (1931, repr. 1961), 89–115. IN THE ARTS: D.C. Allen, *Legend of Noah; Renaissance Rationalism in Art, Science, and Letters* (1949); D.P. Walker, in: *Journal of the Warburg and Courtauld Institutes*, 17 (1954), 204–59; J. Fink, *Noe der Gerechte in der fruehchristlichen Kunst* (1955); M. Roston, *Biblical Drama in England* (1968), index. **ADD. BIBLIOGRAPHY:** EIS[2], 8 (1995), 108–10.

NOAH, BOOKS OF. Although a Book of Noah is not referred to in the Christian canon lists, there is a good deal of evidence that such a work or works existed. In Jubilee 10:1–15 reference is made to a medical and anti-demonic work transmitted by Noah to his descendants after the Flood, when, in spite of Noah's intercession, a tenth of the demons were left on earth, causing trouble and affliction. What appears to be another form of this passage is to be found in the opening paragraphs of the medieval medical treatise *Sefer Asaf ha-Rofe*. Some scholars, such as Charles, would also attribute Jubilees 7:20–39 to a Book of Noah. A second body of Noah material is that discerned by Charles in I Enoch. The chapters which appear assuredly to be drawn from a Noah book are I Enoch 6–11, 60, 65–69, 106–7. Material closely associated with I Enoch 6–11 and 106–7 appears in 1Q19, the so-called "Book of Noah" from Qumran. This text does not appear to be simply the Hebrew original of the I Enoch Noah material, but to be closely associated with it. Yet another group of Noah texts associated with ritual instructions of a priestly character is referred to in Jubilees 21:10, there as part of Abraham's instructions to Isaac. This tradition was also known to the author of the Greek "Fragments of the Testament of Levi," undoubtedly a very ancient text, again directly attributed to Noah and included in Abraham's instructions to Isaac (Greek fragment 57), and in a brief form, without the attribution to Noah, in the Testament of the Twelve Patriarchs, Levi 9:11. The Jewish magical book Sefer ha-*Razim is also ascribed to Noah.

BIBLIOGRAPHY: Charles, Apocrypha, 2 (1913), 168; M.R. James, *Lost Apocrypha of the Old Testament* (1920), 11f.; Barthélemy-Milik, 84–86; M. Margalioth (ed.), *Sefer ha-Razim* (1966).

[Michael E. Stone]

NOAH, MORDECAI MANUEL (1785–1851), U.S. editor, politician, and playwright. Noah, who was probably the most influential Jew in the United States in the early 19th century, was born in Philadelphia. His father, Manuel Noah (c. 1755–1822), was a bankrupt itinerant merchant, and Mordecai Noah was raised by his maternal grandfather, Jonas *Phillips. After apprenticeship as a gilder and carver, Noah became a clerk in the U.S. Treasury through the assistance of Robert Morris (1734–1806), the financier and senator.

Noah began his political career in Philadelphia in 1808 when he, along with other "Democratic Young Men," supported the Republican candidate, James Madison, for president. A year later Noah went to Charleston, where he edited the *City Gazette*. A war "hawk," he strongly supported the War of 1812. In 1813 he was appointed consul at Tunis, but was recalled two years later after he was accused of misappropriation of funds, though the charges were never proved. On his return to the United States, Noah established himself permanently in New York with the help of his uncle Naphtali Phillips, publisher of the *National Advocate*, which ardently supported the Democratic Party of New York County. Noah became the editor of the newspaper in 1817, giving him access to the Tammany Society. He was appointed high sheriff in 1822 and two years later was elected grand sachem of Tammany.

When Phillips sold the *National Advocate* in 1824, Noah became the publisher of the *New York National Advocate*. He broke with Tammany over its opposition to De Witt Clinton, then commissioner of canals, and in 1825 supported Clinton for governor. Noah continued to oppose Tammany in the paper he established, the *New York Enquirer*, published 1826–29.

Critical of Andrew Jackson, particularly of his attack on the U.S. Bank, he associated himself with the newly created Whig Party in 1834, and as publisher and editor of the *Evening Star*, a Whig paper, demonstrated anti-immigrant and anti-Catholic bias. When the Native American Party of 1835–36, the forerunner of the Know-Nothing Party, was created, he was one of its chief supporters. He also supported the Texas revolt of 1836 against Mexico and angrily attacked the abolitionist cause. In 1841, he became a judge of the Court of Sessions.

Noah was a prolific playwright; many of his plays reflected his patriotic fervor. His first play, *Fortress of Sorrento* (written 1808), was followed by, among others, *She Would Be a Soldier* (1819); *Siege of Tripoli* (1820), also produced as *Yuseff Caramalli*; and *Marion, or the Hero of St. George* (1822).

Noah's interest in Jewish affairs drew him into activities on behalf of the congregations of Mikveh Israel in Philadelphia and Shearith Israel in New York. Long taken by the idea of a Jewish territorial restoration, Noah, in 1825, helped purchase a tract of land on Grand Island in the Niagara River near Buffalo, which he named Ararat and envisioned as a Jewish colony. Though the proposal elicited much discussion, the attempt was not a success and Noah's pretensions as ruler were ridiculed. After the failure of the Ararat experience, Noah turned more strongly to the idea of Palestine as a national home for Jews. As the best-known American Jew of his time, Noah in 1840 delivered the principal address at a meeting at B'nai Jeshurun in New York protesting the *Damascus Affair.

BIBLIOGRAPHY: I. Goldberg, *Major Noah: American Jewish Pioneer* (1937); L.M. Friedman, *Pilgrims in a New Land* (1948), 221–32; DAB, s.v.; S.J. Kohn, in: AJHSQ, 59 (1969), 210–4; B.D. Weinryb, in: *The Jewish Experience in America*, 2 (1969), 136–57; R. Gordis, *ibid.*, 110–35; I.M. Fein, *ibid.*, 82–101.

[Leo Hershkowitz]

NOB (Heb. נֹב), priestly town in the territory of Benjamin, near Jerusalem. When David fled from Saul's court, he traveled by way of Nob (I Sam. 21ff.). Pretending to be on a royal mission, he obtained from the chief priest Ahimelech hallowed bread and the sword of Goliath from the local sanctuary for himself and his men. Doeg the Edomite, Saul's chief herdsman, denounced the priest to the king (I Sam. 22:9ff.); on Saul's order, he slew 85 priests and also "men and women, children and sucklings, and oxen and asses and sheep" (I Sam. 22:19). Abiathar son of Ahimelech escaped and later became high priest to David. Nob was the last stopping point, after Anathoth, of Sennacherib's northern army before their assault on Jerusalem (Isa. 10:32). It was one of the cities settled by Jews returning from Babylonian Exile. In the Mishnah, the question of the permissibility of high places at Nob is discussed (Zev. 14:7; Tosef., Zev. 13:5). The ancient city is identified with an Iron Age site near the village of ʿIsawiyya on Mt. Scopus, near the modern campus of the Hebrew University.

BIBLIOGRAPHY: Voigt, in: JPOS, 3 (1923), 79–87; W.F. Albright, in: AASOR, 4 (1924), 139; A. Alt, in: PJB, 21 (1925), 12ff.

[Michael Avi-Yonah]

NOBEL, NEHEMIAH ANTON (1871–1922), German Orthodox rabbi and religious leader. Born in Nagymed (Hungary), he was the son of JOSEPH NOBEL (1840–1917), author of a number of exegetical and homiletical works (*Ḥermon*, 1919[3]; *Levanon*, 1911; *Tavor*, 1899; and others). After being brought up in Halberstadt, where his father was *Klausrabbinner*, Nehemiah Nobel studied at the Berlin *Rabbinerseminar. He served in the rabbinate of Cologne from 1896 to 1899,and then for several months in Koenigsberg. From there he went to the University of Marburg to study under Hermann *Cohen, who had a great influence upon him, although they did not agree about Zionism. Nobel's activity in the Zionist Movement began in Cologne. He was on close terms with Theodor *Herzl and David *Wolffsohn and was one of the original founders of the Zionist Federation in Germany. He also took part in the founding convention of the *Mizrachi movement in Pressburg (1904). Nobel's Zionist activity, motivated by his conviction that religion and nationhood are organically connected in Judaism, stood out in contrast to the united anti-Zionist front of Orthodox and liberal rabbis in Germany at the time. From 1901 he served in the rabbinate of Leipzig, from 1906 in the rabbinate of Hamburg, and finally, from 1910, in the rabbinate of Frankfurt, where he succeeded Marcus *Horovitz. There he prompted closer contacts with Judaism and Zionism in circles that had been drifting away from Judaism. His sermons and preachings, in which he was extraordinarily impressive, tackled topical problems. He influenced such Jewish thinkers as Ernst *Simon, Oscar Wolfsberg (Y. *Aviad), F. *Rosenzweig, and M. *Buber. The last two helped to publish the jubilee book for his 50th birthday (1921). In 1919 he was elected chairman of the Union of German Rabbis and was head of the Akademie fuer die Wissenschaft des Judentums. He died a short time after having been appointed professor of religion and ethics at the University of Frankfurt. A number of his sermons as well as scholarly and halakhic articles, which first appeared in *Festschriften*, have been published in Hebrew as *Hagut ve-Halakhah* (1969). Nobel's younger brother, ISRAEL (1878–1962), rabbi in Schneidemuehl and Berlin, published *Offenbarung und Tradition* (1908) and a Passover *Haggadah* with German translation and notes (1927).

BIBLIOGRAPHY: E.E. Mayer, in: L. Jung (ed.), *Guardians of our Heritage* (1958), 563–79; *Nachrufe auf Rabbiner N.A. Nobel* (1923); O. Wolfberg, *Nehemiah Anton Nobel 1871–1922* (Ger., 1929); idem, *Ha-Rav Neḥemyah Ẓevi Nobel* (Heb., 1944); N.A. Nobel, *Hagut ve-Halakhah* (1969), with biography by Y. Aviad.

[Getzel Kressel]

NOBEL PRIZES, awarded annually to men and women who have "rendered the greatest service to mankind." Since the inception of the prize in 1899 it has been awarded to the following Jews or people of Jewish descent. (See Table: Jewish Nobel Prize Winners.)

Jewish Nobel Prize Winners

Chemistry			
1905	Adolph Von Baeyer	1981	Roald Hoffmann
1906	Henri Moissan	1982	Aaron Klug
1910	Otto Wallach	1989	Sidney Altman
1915	Richard Willstaetter	1992	Rudolph Arthur Marcus
1918	Fritz Haber	1994	George Olah
1943	George Charles de Hevesy	1996	Harold Kroto
1961	Melvin Calvin	1998	Walter Kohn
1962	Max Ferdinand Perutz	2000	Alan Heeger
1972	William Howard Stein (jointly with Dr. Stanford Moore)	2004	Aaron Ciechanover
1979	Herbert Brown	2004	Avram Hershko
1980	Paul Berg	2004	Irwin Rose
1980	Walter Gilbert		

Literature			
1910	Paul Johann Ludwig Heyse	1981	Elias Canetti
1927	Henri Bergson	1987	Joseph Brodsky
1958	Boris Pasternak	1991	Nadine Gordimer
1966	Shmuel Yosef Agnon	2002	Imre Kertész
1966	Nelly Sachs	2004	Elfriede Jelinek
1976	Saul Bellow	2005	Harold Pinter
1978	Isaac Bashevis Singer		

Physiology or Medicine			
1908	Elie Metchnikoff	1972	Maurice Gerald Edelman
1908	Paul Ehrlich	1975	David Baltimore
1914	Robert Bárány	1975	Howard David Temin
1922	Otto Meyerhof	1976	Baruch Samuel Blumberg
1930	Karl Landsteiner	1977	Rosalyn Sussman Yalow
1931	Otto Warburg	1978	Daniel Nathans
1936	Otto Loewi	1980	Baruj Benacceraf
1944	Joseph Erlanger	1984	Cesar Milstein
1944	Herbert Spencer Gasser	1985	Michael Stuart Brown
1945	Ernst Boris Chain	1985	Joseph Leonard Goldstein
1946	Herman Joseph Muller	1986	Stanley Cohen
1950	Tadeus Reichstein	1986	Rita Levi-Montalcini
1952	Selman Abraham Waksman	1988	Gertrude B. Elion
1953	Hans Krebs	1989	Harold Eliot Varmus
1953	Fritz Albert Lipmann	1992	Edmond Fischer
1958	Joshua Lederberg	1994	Alfred Gilman
1959	Arthur Kornberg	1994	Martin Rodbell
1964	Konrad Bloch	1997	Stanley Prusiner
1965	François Jacob	1998	Robert Furchgott
1965	Andre Lwoff	2000	Paul Greengard
1967	George Wald	2000	Eric Kandel
1968	Marshall W. Nirenberg	2002	Sydney Brenner
1969	Salvador Luria	2002	H. Robert Horvitz
1970	Julius Axelrod	2004	Richard Axel
1970	Sir Bernard Katz		

Physics			
1907	Albert Abraham Michelson	1978	Peter Leonidovitch Kapitza
1908	Gabriel Lippmann	1978	Arno Penzias
1921	Albert Einstein	1979	Sheldon Glashow
1922	Niels Bohr	1979	Steven Weinberg
1925	James Franck	1988	Leon Lederman
1925	Gustav Hertz	1988	Melvin Schwartz
1943	Otto Stern	1988	Jack Steinberger
1944	Isidor Isaac Rabi	1990	Jerome Isaac Friedman
1952	Felix Bloch	1992	George Charpak
1954	Max Born	1995	Martin L. Perl
1958	Igor Tamm	1995	Frederick Reines
1959	Emilio Segrè	1996	David Lee
1960	Donald A. Glaser	1996	Douglas Osheroff
1961	Robert Hofstadter	1997	Claude Cohen-Tannoudji
1962	Lev Davidovich Landau	2000	Zhores Alferov
1965	Richard Phillips Feynman	2003	Vitaly Ginzburg
1965	Julian Schwinger	2003	Alexei Abrikosov
1969	Murray Gell-Mann	2004	David Gross
1971	Dennis Gabor	2004	H. David Politzer
1973	Brian David Josephson (jointly with Ivan Giaver and Leon Esoki)	2005	Roy Glauber
1975	Benjamin R. Mottelson (jointly with Aage Bohr)		

World Peace			
1911	Alfred Fried	1986	Elie Wiesel
1911	Tobias Michael Carel Asser	1994	Yiẓhak Rabin
1968	René Cassin	1994	Shimon Peres
1973	Henry Alfred Kissinger	1995	Joseph Rotblat
1978	Menaḥem Begin		

Economics			
1970	Paul Anthony Samuelson	1993	Robert Fogel
1971	Simon Kuznetz	1994	John Harsanyi
1972	Kenneth Joseph Arrow	1994	Reinhard Selten
1975	Leonid Kantorovich	1997	Robert Merton
1978	Herbert Alexander Simon	1997	Myron Scholes
1980	Lawrence Klein	2001	George Akerlof
1985	Franco Modigliani	2001	Joseph Stiglitz
1987	Robert M. Solow	2002	Daniel Kahneman
1990	Harry M. Markowitz	2005	Robert Aumann
1992	Gary S. Becker		

WEBSITE: www.jinfo.org.

°**NOELDEKE, THEODOR** (1836–1930), German Orientalist. Born in Harburg, near Hamburg, Noeldeke taught from 1872 until 1906. Best known for his prizewinning *Geschichte des Qorâns* (1860), he was an acknowledged expert on the comparative philology of the Semitic languages and published grammars of New Syriac (1869), Mandaean Aramaic (1874), and Syriac (1880). His expertise in this field was fully revealed in his *Beitraege zur semitischen Sprachwissenschaft* (1904) and its supplement (1910).

Noeldeke was also a distinguished scholar in the biblical and rabbinic fields. Among his works in this sphere are *Ueber die Amalekiter und einige andere Nachbarvoelker der Israeliten* (1864); "Die Geschichte der Juden in Arabien" (in *Beitraege zur Kenntnis der Poesie der alten Araber*, 1864); *Die alttestamentliche Literatur* (1868), a French edition of which, by H. Derenbourg and J. Soury, appeared in 1873; and *Untersuchungen zur Kritik des Alten Testaments* (1869). Noeldeke, whose pupils included Louis *Ginzberg, was a prolific writer on Islamic history and Arabic and Persian culture, his general works including *Orientalische Skizzen* (1892; *Sketches from Eastern History*, 1892). He also published *Die Inschrift des Koenigs Mesa* (1870), an explanatory work on the Mesha Stele; an essay on the Aramaic papyri of Assuan (1907); and various introductions and annotations to books by other scholars, for example, Friedrich Schulthess' *Grammatik des christlich-palaestinischen Aramaeisch* (1924).

ADD. BIBLIOGRAPHY: M. Frenschkowski, in: *Biographisch-Bibliographisches Kirchenlexikon*, vol. 6 (1993), 979–83.

NOERDLINGEN, city in Bavaria, Germany. Jews were to be found in Noerdlingen from the 12th century, but the sources reflect an organized community only in the 13th century. Eight Jews were martyred there during the *Rindfleisch persecutions (1298), but community life was renewed soon afterward. In 1331 Emperor Louis IV granted four "honorable" Jewish elders the extraordinary privilege of jurisdiction over foreign Jews. There were about 20 Jewish houses in the Judengasse (which was also inhabited by Christians), and the community possessed a synagogue and a cemetery; the Jews made their living as moneylenders. During the *Black Death persecutions of 1348 many Jews were killed or imprisoned; their property and promissory notes were confiscated by the city. Emperor *Charles IV pardoned the burghers and canceled their debts to the Jews. Subsequently he acceded to the city's request to readmit Jews. A synagogue was mentioned in 1357, and in 1378 the community consecrated a cemetery. However, during fresh riots in 1384 about 200 Jews were murdered and the community ceased to exist. After Jews were again admitted into the city in 1401, a new and prosperous community came into being; a new cemetery, which also served the neighboring communities, was put into use in 1415. Taxes were heavy: five **Schutzjuden* ("protected Jews") provided three-eighths of the amount paid by the whole 34-member city council. In 1437 Jews were forbidden to hire Christian servants and ordered to wear the Jewish *badge – though this order does not seem to have been strictly enforced. The Hussite wars resulted in temporary banishment between 1454 and 1459, and hostile agitation by the clergy led to the expulsion of the Jews in 1507. The synagogue was sold in 1517, but refugees who had settled nearby attended Noerdlingen's annual fairs. A community, with 25 families, was organized in 1870, dedicated a new synagogue in 1885, and founded a *ḥevra kaddisha* in 1898. It numbered 489 persons in 1899, and 314 (3.8% of the total) in 1913. By June 16, 1933, only 186 remained; 145 of them left before 1942, when the remnants of the Jewish community were deported. The mayor of the city prevented the destruction of the synagogue in 1938, and in 1952 it was sold to a Protestant group as a community center. The building was rebuilt but, in the process, the architecture of the former synagogue was destroyed. In 1997 the building was demolished and replaced by a new structure. A plaque commemorates the former synagogue.

BIBLIOGRAPHY: L. Mueller, *Aus fuenf Jahrhunderten* (1899); K.O. Mueller, *Noerdlingens Stadtrechte des Mittelalters* (1930), index s.v. *Juden*; K. Puchner and G. Wulz (eds.), *Urkunden der Stadt Noerdlingen 1233–1399*, 2 (1956), 111, no. 529; *Jahrbuch des historischen Vereins fuer Noerdlingen*, 2 (1913), 135; Baron, Social, 11 (1967²), 71; Germ Jud, 1 (1963), 247–8; 2 (1968), 593–7; *Gemeinde-Verzeichnis fuer das Koenigreich Bayern, Volkszaehlung 1890* (1892), 244; *Statistisches Jahrbuch des deutsch-israelitischen Gemeindebundes* (1905), 93; *Handbuch der juedischen Gemeindeverwaltung* (1913), 156; *Fuehrer durch die juedische Gemeindeverwaltung… in Deutschland* (1932/33), 315; T. Oelsner, in; *Transactions of the American Philosophical Society*, 60 (1970); R. Wischnitzer, in: *Chicago Jewish Forum*, 4:1 (1945), 49f.; PK Bavaryah. **ADD BIBLIOGRAPHY:** B. Ophir and F. Wiesemann (eds.), *Die juedischen Gemeinden in Bayern 1918–1945. Geschichte und Zerstoerung* (1979) 486–88; D. Voges, "Zur Geschichte der Juden in Noerdlingen," in: W. Barsig (ed.), *Rieser Kulturtage* (Eine Landschaft stellt sich vor, vol. 3) (1980); G. Roemer, *Der Leidensweg der Juden in Schwaben. Schicksale von 1933 bis 1945 in Berichten, Dokumenten und Zahlen* (1983) 101–6; *Germania Judaica*, vol. 3 1350–1514 (1987), 977–94; I. Schwierz, *Steinerne Zeugnisse juedischen Lebens in Bayern. Eine Dokumentation* (1992²), 259–60. **WEBSITE:** www.alemannia-judaica.de.

NOETHER, family of mathematicians in Germany. MAX NOETHER (1844–1921), born in Erlangen, was professor of mathematics for nearly 50 years. He made important contributions to geometry and was the foremost authority of the algebraic-geometric school in Germany. He wrote many papers on the geometry of hyperspace, Abelian and Theta functions. His son FRITZ NOETHER (1884–1941) became professor of applied mathematics at the Technische Hochschule, Breslau. EMMY (AMALIE) NOETHER (1882–1935), Max's daughter, was born and educated in Erlangen. She went to Goettingen in 1916, but because of the prevailing anti-feminine bias she was unable to obtain an official post. Conditions changed under the Weimar Republic and after much opposition she was appointed "unofficial extraordinary professor" in 1922. She derived an income from a lectureship in algebra. The advent of the Hitler regime forced her to emigrate to the U.S. where she was appointed professor at Bryn Mawr College, Pennsylvania. She was a pioneer in the general theory of ideas, and from 1926 onward initiated advances in non-commutative algebra. A creative mathematician of high caliber, her influence on contemporary mathematics cannot be judged solely by her published work, as she exerted great influence through her students and many of her ideas were developed by them.

BIBLIOGRAPHY: Weyl, in: *Scripta mathematica*, 3 (1935), 201–20; Van der Waerden, in: *Mathematische Annalen*, 111 (1935), 469–76.

[Barry Spain]

NOLA, ELIJAH BEN MENAHEM DA (baptismal name, **Giovanni Paolo Eustachio**; c. 1530–c. 1602), Italian Hebraist and apostate. One of the leading rabbis in Rome during the late 16th century, Da Nola was also a renowned physician and philosopher. When Moses *Alatino was commissioned to translate Hebrew texts into Latin, he received valuable assistance from Da Nola. While acting as a Hebrew tutor to Tommaso Aldobrandini, brother of Pope Clement VIII, Da Nola was induced to convert to Catholicism in 1568, and eventually became a *scrittore* at the Vatican library. He copied Hebrew manuscripts for Cardinal Federigo Borromeo, archbishop of Milan, many such works in his hand being preserved in the Vatican.

Da Nola later published *Sacro Settenario raccolto dalle sacre Scritture…* (Naples, 1579), on the symbolism of the figure 7 in the Old and New Testaments. A collection of sermons, *Salutari discorsi… aggiuntavi un modo utilissimo de la vita che denno tenere i Neophiti* (Naples, 1582), dedicated to Pope Gregory XII, contained an apologia for his apostasy which, the author claimed, had been based on knowledge and conviction, rather than on fear or greed. Like many others who converted during the Renaissance era, Da Nola endeavored to prove the superiority of Christianity over Judaism by judicious manipulation of kabbalistic books, particularly in regard to the significance of the Trinity and the numerical value of selected Hebrew terms.

BIBLIOGRAPHY: C. Roth, *Jews in the Renaissance* (1959), 84, 149–50, 154; F. Secret, *Les Kabbalistes Chrétiens de la Renaissance* (1964), 247–8; U. Cassuto, *I Manoscritti Palatini Ebraici della Biblioteca Vaticana* (1935), index.

[Godfrey Edmond Silverman]

NOM, IBRAHIM (**Avram Naon**, 1870–1947), Turkish poet and lawyer. A successful *Istanbul attorney, he was prominent in Turkish literary life, publishing a review and writing for leading periodicals. A collection of his verse, *Kalbi Şikeste* ("Broken Heart"), appeared in 1901. Other poems, some of which inspired popular Turkish songs, were published from 1938 until 1947 in the Ladino paper *La Boz de Türkiye*. Nom is said to have pioneered the use of the acrostic in Turkish poetry.

[Shmuel Moreh]

NOMADISM, a socioeconomic mode of life based on intensive domestication of livestock which requires a regular movement of the community in an annual cycle in order to sustain the communal ecological system.

Definition

The defining feature of pastoral nomadism is movement, which is neither aimless nor boundless, from pasture to pasture and from watering point to watering point, along well-defined routes, at fixed periods, in rhythm with the rainy and dry seasons, and in greater or lesser comity with adjoining nomadic and settled groups. Little or no agriculture is practiced. Nomads necessarily rely upon trade with or raids upon agriculturalists for food and other necessities or occasional luxuries not supplied by their herds. Pastoral nomads often supply settled peoples with transport services by providing animals and serving as caravaneers. Occasionally, control of routes and specialization in trade lead to settlement of nomad elites in commercial centers such as Palmyra in Syria and Petra in Edom. Ethnographers are generally agreed that pastoral nomadism arose later than the emergence of neolithic agriculture in the Middle East. At first it involved herders of sheep and goats who adapted themselves to the spartan conditions of life on the steppe but who were unable to venture more than one or two days' journey from water. Full nomadism emerged only in about 1500–1000 B.C.E. with the domestication of camels which can go as long as 17 days without water. Introduction of the horse at a somewhat later date allowed for still more flexibility of movement and agility in warfare. Full nomadism never replaced seminomadism altogether and agriculturalists learned how to specialize on the side in pastoralism through a form of nomadism known as transhumance. Actual nomadic groups are extremely varied according to environmental conditions, types of animals bred, communal forms for establishing kinship, wealth, and status, historical fortunes of the group, and relations to surrounding nomadic and settled peoples.

In Ancient Israel

Ancient Israel was in contact with peoples who practiced pastoral nomadism. Some segments of Israel proper were pastoral nomads for varying periods of time in the arid and semiarid zones of Sinai and the Negev, Transjordan, and the rain shadow regions of Canaan, i.e., mostly on the eastern slopes of the central highlands. Excluded from consideration is animal husbandry, which is frequent in agricultural communities in which a few animals raised by farmers are allowed to forage in the human settlement and to graze on farmland stubble and fallow land. The animals referred to in the early Israelite Book of the Covenant (e.g., Ex. 21:28–37; 22:3–4, 9–12; 23:4–5, 12) reveal that the laws applied to resident farmers for whom animal husbandry was a secondary activity and among whom vast pasturage as a special ecological aspect shaping the entire socioeconomic life was absent. Also, we omit all consideration of non-pastoral nomadism, e.g., wild species moving on their own through an annual cycle and nomadic human communities of hunters, fishers, and gatherers. Full or classic pastoral nomadism entailed maximum independence through human symbiosis with the camel and, to a lesser degree, with the horse. It allowed the nomad to keep a safe distance from the settled lands but, when required to trade or raid, he could do so from a position of considerable strength. The occasional camels mentioned in early Israel, if not an outright anachronism, were for transport and were too few in number and insufficiently domesticated to have become the basis for an entire economy. The only full nomadism directly attested in the Bible is non-Israelite, e.g., a caravan of Ishmaelite-Midianite merchants who bought Joseph from his brothers (Gen. 37:25–28); Midianites, Amalekites, and people of the east who carried out camel razzias against Israel in the time of Gideon (Judg. 6:1–5); and Amalekites who raided southern Judah on a smaller scale in the time of Saul (I Sam. 30).

SEMINOMADISM. Seminomadism or partial nomadism (also known as ass nomadism to distinguish the ass from the camel as the chief form of transport) is a mode of pastoral nomadism loosely applied to peoples who are often conceived as midway in the process of settling down after an earlier fully nomadic life. This is misleading in some instances and erroneous in others. In its origins pastoral nomadism was a specific adaptation of animal domestication to desert conditions after it was first developed among agriculturalists. There are of course instances of full nomads reverting to seminomadism and finally to agricultural settlement. But there are also cases of agriculturalists who are "depressed" into seminomadism by geopolitical circumstances. Sometimes this depression is permanent, while in other cases it is temporary. There is some reason to believe that the Israelite groups in the wilderness between Egypt and Canaan were thrown temporarily into a more fully nomadic life than they had known either in Egypt or prior to their entrance into Egypt and, furthermore, that they were consciously seeking a return to a more stable and perhaps even largely agricultural existence. More precisely, seminomadism indicates the relative dependence of herders of sheep, goats, and asses on the settled peoples or on full nomads for the sharing of water rights and for permission to graze. It also refers to their relative military weakness, lacking as they do a striking force of camels or horses. The concomitant of this reality is the high probability that the seminomad will engage in some form of limited agriculture. He is often sedentary for part of the year; fields and pasture are often interspersed; and the herd sizes relative to the human population are much smaller than in full nomadism. Accordingly, the seminomad will often appear to be an incipient peasant who has not yet attained his goal or a decadent farmer who has lapsed into a less secure life. In many cases, however, the seminomad regards his way of life as more satisfying than the softer and more politically lettered existence of the peasant. Traits of seminomadism appear frequently in the patriarchal stories concerning Abraham and Lot (Gen. 12:16; 13:2–12; 18:1–8; 20:14–15; 21:25–26), Isaac (Gen. 26:12–22), Jacob and Esau (Gen. 30:43; 31:17–18; 32:13–15; 33:18–20; 36:6–8), and Joseph (Gen. 37:2, 7; 42:1–5; 43:11; 46:31–34; 47:6). The precise nature of this type (or these types) of seminomadism is difficult to assess in that the movements are not strictly described as regular but are explained largely with reference to famine, intermarriage, religious pilgrimage, and conflicts within and between groups. The Israelites in Egypt are pictured as small stock breeders who also cultivate vegetable gardens (Ex. 10:24–26; 12:1–13, 31–34, 37–39; Num. 11:4–6). Living close to the Egyptian frontier with Sinai (Ex. 1:11; 9:26; 12:37), the holy place of their deity is located a three-day journey away in the desert (Ex. 3:18; 5:3; 8:24). Their relatively self-contained economy was threatened by the recent imperial policy which forced them to work on state building projects and in state-owned fields. One tradition has it that, as they departed Egypt with their flocks, the Israelites despoiled the Egyptians of jewelry and clothing in the manner of a nomadic razzia (Ex. 3:21–22; 12:35–36). In the wilderness the Israelites present a confused picture of a seminomadic people thrust suddenly into conditions where only well-provisioned travel parties or full nomads with camels might normally survive. The Israelites adjusted to this crisis by retaining their flocks for dairy products, wool, and hides. Occasional sacrifice of their animals provided some meat but food staples were supplied by improvising with quail and wild plant products ("manna"). Water was available from oasis to oasis. Even so they seem to have survived only because the Midianites, into whom Moses is said to have married, supplied them with knowledge of the terrain and with basic survival skills; at least some of these Midianites accompanied certain of the Israelite groups into Canaan (Ex. 2:15b–22; 3:1; 18:1ff.; Num. 10:29–32; Judg. 1:16; 4:11). Although unreported, it is reasonable to suppose that the Israelites cultivated small vegetable plots during the time they spent at the oases in the vicinity of Kadesh. All available evidence points to the fact that the component groups in the larger Israelite confederation in Canaan were predominantly agricultural and engaged in supplementary animal husbandry (cf. the laws of the Covenant Code, Ex. 20:24 (19)–23:9 and the descriptions of tribal life in Gen. 49 and Deut. 33). This type of economy characterized a large majority of the population in the highlands of Galilee, Gilead, Samaria, and Judah – the heartland of ancient Israel. However, a significant minority of Israelites, who lived in the semiarid regions to the east and south, sustained a seminomadic economy. A diminishing frequency of references to such seminomadic life in later biblical books suggests that the percentage of seminomadic Israelites relative to the total population steadily declined. Given the marginal rainfall of the land, however, and the abiding attraction of the steppe for certain individuals and groups, seminomadism never ceased in biblical times. In fact, the *Rechabites were one group who made a sectarian virtue of their seminomadism, identifying it with the pure form of Yahwism and refusing adamantly to build houses or to engage in viticulture or grain-growing (Jer. 35). According to one tradition these Rechabites were actual descendants of the Midianite-Kenite group into which Moses married (I Chron. 2:55). A more individualistic version of the tendency to equate holiness with seminomadic culture was the "consecration" of a person as a nazirite, perhaps originally associated with the spontaneous leadership of a war chieftain (Num. 6:1–21; Judg. 13:5, 7; 16:17). While such primitivist equations of Yahwism with seminomadism were not central to biblical traditions, it is nonetheless striking that many of the features of the early religion of Israel, although developed by a predominantly agricultural people, were powerfully indebted to nomadic influences, e.g., the belief that the original home of YHWH was in the wilderness and the decided preference for a mobile shrine over that of a fixed shrine.

CUSTOMS AND WAY OF LIFE. As a congeries of ethnically, geographically, economically, socially, and politically diverse people formed Israel in Canaan, they adopted a framework for their socioeconomic life which drew on the norms, institutions, and practices of pastoral nomadism, with suitable modifications to settled conditions. Among these abiding influences were the practice of blood revenge (Gen. 9:5–6; Num. 35:19; Judg. 8:18–21; II Sam. 3:30; 14:4–7; 21:1–14); protection of the integrity of the patriarchal family (Ex. 20:12, 14, 17; 21:15, 17; 22:15–16, 21; Lev. 18:6–18; Deut. 25:5–10); the institutions of the *ger* – the protected resident alien (e.g., Ex. 22:20; Deut. 10:19); and the asylum (Ex. 21:13–14; Num. 35; Deut. 19), related to the nomad law of hospitality and asylum. Instead of a primitivist attempt to construct seminomadism in Canaan, early Israel was a synthetic socioeconomic formation of loosely federated seminomadic and peasant populations arranged in a socially fictitious kinship network and cemented by a common cult of HWHY. The complex transformation and adaptation of the seminomadic elements in the Israelite confederation are reflected in the ambivalent biblical attitude toward the desert, which is sometimes idealized as the setting for an originally pure Yahwism but which is more often pictured as a place of rebellion and division, in itself a region of waste and horror, the quintessence of death and danger.

Yet another form of pastoral nomadism is transhumance which occurs in communities with developed agricultural specialization where herds are moved to select pastures for a part of the year by herders who specialize in their tasks. A common form of transhumance is to take the herds into mountain ranges for summer upland pasturage after the snows have melted. In Canaan transhumance took at least two forms. Immediately following the winter rains, herds were taken some distance into the steppes to feed on the temporary spring growth. As the summer wore on, and pasturage withered, they were taken to the better watered seaward-facing plains and mountain slopes. There are some biblical data which may be read as evidence for the practice of transhumance nomadism among the Israelites. Joseph and his brothers care for the flocks near Shechem and Dothan while Jacob remains at Hebron (Gen. 37:12–17). Nabal is a man of wealth in Maon whose hired men or slaves care for his large flocks at Carmel (I Sam. 25). Wealthy landowners in Transjordan provision the exiled David with agricultural and pastoral products (II Sam. 17:27–29; 19:31–32). The Job of the prose framework (Job. 1:1ff.; 42:12–17) is a wealthy farmer who also has thousands of domesticated animals cared for by his servants. The region of Bashan in northern Transjordan was well known as a prime cattle-breeding area, to which wealthy Israelites appear to have sent their flocks and herds (Ezek. 39:18; Amos 4:1; Ps. 22:13). Israelite kings capitalized on this process by appointing stewards over royal herds and flocks which were permanently located in the most attractive pastoral regions (II Sam. 13:23; I Chron. 27:28–30; II Chron. 26:10; 32:27–29).

In order to achieve a more exact socioeconomic characterization of early Israel, scholars will increasingly require expertise both in biblical studies and in ethnography and the social sciences. It is evident that the assumption that Arab Bedouin nomadism supplies the nearest surviving approximation to Israel's nomadism, while broadly apt, lacks all exactitude unless care is taken to distinguish among the various subforms and historical constellations of Bedouin existence.

It is necessary to reject the vague notion that full nomadism in the Arabian peninsula was the temporally original base for Middle Eastern socioeconomic evolutionary development. Far from full nomadism having been some simple state from which seminomadism and agriculture grew, almost precisely the opposite occurred in the Middle East over millennia of time as agriculture originated animal domestication was introduced into the sparse conditions of the desert and was elaborated through the eventual introduction of the camel and the horse. Identification of the mutually illuminating affinities between Arab and Israelite nomadism must not obscure the complex web of cultural and historical factors at work in the two different contexts from age to age and from subregion to subregion.

BIBLIOGRAPHY: K. Budde, *The New World*, 4 (1895), 726–45; M. de Goeje, in: EI, 1 (1913), 372–7; J. Flight, in: JBL, 42 (1923), 158–226; L. Febvre, *A Geographical Introduction to History* (1925), 261–94; A. Musil, *The Manners and Customs of the Rwala Bedouins* (1930); M. von Oppenheim, *Die Beduinen*, 1–3 (1939–53); S. Nystroem, *Beduinentum und Jahwismus* (1946); C.S. Coon et al., in: EI^2, 1 (1960), 872–92; de Vaux, Anc Isr, 3–15; A. Jeffery, in: IDB, 1 (1962), 181–4; C. Wolf, *ibid.*, 3 (1962), 558–60; D. Amiran and Y. Ben-Arieh, in: IEJ, 13 (1963), 161–81; S. Talmon, in: A. Altmann (ed.), *Biblical Motifs* (1966), 31–63; L. Krader, in: IESS, 11 (1968), 453–61; M. Sahlins, *Tribesmen* (1968), 32–39.

[Norman K. Gottwald]

NOMBERG, HERSH DAVID (1876–1927), Yiddish essayist and short story writer. Nomberg was born into a family of rabbis and Ḥasidim, in Mszczonow, near Warsaw. Though he traveled widely, Nomberg remained associated with the Polish capital. After both a traditional Jewish and a self-taught secular education, he joined the circle of Y.L. *Peretz (to which Abraham *Reisen and Sholem *Asch also belonged), becoming an ardent and loyal disciple and one of the best interpreters of his works. It was Peretz who persuaded Nomberg to write in Yiddish, his first poem in this language appearing in 1900. Nomberg wrote for the Warsaw Hebrew paper *Ha-Ẓofeh* (1903–5) and was, for a time, its editor. His first collection of Hebrew stories appeared in 1905, followed by five collections in Yiddish. It was under his and Peretz's influence that the struggle between Hebraists and Yiddishists at the *Czernowitz Yiddish Conference in 1908 was resolved and a compromise resolution adopted which proclaimed Yiddish as *a* (not *the*) national language of the Jews. The anonymous hero of his masterful, psychoanalytical tale "Fligelman" ("Winged Man," 1908) served as a symbol for the entire generation of this crucial period. Indeed, most of Nomberg's heroes can be characterized as "winged men."

After 1910 Nomberg almost entirely gave up belles-lettres for politics and journalism. In 1916, he was one of the founders of the Folkspartei ("People's Party") which advocated concentration on Jewish autonomous rights in Poland, though not opposing emigration to Ereẓ Israel. He served in 1919–20 as a member of the Polish *Sejm*. In 1912, however, he published the later often-staged drama, *Di Mishpokhe* ("The Family," 1912), based on the idea of the potential for moral improvement in humans. His interest in the Yiddish theater was also expressed through reviews and translations.

In general he was a controversial figure: his characters often reverse traditional gender roles, while his language is characterized by minimalist, anti-rhetorical traits. In the press of the time he was often compared with the protagonists of his fiction in their cynicism and lack of values. His criticism of progressive movements, such as the New York group, Di *Yunge, contributed to this trend. Even so, Nomberg helped to provide a home for Jewish writers in Warsaw. He was the driving force behind, and for many years the president of, the Society for Jewish Writers and Journalists, which came to be better known as "Tlomatske 13," after the address of its building, a famed center of Yiddish cultural activity until its liquidation by the Nazis. Jewish audiences followed his perceptive articles, especially in the Warsaw Yiddish daily *Der Moment*, with which he was connected for a decade. When he died in 1927, tens of thousands of his readers accompanied him to his grave near that of his friend and preceptor Peretz. His was one of the few tombstones which survived Nazi destruction.

BIBLIOGRAPHY: Rejzen, Leksikon, 2 (1929), 523–33; LNYL, 6 (1965), 160–8; S. Lestchinsky, *Literarishe Eseyen* (1938), 58–63; M. Ravitch, *Mayn Leksikon* (1945), 141–3; S. Mendelson, *Leben un Shafen* (1949), 169–76; J.J. Trunk, *Tsvishn Viln un Onmekhtikeyt* (1930); Jeshurin, in: *Oysgeklibene Shriftn* (1956), 236–52; Kressel, Leksikon, 2 (1967), 443. **ADD. BIBLIOGRAPHY:** M. Meged, in: H. Nomberg, *Sippurim* (1969), 7–41.

[Melech Ravitch / Shifra Kuperman (2nd ed.)]

NONES, BENJAMIN (1757–1826), U.S. patriot and soldier during the American Revolution. Nones, who was born in Bordeaux, France, served as aide-de-camp to his former schoolmate, Marquis de Lafayette (1777), fought in Count Casimir Pulaski's legion during the defense of Charleston and was cited for bravery (1779), and served as aide to General Washington, holding the rank of major. After the Revolution, Nones settled in Philadelphia where he was variously employed as a broker and factor, a notary public, and as government interpreter for French, Spanish, and Portuguese. He was active in Republican politics and, in keeping with his abolitionist sympathies, freed his slaves after the Revolution. Nones served as president of Congregation Mikveh Israel in Philadelphia.

His son JOSEPH B. NONES (1797–1887) was wounded while serving as a midshipman in a battle against Algerian pirates in 1815. At the age of 70, he wrote a colorful account of his adventures in the Navy. He was a pioneer in processing concentrated foods, and in 1829 he proposed a program to combat scurvy in the Navy. In later life, he was an importer in Philadelphia.

BIBLIOGRAPHY: Biogr Dict (1960), 135; AJHSP, 1 (1893), 111–5.

[Abram Vossen Goodman]

NORDAU, MAX (Simon Maximilian Suedfeld; 1849–1923), co-founder of the World Zionist Organization, philosopher, writer, orator, and physician. Born in Pest, the son of Rabbi Gabriel Suedfeld, Nordau received a traditional Jewish education and remained an observant Jew until his eighteenth year, when he became a militant naturalist and evolutionist. In 1875 he earned an M.D. degree at the University of Pest, and he settled in Paris in 1880 as a practicing physician. Nordau's career in journalism dates back to his childhood. In 1867 he joined the staff of the *Pester Lloyd*, and in time he became a correspondent for leading newspapers in the Western world, including the *Vossische Zeitung* in Berlin, the *Neue Freie Presse* in Vienna, and *La Nación* in Buenos Aires, Argentina.

Nordau achieved fame as a thinker and social critic with the publication of *Die Conventionellen Luegen der Kulturmenschheit* (1883; *The Conventional Lies of Our Civilization*, 1884). He sharply criticized "the religious lie," the corruption and oppression of monarchical and aristocratic regimes, the deceptions of political and economic establishments, and the hypocritical adherence to outworn sex mores. He set forth as an alternative what has been called his "philosophy of human solidarity." Nordau's "solidaritarianism" signifies the unity of mind and love. It insists on the intimate connection between free institutions and free inquiry in all areas of human concern. The *Lies* was translated into fifteen languages, including Chinese and Japanese. It raised a storm of controversy and was banned in Austria and Russia. It was followed by *Paradoxe der Conventionellen Luegen* (1885[3]; *Paradoxes*, 1896), which discussed such topics as optimism and pessimism, passion and prejudice, social pressure and the power of love, sham and genuine success. This work also went through several editions and translations.

Even more controversial was *Entartung* (1892; *Degeneration*, 1895), in which Nordau subjected major figures and trends in European art and literature to scathing denunciation. Applying Cesare Lombroso's term "degeneracy" to the works of such men as Nietzsche, Tolstoy, Wagner, Zola, Ibsen, and such phenomena as symbolism, spiritualism, egomania, mysticism, Parnassianism, and diabolism, Nordau predicted the coming of a human catastrophe of unprecedented proportions. An entire literature developed over *Degeneration*, including a rebuttal in book form by George Bernard Shaw. More than 60 years after its first publication, *Degeneration* continued to be the subject of doctoral dissertations accepted by American universities; the book was republished in New York in 1968. Three other works merit perhaps even greater attention than *Lies* and *Degeneration*. The first is *Der Sinn der Geschichte* (1909; *The Interpretation of History*, 1910), which examines man's advance from parasitism through supernaturalist illusion to knowledge and human solidarity. To Nordau, the purpose of man's history was to achieve a lessening of human suffering and to actualize "the ideal of goodness and selfless love." The second, *Biologie der Ethik* (1921; *Morals and the Evolution of Man*, 1922), is a treatise on the natural roots of ethics, the relations between the legal and the moral, and the meaning of "scientific ethics," which aims at the improvement of human life through the cultivation of the twin "solidaritarian" powers of intelligence and compassion. The third, *Der Sinn der Gesittung*; "The Essence of Civilization" (written in 1920), was published in 1932 in an unsatisfactory Spanish version. In this last, fragmentary work, Nordau advocated "the elevation of the independent local community, the free city-republic, to the general type of community" as the best means of redeeming the individual from his bondage. Nordau argued the case of "solidaritarian socialism," which assigns to private property its proper limits without, however, abolishing it. Nordau regarded Communism as entirely unacceptable and, in its Bolshevik form, as "socialism gone mad."

In the field of belles lettres, Nordau's major works are *Der Krieg der Millionen* (1882), *Die Krankheit des Jahrhunderts* (1888; *The Malady of the Century*, 1896), *Seelenanalysen* (1892), *Das Recht zu Lieben* (1894; *The Right to Love*, 1895), *Drohnenschlacht* (1898; *The Drones Must Die*, 1899); *Doktor Kohn* (1899; *A Question of Honor*, 1907); *Morganatisch* (1904; *Morganatic*, 1904), *The Dwarf's Spectacles, and Other Fairy Tales* (1905), and an unpublished biblical tragedy in four acts, *Rahab* (c. 1922).

The Jewish problem was never foreign to Nordau's thoughts. His revulsion against antisemitism is reflected in his essay on Jacques Offenbach entitled "The Political Hep! Hep!" included in *Aus dem wahren Milliardenlande* (an abridged translation entitled *Paris Sketches* appeared in 1884). In the *Lies* Nordau condemned hatred of the Jew as a symptom of the malady of the age. Nordau's upbringing, his piety toward his Orthodox parents (his observant mother lived in his house in Paris until her death in 1900), and the references to Jewish destiny in his general writings all show that the frequent charge of Nordau's alienation from Judaism in his pre-Zionist period is exaggerated.

Nordau met Theodor *Herzl in 1892. As Paris correspondents for German-language newspapers, they witnessed the manifestations of antisemitism in the French capital. In November 1895 Herzl discussed his idea of a Jewish state with Nordau, after Emil Schiff, a friend concerned over his mental condition, advised him to see a psychiatrist. Far from declaring Herzl insane, however, Nordau concluded the consultation by saying: "If you are insane, we are insane together. Count on me!" To Nordau, the idea of a Jewish state appeared as a most welcome means for the implementation of his "solidaritarian" philosophy by Jews in the land of the Jews.

At the First Zionist Congress (1897), Nordau drafted the famed Basle *Program. He served as vice president of the First to the Sixth Zionist Congresses and as president of the Seventh to the Tenth Congresses. In his famed addresses to these Congresses he surveyed the Jewish situation in the world and described and analyzed the physical and material plight of the Jews in Eastern Europe, as well as the moral plight of the emancipated and assimilated Western Jew, who had lost his contact with his fellow-Jews and faced political and social antisemitism, which excluded him from non-Jewish society. These addresses, together with his other Zionist pronouncements, became classics of Zionist literature. At the Congress of 1911 he warned that if current political trends persisted, six million Jews, i.e., those living in the Russian Empire and other East-European countries, were doomed to perish. He was convinced that only political Zionism could forestall the tragedy. Nordau passionately defended Herzl's political Zionism against *Aḥad Ha-Am's cultural Zionism, which he regarded as being pre-Zionist. He believed that his opponent's idea of a "spiritual center" would only obstruct the Zionist effort to rescue large masses of Jews in Ereẓ Israel. Citing a statement of the "cultural Zionists" – that "we are not concerned with Jews but with Judaism" – Nordau told the Sixth Zionist Congress, "'Judaism without Jews' – we know you, beautiful mask! Go with this phrase and join a meeting of spiritualists!"

In loyalty to Herzl, Nordau supported the *Uganda Scheme and coined the phrase *Nachtasyl* (night asylum) to stress the temporary nature of the proposal. He himself was convinced that the idea of a charter for Uganda was a grave error, because Jews who could not go to Palestine would prefer America or Australia. An assassination attempt in Paris, by a young anti-Ugandist, Chaim Selig Luban, who held Nordau responsible for the scheme, failed. Nordau himself defended Luban before the investigating judge.

In his last conversation with Nissan *Katzenelson, Herzl stated that Nordau should be his successor as president of the Zionist Organization, adding, "I can assure you that he will lead the cause at least as well as I did or better." Nordau, however, declined to serve as president when he was offered the post after Herzl's death; he chose to remain outside the organizational hierarchy. His opposition to the cultural Zionism espoused by Aḥad Ha-Am was only matched by his opposition to the practical Zionists led by Chaim *Weizmann. Nordau believed in political action rather than in small-scale, gradual agricultural colonization.

Nordau spent World War I in exile and in relative isolation in neutral Spain. He favored Vladimir *Jabotinsky's idea of a *Jewish Legion, but felt that the Zionist movement should remain neutral, since Zionists lived in countries on both sides of the international conflict. In 1920 he delivered his celebrated Albert Hall address in London, in which he told British statesmen and Zionist leaders that if the *Balfour Declaration of 1917 was to have meaning, that meaning must be made manifest by the swift creation of a Jewish majority and ensuing Jewish political independence in Palestine. In 1919, when a wave of pogroms swept the Ukraine and other parts of Russia, he began advocating the speedy transfer of 600,000 Jews to Palestine within a matter of months. The Zionist leadership rejected his proposal as unrealistic, and in 1921 Nordau retired from active Zionist work. He died in Paris in 1923 and was interred in the Old Cemetery in Tel Aviv in 1926. In the late 1930s, Jabotinsky was to name his own program for the speedy creation of a Jewish majority in Palestine by the mass transfer of Jews from the Diaspora "The Max Nordau Plan."

[Meir Ben-Horin]

His daughter MAXA NORDAU (1897–1991) was a French painter. She was born in Paris, where she studied under Jules Adler. In 1937 she painted mural decorations in the Palestine pavilion at the Paris international exhibition, and during World War II lived in the U.S. A conservative representational artist, her subjects included Israeli landscapes, urban scenes, workyards, nudes, and portraits. Among her portraits are *Max Nordau*, *The Young David*, and *The Pioneers*. She illustrated books, including *Contes pour Maxa* by her father, and collaborated with her mother in writing *Max Nordau, a Biography* (1943).

BIBLIOGRAPHY: N. Sokolow, *History of Zionism*, 2 vols. (1919), index; A. and M. Nordau, *Max Nordau* (Eng., 1943); S. Schwartz, *Max Nordau be-Iggerotav* (1944); Ch. Weizmann, *Trial and Error*, (1949), index; M.P. Foster, "Reception of Max Nordau's 'Degeneration' in England and America" (Ph.D. diss., University of Michigan, 1954); M. Ben Horin, *Max Nordau, Philosopher of Human Solidarity* (1956); idem, *Common Faith – Uncommon People* (1970); M. Gold, "Nordau on Degeneration; A Study of the Book and Its Cultural Significance" (Ph.D. diss., Columbia University, 1957); T. Herzl, *Complete Diaries*, ed. and tr. by R. Patai, 5 (1960), index; M. Heyman, *The Minutes of the Zionist Council, The Uganda Controversy*, 1 (1970).

NORDEN, family of South African pioneers (mid-19th century), consisting of five brothers – Benjamin, Joshua Davis, Marcus, Samuel, and Harry. They were among the 18 Jewish members of the party of settlers sent out by the British government in 1820 to the turbulent frontier of the eastern Cape Colony. The 1820 settlers endured great privations in a wild country exposed to depredations by African tribesmen. After some years many of them, including the Nordens, settled the small towns which had sprung up. BENJAMIN NORDEN (1798–1876), a man of adventurous nature, traveled into the interior, engaged in the ivory trade, and had dealings with the Zulu king, Dingaan. He was a friend of the Boer voortrekker leader, Piet Retief. Norden was interested in plans for the development of Delagoa Bay and Port Elizabeth and joined in a gold prospecting venture. In 1840 he moved from Grahamstown, where he had a trading store with his brother MARCUS, to Cape Town and was associated with the De Pass family in exploiting the guano deposits on the west coast. In Cape Town he was active in civic affairs and was one of the municipal commissioners. He took the lead in forming Cape Town's first Hebrew congregation, Tikvath Israel (1841). When the first synagogue was built in 1849 Norden was president, holding the office until 1857 when he returned to England. JOSHUA DAVIS NORDEN (1803–1846) settled in Grahamstown as an auctioneer after leaving his frontier farm. Like his brother, he served as a municipal commissioner and was leader of the Jewish community. To defend the town from attacks by tribesmen he raised and captained the Grahamstown Yeomanry, which bore his name. In 1846 he was killed at the head of his men in a skirmish during the War of the Axe, one of a long series of "Kaffir wars." As a tribute to his "intrepidity and bravery," his former comrades erected a plaque to his memory on a wall of St. George's Cathedral, Grahamstown. A third Norden brother, SAMUEL, was killed while leading a charge in the Basuto War (1858). A nephew of Benjamin Norden was the famous San Francisco, California eccentric Joshua Davis Norton (1818–1880), known as the "Emperor Norton," who in 1859 proclaimed himself "Norton the First, Emperor of the United States."

BIBLIOGRAPHY: L. Herrman, *History of the Jews in South Africa* (1935), index; G. Saron and L. Hotz, *Jews in South Africa* (1955), index; JC (July 24, 1846), repr. in: *Jewish Affairs* (March, 1953), 23–25; Mendelssohn, in: JHSET, 7 (1915), 192–4; Rosenthal, in: *Zionist Record* (South African, Sept. 30, 1932).

[Louis Hotz]

NORDHAUSEN, city in Thuringia, Germany. The earliest documentary evidence for the presence of Jews in Nordhausen dates from 1290, and by 1300 a Jewish community had come into being. Shortly thereafter a *Judenstrasse, mikveh*, and synagogue were established. A Jewish well is noted in records dating from 1322, and a cemetery is mentioned in 1334. During the course of a disturbance in 1324, the community's synagogue was destroyed. The Jews of the period made their living primarily through moneylending, and their sound economic position brought more Jewish immigrants into the city. In 1333 the municipal council agreed to the adjudication of all disputes between Jews by the rabbinic court. During the course of the *Black Death persecutions of 1349, however, a number of Jews suffered martyrdom. Frederick the Brave was partly responsible for deaths of Jews during this period. (A legendary account published in a Worms prayer book indicates that the entire Jewish community went dancing to its death, willingly submitting to the funeral pyre.) Although refugees from the persecutions fled to *Erfurt and *Frankfurt, by 1350 at least one Jew had already returned to resettle in Nordhausen. Abandoned Jewish property was transferred by King Charles VI to Count Henry von Hohlstein. Despite the upheaval and loss of life and property, by the end of the century a small Jewish community had reestablished itself in Nordhausen, holding its religious services in a private house. In 1391 King *Wenceslaus released the burghers from their debts to the Jews on payment of a fee to the royal chamber.

A small number of Jews continued to live in Nordhausen during the 15th century. In the 16th century they were subject to increasingly restrictive legislation, and they were finally expelled in 1559. They settled in the surrounding towns, however, and continued to trade; the right to trade in Nordhausen itself was granted in 1619. By 1630 there were four *Schutzjuden ("protected Jews") in the city; in the 18th century, however, no Jews were left. A modern community came into being only in 1808, after Nordhausen was annexed by *Westphalia. By 1817 there were 74 Jews in the city; in 1822 there were 100; in 1840 the number was 210; and in 1880, it was 494. A new cemetery was consecrated in 1827 and enlarged in 1854. The first rabbi in Nordhausen was Nathan Meyer, who assumed his post in 1817. A synagogue was dedicated in 1845, and the community was officially recognized in 1847. Among the prominent members of the community in the 19th century was the banker and philanthropist Jacob Plaut (1816–1901). From 1908 until 1925 the community was served with distinction by Rabbi Alfred Sepp. In 1925 the community numbered 438; in 1933 it had 394 members, five cultural and philanthropic organizations, and a religious school. In 1939, under the pressure of Nazi persecution and consequent emigration, the number of Jews declined to 128; in 1942 there were only 19. The community came to an end during World War II. The Jewish cemetery is preserved. In 1988 a memorial was consecrated to the synagogue that had been destroyed in 1938.

BIBLIOGRAPHY: *Germania Judaica*, 1 (1963), 247; 2 (1968), 590–3; H. Stern, *Geschichte der Juden in Nordhausen* (1927); S. Neufeld, *Die Juden im thueringisch-saechsischen Gebiet waehrend des Mittelalters* (1917), passim; E. Carmoly, in: *Der Israelit*, nos. 4–8 (1866); *Der Orient*, 9 (1848), 48, 80; AZJ, 37 (1873), 127–8; A. Lewinsky, in: MGWJ, 49 (1905), 746–51; FJW, 118–9. **ADD BIBLIOGRAPHY:** *Germania Judaica*, vol. 3, 1350–1514 (1987), 994–1000; M. Schroeter, *Die Verfolgung der Nordhaeuser Juden 1933 bis 1945* (1992); J.-M. Junker, "Vom Schicksal der Nordhaeuser Synagoge nach dem Pogrom 1938," in: *Beitraege zur Heimatkunde aus Stadt und Kreis Nordhausen* vol. 18, (1993) 62–66; M. Kahl, *Denkmale juedischer Kultur in Thueringen* (Kulturgeschichtliche Reihe, vol. 2) (1997), 112–15.

[Alexander Shapiro]

NORELL, NORMAN (1900–1972), U.S. fashion designer. Born Norman David Levinson in Noblesville, Indiana, the son of a haberdasher, Norell became the dean of American women's fashion designers in the 1950s and 1960s. At that time, he was the one American whose clothes were held to be the equal of anything created by the Paris couture. One of the first designers whose name appeared on a label, he was the first president of the Council of Fashion Designers of America. After attending military school during World War I, Norell traveled to New York City and studied at the Parsons School of Design in 1918 and Pratt Institute from 1920 to 1922. He returned to Parsons as a teacher in the 1940s and continued mentoring design students there until the end of his life. In 1922 he was hired by the New York studio of Paramount Pictures to create clothes for Gloria Swanson and other stars of the silent screen. He also designed for Broadway shows, including the Ziegfeld Follies. In 1928, he was hired by Hattie *Carnegie, working with her until 1941, when he went into partnership with Anthony Traina to form Traina-Norell. Traina retired in 1960 and Norell formed his own company, Norman Norell Inc. He was known for making clothes with clean, precisely tailored silhouettes and superb workmanship. Breaking with tradition, he conducted his fashion shows for visiting buyers in the evening instead of during the working day – and in front of a black-tie audience. In 1943 he received the first of five Coty Awards for Fashion. In 1956, the same year Parsons gave him its Medal for Distinguished Achievement, he was inducted into the Coty Hall of Fame. He died in October 1972, suffering a stroke on the night before the opening of a retrospective of his work at New York's Metropolitan Museum of Art. In 2000, when New York's fashion industry paid tribute to its top designers by installing bronze plaques on Seventh Avenue, the heart of the garment district, Norell was among the first to be so honored.

[Mort Sheinman (2nd ed.)]

NORFOLK, central city of the Tidewater region of S.E. Virginia, noted for maritime activities and the presence of U.S. military bases. Its Jewish population in 2001 was 11,000.

The first-known Jewish settler in Norfolk, Moses *Myers (1752–1835) arrived in 1787 and became one of the city's leading merchants. The home he erected is on display as part of the city's Chrysler Museum of Art.

From the beginning of their existence as an organized community, Norfolk's Jews created a network of synagogues. German immigrants founded the city's first congregation in 1844, Ohev Sholom. In 1850 a traditionalist faction seceded and founded Beth El congregation, which later became an original member of the United Synagogue of America. East European immigrants created several Orthodox congregations, which united after World War II as B'nai Israel. Migration from the North, connected to the economic growth of Norfolk during World War II, and movement from older neighborhoods into newer and suburban areas, resulted in the formation of new congregations: Temple Israel (Conservative) in 1953 and Beth Chaverim (Reform) in 1982. After a successful, city-sponsored revitalization of Norfolk's downtown commercial and residential areas in the 1980s, the synagogues there rebounded, and a Chabad center, first opened in Virginia Beach in 1980, moved downtown in 2002.

After World War II, Norfolk Jewry, now predominantly American-born, asserted itself by creating a network of communal institutions: the Jewish Family Services in 1948; the Jewish Community Council in 1950, which grew into the United Jewish Federation; the Jewish Community Center, 1952, and the Hebrew Academy of Tidewater, a community day school, in 1954. Later institutions include the Beth Sholom [nursing] Home of Eastern Virginia, founded in 1980, and the Torah Day School, an Orthodox yeshivah, in 2003. Spurred by the philanthropic response to the Six-Day War, the United Jewish Federation grew into the central address of the community by the 1970s.

Postwar Jewish residential patterns, and consequent institutional developments, followed national demographic trends. Small towns close to Norfolk, such as Berkley and

Portsmouth, lost all or most of their Jewish residents, and newer suburbs grew. While some Jews were at the forefront of the local civil rights struggle of the 1950s, many Jews moved into the neighboring suburb of Virginia Beach after court-ordered school desegregation in 1959. In 1974, the Hebrew Academy moved to a Virginia Beach location and in 2004 the United Jewish Federation and the Jewish Community Center of Tidewater, along with the Hebrew Academy, relocated to a Virginia Beach campus.

Although Jews had suffered social discrimination prior to World War II, the Jewish community gained increasing social acceptance in the two generations following. Whereas a descendant of Moses Myers, Barton Myers, Sr., mayor of Norfolk from 1886 to 1888, had been raised as a Christian, the mayor of Virginia Beach from 1988, Meyera Oberndorf, was a professing Jew. Jews were prominently active in Norfolk's urban redevelopment work and a variety of general as well as Jewish philanthropic causes throughout the region.

[Michael Panitz (2nd ed.)]

NORMAN, EDWARD ALBERT (1900–1955), U.S. financier and philanthropist. Norman, who was born in Chicago, attended the U.S. Military Academy at West Point before transferring to Harvard. He worked for *The Survey* (1924–25) and as a research secretary for the Cooperative League of the U.S. (1925–28) before assuming the management of his family's various financial interests. Although a non-Zionist, Norman was extremely interested in the welfare of Palestine and its people and he urged a roof organization to coordinate and funnel the American Jewish aid for Palestinian educational, cultural, and social service institutions. The result was the founding of the American Fund for Israel Institutions (1939), of which Norman was president at his death (see *America-Israel Cultural Foundation).

His other posts in Jewish organizational and communal life included president of the American Economic Commission for Palestine (1939–43); national secretary for the American Jewish Committee (1946–55); non-Zionist member of the Jewish Agency's Executive Council; governor of the Hebrew University (1949–55); and director of the Joint Distribution Committee (1936–55). Norman was also president of the Group Farming Research Institute (1940–55), founded for the purpose of studying cooperative systems throughout the world; treasurer of the Urban League (1928–38); and chairman of the finance commission of the Association of American Indian Affairs.

NORONHA (Loronha), FERNÃO DE (1470?–1540?), New Christian explorer and colonizer of Brazil. Noronha was head of the first of the Portuguese *donatários*, associations formed to lease land for development in Brazil, and his association was composed of *New Christians. Arriving in Brazil in 1503 with six ships, troops, and supplies, he discovered an island near the north coast of the country which he named São João, although it was generally known by his name. Following the terms of his contract, he explored and colonized large areas of Brazil, exploiting them for the benefit of his company. In return for his services, King Manuel I named him Knight of the Crown in 1504 and granted him the captaincy for life of the island he discovered. According to a report of 1505 by the Venetian Lunardo Chá Masser, Noronha acted as the Lisbon agent for the senate of Venice and was a pioneer in the import and export of timber, receiving a monopoly on dyewood from the crown. His contract, originally for three years, was apparently extended to 1512 or 1515. Noronha appears to have been a wealthy Jew, close to the court, who had converted to Christianity prior to 1497. He took his surname from his godfather, a nobleman descended from the royal house of Castile.

BIBLIOGRAPHY: A. Wiznitzer, *Jews in Colonial Brazil* (1960), 5–8; S. Leite, *Os judeus no Brasil* (1923).

[Martin A. Cohen]

NORSA, HANNAH (d. 1784), English actress. The daughter of an Italian Jew from Mantua, who kept The Punch-Bowl tavern in Drury Lane, she went onto the stage and played the part of Polly Peachum in the 1732 production of *The Beggar's Opera* with great success. She subsequently became mistress of the Earl of Orford. Her sister Maria, mistress of the latter's brother, Sir Edward Walpole, is believed to have been the mother of Maria, countess of Waldegrave, whose second husband was the duke of Gloucester, brother of King George III.

ADD. BIBLIOGRAPHY: ODNB online.

NORTHAMPTON, town in central England. Its Jewish community, first mentioned in the 12th century, was one of the most important in medieval England. In 1194 representatives of Anglo-Jewry were summoned there to apportion among themselves a levy of 5,000 marks for ransoming Richard I from captivity (The Northampton Donum). Northampton had its own *archa. Though expelled from Northamptonshire in 1237, Jews were allowed to remain in Northampton itself. In 1263 they were attacked by the baronial rebels and took refuge in the castle. A ritual murder accusation occurred apparently in 1277, the repercussions and consequences of which were much exaggerated by historians. Several local Jews were executed in London in 1278 for coin-clipping. The community continued in existence until the expulsion of 1290. R. Isaac b. Perez of Northampton was one of the most distinguished medieval Anglo-Jewish scholars. A small community was established at the end of the 19th century and in 1969 numbered approximately 300. In the 2001 British census, its population of declared Jews was 322. There was an Orthodox congregation.

BIBLIOGRAPHY: I. Abrahams, in: JHSEM, 1 (1925), lix–lxxiv; A.J. Collins, in: JHSET, 15 (1946), 151–64; Roth, England, index. **ADD. BIBLIOGRAPHY:** M. Jolles, *The Northampton Jewish Cemetery* (1994); idem, *A Short History of the Jews of Northampton, 1159–1996* (1996); idem, "The Presence of Jews in Northamptonshire," in: *Northamptonshire Past and Present*, vol. 57 (2004);

[Cecil Roth]

NORTH CAROLINA, state in S.E. U.S. Its population in 2000 was 8,049,313, of which the Jewish population was estimated at 26,500. Jews appeared in early colonial times, but a community did not develop until the late antebellum era, a trend that accelerated after Reconstruction with the rise of an urban and industrial New South. In the later 20th century, as the state transformed from an agrarian, southern society into the prosperous, multicultural Sunbelt, Jewish population grew dramatically.

North Carolina was the site of the first Jewish settler in a British colony in North America when Joachim Ganz, a native of Prague, arrived in 1585, well before the much heralded date of the 1654 settlement in New Amsterdam, on Raleigh's second expedition to Roanoke Island. Ganz, a metallurgist, returned to England two years later. John Locke's Fundamental Constitutions of 1669 opened the Carolinas to "Jews, heathens, and other dissenters," but the colony, beset by sectarian politics, was inhospitable. The 1776 state constitution included a religious test that restricted public office to Protestants. With few navigable rivers, a swampy coast, and a forested terrain, North Carolina lacked commercial opportunities for Jews.

In the early colonial era a few Jewish settlers followed coastal and inland trade routes from Virginia and South Carolina. A 1702 petition protested illegal votes by undesirables, including Jews. Jewish names appear on Masonic rolls and militia rosters. In the Charlotte area were storekeepers and Revolutionary War veterans Abraham Moses, Solomon Simons, and Aaron Cohen. A 1759 document identifies Joseph Laney as a Jew. Newport merchant Aaron Lopez sent 37 ships to North Carolina between 1761 and 1775. Eighteenth-century Sephardic Jews in Wilmington included Rivera, Gomez, David, and Levy. A rabbi, Jacob Abroo, is reported to have died in New Berne in 1790. The Benjamin family, whose son Judah became a U.S. senator and later a Confederate statesman, lived in Wilmington and Fayetteville after 1813.

The most notable family was the Mordecais who settled in Warrenton in 1792, and in 1808 opened the Warrenton Female Seminary, which pioneered the liberal education of women. Jacob *Mordecai was a Hebrew scholar who later served as lay leader of Richmond's Beth Shalome. His daughter Rachel, married to the Wilmington merchant Aaron Lazarus, was a literary figure, and his son Alfred graduated from West Point in 1823. Mordecai children, including George Washington Mordecai, a railroad builder who served as president of the Bank of North Carolina, largely assimilated into the Christian community.

In 1808 Jacob *Henry of Beaufort was elected to the state legislature, but a year later his constitutional right to serve as a Jew was challenged. After an impassioned speech, Henry was permitted to hold his seat, but the legislature reaffirmed the religious test repeatedly, and it was not removed until 1868. German Jews immigrated after 1835 when the state reformed its constitution and embarked on internal improvements. Jews from Norfolk, Baltimore, Charleston, and Richmond settled in coastal ports and market towns along rivers and rail lines.

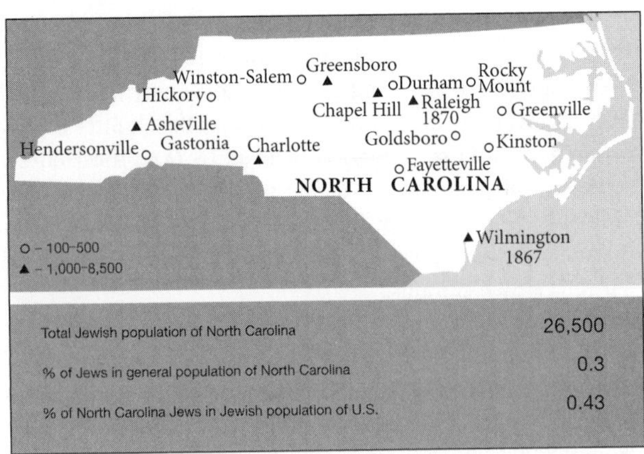

Jewish communities in North Carolina and dates of establishment. Population figures for 2001.

Peddlers, like the Bloomingdale brothers, worked the countryside before opening stores. In the 1850s Lazarus Fels operated a peddler's way station in Yanceyville. In 1858 Herman Weil arrived in Goldsboro, later joined by his brothers, and the family over generations organized the state's Jewry. By 1850 Charlotte had nine Jewish families, and Wilmington claimed 26 Jewish merchants. By 1852 Wilmington supported a burial society, and an Orthodox congregation formed in 1867, which was supplanted by a Reform one in 1872.

When Civil War came, the state's Jews were ardent Confederates. More than 70 Jews served in North Carolina regiments, including six Cohen brothers. Civil War Governor Zebulon Vance, grateful to a courtesy from the merchant Samuel Wittkowsky at war's end, penned a celebrated philo-Semitic speech, "The Scattered Nation," which was delivered and reprinted repeatedly across the South.

As the textile, furniture, and tobacco industries expanded in the New South era, Jews found opportunity in emerging mill and market towns. By 1878, 16 North Carolina towns reported Jews, and the population center began moving from the coastal plain to the piedmont. Country peddlers and urban storekeepers served both a black and a white clientele. Rail lines linked merchants to distribution centers in Baltimore and New York. In 1871 the Wallace brothers of Statesville created the country's largest herbarium. Samuel Wittkowsky, as president of the Board of Trade and founder of the South's first savings and loan, underwrote much of Charlotte's development. In 1895, Moses and Ceasar Cone, traveling agents for the family's Baltimore commercial house, built their first textile factory in Greensboro, and, joined by partners Herman and Emmanuel Sternberger, Cone Mills ranked among the world's largest producers of denim, flannel, and corduroy. In the 1880s Tarboro had 11 Jewish stores and supported a congregation, a B'nai B'rith lodge, a YMHA, and a Jewish Literary Society; in 1885 Henry Morris was mayor. The first synagogue, Temple of Israel, was erected in Wilmington in 1875, followed by Oheb Sholom in Goldsboro (1886) and Temple Emanuel in Statesville (1892). All evolved to Reform. By 1900 congregations could also be found in Asheville, Durham, Lumberton, New Bern, Raleigh, and Winston-Salem. Typically, they accommodated both Reform and Orthodox worship until Jewish population grew sufficiently to form separate congregations.

With an increasing East European immigration, the 820 Jews of 1878 grew to 8,252 by 1927, and congregations increased from one to 22. In the early 1880s J.B. Duke imported more than 100 Jewish immigrants to roll cigarettes in his Durham factory. Jews arrived in family chains, a pioneer drawing relatives and landsleit. Like the Germans before them, they often peddled before opening stores, and they maintained an ethnic economy, mostly in dry goods. The Baltimore Bargain House financed and supplied young immigrants and directed them to towns across the state. In 1929, 53 percent of the state's Jewry was rural. Upward mobility was rapid. Moses Richter of Charlotte earned the title of Peach King for his marketing. William Heilig and Joseph Max Meyers, two Latvian immigrants, expanded their Goldsboro store into the nation's largest furniture chain.

During World War II, Jews headed to North Carolina to serve in military bases and to provide commercial services in camp towns. North Carolina welcomed émigrés from Nazi Europe. The Van Eeden colony, a dairy and agricultural collective on the coastal plain, housed refugee families from the 1930s to 1949. The state's universities offered havens to European scholars. Duke University gave sanctuary to German psychologist Louis *Stern, physicist Fritz *London, and Polish law professor Raphael *Lemkin, author of the Genocide Convention, who coined the very word genocide. In 1981 the state created the North Carolina Council on the Holocaust.

North Carolina's Jews have been notable for their philanthropies and public service. Moses Cone Memorial Hospital in Greensboro was created by a family endowment, and the Brody School of Medicine at East Carolina University in Greenville was named for a local family. The Blumenthals of Charlotte supported the arts, health care, and Jewish causes including the interfaith retreat, Wildacres, and the Jewish Home for the Aged in Clemmons. In 1954 I.D. Blumenthal created a unique Circuit Riding Rabbi program, with a bus outfitted as a synagogue, to serve rural communities. Leon Levine of Charlotte, who created a national network of Family Dollar Stores, has endowed museums, universities, and Jewish facilities. Prominent Jews include Gertrude Weil of Goldsboro, a suffragette leader, who was a tireless advocate for social and racial justice as well as for Jewish and Zionist causes. In 1918 Lionel Weil organized a statewide campaign for the Jewish War Sufferers Fund, and his North Carolina Plan became a national model. Jews have served in the state legislature. Charlotte's Harry *Golden published the *North Carolina Israelite*, which was outspoken in its advocacy of liberalism and civil rights. In 1955 the North Carolina Association of Rabbis passed a resolution calling for rapid integration of the public schools, a stand that they reiterated a year later when the governor called for voluntary segregation.

Solomon Fishblate was elected to his first term as Wilmington mayor in 1878. Jews have also been elected mayors of Chapel Hill, Durham, Fayetteville, Gastonia, Greensboro, Hendersonville, Holly Ridge, Lumberton, Morganton, Tarboro, and Wilmington. E.J. Evans served six terms as mayor of Durham, 1951–1963. Numerous Jews have served in the state legislature.

The success and social acceptance of Jews contrasts with a latent antisemitism that turned occasionally violent. In 1909 a new immigrant to Charlotte, Max Kahn, was murdered, and in 1925 a salesman, Joseph Needleman, was castrated outside Williamston by a mob after he allegedly affronted a woman. In the civil-rights era bombs were planted at synagogues in Gastonia and Charlotte. Jews were generally not accepted into social elites, and the Pinehurst golfing resort maintained antisemitic housing codes. In 1933 University of North Carolina president Frank Graham forced the resignation of the medical-school dean who refused to end a Jewish quota.

North Carolina's Jews maintained communal ties through a network of B'nai B'rith Lodges, Hadassah, and National Council of Jewish Women chapters. The North Carolina Association of Jewish Women, founded by Sarah Weil in 1921, was a nationally unique organization that united communities across ethnic, denominational, and geographical divides. In the 1950s the Jews of High Point sponsored a statewide debutante cotillion. The mountains were home to Jewish summer camps, most notably Blue Star in Hendersonville. Jewish federations, linked to the United Jewish Communities, formed in the Charlotte, Greensboro, Raleigh, and Durham-Chapel Hill areas.

The Sunbelt has welcomed the Jewish doctor, scientist, retiree, and entrepreneur just as the New South welcomed Jewish peddlers, merchants, and industrialists. North Carolina benefited from national demographic trends, which saw Jewish population shift southward. Jewish communities in Charlotte, Wilmington, the Research Triangle (Raleigh-Durham-Chapel Hill), and the Triad (Greensboro-High Point-Winston-Salem) on the high-tech interstate corridor grow while small-town, agrarian communities like Tarboro, Weldon, and Wilson wane or expire. Coastal and mountain resort communities have drawn Jewish retirees. With the breakdown of academic barriers, college towns also have grown dramatically. Jewish studies programs flourish at Duke University, which in 1943 had become the first southern university to establish such a program, and at the University of North Carolina campuses in Asheville, Chapel Hill, and Charlotte. Highlighting the professional migration, Gertrude Elion and Martin Rodbell won Nobel Prizes while working at the Research Triangle Park.

With rapid Jewish population growth, the number of havurot and congregations has grown to more than 40 by 2005. Greensboro is the site of the American Hebrew Academy, a pluralistic boarding school with a global outreach. Charlotte supports the Shalom Park campus that includes a day school, federation headquarters, library, community center, and Reform and Conservative congregations. Lubavitcher Ḥasidim lead congregations in four communities. New or expanded synagogues are arising in all the state's Sunbelt metropolitan areas even as historical Jewish enclaves in mill and market towns struggle to survive.

BIBLIOGRAPHY: E. Bingham, *Mordecai: An Early American Family* (2003); E. Evans, *The Provincials: A Personal History of Jews in the South* (2005); H. Golden, "The Jewish People of North Carolina," in: *North Carolina Historical Review* (April, 1955); L. Rogoff, "Synagogue and Jewish Church: A Congregational History of North Carolina," in: *Southern Jewish History* (1998).

[Leonard W. Rogoff (2nd ed.)]

NORTH DAKOTA, state located in the upper Midwestern part of the U.S. The total population (2004) of 634,366, includes fewer than 500 Jews.

History

At least 800 Jewish individuals filed for land between 1880 and 1916. They generally settled in clusters. Many were aided by the Jewish Agricultural and Industrial Aid Society. In addition several of the earliest settlements, Painted Woods and Devils Lake, were aided by synagogues located in Minnesota's Twin Cities. Homesteaders endured great hardships such as plagues of grasshoppers, prairie fires, blizzards and drought. Most left after acquiring full land title (generally five years). A number settled in market towns along the two railroads that crossed the state and where they operated general stores.

By 1889 the country's growing railroad industry lured people to the eastern community of Grand Forks. A permanent congregation was established in 1892. It was from the pulpit of B'nai Israel Synagogue that President William McKinley urged the Jews to participate in the war with Spain. The city of Fargo also grew near the turn of the century and by 1896 a synagogue was chartered there. The Jews of North Dakota are engaged mainly in retailing. A few, such as Fargo Mayor Herschel Lashkowitz, and Federal Judge Myron Bright, distinguished themselves in politics.

Jews also settled in larger towns such as Fargo, Grand Forks, Bismarck, and Minot where they established synagogues and other elements of Jewish communal life. They have also been included in civic life. One rabbi in particular deserves mention: Benjamin Papermaster was sent to North Dakota by the Chief Rabbi of the Kovno Yeshiva, serving in

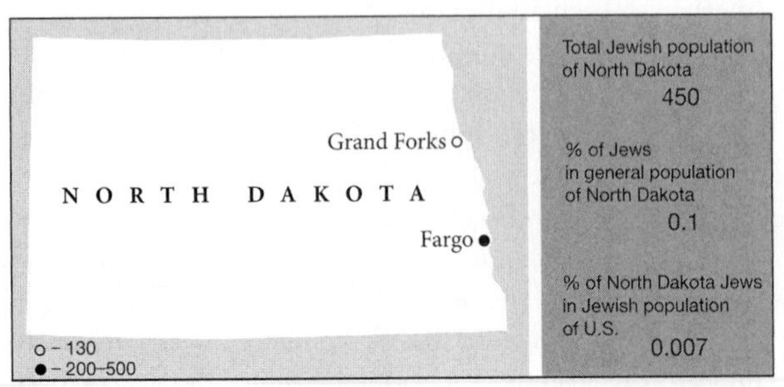

Jewish communities in North Dakota. Population figures for 2001.

Grand Forks from 1891 to 1934. He was also the circuit-riding rabbi for the state, circumcising babies, officiating at weddings and funerals, and even slaughtering cattle. Today, Fargo and Grand Forks rely on student rabbis. In the 1960s the Jewish population of Fargo was some 500 people; it has declined as young people leave and do not return.

BIBLIOGRAPHY: W. Sherman, "The Jews," in: *Plains Folk: North Dakota's Ethnic History.*

[Linda M. Schlof (2nd ed.)]

NORWALK AND WESTPORT, U.S. towns in southeast Connecticut on Long Island Sound, which are joined together with Wilton in a federation. The Jewish population of the communities in 2005 is an estimated 11,500. As early as 1760 there was a small Jewish community in Norwalk. Michael Judah is mentioned in the Connecticut historical annals of that period, and David Judah was a soldier in the Connecticut Line in 1776. In 1776 Norwalk received an influx of Jews from New York, mainly from Congregation Shearith Israel, who were fleeing the British. In 1777 Jews were among the signatories to a petition asking for a patrol vessel for the Norwalk shore. The early community came to an end when Norwalk was burned down by the British in 1779. It was rebuilt in the 1870s by Eastern European immigrants, who were merchants and storekeepers. After 1925 more Jewish families from New York moved to Norwalk, and after World War II many more Jewish families moved to Norwalk in the general move to suburbia and in response to the development of Norwalk as an electronics and engineering center.

Beth Israel Congregation, Orthodox, founded in 1906, was the first synagogue in Norwalk and remained the only one until 1934, when Temple Beth El, Conservative, was organized. The Reform Temple Shalom was formed in 1957. Shortly after World War I, a Young Men's Hebrew Association was founded; it later became the Jewish Community Center. Norwalk has a communal Hebrew school. The United Jewish Appeal drives are sponsored by the Jewish Community Council, formed shortly after World War II to coordinate the efforts of local organizations and fund-raising campaigns.

Participation in community life is extensive. About two-thirds of the Jewish families of Norwalk are affiliated with at least one synagogue; almost 40 percent of the Jewish families belong to the Norwalk Jewish Center; and two-thirds of the adult Jews of Norwalk contribute to the Federated United Appeal Drive. Small Jewish populations in Wilton, Weston, Darien, and Georgetown also participate in Westport and Norwalk's Jewish communal life.

Prominent members of the Jewish community have included Harry Becker, who was superintendent of schools 1952–70; Malcolm Tarlov, the 1967 national president of the Jewish War Veterans; Charles Salesky, who was president of the Hat Corporation of America; and Jack Rudolph, state senator in 1970. Several chairmen of the Board of Education have been Jewish as well. As in most of the United States, most barriers have fallen. There is little discrimination. Employment appears free of anti-Jewish discrimination, but there is still a sense of distinction, though not outright discrimination, in upper-class social clubs.

There are ten synagogues within these towns, which often are joined for Jewish communal activities. Beth Israel Synagogue of Westport/Norwalk, Adat Torah Conservative Congregation, and Beit Chaverim Synagogue of Westport/Norwalk use both towns in their name. Chabad has come to Westport and runs the only Jewish day camp in the towns. There is also a Congregation for Humanistic Judaism in Westport, in which God is not part of the service. Westport itself has a Conservative Synagogue, which is called The Conservative Synagogue of Westport, and a Reform synagogue, Temple Israel, while neighboring Georgetown is the home of Temple B'nai Chaim. There is also a conservative congregation in Wilton, Adat Torah.

The Federation provides all the usual services of a local federation including Family Services and a Home for the Elderly. In addition, it sponsors Kesher, a program for Jewish developmentally challenged adults, which meets to celebrate Jewish holidays with discussion, music and refreshments and Positive Directions (formerly Alcohol and Drug Council), which works with the local Jewish Family Service to offer a 12-step program for Jews in recovery. It belies the myth that Jews don't have these problems.

Many of the Jews are professionals. Some work locally and many commute to neighboring New York City as part of the seamless suburbs of New York in which the Jewish community stretches from the City through Fairfield County and beyond.

[Michael Berenbaum (2nd ed.)]

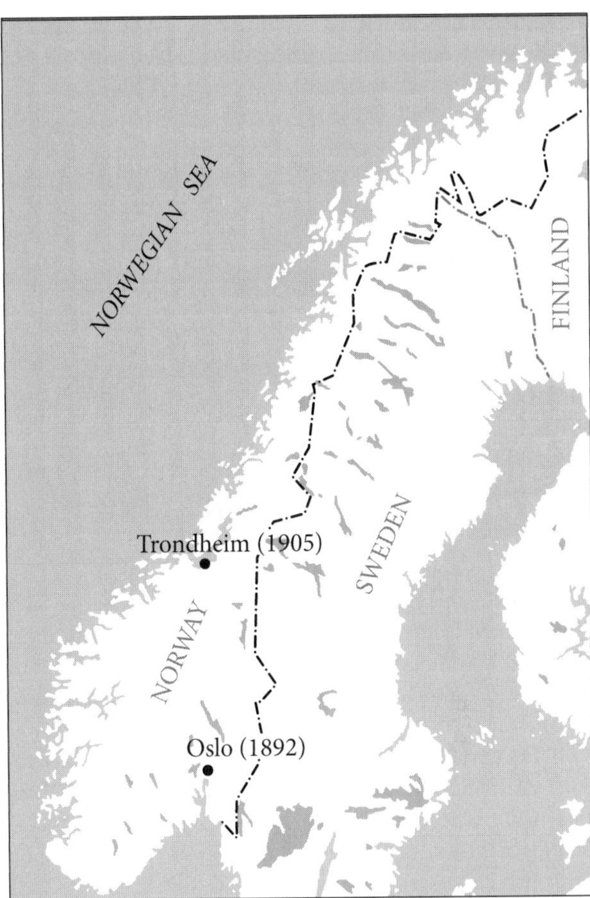

Jewish communities in Norway and dates of establishment.

NORWAY, kingdom in N. Europe. Throughout the 17th and 18th centuries, when Norway and *Denmark were united, most general regulations concerning the Jews of Denmark also applied in Norway. However, according to the Norwegian Legal Code promulgated by King Christian v in 1687 the Jews were barred from admission to Norway without a letter of safe-conduct; without this, a Jew risked arrest, fines, and deportation. As a result of this measure the special regulations allowing free access to the so-called "Portuguese" Jews (issued by the Danish crown in 1657, renewed in 1670, 1684, and 1750) were not consistently adhered to by the Norwegian authorities. An incident which took place in 1734 became notorious: three Dutch "Portuguese" Jews were arrested on their arrival in the country and spent two months in prison. In the 17th and 18th centuries, few Jews stayed in Norway, usually only temporarily, though some Jews in other countries had business connections there, such as Manuel Teixeira from Hamburg who was co-owner of some Norwegian mines. In 1814 Norway became free of the union with Denmark and a Norwegian constitution was produced. Despite the liberal tenor of the Norwegian constitution of 1814, Article Two – stating that Lutheran Protestantism is the official state religion in which all Lutheran children must be brought up – confirmed the exclusion of Jews and Jesuits from Norway; this was strictly enforced. A new union was immediately formed with Sweden. At first this did not interfere with Norwegian politics, but from 1884 the Swedes decided to take an active part in Norway's foreign affairs. This union lasted until 1905. In 1817 a shipwrecked Jew was thrown into jail and then deported. In the 1830s, however, a more liberal spirit gradually emerged. The government issued letters of safe conduct from time to time; one was given to Heinrich *Heine's uncle, Solomon *Heine, who was instrumental in the granting of a loan to the Norwegian state by the Copenhagen banking house of Hambro and Son. In 1844 the Ministry of Justice confirmed the free immigration rights of "Portuguese" Jews. The repeal of the ban on Jewish settlement was largely the result of the efforts of writer Henrik *Wergeland. In 1839 he submitted his first proposal to the Storting, the Norwegian parliament, accompanying his proposal with a lengthy memorandum and publishing his essay on the Jewish question, *Indlaeg i Jødensagen* (1841). This was followed by numerous articles in the press, several of them by Wergeland himself. In 1842 a committee on the constitution dealing with the problem made a notable proposal in which it was stated that the right to free immigration was an international one. The motion to give the Jews free access received a simple majority, i.e., more than 50% of the vote, in 1842, 1845, and 1848, but did not obtain the requisite two-thirds majority until 1851. In that year 93 votes were cast in favor of admitting the Jews with full civil rights, with ten votes against.

The First Communities

The first Jew settled in the country in 1852 and for many years he remained the only representative of his faith; in 1875 only 25 Jews had their permanent residence in Norway. After 1880 immigration increased considerably, and Eastern European Jews gradually became most numerous. In 1890 there were 214 Jews in Norway; ten years later there were 642, most of them in *Oslo, the capital, and in Trondheim. The oldest communities, called "The Mosaic Congregation" (Det Mosaiske Trossamfund), were founded in Oslo in 1892 and in Trondheim in 1905; both congregations are still in existence. (See Map: Jews in Norway). Land for a cemetery was bought in Oslo as early as 1869, and the first burial took place in 1885. For some years there were as many as four congregations in the capital, but only two continued to exist for any length of time. In the 1920s and 1930s, a Jewish orphanage and home for the aged was founded. The census of 1920 recorded 1,457 Jews, of whom 852 lived in the capital. This was the highest number of Jews recorded prior to World War II. In 1930 there were 1,359 Jews in Norway, with 749 resident in Oslo.

In the years before and during World War I, young people's associations, women's groups, Zionist associations and charitable societies were established in Oslo and Trondheim. In the 1930s there were several Jewish theater societies, a choir and other cultural societies, a Norwegian Jewish Youth Society (JUF) that expanded into a Scandinavian Jewish Youth Society (SJUF) as well as an academic society. Two Jewish periodicals were published, *Israelitten* from 1911 to 1927 and *Hatikwoh* from 1929 to 1938. The two synagogue buildings in Oslo and Trondheim, both still in use today, were consecrated in 1920 and 1925 respectively. The second synagogue in Oslo, dedicated in 1921, has not been in use since World War II. (This building was converted into a Jewish museum that opened to the public in 2006.) For many years most Norwegian Jews engaged in trade; gradually they also moved into industry and some entered the professions. Between 1930 and 1940 immigration was comparatively slight.

It is possible to trace the rise of antisemitism in the Norwegian press during World War I and preceding World War II. In the 1930s anti-Jewish race theories were advocated by the Norwegian police, politicians, and press.

Holocaust Period

In 1941–42 the Jewish population of Norway consisted of approximately 1,000 households, numbering a total of 2,173 individuals living mainly in Oslo and Trondheim, but also thinly spread out in other parts of the country. Among these individuals 530 were Jewish refugees from the European continent and were not Norwegian citizens. About 1,800 were registered in the various communities. The number of Jewish refugees was relatively low, Norway being even more restrictive than Denmark and Sweden in the admission of Jewish refugees.

The Jews of Norway were hard-hit during the German occupation in World War II (April 1940–May 1945). Already in October 1940 Jews were prohibited to engage in academic and other professions. In some regions the actual persecution of the Jews began in 1941, but only in the fall of 1942 did it become countrywide. In two raids, on October 25 for all men over 16 and on November 25 for women and children, 767 Jews were seized and shipped via Stettin to *Auschwitz. About 930 Jewish inhabitants succeeded in fleeing to Sweden, while about 60 others were interned in Norway proper. A very small number of Jews managed to remain in hiding, in hospitals, sanatoria or in the Jewish old-age home. Quite a large percentage of Norwegian Jewish men who had managed to escape joined the Norwegian army encampments in Sweden or England and fought with the allied forces throughout the war. Victims of the war, 60% of whom were men (two-thirds of whom were citizens of Norway), totaled 758. Twenty persons perished either through acts of war or were shot in Norway. Of those deported 740 were murdered in extermination camps and only 29 survived. The Germans inflicted heavy damage on the synagogue in Trondheim, and planned to obliterate the Jewish cemetery there. The physical persecution of the Jews by the Germans was facilitated by orders given by *Quisling's government for the forced registration of all Jews (June 1942) and the confiscation of all Jewish property (October 1942). The final arrest was carried out by Norwegian police officers carrying out orders issued by the Nazis. The bishops of Norway sent a protest letter on Nov. 11, 1942 to Quisling. It was also signed by the other Protestant churches of Norway. The letter, in denunciation of the illegal acts, states: "God does not differentiate among people… Since the Lutheran religion is the state religion, the state cannot enact any law or decree which is in conflict with the Christian faith or the Church's confession." The letter was read from the pulpit on Dec. 6 and 13, 1942 and was quoted in the 1943 New Year message. Many Norwegians, with the guidance of the Underground movement, did their utmost to help Jews escape to Sweden, often at the risk of their own lives.

[Leni Yahil / Lynn Claire Feinberg (2nd ed.)]

1945–1970

Most of the survivors of the Holocaust returned to Norway from Sweden after the war. Owing to the liquidation of Jewish property during WWII, most returned to homes that were emptied of all contents or valuables or homes occupied by Norwegians. The same was true of formerly Jewish-owned businesses. Miraculously, one of the synagogues in Oslo, including its Torah scrolls and contents, was untouched. The building had been used to store Nazi literature and property from Jewish homes that the Nazis had confiscated.

The Norwegian government was eager to demonstrate the sympathy of the Norwegian people toward the suffering Jewish people. About 400 Jewish DPs came to Norway in 1947, but many left a while later for North America or Israel. With the abolition of the DP camps in Germany in the 1950s, Norway accepted several scores of "hardcore" cases. By the mid-1950s the Jewish population reached close to 1,000 souls, of whom over 700 resided in Oslo, about 150 in Trondheim, and the rest were scattered throughout the country.

The communities in Oslo and Trondheim were reconstituted: Orthodox services were conducted in the synagogues; a home for the aged that had been in use before the war continued to exist for a few years after the war in Oslo; social work, supported by the American Jewish *Joint Distribution Committee and the Conference on Jewish Material *Claims, was expanded; a *B'nai B'rith lodge was established in Oslo in 1952; a community center was opened in Oslo in 1960; the small community participated in all activities in support of Israel. Rabbi Zalman Aronzon was rabbi of Oslo from 1949 to 1958 and was head of the community's religious instruction. Rabbi Aronzon introduced a bat mitzvah ceremony for girls at the end of their religious instruction. At this time approximately 80 school-age children received regular religious instruction in Oslo and Trondheim; In addition to weekly religious instruction, many children also attended Bnei Akiva, a Zionist youth organization arranging gatherings of a more social nature and summer camps with children from the other Scandinavian countries as well as trips to Israel. During the 1950s and 1960s the Norwegian government, the Church, and all political parties were actively engaged in eradicating antisemitism. Pro-Israel sentiment was very strong and found expression in many actions.

[Chaim Yahil / Lynn Claire Feinberg (2nd ed.)]

1970–2005

POPULATION. The total number of Jews in Norway in 1981 was estimated at 1,100 (0.027% of the total population). In 1992 the number of Jews in Norway was about 1,300–1,400, of which 200–300 were Israelis. More than 1,000 people (including children) were members of the Jewish congregations in the two Jewish communities in Norway: about 900 in Oslo and 135 in Trondheim. This number remained relatively stable throughout the 1990s. There has been a distinct aging process throughout the period with a high percentage of community members older than 65, which explains why there has been a relatively high rate of deaths in proportion to births since the WWII.

Over the years, a small but steady stream of Norwegians have converted to Judaism. There is general tendency among younger members to study and live in places abroad such as Israel, where there are more Jews, and not to return. The number of members of the Oslo Jewish community has traditionally stabilized around the 900 mark but in 2004 there were only about 800 members and in Trondheim only about 100 members. Quite a large percentage of Norwegian-born community members have spouses who are non-Jewish or who have converted. Due to many marriages among Scandinavian Jews, several community members were born in Sweden, Denmark, or Finland. There are also several members who come from other countries.

COMMUNITY. During the late 1970s and 1980s the Jewish community's activities expanded in Oslo. Starting in the 1970s there was a gradual increase in Norwegian school children and other groups visiting the synagogues and learning about Judaism and the fate of the Jews during World War II. Several seminars on Jewish subjects were arranged at the universities of Oslo and Trondheim with Jewish and non-Jewish lecturers. In 1976 Kai Feinberg (1921–1995) became the head of the community, succeeding Harry M. Koritzinsky (1900–1989), who had held this post since 1946. In September 1980 Michael *Melchior (1954–), son of Rabbi Bent Melchior, chief rabbi of Denmark, was inaugurated as rabbi in Oslo by his father after completing his rabbinical studies in Israel. Among those present were representatives of the Lutheran and Catholic Churches, universities, and state and municipal authorities. The community had existed without a rabbi for most of the years following World War II.

In Trondheim religious school instruction recommenced after a break of some years owing to the lack of Jewish children aged 8–13. The community, which celebrated its 75th anniversary in May 1980, had no cantor, and services and religious education were conducted by the community leader.

Moshe Dayan, when foreign minister of Israel, visited Oslo in May 1978, as did his successor Yitzhak Shamir in November 1980. The Jewish community arranged a dinner in the community center for Prime Minister Menaḥem Begin when he received the Nobel Peace Prize in Oslo in 1978.

With Rabbi Michael Melchior the Oslo community experienced a renaissance. Melchior helped make Judaism more visible to the Norwegian public at large and was often cited in newspapers and appeared on national TV. One of his first accomplishments was to open the Jewish kindergarten in Oslo in 1981. The kindergarten received some financial support from the city and soon became an important entry point for Jewish children and their parents into active participation in community life. In 2005 the kindergarten celebrated its 25th anniversary. In collaboration with the synagogue cantor, an Israeli, a children's choir was formed and many new melodies were introduced at the Sabbath morning services encouraging greater participation. Services were followed by a *kiddush*, with refreshments in the community center, also a novelty at this time. This event has since become the weekly meeting place for community members and guests. As a result of Melchior's involvement in the community the frequency of people participating in the Sabbath morning service in Oslo increased. Other services apart from Rosh Ha-Shanah and Yom Kippur were not as well attended. In Trondheim the membership was too small to arrange morning services on Saturday. Services were usually held on Friday afternoons, on Rosh ha-Shanah, Yom Kippur, and some of the other festivals. For many years the service was conducted by the community chairman and superintendent Jacob Kommisar (1922–1995). In recent years the Trondheim community has started holding Friday evening services every two weeks, conducted by one of the community members, often in conjunction with a communal meal. This is in addition to High Holiday services.

With Rabbi Melchior, religious school education was greatly improved; in Oslo in the 1990s the religious afternoon school was taught by the cantor and some community members. There were about 70 pupils in Oslo in the 1990s aged 7–16, and this figure has remained quite stable since. For a number of years, a young member of the Oslo community visited Trondheim every two or three weeks to teach. In recent years several of the teachers at the Trondheim weekly religious school have been recruited from Jewish youth born and raised in Oslo and currently studying at the University of Trondheim. Trondheim also offers weekly religious education for pre-school children.

Beginning in the 1980s, in addition to the ordinary religious school lessons, weekend gatherings (also for the children in the kindergarten) have been arranged once or twice a year in the community vacation home 12 miles (20 km) from Oslo. At regular intervals the community invites children and their parents to spend a weekend at a hotel some 50 miles (80 km) from Oslo and celebrate a full Sabbath. Community members from Trondheim have also participated in these events. The annual summer camps have also been attended by Jewish children from other places in Norway. Bnei Akiva continues to engage members from the ages of 7–18 with weekly gatherings, inter-Scandinavian activities, and trips to Israel.

Twenty apartments for the elderly, partly subsidized by the city of Oslo, were built alongside the synagogue and inaugurated in 1988. A new wing was later added to this building, providing a place for elderly Jews who are too poor to take care of themselves.

The *Jodisk Menighetsblad*, the Jewish community journal, edited by Oskar Mendelsohn, 1976–1991, was succeeded in 1992 by a new publication, *Hatikwa*, which is issued four times a year.

In June 1992 the Oslo Jewish community marked its centenary with various celebrations, seminars and public lectures, while the religious school arranged a walk to and over the Swedish border along one of the fall 1942 escape routes. There was also an exhibition showing the religious holidays and a survey of important events from the past 100 years, which attracted more than 5,000 schoolchildren, and for which a special publication was printed. Jewish children published a paper about Jews in Norway which was distributed to schools. The community published a 230-page jubilee book.

The jubilee, held on June 14, started with a ceremony in the Jewish cemetery at the memorial for Jewish victims of World War II. This was followed by a festive service in the synagogue in the presence of Norwegian authorities and representatives of the other Scandinavian Jewish communities that was broadcast on Norwegian television. Rabbi Michael Melchior spoke and the cantor, the synagogue choir, and Cantor Joseph Malovany of New York conducted the service. There was also a festive concert at which the Norwegian king and queen were present. Rabbi Melchior was honored in 1993 with the Bridgebuilder Prize by the joint council of the Norwegian Church academies. He was granted this award for his significant efforts toward creating a dialogue and building bridges between people of different groups and backgrounds with the aim of counteracting the influence of hatemongers.

In Norway kosher slaughter was made illegal in the 1930s. The community has therefore had to import kosher meat ever since. In 1986 the first shop to sell frozen kosher meat and various kosher food products was opened; until then kosher meat had been sold at appointed times in the community center.

Since 1991 kosher meat has been imported from the U.S. and other kosher foods from Denmark and Israel. In more recent years kosher goods have been imported from Israel and European countries. The import of kosher meat and especially chicken is regularly an issue of concern, due to Norway's strict regulations on the import of agricultural products. The community rabbi has given several Norwegian food products a kosher certificate. The community regularly provides an updated list of kosher products obtainable in Norway.

For a few years starting in 1988, the Oslo community's leadership was divided between the head of the board (administration) and the superintendent of religious affairs. In 2005 Anne Sender was elected the first woman to head the community. Rabbi Michael Melchior, who settled in Israel in 1986, remained the religious leader of the community, spending about four months a year in Oslo until 1999. Since then he has been the chief rabbi of Norway. From 1999 to 2003 the community hired Rabbi Jason Rappoport from England and in 2003 he was replaced by Rabbi Jitzhak Rapoport from Sweden. Over the years the community has had several Israeli cantors serving for an average of two or three years doing service abroad. Services are also conducted by a young Danish Jew who has settled in Oslo and occasionally by local young men from the community.

Antisemitism and Anti-Zionism

There was more evidence of antisemitism during the 1970s and after than in the first decades after World War II, often taking the form of increased anti-Zionism. In January 1979 the synagogue in Oslo was vandalized with swastikas and anti-Jewish slogans in Norwegian and German (*Juden raus!*). The police did not succeed in finding the perpetrators. In autumn 1977 the country's bishops urged a clear and fearless attitude against all forms of antisemitism and aggressive anti-Zionism.

In the 1980s there were numerous articles in the press relating to Israel. Anti-Zionism was on the increase, primarily among political leftists. Pro-Palestinian attitudes, however, were also reflected in youth organizations of the Labor Party and some of the center parties as well as in some trade unions. On the other hand, there were many pro-Israeli articles. In the 1990s there was a tendency to connect anti-Israel and anti-Zionist sentiments with antisemitic statements. The Norwegian press has been increasingly critical of the policy of the State of Israel and many journalists have shown growing sympathy for and bias towards the Palestinians. Many Norwegian

Jews have in later years experienced an increase in antisemitic tendencies, in the guise of anti-Zionist or anti-Israel views. On several occasions newspaper headlines and caricatures have described the Israelis as Jewish aggressors in the Nazi mold. In 2003 the Norwegian head of the Labor Union urged Norwegian shops to stop buying goods from Israel. Several threats have been directed at the Jewish communities.

Renewed Interest in the Holocaust

With a new generation of historians in the 1970s, renewed interest in the Jews and their World War II fate started to emerge. At this time there was a focus on the emergence of Norwegian neo-Nazi youth gangs and ways of taking preventive measures. Many concentration camp survivors began to tell their stories for the first time. "This Concerns You," an account from Auschwitz by Herman Sachnowitz, a Norwegian Jew, was published in 1976 and sold more than 160,000 copies in Norwegian. This was the first of several such accounts written by Norwegian Jewish survivors. In 1978 the television series *Holocaust* led to a whole series of questions related to the fate of the Jews of Norway during the war. Another series about how people were helped to flee to Sweden, among them the nation's Jews, was also aired. One of the questions raised was why persecution of the Jews had received such scant attention in the teaching of history, another related to the complicity of the Church throughout the ages. The *Holocaust* series was succeeded by many information programs on radio and television about events and persecution during the war, including interviews of several of the Norwegian Jewish survivors. Interest was revived in the diary of Anne *Frank. In March 1978 three of the people most active in the resistance movement during the war in helping to rescue Jews were invited by the Jewish community in Oslo to spend a week in Israel and to plant a tree in the Avenue of the Righteous on Har ha-Zikkaron. Several other people who helped Jews during the war have over the years been honored as Righteous Among the Nations by Yad Vashem.

In 1992 the Hvite Busser organization ("White Buses") was formed by Norwegian concentration camp survivors. Their aim has been to arrange field trips to Auschwitz for teenage schoolchildren in order to teach about antisemitism and the Holocaust. Accompanying the groups is a first-hand witness, a Norwegian who survived a concentration camp, and a few of the witnesses are also Jewish. At the 50th anniversary of the end of World War II in 1995, several television programs and films appeared showing interviews with Jewish and non-Jewish Norwegian concentration camp survivors and members of the resistance. There were also several books written by Norwegians depicting the fate of the Jews and putting the role of the Norwegians during WW II in a new light. With the passing of the legislated time period, recently released archive material from the war years was now made available and fresh pages could be written in the nation's history books.

As a result of the focus on Jewish property confiscated by the Nazis during World War II in the Western world, renewed attention was also directed to the fate of the Norwegian Jewish population during the war and their property. In 1996 the Norwegian government formed a committee whose purpose was to ascertain what happened to Jewish property during World War II so as to determine how and to what extent seized assets/property had been restored after the war, and their value. As a result the Norwegian government decided to pay 450,000,000 NOK in restitution. One part was paid as individual compensations to Jewish individuals who had lost one or more relatives in the Shoah and who had been resident in Norway prior to the war. The rest was to be given as collective compensation to the Jewish communities in Oslo and Trondheim. However, in agreement with the Norwegian state some of these funds were to be put aside as the foundation for what has become the Center for Holocaust and Minorities Studies in Norway, a research center and Holocaust museum housed at Villa Grande, the house Vidkun *Quisling used as his home and headquarters during World War II. The Jewish communities also decided to set apart a sum to establish the Fund for Support of Jewish Institutions or Projects outside Norway. The remainder of the restitution money was used to restore the community centers and synagogues in Trondheim and Oslo. Because of the ongoing work that led to the Norwegian restitution, the World Jewish Congress chose to hold its executive meeting in Oslo in November 1996.

As a result of extensive work done by Norwegian Jews and Christians in the former Soviet Union, the Hjelp Jødene Hjem (HJH, Help the Jews Home) organization was founded in 1990 to coordinate all Norwegian contributions to help former Soviet Jews immigrate to Israel. It is a joint venture of a number of Christian organizations in Norway and the Jewish Community of Oslo. HJH also provides information about antisemitism and its consequences. In recent years most of the money collected has been used to support humanitarian projects in Israel.

Since the 1970s Norwegian society has become more multicultural. New immigrants have arrived from many parts of the world, among them many Israelis, bringing their religion and culture with them. The Protestant Norwegian State Church had a tradition of being very homogeneous, the Jews having been one of the very first non-Christian religious minorities in the country. There was now a need to find ways to cope with a new multicultural reality. In 1990 Oslo hosted a conference called "The Anatomy of Hate: Resolving Conflict through Dialogue and Democracy," which was convened by the Foundation and the Norwegian Nobel Committee. Former political prisoners and statesmen, writers and scholars from 30 countries – among them Vaclav Havel, Nelson Mandela, Francois Mitterrand, and Jimmy Carter – discussed ways of living with ethnic and national conflict and managing regional tensions through dialogue. This conference was followed by a series of religious dialogues. The first was held in 1991, called "Common Ethics in a Multicultural Norway." Several smaller and larger interfaith groups followed throughout the country.

From 1991 to 1993 representatives of the Norwegian government were engaged in an ongoing project called "Norway as a Multicultural Society Aiming at Acquiring Knowledge about the Different Minorities' Special Needs."

The Council for Religious and Life Stance Communities in Norway was established on May 30, 1996. The main task of the council is to promote mutual respect and understanding between various religious and humanistic communities. The Council seeks to prevent differences in belief from being used as a basis for prejudice and xenophobia and has received government support for its work since 1998. Representatives from 12 different religious and life stance communities meet regularly to discuss and find resolutions to issues that involve problems arising in the interaction between religious and life stance traditions and Norwegian society at large. Several conferences and dialogue projects have been initiated by this council.

In 1997 the Norwegian government introduced a new subject into the schools: Christianity, Religion and Life Stance – a subject meant to teach different religions against a backdrop of Christian values and religious beliefs. Previously children belonging to religions other than Christianity could be exempt from religious education in school, but now all schoolchildren regardless of their faith were required to learn religion in this way. The various minority religious communities and the humanists lodged strong protests. This was one of the first issues to be dealt with by the Council for Religious and Life Stance Communities in Norway. The strong protest brought about minor alterations in the curriculum and a more lenient approach towards parents who wished to avoid sending their children to these classes. However, despite the negative response to this subject, the effect has also been that all Norwegian schoolchildren regularly learn about Judaism throughout their school years. This has also resulted in a great increase in the number of schoolchildren visiting the synagogues and students contacting the communities for information. There has also been a greater demand to make Jews more visible in society at large.

In 1998 Norway ratified the Council of Europe's convention on acknowledging national minorities. As a result Norwegian Jews were granted the status of a national minority together with several other ethnic minority groups such as Roma (gypsies) and similar groups that have lived in Norway for more than 100 years. Under the new legislation, the Norwegian government is obliged to help its national minorities express, sustain, and develop their individual identities, cultures, and languages. As a result, the two Jewish communities have received government funds for the establishment of Jewish museums. In 1997 a Jewish museum was established in Trondheim and officially opened on May 12, 1997. In 2003 the Oslo Municipality agreed to accept plans to build a Jewish museum in Oslo. This museum was planned to open in 2007 in a building that used to serve as a second synagogue before World War II.

The Restitution Fund from the Norwegian government enabled a major restoration of the synagogue and community buildings of Trondheim and Oslo. In Trondheim the newly restored community center, including a library and multimedia center, was opened in the fall of 2001.

In September 2004 the Oslo Jewish community officially reopened its newly rebuilt community center and redecorated synagogue in the presence of prominent guests from the government.

CULTURE. Many novels and short stories with Jewish motifs and other books on Jewish matters – including the Holocaust – were translated into Norwegian during the 1970s, among them works by Bellow, Heller, Kellerman, Malamud, Potok, Roth, and Wouk. In the late 1970s most of Isaac Bashevis Singer's books were translated as were Eli Wiesel's. In the 1980s and 1990s several books by Amoz Oz and David Grossmann were published in Norwegian as were books by Yoram Kaniuk and in 2004 a book by Etgar Keret.

The Norwegian-Jewish author Eva Scheer published several Jewish folklore collections of tales and stories, with books on 19th-century Jewish life in Lithuania following in the 1970s and 1980s.

Among the many books on Zionism and Israel, *The Right to Survive* (1976), edited by Pater Hallvard Rieber-Mohn and Professor Leo Eitinger – "a book about Israel, Norway and antisemitism" – merits special mention. It includes articles by eleven Norwegians (two of them Jews). Lectures given at the university seminar in Oslo in 1976 in a series called "The Jews and Judaism," with the subtitle "From the Old Testament to the Middle-East Conflict," were published in 1977.

During the 1980s books by Norwegian Jews as well as books on Norwegian Jewry appeared, only some of which are mentioned here. Professor Leo Eitinger edited *Human among Humans: A Book of Antisemitism and Hatred Against Strangers* (1985), the lectures from the Nansen Committee hearing on antisemitism. An autobiography was published by Jo *Benkow; Mona Levin, a well-known author and cultural critic, wrote the biography of her father, the Norwegian Jewish pianist Robert Levin: *Med livet i hendene* ("My Life in My Hands," 1983). Robert Levin (1912–1996), a pianist and professor of piano and interpretation, was one of Norway's most renowned musicians. The author of the two-volume *History of the Jews in Norway during 300 Years* (vol. 1, 1969; vol. 2, 1986; second edition, 1987), Oskar Mendelsohn, was awarded a knighthood, 1st Class, of the Royal Saint Olav Order in 1989 for his work on the history of the Norwegian Jews and in 1993 he received the gold medal of the Royal Norwegian Society of Sciences and Arts, the oldest Norwegian society of science (founded 1760), for his "comprehensive scientific work in the investigation of the history of the Jewish minority in Norway." A concise popular edition of Mendelsohn's work was published in 1992. Mendelsohn died in 1993.

The Holocaust was the subject of many Norwegian books and of several books translated into Norwegian during the 1980s. A Norwegian, Jahn Otto Johansen, wrote *Det hendte også her* ("It Also Happened Here"). In the 1980s came several accounts of concentration camps by survivors still living in Norway: Ernest Arberle, written by Arvid Møller, *Vi må ikke glemme* ("We Must Not Forget," 1980); Robert Savosnik with Hans Melien, *Jeg ville ikke dø* ("I Did Not Want to Die," 1986); Herman Kahan with Knut M. Hansson, *Ilden og lyset* ("The Fire and the Light," 1988); Mendel Szanjfeld, with Simon Szajnfeld, *Fortell hva som skjedde med oss; erindringer fra Holocaust* ("Tell What Happened to Us; Memories From the Holocaust," 1993); Kai Feinberg with Arnt Stefansen, *Fange nr 79108 vender tilbake* ("Prisoner No. 79108 Returns," 1995); Vera Komissar with Sverre M. Nyrønning, *"På tross av alt: Julius Paltiel – norsk jøde i Auschwitz* ("Despite Everything: Julius Paltiel – Norwegian Jew in Auschwitz," 1995). Vera Kommisar also wrote a book about Norwegian Jews who escaped to Sweden in 1942, *Nådetid: norske jøder på flukt 1942* ("Time of Grace: Norwegian Jews on the Run 1942," 1992).

Kristian Ottosen, a Norwegian historian, wrote the account of the deportation of Norwegian Jews during World War II: *I slik en natt* (1994); Karoline Frogner, a Norwegian film producer, did the film and book *Mørketid: kvinners møte med nazismen* ("Time of Darkness: Women's Encounters with Nazism," 1995). It records interviews with several women who survived the Ravensbrueck concentration camp, among them four Jews.

During the late 1990s and early 2000s several books and chapters of books on Judaism were written in Norwegian for all school levels and at university level. As part of a series on religious texts from all religions, central Jewish religious texts were translated and published in Norwegian for the first time. Bente Kahan, a Norwegian Jewish actress and singer, has become known in Norway and Europe for her interpretations of Yiddish songs.

In 2001, the Wergelands Barn (The Children of Wergeland) project was made to commemorate the 150 years since Jews were allowed into Norway in 1851. Brit Ormaasen and Oskar Kvasnes interviewed a number of Norwegian Jews who were alive before the war and collected photographs to depict Jewish life in Norway from the first immigration up until 1945. This work was made into an exhibition that has been shown all over Norway and in 2004–5 in the United States. In 2004 two Norwegian film producers produced a film called *Mannen som elsket Haugesund* ("The Man Who Loved Haugesund"), a story about Moritz Rabinowitz, a Norwegian Jew who lived in Haugesund and who was arrested and killed by the Nazis in 1941.

Relations with Israel

Norway voted for the establishment of a Jewish state in 1947, and Trygve Lie, as secretary-general of the United Nations, used all his diplomatic skill to remove obstacles to the adoption of the resolution. Diplomatic relations between Norway and Israel were soon established, first through nonresident ministers, and since 1961 on the level of resident ambassadors. At the United Nations, Norway frequently came out in support of Israel. The friendly relations found expression in great celebrations of Israel's tenth anniversary and in official visits by prime ministers, foreign ministers and other public figures.

The murder in 1973 of an Arab from Morocco living in Lillehammer temporarily created anti-Israel feelings in the Norwegian press and public. Strained relations developed between Norway and Israel when some of the alleged perpetrators were arrested at the home of an Israeli attaché.

Israel's right to exist within secure borders remained the basic foreign policy of Norway and the Norwegian delegation withdrew from the Geneva Conference on racism in 1978. Israeli policy on the West Bank has been criticized, but all demands for recognition of the PLO were rejected at this time because of the PLO Charter. Representatives of different parties in many cases spoke in favor of Israel, not least those of the Christian People's Party, and Israel has many friends in Christian quarters. However, there is also a smaller Christian pro-Palestinian group.

The group "With Israel for Peace," consisting mostly of non-Jewish youth, including university students, was founded in 1976 for the purpose of disseminating information about Israel and to fight anti-Israel and anti-Zionist propaganda from the Norwegian left-wing.

Cooperation between universities in Norway and Israel was strengthened through technical-scientific symposiums held in Trondheim and in Israel. The organization "Norwegian Friends of the Hebrew University" (reestablished in 1977) raised money for a Norwegian-Israeli research fund. Israeli artists held exhibitions and concerts in Norway, among them the Israel Philharmonic Orchestra. Trondheim and Petaḥ Tikvah became twin towns.

Norway became the center of world attention during the 1990s due to the negotiations that led to the Oslo Accords, a part of the Middle East peace process directly connected with Norway. Due to the close relationship that had developed over the years between the Norwegian and Israeli Labor parties, Norway already had a long-established connection with Israeli officials. During the 1990s Norway also established increasing contacts with the PLO through research projects in the area. Using Norwegian mediators, secret negotiations were conducted between representatives of the PLO and Israel at several locations in Norway. On August 20, 1993, in Oslo, an agreement in principle was signed regarding the establishment of an autonomous Palestinian state. In 1994 Yasser Arafat, Yitzhak Rabin, and Shimon Peres received the Nobel Peace Prize in Norway for this breakthrough. On September 28, 1995, the Oslo II agreement was signed, which was supposed to be the next step in the peace process. Over the years public opinion regarding Israel has changed from being very supportive to being more critical and more in favor of recognizing the Palestinian struggle. Increased hostility towards Israel and its policy continues to characterize the Norwegian press, left-wing intellectuals, and several politicians.

[Oskar Mendelsohn / Lynn Claire Feinberg (2nd ed.)]

BIBLIOGRAPHY: H.M. Koritzinsky, *Jødernes historie i Norge* (1927); O. Mendelsohn, *Jødernes historie i Norge* (1969). HOLOCAUST

PERIOD: H. Valentin, in: YIVOA, 8 (1953), 224–34, passim; B. Höye and T.M. Ager, *The Fight of the Norwegian Church Against Nazism* (1943); *Eduyyot Ha-Yo'eẓ ha-Mishpati la-Memshalah Neged Adolf Eichmann* (1963), 475–80; J.M. Snoek, in: *The Grey Book* (1969), 116–9. **WEBSITES:** www.dmt.oslo.no; www.dmt.trondheim.no.

NORWICH, county town of Norfolk, E. England. The medieval Jewish community is first mentioned in 1144, when the discovery of the body of a boy, William of Norwich, in a wood near the town gave rise to the first recorded *blood libel in Europe. Although this apparently had no immediate effect on the community, there were attacks by citizens on the Jews in the 1230s, the one in 1234 following an accusation that the Jews had kidnapped and circumcised a Christian child. The descendants of *Jurnet of Norwich, who were financiers, patrons of learning, and scholars, dominated the community from 1160 to 1260: the lower part of their stone house still stands in King Street (as part of the "Music House"). The 13th-century community (numbering about 100 to 150) seems, from the considerable documentary evidence surviving, mainly to have consisted of financiers who lent to local traders and the rural gentry and villagers. The community suffered from the "coin-clipping" charges of 1279 and the execution for blasphemy of the local magnate, Abraham fil' Deulecresse; by the time of the general expulsion from England in 1290, it numbered only 50 souls. The poems of *Meir b. Elijah of Norwich (c. 1244) have survived, mainly in a Vatican manuscript.

Individual Jews settled in Norwich in the first half of the 18th century and there was an organized community by 1754 when a quarrel in the synagogue attracted much attention in the press. Continuous communal activity dates from the purchase of a burial ground in 1813 and the opening of a new synagogue in 1828. Local 19th-century families included those of Samuel (father of the first Lord *Mancroft), Haldinstein, and Soman (founder of the *Norwich Argus* newspaper). The community was especially known for shoe manufacture, antique dealing, and the press and printing. The synagogue, which was destroyed by bombing in World War II, was rebuilt in 1948; the community's numbers remained between 100 and 200 (1% of the total population) through most of the 20th century. The 2001 British census found a total of 239 declared Jews in Norwich. The town had an Orthodox and a Reform synagogue.

BIBLIOGRAPHY: V.D. Lipman, *Jews of Medieval Norwich* (1967); C. Roth, *Rise of Provincial Jewry* (1950), 85–87; Roth, England, index; Roth, Mag Bibl, 92, 93, 170; H. Levine, *Norwich Hebrew Congregation 1840–1960*; *Jackson's Oxford Journal* (June 8, 1756). **ADD. BIBLIOGRAPHY:** M. Brown, "The Jews of Norfolk and Suffolk Before 1840," in: JHSET, 32 (1990–92), 219–36.

[Vivian David Lipman]

NORZI, Italian family whose name derives from the Umbrian city of Norcia (where Jews were living from the third century C.E.). The more common forms of the name are de Nursia, da Norcia, da Norsa, Norsa, Norzi. A certain NATHAN (d. 1369) is considered the founder of the family. Many documents attest to the presence of members of the family in Ferrara, in Bondeno, and under the House of Este in the 15th century, mainly in connection with banking activities. Although others lived in Modena, Reggio, Brescia, Verona, and Padua, the *Mantua branch was the wealthiest and most important. According to De Rossi, they came from the regions of Bologna and Turin. The Norzi family played an important part in the life of the community of Mantua. The former synagogue of the family, destroyed when the ghetto was demolished, has been entirely reconstructed on the present community premises, in Via Govi, and is now the only synagogue in Mantua. Many members of the family, pupils of Joseph Colon and Judah b. Jehiel Messer Leon, became rabbis celebrated for their learning beyond Italy.

MANUELE DA NORCIA moved from Rimini to Mantua in 1428 and obtained permission to open a loan bank (*condotta*). LEONE DE NURSIA and others were authorized in 1482 to trade in wool and silk cloths. In 1493 DANIELE DE NURSIA settled in Mantua, where he bought a house which had a painting representing the Virgin on its façade; its erasure by Daniele, although authorized by the bishop, caused a general uproar. Nursia first had to pay 1,100 gold ducats to the painter Andrea Mantegna for a painting of the Madonna, now at the Louvre; he was subsequently evicted, and the house was demolished by order of Marquis Giovanni Francesco II Gonzaga, the ruler of Mantua, who ordered that a church should be built on its premises dedicated to Santa Maria della Vittoria to commemorate his victory over the French at Fornovo. Another work by an unknown painter, now at the Basilica of S. Andrea in Mantua, depicts the ceremony of dedication, with four members of the Norzi family wearing the Jewish *badge; the words *Debellata hebraeorum temeritate* appear at the top of the painting. In 1504 ISAAC BEN DANIEL NORZI was authorized by Gonzaga to engage in moneylending. BENJAMIN BEN IMMANUEL NORZI wrote *Sod La'asot Lu'aḥ* (1477; in Ms.), a study of the Jewish calendar, and commentaries on rulings by R. Isaac Tiburino, and on the Talmud tractates *Pesaḥim, Yoma, Sukkah, Yom Tov, Rosh Ha-Shanah,* and *Megillah* (Wolff, Bibliotheca, 1 (1715), 252).

RAPHAEL BEN GABRIEL (1520–1583?) rabbi at Ferrara and Mantua, was author of various works on rational ethics in religious questions: *Se'ah Solet* (Mantua, 1561); *Marpe la-Nefesh* (Mantua, 1561; Venice, 1571); and *Oraḥ Ḥayyim* (Venice, 1549; Amsterdam, 1557). He exchanged polemics with the rabbi of Ferrara. A *kinah* was published on the occasion of his death (Zunz, Lit, Poesie, 128, 254; C. Bernheimer, *Catalogue des manuscrits et livres rares hébraïques de la bibliothèque du Talmud Tora de Livourne* (1915), no. 27 (1)). ELIEZER BEN DAVID NORZI (16th century), son of a banker from Mantua, cousin of Raphael b. Gabriel, wrote a commentary on Abraham Ibn Ezra's *Sefer ha-Shem* (1834, ch. 6), dealing with the significance of letters and of the Holy Name. The geometrical diagrams in the commentary indicate that he had knowledge of mathematics (Mortara, Indice 45; M. Steinschneider, *Die*

Mathematik bei den Juden (1901), 198; S. Simonsohn, *Toledot ha-Yehudim be-Dukkasut Mantovah* (1964), 458, 474, 528). MOSES BEN JEDIDIAH SOLOMON (d. 1590) was rabbi at Mantua and author of a commentary to tractate *Middot* (Mortara, Indice; Simonsohn, *ibid.*, index). SOLOMON BEN SAMUEL, 16th-century scholar, wrote responsa (Mantua, 1588).

JEHIEL VIDAL BEN JEDIDIAH SOLOMON (d. 1665), son of the rabbi and scholar Jedidiah Solomon Raphael ben Abraham *Norzi, was appointed rabbi of Mantua in 1628 shortly before the expulsion of the Jews from the town, when he led the exiles to San Martino. They resettled in Mantua in 1630 and he devoted himself to the community until his death. He was often at variance with his community. His responsa are scattered in the archives of the community and in works by contemporary authors (Mortara, in: *Corriere Israelitico*, 2–3 (1863–65), 56, 71; S. Wiener, *Mazkerot Rabbanei Italyah* (1898), 40, 66; S. Simonsohn, *ibid.*, index). MOSES BEN JEDIDIAH SOLOMON, rabbi in Mantua in the 17th century, brother of Jehiel, corresponded with Samuel *Aboab (S. Simonsohn, *ibid.*, index). JEDIDIAH SOLOMON BEN ABRAHAM *NORZI (1560–1616) was a rabbi and biblical scholar. ḤAYYIM BEN JEHIEL (d. c. 1698), who sat in the rabbinical tribunal of Mantua in 1665, was a *sofer* in 1677, and became rabbi of the community with the assent of Moses *Zacuto in 1685. With Zacuto and other rabbis he drew up the statutes of the community in 1677, and issued moral precepts for the Jews of Mantua. Some of his responsa were recorded by Zacuto and other *posekim* of that time. He is often confused with another rabbi of the same name of the 16th century (Mortara, Indice, 45; P. Norsa, *I Norsa*, 2 (1959), 122; S. Simonsohn, *ibid.*, 528 and index).

ISAAC BEN MOSES NORSA was rabbi in Ferrara in the 18th century, and author of a ruling on *sheḥitah* as part of a talmudic discussion held at Ferrara and presided over by Isaac Lampronti (*Ittur Bikkurei Kaẓir*, Venice, 1715; Steinschneider, Cat Bod, 140; Fuerst, Bibliotheca Judaica, 3 (1863)). UMBERTO NORSA (1866–1943), scholar, translator from various languages into Italian, including the Psalms (1926, not published), was president of the community of Mantua (G. Bedarida, *Ebrei d'Italia* (1950), index). PAOLO NORSA wrote a history of the Norsa family in the 14th to 16th centuries (*I Norsa*, 2 vols.; 1953–59).

BIBLIOGRAPHY: V. Colorni, in: RMI, 9 (1934/35), 217ff.; P. Norsa, *I Norsa (1350–1950), Contributo alla Storia di una Famiglia di Banchieri*, 2 vols. (1953–59); E. Castelli, *I Banchi Feneratizi Ebraici nel Mantovano (1386–1808)* (1959); S. Simonsohn, *Toledot ha-Yehudim be-Dukkasut Mantovah* (1964); A. Portioli, *Atti e memorie R. Accademia Virgiliana Mantua* (1882), 55–79; Roth, Italy, index; Milano, Italia, index: Milano, Bibliotheca, index; G. Bedarida, *Ebrei d'Italia* (1950), index.

[Alfredo Mordechai Rabello]

NORZI, JEDIDIAH SOLOMON RAPHAEL BEN ABRAHAM (1560–1616), Italian rabbi, biblical and masoretic scholar. Born in Mantua in a well-known family (see *Norzi), he was a pupil of his uncle Moses Cases, and was later appointed a member of the rabbinate of that town. He achieved a great reputation through his critical masoretic commentary on the Bible, a work to which he devoted the greater part of his life. In his research he not only consulted published works, but undertook journeys to many countries to compare various manuscripts. He succeeded in gaining access to the manuscript of Toledo written in 1277 (known as the Codex de Rossi, no. 782). He consulted his friend R. Menahem *Lonzano, the midrashic and talmudic scholar.

Norzi's work, called *Goder Pereẓ*, was completed in 1626. It is in two parts; the first on the Pentateuch and the five Scrolls, and the second on the remaining books of the Bible together with some grammatical treatises. The work was published under the title *Minḥat Shai* (Mantua, 1742–44). The second edition (without the grammatical treatises) was published in Vienna (1816). *Minḥat Shai* is also printed in the rabbinical Bible *Mikra'ot Gedolot*. Norzi's introduction was published in 1819, and in 1876 by A. Jellinek. A commentary to the *Minḥat Shai* called *Or ha-Ḥayyim* (Vilna, 1867) was written by Ḥayyim Ze'ev Bender of Bobruisk.

BIBLIOGRAPHY: Michael, Or, no. 951; S. Simonsohn, *Toledot ha-Yehudim be-Dukkasut Mantovah* (1964), 450, and notes 63, 64; C. Roth, *The Jews in the Renaissance* (1959), 313f.

[Hirsch Jacob Zimmels]

NOSSAL, SIR GUSTAV (1931–), Australian immunologist. He was born in Bad Ischl and emigrated to Australia with his family (1938) because of the Nazi threat. He earned his B.Sc. (1952) and medical degree (1954) from the University of Sydney and Ph.D. (1960) from the University of Melbourne. After clinical training at the Royal Prince Alfred Hospital, Sydney (1955–56), he became Research Fellow at the Walter and Eliza Hall Institute of Medical Research in Melbourne (1957–59) and then assistant professor in the Department of Genetics at Stanford University, Palo Alto, California. He returned to the Hall Institute as deputy director for immunology (1961–65), and became director of the institute and professor of medical biology at the University of Melbourne (1965–96). His research mainly centered on the immune cells which produce antibodies and started with the important original observation that each antibody producing cell only makes one kind of antibody. Subsequently he analyzed the way in which these cells respond to stimulation by antigens, their organization within the immune system, and the mechanisms which prevent antibody producing cells from attacking an individual's own tissues. The practical consequences of these discoveries include a better understanding of autoimmune diseases and the development of diagnostic and therapeutic monoclonal antibodies. He collaborated closely with Israeli immunologists including Dr. Ruth *Arnon. Sir Gustav played a major role in national and international organizations concerned with vaccination programs and education in health and science, including chairing the World Health Organization's Global Program for Vaccines and Immunization. He was especially concerned with training health workers working at the grass roots level. He was president of the International Union of Immunological Societies (1986–89) and of the Australian Academy of Science (1994–98). His leadership of many charitable organizations includes that of the Council for Aboriginal Reconciliation. His many academic honors include election to the Royal Society of London and the U.S. National Academy of Sciences, the Albert Einstein World Award of Science, the Rabbi Shai Schacknai Prize, and the Robert Koch Gold Medal. His many other honors include the CBE (1970), a knighthood (1977), the Companion of the Order of Australia (1989), and election as Australian of the Year (2000).

[Michael Denman (2nd ed.)]

NOSSIG, ALFRED (1864–1943), writer, sculptor, and musician; one of the first supporters of the Jewish national movements and of Zionism. Born in Lemberg, Nossig's diversified talents found expression in literature (poems, plays, essays in literary criticism), music (a monograph on the life of Paderewski and libretto for his opera), sculpture (his works were exhibited in a number of world exhibitions and achieved considerable recognition). In addition, Nossig engaged in various public and social activities. Yet all of his life he was a kind of outsider, despite the wide veneration he enjoyed. In his youth he belonged to the assimilationist Polish Jews and was one of the editors of their Polish-language journal. Later he abandoned them and in 1887 published the first Zionist work in Polish, "An Attempt to Solve the Jewish Problem" (*Próba rozwiązania kwestji żydowskiej*, 1887), in which he proposed the establishment of a Jewish state in Palestine and adjacent countries. This book had a great impact on the Jewish intelligentsia, especially in Galicia. From that time, Nossig was active in the area of political Zionism. During that period he published books and essays on Jewish national problems and critical writings on socialism.

Nossig participated in the first Zionist Congresses but he soon ran into conflict with *Herzl, for his individualistic character prevented his cooperating with other people. From time to time, however, Nossig raised new suggestions and plans for the founding of Jewish and general societies to solve the world's problems in general, and those of the Jews in particular. Thus in 1908 he founded a Jewish colonization organization (Allgemeine Juedische Kolonisations Organization – AIKO), which, like other plans of his, was not implemented. In his works on Jewish statistics (1887, 1903), he laid the basis for the Jewish Statistical and Demographic Institute and thus was among the founders of the scientific study of Jewish statistics. His most famous pieces of sculpture were *Wandering Jew*, *Judas Maccabaeus*, *Nordau*, and *King Solomon*. Nossig lived in Berlin until the Nazi rise to power, when he was expelled to Poland. There he continued his diversified activities, among other things, in the design of a monumental piece of statue called "The Holy Mountain" to be placed on Mount Carmel as a symbol of world peace and the establishment of a national home for the Jews in Palestine. After the Nazi occupation of Poland and the establishment of the Warsaw Ghetto, he drew up plans for Jewish emigration and submitted several memoranda to the German authorities. Upon order of the Nazi authorities, the chairman of the Warsaw *Judenrat*, Adam *Czerniakow, nominated him as a member of the *Judenrat* and head of its Department for Art, which actually existed only on paper. Early in 1943 the Jewish Fighting Organization became convinced that Nossig was collaborating with the Nazis. He was sentenced to death by the Jewish underground and shot on Feb. 22, 1943, by members of the Jewish Fighting Organization.

BIBLIOGRAPHY: J. Friedman, in: JSOS, 21 (1965), 155–8; H. Seidman, *Yoman Getto Varshah* (1947), 204–10; A. Czerniakow, *Yoman Getto Varshah* (1969), index; A. Boehm, *Die zionistische Bewegung*, 1 (1935), index; M. Zylberberg, in: *Wiener Library Bulletin*, 23 (1969), 41–45.

[Getzel Kressel]

NOSTRADAMUS, also known as *Michel de Nostre-Dame* (1503–1566), French astrologer and physician. Both of his grandfathers, Jean de Saint-Rémy and Pierre de Nostra-Donna, were professing Jews, but when Provence became a French possession in 1488, Charles VIII's anti-Jewish policy induced them to convert to Christianity. Consequently Nostradamus was born and raised as a Catholic. In 1529 he graduated from the University of Montpellier as a doctor of medicine. The unorthodox but successful methods of combating the plague which Nostradamus later described in his *Remède très-utile contre la peste* (Paris, 1561) nevertheless failed to save his own wife and children in 1538. For some years thereafter he led a wanderer's existence and, while in Italy, is reputed to have sought out Jews, especially kabbalists.

On his return to France, Nostradamus turned to the occult sciences and, from 1550 onward, published a number of astrological works. The most famous of these, *Les Prophéties de Maistre Michel Nostradamus* (Lyons, 1555), consisted of some 350 quatrains couched in obscure French. The quatrains were arranged in groups of 100, and the work thus acquired its alternative title, *Les Centuries*. Among the many calamities predicted in it was the French king's death in a duel, and the astrologer's fame was assured when Henri II was accidentally killed at a royal tournament in 1559. In 1564 Nostradamus was appointed physician and counselor to Charles IX. The first complete text of the *Centuries* appeared in 1610 and ran to countless editions, not only in French but also in many other languages. Nostradamus uncannily predicts the English and French revolutions and even the rise and fall of a German dictator (whom he calls Hister). The most celebrated astrologer of all time, Nostradamus remains one of the most fascinating and enigmatic figures of the Renaissance.

BIBLIOGRAPHY: J. Boulenger, *Nostradamus* (Fr., 1933); R. Busquet, *Nostradamus, sa famille, son secret* (1950); J. Laver, *Nostradamus* (Eng., 1952); E. Leoni, *Nostradamus, Life and Literature* (1961).

[Godfrey Edmond Silverman]

NOTARIKON (Gr. νοταρικόν; Lat. notaricum, from *notarius*, "shorthand-writer"), a system of abbreviations by either shortening the words or by writing only one letter of each word. This method is used in interpreting the Pentateuch and is the 30th of the 32 hermeneutical rules of the *Baraita of 32 Rules. The word is derived from the system of stenographic shorthand used by the *notarii* in recording the proceedings in the Roman courts of justice (Kohut, Arukh, 5 (1926), 336). The word *notarikon* occurs only once in the Mishnah (Shab. 12:5). Although there is an opinion that the hermeneutic law of *notarikon* has biblical authority (Shab. 105a), the Talmud does not use it for halakhic interpretations. It is only employed in *aggadah* and **asmakhta* (support for the *halakhah*). Nevertheless, there were rabbis who objected to the excessive use of *notarikon* even in *aggadah* (Sif. Deut. 1).

The *notarikon* can be divided into two categories. One kind interprets every letter in a particular word as the abbreviation of a whole word, since "the words of the Torah are written as *notarikon*" (Mekh. Ba-Ḥodesh, 8). Thus the word נִמְרֶצֶת (*nimrezet*, "grievous"; I Kings 2:8) stands for נוֹאֵף, מוֹאָבִי, רוֹצֵחַ, צוֹרֵר, תּוֹעֵבָה (*No'ef, Mo'avi, Roze'aḥ, Ẓorer, To'evah*; "adulterer, Moabite, murderer, oppressor, despised") and the first word of the Ten Commandments, אָנֹכִי (*Anokhi*, "I") was interpreted to mean אֲנָא נַפְשִׁי כְּתָבִית יַהֲבִת (*Anna Nafshi Ketavit Yahavit*; "I Myself wrote (and) gave [them]" (Shab. 105a).

A second and later application of *notarikon* consists of breaking up a word into various components. Through this method the name רְאוּבֵן (*Re'uven*, "Reuben"; Gen. 29:32) becomes ראוּ בֵּן (*re'u ven*, "see (the) son"; PdRE 36) and the word אַבְרֵךְ (*avrekh*, "senior adviser"; Gen. 41:43) changes into אָב בְּחָכְמָה ר"ךְ בְּשָׁנִים (*Av Be-ḥokhmah, Ra-Kh be-Shanim*, "father in wisdom (though) tender in years"; Sif. Deut. 1). Sometimes, one-syllable words are transposed. An example of this is when the noun כַּרְמֶל (*karmel*, "fresh corn"; Lev. 2:14) is taken to mean רַךְ מָל (*rakh mel*, "tender and easily crushed"; Men. 66b). At other times, a word is even transposed although the abbreviation for one of the derived words is missing: מְצוֹרָע (*mezora*, "leper"; Lev. 14:2), is therefore taken to mean מוֹצִיא שֵׁם רַע (*mozi shem ra*, "slanderer"), although there is no letter *shin* in the original word (Tanḥ. Meẓora, 4). Conversely, a letter may not be used at all. Words were interpreted through the principle of *notarikon* even when the words derived from the original did not necessarily correspond to it. Thus *nazuf* ("under divine censure") is connected with *Nezem Zahav be-aF ḥazir* ("a ring of gold in the snout of a pig"; Avot 6:2). The rabbis made extensive use of the *notarikon* and the anagram in the interpretation of dreams (e.g., Ber. 57a), and many analogous usages of them can also be found in Hellenistic writings of the period (S. Lieberman, see bibl.). The use of the *notarikon* was also widespread in medieval homiletical and kabbalistic writings (e.g., *Ba'al ha-Turim* by Jacob b. Asher). Through such methods of interpretation many words in the Bible became *notarikonim*. An example of such kabbalistic interpretation is the taking of the word בְּרֵאשִׁית (*bereshit*, "in the beginning") to refer to the cosmogenic order בָּרָא רָקִיעַ אֶרֶץ שָׁמַיִם יָם תְּהוֹם (*Bara Raki'a Ereẓ Shamayim Yam Tehom*; "He created the firmament, the earth, the heavens, the sea, and the abyss"). Another example is to interpret *bereshit* to mean בְּרָא שִׁית ("created in six primordial days"; Zohar, Gen. Prologue, 3b). According to the Mishnah, Queen *Helena of Adiabene had a golden tablet made for the Temple on which the portion of the **sotah* (see *Ordeal) was written in an abbreviated *notarikon* manner (Yoma 3:10; 37b).

BIBLIOGRAPHY: I.I. Einhorn (ed.), *Midrash Tanna'im*, 2 (1838), 34cff.; Frankel, Mishnah, index; W. Bacher, *Erkhei Midrash* (1923), 86f., 233; S. Krauss, in: *Byzantinische Zeitschrift*, 2 (1893), 512ff.; M. Halperin, *Notarikon, Simanim, Kinnuyim* (1912); S. Lieberman, *Hellenism in Jewish Palestine* (1950), 69ff.; M.D. Gross, *Oẓar ha-Aggadah*, 2 (1961), 796f. (a list of *notarikonim*).

°NOTH, MARTIN (1902–1968), German Bible scholar, disciple of Albrecht *Alt, to whose ideas Noth was deeply indebted. Noth was born in Dresden and served as professor at Koenigsberg (1930–45) and Bonn (1945–65). He edited *Zeitschrift des deutschen Palaestina-Vereins* from 1929 to 1964 and was director of the Deutsches Evangelische Institut in Jerusalem from 1965 until his death, Noth brought his extensive topographical studies, mainly published in *Palaestinajahrbuch* and *Zeitschrift des deutschen Palaestina-Vereins*, linguistic research (in particular, *Die israelitischen Personennamen*, 1928), and form-criticism studies to bear on problems of Israelite history. Of primary importance was his thesis that from the time of the settlement, Israel was organized into a 12-tribe confederation, similar to the Greek amphictyony (in his *Das System der zwoelf Staemme Israels*, 1930). He felt that virtually nothing can be known about pre-settlement history.

Noth was one of the foremost representatives of the form-critical approach, and his studies of pentateuchal traditions, *Ueberlieferungsgeschichte des Pentateuchs* (1948, 19602), and Deuteronomy (*Ueberlieferungsgeschichtliche Studien*, 1 (1943, 1957[2])), had widespread influence on biblical research. In the former work he examined the themes of the pentateuchal narrative and the history of its traditions and presented the idea that both J and E go back to a common source, G (*Grundlage*). In the latter he originated the idea of the Deuteronomic history work, a unified history extending from Deuteronomy to II Kings (minus insertions), in which previously independent units were joined and unified by a distinctive theology and philosophy of history. In *Die Gesetze im Pentateuch* (1940) he linked Hebrew law to the religious confederation rather than to the monarchy. He wrote commentaries to individual books of the Bible: Exodus (1959[2], Eng. tr. 1962), Leviticus (1962, Eng. tr. 1965), Numbers (1966), Joshua (1953[2]), and I Kings 1–16 (1964). He also wrote *Geschichte Israels* (1954[2], 1961[5]; *The History of Israel*, 1960[2]); and *Die Welt des Alten Testaments* (1946, 1957[3]). Some of his articles were collected in his *Gesammelte Studien* (1957, 19602). *The Laws in the Pentateuch and Other Studies* (1966) is an English translation of some of his works.

[Michael V. Fox]

NOTKIN, NATA (**Nathan Note of Shklov**, also **Nathan Shklover**; d. 1804), Russian merchant and army contractor.

Notkin was a champion of the improvement of the status of Jews in Russia at the beginning of the 19th century. Born in Shklov, he lived in Mogilev and later in Moscow and St. Petersburg. He was introduced by General Zorich, the squire of Shklov, to Count Kurakin, and used this opportunity to act in behalf of his fellow Jews. He presented the count with a project for the establishment of large-scale agricultural colonies for the Jews of "New Russia" as well as plans for industrial plants near the ports of the Black Sea, which he hoped would direct the Jews to productive labor. Toward the end of 1802 he was invited by G.R. *Derzhavin to be a member at the Committee for the Betterment of the Jews. In all of his writings and projects Notkin tried to demonstrate to the government ways to improve the condition of the Jews, e.g., the gradual removal of Jews from the liquor business, the establishment of Jewish schools, and the direction of Jews toward productive labor. Notkin was one of the founders of the St. Petersburg Jewish community.

[*Encyclopaedia Judaica* (Germany)]

NOTOVICH, OSIP KONSTANTINOVICH (1849–1914), journalist and playwright. Notovich was a graduate of the University of St. Petersburg. In his youth he converted to the Greek Orthodox Church. Acquiring the small daily *Novosti* in 1876, in time he developed it into an important political journal. Although Notovich published facts about the persecution of Jews, he did not come to their defense for fear of losing his Russian readers. Notovich wrote several philosophical works and plays, some of which were performed on the stages of the imperial theaters of Moscow and St. Petersburg. His translation of H.T. Buckle's *History of Civilization in England* (1890) was especially popular. In 1905 Notovich published a revolutionary appeal for a trade union. As a result, his newspaper was confiscated and he was summoned to court. Subsequently, he fled the country and died abroad.

BIBLIOGRAPHY: S. Ginsburg, *Historishe Verk*, 2 (1946), 203–4.

NOTTINGHAM, industrial city in the E. Midlands, England. In the 13th century Nottingham was one of the 27 centers in which an *archa was established for the registration of Jewish debts. An attack was made on the Nottingham Jews during the Barons' Revolt in 1264. From the resettlement until the 19th century only individual Jews settled in the city. By 1805 there was a small, organized community; a cemetery was acquired in 1822; and by 1880 there were about 50 Jewish residents, though a synagogue was not built until 1890. The Nottingham lace-curtain industry was founded by a Jewish immigrant from Germany, Lewis Heymann. By 1939, the community had increased to 180, but World War II brought an influx of new residents. In addition to an Orthodox synagogue there was a Progressive congregation; communal institutions included a Zionist Association and a University Jewish Society. In 1969 the community was estimated at 1,500 (out of a total population of 310,000), and in the mid-1990s it was estimated at about 1,050. The 2001 British census found 627 Jews by religion in Nottingham. There is a Nottingham Representative Council and an Orthodox and a Progressive synagogue.

BIBLIOGRAPHY: C. Roth, *The Rise of Provincial Jewry* (1950), 27–89; J. Spungin, *A Short History of the Jews of Nottingham* (1951).

[Vivian David Lipman]

NOVAK, DAVID (1941–), U.S. theologian, rabbi, and leading authority on Jewish law. Born in Chicago, Novak received his bachelor of arts degree from the University of Chicago in 1961, his rabbinical ordination from the Jewish Theological Seminary of America in 1966, and his doctorate in philosophy from Georgetown University in 1971. From 1966 to 1969 he was Jewish chaplain at St. Elizabeth's Hospital, National Institute of Mental Health, in Washington, D.C., and he served as rabbi to congregations in Maryland, Oklahoma, Virginia, and New York City from 1966 to 1989. He taught at Oklahoma City University, Old Dominion University, the New School for Social Research, the Jewish Theological Seminary of America, and Baruch College of the City University of New York. From 1989 to 1997 he was the Edgar M. Bronfman Professor of Modern Judaic Studies at the University of Virginia. In 1997 he joined the University of Toronto, holding the J. Richard and Dorothy Shiff Chair of Jewish Studies as professor of the study of religion, professor of philosophy, and director of the Jewish Studies Programme.

Novak wrote primarily on the philosophical aspects of Jewish legal tradition; his work concerns the foundations of Jewish theology and its application to contemporary problems, especially those involving ethics. His books include *Law and Theology in Judaism* (1974, 1976), *Suicide and Morality* (1975), *The Image of the Non-Jew in Judaism: An Historical and Constructive Study of the Noahide Laws* (1983), *Jewish-Christian Dialogue: A Jewish Justification* (1989), *Natural Law in Judaism* (1998), and *Covenantal Rights: A Study in Jewish Political Theory* (2000). He contributed numerous articles to theology, law, and philosophy journals, and he was a contributing editor of *Sh'ma: A Journal of Jewish Responsibility.*

Novak was a founder of the Panel of Inquiry on Jewish Law of the Union for Traditional Judaism and a founder of the Institute of Traditional Judaism in Teaneck, N.J. He is a fellow of the American Academy for Jewish Research and of the Academy for Jewish Philosophy, and he was a member of the international advisory board to the government of Poland concerning the Auschwitz-Birkenau site. Novak was a fellow of the Woodrow Wilson International Center for Scholars in Washington, D.C., and in 1996 delivered the Lancaster/Yarnton Lectures in Judaism and Other Religions at Oxford University. He lectured extensively throughout North America, Israel, Europe, and South Africa. He spoke Hebrew, Yiddish, and German, and had a knowledge of Aramaic, Greek, Latin, and French.

[Dorothy Bauhoff (2nd ed.)]

NOVAK, ROBERT (1931–), U.S. journalist. Born in Joliet, Illinois, Novak graduated from the University of Illinois in 1952 with a bachelor of arts degree. His journalism career began when he wrote for local newspapers while in college. During the Korean War, Novak served in the Army, attaining the rank of lieutenant. After the war, he joined the Associated Press and became a political correspondent in Indianapolis. In 1957 Novak was transferred to Washington, where he reported on Congress. He left the AP to join the capital bureau of *The Wall Street Journal*, covering the Senate, and in 1961 he became the newspaper's chief congressional correspondent. In 1966 Novak teamed up with Rowland Evans to create the Evans-Novak Political Report, a nationally syndicated column. After Evans's death in 2001, Novak continued the column on his own. By that time, Novak had also become a television personality, appearing on many interview and opinion programs on CNN, most notably *The Capital Gang, Crossfire* and *Evans, Novak, Hunt and Shields*. While he held centrist views early in his career (he supported the Democratic presidential candidacies of John F. Kennedy and Lyndon B. Johnson), he moved to the right and his feisty personality earned him the nickname the Prince of Darkness.

As his career evolved in the 1980s and into the early years of the 21st century, Novak became embroiled in a number of controversies for his public comments and actions. He was frequently criticized as acting as a political operative for the Republican Party while posing as a journalist. He was implicated in a number of political scandals and violations of journalistic ethics and standards. Twice Novak was reportedly involved in situations that led to the dismissal of Karl Rove, later the architect of George W. Bush's presidential victories, from George H.W. Bush's vice presidential campaign and in 1992 while working for Bush's re-election campaign. Both times Rove was dismissed for leaking campaign information to Novak, a charge they both denied. Novak's loyalty to his sources was called into question after he revealed Robert Hanssen as the confidential source for some of his articles. Hanssen was later found guilty of selling state secrets, including the identities of covert operatives, to the Soviet Union. In 2003, Novak disclosed the identity of Valerie Plame, an agent of the Central Intelligence Agency, in his newspaper column. Novak reported that the information had been provided to him by "senior administration officials." Plame was the wife of Joseph Wilson, a former ambassador, who wrote an article charging that the Bush administration twisted intelligence to explain its rationale for going to war against Iraq. The leak and allegations of a possible cover-up were investigated by a special prosecutor and a grand jury. I. Lewis Libby, chief of staff to Vice President Dick Cheney, was indicted on five counts in the case and resigned. Rove was questioned by the grand jury at least four times.

Novak was born Jewish but said he lost his faith while in college. He converted to Roman Catholicism in 1998 and was a member of the ultra-conservative Catholic organization Opus Dei. He was an avid supporter of a Palestinian state and was a fierce critic of the State of Israel and most especially of Ariel *Sharon, whom he deliberately called General Sharon, well after he became prime minister.

[Stewart Kampel (2nd ed.)]

NOVAYA USHITSA, town in Khmielnitskii (Kamenets-Podolski district until 1954), Ukraine. The Jewish community in Novaya Ushitsa and its environs dates from the beginning of the 18th century. In 1765 there were 203 poll tax payers. From 1838 to 1840, 80 Jews of the Novaya Ushitsa region, including rabbis and community leaders, were tried in what became known as the Oyshits Incident. They were accused by the governor of Kiev, General Gurayev, of the murder of two Jews who had informed on "absconders" (unregistered persons who had avoided paying taxes and doing military service) to the authorities. Most of the accused were sentenced by a military court to flogging and exile to Siberia.

The 1847 census records 725 Jews living in Novaya Ushitsa, with 1,235 in the communities of the district. The Jewish population numbered 2,213 in 1897 (34.5% of the total). After the Bolshevik Revolution and the civil war, their sources of livelihood were drastically curtailed. In 1926 there were 1,844 Jews in the town (28.4% of the total), and in 1939 they numbered 1,547 (55% of the total population). In the 1920s there existed a rural Jewish Council (Soviet). Germans entered the town on July 14, 1941. In September a closed ghetto was instituted and in spring of 1942 Jews from the environs were herded there. On August 20, 1942, an *Aktion* was conducted, and 3,222 were murdered. A group was taken to the labor camp in Letichev and perished there. Those remaining in the town ghetto were killed on October 16, 1942. After the *Holocaust the community ceased to exist.

BIBLIOGRAPHY: *Perezhitoye*, 1, pt. 2 (1908), 1–7; M. Kiper, *Dos Yidishe Shtetl in Ukraine* (1929); S. Ginzburg, *Historishe Verk*, 3 (1937), 178–9; *Yidn in Ukraine*, 1 (1961), 164–78; V.B. Antonovich (comp.), *Arkhiv yugo-zapadnoy Rossii*, 2, pt. 5 (1890).

[Arthur Cygielman]

NOVE, ALEC (1915–1994), British historian and economist. Born Alexander Novakovsky in St. Petersburg, the son of left-leaning middle-class parents, Nove came with his family to Manchester in the 1920s, when his father, a Menshevik, was given the choice of emigration or Siberia by the Bolshevik government. Nove was educated at the London School of Economics and, after serving in the British civil service, became a senior academic in 1958 with a readership at the LSE and, subsequently, a chair at Glasgow University. Nove was regarded as one of the foremost experts in the West on the Soviet economy, publishing *An Economic History of the U.S.S.R.* (1969) and many other works on the realities of the Soviet economic system. He was one of the few Western experts on the Soviet Union to predict the possibility of the reform of the system from within, as actually occurred in the 1980s.

BIBLIOGRAPHY: ODNB online.

[William D. Rubinstein (2nd ed.)]

NOVECK, SIMON (1914–2005), U.S. rabbi. Born in Atlanta, he earned a B.A. from Yeshiva College and then moved to the Jewish Theological Seminary where he was ordained in 1941. He earned a Ph.D. from Columbia University in 1955.

He entered the pulpit upon ordination serving Baldwin Jewish center during the early war years (1940–44) and as acting rabbi in Temple Beth El in Cedarhurst during the last part of World War II and rabbi in B'nai Israel in Freeport, Long Island (1946–49). He then assumed the assistant rabbi position at Park Avenue Synagogue under Milton *Steinberg and became rabbi upon his passing in 1950.

Noveck had an active interest in adult education and was director of the National Academy for Adult Jewish Studies (1952–57) that became part of United Synagogue of America. He resigned from Park Avenue to head the Adult Jewish Education Department of B'nai B'rith and initiated the B'nai B'rith Great Books Series (1959–63) which added significantly to the classical texts available in the English language at that time.

Having once succeeded a legendary rabbi in Manhattan, he returned to the pulpit to succeed Morris *Silverman in Hartford, Connecticut. Silverman was the editor of the Conservative Movement Sabbath and Holiday Prayerbook. Noveck helped plan the congregation's move from its imposing sanctuary in Hartford to West Hartford, where it has remained for over a generation.

Among his works are: *Judaism and Psychiatry: Two Approaches to the Personal Problems and Needs of Modern Man* (1956); *Great Jewish Personalities in Modern Times* (1960); *Great Jewish Thinkers of the Twentieth Century* (1963); *Contemporary Jewish Thought: A Reader* (1963); *Creators of the Jewish Experience in Ancient and Medieval Times* (1985); *Milton Steinberg: Portrait of a Rabbi* (1978); and *Creators of the Jewish Experience in the Modern World* (1985).

BIBLIOGRAPHY: P.S. Nadell, *Conservative Judaism in America: A Biographical Dictionary and Sourcebook* (1988).

[Michael Berenbaum (2nd ed.)]

NOVE MESTO NAD VAHOM (Slovak, **Nové Mesto nad Váhom**; Hung, **Vágúhely**), town in western Slovakia, since 1993 Slovak Republic. During the reign of King Luis the Great (1342–1382), Jews lived there, were expelled, and later permitted to return. In 1465 there were 10 Jews; the community was expelled again in 1514. In 1683, many Jews died in the Kuruc massacre in the Moravian city of *Uhersky Brod. The surviving 11 families received permission to settle in Nove Mesto and engage in trade and craft. They belonged to the Uhersky Brod congregation and were obliged to pay taxes. The community continued to grow, with more Moravian Jews arriving. They were subject to the "Familiants" law of the Emperor Charles VI (1711–1740), which permitted only one Jew per family to marry and limited the number of Jews in a city. The others immigrated to upper Hungary.

By 1735 there were 372 Jews in Nove Mesto. In 1780 they built their first synagogue. In 1785 there were 2,320 Jews; it was the second most important Jewish city in upper Hungary, after *Pressburg (Bratislava). In 1830 there were 2,495; in 1840 there were 2,050; in 1880 there were 1,850; and in 1910 they numbered 1,553. In 1930 there were 1,581; in 1940 the number fell to 1,209.

In 1754 the community hired its first rabbi, Moses Hamburger (1754–1764). In 1780 a *talmud torah* was opened. Following the order of Emperor Joseph II (1780–1790), a school was founded in 1783, with German as the language of instruction. During the Hapsburg Empire, the Jews lived undisturbed until the Spring of Nations (1848–49). In May 1848, a massive pogrom claimed many Jewish lives. During the Magyar war of independence, nine Jews enlisted in the Magyar army. Thus Jews clashed with the Slovak national interest, which wanted self-rule. A fire in 1856 destroyed a large part of Nove Mesto. In 1848 a primary school opened, still using German; in the 1860s it switched to Magyar. In 1856 Rabbi Joseph Weisze (1855–1897) founded a government-supported Jewish high school, the first of its kind in Jewish Hungary. When support was lost in 1919, the school was taken over by the authorities and it ceased to be Jewish. In 1860 a school for girls was established, operating until 1919.

After the 1868 Hungarian Jewish Congress many congregations split, but Nove Mesto continued its old tradition, called "Status Quo Ante." In 1921, several families established an Orthodox congregation. They hired a rabbi, built a synagogue, and founded a *ḥevra kaddisha* and a *talmud torah*. In 1928 Rabbi Lipmann Donath established a small yeshivah. The two rival congregations made peace in 1932.

During World War I dozens of Jews were recruited into the army. At the end of the war there was a wave of pogroms in Slovakia, and Nove Mesto was one of the hardest hit. Jews tried to defend themselves, using the rifles they had kept from the army; Hungarian soldiers came to their rescue. Nationalist and Catholic elements continued to persecute Jews. Pro-Czechoslovak and Social-Democratic figures protested, serving to calm the situation.

In the New Czechoslovak Republic, Jewish entrepreneurs helped industrialize Nove Mesto. They established food, metal, wood, and textile industries; Jewish physicians, lawyers, and teachers contributed to intellectual life, and Jews figured largely in retail and handicrafts. The Jewish party played an important role in local political life, and its members were regularly elected to the municipal council and as deputy mayor. The Zionist movement was well established.

With the support of the Third Reich, Slovakia proclaimed independence on March 14, 1939. A wave of antisemitism ensued, culminating in 1942 with the deportation of 1,300 of the city's 2,215 Jews to Sobibor and Treblinka. In August 1944 there was an anti-Nazi uprising in Slovakia in which Jewish youth participated, but the invading German army deported the surviving Jews to Auschwitz.

In 1947 there were 266 Jews in Nove Mesto; most emigrated. In 1965 there were 25. In 1975 the Communist authorities destroyed the ancient cemetery. The synagogue was destroyed during the war, and Jewish communal buildings were expropriated.

BIBLIOGRAPHY: J.J.(L.) Greenwald (Grunwald), *Mekorot le-Todedot Yisrael* (1934), 53–72; L. Rothkirchen, in: Yad Vashem, *Pinkas ha-Kehillot* (1963), 35–39; Y. Toury, *Mehumah u-Mevukhah be-Mahpekhat 1848* (1968), index; M. Lányi and B.H. Propperné, *Szlovenskói Zsidó Hitközségek Története* (1933), 279–80; E. Bàrkàny and L. Dojč, *Židovské náboženské obce na Slovensku* (1991), 225–32.

[Yeshayahu Jelinek (2nd ed.)]

NOVE ZAMKY (Slovak. **Nové Zámky**; Hung. **Ersekújvár**; Ger. **Neuhaeusel**), town in S. Slovakia, since 1993 the Slovak Republic. Until 1840, Jews were not permitted to live in Nove Zamky. They attended markets in the town and lived in nearby Surany (Nagysuran). In 1840, when the Hungarian Parliament passed the law permitting Jewish settlement, the first Jewish families moved there, where they traded in grain and horses. In 1855 the community numbered 85. In 1857 they founded a *ḥevra kaddisha* and in 1858 consecrated a cemetery. In 1860 the first synagogue was erected. Railway connections with Budapest and Vienna increased the economic importance of the town, and the Jewish population grew accordingly. In 1857 there were 892 Jews; in 1890 there were 1,491; and in 1910 there were 1,540. The first Czechoslovak census of 1921 recorded 2,087 Jews; the 1930 census recorded 2,535. On the eve of the deportations in 1940 there were 3,000 Jews in Nove Zamky.

In 1842 the first school was founded. The language of instruction was German; it changed to Magyar in 1869, by which time the school was a regular elementary school. In 1920, courses in Slovak and Hebrew were added to the curriculum. After the 1868 Jewish Congress, an Orthodox congregation was founded as well. They built a synagogue and organized a *ḥevra kaddisha*, a primary school, a *talmud torah*, a cemetery, and a yeshivah. In 1927 the community established a Jewish high school and, later, a Beth Jacob elementary school for girls. The Neolog Rabbi Dr. Samuel Klein (1866–1940) as well as his son and heir in the rabbinate, Dr. Ernst Klein, advocated speaking Slovak in daily life.

During World War I, some 85 Jews enlisted in the army. Nove Zamky suffered less than other cities from the wave of pogroms and looting that swept Slovakia in 1918–1919, probably because of the presence of the Hungarian army. However, Czechoslovak troops occupying the region faced Magyar armed resistance; fighting also took place during the Bolshevik Commune in 1919, causing considerable damage.

The Czechoslovak Republic signified prosperity for the Jewish community. Both congregations expanded in number and affluence. The American Jewish Joint Distribution Committee assisted in establishing a credit society that served the entire region; at its peak it held 684 deposits (totaling more than 3,000,000 crowns); 1937 was the society's best year. Jews participated in municipal life and were elected to the city council. The Jewish party and the Zionist movement had important branches in the town. The local branch of Ha-Shomer ha-Ẓa'ir was one of the largest in the country, and Brit Trumpeldor thrived.

In November 1938 Nove Zamky was ceded to Hungary. The Hungarian anti-Jewish laws were applied immediately, and the local authorities added their own. They curtailed Jewish economic activity, forbidding them to do business on certain streets. When Hungary introduced the Labor Service System (*Munkaszolgalat*) in 1939, Nove Zamky Jews were recruited. After the German occupation of Hungary in March 1944, the deportation of Hungarian Jewry to Auschwitz began. Nove Zamky's Jews were concentrated in a temporary ghetto comprised of several shabby streets, while neighboring Jews were moved to the Kurzweil Brick Works. On June 12 and 15, 1944, two transports of Jews were sent to Auschwitz. The entire local Jewry was deported; only a few managed to return after the war.

In 1947 there were 501 Jews in Nove Zamky. After the war, the surviving Jews worked hard to revive their congregation. They abolished the division by rite, and reconstructed the Orthodox synagogue (the Neolog synagogue had been bombed), both cemeteries, and the *mikveh*. The congregation remained active during the entire Communist regime, one of the few that retained its religious life. In 1990, there were 70 Jews in the city. A plaque bearing the names of the Nove Zamky Holocaust victims was mounted in the synagogue in 1999. Slovakia has maintained the synagogue and other Jewish communal buildings.

Peter *Ujvary, the author of *Zsido Magyar Lexicon* (Budapest 1929), was born in Nove Zamky.

BIBLIOGRAPHY: R. Iltis (ed.), *Die aussaeen unter Traenen mit Jubel werden sie ernten* (1959). E. Barkany-L. Dojc, *Zidovské nábozenské obce na Slovensku* (1991), 176–78. S. Strba and T. Lang, *Az ersekújvary zsidoág toertenete* (2004).

[Yeshayahu Jelinek (2nd ed.)]

NOVGOROD-SEVERSK, city in Chernigov district, Ukraine. During the 14th century, Novgorod-Seversk was conquered by the princes of Lithuania; in the 16th and 17th centuries it was alternately in the hands of the Poles and the Russians; and in 1667 it was definitively annexed by Russia. A Jewish settlement is mentioned for the first time in a residence permit granted to the townspeople by King Sigismund III Vasa (1587–1632) of Poland. According to the permit Jews were forbidden to sell meat in the town, except in the courtyard of the synagogue. Also included were several tax levies which Jews were ordered to pay. During the *Chmielnicki persecutions of 1648 many Jews in Novgorod-Seversk were massacred by the Cossacks. The community was renewed only in the late 18th century. In 1847 1,336 Jews were registered in the community; by 1897 the number had risen to 1,956 (32% of the total population). The community suffered in the wave of pogroms which swept over Russia in 1905. On April 6, 1918, units of the Red Army retreating before the German army savagely attacked the Jews of Novgorod-Seversk and 88 Jews (including the author A.J. Slutzky) lost their lives. In 1926 there were 2,089 Jews (22.8%

of the total population) in the town, and in 1939 it dropped to 982 (8.56% of the total population). The Germans arrived there on August 26, 1941, and they found 200 Jews in the town. On November 7, 174 were murdered; others were executed some days later. There is no information on a Jewish community after World War II.

BIBLIOGRAPHY: *Die Judenpogrome in Russland*, 2 (1910), 295–300; E. Tcherikower, *Yehudim be-Ittot Mahpekhah* (1957), 529–31.

[Yehuda Slutsky]

NOVI SAD (Hung. **Ujvidék**; Ger. **Neusatz**), city on the Danube in Vojvodina, Serbia. Some Jews from Belgrade seem to have settled at the foot of the later Petroraradin fortress in the 16th century. Under Ottoman rule (16th–17th centuries) they were treated well and engaged in trade on the Danube. During the Austro-Turkish war of 1683–99, Ashkenazi Jews were among the *contractors to the Austrian army. When the region passed under Austrian rule in 1699, it was devastated and depopulated. Jews were therefore exceptionally authorized to settle in the new town of Neusatz opposite the fortress but were not allowed to form a recognized community. Austrian archives mention Salomon Hirschl, probably the first *rosh kehillah* of Novi Sad. At the beginning of the 18th century three Jewish families are known to have lived in Novi Sad; however, there were probably more, as only owners of real estate were registered. Most Jews came from Nikolsburg in Moravia. All Jews had to pay the Jewish tax (until the end of the 18th century). They were subject to limitations, such as the interdiction of acquiring real estate; as only the eldest son of each family could marry in the same town (see *Familiants Laws), others had to leave and settle elsewhere. The *ḥevra kaddisha* was founded in 1729 as a "Holy Welfare Society." Under Joseph II the teaching of German or Hungarian became obligatory, and in order to open a business or marry, Jews had to have some formal education. A Jewish school was built in Novi Sad in 1802 and a synagogue in 1829. During the Hungarian revolution of 1848–49 all Jewish property was destroyed, but in 1851 the synagogue was rebuilt, and a new, monumental one was built in 1901 (still standing in the 1970s). Previously all Vojvodina belonged to Hungary (within Austria-Hungary); however, in 1918, when Vojvodina became a part of the new Yugoslav kingdom, it formed a province closely linked with Serbia.

Between the two world wars communal life was intensive and diversified. There was a Jewish school, a home for the aged, a modern community center, widespread Zionist activities, and Jewish newspapers were published (*Juedisches Volksblatt*, later *Juedische Zeitung Jevreyske Novine*).

Until the Holocaust, in 1941, there were 4,000 Jews in Novi Sad, out of a total population of 80,000. The extermination of the Jews of Novi Sad was carried out in successive waves, initially under the Hungarian occupation and later by German troops. It began with individual arrests, torture, and murders. On Jan. 21–23, 1942, a small rebellion near Novi Sad served as a pretext for the so-called "*razzia*," when total curfew was ordered and Jewish homes were searched and plundered while their occupants were murdered in the streets. On January 23 more than 1,400 Jews were marched to the Danube and lined up in four rows. The ice in the frozen river was broken and throughout the day Jews, including women and children, were shot in the back, disappearing in the waters, which carried corpses down to Belgrade and beyond for weeks. Among the victims were also some 400–500 Serbs. The "*razzia*" caused an upheaval even in Hungarian circles, and cabled orders arrived from Budapest to stop the massacre on the evening of January 23. Several hundred survivors, half frozen and frightened to death, were released. The extermination policy continued, however. During 1942 all male Jews between the ages of 18 and 45 were gathered into "labor battalions," maltreated, and starved (first in Hungary), and then sent to the Ukrainian front, where they perished. The last phase came with the German occupation in March 1944. With the aid of Hungarians, the Germans sought out all remaining Jews and transported about 1,600 to Auschwitz in April 1944. Jewish property was plundered completely, except for personal and worthless items, which were gathered in the synagogue. About 1,000 Jews survived the Holocaust; 700 left for Israel and about 200 remained in Novi Sad in 1970, most of them survivors of POW camps. Subsequently the community grew to around 630 with the addition of former residents returning from abroad and Jews arriving from places depleted of their Jewish inhabitants. Restoration of the synagogue and of community offices was undertaken and legal proceedings initiated for the return of Jewish public buildings like the community center and the Jewish orphanage. The chapel of the cemetery was also renovated. The pre-Holocaust choir was reconstituted and an art club was set up in addition to regular cultural gatherings. The synagogue was used only for holiday services.

The presidents of the community were Pavle Šosberger, Prof. Theodore Kovać, and Tihomir Ungar.

BIBLIOGRAPHY: Radó and J. Major, *A noviszádi zsidók története* (1930); *Magyar Zsidó Lexikon* (1929), s.v. *Ujvidék; Zločini fašističkih okupatora i njihovih pomagača protiv Jevreja u Jugoslaviji* (1952, 1957[2] with Eng. text, pp. 1–43), ch. 5; J. Buzási, *Az ujvidéki "razzia"* (1963). **ADD. BIBLIOGRAPHY:** I. Radó and J. Major, *Istorija novoasadskih Jevreja* (1930; enlarged ed., Tel Aviv, 1972); Z. Loker (ed.), *Yehudei Vojvodina be-Et he-Ḥadashah* (1994), with Eng. summary; P. Šosberger, *Novosadski Jevreji* (1988); idem, *Jevreji Vojvodine* (2001).

[Zvi Loker]

NOVITCH, MIRIAM (1908–1990), Holocaust historian. Novitch was born in Yurtishki, White Russia. She studied at the gymnasium in Vilna and at the Superior School for the Languages of Eastern Europe. She traveled to France before World War II and as a French resistance fighter was arrested in June 1943 and taken to the Vittel camp in France. After being liberated by the Americans in 1944, she devoted her life to Holocaust research. She arrived in Ereẓ Israel in 1946 and was a founder of kibbutz Loḥamei ha-Getta'ot, and its Holocaust museum in 1949. She was the first curator of the museum. She was also a pioneer in collecting film on the Holocaust.

She brought archival material from Eastern and Western Europe to the museum, collecting material in Poland, Germany, Czechoslovakia, Spain, Belgium, Italy, and Switzerland. She did pioneering research soon after World War II on the Sobibor death camp, Greek Jewry in the Holocaust, and the confiscation of Jewish art. She was a model to many younger researchers and helped them with scholarships and research. She made many trips to Europe in the early years following the Holocaust when research was difficult and countries were closed to such initiatives.

She published the following books: *Women and The Holocaust, Personal Reflections* (1965); *Le Passage Des Barbares, Contribution a l'Histoire de la Deportation et de la Resistance des Juifs Grecs* (1967, 1982); *La Verite sur Treblinka* (1967); *Sobibor – Camp of Death and Revolt* (1979); *Spiritual Resistance: Art from Concentration Camps 1940–1945 – A Selection of Drawings and Paintings from the Collection of Kibbutz Lohamei Haghetaot* (1981); and *Le Genocide des Tziganes sous le Regime Nazi* (1968).

[Yitzchak Kerem (2nd ed.)]

NOVOGRUDOK (Pol. **Nowogródek**; also referred to by Jews as **Novaredok**), city in Grodno district, Belarus. Novogrudok was within Poland-Lithuania until the third partition of Poland (1795), when it passed to Russia, from 1842, and a county capital in the province of Minsk. It reverted to Poland in 1921, but passed to the Soviet Union in 1939. The Jewish community of Novogrudok, one of the oldest in Lithuania, is first mentioned in documents in 1529. In 1563, at the request of the townspeople, King Sigismund II Augustus ordered that the Jews were to move to one of two streets at a distance from the center, where space had been allocated to them for building houses. In 1576 King Stephan Báthory confirmed all the former rights of the Jews of Novogrudok and of the other Jews in Lithuania. According to a decision of the Council of the Province of Lithuania (see *Councils of the Lands) of 1623, Novogrudok Jews were subject to the jurisdiction of the *Brest community. There were 893 poll tax payers in the community and surrounding villages attached to it in 1765. There were 2,756 persons in 1847 and 5,105 in 1897 (63.5% of the total population). In the 19th century two of Russia's leading rabbis, Jehiel Michael *Epstein and Isaac Elhanan *Spektor, officiated in Novogrudok. At the end of the 19th century the city became one of the centers of the *Musar movement after a *yeshivah and **kolel* had been founded there in 1896 by Joseph Hurwitz, one of the most prominent disciples of Israel *Salanter and a leader of the Musar movement. During World War I the yeshivah was transferred to *Gomel. The Zionist movement and the Bund were active before World War I and after. The community decreased considerably after that war, numbering 3,405 (53.4% of the total) in 1921 and increasing to 6,309 in 1931. There were a Hebrew Tarbut school, a Yiddish CYSHO school that operated for 4 years, and a religious Tushia school (of the Mizrachi). In the 1930s the Yiddish weeklies *Novaredok Life* and *Novaredok Week* appeared in the town.

[Yehuda Slutsky]

Holocaust Period

In 1939 after the outbreak of the war (September 1939) refugees from western Poland settled in town. During the period of Soviet rule (1939–41), the institutions of the Jewish community were destroyed, enterprises were nationalized, small trade was drastically reduced, and artisans were organized in cooperatives. The Jewish schools were closed and a Yiddish one with a Soviet curriculum was opened. There were arrests among the "bourgeois" Jews. With the outbreak of the war between Germany and the U.S.S.R. on June 22, 1941, groups of Jews attempted to reach Soviet territory but the Soviet guards prevented them from crossing the border and they returned to the city. Germans entered the city on July 3, and as early as July 10 they had murdered about 50 men. On December 7 the Jews were ordered to assemble in the courtyard of the district courthouse. About 1,896 skilled laborers with their families (only two children per family) were concentrated in a ghetto, and the others, about 4,500, were murdered outside the town. The *Aktion* was carried out by Einsatzkommando 8, with the help of local policemen. The survivors were concentrated in the ghetto that was set up in the suburb of Peresieka immediately after this *Aktion*. The first chairman of the Judenrat was the lawyer Ciechanowski, and the second was Chaim Ajzykowicz. Jews from the surrounding communities were also brought into the ghetto; they came from Weielub, Korelicze, Iwieniec, Rubiezewicze, Lubcz, and Naliboki.

The second *Aktion* was carried out on Aug. 7, 1942, and about 2,000 Jews perished in it. Only 1,240 artisans survived. They were concentrated in two places: construction workers in Peresieka and the others in a camp that was set up at the district courthouse. In October 1942 a group of about 50 Jews succeeded in escaping to the forests. Contact was made with a partisan unit headed by a Jew, Tuvia *Bielski. On Feb. 4, 1943, the Germans liquidated the camp of construction workers. In another *Aktion* on May 7, about 375 people were killed including the last of the women and children, and 300 skilled workers were left. At the beginning of 1943 a resistance group was created by Berko Joselewicz, Yasha Kantorowiez, and others, and headed by Dr. Yaakov Kagan. They decided to break out of the camp in which they were imprisoned and join the partisans. They dug a tunnel, and about 323 Jews escaped, but only 200 succeeded in reaching the forests; most of them joined the Jewish Battalion commanded by the Bielski brothers. Many of them took part in the fighting against the Nazis, Belorussian collaborators, and others. After the war about 1,200 Jews returned to Novogrudok from hiding in the forests. In 1970 the Jewish population was estimated at about 75 (15 families).

[Aharon Weiss]

BIBLIOGRAPHY: S.A. Bershadski (ed.), *Russko-Yevreyskiy arkhiv*, 2 (1882), 183, 202; *Nedelnaya Khronika Voskhoda*, no. 47 (1887); *Ha-Ẓefirah*, 280 (1887); *Regesty i Nadpisi*, 1–2 (1899–1910), indexes; M.Z.H. Walbrinski and S.Z. Markovitz, *Le-Korot Ir Novohredak ve-Rabbaneha* (1913); A. Harkavy, *Novoredak* (1921); idem, *Perakim me-Ḥayyai* (1938), 4–18; J. Źmigródski, *Nowogródek i okolice* (1927); M. Schalit (ed.), *Oyf di Khurbons fun Milkhomes un Mehumes* (1913),

393–411, 1093–101; A. Gumener (ed.), *15 Yor Kinder-Heym in Novogrudek* (1933); *Yahadut Lita*, 1 (1959), index; *Sefer Novorodek* (1963). HOLOCAUST PERIOD: T. and Z. Belski, *Yehudei Ya'ar* (1946); B. Ajzensztajn, *Ruch podziemny w gettach i obozach* (1946), 182–3; Y. Jaffe, *Partizanim* (1951); M. Zuckerman and M. Bassok (eds.), *Milḥamot ha-Getta'ot* (1954), 63, 492–3; M. Kahanowitz, *Milḥemet ha-Partizanim ha-Yehudim be-Mizraḥ Eiropah* (1954), index; *Sefer ha-Partizanim ha-Yehudim*, 1 (1958), 415–6.

NOVOMEYSKY, MOSHE (1873–1961), industrial pioneer in Ereẓ Israel. Born in Barguzin, a village on Lake Baikal in Siberia, Novomeysky attended a secondary school in Irkutsk, graduated as a mining engineer in Germany, and engaged in gold mining in Siberia. He received a Jewish upbringing and became involved in Zionism, although the Russian revolutionary movement also attracted him and he spent some time in prison. While in Germany in 1906, he became interested in a study of the potentialities of the Dead Sea as a source of valuable chemicals for industrial use. He visited Ereẓ Israel before World War I and participated in the establishment of the Palestine Industrial Syndicate in Berlin. During the war and the Russian Revolution, he was active in Jewish affairs in Siberia and became head of the National Council of Siberian Jews and of the regional Zionist Organization. When the Bolsheviks came to power he left Siberia and settled in Palestine in 1920, where he took first steps toward the realization of his plans for the exploitation of the Dead Sea. It took some ten years to obtain the necessary concession in the face of opposition in the British Parliament; but eventually his Palestine Potash Company became the most important enterprise of its kind in the Middle East. During the Israel War of *Independence (1948), the Potash Works on the north of the Dead Sea were evacuated and totally destroyed by the Arab forces, and only the plant erected in the south, near Sedom, survived. After the establishment of the State of Israel, the Potash Company, registered in Britain, was replaced by an Israel company under government control. Novomeysky was also a founder of Fertilizers and Chemicals, another large chemical enterprise in Haifa.

Apart from his intensive work in the economic field, Novomeysky devoted much time to public affairs. For a time after he settled in Palestine, he acted as treasurer of the *Haganah. He was a founder of the Palestine Economic Society for the study of the country's economic problems. Deeply interested in the Arab question, he succeeded in establishing good relations with the Trans-Jordanian authorities and the hundreds of Arabs employed by his company. In later years he devoted his time to writing his reminiscences, *My Siberian Life* (1956), and the story of the Dead Sea concession, *Given to Salt* (1958). He died in Paris and was buried in Tel Aviv.

[Moshe Medzini]

NOVOSELITSA (Rom. **Nouă Sulița** or **Sulița**), town in the Khotin district, region of Bessarabia, Moldova. As a result of the large emigration of Jews to Bessarabia, Novoselitsa developed in the first half of the 19th century from a rural into an urban community. There were 3,898 Jews living there (66% of the total population) in 1897 and 4,152 (86.2%) in 1930. Among the 875 members registered in the loan fund in 1925, were 461 merchants, 213 craftsmen, and 65 farmers. Prior to World War II, community institutions included a *talmud torah*, a kindergarten, and a school, all belonging to the *Tarbut network, and an old-age home. The town was annexed on June 29, 1940, to the Moldavian S.S.R.

[Eliyahu Feldman]

Holocaust Period

The town was captured by Romanian forces on July 2, 1941. On the same day, 800 Jews were murdered on the pretext that Jews had shot at the Romanian troops. Sixty Jews were arrested and taken to the local spirits factory, where they were shot to death. The surviving Jews, as well as others gathered from the entire district, were rounded up and put into the factory. On July 5, the old men, the women, and children were forced into a ghetto in the town. On July 20, all the Jews were put on the road to *Transnistria. En route they were exposed to constant brutality, and the old and weak among them were put to death. They reached *Ataki, on the banks of the Dniester, on August 6, by which time the Germans had closed the Ukrainian border, and the deportees were sent back to *Secureni. In a report by the gendarmerie commander at Cernauti, dated August 11, 2,800 Jews from Novoselitsa are mentioned among the prisoners of the Secureni camp. Their fate was the same as that of the other Jews in that camp; many were killed and others buried alive. Only 200 returned from Transnistria after the war. In 1959 the authorities closed down the community's two synagogues, one of them being converted into a club. In 1970 the Jewish population was estimated at about 1,000.

[Jean Ancel]

BIBLIOGRAPHY: M. Carp, *Cartea Neagra*, 3 (1947), index; N. Kahn in: *Eynikayt* (Sept. 11, 1945); BJCE. **ADD. BIBLIOGRAPHY:** *Pinkas Hakehillot, Romanya*, vol. 2 (1980).

°**NOVOSILTSEV, NICOLAI NIKOLAYEVICH** (1761–1836), Russian politician. As the czar's adviser in the Polish kingdom (1815), he took charge of Jewish questions. He recommended that the Polish government should gather material on the conditions of the Jews in the kingdom so that the czar could decide how to improve their situation and "make them more useful to the country." He was the author of a project which forbade the Jews to manufacture or trade in alcohol, but at the same time proposed granting them self-government, with the aim of modernizing Jewish life and promoting science and the arts, so that ultimately they would be awarded political rights. However Novosiltsev, head of the secret police, was implacably opposed to Polish nationalism, and the true purpose of this project was to sow dissension between the Jews and the Poles.

BIBLIOGRAPHY: *Perezhitoye*, 1 (1910), 164–221; 2 (1910), 78–93; YE, 11 (c. 1912), 765–6; *Bolshaya Sovetskaya Entsiklopediya*, 30 (1954), 104; R. Mahler, *Ḥasidut ve-Haskalah* (1961), index; *Wielka Encyklopedia Powszechna*, 8 (1966), 55.

NOVOZYBKOV, town in Oriol district, Russian Federation. Before the 1917 Revolution, Novozybkov was a district town in the province of Chernigov in the *Pale of Settlement. Although the town was founded at the beginning of the 19th century, it was not until the middle of that century that Jews were permitted to live there. In 1847 they numbered 446, and in 1897 there were 3,836 Jewish residents (about 25% of the total population). A *talmud torah* existed there. In October 1905 the town was subjected to pogroms. In 1926, 4,825 Jews (22.4% of the total) lived there, with the number dropping to 3,129 in 1939 (13% of the total population.). The Germans occupied the town on August 16, 1941, and on February 18, 1942, they murdered the 950 remaining Jews in a forest near the railway station. There is no subsequent information on any Jewish life in the town.

[Yehuda Slutsky / Shmuel Spector (2nd ed.)]

NOVY, JIM (1896–1971), U.S. business executive. Novy, who was born in Knyszyn, Poland, went to the U.S. in 1913 and settled in Austin, Texas, where he played a leading role in the metal industry. A member of many Jewish organizations, he was especially active on behalf of the State of Israel. In December 1963 his long-time friend President Lyndon B. *Johnson took part in the dedication of the newly erected synagogue of Novy's congregation, Agudas Achim in Austin, Texas, the first time a United States president ever helped dedicate a Jewish place of worship. In fact, Johnson may well have saved Novy's life 25 years earlier. In 1938, Novy was planning to take his son to Palestine to celebrate his bar-mitzvah and, on the way over, stop in Poland and Germany to visit relatives. But the first German-Czechoslovakian crisis had occurred and Nazism was on the rise, and Johnson, then a Congressman, warned Novy to try to get as many Jews as possible out of the two countries. To that end, as part of "Operation Texas," he supplied Novy with a letter of introduction to the diplomats in the U.S. Embassy in Warsaw and a large number of signed immigration papers. When he reached the embassy, Novy learned that Johnson had already called the consul and asked him to process the visas immediately. Forty-two Jews from Poland and Germany, including four of Novy's relatives, received the documents and safely fled Europe. Novy and his son went on to Paris, but Johnson tracked them down and insisted that they return to the U.S., as the second German-Czech crisis was imminent.

[Ruth Beloff (2nd ed.)]

NOVY BOHUMIN (Czech **Nový Bohumín**; Ger. **Neuoderberg**), town in N.E. Moravia, Czech Republic. In 655 the local lord permitted a Jewish soap-maker and a Jewish distiller to settle under his jurisdiction. In 1751 six Jewish families lived in various localities of the Oderberg domain. Jews settled in the town early in the 19th century, attracted primarily by the fact that Novy Bohumin, a border town, was one of the important railway-crossings in central Europe, and was later the site of an oil refinery. The Jews there first came under the administration of the *Teschen and later of the *Ostrava community. A synagogue was built in 1900; an independent community established in 1911; and a Jewish center opened in 1924. In 1933 a large Maccabiah (sports festival) was held in Novy Bohumin. The Jewish community numbered 722 (6.6% of the total population) in 1931. During the German occupation the Jews were put to work rebuilding a bridge blown up by the Poles. The synagogue was burned on Rosh Ha-Shanah 1939. Later that year most of the Jews were deported to Nisko. The community was not revived after the Holocaust.

BIBLIOGRAPHY: *Dr. Bloch's Oesterreichische Wochenschrift*, 28 (1911), 157; G. Wolf, in: ZGJD, 4 (1890), 193–4; B. Brilling, in: *Judaica Bohemiae*, 4 (1968), 101–18 passim, *Jews of Czechoslovakia*, 1 (1968), 199, 240–2.

[Meir Lamed]

NOVY BYDZOV (Czech **Nový Bydžov**; Ger. **Neubitschow**), town in N.E. Bohemia, Czech Republic. Jews are first mentioned in town records of 1514; they acquired a cemetery in 1520, the oldest tombstones dating from the mid-17th century. A synagogue was mentioned in 1559 (renovated in 1660 and 1838) and ten Jewish families were recorded in 1570 and 1620. In 1650, after the Swedish invasion of the Thirty Years War, 18 Jewish families were living there. Between 1656 and 1670 Jews sold salt. After a case of plague, the community was temporarily expelled, some of its members founding communities in surrounding villages. There were 90 Jewish families in Novy Bydzov in 1724. Three years later they were segregated from Christians in a special quarter. Expellees from Prague in 1744 reinforced the community. In 1750 Mendel of Novy Bydzov was burnt at the stake in connection with the emergence of the sect of the *Abrahamites. There were 37 Jewish houses in 1786. A new cemetery was consecrated in 1885 (still in existence). Some of the 838 members of the community in 1893 lived in the 35 surrounding villages. The old Jewish quarter burned down in 1903. In 1930 the community numbered 148 (2.1% of the total population). During the Holocaust 98 Jews were deported to *Theresienstadt and from there to the death camps in 1942; one only returned. Synagogue equipment and documents were transferred to the Central Jewish *Museum in Prague. No congregation was reestablished after the Holocaust. The synagogue dating from the mid-16th century was remodeled in 1660, 1838, and 1902. It was last restored in 1985 and subsequently used by the Czech Brethren Protestant Church.

BIBLIOGRAPHY: J. Koudelka, in: H. Gold (ed.), *Juden und Judengemeinden Boehmens* (1934), 416–9; J. Prokeš, in: JGGJČ, 8 (1936), 147–308; J. Hráský, *ibid.*, 9 (1938), 246, 259; AZDJ, 2 (1838), 562, 600; Bondy-Dworský, 299. **ADD. BIBLIOGRAPHY:** J. Fiedler, *Jewish Sights of Bohemia and Moravia*, (1991),124–25.

[Jan Herman]

NOVY DVOR (Rus. **Novyi Dvor**), small town in the Grodno district (county of Sokolka), Belarus. The first Jews settled there during the first half of the 16th century. During the second half of the 16th century there was an organized Jewish community with a synagogue and cemetery. In 1561 12 houses and a number of orchards were owned by Jews. During the following decades Jews from Grodno joined the local community and, according to the decisions of the Council of Provinces of Lithuania (*Councils of the Lands; 1623), the community of Novy Dvor was subordinated to that of Grodno. In 1648 Jewish refugees from Ukraine arrived in Novy Dvor. A few years later local Jews suffered the onslaught of the Russian and Swedish armies. In 1765 there were 299 poll-tax paying Jews in Novy Dvor and the surrounding villages. During the 19th century the sources of livelihood of the Jews of Novy Dvor were cut off and a period of economic stagnation ensued. In 1847 there were 394 Jews and in 1897, 490 (38% of the total population). In 1900 a new synagogue was erected, and during the first weeks of the Polish rule (1918) a Jewish self-defense organization was active. In 1921 there were 402 Jews (33% of the population) in Novy Dvor. From 1925 there was a *Tarbut school. The last rabbi of the community was Isaac Kamieniecki, who perished in the Holocaust.

Holocaust Period

At the end of June 1941, a few days after the Nazis entered the town, 50 Jewish men were deported to concentration camps. In October 1941 the Jews of Novy Dvor were sent to the ghetto at Ostryna, and in the spring of 1942 to the ghetto in Sukhovolia, and finally to the extermination camp of Auschwitz. Only six Jews of the community survived, three of them having joined the partisan movement. No Jews returned to Novy Dvor after World War II.

BIBLIOGRAPHY: *Dokumenty i regesty k istorii utovskikh yevreyev*, 1 (1882), nos. 235, 236, 241, 243; Dubnow, Pinkas, 17; B. Wasiutyński, *Ludność żydowska w Polsce…* (1930), 83; S.A. Bershadski, *Litouskiye yevrei* (1883), 331, 347; *Sefer Zikkaron li-Kehillot Sczuczyn, Wasiliszki, Ostryna, Novy Dvor. Różana* (n.d.), 379–434. PK Poland, vol. 7, North-East (2005).

[Arthur Cygielman]

NOVY JICIN (Czech, **Nový Jičín**; Ger. **Neutitschein**), town in Moravia, Czech Republic. Jews are recorded in Novy Jicin in the middle of the 14th century as owners of houses, and as cloth merchants. The Jewish lane (*Judengasse*), which in 1581 contained 46 houses, was situated next to the castle, but Jews resided in other streets as well. When the community was expelled in 1562, its leaders sold the synagogue to the mayor and presented the city with the cemetery, requesting that it should not be damaged. The expellees settled in the neighboring villages. In the late 18th and early 19th centuries Jews returned to the vicinity of the town, and by 1828 a few privileged families were again residing in it. Full freedom of settlement was granted only in 1848, and in July 1850 the authorities quelled an attempt to organize anti-Jewish riots. In 1868 the statutes of a *Kultusverein were confirmed, and by 1892 it was acknowledged as a community. The cemetery dates from 1875 and the synagogue from 1908. The Jews of Novy Jicin were active in the local textile industry and in trade. The community numbered 14 in 1847, 155 in 1868, 275 in 1880, 253 in 1900, and 206 (1.4% of the total population) in 1930. Novy Jicin was the site of the first *hakhsharah* farm in Czechoslovakia, organized in 1921. At the time of the Sudeten crisis in 1938, the community dispersed, and it was not revived after World War II.

BIBLIOGRAPHY: S. Mandl, in: H. Gold (ed.), *Juden und Judengemeinden Maehrens…* (1929), 404–16; P. Ziegler, *Zur Geschichte der Juden in Neu-Titschein* (1939); Bondy-Dworský, no. 649; Ch. D'Elvert, *Zur Geschichte der Juden in Maehren…* (1895), 110–3.

NOVY OLEKSINIEC, small town in Kremenets (Krzemieniec), today in Tarnopol district, Ukraine, noted for leather products. In 1765, 203 Jewish taxpayers were registered in Oleksiniec and its suburb (Oleksiniec Stary). The printing press established there in 1760 was one of the first Hebrew presses in Russia. H. Margolis, active between 1766 and 1776, printed some 18 rabbinical works there. Noteworthy is *Zemir Ariẓim ve-Ḥarvot Ẓurim* (1772), a collection of anti-ḥasidic proclamations. Rabbis of Oleksiniec include Mordecai ha-Kohen Rappoport, son of Shabbetai, author of *Imrei No'am* (Oleksiniec, 1767), and Jacob Joseph ha-Levi Horovitz of Brody, installed in 1790.

BIBLIOGRAPHY: *Yalkut Vohlin*, 1 (1945), 9; B. Friedberg, *Toledot ha-Defus ha-Ivri be-Polanyah* (1950²).

°**NOWACK, WILHELM GUSTAV HERMANN** (1850–1928), German Bible critic. Nowack was professor at Halle, and from 1881, of biblical exegesis and Hebrew in Strasbourg.

Among his writings, the *Lehrbuch der hebraeischen Archaeologie* (2 vols., 1894) represents a classical armchair approach to Palestinian archaeology in its description of ancient Israelite realia. He prepared the second edition of E. Bertheau and F. *Hitzig's commentaries on Ecclesiastes for the *Kurzgefasstes exegetisches Handbuch zum Alten Testament* (1883²) and the third edition of H. *Hupfeld's commentary on Psalms (2 vols., 1888). He also wrote commentaries on Amos and Hosea for the *Religionsgeschichtliche Volksbuecher* (vol. 9, 1908). From 1892 to 1903 he served as editor of *Goettinger Handkommentar zum Alten Testament*, to which he contributed the sections on the Minor Prophets (1897; 1922³); Judges (1902); Ruth (1902); and Samuel (1902). He also wrote on the religious development of ancient Israel (*Die sozialen Probleme in Israel und deren Bedeutung fuer die religioese Entwicklung dieses Volkes*, 1892), and on Israel's role against the background of the Assyrian Near East (*Die Zukunftshoffnungen Israels in der assyrischen Zeit*, 1902). His other studies on the Bible are: *Die Bedeutung des Hieronymus fuer alttestamentliche Textkritik* (1875); *Die assyrisch-babylonischen Keil-Inscripten und das Alte Testament* (1878); and *Der Prophet Hosea erklaert* (1880). He also prepared the masoretic text of the Minor Prophets for R. *Kittel's *Biblia Hebraica* (1906).

[Zev Garber]

NOWACZYNSKI, ADOLF (1876–1944), Polish playwright and satirist. The son of a Catholic aristocrat and of a Jewess, Nowaczyński (who used the pen name Neuwert) joined the right-wing, antisemitic pamphleteers and wrote many satirical attacks on the Jews and the Polish bourgeoisie. His historical dramas include *Wielki Fryderyk* ("Frederick the Great," 1910), *Pułaski w Ameryce* ("Pułaski in America," 1917), and *Cezar i Człowiek* ("Cesare Borgia and Copernicus," 1937). Nowaczyński was killed during the anti-German Warsaw Uprising.

NOWAKOWSKI, DAVID (1848–1921), Russian choirmaster and cantor. Born in Malin near Kiev, Nowakowski went to Odessa at the age of 21. There he was choirmaster and assistant to Chief Cantor Nissan *Blumenthal in the Brody Synagogue; and then to Blumenthal's successor, Pinḥas *Minkowski. He trained the Brody Synagogue choir, long noted for its quality, and the 30 years during which he worked with Minkowski became a brilliant period in the development of synagogue music. He left printed works and hundreds of compositions in manuscript which continued to be sung by many cantors and choirs. Two volumes of his work, *Shirei David*, were published during his lifetime: *Sabbath Eve and Evening Services* (1901) and *Ne'ilah* for the Day of Atonement (1895). He employed to a large extent the traditional chants of the cantors, integrating them into the choral sections.

BIBLIOGRAPHY: Friedmann, Lebensbilder, 3 (1927), 41–43; Sendrey, Music, index.

[Joshua Leib Ne'eman]

NOWY DWOR MAZOWIECKI, town in Warszawa province, central Poland. The Jewish settlement appears to have been founded at the close of the 17th century. From the beginning of the 18th century there was an organized Jewish community owning a synagogue and a cemetery (which until 1780 was also used by the Jews of Praga, a suburb of Warsaw). In 1768–69, a number of Jews fleeing from the *Haidamack massacres in Podolia found refuge in Nowy Dwor, bringing the ḥasidic teachings with them. During that period the Jews earned their livelihood primarily from innkeeping and by trading in wood. A woolen cloth factory established in the 1780s by the Poniatowski family (owners of the town) was to a considerable extent dependent on Jewish merchants for its financing, for supplying its raw materials, and for taking on the bulk of its orders. Jewish craftsmen and merchants earned their livelihood from tailoring, shoemaking, carpentry, construction, innkeeping, and the supply of building materials and food to the military units stationed in the district. In 1808, 183 Jews formed 25% of the town's population; in 1827 there were 334 Jews (28% of the total population), increasing to 1,305 (49%) in 1857. A German editor, J.A. Krieger, had taken over a Hebrew printing privilege from the Warsaw printer and bookseller Du Four, so that between 1781 and 1816 Nowy Dwor had one of the most active Hebrew presses in Eastern Europe, issuing well over 100 works. The driving powers behind the business were Eliezer b. Isaac of Krotoszyn and his son-in-law, Jonathan b. Moses Jacob of Wielowicz, who had also acted as proofreader and later as manager of Krieger's bookshop in Warsaw. An ambitious project of a Talmud edition did not proceed beyond the publication of the first two volumes in 1784, and subsequently the Napoleonic wars put an end to Krieger's enterprise.

During the middle of the 19th century Jews of Lithuanian origin, who were principally employed as purveyors to the Russian authorities, settled in the town. As a result of their powerful economic status they rapidly gained control of most of the community's institutions. During the last third of the 19th century the rabbinical office was held by Jacob Moses *Teomim and until 1904 by R. Menahem Mendel Ḥayyim Landau, a leader of Agudat Israel, later a rabbi in Detroit, Michigan. Landau was succeeded by Moses Aaron Taub, and between the two world wars Judah Reuben Neufeld served as the last rabbi of the town.

Industralization, the departure of Jews from regions suffering pogroms, and the expulsion of Jews from Moscow (1891) caused a rapid increase in the Jewish population of Nowy Dwor. In 1897 there were 4,735 Jews (c. 65% of the population) in the town. In 1905–06 Jewish trade unions gained in strength under the influence of the *Bund and the *Po'alei Zion. In addition to retail trade, the Jews of Nowy Dwor engaged in shoemaking, millinery, carpentry, locksmithing, tailoring, and portage; about 300 Jewish women were employed in embroidery workshops. A general conflagration in 1907, in which more than half the town's houses were destroyed, led many Jews to move to Warsaw or to emigrate to the United States. In 1920, during the war in Soviet Russia, the Polish army expelled hundreds of Jews from the town and desecrated its synagogue. In 1921 there were 3,916 Jews (50% of the population) in Nowy Dwor and 3,961 (42%) in 1931. In the municipal elections of 1927, four Jewish delegates won seats in the town's administration and the delegate of the Bund was appointed vice mayor. For a number of years the CYSHO (Central Yiddish School Organization) and *Tarbut schools as well as the Shalom Aleichem Library were subsidized by municipal funds. In the early 1930s Jewish haulage workers organized a self-defense movement against antisemitic rioters.

[Arthur Cygielman]

Holocaust Period

At the outbreak of World War II there were about 4,000 Jews in Nowy Dwor. The German army entered the town on Sept. 30, 1939. The ghetto was established at the beginning of 1941. In May 1941, 3,250 Jews were deported to Pomiechowek camp, where most of them perished. In November 1942 two deportations to *Auschwitz took place. The ghetto was liquidated on Dec. 12, 1942, when 2,000 Jews from Nowy Dwor and nearby Czerwinsk were sent to Auschwitz. After the war the Jewish community of Nowy Dwor was not reconstituted.

BIBLIOGRAPHY: Warsaw, Archiwum Glówne Akt Dawnych, KRSWI-D 6651 (= CAHJP, HM/3652); B. Wasiutyński, *Ludność żydowska w Pólsce w wiekach XIX i XX* (1930), 23; I. Schiper (ed.), *Dzieje handlu żydowskiego na ziemiach polskich* (1937), index; J. Shatzky, *Geshikhte fun Yidn in Varshe*, 1 (1947), 134, 137, 234; I. Ringelblum, in: *Kapitlen Geshikhte fun Amolikn Yidishn Lebn in Poyln* (1953); *Pinkas Nowy*

Dwor (1965). PRINTING: Weinryb, in: MGWJ, 77 (1933), 214ff.; Yaari, in: KS, 9 (1933), 436ff.; 10 (1933/34), 372ff.; 19 (1942/43), 204, 216f.; B. Friedberg, *Toledot ha-Defus ha-Ivri be-Polanyah* (1950²), 75ff.

NOWY DZIENNIK ("The New Daily"), first Zionist Polish-language journal. It appeared daily in Cracow from the end of 1918. The paper was representative of the climate of linguistic assimilation current in certain nationalist Zionist circles in the region. Its founding was to some extent the result of the murder of a Jew: since, to the dismay of the Jewish community, the incident was glossed over by the Polish press, a need was felt for some independent means of expression. For technical reasons and because of censorship, the early editions of *Nowy Dziennik* were published in Moravska-Ostrava. However, by the beginning of 1919, the paper had its own building and presses in Cracow. Dr. Wilhelm Berkelhammer, who served as editor for many years, not only set an example of polished newspaper style but fought numerous and continuous battles against antisemitism. Other noted editors were Isaac Ignacy Schwarzbart, Elijah Tisch, and David Lazar, the last serving until the paper's demise during the Holocaust. Among the regular contributors were Osias (Joshua) *Thon, who set the tone of the paper and gave it its political direction, and Moses Kanfer, literary and artistic critic, who was particularly devoted to the Yiddish theater. Other such well-known personalities as Isaac *Deutscher, Hersch *Lauterpacht, and Ezriel *Carlebach also contributed to the paper. Particularly noted for his essays on antisemitism was Matthias *Mieses. One important role played by the journal was its publication from time to time of a list compiled by the community leaders of Jews who had converted to Christianity but who sought to keep this secret from the Jewish community. Despite governmental interference and the bombing of its building by Polish nationalist extremists in 1923, the paper prospered. Carefully organized and efficiently run by Sigmund Hochwald, it grew from its initial four to a format of 32 pages. While ideologically the journal served as an organ of the Zionist Movement, its scope was quite wide, serving the general Cracow community as well as the region of western Galicia and Silesia.

BIBLIOGRAPHY: I. Schwarzbart, *Tvishn beyde Velt Milkhomes* (1958), 128–42. **ADD. BIBLIOGRAPHY:** J. Gothelf (ed.), *Ha-Ittonut ha-Yehudit she-Hayeta* (1973), 270–80.

[Moshe Landau]

NOWY SACZ (Pol. **Nowy Sącz**; Ger. **Neu Sandec**; in Jewish sources **Zanz, Naysants**), city in the province of Cracow, S. Poland. Jewish settlement is mentioned in a document of 1469; in 1503 a Jewish eye doctor, Abraham, practiced in Nowy Sacz. The Jews participated in the reconstruction of the town after the invasion of the Swedes. The royal privilege of 1676 (ratified in 1682 by King John III Sobieski) accorded them the right to build their houses on the town's empty lots and to engage in commerce (mainly with Hungary) and weaving. The Great Synagogue, renowned for its beautiful frescoes, was completed in 1746. In 1765 there were 609 Jews (154 families) in Nowy Sacz paying the poll tax and owning 70 houses (595 additional Jewish poll tax payers lived in 103 surrounding villages). At the beginning of the 19th century Austrian authorities compelled the Jews to live in a special quarter. During the first half of the 19th century the ḥasidic dynasty of the Zanzer Ḥasidim was established (see *Halberstam). In 1880 there were 5,163 Jews (46% of the total population) living in the town, earning their livelihoods from the sale of wood, agricultural produce, and clothing, or engaging in such trades as tailoring, carpentry, shoemaking, and engraving. By 1890 the number of Jews had decreased to 4,120 (32%), to rise again to 7,990 (32%) in 1910. Between 1900 and 1914 a Jewish school was established by the *Baron de Hirsch fund, which in 1907 was attended by 204 pupils. In 1921 the Jewish community numbered 9,009 (34%). *Tarbut and Beth Jacob schools, a yeshivah, and sport clubs were supported by the community. Over 10,000 Jews lived in Nowy Sacz before the outbreak of World War II, with another 5,000 living in smaller towns of the county.

[Arthur Cygielman]

Holocaust Period

The German army entered the town on Sept. 5, 1939, and the anti-Jewish terror began. In March 1940 about 700 Jews from Lodz were forced to settle there; in August 1941 a ghetto was established. Two forced labor camps for Jews were built by the Germans near the town: one, in Roznow, existed from the spring of 1940 until December 1942, and the second, in Lipie, from the autumn of 1942 until July 1943. Over 1,000 Jewish prisoners perished in these camps. In April 1942 a few score members of the underground *Po'alei Zion organization fell into German hands and were executed on the site of the town's Jewish cemetery. In Aug. 24–28, 1942, the entire Jewish population was deported to the *Belzec death camp and killed there.

[Stefan Krakowski]

BIBLIOGRAPHY: R. Mahler, *Yidn in Amolikn Poyln in Likht fun Tsifern* (1958), index; B. Wasiutyński, *Ludność żydowska w Pólsce w wiekach XIX i XX* (1930), 112, 146, 150, 156; J. Sygański, *Historya Nowego Sącza*, 3 vols. (1901–02); I. Schiper, *Studya nad stosunkami gospodarczymi Żydów w Polsce podczas średniowiecza* (1911), index; idem (ed.), *Dzieje handlu żydowskiego na ziemiach polskich* (1937), index; R. Mahler, *Sefer Zanz* (1970). HOLOCAUST: E. Podhorizer-Sandel, in: BZIH, 30 (1959), 87–109.

NOY, DOV (1920–), scholar in Jewish folklore. Born in Kolomyja, Poland, he graduated from a Polish secondary school, and then immigrated to Palestine where he began his academic studies at the Hebrew University of Jerusalem. He interrupted his studies to volunteer for military service in the British Army Royal Engineers during World War II, returning to the Hebrew University to complete his master's degree in Talmud, Jewish History, and Bible studies in 1946. He directed educational and cultural activities in the Cyprus Detention camps of Jewish refugees and worked there until the camps' liberation in 1948. For the next three years he served as editor of the leading Israeli children's weekly, *Davar le-Yeladim*.

Returning to his studies, he received his post-graduate education in folklore, comparative literature, and anthropology at Yale University and at Indiana University, from which he obtained his doctorate in 1954, studying under Stith Thompson.

In 1955 he began his teaching career at the Hebrew University of Jerusalem where he taught *aggadah*, folk literature, general folklore, and Yiddish. He became professor and incumbent of the Chair of Folklore and Hebrew Literature. Noy's contribution to Jewish folklore has been pioneering. He founded and directed the Haifa Ethnological Museum and Folklore Archives (1956–82) and edited the Israel Folktale Archives Publications series until 1981. He founded the Israel Folklore Archives, the largest treasure of Jewish folktales recorded in Israel. He was director of the Hebrew University Folklore Research Center from 1968 and edited *Studies*, its journal. He served as the *Encyclopaedia Judaica* departmental editor for folklore. He also trained a generation of researchers and students to tape and collect folk stories from all the various Jewish ethnic groups. He started the folklore section at Haifa University within the department of Hebrew Literature. From 1985 to 1992, he served as professor of Yiddish Folklore at Bar-Ilan University. In 1992–93 he served as professor of folk literature at Ben-Gurion University and in 1995–96 professor of folklore at Haifa University. In addition to teaching in Israeli universities, Noy devoted himself to spreading Jewish folk culture all over the world. He also wrote and edited about 60 books, covering a wide range of Jewish folklore: European, North African, Yemenite, and others. In 2004 he was awarded the Israel Prize for literary research.

[Elaine Hoter]

NOY, MEIR (1922–1998), Israeli musician, composer, and song collector. Born in Kolomea, Galicia, Noy received a Jewish and musical education. He studied violin and engineering. During World War II he escaped his town's ghetto and joined the Red Army, where he served as a musician and directed a musical ensemble. After the war he emigrated to Israel. On his way, he was interned in a Cyprus British Mandatory camp where he decided to collect Yiddish songs to commemorate the lost Yiddish musical folklore. In Israel, he first joined the army music entertainment troupe, the Tshisbatron, as an accordionist. He also composed his first Hebrew songs, such as "*Ba-Derekh le-Eilat*" (1949) and "*Ha-Pegishah*" (1949), for this troupe, and later composed for other troupes. Other popular songs he composed are "*Ha-Zekankan*" (1956) and "*Al Rosh ha-Djindji Bo'er ha-Kova*" (1957). After his army service, he taught music in a school in Tel Aviv for 30 years. From 1949 until his last day, he collected Yiddish and Hebrew songs from written and oral sources, which he transcribed and catalogued. His collection includes about 100,000 Hebrew songs and 30,000 Yiddish songs. This collection is one of the most complete collections of this sort and contains unique and accurate information about the creation and continuity of Israeli popular song. The collection was donated with the assistance of the Wachs family to the Music Department of the Jewish National and University Library in Jerusalem. The collection was recatalogued and is open to the public and serves scholars from all over the world. Meir Noy also published two books of songs from his collection, *Otiyyot ha-Alef Bet* and *Ma'ayanei ha-Zemer*, in which he compares Yiddish and Hebrew songs with the same melody.

[Gila Flam (2nd ed.)]

NUDEL, IDA (1931–), Russian Jewish activist and *refusenik*. Born in the Crimea, she was trained in Moscow as an economist. Under the impact of the 1967 Six-Day War and the 1970 Leningrad Trial, she and her sister – her sole relative – decided to leave for Israel in 1971. Her sister and her family were permitted to emigrate but Nudel was refused permission on the ground that she was privy to state secrets (she had been working as an accountant in a planning institution which was totally non-secret). Dismissed from her job, she became extremely active in the Jewish Emigration movement and was known as the "guardian angel," caring for Jewish prisoners and their families. Through demonstrations, correspondence, and meetings with foreigners visiting Moscow, she brought the plight of the prisoners to public attention. She was arrested on many occasions, placed under house arrest, harassed frequently and physically abused.

In 1978 she hung a banner on the balcony of her apartment reading "KGB – GIVE ME MY EXIT VISA," as a result of which she was sentenced to four years' exile in Siberia on charges of malicious hooliganism. There she suffered great hardships and after her release in 1982 was refused the right to live in a major city and moved from one place to another. In the Western world she became the best-known woman *refusenik*, winning the active support of many public figures such as Jane Fonda (who visited her in her exile) and Liv Ullmann (who portrayed her in a movie). Finally in 1987 she was permitted to leave for Israel where she settled near her sister in Reḥovot.

NUDELMAN, SANTIAGO ISRAEL (1904–1961), Argentine politician. Born in the colony of Médanos in the province of Buenos Aires, Nudelman graduated in both medicine (1930) and law (1936) from the University of Buenos Aires. He was a member of the Federal Chamber of Deputies representing the Unión Cívica Radical (1946–55) and championed the cause of civil liberties in parliament. In 1958 he became director of the daily newspaper *Critica*. He wrote *El radicalismo al servicio de la libertad* (1947) and *El régimen totalitario – Torturas, presos políticos, negociados* (1960).

NUISANCE. The owner or person in possession of land is not at liberty to use it as he pleases. Land, even if unencumbered, may not be used in such manner as to harm or disturb one's neighbors. Any neighbor can require the offending landowner to abate the nuisance or to have the cause thereof removed from their common boundary.

Among the restraints imposed on the use of land, the Mishnah (BB 2) makes mention of the following: A person may not dig a cistern near to his neighbor's cistern or wall, since they would thus be damaged, and he must remove lime from the vicinity of his neighbor's wall; he may not open a bakery or stable under his neighbor's barn, nor a shop on residential premises where the customers will disturb the neighbors; he may not build a wall so close to his neighbor's windows as to darken them; he must not keep his ladder near his neighbor's dovecote since it will enable a weasel to climb it and devour the pigeons; his threshing floor must not be too near a town or his neighbor's field lest the chaff harm the vegetation. There are further instances of the potentially harmful use of land enumerated in the Talmud.

The *tanna*, R. Yose, is of the opinion that the person creating a nuisance cannot be obliged to abate it and is free to act as he pleases and the injured party must keep his distance if he wishes to avoid suffering harm. The *halakhah* of the Talmud was decided in accordance with R. Yose's view, but the latter was interpreted as admitting that the tort-feasor must abate a nuisance if the interference with his neighbor's use of his property arises from his own harmful act (i.e., an act of his own body, as if he had "shot arrows" into his neighbor's domain; BB 22b). The scope of this qualification is not clear and some scholars hold that most of the injuries enumerated in the Mishnah (above) are of the kind qualified by R. Yose, which the latter concedes must be abated by the tort-feasor. Other scholars hold that R. Yose disagrees with the above-mentioned *mishnayot* and obliges the tort-feasor to abate a nuisance only when damage is actually (and directly) caused by his own act (see Rashi and Tos. *ibid.*). In fact, in the post-talmudic period, the instances in which R. Yose was considered to have conceded the existence of tort-feasor's obligation to abate a nuisance were extended as far as possible (see *Asher b. Jehiel (Rosh), quoted in Tur, ḤM 155:20–23). The Talmud (BB 17b) also records the dispute over the question whether the obligation – when it exists – of abating a nuisance applies even if the offender's particular use of his land preceded that of his neighbor – the latter suffering no damage until the time of such conflicting use by him – or whether prior use takes precedence. Thus if the injured party's particular use of his land preceded his neighbor's conflicting use of his land, the latter must curtail his use, but if the other way round the obligation rests upon the injured party. There is an opinion (Tos. *ibid.*, 18b), which holds that the rule of precedence by virtue of prior use is universally accepted and that there is no dispute save with regard to a single case, that of digging a cistern in the vicinity of a common boundary with a neighbor.

Which Nuisance Must Be Abated

An analysis of the cases of nuisance referred to in talmudic literature and the reasoning behind them suggests that all cases of nuisance may be divided into four categories:

(1) An interference arising when land is used in a manner usual for that particular place and time, but the neighbor suffers injury in an unusual manner, either because of the unusual use of his own land or because he is uncommonly sensitive to the disturbance. It is unanimously agreed that in this event the alleged tort-feasor is at no time obliged to abate the so-called nuisance.

(2) The tort-feasor uses his land in an unusual manner for that particular place and time, while the injured neighbor uses his land in the usual manner, in the same way as other people do, and is neither more sensitive nor anxious than most people. In this event all agree that the tort-feasor must always abate the nuisance he has created.

(3) Both parties use their land in the usual manner and the injured party is not uncommonly sensitive.

(4) The tort-feasor uses his land in an unusual manner, and the injured party does so too or is uncommonly sensitive.

The latter two categories are the subject of the dispute mentioned above between R. Yose and the sages, as to whether the party causing the nuisance is obliged to abate it or whether it must be suffered by the injured neighbor; and of the dispute whether the injuring party must always abate the nuisance or whether it is a matter of prior use taking precedence. Most acts of nuisance referred to in the Talmud fall into the third of these categories (see Albeck, bibliography).

The Rules of Nuisance as Part of the Law of Property

The prohibition against using land in a manner interfering with a neighbor's enjoyment of his own property is inherent in the proprietary rights over that immovable property, and the right to the undisturbed use of one's property may be sold like any other proprietary right. A person may sell or transfer part (or all) of his right to the undisturbed enjoyment of his property by agreeing to a particular use of his neighbor's property, whereupon the neighbor may make such use of his land regardless of any nuisance thereby caused to the former. Thus, for instance, a person may become entitled to erect a dovecote alongside this common boundary and may transfer this right, together with the land itself, to a new owner. Furthermore this right is retained by the owner of the disturbing property even when the adjacent land is sold to a new owner (see Sh. Ar., ḤM 155:24). A nuisance which is continued for a period of three years (or even from the outset, according to some scholars), if supported by a plea that the right was granted to him by the injured neighbor (or even without such a plea, according to some scholars), constitutes evidence of such right of user. However, these rules apply only when the nuisance is not so severe as to be insufferable (*ibid.*, 155:35–36.)

Relationship of Nuisance to the Laws of Tort

A person suffering a nuisance may oblige his neighbor to abate the nuisance and if physical damage results from the nuisance which itself was the result of the neighbor's negligence, he is also entitled to be compensated for such damage (BB 20b). If the nuisance is of a kind which the law does not require the tort-feasor to abate, the neighbor cannot oblige the tort-feasor to do so, nor, according to some scholars, can he recover compensation for damage of a physical nature even when caused by negligence, because he, in turn, is expected to take precautions. Other scholars, however, hold the tort-feasor liable for resulting damage. If a person's use of his land is such that it may cause his neighbor damage for which compensation is payable but it is not likely that such damage will result, the neighbor cannot demand the abatement of the nuisance because people are not normally afraid of or disturbed by an unlikely risk; but if in fact the damage does result from the landowner's negligence he is obliged to compensate his neighbor. If such use of the land habitually causes damage for which compensation is payable, people will usually be disturbed thereby and the neighbor can require the abatement thereof. If the damage is of a kind which is foreseeable, the landowner will be deemed negligent, but if the damage was unforeseeable, he is exempt from liability. The law of the State of Israel (Civil Wrongs Ordinance, 1947) defines private nuisance as any conduct which causes a material interference with the reasonable use and enjoyment of another's immovable property. The injured party is entitled to compensation and the court may order the abatement of the nuisance.

[Shalom Albeck]

Visual Trespass (*hezzek re'iyyah*)

The damage occasioned by a neighbor's ability to "look" into another person's home (*hezzek re'iyyah*) is a nuisance bearing unique characteristics. It occurs as a result of the neighbor's ability to observe another person's activities in his home. The damage may be caused when a person builds a window opposite his neighbor's window in a way that enables him to see into his neighbor's home, and the "trespasser" may be compelled to remove the potential source of damage – i.e., his visual trespass into another person's private domain – by requiring him to close off the window (Mish., BB 3:7; Yad, Shekhenim 5:6; Sh. Ar., ḤM 154:3). In the case of partners sharing the same courtyard, the possibility of this kind of trespass, occasioned by the proximity of their dwellings, imposes on each of the parties the advance (financial) obligation of erecting a partition between the separate parts of the courtyard (BB 2:2; Yad, Shekhenim 2:14; Sh. Ar. ḤM 157:1).

Regarding partners to the same courtyard, the *posekim* agree that one cannot acquire a *ḥazakah,* i.e., a right established by ongoing practice, to visually trespass in another person's domain. Hence both parties are entitled at all times to force the other to participate in the construction of the partition, and the other cannot argue that a waiver may be inferred from the length of time that has elapsed without protest (Maim., Yad, Shekhenim 11:4; Sh. Ar., ḤM 155:36). The *posekim* however dispute the question of visual trespass created by the construction of a window. The issue is whether visual trespass under these circumstances establishes a *ḥazakah* (in the sense referred to above) so that in the absence of protest by the other party, the builder of the window gains the right to perpetuate the existing situation, and what length of time must elapse after the window's construction for a lack of protest to be deemed as a waiver on the neighbor's part. This dispute is based on the various tannaitic views cited in the Talmud (BB 59b), and indicates the uniqueness of this type of nuisance. Certain *posekim* view this form of trespass as analogous to any other nuisance, so that if protest is not expressed from the outset, it may be seen as consent and the person causing it will acquire a *ḥazakah* with respect thereto (Yad, Shekhenim 5:6; *Kesef Mishneh*, ad loc.; Yad, Shekhenim 11:4; *Maggid Mishneh*, ad loc.). Other *posekim* classify it as a nuisance in respect of which there can be no *ḥazakah* based on waiver because it falls into the category of nuisance caused without any action being taken and, as such the nuisance is a permanent one and the evidentiary presumption is that others do not pardon it. Nevertheless, if one of the parties waived his right to the other by a formal *kinyan,* his waiver is effective and he cannot retract it (Rif, quoted in *Nimukkei Yosef,* BB 1b; for a general discussion of waiver of obligations, see *Acquisition; *Meḥilah). A third view is presented by the Rashba (Resp. Rashba, vol. 2. no. 268; see also *Ḥiddushei ha-Ramban* to BB 59a). Rashba states that visual trespass is forbidden, not only in terms of civil law, but in order to preserve modesty, which a Jew is not at liberty to waive, and should he do so his waiver is invalid. Rashba finds support for this opinion in the words of Rabbi Johanan in the Talmud (BB 60a), who states that the law of *hezzek re'iyyah* is based on the Biblical verse (Numbers 24:2): "And Bilaam lifted up his eyes and he saw Israel dwelling according to their tribes," which emphasizes the modesty of Israel. In light of this ruling, Rashba stated that a custom accepted by the people in a place not to insist on matters involving visual trespass is an erroneous custom and of no validity (see *Minhag; *Mistake). Some consider Rashba's statement as the source for protection of privacy in Jewish law (see *Rights, Human).

[Menachem Elon (2nd ed.)]

BIBLIOGRAPHY: Gulak, Yesodei, 1 (1922), 134, 146f; ET, 8 (1957), 659–702; 10 (1961), 628–96; S. Albeck, in: *Sinai,* 60 (1967), 97–123. **ADD. BIBLIOGRAPHY:** M. Elon, *Ha-Mishpat ha-Ivri* (1988), 1:763f.; 879ff.; idem, *Jewish Law* (1994), 2:942f.; 1073ff.; *Enẓiklopedyah Talmudit,* 8, 659.

NULMAN, MACY (**Moshe**; 1923–), *ḥazzan.* Born in Newark, New Jersey, Nulman held cantorial positions in Anshei Sefard Congregation of Boro Park, Etz Chaim of Flatbush, and various other congregations in the United States. He acted as principal of the Philip and Sarah Belz School of Jewish Music of Yeshiva University until he retired in 1983. From 1970 to 1972 he taught Jewish music in Brooklyn College and appeared on educational programs on radio and television. He was among the founders of the Cantorial Council of America of Yeshiva University. Nulman published "Wedding Service" (1948), "Sabbath Chants"(1958), "*Ma'ariv* Chants" (1965). He was editor of the *Journal of Jewish Music and Liturgy.* His other publications included *Concise Encyclopedia of Jewish Music* (1975), *Concepts of Jewish Music and Prayer* (1985), and *Encyclopedia of Jewish Prayer: Ashkenazic and Sephardic Rites* (1993), an award-winning volume with comprehensive information on every prayer recited in the Ashkenazi and Sephardi traditions.

[Akiva Zimmerman / Raymond Goldstein (2nd ed.)]

NUMBERS, BOOK OF (Heb. בְּמִדְבַּר; "in the wilderness"), the fourth book of the Pentateuch. Like the other books of the Pentateuch, its name in Hebrew is taken from the first significant word in the book (the fifth word in chapter 1), which also reflects its theme, the wilderness wanderings. The English name Numbers derives from the Greek translation, the Septuagint, which titled the book thematically after the censuses mentioned in the first four chapters. The Greek name corresponds to an earlier Hebrew name in the Talmud, *Ḥummash* (properly, *homesh*) *ha-Pekudim*

Jewish tradition divides the book into 10 *parashiyyot,* "annual pericopes"; based on the Vulgate system the book is divided into 36 chapters.

Contents and Sequence

Numbers is a complex collection of texts woven of a variety of literary genres: legal material; ritual prescriptions; historical narratives; and poetic folk traditions. Its present form reflects a long and intricate literary history. The book can easily be divided by subject matter and other criteria into three major sections; these can be further subdivided into smaller segments. Often it is difficult, however, to determine any meaningful relationship between contiguous segments, though certain structural patterns do exist. Numbers has a broad outline, with the main thread leading from preparations for the departure from Sinai and ending with the stay in Shittim in Moab opposite Jericho. Three main units reflect a literary sandwich of sorts:

(1) 1:1–10:10: Final encampment at Sinai.

(2) 10:11–22:1: Generation-long march in the wilderness from Sinai to Moab.

(3) 22:2–36:13: Encampment on the plains of Moab and preparation to enter Canaan.

According to the chronology in Numbers, the 40 years in the wilderness are divided as follows: 19 days at Sinai (unit 1); approximately 38 years from Sinai to Moab (unit 2); and five months of the 40th year on the plains of Moab (unit 3).

(1) FINAL ENCAMPMENT AT SINAI (1:1–10:10). The first ten chapters conclude the bloc of priestly material dealing with the portable sanctuary, given in the previous books of the Pentateuch. Where *Exodus (25–31 and 35–40) gives the details of the preparation of a portable sanctuary, and *Leviticus the consecration of the officiating clergy and the sacrificial ritual, Numbers 1–10 concentrates on the movement of the sanctuary. The functionaries featured are Levites, who lend logistical support to the priests. This first unit focuses on preparations, practical and cultic, for the desert marches and encampments. Maintenance of cult purity within the camp is stressed, as it assures God's presence. In chapters 1–4 the subject is the group service (*ẓava*, usually military service, but not exclusively; cf. Akk. *ṣābu*, and see Naḥmanides to Num. 1:2). The laic tribes must prepare to engage in battle; the Levites carry the components of the portable sanctuary. The numbers of the able-bodied males are given; and the order in which they camped and marched with the 12 tribes ranged around the sanctuary, three on each side. This first census, oriented to military preparedness as well as procedures for the march, has the same total as Exodus 38:26, namely 603, 550 (Num. 2:32). The numbers are not easy to interpret in detail, but they reflect an effort to clothe the schematic number 600,000 (see *Exodus) with the details of a tribal breakdown. Topics that focus on the Levites include their consecration in place of first-born Israelites, two censuses, and their familial relationships and duties (ch. 3–4).

The next section switches focus from camp organization to maintenance of camp purity. Conditions are outlined for the removal and readmission of persons who have become impure (parts of ch. 5). The procedures for the *Nazirite follow (6:1–21). As seen here in its aspect of supererogatory piety, the institution offers an outlet to the zealous Israelite; he may take on, for a limited time, additional personal restrictions. This part of the book, concentrating on the protection of the Tabernacle, culminates with the Priestly Blessing (6:22–27). Chapter 7, which describes the presents offered by the tribal leaders for the service of the Tabernacle, jointly (six wagons and 12 oxen) and individually, is the longest chapter in the Torah. Each tribal leader is assigned a day for his presentation (following the order in ch. 2), and the formula is scrupulously repeated without variation. The first Passover is celebrated in the wilderness (9:1–14) and Moses makes provisions for ritually impure persons to celebrate a second Passover one month later. In final readiness for the march, two silver trumpets are fashioned (10:1–10), and instructions are provided for their use, in battle and on festive occasions.

(2) GENERATION-LONG MARCH IN THE WILDERNESS FROM SINAI TO MOAB (10:11–22:1). The middle unit is woven of narratives interspersed with sacrificial law, various prohibitions, and expiation processes. Recurring rebellions and murmuring against God and Moses characterize these narratives. Ultimately, all the preparations for the imminent entry into the Promised Land came to naught as a result of the moral degeneration of the people that resulted in the decree that all those who were 20 years and older when they left Egypt, with the sole exception of Joshua and Caleb, were to die in the wilderness. The "murmuring" which runs throughout this part of the book is probably a technical term for disloyalty, in the terminology of a treaty between suzerain and vassal (see *Covenant). Even Moses, Aaron, and Miriam have moments of disloyalty to God. The unit opens with a description of the departure from Sinai on 20 Nisan, year 2 of the Exodus (10:11). It is followed immediately by a litany of grievances and their resolutions (ch. 11); a key complaint is the monotony of the people's staple food, manna, which is then supplemented by the delicacy of quail meat (as in Ex. 16). In satisfying their hunger for substantial food, the people gorge themselves and

are punished by a plague. Woven into this story is the initiation of 70 elders to share the burden of the people of Israel, the prerequisite for such service being an experience of prophetic ecstasy occasioned by the presence of Moses in the vicinity of the Tent. Probably the original number was 72, six from each tribe; the failure of *Eldad and Medad to report to the Tent resulted in the installation of only 70. The next account treats the loss of faith of Miriam and Aaron (ch. 12). The occasion is Moses' marriage to a Kushite, although the laconic account gives no indication of whether the pigmentation of the woman is an issue. The affliction of Miriam with leprosy, which turns her skin white, may be a poetic judgment because she slurred a black woman.

The nadir in the loss of faith is the story of the refusal to invade Canaan from the south (chs. 13–14). Twelve men, eminent representatives of each tribe, reconnoiter the land that has been promised to the Israelites. It is this incident which brings the decree of the death of that generation in the wilderness. The story is of major importance in Israelite tradition. It is similar in many points to the other great act of treason, the episode of the Golden Calf (Ex. 32–34). It has a military context, which is central to the wilderness experience and the conquest of the Promised Land. Chapter 15 is an aggregate of prescriptions, which are apparently placed here as a pause in the drama. It begins with cultic ordinances for Canaan, which serve as a placebo after the dire punishment. Then come prescriptions relating to errant behavior, climaxed by the execution of the man who gathered firewood on the Sabbath. The final section ordains the use of a garment fringe with an azure thread, to serve as a reminder of the Covenant. In pre-Israelite times the fringe had an apotropaic function, the warding off of demonic harm, and was regarded as an extension of the person. As with the *phylacteries, the fringe was transvalued by the Bible, to serve as a reminder to the Israelites that they are a Covenant community. This is a fitting epilogue to the account of the treason in chapters 13–14, as well as to the ordinances of errancy attached to it. The rebellion of Korah (chs. 16–17) blends two (or three) attacks on the authority of YHWH as vested in Moses and Aaron. One reflects the dissatisfaction of a group of laymen from the tribe of Reuben. Another shows the dissatisfaction of a Levite, from the most important family (Kohath) of the Levites with the assignment of Levites to the subordinate service of supporting the priests, who alone are authorized to officiate in the Tent. Through divine intervention both parties are punished. The subsequent murmuring of the Israelites against Moses and Aaron leads to punishment by plague, which is stopped when Aaron carries a pan with burning incense into the midst of the dying. In this way, the authority of Aaron is brought home strikingly, and is underscored by the contest of the staves. This is followed by a restatement of the relationship between the priests and the Levites (ch. 18), including the perquisites due to each group (*terumah* and *tithe). Then comes the prescription of the *red heifer (ch. 19), the ashes of which serve to decontaminate those in a state of ritual pollution; the ashes also contaminate the uncontaminated. This double nature of sanctuary taboo may reflect the attitude toward a superhuman power source, which can electrify or electrocute, as dramatized in the Korah story. Possibly this explains the location of chapter 19. The death of the leadership is the theme of chapter 20, which opens with the death of Miriam and ends with the death of Aaron. The cause of the death of Aaron and the doom of Moses is reported in the laconic account of water from the rock (cf. Ex. 17:1–7): they demonstrate loss of faith, which fits into the catalog of acts of disobedience.

The narrative now moves to the end of the 40 years in the wilderness. The generation of the Exodus is coming to an end. It is here that the Israelites anticipate the move into the area of Transjordan, and they ask for peaceful passage through the southern state of Edom, but permission is refused (20:14–21). They gain a victory over the Canaanite king of Arad (21:1–3), and turn south, to avoid Edom. Another incident of dissatisfaction is recorded, which is met by God with venomous snakes, followed by an antidote in the form of a bronze serpent. Reports of the Israelite itinerary are interspersed with two fragments of poetry supposedly derived from an ancient source, the Book of the Wars of YHWH. Then follows the victory of Israel over the Amorite king Sihon, which results in the first acquisition of territory, and a second victory, over Og king of Bashan. *The unit ends with the Israelites encamped on the plains of Moab.*

(3) ENCAMPMENT ON THE PLAINS OF MOAB AND PREPARATION TO ENTER CANAAN (22:2–36:13). Unit three finds the Israelites encamped on the eastern side of the Jordan River, opposite Jericho. This unit too, is composed of narratives, legislation, and folk tales. Its theme centers on final preparation to inherit the promised land. The first section (chs. 22–24) tells the story of *Balaam, an expert seer who is hired to curse the Israelites (damnation of one's enemies before battle is a practice well known from the ancient Near East). He is summoned in desperation by Balak, king of Moab, with the concurrence of his Midianite overlords. Repeatedly Balaam tries to curse the Israelites but God thwarts his mission and he is able only to bless them. Finally, Balaam is expelled angrily by Balak. The tale of Balaam, recorded in prose and poetry, seems to be an independent composition inserted at this juncture because its outcome determines if Israel will indeed inherit Canaan. Ultimately, it demonstrates the invincibility of Israel under the protection of YHWH, impervious to the greatest outside powers, human or magical. A non-biblical inscription from the site of Deir Alla in Jordan reveals an account of a seer by the same name, indicating at least an ancient tradition surrounding one Balaam known for his prophecies (see Levine, Balaam). Another act of treason follows at the heels of Israel's rescue from Balak's intended curses at Baal-peor. There, the people are enticed by Moabite women, and are attracted to their cultic worship; a (Simeonite) tribal leader is beguiled by a Midianite woman of high position and the two parade their liaison in the presence of the whole camp. Phinehas kills

them, earning for his descendants the right of perpetual priesthood (25:1–15). As revenge for the supposed trickery, the Israelites are enjoined to assail the Midianites. Here the catalog of treacherous acts ends.

The latter part of the book begins with a second census and the apportionment of the land to the tribes. The census of chapter 26 follows the pattern of chapter 1, with a slightly lower total, reflecting the losses resulting from punishment, which offset the natural increase. It also serves to introduce the theme of the remainder of the book and the preparation for the conquest of Canaan. Arising from the tribal allotment is the special case of Zelophehad's daughters, who petition Moses for the right to inherit, since their father *Zelophehad had no sons. Their claim is allowed (27:1–11), with the stipulation, in a later supplemental narrative, that they marry within their own tribe, so as not to disturb the tribal divisions (ch. 36). The promise of the land is the subject of the remaining material. Into this outline is set, first, the ceremony of succession, so that the people have Joshua to command them during the conquest. Again the narrative is suspended, by the insertion of prescriptions concerning festival sacrifices (chs. 28–29). There is no clear reason for the placement of these cultic regulations here, except that they are part of the testamentary matter that preceded the death of Moses, as the subscription (30:1) indicates. The same is true for chapter 30, the regulations governing the validity of vows made by a woman. The defeat of Midian, allegedly in retaliation for the seduction of the Israelites at Baal-peor, is recorded in chapter 31. Chapter 32 records the approval of the request of two and a half tribes to settle in the territory of the Amorites. Chapter 33 contains a list of the stations in the wilderness trek, most of which are unidentified, and many of which are not mentioned elsewhere. It is followed by the command to conquer Canaan and distribute the land among the tribes. There follows an outline of the ideal borders of the territory designated for Israelite settlement, and then the names of the men who will effect the division of the land by lot (ch. 34). Chapter 35 calls for the assignment of cities for special inhabitants: for the Levites, who have no share in the land allotment, and for the unwitting manslayer, to find refuge from the blood-avenger (cf. Ex. 21:12–14). The book ends with the resumption of the subject of Zelophehad's daughters, whose case serves as a model for marriage regulations enjoined on female heirs. The final verse of Numbers (v. 13) forms an inclusio with 22:1, stating the place where the precepts of this unit were given to the Israelites.

Critical View

The problems of the composition of Numbers must be viewed in the broader framework of Bible criticism. Modern critical scholarship – based on stylistic, linguistic, and contextual criteria – identifies separate sources underlying the final version of the book. Primarily, the texts of Numbers derive from various layers of the Priestly source (P); additional texts are identified with two older sources, the Yahwist (J) and the Elohist (E) (see *Pentateuch). The predominant Priestly material frequently serves to expand, supplement, or recast ideologically the earlier *je* texts to fit the agenda of the Priestly writers. The Balaam pericope, both the prose and poetry, seems to derive from a different author altogether. Dating the varying sources in Numbers, as in the rest of the Bible, remains incredibly difficult. Even the priestly material, which Bible scholars at an early date assigned to the post-Exilic period, seems to contain earlier layers. Numerous pre-Mosaic cultic texts from the Ancient Near East have been discovered, which display the same characteristics of the repetition of formulas and scrupulous detail. The argument from exaggerated and schematic numbers is similarly neutralized; earliest texts, such as the Sumerian Kings List, have exactly these features. The prodigious cultic requirements in the priestly material are also found in other early cultures, notably in Hittite sources. The theory that the Priestly legislation reflects the post-Exilic theocracy is still widely held, but has been challenged by a number of scholars. Even the dating of the narrative material of J and E, once believed to be securely dated to the pre-Exilic period, is debated. Essentially, one may recognize various narrative traditions, not necessarily consistent throughout Numbers, combined with Priestly material, narrative and cultic, which is of diverse dates and origins.

Jewish tradition, however, views the apparently disparate texts of Numbers as a single work written by Moses. Even so, the attempt to descry principles and patterns of arrangement is as early as the rabbis of the Talmud. They pursued the question of juxtaposition (or sequence), and it was they who implied an order other than the simple chronological thread: "There is no earlier and later in the Torah" (see Rashi on Num. 9:1). Although critical scholarship does not recognize Mosaic authorship, certain modern approaches have emphasized a kind of literary study that focuses on the final form of the text (synchronic approach) rather than its layers (diachronic approach). This method views the preserved text as an organic unit and searches for techniques of style and structure that bind the individual literary units into a whole (Milgrom, 1990). Finally, redaction criticism demonstrates the interaction of the different parts of the text. Milgrom highlights the literary style of Numbers. His structural analysis focuses on the device of chiasm and introversion as well as the prevalence of repetitive subscripts and resumptions, septenary repetitions, and recapitulations.

Religious Values

According to the critical view it is virtually certain that the Book of Numbers as we now have it is considerably later than Moses. In addition, the historical value of its accounts is considered minimal by most modern scholars, not only because of the late date of the written version, but because the agenda of its authors was to write a redemption history of Israel that focuses on ideology rather than historically accurate records in the modern sense. Several religiously motivated messages can be uncovered in the texts of Numbers and in their interaction with those in other books of the Pentateuch. The treatment of the traditions from the wilderness experience in Numbers has many points of contact with the wilderness journey in Exodus (especially 16–17). According to Abrabanel, the two collections are sharply distinguished: in Exodus, prior to Sinai, the Israelite failure of faith was not punished; in Numbers, after the revelation, it was punished. It seems that the Israelite traditions of the wilderness experience were largely used in duplicate, to convey the implications of the Covenant. Numbers 1–26 stresses the failure of faith even after the elaborate sanctuary ritual is instituted. The peroration comes in Deuteronomy 31:16–21. This reveals the (or a) Torah view regarding humankind: humans are constitutionally capable of rising above the realities of everyday life, but consistently do not. Confronted with circumstances, the theoretical supports of religious experience desert a person, who reacts to human situations with human behavior, which is not the standard set by the deity. On the whole, this is a depressing message. But while individuals and communities fail, the people, chosen by God, survives, always to find another chance to live up to the Covenant standards. God's fidelity, in contrast, remains constant. This hopeful note of recurrent opportunity is muted but audible in the latter section of Numbers. The failures of the wilderness experience are tied off: Israel is ensconced in the territory east of the Jordan. Perhaps in the land of the Covenant, the people of the Covenant will fulfill the terms of the Covenant.

For the traditional view, see *Pentateuch: The Traditional View.

BIBLIOGRAPHY: COMMENTARIES: H.L. Strack (Ger., 1894); B. Baentsch (Ger., 1903); G.B. Gray (Eng., ICC, 1903, 1955); H. Holzinger (Ger., 1903); A.H. McNeile (Eng., 1911); H. Gressmann (Ger., 1922); L.E. Elliott-Binns (Eng., 1927); P. Heinisch (Ger., 1936); J.G. Greenstone (Eng., 1948); H. Schneider (Ger., 1952); J. Marsh (Eng., 1953); M. Noth (Eng., 1966). STUDIES: M.H. Segal, in: *Eretz-Israel*, 3 (1954), 73–83; E.A. Speiser, in: BASOR, 149 (1958), 17–25; R.C. Dentan, in: IDB, 3 (1962), 567–71; B.A. Levine, in: JAOS, 85 (1965), 307–18; O. Eissfeldt, in: JBL, 87 (1968), 383–93; W.F. Albright, *Yahweh and the Gods of Canaan* (1968). **ADD. BIBLIOGRAPHY:** J. Milgrom, *JPS Torah Commentary Numbers* (1990); idem, in: ABD, 4:1146–55 (incl. bibliography); T. Dozeman, in: DBI, 2:214–18 (incl. bibliography); B. Levine, *Numbers 1–20* (AB; 1993; bibliography 111–21); idem, *Numbers 21–36* (AB; 2000; bibliography 61–76); N. Fox, in: *Jewish Study Bible* (2004), 281–355.

[Ivan Caine / Nili S. Fox (2nd ed.)]

NUMBERS, TYPICAL AND IMPORTANT. Biblical numbers are primarily based on the decimal system, which is of Hamito-Egyptian origin. The sexagesimal system, however, which ultimately derives from Sumerian usage, also plays an important role in Scripture, and since 60 is divisible by ten and five, the two methods of reckoning easily coalesce. The numbers in the Bible range from one (Gen. 1:5) to 100,000,000 (Dan. 7:10), though the latter figure is to be regarded as a hyperbole rather than a literal numerical expression. The largest number to be understood literally is that given in I Chronicles 21:5 in connection with David's census: 1,100,000 men from Israel plus 470,000 from Judah that drew the sword (but cf. the smaller figures in II Sam. 24:9). The idea of infinity in the mathematical sense (in contrast to the theological concept of God's unlimited powers) is not found in the Bible. However, it is recognized that there are limits to the human ability to count (Gen. 13:16; 41:49).

Biblical Arithmetic

The Israelites in biblical times did not take a special interest in mathematics. Their knowledge was confined, it seems, to their essential needs and was based on Egyptian and Babylonian methods of calculation. The four basic arithmetical operations are represented in the Bible, but only the results – not the method of calculating – are given. Thus there are examples of simple addition (Num. 11:26), subtraction (Gen. 18:28–33), multiplication (Lev. 25:8; Num. 7:84–86), and division (Num. 31:27). More complicated operations, involving "the rule of three," are exemplified in Leviticus 25:50ff.; 27:18, 23. The Hebrews also had an elementary control of fractions, but they seem to have avoided, as did other peoples of antiquity, the problem of converting mixed fractions to a common denominator. The biblical use of complementary fractions (i.e., fractions in which the numerator is one less than the denominator, e.g., 2/3, II Kings 11:7; 4/5, Gen. 47:24; 9/10, Neh. 11:1) shows Egyptian and Mesopotamian influence. Of particular interest is the use of certain parts of the body to express fractions or multiplication, e.g., *yad*, "hand" (fractions: *ibid.*; multiplication: Gen. 43:34); *regel*, "foot" or "times" (multiplication: Num. 22:28); *pi*, "mouth" (fraction: Zech. 13:8; multiplication: Deut. 21:17, according to many exegetes). The term *pi shenayim* originally meant two-thirds but subsequently came to signify "twice as much" (II Kings 2:9). The latter is the meaning it always has in the Mishnah and Talmud. In Deuteronomy 21:17 the sense is uncertain: the expression could mean either two-thirds of the inheritance or a double portion. *Rosh*, "head," frequently occurs in the sense of "sum, total" (Ex. 30:12; Num. 1:2), or "capital" (Lev. 5:24). The curious psychological approach that enables *yad*, for example, to serve both for division and multiplication is also reflected in the use of certain denominative verbs (in the *pi'el*) derived from numbers. Thus *shillesh* denotes "to divide into three" (Deut. 19:3) and "to repeat an action three times" (I Kings 18:34). The value of π was taken to be 3 (I Kings 7:23). Even the Mishnah in *Eruvin* 1:5 retains this approximate value, but *Mishnat ha-Middot* (second century) estimates π as 22/7.

Method of Expression

Biblical numbers are expressed by words denoting units, tens, 100, 200, 1,000, 2,000, 10,000, 20,000, and by combinations of these. There is no real evidence of the use of arithmetical symbols either in Scripture or in monumental inscriptions of the biblical period, like the *Siloam Inscription (c. 700); cf. also the *Mesha Stele of the ninth century. However, the use of figures in everyday documents, chiefly for small numbers, is demonstrated by the *Samaria ostraca (eighth century), where both words and figures are employed for numerals. The *Lachish Letters (sixth century) likewise contain numerical symbols. But, whereas these figures appear to be based on Egyptian models, other Samarian inscriptions display symbols that correspond to the Phoenician-Aramaic tradition. The *Elephantine papyri (fifth century) also use arithmetical signs (chiefly vertical strokes for units and horizontal lines for tens). In later times (the Hasmonean period and throughout the talmudic age), following the Greek example, the letters of the alphabet were given numerical values. The letters *alef* to *tet* represent the digits one to nine; *yod* to *ẓade*, the tens to 90; and *kaf* to *tav* 100 to 400; thousands are expressed by the letters for units with two dots above. The system eventually gave rise to the numerological method called **gematria*, which R. Eliezer b. R. Yose made the 29th of his 32 hermeneutical rules, and examples of which are to be found already in the New Testament (Rev. 13:18), as well as in the Talmud and Midrash; while the kabbalists went to fantastic lengths in the application of this exegetical device. In modern times, G.R. Driver has revived the idea that even in the Bible, numbers are occasionally indicated by the first letter of their name (acrophonic system) or by the numerical value of letters of the alphabet. Thus the number 318 in Genesis 14:14 represents אליעזר (Eliezer) (cf. Gen. R. 43:2, and the *Epistle of Barnabas*).

Symbolic and Rhetorical Use

Biblical numbers are not always intended to be taken at their face value. They are often used indefinitely – as round figures – or rhetorically, for emphasis or in a hyperbolic sense. At times the rhetorical effect is achieved through a latent number, i.e., certain words or names occur a given number of times, although the actual figure is not specified. Many numbers are noteworthy for their symbolic nuances. Hebrew literature is not altogether unique in this regard; analogues are to be found in Egyptian, Sumerian, Akkadian, Canaanite, and Hittite writings. Ugaritic, in particular, provides many examples of the rhetorical and symbolic use of numbers. Especially significant is the biblical use of sacred numbers, which play an important religious role. There is, in addition, a distinct tendency in Scripture to achieve numerical harmony or symmetry. This aspect has been worked out in considerable detail for Genesis, notably its early chapters, by U. Cassuto (see bibliography).

ONE. One is sometimes used as the indefinite article (I Sam. 24:14), and often as an indefinite pronoun, "someone, anyone, a certain man" (II Kings 4:39). Though a cardinal number, it is also used as an ordinal (Gen. 1:5; 8:5, 13; Ruth 1:4). It also signifies uniqueness and indivisibility. Hence it is expressive of the unity of marriage (Gen. 2:24) and of the doctrine of monotheism (Deut. 6:4).

TWO. The fact that various organs and limbs of the body occur in pairs (eyes, hands, etc.) invested the number two with a certain importance. The animals entered the ark in pairs; the Decalogue was inscribed on two tablets of stone. Often two sacrifices were ordained (Lev. 14:22). The fraction one-half is also common in the Bible: the half-tribe of Manasseh (Num. 32:33) and the half-shekel (Ex. 30:13). The Hebrew preference for the concrete to the abstract finds expression, inter alia, in the idiomatic use of two for "a few" (Num. 9:22; I Kings 17:12). Sometimes "three" is added to emphasize the approximate character of the number (II Kings 9:32; Job 33:29; Isa. 17:6). Mention may also be made here of the idiom *temol shilshom*, "hitherto" (literally: 'yesterday, the third day back'). A not uncommon device for achieving emphasis is the repetition (latent two) of a word or phrase (I Kings 13:2; Isa. 43:25).

THREE. Three is a very common biblical number. At times it is difficult to tell whether it is used with precision or as a small round number (Gen. 30:36; Ex. 2:2); but the addition of the next high number establishes its approximate character (Ex. 20:5; Jer. 36:23). Of special importance is its use in sacred contexts. It conveys the idea of completeness, having a beginning, middle, and end. Even in remote antiquity the pagan peoples worshiped triads of gods (in Babylonia: Anu, Bel, and Ea; in Egypt: Isis, Osiris, and Horus). The universe was divided into heaven, earth, and the abyss (or the netherworld), which the three deities represented. The family group of father, mother, and child, without doubt, also contributed to the significance of the number. In the Bible three has various religious associations: a three-year old (or third-born) sacrifice in Genesis 15:9; three feasts (Ex. 23:14); for three years the fruit of a newly planted tree was forbidden (Lev. 19:23); ritual purification on the third day (Num. 19:12; 31:19); Daniel kneeled and prayed three times a day (Dan. 6:11). The following occurrences of three are also of interest: In Genesis 40, three has symbolic significance. It exercises a mystic power in the story of Elijah's revival of the child (I Kings 17:21). Three cities of refuge are mentioned in Deuteronomy 19:7, 9. Three daughters (plus seven sons) seem to be an ideal number (Job 1:2; 42:13). Three is latent in a number of passages where it expresses a complete and perfect number or is used for emphasis. The expression "and God blessed" occurs, for example, three times in Genesis 1:22, 28; 2:3. The Sanctuary has three divisions: a court, a holy place, and a Holy of Holies (Ex. 26:33; 27:9; I Kings 6:16–17). In Aaron's benediction (Num. 6:24–26) the Tetragrammaton occurs thrice, and three pairs of blessings are pronounced. On the other hand, the trisagion in Isaiah 6:3 is a form of superlative (in the Qumran scroll, 1QIsa, "holy" is found only twice); while the occurrence of "temple of the Lord" three times in Jeremiah 7:4 merely lends emphasis to the prophet's mocking rebuke.

FOUR. The importance of the number four is probably derived from the four cardinal points of the compass (some scholars point to the square). It is regarded as sacred in various parts of the world, and signifies completeness and sufficiency. Four rivers issued from the Garden of Eden (Gen. 2:10). Jephthah's daughter was lamented annually for four days (Judg. 11:40). In Jeremiah 15:2 the people is divided into four groups, each subjected to a different type of disaster; in the next verse the category of "the sword" is itself divided into four phases. There are four winds; four quarters of heaven (Jer. 49:36); four sore judgments (Ezek. 14:21); and four horns that scatter Judah (Zech. 2:1 [1:18]). The number four frequently occurs in the measurements of the furniture of the Tabernacle (Ex. 25ff.; 36ff.) and of the Temple (I Kings 7). The bearers of God's throne are four (Ezek. 1, 10), and four chariots issue from two mountains (Zech. 6:1–8). Multiples of four are discernible in the length of the Tabernacle curtains – 28 cubits (Ex. 26:2); in the large round number 400 (Gen. 15:13; Judg. 21:12), and in the still larger figure of 400,000 (Judg. 20:2, 17; II Chron. 13:3).

FIVE. Five probably means simply "a few" in II Kings 7:13, perhaps also in Genesis 43:34; 47:2 (cf. Er. 6:6, 8). Five as a basic number goes back to remote antiquity. There was a primitive Hamitic system based on the number five before the decimal system. It is obviously derived from the fingers of the hand used by early man in his simple calculations. In the Bible, five is related to both the decimal and sexagesimal systems. It is a feature of sacred architecture (I Kings 7:39, 49). It is also found in connection with penalties (Ex. 21:37), redemption (Num. 3:47; 18:16), and gifts (Gen. 43:34; 45:22). The fraction one-fifth is likewise common (Lev. 5:16; 22:14). It is often used as a small round number (Lev. 26:8; I Sam. 17:40; Isa. 19:18). For the multiple 50 see below. Other multiples up to 500,000 occur frequently (Gen. 5:32; Ex. 30:23–24; II Chron. 13:17, et al.).

SIX. Six is part of the sexagesimal system but has little symbolic value. Examples of its occurrence are: the working days of the week (Ex. 20:9); the maximum years of servitude for a Hebrew slave (Ex. 21:2); the steps of Solomon's throne (I Kings 10:19–20); the wings of the seraphim (Isa. 6:2); the six-cubit measuring reed of Ezekiel's vision (Ezek. 40:5; 41:8).

SEVEN. Seven played an exceptionally important role in antiquity. It was sacred to Semitic and other peoples, including the Egyptians, Assyrians, Persians, and the Vedic folk in India. Its importance is often derived from the worship of the seven heavenly bodies: the sun, moon, and the five planets. It is also pointed out that the seven-day week was approximately a quarter of the lunar month (29½ days), and that the Pleiades (Amos 5:8) were thought to comprise seven stars. Others see the origin of the number's prominence in the fact that it is composed of the sacred numbers three and four, or in the "unrelated" character of seven in the series one to ten. Like the Sumerians, the biblical writers often add seven to a large number to indicate a very big figure. U. Cassuto writes: "It clearly follows that the chronology of the Book of Genesis as a whole is also founded on the dual principle of the sexagesimal system and the addition of seven" (*From Adam to Noah*, in bibl., 259). In the Bible the number seven is connected with every aspect of religious life in every period: e.g., the clean beasts in the ark (Gen. 7:2ff.); Abraham's covenant with Abimelech (Gen. 21:28–30); cleansing from leprosy (Lev. 14); the festivals (Lev. 23; Deut. 16:9); Balaam's altars (Num. 23); the induction of the priests and the consecration of the altars (Ex. 29:35–37); sacrifices (Gen. 8:20; Num. 28:11; Job 42:8; I Chron. 15:26); the Temple furnishings (I Kings 7:17); the *menorah* (Ex. 25:31–37; Zech. 4:2); the Temple steps (Ezek. 40:22); the width of the Temple entrance (Ezek. 41:3); the sprinkling of blood (Lev. 4:6, 17;16:14; Num. 19:4) and the like. The innate, mystic power of seven is exemplified in Joshua 6:4, 8, 13 (Jericho); Judges 16:13, 19 (Samson); and II Kings 5:10 (Naaman). It also occurs in connection with punishment (Gen. 4:24; Lev. 26:18; Deut. 28:7, 25; II Sam. 21:6; Prov. 6:31; Dan. 4:13, 20, 29; 9:27). In relation to time, seven represents a fitting (or sacred) period (Gen. 1:3ff.; 8:12; 50:10; Ex. 7:25; Lev. 8:33; Josh. 6). More generally it indicates a complete or round number of moderate size (Isa. 4:1; 11:15; Micah 5:4; Ps. 12:7 [6]; Prov. 26:16, 25; Job 1:2; Esth. 1:10; 2:9). In Deuteronomy 7:1 it is equated with "many." Other interesting references are: Genesis 29:20, 27, 30 and Judges 14:12, 17 (marriage); Ezekiel 9:2 (angels); II Kings 4:35 (sneezes of revival); Genesis 41; II Kings 8:1 (famine and plenty); Genesis 33:3 (prostrations; parallels are found in the Tell El-Amarna Letters and in Ugaritic writings). Multiples of seven bear the same character with added emphasis (Lev. 12:5; Num. 29:13; I Kings 8:65). For 70 see below. The half of seven, three and a half, also has special significance. "Times, time, and half a time" occurs in Daniel 7:25 and 12:7. "Half of the week" in Daniel 9:27 is explained by CH Cornill to mean 3½ years and to have its origin in the 3½ years of Antiochus' persecution. H. Gunkel, however, traces the expression to Babylonia (half Kislev, Tevet, Shevat, and Adar), the references being to the 3½ months between the winter solstice and the festival of Marduk, i.e., the period of the supremacy of Tiamat.

EIGHT AND NINE. The numbers eight and nine do not appear to have any intrinsic symbolic import. Their significance seems to be related to seven and ten, respectively. The eighth day of circumcision (Gen. 17:12), of the consecration of first-born beasts (Ex. 22:29), of the sacrifices of the defiled Nazirite (Num. 6:10), and of the holy convocation (Lev. 23:36) is simply the day after the important period of seven days. Noteworthy, however, is Ezekiel's predilection for the number eight in the Temple structure (Ezek. 40:9, 31, 34, 37). Nine is at times significant insofar as it is one less than the important number ten (Neh. 11:1).

TEN. Like five, ten is clearly derived from the use of the fingers in counting (the Sefirot, it may be noted, emanate from the fingers according to *Sefer Yeẓirah*) and is the basis of the numeral system chiefly, though not solely, used in the Bible. It expresses completeness and perfection (Gen. 24:10, 22; Josh. 22:14; Judg. 17:10; II Kings 20:9–11; Jer. 41:8; Job 19:3). Its sacred character, which may derive from the fact that it is the product of three and seven (both sacred numbers), is exemplified in the Decalogue (Ex. 20:2ff.), where it may also serve as a mnemonic; the tithes (Gen. 14:20; Num. 18:21, 26; Deut. 26:12); the Tabernacle and Temple furnishings, including multiples of ten (Ex. 26; I Kings 6–7; Ezek. 45; II Chron. 4); and the minimum number of righteous men required to save Sodom. It also occurs in latent form: e.g., there are ten patriarchs from Adam to Noah (Gen. 5), and ten from Noah to Abraham (Gen. 11:10–27). It is stated that the Israelites put the Lord to test ten times (Num. 14:22). In ritual observances the fraction one-tenth occurs frequently (Num. 28).

TWELVE. The number 12 may have derived its importance from the division of the lunar year into 12 months, and from the 12 signs of the Zodiac. It should also be noted that it can be broken down into the significant numbers five (+) seven or three (×) four. But undoubtedly its divisibility and its role in the Sumerian sexagesimal system gave it a special status. In the Bible the fact that the tribes numbered 12 (Gen. 35:22; 42:13, 32; 49:28; Num. 1:44) endowed the number with special religious significance (cf. the Greek amphictyonies). To maintain the number 12, Ephraim and Manasseh were counted as two tribes when Levi was omitted. The tribes of Ishmael likewise numbered 12 (Gen. 17:20). Representative persons and objects often correspond to the number of the tribes (Ex. 24:4; 28:21; Lev. 24:5; Num. 7:3; 17:17, 21; Josh. 4:2; I Kings 10:20; 18:31; Ezek. 48:31ff.; Ezra 6:17; 8:35). Multiples of 12 are found in the 24 classes of priests and Levites (I Chron. 24:4; 25:31); the 48 levitical cities (Num. 35:7); the 24,000 men in the monthly courses that served King David (I Chron. 27:1–15). The male descendants of Adam listed in Genesis 4:1–26 numbered 12, and the verb *yalad* ("to bear") occurs there 12 times.

TWENTY. Twenty marks a distinctive period in human life. Isaac's sons were born 20 years after marriage (Gen. 25:20, 26). Also, the age for army service was 20 (Num. 1:3).

FORTY. Forty is an important round number, indicating a fairly long period. The length of a generation is approximately 40 years. A man reaches full adulthood at 40 (cf. Josh. 14:7; II Sam. 2:10). Isaac and Esau married at 40 (Gen. 25:20; 26:34). The complete span of human life is thrice 40 (Gen. 6:3; Deut. 34:7), while twice 40 represents advanced old age (II Sam. 19:33–36; Ps. 90:10). The Israelites wandered 40 years in the wilderness (Ex. 16:35; Deut. 2:7), in which time an entire generation died out (Num. 14:33; 32:13). In I Kings 6:1 (cf. I Chron. 5:29–36 [6:3–10]) 480 years represents 12 generations. At various periods the land had rest for 40 years (Judg. 3:11; 8:28; I Sam. 4:18; 80 years in Judg. 3:30 is the equivalent of two generations) and David, Solomon, and Joash reigned for 40 years (II Sam. 5:4; I Kings 2:11; 11:42; II Chron. 24:1). This was a sign of divine grace. It is noteworthy that, according to the Mesha Stele, Israel oppressed Moab for 40 years. Periods of special significance often consist of 40 days (Gen. 7:4, 12; 8:6; Ex. 24:18; 34:28; Num. 13:25; Deut. 9:9ff.; 10:10; I Sam. 17:16; I Kings 19:8; Ezek. 4:6; 29:11–13; Jonah 3:4). Other interesting examples of the occurrence of 40 are: 40 lashes (Deut. 25:3); sons (Judg. 12:14); camel loads (II Kings 8:9); shekels (Neh. 5:15); Temple measurements (Ezek. 41:2; 46:22). Forty thousand indicates a very large number (Josh. 4:13; Judg. 5:8; II Sam. 10:18; I Chron. 12:37).

FIFTY. Fifty, a multiple of ten, occurs in measurements (Gen. 6:15; Ezek. 40:15); in compensation (Deut. 22:29); and in civil and military organization (Ex. 18:21; Deut. 1:15). Other multiples of ten, up to 500,000, are frequently encountered (Gen. 5:32; Ex 30:23–24; II Chron. 13:17).

SIXTY. Sixty, the basis of the sexagesimal system, is a heritage from the Sumerians, whose method of calculation has left its mark on the civilized world to this day. The division of the circle into 360 degrees, of an hour into 60 minutes, the minute into 60 seconds, and counting by the dozen and the gross are derived from this ancient people. The system originated, it is suggested, "in a mythical addition of zenith and nadir to the four points of the compass" (Mc-Gee). Although the biblical method of reckoning is based mainly on the decimal system, many scriptural (and likewise talmudic and midrashic) numbers show a sexagesimal structure. Thus the total ages of the patriarchs from Adam to Noah and their ages at the birth of the first son are either exact multiples of five or of five with the addition of seven (see Seven above), in accordance with a stylistic Sumerian usage. All the ages in Genesis 5 are to be analysed in the same way, as U. Cassuto has shown in his commentaries to Genesis (see bibl.). The sexagesimal method of calculation applies to other parts of the Bible, too.

SEVENTY. Seventy (the product of two sacred numbers, seven times ten) is used as a round figure, with symbolic or sacred nuances. It occurs in various contexts; it is the number of the family of Jacob that went down to Egypt (Ex. 1:5; Deut. 10:22); of the palm trees at Elim; of the elders that went up with Moses, Aaron, Nadab, and Abihu (Ex. 24:9); of the elders set round about the Tent (Num. 11:24); of the years that the nations will serve the king of Babylon (Jer. 25:11ff.); and of the weeks mentioned in Daniel 9:24ff. The nations enumerated in Genesis 10 total 70 (or 71, or 72, according to others); cf. also the 77-fold of Lamech's vengeance (Gen. 4:24). In Ugaritic literature 70 funerary offerings for Baal are mentioned, and the gods are referred to as "the 70 children of Asherah."

A THOUSAND. A thousand and its multiples are frequently used in the Bible as round numbers indicating a large amount. Etymologically the Hebrew word *elef* ("thousand") denotes "a crowd," and hence at times has the sense of "tribe," "clan," or designates a military unit, which does not necessarily comprise 1,000 (Ex. 18:21; Deut. 33:17; Judg. 6:15). Flinders Petrie (*Researches in Sinai*), interpreting *elef* to mean a family or tent, reduced the figure for the first census to 5,500, and to 5,730 for the second. Multiples of 1,000 are often hyperbolic expressions (Lev. 26:8; Deut. 32:30; I Sam. 18:7; Ps. 3:7[6]; Song 5:10). Seventy thousand (II Sam. 24:15) and 1,000,000 (Dan. 7:10; I Chron. 21:5; 22:14; II Chron. 14:8) are globular figures indicative of a vast number, while "thousands of ten thousands" (Gen. 24:60) and "ten thousand times ten thousand" (Dan. 7:10) are imaginative numerical ultimates. Similarly high figures are found in Ugaritic literature.

Accuracy

The question of the accuracy of biblical numbers is an exegetical problem. There are actual contradictions within the Bible itself (cf. II Sam. 24:9 with I Chron. 21:5). The correctness of other figures is doubted on other grounds. Unquestionably, some excessively large numbers must be regarded as symbolic or hyperbolic figures. In certain cases critics suppose that estimates – especially of enemy forces – are only rough, and possibly exaggerated, guesses. However, errors in transmission and copying must be taken into account. Manuscripts generally show that they are particularly prone to corruption where numbers are concerned. In Hebrew a single letter could change five to 50, for example. It is interesting to note that one Hebrew Ms. of the Bible (no. 9 of Kennicott) reads in Numbers 1:23, 1,050 for 59,300 (MT); Numbers 2:6, 50 for 54,400; and in Numbers 2:16, 100 for 151,450. There are also considerable divergences between the Masoretic Text, the Septuagint, and the Samaritan versions. For example, the years between the Creation and the Flood are 1,656 in the Hebrew Bible, 2,262 in the Septuagint, and 1,307 in the Samaritan recension.

Ascending and Descending Numbers

The manner in which large numbers are arranged is subject to interesting variations: sometimes they are arranged in ascending order (Gen. 5:17), at other times in descending order (Gen. 23:1; Ex. 38:26), and occasionally a combination of both (Num. 3:43). The conventional explanation is that J, E, and D prefer the descending order, while P favors the ascending order. Cassuto, however, has argued that not a documentary criterion but a linguistic principle is operative here: "When the Bible gives us technical or statistical data and the like, it frequently prefers the ascending order, since the tendency to exactness in these instances causes the smaller numbers to be given precedence and prominence. On the other hand, when a solitary number occurs in a narrative passage or in a poem or in a speech and so forth, the numbers are invariably arranged, save in a few cases where special circumstances operate, according to the more natural and spontaneous order, to wit, the descending order" (*The Documentary Hypothesis*, in bibl., 52).

Numerical Harmony

Another question to which Cassuto has given special attention is that of numerical harmony. He demonstrates, for instance, that heptads repeatedly occur in Genesis 1:1–2:3, leaving no doubt that these literary variations on the theme of seven were carefully designed so as to achieve a harmony of numbers. "This numerical symmetry," he writes, "is, as it were, the golden thread that binds together all the parts of the section and serves as a convincing proof of its unity" (*From Adam to Noah*, in bibl., 15).

Graded Numbers

Another interesting feature of biblical style is the use of graded numbers. This consists of the collocation of two consecutive numbers for rhetorical purposes. The usage may be divided into three categories:

(a) In prose it expresses approximation and, as a rule, fewness, and has a colloquial character (II Kings 9:32; 13:19).

(b) In poetry the two numbers form a parallelism and also express inexactness (Micah 5:4; Job 5:19). A similar usage is found in Sumerian and Akkadian, and, especially, in Ugaritic epic poetry. Since numbers are involved, the parallelism cannot be expressed through synonyms, and consecutive numbers are the only alternative (cf. the parallelism between 1,000 and 10,000 in Ps. 91:17). A combination of the idiom for fewness and poetic parallelism is seen in Isaiah 17:6.

(c) In proverbial sayings a schematic device is employed in which two successive numbers are given of things that share a common characteristic, and the actual items subsequently enumerated conform to the second, i.e., the higher, number (Prov. 30:15–31). The use of numbers in Proverbs (including single numbers as in Prov. 30:15a) is intended as an aid to memory. In Amos 1:3–2:6, where three and four are repeatedly mentioned but only one example is cited, the prophet apparently uses surprise as a rhetorical factor.

Reviewing the facts adumbrated above, it appears that numbers are used in the Bible not solely for statistical or arithmetical purposes. They are also employed as stylistic devices to express symbolically the idea of completeness and perfection, to convey the concept of sanctity, to provide mnemonics, and are often arranged so as to give numerical symmetry or harmony to a passage. They are used both expressly and latently to emphasize the leading thought of a text, and thus often establish its intrinsic unity. The rhetorical uses of numbers in Scripture unquestionably constitute a highly valuable aid to biblical exegesis. Furthermore, the biblical approach to numbers strongly influenced the thinking of later ages. Philo and other Hellenistic writers, the Apocryphal literature, the New Testament, the Talmud and Midrash, and especially the kabbalistic writers laid great stress on numerology in various forms. In this way, numbers became an integral part of both literature and theology.

BIBLIOGRAPHY: D. Curtis, *A Dissertation upon Odd Numbers* (1909); H. and J. Lewy, in: HUCA, 17 (1943), 1–52; U. Cassuto, *From Adam to Noah* (1961); idem, *From Noah to Abraham* (1964); idem, *The Documentary Hypothesis* (1964); idem, *Exodus* (1967).

[Israel Abrahams]

NUMBERS RABBAH, aggadic Midrash to the Book of Numbers, also called *Va-Yedabber Rabbah* in medieval literature. (For the name "Rabbah" see **Ruth Rabbah*.)

Structure

The book is divided into 23 sections. The Midrash on chapters 1–8 of the book of Numbers, which are the first two weekly portions as read today – *Ba-Midbar* and *Naso* – is two and a half times longer than the remaining Midrash on chapters 9–36, which cover the eight remaining portions. This disproportion – five sevenths of the Midrash applying to one fifth of the book of Numbers – is in itself sufficient indication that there are here two different Midrashim: *Numbers Rabbah I*, consisting of sections 1–14, and *Numbers Rabbah II*, consisting of sections 15–23.

Numbers Rabbah I

This appears at first sight to be an exegetical Midrash, since (with certain omissions) it forms a kind of consecutive interpretation to Numbers 1–8, chapter by chapter and verse by verse. Nevertheless, many of its long expositions deal with one single theme and are typical of homiletic Midrashim. The division into sections is at times determined by the open and closed sections of the Torah (see *Masorah) and at times by the weekly division of the reading of the law according to the triennial cycle once customary in Ereẓ Israel. In general each section begins with an anonymous proem, either an imitation (not always successful) of the classical proem typical of the amoraic Midrashim (see *Midrash; *Homiletics), or of the type combining *halakhah* and *aggadah* common in the *Tanḥuma Yelammedenu* Midrashim. Some sections have epilogues of consolation or of future destiny. The language of the Midrash is Hebrew, in part mishnaic and in part of the early medieval period. It contains a little Galilean and also Babylonian Aramaic and a few Greek words.

In the light of the many parallels between *Numbers Rabbah I* on the one hand, and *Genesis Rabbati* and *Midrash Aggadah* (see Smaller *Midrashim) which are of the school of Moses ha-Darshan, the 11th-century scholar of Narbonne, on the other, it seems that *Numbers Rabbah I* is also based on Moses ha-Darshan's Midrash to the Pentateuch, of which it preserved not only the contents but even the terminology. This conclusion follows also from the fact that quotations by medieval scholars from the work of Moses ha-Darshan are found in *Numbers Rabbah I*. Since, however, the parallel part of *Midrash Aggadah* (to Num. 1–8) contains many homilies not in *Numbers Rabbah I*, it is obvious that *Numbers Rabbah I* is not an actual part of the work of Moses ha-Darshan, but his book served as the main source for its editor and compiler. The basis of *Numbers Rabbah I* was a Midrash of the *Tanḥuma Yelammedenu* type (which is the reason for the many parallels to these Midrashim and for the homilies which mix *halakhah* with *aggadah*), but the late compiler broke down and reconstructed its homilies, changing its character by greatly enlarging it (particularly in the case of the homilies to *Naso*, sections 6–14, which themselves constitute four sevenths of the whole Midrash *Numbers Rabbah*), adding to it from various sources, especially from the work of Moses ha-Darshan. That work was a combination of biblical commentary, *aggadot* and homilies, and halakhic topics, and included old and new sources (the greater part of which had been revised), together with original novellae. Among the works utilized by Moses ha-Darshan were the *Apocrypha and *Pseudepigrapha of the Second Temple period, especially those of the *Enoch circle (see also *Jubilees; the *Testaments of the Twelve Patriarchs), of which he seems still to have had Hebrew versions. He used all the tannaitic literature, the Jerusalem Talmud, the early amoraic Midrashim, the *Tanḥuma Yelammedenu*, Midrashim (including *Pesikta Rabbati*), *Seder Eliyahu Rabbah* and *Seder Eliyahu Zuta*, the Babylonian Talmud, and even late Midrashim like the *Midrash Tadshe*; his work also contains pseudepigraphic material. *Numbers Rabbah I* also makes use of the *piyyutim* of *Kallir and of *Sefer *Yeẓirah*, and contains topics of esoteric lore, mysticism, and combinations of numbers and calculations. Hence its comparatively late Hebrew is understandable. As the compiler was apparently acquainted with the Midrash *Lekaḥ *Tov*, which like the work of Moses ha-Darshan dates from the end of the 11th century, the middle of the 12th century seems to be indicated as the earliest possible date for the compiling of *Numbers Rabbah I*. It is of interest that the Paris manuscript (no. 149) of 1291 only includes sections 1–5 of *Numbers Rabbah* (on the reading of the law for Numbers), while the Munich manuscript (97, 2) of 1418 includes the whole of *Numbers Rabbah I* but not *Numbers Rabbah II*.

Numbers Rabbah II

This homiletical Midrash of the *Tanḥuma Yelammedenu* type is identical in all respects with the part parallel to it in the printed *Tanḥuma* and in Buber's edition of the *Tanḥuma*. Moreover a much better version has at times been preserved in *Numbers Rabbah II* than in the parallel passages of both the above-mentioned *Tanḥuma* Midrashim. Thus, for example, it has not the Babylonian *She'ilta*, added to the *Tanḥuma* Midrashim *Ḥukkat*, 2. Instead of the expression *Yelammedenu Rabbenu* ("teach us, our master") found in the *Tanḥuma*, it has *halakhah* (in the manuscripts, however, *Numbers Rabbah II* too has *Yelammedenu Rabbenu*). Many of the halakhic proems found in the *Tanḥuma* have been abridged in *Numbers Rabbah II*, as for example the first. However, they are found in full in the manuscripts. The division of *Numbers Rabbah II* into sections, not found in the manuscripts, is, as in the *Tanḥuma*, almost identical with the division of the triennial cycle. The view accepted by the majority of critical scholars is that *Numbers Rabbah II*, which is apparently the second half of a complete Midrash whose first half, which served as the original basis, was lost, was compiled in the ninth century, like most of the *Tanḥuma Yelammedenu* Midrashim. It has, however, also some late additional interpolations from the book of Moses ha-Darshan (18:15–18; 20:5–6, lacking in the *Tanḥuma*; and 18:29 found also in the printed *Tanḥuma*).

The union of *Numbers* Midrashim *Rabbah I* and *Rabbah II* is the work of a copyist of the beginning of the 13th century. The complete Midrash was not yet known to the author of the *Yalkut Shimoni*; it seems that the first to cite it was Naḥmanides. The earliest manuscripts of the whole of *Numbers Rabbah* date only from the 15th century, but they are nevertheless much better than the printed versions.

BIBLIOGRAPHY: Zunz-Albeck, Derashot, 125–7, 397–400.

[Moshe David Herr]

NUMENIUS, son of Antiochus, Jewish envoy sent by the high priest *Jonathan to renew the Hasmonean pact with Rome. Numenius, together with Antipater the son of Jason, was instructed at the same time to deliver a pledge of friendship to the Spartans, who, according to Josephus, "received the envoys in a friendly manner" and reciprocated with a decree of their own "concerning a friendly alliance with the Jews" (Ant., 13:169–70). It appears that both envoys were used in a similar capacity by Jonathan's successor, *Simeon, and the Spartan reply to Simeon is quoted in I Maccabees 14:20ff. It has been suggested, however, that the two representatives were in fact sent to Rome and Sparta by Jonathan, who died during their mission, and therefore the Spartan correspondence is addressed to Simeon. In any event, Numenius was subsequently sent again to Rome by Simeon, taking with him on this occasion a golden shield in honor of the renewed pact. Numenius participated in yet another mission to Rome, for a similar purpose, during the early years of John *Hyrcanus. The document to this effect, however, was erroneously inserted by Josephus into the priesthood of Hyrcanus II (Jos., Ant., 14:143ff.).

BIBLIOGRAPHY: Schuerer, Hist, 53, 63; Klausner, Bayit Sheni, 3 (1950^2), 62, 76f.; M. Stern, *Ha-Te'udot le-Mered ha-Ḥashmona'im* (1965), 111, 113, 127–9, 147f., 157.

[Isaiah Gafni]

°**NUMENIUS OF APAMEA** (c. 150–200 C.E.), Greek philosopher, author of a lost work "On the Good" where he introduced the Jews to support his Platonic-Pythagorean view of God as incorporeal. A quotation in Eusebius, *Praeparatio Evangelica* 9:8, praises Moses; according to *Clement of Alexandria Numenius called Plato, whom he revered, "Moses speaking pure Greek."

NUMERUS CLAUSUS ("closed number"), amount fixed as maximal number in the admission of persons (or certain groups of persons) to specific professions (in particular the liberal professions), institutions of higher learning, professional associations, positions of public office, etc.; frequently applied to Jews. The numerus clausus on the admission of Jews to institutions of higher learning was applied in the 19th century, and extended in the 20th century, in particular in the countries of Eastern Europe, but also in others. It assumed its most characteristic form in czarist Russia (see below) as the *protsentnaya norma* where the restrictions and limitations on the admission of Jews were established by special legislation. In countries such as Poland and Romania (see below) the numerus clausus was introduced as a quasi-legal means, or was applied in practice, as part of an antisemitic policy. However, in democratic countries the numerus clausus was also tacitly applied, at least in some institutions of higher learning, for social or prestige reasons. A numerus clausus of this type was applied not only to students but also (sometimes principally) to teaching staff in the universities or in admission to the civil or public services where higher professional qualifications were required. It was also applied in admission to positions which carried a special status, as in the higher ranks of the civil service, the diplomatic service, army, etc.

In Czarist Russia

During the first half of the 19th century, the policy of the Russian government toward the Jews, as formulated in the statutes concerning the Jews ("*polozheniya*") of 1804, 1835, and 1844, was to attract the Jewish youth to Russian schools. This ambition encountered strong opposition from the Jewish masses who regarded education in these schools as a step toward the alienation of Jewish youth from its people and its religion. They also viewed the network of Jewish state schools established by the government to promote general education among the Jews with suspicion. In 1853 there were 159 Jewish pupils in all the secondary schools of Russia (1.3% of the total student roll), while in the universities there were a few dozen. On the other hand, the *maskilim* advocated education in the Russian schools as a means of rapprochement with the Russian people.

During the reign of Alexander II, a radical change occurred in the attitude of the Jews, especially those of the middle and upper classes, toward the Russian schools. This was due to the privileges granted to educated Jews (extension of the right of residence in 1865; important concessions with regard to military service in 1874). In 1880 the number of Jewish pupils in the secondary schools rose to 8,000 (11.5% of the total) and in the universities to 556 (6.8% of the total). These numbers increased yearly. In the educational region of Odessa (which included southern Russia) the proportion of Jewish students rose to 35.2%, and in the region of Vilna (Lithuania) to 26.7%. A Russian-Jewish stratum of intelligentsia rapidly became prominent. As service in the government and administration was closed to them, this intelligentsia concentrated in the liberal professions – medicine, law, and journalism. The members of these professions soon became aware of growing competition from Jews. A propaganda campaign was instigated against the admission of Jews into the class of the intelligentsia; this was sparked off in 1880 by a letter to the editor entitled *Zhid Idyot* ("The Jew Is Coming") which was published in the widely influential newspaper *Novoye Vremya*.

Of their own initiative, higher and secondary schools in various parts of the country began to restrict the admission of Jews within their precincts. This coincided with the general policy of the government of Alexander III which sought to prevent the admission of children of the poorer classes into the higher and secondary schools. It was claimed that the Jewish students introduced a spirit of rebellion and revolution into the schools and thus had a deleterious influence over their Christian fellow students. In July 1887 the Ministry of Education decided that the proportion of Jews in all secondary schools and higher institutions subject to its jurisdiction was not to surpass 10% in the towns of the *Pale of Settlement, 5% in the towns outside it, and only 3% in the capitals of St. Petersburg and Moscow. Many schools were completely closed to Jews. In time, this regulation also spread to schools which were under the supervision of other government ministries (ministry of communications, ministry of finance, etc.). There were individual cases, after the Revolution of 1905, where the restrictions and admission prohibitions were also applied to converted Jews.

These restrictions were introduced during a period when masses of Jewish youth were besieging the Russian schools, and had severe repercussions on Jewish life. Only those who had obtained the highest marks and distinctions were likely to be admitted to Russian secondary and high schools. There were naturally instances of bribery and corruption, or parents who baptized their children so that they could enter the schools. Secondary school graduates began to convert for this end, and during the years 1907 to 1914 this became commonplace. The Lutheran clergyman Piro of Finland became known for selling baptismal certificates at a low price to all those who desired them (*"pirovtsy"*). The Jewish national and Zionist movements fought this phenomenon. These regulations also resulted in the emigration of thousands of Jewish youths to study at the universities of Western Europe (Switzerland, Germany, France, etc.). Jewish students formed the majority of the "Russian" colonies in the university towns of the West. In 1892 the number of Jewish pupils in the secondary schools had decreased to 5,394 (7% of the pupils).

Jewish youths took advantage of the possibility of completing their studies by means of external examinations. In Jewish society, the "extern" studied under the guidance of private teachers and then sat for the state examinations. The antisemitic examiners were severe and failed many of them. In 1911 it was decided that the numerus clausus would also apply to external students, and since the number of non-Jewish external students was very limited this system was brought to an end. During the period of the Russian Revolution of 1905, when autonomy was granted to the institutions of higher learning, the numerus clausus was abolished, but immediately upon the repression of the Revolution the practice was restored. The proportion, however, was increased (to 15% in the Pale of Settlement, 10% beyond it, and 5% in the capital cities). Accordingly, the number of Jewish pupils in the secondary schools rose to 17,538 (9.1% of the pupils), and of Jewish students at the universities to 3,602 (9.4%). In the overwhelming majority of secondary schools for girls, the numerus clausus was not introduced. In 1911 about 35,000 Jewish girls studied at Russian secondary schools (13.5% of the pupils). In the educational region of Vilna (Lithuania) the proportion of Jewish girl pupils rose to 49%, in the region of Warsaw to 42.7% and in the regions of Kiev and Odessa to 33.3% (these four educational regions encompassed the whole of the Pale of Settlement). The numerus clausus served as an impetus for the establishment of private Jewish secondary schools, several of which evolved the beginnings of a national Jewish education.

All restrictions on the admission of Jews to the secondary schools and institutions of higher learning were abolished with the Revolution of February 1917. In 1919, during the brief period when the armies of *Denikin (the "White Army") gained control of large regions of southern Russia, the numerus clausus was temporarily reinstated in many towns under their control.

[Yehuda Slutsky]

In the Soviet Union

There are no indications of any official or unofficial numerus clausus existing in the Soviet Union until the last "Black Years" of Stalin's rule (1948–53). Even then discrimination against Jews seeking admission to Soviet universities seems to have been related to the general atmosphere of distrust and enmity, engendered by the anti-Jewish trend of official policy, rather than the result of a regulated system of limited percentages. Though legally and openly there has never been a numerus clausus for Jews in the U.S.S.R., young Jews seeking admission to certain prestige universities, or to studies leading to positions entailing use of classified information or representative status in the state or on its behalf, increasingly encountered unexpected artificial difficulties in the 1950s and 1960s. Many young Jews complained of having been rejected despite brilliant achievements in the entrance examinations in favor of non-Jews with fewer scholastic qualifications. A number of statements were made by Prime Minister Nikita Khrushchev (for instance to a French socialist delegation in 1957; see *Réalités*, May 1957) or by the minister of culture, Yekaterina Furtseva (to a correspondent of the pro-Communist American magazine, *National Guardian*, June 25, 1956) confirming the existence of a general policy to regulate cadres according to nationality – particularly and explicitly by reducing the proportion of Jews in the intelligentsia and in government departments. These statements seemed to validate the assumption of many Soviet citizens as well as of scholars abroad that, as W. Korey affirms in his study on the legal position of Soviet Jewry (1970), "unpublished governmental regulations appear to have been issued, whether in written or oral form, which establish quotas limiting educational or employment opportunities for Jews." In 1959 the minister for higher education, U.P. Yelyutin, vehemently denied the existence of such quotas, and in 1962 the U.S.S.R. ratified the UNESCO Convention against Discrimination in Education. However, some evidence to the contrary was found in 1963 in Soviet journals such as *Kommunist* and, particularly, the "Bulletin of Higher Education," which acknowledged the existence of "annually planned preferential admission quotas." An American specialist on Soviet education, N. de Witt, reached the conclusion in 1961 that a quota system existed "to the severe disadvantage of the Jewish population." According to de Witt the principle applied makes "the representation of any national or ethnic grouping in overall higher education enrolment" proportional to its size in the total Soviet population. He presented statistical data which showed that between 1935 and 1958 "the index of representation (in higher education) rose for most nationalities, but fell for Georgians and all national minorities, with a very drastic decline for the Jews."

The official statistics on the number of Jewish students, which apparently contradicted this assertion, were misleading (as some scholars, like Alec Nove and J.A. Newth, have found after a meticulous analysis, published in 1970), mainly because these overall numbers included not only students in every kind of "institute" and field of study, but also external (i.e., correspondence) students. The question whether Jews were "able to get into universities of their choice on equal terms with competitors of other nationalities" remained open. The percentage of Jewish students (including evening and correspondence students) fell from 14.4% in 1928–29 to 3.2% in 1960–61. Though the official percentage of Jews in the total population was in 1960–61 approximately 1.1% and in the urban population 2.2%, the above-mentioned percentage of Jewish students should be considered, according to A. Nove and J.A. Newth, to be proportionately low.

The majority of the Jewish proletariat perished during the German invasion in World War II, and there seems to be no doubt that, as a purely urban element consisting of white-collar workers, professional men, engineers, scientists, and people occupied in retail trade "a much larger proportion of Jews than of other nationalities endeavors to obtain higher education. It is this fact that may well give rise to discrimination. Some officials may feel that it is wrong for Jews to be so overwhelmingly non-proletarian in their composition. Others, particularly in the national republics, are concerned to provide special educational advantages for the relatively backward peoples of their own nationality." This conclusion of A. Nove and J.A. Newth seems to be borne out by a large number of case histories related by Soviet Jews themselves.

[Binyamin Eliav]

In Poland

The numerus clausus was one of the manifestations of the widespread antisemitism in Poland between the two world wars. The Polish government made use of the numerus clausus as a quasi-legal means to limit the number of Jewish students in the institutions of higher education to the minimum. The total number of students in Poland increased continuously between 1920 and 1935. From 34,266 students in 1921–22, it rose to 47,200 in 1935–36. In the same period both the number of Jewish students and their proportion in the total declined. In 1920–21 there were 8,526 Jewish students in Poland; in 1923–24 their number reached its peak figure of 9,579; but in 1935–36 their number dropped to 6,200, i.e., a decrease of about 35%. The proportion of Jewish students in the total number of students was 24.6% in 1921–22, 20% in 1928–29, and only 13.2% in 1935–36.

The results of the numerus clausus are especially instructive if the fluctuations in the number of Jewish students in the various faculties are noted. The most striking instance is the faculty of medicine. In 1923–24 there were still 1,402 Jewish medical students, forming 30.2% of the total. In 1926–27 their number dropped to 698 (18.6%), and in 1935–36 Jewish medical students formed only 13.8% of the total number. In the faculty of law their percentage in 1923–24 was 24.6%, while in 1935–36 it was only 12.5%. In the humanities the numbers for the corresponding years were 35.4% and 18.3%, and in the faculty of chemistry 25% and 12%. This tendency to a continuous decrease in the number of Jewish students in all faculties, especially in the professions of medicine, law, and engineering, was an outcome of the numerus clausus policy. It hindered the admission of Jewish students to the institutions of higher education, although the number of Jewish applicants increased in Poland and a growing number of Jewish youths wished to enter academic professions.

In Poland up to World War II there were 14 state institutions of higher education, and nine nongovernmental (e.g., the Catholic University in Lublin; commercial colleges in Warsaw, Cracow, Lvov, Lodz, etc.). Almost all of these institutions applied the numerus clausus as the leading criterion in admitting new students, though some applied it more strictly than others. In the University of Lvov, for instance, the Jewish students comprised 46.6% of the total number of students in 1921–22, while in 1930–31 (there are no statistical data for later years) they comprised only 31.9%; in the University of Warsaw the figures for the corresponding years were 31.4% and 23.8%; in the Warsaw Polytechnic 15.5% and 10.2%; in the Veterinary College in Lvov 13% and 5.4%; and in the institute of Dentistry, 70.4% and 19.7%.

The proportion of females among Jewish students throughout this period was higher than that among non-Jewish students. The percentage of Jewish females was 33.3% in 1923–24 and 39% in 1930–31, while the numbers among non-Jews for these years were 15% and 26%. The authorities of the academic institutions were more willing to admit Jewish female students than Jewish males, since many left the universities before graduating. Another reason for not strictly applying the numerus clausus toward Jewish women was that the majority studied in the faculty of humanities (philosophy, history, literature), instead of the more demanding professions. Thus, for instance, in 1930–31, 50% of the male students studied law; 11% medicine; 16.4% philosophy; and 14.6% sciences, while 11% of the female students studied law; 3.4% medicine; 63.2% philosophy; and 1.7% sciences. In the last few years preceding World War II the authorities took even stronger discriminatory measures against the Jewish students. They introduced the system of "Jewish benches," which allocated special benches at the back of the auditoriums and classrooms to be used only by Jews. The Jewish students revolted against these regulations and refused to sit there. This frequently led to serious clashes in the universities, resulting in bloodshed and tragedy.

[Shaoul Langnas]

In Romania

In Romania in 1922 a numerus clausus of the admission of Jewish students was advocated by Romanian students in the University of *Cluj. These were members of the Association of Christian Students, founded by adherents of A.C. *Cuza in Jassy earlier that year. It was adopted also by the students in the universities of Jassy, Bucharest, and Cernauti (Chernovtsy). December 10, the day of its announcement by the students in Cluj, was declared a holiday throughout Romania by the students, who every year took the opportunity to attack Jewish students on that day. The numerus clausus in Romania was not introduced by law. However, in practice the Christian students, by using force, prevented the Jewish students from regular studies. The position of the science and medical students was especially serious since they were prevented from using the laboratories, taking part in autopsies, etc. In the late 1920s Jewish students in this sphere were forced to go abroad, especially to France and Italy, in order to complete their studies.

At first the majority of teachers in the universities were opposed to the students' antisemitic activities, but with the rise of National Socialism in Germany many professors supported the numerus clausus movement. In 1933 special entrance examinations were introduced and Jewish candidates were deliberately failed. The few who were accepted were prevented by the Christian students from taking part in the studies, and in some faculties there were no Jewish students at all. Thus the numerus clausus became a numerus nullus. The Association of Christian Students was subsidized by all ministers of the interior throughout this period.

In 1935 the Romanian statesmen A. Vaida-Voevod declared a "numerus valahicus" (a "Walachian numerus"), a disguised form of the numerus clausus. The head of the Orthodox Church in Romania, the patriarch Miron Cristea, declared his support of the numerus valahicus in the Romanian senate.

A law on the employment of Romanian employees was passed in 1934, which fixed a proportion of 80% for Romanian workers in every place of employment, and 50% for Romanians in their management. This law was felt especially in the textile industry, banking, and commerce, where a large number of Jews was employed. Professional and trade unions, such as the lawyers', accountants', clerical workers', etc., began to evict the Jews from their membership and refused to accept new Jewish members.

At the beginning of the pro-Nazi regime of Ion Antonescu in 1940, all Jewish students were officially expelled from the schools and universities. This was also the fate of the Jewish workers in the private economic sector.

[Theodor Lavi]

In Hungary

Restrictions affecting the admission of Jewish students into the institutions of higher learning in Hungary were passed as a law in 1920. This laid down that no new students should be accepted in the universities unless they were "loyal from the national and moral standpoint," and that "the proportion of members of the various ethnic and national groups in the total number of students should amount to the proportion of such ethnic and national groups in the total population." According to the official ground for this enactment, the law was intended to prevent a surplus of persons in the liberal professions, which the dismembered country was unable to integrate. But it was clear that the law was directed against the Jews only.

The leaders of the *Neologists in Hungarian Jewry who considered the law a severe blow to Jewish equal rights, as well as the liberal opposition and especially its Jewish representatives, attempted to combat the law, but without success. Jewish students who were not admitted to institutions of higher learning were forced to go abroad to study in Germany, Austria, Czechoslovakia, Italy, France, and Belgium. The Jewish students who were admitted despite the restrictions were often insulted and sometimes beaten up by the non-Jewish students, whose "ideal" was to achieve a "numerus nullus."

Outside Hungary a number of Jewish organizations initiated a struggle against the law on the international level in 1921, basing their claims on the peace treaty of Trianon, in which Hungary had guaranteed that all its citizens should "be equal before the law … without distinction of race, language, or religion." The Jewish organizations sent a petition based on these lines to the *League of Nations. However, the official leadership of Hungarian Jewry refrained from cooperating with these Jewish organizations. Nevertheless the international Jewish organizations received support from Jews in Hungary as well as from the Hungarian Jewish students studying abroad.

The Hungarian government, when asked by the League of Nations to supply information concerning this question, avoided the issue by providing statistical data showing that the Jews were not discriminated against by this law. In 1925 the Joint Foreign Committee and the Alliance Israélite Universelle, fearing that other countries would adopt the numerus clausus, appealed to the Permanent Court of International Justice. This time Hungary was compelled to give a relevant answer. The Hungarian minister of education claimed in 1927 that the law was merely temporary, arising from Hungary's difficult situation, and undertook that the law would shortly be amended. When the amendment was not forthcoming Hungary was asked to hasten the procedure, and in 1928 the bill was submitted to the Hungarian parliament. According to this amendment racial criteria in admitting new students were removed and replaced by social criteria. Five categories were set up: civil servants, war veterans and army officers, small landowners and artisans, industrialists, and the merchant classes. The result was much the same. According to the new socioeconomic criteria the Jews had approximately the same status as before. The theoretically nonracial character of the amended law was a temptation to convert to Christianity. Indeed many Jews did so, like their predecessors of an earlier period, for the sake of office. The numerus clausus remained in force despite the protests of Jews and liberals.

By the second anti-Jewish law passed in 1939 the admission of new students was again put on a racial and not a confessional basis. Students of the rabbinical seminary were exempted from the law's application, since according to the government regulations of this institution its students required a doctorate in philosophy in order to obtain their rabbinical diploma, and were restricted in their choice of subject to Oriental studies and philosophy. The Hungarian constituent national assembly which convened in Debrecen in December 1944 abolished the numerus clausus among the rest of the discriminatory racial legislation.

[Baruch Yaron]

In the United States

In the United States mass immigration after 1881 resulted in the partial exclusion of Jews from many of the professions. There were very few Jews in the teaching profession before 1930. In 1920 there were 214 Jewish students in the medical schools of the State of New York; by 1940 there were only 108 in the same schools. In its Annual Report in 1932, the American Jewish Committee was willing to accept the proposition that this exclusion was not entirely due to antisemitism but that there was "overcrowding in an already overcrowded profession" and that Jews needed to be redirected to other pursuits. This was a vain hope in an era when the opportunities for Jews in the professions were constantly decreasing, so that, for example, the proportion of Jews in veterinary medicine decreased from almost 12% to less than 2% between 1935 and 1946. The situation was somewhat better in dentistry, where by the mid-1930s about one-fifth of the students in the dental schools were Jews, but even here the leaders of the profession tried to keep Jews out.

This trend of exclusion during most of the first half of the 20th century reached down into the undergraduate schools. There was a famous incident in 1923 when President Lowell of Harvard advised that the enrollment of Jews should be limited at his school, in order to preserve the representative character of the leading academic institution of the United States. The committee that he appointed at Harvard was unanimous in opposing him and in insisting that places be given to applicants solely on the basis of merit. Lowell was denounced by the American Federation of Labor, the Boston city council, and the legislature of the State of Massachusetts, which body threatened to remove the tax exemptions that Harvard enjoyed if a discriminatory policy were followed. Despite the storm an unofficial numerus clausus continued until after World War II in most of the major American colleges and universities. In 1931 Rutgers College admitted that it was limiting the number of Jews in order "to equalize the proportion" and to prevent the university from becoming denominational. In the spring of the following year the college authorities withdrew from this position, which had been vehemently attacked by local and national Jewish agencies. Nonetheless, at the end of a generation of struggle a B'nai B'rith survey in 1946 found that Jews indeed formed about 9% of a U.S. college population that was then slightly over two million, but that they were concentrated (77%) in 50 of the largest schools, and the best smaller schools were still discriminating against them. The proportion of Jews in the professional schools was only 7%, thus indicating that discrimination was still high.

The turning point came that year. Rabbi Stephen S. *Wise mounted an attack on Columbia University for practicing unofficial discrimination against Jews by petitioning the city council of the City of New York to withdraw its tax exemption. Columbia had no choice but to announce that the question of religion would no longer figure on any of its application forms. For the flood of soldiers returning from World War II the national government was providing the funds with which to complete their education and the colleges and universities boomed in the next decade. Discrimination against Jews was hard to practice in an era when the educational institutions were seeking the maximum of government funds. In the post–World War II era, faculties were doubling and redoubling, and place was therefore available for Jews. The new postwar industries, especially electronics, required a whole new corps of technicians, and these jobs were staffed without regard to earlier exclusions. By 1968 some opinions were being expressed that the marked presence of Jews everywhere in the professions and the academic world was "arousing some resentment, envy, and discontent among less successful non-Jewish faculty members."

It was estimated that by 1971 Jews formed at least 10% of the faculties of all American institutions of higher learning, and that the more highly regarded a school the more nearly likely would it have a Jewish proportion in its faculty reaching 25–50%, the Harvard faculty being probably one third Jewish. Attacks on Jews in academic life and in the professions were mounted largely from within the black community, which was demanding place for itself consonant with its proportion in the total population (about 10%), regardless of the results of tests or other screening devices. In this demand blacks have come into conflict with Jews who have found what contemporary sociologists have called the "meritocracy" useful and convenient. Blacks have succeeded in obtaining a quota of their own, perhaps to some extent at the expense of Jews, in many of the best colleges.

[Arthur Hertzberg]

BIBLIOGRAPHY: CZARIST RUSSIA: Dubnow, Hist Russ, index; L. Greenberg, *Jews in Russia: The Struggle for Emancipation* (1965); S. Baron, *Russian Jews under Tsars and Soviets* (1964); J. Kreppel, *Juden und Judentum von heute* (1925), para. 77, 501–4. SOVIET UNION: W. Korey, in: L. Kochan (ed.), *The Jews in Soviet Russia since 1917* (1970), 90, 94–95; A. Nove and J.A. Newth, *ibid.*, 145, 154–6. POLAND: S. Langnas, *Żydzi a studja akademickie w Polsce* (1933); M. Mirkin, in: *Yidishe Ekonomik*, 2 (1938), 272–6; *Polscki Rocznik statystyczny* (1921–38). HUNGARY: N. Katzburg, in: *Sefer ha-Shanah shel Universitat Bar Ilan*, 4–5 (1956–65), 270–88 (with an English summary); *The Jewish Minority in Hungary. Report by the Secretary and Special Delegate of the Joint Foreign Committee…* (1926). UNITED STATES: AJYB, passim; O. and M.F. Handlin, in: AJYB (1955), 75–77.

NUMISMATICS. Interest in Jewish coins arose already in the late Middle Ages, e.g., with *Maimonides and Estori *ha-Parḥi. Special studies, however, were carried out only considerably later. For geographical reasons and due to the fact that Jewish coins bear partly Greek legends, these have been generally classified as Greek coins. Among the earliest studies is one by F. Perez Bayer (*De numis hebraeo-samaritanis*, 1781). Bible research gave Jewish numismatics a special interest. One of the first in the field was the English scholar J.Y. Akerman ("Numismatic Illustration of the Narrative of Portions of the New Testament," in: *Numismatic Chronicle*, 1846/47). Another important work was written by the Italian C. Cavedoni (*Numismatic Biblica*, 1850), followed by F. de Saulcy's *Recherches sur la Numismatique Judaïque* (1854). The first work that may claim scientific value was published by F.W. Madden (*History of Jewish Coinage…*, 1864; repr. with introd. by M. Avi-Yonah, 1967). *Coins of the Jews* (1881) was the second edition of the former. Though the research on Jewish numismatics has since greatly advanced, Madden's study remains of basic value even today. T. Reinach's noteworthy book, *Jewish Coins*, appeared in 1903. In 1914 G.F. Hill published his *Catalogue of the Greek Coins of Palestine in the British Museum*. It is an excellent summary of the material then known, based on the almost complete collection of the British Museum. Hill's own critical observations add to the value of this catalog, which is indispensable for the student of Jewish numismatics. In Ereẓ Israel numismatic interest has developed in the 20th century. The first book on Jewish coins was S. Raffaeli's *Matbe'ot ha-Yehudim* (1913). This was followed by M. Narkiss' *Matbe'ot Ereẓ Yisrael* (3 vols., 1936–39). In 1940 A. Reifenberg published his *Ancient Jewish Coins* (Heb. ed., *Matbe'ot ha-Yehudim*, 1947, 1963^2). In 1945 the Israel Numismatic Society was founded, and since then its members have contributed to the progress of numismatic research. Foremost among them was its second president, L. Kadman, who founded the Israel Numismatic Research Fund and published himself four volumes of the *Corpus Nummorum Palestinensium* (1956–61; Aelia Capitolina, Caesarea Maritima, Jewish-Roman War, and Akko-Ptolemais). Kadman was also the sponsor of the Kadman Numismatic Museum in Tel Aviv, which was inaugurated in 1962 and houses the largest numismatic library in Israel. The *Publications of the Israel Numismatic Society* have appeared since 1954. L. Kadman published in co-authorship with A. Kindler a numismatic handbook (Heb., 1963). The latter published, besides many articles on special subjects, the *Oẓar Matbe'ot Ereẓ Yisrael* (with an English summary, 1958); *The Coins of Tiberias* (Heb. and Eng., 1962); and a catalog of the collection of Jewish coins of the Bank of Israel (1969). Y. Meshorer published his corpus of *Jewish Coins of the Second Temple Period* in 1967 (Heb., 1966) with an almost up-to-date listing of all types of Jewish coins known to date.

In 1963 an International Numismatic Convention was held in Jerusalem, and its proceedings were published by the Israel Numismatic Society. The latter holds monthly meetings and seminaries, and annual conventions for its membership of 250. It also publishes a quarterly, *Israel Numismatic Journal*. The American Israel Numismatic Society, based in North Miami, Florida, publishes *The Shekel* six times a year. Numismatic research is not confined to books. Hundreds of articles and minor monographs have been written by various scholars. L.A. Mayer published a Bibliography of Jewish Numismatics which counts 882 items until 1963. In the framework of archaeological research in the Hebrew University and in the Museum of Jewish Antiquities, E.L. *Sukenik built up an extremely important collection of Palestinian coins. He was the first to identify the earliest Jewish coins by correctly reading the legend *Yehud* on them. Other important numismatic collections in Israel are in the Department of Antiquities of the Hebrew University, in the Jewish Museum, in the Bank of Israel, in the Franciscan Biblical School, and in the Pontifical Biblical Institute, all in Jerusalem. Private collections of importance are those of the late A. Reifenberg, Jerusalem, on loan to the Israel Museum; of A. Spaer, Jerusalem; of R. Hecht, Haifa; of J. Meyshan and of J. Willinger, Tel Aviv. Outside Israel the collections of the American Numismatic Society, as well as the private ones of A. Klaksbald, Paris, D. Littman, Geneva, and W. Wirgin, New York, are of importance.

BIBLIOGRAPHY: L.A. Mayer, *Bibliography of Jewish Numismatics* (1966).

[Arie Kindler]

NUN (Heb. נוּן; ן ,נ), the fourteenth letter of the Hebrew alphabet; its numerical value is 50. The earliest representation of this letter is a pictograph of a serpent 𓆓, which developed into the early Phoenician 𐤍. The later variants are Hebrew 𐤍 (Samaritan ࠍ), Phoenician 𐤍, and Aramaic ן. During the late fifth century B.C.E. and after, in Aramaic cursive in the medial position the downstroke bent leftward J. Thus the Jewish medial נ and final ן *nun* forms developed. The Nabatean cursive medial *nun* J became more and more similar to medial *bet, yod,* and *taw;* in Arabic diacritic marks distinguish *nun* ن from *ba* (ب), *ya* (ي), and *ta* (ت). The ancestor of the Latin "N", the Archaic Greek 𐌍, developed from the early Phoenician *nun*. See *Alphabet, Hebrew.

[Joseph Naveh]

NUNBERG, HERMAN (1884–1970), U.S. psychiatrist. Born in a Polish Jewish townlet, Nunberg studied psychiatry with Eugen Bleuler and in 1914 joined the Vienna group of psychoanalysts. At the Psychoanalytic Congress in Budapest (1918) Nunberg maintained the necessity for personal analysis in the training of its practitioners. In 1932 he went to the United States. Nunberg's earliest writings were concerned with psychoanalytic interpretation of psychotic conditions. In 1932 his first book *Allgemeine Neurosenlehre auf Psychoanalytischer Grundlage* appeared. In his preface Sigmund *Freud considered it the most accurate presentation at that time of the psychoanalytic theory of neurotic processes.

In 1949 Nunberg published his monograph, *Problems of Bisexuality as Reflected in Circumcision*, in which he collated psychoanalytic experience, especially with the dreams of a patient who had undergone circumcision after infancy, with mythological and anthropological knowledge. Freud and T. *Reik had recognized the interrelation between circumcision and castration. According to Nunberg circumcision stimulates the feminine as well as the masculine strivings of the boy. Some Jewish tradition states that Adam was created both male and female and that the creator separated his female half. This belief is reminiscent of myths and infantile speculation on the origin of the two sexes. The female is made by castrating (circumcising) the male. An afterthought in this book dwells on the "question of German guilt." The Germans submitted unconditionally to their Fuehrer. By licensing murder the Fuehrer relieved the Germans of their sense of guilt for their inability to restrict their aggression. His book *Curiosity* (1961) was based on a lecture given at the New York Academy of Medicine. He served as a member of the Committee for the Study of Suicides. In later years he was noted for his psychoanalytic elucidation of dreams. As a teacher, researcher, and clinician Nunberg was recognized for the integration of theoretical contributions and clinical observations.

BIBLIOGRAPHY: P. Neubauer et al. (eds.), *Herman Nunberg: Memoirs* (1969).

[Louis Miller]

NUNES VAIS (Nunez-Vaez), rabbinical family of Marrano extraction in Leghorn (Italy). ISAAC JOSEPH NUNES VAIS (d. 1768) was one of the rabbis of the community and colleague of *Malachi b. Jacob ha-Kohen. His *Si'aḥ Yiẓḥak* (Leghorn, 1766; 2nd vol. 1768) comprised glossaries on the talmudic tractates *Shevu'ot, Yoma*, and *Ḥagigah* (forming the acrostic of *Si'aḥ*). His son JACOB (d. 1814) became chief rabbi of the consistory established at Leghorn during the period of French occupation, and taught what was termed "practical theology" in the Talmud Torah when it was reorganized in 1812. He edited *Da'at Zekenim* (Leghorn, 1783) comprising amplifications of the tosafists on Rashi's pentateuchal commentaries, and *Amar Neke* (Pisa, 1810), comprising the glosses of Obadiah of *Bertinoro on Rashi. To the same family belonged ABRAHAM JOSEPH NUNES VAIS (1811–1898), physician to the bey of Tunis, and the former's son, the painter ITALO NUNES-VAIS (1860–1932) of Florence.

BIBLIOGRAPHY: A. Lattes and A.S. Toaff, *Gli studi ebraici a Livorno* (1909), 14; M. Monteverdi, *Italo Nunes-Vais* (1969); M. Benayahu, *Rabbi Ḥayyim Yosef David Azulai* (1959), index.

[Cecil Roth]

NUÑEZ (Nuñes), family name of Portuguese Marranos, prominent in the Sephardi Diaspora, particularly in the American colonies. PEDRO NUÑEZ (1492–1577) was a geographer with a strong attachment to Judaism. Born in Alcarcer do Sal, Portugal, he was professor of mathematics at Coimbra University, and in 1529 was appointed cosmographer to the crown. Credited with being the father of modern cartography for his treatise on the sphere (1537), he was also author of *De crepusculi* (1542) and *De arte atque ratione navigandi* (1546). His complete works were published in 1592 at Basle. HENRIQUE NUÑEZ (d. 1524), who was born in Barba, was baptized in Castile. Enlisted by King John III of Portugal to inform on the *New Christian Judaizers, he provided the monarch with a list of persons secretly conforming to Judaism, even denouncing his own younger brother. When the *Marranos discovered that Henrique was the informer in their midst, they dispatched two men, André Dias and Diego Vaz, to assassinate him. Disguised in Franciscan habit, the two succeeded in stabbing Henrique to death but were apprehended, tortured into confessing, and executed. Henrique was then declared a martyr of the church and dubbed Firme Fé. Another HENRIQUE NUÑEZ, a physician by profession, headed a tiny Marrano group that found respite at *Bristol, England, from at least 1553 to 1555, at which time the new religious policies of Queen Mary Tudor forced him to seek refuge in France. HECTOR *NUÑEZ (1521–1591) was lay head of London's Marrano community during the reign of Elizabeth; through his business agents on the continent he was a source of intelligence for the queen.

BEATRICE NUÑEZ (c. 1568–1632) was martyred at the *auto-da-fé held in Madrid on July 4, 1632. Burned at the same time was ISABEL NUÑEZ ALVAREZ of Viseu, Portugal, who married Miguel Rodriguez of Madrid, and held title to one of Madrid's synagogues. On the same occasion, HELEN and VIOLANTE NUÑEZ both received sentences of life imprisonment. That year saw the death of still another member of the family, CLARA, at an auto-da-fé in Seville, Spain. More fortunate was the beautiful MARIA NUÑEZ (b. 1575 or 1579) who, together with a group of fellow-Marranos, escaped from Portugal in about 1593 aboard a ship bound for Holland. While at sea they were captured by a British vessel and diverted to London. En route, the British captain became infatuated with Maria and proposed marriage. A contemporaneus account tells of how Queen Elizabeth's curiosity was aroused and how Maria was presented to the queen, who then accompanied Maria on a tour of London. Maria insisted on rejoining her Jewish comrades, who went on to Amsterdam to found a community which was to become the major Marrano haven. Communal records of that period in Amsterdam list the marriage of a Maria Nuñez, aged 19, in August 1598, and the marriage of another Maria Nuñez, aged 23, in November 1598. Living in Amsterdam some time around 1700 was DAVID NUÑEZ-TORRES (1728), talmudist and a director of the Abi Yetomim orphanage. He was called to the Hague as *ḥakham* of the Spanish and Portuguese community. Actively engaged in publishing Jewish classics, he also prepared two editions of the Bible and co-edited the 1697 edition of the Shulḥan Arukh, as well as the 1702 edition of Maimonides' code. A catalog of his extensive personal library was published after his death.

The name Nuñez was also prominent in colonial America. J.R. Rosenbloom in his *Biographical Dictionary of Early American Jews* (1960) lists 19 members of the Nunes (Nuñez) family, mostly relatives and descendants of the Marrano SAMUEL RIBEIRO NUÑEZ, who was born in Lisbon where he became a doctor of renown and was appointed to serve the crown. Neither this appointment, however, nor his wealth guaranteed him safety from the menacing surveillance of the Inquisition. In 1732/33 he escaped on a chartered English vessel which he and his family secretly boarded while a lavish dinner party was being held at the Nuñez family mansion. Samuel was able to take some of his wealth with him to London, where he joined a group of Jews embarking for the new settlement of Savannah, *Georgia. There Governor Oglethorpe took note of the man's eminence and went on record as acknowledging that upon landing Dr. Nuñez had saved the colony from a raging epidemic. Accordingly, Oglethorpe suggested to the colonial directors that the usual Jewish disabilities might be waived in this case. With Samuel in Georgia were his mother, ZIPPORAH (b. c. 1680), his sons DANIEL (1704–1789) and MOSES (1705–1787), and his daughter ZIPPORAH (1714–1799). Families of some of the original Jewish settlers continue to live in Savannah. Elsewhere in the Americas, the Nuñez family included ROBERT NUÑEZ (1820–1889), born in *Jamaica, a leading figure there in both business and politics and founder of the journal *The Political Eagle* in 1850. Active in matters of finance, from 1863 until his death he filled a variety of government posts, ranging from member of the Jamaica House of Assembly to magistrate. He also had diplomatic contacts with the United States, Spain, Norway, and Sweden.

BIBLIOGRAPHY: Roth, Marranos, index; J.R. Marcus, *Early American Jewry 1655–1790*, 2 (1955), index; idem, *Memoirs of American Jews 1775–1865*, 1 (1955), index; Rosenbloom, Biogr Dict, s.v.; M. Kayserling, *Geschichte der Juden in Portugal* (1867), 171–2.

[Aaron Lichtenstein]

NUÑEZ, HECTOR (1521–91), leader of the Marrano community in England. A distinguished physician and successful merchant, Nuñez was born in Portugal and arrived in London about 1550; he was admitted a Fellow of the Royal College of Physicians and of the Royal College of Surgeons in 1554. His large-scale trading activities in the Mediterranean enabled him to provide information for the government, and it was he who brought Sir Francis Walsingham, whose friendship he enjoyed, the first news of the arrival of the Spanish Armada at Lisbon. His wife, Leonara Freire, subscribed to the upkeep of the secret synagogue in Antwerp.

BIBLIOGRAPHY: Roth, England, 140ff., 283; idem, *Anglo-Jewish Letters* (1938), 23–26; Wolf, in: JHSET, 11 (1924–27), 6f., 23f., 37–48, 50–55.

[Vivian David Lipman]

NUREMBERG (Ger. **Nuernberg**), city in Bavaria, Germany. A report of 1146 records that many Jews from Rhenish towns fled to Nuremberg, but Jews are first mentioned in the city in 1182. By the 13th century a large number of Jews were resident there. In reply to an enquiry from Weissenburg in 1288, the mayor and council of Nuremberg pointed out the laws then governing Jewish moneylending in the city. The *memorbuch* ascribed to Nuremberg by S. *Salfeld (see bibl.) would prove that a synagogue was consecrated there in 1296. Two years later, 728 Jews were victims of the *Rindfleisch persecutions, among them *Mordecai b. Hillel, author of the *Mordekhai*. Jews are mentioned in Nuremberg again in 1303. In 1313 Henry VII allowed the *Schultheiss* ("mayor") to admit more Jews and granted him their protection dues. However, two years later King Louis IV of Bavaria (1314–47) allowed the council to demolish the houses that the Jews had rebuilt. In 1322 the Jews of Nuremberg, and their taxes, were pledged to the burgrave Frederick IV. Although King Louis promised in 1331 to protect the Jews against oppression and demanded an annual payment of 400 florins for three years in lieu of all taxes, he allowed the council to increase this sum according to the Jews' ability to pay. The council exerted strong pressure on the Jews, and many of them fled the town. Two years later, the king declared himself willing to readmit them: a list of 1338 shows that 212 authorized Jewish families (indicating a total of about 2,000 persons) were resident in the city. In 1342 Nuremberg Jews were compelled to pay the *gueldener *Opferpfennig* tax. The council continued to fight an increase in Jewish ownership of houses, and in 1344 Louis IV was obliged to promise that the Jews would no longer be permitted to purchase houses owned by Christians. In the *Black Death massacres 560 Jews were burnt to death on December 5, 1349; the rest fled or were expelled. *Charles IV (1346–76) exonerated the town council: promising the property of the Jews to the burgrave of Nuremberg and the bishop of Bamberg, he allowed the majority of Jewish houses to be demolished to make room for the markets; the St. Mary Church (the Frauenkirche) was built on the site of the synagogue.

However, soon afterward, growing short of money, the city authorities were anxious to attract the Jews back, and in 1351 Charles IV permitted the burgrave to admit them and ordered the officials and knights to assist them. The Jewish community in Nuremberg increased rapidly. A contract concluded in 1352 between the city council and the Jews obliged the latter to live in a special quarter (the present *Judenstrasse*), and all debts of the citizens were cancelled. A tax list of 1382 indicates that the Jewish population then numbered more than 500.

In 1310 King Henry VII had restricted their commerce in the market and established a fixed interest rate. In the 14th–15th centuries the right to live in Nuremburg could be acquired only by the head of a family, on payment to the council of a fee that was probably assessed according to the financial situation of the applicant. In addition, he had to provide guarantors and take an oath of loyalty. If a Jew wished to leave the city, he had to notify the council, pay all taxes and dues for the following year, hand over his pledges to a Jew of Nuremberg, and sell his property only to a citizen. Foreign Jews, with the exception of yeshivah students, could not be given accommodation in any house. If a Nuremberg Jewish couple married, they were allowed to stay four weeks only and during that period had to apply for admittance. Jews and Christians were forbidden to use each other's bathhouses. *Moneylending by Jews was regulated in substantially the same fashion as throughout Germany. Trading was forbidden to Jews in the 13th to 14th centuries except in horses and meat. The latter had to be sold at special stalls, separated from those of the Christians, who were not allowed to buy meat slaughtered by Jews. Jews were also forbidden to sell wine, beer, and some other foodstuffs to non-Jews.

As in other towns in Germany, the protection of the Jews (a profitable source of income) became a bone of contention between the municipality and the king. In 1352 the king granted the city council the right to admit Jews and promised not to pledge or to cede to anyone else the taxes payable by the Jews. However, by 1360 Charles IV admitted Jews to Nuremberg on his own accord and obtained one-third of the receipts for the transference of their protection dues to the municipality; in 1371 he demanded a further 400 florins for 20 years. In 1382 King Wenceslaus IV (1378–1419) again ceded to the city the protection of the Jews and their taxes for 19 years, against an annual payment of 400 florins. Nuremberg shared with Emperor Wenceslaus in the gains from the cancellation of debts to Jews (1385). Jews in Nuremberg were arrested and released only after handing over the pledges they held and promising the city council still larger sums. The council appointed a special commission to collect the debts (without interest in the case of recent debts and with a deduction of one quarter in the case of old ones). The commission kept special accounts of "the Jews' money." Total extortion from the Jews approximated 95,000 florins at that time and a similar sum in 1390. In 1412 King Sigismund (1411–37) handed over to the burgrave in Nuremberg his share of the Jewish taxes. However, in 1414 he forced the Jews to contribute 12,000 florins to the Church Council of Constance, and in 1416 obtained an annual payment of 10% of their movable assets for three years against a promise of leaving their other assets untouched and renouncing new taxes. At times the city council prevented the king from extorting large sums (Frederick III, in 1442, had to content himself with 7,000 florins) since they wanted to retain for themselves the income from the Jews. When the Synod of Bamberg prohibited the Jews from engaging in moneylending, the council intervened to have the decree revoked. The council also saw to it that the regulation requiring Jews to wear a distinguishing *badge and headdress was not strictly enforced; only foreign Jews were obliged to wear *Gugeln*, i.e., tall white caps.

With their increasing indebtedness to them, the common citizens' hatred of the Jews also grew. The position of the Jews was aggravated by the appearance in Nuremberg of John of *Capistrano in 1454; the Jews were compelled to attend his conversionist sermons (as they were in 1478 the sermons of Peter *Schwarz). In 1467, 18 Jews were burnt to death, accused of having killed four Christians. In 1470 the Jews obtained permission from Frederick III to continue moneylending for six years; three years later the council began to agitate for their expulsion. A new municipal code of 1479 forbade them to charge interest and enforced a humiliating Jewish *oath. The Jews refused to obey the council's regulations, and relations between the townspeople and the Jews worsened. Around 1499 the city obtained a legal opinion from the synod that lending on interest to Christians was forbidden to Jews according to the Torah and Canon Law (W. Pirckheimer, *Briefwechsel*, 1, no. 89 (1940), 295–6). In 1498 Maximilian I (1485–1519) at last approved the expulsion of the Jews from Nuremberg forever. In March 1499 they left the city, some settling in the surrounding villages. Their houses and the synagogue were confiscated by the mayor in favor of the emperor and then purchased by the town for 8,000 florins. The cemetery was destroyed and the tombstones used for building purposes; one of these stones is located in the spiral staircase of the St. Lorenzkirche.

Jewish communal *autonomy in Nuremberg was active and in the main respected. Internal Jewish matters, particularly of taxation, were decided by the rabbi (*Judenmeister*) and the council of the Jews (Judenrat); the five members of the latter were appointed every year by the town jurors. Attempts by the Jews to select their own council members were frustrated by the town authorities. The Judenrat apportioned the taxes payable by the community and administered its assets. Several noted personalities taught at the yeshivah in the city and were the community's rabbis: Mordecai b. Hillel, Jacob ha-Levi, Jacob *Margolioth, Jacob *Weil (1430–50), and Jacob *Pollack (from 1470). During Weil's period of office a synod of rabbis was convened in Nuremberg. Meir b. Baruch of Rothenburg is said to have been rabbi of Nuremberg. Some Hebrew was printed in Nuremberg (by non-Jews) during the 16th century, first on an engraved bookplate designed by Albrecht Duerer in 1503, and in J. Boeschenstein's *Vil gutter Ermanungen* (1525) and W. Fugger's *Ein nutzlich und wolgegrundt Formular* (1553). Between 1599 and 1602 large parts of a polyglot Bible were issued by Elijah Hutter; J.L. Muehlhausen's *Sefer Nizzaḥon* (with a Latin translation) appeared in 1644, printed by W. Endler.

Return and Settlement

It was not until the end of the 17th century that Jews were allowed to enter Nuremberg to purchase goods on payment of a body tax (*Leibzoll*), but they were not allowed to remain there. In the first half of the 19th century individual Jews occasionally succeeded in staying for shorter or longer periods. At the end of the 1840s, a few Jews were living there, but it was only in 1850 that a Jew (Josef Kohn) was accepted as a citizen by the town council. A community began to form in 1857, subject to the rabbi of Fuerth. In 1859 the *Israelitischer Religionsverein* (Jewish Religious Association) was formed, legalized as the *Kultusgemeinde* five years later. In the same year the cemetery was opened and ten years later (1874) the synagogue was consecrated. In 1875 the Orthodox members founded the Adass Israel community, which opened its own synagogue in 1902 and a primary school in 1921. The Jewish population of Nuremberg increased from 11 in 1825, to 219 in 1858, and 3,032 in 1880. It continued to rise from 5,956 in 1900 to 8,603 in 1915, and 9,000 in 1933, making it the second largest community in Bavaria.

The Nazi Period

Between the two world wars, Nuremberg became the center of the Nazi Party; the molesting of Jews in the streets became an everyday occurrence. Julius *Streicher established one of the first branches of the nascent Nazi Party there in 1922 and edited the notorious antisemitic paper *Der *Stuermer*. Between 1922 and 1933 about 200 instances of cemetery desecration were reported in and around Nuremberg. While the Nazi Party annual rallies were in progress in the city, the Jews lived in fear of humiliation and attack. The reign of terror began in 1933 when Streicher was made *Gauleiter* of Franconia.

On July 30, 400 wealthy and distinguished Jewish citizens were arrested and publicly maltreated; some were forced to trim grass with their teeth. In succeeding years, boycotts and excesses continued without abating. On August 10, 1938, the synagogue and communal center were demolished. Exactly three months later, a systematically organized pogrom broke out. The two remaining synagogues and numerous shops were burned to the ground. Of the 91 Jews in Germany who met their deaths on *Kristallnacht*, 26 (including ten suicides) were in Nuremberg. Immediately afterward, between 2,000 and 3,000 Jews left the city. In 1939 only 2,611 Jews remained. In 1941 there were 1,800. A total of 1,601 were deported during the war (Dr. Benno Martin, head of the police, rescued many Jews from death and alleviated the suffering of others); the three main transports were 512 to *Riga on November 29, 1941 (16 survived); 426 to *Izbica on March 25, 1942 (none survived); and 533 to *Theresienstadt on September 10, 1942 (27 survived).

About 65 of the former inhabitants returned after the war and a community was reorganized, which numbered 181 in 1952 and 290 in 1970. In 1984 a new community center with a synagogue was opened. The Jewish community numbered 316 in 1989; 200 in 1990; and about 1,450 in 2005. More than 80 percent of the members are immigrants from the former Soviet Union.

BIBLIOGRAPHY: A. Mueller, *Geschichte der Juden in Nuernberg* (1968). MEDIEVAL PERIOD: M. Wiener, *Regesten zur Geschichte der Juden in Deutschland waehrend des Mittelalters* (1862); O. Stabbe, *Die Juden in Deutschland* (1866), 49–66, 135–41, 211, 221, passim; H.C.B. Briegleb, in: J. Kobak's *Jeschurun*, 6 (1868), 1–28, 190–201; S. Taussig, *Geschichte der Juden in Bayern* (1874), 12, 23–24, 27, 32; M. Stern, *Die israelitische Bevoelkerung der deutschen Staedte*, 3 (1896); Salfeld, Martyrol; Aronius, Regesten; A. Suessmann, *Die Judenschuldentilgungen unter Koenig Wenzel* (1907); G. Caro, *Sozial-und Wirtschaftsgeschichte der Juden*, 2 vols. (1908–20), index; I. Schiper, *Yidisher Geshikhte*, 2 (1930); G. Kisch, in: HJ, 2 (1940), 23–24; A. Kober, in: PAAJR, 15 (1945), 65–67; Z. Avneri, in: *Zion*, 25 (1960), 57–61; Germ Jud, 1 (1963); 2 (1968); G. Michelfelder, in: *Beitraege zur Wirtschaftsgeschichte Nuernberg* (1967), 236–60. MODERN PERIOD: H. Barbeck, *Geschichte der Juden in Nuernberg und Fuerth* (1878); B. Ziemlich, *Die israelitische Kultusgemeinde in Nuernberg* (1900); R. Wassermann, in: *Zeitschrift fuer Demographie und Statistik der Juden*, 3 (1907), 77; M. Freudenthal, *Die israelitische Kultusgemeinde Nuernberg 1874–1924* (1925); ZGJD, 2 (1930), 114, 125; J. Podro, *Nuremberg, the Unholy City* (1937); Nuernberger Stadtarchiv und Volksbuecherei, *Schicksal juedischer Mitbuerger in Nuernberg 1850–1945* (1965); E.N. Peterson, *The Limits of Hitler's Power* (1969), 224–94; Yad Vashem Archives. HEBREW PRINTING: L. Loewenstein, in: JJLG, 10 (1912), 53, 168–70; A. Marx, *Jewish History and Booklore* (1944), 318; A. Freimann, *Gazetteer of Hebrew Printing* (1946), 54–55. **ADD BIBLIOGRAPHY:** *Germania Judaica*, vol. 3 1350–514 (1987), 1001–44; A. Eckert and H. Rusam, *Geschichte der Juden in Nuernberg und Mittelfranken* (Beitraege zur politischen Bildung, vol. 7) (1995^2) ; J. Kammerling, *Andreas Osiander and the Jews of Nuremberg. A Reformation Pastor and Jewish Toleration in 16th-Century Germany* (1998); M. Janetzko, *Haben Sie nicht das Bankhaus Kohn gesehen? Ein juedisches Familienschicksal in Nuernberg 1850–1950* (Nuernberger Stadtgeschichten, vol. 1) (1998); M. Diefenbacher and W. Fischer-Pache (eds.), *Mitten in Nuernberg. Juedische Firmen, Freiberufler und Institutionen am Vorabend des Nationalsozialismus* (Quellen zur Geschichte und Kultur der Stadt Nuernberg, vol. 28) (1998); idem, *Gedenkbuch fuer die Nuernberger Opfer der Schoa*, vol. 1 and 2 (Quellen und Forschungen zur Geschichte und Kultur der Stadt Nuernberg, vol. 29, 30) (1998, 2002); L. Rosenberg, *Spuren und Fragmente. Juedische Buecher, juedische Schicksale in Nuernberg* (Ausstellungskatalog der Stadtbibliothek Nuernberg, vol. 102) (2000).

NUREMBERG LAWS, anti-Jewish statutes enacted by Germany on September 15, 1935, marking a major step in clarifying racial policy and removing Jewish influences from Aryan society. These laws, on which the rest of Nazi racial policy hung, were written hastily. In September 1935, Hitler decided that the time was ripe for more restrictions on Germany's Jews, especially since many Party militants had expressed their disappointment with the *Arierparagraph*. He outlined new laws for the protection of German blood and honor. These laws would "regulate the problems of marriage between 'Aryans' and 'non-Aryans.'" On September 13, 1935, he called on the desk officer for racial law, Bernhard Loesener, in the Reich Ministry of the Interior (RMI), and on others, among them state secretaries Hans Pfundtner and Dr. Wilhelm Stuckart, to formulate the legal language. Hitler wanted to present these new laws at the Nuremberg Party rally on September 15, leaving only two short days to write them. During these two days, several of the men involved in the drafting process did not sleep. Much preliminary work had been done for the drafting of such laws prior to September 13, but they still had to agree on their severity and language. They wrote notes at mealtimes on menu cards as they threw together the laws that would decide the fate of millions. Hitler had asked these men to translate racial ideology into law. Remarkably, the head of Reich Office for Genealogy Research, Dr. Kurt Mayer, heard about these new laws for the first time when they were officially announced. He openly expressed his anger, humiliation, and surprise at not having been consulted during the drafting process. Hitler made no pretense of basing these laws on any "scientific truths" discovered by his "racial scientists." His driving force was not reason but rather the need for an enemy. Hitler had said that if the Nazis had not had Jews, they would have had to invent them. Since Hitler believed he was the sole authority on racial policy, he had the final say about what the law stated.

The laws issued on September 15, 1935, approved by Hitler personally, deprived Jews of citizenship, prohibited Jewish households from having German maids under the age of 45, prohibited any non-Jewish German from marrying a Jew, and outlawed sexual relations between Jews and Germans. These laws enforced a new morality on Germans. Hitler claimed during a Reichstag session that the Nuremberg Laws would actually help the Jews by creating "a level ground on which the German people may find a tolerable relation with the Jewish people." Hitler's statement was a "blatant deception, aimed at the outside world." Regardless of what Hitler said, he implemented these laws to ostracize, discriminate, and expel Jews from society. This was quickly gleaned from his speech when he next said that if this "tolerable situation" was not found and if the Jewish agitation both within Germany and abroad continued, then the position must be reexamined. In other words, Hitler would then implement further laws and policies to persecute the Jews. The Nuremberg Laws, according to Hitler, were just a precursor to other more degrading decrees. To create his homogeneous and harmonious Aryan society, Hitler had first to discard the Jews, a "people" incompatible with "true Germans." The Nuremberg Laws helped Hitler take the first step toward getting rid of "these parasites" and imposing racial conformity on society.

The Nuremberg Laws issued on September 15, 1935 prohibited marriages between Jews and Germans but failed to specify who counted as a Jew. Years of German-Jewish assimilation made this a difficult question to answer. The debate raged for the next several months. Hitler wavered between declaring half-Jews the same as Jews or keeping them separate as half-Jews. Many issues about *Mischlinge* (partial Jews) and intermarriage were discussed. For example, Nazi hard-liners thought the *Arierparagraph* had been too lenient. Dr. Gerhard Wagner, Reichsaerztefuehrer (Reich doctors' leader) and a fanatical antisemite, had many talks with Hitler during the drafting of the racial laws. He wanted to equate all half-, quarter-, and even one-eighth-Jews with full Jews. Such extremists argued that partial Jews were more dangerous than full Jews because their mix of German and Jewish blood would enable them to lead the state's enemies with the skill of Aryans.

The racial theorist Dr. Achim Gercke in the RMI introduced another argument when he wrote in September 1935 that *Mischlinge* could really be disguised Jews. Anyone who mathematically defined "50 percent, 25 percent, 12.5 percent, 6.25 percent, etc., *Mischlinge*" had not understood Mendel's laws of genetics, Gercke maintained. Gercke warned that *Mischlinge* could also "mendel out pure Jews." At this time, Hitler refused to give his decision on whether to declare half-Jews as Jews. Hitler's wavering was typical of his style of rule. He often avoided giving a final decision that involved choosing different options proposed by two or more of his trusted underlings. And being the good politician that he was, Hitler probably did not declare half-Jews as Jews because he did not want to alienate the Aryan families of *Mischlinge* too much.

The Nazis not only persecuted people of Jewish descent, but Aryan Germans with Jewish spouses as well. Stuckart in the RMI argued that anyone who married a Jew was an inferior German. Any children born to such parents did not deserve any better treatment than Jews, since their German half was not really worth protecting. Julius *Streicher, the editor of the notoriously antisemitic and vulgar newspaper *Der *Stuermer*, tried to convince Frick that Jewish semen permanently polluted an Aryan woman to such an extent that later, although married to an Aryan, she could not bear "pure-blooded Aryan babies." Men like Loesener, who were responsible for drafting these laws, did not take Gercke's or Streicher's beliefs too seriously.

Throughout this process of defining Jewishness, Loesener realized the problems inherent in labeling as un-German people who felt German, thereby marking them for persecution. Loesener feared the disastrous social repercussions that would result from branding as Jews several highly decorated half-Jewish World War I veterans (one a Pour le Mérite recipient) and distinguished supporters of the Nazi movement. Loesener argued that since most felt German and rejected Judaism, their suicide rate would climb dramatically if the government labeled them as Jews. Loesener also cautioned that if they treated half-Jews as Jews, the armed forces would probably lose 45,000 soldiers. He felt that the "laws transformed dissimulation into an established fact [and] would minimize racial hatred," and he "stressed that legal segregation meant legal protection." After the war, Loesener explained his reasoning: "One could no more achieve any movement on the Jewish question in the narrow sense, i.e., the full-Jews, than one could move a mountain. It would also have been tactically the most stupid thing I could possibly have done because it would have removed any further possibility of making use of my position [in helping half-Jews]." He knew the Jews were doomed but felt that he could save the *Mischlinge* from meeting the same fate if he could prevent the authorities from labeling them as Jews. In this battle between the Party, led primarily by Wagner, and the RMI, led by Stuckart and Loesener, the RMI won. Hitler had been content to let these two factions fight it out. Hitler apparently allowed the RMI to enact its version of the law because he feared the unrest in society that the harsh law of the Party fanatics would cause. According to historian Nathan Stoltzfus, Hitler was only concerned "for his popularity" in permitting RMI to get its way.

As Raul Hilberg pointed out, the task of explaining the laws and fully articulating them was left to the bureaucracy. On November 14, 1935, the RMI issued a supplement to the Nuremberg Laws of September 15, 1935, which created the racial categories of German, Jew, half-Jew (Jewish *Mischling* first degree), and quarter-Jew (Jewish *Mischling* second degree), each with its own regulations. Apparently, Hitler decided for the time being to keep half-Jews as such rather than treating them as full Jews. Full Jews had three to four Jewish grandparents. According to Hitler, when someone was more than 50 percent Jewish, he was beyond the point of saving and was evil (*uebel*). Half-Jews had two Jewish grandparents, and quarter-Jews had one Jewish grandparent. The Nazis had to resort to religious criteria to define these racial categories, ultimately determined by birth, baptismal, marriage, and death certificates. Often stored in churches and courthouses, these records indicated what religion one adhered to or had left. When a *Mischling* belonged to the Jewish religion or was married to a Jew, the Nazis counted him as a full Jew. Jews could only marry Jews or half-Jews, and half-Jews could only marry Jews or other half-Jews. Quarter-Jews could only marry Aryans, although in practice they experienced difficulties in doing so. Marriages between a Jew and an Aryan that had occurred before 1935 were called "privileged mixed marriages" and provided some protection for the Jewish spouse. Most Jews who survived the Holocaust in Germany were married to non-Jews. At the same time, Hitler allowed some *Mischlinge* to apply for exemptions under section 7 of the supplementary decrees of November 1935. In some cases, if Hitler approved, the *Mischling* was allowed to call himself or herself an Aryan.

The Nuremberg Laws of 1935 laid the foundation for the next 10 years of racial policy. Subsequent official documents usually replaced the term non-Aryan with the more specific "Jewish *Mischling* first or second degree" and Jew. Although by 1938 Hitler felt the Nuremberg Laws had been too "humane," he never changed them.

As Loesener had predicted, these laws calmed many individuals of Jewish descent by clarifying their situation somewhat. Half-Jew Peter Gaupp, who called the time from 1933 until the racial laws of 1935 the "lawless years," said:

> In 1935, the laws came out, the Nuremberg Laws. That was the first time you knew where you stood legally.... Before it was all guesswork. You could meet a Nazi in some office and he could exterminate you or you could meet a Nazi that was very human and he could help you.... Before 1935, before the laws came out of Nuremberg, you swam your way through.... You know, there was no regulations. The laws of Nuremberg was the first, ah, form, legal shape where you knew where you stood.

Mischlinge felt oppressed, but at least they knew where they belonged. Some Jews welcomed the laws because they felt that now they could live an "orderly existence." Moreover, for a few years after these laws, most *Mischlinge* continued to live fairly "normal" lives – that is, they were able to study, date, serve in the armed forces, and so on. Most felt pleasantly surprised that the majority of their Aryan friends and acquaintances did not treat them differently after the issuance of these laws. Ian Kershaw wrote, "Between the promulgation of the Nuremberg Laws and the summer of 1938, it would not be going too far to suggest that the 'Jewish Question' was almost totally irrelevant to the formation of opinion among the majority of the German people." Many people did not take the new laws seriously. "[The Nuremberg Laws] appear to have passed by much of the population almost unnoticed." It seems that those who did know about these laws, including *Mischlinge*, accepted them without objection.

Stuckart and his assistant, Dr. Hans Globke, in the RMI claimed that Nazi racial laws differed little from Jewish law: "The German people want to keep their blood pure and their culture together just like the Jews have done since the prophet Ezra ordered them to do so." Regardless of what Nazi officials said, these laws inflicted humiliation and suffering on Jews and *Mischlinge*. Quarter-Jew Hans Ranke said, "I was shocked [by these laws]. I no longer felt like a worthy German." The Reichstag felt it had secured the purity of blood essential for the German people's future existence. Lammers wrote Frick on February 20, 1936, that Hitler's goal in *Mischling* politics was to make the "mixed race disappear" and to force *Mischlinge* to lose their citizenship rights. The Nazis used these Nuremberg Laws to define, control, and dehumanize Jews and *Mischlinge* and eventually to expel them from "Aryan" society.

BIBLIOGRAPHY: PRIMARY SOURCES: *Akten der Parteikanzlei der NSDAP: Rekonstruktion eines verlorengegangenen Bestandes*, Bundesarchiv (Akten-NSDAP), Microfiches, hrsg. v. Institut fuer Zeitgeschichte, Munich, 1983; BA-B (Bundesarchiv-Berlin), *Bestände aus der Zeit von 1867 bis 1945: Zivile Behoerden und Einrichtungen des Deutschen Reiches*; BA-B, R 18/5514; BA-B, 15.09/52; BA-MA (Bundesarchiv/Militaerarchiv – Freiburg), RH 53-7/627; BA-MA, BMRS (Bryan Mark Rigg Sammlung), interview Peter Gaupp; BA-MA, BMRS, interview Hans Koref; BA-MA, BMRS, interview Hans Ranke; Das Reichsbürgergesetz vom 15.09.1935 (RGBL. 1935, Teil 1, Nr. 100, p. 1,146); Erste Verordnung zum Reichsbürgergesetz vom 14.11.1935 (RGBL, Teil 1, 1935, Nr. 125, pp. 1,333–36); Institut fuer Zeitgeschichte (IfZ), N-71-73. SECONDARY SOURCES: H.G. Adler, *The Jews in Germany* (1969); W. Benz, *The Holocaust: A German Historian Examines the Genocide* (1999); Y. Bauer, *A History of the Holocaust* (1982); N.H. Baynes (ed.), *The Speeches of Adolf Hitler*, vol. 2 (1942); D. Cesarani (ed.), *The Final Solution: Origins and Implementation* (1994); C. Essner, *Die "Nuernberger Gesetze" oder Die Verwaltung des Rassenwahns 1933–1945* (2002); S. Friedlaender, *Nazi Germany and the Jews*, vol. 1, *The Years of Persecution, 1933–1939* (1997); H. Globke and W. Stuckart, *Kommentare zur Deutschen Rassengesetzgebung* (1936); *Heeresadjutant bei Hitler, 1938–1943. Aufzeichnungen des Majors Gerhard Engel*, Hrsg. u. kommentiert v. Hildegard von Kotze (= Schriftenreihe der Vierteljahreshefte fuer Zeitgeschichte Nr. 29; 1974); R. Hilberg, *Destruction of the European Jews* (1961, 1985, 2003); A. Hitler, *Mein Kampf* (1971); *The Holocaust*, vol. 1, *Legalizing the Holocaust – The Early Phase, 1933–1939*, intr. by John Mendelsohn (1982); H. Kammer and E. Bartsch (eds.), *Nationalsozialismus: Begriffe aus der Zeit der Gewaltherrschaft, 1933–1945* (1992); M.A. Kaplan, *Between Dignity and Despair: Jewish Life in Nazi Germany* (1998); I. Kershaw, *Hitler, 1889–1936: Hubris* (1999); idem, *Hitler, 1936–1945: Nemesis* (2000); idem, *The Hitler Myth: Image and Reality in the Third Reich* (1987); idem, "Popular Opinion in the Third Reich," in: J. Oakes (ed.), *Government, Party, and People in Nazi Germany* (1980); idem, *Profiles in Power: Hitler* (1991); B. Lösener, "Als Rassereferent im Reichsministerium des Innern," in: Das Reichsministerium des Innern und die Judengesetzgebung, *Vierteljahreshefte fuer Zeitgeschichte*, vol. 9 (1961); J. Noakes, "The Development of Nazi Policy towards the German-Jewish '*Mischlinge*,' 1933–1945," in: *Leo Baeck Yearbook*, 34 (1989); R. Pommerin, *Sterilisierung der Rheinlandbastarde. Das Schicksal einer farbigen deutschen Minderheit, 1918–1937* (1979); F. Redlich, *Hitler: Diagnosis of a Destructive Prophet* (1998); B.M. Rigg, *Hitler's Jewish Soldiers: The Untold Story of Nazi Racial Laws and Men of Jewish Descent in the German Military* (2002); idem, *Rescued From the Reich: How One of Hitler's Soldiers Saved the Lubavitcher Rebbe* (2004); N. Stoltzfus, *Resistance of the Heart: Intermarriage and the Rosenstrasse Protest in Nazi Germany* (1996); R. Vogel, *Ein Stueck von uns* (1973); L. Yahil, *The Holocaust* (1987).

[Bryan Mark Rigg (2nd ed.)]

NUROCK, MORDECHAI (**Max**; 1884–1962), Religious Zionist and Israeli politician, member of the First to Fifth Knessets. Nurock was born in Tukum in the Courland district of Latvia. His father, Zvi Hirsch Nurock, was rabbi in the capital of the Courland district, Mitau (Jelgava). Nurock was first taught religious studies by his father, and was eventually ordained a rabbi himself. He later studied at a gymnasium in Mitau. In 1902 Nurock attended the Russian Zionist

Conference in Minsk as a delegate from Courland. In 1903 he participated in the Sixth Zionist Congress, at which he took a stand against the *Uganda Plan. At the same time he was instrumental in gaining an important concession from the czarist government which made possible the settlement of more Jews in Courland and in Riga, though these areas were outside the Pale of Jewish settlement. In 1913 Nurock succeeded his father as the official government-appointed rabbi of Mitau. In 1915, when the Russian military command expelled the Jews from Courland, accusing them of spying for the Germans, Nurock was invited to remain in Mitau as a military censor, but he declined the offer, and left for St. Petersburg, where he attended university. In later years he studied at German and Swiss universities, and received a Ph.D. He eventually settled in Moscow, where he lived until 1921, becoming deputy chairman of the Jewish community. Between the February and the October Revolutions of 1917, he was engaged in preparing for the All-Russian Jewish Congress, establishing a united religious front of Zionists and non-Zionists called Masoret ve-Ḥerut (Tradition and Freedom). However, the Congress never met, due to opposition by the new Bolshevik regime. In 1921 Nurock left the Soviet Union and settled in Riga, where he was elected to the Latvian Sejm on a religious Zionist ticket. Five years later, as head of the Minorities' Bloc (Jews, Germans, Russians) in the Sejm, Nurock was formally entrusted with the task of helping form a left-of-center government, which he himself did not join. He was an active defender of the rights of national minorities and participated in the meetings of the Congress of National Minorities. He was a member of the Sejm until it was disbanded in 1934. Nurock was one of the founders of the World Jewish Congress in 1936, and until World War II was a delegate on behalf of *Mizrachi to most of the Zionist Congresses, at which he traditionally served as chairman of the closing session. In addition to his activity in the world leadership of Mizrachi, Nurock was a member of the Zionist General Council, the World Council of HICEM – an organization founded in 1928 by HIAS, ICA and Emig-Direkt to deal with Jewish migration – and other Jewish bodies.

After Latvia was annexed by the Soviet Union, Nurock was arrested in 1941 for his Zionist activities, and sent to Turkestan. He was released the following year. His wife and two sons, who had remained in Riga, perished in the Holocaust. In 1945 Nurock left the Soviet Union, visited Norway, where he was received by King Haakon, and traveled to New York. In 1947 he settled in Palestine. He was elected to the First Knesset on the United Religious Front list, and in the Second to Fifth Knessets on behalf of Mizrachi and then the National Religious Party. Nurock strongly opposed the restitution agreement with West Germany, and the establishment of any sort of formal relations with it, often voting independently from his parliamentary group on this issue. In 1952 he was appointed minister of posts and was a candidate for the presidency of the State opposite Yitzhak *Ben-Zvi in 1952. He passed away in the course of the Fifth Knesset.

He wrote *Ve'idat Ẓiyyonei Rusya be-Minsk, Elul 5662, August/September 1902* (1963).

BIBLIOGRAPHY: A. Tartakower (ed.), *Zekher Mordechai – Mukdash le-Ḥayyav u-Po'alo shel ha-Rav Mordekhai Nurock* (1967).

[Mendel Bobe / Susan Hattis Rolef (2nd ed.)]

NUSAḤ (Heb. נֹסַח, נוּסַח, נֻסָּח, Nosaḥ), musical term (for its use in liturgy, see *Liturgy). The common meaning of the Hebrew noun *nusaḥ* is adapted to musical contexts both in a more general and in a very specific way. Expressions like "biblical chant *nusaḥ Sefarad*" (the Sephardi version of melodical Bible-reading; see *Liturgy), or "this cantor has a good *nusaḥ*" (he executes the traditional tunes in good taste) are easily understood as an application of the term in its normal meaning. The word *nusaḥ*, however, is also used as a technical term of synagogue music. In combinations such as *Nusaḥ ha-Tefillah, Nusaḥ Yamim Nora'im, Nusaḥ Shabbat* it denotes the specific musical mode to which a certain part of the liturgy is sung. The musical characteristics of these modes are defined by the following elements: (1) each is based upon a particular series of notes which may simply be a tetrachord, more often a combination of several overlapping tetrachords, or another scale of less or more than eight notes; (2) each contains a stock of characteristic motives which undergo constant variation; (3) each combines these motives in a completely free order, forming an "irrational" pattern; (4) the association of each *nusaḥ*, as defined by the above-mentioned three elements, is with a particular section of a specific holiday liturgy as, for instance, the *Musaf* prayer of the Penitential Feasts, the Morning Prayer on weekdays, and so on.

The musical definition of a *nusaḥ* and its close connection with a certain time and occasion exhibit a strong resemblance to the characteristics which are ascribed to the Oriental **maqām*, the Indian *raga*, and to certain ancient parts of Roman plainsong and Byzantine hymnody (where it is defined by research as "migrating motives" or "a mosaic of motives"). It is worth noting that the *nusaḥ*-principle is known to European as well as to Eastern Jewish communities and may be regarded, therefore, as a very old musical trait in synagogue song.

Other Musical Meanings of Nusah

The plural form *nusaḥim* denotes the particular tunes to which some prominent chapters of the Pentateuch are read, such as Genesis 1, the Song of the Sea (Ex. 15), or the Decalogue. The *nusaḥim* of these chapters are florid variants of the common mode of reading. Furthermore, the Aramaic plural form *nusḥa'ot* ("formulas") is sometimes used by Ashkenazi cantors for denoting a vocal "prelude" without words which introduces important prayers.

[Hanoch Avenary]

NUSINOV, ISAAC (**Yitzhak**; 1889–1952), Russian literary critic and historian. Born in Chernikhov, Volhynia, he studied at universities in Switzerland and Italy, returning in 1917 to Russia, where he became active in cultural life. From 1925 he taught literature at the University of Moscow and at the

Yiddish department of the Western University, Moscow, and participated in the work of the Institute for Jewish Proletarian Culture of the Ukrainian Academy of Sciences, Kiev. Nusinov published many studies, essays, and papers in Yiddish journals; he also contributed to the *Bolshaya Sovetskaya Entsiklopediya* ("Great Soviet Encyclopedia") and to the *Literaturnaya Entsiklopediya* ("Literary Encyclopedia"). His books include *Teories* (1926), articles of literary criticism; *Problemen fun der Proletarisher Literatur* (1932); and *A History of Yiddish Literature*, scheduled for publication in 1927 but never published, though the manuscript was completed. Nusinov was arrested in 1948 and executed in August 1952.

BIBLIOGRAPHY: Rejzen, Leksikon, 2 (1927), 537–9; LNYL, 6 (1965), 183; E.I. Simmons, *Through the Glass of Soviet Literature* (1953), 146.

[Elias Schulman]

NUSSBAUM, ARTHUR (1877–1964), professor of law. Born in Berlin, Nussbaum published *Der Polnaer Ritualmordprozess* (1906), an attack on the procedure of the prosecution at the trial of Leopold *Hilsner, the man tried after the Polna blood libel. The book led to renewed efforts on Hilsner's behalf and gained Nussbaum considerable distinction as a lawyer. In 1914 he became a lecturer at the University of Berlin and was made professor of law in 1921. Following the advent of Hitler, Nussbaum was forced to relinquish his post and he immigrated to the United States. He was research professor of public law at Columbia University from 1934.

A prolific writer in German and English, Nussbaum was an authority on commercial and private international law and his works were translated into several languages. His principle writings include: *Das Geld in Theorie und Praxis des deutschen und auslaendischen Rechts* (1925; republished as *Money in the Law*, 1939); *Deutsches internationales Privatrecht* (1932); *Principles of Private International Law* (1943); *A Concise History of the Law of Nations* (1947, 1954^2); and *A History of the Dollar* (1957). He also contributed to numerous legal journals and was editor of the *Internationales Jahrbuch fuer Schiedsgerichtswesen in Zivil- und Handelssachen* (1926–34).

BIBLIOGRAPHY: *Kuerschner's Deutscher Gelehrten-Kalender* (1966), s.v., incl. bibl.; *New York Times* (Nov. 23, 1964).

NUSSBAUM, FELIX (1904–1944), German painter and graphic artist. Nussbaum was born in Osnabrueck, Germany. In 1922 he left home to study at the Hamburg School for Arts and Crafts under Cesar Klein, Hans Meid, and Paul Plontke. From 1924 to 1929 he took classes at the Vereinigte Staatsschulen fuer freie und angewandte Kunst in Berlin. Some of his paintings in the style of the Neue Sachlichkeit, also revealing the influence of Karl Hofer and Henry Rousseau, were exhibited in the Berlin *Sezession*. In 1932 Nussbaum was awarded a scholarship at the Deutsche Akademie Villa Massimo in Rome. In Italy he started to paint neorealist landscapes. After some antisemitic incidents in the academy he left for Alassio and in 1935 moved to Belgium. During the German invasion of Belgium in 1940, Nussbaum was caught in Brussels but he was able to flee about four months later. He returned to Brussels, where he and his wife, Felka Platek, went into hiding. It was during this life of despair that he created the bulk of his most impressive paintings and self-portraits foreshadowing the extermination of the Holocaust in a surrealist manner, such as *Soir* (a self-portrait with his wife, 1942), *Self-Portrait with ID Card*, marked "J" for "Jewish," and *Self-Portrait at the Easel*, both painted 1943 (all in the Kulturgeschichtliches Museum, Osnabrueck). In his last known work, *Die Gerippe spielen zum Tanz* (1944, Kulturgeschichtliches Museum, Osnabrueck), a danse macabre reflects his hopeless situation. In 1944 he and his wife were caught by the Nazis and deported to Auschwitz in one of the last trains leaving Belgium. Nussbaum and his wife did not survive the extermination camp. Only his paintings have survived and were retrieved after World War II. In 1998 his native city Osnabrueck opened a museum solely dedicated to his work, the Felix Nussbaum Haus, which was designed by the American architect Daniel *Libeskind.

BIBLIOGRAPHY: E.D. Bilsky, *Art and Exile, Felix Nussbaum 1904–1944* (1985); H. Guratzsch, *Felix Nussbaum, 1904–1944* (2004); R. Heidt and Ch. Ebers, *Felix Nussbaum* (1988); P. Junk and W. Zimmer, *Felix Nussbaum – Leben und Werk* (1982); R. Neugebauer, *Zeit im Blick – Felix Nussbaum und die Moderne* (2004).

[Philipp Zschommler (2nd ed.)]

NUSSBAUM, HILARY (**Hillel**; 1820–1895), Polish historian, educator, and communal worker. Born in Warsaw, he was educated in the rabbinical seminary there and as a young man was active in communal affairs. He became a member (*"dozor"*) of the community council, and was instrumental in building the progressive synagogue of Warsaw. Nussbaum may be considered a moderate assimilationist, influenced by the positivist tendencies in the Polish society of his time.

A prolific writer, Nussbaum contributed to the Polish-Jewish periodical *Izraelita*. He was also a writer of apologetics. He published a German translation of a Hebrew treatise by his father-in-law, the Hebrew *maskil* Moses Tenenboim, under the title *Der Talmud in seiner Wichtigkeit* (1880), which was a refutation of *Der Talmud in seiner Nichtigkeit* by a radical assimilationist Abraham *Buchner, an associate of the antisemitic Catholic priest L. *Chiarini. Nussbaum is, however, remembered mostly as an author of popular historical works, namely *Szkice historyczne z życia Żydów w Warszawie* ("Historical Sketches from the Life of Jews in Warsaw," 1881); *Historya żydow od Mojźesza do epoki obecnej* ("History of the Jews from Moses to the Present," 5 vols., 1888–90). The works of Nussbaum, although outdated, still have some value for the history of the Jews in Poland. He attempted to stress their great antiquity and their glorious past. Nussbaum, who knew Hebrew well, also published poems and articles in that language.

BIBLIOGRAPHY: J. Shatzky, *Yidishe Bildungspolitik in Poyln fun 1806 biz 1866* (1943), index; idem, *Geshikhte fun Yidn in Varshe*, vols. 2–3 (1948–53), indexes.

[Judah M. Rosenthal]

NUSSBAUM, JAKOB (1873–1936), German painter. Nussbaum was born in Rhina near Kassel, Germany. His family moved to Frankfurt-on-the-Main ten years later and he was educated for a career in commerce. From 1893 to 1896, however, he studied art in Munich, first at the private academy of arts run by the Hungarian painter Simon Hollósy and later at the Academy of Fine Arts under Gabriel von Hackl. Following the example of French impressionism Hollósy instructed his pupils to emulate nature as the only source of true beauty and paradigm for artistic expression. Nussbaum and several other artists went so far as to accompany Hollósy to Hungary, where he intended to establish a colony of artists devoted solely to plein-air painting. The tenor of impressionist plein-air painting remains visible in Nussbaum's work, even after he had turned to expressionism. In 1902 he returned to Frankfurt, where he had a successful career as a painter of landscapes, still lifes, and portraits, such as the one of Georg Swarzenski (1928, Staedelsches Kunstinstitut, Frankfurt-on-the-Main). He joined the Berlin Secession and together with Corinth, Slevogt, and Liebermann became one of the leading representatives of German impressionism. He also made several trips, such as to Holland together with Max Liebermann in 1908, to Tunisia in 1903/4, and to Palestine and Egypt in 1925, which is reflected in his painting *Street of Tiberias in 1925* (Staedelsches Kunstinstitut, Frankfurt-on-the-Main). During World War I he was drafted to document the war as an artist. In 1932 he became a teacher at the Frankfurt School of Arts and Crafts. He also became an honorary member of the Frankfurt Kuenstlerbund but lost all positions after the Nazi takeover in 1933. As a devoted Zionist he decided to immigrate to Palestine together with his wife and his children shortly after 1933, and settled at Lake Kinneret, where he continued to paint expressionist landscapes.

BIBLIOGRAPHY: C.C. Mueller, *Jakob Nussbaum (1873–1936), with Catalogue Raisonné* (2002).

[Philipp Zschommler (2nd ed.)]

NUSSBAUM, MAX (1908–1974) U.S. Reform rabbi and Zionist leader. Nussbaum was born in Suczawa, Bukovina, and was ordained in 1933 at the Jewish Theological Seminary in Breslau, Germany, where he also earned a Ph.D. He served as a rabbi in Berlin until 1940, when he came to the United States at the invitation of Stephen S. *Wise, who had been introduced to the young Zionist activist by Chaim *Weizmann. Immediately upon Nussbaum's arrival in New York, Arthur *Sulzberger dispatched him to Washington, D.C., to brief Secretary of the Treasury Henry *Morgenthau on the situation of Jews in Nazi Germany.

Nussbaum's first position in the United States was as rabbi of Temple Beth Ahaba in Muskogee, Oklahoma. In 1941, he was invited to join the faculty of Oklahoma State University in Norman, where he also founded the Jewish Students' Center, which was converted into the campus Hillel organization; Nussbaum was installed as its first director by Abraham *Sachar.

In 1942, he was appointed rabbi of Temple Israel in Hollywood, California, where he remained until his death. An admirer of Mordecai Kaplan, he formed a Reconstructionist group within the temple, which grew considerably during his tenure. His eloquence also shifted the orientation of the congregation from non-Zionist to pro-Zionist. As the charismatic rabbi of a high-profile congregation in the center of the movie industry, Nussbaum conducted numerous celebrity weddings (including that of Elizabeth Taylor and Eddie Fisher) and funerals (Samuel Goldwyn, Al Jolson, Edward G. Robinson, and more). He was one of the first West Coast rabbis to hold the highest offices of major national Jewish organizations, including vice president of the *American Jewish Congress (1946), chairman of the National Executive Committee of the *Zionist Organization of America (1958–62), president of the ZOA (1962–65), chairman of the *American Zionist Council (1964–66), and chairman of the American Section of the *World Jewish Congress (1964–68). He also served as president of both the Southern California Association of Liberal Rabbis and the Western Association of Reform Rabbis. A board member of the National Conference of Christians and Jews, Nussbaum was an active supporter of the civil rights movement; Martin Luther King shared the pulpit with him at one memorable Temple Israel service.

Nussbaum was instrumental in establishing the Los Angeles campus of HUC-JIR, serving as its first vice president. He was the first West Coast recipient of both the Eleanor Roosevelt Humanities Award (from the State of Israel Bonds Organization) and the ZOA's Brandeis Award – shared with his wife Ruth, who became a Zionist leader in her own right as one of the founders of ARZA (Association of Reform Zionists of America) and a member of the boards of Hadassah, the Jewish National Fund, and the State of Israel Bonds. She was also a leading activist in Youth Aliyah.

[Bezalel Gordon (2nd ed.)]

NUSSBAUM, PERRY (1908–1987), U.S. rabbi and activist. In the midst of a somewhat lackluster career, Rabbi Perry Nussbaum found himself thrust into the national spotlight during the Civil Rights era. Nussbaum was raised as an Orthodox Jew in Toronto. He later joined the Reform movement, and was ordained by Hebrew Union College in 1933. Throughout the first 20 years of his career, Nussbaum bounced around between small congregations across the country, at least partly due to his outspoken and sometimes difficult personality.

Nussbaum took the pulpit at Beth Israel Congregation in Jackson, Mississippi, in 1954, not long after the Supreme Court's landmark decision Brown v. Board of Education which mandated school integration. From his arrival, Rabbi Nussbaum was caught up in the civil rights issue. Though he was morally appalled by Mississippi's system of racial discrimination, he faced a congregation that largely did not want to challenge the status quo and wished their rabbi to remain quiet on the issue. At first, Nussbaum avoided getting involved in the burgeoning civil rights movement, though he did occasionally sermonize on the issue.

In the summer of 1961, waves of freedom riders arrived in Jackson protesting segregation in interstate bus travel. These activists, many of whom were Jewish, were arrested and sent to Parchman State Prison. Nussbaum tried to organize the state's rabbis to visit these Jewish protestors regularly, but none of his colleagues would agree to do it. Nussbaum shouldered this burden himself, driving 150 miles each way once a week to visit them, deliver personal supplies and cigarettes, and lead a short worship service. Perhaps most importantly, he took down the names and addresses of the activists' families, and wrote them letters assuring them that their sons and daughters were okay. Although Nussbaum received attention and support from Jews around the country for his work, the rabbi did not publicize his visits to his congregation. He paid his own expenses for these trips.

As the backlash against civil rights became more violent in Mississippi, Nussbaum became more outspoken. In 1964, he helped found the Committee of Concern, an interracial group of ministers that sought to raise money to rebuild bombed or burned churches. At the dedication of Beth Israel's new temple in 1967, both black and white ministers participated. On September 18, 1967, Nussbaum's own house of worship was bombed by local Ku Klux Klan members. Two months later, the same group bombed Nussbaum's home. Though the rabbi was home with his wife at the time, no one was seriously hurt.

Shaken by these attacks, Nussbaum initially tried to leave Jackson, but ended up staying at Beth Israel until his retirement in 1973. Nussbaum's career in Jackson reflected the tremendous pressures that southern rabbis felt in balancing their religious and moral ideals with societal demands to conform to white supremacy. Though they were not as outspoken as their northern colleagues who did not face the same threat of violence, Nussbaum and many of his fellow rabbis in the South helped lay the difficult groundwork for constructing a new South based on racial equality.

[Stuart Rockoff (2nd ed.)]

NUSSENBLATH, TULO (1895–1943), researcher into *Herzl's life. Born in Stryj, Galicia, Nussenblath was an officer in the Austrian army in World War I. After the war he studied law in Vienna, but instead of working as a lawyer he engaged in historical study, concentrating in particular on the life of Theodor Herzl. He published his findings in three books: *Zeitgenossen ueber Herzl* (1929), a collection of contemporary records; *Ein Volk unterwegs zum Frieden* (1933), about the endeavors to found a peace movement, which includes Herzl's correspondence with the Zionist sympathizer Berta von Suttner; and *Herzl Jahrbuch* (1937), which was intended to become a regular annual for researches concerning Herzl's life and era, based primarily on documents not yet published. After the German occupation of Austria in 1938, Nussenblath was expelled to Poland, and when it too was conquered by the Germans, he lived in the Warsaw Ghetto, working there as a communal leader. In the spring of 1943 he was taken to a concentration camp, where he was murdered.

BIBLIOGRAPHY: N. Eck (Eckron), *Ha-To'im be-Darkhei ha-Mavet* (1960), 228–33; N. Kudish et al., *Sefer Stryj* (1962), 120–1.

[Getzel Kressel]

NUT (Heb. אֱגוֹז), in the Bible and Talmud – the walnut, *Juglans regia*, which grows wild in Greece, Asia Minor, and Central Asia. It is mentioned once only in the Bible, but frequently in rabbinic literature. Song of Songs (6:11) refers to "a garden of nuts" where also grew the vine and pomegranates. The verse was regarded as an allegory referring to the Jewish people and the many interpretations afford much information about the growth of the tree, its characteristics, and its fruits: just as regular pruning of this tree assists its development, so does the pruning of the wealth of the Jews by giving charity to those who labor in the Torah (Song R. 6:11); when the walnut tree is smitten with disease, its roots should be exposed, so when Israel suffers, it must examine itself from the foundation (Yal, Song 6:cf. Song R. 6:11); it is a tall tree with a smooth trunk so that a careless person is liable to fall from it and be killed, such too is the fate of a leader of Israel who is not careful (*ibid.*); the walnut has species with shells of varying thickness, so too in Israel some have a soft charitable heart, some are average, and some are hard (*ibid.*); the walnut has "four compartments and a central carina" like the camp of Israel in the wilderness which had "four camps with the tent or meeting in the center" (*ibid.*; see Num. 2); just as if one nut is taken from a heap, all the rest roll, so if one Israelite is smitten, all feel it.

Walnut trees were abundant in Ereẓ Israel in the talmudic period, but because of the great demand for the nuts, they were also imported (Tosef., Dem. 1:9). It flourishes mainly in the cooler regions of Israel. Josephus stresses the exceptional fertility of the valley of Gennesareth which produces trees needing heat like palms, but also walnuts that require a cool climate (Jos., Wars, 3:517). As its wood is highly combustible, it was used for the altar fire in the Temple (Tam. 2:3). Because of the excellence of the timber, it was used to make objets d'art (BB 89b). Its green outer skin supplied material for dyeing (Shab. 9:5) and writing (Tosef., Shab. 11:8). The fruit was regarded as of high nutritional value (Er. 29a). It was particularly beloved by children who played games with the shells. Women too used to play with them (Er. 104a) and walnut shells were also thrown in front of the bride and groom (Ber. 50b). Nowadays walnuts are chiefly to be found in Israel in the gardens of Arabs, very few walnuts being planted in Jewish settlements. The tree is sensitive to pests, but there are giant trees which produce fine crops (like the old walnut tree near the Byzantine church in Abu Ghosh).

BIBLIOGRAPHY: Loew, Flora, 2 (1924), 29–59; H.N. and A.L. Moldenke, *Plants of the Bible* (1952), index, s.v.; J. Feliks, *Olam ha-Ẓome'aḥ ha-Mikra'i* (1968²), 71–73. ADD. BIBLIOGRAPHY: Feliks, Ha-Ẓome'aḥ, 17.

[Jehuda Feliks]

NUZI, ancient city in N.E. Iraq at the present site of Yorghan Tepe, about 10 miles (16 km.) S.W. of Arrapha, modern Kirkuk, near the foothills of southern Kurdistan. Excavations were begun at Nuzi in 1925 by E. Chiera and were continued through 1931 under the joint auspices of the American School of Oriental Research, Harvard University, and the University Museum of Pennsylvania. The earliest occupation of the site can be traced to prehistoric times. During the middle of the third millennium B.C.E. the place was called Gasur (Foster 1987). The city reached the height of its importance during the 15th–14th centuries B.C.E., when it was called Nuzi and was part of the Mitanni Empire centered in northern Syria; its population largely spoke the Hurrian language, though they wrote in Akkadian. It was destroyed by the Assyrians in the 14th century B.C.E.

Interest in Nuzi arose because of apparent parallels between situations discussed in the approximately 7,000 cuneiform tablets from the site with biblical materials especially from Genesis about the Patriarchal Age (Speiser 1962). The tablets reveal activities of perhaps six generations of citizens over fewer than 100 years from 1440 to 1340. The king of nearby Arrapha had a palace in the town, and he was a vassal of Mitanni. But the contacts with the outside world were minimal, and the main story to be derived from the texts is the gradual impoverishment of most of the population and the growth in power of the rich and the large estates they were putting together (Morrison 1992; Maidman 1995; Wilhelm and Stein 2001). Archaeologically the site is of interest because of the regular layout of the streets around the palace and temple, and within the palace and another rich house there were frescoes preserved that show Aegean and Egyptian influence (Wilhelm and Stein 2001, Stein 1997).

It is not so clear that the practices in Nuzi really reflect practices depicted among the Patriarchs. Partly this is because other sites have provided insights into nomadic life in the second millennium and partly this is because the historical memory in the Genesis stories has been affected by much later events. Also customs seen at Nuzi are known now to be widespread in the Ancient Near East, and some persist today (Morrison 1992: 1160–61).

Among parallels that still are of interest is the fact that apparently land could only be sold within families in Nuzi. This recalls the biblical preoccupation with redeeming land and trying to keep it within the same extended family. The Nuzi wheelers and dealers got around the prohibition by having themselves adopted into families (Zaccagnini 2003, 594–96). The biblical material knows nothing of adoption, though it seems that before Isaac's birth Abram assumed his house-born slave would be his heir (Gen. 15:3).

Rachel's theft of her father Laban's household gods (Genesis 31:19) may be explained by the idea that possession of household gods could be part of a legal title to the paternal estate. This interpretation is based on the following tablet from Nuzi: "Tablet of adoption belonging to N., the son of A.; he adopted W., the son of P. As long as N. is alive, W. shall provide food and clothing. When N. dies, W. shall become the heir. If N. has a son of his own, he shall divide [the estate] equally with W., but the son of N. shall take the gods of N. However, if N. does not have a son of his own, then W. shall take the gods of N. Furthermore, he gave his daughter N. in marriage to W. and if W. takes another wife, he shall forfeit the lands and buildings of N." (Meek 1969: 219–20; Zaccagnini 2003, 602–3). Clearly the nature of the material from the Hebrew Bible and from Nuzi is quite different, but the cultural milieus may reflect similar concerns.

BIBLIOGRAPHY: B. Foster, "People, Land, and Produce at Sargonic Gasur," in: D. Owen and M. Morrison (ed.), *Studies on the Civiliation and Culture of Nuzi and the Hurrians* (1987), 2: 89–107; M. Maidman, "Nuzi: Portrait of an Ancient Mesopotamian Provinical Town," in: J. Sasson (ed.), *Civilizations of the Ancient Near East* (1995), 931–47; T. Meek, "Nuzi Akkadian," in: J. Pritchard (ed.), *Ancient Near Eastern Texts* (1969), 219–20; M. Morrison, "Nuzi," in: *Anchor Bible Dictionary* (1992.), 4: 1156–62; E.A. Speiser, "Nuzi," in: *The Interpreter's Dictionary of the Bible* (1962), 3:573–74; D. Stein, "Nuzi," in: E. Myers (ed.), *The Oxford Encyclopedia of Archaeology in the Near East*, 4: 171–75; C. Zaccagnini "Nuzi," in: R. Westbrook (ed.), *A History of Ancient Near Eastern Law* (2003), 1: 565–617; G. Wilhelm and D. Stein "Nuzi," in: *Reallexikon der Assyriologie* (2001), 9: 7/8: 636–47.

[Daniel C. Snell (2nd ed.)]

NYIREGYHAZA (Hung. **Nyiregyháza**), town in N.E. Hungary. Jews were living in the district in the 18th century, but were excluded from Nyiregyhaza itself until 1840, when they were authorized to settle in the towns. By 1848–49, 71 Jews lived in the town. In 1865 they became affiliated to the community of Nagykallo. After the general Jewish Congress of 1868–69 the community remained within the framework of the *status quo ante communities. In 1904 the Orthodox members formed a separate community. The first synagogue of the congregation was built in 1880, when the Orthodox also built their own synagogue. A Jewish elementary school serving the whole community was established in 1868 and existed until the Holocaust. Rabbis of the community included Jacob K. Friedman (officiated 1856–1905), who participated in the Congress of 1868–69 as representative of the whole district; and the historian, Bela *Bernstein (1900–1944), who was deported with his congregation in the Holocaust. The court hearings of the *Tiszaeszlar blood libel case were held in Nyiregyhaza. The Jewish population numbered 60 in 1850; 1,128 in 1869; 2,097 in 1880; 2,159 in 1890; 3,008 in 1900; 5,066 in 1920; 5,134 in 1936; and 4,993 in 1941. Their economic position was favorable.

Holocaust Period and After

When World War II broke out, refugees from Poland arrived in Nyiregyhaza and were assisted by a special communal committee organized for that purpose. The community also supported refugee children from Slovakia. After the imposition by the Hungarian authorities of anti-Jewish laws and forced labor from 1938 to 1944, the Germans occupied the town on March 19, 1944. During Passover (April 17, 1944) SS units herded the Jews of the town and from 36 surrounding villages, totaling 11,000, into the ghetto. At the end of May and beginning of June, more than 5,000 Jews were deported in the most inhumane conditions in closed cattle wagons. Some days later the synagogue was blown up.

The two congregations in Nyiregyhaza reorganized after the war and opened a yeshivah. The number of the Jewish population decreased from 1,210 in 1946 to 180 in 1970 as most left for Israel after 1956.

BIBLIOGRAPHY: *Zsidó Világkongresszus Magyarországi Képviselete Statisztikai Osztátyanak Közleményei*, 4 (1947), 8–9 (1948), 13–14 (1949); S. Gervai, *Nyiregyháza zsidósága élete* (1963); B. Bernstein, in: *Semitic Studies in Memory of Immanuel Loew* (1947), 57–62.

[Laszlo Harsanyi]

NYONS, town in *Dauphiné, in the department of Drôme, S.E. France. Like the other Jews of Dauphiné, those of Nyons were not affected by the expulsions of the Jews from the Kingdom of France in 1306 and 1322. During the latter year, a number of Jews expelled from *Comtat Venaissin joined the Jews already established in Nyons. Their situation was quite satisfactory; a Jew held public office in Nyons and another was in the service of the dauphin. At the time of the *Black Death in 1348, the community suffered violent persecution. It was reconstituted about 1364 and then occupied the present Rue Juiverie. The synagogue, whose dilapidated building still existed toward the end of the 19th century, appears to have belonged to this second community. There were no Jews in Nyons by the end of the 15th century. Known among the scholars of Nyons are Isaac b. Mordecai *Kimḥi, named Petit, a liturgical author, and Ḥayyim of Vienne. At the beginning of World War II about 50 Jewish families, many of them from the Saar, lived in Nyons. Nyons has no organized community.

BIBLIOGRAPHY: Gross, Gal Jud, 384ff.; C. Brechet, *Pages d'histoire nyonsaise* (1927), 90ff.; Z. Szajkowski, *Analytical Franco-Jewish Gazetteer 1939–1945* (1966), 186.

[Bernhard Blumenkranz]

Initial letter "O" of the word Ozias *at the beginning of the prologue to the Book of Amos in a Latin Bible, France, 13th century. The illumination shows Amaziah, the priest of Beth-El (Amos 7:10–17) waving an incense burner. Lyons, Bibliothèque Nationale, Ms. 411 fol. 160v.*

OA-OZ

OAK (Heb. אַלּוֹן), the main trees of Israel's natural groves and forests. The three species which grow there have in common their strong and hard wood and all attain a great height and reach a very old age. The Hebrew name, *allon*, means strong (Amos 2:9). Extensive oak forests still exist in Bashan, and these, together with the cedars of Lebanon, symbolized pride and loftiness (Isa. 2:13; Zech. 11:2). The people of Tyre made the oars for their ships from the oaks of Bashan (Ezek. 27:6). Some oaks served as sites for idol worship (Hos. 4:13), and burial took place under them (Gen. 35:8). The oak is long-lived and when it grows old or is cut down it has the ability to renew itself, putting out new shoots from the stump or roots that in time develop into a strong tree. In his prophecy describing the fate of the Jewish people, for whom it was decreed that they should suffer great losses, the prophet Isaiah uses the image of the old oak (together with an *elah*, *terebinth) standing near the gate Shallekhet in Jerusalem that frequently had its branches and trunk cut down, only its stump remaining; yet no sooner was it felled, than the stump put forth "holy seed," sprouting new shoots (Isa. 6:13). Possibly Isaiah 11:1: "And there shall come forth a shoot out of the stock of Jesse, and a twig shall grow forth out of his roots" is a continuation of this chapter.

Evidence of this phenomenon can be seen in many oaks in Israel today. The most famous, and apparently the oldest of them, is "the oak of Abraham" in Hebron. This oak, or one of its ancestors, is mentioned in the Apocrypha – Jubilees and Tobit – as the tree under which Abraham received the kings. Josephus (Ant., 1:186; cf. Wars, 4:533) also speaks of it. *Jerome notes that Titus sold 10,000 Judean captives under this tree. Since the third century many Jewish and Christian pilgrims have mentioned that this tree is considered sacred. It is an evergreen of the species *Quercus calliprinos*, which constitutes most of the groves in the hills of Judea and Galilee. Most of them look like shrubs as a result of continuous felling and of being gnawed by goats. Some giant trees still survive (as for example at Aqua Bella, now called Ein Ḥemed). The other two species of oak growing in Israel are deciduous. On the hills of Lower Galilee (in the vicinity of Tivon and Allonim) there exist groves of the Tabor oak (*Quercus ithaburensis*). This tree is also to be seen in the Ḥurshat Tal in the Ḥuleh valley where there are about 200 giant trees (50 ft. high with trunks of 16 ft. or more in circumference). The third species is the *Quercus infectoria* (*Quercus boissier*), called in Hebrew by the corresponding name *tola* oak because of the *crimson worm (*tola*) which lives off its branches (as it does off the Tabor oak). This tree, which has a tall straight trunk, is called in the Mishnah *milah* or *milast* (Mid. 3:7).

BIBLIOGRAPHY: Loew, Flora, 1 (1928), 621–34; Feliks, in: *Sinai*, 38 (1956/57), 85–102; idem, *Olam ha-Ẓome'aḥ ha-Mikra'i* (1968²), 107–9; H.N. and A.L. Moldenke, *Plants of the Bible* (1952), index. **ADD. BIBLIOGRAPHY:** Feliks, Ha-Ẓome'aḥ, 27, 99.

[Jehuda Feliks]

OAKLAND, city located on the east shore of San Francisco Bay, California. The 1969 metropolitan Jewish population (including Alameda and Contra Costa Counties) of Oakland was 18,000. It is estimated that the 2005 metropolitan Jewish population (including Alameda and Contra Costa Counties) of the East Bay was 60–80,000.

The first Jewish organization was the Oakland Hebrew Benevolent Society (1862), which owned a cemetery and served the religious and cultural needs of the Jewish community until the founding of the First Hebrew Congregation (now Temple Sinai) in 1875. These two organizations merged in 1881. The Oakland lodge of B'nai B'rith was founded in 1875 and many local relief societies followed. The Jewish population of the city in 1880 was 227, with 68 in the suburbs. Congregation Beth Jacob, Orthodox, was founded by Eastern Europeans in 1887 and Temple Beth Abraham, Conservative, by Hungarians in 1907. The Jewish Welfare Federation of Alameda and Contra Costa Counties was organized in 1918 and the Oakland Jewish Center was built in 1958.

The Jewish Community Federation of the Greater East Bay has its main office in Oakland and an auxiliary office in Walnut Creek. The East Bay Jewish community covers a two-county area (Contra Costa and Alameda) and is comprised of both urban as well as suburban areas, including the cities of Oakland, Berkeley, Richmond, Fremont, Lafayette, Walnut Creek, Danville, San Ramon, and Pleasanton. The East Bay is an active Jewish community. There are now four synagogues in Oakland (one Reform, one Conservative, one Orthodox, and one Renewal), as well as four in Berkeley and 17 in the surrounding areas. Many of the congregations maintain religious schools. There are three day schools, 12 Jewish preschools, and a successful Midrasha program (grades 8–12) that offers weekly educational classes as well as retreats. The Center for Jewish Living and Learning of the Jewish Community Federation coordinates the four Midrashot, special education programs, Holocaust education as well as professional development for both the congregational and early childhood educators. The Jewish Community Federation sponsors a Volunteer Action Center, an Israel Center that runs the largest Federation-based teen trip to Israel each summer, and an active Young Leadership Division. The Federation also supports Building Jewish Bridges, that helps interfaith couples find their place in the Jewish community.

The East Bay Jewish community maintains a *mikveh*, kosher butcher and bakery shops, a synagogue council, a home for seniors and local chapters of the national Jewish organizations. Most of the Jews are in the professions or in mercantile activity. The East Bay Jewish population participates in the social and cultural life of the region and is especially active in social action/Tikun Olam issues as well as those that address educational and environmental concerns. The Jewish community is noted for the good relations between the different religious movements as well for its diversity of population, which includes Jews of different racial and religious backgrounds. To the north of Oakland is Berkeley, containing the main campus of the University of California, which has a Hillel Foundation and many distinguished Jews on the faculty and an important Judaic Studies Program including such scholars as Robert *Alter and Daniel *Boyarin. Also located in Berkeley is the Judah L. Magnes Memorial Museum, which was organized in 1961, and the headquarters of Lehrhaus Judaica, the Bay Area's largest adult school for Jewish studies.

[Riva Gambert (2nd ed.)]

OATH.

IN THE BIBLE

Definition and Form

The truth or inviolability of one's words was commonly attested in ancient Israel by oath – a self-curse made in conditional form that went into effect if the condition was fulfilled; e.g., "May harm befall me if I do so and so" (cf. Eng. "I'll be damned if I will!"). The full form, including the curse, is only rarely found, as, e.g., in the adjuration of the suspected adulteress: "'If no man has lain with you … be immune to harm from this water of bitterness that induces the spell. But if you have gone astray while married to your husband … may YHWH make you a curse and an imprecation among your people as YHWH causes your thigh to sag and your belly to distend'… and the woman shall say, 'Amen, amen'" (Num. 5:19–22). The oath might be accompanied by a gesture expressive of the curse: "Then I called the priests and made them take an oath to act on their word. I also shook out the bosom of my garment and said, 'So may God shake out every man from his house and from the fruit of his labor who does not fulfill his word. So may he be shaken out and emptied!' And all the assembly said, 'Amen'" (Neh. 5:12–13). As a rule, the condition alone appears in oath statements, the self-curse being omitted for superstitious reasons. Thus a negative oath normally is framed as an affirmative conditional statement with aposiopesis: "Swear to me by God, if you will kill me or if you will deliver me to my master […]" (= that you will not kill or deliver me to my master; I Sam. 30:15); "By YHWH's life! if guilt shall come upon you for this […]" (= no guilt shall; *ibid.* 28:10). Less often the self-curse is couched in vague terms (perhaps accompanied by a meaningful gesture): "May God do thus to me and more so, if before sunset I taste bread or anything else!" (II Sam. 3:35). So essential was the curse that the oath might be cited in the form of a curse: "The Israelites had sworn, 'Cursed be he who provides a wife for the Benjamites'" (Judg. 21:18); "Your father adjured the army, 'Cursed be the man who eats bread today'" (I Sam. 14:28). Moreover, the term "curse" (*ʾalah*) freely interchanges with "oath" (*shevuʿah*): cf.

Genesis 24:8 with 24:41; the exchange of the related verbs in I Samuel 14:23 and 14:28; and the pair yoked in Numbers 5:21; Daniel 9:11; and Nehemiah 10:30. That too is the basis of the contrast in Isaiah 65:16, between "one who invokes a blessing on himself" (*mitbarekh*) and "one who swears" (i.e., one who invokes a curse upon himself). A strong malediction consisted of condemning someone to such exemplary misfortune as would make him citable in an oath: "You shall leave your name for my chosen ones to use in oaths" (Isa. 65:15; cf. Num. 5:21; Ps. 102:9). The close link between oath and curse lends color to the suggested derivation of the terms *hishbi'a'*, "adjure," *nishba'*, "swear," and *shev'uah*, "oath," from *sheva'*, "seven" – based on the use of seven in maledictions: e.g., Leviticus 26:18, 21, 24, etc.; Deuteronomy 28:7; II Samuel 24:13; Job 5: 19; cf. too the repeated sevens in the curses of the Sfire treaty (eighth century B.C.E., Pritchard, Texts[3], 659–60). The original sense might have been "to lay [curses in] sevens on someone" or "to take [curses in] sevens on oneself." (Sevens are also associated with oaths and maledictions in Gen. 21:27–31 and Num. 23; but neither these nor the aforementioned texts support the theory that seven animals were slaughtered at oath-taking, the taker accepting their fate for himself if he broke his word (Lehmann). Biblical and extrabiblical evidence of the symbolic killing of animals at treaty ceremonies never shows so many as seven animals: Gen. 15; Jer. 34:18; Pritchard, Texts[3], 482 no. c, 532.)

Oaths were associated with an invocation of God, or some sacred and powerful equivalent, as the king (Gen. 42:15; both in II Sam. 15:21), either as witness (I Sam. 20:12 [?], 42, cf. Targ.) or in order to convict the perjurer of sacrilege – desecration of the divine name (Lev. 19:12). The terms for such invocation were *nasa' shem/nefesh* YHWH, "take up, utter the name/life of YHWH" (Ex. 20:7; Ps. 16:4; 24:4; 50:16) or simply *hizkir be-[shem] 'elohim*, "mention [the name of] God" (Josh. 23:7; Isa. 48:1). The commonest formula or invocation is *ḥai YHWH* (Judg. 8:19; I Sam. 14:39), a problematic phrase whose most likely meaning is "[By] the life of YHWH!" (Greenberg). Additions to the repertoire of invocations may be gleaned from oaths ascribed to God. His swearing "by Himself" (Gen. 22:16), "by His great name" (Jer. 44:26), "His life" (Amos 6:8), "His holiness" (Amos 4:2; Ps. 89:36), "the pride of Jacob" (Amos 8:7 [= Himself? cf. Ibn Ezra]) presumably echo man's language. His oath "by His right hand and His mighty arm" (Isa. 62:8) recall later Hebrew formulas where the swearer stakes something precious (e.g., "the life of my head" [Sanh. 3:2]) as a guarantee of his word. The unique adjuration "by gazelles and hinds of the field" (Song 2:7; 3:5) suggests that these animals symbolized love or beauty (cf. Prov. 5:19). "Raising the hand to YHWH" (Gen. 14:22) was an oath-gesture (another time it is "lifting the right and left hands to heaven" [Dan. 12:7]). Of God too it is said that he "lifts His hand [to heaven]" (Ex. 6:8, Num. 14:30; Deut. 32:40; Ezek. 20:5) – meaning that He swears. The origin of the gesture is obscure, as is that of the twice-recorded patriarchal oath-gesture of the swearer's placing his hand under the thigh of his adjurer (Gen. 24:2–3, 9; 47:29). The latter was understood by the rabbis as an oath by circumcision (Gen. R. 59:8).

The Use of Oaths in Ancient Israel

Oath-taking was very common, occasions for oath-taking ranging from the personal and the trivial to the most solemn public undertakings: e.g., Judges 21:1; I Samuel 14:28; 17:55; 20:3; II Samuel 14:19; I Kings 17:1; II Kings 2:2; and Nehemiah 13:25. Personal (Gen. 21:23; I Sam. 20:42) and state or communal (Josh. 9:18; II Sam. 21:2; Ezek. 17 [cf. II Chron. 36:13]) alliances were solemnized by oaths – the parties being termed *ba'ale shevu'ah*, "oath-partners" (Neh. 6:18). Israel's covenant with God involved the people in oath-like sanctions (e.g., Lev. 26; Deut. 27–28); however, the covenant sanction is only seldom expressly called an oath (of allegiance) to God, as in II Chronicles 15:12–15, which in turn evokes Nehemiah 10:30. Eschatological acceptance of God by non-Israelites is also expressed through an oath of allegiance to Him (Isa. 19:18; 45:23). The laws of the Torah reckon with the following kinds of oaths:

(a) The exculpatory oath, exacted by the plaintiff from the defendant to back the latter's plea of innocence when no witness to the facts was available; the oath was taken at the Sanctuary (Ex. 22:7, 10; the procedure is described in I Kings 8:31). If the defendant took the oath, the suit was decided in his favor (Ex. 22:10; cf. the effect of the exculpatory oath in the Old Babylonian lawsuits in Pritchard, Texts[3], 218 [E, 1], 545 [no. 10]). On the other hand, if he refused to swear, his plea was automatically rebutted and he lost the suit (cf. Pritchard, Texts[3], 545 [no. 11]). Such a self-convicted liar is referred to in Ecclesiastes 9:2 as "he who is afraid of the oath" (note esp. his position as the second, pejorative member of his pair, paralleling "the wicked," "the impure," etc. of the preceding pairs). A perjurer who repents and wishes to clear himself before God and man must follow the prescription of Leviticus 5:20–26. A special case of exculpatory oath is that of the suspected adulteress; its curse is effected through the ordeal of the "bitter waters that induce the spell" (Num. 5). See *Ordeal of Jealousy.

(b) The adjuration to give testimony or information – uttered by the party interested in the testimony and directed to the community at large or against a particular party (Lev. 5:1; Judg. 17:1–3 [an example of its effectiveness]; I Kings 18:10; Prov. 29:24). One who defied the adjuration and withheld information and later wished to expiate his guilt must follow the prescription of Leviticus 5:6–13.

(c) The voluntary obligatory oath, binding the taker to do or not to do something (Lev. 5:4). The standard of righteousness was to fulfill such oaths even when they resulted in harm to the taker (Ps. 15:4). How to expiate unwitting violations of these oaths is the subject of Leviticus 5:6–13. The oath of self-denial (closely related to the vow) discussed in Numbers 30 belongs to this class. The chief concern of the law is to subject such an oath taken by a woman to the approval of her father or husband. The oath is nicely illustrated in Psalms 132:2–5.

Prohibitions against taking false oaths occur in Exodus 20:7 (Deut. 5:11) and Leviticus 19:12.

Sanctions

The Bible provides no external legal sanctions for oaths; punishment for false oaths is in the hands of God "who will not hold guiltless one who swears falsely by His name" (Ex. 20:7). The perjurer "desecrates" the name of God (Lev. 19:12); he may not have access to God's holy place and its blessings (Ps. 24:4). How the divine sanction was thought to operate may be illustrated from the failure of the oracle due to Jonathan's violation of Saul's adjuration (I Sam. 14:36ff.); from the famine ascribed to Saul's violation of the oath made to the Gibeonites (II Sam. 21:1–2); and from the death of Hiel's sons ascribed to his defiance of Joshua's adjuration not to rebuild Jericho (I Kings 16:34; cf. Josh. 6:26). The divine sanctions of the oath were personified almost as demons: upon the man who was disloyal to God the curses of the covenant would "couch" (Deut. 29:19). Zechariah 5:2–4 speaks of a visionary flying scroll bearing a curse that will destroy perjurers (among others); and Daniel 9:11 speaks of the oath-curses of the Torah "pouring down" upon sinful Israel.

Appreciation of Oaths

The estimate of the biblical period that there was nothing amiss in oaths is manifest in the frequency with which God is represented as swearing. Indeed, the invocation of God in oaths was highly appreciated for its confessional value: "You must revere YHWH your God: Him shall you worship, to Him shall you hold fast, by His name shall you swear" (Deut. 10:20; cf. 6:13). So much was this so that swearing by YHWH could be used as a synonym of adhering to Him: Psalms 63:12; Isaiah 19:18 (cf. Targ. and Radak); 48:1; Jeremiah 44:26; Zephaniah 1:5 (cf. Targ.). Contrariwise, apostasy is expressed through swearing by other gods: Joshua 23:7 (cf. Ex. 23:13); Amos 8:14; Jeremiah 5:7; 12:16. Ibn Ezra's comment to Hosea 4:15 illuminates the sentiment: "Adhering to God carries with it the obligation to make mention of Him in all one's affairs, and to swear by His name, so that all who listen may perceive that he adheres lovingly to God, the name and mention of Him being always on his lips." The only offense recognized in connection with oaths by YHWH was, "Though they may swear, 'By the life of YHWH,' yet they swear falsely" (Jer. 5:2). Ecclesiastes is the only biblical writer who is wary of oaths. In 8:2–3a, he cites a proverb, "Do not rush into uttering an oath by God" (cf. a parallel wariness of vows in 5:1–6). From here it is but a step to Ben Sira's warning against addiction to oaths (23:9ff.), and Philo's recommendation to avoid them entirely (Decal. 84).

[Moshe Greenberg]

TALMUDIC LAW

General Rules

(1) The oath, as here understood, is a mode of judicial proof. It is applicable only in civil and not in criminal cases. (For non-judicial oaths, see *Vows.)

(2) The oath is a residuary proof only: it is admitted only where no sufficient evidence is available (Shev. 45a, 48b). Where an oath had been taken and judgment pronounced, and then witnesses came forward and testified that the oath had been false, the judgment is quashed and any money recovered thereon restituted (BK 106a; Yad To'en ve-Nitan 2:11).

(3) The oath is a party oath, originally administered as purgatory oath to the defendant, but later admitted in special cases also as confirmatory oath of the plaintiff (Shevu. 7:1). (For witnesses' oaths, see below under Post-Talmudical Law.)

(4) The oath is admissible to deny, or confirm, a liquidated and valid claim only: where (or insofar as) the claim does not disclose a cause of action and could be dismissed *in limine*, no oath may be administered (BM 4b–5a; Yad, loc. cit. 1:15). An exception to this rule is made in respect of unliquidated claims for accounts against trustees, partners, and agents (Shevu. 7:8).

(5) The oath need not be confined to one particular cause of action: once the oath is administered to a defendant, he may be required to incorporate in it any number of additional claims in respect of other debts allegedly due from him to the same plaintiff ("*Gilgul Shevu'ah*"; Shevu. 7:8; Kid. 28a; Yad, loc. cit., 1:13; Sh. Ar., ḤM 94, passim).

(6) No oath is administered to suspected liars, such as gamblers, gamesters, usurers, and the like, or to people who have once perjured themselves (Shevu. 7:4; Yad, loc. cit., 2:1–2; ḤM 92:2–3), or who are otherwise disqualified as *witnesses for their wickedness (Yad, loc. cit.; ḤM 92:3).

(7) Not only is no oath administered to minors, or to the deaf and dumb, or insane persons (Yad, loc. cit., 5:12; ḤM 96:5), but originally none would be administered even to rebut the claim of any such person (Shevu. 6:4; Yad, loc. cit., 5:9; ḤM 96:1), until the law was reformed to allow such claims to be presented and require them to be rebutted on oath (Yad, loc. cit., 5:10; ḤM 96:2).

(8) Originally, oaths were admitted to rebut, or confirm, claims in respect of movable property only, excluding lands, slaves, and written deeds (Shevu. 6:5; BM 56b); but the law was later extended to allow, and require, the administration of oaths also in claims for immovables and deeds (Yad, loc. cit., 5:1; ḤM 95:1).

(9) The right to have an oath administered to one's debtor is enforceable in a separate action (BM 17a; Yad, loc. cit., 7:5). The right may, however, be contracted out (Ket. 9:5). Opinions are divided as to whether this right devolves to one's heirs (Shev. 48a; Yad, Sheluhin, 9:3). Like all other enforceable debts, the liability to take an oath lapses in the seventh year of remission (Deut. 15:1; Shevu. 7:8).

(10) The duty to take an oath is personal and does not devolve on the debtor's heirs: if the debtor died after the death of the creditor, the creditor's heirs inherit the chose in action and may recover on taking the oath that the claim is still unsatisfied; but where the creditor died after the debtor's death, the claim is extinguished if it cannot be enforced otherwise than by tendering the oath (Sh. Ar., ḤM 108:11).

Classes of Oaths

The Talmud classifies the judicial oaths chronologically, the classes varying in sanctity and gravity in descending order – the earlier, the more severe.

THE PENTATEUCHAL OATH (SHEVU'AT HA-TORAH). (1) The oath of bailees: where property was entrusted to the defendant for bailment, safekeeping, or other custody, and the defendant claimed that it was lost or stolen, or that it depreciated without his fault, the oath is imposed on him to verify his defense (Shevu. 5 and 8, BK 107b; BM 93a; Yad, Shevu'ot 11:5 and She'elah uFikkadon, 4:1; Sh. Ar., ḤM 87:7; see also *Shomerim*).

(2) Where the defendant admits part of the claim, he will be adjudicated to pay the amount admitted and to take an oath that he does not owe more (Shevu. 6:1; BM 3a; Yad, Shevu'ot 11:5, and To'en ve-Nitan, 1:1; Sh. Ar., ḤM 87:1; see also *Admission).

(3) Where the defendant denies the claim in whole, and the plaintiff could adduce only one witness to prove his claim (for the two-witnesses-rule, see *Witness), the defendant will have to take the oath that he owes nothing (Shevu. 40a; Yad, Shevu'ot 11:5, To'en ve-Nitan, 1:1 and 3:6; Sh. Ar., ḤM 87:1 and 7).

THE MISHNAIC OATH (SHEVU'AH MI-DIVREI SOFERIM). The following are plaintiff's oaths ("they swear and take"):

(1) The laborer's oath: On a claim for wages, the plaintiff is entitled to judgment on taking the oath as to the amount due to him (Shevu. 7:1), provided the contract of employment is uncontested or has first been duly proved, and provided the claim is made promptly (Shev. 45b; Yad, Seḥirut, 11:6; Sh. Ar., ḤM 89:1–3). See also *Labor Law.

(2) The shopkeeper's oath: Where the plaintiff claims to have advanced money or goods to a third party upon the defendant's request, and the request is uncontested or has first been duly proved, the plaintiff may recover on taking the oath as to the amount so advanced and due to him (Shevu. 7:5; Yad, Malveh ve-Loveh, 16:5; Sh. Ar., ḤM 91:1). The fact that a debt was entered in the shopkeeper's books was not originally sufficient in itself to entitle him to recover even on taking the oath (Yad, loc. cit., 16:6); later the rule was established that where a merchant kept regular books on account, his oath would be accepted to verify his books (Rosh, Resp. nos. 86:1–2 and 103:2; Sh. Ar., ḤM 91:4–5).

(3) The landlord's oath: Where it was duly proved, or admitted, that the defendant entered the plaintiff's house empty-handed and left it with chattels in his hands, the plaintiff may recover upon his oath as to what it was the defendant had taken away (Shevu. 7:2; Shev. 46a; Yad, Gezelah va-Avedah, 4:1–2; Sh. Ar., ḤM 90:1). In the absence of the landlord himself, his wife or any other person in charge of the premises could take the oath (Shev. 46b; Yad, loc. cit., 4:6; Sh. Ar., ḤM 90:4; *Sefer Teshuvot ha-Rashba ha-Meyuḥasot le-ha-Ramban*, no. 89). The oath was later extended to all cases where it was proved, or admitted, that some monetary damage had been caused by the defendant, for instance where he had been seen to throw the plaintiff's purse into the water or into fire: the plaintiff would be entitled to recover damages on taking the oath as to what had been the contents of the purse, provided the claim did not exceed what would normally be kept in a purse (BK 62a; Yad, Ḥovel u-Mazzik, 7:17; Sh. Ar., ḤM 388:1).

(4) The injured's oath: Where it was duly proved, or admitted, that the plaintiff had been whole and sound when encountering the defendant, and when he left him he was found injured, the plaintiff is entitled to recover damages on taking the oath that it was the defendant who had injured him (Shevu. 7:3; Yad, loc. cit., 5:4; Sh. Ar., ḤM 90:16). Where the injury could have been neither self-inflicted nor caused by a third party, however, the plaintiff was allowed to recover without taking the oath (Shev. 46b; Yad, loc. cit., 5:5; Sh. Ar., ḤM 90: 16; see also *Damages).

(5) The billholder's oath: While a bill duly proved to have been made by the defendant is normally sufficient evidence of the debt (see *Shetar*), where the plaintiff "detracts" from the bill by admitting to have received part of the debt evidenced by it, he has to take the oath that the balance is still due to him (Tosef., Shevu. 6:5; Shev. 41a; Yad, Malveh ve-Loveh, 14:1; Sh. Ar., ḤM 84:1). The same rule applies to the widow's claim on her *ketubbah* (Ket. 9:7); but the widow's oath was later required even where she did not expressly admit any part payment, so as to establish that she had not received anything on account of her *ketubbah* during her husband's lifetime (Git. 4:3; Sh. Ar., EH 96:1).

(6) The shifted oath: Where the defendant is a suspected liar and cannot therefore be sworn (see above), the oath is shifted to the plaintiff to verify his claim (Shev. 7:4; Yad, To'en ve-Nitan, 2:4; Sh. Ar, ḤM 92:7). If the plaintiff is a suspected liar, too, the liability to take the oath reverts to the defendant, but as he will not be allowed to take it, judgment will anyhow be entered against him (*ibid.*). This highly unsatisfactory result was sought to be avoided by applying the general rule that the burden of proving his claim always rested on the plaintiff (see *Evidence), and as the plaintiff would not be allowed to take the shifted oath, his claim ought to be dismissed (cf. *Rema* Sh. Ar., ḤM 92:7), the more so where the plaintiff had known that the defendant was a suspected liar and ought therefore to have abstained from doing business with him (Rosh, Resp. no. 11:1).

The following is a defendant's oath ("they swear and do not pay"):

(7) The Pentateuchal oath of the bailees was in the Mishnah extended to partners, tenant farmers, guardians, married women (in their capacity as agents of their husbands), and self-appointed administrators of estates (Shevu. 7:8; Yad, Sheluhin ve-Shuttafin, 9:1; ḤM 93:1). The same oath is imposed by the husband on his wife in respect of any business carried on by her (Ket. 9:4).

THE POST-MISHNAIC OATH (SHEVU'AT HESSET). The presumption has been raised that plaintiffs will not put forward unfounded and vexatious claims; and the rule evolved (in the third century) that a plaintiff who could not otherwise prove his claim, was entitled to have an oath administered to the defendant that he did not owe anything (Shevu. 40b; Yad. To'en ve-Nitan, 1:3; Sh. Ar., ḤM 87:1). A defendant unwilling to take this oath, but still persisting in his denial of indebtedness, had the right to shift the oath to the plaintiff who, upon taking it, would be entitled to recover (Shevu. 41a; Yad, loc. cit., 1:6; Sh. Ar., ḤM 87:11); but the Pentateuchal and mishnaic oaths could not be so shifted except as set out above (see the shifted oath). In the event of the plaintiff's refusing to take the shifted oath, the claim will be dismissed (Sh. Ar., ḤM 87:12).

Administration of Oaths

The Pentateuchal and mishnaic oaths are taken by holding the Scroll of the Torah in one's hand and swearing by God (Shevu. 38b; Yad, Shevu'ot, 11:8; ḤM 87:15). God need not be mentioned by name but may be described by one of His attributes. The oath is taken standing up (Shevu. 4:13; Sh. Ar., ḤM 87:16, 17). The post-mishnaic oath is taken without holding the Scroll and without mentioning God (Sh. Ar., ḤM 87:18; a contrary rule is given by Yad, Shevu'ot, 11:13, to the effect that the Scroll should at least be held out to the deponent so as to instill fear into him). The oath is pronounced either by the person taking it or by the court administering it; in the latter case, the deponent responds with "Amen" (Shevu 9:11; Yad, Shevu'ot 11:10). There was a rule to the effect that oaths must always be taken in Hebrew (Yad, Shevu'ot 11:8), but it was later mitigated so as to allow the oath to be taken in the language best understood by the deponent (*ibid.*, 11:14; Sh. Ar., ḤM 87:20).

Before administering the oath, the court warns the deponent of the gravity of the oath and the inescapability of divine punishment for any false oath. This warning is not required for the post-mishnaic oath (Shevu. 39a; Yad, Shevu'ot 11:16; Sh. Ar., ḤM 87:20–21). The court also warns the party at whose instance the oath is administered that he should abstain if his case was wrong, so as not to have the oath administered unnecessarily, whereupon that party has to say "Amen" to confirm his own good faith (Yad, To'en ve-Nitan, 1:11; Sh. Ar., ḤM 87:22).

Sanctions

(1) Where a defendant was by law required to take the Pentateuchal oath and refused, judgment would be entered against him and execution be levied against his property forthwith (Shevu. 41a; Yad, loc. cit., 1:4; Sh. Ar., ḤM 87:9).

(2) Where a plaintiff was by law allowed to take the mishnaic oath and obtain judgment, he could forego his privilege and have the post-mishnaic oath administered to the defendant (Yad, loc. cit., 1:4; Sh. Ar., ḤM 87:12). However, the defendant would then shift the post-mishnaic oath back to the plaintiff (see above), and if the plaintiff still refused to take the oath, his claim would be dismissed (Sh. Ar., ḤM 87:12); but it must be borne in mind that the refusal or reticence to take the much severer mishnaic oath did not necessarily entail such refusal or reticence in respect of the much lighter post-mishnaic oath.

(3) Where a defendant refused to take the mishnaic or post-mishnaic oath, a **ḥerem* (ban) lasting 30 days would be pronounced against him (Yad, loc. cit., 1:5; Sh. Ar., ḤM 87:9); for refusal to take the oath, he would also be liable to *flogging (Yad, loc. cit., 1:5); but judgment would not be entered against him so as to authorize execution upon his goods or lands (Shevu. 41a; Yad, loc. cit.; Sh. Ar., ḤM 87:9).

POST-TALMUDIC LAW

To the classes another class was added at a much later period (as from the 14th century), namely, the testimonial oath. Originally, potential witnesses could be sworn only to the effect that they were, or were not, able to testify on a given matter (Shevu. 4:3) – the purpose of such "oath of the witnesses" was solely to avoid suppression of testimony. It was an innovation to have witnesses, who were prepared and about to give evidence, swear first that they would testify to the truth; but the swearing in of witnesses became a widespread practice (Ribash, Resp. no. 170; Tashbeẓ 3:15; Resp. Joseph ibn Lev 4:1), though not a binding rule of law (*Ḥatam Sofer*, Resp. ḤM no. 207). It is not practiced in the rabbinical courts of today. The rule appears to be that it is in the free discretion of each particular court to administer the testimonial oath whenever in its opinion circumstances so require (cf. *Beit Yosef* ḤM 28:1; *Rema* Sh. Ar., ḤM 28:2; *Urim ve-Tummim* ḤM 28:2; and *Sma*, Sh. Ar., ḤM 28 n. 16); but it has been said justifiably that a witness who cannot be believed without being first sworn, cannot be believed at all (Tos. to Kid. 43b s.v. *Hashta*).

JURAMENTUM JUDAEORUM, MORE JUDAICO (THE JEWRY OATH)

As from the fifth century and throughout the Middle Ages, Jews testifying in non-Jewish (Christian) courts were required to take an oath which was invariably so formulated as to be binding upon them under Jewish law. Its essential elements were the solemn invocation of God; the enumeration of certain miraculous events from biblical history in which God's omnipotence was especially manifest; and curses to discourage perjury (Kisch, Germany, 275). Most medieval lawbooks and statutes contain elaborate provisions and formulae for the Jewry Oath. Many provided for concomitant degradations and insults, such as having Jews take their oaths while standing on a pigskin (*ibid.*, 278 et al.).

[Haim Hermann Cohn]

Oath in Market Overt

The Sages also enacted an oath in the framework of market overt rules (Mish., BK 10:3; see *Theft and Robbery). If a person identifies an article belonging to him in the possession of another person, who bought the article on the open market, and the former brings evidence that the article is his, claiming it was stolen from him – according to Jewish law the buyer must return the article to the owner without compensation, even if he bought it in good faith. This law proved very onerous for commercial life: every buyer had to be concerned that a person might turn up and prove his ownership of the article he had bought, and he would thus lose his money. Therefore, a regulation was enacted that, if the word had spread in town that an article belonging to a person had been stolen, the buyer – who was in possession of the article – must swear to the owner as to the amount he had paid for it, and receive that amount from the owner; he is then obliged to return the article to the owner. Even though the buyer is in possession of the article, and apparently the burden of proof should be on the owner, the buyer is considered trustworthy with respect of the amount he paid *only after taking an oath*. The rationale for this practice is to cause buyers to take care not to buy from thieves, for a buyer will receive his money back from the owner only against the taking of an oath (TJ, BK 10:3; *Penei Moshe, ibid.*)

IN POST-TALMUDIC LAW. *Oath of Insolvency.* The basic approach of Jewish civil execution law is characterized by rigorous protection of the debtor's liberty and dignity (see *Execution, Civil). The Torah commands the lender: "Thou shalt not be to him as a creditor" (Ex. 22, 24). Therefore, according to the original law, when the debtor is not able to repay his debt, the creditor is precluded from imprisoning him (see *Imprisonment for Debt), or from demanding that he should show evidence that he is insolvent, and he is not even entitled to require the debtor to swear to that effect (Yad, Malveh ve-Loveh 2:1). However, during the period of the *geonim*, with the development of economic and commercial life and the concomitant rise in the phenomenon of swindlers – who used to claim falsely that they were insolvent – it became necessary to ensure the continued provision of loans by lenders, and to devise an efficient way of collecting debts. One means enacted for facilitating this process was the "oath of insolvency," or "oath of suspicion." The debtor was compelled to take a solemn oath, similar to the oath on the Torah, in which he holds an object, stating that he is in fact insolvent, and that he has not acted deceitfully by transferring his property to others, in order to avoid the obligation to pay his debt. This oath also included a future commitment to the effect that everything he earns in the future, beyond the minimum required for himself and his family for their livelihood, will be given to the creditor, until the entire debt is repaid. (Yad, *ibid.* 2:2). However, this measure was qualified by Maimonides (Yad, 2:4), who ruled that the court must prevent the creditor from imposing such an oath upon a debtor who claims insolvency, when it is clear and obvious to the court and to the public that in fact that debtor is poor and has no means of payment, and the purpose of the creditor in imposing the oath on the debtor is only to inflict pain and humiliation on him, or to make him "go and borrow from the Gentiles, or to take his wife's property (which is not mortgaged to the creditor) and give it to him (the creditor) in order to be saved from this oath": that is forbidden and constitutes a transgression of the biblical admonition, "Thou shalt not be to him as a creditor." On this issue, see the decision of the Israeli Supreme Court (HC 5304/92 *Perach* v. *Minister of Justice*, PD 47(4) 715, 736ff. per Justice Menachem Elon).

The "oath of insolvency" is also invoked in the field of public law, in tax laws, and with respect to the option of taking an oath and avoiding payment of a tax that a person owes the community (Resp. Or Zaru'a, 222).

OATH OF THE WITNESSES. In principle, Jewish law does not exact an oath from a witness with respect to the truthfulness of his testimony, since perjury was one of the prohibitions in the Ten Commandments: "Thou shalt not bear false witness against thy neighbor" (Ex. 20:14), and therefore every witness "is sworn since Mount Sinai" to testify only truthfully. Originally, Jewish law required only that witnesses be warned, before testifying, of their obligation to testify truthfully, of the strict prohibition on perjury and of the punishment prescribed for perjury (Yad, Edut, 17:2; Sanh., 12:3), without swearing them in. However, the popular prevalent assumption was that the prohibition on testifying falsely was less severe than taking a false oath. At the beginning of the 15th century, the halakhic sages in Spain and North Africa, aware of the common conception, and recognizing that "the generation makes light of false testimony" (Resp. Tashbeẓ 3:15), introduced into their courts the possibility of imposing an oath upon those witnesses who were suspected of having transgressed (Resp. Ribash 170), or at the court's discretion. This practice was enacted as *halakhah* by Rabbi Moses Isserles (in his gloss on the Sh. Ar., ḤM. 28:2): "Should the court perceive a need to impose an oath on them so that they shall say the truth – it may do so."

The approach of Jewish law to the issue of imposing an oath on witnesses formed the basis of the law in the State of Israel, and we shall briefly follow the stages of its development: this provides an instructive example of a case in which Israeli legislation has adopted Jewish law. The Civil Procedure Regulations, 5723 – 1963, state that prior to hearing testimony, the Court must warn the witness that he must state the truth, and the witness must swear to testify the truth. However, the witness is entitled not to swear, and, instead, to make a declaration, for reasons of religion or conscience. A similar route was adopted by the legislator with respect to testimony on criminal issues, in the Criminal Procedure Law, 5725 – 1965. In the discussions prior to passage of the Law, it was emphasized that the Law adopts the requirement of an oath as a compromise with the prevailing reality, on the basis of the assumption that the population needs a deterrent factor, in the form of an oath, to prevent false testimony.

In 1978 the Supreme Court considered this issue in the context of the Becker affair (HC 172/78 *Becker* v. *Judge Eilat*, PD 32(3) 370, as per Menachem Elon). In that case, a witness refused to swear when testifying in the Magistrates' Court, as he said, for reasons of religion and conscience, and consequently the Judge did not allow him to testify. The Supreme Court pointed out that the roots of the existing law lie in the principles of Jewish law, and it discussed the aforementioned sources as well as others extensively. It ruled that the appropriate policy is to allow whoever refuses to swear to simply make a declaration, for a number of reasons: the desire to protect freedom of religion and conscience, which requires that a non-religious person not be compelled to take an oath; the serious doubts with respect to the advantages of the oath over a person's declaring upon his honor, as a means of facilitating truthfulness; and the rampant flippancy and affront, "as we see on a daily basis how the act of taking an oath, which has a deep significance specifically for religious persons, becomes a mere insignificant muttering and an object of scorn due to its routine use" (p. 386 of the decision). Because of this, the appropriate policy is to allow the person who refuses to swear to suffice with declaration.

Following this decision, in 1980 the Knesset approved an amendment to the Rules of Evidence Amendment (Warning of Witnesses and Abolition of Oath) Law, 5740 – 1980, canceling the mandatory oath that had prevailed in the legal procedure in the State of Israel, and determining that in every legal proceeding the witness must be warned that he is obliged to tell the truth, but without taking an oath. Section 5 of the Law further states that "should the Court have basis to assume that administering an oath could assist the witness in revealing the truth, then the Court is entitled, at its own initiative or in response to a request by one of the litigants, to make him swear. However, the witness is entitled, having stated that he does so on account of religious or conscientious reasons, not to swear, but rather to affirm upon his honor…" This law complies with the position of Jewish law, and in the explanatory notes to the Bill, the position of Jewish law with respect to the warning and oaths of witnesses, as it developed over the generations and as presented in the aforesaid, was elucidated (HH 5740, 327).

Regarding the mode according to which an oath was administered during the era of the *geonim*, and alternative modes adopted by the *geonim*, see the entries "Gezirta," Ḥerem Setam; and bibliography there.

[Menachem Elon (2nd ed.)]

BIBLIOGRAPHY: IN THE BIBLE: J. Pedersen, *Der Eid bei den Semiten* (1914); M.H. Segal, in: *Leshonenu*, 1 (1929), 215–27; S. Blank, in: HUCA, 23 (1950/51), 73–95; N.H. Tur-Sinai, *Ha-Lashon ve-ha-Sefer*, 3 (1957), 177–86; M. Greenberg, in: JBL, 76 (1957), 34–39; H. Silving, in: *Yale Law Journal*, 68 (1959), 1329–48; M.R. Lehman, in: ZAW, 81 (1969), 74–91. POST-BIBLICAL: J. Seldenus, *Dissertatio de Juramentis (Excerptio ex eius libro secundo de Synedriis)* (1618); K.F. Goeschel, *Der Eid…* (1837); Z. Frankel, *Die Eidesleistung der Juden in theologischer und historischer Beziehung* (1847[2]); L. Zunz, *Die Vorschriften ueber Eidesleistung der Juden* (1859); L. Loew, in: *Ben Chananja*, 9 (1866), suppl., 17–25, reprinted in his *Gesammelte Schriften*, 3 (1893), 335–45; T. Tonelis Handl, *Die Zulaessigkeit zur Zeugenaussage und zur Eidesablegung nach mosaisch-rabbinischem Rechte* (1866; Ger., and Heb. *Edut le-Yisrael*); J. Blumenstein, *Die verschiedenen Eidesarten nach mosaisch-talmudischem Rechte und die Faelle ihrer Anwendung* (1883); R. Hirzel, *Der Eid* (1902); F. Thudichum, *Geschichte des Eides* (1911); D. Hoffmann, in: *Jeschurun*, 1 (1914), 186–97 (Ger.); J. Pedersen, *Der Eid bei den Semiten* (1914); Gulak, Yesodei, 4 (1922), 129–49; H. Tykocinsky, *Die gaonaeischen Verordnungen* (1929), 67–99; T. Bernfeld, *Eid und Geluebde nach Talmud und Schulchan Aruch* (1930[3]); S. Rosenblatt, in: PAAJR, 7 (1935/36), 229–3; Herzog, Instit, 1 (1936), 11–13; Kisch, Germany, 275–87, 506–15; idem, in: HUCA, 14 (1939), 431–56 (Ger.); Z. Warhaftig, in: *Yavneh*, 3 (1949), 147–51; ET, 1 (1951[3]), 267f.; 5 (1953), 522–4, 528; 6 (1954), 37–61; 8 (1957), 741–3; B. Cohen, in: HJ, 7 (1945), 51–74, reprinted in his *Jewish and Roman Law*, 2 (1966), 710–33, and addenda 797–800; idem, in: *Goldziher Memorial Volume*, 2 (1958), 50–70, reprinted op. cit., 734–54 and addenda 801; Elon, Mafte'ah, 310–26; idem, in: ILR, 4 (1969), 106–8. **ADD. BIBLIOGRAPHY:** M. Elon, *Ha-Mishpat ha-Ivri* (1988), 1:106, 112, 132, 193, 276, 348, 364, 366, 371, 376, 380, 436, 490f, 497, 504ff., 535f., 564, 568f., 570f., 574, 579, 583, 591f., 594f., 604f., 617f., 638, 646, 655, 659, 743, 817, 821; 2:842, 991, 1001f., 1069, 1106, 1285; 3:1340, 1424ff., 1452, 1628; idem, *Jewish Law* (1994), 1:120, 126, 149, 217, 325, 419, 440, 443, 449, 455, 461; 2:533, 596, 606, 614ff., 651f., 685, 698f., 701f., 707, 713, 718, 731f., 734f., 748f., 763f., 790, 800, 811, 815, 916, 1001, 1006; 3:1030, 1199, 210f., 1289, 1330, 1533; 4:1600f., 1697ff., 1726, 1939; idem, *Jewish Law (Cases and Materials)* (1999), 189–200; idem, *Kevod ha-Adam ve-Ḥeruto be-Darkehi ha-Hoẓa'ah le-Poal* (2000), 38–43; M. Elon and B. Lifshitz, *Mafte'aḥ ha-She'elot ve-ha-Teshuvot shel Ḥakhmei Sefarad u-Ẓefon Afrikah* (legal digest) (1986), 2:474–83; B. Lifshitz and E. Shochetman, *Mafte'aḥ ha-She'elot ve-ha-Teshuvot shel Ḥakhmei Ashkenaz, Ẓarefat ve-Italyah* (legal digest) (1997), 316–26; Z. Shteinfeld, *Modeh be-Mikẓat – Meḥkar be-Sugyot min ha-Mispat ha-Talmudi* (1978), 79–154; G.Libson, "The Use of the '*Gezerta*' during the Geonic Period and the Early Middle Ages," in: *Shenaton ha-Mishpat ha-Ivri*, 5 (1978) 154–79; idem, "'*Ḥerem Setam*' during the Geonic Period and the Early Middle Ages," in: *Shenaton ha-Mishpat ha-Ivri*, 22 (2004) 107–232; B. Lifshitz, "*Gilgulah shel Shevu'at Bet Din be-Ala*," in: *Mishpetei Erez*, 2 (collection) (2005); *ibid.* (in general), 381–511.

OATH MORE JUDAICO or **JURAMENTUM JUDAEORUM**, the form of oath which Jews in the Middle Ages were compelled to take in lawsuits with non-Jews. Both the text of the oath and the symbolic ritual involved in taking it were intended to give it the explicit character of a self-imposed curse, entailing detailed punishment if it were falsely taken. The ceremonial and symbolism were intended to strengthen and make vivid the curse as well as to stress the distrust of the Jew and the wish to humiliate him that were at the root of this special oath ritual. In various formulas, an oath of this kind was the rule in Europe from the early Middle Ages until the 18th century and in some places persisted even later. One such formula is found in a capitulary ascribed to Charlemagne, though it may have been composed at a somewhat later date. The Byzantine emperor Constantine VII (913–959) promulgated such an oath, which was probably patterned after earlier rulings on the subject. Jewish oath formulas written in German are preserved in 12th-century manuscripts from Erfurt and Goerlitz. The oath was taken on the Hebrew Bible. The text of the German *Schwabenspiegel* (c. 1275) exemplifies most of its main characteristics.

> About the goods for which this man sues against thee, that thou dost not know of them nor have them, nor hast taken them into thy possession, neither thyself nor thy servants…
>
> So help thee God, who created heaven and earth, valleys and mountains, wood, foliage, and grass, that was not before;
>
> So help thee the Law that God wrote with His hand and

gave to Moses on Mount Sinai;… And that so [if] thou eatest something, thou will become defiled all over, as did the King of Babylon; And that sulphur and pitch rain upon thy neck, as it rained upon Sodom and Gomorrah;

…And that the earth swallow thee as it did Dathan and Abiram; … So art thou true and right.

And so help thee Adonai; thou art true in what thou has sworn.

And so that thou wouldst become leprous like Naaman: it is true..

And so that the blood and the curse ever remain upon thee which thy kindred wrought upon themselves when they tortured Jesus Christ and spake thus:

His blood be upon us and upon our children: it is true.

So help thee God, who appeared to Moses in a burning bush.

It is true the oath thou hast sworn:

By the soul which on doomsday thou must bring to judgment.

Per deum Abraham, per deum Isaac, per deum Jacob it is true.

So help thee God and the oath which thou hast sworn
Amen.

Not all formulas were as detailed or as harsh; most made no reference to the Jews as Christ-killers, yet all were intended to frighten the Jewish deponent in one way or another and to demonstrate visibly his inferior status.

The ceremonies attached to taking the oath were often even more degrading than the text. While Magdeburg jurors simply required that the deponent place his hand on the Pentateuch during the ceremony, many others insisted on ceremonials calculated to humiliate by their ludicrous and fantastic elements. According to old German custom the plaintiff or the judge held out a staff to be touched by the Jewish defendant while the oath was administered. One ritual made the Jew stand on a sow's skin, and in another he was obliged to stand on a hide of an animal that had brought forth young during the preceding fortnight: "The skin shall be cut open along the back and spread on [displaying] the teats; on it the Jew shall stand barefoot and wearing nothing but nether garment and a haircloth about his body." In yet another ceremonial the Jew had to stand on a stool, wearing his cloak and "Jew's hat" and facing the rising sun. The oath was administered either within or outside the synagogue or, less frequently, in the Christian courtroom. Yet in spite of these extravagant aspects of both ceremonial and formula, fundamentally the oath *more judaico* was patterned after Jewish religious law.

BIBLIOGRAPHY: Baron, Community, 3 (1942), index; Kisch, Germany, 275–87; J.R. Marcus, *Jew in the Medieval World* (1938), 49f.; J.E. Scherer, *Die Rechtsverhaeltnisse der Juden in den deutsch-oesterreichischen Laendern*, 1 (1901); O. Stobbe, *Die Juden in Deutschland waehrend des Mittelalters in politischer, sozialer und rechtlicher Beziehung* (1923[3]), 7, 153–9, 262–5.

[Isaac Levitats]

OBADIAH, king of the Khazars, a descendant of Būlān, and collateral ancestor of *Joseph according to the *Reply of Joseph* (see *Khazars). Obadiah is mentioned in the correspondence as a reformer in Khazaria who "renewed the state, established the [Jewish] religion, built synagogues and colleges, sent for many of the wise men of Israel and gave them much silver and gold, and they explained to him the books of the Bible, Mishnah and Talmud, and the whole liturgy" (*Reply*, short version). This reform probably took place in about 800 C.E., i.e., about the time when, according to Masʿūdī (*Murūj al-Dhahab*, vol. 2, 8–9), the Khazar king accepted Judaism (see *Būlān).

BIBLIOGRAPHY: D.M. Dunlop, *History of the Jewish Khazars* (1954), 144, 148; M.I. Artamonov, *Istoriya Khazar* (1962), 278–80.

[Douglas Morton Dunlop]

OBADIAH, BOOK OF (Heb. עֹבַדְיָה; "Servant of the Lord"). Obadiah, author of the shortest book in the Bible, is the fourth of the Minor Prophets. The same name is not necessarily a later pseudonymous designation of the book, for other persons in biblical times also had this name, including the father of an individual mentioned in Arad letter 10 (Ahituv, p. 68). The Rabbis identified Obadiah with the man of the same name who lived during Ahab's reign (I Kings 18:3–4), and they considered him an Edomite proselyte (Sanh. 39b). However, it should be noted that there is a clear similarity between Jeremiah 49:7–22 and Obadiah 1–11 (cf. Obad. 1–4, 5–6, 8 with Jer. 49: 14–16, 9–10a, 7). A careful comparison of the two recensions seems to indicate that the common elements have been derived from an older source. It may therefore be inferred that in his oracle on Edom the author of Jeremiah 49:7–22 incorporated passages from an anonymous source, which was still later included in the Book of Obadiah. This view, however, does not preclude the Obadian authorship of the second part of the book. Indeed, though its 21 verses are concerned almost entirely with Edom, its unity is disputed quite independently from its relationship with Jeremiah 49.

Some scholars (e.g., A. Condamin, C. von Orelli, S.O. Isopescul, J. Theis, A.H. Edelkoort, G.C. Aalders, M. Bič, and J. Scharbert) regard the book as one single prophetic speech. J. Scharbert takes it as a prophetic liturgy composed by a cultic prophet after the fall of Jerusalem in 587 B.C.E. (verses 1–18), whereas M. Bič interprets it as an expanded oracle for the enthronement festival of the Lord. A liturgical setting is also urged by Woolf, who sees the book as an oracle of assurance delivered by a cult prophet. J.A. Bewer and R. Augé assume that there are two sections, verses 1–14, 15b, and 15a, 16–21, both belonging to the same prophet. This literary division of the text corrects somewhat the view of J. Wellhausen who ascribed verses 1–14 to the prophet Obadiah and considered verses 15–21 as a later addition. G. Wildeboer and J.A. Thompson assume that verses 1–9 constitute a pre-Exilic oracle, and verses 10–21 are a post-Exilic complement. Part of the problem is due to the ambiguity of the prohibitions in vss. 12–14; some scholars interpret them as a reference to future events, while others refer them to the past in the sense "you should not have?" Some scholars divide the book into three (C. Steuernagel, W. Rudolph, D. Deden, M. Vellas, O. Eissfeldt), four (E. Sellin), five (C.-A. Keller), six (G. Fohrer), seven (W.O.E. Oesterley), or eight (T.H. Robinson) sections. There are some formal and stylistic reasons for a division into six oracles. The first is an oracle of woe against Edom (Obad. 1b-4), paralleled in Jeremiah 49:14–16, where, in some passages, more of the original text seems to have been preserved. It mentions the Edomite fortress of Sela ("Rock"; Obad. 3) captured by King Amaziah of Judah c. 800 B.C.E. (II Kings 14:7). The second oracle of woe (Obad. 5–7) is paralleled in Jeremiah 49:8–10a, where the beginning of the poem (Jer. 49:8) is also preserved. It announces that the invader will this time penetrate the dwellings of Edom, identified there with Esau (Obad. 6), and that her allies will abandon her. Obadiah 7 refers to the displacement of Edom by a foreign (*mazor*) population (McCarter). In the third oracle (Obad. 8–11) the prophet first declares that YHWH has deprived Edom of her proverbial wisdom so that she is unable to prevent the ruin awaiting her (Obad. 8–9). Verses 10–11 state the reason for the curse, namely, the violence and outrage of which Edom had been guilty during Jerusalem's calamity in 587 B.C.E. Elements from the beginning (Obad. 8) of this poem are employed as an introduction to the oracles on Edom in Jeremiah 49:7–22. Another curse against Edom, related to the same events, is found in Obadiah 12–14, 15b. (Most scholars now think that verse 15a belongs to the following oracle, and verse 15b to the foregoing one.) In a series of eight imperative prohibitions the prophet summons Edom to desist from her inhuman delight at Judah's ruin, and he concludes with a threat expressed in the form of a law of retaliation.

The first four sections (Obad. 1–14, 15b) address Edom in the second person plural, proclaiming the "Day of the Lord" and announcing salvation on Zion (cf. Joel 3:5) and judgment on the nations, especially on Edom (Obad. 18). The clear mention of Edom, "the House of Esau" which will be exterminated on that Day, reveals that this oracle too reflects the situation after 587 B.C.E. The aid which the Edomites gave the Babylonians against Jerusalem in 587, and which is alluded to in Arad ostracon 24 (Ahituv, p. 78), could not be forgiven. The Edomites not only exulted at the humiliation of the Judahites but actively assisted their foes and sought to intercept and cut off the fugitives. The remembrance of these events inspires the fifth section, as well as the preceding ones, and also Isaiah 34; Jeremiah 49:7–22; Ezekiel 25:12–14; 35; Malachi 1:2–5; Psalms 137:7; Lamentations 4:21–22. These texts all seem to refer to the same events; their dominant thought is that at last Edom will receive its due punishment at the hand of the Lord. The actual disaster that befell Edom was most likely its invasion by the neighboring Arab tribes, which seem to have entirely taken over the land of Edom toward the end of the sixth century B.C.E. so that Edom remained without settled population throughout the Persian period. If so, the oracles of Obadiah 8–18, and 1–7 as well, which are not explicitly motivated by Edom's violence against Judah, may be assumed to belong to the end of the sixth century B.C.E. The opinion of scholars such as E. Sellin and J. Theis, who assign Obadiah 1–10, and especially 1–7, to the time of King Amaziah, about 800 B.C.E. (II Kings 14:7; cf. II Kings 8:20–22; Ps. 60:11–14), is based upon the fact that these verses contain no allusions to the special circumstances of 587 B.C.E. But the invitation addressed to "the nations" in Obadiah 1, the image of "robbers" in verse 5, and the probable allusion to the Babylonian allies of Edom in verse 7, may also suggest a connection between verses 1–7 and the Arab incursion of the sixth century. However, since the author of Jeremiah 49:7–22 seems to have known only Obadiah 1b-11, these verses may have been composed somewhat earlier than verses 12–18. The date and the composition of the last section (verses 19–21) are not known. Many scholars regard it as a later appendix, in which the fate of Edom is reduced to an episode of the eschatological triumph of the Jews: the territory of Judah is to be enlarged on all sides, with the inhabitants of the Negev possessing Edom, and Benjamin overflowing into Gilead. The victorious Israelites (read *noshaʿim*) will ascend Mount Zion to judge the Mountain of Esau, and the Lord's kingdom will be established.

BIBLIOGRAPHY: W. Nowack *Die Kleinen Propheten* (1922[3]); J. Wellhausen, *Die Kleinen Propheten* (18983); A. Cohen, *The Twelve Prophets* (1948); J. Trinquet, in: *La Sainte Bible de l'Ecole Biblique de Jérusalem* (19603); Th. Laetsch, *The Minor Prophets* (1956); J.A. Thompson, in: *The Interpreter's Bible*, 6 (1956); G.C. Morgan, *The Minor Prophets. The Men and their Message* (1960); E.G. Kraeling, *Commentary on the Prophets*, 2 (1966). SPECIAL STUDIES: W.W. Cannon, in: *Theology*, 15 (1927), 129–40; 191–200; W. Rudolph, in: ZAW, 49 (1931), 222–31; S. Loewinger, in: REJ, 111 (1951), 93–94; M. Bič, in: VT Suppl., 1 (1953), 11–25; J. Gray, in: ZAW, 65 (1953), 53–59; W. Kornfeld, in: *Mélanges bibliques rédigés en l'honneur d'André Robert* (1957), 180–6; Kaufmann Y., Toledot, 4 (19675), 363–5. **ADD. BIBLIOGRAPHY:** E. Lipiński, in: VT, 23 (1973), 368–70; H. Wolff, *Obadiah and Jonah* (1976); P.K. McCarter, in: BASOR, 221 (1976), 87–91; D. Stuart, in: idem, *Hosea- Jonah* (Word; 1987), 402–22; M. Cogan, in: idem and U. Simon, *Obadiah and Jonah* (1992), 3–39; S. Ahituv, *Handbook of Ancient Hebrew Inscriptions* (1992); P. Ackroyd, in: ABD, 5:2–4; R. Marrs, in: DBI, 1:219–21 (extensive bibl.); P. Raabe, *Obadiah* (AB; 1996); E. Ben Zvi, *A Historical-Critical Study of the Book of Obadiah* (1996).

[Edward Lipinski / S. David Sperling (2nd ed.)]

OBADIAH, THE NORMAN PROSELYTE (third quarter 11th century–first half 12th century). Catholic priest who converted to Judaism. Obadiah later wrote religious works and became a prominent figure in the Near Eastern Jewish communities. He was born in Oppido Lucano (Italy) as Johannes, the son of a Norman aristocrat named Dreux (Dreu, Drogo, Droco); his twin Roger was destined for knighthood. As a youth he was influenced by the conversion of Andreas, archbishop of Bari, who adopted Judaism in Constantinople and subsequently departed for Egypt. Obadiah's conversion (c. 1102) was inspired by a dream shortly after he took priestly vows and was influenced by the study of the Bible and the persecutions of Jews in Europe by precursors of the Crusaders. He left for Constantinople, where he probably began his studies, and was wounded by Crusaders. Obadiah subsequently moved to Baghdad, where he lived in a *hekdesh* ("poorhouse") in the synagogue and studied Hebrew, the Pentateuch, and the Prophets. There he became acquainted with the poverty and the desperate circumstances of Baghdad Jewry and the tragic end of two recent pseudo-messianic movements. In 1113 he left for Aleppo, where he received a letter of recommendation from R. Baruch b. Isaac, head of the yeshivah, verifying the details of his conversion. Later he traveled to northern Palestine and met the Karaite Solomon ha-Kohen, a false messiah, in Banias (Dan) in 1121. The latter invited him to Jerusalem. Obadiah, however, departed for Egypt by way of Tyre and settled in Fostat. The main source of information concerning Obadiah is his autobiography, the so-called "Obadiah Scroll," written in biblical Hebrew. All writings related to him have been found in the Cairo *Genizah*. Only the following fragments are extant:

(1) a chronicle (seven leaves);

(2) a prayer book (one leaf);

(3) music notes (three leaves);

(4) religious poems (one leaf); and

(5) the letter of recommendation by Baruch b. Isaac, part of it in Obadiah's handwriting (one leaf).

CHRONOLOGICAL ANNOTATED BIBLIOGRAPHY: The record of the discovery of Obadiah's existence and works dates from the early 20th century. The beginning of the letter by Baruch b. Isaac was published by S.A. Wertheimer in *Ginzei Yerushalayim* (2 (1901), 16a–17a) and the first page of Obadiah's diary was printed by E.N. Adler (REJ, 69 (1919), 129–34). Two fragments discovered in Cambridge and a page of a prayer book written by Obadiah, found in Cincinnati, were presented by J. Mann (REJ, 89 (1930), 245–59). S.D. Goitein published another fragment containing Obadiah's original name, Johannes (JJS, 4 (1953), 74–84) and A. Scheiber, a piece of Obadiah's diary (KS, 30 (1954/55), 93–98). A *piyyut* with musical notation in Obadiah's handwriting is included in the Adler collection. Its discovery was made independently by A. Scheiber (*Tarbiz*, 34 (1964/65), 366–71) and by N. Golb (JR, 45 (1965), 153–6). The continuation of the booklet of music notes was published by N. Allony in *Sinai* (57 (1965), nos. 1–2, 43–55). A. Scheiber also published a *piyyut*, an acrostic of the name Obadiah (*Tarbiz*, 35 (1965/66), 269–73), and the original of a Hebrew fragment (HUCA, 39 (1968), 168–75, Ger.). See also: Prawer, Ẓalbanim, 1 (1963), 423–5 and J. Mann, in: *Ha-Tekufah*, 24 (1928), 335–58.

[Alexander Scheiber]

As Musician

Obadiah's main importance for Jewish studies are his notations of synagogal chant, which are the oldest discovered to date. Two chants and the terminal fragment of a third have been preserved:

(1) Ms. NY, JTS, Adler collection, no. 4096b, one leaf recto-verso, contains a *piyyut, Mi al Har Horev*, together with its melody written in neumes; the text is a eulogy on Moses, intended for *Shavuot or Simḥat *Torah, and its acrostic reveals the name of the author, a certain ʿAmr.

(2) Ms. Cambridge, Univ. Libr. TS K5/41, one leaf containing two chants, also in neumatic notation; the recto, beginning with the words *Va-eda mah*, contains the final fragment of a non-identified *piyyut*; the verso, beginning with the words *Barukh ha-gever*, contains five biblical verses from Jeremiah, Proverbs, and Job. The chants notated in manuscript 1 and on the recto of manuscript 2 are a composition of unknown authorship in the style of the Western monodic chant of the Middle Ages. The chant on the verso of manuscript 2 is not a contemporary composition but a faithful transcription of a traditional synagogal cantillation, which Obadiah must have learned in one of the Oriental communities in which he lived after his conversion. The same cantillation style is preserved up to modern days in the oral tradition of several Jewish communities in the Near East and Mediterranean areas.

[Israel Adler]

BIBLIOGRAPHY: For studies until 1965 see I. Adler, *Revue de musicologie*, 51 (1965), 19–51; H. Avenary, in: JJS, 16 (1966), 87–104; N. Golb, *ibid.*, 18 (1967), 43–63; A. Scheiber, in: HUCA, 39 (1968), 163–75.

OBADYA, ABRAHAM (1923–), Iraqi poet. His verse collections, published in Baghdad and Cairo, include *Wabīl wa-Tal* ("Shower and Dew," 1949) and *Fī Sukūn al-Layl* ("In the Stillness of the Night," 1947), both dedicated to King Faisal II. He immigrated to Israel in 1951.

[Shmuel Moreh]

OBED (Heb. עוֹבֵד; "worshiper"; perhaps shortened from עֹבַדְיָה), son of Boaz and Ruth; father of Jesse; grandfather of King David (Ruth 4:17, 21–22; I Chron. 2:12).

°OBEDAS, the name of two Arabian kings.

OBEDAS I, Arabian king during the reign of Alexander Yannai (103–76 B.C.E.). Alexander's expansionist tendencies brought him into armed conflict with a number of neighboring rulers, including Obedas. The latter, however, successfully laid an ambush for the Judean king in the Gaulan. Alexander, falling into the trap, lost an entire army which, according to Josephus, "was cooped into a deep ravine and crushed under a multitude of camels." Alexander barely escaped with his life, and his overwhelming defeat rekindled the Jewish nation's hatred toward its monarch (Jos., Wars, 1:90; Ant., 13:375).

OBEDAS II (d. c. 9 B.C.E.), Arabian king during the reign of Herod the Great. Josephus describes Obedas as "inactive and sluggish by nature; for the most part his realm was governed by Syllaeus," who at one time had been on the point of marrying Herod's sister, Salome. Syllaeus eventually became a bitter enemy of Herod. This aroused the Judean king to demand immediate repayment of 60 talents loaned to Obedas, through Syllaeus, with the claim that the time limit on the loan had expired. It is evident, however, that the feeble Obedas had little to say in the matter, and Syllaeus refused. With the death of Obedas his successor Aretas sent a letter to the Roman emperor Augustus, accusing Syllaeus of poisoning the king. This claim was probably correct, and it subsequently became known that most of Obedas' friends perished together with him (Jos., Wars, 1:487; Ant., 16:220, 279ff., 337). See *Nabateans.

BIBLIOGRAPHY: OBEDAS I: Schuerer, Hist, 86f.; Klausner, Bayit Sheni, 3 (1950²), 150, 153. OBEDAS II: Schuerer, Hist, 154; Klausner, Bayit Sheni, 4 (1950²), 38; A. Schalit, *Koenig Herodes* (1969), 253, 599, 614f.

[Isaiah Gafni]

OBED-EDOM (Heb. עֹבֵד אֱדוֹם; "the servant of *Adam [the deity?]"), the name of two biblical figures.

(1) The Gittite to whose house the *Ark of the Lord was transferred after the death of Uzzah (II Sam. 6:10ff.; I Chron. 13:13–14). Uzzah had died after touching the Ark while it was being brought by David to Jerusalem. In order to prevent further calamities, the Ark was brought to the house of Obed-Edom, which was apparently situated between Kiriath-Jearim and Jerusalem. When it was reported to David three months later that the Lord had blessed Obed-Edom and his house, David brought the Ark up to Jerusalem with rejoicing. As a temple gatekeeper for the Ark, Obed-Edom is mentioned several times among the Levites (I Chron. 15:18, 21, 24; 16:5, 38), as are his descendants (I Chron. 26:8, 15).

(2) A descendant of Obed-Edom the Gittite, who was in charge of the gold, the silver, and all the vessels in the Temple in Jerusalem in the days of Amaziah king of Judah (798–769 B.C.E.; II Chron. 25:24).

BIBLIOGRAPHY: M. Dahood, in: CBQ, 35 (1963), 123–4; W.F. Albright, in: *Biblica*, 44 (1963), 292; idem, *Yahweh and the Gods of Canaan* (1968), 122.

OBERMANN, JULIAN JOËL (1888–1956), Orientalist. Born in Warsaw, Obermann taught Semitic languages at the University of Hamburg from 1919 to 1922, achieving recognition with the publication of his work on the philosophy of Al-Ghazālī in 1921. He subsequently became professor of Semitic philology at the Jewish Institute of Religion in New York, where he taught from 1923 to 1931. From 1933 to 1935 Obermann was visiting professor of Semitic languages at Yale University; he became professor in 1935. He served as coeditor of the *Journal of Biblical Literature* (1933–36). In 1944 Obermann became director of Judaic research and editor of the Yale Judaica Series, in which capacity he served until his retirement.

In the course of his career, Obermann made contributions in Semitic philology and epigraphy, Old Testament and Ugaritic studies, Islamic culture, and Arabic philosophy. His works include: *Das Problem der Kausalitaet bei den Arabern* (1916); *Der philosophische and religioese Subjektivismus Ghazalis* (1921); *The Arabic Original of Ibn Shahin's Book of Comfort* (1933); and *Ugaritic Mythology* (1948). He also edited H. Gressman's *Tower of Babel* (1928) and Gandz's translation of Maimonides' *Sanctification of the New Moon* (1956) after the death of the authors.

BIBLIOGRAPHY: *New York Times* (Oct. 18, 1956); JAOS, 77 (1957),

[Raymond P. Scheindlin]

OBERMEYER, JACOB (1845–1935), traveler, scholar, and teacher. Obermeyer was born in Steinhardt, Bavaria. He toured North Africa from Morocco to Egypt in 1868, proceeded to Palestine, and from there traveled to Damascus and Baghdad. He taught French at the Baghdad school of the Alliance Israélite Universelle during 1869–72, and from 1872 to 1881 he was the teacher of Prince Naib Alsultana, contender to the throne of Persia, who had been compelled to flee his native country. With his student, Obermeyer toured the whole of Mesopotamia and then accompanied the prince when he signed a peace treaty with his brother the king and returned to Persia. Obermeyer's *Die Landschaft Babylonien*... (1929) is a standard work which includes his personal observations during his years of travel, as well as the works of medieval Arab geographers and various Hebrew sources. From 1884 to 1915 Obermeyer taught Arabic and Persian in Vienna.

BIBLIOGRAPHY: S. Assaf, in: KS, 7 (1930), 60–62; Sassoon, *History of the Jews of Baghdad* (1949), 153–6.

[Zvi Avneri]

OBERNAI (Ger. **Oberehnheim**), town in the department of Bas-Rhin, E. France. The first evidence for the presence of Jews in Obernai dates from 1215. In 1349 a Jewish woman who had been sentenced to death for coin clipping accused the Jews of propagating the *Black Death, whereupon all the Jews of Obernai were burned at the stake. Jews were recorded as living in Obernai again between 1437 and 1477 and from 1498 to 1507. Subsequently Jews were rarely even allowed to travel through Obernai or permitted to visit the local market. Only in 1647, when the town passed under French rule, were Jews again permitted to settle there. In 1784 the number of Jews in Obernai was 196. Many more were recorded as living there on the eve of World War II. About 60 lived there in 1970.

BIBLIOGRAPHY: J. Gyss, *Histoire... d'Obernai* (1866); Germ Jud, 1 (1937), 93f.; 2 pt. 2 (1968), 614f.

[Bernhard Blumenkranz]

OBERNIK, JUDAH (d. c. 1520), talmudist, rabbi of Mestre. Judah was a pupil of Israel Isserlein whose rulings and expositions, both heard directly and reported by others, he entered in his notebook, along with rulings of Jozman Katz, responsa of Sar Shalom of Vienna, expositions of Jacob *Moellin, glosses on the *Tashbaẓ* (Cremona, 1556) by *Perez b. Elijah of Corbeil and other material. *Joseph b. Moses, Judah Obernik's pupil, made abundant use of this notebook in his work *Leket Yosher* (ed. by J. Freimann, 2 vols., 1903–4), which he quotes at length. He conducted a halakhic correspondence with Isserlein and engaged in learned discussions with Judah *Muenz and Joseph *Colon. He was also the author of *Seder Pesaḥ*.

BIBLIOGRAPHY: Joseph b. Moses, *Leket Yosher*, ed. by J. Freimann, 2 (1904), xxx–xxxi.

[Samuel Abba Horodezky]

OBLIGATIONS, LAW OF. This law is concerned with the rights of one person as against those of another (*jus in personam*), as distinguished from the law of property, which is concerned with a person's rights in a chattel or other property as against the world at large (*jus in rem*). Unlike Roman law, in Jewish law the mere existence of the obligation automatically creates in favor of the creditor a *lien (*shi'bud*) over his debtor's property, a real right attaching to the obligation, which for a very long time was regarded as stronger than the personal right afforded by the obligation. The term *ḥiyyuv* originates in the word *ḥov*, meaning both the obligation which is imposed on the debtor (e.g., BB 10:6) and the right to which the creditor is entitled (Bik. 3:12; Git. 8:3). However, *ḥov* generally refers to a pecuniary obligation only, whereas *ḥiyyuv* has come to be used in a wider sense to include also the duty to perform an act, etc., comparable to the Roman law concept of *obligatio*.

The two parties to an obligation are the debtor (*ḥayyav*, BM 12b) – on whom the duty of fulfilling the obligation is imposed – and the creditor (*ba'al ḥov*) – who has the right to claim that the obligation be fulfilled. The term *ba'al ḥov* is sometimes used in the sources to describe the debtor as well (see Elon, *Ha-Mishpat ha-Ivri.*, 1, p. 483), which makes it necessary to exercise care in the use of these terms. It may be noted, too, that in Jewish law the term *malveh* ("lender") and *loveh* ("borrower") are not invariably used to denote an obligation arising from the transaction of a loan, but also to describe the parties to an obligation arising from any other transaction. This follows from the tendency in Jewish law to express a plain legal norm in concrete terms (e.g., *keren, shen, bor*, etc.; see *Avot Nezikin; *Mishpat Ivri), and thus the transaction of loan (*halva'ah*) is used as a concrete illustration of a clear and common obligation (e.g., sections 97–107 of Sh. Ar., ḤM are grouped under the heading *Hilkhot Geviyyat Milveh*, even though they are not confined exclusively to the recovery of debts originating from loan) (Elon, *Ha-Mishpat ha-Ivri.*, 1, p. 483).

Creation of the Obligation

As in other legal systems, Jewish law recognizes the creation of obligations in two principal ways:

(1) arising from *contract, whereby one party acquires a claim of right against another which the latter is obliged to honor; and

(2) arising from an act of tort (*nezek*; see *Torts), whereby the conduct of one party causes another to suffer damage, so that the latter acquires a claim of right against the tortfeasor for indemnification in respect of the damage, which the law obliges the tortfeasor to honor. The first talmudic tractate of the order of **Nezikin*, namely *Bava Kamma*, deals mainly with the laws of obligations arising from tort, i.e., harm inflicted by one man on another's person (e.g., *assault) or property (e.g., *theft and robbery), as well as harm inflicted by means of one man's property (*mamon*) on the person or property of another. In this case the owner of the property is obliged to compensate the injured party for the damage suffered through his negligence in preventing harm arising by means of his property. The other two tractates, *Bava Meẓia* and *Bava Batra*, deal largely with obligations arising from contract. Jewish law distinguishes between the obligations arising from these two different sources, particularly from the point of view of the manner of recovery of the debt on the debtor's failure to make due payment of it in cash or chattels. Thus obligations arising from tort are recoverable from the best of the land (*idit*), whereas contractual obligations are recoverable only from land of average quality (*beinonit*), and the **ketubbah* obligation from the worst (*zibburit*; Git. 5:1; see also *Execution, Civil). Roman law, in addition to a similar distinction between *obligationes ex contractu* and *obligationes ex delicto*, further subdivides the obligations into those which are quasi-delict and quasi-contract. Although Jewish law also recognizes quasi-contractual obligations, it does not employ the legal fiction of regarding these as arising, as it were, from a contract between the parties (as, e.g., in the case of the *negotiorum gestio*); the degree of liability imposed on the owner of a field toward one who "goes down to his field" and plants there without permission extends to the latter's expenses and, at most, to the value of the improvement from which the field has benefited (Tosef., Ket. 8:8; BK 10:3; Ket. 80a).

Fines (*Kenasot*)

In the case of obligations arising from both contract and tort, the degree of liability is coextensive with the respective objective value of the contractual transaction or with the extent of the loss sustained as a result of the damage inflicted; this liability is called *mamon*. When the measure of liability does not correspond to the value or loss it is called *kenas* ("a fine"; e.g., BK 15 a–b and see *Fines). Liability for such a fine may exist:

(1) by the consent of the parties, i.e., their agreement to pay a certain liquidated sum upon breach of the contract; or

(2) by operation of law, i.e., when the law provides for a measure of compensation that does not correspond to the actual loss caused by the act of tort (BK 15a–b).

Such a fine by operation of law can take three possible forms:

(1) the liability exceeds the actual damage (e.g., a thief being liable to pay double and four-or fivefold compensation: see *Theft and Robbery);

(2) the liability is less than the actual damage (e.g., where only half-damages are payable for a *shor tam* that has gored: see *Avot Nezikin); and

(3) the liability is for a fixed and pre-determined amount (e.g., in the case of defamation of a virgin: Deut. 22:19 and see also 29).

Imperfect (i.e., Unenforceable) Obligations

Jewish law recognizes the existence of two kinds of imperfect obligations. In the first category a legal obligation exists, but the court will provide no remedy for the party seeking its enforcement. Thus in the case of fixed (direct) interest (*ribbit keẓuẓah*; e.g., 100 are lent so that 120 shall be repaid), which is prohibited by Pentateuchal law, the lender is obliged to return the interest paid, and it may even be reclaimed by the borrower through the court; if, however, the interest is indirect (*avak ribbit*, lit. "dust of interest"), which is forbidden by rabbinical law only, the borrower cannot reclaim the interest in court (BM 61b; Yad, Malveh 6:1; Sh. Ar., YD 161; and see *Usury). Similarly, in all cases which are regarded as robbery according to rabbinical law only – e.g., when a person wins money in a game of chance (which is regarded as unjustified even if the loser consents) – the loser cannot reclaim the money in court (Sanh. 25b; Yad, Gezelah 6:6–16, and other *posekim*; see Elon, *Ha-Mishpat ha-Ivri,* 1, p. 194). The second category of imperfect obligations derives from tort; regarding this it was prescribed that "the offender is exempt from the judgments of man but liable to the laws of heaven" (BK 55b), as for example, in the case of a man who bends his neighbor's standing grain toward a fire in such a way that the grain will catch fire if the wind changes or strengthens unexpectedly, although there is no such danger as long as the wind does not alter (BK 55b and codes; see further Law and Morality for obligations carrying a moral or religious sanction only) (see Elon, *Ha-Mishpat ha-Ivri*, 1, p. 129).

The Personal and Proprietary Aspects of Obligation in Jewish Law

Many ancient systems of law (e.g., Babylonian law, Assyrian law, the laws of Eshnunna) provided for the creditor's being able to secure repayment of his debt by enslaving the debtor or the members of his family (see Elon, *Kevod ha-Adam ve-Ḥeruto,* pp. 3–8). According to the early Roman "XII Tables" and by means of the *legis actio per manus injectionem*, the creditor was even afforded the right, after certain preliminary procedures, of putting the defaulting debtor to death and taking his proportionate share of the body if there were several creditors. This "right" was abrogated by the *Lex Poetelia* and replaced by the possibility of imprisoning the debtor (see *Imprisonment for Debt on the position in Jewish law).

On the other hand, Jewish law did not recognize any form of enslavement of the debtor's person (the bondsmanship referred to in the Bible is confined to two cases: one of the thief who lacks the means to make restitution (Ex. 22:2); the other of a person who voluntarily sells himself on account of utter poverty (Lev. 25:39)). The creditor is strongly adjured to act mercifully toward the borrower and not to take in pledge the latter's basic essentials, nor to enter his house for the purpose of seizing a pledge (Ex. 22:24–26; Deut. 24:6, 10–13). If in practice the law was not always strictly observed and there were cases – due to the influence of surrounding legal customs – of enslavement for debt (II Kings 4:1; Isa. 50:1, etc), such cases were roundly condemned by the prophets (Amos 2:6; 8:4–6), and it appears that after the sharp reaction of Nehemiah (Neh. 5:1–13) enslavement for debt was abolished in practice as well (Elon, *Kevod ha-Adam ve-Ḥeruto,* 8–10).

The uncertain personal nature of an obligation in Jewish law led, in the second half of the fourth century, to fundamental differences of opinion on the substance of the borrower's personal liability to repay money to the lender. In the opinion of all scholars, restitution in the case of bailment or robbery constituted a clear legal obligation – since the bailor or the person robbed had a proprietary right in the property concerned. In the case of a loan of money, however, given in the first instance so that it could be used and expended by the borrower, in the opinion of R. Papa, the liability to repay the debt was no more than a religious duty (i.e., it was a *mitzvah* for a person to fulfill his promise and give effect to his statements (Rashi Ket. 86a)) and not a legal obligation. R. Huna, however, expressed the opinion – which was shared by the majority of the scholars and according to which the *halakhah* was decided – that the duty of repaying a debt was also a legal obligation. This personal aspect of the obligation is termed *shi'bud nafsheih* in the Talmud (i.e., pledging personal responsibility; see, e.g., Git. 13b, 49b; BK 40b; BM 94a; BB 173b). From the 11th century onward it seems, it was referred to as *shi'bud ha-guf* ("servitude of the person"), a term apparently mentioned for the first time in the statements of Alfasi (quoted in the Resp. Maharam of Rothenburg, ed. Cremona, no. 146, and in greater detail in the statements of Jacob *Tam cited in the commentary of Nissim Gerondi on Rif, to Ket. 85b; see also *Contract).

The impossibility of securing repayment of a debt by enslaving the debtor created a need for the establishment of an adequate security, i.e., by charging the debtor's assets: land was well suited for this purpose since it could not be carried away and was not subject to loss or extinction. Hence the rule that, immediately after a debt was created, the creditor acquired a lien over all the real estate possessed by the debtor in such a manner that the debt afforded the creditor not only a personal right of action against the debtor but also a right in the form of a lien over all his land. Land was accordingly termed "assets bearing responsibility" (*nekhasim she-yesh lahem aḥarayut*; i.e., guaranteeing the obligation of the debtor; Kid. 1:5; BM 1:6; BB 174a) and recovery therefrom was based on the creditor's charge and not on his right of recourse against the debtor personally. On the other hand, the debtor's chattels, being subject to loss and depreciation, were incapable of "bearing responsibility" for his obligation and were so termed (*nekhasim she-ein lahem aḥarayut*; Kid. 1:5), and the right of recovery from such assets was based on the creditor's personal right of recourse against the debtor (BK 11b; see also *Lien). The demands of developing commerce resulted in a substantive change in the concept of the contractual obligation in post-talmudic times; from an essentially real or property obligation it became an essentially personal one, with the property aspect subordinate to the personal (see Elon, *Ha-Mishpat ha-Ivri*, 1, p. 484).

Recovering Payment out of "Encumbered and Alienated" Assets (i.e., in the hands of a third party)

The creditor's above-mentioned lien over his debtor's property did not preclude the debtor from transferring the encumbered assets to a third party, except that any such transfer could be subject to the creditor's right to seize the assets from the transferee when seeking to enforce payment of the debt. At first this right did not extend to the debtor's chattels, since the creditor had no property right in them and his right of recovery from them derived merely from the debtor's personal obligation (see *Beit ha-Beḥirah*, BB 175b); thus they were beyond the creditor's reach once they had been transferred from the debtor's ownership (Ket. 92a). However, in the course of time, and with the changes in the economic circumstances of Jewish life, this distinction between land and chattels underwent substantial changes. Similarly, the general lien on the debtor's assets gave rise to many problems, concerning both the need to protect trade (*takkanot ha-shuk*) and the rights of third party purchasers, as well as the question of securing debts for the benefit of creditors, concerning which various **takkanot* were enacted at different times (see *Lien).

Verbal and Written Obligations

Jewish law distinguishes between a verbal and a written obligation, termed in the Talmud a *milveh be-al peh* and a *milveh bi-shetar*, respectively (BB 175a; see also Sh. Ar., ḤM 39:1, et al.). Although phrased in the language of loan, these terms are intended to embrace all obligations of whatever origin (see above). The distinction between the two forms of obligation relates to the weight of consequence accorded each one rather than to the substance of the obligation. This finds expression in two main respects:

(1) a written obligation entitles the creditor to recover payment out of the debtor's encumbered assets which are in the hands of a third party, a right unavailable in the case of a mere verbal obligation, since here the obligation or debt has no *kol* ("voice") and does not provide notice that will put prospective purchasers on their guard;

(2) in the case of a written obligation, a plea by the debtor that he has repaid the debt is not accepted without proof, whereas a plea of this kind is accepted without proof in the case of a verbal obligation (Shevu. 41b; Yad, Malveh 11:1, 15:1; Sh. Ar., ḤM 70:1, 82:1; see also *Pleas).

The distinction between the two is not characterized by the mere fact of writing or its absence, and the fact that an obligation is recorded in a document does not of itself ensure the application of the special consequences attaching to a *milveh bi-shetar*. Thus, for example, an undertaking even in the debtor's own handwriting, but not signed by witnesses, will be treated as a *milveh be-al peh*, since only a properly written, witnessed, and signed obligation carries a "voice" and constitutes notice (BB 175b and codes). Similarly, since a written obligation affects the rights of the parties, it is not considered as such unless it has been drawn up and signed in accordance with the instructions of the parties (BB 40a and codes), and with the prior intention of constituting it a *milveh bi-shetar* and not simply an aide-memoire (Sh. Ar., ḤM 61:10). Contrariwise, it is possible that a wholly verbal obligation can be treated as a written one, as in the case of sale of land before witnesses, when the purchaser from whom the land is seized may in turn exact the seller's responsibility to him out of encumbered and alienated assets sold by the latter (BB 41b). So too all verbal obligations claimed through, and upheld by, judgment of the court are treated as obligations by deed (BM 15a) which may be recovered out of encumbered and alienated assets, since in these circumstances they have a "voice" and constitute notice even if they are not evidenced in writing.

The Parties to an Obligation

On the capacity of the parties to an obligation see *Legal capacity (see *Deaf Mute); *Embryo; *Legal Person.

From various scriptural sources it may be inferred that it is possible that an obligation may subsist toward a person unknown at the time (Josh. 15:16; I Sam. 17:25). This principle is also illustrated in this way: "he who says 'whoever shall bring me the tidings that my wife gave birth to a male child shall receive two hundred; that she gave birth to a female child a *maneh*'; [then] if she gives birth to a male he shall receive two hundred and if to a female child, he shall receive a *maneh*" (Tosef., BB 9:5; BB 141b). It was also followed in practice, in the case of a deed granted by the community in respect of the right to collect a tax, in which the name of the grantee was not specified at the time of signature, it being provided that certain communal officials would determine the person to acquire the right (Resp. Rosh no. 13:20).

Plurality of Creditors and Debtors

Both possibilities are allowed for in Jewish law. Most sources indicate that each of the co-debtors is responsible for his proportionate share only; e.g., if they borrow in a common deed (Tosef., BM 1:21), or guarantee a single debt (Tosef., BB 11:15; but cf. Yad, Malveh 25:10 and Sh. Ar., ḤM 77:3 and commentators). In the same way a judgment of the court against one of the debtors does not of itself render the others liable (Rema, ḤM 176:25). Some scholars sought to infer from another source that each of the debtors is liable for the whole amount of the debt (R. Yose, TJ, Shevu. 5:1, 136a; *Piskei ha-Rosh*, ad loc., 2); but most of the *posekim* interpreted this source as prescribing that each of the debtors, in addition to the principal obligation for his proportionate share, is also liable as surety for the remainder of the debt upon default of the other debtors (Yad, Malveh 25:9; Tur and Sh. Ar., ḤM 77:1, and see also commentators); the *halakhah* was decided accordingly.

A similar rule prevails with regard to liability for damage jointly caused by several tortfeasors, namely the apportionment of liability according to the degree of participation of each (BK 10b and codes). Opinions are divided in the codes on the question of whether each of the tortfeasors is also liable as surety for the shares of the others (Tur, ḤM, 410:29 and Sh. Ar., ḤM 410:37). Similarly, when a debt is owed to a number of creditors jointly, each of them is entitled to his proportionate share. Any one of them may claim payment of the whole amount in circumstances where it can be presumed that he is acting as an agent for his fellow creditors with regard to their shares (Ket. 94a and codes). Where there is no room for this presumption and one creditor wishes to claim recovery of his share alone, two possibilities exist: if the share of each of the creditors is known, each may separately claim his own share, e.g., in the case where a creditor is survived by a number of heirs, each claiming his known share; if the proportionate share owing to each creditor is unknown, none may separately claim recovery but must be joined in his claim by the remaining creditors (Sh. Ar., ḤM 77:9–10 and *Siftei Kohen* ad loc., n. 25; Sh. Ar., ḤM 176:25). This is also the law when the debt derives from tort.

Extinction of Obligation

An obligation is extinguished when it is fulfilled by the debtor, whether voluntarily or under compulsion by way of civil execution. (For the consequences of nonfulfillment of an obligation deriving from tort or contract see *Damages; *Tort; and *Contract.) An obligation also becomes extinguished, even if unfulfilled, when a release is granted by the creditor to the debtor (see **Meḥilah*). According to Pentateuchal law, a *Jubilee year terminates certain obligations. *Hillel the Elder and his court instituted the prosbul, whereby the obligation continues to exist and is not wiped out in the seventh year (see also *Loans).

In the State of Israel

The law of obligations in the State of Israel is derived from numerous different sources: Ottoman and mandatory laws, as well as Israel legislation. English common law and equity is a further source of the Israel law of obligation whenever there is a "lacuna" in the existing law (s. 46, Palestine Order in Council, 1922–47). In recent years there has been increasing legislation in this field, showing to a certain extent the influence of Jewish law. (See also *State of Israel, Jewish Law in.) In some of these laws it is stated that the abovementioned section 46 no longer applies to them. See *Contract and Introduction.

See further: *Admission; *Assignment; Bailment; Gifts; Labor law; Lease and Hire; Maritime Law; Partnership; Sale; Servitude; *Shetar*; Suretyship.

[Menachem Elon]

The Obligation as an Undertaking

In the framework of the laws of obligations, a distinction is drawn between a statutory obligation (such as a tort) and a contractual obligation. In the framework of the contractual obligation, a distinction should be drawn between an obligation relating to price – consideration for the purchase of an object or a legal right (such as the obligation of the purchaser or the lessee to pay) and an obligation (or undertaking) that a person takes upon himself for his fellow, with no consideration. In the Talmud, we find several examples of such an obligation. Let us mention a few of them:

1. *Ketubbah's* Increment (*tosefet ketubbah*): a person undertakes to add to the minimum sum prescribed by law for his wife's *kettubah* (M. Ket. 5:1; Ket. 54b).

2. Obligation to Pay Maintenance: The undertaking of a person who marries a divorced woman or a widow to maintain her daughter (M. Ket. 11:1; Ket. 101b).

3. Obligation of a Tenant Farmer: The obligation of a tenant farmer, who undertook to work the field, to compensate the owners if he should leave the field untended. This is a type of obligation to pay a fine for violation of contract (M. BM 9:4; BM 104a).

4. Obligation of Bailees: The undertaking of a bailee to deviate from the biblical laws of bailees, for example an unpaid bailee who undertakes to pay even in the case of theft.

5. Guarantee (surety): A guarantor for a loan undertakes to pay the borrower's debt if the borrower does not pay himself (BB 173b, see *Surety).

This undertaking gives rise to a number of questions, some of which have been discussed in other entries, as will be mentioned below.

THE MODE OF EXECUTION. A transaction is not concluded by words but by an act of acquisition (BM 49a; Yad, beginning of *Hilkhot Mekhirah*). What is the law in the case of an obligation: does it require an act of acquisition, and if so – what is the nature of the act? In several places, the *gemara* requires an act of acquisition in respect to obligations (see BM 58a; 94a; BB 3a). However, from the passage in Ket. 101b, we see that in the case of a person who says to another: "I owe you a certain amount by virtue of a deed," the debt is valid. The *rishonim* disagree as to the meaning of the passage. Rashi explains that it refers to a new obligation, and Ramban and Rashba interpret the passage as referring to an obligation by virtue of a deed. This is also the approach of Rabbenu Tam (Tos. to Ket. 102a, s.v. *aliba*). Maimonides, however, says that the reference is to an oral obligation, if it is uttered according to a certain formula in the presence of witnesses (Yad, Mekhirah 11:15). Accordingly, an oral obligation is also possible (see Sh. Ar., ḤM 40:1), and only a conditional obligation requires an act of acquisition (*Siftei Kohen, ibid.* 3–4). *Keẓot ha-Ḥoshen ad loc.*, however, explains that Maimonides is referring to an acquisition by way of admission (see: *Admission, *Wills), which is one of the modes of acquisition, when it is said, in terms of an admission: "I am indebted"; however, if the person says, "I undertake," an act of acquisition or a deed is required. The normal form of acquisition in relation to an obligation is *kinyan sudar* – acquisition by symbolic barter (see *Acquisition).

"THE PARTICULAR BENEFIT." In several places, the *gemara* indicates that an obligation is valid following a benefit derived by the obligee. For example, parents-in-law may make a mutual undertaking when they negotiate over what they each will supply for their children's needs, and the *gemara* states that "these are in the category of things that are acquired orally" because of the mutual benefit of the parties from the union between them (see Ket. 102b). Similarly in the case of the above-mentioned bailee who takes upon himself a liability beyond that specified by law, the *gemara* cites an opinion, which acquired the status of *halakhah*, that his obligation is effected without *kinyan* due to the benefit of the trust that was placed in him (see BM 94a). The same applies in relation to a guarantee: the obligation is valid without an act of acquisition because of the benefit to the effect that the lender relied upon him (BB 173b).

Ritba, one of the great *rishonim*, extends this idea to other obligations that a person takes upon himself, when he is determined to pay even though there has been no act of acquisition, due to his benefit from the fact that the other person laid out money and relied on him that he would not lose his money. Thus he explains the obligation of an employer to pay the employee if he retracted and caused the latter a loss, even in the absence of a specific contract relating to violation (Nov. Ritba BM 74a.)

Other commentators had recourse to this approach in extending the ambit of obligations. Let us cite a contemporary example. In the case of parents who adopt a child, even if they have not performed an act of acquisition which requires them to maintain him, some authorities obligate them to maintain him by virtue of their benefit in receiving the child (see *Teḥumin* 15, p. 278).

THE CONTENTS OF THE OBLIGATION. Is it possible to obligate oneself with respect to all things, or only with respect to a transfer of money in which a charge is placed on the obligee's property? The *gemara* (BB 3a) explains that a contract made by partners for division in a courtyard is not valid, because it falls within the category of *kinyan devarim be-alma* – a *kinyan* over mere words, a promise which has no legal validity, and which does not apply to anything (see Rashi and Rosh *ad loc.*) At the same time, other sources indicate that an obligation can have validity even when no property is charged, such as a poor groom who undertakes to pay more than the required minimum for his wife's *kettubah* (marriage deed), even though he has no money. On this basis, some understood that the person making the obligation pledges his body, like a worker who pledges his body to his work (see Tos. to Ket. 54b). On the tension between the *in rem* element and the *in personem* element of the obligation, and the transition to the personal aspect, see *Obligations. In any case, according to many opinions, the monetary undertaking is valid, and therefore an undertaking to divorce falls within the category of an oral act of acquisition (*Terumat Hadeshen, Pesakim* 163; *Sema*, ḤM 195:16). Consequently, an undertaking to marry is not valid (*Sema*, ḤM 243:12; *PDR* 4, p. 374, 377). Similarly, a negative undertaking, to desist from an action, is problematic (see Resp. Divrei Ḥayyim 31; *PDR* 3 p. 336.).

BYPASS SOLUTIONS. In order to overcome the constraints of the contract, and particularly the problem of oral acts of acquisition, certain bypass routes were devised:

Making the Act Contingent upon a Monetary Obligation. The prospective groom does not undertake to marry, but rather, to pay a sum of money if he should not marry by the set date. Thus, for example, Tashbez (1:94) explains the validity of the undertaking of a husband not to marry a second wife without his (first) wife's approval, even if it should transpire that she is barren. This is not a negative obligation – an obligation not to marry the (second) woman – but rather an undertaking to pay the first wife compensation if he should marry another woman in addition to her. The practice, in a matchmaking agreement, is to undertake to pay a fine for violation of the agreement, since the agreement to marry is considered to be an oral act of acquisition (*Sema, ibid.*). This is how the Maggid Mishneh explains the position of Maimonides (Yad, *Malveh ve-Loveh* 25:14) whereby a guarantor for a body – to bring the debtor to the creditor – actually means only that the person guarantee to pay if he does not produce the debtor. In our times, there are those who propose adopting this approach as a means of exerting pressure on a recalcitrant husband, by means of signing a pre-nuptial agreement, in which the husband does not undertake to divorce, but to pay a large amount of maintenance if he should separate from his wife under certain circumstances (see *Naḥalat Shiva* 9; *Teḥumin* 21 pp. 279–339; and see **Ketubbah*).

Oath and Ḥerem (excommunication). Even if a non-monetary obligation is not valid, an oath or vow to the same effect is valid. These are religious undertakings to stand by one's word vis-à-vis Heaven. Therefore, some authorities had recourse to this legal institution in order to validate several kinds of contracts. According to Rema, for example (YD. 264:1), the undertaking of a father to hand over his son to a particular *mohel* (circumcisor) for circumcision should be strengthened by a *ḥerem* or a handshake which is similar to an oath. To this day, the practice in Sephardi marriage deeds is that the husband takes upon himself not to marry a second wife without the (first) wife's consent (see Resp. *Yabia Omer* 7:2). The *ḥerem*, which is like an oath, was also invoked in relation to a violation of a matchmaking agreement, as mentioned above. Now, a vow or an oath to another must be formulated appropriately, and not in terms of a promise, but if a person promises a contribution to a dedicated fund or to a charity for the poor, even if what he promises does not yet exist, the promise is valid even without an act of acquisition, like an oath (see Yad, *Mekhirah* 22:17, and Tur, Sh. Ar., ḤM 212:7–9). A promise to fulfill a *mitzvah* also is valid by virtue of the laws of vows or oaths (see Rema, YD. 213:2).

OBLIGATION BY VIRTUE OF CUSTOM. On the force of custom, see *Custom. Some authorities hold that even a contract which is not binding, such as one secured by an oral *kinyan*, will be binding if it is acted upon as if binding. Some authorities thus validated the father's undertaking to hand over his son to a particular circumcisor by virtue of custom (see *Pitḥei Teshuvah*, ḤM. 201:2 and *PDR* 6 pp. 315–23). This approach is particularly important in relation to the sale of "a thing which is not concrete." Objects may be sold, but it is not simple to sell rights, and in particular, intangible rights such as the right of passage or right of residence or copyright. Nevertheless, some authorities allowed these transactions by virtue of custom: see *Pitḥei Teshuvah* (ḤM 212:1–2).

A PUBLIC ACT. The statements of a number of *rishonim* indicate that a contract, one of the parties to which is a plurality or a public representative, is not bound by the normal rules of Contract law. Not only is an act of acquisition unnecessary, but there are also no other constraints, such as those relating to something which does not yet exist, or an oral *kinyan*. Therefore, a group that hired a tutor – without any act of *kinyan* – may not retract (see Resp. Rosh. Nos. 6, 19, 21; ḤM 204:9; Rema, ḤM 22:1; 81:1; 163:6). For this reason, the undertaking of a member of the City Council to resign under certain circumstances, despite constituting an oral *kinyan*, is valid, for it relates to the public (*PDR* 6, p. 166).

BREACH OF CONTRACT. What relief is available to a party injured by breach of contract? In some cases, he is entitled to void the contract (see Sh. Ar., YD. 236:6). According to some authorities, this applies only in the case of breach of a fundamental clause (*Taz, ibid.* 13), such as a person who purchased goods in order to sell them at a fair, but the seller was late in delivery. There are others who disagree and hold that the criterion is whether the person making the undertaking made his debt contingent upon the fulfillment of this condition, and in that case, he is exempt, even though the other party did not fulfill his obligation as a result of coercion. If this is not the case, however, he must fulfill his obligation (*Siftei Kohen* on *Nekudot ha-Kessef, ibid.*).

Specific Performance or Compensation. What is the relief for breach of contract? If the contract is valid, an obligation exists to execute it. At times, it is difficult to execute, and money may be obtained from the party in breach. Thus, for example, an employer or employee who violates an employment contract will be obligated to pay (monetary compensation to) the injured party, see *Employment. When a person undertook to sell his house to one person but proceeds to sell it to another, then according to some authorities, the sale to the second person is valid, for a real right takes precedence over an obligation, but the seller must pay compensation to the first "buyer" in respect of whom he breached the contract (*Netivot ha-Mishpat* 39:17). There is, however, an opinion whereby the first undertaking prevails (Resp. Mahara Sasson, 133). Indeed, some authorities hold that this obligation falls within the category of an oral *kinyan*, unless he took upon himself responsibility for the members of the household (*Keẓot ha-Ḥoshen* 203:2).

If a person says that he will sell his house but did not obligate himself expressly to do so, we are faced with the question that was disputed by the *rishonim* as to whether acquisition through uttering the words "I will give" is valid. Some authorities hold that it is not valid, and it is only a vague promise (Resp. Rif, Leiter edition 14), and others hold that the contract is valid, because the assessment is that the person intended to obligate himself (Resp. Rashba 1:1003).

INHERITING OBLIGATIONS. With respect to an obligation to make a payment, a charge is placed on the property, and therefore the heir repays the debts of the deceased from that property. However, the Shulḥan Arukh rules that the heir also pays up from land that he inherited even if it was not mortgaged during the lifetime of the legator, for "a son stands in place of his father" (see Sh. Ar., ḤM 107:1; Sema and *Be'ur ha-Gra ibid.*) There is also a commandment – one which is not forced upon a person – to pay out of movable property that was inherited, by virtue of the law of honoring one's parents. Indeed, the *geonim* made an enactment whereby a debt could be claimed from movable property, even if the property was not charged to the debt (Shulkhan Arukh, *ibid.*), and see also the entry: *Succession.

COERCION. An obligation which was made as a result of coercion, without absolute volition, is not valid (*Sema*, ḤM 205:28). However, if consideration was promised by the coercer, some authorities hold that it will be valid (Maharik, no. 118), and others say that it will not be valid (Resp. Ḥemdat Shelomo 13).

"I was not serious." Sometimes, a person makes an undertaking in the heat of the moment, and he is in something like a situation of coercion, e.g., a person who escapes from prison and reaches the banks of the river, where a barge is moored, and the boatman negotiates with him a higher price than normal: the debtor can later say, "I was not serious." The same applies in relation to a *yevamah* (a woman obliged to undergo *levirate marriage) whose brother-in-law was corrupt and demanded that she pay him an amount of money in order that he release her: she is entitled to retract her obligation with the same claim (Yev. 106a; ḤM 264:7). According to some authorities, this applies only when the other person is commanded to act in this way on his behalf; but where there is no commandment, he is obligated to the full extent of his undertaking (*Mordekhai* on BK 174, and see *PDR* 14, p. 43). Some authorities hold that if there was an act of acquisition, he cannot say, "I was not serious"; others disagree (see *Keẓot ha-Ḥoshen* 81:4, and *Netivot ha-Mishpat* 264:8).

In the case of a person who made an undertaking towards another person, and due to an unusual accident (i.e., a situation of coercion), he cannot uphold his undertaking, some authorities exempt him, as if he had made a condition to that effect (Taz, EH 114:2); others hold that coercion does not constitute grounds for exemption from an obligation, and he is like a borrower who became impoverished, since a charge had already been placed on his property (*Avnei Millu'im, ibid.* 2).

FRUSTRATION OF CONTRACT. In the case of a person who undertook to work, but it became impossible to do so, and he is not able to fulfill his obligation; for example, he undertook to water a field from the river, and the river dried up, or conversely, the river flooded the field by itself, or he undertook to transfer barrels from a ship and the ship sank, several opinions have been voiced on the question of who should bear the loss (see Sh. Ar., ḤM. 334; and see *Employment).

TIME IN THE CONTRACT. A continuing contract in which no particular time has been set for execution is a subject of dispute amongst the *rishonim*. For example, if a person undertakes the maintenance of another person, some authorities hold that he is required to support him as long as he is in need, but others say that he is exempt from his obligation after one year (Rema, ḤM 60:3).

If no time has been specified for execution of the contract, it must be executed at the first opportunity, e.g., a person who undertakes to maintain his wife's daughter for five years must do so in the first five years (*Siftei Kohen*, ḤM 42:19).

[Itamar Warhaftig (2nd ed.)]

BIBLIOGRAPHY: L. Auerbach, *Das juedische Obligationsrecht*, 1 (1870), 159ff.; I.S. Zuri, *Mishpat ha-Talmud*, 5 (1921); Gulak, Yesodei, 2 (1922), 3–30, 83–88, 105–18; idem, in: *Madda'ei ha-Yahadut*, 1 (1925/26), 46–48; idem, *Toledot ha-Mishpat be-Yisrael bi-Tekufat ha-Talmud*, 1 (*Ha-Ḥiyyuv ve-Shibudav*, 1939), 1–2, 15–52, 88–96; Herzog, Instit, 2 (1939); M. Silberg, *Kakh Darko shel Talmud* (1961), 71–75. **ADD. BIBLIOGRAPHY:** M. Elon, *Kevod ha-Adam ve-Heruto be-Darkhei Hoza'ah le-Po'al* (2000); idem, *Ha-Mishpat ha-Ivri* (1988), 1: 69f, 97, 104, 129f., 193, 195f., 327f., 354, 405, 417, 476, 479, 482f., 486f., 487f., 562, 572, 581, 596, 610, 623, 653, 663, 666, 715, 740f., 766; 2:867; idem, *Jewish Law* (1994), 1:76f., 109, 117, 145f., 217, 219f., 391f., 427; 2:495, 509, 586, 584, 587f., 591f., 593f., 683, 705, 715, 737, 754, 770, 808, 820, 823, 883, 912f., 943; 3:1059; A. Gulak, *Ha-Ḥiyyuv ve-Shi'abudav* (1939); S. Warhaftig, *Dinei Ḥozim ba-Mishpat ha-Ivri* (1974); B. Lifshitz, *Asmakhta – Ḥiyyuv ve-Kinyan ba-Mishpat ha-Ivri* (1988); Y. Bloi, *Pitḥei Ḥoshen – (Dinei Kinyanim)* (2004), ch. 18; I. Warhaftig, *Ha-Hitḥayyevut* (2001).

OCAÑA, town in central *Spain, in New Castile. Its community maintained close relations with the city of *Toledo. The *Fuero Juzgo* laws on the settlement of debts owed by Christians to Jews did not apply to Ocaña, and King Ferdinand IV prohibited their enforcement in the town (1296). In 1313 King Alfonso XI granted the income from the taxes of the Jews of Ocaña to the commander of the Order of Santiago for life; previously they had paid their taxes together with the community of Toledo. A similar income, amounting to 4,000 maravedis benefiting this order, was ratified in 1386 by King John I. The community of Ocaña suffered during the riots of 1391, but it recovered soon after. Subsequently, there was also a group of Conversos which maintained close links with the local Jews. Some of the Jews who were expelled from Andalusia in 1483 found refuge in Ocaña. Among the refugees was Judah ibn Verga, one of the last Jewish tax-farmers, who lived in Ocaña from 1488 to 1491. He may have been identical with the Rabbi Judah ibn Verga portrayed by Solomon *Ibn Verga in his *Shevet Yehudah*. The rabbi of Ocaña at that time was Isaac de *Leon, one of the last distinguished Spanish rabbis. It was he who maintained relations with Don Alfonso de la Cavallería, when the latter stayed in the town from 1488 to 1489 along with the king's retinue. Information is available on ten Inquisition trials held in Ocaña at the close of the 15th century and the beginning of the 16th; from this, close contact between the Jews of the town and the Conversos from the pre-Expulsion period can be inferred. Ocaña also attracted Conversos during the 16th and 17th centuries.

BIBLIOGRAPHY: A. Jellinek, *Philosophie und Kabbala* (1854), 15; Baer, Urkunden, index; Baer, Spain, index; Suárez Fernández, Documentos, index.

[Haim Beinart]

OCHBERG, ISAAC (1879–1938), South African philanthropist and Zionist. Ochberg was born in the Ukraine and went to South Africa in 1894. A successful Cape Town businessman, he was best known for his humanitarian project in bringing some 200 Jewish pogrom orphans from the Ukraine and Poland to South Africa after World War I. In 1921 he traveled to Russia on his own initiative, personally selected the children and organized their transportation to South Africa, where they were cared for by the Jewish orphanages in Cape Town and Johannesburg and the South African Jewish War Victims Fund. He returned to Russia the following year and distributed food, clothing, and medicines to the starving people in the war-afflicted areas. Ochberg served on the Cape executive of the South African Jewish Board of Deputies and other communal bodies. Among his benefactions were bequests to the Isaac Ochberg Fund for bursaries and to the Hebrew University for extensions and scholarships. In Israel the kibbutz Galed was also called Even Yizḥak in his honor, and his estate was used to purchase the land of kibbutz Daliyyah, where a monument to him was erected.

[Louis Hotz]

OCHRIDA (ancient **Lychnidos**), town on Lake Ohrid/Ochrida in the former Yugoslav Republic of Macedonia. There were Jews living in Ochrida during the Middle Ages. The scholar Judah Leon *Mosconi lived in Ochrida. He studied under Shemariah ha-Ikriti (the Cretan) and authored *Even Ha-Ezer*, a commentary on Abraham ibn Ezra's Torah commentary. Jews were probably moved from there under the Ottoman system of sorgun. It is therefore not surprising to find in Constantinople a Romaniot synagogue named after Ochrida. The Jews of Ochrida engaged in the preparation of furs and those of them who settled in *Kastoria developed the same profession there. There is no information on the Jews of Ochrida in recent times.

BIBLIOGRAPHY: Perles, in: *Byzantinische Zeitschrift*, 2 (1893), 569–84. **ADD. BIBLIOGRAPHY:** V.S. Bowman, *The Jews in Byzantium 1204–1455* (1985).

[Simon Marcus]

OCHS, U.S. family of newspaper publishers. JULIUS OCHS (1826–1888), founder of the family, was an immigrant from Bavaria who went into business in Louisville, Kentucky, and then in Knoxville, Tennessee. He became a communal leader and served as volunteer rabbi to the Jewish community for 25 years. His three sons rose to prominence as publishers and editors. ADOLPH SIMON OCHS (1858–1935) was the eldest and most distinguished. His career began at the age of 11, when he left school to become an office boy for the *Knoxville Chronicle*. At 17 he became a compositor for the *Louisville Courier-Journal*, and three years later he gained control of the decrepit *Chattanooga Times* for $250. He soon put it on its feet and made it one of the leading papers in the South. In 1896 he went to New York to take over the declining *New York Times*. He revitalized it, and in his 39 years as its publisher he strengthened it all round. Before he died, he saw its circulation rise from 9,000 to 466,000 daily and 730,000 on Sunday. When he went to New York, "yellow journalism" was at its height; he adopted the slogan "All the news that's fit to print" and appealed to intelligent readers with trustworthy and comprehensive coverage. He raised the standards of printing and advertising, and brought responsible journalism to a high level. In 1902 he bought *The Times* and *The Ledger* of Philadelphia, amalgamated them and installed his brother GEORGE WASHINGTON OCHS (1861–1931) as editor. When the company was sold in 1913, George Ochs stayed on for two more years and then became editor of *Current History*, a monthly magazine published by the *New York Times*. He continued in that post until his death. He also served as mayor of Chattanooga, Tennessee (1894–98). In 1917, out of anger at the German atrocities during World War I, he anglicized his Germanic-sounding family name Ochs to Ochs-Oakes. His son, John B. OAKES (1913–2001), a Rhodes scholar who worked as a political reporter for the *Washington Post*, took charge of the editorial page of the *New York Times* in 1961, until 1976. He conceived the concept of the op-ed page and was a pioneer of environmental journalism. In 1993, the John B. Oakes Award for Distinguished Environmental Journalism was established by Oakes' family and friends to promote the highest standards in environmental journalism. The award is housed at the Natural Resources Defense Council, an environmental public policy organization of which Oakes was a founding trustee. MILTON B. OCHS (1864–1955), the youngest brother, served with his brothers in high executive positions in Chattanooga and Philadelphia, and ultimately became vice president of the New York Times Publishing Company.

[Irving Rosenthal / Ruth Beloff (2nd ed.)]

OCHS, PHILIP DAVID (**Phil**; 1940–1976), U.S. topical protest singer/songwriter of the 1960s, perhaps best known for his songs "Power and Glory," "There but for Fortune," "Changes," "Small Circle of Friends," "When I'm Gone," "Pleasures of the Harbor" and "Love Me, I'm a Liberal." Ochs was born in El Paso, Texas, the second of three children to Jacob, a doctor, and Gertrude, who came from Scotland. Ochs' father was driven mad by his World War II experiences in Europe, and beginning when Ochs was five, spent two years away from the family in a mental institution diagnosed as manic-depressive. Ochs grew up in New York and Ohio, attended the Staunton Military Academy in Virginia, from where he graduated in 1958, and then Ohio State University, where he studied journalism, became involved in protesting campus ROTC training, and started writing for *The Lantern*, the student newspaper. In 1962, Ochs dropped out of college one semester shy of graduation and headed for New York, where he became an integral part of the Greenwich Village folk music scene. In the tradition of Woody Guthrie and Pete Seeger, Ochs was one of the premier "protest singers" of the era: He played at voter-registration drives in the Deep South during the early days of the civil rights movement, campaigned for striking coal miners in the hills of West Virginia and Kentucky, and was a leading figure in demonstrations against the Vietnam War. A self-styled "singing journalist," Ochs' first album was *All the News That's Fit to Sing* (1964), followed by *I Ain't Marching Anymore* (1965), which gave the anti-war movement two anthems with the title track and "Draft Dodger Rag," and a moving civil-rights piece, "Here's to the State of Mississippi," which he later re-recorded as "Here's to the State of Richard Nixon" to protest Nixon-era politics. In 1966, Ochs sold out Carnegie Hall for a solo concert. On January 16, 1968, Ochs along with seven others including Abbie Hoffman, founded the Youth International Party (Yippies), a theatrical political party that used guerrilla street theater to attract media attention to their causes. They were most successful at the 1968 Democratic Convention in Chicago, where they promoted the Yippie candidate for president – a pig named Pigasus, which Ochs selected and purchased, as he testified at the Chicago 7 trial. Ochs recorded eight albums in 12 years (1964–75), but disappointment over his lack of commercial success coupled with alcoholism, writer's block and depression led Ochs to hang himself in his sister's home at age 35. He is the subject of *Death of a Rebel* by Marc Elliot (1977) and *There but for Fortune – The Life of Phil Ochs* by Michael Schumacher (1996).

[Elli Wohlgelernter (2nd ed.)]

OCHS, SIEGFRIED (1858–1929), conductor and composer. Born in Frankfurt, Germany, Ochs founded the Berlin Philharmonic Choir in 1882, revived neglected works by Bach and Handel, and promoted the music of Bruckner and Hugo Wolf. He later became professor at the Berlin Hochschule fuer Musik. He wrote a comic opera, *Im Namen des Gesetzes* (1888); an autobiographical work, *Geschehenes, Gesehenes* (1922); and *Der deutsche Gesangverein* (4 vols., 1923–28), a history of German choral singing. His humorous piano variations on the German children's song, *S'kommt ein Vogel geflogen*, imitating the style of the masters, started a trend which remained popular.

OCTOBRISTS, constitutional-monarchist party in czarist Russia founded after the issue of the Manifesto of *Nicholas II of Oct. 30, 1905. The goal of the Octobrists was to attain certain limited freedoms, i.e., the freedom of speech, of assembly, and organization. The party also demanded the right to a legislative assembly (*Duma), elected democratically as had been promised to the Russian people in the Manifesto. In the First Imperial Duma (1906), composed mostly of constitutional-democratic factions, the Octobrists did not occupy a significant place, having only 16 seats out of a total of 500. In the Second Duma (1907) they had 44 representatives. The strength and influence of the party rose in the Third Duma (1907–1910) which was elected after electoral reforms had been introduced, conferring preferential rights on the aristocracy and restricting the electoral rights of the broader levels of the social strata. The Octobrists drew close to the reactionary right wing of the Duma which unreservedly supported the czar and his government; the leader of the faction, A. Guchkov, was elected as chairman of the Duma.

On the Jewish question the Octobrists from the very outset adopted an evasive policy. When compelled to take a clear stand, they supported the retention of restrictions on Jewish rights and did not refrain from open antisemitic attacks. In connection with the bill permitting greater freedom of residence outside the *Pale of Settlement (1908), the Octobrists supported the restricting amendment introduced by the reactionary majority of the Duma, which sought to intensify the restrictions. In military affairs the Octobrists demanded that the Jews be withdrawn from army service, since in their opinion the loyalty of Jews could not be relied upon in the event of war. Their opposition to the appointment of Jews as justices of the peace was rationalized on the ground that to place a Jew in such a position was contrary to the principles of a Christian state (1909). By agreement with the reactionary representatives of the Polish faction in the Third Imperial Duma, the Jews were deprived of their municipal rights in the cities of Poland. A slight relaxation in the stand taken by the Octobrists on the Jewish question was evidenced when 26 of its members in the Duma signed a bill submitted by the opposition to abolish the Pale of Settlement (1910).

[Simha Katz]

ODENATHUS AND ZENOBIA. Odenathus ("little ear") Septimius (258–67 C.E.) was a Palmyrene vassal of Rome; Zenobia Julia Aurelia Septimia, his wife, succeeded him as regent for their minor son Vaballathus (267–71 C.E.). Odenathus maintained at least a nominal loyalty to Rome, slaying Callistus and Quietus, the rival pretenders to the throne of the emperor Gallienus and warring against the Persians who had invaded the Roman east. Palmyra reached the zenith of her affluence when Gallienus conferred the title *corrector totius orientis* upon Odenathus, legitimizing him as the virtual viceroy of Rome over the east. His assassination left Zenobia, famous for her beauty and political acumen, the ruler of Palmyra, since their son Vaballathus was still a minor. Zenobia, controlling Syria, Egypt, and Palestine, aimed at political independence from Rome and in 271 openly assumed the title of Augusta. In the ensuing war the Roman emperor Aurelian reconquered all her territory and took her prisoner. According to Zosimus, *Historiae* (1:59, 3), Zenobia perished while crossing the Bosphorus, but most scholars accept the account of Flavius Vopiscus (Aurelian 34, 3) and Trebellius Pollio (The Thirty Pretenders 30, 24, 6) that after being exhibited in Aurelian's march of triumph, she ended her life as a Roman matron on an estate in Tibur (Tivoli).

Graetz was the first to identify Odenathus as the Ben Naẓer of the Talmud, which regards him as half king, half robber (Ket. 51b). Funk, on the other hand, identifies him with "Adi the Arab" (Av. Zar. 33a; Men. 69b). According to the Midrash (Gen. R. 76:6), he succeeded (the pretenders) Macrianus, Carinus, and Quietus (or Cyriades) and was merely an agent of Rome, the "little horn" predicted by Daniel 7:8. If Odenathus is identical with Ben Naẓer, who according to Sherira Gaon (*Iggeret*, p. 82, ed. Lewin) destroyed Nehardea, it becomes clear why the daughters of Samuel who were captured there could be taken to Palestine to be redeemed (Ket. 23a). Zenobia is reported to have pardoned a Jewish prisoner, probably political, when shown the bloody sword with which the prisoner's brother was killed by Ben Naẓer (TJ, Ter. 8:10, 46b; Funk takes this story as a confirmation of Zenobia's collaboration in Odenathus' assassination).

Athanasius (298–373) states that Zenobia was Jewish (*Historia Arianorum ad Monachus* 71, PG 25, 777b). Though this statement is repeated by Theoredet (386–457) and Photius (820–891), scholars (S. Brady, J. Fevrière, etc.) give little credence to it. Her patronizing of Paul of Samosata, a Christian-Jewish thinker, has erroneously been given religious significance. However, recently discovered inscriptions, containing dedications such as "*levarekh shemah le-alma alma*" ("to the One whose name is blessed forever," etc.) as well as expressions from the Psalms, do testify to the penetration of Jewish ideas into the syncretistic religion of the Palmyrene population. Zenobia herself rebuilt a synagogue in Egypt. Both Odenathus and Zenobia figure in Arab legends, which may contain kernels of truth (see T. Noeldeke).

BIBLIOGRAPHY: T. Noeldeke, *Geschichte der Perser und Araber… des Tabari* (1879), 22f., 25 n. 1; S. Funk, *Die Juden in Babylonien* (1902) 75–78; G. Bardy, *Paul de Samosate* (1923), 172–4; J.G. Février, *Essai sur l'historie politique et économique de Palmyre* (1931), 79–141; idem, *La religion des Palmyréniens* (1931); Lieberman, in: JQR, 37 (1946/47), 32–38; M. Avi-Yonah, *Bi-Ymei Roma u-Bizantiyyon* (1952), 81–83; E. Kornemann, *Grosse Frauen des Altertums* (1952[4]), 288–313; Baron, Social[2], 3 (1957), 62f.; Alon, Toledot, 2 (1961[2]), 168–78; Neusner, Babylonia, 2 (1966), 48–52 (which questions Sherira's date for the destruction of Nehardea in the year 258 and contains further bibliography).

[Hugo Mantel]

ODESSA, capital of Odessa district, Ukraine. In the 19th century it became the industrial and commercial center for southern Russia. In 1865 a university was founded. Odessa was an important center of the Russian revolutionary movement. Under the Soviet regime it lost some of its importance. In October 1941 Odessa was occupied by the German and Romanian armies and was under Romanian military rule until its liberation in April 1944.

From the 1880s until the 1920s the Jewish community of Odessa was the second largest in the whole of Russia (after *Warsaw, the capital of Poland, then within czarist Russia) and it had considerable influence on the Jews of the country. The principal characteristics of this community, and responsible for its particular importance, were the rapid and constant growth of the Jewish population and its extensive participation in the economic development of the town, the outstanding "Western" character of its cultural life and numerous communal institutions, especially educational and economic institutions, the social and political activity of the Jewish public, the mood of tension and struggle which was impressed on its history, and the Hebrew literary center which emerged there.

Beginnings of the Community

The Russians found six Jews when they took the fortress of Khadzhi-Bei in 1789; the oldest Jewish tombstone in the cemetery dates from 1793. Five Jews were among those who in 1794 received plots for the erection of houses and shops and the planting of gardens. The Gemilut Ḥesed Shel Emet society (*ḥevra kaddisha*) was founded in 1795. In 1796 Jews participated in the administration of the town. The *kahal* (community administration) was already in existence in 1798, when the first synagogue was built; the first rabbi to hold office, in 1809, was Isaac Rabinovich of Bendery.

Growth of the Jewish Population

There were 246 Jews (out of a total population of 2,349) in 1795, 6,950 (out of 41,700) in 1831, 51,378 (out of 193,513) in 1873, 138,935 (out of 403,815) in 1897. During the Soviet period the Jewish population continued to grow: in 1926, 153,243 (of a total population of 420,862), and 200,981 in 1939 (out of 604,217). It was then the second largest Jewish population in Ukraine, after Kiev. After World War II 108,900 Jews lived in Odessa (12.1% of the total) in 1959, and 86,000 (8.4% of the total) in 1979.

Economic Status

From the start, the Jews of Odessa engaged in retail trade and crafts. Their representation in these occupations remained important. In 1910, 56% of the small shops were still owned by Jews; they also constituted 63% of the town's craftsmen. Jewish economy in Odessa was distinguished by the role played by Jews in the export of grain via the harbor, in wholesale trade, banking and industry, the large numbers of Jews engaged in the liberal professions, and the existence of a large Jewish proletariat in variegated employment.

During the first half of the 19th century, the participation of Jews in the grain export trade was limited to the purchase of grain in the villages and estates, and to brokerage and mediation in the capacity of subagents for the large export companies, which were Greek, Italian, and French. By 1838 Jews were well represented among the officials of the exchange, and as classifiers, sorters, weighers, and even loaders of grain. From the 1860s, however, Jewish enterprises won a predominant place in the grain export and succeeded in supplanting the export companies of foreign merchants from their monopolist positions. During the early 1870s, the greater part of the grain exports was handled by Jews, and by 1910 over 80% of grain export companies were Jewish owned, while Jews were responsible for almost 90% (89.2%) of grain exports. This success in Jewish trade was not only due to greater efficiency in the organization of purchases and rapidity in their expedition, but was also connected with the constant rise of grain prices and the decline of commercial profit rates, which resulted in a tremendous increase of the grain exports which passed through the port of Odessa.

Jews also held an important share of the wholesale trade; about one-half of the wholesale enterprises were owned by Jews in 1910. During the 1840s most of the bankers and moneychangers were Jews, and at the beginning of the 20th century 70% of the banks of Odessa were administered by them. Among the industrialists, Jews formed 43%, but their manufactured products amounted only to 39%. In 1910, 70% of those engaged in medicine were Jews; about 56% of those engaged in law, and about 27% of those engaged in technical professions (engineers, architects, chemists, etc.). About two-thirds of the Jewish population were engaged in crafts and industry, in transportation and services, and in other categories of labor. More than one-half of these (about one-third of the Jewish population) belonged, from the social point of view, to the proletariat – industrial workers, apprentices in workshops, and ordinary laborers. During the 1880s these formed a considerable part of the Jewish proletariat (about one-third), and their standard of living, as that of the poorer classes, was very low. With the progress of industrialization in Odessa, many of them were integrated in new enterprises and the number of unskilled workers decreased.

The October Revolution of 1917 brought a decline in the commercial status of Odessa as well as the process of socialization. While this affected the means of livelihood of the majority of Jews, much of their experience and skills were utilized in the new social and economic structure under different designations. In 1926 Jews formed the overwhelming majority of the commercial clerks (in government stores and cooperatives), about 90% of the members of the tailors' union, 67% of the members of the printing workers' union, about 53% of those employed in the timber industries, about 48% of the municipal workers (which also included drivers, electricians, etc.), and about 40% of the members of the free professionals' union. Thousands of Jewish workers found employment in heavy industry (metal industry, sugar refineries, ship building), in which Jews had formerly been absent, and of which only 27% were members of the trade unions: during the same year, the Jews formed up to 64% of those engaged in the smaller private industries which occupied some of those thousands who had remained unemployed and had not been successfully integrated within the new economic regime.

Cultural Trends

From the cultural aspect the Odessa community was the most "Western" in character in the *Pale of Settlement. Its population was gathered from all the regions of Russia and even from abroad (particularly from *Brody in Galicia and from Germany, during the 1820s–30s), and the throwing off of tradition became a quite familiar occurrence. This situation was expressed by a popular Jewish saying: "The fire of Hell burns around Odessa up to a distance of ten parasangs." The low standard of Torah learning within the community and the general ignorance and apathy of the Odessa Jews in their attitude to Judaism were depicted in popular witticisms as well as in literature (Y.T. *Lewinsky). Linguistic and cultural Russian assimilation encompassed widespread classes and thus formed a social basis for the community's role as an active and organized center for the spread of Russian education among the Jews of southern Russia. The social and economic position of the *maskilim* of Odessa (the "Brodyists") drew them closer to the authorities and enabled them to gain considerable influence within the community and the shaping of its institutions. Odessa was thus the first community in Russia to be directed by *maskilim*, who retained their control over its administration throughout its existence: the "Council of the Wealthy and Permanently Appointed Jews" and later the "Commission of the Twenty" (which also included the delegates of the synagogue officials), which was organized as an opposition to the leadership of the community after 1905.

Educational and Communal Institutions

The cultural character of the community was reflected in its educational institutions. At the beginning of the 20th century, there were still about 200 *ḥadarim*, attended by about 5,000 pupils, in Odessa; 97% of these pupils came from the masses of the poor, and the *ḥadarim* were generally not of high standing. At the same time, about 6,500 pupils (boys and girls) attended 40 Jewish elementary schools (of which three were *talmudei torah* and 13 of the *Society for the Promotion of Culture among the Jews of Russia) of public, governmental, or semipublic categories. The language of instruction in these schools was Russian, while Jewish subjects held an insignificant place or were hardly studied at all. Many Jewish pupils studied at the government municipal schools (in 1886, over 200 pupils – 8%) and government secondary schools (about 50% of the male and female pupils in 1910), about 2,500 pupils in private secondary schools, and about 700 pupils in Jewish vocational schools (for boys and girls); there were also many hundreds of Jewish students at the university (the maximum figure in 1906 was 746). In addition, Jews studied at the governmental college for music and arts (60%) and the advanced private professional colleges (for dentistry, midwifery, etc.). There were also numerous evening classes and courses for adults. Of the Jewish schools, noteworthy was the vocational school Trud ("Labor") which was founded in 1864 and was the best of its class, and the yeshivah (founded 1866) which after 1906, when it was headed by Rav Ẓa'ir (Ḥayyim *Tchernowitz) and its teachers included Ḥ.N. *Bialik and J. *Klausner, attracted excellent pupils and achieved fame.

The educational institutions of Odessa became examples and models for other communities from the foundation of the first Jewish public school (in 1826), in which an attempt was made to provide a general and modern Hebrew education (with modern literature as a subject of study) under the direction of Bezalel *Stern; it had considerable influence within the Haskalah movement of Russia. Other institutions which also served as models included the synagogue of the "Brodyists," where a choir and modern singing were introduced during the 1840s, and in 1901, an organ; orphanages; agricultural training farms; summer camps for invalid children; and a large and well-equipped hospital.

Social and Political Activities

The prominent social and political activities of the Jews of Odessa had considerable influence on the rest of Russian Jewry. The community leaders and *maskilim* showed considerable initiative and made frequent representations to the authorities to obtain improvements in the condition of the Jews and their legal equality with the other inhabitants during the 1840s, 1850s, and 1870s, and called for the punishment of those who took part in the pogroms of 1871, 1881, and 1905 (see below). They were the first in Russia to adopt the system of publicly and courageously defending the Jews in the Russian-Jewish press which they had established (**Razsvet* (1860), of Joachim H. Tarnopol and O.A. *Rabinovich; *Zion* of E. Soloveichik and L. *Pinsker; *Den* (1869), of S. Orenstein with the permanent collaboration of I.G. *Orshanski and M. *Morgulis), while the criticisms they published of internal Jewish matters were also sharp and violent in tone. The Hebrew and Yiddish Haskalah press (**Ha-Meliẓ*, 1860; **Kol Mevasser*, 1863) which had been born in Odessa (under the editorship of A. *Zederbaum) also adopted this "radical" attitude to some extent. Jews of Odessa contributed largely to the local press, where they also discussed Jewish affairs. At the beginning of the 20th century, a style of Jewish awareness became apparent in discussions of Russian-speaking and Russian-educated Jews (V. *Jabotinsky and his circle) which was widely echoed within the Jewish public, particularly in southern Russia. The social and political awakening of the Jewish masses was also widespread in Odessa. Odessa Jews played an extensive and even prominent part in all trends of the Russian liberation movement. The Zionist movement also attracted masses of people.

The Pogroms

This social and political awakening of the masses arose in the atmosphere of strain and struggle surrounding the life of the community. Anti-Jewish outbreaks occurred on five occasions (1821, 1859, 1871, 1881, 1905) in Odessa, as well as many attempted attacks or unsuccessful efforts to provoke them. Intensive anti-Jewish agitation shadowed and accompanied the growth of the Jewish population and its economic and cultural achievements. Almost every sector of the Christian population contributed to the agitation and took part in the pogroms: the monopolists of the grain export (especially the Greeks in 1821, 1859, 1871) in an attempt to strike at their Jewish rivals, wealthy Russian merchants, nationalist Ukrainian intellectuals, and Christian members of the liberal professions who regarded the respected economic position of the Jews, who were "deprived of rights" in the other towns of the country, and their Russian acculturation as "the exploitation of Christians and masters at the hands of heretics and foreigners" (1871, 1881). The government administration and its supporters favored the *pogroms as a means for punishing the Jews for their participation in the revolutionary movement; pogroms were also an effective medium for diverting the anger of the discontented masses from opposition to the government to hatred of the Jews (1881, 1905); the masses, the "barefoot," the destitute, the unemployed, and the embittered of the large port city were always ready to take part in robbery and looting.

The severest pogroms occurred in 1905, and the collaboration of the authorities in their organization was evident. In this outbreak, over 300 Jews lost their lives, whilst thousands of families were injured. Among the victims were over 50 members of the Jewish *self-defense movement. Attempts to organize the movement had already been made at the time of the pogroms of the 1880s, but in this city inhabited by Jewish masses it had formed part of their existence before then and on many occasions had deterred attempted pogroms. After the Revolution, during 1917–19, the Association of Jewish Combatants was formed by ex-officers and soldiers of the Russian army. It was due to the existence of this association that no pogroms occurred in Odessa throughout the Civil War period.

Zionist and Literary Center

From the inception of the *Ḥibbat Zion movement, Odessa served as its chief center. From here issued the first calls of M.L. *Lilienblum ("The revival of Israel on the land of its ancestors") and L. Pinsker ("Auto-Emancipation") which gave rise to the movement, worked for its unity ("Zerubbavel," 1883), and headed the leadership which was established after the *Kattowitz Conference ("Mazkeret Moshe," 1885–89). The *Benei Moshe society (founded by *Aḥad Ha-Am in 1889), which attempted to organize the intellectuals and activists of the movement, was established in Odessa. Odessa was also chosen as the seat of the settlement committee (the *Odessa Committee, called officially The Society for the Support of Agricultural Workers and Craftsmen in Syria and Palestine), the only legally authorized institution of the movement in Russia (1890–1917). Several other economic institutions for practical activities in Palestine (Geulah, the Carmel branch, etc.) were associated with it. Jewish emigration from Russia to Ereẓ Israel also passed through Odessa, which became the "Gateway to Zion."

The social awakening of the masses gave rise to the popular character of the Zionist movement in Odessa. It succeeded in establishing an influential and ramified organization, attracting a stream of intellectual and energetic youth from the townlets of the Pale of Settlement to Odessa – the center of culture and site of numerous schools – and provided the Jewish national movement with powerful propagandists, especially from among the ranks of those devoted to Hebrew literature. The group of authors and activists which rallied around the Zionist movement and actively participated in the work of its institutions included M.L. Lilienblum and Aḥad Ha-Am, M.M. *Ussishkin, who headed the Odessa Committee during its last decade of existence, and M. *Dizengoff, Zalman *Epstein and Y.T. Lewinsky, M. *Ben-Ammi and H. *Rawnitzky, Ḥ.N. Bialik and J. *Klausner, A. *Druyanow and A.M. Berakhyahu (Borochov), Ḥ. *Tchernowitz, S. Pen, M. *Gluecksohn and V. Jabotinsky. These had great influence on this youth, who were not only initiated into Jewish national activity, but were enriched in Jewish culture and broadened in general education. Important literary forums were established in Odessa (*Kavveret*, 1890; *Pardes*, 1891– 95; **Ha-Shilo'aḥ*, 1897–1902; 1907–17; **Haolam*, 1912–17); their editors (Aḥad Ha-Am, Y.H. Rawnitzky, Ḥ.N. Bialik, J. Klausner, A. Druyanow, and M. Gluecksohn) not only succeeded in raising them to a high literary standard but also won considerable influence among the public through the ideological integrity of their publications. The publishing houses established in Odessa (Rawnitzky, Moriah; Ḥ.N. Bialik and Y.H. Rawnitzky, S. *Ben-Zion and Y.T. Lewinsky, *Devir, founded by Bialik and his circle, from 1919) were also systematic in their standards and consistently loyal to their ideology. A Hebrew literary center and "Hebrew climate" was created in Odessa. It united the Hebrew writers by an internal bond more closely than in any other place; it attracted toward Hebrew literature authors who had become estranged from it or who had never approached it (Mendele Mokher Seforim, S. *Dubnow, Ben-David, M. Ben-Ammi, S.S. *Frug, V. Jabotinsky); it produced new authors who were to play an important and valuable role in literature (S. *Tchernichowsky, J. Klausner, N. *Slouschz, etc.); it attracted talented young authors (S. Ben-Zion, Y. *Berkowitz, J. *Fichmann, Z. *Shneour, A.A. *Kabak, E. *Steinman, and many others) who sought the benefit of this congenial literary meeting place refecting the spirit of its distinguished founders (Aḥad Ha-Am and Ḥ.N. Bialik). The arguments between the leaders of the national movement (Aḥad Ha-Am and S. Dubnow, M.M. Ussishkin and V. Jabotinsky) and its opponents, grouped around the local branch of the Society for Promotion of Culture among the Jews of Russia who stood for "striking civic roots, linguistic-cultural assimilation, and general ideals" (M. Morgulis, J. *Bikerman, etc.), were published at length and grew in severity from year to year, their influence penetrating far beyond Odessa. With the advent of the Soviet regime, Odessa ceased to be the Jewish cultural center in southern Russia. The symbol of the destruction of Hebrew culture was the departure from Odessa for Constantinople in June 1921 of a group of Hebrew authors led by Bialik. The *Yevsektsiya chose *Kharkov and *Kiev as centers for its activities among the Jews of the Ukraine. Russian-oriented assimilation prevailed among the Jews of Odessa in the 1920s (though the city belonged to the Ukraine). Over 77% of the Jewish pupils attended Russian schools in 1926 and only 22% Yiddish schools. At the University, where up to 40% of the student role was Jewish, a faculty of Yiddish existed for several years which also engaged in research of the history of Jews in southern Russia. The renowned Jewish libraries of the city were amalgamated into a single library named after Mendele Mokher Seforim. In the later 1930s, as in the rest of Russia, Jewish cultural activity ceased in Odessa and was eventually completely eradicated. The rich Jewish life in Odessa found vivid expression in Russian-Jewish fiction, as, e.g., in the novels of *Yushkevich, in Jabotinsky's autobiographical stories and his novel *Piatero* ("They Were Five," 1936) and particularly in the colorful *Odessa Tales* by Isaac *Babel, which covered both the pre-revolutionary and the revolutionary period and described the Jewish proletariat and underworld of the city.

[Benzion Dinur (Dinaburg)]

The Interwar Period (1920–1941)

After 1920 the export of grain almost stopped, and since most of this trade was in Jewish hands, they suffered. In the years 1922–1923 there was great hunger, and in January–June 1922, 12,552 Jews died from hunger or plagues that resulted from it. To overcome it, the authorities started to build food factories and other consumer branches. There were still 34,000 unemployed in 1929. According to the 1926 census, among 77,362 workers, there were 18,789 Jews (27.7%); 7,285 were white collar workers, 5,774 worked in the food industry, 4,354 in the medical branch, 2,317 were teachers, and 1,574 artisans. By the 1930s unemployement was almost eradicated. In 1934 there were 60,000 Jewish workers; a couple of thousand of them worked in big factoriees. The earnings of the workers and artisans were quite low or poor, and the American journalist Hirsh Smolar, who visited the suburb of Moldavanka (7,000 Jews lived there) in 1932 reported on the hunger and poverty. According to him, it looked like a community after a big fire. In the 1926 census only 54% declared Yiddish their mother tongue. Most Jewish children studied in Russian schools. In 1929 there were 15 Yiddish primary schools, 4 nurseries, 3 vocational schools, 1 high school, and a department of Yiddish language and literature in the local university. There was an active Jewish theater, the only museum in U.S.S.R. (which was closed in 1933), and a department of Yiddish books (32,000 volumes) in the city academic library. From 1926 the Yiddish weekly *Odesser Arbeter* ("Odessa Worker") appeared.

Holocaust Period

Odessa was occupied by the Germans on October 16, 1941, after a long siege. Nearly half of the local Jews were evacuated or fled, but their place was taken by thousands of refugees from Bessarabia and South Ukraine. The city was annexed to Transnistria as its capital. On October 22, 1941, the Romanian Army HQ building exploded and many Romanians were killed or wounded. In retaliation 5,000 citiziens were hanged, most of them Jews. On October 24 some 5,000 Jews were concentrated in four stores in the Dalnik suburb – all were burnt down. About 25,000 Jews registered in Dalnik and were taken to Bogdanovka in terrible condition. Until December 20 about 50,000 gathered there. On December 21–23 and 27–29, 1941, almost all of them were murdered. On November 7, 1941, all Jewish males were ordered to report to the city prison, and 1,000 were executed. An order to wear the yellow badge was also given, On December 28 Marshal Ion Antonescu ordered the expulsion of the Jews from the city. On January 10, 1942, the Romanian city commandant ordered the Jews to move to the Slobodka suburb of Kovno, Lithuania, within two days. From there during January and February 1942 they were sent in transports of over 1,000 persons to the villages in the nearby counties, where they were murdered by Romanian policemen, local Germans, and subunits of the *Einsatzkommandos* 10 and 10a. By May 12, 1942, some 28,000 Jews had been killed, and several thousand more died from hunger, cold, and diseases. About 3,000 Jews were concentrated in the ghettos of Domanievka and Akhmetevka and were used for forced labor. The ghetto in the Slobodka suburb existed until June 10, 1942, when the last 400 were deported.

Jews took part in the anti-Nazi underground and partisan units, which were mainly concentrated in the city catacombs. Among 35 underground members caught by the Romanians, there were 6 Jews. In the catacombs a Jewish group of 33 fighters also operated. Among the commanders of the resistance were Robert Sofer and Professor Tatiana Bragarenko-Fridman.

After the last convoy left on Feb. 23, 1942, Odessa was proclaimed *judenrein*. The local inhabitants and the occupying forces looted Jewish property. The old Jewish cemetery was desecrated and hundreds of granite and marble tombstones were shipped to Romania and sold. The gravestone of the poet Simon Frug was recovered and after the war laid in the Jewish cemetery of Bucharest. The Mendele Mokher Seforim Library was sacked and the building demolished. In August 1942 Alexianu and SS-Brigadefuehrer Hoffmeyer – head of *Sonderkommando* R – signed an agreement transferring to the 7,500 Volksdeutsche living in Odessa all the local Jewish-owned apartments, including the furniture. The Jewish Theater became the Deutsches Haus for entertaining German troops in Odessa. In the summer of 1942 the Romanian authorities organized various handicraft workshops for their employees' service for which they brought 50 of the best Jewish artisans from the Transnistrian ghettos (deportees from Romania). They were segregated in ghetto-like quarters in a building on Adolf Hitler Street (formerly Yekaterinovskaya Street). A delegation of the Relief Committee from Bucharest, authorized by the government to visit the ghettos of Transnistria, succeeded in January 1943 in sending them some funds.

Soviet troops under General Malinovsky returned to Odessa on April 10, 1944. It is estimated that at the time of liberation, a few thousand Jews were living in Odessa, some of them under false documents or in hiding in the catacombs. Others were given shelter by non-Jewish families. There had been numerous informers among the local Russians and Ukrainians but also persons who risked their liberty and even their lives to save Jews.

[Dora Litani-Littman / Shmuel Spector (2nd ed.)]

Contemporary Period

After the Jewish survivors returned, Odessa became one of the largest Jewish centers of the Soviet Union. However there was no manifestation of communal or cultural life. In 1959 the Jews numbered 108,900 (12.1% of the total). It dropped to 86,000 (8.4% of the total) in 1979. Until 1956 Israeli vessels visited the port of Odessa for loading and unloading, and Israeli sailors visited the harbor club and were seen in the city's streets. In 1962 private prayer groups were dispersed by the authorities, and religious articles found among them were confiscated. A denunciation of the Jewish religious congregation and its employees appeared in the local paper in 1964. *Matzah* baking by the Jewish congregation was practically prohibited during

1959–65. It was again allowed in 1966. In 1968 the synagogue burned down, but was later rebuilt. While it was still in ruins, thousands of Jews, many of them youngsters, came to the site on *Simḥat Torah* eve to dance and sing. In the 1959 census 102,200 Jews were registered in Odessa, but the actual number has been estimated at about 180,000 (14–15% of the total population). There remained only one synagogue in Odessa, on the outskirts of the city. The old Jewish cemeteries were in disrepair. From 1968 several Jewish families were allowed to immigrate to Israel, following the increased demand for exit permits of Soviet Jews in the wake of the Six-Day War (1967). In the 1990s most Jews emigrated. Those remaining enjoy a full range of community services, including a yeshivah, *mikveh*, and Chabad television.

BIBLIOGRAPHY: *Eshkol, Enẓiklopedyah Yisre'elit*, 1 (1929), 809–26; B. Shohetman, in: *Arim ve-Immahot be-Yisrael*, 2 (1948), 58–108 (incl. bibl.); J. Lestschinsky, *Dos Sovetishe Yidntum* (1941; Heb. tr. *Ha-Yehudim be-Rusyah ha-Sovyetit*, 1943); A.P. Subbotin, *V cherte yevreyskoy osedlosti*, 2 (1888); J.J. Lerner, *Yevrei v Novorossiyskom kraye-istoricheskiye ocherki* (1901); A. Dallin, *Odessa 1941–1944…* (1957); Litani, in: *Yedi'ot Yad Vashem*, no. 23–24 (1960), 24–26; idem, in: *Yad Vashem Studies* (1967), 135–54; A. Werth, *Russia at War, 1941–1945* (1964), 813–26; S. Schwarz, *Jews in the Soviet Union* (1951), index, I. Ehrenburg et al. (eds.), *Cartea Neagr…*, 1 (1946), 92–107; M. Carp (ed.), *Cartea Neagr…* 2 (1948); 3 (1947), indexes; *Procesul Marii Trădări Nationale* (1946), index; PK Romanyah (1969), 390–4.

ODESSA COMMITTEE, shortened name for the Society for the Support of Jewish Farmers and Artisans in Syria and Palestine, the legalized framework of the *Ḥibbat Zion movement. It was founded in Odessa in 1890, with the permission of the Russian government, and continued the work of Ḥovevei Zion in Russia until 1919. Its official aim was to help Jews who settled in "Palestine and Syria" to earn their living by productive work, especially agriculture. Leon *Pinsker, Abraham *Gruenberg (from 1891), and Menaḥem *Ussishkin (from 1906) served successively as chairmen of the committee. It had an executive committee in Jaffa. When Jewish immigration to Ereẓ Israel increased, as a result of the worsening conditions of Russian Jewry, particularly after the expulsion of Jews from Moscow, the committee assisted settlement societies in the purchase of lands. Vladimir *Tiomkin, chairman of its executive committee in Jaffa, was active in organizing and planning the purchase of lands. When emigration from Russia was forbidden by the Turkish authorities, the purchases were discontinued and the Jaffa committee went bankrupt. The Russian Jews were discouraged and the income of the Odessa Committee decreased, but it gradually increased again, particularly when *Herzl began his activities and the Odessa Committee became the only legal Zionist body in Russia. The committee also received donations for special projects, such as supporting the Hebrew school in Jaffa and the workers' fund. In 1900, after the transfer by Baron Edmond de *Rothschild of the management of the supported settlements to the *Jewish Colonization Association (ICA), the Odessa Committee sent Aḥad *Ha-Am and the agronomist Abraham Sussman to investigate the situation. Their reports spoke of the harm caused by the paternalistic methods of the Baron's bureaucracy. A year later Aḥad Ha-Am took part in a delegation to the Baron, but his reply was not satisfactory.

Following the suggestions of the agronomist Akiva *Ettinger, whom the Committee sent to Ereẓ Israel in 1902, it ceased its support of individuals, encouraging private and public initiative instead. In 1903 a delegation led by Ussishkin was sent by the committee to Ereẓ Israel in order to organize the new *yishuv*. The settlers' delegates held several meetings in Zikhron Ya'akov and laid the foundations for an "Organization of the Jews in Ereẓ Israel" and the Teachers' Association. The former failed, but the latter developed.

The Odessa Committee maintained a network of information bureaus for immigrants in Odessa, Constantinople, Beirut, Jaffa, Jerusalem, and Haifa. It established moshavot and smallholdings for agricultural workers (*Be'er Ya'akov in 1908, *Ein Gannim near Petaḥ Tikvah, and *Naḥalat Yehudah near Rishon le-Zion). It aided in the establishment of the Carmel winegrowers cooperative and Geulah Company for land purchase and supported schools, book publishing, and periodicals in Ereẓ Israel. It gave the first donation for purchasing a plot for the Hebrew University in Jerusalem.

BIBLIOGRAPHY: I. Klausner, *Mi-Kattowitz ad Basel*, 2 vols. (1965), index; *Reports of the Odessa Committee* (Heb. and Rus., 1890–1919).

[Israel Klausner]

ODETS, CLIFFORD (1906–1963), U.S playwright. Born in Philadelphia and raised in the Bronx, New York, Odets became an actor at the age of 15. He was a cofounder of the Group Theater, where his one-act play, *Waiting for Lefty* (1935), based on the New York taxi strike of 1934, brought him early success. Two more plays were staged in the same year: *Awake and Sing!*, a drama about poor New York Jews, marked an important turning point in the portrayal of the Jew on the American stage; and *Till the Day I Die* dealt with left-wing German opposition to the Nazis. These brought Odets to the fore as the most promising playwright of the new generation. He expressed perhaps better than any dramatist of his time the hardships of the great depression of the 1930s, and while his works have lost some of their original appeal, they were in their day of considerable social significance. Their impact owed much to their vivid dialogue and characterization. Probably the finest example of the latter quality is *Golden Boy* (1937), the story of a musician turned prizefighter, which was made into a musical in 1964. Odets also wrote *Rocket to the Moon* (1938), and *Clash by Night* (1941). After spending many years as a screenwriter in Hollywood, he returned to Broadway with *The Big Knife* (1949), a play dealing with the corrupting influence of the film colony. Two later plays were *The Country Girl* (1950) and *The Flowering Peach* (1954), a new version of the biblical story of Noah in terms of Jewish family life.

BIBLIOGRAPHY: E. Murray, *Clifford Odets: The Thirties and After* (1968); R.B. Shuman, *Clifford Odets* (1962); J. Gould, *Modern*

American Playwrights (1966), 186–203; S.J. Kunitz (ed), *Twentieth Century Authors*, first suppl. (1955), incl. bibl.

[Joseph Mersand]

°ODO OF CAMBRAI (d. 1113), bishop and theologian. Among Odo's works was the polemic text *Disputatio contra Judaeum Leonem de adventu Christi*, which he claimed was an account of a disputation held in *Senlis during the Christmas season of 1106 between himself and a Jew named Léon. The disputation deals mainly with the virginal birth and the incarnation, and in some places it is clear that Odo borrowed from *Anselm of Canterbury. Odo dedicated this text to a certain Acardus, a monk from the abbey of Fémy, near Cambrai, in commemoration of his visit to this abbey, where he had already expounded the subjects covered by the *Disputatio*.

BIBLIOGRAPHY: P. Browe, *Judenmission im Mittelalter* (1942), 63, 101, 115; F. Cayre, *Patrologie…*, 2 (1945^3), 386; J. de Ghellinck, *L'essor de la littérature latine*, 1 (1946), 164; PL, 160 (1880), 1103–12.

[Bernhard Blumenkranz]

°ODO (Eudes) OF CHÂTEAUROUX (d. 1273), chancellor of the University of Paris from 1238. Odo was probably one of the judges at the public trial of the Talmud in 1240. Appointed cardinal bishop of Tusculum (Frascati) in 1244, he returned as papal legate to France in 1245 to preach the Crusade. A violent opponent of the Talmud, Odo was incensed by a letter from Pope Innocent IV (1247) instructing him to give back to the Jews any copies which had survived the *auto-da-fé* of 1242 (see *Talmud, Burning of). Adopting a high moral tone in his reply, Odo reproached the pope with having been duped by the wiles of the Jews, and repeated the verdict of Gregory IX that the Talmud prevented Jews from becoming Christians. It would be disgraceful, he said, for books which had been solemnly and justly burned in public to be returned to the Jews at the instance of the pope. On May 15, 1248, he issued a formal condemnation of the Talmud, forbidding copies to be returned.

BIBLIOGRAPHY: S. Grayzel, *Church and Jews in the XIIIth Century* (1966^2), index; idem, in: W. Jacob et al. (eds.), *Essays in Honor of Solomon B. Freehof* (1964), 220–45.

[Nicholas de Lange]

°ODO (Eudes) OF SULLY (c. 1160–1208), bishop of Paris from 1196. In several paragraphs of his synodal statutes (par. 15, 37–38, 60, and addenda 1–3), Odo of Sully attempted to restrict relations between Jews and Christians. Particular decrees prohibited priests from standing security for a Jew or giving him church vessels or books in pledge, and forbade Christians to use the skins of grapes which had been pressed by Jews, except as food for pigs or as fertilizer. Here, for the first time, laymen were forbidden – on pain of excommunication – to debate articles of Christian faith with the Jews. These decrees are thought to have been drawn up around 1200, but they were probably issued after July 15, 1205, the date of the letter from Pope *Innocent III to Odo calling for greater severity toward the Jews.

BIBLIOGRAPHY: S. Grayzel, *Church and the Jews in the XIIIth Century* (1966^2), 114f., 300f.; T. de Morembert, in: *Dictionnaire d'histoire et de géographie ecclésiastique*, 15 (1963), 1330f.

[Bernhard Blumenkranz]

°OENOMAUS OF GADARA, pagan philosopher of the school of younger Cynics, who lived during the reign of Hadrian (117–38). He composed a number of works, only little of which has survived. His most famous Γοήτων θώρα (*Kata Chresterion*), fragments of which are preserved in Eusebius (Praeparatio Evangelica 1:7ff.), was a lively attack on the belief in oracles. The argument was based on the belief in free will, and it seems to have had some measure of success, because Julian, in the middle of the fourth century, upbraids him for destroying reverence for the gods (*Orationes* 7:209, also 6:199). Oenomaus aimed at a cynicism which did not slavishly follow either Antisthenes or Diogenes, defining it as "a sort of despair, a life not human but brutish, a disposition of the soul that reckons with nothing noble or virtuous or good." Oenomaus is generally identified with Avnimos ha-Gardi, who appears in rabbinic literature as a philosopher friendly toward the rabbis. He once asked them how the world was first created. Declaring themselves not versed in such matters, they referred him to Joseph the builder, who satisfied him with his reply (Ex. R. 13:1).

He was particularly friendly with R. Meir and once asked him; "Does all wool rise that is placed in the dyeing-pot?" Meir replied, "What was clean upon the body of the mother rises, what was unclean upon the body of the mother does not rise" (Ḥag. 15b). This enigmatic dialogue probably refers to the fact of Meir's teacher, *Elisha b. Avuyah, having become an apostate, and the dangers involved in Meir's learning from him (see TJ, Ḥag. 2:1, 77b). Avnimos' question is indicative of an intimate understanding of Jewish problems. This positive attitude is reflected in an episode according to which the pagans asked him whether they could overcome the Jews, and he replied that if they heard the chirping (i.e., studying) of children in the synagogues and academies, they would be unable to overcome the Jews (Gen. R. 65:20). He had some knowledge of the Bible (Ruth R. 2:13), but it is most significant that the rabbis regarded him as the greatest heathen philosopher of all ages (with Balaam, Gen. R. 65:20). This is due to his gibes at the gods and oracles, coupled with his sympathy and closeness to rabbinic circles, but also indicates the measure of their unfamiliarity with Greek philosophy (see S. Lieberman, in *Biblical and other Studies*, ed. by A. Altmann (1963), 129–30).

BIBLIOGRAPHY: Hyman, Toledot, 946; 261; Pauly-Wissowa, 17 (1937), 2249–51.

[Daniel Sperber]

°OESTERLEY, WILLIAM OSCAR EMIL (1866–1950), English Semitics scholar. Oesterley, who was born in Calcutta, was ordained a clergyman and taught Hebrew and Old Testament exegesis at King's College, London, from 1926. In his work he endeavored to demonstrate talmudic influence on New Testament form and content.

Among his published writings are: *The Jewish Background of Christian Liturgy* (1925); (with T.H. Robinson) *A History of Israel* (vol. 2; *From 586 B.C.E. to A.D. 135*; 1932 and many reprints); *Introduction to the Books of the Old Testament* (with T.H. Robinson, 1934) and *An Introduction to the Books of the Apocrypha* (1935); *The Jews and Judaism During the Greek Period* (1941). Oesterley also wrote commentaries to Psalms (1939; repr. 1962) and Proverbs (1929), *A Fresh Approach to the Psalms* (1937) and a metric translation of the Song of Songs, *Ancient Hebrew Poems* (1938). Together with G.H. Box he wrote an outline of Jewish literature, *A Short Survey of the Literature of Rabbinical and Mediaeval Judaism*, 1920.

OESTERREICHER, TOBIAS VON (1831–1893), Austro-Hungarian rear-admiral. After serving in wars in Hungary, Italy, France, and Prussia, in which Oesterreicher commanded vessels and was decorated, he became a naval captain at the age of 38 and commanded a battleship. He was raised to the nobility and in 1881 he became a rear admiral. Until 1883 he occupied a key position in the Ministry of War and on his retirement received the personal thanks of Emperor Francis Joseph I for his services. On his death, he was given a state funeral.

OESTERREICHISCHE NATIONALBIBLIOTHEK, Austrian government library in Vienna, court library of the Austro-Hungarian Empire until 1918. The Oesterreichische Nationalbibliothek is a major European library founded in 1526.

It possesses 224 Hebrew manuscripts dating from the 13th through the 18th centuries, of which 41 are illustrated. It also has a considerable number of Hebrew incunabula, mostly Bibles, including the first complete Hebrew Bible, printed by the Soncino family in 1488. The library's papyrus collection contains 191 Hebrew texts written on papyri, parchment, and paper. Also among its holdings are a few fragments from the Cairo **Genizah*, including some written in Judeo-Arabic. The library contains an unusually complete collection of rabbinic literature from Galicia and the other eastern portions of the Austro-Hungarian Empire, since a copy of every work published under the empire had to be deposited at the Nationalbibliothek.

The printed volumes of Judaica in the library are part of the Orientalia collection, estimated at about 5% of the library's total holdings. Of the library's Judaica, in 1970 only the incunabula were catalogued separately.

BIBLIOGRAPHY: A.Z. Schwarz, *Hebraeische Handschriften der Nationalbibliothek in Wien* (1925); F. Unterkircher, *Inventar der illuminierten Handschriften…*, 2 (1959).

[Michael A. Meyer]

OESTERREICHISCHES CENTRAL-ORGAN FUER GLAUBENSFREIHEIT, CULTUR, GESCHICHTE UND LITERATUR DER JUDEN, German-language Jewish weekly published in Vienna immediately after freedom of the press was granted at the beginning of the 1848 revolution. Its 49 issues appeared from April 4, 1848 to Oct. 25, 1848. The publisher and editor was Isidor *Busch, and Max (Meir) *Letteris also contributed to the first four issues. A Hebrew supplement, *Meged Geresh Yeraḥim*, edited by Isaac Samuel *Reggio, appeared once (Nisan 5408/1848). Leopold Kompert and Simon Szanto were among its contributors and Busch had many correspondents throughout the Hapsburg monarchy. At first the *Central-Organ* enthusiastically supported the revolution, taking it for granted that Jewish rights would be secured within the framework of general civic rights. Dealing at length with the legal status of the Jews in various countries, the paper was also sensitive to the social discrepancies within Jewish society and attacked leading Jewish capitalists, Rothschild in particular. The outbreak of the anti-Jewish riots in Hungary, Bohemia, Posen, and Alsace brought about a sharp change in its position. After Kompert had published his article *Auf nach Amerika!* (May 6, 1848, No. 6), the *Central-Organ* energetically campaigned for Jewish immigration to the United States, where the Jews were assured of civic equality. Emigration, organization of groups of emigrants, and information for families who intended to emigrate became one of the central themes of the newspaper. The last issue of the newspaper appeared on Oct. 25, 1848, and it probably came to an end as the result of the capture of the city six days later, following the failure of the revolution. Busch himself emigrated to the U.S.

BIBLIOGRAPHY: J.A. Helfert, *Die Wiener Journalistik im Jahre 1848* (1877), index; G. Kisch, in: Historia Judaica 2 (1940), 65–84; idem, in: PAJHS 38 (1948/49), 185–235. **ADD. BIBLIOGRAPHY:** D. Weiss, "Der publizistische Kampf der Wiener Juden um ihre Emanzipation in den Flugschriften und Zeitungen des Jahres 1848" (Ph. D. diss., Vienna University, 1971); J. Toury, *Die Juedische Presse im Oesterreichischen Kaiserreich* (1983), 12–16, index; B.F. Abrams, in: *Bohemia*, 31 (1990), 1–20; E. Friesel, in: LBIYB, 47 (2002), 117–149; E. Campagner, *Judentum, Nationalitätenprinzip und Identität…* (2004), 12, 55–61, 381.

[Avyatar Friesel]

OETTINGEN, town in *Bavaria, Germany. Jews were to be found in Oettingen from the second half of the 13th century. The Jewish settlement suffered in 1298 during the *Rindfleisch persecutions, and during the *Black Death persecutions of 1348 almost all the Jews were massacred. Emperor *Charles IV then transferred their property to Duke Albrecht of Oettingen. A new Jewish community, consisting mainly of money-lenders maintaining strong commercial and familial ties with *Noerdlingen, was soon reorganized. Privileges were issued for 1383–88, and a *Judenstrasse* was mentioned in 1457. The community absorbed an influx of refugees after clerical agitation resulted in the expulsion of the Jews from Noerdlingen and other Bavarian cities in 1507. Oettingen was the capital of the rival duchies of Oettingen-Spielberg and Oettingen Wallerstein and had two synagogues (a "Catholic" and a "Lutheran" one, so named after the two branches of the Oettingen ruling house) and separate district rabbinates and communal organizations. There were many rural Jewish communities in the villages and towns of the duchies of considerable economic importance; their members were engaged in livestock dealing, peddling, and even farming. The duchies were incorporated into *Bavaria in 1806.

In the 17th and 18th centuries, the Oettingen communities benefited from the patronage of several influential *Court Jews, including Hirsch Neumark, David Oppenheim, and the *Model family, who originated in Oettingen. A pogrom resulting from a *blood libel was narrowly averted in 1690 when the murderer of a young child was discovered to be a Christian; the event was commemorated by a fast day each year thereafter on the 17th of Iyyar. The most distinguished rabbi of Oettingen-Wallerstein was Asher Loew (1789–1809), later rabbi of Metz, who opposed Moses *Mendelssohn's proposal to use a burial hall in the cemetery in order to comply with government regulations requiring corpses to be buried three days after death. Of comparable distinction in Oettingen-Spielberg was Jacob Phinehas Katzenellenbogen (1764–95). The Jewish community of Oettingen numbered about 300 in the 18th century (about 10% of the total population). A cemetery was opened in 1850 and a new synagogue built in 1853. The rural community declined from 430 persons (13.4%) in 1837 to 102 in 1910 and only 66 in 1933. On November 10, 1938, Jewish homes and shops were demolished and the synagogue sacked. The rabbi was beaten and hospitalized and all Jewish men deported to *Dachau. Ten of the 11 Jews still living in Oettingen in 1942 were deported. In 2005 the former synagogue was used to house a medical practice. There are commemorative plaques at the building of the former synagogue and at the Jewish cemetery.

BIBLIOGRAPHY: Germ Jud, 2 (1968), 633–5; L. Lamm, in: JJLG, 22 (1931–32), 147–59; J. Mann, in: ZGJD, 6 (1935), 32–39; L. Mueller, *Aus fuenf Jahrhunderten* (1900); S. Stern, *The Court Jew* (1950), index; PK, Bavaria. **ADD BIBLIOGRAPHY:** B. Ophir and F. Wiesemann (eds.), *Die juedischen Gemeinden in Bayern 1918–1945. Geschichte und Zerstoerung* (1979), 489–90; *Germania Judaica*, vol. 3 1350–1514 (1987), 1061; *Die Juden in Oettingen. Ein Beitrag zur Heimatgeschichte* (Oettinger Blaetter, vol. 2/1989) (1989); T. Harburger, *Die Inventarisierung juedischer Kunst- und Kulturdenkmaeler in Bayern*, vol. 3 (1998), 636–41.

[Henry Wasserman]

OFAKIM (Heb. אֳפָקִים; "Horizons"), development town, with municipal council status in southern Israel, 15 mi. (25 km.) N.W. of Beersheba. Ofakim was founded in 1955 as a regional center for the "Merḥavim" development region. The new immigrants who settled there suffered in the initial years from unemployment, low cultural standards, and severe social problems. The population, numbering 631 in the first year, grew to 9,200 by 1970. The majority (71%) of the inhabitants in 1965 were from Morocco and Tunisia; 5% came from India, 9% from Persia, 5% from Egypt, and the rest were from Europe or Israel-born. Families were large and the median age low, with 57.2% of the population below 20 years of age. With the opening of industrial enterprises in the 1960s (textiles, diamond polishing, bakery, basketmaking) Ofakim's economic situation improved and a manpower shortage developed. In the mid-1980s, 42% of Ofakim's employees worked in public and community services and another 20% in industry, mainly textile factories. Others were engaged in seasonal agricultural work. In the 1990s, the city's economic resources ran dry and unemployment increased as the population rose to 18,800 in the mid-1990s and then to 23,200 in 2002. The population increase was due to the absorption of new immigrants from the former Soviet Union and Ethiopia. Ofakim received city status in 1995, occupying an area of 4 sq. mi. (10 sq. km.). Income was about half the national average.

[Efraim Orni / Shaked Gilboa (2nd ed.)]

OFEK, AVRAHAM (1935–1990), Israeli painter and sculptor. Ofek was born in the town of Borgos, Bulgaria. When he was seven years old, his father, Jacob Rubanov, and his mother, Dina, passed away, and Miriam and Leon Algem adopted him. Only when he was 22 years old did Ofek uncover the story of his life and find out that he had two older brothers. After World War II, under Ofek's influence, the family immigrated to Israel. Ofek chose to live in kibbutz Ein ha-Mifraẓ, in order to assimilate into Israeli society. In the kibbutz he painted the vistas that surrounded him, guided by the artist Arie Roitman. During the 1950s Ofek's art style was influenced by modern Italian artists as well as by his social involvement; he chose to draw in a Social Realist style. He described the life of the workers, Jews and Arabs, as monumental figures with bulging muscles.

Ofek, who studied art in Italy, learned the technique of wall painting. In 1963 he and his wife, Talma, moved to Jerusalem, where he became a teacher at the Bezalel Academy of Art and Design. In 1972 he exhibited in the Israeli pavilion in the Venice Biennale. In the 1980s Ofek taught art at Haifa University and, during 1981–83, he was consul for sculpture and science in the Israeli embassy in Rome.

Ofek's first wall painting was created in 1970 in Kefar Uriyyah. From then on he was commissioned for many wall paintings all over the country, most of them dealing with the history of Israel (1972, Post Office, Jerusalem). Ofek's social views were appropriate for the public art of that genre.

In 1976 he was one of the founders of the Leviathan artistic group. The group proclaimed its belief in the need to create, in Israel, art that would be connected with Jewish mysticism. They looked for a primitive and symbolic style with a deep connection to the spirit of modernism. They organized art happenings in the Judean Desert. Ofek screened Hebrew letters and geometric forms made of light on the rocks of the desert. Emphasis was placed on the symbolic meaning of the letters and their forms through the media, their huge size, and the desert space.

Ofek was also involved in sculpture. He preferred the carving technique, usually very flat carving, so the stone stayed in its natural form with a relief on the surface. One of the sculpture series dealt with the *Sacrifice of Isaac*, a subject that combines the Jewish mythos and the history of Israel's wars (1987, Safra Square, Jerusalem).

BIBLIOGRAPHY: G. Efrat, *Home – Avraham Ofek Works 1956–1986* (1987); Tefen, The Open Museum, *Ofek Avraham 1935–1990* (2001).

[Ronit Steinberg (2nd ed.)]

OFEK, URIEL (1926–1987), Hebrew writer. Born in Tel Aviv, Ofek served in the Palmaḥ (1944–48). From 1951, he was coeditor, and from 1971 editor of the children's weekly *Davar li-Yladim*. His poems, stories, articles, and studies on children's literature appeared in various publications, and his plays were staged in children's theaters. He published many books for children, stories, verse, and anthologies of world children's literature. He also translated many children's books and folksongs into Hebrew. He edited memorial volumes to the soldiers who fell in Israel's War of Independence: *Benei Kiryat Ḥayyim be-Milḥemet ha-Shiḥrur* (1950) and *Le-Vaneinu* (1952). His encyclopedia on children's literature, *Olam Ẓa'ir*, appeared in 1970. Ofek's *Smoke over Golan* was selected as the Israel Honor Book of the International Board on Books for Young People at its congress held in May 1977. Ofek was also chosen to deliver the 1978 Arbuthnot Honor Lecture.

BIBLIOGRAPHY: Kressel, Leksikon, 1 (1965), 48. **ADD. BIBLIOGRAPHY:** G. Kressel, "*Ha-Nizzanim ha-Rishonim shel Sifrut ha-Yeladim be-Ivrit*," in: *Hadoar*, 59:2 (1980), 27–28; Z. Shamir, in: *Haaretz* (May 11, 1984); M. Regev, "*Ha-Kirvah ve-ha-Riḥuk: Al Sippurav ha-Otobiyografiyim shel U. Ofek*," in: *Sifrut Yeladim va-No'ar*, 14:2 (1988), 12–20; Y. Hadas, "*Izzuvo shel Paḥad: Iyyun be-Sifro shel U. Ofek*," in: *Sifrut Yeladim va-No'ar*, 14:2 (1988), 8–11.

[Getzel Kressel]

OFER, AVRAHAM (1922–1976), Israeli politician. He was born in Poland and taken to Jerusalem in 1933. In 1941 he was a founder of kibbutz Ḥamadyah. He served with the Israel Navy during the War of Independence, becoming lieutenant-colonel and first commander of a Navy base in Eilat. He was founder and director of Tel Aviv's Mapai Young Guard, 1950–61. After managing Kefar Yarok youth village near Tel Aviv he was secretary of the Egg Marketing Council in 1958 and of the Vegetable Marketing Board in 1961 and deputy director-general of the Ministry of Agriculture, 1960. He resigned his government post in 1963 to become manager of AGREXCO, the agricultural export company. In 1965 he was elected deputy mayor of Tel Aviv. He headed *Shikun Ovdim* in 1967, and also became chairman of the Mashkantaot Leshikun bank. A member of the Knesset from 1969, he headed the Alignment's election campaign in 1973, and was appointed minister of housing in 1974.

In 1976, accusations of corruption were leveled against him and he was dismissed by Prime Minister Rabin but committed suicide before the charges were investigated.

OFFENBACH, city in Hesse, Germany. The Jewish community of Offenbach is mentioned in the list of communities whose members were martyred at the time of the *Black Death persecutions (1348). Individual Jews lived in Offenbach only until after the expulsion of the Jews from *Frankfurt on the Main (1614); fleeing to Offenbach, they founded a small community, which in time developed and grew in strength. In 1702 one of the town's streets was called the *Judenstrasse*. The community was officially constituted in 1707; in the community regulations of that year and in the letters of privileges granted by the authorities in 1708, the organization of the synagogue and all matters of taxation, commerce, and labor were regulated. In 1708 a second *Judenstrasse* was set aside.

From 1788 to 1791 Jacob *Frank lived in the town, and his daughter Eva until 1817. During those years, thousands of Frank's adherents came to Offenbach in order to express their devotion to him and his daughter. Between 1803 and 1806 Wolf *Breidenbach of Offenbach endeavored to obtain the abolition of the body tax (*Leibzoll*) in several of the German states. The Jewish community remained numerically stable at about 1,000 persons throughout the 19th century, while its proportion in the total population declined from about 10% to 3%. It attained a peak of 2,361 in 1910 and totaled 1,435 (1.8%) in 1933. In October 1936 large numbers of Polish Jews were expelled, and on November 10, 1938, the synagogue, built in 1913–16, was burned down. The last rabbi of the community, Dr. Max *Dienemann (served 1918–39), was attacked by the mob and imprisoned. Of 554 Jews who remained on May 17, 1939, 205 were deported in October 1942 and the rest soon after. Seven former inhabitants returned after the war and, with the aid of refugees, rebuilt the community. In June 1956 a new synagogue was consecrated, although in that month 70 tombstones were desecrated. In January 1970, there were 662 Jews living in Offenbach. The Jewish community numbered 829 in 1989 (together with Hanau) and 960 in 2005 (without Hanau, where an independent Jewish community was founded in 2005). About half the members are immigrants from the former Soviet Union. In 1997 a new community center was opened. The synagogue, which was built in 1956, is integrated into the new center. In the mid-1990s the community hired a rabbi, officiating in Offenbach and Hanau.

[Zvi Avneri / Larissa Daemmig (2nd ed)]

Hebrew Printing

The Frankfurt bookseller Seligmann Reiss and his son Herz set up a Hebrew press in Offenbach and issued a variety of Hebrew and Judeo-German books between 1714 and 1721, among them *Beit Yisrael* by Alexander b. Moses Ethausen (1719); *Historie vom Ritter Siegmund* (1714); and similar medieval tales. Israel b. Moses Halle printed Hebrew books in Offenbach with interruptions from 1718 to at least 1738. In 1767 Hirsch Spitz of Pressburg (Bratislava) set up a Hebrew printing press in Offenbach; the press continued to operate until 1832, when competition from *Roedelheim became too strong. The well-known Amsterdam printer Abraham *Proops published Nathan Maz's *Binyan Shelomo* in Offenbach in 1784.

BIBLIOGRAPHY: Silberstein, in: ZGJD, 5 (1892), 126–45; *Zeitschrift fuer Demographie und Statistik der Juden*, 4 (1908), 92; MGADJ,

1 (1909), 49–66; Z. Rubashov, *Al Tillei Beit Frank* (1923); S. Guggenheim, *Aus der Vergangenheit der israelitischen Gemeinde zu Offenbach* (1915); M. Dienemann-Hirsch, *Max Dienemann, ein Gedenkbuch* (1946); *Mitteilungen des Gesamtarchivs der deutschen Juden*, 1 (1909), 49–64; P. Arnsberg, *Von Podolien nach Offenbach* (1965); *Germania Judaica*, 2 (1968), 625; Ḥ.D. Friedberg, *Toledot ha-Defus ha-Ivri… be-Eiropah* (1937), 101–4; M. Steinschneider and D. Cassel, *Juedische Typographie* (1938), 261 (repr. from Ersch und Gruber, *Allgemeine Encyclopaedie…*, 28, 1851). **ADD BIBLIOGRAPHY:** P. Arnsberg, *Die juedischen Gemeinden in Hessen. Bilder, Dokumente*, vol. 3 (1973), 170–6; *ibid.*, *Anfang, Untergang, Neubeginn*, vol. 1 (1971); *ibid.*, vol. 2 (1971), 1160–80; K. Schild and W. Woell, *Judenpogrom in Offenbach* (1978); *Zur Geschichte der Juden in Offenbach am Main*, vols. 1–3 (1988–1994); H. Guttmann, *Vom Tempel zum Gemeindezentrum. Synagogen im Nachkriegsdeutschland* (1989), 23–29.

OFFENBACH, ISAAC (1779–1850), *ḥazzan*. Isaac ben Judah, surnamed Eberst, was born in Offenbach near Frankfurt. After he left his native town in 1799 to become a wandering *ḥazzan* and musician, he began to be called, "der Offenbacher," which soon became his official family name. In 1802 he settled in Deutz as a tavern musician, and in 1816 moved to Cologne, where he became a music teacher and in about 1826 the town *ḥazzan*, a post he held until shortly before his death. The seventh of his nine children, Jacob, was the composer Jacques *Offenbach.

Isaac Offenbach was a versatile musician, a prolific composer (mainly of synagogal works), and a writer and translator of merit. His historical importance stems from the fact that the documentation of his life and work has survived almost in full.

His publications are a *Haggadah* with German translation and six appended melodies, some traditional and some composed by him (1838); a Hebrew-German youth prayer book (1839); and a number of guitar pieces. His manuscripts were given by his granddaughters to the Jewish Institute of Religion in New York, and some items also reached the Birnbaum Collection at the Hebrew Union College, Cincinnati, and the Jewish National and University Library, Jerusalem. The material includes reminiscences by his daughter, and about 20 fascicles and folders of cantorial compositions and notations of traditional melodies. Over and above their value as "cantorial" antecedents of his famous son's work, these manuscripts provide both a treasure trove of the "great tradition" of Ashkenazi *ḥazzanut* and an instructive picture of the development of a *ḥazzan* at the beginning of the Emancipation.

BIBLIOGRAPHY: B. Bayer, in: *Proceedings of the World Conference of Jewish Studies* (Heb., 1971); A. Henseler, *Jakob Offenbach* (Ger., 1930), 16–31 and passim; P. Nettl, *Forgotten Musicians* (1951), 41–46; H. Kristeller, *Der Aufstieg des Koelners Jacques Offenbach… in Bildern* (1931), plates 7–11; A.W. Binder, in: *Jewish Music Journal*, 2:1 (1935), 4–6 (augmented in YLBI, 16, 1971); Sendrey, Music, index.

[Bathja Bayer]

OFFENBACH, JACQUES (1819–1880), French composer of comic operas and operettas. Born in Cologne, Offenbach was the son of Isaac *Offenbach. At the age of 14 young Jacob, as he was then called, was sent to study the cello at the Paris Conservatoire, but after a year, poverty compelled him to earn his living as a cellist in theater orchestras. He received basic instruction in the art of composition from the composer, Jacques *Halévy, and in 1835 took to writing short, sentimental pieces. He attracted attention more because of his eccentric behavior than the quality of his music and his first theatrical works met with little success. They were followed by years of hardship and struggle for recognition. For a time he was a conductor at the Théâtre Français and gradually built a reputation with works such as *Pépito* (1853) and *Oyayayie ou la Reine des Iles* (1855). It was the Paris World Fair of 1855 that proved a turning point in Offenbach's career. He obtained the lease of a small theater in the Champs-Elysées and opened it in time for the Fair under the name of *Les Bouffes Parisiens*. Its success surpassed his expectations. He took Paris by storm with musical plays such as *Les Deux Aveugles* and *Le Violoneux* and had to move to a larger theater in the Passage Choiseul. During the ensuing years he wrote about 100 stage works, many of them of enduring brilliance. Among them were *Orphée aux Enfers* (1858), *La Belle Hélène* (1864), *La Vie Parisienne* (1866), *La Grande-Duchesse de Gérolstein* (1867), *La Périchole* (1868), *Madame l'Archiduc* (1874), and finally his grand opera, *Contes d'Hoffmann*, which was first performed in 1881.

Rossini called Offenbach "our little Mozart of the Champs-Elysées"; others summed him up as "the entertainer [*amuseur*] of the Second Empire." All Europe sang his melodies and danced to his rhythms. He was not as happy, however, in his business dealings. In spite of profitable tours to Berlin, Prague, Vienna, London, and New York, he was frequently in debt and had to face harassing lawsuits. In about 1844 he converted to Catholicism. After the fall of the Empire in 1870, Offenbach's reputation declined, and during the last few years of his life he was a sick man. He did not live to see his *Contes d'Hoffmann* on the stage; when he died it existed only in an annotated piano score, on the basis of which E. Guirard made the orchestration. Together with his librettists, particularly Ludovic *Halévy and Henri Meilhac, Offenbach created a world of fantasy and joy in which, as the critic Karl *Kraus expressed it, "causality is abolished and everybody lives happily under the laws of chaos…."

BIBLIOGRAPHY: J. Brindejont-Offenbach, *Offenbach, mon grandpère* (1940); S. Kracauer, *Orpheus in Paris: Offenbach and the Paris of his Time* (1938); A. Decaux, *Offenbach, roi du Second Empire* (1958); A. Moss and E. Marvel, *Cancan and Barcarolle: the Life and Times of Jacques Offenbach* (1954).

[Frank Pelleg]

OFFENBURG, town in Baden, Germany. It appears that there were Jews in Offenburg during the 13th century. A *Judenbad* (*mikveh*), 39 ft. (12 m.) deep, dating from this period was discovered in 1857. At the time of the *Black Death (1348–49), three Jews "confessed" under torture that they had poisoned the wells. Although the well was later examined and no signs of poison were found, the Jews were expelled. The town gates were not reopened to Jews until 1862. A community was formally established in 1866. The number of Jews increased from 37 in 1863 to 337 in 1900. An inn was transformed into a synagogue in 1875 and renovated in 1922. There were 271 Jews in Offenburg in 1933. Offenburg was the seat of the district rabbinate serving dozens of rural localities, the last rabbi being Siegfried (Sinai) *Ucko. On November 9/10, 1938, the interior of the synagogue was demolished, and 91 Jews were deported to *Gurs on October 22, 1941. In 1967 there were four Jews in Offenburg. The Oberrat – the association of Jewish communities in Baden – sold the synagogue to a private owner. In 1997 it was purchased by the municipality of Offenburg. It was restored with public funding and has served as a municipal cultural center since 2002. A small exhibition is dedicated to the history of the building and the Jewish community. The former *mikveh* is open to the public.

BIBLIOGRAPHY: *Germania Judaica*, 2 (1968), 625–6; F. Hundsnurscher and G. Taddey, *Die juedischen Gemeinden in Baden* (1968), passim; FJW, 351–2; O. Kaehni, in: *Veroeffentlichungen des historischen Vereins fuer Mittelbaden*, 49 (1969). **ADD BIBLIOGRAPHY:** M. Ruch (ed), *Juedische Stimmen. Interviews, autobiographische Zeugnisse, schriftliche Quellen zur Geschichte der Offenburger Juden in der Zeit von 1933–1945* (Veroeffentlichungen des Kulturamtes der Stadt Offenburg, vol. 21) (1995); M. Ruch, *Verfolgung und Widerstand in Offenburg 1933–1945. Dokumentation* (Veroeffentlichungen des Kulturamtes, vol. 20) (1995); idem, *In staendigem Einsatz. Das Leben Siegfried Schurmanns. Juedische Schicksale aus Offenburg und Suedbaden 1907–1997* (1997); idem, *Aus der Heimat verjagt. Zur Geschichte der Familie Neu. Juedische Schicksale aus Offenburg und Suedbaden 1874–1998* (1998); idem, *Juedisches Offenburg. Einladung zu einem Rundgang* (1999); S. Dzialoszynski and M. Ruch, *Der gute Ort. Der juedische Friedhof in Offenburg* (2000); M. Ruch, *Der Salmen. Geschichte der Offenburger Synagoge. Gasthof – Synagoge – Spielstaette* (2002). **WEBSITES:** M. Ruch, *Quellen zur Geschichte der Offenburger Juden im 17. Jahrhundert* (www.freidok.uni-freiburg.de/volltexte/301/); www.jakob-adler-zentrum-offenburg.de.

[Zvi Avneri / Larissa Daemmig (2nd ed.)]

OFFICE OF SPECIAL INVESTIGATIONS. The United States Department of Justice's Office of Special Investigations (OSI) was established in 1979 for the purpose of investigating and bringing suit to denaturalize and deport persons who took part in Nazi-sponsored acts of persecution, and to exclude from entry into the United States any person listed on OSI's "watch list" of suspected Nazi and Axis persecutors. Since its inception through 2004, OSI has denaturalized 98 individuals and brought action against an additional 34 suspected persecutors; it has also assembled a list of nearly 70,000 foreign individuals whose names it added to the United States Government's "watchlist" to be denied entry into the country. The targets of OSI's activities are largely Americans who entered the United States under false pretenses by hiding their Nazi past when applying for residency or citizenship; many have been deported. Since 2004, OSI's mandate has been expanded, and the agency is now also responsible for investigating and taking legal action to denaturalize American citizens who took part in war crimes, crimes against humanity, genocide, or torture outside of the United States.

OSI has handled several high-profile cases, including placing former Austrian President and United Nations Secretary General Kurt Waldheim on the "watch list," based on Waldheim's service in the Wehrmacht while in the Balkans and Greece as Jews were being deported and murdered there. OSI also successfully prosecuted Arthur Rudolph, the former project director of NASA's Saturn V moon rocket program, who left the country in 1984 when OSI proved he served from 1943 to 1945 as director of the Mittelwerk slave labor V-2 rocket factory. In 1981, Karl Linnas was stripped of his citizenship when OSI shed light on his notorious past as commander of the Tartu, Estonia, concentration camp and his personal involvement in the killing of thousands of Jews.

One case in which OSI found itself enmeshed in controversy was that of John Demjanjuk, a retired Cleveland, Ohio, auto worker. In news that attracted international headlines, the Justice Department accused Demjanjuk of being "Ivan the Terrible," an infamous and brutal Ukrainian guard at Treblinka. In 1982, Demjanjuk was stripped of American citizenship and deported by OSI to Israel, where he was convicted of murder, though his conviction was overturned by the Israeli Supreme Court in 1993 for lack of evidence. The United States Court of Appeals for the Sixth Circuit subsequently ruled that OSI had "acted with a reckless disregard for the truth" in the case. Nonetheless, in a separate legal case brought by OSI, Demjanjuk was eventually stripped of his citizenship for his activities in the Sobibor death camp and several concentration camps.

The directors of the OSI have included Walter Rockler (1979–80), a former Nuremberg prosecutor, Allan A. Ryan, Jr. (1980–83), Neal M. Sher (1983–94), and Eli M. Rosenbaum (1994–).

[Ralph Grunewald (2nd ed.)]

OFFICIAL, NATHAN BEN JOSEPH AND JOSEPH, leading polemicists of Franco-German Jewry of the 13th century. Both were in the service of the archbishop of Sens as financial agents, and hence the name Official. Joseph, the son of Nathan, is also known as Joseph the Zealot (Joseph ha-Mekanne), because he was zealous in the defense of Judaism and compiled a book under this name. Nathan came from a long line of scholars and communal leaders, many of whom were known for their passionate and indefatigable activities in defense of Judaism. Nathan conducted frequent debates with dignitaries of the Church and also with fanatical converts to Christianity. He was an eloquent debater. Joseph calls his father "the chief spokesman in everything." Among his challengers were a cardinal, archbishops, bishops, priests, monks of various orders, and zealous and fanatical converts. The debates are fully described by his son in his *Yosef ha-Mekanne*. Joseph was a pupil of *Jehiel b. Joseph of Paris and was the author of the Hebrew report of the historic disputation of 1240. Joseph, like his father, was an "Official" and continued the tradition of the family as a defender of Judaism. His book *Yosef ha-Mekanne* is a polemical commentary on the Bible, and contains a large collection of Christological passages which were discussed and refuted by Jewish exegetes and polemicists, most of them members of the Official family. Its purpose was to refute the Christological interpretation of the Bible, verse by verse, as a ready handbook of Jewish answers to the challenge of the Church. At the end of the book Joseph added a short criticism of the life of Jesus according to the Gospels, which contains a Jewish challenge to Christianity. Over 40 Jewish disputants, including some proselytes, and ten Christian disputants, including some converts, are mentioned in the book. Noteworthy is the high degree of freedom in the debates and the courage of the Jewish disputants, who accepted all challenges. This fact is especially surprising since the activities of the Officials fall in the period after the Fourth Lateran Council of 1215 with its severe anti-Jewish resolutions. The close familiarity of the Officials with Christian rites and liturgy is also remarkable. The book sheds light on Jewish-Christian relations in day-to-day life in 13th-century France and Germany, reflecting an atmosphere of relative tolerance, in which the Jew is able to accept the challenge and counter with his own challenge. The book is also important for the history of Hebrew translations of the New Testament. *Yosef ha-Mekanne* was also known under the name of *Sefer ha-Nizzaḥon* ("Book of Disputation"). It influenced similar polemical works of collections of Christologies and their refutations according to biblical order, the best known being the *Sefer ha-Nizzaḥon* of Yom Tov Lipmann *Muelhausen.

BIBLIOGRAPHY: Z. Kahn, in: REJ, 1 (1880), 222–46, 3 (1881), 1–38; *Mi-Mizraḥ u-mi-Ma'arav*, 4 (1899), 17–25; idem, in: *Festschrift... A. Berliner* (1903), Heb. pt., 80–90; E.E. Urbach, in: REJ, 100 (1935), 49–77; Joseph Official, *Yosef ha-Mekanne*, ed. by J. Rosenthal (1970), introd.

[Judah M. Rosenthal]

OFFNER, STACY (1955–), U.S. Reform rabbi. A *magna cum laude* graduate of Kenyon College in Gambier, Ohio (1977), she received her M.H.L. (1982) and was ordained at Hebrew Union College in New York City (1984). She then went to the Twin Cities where she was the first woman rabbi in the state of Minnesota and went on to be the first openly gay woman rabbi in the United States. She was the founding rabbi of Shir Tikvah (1988). Involved in many community-wide endeavors, Offner also served as adjunct professor of Jewish Ethics at Hamline University for over a decade and served on the Ethics Committee of Children's Hospital and as chair of the Socially Responsible Investing Committee of the Reform Pension Board.

She was president of the Midwest Association of Reform Rabbis, and was the first rabbi ever to serve a term as the officially elected chaplain of the Minnesota State Senate.

Among other activities she is a founding member of Feminists in Faith, Mpls.-St. Paul, 1984–88; a member of the Task Force on Sexual Exploitation Minn. Dept. Corrections, St. Paul, 1985–87; a member of the Disability Services Panel of the United Way, St. Paul, 1985–86.

She is the recipient of the Clergy Appreciation award, Civitan, 1990; Founding Feminist award, Women's Political Caucus, 1988; Sherrill Hooker Memorial Award, Lesbian and Gay Community, 1989.

Among her more innovative ideas for social justice, Rabbi Offner, as chair of the social responsibility subcommittee of the Reform Rabbinic Pension Fund, first responded to the idea of a national campaign to organize Jewish investment in community development financial institutions. The Pension Fund's 1995 investment of $200,000 in four community development banks was the first "mainstream Jewish" investment that the Shefa Fund could say it leveraged.

[Michael Berenbaum (2nd ed.)]

OFIR, ARIE (1939–), Israeli designer and silversmith. Ofir was born in Tel Aviv and was a member of kibbutz Bet Nir. During rehabilitation from wounds received during his military service, he developed an interest in metalcraft, and from 1961 to 1964 studied at the *Bezalel Academy of Art and Design and later worked at the studio of D.H. Gumbel, a silversmith in Jerusalem, 1964–66, and from 1966 to 1968 at the workshop of Georg Jensen in Copenhagen, where he was granted a scholarship by the Danish Ministry of Education. On his return to Israel in 1969 he opened his own studio in Jerusalem. In 1969 he was appointed lecturer at the gold- and silversmithing department of Bezalel, its head in 1972, and in 1977 professor of fine arts.

He has held exhibitions at art museums in many countries, and was guest lecturer at various universities. His works are included in many private and public collections. Exhibitions have included the Jewish Museum, New York; Spertus Museum, Chicago; Yeshiva University Museum, New York; Israel Museum, Jerusalem; Schmucksmuseum Pforzheim, Germany; and a Torah crown, breastplate and *yad* at the Victoria and Albert Museum, London (Anglo-Jewish Exhibition 1978). In 1976 Ofir designed and executed a memorial for Jerusalem soldiers killed in the Yom Kippur War, which stands in the Peace Forest between Armon Ha-Naẓiv and Abu Tor. Later he produced striking functional lighting elements by transferring two-dimensional images onto glass. In 1992 he was awarded the Jesselson Prize for Contemporary Judaica Design by the Israel Museum. He is the author of *Yesodot Ha-Ẓorfut* ("Basics of Gold and Silversmithing," 1977).

[Amia Raphael]

OFIR, SHAIKE (Yeshayahu; 1929–1987), Israeli actor, comedian, and pantomimist. Ofir was born in Jerusalem as Yeshayahu Goldstein. At the age of 14 he joined the *Palmaḥ, but left to join the Ohel theater. In the War of Independence he rejoined the Palmaḥ. During his service, the Chizbatron, the Palmaḥ's entertainment troupe was created and Ofir joined it. After his service, he went to Paris to study pantomime under Atiene Decrot, the father of modern pantomime. After three years of study and half a year of performing with Marcel *Marceau, he returned to Israel and joined the Cameri Theater. While there, he founded a Cameri pantomime group. In 1956 he went to the United States, working there for four and half years and performing with Marlene Dietrich. In the beginning of the 1960s he returned to Israel. He wrote and directed the first two shows of *Ha-Gashash ha-Ḥiver and was recognized as an established actor, both in theater and film. Of his 28 films, the best known is the award-winning *The Policeman Azulai* (1971), written and directed by Ephraim *Kishon, where he plays a blundering policeman so inept that criminals try to boost his arrest record so that he will remain on the beat. Other Kishon films include *Ervinka* (1967), *The Blaumlich Canal* (1970), and *The Fox in the Chicken Coop* (1978), and Ofir also starred in *Hole in the Moon* (1965) and *Abu al Benat* (1973). His movie career garnered him three Kinor David prizes. He also put on one-man shows such as *A Thousand Faces* and *The Joy of the Poor*, portraying an entire gallery of Israeli types, none more hilarious than the fiery *Histadrut orator eating a sandwich as he delivers a speech. Ofir was called "the king of Israeli entertainment." In 2004, the Israeli film academy named its equivalent of the Oscar the Ofir in his honor

[Shaked Gilboa (2nd ed.)]

OFNER, FRANCIS-AMIR (1913–), journalist. Born in Novi Sad, Yugoslavia, he studied law at Besançon, Lausanne and Zagreb (where he obtained the degree of Juris Doctor in 1938). During 1940–41 he was active in the Yugoslav Zionist-Revisionist movement, acting as Netziv Betar (lit. commissioner, i.e., head of the Berit Trumpeldor youth organization). His endeavors at that time included the fostering of illegal immigration of Jewish refugees from Nazi-occupied Europe to Palestine across the Danube.

During 1942–45, he worked in Istanbul at the U.S. Office of War Information, in the capacity of Balkan press liaison officer. Settling in Tel Aviv in September 1945, he started a productive career in international journalism. He worked mainly for the *Christian Science Monitor* of Boston and for the London *Observer* (writing a column syndicated in 300 newspapers). He contributed articles to the German and Swiss press; also to the International News Service, New York. In Israel, he contributed to the *Jerusalem Post* and to *L'Information*; in later years, he acted as senior lecturer on international media at Tel Aviv University. He founded, and for a while chaired, the Foreign Correspondents Association in Israel. He covered major milestones of Israel's history.

In the early 1960s, Ofner occupied the post of press counselor at the Israel Embassy, Washington, D.C. and the Israeli delegation to the United Nations, New York.

On professional missions he traveled to many countries, interviewing leading statesmen, such as the Shah of Iran, Emperor Haile Selassie of Ethiopia, King Hassan of Morocco, and David Ben-Gurion.

Ofner acted as vice chairman of the Israel-German Friendship Society and as Middle East consultant to the Alex Springer Foundation, Berlin and Hamburg.

[Zvi Loker (2nd ed.)]

OFNER, JULIUS (1845–1924), Austrian lawyer and politician. Born in Horschenz/Hořenice, Bohemia, Ofner qualified as a lawyer in Vienna and acquired a considerable reputation as a jurist through his writings on law and philosophy. These included *Das Recht auf Arbeit* (1885) and *Der Urentwurf und die Beratungsprotokolle des oesterreichischen Allgemeinen Buergerlichen Gesetzbuches* (1887–88). He was elected to the Lower Austrian Diet in 1896 and, five years later, to the Reichsrat (1901–18). Later he joined the Austrian Liberal Party and fought for comprehensive social legislation, including the extension of women's rights and the granting of suspended sentences in criminal cases. He also initiated a law preventing criminal prosecution for petty larceny known as the *Lex Ofner*.

In 1913 Ofner was appointed to the Austrian Supreme Court (*Reichsgericht*) and in 1919 was made permanent referee of its successor, the Austrian Constitutional Court (*Verfassungsgerichtshof*). Ofner was instrumental in obtaining the release of Leopold *Hilsner. He advocated the abolition of ecclesiastical jurisdiction in matters of marriage and divorce, and thereby aroused the hostility of the Roman Catholic majority in Vienna. The Catholics particularly resented the fact that it was a Jew who pressed for this measure, and the Jews were afraid that the intervention of a Jew in Christian affairs would lead to antisemitism. In the 1919 elections to the Constituent Assembly, Ofner was defeated but the seat went to another Jew, the Zionist candidate, Robert *Stricker.

BIBLIOGRAPHY: *Julius Ofner zum 70sten Geburtstage* (1915), includes a list of his books; W. Herz, in: *Neue Oesterreichische Biographie*, 13 (1959), 104–11. E. Lehmann, "Julius Ofner. Ein Kaempfer für Recht und Gerechtigkeit" (Ph.D. thesis Vienna University, 1931). **ADD. BIBLIOGRAPHY**: E. Fraenkel, *The Jews of Austria…* (1976), 31–34.

[Josef J. Lador-Lederer]

OFRAN (**Ifrane**), the provincial capital of the Centre Sud region, north central Morocco, is situated in the Middle Atlas Mountains. It is Morocco's winter and summer premier resort area. According to Judeo-African tradition Ofran is regarded as the first site of Jewish settlement in Morocco. Many legends have been created about the ancient community of Ofran, whose first members are said to have arrived from Ereẓ Israel before the destruction of the First Temple in Jerusalem. A Jewish kingdom was set up there which was governed by the Afriat family – then named Efrati. The Jews of this kingdom are said to have belonged to the tribe of Ephraim – one of the lost Ten Tribes of Israel. Indeed, in the modern era the Afriat family administered the affairs of the community of Ofran and of all the communities of the region.

The Jewish cemetery of Ofran is very old, and there are many tombstone inscriptions dating from the Middle Ages. Local tradition ascribes some of them to the first century B.C.E. Pilgrimages were made from every part of Morocco to this cemetery, which contains the remains of revered rabbis and martyrs.

According to local traditions there was a terrible persecution following the destruction of the community by the Byzantine Christians (sic). Other persecutions have been historically proven, the last of which took place in 1792 when the pretender Bou-Hallais, who sought to be proclaimed sultan, arrived in Ofran. He seized 50 Jewish notables and gave them the alternative of converting to Islam or death by fire. Under the guidance of their leader, Judah Afriat, they jumped one after the other into the huge furnace which had been lit for the occasion. Judah Afriat remained to the end in order to encourage those who faltered. The remains of these martyrs, known as the *Nisrafim* ("Burnt Ones"), were piously gathered and interred in the cemetery of Ofran. The account of their martyrdom was copied on parchment and circulated throughout the country. A popular etymology explains the name Ofran as a combination of *efer* ("the ashes of") and the letter *nun* (= 50). Their descendants were greatly esteemed and to the present day they commemorate the anniversary of the event (the 17th of Tishri) by refraining from lighting fires in their homes.

The community of Ofran was prominent and wealthy and a large part of the trans-Sahara trade passed through its hands. After 1792 its members dispersed. They played an important role in the community of *Mogador, especially the members of the Afriat family, and during the 19th century they established a commercial house in London. For more than 50 years the Afriat house was the most important family in Anglo-Moroccan trade. The community of Ofran was reorganized in the 19th century by a few Jewish families of the region (58 families in 1820, 34 in 1883, 122 persons in 1936, and 141 persons in 1951). The community never regained its former prosperity but its members nevertheless lived in security until 1955, when they all immigrated to Israel.

BIBLIOGRAPHY: J.M. Toledano, *Ner ha-Ma'arav* (1911), 3–5, 95, 219; J. Ben-Naim, *Malkhei Rabbanan* (1931), s.v. *Judah Afriati*; V. Monteil, in: *Hesperis*, 35 (1948), 151–62; A.I. Laredo, *Berberes y Hebreos en Marruecos* (1954), 126–44.

[David Corcos]

OG (Heb. עֹג, עוֹג), ruler of *Bashan, one of the Amorite kings in the Transjordan area during the time of Moses. The Bible remembers Og as belonging to the race of giants "who was left of the remaining Rephaim," and special attention is paid to the description of his huge iron bedstead (Deut. 3:11). The kingdom of Og comprised Bashan and the Hermon region, and extended to the Jordan river to the west (Josh. 12:4–5). Three or four of the cities of his kingdom are mentioned in the Bible – *Ashtaroth, which was apparently his capital and known as the capital of the realm (Tell el-Amarna letters, no. 197, possibly also Karnaim, cf. Gen. 14:5); Salcah (Josh. 12:5; 13:11, et al.); and *Edrei (Num. 21:33; Josh. 13:12, 31). From this it would appear that his kingdom was one of the remaining *Hyksos kingdoms whose cities at that time were scattered in Palestine. It is also possible that this kingdom was established by Amorites who invaded the area in the time of the Egyptian-Hittite struggle during the reign of Ramses II (13th century). Og was defeated by the Israelites when the eastern side of the Jordan was conquered by those who left Egypt (Num. 21:33, 35; Deut. 3:1ff.). Half of the tribe of Manasseh took Og's land as their inheritance (Josh. 13:31). This victory greatly strengthened the spirit of the people. "Sixty towns … fortified with high walls, gates, and bars" were then conquered (Deut. 3:4–5). Echoes of this victory, which was of exceptional importance, are also encountered in later passages (Josh. 13:12; Ps. 135:11; 136:20; Neh. 9:22).

[Josef Segal]

Og and Sihon in the Aggadah

Sihon and Og were the sons of Ahijah, whose father was the fallen angel Shamḥazai (Nid. 61a), and of Ham's wife (Yal. Reub. on Gen. 7:7). Og was born before the Flood and was saved from it by Noah on the promise that he and his descendants would serve Noah as slaves in perpetuity (PdRE 23). Sihon and Og were giants, their foot alone measuring 18 cubits (Deut. R. 1:25). Og is identified with Eliezer, the servant of Abraham, who received him as a gift from Nimrod. So that he could not claim reward in the world to come for his services to his master, God paid him in this world by making him a king (Sof. 21:9; ed. M. Higger (1937) 366 and PdRE 16). During his reign he founded 60 cities, which he surrounded with high walls, the lowest of which was not less than 60 miles in height (Sol. *ibid.*). When Og, who was present at the feast Abraham made on the occasion of Isaac's weaning, was teased by all the great men assembled there for having called Abraham a sterile mule, he pointed contemptuously at Isaac, saying, "I can crush him by putting my finger on him," whereupon God said to him, "Thou makest mock of the gift given to Abraham – by thy life thou shalt look upon myriads of his descendants, and thy fate shall be to fall into their hands" (Gen. R. 53:10). Sihon, appointed by the other kings as guardian of Ereẓ Israel, extracted tribute from them (Num. R. 19:29). Sihon and Og were even greater enemies of Israel than was Pharaoh (Mid. Ps. 136:11). When Moses was about to attack them, God assured him that he had nothing to fear, for He had put their guardian angels in chains (*ibid.* and Deut. R. 1:22). Though Moses was undaunted by Sihon, he did fear Og because he had been circumcised by Abraham (Zohar, Num. 184a) and because of the possibility that the latter's merit might stand him in good stead for having been the "one who escaped and told Abraham" (Gen. 11:13; Nid. 61a). Moses' fears were unfounded, however, in that Og's real motive had been to bring about the death of Abraham so that he could marry Sarah (Deut. R. 1:25).

Sihon was left to his own resources by Og, who was confident of his brother's ability to conquer Israel unaided (Song R. 4:8). Og himself met his death when a mountain three parasangs long, which he had uprooted to cast upon the camp of Israel, was invaded by ants dispatched by God as he carried it upon his head toward his destination. The perforated mountain slipped from Og's head to his neck, whereupon Moses struck him upon the ankle with an ax and killed him (Ber. 54a–b). Though the victory over Sihon and Og was as important as the crossing of the Red Sea, Israel did not sing a song of praise to God upon it as they had upon Pharaoh's destruction, the omission not being made good until the time of David (Mid. Ps. 136:11).

BIBLIOGRAPHY: Aharoni, Land, 191; Noth. Hist Isr, 159–60; idem, in: BBLA, 1 (1949), 1ff.; Bergman (Biran), in: JPOS, 16 (1936), 224–54; Y. Kaufmann, *Sefer Yehoshu'a* (1959), 166. IN THE AGGADAH: Ginzberg, Legends, index.

OHEL (Heb. אֹהֶל; "Tent"), Israel theater company, originally known as the Workers' Theater of Palestine, founded in 1925 by Moshe *Halevy. It was the company's original intention to create a socialist theater whose members combined work in the theater with agricultural and industrial labor. After about two years, however, it became clear that to reach a high level of accomplishment actors must devote themselves fully to their profession. Furthermore, from the outset Ohel found it difficult to procure ideologically suitable plays. The theater's inaugural production was an adaptation of stories by I.L. *Peretz (1926) that was received with great enthusiasm, especially in the rural settlements for which Ohel's work was primarily intended. This was followed by *Dayyagim* ("Fishermen," 1927), a socialist play about the exploitation of fishermen by entrepreneurs. Thereafter, the company turned to biblical plays and the standard international repertoire.

In 1934 Ohel had reached the climax of its development. The early years of the 1930s witnessed its struggle between being a "proletarian" theater and a "national" one. It sometimes even presented "proletarian" plays that were criticized for being incongruent with the actual social and labor situation in Palestine. On its highly successful European tour in 1934, however, Ohel staged mainly biblical and national plays. Upon its return to Palestine, it produced some of its greatest successes, including "The Good Soldier Schweik" (1935), mostly due to the talents of Meir Margalit (d. 1974), a comedy actor. Two years later it also staged *Yoshe Kalb*, adapted from a novel by the Yiddish author I.J. Singer and directed by Maurice *Schwartz.

The theater progressed until 1958, when it faced a crisis over being suddenly divorced from the Histadrut (General Federation of Labor), which had been its parent body. The motivating factor behind the split was the theater's decline in both quality and audience-drawing power. The decline continued until 1961, when Ephraim *Kishon brought his comedy *Ha-Ketubbah* ("The Marriage Contract") to the Ohel. With Margalit in the lead, the play proved to be such a success that it revived the theater for three seasons. Under the new artistic director, Peter Frye (d. 1991), the theater experienced another major hit, Shalom Aleichem's *Ammekha* (1964), and proceeded to produce works by Ionesco, Brecht, and young British playwrights, using actors from outside the repertory company and the aid of foreign directors. The period of revival was short-lived, however, and the theater closed in 1969.

BIBLIOGRAPHY: M. Kohansky, *The Hebrew Theatre* (1969), 96–106 and index; M. Halevy, *Darki alei Bamot* (1955).

[Mendel Kohansky]

OHEV BEN MEIR HA-NASI (late 11th–early 12th century), liturgical poet in Spain. Abraham *Ibn Daud mentions him in his *Sefer ha-Kabbalah* (ed. G.D. Cohen (1967), 73, 102) together with the poet Moses *Ibn Ezra, and refers to him by his Arabic name Ibn Shortmeqas.

Three of Ohev's *piyyutim* were published in *Ḥizzunim* (Constantinople, 1585), a collection of *piyyutim* which were recited in the rite of the "Westerners" who lived in Sicily. One of these, the *ofan "Erelim ve-Ḥashmalim"* (i.e., various kinds of angels) resembles in several details the famous *piyyut "Malakhim mamlikhim"* ("The Angels Enthrone") of Moses Ibn Ezra. One of his *piyyutim* on the Ten Commandments was discovered in the Cairo *Genizah and published by J. Schirmann.

BIBLIOGRAPHY: J. Schirmann, in: YMḤSI, 4 (1938), 277–82; 6 (1945), 332–6; Schirmann, Sefarad, 1 (1961²), 327f.; Davidson, Oẓar, 4 (1933), 360; M. Zulay, in: *Sinai*, 25 (1949), 47–49.

OHIO, industrial state in eastern central United States. In 2001, the Jewish population of Ohio was 149,000 of a total population of 11,353,140, or 1.3%. Jewish settlement in Ohio paralleled the opening of new lands to the west of the Allegheny and Appalachian Mountains, the development of canals, roads, and later, railroads. The first documented Jewish settler in Ohio was an English watchmaker named Joseph Jonas, who settled in Cincinnati in 1817. His presence, something of a curiosity to the locals who had never seen a Jew, was well tolerated. As his relatives joined him, and new settlers made their way to *Cincinnati, there was a large enough group to establish Ohio's first congregation, Bene Israel, in 1824. *Cleveland, in the northeastern portion of the state, also attracted Jewish settlers. Daniel Maduro Peixotto arrived in 1835 to teach at Willoughby Medical College, and in 1839 a group of 15 men and women from Unsleben, Bavaria, joined Simson Thorman and founded the Israelitic Society. Prior to the Civil War, five other Jewish communities were founded: *Columbus (1838); *Dayton (1850); Hamilton (1855); Piqua (1858); and Portsmouth (1858). Throughout the German Jewish immigration period (through the 1870s) communities were also established in Youngstown, *Akron, *Toledo, and Canton. With little overt antisemitism, Jews were elected to public office. Marcus Frankel served as mayor of Columbus, and William Kraus and Guido Marx were mayors of Toledo.

Cincinnati's Jewish community played a significant national role in the development of the Reform movement. Rabbi Isaac Mayer *Wise founded *The Israelite* in 1854, the first English language newspaper published west of the Allegheny Mountains. In 1855 he convened a national conference in an attempt to unify American Jewry, which, while unable to achieve that goal, was successful in producing *Minhag America*, a new prayer book co-edited by Rabbi Isador *Kalisch, then rabbi of Cleveland's Tifereth Israel. Wise organized the Union of American Hebrew Congregations in 1873 and in 1875 founded the first American rabbinical seminary, Hebrew Union College.

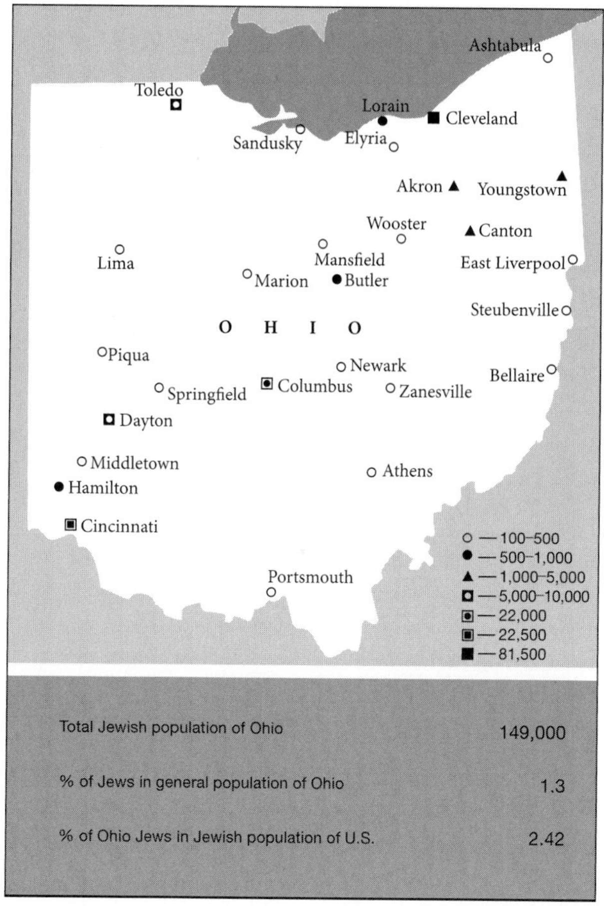

Jewish communities in Ohio. Population figures for 2001.

With the influx of eastern European immigration beginning in the 1880s, the largest of Ohio's Jewish communities created complex organizational structures, which often included federations, social settlements, educational bureaus, hospitals, homes for the aged, schools, labor unions, and social and benevolent societies. Economically, peddling and small businesses led to larger enterprises and the professions. Some nationally known businesses emerging from Ohio were the B. Manischewitz Company and the Federated Department Stores, founded in Cincinnati, and the Cleveland-based American Greetings Corporation and Forest City Enterprises.

In the 20th century there were six Jewish mayors in Cincinnati; Howard M. Metzenbaum, a Democrat from Cleveland, was a United States senator for 17 years; Gilbert Bettman and Lee Fisher were state attorneys general. Pauline Steinem, a suffragist from Toledo, was the first woman to serve on the Toledo Board of Education, and Mary Belle Grossman, an attorney from Cleveland, was the first woman municipal judge in the United States. Sally *Priesand, raised in Cleveland and ordained at Hebrew Union College in 1972, was the first woman rabbi in the United States. Rabbi Abba Hillel *Silver was a leader in the international Zionist movement; rabbis Arthur J. *Lelyveld and Sylvan Ruslander were active in the civil rights movement.

After World War II, there was increased movement of Jewish populations to the suburbs of Roselawn, Golf Manor, and Amberley Village of Cincinnati; Bexley of Columbus; and the "Heights" – Shaker, Cleveland, and University – of Cleveland, as well as Beachwood, which became about 80 percent Jewish.

In 2001 the major Jewish communities in Ohio were in the metropolitan areas of Cleveland (81,500), Cincinnati (22,500), Columbus (22,000), Dayton (5,000), Akron (3,500), Toledo (5,900), Youngstown (3,200), and Canton (1,500). These eight cities and their suburbs all have federations or community councils. The eight federations work together on a state-wide basis to support the Government Affairs Committee of Ohio Jewish Communities, located in Columbus, the state capital. There are more than 100 synagogues in the state, 14 day schools, and seven Anglo-Jewish newspapers: *Akron Jewish News*, *American Israelite* (Cincinnati), *Cleveland Jewish News*, *Dayton Jewish Observer*, *Jewish Journal* (Youngstown), *Ohio Jewish Chronicle* and *The New Standard* (both Columbus), *Stark Jewish News* (Canton area), and the *Toledo Jewish News*.

There are three institutes of higher Jewish learning in Ohio: the Hebrew Union College-Jewish Institute of Religion, mentioned above; the Laura and Alvin Siegal College of Judaic Studies in Beachwood; and the Telshe Yeshiva (Wickliffe). All three train either rabbis or educators. Several of Ohio's universities offer Jewish studies majors and graduate level degrees, as well as provide Hillel Foundation meeting centers for students. In addition, a number of prominent families have established foundations that support local, national and international educational efforts, including the Melton, Schottenstein, and Wexner families of Columbus, and the Mandel and Stone families of Cleveland. The Klau Library and the Jacob Rader Marcus Center for the American Jewish Archives (AJA) are located on the campus of Hebrew Union College-Jewish Institute of Religion in Cincinnati. A major repository of written and audio-visual American Jewish history, the AJA publishes the *American Jewish Archives Journal*. A second source of Jewish archives material in the state, focusing on northeast Ohio, is at the Western Reserve Historical Society in Cleveland. There are two Jewish museums: the Skirball Museum at the Hebrew Union College, which also houses the Center for Holocaust and Humanity Education; a second, the Milton and Tamar Maltz Museum of Jewish Heritage, opened in 2005 in Beachwood. It is to include The Temple-Tifereth Israel's distinguished collection of international Judaica and a new interactive presentation of local American Jewish history.

BIBLIOGRAPHY: J.A. Avner, "Judaism," in: T.S. Butalia and D.P. Small (eds.), *Religion in Ohio* (2004).

[Jane Avner (2nd ed.)]

OHOLIAB (Heb. אָהֳלִיאָב; "the [divine] father is a [or "my"] tent," or, "tent of the father"), son of Ahisamach; of the tribe of Dan. Oholiab was appointed, together with *Bezalel, to construct the Tent of Meeting and its furnishings (Ex. 31:6; 35:34;

36:1–2; 38:23). He is said to have been a "carver and designer, and embroiderer in blue, purple, and crimson yarns, and in fine linen" (Ex. 35:35; 38:23).

BIBLIOGRAPHY: Noth, Personennamen, 158–9.

OHOLOT (Heb. אָהֳלוֹת; "tents"), the second tractate in the Mishnah order of **Tohorot*. It deals with the ritual impurity conveyed by a corpse (or parts of it) either through physical contact, or through being under a common roof. There are 18 chapters both in the Mishnah and the Tosefta. The original name of the tractate was *Ahilot* (literally, "overtenting"), by which name it is called both in the Tosefta and when it is mentioned in the *Gemara*. It also occurs in several manuscripts of the Mishnah. The name *Oholot* is a popularization attributable to the influence of the passage in Numbers 19:14: "Whoever dies in a tent." There is no *Gemara* to this tractate either in the Palestinian or Babylonian Talmud. Nevertheless, the great amount of commentary on it scattered in both Talmuds is reflected in the fact that G. Leiner published a large "synthetic" *Gemara* on the tractate by assembling and arranging all this material in an orderly manner. The Talmud (Ḥag. 11a) itself notes that the biblical treatment of the subject, consisting as it does of only four verses (Num. 19:11, 14, 16, 22), is very meager, yet rabbinic exposition has made *Oholot* one of the larger tractates of the Mishnah. The ritual uncleanness conveyed by a corpse is of the severest degree (lasting seven days) and requires sprinkling with water mixed with the ashes of the *Red Heifer (see **Parah*) as part of the purification procedure. With the destruction of the Temple, this type of ritual purification became impossible to observe and it lapsed a century or so later. The laws of the tractate, however, retained their relevance for those of priestly descent, who, except in the case of close relatives, must avoid contact with the dead.

Like most tractates of the Mishnah, *Oholot* is composed of several layers. The basic layer (although not the earliest) reflects the teaching of R. Akiva, primarily as taught by his disciple R. Meir. Other sections reflect the interpretation of R. Akiva's teachings by other pupils: Judah, Simeon, and Yose. Because the greater part of the first tractate, *Kelim*, in this same Mishnah order is rightly attributed to R. Yose, several scholars were formerly of the opinion that *Oholot* was also largely written by him. It has been recently demonstrated, however, that the role of R. Yose in this tractate is even less than of his colleagues. English translations of the Mishnah were published by H. Danby (1939) and P. Blackman (1955), and J. Neusner published a translation of both the Mishnah (1991) and the Tosefta (2002) of *Tohorot*.

BIBLIOGRAPHY: G. Leiner, *Sidrei Tohorot*, 2 (1903); H.L. Strack, *Introduction to the Talmud and Midrash* (1945), 60f.; A. Goldberg (ed), *Massekhet Oholot* (1955). **ADD. BIBLIOGRAPHY:** J.N. Epstein, *The Gaonic Commentary on the Order Toharot* (Heb.) (1982); S. Lieberman, *Tosefet Rishonim*, vol. 3 (1939); J. Neusner, *A History of the Mishnaic Laws of Purities* (1974–77), vol. 4–5; idem, *From Mishnah to Scripture* (1984), 45–51; idem, *The Mishnah Before 70* (1987), 269–90; idem, *The Philosophical Mishnah 3* (1989), 47–59; idem, *Purity in Rabbinic Judaism* (1994), 88–95.

[Abraham Goldberg]

OHRBACH, family of U.S. department store founders and owners. NATHAN M. OHRBACH (1885–1972) was born in Vienna and taken to the United States at the age of two. He went into the retail dry goods business and opened his own store in 1911. He established his first department store in New York City in 1923 and another in Newark in 1930. In 1935 he published his memoirs, *Getting Ahead in Retailing*. After his retirement in 1940, his son JEROME KANE OHRBACH (1907–1990), who was born in Brooklyn, became the head of the firm and its affiliates. In 1948 he added the Los Angeles store to the two his father had founded. Both father and son were prominent in numerous general and Jewish public organizations, including New York's Federation of Jewish Philanthropies, the American Jewish Committee, the Boy Scouts, and the City University of New York.

The Orbach's chain had branches across the country until 1987, when the New York store went out of business. The company was bought out by Howland-Steinbach, and the stores reopened under that name.

BIBLIOGRAPHY: T. Mahoney and L. Sloane, *Great Merchants* (1966), 310–23.

[Joachim O. Ronall / Ruth Beloff (2nd ed.)]

OIL OF LIFE. There appears to have been a tradition in certain circles according to which the tree of life in the Garden of Eden was an olive tree (a tradition which is not found in Talmud or Midrash, cf. Ber. 40a; Gen. R. 15:7). As a result there emerged the belief that immortality is gained by anointing with oil. According to *Apocalypsis Mosis* 9:3, 13:1–2, when Adam fell ill Seth went to the garden to request "the oil of mercy" with which to anoint Adam and restore his health. His entreaty was refused, but the angel Michael promised that oil would be granted to the righteous at the end of days. In the parallel passage in the Latin *Vitae Adae* the oil is referred to as "the tree of mercy from which the oil of life flows" (ch. 36, cf. 40, 41). The same tradition is to be found in the Acts of Pilate (Gospel of Nicodemus III (XIX). This oil is perhaps to be identified with the heavenly oil with which Enoch is anointed and which transforms him into a heavenly being. Called "the good oil," it is shining and fragrant (II En. 9 = 22:8–9, cf. 14 = 56:2). A further reference to the tree of life in the Garden of Eden as an oil-yielding tree may be found in IV Ezra 2:12 – "*lignum vitae erit in illis in odorem unguenti*" – and this idea is also perhaps to be discerned in the Acts of Thomas §157. The furthest circulation of this concept is to be observed in Pseudo-Clement, *Recognitiones* 1:45 which again refers explicitly to the oil of the tree of life. The legend of Seth's quest for the oil had various later developments and acquired considerable importance in Christian legend and art.

BIBLIOGRAPHY: Ginzberg, Legends, 5 (1925), 119; E.M.C. Quinn, *Quest of Seth for the Oil of Life* (1962).

[Michael E. Stone]

OILS (Heb. שֶׁמֶן; יִצְהָר, "new oil"; תַּמְרוּק, מֶרְקָחָה, "ointment"), unctuous, inflammable substances, usually liquid, obtained from animal, vegetable, or mineral matter. In Job 29:6 and Deuteronomy 32:13, the references to oil flowing from rocks are hyperboles for fertility or prosperity.

Regarded as one of the characteristic products of the Land of Israel (II Kings 18:32; Jer. 40:10), oil served as an element in food (I Kings 17:12), as a cosmetic (Eccles. 9:7–8), as a fuel for lamps (Ex. 25:6), as a medicine (Isa. 1:6), and as a principal export in foreign trade (I Kings 5:25). As oil was apparently applied to leather shields to keep them supple, the expression "to oil a shield" (*mashaḥ magen*) came to be an idiom for "to make war" (Isa. 21:5). As an extension of its use in the preparation of food, oil occupied a place in sacrifices. As an extension of its cosmetic function, it played a role in various investiture proceedings.

The olives were beaten down from the tree with poles (Isa. 17:6) and were pounded into pulp in mortars or by the feet (Micah 6:15). The pulp was placed in wicker baskets from which the lightest and finest oil could easily run off. This grade of oil, known as beaten oil (Heb. *shemen katit*), is mentioned five times in the Bible. It served as fuel for the lamp in the Tabernacle (Ex. 27:20; Lev. 24:2) and as an element in the obligatory daily meal offerings (Ex. 29:40; Num. 28:5). King Solomon traded this type of oil with Hiram of Tyre in exchange for cedar and cypress wood (I Kings 5:25). After the removal of the beaten oil, a second grade was produced by heating and further pressing the pulp (for the method of extraction in the talmudic period see Mishnah Men. 8:4–5 and *Olive). Ointments were made by boiling aromatic substances in oil (Job. 41:23).

Oil was one of the three staples of life. Thus while Jacob prayed for bread to eat and clothing to wear (Gen. 28:20), Hosea described Israel's basic needs as bread and water, wool and flax, oil and drink (Hos. 2:7). As a typical product of Palestine and as a necessity, oil is listed, particularly in Deuteronomy, among the three blessings of the land in time of God's favor – grain, wine, and oil (Deut. 11:14, etc.) The same three shall be consumed by the nation that will rise against Israel from afar if Israel should lose God's favor through disobedience to His laws (Deut. 28:38–40, 51). S.M. Paul calls attention to the triad of basic needs – food, clothing, and oil – mentioned throughout the Mesopotamian legal tradition, and supports that the three necessities with which a master must provide a slave-girl, referred to in Exodus 21:7–11 are meat, clothing, and oil.

In addition, anointing with oil provided protection from the sun. As an element in baking (Num. 11:8; I Kings 7:12), oil played a role also in sacrifices, which are called God's bread (Heb. *leḥem 'Elohim*, Lev. 21:6). The obligatory daily morning and evening burnt offerings included a tenth of a measure of choice flour mixed with a quarter *hin* of beaten oil (Ex. 29:40; Num. 28:5). An individual's voluntary meal offering could be of five types, all of which included oil. These were (1) raw flour on which oil and frankincense were poured; (2) unleavened cakes mixed with oil; (3) unleavened wafers spread with oil; (4) broken griddle cakes on which oil was poured; and (5) choice flour fried in oil (Lev. 21:1–7).

The amount of oil and flour for the personal offering was determined in proportion to the size of the accompanying animal sacrifice according to the following scale: sheep, a tenth of a measure of fine flour and a quarter *hin* of oil; ram, two-tenths of a measure of flour and one-third of a *hin* of oil: ox, three-tenths of a measure of flour and a half *hin* of oil.

Oil was regarded as a symbol of honor (Judg. 9:9), joy (Ps. 45:8), and favor (Deut. 33:24; Ps. 23:5). Therefore, oil was to be withheld from offerings associated with disgrace, sorrow, and disfavor, just as it was withheld from the body in time of mourning (II Sam. 12:20; Dan. 10:3; see *Mourning). Thus it is stated with reference to the special sacrifice offered when a man suspects his wife of adultery: "No oil shall be poured upon it and no frankincense should be laid on it, for it is a meal offering of remembrance which recalls wrong doing" (Num. 5:15). Likewise the choice flour of a sin offering is to be free of both oil and frankincense (Lev. 5:11).

In the ritual purification of a person who has recovered from leprosy oil plays a major role. The sacrifice offered on the eighth day of the procedure includes an offering of choice flour mixed with oil and the presentation of a *log* of oil – the largest measure of oil called for in any biblical rite. Some of the oil is sprinkled "before the Lord" seven times, as was blood. Some is placed on the right ear, right thumb, and right big toe of the recovered leper, where blood has already been placed; that which is left over is poured on his head. These rites symbolize the restoration of God's favor and the return of honor and joy to a man who had previously been disgraced and who had observed rites characteristic of mourning (Lev. 13:45). From the association of oil with vigor and fertility (Ps. 36:9), as, for example, in the term "son of oil" (Heb. *ben shemen*) for "fertile" (Isa. 5:1), it may be surmised that the sprinkling of the leper with oil is also symbolic of his restoration to life since the Talmud regards the leper as "a dead person" (Ned. 64b).

Virtue is frequently likened to fragrant oil (Ps. 133:2; Song 1:3; Eccles. 7:1) because both are so costly to obtain. Thus wisdom writers warn against extravagant use of oil (Prov. 21:17, 20), while the historical books of the Bible testify to its having been guarded as were silver and gold (I Chron. 9:29; 27:28). Perfumed oil was among the treasures which Hezekiah revealed to Merodach-Baladan (II Kings 20:13; Isa. 39:2). As a symbol of affluence, Isaiah (28:1, 4) associates oil with arrogance.

As an element in the normal grooming of all classes of people in the Ancient Near East, anointing with oil, like the washing that preceded and the dressing that followed it (Ezek. 16:9–10; Ruth 3:3), was symbolic of a change in status throughout the Ancient Near East. The practice of anointing in legal and cultic proceedings is to be understood in the light of the role of ablutions and the changing of garments. The Bible speaks frequently of donning victory (e.g., Isa. 59:7), honor (Ps. 104:1), disgrace (Job 8:22), etc. Likewise, it prescribes washing as the key to ritual purity (Ex. 30:20; Lev. 22:6, etc.).

It is not surprising, therefore, that the consecration of Aaron to the priesthood included washing (Lev. 8:6), donning special garments (Lev. 8:7–9), and anointing his head with oil (Lev. 8:12). The consecration of Aaron's sons as priests also included these three elements (Lev. 8:6, 13, 30).

Akkadian documents from Ugarit mention the anointing of manumitted slave girls, while the Middle Assyrian laws (sections 42–43; Pritchard, Texts, 183–4) prescribe the anointing of the bride prior to marriage. In the Bible, God instructs Elijah to appoint Elisha a prophet by anointing him with oil (I Kings 19:16). Similarly, the spirit of the Lord is said to have come upon King David from the time he was anointed (I Sam. 16:13). Both in Ugarit (V AB, B 31ff.; Pritchard, Texts, 136) and in the Bible (Lev. 8:10–11), anointing with oil is associated with the dedication of temples as well as of people. Thus Jacob dedicates an altar at Beth-El by anointing it with oil (Gen. 28:18).

The anointing of kings, attested among peoples of the Ancient Near East only in Israel and among the Hittites, is mentioned in the Bible in connection with Saul (I Sam. 10:1), David (I Sam. 16:1), Solomon (I Kings 1:39), Absalom (II Sam. 19:11), Jehoash (II Kings 11:12), Jehoahaz (II Kings 23:30), and Hazael of Aram and Jehu son of Nimshi of Israel (I Kings 19:15–16). While Saul, David, Hazael, and Jehu were anointed by prophets, Solomon and Jehoash were anointed by priests. Of Absalom and Jehoahaz it is simply stated that "they anointed him." This last expression may be simply an idiom meaning "they made him king." It is certainly in this sense that Jotham employs the phrase in Judges 9:8: "the trees went to anoint (Heb. *limshoaḥ*) over them a king." Likewise the noun "anointed one" (Heb. *mashi'aḥ*) is employed as a poetic synonym for "king" (Heb. *melekh*; II Sam. 22:51). Deutero-Isaiah thus calls Cyrus the Lord's "anointed" (Isa. 45:1), while he refers to the rulers whom the Lord will subdue for Cyrus simply as "kings." Psalm 2:2 similarly contrasts the Lord's "anointed," the Davidic king of Zion, with the "kings of the earth." It is understandable, therefore, that "anointed" should eventually be the term for the human instrument of eschatological redemption (see *Messiah and *Anointing).

As a typical product of the land of Israel with so many diverse uses, oil played an important part in Israel's relations with her neighbors. Thus King Solomon traded 1,000 *kor* of wheat and 20 *kor* of beaten oil annually in exchange for a steady supply of cedar and cypress wood from Sidon (I Kings 5:24–25; II Chron. 2:14–15). Likewise, the same trade was revived in the sixth century by those who returned in the days of Zerubabbel and Jeshua (Ezra 3:7). Hosea 12:2 mentions sending oil to Egypt. D.J. McCarthy notes that the expression "oil is sent to…" in that context appears to be a synonym for "conclude a treaty." If so, the idiom is typical of treaty terminology like "to dissect a calf" (Jer. 34:18), "covenant of salt" (Num. 8:19) and the Greek σπονδη "treaty," "libations" – all examples of synechdoche.

[Mayer Irwin Gruber]

In the Talmud

Although, as stated above, the only oil employed to any extent in biblical times was *olive oil, in the period of the Talmud, many other oils (and fats) were in common use. Those oils and fats were animal, mineral, and especially vegetable. The first two Mishnayot of the second chapter of tractate *Shabbat* give a comprehensive list: pitch, wax, *kik*-oil, tail fat, tallow, both melted and solid, sesame oil, nut oil, fish oil, colocynth oil, tar, and naphtha. The wax was the residue from honey. There is a controversy as to the identity of *kik*. The identification accepted today is that it is identical with the *kikayon* of Jonah 4:6, i.e., castor oil, which is mentioned in the Talmud (Shab. 21a), but two alternative suggestions are made: one that it is produced from a fish of that name (despite the fact that fish oil is specifically mentioned in the next Mishnah) while another opinion is that it is cottonseed oil. In the Jerusalem Talmud (Shab. 2:1, 4c) it is also regarded as of animal origin, but derived from a bird and it is even identified with the *ka'at* (JPS "pelican") of Leviticus 11:18. Symmachus declares that the only animal oil which may be used for the Sabbath lamp is fish oil and there is no doubt that other oils of animal origin were known and used for secular purposes (Shab. 25b).

An account of the availability of various oils is given in a protest against the opinion of Tarfon that only olive oil may be used for the Sabbath lamp: "What shall the Babylonians then do, who have only sesame oil, or the people of Medea who have only nut oil, or the Alexandrians who have only radish oil, or the people of Cappadocia who have none of these, but only naphtha?" (Shab. 26a). Sesame oil was, as is suggested in this passage, the most common oil in Babylonia, as olive oil was in Ereẓ Israel. As a result, if a man took a vow to abstain from oil without specifying which, in Ereẓ Israel it was taken to refer to olive oil, but in Babylonia to sesame (Ned. 53a). They fulfilled the same needs, for fuel, light, and food. Although extensively cultivated (BB 106a, Git. 73a), they were comparatively expensive and stated to be dearer than wheat, dates, or pomegranates (BM 21a, 104b). Oil presses are mentioned in Nehardea and Pumbedita (BK 27b).

To a different category belong balsam oil and rose oil, which were used as unguents. The former was too volatile and inflammable to be used as fuel, and a case is actually cited of a mother-in-law planning and carrying out the murder of her daughter-in-law by telling her to adorn herself with it and then light the lamp (Shab. 26a). Rose oil was so expensive in Ereẓ Israel that its use was limited to "princes"; in Sura in Babylonia, however, it was in plentiful supply and therefore used by all (Shab. 111b).

[Louis Isaac Rabinowitz]

BIBLIOGRAPHY: E. Kutsch, *Die Salbung als Rechtsakt im Alten Testament und im alten Orient* (ZAWB, 87, 1963); D.J. McCarthy, in: VT, 14 (1964), 215–21; J.S. Licht, in: EM, 5 (1968), 526–31; S.M. Paul, in: JNES, 28 (1969), 48–53; Krauss, Tal Arch, 1 (1910), 234–7; 2 (1911), 211–27; J. Newman, *Agriculture Life of the Jews in Babylonia* (1932), 101–4.

OISTRAKH, DAVID FEDOROVICH (1908–1974), Russian violin virtuoso. Born in Odessa, Oistrakh studied the violin from the age of five with *Stoljarsky, made his first public appearance in 1914, and attended the Institute of Music and Drama in Odessa, 1923–26. After winning other prizes he gained international attention when he won the first prize at the Queen Elizabeth competition in Brussels in 1937. Attached to the Moscow Conservatory, he became professor in 1939 and head of the violin department in 1950. On his subsequent world tours he performed in Paris and London in 1953, in the U.S. in 1955, and was acknowledged everywhere as a master. From 1961 he also appeared as a conductor. Foremost Soviet composers (Prokofiev, Miaskovsky, Shostakovich, Khachaturian) wrote violin works for him, and he received many Soviet awards. His son IGOR OISTRAKH (1931–), also a violinist, studied with his father at the Moscow Conservatory (1949–55). Winner of the International Festival of Democratic Youth in Budapest (1949) and the Wieniawski International Contest in 1952, he became a teacher of violin at Moscow Conservatory in 1958, and often appeared in duets with his father.

BIBLIOGRAPHY: Baker, Biog Dict; MGG; Riemann-Gurlitt; V. Bronin, *David Oystrakh* (Rus., 1954); D. Oistrakh, in: *Sovetskaya Muzyka*, 22:9 (1958), 98–105.

[Michael Goldstein]

OKHLAH VE-OKHLAH (Heb. אָכְלָה וְאָכְלָה), early collection of masoretic notes to the Bible text, arranged partly alphabetically and partly in the order of the books of the Bible. Its date and author are unknown but it was mentioned for the first time by Jonah ibn Janāḥ in the tenth century (Abu al-Walīd Marwān ibn Janāḥ, cf. חלך), by whom it was considered the most important book on the subject. Originally called *Ha-Masoret ha-Gedolah* by Rashi and R. Jacob Tam, its present name, first mentioned by R. David Kimḥi (*Sefer Shorashim*, ed. Biesenthal-Lebrecht (1864), 334 cf. קרב), derives from the opening words of the first section, which is an alphabetic list of pairs of words occurring only twice in the Bible (once with *waw* and once without), i.e., *okhlah* (1 Sam. 1:9) and *ve-okhlah* (Gen. 27:19). Jacob b. Ḥayyim gained most of his information for the *masora finalis* (list of masoretic notes found at the end of a Bible, as opposed to the *masora marginalis* written on the sides of its pages) from *Okhlah ve-Okhlah* for his Bomberg edition of the Bible (Venice, 1524/5).

After lying in obscurity for over 300 years it was rediscovered and published by S. Frensdorff (*Das Buch Ochlah W'ochlah*, 1864), and shortly afterwards a second manuscript was discovered by H. Hupfeld. Hupfeld's manuscript contains 120 citations more than Frensdorff, and it is concluded that the book was expanded over the centuries (see Graetz, bibl.). In 1954 F. Diaz Esteban prepared a critical edition of the work as a Ph.D. dissertation and published it later, in 1975.

BIBLIOGRAPHY: E. Wuerthwein, *The Text of the Old Testament* (1957), 21–22; S. Frensdorff, *Das Buch Ochlah W'ochlah* (1864), introd.; H. Hupfeld, in: ZDMG, 21 (1867), 201–20; Graetz, in: MGWJ 36 (1887), 1–34. **ADD. BIBLIOGRAPHY:** F. Diaz Esteban, *Sefer 'Oklah we-'Oklah* – Colección de Listas de Palabras Destinadas a Conservar la Integridad del Texto Hebreo de la Biblia entre los Judios del a Edad Media (critical edition,1975).

OKLAHOMA, state in south central United States. The Jewish population in 2001 was about 5,000 out of a general population of 3,453,000. The vast majority resided in Tulsa and Oklahoma City, the two large metropolitan areas of the state. Extensive white settlement began with the famous "run" of April 22, 1889. Jews began coming to Oklahoma and Indian Territory as early as 1875. There were also Jews in the "run" of 1889. Leo Meyer of Tulsa was active in state political offices in the early territorial and statehood days. In 1890 High Holiday services were conducted in Oklahoma City. In Ardmore there were 50 Jewish people in 1890 and about 100 in 1907, when a Reform congregation, Temple Emeth, was organized. In the 1890s Jake Katz went to Stillwater and prospered. In Perry, a Jew named Kretsch arrived in 1892 from his native Bohemia. Subsequently he served as mayor of the town for three or four terms. Seymor C. Heyman arrived in Oklahoma City in 1901, eventually served as president of the local Chamber of Commerce, and later became president of the school board, the only Jew to hold these offices in Oklahoma. Sam and Dave Daube of Ardmore and the Sondheimer family of Muskogee were famed for their philanthropy. Dave Schonwald, a Hungarian immigrant, came to Oklahoma Territory before the turn of the 20th century, served as a penniless section hand on the Santa Fe Railroad in Guthrie, and subsequently became president of a gas and oil company and a bank in Blackwell, ending his days as a prominent Oklahoma City businessman and Jewish leader.

Enid Jewish history began with the Cherokee Strip opening in 1885, when Marius Gottschalk made the "run." In Tecumseh the Krouch brothers, German immigrants, came from Kansas and Colorado to establish a business in the early 1890s. A new elementary school building stands as a memorial to the philanthropy of Max Krouch, while his brother, Julius, who was elected county commissioner in Pottawatomie County in 1916, and sister Erna, who survived Max, continued to contribute lavishly to Jewish and non-Jewish causes. Julius Krouch was a delegate to the Democratic Convention in Denver in 1908 which nominated William Jennings Bryan for president. Max Krouch was chairman of the Excise Board in Pottawatomie County under three governors (Bill Murray, Phillips, and Kerr), until he died in 1948. He also was chairman of the Draft Board in Pottawatomie County during World War II.

In Oklahoma City a Reform congregation, Temple B'nai Israel, was chartered in 1903. Gus Paul, who came from Evansville, Indiana, was a moving figure in the life of the congregation for many years. He was a prominent civic leader and served the municipal government as city attorney. The first ordained rabbi to serve a congregation in Oklahoma was Joseph Blatt. He came in 1906 to minister to the 35 families of Temple B'nai Israel. The Jewish population did not expand in proportion to the growth of the general population. In 1967 the temple's membership numbered 325 families, representing about

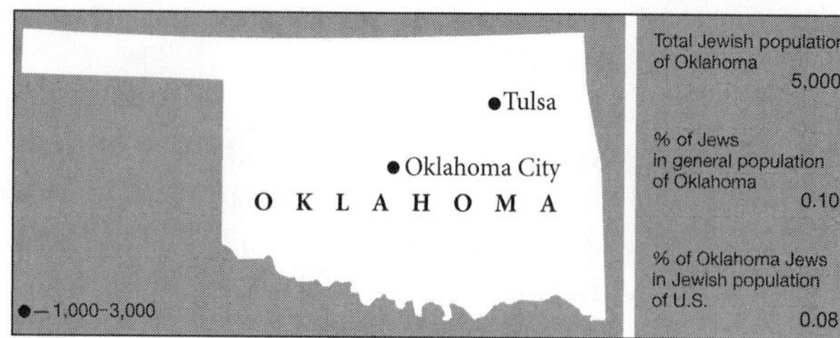

Jewish communities in Oklahoma. Population figures for 2001.

half of the Jewish population of the city. In 1904 Emanuel Synagogue was organized as an Orthodox congregation. It is now affiliated with the Conservative movement and also embraces about half of the Jewish population of Oklahoma City in its membership. A Jewish community council was organized in 1941 to serve as a fund raising and social service agency.

In Tulsa, Temple Israel (Reform) was organized in 1914. Its first rabbi came in 1917. Orthodox congregation B'nai Emunah has its origins in a *minyan* begun by Latvian immigrants in 1903. The Jewish community council of Tulsa was founded in 1938 to raise funds for national and overseas relief. Early Tulsa Jewish life sponsored the Federation of Jewish Charities – taken over by the Tulsa Community Fund – a Mutual Aid Bank, and a Hebrew Free Loan Society.

Muskogee Jewish history began with the arrival of Joseph Sondheimer in 1881. Alexander, the former's son, was the first court reporter in Oklahoma in 1891. Temple Beth Ahabah, the Reform congregation, was founded in 1905 and was heavily supported and endowed by the Sondheimer family.

Oklahoma Jewry, small though it has been, has participated significantly in the development of every aspect of the state's life. Jews were representatives in the first territorial legislature. There were also Jews in the convention which decided that the Indian Territory and Oklahoma Territory should enter the Union as a single state. A number of Jews served in the state legislature through the years. Some have been elected judges and county commissioners, and have held important state and municipal appointive positions. There are Reform synagogues in Ardmore and Muskogee, as well as Ponca City and Seminole. Oklahoma City, which includes the University of Oklahoma at Norman, has three synagogues: Conservative, Reform, and Chabad, as well as a *mikveh* and a Jewish population of some 2,600 people. Tulsa supports the Charles Schusterman JCC, the Sherwin Miller Museum of Jewish Art; a Conservative Congregation B'nai Emunah, as well as a Reform and Chabad Congregation. The Tulsa *Jewish Review* is published monthly, and the Heritage Hebrew Academy is the Tulsa day school. Although small in number, the Oklahoma Jewish community has had national influence. In the early part of the 20th century, Yeshiva University president Bernard Dov *Revel had business interests and spent considerable time in Tulsa. Irvin Frank was an early chairman of the National Jewish Conference Center, the precursor of CLAL, and Charles Goodall, established the small cities program on the Council of Jewish Federations. The Charles and Lynn Schusterman family are among the mega givers who support Jewish life throughout the country, and their family foundation is among the most important in the United States. The scope of their philanthropic work has given them international outreach. Among their largest gifts were $11.25 million to Synagogue Transformation and Renewal (STAR), a Chicago-based philanthropic partnership committed to enhancing synagogues and increasing their potential to connect and inspire Jews in North American Jewish communities; $10 million to the University of Oklahoma to establish the Schusterman Center at the University of Oklahoma in Tulsa, expanding the OU presence and providing the cohesiveness, facilities, and organizational identity to aid in future program development for the Tulsa campus; $5 million to the World Union of Progressive Judaism to help complete Mercaz Shimshon (Samson Center), a new cultural center in Jerusalem named in honor of Mr. Schusterman's father; $1.5 million to the Partnership for Excellence in Jewish Education (PEJE); an initiative designed to meet the challenge of providing excellent Jewish education for K-12 with the goal of ensuring a Jewish presence into the next century.

They helped build Succat Shalom: The Jerusalem Center for Children and their Families, the Parent-Child Center of Tulsa, and the Schusterman-Benson Library in Tulsa.

BIBLIOGRAPHY: C.I. Cooper, in: *Oklahoma Jewish Chronicle* (Dec. 1929 and March 1930).

[Joseph Levenson / Michael Berenbaum (2nd ed.)]

OKO, ADOLPH S. (1883–1944), librarian and expert on Spinoza. Born near Kharkov, Russia, Oko received his education in Germany and went to the United States (1902), where he worked in the Astor Library, New York. In 1906 he was appointed librarian of Hebrew Union College, Cincinnati, retaining the position until 1933 when he resigned. Under his administration the college library was transformed. A new building, designed to hold 40,000 volumes, was opened in 1913, but so great was the rate of expansion that a second building was needed in 1931. In 1911 he began a collection of Spinozana, which he brought to unusual completeness. He also began the development of the college museum. Shortly after World War I Oko visited Europe and purchased 18,000 items, including the Edward Birnbaum music collection as well as manuscripts and printed books. Throughout his life Oko was a devoted student of Spinoza. He was a trustee of the Domus Spinozana at The Hague and a founder and U.S. secretary of the Societas Spinoza. From 1933 to 1938 he devoted himself to research on Spinoza in England, resulting in *The Spinoza Bibliography* (1964). In addition he wrote several bibliographies, among them: *Solomon Schechter, a Bibliography* (1938) and *Bibliography of… Kaufman Kohler* (1913). He also wrote many articles in *Menorah-Journal*, of which he was associate editor for many years. After returning to the United States he joined the staff of the American Jewish Committee and was associate editor of the *Contemporary Jewish Record* in 1943/44.

OLAH, GEORGE A. (1922–), U.S. chemist and Nobel laureate. Born in Budapest, Hungary, he was educated at the Gymnasium of the Piarist Fathers. After surviving the last months of World War II in hiding in Budapest, he graduated in chemistry from the Technical University, Budapest (1954). He worked in the Central Chemical Research Institute of the Hungarian Academy of Sciences until the failed uprising, when he left Hungary in December 1956 first for London, where he was sympathetically received, and in 1957 for North America. He worked initially in Sarnia, Ontario, and subsequently in Framingham, Mass., for Dow Chemical. In 1965 he joined Western Reserve University in Cleveland, Ohio, and later became chairman of its chemistry department when it merged with that of Case Institute of Technology. In 1977 he moved to the University of Southern California in Los Angeles to head its newly established Loker Institute of Hydrocarbon Research, a center for research and graduate training. He was director of research and Donald P. and Katherine B. Loker Distinguished Professor of Chemistry. Olah's initial research concerned carbocation, the process by which hydrocarbons, consisting of carbon and hydrogen, become positively charged. However the instability of these short-lived intermediate products made them very difficult to study. He faced formidable practical difficulties in impoverished post-war Hungary and scientific scepticism. However, he was able to pursue this research after he joined Dow Chemicals. He succeeded in preparing a wide range of carbocations that were sufficiently stable for detailed analysis by using extremely strong "superacids." His findings launched a very active field of research which led to the synthesis of many new, more complex hydrocarbons. He was awarded the Nobel Prize for chemistry in 1994 for his work on carbocations. His research has greatly influenced the study of bond making and breaking in organic chemistry and the development of "superelectrophiles" with increased reactivity. His findings also have practical applications of major importance for hydrocarbon technology, which he continued to explore at the Loker Institute. These include the more efficient utilization and extraction of fossil fuels and the recycling of carbon dioxide into useful products while reducing the build-up of carbon products in the atmosphere. Other projects include the conversion of methane and methanol into fuels and the production of new materials for use in electrical engineering, optics, and biomedical devices. He was the author or co-author of many standard texts on these subjects. His many honors include election to the U.S. National Academy of Sciences (1976), the American Academy of Arts and Sciences (2002), and the American Philosophical Society (2002), and the award of the Einstein Medal of the Russian Academy of Sciences (2002) and the Priestley Medal of the American Chemical Society (2005).

[Michael Denman (2nd ed.)]

OLAM HA-BA (Heb. עוֹלָם הַבָּא). The term *olam ha-ba* (literally, "the coming world") in contrast to *olam ha-zeh* (literally "this world") refers to the hereafter, which begins with the termination of man's earthly life. This meaning of the expression is clearly implied in the statement of R. Jacob, quoted in *Avot* (4:17): "One moment of repentance and good deeds in this world is better than the entire life of the world to come." The earliest source in which the phrase occurs is Enoch 71:15, which is dated by R.H. Charles (Charles, Apocrypha, 2 (1913), 164) between 105 and 64 B.C.E. A synonym frequently used in place of "the world to come" is *atid lavo* ("What is to come" or "the future") as in Tosefta *Arakhin* 2:7. Often also "the days of the Messiah" are contrasted with the life of this world. An example is the comment by the colleagues of Ben Zoma (1:5) on the phrase "all the days of thy life" (Deut. 16:3) that it includes in addition to this world the era of the Messiah.

Strictly speaking the period referred to by the phrase *olam ha-ba* or its equivalent *atid lavo*, between which and the present order of things comes the age of the Messiah (cf. Zev. 118b; Tosef. Ar. 2:7; also Ar. 13b), is the final order of things beginning with the general resurrection and the last judgment. According to the Palestinian *amora* R. Johanan, the golden age of the future pictured by the prophets concerned only the days of the Messiah. As for the world to come, it is said of it, "Eye hath not seen" (Isa. 64:3). His older contemporary, the Babylonian *amora* Samuel, however, held the view that the only difference between the present time and the Messianic era lay in the fact that Israel's current subjection to the rule of alien empires would cease. The new order of things would, therefore, according to him, first commence after the age of the Messiah was over (cf. Sanh. 99a; Ber. 34b).

A cardinal eschatological doctrine of rabbinic Judaism connected with the world to come was that of the restoration to life of the dead. It is listed as a dogma at the beginning of the tenth chapter of Sanhedrin. "Whoever says that the revivification of the dead is not proved from the Torah," so it is remarked there, "has no portion in the world to come." The matter was, according to Josephus (Wars, 2:8, 14 and Ant. 18:1, 4), one of the chief points of difference between the Pharisees and the Sadducees, the latter asserting that the soul died together with the body. I *Maccabees, which records events down to the time of John Hyrcanus, whose reign began in the year 135 B.C.E., contains no allusion to it. The first definite historical reference to the Pharisees is that which speaks of the rift which took place between them and the aforementioned John Hyrcanus toward the end of his rule (Jos. Ant. 8:10). The Talmud (Kid. 66a) attributes the incident to his son Alexander Yannai. In the canonical Scriptures the first allusion to a return of the dead to life is made in Isaiah 26:19. However, the Sadducees contended (Sanh. 90b) that the statement "Thy dead shall live, my dead bodies shall stand up" might have referred to the dead whom Ezekiel (37:5ff.) had brought back to life in his vision, not to the general resurrection. An unequivocal reference to resurrection is contained in the last chapter of Daniel (7:2), where it is stated: "And many of those that sleep in the dust will wake, these to eternal life, and those to ignominy and eternal abhorrence." The 11th chapter of the Book of

Daniel (21ff.), however, describes events that took place during the rule of Antiochus IV of Syria.

As far as the older books of the Hebrew Scriptures are concerned, man's sojourn on earth is followed by a descent to *Sheol*, which is equivalent to the grave. The patriarch Jacob, upon hearing that his favorite son Joseph had been torn to pieces by a wild beast, moaned that he "would go down in grief to his son in Sheol" (Gen. 37:35). Isaiah (14:3–21) and Ezekiel (31:15–18; 32: 17–32) picture it as a dreary, gloomy place, a land of the shades (Isa. 26:19). In the Book of Job (17:13–16) it is portrayed as an abode of worms and decay. This was also, according to Akavyah b. Mahalalel (Avot 3:1), man's destiny after the termination of his life on earth. "The dead do not praise the Lord," said the Psalmist (115:17), "nor those that go down to the silence [of the grave]." Job entertained no hope of revivification. "But when man lieth down," he remarked gloomily, "he does not rise. Till the heavens be no more they will not awake nor be roused out of their sleep" (14:12).

The rewards and punishment promised in the Hebrew Scriptures as requital for man's actions, as for example in Deuteronomy 13ff. and Jeremiah 3:10ff. were, as *Saadiah Gaon already noted (*Book of Beliefs and Opinions*, 9:2), all of this world. It was in order to reconcile the sufferings of the righteous with divine justice that R. Jacob remarked (Kid. 39b) that "there was no reward for virtue in this world" and that R. Tarfon assured those who would occupy themselves with the study of the Torah that the (full) reward of the righteous would be meted out in the hereafter (Avot. 2:16). As for the nature of man's existence in the world to come, the Babylonian *amora* Rav, who lived at the beginning of the third century B.C.E., was of the opinion that it was quite unlike life in this world. "There is there," he said, "neither eating, nor drinking, nor any begetting of children, no bargaining or jealousy or hatred or strife. All that the righteous do is to sit with their crowns on their heads and enjoy the effulgence of the [divine] Presence" (Ber. 17a). However, no tannaitic parallel to Rav's conception of the world to come has been found; most of his contemporaries and followers believed in the restoration of the souls into the bodies of the resurrected and their rising from their graves fully clothed (Ket. 111b). Even so bold a thinker as Saadiah Gaon, who lived centuries after the redaction of the Talmud, accepted the dogma of physical resurrection. Moses Maimonides included the bodily revivification of the dead among the Thirteen Articles of the Faith in his commentary on the tenth chapter of Mishnah Sanhedrin, though in his *Guide of the Perplexed* he speaks only of the immortality of the soul, which is an incorporated state, and passes over physical resurrection in silence. The traditional Jewish book of prayers includes a praise of God as the revivifier of the dead. The Reformist prayer book omits it completely. As it is expressed in the tenth chapter of the Mishnah of Sanhedrin, all Israelites, with certain notable exceptions, had, in the view of the *tannaim*, a share in world to come. In the opinion of R. Joshua b. Hananiah the righteous among the gentiles were also to be included (Tos. 13:2). Moses Maimonides incorporated his pronouncement in his code, which states: "The pious of the nations of the world have a portion in the world to come" (Yad, Teshuvah 3:5). It is futile to attempt to systematize the Jewish notions of the hereafter. Since its conception belonged to the realm of *aggadah*, great latitude was allowed the individual imagination. It is on this account that there exists considerable ambiguity about the meaning of the phrase *olam ha-ba*. Did it refer to the final state of man or to the one intermediate between the life of this world and the disposition of his soul in either the *Garden of Eden, which is the eternal abode, after the last judgment, of the righteous, or the *gehinnom* (gehenna), the miserable dwelling place of the wicked (Ber. 28b). The question was also asked where the souls of human beings were kept between the time of their death and the resurrection, which is supposed to take place prior to the last judgment. The answer given by R. Yose ha-Gelili was that there were special store-chambers where the souls of the righteous were deposited, as it is stated (I Sam. 25:29): "The souls of the wicked, on the other hand, would, as the verse goes on to say, "be slung away in the hollow of the sling" (Shab. 152b).

BIBLIOGRAPHY: G.F. Moore, *Judaism in the first Centuries of the Christian Era*, 2 (1946), 377–95; Saadiah Gaon, *The Book of Beliefs and Opinions*, tr. by S. Rosenblatt (1948), 323–56; Moses Maimonides, *The Guide of the Perplexed*, tr. by S. Pines (1963), passim; C. Montefiore and H. Loewe, *Rabbinic Anthology* (1938), ch. 31 and index, s.v. *World to Come*; A. Cohen, *Everyman's Talmud* (1932), ch. 11 and index, s.v. *World to Come*; M. Kadushin, *The Rabbinic Mind* (1952), index, s.v. *Olam ha-Ba; World to Come.*

[Samuel Rosenblatt]

OLAN, LEVI ARTHUR (1903–1984), U.S. Reform rabbi and theologian. Olan was born in Russia and immigrated to Rochester, New York, in 1906. He received his B.A. from the University of Cincinnati in 1925 and was ordained by the *Hebrew Union College in 1929. He was awarded a D.D. by HUC-JIR in 1955, and a D.H.L. by Austin College in 1967 and by Southern Methodist University in 1968. He served as rabbi of Temple Emanu-El in Worcester, Massachusetts (1929–49), where he was also president of the United Jewish Charities and an organizer of the People's Forum, sponsoring such speakers as Norman Thomas and Clarence Darrow. In 1949, he was named rabbi of Temple Emanu-El in Dallas, Texas, becoming emeritus in 1970. He also lectured at Southern Methodist University's Perkins School of Theology and at Texas Christian University.

In Dallas, Olan was the host of a popular weekly radio program, which later expanded to television, on the religious issues of life. His courageous attacks on racial segregation earned him the sobriquet "the conscience of Dallas." He was appointed chairman of the city's Housing Authority, a director of the Human Relations Commission, and a regent of the University of Texas.

In the *Central Conference of American Rabbis, Olan was instrumental in establishing a Special Interest Group in Jewish Theology, which he chaired from 1961 to 1965. He also served on the executive board (1946–48, 1969–71) and was elected vice president (1965–67) and then president of the CCAR (1967–68). Additionally, he was vice president of the World Union for Progressive Judaism (1967–68).

As a theologian, Olan described himself as a religious liberal, a rationalist who stressed the role of reason and experience in the search for truth. A philosopher who sought to narrow the gap between conflicting religious and secular points of view, his thinking influenced colleagues, as reflected in the book *A Rational Faith, Essays in Honor of Levi A. Olan* (1984). Olan himself wrote *Judaism and Immortality* (1942, 1971), *Prophetic Faith and the Secular Age* (1982), and *Maturity in an Immature World* (1984; an anthology of his broadcasts).

[Bezalel Gordon (2nd ed.)]

OLBRACHT, IVAN (pseudonym of **Kamil Zeman**; 1882–1952), Czech author and publicist. Olbracht was born in Semily, Bohemia. His mother was Jewish; his father, a non-Jewish writer. Olbracht's early works, *O zlých samotářích* ("Of Evil Lonely Men," 1913), *Žalář nejtemnější* ("Darkest Prison," 1918), and *Podivné přátelství herce Jesenia* ("The Strange Friendship of the Actor Jesenius," 1919), were psychological masterpieces. He became a Communist after a visit to the U.S.S.R. which inspired his *Obrazy ze současného Ruska* ("Pictures from Contemporary Russia," 1920). Later he concentrated on social themes, without, however, embracing "socialist realism."

His *Anna proletářka* ("Anne the Proletarian," 1928) is both a psychological and a social novel, while *Nikola Šuhaj loupežník* ("The Bandit Nikola Šuhaj," 1933) remains, despite its social-revolutionary tendency, a delightful ballad about a "Robin Hood" hero from sub-Carpathian Ruthenia. This poor, eastern region of pre-war Czechoslovakia also provides the setting for three more works by Olbracht: *Země beze jména* ("Land Without a Name, 1932), *Hory a staletí* ("Mountains and Centuries," 1935), and *Golet v údolí* ("*Galut* in the Valley," 1937), the last serving as a literary memorial to ḥasidic life in the sub-Carpathian region. One of his children's books, *Biblické příběhy* ("Bible Tales," 1939), is a modern treatment of Old Testament stories. Olbracht also translated Marx and Engels' *Communist Manifesto* into Czech. He was for some years a member of the Czechoslovak parliament.

BIBLIOGRAPHY: P. Váša and A. Gregor, *Katechismus dějin české literatury* (1925); B. Václavek, *Česká literatura XX. století* (1935); J. Kunc, *Slovník českých spisovatelů beletristů* (1957). **ADD. BIBLIOGRAPHY:** V. Hnízdo, *Ivan Olbracht* (1977): *Lexikon české literatury*, 3/1 (2000); J. Podlešák, *Židé v díle Ivana Olbrachta*, in.: Židovská ročenka (1982–83); *Slovník českých spisovatelů* (2000).

[Avigdor Dagan]

OLDENBURG, city and former state in Lower Saxony, Germany. Jews lived in the city of Oldenburg in the early 14th century. In 1334 the municipal council decided to cease issuing letters of protection (*Schutzbriefe*) to Jews; however, they continued to reside there under the protection of the duke of Oldenburg, who agreed that they be allowed to deal only in money lending. The community ceased during the *Black Death persecutions (1348). Jews must have returned soon after, for a privilege of 1365 granted them the same rate of interest as had been accorded the Jews of Bremen. Between 1667 and 1773 Oldenburg belonged to Denmark. In this period the dukes made use of the services of Sephardi *Court Jews and financiers from Hamburg, such as Jacob Mussaphia and his sons. A few Jews from Oldenburg attended the Leipzig fairs. Three Jewish families lived in Vechta, in the duchy of Oldenburg, in the middle of the 18th century. Their number increased during French occupation after 1810. A law of August 25, 1827, organized communal affairs, made German names and language compulsory, regulated the conditions of their inferior civil status, and ordered a *Landrabbiner* to be appointed for Oldenburg. The first to hold this office was Nathan Marcus *Adler, who took office in 1829 and moved to Hanover in 1831. Samson Raphael *Hirsch succeeded him until 1841 and there he wrote his *Choreb*. His successor was Bernhard Wechsler (d. 1874), who consecrated the new synagogue in the city in 1835. In 1859 Jewish affairs were reorganized by a new comprehensive law. The Jews of the duchy numbered 1,359 in 1900; by 1925 their number had declined to 1,015 (of which 250 lived in the city of Oldenburg). In 1933 there were 279 Jews. Sizable communities existed in the towns of Delmenhorst, Jever, Varel, Vechta, and Wildeshausen; and in the region of Birkenfeld, Bosen, Hoppstaedten, Oberstein, Idar, and Soetern. The synagogue of Oldenburg was destroyed on November 9/10, 1938, and the last *Landrabbiner*, Leo Trepp, was deported to *Sachsenhausen. The community was annihilated during the war. In 1959, 35 Jews were again living in Oldenburg, and in 1967 a memorial was erected on the site of the synagogue. In 1992 the Jewish community was refounded. From the beginning it was egalitarian, counting women and men for the *minyan*. In 1997 there were 150 Jewish residents. From 1995 to 2004 Bea Wyler – a graduate of the Jewish Theological Seminary in New York – officiated as a rabbi in Oldenburg (and Brunswick and Delmenhorst until 2000 as well). Born in Switzerland, she was the first woman rabbi in Germany after the Shoah. In 1995 a new synagogue was consecrated in the presence of Rabbi Leo Trepp. In 2002 a new community building and in 2002 a *mikveh* were inaugurated. In 2005 the community numbered 330. More than 90% of the members are immigrants from the former Soviet Union.

BIBLIOGRAPHY: L. Trepp, *Die Landesgemeinde der Juden in Oldenburg* (1965); idem, *Eternal Faith, Eternal People* (1962), 294–7; D. Mannheimer, *Gesetzessammlung betreffend die Juden im Herzogtum Oldenburg* (1918); Germ Jud, 2 (1968), 627–8; FJW (1932/33), 410–4; H. Schnee, *Die Hoffinanz und der moderne Staat*, 3 (1955), 124–7; *Zeitschrift fuer Demographie and Statistik der Juden*, 4 (1908), 14. **ADD. BIBLIOGRAPHY:** L. Trepp, *Die Oldenburger Judenschaft. Bild und Vorbild juedischen Seins und Werdens in Deutschland* (Oldenburger Studien, vol. 8) (1973); E. Meyer, *Die Reichskristallnacht in Oldenburg* (1979); J.-F. Toellner et al., *Die juedischen Friedhoefe im Oldenburger Land* (1983); E. Meyer (ed.), *Die Synagogen des Oldenburger Landes* (Oldenburger Studien, vol. 29) (1988); U. Elerd (ed.), *Die Geschichte der Oldenburger Juden und ihre Vernichtung* (Veroeffentlichungen des

Stadtmuseums Oldenburg, vol. 4) (1988); D. Goertz, *Juden in Oldenburg. Struktur, Integration und Verfolgung. 1930 – 1938* (Oldenburger Studien, vol. 28) (1995[2]); J. Paulsen, *Erinnerungsbuch. Ein Verzeichnis von der nationalsozialistischen Judenverfolgung betroffenen Einwohner der Stadt Oldenburg 1933–1945* (2001); S. Schumann (ed.), *Juedische Gemeinde zu Oldenburg 1992–2002* (2002).

[*Encyclopaedia Judaica* (Germany) and Zvi Avneri / Larissa Daemmig (2nd ed.)]

OLEANDER (Heb. הַרְדּוּף mishnaic (*harduf*) or הַרְדּוּפְנִי (*hirdufeni*)), the evergreen shrub with rose-colored flowers that grows wild in Israel on the banks of rivers. Cultivated varieties having flowers of various colors are also grown. Its leaves are arranged at the nodes of the stalk in groups of three. In this respect it resembles the three-leaved *myrtle. The Talmud (Suk. 32b) raises the possibility that by *eẓ avot* ("plaited tree"), one of the four species taken on the Feast of Tabernacles (Lev. 23:40), the oleander may be intended, but the suggestion is rejected on the grounds that the Bible would not have required a plant containing a dangerous poison to be taken (see Rashi, Suk. 32b). A fowl that has eaten oleander "is forbidden because of danger to life" (Ḥul. 3:5). It is, in fact, very poisonous and its ground leaves are sometimes used as mouse poison. One *tanna* held that it was because of its bitterness that this tree was used by Moses to sweeten the bitter waters (Ex. 15:25) "for God heals with that with which he wounds" (Ex. R. 50:3). The Talmud (Pes. 39a) mentions a bitter plant called *hardufenin* which is not poisonous and was eaten as a salad. The reference is apparently to the *Scorzonera*, to which the name *hardufenin* is given in modern Hebrew.

BIBLIOGRAPHY: Loew, Flora, 1 (1924), 206–12; H.N. and A.L. Moldenke, *Plants of the Bible* (1952), index; J. Feliks, *Ẓimḥiyyat ha-Mishnah*, in: *Marot ha-Mishnah, Seder Zera'im* (1967), 38. **ADD. BIBLIOGRAPHY:** Feliks, Ha-Ẓome'aḥ, 52.

[Jehuda Feliks]

OLEI HA-GARDOM ("Those Who Went to the Gallows"). A collective name for the 12 members of the organizations who fought actively against the British Mandatory Government in the struggle for the emergence of the State and were sentenced to death and executed (with the exception of two who cheated the gallows by taking their own lives). All belonged either to the Irgun Ẓeva'i *Le'ummi (Eẓel) or the Loḥamei Ḥerut Israel (Leḥi), with the exception of Shlomo ben *Yosef, who was hanged before the founding of these two militant organizations. Most of them turned their trials into a defiant "J'accuse" against the alleged illegality and brutality of the British Mandatory Government, and all marched proudly to their deaths with heads erect and singing patriotic songs.

In 1974 the municipality of Jerusalem named a street in the new suburb of East Talpiyyot after the Olei ha-Gardom collectively, and others after each individual member. Symbolically enough, the suburb is adjacent to the building which at the time was the official seat of the British High Commissioner (and is now the seat of the UN organization in Israel).

After their return from Kenya in 1947, where they were exiled by the British, members of Eẓel and Leḥi founded a synagogue, Aḥdut Israel in Jerusalem, in the name of the Olei Ha-Gardom, of which Rabbi L.I. *Rabinowitz was appointed rabbi in 1972.

BIBLIOGRAPHY: Nedava, J., *Olei ha-Gardom* (1966); Gurion, Y., *Ha-Nizzaḥon Alei Gardom* (1971).

OLESKO, town in Tarnopol district, Ukraine (E. Galicia). Twelve buildings in Olesko were owned by Jews in 1628. The provincial council of *Bratslav (see *Councils of Lands) convened here in the 18th century. In 1765, 771 Jewish taxpayers were registered in Olesko and its "boroughs." The Jewish population numbered 832 (20% of the total) in 1910, and 636 in 1920 (10.7% of the total population). Noted rabbis who lived in Olesko include Ze'ev (Wolf) b. Samuel, author of *Ḥiddushei ha-Razah* (Zolkiew, 1771). *Ḥasidism had a following in Olesko which was the residence of *ẓaddikim*; one of them opposed the establishment of a modern Jewish school there by the *Israelitische Allianz of Vienna; it was eventually opened in 1910 after a fierce struggle.

[Nathan Michael Gelber]

In 1931 some 600 Jews lived in Olesko. Soon after the outbreak of World War II and until June–July 1941 the whole of the district of Tarnopol, in which Olesko was situated, was under Soviet administration. After the Nazi occupation the town belonged to the "District Galizien" created in August 1941 by the German authorities and incorporated into the General Government. The majority of the 472 Jews remaining in Olesko were deported to the *Belzec concentration camp on Aug. 28, 1942. A Jewish labor camp, where "selected" men were employed by the Nazis, was situated in the town or in its vicinity; it was liquidated in June 1943.

[Danuta Dombrowska]

BIBLIOGRAPHY: T. Brustin-Bernstein, in: *Bleter far Geshikhte*, 6:3 (1953), passim.

OLESNICA (Ger. **Oels**), town in Silesia, Poland. The first mention of a synagogue dates from 1417. Five members of the local community were accused of desecration of the *Host in *Breslau in 1453. The Jews were expelled in 1492, but by 1521 seven families were again resident. Hebrew printing in Olesnica is mainly connected with the well-known 16th-century Jewish printer Ḥayyim *Schwarz, who, in 1530, produced the first Hebrew book printed by a Jew in Germany, a handsome Pentateuch (with the Five Scrolls and *haftarot*), of which only two copies have been preserved. In 1535 a violent storm destroyed the press, bringing financial ruin to Schwarz's successors – Samuel Ester and Eliakim Herliz – and to the many members of the community who were employed by them. In the same year the community also tried in vain to intercede on behalf of their persecuted brethren in Jaegerndorf. With the destruction of the press, the community gradually dispersed and the synagogue was converted to a church (consecrated in 1695). In 1758 24 Jews were again living in the town. A synagogue served 121 persons when it was consecrated in 1840 and 330 in 1880. By 1933 144 remained, but by 1939 the number had fallen as a result of Nazi persecution.

BIBLIOGRAPHY: M. Brann, *Geschichte der Juden in Schlesien* (1917), 205, n. 8, passim; A. Grotte, *"Synagogen," Kirchen in Schlesien* (1930), 3–12; idem, *Synagogenspuren in schlesischen Kirchen*, 1 (1937), 12–20; FJW, 95; M. Brann, in: *Jahresbericht des juedisch-theologischen Seminars* (Breslau; 1910), 167–73; A.M. Habermann, in: KS, 33 (1957/8), 509.

°OLEŚNICKI, ZBIGNIEW (1389–1455), bishop of Cracow. During the reign of Ladislau II Jagello of Poland, Oleśnicki was the power behind the throne of Wladislaw Warnenczyk and the spiritual agitator of contemporary hatred of the Jews. He was also the patron of Jan *Dlugosz, the anti-Jewish Polish chronicler. Oleśnicki invited John of *Capistrano to Poland in 1453, and his arrival coincided with the Jews' endeavor to have their general privileges agreed upon by the king. In the resulting riots of Cracow many Jews fled and a few converted to Christianity. Oleśnicki personally took care of some of the converts. He charged Casimir IV Jagello with favoring the Jews, stating that their privileges included articles which were against Christian religious principles. In a letter addressed to the Sejm at Leczyca he called these privileges "disgusting and abject." He demanded the introduction of the Jewish *badge in Poland. After the Polish armies had been defeated by the Teutonic Order at Chojnice, Oleśnicki increased his pressure on the king. At the congress of Great Poland's nobility at Cerekwica in 1454, the king agreed to issue anti-Jewish laws. The knights, facing a new military expedition, forced the king to keep his promise, and in the same year Casimir IV Jagello issued the Nieszawa statutes which canceled the general privileges accorded to the Polish Jews and reinstated the Warta statute of 1423 making moneylending by Jews to Christians more difficult.

BIBLIOGRAPHY: M. Balaban, *Historia Żydów w Krakowie i na kazimierzu 1304–1868*, 1 (1931); E. Maleczynska, *Społoczeństwo polskie pierwszej połowy XV wieku wobec zachodnich agadnień* (1947).

[Jacob Goldberg]

OLEVSKI, BUZI (1908–1941), Soviet Yiddish writer. Born in Volhynia, Olevski graduated in 1930 from the Yiddish department at the Second Moscow State University, where he later defended his doctoral thesis on David Hofstein's oeuvre. In 1926 he debuted as a poet in the Minsk-based journal *Shtern*, eliciting the favorable reaction of critics. He published stories and poems in various Soviet periodicals and anthologies. In the early 1930s he moved to Birobidzhan. His stories depict people in the Civil War and in the air force, the destruction of the Jewish *shtetl*, and the heroism of the Red Army. He also wrote children's literature. Among his books are *In Vuks* ("Growing," 1930), *Shakhte* ("Mines," 1933), *Alts Hekher un Hekher* ("Higher and Higher," 1933), *Birobidzhaner Lider* ("Birobidzhan Poems," 1938), and *Onheyb Lebn* ("In the Beginning of Life," 1939). He was killed in action on the Soviet-German front.

BIBLIOGRAPHY: LNYL, 1 (1956), 103–4.

[Israel Ch. Biletzky / Gennady Estraikh (2nd ed.)]

OLGIN, MOSHE J. (adopted name of **Moses Joseph Novomsky**; 1878–1939), writer, editor, and translator. Born near Kiev, Olgin studied there. He joined a student revolutionary group which developed in the Kiev branch of the Jewish Labor Bund. After leaving Kiev University in 1904, he lived in Vilna where he joined the editorial board of the Bundist *Arbeter Shtime* and the legal publication *Der Veker*. At the end of 1906, Olgin left Russia and settled in Germany, where he studied at the University of Heidelberg. He returned to Russia in 1909 and became active as a teacher and lecturer. In 1913 Olgin moved to Vienna and became the coeditor of the Bundist weekly *Di Tsayt* which was published in St. Petersburg. In 1914 he went to New York, and became a staff member of the *Jewish Daily Forward*. After the split in the Jewish Socialist Federation in 1921, he joined the Workers' Party. He was one of the founders of the Communist Yiddish Daily *Freiheit* (later *Morning Freiheit*) and remained its editor until his death. He was also the editor of the monthly *Der Hamer* (1926) and from 1932, New York correspondent of the Moscow *Pravda*. A prolific writer, he followed the Communist party line and justified Arab riots and pogroms in Palestine. Olgin wrote about political affairs, literature, and the theater.

His books include: *Mayn Shtetl in der Ukrain* (1921); *Fun Mayn Togbukh* (1926); and a posthumous collection of essays *Kultur un Folk* (1949). His books in English include: *The Soul of the Russian Revolution* (1917); *A Guide to Russian Literature* (1920); and *Gorki, Writer and Revolutionist* (1933). Olgin translated Lenin into Yiddish as well as Jack London's *The Call of the Wild* (1919) and John Reid's *Ten Days that Shook the World* (1920).

BIBLIOGRAPHY: Rejzen, Leksikon, 1 (1926), 92–97; *Tsum Ondenk fun M. Olgin* (1939); LNYL, 1 (1956), 88–91.

[Elias Schulman]

OLGOPOL, townlet in Vinnitsa district, Ukraine. Before the 1917 Revolution, Olgopol was a county capital in the province of Podolia. Jews are mentioned in 1799, and by 1847 the Jewish population was 247; by 1897 the number had increased to 2,473 (30% of the total population). Olgopol suffered heavily in 1919 at the hands of the Ukrainian bands which were active in the surroundings. Jews were also attacked by the armies of *Denikin. In 1926 the Jewish population numbered 1,660 (76.4% of the total), and it dropped to 660 in 1939. In the Soviet period there was a kolkhoz most of whose members were Jews. Yiddish was the official language (beside Ukrainian) in the local council in the 1920s. Olgopol was taken by the Germans on July 26, 1941, and later attached to Romanian Transnistria. A ghetto was set up with a few dozen local families who remained, plus hundreds of people expelled from Bessarabia and Bukovina. The fate of the local Jews is unknown, but on the day of liberation (March 22, 1944) there were still 164 Jews from Bessarabia and 27 from Bukovina there. There was no information on the presence of Jews in Olgopol in 1971.

[Yehuda Slutsky / Shmuel Spector (2nd ed.)]

°OLIPHANT, LAURENCE (1829–1888), English writer and traveler, Christian mystic, and active supporter of the return of the Jewish people to Ereẓ Israel. Born of a Scotch family in the Cape of Good Hope, Oliphant traveled in many countries and wrote impressive travel books. From 1865 to 1867 he was a member of parliament. During the Russo-Turkish War (1878) he began to take an interest in the Holy Land and Jewish settlement there, in a blending of political, economical, and religious-mystic considerations. He supported Turkey and thought that the best way to revive it was by improving the condition of its Asian regions, first and foremost Palestine. He decided to submit to the sultan a plan for large-scale Jewish settlement in Palestine, supported by resources from abroad. With letters of recommendation from Lord Beaconsfield and Lord Salisbury, who approved his plan and a letter from the French minister of foreign affairs, William Henry Waddington, he went to Palestine in 1879. He investigated the country and arrived at the conclusion that the best place to start Jewish settlement was the Gilead region in Transjordan. Consequently, he negotiated with the authorities in Constantinople concerning tenancy rights and a concession for settlement. The Turkish cabinet approved the proposal, but the sultan Abdul Ḥamid rejected it for fear that it was a British intrigue. The pogroms of 1881 in Russia moved Oliphant to new undertakings. He established a group of influential Christians in London for the purpose of bringing them closer to his idea. In the same year he provided assistance to Russian Jewish refugees in Galicia by means of the mayor of London's Mansion House Relief fund. In opposition to the representatives of the Alliance Israélite Universelle who directed the emigration to the United States, he advised the Jews to go to Palestine and tried to persuade Alliance spokesmen to do the same. He also decided to renew his negotiations in Constantinople. The Turkish foreign minister, Said Pasha, regarded his plan as practical and wanted to connect it with the project of constructing a railroad in Palestine. But the negotiation could go no further, especially when the Turkish-British relations deteriorated because of Egypt, and Oliphant's efforts came to nothing. He settled in Haifa and engaged in religious and mystic contemplation. Yet he always remained attached to the Zionist idea and provided advice and assistance to the first Jewish settlers in Ereẓ Israel. His Hebrew secretary in Haifa was the poet, N.H. *Imber. Oliphant was the most important Christian figure of his time supporting the idea of the Jewish Return to Zion. The *Bilu'im and Ḥovevei Zion had great hopes for his negotiations in Constantinople, and his firm position on their behalf was encouraging, even though his political undertakings failed. His writings included the programmatic book *Land of Gilead* (1880; Heb. trans. by Nahum *Sokolow as *Ereẓ Ḥemdah*, 1886) and *Haifa, or Life in Modern Palestine* (1887). Oliphant was one of the most famous of British gentile proto-Zionists.

BIBLIOGRAPHY: M.O.W. Oliphant, *Memoir on the Life of Laurence Oliphant…*, 2 vols. (1891); P. Henderson, *The Life of Laurence Oliphant* (1956); N. Sokolow, *Hibbath Zion* (1935), 275–9 and index; idem, *History of Zionism*, 2 (1919), index; S. Jawnieli, *Sefer ha-Ẓiyyonut*, 2:1 (1942), 9–11, 90–95; I. Klausner, *Be-Hitorer Am* (1962), 72–78, 199–202, and index; G. Yardeni, *Ha-Ittonut ha-Ivrit be-Ereẓ Yisrael* (1969), index. **ADD. BIBLIOGRAPHY:** ODNB online; A. Taylor, *Laurence Oliphant* (1982).

[Alexander Bein / Nathan Michael Gelber]

OLITSKI, JULES (1922–), U.S. painter, sculptor, and printmaker. Born Jules Demikovsky in Russia, Olitski immigrated to the United States in 1923 and grew up in New York. He studied painting and drawing at the National Academy of Design (1940–42) and sculpture at the Beaux-Arts Institute of Design (1940–42) in New York. He served in the Army during World War II (1942–45), before which he became an American citizen and adopted his stepfather's surname. In 1947 Olitski studied sculpture at the Educational Alliance with Chaim *Gross. Under the GI Bill, Olitski received additional art instruction at the Académie de la Grande Chaumiére (1949–50) and with the sculptor Ossip Zadkine (1949) in Paris. In an effort to transcend his academic training, Olitski made a series of vigorously rendered paintings while blindfolded. He had his first solo exhibition in Paris (1951), where he showed partially abstract, brightly colored paintings. Upon his permanent return to the United States he received a B.S. (1952) and an M.A. (1954) in art education from New York University. Responding to his vibrantly hued Parisian works, during this transition period Olitski made monochrome abstractions and experimented with heavily impastoed imagery in the late 1950s.

Throughout Olitski's career he explored varied modes of color field painting. Adopting a technique made popular by Helen *Frankenthaler and Morris *Louis, in 1960 Olitski started to stain large canvases with hard-edge, oblong shapes; *Born in Snovsk* (1963, Art Institute of Chicago) is one of several paintings in the Core series. In 1964 Olitski applied paint to canvases with spray cans and later with a spray gun. Color mists hover and subtle hues of pink dissolve into each other in *Ishtar Melted* (1965, Princeton University Art Museum). During the 1970s, Olitski reacted against the spray technique and composed abstractions with tactile, dense, often dull-colored paint. Iridescent paintings followed, in which he applied gobs of paint with mittened hands. *Temptation Temple* (1992, collection unknown) exemplifies this period with the energetic texture and sense of relief created by the thick metallic brown color interwoven with highlights of green, purple, and blue.

Olitski began making prints in 1954. His forays into printmaking yielded a wide range of imagery from representational self-portraits to abstractions. Colored silkscreens from the early 1970s are pure abstractions of color akin to his paintings of the period. In 1968 Olitski designed his first sculptures – aluminum abstractions colored with a spray gun. His sculptures are typically produced in series, such as the Ring series (1970–73), a group of works comprised of concentric circles made of thin sheet steel. Olitski's art has been publicly exhibited on numerous occasions. Notably, Olitski represented the United States at the 1966 Venice Bienniale; he was the first living American artist to have a one-person show at the Metropolitan Museum of Art (1969); and in 1973 he enjoyed a retrospective at the Museum of Fine Arts in Boston.

BIBLIOGRAPHY: K. Moffett, *Jules Olitski* (1981); K. Wilkin and S. Long, *The Prints of Jules Olitski: A Catalogue Raisonné, 1954–1989* (1989); B. Rose, *Jules Olitski: Recent Paintings* (1993).

[Samantha Baskind (2nd ed.)]

OLITZKI, ARYEH LEO (1898–1983), Israeli bacteriologist. Born in Allenstein (E. Prussia), he was an assistant in the Institute of Hygiene of the University of Breslau before moving to Palestine in 1924. He continued his serological research at Hadassah Hospital, Jerusalem, and for some years headed the bacteriology laboratories at the Hadassah hospitals in Jerusalem and Safed. He taught at the Hebrew University from 1928, becoming professor in 1949 and dean of the Medical School from 1961 to 1965. In the course of investigating problems of serology and immunology, especially in relation to infectious diseases peculiar to Israel, he discovered a method of inoculating humans against Brucellosa infection from sheep and cattle. His major breakthrough was the laboratory cultivation (with Zipporah Gershon) of the Lepra bacillus, thus paving the way toward early diagnosis of the disease and the possibility of more effective treatment. Olitzki published many scientific papers and co-authored (with N. Grossowicz) a Hebrew textbook on microbiology and immunology (*Yesodot Torat ha-Ḥaidakkim ve-ha-Ḥasinut*, 2 vols., 1964–68). He was awarded the Israel Prize in Medicine in 1967.

[Lucien Harris]

OLITZKY, family of three brothers, all Yiddish authors. LEIB (1897–1975) was poet, short-story writer, and translator. He taught in Yiddish schools in his native Trisk and in Warsaw until 1939. Fleeing eastward from the German invaders, he spent the war years in Soviet Russia, but returned to Poland in 1946. In 1959 he settled in Israel. His first stories and his first novel, *In an Okupirt Shtetl* ("In an Occupied Town," 1924) dealt with Jewish life under the German occupation of World War I and during the early years of the Polish Republic. There followed juvenilia, books of parables, short stories, and poems. During his years in Russia and in Communist Poland, he translated Pushkin and Krylov, published 10 volumes of prose and poetry, and edited the lyrics of his brother Baruch Olitzky, who had perished under the Nazis. Seven collections of Leib's lyrics were published in Israel (1960–76), as well as a volume of his and his brother Mattes' poems, *Lider tsu a Bruder* ("Songs to a Brother," 1964), a volume of tributes to Baruch Olitzky, some of whose lyrics were also included. Some of Leib's poems and fables have been translated into Polish, Hebrew, and English. BARUCH (1907–1941), was also a poet. Born in Poland, he became a teacher in the Yiddish schools of Volhynia. He made his literary debut in *Literarishe Bleter* in 1925 and subsequently published poems in various newspapers in Poland and Soviet Russia. He was strongly influenced by the poetry of the **Khalyastre*. He perished during the Holocaust in Poland. His brothers Leib and Mattes edited a posthumous volume of his poetry, *Mayn Blut iz Oysgemisht* ("My Blood is Mixed," 1951). MATTES (1915–) published his first book of poems, *In Fremdn Land* ("In Alien Land," 1948), while still in a postwar refugee camp in Germany. His second book, *Freylekhe Teg* ("Happy Days," 1962), the outcome of his experiences as a teacher of Jewish children in New York, consisted mainly of songs which aimed at bringing life and immediacy to Bible stories, and the joys of the Sabbath and Holy Days which he was teaching his pupils, but also included poems recalling Jewish children whom the Nazis summoned from classrooms to death-marches. His other books are *Lider far Yugnt* ("Songs for the Youth," 1974), *Lider fun Frier un Itst* ("Songs From Then and Now," 1980), which include additional poems by his brother Baruch, and *Lid un Esey* ("Song and Essay," 1988). He joined his brother Leib Olitzky in *Lider tsu a Bruder*. His *Geklibene Lider* ("Selected Poems," 1967) covered a wide range of scenes and experiences, from a golden childhood in Poland, through tragic war years, to a calm existence in New York.

BIBLIOGRAPHY: LNYL, 1 (1956), 104–6. **ADD. BIBLIOGRAPHY:** B. Kagan, *Leksikon* (1986), 28–30; J. Glatstein, *Prost un Poshet* (1978), 278–83; I. Yanasowicz, *Penemer un Nemen* (1971), 34–9.

[Sol Liptzin / Tamar Lewinsky (2nd ed.)]

OLITZKY, KERRY M. (1954–), U.S. Reform rabbi, educator, administrator, and author. Olitzky was born in Pittsburgh, Pennsylvania, and earned his B.A. (1974) and M.A. (1975) from the University of South Florida. He received his M.H.L. from Hebrew Union College in 1980, where he was ordained in 1981 and earned a D.H.L. in 1985. He served as assistant rabbi and director of religious education at Congregation Beth Israel in West Hartford, Connecticut (1981–84), before returning to Cincinnati, Ohio, to become director of the school of education at HUC-JIR (1984–96). In 1991, his title was expanded to National Director for Research and Educational Development, and responsibility for development efforts related to institutional grants was added to his administration of degree programs, as well as of all HUC-JIR programs related to alumni and continuing education. In 1996, he was named National Dean of Adult Jewish Learning and Living, in charge of adult educational programs on all four campuses of HUC-JIR, including the Kollel in New York, the Beit Midrash in Jerusalem, and the Academy for Interfaith Studies in Cincinnati. He also supervised national and regional programs co-sponsored with other branches of the Reform movement and served on the Executive Committee of the CCAR-UAHC-NATE Joint Commission on Jewish Education. In 1998, Olitzky left HUC-JIR to become vice president of the *Wexner Heritage Foundation, with particular responsibility for alumni programs and institutes and for editing the foundation's publications.

In 1999, Olitzky was appointed executive director of the Jewish Outreach Institute in New York City, an independent national organization dedicated to bringing Judaism to interfaith families and the unaffiliated. In addition, he has continued his pioneering work in the area of Jewish twelve-step spirituality, serving as rabbinic adviser to the Jewish Alcoholics, Chemically Dependent Persons, and Significant Others Council (JACS) and as a member of the editorial board of the *Journal of Ministry in Addiction and Recovery.* Olitzky was also the founding editor of the *Journal of Aging and Judaism* and a member of the American Society of Aging Forum on Religion and Aging.

Olitzky was a contributing editor for *Shma: A Journal of Jewish Responsibility* and a consultant to Capstone Press. His books include *An Interfaith Ministry to the Aged: A Survey of Models* (1989); *Recovery from Codependence: A Jewish Twelve Steps Guide to Healing Your Soul* (1993); *The American Synagogue: A Historical Dictionary* (1996); *Grief in Our Seasons: A Mourner's Companion for Kaddish* (1998); *From Your Father's House … Reflections for Modern Jewish Men* (1999); *American Synagogue Ritual* (2000); and *Jewish Paths Toward Healing and Wholeness: A Personal Guide to Dealing with Suffering* (2000). After collaborating with Leonard Kravitz on a critically acclaimed annotated translation with commentary of *Pirke Avot* (1993), Olitzky teamed up with Kravitz to embark on a series of similarly new translations of books of the Bible: *The Book of Proverbs, Kohelet, Song of Songs, Ruth, Jonah* and *Lamentations* (2000–06).

[Bezalel Gordon (2nd ed.)]

OLIVE (Heb. זַיִת), the *Olea europaea* tree and its fruit. The wild olive grows in the groves of Upper Galilee and Carmel. It is a prickly shrub producing small fruits. There are many varieties of cultivated olives, some being suitable for oil, and some for food as preserved olives. Its foliage is dense and when it becomes old, the fairly tall trunk acquires a unique pattern of twists and protuberances on its bark. There are trees in Israel estimated to be 1,000 years old that still produce fruit. In old age the tree becomes hollow but the trunk continues to grow thicker, at times achieving a circumference of 20 ft. (6 m.). The olive tree blossoms at the beginning of summer and its fruit ripens about the time of the early rains in October. The fruit, which is rich in oil, is first green, but later becomes black. Olive trees have always been the most extensively distributed and the most conspicuous in the landscape of Israel. The olive is numbered among the seven species with which Ereẓ Israel is blessed (Deut. 8:8). The Rab-Shakeh, who besieged Jerusalem, also made use of a similar description for Ereẓ Israel when promising the inhabitants of Jerusalem that he would exile them to a country of like fertility (II Kings 18:32). The bounty of Israel is frequently described by "corn, wine, and oil" (Deut. 7:13, et al.); grain, vines, and olives, which formed the basis of Israel's economy. The olive flourishes throughout the country. Its cultivation dates from early times. When the Israelites conquered the land they found extensive olive plantations (Deut. 6:11). Western Galilee, the territory of Asher, was especially rich in olives (33:24), as it is today. They flourish in mountainous areas, even among the rocks, thus producing "oil out of the flinty rock" (32:13). "The Mount of Olives" (Zech. 14:4) near Jerusalem is Har ha-Mishḥah, "the mount of Oil" of the Mishnah (Par. 3:6). The olive also develops well in the *Shephelah Lowland, where it grows near *sycamores, and David appointed a special overseer over these plantations (I Chron. 27:28).

The olive was the first to be chosen by the trees when they went "to anoint a king over themselves" in Jotham's parable (Judg. 9:8–9). The tree is full of beauty, especially when laden with fruit: "a leafy olive-tree, fair with goodly fruit" (Jer. 11:16). It is an evergreen, and the righteous who take refuge in the protection of God are compared to it (Ps. 52:10). The "olive plants" of Psalm 128:3 are the shoots that sprout from its roots and protect the trunk and, if it is cut down, they ensure its continued existence. This is the simile referred to in the words "thy children like olive saplings round about thy table." The wood is very hard and beautifully grained, making it suitable for the manufacture of small articles and ornaments, the hollow trunk of the adult tree, however, rendering it unsuitable for pieces of furniture. The olive cannot therefore be the *eẓ shemen* from which the doors of the Temple were made (I Kings 6:31).

In spring the olive tree is covered with thousands of small whitish flowers, most of which fall off before the fruit forms (cf. Job 15:33). After the fruit is formed the tree may be attacked by the olive fly, causing the fruit to rot and fall off (Deut. 28:40). The fruits are arranged upon the thin branches in parallel rows like ears of corn (Zech. 4:12). Two such olive branches at the side of the candelabrum symbolize the State of Israel, because "an olive leaf" symbolizes peace (cf. Gen. 8:11). After ripening, the fruit is harvested in two different ways, by beating the branches with sticks or by hand picking. The former way is quicker but many branches fall off and this diminishes successive harvests. This method was used in biblical times, the Bible commanding that the fruit on the fallen branches are to be a gift to the poor (Deut. 24:20). The second method was the more usual in mishnaic times and was termed *masik* ("harvesting olives"), the fingers being drawn down the branches in a milking motion so that the olives fall into the hand. By this method the "harvested" olives remained whole, whereas the "beaten" olives were bruised by the beating (Ḥal. 3:9). The best species for preserving are called *kelofsin* (Tosef., Ter. 4:3) or *keloska* olives (Av. Zar. 2:7). Though there were olives of different varieties and different sizes, the olive was designated as a standard size for many *halakhot*, and the expression "land of olive trees" was interpreted as "a land whose main standard of measurement is the olive" (Ber. 41b). Rabbinic literature contains innumerable details about the oil, its types and methods of extraction; the Midrash (Ex.

R. 36:1) summing it up as follows: "The olive is left to fully ripen while it is yet on the tree after which it is brought down from the tree and beaten,… it is then brought up to the vat and placed in a grinding mill, where it is ground and then tied up with ropes [through which the oil is filtered], and then stones are brought [which press upon the olives] and then at last it yields its oil."

[Jehuda Feliks]

In Israel

Limited Jewish attempts to grow olives date back to the small Jewish settlements established during the First Aliyah. The planting of olive groves on a wider scope began at the Ben Shemen farm in 1905–06, and from then on grew steadily. From the establishment of the State of Israel (1948) there was a decline in the area covered by olives: in 1948–49 there were 137,000 dunams (34,000 acres); in 1959–60, 123,000 dunams; and in 1968–69, 107,000 dunams, of which 82,000 were on non-Jewish farms, especially in Arab villages in the Galilee. The amount of olive produce fluctuated substantially in those years, despite the fact that the area of land under cultivation remained fairly steady. In the most productive year, produce reached a peak of 24,500 tons (1966–67), and in the low years it reached the level of 3,800 tons (1949–50) and 2,800 tons (1954–55). In the peak year of 1966–67, 18,950 tons of olives went for food processing and another 5,550 tons yielded 3,000 tons of olive oil. In the same year the value of the olives produced and processed came to IL 17,998,000. A survey carried out by the Ministry of Agriculture after the Six-Day War (1967–68) revealed 477,600 dunams of land under olive cultivation in Judea and Samaria and 3,000 dunams in the Gaza Strip. Within the borders set by the 1949 Armistice Agreements, the Galilee and the area around Lydda were the main centers of olive cultivation. After the Six-Day War, however, the mountains of Samaria and northern Judea took the lead in olive production within the cease-fire lines.

Since that time a large-scale olive oil industry has been developed in Israel, such that between 1995 and 2002 the consumption rose from 6,000 tons to 14,000 tons of olive oil per year. The increase in olive oil consumption was due to the public's recognition of its medical virtues. This trend led the Ministry of Agriculture to encourage farmers to raise olives for oil instead for eating, and to increase their yields by using advanced irrigation techniques. The majority of olive plantations held by Arab farmers are designated for olive oil, and include 180,000 dunams producing 5,000–6,000 tons of oil a year. Most of these plantations are not irrigated due to water recycling problems in the Arab sector. The main species in these plantations is the Syrian, which yields large quantities of oil and is raised in the Galilee. Jewish farmers hold another 22,000 irrigated dunams designated mainly for eating, yielding 15,000 tons of olives per year and located in central and southern Israel. They raise the Manzileno for eating and the Barnea for oil. Two institutions are responsible for regulating the olive sector in Israel: the Fruit Council is responsible for olives for eating, while the Olive Board is responsible for the development of the farming, production, and marketing of olive oil and the branding of the various oils.

[Shaked Gilboa (2nd ed.).]

BIBLIOGRAPHY: F. Goldmann, *Der Oelbau in Palaestina zur Zeit der Mišnâh* (1907); Krauss, Tal Arch, 2 (1911), 214–26; Loew, Flora, 2 (1924), 287–95; G. Dalman, *Arbeit und Sitte in Palaestina* 4 (1935), 153–290; H.N. and A.L. Moldenke, *Plants of the Bible* (1952), 317 (index), s.v.; J. Feliks, *Ẓimḥiyyat ha-Mishnah*, in: *Marot ha-Mishnah, Seder Zera'im* (1967), 41; idem, *Kilei Zera'im ve-Harkavah* (1967), 155f.; idem, *Olam ha-Ẓome'aḥ ha-Mikra'i* (1968²), 25–32. **ADD BIBLIOGRAPHY:** Feliks, Ha-Ẓome'aḥ, 55. **WEBSITE:** www.moag.gov.il; www.oliveboard.org.il; www.fruit.org.il.

OLIVERO, BETTY (1954–), Israeli composer born in Tel Aviv. Her parents, who were born in Greece, emigrated to Palestine in 1932. Her Sephardi-Mediterranean cultural background was the most powerful element in the crystallization of her personality as composer. At the same time, her musical training was completely Western. She graduated from the Rubin Academy of Music in Tel Aviv in 1979, having studied composition with Yitzhak *Sadai and Leon *Schidlowsky. In 1982 she completed graduate studies at Yale University with Jacob Druckman and Gilbert Amy. In 1986 she won the Leonard Bernstein Fellowship at Tanglewood, where she commenced three years of studies with Luciano Berio, which led to a prolonged stay in Italy. In October 2002 she was appointed to the position of professor of composition at Bar-Ilan University, Israel. She won the Koussevitzky Award (2000), the Prime Minister's Prize (2001), the Rosenblum Award (2003), and the Landau Award for the Performing Arts (2004).

Betty Olivero developed a unique personality as a distinctly local Israeli composer who is at the same time deeply identified with contemporary trends in Western music. While highly individual, her communicative and intensive expression represents the most convincing realization of the ideological trend in early Jewish music in Palestine and early Israel, defined as the collective ideology (Hirshberg, 1995, 241–272). Olivero commented that her "thought of the form and the development or way of making decisions, is in completely Western terminology and the precise notation. At the same time the harmony, the melody, the colors, the timbre – are derived from oriental music that I was surrounded by" (Fleisher, 1997, 275). Nearly all of her many vocal compositions use texts from Jewish prayers and folk songs in Hebrew, Ladino, and Arabic. She collaborated for many years with the singer Esti Kenan-Ofri, who specialized in performing Sephardi and Arabic vocal rendition, as well as with clarinetist Giora *Feidman, who has been the most salient performer of ḥasidic music. Olivero's music stresses that which is common to the Jewish heritage rather than that which is specific to different Jewish ethnic groups. For example, in her *Mizraḥ* (East), Feidman smoothly moves from quotes of ḥasidic music to a Sephardi folk song. Her vocal works range from nearly direct quotes of Hebrew, Yemenite, and Beduin folk songs as in *maqamat* to the stylized, powerful expression of intense pain in her *Hosha'anot*.

BIBLIOGRAPHY: J. Hirshberg, *Music in the Jewish Community of Palestine 1880–1948* (1995); R. Fleisher: *Twenty Israeli Composers: Voices of a Culture* (1997), 271–81.

[Jehoash Hirshberg (2nd ed.)]

OLIVER Y FULLANA, NICOLÁS DE (fl. c. 1670), Marrano soldier and writer. Born in Majorca, he pursued a military career, rising from sergeant major in the Spanish army in Catalonia to the rank of colonel in Flanders, where he distinguished himself in action against the French. It was probably while in the Low Countries that Oliver y Fullana became a Jew and took the name of Daniel Judah. Nevertheless, he still maintained friendly relations with the Spanish military establishment in Brussels in the 1670s. His second wife, Isabel de *Correa, was a poet in Amsterdam. Oliver y Fullana, who wrote in three languages, exchanged laudatory verses with Miguel de *Barrios. He completed a part of the *Atlas Mayor* (1641) of Jan Blaeu and was cosmographer-royal to the king of Spain.

BIBLIOGRAPHY: Kayserling, Bibl, 79; Scholberg, in: JQR, 53 (1962), 145; I. Da Costa, *Noble Families among the Sephardic Jews* (1936), 94.

[Kenneth R. Scholberg]

OLIVETTI, Italian family of industrialists of Piedmont. CAMILLO OLIVETTI (1868–1943), who founded the firm, started a small industry in his native Ivrea for the production of instruments of electrical measurement, the first of its kind in Italy (subsequently the CGS of Milan). In 1909 he introduced the production of typewriters in Italy, founded the "Ing. C. Olivetti and Co." at Ivrea and invented the typewriter bearing his name. A patriarchal figure, he strove to make his firm one of the most advanced in Europe, both technically and socially, caring especially for the welfare and education of the workers. His son ADRIANO (1901–1960), like his father an outspoken anti-Fascist, was responsible for a radical transformation of the Ivrea plant leading to notable production increases. In 1933, as the general director of the firm, Adriano Olivetti started production on a world scale at Ivrea, Turin, and Pozzuoli, of metal furniture, typing and calculating machines, and telescriptors. He initiated a huge housing scheme at Ivrea and built free holiday resorts. Dedicated to advanced urbanism he initiated the "Movimento di Communità," on behalf of which he sat in the Italian parliament in 1958. In 1959 he took world-wide control over the Underwood Corporation. He wrote *L'ordine politico della Communità* (1946), *Società stato communità* (1948), and *Città dell' Uomo* (1960), which set out his aspirations for social renewal through decentralized economy based on a system of communal cooperatives, each autonomous with its own government, industries, and educational and cultural institutions.

BIBLIOGRAPHY: N. Ginzburg, *Lessico famigliare* (1963), passim; E. Mann Borgese, in: *Il Ponte*, 6 (1960), 244–8; Edizioni di Communità, *Ricordo di Adriano Olivetti* (1960); B. Hirschman, in: *South African Jewish Times* (Nov. 28, 1969), 31–32.

OLIVEYRA, SOLOMON BEN DAVID DE (d. 1708), rabbi, philologist, and poet. Oliveyra was born in Lisbon, but lived in Amsterdam where he served as teacher of the Keter Torah association and as a member of the rabbinical council, over which he presided after the death of Jacob *Sasportas (1698).

He wrote a number of works in Hebrew and Portuguese, including grammatical treatises, lexicons and translations, of which the following may be noted: *Sharshot Gavlut* (Amsterdam, 1665), consisting of a dictionary of rhymes with chapters on meter; *Ayyelet Ahavim* (*ibid.*, 1665), an account of Abraham and the sacrifice of Isaac in prose and poetry; *Darkhei No'am* (*ibid.*, 1688–89), a guide to the study of the Talmud.

BIBLIOGRAPHY: M. Hartmann, *Die hebraeische Verskunst* (1894), 75–79; M.B. Amzalak, in: *Revista de Estudos Hebráicos*, 1 (1928), 96–118; Kayserling, Bibl, 79–81.

OLKUSZ (Heb. עלקיש), town in Kielce province, Poland. There was a Jewish settlement in Olkusz by the time of Casimir the Great (1333–70), who expropriated the gold and silver mines in Olkusz belonging to his Jewish banker Levko. In 1374, however, Olkusz obtained the privilege *de non tolerandis Judaeis*; Jews were barred from residing there and left for Cracow. During the reign of John Casimir (1648–69), a Jew, Marek Nekel, was granted the first concession to quarry in the hills and was allowed to trade in metals (1658). An agreement between the Jews and the municipality concluded in 1682 granted Jews domiciliary and trading rights on condition that they helped to defray the town debts; they were accordingly granted the customary privileges by John Sobieski (Dec. 3, 1682) to enable their settlement. The Olkusz community came under the jurisdiction of the Cracow *kehillah*, but in 1692, the community of Olkusz and other towns in the district seceded from Cracow, a decision endorsed by the *Council of the Four Lands. In 1764 there were 423 Jews living in Olkusz. The economic position of the town deteriorated in the 18th century after copper mines in the district had been ruined by the Swedish invasion. A *blood libel involving the Jews in Olkusz in 1787 was the last such case to occur in Poland before its partition. The principal Jew accused, a tailor, was sentenced to death, but the leaders of the community managed to obtain the intervention of King Stanislas Poniatowski and secure a reprieve. Under Austrian rule (1796–1809), the number of Jews living in Olkusz diminished, and when it was annexed to Russia the prohibition on Jewish settlement in border districts applied. However, there were 746 Jews living in Olkusz in 1856 (83.4% of the total population), 1,840 in 1897 (53.9%), 3,249 in 1909 (53%), 2,703 in 1921 (40.6%), and in 1939 about 3,000.

[Nathan Michael Gelber]

Holocaust Period

The Germans entered the town on Sept. 5, 1939, and subjected the Jews to beating and torment, plundering of property, kidnapping in the streets for hard labor, and religious persecution. The Judenrat, created in October 1939, had to take care particularly of 800 deportees who came from other localities in

Upper Silesia. Transports of men to labor camps in the Reich commenced in October 1940 with the dispatch of 140 Jews. A second transport with 130 Jews left Olkusz in January 1941; the third, composed of 300 women, left in August 1941. In the spring of 1942, shortly before the liquidation of the community, the number of transports increased. In March 1942, 150 women were shipped out, followed on April 20, 1942 by 140 men. One month later during Shavuot (May 21–23, 1942) about 1,000 Jews, including women, were sent out. The victims of these transports were mainly the poor, particularly refugees and deportees; those with means could temporarily avoid such transports. In the latter half of 1941 a ghetto was established in a suburb. It was open and probably not fenced off, but leaving the ghetto was forbidden and the entrances were watched by German and Jewish police. There were, together with the new arrivals, about 3,000 Jews interned in the ghetto. In the last few months prior to the liquidation, transports to labor camps increased, and the German police on March 6, 1942 publicly hanged three Jews for illegally leaving the ghetto and smuggling food. Local Jews were forced to build the gallows and carry out the hanging. The final liquidation took place in June 1942. A *Selektion* ("selection") was carried out to separate the most able-bodied men for labor camps from the rest of the inhabitants, among them the local rabbi; the latter were all sent to *Auschwitz. A group of some 20 Jews was left to clear up the ghetto; they were afterward deported and exterminated. The community was not reconstituted after the war.

[Danuta Dombrowska]

BIBLIOGRAPHY: K. Leszczyński, in: *Biuletyn Głównej Komisji Badania Zbrodni Hitlerowskich w Polsce*, 9 (1957), 157; Balaban, in: *Yevreyskaya Starina*, 7 (1914), 163–81, 318–27. **ADD. BIBLIOGRAPHY:** *Sefer Zikkaron le-Kehillat Olkusz*,(1972).

OLLENDORFF, FRANZ (1900–1981), Israeli engineer. Born in Berlin, Ollendorff in 1924 joined the Siemens research department in Berlin, working under Reinhold Ruedenberg. From 1928 he taught in the engineering faculty of the Berlin Technische Hochschule. After being dismissed from his post by the Nazis in 1933, he joined the teaching staff of the Jewish public school in Berlin, moving to Jerusalem when the school and staff transferred there in 1934. Ollendorff returned to Germany in the following year to organize the transfer of Jewish children to Ereẓ Israel within the framework of the newly established Youth Aliyah. In 1937 he was finally expelled by the Gestapo and, on his return to Palestine, joined the staff of the Haifa Technion. Ollendorff was a professor there from 1939. He became research professor in the faculty of electrical engineering and worked in the field of biomedical electronics and physics. He was a member of the Israel Academy of Science and was awarded the Israel Prize for his research in magnetic fields (1954). He was elected a fellow of the American Institute of Electrical Engineers in 1963 and served as the Institute's vice president. His interest in the education of teenagers made him a keen supporter of the Technion's vocational high school. Ollendorff wrote books and papers on electronics, physics, mathematics, acoustics, medical electronics, technical education, and other specialized fields. His publications include *Die Grundlagen der Hochfrequenztechnik* (1926); *Erdstroeme* (1928); *Die Welt der Vektoren* (1950); and *Innere Elektronik* (1955).

[Carl Alpert]

OLLENDORFF, FRIEDRICH (1889–1951), German social welfare expert. Born in Breslau, Germany, Ollendorff studied law. After service in the German army in World War I, he was appointed legal adviser to one of the district municipalities of Berlin. He later turned to social welfare work and was one of the highest officials in the youth welfare and welfare administration of the Berlin municipality. He played an active role in preparing modern welfare legislation in Germany. In 1924 he left his post to become director of the "Zentralwohlfahrtsstelle der deutschen Juden" (Central Office for Social Welfare of German Jewry) and co-editor, with Max Kreuzberger, of the Collection of Welfare Legislation. Ollendorff introduced many new ideas and practices in Jewish welfare work in Germany. In 1934 he immigrated to Palestine and together with his wife, Fanny, a trained social worker, became an adviser to Henrietta *Szold, then director of the social welfare department of the Vaad Leummi (General Council of Palestine Jewry). He introduced the *Kartis ha-Kaḥol* (the blue contribution card) as a means of collecting regular contributions for social welfare. He became the first honorary secretary of the Jerusalem social welfare council, which was composed of the director of social welfare of the Palestine government and representatives of Jewish, Christian, and Muslim welfare institutions. He was also one of the initiators of the International Conference of Jewish Social Work, which held its first meeting in 1928 in Paris.

ADD. BIBLIOGRAPHY: *Biographisches Handbuch der deutschsprachigen Emigration…* (1999), 540 (with bibliography).

[Giora Lotan]

OLMEDO, small town near Medina del Campo, in Old Castile, N. central Spain. The date when Jews first settled there is unknown. The town was captured by Alfonso VI a short while before 1085. In 1095 it was again inhabited and was granted a *fuero* (charter). The community grew particularly during the 13th century. No information is available on Olmedo Jewry throughout the 14th century. In 1458 King John II granted the community an exemption from payment of certain taxes and levies.

Olmedo was the scene of a severe battle fought between the brothers Henry IV and the infante Alfonso in 1467. Although there is no detailed information about the community, it presumably suffered as a result of the war. In 1474 the community taxes amounted to 500 maravedis, while in 1491, immediately before the expulsion from Spain, they increased to 108,500 maravedis, the number of the community having probably increased by refugees from the south. In 1480 the Catholic monarchs ordered an inquiry into the complaint made by the community concerning the closure of the street between the Jewish quarter and the town square. This indicates that the attempts to apply restrictions against the Jews in other Spanish towns were also enforced in Olmedo. After the expulsion of the Jews from Spain in March 1492, Luis de Alcalá and Fernań Núñez Coronel (Abraham *Seneor) were authorized to collect the outstanding debts owed by the Christian population to the Jews who had left because of the expulsion.

BIBLIOGRAPHY: Baer, Urkunden, 2 (1936), 81, 135f., 325; Baer, Toledot, 396; D. de Valera, *Memorial de diversas hazañas*, ed. by J. de M. Carriazo (1941), 123ff.; Suárez Fernández, Documentos, index; P. León Tello, *Los judíos de Palencia* (1967), 193.

[Haim Beinart]

OLMERT, EHUD (1945–), Israeli politician, mayor of Jerusalem 1993–2003, member of the Eighth to Fourteenth and Sixteenth Knessets, and prime miniter from 2006. Olmert was born in Nahalat Jabotinsky. His father, Mordechai Olmert, was a Knesset Member on behalf of the Ḥerut Movement in the Third and Fourth Knessets. Ehud Olmert went to school in Binyaminah. He served in the Golani brigade and was a military correspondent for the army weekly *Ba-Maḥaneh*. He studied psychology, philosophy, and law at the Hebrew University of Jerusalem, and as a student became active in the Ḥerut Movement. At the eighth Ḥerut conference in 1966, he was part of the opposition to Menaḥem *Begin. In 1967 he left the Ḥerut Movement and joined the Merkaz ha-Ḥofshi Party founded by Shmuel *Tamir. He was first elected to the Eighth Knesset in 1973 on the Likud list, of which the Merkaz ha-Ḥofshi was one of the founders. In that Knesset he was especially active on the issue of organized crime in Israel. In 1975 he broke away from the Merkaz ha-Ḥofshi faction within the Likud together with Eliezer *Shostak, and formed Ha-Merkaz ha-Aẓma'i. The following year Ha-Merkaz ha-Aẓma'i joined the La-Am block, and in 1985 La-Am joined the Ḥerut Movement.

Simultaneously with his service in the Knesset, Olmert continued to work as a lawyer, representing *inter alia* clients against state authorities. In 1988 he was appointed minister without portfolio by Yitzhak *Shamir, and after the Labor Party left the National Unity government, he was appointed minister of health. In this capacity he appointed the Netanyahu Commission of Inquiry, to investigate the situation in the health system, and planned to present a national health insurance bill. After the Likud had lost the elections to the Thirteenth Knesset, he ran for election as mayor of *Jerusalem, defeating Jerusalem's long-time mayor Teddy *Kollek with the support of the **ḥaredi* vote. He continued to serve simultaneously as a Knesset member, but resigned from the Knesset in November 1998 after the law had been amended, making it impossible to serve both as a Knesset member and mayor. In the course of the Fourteenth Knesset Attorney General Michael Ben-Ya'ir announced that charges would be brought against Olmert regarding alleged felonies that he had committed while he had served as treasurer of the Likud before the elections to the Twelfth Knesset. His immunity was lifted in October 1996 at his own request, and in September 1997 he was exonerated by the Tel Aviv district court from all the charges against him. As mayor, Olmert supported projects for Jewish construction in various parts of East Jerusalem, in the face of mounting international criticism. He also favored expanding the boundaries of Jerusalem westwards in order to ensure the maintenance of the demographic balance in favor of the Jews in the city, despite the departure of many secular Jews, and the high birthrate among the Arabs.

Olmert did not run in the elections to the Fifteenth Knesset, but decided to run again in the elections to the Sixteenth Knesset, after resigning his post as mayor of Jerusalem. As one of the loyal supporters of Ariel *Sharon, in the government formed by him after the elections to the Sixteenth Knesset, Olmert was appointed vice prime minister and minister of industry and trade, to which was added the labor portfolio, responsibility for the Israel Broadcasting Authority, and additional functions. In this government, until the National Religious Party, the National Union, and Shinui left it, Olmert was one of the more moderate ministers, strongly supporting Sharon's Gaza Strip disengagement plan. Almost singlehandedly he campaigned for the plan when it was brought to a vote in the Likud Conference, and he continued to support it after the plan was defeated there. Following the resignation of Binyamin *Netanyahu in August 2005, Olmert was appointed acting minister of finance; in November 2005 he became minister of finance.

In January 2006, after Prime Minister Sharon was disabled by a stroke, Olmert became acting prime minister. He headed the Kadimah list, the party newly formed by Sharon, in the March 2006 elections. In the elections themselves the Kadimah list won 29 seats, making it the largest party in the Knesset. Olmert was able to form a government along with the Labor Party, Shas, and the newly formed Pensioners list. Olmert vowed to fix Israel's final borders during his term of office, either through negotiations with the Palestinians or unilaterally.

[Susan Hattis Rolef (2nd ed.)]

OLMO, JACOB DANIEL BEN ABRAHAM (c. 1690–1757), Italian rabbi and poet. Born in Ancona, his family moved to Ferrara, where he became a student of Isaac *Lampronti. He served as a teacher and later as head of the yeshivah of Ferrara and as rabbi of the Ashkenazi synagogue there. A student of the Kabbalah, he founded a society of *Shomerim la-Boker* ("Morning Watchers") to pray for the return to Zion. With the death of Lampronti, he became head of the local rabbinical court.

Some of Olmo's legal decisions are included in Lampronti's *Paḥad Yiẓḥak*. A collection of his decisions, entitled *Pi Ẓaddik*, is still in manuscript. His *Eden Arukh* is a poetic drama of 274 stanzas which both in form and content is a continuation and imitation of Moses *Zacuto's *Tofteh Arukh*; the two works were published in one volume (Venice, 1743). *Eden Arukh* is based on talmudic, midrashic, and kabbalistic literature. It was translated into German and into Italian by Cesare Foa (1904). He compiled a work on the sages of the Ashkenazi synagogue of Ferrara and wrote occasional poems and hymns included in various Italian liturgical works. One of his poems, in honor of the wedding of a pupil, consisted of 35 stanzas in Hebrew with Italian words echoing the last Hebrew word at the end of each stanza.

BIBLIOGRAPHY: C. Roth, in: *Melilah*, 3–4 (1951), 204–23; U. Cassuto, in: *Eshkol-Enẓiklopedyah Yisre'elit*, 1 (1929), 890–1; F. Delitzsch, *Zur Geschichte der juedischen Poesie…* (1836), 73, s.v. *Ulamo*; Rhine, in: JQR, 2 (1911/12), 39–42.

[Yonah David]

OLOMOUC (Ger. **Olmuetz**), city in Moravia, Czech Republic. Jews are first mentioned there by *Isaac b. Dorbelo (c. 1140; a 1060 reference by a later chronicler is unreliable). In 1273 the bishop reported disapprovingly to Pope *Gregory x on the Jews of Olomouc. In 1278 Rudolph I of Hapsburg decreed that the Jews must participate in all payments to the city on the same footing as all other citizens. A 1413–20 register of the Jews (*liber fatalis*) and their transactions is extant. There was a *platea Judaeorum* (*Jewish quarter), but the Jewish community was expelled in 1454 and their property ceded to the municipality, which had to assume the taxes previously paid by the Jews. Some individual Jews, however, continued to be tolerated in the town on weekdays. The Jewish community was reconstituted in 1848 and Jews from *Prostejov (Prossnitz) and *Kromeriz transacted business there. The first Jew permitted to resettle was seized by a mob and transported out of the town on a hearse. In 1863 a congregation (*Kultusverein) was founded, in 1867 a cemetery was established, and in 1891 the community was approved. In 1897 a magnificent synagogue was dedicated and in the same year the first Zionist convention of Austria met at Olomouc. In 1900 part of the new municipal cemetery was allotted to the community. Olomouc absorbed many World War I refugees. Jews were instrumental in its economic development, mainly that of the malt industry. In 1903 there were 2,198 Jews (3.3% of the total population) and in 1941, 4,015. With the German occupation, the synagogue was burned down (on March 15, 1939). Jews from the surroundings were concentrated in the city, and of the 3,445 deported to the extermination camps through *Theresienstadt in June–July 1942, there were 232 survivors. After World War II a small community was reestablished. In 1949 a memorial to the victims of the Holocaust was dedicated in the cemetery and in 1955 a synagogue was established. In 1959 the community numbered 450, and was guided by the district rabbi of *Brno. It remained an active community, becoming part of the Czech Republic in 1993. Olomouc was well-known among East European Jewry as a center for the livestock *trade.

BIBLIOGRAPHY: B. Oppenheim, in: H. Gold (ed.), *Die Juden und Judengemeinden Maehrens…* (1929), 451–6; B. Bretholz, *Quellen zur Geschichte der Juden in Maehren… (1067–1411)* (1935), index; idem, *Geschichte der Juden in Maehren im Mittelalter* (1934), index; Germ Jud, 1 (1963), 254–5; 2 pt. 2 (1968), 628; R. Iltis (ed.), *Die aussaeen unter Traenen, mit Jubel werden sie ernten* (1959), 66ff.; K. Hudeczek, *Die Juden in Olmuetz* (1897); W. Haage, *Olmuetz und die Juden* (a Nazi publication, 1944); W. Mueller (ed.), *Urkundliche Beitraege zur Geschichte der maehrischen Judenshaft im 17. und 18. Jahrhundert* (1903); A. Engel, in: JGGJČ, 2 (1930), 58–59.

[Meir Lamed]

OLSCHWANGER, ISAAC WOLF (1825–1896), one of the first rabbis in Russia to join the Ḥibbat Zion movement. Born in Plunge, Lithuania, he was ordained as rabbi in 1845 and held an office in the rabbinate of Taurage (Lithuania). From 1876 until his death he served as rabbi in St. Petersburg. Throughout his life he took part in various public activities and sympathized with the moderate Haskalah movement. At the outset of the Ḥibbat Zion movement in the 1880s, he enthusiastically accepted its tenet of restoring the Jewish people to its homeland and became actively engaged in the movement's undertakings in St. Petersburg, when it still had only a few followers. Later, when the majority of rabbis expressed their opposition to the movement, Olschwanger criticized those rabbis who did not actively strive to bring about the redemption, waiting instead for a divine miracle. Unlike many rabbis, he permitted work on the land in the sabbatical year, when the issue arose for the first time in the settlements in Ereẓ Israel (1889).

BIBLIOGRAPHY: EẒD, 1 (1958), 58–59; N. Sokolow, *Hibbath Zion* (1935), 230–1.

[Getzel Kressel]

OLSEN, TILLIE (1913–), U.S. author. Born Tillie Lerner in Omaha, Nebraska, the daughter of Russian immigrants, her stature rose steadily over the years and she became regarded as one of America's leading writers. Self-taught, with little formal education, she writes about the world with which she is most intimately familiar – the struggles of working people, particularly women.

She was raised in a socialist background and developed her passion for writing as a young girl. In the 1930s she became involved in a variety of political and trade union movements. After dropping out of high school, she was briefly jailed in Kansas City for trying to organize packing-house workers. She then worked full time in various trade unions while writing for left-wing journals.

Married in 1945, she thereafter devoted herself to raising her four daughters, while employed in various menial jobs. A novel begun in the 1930s was finished only 40 years later, and her first book, *Tell Me a Riddle* (1962), a collection of four stories exploring human relationships, was published when she was nearly 50. The title story, published separately in 1961, received the O. Henry Award. It deals with the last months of a terminally ill elderly woman and her attempts to resolve deep-rooted marital conflicts. Another much anthologized story in the collection, "I Stand Here Ironing," explores the relationship of mothers and daughters and the repression of women.

As a result of her publication, Olsen began receiving writing fellowships, including grants from the National Endowment of the Arts, and served as a visiting professor at several universities. In 1974, her novel, *Yonnondio: From the Thirties* was finally published to widespread acclaim. The novel deals with the struggles of a midwestern family during the Depression.

Olsen has also written a biographical and literary commentary of the writer Rebecca Harding Davies who was an early influence on her writing, and a collection of essays, *Silences* (1978). In her 1981 play *I Stand Here Mourning* – a monologue – a mother mourns the blighting of her 19-year-old daughter's life.

[Susan Strul (2nd ed.)]

OLSHAN, ISAAC (1895–1983), Israeli jurist. Born in Kovno, Lithuania, Olshan immigrated to Ereẓ Israel in 1912. He studied at the University of London and served in the Jewish Legion during World War I. From 1927 to 1948 he worked as a lawyer in private practice in Palestine, and after the creation of the State of Israel was one of the original five justices appointed to the Supreme Court. Olshan became president of the Supreme Court in 1953 and served until his retirement in 1965. During his tenure of office he repeatedly emphasized that the state was as much bound by the rule of law as the individual and that respect for the rule of law was one of the foundations of a democratic society.

BIBLIOGRAPHY: *Ha-Peraklit*, 21 (1965), 381–8.

°**OLSHAUSEN, JUSTUS** (1800–1882), German Orientalist, theologian, and Bible scholar. He was born in Schleswig-Holstein and from 1830 to 1852 was professor of Oriental languages at the University of Kiel, and from 1853 professor at the University of Koenigsberg. From 1858, he was adviser to the Prussian Ministry of Religion and Culture. Olshausen was one of the first scholars who used modern philological and comparative linguistic methods in explanation of obscure passages in the Bible. He also applied modern studies in Assyriology to Bible research, and pioneered in the "Arabian School" which employs Arabic as a key to the elucidation of the Bible and the understanding of the Hebrew language and its radicals (in opposition to Ewald's system). In 1826, Olshausen published *Emendationen zum Alten Testament*, giving grammatical and historical explanations to the Old Testament. His theses on the geography, people, and culture of Mesopotamia were confirmed by the findings of later Assyriologists.

Other published works are: *Observationes criticae ad Vetus Testamentum* (1836); *Ueber das Vocalsystem der hebraeischen Sprache nach der sogenannten assyrischen Punktuation* (1865); and *Beitraege zur Kritik des ueberlieferten Textes im Buche Genesis* (1870). His critical method is explained in the second edition of Hirzel's commentary on Job which Olshausen edited (1852), and in his commentary on Psalms (1853), where he stated that most of the psalms were composed in the Maccabean period; this assertion was sharply criticized. His *Zur Topographie des alten Jerusalem* (1833) has been superseded by later discoveries; but *Ueber den Ursprung des Alphabetes und ueber die Vocalbezeichnung im Alten Testamente* (1841), a study on the origin of the Hebrew alphabet and its vocalization, is still important. *Lehrbuch der Hebraeischen Sprache* (1861) is probably his major work. It is a Hebrew grammar; the third volume, devoted to Hebrew syntax, was, however, not published.

BIBLIOGRAPHY: Kamphausen, in: J. Herzog and A. Hauck (eds.), *Realencyklopaedie fuer protestantische Theologie und Kirche*, 14 (1904^3), 368–71; ADB, 24 (1887), 328–30.

OLSVANGER, IMMANUEL (1888–1961), folklorist and Hebrew translator. Born in Poland, he was active in the Zionist movement and was a founder of the student Zionist organization He-Ḥaver. He emigrated to Ereẓ Israel in 1933.

Bein Adam le-Kono, his book of verse, was published in 1943. Olsvanger was among the first to translate Far Eastern literary texts (especially Sanskrit and Japanese) from the original into Hebrew; he also translated poems by Goethe, Dante's *Divine Comedy* (*Ha-Komedyah ha-Elohit*, 3 vols., 1944–56) to which he added notes and wrote an introduction, and Boccaccio's *Decameron* (1947). The two collections of Yiddish proverbs and anecdotes he edited were printed in Latin characters, *Rőyte pomerantsen* (1947) and *L'chayim*! (1949).

BIBLIOGRAPHY: D. Lazar, *Rashim be-Yisrael*, 2 (1955), 267–71.

[Getzel Kressel]

OLYKA, town in Volhynia, Ukraine, formerly in Poland-Lithuania. Jews are first mentioned in the mid-16th century. During the Chmielnicki massacres of 1648–49, they found refuge in the local fortress. In the late 17th–18th centuries the Olyka community was the leading member of the Volhynian Council (one of the *Council of Four Lands). It was one of the principal communities of the council for the province of Volhynia (see *Councils of the Lands), with the right of veto in taxation deliberations. In 1703 the Olyka community protested that these rights had been violated by the leaders of the Volhynian council. In 1765 there were 645 poll tax payers in the Olyka congregation; the Jewish population numbered 2,381 in 1847; 2,606 in 1897 (62% of the total population); 2,086 in 1921 (48.1%); and according to figures of the Jewish Colonization Association, 2,500 in 1924. During WWI Jews suffered from Cossack troops and after the October 1917 revolution from various gangs that operated in the vicinity. In the interwar period the Zionist movement flourished, and it controlled the leadership of the community. A Hebrew school and kindergarten existed in Olyka. All these ceased functioning with the Soviet annexation in September 1939. The Germans occupied the town on July 1, 1941, after having bombed and destroyed 70% of the houses and killing 100 Jews. In August 1941 they murdered 700 Jews, and in March 1942 a ghetto was established, housing 3,500 persons, including many refugees. On August 29, 1942, most of them were executed near the old Radziwill castle. The 130 artisans who had been spared were subsequently murdered in early 1944; 23 young Jews escaped into the woods and were engaged in partisan warfare.

[Mark Wischnitzer / Shmuel Spector (2nd ed.)]

OLYMPIC GAMES. Between 1896 and 2004, Jews won 306 medals (137 gold, 79 silver, 90 bronze) in Olympic competition. (See Table: Jewish Olympic Medal Winners.) In addition, Alfred Hajos (Guttmann) of Hungary, a winner of Olympic swimming medals, was awarded a silver medal in architecture in 1924, and Ferenc Mezo (1885–1961) of Hungary received a 1928 gold medal in literature. As the official historian of the Olympic Games, Mezo wrote numerous articles and books on the subject. He served as a member of the International Olympic Committee and president of the Hungarian Olympic Committee.

[Jesse Harold Silver]

Jewish Olympic Medal Winners: G=Gold S=Silver B=Bronze

	G	S	B
1896			
Alfred Flatow, Germany, gymnastics	3		
Felix Schmal, Austria, cycling.	1		
Felix Flatow, Germany, gymnastics	2		
Alfred Hajos-Guttmann, Hungary, swimming	2		
Dr. Paul Neumann, Austria, swimming	1		
Alfred Flatow, Germany, gymnastics		1	
Felix Schmal, Austria, cycling.		2	
Otto Herschmann, Austria, swimming			1
1900			
Myer Prinstein, USA, track	1		
Myer Prinstein, USA, track		1	
Otto Wahle, Austria, swimming		2	
Edouard Alphonse de Rothschild, France, polo			1
Siegfried Flesch, Austria, fencing			1
1904			
Myer Prinstein, USA, track	2		
Samuel Berger, USA, boxing	1		
Daniel Frank, USA, track		1	
Otto Wahle, Austria, swimming			1
1908			
Dr. Jeno Fuchs, Hungary, fencing	2		
Dr. Oszkar Gerde, Hungary, fencing	1		
Lajos Werkner, Hungary, fencing	1		
Alexandre Lippmann, France, fencing	1		
Richard Weisz, Hungary, wrestling	1		
Jean Stern, France, fencing	1		
Alexander Lippmann, France, fencing		1	
Harald Bohr, Denmark, soccer		1	
Edgar Seligman, Great Britain, fencing		1	
Odon Bodor, Hungary, track			1
Otto Scheff, Austria, swimming			1
Clair S. Jacobs, USA, track			1
1912			
Dr. Jeno Fuchs, Hungary, fencing	2		
Dr. Oszkar Gerde, Hungary, fencing	1		
Lajos Werkner, Hungary, fencing	1		
Gaston Salmon, Belgium, fencing	1		
Jacques Ochs, Belgium, fencing	1		
Edgar Seligman, Great Britain, fencing		1	
Dr. Otto Herschmann, Austria, fencing		1	
Abel Kiviat, USA, track		1	
Alvah T. Meyer, USA, track		1	
Ivan Osiier, Denmark, fencing		1	
Imre Gellert, Hungary, gymnastics		1	
Josephine Sticker, Austria, swimming			1
Mor Kovacs (Koczan), Hungary, track			1
1920			
Samuel Mosberg, USA, boxing	1		
Alexandre Lippmann, France, fencing		1	
Samuel Gerson, USA, wrestling		1	
Gerard Blitz, Belgium, waterpolo		1	
Maurice Blitz, Belgium, waterpolo		1	
Fred Meyer, USA, wrestling			1
Montgomery "Moe" Herzowitch, Canada, boxing			1
Gerard Blitz, Belgium, swimming			1
Alexandre Lippmann, France, fencing			1
1924			
Harold Abrahams, Great Britain, track	1		
Elias Katz, Finland, track	1		
Alexandre Lippmann, France, fencing	1		
Louis A. Clarke, USA, track	1		
Jackie Fields, USA, boxing	1		
Janos Garai, Hungary, fencing		1	
Harold Abrahams, Great Britain, track		1	
Elias Katz, Finland, track		1	
Gerard Blitz, Belgium, waterpolo		1	
Maurice Blitz, Belgium, waterpolo		1	
Alfred Hajos-Guttmann, Hungary, architecture		1	
Baron H.L. De Morpurgo, Italy, tennis			1
Janos Garai, Hungary, fencing			1
Sydney Jelinek, USA, crew			1
1928			
Fanny Rosenfeld, Canada, track	1		
Attila Petschauer, Hungary, fencing	1		
Hans Haas, Austria, weightlifting	1		
Dr. Sandor Gombos, Hungary, fencing	1		
Janos Garai, Hungary, fencing	1		
Dr. Ferenc Mezo, Hungary, literature	1		
Fanny Rosenfeld, Canada, track		1	
Attila Petschauer, Hungary, fencing		1	
Lillian Copeland, USA, track		1	
Fritzie Burger, Austria, figure skating		1	
Ellis R. Smouha, Great Britain, track			1
Harry Devine, USA, boxing			1
Harry Isaacs, South Africa, boxing			1
S. Rabin, Great Britain, wrestling			1
1932			
Attila Petschauer, Hungary, fencing	1		
Endre Kabos, Hungary, fencing	1		
Gyorgy Brody, Hungary, waterpolo	1		
Miklos Skarnay, Hungary, water polo.	2		
Irving Jaffee, USA, speed-skating	2		
Lillian Copeland, USA, track	1		
George Gulack, USA, gymnastics	1		
Hans Haas, Austria, weightlifting		1	
Abraham Kurland, Denmark, wrestling		1	
Dr. Philip Erenberg, USA, gymnastics		1	
Fritzie Burger, Austria, figure skating		1	
Rudolf Ball, Germany, ice hockey			1

	G	S	B
Endre Kabos, Hungary, fencing			1
Nikolaus Hirschl, Austria, wrestling			1
Nathan Bor, USA, Boxing			1
Albert Schwartz, USA, swimming			1
Jadwiga Wajsowna (Weiss), Poland, track			1
1936			
Gyorgy Brody, Hungary, water polo	1		
Miklos Skarnay, Hungary, water polo.	2		
Endre Kabos, Hungary, fencing	2		
Samuel Balter, USA, basketball	1		
Irving Meretsky, Canada, basketball		1	
Helene Mayer, Germany, fencing		1	
Jadwiga Wajsowna (Weiss), Poland, track		1	
Gerard Blitz, Belgium, waterpolo			1
1948			
Frank Spellman, USA, weightlifting	1		
Henry Wittenberg, USA, wrestling	1		
Agnes Keleti, Hungary, gymnastics		1	
Dr. Steve Seymour, USA, track		1	
James Fuchs, USA, track			1
Norman C. Armitage, USA, fencing			1
1952			
Maria Gorokhovskaya, USSR, gymnastics	2		
Boris Gurevich, USSR, wrestling	1		
Mikhail Perelman, USSR, gymnastics	1		
Agnes Keleti, Hungary, gymnastics	1		
Judit Temes, Hungary, swimming	1		
Eva Szekely, Hungary, swimming	1		
Claude Netter, France, fencing	1		
Dr. Gyorgy Karpati, Hungary, waterpolo	1		
Sandor Geller, Hungary, soccer	1		
Grigori Novak, USSR, weightlifting		1	
Agnes Keleti, Hungary, gymnastics		1	
Maria Gorokhovskaya, USSR, gymnastics		1	
Henry Wittenberg, USA, wrestling		1	
Lev Vainshtein, USSR, shooting			1
Agnes Keleti, Hungary, gymnastics			2
Judit Temes, Hungary, swimming			1
James Fuchs, USA, track			1
1956			
Alice Kertesz, Hungary, gymnastics	1		
Leon Rottman, Romania, canoeing	2		
Laszlo Fabian, Hungary, canoeing	1		
Isaac Berger, USA, weightlifting	1		
Agnes Keleti, Hungary, gymnastics	4		
Dr. Gyorgy Karpati, Hungary, waterpolo	1		
Boris Razinsky, USSR, soccer	1		
1960			
Mark Midler, USSR, fencing	1		
Allan Jay, Great Britain, fencing		2	
Vladimir Portnoi, USSR, gymnastics		1	
Isaac Berger, USA, weightlifting			1
Boris Goikhman, USSR, waterpolo		1	
Ildiko Uslaky-Rejto, Hungary, fencing		1	
Klara Fried, Hungary, canoeing			1
Moses Blass, Brazil, basketball			1

	G	S	B
Albert Axelrod, USA, fencing			1
Vladimir Portnoi, USSR, gymnastics			1
David Segal, Great Britain, track			1
Robert Halperin, USA, yachting			1
Rafael Grach, USSR, speed-skating			1
Leon Rottman, Romania, canoeing			1
Imre Farkas, Hungary, canoeing			1
Dr. Gyorgy Karpati, Hungary, waterpolo			1
1964			
Lawrence Brown, USA, basketball	1		
Gerald Ashworth, USA, track	1		
Grigory Kriss, USSR, fencing	1		
Mark Rakita, USSR, fencing	1		
Dr. Gyorgy Karpati, Hungary, waterpolo	1		
Tamas Gabor, Hungary, fencing	1		
Mark Midler, USSR, fencing	1		
Arpad Orban, Hungary, soccer	1		
Ildiko Uslaky-Rejto, Hungary, fencing	2		
Irena Kirszenstein, Poland, track	1		
Yakov Rylsky, USSR, fencing	1		
Irena Kirszenstein, Poland, track		2	
Alain Calmat, France, figure skating		1	
Marilyn Ramenofsky, USA, swimming		1	
Isaac Berger, USA, weightlifting			1
Vivian Joseph, USA, figure skating			1
Ronald Joseph, USA, figure skating			1
James Bregman, USA, judo			1
Yves Dreyfus, France, fencing			1
1968			
Irena Kirszenstein-Szewinska, Poland, track	1		
Mark Spitz, USA, swimming	2		
Victor Zinger, USSR, ice hockey	1		
Boris Gurevich, USSR, wrestling	1		
Valentin Mankin, USSR, yachting	1		
Mark Rakita, USSR, fencing	1		
Eduard Vinokurov, USSR, fencing	1		
Mark Spitz, USA, swimming		1	
Mark Rakita, USSR, fencing		1	
Grigory Kriss, USSR, fencing		2	
Josef Vitebsky, USSR, fencing		1	
Semyon Belits-Geiman, USSR, swimming		1	
Ildiko Uslaky-Rejto, Hungary, fencing		1	
Irena Kirszenstein-Szewinska, Poland, track			1
Mark Spitz, USA, swimming			1
Semyon Belits-Gieman, USSR, swimming			1
Naum Prokupets, USSR, canoeing			1
Ildiko Uslaky-Rejto, Hungary, fencing			1
1972			
Mark Spitz, USA, swimming	7		
Valentin Mankin, USSR, yachting	1		
Faina Melnik, USSR, track	1		
Neal Shapiro, USA, equestrianism		1	
Ildiko Sagine-Rejto, Hungary, fencing		1	
Mark Rakita, USSR, fencing		1	
Eduoard Vinokurov, USSR, fencing		1	
Andrea Gyarmati, Hungary, swimming		1	

Oil lamp, provenance unknown, 5th–6th century C.E. Bronze, 10.5 x 9.5 x 17.0 cm. 89.114/1.
Schloessinger collection, Institute of Archaeology, The Hebrew University, Jerusalem, exhibited at The Israel Museum, Jerusalem. Photo © The Israel Museum, Jerusalem, by David Harris.

The production of ceremonial objects was a major venue through which Jews expressed their artistic abilities, despite the partial prohibition against sculpture. The focus centered on items related to the synagogue and prayers, festivals, and home rituals. Materials and styles for the same function varied among the dispersed Jewish communities, lending a rich texture to the overarching Jewish civilization.

CEREMONIAL OBJECTS

Esther scroll and case. Scroll: Baghdad, Iraq, 19th century. Pen and ink, tempera on parchment, 103 X 1240 cm. Case: Germany, 19th century. Silver, etched, engraved, pierced and cast, partly gilt, 190 cm x 32 cm. *Collection, The Israel Museum, Jerusalem. Photo © Israel Museum, Jerusalem, by Avi Ganor.*

Tevah (prayer stand) for Torah reading. A bench can be drawn out for little boys to stand on while reciting the Targum in Aramaic. San'a, Yemen, 18th century. Wood, carved, painted, and lacquered. 100 x 34 x 30 cm. *Collection, The Israel Museum, Jerusalem. Photo© The Israel Museum, Jerusalem, by David Harris.*

Torah binders, Turkey, 19th–20th century. Brocade, silk, linen, satin. Sephardi Torah binders often included the name of the embroiderer. *Collection, The Israel Museum, Jerusalem. Photo © The Israel Museum, Jerusalem, by Nahum Slapak.*

(opposite page): **Ornate, multi-colored *Havdalah* candles, Bohemia, 20th century.** *State Jewish Museum of Prague.*

Spice box and *Havdalah* cup, Poland, early 19th century. Silver, filigree, repoussé and engraved, partly gilt. H 310cm; W 70cm. *The Stieglitz Collection was donated to the Israel Museum with the contribution of Erica and Ludwig Jesselson, New York, through the American Friends of the Israel Museum. Collection, The Israel Museum, Jerusalem. Photo © The Israel Museum, Jerusalem, by Avi Ganor.*

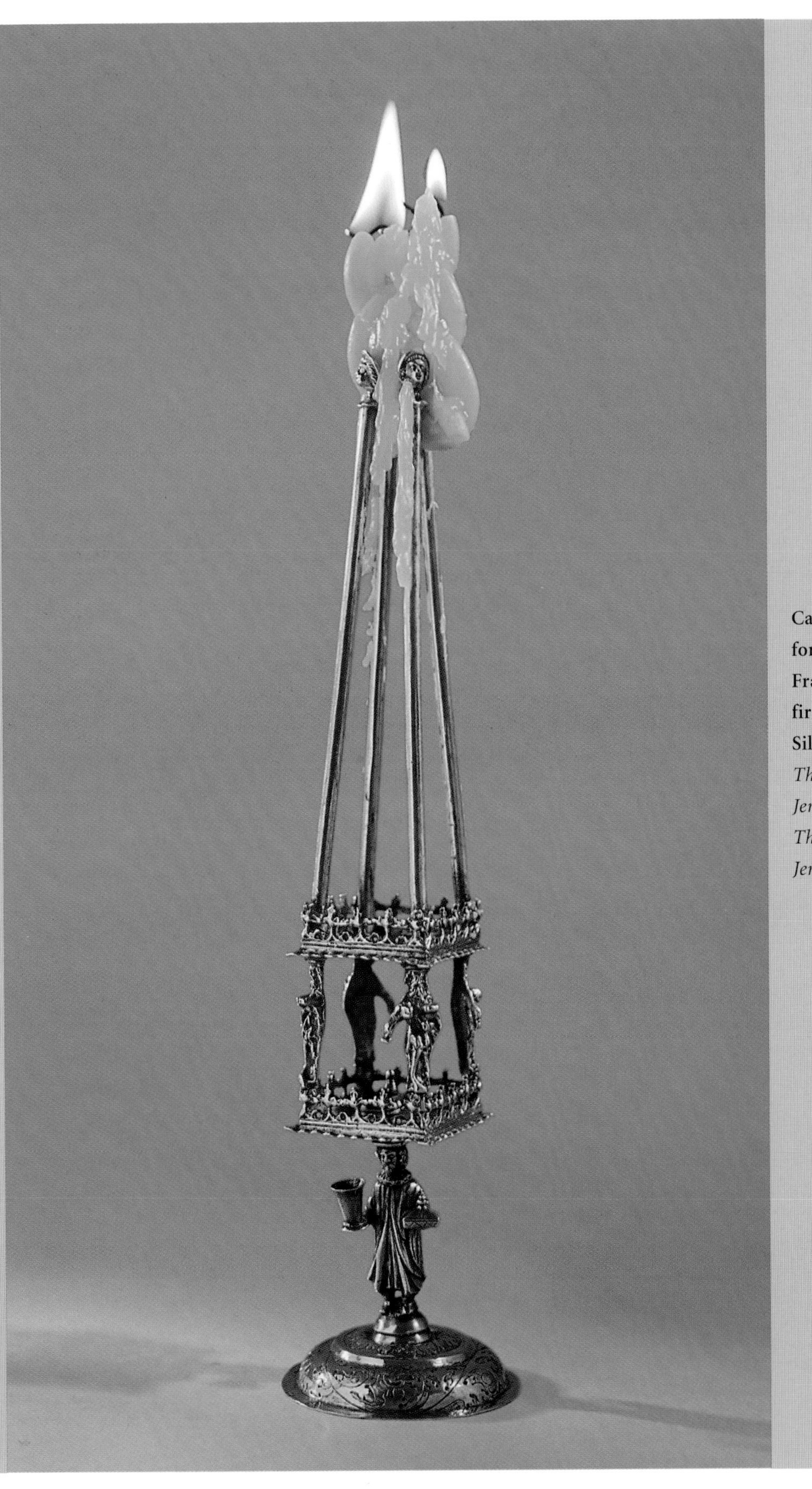

Candle Holder for *Havdalah*, Frankfurt, Germany, first half 18th century. Silver. *Collection, The Israel Museum, Jerusalem. Photo © The Israel Museum, Jerusalem.*

Mezuzah cases (*from left to right*): Germany 19th century; silver, repoussé, engraved and pierced; Central Europe, 19th century, silver, engraved; Slovakia; 19th century, carved wood; Germany, early 19th century, carved wood; Bombay, India, 19th century, brass, cast; United States, 20th century, pierced (by Ludwig Wolpert). *Collection, The Israel Museum, Jerusalem. Photo © The Israel Museum, Jerusalem, by David Harris.*

	G	S	B
Neal Shapiro, USA, equestrianism			1
Grigory Kriss, USSR, fencing			1
Andrea Gyarmati, Hungary, swimming			1
Irena Kirszenstein-Szewinska, Poland, track			1
Donald Cohan, USA, yachting			1
Peter Asch, USA, water polo			1
1976			
Irena Szewinska, Poland, track	1		
Ernest Grunfeld, USA, basketball	1		
Eduard Vinokurov, USSR, fencing	1		
Yuriy Liapkin, USSR, ice hockey	1		
Valentin Mankin, USSR, yachting		1	
Wendy Weinberg, USA, swimming			1
Victor Zilberman, Romania, boxing			1
Edith Master, USA, equestrianism			1
Ildiko Sagine-Rejto, Hungary, fencing			1
1980			
Valentin Mankin, USSR, yachting	1		
Svyetlana Krachevskya, USSR, track and field		1	
1984			
Johan Harmenberg, Sweden, fencing	1		
Mitch Gaylord, USA, gymnastics	1	1	
Carina Benninga, Netherlands, field hockey	1		
Dara Torres, USA, swimming	1		
Robert Berland, USA, judo		1	
Mitch Gaylord, USA, gymnastics			1
Bernard Rajzman, Brazil, volleyball		1	
Mitch Gaylord, USA, gymnastics			2
Mark Berger, Canada, judo			1
1988			
Dara Torres, USA, swimming			1
Brad Gilbert, USA, tennis			1
Carina Benninga, Netherlands, field hockey			1
Seth Bauer, USA, rowing			1
1992			
Joseph Jacobi, USA, canoeing	1		
Dara Torres, USA, swimming	1		
Valeri Belenki, Unified Team, gymnastics	1		
Yael Arad, Israel, judo			1
Arbital Selinger, Netherlands, volleyball		1	
Shay Oren Smadga, Israel, judo			1
Valeri Belenki, Unified Team, gymnastics			1
Dan Greenbaum, USA, volleyball			1
1996			
Sergei Sharikov, Russia, fencing	1		
Kerri Strug, USA, gymnastics	1		
Yanina Batrichina, Russia, rhythmic gymnastics		1	
Sergei Sharikov, Russia, fencing		1	
Myriam Fox-Jerusalmi, France, canoe			1
Gal Fridman, Israel, sailing			1
Maria Mazina, Russia, fencing			1
2000			
Anthony Ervin, Hungary, gymnastics	1		
Lenny Krayzelburg, USA, swimming	3		
Dara Torres, USA, swimming	2		
Sergei Sharikov, Russia, fencing	1		

	G	S	B
Maria Mazina, Russia, fencing	2		
Adriana Behar, Brazil, beach volleyball		1	
Anthony Ervin, USA, swimming		1	
Scott Goldblatt, USA, swimming		1	
Jason Lezak, USA, swimming		1	
Yulia Raskina, Belarus, rhythmic gymnastics		1	
Sara Whalen, USA, soccer		1	
Dara Torres, USA, swimming			3
Robert Dover, USA, equestrian			1
Michael Kalganov, Israel, canoe/kayak			1
2004			
Gal Fridman, Israel, sailing,	1		
Lenny Krayzelburg, USA, swimming	1		
Jason Lezak, USA, swimming	2		
Scott Goldblatt, USA, swimming	1		
Nicolas Massu, Chile, tennis	2		
Adriana Behar, Brazil, beach volleyball		1	
Gavin Fingleson, Australia, baseball		1	
Arik Ze'evi, Israel, judo			1
Deena Kastor, USA, athletics			1
Robert Dover, USA, riding			1
Sada Jacobson, USA, fencing			1
Jason Lezak, USA, swimming			1
Sarah Poewe, Germany, swimming			1
Sergei Sharikov, Russia, fencing			1

OMAHA, city in the state of Nebraska, whose total population is 390,000 and Jewish population approximately 6,500. A few Jews went to Omaha, along with Christian pioneers, when the city was first settled in the mid-1850s. The first two Jews to become permanent residents were Aaron Cahn and his brother-in-law Meyer Hellman, who opened a clothing store and eventually became well-known merchants and citizens. Another early arrival, and perhaps the most prominent early Omaha Jew, was Edward Rosewater, founder and editor of the newspaper the *Omaha Bee*. Another pioneer was Julius Meyer who arrived in 1866 and became friendly with the Ponca Indian chief Standing Bear; he learned to speak six Indian dialects and was adopted by the tribe. The Meyer family was interested in music and was instrumental in establishing the first opera house (1885). The Jewish population of Omaha remained small until after the Civil War. The year 1882 marked the arrival of the first contingent of Jewish refugees from Russia, and from that time until World War I the population increased markedly. Omaha Jews have been particularly active in the retail field.

Jonas L. Brandeis, who came to Omaha in 1881, founded the state's largest department store, and a number of other large retail establishments were founded by Jews. Omaha has had two Jewish mayors, Harry Zimman, who served temporary terms in 1904 and 1906, and John Rosenblatt, mayor from 1954 to 1961. Also active politically was Harry Trustin, who served many terms on the city council and was one of the drafters of the present city charter. Jews as a group have been politically influential since the 1890s.

The earliest recorded Jewish services were held in 1867; the Congregation of Israel was formally organized in 1871. Traditional services were held in the 1880s and a Conservative congregation was begun in 1929. Omaha has four congregations, one Orthodox, one Chabad, one Conservative, and one Reconstructionist. The Associated Jewish Charities was established in 1903 and the Jewish community was federated in 1914. Aleph Zadek Aleph, international junior B'nai B'rith lodge, originated in Omaha in 1924; Henry *Monsky, an Omaha citizen and civic leader, served as national president of B'nai B'rith. Edward Zorinsky was the popular Republican mayor of Omaha before being elected as a Democrat to the United States Senate. Omaha Jewry, generally influential in the community as a whole, has been characterized by a large degree of cohesion and cooperation since shortly after the turn of the century, when Orthodox and Reform Jews joined together to work for their common welfare. Rabbi Myer Kripke, the long-time rabbi of Congregation Beth El, maintains a modest lifestyle. Rabbi Kripke, who drove a three-year-old Chevrolet and lived in a $900 a month apartment, shocked his *Jewish Theological Seminary colleagues – who knew the size of his congregation and had a rough idea of his salary – when his contributions made the Slate 60, the 60 largest contributions of 1997, the year that he gave $7 million toward the reconstruction of the Seminary tower and $1 million to the *Reconstructionist Rabbinical College to fund scholarships. Myer and Dorothy Kripke met while both were students at the seminary in the 1930s. They married and moved to Omaha in 1946. The Kripkes became friendly with investor Warren Buffett, the sage of Omaha and one of the most widely admired investors in the United States. Dorothy Kripke, a writer of children's books, urged her husband to invest with Buffett. Myer Kripke finally agreed in 1966, despite his concern that he had so little money to invest that he would look silly. Over the years, Myer Kripke continued as rabbi and Dorothy to write books and raise their three children. When Buffett closed his limited partnership in 1969, "suddenly we found ourselves wealthy people," the couple told the *Omaha World Herald*. Among the other charities they funded was the Rabbi Myer and Dorothy Kripke Center for the Study of Religion and Society at Creighton University. Rabbi Kripke's son is the preeminent Princeton philosopher Saul *Kripke.

BIBLIOGRAPHY: N. Bernstein, in: *Reform Advocate*, 35 (May 2, 1908), 10–52.

[Carol Gendler / Renee Corcoran and Michael Berenbaum (2nd ed.)]

OMAR, COVENANT OF (Ar. *ʿahd /ʿaqd* - "covenant," or *shurūṭ* – "stipulations"), the series of discriminatory regulations of *Islam applied to the *dhimmī, the protected Christians and Jews, and attributed to the second caliph, Omar (634–644). In various versions it is said that when the Christians of Syria sought their security from Omar, they offered to abide by these conditions. M.J. de Goeje and Caetani have pointed out that this is unlikely because Omar was known for his tolerant and friendly attitude toward the protected subjects who subordinated themselves to him. Furthermore, during the first 50 years of the rule of the *Umayyad Dynasty the protected subjects did not complain of any restrictions, and some of them attained high positions in the administration, while churches were built with the protection of the caliphs. A second reason for doubting the authenticity of the document, as A.S. Tritton wrote, is that "[i]t is not usual for a conquered people to decide the terms on which they shall be admitted to alliance with the victors" (*The Caliphs and their Non-Muslim Subjects*, 8).

Recent research on the Covenant of Omar sees the document in a different light and considers many of its provisions to be consistent with the early years of the conquest, which began in earnest under the caliph Omar. Albrecht *Noth argued that many of the "stipulations" have their source in the conquest treaties or otherwise reflect the reality of Muslim–non-Muslim relations in the earliest period of the conquest. He contended that the *terms* in the covenant originally did not have the restrictive, discriminatory purpose that is so obvious in the actual *text* of the covenant as it existed later on. Many of the stipulations were devised, Noth claimed, to create boundaries between the Muslims and their subjects and protect the fragile identity of the conquerors.

Mark Cohen discussed numerous versions of the covenant, including new ones from the beginning of the tenth century, and addressed the mysterious literary form of the document. Extending Noth's insight, and paying attention to the structure of the texts (as opposed to their content), he explained the document as a petition from the conquered, in which they offered submission in return for protection. In turn, they received confirmation (a decree) from the caliph Omar. This conformed with the normal procedure in Islamic administration and would have been recognized as "authentic" by medieval Muslims. In addition, by placing the restrictive stipulations in the mouth of the dhimmīs, the Muslim case for enforcing the laws and for answering the dhimmīs whenever they violated the rules and claimed ignorance of them was strengthened.

Arabic historical sources indicate that the first caliph to issue discriminatory regulations was Omar ibn ʿAbd al-ʿAzīz (717–720) (Omar II), a zealous ruler who ordered the governor of Khurasan not to authorize the erection of synagogues and churches, to compel "them [Christians and Jews?] to wear special hats and mantles which would distinguish them from the Muslims, and to prohibit them from using a saddle, and from employing a Muslim in their service." These conditions, in addition to the obligation of paying the poll tax, expressed the degradation of the protected subjects according to the principle defined in the *Koran (Sura 9:29), where the word "*ṣāghirūn*," "kept low," appears, and in keeping with the concept of *ghiyār*, "segregation." Several of the stipulations themselves are identical with the anti-Jewish laws of the Byzantine emperors.

The conditions of the covenant and related texts are not uniform but consist of a collection of regulations and administrative restrictions which were promulgated or repromulgated by caliphs and sultans over the generations whenever religious fanaticism or envy of the status of the protected subjects was in the ascendant. There are various versions of these conditions, ranging from the early *kitāb al-ʾUmm* of Muḥammad ibn Idrīs al-Shāfiʿī (767–820), the founder of the *Shāfiʿī* school, and *fatwās* (responsa) of Aḥmad ibn Ḥanbal (d. 855) to the writings of the chroniclers of the *Abbasid and especially the *Mamluk periods, including that of Ibn Khaldūn (1322–1406) and those of two other versions, a short one and a lengthy one brought by Qalqashandī of the 15th century in Egypt. There is also a Hebrew adaptation in the *Divrei Yosef* of Joseph b. Isaac *Sambari who lived in Egypt (1640–1703).

The following points may be summarized from the various versions: (a) The erection or repair of churches and synagogues which did not exist during the pre-Muslim period was prohibited. (b) The Koran was not to be taught to protected subjects. (c) Protected subjects were not to shelter spies. (d) They were not to buy a Muslim slave or maidservant, nor such as were formerly owned by a Muslim. (e) They were not to sell intoxicating liquors to Muslims, nor carcasses of animals not ritually slaughtered, or pork. (f) They were not to employ a Muslim in their service, and in partnerships with non-Muslims they were restricted to the role of the "silent" rather than the trafficking partner. (g) Protected subjects were to honor the Muslims and stand in their presence. They could not deceive or strike them. (h) They were to accommodate Muslim travelers for three days. (i) They were not to prevent anyone from converting to Islam. (j) They were not to resemble Muslims in their clothing or hairdressing. The Jews were to wear yellow clothes, girdles, and hats, the Christians, blue. The girdles were not to be of silk. The color of their shoes was to differ from that of the Muslims. (k) They were not to be called by Muslim names or appellations. (l) Entry into bathhouses was only to be authorized when a special sign was worn on the neck which would distinguish them from Muslims. Special bathhouses were to be built for women so that they would not bathe together with Muslim women. (m) They were forbidden to carry arms. (n) They were not to ride on horses or mules but only on asses, and then on packsaddles without any ornaments, and not on saddles. They were to ride sidesaddle. (o) Their houses were not to be higher than those of the Muslims. (p) Their tombs were not to be higher than those of the Muslims. (q) They were not to raise their voices in their churches or be seen in public with crosses. (r) They were not to be employed as government officials or in any position which would grant them authority over Muslims. (s) The property of the deceased was to belong to the authorities until the heirs proved their right to it according to Islamic law. If there was no heir, the property would be transferred to the authorities.

The head of the religious community was responsible for the enforcement of these conditions. Ibn al-Jawzī (d. 1200) relates that in 1031 the Christian catholics and the Jewish exilarch were ordered to supervise the members of their communities and ensure that they wore the special garb which had been imposed on the protected subjects. Other sources mention that it was the duty of the *raʾīs al-yahūd*, "head of the Jews" (in Hebrew, the **nagid*), "to protect the Muslims from the Jews" by assuming responsibility for the execution of these conditions. The rights which stemmed from the upholding of the Covenant of Omar were security of life and property, freedom of religion, and internal autonomy. Anyone transgressing the covenant or related prohibitions forfeited his right to security, especially in the case of one of the following conditions: failure to pay the poll tax; refusal to accept a Muslim legal decision; the murder of a Muslim by a protected subject; immoral relations with a Muslim woman; spying on behalf of the enemy; and cursing the Prophet in public, which was punishable by death.

The fact that instructions for upholding the covenant were repeatedly issued during various periods, and sometimes at short intervals, shows that most of the conditions were not respected. The Abbasid caliphs also issued discriminatory laws against the Christians and Jews, e.g., Hārūn al-Rashīd (786–809), al-Maʾmūn (813–833), al-Mutawakkil (847–861), who was the most extreme and published a series of restrictions in 850 and 854, and finally al-Muqtadir (908–932). The rulers required the services of physicians, clerks, specialists in minting coins, and other professionals who served them faithfully. They explained that these people were even authorized to serve as viziers upon the condition that their function consisted merely of the execution of orders (*tanfīdh*) and that they were not empowered with any personal initiative (*tafwīḍ*). During periods of religious fanaticism, churches and synagogues were destroyed under the pretext that it had been forbidden to build them (see above, regulation (a)). The most outstanding example was the act of the *Fatimid caliph al-Ḥākim bi-Amr Allah (996–1021) who, as the result of extreme religious fanaticism, ordered – in Egypt from 1004 and in other countries from 1008 – the destruction of all churches, including that of the Holy Sepulcher in Jerusalem, and of all the synagogues throughout the Fatimid empire, in addition to a series of restrictions, which included the choice between forced conversion to Islam or departure from the country. But this was exceptional during the period of Fatimid rule, which was generally characterized by tolerance and during which Jews and Christians rose to important public positions.

The Decrees of the Almohads

Under the rule of the fanatical *Almohads in Spain and Northern Africa during the 12th century, the alternative was placed before the Jews of conversion to Islam, death, or leaving the country, and restrictions in the spirit of the Covenant of Omar were also imposed on the converts to Islam, who were suspected of only having converted outwardly. They were prohibited from possessing slaves and were disqualified from acting as guardians of orphans; the latter were removed from their families and handed over to Muslims. They were also forbidden to engage in commerce. The purpose of these restrictions was also to separate them from the Muslims by special dress. They were not allowed to wear the *ʿimāma* and *iḥrām* (kinds of headgear). Instead, they were requested to cover their heads with a kind of cap known as a *qalansuwa*. They were ordered to wear black clothes with particularly wide hems. These restrictions were in force until the reign of Abdallah ibn Manṣūr (1199–1214). Even after the decrees of the Almohads were abolished from the 13th century onward, the *ghiyār* decrees governing dress were not completely annulled, but were not enforced as strictly as previously.

The Mamluks

Religious fanaticism intensified during the period of the wars against the crusaders; this was evident from the campaign of incitement and pressure for the application of the Covenant of Omar, and even harsher restrictions during the *Mamluk period (1250–1516). This situation was connected with the fact that the foreign ruling class (the Islamized Mamluk slave dynasty) desired to appear as the protector of Islam and thus came under the influence of religious fanatics. It is known that the regulations concerning distinctive dress and the prohibition of riding horses were enforced with more severity than the other restrictions. The Mamluk rulers, nevertheless, could not dispense with the employment of the protected subjects as officials, among them some of whom attained respected positions. This fact and their obvious economic success occasionally gave rise to waves of jealousy and hatred which resulted in the publication of decrees concerning the enforcement of the laws, especially the exclusion of Jews and Christians as public officials. This was the case in 1290, when a decree in this spirit was issued by Sultan Ṣalāḥ al-Dīn Khalīl ibn Qalāʾūn. In 1301 churches and synagogues throughout the empire were closed down for a year. There was even a tendency to destroy them, and this was only averted after it was "proved," with the support of bribery, that they had been erected during the pre-Muslim period. During the middle of the 14th century there was a renewed wave of fanaticism which brought about very severe legislation in 1354, not only including the previous restrictions of the Covenant of Omar but also new restrictions which also affected converts to Islam, e.g., the prohibition of their employment as officials and physicians, the severance of all relations with their nonconverted relatives, and their obligatory presence five times a day at the mosque.

The Ottoman Empire, the Maghreb, and Iran

In the *Ottoman Empire (and in *Iran, with stricter, Shiite embellishments) the Covenant of Omar was in force until the middle of the 19th century. The authorities imposed special dress, and Jews and Christians were forbidden to acquire slaves. There was a prohibition on the construction of synagogues and churches, which could only be circumvented by bribery and special authorization. During the 17th century synagogues and churches in the empire were destroyed on a number of occasions. The *jizya* (poll tax) was also paid, except for those connected with the royal court, e.g., court physicians, who were exempted and who were the only Jews authorized to ride on horses and wear clothing in keeping with their status.

In the 19th century, under the pressure of European countries, especially Britain, France, and Austria, firmans were issued which abolished the discriminatory measures against the Christians. The first of these abolished the poll tax (1839). It was not enforced, and under further pressure an additional firman was issued in 1855, and again in 1856 when the prohibition on the carrying of arms by non-Muslims was also abolished and they were exempted from military service. As an alternative to military service a ransom tax known as *bedel askeri*, which in practice replaced the poll tax, was imposed. This tax was not abolished until the revolution of the Young Turks in 1909, when non-Muslims were also ordered to serve actively in the army.

In the countries of the Maghreb, the Covenant of Omar remained in effect until more recently. The *jizya* was taken into consideration in the Tunisian Constitution of 1857. In the *capitulation treaties between Morocco and the European countries in the second half of the 19th century certain persons are mentioned who were exempted from this tax.

Even though in principle the Covenant of Omar applied equally to Christians and Jews, the position of the former within society was generally more favorable as a result of the backing they received from European states. Thus, in 1664 all the European Christians in Egypt were exempted from the poll tax. Similarly, in the emirate of Bukhara only the Jews paid this tax.

It may be said that in principle protected subjects were bound by the Covenant of Omar, but that its enforcement was conditioned by internal factors of the Muslim countries; it was dependent on the internal struggles and the conflicts between religious and economic interests, on the one hand, and the influence and the status of the protected subjects themselves and their ability to lessen the severity of the decree, on the other. The execution of the restrictions was dependent on the will of the ruler, who generally gave preference to economic interests over religious law. Rarely was the covenant enforced against Jews alone. Exceptions to this were in North Africa in the post-Almohad period, when converted Christians, unlike converted Jews, failed to revert to their former religion, and in the Yemen, where very few Christians dwelled. The so-called "pogrom" against the Jews of Granada in 1066 was also an exception proving the rule.

BIBLIOGRAPHY: M. Steinschneider, *Polemische und apologetische Literatur in arabischer Sprache…* (1877), 165–87; M.J. de Goeje, *Mémoires d'histoire…*, 2 (1886), 143; R. Gottheil, in: *Old Testament and Semitic Studies in Memory of W.R. Harper*, 2 (1908), 353–414; idem, in: JAOS, 41 (1921), 383–457; L. Caetani (ed.), *Annali dell' Islam*, 3 (1911),

957; A. Tritton, *The Caliphs and their Non-Muslim Subjects* (1930); L.A. Mayer, in: *Sefer Magnes* (1938), 161–7 (English summary); W.J. Fischel, *Jews in the Economic and Political Life of Mediaeval Islam* (1969[2]); idem, in: *Zion*, 5 (1940), 209–13; Ashtor, *Toledot*, 1 (1944), 305–7; idem, in: *Sefer Zikkaron… G. Hirschler* (1940), 73–94; A.S. Halkin, in: *Joshua Starr Memorial Volume* (1953), 101–10 (Hebrew); Dinur, Golah, 1 pt. 1 (1958[2]), 60–70; M. Khadduri, *War and Peace in the Law of Islam* (1955), 175–201; A. Fattal, *Le Statut légal des non-Musulmans en pays d'Islam* (1958); B. Lewis, *Emergence of Modern Turkey* (1966), 114, 331; H.Z. Hirschberg, in: A.J. Arberry (ed.), *Religion in the Middle East*, 1 (1969), 150–60. **ADD. BIBLIOGRAPHY:** A. Noth in: *Jerusalem Studies in Arabic and Islam* 9 (1987), 290–315. M.R. Cohen, in: ibid. 23 (1999), 100–57; idem, *Under Crescent and Cross: The Jews in the Middle Ages* (1974). B. Lewis, *Islam: From the Prophet Muhammad to the Capture of Constantinople* (1974), vol. 2, chap. 11; idem, *The Jews of Islam* (1984); D. Tsadik, in: *Islamic Law and Society* 10, 3 (2003).

[Eliezer Bashan (Sternberg) / Mark R. Cohen (2nd ed.)]

°OMAR IBN AL-KHAṬṬĀB, second caliph (634–644), conqueror of Ereẓ Israel, Syria, Iraq, Persia, and Egypt. Omar organized the Muslim empire, established the rules assuring the conquerors of their special status (in spite of their numerical inferiority), fixed the calendar on the basis of the Hegira, and laid the foundations of the legal system. The administrative practices that he introduced were based on Persian and Byzantine models. A man of simple manners and approach, he adopted a humane attitude to non-Muslims as well, and earned the epithet of al-Fārūq ("he who can distinguish truth from falsehood"); according to one tradition, the Jews gave him that name. Balādhurī (d. 862) reports that the Jews of *Khaybar, the last Jewish community in the Hejaz, who had been permitted by *Muḥammad to remain on their land in exchange for one half of their yearly crop, were expelled to Tayma and Jericho by Omar; Ibn al-Athīr (Mosul, 1160–1233) adds that Omar reimbursed them with one half the value of their land. According to Jewish sources, Omar, after the conquest of Persia, gave the Persian king's daughter to *Bustanai in marriage and appointed him to the office of exilarch. A Jewish convert to Islam, *Kaʿb al-Aḥbār, who was a member of Omar's entourage at the time of the conquest of *Jerusalem, is said to have pointed out to Omar the site of the "*Sakhra*," the "**Even Shetiyyah*" ("world's cornerstone") on the Temple Mount; Omar ordered the clearing of the Rock and the site served as a place of prayer until the time of ʿAbd al-Malik (685–705), who built the Dome of the Rock (which became popularly known as the "Mosque of Omar") on this spot. Some Christian and Arab sources report that one of the conditions set by the Christian residents of Jerusalem for their surrender to Omar was a prohibition on the residence of Jews in Jerusalem; the truth of these reports seems doubtful, since Jews did in fact live in Jerusalem during the Arab period. Omar permitted the Jews to reestablish their presence in Jerusalem – after a lapse of 500 years –and also seems to have allotted them a place for prayers on the Temple Mount (from which they were driven out at a later date). Jewish tradition regards Omar as a benevolent ruler and the Midrash (*Nistarot de-Rav Shimon bar Yoḥai*) refers to him as a "friend of Israel." According to Ṭabarī, a Jewish sage told Omar that he was destined to become the ruler of the Holy Land. Omar has been described as the author of the rules discriminating against minorities in Muslim lands (see *Omar, Covenant of), but this allegation does not stand up to scientific investigation.

BIBLIOGRAPHY: G. Weil, *Geschichte der Chalifen* (1846), 54–148; A. Kremer, *Culturgeschichte des Orients unter den Chalifen*, 1 (1875), 14–16, 65–71, 99–105; W. Muir, *Annals of the Early Caliphate* (1883), 125–285; Ch. Tykocinski, in: *Devir*, 1 (1923), 145–79; Assaf, Mekorot, 12–22; S.D. Goitein, in: *Melilah*, 3–4 (1950), 156–65; Dinur, Golah, 1 pt. 1 (1959), 31–42; B. Zoltak, in: H. Lazarus Yafeh (ed.), *Perakim be-Toledot ha-ʿAravim ve-ha-Islam* (19682), 105–17; H.Z. Hirschberg, *ibid.*, 269–70; A. Fattal, *Le Statut légal des non-Musulmans en pays d'Islam* (1958), 60–68. **ADD. BIBLIOGRAPHY:** EIS[2] 10 (2000), 818–21.

[Eliezer Bashan (Sternberg)]

OMER (Heb. עֹמֶר), urban community in southern Israel. Omer is located 4 mi. (6 km.) northeast of Beersheba. It was established in 1961 by a group of Beersheba residents. Some proceeded to earn their livings as farmers and others worked in the nearby settlements and factories. Over the years, agriculture languished and the settlement was further urbanized. In 1974 it received municipal status. In 2002 its population reached 5,840, occupying a land area of 5.4 sq. mi. (14 sq. km.). Seventy percent of Omer's population held an academic degree. Women enjoyed the highest average earnings in the country and men the second highest. The settlement has a nearby industrial park housing such hi-tech companies as Motorola. The name Omer derives from the El Omri hill located in the industrial park area.

WEBSITE: www.omer.muni.il; www.cityindex.co.il.

[Shaked Gilboa (2nd ed.)]

OMER (Heb. עֹמֶר, lit. "sheaf"), an offering brought to the Temple on the 16th of Nisan and thus the name of the period between Passover and Shavuot.

The Bible (Lev. 23:9ff.) prescribes that "when you enter the land which I am giving to you and reap its harvest, you shall bring the first sheaf of your harvest to the priest… the priest shall wave it on the day after the sabbath." After the waving, a burnt offering together with a meal offering and a libation were made at the altar and after that had been done it was permissible to eat of the new harvest: "Until that very day, until you have brought the offering of your God, you shall eat no bread or parched grain or fresh ears." The exact meaning of "the day after the sabbath" in the biblical passage was a major point of controversy between the rabbis and the *Boethusians (Men. 65a–b) and, later, the *Karaites. The latter argued that the ceremony was to be performed on the day after the Sabbath immediately following the first day of Passover whereas the rabbis argued that in this context the word "sabbath" was to be understood not as the weekly Sabbath but as a "holy day" and meant the first day of Passover itself. Since the passage quoted continues with the law "And from the day on which you bring the sheaf of wave offering – the day after the Sabbath – you shall count seven weeks" and the fiftieth day is Shavuot it follows that according to the sectarians the festival of Shavuot always fell on a Sunday. It has been suggested (L. Finkelstein, *The Pharisees* (1962[3]), 2, 641 ff.) that this was a major factor in the dissidents' view, as having the festival always on a Sunday was far more convenient for the Temple cult.

The rabbis, in the light of Exodus 16:36 – "The *Omer* is a tenth of an *ephah*" – interpreted the word as a measure of grain and also ruled that it was to be brought of barley only. The *ephah* was three *se'ot* and thus on the 16th of Nisan three *se'ot* of barley were reaped, brought to the Temple, ground and sifted, and of this, one tenth (the *Omer*) was "waved" by the priest. The Mishnah (Men. 10) describes the ritual in detail. It was celebrated with a great deal of ceremony and festivity in order to stress the opinion of the rabbis that the 16th of Nisan was the correct date. The ceremony, including the reaping, took place even if the 16th of Nisan was a Sabbath; one opinion has it that on a weekday five *se'ot* were reaped since after sifting only three would remain but that on a Sabbath only three were reaped so as to avoid unnecessary work (Men. 10:1). If the barley was ripe it was taken from the vicinity of Jerusalem; otherwise it could be brought from anywhere in Israel. It was reaped by three men, each with his own scythe and basket. The grain was then brought to the Temple where it was winnowed, parched, and ground into coarse flour. It was then sifted through 13 sieves and one tenth was given to the priest who mixed it with oil and frankincense for "a pleasing odor to the Lord" and "waved" it "before the Lord." This was done by the priest taking the offering on his outstretched hands and moving it from side to side and up and down. This ceremony was interpreted as a prayer to God to protect the harvest from injurious winds and other calamities (Men. 62a). After the waving ceremony a handful was burnt on the altar and the rest was eaten by the priests.

Counting the Omer

(Heb. סְפִירַת הָעֹמֶר, *Sefirat ha-Omer*). The injunction to count the 49 days from the 16th of Nisan until Shavuot is considered to be of Pentateuchal authority as long as the *Omer* itself was offered; thus at present time it is of rabbinic authority only. The 49 days themselves are commonly known as the *sefirah*.

The counting is preceded by a special benediction "… concerning the counting of the *Omer*." Since the Bible states that "You shall count off seven weeks. They must be complete" and "You must count… fifty days," the counting must mention both the number of days and the number of weeks (Men. 65b–66a). Hence the standard formula runs as follows: on the first day, "Today is the first day of the *Omer*"; on the eighth day, "Today is the eighth day, making one week and one day of the *Omer*," and so on. The time for the counting, which is to be done standing, is after the evening service, that is, when the new day begins (Sh. Ar., OḤ 489:1). One who forgets to count in the evening may count during the following day, without however reciting the blessing. He may then count again the same evening, using the blessing. But if he fails to count for one complete day, he is not permitted to resume the utterance of the blessing for the whole duration of the *Omer* (Sh. Ar., OḤ 489:7–8). And since the sole stipulation of the commandment is that the number of the particular day of the *Omer* is to be spoken aloud, one should avoid uttering it inadvertently once the time for counting has arrived; for example, if one has not yet counted and is asked what the number of the day is, one should reply by giving the number of the previous day (Sh. Ar., OḤ 489:4).

The kabbalists used the 49 days (7×7) to form permutations of various *sefirot* denoting the ascent out of the 49 "gates" of impurity of the Egyptian bondage to the purity of the revelation at Sinai. In many prayer books these combinations are printed at the side of each day listed. Because the days counted "must be complete" it has become customary not to recite the evening service for Shavuot until after nightfall of the 49th day, whereas for other festivals it is permissible to start some time before nightfall (see *Day and Night).

In order not to forget the count of the day it was fairly common practice to have an "*Omer* calendar" in the home with movable numbers on it. These "calendars" even developed into an art form and several early specimens show intricate work and lettering.

A Time of Mourning

From an unknown date during the talmudic period, the days of the *Omer* began to take on a character of semi-mourning; the solemnization of marriages was prohibited, then haircutting, and, later still, the use of musical instruments was banned. The mourning is normally associated with a plague said to have decimated the disciples of Rabbi kiva, who died "because they did not treat each other with respect" (Yev. 62b; cf. Sh. Ar., OḤ 493:1). But this reason for the mourning is among the many uncertainties connected with the *Omer* period and with *Lag ba-Omer, the minor festival celebrated on its 33rd day. The Talmud alludes to the plague, but makes no mention of any commemorative mourning. This is first recorded in the eighth century, when Neutrino Gone issued a responsum confirming both the practice of mourning and the accepted reason for it (Levin, Oẓar, Yevamot, 141). Subsequent codes and compilations of custom up to and including the Shulḥan Aruch (OḤ 493) cite this reference; and most, although not all (e.g., *Toledot Adam ve-Ḥavvah*, 5, 4; *Abudraham ha-Shalem* (1959), 245), presume that the custom did in fact originate with the death of Akiva's disciples. On the other hand, Maimonides' *Mishneh Torah* and the Ashkenazi *Maḥzor Vitry* appear unaware of its very existence.

Lag ba-Omer

The origin of Lag ba-Omer is likewise shrouded in mystery. It is not explicitly mentioned any earlier than the 13th century, when Meiri in his commentary to *Yevamot* (*Beit ha-Beḥirah*, Yev. 62b) described it as the day when, "according to a tradition of the *geonim*," the "plague" surceased. Moreover there are differences of opinion as to how the date of Lag ba-Omer is to be calculated. Fundamentally, there are two approaches to the question, which in turn account for the different periods of time (according to various rites) when the mourning restrictions are held to be in force.

One school of thought sees the 33rd day of the *Omer* as the anniversary of the termination of the plague. The authority for this view derives from a Midrash, no longer extant, which was handed down by Joshua ibn Shu'aib in the 14th century, or possibly based on an unknown "Spanish manuscript" cited by Zerahiah b. Isaac ha-Levi of the 12th century (see Tur, OḤ 493). In place of reading "they died from Passover to Shavuot," this Midrash adds the word "*pros*," i.e., "they died from Passover until before (*ad pros*) Shavuot." Pros" is taken to mean 15 days before; and thus implies that the plague terminated a fortnight before Shavuot, and Lag ba-Omer is the anniversary of that day. Strictly speaking, however, 15 days before Shavuot would be the 34th day of the *Omer*, as indeed the Shulḥan Arukh concedes.

The present custom, then, must be attributed to a different calculation which is given by Isserles in his gloss to the Shulḥan Arukh. The explanation stems from a *tosafot*, also no longer extant, cited by Ibn Shu'aib and most fully elaborated on by Jacob b. Moses Moellin in the 15th century in his *Sefer Maharil* (1873), 21b. In this work, Lag ba-Omer appears not as an anniversary at all but as a symbol of the 33 weekdays that occur during the course of the 49 days of the *Omer*. After subtracting the days of Passover, and those of the Sabbath and of Rosh Ḥodesh, only 33 are left from the 49 in which mourning is permissible; this fact is symbolically observed by constituting the 33rd day as a minor festival. This second mode of interpretation gave rise to three divergent customs regarding the mourning period. Some communities observed it for the 33 days from Passover to Shavuot omitting the special days, others for the 33 between Passover and Lag ba-Omer, and others for the 33 from after Rosh Ḥodesh Iyyar to Shavuot excluding Lag ba-Omer itself. The kabbalists took an entirely different approach to the matter. As to *sefirah* days, they stressed the idea of spiritual preparation for Shavuot, the anniversary of the revelation on Mt. Sinai (*Ḥemdat Yamim*, 3, 41d). Lag ba-Omer itself marked the **hillula* – the *yahrzeit* of *Simeon. b. Yoḥai, by tradition the author of the Zohar. It was either the day on which he was ordained by Rabbi Akiva, or when he emerged from the cave in Meron where he had been hiding from the Romans (Shab. 33b), or the day on which he died; and it is observed as a *hillula* – a festivity or a "wedding between heaven and earth." Hence the grand celebrations which take place at Meron (*Zohar Idra Zutra*, end of *Ha'azinu*). However, although the Zohar does speak of Simeon's death as a *hillula*, there is no recorded reference to its date earlier than that in *Peri Ez Ḥayyim* by Ḥayyim b. Joseph Vital (16/17th century; *Sha'ar Sefirat ha-Omer*, ch. 7).

While the celebrations at Meron excited enthusiasm among all sections of Jewish society and particularly from the kabbalists, they also provoked severe criticism. R. Moses *Sofer of Pressburg (d. 1839), after opposing the popular observance of lighting bonfires and questioning all of the reasons given above for the observance of Lag ba-Omer, offered his own explanation for the holiday. Lag ba-Omer is the day when manna began to fall in the wilderness (*Resp. Ḥatam Sofer*, YD 236). Since, however, the Talmud (Shab. 87b) and the *Sefer Olam* calculate that this happened two days earlier, there is, in the last resort, no unassailable determination of what actually took place on Lag ba-Omer; the only definite tradition is that the day is a holiday.

It has for a long time been considered – Nachman Krochmal (d. 1840) being the most notable to express this view – that the cryptic reference in the Talmud to the disciples of R. Akiva and their mysterious death is in fact a veiled report of the defeat of "Akiva's soldiers" in the war with Rome (cf. Maimonides, *Yad Melakhim* 11:3; probably based on TJ, Ta'an. 4:5). As a result, a variety of new theories have arisen among modern writers as to the origin of Lag ba-Omer. R. Isaac Nissenbaum of Warsaw, author of several books on religious Zionism, suggested that Lag ba-Omer is the anniversary of some great but brief triumph by the Judeans in their forlorn war with the Romans – possibly the recapture of Jerusalem, for which special coins were struck (*Hagut Lev* (1911), 181). Y.T. Levinsky, in *Sefer ha-Mo'adim* (1955), 340–2, pursues this line further; he cites Josephus (Wars 2:402ff.) as authority for the fact that a Judean uprising commenced in 66 C.E. in the days of the procurator Florus. At the same time he concurs with the tradition associating the victory on Lag ba-Omer with Bar Kokhba 70 years later, as well as with the story that Julius Serverus' campaign against the insurrectionist Judeans was most severe during the period between Passover and Shavuot.

Eliezer Levi (*Yesodot ha-Tefillah* (1952), 232) advanced a hypothesis endeavoring to resolve another problem sensed by earlier writers; namely why we should mourn for the disciples of Rabbi Akiva, since they died as a punishment for their unseemly conduct? In view of the veiled references to the war with the Romans, he suggests, the judgment of the Talmud is to be understood not as condemning Akiva's disciples and their lack of respect for one another, but on the contrary as praising their dedication and teamwork. On the other hand, it may be that the phrases in the Talmud are to be understood in their literal sense: "Akiva's soldiers" were defeated due to a lack of coordination and unified command (see *Panim el Panim*, no. 574, May 22, 1970). The earlier traditions surrounding Bar Yoḥai's connection with Lag ba-Omer are entirely in accord with these theories, and one might then draw up a summary or composite theory in the following vein: Bar Kokhba's (i.e., Akiva's) men suffered an overwhelming defeat during the weeks between Passover and Shavuot; on the 33rd day of the *Omer* they enjoyed an important, though brief, change of fortune; and on this day Bar Yoḥai, one of the leading fighters in the uprising, either emerged from hiding in Meron, or lost his life in securing the victory.

Other Explanations

Extra-rabbinic sources do not help to clarify the matter. Some students of folklore trace the mournful nature of the days of the *sefirah* to the Roman superstition against marriages in May. The fullest statement of this theory was made in the 19th century by Julius Landsberger of Darmstadt (see bibl.). The author cites Ovid (Fast 5: 419ff.), who explains that the Romans did not solemnize marriages in May due to the fact that this was the month of the *Lemuria* when the souls of the departed returned to wander over the earth and disturb the peace of the living. Funeral rites (*Lemuria*) were held to appease the spirits, and no Roman maiden would jeopardize her happiness by marrying during a month associated with funeral ceremonies. According to Landsberger, the Roman superstition was adopted by the Jews, who subsequently lost all recollection of its origin and found a new rationale for it in the tragedy of Akiva's disciples. Landsberger's theory leaves many questions unanswered. It does not explain why there is a ban on haircutting during the *Omer* as well as on marriage, or why the custom prevailed in geonic countries. But it does, however, offer an ingenious explanation of the origin of Lag ba-Omer. Among the Romans, the period of superstitious fear lasted for 32 days starting from Walpurgis Night (the last night of April) and continuing throughout the 31 days of May. In commemoration of this period of 32 days, its conclusion on the 33rd day was celebrated as a festival.

Theodor H. Gaster (*Festivals of the Jewish Year* (1953), 52) suggests that Lag ba-Omer, especially with its custom of children going forth with bows and arrows, is a Jewish version of the English and German custom of shooting arrows at demons on May day, i.e., the day after Walpurgis Night. In the view of Joseph Naphtali Derenbourg (in REJ, 29 (1894), 149), Lag ba-Omer is a day in the middle of the *sefirah* period when mourning is to be relaxed, comparable to *mi-carême* observed midway during Lent. There were 34 (twice 17) bad days during the *sefirah*; a respite was needed and the first day of the second half was chosen. J. Morgenstern (in: HUCA, 39 (1968), 81–90) points out that the date of Lag ba-Omer is the approximate midpoint of the 49-day period for those dissidents who begin their *Omer* offering the day after Passover. L.H. Silberman (see bibl.) following H. Grimme, regards the day as commemorating an anniversary celebrated in honor of Marduk; and Gustav Dalman conjectured that it may have marked the first day of summer between the 13th and 25th of May, which was distinguished by the early rising of the Pleiades (cf. RH 11b).

Later Events During the Omer

If the origins of the mourning during the *sefirah* period remain obscure, more identifiable subsequent events add justification for its observance today. According to 13th-century authorities, the melancholy of the season was in remembrance of the victims of the Crusades in the Rhineland in 1096 and 1146 (*Sefer Minhag Tov, Sefer Asufot*). These Crusades are recollected in *piyyutim* of lament during the Sabbaths of the *sefirah*, together with mention of another series of massacres that took place in the springtime, i.e., those perpetrated in 1648–49 by the Cossacks and the Poles. Later and modern sources, such as the *siddur* of Jacob Emden and the *Arukh ha-Shulḥan* (OḤ 493:1) include these together with the earlier events. And in J. Vainstein's *Cycle of the Jewish Year* (1953), 131–2, the revolt of the ghettos against the Nazis in the month of Nisan is included in the discussion of the *sefirah* and mention is made of the Knesset's decision to fix the 27th of that month as a memorial day for the victims. On the other hand, Israel Independence Day (5th of Iyyar) has the status of a half-holiday, and has been included among the days on which mourning restrictions are suspended (Resp. *Kol Mevasser pt.* 1, no. 21).

BIBLIOGRAPHY: S. Goren, *Torat ha-Mo'adim* (1964), 346–58; J. Landsberger, in: JZWL, 7 (1869), 81–96; L.H. Silberman, in: HUCA, 22 (1949), 221–37; J. Morgenstern, in: HUCA, 39 (1968), 81–90; D.M. Feldman, in: *Proceedings of the Rabbinical Assembly* (1962), 201–24; E. Munk, *World of Prayer*, 2 (1963), 137–42; S.Y. Zevin, *Ha-Mo'adim ba-Halakhah* (1963[10]), 292–304.

[David M. Feldman]

OMER (Ayin), HILLEL (1926–1990), Hebrew writer and poet. Born and educated in the kibbutz Mishmar *ha-Emek, Hillel fought in the *Palmaḥ during the Israel War of Independence. After the war he studied horticulture in Paris. His first poems were published when he was 18, and his first collection, *Ereẓ ha-Ẓohorayim*, appeared in 1950. His books of stories and verse for children include *Boker Tov* (1961) and *Dodi Simḥah* (1964). In 1968, he was appointed director of the Department of Landscape and Gardening of the Tel Aviv municipality.

BIBLIOGRAPHY: M. Shamir, *Be-Kulmos Mahir* (1960), 148–52; M. Avishai, *Bein Olamot* (1962), 174–84; S. Burnshaw et al. (eds.), *The Modern Hebrew Poem Itself* (1965), 174–7.

[Getzel Kressel]

OMNAM KEN (Heb. אָמְנָם כֵּן; "Yes, it is true"), initial words and name of a penitential *piyyut* for the *Kol Nidrei service on the eve of the Day of Atonement, known only in the Ashkenazi (German and Polish) ritual. This *piyyut*, of an alphabetical acrostic pattern, was composed by R. *Yom Tov of Joigny, who died as a martyr in the York massacre in 1190. The *piyyut* emphasizes the sinfulness of man who fails because of his evil inclinations, and pleads for God's forgiveness and mercy. Each of its 11 stanzas ends with *salaḥti* ("I have pardoned"), derived from Numbers 14:20.

Text and English translation printed in *High Holiday Prayerbook*, ed. by Morris Silverman (1954[2]), 233; *Service of the Synagogue, Day of Atonement*, 1 (1955), 38.

BIBLIOGRAPHY: Davidson, Oẓar, 1 (1924), 263, no. 5764.

OMRI (Heb. עָמְרִי), king of Israel (c. 882–871 B.C.E., I Kings 16:16–28), contemporary of King Asa of Judah. Omri's father's name is not mentioned in sources. According to II Kings 16:23, Omri reigned over the Kingdom of Israel for 12 years, six of them in Tirzah. But according to the synchronism with the king of Judah, it would seem that he reigned only eight years (I Kings 16:23, 29). The background of Omri's ascent to the throne at Tirzah was the extinction of *Baasha's dynasty and struggle for power among the high officers of the army, When the report was received that *Zimri had liquidated *Elah, son of Baasha, "all Israel" made Omri "the captain of the host," king of Israel. At that time Omri was on the field of battle, fighting the Philistines at the border town of Gibbethon (I Kings 16:15, 17; cf. 15:27). Omri and "all Israel" with him turned north to Tirzah, which they besieged and captured. After Zimri's death, the struggle for the throne continued between Omri and *Tibni son of Ginath (I Kings 16:21–22), each respectively having the support of "half of the people," and ended with the latter's death.

Of all Omri's deeds after he became king of Israel, only one item is mentioned in the Bible, which concerns his founding of the city of *Samaria. Omri left Tirzah, which had been the royal capital since the reign of *Jeroboam the son of Nebat (14:17), and built himself a new capital on land which he bought from Shemer, "the owner of the hill Samaria" (16:24). Samaria remained the capital of the Kingdom of Israel for the rest of its existence. The name Omri became an established term to indicate the Israelite kings (in the Assyrian documents *Bît Ḥumri*) even after the death of Omri and his descendants. According to archaeological evidence, the building of the Samarian acropolis and the royal palace within, begun in Omri's reign, was only completed in the time of his son *Ahab. The removal of the capital from Tirzah to Samaria marks a new chapter in the history of the Israelite kingdom. Omri achieved stability in internal affairs, after a prolonged period of riots and tumult in the court, and founded a dynasty which remained in power for nearly 50 years. The stabilization of the central government brought in its wake a general improvement in Israel's military and political standing. In the stele of *Mesha king of Moab, it is related that Omri gained possession of Madaba in the northern section of the plain north of the Arnon. Omri's successes in southern Transjordan were the result of a policy of mending quarrels and establishing peaceful relations with neighbors in the north and in the south. In Omri's time the prolonged war between Judah and Israel was discontinued. The Davidids accepted (at least temporarily) the existence of the northern kingdom, and the two royal houses made a pact (see: *Ahab, *Jehoshaphat). Israel enjoyed great economic prosperity in the time of Omri as a result of the treaty with Ethbaal king of Sidon, which was sealed by the marriage between Jezebel, Ethbaal's daughter, and Ahab, apparently while Omri was still alive (cf. Amos 1:9, "the brotherly covenant"). The triple alliance between Israel, Judah, and Phoenicia served at the same time as a counterweight to the threat of Aram-Damascus, whose aim was to gain possession of the northern part of Ereẓ Israel and to establish hegemony in Syria and Ereẓ Israel (see: *Ben-Hadad). The triple alliance countered the Aramean threat but could not reduce it entirely. From I Kings 20:34 it becomes apparent that Aram-Damascus had some advantage over the Samarian kingdom. There were "bazaars" in Samaria belonging to Damascus already in Omri's time, and Israel was forced to grant special privileges to Aramean merchants in Samaria. In spite of the relative stability which Omri achieved in internal affairs and his improvement of Israel's political status externally, the biblical historiographer finds fault with Omri (I Kings 16:25–26). This negative assessment stems from the religious and social viewpoint and is in accordance with the Deuteronomic school. Indeed Omri did not abolish the worship of the golden calves which Jeroboam the son of Nebat had introduced. Moreover, the politico-economic alliance with Phoenicia had far-reaching results in cultural, religious, and social spheres – the cult of the Tyrian Baal took root among the royal courtiers, royal officers, and the urban population. The economic prosperity was not felt equally by all groups of the population, and thus the economic rift in Israelite society was widened. The increasing sway of the foreign cults on the one hand, and the social oppression (cf. "the statutes of Omri" in Micah 6:16) on the other, caused the formation of a strong opposition movement to Omri and his house, at the head of which stood the prophets, such as *Elijah and *Elisha, and those who had remained faithful to the Lord.

BIBLIOGRAPHY: Bright, Hist, 219ff.; J. Gray, *A History of Israel* (1960), 220–3; A. Parrot, *Samaria, the Capital of the Kingdom of Israel* (1958); Morgenstern, in: HUCA, 15 (1940), 134–66; Whitley, in: VT, 2 (1952), 137–52; H.L. Ginsberg, in: *Fourth World Congress of Jewish Studies*, 1 (1967), 91–93.

[Bustanay Oded]

OMSK, town in S.W. Siberia, Russian Federation. The first Jewish settlers in Omsk were exiles to Siberia. During 1828–56 Jewish children who had been seized for military service were sent to the *Cantonist regiment in Omsk. The community was formed by the exiles and ex-servicemen of the Russian army. In 1855 the first synagogue was founded and a second in 1873. The Jewish population numbered 1,138 Jews (3% of the population) in 1897. There were 4,389 Jews in the province of Omsk in 1926; 2,135 in the city (1.6% of the total) in 1939; and 9,175 Jews in 1959. In 1970 the Jewish population was estimated at about 10,000. In 2002 there were 2,400 Jews in the entire Omsk district, with Jewish life reviving from the 1990s, including Jewish clubs, a Chabad kindergarten, and an active synagogue in the city.

[Yehuda Slutsky]

ONA'AH (Heb. אוֹנָאָה; "overreaching"), the act of wronging another by selling him an article for more than its real worth or by purchasing from him an article for less than its real worth.

Origin and Nature of the Prohibition

The prohibition against *ona'ah* has its origin in the Pentateuch, "And if thou sell aught unto thy neighbor, or buy of thy neighbor's hand, ye shall not wrong one another" (Lev. 25:14). The passage was construed by the scholars as relating to overreaching in monetary matters, and they distinguished three degrees of this, according to whether the discrepancy amounts to one-sixth, less than one-sixth, or more than one-sixth of the value of the article (see below). The law of *ona'ah* applies to undercharging as well as overcharging (Sh. Ar., ḤM) 227:2). The prohibition against *ona'ah* is a separate one but is also embraced within the wider prohibition against robbery. Despite the express enjoinder of the prohibition as a negative command, transgression is not punished by *flogging since the overreaching is remediable by restitution, and the person who has overreached – whether wittingly or unwittingly – is obligated to make good the discrepancy (Yad, Mekhirah 12:1; Sh. Ar., ḤM 227:2).

Three Degrees of Ona'ah

In the case where a person has overreached by one-sixth, the transaction is valid, but he must make good the discrepancy to the injured party (BM 50b). The discrepancy of one-sixth is calculated on the market value. If the discrepancy amounts to less than one-sixth, the transaction is valid and the difference need not be made good (Yad, loc. cit. 12:3). As regards sales and purchases transacted by minors, the scholars, having noted that their transactions shall be valid for the sake of insuring their vital needs, also laid down that, even though minors have no legal capacity to waive their rights, their mistake shall nonetheless be treated in the same way as the mistake of an adult (Sh. Ar., ḤM 235:3), and they must be deemed to waive their right in respect of overreaching amounting to less than one-sixth. If the discrepancy amounts to more than one-sixth, the transaction is void, but the injured party may waive his right in respect of the overreaching and uphold the transaction (Yad, *loc. cit.* 12:4). Some scholars held that the party who has overreached may insist on voiding the transaction even though the injured party is willing to waive his rights in the matter (Tos. to BM 50b).

Contracting Out of the Law of Overreaching

A stipulation between the parties stating, "on condition that there is no overreaching therein" (i.e., in the transaction), or "on condition that you have no claim of overreaching against me," is invalid (Sh. Ar., ḤM 227:21), since the language used implies a stipulation contrary to a prohibition laid down in the Torah and one may not stipulate to set aside the Pentateuchal law; however, when the amounts involved in the transaction are specified, a stipulation of this nature is valid, since the injured party knows the precise amount of the overreaching to which he waives his right, and all stipulations in monetary matters are valid (*ibid.* (*mamon*) see also *Contract). If the parties agreed that the purchase price be determined by the valuation of a third party, the parties to the transaction will have a claim against each other for overreaching if it is later found that the valuer erred in his valuation (Sh. Ar., ḤM 227:25).

Property Not Subject to the Law of Overreaching

Four items are not subject to the law of overreaching: land, slaves, deeds, and consecrated property (*hekdesh*; BM 56b). "Even though it is a decree of the Torah, yet the matter must to some extent be amplified by logical reasoning. For a person sometimes buys land for more than its worth, and the scholars called land something that is always worth the money paid for it. Contrariwise, when a person is in need of money but finds no purchaser, he sells it (land) for much less than its worth, since it is impossible to carry land from place to place. Similarly, slaves are sometimes the source of trouble, yet a person who is in need of a slave may be prepared to pay a high price for him. As regards deeds which are due for payment, these are sometimes subject to depreciation because of the financial position of the debtor or his aggressiveness. Concerning consecrated property in the Temple period, it was decided that 'if *hekdesh* worth a *maneh* had been redeemed for the equivalent of a *perutah*, the redemption was valid' – hence, in the sale of consecrated property also there is no law of overreaching, even though the Temple treasury be wronged, so that the buyer cannot retract since 'a verbal undertaking in favor of the Temple treasury is as a delivery to the common man'" (*Arukh ha-Shulḥan*, ḤM 227:34).

LAND. The law of overreaching applies neither to the sale nor the leasing of land (Yad, Mekhirah 13:14). Anything which is attached to the land is subject to the same law as the land itself, provided that it is dependent on that land itself (Sh. Ar., ḤM 193). An opinion was also expressed that the same law applies to both, even when the article attached to the land is not dependent on that land itself (*Rema*, ad loc.). A very early opinion that land outside Ereẓ Israel is considered as movable property and subject to the law of overreaching was rejected (Tur., ḤM, 95:4).

SLAVES. There is no overreaching as regards slaves, since the law of slaves is analogous to the law of land (BM 56b. See *Slavery). Hence it was laid down as *halakhah* that the law of overreaching does not apply to the hire of laborers, because it is as if the employer buys the laborer for a limited time and the latter's position is assimilated to that of a slave required for a limited period (Yad, Mekhirah, 13:15). The opinion that the law of overreaching applies to a contractor (*kabbelan*; Yad, loc. cit. 13:18) is disagreed with by certain scholars (Nov. Ramban, BM 55a; Maggid Mishneh, Mekhirah 13:15). A minority opinion that the hire of a laborer is subject to the law of overreaching was rejected (Resp. Maharam of Rothenburg, ed. Prague, no. 749; see also *Labor Law). There is no law of overreaching as regards a Hebrew slave (*Minḥat Ḥinnukh*, no. 337).

DEEDS. There is no overreaching as regards bonds, but money bills issued in different countries at the instance of the government are treated as money in all respects since they are officially issued and are taken in payment; however, shares and the like which are not officially issued are apparently like deeds and not subject to the law of overreaching (*Pitḥei Teshuvah*, YD 305, n. 7 and ḤM 95, n. 1).

The scholars expressed differing opinions on the question of whether enormous overreaching gives ground for invalidating a transaction relating to land, slaves, or deeds; one view is that the transaction may be invalidated when the overreaching exceeds one-sixth of the price (*Halakhot*, Rif, BM 57a); another is that this may be done if the overreaching reaches one-half of the purchase price (Rif, loc. cit.); and a third is that the sale is only invalidated when the limit of one-half has been exceeded (*Rema*, ḤM 227:29; *Sma, Siftei Kohen* and *Ha-Gra*, ad loc.). However, the accepted opinion is that, with regard to land, slaves, and deeds, the law of overreaching never applies nor does it ever serve to invalidate the transaction (Sh. Ar., ḤM 227:29; *Siftei Kohen*, ḤM 66, n. 122).

CONSECRATED PROPERTY. In the Temple period the law of overreaching did not apply to consecrated property (BM 56b; Yad, Mekhirah 13:8), but "in these times" the law of overreaching does apply in respect of consecrated property and property dedicated to the poor (ḤM 227, n. 48; see **Hekdesh*). Although it was enjoined, "if you shall sell" the law of overreaching applies to coins (BM 51b), despite the fact that a coin is not something that is sold (ḤM 227, n. 26).

Further Cases of Exclusion from the Law of Overreaching

BARTER. The accepted opinion is that the law of overreaching does not operate in a transaction of barter (see *Acquisition, Yad, Mekhirah, 13:1; Sh. Ar., ḤM 227:20). In the opinion of some scholars, utensils and animals that are stock in trade are subject to the law of overreaching even when bartered, and the rule excluding overreaching in barter was laid down solely in respect of property traded by a layman (Resp. Radbaz, no. 1340, and see below).

"ONE WHO TRADES ON TRUST." There is no overreaching as regards "one who trades on trust" (BM 51b). "How so? If the seller said to the purchaser 'I purchased this article for so and so much and I wish to earn thereon so and so much,' the purchaser will have no claim against him for overreaching" (Arukh ha-Shulḥan 227:28), "even if the overreaching amounts to more than one-sixth" (Yad, Mekhirah 14:1). On the other hand, the scholars laid down that raising the prices of commodities beyond the accepted level, or beyond those fixed by the competent authority, amounts to a transgression of the prohibition against profiteering.

PERSONAL APPAREL. The law of overreaching does not apply to the sale of apparel because the owner would not sell such articles except if he received the price he demanded (BM 51a), and this is so even when he is known to have sold these items on account of financial hardship (Resp. Rosh, no. 105:3). The scholars differed as to whether or not the "layman" has a claim in respect of overreaching (*Shitah Mekubbeẓet* loc. cit.; *Maggid Mishneh*, Mekhirah 13:2). It was held that if he has sold articles which are normally traded, he will have a claim in respect of overreaching (*Ḥananel*, BM 51a).

AGENCY. The law of *ona'ah* does not operate in respect of property sold through an agent. If the agent is overreached in any manner, the sale is void since his principal may say, "I delegated you to act to my advantage and not to my detriment" (Kid. 42b; Yad, Mekhirah 13:9). If the purchaser is the injured party, some scholars hold that the sale is void, as it is in the reverse case, but the accepted opinion is that in this case the law applies as if the agent were acting independently and the purchaser waives a discrepancy of less than one-sixth (Rosh, loc. cit.; Sh. Ar., EH 104:6). When the fact that a party was acting as an agent remained undisclosed, the sale will be valid as long as the overreaching did not reach the stipulated measure (Yad, Sheluḥin 2:4). The principal has the right to retract on account of overreaching even in matters which are not otherwise subject to the law of overreaching (Sh. Ar., ḤM, 227:30). He has the right either to void the sale or to uphold it, but the purchaser is not entitled to seek its invalidation (*Netivot ha-Mishpat, Mishpat ha-Urim* 185, n. 8).

The law of overreaching is the same for a guardian (see *Apotropos) as it is for a principal (Sh. Ar., ḤM 227:30), even when the former is appointed by the court (Mekhirah 13:9). A partner who has bought or sold is subject to the same law as a person who has bought or sold his own property, since this is not a case in which it may properly be said, "I have delegated you to act to my advantage and not to my detriment" (*Siftei Kohen*, ḤM 77, 19). A broker who has an interest in the property sold is held by some scholars to be in the same position as an agent (*Netivot ha-Mishpat, Mishpat ha-Urim*, 222, n. 16), while another opinion is that his position is equated with that of a partner (ḤM 227, n. 42; see also *Shalish). The law of overreaching does not apply to transactions negotiated by the "seven senior citizens" (i.e., public representatives) on behalf of the community (Ran on Rif, Meg. 8a; *Rema*, OH 153:7; *Taz*, thereto, n. 8).

Division of Property by Brothers or Partners

The law of overreaching applies to the division of inherited property by brothers or partners, since their position is assimilated to that of purchasers. This rule applies to partners in respect of the partnership property only and not to a mere profit-sharing or business partnership (*Arukh ha-Shulḥan*, ḤM 8, 227:338; see also *Ownership).

Claim for Restitution or Invalidation of a Transaction

A purchaser who wishes to claim restitution or to invalidate a transaction on the grounds of overreaching must do so within the time it would take for him to show the article to a merchant or other person from whom he may ascertain its market price (Sh. Ar., ḤM 227:7). Longer delay entails forfeiture of his right, but he need not pay the price if he has not yet done so (*Siftei Kohen*, thereto). If the injured party is the seller, he may retract at any time since he no longer holds the article and cannot show it to a merchant (BM 50b; Yad, Mekhirah 12:6; Sh. Ar., ḤM 227:8). However, if the seller should ascertain the value of the article and thereafter fail to claim restitution of the amount of the overreaching or invalidation of the sale, he will forfeit his right to do so (Yad and Sh. Ar., loc. cit.), but another opinion is that the seller retains this right at all times (*Maggid Mishneh*, Mekhirah 12:6).

[Shmuel Shilo]

Further Remarks on the Nature of Ona'ah

In addition to comments above regarding the nature of the law of overreaching, it may be regarded as derivative of the prohibition of robbery, and the Talmud indeed discusses the relationship between overreaching and theft (BM 61a). However, it is more likely that this law was an innovation of Jewish law, being a separate prohibition in its own right, since the prohibition of overreaching has many unique characteristics, as indicated by the details of the laws discussed above, and because the prohibition does not apply to a sale to non-Jews (Yad, Mekhirah 13:7; Sh. Ar, ḤM 227:26), whereas the prohibition of theft applies to the non-Jew as well.

Certain authorities even regard the prohibition as being religiously based, unrelated to civil law (Rabbenu Hanannel, BM 51b; Asheri, BM 4:7), indicating that this law originated from the ethical imperative of conducting business fairly and amicably, based on the verse "that your brother may live with you" (Lev. 25:36).

The unique nature of the prohibition against overreaching is expressed by the conditions of its application: (1) The article to be sold must have a known market value; (2) the buyer must be unaware of this market value. These conditions severely impede the implementation of the law in our times, as the vast majority of items sold do not have a fixed, uniform price, and prices may vary considerably from place to place and among different vendors. Furthermore, a buyer would have difficulty in convincing a court that he did not know that prices of goods are likely to vary.

The Law of Overreaching and Acts of Public Authorities

Actions of a public authority in the areas of finance and commerce differ from those of the private person, in that a public authority must exercise a higher degree of seriousness, integrity, and fairness. One of the manifestations of the special standing of the public authority is that the law of *ona'ah* does not apply to public authorities. Where a public authority sells something, it cannot revoke the sale by claiming that the consideration for the sale was too low, to the extent of constituting *ona'ah* – invoking the talmudic rule that where the contract price was a sixth below the fair price, the seller, who is the injured party in this case, cannot rescind the transaction.

The rationale given for this principle is that "it is unseemly for the community to say: We have made a mistake" (R. Solomon b. Simeon Duran, Algiers, 15th century – Resp. Rashbash, no. 566). This principle and its sources in Jewish law were cited and relied upon in the Israeli Supreme Court in the *Lugasi* case (HC 376/81 *Lugasi v. Minister of Communications*, 36 (2) PD, 449, pp. 465–471, per Justice Menachem Elon, in the context of the obligations of a public authority in its business dealings.

[Menachem Elon (2nd ed.)]

BIBLIOGRAPHY: J.S. Zuri, *Mishpat ha-Talmud*, 5 (1921), 70–76; Gulak, Yesodei, 1 (1922), 64–66; 2 (1922), 153–60; P. Dickstein, in: *Ha-Mishpat ha-Ivri*, 1 (1925/26), 15–55; Herzog, Instit, 1 (1936), 112–7; 2 (1939), 121–4; E.Z. Melamed, in: *Yavneh*, 3 (1942), 35–56; ET. 1 (1951³), 153–60; B. Rabinowitz-Teomim, *Ḥukkat Mishpat* (1957), 113–40, Elon, Mafte'aḥ, 1f. **ADD. BIBLIOGRAPHY:** M. Elon, *Ha-Mishpat ha-Ivri* (1988), 1:113, 574, 642; 2:1101, 1106; idem, *Jewish Law* (1994), 1:127; 2:707, 795; 3:1324, 1330; idem, *Jewish Law (Cases and Materials)* (1999), 274–75; S.Warhaftig, *Dinei Misḥar ba-Mishpat ha-Ivri* (1990), 51–94; I. Warhaftig, "*Halikhot Misḥar – Ona'ah u-Mekkaḥ Ta'ut*," in: *Teḥumin*, 2 (1981), 471–92; Y. Ahituv, "*Kalkalah ve-Halakhah*," in: *Teḥumin*, 12 (1991), 145–70.

ONAGER (Heb. פֶּרֶא, Wild Ass; Job 39:5, also עָרוֹד). Two subspecies of the wild ass, the *Equus hemionus hemihippus*, the Syrian onager, and the *Equus hemionus onager*, the Arabian onager, existed in the Syrian desert up to the present century. The onager is described as loving freedom (Jer. 2:24) and fearless (Job 39:5–8). Its habitat is in waste places (Isa. 32:44 and Job 39:6), and Ishmael who was to dwell in the desert is called a wild ass of a man (Gen. 16:12). It appears that from time to time efforts were made to domesticate the wild ass. An ancient Sumerian picture shows it harnessed to a wagon, and the Tosefta (Kil. 5:5) forbids the yoking of an ass with an onager. It was sometimes employed for turning millstones (Av. Zar. 16b). It would appear that the wild ass flourished in the talmudic period, and its flesh was used to feed animals in the arena (Men. 103b). In Babylon fields were fenced in to prevent the onagers from doing damage (BB 36a).

BIBLIOGRAPHY: Y. Aharoni, *Torat ha-Ḥai*, 1 (1923), 99–101; Lewysohn, Zool, 143; J. Feliks, *Animal World of the Bible* (1962), 29–30. **ADD. BIBLIOGRAPHY:** Feliks, Ha-Ẓome'aḥ, 264.

[Jehuda Feliks]

ONAN (Heb. אוֹנָן; "power," "wealth"), second son of Judah and Shua (Gen. 38:2–4; 46:12; Num. 26:19). After the death of his elder brother Er, Onan was instructed by his father to contract a levirate marriage with his childless sister-in-law Tamar (Gen. 38:7–8). Onan refused to fulfill his fraternal duty, and whenever he had relations with Tamar he would let the semen go to waste (presumably by *coitus interruptus*, although the term *onanism can be actually applied to masturbation), thereby avoiding effective consummation of the marriage (38:9). Onan's offensive conduct was motivated by the fact that the son born of a levirate marriage was accounted to the dead brother (Deut. 25:5–6). His uncharitableness was displeasing to the Lord, who took his life (Gen. 38:10). The Judahite genealogy in I Chronicles 2:3 does not mention the death of Onan.

This story may possibly contain a historical nucleus reflecting the extinction of two clans of the tribe of Judah.

BIBLIOGRAPHY: EM, 1 (1955), 155 (incl. bibl.); D.M. Feldman, *Birth Control in Jewish Law* (1968), 111–2.

ONANISM, term derived from the biblical narrative of Onan, son of Judah (Gen. 38, 7–10), who "spilled" his seed "on the ground." Onanism refers to the thwarting of the sexual process in one of several ways. In Hebrew, it is called more fully *ma'aseh Er ve-Onan* ("the act of Er and Onan") and is taken by the Midrash (Gen. R. 85:5; and by Rashi to the Pentateuch) to mean *coitus interruptus* and by the Talmud (Yev. 34b) to refer either to unnatural intercourse or (cf. Nid. 13a) to masturbation. The Zohar (*Va-Yeshev*, p. 188a; *Va-Yeḥi*, p. 219b) expatiates on the evil of onanism in the last sense, which condemnation then entered the Shulḥan Arukh (EH, 23:2) to underscore the gravity of the sin of *hashḥatat zera* ("improper emission of seed"). Halakhically, there is a question whether the prohibition against onanism, in any sense, is a prohibition of biblical or of rabbinic force. A 16th-century legal work by R. Moses Trani, *Kiryat Sefer* (on Yad, Issurei Bi'ah, 21), whose express purpose is to determine which of the commandments are biblical and which rabbinic, did not reach a decision about onanism. The Onan narrative in the Bible is pre-Sinai, and the context makes it sufficiently doubtful whether Onan's sin is his contraceptive act or his frustration of the purpose of levirate marriage, i.e., to establish progeny for his brother. Other biblical bases for onanism or *hashḥatat zera* (Gen. 1:28; 6:12; Ex. 20:13; Lev. 18:6; Isa. 1:15; 57:5) are variously regarded as deductive, or "intimations" (*remez*), from the standpoint of their biblical derivation, though the prohibition is nonetheless clear. The question is of more than academic interest, as evidenced by the circumstances under which onanism is condoned. *Coitus interruptus*, for example, is actually recommended by R. Eliezer in the Talmud (Yev. 34b) as a contraceptive procedure to prevent dilution of the mother's milk during nursing, but is rejected by the other sages and is forbidden by all the law codes, beginning with that of Maimonides (Yad, Issurei Bi'ah 21:18). Yet the factors of intent and constancy (as was indeed the case with Onan) are considered, and the responsa would permit, for example, the continuance of marital relations where interrupted coitus is unintentional or irregular. On the other hand, the deviations of "unnatural" coitus (*she-lo kedarkah*) are objected to on moral grounds (Maim. Comm. to Sanh. 7:4), though legally permitted (Ned. 20b; Sanh. 58b). R. Isaac in *tosafot* (Yev. 34b) reconciled the leniency of the sages in law with what they condemned in Er and Onan, by distinguishing between the corrupt intent of Onan and legitimate heterosexual intent in ordinary marital relations. The responsa, too, ruled in accordance with the latter interpretation – despite the reaction that set in against this point of view after the Zohar appeared, leading R. Joseph Caro to claim that R. Isaac would not have ruled so permissively had he seen what the Zohar says on the subject (*Bedek ha-Bayit* to *Beit Yosef*, EH, 25). Other medieval mystical works sided with the Zohar in this matter, but the legal tradition affirmed the permissibility of *she-lo kedarkah* in marital relations. A post-medieval mystic, R. Jacob Emden (d. 1776), addressed himself to the difference between the talmudic and zoharic attitudes toward onanism in the sense of masturbation, which has consequences for the question of birth control. He prefers the attitude of the Talmud, and calls that of the Zohar "exaggeration" (*Mitpaḥat Sefarim* (Altona, 1768), 1:20). More important, he emphasizes a doctrine, articulated by earlier legal authorities, that the prohibition against onanism in method is not applicable to marital contraception; that when contraception is necessary and abstinence would be the alternative, then possible onanism in the use of a contraceptive device is neutralized by the positive *mitzvah* of marital sex. In the voluminous responsa literature on birth control, the dominant tendency is to rule in this manner; namely, that Onan's marriage to his brother's widow, ordinarily prohibited, was exceptionally permitted in order to produce progeny – a purpose his act frustrated. But in ordinary marriages, the sexual relation without procreative possibility is allowable; and, where contraception must be practiced, the use of a device which smacks of Onan's method but is free of his intent (*Tosefot Ri-D* to Yev. 12b) is preferable to abstinence, so that the *mitzvah* of marital sex can be continued. For reasons such as this, an oral contraceptive – such as the pill, or its talmudic prototype, the *kos shel ikkarin* ("cup of barrenness") – is preferable to other contraceptive devices, for an oral contraceptive is onanistic neither in intent nor in method. Because of the objectionable methods of contraception available, rabbinic responsa by and large allowed contraception only for medical reasons. However, where oral contraception is possible, the responsa would be more permissive – but only in a way consistent with the overriding *mitzvah* of procreation.

BIBLIOGRAPHY: D.M. Feldman, *Birth Control in Jewish Law* (1968, 1970).

[David M. Feldman]

ONDERWIJZER, ABRAHAM BEN SAMSON HAKOHEN (1862–1934), Dutch rabbi. Born in Muiden, near Amsterdam, Onderwijzer studied at the rabbinical seminary of Amsterdam under Rabbi J. *Duenner. In 1888 he was appointed rabbi of the Ashkenazi community in Amsterdam and in 1917, chief rabbi of the town and of the province of North Holland. Onderwijzer translated the Pentateuch with Rashi's commentary into Dutch and added his own explanations (1895–1901). In 1895 he founded Bezalel, an organization of Jewish workers, for the amelioration of the religious and economic conditions of the Jewish workers in Amsterdam, most of whom worked in the diamond industry. Bezalel acted in conjunction with the general diamond workers' trade union (A.N.D.B.B.) in Holland.

BIBLIOGRAPHY: *Orde van den Dienst ter Gelegenheid van de plechtige Bevestiging... A.S. Onderwijzer* (1917), S. Seeligmann, *Opperabbijn A.S. Onderwijzer* (1935).

[Yehoshua Horowitz]

ONES (Heb. אֹנֶס), either (1) compelling a person to act against his will, or (2) the occurrence of an unavoidable event that prevents or obstructs the performance of certain acts, or causes them to occur. Both categories of *ones* are derived exegetically from the verse in the Pentateuch dealing with *ones* in the sense of compulsion. With regard to the rape of a betrothed maiden, it states (Deut. 22:26): "But unto the damsel thou shalt do nothing." From this the sages inferred that in all cases of "*ones* the merciful [Torah] exempts" (Ned. 27a; BK 28b).

Compelling a Person to Act against His Will

CATEGORIES OF ONES OF COMPULSION. *Ones* of compulsion comprises three categories: the threat of death, physical torture, and financial loss. Compulsion by threat of death or as a result of physical torture is adjudged as *ones* in all cases (Ket. 33b; see Tos. ad loc.). Financial pressure is not considered as *ones* in cases of transgression or **issur* (acts forbidden by the Torah), but as regards money matters, divorce, or an oath, the authorities differ (see below). The threat of duress (*le'enos*) counts as *ones* if the threatener possesses the power to execute the threat himself or through the agency of others (Sh. Ar., ḤM 205:7), but some scholars do not permit the extension of *ones* to such a threat (*Rema*, ad loc). If the threat is made to a kinsman, for example, it is generally counted as *ones* of compulsion (Resp. Rashbash no. 339; *Haggahot Mordekhai Git.* no. 467; Resp. Bezalel Ashkenazi no. 15), but other scholars differ (*Tashbeẓ* 1:1; *Rema*, EH 134:5).

IN COMPULSION TO WRONGDOING. Anyone who commits a transgression through *ones* is exempt (Tos. to Yev. 54a; Yad, Yesodei ha-Torah 5:4) even from the judgment of heaven (Resp. Ribash 4 and 11). Even though a person commits one of the three transgressions of which it is said that he should choose death rather than commit them, he will not be punished if he acted under duress. He is obliged, however, to expend money to enable himself to escape from a situation where otherwise he would be forced to transgress (Resp. Ribash 387; and see *Penal Law).

IN KIDDUSHIN. If a man was compelled under duress to betroth a woman, some authorities hold that the *kiddushin* (see *Marriage) is valid (Yad, Ishut 4:1 and *Maggid Mishnah* ad loc. in the name of Rashba), but others maintain that it is of no effect (Sh. Ar., EH 42:1). Those who hold that the *kiddushin* is valid base their opinion on the fact that a man can *divorce his wife without her consent (*Maggid Mishneh* loc. cit.; *Beit Shemu'el* 42, n. 1) – even after the ban of Rabbenu Gershom prohibiting divorce against the woman's will – should he have been compelled to betroth her under duress (*Beit Shemu'el, loc. cit.*). If a woman is compelled under duress to be betrothed, the *kiddushin* is as valid as if she had acted willingly (BB 48b), but nevertheless the rabbis nullified it because of her partner's improper behavior (*ibid.*; see *Marriage).

IN DIVORCE. A husband divorcing his wife must act freely (Yad, Gerushin 1:1–2), and a divorce given by the husband against his will is divorce under duress and therefore invalid. There are, however, cases in which the court may compel the husband to grant a divorce, and in such cases it is valid (Git. 9:2; see *Divorce). Some authorities are of the opinion that in such cases the husband must say, "I am willing" (*Netivot ha-Mishpat, Mishpat ha-Urim* 205, n. 1), but others say that if he gives the divorce without making any remark then this is tantamount to saying, "I am willing" (*Ḥavvot Ya'ir* nos. 55 and 56). Various explanations are given for the validity of this divorce despite its being given under duress. Some explain that just as in a *sale under duress the sale is valid because of the assumption that in the end the seller made up his mind to sell (under certain conditions; see below), this is also the case in a divorce given under duress when compulsion is legally permitted (Tos. to BB 48a); others say that as it is a religious precept to obey the sages, the husband is reconciled to the divorce (*Rashbam* BB 48a); while others hold that the laws of *ones* are not applicable to one legally bound to act in a particular way, even though his act results from compulsion (Yad, Gerushin 2:20). Financial duress counts as *ones* with regard to compulsion to divorce (Resp. Rashba vol. 4 no. 40; Nov. Ritba Kid. 49b s.v. *ve-ha*), but some authorities disagree and do not regard it as *ones* (*Toledot Adam ve-Ḥavvah*, Ḥavvah 24:1).

IN SALE. If a purchaser snatches the property of the seller through giving him the purchase price against his will, then this is an invalid sale. In this case the purchaser is treated as a predator, and he is obliged to restore the article he took as if he were a robber (BK 62a; Yad, Gezelah 1:9; see *Theft and Robbery). In certain circumstances, however, though the seller sells under duress, it is assumed that in the end he agreed to the sale, for he accepted money in consideration of the transferred property. Therefore, if he was given the monetary value of the property for sale and took it into his hands, the sale stands (Sh. Ar., ḤM 205:1). Some hold the sale to be valid only if he took the money at the time of the actual transaction (Yad, Mekhirah 10:1, see *Mishneh le-Melekh*), while others hold it to be valid even if the money was taken afterward (*ibid.*). If he was compelled to reduce the price, the sale is void (Sh. Ar., ḤM 205:4), but some scholars disagree (Resp. Maharik 185). If a man is compelled to purchase, the transaction is void and the purchaser may withdraw (*Rema* ḤM 205:12), but here too there are dissident opinions (*Ha-Gra, ibid.*, n. 32). In the event of the purchaser's becoming reconciled to the sale, the seller is unable to withdraw (*Netivot ha-Mishpat*, Mishpat ha-Urim 205, n. 18). In the case of a business transaction that resembles a sale, such as a compromise when it is uncertain where the legal right lies, if the compromise is agreed upon under duress, then the same ruling applies as for sale and the compromise prevails (*Beit Yosef* ḤM 205:16).

IN GIFTS. If a man is compelled to assign a *gift, the gift is void (*Rashbam* BB 47b). A transaction that resembles a gift, such as a compromise when the litigant would have succeeded at law but was forced to compromise, counts as a gift and the compromise is void (*Beit Yosef, loc. cit.*). Similarly, an obligation undertaken through an acknowledgment of liability where none exists rates as a gift in regard to *ones*, and the obligation cannot be enforced (*Beit Yosef, loc. cit.*).

MODA'AH ("NOTIFICATION"). If the person under duress discloses in advance that the transaction he is about to acquiesce to will be effected against his will and that he has no intention of executing it, the subsequent transaction is void through lack of intent. Such a declaration to witnesses is termed *mesirat moda'ah* ("making a notification"). The witnesses usually wrote a deed of *moda'ah*, but this was not imperative (BB 40a–b; ḤM 205). If the seller makes a *moda'ah*, the sale is void even though he accepts the purchase price (ḤM 205:1). A *moda'ah* made before a single witness is ineffective even if the compeller admits the duress, for, since the person under duress knows that he cannot prove that he made a *moda'ah*, he acquiesces in the transaction (*Sha'ar Mishpat* 46, n. 21). If, however, he made the *moda'ah* in the presence of two witnesses separately, it is effective (*Keneset ha-Gedolah*, ḤM 46, Tur no. 36). Where the sale is void because a *moda'ah* has been made, the purchaser too has the right to withdraw on becoming aware that the seller made a *moda'ah* prior to the sale (*Ḥavvot Ya'ir* no. 40).

A deed of *moda'ah* may not be written in the first instance unless the witnesses know the duress (Sh. Ar., ḤM 205:5), and the witnesses must write "we the witnesses know the *ones*" (Sh. Ar., ḤM 205:1). If they write that the person concerned made a *moda'ah* in their presence, although they were unaware of the duress, the transaction will be void if he subsequently proves that there was *ones*. If witnesses testify to, or write, the *moda'ah* without knowing the *ones*, and other witnesses testify to the *ones*, these are combined and the transaction is void (*ibid.*). In a case where there is duress but the man under it is not able to make the *moda'ah*, if witnesses know of the *ones*, this has the same effect as a *moda'ah* (*Tashbez* 2:169; *Matteh Shimon* 205, Tur no. 39). The deed of *moda'ah* may be written before or after the transaction, providing the one under duress makes the notification before the transaction (*Netivot ha-Mishpat*, Mishpat ha-Urim 205 n. 6; *Kezot ha-Ḥoshen* 205, n. 1; *Haggahot Maimuniyyot*, Mekhirah 10:2). If the deed of *moda'ah* is undated and it is not known whether notification was made before or after the transaction because the witnesses are not available, it is valid and the transaction is void (*Rema* ḤM 205:9), for since the witnesses knew of the *ones* it is to be assumed, unless there is evidence to the contrary, that the notification was made beforehand (*ibid.*). In the case of gifts and similar dealings, such as remission of *debt, the witnesses may write the *moda'ah* without knowing the *ones*; the *moda'ah* will then testify to lack of intent (Tur ḤM 205:12 and *Beit Yosef* thereto). The authorities differ as to why this should be so, some holding that the *moda'ah* is effective as regards a gift even without the witnesses' knowledge of the *ones*, because if there is no *ones*, why should anyone confer a gift and make a *moda'ah*? It is therefore assumed that there must be *ones*. Accordingly, if it is known with certainty that there is no *ones*, the *moda'ah* may not be written. Others hold, however, that, in the case of a gift, manifestation of lack of proper intent is effective even without *ones* (see Gulak, Yesodei, 1 (1922), 61).

If after making the *moda'ah* the one under duress decides to effect the transaction and cancels his *moda'ah*, the transaction prevails (Sh. Ar., ḤM 205:11 and *Sma* thereto). It is possible, however, to make a *moda'ah* canceling ab initio such a *moda'ah* and declaring that the cancellation all the time of the transaction will result from *ones* and lack of intent. Such a notification, called "*moda'ah de-moda'ah*," cancels the transaction. To make certain that an action was not voided through a *moda'ah*, it became customary at the time of the transaction to cancel every *moda'ah* and every *moda'ah* canceling a *moda'ah ad infinitum*, or alternatively for the party involved to disqualify the witnesses before whom he made any *moda'ah* with regard to the transaction at hand, thus making them unfit to testify on his behalf. By these methods the previous *moda'ot* are voided and the act subsists (*ibid.*; *Beit Yosef* ḤM 205:15).

ACTS COUNTING AS *ONES*. A man who performs an act under an erroneous impression of the facts is described as "forced by his heart"; since his understanding of the case was in error, it is included in *ones*. This *halakhah* occurs especially in connection with an oath pledged under a mistaken impression. The one who swore the oath is delivered from it and exempted from offering a sacrifice, since he swore in error (Shevu. 26a; Ned. 25b; Maim. Yad, Shevuot 1:10; see *Mistake). Forgetting rates as *ones* (BK 26b and *Nimmukei Yosef*, *ad loc.*), as does an act performed as the result of an overpowering impulse. Hence, for example, a woman who is forced to have sexual intercourse is regarded as having been raped, even though she yielded willingly during the final stages of the act, since she had not the power to resist to the end because her natural impulse compelled her desire (Yad, Sanhedrin 20:3, Issurei Bi'ah 1:9; Resp. Ḥatam Sofer, EH pt. 1, no. 18). A minor girl who commits *adultery, even willingly, is regarded as acting under duress, since "the seduction of a minor is deemed *ones*" because she has no will of her own (Yev. 33b, 61b; TJ, Sot. 1:2, 16c). Some hold that adultery committed by a deranged woman also counts as *ones* (*Mishneh le-Melekh*, Ishut 11: 8), but others are doubtful about this (see *Rape).

ACTS COUNTING AS VOLUNTARY. A man compelled to incestuous or adulterous intercourse (see *Incest) is guilty of a capital offense, since "an erection can only take place voluntarily" (Yad, Issurei Bi'ah 1:9), but some hold that he is not liable for the death penalty (*Maggid Mishneh*, *ad loc.*). Duress arising from the person's own situation, as in the case of a man who sells his property because of financial distress, does not count as *ones* (Sh. Ar., ḤM 205: 12). Similarly, if the duress was related to some other action and he was compelled to act as a cause of this – e.g., if he was compelled to give money and because he did not have it was compelled to sell – this is not *ones* (*ibid.*).

Unavoidable Causes

CATEGORIES OF CAUSES COUNTING AS ONES. The scholars developed a threefold division of the types of *ones*, a classification which was made especially in connection with the laws of divorce; a somewhat similar one was made in connection with the law of *obligations, particularly with reference to *torts. The three categories relating to divorce (see below) are (1) an *ones* of common occurrence; (2) an *ones* neither common nor uncommon; and (3) an uncommon *ones*.

The classical examples of these are (1) if a man returning home was delayed because the ferry was on the opposite bank of the river and so he could not cross it; (2) illness; and (3) if a man was killed when a house collapsed, or he was bitten by a snake, or devoured by a lion (Tos., *Piskei ha-Rosh* and *Mordekhai* to Ket. 2b and 3a and to Git. 73a; Sh. Ar., EH 144:1).

A general *ones* not arising from human agency is termed *makkat medinah* ("regional mishap"; BM 9:6). As regards liability in the laws of obligation, the division is made between an absolute *ones* and one which is relative. In the words of the *rishonim*, the distinction is between an *ones* "like theft" and one "like loss." The Talmud (BM 94b) has a dictum that "loss is close to negligence" while "theft is near to *ones*" (Tos. to BK 27b and to BM 82b).

NONFULFILLMENT OF OBLIGATION RESULTING FROM ONES. A man bears no liability for the nonfulfillment of his obligations if he is prevented from doing so by *ones* (BK 28b; Ned. 28a), with the exception of the borrower (BM 93a; see *Bailees). It is possible that a tortfeasor too is excluded from this rule, since "man is always liable, whether acting inadvertently or willingly, whether awake or asleep" (BK 2:6), or in another version, "whether acting inadvertently or willingly, accidentally or deliberately" (Sanh. 72a). It has, however, been ruled that there are kinds of *ones* which exempt even tortfeasors (Tos. to Sanh. 76b). A man accepting liability for every *ones* is not liable for an uncommon one (Resp. Ribash no. 250; Resp. Moharik no. 7; Sh. Ar., ḤM 225:4).

NONFULFILLMENT OF OBLIGATION BY REASON OF ONES. If a man was to execute an act on certain conditions and his nonfulfillment of these conditions was due to *ones*, the *amoraim* differ as to whether the act counts as not having been executed because the condition was not fulfilled, although the nonfulfillment was caused by *ones*, or whether the act stands since it was *ones* that prevented fulfillment of the condition (TJ, Git. 7:6, 49c; see *Beit Yosef* and *Baḥ* ḤM 21; *Siftei Kohen* ḤM 21). Some explain the former opinion as follows: The rule is that "the merciful [Torah] exempts in cases of *ones*" and not that "in cases of *ones* the merciful [Torah] obligates" the other person. For in what way is he concerned with the *ones* of the other? His obligation was dependent on the other's fulfillment of the condition, which in fact was not done (*Siftei Kohen* loc. cit.; Resp. Ḥatam Sofer, ḤM no. 1; for other explanations see the ḤM and *Malbushei Yom Tov*, Kuntres Mishpetei ha-Tanna'im 2). The *halakhah* follows the first view (*Avnei Millu'im*, EH 38:1).

ONES IN DIVORCE. Contrary to the principle "the merciful [Torah] exempts in cases of *ones*," the rabbinic regulation lays down "accident is no plea in divorce." Hence, if a man says to his wife, "This is your bill of divorce if I do not return by such a date," and he does not come back in time because of *ones*, the divorce is effective and he is unable to have it set aside on the plea that he was delayed by *ones*. There were two considerations behind this regulation. If the divorce was regarded as ineffective in a case of *ones*, a chaste woman, when her husband did not arrive on the stated day, would always consider that an accident might have befallen him, even when his absence was deliberate, and thus would remain unable to remarry. A loose woman, on the other hand, would always claim that her husband's failure to return was not due to *ones* and would contract a second marriage; then, when subsequently his nonreturn was found to be due to *ones*, the divorce would be invalid and her children from the second marriage **mamzerim*. As a result the rabbis enacted that the divorce must always take effect, even though the husband's failure to return is due to *ones*, and even though he stands on the other bank of the river and cries aloud, "See I have returned and am not responsible because of *ones*" (Ket. 2b–3a; Tos. to Ket. 3a; Sh. Ar., EH 144:1). The *rishonim* ruled that this *halakhah* applies to *ones* of common occurrence and to *ones* neither common nor uncommon, but not at all to uncommon *ones* (Tos., *Piskei ha-Rosh*, and *Mordekhai* to Ket. 2b–3a and to Git. 73a and codes).

ONES ON THE DUE DATE. A man who was obliged to perform an action within a certain period of time and relied on the fact that he still had the time to do it until the end of the period, who was then overtaken by *ones* at the very end of the period, is regarded as subject to *ones* (Sh. Ar., OH 108:8 and *Magen Avraham* thereto n. 11), but others do not consider this *ones* (*Rema* YD 232:12).

[Shmuel Shilo]

Moda'ah ("Notification")

The *Green* case (CA 457/61 *Green v. Green*, 16 (1) PD 318) concerned a husband who went abroad, left his wife, and for a long period of time refused to give her a *get* (see *Divorce). The husband finally agreed to give her a *get*, but only after the wife had waived all her financial claims, including her right to claim child support for their daughter. In addition the wife gave a declaration, on the basis of which the Rabbinical Court gave its decision, that should the husband nevertheless be forced to pay child support for the daughter, the wife would be obliged to reimburse the husband for any sum he paid as child support. The District Court ruled that this declaration was invalid, because the husband was obliged to pay child support for his child, and that the wife's undertaking to waive child support payments for the child, and compensate the husband for any sum he paid in child support was void, and hence the verdict of the Rabbinical Court was void. In the Supreme Court the husband claimed that the District Court should have adjudicated the matter in accordance with Jewish Law, since it concerned child support which, according to the law, must be decided according to Jewish Law (see *Maintenance). Justice Haim Cohn ruled that, even if the matter ought to be decided in accordance with Jewish law, under Jewish Law the wife's agreement was invalid as it was given under duress. Justice Cohn explained the difference between duress in the case of sale – in which one must give "notification" during the course of the sale in order to void it – and duress in a gift, where there is no need to give "notification" at the time of giving the gift, "for one does not follow anything in a gift except the expressed will of the giver, since if he does not want to give it with all his heart, the recipient of the gift has not acquired it" (Maim., Yad, Mekhirah 10:3). In his opinion, the husband's threats to refuse to grant a divorce to his wife if she did not waive all her rights constituted duress (see *Agunah) and, in the instant case the wife had given her husband remission from all his debts to her without receiving anything in return. Hence the wife's waiver should be considered as a gift from the wife to the husband, and, therefore, according to Jewish Law, the wife is entitled to retract her undertaking to her husband.

Justice Moshe Silberg opined that the circumstances of this case involved neither waiver nor a gift, since the wife did in fact receive a return for what she waived. Rather, it involved a compromise, in which both sides waived something, and hence is considered a sale according to Jewish Law. In the case of a sale, as noted, since the wife did not give "notification" when making her declaration of waiving the rights due her from her husband, it was impossible to void her undertakings on the grounds of duress according to Jewish law. Nevertheless, Justice Silberg ruled that in this case Jewish law did not apply, as the matter did not concern the laws of maintenance but an ordinary compensation agreement, governed by civil law, under which the wife's undertakings to her husband are void, since she was forced to sign the agreement for fear that her husband would not grant her a divorce and leave her an *agunah*.

Duress in Israeli Law

Section 17(a) of the Contracts (General Part) Law, 5733 – 1973, which bears certain similarities to duress in Jewish Law with respect to contracts, provides that "A person who has entered into a contract in consequence of duress – by force or by threats – applied to him by the other party or a person acting on his behalf may rescind the contract." According to this section, there is no need to give "notification" in order to void undertakings given under duress, the circumstance of duress itself constitutes sufficient grounds to entitle the aggrieved party to rescind the contract.

[Menachem Elon (2nd ed.)]

BIBLIOGRAPHY: Gulak, Yesodei, 1 (1922), 57–62; 2 (1922), 70f.; M. Higger, *Intention in Talmudic Law* (1927); Herzog, Instit, 1 (1936), 101–7; 2 (1939), 130–2, 240–3, 248–75; ET, 1 (1951³), 162–72; 5 (1953), 698–707; Z. Karl, in: *Mazkeret Levi... Freund* (1953), 29, 45f.; B. Rabinovitz-Teomim, *Ḥukkat Mishpat* (1957), 182–91; B. Lipkin, in: *Sinai – Sefer Yovel* (1958), 394–402; S. Albeck, *Pesher Dinei ha-Nezikin ba-Talmud* (1965), 175–82; Elon, Mafte'aḥ, 2–4; Sh. Warhaftig, *Dinei Avodah ba-Mishpat ha-Ivri*, 2 (1969), 721–96, 829–66. **ADD. BIBLIOGRAPHY:** M. Elon, *Ha-Mishpat ha-Ivri* (1988), 1:72, 254, 293, 296, 427, 505, 518, 520, 522, 523, 524, 542, 618, 790ff., 808ff.; idem, *Jewish Law* (1994), 1:80, 297, 348–349, 353, 521, 615, 630, 633, 636ff., 638, 659, 764, 969ff., 990ff.; M. Elon and B. Lifshitz, *Mafte'aḥ ha-She'elot ve-ha-Teshuvot shel Ḥakhmei Sefarad u-Ẓefon Afrikah* (legal digest), 1 (1986), 2–3; B. Lifshitz and E. Shochetman, *Mafte'aḥ ha-She'elot ve-ha-Teshuvot shel Ḥakhmei Ashkenaz, Ẓarefat ve-Italyah* (legal digest), (1997), 2–3; S.Warhaftig, *Dinei Ḥozim ba-Mishpat ha-Ivri* (1974), 117–31; S. Deutch, "*Hora'at Ha-Oshek be-Ḥof ha-Ḥozim*," in: *Meḥkarei Mishpat*, 2 (1982), 1, 25–32; *Enẓiklopedyah Talmudit*, s.v. "*ones*," vol. 1, 162ff.

ONIAS, the name of four high priests of the Second Temple period (corresponding to the Hebrew חוֹנְיוֹ).

ONIAS I lived at the end of the fourth century B.C.E. I Maccabees 12:20–23 relates that Areios, king of Sparta, sent a letter to the high priest Onias, claiming that the Spartans and the Jews were brethren being descended from Abraham. Although most scholars consider the high priest referred to was Onias I, and the king, Areios I, who reigned 309–265 B.C.E., they regard the letter itself as unhistorical. There is no sufficient reason, however, to cast doubt upon the essential veracity of the incident, and it is probable that the Areios referred to is Areios I, since Areios II came to the throne about 255 B.C.E. and died while still a child. On the other hand, Onias II was not contemporary with any Areios. According to Josephus (Ant. 12:226–7), the letter was sent to Onias III, the grandson of Onias II, but this is clearly erroneous, since there is no knowledge of a Spartan king named Areios at this time.

ONIAS II, son of *Simeon the Just and grandson of Onias I, lived in the second half of the third century B.C.E. According to Josephus (Ant. 12:44) he was a minor when his father died, and his uncle Eleazar officiated for him during his minority. When Eleazar died, another uncle, Manasseh, took his place until Onias was old enough to assume the high priesthood. In his account of Joseph b. Tobiah (*ibid.*, 12:158), Josephus depicts Onias as miserly and foolish, and careless of the dignity of his rank, thereby allowing the rise of Joseph the tax collector. The truth would appear to be otherwise. Onias was involved in the political events connected with the war between Ptolemy III (Euergetes I) and Queen Laodice, the wife and murderess of Antiochus II Theos. Wishing to throw off the yoke of Ptolemaic Egypt, he conspired with the enemies of Ptolemy and refused to pay taxes. Ptolemy threatened to drive the Jews from their land if the tax was not paid. It would appear that Onias was high priest until the close of the second century B.C.E.

ONIAS III, a son of Simeon II and grandson of Onias II, knew how to preserve both the religious and secular authority of the house of Onias. This is demonstrated in the quarrel he had with Simeon, the head of the Temple (II Macc. 3:4). Simeon, an important official in the administration of the Temple, demanded from Onias the post of market commissioner (*Agoranomos*) which Onias refused because the *Agoranomos*, by virtue of his control over such things as the market, the price of goods, and employment, in effect exercised all real authority in the city. When his demand was rejected, Simeon turned to Apollonius, the commander of the Syrian army, and told him that vast treasures belonging to the king were preserved in the Temple vaults. Apollonius informed Seleucus who sent his chancellor, *Heliodorus to remove the treasure. Heliodorus, however, failed to do so, and having thus lost face, had to leave Jerusalem. Thereafter Onias was hated by the Seleucid ruler who suspected him of having brought about the failure of the mission. When Antiochus IV ascended the throne (175 B.C.E.), Onias was summoned to Antioch, and his brother *Jason was appointed high priest in his place, having apparently promised a large sum of money for the appointment. After three years Jason was displaced by *Menelaus, who obtained the appointment by offering a larger sum. Menelaus, an extreme Hellenizer, brought about a rebellion in Jerusalem by the contempt with which he treated the sacrifices of the people. He went to Antioch, apparently in an attempt to restore his standing. He feared the influence of Onias who was living in Daphne, near Antioch, and persuaded Andronicus, a favorite of Antiochus, to murder the exiled high priest. There seems to be a reference to the death of Onias III in Daniel 9:26.

ONIAS IV, son of Onias III, was a candidate for the high priesthood after his father's death, but was ousted by *Alcimus. For this reason and because of the edicts of Antiochus, he left Judea, and went to Egypt. The works of Josephus present contradictory traditions (cf. Wars, 1:33; 7:423–4, and Ant., 12:387–8; 13:62). According to *The Jewish War*, it was Onias III who fled to Egypt because of the persecutions of *Antiochus Epiphanes, whereas according to the *Antiquities*, it was Onias IV, in the time of Antiochus V Eupator. In about 145 B.C.E., Ptolemy VI Philometer granted Onias authority to build a temple in Leontopolis, the Temple of Onias. The view of Tcherikover that the erection of the temple was a political act, of interest to both Onias and Ptolemy, and that it was intended merely as a local center of worship for the Jewish military settlement is a plausible one. This emerges from the fact that the temple fulfilled no religious function in the Jewish community of Egypt whose loyalties were solely to the Temple in Jerusalem. The Mishnah (Men. 13:10) mentions "the Temple of Onias," emphasizing that it had not the same religious status as the Temple in Jerusalem. Josephus regarded Onias' deed as an act of desecration. The priests of Jerusalem regarded the sacrifices in the Temple of Onias as invalid and refused to recognize the priests and levites who ministered there (Jos., Ant., 13:73; Wars, 7:431). Many Jewish soldiers came to Egypt together with Onias, and, as military settlers, were given land between Memphis and Pelusium by Philometor. This region was known from that time as "the land of Onias." Hilkiah and Hananiah, the sons of Onias, served as commanders in the army of Cleopatra III, and participated in the queen's military campaign in Israel and Syria against Ptolemy Lathyrus. They influenced Cleopatra to such an extent that she desisted from annexing Judea to Egypt (Jos., Ant., 13:284–7, 349, 354–5). In the struggle between Cleopatra and Ptolemy Physcon, after the death of Ptolemy Philometor, Onias and his sons supported the queen (Jos., Apion, 2:50). During the reign of Hyrcanus II the Jews of Onias still retained a certain military importance (Jos., Ant., 14:131–2, and Wars, 1:189 state that Pelusium was taken by force from the garrison army). The Temple of Onias was closed in 73 C.E. by order of *Vespasian.

BIBLIOGRAPHY: II Macc. 3:1–4; 5:32–35; A. Buechler, *Die Tobiaden und die Oniaden* (1899), 74ff.; Schuerer, Hist, 24f., 54, 274; Schuerer, Gesch, 3 (1909[4]), 42, 131, 144–7; Klausner, Bayit Sheni, index, s.v. *Ḥonyo*; F.-M. Abel, *Histoire de la Palestine*, 1 (1952), 105ff.; A. Tcherikover, *Hellenistic Civilization and the Jews* (1959), 138f., 156ff., 172–4, 276ff., 389f.

ONIAS, TEMPLE OF, temple of the Hellenistic and Roman period established in Egypt for Jewish worship and sacrifice. Its location is given by Josephus as being in the district of Heliopolis, where it was built over an earlier ruined temple to Bubastis, the lioness-goddess; hence the area's other name Leontopolis. It was established for the worship of "God the most High," as that at Jerusalem (Ant., 13:62–68). The location is presumed to be at Tel el-Yehudiyah (Mound of the Jewess), the name serving as a clue to its identity. It was first investigated by E. Naville in 1887 and in more detail by Flinders Petrie in 1905. The site is part of an earlier Hyksos encampment outside the present town of Shirban el-Qanatir, 25 km. north of Cairo. Petrie found a towered structure beside a small temple-like enclosure, accessed by a long staircase and surrounded by a mudbrick wall, triangular in plan. He showed a model of his finds to a meeting of the Jewish Community in London in 1906, but the model has since disappeared. The location in Egypt has been visited by a number of archaeologists, including the writer, who have been unable to confirm Petrie's findings, though it is clear that the alleged site is close to a necropolis of Jewish burials in the area known as Leontopolis.

The temple is mentioned several times by Josephus and twice in some detail, but each time differently. He describes it first as being modeled on the Temple of Jerusalem (Ant., 13:72), while the second time he says it was built like a fortress in the form of a tower 60 cubits high, unlike Jerusalem (Wars, 7:426–432). It is presumed that the second description is a correction of the first. Josephus claims that it stood for 343 years (ibid., 436), but this is unlikely; 243 years would be nearer the mark. It was destroyed in 73 C.E. on the orders of Titus or Vespasian (ibid., 421), who feared that it might become the focus of further revolt after the destruction of the Temple of Jerusalem in 70 C.E. At the earliest it could have been built in 170 B.C.E., shortly before the Hasmonean Revolt, because it is always referred to as the Temple of Onias (*Ḥonia* in Hebrew). There are two candidates for that honor, *Onias III (son of Simon II, the Just), who was high priest some time after 200 B.C.E., or his son *Onias IV. It is generally accepted that the earlier Onias, who was ousted by his Hellenizing brother Jason, was murdered in Antioch (II Macc. 4:34), so Onias IV is the more likely candidate. When he saw that his legitimate right to the High Priesthood had been usurped by the Hellenistic party, friendly to the Seleucids, Onias set up a rival sanctuary in Egypt, under the protection of their enemies, the Ptolemies.

It is unlikely that he did this to serve the Jews of Egypt as a whole, who may have had some difficulty in reaching Jerusalem under the Seleucids, as the temple is never mentioned by Philo or other Judeo-Egyptian sources; nor was it located in or near Alexandria, the chief center of Egyptian Jewry. It is more likely that the temple served a military colony under the direction of this Onias, acting in the capacity of an officer willing to bring manpower and troops over to Ptolemy VI Philometor and his queen, Cleopatra II. Josephus records that two sons of Onias acted as generals in assisting Cleopatra in her fight against her son Ptolemy Lathyrus (Ant., 13:285–287 and 348–349). In that role the temple was similar to the earlier fifth century B.C.E. temple serving the Jewish mercenaries at Elephantine, at the southern border of Egypt.

The Talmud takes a somewhat relaxed view of this temple. It claims that it was not an "idolatrous shrine" because Onias had based himself on Isaiah 19:18, which says that, "One day there will be an altar to the Lord in the midst of the land of Egypt," and because he was a legitimate Zadokite priest, a descendant of the high priest Simon the Just (Men. 109b). The Mishnah states that some vows made in the Temple of Jerusalem could be redeemed in the Temple of Onias and, while a priest who served at Onias was precluded from serving in Jerusalem, he could nevertheless eat the *terumah* (consecrated food) there together with his priestly brethren (Men. 13:10).

BIBLIOGRAPHY: M. Delcor, "Le Temple d'Onias en Egypte," in: *Revue Biblique*, 75 (1968), 188–203.; R. Hayward, "The Jewish Temple of Leontopolis: a Reconsideration," in: *Journal of Jewish Studies*, 33 (1982), 429–43; J.M. Modrzejewski, *The Jews of Egypt, from Rameses II to Emperor Hadrian*, trans. R. Cornman (1995), 124–29; E. Naville, *The Mound of the Jews and the City of Onias* (1890), 13–21; W.M. Flinders Petrie, *Hyksos and Israelite Cities* (1906), 19–27; E. Schuerer, *The History of the Jewish People in the Age of Jesus Christ* (rev. English edition, G. Vermes, F. Millar, M. Goodman, 1986), vol. 3:47–48, 145–47; V. Tcherikower, *Hellenistic Civilisation and the Jews*, trans. S. Applebaum (1959), 275–81.

[Stephen G Rosenberg (2nd ed.)]

ONION (Heb. בָּצָל), the *Allium cepa*, one of the earliest cultivated plants. It is mentioned only once in the Bible as one of the vegetables eaten in Egypt for which the Israelites longed when they were in the wilderness (Num. 11:5). Onion growing was widespread in Egypt and drawings of it are found on the pyramids. The onion, with its concentric skins, symbolized in Egypt the stellar and planetary system, and was an object of idol worship, some swearing by its name (Pliny, *Historia naturalis*, 19:101). The word appears in family names. Among the Nethinim (see *Gibeonites and Nethinim) who went from Babylon to Ereẓ Israel, a family of the children of Bazluth is mentioned (Ezra 2:52), and the Jerusalem Talmud (Ḥag. 2:2; 77d) mentions a Miriam bat Alei Beẓalim ("onion leaves") which may be a reference to Miriam the mother of Jesus.

The onion is frequently mentioned in rabbinic literature. R. Judah used to say "Eat *bazal* [onions] and sit *ba-ẓel* [in the shade], and do not eat geese and fowl" (Pes. 114a), i.e., do not desire luxuries but be content with little. They made a distinction between "rural onions" (TJ, Shev. 2:9, 34a) and "urban onions which were the food of city folk" (Ter. 2:5). A species very near to the onion was called *beẓalẓul* (Kil. 1:3), which is possibly the shallot, the Ashkelon onion, and therefore sometimes called "scallion" which was praised by Theophrastus, Strabo, and Pliny. The onion was usually pulled up before it flowered and some of the plants were left to flower and produce seed (Pe'ah 3:3 and TJ, Pe'ah 17c). Many species of *Allium* of the same genus as the onion grow wild in Israel, where the climate and soil are very suitable for onion plants. To the Liliaceae family of onion belong some of the most beautiful of Israel's flowers (see *Flowers of the Bible).

BIBLIOGRAPHY: Loew, Flora, 2 (1924), 125–31; H.N. and A.L. Moldenke, *Plants of the Bible* (1952), index; J. Feliks, *Olam ha-Ẓome'aḥ ha-Mikra'i* (1968²), 169–71. **ADD. BIBLIOGRAPHY:** Feliks, Ha-Ẓome'aḥ, 38.

[Jehuda Feliks]

ONKELOS AND AQUILA (second century C.E.), two translators of the Bible, the one into Aramaic and the other into Greek, both of whom were proselytes. Although there is no doubt of their separate existence, the translation of Onkelos being preserved in its entirety, and that of Aquila in fragments (see *Aramaic (Middle Aramaic) and *Bible, Translations), the similarity of the names has caused considerable confusion. Similar or identical incidents are given in the Babylonian Talmud and the Tosefta as applying to Onkelos, and in the Jerusalem Talmud and the Palestinian Midrashim to Aquila (Akilas). It is therefore convenient to treat both of them primarily as one, while indicating where possible where they can be distinguished from one another. Fact and legend are inextricably interwoven.

According to Epiphanius, Aquila was a native of Pontus and a relative of the emperor *Hadrian, who in about 128 appointed him to an office connected with the rebuilding of Jerusalem as Aelia Capitolina. The Midrash (Tanḥ. 41a, Mishpatim 3) also refers to him as the son of the sister of Hadrian, although the Babylonian Talmud refers to him as "Onkelos the son of Kalonikus [v. Kalonymus] the son of the sister of Titus." He became converted to Judaism, but before doing so he raised the spirits of Titus, Balaam, and Jesus (this last was expurged by the censor from the printed editions), all of whom confirmed that the people of Israel is held in the highest repute in the world to come (Git. 56b, 57a). According to the Tanḥuma, when he formed the intention of converting to Judaism, fearing the anger and opposition of Hadrian, he informed him that he wished to travel (to Ereẓ Israel) on business, and Hadrian offered him all the money he needed to remain in Rome. In any case, he must have been a person of wealth, and this lends point to the comment of the Midrash (Gen. R. 70:5), to the effect that he asked R. Eliezer b. Hyrcanus whether there was no greater reward for the proselyte than that stated in the Bible, that God "loveth the stranger [*ger*, in mishnaic Hebrew a proselyte] in giving him food and raiment" (Deut. 10:18), pointing out that he was short of neither of these things. Eliezer's brusque reply might have discouraged him, but he went to R. Joshua with the same question and Joshua replied that it refers to spiritual benefits. His conversion met with the vigorous opposition of the emperor. According to the Tanḥuma he "smote him on the cheek"; according to the Talmud (Av. Zar. 11a) he sent four successive contingents of soldiers to arrest him, but he succeeded in converting them all to Judaism. Onkelos was a contemporary of Rabban Gamaliel of Jabneh and a colleague and pupil of Eliezer b. Hyrcanus and Joshua b. Hananiah (cf., above). His relationship with Gamaliel was a close one, and when Gamaliel died Onkelos arranged a costly funeral for him, such as was usually reserved for royalty (Tosef., Shab. 7 (8):18; Av. Zar. 11a). He conducted himself with the utmost piety and was particularly meticulous in adhering to the laws of ritual purity, surpassing in this respect even Rabban Gamaliel, applying to ordinary food the rules enjoined for partaking of sacrifices (Tosef., Ḥag. 3:2 and 3). On one occasion he refused to bathe in the ritual baths of Ashkelon (since he regarded it as heathen territory) and made his ablutions in the sea, while Gamaliel (according to one opinion) was not so particular (Tosef., Mik. 6:3). There is one talmudic statement attributed to him (BB 99a) that the faces of the *cherubim were turned sideways "as a pupil taking leave of his master."

The two translators are differentiated from one another in two passages of the Talmud. Where the Babylonian Talmud (Meg. 3a) states that Onkelos the Proselyte translated the Pentateuch into Aramaic (Targum) under the guidance of R. Eliezer and R. Joshua, the parallel passage in the Jerusalem Talmud (*ibid.* 1:11, 71c) clearly refers to the translation of Aquila the Proselyte into Greek, and there are some quotations in the Talmud which clearly refer to a translation into Greek. Since Azariah de *Rossi, attempts have been made to disentangle the confusion between the Aramaic translator Onkelos and the Greek translator Aquila. The prevalent opinion tends to ascribe the talmudic passages to Aquila, but when, in Babylonian sources, the name was corrupted to Onkelos, the existing anonymous translation of the Pentateuch into Aramaic was ascribed to "Onkelos the Proselyte."

BIBLIOGRAPHY: A. Silverstone, *Aquila and Onkelos* (1931); Zunz-Albeck, Derashot; Kohut, Arukh, 1 (1926), 158, and note. For further bibliography see *Bible, Translations.

[Louis Isaac Rabinowitz]

ONO (Heb. אוֹנוֹ), town in Judea, first mentioned in Thutmosis III's list of conquered towns in Canaan (No. 65). It was apparently settled originally by descendants of Benjamin (I Chron. 8:12). It appears with Lod and Hadid in the list of places resettled after the return from Babylonian Exile (Ezra 2:33; Neh. 7:37). It was situated near the border of Samaria, for Sanballat offered to meet Nehemiah in one of the villages of the Plain of Ono as on neutral ground (Neh. 6:2). According to Nehemiah 11:35, it was located in the Ge-Harashim ("Valley of Craftsmen"). Ono is frequently mentioned in talmudic sources. According to the Mishnah (Arak. 9:6), it had been fortified "from the days of Joshua"; the Babylonian Talmud locates it 3 mi. (c. 5 km.) from Lod, but relations between the two towns were unfriendly (Lam. R. 1:17, no. 52). Sometime in the third century, it was made an independent municipality: a councilor of Ono is mentioned in a papyrus from Oxyrrhynchus dated 297 (no. 1205). It appears as an independent town in Byzantine town lists of the fifth and sixth centuries (Hierocles Synecdemus 719:4; Georgius Cyprius 1006). The former Arab village of Kafr ʿAnā occupied the spot until 1948. An urban settlement called *Kiryat Ono now exists nearby.

BIBLIOGRAPHY: S. Klein, *Ereẓ Yehudah* (1939), 7–8, 20; Mazar, in: BJPES, 8 (1941), 106; Noth, in: ZDPV, 61 (1938), 46; EM, S.V. (incl. bibl.).

[Michael Avi-Yonah]

°ÓNODY, GÉZA (1848–?), Hungarian antisemitic leader born in Tiszaeszlar. A member of the gentry, he was elected to the lower house of parliament as a delegate of the opposition Independence Party in 1881. At first, Ónody's antisemitic activities were connected with the blood libel of 1882 in *Tiszaeszlar where he owned an estate. Raising the matter in parliament in May 1882, he opened the public campaign around the libel. From that time, he was one of the leading spokesmen of the group responsible for the anti-Jewish agitation which followed in the wake of the libel. In his work, *Tiszaeszlar in der Vergangenheit und Gegenwart* (1883, orig. in Hung.), Ónody sought to "prove" the authenticity of the blood libel against a historic background. When the antisemitic party was organized in Hungary in 1883, he became one of its leaders, together with Istóczy Cyőző. Because of his activity in the blood libel affair and his work on the subject, he also became renowned among antisemites abroad, especially in Germany. He was among the leaders of antisemitic unions which convened the First International Anti-Jewish Congress (Dresden, 1882) and one of its most prominent participants. In 1884 he was reelected to parliament, this time on an antisemitic platform, and became one of the leaders of the antisemitic faction.

BIBLIOGRAPHY: *Istóczy und Ónody* (1882); Z. Bosnyák, *A magyar fajvédelem uttöröi* (1942), 63–102; N. Katzburg, *Antishemiyyut be-Hungariyah 1867–1914* (1969).

[Nathaniel Katzburg]

ONTARIO, Canada's second largest province, a vast territory of more than one million square kilometers (415,000 square miles) – an area larger than France and Spain combined. It borders on Quebec to the east and Manitoba to the west, and to the south the St. Lawrence River and Great Lakes form a water border with a series of neighboring northeastern American states running from New York to Minnesota. With a population of more than 12 million, Ontario is today home to about one in three Canadians. Largely English-speaking, 80 per cent of all those who live in Ontario live in urban centers, with the largest concentration in the "Golden Horseshoe" that arcs along the western end of Lake Ontario and includes the Greater *Toronto Area, Hamilton, St. Catharines, and Niagara Falls. About five million people live in the "Golden Horseshoe." In southwestern Ontario, significant populations live in Kitchener-Waterloo, London, and Windsor. In eastern Ontario, Ottawa and Kingston are the predominant cities. In more sparsely settled northern Ontario, smaller municipalities have grown at strategic points along the railway lines that opened up the vast wilderness to mining and logging. The cities that have evolved include Hearst, Moosonee, Kenora, Sudbury, North Bay, Sault Ste. Marie, Thunder Bay, and Timmins.

Ontario's economy had its beginnings in exploitation of natural resources: fur, timber and minerals. The province's many rivers and lakes, particularly the Great Lakes, made for natural transportation routes. As the population of Ontario increased, people started new industries and surveyed, cleared and farmed the rich agricultural land. Today, northern Ontario's economy is still highly dependent on natural resources while southern Ontario, with its proximity to the enormous American market, is heavily industrialized. However, in the 21st century, more Ontarians are employed in service industries than on assembly lines. The fastest-growing sectors are business services, finance, tourism, and culture. Ontario is the economic engine that powers the Canadian economy. This one province contributes about 40 per cent of Canada's total employment. Ontario has relatively high employment in manufacturing and financial and business services, and relatively less employment in agriculture, forestry and mining.

Today Ontario's Jewish population stands at about 212,000, almost 60 percent of all Jews in Canada. Nearly 180,000 of those Jews are concentrated in the greater Toronto area, which is rich in Jewish organizational and religious life. While there are about 25 centers that have synagogues, only *Ottawa, Canada's capital city, *Hamilton, London, Windsor, and Kingston have populations large enough to sustain local Jewish federations, with professional staff.

History

While Ontario was still a British colony, first called Upper Canada and then Canada West from 1841 to 1867, a tiny number of Jews was attracted by the colony's economic opportunities. Many of these Jews, mainly of English or German origin, were merchants or wholesalers involved in the import of manufactured goods. Some had kinship connections to Jewish merchant families in Montreal, New York, or London. But as the number of Jews in Ontario continued to grow slowly through the 1800s only a few Ontario communities had sufficient Jewish population to support synagogues or other Jewish institutions. By the mid-1800s, the largest Jewish community was in Toronto, where community members organized services in private homes or rented space until 1859 when the first Jewish congregation, Holy Blossom, was formed. However, 10 years earlier, in 1849, land was bought and a Jewish cemetery consecrated. The first burial took place in 1850.

After Canadian confederation in 1867, and with the surge of mass immigration of Yiddish-speaking East European Jews to North America starting in 1882, the Jewish population of Ontario began to grow more rapidly. Most new arrivals, looking for both economic opportunity and the comfort of a familiar Jewish community, settled in larger centers like Toronto and Hamilton. But here and there Jews also found their way into smaller towns and villages. By World War I, rare was the Ontario town of any size, even one in a more remote area of northern Ontario, that was not home to one or more Jewish families hoping to make a living as shopkeepers or peddlers or, in some cases, by trading with members of Canada's First Nations. Where numbers warranted, Jews in smaller communities organized synagogues – mostly Orthodox in liturgy – and religious schools for their children. In later years it was not uncommon to find active chapters of Hadassah, Young Judaea, and B'nai B'rith in smaller towns. Some small-town Jewish communities were able to employ rabbis who also often served as the communities' Jewish teachers, *shoḥets* and perhaps even *mohels*. Other communities got by without Jewish professionals, importing rabbis or *mohels* from far away as need arose.

In the years following World War II Jewish populations in smaller communities began to gradually decline as many younger and Canadian-born Jews began leaving, sometimes in search of better job prospects or university education or of Jewish marriage partners – and often all three – in larger centers. Once married and with university degrees and good jobs, many did not return to the smaller centers from which they came but remained in larger cities where, in an atmosphere of declining antisemitism and rising economic prosperity, the opportunities for a rich Jewish communal life were far greater than they had previously known. And as a younger generation of Jews from smaller communities relocated to larger cities, in many cases their parents followed. The result has been a gradual but steady decline in Jewish population in smaller Ontario centers and a rapid growth of urban Jewish population, especially in Toronto and, to a lesser extent, Ottawa.

But this exodus from small-town Ontario since the end of World War II has not been the only reason for the growing concentration of Ontario Jews in centers like Toronto and Ottawa. Two other factors have been at work: a shift in Jewish population from Montreal to Toronto and Jewish immigration to Canada collecting in Toronto. In the wake of a rise in separatist sentiment in Quebec through the 1960s and 1970s, and the first election of an avowed pro-separatist government in Quebec in 1976, fear that Quebec might eventually leave Canada grew among Montreal's overwhelmingly pro-federalist and English-speaking Jewish community. While this has not happened, by the late 1970s a migration of Jews out of Montreal, many to Ontario, and particularly to Toronto, Ottawa, and other larger Ontario cities was underway. As a consequence, Toronto has now replaced Montreal as Canada's largest Jewish center. In addition, since the end of World War II, Ontario and Toronto in particular have been magnets for immigration from around the world. This includes Jewish immigration. Toronto has absorbed more than half of all Jewish immigrants arriving in Canada – including, during the past several decades, new arrivals from the former Soviet Union, Israel, Europe, the United States, and, of late, Latin America.

The figures tell the tale. In 1931 approximately 70 percent of all Jews in Ontario lived in Toronto. By 1961 that number had grown to more than 80 percent. Today more than 85 percent of all Jews live in the greater Toronto area and the Jewish population of Toronto continues to grow both as a percentage of Ontario's Jewish population and in absolute numbers.

Jews and Provincial Politics

Jews have had an important stake in areas that are, in the Canadian federal system, under provincial jurisdiction, most notably in the areas of human rights legislation and education. Faced with a rising tide of antisemitism during the Depression of the 1930s, the revitalized and reorganized *Canadian Jewish Congress maintained an office in Toronto, the seat of the Ontario provincial legislature. It immediately began to lobby the Ontario legislature, at first without much success, for laws to bar discrimination on account of race, religion, or national origin, particularly in employment and housing, and also to limit and prosecute the distribution of hate propaganda. In 1932, one of the Jewish pioneers of provincial politics, the Conservative Party member of the provincial legislature E.F. Singer, did manage to introduce a bill to prevent insurance companies from charging higher premiums to certain minorities. More successful were the activities of the Joint Public Relations Committee, a joint agency of the Canadian Jewish Congress and B'nai B'rith committee during the 1940s and 1950s. Working in cooperation with liberal churches, the labor movement, progressive media, and sympathetic politicians, it played a prominent role in the passage of the 1944 Ontario Racial Discrimination Act and the Fair Employment Practices Act of 1951. They also successfully went to court to end the practice of restrictive covenants. These victories helped pave the way for the wide-ranging human rights protections that are today enjoyed by all residents of Ontario and Canada, including those rights enumerated in the Canadian Charter of Rights and Freedoms.

For all these successes, the organized Jewish community has experienced some frustrations in the arena of education, albeit for significantly different reasons. Arguing for the separation of religion and state, the organized Jewish community protested against the 1944 introduction of prayer and mandatory religious instruction into Ontario public schools. While they were eventually successful in winning exemptions for individual Jewish children who did not wish to receive religious instruction, and later won exemptions for schools in Jewish neighborhoods, it was not until Canada adopted a Charter of Rights and Freedoms with protection of religious freedom and equal treatment that the courts declared the 1944 legislation unconstitutional.

On another educational issue Jewish groups have remained unsuccessful in changing Ontario practice. With a major proportion of Jewish children in larger communities attending Jewish day schools, the organized Jewish community has lobbied the provincial government to deepen its involvement in religious matters by extending to Jewish schools the public funding that Catholic schools have enjoyed since the time of Confederation, which to this day remains protected by the British North America Act under which the Canadian federation was formed. However, neither Jewish political pressure nor resorting to the courts has yet led the provincial government to offer financial support for Jewish schools.

Jews in Ontario today participate in all areas of economic, cultural, and public life and by every measure public attitudes towards Jews in Ontario have, on balance, become far more positive during the past several decades. These positive attitudes are reflected in the makeup of the popularly elected Ontario Legislature. The first Jewish cabinet minister appointed by any Ontario government was Allan *Grossman, who was appointed minister of correctional services in the Ontario cabinet in 1970. Since then, all major parties have not only had Jews serve in the cabinet but have also chosen Jews to lead their parties. Today, the presence of Jews in provincial politics has become so widespread as to not draw attention.

BIBLIOGRAPHY: G. Tulchinsky, *Taking Root* (1992); idem, *Branching Out* (1998).

[Richard Menkis and Harold Troper (2nd ed.)]

ONYCHA (Heb. שְׁחֵלֶת), aromatic substance. According to the ancient translations, the *sheḥelet* included among the ingredients of the incense (Ex. 30:34) is onycha. An early *baraita* dating from Temple times has צִפֹּרֶן ("fingernail") instead of *sheḥelet* (Ker. 6a). The reference to the shell of a mollusk, the *Unguis odoratus* (shaped like a fingernail and hence its name) which is found in the Indian Ocean, and, like several other mollusks found in the Red Sea, emits a pleasant smell when burned. Ben Sira 24:15 also includes onycha (in Greek ὄνυξ as one of the ingredients of the incense in the Temple, while in Ugaritic writings it is mentioned among several spices and foods.

BIBLIOGRAPHY: Loew, Flora, 1 (1928), 313; H.L. Ginsberg, *Kitvei Ugarit* (1936), 103; H.N. and A.L. Moldenke, *Plants of the Bible* (1952), 223f., no. 209.

[Jehuda Feliks]

OPATOSHU, JOSEPH (originally **Opatovsky**; 1886–1954), Yiddish novelist and short-story writer. Born near Mlave (Poland), Opatoshu immigrated to the U.S. in 1907, where he studied engineering at Cooper Union at night, while supporting himself by working in a shoe factory, selling newspapers, and teaching in Hebrew schools. In 1914 he graduated as a civil engineer, but soon found literature a more congenial profession. From 1910 he contributed stories to periodicals and anthologies, and in 1914 edited an anthology of his own, *Di Naye Heym* ("The New Home"), which included his story of American Jewish life, "Fun Nyu Yorker Geto." When the New York daily *Der Tog* was founded (1914), he joined its staff and for 40 years contributed stories, sketches, and serials, most of which were later reprinted in book form.

Opatoshu's early work was naturalistic, depicting scenes from contemporary life. Thus his *A Roman fun a Ferd Ganev* ("A Novel about a Horse Thief," 1912), his first novel to attract wide attention, was based on his boyhood acquaintance with an unusual Jewish thief who made a living by smuggling horses across the border from Poland to Germany and who was killed while defending fellow Jews against their hostile neighbors. Opatoshu expressed his reaction to romanticism by creating thieves, smugglers, and drunkards who were a distinct contrast to the figures in the writings of Sholem *Aleichem or Y.L. *Peretz. Opatoshu was one of the first Yiddish writers to depict American Jewish experience in his works. After reading some of his American stories, Sholem Aleichem encouraged Opatoshu to continue writing about the subject. Opatoshu heeded this suggestion and gave literary expression to the conflicts created by the Americanization of the Jewish immigrant in such works as *Hibru* ("Hebrew," 1919), a naturalistic novel that deals with the problems of Jewish education in New York; *Di Tentserin* ("The Dancer," 1929) portrays declining Ḥasidism in New York; *Arum Grand Strit* ("Around Grand Street," 1929) focuses on the immigrant Jews on the Lower East Side; and *Rase* ("Race," 1923), a short-story collection that portrayed the conflict between varying ethnic and religious groups.

Fascinated by the Jewish past, he sought to revivify segments of it in historical novels, based on extensive research and guided by an insight, gained through Simon Dubnov's work in Jewish history, that the narrative of Jewish oppression and life in the ghetto that dominated Jewish history as written by Jews could mislead through its onesidedness. Opatoshu sought descriptions of a vital, interactive, and hopeful daily life among Jews. In his novel *In Poylishe Velder* (1921; *In Polish Woods*, 1938, the first volume of a trilogy), Opatoshu described the decay of the ḥasidic court of Kotzk during the post-Napoleonic generation and presented a rich panorama of Polish-Jewish interrelations up to the Revolt of 1863. Often reprinted, and translated into eight languages, it established Opatoshu's fame internationally, though its sequel, *1863*, made less of an impact; the last volume of the trilogy, *Aleyn* ("Alone") was the first to be published (1919). In his Falstaffian narrative, *A Tog in Regensburg* ("A Day in Regensburg," 1968), and *Elye Bokher* (dealing with the author of the Yiddish romance, the *Bove Buch), both published in 1933, Opatoshu portrays the vanished world of 16th-century Jewish patricians and Yiddish minstrels in a stylized language that utilizes older stages of Yiddish. In his final historical epic, *Der Letster Oyfshtand* (2 vols. 1948–52; *The Last Revolt*, 1952), Opatoshu attempted an imaginative reconstruction of daily life in 2nd-century Judea, when the last desperate revolt of the Jews against Roman rule flared up and was crushed.

His son DAVID (1919–1996) worked extensively in the Yiddish theater and starred in the classic Yiddish film *Di Klyatshe/ The Light Ahead* (1939; adapted from S.Y. *Abramovitsh's *Fiske der Krumer*). Over the course of four decades he appeared in numerous Broadway productions and Hollywood films, and hundreds of television productions, winning an Emmy in 1990. He published short stories and television scripts, and directed and produced for theater, film, and television.

BIBLIOGRAPHY: *Opatoshu Bibliografye*, 1 (1937), 2 (1947); LYNL, 1 (1956), 145–9; B. Rivkin, *Yoysef Opatoshus Gang* (1948); I. Freilich, *Opatoshus Shafungsveg* (1951); J. Glatstein, *In Tokh Genumen* (1956), 145–56; S. Bickel, *Shrayber fun Mayn Dor* (1958), 304–16; C. Madison, *Yiddish Literature* (1968), 326–47; N. Mayzel, *Yoysef Opatoshu* (1937); S. Liptzin, *Maturing of Yiddish Literature* (1970), 10–18.

[Sol Liptzin / Shifra Kuperman (2nd ed.)]

OPATOW (Pol. **Opatów**; Yid. **Apta, אַפּטאָ**), town in Kielce province, E. Poland. A Jewish settlement existed in Opatow from the 16th century. In 1634 the town was divided into two sectors, the Christian and the Jewish, the latter known as the "Street of the Jews." According to Samuel Feivish in *Tit ha-Yaven* (Venice, 1670) over 200 Jewish families perished there during the Swedish invasion of Poland in 1656. Conditions became so difficult that in 1687 the *Council of the Four Lands issued an ordinance prohibiting other Jews from settling in Opatow without obtaining express permission from the community board (*kahal*). The community in Opatow was efficiently organized at this period, and its diverse activities, including collection for the needy of Ereẓ Israel, were administered by various officers (*ne'emanim* and *gabba'im*). In the 18th century its economic position deteriorated and it became dependent on the whims of the overlords of the town and the governor. The minute book (*pinkas*) of the Opatow community was an important source of information for the history of Polish Jewry; a copy was preserved in the communal archives in Warsaw up to 1939.

The Jewish population in Opatow increased in the 19th century, numbering 2,517 in 1856 (out of a total population of 3,845), and 4,138 in 1897. Among the noted personalities who lived in Opatow the best known is the ḥasidic *ẓaddik*, Abraham Joshua *Heshel, "the rabbi of Apta."

Holocaust Period

Before World War II 5,200 Jews lived in Opatow. The town came under the Radom District of the General-Government during the Nazi occupation. Many Jews fled before the Germans entered, young Jewish men in particular escaping to Soviet-occupied territory. After the capitulation of the town, the Germans set fire to the market place where mainly Jews lived. Over the next days 200 men, Poles and Jews, were deported and never returned. A "contribution" (fine) of 60,000 marks was exacted, and Jews were evicted from the better residences, which were handed over to German officers. A ghetto was officially established in the spring of 1941. It was open and without fence or guard, but Jews were forbidden to leave it on pain of death. Food, however, was available illegally in the open ghetto for high prices, so that Jews with means did not suffer from hunger. The poor (among them deportees and refugees from other places), who had no property or could not get work or were not hardy enough to get on in these difficult conditions, suffered misery and hunger, being left only with the meager official food rations. Among the poor an epidemic of typhus broke out and a hospital was set up in the synagogue, which also served the surrounding Jewish towns. Jews engaged in hard labor in the vicinity of Opatow, on road construction and in quarries.

The number of Jews in Opatow grew continually because of the influx of refugees from surrounding townlets and villages, as well as from distant towns – *Konin, *Lodz, and *Warsaw. In September 1940 there were 5,800 Jews, 600 of them newcomers; by September 1942 there were about 7,000 Jews, 1,800 of them deportees. Shortly before the liquidation a number of Jews from Silesia settled in Opatow Ghetto, which from June 1, 1942, was one of the 17 ghettos officially left in the country.

In July 1941 the German police began abducting young men for labor camps. Raids were carried out by German police with the help of Jewish police. Jews found in hiding were often executed. Until the liquidation of the ghetto, about 1,900–2,100 Jews were sent to the labor camps. A group of youth planning armed resistance bought weapons from Poles and stored them in the garret of the synagogue. The German police, who were informed, seized the weapons and shot a group of girls who were found there. The Judenrat was composed of well-known persons, mainly Zionists. The president, Mordekhai Weissblum, is reported to have taken care of the Jewish population, organized Jewish life, and alleviated German persecution and repression by personal diplomacy and bribery. But the Judenrat was also reproached for having prepared lists of candidates for labor camps, although it also sent parcels with food and clothing to the camp inmates.

The liquidation of the ghetto took place on Oct. 20–22, 1942. German police and Ukrainians surrounded the ghetto and carried out a mass *Selektion* in the square. Six thousand Jews were driven on foot to the Jasice station near Ostrow, loaded onto wagons, and taken to *Treblinka. Another 500 to 600 Jews were taken to a labor camp in Sandomierz. During the three-day *Aktion* several hundred Jews were killed in the town. The Germans left a few score Jews in Opatow to clear the terrain and sort out Jewish property. After the work was completed the Jews were shot at the Jewish cemetery, with the exception of a few individuals, among them the president of the Judenrat, who reached labor camps in Sandomierz. The community was not reconstituted after the war.

BIBLIOGRAPHY: *Apt (Opatov), Sefer Zikkaron...* (Heb. and Yid., 1966); A Rutkowski, in: BŻIH, no. 15–16 (1955), 75–182 passim; Yad Vashem Archives.

[Danuta Dombrowska]

OPAVA (Ger. **Troppau**), city in N. Silesia, Czech Republic. A tale about 27 Jews being executed for well-poisoning in Opava in 1163 is probably unreliable. A Jewish community is first mentioned in 1281. Although their expulsion is not documented it is recorded that in 1501 Jews were permitted to return and buy back their houses. Jews from *Osoblaha (Hotzenplotz) traded in Opava. In 1737, 20 Jewish families lived in the duchy. Several Jewish families lived in Opava at the beginning of the 19th century, and their number increased after the 1848 Revolution. At the end of the 19th century Opava became a center of the *Schoenerer brand of German nationalism, and the community suffered from antisemitic attacks. The community developed, inspired by its rabbi, Simon Friedmann, an ardent Zionist from his student days. In 1923 a progressive community statute was introduced. On the outskirts of Opava in the 1920s the training farm, Komorau, was a center of the He-Ḥalutz movement. The community numbered 134 in 1867, 1,127 in 1921, and in 1931, 971 (2.6% of the total population), 502 of whom declared their nationality as Jewish. At the time of the Sudeten crisis the community dispersed, sharing the fate of the Jews of the Protectorate. The synagogue was set on fire by the Nazis. After the war the community was revived, mainly by Jews from Subcarpathian Ruthenia. In 1959 it was affiliated with the Ostrava community and it was still active in 1970 as a synagogue congregation. Virtually no Jews lived there at the turn of the century.

BIBLIOGRAPHY: Germ Jud, 1 (1963), 387–8; 2 (1968), 834; Bondy-Dworský, nos. 305, 309, 1110; A. Engel, in: JGGJČ, 2 (1930), 59, 84; A. Cassuto, in: *Zeitschrift fuer Geschichte der Juden in der Tschechoslowakei*, 1 (1930), 81–90; J. Nirtl, *ibid.*, 4 (1934), 41–43; B. Brilling, in: *Judaica Bohemiae*, 4 (1968), 101–18, passim; B. Bretholz, *Quellen zur Geschichte der Juden in Maehren* (1935), index; Yad Vashem Archives.

[Meir Lamed]

OPFERPFENNIG, a poll tax introduced in 1342 by Emperor Louis IV the Bavarian, who ordered all Jews above the age of 12 and possessing 20 gulden to pay one gulden annually so that he would be better able to protect them. The original name was *Guldenpfennig*, changed in later generations to *Opferpfennig*. The practice was motivated by sheer economic necessity and justified by Christian chroniclers on the grounds that the German emperor, as the legal successor of the Roman emperors, was the rightful recipient of the traditional Temple tax which Jews paid after the destruction of the Second Temple. The *Opferpfennig* (called *donatio* by the exchequer) was collected on Christmas day, giving the levy the ignominy of a degrading poll tax. By 1346 the emperor was already disposing of the *Opferpfennig* of *Frankfurt, *Friedberg, *Gelnhausen, and *Wetzlar. *Charles IV ordered the income of the 1348 tax to be delivered to the archbishop of Triers. The *Opferpfennig*, like other taxes, was a readily transferable source of income but never grew to sizable proportions. This poll tax was sometimes replaced by an overall fixed communal tax. Rich and powerful Jews often succeeded in buying or obtaining exemption from the tax, a symbol of servitude.

BIBLIOGRAPHY: T. Roesel, in: MGWJ, 54 (1910), 208–10; Kisch, Germany, 167–8; Baron, Social², 9 (1965), 156. **ADD. BIBLIOGRAPHY:** H. Duchhardt, in: *Zeitschrift fuer historische Forschung*, 10 (1983), 149–67; P. Rauscher, in: *Aschkenas*, 14 (2004), 313–63.

OPHEL, rocky protuberance north of the city of David in Jerusalem. Its wall is mentioned in the time of Jotham (II Chron. 27:3), Manasseh (II Chron. 33:14), and Nehemiah (3:27); it formed part of the eastern fortifications of Jerusalem. In the time of Nehemiah, the Temple servants (*Nethinim*) lived there. According to Nehemiah 3:27, the Ophel was situated between the "tower that standeth out" of the royal palace and the water gate. The name Ophel in a general sense was applied to a city hill in Micah 4:8 and Isaiah 32:14, and specifically to a hill in Samaria (II Kings 5:24). In modern times, the name Ophel has been extended to the whole eastern hill of Old Jerusalem, including David's City. Excavations in this area were begun by Ch. Warren in 1867 and continued by C. Schick (1880, 1886), H. Guthe (1881), F.J. Bliss and A.C. Dickie (1894–97), M. Parker (1909), R. Weill (1913–24), F.J. Macalister (1923–25) and J.W. Crowfoot (1927–28). For their results, see *Jerusalem.

[Michael Avi-Yonah]

OPHIR (Heb. אוֹפִיר, אוֹפִר), a country in the biblical period, well known for its gold. Trade between Palestine and Ophir was possible by sea from the port of Ezion-Geber, but only in the time of Solomon was an attempt made to reach Ophir and take gold, precious stones, and sandalwood from there (I Kings 9:28; 10:11; II Chron. 8:18; 9:10). An attempt made during the reign of Jehoshaphat to reach Ophir did not succeed, as the ships prepared for this undertaking in Ezion-Geber broke on the rocks (I Kings 22:49). Sailing to Ophir apparently required much preparation, and could not be accomplished without outside help. In the days of Solomon the voyage was undertaken with the assistance of Tyrian sailors. Even in the days of Jehoshaphat, lengthy negotiations had been carried on between Jehoshaphat and Ahaziah king of Israel for the purpose of preparing the journey to Ophir, and still it did not succeed. The author of II Chronicles (20:35–37) mistakenly indicates Tarshish as the goal of Jehoshaphat's voyage. However, the evidence recorded in the book is indeed correct, namely, that the negotiations between Jehoshaphat and Ahaziah aroused bitter opposition in Judah, no doubt because of the rights Jehoshaphat granted Ahaziah – as payment for his help in preparing the trip to Ophir – in the region of Ezion-Geber, which was located within the area of Judah's sovereignty. These negotiations also testify not only that the region of Ophir was distant from Palestine and that the voyage involved much preparation and special technical, professional training in navigation, but also that the mining of gold entailed many difficulties that the Kingdom of Judah could not overcome itself. According to information preserved in the Bible, Solomon's fleet sailed to Ophir only once. The plentiful information concerning the value of the gold of Ophir which was found in Palestine corroborates the assumption that this gold reached Palestine by way of gold markets which existed throughout the world at that time. The fact that the port of Ezion-Geber served as a point of departure for ships sailing to Ophir indicates that it was also possible to reach Ophir from the coastal regions of the Red Sea; and consequently, it is reasonable to suppose that Palestine served as a channel for the transportation of gold from Ophir to Syria, Babylonia, and Asia Minor. The use of the gold of Ophir in Palestine is attested to in the inscription: [ז]הב אפר לבית חרן ("Gold of Ophir for Beth-Horon") which was found on an earthern vessel discovered in the excavations at Tell Qasile.

There are many assumptions concerning the location of Ophir. Eupolemus was of the opinion that Ophir is an island in the Red Sea (in Eusebius, *Praeparatio Evangelica*, 9:30, 7). Josephus (Ant., 1:147; 8:164; cf. Eusebius, Onom. 176:13) locates Ophir in India – in the regions between one of the tributaries of the Indus River and China. It has also been suggested that Ophir should be located along the coast of the Arabian Peninsula, since the location of Ophir the son of Joktan the son of Eber was between Sheba and Havilah (Gen. 10:28–29), which were also famous in the biblical period for their gold (Gen. 2:11; Isa. 60:6; Ezek. 27:22; Ps. 72:15). The most likely location of Ophir to have been suggested so far is the region of Somalia on the East African coast, possibly extending to the neighboring coast of South Arabia. The products of Ophir are characteristically African and are similar to those of Punt, which suggests that Ophir and Punt were located in the same region. It is certain that Punt was in the area of Somalia, and it is thus likely that Ophir was situated there as well.

BIBLIOGRAPHY: K. Peters, *Ofir nach den neuen Entdeckungen* (1908); Pauly-Wissowa, s.v. *Saba*; B. Moritz, *Arabien* (1923), 63ff.; J.A. Montgomery, *Arabia and the Bible* (1934), 38ff.; J. Eitan, in: HUCA, 12–13 (1937–38), 61; G.W. Van Beck, in: JAOS, 78 (1958), 141–52; R.D. Barnett, *A Catalogue of the Nimrud Ivories* (1957), 59ff., 168.

[Joshua Gutmann]

OPHRAH (Heb. עָפְרָה), name of two places mentioned in the Bible.

(1) A locality in the northern part of the territory of the tribe of Benjamin near Beth-El (Josh. 18:23). Ophrah was one of the places attacked by Philistine "spoilers" shortly before the battle of Michmas (I Sam. 13:17). Abijah of Judah captured it together with Beth-El (II Chron. 13:19 as Ephrain). It was the capital of a district ceded by Samaria to Judea in 145 B.C.E., when it was called Aphaerema (I Macc. 11:34). It appears as Ephraim in the New Testament (John 11:54) and as Ephron in Eusebius (Onom. 28:4; 90:19) and on the Madaba Map. Ophrah is identified with al-Ṭayyiba, 4 mi. (6.4 km.) northeast of Beth-El.

(2) Gideon's home town, which belonged to the Manassite clan of Abiezer (Judg. 6:11, 24; 8:27, 32; 9:5). Here God called on Gideon to fight the Midianites and here he ruled, died, and was buried. The identification of the place is uncertain. Most scholars locate it in the vicinity of Mt. Tabor (cf. Judg. 8:18) and the Jezreel Valley, the site of Gideon's encounter with the Midianites. Suggested sites in this region are either al-Ṭayyiba to the northeast of the hill of Moreh (the Crusader Effraon or Forbelet which is, however, also considered for Hapharaim of Issachar (Josh. 19:19)) or the tell of Affuleh which has traces of the Canaanite and Israelite periods.

BIBLIOGRAPHY: (1) Abel, Geog, 2 (1938), 402; Aharoni, Land, index. (2) Abel, in: JPOS, 17 (1937), 31ff.; Press, Ereẓ, 4 (1955), 746; Aharoni, Land, index.

[Michael Avi-Yonah]

OPHUELS, MAX (1902–1957), film director. He was born in Saarbruecken, Germany, as Max Oppenheimer. He directed plays in many German theaters and, starting in 1925, worked at the Vienna Burgtheater. Antisemitic letters made the head of the Viennese theater fire him, and in 1926 he moved back to Frankfurt am Main together with his wife, the actress Hilde Wall. There he directed and wrote plays and, after 1931, also made films. Ophuels became an antifascist before the Nazi rise to power, and his engagement grew after 1933. In 1935 the business of the Oppenheimer family in Saarbruecken was "aryanized," and the family emigrated to Paris. Ophuels received French citizenship in 1938 and worked in Paris as a filmmaker and writer of radio plays. After the occupation of

France in 1940 Ophuels escaped to unoccupied France and later to the United States. In 1941 he settled in Los Angeles where he continued to direct movies in Hollywood. He returned to Germany in 1949, where he stayed for the rest of his life. Among his works are the early successes *Liebelei* (1933) and *La Signora di Tutti* (1934). Other films were *Letter from an Unknown Woman* (Hollywood, 1948), the French *La Ronde* (1950), and *The Earrings of Madame de...* (1953). His expressionist film *Lola Montez* (1955) aroused controversy among film critics in the United States after the showing of its complete version there in 1969.

BIBLIOGRAPHY: H.G. Asper, in: *Max Ophuels* (1989), 73–108; L. Bacher, *Max Ophuels in the Hollywood Studios* (1996); H.G. Asper, *Max Ophuels: Eine Biographie* (1998).

[Noam Zadoff (2nd ed.)]

OPLER, MARVIN KAUFMANN (1914–1981), U.S. anthropologist and social psychiatrist; brother of Morris Edward *Opler. Opler was born in Buffalo, New York. He received an A.B. degree in social studies from the University of Michigan in 1935 and a Ph.D. in anthropology from Columbia University in 1938. He did anthropological fieldwork among Eastern Apache tribes, such as the Mescalero Indians in New Mexico, as well as Eskimo and Northwest Coast Indians in Oregon. Between 1943 and 1946, he served as a community analyst at the Tule Lake Japanese internment camp in Newell, California. That experience and the complex issues inherent in the segregation program led him to co-author the book *Impounded People (1946).* After teaching anthropology, sociology, and social psychiatry at various American universities, Opler was appointed professor of social psychiatry at the University of Buffalo School of Medicine in 1958. He remained there for the rest of his teaching career, serving as chairman of the anthropology department from 1969 to 1972. He also served as professor of sociology and anthropology at the Graduate School of the State University of New York at Buffalo. Opler was, with Thomas A.C. Rennie, a principal investigator in the Midtown Manhattan Mental Health Research Study, 1952–60. On this topic, he wrote *Mental Health in the Metropolis: The Midtown Manhattan Study* (1962).

He was an associate editor of the *International Journal of Social Psychiatry* from 1958 and associate editor of *American Anthropologist* from 1962.

His principal interests were social theory, world areas research, psychoanalytic techniques in social analysis, and social psychiatry. Opler researched groups extending from the Ute Indians to modern social groups. He pioneered research on psychotic disorders among different ethnic groups to illuminate cross-cultural perspectives in mental disease and to establish the need for the collaboration of psychiatry and anthropology in defining contexts and differentials of mental disease. This is exemplified by his book *Culture and Social Psychiatry* (1967), originally *Culture, Psychiatry, and Human Values* (1956). He was editor of the book *Culture and Mental Health* (1959).

Opler was active in such professional organizations as the American Anthropological Association, the American Sociological Association, and the International Association of Social Psychiatry, and was the co-organizer of the First International Congress on Social Psychiatry held in London in 1964.

[Ephraim Fischoff / Ruth Beloff (2nd ed.)]

OPLER, MORRIS EDWARD (1907–1996), U.S. anthropologist and brother of Marvin Kaufmann *Opler. Born in Buffalo, New York, Opler received a bachelor's degree in sociology (1929) and a master's degree in anthropology (1930) from the University of Buffalo; he received a Ph.D. in anthropology (1933) from the University of Chicago. Opler taught at the University of Chicago (1933–35); he worked at the Bureau of Indian Affairs (1936–37); and taught at Reed College (1937–38) and Claremont College (1938–42). During World War II, he worked as a social science analyst at a Japanese-American internment camps and then with the War Office.

In 1948 he was appointed to Cornell University as professor of anthropology and Asian studies, and director of its South Asia Program, 1948–66, and the India Program 1952–66. He served as president of the American Anthropological Association (1962–63). In 1969 he joined the anthropology faculty at the University of Oklahoma, retiring in 1977 as professor emeritus.

His primary research interests were the ethnology of the Apache tribes, the cultural history of the Southwest, and the culture of India, as set out in *An Apache Way of Life* (1941). He was also author of *Social Aspects of Technical Assistance in Operation* (UNESCO, 1954). In later years he, like his brother, became interested in the relation between psychiatry and anthropology, and disturbed behavior and treatment in primitive and modern cultures.

Other books by Opler include *Myths and Tales of the Chiricahua Apache Indians* (1942), *Childhood and Youth in Jicarilla Apache Society* (1964), *Apache Odyssey* (1969), and *Myths and Tales of the Jicarilla Apache Indians* (1994).

[Ephraim Fischoff / Ruth Beloff (2nd ed.)]

OPOCZNO, town in central Poland. Opoczno was the birthplace of Esterka, according to legend the mistress of Casimir the Great (1333–70). In 1588 the Polish sovereign authorized the town to expel the Jews living there, but a Jewish community had resettled in the environs by 1646. The settlement was not permanent: a judgment of the supreme tribunal in 1714 again prohibited Jews from living in the town. According to the census of 1765, however, there were 1,349 Jews in Opoczno and the vicinity (excluding infants under one). They owned 12 plots of land outside the town and 41 houses within it. A number of crafts were exclusively pursued by Jews. Judah Leib, son of Eliezer b. Solomon *Lipschutz, author of responsa *Dammesek Eliezer*, officiated as rabbi of Opoczno at the end of the 18th century. The community numbered 1,469 in 1856, 2,425 in 1897, and 4,025 in 1909 (compared with 2,387 Christians).

The 1921 census shows a marked decrease to 3,135 Jews (46.9% of the total population).

[Nathan Michael Gelber]

Holocaust Period

In 1939 there were about 3,000 Jews in Opoczno. The German army entered the town on Sept. 6, 1939. In November 1940 a ghetto was established and the town's Jewish population was crowded into 115 small houses. In June 1942 about 1,200 Jews from nearby villages were deported to Opoczno Ghetto which grew to over 4,200. In July 1942 about 400 men were deported to the Hasag slave labor camp in Skarzysko-Kamienna and on Oct. 27, 1942 the ghetto was liquidated and all its inmates deported to *Treblinka death camp. Only 120 men were left by Jan. 3, 1943, and they were then exterminated. At the time of the mass deportation in October 1942, scores of Jews fled to the forests and organized partisan units there. The best-known unit, "Lions," under the command of Julian Ajzenman-Kaniewski, conducted a number of successful guerilla actions against Nazi forces and the Opoczno-Konskie railway line. After the war, the Jewish community of Opoczno was not reconstituted.

[Stefan Krakowski]

BIBLIOGRAPHY: BZIH, no. 15–16 (1955), 82, and no. 65–66 (1968), 55–57.

OPOLE LUBELSKIE, small town in Lublin province, S.E. Poland. A silver merchant named Manasseh is known to have resided in Opole in 1626 and carried on business there. The administration of the Opole community came under the jurisdiction of the Lublin *kahal* (see *Councils of the Lands). There were 487 Jews living in Opole in 1765. The community increased substantially during the 19th century, numbering 1,799 in 1856 (nearly twice the number of gentiles), and 3,323 in 1897 (60.1% of the total). The Jewish population numbered 3,766 in 1921 (66.7%).

[*Encyclopaedia Judaica* (Germany)]

Holocaust Period

About 4,000 Jews were living in Opole Lubelskie on the eve of World War II. The number was more than doubled when about 2,500 Jews from Pulawy and over 2,000 Jews from Vienna were deported there in December 1939 and February 1941, respectively. In May 1942 an additional few hundred Jews from nearby smaller places and Slovakia were brought to the town. Jews were deported from Opole to death camps on three occasions: on March 31, 1942, to Belzec, and in May and October 1942 to Sobibor. The community was not revived after the war.

[Stefan Krakowski]

BIBLIOGRAPHY: T. Brustin-Bernstein, in: *Bleter far Geshikhte*, 3:1–2 (1950), 51–78, passim; Yad Vashem Archives.

OPORTO, port city in northern Portugal, on the Douro River. Oporto had a vibrant Jewish community before the establishment of the Portuguese kingdom in 1143. One of its three Jewish neighborhoods was called Monte dos Judeus (Jews' Hill). The ancient synagogue structure – approved by King John in 1388 – was confiscated in 1554 for use by the Order of Santa Clara. Stairs adjoining the ruins are still known as *Escadas de Esnoga* ("the Synagogue Steps"), and an inscription unearthed in 1875 reveals that the synagogue had been dedicated by Don Judah. With the expulsion of the Jews from Spain in 1492, Oporto received an influx of Spanish Jews, including some 30 families who arrived as a group under the illustrious rabbi Isaac *Aboab. When Portugal ousted its Jews in 1497, Jewish communal life in Oporto was reduced to underground *Marrano activities. The Inquisition was active in the city and an auto-da-fé took place on Feb. 11, 1543. Local public opinion was so adverse, however, that no additional inquisitorial spectacles were permitted. In 1920 when Arturo Carlos de *Barros Basto set out to revive Judaism among the Marranos, Oporto became the center of his activities. The congregation Mekor Ḥayyim was organized there in 1927. In 1929 the imposing Kadoorie Synagogue was erected, housing both the congregation and an affiliated seminary for religious studies. In 1970 the Jewish community of Oporto numbered about 100 persons.

BIBLIOGRAPHY: N. Slouschz, *Ha-Anusim be-Portugal* (1932), index; Pinho Leal, *Portugal, antigo e moderno* 12 vols. (1873–90); L. Piles Ros, in: *Sefarad*, 6 (1946), 139; 7 (1947), 357; H. Beinart, in: *Sefunot*, 5 (1961), 75–134. **ADD. BIBLIOGRAPHY:** H. Baquero Moreno, in: *Revista de história* (Pôrto) 1 (1978), 7–38 [rep. in idem, *Marginalidade e conflitos sociais em Portugal nos séculos XIV e XV* (1985), 133–60]; A. Paulo, in: *Miscelánea de estrudios árabes y hebraicos* 23:2 (1974), 93–102; idem, in: *Proceedings of the 6th World Congress of Jewish Studies*, vol. 2 (1976), 61–69; G.J.A. Coelho Dias, in: *Humanística e teología* 4 (1983), 321–58; H. Vasconcelos Vilar, in: *Revista de história económica e social*, 21 1987), 29–37.

[Aaron Lichtenstein]

OPPÉ, ADOLPH PAUL (1878–1957), British art historian and collector. Born in London, the son of a silk merchant, Oppé was educated at the Charterhouse school, St. Andrews University, and Oxford. A senior civil servant, he became one of the greatest British art scholars of his time, specializing in studies of Renaissance Italian artists such as *Raphael* (1909) and *Botticelli* (1991). Universally respected, he was made a fellow of the British Academy in 1952. Oppé built up one of the greatest collections of drawings and watercolors of his time, having an uncanny eye for buying unappreciated works for virtually nothing. His collection was acquired by the Tate Gallery after his death.

BIBLIOGRAPHY: ODNB online.

[William D. Rubinstein (2nd ed.)]

OPPEN, GEORGE (1908–1984), U.S. poet. Oppen's life is exemplary of Jewish American culture and poetry in the 20th century. Born in New Rochelle, N.Y., Oppen was the child of George August Oppenheimer, a diamond merchant, and Elsie Rothfeld. His mother committted suicide when George was four; his father remarried in 1917 and moved to San Francisco, changing the family name to Oppen in 1927. Raised in a highly assimilated, wealthy milieu, the young Oppen's early years were not happy, and he eventually rejected the world in which he grew up. His stepmother was abusive, and he was expelled from high school for drinking just prior to graduation when a car that Oppen was driving had an accident and one of the passengers was killed. On a whim, Oppen entered Oregon State University at Corvallis the next year. In a class on modern poetry, he met his future wife, Mary Colby. When the two stayed out one night, George was suspended and Mary expelled. The two traveled together across the country, hitchiking, sailing, and working at odd jobs. Soon after their arrival in New York City, the Oppens made the acquaintance of Louis *Zukofsky and Charles *Reznikoff. With connections to older modernists, including Ezra Pound and William Carlos Williams, the Objectivists (the term was coined by Zukofsky when he edited a special issue of *Poetry* in 1931) were active through the mid-1930s, first through Oppen's To Publishers and then through the Objectivist Press, which published Oppen's first book, *Discrete Series*, in 1934. But a year later, the Oppens joined the Communist Party, abandoning their cultural activities and immersing themselves in political organizing. When the U.S. entered World War II, Oppen enlisted; serving in the infantry, he was seriously wounded in the Battle of the Bulge. After the war, the Oppens, with their daughter Linda (born in 1939), moved to California, but upon being investigated for their earlier political activities, they moved to Mexico and did not return to the U.S. until 1958, settling in Brooklyn in 1960. Oppen had by then returned to poetry, and entered into an extraordinary period of artistic productivity. Reconnecting with some of his old Objectivist colleagues, and meeting many younger poets, he published *The Materials* (1962), *This In Which* (1965), and *Of Being Numerous* (1968), which won the Pulitzer Prize. The Oppens moved to San Francisco in 1966. Oppen's *Collected Poems* appeared in 1975 (the same year he and Mary visited Israel); his final volume, *Primitive*, in 1978, by which time Oppen was evincing symptoms of Alzheimer's disease. His mental and physical condition gradually deteriorated but he continued to write in the fragmentary style out of which nearly all his poems emerged. *New Collected Poems* was published in 2002.

Oppen has gradually come to be recognized as one of the most important American poets of his time, as a growing body of critical and biographical studies attest. His work forms a crucial bridge between modernism and more recent tendencies in American poetry, and his years of poetic silence, during which he lived, in effect, the crisis of midcentury American history, resonate with extraordinary force and gravitas in his lyrics of the 1960s, culminating in his masterpiece, the serial poem "Of Being Numerous." Yet Oppen, following the dicta of Objectivism, always wrote with great humility, insisting on his poetry as a "test of truth" or "test of sincerity" and devoting himself to intense scrutiny of "the materials" of everyday life, its social fabric and physical being. It is out of this scrutiny, supported on the one hand by Marxism and on the other by Heideggerian phenomenology, that a profoundly philosophical, formidably compressed, and beautifully constructed poetry emerges.

Given his completely secular upbringing and lifestyle, and the relative lack of Jewish references in his poetry, it is difficult to consider Oppen in the light of a specifically Jewish literature. Yet a number of Oppen's most important poems may be understood in terms of Jewish themes and identity. "Psalm," one of his most frequently anthologized poems, celebrates the natural world and the way it almost kabbalistically folded into language. "Of Hours" addresses Oppen's vexed relationship to the antisemitic Ezra Pound, one of his most important mentors. "Exodus" beautifully recalls Oppen's reading about "The children of Israel" to his young daughter, while in "Semite" the poet insists on "my distances neither Roman / / nor barbarian."

BIBLIOGRAPHY: R.B. DuPlessis and P. Quartermain, *The Objectivist Nexus* (1999); R.B. DuPlessis (ed.), *Selected Letters of George Oppen*, (1990); B. Hatlen, *George Oppen: Man & Poet*, (1981); N. Finkelstein, "Political Commitment and Poetic Subjectification: George Oppen's Test of Truth," in: *Contemporary Literature*, 22:1 (Winter 1981), 24–41; M. Heller, *Conviction's Net of Branches: Essays On the Objectivist Poets and Poetry* (2002).

[Norman Finkelstein (2nd ed.)]

OPPENHEIM, town in Germany. Jews are first mentioned there in the tax register of 1241, according to which they were obliged to pay the emperor an annual tax of 15 marks. The Jews of the town, legally the property of the emperor, were placed under the protection of the officers in charge of the local fortress, to whom they paid their taxes. They also paid a house tax to the archbishop of Mainz. *Rudolf of Hapsburg and other kings gave letters of credit to various noblemen which were to be defrayed from the taxes paid by the Jews of Oppenheim; at times, they also leased these taxes. The burden of their taxes appears to have caused several Jews of Oppenheim to join the group that fled from the Rhineland and, under the leadership of *Meir b. Baruch of Rothenburg, attempted to emigrate to Ereẓ Israel (1285). At the end of July 1349, during the persecutions that followed the *Black Death, most of the Jews of Oppenheim were murdered, while others chose martyrdom (**kiddush ha-Shem*) and burned themselves to death in order to escape forced conversion at the hands of the mob. Among the martyrs was the rabbi Joel ha-Kohen.

Some time later the community was reestablished. After 1400 the right of residence was made renewable at the end of every six years, and the amount of taxes to be paid was fixed. In 1422 a plot by two Christians to kill the Jews of the town was frustrated by the municipal council. Certain protection fees and "gifts" that the Jews of Oppenheim were compelled to pay weighed upon them so heavily that despite the additional support of such communities as Worms, Mainz, and Frankfurt, Oppenheim Jewry could not meet their payments and were therefore penalized (1444). In 1456, R. Seligmann Bing (or R. Seligmann Oppenheim) attempted to establish a union of the communities of the Upper Rhine, but because of community opposition and that of R. Israel Isserlein (c. 1390–1460), the project was abandoned.

The community suffered during the wars of Louis XIV, and by 1674 only three families remained in the town. By 1722 the number had grown to eight. Many Oppenheim Jews settled in Frankfurt and other south German cities, where they were known as "Oppenheim" or "Oppenheimer," and the name became widespread. The community numbered 20 families in 1807; 257 in 1872; 189 in 1880; and 56 in 1933. Of the 17 Jews who remained during World War II, 16 were deported. In 1970 no Jews lived in Oppenheim. A memorial plaque commemorates the destroyed synagogue and the Oppenheim Jews who were victims of the Holocaust. The municipality organized two meetings of "Oppenheims" and "Oppenheimers" in 2000 and 2003.

BIBLIOGRAPHY: FJW, 405; P. Lazarus, in: ZGJD, 5 (1934), 200–4; *Germania Judaica*, 1 (1963), 255–6; 2 (1968), 629–32; E.L. Rapp and O. Boecher, in: *Festschrift 1200 Jahre Oppenheim* (1965), 91–105. **ADD. BIBLIOGRAPHY:** P. Arnsberg, *Die juedischen Gemeinden in Hessen*. Volume 1: Anfang, Untergang, Neubeginn, vol. 2 (1971), 180–87; *Germania Judaica*, vol. 3. 1350–1514 (1987), 1068–76; F.-J. Ziwes, *Studien zur Geschichte der Juden im mittleren Rheingebiet waehrend des hohen und spaeten Mittelalters* (Forschungen zur Geschichte der Juden. Abteilung A, Abhandlungen, vol. 1) (1995).

[Paul Lazarus / Zvi Avneri / Larissa Daemmig (2nd ed.)]

OPPENHEIM, name of a German family derived from the Rhenish town of that name. In Hebrew works the members of the family are always called Oppenheim. Later some of them, especially the Vienna branch, were called Oppenheimer. Another branch of the family settled in Heidelberg and assumed the name of that town. The earliest known mention of the name is that of R. Isaac Oppenheim and R. Joel Oppenheim, both mentioned in the responsa of R. Meir of Rothenburg (d. 1293). In Worms the family early achieved distinction, providing the community with a long line of leaders and representatives, while its members were also to become founders of the Vienna Oppenheimer branch. In 1531 this family appeared in Frankfurt, where they had come from Heidelberg. After the expulsion of the Jews from Frankfurt in 1614, part of the family again settled in Heidelberg. In Frankfurt, too, it was one of the most prominent families, many of its members serving the community as *parnasim* and *shtadlanim*, and producing many rabbis, financiers, and successful merchants. More than 200 tombstones bearing this family name are to be found in the old Jewish cemetery in Frankfurt.

[Heinrich Flesch]

OPPENHEIM, family of German bankers, originally from Frankfurt, and later from Bonn, where in 1789 SOLOMON OPPENHEIM, JR. (1772–1828) established a commission and forwarding business. From 1798 Cologne was the headquarters of the banking house of Sal Oppenheim Jr. & Cie. Proximity both to West European financial centers and to the Rhine-Ruhr industry determined its rise after World War II to the position of Federal Germany's second largest private banking concern. The firm promoted railroad construction, river transportation, insurance, and corporate banks in Germany and abroad, participated in syndicates for the public sector, and supplied industrial credit. Solomon Oppenheim Jr. helped to establish the Paris bank of B.L. Fould et Fould-Oppenheim (now Heine & Co.). His daughter Helene married the banker Bénoît *Fould. Solomon Oppenheim Jr.'s sons, SIMON (1803–1880) and ABRAHAM (1804–1878) were ennobled and their descendants converted. Simon's great grandsons WALDEMAR (1894–1952) and FRIEDRICH CARL (1900–?), "quarter-Jews" by Nazi reckoning, had to change the firm's name to Pferdmenges (a non-family partner) & Co. in 1938. Friedrich Carl Oppenheim was imprisoned in 1944, following the abortive attempt on Hitler's life. After World War II, the bank resumed its original name and Oppenheim partnership interests. Two descendants of Solomon Oppenheim Jr. were active in public affairs: Simon's brother DAGOBERT (David; 1809–1899), who converted to Christianity, was a co-founder and co-director of the progressive daily *Rheinische Zeitung* (1841–43). Simon's baptized grandson MAX OPPENHEIM (1860–1946), a German career diplomat and Orientalist, founded the Deutsches Orient Institut.

BIBLIOGRAPHY: K. Grunwald, in: YLBI, 12 (1967), 201–2, 207; W. Treue, in: *Rheinisch-Westfaelische Wirtschaftsbiographien*, 8 (1962); idem, in: *Tradition, Zeitschrift fuer Firmen-Geschichte und Unternehmerbiographie*, 9 (1964).

[Hanns G. Reissner]

OPPENHEIM, BEER BEN ISAAC (1760–1849), German rabbi and scholar. In his early youth Oppenheim studied at the yeshivah of Fuerth and then proceeded to Berlin where he apparently made contact with the followers of the Haskalah movement. His contributions to *Bikkurei ha-Ittim are written in an attractive Hebrew style, and he carried on correspondence with Moses Israel *Landau, Isaac Samuel *Reggio, and Solomon Judah Loeb *Rapoport. He later settled in Pressburg (Bratislava), living there in favorable financial circumstances and engaging mainly in talmudic studies. In 1829 he published *Mei-Be'er*, a collection of his responsa to Moses *Muenz, Samuel b. Ezekiel *Landau, Solomon Margolis, Baruch b. Josiah *Jeiteles, his brother Ḥayyim, and other contemporary scholars. It appeared with an appendum entitled *Palgei Mayim*, containing a number of his talmudic novellae.

BIBLIOGRAPHY: Oppenheim, in: MGWJ, 1 (1874), 63; Loewenstein, in: *Gedenkbuch… D. Kaufmann* (1900), 551; Ḥ.N. Dembitzer, *Kelilat Yofi*, 2 (1893), 58b; J.K. Duschinsky, *Toledot ha-Ga'on R. David Oppenheimer* (1922), 83f.

[Heinrich Flesch]

OPPENHEIM, DAVID (1816–1876), Hebrew scholar. Born in Leipnik, Moravia, he was a rabbi in his native land and in Hungary. He published articles and studies in Hebrew and other languages, which encompassed a broad range of Hebrew literature and culture. A zealot for the Hebrew language, he fought the movement to eliminate Hebrew in the synagogue. His Hebrew studies were published in the periodicals *Bet ha-*

Midrash and *Yeshurun*, and especially in *Ha-Maggid*, to which he contributed critiques of Judaica.

BIBLIOGRAPHY: Zeitlin, Bibliotheca, 256.

[G.K.]

OPPENHEIM (Oppenheimer), DAVID BEN ABRAHAM (1664–1736), rabbi. Born in Worms, his teachers were Gershon *Ashkenazi of Metz, Jacob Ashkenazi, Benjamin Wolf Epstein of Friedberg, and *Isaac Benjamin Wolf b. Eliezer Lipman of Landsberg. While he was still a boy, he maintained a scholarly correspondence with Jair Ḥayyim *Bacharach. At the age of 17 he married Genendel, daughter of the Hanoverian Court Jew Leffman *Behrends. A nephew of Samuel *Oppenheimer, he inherited a fortune from him. At the age of 20 Oppenheim was ordained rabbi by his teachers in Metz and Landsberg, as well as by the rabbi of Worms, Aaron b. Moses *Teomim. While his noble descent, his wealth, and the influence of his family may have helped him, as a scholar of repute he was entitled to recognition in his own right. When 25 he was called to the rabbinate of the highly respected community of Nikolsburg (*Mikulov), thus becoming *Landrabbiner of Moravia. There he gathered many students around him, founding a *bet midrash* which he endowed with large funds to ensure its continued existence for many years. In 1698 he received a call from the community of Brest-Litovsk and, although he declined, from this time he called himself rabbi of Brest. He also declined the call to become *Landrabbiner* of the Palatinate (1702). The community of Jerusalem honored him with the title "rabbi of the Holy City," which explains the use of the title "rabbi of Israel and of many communities and districts of the Diaspora" in the heading of his introduction to the Pentateuch (Berlin, 1705). Appointed *nasi Ereẓ Israel* by Samson *Wertheimer, Oppenheim became responsible for the collection and transference of sums collected throughout Europe for the benefit of Jews in Jerusalem (see *Hierosolymitanische Stiftung, **Ḥalukkah*). Many communities turned to him for help in regularizing their internal affairs; he prepared the statutes of the community of *Hildesheim, which were partially accepted. After 12 years of successful activity in Nikolsburg, Oppenheim became rabbi of Prague, a community rich in talmudic scholarship. His munificence and liberality attracted many scholars. His wife Genendel died in 1712, and in her memory he donated a valuable Ark curtain to the Altneu synagogue. In 1713 he was appointed *Landrabbiner* of half of Bohemia, while the other half remained under the leadership of Benjamin Wolf Spira, whose daughter Shifrah, widow of Isaac b. Solomon Zalman Bondi of Prague, became Oppenheim's second wife. When Benjamin Wolf Spira died in 1715, he also became *Landrabbiner* of the other half of Bohemia.

Regarded as a man who was familiar with all branches of rabbinical and halakhic literature, Oppenheim also had a reputation as a mathematician, and many rabbis of the day turned to him with difficult questions of religious law. Many demands for his approbations (**Haskamot*) were made; Loewenstein has traced more than 70 of these. Oppenheim was reluctantly drawn into contemporary quarrels. Judah Leib *Prossnitz vilified his name in an unprecedented manner – with his agreement, the rabbinate of Prossnitz (*Prostejov) had excommunicated Judah Leib – but on the other hand he was accused by Ẓevi Ashkenazi of having given material and moral support to Nehemiah *Ḥayon. It would appear that he had approved one of Ḥayon's works but that Ḥayon had printed the approbation in another. Oppenheim also had serious differences with Jonathan *Eybeshuetz, who also worked in Prague. When Eybeshuetz's students slandered him in a most vulgar fashion, serious disturbances arose between the students of their respective yeshivot, prompting the authorities to intervene. In a decree of June 16, 1722, Emperor Charles VI ordered that the students responsible for the upheaval were not to remain in Prague and that "in future, Jewish studies be under the control of the said chief rabbi Oppenheim," and that no other Prague rabbi might maintain a house of study.

From his early youth a lover of books, Oppenheim undertook long journeys in order to obtain rare manuscripts or prints. He visited the fairs at Leipzig, was in close touch with printers and book dealers, and published lists of works he sought, in order to obtain books from all lands. He used his wealth (inherited and received from his wives) to establish a library. J.C. Wolf, who obtained most of the material for his Bibliotheca Hebraea from Oppenheim's library, estimated that it contained 7,000 volumes, including 1,000 manuscripts. An incomplete catalog of Oppenheim's library appeared in 1764, a second, by Israel Bresslau, was published in Hamburg in 1782, and a third, entitled *Kohelet David*, by Isaac Metz appeared in Hamburg/Altona in 1826 with a Latin translation by Lazarus Emden. A supplement to the latter was issued by J. Goldenthal in Leipzig in 1845. Because of censorship problems, the library was kept in Hanover; on Oppenheim's death it was inherited by his only son, Joseph, who married a daughter of Samson *Wertheimer. After Joseph's death it passed to his nephew Isaac Seligman Cohen. One of Oppenheim's grandchildren, the widow of R. Hirsch Oppenheim of Hildesheim, put the library up for sale. M. Mendelssohn valued it at between 50 and 60,000 thaler, and it was later taxed for 150,000 thaler, but in 1829 it was finally sold for the ridiculously low sum of 9,000 thaler to Oxford, where it forms the substantial part of the Hebrew section of the *Bodleian Library. Oppenheim was a patron of Jewish scholarship and gave many editors and publishers of talmudic and halakhic works grants toward publishing costs. He willingly put manuscripts that he had obtained at great expense at the disposal of publishers, in order to make them available to the wider public. Although Oppenheim himself wrote a great deal, the greatest part of his works lies unpublished in Oxford and other libraries. His responsa were published in the collections of responsa of Jair Ḥayyim Bacharach, Jacob b. Joseph *Reicher-Backofen, Ezekiel *Katzenellenbogen, *Eliakim Goetz b. Meir, and Eliezer Lipschuetz.

BIBLIOGRAPHY: M. Grunwald, in: MGWJ, 40 (1896), 425–8; D. Kaufmann, *ibid.*, 42 (1898), 322–5; M. Freudenthal, *ibid.*, 262–74;

L. Lowenstein, in: *Gedenkbuch… David Kaufmann* (1900), 538–59; M. Freudenthal, in: MGWJ, 46 (1902), 262–74; C. Duschinsky, in: *Ha-Ẓofeh le-Ḥokhmat Yisrael*, 5 (1921), 30–45, 145–55; 6 (1922), 26–37, 160–5, 205–56; *Soncino-Blaetter*, 2 (1927), 59–80; 3 (1929/30), 63–66; J. Rivkind, in: *Reshummot*, 4 (1929), 321–4; A. Marx, in: *Mélanges Israel Lévi* (1926), 451–60 (Eng.); S.H. Lieben, in: JJLG, 19 (1928), 1–38; C. Duschinsky, in: JQR, 20 (1929/30), 217–47; S.H. Lieben, in: JGGJC, 7 (1935), 437–83; D. Feuchtwang, in: *Gedenkbuch… [des Juedischen Museums in Nikolsburg]* (1936), 51–58; A. Marx, *Studies in Jewish History and Booklore* (1944), 213–9, 238–55; D. Brilling, in: *Zion*, 12 (1946/47), 89–96; Y.Z. Cahana, in: *Sinai*, 21 (1947), 327–34; idem, in: *Arim ve-Immahot be-Yisrael*, 4 (1950), 268–72; Yaari, Sheluḥei, index; M. Benayahu, in: *Yerushalayim*, 3 (1951), 108–29; idem, in: *Sefunot*, 2 (1957/58), 131; 3–4 (1959/61), index; M. Friedmann, *ibid.*, 10 (1966/67), 496–8; B. Nosek and V. Sadek, in: *Bohemia Judaicae*, 6 (1970), 5–27.

[Heinrich Flesch]

OPPENHEIM, ḤAYYIM (1832–1891), Hebrew scholar. Born in Moravia, a brother of David *Oppenheim, he received his academic degree as well as a teaching certificate in Vienna in 1857. He also served as rabbi in various communities. His studies and articles encompassed the entire range of talmudic, religious, and philosophic literature of the Middle Ages. Most of his studies were written in Hebrew and appeared in scholarly publications during the latter half of the 19th century. He was among the first to introduce into Hebrew scholarship the early findings of Assyriology. He also contributed to German scholarly periodicals devoted to Judaic studies.

BIBLIOGRAPHY: Kressel, Leksikon, 1 (1965), 46.

[Getzel Kressel]

OPPENHEIM, HERMANN (1858–1919), German neurologist and researcher of the nervous system. Oppenheim, born in Warburg, published many studies on the anatomy and pathology of the brain, the spinal cord, and the peripheral nerves. He improved the methods for examining patients with nervous disorders, and introduced many important innovations in diagnostic and therapeutic procedures, especially in the diagnosis of brain tumors and their localization, as well as in meningitis aphasia. A congenital disease of the brain stem and spinal cord in infants is named after him. The fruits of his rich experiments were assembled in his work *Lehrbuch der Nervenkrankheiten fuer Aerzte und Studierende*, which was published in seven editions (first in 1894) and translated into many languages. It became the textbook for neurologists throughout the world for decades. Oppenheim was the founder and organizer of the German Neurological Association and its chairman for many years. Despite his international reputation and a unanimous recommendation by the medical faculty of Berlin University that he be appointed to the chair in neurology, the Prussian government refused to sanction this unless he be converted to Christianity, which Oppenheim resolutely refused.

BIBLIOGRAPHY: A. Stern, *In bewegter Zeit* (1968), 55–60.

[Joseph Prager]

OPPENHEIM, JACQUES (1849–1924), Dutch jurist. Oppenheim was born in Groningen, where he became secretary of the municipality in 1873. In 1885 he was appointed professor of constitutional and administrative law at Groningen University and became professor of public and international law at Leiden University in 1893. He was an important figure in several state commissions and was a member of the Council of State from 1907 until 1924. He was a member of the Netherlands Royal Academy of Sciences (1902–24) and curator of Leiden University (1916–24). Of his many books, *Het Nederlandsche Gemeenterecht* (2 vols., 1895) is an important standard textbook on Dutch municipal law. Active in Jewish affairs, Oppenheim served as chairman of the Ashkenazi rabbinical seminary in Amsterdam and as a member of the board of the Jewish community in The Hague. During World War I he was also president of the European committee of the *American Jewish Joint Distribution Committee. Through his wife he was connected to the Van *Nierop family.

BIBLIOGRAPHY: W.M. Peletier, in: *Biografisch Woordenboek van Nederland* (1979), s.v.

[Henriette Boas / Bart Wallet (2nd ed.)]

OPPENHEIM, JAMES (1882–1932), poet. Oppenheim's books of poetry were *Monday Morning and Other Poems* (1909), *Songs for the New Age* (1914), and *The Sea* (1924). The stories of *Doctor Rast* (1909) dealt with Jewish immigrants and their Americanized children whom he first met as a social worker on New York's Lower East Side. As editor of *Seven Arts*, which he founded together with Waldo *Frank and Paul *Rosenfeld in 1916, he stimulated many young poets.

OPPENHEIM, JOACHIM (**Ḥayyim**; 1832–1891), Austrian rabbi. Oppenheim was born in Eibenschitz (Moravia) where his father, Dov Baer, was a rabbi. He took over his brother David's position in the rabbinate at Jamnitz and after the death of his father (1859) he became rabbi in Eibenschitz (1860). From 1868 until his death, he served as rabbi of Thron. Oppenheim was a prolific scholar.

He had a profound knowledge of biblical, talmudic, and midrashic literature. The results of his studies in these areas were published, mostly in Hebrew, in the learned periodicals of the time. His *Toledot ha-Mishnah* (1882), an introduction to the Mishnah, was originally published in *Beit Talmud*, edited by his brother-in-law, I.H. *Weiss. Two of his sermons were published under the title *Das Tal-Gebet* (1862).

BIBLIOGRAPHY: N. Sokolow, *Sefer Sokolow* (1943), 126–7; idem, in: *Ha-Asif*, 6 (1894), 143f. (1st pagination); C.D. Lippe, *Bibliographisches Lexicon…*, 1 (1881), 354f.

OPPENHEIM, LASSA FRANCIS LAWRENCE (1858–1919), international lawyer. Oppenheim, one of the greatest authorities in his field, was born in Windekken, Germany. In 1886 he was appointed lecturer at the University of Freiburg, but because he was Jewish was precluded from advancing in the academic field. He therefore left Germany and went to

Switzerland, where he lectured at Basle University, and then, in 1895, to England. From 1898 to 1908 Oppenheim taught at the London School of Economics, and in 1908 became Whewell professor of international law at Cambridge, a position he held until his death. He was an adviser to the British government on questions of international law and collaborated on the British Army manual *Land Warfare* (1912). He also prepared memoranda for the British delegates at the Paris Peace Conference in 1919. Oppenheim's authoritative treatise, *International Law*, 2 vols. (1905–06), subsequently edited by Hersch *Lauterpacht, was accepted as the principal textbook for English-speaking countries. He became leader of the positive school in international law and a supporter of the League of Nations concept. Oppenheim was the principal founder of the *British Yearbook of International Law.*

BIBLIOGRAPHY: Whittuck, in: *British Year Book of International Law*, 1 (1920–21), 1–10. **ADD. BIBLIOGRAPHY:** ODNB online.

[Guido (Gad) Tedeschi]

OPPENHEIM, MORITZ DANIEL (1799–1882), German painter. Oppenheim was born in Hanau and, after studying art at Frankfurt and Munich, he went to Paris and in 1821 to Rome, where he stayed four years. There he came under the influence of the Nazarenes, a group of fervently Christian artists who painted New Testament scenes. In 1825 Oppenheim returned to Frankfurt. His paintings of Old and New Testament scenes were soon widely appreciated. His most loyal patrons were the Rothschilds and he was known as "painter of the Rothschilds" and – on account of his financial success – as "the Rothschild of the painters." He earned praise from Goethe to whom he sent two drawings based on Goethe's *Hermann und Dorothea*. Goethe, whom Oppenheim visited in Weimar and whose portrait he painted, persuaded the grand duke of Weimar to bestow upon the painter the title of honorary professor. In 1833 a picture with the narrative title "Return of a Jewish Volunteer from the Wars of Liberation to his Family Still Living According to the Old Tradition" brought the artist further renown. Encouraged by its wide success, Oppenheim painted 19 other canvases on Jewish motifs. These were eventually published in an album, *Bilder aus dem altjuedischen Familienleben* (1865) which appeared in the United States as *Family Scenes from Jewish Life of Former Days* (1866). These genre scenes, realistic yet tinged with romanticism, were much appreciated. They show excellent composition, and real skill in the grouping of the *dramatis personae*. They have been frequently reproduced to illustrate books on Jewish topics. He produced a series of large pictures on confrontations between Jews and Christians, e.g., Moses Mendelssohn and Lavater, Mendelssohn and Frederick the Great. Undoubtedly, Oppenheim's best works are his numerous portraits, pencil sketches as well as oils, including portraits of Ferdinand Hiller and Gabriel Riesser. He illustrated works by Berthold Auerbach and Solomon Hermann von Mosenthal. The city of Frankfurt commissioned him to paint portraits of past emperors for the Kaisersaal (Emperor's Hall) in the Roemer, the medieval town hall. Admirers came from all parts of Europe to visit his studio in Frankfurt. He continued to paint in his skillful, charmingly naive manner until a few days before his death, unconcerned with the changes in art and taste since his student days in Rome. His autobiography was published posthumously: *Erinnerungen*, ed. by A. Oppenheim (1924).

BIBLIOGRAPHY: L.A. Mayer, *Bibliography of Jewish Art* (1967), index; Roth, Art, 544, 522–5. **ADD. BIBLIOGRAPHY:** R. Droese, F. Eisermann, M. Kingreen, A. Merk (ed.), *Der Zyklus "Bilder aus dem altjuedischen Familienleben" und sein Maler Moritz Daniel Oppenheim* (1996); G. Heuberger and A. Merk (eds), *Moritz Daniel Oppenheim: Die Entdeckung des juedischen Selbstbewusstseins in der Kunst* Exhibition catalogue, Juedisches Museum Frankfurt (1999; with catalogue of works); C. Praeger (ed.), *Moritz Daniel Oppenheim: Erinnerungen eines deutsch-juedischen Malers* (1999).

[Alfred Werner]

OPPENHEIM, PAUL LEO (1863–1934), German geologist and paleontologist. Oppenheim worked as a private scientist in Berlin, only occasionally cooperating with academic or governmental scientific institutions. In 1907 the Prussian Ministry of Education awarded him the title of "professor" in appreciation of his outstanding achievements.

During nearly 50 years of research, Oppenheim published several monographs and many papers in various fields of geology and paleontology. He was particularly interested in the study of tertiary fossils, especially those of Italy and other countries of southern Europe, as well as of the Levant regions of Turkey, Syria, Palestine, the former German colonies of East and West Africa, and Egypt. He was internationally known as an expert of almost all groups of fossil invertebrates, but his special interest was directed to nummulites, echinoids and mollusks, and particularly to corals. Oppenheim bequeathed his unique collection of fossils and his comprehensive library to the Geology Department of the Hebrew University of Jerusalem. His numerous works advanced the stratigraphy of the Tertiary and Cretaceous formations. His longer monographs on the "Niemitzer Schichten" of Bohemia (1924) and on the "Anthozoae der Gosauschichten" of the Alps are outstanding paleontological presentations of text and illustrations.

[Moshe A. Avnimelech]

OPPENHEIM, SALLY, Baroness Oppenheim-Barnes (née **Viner**; 1928–), British politician. Born in Dublin and educated in Sheffield, where her father was a diamond cutter, Sally Oppenheim worked as a social worker in London before serving as a Conservative member of Parliament from 1970 to 1987, and was minister of state for trade and consumer affairs under Margaret Thatcher in 1979–82. She was chairman of the Conservative Party in 1973–74 and served as chairman of the National Consumer Council. She was made a life peeress in 1989.

[William D. Rubinstein (2nd ed.)]

OPPENHEIMER, CARL (1874–1941), German biochemist. Born in Berlin, Oppenheimer was the second son of a reform rabbi, and brother of the economist Franz Oppenheimer. In 1902 he joined the Berlin Agricultural Academy, and was professor there from 1908 until dismissed by the Nazis in 1936. In 1938 he went to Holland as head of the agricultural department of a company in The Hague. He died in Zeist, Holland, probably murdered by the Nazis.

As a young man Oppenheimer wrote textbooks which were translated into many languages and became the most popular chemical books for medical students all over the world: *Grundriss der organischen Chemie* (1895, 1930[14]); *Grundriss der anorganischen Chemie* (1898; 1934[145]). His *Die Fermente und ihre Wirkungen* (1900; 4 vols., 1925–30[5], suppl. 2 vols., 1935–38) gave enzymology its form and structure, and was followed by *Toxine und Antitoxine* (1904). Oppenheimer held that the study of living matter needed a knowledge of both the medical and the exact sciences. From 1909 to 1936 he published numerous basic texts in biochemistry as well as founding and editing the journals *Zentralblatt fuer Biochemie und Biophysik* (1910–21) and *Enzymologia* (1936–41).

[Samuel Aaron Miller]

OPPENHEIMER, SIR ERNEST (1880–1957), South African financier. Born in Friedberg, Germany, he went to London at the age of 16 to work for a firm of diamond merchants, which in 1902 sent him to represent them in Kimberley. He was very successful in the diamond business and in 1917 founded the Anglo-American Corporation. He gained control of several other companies, and in 1929 became chairman of the great diamond firm of De Beers and thus the acknowledged head of the industry. During the 1930s Oppenheimer steered the diamond trade through the difficulties of the great depression, ultimately establishing control of world marketing through the Diamond Corporation. His foresight also contributed to the discoveries which extended the Rand goldfields after World War II. Mayor of Kimberley from 1912 to 1915, he helped to raise the 2nd Battalion, the Kimberley Regiment, in World War I and was knighted in 1921. He represented Kimberley in Parliament as a supporter of Smuts from 1924 to 1938. He and his first wife, Mary Lina née Pollak, were liberal supporters of Jewish charities and interested themselves in Jewish communal affairs. After her death in 1934, he married a Catholic and converted to Christianity. In the development of the Orange Free State goldfields, Ernest Oppenheimer set high standards of town-planning and did much to promote better hospital and recreation services and housing for the Africans there and on the Witwatersrand. He was a gracious patron of the arts and sciences.

His son HARRY FREDERICK OPPENHEIMER (1908–2000), widely known as "H.F.O.," was educated at Charterhouse school in England and at Oxford. He succeeded his father as head of the diamond industry and of more than 150 mining, manufacturing, and investment companies. His birth in Kimberley was recorded in the Jewish communal records, but later he became a member of the Anglican Church. He entered the Anglo-American Corporation, eventually succeeding his uncle, Leslie Pollak, as manager. During World War II, he saw service as an intelligence officer in the Western Desert. After the war he helped his father develop the new Orange Free State goldfields. "H.F.O." was chairman of the Anglo-American Corporation (1957–82) and of DeBeers Consolidated, the great diamond and minerals mining giant, from 1957 to 1984. In 1948 he entered Parliament, winning his father's former Kimberley constituency for the United Party. Oppenheim was a consistent opponent of Apartheid. At the end of 1957 he retired from politics to devote himself entirely to his business interests. Harry Oppenheimer assisted materially in the development of the diamond industry in Israel. He was one of the richest men in South Africa, reputedly worth $2.5 billion at his death.

BIBLIOGRAPHY: T.E. Gregory, *Ernest Oppenheimer and the Economic Development of South Africa* (1962); A.P. Cartwright, *Golden Age* (1968); Oppenheimer, in: *Optima* (Sept. 1967); J.M. White, *The Land God Made in Anger* (1969). **ADD. BIBLIOGRAPHY:** G. Wheatcroft, *The Randlords* (1985), 240–59.

[Lewis Sowden]

OPPENHEIMER, FRANZ (1864–1943), German sociologist and economist, an initiator of cooperative agriculture in Ereẓ Israel. The son of a reform rabbi, Oppenheimer was born in Berlin and studied medicine in Freiburg and Berlin. He started his career as a practicing physician, but after graduating in economics at the University of Kiel (1908), he became *Privatdozent* at the University of Berlin in 1909 and professor at the University of Frankfurt in 1917, where he occupied a newly established chair of sociology from 1919 to 1929. After Hitler's advent to power in 1933, Oppenheimer lectured in Berlin at the Hochschule fuer die Wissenschaft des Judentums. In 1938 he left Germany for the U.S. He died in Los Angeles.

Oppenheimer's sociology is developmental in character, combining in an independent way elements from the theories of Marx, Spencer, Gumplowicz, and also from the instinct theory of McDougall; to these is added a melioristic intention. Oppenheimer considered accumulation of wealth and power, and hence gross inequality among men, as originating from social conflict, exemplified in earliest times chiefly by the subjugation of peaceful farmers, craftsmen, and traders by conquering nomads and pirates. The "economic means" of accumulation through one's own work is thereby replaced by "political means," i.e., force of arms, starting with payment of tribute, then leading to serfdom, feudalism, and finally to the development of antagonistic classes under capitalism. The central evil is the monopolization of land, which forces rural populations into urban areas, and creates what Marx had defined as the "industrial reserve army." Consequently, if the monopolization of land were replaced by an agrarian cooperative system of independent farmers, free competition could be restored and a "liberal socialism" established. Oppenheimer's belief that the removal of evil institutions would do away with the domination of man by man and lead to social harmony has a dogmatic ring.

Oppenheimer's interest in Zionism and Jewish affairs dated from 1902, when Oskar *Marmorek and Johann *Kremenetzky introduced him to Theodor *Herzl. Herzl asked Oppenheimer to elaborate the economic and agricultural parts of the Zionist program, which he did in 1903 at the Sixth Zionist Congress in Basle. In 1911 the Palestine Office of the Zionist Organization in Jaffa established at *Merḥavyah a cooperative settlement based on Oppenheimer's ideas. Although it did not prove successful and had to be reorganized, the Merḥavyah experiment laid the foundation for cooperative agricultural settlement in Ereẓ Israel.

As an opponent of nationalism, Oppenheimer became alienated from the Zionist movement, and in 1913 he withdrew from any official participation. Nevertheless, he maintained his interest in the development of Ereẓ Israel and in Jewish social problems. During World War I he became aware of the misery of the Jewish population in Eastern Europe. In 1934–35 he visited Palestine and explained his concepts to Jewish labor leaders, but his ideas were not enthusiastically received.

His most important works are *Der Staat* (1907; *The State*, 1914) and *System der Soziologie* (4 vols., 1922–35). Some of his articles on the Merḥavyah experiment were included in the books *Genossenschaftliche Kolonisation in Palaestina* (1915); *Merchavia* (1914); and *Wege zur Gemeinschaft* (1924). He also published an autobiography, *Erlebtes, Erstrebtes, Erreichtes* (1913, 1964). In later years his collected works were published in three volumes edited by J.H. Schoeps, A. Silbermann and H. Suessmuth: vol. 1, *Theoretische Grundlegung* (1995); vol. 2, *Politische Schriften* (1996), vol. 3, *Schriften zur Marktwirtschaft* (1998).

BIBLIOGRAPHY: K. Werner, *Oppenheimers System des liberalen Sozialismus* (1928); Fuss, in: *American Journal of Economics and Sociology*, 6 (1946), 95–112; 7 (1947), 107–17; H.E. Barnes (ed.), *Introduction to the History of Sociology* (1948); J.H. Bilski (ed.), *Means and Ways Towards a Realm of Justice* (1958); A. Bein, *Return to the Soil* (1952), index; A. Granott, *Ishim be-Yisrael* (1956), 79–109. **ADD. BIBLIOGRAPHY:** A. Loewe, in: YBLBI, 10 (1965), 137–49; A. Bein, in: *Herzl Yearbook*, 7 (1971), 71–127; G. Kressel, *Franz Oppenheimer* (Heb., 1972); V. Caspari and B. Schefold (eds.), *Franz Oppenheimer und Adolf Lowe* (1996); H. Oppenheimer, *Mabat Aḥorah: Zikhronot* (2004).

[Joachim O. Ronall and Werner J. Cahnman / Noam Zadoff (2nd ed.)]

OPPENHEIMER, FRITZ E. (1898–1968), U.S. international lawyer and diplomat. Born in Berlin, Oppenheimer served in the German Army in World War I and was wounded three times. He practiced as a lawyer in Berlin until 1936, when he was forced to leave Germany and went to London. There he acted as an adviser to the attorney general and the British Treasury and was admitted to the English bar. In 1940, Oppenheimer went to the United States where for two years he worked in a private law firm. In 1942 he enlisted in the U.S. Army and rose to become a lieutenant colonel. At the headquarters of the Supreme Allied Command, he was in charge of the reform of the German law and court system after the war. He also helped to prepare the documents relating to Germany's surrender and to draft military government and control council legislation.

On his return to the United States, Oppenheimer became special assistant to the State Department for German and Austrian affairs and adviser to the secretary of state at the meetings of the Council of Foreign Ministers (1947 and 1948). He played an important part in Germany's rehabilitation in the 1950s, helping to reorganize the German coal, iron, and steel industries, and to draft the U.S.-German treaty for the validation of German dollar bonds.

BIBLIOGRAPHY: *New York Times* (Feb. 6, 1968), 43.

OPPENHEIMER, HILLEL (Heinz) REINHARD (1899–1971), Israeli plant physiologist. Born in Berlin, son of the sociologist and economist Franz *Oppenheimer, Hillel Oppenheimer became assistant in plant physiology at the Geisenheim experimental station in 1923. After a year's work in Berlin he went to Palestine in 1926 as keeper of the Aaron Aaronsohn Herbarium at Zikhron Ya'akov, where he arranged and cataloged the famed botanical collection. He was head of the plant physiology section at the Hebrew University of Jerusalem in 1931–32, and in 1933 established the horticultural, physiological, and genetics station at the Jewish Agency's Agricultural Experiment Station at Reḥovot, which he directed for twenty years. From 1952 until his retirement in 1967, he was professor of horticulture and of plant physiology at the Hebrew University, and dean of its agricultural faculty, 1952–54. In 1959 he was awarded the Israel Prize in Agriculture.

Oppenheimer contributed notably to the knowledge of the theory of irrigation, plant-water relations, and the mineral and irrigation requirements of plantation crops, especially citrus, which was his special interest and on which he was a world authority. His research encompassed germination inhibitors in fruits, the osmotic and elastic properties of plant cells, and drought tolerance of plant cells; and citricultural physiology, including timing of irrigation, foliar analysis, rootstock selection, response to pruning and fruit production. He was also concerned with forestry and tree physiology, including water relations in semiarid surroundings, root structure and growth, and the action of the cambium. His work helped to bridge the gap between plant-physiology and plant-geography. Oppenheimer's books include *Giddul Aẓei Hadar* ("Citrus Growing," 1957). In 1935 he founded *The Palestine Journal of Botany*, which he edited until 1953.

BIBLIOGRAPHY: I. Reichert, in: BRCI, section D Botany, 8D (April 1960), i–vi (includes biography, portrait, and list of publications); A. Halevy, in: *Madda*, 14 (1969), 193 (Heb.).

[Julian Louis Meltzer]

OPPENHEIMER, JOSEPH (1876–1966), German impressionist painter born in Wuerzburg, Bavaria. In 1891 he started his artistic training in Munich, first at the private school of Conrad Fehr and then from 1893 to 1895 at the Munich Royal Academy of Fine Arts. He traveled to Italy in 1895 and in Rome painted his first impressionist painting, *Horses and Carriage on the Monte Pincio* (Private Collection).

After his return to Munich, in 1896, he set up his studio in the domicile of the archaeologist Adolf Furtwaengler and in 1899 became a member of the German secessionist movement. From then on he earned a reputation as a modern portrait painter in an impressionist style related to Max *Liebermann, and he exhibited on a regular base. After several journeys, among them a six-month stay in New York and a trip to England, he settled in Berlin in 1902 and exhibited at the Hamburg art gallery of Paul Cassirer, who was associated with the Berliner Secession and who arranged various portrait commissions for Oppenheimer. From 1902 to 1908 Oppenheimer lived in England, where Julius Spier also helped him obtain commissions. In addition he became a member of the Chelsea Arts Club. In 1908 he married Fanny Sternfeld and in the same year they returned to Berlin. He continued to work as a portrait painter also after World War I and accepted hundreds of commissions in Germany and abroad. His models were from the upper class and from the cultural and intellectual elite, such as Aby Warburg, Max J. Friedlaender, Adolf Harnack, Albert Einstein, Paul Cassirer, and Max Liebermann among others. In addition, he designed the covers of glossy magazines in Germany, where several of his plein-air studies were reproduced.

In 1933 Oppenheimer and his family immigrated to London, where he obtained British citizenship in 1939 and could resume his work as portraitist and designer of covers for magazines after World War II. From 1934 to 1965 he was a member of the Royal Society of Portrait Painters in London, where he produced works adapted to the British impressionist style that were accepted for exhibition on a regular base. Owing to World War II many of Oppenheimer's paintings disappeared or were destroyed. Some of them, among them paintings of Wuerzburg, are exhibited, but the vast majority of his paintings are in private collections.

BIBLIOGRAPHY: M. Lauter (ed.), *Joseph Oppenheimer (1876–1966). Leben und Werk, mit Beitraegen von Beate Reese und Hélène Sicotte* (1998; with catalogue raisonné).

[Jihan Radjai-Ordoubadi (2nd ed.)]

OPPENHEIMER, JOSEPH BEN ISSACHAR SUESSKIND (also known as **Joseph Suess** or "**Jud [Jew] Suess**"; 1698 or 1699–1738), Court Jew and confidential financial adviser to the duke of *Wuerttemberg. His father was a prominent merchant in Heidelberg and collector of taxes from the Jews of the Palatinate. In his youth, Oppenheimer was sent to Frankfurt, Amsterdam, Prague, and Vienna, where he became familiar with business methods within the circle of his wealthy relatives, the family of Samuel *Oppenheimer. He later engaged in commerce in Mannheim and Frankfurt. In 1732 he became the court factor of the Prince of Wuerttemberg, Charles Alexander, and a year later he was also appointed court factor to the ruler of Hesse-Darmstadt, the elector of Cologne, as well as tax collector of the elector of the Palatinate. When Charles Alexander, who in 1733 became duke of Wuerttemberg, decided to introduce an absolute and mercantile form of government within the territory under his control, Oppenheimer was appointed state counselor and was made responsible for the direction of financial affairs. In order to free the duke from his dependence on the allocations of the states, he endeavored to establish new economic foundations for the state income. He leased enterprises and properties to Christians and Jews, at the same time authorizing Jews to settle in the country. Through his supervision of the division of private property in cases of marriage or inheritance and his control over the appointment of government officials, Oppenheimer sought to enrich the state treasury and concentrate governmental power in the hands of the duke. Exercising his authority in an autocratic fashion, he imitated the life of a contemporary nobleman, dwelling in luxury and splendor; accusations of licentiousness seem to have had some foundation. With the support of the duke, he even made two unsuccessful applications for noble status to the emperor. His efforts to establish an absolute rule based on a system of mercantile economy aroused the fierce opposition of the conservative elements in the country, an opposition that was fanned by the fact that the duke was a Catholic while the country was Protestant, and that the change in the system of government had been assisted by the Jesuits and the army.

On March 19, 1737, the duke died suddenly before his projects could be executed. On the same day, Oppenheimer was arrested and charged principally with having endangered the rights of the country and embezzled the incomes of the state. Although the charges were not adequately substantiated, his property was confiscated and he was condemned to death. After the German Jewish communities had vainly attempted to obtain his release against a ransom, Oppenheimer was hanged on April 2, 1738, and his remains were publicly exhibited in an iron cage. While he was in prison, Oppenheimer, who during the period of his greatness had treated his religion with scant respect, rejected the offers of the clergy to save his life if he would accept baptism, proclaiming his intention of dying as a martyr. He died reciting the *Shema*. In the year after his death, the German Jewish communities lit memorial candles for him.

Contemporary legal authorities considered that Oppenheimer's death was an act of murder. Historians, too, have viewed it as judicial murder, the result of the conflict between various interests during the transition period from medieval to modern forms of government, in which Oppenheimer played a significant part. Traditional hatred of the Jews also served to bring about the downfall of a man who rose to considerable power in a Christian state at a time when the very idea of civic emancipation for the Jews was far distant. Joseph Suess Oppenheimer was the subject of a story by M. *Lehmann, and a novel, *Jud Suess*, by L. *Feuchtwanger, both of which were translated into several languages, including English.

BIBLIOGRAPHY: M. Zimmermann, *Joseph Suess Oppenheimer* (1874); H. Schnee, *Die Hoffinanz und der moderne Staat*, 4 (1963), 109ff., 251–4; 6 (1967), 57ff.; S. Stern, *Jud Suess* (1929); idem, *The*

Court Jew (1950), index; F. Baer, in: KS, 7 (1930/31), 390–3; D. Kahana, in: *Ha-Shilo'aḥ*, 4 (1898), 134–42, 239–46; H. Pardo, *Jud Suess; Historisches und juristisches Material zum Fall Veit Harlan* (1949). **ADD. BIBLIOGRAPHY:** B. Gerber, *Jud Suess* (1990); C. Singer, *Le juif Suess et la propagande nazie* (2003); A. von der Heiden, *Der Jude als Medium* (2005).

[Zvi Avneri]

OPPENHEIMER, J. ROBERT (1904–1967), U.S. physicist. Oppenheimer was in charge of the construction of the first atomic bomb as director of the laboratories at Los Alamos, New Mexico. Born in New York City, Oppenheimer was the son of a cultured and successful businessman, who had immigrated to the U.S. from Germany. His mother, a painter and teacher, died when he was nine years old. He was a child prodigy and at the age of five was collecting geological specimens. At Harvard University, he studied physics and chemistry, Greek and Latin. He worked under the world-famous scientist Ernest Rutherford at Cambridge, England (1925–26), and went to Goettingen at the invitation of Max *Born in 1927. On his return to America he became professor simultaneously at the California Institute of Technology at Pasadena and at the University of California at Berkeley (1929–47). He was a brilliant teacher, intense and dedicated – reading no newspaper, owning no radio, and learning Sanskrit as a diversion. He became director at Los Alamos in 1943 and during World War II was hailed as a world figure for the creation of "the bomb." In October 1945 he resigned as director at Los Alamos, and in 1947 became director of the Institute of Advanced Study at Princeton (1947–66). As chairman of the General Advisory Committee of the Atomic Energy Commission he continued to influence policy. He was greatly concerned with international control of atomic weapons. He was involved in the great debate with scientist Edward *Teller and the chairman of the Atomic Energy Commission Lewis *Strauss on the construction of the thermonuclear bomb. In 1954, his security clearance was cancelled because of his early association with communists in the late 1930s and his opposition to the H-Bomb (the subject of a play *In the Matter of J. Robert Oppenheimer* based on the documents by H. Kipphardt, and translated by R. Speirs, 1954). After a hearing before a special board he was declared "a loyal citizen but not a good security risk." In 1963, as a sign of restored confidence, he was given the Fermi Award for his contribution to nuclear research by the Atomic Energy Commission.

BIBLIOGRAPHY: J. Alsop and S. Alsop, *We Accuse* (1954); J. Boskin, *The Oppenheimer Affair* (1968); H.M. Chevalier, *Oppenheimer: The Story of a Friendship* (1966); C.P. Curtis, *The Oppenheimer Case* (1955); M. Rouzé, *Robert Oppenheimer; the Man and His Theories* (1964); J.L.C. Vilar, *Le dossier Oppenheimer* (1965); N.P. Davis, *Lawrence and Oppenheimer* (1968); R. Serber et al., *Oppenheimer* (Eng., 1969); I.L. Rabi et al., *Oppenheimer* (Eng., 1969); P. Michelmore, *The Swift Years, Robert Oppenheimer's Story* (1969); J.R. Soyer, *The Oppenheimer Case: Security on Trial* (1969).

[J. Edwin Holmstrom]

OPPENHEIMER, KARL (1864–1926), pioneer of infant and child welfare in Germany. Born in Bruchsal in Baden, he settled in Munich in 1890 and became a leading pediatrician. During more than 30 years of practice, he personally financed an extremely successful child welfare clinic. Oppenheimer considered the main purpose of this extensive free advisory service to be an attempt to achieve a decrease in the infant mortality rate, by educating and instructing indigent mothers. Largely on his initiative, the payment of maternity benefits and the training and recruitment of welfare workers were introduced. Oppenheimer was also responsible for the realization of a school meal service and the founding of the Jewish Country Home in Wolfratshausen. Oppenheimer published numerous articles on infant feeding; his proposals and improvements in regard to the composition and preparation of artificial infant food were vigorously contested at first but met with increasing acceptance.

BIBLIOGRAPHY: Wininger, Biog, s.v.

OPPENHEIMER, SAMUEL (1630–1703), Austrian *Court Jew and military contractor. He began his career in Heidelberg as purveyor to the elector, Karl Ludwig, and tax collector of *Palatinate Jewry. Subsequently he moved to *Vienna where he received the right of unlimited residence and extraordinary trade privileges. Like other Jews, he was affected by the 1670 expulsion from Vienna but from 1672 he was in the business of supplying the Austrian army. Officially allowed to settle in 1676, he was the first Jew to be granted such a privilege after the 1670 expulsion, and his entourage became the core of the reestablished Jewish community. Although his request to open a synagogue was turned down by the authorities, services were held in his home. At the time of his resettlement he was given the title of Imperial War Purveyor. During the 1673–79 war against France he organized a consortium to supply Austrian armies in the west. After the Peace of Nijmegen (1679), the treasury refused to honor a 200,000 florin debt to him, and it was only through a personal appeal to the emperor that he even received partial payment. Shortly thereafter, he and his entourage were imprisoned for allegedly defrauding the state, although a subsequent investigation proved the accusations to be groundless. The outbreak of the Austrian-Turkish War (1682), however, forced the state to release him and to come to terms with his pecuniary demands, which were surprisingly lenient, and it further decided to put to the test his boast of being able to supply the Austrian armies single-handedly. The emperor approved the contract just before he fled Vienna to escape from the advancing Turkish armies; nevertheless, he declared that it was dangerous to give so important a position to a Jew. Oppenheimer fulfilled the contract during the desperate siege of Vienna in 1683 and, thereafter, took on all the logistic problems raised by the war: the supply of uniforms, food, and salaries for the troops, livestock for the cavalry and artillery and fodder for the beasts, as well as seeing to supplies for hospitals for the wounded. Conducting business throughout the empire, his coup was building the Danube fleet of rafts for the relief of besieged Ofen (see *Budapest).

Oppenheimer's success may be attributed to his business acumen and persistence despite the many difficulties which beset his enterprises, and especially to his organizational talents. He set up a network of contractors and subcontractors throughout central Europe, many of whom were Court Jews in their own right and some of whom established themselves by their business connections with him. A good part of his success was due to his family and its far-flung business connections. His wife, Sandela Carcassone, daughter of a Sephardi Jew of Mannheim, bore him nine children. His son Wolf married a daughter of Leffmann *Behrens, a business associate. Oppenheimer also had an entourage of secretaries and agents whom he placed in all the financial and commercial centers of Europe. One of them was his nephew and future competitor, Samson *Wertheimer. Oppenheimer raised money from many sources, not only from his fellow Jews but also from Christian merchants and bankers.

The Turkish menace was barely repulsed when *Louis XIV invaded the Palatinate in 1688 and Oppenheimer was at once called upon for assistance. Although the field commanders, Eugen of Savoy and Margrave Louis of Baden, both praised his efficiency and contributions in the country's dilemma, the court in Vienna, and particularly Bishop *Kollonitsch, viewed his monopolistic position with misgivings, pointing out that not only was he Austria's sole military purveyor but that a disproportionate part of the state income was being earmarked solely for him as payment for his services. All attempts to dispose of his services failed, however, for few others were in possession of sufficient capital to assume his place, and none was prepared to extend credit to the state with its chronically empty treasury. The state's debts to Oppenheimer grew from 52,600 florins in 1685 to 700,000 in 1692, and to 3,000,000 in 1694, at which point it remained stable for a few years until it increased during the War of the Spanish Succession.

Bishop Kollonitsch, appointed head of the treasury in 1692, frustrated by his unsuccessful attempts to dispense with Oppenheimer's services, tried to undermine Oppenheimer by falsely accusing him of attempting to murder Samson Wertheimer. As a consequence, Oppenheimer was forced to buy his freedom and establish his innocence with the sum of 500,000 florins. In 1700 when his sumptuous home was stormed and plundered by a mob, order was reluctantly restored by the authorities and the two instigators hanged. It has been suggested that the cause of the attack was Oppenheimer's intervention in suppressing an anti-Jewish book of *Eisenmenger.

When Oppenheimer died, the state refused to honor its debts to his heir Emanuel and had his firm declared bankrupt. His death brought deep financial crisis to the state; it experienced great difficulty in securing the credit necessary to meet its needs. Emanuel appealed to European rulers to whom the state owed money and who intervened on his behalf. After deliberate procrastination, the state refused Emanuel's demand for 6 million florins and instead demanded 4 million florins from him. This amount was based on a sum which (with compound interest), according to the state, Oppenheimer had allegedly obtained by fraud at the beginning of his career. Emanuel died in 1721 and the Oppenheimer estate was auctioned in 1763.

Although Oppenheimer was not himself learned, he was a benefactor on a scale hitherto unknown, building many synagogues and yeshivot and supporting their scholars. He also paid ransom for the return of Jews captured during the Turkish wars and supported as well R. Judah he-Ḥasid's voyage to Ereẓ Israel in 1700. Known as "*Judenkaiser*" by his contemporaries, he was a man whose complex personality, a mixture of pride and reserve, defied historical analysis. Twenty years after his death it was estimated that more than 100 persons held residence in Vienna by virtue of their being included in Oppenheimer's privileges.

BIBLIOGRAPHY: M. Grunwald, *Samuel Oppenheimer und sein Kreis* (1913); idem, *Vienna* (1936), index; S. Stern, *Court Jew* (1950), index; H. Schnee, *Die Hoffinanz und der moderne Staat*, 3 (1955), 239–45; MHJ, 2 (1937); 5 (1960); 9 (1966); 10 (1967), indexes; **ADD. BIBLIOGRAPHY:** J. Bérenger, in: *XVIIe siècle* 46 (1992), 303–20.

[Henry Wasserman]

OPPENHEJM, RALPH GERSON (1924–), Danish author. During the Nazi occupation, Oppenhejm was deported to Theresienstadt but, together with his family and many other Danish Jews, was eventually sent home as a result of the *Bernadotte rescue operation. Oppenhejm's experiences are recorded in the form of a girl's diary entitled *Det skulle så være: Marianne Petits dagbok fra Theresienstadt* (1945; *The Door of Death*, 1948). In *Alt dette – og Bevin med. ABC for Englandsresende* (1948) he attacked Britain's Palestine policy. He also wrote travel books about Europe and Asia.

OPPER, FREDERICK BURR (1857–1937), U.S. political cartoonist; an originator of the comic strip. Opper left Madison, Ohio, for New York, where he worked for 18 years on the weekly *Puck*. He joined Hearst's *New York Journal* in 1899, and his work was then syndicated through the *International News*. Opper depicted suburban types which became familiar to almost every American household. He also became Hearst's leading political caricaturist, lampooning the eccentricities of public figures, particularly during election campaigns.

A volume of his political drawings, *Willie and his Papa*, was published in 1901. His cartoons on England, *John Bull*, appeared in 1903. Other collections were *Alphabet of Joyous Trusts* (1902), *Our Antediluvian Ancestors* (1903), two volumes of his character *Happy Hooligan* (1902–07) and *Maud and the Matchless* (1907). Opper also illustrated the work of some of his contemporary humorists, including Mark Twain, Peter Finley Dunne, Bill Nye, and George V. Hobart.

BIBLIOGRAPHY: DAB, 23 (1958), 504f. (incl. bibl.).

OPPERT, GUSTAV SALOMON (1836–1908), German Orientalist and Indologist. Born in Hamburg, younger brother of the assyrologist Julius (Jules) *Oppert and of Ernst Jacob Oppert, merchant and traveler, Oppert studied languages, literature, philosophy, and history in Bonn, Leipzig, and Berlin. He worked in the Bodleian Library, Oxford, and was appointed assistant librarian at Queen Victoria's Library in Windsor. In 1872 he was appointed professor of Sanskrit and comparative philology at the Presidency College in Madras, India where from 1878 to 1882 he also served as editor of the *Madras Journal of Literature and Science.* After traveling through India, the Far East, and the U.S. he accepted a teaching post at Berlin University in Dravidian languages.

He also produced a number of works in folklore, general philology, ancient Hindu culture, studies of South Indian manuscripts; travel accounts, and editions of various classics of Sanskrit culture in the areas of philosophy, poetry and philology.

Like his brother Jules, Gustav Oppert devoted himself to various Jewish causes. He was a trustee of the Hochschule fuer die Wissenschaft des Judentums and bequeathed his estate to this organization.

BIBLIOGRAPHY: JC (March 20, 1908), obituary. **ADD. BIBLIOGRAPHY:** DBE, 7 (1998) 501; J. Jacobson, in: YBLI, 7 (1959), 67–72; 8; L.H. Grey, in: JE, 9 (1903), 419–420; *Lexikon der hamburgerischen Schriftsteller bis zur Gegenwart*, 5 (1870), 610–611; G. Pelger, in: *EAJS Newsletter*, 11 (2001–2002), 15–23; V. Stache-Rosen, *German Indologists. Biographies of Scholars in Indian Studies* (1990), 81–82; *Sechsundzwanzigster Jahresbericht der Lehranstalt fuer die Wissenschaft des Judentums zu Berlin* (1908), 63–67; Wininger, in: JNB, 4 (1979), 584; *Zeitschrift fuer Ethnologie*, 40 (April 23, 1908), obituary, 260.

[Ephraim Fischoff / Gregor Pelger (2nd ed.)]

OPPERT, JULES JULIUS (1825–1905), French philologist, Orientalist, and archaeologist. Born in Hamburg, he studied law but changed to Oriental languages. He migrated to France where he continued his research on Old Persian and Assyrian and became a recognized authority in his field. In 1851 he was invited to join a sponsored expedition to explore Mesopotamia. The results of this expedition contained Opper's definite identification of the site of ancient Babylon, and appeared in a two-volume report, *Expédition Scientifique en Mesopotamie* (1859–63), which received a prize for the most significant discovery of the year. In 1869 Oppert joined the Collège de France, first as instructor in Assyriology, and then in 1874 as professor of Assyrian philology and archaeology.

His studies in various branches of Oriental learning included Indo-Iranian, Sumerian, Elamitic, and Assyriology, in which he became a founder and preeminent authority. He discovered and deciphered numerous historical, astronomical and religious inscriptions, juridical documents, contract tablets, and collected material for his history of the Chaldean and Assyrian civilizations.

He made decisive contributions to the decipherment of cuneiform inscriptions and together with E. Hinds, H. Rawlinson, and F. Talbot was one of the pioneers in the recovery of Babylonian cuneiform. His profound knowledge of Assyriology was signified by his participation together with the scholars mentioned above in the historic experiment arranged by the Royal Asiatic Society in 1857 when a separate decipherment made by them of one identical Assyrian Royal Inscription proved the sound basis of Assyriology. Oppert continued to be most active in the field and participated in the lively dispute on the origins of the Sumerian language (see also *Mesopotamia, Assyriology). He also interpreted Assyrian, Median, and Persian history and mythology. He was one of the founders and an editor of the *Revue d'Assyriologie et d'Archéologie Orientale* (1884–) and one of the contributing editors of the *Zeitschrift fuer Assyriologie* on its establishment in 1886. Among the honors that came to him was election to the Académie des Inscriptions et Belles-Lettres in 1881, and later to the presidency of this body.

Both he and his younger brother Gustav Salomon *Oppert, philologist and Indologist, had a strong interest in Jewish affairs. Jules *Oppert was a member of the administrative executive committee of the Société des Etudes Juives and contributed to its journal, the *Revue des Etudes Juives.* He was also involved in the activities of the *Alliance Israélite Universelle and the Jewish Central Consistory. He was interested in biblical scholarship and wrote studies on the Book of Esther and Judith and the chronology of Genesis (1877).

BIBLIOGRAPHY: Muss-Arnolt, in: *Beitraege zur Assyriologie und semitischen Sprachwissenschaft*, 2 (1894), 523–56, incl. bibl. to 1891; K. Bezold, in: ZA, 19 (1905), 169–73.

[Ephraim Fischoff]

OPPRESSION (Heb. עֹשֶׁק), an offense against property, standing midway between *theft and robbery and *fraud and often overlapping with either of them. The injunction, rendered in English as "Thou shalt not oppress thy neighbor" (Lev. 19:13), really means (like the injunction immediately following: "nor rob him") that you must not try to enrich yourself by, or derive any material benefit from, any violation of your neighbor's rights. The exact dividing line between oppression (coercion) and robbery gave rise to a discussion among talmudic scholars: where a man failed to restore property to its lawful owner, some held that it was oppression if he admitted the other's ownership, and robbery if he denied it; others held it to be oppression if he asserted that he had already returned it, and robbery if he refused to return it; a third opinion was that it was oppression if he denied that he had ever received the property, and robbery if he asserted that he had already returned it; a fourth scholar held that oppression and robbery were essentially identical terms (BM 111a). The proximity in the Bible of the offenses of stealing, deceit, perjury, oppression, and robbery (Lev. 19:11–13) led an ancient authority to observe that he who steals will eventually commit deceit, perjury, oppression, and robbery (Sifra 3:2); and it is in reliance on the same authority that oppression per se has been held by some to be limited to the crime of withholding a laborer's wages (*ibid.* 3:2; cf. Rashi to Lev. 19:13). The particular oppression of laborers, in withholding their wages, is the subject of a special prohibition, accompanied by a mandatory injunction that the payment of such wages may not be delayed even for one night (Deut. 24:14–15; see *Labor Law). The definition of oppression, as it eventually emerged, is given by Maimonides in the following terms: "Oppression is the forceful withholding and not restoring of money which had been received with the owner's consent, as, for instance, where a man had taken a loan or hired a house and, on being asked to return the same, is so violent and hard that nothing can be got out of him" (Yad, Gezelah va-Avedah 1:4; and cf. ḤM 359:8). Although it is in the nature of a criminal offense, no punishment can be inflicted for such oppression, as the proper remedy is an order for the payment of the money due, and civil and criminal sanctions are mutually exclusive (see *Flogging). But the guilt before God subsists even after payment, hence a sacrificial penalty is imposed on the oppressor (Lev. 5:23–26). Oppressors are also regarded as criminals so as to disqualify them as witnesses before the court (Sanh. 25b; Yad, Edut 10:4). As against strangers, the prohibition of oppression is extended to cover also intimidations and importunities (Ex. 22:20; 23:9), even where no violation of monetary rights is involved (BM 59b and Rashi *ibid.*). Monetary oppression has frequently been denounced as one of the most reprehensible of offenses (Jer. 21:12; 22:17; Ezek. 22:29; Zech. 7:10; Mal. 3:5; Ps. 62:11; 72:4–5; et al.), and its elimination as one of the conditions precedent to national and religious survival (Jer. 7:6).

In the State of Israel, the offense consists of taking advantage of the distress, the physical or mental weakness, or the inexperience or lightheadedness of another person in order to obtain something not legally due, or profiteering from services rendered or commodities sold (Sect. 13, Penal Law Amendment (Deceit, Blackmail and Extortion) Law, 5723 – 1963).

BIBLIOGRAPHY: M. Elon, *Ha-Mishpat Ha-Ivri* (1988), III, 1464; Ibid., *Jewish Law* (1994), IV, 1739; Section 431 of the Penal Law, 5737–1937; C.A. 719/78, *Ilit Ltd et al v. Alko Ltd*, 34 (4), 673, 686–187.

[Haim Hermann Cohn]

ORABUENA, noted family of Navarre in the 13th and 14th centuries. ISHMAEL ORABUENA and his son JOSEPH are mentioned as important personalities in the kingdom of Navarre in 1265. Members of the family were among the signatories of the *takkanot* of Tudela (1305). The Orabuena family maintained close relations with the foremost Jewish families of the Iberian peninsula. JOSEPH, grandson of the above-mentioned Joseph, leased the tax collection for Tudela in 1367. He was the physician to King Charles III of Navarre, accompanied him on several journeys to France, and advised him in political matters of importance. He was chief rabbi of Navarre Jewry and it was to him that Solomon ha-Levi (*Pablo de Santa María), rabbi of Burgos, wrote announcing his intention of converting to Christianity. Joseph was still active in 1399, granting loans to the crown and providing medical services to the king.

BIBLIOGRAPHY: M. Kayserling, *Juden in Navarra* (1861), index; Baer, Urkunden, 1 (1929), index; Baer, Spain, index.

[Haim Beinart]

ORACH (Heb. מַלּוּחַ, *mallu'aḥ*), the species *Atriplex halimus*. This shrub grows wild in the saline soil of the lower Jordan valley, in the Negev, and in the Arabah; it is also found in the sandy lands of the Sharon and in the beds of rivers. There is a concentration of the shrub at Abu-Tor in Jerusalem, close to the remains of a Byzantine church, where it may possibly have been cultivated formerly. Some Bedouin eat the leaves cooked or as salad, and they have a popular saying that "were it not for the orach the Bedouin would suffer from sores," and in fact it is rich in the vitamins which prevent skin disease. The Hebrew name *mallu'aḥ* is derived from its salty taste (*melaḥ*, "salt"). The shrub can grow in soil with a 20% salt concentration; some of the salt is excreted by the leaves and the granules cover them with a silvery layer. The massed plants in various parts of the Arabah give it its silvery gray landscape. Job (30:4) describes the food of the wretched people living in the wilderness "who pluck *mallu'aḥ* with wormwood," i.e., who feed on the leaves of the orach which they eat directly from the shrub without first preparing them (see *Wormwood). According to an ancient tradition the children of Israel ate the orach when traveling in the wilderness, and after Alexander *Yannai was victorious in the wilderness he ordered this tradition to be respected, "and they served orach on golden tables and ate it" (Kid. 66a). In talmudic times the cultivated species, *Atriplex hortensis*, which was named *kerosalkinon*, was grown and thought to be a hybrid of beet and amarynth (TJ, Kil. 1:4, 27a; Rome Ms.).

BIBLIOGRAPHY: Loew, Fora, 1 (1924), 345–6; J. Feliks, *Kilei Zera'im ve-Harkavah* (1967), 108–9; idem, *Olam ha-Ẓome'aḥ ha-Mikra'i* (1968^2), 186–7).

[Jehuda Feliks]

ORADEA (formerly **Oradea Mare**; Hung. **Nagyvárad**, also **Várad**; Ger. **Grosswardein**; in Hebrew and Yiddish texts the German name was used), city in Transylvania, W. Romania; until 1918 and between 1940 and 1944 in Hungary. Although documents dating from 1407 and 1489 mention several Jews in connection with the city, the only reliable evidence of Jews residing there dates from the early 18th century, but there are several popular legends that speak about a Jewish presence starting with the 10th century. Officials in the four different constituent parts of the city had different policies concerning the settlement of Jews. In 1722 four Jews are listed as residents. A *ḥevra kaddisha* was formed in 1731. Ten Jewish families were registered in 1736, including one *ḥazzan*. The Jewish residents in Oradea were immigrants from Moravia, Bohemia, and Poland. As the fort of Oradea lost its strategic importance after the end of the Turkish wars (1692), the Jews were later permitted to live in the adjacent Váralja quarter. In 1787 the Jews were permitted to build a synagogue; a second synagogue was built in 1812. The whole city, including the Jewish population, expanded rapidly from the end of the 18th century. The number of Jews increased from 104 taxpayers in 1830 to 1,600 persons in 1840; 10,115 (26.2% of the total population) in 1891; 12,294 (24%) in 1900; 15,115 (23.6%) in 1910; 20,587 (21%) in

1930; and 21,337 (22.9%) in 1941. The Jews in Oradea, as elsewhere, actively participated in the economic life of the city but were seen by some of the local population as endangering their livelihoods. During mostly the second half of the 19th century some Jews succeeded in being accepted socially by a part of the local Hungarian population, who saw in the Jews potential helpers in their struggle against what was perceived to be Romanian nationalism (that is, the Romanian fight for their rights, not recognized by the Hungarian authorities). Many local Jews actively participated in the Hungarian revolution of 1848–49.

The Jews of Oradea adopted the Hungarian language and culture earlier than any other Jewish community in Hungary. The contribution of the Oradea Jews to the development of Hungarian literature and culture, as well as Hungarian journalism, was very significant even after 1919, when the new Romanian authorities tried to make the Jews change their Hungarian allegiance. The Reform congregation, organized in 1847, was disbanded in 1848. During the Hungarian revolution in that year the Jews supported the rebels and some served in their ranks. Austrian oppression during the following decade weighed heavily on the Jews.

Conflicts between Orthodox and Reform elements within the Oradea community characterized the latter half of the 19th century. After the schism following the Hungarian Jewish Congress (see *Hungary), the Oradea community divided in 1870 into *Orthodox and *Neolog congregations, each developing separate institutions which remained active until after World War II. A Neolog temple, with an organ, was built in 1878, and an Orthodox synagogue in 1891. In both congregations well-known rabbis officiated, including the Orthodox rabbis Aaron Isaac Landsberg (1853–79), and Moses Ẓevi *Fuchs and his son Benjamin (1915–36). Rabbis of the Neolog congregation included Alexander *Kohut (1880–84), Lipót *Kecskeméti (1897–1936), the most influential, and István Vajda (1939–44), the last Neolog rabbi, who perished in *Auschwitz with the rest of his community. During World War I several ḥasidic rabbis from Bukovina and Galicia of the *Vizhnitsa and *Zhidachov dynasties found refuge in Oradea and attracted Ḥasidim from the district.

Jewish institutions in Oradea included a hospital. Jewish public schools were opened early in the 19th century. An Orthodox high school with four classes, founded in 1888, remained open until the Holocaust. A Neolog high school, founded in 1920, also continued until the Holocaust.

In the cultural and economic spheres Oradea Jewry was the most active of all the communities in Hungary or Romania. Jews were prominent in Hungarian journalism. Hebrew printing houses operated in the city. The leading Jewish newspaper was the religious Zionist weekly *Népünk* ("Our People"; 1929–40). Branches of the Zionist movement were active in Oradea between the world wars. The National Jewish Party had supporters in Oradea, although some Jews supported the party of the Hungarian nationalists. Jews joined the Communist Party when it was still legal and were even elected as city councilors. In 1927 several Romanian nationalist student leaders organized anti-Jewish riots in which several Jews were killed and synagogues were despoiled. Marked antisemitic manifestations made the lives of the Jews difficult both under Romanian rule (1919–40) and, after that, under the new Horthiite regime, which had its climax in their being ghettoized after the German occupation of March 1944, and subsequently deported to Auschwitz.

After the end of the war, in 1947, the Jewish population numbered 8,000, including survivors from the camps, the Hungarian labor battalions, and Jews who had arrived there from other areas. Their number decreased through emigration to Israel and other countries, falling to 2,000 in 1971. The only Jewish institutions still functioning then were the three synagogues, which held services on the Sabbath and holidays. There was a *kosher* restaurant in the city.

BIBLIOGRAPHY: L. Lakos, *A váradi zsidóság tőrténete* (1912); MHJ, 3 (1937); 5 pt. 1 (1959); 7 (1960), index. s.v. *Nagyvárad, Várad*; P. Adorján, *A halott város* (1941); B. Katona, *Várad a viharban* (1946); S. Yitzhaki, *Battei Sefer Yehudiyyim bi-Transylvanyah Bein Shetei Milḥamot Olam* (1970), 102–77.

[Yehouda Marton / Paul Schveiger (2nd ed.)]

OR AKIVA (Heb. אוֹר עֲקִיבָא; "Light of R. Akiva"), immigrant development town in the northern Sharon, 1½ mi. E. of *Caesarea. Construction of the town began in 1951 with the aim of providing permanent housing for the inhabitants of the Caesarea *ma'barah* (immigrant transit camp). In 1968, Or Akiva had 6,000 inhabitants, as compared with 3,208 in 1961. In the mid-1990s the population was approximately 11,500, increasing to 15,700 in 2002 and occupying an area of 1.2 sq. mi. (3 sq. km.). In 2001 Or Akiva received city status. A new Performing Arts Center produced a cultural awakening in the town. Its economy was based mainly on medium-size industry (carpet weaving, silk weaving; fur coats, rubber mattresses, etc.). Further employment was provided by the tourist enterprises of Caesarea. Income was about half the national average.

[Shlomo Hasson / Shaked Gilboa (2nd ed.)]

ORAL LAW (Heb. תּוֹרָה שֶׁבְּעַל־פֶּה), the authoritative interpretation of the Written Law (*Torah, which is the text of the *Pentateuch) which was regarded as given to Moses on Sinai, and therefore coexistent with the Written Law. This view of the Oral Law was a fundamental principle of the rabbis. The Written and Oral Laws constitute together "two that are one." "It is related that a certain man stood before Shammai and said 'Rabbi, How many Torahs have you?' The rabbi replied 'Two – one written and one oral'" (ARN[1] 15, 61; cf. Sif. Deut. 351). There is a strong and close bond between the Written Law and the Oral Law, and neither can exist without the other – both from the dogmatic point of view and from that of historical reality. The Oral Law depends upon the Written Law, but at the same time, say the rabbis, it is clear that there can be no real existence for the Written Law without the Oral. The need for the positing of the existence of the Oral Law is inherent in the very character and nature of the Torah. The statutes of the Written Law could not have been fulfilled literally even in the generation in which they were given, since "that which is plain in the Torah is obscure, all the more that which is obscure" (Judah Halevi, *Kuzari*, 3, 35; cf. Moses of Coucy in *Semag*, introduction: "For the verses contradict and refute each other," and "the statements in the Written Law are vague"). Even those statutes of the Torah that appear to be clearly formulated and detailed contain more that is obscure and requires explanation than what is manifest and understandable. The reasons given for this are many and various. The Written Law contains contradictions (cf., e.g., Deut. 16:3–4 with 16:8), and there is a lack of clarity and definition: The law "he shall surely be put to death" (Ex. 21:12 et al.) does not state whether by stoning, burning, or some other method not mentioned in the Torah. "And ye shall afflict your souls" (Lev. 16:31) does not indicate whether it means by mortification of the body through ascetic practices, by fasting, or in some other manner. The prohibition against doing work on the Sabbath does not specify the nature of work (see below). "And if men strive together and hurt a woman with child so that her fruit depart and yet no harm follow… But if any harm follow…" (Ex. 21:22–23) does not make it clear whether the "harm" refers to the woman or her embryo. Dimensions and quantities are not given, e.g., in the precepts of leket, *shikhḥah, and *pe'ah, or *terumah (the priestly portion), etc. Individual laws are given without any indication of whether the law is confined to that particular case or whether it is to be regarded merely as an example of a category of laws, e.g., the law that a slave goes free if his master destroys his eye or his tooth (Ex. 21:26–27).

There are lacunae, and laws which are not explicitly stated but to which mere passing reference is made (thus the only reference to the laws of sale and acquisition is the prohibition against overreaching – *ona'ah); there is no reference to the laws of marriage, while the law of divorce is mentioned only incidentally in connection with the injunction that a man may not remarry his divorced wife after she has remarried and become divorced again (Deut. 24:1–4); the Torah enjoins that one sentenced to be flogged may not have more than the fixed number of lashes inflicted (Deut. 25:1–3), but nowhere does it specify which transgressions involve the punishment of a flogging. From the above it seems clear that it was impossible for life to be regulated solely in accordance with the Written Law ("and I should like someone to adjudicate between two litigants on the basis of the weekly portions, *Mishpatim* [Ex. 21–24] and *Ki Teẓe* [Deut. 21:10–25:19]" – Judah Halevi, *Kuzari*, 3:35). It may even be inferred from the Written Law itself that immediately after it was given there already was difficulty in understanding it. Thus, e.g., it is apparent that until he heard it explicity from God, Moses did not know what the penalty was for the transgression of gathering wood on the Sabbath (Num. 15:32–35; cf. Sif. Zut. 15:34: "Eliezar b. Simeon says: Moses did not know that he was liable to death, nor did he know how he should be executed, as can be inferred from the reply given: 'And the Lord said unto Moses: the man shall be put to death,' i.e., he is liable to death; how shall he put to death? He [God] replied: by stoning"; cf. also the case of the blasphemer in Lev. 24:10–23). As stated above, there is no definition in the Pentateuch of what constitutes work in connection with the Sabbath (or the Day of Atonement), only some of the things forbidden being explicitly mentioned (plowing, reaping, kindling fire). Furthermore, in connection with the desecration of the Sabbath, in one and the same verse (Ex. 31:14) two different punishments – death and *karet – are given. From the point of view of its judicial literary form, the Written Law is in fact no different from other early Oriental statutes which never exhausted or aimed at exhausting all the details of the laws given.

If, therefore, the statutes of the Torah could not be properly understood in the generation in which it was given, how much less could it be understood by later generations? In addition to this consideration, it was a fundamental doctrine of the rabbis that the Torah was given by God for all time, that it would never be exchanged for another Torah and certainly never rescinded, and that it provided for all possible circumstances which might arise at any time in the future. Nevertheless, in practice, changing conditions – social, economic, etc. – raised many new problems, as well as the question of their solution in accordance with the Torah. The new situations and spheres of human activity which arose, for which the Written Law did not provide, could not be ignored. In fact, from the beginning the Written Law was the basis of authority of the Oral Law for the future (Deut. 17:8–11 and see below). It can thus be regarded as a historical fact that the Oral Law existed not merely from the moment the Written Law was given (and in this sense it is correct to say that the Written and Oral Laws were given together to Moses at Sinai), but it may even be maintained that the Oral Law anticipated the Written Law, as the Written Law not only assumes the observance of the Oral Law in the future but is in effect based on its previous existence. Since the written law relies – by allusion or by its silence – on statutes, customs, and basic laws not explicitly mentioned in it (marriage, divorce, business; see above), these statutes are ipso facto converted into a part of the Oral Law.

The impossibility of the Written Law existing without an Oral Law can also be demonstrated from Jewish history. The development of the Oral Law can be traced throughout the books of the Bible, especially in the prophets and the hagiographa, in the Jewish literature of the time of the Second Temple (Apocrypha and pseudepigrapha, in Jewish Hellenistic *literature, and in the early Targums of the Bible), the talmudic literature and the rabbinical literature throughout the generations (see *Halakhah). Even the dissenting sects outside normative Judaism, as long as they did not abandon Judaism completely, did not maintain the Written Law without an Oral Law: the *Sadducees possessed a "Book of Decrees – who were to be stoned, who burnt, who beheaded, and who strangled" (the scholium to Megillat *Ta'anit); the

Judean desert sect developed, especially by means of biblical exegesis, a most ramified *halakhah* which has survived in its works (in particular in the Damascus Covenant, the Manual of Discipline and other works; see Dead Sea *Scrolls); and a most ramified *halakhah* also developed among the *Karaites. In the relationship of the Written to the Oral Law there exists a kind of paradox, both interesting and characteristic. From the dogmatic point of view the Oral Law has its basis in, and derives its validity from, explicit verses in the Written Law, but at the same time the Written Law itself obtains its full validity and its authority for practical *halakhah* from the Oral Law. The Written Law in fact establishes the authority of the Oral Law by laying down that "if there arise a matter too hard for thee, thou shalt turn unto the judge that shall be in those days," and "according to the tenor of the sentence which they shall declare unto thee from that place… According to the law which they shall teach thee, and according to the judgment which they shall tell thee shalt thou do; thou shalt not turn aside from the sentence which they shall declare unto thee, neither to the right hand, nor to the left" (Deut. 17:8–11). Yet it follows precisely from those very verses themselves that it is the Oral Law itself which determines what the *halakhah* of the Written Law is in practice, including the true meanings (as distinct from the theoretical philological meanings) of those very verses (Deut. 17:8–11) themselves.

Furthermore the Oral Law lays down explicitly that from the moment of the giving of the Written Law – "from Heaven," at Sinai, but in the language of men and to men – it is handed over absolutely to the judgment of the human intelligence of the scholars of the Oral Law, who accept the "yoke of the kingdom of Heaven" but give halakhic ruling according to their understanding ("henceforth no prophet can innovate anything" – Sifra, *Be-Ḥukkotai*, 13:7; cf. Shab. 104a), since "it is not in Heaven" (TJ, MK 3:1, 81d; BM 59b – based upon Deut. 30:12). Though indeed this rule was not accepted without protest, yet those who objected belonged to the fringes of Judaism, and it was not they who determined the *halakhah*. The Oral Law is able to circumvent the Written Law (see TJ, Kid. 1:2, 59d). In consequence of this provision, Maimonides, following the talmudic sages, ruled that "in an emergency any *bet din* may cancel even the words of the (written) Torah… in order to strengthen religion and to prevent people from transgressing the Torah. They may order flagellation and punish for breach of law, but such a ruling may not be effected permanently. Similarly, if they see a temporary need to set aside a positive precept, or to transgress an injunction in order to bring many back to religion, or in order to save many Israelites from grief in other matters, they may act in accordance with the needs of the time; just as the physician amputates a hand or a leg in order to preserve the life, so the *bet din* may rule at some particular time that some precept of the Torah may be transgressed temporarily in order that it may be preserved" (Yad, Mamrim 2:4). Then the sages rightly maintained that the Oral Law is the major and the main part (i.e., both in quantity and quality) of the Torah. "The Holy One made a covenant with Israel only for the sake of that transmitted orally" (Git. 60b; cf. TJ, Pe'ah 2:6, 17a: those given orally are beloved"). The Oral Law, which is well-nigh sovereign in relation to the Written Law, is the "mystery" (μυστήριον) of the Holy One (Tanḥ. Ki Tissa 34, et al.; though the sources speak of the *Mishnah, it is certain that the whole oral law is intended) because of the essential nature of its being given orally. It is this nature of the Oral Law – that it was given orally – that determines its vitality and organic development; it is not immutable and fossilized but alive and evolving. This vitality, however, could only be preserved in words not fixed in writing and in a binding and unchangeable form but in words developing continually and unceasingly. As mentioned, the Sadducees had a book of decrees in writing which was their "Oral Law" (the scholium to Meg. Ta'an.), and therefore according to their outlook the whole of the Torah too was "prepared in writing" (Kid. 66a – according to early printed versions and *Haggadot ha-Talmud*, Constantinople, 1511, 56d), i.e., the written word obligates. The Pharisees, however, claimed that the distinguishing feature and authority of the Oral Law is embedded in the fundamental rule (Deut. 31:19), "put it in their mouths" (the scholium to Meg. Ta'an.). The Oral Law was handed over to the sages, by means of whose words it is fixed and evolves from generation to generation. It is this nature and this sovereignty that are the real will of the Written Law, which was given on the basis that it be explained by means of the Oral Law. This, apparently, is the reason that although there is a disciple who expounds "more than was spoken to Moses at Sinai" (ARN2 [13], 32), yet "even what a distinguished disciple will rule in the presence of his teacher was already conveyed to Moses at Sinai" (TJ, Pe'ah 2:6, 17a; cf. Meg. 19b and SEZ 2:171 "Surely both the Bible and Mishnah were communicated by the Almighty"). The meaning of all these and of similar sources is that from the point of view of its functional essence, the whole of the Oral Law was given to Moses at Sinai, since "the Torah itself gave the sages a mind to interpret and to declare" (Sif. Num. 134; cf. "matters not revealed to Moses were revealed to Akiva" – (Tanḥ. B. Num. 117; for its true meaning cf. Men. 29b – the *aggadah* of Moses entering the yeshivah of *Akiva – "and he did not know what they were saying," not even a detail of a *halakhah* given to Moses at Sinai). Even the Holy One repeats, as it were, a *halakhah* as spoken by the sages (PdRK, ed. by D. Mandelbaum (1962), 73, et al.).

[Moshe David Herr]

Attitude of Reform Judaism

In the approximate century and a half of Reform *Judaism's existence, the development of its attitude toward the Oral Law has undergone three fairly distinct phases. In the initial stage, in the early 19th century, most Reform rabbis invoked the Oral Law itself in calling for change in halakhic practice and usage. Thus Aaron *Chorin justified the changes in the liturgy of the Reform congregation of Hamburg (established 1818) by extensive citation of the Talmud and codes. Abraham *Geiger expressed the spirit of the leaders of Reform Judaism of his time in the opening article of the first issue of his publication

(*Wissenschaftliche Zeitschrift fuer juedische Theologie*, 1835) when he wrote: "Salvation lies not in the violent and reckless excision of everything which has descended to us from the past, but in the careful search into its deeper meaning, and in the aim to continue to develop historically from that which has grown historically… much which is now believed and observed is not tradition… but is a product of a certain age, and therefore can be removed by time." Geiger frequently quoted rabbinic sources to justify the abolition of rituals which he deemed a hindrance to "true" religion. This qualified appeal to talmudic tradition is reflected in Michael Creizenach's statement that the unanimous decisions of the Talmud are to be regarded as binding. In a case of divided opinion, "we follow the less strict version so long as it does not contradict our own conviction." The Breslau Synod of Reform Rabbis (1846) centered on the question of modifying Sabbath observance in the light of changed social and economic conditions. The participants buttressed their views by frequent citations from the Talmud and the standard rabbinic codes. The attitude finds expression in the declaration of David *Einhorn, which reflected the position of the majority of Reform rabbis of his age (1839): "We address the Talmud in these words, 'Israel believes thee, but not in thee; thou art a medium through which the divine may be reached but thou art not the divine.'"

This trend of introducing changes in current religious practice on the basis of halakhic precedent interpreted in liberal fashion met with strong dissent within the ranks of early Reform Judaism itself in the person of Samuel *Holdheim, one of the dominant personalities of the movement. He may be said to have spiritually fathered the anti-halakhic stance that marked the second phase of the development of Reform Judaism. His views were set forth in his book *Das Ceremonialgesetz in Messiasreich* (1845). According to Holdheim, the basic purpose of the ritual law was to safeguard the holiness of the people of Israel in a pagan world. As paganism vanishes, the ritual laws are needed less and less, and with the arrival of the messianic age they will become totally superfluous. "The time has to come when one feels strong enough vis-à-vis the Talmud to oppose it, in the knowledge of having gone beyond it." Accordingly, Holdheim advocated the abolition of circumcision and changing the Sabbath to Sunday. David Einhorn, deeply influenced by Holdheim, limited the authority of the Talmud to those aspects which were attributable to the Men of the Great Assembly.

The anti-halakhic mood of Reform Judaism, a minor strain in the incipient stage of the movement, gained increasing ascendancy as the 19th century progressed and the major scene of the Reform movement's activity shifted to the United States. Bernard Felsenthal summed up the dominant mood of most of his colleagues toward the *halakhah*: "There is but one class of laws biblical or post-biblical which have eternal validity and these are the moral laws engraved by the finger of God with ineradicable letters in the spirit and nature of man" (*Kol Kore Be-Midbar*, no. 11, 1858). The official attitude of 19th-century American Reform Judaism found expression in the platform adopted in 1885 by the Conference of Reform Rabbis in Pittsburgh. The fourth paragraph of the platform reads in part: "We hold that all such Mosaic and rabbinical laws as regulate diet, priestly purity and dress originated in ages and under the influence of ideas entirely foreign to our present mental and spiritual state… their observance in our day is apt rather to obstruct than to further modern spiritual elevation." In this spirit, the annual meeting of the Central Conference of American Rabbis (CCAR) in 1892 declared that no initiatory rite (circumcision, ritual immersion) was required for admission into Judaism. In his work *Jewish Theology* (1928) Kaufman *Kohler formulated the position of this second phase of Reform Judaism in these words: "To them (the prophets) and to us the real Torah is the unwritten moral law which underlies the precepts of both the written law and its moral interpretation" (p. 45). "It [the Oral Law] fostered hair-splitting casuistry and caused the petrifaction of religion in the codified Halakhah" (p. 47).

In the past few decades, Reform Judaism has displayed a sharp veering away from the anti-halakhic spirit described above. The depreciation of the Shulḥan Arukh and other legal works characteristic of discussions on the subject as reported in the early *Annuals of the CCAR* have been replaced by regret that Reform Judaism lacks the sense of *halakhah* (Introd. to *Current Reform Responsa*, Solomon B. Freehof, 1969). Repeatedly, in the recent past, the demand for a specific code of practice has been raised. Though opposed to the formulation of a binding code for Reform religious practice, Solomon B. Freehof has been active, as chairman of the Responsa Committee of the CCAR, in responding to questions relating to Reform religious practice. While written in the style of traditional responsa, citing the recognized codes and legal authorities, the answers given are intended, with a few exceptions, to be merely advisory in nature. The turn toward traditional practice in Reform congregations is to be seen in the reintroduction of the bar mitzvah, calling to the Torah (*aufrufen*), *Havdalah*, etc. The revision of the anti-halakhic attitude of classic Reform Judaism is a process whose outcome can hardly be anticipated at this writing, but that it is one of the major concerns of contemporary Reform Judaism is evidenced by the prominent place it occupies in Reform thought and writing.

Attitude of Conservative Judaism

Zacharias *Frankel's demonstrative withdrawal from the Synod of Reform Rabbis (Frankfurt, 1845) and his enunciation of Positive-Historical Judaism are regarded as the point of departure for the subsequent founding of the distinct trend in modern Judaism commonly known as *Conservative. The doctrine of Positive-Historical Judaism received considerable elaboration by Solomon *Schechter, who regarded himself as a disciple of Frankel, Leopold Zunz, and Heinrich Graetz when he wrote: "It is neither Scripture nor primitive Judaism but general custom which forms the real rule of practice… Liberty was always given to the great teachers of every generation to make modifications and innovations in harmony with the spirit of existing institutions. The norm as well as the sanction of Judaism is the practice actually in vogue. Its consecration is the consecration of general use or, in other words, of Catholic Israel" (*Studies in Judaism*, 1 (1896), 17–19). While the ideological leaders of Reform Judaism interpreted the thesis of the Oral Law's historical conditioning as implying its dispensability, for Schechter and his disciples the thesis, originally propounded by the Wissenschaft Des *Judentums, served as one of the touchstones of the authority of the Oral Law. The divergence in viewpoint is to be attributed to the preponderant weight ascribed to tradition by the spokesmen of Conservative Judaism. In contrast to Orthodoxy, the divine origin of the Oral Law as the basis of its authority is interpreted in Conservative circles in non-literalistic fashion (see Robert Gordis, in *Tradition and Change*, ed. by Mordecai Waxman (1958), 377ff.). The frequent appeals for loyalty to the Oral Law to be found in the writings of Schechter ("It – Judaism – insists upon the observance both of the spirit and the letter… Judaism is absolutely incompatible with the abandonment of the Torah" (*Seminary Addresses and Other Papers* (1915), 21–22).) find their final validation in the fact that Jewish religious usage had won acceptance from the religious conscience of the overwhelming majority of the Jewish people (the concept of Catholic Israel).

Louis *Ginzberg viewed *halakhah* as constituting the mainstream of Judaism. Through his teaching and writings, he made the *halakhah* one of the central concerns of Conservative Judaism, always insisting, however, that the *halakhah* of the Talmud constituted an organic growth that retained its vitality by reason of its responsiveness to changing locale, and social and economic conditions. Yet, with a single exception – a responsum on the permissibility of the use of grape juice for sacramental purposes during the prohibition era in America – he proved reluctant to apply his theoretical understanding of the *halakhah* to the exigent problems of Jewish life in the 20th century. (For the responsum in English translation, see AJYB, 25 (1923–24), 401–25.)

The practical implications of this approach to the *halakhah* underlay the work of the Committee on Jewish Law of the Rabbinical Assembly. Established in 1927, it has issued a large number of halakhic decisions recorded in brief or in detail in the annual Proceedings of the Rabbinical Assembly. Prior to 1948, none of these decisions reflected any significant departure from traditional Orthodox practice. In 1948, the annual convention of the Rabbinical Assembly rejected a proposal that its Committee on Jewish Law "shall be instructed to hold itself bound by the authority of Jewish law and within the frame of Jewish law to labor toward progress and growth of the law to the end of adjusting it to present-day religious needs and orientation, whether it be on the side of severity or leniency." The defeat of the proposal was motivated by a desire on the part of the majority to reckon with non-halakhic factors, such as contemporary social realities and moral standards, in determining the point of view of Conservative Judaism on any specific question. Hence, in 1949 the concept was formally accepted that "decisions of the Law Committee shall be presented in the form of a traditional responsum indicating its relationship to relevant halakhic and other material."

To reflect this change in basic position, the name of the committee was changed to Committee on Jewish Law and Standards. It was reorganized and increased to 23 members, so as to offer representation for the diversity of viewpoint to be found among members of the Rabbinical Assembly. A rule of procedure was adopted whereby a member of the Rabbinical Assembly could accept either the majority or minority view of the committee. In instances where decisions were unanimous, such decisions were to be regarded as binding. Two responsa were published by the committee on Sabbath observance, in the course of which divergent views were expressed on the permissibility of riding to attend synagogue service on the Sabbath in instances where one lived beyond reasonable walking distance and the use of electricity on the Sabbath for purposes of illumination (for the responsa in question, see *Tradition and Change*, ed. by M. Waxman (1958), 349–409). To obviate the problem of the *agunah, a woman who though divorced civilly cannot obtain a *get* (writ of divorcement), the Joint Law Conference of the Rabbinical Assembly and the Jewish Theological Seminary adopted in 1954 a *takkahah* (enactment) to be inserted in the *ketubbah* (marriage document). Latterly, the committee has adopted, and in specific instances exercised, the long-dormant halakhic principle of *hafka'at kiddushin* (annullment) where, for one or another circumstance, the writing of the traditional *get* is impossible. Another halakhic decision of far-reaching consequence is that of rendering the observance of *Yom Tov Sheni* (the second days of the three festivals) a matter of option to be exercised by the rabbi of the local congregation (some members of the committee vigorously dissented on the decision; see *Conservative Judaism*, 24, no. 2 (1970), 21–59). Various responsa by the committee are to be found in the annual *Proceedings of the Rabbinical Assembly* and deal with such matters as the use of the organ on Sabbaths and festivals, the use of gentile wine (*yayin nesekh*), the donation after death of the cornea of the eyes for purposes of transplant, ritual circumcision by a Jewish physician, cremation, synagogue membership for a Jew who has intermarried, etc.

[Theodore Friedman]

BIBLIOGRAPHY: N. Krochmal, *Moreh Nevukhei ha-Zeman*, in: S. Rawidowicz, *Kitvei Rabbi Naḥman Krochmal* (1924), 189–93; W. Bacher, *Die exegetische Terminologie der juedischen Traditionsliteratur*, 1 (1889), 89f., 197; S. Kaatz, *Die muendliche Lehre und ihr Dogma* (1922–23); J. Heinemann, in: HUCA, 4 (1927), 149–72; Y. Kaufmann, *Golah ve-Nekhar* (1929–32), index s.v. *Torah*; H. Tchernowitz, *Toledot ha-Halakkah*, 1 (1934), 1–10, 67–136, 197–324; E.E. Urbach, in: *Tarbiz*, 17 (1945/46), 1–11; 18 (1946/47), 1–27; 27 (1957/58), 166–82; idem, Ḥazal, *Pirkei Emunot ve-De'ot* (1969), 254–78; G.F. Moore, *Judaism*, 1 (1927), 251–80; 3 (1930), 73–88; Z.H. Chajes, *Kol Sifrei… Ḥayyot*, 1 (1958), 1–176, 283–91; Ḥ. Albeck, *Mavo la-Mishnah* (1959), 3f.; B. De Vries, *Hoofdlijnen en Motieven in de Ontwikkeling der Halachah* (1959); M.D. Herr, in: J. Eisner (ed.), *Hagut ve-Halakhah* (1968), 131–44. ATTITUDE OF REFORM JUDAISM: D. Philipson, *Reform Movement in Judaism* (1928); W.G. Plaut, *Rise of Reform Judaism* (1963); idem, *Growth of*

Reform Judaism (1965); idem, in: *Contemporary Jewish Thought*, ed. by B. Martin (1968); J. Petuchowski, *ibid.*; S.B. Freehof, *Current Reform Responsa* (1968); E. Mihaly, in: CCAR Annual, 44 (1954), 214–26; A. Guttman, *ibid.*, 48 (1958), 246–55. ATTITUDE OF CONSERVATIVE JUDAISM: B. Cohen, *Law and Tradition in Judaism* (1959); M. Davis, *Emergence of Conservative Judaism* (1963); H. Parzen, *Architects of Conservative Judaism* (1964); S. Dresner, in: *Conservative Judaism*, 16 no. 1 (1961), 1–27; S. Greenberg, *ibid.*, 19 no. 1 (1964), 36–50; D. Aronson, *ibid.*, 26 no. 1 (1969), 34–48.

ORAN (Ar. **Waharan**), seaport on the Mediterranean coast, the second largest city in *Algeria and a key trading and industrial center. Oran as a city (and an administrative unit or region since the 1870s known as a *department*), is located in western Algeria and is contiguous to the border with *Morocco at a point where Algeria is closest to the Spanish coast. Oran was founded in the 10th century by Andalusian merchants and incorporated into the Kingdom of Tlemcen, serving as its main seaport since the 15th century.

Jews began settling the area mainly in 1391, when they arrived there as refugees from Spain (first wave of expulsion). This population swelled in 1492 and 1502, when Oran afforded refuge to Jewish and Muslim expellees from Spain in the wake of the fall of Granada. As was the case with other parts of the Maghreb in the Atlantic and Mediterranean coasts, where Spanish and Portuguese influences became supreme, the Spaniards conquered Oran in 1509. Initially the Spanish forces were inclined to expel the Jews from the city, but refrained from doing so in the final analysis. For the next 300 years or more Spain and its colonists remained in control of Oran. Although Jews had been forced to leave Spain (after 1492), the Spanish authorities in Oran learned to tolerate local Jewry and some of the latter engaged in influential trade activity, until the 1760s

In 1669 or 1670, however, the Spanish Queen Maria of Austria expelled the overwhelming majority of the Jews of Oran and its environs. The expellees resettled in Nice, then under the suzerainty of the Dukes of Savoy; from there they made their way to Italian Livorno and reinforced the thriving community that existed there. Jews did return to Oran at the beginning of the 18th century, when the Muslims, led by the Bey of Mascara, captured the city from the Spaniards. But the Spaniards regained control of the area in the 1730s, although this time there was no indication that Jews were barred from Oran. Spanish rule lingered into the last decade of the 18th century and abandoned it in the wake of a devastating earthquake of the early 1790s. Authority passed once again to Muslim hands. This "restoration" period proved advantageous to the Jews. The Muslim authorities now invited Jews from nearby Mostaganem, Mascara, and Nedrona to settle in Oran. The arrival from Morocco of additional Jews only strengthened the Jewish community, transforming it into the second largest Algerian community after Algiers. Many among the Jews plunged into trade activity between the port of Oran and British-controlled Gibraltar, Malaga, and Almeria, as well as Italy and France.

The Jewish community was presided over by a *mukkadem*, or **nagid*, an administrative head. His functions were diversified by local leaders (**parnassim* or *tovei ha-ir*). All disputes among Jews, including marriages and divorce, were decided by the *dayyanim* (religious judges), the noted exception being criminal matters or disputes between Muslims and Jews, which were referred to the Muslim *Shari'a* courts run by the *qadis*. By then the Ottoman Empire was well entrenched in Algeria, in charge of parts of *Algiers and Oran.

Ottoman Turkish rule collapsed in 1830 following the French conquest of Algeria. The French administration gradually removed the Jews from the jurisdiction of both the Muslim and Jewish courts, in the latter case including matters relating to personal status. This applied to Oran. The community of Oran, like those in the regions of Algiers and *Constantine, was administered from the 1840s by a consistoire, a new communal administrative apparatus modeled on the French-Jewish community leadership bodies. The consistoire, which encouraged Jews to modernize, orient themselves to new professions such as agriculture, and send their children to French-type schools, was led by a president and a dozen lay and rabbinic leaders elected by local notables.

From the French occupation of 1830 until France achieved stability over its domination of Algeria (the 1870s), the Jewish community of Oran thrived and its synagogues mushroomed throughout the region. In addition to *talmudei torah* religious schools, French schools emerged in the community as early as the late 1840s, while in subsequent years Jewish youths frequented French public schools. This was all the more so once France granted Algerian Jewry French citizenship collectively in the spirit of the Crémieux Decree of October 24, 1870. Jews could now serve in the French army and participate in local municipal elections as well as elections to choose local representatives among the European settlers to the French parliament. The Muslims shunned French privileges of naturalization fearing it would run counter to their religious obligations and personal status matters ingrained in the *Shari'a*. It was then that the local Jewish press in the French language had its inception, though Oran's Jews still continued to disseminate publications in Hebrew and Judeo-Arabic as well.

During the latter half of the 19th century, Oran's Jewry consisted of a heterogeneous population that included indigenous Jews who originated from Mascara, Mostaganem, and Tlemcen. They were reinforced by immigrants from Algiers and Moroccan Jews – émigrés from the mountainous Rif area in northern Morocco, and other northern and western Moroccan regions such as *Tetuan, Figuig, Tafilalet, Oujda, and Debdou. Oran's Jews spoke a variety of jargons, among them Moroccan Judeo-Arabic (a mélange of Hebrew, Arabic, and Aramaic expressions), Algerian Judeo-Arabic, and Tetuani Judeo-Spanish known as Hakitia – resembling somewhat the Ladino of Sephardi Jews in *Turkey, the Balkans, and *Egypt. Increasingly, however, French became the dominant language among Oran's Jews after World War I.

Until modernization crept in after World War I, Jews engaged in the traditional occupations of crafts and worked as tailors, goldsmiths, carpenters, and shoemakers. By the 1950s numerous Jews had entered the liberal professions. Others established themselves as large-scale merchants and exporters of cereals and cattle to Spanish Malaga and Algeciras, British-controlled Gibraltar, and France.

The Dreyfus Affair and later manifestations of an antisemitic nature in metropolitan France affected the Jews of Oran and the rest of French Algeria. These led to riots and assaults on Jews and their properties. The emergence of the Vichy regime in France (1940) meant that pro-German French influences extended to that country's colonial possessions. Algerian Jews, including those of Oran, were subjected to discriminatory racial laws, stringent quotas in government employment, expulsion of their students and teachers from the public schools, and the temporary abrogation of the Crémieux Decree, leaving the Jews without citizenship status. After the liberation of Algeria by Allied Forces in November 1942, the Crémieux Decree was reestablished. Then, in November 1954, the Algerian war of Muslims against lingering French colonial rule placed the Jews of Oran, Algiers, and Constantine between the hammer and the anvil. They were placed in the awkward position of having to choose between support for the Muslims or for the French. They chose neutrality, even though it was quite evident to the Muslim rebels that deep in their hearts the Jews remained loyal to France and to its colonial policies. From spring 1956 until France granted Algeria national independence in July 1962, the situation of the Jews deteriorated and they were frequent victims of violence. In 1962, of the nearly 30,000 Jews in Oran (out of some 140,000 Algerian Jews), the great majority emigrated to France with only several thousand at the very most making *aliyah*. In 1963, a year after Algeria's independence, only 850 Jews dwelt in the region of Oran. The Great Synagogue, the most impressive symbol of the Oran community, was transformed into a mosque in the mid-1970s. By 2005, there were apparently no Jews left there.

BIBLIOGRAPHY: R. Ayoun, "Problématique des conflits internes de la communauté juive: Simon Kanoui, président du Consistoire Israélite d'Oran," in: *Congress of Jewish Studies in Jerusalem*, 9, B3 (1986), 75–82; J.I. Israel, "The Jews of Spanish Oran and Their Expulsion in 1669," in: *Mediterranean Historical Review*, 9:2 (1994), 235–55; M.M. Laskier, *North African Jewry in the Twentieth Century: The Jews of Morocco, Tunisia, and Algeria* (1994); *Museum of the Jewish People: Bet ha-Tefutsoth: The Database of Jewish Communities: The Jewish Community of Oran, Algeria*; G. Nahon, "Le Consistoire Israélite d'Ooran et le décret du 16 septembre 1867: documents et correspondances," in: *Michael*, 5 (1978), 98–129; J.-F. Schaub, *Les Juifs du Roi d'Espagne* (1999); S. Schwarzfuchs, *Les Juifs d'Algérie et la France 1830–1855* (1981).

[Michael M. Laskier (2nd ed.)]

ORANGE, previously a principality and later a town in Vaucluse department, S.E. France. The earliest evidence of the presence of Jews in Orange dates from 1282 and in the locality of Courthézon from 1328, at the latest. In 1353 Raymond V, prince of Orange, granted the Jews of his principality a charter which in effect constituted a series of privileges which were remarkable, indeed almost exceptional, for the 14th century. Even before Raymond's time, however, some precedent had been set in this direction by other princes of Orange, who had, for example, already employed Jews as toll collectors. Because of these favorable conditions, a constant stream of Jews came from *Comtat Venaissin to Orange, among them the physician Durand de Cavaillon who arrived there in 1387. This situation lasted until the latter half of the 15th century. In 1477 the municipal council sought to remove Jews from the grain trade in which they were engaged in addition to moneylending (Jews frequently acted as brokers for the wealthy burghers of Orange or for Italian financiers). When the council demanded the expulsion of the Jews in 1484, the prince of Orange refused unless the town could indemnify him for the taxes that would be lost by such an action. Jewish houses were openly attacked in 1490 and the expulsion was carried out in 1505.

On several occasions during the first half of the 17th century the parliament of Orange renewed the expulsion decree. Despite this, by 1643 several Jewish families had "clandestinely" resettled in Orange. Their numbers slowly increased, until by 1731 there were 21 families (16 in Orange, 4 in Courthézon, 1 in Jonquières). The new expulsion orders were only partially applied, and from 1774 on there was a massive influx of Jews from Comtat Venaissin. With the onset of the French Revolution, however, the departure of the Jews was almost as rapid. Using their newly acquired liberties, they left Orange for more important towns. In 1808 only 36 Jews remained in Orange and almost all of them bore the name Mossé. The Jewish community rapidly dissolved and was never reconstituted.

Several eminent scholars, particularly *Levi b. Gershom, lived in Orange for varying lengths of time. Another such scholar was Mordecai, also named En Crescas, or Ezobi, of Orange, who settled in Carcassonne toward the close of the 13th century. The surname Ezobi, borne by a large number of other scholars, points to a more or less distant origin in Orange. An anonymous scholar and translator of the late 12th century and one Gershon b. Hezekiah, author of medical books in the first half of the 15th century, are intimately connected with the town of Orange.

BIBLIOGRAPHY: Gross, Gal Jud, 18ff.; I. Loeb, in: REJ, 1 (1880), 72ff.; J. Bauer, *ibid.*, 32 (1896), 236ff.; D. Wolfson, *ibid.*, 57 (1909), 93ff.; H. Chabaut, *ibid.*, 100 (1936), 62ff.; L. Barthélemy, *Inventaire… Maison de Baux* (1882), index.

[Bernhard Blumenkranz]

ORANGE COUNTY, county in California, U.S. In 2005 there were some 3 million people living in Orange County, with the Jewish population estimated at 60,000–80,000.

Orange County Jewish communities include Orange, Anaheim, Santa Ana, Irvine, Yorba Linda, Garden Grove, Laguna Beach, Laguna Hills, Huntington Beach, Tustin, Fountain Valley, Newport Beach, Westminster, Fullerton, Mission

Viejo, and Costa Mesa. Most Jews live in Irvine, Newport Beach, Mission Viejo, and Aliso Viejo.

Southern California or California Southland Jewry is an interrelated community in Santa Barbara, Ventura, Los Angeles, Orange, Riverside, San Bernardino, Imperial, and San Diego counties. In climate, water supply, politics, agriculture and industry it differs from the rest of California. Rivalry has long existed between the northern and southern areas of California. There is a virtual seamlessness between Orange County and neighboring Los Angeles. It seems at points like one endless community.

The primary motivation for settlement in Southern California was not a search for religious freedom but economic opportunity. Many Jews who came to the Southland in the early days had first gone to San Francisco, from which place Jews quickly dispersed throughout the entire American and Canadian West. The Gold Rush brought Jews to Southern California more for trade and agriculture than for mining. The area was known in biblical language as the place of "cattle on a thousand hills."

French Jews were perhaps 10% of all the Jews who arrived during the Gold Rush decades. They came from Alsace, Marseilles, and Paris. Among them were Algerian Jews such as Hippolyte Cohen in Anaheim in 1878.

In the beginning of the 20th century Sephardi Jews from the island of Rhodes immigrated to Southern California. Other Sephardim arrived during the 1910s and 1920s. Most of the newcomers did not speak English, but the Ladino they spoke was close to the Mexican Spanish of California. Sephardi Jews generally moved first to Seattle, Washington, then later on to California.

Orange County Jewry began in the 1870s. Santa Ana was platted in 1870, and in 1872 Jews were located there as merchants. In 1876 the first Jew reached Tustin. The community of Anaheim was quiet in 1880 when Jewish stores were closed for Rosh Hashanah, the local press reported. In the early period the best known Jewish citizen of Orange County was Benjamin Dreyfus, the vintner, general agriculturalist, and mayor of Anaheim in 1881 and 1882. Three Jews held the first High Holy Day services in 1874. In that year Jews were also found in the nearby mission town of San Juan Capistrano. Santa Ana and Tustin Jewry – 25 families in all – began establishing a congregation in 1919, to meet the needs of their children for Jewish education.

From the 1930s onward there has been a massive influx of population to Southern California, and Orange County has benefited from the post-World War II development of the region as well as the movement of major corporations and hi-tech industries to Southern California. Jewish life was stimulated by a large influx of British, Canadian, Israeli, Latin American, North African, Russian, South African, and Iranian Jews, who established their own organizations as well as integrating into the older communities. A large number of Hungarian Jews reached the Southland after the Soviets crushed the movement to liberalization in that country in 1956. Iranian Jews have sent their children to all-day schools and have a higher rate of synagogue affiliation than the average. Russian and Israeli non-Orthodox immigrants tend to be High Holiday Jews.

The Merage Jewish Community Center, one of the largest in the United States, with its impressive community campus in Irvine, is an important presence in the community. The Federation sponsors all the activities of a Jewish Federation, including a Board of Jewish Education and the Jewish Family Service.

Synagogue life is local and Jews are spread throughout the county, but communal life is concentrated in the areas of greatest populations.

There are 35 synagogues in Orange County of every denomination. There are Conservative congregations in several cities: B'nai Israel in Tustin, Congregation Eilat in Mission Viejo, Surf City Synagogue of Huntington Beach, Temple Beth Emet of Anaheim, Temple Isaiah of Newport Beach, Temple Judea of Laguna Woods. Reform congregations are also found throughout the county: B'nai Tzedek in Fountain Valley, Congregation Kol HaNeshamah in Irvine, Congregation Shir Ha Ma'alot also in Irvine, Temple Bat Yahm in Newport Beach, Temple Beth David in Westminster, Temple Beth El of South Orange County in Aliso Viejo, Temple Beth Ohr in La Mirada, Temple Beth Sholom in Santa Ana, Temple Beth Tikvah/Adat Ari in Fullerton. There are Orthodox Congregations: Beth Jacob Cong. of Irvine, Beth Torah Synagogue of Laguna Hills that meets at Leisure World, which also hosts a Reform Congregation.

Chabad has established a presence in Costa Mesa, Huntington Beach, Irvine, Laguna Beach, Los Alamitos, Mission Viejo, Newport Beach, San Clemente, Tustin, and Yorba Linda. The Sephardi community maintains Ohr Yisrael Sephardic Congregation of Orange County in Irvine.

Rabbi Arnold Rachlis, a former White House Fellow and a leading voice in the Reconstructionist movement, is the rabbi of University Synagogue in Irvine, the sole Reconstructionist congregation and one of the largest synagogues in Orange County.

Secular Humanists are represented in Pacific Community of Secular Humanistic Jews and Society of Humanistic Judaism. There is also a non-denominational Congregation Kol Simcha for Gay and Lesbian Jews.

There are three day schools in the community: Tarbut V'Torah Community Day School in Irvine, the Hebrew Academy in Huntington Beach, and the Morasha Day School in Rancho Santa Margarita.

Among the national organizations that have established offices in Orange County are the American Jewish Committee (AJC) and the Anti-Defamation League (ADL), which have a large presence. The American Israel Public Affairs Committee (AIPAC) and B'nai B'rith Youth Organization are also present.

Hillel serves all the campuses in Orange County, including UC Irvine, Chapman University, Cal State Fullerton, and the surrounding colleges. Chapman University has a strong Holocaust education program that not only serves the campus but the community at large and sponsors annual activities in the schools, including a writing contest and teacher training. It recently established a Holocaust Center, sponsored by the Samueli Family, local philanthropists, in its new library, including a small display of Holocaust artifacts.

Heritage Pointe provides care for the elderly.

Although Jews are an accepted part of Orange County life, the county used to have the reputation of being the center of significant antisemitism. In the late 1970s, The Institute for Historical Review, a Holocaust denial organization, once posted a $50,000 reward for anyone who could prove that the Holocaust happened. Much to their chagrin, Auschwitz survivor and Newport Beach resident Mel Mermelstein took up the challenge and prevailed in court. Mermelstein went against the common advice of the Jewish professional community to quarantine the hate groups and not to engage in discourse. The case drew national attention and was the subject of a television movie. Several mayors have been Jewish; two in Irvine and others in Orange County.

[Michael Berenbaum and Arnold Rachlis (2nd ed.)]

ORANIT (Heb. אֳרָנִית), urban settlement in Samaria. It is located on the western slopes of the Samarian Hills, northeast of *Petaḥ Tikva, and southeast of *Kefar Sava. Oranit was established by private initiative authorized by the government. In 1985 the first settlers arrived. In 1990 it received municipal council status. In 2002 the population was 5,190, occupying 0.65 sq. mi. (1.750 sq. km.). Residents work outside the settlement. The name of the settlement derives from the pine (Heb. *oren*) forests nearby.

[Shaked Gilboa (2nd ed.)]

ORDEAL, the generic term for the various ways and means by which divine judgment would be ascertained. The most common form of ordeal, which survived long into the Middle Ages and beyond, was entirely unknown to biblical as well as to later Jewish law: namely, the exposing of an accused person to physical dangers which were supposed to be harmless to him if he were innocent but which were considered conclusive proof of divine condemnation if he suffered harm. The only remnant of this kind of ordeal may be found in the *Ordeal of Jealousy. It is an early talmudic tradition (Sot. 9:9) that these "waters of bitterness" ceased to be effective when adulterers proliferated. Traces of a similar ordeal by water may be found in the water that Moses made the Israelites drink after he had sprinkled it with powder ground from the golden calf (Ex. 32:20), the talmudic tradition being that this was the method used to detect the guilty. Another widespread method of ascertaining God's judgment was the curse. A written curse had first to be erased into the "water of bitterness" to be swallowed by the woman suspected of adultery (Num. 5:23), so that either the curse or the water or both could be instrumental in the ordeal. The curse is interchangeable with, and a forerunner of, the *oath: he who takes the oath before God (cf. Ex. 22:7–8, 10) brings God's curse on himself if he perjures himself (cf. I Kings 8:31–32; II Chron. 6:22–23). On hearing the oath sworn at His altar, God judges – condemning the wicked and justifying the righteous (see also Zech. 5:3–4; et al.). There is a statement that when atonement was made for general sinfulness (Lev. 16:21–22), God would, by changing red into white, reveal His forgiveness, or by not changing the color indicate unforgiveness (Yoma 6:8; 67a). In many instances, God's judgment was, of course, executed directly, manifesting itself in the very act of divine punishment (e.g., Num. 16:5–7, 31–35; Deut. 11:6; I Kings 18:38).

BIBLIOGRAPHY: J. Kohler, in: *Zeitschrift fuer vergleichende Rechtswissenschaft*, 5 (1884), 368–76; J.G. Frazer, *Folklore in the Old Testament*, 3 (1919), 304–414; J. Morgenstern, in: HUCA *Jubilee Volume 1875–1925* (1925), 113–43; R. Press, in: ZAW, 51 (1933), 121–40, 227–55; ET (1951³), 182–5; EM, 1 (1950), 179–83; 5 (1968), 1003f.

[Haim Hermann Cohn]

ORDEAL OF JEALOUSY. According to Numbers 5:11–31, a woman suspected of adultery that cannot be legally proved is to be brought by her husband to the priest for an ordeal of jealousy. The priest takes "holy water" (according to Sot. 2:2, from the laver) and mixes into it some earth from the floor of the Tabernacle. He then assures the woman that if she is innocent she will be immune to harm from the water, but warns her that if guilty her "belly shall distend" from the potion and "her thigh sag" (the exact sense is unknown). After this adjuration, he writes down the oath, dissolves the writing in the water, and makes the woman drink of it. Accordingly, the water is called *mayim me'arerim*, "the water that induces the spell." The ordeal has to be accompanied by a meal offering of a specific type. It is composed of barley without oil and frankincense (cf. Lev. 5:11) and is called "an offering of remembrance which recalls wrongdoing" (Num. 5:15).

Critical View

The law in its present form contains repetitions (16b = 18a, 19a = 21a, 21b = 22a, 24a = 26b = 27a), which appear to be redundant, and seeming inconsistencies. Thus verse 21, inserted between the protasis and apodosis, disrupts the adjuration, while verse 24, which prescribes giving the drink before offering the meal (5:25), contradicts the express order of verse 26. These inconsistencies are reflected in the Mishnah. Whether the meal offering precedes drinking the water, as stated in verse 26, or the drinking comes before the meal offering, as in verses 24–25, is a matter of dispute (Sot. 3:2). Moreover, the interpolation in verse 21a gave rise to a disagreement over the extent of the written oath (Sot. 2:3). According to R. Judah, the priest had to write down only the oath appearing in verses 21–22; according to R. Yose, all of verses 19–22 had to be written; the prevailing opinion, however, is that the priest wrote down the adjuration of verses 19, 20, and 22 and the oath in verse 21 without the introductory directions concerning the priest (*we-hishbiaʿ ha-Kohen et ha-ʾishah*) and the woman (*we-ʾamerah ha-ʾishahʾ amen*, 22).

These textual difficulties suggest that two literary strands have been interwoven in this chapter. One strand prescribed only an oral conditional adjuration (5:19–20, 22), whereas the other prescribed the recital of a curse and its writing, and the dissolving of the written curse in the water (5:21, 23). The latter strand also prescribed the offering of the meal (5:15, 25–26). The beginning of verse 27 is an editorial resumption (*Wiederaufnahme*) of verse 24, necessitated by the interpolation of verses 25–26. There is no way of deciding which of the two strands is original or earlier. It may be that the author had both before him when he composed the law. Yet the strand prescribing the writing of the curse shows signs of more advanced religious conceptions. God is made responsible for the curse (5:21), whereas according to the other source the water itself induces it (5:22). Furthermore, the word of God is made the agency of the curse, in the form of the writing dissolved in the water.

An ancient water ordeal consisting of an oral adjuration but no written oath is attested in a Mari text (Archives Royales de Mari, x, no. 9, lines 9–15). A heavenly scene is described in which a command is given to dissolve some earth from the gate in water and give it to drink to the (minor) gods who take an oath not to harm (or betray) Mari and its commissioner. Another analogue is found in the so-called "Hittite instructions for the temple officials." Somebody suspected of having used up the firstlings before giving them to the gods has to "drink the horn of the god of life"; if he is found guilty he will perish together with his family (Sturtevant-Bechtel in bibl., 164–165, no. 18, 4:52–53). In Mesopotamia a water ordeal consisted of being thrown into the river: the guilty sank, the innocent floated (cf. Code of Hammurapi; in Pritchard, Texts, 166, law 2). A similar procedure is attested in a letter from Mari where two suspected persons are to be submitted to the ordeal by river (see Dossin in bibl.). The river ordeal is actually applied in Mesopotamia to the case of jealousy. Thus the Code of Hammurapi (Pritchard, Texts, 171, law 132) states that "if a finger has been pointed at a married woman with regard to another man and she is not caught lying with the other man she shall leap into the river for her husband." The specification of "not being caught lying with the other man" is instructive for the understanding of the Hebrew clause: *we-hiʾ loʾ nitpasah* (Num. 5:13b). The Babylonian parallel inclines the balance in favor of the rendering "she had not been caught in the act" (cf. Ibn Ezra to 5:13b) rather than "she had not been forced" (cf. Rashi to 5:13b).

BIBLIOGRAPHY: R. Press, in: ZAW, 51 (1933), 122–6; E.H. Sturtevant and G. Bechtel, *A Hittite Chrestomathy* (1935), 164–5; G.R. Driver and J. Miles, *The Babylonian Laws*, 1 (1952), 63–65, 284; G. Dossin, in: *Comptes rendus Académie des Inscriptions et Belles-Lettres* (1958), 387ff.; W.L. Moran, in: *Biblica*, 50 (1969), 50–52.

[Moshe Weinfeld]

ORDMAN, JEANNETTE, Israeli ballet dancer and teacher; director of the Bat-Dor Dance Company and school. Born in Germiston, South Africa, her family moved to Johannesburg where she studied dance with Reina Berman and later with Marjorie Sturman, founder of the Johannesburg Festival Ballet (which became the Pact Ballet). She was still in her teens when Anton Dolin who had come to advise on dance selected her to dance the title role in *Giselle*.

Moving to London, she danced with the Sadler's Wells Opera Ballet and on television. In 1965 she went to Israel as principal dancer of a touring company. When the tour ended abruptly, she opened a studio. Her dancing had already made an impression and pupils flocked to her. At that time Batsheva de Rothschild, who had settled in Israel in 1958 and founded the Batsheva Dance Company in 1964, was looking for a suitable director to open a dance school. With her friend Martha Graham, then visiting Israel, she saw Ordman's classes. The result was the opening of the Bat-Dor Dance School in 1967 and of the Bat-Dor Dance Company in 1968, with Ordman as director and principal dancer.

From then on, the studio grew in importance and the company is one of the major dance companies in Israel and has toured widely. It was the first professional Israeli company to go to Poland (1987) and to Russia (1989).

After her great success in the Polish tour, Ordman developed hip trouble. After two operations, she made a successful comeback (1989) in Rodney Griffin's *Piaf Vaudeville*. She was invited a number of times to serve on the jury of the International Ballet Competition at Jackson, Mississippi (held every fourth year).

[Dora Leah Sowden]

ORDZHONIKIDZE (until 1932 **Vladikavkaz**; 1944–54 **Dzaudzhikau**), capital of the N. Ossetian Autonomous Republic in the Russian Federation. The city is situated in the N. Caucasus. In 1784 the Russian government erected a fortress which dominated the road crossing the Caucasus; from the 1830s there were always some Jewish soldiers in the fortress and it was, in fact, demobilized soldiers who founded the community. A prayer room was erected in 1865, and about 10 years later authorization for the construction of a synagogue was obtained. A community of Subbotniki (*Judaizers) also existed in the town. During the 1890s the administration began to oppress the Jews. There were 1,214 Jews (about 2.8% of the total population) in 1897, in 1926 about 1,000 (1.3% of the population), and 1,517 (1.16% of the total) in 1939. When the Germans invaded the Soviet Union, they were brought to a halt on the outskirts of the town, so the Jewish inhabitants were saved. In 1959 about 2,000 Jews lived in the town.

[Yehuda Slutsky]

OREB AND ZEEB (Heb. עֹרֵב, עוֹרֵב, "raven"; זְאֵב, "wolf"), two Midianite princes captured by the Ephraimites during a battle led by Gideon the judge (Judg. 7:25; 8:1–3). To commemorate the event, the places where the capture occurred were called "The Rock of Oreb" (Ẓur Orev) and "The Winepress of Zeeb" (Yekev Ze'ev). Their exact location is uncertain. The narrative relates that the two princes were decapitated and their heads brought across the Jordan to Gideon, apparently as testimony to the great valor and glory of the Ephraimites (7:25; 8:2–3). The defeat and execution of Oreb and Zeeb became proverbial as a paradigm for the annihilation of the enemies of Israel (Isa. 10:26; Ps. 83:11).

BIBLIOGRAPHY: Y. Kaufmann, in: *Tarbiz*, 30 (1960/61), 139–47 (Heb.), 45 (Eng. summary); A. Malamat, in: PEQ, 85 (1953), 61–65; C.F. Whitley, in: VT, 7 (1957), 157–64.

[Nili Shupak]

OREGON, Pacific N.W. state of the U.S. with some 35,000 Jews (out of a total of 3,594,586) according to 2004 figures. Jewish communal life in the Oregon Territory began with the arrival of Jacob Goldsmith and Lewis May, young German-born immigrants who opened a general store in Portland in 1849. Two years later, a thriving mining camp developed along southern Oregon's gold laden Jackson Creek. Within months, miners streamed northward from the Sacramento Valley bringing Jews, mostly from San Francisco. In 1852, seven Jewish residents were listed on the Jacksonville census, all young men involved in store keeping, supplying mining equipment, dry goods, and groceries. German Jews expanded their mercantile skills into Oregon's more remote areas by exploiting family networks, importing goods from associates in San Francisco or even New York, and then sending younger relatives to towns like Albany, Eugene, or The Dalles to open general stores.

The first Jewish arrivals emigrated from Germany to the U.S., followed by co-religionists originating from, successively, the Russian empire, the Isle of Rhodes, and Turkey. The greatest number came from the Russian empire beginning in the 1890s and made an impact on the already established German Jewish community. Most settled in Portland, where they found inexpensive housing, synagogues, and kosher groceries that helped to create a familiar community. Whereas the central European Jews integrated very quickly and expanded to smaller towns across the state, the first generation Eastern European Jews remained close-knit, residing primarily in Portland until the second generation. The Sephardim founded a synagogue in Portland in 1910, still existing today. Following the collapse of the Soviet Union in the 1980s, another wave of immigrants came to Oregon.

From the early years of settlement in Oregon, Jews despite their minute numbers distinguished themselves in prominent political, judicial, civic, business, and cultural positions: Solomon Hirsch, minister to Turkey; Joseph *Simon, Richard *Neuberger, Ron *Wyden (in 2005), U.S. senators; Julius *Meier, Neil *Goldschmidt, governors; Henry Heppner, founder of the town of Heppner; Samson Friendly, regent of the University of Oregon; Joseph Shemanski, Ben Selling, philanthropists; Gus Solomon, federal district court judge; Bernard Goldsmith, Philip Wasserman, Neil Goldschmidt and Vera Katz among at least 21 Jewish mayors; Stewart Albert, co-founder of the Yippie Movement. Russian-born artist Mark *Rothko (1903–1970) spent part of his youth in Portland; Dr. Albert Starr, inventor of the first artificial heart valve, performed the first successful valve implant in 1965; Bernard *Malamud taught at Oregon State University 1949–61; Phillip Margolin is a best-selling mystery writer. Mel *Blanc, the "Man of 1,000 Voices," was the voice of Bugs Bunny and other animated characters. In the field of music, Jacques Gershkovitch founded the Portland Junior Symphony (today the Portland Youth Philharmonic), succeeded by Jacob Avshalomov. Ernest *Bloch, who made Oregon his home, wrote his famous *Sacred Service* on the Oregon coast. Jacques Singer conducted the Oregon Symphony Orchestra and Carlos Kalmar was conductor in 2005; composer David Schiff taught at Reed College.

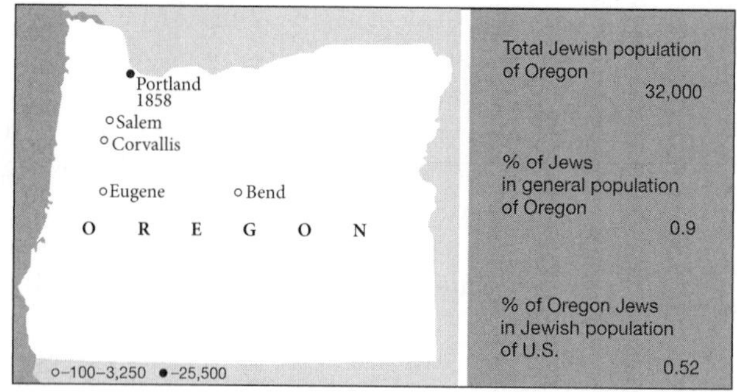

Jewish communities in Oregon with date of establishment. Population figures for 2001.

In 2005 Oregon had 36 congregations throughout the state, including Portland (17 congregations), Ashland, Bend, Corvallis Eugene, Klamath Falls, Roseburg and Salem, and the central and north coasts. Portland, Oregon's largest Jewish community, has two Jewish day schools, a Jewish Community Center, Jewish Federation, a Jewish facility for the elderly, a Jewish family counseling service, and the Oregon Jewish Museum. The Oregon Holocaust Resource Center is on the campus of Pacific University in Forest Grove. Jewish students participate in Hillel at the University of Oregon (Eugene) and Oregon State University (Corvallis), and Jewish Student Unions at Lewis and Clark College, Reed College and Portland State University. The University of Oregon, Portland State University and Reed College have Jewish Studies programs. Indeed, the president (in 2005) of the AJS taught at the University of Oregon.

[Judith Margles (2nd ed.)]

OREL, capital of a district in the Russian Federation. Orel lay outside the *Pale of Settlement. A small Jewish community was founded there during the second half of the 19th century; in 1876 it was authorized to build a synagogue. In 1897 the Jews of Orel numbered 1,750 (2.5% of the total population). Anti-Jewish riots broke out on Oct. 18, 1905, many were injured and shops looted. During World War I, many refugees from the battle areas came to the town. In 1926 there were 3,597 Jews (4.6% of the total population); and their number dropped slightly to 3,143 (2.84% of the total) in 1939. The Germans took the city on October 3, 1941. Most of the remaining Jews were killed in August–December 1942. The last were murdered during February–July 1943.

BIBLIOGRAPHY: B. West (ed.), *Be-Ḥevlei Kelayah* (1963), 52–54.

[Yehuda Slutsky / Shmuel Spector (2nd ed.)]

OREN, RAM (1958–2005), Israeli novelist. Oren was born in Tel Aviv. He graduated from the Faculty of Law at the Hebrew University and was a member of the Lawyers Association. Oren worked for many years as a journalist and senior editor of the daily *Yedioth Aharonoth*. He was the founder and owner of Keshet Publishing House and is known as the author of thrillers, all of which were commercial bestsellers in Israel. His first novel *Pitui* ("Seduction") was published in 1994. *Ot Kain* (1996; *The Mark of Cain*, 1998) tells the story of Michael, head of the Israeli Mossad, who discovers that he and Elsa, a rabid Nazi planning terrorist attacks, are the children of a notorious commander of a concentration camp. *Esh Ḥayah* ("Live Ammunition," 1999) is the story of intrigues, blackmail, and love revolving around the hopes of Amos Gonen to become the new chief of staff. Among Oren's other works are the historical novel *Latrun* (2002) and *Nesikhah Afrikanit* ("African Princess," 2003).

[Anat Feinberg (2nd ed.)]

OREN, YIZḤAK (pen-name of **Yizḥak Nadel**; 1918–), Israeli writer. Born in Ulan-Ude, Siberia, Oren received a thorough Jewish education from his father, who was a Hebrew teacher and an active Zionist from Latvia. In 1924 the family moved to Harbin, China, where Oren graduated from a Russian high school. There he joined the *Betar movement and in 1936 went to Ereẓ Israel, later becoming a member of the *Irgun Ẓeva'i Le'ummi. He studied Hebrew literature, history, and philosophy at the Hebrew University. His first stories were published in literary supplements of the Hebrew daily press, but later he contributed frequently to such literary journals as *Molad, Moznayim, Keshet*, and *Ha-Ummah*. He translated Russian classics into Hebrew (e.g., Goncharov's *Oblomov*) as well as Hebrew prose and verse (e.g., Agnon and Alterman) into Russian. He was editor of the educational programs of Israel's Russian-language broadcasts. Among his published works are *Ei-Sham* ("Somewhere," 1950), *Ba-Oref* ("Behind the Lines," 1953), *Massot Binyamin ha-Ḥamishi* ("Adventures of Benjamin the Fifth," 1958), *Avot u-Boser* ("Fathers and Sour Grapes," 1964), *Penei Dor ke-Kelev* ("The Dog-like Generation," 1968), *Konei Shamayim va-Areẓ* ("Possessors of Heaven and Earth," 1970), *Etgarim* ("Challenges," 1972), *Ha-Har ve-ha-Akhbar* ("The Mountain and the Mouse," 1972), *Ḥamesh Megillot Afot* ("Five Flying Scrolls," stories, 1985) and *Yeẓarim vi-Yẓirot* ("Passions and Creations," stories and essays, 1997). Though not religious in any formal sense, in his very personal, somewhat surrealistic, narrative style and structure, Oren expresses a mystical belief in man and particularly his spiritual creativity as a central element in the cosmic design, stressing thereby the specific significance of the history and renaissance of the Jewish people. The author of "Jabotinsky and Me" (1980), Oren was awarded the Jabotinsky Prize in 1999. He also received the Newman Prize (1989) and the President's Prize (1999). The English translation *The Imaginary Number* appeared in 1986. For further information concerning translations see the ITHL website at www.ithl.org.il.

BIBLIOGRAPHY: S. Halkin, *Derakhim ve-Ẓiddei Derakhim ba-Sifrut*; M. Dor, in: *Ma'ariv* (May 26, 1972). **ADD. BIBLIOGRAPHY:** A. Zehavi, *"Al Jabotinsky va-Ani,"* in: *Yedioth Aharonoth* (October 24, 1980); Y. Friedlander, *"Al Jabotinsky va-Ani,"* in: *Be-Ereẓ Yisrael*, 110 (1981), 14; G. Shaked, *Ha-Sipporet ha-Ivrit*, 3 (1988), 164–78; O. Bartana, *"Ẓava'ah ke-Sippur Merkaz bi-Yẓirat Y. Oren,"* in: *Biẓaron*, 43–44 (1989), 41–51.

ORENSE, city in Galicia, N.W. Spain. Jews had apparently settled there by the 11th century, and in 1044 were living in the nearby fortress. Until the 1460s, no further information is available on the community which during that period probably consisted of some 30 to 40 families. In 1474, its annual tax, together with that paid by the Jews of Rivadabia, Monforte, and Allariz, amounted to 2,000 maravedis. This decreased to 1,000 maravedis in 1482, and rose to 13,500 maravedis in 1491, apparently because of the obligation to contribute to the expenses of the war against Granada. In 1489 a writ of protection was granted to the community of Orense against the attempts of several knights to attack the Jews of the town; the governor of Galicia was ordered by the Catholic monarchs to protect them. The Jewish quarter, which until 1488 bordered upon the Rua Nova, was then transferred to another site next to the Fuente del Obizpo, and the local Jews were given a period of grace to settle there. A fine of 3,000 maravedis was to be imposed on those who refrained from obeying this order. The quarter remained on that site until the expulsion in 1492.

BIBLIOGRAPHY: F. Fita, in: *Boletín de la Academia de la Historia, Madrid*, 22 (1893), 171; Baer, Urkunden, 2 (1936), 307, 387; SuáRez Fernández, Documentos, index. **ADD. BIBLIOGRAPHY:** A. López Carreira, in: *Boletín avriense*, 13 (1983), 153–72.

[Haim Beinart]

ORENSTEIN, ALEXANDER JEREMIAH (1879–1972), South African medical scientist. Of Jewish origin, Orenstein was one of the teams of experts who, under W.C. Gorgas, cleared the Panama Canal Zone of yellow fever and malaria (1905–12). His experience of tropical and subtropical diseases led to his appointment in 1913 in the health services of German East Africa. In 1914 he was taken to South Africa by a Rand mining company to help reduce the incidence of pneumonia and tuberculosis which were taking a heavy toll among miners in the goldfields. Over the years, spectacular results were achieved in reducing the death rate, especially among African mine workers. Orenstein was director of the pneumoconiosis research unit of the South African Council for Scientific and Industrial Research when he retired in 1959. He had an international reputation and often represented South Africa at world health and labor conferences. Orenstein was director-general of medical services in the South African defense forces in both world wars, with the rank of brigadier (later major-general).

BIBLIOGRAPHY: A.P. Cartwright, *Golden Age* (1968); *South Africa's Hall of Fame* (1960).

[Louis Hotz]

ORENSTEIN, ARBIE (1937–), U.S. musicologist and pianist. Born and raised in New York City, he attended the High School of Music and Art, Queens College, and the Graduate School of Columbia University, where he received a Ph.D. in musicology. He was professor of music at the Aaron Copland School of Music at Queens College, where he also taught a course in Jewish music.

Arbie Orenstein is the author of two major books on Ravel: *Ravel: Man and Musician*, published by Columbia University Press, 1975 (reissued as a Dover paperback in 1991), and *A Ravel Reader* (Columbia University Press, 1990; reissued as a Dover paperback in 2003). The latter was originally written in French as *Ravel: Lettres, Écrits, Entretiens*, published by Flammarion in 1989. As a pianist, Orenstein accompanied many outstanding cantors and recorded the world premieres of several works by Ravel, which he discovered in France while on a United States Government Fulbright grant. Orenstein also wrote an introductory essay on the life and work of A.Z. *Idelsohn for the Dover reprint of Idelsohn's classic text, *Jewish Music in Its Historical Development*. The French knighted him, awarding him the medal of Chevalier of the Order of Arts and Letters. He was the coeditor, with Israel J. *Katz, of the scholarly annual journal *Musica Judaica*, sponsored by the *American Society for Jewish Music.

[Amnon Shiloah (2nd ed.)]

ORGAD (Bueshel), BEN ZION (1926–2006), Israeli composer. Born in Germany, Orgad was brought to Ereẓ Israel in 1933. He studied composition with Paul *Ben-Haim and Josef *Tal, and graduated from the Jerusalem Academy of Music in 1947. In 1952 he won the UNESCO *Koussevitzky Prize, which enabled him to study in the United States with *Copland and Irving Fine. He obtained a degree (M.F.A.) from Brandeis University (1961).

Orgad was supervisor (1956–74) and chief supervisor (1975–88) of music at the Israel Ministry of Education and Culture. Deeply involved in Hebrew literature, he published a book of poetry. In 1997 he won the Israel Prize.

Among Israeli composers Orgad has been the most consistent in his commitment to the ideology of creating a modern Israeli musical style ingrained in ancient Jewish culture. He regarded the Hebrew language as "a bridge to tradition and its origins" (Fleisher, p. 131). His compositions derive their inspiration from two principal sources: The first is the melos of biblical Hebrew as expressed in the *Masoretic accents (*Ta'amei ha-Mikra*), as, for example, in his cantata *Ve-Zot ha-Berakhah* ("And This Is the Blessing"). The second principle is the irregular rhythmic values emanating from the meters of medieval Sephardi Jewish poetry, such as the piano composition *Rashuyot*.

Among his other works are *Ha-Ẓevi Yisrael*, symphony for baritone and orchestra (1949; revised 1958); *Out of the Dust*, for mezzo-soprano and four instruments (1956); *Monologue for Viola* (1957), a string trio (1961); *Mizmorim* for soloists and chamber orchestra (1966–68); *Hityaḥadut* (Individuations no. 1), for clarinet and chamber orchestra (1981); *Hityaḥadut* no. 2, for violin, cello, and chamber orchestra (1990); *Continuous Presence*, for chamber orchestra (2002). He wrote "*Ha-Potenẓi'al ha-Musikali shel ha-Safah ha-Ivrit*" ("The Musical Potential of the Hebrew Language"), in: *Proceedings of the World Congress on Jewish Music*, Jerusalem, 1978, ed. Judith Cohen (Tel Aviv, 1982), 21–47.

ADD. BIBLIOGRAPHY: NG[2]; S. Weich, "Musical Works of Ben-Zion Orgad," doctoral thesis (1971); A. Tischler, *A Descriptive Bibliography of Art Music by Israeli Composers* (1989), 178–81; R. Fleisher, *Twenty Israeli Composers* (1997), 128–35.

[Uri (Erich) Toeplitz and Yohanan Boehm / Jehoash Hirshberg (2nd ed.)]

ORGAN.

Antiquity

In its conventional form, an organ is basically a set of pipes activated by compressed air, under the control of a keyboard. It is thought to have been invented in Hellenistic Alexandria around the beginning of the second century C.E., and was called *hydraulos* (ὑδραυλός – water pipe) since the air was compressed by a water-pressure mechanism. During the first centuries C.E. this mechanism came to be replaced by bellows, but the name *hydraulos* or *hydraulis* remained. The instrument spread through the Roman and Byzantine Empires as a crude but effective accompaniment to games and ceremonies in the circus and at court. Byzantine influence brought the organ both to the Persian court and to Europe in the eighth or ninth centuries.

It was the late Roman and Byzantine organ, with its multiplicity of pipes and – for that time – astounding tone-volume, that gave rise to the late talmudic identification of the *magrefah* ("rake") as an organ supposed to have been used in the Second Temple. The development of the legend, for such it is, can easily be traced. The Mishnah (Tam. 2:1; 3:8, and 5:6) states that a *magrefah* was among the implements used for cleaning the altar in the morning before the new daily sacrifice; and that the noise of its being thrown on the floor was one of several "noise-cues" which the priests used to ensure the smooth running of the ceremony (cf. *The Letter of Aristeas* 92; 94–96) in the absence of perceptible orders during the service. A hyperbole states that all these noises were audible "unto Jericho" (Tam. 3:8). The equating of *magrefah* with *hydraulis* must have occurred in the time of the *Tosefta, since Tosefta Arakhin 1:13–14 quotes R. Simeon b. Gamaliel as saying: "There was no *hydraulis* [הדראוליס] in the Temple since it confuses the voice and spoils the tune." The Jerusalem Talmud (Suk. 5:6, 55c–d) quotes R. Simeon b. Gamaliel, and then goes on to identify the biblical *ugav* with *ardablis*, and states that the *magrefah* had ten holes (or pipes) each emitting a hundred tones, or a hundred holes (or pipes) each emitting ten tones. Finally, in *Arakhin* 10b the identification *magrefah-hydraulis* appears as a categorical statement. Henceforth the identification of *magrefah* with organ remained practically unquestioned by most commentators and musicologists, although there is Rashi's compromise-exegesis to *Arakhin* 10b: "but it seems that there were two *magrefot*, one for [raking] the altar-remnants and one for song/music."

[Bathja Bayer]

The Organ in the Synagogue Before the 19th Century

Little is known about the use of the organ in the synagogue before its introduction by Reform Judaism in the 19th century. The earliest evidence of its use is in Italy in the 17th century. Giulio *Morosini (Samuel Nahmias, Leone *Modena's pupil, who converted to Christianity) tells in his *Via della Fede* (Rome, 1683, p. 793) about the performance of the Jewish Academy of Music (*Accademia degli impediti*) in the Spanish synagogue of Venice, about 1628. On one occasion (Simḥat Torah) there was an organ among the instruments used but the Venetian rabbis disapproved of it because of its close association with Christian worship. But another Italian source of the 17th century indicates that the organ was not frowned upon by some Italian rabbis of this period. Abraham Joseph Solomon *Graziano, rabbi of Modena (d. 1683) observed in glosses on the Shulḥan Arukh (OḤ 560:3): "... Jewish musicians should not be prevented from playing on the organ [to accompany] songs and praises performed [in honor of] God..." He went on to suggest that the argument of *ḥukkot ha-goyim* ("customs of the gentiles") was not relevant: no competent rabbinic authority would forbid organ playing; only ignorant people would oppose it.

The existence of a synagogue organ in Prague in the late 17th and 18th centuries is indicated by several writers. The use of the organ seems to have been linked mainly with the musical "inauguration of the Sabbath." The earliest mention is by Shabbetai *Bass, who uses the term *ugav* in the prayer book printed as a supplement to his Hebrew bibliography, *Siftei Yeshenim* (Amsterdam, 1680, 21b:3). Two later sources are J.J. *Schudt, (1664–1722) and Abraham Levi b. Menahem Tall (early 18th century). The broadsheet *Naye Tsaytung un Yudisher Oyftsug* (1716) reveals the name of the Jewish builder of the "new organ" (Meir Mahler) employed during the celebrations of the Jewish community of Prague in honor of the birth of Prince Leopold, son of the German emperor, Charles VI.

[Israel Adler]

In the 19th and 20th Centuries

The organ was introduced by *Reform Judaism into the synagogue services as part of its stress on the aesthetic aspects of Jewish worship. The controversies surrounding the use of the organ began when Israel *Jacobson placed an organ into the temple he opened for his boys' school in Seesen, in 1810. He also employed the organ in the services which were held in private homes in Berlin from 1815 on. The Hamburg Temple, which opened in 1818, held services with organ accompaniment. From that time, this became the distinguishing feature of all Reform congregations. Of all the liturgical reforms introduced in the 19th century, none has proved to be as divisive as the introduction of the organ. The introduction of an organ into a synagogue was usually followed by an exodus of the more traditionalist members who organized services for themselves without organ accompaniment. As the shibboleth of Reform, the organ figured primarily in Germany and, in the 19th century, in America. French and Italian synagogues, not otherwise departing from traditional usage, introduced the organ without giving rise to controversy. For wedding ceremonies, the organ is played in some modern Orthodox synagogues. Many American Conservative synagogues also play it on the Sabbath. To justify their innovation, the Reformers published a collection of responsa, entitled *Nogah ha-Ẓedek* ("The Splendor of Justice," 1818). The Orthodox replied with a responsa collection of their own, *Elleh Divrei ha-Berit* ("These are the words of the Covenant," 1819). Since then, a vast literature has accumulated around the subject, consisting mainly of restatements and reformulations of the arguments used in 1818 and 1819.

Basically, three halakhic objections have been raised: (1) Playing the organ on the Sabbath, even by a non-Jew, is prohibited "work" – if not biblically forbidden, at least falling into the rabbinic category of *shevut* (occupations forbidden on Sabbaths and festivals); (2) as a sign of mourning for the destruction of the Temple, music in general is prohibited; (3) the organ is so closely associated with worship in the Christian churches that it would be a case of the prohibited "imitation of gentile customs" (*ḥukkot ha-goyim*) to play it in the synagogue.

The Reform justification has taken the following form: (1) the Shulḥan Arukh (OḤ 338:2) permits the playing of music by a non-Jew on the Sabbath for the purpose of entertaining a wedding party. What is permitted for a wedding party should be permitted all the more for the enhancement of worship. Moreover, just as the rules of *shevut* did not apply to the Temple, so they should not apply to the synagogues which have taken its place; (2) the prohibition of music as a sign of mourning for the destruction of Jerusalem includes vocal no less than instrumental music. Yet tradition has obviously accepted vocal music for religious purposes (Sh. Ar., OḤ 560:3). Reform is merely extending the compromise to instrumental music as well. Beside, instrumental music was used in some pre-modern synagogues, although not on the Sabbath; a synagogue in Prague even had an organ; (3) the organ is not universal in Christian worship. Since there can be Christian worship without an organ, it follows that the instrument is by no means "essential" to that worship. Joel *Sirkes, in his responsum (Resp. Bah Yeshanot, no. 127) made a distinction between melodies which are an integral part of Christian worship and those which are not. The Reformers extended that distinction to musical instruments as well. In addition, they claimed instrumental music in the church is itself a borrowing from the Temple, in which there was an organ-like instrument, called *magrefah* (Ar. 10b–11a). While the use of the organ, particularly when played by non-Jewish musicians, has frequently led to the introduction of melodies akin to the traditional Jewish worship, it has likewise led both to a renaissance of modern synagogue music and to a revival of old Jewish modes. Hermann Heymann *Steinthal said: "The organ has restored to us the old *ḥazzanut*. It will preserve it, and transmit it to our children" (*Ueber Juden und Judentum*, 272). But Leopold *Zunz, a friend of the organ, cautioned: "Unity is the sweetest harmony. It is, therefore, better to refrain from the use of the organ…, if that should be the sole cause for a serious split in the congregation" (Zunz-Albeck, Derashot, 219).

[Jakob J. Petuchowski]

BIBLIOGRAPHY: ANTIQUITY: Idelsohn, Music, 14, 19, 242–4, 496; J. Yasser, in: *Journal of the American Musicological Society*, 13 (1960), 24–42; J. Perrot, *L'orgue, de ses origines hellénistiques à la fin du* XIII*e siècle* (1965), 14–19; H. Avenary, in: *Taẓlil*, 2 (1961), 66; C. Sachs, *The History of Musical Instruments* (1940), 124. MODERN TIMES: Sendrey, Music, nos. 2537–86; Adler, Prat Mus, 28–30, 65, 74, 112, 263; A. Berliner, *Zur Lehr' und zur Wehr, ueber und gegen die kirchliche Orgel im juedischen Gottesdienste* (1904); S. Krauss, *Zur Orgelfrage* (1919), incl. bibl.

ORGELBRAND, SAMUEL (1810–1868), Polish publisher. A graduate of the rabbinical seminary of his native Warsaw, he taught for a few years, and in 1836 he opened a shop specializing in the sale of manuscripts and old and rare books. Exploiting the demand for Jewish books because of the restrictions on their publication in Russia, he opened a publishing house for both Hebrew and Polish books. In 1844 he acquired the publishing firm of Jozef Krasinski, which he expanded and improved, becoming the most important publisher in Warsaw. For a while he was in partnership with Henryk Natanson. In 1860 he appointed the conservative *maskil* Daniel *Neufeld to head the department for Hebrew books. In 30 active years, Orgelbrand published over 250 works in 520 volumes, of which about 100 volumes were Hebrew works, sold mostly to subscribers. Between 1860 and 1864 he published the Babylonian Talmud in 20 volumes. Despite the competition of the *Romm edition of Vilna and the Zusman Javetz edition of Berlin, 12,000 copies of this edition were sold. Orgelbrand also published fine editions of the Pentateuch with commentaries, *Ein Ya'akov*, prayer books, *Ẓe'enah u-Re'enah* (1867), and other works. Between 1842 and 1850 he financed the weekly *Kmiotek* ("Peasant"), the first Polish periodical for the masses. Between 1858 and 1868 he published the first Polish general encyclopedia (*Encyklopedja Powszechna*), in 28 volumes, which he financed from the profits of the Talmud. A large section on Judaica, edited by Daniel Neufeld and Fabian Streuch (1820–1884), was included in the encyclopedia. Orgelbrand also published a series of works by Polish authors as well as Polish translations of classical works. During the 1860s he was a member of the executive board of the Warsaw community.

His sons, HIPOLIT (1843–1920) and MIECZYSLAW (1857–1903), took over the publishing house, keeping the Polish department in operation but discontinuing the Hebrew department in 1901. Both brothers belonged to extreme assimilationist circles and converted to Christianity during the 1890s. Before closing down the Hebrew department, they invited their brother-in-law, the learned *maskil* and author Hershel Rundo, to be their partner in the publication of Hebrew works.

Samuel's brother, MAURYCY (Moses; 1826–1904), was also a publisher, active in assimilationist circles in both Warsaw and Vilna. In Vilna he published a practical dictionary of the Polish language in two volumes, *Słownik jézyka polskiego do podrécznego użytku* (1861). Ordered to leave Vilna in 1865 by the Russian governor, Muravyov, he returned to Warsaw in 1873, establishing a publishing house in partnership with Gebethner and Wolff, and Michael Gluecksberg. From 1878 to 1885 he was the publisher and editor of the popular Polish weekly, *Tygodnik Powszechny*.

BIBLIOGRAPHY: B. Prus, in: *Kurier Warszawski*, 97 (1833); B. Weinryb, in: MGWJ, 77 (1933), 273–300; S. Rosencweig, in: *Nasz Przegląd* (Nov. 7–13, 1937); Z. Kobryński, in: *Miesięcznik graficzny*, 1 (1938); J. Bartosiewicz, in: *Tygodnik Ilustrowany*, 51 (1922); J. Shatzky, *Geshikhte fun Yidn in Varshe*, 3 (1953), index.

[Arthur Cygielman]

ORGEYEV (Rom. **Orhei**), city in Bessarabia district, Moldova. Jews are first mentioned in Orgeyev in 1741. The community developed after the Russian annexation of Bessarabia in 1812 when many Jews immigrated to the region. There were 3,102 Jews registered in 1864 and 7,144 (57.9% of the total population) in 1897. They established educational and welfare institutions, and in 1865 a *talmud torah* was opened where secular studies were also taught; in 1877 a hospital and an old age home were founded. The Jews of Orgeyev were mostly businessmen and craftsmen, but some were viniculturists on the outskirts of the town. In the late 1890s an agricultural training school was founded and it was active until 1902, receiving support from the Jewish Colonization Association (ICA). Among the 1,480 members registered in the loan fund in 1925 there were 286 farmers. In 1919 a training farm was opened. Owing to the influence of the Zionist movement Hebrew was taught in many schools. In 1927 ORT started a vocational woodworking school for boys, and a vocational tailoring school for girls. In 1930 there were 6,408 Jews (41.9% of the total population).

[Eliyahu Feldman]

Holocaust Period and After

When war broke out (June 1941) the Soviet army, which had been in Orgeyev from the previous June, helped Jews to escape. Some got to Kryulyany (Criuleni) and wandered from there. One group roamed through southern Russia on foot; of these, some were killed in German air raids, while others succumbed to the cold or died from starvation and disease. The survivors eventually reached Stalingrad, where the authorities dispersed them among the kolkhozes. When the front drew near, they were sent on to the Ural Mountains, central Asia, and Uzbekistan. One large group of Orgeyev Jews was located at Tashkent and the surrounding area. Those Jews who remained in Orgeyev came to a bitter end. When the German-Romanian forces entered on July 8–10, a Jewish delegation presented itself before them to welcome them with bread and salt, but all its members were murdered on the spot. The Jewish population was enclosed in a ghetto, where it lived under extremely crowded conditions and was exposed to constant maltreatment and daily murders. On August 6, about 200 Jews were murdered by the 25th Romanian regiment and their bodies were thrown into the Dniester. In 1942 all the survivors were deported to the concentration camp at Tiraspol, Transnistria; their exit from the city was accompanied by the music of a gypsy band and the old people were forced to dance in the streets. When the transport reached a nearby forest, the young men among the deportees were taken to an open field where they underwent torture and where many were shot to death by the soldiers. Others died on the way to Tiraspol and others in the Transnistrian camps. Only a few lived to see the end of the war.

There was little Jewish life after the war. The only synagogue in Orgeyev was closed down by the authorities in 1960, after they had organized a "petition" claiming that its presence was disturbing the neighbors. The Jewish population in 1970 was estimated at about 3,000. Most left in the 1990s.

[Jean Ancel]

BIBLIOGRAPHY: *Orheiyov be-Vinyanah u-ve-Ḥurbanah* (1959); M. Mircu, *Pogromurile din Basarabia…* (1947), 9–10.

OR HA-NER (Heb. אוֹר הַנֵּר), kibbutz in the southern Coastal Plain of Israel, north of Sederot, affiliated with Iḥud ha-Kevuẓot ve-ha-Kibbutzim. Or ha-Ner was founded initially as an administered farm of the "Yiẓẓur u-Fittu'aḥ" company belonging to Iḥud ha-Kevuẓot ve-ha-Kibbutzim, in 1955. It was taken over in 1957 by the kibbutz which had previously settled in Givot Zaid near *Kiryat Tivon. Pioneers from Brazil, Mexico, Chile, and Uruguay made up the majority of the 284 inhabitants in 1970. In 2002 the population was 394. Or ha-Ner engaged in intensive farming with citrus groves, poultry, cattle, and field crops in partnership with nearby Kibbutz Erez. It manufactured metal, aluminum, and steel products for the auto industry and ran a catering service specializing in South American food. The name, "Light of the Candle," referring to nearby Beror Ḥayil, is taken from Sanhedrin 32b (see *Beror Ḥayil).

[Efraim Orni / Shaked Gilboa (2nd ed.)]

ORḤOT ḤAYYIM (Heb. אָרְחוֹת חַיִּים; "Ways of Life"), or **Zavva'at Rabbi Eliezer** (Heb. צַוָּאַת רַבִּי אֱלִיעֶזֶר; "The Ethical Will of Rabbi Eliezer"), one of the most popular and best-known short treatises on ethics and moralistic behavior in medieval Hebrew literature. *Orḥot Ḥayyim* is arranged in the form of an ethical will (*Wills, Ethical), and owing to the fact that it begins with the talmudic story about the illness of Rabbi *Eliezer b. Hyrcanus, was conventionally attributed to him. However, as early as the Middle Ages, doubts arose as to whether he was in fact the author, and Menahem b. Judah de *Lonzano and other scholars after him ascribed the work to *Eliezer b. Isaac Ashkenazi of the 11th century. *Orḥot Ḥayyim* was first printed, together with other works, in Venice in 1544; and it has been reprinted many times. There are two commentaries to it – one by Abraham Mordecai Virnikowski (1888), and one by Gershon Hanoch Leiner of Radzyn (1891).

There are several bibliographical problems in connection with *Orḥot Ḥayyim* which have been studied by Israel Abrahams and Gershom Scholem. The work consists of two parts: the first is the ethical will, comprising short paragraphs of moralistic advice given by a father to his son; and the second, called *"Seder Gan Eden,"* is a treatise on the structure of and the different palaces (*heikhalot*) in the garden of Eden. The two parts were printed as a single entity and are found together in early manuscripts; Scholem noted that the work as a whole usually appears in manuscript collections of kabbalistic material, often in close proximity to works written by *Moses b. Shem Tov de Leon, the reputed author of the Zohar.

There is virtually no doubt about the date of the second part of *Orḥot Ḥayyim*; its descriptions of the *heikhalot* of the garden of Eden bear a close resemblance to the descriptions found in the Zohar, and various other motifs are common to both works. Scholem has suggested that if the author of the Zohar had written his work in Hebrew, the result would have been very similar in style to the *"Seder Gan Eden."* Hence it must have been written by a member of the kabbalistic circles of the end of the 13th century, very probably by Moses de Leon himself.

The problem is whether the same can be said about the first part of *Orḥot Ḥayyim*, the ethical will attributed to Rabbi Eliezer. Scholem believes that it is impossible to make any distinction between the two parts; nonetheless, there are great differences in style between them, and it is difficult to discover any hint of mystical speculation in the first part. It is possible that the first part is in fact an Ashkenazi work dating from the 11th century or later, whereas the second part was added at a later period. However, the question must be regarded as an open one.

BIBLIOGRAPHY: I. Abrahams, *Hebrew Ethical Wills*, 1 (1926), 30–49; A. Jellinek, *Beit ha-Midrash*, 3 (1938²), xxvi–xxviii, 131–40; G. Scholem, in: *Le-Agnon Shai* (1959), 293ff.

[Joseph Dan]

ORḤOT ẒADDIKIM (Heb. אוֹרְחוֹת צַדִּיקִים "The Ways of the Righteous"), an anonymous work in Hebrew probably written in Germany in the 15th century. *Orḥot Ẓaddikim*, one of the most important works in Hebrew ethical literature, has always been published anonymously and though an attempt was made to identify the author with the 15th-century moralist and polemical writer, Yom Tov Lipmann Muelhausen, the hypothesis seems to be without foundation. The only historical fact cited in the work is the expulsion of the Jews from France in the 14th century. Since *Orḥot Ẓaddikim* follows the teachings of the *Ḥasidei Ashkenaz in many ways, it is possible that the author, in keeping with the admonishment of *Judah b. Samuel he-Ḥasid of Regensburg in *Sefer *Ḥasidim* (also published anonymously) for writers not to identify their work so that their descendants might not pride themselves with the accomplishments of their fathers, purposely kept the book anonymous. Despite its anonymity *Orḥot Ẓaddikim* became one of the most popular works in traditional Hebrew literature and since the 16th century nearly 80 editions, including abridged versions and translations, have been published. The first was a shortened version in Yiddish (Isny, 1542); the full Hebrew text appeared for the first time in Prague some years later (1581, latest publication 1969).

The original title is probably not *Orḥot Ẓaddikim*, apparently given to it by the copyists and publishers. The Isny edition (1542) is called *Sefer ha-Middot* ("The Book of Ethical Qualities"), a name traditionally bestowed on Hebrew ethical works. In the introduction the author refers to the book as *Sefer ha-Middot* and in the concluding paragraph of the introduction he states "this *Sefer ha-Middot* was written and sealed with the seal of wisdom." The title is also appropriate to the structure of the work since it enumerates ethical qualities and their characteristics.

Orḥot Ẓaddikim, to a large extent a compendium of earlier Hebrew ethical thought, is based on philosophical and ethical works written in Spain, and on Ashkenazi ethical writings. The author also drew on some works written in Italy which he copied verbatim. The language and style, though mainly patterned after the philosophical-ethical literature of Spain, is also fused with stylistic and structural elements of the Ashkenazi ethical school. *Ḥovot ha-Levavot* by Baḥya ibn Paquda, the classical work of Jewish ethics, is one of the main sources of *Orḥot Ẓaddikim* both in its basic ideas and the many proverbs and parables which the author culled from it. *Orḥot Ẓaddikim*, more than any other medieval Hebrew ethical treatise, used proverbs and parables for elucidation. The structure of the work seems to have been influenced by Solomon ibn *Gabirol's *Tikkun Middot ha-Nefesh* which sets up pairs of ethical qualities (usually conflicting) and by *Mivḥar ha-Peninnim*, a work also attributed to Ibn Gabirol. The last chapter of *Orḥot Ẓaddikim* draws extensively on *Saadiah b. Joseph Gaon's concept of the desired harmony between the various ethical qualities in *Emunot ve-De'ot*. The influence of the ethical works of Maimonides is also marked and the author sometimes quotes whole passages verbatim. He also copied sections from *Ma'alot ha-Middot*, an ethical work by Jehiel b. Jekuthiel *Anav of Rome.

Despite the major influence that the above works had on the ideas, style, and structure of *Orḥot Ẓaddikim*, in its ethical outlook and approach the book follows the teachings of the Ḥasidei Ashkenaz, *Sefer Ḥasidim* and *Sefer ha-Roke'aḥ* by *Eleazar b. Judah of Worms, and is mainly interested in the practical and immediate meaning of the ethical qualities. Though the author also deals in generalizations and often divides every subject into sections and subsections, following the structure of medieval philosophical works, primary significance is given to practical behavior. The last chapter describes how a full religious life may be realized. This realization is not seen in the achievement of wisdom, or the unity with God through love, as is common in philosophical-ethical literature, but in the awe of and obedience to heaven, the supreme quality posited by the Ḥasidei Ashkenaz.

In the introduction, the author gives a theoretical and anthropological basis for his theory of ethics; the book is divided into *she'arim* (portals, i.e., sections), most of which are short, each devoted to a discussion of the ethical merits and demerits of a specific moral quality. The author apparently tried to arrange the chapters into pairs of contradictory qualities, but this was not followed through. Some of the major sections are devoted to pride, modesty, love (not exclusively the love of God, but all aspects of love in human life), hatred, compassion or mercy (*raḥamim*), cruelty, joy (including a long discussion on faith in God, to which, strangely enough, a special portal was not devoted). The author discusses the negative characteristics of non-religious joy, and extols the joy found in the love of God and obedience to him. Other sections treat worry, anger, envy, zeal and laziness, truth and falsehood, flattery, gossip, and repentance. (The section on repentance is the longest and most detailed section in the work.) The last two chapters are on the Bible and the study of Torah, discussing problems of religious knowledge and wisdom, and the awe of heaven, which, to the author, is the most important quality. Awe of heaven expresses itself in man's attitude toward God in everyday life.

Orḥot Ẓaddikim greatly influenced later Hebrew ethical works. The Hebrew moralists in Safed, though kabbalists and though there is no kabbalistic element in *Orḥot Ẓaddikim*, drew on its teachings. The work also influenced ethical writers of Eastern Europe. It is even possible that the manner in which the merits and demerits of every quality are enumerated influenced Moses Ḥayyim *Luzzatto in his *Mesillat Yesharim*.

BIBLIOGRAPHY: S.J. Cohen, *The Ways of the Righteous* (1969); Guedemann, Gesch Erz, 3 (1888), 223ff.; J. Kaufmann (Even Shemuel), *Rabbi Yom Tov Lipmann Muhlhausen* (Heb., 1927).

ORIA, small town near Brindisi in Apulia, S. Italy, formerly of great importance. The Jewish settlement probably went back to classical times, and Jewish sepulchral inscriptions have been found there. During the period of Byzantine rule, from the eighth century, the community was one of the most important in southern Italy, and a great deal is known about it because of the wealth of information contained in the chronicle of *Ahimaaz. This deals largely with the family of the synagogue poet Amittai of *Oria and his son *Shephatiah, who was inducted into practical mysticism in Oria by Aaron of *Baghdad. Shephatiah went on a mission to Constantinople in 873–74 to obtain the cancellation, at least so far as Oria was concerned, of the edict of conversion issued by the emperor Basil *I. In 925 the city was attacked by Arab marauders; some Jews were killed and many were enslaved, including the young

Shabbetai *Donnolo. Other attacks followed during the same century. The Jewish community remained important until the 15th century, but thereafter it declined. The Porta degli Ebrei ("Jew's Gate") still stands at the entrance of the Jewish quarter (now Piazza Donnolo).

BIBLIOGRAPHY: Roth, Dark Ages, index; Milano, Bibliotheca, index; idem, in: RMI, 32 (1966), 414ff.; P.B. Marsella, *Da Oria viene la parola di Dio, saggio storico-critico…* (1952); Marcus, in: PAAJR, 5 (1933/34), 85–94.

[Cecil Roth]

ORIENTALISTS. Orientalism is the study of the languages, history, and civilization of the peoples of Asia and, due to the expansion of *Islam, the northern parts of Africa. As Islam, almost from its beginning, widely influenced Jewish thought, Jewish religious and philosophical literature from the 8th century C.E. onward displays a more or less intimate knowledge of Islamic theology, philosophy, and even religious law, not to speak of the subtleties of Arabic language and literature, which did not fail to leave their mark on the corresponding Hebrew and Jewish scholarly productions. The works of men such as *Saadiah, *Judah Halevi, *Maimonides, Abraham *Ibn Ezra, *Baḥya ibn Paquda, Shem Tov b. Joseph *Falaquera, and many others on the above-mentioned subjects, as well as on biblical exegesis and Hebrew grammar and lexicography, were inconceivable without their knowledge, either receptive or polemical, of Arabic and Islam. *Ibn Kammuna even wrote a kind of history of the religions – Judaism, Christianity, and Islam – in which he betrays detailed knowledge of the internal controversies of Christianity and Islam respectively. Jewish scholars occupied themselves with comparative Semitic linguistics long before Christian scholars did. The translators of Arabic works by Jews and of an immense number of books by Muslim authors on Islamic and scientific subjects still await adequate evaluation as Orientalists. Noteworthy were the achievements of the Ibn *Tibbon family and Judah *Al-Ḥarizi. Apart from their own translations, Jews served as mediators between Arabic and Latin from the time that Christian scholars began to study Islamic science. The assessment of the Jewish share in these studies has been enormously facilitated by the bibliographical studies of Moritz *Steinschneider and later scholars, not only as a consequence of many newly discovered literary texts, but especially of the investigation of the thousands of documents of all kinds found in the Cairo *Genizah*.

Along with the rise of the "Wissenschaft des Judentums" in the last two centuries, an ever increasing number of Jews studied Orientalia at the universities not only as training for the rabbinate, but also as secular historians, philosophers, and philologists. The pioneers in this field were Abraham *Geiger, Moritz *Steinschneider, Simon *Eppenstein, Samuel *Poznanski, Solomon *Munk, Adolf *Neubauer, Leopold *Dukes, and Alexander *Harkavy. Among their followers were Joseph and Hartwig *Derenbourg, Wilhelm *Bacher, David *Kaufmann, Israel *Friedlaender, Samuel *Landauer, Z. *Fraenkel, Hartwig and Leo *Hirschfeld, Ignaz *Goldziher, Herman *Reckendorf, Jakob *Barth, Gotthold *Weil, Martin *Schreiner, Friedrich Kern, A.S. *Yahuda, Jacob *Mann, Daniel *Chwolson, Eugen *Mittwoch, Saul *Horovitz, Joseph *Horovitz, S.M. *Stern, Kurt Levy, Joseph *Halévi and Eduard *Glaser were among the pioneers of the search for South Arabian inscriptions. Unparalleled in his mastery of the whole field of Oriental studies was Giorgio Levi della Vida. J. Blau, C. Rabin, and M. Goshen-Gottstein all made important contributions to the study of Semitic languages. Julian Joel *Obermann III, Max Meyerhof, Immanuel *Loew, Paul *Kraus, Franz *Rosenthal, Georges *Vajda, Richard *Walzer and H. Kroner who edited many of the medical works of *Maimonides in their original Arabic, deserve special mention as historians of Arabic literature, philosophy, and sciences. The investigation of Islamic arts owes many of its most valuable achievements to Ernst *Herzfeld, Leo Ary *Mayer, and R. Ettinghausen. Bernard *Lewis, S.D. *Goitein, and H.Z. *Hirschberg excelled in the field of Islamic history, including that of Jewish communities in Islamic lands.

During the 19th century, when the deciphering of the hieroglyphs and the cuneiform scriptures enlarged the field of "Bible Lands," Jewish scholars also turned to these philologies. Morris *Jastrow and Heinrich Zimmern were among the leading Assyriologists, and the unrivaled master of this field was Benno *Landsberger. Other important contributions were made by Herman *Pick and Julius and Hildegard *Lewy.

Among the leading Egyptologists rank Georg Ebers, Georg Steindorff, Ludwig *Borchardt, A. *Ember, and H.J. *Polotsky, who also played an important part in the interpretation of the Coptic Manichaic texts discovered in Egypt. Knowledge of the Mandaic religious literature is due almost entirely to Mark *Lidzbarski, who also was the main cultivator of Semitic epigraphics. The investigation of the Ugaritic texts was greatly furthered by H.L. *Ginsberg and Umberto *Cassuto. Aramaic studies in general were cultivated by Alexander Sperber and E.Y. *Kutscher. Noted Iranists were James *Darmesteter, Isidor *Scheftelowitz, Alexander *Kohut, and Sir Marc Aurel *Stein. Gotthold *Weil and Uriel *Heyd excelled in Turkish philology and history. Some of the leading Indologists were G.S. *Oppert and Moritz *Winternitz. Far Eastern languages were studied by B. Laufer and Arthur *Waley. Israeli scholars who received the prestigious Israel Prize in Oriental studies were Joshua *Blau, linguist in Judeo-Arabic; David *Ayalon, historian of Mamluk society in Egypt; M.J. *Kister, historian of early Islam; Gabriel *Baer, historian of Egyptian society; Havah *Lazarus-Yafeh, philologist; Moshe *Piamenta, researcher of Arabic dialects; Shmuel *Moreh, researcher of Arabic literature; Sasson *Somekh, researcher of Arabic language and literature; and Jacob M. *Landau, political scientist researching the modern Middle East and Central Asia.

[Martin Meir Plessner]

ORIENTAL LITERATURE. In the vast area between Morocco and the Pacific, Jewish writers were mainly active in areas of Islamic culture; this survey is mainly concerned with the Middle East.

Writers in the Arab World

Few Jewish writers gained a place in the history of Arabic literature from the pre-Islamic period until modern times, yet the number of Jewish authors in the Islamic world greatly exceeds that mentioned by Arab historians. Jews gained fame mainly in the pre-Islamic period (the *Jāhiliyya*); during the period of Islamic rule in *Baghdad and *Spain; and in the 19th and 20th centuries. In the pre-Islamic period Jewish poets were prominent in *Arabia, notably the warrior-poet *Samuel ibn Adiyā, "The Faithful," and members of his family, and the Jewish poetess Sārā al-Qurayẓiyya, who was famous for her elegy over the dead of her tribe, which was betrayed by its Arab allies. After the rise of *Islam, because of the animosity between *Muḥammad and the Jewish communities and tribes of his day, Jewish poets and writers – with the notable exception of *Marḥab al-Yahūdī, the Arabian warrior poet – ceased to be mentioned, although Arabic-speaking Jews are known to have been prominent in science. It was only during the period of Islamic rule in Spain that Jewish writers reappeared in the accounts of Arab historians. Outstanding among these was the Spanish poet *Ibrāhīm ibn Sahl. Jewish scientists who wrote in Arabic gained fame at this time in Spain, North Africa, and Baghdad. Jews rarely distinguished themselves in Arabic poetry of the period, since they did not usually show great interest in the study of Arabic grammar, literature, and rhetoric. Blau (*The Emergence and Linguistic Background of Judaeo-Arabic*, 1965) has shown that Jews shunned Arabic poetry because of the difficulties involved in the study of Arabic literature and language, and mostly preferred to compose Hebrew verse. Muslim historians explain the emergence of Ibn Sahl and his fellow Jewish poets by claiming that Spanish Jews began to study Arabic grammar and literature. In the 19th and 20th centuries Jews were active in Arabic culture. Many won praise from their Muslim colleagues and some were considered by Arab literary historians to be leading pioneers of modern Arabic literature. The cultural and social revival of Arabic-speaking Jewry resulted from a number of factors. These include growing commercial prosperity, the equality in civil rights granted to ethnic minorities in the Ottoman Empire, and the competition between the European powers to gain a political and economic foothold in the region. Other factors were the demand for a multilingual intelligentsia and an efficient governmental administration, the awakening of East European Jewry and its interest in the Jewish communities of the East, the opening of Jewish schools by the *Alliance Israélite Universelle, and the intensification of Zionist activity. With the termination of Ottoman rule in the Arab lands, the establishment of the French and British mandates and the institution of Arabic as the official language of the newly emergent Arab states brought about a revolutionary revival of Arabic. Active Jewish participation in the revival of Arabic literature during the second half of the 19th century was spurred by the wish to safeguard Jewish rights in the Arabic-speaking countries. In fact, the use of literary Arabic by Jews in the 19th century was confined mainly to the lands of the Fertile Crescent. Jews actually lagged behind other religious minorities in these countries, notably the Christians, who had adopted Arabic for liturgical and literary purposes in the 18th century. In North Africa, *Yemen, and *Aden, Jews preferred to use either Hebrew and their own *Judeo-Arabic dialect, or else the language of the ruling power. The prevailing attitude of Jewish writers in the Muslim countries toward Arabic was therefore utilitarian and didactic. Jews were also activated by apologetic considerations, defending the position of their people and religion against false accusations. With the rise of *Zionism, the level of Jewish-Arabic cultural life was greatly enhanced. Zionism brought new vitality to the Jewish communities of the Arab lands, developing their national pride, sense of security, and consciousness of progress. Jewish writers began to demand an improvement of existing educational facilities and the furtherance of, and an increased respect for, their national uniqueness and autonomy. These trends were supported by the British and French mandatory administrations, which favored the autonomy of national and religious minorities in the area. It is thus not surprising that most of the Arabic-Jewish press was usually pro-Zionist. Any survey of Jewish literary activity in Muslim lands during the 19th–20th centuries faces a number of serious handicaps. The most serious of these are: (1) the fact that Arab writers mainly overlooked their Jewish colleagues; (2) the lack of any systematic collection of Jewish literary works in Arabic, mainly due to the low regard in which the Jews themselves held the study of Arabic language and literature (in many Jewish schools Hebrew and foreign languages entirely replaced Arabic in the curriculum); and (3) the immense difficulty involved in obtaining the necessary source material as a result of the Middle East conflict. Jewish writers were first attracted to the theater and journalism, since the former offered virtually unlimited scope for education, and the latter scope for apologetics, despite the danger of clashes with government authorites and other pressure groups.

PLAYWRIGHTS. The theater was a most effective mass medium for the purpose of education, enlightenment, and social criticism, since its aim could easily be concealed behind the camouflage of entertainment. Among the first Jewish journalists and writers to enter the field was the versatile Yaʿqūb *Ṣanūʿ, known also as Abu Naẓẓāra ("The Bespectacled"). An outstanding pioneer actor, stage producer, playwright, and journalist, he established his first theater in one of *Cairo's large cafés. Sanuʿ was much influenced by Molière, Sheridan, and Goldoni, but his Arabic operettas were more to the taste of his public, which preferred lighter entertainment. One of the first stage producers in the Arab countries to employ actresses, he wrote 32 plays (mainly short comedies) and translated many others. Ṣanūʿ's criticism of the khedive Ismāʿīl and his ministers in the Egyptian paper *Abū Naẓẓāra Zarqā'* ("The

Man with the Blue Spectacles") led to the closing down of his paper and his self-exile to France in 1878. While the Arab national theater flourished in Egypt, enjoying government support and the visits of Syrian and Lebanese stage companies, the Jewish theater was mainly confined to amateur activity in Jewish schools. Nevertheless, premiers, ministers of education, and even the khedive Ismāʿīl and King Fayṣal I of Iraq attended its performances. Jewish amateur theater also flourished in *Lebanon. The plays of Salīm Zakī Kūhīn, the son of Rabbi Zakī Kūhīn of *Beirut, were staged in 1894–95. In *Iraq, the Jewish schools of Baghdad and the Baghdad Jewish Literary Association promoted Arabic-Jewish theater. Original works by Jewish playwrights were also staged. In Egypt Raḥamīm Kūhīn wrote and translated many plays performed on the stage during the 1930s. His *al-Malik Dāʾūd* ("King David") was published in the Cairo Arabic-Jewish weekly *al-Shams* ("The Sun") in 1944.

JEWISH RELIGIOUS LITERATURE IN ARABIC. With the rise of the Zionist movement, Arabic-speaking Jewry experienced a cultural revival. This led both to the establishment of new Hebrew periodicals and publishing houses and to the intensive translation into Arabic of Hebrew books, including many religious works. Selections of the Babylonian Talmud were translated into Arabic under an English title by Shimon Joseph Moyal (*The Talmud, Its Origins and Its Morals*, 1909) and Hillel *Farḥi published Hebrew-Arabic liturgical works, including the high holiday *maḥzor*, prayer books, and Passover *Haggadot*. Farḥi also wrote religious tales in both languages. The *Karaite scholar Murād *Faraj published an Arabic commentary on the Pentateuch and other works, including translations of Proverbs and Job. Such activity encouraged the compilation of Hebrew-Arabic lexicons, notably the Hebrew–Arabic dictionary of Murād Faraj (1925), the Hebrew–Arabic–English dictionary of Hillel Farḥi, and the pocket Hebrew–Arabic dictionary of Nissim Mallul.

NOVELISTS AND PROSE WRITERS. Very few Jewish writers in the Islamic world produced original novels, although many engaged in the translation of novels from various European languages. Outstanding in this field was Esther Azharī *Moyal, who translated nearly a dozen novels by European writers. With the exception of Najīb Ashaʿyā, who wrote in Egypt, all the Jewish writers of Arabic novels were Iraqis who immigrated to Israel during the 1950s. Ezra Menasheh ʿAbid, an editor, wrote the novel *al-ʿĀlam al-Saʿīd* ("The Happy World," c. 1952); and Ezra *Ḥaddad, who translated from English and Hebrew, wrote *Fuṣūl min al-Kitāb al-Muqaddas bi-Uslūb Qaṣasī* ("Chapters from the Holy Bible in Narrative Form," 1947). The outstanding Jewish novelist in Arabic was Ibrāhīm Mūsā Ibrāhīm, whose works include *Asmahān* (1961) and who joined the editorial staff of the Mapam Arabic paper *al-Mirṣād*. Greater distinction was gained in the field of the short story. Saʿd Litto Malkī, an Egyptian pioneer of the genre, published some of his work in *al-Shams*. His first collection of short stories, *Yarāi al-Awwal* ("My First Pen," 1936), contained one piece about Egyptian Jewish life, on antisemitism in Muslim schools. The Jewish role in this genre was more significant in Iraq, where the Arabic short story was virtually created by the Jews. Those who published fiction of this type include Meer Baṣrī; Yaʿqūb Bilbūl, who was author of *al-Jamra al-Ūlā* ("The First Ember," 1937); Shalom Darwīsh; and the versatile Anwar Shaul, whose works called for social reform. Shimon (Balāṣ) Ballas (1930–), who eventually switched to Hebrew, published the novel *Ha-Maʿbarah* ("The Transit Camp," 1964) and a collection of short stories, *Mul ha-Ḥomah* ("Opposite the Wall," 1969). Esperance Cohen (1930–) published stories in the semiofficial paper *al-Anbāʾ* and in the Histadrut daily *al-Yawm*, later joining the editorial boards of the Histadrut journals. Most of these writers immigrated to Israel in the 1950s, two exceptions being Meer Baṣrī and Anwar Shaul, both anti-Zionists and Iraqi nationalists.

Poets. Modern Arabic poetry by Jews is again an almost exclusively Iraqi preserve. However, there were two notable exceptions to this rule – the Egyptian Karaite Murād Faraj and the Palestinian ʿAbdallah Nadīm Moyal. The latter belonged to a distinguished Sephardi family which settled in Ereẓ Israel. Moyal mainly wrote love poems, his lyrical collection *Ḥanīn al-Nadīm* ("The Yearning of Nadīm," 1934) being published in Beirut. At one stage of his career Moyal wrote narrative verse, producing a poetic biography of *Maimonides. Iraqi Jews have played an important part in the development of modern Arabic poetry. In style, form, and idea they have tended to follow the Christian Lebanese poets active in the North American Lebanese diaspora. Those Iraqi Jewish poets of note include Anwar Shaul, Murād *Mīkhāʾīl, Yaʿqūb Bilbūl, Abraham *Obadya, Salīm Shaʿshūʿ, Shalom Katav, Shmuel *Moreh, Benjamin Aaron Zakkay, David Semah, and Sasson *Somekh. Bilbūl's highly introverted poems, which bear the imprint of French writing, include a sonnet collection, and Shalom Katav (1931–) wrote prose poems collected in *Mawākib al-Ḥirmān* ("The Convoys of Frustration," 1949) and *Washwashāt al-Fajr* ("Dawn's Whispering," 1958). David Semah's leftist verse appeared first in Iraqi and later in Israel periodicals. The first part of his collection *Ḥattā Yajiʾu al-Rabīʿ* ("Till Spring Comes," 1959) contained tender love poems, while the second expressed the author's support for the Algerian war of liberation against the French and the 1959 anti-royalist coup in Iraq. Sasson Somekh (1933–), another leftist poet, also began his career as poet and translator in the Iraqi press, later writing for the Israeli Communist monthly *al-Jadīd*. Like most of these Iraqi poets who had settled in Israel, Somekh eventually wrote mainly in Hebrew.

Jewish Writers in Other Oriental Cultures

Though technically part of the Islamic world, some Jewish writers actually belonged to separate cultural traditions. Thus the Tunisian author *Ryvel, who wrote sensitive tales about his life in the Tunisian *ḥāra* (ghetto), chose French as his literary medium. This was also true of the Tunisian-born French novelist Albert *Memmi, the Egyptian-born novelist Élian-J. Finbert, and the Egyptian-born poet Édmond Jabès. Elsewhere in the Near East, Jews contributed to Turkish literature, notably the poetess Matilde Alçeh, the poet Jozef Ḥabib *Gerez, and the poets Ibrahim Nom and Robert Sezer. Further to the east, Jewish writers made their appearance in India, one of the earliest being Sarmad the Jew, a 17th-century poet of Hyderabad, who converted to Islam. Indian Jews of Baghdadi origin wrote in Hebrew, Arabic, or English, only Bene-Israel authors using native languages, such as Marathi. Most of the works by Bene Israel writers were liturgical, historical, or didactic; but a few produced original works of fiction. These include Bahais Joseph Talker's short novel *Gul ani Sanobar* ("Gul and Sanobar," 1867), the first of its kind in Marathi, and *Jagha che Chamatkar* ("Wonders of the World," 1869); Moses Daniel Talker's novels *Bago-Bahar* ("A Beautiful Garden," 1869) and *Premal Shushila* ("Lovely Sushila," 1872) and his Hindi play *Chhel Batao Mohana Rani* ("Stage Your Play, Mohana Rani," 1872); and S.R. Bunderker's drama *Ayushache Chitre* ("Life Picture," 1956). Other Indian authors were the prolific poet and prose writer Benjamin Samson Ashtamker, who wrote over 30 works from 1868 onward; the Baghdadi novelist Judah Aaron; and the Baghdadi poet Nissim Ezekiel, who was also a journalist. In the Far East, Chinese verse on Jewish themes was composed by three members of the *Kaifeng-Fu community during the 17th century – Ai-Shih-Tê, Chao Ying-Tou, and Shên Chu'üan.

BIBLIOGRAPHY: Y. ben-Ḥanania, in: *Hed ha-Mizraḥ* (Sept. 29, 1943), 12; (Oct. 13, 1943), 6–7; (Oct. 29, 1943), 7; (Nov. 12, 1943), 6–7; idem, in: *Yad la-Koré*, 4 (1958), 14–21, 119–27; E. Marmorstein, in: JJSO, 1 (1959), 187–200; S. Moreh, in: *Middle Eastern Studies*, 3 (April 1967), 283–94; idem, in: *Ha-Mizraḥ he-Ḥadash*, 14:2–3 (1964), 296–309; Ezekiel, *History and Culture of the Bene-Israel in India* (1948), 76–82; D. Salloum, *Change of Thought and Style in Iraqi Literature in the 19th and 20th Centuries* (Ar., 1959); S. Idris, in: *al-Ādāb* (Feb., March, April, Dec., 1953)

[Shmuel Moreh]

°**ORIGEN** (c. 184–c. 254 C.E.), Christian biblical critic, exegete, and homilist. Origen was a contemporary of Judah ha-Nasi in Roman Palestine. In his native Christian Alexandrian home, Origen learnt the Psalms in Hebrew and studied Greek and Bible. His father's martyrdom in 202 led Origen to become a teacher first in Alexandria and, after his expulsion by Bishop Demetrius in 213, in Caesarea Maritima. Having encountered personally the Jewish teachers of his time, Jewish customs, and Jewish relations with non-Jews, he interspersed his works with knowledge about Judaism, including non-rabbinic Judaism. As was customary for scholars then, he traveled to Greece, Asia, Syria, Rome, and Arabia to lecture, debate, and study. Famous and at the height of his activities, he was among other Christians imprisoned and tortured under Decius (249–51 C.E.). Set free at the emperor's death, Origen died soon after from the consequences of the ordeal.

Of this very fertile author's works only a fraction has survived. Its greater part is extant as Rufinus' and Jerome's Latin renditions often adapted to the Latin mind, its smaller part survived in Greek catena. The existing material belongs to two groups, thematic reflections and biblical studies. Of the thematic works, *On Principles* in four books belongs to Origen's early Alexandrian period. It speculates about God and the heavenly beings, man and the material world, free-will and its consequences, and Holy Scripture. The composition indicates detailed knowledge of Jewish observances, such as phylacteries and the Passover search for leaven, and also of some detailed halakhic rules. In a few cases it supplements the *halakhot* preserved in the Mishnah, as in regard to the *eruv* and to carrying on the Sabbath. Best known of the biblical studies, all composed during Origen's final 20 years, is the *Hexapla*, setting the Hebrew Bible in six columns: Hebrew, in Hebrew and Greek characters, followed by the Greek versions of Aquila, Symmachus, the Septuagint, and Theodotion. For some books there exist supplementary versions, called fifth, sixth, seventh. Comparing the Greek versions meticulously with the Hebrew, Origen marked additions and lacunae in the Greek with graphic symbols borrowed from the Alexandrian grammarians.

Of his commentaries to almost every book of the Bible, substantial remnants are extant for those on the Psalms, Song of Solomon, John, Matthew, and Romans. Some 279 homilies, mostly on the Hebrew Bible, have survived. Both these genres demonstrate Origen's close attention to the work of the Greek literary critics and of Hellenistic religious traditions. Origen occasionally rebukes Jewish literalism but also defends Jews against abuse. His distinction of three senses of scripture anticipated the Jewish distinction of four senses; in this regard, Jews borrowed from Christians rather than the reverse.

BIBLIOGRAPHY: The works of Origen have been published in the GCS collection (*Die Griechischen Christlichen Schriftsteller*) of various authors in 12 vols. (1899–1983), 4 additional vols. are in preparation. English translations include ANF (*Ante-Nicene Fathers*), vols. 4, 6, 9. STUDIES: N. de Lange, *Origen and the Jews. Studies in Jewish-Christian Relations in Third-Century Palestine* (1976); C.P. Bammel, "Adam in Origen," in: R. Williams (ed.), *The Making of Orthodoxy. Essays in Honour of Henry Chadwick* (1989); H. Crouzel, *Origen* (1989).

[Petra Heldt (2nd ed.)]

ORIHUELA, city in Valencia, E. Spain. When it was captured during the Christian Reconquest by Alfonso x of Castile, the Jew, Jacob ibn Dino, was taken captive by a Christian knight. Abraham ibn Baḥya collected the taxes in Orihuela and nearby Elche between 1381 and 1384. The Jews in Orihuela were evidently baptized during the persecutions of 1391. The movement led by Inés, "the Maiden of *Herrera," in 1500 found adherents among the *Conversos in Orihuela.

BIBLIOGRAPHY: Baer, Spain, 1 (1961), 114; Baer, Urkunden, 2 (1936), 536; García Serrano, in: *Boletín de la Academia de la Historia, Madrid*, 104 (1934), 216; López de Meneses, in: *Sefarad*, 14 (1954), 111; Bellot, in: F. Torres Fontes (ed.), *Anales de Orihuela* (1954). **ADD. BIBLIOGRAPHY:** J.B. Vilar, in: *Sefarad*, 36 (1976), 337–39; idem, in: *Boletín de la Asociación Española de Orientalistas*, 13 (1977), 175–86.

[Haim Beinart]

ORLAH (Heb. עָרְלָה; "uncircumcised"), tenth tractate in the order *Zera'im* in the Mishnah, Tosefta, and Jerusalem Talmud. It deals with the law prohibiting the fruit of trees during the first three years after their planting (Lev. 19:23–25). The subject matter of *orlah* being scanty, the tractate includes in its discussions the laws concerning the admixture of many other forbidden products.

The tractate has three chapters. Chapter 1 deals with intention affecting the application of the law; the kind of trees subject to the law; when a tree counts as replanted; if an unidentifiable *orlah* tree grows among other trees; edible parts of a tree not counting as fruit; and the planting or grafting of *orlah* shoots. Chapter 2 discusses the effect on produce of an admixture of *orlah, terumah*, etc., both as regards eating and uncleanness. Chapter 3 deals with garments dyed with the shells of *orlah* fruit; when threads of such dyed fabric are woven into a garment; the effect on ovens and food if *orlah* shells are used for fuel; difference between Ereẓ Israel, Syria, and other lands with regard to doubtful *orlah*. Mishnah 2:4 is an early one, apparently predating Shammai since he disagrees about its interpretation (*ibid.* 5), and 2:12 contains a comment by Joezer Ish ha-Birah, who lived during the period of the Second Temple. In the Tosefta *Orlah* consists of a single chapter which corresponds to *mishnayot* 1:1–5, and 3:1, 3, 5, 9. Nevertheless, the *mishnayot* 1:7, 13–15; 2:6; and 3:8 are complemented by Tosefta *Terumot* 5:9–10; 6:5–11; and 8:3, 15ff. Despite this, 17 *mishnayot* in *Orlah* remain without corresponding Tosefta (1:6–8; 2:2–6, 8–12, 17; 3:2, 4, 6). The Jerusalem Talmud deals only with the halakhic aspect of *orlah*. It contains no aggadic material. It was translated into English by H. Danby, in his *The Mishnah* (1933).

BIBLIOGRAPHY: H. Albeck, *Shishah Sidrei Mishnah, Seder Zera'im* (1958[2]), 291f.

[David Joseph Bornstein]

ORLAND, HERSHL (1896–1946), Soviet Yiddish writer. Born near Kiev, Orland moved to the city at the age of 22, and began his literary career with the publication of his first short stories, on the life of workers, in the Kiev newspaper, *Komunistishe Fon*. He was a dedicated Communist writer, whose narrative talent was fully appreciated. He wholeheartedly immersed himself in the reconstruction of the socio-economic framework of Jewish life, the main theme of his work. Orland also co-edited Yiddish periodicals, notably the Kiev journal, *Sovetishe Literatur.* When the Jewish *Anti-Fascist Committee was founded, Orland was one of its writers. His books include the novels *Hreblies* ("Dikes," 1929), and *Aglomerat* ("Agglomerate," 1935), both dealing with Sovietization of the shtetl population. While *Dikes* portrays the melioration of Polesie, Ukraine, *Agglomerate* is set in the Crimean industrial center of Kerch.

BIBLIOGRAPHY: LNYL, 1 (1958), 174–5.

[Israel M. Biderman / Gennady Estraikh (2nd ed.)]

ORLAND, YAAKOV (1914–2002), Hebrew writer. Born in the Ukraine, Orland was taken to Ereẓ Israel in 1921. In 1933 he began publishing poems, critical articles, and translations from English, German, and Yiddish. Several of his plays, both original and translations, were performed in Israel's theaters, including *Hershele Ostropoler* (1966). He also wrote lyrics for songs and was an editor of the periodicals *Ashmoret* and *Sifrut Ẓe'irah*. His books of poetry include *Ilan ba-Ru'aḥ* (1939), *Shirim al Ayit ve-al Yonah* (1946), and *Shirim me-Ereẓ Uẓ* (1963). He translated works by Byron, Oscar Wilde, Edgar Allan Poe, A.A. Milne, George Bernard Shaw, John Galsworthy, Erich Maria Remarque, and I. Manger. Orland served as chairman of the Hebrew Writers Association and was awarded the Alterman Prize for poetry as well as the Israel Prize for lyrics. A volume of selected works (*Mivḥar Ketavim*) was published in 1997 with an essay by Dan Miron. Several of his poems have appeared in English translation (for a complete list see Goell, Bibliography, index).

BIBLIOGRAPHY: Kressel, Leksikon, 1 (1965), 53. **ADD. BIBLIOGRAPHY:** S. Weissblit, "*Yom Tel Faher shel Sifrut Y. Orland*," in: *Ha-Ummah*, 49 (1977), 56–62; H. Shaham, "*Shirat Y. Orland be-Zikatah le-Shirat Alterman*," in: *Dappim le-Meḥkar be-Sifrut*, 9 (1994), 75–100; A. Lipsker, "*Homeland of the Pomegranate: Ereẓ Yisrael in the Verse of Y. Orland*," in: *Homeland of the Pomegranate* (1999), 104–114; Z. Luz, '"*Al ha-Yesod ha-Epi be-Shirato ha-Me'uḥeret shel Y. Orland*," in: *Ẓafon*, 6 (2000), 83–95; A. Lipsker, "*A Commitment to an Ancient Covenant: Biblical Sights and Biblical Language in the Poetry of Y. Orland*," in: *Terumah*, 10 (2001), 81–98; G. Halili, *Iyyun ba-Meḥazeh Ahavat Kuimbrah le-Yaakov Orland: Mitos, Historiyyah u-Meẓi'ut Akhshavit* (2002); R. Leket, "*Y. Orland Metargem Shirei Yeladim*," in: *Olam Katan*, 2 (2004), 141–168.

[Getzel Kressel]

ORLANDO (and the **Central Florida** area). Drawn by cotton and cattle in the 1850s–1860s, some Jews came to Orlando with other pioneers to this "old west" style town. Records show that after the Civil War there were about 16 Jewish families. A Jew, Jacob Raphael Cohen, bought a store in 1873, and in 1875 he helped write the city charter and was elected an alderman. Merchant A.H. Birnbaum was a member of Orlando's first fire department and was elected alderman in 1886. In the beginning the Sanford Jewish community was larger than Orlando's. Jews arrived in Sanford by 1892. Kanner Highway (Route 76) in Martin County was named for Abram Otto "A.O." Kanner, son of Charles and Pauline of Sanford, who arrived from Romania. A.O. was born in 1893 in Sanford, attended Stetson University Law School, and then had a 40-year political career in Florida.

The citrus industry played a significant role in the development of central Florida. Dr. Philip Phillips arrived in Orlando in 1897 to buy land for citrus groves; his empire grew to over 5,000 acres, and in 1954 the business was sold to Minute Maid. Pauline and Nat Berman settled in 1908. Active civically and Jewishly, Pauline had her own radio show and was the nation's first woman radio news commentator. The Benedict, Phillips, Kanner, Salomon, and Berman families comprised the Jewish community of Orlando from 1900 until the Pittsburgh migration in 1912 (Wittenstein, Shader, Meitin,

Levy, and Levine families). By 1915 other families settled and religious services were held in a citrus grove. Prior to the entry of the U.S. into World War I, a parade and rally drew every organization in the city as participants. After it was publicly noted that no Jewish group was present, Pauline Berman gathered the community at the home of Harry Kanner and spoke out that Orlando Jewry needed to organize a congregation. On August 30, 1918, Congregation Ohev Shalom was chartered and a church was purchased at the corner of Terry and Central Avenues; the dues were $1.00 per month. In 1926 B'nai B'rith was chartered and a cemetery opened in 1928. Prior to this, Jews were taken to Jacksonville (1857) or Tampa (1894) for burial. Jewish families from Paterson, New Jersey, and other northeastern cities, as well as other Florida cities, came to Orlando. Jews formed their own social and recreational clubs since they were denied memberships in others.

Harry and Minerva Nirenberg moved in 1937 with children Joan and Marshall because Marshall had rheumatic fever. Harry bought a dairy, was active at Ohev Shalom, and then was a founder of Congregation of Liberal Judaism. When he was a youngster, Marshall collected bugs from the swamp and sent specimens to a museum. He graduated from Orlando High School in 1944 and the University of Florida four years later. In 1968 Dr. Marshall Warren *Nirenberg received the Nobel Prize in medicine and physiology for being the first to discover a code equivalence between a nucleic acid component and an amino acid.

Some families who settled in the 1930s and 1940s were fruit and vegetable growers and buyers. Well-known citrus labels were: Select-O-Sweet, Lady in Red, Richfruit, Emerald Fruit, Moto-Cop, MEG and Babijuice. Albertson, Heller, Jacob, Meitin, Shader, Morrell, Bornstein, Echelman, Willner, Arost, Miller, and Zimmerman were among the Jewish people who grew, packed, and shipped fruit nationwide over the second half of the 20th century. In 1940 Orlando became the air capital of the armed forces, which brought more Jewish families to the area. Many who were stationed or received training there returned to make their homes in the central Florida area. After twice escaping from Siberian concentration camps during World War I, George Terry arrived at Ellis Island in 1920 with $40. The advent of World War II brought him to Florida, where he bought 70,000 acres in southeast Orange County to raise cattle.

After World War II, Orlando experienced a population boom. The Martin Company moved there in 1956 to manufacture missiles for Cape Canaveral. Martin employed hundreds of Jews in many occupations and at every level and has been a major supplier of defense systems to Israel. Housing was needed, which brought more Jews as builders and developers. By 1960 the population had doubled. New organizations were formed to address the needs of the larger Jewish community (Hadassah in 1948; Jewish Community Council in 1949; Congregation of Liberal Judaism in 1950; Temple Israel in 1954; and Women's American ORT in 1964). Jews entertained in their homes because "everyone knew everyone else" and assumed roles in the business, civic and cultural life of the city.

Supercalifragilisticexpialidocious: When Disney World opened in October 1971, the Central Florida area was changed forever. Orlando has become a "crossroads" of the state, with industry diversification and a distribution and service hub. Tourism and the hotel industry took giant leaps, and Jewish professionals, business people and service people – young and old – have made the Jewish community diverse and dynamic. Orlando is the #1 vacation capital and many visitors stay on to become residents. This was the greatest period of growth – from 4,000 Jews in 1971 to approximately 35,000 Jews in Central Florida in 2005. Agencies created include Kinneret (senior housing) in 1968 and 1979, Jewish Community Center in 1973, Hebrew Day School in 1976, Jewish Family Services in 1978, and Holocaust Memorial Resource and Education Center in 1981. The Jewish campus grew from one room in an old house on the original JCC property in 1973 to a 53,000 square foot facility in Maitland that also houses the Jewish Federation, Hebrew Day School, and Holocaust Center. *HERITAGE Central Florida Jewish News* was started in 1976, by Gene Starn "to provide a Jewish 'ta'am' so that the community will know what is going on in Jewish life, both here at home and worldwide." In 1982 Starn sold the paper to Jeff Gaeser who continued as the editor. In 2005 there were eight constituent agencies of the Federation: Central Florida Hillel, Jewish Pavilion (providing services to Jews in nursing homes), and TOP Jewish Foundation (in addition to those already mentioned). In the Central Florida area there were three Orthodox congregations, five Conservative, seven Reform, and two Reconstructionist. There were Judaic Studies Programs at University of Central Florida and Rollins College, Chevra Kadisha, Florida Kosher Services, Hadassah, ORT, Israel Bonds, Jewish National Fund and Jewish War Veterans. The Central Florida area was thriving Jewishly, with strong expansion in the southern part of town.

[Marcia Jo Zerivitz (2nd ed.)]

ORLÉANS, town in France, S. of Paris. A Jewish community was established in Orléans before 585. During that year, the Jews of Orléans participated in the welcome which was given to King Gontran and appealed to him to be allowed to rebuild the synagogue, which had previously been destroyed. The community may well have existed earlier, for the second, third, and fourth Councils of Orléans, held in 533, 538, and 541 respectively, had already passed legislation concerning the Jews. During the tenth century, an apostate Orléans Jew, Gautier (Walterius), owned houses in the town. At the beginning of the 11th century, the Jewish community, then quite numerous, was accused of having established relations with Caliph El Ḥakim in order to instigate persecutions of Christians in Jerusalem. The ensuing general persecution of the French Jews struck first in Orléans, from which Jews were expelled for several years. The importance of the Orléans Jewish community is again attested when in 1171 it attempted to succor the *Blois Jewish community at the time of the blood libel. After the expulsion of Jews from the French kingdom in 1182, the synagogue of Orléans was transformed into the St. Sauveur Chapel. The community was reconstituted after Jews were permitted to return to France in 1198; among the Jewish notables imprisoned in the Châtelet of Paris in 1204 were two from Orléans. The Jewish cemetery of Orléans was also used by the small surrounding communities.

The large taxes paid by the Jews of Orléans point to the numerical and economic importance of the community (although the customers for their loans were essentially drawn from among the common people), as well as to the size of the Jewish quarter (Grande Juiverie during the 13th century) and its numerous institutions, especially its two synagogues. After the expulsion of 1306, a new, smaller, community was formed between 1315 and 1322 (or 1323) and again in 1359. As a result of the complaints of the Christian inhabitants, the Jews were confined to a narrow quarter. As was the case in several other cities, notably Paris, the Jews of Orléans were the victims of a popular uprising in February 1382, later crushed by King *Charles VI. It was, however, this same king who in 1394 refused to prolong the residence of Jews in France, thus ending the medieval Jewish community of Orléans. Early in its history Orléans became an important center of Jewish learning. Isaac b. Menahem, second half of the 11th century, was cited by *Rashi for his talmudic commentaries and was also known as a legal authority. The hymnologist Meir b. Isaac, late 11th century, was, most probably, his son; the latter's son was the biblical commentator Eleazar b. Meir b. Isaac. The most renowned scholar of Orléans was Joseph b. Isaac *Bekhor-Shor. After 1171 the tosafist *Jacob of Orléans emigrated to London, where he became one of the victims of the massacre of 1189. A Jewish community was again established at the beginning of the 19th century; it possessed a small synagogue and, by the close of the century, had about 40 members.

Contemporary Period

In 1971 there were about 500 Jews in Orléans with a synagogue-community center. In May 1969, the Jewish owners of fashion shops in Orléans suddenly found themselves in the midst of a turmoil of strange gossip, which claimed that Christian women who had been trying on dresses had been drugged and spirited away to exotic brothels. The police had absolutely no knowledge of the alleged kidnapping of any female citizen in Orléans, and yet the rumor spread like wildfire that they had been abducted from six shops, all of which were owned by Jews. Schoolgirls were warned by their teachers not to enter the suspect places and husbands would not allow their wives to go into such shops unaccompanied. The rumor persisted for several weeks, dying out only when a full-scale campaign was organized by the national press, and after conferences held by leading personalities both within and outside of Orléans.

BIBLIOGRAPHY: Gross, Gal Jud, 30ff.; B. Blumenkranz, *Juifs et chrétiens…* (1960), index; E. Morin, *Rumour in Orleans* (1971).

[Bernhard Blumenkranz]

ORLEV, URI (1931–), Israeli writer. Orlev was born in Warsaw and spent the first years of World War II in the Warsaw Ghetto. After his mother was killed by the Nazis, he and his younger brother were smuggled out of the ghetto. For a while, they lived in hiding and in 1943 were sent to Bergen-Belsen where they were liberated by American soldiers. When he finally came to Israel, Orlev lived for a while in a kibbutz, before he was reunited in 1954 with his father, who had been captured on the Russian front. Until 1976, Orlev wrote prose for adults. *Ḥayalei Oferet* (1956; *The Lead Soldiers*, 1979) is an autobiographical novel, telling the story of Yorik and his younger brother against the backdrop of the Holocaust in Warsaw. Orlev's worldwide reputation rests, however, on his books for young readers, and he is one of the first authors who confronted the Holocaust in books for children, avoiding sentimentality and kitsch and always maintaining high literary quality (for instance, *The Island on Bird Street*, 1981; English translation, 1984; *Run, Boy, Run*, 2001; English translation, 2003). *Aḥ Boger* ("Big Brother," 1983) is the story of ten-year-old Yossi whose father is killed in the war, while *Shirat ha-Livyatanim* (1997; "The Song of the Whales," French translation 2003) recounts the special bond between a grandfather and his grandson. Author of novels and stories for children, which have been translated into many languages, Orlev received the prestigious Hans Christian Andersen Award (1996). In 2002, he was awarded the Zeev Prize in Israel for his life's work. Information concerning translations is available at the ITHL website at www.ithl.org.il.

BIBLIOGRAPHY: L. Hovav, "*Ḥavayat Yaldut bi-Yẓirah Otobiyografit u-vi-Yẓirah li-Yeladim*," in: *Sifrut Yeladim va-No'ar*, 5:3–4 (1979), 26–31; D. Stern, "*Nose ha-Shoah be-Sippurei Uri Orlev*," in: *Sifrut Yeladim va-No'ar*, 14:3 (1988), 40–48; M. Regev, "*Ke-ilu ani Ḥai be-tokh Eyzeh Sippur*," in: *Teḥushato shel Adam ha-Mitganev el Yalduto* (2002), 279–299; R. Shichmanter, "*Bekhi Medabek, be-diyyuk kemo Ẓeḥok*," in: *Olam Katan*, 2 (2004), 169–179; D. Prior, *Melekhet Maḥshevet, Ma'aseh Ḥoshev*, in: *Masad*, 2 (2004), 62–70.

[Anat Feinberg (2nd ed.)]

ORLIK, EMIL (1870–1932), German painter and graphic designer. Orlik was born in Prague, son of a highly assimilated German Jewish family, and baptized in his youth. He studied in Munich and traveled widely in three continents. From 1903 until his death he was a teacher at the Arts and Crafts Academy in Berlin. Though he made numerous paintings, he was primarily a master draftsman and an accomplished printmaker, who excelled in woodcuts, etchings, and lithographs. Orlik was particularly successful in his portraits of celebrated contemporaries. Orlik is also known as graphic artist and stage designer. Furthermore, because of his East Asia and Japan journeys in 1900/01 and in 1912, he paved the way for the modern color woodcut in Germany. A prolific and indefatigable worker, he left hundreds of prints and thousands of drawings. After his death, the *Kunstverein* in Cologne honored him with a memorial exhibition, despite the fact that the Nazi era had already begun. Orlik's estate might have been destroyed had not his brother-in-law, a banker of

Prague, managed to transfer the works to Czechoslovakia, where they were hidden in a house in the woods near Prague for many years. His better-known graphic works are collected in *95 Koepfe von Orlik* (1920), *Handzeichnungen* (1924), and *Kleine Aufsaetze* (1924).

BIBLIOGRAPHY: M. Osborn, *Emil Orlik* (Ger., 1920). **ADD. BIBLIOGRAPHY:** B. Ahrens, *"Denn die Bühne ist der Spiegel der Zeit," Emil Orlik (1870–1932) und das Theater* (2001); Juedisches Museum Wien and O. Rychlik, *Emil Orlik. Prag, Wien, Berlin*, Exhibition Catalog Vienna (1997); S. Kuwabara, *Emil Orlik, ein Porträtist des geistigen Berlin* (1998); E. Otto and B. Ahrens (eds.), *Emil Orlik* (1997); E. Otto and B. Ahrens (eds.), *Emil Orlik* (1997).

[Alfred Werner / Jihan Radjai-Ordoubadi (2nd ed.)]

ORLIKOW, DAVID (1918–1998), Canadian pharmacist, politician, labor activist. Orlikow was born in Winnipeg to Louis Orlikow, founder of the "firmly anti-communist, democratic socialist group" Arbeiter Ring, and Sarah Cherniack. In 1941 he graduated in pharmacy from the University of Manitoba but his passion was for progressive politics. At age 16, David was a guest speaker at a youth group meeting against war and fascism. In 1946 he was hired as Western Canada Secretary of the Jewish Labour Committee of Canada and later served as national director, working to expose racial discrimination. He was also a member and local president of the Officer Employees International Union, secretary of the Manitoba Labour Committee for Human Rights and board member of the John Howard & Elizabeth Fry Society which worked to aid those in prisons.

For 43 unbroken years Orlikow also held electoral office. He was a Winnipeg School trustee (1945–50), Winnipeg alderman (1951–58), CCF/NDP member of the Manitoba Legislature (1958–62), and, finally, for 26 years, the NDP member of the House of Commons for Winnipeg North (1962–88). When he died all parties in the House paid Orlikow tribute, but it fell to Deborah Grey of the Official Opposition (Conservative Alliance) to praise him for "faithfulness to his political roots … in the eastern European tradition."

Orlikow said that both his Jewishness and political views came from his early education at Winnipeg's Yiddish Arbeiter Ring school which rejected Orthodoxy and inspired his "lifelong bent toward the secular humanism of the left." His background was "non-Zionist," but the Holocaust compelled him "to do some rethinking." He came to support Israel as a "place of refuge" for Jews denied a home but he was more comfortable when Israel's leadership "was vested in people … grounded in European socialism." Jews in Canada, he hoped, would help build a progressive and welcoming society. He expressed great hope for Canadian multiculturalism.

[Abraham Arnold (2nd ed.)]

ORLINSKY, HARRY MEYER (1908–1992), U.S. biblical scholar and philologist. Orlinsky was born in Owen Sound, Ontario, Canada and went to the U.S. in 1931, later becoming a fellow at Dropsie College (1931–35) and Johns Hopkins University (1936–41). He was professor of Bible at the Hebrew Union College-Jewish Institute of Religion in New York City from 1943, chairman of the Society for Biblical Literature (president 1969–70), and chairman of the American Friends of the Israel Exploration Society from 1954.

Orlinsky was co-translator of a five-volume English translation of Rashi's commentary on the Pentateuch, 1949–50; the only Jewish consultant of the Protestant Revised Standard Version (Old Testament, 1952); and editor of the *Library of Biblical Studies* published by Ktav Publishing House. He was editor in chief of the Jewish Publication Society's new translation of the Pentateuch (1962), to which he wrote a companion volume, *Notes on the New Translation of the Torah* (1969). His other works include *Ancient Israel* (1954; 1969[9]) and *The So-called "Servant of the Lord" and "Suffering Servant" in Second Isaiah 53* (1964), in which he argues that a servant of YHWH, originally innocent of sin and who dies for the punishment of others, is unknown in Jewish thought until the first century. His textual studies of the scrolls from the Judean Desert argue that the St. Mark's Isaiah Scroll (1QIsaa) was copied from memory and is not to be given independent value.

[Zev Garber]

ORLOFF, CHANA (1888–1968), French sculptor. Born in Staro-Konstantinov, Ukraine, Orloff left her native country at the age of 16 for Palestine, but six years later moved to Paris where she remained. She studied at the Ecole des Arts Décoratifs, and her work was exhibited, for the first time, at the Salon d'Automne of 1910. *Modigliani made a portrait of her in 1912. Chana Orloff visited the United States in 1929 and 1938 and exhibited there at the Marie Sterner Gallery, New York, and at the School of the Museum of Fine Arts, Boston. She managed to survive in France during the Nazi occupation although her studio was raided and most of her works there were stolen or destroyed. After the war, she paid several visits to Israel where she made two public monuments: a bronze statue in Ramat Gan depicting the struggle of the Jewish underground and a stone group in Ein Gev. In 1961, the museums in Tel Aviv, Jerusalem, Haifa, and En-Harod honored her with a retrospective exhibition, covering 50 years.

She made many portraits in bronze of well-known contemporaries, such as David Ben-Gurion, Sholem Asch, Shmarya Levin, the actress Hanna Rovina, and the painter Reuven Rubin. She also carved subjects in wood. These include female nudes, mothers with children, men and women sitting or standing, and a variety of birds. Though a contemporary of the cubists, she did not eliminate realistic detail. Her work was realistic and heavily stylized. A mild swing toward abstraction was noticeable in the bronzes she did in the 1950s and 1960s. She could be tenderly lyrical, but also very ironic, especially in her portrait busts. She created for herself an entirely individual mode of expression.

BIBLIOGRAPHY: L. Werth, *Chana Orloff* (Fr., 1927); H. Gamzu, *Chana Orloff* (Heb., 1949); G. Talpir, *Chana Orloff* (Heb., 1950).

[Alfred Werner]

ORMANDY, EUGENE (1899–1985), conductor. Born in Budapest and a child prodigy, Ormandy studied the violin with Hubay and became a teacher at the Budapest Academy, later playing as first violinist with the Bluethner Orchestra in Berlin. After touring in the United States in 1921, he settled there and in 1924 began a career as conductor in New York. After conducting the New York Philharmonic and Minneapolis orchestras, among others, he became first the associate conductor of the Philadelphia Orchestra (with Leopold Stokowski; 1936–1938) and then its permanent conductor, raising it to the status of one of the major orchestras of the world. He retired in August 1980 after 44 years as its musical director, but was appointed conductor laureate. He specialized in 19th-century and modern music, and always conducted from memory.

ORMIAN, ḤAYYIM (1901–1982), educationalist. Ormian was born in Galicia, where he received both a religious and a secular education and was active in the Jewish youth movement. He studied psychology and education at Vienna University and Jewish studies at the Vienna Hebrew Paedagogium, then under the directorship of H.P. Chajes. From 1925 he taught child psychology at the Free Polish University in Lodz. In 1936 he immigrated to Ereẓ Israel, where until 1950 he taught at the Hebrew University Secondary School, at the Teachers' Training College in Beit ha-Kerem, and for some years at the Hebrew University. He was a founder of the psychological clinic at Hadassah Hospital, Jerusalem, and the Israel Psychology Association. He represented Israel at international psychological and pedagogical conferences and was a member of the committee on psychological terminology of the Academy of the Hebrew Language. From the 1950s he was editor of the *Enẓiklopedya Ḥinnukhit* (together with M. Buber). He was awarded the Israel Prize for education in 1971.

ORMÓDY, BERTALAN (1836–1869), Hungarian poet and journalist. One of the first Jewish poets in Hungary, Ormódy wrote patriotic verse and, unlike many Jewish authors of the time, described his fellow Jews in a realistic and sympathetic manner. His works include *Magyar Romanzero* ("Hungarian Romances," 1859) and *Magyar hon ébredése* ("The Awakening of the Hungarian Homeland," 1860).

ORNEST, OTA (**O. Ohrenstein**; 1913–2002), Czech theater director and translator. Ornest was born in Kutná Hora, Bohemia. During World War II, he worked in the Czech section of the BBC, London. On his return to Prague, 1945, he became director of Realistické divadlo ("Realistic Theater"), and from 1950 was simultaneously in charge of three theaters in Prague, the Komorní divadlo ("Chamber Theater"), Divadlo Komedie, and Divadlo ABC. He was also lecturer on theater production at the Academy of Arts, and translated many plays from English. After 1968 Ornest ran afoul of the Communist regime and he was even imprisoned in 1977–78. Ornest's brother, the poet, Jiří *Orten, was killed by the Germans at the beginning of World War II.

ORNITZ, SAMUEL BADISCH (1890–1957), U.S. author. Born in New York City, Ornitz was a social worker from 1908 to 1920, and was also employed by the New York Prison Association. In 1919 he wrote a one-act play, *The Sock*, under a pseudonym, but his name became familiar with the success of his novel *Haunch, Paunch, and Jowl* (1923), one of the best-known works produced by the left-wing "proletarian" literary movement in the United States. Its anti-hero, Meyer Hirsch, is an an East Sider who rises from poverty to become a shady lawyer, crooked politician, and corrupt judge. Ornitz, a professed atheist, saw no virtues in Jewish immigrant life and wished to end Jewish isolation by a policy of outright assimilation. He defied Jewish opinion with his violently hostile portrayals of Jewish types, notably the money-chasing "allrightniks" detested by contemporary leftists and antisemites. Ornitz also depicted the Jewish immigrant generation of the 1880–1914 era in other novels. His books include *Round the World with Jocko the Great* (1925), *A Yankee Passional* (1927), and *Bride of the Sabbath* (1951). In later life Ornitz went to Hollywood, where he wrote scripts for motion pictures.

BIBLIOGRAPHY: S. Liptzin, *The Jew in American Literature* (1966), 131–3.

[Milton Henry Hindus]

ORNSTEIN, ABRAHAM FREDERICK (1836–1895), London-born pioneer minister in Australia and South Africa. (His surname is sometimes spelled "Ornstien.") After serving the Melbourne Hebrew congregation (1866–75) and being principal of Aria College for training Jewish ministers in Portsmouth, England, Ornstein went to Cape Town in 1882 and headed the congregation there for 13 years. He was particularly interested in education. His efforts to establish a Jewish public school in Cape Town did not meet with enough support, so in 1884 he started a private "Collegiate School" for Jewish boys, which provided both Jewish and general education. Its boarding house also accepted girls from other schools in town. Ornstein ran the school successfully. It closed down after his death. Despite his abilities and sense of dedication, his ministry was marred by a number of controversies resulting from his somewhat inflexible personality, and especially from the clash between his "English" outlook and that of the Eastern European immigrants who were arriving at the Cape in increasing numbers.

BIBLIOGRAPHY: L. Herrman, *History of the Jews in South Africa* (1935), 234, 257–66, 269; G. Saron and L. Hotz, *The Jews in South Africa* (1955), 23–26, 28–31, 124; I. Abrahams, *The Birth of a Community* (1955), index. **ADD. BIBLIOGRAPHY:** H.L. Rubinstein, Australia I, 256–57; M. Turnbull, "Rev. Abraham Ornstien [sic]," in: *Australian Jewish Historical Society Journal*, XII (1993–95), 443–66.

[Lewis Sowden]

ORNSTEIN, JACOB MESHULLAM BEN MORDECAI ZE'EV (1775–1839), Galician rabbi and halakhist, son of Mordecai Ze'ev b. Moses *Ornstein. Ornstein, as a young man, married the daughter of Ẓevi Hirsch Wahl of Jaroslaw, who contributed greatly toward his material needs. After Wahl's death Ornstein was proposed as his successor, but because of the violent conflict that the suggestion aroused, he refused to accept the appointment. In 1801 he moved to Zolkiew, where he was appointed rabbi of the town and district. In 1805 he was appointed rabbi of Lemberg (Lvov) and remained there until his death. During his lifetime the Haskalah movement began to spread in Galicia. On the other hand, the ḥasidic movement also gained strength as a result of the establishment of new ḥasidic centers. Although Ornstein, who found himself at the center of these two opposing trends, did not incline to Ḥasidism and was regarded as a *Mitnagged*, he was at the same time opposed to the Haskalah movement and conducted a resolute campaign against it. He was supported in this struggle by his only son, Mordecai Ze'ev, an extremist who was regarded as the driving force in the war against the *maskilim*. Ornstein distrusted the circle of *maskilim* that was formed in Lemberg around Solomon Judah *Rapoport which included N. Krochmal, I. Erter, F. Mieses, and M. Letteris. As a result of the mounting tension between the two sides caused by Rapoport's sharp criticism of Ornstein's *Yeshu'ot Ya'akov* (see below), a ban of excommunication against Rapoport and the leaders of the *maskilim* in Lemberg was issued in 1816. It has been assumed that Ornstein's son Mordecai Ze'ev was its author but that it had his father's approval. The text of the ban refers to the "sins" of the *maskilim* in studying German and studying the Bible with Mendelssohn's commentary. The *maskilim* who ridiculed Ornstein by referring to him as "the Great Inquisitor of Galicia" translated the ban into German and complained to the government that it was illegal, since it had been forbidden to issue such bans in Austria from the time of Emperor Joseph II. As a result Ornstein was compelled publicly to rescind the ban. Rapoport and the *maskilim* reacted to Ornstein's persecution with scathing articles and satires.

Ornstein was regarded as one of the great halakhists of his era, but his main fame rests on his *Yeshu'ot Ya'akov*, novellae and talmudic disquisitions on the whole of the Shulḥan Arukh (OḤ, Zolkiew (1828); YD, *ibid.* (1809); EH, *ibid.* (1809–10)). The four parts of the work, with additions from the author's manuscript and the glosses of his grandson Ẓevi Hirsch, were published in Lemberg (1863). The work is divided into a long and a short commentary; in the latter he merely gives explanations of the Shulḥan Arukh, but in the former he summarizes the views and arguments of the *posekim* while resolving the difficulties of the different novellae by casuistic arguments. Ornstein also wrote, under the same title (which he also used for his Bible commentary), responsa on the four parts of the Shulḥan Arukh (Pietrkov, 1906). Among the questioners and respondents mentioned in it are Moses Sofer (YD, 33; EH, 2) and Aryeh Leib *Horowitz (EH, 20, 26, 29, 30). Ornstein's commentary on the Pentateuch was published in 1907.

His son MORDECAI ZE'EV refused to accept a rabbinical post for many years. He finally accepted an invitation from the Przemysl community to become its rabbi, but died in 1837, before he was able to take up his post. His responsa and novellae are to be found in his father's *Yeshu'ot Ya'akov*.

Mordecai Ze'ev's son, ẒEVI HIRSCH, was appointed *av bet din* of Brest-Litovsk, and remained there until 1874, when he had to leave by order of the Russian government on the grounds that he was a foreign national. He was then appointed *av bet din* of Rzeszow. On the death of Joseph Saul *Nathanson in Lemberg, Ẓevi Hirsch was appointed to succeed him and remained there until his death in 1888. Apart from being an outstanding talmudist he also had a wide general education. He treated the *maskilim* and progressives tolerantly and succeeded in attracting them. On the other hand, he was disliked by the Ḥasidim. At the great rabbinical convention of 1882 in Lemberg, he opposed the demands of the extremists (instigated by Simeon Sofer of Cracow) to confirm the text of a statute that would rescind the right of anyone to be elected to the committee of the community if he transgressed the laws of the Shulḥan Arukh, and as a result the proposed statute was rejected. He attempted to explain to Orthodox circles in 1884 that since the Austrian government was about to introduce compulsory general education, it was desirable to organize religious schools. Because of the extremist opposition to any change in the method of the *ḥeder* and its organization, however, the previous educational structure remained in force. Some of his novellae and responsa were published in the second edition of *Yeshu'ot Ya'akov* on the Shulḥan Arukh. After his death, his son-in-law Aryeh Leib Broda published a collection of his responsa under the title *Birkat ReẒe-H* (Lemberg, 1889; Jerusalem, 1965^2), together with his own additions and glosses, *Milḥamot Aryeh*, and containing his responsa from the years 1864–79.

BIBLIOGRAPHY: Ḥ.N. Dembitzer, *Kelilat Yofi*, 1 (1888), 1506–56a; S. Buber, *Anshei Shem* (1895), 111f., 151, 199; idem, *Kiryah Nisgavah* (1903), 39; M. Weissberg, in: MGWJ, 57 (1913), 519–22; S.M. Chones, *Toledot ha-Posekim* (1910), 286f.; Z. Horowitz, in: *Oẓar ha-Ḥayyim*, 5 (1929), 207f.; M. Balaban, in: *Sefer ha-Yovel... M.Z. Brode* (1931), 29–32; A. Kamelhar, *Dor De'ah* (1935), 188–96; M.Z. Brode, in: *Keneset... le-Zekher Ḥ.N. Bialik*, 8 (1943–44) 104f., 109; Z. Karl, in: *Arim ve-Immahot be-Yisrael*, 1 (1950), 332f., 336; R. Margalioth, in: *Sinai*, 27 (1950), 357–60; 29 (1951), 220; EG, 4 (1956), 217–19, 221, 249, 257, 314–17, 416–18; Klausner, Sifrut, 2 (1952^2), index; Zinberg, Sifrut, 6 (1960), index.

[Josef Horovitz]

ORNSTEIN, LEO (1892–2002), composer. Born in Kremenchug, Russia, Ornstein emigrated to the United States in 1907. He was a piano prodigy, giving recitals of modern music, including his own compositions with colorful titles, which impressed audiences and critics as extreme examples of "futuristic" music. After a period of notoriety, he withdrew from the concert stage without ever having been recorded. He taught in Philadelphia until his retirement in the 1950s but continued to compose until 1990. His stylistically eclectic compositions, characterized by wild rhythms and jarring shifts in tonality, include piano works, chamber music, songs, and orchestral works.

BIBLIOGRAPHY: F.H. Martens, *Leo Ornstein: The Man, His Ideas, His Work* (1918). **ADD. BIBLIOGRAPHY:** C. Oja, *Making Music Modern* (2000), 11–24

[Jerold C. Frakes (2nd ed.)]

ORNSTEIN, LEONARD SALOMON (1880–1941), Dutch Zionist and physicist. Born in Nÿmegen, Ornstein became in 1915 professor of mathematical physics and in 1925 of experimental physics at Utrecht University and in 1921 director of the Utrecht Physical Laboratory. In 1929 he was made a member of the Netherlands Academy of Sciences, and in 1939 a knight in the Order of the Netherlands Lion. He was for several years a member and in 1918–1922 chairman of the Executive of the Netherlands Zionist Organization. During the same period he was also a member of the Zionist General Council. From 1925 to 1940 Ornstein was a member of the Board of Governors of the Hebrew University, and in 1933 the first chairman of *Youth Aliyah in Holland.

[Henriette Boas]

ORNSTEIN, MORDECAI ZE'EV BEN MOSES (d. 1787), Polish rabbi and kabbalist. His father, Moses b. Joske (d. 1764), known as "Rabbi Moses b. Rabbi Joskes," was a member of the community council of Zolkiew. Previously rabbi of Satinov, Kamenka, and Yampol, Podolia, Ornstein was appointed rabbi of Lvov in succession to Solomon b. Moses of Chelm, the author of *Mirkevet ha-Mishneh* (Frankfurt on the Oder, 1851), who moved to Ereẓ Israel. According to Ornstein's tombstone, he had been appointed rabbi of Fuerth just before he died (1787). Ornstein applied himself to the study of Kabbalah and was close in spirit to Ḥasidism, and so was referred to as "the kabbalist and Ḥasid." He is reputed to have studied for a while under Rabbi Dov Baer of Mezhirech. He was known in Lemberg as "The Great Rabbi Mordecai Ze'ev" to distinguish him from his grandson, Mordecai Ze'ev Ornstein. Ornstein did not publish any halakhic works, but his novellae are quoted by his descendants. He gave approbations to many of the works of his contemporaries, and he is referred to in terms of the greatest reverence. Of his sons, the best known are Jacob Meshullam *Ornstein, author of *Yeshu'ot Ya'akov* (1828), and Moses Joshua Hoeschel, rabbi of Taringrad and author of *Yam ha-Talmud* (Lemberg, 1825). Two of his sons-in-law are well known, Aaron ha-Levi Ittinga (the first) and Dov Berish Halperin of Berzan (Brezhany). For over a century, except for a brief gap, all the incumbents of the rabbinate of Lvov were his descendants.

BIBLIOGRAPHY: Ḥ. N. Dembitzer, *Kelilat Yofi*, 1 (1888), 144b–146a; S. Buber, *Anshei Shem* (1895), 149–51; idem, *Kiryah Nisgavah* (1903), 59f.; M. Balaban, in: *Sefer ha-Yovel... M.Z. Brode* (1931), 25; Z. Karl, in: *Arim ve-Immahot be-Yisrael*, 1 (1950), 329; EG, 4 (1956), 413f.

[Itzhak Alfassi]

OROBIO DE CASTRO, ISAAC (**Balthazar**; 1620–1687), philosopher and physician, born in Braganza, Portugal, of Marrano parentage. After studying medicine and philosophy in Alcalá de Henares, Orobio became a leading physician and professor of medicine in Seville and professor of metaphysics at Salamanca. In Alcalá he was the student of the Carmelites and the Franciscans. He was subsequently arrested by the Inquisition and charged with secretly practicing Judaism. Orobio was incarcerated for three years, tortured, and finally confessed. Upon his release, he fled to France, where he became professor of pharmacy at Toulouse. In 1662 he moved to Amsterdam where he joined the Jewish community, changed his name to Isaac, and practiced medicine. During the 17th century he was one of many Conversos who returned to Judaism in communities which were mainly established by such people. Orobio, who soon became one of the leading intellectual figures among the Spanish and Portuguese refugees, wrote poetry and philosophical treatises in defense of Judaism.

Orobio experienced a variety of religious and cultural encounters before he joined the Amsterdam Portuguese Jewish community. In Braganza he lived in fear of the Inquisition. From Portugal his family moved to Andalusia where he learned to live a double life. In Spain he moved from one place to another in search of a safe haven. In France he was able to reveal his Jewish identity and decided to move to Amsterdam.

His first important work consists of letters against the rationalistic defense of Judaism in answer to Alonso de Cepeda of Brussels. Among his best-known works is *Certamen philosophicum propugnatae veritatis divinae ac naturalis* (1684), a rationalistic and scholastic attempt to refute the philosophy of *Spinoza, and like Spinoza's *Ethics* written in a series of theorems. The work was also published in Fénelon's *Refutation des erreurs de Benoît de Spinosa* (1731). Orobio became acquainted with the Dutch Protestant liberal preacher, Philip van Limborch, in Amsterdam, who, impressed by Orobio's accounts of how the Spanish Inquisition functioned, used them as the chief case history in his Latin history of the Inquisition. Limborch, however, was disturbed by Orobio's anti-Christian arguments. They held a debate in the presence of John Locke which was published in 1687 (*Pauli a Limborch de Veritate Religionis Christianae, amica collatio cum erudito Judaeo*) along with the first issue of Uriel da *Costa's autobiography. Locke wrote a long review of the debate for the *Bibliothéque universelle* (vol. 7). Orobio's major anti-Christian work is *Prevenciones divinas contra la vana idolatria de las Gentes*; portions of this were published by Baron d'Holbach in French, as part of his anti-religious campaign, under the title *Israel vengé* (London, 1770). A greatly toned-down version, translated by Grace *Aguilar, was printed in English in 1842 as *Israel Defended*.

Most of Orobio's works were not published but circulated in manuscript among the European Jewish communities. The largest collection exists in the Biblioteek Ets Ḥayyim in Amsterdam; others are in the Rosenthaliana collection in Amsterdam, in Paris, London, Oxford, and New York. An acute metaphysician, Orobio de Castro utilized materials from the Spanish scholastics of the 16th and 17th centuries to defend Judaism against freethinkers like Juan de *Prado and Spinoza, against orthodox Christians, and against religious liberals like

Limborch. Certain of Orobio's arguments against Christian theology are very close to some of Spinoza's against the plurality of substance. He made interesting efforts to provide a philosophical justification for Judaism in 17th-century terms, and, in contrast to Spinoza, to show the compatibility of reason with the traditional faith.

BIBLIOGRAPHY: Kayserling, Bibl, 81–83; Graetz, in: MGWJ, 16 (1867), 321–30; Orobio de Castro, *La Observancia de la Divina Ley de Mosseh*, ed. by M.B. Amzalak (1925), xviii–xxxix; J. de Carvalho, *Oróbio de Castro e o espinosismo* (1937); I.S. Revah, *Spinoza et le Dr. Juan de Prado* (1959), 84–153; Roth, Marranos, index. **ADD. BIBLIOGRAPHY:** G. Nahon, in: *Yod*, 26 (1987), 57–62; Y. Kaplan, *From Christianity to Judaism: The Story of Isaac Orobio de Castro* (1989).

[Richard H. Popkin / Yom Tov Assis (2nd ed.)]

°OROSIUS, PAULUS (b. c. 385), Christian author of *Historiarum adversum paganos libri septem* ("Seven Books of Histories Against the Pagans"), a history of the world from the Creation to 417, written at the suggestion of St. Augustine as a supplement to the latter's *De civitate Dei* (book 3). It attempted to prove that the Roman Empire had suffered as many calamities before the rise of Christianity as it did afterward.

Among details concerning the Jews which he mentions are the reasons given by Pompeius Trogus and Tacitus for the expulsion of the Jews from Egypt; the establishment of a sizable Jewish community in Hyrcania near the Caspian Sea in the fourth century B.C.E.; the capture of Jerusalem by Pompey; the plundering of the Temple by Crassus Licinius; the embassy to Caligula led by Philo; the relief of a famine (of Christians, surprisingly) in Jerusalem by Helena, queen of Adiabene (who, according to Orosius, was a Christian convert); the expulsion of the Jews from Rome by Claudius; the Jewish revolt against the Romans in 66–73 (Orosius, in common with Sulpicius Severus and in opposition to Josephus, claims that Titus gave the order to set fire to the Temple); Domitian's persecution of the Jews; the Jewish revolt against Trajan (important for confirming and supplementing Eusebius' account and now verified by inscriptions and papyri); the Bar Kokhba rebellion (in connection with which it is stated that the Jews tortured the Christians because they would not join the revolt); and the suppression of a Jewish, Samaritan, and Adiabenian revolt by Septimius Severus. Orosius' aim is essentially apologetic and his work is superficial and fragmentary. It is heavily indebted to others, especially Livy, Pompeius Trogus, Josephus, Tacitus, Eusebius, and Eutropius. His history is of limited value, except for contemporaneous events or where, as in the case of a large part of Livy, his sources are lost.

The following are the English translations of his writings: I.W. Raymond, *Seven Books of History against the Pagans* (1936); R.J. Deferrari, *Seven Books of History against the Pagans* (1964).

BIBLIOGRAPHY: Reinach, Textes, 325, n. 1; Pauly-Wissowa, 35 (1939), 1185–95.

[Louis Harry Feldman]

OROT (Heb. אוֹרוֹת; "Lights"), moshav in southern Israel near Kiryat Malakhi, affiliated with Tenu'at ha-Moshavim. Founded in 1952 by members of Ha-Ikkar ha-Oved Organization from the United States, the moshav cultivated irrigated field and garden crops and dairy cattle, but many liquidated their farms and the moshav was one of the many riddled with unmanageable debts in the inflationary 1980s. In 1970 it had 240 inhabitants, growing to 420 in 2002.

[Efraim Orni / Shaked Gilboa (2nd ed.)]

ORPAH (Heb. עָרְפָּה), Moabite woman. Elimelech and Naomi, driven by famine from Beth-Lehem in Judah, settled in Moab. After Elimelech's death, their two sons, Mahlon and *Chilion, married Orpah and *Ruth. After her two sons died, Naomi set out for home and tried to persuade her daughters-in-law to remain behind in Moab, their native land. Orpah obeyed, while Ruth insisted on accompanying her mother-in-law (Ruth 1:4–14).

[Nahum M. Sarna]

In the Aggadah

Orpah was a daughter of Eglon, king of Moab (Ruth R. 2:9). She was called Orpah because she turned her back (*oref*, "nape of the neck") on her mother-in-law (Ruth R. 2:9). She is identified with Harafu, the mother of four Philistinian giants of whom Goliath was one (II Sam. 21:18). They were vouchsafed to her because she shed four tears for Naomi, but all of them were slain by David (Sotah 42b). Goliath's punishment was delayed for 40 days (I Sam. 17:16), as a reward for Orpah's accompanying Naomi on the way for 40 paces (Ruth R. 2:20).

Orpah was killed by David's general, Abishai, when she attempted to prevent him from reaching her son Ishbibenob (Sanh. 95a).

BIBLIOGRAPHY: Ginsberg, Legends, index; I. Ḥasida, *Ishei ha-Tanakh* (1964), 353.

ORPAZ AVERBUCH, YITZHAK (1923–), Israeli writer. Orpaz was born in Zinkov, in the former Soviet Union. At the age of 17 he reached Ereẓ Israel and joined a group called Yas'ur in the settlement of Magdiel. In 1942 he learned about the death of his parents and sister in the Holocaust, and he then joined the British army in Europe. Upon his return to Ereẓ Israel in 1946, he worked as a diamond polisher and shortly thereafter took part as an artillery officer in the War of Independence (1948). His literary career began in 1949, when he had his first story published in the military journal *Ba-Maḥaneh*. In order to read his story on the radio he was asked, typically for that time, to change his last Diaspora-sounding name – Averbuch – to the Hebrew one, Orpaz.

Orpaz studied philosophy and Hebrew literature at Tel Aviv University, and after serving 13 years in the Israeli Army, he became a night editor in the *Al ha-Mishmar* daily newspaper. His first collection of stories, *Isbei Pere* (Wild Grass), appeared in 1959 and may be considered as the nucleus for his novel, *Or be'ad Or* (1962). During these years his writing was naïve, influenced by the Socialist Realism genre.

In 1964 he published his novella *Mot Lisanda* ("The Death of Lysanda"), a dramatic political shift from the naïve style to symbolic writing. In the article "*Impresiyya al ha-Sippur ha-Nisyoni*" (1965; "Impression on the Experimental Story"), Orpaz underlines three major features: breaking away from narrative continuity, narrative naiveté and moral message. The stories *Ẓed ha-Ẓeviyah* (1966), the *Mot Lysanda*, *Nemalim* ("Ants," 1963), *Madregah Ẓarah* (1972), and the stories of *Ir she-Ein ba Mistor* (1973) reflect these features. The novel *Masa Daniel* ("Daniel's Trials," 1969), set against the Six-Day-War, links materialistic reality and historical, social relevance. *Bayit le-Adam Eḥad* (1975) turns to the form of an autobiographical, confessional journal. Orpaz gives an intimate testimony, interweaving personal trauma – the death of his nephew in the Yom Kippur War – and the national one. "For me the Yom Kippur War was a shock and a catalyst mixed together," Orpaz maintains. The author goes back to the world of Jewish symbols and to Yiddish, his mother tongue. Consequently, in 1982 Orpaz added his former surname to the Hebrew one. By doing so he underlined his Jewish identity. At 56, Orpaz left Israel for the first time. His encounter with the Diaspora, a world lost forever, is reflected in the stories of *Reḥov ha-Tomojna* (1979), which describes a journey to a mythical childhood in a miraculous street. The novels *Bayit le-Adam Eḥad*, *Ha-Gevirah* (1983) and *Ha-Elem* (1984) constitute the Tel Aviv trilogy (*Maḥzor Ataliyah*), in which Orpaz highlights the tensions between Israeli and Jewish identity.

The novel *Ha-Kalah ha-Nitzḥit* ("Eternal Bride," 1987) highlights mystical elements from the Jewish world. Orpaz confronts Judaism with Christianity throughout history, expressing his longing for the Jewish world. In the 1990s Orpaz went back to look at Israeli reality. The collections *Ahavot Ketanot, Terufim Ketanim* (1992), and *Laylah be-Santa Poalina* (1997) reflect this tendency.

Orpaz published a book of poems, *Lizlo'aḥ et ha-Me'ah* ("Cruising the Century," 1983), and a philosophical essay, *Ha-Ẓalyan ha-Ḥiloni* (1982), which constitutes the spiritual, poetic infrastructure of his writing. Orpaz's heroes are religious pilgrims who go on a secular journey, yearning for existential values.

Orpaz was awarded the Bialik Prize (1986), the Prime Minister's Award (2004), and the Israel Prize (2005). Many of his stories and novels have been translated into various languages. These include *The Death of Lysanda* (1970), and translations into French of *The Eternal Bride* (1991) and *A Narrow Stair* (1993).

BIBLIOGRAPHY: H. Barzel, in: *Moznayim*, 42 (1976), 119–126; R. Furstenberg, in: *Modern Hebrew Literature* 5:3 (1979), 12–15; O. Bartana, in: *Akhshav*, 51–54 (1987), 142–157; O. Bartana, in: *Apiryon*, 16–17 (1990), 26–31; G. Shaked, *Ha-Sipporet ha-Ivrit*, 5 (1998), 147–158; H. Zemiri, in: *Dimmui*, 19 (2001), 105–112.

[Kochava Petal Benyamin (2nd ed.)]

ORPHAN, ORPHANAGE.

Treatment of Orphans

Communal concern for orphaned children has deep roots in Jewish tradition, and numerous biblical commandments stress the importance of providing for them. Along with the widow (*almanah*), resident alien (*ger*), and Levite (*Levi*), orphans are to be protected and treated with justice and compassion (Deut. 16:11 and 14; 24:19–21; 26:12–13). Psalm 68:6 describes God as a "father of the fatherless."

Rabbinic Judaism reinforced the individual and communal obligation to meet the needs of orphans. "Whoever brings up an orphan in his home," Sanhedrin 19b states, "it is as though he had begotten him." According to Ketubbot 50a, a man who brings up an orphan boy or orphan girl in his house and enables them to marry, is performing righteousness at all times. The rabbis considered the community responsible for supporting impoverished orphans, including educating them and preparing them for marriage.

Maimonides summed up biblical and rabbinic discussions regarding the treatment of orphans in the *Mishneh Torah* (De'ot 6:10), specifying the need for sensitivity and courtesy: "Whoever irritates them, provokes them to anger, pains them, tyrannizes over them, or causes them loss of money, is guilty of a transgression .... If a teacher punishes orphan children in order to teach them Torah or a trade, or lead them in the right way – this is permissible. And yet he should not treat them like others, but make a distinction in their favor. He should guide them gently, with the utmost tenderness and courtesy…."

In Jewish Law

The meaning of the word *yatom* ("orphan"), as found in the traditional literature, varies in accordance with the context. In terms of the social treatment of the orphan, no distinction is made as to whether the child has been orphaned of father or mother (Yad, De'ot 6:10). If, however, reference is being made to the special privileges accorded the orphan by the civil code, then only the fatherless child is meant (Resp. Mahayashdam, nos. 196, 454).

The Talmud shows great concern for the claims of minor children to support from their father's estate. The rabbis recognized no legal differences between children of "privileged" or "secondary" wives, and extended protection even to a man's proven illegitimate offspring (see *Maintenance, *Parent and Child, **Yuḥasin*). They also extended the legal protection of orphan girls by seeing to it that each *ketubbah* should specifically pledge the bridegroom's estate for the support of his surviving minor daughters (*ketubbat benan nokevan*), and, in the absence of his pledge, by construing the omission as an error. Ultimately, the right of female orphans to support came to overshadow the claims of all other heirs, and, if need be, the entire estate was used for this purpose (M. Ket. 4:11; 13:3; TJ Git. 5:3–4; and commentaries; see *Succession.).

In the case of impoverished orphan children whose father left little or no property, the Talmud holds the community responsible for their support, for marrying them off, and for providing them with the means to live economically independent lives. Communal funds were to be used to rent and furnish a house for a young man, and to fit out a girl with clothing and a minimum dowry. If the communal funds were low, the orphan girl was given priority over the boy. If the community chest could afford to do so, the provisions provided for the orphan were made in accordance with his social position and the former manner of life to which he had been accustomed (M. Ket. 6:5 and TB Ket. 67b).

In the case of a man who died without appointing a guardian for his minor children, the court must do so (*Mishneh Torah*, Nahalot 10:5; *cf.* BK 37a). For more particulars see *Apotropos. Minor orphans and their property are exempt from the ordinary laws of overreaching (*ona'ah*; Sh. Ar., ḤM 109:4–5), usury (*ribbit de-Rabbanan*; YD 160:18), the seventh-year recession of debts (prosbul; ḤM 67:28), and communal taxation for the charity fund (*ẓedakah*), with specified exceptions (TB BB 8a and Sh. Ar., YD 248:3; for further particulars see *Taxation).

Whenever orphans of any age are involved in litigation regarding their father's property or transactions, judicial practice is to enter on their behalf all pleas and all arguments that their father could have entered (b. BB 23a; see *Pleas; *Practice and Procedure).

[Aaron Kirschenbaum]

Communal Care of Orphans

Orphan care was a major concern of all medieval European Jewish communities. Many Cairo *Genizah* letters express the anguish of destitute widows and their children who appealed for help to alleviate their distress. Orphaned children in this milieu were sheltered by relatives or, when this was not possible, by other families, especially those of teachers or cantors, and the community assumed responsibility for the education of such youngsters. Individuals were encouraged to marry off the orphaned daughter of a poor relative, and to provide dowries for poor brides, particularly orphans. Jewish philanthropists left large sums for this purpose. In Saragossa, Spain, the general charitable society for the poor, including orphaned girls, was known as *Hoce Hece* (probably a corruption of the Hebrew *osei ḥesed*). In Rome, during the 17th century, two societies supplied minimum dowries and trousseaus to needy brides. A wide ranging society, the *Hasi Betulot*, founded in 1613 (based in Venice, but extending to several other cities), and a similar one, based in Amsterdam and known as the *Dotar* (established in 1615), provided dowries and financial assistance to impoverished girls, including orphans.

The first Jewish orphanage is thought to have been established by members of the Spanish-Portuguese community in Amsterdam in 1648, and was administered by a society known as *Aby Yetomim* (Father of Orphans). Its founders may have been inspired by similar institutions under non-Jewish auspices. The Jewish orphans' home in Fuerth, established in 1763 with a donation from a private businessman, was the first of its kind in Germany. These institutions were part of the "extraordinary expansion of Jewish philanthropic societies in the eighteenth century," described by Salo Baron.

Jewish orphanages were founded in many European cities during the 19th century. In London, Jews' Hospital opened in 1807 to care for the aged Jewish poor and to provide education and industrial employment for youngsters, including orphans. An orphanage already served destitute children in the Sephardi community, and a society to care for orphaned Ashkenazi children, known as *Honen le-Yetonim*, existed from 1818. In 1831, the Orphan Asylum was established in response to needs arising from a severe cholera epidemic the year before. Children in the orphanage were educated, taught a trade, and apprenticed outside the institution. Eventually, Jews' Hospital and the Orphan Asylum merged to form the Jews' Hospital and Orphan Asylum, later known as the Norwood Home for Jewish Children. In Germany, the number of Jewish hospitals and orphanages increased significantly after the nation's unification in 1871. This trend was linked to the rationalization of philanthropy and development of the social work profession throughout Europe, as well as the influx of eastern European Jewish immigrants into Germany during these years. The growing number of Jewish orphanages, many with modernized buildings, joined the extensive network of German Jewish charitable organizations.

By the late 19th and early 20th centuries, many cities and towns in Poland, including Warsaw, Bialystok, Radom, Tarnow, Chelm, Lomza, and Brody, had at least one, and often several, Jewish orphanages. Children admitted to these asylums were either actual orphans or from impoverished families. The orphanages housed and fed their wards, educated them in general and Jewish subjects, and taught them trades. Following their discharge, youngsters were often apprenticed, sent to Jewish vocational schools, or continued their education in yeshivot or other schools

The number and size of East European Jewish child care institutions increased significantly during and following World War I in order to serve the large number of children orphaned during the war and in subsequent pogroms. An orphan home for boys was established in Warsaw in 1917, and another orphanage, *Ezrah ve-Hazzalah* (Help and Rescue), was founded in Stanislawow in 1919. These orphan homes were funded by private individuals (especially through bequests), donations, fundraising activities, grants from the municipal authorities and, in several cases, contributions from the American Jewish Joint Distribution Committee (JDC). Many Jewish orphanages continued to function into World War II. Probably the best known of that period was the one on Krochmalna Street in Warsaw. Dr. Janusz *Korczak, the famous Polish Jewish physician, educator, and writer, had directed that institution since 1912, while at the same time lecturing and publishing many books on child development and welfare. During the final deportation from the Warsaw Ghetto, in August 1942, he refused to abandon his children and led 200 of them on a dignified and poignant march to the train station, after which they were transported to Treblinka and murdered.

Jewish Orphanages in the United States

Societies for the care of orphaned Jewish children in the U.S. date back to the early 19th century. The Society for the Relief of Orphans and Children of Indigent Parents in Charleston, South Carolina, created in 1801, which maintained orphans in private homes (and later established an orphan asylum) was an important pioneer. In 1855, the first actual Jewish orphanages, the Jewish Foster Home of Philadelphia and the Association for the Relief of Jewish Widows and Orphans of New Orleans, were established.

Before the mid-19th century, most dependent children had been maintained through charity in their own homes, placement with other families, indenture, apprenticeship, or placement in public almshouses, along with adult poor. The decades following the Civil War witnessed campaigns in several states to remove children from the often unwholesome atmosphere of such almshouses. The number of American orphanages mushroomed in response to the needs of children orphaned by the Civil War and, later, to the hardships of impoverished, largely immigrant, families in America's crowded cities. Many Catholic and Jewish child care institutions were established in this era due to concerns that children housed in so-called non-sectarian institutions were subject to Protestant proselytizing. Jewish orphanages were founded in New York, Cleveland, San Francisco, Baltimore, Newark, New Jersey, Brooklyn, Rochester, New York, Atlanta, Boston, and Chicago, among other cities, part of a constantly expanding network of Jewish child care institutions (also including juvenile reformatories and foundling asylums). Some of the largest and most influential of these were the Hebrew Orphan Asylum of New York (1860), the Cleveland Jewish Orphan Asylum (1868), and the Hebrew Sheltering Guardian Society of New York (1879).

Jewish orphanages in the U.S. provided their wards with general and Jewish education, vocational training, and placement services ("after-care") once they left the orphanage. By 1900, according to estimates at the time, the majority of children served by these institutions were not full orphans, but rather half-orphans or the children of ill or destitute parents. While most Jewish orphanages had been founded by Central European Jews, initially to serve the poor of their own communities, they subsequently aided impoverished eastern European Jewish immigrants. However, such Jews in many cities also created their own child care institutions (such as the Hebrew National Jewish Orphan Asylum in New York, the Home for Hebrew Orphans in Brooklyn, the Orthodox Jewish Orphan Asylum in Cleveland, and the Marks Nathan Orphan Asylum in Chicago), which offered more traditional religious education and training. In the 19th century, larger Jewish institutions, like many other child care asylums of the time, tended to be highly regimented and impersonal; however, by the early years of the 20th century, many liberalized their policies due to the influence of a "new breed" of orphanage managers and in keeping with changing theories of child development.

Although foster care gradually superseded institutional care as the preferred means of providing for dependent children in the early 20th century, Jewish orphanages retained their vitality in many communities. Quite a few institutions reorganized themselves structurally so as to create more homelike environments for their wards. The so-called "cottage plan" (originating in France, Germany, and England) was first introduced in a Jewish institution in 1912 by the Hebrew Sheltering Guardian Society of New York, which became known as Pleasantville. This model, which grouped youngsters of mixed ages in small cottages on a rural property, was later adopted by Jewish orphanages in San Francisco, Los Angeles, and Cleveland as well. In the mid-1930s, according to one estimate, there were about 100 organizations serving approximately 10,000 dependent Jewish children (including, but not limited to, full and half orphans) in the U.S., either in institutions or foster homes. Some Jewish orphanages, such as the Cleveland Jewish Orphan Asylum, renamed Bellefaire in 1929, gradually focused more attention on youngsters with social, emotional, and behavioral problems, rather than orphans. By the 1940s, most American Jewish orphanages had closed their doors, and had been absorbed into city-wide Jewish Child Care Associations or similar agencies, which allocated children to various types of care, including group homes, foster care, and adoption.

Orphanages in the Yishuv and in Israel

The first Jewish orphanage in the *yishuv* was the Diskin Orphan Home in Jerusalem, founded in 1881 to assist those fleeing the pogroms in Russia. The Zion Orphanage (1900) and the General Israel Orphans' Home for Girls (1902) followed. Not all of the children in these institutions were orphans; some were placed there because their parents were temporarily unable to care for them.

During and following World War I, the need for orphan care increased dramatically due to war-time conditions, cholera and typhus outbreaks, as well as Arab riots during the 1920s. About 4,500 of the 20,000 children under 15 in the *yishuv* between 1918 and 1928 were orphaned of one or both parents, primarily as a result of the war. In 1918, there were three orphanages in Jerusalem (accommodating about 500 children), as well as the *Mikveh Israel agricultural training school near Tel Aviv (which housed Sephardi, Ashkenazi, and Yemenite orphans from abroad, and admitted 150 war orphans after the war). In 1919, The Palestine Orphan Committee was formed (at the initiative of American and British Zionists, but later including board members from the *yishuv* as well) to provide for the large numbers of children orphaned during the war. Although the committee, which functioned until 1928, initially favored home placement (through grants to mothers, relatives, and foster homes), it also established 12 small, short-lived institutions and two larger, more permanent institutions. Over 700 children were cared for in Jerusalem orphanages during the 1920s. Among these were the General Orphanage (a religious institution) and the WIZO (Women's International Zionist Organization) Baby Home for orphans and abandoned children. Another WIZO home for infants was founded in Tel Aviv in 1929, and the two housed over 250 infants during the 1930s. By 1945, there were 21 orphan homes in the country.

Emerging in the 1920s, and gaining strength in the 1930s and 1940s, was the Children's Village model, i.e., rural communities of children (many of whom were orphans and, increasingly, refugees from Europe) who lived together and learned agricultural skills. The first such village was Me'ir Shefeyah for orphan girls, founded near Zikhron Ya'akov in 1923. Another early, well known institution of this type was Ben Shemen, founded in 1925, which took in all 200 children from a model Jewish orphan home in Kovno, Lithuania. A third children's village was created in Haifa for 120 children arriving in 1934 from the Ahava Orphan Home in Berlin. During the 1930s, these youth villages served as the foundation of the remarkable *Youth Aliyah program, which rescued 16,167 youngsters from Europe by 1945, and assisted another 14,000 children in the immediate postwar period. Children who arrived in Palestine with their parents were cared for by the *yishuv*'s Social Work Department, while orphans and partial orphans were cared for by Youth Aliyah.

In the early years, many child welfare workers in the *yishuv*, particularly Henrietta *Szold, had favored home-based or foster care for orphaned children, However, by the early 1930s, institutional care emerged as the preferred method, generally for economic reasons; it was easier to raise funds for orphan homes than for family settings. Such institutions, influenced by European models and meshed with the collectivist orientation of Israeli society, appeared best suited to accommodate massive waves of immigrants, and were viewed as more stable environments for children than many home settings. In the 1980s, approximately 10,000 children under the age of 14 (including orphans as well as children with problematic family situations) lived in about 200 residential institutions in Israel.

The Role of Women

Women played a significant role in the history of Jewish orphanages, both as founders, managers, and supporters of orphanages, and as recipients of aid. Orphanage work was considered to be an appropriate sphere of activity for women, who served these institutions in both volunteer and professional capacities.

Women volunteers took active roles in fundraising for orphanages, and also provided children with food, clothing, and entertainment. In both Europe and the U.S., women founded and/or directed Jewish orphanages, although sometimes the original women directors were later replaced by men. This pattern was evident, for example, in the Jewish Foster Home of Philadelphia and the Hebrew Sheltering Guardian Society of New York. In Poland, several Jewish orphanages were administered by women's committees in the late 19th and early 20th centuries, including those in Czenstochowa, Wloclawek, and Biala-Podlaska. Orphanage work was in keeping with popular views of womanhood at the time, which legitimized women's involvement in charitable causes, particularly those assisting other women and children.

Women also worked as paid matrons, teachers, and other staff members in many Jewish orphanages. For example, Simha Peixotto, a prominent Jewish educator at the Hebrew Sunday School Society of Philadelphia, was also a beloved teacher in that city's Jewish Foster Home, where she taught Hebrew and prepared boys for bar mitzvah from 1863 to 1878. In addition, Bertha *Pappenheim, the well-known leader of the Jewish women's movement in Germany in the early 20th century, served as housemother of a Jewish orphanage for girls in Frankfurt from 1895 to 1907.

Finally, Jewish orphanages assisted large numbers of desperate mothers, and provided education and training for young girls who might not otherwise have had such opportunities. Most of the youngsters admitted to these institutions, at least in the U.S. in the late 19th and early 20th centuries, were half-orphans, especially the children of widowed or deserted mothers. In most child care institutions, boys and girls received training considered suitable for their sex, for example, woodworking and carpentry for boys, and sewing and embroidery for girls. However, by the early 20th century, orphanage directors, at least in the United States, attempted to provide all of their wards, male and female, with broader educational opportunities, based on their individual talents and abilities.

Contemporary Efforts

The greatest growth in Jewish group child care in recent years has probably been in the former Soviet Union, especially Ukraine, where orphanages funded by the JDC and religious groups (such as *Chabad, the Lubavitch organization) have been established to meet the needs of orphaned and destitute children. Concerned about the significant number of Jewish children housed in general orphanages in Ukraine (where they were subjected to terrible living conditions, abuse, and antisemitism), the JDC, for example, helped support the opening of a Jewish Children's Home in Odessa in 1996, which is currently sheltering more than 100 children.

Sources of Communal Support

In pre-modern times, the *kuppah* (Jewish community chest) supported orphans along with other impoverished people. Once institutions for the care of Jewish orphans were established, they received funding from many sources. These included: private donations (including bequests), membership dues (i.e., groups of individuals who supported particular institutions), grants or subsidies from the municipal authorities, specific fund-raising events and drives (e.g., "Purim Balls"), solicitations of funds from abroad, and pledges made in synagogues (especially during the Torah reading on specific holidays). In addition, individuals or local merchants often made donations of food, clothing, equipment and entertainment, and Jewish organizations, such as *B'nai B'rith, the *Joint Distribution Committee, or *ORT (Organization of Rehabilitation through Training) provided financial support. In some cases, these organizations played major roles in establishing the institutions; for example, the western division of the International Order of B'nai B'rith founded the Cleveland Jewish Orphan Asylum in 1868, and the *Bund (the General Union of Jewish Workers in Lithuania, Poland and Russia) founded a children's home in Chelm during World War I.

Standards of Care

Jewish child care institutions in all parts of the world were influenced by prevailing trends in child welfare in the larger society. However, there were also instances in which the Jewish institutions pioneered in certain areas and made important contributions to the child welfare field as a whole. In America, even in the 19th century, the era of the so-called "total institution," Jewish orphanages were known for progressive measures, such as the official prohibition against corporal punishment (before this became public policy in many states), quality medical care systems (including staff physicians, dental care, and accurate record-keeping), widespread advocacy of public school education for institutionalized youngsters, and sponsorship of "boarding out" and widows' pension programs.

[Reena Sigman Friedman (2nd ed.)]

BIBLIOGRAPHY: M. Cohn, in: *Zeitschrift fuer vergleichende Rechtswissenschaft*, 37 (1919–20), 417–45; Gulak, Yesodei, 1 (1922), 37, 154 n. 11; 3 (1922), 147ff.; 4 (1922), 43, 140; L.M. Epstein, *The Jewish Marriage Contract* (1927), 121–43, 175–92; Herzog, Instit, 1 (1936), 173f.; Baron, Social², 2 (1952), 253, 271; 5 (1957), 321 n. 81. **ADD. BIBLIOGRAPHY:** I. Abrahams, *Jewish Life in the Middle Ages* (rep. 1969); S. Baron, *The Jewish Community* (1942); M. Bodian. *Hebrews of the Portuguese Nation* (1997); B. Bogen, *Jewish Philanthropy* (1917), E. Conway. "The Origins of the Jewish Orphanage," in: *The Jewish Historical Society of England. Transactions*, Sessions 1968–1969, Vol. 22 & Miscellanies Part 7 (1970), 53–66; R.S. Friedman. *These Are Our Children: Jewish Orphanages in the United States, 1880–1925* (1994); W. Glicksman, *Jewish Social Welfare Institutions in Poland* (1976); S.D. Goitein. *A Mediterranean Society*, 3 (1978); E. Jaffe, *Child Welfare in Israel* (1982), M. Karpf, *Jewish Community Organization in the U.S.* (1938); M. Smilansky et. al. *Child and Youth Welfare in Israel* (1960); E. and A. Weiner, *Expanding the Options in Child Placement* (1990); B. Weinryb, *A Social and Economic History of the Jewish Community in Poland from 1100–1800* (1982). **ADD. BIBLIOGRAPHY:** IN JEWISH LAW: M. Elon, *Ha-Mishpat ha-Ivri* (1988), 1:354, 461, 502, 514, 531f., 551, 569, 600, 649, 661, 669, 680, 730, 764, 787f.; 2:1231; idem, *Jewish Law* (1994), 1:427; 2:562, 611, 626, 646f., 671, 699, 743, 803, 817, 827, 839, 901, 941, 966f.; 3:1475.

ORSHA, city in Vitebsk district, Belarus. Already in existence during the 16th century, the community of Orsha was subordinated to that of *Brest-Litovsk. In 1643 Isaiah Nahumowicz of Orsha was mentioned among the tax lessees of Lithuania. In the charter of privileges granted by King Jan II Casimir to the Jews (1649), Orsha is numbered among the large communities of the country. In 1765, 368 Jews in Orsha paid poll tax. There were 1,662 Jews in 1847 and 7,383 (56% of the total population) in 1897. Most of the town artisans were Jews. There were 4 Jewish schools, a *talmud torah*, and many *ḥadarim*. In October 1905 over 30 Jews in the town lost their lives in a pogrom. Although in 1910 there were 9,842 Jews in Orsha, the community began to decline under the Soviet regime. In 1926 there were 6,780 Jews (30% of the total population), and 7,992 (21.3% of the total population) in 1939. In the Soviet interwar period two Jewish elementary schools existed, but they were closed by the authorities in the mid-1930s. At that time 95% of Jewish artisans were organized in cooperatives. The Germans occupied Orsha on July 16, 1941. Many Jews succeeded in escaping to the East. A Judenrat was appointed, the main purpose of which was to collect tribute for the Germans. In September 1941 two ghettoes were organized, with about 2,000 people in each. On November 26, 1941, all Jews – some 5,000 (including from the environs) – were murdered in the Jewish cemetery. The Jewish population was estimated at about 1,000 in 1970, with most leaving in the 1990s.

BIBLIOGRAPHY: *Delo o pogrome v Orshe* (1908); *Die Judenpogrome in Russland*, 2 (1909), 467–87.

[Yehuda Slutsky]

ORSHANSKI, ILYA (Elijah) GRIGORYEVICH (1846–1875), journalist, jurist, and historian in Russia. Orshanski, who was born in Yekaterinoslav (now Dnepropetrovsk), received both a traditional Jewish and a general education. He completed law studies at the University of Odessa in 1868 and was subsequently offered a professorship there on condition that he embrace Christianity, a condition which he unhesitatingly rejected. Orshanski's first literary endeavors appeared in the Hebrew newspapers **Ha-Meliẓ* and **Ha-Karmel*. From 1869 to 1871 he served as assistant editor of the Russian-Jewish newspaper *Den*, which was closed down in 1871 by government decree because of an article Orshanski wrote on the pogroms in Odessa of that year. In his article he openly accused the government of responsibility for the pogroms and urged the Jews to demand legal satisfaction and compensation for injuries sustained.

Before the newspaper was closed down, Orshanski published in it a series of articles on the legal status of the Russian Jews and their economic and social condition. These essays, among others, were published in two volumes entitled *Yevrei v Rossii* ("The Jews in Russia," 1872, 1877²) and *Russkoye zakonodatelstvo o yevreyakh* ("Russian Legislation Affecting the Jews," 1877). Despite their contemporary propagandist objectives, these studies are among the most noteworthy contributions to the history of the Jews in Russia. When discussing the economic structure of the Jews in Russia, Orshanski was the first to refrain from indulging in the defense, apology, and criticism customarily leveled by authors of the Enlightenment (*Haskalah) at Russian Jewry. His impartial, scientific analysis clarified the economic foundations of Jewish life in Russia and enabled him to determine from a historical point of view the place of the Jew in the national economy, while his keen legal mind enabled him to examine the Russian legislation affecting Jews, to trace its origins and motivations, and to demonstrate its medieval character and spirit. His "Russian Legislation Affecting the Jews" not only contains a vast amount of legal information but is also a first attempt to describe systematically the historical development of Russian legislation.

Orshanski also wrote a comprehensive, if critical essay, *"Mysli o khasidizme"* ("Reflections on Ḥasidism," in his *Yevrei v Rossii* (1877[2]), 311–46, and also in *Yevreyskaya Biblioteka*, vol. 1, 1871), examining the growth and development of Ḥasidism against the economic and social background of the Jews in Ukraine in the 18th century.

In the last years of his life, Orshanski devoted his time and his pen to research and writing on general Russian law. The resultant studies, published posthumously in three volumes, gained a high reputation in the field of Russian jurisprudence, and are still considered among the finest examples of Russian juridical literature of the time. Because of his failing health Orshanski went to Germany, where he spent several years before he returned to Russia in the spring of 1875.

BIBLIOGRAPHY: M.G. Morgulis, *Ilya Grigoryevich Orshanski i yego literaturnaya deyatelnost* (1904); E.M. Morgulis, *I. Orshanski, 1846–1875: Yego zhizn i literaturnaya deyatelnost* (1898).

[Simha Katz]

ORSOVA (Rom. **Orşova**), town in Severin province, S.W. Romania; until 1918 part of Hungary. Since Orsova was a border town between Hungary and Romania, settlement of Jews was prohibited until the first half of the 19th century. After the prohibition was lifted, Jewish merchants and craftsmen, mainly from western Hungary, began to settle there. A community was founded in the old town in 1876, affiliated with the organization of Neologist communities. A synagogue was erected in 1878. The oldest tombstone in the Jewish cemetery dates from 1879. Between the world wars the community was prosperous, its members including merchants, craftsmen, physicians, and lawyers. This period saw the development of ramified Zionist activity. Activities were guided by the local rabbi, K. Löwenkopf, who held office from 1928 until 1945, when he emigrated to Palestine. In September 1942 Jewish property was confiscated by the Fascist regime, and many of the men were conscripted for forced labor, while others were expelled to *Transnistria. The Jewish population, 192 in 1930, fell to 135 in 1942 and 10 in 1947. By 1970 emigration to Israel and other places had reduced it to 20.

BIBLIOGRAPHY: E. Deutsch, in: *Almanahul Evreesc*, 3 (1938), 141–52 (Ger.); K. Löwenkopf, in: *Uj Kelet* (Feb. 17, 1967).

[Yehouda Marton]

ORT (initials of Rus. **Obshestvo Remeslenofo zemledelcheskofo Truda**, originally meaning "The Society for Handicrafts and Agricultural Work"), organization for the promotion and development by vocational training of skilled trades and agriculture among Jews. It was initiated by a "private letter" sent out in April 1880 to the Jews of the towns of Russia. It was signed by S.S. *Poliakov, Baron Horace *Guenzberg, A.J. Zak, L.M. *Rosenthal, and M.F. Friedland, and concerned the permission granted by Czar Alexander II "to collect a fund for a philanthropic purpose…" The Jewish population in all parts of the country was called upon to contribute to the fund, which was intended "to support and develop the existing vocational schools for Jews, to help open new schools, to help the Jewish agricultural colonies, model farms, and agricultural schools." Response to the letter was widespread. A capital of 204,000 rubles was quickly collected. Over 25 years (1880–1905), ORT raised the sum of one million rubles. The interest from this sum and the dues paid by its wealthy members supported ORT in that period. The sum was lost in the 1917 Revolution. During this initial period ORT's legal status was uncertain. It was not until 1906 that it received regular legal authorization.

The 125-year history of ORT can be divided into five (principal) periods:

1880–1920

At first ORT functioned in Russia only, on a small scale. One of its aims in this period was to assist craftsmen by transferring them from the *Pale of Settlement to the Russian interior. The committee of ORT decided upon the establishment of small workshops for trades such as tailoring, shoemaking, or carpentry within a *talmud torah* or orphanage, or settled requests from needy persons. A large-scale campaign "Help Through Work" was launched between 1914 and 1916, helping needy Jews who had been driven out of their homes in wartime to find employment in the new places where they settled.

1920–1945

In 1921 ORT was established in Berlin as an international organization with the name World ORT Union. From a purely philanthropic organization it increasingly became a basic social movement in Jewish life. Subsequently ORT was active in the areas formerly within the Russian Empire – Poland, Lithuania, Latvia, and Bessarabia – as well as in Germany, France, Bulgaria, Hungary, and Romania. This work by ORT had a considerable influence not only on the masses most directly involved but also on Jewish communities of the so-called "helping countries," which had been invited to join the ORT movement, to support it financially and to help it expand and consolidate its activities. Between the two wars, ORT's global work was directed by an international committee headed by Leon *Bramson, former member of the *Duma, with the help of David *Lvovich and Aaron *Syngalowski. The latter inspired the ideology of ORT and spread the idea of manual work among Jews, stressing the need for a change in the economic structure of Jewish life. The committee established ORT organizations in the United States, South Africa, Canada, South America, and many other places.

Until 1938, the Soviet Union was also an important area of ORT activity. ORT was the first organization in the Soviet Union to assist (from 1922) in the rehabilitation of Jewish farmers in the Ukraine, who had suffered severe losses, both in lives and to their farms, during World War I and the Civil War. ORT then cooperated with Komzet (see *Russia, under the Soviet regime). It assisted in the transference of many

Jews in Belorussia to occupation in agriculture. Assistance to Jewish settlers was provided in Bessarabia, where ORT's activities in 1928 extended to 604 families in 37 agricultural settlements. By this year ORT had aided a total of 141 settlements with 4,737 families (c. 20,000 persons) cultivating agricultural land amounting to approximately 40,000 dessiatine (c. 108,000 acres), as shown by Table: ORT Aid.

A report of 1934 shows that in the Soviet Union ORT operated 67 agricultural colonies, with 3,100 families or almost 10,000 persons, 47 factories and cooperatives in cities and kolkhozes, employing more than 5,000 persons, as well as many adult courses and workshops. In Poland there were 49 schools for adolescents and adult courses with over 2,000 students in addition to 12 agricultural colonies. There was also an ORT network in Romania, Lithuania, Latvia, Hungary, Bulgaria, France, and Germany.

One of the problems which ORT tackled was to help working Jewish youth and craftsmen to integrate into the industrialization especially affecting the Eastern European countries after World War I. ORT also undertook to provide specialist training for certain professions in which, under the legislation approved by the countries of Eastern Europe (as in Poland in 1927), it was necessary to pass an examination. In the Soviet Union assistance was given to Jews who, as a result of the changed Soviet economic structure, were deprived of their occupational status (*lishentsi*) and were compelled to turn to new sources of livelihood, especially crafts.

An important sphere of ORT activity was to provide Jewish craftsmen with necessary implements. In 1920–23 ORT established a central buying agency for providing implements and machines to craftsmen who had lost them during and after World War I, as well as new materials. In 1924 a similar institution to replace the buying agency was opened in London named the ORT Tool Supply Corporation, with branches in Warsaw, Kovno (Kaunas), Riga, and Czernowitz (Chernovtsy), and in the Soviet Union.

This was a difficult period for World ORT. The deepening world economic crisis reduced its income from the West, and the organization faced increasing antisemitic discrimination in almost every country in which it operated. With the rise of Nazism in Germany, the Berlin headquarters no longer seemed safe. In October 1933 the office was transferred to Paris, which had become a refugee center for thousands of German Jews. World ORT soon organized vocational retraining programs to help refugees integrate into French society or prepare for careers in other countries.

Most of World ORT's programs continued throughout 1939 and beyond the start of World War II. This included the transfer of most of the Berlin ORT School to Leeds, England, just days before the war. As the war progressed, communication between World ORT and its European operations was frequently cut, but individual schools and programs continued to operate in isolation, often with former ORT directors and teachers working within their camps and ghettos. In Kovno, Lithuania, for example, the ORT training workshop continued to function until 1944, when the ghetto was destroyed and the surviving occupants deported. Similar activities took place in the ghettos of Warsaw and Vilna.

In occupied France, ORT was permitted to continue working until 1942–43. Courses originally set up for German refugees were now serving French Jews. ORT ran programs in 20 cities throughout the country and provided tools, materials, and training to a number of internment camps. Eventually World ORT's headquarters had to move from France to neutral Switzerland, where it established many training programs for the thousands of Jewish refugees who managed to escape there.

The movement of Jewish refugees also led to the development of ORT programs beyond Europe. Some of these new operations were temporary – such as that in Shanghai, China (1941–1950) – but many laid the foundations for continuing programs, especially in South America. During the 1930s and early 1940s many thousands of refugees from Europe arrived in South America, many of them en route to the United States. Communities were formed in Argentina, Brazil, Chile, Cuba, Mexico, Uruguay, and other countries of the region. ORT rapidly established operations throughout the subcontinent to provide vital training courses that would help the newcomers to rebuild their lives.

1945–1960

The programmatic and, in particular, the geographical changes which ORT experienced during these 15 years were a result of the constantly changing economic and political situation, and especially the migration affecting the Jewish communities in various countries. In accompanying the masses of Jewish refugees and emigrants to the countries where they found new homes, ORT entered into yet more Jewish communities in Europe, Africa, Asia, and the Americas.

World ORT's largest refugee program took place at the war's end, training tens of thousands of survivors and displaced persons (DPs) from the Jewish communities of Europe. Working with UNRRA (the UN Relief and Refugee Agency), ORT became the recognized vocational agency for the camps, working throughout Europe to support Jewish survivors. This work was completed by the mid-1950s, when most of the DP programs were closed. It is estimated that a quarter of all Jewish DPs – some 80,000 people – had passed through ORT's vocational centers, many on their way to the new State of Israel.

In addition to its work in the DP camps, ORT ran programs for survivors in Switzerland, the United Kingdom, the Netherlands, Belgium, and, especially, France. Most of these West European operations were created as temporary responses to prevailing needs, closing in the late 1940s or early 1950s. The work in France, however, continued, forming the basis of today's flourishing ORT France school system.

After World War II, ORT turned its attention to the needs of "forgotten" Jewish communities in North Africa, Iran, and India and, somewhat later, Ethiopia. Jews in these countries earned a meager living as peddlers and semi-skilled artisans, but had no way of acquiring the necessary skills to improve their situation. Many faced harsh conditions, with widespread poverty and disease. World ORT set up vocational courses and schools, teaching a range of skills that allowed young people – for the first time – to seek and obtain gainful employment. Political changes and civil unrest in North Africa (late 1950s and early 1960s) and Iran (late 1970s) made life too difficult for the local Jewish populations. Most immigrated to Israel, France, and other Western countries, marking an end to ORT's activities in these countries.

In France, ORT's main efforts in the immediate post-war years were devoted to helping Holocaust survivors from all over Europe rebuild their lives. In the late 1950s and early 1960s this program drew to a close and a new one began as thousands of Jewish families began to arrive from the newly independent and now unsafe Muslim countries of North Africa. Their children needed to be educated and prepared for their adult lives. ORT mobilized its resources and accepted many hundreds of these children into its schools. All the schools were enlarged during this period, and several added dormitory blocks to accommodate students. Between 1950 and 1970, ORT France student numbers rose from 1,700 to more than 5,000.

IN ISRAEL. Israel was the only country where the ORT idea of manual work did not need to be propagated, as it was deeply rooted there by the pioneers of the First and Second Aliyah, as well as by the *halutzim* who arrived in Erez Israel between the two wars. The establishment of ORT in Israel followed rapidly after the creation of the state, but former students of ORT had been settling in Palestine from the 1920s. A Tool and Supply Corporation, which provided machinery and tools to new immigrants, kibbutzim and kevuẓot, was set up as early as 1946. Workshop equipment from DP camps was transported to Palestine following the DPs' immigration there. In 1949, ORT opened vocational courses for new immigrants in Pardes Ḥannah, manual-training workshops in the children's village of *Ben Shemen, and the first vocational school sections in Jerusalem, Tel Aviv, Reḥovot, Ramleh, Jaffa, and the yeshivah in Kefar Avraham.

From the beginning ORT paid special attention to the needs of disadvantaged communities, bringing them high-quality education and training programs that gave them a foothold on the ladder to self-sufficiency and growth. Thus, apart from its schools in the main conurbations, ORT has always worked in deprived areas, in development towns and with successive waves of immigrants from North Africa, Ethiopia, and the former Soviet Union.

Today, ORT Israel is the country's largest vocational training organization, operating some 150 schools and technological colleges. Supported by development teams, teacher training programs, and its own publishing house, ORT offers vocational, technological, and academic training to almost 100,000 students aged between 5 and 80. In modern Israel there are over half a million ORT graduates who are making a vital contribution to their nation's industry and economy.

1960–1990

The basic idea and aims of ORT had remained unchanged in the years between the 1920s and the 1950s. Minor changes occurred in form and work methods, varying with the standard of living and technical development in the countries of operation and, to an even larger extent, with the economic condition and mentality of the Jewish communities there. In those years ORT carried out an important educational task. It spread its principles of work among the Jews of Algeria, Morocco, Tunisia and Iran, helping to convince them that learning a trade was the surest means to acquire economic independence.

In 1960, the ancient *Bene Israel community of India appealed to World ORT for help. Depleted by immigration to Israel in the 1950s, the Bombay-based community was poor and unskilled. A health and welfare program was established in 1961 and then, in 1962, a Polytechnic was created on the campus of a Jewish school. The impact of ORT's work was quickly felt, and its operations continue today.

ORT's work of enlightenment, and the ever-improving situation of the qualified tradesman, as well as the good reputation achieved by ORT schools, made vocational training for youth accepted even in the most distant Jewish communities. By the mid-1950s there were so many applications for admission to ORT vocational schools that there were not enough vacancies.

The late 1960s saw ORT Israel beginning to move away from trade training for manual labor to a more comprehensive education network, providing general academic education as well as vocational training. Increasingly, following the demands of the local economy and employment market, science and technology education was being introduced into more and more schools. Subjects such as electronics, automation, pneumatics, hydraulics, and plastics technology became very popular. The Harmatz School of Engineering, which opened in Jerusalem in 1976, typifies this shift. It was ORT's first school to provide post-secondary technical education leading to a practical engineering degree.

To enable the change in its programs ORT Israel developed its own teacher training scheme in dedicated institutions alongside its schools. One such institution was the ORT Moshinsky Center in Tel Aviv, where teaching materials and methodology were developed and teachers were trained in the application of new technologies. Textbooks and learning aids were produced for both teachers and students. These were then translated for use across the entire World ORT network.

During the 1980s ORT schools around the world continued to grow – especially so in Israel and Latin America. In 1988 ORT Israel opened its next purpose-built, flagship institution, the ORT Braude College of Engineering. Like the Harmatz School of Engineering before it, this was a direct result of a dedicated fundraising campaign. Following ORT Israel's example, schools in France and Latin America introduced advanced courses of study that would lead to university entrance and employment at the higher levels of engineering and technology. In France, new adult training programs were added and junior colleges established. The schools of ORT Argentina were acknowledged to be among the best in the country, while in Uruguay the ORT Montevideo school became a degree-conferring university in 1988.

In addition to the training programs for Jews, in 1960 World ORT was asked by the U.S. Agency for International Development (USAID) to undertake technical training programs in Africa. Seeing this as an integral part of its mission, World ORT took up the challenge, and so began a new phase of humanitarian activities, outside the Jewish community.

Since that time, ORT has carried out over 350 economic and social development projects in more than 90 countries in Africa, Eastern Europe, Latin America, and Asia.

These projects bring basic life-skills to urban and rural populations in developing and emerging countries, helping these communities to achieve independence and self-sufficiency. The range of subjects that has been covered includes health and nutrition, transportation, mother and child care, rural development, agriculture, forestry, democracy development, and information technology. Literally millions of people in some of the most disadvantaged regions of the world have benefited from these projects.

In each project that it undertakes, ORT consultant teams evaluate the needs of the local community, devise specific training programs, and implement them "on the ground." All ORT's International Cooperation projects are designed to become self-sustaining, with local staff learning how to continue the operation once ORT has withdrawn. Funding for all these projects is provided by international agencies and private foundations.

From 1990

In the 1990s ORT was among the first to perceive the advantages of Information Technology. The World ORT IT department established its first Internet connection in 1992 and the ort.org domain name was registered in 1994. By 1998 all ORT schools had an Internet connection, and many had their own websites. ORT's curricula reflected the changing needs of a modern technological society, providing high-tech courses as well as general, Jewish, science and management programs. ORT began to develop projects that would link communities across continents and provide general and Jewish knowledge and resources to people everywhere. In 1996 it launched Navigating the Bible, an online Bar/Bat Mitzvah tutor. This was followed by several other projects, including: DO I.T., an online foundation course in Information Technology; English Space, an interactive and collaborative English as a second language tutor; Learning about the Holocaust through Art, a unique resource for those teaching and wanting to learn about the Holocaust through art; and Yizkor, a *yahrzeit reminder service and memorial website. ORT continues to develop online resources that benefit large numbers of people worldwide.

The collapse of the Soviet Union and East European communism enabled the return of ORT to these areas. In 1991, after an enforced absence of 53 years, ORT was able to return to the country of its birth. The political changes ushered in a new market-driven economy for the region, and ORT's first task was to provide computer and technology courses for the local community to enable them to prepare for employment in the new conditions. To facilitate its work, ORT established relationships at the highest level with the Russian authorities – and later, with each of the new independent states – gaining their recognition and their trust. In 1993, ORT signed a collaboration agreement with the Ministry of Education of the Russian Federation. In 1995, the ORT Technology School in Moscow was inaugurated. This was quickly followed by other agreements and the opening of ORT schools and centers throughout the CIS and Baltic States.

By 2005, there were 58 ORT schools and educational institutions in the CIS and Baltic States serving more than 25,000 students each year and considered by the local authorities to include the finest educational establishments available in the region.

While many Jews remained in the CIS and Baltic States following the dismemberment of the Soviet Union, a great number chose to immigrate to Israel. At the same time Operation Solomon brought the second, larger wave of immigrants from Ethiopia to Israel. ORT Israel opened thousands of high-school places to accommodate the new arrivals. It also created courses for adults, providing the necessary knowledge and skills to obtain employment.

In 2005, More than 90,000 students – Jews, Israeli Arabs, Druze, Bedouins, and new immigrants – are educated at ORT Israel schools, colleges, and institutions. ORT graduates comprise 25 percent of Israel's high-tech workforce.

In Latin America ORT continued to expand, offering its expertise to both the Jewish and the wider community. In Brazil, two new schools, specializing in life sciences and technology were opened during the 1990s. In Mexico, a state-of-the-art technology and science resource center opened in 1998. While providing courses in computer programming, biotechnology, and business administration in its schools and centers throughout the region, ORT also addressed the needs of poorer local communities. Vocational training and Mother and Child projects were undertaken by ORT's International Cooperation department in several Latin American countries.

By 2005 ORT Argentina has become ORT's third largest operation, with over 7,300 students enrolled in its institutions. Across Latin America ORT provides Jewish communities the high standard of education they require in the 21st century.

ORT has been active in more than 100 countries past and present with current operations in Israel, the CIS and Baltic States, Latin America, Western Europe, Eastern Europe, North America, Africa, Asia, and the Pacific. It has a student body of some 270,000 each year worldwide and offers its experience on a non-sectarian basis. Since its inception in 1880, more than 3,000,000 people have graduated from ORT programs worldwide. In 2000 ORT changed its name from World ORT Union to World ORT.

The World ORT administrative office moved from Geneva to London in 1979, but the headquarters remain in Geneva. In 2005 Robert Singer was director general, Sir Maurice Hatter (U.K.) was president, Jean de Gunzburg (France) was deputy president, Mauricio Merikanskas (Mexico) was chairman of the Executive Committee, and Robert Sill (U.S.A.) was chairman of the Board of Directors.

BIBLIOGRAPHY: *80 Years of ORT*, Historical Materials, Documents and Reports (1960); J. Rader, *By the Skill of their Hands, the Story of ORT* (1970). **ADD. BIBLIOGRAPHY:** L. Shapiro, *The History of ORT, A Jewish Movement for Social Change* (1980); *Facing the Future: ORT 1880–2000* (2000).

[Vladimir Seev Halperin / Rachel Bracha and Judah Harstein (2nd ed.)]

ORTA, GARCIA DE (c. 1500–1568), Portuguese Marrano scientist and physician. Born in Castelo de Vide, he studied medicine at Salamanca and Alcalá and taught at Lisbon University. Garcia de Orta left for India in 1534. During his long stay in Goa, he served as physician to the Portuguese viceroys and leading Christian dignitaries, as well as the Muslim ruler Burhā n al-Dīn Niẓām al-Mulk. In recognition of his services, the Portuguese viceroy bestowed on him, probably in 1548, the island of *Bombay, then a small fishing village.

Garcia de Orta's great work, *Coloquios dos Simples e drogas he Cousas Medicinais da India* (Goa, 1563; "Colloquies on the Simples and Drugs of India" 1913), made him "the first European writer on tropical medicine and a pioneer in pharmacology." This work, written in Portuguese in the form of a dialogue, was approved by the Inquisition and recommended by the official physician of the viceroy, Luiz de Camões. It was hailed as one of the chief cultural achievements of the 16th century, a work which brought the greatest honor to the author's country, Portugal. Garcia de Orta was long believed to be Christian, but the *Acts of the Inquisition*, published in 1934, made it clear that he was a militant Converso who had lived a dual religious life throughout his 30 years in Goa and had possibly gone there in the hope of escaping the Inquisition. He was posthumously condemned by the Inquisition in 1580, and his remains exhumed and cast into the sea.

BIBLIOGRAPHY: W.J. Fischel, *Garcia de Orta and the Exodus of Jews from Spain and Portugal to India* (1970); Carvalho, in: *Revista da Universidade de Coimbra*, 12 (1934), 61–246; Revah, *ibid.* (1960); H. Friedenwald, *The Jews and Medicine* (1944), index; C.R. Boxer, *Two Pioneers of Tropical Medicine* (1963).

[Walter Joseph Fischel and Joshua O. Leibowitz]

ORTEN, JIŘÍ (pseudonym of **Jiří Ohrenstein**; 1919–1941), Czech poet. Orten was born in Kutná Hora, Bohemia. His first poems, published in literary reviews before 1939, attracted immediate attention because of their novel existentialist approach and surprisingly mature form. After the Nazi invasion, his works were published under pseudonyms. Within two years, he managed to complete four books of poetry: *Čítanka jaro* ("Primer of Spring," 1939), *Cesta k mrazu* ("The Road to the Frost," 1940), *Ohnice* (1941), and *Jeremiášův pláč* ("Jeremiah's Lament," 1941). Orten's friends arranged their publication, ascribing their authorship to "Karel Jílek" or "Jiří Jakub." He was run over and killed by a German army vehicle on a Prague embankment. Two other volumes of Orten's poetry, *Zcestí* ("The Wrong Way") and *Elegie* ("Elegy"), appeared in the definitive edition of his verse after World War II. His prose works appeared later: *Eta, Eta, žlutí ptáci* ("Eta, Eta, Yellow Birds," 1966). Also appearing was *Deníky* (1958; "Diaries," 1958), published in full as *Modrá kniha* ("The Blue Book," 1992), *Žíhaná kniha* ("The Striped Book," 1993), and *Červená kniha* ("The Red Book," 1994). His brother was Ota *Ornest.

BIBLIOGRAPHY: V. Černý, in: *Dílo Jiřího Ortena*, 1 (1947), 443–7; J. Kunc, *Slovník českých spisovatelů beletristů* (1957); Eisner, in: *Věstník židovské náboženské obce v Praze* (1948), 236. **ADD. BIBLIOGRAPHY:** J. Kocián, *Jiří Orten* (1966); A. Mikulášek et al., *Literatura s hvězdou Davidovou*, vol. 1 (1998); *Lexikon české literatury* 3/I (1985); O. Ornest, "My Brother Jiří Orten," in: *Review of the Society for the History of Czechoslovak Jews*, Vol. 6, 1993–94; *Slovník českých spisovatelů* (1982).

[Avigdor Dagan / Milos Pojar (2nd ed.)]

ORTENBERG, ARTHUR (1926–) and **CLAIBORNE, LIZ** (1929–), U.S. apparel manufacturers, environmentalists. Ortenberg and his non-Jewish wife, fashion designer Liz Claiborne, had each been in the textile and apparel industry for more than 20 years when they decided to go into business together. By the time they retired 14 years later, Liz Claiborne Inc. was a $1.3 billion corporation and one of the fashion industry's most spectacular success stories. Ortenberg provided the management know-how, while Claiborne was the creative force. Their target customer was the working woman who wanted moderately priced, well-made, stylish sportswear that could be worn to the office. Ortenberg, a New Yorker, met Claiborne, born in Brussels to American parents, in the mid-1950s. He was running the junior dress division of a sportswear company and hired her as a designer. They each went through divorces and married in 1957. Claiborne moved to Youth Guild, a junior dress manufacturer, as chief designer and Ortenberg became president of Fashion Products Research, a textile and consulting firm. In 1976, after scraping together $50,000 in savings and raising $200,000 more from family, business associates, and friends, they launched their own business. Claiborne was president and Ortenberg was executive vice president of operations. Claiborne's designs were so popular that the company went public in 1981. Ortenberg became a vice chairman in 1985, together with Jerome Chazen, who had been executive vice president of marketing and who had been with the company since its start. The product line expanded to include men's clothing, a more extensive sportswear line, accessories, cosmetics, and fragrances. In 1986, revenues reached $800 million and Claiborne appeared on the Fortune 500 list of the biggest industrial firms in the U.S. Citing a desire to do other things with their lives, Ortenberg and Claiborne retired from active management roles in 1989, remaining directors for another year. The Liz Claiborne and Art Ortenberg Foundation, created in 1984, is devoted to "the conservation of nature and the amelioration of human distress" and pursues environmental and social interests from the U.S. to Europe, Africa, and Central and South America. "Liz and I have long had numerous environmental projects in mind and not enough time to address them," Ortenberg said. "Now we have the time and the wherewithal through the Foundation to do just that. We want to make this world a better place for our grandchildren." Claiborne was honored by the Council of Fashion Designers of America in 1986 and Ortenberg and Claiborne were inducted into the National Sales Hall of Fame in 1991.

[Mort Sheinman (2nd ed.)]

ORTHODOXY. The term "Orthodoxy" first appeared in respect to Judaism in 1795, and became widely used from the beginning of the 19th century in contradistinction to the *Reform movement in Judaism. In later times other terms, such as "Torah-true," became popular. Yet, in general, Orthodox came to designate those who accept as divinely inspired the totality of the historical religion of the Jewish people as it is recorded in the Written and Oral Laws and codified in the Shulḥan Arukh and its commentaries until recent times, and as it is observed in practice according to the teachings and unchanging principles of the *halakhah*. Orthodoxy as a well-defined and separate phenomenon within Jewry crystallized in response to the challenge of the changes which occurred in Jewish society in Western and Central Europe in the first half of the 19th century: Reform, the *Haskalah, and trends toward secularization. Those who opposed change and innovation felt it necessary to emphasize their stand as guardians of the Torah and its commandments under altered conditions and to find ways to safeguard their particular way of life.

[Nathaniel Katzburg]

Orthodox Judaism considers itself the authentic bearer of the religious Jewish tradition which, until *Emancipation, held sway over almost the entire Jewish community. The term Orthodoxy is actually a misnomer for a religious orientation which stresses not so much the profession of a strictly defined set of dogmas, as submission to the authority of *halakhah*. Orthodoxy's need for self-definition arose only when the mold into which Jewish life had been cast during the period of self-sufficient existence of Jewish society had been completely shattered. Orthodoxy looks upon attempts to adjust Judaism to the "spirit of the time" as utterly incompatible with the entire thrust of normative Judaism which holds that the revealed will of God rather than the values of any given age are the ultimate standard.

At the very dawn of Emancipation, many Orthodox leaders foresaw the perils which the breakdown of the ghetto walls incurred for Jewish survival. Some of them were so apprehensive about the newly available political, social, and economic opportunities, which they felt would make it almost impossible for the Jew to maintain his distinctive national and spiritual identity, that they went so far as to urge the Jewish communities to reject the privileges offered by Emancipation. Others, while willing to accept the benefits of political emancipation, were adamant in their insistence that there be no change in the policy of complete segregation from the social and cultural life of the non-Jewish environment. R. Ezekiel *Landau was so fearful that exposure to the culture of the modern world might ultimately result in total assimilation of the Jew that he proclaimed a ban on the reading of Moses *Mendelssohn's translation of the Pentateuch, even though Mendelssohn had advocated strict observance of the *halakhah*. Fear of assimilation was intensified by a number of developments, seen as alarming, ranging from numerous instances of outright conversion to Christianity to the efforts on the part of the Reform movement to transform radically the character of Judaism in order to facilitate the total integration of the Jew within modern society.

The Orthodox leadership believed that the aesthetic innovations which characterized the first phase of the Reform movement were motivated by the desire to model the synagogue on the pattern of the Protestant Church – a move that was regarded by its advocates as indispensable for gaining for the Jew full acceptance by his Christian neighbors. The claim that the introduction of organ music or the substitution of prayers in the vernacular for those in Hebrew did not violate talmudic law was refuted by 18 leading rabbinic authorities who joined in writing the book *Elleh Divrei ha-Berit* (Altona, 1819). The Orthodox community, intuitively realizing that liturgical reforms were only the beginning of a long-range process designed to change the tenets and practices of Judaism so as to remove all barriers against full immersion in the majority culture, reacted with an all-out effort to preserve the status quo. The slightest tampering with tradition was condemned.

Orthodoxy in this sense first developed in Germany and in Hungary (see Samson Raphael *Hirsch; *Neo-Orthodoxy). As its religious and political ideology crystallized, it emphasized both its opposition to those who advocated religious reform and the essential differences in its outlook and way of life from that of the reformers. At the same time, it refused to countenance any possibility of cooperation with those advocating different viewpoints. Herein lay Orthodoxy's main impetus toward organizational separation, a trend epitomized in Germany after 1876 when separation from the established community became legal, thus permitting the formation of the "separatist Orthodoxy" (*Trennungsorthodoxie*). This trend was opposed by R. Isaac Dov *Bamberger, one of the outstanding German Orthodox rabbis of his day. Underlying the opposition to secession was the reluctance to jeopardize the unity of the Jewish people. Historically, membership in the Jewish community was never regarded merely as a matter of voluntary identification with a religious denomination. One's status as a Jew was not acquired through the profession of a particular creed. With the exception of converts, the privileges and responsibilities devolving upon a member of the people of the Covenant derive from the fact that he was born a Jew. To this day Orthodoxy has not been able to resolve the dilemma that a considerable section of Jewry today no longer obeys the *halakhah*. There are those who lean toward a policy of withdrawal, lest they be responsible for the implicit "recognition" of the legitimacy of non-Orthodox ideologies. Others, concerned with preserving the unity of the Jewish people, advocate involvement of Orthodoxy in the non-Orthodox Jewish community even at the risk that their policies might be misconstrued as a willingness to condone non-Orthodox approaches. It was, ironically, the issue of separation that precipitated most of the internal conflict that has plagued Orthodoxy. In its early history, *Agudat Israel was torn asunder by the controversy over whether Orthodox Jews should be permitted to take a leading part in the organization if they, at the same time, also belonged to groups in which non-Orthodox Jews were allowed to play a prominent role. The influence of the Hungarian element finally swayed Agudat Israel to adopt a resolution barring its members from participation in non-Orthodox movements. Isaac *Breuer, a grandson of Samson Raphael Hirsch and one of the leading Agudat Israel ideologists, formulated in his *Der neue Kuzari* a philosophy of Judaism in which refusal to espouse the cause of separation was interpreted as being equivalent to the rejection of the absolute sovereignty of God.

*Mizrachi, on the other hand, espoused a policy of cooperation with non-Orthodox and secular elements. It is also noteworthy that in eastern Europe most Agudat Israel circles frowned upon secular learning, while Mizrachi, as a general rule, adopted a far more sympathetic attitude toward worldly culture. In central and western Europe, however, Agudat Israel circles were guided not only by Hirsch's separationist policy toward the non-Orthodox community, but also subscribed to his philosophy of *Torah im derekh ereẓ* (Torah with secular education), and espoused the synthesis of Torah with modern culture. In Israel, the split between the two approaches is especially noticeable. Mizrachi and Ha-Po'el ha-Mizrachi have favored full participation in the political life of the *yishuv* and subsequently in the sovereign State of Israel. Agudat Israel circles, however, refrained from joining the Keneset Yisrael (the recognized community of the Jews in Palestine) and refused to recognize the official rabbinate appointed by that body. After the establishment of the State of Israel, Agudat Israel participated in elections to the Knesset and for some time even participated in a coalition government. A far more extreme position was adopted by *Neturei Karta. They have categorically refused to recognize the authority of a secular Jewish state which, in their opinion, came into being only through the betrayal of the religious values of Jewish tradition.

Although the followers of the *Torah im derekh ereẓ* approach advocated openness to modern culture and discouraged the insulation of the Jew from the intellectual currents of his time, they nonetheless unequivocally rejected any doctrine which in the slightest manner would jeopardize the binding character and validity of the *halakhah*. They were unbending in their insistence that the traditional belief in *Torah min ha-Shamayim* entailed: that the Masoretic text represents an authentic record of divine communication of content; and that the Oral Torah represents in essence the application and extension of teachings and methods that are ultimately grounded in direct divine revelation (see *Oral Law). This view not only clashed with Abraham *Geiger's radical doctrine of "progressive revelation," according to which even the Bible was the product of the religious genius of the Jewish people, but also with the more moderate theory of "continuous revelation" as formulated by the positivist historical school. According to Zacharias *Frankel (considered by some to be the spiritual father of Conservative Judaism), the original Sinaitic revelation was supplemented by another kind of revelation – the ongoing revelation manifesting itself throughout history in the spirit of the Jewish people. Orthodoxy balked at Frankel's thesis that the entire structure of rabbinic Judaism was the creation of the scribes, and subsequently of the *tannaim* and the *amoraim*, who allegedly sought to adapt biblical Judaism to a new era by inventing the notion of an Oral Torah. From the Orthodox point of view, rabbinic Judaism represents not a radical break with the past, but rather the ingenious application and development of teachings which ultimately derive their sanction from the Sinaitic revelation. Whereas for the positivist historical school the religious consciousness of the Jewish people provided the supreme religious authority, the Orthodox position rested upon the belief in the supernatural origin of the Law which was addressed to a "*Chosen People."

[Walter S. Wurzburger]

German Orthodoxy exerted a significant influence upon Jews in Western lands, especially Holland (to which Reform had not yet spread) and Switzerland. Hungary became the center of a specific type of Orthodox development. The spread of Haskalah there and the reforms in education and synagogue worship led to tension within the communities, especially from the 1840s on (see Aaron *Chorin). Orthodoxy became very much aware of its distinctive character, especially under the influence of R. Moses *Sofer and his school. Later the call for independent organization became more pronounced. Preparations for a nationwide congress of Hungarian Jews at the end of the 1860s gave this trend an organizational and political expression in the formation of the Shomrei Hadass Society (*Glaubenswaechter*, "Guardians of the Faith"), founded in 1867 to protect and further the interest of Orthodoxy, thus becoming the first modern Orthodox political party. In a congress held from December 1868 to February 1869, the Orthodox and Reform camps split; afterward the Orthodox withdrew, announcing that the decisions of the congress were not binding on them. Independent Orthodox communities were set up in those areas where the established communal leadership had passed to the Reform camp, and a countrywide organization of these separate communities was set up. Orthodox autonomy was confirmed by the government in 1871. Approximately half of Hungarian Jewry joined the Orthodox communities.

Within Hungarian Orthodoxy, two strands can be discerned:

(1) traditional Orthodoxy, encompassing the ḥasidic masses in the northeastern districts; and

(2) non-ḥasidic Orthodoxy, which contained a segment that bore the marks of modern Orthodoxy – a measure of adaptation to its environment, general education (without the ideology of *Torah im derekh ereẓ*), and use of the language of the country. Non-ḥasidic Orthodoxy was shaped by the school of R. Moses Sofer.

In eastern Europe until World War I, Orthodoxy preserved without a break its traditional ways of life and the time-honored educational framework. In general, the mainstream of Jewish life was identified with Orthodoxy while Haskalah and secularization were regarded as deviations. Hence there was no ground wherein a Western type of Orthodoxy could take root. Modern political Orthodox activity first appeared in eastern Europe at the beginning of the 20th century with Agudat Israel. Orthodoxy's political activity was especially noticeable in Poland. During the period of German conquest at the time of World War I, an Orthodox political party was organized (with the aid of some German rabbis), the Shelomei Emunei Israel. In the communal and political life of the Jews in the Polish republic, Orthodoxy was most influential in the townlets, and was supported by the ḥasidic masses. The central political aim of Orthodoxy was to guarantee its autonomy in all religious matters. After World War I, a definite shift may be detected in Orthodoxy in Poland toward basic general education to a limited degree. Agudat Israel established an educational network, with Horeb schools for boys and Beth Jacob schools for girls.

European Orthodoxy, in the 19th and the beginning of the 20th centuries, was significantly influenced by the move from small settlements to urban centers (within the same country), as well as by emigration. Within the small German communities there was a kind of popular Orthodoxy, deeply attached to tradition and to local customs, and when it moved to the large cities this element brought with it a vitality and rootedness to Jewish tradition. From the end of the 19th century, countries in western Europe absorbed newcomers from the East, who either constituted an important addition to the existing Orthodox congregations or set up new communities. After World War I, scholars from eastern Europe (among them the rabbis Abraham Elijah Kaplan and Jehiel Jacob *Weinberg) went to Germany and other western countries. They exerted a perceptible influence on western Orthodoxy, providing it with a direction in scholarship and drawing it closer to the world of talmudic learning. In the interwar period, young Orthodox students from the West went to the yeshivot of Poland and Lithuania, and yeshivot of the traditional type were later established in western Orthodox centers.

In the United States, Orthodoxy constituted one of the mainstreams of life and thought within Jewry. Different varieties of Orthodoxy coexisted. In 1898 the *Union of Orthodox Jewish Congregations of America was founded. Its declared aims were to accept "the authoritative interpretation of our rabbis as contained in the Talmud and codes." Among the leaders and teachers prominent in American Orthodoxy were the rabbis Bernard *Revel, Joseph D. *Soloveichik, and Joseph H. *Lookstein. One of the influential Orthodox centers in the United States, *Yeshiva University, inspired the establishment of many other schools offering instruction in both Jewish and secular subjects on the elementary and high school levels. This trend of U.S. Orthodoxy published the periodicals *Jewish Life, Jewish Forum, Tradition*, and *Intercom* (publication of the Association of Orthodox Jewish Societies). The differences within American Orthodoxy were evidenced by the establishment of different rabbinic bodies there. Rabbis from eastern Europe, representing traditional Orthodoxy, make up the *Union of Orthodox Rabbis of the United States and Canada (founded in 1902), while rabbis educated in America united to form the *Rabbinical Council of America (in 1923; reorg. 1935). Ḥasidic groups, who became influential chiefly after World War II, constitute a separate division within American Orthodoxy. Especially well known are those associated with Menahem Mendel *Schneersohn of Lubavitch and Joel *Teitelbaum of Satmar. Rabbis, scholars, and the heads of yeshivot who came after World War II and built yeshivot according to the Lithuanian tradition added their special quality to American Orthodoxy. Most prominent among them was Rabbi Aaron *Kotler.

The senior central organization of the Jews of England, the *United Synagogue, is an Orthodox body in its constitution and rabbinic leadership. However, the lay leaders and congregants are not necessarily all observant in the light of the accepted Orthodox standard. Those who were dissatisfied with the degree of observance and religious spirit prevailing in the United Synagogue founded separate congregational organizations. The Federation of Synagogues, which in composition was more suited to the spirit of those who came from eastern Europe, was founded in 1887, and its numbers multiplied with the extensive Jewish emigration to England. In 1891 the society known as Machzike Hadath ("The Upholders of the Faith"), was formed, and immigrants from western Europe founded the congregations known as Adath Yisroel in the spirit of German Orthodoxy. In 1926 R. Victor Schonfeld established the Union of Orthodox Hebrew Congregations which attempted to unite the various branches of western traditional Orthodoxy.

[Nathaniel Katzburg]

Trends within Modern Orthodoxy

In spite of the new impetus given to Orthodoxy by the success of the day school and improved methods of organization and communication, evidence of grave dangers cannot be ignored. The rapid polarization within the Orthodox camp seriously threatens to split the movement completely.

While much of the controversy seems to revolve around the question of membership in religious bodies containing non-Orthodox representation, the real issue goes far deeper. The so-called "modern Orthodox" element is under severe attack for allegedly condoning deviations from halakhic standards in order to attract non-observant Jews. On the other hand, there constantly come to the fore mounting restlessness and impatience on the part of significant elements that are dismayed over the slowness with which Orthodoxy has responded to the upheavals of Emancipation, the Enlightenment, and the establishment of the State of Israel. The charge has been made that, instead of coming to grips with these events which have confronted the Jew with entirely new historic realities, Orthodoxy has been satisfied with voicing its disapproval of those who have reacted to them.

Some of the more "radical" thinkers regard the Hirsch type of synthesis between Torah and culture as an invaluable first step, but it must be developed much further if it is to meet contemporary needs. They look askance at the feature of "timelessness" which in Hirsch's system constitutes a hallmark of Torah and which, in their opinion, ignores the dynamic character inherent in the processes of the Oral Torah. They contend that, as long as the domain of Torah remains completely insulated from the culture of a given age, the authorities or the *halakhah* cannot creatively apply teachings of Torah to ever-changing historic realities. What, therefore, is needed is not merely the coexistence but the mutual interaction of the two domains. This view, of course, runs counter to the basic tenets of "right-wing" Orthodoxy, which frowns upon the intrusion of elements derived from secular culture as a distortion of the authentic teachings of the Torah. The exponents of the more radical positions of "modern Orthodoxy" are frequently charged with cloaking under the mantle of Orthodoxy what essentially amounts to a Conservative position. This argument, however, is countered by the claim that no modifications of the *halakhah* are condoned unless they are sanctioned by the methods governing the process of halakhic development. There is no thought of "updating" the *halakhah* in order to adjust it to the spirit of the time. What is advocated is only that its meaning be explicated in the light of ever-changing historic conditions. The contention is that, as long as halakhic opinion is evolved in conformity with the proper procedures of halakhic reasoning, its legitimacy as a halakhic datum is assured.

To bolster their case, the proponents of this "left wing" frequently claim to derive the basic elements of their position from the teachings of Rabbi *Kook, as well as from the philosophy of the most influential contemporary Orthodox thinker, R. Joseph B. Soloveichik. Neither of these two seminal thinkers has in any way identified himself with the views advanced by the more "progressive" wing. But Kook's readiness to attribute religious value to modern secular movements, as well as his positive stance toward cultural and scientific developments, provide a key element to a philosophy that seeks to integrate the positive contributions of the world within the fabric of Judaism. Similarly, Soloveichik's characterization of the man of faith in terms of the dialectical tension between a commitment to an eternal "covenantal community" and the responsibilities to fulfill socio-ethical tasks in a world of change is widely hailed as an endorsement of the thesis that the Jewish religious ideal does not call for withdrawal from the world but for the confrontation between human culture and the norms and values of the Torah.

Obviously, such a conception of the nature of the commitment of the Jewish faith completely disposes of the charge of "moral isolationism" that time and again has been hurled at Orthodoxy because its alleged preoccupation with the minutiae of the Law renders it insensitive to areas which do not come within the purview of formal halakhic regulation. Actually, the covenantal relationship between man and God embraces all aspects of life and cannot be confined to a mere adherence to a set of legal rules. The observance of the *halakhah*, far from exhausting the religious task of the Jew, is designed to make him more sensitive and "open" to social and moral concerns.

THE DILEMMA OF ORTHODOXY IN THE MODERN WORLD. Although many segments of Orthodoxy have veered away from the course of "splendid isolation" which has been espoused by the "right wing," they have not as yet been able to formulate a systematic theology capable of integrating the findings of modern science and historic scholarship. For that matter, there has not yet been developed a theory of revelation which would satisfy the demands of modern categories of thought. There are some isolated voices clamoring for less "fundamentalist" or "mechanical" approaches to revelation which would utilize some of Martin *Buber's notions and assign a large role to man's subjective response to the encounter with the Divine. But it remains to be seen whether such a solution is feasible within the framework of Orthodoxy. At any rate, some of the widely recognized Orthodox authorities unequivocally reject any approach which compromises in the slightest with the doctrine that divine revelation represents direct supernatural communication of content from God to man.

Even more serious is the problem of the increasing resistance to the Orthodox emphasis on the authoritative nature of the *halakhah*. This runs counter to the prevailing cultural emphasis upon pluralism and the individual's free subjective commitment, a freedom which challenges acceptance of objective religious values or norms imposed upon the individual from without. What renders the problem even more acute is the paradox that the Orthodox community, which places so much emphasis upon the authority of the rabbis to interpret the revealed word of God, is the one that has been plagued most by conflicting claims of competing authorities. Characteristically, all efforts to establish some central authority have failed dismally. The proposal to revive the Sanhedrin, far from promoting cohesiveness, has actually precipitated considerable disharmony within the Orthodox camp. The latter, so far, has not even succeeded in evolving a loose organizational structure which would be representative of the various ideological shadings within the movement.

[Walter S. Wurzburger]

Developments in Modern Orthodoxy

Orthodox Judaism is by no means monolithic; the diversity in faith and practice is legion; it has no ultimate authority or hierarchy of authorities; and it has never been able to mobilize even one national or international organization in which all of its groups would speak as one. The diversity in halakhic rulings is typical of most legal systems. It stems principally from reliance on different sources, all of which are deemed authoritative, or from methods of reasoning, applied to the sources, which are also deemed normative by all halakhists. Philosophy or teleology plays little part in the decision-making process, except for a few among the Modern Orthodox.

The Modern Orthodox constitute neither sect nor movement. They convene no seminars and no colloquiums. They have no organized group and no publication of their own. There is no list of rabbis or laymen who call themselves "Modern Orthodox." They are at best represented by a group of rabbis who see each other from time to time and share the same commitment, namely that the Torah does not have to be afraid of modernity since there is no challenge that the Torah cannot cope with. Some prefer the word "centrist" because the word "modern" is too often associated with permissiveness. Others reject the term "centrist" because it suggests being in the center on all issues. But the Modern Orthodox are extremists on the positive side of many issues, such as the centrality of ethics in religious behavior and the need for improving the status of women in *halakhah*.

The diversity among all Orthodox Jews that evokes the most acrimony revolves around three issues: the nature and scope of Revelation; attitudes toward secular education and modern culture; and the propriety of cooperation with non-Orthodox rabbis. To systematic theology very little attention is given. The writings of the medieval Jewish philosophers are studied and expounded, but they appear to stimulate no new approaches. Orthodox Jews are still rationalists or mystics; naturalists or neo-Hegelians; and, even existentialists, most notably Joseph D. *Soloveitchik. Starting with the premise that all the Torah is God's revealed will, he holds that logically all of it must have theological significance. Therefore, he sees the totality of Torah as the realm of ideas in the Platonic sense, given by God for application to the realm of the real. Just as the mathematician creates an internally logical and coherent fabric of formulas with which he interprets and integrates the appearances of the visible world, so the Jew, the "Man of Halakhah," has the Torah as the divine idea that invests all of human life with direction and sanctity. "The *halakhah* is a multidimensional, ever-expanding continuum that cuts through all levels of human existence from the most primitive and intimate to the most complex relationships." And though the *halakhah* refers to the ideal, its creativity must be affected by the real. "Man's response to the great halakhic challenge asserts itself not only in blind acceptance of the divine imperative, but also in assimilating a transcendental content disclosed to him through an apocalyptic revelation and in fashioning it to his peculiar needs. It is rather the experiencing of life's irreconcilable antitheses – the simultaneous affirmation and abnegation of the self, the simultaneous awareness of the temporal and the eternal, the simultaneous clash of freedom and necessity, the simultaneous love and fear of God, and His simultaneous transcendence and immanence."

As for conceptions of the hereafter and resurrection of the dead, Soloveitchik holds with earlier authorities that no man can fathom or visualize precisely what they signify in fact, but the beliefs themselves can be deduced logically from the proposition that God is just and merciful. God's attribute of absolute justice and mercy require that he provide rewards and punishments and that He redeem Himself by being merciful to those most in need of mercy – the dead. Soloveitchik holds with many earlier philosophers that the immortality of the soul after death is to be distinguished from a this-worldly resurrection of the dead in a post-Messianic period; the Messianic period itself will produce only international peace and order.

Essentially the doctrines represent fulfillment of Judaism's commitment to an optimistic philosophy of human existence. In Soloveitchik's intellectual development there was a period when there was a clash, a confrontation between two ways of life and modes of thought: that of Brisk (Brest-Litovsk), where he became the great Talmudist, and that of Berlin, where he later became the great philosopher.

For many of his disciples who call themselves Modern Orthodox there was no such clash. They grew up in both cultures simultaneously, and the synthesis they sought and attained was a gradual achievement over a long period, virtually from elementary school days through graduate study. What little they achieved was not born altogether from anguish but more by the slow natural process of intellectual and emotional maturation. That is why they often part with the master in whose thought existentialism plays the major role, and they are more likely to embrace a more naturalist theology.

Theology and eschatology generally receive very little attention from Orthodox Jewish thinkers. The case is not so with Revelation, on which the range in views is enormous. There are those who hold literally that God dictated the Torah to Moses, who wrote each word as dictated, and there are those who maintain that how God communicated with Moses, the Jewish people, the Patriarchs and the Prophets will continue to be a matter of conjecture and interpretation, but the crucial point is that He did it in history. As creation is a fact for believers, though they cannot describe how, so Revelation is a fact, though its precise manner is not clear. This less fundamentalist approach would not deny a role to man's subjective response to the encounter with the divine, but all Orthodox Jews would agree that the doctrine of divine Revelation represents direct supernatural communication of content from God to man.

There are those who hold that every event reported in the Torah must be understood literally; some are less rigid in this connection and even regard the Torah as the ultimate source for a Jewish philosophy of history rather than Jewish history itself. This accounts for the fact that presently some authorities insist that Orthodox Jews must hold the age of the earth to be some five thousand years plus, while others have no difficulty in accepting astronomical figures.

The head of the Lubavitch movement, Rabbi Menachem *Schneersohn, insisted that the age of the earth was what the tradition holds it to be. The Modern Orthodox are more likely to hold with Rabbi Menaḥem Mendel *Kasher that it is not imperative that one so hold, and he thus advised scientists who sought his definitive opinion on the issue. He made no dogma of the traditional view. There are many Orthodox scientists, researchers, and academicians, who bifurcate their position. They hold to the traditional view as believers and to the scientific views in their professional pursuits – and this schizoid position does not disturb them.

With regard to the legal portions of the Torah, many Orthodox Jews still insist that they are eternal and immutable. Others maintain that the Oral Torah itself affords conclusive proof that there are laws that are neither eternal nor immutable. In the Oral Torah one also finds that some commandments were deemed by one authority or another never to have been mandatory but, rather, optional. Such were the commandments with regard to the blood-avenger and the appointment of a king. However, exponents of Orthodox Judaism generally affirm eternity and immutability, even though they engage in halakhic development without regard to the fiction they verbalize. The Modern Orthodox are more likely not to articulate the fiction as they explore ways to make the eternal law cope with the needs of the period.

With regard to parts of the Bible other than the Pentateuch, some hold that all of them were written because of the Holy Spirit; others are more critical and do not dogmatize with regard to their authorship, accuracy of texts, dates of composition, or literal interpretation. Some extend the doctrine of the inviolability of the Torah to all the sacred writings, including the Talmud and the Midrashim, and do not permit rejection even of any of the most contradictory legends or maxims. Others are "reductionists" and restrict the notion of inviolability to the Five Books of Moses.

Many of these views were expressed before the modern period. They are found in the writings of Jewish philosophers of the Middle Ages, and some are clearly expressed in the Talmud and Midrashim. The so-called Modern Orthodox are more likely to be found among those who hold the more liberal views with regard to these issues. Similarly, on the basis of tradition, the Modern Orthodox differ with their colleagues with regard to secular education and modern culture and the cooperation of Orthodox Jews with non-Orthodox Jews.

There were Orthodox rabbis who bemoaned the collapse of the ghetto walls because they fathomed what this would mean to the solidarity of the Jewish community and especially the future of its legal autonomy. *Halakhah*, which had always been applicable to the personal, social, economic, and political existence of Jews, would thereafter be relevant to very limited areas in the life of the Jew. These rabbis opposed any form of acculturation with their non-Jewish neighbors. Others advocated acculturation in social and economic matters but retained commitment to a Judaism totally unrelated to, and unaffected by, the ideas and values that dominated the non-Jewish scene. Others advocated the fullest symbiosis, outstanding among them, Rabbis Abraham Isaac Hacohen *Kook and Joseph D. *Soloveitchik. Rabbi Kook maintained a very positive attitude to all modern cultural and scientific developments; Rabbi Soloveitchik described the believing Jew as one who is forever in dialectical tension between his being a member of the covenanted community and his obligation to fulfill his socio-ethical responsibilities with and for all humanity in a rapidly changing world. Disciples of theirs even find that their secular education and exposure to modern culture deepen their understanding and appreciation of their own heritage, even as it helps them to evaluate modernity with greater insight and a measure of transcendence.

Because of differences of opinion, one finds contemporary Orthodox Jews holding many different views with respect to their own mode of living, their careers, and the education of their children. Those who want no part of modernity prefer to live in isolation and earn a livelihood by pursuing "safe" careers in business. They want the same for their offspring. Others seek to bifurcate their existence. They are modern in dress, enjoy the culture which surrounds them, but avoid intellectual challenges, and build a protective wall around their religious commitment, forbidding the environment to encroach upon their faith and ancestral practice. Usually they too want for their children what they enjoy, and they also encourage their young to pursue "safe" careers at college-courses in business, law, medicine, accounting, but rarely the social sciences or the humanities.

Then there are those who are determined to cope with all the challenges that modernity can offer. Some, like Samuel *Belkin, held to this view but spoke of the "synthesis" between modernity and traditional Judaism as a merging of the two cultures in the personality and outlook of the Orthodox Jew. His predecessor, Bernard *Revel, the first president of Yeshiva University, had a more exciting goal – a genuine synthesis of the best in both worlds. He craved the sanctification of the secular as did Rabbi Kook; the integration of the best that humanity has achieved with the eternal truths of Judaism; the greater appreciation of Judaism because of its differences from other religions and cultures; and the reformulation of the cherished concepts and practices of Judaism and their rationalization in modern terms. This goal has been achieved by only a few, but most of the intelligentsia among the Modern Orthodox share Revel's dream rather than the less difficult goal of Belkin.

The attitudes of Orthodox Jews to their non-Orthodox co-religionists also range from one end of the spectrum to the other – from hate, presumably based on revered texts, to toleration, total acceptance, and even love, similarly based on revered texts. Those indulging in hate are responsible for the physical violence occasionally practiced against any who deviate from the tradition. Theirs is a policy of non-cooperation in any form whatever with any who disagree with them, and they not only pray for the destruction of the State of Israel but even take measures to achieve that end. Others simply desire total separation from those who deviate from their customs and practices, even in the matter of dress.

A further group is reconciled to the fact of pluralism in Jewish life but has no affinity whatever for the non-Orthodox. A fourth group loves all Jews irrespective of how they behave, but does not accord even a modicum of tolerance to organizations that represent non-Orthodox rabbis and congregations. It is more tolerant of secular groups – no matter how anti-religious. A fifth group is even willing to cooperate with non-Orthodox groups in all matters pertaining to relationships between Jews and non-Jews, at least in the United States. They are even less open-minded with regard to the situation in Israel. Only a very small group goes all the way with the inescapable implications of the thought of Kook and Soloveitchik and welcomes the challenge of non-Orthodoxy, even as it views secular education and modern culture as positive factors in appreciation of the tradition.

It is also in this last group, Modern Orthodox, that one is likely to find those who will project halakhic decisions that are based on the sources but not necessarily the weight of the authorities. Especially with respect to the inviolability of the persons of all human beings, including Jewish dissenters, they are zealots. Thus they encourage dialogue with all Jews, solutions to the painful problems in Jewish family law, more prohibitions with community sanctions against the unethical behavior of Jews in business, in the exaction of usury, in the evasion of taxes, and in the exploitation of the disadvantaged. They propose the use of more theology and teleology in the process of halakhic decision. Their principal difference with so-called right-wing Conservative rabbis is that they do not wish to "update" the *halakhah* to adjust it to the spirit of the time but rather within the frame and normative procedures of the *halakhah* – its sources and its method of reasoning – to express the implications of the *halakhah* for the modern Jew and his existential situation.

The Modern Orthodox are especially attentive to historical, psychological, sociological, and teleological considerations. A few illustrations may be of interest.

They oppose any form of religious coercion by Jews against Jews and not by resort to the legal fiction that every Jew is now to be considered the equal of one who was taken captive in his early childhood and never raised as a Jew.

The tradition exempts such a person from religious coercion. The Modern Orthodox prefer the approach which says that religious coercion was only permitted when it might truly change the attitude and inner feeling of its victim. However, coercion now only angers the victim more and makes him or her more hostile to Judaism. Therefore, it defeats rather than advances its original purpose. Similarly, Jewish family law developed to give dignity and sanctity to the status of every member of the family, with every individual enjoying the right freely to serve God and fulfill his or her responsibilities as a member of the family. When Jewish law, however, no longer serves this purpose and becomes an instrument for exploitations of one by another and the literal enslavement of spouses or offspring, then there must be legislation and the sooner the better. Therefore, the Modern Orthodox especially favor antenuptial agreements anticipating certain unfortunate events and the reactivation of the annulment of marriages – all of which has ample sources in the halakhic literature. Last but not least, the Modern Orthodox are more likely than others to lend a sympathetic ear to halakhic changes in the face of developments in modern medicine – especially the right to volunteer one's organs for transplanting. This is a field in which very little creative work has been accomplished by rabbis, except to assemble ancient sources with little or no philosophical analysis. Because of the enormous diversity among Orthodox Jews in both creed and practice, there is a tendency at present to speak of the ultra-Orthodox, the Orthodox, and the Modern Orthodox. Yet in each of these groups there is substantial diversity, and the outlook in a free world and open society is for more, rather than less, of it.

[Emanuel Rackman]

(For the political and ideological expression of right-wing Orthodoxy in Israel, see *Gush Emunim.)

BIBLIOGRAPHY: E. Schwarzschild, *Die Gruendung der israelitischen Religionsgesellschaft zu Frankfurt am Main* (1896); J. Wohlgemuth, in: *Festschrift... David Hoffmann* (1914), 435–53; S. Japhet, in: HJ, 10 (1948), 99–122; I. Heinemann, *ibid.*, 123–34; J. Rosenheim, *ibid.*, 135–46; H. Schwab, *History of Orthodox Jewry in Germany* (1950); B. Homa, *A Fortress in Anglo-Jewry; the Story of the Machzike Hadath* (1953); E. Rackman, in: *Judaism*, 3 (1954), 302–9; 18 (1969), 143–58; Y. Wolfsberg, in: YLBI, 1 (1956), 237–54; S. Federbush (ed.), *Ḥokhmat Yisrael be-Ma'arav Eiropah*, 3 vols. (1958–65); S.K. Mirsky (ed.), *Ishim u-Demuyyot be-Ḥokhmat Yisrael be-Eiropah ha-Mizraḥit Lifnei Sheki'atah* (1959); I. Grunfeld, *Three Generations: The Influence of Samson Raphael Hirsch on Jewish Life and Thought* (1959); S. Poll, *The Ḥasidic Community of Williamsburg* (1962); C.S. Liebman, in: AJYB, 66 (1965), 21–97; D. Rudavsky, *Emancipation and Adjustment* (1967); N. Lamm, *Faith and Doubt: Studies in Traditional Jewish Thought* (1986[2]); idem, in: *Jewish Life* (May–June, 1969), 5–6; N. Katzburg, in: R. Braham (ed.), *Hungarian Jewish Studies*, 2 (1969); S. Belkin, *Essays in Traditional Jewish Thought* (1956); M. Davis, in: L. Finkelstein (ed.), *The Jews, their History, Culture and Religion*, 1 (1960[3]), 488–587; I. Epstein, *The Faith of Judaism* (1954); I. Grunfeld, *Judaism Eternal* (1956); S.R. Hirsch, *The Nineteen Letters on Judaism* (1960, 1969); N. Lamm and W.S. Wurzburger (eds.), *A Treasury of Tradition* (1967). **ADDITIONAL BIBLIOGRAPHY:** L. Bernstein, *Challenge and Mission: the Emergence of the English Speaking Orthodox Rabbinate* (1982); S. Bernstein, *The Renaissance of the Torah Jew* (1985); M. Breuer, *Modernity Within Tradition: the Social History of Orthodox Jewry in Imperial Germany*, tr. E. Petuchowsky (1992); R.P. Bulka (ed.), *Dimensions of Orthodox Judaism* (1983); M.H. Danziger, *Returning to Tradition: the Contemporary Revival of Orthodox Judaism* (1989); D.H. Ellenson, *Rabbi Esriel Hildesheimer and the Cre-*

ation of a Modern Jewish Orthodoxy (1990); T. Frankiel, *The Voice of Sarah: Feminine Spirituality and Traditional Judaism* (1990); J.S. Gurock, *The Men and Women of Yeshiva: Higher Education, Orthodoxy, and American Judaism* (1988); S.C. Heilman, *Defenders of the Faith: Inside Ultra-Orthodox Jewry* (1992); S.C. Heilman and S.M. Cohen, *Cosmopolitans and Parochials: Modern Orthodox Jews in America* (1989); W.B. Helmreich, *The World of the Yeshiva: an Intimate Portrait of Orthodox Jewry* (1982); H.C. Schimmel & A. Carmell (eds.), *Encounter: Essays on Torah and Modern Life* (1989); Z. Kurzweil, *The Modern Impulse of Traditional Judaism* (1985); L.J. Kaplan & D. Shatz (eds.), *Rabbi Abraham Isaac Kook and Jewish Spirituality* (1994); B. Kraut, *German Jewish Orthodoxy in an Immigrant Synagogue: Cincinnati's New Hope Congregation and the Ambiguities of Ethnic Religion* (1988); A. Rakeffet-Rothkoff, *The Silver Era in American Jewish Orthodoxy: Rabbi Eliezer Silver and his Generation* (1981); N.H. Rosenbloom, *Tradition in an Age of Reform: the Religious Philosophy of Samson Raphael Hirsch* (1976); J. Sacks, *Arguments for the Sake of Heaven: Emerging Trends in Traditional Judaism* (1991); N. Solomon, *The Analytic Movement: Hayyim Soloveitchik and his Circle* (1993); J.D. Soloveitchik, *The Halakhic Mind* (1986); idem, *Reflections of the Rav: Lessons in Jewish Thought* (1979); W.S. Wurzburger, *Ethics of Responsibility: Pluralistic Approaches to Covenantal Ethics* (1994).

ORVIETO, town in Umbria, central Italy. Jewish loan bankers appeared there as early as 1297, being given citizenship rights and permitted to carry weapons. In 1334 one of them was sent as envoy to a neighboring town. The prosperity of the Jewish community induced many families from outside to settle there, as did a group of Jews from Viterbo in 1396. The anti-Jewish sermons of the *Franciscan friars later caused the position of Jews to deteriorate. However, Jewish moneylending activities continued until a *monte di pietá* was established in 1464. After Orvieto came under the rule of the Church in the second half of the 16th century, anti-Jewish legislation was strictly enforced. When in 1569 Pius v decreed the expulsion of the Jews from the Papal States, the Jewish community effectively ceased to exist, although some families came back for a short time under Sixtus v (1585–90). The name of the church of St. Gregorio nella Sinagoga in Orvieto still commemorates the former Jewish settlement.

BIBLIOGRAPHY: Roth, in: RMI, 17 (1951), 430ff.; Milano, Italia, index.

[Ariel Toaff]

ORVIETO, ANGIOLO (1869–1967), Italian author and editor. A nephew of Alberto *Cantoni, Orvieto was a member of an old, traditionalist family. He was born and educated in Florence and, during the years preceding World War I, took an active part in the cultural life and literary disputes of the city, which was then the main center of Italian intellectual activity. With his brother Adolfo, he founded the literary review *Il Marzocco* (1896–1932), giving it a classical trend in keeping with the formalism of Italian style. At the same time, Orvieto sought the collaboration of famous writers such as Luigi Pirandello and his friends Giovanni Pascoli and Gabriele D'Annunzio. Orvieto and his journal became the center of an intellectual circle consisting of the major Italian writers. He also initiated many cultural associations, including the Società dei papiri greci e latini, and the Società Leonardo da Vinci, and was among the founders of the British Council; he founded the reviews *Vita Nuova* and *Nazione Letteraria*; and was for many years superintendent of the Istituto di studi superiori in Florence.

As a poet, Orvieto tried to give new life to the traditional Italian sonnet: his collections of verse include *La sposa mistica* (1893), *Il velo di Maia* (1898), *Verso l'Oriente* (1912), *Le sette leggende* (1912), *Primavera della cornamusa* (1925), and *Il gonfalon selvaggio* (1934). *Il Vento di Sion* (1928) is a book written after a spiritual crisis and a return to Jewish tradition, in which he achieved a more personal tone. In this Orvieto pretends to be a 16th-century Florentine Jewish poet who tries in vain to reconcile his love for Zion with his equally sincere love for Renaissance Florence. His *Canti dell' escluso*, written during and after the Nazi persecutions and published in a single volume with *Il Vento de Sion* in 1961, is similar in tone. He also wrote impressions of his travels, a collection of translations of English poetry, and three librettos set to music by the Jewish composer G. Orefice: *Chopin* (1901), *Elena alle porte Scee* (1904), and *Mosè* (1905). After 1928 Orvieto was active in Jewish communal life and in extreme old age became deeply observant of religious tradition. His wife, Laura Cantoni Orvieto (1876–1953), was well known as a writer of storybooks and history books for children, among which were *Leo e Lia* (1908) and *Storie di bambini molto antichi* (1951). During the Nazi occupation of central Italy, the Orvieto couple was hidden in a Christian home for the elderly.

BIBLIOGRAPHY: G.L. Luzzatto, in: RMI, 27 (1961), 454–61; 28 (1962), 32–39, 83–88; A. Bobbio, *Le riviste fiorentine del principio del secolo, 1903–1916* (1936). **ADD. BIBLIOGRAPHY:** C. Del Vivo, in: RMI, 34 (1968), 97–113; idem, in: *Rassegna della letteratura italiana* 106:2 (2002), 482–98; A. Arslan and P. Zambon, *Il sogno aristocratico. Angiolo Orvieto e Neera. Corrispondenza (1899–1917)* (1990); G. Sciloni, in: *Italia Judaica*, 4 (1993), 97–113; L. Orvieto, *Storia di Angiolo e Laura* (2001).

[Giorgio Romano]

OR YEHUDAH (Heb. אוֹר יְהוּדָה), Israel urban community with municipal council status, 8 mi. (13 km.) E. of Tel Aviv. Or Yehudah comprises the site of biblical *Ono. Prior to the Israeli *War of Independence, two Arab villages existed on its area, Sākiyya (Sāqiyya) and Kafr Ānā, which were abandoned by their inhabitants before being taken by Israeli forces in June 1948. In 1949, immigrants from Libya and Turkey settled there under primitive conditions. In 1950 and 1951, two large *ma'barot* (tent and hut camps) were set up, mainly for newcomers from Iraq and Romania. Living conditions continued to be difficult until 1958, when permanent housing projects were started. The population declined from its 1958 figure of 12,500 to 10,100 in 1963, and rose to 12,300 in 1970 when more than half the total population were immigrants (over half from Iraq, and one-third from other Middle Eastern and North African countries). Or Yehudah had a large average family size and a low average age of population (52% below 20 years of age). It had 11 factories, the largest of which was a weaving factory for export. Other local enterprises engaged in metal, diamonds, and food processing. In the mid-1990s the population was approximately 23,300, and by 2002 it was 28,600. In 1988 Or Yehudah received city status, with an area of about 2 sq. mi. (5 sq. km.). The name "Light of Judah" commemorates Rabbi Judah *Alkalai.

[Efraim Orni / Shaked Gilboa (2nd ed.)]

°ORZESZKOWA (Orzeszko), ELIZA (1841–1910), Polish novelist. Born in Grodno, Eliza Orzeszkowa was a member of the Polish landed gentry. A leading prose writer of the late 19th century, she was an advocate of social reform and endeavored to destroy the barriers separating the Poles and the Jews. Of all Polish writers, she took the greatest interest in the Jews, studying their history and even learning Hebrew and Yiddish (in spite of which there are in her writings some serious mistakes, as regards Jewish customs, etc.). An opponent of antisemitism, Orzeszkowa nevertheless attacked Jewish religious separatism and Zionism in the hope that Polish Jewry might ultimately be assimilated into the mainstream of Polish culture and diverted from any identification with the Germans or Russians. These ideas were propagated in her novels and short stories and in the pamphlet "*O żydach i kwestyi żydowskiej*" ("On the Jews and the Jewish Question," 1882), published after the Warsaw pogrom of December 1881. Her opposition to Zionism was expressed in an article "*O nacyonaliżmie żydowskim*" (1911; published posthumously in *Kuryer Warszawski*, 1911).

One of her early novels, *Pan Graba* ("Mr. Graba," 3 vols., 1872) sympathetically described a Jewish moneylender who amasses his wealth with the sole intention of building schools for the Jews in Jerusalem; while *Eli Makower* (2 vols., 1875), shows how another Jew assists a decent Polish landowner and works for mutual understanding between their two peoples. *Meir Ezofowicz* (1878; Eng. trans. 1898), Orzeszkowa's most important Jewish work, describes a young Jew's struggle for enlightenment and human brotherhood in face of Jewish narrowness and fanaticism. This novel is remarkable for its understanding of Orthodox motivation and for its censure of those Jews, who, touched by shallow assimilation, try to imitate some of the customs of the gentiles. In *Mirtala* (1886), a historical novel set in Rome two years after the destruction of Jerusalem (i.e., 72 C.E.), the novelist portrays the life of the Jewish exiles and their relations with the gentiles. Her short stories – notably "*Silny Samson*" ("The Strong Samson," 1878); "*Gedali*" (1884), and *Rotszyldówna* ("The Rothschild Girl," written before 1891, publ. 1921) – contain sympathetic descriptions of poverty-stricken Jews. In 1905 Orzeszkowa edited an anthology of 16 short stories about Jews by ten Polish writers, entitled *Z jednego strumienia* ("From One Source").

BIBLIOGRAPHY: I. Butkiewiczówna, *Powieści nowele żydowskie Elizy Orzeszkowej* (1937), incl. bibl.

[Yehuda Arye Klausner]

OSBORN, MAX (1870–1946), German art critic and author. He was art critic for the *Vossische Zeitung* 1914–33. From 1938 he lived in Paris, and in 1941, at the age of 72, he was forced to flee from France and emigrate to the United States. His books include *Kunst im Leben des Kindes* (1902); a study of Duerer's literary legacy, *Duerer's Schriftliches Vermaechtnis* (1905); a work on woodcarving, *Der Holzschnitt* (1905); *Berlin* … (1902, 1926[2]); and *Die Kunst des Rokoko* (1929). He also wrote a work on the 16th-century literature of demonology.

BIBLIOGRAPHY: S. Stompor, *Kuenstler im Exil*, 6:1–2 (1994).

[Jihan Radjai-Ordoubadi (2nd ed.)]

OSCHINSKY, LAWRENCE (1921–1965), U.S. physical anthropologist. Born in New York, he taught physical anthropology at the University of Pennsylvania graduate school of medicine, and from 1956 at Howard University Medical School. His special interest was in the anatomy of the nervous system, the races of Africa and Asia, and human evolution and the physical anthropology of the Eskimos of Siberia and Canada. His books include *Most Ancient Eskimos* (1964) and *Racial Affinities of the Baganda and Other Bantu Tribes of British East Africa* (1954).

[Ephraim Fischoff]

OSHAIAH (Hoshaiah) RABBAH (first half of the second century C.E.), Palestinian *amora*. Oshaiah was born in southern Palestine (TJ, Nid. 3:2), where he studied under *Bar Kappara (MK 24a) and *Ḥiyya (TJ, Shab. 3:1), eventually becoming the latter's assistant. The Jerusalem Talmud (Nid. 3:2, 50c) reports that Bar Kappara and Oshaiah's father *Ḥama were found together in "the south" (= Lydda), and that Oshaiah himself disseminated Bar Kappara's Mishnah (TJ, Shev. 5:2, 35b) which he brought from Lydda. According to S. Lieberman (Sifre Zuta, 123), Oshaiah eventually established his *bet midrash* in Lydda, not far from that of Bar Kappara. The Talmud reports that his father, *Ḥama, left the family when Oshaiah was a child in order to study. When after several years Ḥama finally returned, he found that the young stranger with whom he had discussed *halakhah* on the way was his own son (Ket. 62b). When father and son disputed a particular issue, Oshaiah's grandfather, Bisa, ruled in his grandson's favor (BB 59a). Oshaiah was apparently a member of *Judah Ha-Nasi's council in Sepphoris and was entrusted with examining the witnesses of the new moon (TJ, Ned. 6:8). After Judah ha-Nasi's death, he founded his own academy at Caesarea (TJ, Ter. 10:2). He was famed for his collection of *baraitot*, called *Mishnayot Gedolot* ("Great *Mishnayot*"; TJ, Hor. 3:5) and for the ability with which he explained them. As a result he was called *Av ha-Mishnah* ("Father of the Mishnah"; TJ, BK, 4:6). The collection was respected in Babylon, too, and *Ze'eira remarked, "Every *baraita* that was not taught in the school of Ḥiyya and Oshaiah is not authentic" (Ḥul. 141a–b).

Oshaiah was particularly strict in requiring from a prospective proselyte both circumcision and immersion in the presence of three rabbis (Yev. 46b), a decision which was possibly prompted in opposition to the widespread conversion of gentiles by Christian Jews. R.T. Herford (*Christianity in Talmud and Midrash* (1903), 247ff.) suggests that Oshaiah's maxim, "The Almighty dwelt kindly with Israel in scattering them" (Pes. 87b), may also have been directed against them. Bacher (JQR. 3 (1891), 357–60) maintains that Oshaiah had certainly heard of Origen, if not read his works, and associates the latter with "the philosopher" who asked Oshaiah, "Why was not man created circumcised?" Oshaiah replied, "Man, together with all creations, needs perfecting, and circumcision brings perfection" (Gen. R. 11:6). He was also the author of the phrase, "Custom overrides law" (TJ, BM 7:1). According to one reading, Oshaiah was poor (Meg. 7a). His kindness and consideration for his fellow men is illustrated by his apology to his son's blind teacher, whom he had not invited to a particular meal for fear that he would be embarrassed by other guests (TJ, Pe'ah 8:9, 21b). His son, Merenos, was a scholar (TJ, Git. 4:6). Among his pupils were Ammi (TJ, Shab. 3:7) and *Johanan b. Nappaḥa (TJ, Ter. 10:2). The latter continued to visit Oshaiah even when he himself became a great scholar (TJ, Sanh. 11:6, 30b). He once said, "Oshaiah in his generation is like *Meir was in his" (Er. 53a).

BIBLIOGRAPHY: Hyman, Toledot, 110–6; Bacher, Pal Amor; Ḥ. Albeck, *Mavo la-Talmudim* (1969), 163f. S. Lieberman, *Sifrei Zuta* (1968), 123.

[Stephen G. Wald (2nd ed.)]

OSHEROFF, DOUGLAS DEAN (1945–) U.S. physicist and Nobel Laureate. Osheroff was born in Aberdeen, Washington, and graduated from the California Institute of Technology before gaining his Ph.D. in physics from Cornell University. He joined the Department of Solid State and Low Temperature Research of Bell Research Laboratories in Murray Hill, New Jersey, in 1972 and was head of this department from 1982–87. He moved to Stanford University as professor of physics and was appointed J.G. Jackson and C.J. Wood Professor of Physics in 1992 and chairman of the department of physics (1993–96). Osheroff's research concerns low temperature physics and led to the discovery of three new superfluid forms of helium-3 resulting from pair forming by the super-cooled 3He atoms. This work influenced the future course of low temperature research and has important theoretical implications for understanding superconductivity and its practical applications. He was awarded the Nobel Prize in physics (1996), shared with his collaborators David Lee and Robert Richardson. His subsequent research continues to focus on the behavior of condensed matter at very low temperature. His awards include the Sir Francis Simon Memorial Prize of the British Institute of Physics (1976) and election to the American Academy of Arts and Sciences and the U.S. National Academy of Sciences. In recognition of his teaching expertise, he received Stanford University's Walter J. Gores Award. He married Phyllis S.K. Liu in 1970.

[Michael Denman (2nd ed.)]

OSHEROWITCH, MENDL (pseudonyms: **A. Glan, M. Glebovitch, Menakhem Podolyer, M. Ovodovski**; 1888–1965), Yiddish journalist and author. Born in Trostyanets, Ukraine, Osherowitch immigrated to the U.S. in 1909. From 1914 on he was a staff member of the New York daily *Forverts* which printed most of his profuse production before parts of it appeared in book form. His writings include stories, plays, historical novels, numerous biographies, popular history, travel impressions, theater history, a history of *Forverts*, criticism, and autobiography. He also translated widely from Russian and English, and wrote the scenario of the popular Yiddish film *A Brivele der Mamen* ("A Letter to Mother," Poland, 1938). His book on David *Kessler and Paul *Muni, *Dovid Kesler un Muni Vayzenfraynd* (1930), his memoirs, and his studies of Ukrainian Jewish towns are of great interest.

BIBLIOGRAPHY: Rejzen, Leksikon, 1 (1926), 186–8; Z. Zylbercweig, *Leksikon fun Yidishn Teater* (1931), 113–4; LNYL, 1 (1956), 195–6. **ADD. BIBLIOGRAPHY:** M. Shtarkman, in: *Di Goldene Keyt*, 37 (1960), 203–6.

[Leonard Prager]

OSHMYANY (Pol. **Oszmiana**), town in Grodno district, Belarus. Oshmyany, one of the oldest settlements in Lithuania, was granted municipal status in 1537. A Jewish community developed there at the beginning of the 18th century. In 1765 there were 376 Jewish poll-tax payers in Oshmyany and the surrounding villages. In 1831, after a battle against Polish rebels, Russian soldiers set fire to Oshmyany and killed many of the town's inhabitants, including many Jews. In 1847 the community numbered 1,460, and by 1897 the number had increased to 3,808 (about 53% of the population). Jews earned their livelihood from small trade and crafts, essentially from tanning, shoemaking, tailoring, and carpentry. At the beginning of the 20th century most of the Jewish workers organized themselves into a trade union. There were seven synagogues in the town, three of them belonging to the unions of the tanners, shoemakers, and tailors. Prominent rabbis served the community during the 19th and the beginning of the 20th centuries, among them R. Meir Michael Kahana (1883), R. Mordecai b. Menahem *Rosenblatt (author of *Aleh Ḥavaẓẓelet*, 1891–1906), and R. Judah Leib Fein 1906–14).

The Great Synagogue of Oshmyana was erected in 1902. In the battles between the Red Army and the Polish Army in 1920, many Jews fell victim to the fighting. Between the two world wars (under Polish rule) the office of vice mayor was held by a Jewish delegate. During this period branches of all the Jewish parties were active in the town. The leading educational and cultural institutions were the Tarbut and Yavneh Hebrew schools, the CYSHO Yiddish school, a Hebrew library, and a drama circle. Between the years 1922 and 1925 a Jewish agricultural cooperative with 30 members functioned in the surroundings of Oshmyany.

[Arthur Cygielman]

Holocaust Period and After

The Germans occupied the town on June 26, 1941. On July 25 they ordered all male Jews to assemble in the square. The assembled, who numbered about 700, were taken to Bartel and murdered. In October 1941 a ghetto was established of 1,800 inhabitants; Jews from the neighboring towns of Olshan, Smorgon, and Krawo were brought in, and disease and hunger took many lives. On June 16, 1942, about 350 youths were transferred to a camp in Miligany. In October the Germans announced that too many Jews were still living in the ghetto and that the population must be decreased, which meant extermination for some of its occupants. Receiving the information, the *Judenrat in Vilna claimed that if it performed the *Aktion* the number of victims would be reduced. Headed by Salek Dresler, members of the Vilna Jewish police participated in the *Aktion* on Oct. 19, 1942, making their *Selektion* and kidnapping 406 Jews, who were taken in the direction of Oglyovo, about 4 mi. (7 km.) from Oshmyana, and murdered there.

This episode roused the Jews against both the Judenrat and the Vilna Jewish police. Jacob Gens, head of the Judenrat in Vilna, took full responsibility for the *Aktion*, claiming that by sacrificing part of the Jewish population there was a chance to save the rest. Early in 1943 an underground organization was established in the ghetto, and its members left for the forests to join the partisans. On April 28, 1943, the ghetto was liquidated. Some of its 2,500 inhabitants were transferred to the Vilna ghetto, some were deported to labor camps in the vicinity, and others were killed at Ponary. After World War II Jewish life in Oshmyany did not fully revive. In 1965 there were some 25 Jewish families living there, most of whom had not previously been residents of the city. A monument to Jewish martyrs murdered by the Nazis, erected outside the city, was repeatedly desecrated. In 1970 some 300 families from Oshmyany lived in Ereẓ Israel.

[Aharon Weiss]

BIBLIOGRAPHY: B. Wasiutyński, *Ludność żydowska w Polsce w wiekach XIX i XX* (1930), 82; *Żydzi a powstanie styczniowe, materiały osijek i dokumenty* (1963), index; *Sefer Zikkaron li-Kehillat Oshminah* (Heb., Yid., and some Eng., 1969).

OSHRY, EPHRAIM (1914–2003), rabbi and halakhic authority. Oshry was born in Kupiskis, Lithuania, and studied at the Slobodka Yeshivah. During the Nazi occupation of Lithuania, he became the rabbi of the Kaunas (Kovno) ghetto, and issued responsa to halakhic questions concerning Jewish practice under unprecedented conditions. These responsa constitute one of the most interesting religious documents to emanate from the Holocaust era. He hid the written responsa, and was able to retrieve them after the war. They were eventually published in five volumes in Hebrew as *She'elot u-Teshuvot mi-Ma'amakim* (1959–74), and in English summary as *Responsa from the Holocaust* (1983)

When the Kaunas ghetto was liberated in 1944, Oshry went to Rome, where, in 1945, he founded Yeshivat Meor ha-Golah for young Holocaust survivors. He transferred the yeshivah to Montreal, Canada, in 1950, and eventually moved it to New York, where he became rabbi of the Beit Midrash Hagodol on the Lower East Side in 1952.

Beside his volumes of responsa, which won two National Jewish Book Awards, he published a number of studies on rabbinic and halakhic literature including *Divrei Efraim* (1949), *Oẓar ha-Pesaḥ* (1965), *Imrei Efraim* (1968), and *Hasidei Efraim* (1975). He wrote an account of the destruction of Lithuanian Jewry, *Khurbn Lite* (Yid. 1951; Eng. tr. 1995).

BIBLIOGRAPHY: *New York Times* (Oct. 5, 2003).

°OSIANDER, ANDREAS (1498?–1552), German theologian, religious reformer, and *Hebraist. Born in Gunzenhausen (Franconia), Osiander was ordained a priest in 1520, but shortly thereafter converted to Protestantism, becoming one of the most influential reformers of the time. He was a Hebrew tutor at Nuremberg and continued his studies with a Jew, Woelfflein of Schnaittach, who was given the extraordinary privilege of visiting Nuremberg for that purpose. In the wake of the *Pezinok blood libel of 1529, Osiander published an anonymous refutation of the ritual murder charge, which led to a literary dispute with Johannes Eck. Although Osiander was himself a Lutheran theologian, in a private letter to Elijah *Levita he vehemently denounced Martin *Luther's anti-Jewish *Vom Schem Hamphoras* (1544). In 1548 Osiander left Nuremberg and was made professor of Hebrew at the then newly founded University of Koenigsberg, where he died a few years later.

BIBLIOGRAPHY: M. Stern, *Andreas Osianders Schrift ueber die Blutbeschuldigung* (1893); Baron, Social², 13 (1969), 228, 232f., 431f. **ADD. BIBLIOGRAPHY:** A. Osiander d.Ä., *Gesamtausgabe*, 10 vols. (1975–1995); G. Seebaß, *Das reformatorische Werk des Andreas Osiander* (1967); M. Stupperich, *Osiander in Preußen, 1549–1552* (1973); G. Ph. Wolf, in: *Zeitschrift fuer Bayerische Kirchengeschichte*, 53 (1984), 49–77; B. Haegler, *Die Christen und die "Judenfrage" am Beispiel der Schriften Osianders…* (1992); H. Schreckenberg, *Die christlichen Adversus-Judaeos-Texte …* (1994), 612–5 (with bibliography).

[Yehoshua Amir (Neumark) / Aya Elyada (2nd ed.)]

OSIJEK (Hung. **Eszék**, Ger. **Esseg**), town in E. Croatia; until 1918 in Austria-Hungary. Jews were first mentioned in Osijek after the Austrian conquest of Belgrade in 1688, when some 500 Jewish prisoners were taken to Osijek where they had to wait until they were ransomed by European Jewish communities (Moses Sofer, *Et Sofer*, Fuerth, 1691). Jews from the Austrian Empire began settling in Osijek under difficult conditions in the middle of the 18th century. They had no official right of residence until 1792. Religious services were held in the town from 1830, and the community was founded in 1845; it had 40 members in 1849. The congregation school and *ḥevra kaddisha* were founded in 1857; a synagogue was built in 1867. When emancipation was granted to Jews in Croatia in 1873, the community prospered and was the largest one in Croatia until 1890. In 1900 there were 1,600 Jews in Osijek. In the 20th century Osijek had two Jewish communities – one in the upper and another one in the lower town – and communal life was intensive. In 1940 there were 2,584 Jews in the two communities.

Holocaust Period

After the German conquest of Yugoslavia in April 1941, Croatia became the "Independent Croatian State" under A. *Pavelić. On April 13 Germans, *Volkdeutsche* (very numerous in this region), and Pavelić's *ustaše* (paramilitary collaborators) looted Jewish property, imposed a contribution of 20,000,000 dinars, and made all economic activity impossible for Jews; Jewish families were evicted from the center of town. On April 13 a mob of Germans, *Volkdeutsche*, and *ustaše* burned the main synagogue and destroyed the Jewish cemetery, but mass persecution did not start until June 1942. In December 1941 a camp for 2,000 Jewish women and children was established in an old mill in Djakovo, near Osijek. In February 1942 approximately 1,200 women and children from the Stara Gradiška camp were transferred to Djakovo until, because of an epidemic, the camp was liquidated and its inmates sent for extermination to Jasenovac. In June 1942 the community was ordered to build a settlement on the road to Tenje, a nearby village, where the Jews would be left unmolested. The leaders of the community were hoodwinked into building the settlement and organizing the life in it. Three thousand Jews from Osijek, and later from other places in the region, were confined there; by August 1942 they had all been sent either to Jasenovac or Auschwitz. Only Jews married to gentiles and a few who were in hiding remained in Osijek; ten managed to return from the death camps.

Contemporary Period

In 1947 there were 610 Jews in the community, including the surrounding area, and in 1949, after the immigration to Israel, 220. In 1965 a monument to Jewish fighters and victims of Nazism from Osijek and Slavonia was dedicated in a square in Osijek; it was created by Oscar Nemon of London, a former native of Osijek. At the beginning of the 21st century the Jewish population of Osijek was around 200.

BIBLIOGRAPHY: Schwarz, in: *Jevrejski almanah*, 3 (1927/28), 193–6. **ADD. BIBLIOGRAPHY:** *Dva stoljeća židovske povijesti i kulture u Zagrebu i Hrvatskoj* (1998), issued by Zagreb Jewish community.

[Zvi Loker (2nd ed.)]

OSIPOVICH, NAHUM (1870–?), Russian writer. While preparing for the entrance requirements of the University of Odessa he joined the Narodnaya Volya (the "People's Will" movement) circles, was arrested by the czarist authorities, and spent 18 years in prisons and in exile. Osipovich started his literary activity in 1902. On the recommendation of the *Society for the Promotion of Culture among the Jews of Russia, he studied the educational problem of the Jews in *Bessarabia (in *Voskhod*, no. 12, 1902). His short story "*Za chto?*" ("Why?") was refused publication by the censors. Osipovich wrote many short stories devoted mainly to Jewish types and Jewish life. His works are filled with love for nature, humanity, and the Jewish people in particular. His short story "*U vody*" ("At the Water") shows his devotion to the Jewish Black Sea fishermen whom he knew so well. Soviet critics consider him representative of the Jewish petit-bourgeois intelligentsia who were unable to adapt to the new Soviet reality.

BIBLIOGRAPHY: YE, 13 (c. 1910), 144–5; *Literaturnaya Entsiklopediya*, 8 (1949), 340.

OSIRIS, DANIEL ILLFA (1825–1908), French philanthropist and art patron, member of a Sephardi family of Bordeaux. He gave large sums for the promotion of technology (radio, telegraphy) and medicine (Institut Pasteur) and bequeathed his valuable art collection to the Louvre. He bought La Malmaison and part of the field of Waterloo and gave them to the French nation. He also built several synagogues.

OSLO, capital of Norway. When the law of 1814 prohibiting the admission of Jews to Norway was revoked in 1851, a Jewish community began to develop in Oslo; it acquired land for a cemetery in 1869 and was officially established in 1892 with 29 dues-paying members. In 1917, the community split up, and two synagogues were opened in 1920. In 1909, a "Jewish Youth Society" (*Israelitisk Ungdoms Forening*) was formed, which published a monthly journal, *Israelitin* (1909–12). A Zionist Association was formed in 1910 and from 1929 published a monthly, *Ha-Tikvah*. There were 852 Jews in Oslo in 1930, mainly engaged in commerce and industry. During World War II, more than half of the Jews in Oslo managed to escape to Sweden. The rest perished in Nazi concentration camps. The refugees who returned united into a single community. They were joined by several hundred displaced persons whom the Norwegian government had brought to Oslo, most of whom later emigrated to Israel or the United States. The Oslo Jewish community (Det Mosaiske Trosamfund, DMT) holds its services in the synagogue that was built in 1920 in Bergstien and was miraculously left untouched by the Germans during the war. A B'nai B'rith Lodge was established in 1952 and a new communal center was built in 1960. In 1968, there were 650 Jews in Oslo, a synagogue, and two cemeteries. The Jewish community of Oslo experienced a renaissance in the 1980s when the young rabbi Michael *Melchior, son of rabbi Bent Melchior of Denmark, became the community rabbi. A Jewish kindergarten was established. A children's choir was formed and many new melodies introduced in the Sabbath morning services. In 1988 a Jewish home for the aged was built next to the synagogue and community center, and later a new wing for those in need of extended care was added. In 1992 the community celebrated its 100th anniversary; this contributed to increased activities in the Jewish community. Since the 1970s Norwegian society has tended toward multiculturalism. This has also affected the way religion is taught in schools. Now all children must learn about the major religions, Judaism being one of them. Schoolchildren regularly visit the synagogue to learn more about the Norwegian Jews.

As a result of the Norwegian government's decision to make restitution in compensation for the Nazi government's liquidation of Jewish property and assets during World War II, the Jewish community of Oslo was given the means to renovate the community center. The restored and renewed community center was officially opened in September 2004. As a result of the Jewish restitution, the Center for Holocaust and Minorities Studies in Norway has been established. The Center, including a Holocaust exhibition, was opened in 2006 at Villa Grande, Vidkun *Quisling's former villa at Bygdøy in Oslo. A building in Oslo used as a synagogue before World War II is presently converted into a Jewish museum. Many of the new members of the Jewish community are Jews from various countries who have come to live in Norway or Norwegians who have converted to Judaism. Throughout the 1990s there was a gradual increase in community members, reaching around 900. However, in 2004 the number was only about 800.

BIBLIOGRAPHY: H.M.H. Koritzinsky, *Jødernes Historie i Norge* (1922), passim. **Website:** www.dmt.oslo.no.

[Lynn Claire Feinberg (2nd ed.)]

OSNABRUECK, city in Lower Saxony, Germany. Jews are mentioned as living in Osnabrueck during the 13th century, and the formula of the Jewish *oath from this period is extant. From a letter of Bishop Engelbert II to the municipal council in favor of the Jews (1309), it appears that there were then ten or 13 Jewish families in Osnabrueck. As in the other towns of Germany, here too the Jews engaged in moneylending. In 1312 the bishop issued a regulation fixing the rate of interest at 36.1/9%. All offenders against this regulation had to pay a fine to the bishop and the municipal council, suggesting that at this time the Jews were dependent on the benevolence of both the bishop and the townsmen. In 1327, however, the 15 Jewish families were placed under the protection of the bishop. In 1337 Emperor Louis the Bavarian submitted the Jews to the authority of Baron Henry von Valdeck. At the time of the *Black Death (1350), the Jews of Osnabrueck were all martyred and their property confiscated. After a few years, eight Jewish families only were permitted to settle in exchange for an annual payment of 30 marks. As was customary in other localities, this privilege was valid for only six years. They were authorized to purchase a tract of land for a cemetery in 1386 (an "old" cemetery had been mentioned in 1343). By 1424, there were only two families who were able to pay the annual tax of seven to eight guilders. The remaining Jews were expelled, and Osnabrueck received the privilege of "*non tolerandis Judaeis*" which remained in force, with the exception of three families, until the French Revolution. The townsmen were, however, jealous of the income of even these few Jews, and in 1716 a law forbade them to engage in commerce without the authorization of the municipal council. The number of Jews increased under French occupation. In 1825 there were five families and a teacher, affiliated to the Emden rabbinate. The community subsequently grew from 138 in 1871 to 379 in 1880 and 450 in 1925. A large synagogue was consecrated for the community of wealthy merchants in 1906. Antisemitic movements flourished in Osnabrueck, and in 1927 the synagogue and cemetery were desecrated. Between 1933 and 1938 about 350 Jews emigrated; on May 17, 1939, only 119 remained. On **Kristallnacht* the synagogue was set on fire and shops and homes were looted. During the Holocaust, 134 former citizens of Osnabrueck lost their lives. During the war, 400 Jewish Yugoslav officers were placed in a special P.O.W. camp in Osnabrueck. In August 1945 services were renewed in a prayer room. In 1969 a synagogue and community center for the community of 69 persons were consecrated. The Jewish community numbered 61 in 1989 and 942 in 2005. The increase is explained by the immigration of Jews from the former Soviet Union. In 1998 the Felix Nussbaum Museum was inaugurated. Built by American Jewish architect Daniel *Libeskind, it houses a collection of German Jewish artist Felix *Nussbaum (1904, Osnabrueck–1944, Auschwitz).

BIBLIOGRAPHY: M. Wiener, in: *Ben Chananja*, 5 (1862), 325–7; FJW, 136; *Germania Judaica*, 2 (1968), 634–6; Z. Asaria, *Zur Geschichte der Juden in Osnabrueck* (1969). **ADD. BIBLIOGRAPHY:** K. Kuehling, *Die Juden in Osnabrueck* (1969); *Germania Judaica*, vol. 3. 1350–1514 (1987), 1079–81; Z. Asaria, *Die Juden in Niedersachsen. Von den aeltesten Zeiten bis zur Gegenwart* (1979), 301–19; H. Guttmann, *Vom Tempel zum Gemeindezentrum. Synagogen im Nachkriegsdeutschland* (1989), 64–73.

[Azriel Shochat / Larissa Daemmig (2nd ed)]

OSOBLAHA (Ger. **Hotzenplotz**), village in Silesia, Czech Republic. Osoblaha was the seat of an important Jewish community during the Middle Ages, under the protection of the bishopric of *Olomouc (Olmuetz), and had its own municipal administration (see *Politische Gemeinden) until 1849. In 1415 a decree of the bishop urged the town to treat the Jews fairly. In order to revive the town, which had been devastated by the *Hussites, in 1514 land lots were sold to Jews of Leobschuetz (Glubczyce). Twelve families from Prudnik (now Poland) settled in Osoblaha in 1570, and the community then numbered 132 families in 22 houses. They traded in Silesia and Poland and the community as such leased the distillery. A few years before the Thirty Years' War (1618–48), the *Council of the Lands succeeded in averting the community's threatened expulsion. In 1670 the Jewish community of Osoblaha absorbed several Jews expelled from Vienna. It suffered during the Seven Years' War (1756–63) and many left. There were 596 Jews living in 30 houses in 1788. The *Familiants Law of 1798 limited the community to 135 families, but in 1802 there were 153 families (845 persons); the number had fallen to 589 persons in 1830 when the Jewish quarter was destroyed by fire. It had a German-language elementary school (1803–70). During the Middle Ages important rabbis held office in Osoblaha, among them the future Moravian chief rabbi, Gershon Ḥayyot Manasse of Hotzenplotz (see *Mintmasters), who was the first purveyor to the Silesian mint (1622–24). The village was a Moravian enclave situated in Silesia. When in the 16–18th centuries Jews were not permitted to reside in Silesia, they took refuge in Osoblaha.The community declined quickly during the 19th century when most of its members moved to nearby Krnov (Jaegernodorf). In 1921 there were 37 Jews in

Osoblaha and only one in 1934. The dilapidated synagogue was demolished in 1933, and the records and ritual objects were transferred to Krnov. What remained of the old Jewish quarter and the Jewish cemetery were destroyed in World War II. The cemetery was renovated by a grant from the Czechoslovak government in the 1950s.

BIBLIOGRAPHY: E. Richter and A. Schmidt, in: *Mitteilungen zur juedischen Volkskunde*, 14 (1911), 29–36; Marmorstein, *ibid.*, 81; B. Brilling, in: *Zeitung fuer die Geschichte der Juden*, 2 (1965), 53–57; idem, in: JGGJČ, 7 (1935), 387–98; R. Iltis (ed.), *Die aussaeen unter Traenen…* (1959), 80–81; S. Rubaschow, in: *Ost und West*, 16 (1916), 199ff. **ADD. BIBLIOGRAPHY:** J. Fiedler, *Jewish Sights of Bohemia and Moravia* (1991), 128, 129.

[Meir Lamed]

OSROENE (Osrhoene), district within the Seleucid Empire, occupying the N.W. portion of Mesopotamia. The capital city of the district, Edessa (modern Urfa), became a Greek *polis* under Seleucus I Nicator, but during the reign of Antiochus VII Sidetes (c. 136 B.C.E.) the area was conquered by Arab tribesmen, sons of Orhai (Osroes). Thereafter the capital and the state were known as Orhai or Urhai (Orrhoene being the form given by Pliny the Elder). Situated between the Roman and Parthian Empires, the Arab kingdom tended to support the latter, and thus during the temporary Roman conquest of Mesopotamia under Trajan (116 C.E.) the reigning monarch, Abgar VII, was deposed. Although the king was eventually returned under Hadrian, total autonomy was short-lived, and in 216 the area became a Roman colony. Jews probably resided in Osroene from the late Persian and early Hellenistic periods. By the end of the Second Temple period their influence carried over to the neighboring kingdom of *Adiabene, whose royal family converted to Judaism. Christianity was also introduced into Osroene by means of the local Jewish community, and according to one legend the Jew Hananiah supposedly conveyed a letter from Jesus to King Abgar V. By the end of the second century Christianity was officially recognized in Osroene, and thereafter the office of bishop of Edessa was considered of utmost importance for Eastern Christianity.

BIBLIOGRAPHY: A. von Gutschmid, in: *Mémoires de l'Académie de St. Petersbourg*, 35 (1887); J. Neusner, *History of the Jews in Babylonia*, 1 (1965), 166–9.

[Isaiah Gafni]

OSSOWETZKY, O. YEHOSHUA (1858–1929), senior official in Baron Edmond de *Rothschild's administration in Ereẓ Israel. Born in Kiev, in 1883 Ossowetzky was appointed chief administrator in *Rishon le-Zion by Baron de Rothschild. There he induced the farmers to plant vines and doubled the settlement's land area. The "free" farmers not subsidized by the Baron clashed with Ossowetzky; their leaders were forced to leave Rishon le-Zion after the "free" farmers' revolt, while Ossowetzky was replaced by an even harsher official. In 1887 he bought 7,000 dunams (1,750 acres) of land in Kastina (later *Be'er Toviyyah), and two years later he was appointed chief official of the Baron de Rothschild in Galilee and moved to *Rosh Pinnah. There he gained great influence in Turkish circles with the aid of bribes and gifts. He used to ride in a carriage, preceded by armed Jewish horsemen. Ossowetzky extended the area of Rosh Pinnah and tried to base its economy on plantations and the silk industry. He also established three settlements of *Metullah on land he had purchased. In the 1890s Ossowetzky purchased large tracts of land in the Golan and other areas east of the Jordan River and also began purchasing land in Lower Galilee (*Sejera). When the management of the settlements was handed over to the *Jewish Colonization Association (ICA) in 1900, Ossowetzky left the country and lived in Paris until his death.

BIBLIOGRAPHY: M. Smilansky, *Mishpaḥat ha-Adamah*, 2 (1944), 120–5; Tidhar, 3 (1949), 1318–9.

[Yehuda Slutsky]

OSSUARIES AND SARCOPHAGI. Ossuaries are small chests in which the bones of the dead were placed after the flesh had decayed. Sarcophagi are body-length coffins made of stone or marble, clay and marble, which were used for primary burials (the term is from the Greek meaning "flesh-eater"). The earliest ossuaries found in Ereẓ Israel are from the Chalcolithic period. Ceramic ossuaries have been found at Ḥaderah, Bene-Berak, Azor, and Peqi'in. Some are shaped like a four-legged receptacle with a vaulted roof, a door with a bolt in the facade, and windows in the rear, and are thought to resemble dwellings of the period. The ossuaries have painted decorations and some of their facades are given the appearance of a human face. Ceramic anthropoid coffins dating to the transitional period between the end of the Bronze Age and the beginning of the Iron Age, which imitate the shape of Egyptian mummies, have been found at Deir el-Balah (near Gaza) and at Beth-Shean. During the Iron Age neither ceramic nor stone coffins were used for burial purposes.

Sarcophagi

Known in Ereẓ Israel particularly from the Second Temple period and onwards, elongated sarcophagi decorated with plant motifs have been uncovered in "Herod's family tomb" and in the "Tombs of the King" in Jerusalem, and also in a large tomb on the Mount of Olives. Especially remarkable is the ornamentation of the vaulted lid of a sarcophagus from the "Tombs of the Kings," which is carved with plants common to the country, vine and olive branches, etc. Wooden coffins from this period have been found at Ein-Gedi, one of which was inlaid with bone. In the Roman period, many carved sarcophagi made of marble were introduced into the country from abroad. A sarcophagus discovered near Caesarea portrays a battle between Greeks and Amazons, another from Turmus Aiya is carved with representations of the seasons. Sarcophagi are also known from tombs in Samaria (in a third-century C.E. tomb), one depicts peasants taking their produce to market. A sarcophagus with mythological scenes (Achilles among the daughters of Lycomedes; Leda) was found in the Bet She'arim cemetery (possibly in secondary use). Lead coffins which were cast in Tyre, Ashkelon, and Jerusalem were common in the third-fourth centuries; molds were employed for their decorations. Early Christian sarcophagi bear reliefs depicting scenes from the Bible and the Gospels. In the Byzantine period, the use of sarcophagi died out.

Ossuaries

Small stone chests, used for the secondary interment of human bones, were extremely popular among the Jewish population during the Second Temple period, i.e., between c. 40 B.C.E. and 135 C.E.. Ossuaries found by Hachlili at Jericho are dated to a more restricted time period: 10–68 C.E. They are mainly known from tombs in the vicinity of Jerusalem, but examples are known from Galilee (e.g., Nazareth), the Shephelah (e.g., Modi'in), and the lower Jordan River region (e.g., Jericho). A typical ossuary had a length of about 2.5 ft., so that it might accommodate the long bone of an adult leg, which is the longest bone in a human body. The ossuaries taper slightly toward the bottom; some stand on four low legs; they are made of soft limestone with flat or vaulted lids. Many contain scratched inscriptions on their sides in cursive Hebrew, Aramaic, or Greek, or in two languages (a few inscriptions were made with charcoal). In most cases only the name of the deceased or his family status is given, e.g., "Mother"; some inscriptions, however, are longer, e.g., "Dostos our father – do not open," or "The bones of the sons of Nicanor, who made the doors" (i.e., those of the *Nicanor gate in the Second Temple). In some cases (mostly in the burial of small children) one ossuary served for the bones of more than one body. The chests are sometimes decorated with a red or yellow wash of paint, but the usual decorations are chip-carved and chiseled decorations, with some designs executed using a compass. The surface of the ossuary was generally divided into two fields by square frames formed by a wavy line between two straight ones. The squares were filled with a rosette motif, usually with six leaves, but there are considerable variations in its form, as well as in the decoration of the surrounding surface, by the use of dots, wreaths, etc. The double-rosette motif is a very common decoration on ossuaries, and Wilkinson has suggested they might have been symbols used to invoke cherubim – the winged creatures on the inner curtain of the Tabernacle (Ex. 26:31). Some ossuaries are decorated with representations of plants, buildings, or parts of them (columns, capitals), gates. Various cross-like scratches and other marks sometimes appear on ossuaries and their lids (erroneously regarded by early scholars as Judeo-Christian symbols), and these were probably made by the stone craftsmen who carved the chests and wished to ensure their proper closure.

BIBLIOGRAPHY: Y. Brand, *Kelei ha-Ḥeres be-Sifrut ha-Talmud* (1953), ch. 12, 20; Clermont-Ganneau, Arch, 1 (1899), 381ff.; R. Schutz, in: MGWJ, 75 (1931), 286ff.; L.H. Vincent. in: RB. 43 (1934), 564ff.; Watzinger, Denkmaeler, 2 (1935); Galling, Reallexikon, s.v. *Sarkophag, Ossuar*; Frey, Corpus, 2 (1952), 245ff.; A.G. Barrois, *Manual d'archéologie biblique*, 2 (1953), 308ff.; Goodenough, Symbols, 1 (1953), 110ff.; 3 (1953), nos. 105–230; Perrot, in: *Atiqot*, 3 (1961), 1ff. **ADD. BIBLIOGRAPHY:** E.M. Meyers, *Jewish Ossuaries: Reburial and Rebirth* (1971): I. Singer (ed.), *Graves and Burial Practices in the Ancient Period* (1994); L.Y. Rahmani, *A Catalogue of Jewish Ossuaries* (1994); R. Hachlili and A. Killebrew, *Jericho: The Jewish Cemetery of the Second Temple Period* (1999); Y. Billig, "The Use of Ossuaries for Secondary Burial During the Second Temple Period," in: *Judea and Samaria Research Studies*, 13 (2004), 51–55; A.M. Berlin, "Jewish Life Before the Revolt: The Archaeological Evidence," in: *Journal for the Study of Judaism*, 36 (2005), 453ff.

[Michael Avi-Yonah / Shimon Gibson (2nd ed.)]

OSTFELD, BARBARA JEAN (1952–), one of the first U.S. women invested as a cantor. Born in St. Louis, Missouri, one of three children of Dr. Adrian Ostfeld, an epidemiologist, and Ruth Vogel Ostfeld, Barbara was musical from very early childhood and knew from an early age that she wanted to be a cantor. Ostfeld's decision to apply to the sacred music undergraduate program at HUC-JIR was not motivated by a particular political or feminist viewpoint. Initially, she was unaware that women had not previously been admitted to the school. At HUC-JIR Ostfeld was profoundly influenced by Arthur Wolfson, cantor at Temple Emanuel in New York City, who taught her both contemporary Reform music and traditional *nusaḥ*. She graduated in 1975, receiving ordination at age 22. She also met and married her first husband, Frederick Herman, during her years of study. This marriage was not successful and Ostfeld later married Todd M. Joseph, with whom she had two daughters.

Ostfeld served congregations in Great Neck, Rochester, and Buffalo, New York, where she fulfilled the full range of cantorial responsibilities, including funerals, weddings, leading services, and directing a children's choir. Early on her talents were recognized by the Reform cantors' professional organization, the American Conference of Cantors (ACC). She served on board positions of the ACC, as Secretary (1978–80), as vice president (1980–82), as a Northeast regional representative (1994–96), and several terms on the board of directors. From 1996 to 1998, she chaired the Joint Cantorial Placement Commission. She received an honorary doctorate in sacred music in 2000. In 2002, she accepted the directorship of the Placement Commission of the ACC.

[Judith S. Pinnolis (2nd ed.)]

OSTIA, city in central Italy, near the mouth of the River Tiber; it was one of the harbors of Rome and became at the end of the Republic an important commercial center. However, Ostia flourished mainly under the Flavian and Antonine Dynasties. From the middle of the 3rd century C.E. its slow decline began.

At the end of the 19th century the site was excavated and a few epitaphs in Greek and Latin were discovered, which seemed to indicate the presence of a Jewish community (*universitas Judaeorum*). In 1961 the remains of a synagogue found near Ostia provided definite proof that a Jewish community had existed there. The excavations have shown that part of the building was constructed at the end of the first century, underwent alterations and enlargements during the second and third, and was considerably enlarged and partly rebuilt at the beginning of the fourth. As a result of the diminished population of the city, the synagogue fell into ruins at the end of the fourth or during the fifth centuries.

The building, which is of the basilica type, stands between the ancient seashore and the coastal road (*Via Severiana*), and faces east-southeast, in the direction of Jerusalem. It has three entrance doors, recalling the synagogues of Galilee. From the door in the center a step leads down to the synagogue proper, a large rectangular hall about 81.6 × 41.0 ft. (24.9 × 12.5 m.). This is divided into three aisles with four marble columns surmounted by finely worked Corinthian capitals. It has been suggested that the lateral sections, which are divided by stone balustrades, were reserved for women. The wall at the back is slightly curved. In the oldest hall the seats were of stone, set against the walls. An inscription of the second or third century, partly in Latin, partly in Hebrew, refers expressly to the ark: "For the Emperor's health Mindis Faustos (with his family) built and made (it) from his own gifts and set up the ark for the Holy Law."

In the later fourth-century building the Tabernacle for the Ark, shaped as an aedicula, rises behind the pulpit in the left aisle along its entire length, a few steps leading to it. Jewish symbols, which can be found also in other synagogues of that period, are carved on the corbel of the aedicula's architrave: a seven-branched *menorah*, a *shofar*, and a *lulav* and *etrog*.

The floor is covered with a bichrome mosaic decorated with floral motifs.

It is thought that a stove for baking *maẓẓot* can be identified in one of the surrounding rooms, as well as a *mikveh*, and a spacious hall which served for religious instruction or as a resting place for pilgrims. The building of the synagogue of Ostia is the first ancient synagogue known in Italy and Western Europe.

In the area of the synagogue were found various terracotta oil-lamps with an obvious Jewish character. Most were decorated with a *menorah* and one with a Torah ark.

The community must have numbered several hundred Jews.

BIBLIOGRAPHY: G. Calza, in: Pauly-Wissowa, 36 (1942), 1654–64; P.L. Zovatto, in: *Memorie storiche forogiuliesi*, 49 (1960); F. Squarciapino, in: Ministero della publica istruzione, *Bolletino d'arte* (1961), 326–37; idem, in: *Studi Romani*, 11 (1963), 129–41; idem, in: *Archaeology*, 16 (1963), 194–203. **ADD. BIBLIOGRAPHY:** M. Floriani-Squarciapino, "Plotius Fortunatus archisynagogus," in: RMI, 36 (1970), 183–91; M.T. Lazzarini, "Appendice: iscrizioni da Ostia e Porto," in: *La cultura ebraica nell'editoria italiana* (1992), 185–87; B. Olsson, D. Mitternacht and O. Brandt, *The Synagogue of Ancient Ostia and the Jews of Rome, Interdisciplinary Studies*, Acta Instituti Romani Regni Sueciae, Series IN 4, 57 (2001).

[Alfredo Mordechai Rabello / Samuel Rocca (2nd ed.)]

OSTRACA (Gr. ὄστρακον, plural ὄστρακα), ancient inscribed potsherds. Ostraca were common writing materials in antiquity which were used mainly for writing receipts, temporary records, lists of names, etc., but some letters written on potsherds have also been found. Ostraca from the Middle Bronze Age II (c. 1788–1550 B.C.E.) have been found in Ereẓ Israel; the earliest one comes from the pile of debris left by *Macalister after his excavations at Gezer. It appears to represent a transitional stage between the proto-Sinaitic script and Hebrew-Phoenician alphabetic writing and has been deciphered as *klb* ("Caleb"). A later example of this transitional stage of writing appears on an ostracon from Tell el-Ḥesi discovered in the stratum attributed to the beginning of the Late Bronze Age II (c. 1400–1200 B.C.E.) which Sayce proposed reading *bla*. Three inscribed potsherds from Lachish, probably dedicatory inscriptions, and one from Tell al-ʿAjjūl, are dated to the 13th century B.C.E. An ostracon found at Beth-Shemesh belongs to the transitional period between the Middle and Late Bronze Age but since it is written in ink, the potsherd and the inscription cannot be definitely dated to the same period. It seems to date to the beginning of the 12th century B.C.E. and apparently contains a list of names of workers, the number of their work days, and names of the employers. It is the first ostracon found in Ereẓ Israel which contains numerals. The latest ostracon from Ereẓ Israel was found at Tell ab-Ṣarim in the Beth-Shean Valley and probably dates to the beginning of the first century B.C.E.

These ostraca are most valuable for tracing the development of the alphabet. Ostraca from the Israelite period have been found in the royal storehouse of the Israelite kings at *Samaria. These sherds, written in ink, are receipts for taxes and contain the year of payment, the name and provenance of the payer, the kind of tax (wine or oil), and some also have the name of the tax collector or the official in charge of the storehouse. These ostraca seem to date from the time of the Israelite king Jehoahaz, son of Jehu (c. 3–800 B.C.E.). Near the wall outside the city several other inscribed potsherds were found which were incised, and not written in ink. The "Ophel Ostracon" found in the City of David is assigned to the end of the period of the kingdom of Judah. It apparently contains the names of persons and their provenances. From the same period is a group of potsherds written in ink from Lachish (Tell al-Duwayr); 18 were found in the city gate and three in the latest Israelite stratum inside the city near the inner wall. In the excavations at Arad, ostraca were found written in Hebrew and Aramaic and one in Egyptian. They are assigned to the end of the kingdom of Judah and early Persian period and are mostly orders to the official in charge of the fortress to provide supplies to the soldiers of the Judean kings. Several fragmentary ostraca from the Persian period were discovered in the upper stratum (sixth–fifth century B.C.E.) at Tell al-Khalayfa (cf. *Ezion-Geber, *Elath) on the coast of the Gulf of Akaba. They are written in Aramaic and are apparently receipts for wine.

Ostraca were commonly used in Egypt; those found at Elephantine are written in Aramaic in a script similiar to that appearing on the ostraca from Tell al-Khalayfa. The Egyptian ostraca, mostly tax receipts, are an important source of information on the economic history of the Ptolemaic and Roman periods in Egypt, and include records of the taxes levied on the Jews from the time of Vespasian onward.

BIBLIOGRAPHY: S. Yeivin, *Toledot ha-Ketav ha-Ivri* (1939); R.B. Kallner, in: *Kedem*, 2 (1945), 11ff.; E.L. Sukenik, *ibid.*, 15; idem, in: PEFQS, 65 (1933), 152ff.; Y. Sukenik (Yadin), *Yedi'ot ha-Ḥevrah la-Ḥakirat Ereẓ Yisrael ve-Attikoteha*, 13 (1947), 115ff.; N.H. Torczyner, *Te'udot Lakhish* (1940); B. Maisler, in: JPOS, 21 (1948), 117ff.; U. Wilcken, *Griechische Ostraka*, 2 vols. (1899); P. Jouguet, in: *Bulletin de l'Institut Français d'Archéologie Orientale*, 2 (1902), 91ff.; E. Sachau, *Aramaeische Papyrus and Ostraka*..., 2 vols. (1911); D. Diringer, *L 'alfabeto nella storia della civiltà* (1931); Diringer, Iscr, 21–79; Moscati, Epig, 27–39, 44–46, 111–3; Y. Aharoni, in: IEJ, 16 (1966), 1–17; Tcherikover, Corpus, 2 (1960), 108–76.

[*Encyclopaedia Hebraica*]

OSTRAVA (until 1929 **Moravska Ostrava**; Ger. **Maehrisch-Ostrau**), city in N. Moravia, Czech Republic; after Prague and Brno the third largest Jewish community in Czechoslovakia between the two world wars. The town was prohibited to Jews in the Middle Ages. In 1508 the local lord permitted one Jew to settle, against the wishes of the town. He was followed by others, resulting in an expulsion order of 1531, although it was only partly carried out. Jews mainly from *Osoblaha (Hotzenplotz) later did business in Ostrava. In 1786 the municipality leased its distillery to a Jew. Other Jews subsequently arrived and in 1832 a *minyan* was organized. When in 1837 the city council was in session deciding on whether to grant a Jew right of sojourn, the mob rioted and the council did not dare to decide in the affirmative. A *Kultusverein was organized in 1860 under the guidance of the *Teschen community. A cemetery was consecrated in 1872 and a community authorized in 1875; it then numbered 58 persons. The Jewish population was divided between the different parts of the city; Polnisch-Ostrau (after 1918, Slezska Ostrava), which was then under Silesian administration, and Maehrisch-Ostrau, which was under Moravian administration. After a prolonged conflict over where the community's institutions would be located, Maehrisch-Ostrau became the center.

With the rapid development of the city, caused by the development of mines and the founding of the Vitkovice steelworks by the *Gutmann brothers, the community thrived, absorbing Jews from older Moravian communities and many from Galicia. In 1879 the main synagogue was consecrated. While in 1880 there were 1,077 Jews in Ostrava, in 1900 there were already about 5,000 and in the census of 1930, 7,189 Jews. In 1937 the Jewish population was around 10,000, making Ostrava the third largest Jewish community in Czech-speaking lands. On the eve of World War II there was a wave of emigration to Ereẓ Israel. Several leaders of the Czechoslovak Zionist movement who resided in Ostrava, like Joseph *Rufeisen and Paul Maerz, also left. On the other hand, there was a steady influx of Jews to the city, from Galicia across the border and from Carpatho-Russia; consequently the religious community in the town was strengthened and successfully rivaled the liberal-minded local congregation. By 1875 a religious congregation had been established, and a rabbi was invited in 1890. Later a "Sephardi," i.e. ḥasidic, congregation was established as well. Alois Hilf was president of the community. Additional synagogues were opened in the suburbs of Privoz (1904), Vitkovice (1911), Hrusov (1914), and Zabreh, among others. In 1912 the community built a vacation home for Jewish children. After 1918 Ostrava became a main center of Jewish life, where the regional offices of the Zionist Organization and of *He-Ḥalutz were located. The *Maccabi sport club was strong there, and in 1929 a *Maccabiah was held in Ostrava with the participation of some 2,000 men and women. Other organizations like Maccabi ha-Ẓa'ir and *Blau-Weiss thrived there. A Jewish technical school was founded in 1919. The communal statute adopted in 1921, based on universal, proportional, and direct suffrage for men and women without regard to their citizenship, served as an example for many other communities. Among the new communal institutions opened in the 1920s were the Kedma, a home for Jewish apprentices (1924), and a new Orthodox synagogue (1926). In the community's elementary school, teaching was in German in the lower grades and in Czech in the upper grades. The community increased from 4,969 in 1921 to 6,865 in 1931 (5.4% of the total population). There were some very active communities on the outskirts and in the vicinity of Ostrava, e.g., Frystat (Ger. Freistadt; 322 in 1930), Karvinna (172 in 1930), Orlova (Ger. Orlau; 394 in 1930), and Frydek (Ger. Friedeck; 237 in 1930), Mistek (195 in 1930), Hrusov (Ger. Hruschau; 219 in 1930). Jewish life in Ostrava was depicted in the writings of Joseph Wechsberg, a native of the town who later emigrated to the United States.

Holocaust Period

Immediately after the German occupation, the Jewish old-age home was confiscated and most of the synagogues in the city and in the suburbs of Vitk, Privoz, Hrusov and Zabreh were set on fire. On Oct. 17, 1939, about 1,200 Jews were transferred to Zarzecze, where a forced-labor camp, Nisko nad Lanem, was erected; the Ostrava community was forced to supply the materials for the building of this camp, which was known as *Zentralstelle fuer juedische Umsiedlung* ("central office for Jewish resettlement"). The Nisko camp was part of a projected plan to create a Jewish reservation in Poland, but it was soon abandoned. In March 1940, 600 Jews were driven over the border into Poland; another 500 were returned to Ostrava. Many of those driven east survived the war while those who remained, 3,903 in 1941, were subjected to deportations. Between Sept. 17 and Sept. 29, 1942, 2,582 Jews were deported in three transports. In all, a total of 3,567 Jews were deported from Ostrava; 253 survived.

After World War II the Jewish congregation was reestablished, with numerous Jews from Carpatho-Russia who had chosen to settle in Czechoslovakia instead of their native land ruled by the Soviets. A prayer room was active in the city from 1978. A new cemetery was opened in neighboring Sliezska Ostrava and a ceremonial hall was added in 1988. Few Jews lived there in the early 21st century.

BIBLIOGRAPHY: H. Gold (ed.), *Juden und Judengemeinden Maehrens...* (1929), index s.v. *Maehrisch-Ostrau*; R. Iltis (ed.), *Die aussaeen unter Traenen...* (1959), 77–82; M. Kreutzberger (ed.), *Bibliothek und Archiv*, 1 (1970), 173. **ADD. BIBLIOGRAPHY:** J. Fiedler, *Jewish Sights of Bohemia and Moravia* (1991), 129, 130.

[Meir Lamed and Henry Wasserman / Yeshayahu Jelinek (2nd ed.)]

OSTRICH, the largest of the birds. The ostrich, in its habits and bodily structure, has features similar to those of a camel (its Latin name is *Strutio camelus*). It was formerly commonly found in eastern Transjordan but by reason of being intensively hunted has disappeared almost entirely from the Middle East region; individual ostriches are only seldom found in eastern Transjordan, to which they apparently come from the Arabian deserts where the ostrich has also become rare. In the Bible the ostrich is called *ya'en* (יָעֵן) and *kenaf-renanim* (כְּנַף רְנָנִים; AV, JPS "the wing of the ostrich"). The former name occurs once, in Lamentations (4:3): "The daughter of my people is become cruel, like the ostriches in the wilderness." Its description as cruel is apparently connected with the fact that when in danger it is liable in its flight to hurt its chicks and also to the fact that the female often hatches only some of the eggs, the rest being abandoned and used as food for the newly hatched chicks. Job (39:13–18) contains an extensive description of the ostrich, there called *kenaf-renanim*, that is, "the wing that delights the eye with its beauty." There an account is given of the way it hatches its eggs on the ground (*ibid.*, 14–15); of the male who confuses the chicks of other females and is their leader (*ibid.*, 16); of the ostrich's meager understanding; "Because God hath deprived her of wisdom, neither hath He imparted to her understanding" (*ibid.*, 17; cf. the expression *Vogelstrausspolitik*); of its ability to escape from hunters mounted on horses (*ibid.*, 18). The translations have identified the *bat-ya'anah* (בַּת יַעֲנָה), included among the unclean birds and mentioned several times as inhabiting desolate places (Isa. 13:21; Micah 1:8; et al.), with the *ya'en*. The *bat-ya'anah* was originally a species of *owl but the name is used for ostrich in modern Hebrew. In the Mishnah the ostrich is called *na'amit* (נַעֲמִית; in Ar.: *na'ama*); in mishnaic and talmudic times the ostrich was well known. Vessels were made from its eggshells (Kel. 17:14), while some people bred it as an ornamental bird (Shab. 128a). Its ability to swallow anything was exploited; fed pieces of gold covered with dough, it evacuated them after the action of its gastric juice had refined the gold (TJ, Yoma 4:4, 41d).

BIBLIOGRAPHY: Lewysohn, Zool, 188f., no. 240; I. Aharoni, *Zikhronot Zo'olog Ivri*, 1 (1943), 20, 33; F.S. Bodenheimer, *Animal and Man in Bible Lands* (1960), 59f.; J. Feliks, *Animal World of the Bible* (1962), 91.

[Jehuda Feliks]

OSTRIKER, ALICIA (1937–), U.S. poet and literary critic. Born in Brooklyn, New York, the second daughter of Beatrice (Linnick) and David Suskin, Ostriker was raised in a secular left-wing home. While studying English literature at Brandeis University (B.A. 1958), Alicia met Jeremiah P. Ostriker, a student at Harvard and a Reconstructionist Jew, who encouraged her to read the Bible. This first encounter with biblical literature created a complicated connection to Judaism that she would pursue in her subsequent creative and scholarly writing. The couple married in 1958. While her husband earned a doctorate in astrophysics at the University of Chicago, Ostriker pursued graduate work in English at the University of Wisconsin, earning an M.A. (1961) and Ph.D. (1964). Her dissertation focused on William Blake. In 1965, she joined the faculty of Rutgers University, teaching English and creative writing. She was promoted to full professor in 1972 and named distinguished professor in 1982.

Known for her strongly feminist perspective, Ostriker published numerous essays and five volumes of literary criticism, including *Writing Like a Woman* (1983) and *Stealing the Language: The Emergence of Women's Poetry in America* (1986). Her 11 volumes of poetry draw from her personal life. Once unaffiliated with any Jewish institution, Ostriker began to study Hebrew and Bible in the 1980s and went on to offer workshops on feminist Bible reading and Midrash at the National Havurah Institute. Both her scholarly and creative work reflect feminist readings of the Bible and of Jewish liturgy and tradition. The essays in *Feminist Revision and the Bible* (1992) and *The Nakedness of the Fathers: Biblical Vision and Revision* (1994) reimagine characters and narratives of the Hebrew Bible from a contemporary, post-Holocaust, and feminist perspective. Her poems reflect similar concerns. *Green Age* (1989) addresses women's aging, spiritual development, and creativity, while offering a critique of patriarchy in Jewish tradition. *The Crack in Everything* (1996) charts her battle against breast cancer and includes several moving poems reflecting on the Holocaust. *The Volcano Sequence* (2002) probes Jewish texts, history, liturgy, and theology, revealing Ostriker's growing knowledge of classic rabbinic writing and modern Jewish philosophy, while *No Heaven* (2005) explores issues of Jewish identity as well as art.

Ostriker received many prestigious awards and grants, including a National Endowment for the Arts Fellowship (1976–77); a Rockefeller Foundation Fellowship (1982); a Guggenheim Foundation Fellowship (1984–85); the Pushcart Prize (1979 and 2000); Poetry Society of America's William Carlos Williams Prize for *The Imaginary Lover* (1986); Strousse Poetry Prize (1986); Edward Stanley Award (1994); Anna David Rosenberg Poetry Award (1994); Paterson Poetry Award (1996); San Francisco State Poetry Centre Award (1996); Readers' Choice Award (1998); and Bookman News Book of the Year (1998).

[Sara R. Horowitz (2nd ed.)]

OSTROG (Heb. אוסטרהא, אוסטרא), city in Rovno district (Volhynia), Ukraine; formerly in Poland. Evidence of the beginnings of Jewish settlement in Ostrog dates from the 15th century; inscriptions on two Jewish tombstones in the ancient cemetery date from 1445, and the archives of Lvov contain documents of 1447 relating to Ostrog Jewry. In 1495 the Jews were expelled from Ostrog, during the general expulsion of Jews from the grand duchy of Lithuania, but they were able to return after a short interval. Their trading activities were opposed by the burghers who in 1502 complained to the Polish king that the Ostrog Jews were depriving them of their profits from the transit trade through Lvov to Podolia and Russia. Sigismund I adjudicated a case relating to customs dues in which Ostrog Jews were involved in 1536. The growth of the Ostrog community was linked to the expansion of trade with Walachia, Walachian cattle being exchanged for cloth and other goods which the Ostrog Jews sold in Poland. They also exported timber, wax, potash, leather and leather goods via the Bug River to Danzig. The Ostrog community was one of the four original leading communities in Volhynia represented on the *Council of the Four Lands. The community perished during the Cossack uprising under *Chmielnicki in 1648–49 when 1,500 families (about 7,000 persons) were massacred. In 1661 there were only five Jewish families in the town. Later the community revived, to regain its former leading position in Volhynia, with jurisdiction over a number of communities in the vicinity. The Jews of Ostrog were miraculously saved during the *Haidamack raids in the middle of the 18th century, with the help of their Tatar neighbors. They also emerged unscathed when Russian troops in 1792 attacked the synagogue of Ostrog, believing it to be a fortress, in the fighting that preceded the second partition of Poland. In commemoration of their deliverance the Ostrog Jews instituted a "Purim of Ostrog," and the *Megillat Tammuz* was read in the synagogue on the 7th of Tammuz. At the end of the 18th century the Jewish population numbered under 2,000 and in 1830 2,206. By 1847 it had increased to 7,300, a similar figure to that in the period preceding the 1648 massacres, an influx evidently following the decree of *Nicholas I of 1843 ordering the expulsion of Jews from western border settlements (see *Russia). In 1897, the Jews numbered 9,208 out of a total population of 14,749; and in 1921 7,991 (out of 12,975). By 1939 nearly 10,500 Jews were living there.

Ostrog was one of the most important centers of Jewish religious learning in Poland, its name being interpreted in Hebrew as *Os Torah* ("the letter of the Law"). Some of Poland's most eminent scholars served as rabbis and principals of the Ostrog yeshivah, which was already in existence by the beginning of the 16th century. The first-known rabbi of the congregation and principal of the yeshivah was Kalonymus Kalman Haberkasten. Among his notable successors were Solomon *Luria (Maharshal), Isaiah *Horowitz, author of *Shenei Luḥot ha-Berit* (first quarter of the 17th century), Samuel *Edels (Maharsha), and *David b. Samuel ha-Levi (Taz). According to the last, the Ostrog yeshivah was probably the greatest in Poland: "Never have I seen so important a yeshivah as this." Ostrog was the "great town of scholars and writers" according to Nathan Nata *Hannover. The yeshivah was restored soon after the Cossack destruction through the efforts of Samuel Shmelke, who loaned a large sum to the Council of the Four Lands for its reestablishment and the maintenance of students. Its rabbis included many distinguished scholars and its graduates provided rabbis, principals of yeshivot, *dayyanim*, and *maggidim* for numerous communities. Ostrog also became celebrated as a center of *Ḥasidism which was disseminated there by several disciples of *Israel b. Eliezer (the Ba'al Shem Tov). A number of benevolent societies and foundations functioned in Ostrog, the most important being the burial society. During the Russian rule the Jewish population grew from 1,829 in 1787 to 7,300 (including nearby settlements) in 1847, and 9,208 in 1897 (total population – 14,749). Jews were active in the trade of lumber, cattle, and farm products. They owned sawmills, hide-processing and furniture factories, and two banks. After World War I Ostrog turned into a border town within Poland, and was cut of from the Eastern market. This led to an economic decline. The number of Jews fell to 7,991 (total population – 12,975) in 1921, and 8,171 (total population – 13,265) in 1931. The Zionist movement and the Bund flourished. There was a Hebrew elementary and junior high school, and a kindergarten.

[Azriel Shochat / Shmuel Spector (2nd ed.)]

Holocaust Period

Under Soviet rule (1939–41), the Jewish communal bodies were disbanded. A number of Zionist youth left for Vilna in the hope of reaching Palestine from there. In the summer of 1940 some Jewish families were sent into exile to the Soviet interior. When war broke out between Germany and Russia on June 22, 1941, groups of Jewish youth left the town with the retreating Soviet army. About 1,000 Jews from Ostrog reached the Soviet Union, leaving about 9,500 Jews in Ostrog itself. During the heavy fighting 500 Jews were killed. The German forces entered Ostrog on July 3, 1941, and immediately embarked upon a campaign of murder and plunder among the Jewish population. On Aug. 4 2,000 Jews were rounded up and murdered in the woods in the New City, followed on September 1 by a similar action against 2,500 more victims. The members of the first *Judenrat headed by Rabbi Ginzburg were murdered in the first murder *Aktion* in August. A second Judenrat was set up, headed by Avraham Komedant and including Chaim Dawidson, Yakov Gurewitz, and Yakov Kaplan. A ghetto was established in June 1942, where the remaining 3,000 Jews were concentrated. The third and final *Aktion* came on Oct. 15, 1942, in which 3,000 persons were taken and murdered on the outskirts of the town. About 800 Jews escaped to the forest, but few of them survived, as they were often attacked or betrayed by the Ukrainian peasants, or were murdered by gangs of the Bandera Ukrainian nationalists. Some of the escapees organized partisan units operating in the vicinity. Among the outstanding partisans were Yakov Kaplan, Mendel Treiberman, and Pesach Eisenstein. When the Soviet forces returned to Ostrog on Feb. 4, 1944, about 30 Jews emerged from the partisan ranks. Approximately another 30 came out of hiding. Later on, former Jewish inhabitants who had fled to the Soviet Union also returned, but the vast majority left Ostrog for Poland, on their way to Ereẓ Israel or other countries abroad. The community was not reconstituted after World War II.

[Aharon Weiss]

BIBLIOGRAPHY: M.M. Biber, *Mazkeret li-Gedolei Ostraha* (1908); *Arim ve-Immahot be-Yisrael*, 1 (1946), 5–40; Halpern, Pinkas; *Pinkas Ostrah: Sefer Zikkaron li-Kehillat Ostraha* (1960). **ADD. BIBLIOGRAPHY:** *Pinkas ha-Kehillot Poland*, vol. 5 –Volhynia and Polesie (1990).

OSTROGORSKI, MOSES (1854–1917), scholar of political law and community leader. Born in Grodno, Belorussia, Ostrogorski finished his studies at the University of St. Petersburg and worked in the Ministry of Justice. In 1882 he was appointed head of the legislation department, but when the czarist reaction increased its power he was forced to resign and leave the country. His book, *La femme au point de vue du public*, published in 1892, was awarded a prize from the law faculty in Paris and was translated into English, German, and Polish. His most important book, *La démocratie et l'organisation des partis politiques* (translated into English in 1903), severely criticized the democratic regimes of England and the United States, whose main fault was that the power of the political parties suppresses individual freedom. On the basis of this book Ostrogorski became renowned among American and Western European thinkers. In 1904 he returned to Russia, where he was elected to the first *Duma in 1906 by the Jewish voters as the representative of the Grodno district. He was one of those who determined the Duma's work procedures. He also served as a member of the committee for equal rights, and with M. *Vinaver presented the case of the Jews. He was one of a six-member delegation sent by the Duma to visit the British Parliament. Although he did not formally join any political party, he always took the side of the Constitutional Democrats. As a member of the Jewish Popular Group, founded by Vinaver and *Sliozberg, he vehemently objected to the establishment of an organized group of Jewish representatives to the Duma which was demanded by the Zionists and *Dubnow.

[Eliezer Margaliot]

OSTROLEKA (Pol. **Ostrołęka**; also **Ostrolenka**), town in Warsaw province, Poland. A permanent Jewish settlement in Ostroleka is not recorded before the 19th century, although Jews are mentioned in connection with the town in a document of 1622. An ordinance of 1826 prescribed certain areas for Jewish residence, only those with special privileges being permitted to live outside. The restriction was removed in 1862. The community, which numbered approximately 560 in 1827 (16.3% of the total population), increased to 1,129 (36.8%) in 1856; 4,832 (37.2%) in 1897; and 6,219 (53.5%) in 1909; decreasing to 3,352 (36.6%) in 1921. The 708 members of the loan society (founded in 1909) of the Ostroleka community in 1924 comprised 359 artisans, 259 small traders, 11 agriculturalists, and 79 members of other professions.

[Nathan Michael Gelber]

Holocaust Period

Ostroleka was occupied by the Germans in September 1939. Jews were physically attacked and Jewish property confiscated. On Simḥat Torah all Jews were ordered to cross into the Soviet sector within three days. During the expulsion many were killed and their property stolen. The Jews of Ostroleka were scattered throughout the Soviet sector and found temporary asylum in Bialystok, Slonim, Lomza, and other cities. Administrative restrictions were placed upon them, and in 1940 many families were deported to the Soviet interior. Those who remained in the Soviet-occupied sector of Poland fell into the hands of the Germans after the outbreak of the German-Soviet war (June 22, 1941) and suffered the same persecutions as the local Jews – forced labor, starvation, disease, and finally extermination. Jews from Ostroleka were active in the resistance movements in the Vilna and Baranovichi ghettoes. Some also joined the partisans and fought in the Puszcza Naliboki and the surrounding area.

[Aharon Weiss]

BIBLIOGRAPHY: *Sefer Kehillat Ostrolenka* (Heb. and Yid., 1963).

OSTROLENK, BERNHARD (1887–1944), U.S. economist. Ostrolenk, who was born in Warsaw, received his early schooling in Berlin, and was taken to the United States in 1897. After holding several teaching posts, he became professor of economics at the School of Business and Civic Administration at the City College of New York where he taught until his death. He also wrote for many magazines including *Current History* and *Business Week*. His major publications include: *Economic Geography* (1941); *The Surplus Farmer* (1932); and *The Economics of Branch Banking* (1930). His main interests were scientific farming and the economic problems of agriculture. During World War II, he became interested in immigration problems and the Zionist movement.

[Joachim O. Ronall]

OSTROPOLER, HERSHELE (late 18th century), Yiddish jester. Although biographical facts concerning him are based on oral tradition intermingled with folklore, he was probably born in Balta, Podolia, and lived and died at Medzibezh. He derived his name from the townlet of Ostropol, Poland, where he served as *shoḥet* ("ritual slaughterer"), until his satiric wit offended the communal leaders. He then wandered through Podolia townlets becoming a familiar figure in the inns of the district. His poverty was proverbial. According to a folk legend, he was called to the ḥasidic court of Medzibezh to cure the *Ba'al Shem Tov's grandson, Reb Baruch Tulchiner, of his fits of depression by serving as his jester. His satiric barbs shocked the rich and delighted the simple folk. Booklets recording his tales, anecdotes, and witticisms appeared posthumously and were widely disseminated until the mid-20th century. He was the subject of lyrics by Ephraim *Auerbach and Itzik *Manger, a novel by I.J. *Trunk, a comedy by M. Livshitz performed by the *Vilna Troupe in 1930, a comedy by Jacob Gershenson, and a folkplay by Jacob Zonshein.

BIBLIOGRAPHY: D. Sfard, *Shtudyes un Skitzen* (1955), 176–9; A. Holdes, *Mayses, Vitsn un Shpitslekh fun Hershele Ostropolier* (1960); Several stories of Hershele Ostropoler in English appear in I. Howe and E. Greenberg, *A Treasury of Yiddish Stories* (1953), 614–20; E. Sherman, *Hirshele Ostropoler* (Heb., 1931) includes bibliography.

[Sol Liptzin]

OSTROPOLER, SAMSON BEN PESAḤ (d. 1648), kabbalist. No details are known about Ostropoler's life except those few that can be deduced from his own writings. During his lifetime, in the second quarter of the 17th century, he became widely known throughout Poland as the greatest kabbalist in the country, and the tradition about his outstanding rank lived on for several generations after his death. Considered one of the principal proponents of Lurianic Kabbalah in Poland, he corresponded with many kabbalists of his day. While serving as preacher and *Maggid* in Polonnoye (Volhynia), he died a martyr's death at the head of the Jewish community (July 22, 1648) during the *Chmielnicki massacres. None of his writings was published during his lifetime and it is not until the following generation that scattered quotations in his name are found in various kabbalistic books. In 1653 Ẓevi Horowitz (or Hurwitz) ha-Levi copied in Grodno a collection of Ostropoler's kabbalistic notes (preserved in Ms. Oxford Neubauer Cat. Bod. no. 1793). His grandson incorporated this collection into his commentary on the Zohar, *Aspaklarya Me'irah* (Fuerth, 1776), dispersing it throughout many passages; only some portions were omitted. Moses Meinsters from Vienna published (Amsterdam, 1687) a small pamphlet containing *Ketavim* by Ostropoler. In 1709 the latter's nephew published in Zolkiew the book *Karnayim* with Ostropoler's commentary, *Dan Yadin*, and another batch of collectanea (*likkutim*) from his papers which also contained some of his letters on kabbalistic matters. *Karnayim*, attributed by Ostropoler to an unknown Aaron from the unknown city of Kardina, consists mainly of extremely obscure hints which are so cleverly expounded in the commentary that during the 18th century it was suggested that the book and the commentary were written by the same man. An analysis of all Ostropoler's remaining writings makes this virtually certain.

Ostropoler lived in a world of numerological mysticism and was deeply concerned with demonology, on which his writings abound in the most extraordinary statements. In the main his frequent references to Lurianic writings have no basis in Ḥayyim *Vital's texts and are only loosely connected with Israel *Sarug's brand of Lurianism. Many other quotations are equally fictitious, imitating Moses *Botarel's methods in his commentary on *Sefer Yeẓirah*. Ostropoler was apparently closely connected with two of his kabbalistic contemporaries, Nathan Shapira in Cracow and Aryeh Loew Prilik, who had similar interests but did not employ pseudepigraphy. Whereas the Lurianic writings speak of the power of evil, the *kelippot*, at great length but in a general, impersonal manner, Ostropoler liked to give each and every one special and previously unknown names, many of them obviously constructed on numerological principles. There is no doubt that he presents a psychological enigma. Anti-Christian and elaborate messianic hints appear in his writings. His main work, which is often referred to, was a commentary to the Zohar, *Maḥaneh Dan*, but no trace of this has been found. The unique character of Ostropoler's writings led to their being widely quoted in later kabbalistic literature, and they were reprinted several times. Two other commentaries on *Karnayim* were published, one by Eliezer Fischel from Stryzow (Zhitomir, 1805) denouncing those who suspected Ostropoler of being the author, and one by Samuel Samama of Tunis (Leghorn, 1825).

BIBLIOGRAPHY: Nathan Hanover, *Yeven Meẓulah* (Venice, 1653), 7a; N. Bruell, in: *Oẓar ha-Sifrut*, 4 (1888), 468–72; G. Scholem, in: *Revue de l'Histoire des Religions*, 143 (1953), 37–39.

[Gershom Scholem]

OSTROWER, FAYGA (1920–2001), Brazilian graphic artist, born in Lodz, Poland. Ostrower lived in Germany from 1921 until 1934 when she immigrated to Brazil. After 1944 she specialized in the graphic arts, producing book illustrations, fabric designs, and carefully composed, delicately colored prints.

OSTROWIEC (also **Ostrowiec Swietokrzyski**), town in Kielce province, Poland. In 1755, the rabbi of Ostrowiec, Ezekiel b. Avigdor, took part in an assembly of the *Council of the Four Lands. Previously Eliezer b. Solomon Zalman Lipschuetz, author of responsa *Heshiv R. Eliezer ve-Si'aḥ ha-Sadeh* (Neuwied, 1749), had served as rabbi there. The community increased from 1,064 in 1827 to 2,736 in 1856 (80% of the total population) and 6,146 in 1897 (62.8%). In 1921 it numbered 10,095 (51%). Most of the Jews in Ostrowiec lived in conditions of extreme poverty. A pogrom was instigated there by factory workers in 1904. The Jewish loan fund in Ostrowiec had a membership of 474 in 1924, of whom 344 were storekeepers, tradesmen or peddlers, 97 artisans, and 33 in miscellaneous professions.

[Nathan Michael Gelber]

Holocaust Period

At the outbreak of World War II there were about 8,000 Jews in Ostrowiec. The first *Aktion* took place on Oct. 11–12, 1942, when 11,000 Jews from Ostrowiec and the vicinity were deported to the *Treblinka death camp. In October 1942 a forced-labor camp for Jews was established in Ostrowiec. On Jan. 16, 1943, 1,000 Jews were deported to the *Sandomierz forced-labor camp. The Jewish community was liquidated on June 10, 1943, when the remaining 2,000 Jews were transferred to Ostrowiec forced-labor camp, which was itself liquidated on Aug. 3, 1944, when the inmates were deported to *Auschwitz. An underground organization, headed by the brothers Kopel and Moshe Stein, and David Kempinski, was active in Ostrowiec. They established contact with the leaders of the Jewish Fighting Organization in *Warsaw. A few groups of prisoners escaped and started guerrilla activities in the vicinity. Those who fled in July 1944 conducted guerrilla activities until the liberation of the region in July 1945. After the war the Jewish community of Ostrowiec was not reconstituted.

BIBLIOGRAPHY: S. Krakowski, in: BŻIH, no. 65–66 (1968), 66–68; Yad Vashem Archives; BJCE; PK.

OSTROW MAZOWIECKA (Pol. **Ostrów Mazowiecka**; Russ. **Ostrov Lomzinsky**), town in the province of Warszawa, N.E. Central Poland. The intolerant attitude of the authorities of Masovia prevented the settlement of Jews for several centuries, and it was only during the 18th century that Jews succeeded in establishing themselves there permanently. In 1765 there were 68 Jews (20 families) paying the poll tax and owning 15 houses in the town, and another 45 Jews in six surrounding villages. Seven heads of families earned their livelihood from crafts; the remainder engaged in retail trade or held leases. In 1789 a Polish tribunal issued a restriction against Jewish settlement in the town, which remained in force until 1862. Jews who succeeded in settling in Ostrow Mazowiecka came mostly from central Poland and Lithuania, developing a special Yiddish dialect which combined the Yiddish language features of both areas. In spite of prohibitions there were 382 Jews living in Ostrow Mazowiecka in 1808 (34% of the total population). In 1827 they numbered 809 (39%). Jews engaged essentially in retail trade, peddling, haulage, and tailoring. In 1857 the community numbered 2,412 (61% of the population). A few wealthy families traded in wood and grain, and worked flour and saw mills. From 1850 the community supported a yeshivah. During the second half of the 19th century (somewhat later than in most other places) a dispute broke out between the Ḥasidim and the *Mitnaggedim in the community. Rabbis of the two factions officiated alternately, notably David Solomon Margolioth, Judah Leib *Gordon, and the *ẓaddik* Gershon Ḥanokh of Radzyn. The majority of the local Ḥasidim belonged to the Gur (*Gora Kalwaria) and *Warka dynasties. In 1897 the Jewish community numbered 5,910 (60% of the population). Although at the beginning of the 20th century religious and secular Jewish educational institutions were established, it was not until the end of World War I that the community's institutions were organized to their fullest extent. In 1921, 6,812 Jews (51% of the total) made up the community's population. In 1934 the Jews of Komorowo were incorporated into the community of Ostrow Mazowiecka, and the yeshivah Beit Yosef was transferred to the town in 1922.

[Arthur Cygielman]

Holocaust Period

In 1939 over 7,000 Jews lived in Ostrow Mazowiecka. The German army entered on Sept. 8, 1939, and two days later initiated a pogrom, killing 30 Jews. At the end of September 1939 the German army withdrew for a few days and the Soviet army reached the town's suburbs since, according to the Soviet-German agreement, Ostrow Mazowiecka became a frontier town on the German side. Almost all the Jews crossed over to the Soviet side. On Nov. 11, 1939, the Germans assembled the remaining 560 Jews, drove them to a forest outside the town, and murdered them. Most of the Jewish refugees from the town settled in Bialystok but many did not succeed in leaving when the Germans invaded the Soviet Union (June 1941), and they shared the tragic plight of the Jews in Bialystok. After the war the Jewish community in Ostrow Mazowiecka was not rebuilt. Organizations of former residents of Ostrow Mazowiecka are active in Israel, the U.S., and France.

[Stefan Krakowski]

BIBLIOGRAPHY: R. Mahler, *Yidn in Amolikn Poyln in Likht fun Tsifern* (1958), index; B. Wasiutyński, *Ludność żydowska w Polsce w wiekach XIX i XX* (1930), 36, 66, 72, 77, 79; I. Schiper (ed.), *Dzieje handlu żydowskiego na ziemiach polskich* (1937), index; *Sefer ha-Zikkaron li-Kehillat Ostrów Mazowieck* (Heb. and Yid., 1960); *Ostrow Mazowieck* (1966), a memorial book publ. in Heb.

OSTRYNA (in Jewish sources אוֹסְטְרִין), town in Grodno district, Belarus. Jews are first mentioned in Ostryna some time before 1569 as contractors of customs and taxes. In 1623 the Lithuanian Council (see *Councils of the Lands) placed Ostryna under the jurisdiction of the Grodno community. The number of Jewish poll tax payers in the town and surrounding communities was 436 in 1765. There were 405 Jews in Ostryna in 1847, 1,440 (59% of the total population) in 1897, and 1,067 (67.3%) in 1921. The Jews engaged mainly in trading, forestry, crafts, peddling, and agriculture; in the early 1920s there were 60 Jewish farmers in Ostryna. When the Germans evacuated Ostryna in 1919 the Jewish youth and military veterans established a Jewish police force to guard against peasant attacks. A Jewish self-defense group, which was organized in 1934, acted effectively against peasants who, incited by Polish students, were attempting to loot Jewish shops. A Jewish savings and loan fund was established in 1912 with 214 members; it was dissolved in World War I and later renewed as a cooperative bank which had 168 members in 1921.

A Hebrew school, in which the "direct method" (*Ivrit be-Ivrit*) was used to teach Hebrew, was established by the Zionist M. Gornilki. The first coeducational school was founded in 1913. In 1921 the CYSHO (Central Yiddish School Organization) established a Yiddish school which operated a club to promote cultural activities in the spirit of the *Bund. From the earliest days of the movement Zionists were active in Ostryna. In 1923 they opened a *Tarbut school. There was a Jewish public library in the town. In 1923 a branch of *He-Ḥalutz was organized and in 1928 of He-Ḥalutz ha-Ẓa'ir. An attempt was made to establish a training center (*hakhsharah*), based on forestry in the area. A training center of *Ha-Shomer ha-Ẓa'ir was established in 1927. Many ḥalutzim from Ostryna emigrated to Ereẓ Israel and some of them settled in kibbutzim. Among Ostryna's rabbis were Jacob Ẓevi Shapiro, author of *Tiferet Ya'akov* on the Mishnah; Jacob Tabszunsky, who during World War I gathered a group of students around him; and S. Gerszonowicz, the last rabbi, who was murdered along with his congregation by the Nazis. Harry Austryn *Wolfson was a native of Ostryna.

Holocaust Period

During World War II, when the Germans entered Ostryna on June 25, 1941, all the Jews were ordered to wear the yellow badge, and shortly after a Judenrat was established. The week after the invasion, the first Jews were killed. In October 1941 the Jews of Ostryna, together with those of Nowy-Dwor, numbering 1,200, were concentrated in two small ghettos. On Nov. 2, 1942, all the Jews from the Ostryna ghetto were deported to the Kelbasin forced-labor camp near Grodno, and at the end of the month were deported to *Auschwitz. A few young people succeeded in escaping from the trains going to Auschwitz and joined partisan units.

BIBLIOGRAPHY: S. Dubnow (ed.), *Pinkas... Medinat Lita* (1935), 17, 96; *Sefer Zikkaron li-Kehillot... Ostrin* (1966); *Unzer Hilf* (1921–23); *"Ort" – Barikht* (Berlin, 1923); **ADD. BIBLIOGRAPHY:** *Pinkas Kehillot Poland*, vol. 8 – North-East (2005).

[Dov Rabin]

OSVÁT, ERNÖ (1878–1929), literary critic and editor. From 1902, when he began editing *Magyar Géniusz*, Osvát devoted himself to widening the horizons of Hungary's literary press. He founded *Figyelő* in 1905 and three years later also joined the staff of *Nyugat*, where he promoted talented young writers, especially the poet Endre Ady. The tragic death of his only daughter led him to commit suicide.

OSWIECIM (Ger. **Auschwitz**), town in S. Poland and site of the notorious death camp. In the Middle Ages it was the capital of the duchy of that name, which in 1457 was purchased by Poland. Fairs, which attracted widespread interest, were held there in the 16th century. That Jews were living in Oswiecim as early as 1563 is attested by a charter of privileges granted by King Sigismund II Augustus which denied them residence rights near the marketplace or in the main streets and barred new Jewish settlers from the city. In 1564, when the Oswiecim regional council was undergoing reorganization, the Jews declared to the authorities concerned that the city had been inhabited by Jews since its foundation. In 1588 the community built a synagogue on grounds acquired from a burgher and established a cemetery. The transaction was confirmed by the royal chancellery. The Jews in Oswiecim suffered severely during the war between Sweden and Poland, 1656–58. Twenty houses are recorded in Jewish ownership in 1666, the number being equally small in the 18th century. According to a census of 1765 there were 133 Jewish residents. The community (*kahal*) of Oswiecim, whose jurisdiction extended over all the Jewish population in the area of the former duchy, had a membership of 862. In matters of Jewish communal administration it was subordinate to the *kahal* of Cracow. In 1773 Oswiecim came under Austrian rule. The tax levied on the community was so high that for a considerable time it was unable to meet its obligations. Two synagogues in Oswiecim, among other buildings, were destroyed by a fire in 1863. The last Austrian census in 1910 records 3,000 Jews residing in Oswiecim. The number had increased to 4,950 in 1921 (40.3% of the total population). The community was destroyed in World War II. For details of that period, see *Auschwitz.

BIBLIOGRAPHY: M. Berson, *Dyplomataryusz* (1910), 69; M. Balinski and T. Lipinski, *Starożytna Polska*, 2 (1843); S.A. Bershadski, *Russko-Yevreyskiy Arkhiv*, 3 (1903), 228–30; M. Balaban, *Dzieje żydów w Galicji* (1914), index.

[Mark Wischnitzer]

OTHNIEL (Heb. עָתְנִיאֵל), son of Kenaz, the first judge of Israel. He is first mentioned as a hero of the tribe of Judah during the period of the conquest of the land. As a reward for capturing Debir, he received in marriage Achsah, the daughter of *Caleb. At his wife's request Othniel also obtained from Caleb springs of water (Josh. 15:15–19; Judg. 1:11–15). As a motif, this narrative is reminiscent of the action of *Saul in promising his daughter to the one who would defeat Goliath (I Sam. 17:25). Historically, it presents a difficulty in that the capture of Debir is earlier attributed to Joshua himself (Josh. 10:38–39). The next reference to Othniel is as a divinely sent national hero who delivered Israel from the eight-year oppression of Cushan-Rishathaim, king of Aram-Naharaim, and so enabled the land to enjoy a respite from its enemies for a whole generation (Judg. 3:8–11). He was the only judge to come from a southern tribe. Othniel is described as being "the son of Kenaz, Caleb's [younger] brother" (Josh. 15:17; Judg. 1:13; 3:9). The ambiguity in the relationship is most likely to be resolved, on the basis of the genealogy of I Chronicles 4:11–15, in favor of his being Caleb's nephew. However, the problem of Othniel's identity is complicated by the fact that Kenaz is also the name of a clan. Caleb is a Kenizzite (Num. 32:12; Josh. 14:6, 14) and Kenaz is also the name of an Edomite tribe (Gen. 36:11, 15, 42; I Chron. 1:36, 53). Many scholars believe that Caleb and Othniel were respectively the eponymous ancestors of older and younger clans of the tribe of Kenaz that became absorbed within Judah. The importance of the clan of Othniel is indicated by the fact that one of David's divisional commanders in charge of the 12 monthly relays was "Heldai the Netophathite of Othniel" (I Chron. 27:15; cf. 11:30; II Sam. 23:28–29).

[Nahum M. Sarna]

In the Aggadah

Othniel is identified with Jabez (I Chron. 2:55), and was so called because he counseled (Heb. *ya'az*; יעץ) and fostered the study of Torah in Israel. He restored the knowledge of the Torah, particularly the Oral Law, which had been forgotten in the period of mourning for Moses (Tem. 16a). He assumed the leadership of the people of Israel while Joshua was still alive (Gen. R. 58:2) and judged Israel for 40 years (SOR 12). According to the Alphabet of Ben Sira (II, 29a and 36a), he was one of those who was vouchsafed to enter Paradise alive.

BIBLIOGRAPHY: E. Taeubler, in: HUCA, 20 (1947), 137–42; A. Malamat, in: JNES, 13 (1954), 231–42; Noth, Hist Isr, 56ff.; S. Yeivin, in: *Atiqot*, 3 (1961), 176–80; E. Danelius, in: JNES, 22 (1963), 191–3. For further bibl. see *Cushan Rishathaim. IN THE AGGADAH: Ginzberg, Legends, index; I. Ḥasida, *Ishei ha-Tanakh* (1964), 359–60.

OTRANTO, town in Apulia, S. Italy. Tombstone inscriptions dating from the third century onward are proof of the existence of an early Jewish settlement in Otranto. The *Josippon chronicle (10th century) states that Titus settled a number of Jewish prisoners from Ereẓ Israel in the town. In the Middle Ages Otranto became one of the most prosperous Jewish centers in southern Italy. At the time of the forced conversion under the Byzantine emperor Romanus I *Lecapenus, one communal leader committed suicide, one was strangled, and one died in prison. When Benjamin of *Tudela visited Otranto in about 1159, he found about 500 Jews there. It was considered one of the most important rabbinical centers in Europe. In the *Sefer ha-Yashar*, Jacob *Tam (12th century) quotes an old saying parodying Isaiah 2:3: "For out of Bari shall go forth the Law and the word of the Lord from Otranto." When the Turks besieged Otranto in 1481, the Jews contributed 3,000 ducats for the defense of the town. In 1510, with their expulsion from the kingdom of *Naples, the Jews had to leave Otranto. A number of them settled in Salonika, where they founded their own synagogue.

BIBLIOGRAPHY: Roth, Dark Ages, index; Frey, Corpus, 1 (1936), no. 632; Milano, Bibliotheca, index; Milano, Italia, index; N. Ferorelli, *Ebrei nell' Italia meridionale…* (1915); Cassuto, in: *Giornale della società asiatica italiana*, 29 (1921), 97ff.

[Ariel Toaff]

OTTA, FRANCISCO (1908–1999), Chilean artist. Born in Czechoslovakia, Otta emigrated to Chile in 1939. After a youthful period of realistic portraits in which he searched for common features in ethnological communities such as Peruvian Indians, Sicilian peasants, or Ukrainian Jews, he became an expressionist. Later he moved to semi-abstract paintings and finally to a new figuratism with some pop elements.

OTTAWA, city in the province of Ontario and capital of Canada, situated at the junction of the Ottawa and Rideau rivers. Settled in the early 1800s, Ottawa was originally called Bytown (1826) after Colonel John By, who supervised the building of the Rideau Canal. In 1855 it was incorporated as the city of Ottawa, and in 1857 Queen Victoria chose Ottawa as the capital of Canada. The current city of Ottawa, population 774,072 (2001 census), was created in 2001 out of the amalgamation of Ottawa with 11 surrounding local municipalities.

The development of a Jewish community in Ottawa began in the latter half of the 19th century. According to census records, there were no Jews in Bytown in 1851. Moses Bilsky first went to Ottawa in 1857 or 1858, though he did not permanently settle there until some years later. In 1861 the census showed six Jews residing in Ottawa; for 1871 none is shown and in 1881 there were 20 Jews, more than half of whom were members of the families of John Dover, a dry goods merchant, and Aaron Rosenthal, a jeweler and silversmith. By 1891 the number of Jews had more than doubled to 46. There has been growth in Ottawa's Jewish population in every decade since. In 1901 there were almost 400 Jews in Ottawa. The number increased more than tenfold to approximately 5,000 at the end of World War II. In 2001 Ottawa had almost 13,500 Jews, making it home to the fifth largest Jewish population in Canada. Between 1881 and 1921 Jews arriving from the pogroms and restrictions in Russia and Eastern Europe contributed to the rapid rise in the size of Ottawa's Jewish community. A second period of rapid growth occurred between the 1960s and 1980s when the rise of French-Canadian nationalism in Quebec and election of the separatist Parti Québécois government led many Jews to leave Montreal for Toronto, Ottawa, and other Canadian cities.

Organized congregational life in Ottawa began in 1892 when Moses Bilsky and John Dover helped found Adath Jeshurun. In 1895, the congregation's first synagogue was completed and within a decade it moved to a new building. Adath Jeshurun's first religious functionary was the Rev. Jacob Mirsky and local businessman A.J. *Freiman served as the congregation's president from 1904 to 1930. In 1902 a second Ottawa congregation, Agudath Achim, was founded. Its services were held in a congregant's house until a synagogue was erected in 1912. The Machzikei Hadas congregation was founded in 1906 by newly arrived immigrants who desired their own Orthodox synagogue. The congregation has changed location several times, and its rabbi at the outset of the 21st century, Reuven Bulka, has served as spiritual leader since 1967.

B'nai Jacob synagogue was founded in 1911 for Jews living in Ottawa's west end. Services were first held in a public hall or in a private home, but in 1914 the congregation bought a house which they turned into a synagogue. In 1936 the Agudath Israel Congregation, also in the city's expanding west end, was organized and two years later converted a former Anglican church into its synagogue. In 1948, Agudath Israel bought a new property on which it built a synagogue. Agudath Israel affiliated with the Conservative movement in 1951. Its current home was dedicated in 1960, and a new 400-seat sanctuary added in 1966. In 2005 Agudath Israel was the largest congregation in Ottawa, with a membership of approximately 850 families. In 1956 Ottawa's first two congregations, Adath Jeshurun and Agudath Achim, both Orthodox and both located near one another, merged to form Beth Shalom. Faced with declining membership, the B'nai Jacob amalgamated into Beth Shalom in 1971.

Since the 1960s, Ottawa's Jewish religious life has demonstrated both growth and increasing pluralism of expression. In 1966, the Young Israel Congregation was founded to serve the needs of Orthodox worshipers living in Ottawa's west end. A new sanctuary was dedicated in 1980. In 1966 Ottawa's Reform congregation, Temple Israel, was organized and, after first holding services in a public school, acquired its own home in 1971. After a destructive fire less than a year later, a new synagogue was built and dedicated in 1975. Adath Shalom, an egalitarian Conservative havurah, was established in 1978 and Beth Shalom West, a modern Orthodox congregation, was created as a west end satellite of Beth Shalom. Its new synagogue was completed in suburban Nepean in 1985.

The Ottawa Reconstructionist Havurah and the Sephardi Association both organized in 1987, and the Ottawa Torah Center Chabad was established in Barrhaven in 1997. Ottawa's newest congregation, the Orthodox Community Ohev Yisroel, held its first service in 2004 near the University of Ottawa.

The Ottawa Jewish community's first cemetery was established in 1893 but by the early 1970s a new cemetery was needed. In 1976 the New Jewish Community Cemetery of Ottawa was consecrated. Originally each synagogue had its own burial society, but in 1918 all the burial societies amalgamated to form the Ottawa Chevra Kadisha. In 1953 the Chevra Kadisha purchased a vacant synagogue building and in 1957 dedicated the building as the Jewish Community Memorial Chapel. In 1997 it relocated to newer facilities.

In 1934 the city's Orthodox synagogues formed a *kehillah*, a unified Jewish community organization called the Jewish Community Council of Ottawa / Vaad Ha'Ir. A.J. Freiman served as its president until his death on June 4, 1944. The day-to-day operations of the Vaad Ha'Ir were directed by Hy Hochberg from 1946 until his death in 1985. The Jewish Community Council continues to serve as the central planning, coordinating, community relations, and fundraising body for the Ottawa community.

Jewish education is served by several day and afternoon schools. Hillel Academy, established in 1949, is the largest of three community Hebrew day schools, offering study from junior kindergarten to grade eight. Cheder Rambam School and the Torah Academy offer a more Orthodox early childhood education. Jewish schools offering afternoon programs include the Ottawa Talmud Torah, Star of David, Temple Israel, and Ottawa Modern Jewish School. The Ottawa Torah Institute is the community yeshivah high school for boys. Founded in 1982, it was Ottawa's first full-time Jewish high school. A sister institution, Machon Sarah High School for Girls, was founded in 1990 and shares the Ottawa Torah Institute's teaching staff, albeit at a different campus. Two other Jewish high schools are Yitzhak Rabin, a day school, and Akiva Evening High School. The Kollel of Ottawa, located adjacent to the Soloway Jewish Community Centre, is a center for advanced study of Torah, talmudic law, and Judaic studies by committed adult learners.

Ottawa has contributed a number of national Jewish community leaders including A.J. Freiman, national president of the Zionist Organization of Canada from 1920 to his death in 1944; his wife, Lillian Freiman, a leader of Canadian Hadassah; their son Lawrence Freiman, president of the Zionist Organization of Canada for several terms, and Hyman Bessin, head of the Canadian Mizrachi movement and from 1970 president of the Federated Zionist Organization of Canada. Ottawa Jews have also played an active role in Ottawa municipal affairs. In 1902 Samuel Rosenthal was the first of several Jewish aldermen in Ottawa and in 1975 Lorry Greenberg was the first Jew elected mayor of Ottawa, a position he held until he retired in 1978. Jews have also served on the Ottawa Board of Control and on the Ottawa Public School Board and a Jew was elected mayor of South Hull, a Quebec municipality across the Ottawa River from Ottawa.

Ottawa's Jewish community supports a wide array of programs and services. The *Ottawa Jewish Bulletin*, founded in 1938, is the community's official newspaper. The Jewish Community Centre was established in 1951. By 1960 the JCC complex included Beth Shalom Synagogue, the Talmud Torah, and a gymnasium. Founded in 1953, the Ottawa Home for the Aged opened its Hillel Lodge in 1965. With the growth and westward shift of the Jewish community, a new Jewish community campus was developed in the city's west end. In 1983 a 7.8 acre site and high school building was purchased and is today home to the Hillel Academy, Talmud Torah Afternoon School, Ottawa Modern Jewish School, and Akiva Evening High School. In 1998, the Jewish Community Centre moved to more modern facilities and now houses a library, archives, athletic facilities, social halls and meeting rooms, a mikveh, kosher restaurant, and offices of many Jewish communal organizations, including those of the Vaad Ha'Ir. Hillel Lodge also relocated in 2000 to a new long-term care facility built across from the JCC, and the Tamir Foundation operates a nearby home for Jewish adults with developmental disabilities.

As Canada's capital, Ottawa is home to the Parliament Buildings, Supreme Court, Royal Mint, Bank of Canada, National Research Council, National Gallery, Canadian Museum of Civilization, War Museum, National Arts Centre, and many other administrative and cultural institutions. One of these, the Library and Archives of Canada, houses numerous publications, documents, and archival collections of significance to the study of Canadian Jewry, as well as the Jacob M. Lowy Collection of rare incunabula, Hebraica, and Judaica. Ottawa's Jewish community continues to grow, spurred on by Ottawa's economic development as an important center of high-tech industry and the administrative seat of the federal government.

BIBLIOGRAPHY: M.H. Arnoni, in: V. Grossman, *Canadian Jewish Year Book*, vol. 2 (1940–1941): 115–20; S. Berman in: *Pathways to the Present: Canadian Jewry and Canadian Jewish Congress* (1986), 50–56; M. Bookman, in: E. Gottesman (ed.), *Canadian Jewish Reference Book and Directory, 1963* (1963), 387–405; H.S. Roodman, *The Ottawa Jewish Community: Looking Back, an Historical Chronicle of Our Community for the Years 1857–1987, 5617–5747* (1989).

[Gerald Stone (2nd ed.)]

OTTENSOSSER, DAVID (1784–1858), Hebrew scholar. Born in Germany, he was a teacher at Fuerth yeshivah. Ottensosser devoted himself mainly to the study of Maimonides, upon whose works he drew in his Bible commentaries. His editions of Maimonides' works are among the best of his volumes of ancient texts, and he published Maimonides' letters with a German translation (*Iggerot ha-Moreh*, 1846) and an anthology of his teachings (*Imrei Da'at Rambam*, 1848). His explication and translation into German of Isaiah (1807) was his first effort in this field. He published a corrected edition of Mendelssohn's Bible, in which he improved upon the Pentateuch translation. He also edited Abraham Bedersi's *Olelot ha-Boḥen*, Jedaiah Bedersi's *Beḥinot Olam*, and the travelogue of Pethahiah of Regensburg, *Sibbuv ha-Olam* (with a German translation, 1854), as well as a German version (with Hebrew commentary) of the liturgy (1811).

BIBLIOGRAPHY: Zeitlin, Bibliotheca, 258–60; Kressel, Leksikon, 1 (1965), 36.

[Getzel Kressel]

OTTINGER, ALBERT (1878–1938), U.S. lawyer, politician, and communal leader. Ottinger, who was born in New York City, was admitted to the bar in 1900. Active in Republican politics, he became Republican leader of Manhattan's 15th Assembly District (1912), was elected to the New York State Senate (1916), and was appointed assistant U.S. attorney general by President Harding (1921). Twice elected New York State attorney general (1924, 1926), Ottinger vigorously prosecuted food profiteers, loan sharks, and stock swindlers, and earned the Republican nomination for governor in 1928. He lost that election to Franklin Delano Roosevelt by 25,000 votes. A staunch opponent of Tammany Hall, he urged the probe into the Tammany activities that became known as the Seabury investigation. Active in Jewish affairs, Ottinger was chairman of New York City's Joint Distribution Committee drive (1931) and was associated with the Hebrew Orphan Asylum and the Young Men's Hebrew Association.

°OTTO, RUDOLPH (1869–1937), German Protestant theologian and historian of religion. Otto's major contribution to the study of comparative religion was his emphasis on, and analysis of, the notion of the "holy" as the specific and characteristic feature of religious experience. The "holy" is not identical with the true, the beautiful, or the moral. It is "awesome" in its grandeur and mysterious majesty. It is "wholly other" and causes ambivalent reactions, inspiring love as well as fear and producing confidence and joy as well as trembling. To express the range of meaning of the idea of the holy, Otto coined the term "numinous" (from Lat. *Numen*, "divine power"). While Otto's analysis may not apply to all religions, it well describes the religious consciousness of biblical religion and the religions influenced by it. The various aspects of the numinous as described by Otto correspond to the complementary categories of "love of God" and "fear of God" in Jewish thought, and more especially to the feelings evoked and emphasized by the liturgy of Rosh Hashanah and the Day of Atonement (the "Days of Awe"). In fact, Otto illustrated his argument by quoting not only from the Bible but also from the *piyyutim* in the prayer book for the High Holidays. Among Otto's important works are *West-oestliche Mystik* (1926; *Mysticism, East and West*, 1932) and *Reich Gottes und Menschensohn* (1934; *The Kingdom of God and the Son of Man*, 1938), but his best-known work is *Das Heilige* (1917; *The Idea of the Holy*, 1923).

ADD. BIBLIOGRAPHY: M.J.H.M. Poorthuis, in: *Purity and Holiness* (2000), 107–27; J.A. Levisohn, in: *Journal of Jewish Education*, 70:1–2 (2004), 4–21.

[R.J. Zwi Werblowsky]

OTTOLENGHI (Ottolengo), Italian family of Piedmont, apparently originating in Germany, the name being an Italian form of Ettlingen. Its prominent members include: Joseph b. Nathan *Ottolenghi (d. 1570), rabbi of Cremona; SAMUEL DAVID B. JEHIEL *OTTOLENGO (d. 1718), scholar and kabbalist, born in Casale Monferrato. ABRAHAM AZARIAH (BONAIUTO) OTTOLENGHI (1776–1851), rabbinical scholar born in *Acqui. When the French revolutionary army entered Acqui in 1796, he gave a public address on the significance of the tree of liberty erected in Acqui, as everywhere else, as a symbol of the new era. With the defeat of the French following the battle of Novi in 1799, Abraham had to flee to Genoa. After the return of the French in 1800, he returned to Acqui, and was appointed rabbi of the community, which position he held until his death. He wrote *Shir li-Khevod ha-Torah* (Leghorn, 1808). NATHAN (DONATO) OTTOLENGHI (1820–1883), the last outstanding member of the once-famous community of Acqui. On friendly terms with noted political figures of the period, including Massimo *d'Azeglio, Vincenzo Gioberti, and Cesare Balbo, he did much to better the position of both Jews and non-Jews and to improve the condition of the poor. ELEAZAR (LAZZARO) OTTOLENGHI (1820–1890), rabbi, born in Acqui. He held rabbinical office in Turin, Moncalvo, and Acqui, settling in Rome a year before his death. Author of a number of *piyyutim*, he also wrote a comedy, *Matrimonio misto* (1870), and *Dialoghi religiosomorali* (1873). In his youth, he also wrote several tragedies, one of which, *Etelwige*, was presented in Acqui in 1852. EMILIO OTTOLENGHI (1830–1908), philanthropist, born in Acqui. In 1848 he moved to Alessandria and was elected member of the municipal council in 1882. He served as president of the community for a long period and was made a count by King Humbert I in 1883. GIUSEPPE *OTTOLENGHI (1838–1904), was an Italian general, minister of war in 1902–03, veteran of the Italian War of Liberation. MOSES JACOB *OTTOLENGHI (1840–1901) was a writer and educator. JOSHUA (SALVATORE) OTTOLENGHI (1861–1934), physician. He studied in Turin, was assistant of Cesare *Lombroso, and taught at Rome University. A pioneer in modern criminology, Ottolenghi founded (1902) the Scuola di Polizia Scientifica in Rome, the first of the kind in Italy. DONATO OTTOLENGHI (1874–?1940) was professor of general pathology and hygiene at the universities of Pisa, Cagliari, and Bologna. ADOLFO OTTOLENGHI (?1880–1943) served as rabbi in Venice from 1919 to 1943. During the Holocaust he was arrested by the Nazis and deported to Germany, where he perished. He was remembered in his community for his sincerity and his devotion to their needs. He wrote several historical essays, including *Leon da Modena e spunti di vita ebraica del ghetto nel sec. XVII* (1929) and *Abraham Lattes nei suoi rapporti colla republica di Daniele Manin* (1930). RAFFAELE OTTOLENGHI (?1887–1917), lawyer and publicist, devoted to the Jewish cause and to Zionism. He wrote *Voci d'Oriente* (2 vols.), a study of Oriental influences in literature and of Hebrew proselytism. MARIO OTTOLENGHI (1904–1978), economist and secretary of the Italian Zionist Federation (1933–39), settled in Israel in 1938. His son MICHAEL (1934–) was professor of physical chemistry at the Hebrew University of Jerusalem.

BIBLIOGRAPHY: Mortara, Indice, 46; E. Foa, in: *Il Vessillo Israelitico*, 31 (1883), 327–9, 343ff.; F. Servi, *ibid.*, 38 (1890), 137–9; Ghirondi-Neppi, 330, 332; Roth, Italy, index; Milano, Italia, index.

OTTOLENGHI, GIUSEPPE (1838–1904), Italian general and minister of war. Born in Sabbioneta, Lombardy, Ottolenghi studied at the Turin military academy and fought with the Italian army in the war against Austria in 1859. In the following year he was transferred to the general staff, the first Jew to serve in that capacity in Italy. Ottolenghi was promoted to captain in 1863 and lectured on military tactics at the Modena military academy. During the Franco-Prussian War of 1870–71 he was Italian military attache in France and in 1878 was a member of the international commission to fix the boundary between Turkey and Montenegro. In 1902 he became commander of the 4th army corps with the rank of lieutenant general. In the same year he was made minister of war (the first Jew in Europe to hold this position) and a member of the senate. Ottolenghi was the recipient of many honors, including the silver medal for military valor and the Cross of Savoy. He remained a loyal Jew all his life.

ADD. BIBLIOGRAPHY: A. Rovighi, *I Militari di Origine Ebraica nel Primo Secolo di Vita dello Stato Italiano*, Roma (1999), 85–86.

[Mordechai Kaplan]

OTTOLENGHI, JOSEPH BEN NATHAN (d. 1570), rabbi of *Cremona, Italy. As head of the yeshivah, he made Cremona famous as a center of talmudic learning. Between 1558 and 1562 Ottolenghi published about 20 Hebrew works at the celebrated Riva di Trento press. He wrote novellae on the code of Isaac *Alfasi and compiled an index to the *Mordekhai* (the code of *Mordecai b. Hillel). Some of his contemporaries (among them the historian *Joseph ha-Kohen) considered that the burning of the Talmud and Hebrew legal works in Cremona in 1559, when over 10,000 volumes were destroyed, was the consequence of a dispute between Ottolenghi and a certain Joshua de Cantori, aggravated by the interference of the apostate Vittorio Eliano.

BIBLIOGRAPHY: Roth, Italy, 221, 303; Milano, Italia, 265, 620; J. Bloch, *Hebrew Printing in Riva di Trento* (1933), 3; I. Sonne, *Expurgation of Hebrew Books – the Work of Jewish Scholars* (1943), 21–38.

[Giorgio Romano]

OTTOLENGHI, MOSES JACOB (1840–1901), Italian Hebrew writer and educator and pupil of Elijah *Benamozegh. He was born in Leghorn and died in Salonika. His works include *Degel ha-Torah* (an entertainment in seven acts, to be played on commencement day in houses of learning for the sons of Israel) printed in Hebrew and Ladino (Salonika, 1885), and *Ẓemaḥ David*, a collection of poems (1887). He also translated into Hebrew an Italian Jewish religious catechism, *Mishpat le-Ya'akov* (1892–95).

[Getzel Kressel]

OTTOLENGO, SAMUEL DAVID BEN JEHIEL (d. 1718), Italian rabbi, kabbalist, and poet. Samuel was born in Casale Monferrato and studied under Moses *Zacuto and Benjamin Cohen. He served as chief rabbi of Padua and later of Venice.

His published works are *Kiryati Ne'emanah* (Venice, 1715?), a digest of *Ma'avar Yabbok* of Aaron Berechiah of Modena; and *Me'il Shemu'el* (*ibid.*, 1705), an abridgement and index to the *Shenei Luḥot ha-Berit* of Isaiah *Horowitz. He also wrote a supplement to the *Tikkun Shovavim* (the initial letters of the first six weekly portions of the Book of Exodus) of Moses Zacuto that was published (*ibid.*, 1708) with the text. He founded a "Malbish Arumim" Society to assist the needy during those six weeks. Responsa, novellae, *piyyutim*, and kabbalistic articles by Ottolengo have remained in manuscript.

BIBLIOGRAPHY: Ghirondi-Neppi, 330–2, 335; Steinschneider, Cat Bod, 2473, no. 7065.

OTTOMAN EMPIRE, Balkan and Middle Eastern empire started by a Turkish tribe, led by ʿUthmān (1288–1326), at the beginning of the 14th century. This entry is arranged according to the following outline:

The Ottoman Empire spread through Asia Minor, and until 1922 the realm built by ʿUthmān and his descendants was called by his name: the Ottoman-Turkish Empire. The Ottoman Turks continued to extend the areas of their conquests, and in this way the Jewish communities in the region came under their rule (for the earlier period, see *Byzantine Empire).The rule of the Ottoman Empire in North Africa was very loose. Therefore the history of the Ottoman Empire as presented in this entry relates chiefly to Turkey, Greece, the Balkans, Egypt, Syria, and Iraq (see also the individual countries).

SOURCES

Our knowledge of Ottoman Empire Jewry is based on a wide range of sources, Ottoman, Arabic, European, and Jewish. The Ottoman documents include those of the Ottoman archives, especially the Prime Minister's Archives in Istanbul, which shed light on forms of taxation and on demographic and economic matters, as well as containing collections of orders issued by the Sublime Porte to the various provincial governors. Other Ottoman sources on Jews include travel literature, such as concern the Turkish traveler Evliya Çelebi, and some Ottoman chronicles. Other Ottoman historical material relating to the Jews exists in the Muslim courts of law in many cities throughout the empire. The majority of the Arabic historical sources on the Ottoman period are chronicles written in the Arab provinces of the empire. The European material includes diplomatic reports submitted to their governments by foreign ambassadors and consuls, archives of trade companies such as the Levant Company, and letters of merchants and European Itinerary literature. The Jewish sources contain some significant chronicles, letters written by Jews, marriage contracts, records of Jewish courts of law, and especially the vast halakhic literature including hundreds of books. The main considerable historical material is included in the responsa literature. In the last century, the publication of a large part of these sources, and especially new research since the 1950s and its conclusions, has enabled one to portray the history, demography, and social and economic life of the Jewish communities in the Ottoman Empire from the 15th to the 20th centuries.

GROWTH OF THE OTTOMAN EMPIRE UNTIL THE CONQUEST OF CONSTANTINOPLE (1453)

The first Jewish community to come under Ottoman protection was that of *Bursa (Brusa), captured in 1326 by Orhan (1326–1359), the son of ʿUthmān. In accordance with the pact made between the inhabitants of the town and the victors, the Greek inhabitants were removed; the Jews returned to the town by themselves and settled in a special district, *Yahudi mahallesi* (Jewish quarter). The conquest was a blessing for the Jews after the experience of servitude under Byzantium, which had decreed harsh laws upon them. The Jews were permitted by the sultan, who issued a firman (royal order), to build a synagogue (Eẓ Ḥayyim). They were also allowed to engage in business in the country without hindrance and to purchase houses and land in the towns and villages. On the other hand, they were obliged to pay the government the poll tax, called here **kharāj* (or **jizya*). At a later period this tax was imposed by district, and the community leaders of every district apportioned it in accordance with the members of each. The Jews of Bursa were all old inhabitants of the country and were called *Romaniots (or Gregos); during the 15th century they were joined by Jews from *France and *Germany, as well as refugees from *Spain and *Portugal. The son of the sultan Orhan, the vizier Suleiman Pasha, proceeded to Europe, capturing *Gallipoli, which from early times had a small Jewish community. With the beginning of Ottoman rule the community grew, however, through the addition of local Jews. Angora (*Ankara) and *Adrianople (Edirne) were captured by the sultan Murad I (1360–89). In Angora there was a Jewish community from early times. Adrianople, which the sultan turned into his capital in 1365 – instead of Bursa – became the largest town in the empire and contained the largest Jewish community in the Balkan Peninsula. Jews from Germany, Italy, and France lived there, as well as *Karaites. The Ottomans continued their conquests taking Philippopolis (*Plovdiv), *Sofia, and other towns. Nicopolis (*Nikopol) and Vidin were captured by the sultan Beyazid I (1389–1403). These towns contained various Jewish communities. Besides the Romanian and Bulgarian Jews, who were early inhabitants, there were also recent settlers from Hungary who had been driven out in 1376 by order of the Hungarian king Ludwig I and admitted to Walachia near Nicopolis. They continued from there, settling in Nicopolis itself and in Vidin. Beyazid conquered all *Bulgaria and fought the *Mongols near Angora. The town of *Izmir (Smyrna) was captured by Sultan Mehmed I (1413–21). Before this conquest not many Jews lived there. The community of Izmir flourished from the 17th century on.

*Salonika was captured by the Ottomans in 1387, but in 1403 the city returned to the hands of the Venetians, and was recaptured by Sultan Murad II (1421–51) in 1430. Salonika had an ancient Romaniot community which was transferred to Istanbul after 1453. *Ioannina was captured two years later, together with other places in *Albania where Jews lived. The Jews were well treated. Many were enrolled in the troop of foreigners called *gharība* (aliens) which was then established. Murad II was the first Ottoman ruler to introduce special clothes for Jews (*ghiyār*; see Covenant of *Omar). They were compelled to wear long garments like other non-Muslims (Greeks and Armenians); their headgear was yellow to distinguish them from other non-Muslims, while the Turks wore green headwear and were called "green ones" by the Jews. A large part of the Peloponnesus was captured by Murad; Jews had lived there from the earliest times (see *Greece). Murad's attitude toward them was expressed by his appointment of a Jew as personal physician.

THE OTTOMAN EMPIRE AFTER THE CONQUEST OF CONSTANTINOPLE: THE MIGRATION OF THE REFUGEES

*Constantinople was captured in 1453 by Mehmed II, the Conqueror (1451–81), who changed the name of his new capital to *Istanbul. Immediately after the conquest, in which many Jews, who did not flee in time, were killed, Mehmed II adopted the transfer policy. In order to renovate the town, populate it, and convert it rapidly into a flourishing and prosperous capital, he adopted a policy of transferring Muslim, Christian, and Jewish inhabitants, most of them merchants and craftsmen, from various regions of the empire – principally from Anatolia and the Balkans – to the new capital. All the transferred Jews were Romaniot and were called by the Ottoman authorities "*sürgün*" from the Turkish word for "those who were exiled," to distinguish them from other Jews, principally from Spain, Portugal, Ashkenaz (Germany), and other European lands who were named "*kendi gelen*," meaning "those who came of their own free will." The sürgüns also included survivors and escapees, Jews from the city who resettled in the city as sürgün. All the Jewish population of Asia Minor and many communities in Greece, Macedonia, and Bulgaria, and also a large group of Karaites from Adrianople were deported to Istanbul over a period of 20 years and established synagogues called congregations (*kehalim*). All these congregations bore the name of their original communities. The chronicler Elijah Capsali described the new Jewish settlement in Istanbul in his book *Seder Eliyahu Zuta:* "There came into being in Constantinople splendid communities; Torah, wealth, and glory increased in the congregations". The sürgün congregations paid taxes separately from the kendi gelen, and had a special status forbidding their members to leave Istanbul without a permit from the Ottoman authorities. All the Jews of Salonika were transferred as sürgün to Istanbul, so that the Ashkenazim who settled in the city in the second half of the 15th century found no Jewish community there. After a short time the Spanish expellees joined them. The Ottoman censuses and documents and many Jewish sources enable us to evaluate the demographic, social, and economic strength of every ethnic group in the Jewish communities during the Ottoman period. Mehmed II needed Jews to develop business and crafts, and also imposed taxes upon the Jews: *kharāj*, those paying it being registered in the sultan's ledger; *rab akçesi* (rabbi tax), which permitted them to appoint rabbis; and *ʿavāriḍ*, household tax. The following sultans imposed many other taxes on the Jew-

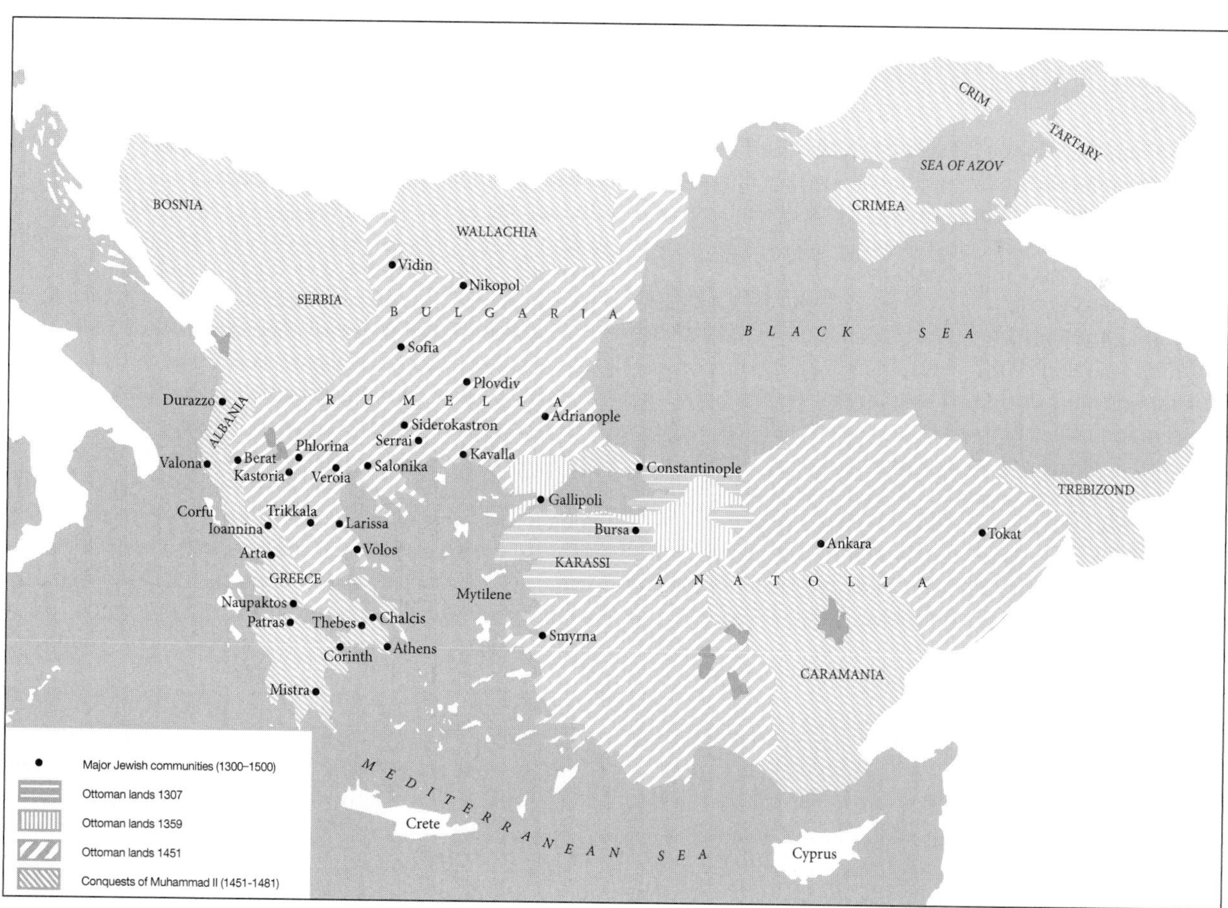

Map 1. Growth of the Ottoman Empire from the beginning of the 14th century until the end of the 15th century.

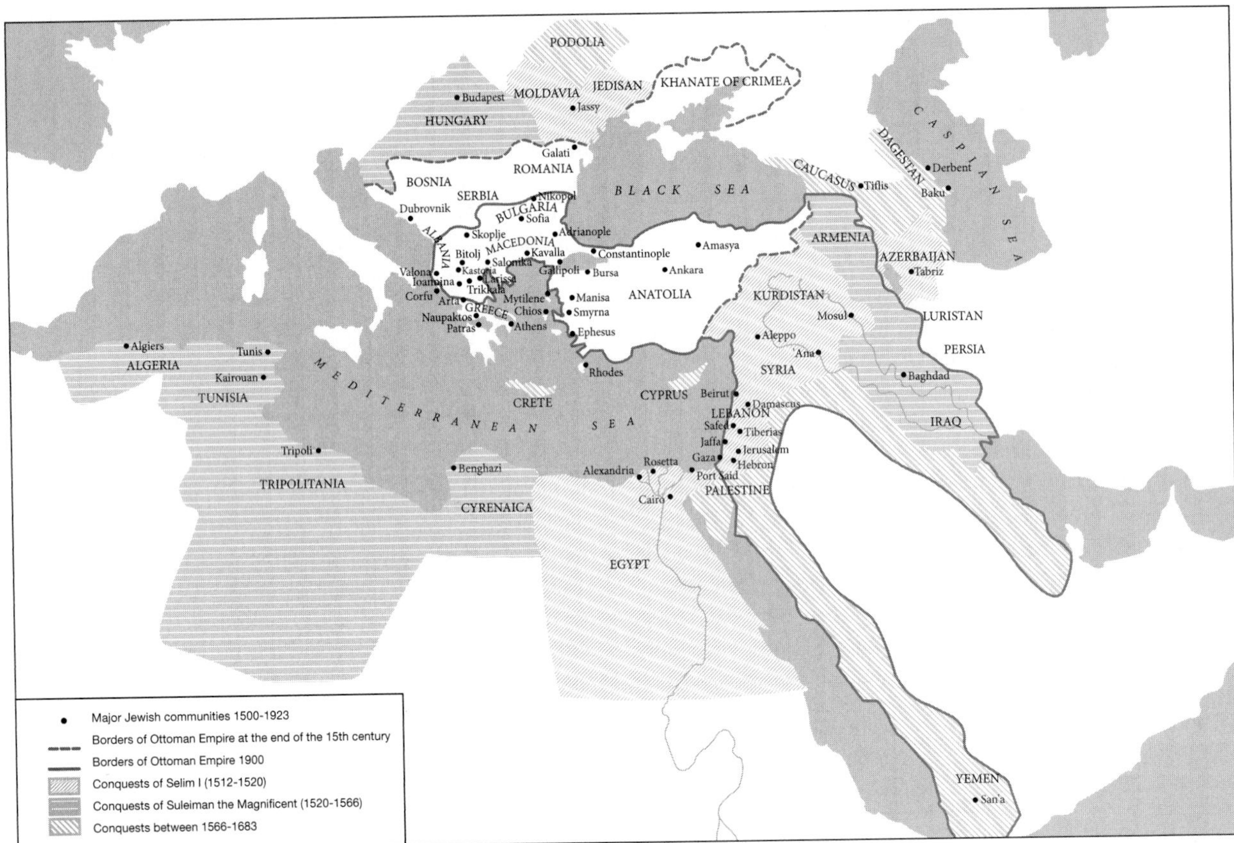

Map 2. Decline of the Ottoman Empire from the conquests of the 16th–17th centuries until the end of the 19th century.

ish communities, which considered them difficult. There were many appeals by the Jewish communities to the Ottoman authorities to reduce the taxes. There were also many disputes within the Jewish communities about the division of the tax burden between the congregations.

In the second half of the 15th century, refugees from Germany, as well as French families, came to settle in Adrianople (Edirne). Isaac Sarfati, the rabbi of the congregation, became well known for the letter he sent to the refugees from Germany and Hungary, informing them of the advantages of the sultanate and of its liberal attitude toward Jews. Seven years after the conquest of Istanbul, the entire Peloponnesus, Serbia, Bosnia, Herzegovina, Albania, the Crimea, and the Aegean islands, including the large island of Euboea, were conquered by the sultan Mehmed II; thus all their Jews came under Ottoman rule. In 1462 he conquered Walachia.

The Settlement of the Spanish and Portuguese Refugees in the Empire

*Beyazid II (1481–1512) settled many of the Spanish and Portuguese refugees in Istanbul. The communities of Turkey assisted the refugees to settle down: "Then the communities of Turkey performed innumerable and unlimited great deeds of charity, giving money as if it were stones, to redeem captives and restore Jews to their environment" (Capsali, *ibid.*). According to Jewish sources, Beyazid wanted to enrich his Empire by giving economic rights to the refugees, but at the same time he closed new synagogues and forced Jews to convert to Islam. In 1499 the sultan captured Lepanto and Patras. The overall total of Jewish families who arrived in the Ottoman Empire soon after 1492 is estimated at 12,000, which represents approximately 60,000 persons. Some estimates suggest a figure of 50,000 for the whole Jewish population of the Empire at the end of the first quarter of the 16th century, and others put the figure at 150,000. The Ottoman statistics were used for levying taxes, and the real figures could well have been higher than the official count. Most of the refugees settled in Istanbul, Salonika, Edirne, in towns in the Peloponnesus, Egypt, etc. They founded separate synagogues, also called congregations (*kehillot*) and named after the country or town from which they had departed. In the Ottoman documents the community or congregation is called *cemaat* or *taife*, and later, *millet*. Those who wandered to smaller towns, and in smaller numbers, founded one general Spanish congregation (*Kehilah, Kahal Kadosh*). Spanish congregations were also established in *Kastoria, Bursa, *Manissa (Magnesia), Gallipoli, *Tokat, *Amasya, *Ephesus, Siderokastron (Serres), *Patras, *Naupaktos (Lepanto), *Arta, *Trikkala, *Larissa, *Valona, *Monastir, *Skoplje, Ioannina, Serres, *Corfu, *Chios, *Cairo, *Safed, and other cities. A small number of refugees settled in *Jerusalem. Among the leaders of the refugees who settled in the empire soon after 1492, were Abraham *Saba, Abraham ibn Shoshan, Baruch

*Almosnino, David ibn Vidal Benveniste, Judah Benveniste, Judah ibn *Bulat, Joseph Fasi, Meir ibn Verga, Isaac Don Don, Samuel Franco, Isaac *Levi (Bet Halevi), Moses ha-Levi ibn Alkabeẓ, Moses ben Isaac *Alashkar, Solomon Attia, Samuel ibn Sid, Samuel Ḥakīm-Ḥaqan ha-Levi, *David ibn Abi Zimra, Joseph Saragossi, and Abraham ben Eliezer ha-Levi.

The Spanish refugees were followed by immigrants from Portugal (most of whom were Spanish Jews) in several waves (1497, 1498, and 1506 until 1521). They brought with them wealth and prosperity, in contrast to those coming from Spain, most of whom came with almost nothing. Among the leaders who came from Portugal were Ephraim Caro and his young son Joseph *Caro, David b. Solomon ibn *Yaḥya and his son *Tam Ibn Yaḥya, Jacob Abraham ibn Yaish, Joseph *Taitaẓak and his brother Samuel, Jacob ibn Ḥabib and his young son *Levi ibn Ḥabib, and Solomon *Taitaẓak. These Portuguese refugees founded separate Spanish and Portuguese congregations in Istanbul, Edirne, Salonika, Safed, and other towns. Among those who came were *Conversos (Crypto-Jews) and the children of Conversos who fled to Turkey and returned to their ancestral faith. The Iberian immigrants were motivated by strong religious feelings and had to cope with many religious and economic problems, including the halakhic meaning of betrothal and the betrothal gifts, the *sivlonot,* to decide about many questions of marital status and personal problems and tragic situations resulting from the expulsion, such as the loss of their children, the problems of *yibbum, ḥaliẓah,* and *agunot.* There were many expellees who lost their families and were anxious to rebuild their lives in the communities of the Ottoman Empire.

THE SPREAD OF THE OTTOMAN EMPIRE

The Conquest of Syria, Ereẓ Israel, Egypt, Hungary, North Africa, Iraq, and Yemen

Selim I (1512–20), called "the Grim," began a new era in the great conquests of the Ottoman Empire. Instead of continuing conquests in Europe, he turned to the East, and because of this was called "the man of the eastern front." In his time the Ottoman Empire doubled its area by conquests in Asia. He built a Turkish fleet, established a cavalry corps and mercenary bands, in addition to the *sipahi*, the feudal cavalry army. His aim in doing this was to overpower the *Mamluks, whose kingdom extended over Egypt, Ereẓ Israel and Syria. The war between the Ottomans and the Mamluks commenced in 1516; the Ottomans were victorious due to their superior use of firearms, their good organization, their strict discipline and, to a certain extent, the treachery of some leading Mamluks. Before the end of 1516 Syria and Ereẓ Israel were conquered, thus beginning a new era in the empire's history, lasting 400 years.

Selim I seized control of Egypt in January 1517 and was acclaimed in Cairo as the ruler of two continents (Europe and Asia) and two seas (the Black and the Mediterranean), the destroyer of two armies (the Persian and the Mamluk) and the "servant" of two temples (Mecca and Medina). For Jews the conquest was a salvation, as their situation in the 14th and 15th centuries under Mamluk rule had deteriorated. After the Ottoman conquest of Egypt, the office of *nagid, which had existed under *Fatimid and Mamluk rule, was abrogated. The last nagid, Isaac ha-Kohen *Sholal, was removed from office and settled in Jerusalem. It seems that in Cairo under Ottoman rule a chief dayyan served and with him a secular leader, a wealthy person who also fulfilled political functions. It seems that the first to serve in that office in the 1520s was Abraham *Castro, the master of the mint in Egypt, who is called in an Ottoman document *ra'is al-yahud* (the head of the Jews). Until 1769 the Jewish masters of the mint in Egypt functioned as *sarrāf bashis*, fulfilling de facto the office of the supreme leader of the Jews in Egypt. The Egyptian pashas also had Jewish physicians who were appointed to high positions in the government. The economic situation of Egyptian Jews, like that of the other inhabitants of Turkish lands, was good. Among the best-known wealthy persons in Egypt in the 16th century were Solomon *Alashkar, who maintained yeshivot in Egypt and Ereẓ Israel; Samuel ha-Kohen (Kahana); Abba Iscandari and his son the physician Abraham Iscandari; Joseph Bagliar, who maintained the yeshivot of Ereẓ Israel for a period of ten years; and in the 17th century Raphael b. Joseph, who was executed in 1669. After the Ottoman conquest refugees from Spain settled in Egypt (in Cairo, *Alexandria, Rosetta, etc). They found the old congregations of *Mustʿarabs (Moriscos), *Maghrebis (North Africans), Shāmīs (from Syria or *Damascus). Among the Spanish refugees who settled in Egypt, or lived there for a time, were Samuel b. Sid, Abraham b. Shoshan, Moses b. Isaac Alashkar, Samuel Ḥakīm-Ḥaqan ha-Levi, David ibn Abi Zimra, and Jacob *Berab. They founded yeshivot and the study of Torah developed. Well-known rabbis of the next generation included Bezalel Ashkenazi, Isaac *Luria (Ha-Ari), the pupils of David ibn Abi Zimra, Simeon Kastilaẓ, Jacob *Castro, Ḥayyim *Capusi, Abraham *Monzon. In *Syria, Spanish refugees settled in Damascus, Kfar *Jubār (near Damascus), and in *Aleppo. In all these localities there were Mustʿarab communities. The *Sephardim surpassed them in knowledge and culture, however, and sometimes were unable to live in peace with these veteran inhabitants. Prominent among the rabbis of Damascus were Moses *Najara, the chief rabbi, and his son Israel *Najara, the poet Jacob *Abulafia and his pupil Josiah *Pinto, Moses *Galante, Ḥayyim *Vital. Prominent among the rabbis of Aleppo were Samuel *Laniado, Moses Laniado, Abraham Laniado, Ḥayyim ha-Cohen, Mordecai ben Isaac ha-Cohen, Moses Dayyan, Mordecai Dayyan, Abraham Berabi Asher, Moses ben Solomon Ibn Alkabatz, R. Samuel ha-Cohen, Daniel Pinto, and others.

When *Suleiman the Magnificent (1520–66) ascended the throne, the rebellious governor of Syria and Ereẓ Israel was defeated by him and his head sent to Istanbul. Moreover, the Jerusalem community suffered from this rebellion. Later, the Turks learned the lesson of this rebellion and changed all the governors of these regions, replacing them with Ottomans. The local Mamluk troops were disbanded, and the land then became quiet. The civil and military administration was organized in accordance with the political system of Sultan Suleiman. He ordered the erection of the walls of *Jerusalem and he repaired the water conduits and the pools; as a result of these actions the security of the city was improved.

During his rule the Ottoman Empire attained its greatest power and extent. For more than 50 years Ereẓ Israel benefited from the peace and security which prevailed. Its population grew and its agricultural economy was expanded. This sultan introduced the *capitulations, i.e., pacts or contracts between the Ottoman sultans and the Christian states of Europe concerning the rights to be enjoyed by the subjects of each when dwelling in the country of the other. Many Jews who had immigrated from abroad benefited from these agreements, which had great influence on their legal standing. They acquired the status of protected persons and were granted extraterritorial rights and protection from attacks on property and life. *Venice was the first to come to such an arrangement in 1521 and was followed by François I, king of France, in 1535. After Suleiman's death, the capitulations were renewed during the time of his heir Selim II (1566–74), and also in the time of Murad III, Mehmed III, and Ahmed I. The era of Suleiman is considered to be the most prosperous period of Ereẓ Israel, and its Jewish communities were extended. Dona Gracia Mendes became the *multazima* (lessee) of the city of Tiberias and its environs during the years 1560–66 and was permitted to build the walls of the city. Details about this agreement are written in the orders of Suleiman to the governor of Damascus and to other Ottoman officials. The chronicler Joseph ha-Cohen writes about the important role of Joseph Nasi, the adviser of Suleiman and the son-in-law of Gracia Mendes, in developing the city of Tiberias. According to Jewish sources Joseph Nasi wanted to turn the locality into a great Jewish center, both spiritually and economically, and he sent his steward, Joseph b. Ardit, who was a representative of the sultan, there. There is no proof that Nasi had the aspiration to establish in Tiberias a Jewish state under the patronage of the sultan, or to become a Jewish king in Ereẓ Israel or later in Cyprus. Gracia Mendes and Nasi did not visit Tiberias themselves. With the support of Gracia, *Nasi founded a yeshivah of scholars in Tiberias and supported its students. The wall of Tiberias was built, people were brought from Safed, and foundations for the development of the site were laid. On Joseph Nasi's death the enthusiasm evaporated. He was followed by a new benefactor, Don Solomon ibn Yaish, who was also a counselor of the sultan Murad III (1574–95). The sultan gave Solomon a renewed concession for Tiberias, and sent his son Jacob ibn Yaish there. For want of organizational ability, however, he devoted himself to Torah study, but did not succeed in his task and the settlement in Tiberias failed to continue.

Toward the end of the 16th century, signs of decline manifested themselves in the Jewish settlement of Ereẓ Israel. Security deteriorated, especially after the period of Safed's eminence, which lasted three generations. The ruler of the town treated the Jews poorly and the sultan was unable to supervise his rulers. Sultan orders in 1576 demanded the expulsion of wealthy Jews from Safed to Cyprus, but it seems that the orders were not implemented. The Ottoman Jewish communities during this period, especially in Istanbul, began to send assistance to the Jewish population of Safed. The rabbis Yom Tov *Zahalon, Joseph of *Trani, Abraham *Shalom, Moses Alsheikh, and Bezalel Ashkenazi traveled to Istanbul, Syria, and Persia to collect financial aid for the Jews of Safed and Jerusalem, as well as to beg the viziers to ease the burden imposed on them by the local governors. Emissaries (*sheluḥei Ereẓ Israel*) also departed for North Africa, Italy, and Germany. Tiberias was evacuated, and Safed's community lost its hegemony and experienced an economic and social crisis in the last quarter of the 16th century and during the 17th century. The center of the Jews of Ereẓ Israel passed to Jerusalem. In the 17th century many Sephardi, Italian, and Ashkenazi scholars settled in Jerusalem. The most famous Ashkenazi scholar was Rabbi Isaiah ha-Levi *Horowitz, who settled in Ereẓ Israel in 1620. Another rabbi, Jacob Hagiz from Morocco, established a yeshivah in Jerusalem called the Beit Ya'akov Viga Yeshivah. In 1522 Suleiman captured Rhodes, and then defeated the Hungarians in the battle of Mohacs in 1526, conquering *Hungary and its capital Buda (Budon), but the final conquest of the city was only in 1541. In 1526 its other inhabitants had fled, but the Jews remained. The leader of the Jewish community, who handed the keys of the city to the sultan, was Joseph b. Solomon Ashkenazi of the Alaman family. The sultan dealt charitably with him and also with his children, giving them a deed exempting them and their descendants from taxes. The Jews of Buda frequently defended the city from enemies and were faithful to the Ottoman sultans. It contained both Ashkenazi and Sephardi congregations. Suleiman transferred the majority of the Buda Jews and settled them in Sofia, Kavalla, Edirne, Salonika, Istanbul, and perhaps even in Safed. They were dispatched as sürgün in the category of craftsmen and tradesmen. But it seems that in the 16th century not all the Hungarian Jews in the Ottoman Jewish communities were sürgün. A Jewish community in Buda existed during the Ottoman rule over Buda until 1686.

The struggle of the Ottoman sultans to extend their domain west of Egypt lasted almost 60 years (1518–74), but their success was incomplete. The Turks were unable to seize control of *Morocco, which preserved its independence. They forced their sovereignty upon Tripolitania (see *Libya), *Tunisia, and *Algeria, three of the *Berber countries. Each of these developed a different administration and legal system that also differed from those in the Ottoman Empire in Asia, Egypt, and Europe. The rule of the Ottomans in these countries was very loose, and during the long period until the French occupation of Algeria and Tunisia in the 19th century local rulers reigned in these lands. With the consolidation of Ottoman rule, descendants of Spanish refugees and *anusim*, who had succeeded in escaping from Spain, began to settle in three Berber countries. The condition of Jews changed from country to country and was dependent upon the goodwill or whim of the local ruler. In Algeria the establishment of a new synagogue was dependent on giving bribes. In the 17th century, a new wave of descendants of the refugees arrived in these countries, who had first settled in *Leghorn (Italy). Rabbis who were descendants of Simeon b. Ẓemaḥ *Duran lived in Algiers, and in the second half of the 16th century members of the sixth generation of the family headed the congregation. Apparently, Abraham b. Jacob ibn Tāva was also a descendant of the Duran family. The Algiers scholars in the 18th century included Raphael Jedidiah, Solomon *Seror, Judah *Ayash, and Jacob ibn Naʿim. In Libya an improvement in the situation of the Jews took place when the Sublime Porte in Istanbul reestablished direct rule over it (1835–1911). This improvement was manifested primarily in the appointment of *valis* (*pashas,* governors) charged with administration of the country and their periodic replacement, as was customary in other provinces of the empire. The Ottoman *valis*, who did not succeed in getting to know the conditions of the country and its language, were to a great extent dependent upon the help of Jewish secretaries. The influence of foreign consuls also increased and, as a result, the status of the Jews improved, especially in the city of *Tripoli.

THE CONQUEST OF IRAQ (1534–1623, 1638–1917). In 1534 Suleiman captured *Tabriz, the capital of Persia, through the efforts of the vizier Ibrahim Pasha. From there he sent the vizier to take Baghdad from the Persians. It fell on Dec. 31, 1534. The Jews of Baghdad, who had suffered under Persian rule, helped the Turks in this victory. Baghdad remained in Turkish hands for almost 90 years. In the 16th century it had a large Jewish population, including wealthy people and great scholars. There was another community in Ana, which had strong ties with the *Aleppo community and contained "Ma'raviyyim" and "Mizraḥiyyim" congregations. The economic situation of the two communities in Baghdad and in Ana was good. At the beginning of the 16th century there was a large yeshivah in *Mosul, headed by Asenat *Barazani, wife of the ḥakham Jacob b. Judah Mizraḥi. She was a daughter of Samuel Adani (Barazani). At the request of the local Jews, she sent her son Samuel to Baghdad, where he established a yeshivah. Murad IV (1623–40) captured Baghdad from the Persians. Among his 15,000 troops were 10,000 Jews – as a result of their great suffering in the period of Persian rule, the Jews helped the Turks conquer the city. After its capture, Murad rewarded the Jews accordingly. They considered the capture of the city a miracle from heaven and named the 16th of Tevet, 1638, as the day of the miracle. For a period of 280 years (until 1917), Baghdad remained in Turkish hands. The sultans appointed *valis,* and the condition of the Jews depended upon their favors. Baghdad had wealthy Jews, among them the banker Ezekiel *Gabbai, who was from a philanthropic and charitable family that supported *Talmud torahs*, yeshivot, the printing of books, etc. The sultan Mahmud II (1808–39) appointed him chief banker and money changer (*sarrāf bashi*) and a member of his government. After Gabbai's death, the pasha of Baghdad severely persecuted the Jews, and as a result of his actions, many left the city and fled to neighboring countries, including Syria and Egypt. He was followed by two more oppressive rulers.

*The *Nasi in Babylon.* It was customary for the pasha to appoint a wealthy and respected Jew as his banker and also as *nasi* of his community. This functionary acted as an intermediary between the community and the government, and his influence extended beyond Babylon to Persia and Yemen. As in Baghdad he had complete authority over the communities in the other towns of the country. In 1890 the Jewish population in Baghdad numbered 30,000 people, which means that it was one of the largest Jewish communities in the Ottoman Empire, after those of Salonika and Istanbul.

Yemen was conquered by the Turks in 1546. In the days of Suleiman I the Turks ruled over *Sanʿa and part of *Yemen: their sovereignty continued until 1628. There are only a few extant details on the situation of the Jews at the time of their rule, except for *Zechariah al-Ḍāhiri's introduction to his *Sefer ha-Musar*. The imam al-Muṭahhar drove the Turks from Sanʿa in 1569. After his victory he falsely accused the Jews of assisting the Turks in their conquest and expelled them to *Mowzaʾ. The Jews, who wished to redeem themselves from oppressive rule, longed for the Turks and assisted them in their conquests. The Turks, who nominally ruled Yemen, were however unable to dominate the country. They held part of Hodeida, but the road to Sanʿa and the district were under the influence of the local sheikhs. In 1872 the Turks conquered Yemen again. During the period of their rule – up to World War I – the Jews generally experienced a certain degree of well-being in the district towns.

THE ERA OF STAGNATION AND DECLINE OF THE OTTOMAN EMPIRE (THE 16TH-18TH CENTURIES)

After the peak military, political, and economic era of the sultans Selim I, Suleiman the Magnificent, and Selim II, the gradual eclipse of the empire began during the rule of Murad III and his son. The strict discipline introduced into the janissary army by Selim I was destroyed, and the military became a constant source of danger to the sultans because of frequent revolts and exaggerated demands for remuneration and bonuses. Breaches occurred in the feudal arrangements of the army of *sipahis*. The tax burden increased and the foundations of rule and order were undermined. In the courts of the sultans and the pashas, luxuries and extravagance spread. The cruel exploitation of the conquered regions caused revolts in many parts of the empire, which the rulers succeeded in crushing only with difficulty. Bribery was one of the most certain methods of arranging all matters at the court, as well as with its representatives in the provinces. Sheikhs and minor rulers enriched themselves on the ruin of the Ottoman Empire. When the sultan Murad III learned that Sephardi girls were wearing choice garments and ornaments with precious stones, he issued a decree to exterminate all Jews throughout all the provinces of his empire. Through the influence of the sultan's mother, the decree was revoked, but an order was issued that Jews must wear, in place of the yellow turban, a peculiar and strange tall hat, pointed above and wide below, like those of the Spaniards. Jewish women were forbidden to walk in the streets of Turkish towns wearing silk gowns and elegant clothes. As a result of this decree, the rabbis issued an ordinance which added to the royal decree: "women and girls are not to go out wearing velvet garments and ornaments of gold and precious stones." The situation of Jews in Istanbul and throughout the empire deteriorated. Murad IV (1623–40), known for his cruelty and bloodshed, ordered the execution of Judah Kovo, the chief of the Salonika delegates who came to pay "the clothes tax" (paid annually), in 1636; there was no Jew powerful enough to influence the sultan to rescind the decree.

During the rule of Ibrahim I (1640–48) the Turks attacked the island of *Crete, which belonged to Venice, and conquered part of it (1646); the war for its complete capture was a prolonged one. The sultan's court was transferred from Istanbul to Edirne, and as a result of this transfer many Jews who had business dealings with the sultan also moved their residences there. Nevertheless, the political and economic situation of the Jews deteriorated during the 17th century.

The Turkish Empire gradually lost the areas it had conquered. In July 1703 the Janissary rebellion which dethroned Sultan Mustafa II in Istanbul was followed by large-scale sacking of the Jewish quarter of Salonika by the Janissary garrison and the local Greek population. The Janissary troops had a long anti-Jewish policy from the 15th century onward, in spite of the fact that Jews had economic relations with the Janissaries. In the time of Ahmed III (1703–30) a decree was issued (1728) that all the Jews living in the capital in the street of the fish market – near the mosque of the sultan's mother – must sell their houses and possessions to Muslims in order not to contaminate the street. In 1730 the Janissaries massacred Jews in Istanbul, Salonika, Izmir, Bursa, and cities in Macedonia. During the rule of 'Uthmān III (1754–57), the Ottoman authorities oppressed the Jews and limited their rights. An ancient decree was renewed which stated that Jews could not build houses above the height of 18 feet (c. 5.4 m.), while Turks could build up to 24 feet (c. 7.2 m). In October 1757, Jews, Greeks and Muslims were the objects of exactions on the part of the military garrisons in most Ottoman cities and towns in Europe. The Janissaries invested their wealth in lands and tax farms, using Jewish agents who collected their taxes. In 1758, Mustafa III issued a decree, renewing the decree of 1702 that Jews could not wear clothes and hats like those of Muslims. The weakness of the central government in the 18th century encouraged local strongmen to establish themselves as independent or semi-independent rulers, and some of them targeted the Jews for particular oppression. For example, in Egypt the rebellious Mamluk ruler Ali Bey al-Kabir (reigned 1760–73) oppressed the Jews with particular vehemence. He executed and seized the property of the wealthiest Jews, Joseph Levi, who administered the Alexandria customs house, and Isaac al-Yahudi, who held the tax farm on the customs house in Bulaq in 1768 and 1769. He systematically purged Egypt's financial administration of Jews, replacing them with Syrian Catholics, and he imposed on the Jewish merchants heavy fines. The Jewish population in the 17th and 18th centuries suffered a lot from the decline of the Ottoman cities, a result of the political situation and of anarchy, hunger, numerous epidemics, and fires. In about 1800 the Jewish population in the Ottoman Empire numbered around 100,000 people.

Decline of the Political and Economic Status of the Jews

STATUS OF THE JEWS IN THE EMPIRE IN THE 19TH CENTURY. Sultan Mahmud II (1808–39), in his desire to inaugurate reforms in the empire, fought the Janissaries, and the vizier Bayrakdar Mustafa Pasha spoke out harshly against the wealthy Jews of the capital who conspired with the Janissaries, among them the *çelebi* Bekhor *Carmona, the brothers Adjiman, and Gabbai. These supported the Janissaries in order to defend themselves and their property; nevertheless, they were sentenced to death in 1826. The reforms continued at a quicker pace in the time of Abdul Mejid (1839–61), who was concerned with the modernization of the judiciary and removal of the restrictions on Christians. Reforms were introduced in internal government, in the collection of taxes and in the granting of some equal rights to non-Muslims. The Jews received the same rights and liberties as the other non-Muslim inhabitants (Greeks, Armenians, Bulgarians, etc.) as a result of the Ottoman proclamation – known as *haṭṭi-i sherif* of the *Gül-Khane* (The Rose Law or The Rescript of the Rose Chamber) – of Nov. 3, 1839; according to it, the sultan instituted the *Tanzimat* (reforms): He vouched for the security of the lives, property, and regularization of taxation for the subjects of the empire without distinction of religion; religious and personal freedom, as well as equality of rights and military service for non-Muslim citizens, were also guaranteed. The ceremony which took place in the above-mentioned Rose Chamber was also attended by the *ḥakham bashi* R. Moses Fresco and the delegates of the Jewish community of Istanbul. These rights were again reconfirmed in 1843 by the grand vizier Riza and in 1846 by the grand vizier Reshid. Some time in the mid-19th century, and perhaps as early as 1835, a new political term, *millit-I erba'a* ("The Four Communities"), entered the Ottoman political lexicon. It came to denote the officially recognized four religious communities: Muslims, Jews, Armenians, and Greeks, and to suggest that the empire was at the same time also a pluralistic society in which the minorities' special status was officially recognized. The *Gül-Khane* Edict of 1839 was renewed in 1856 by the proclamation of the *Haṭṭ-i Hümayun* (imperial rescript), which was a charter of tolerance the sultan granted to all protected subjects and whose first lines were written by the sultan himself. A solemn ceremony was attended by ministers, patriarchs, and the *ḥakham bashi* of the Jews of Turkey, R. Jacob Bekhar David. It was stipulated in this legislation that there was to be no distinction between sects, races, and religions; liberties were granted to all; non-Muslims were to be admitted to the government, civil, and military schools; the security of life and property were guaranteed; equality before the law was instituted; every citizen was eligible for public or military office; and religious freedom, equal taxation, and jurisdiction and representation in the municipal councils were guaranteed. The Jews of Turkey received the same rights as the other minorities. As formerly, they secured positions in Ottoman society and participated in the cultural and economic life. They did not, however, regain their past importance, and their positions were of a secondary nature. Jews began to hold such government functions as administrative directors, judges, physicians of ministers, military doctors, officers, consuls, etc. Every Jew was authorized to wear the national hat (fez). Rabbis were authorized to add a scarf of blue silk to their headdress, and the turban of the rabbis was of the same color as that of the Muslim imam. In 1847 the sultan Abdul Mejid visited the military medical school. When he observed that there were no Jewish students, he decided that their entry should be encouraged and ordered the director of the school to install a *kasher* kitchen under the supervision of a Jewish cook and supervisor; he exempted Jewish students from studies on the Sabbath and authorized the organization of Jewish prayers on the premises. When the sultan visited Salonika, the children of the Jewish schools, led by the *ḥakham bashi* R. Asher Kovo, welcomed him; he contributed 25,000 piasters to the Jewish schools and 26,000 piasters to the poor of the community. In spite of the sultan's proclamations, which should have increased the rights of the empire's Jews, certain internal events in the Jewish community in the capital caused a delay in confirming the regulations for the Jewish *millet. This delay was caused by the following internal struggle within the Istanbul Jewish community. The Gabbai, Adjiman, and Carmona families, the most prominent in the capital, maintained close relations with the Janissaries and they, as bankers and farmers of taxes, maintained their high position in the Jewish community. As mentioned above, the massacre of the Janissaries in 1826 was accompanied by the execution of the major figures of these families and a consequent decline in their importance. In the 1830s Abraham de *Camondo assumed the leadership, as he was from a family of noted scholars and wealthy businessmen. He was influential in court circles, and the confirmation of the first *ḥakham bashi* of Jerusalem in 1841 was in a large part due to his efforts. He also led the group which attempted to strengthen the community's economic position vis-à-vis the Armenians and the Greeks, who for many years past had held the upper hand due to their better general education, ready acceptance of European influence, and connections with the court. Aware, as a result of his business experience and travels, of the progress made in Europe, Camondo undertook the establishment and a large part of the financing of a modern school in the capital. In 1856 the *Haṭṭ-i Hümayun* further influenced these modernization trends and brought about the formation of a "committee of notables" comprised of wealthy and reform-minded persons under Camondo's leadership. The constitution of this committee in 1860, which included members of the Hamon, Adjiman, and Carmona families, was to some degree an irregular response to the appeal by the *Haṭṭ-i Hümayun* for non-Muslim communities to offer the sultan suggestions for their reorganization in accord with the times. Progressive and conservative circles in the community split over the matter, and the conflict was heightened after the modern school was established (French was taught there). An attempt was made to avoid elections to the ruling bodies by establishing a rabbinical grand court and a lay "committee of notables," which was attended by the *ḥakham bashi*, Jacob Avigdor. However, the rabbis Isaac Akrish and Solomon Kimḥi led an anti-Camondo propaganda and claimed that the modern school encouraged children to become Christians. This sort of propaganda easily inflamed the common people. Camondo was subsequently excommunicated by Akrish and some scholars. The *ḥakham bashi* had Akrish imprisoned, but he was released on the order of the sultan Abdul-Aziz (1861–76) following demonstrations by those who wanted Jacob Avigdor to be dismissed. The grand vizier then convened a special rabbinical court on which the *ḥakham bashi* of Izmir and his colleagues from Edirne and Salonika sat. The court heard the opponents of *ḥakham bashi* Avigdor who wanted him removed and the notables who supported him. The court cleared Avigdor of all charges and threatened excommunication to those who repeated such charges, but Avigdor was unable to continue in his position and resigned the next year (1863); he continued to serve as *rav ha-kolel* for the next 11 years. Carmona and Camondo were also exonerated and their attackers were compelled to apologize. Camondo moved in 1866 to Europe and died in Paris in 1873, so new forces entered politics in the Jewish community of Istanbul.

The new *ḥakham bashi* was Yakkir Gueron, who had held the same position in Edirne. He was ordered to draft regulations immediately for the community (*niẓām-name*), but they were only confirmed, after close scrutiny and some changes, in 1865. The "Organizational Regulations of the Rabbinate" (*ḥakham-khane niẓām-namesi*) were divided into five parts, as follows: (1) the status of the *ḥakham bashi* as head of Jewry in the empire; his qualifications and election (clauses 1–4); (2) his powers and replacement in the event of resignation or removal from office (clauses 5–15); (3) the "general committee" (*mejlis umūmī*), its election and powers. It consists of 80 members and is presided over by the permanent deputy of the *ḥakham bashi*. Sixty secular members are elected by the inhabitants of Istanbul according to city districts, and they in turn elect 20 rabbinical members. These 80 members elect the seven rabbis forming the spiritual committee (*majlis rūḥānī*) and the nine members of the secular committee (*majlis jismānī*). These elections require the approval of the Sublime Porte. At the election of the *ḥakham bashi* for the entire empire, the general committee is temporarily reinforced by 40 members from eight districts where they officiated as provincial *ḥakham bashis*: Edirne, Bursa, Izmir, Salonika, Baghdad, Cairo, Alexandria, and Jerusalem (clauses 16–19). It is to be noted that clause 16 fails to prescribe the committee's term of office; only in 1910 was it fixed at ten years; (4) the powers of the spiritual committee. The seven rabbis are to concern themselves with religious and other matters referred to them by the *ḥakham bashi*. The committee is not to prevent the publication of books or spread of science and art unless prejudicial to the government, the community, or religion. The committee is to supervise the activities of the city-district rabbis (*marei de-atra*), who act under its instructions. The committee is headed by a president, who is also the head of the rabbinical court; he is to have two deputies (clauses 20–38); (5) the powers of the secular committee regarding management of communal affairs and carrying into effect government orders. It has to apportion communal taxes and supervise the property of orphans and endowments (clauses 39–48).

No changes in the status of non-Muslim subjects of Muslim rulers took place until the middle of the 19th century. Restrictions and tax laws on changing the shape of existing synagogues or constructing new ones remained in effect (see Covenant of *Omar). The authorities also closely regulated the *ghiyār* – distinctive apparel and footwear. Certain individuals, physicians in particular, were granted dispensations such as tax exemptions – by imperial *firmans* – and were allowed to ride horses and dress normally. Those who were employed by European powers covered by capitulation agreements also enjoyed privileges and were exempt from special clothes. In their legal status within the empire the Jews were not essentially on a different footing from Christians, except for the fact that veteran Jewish inhabitants could not find support from the European powers which saw as their duty to protect Christianity in Muslim countries.

THE POLL TAX. The **jizya* (also **kharāj* or *jawālī*) was generally collected from small income earners, the middle class, and the wealthy at a ratio of 1:2:4. Agents, interpreters, or other employees of European powers who worked at consulates or embassies were completely, or substantially, relieved from paying the poll tax, under capitulation agreements. The Ottoman reforms abolished the poll tax and ordinances in 1855 and in 1856 replaced it with a military service exemption tax for non-Muslims (*bedel-i ʿaskeri*). It was abolished in 1909, when non-Muslims were drafted into the army. No complaints were voiced about the existence of the poll tax, but there were numerous ones over the manner of its collection. In the Jewish communities many discussions were held between rich and poor Jews about the internal assessment of this tax and also about other taxes.

RESTRICTIONS ON BUILDING NEW SYNAGOGUES, CLOTHES, HEADGEAR, AND SLAVES. In spite of the fact that non-Muslims were limited in their use of buildings for religious worship to those constructed prior to the Arab conquest, they found ways to circumvent this restriction. Indeed, many hundreds of buildings for worship were constructed in cities founded under Islam, e.g., in *Kairouan, Baghdad, Cairo, and *Fez; R. Obadiah of *Bertinoro states in the last decade of the 15th century that a Jew was prohibited "from rebuilding his house and yard [in Jerusalem] without permission, even if they were falling down, and the permit was sometimes more costly than the rebuilding itself" (A. Yaari, *Letters from Palestine*, 130). This was the state of affairs in Jerusalem, which was then ruled by the Mamluks. The Ottoman sultan Mehmed II, at about the same time, allowed the use and repair of old synagogues, even though he prohibited the construction of new ones. About a generation or two later, Jacob ibn Habib described the situation in Turkey as follows: "We are not permitted to obtain permanent quarters for a synagogue, let alone build one: we are compelled to hide underground, and our prayers must not be heard because of the danger" (quoted by Joseph Caro, *Beit Yosef*, Tur *Oraḥ Ḥayyim*, 154). These regulations were used by zealous officials and fanatical muftis and qadis to frustrate the Jews in their efforts to worship, for example in Jerusalem, but in spite of this, many synagogues were built during Ottoman rule due to both tolerance and greed on the part of the authorities. In 1554 a complaint was lodged with the sultan concerning the large number of synagogues in Safed; it reported that in the town there were only seven mosques, while Jews, who in olden times had had three synagogues (*kanīsa*), then had 32 synagogues, built very high. The sultan ordered an investigation of the matter (U. Heyd. *Ottoman Documents on Palestine*, 1552–1615 (1960), 169). As the results of the inquiry and the action taken are unknown, the matter may possibly have been taken care of by a bribe. This state of affairs continued there until the middle of the 19th century, and every major or minor repair demanded the appropriate bribe for the official who had to rule on the necessity of the action. The condition of synagogues in Jerusalem was poor, and in 1586 the old synagogue was closed by the governor; change only came during the rule of Muḥammad ʿAlī. His son *Ibrāhīm Pasha allowed two important synagogues in the Old City of Jerusalem to be both enlarged and repaired.

Since the situation of bribes continued to get worse, the Turkish authorities were unable to overlook such a cause of corruption, and in about 1841 a *berāt* of the *ḥakham bashi* was issued which stated that the reading of the Scroll of the Law (during services) in the house of the *ḥakham* and in other houses was in accord with Jewish religious practice; consequently it was allowed that veils be hung and candelabra be placed in houses where the services took place. Thus, synagogues and their property gained immunity and could not be confiscated or held in security for debts. Generally, Jews were careful in most other Muslim countries in building their places of worship so that they were not readily noticeable – and as they lived in special quarters – there were only a few mentions of trouble from the authorities. In addition, there was little likelihood that the feelings of Muslims would be hurt. Refugees in North Africa seem to have encountered little difficulty in building their synagogues. Nonetheless, D'Arvieux, who was the French consul in Algiers in 1674 and 1675, says that the Jews of that city had to pay large sums to the Ottoman authorities in order to construct additional places of worship. At times savage attacks were made upon synagogues by incited mobs of Muslims or troops. Various sources relate that Scrolls of the Law were desecrated, religious articles stolen, furniture burned and buildings destroyed. Nevertheless, these events were not connected with the regulations of the Covenant of Omar, as they were in fact violations of them.

Middle Eastern Jewish quarters are frequently mentioned in the writings of European travelers from the 16th century on, laying stress on the conditions of overcrowding and poor sanitation, dirty narrow streets, and indifferent state of health of the inhabitants. Nevertheless, it should be realized that these sources were often not sufficiently objective in their presentation. Even though the special dress of non-Muslims in the East (*ghiyār*) is described in detail by European tourists, Jewish sources were more concerned to determine deviations from the regulations and whether they existed due to tolerance on the part of the authorities or to a lax enforcement of the law. Difference in dress was the most common and at the same time striking phenomenon. In Algiers the refugees from Spain after 1391 wore the *capos* or *caperon*, as distinguished from the veteran inhabitants who wore the cap (*shāshiyya*). As there were no Christians in the region at the time and the Muslims wore no European clothes, the *capos* was also a sign of the Jewishness of the wearer. The chief rabbi of Istanbul prohibited the wearing of the *caperon*, which was the cloak of the Sephardi *ḥakhamim*, in the late 15th century. D'Arvieux gave the following description of the clothing of the Jew, in Algiers: "the residents wore a bournous over a black shirt of light-weight fabric and covered their heads with a black woolen *shāshiyya*; those from other Muslim countries wore a turban of different shape, ending in a tassel descending upon the shoulders; all wore sandals without stockings. Livornese (from Leghorn) and Alexandrian Jews wore hats and clothes like the Italians or Spaniards, whose customs they even preserved" (L. D'Arvieux, *Mémoires du... envoyé extraordinaire* (Paris, 1735), vol. 5, 288).

A number of orders (which are in the archives in Istanbul) were issued by the kadi of the capital between 1568 and 1837 to the official in charge (*muḥtasib*) of non-Muslims concerning the headgear and clothes of Jews and Christians; in one particular instance such an order, which was issued to the chief rabbi, is extant. In 1599 the sultan ordered the Jews to change the color of their headgear to red. In 1595 the sultan ordered the kadi of Istanbul not to hurt the Jews because of their dress and headwear. These particular orders stressed the headwear, that if it was replaced by the turban of the Turks, it was considered as evidence of a change of religion on the part of the wearer. Jews in the East generally had to wear dark apparel, and light or colored clothes were allowed only on the Sabbath and festivals, and then only within their own quarters. Particular stringency existed concerning the prohibition of the wearing of green (green headgear was a sign of descent from the Prophet *Muhammad) and purple. Nevertheless, there is evidence that the above-mentioned Ottoman decrees were not strictly enforced, as 18th-century sources mention that many Istanbul Jews wore green turbans and the same kind of shoes as the Muslims. There seems to have been some doubt on the part of the Jews as to the halakhic permissibility of this kind of dress, and a discussion of the problem is preserved in rabbinic literature. The *ghiyār* continued to be mentioned in official Ottoman sources until almost the middle of the 19th century. In 1702 and in the 1750s the sultans renewed the orders about clothing, and forbade Jews to put green on shoes and wear red headgear with red strings. They were ordered to wear black shoes and black clothes. In 1837 a decree stated that Jews and Christians permitted to wear the tarbush had to use special marks on it so that it could be distinguishable from that of Muslims. The *berāt* which was issued to the first *ḥakham bashi* of Jerusalem in 1841 states that his official emissaries are held to be exempt from the *ghiyār* so that they might travel without being molested. In addition, they were allowed to carry arms to defend themselves from attack. In the 17th and 18th centuries the sultans issued orders which forbade the Jews to sell wine to Muslims, and threatened those who did not obey. The upper middle class Jewish households in Ottoman cities had slaves bought in the slaves markets, and in the 16th century there were immigrants from Portugal who brought their own slaves into the Ottoman Empire. Most of the slaves in Jewish homes were Christians from Europe and pagans from Africa. The Ottoman authorities tried to limit the number of slaves held by Christians and Jews. Jews did not stop buying slaves but paid a tax for the right to own slaves. Jews kept slaves until the 19th century.

BLOOD LIBELS. Until the *Damascus Affair of 1840 accusations of ritual murder were very rare in the Ottoman Empire. The majority of blood libels broke out as a result of the hostility of the Greek and Armenian populations toward the Jews. The first blood libel is mentioned in a firman (sultanic decree) issued in the time of Mehmed II. Orders were given that henceforth such cases should be brought before the imperial *divan* in Istanbul. During the reign of Suleiman I such an accusation was again made, between December 1553 and June 1554, and the firman to hear such cases in the divan only was renewed. The order was renewed by Selim II and Murad III. It seems that Suleiman's decree was obtained by the sultan's chief physician, Moses Hamon after a blood libel in the Anatolian cities of *Amasia and *Tokat. The firman removed the prosecution of such cases from the jurisdiction of the local kadis and assigned them to the sultan's jurists. In 1592 two firmans were issued which dealt with a ritual murder accusation in Bursa. The accused Jews were tortured, and Murad III ordered them to be exiled to Rhodes. It is not clear if they remained in Rhodes or were punished and sent to serve in the Ottoman naval galleys. In the beginning of the 17th century a blood libel broke out in Thebez (Thebatai) in Greece. The Jews had to pay to end the libel and asked the Jews of Chalkis to contribute money for that purpose. The ill-famed blood libel against *Damascus Jewry (1840) was followed by another on the island of *Rhodes. In order to protect the Jews from slanderous accusations, Moses *Montefiore, A. *Crémieux, and the well-known Orientalist S. *Munk traveled to Egypt to meet Muhammad Ali, who ruled Syria at that time. The blood libel was not quashed, but the Jewish prisoners were freed so that Muslim public opinion in Syria considered the accusations true. Montefiore went to meet the Sultan Abdul Aziz in Istanbul, and on October 28, 1840, after an audience with the sultan, obtained a firman which could be regarded as a bill of rights for the Jews. It mentions the deep emotions that the blood libels had stirred in Europe and recommends the issuing of a firman that would exonerate the Jews of all ritual murder accusations, and to translate the firman into European languages. All the recommendations of this document were indeed carried out. In 1844 a blood libel occurred in Egypt when the Jews of Cairo were accused of murdering a Christian. Only the firmness of Muhammad Ali prevented the outbreak of violence. Between 1840 and 1860 there occurred 13 blood libels in Damascus and Aleppo. In February 1856, three days after the Ottoman Reform Decree was made public, a blood libel reappeared in Istanbul in the Balat quarter. A mob consisting of Greeks, Armenians, and Turks started attacking Jews. French Jewish leaders who visited the city, including Alphonse de Rothschild, immediately alerted the Ottoman authorities, who put a stop to the disturbances. In 1864 and 1872 the Jews of Izmir were accused of kidnapping Christian children before Passover. There were similar conspiracies in Istanbul in 1868, 1870, and 1874. In 1872 there were blood libels in Edirne, Marmara, Ioannina, and La Canee. All these cases required the intervention of the *ḥakham bashi* R. Yakkir Gueron and *ḥakham bashi* R. Moses ha-Levi, as well as that of the *Alliance Israélite Universelle. The Alliance in Istanbul or its headquarters in Paris called upon the Ottoman government to investigate this affair and punish the rioters. A blood libel also occurred in 1880 in the island of Mytilene. In 1884 there was a blood libel in a village located near the Dardanelles, where about 40 Jewish families lived. When a non-Jewish boy servant was sent to fetch something and failed to return, it was rumored that the Jews had murdered him. The Jews were fortunate that the boy reappeared once the riots broke out. In 1887 the municipality of Salonika accused the Jews of ritual murder. The representative of the government condemned the libel and mentioned the firman according to which the propagators of such rumors would be prosecuted. In Beirut, Jews were molested by Christian youths but the Ottoman authorities punished the assailants. Other blood libels occurred in Aleppo (1891), Damascus (1892), *Manissa (1893), Kavalla, and *Gallipoli (1894). There were also blood libels in Jimlitoh near Bursa (1899), in Monastir (Bitola) (1900), and in Izmir (1901). All these were based on the disappearance of a child who was subsequently found. In general, Ottoman government officials defended the Jews, and the Jews also received help from Jewish organizations such as the Alliance Israélite Universelle, European ambassadors and consuls, and even Protestant missionaries. Many blood libels occurred also in Egypt during the 19th century. In Cairo blood libels occurred in the years 1844, 1890, and 1901–2.

In Alexandria an elderly Jew named Sasson was arrested in 1870. He was imprisoned for a month, during which period the press emphasized his Jewish identity in an attempt to have him accused of having sought to kidnap a child to strangle and to utilize his blood for the baking of the Passover *matzoh*. The fall of a Christian child (1880) from a balcony into the courtyard of a synagogue in Alexandria served as a pretext for the Greeks to accuse the Jews of ritual murder. The Greeks, with the assistance of Arabs who had joined them, attacked the Jews in spite of the fact that the doctors who had examined the child testified that he did not bear any wounds. In 1880 the Jews were accused of having raped a local girl. In 1881, again in Alexandria, it was rumored that they had employed the blood of a ten-year-old Greek child who had disappeared from his home. The Greek mob threatened to attack the Jewish quarter and burn it down. The British consul then called on the governor of Alexandria to intervene on behalf of the Jews. During the same year a nine-year-old child of Cretan origin disappeared there. The corpse of the child was retrieved from the sea and no wounds were found on it. In Mansura a blood libel occurred in 1877 and in Damanhur in 1871, 1873, 1877, and 1892. In Port Said a girl disappeared in 1882. She was found dead in the Arab quarter but rumors were immediately circulated that the Jews had assassinated her in order to use her blood for the preparation of *matzoh*. The Jews were the victims of many attacks and the French consul was influential in calming the passions. During the same year the Jews of Cairo were accused of having killed a girl. There were antisemitic accusations in the Arabic press, and newspapers of the Syrian Christians played a prominent role in this campaign of agitation; they claimed that the Jews lent money for interest and were thus usurers. The foreign consuls assisted the Jews by intervening with the Ottoman authorities. The libels in Egypt and throughout the empire were largely due to commercial rivalry between Greeks and Jews. Everywhere Greeks were the foremost agitators. The Jews were also hated by Christian Syrians, Christian Arabs, and Armenians both for religious reasons and competition. In Egypt there were also local circumstances: there was a period of extreme tension as a result of the deposing of the ruler of the country, Ismail, by the Ottoman sultan and the accession of his son Taufik. The inhabitants of Egypt were also embittered against foreigners. Many articles imbued with hatred and defamation of foreigners appeared in the local press; Jews became the scapegoats for the hostility of the masses. With the establishment of British rule in Egypt (July 1882) the Jews lived there in greater security. In spring 1862 a blood libel occurred in Benghazi. Four Jews, including British and French subjects, were accused by Christians that on their return from "Blessing the Trees" out of town during Passover, they had mockingly raised the image of Jesus covered with blood. Following mass agitation by the Christian and Muslim population, both the British and the French local consular agents collaborated against the Jews, although some of these were their own subjects. The intervention of the British consul in Tripoli put an end to this libel. The imprisoned

Jews were released and the local consular agents were ordered to leave town. A blood libel broke out also in Ereẓ Israel during the lifetime of the *rishon le-Ẓion, ḥakham bashi* Raphael Meir *Panigel, in 1890, when two Jews of *Gaza were brought to Jerusalem and accused of ritual murder. These men had employed an Arab lad as a servant. The lad went to play with another Arab who owned a camel and as he toyed with a rifle, a bullet was fired from it and the camel owner was killed. The next-of-kin seized the lad and slaughtered him. The Jews then informed the tribunal of the details of the murder but some Muslims accused the Jews of the murder. They were arrested by the police, imprisoned in Jerusalem, and after interrogation were set free as they were foreign subjects. In 1892, Ereẓ Israel was stirred up by the publication of a work entitled "The Sounding of the Horn of Liberty by the Innocent," which was circulated in Egypt in Arabic and French and propagated anti-Jewish hatred. This book described how a Jewish rabbi was about to slaughter a Christian child to take his blood, which was to be employed for kneading the Passover *matzoh*. The pamphlet was also widely circulated in Palestine and came into the hands of many government officers and officials in Jerusalem. The *ḥakham bashi* R. Elijah M. Panigel, accompanied by a delegation, intervened with the pasha; the pasha ordered the immediate destruction of the pamphlet and prohibited reading it and spreading such rumors, as it was claimed that a child had also disappeared in Jaffa and his blood was to be employed for religious requirements. A Catholic publicly proclaimed that a famous rabbi who had converted had confirmed that Jews indeed employed Christian blood for the Passover ceremonies. The pasha immediately sent out orders to every town that this report was to be suppressed so as to prevent the outbreak of riots and disorders. The sultan then ordered his minister of education to extirpate this evil, as he was shocked that in his empire, a land of peace and tranquility, there were conspirators who incited Greek citizens against Jews who enjoyed his protection and published slanderous pamphlets whose contents were unfounded. All the pamphlets that were subsequently found were burned.

CONVERSION. Jews converted to Islam and, to a much lesser extent, to Christianity throughout the duration of the Ottoman Empire. Beyazid II compelled Jews to adopt Islam, but we do not know the precise number of these converts. His son, Selim I, gave them permission to return to Judaism, an irregular decision in a Muslim state. It seems that during the Ottoman period not more than 5% of the Jewish population converted to Islam, and only a few Jews converted to the Greek Orthodox and Catholic faiths. Some Jewish men converted to Islam for economic reasons or to enhance their professional status, while some women converted mainly to resolve social and personal problems or to marry non-Jews. In the 19th century the American Mission, the London Society for Promoting Christianity amongst Jews, and the Church of Scotland Mission were active in the larger Jewish communities of the Ottoman Empire, but only a few Jews converted. It seems that in the 19th century conversion to Islam and Christianity rose, apparently by about one percent. In that century, apart from one document that mentions fear of a mass conversion to Protestantism in the community of Izmir, around the year 1847, no other source indicates that there was any cause for concern. The converts came from all strata of society, but mainly from the lower classes. Some migrants were easy targets for conversion. Notwithstanding the increasing secularization of Jewish society in the second half of the 19th century, it would be fair to conclude that Jewish tradition and the traditional education most Jewish children received prevented the large-scale conversion of Jews. In the cases of forced conversion, the Ottoman policy was precise and further strengthened by the Tanzimat reforms. Local officials were ordered to prevent forced conversion, and forced converts were freed through government intervention.

Economic Life

The large Ottoman Empire, spread over three continents, with its maritime and land routes which connected it with many countries, provided extraordinary facilities for the activities of its Jewish inhabitants. All fields of economic activity, except the functions performed by members of the *askeri* class, were open to Jews. Jews could not be governors, military officials, and judges in the system of law and justice of the empire, but otherwise there was hardly any activity in which Jews did not participate. The sultans offered the old settlers, the refugees, and immigrants from Christian Europe all the facilities necessary to carry on commerce, foreign trade, industrial enterprises, and the development of firearms. Their knowledge of the foremost European languages – German, Italian, Spanish, and French – was an asset in commercial relations with Europe. Another important asset were the old established Jewish merchant firms in Muslim ports and capitals, like Alexandria, Cairo, Baghdad, Damascus, and Basra. This Ottoman economic policy explains the growth of Salonika, Safed, Izmir, Tunis, Algiers, and other cities as centers of Jewish trade and industry. The communities in these towns served in international commerce as new centers for the import of finished foreign goods and for the export of raw products and manufactures. Jewish merchants settled in Izmir only from the last quarter of the 16th century. The community particularly increased in the 17th century and the city became an entrepôt for international trade. Many *anusim* and Jews from Anatolia and Salonika settled in the city. The Levant trade carried on by the Jews of the Ottoman Empire by sea and land reached its height in the 16th century. Many Levantine Jews of Iberian origin settled in Italian cities, especially in Venice, and had the patronage of the Ottoman Empire. In 1534 the Pope gave those Jews trading rights in the town of Ancona, trying to attract the trade between Italy and the Ottoman Empire from Venice to his realm. At the end of the war between Venice and the Ottoman Empire in 1540, the Venetians officially recognized the presence of the Levantine merchants in Venice for the first time. The Jewish merchants also followed their trade with Ancona. In 1555 the new Pope, Paul IV, annulled the privileges of the Portuguese Jews in Ancona, and 24 of them were burnt after being tortured for months. Gracia Mendes and Joseph Nasi made efforts to put a Jewish ban on the city of Ancona, but Levantine Jews continued to trade there. Similar rights were granted to them in Florence, Ferrara, and Urbino in the middle of the 16th century. In this century the Ottoman Turks relied very heavily in commerce, diplomacy, and many fiscal matters on the Jews – the only community which possessed the necessary aptitudes and yet was not suspected of having treasonable sympathies for Christian powers. The commercial routes were under Jewish control, and ships loaded with goods belonging to Jews passed through the ports of the Mediterranean. The Jews used to insure their goods against piracy and shipwreck. A peculiarity of Jewish commerce was family partnership. Rich merchants with widespread commercial connections used to extend their business affairs by opening branches managed by their closest relatives, brothers, brothers-in-law, etc., in large ports and towns, even in foreign countries. A classic example is the firm of *Bacri and *Busnach in Algiers, who were the grain suppliers of France during the French Revolution. Also widespread were the occupation of agents (fattors); they received a fixed commission for their activities as buyers of raw materials or sellers of manufactured products. These agents used bills of exchange, "*polizza di cambio.*" Many Jews were employed in international trade as clerks, interpreters, accountants, dealers, and criers. The Jews of the Ottoman Empire developed trading techniques which enabled them to expand their activities both geographically and financially, and gave them an advantage over Muslim and Christian merchants. The existence of Jewish communities almost in every place gave the Jewish merchants possibilities to remain for long in Jewish communities afar and get help from them in difficult times.

Many Ottoman Jews bought from the embassies *berāts*, i.e., certificates, originally intended to protect locally recruited interpreters and consular agents. Such practices were extended especially in Egypt. However, the majority of Jews in the empire were not rich. In fact, the majority of the employees in the textile industry were poor home workers. The suppliers of export goods and distributors of imported products (fancy goods and the like) were small traders and peddlers who set up trade relations on a barter principle with the farmers in villages or made payments in advance and received their products at low cost. In a few communities, such as Aleppo, Cairo and Alexandria there were Jews who leased or managed agricultural property in the town's vicinity while other Jews were directly involved in farming. There existed also in some remote provinces such as eastern Anatolia, northern Iraq, Yemen and North Africa Jewish peasants and peasant communities. In the Galilee region of Ereẓ Israel in the 16th century there existed peasant Jews in 12 villages, such as Peki'in, Kefar Kanna, and Kefar Yasif. Among the trades in which the Jews in Spain had engaged, weaving took first place. The refugees found excellent opportunities in the Ottoman Empire with its backward industry – and manufactured cloth, which previously had had to be brought from abroad. This explains the rapid growth of Salonika, the largest center of the Spanish refugees, and the even more astonishing rise of Safed, the largest and most developed town in Ereẓ Israel in the 16th century, with a concentration of the second-largest Jewish population in Asia. The development of both communities was based on the manufacture of textiles and ready-made garments, although the raw material – wool – had to be imported, sometimes from abroad, and the product – the cloth and the garments – exported. The wool used in Salonika was sometimes bought in Macedonia and in other districts of the Balkans. This kind of wool was also brought to Edirne, and then forwarded to ports in the Sea of Marmara. From there it was sent once a year in a special ship to Safed by way of *Sidon or *Tripoli (Syria).

Other communities in the empire had their textile factories. The textile industry was mainly a domestic one. Spinning was done by women at home; weaving, in larger workshops. Dyeing had been a traditional Jewish occupation from the earliest times, and the art was more developed than in Europe. The wool industry of Salonika produced thousands of bolts of cloth for the Ottoman army, the palace, and export. The decline of this industry in Salonika and Safed impoverished the two communities from the last quarter of the 16th century. The Jews of Bursa played a prominent role in the city's international trade in silk and spices. A considerable number of Jews throughout the Middle East were engaged in the leather trade. They bought raw hides and exported them to Europe or finished them into leather, and Jewish tanners were famous for their products. The production of wine was a specifically Jewish occupation. As Muslims were the main consumers of alcoholic beverages, prohibited to them by the *Koran, dealing in that commodity was dangerous and was prosecuted by governmental authorities. Thus, very often in rabbinic literature there are references to ordinances promulgated by the Jewish authorities against the selling of wine to gentiles (Muslims). Another old Jewish occupation was dealing in precious stones, gold, silver, jewelry, and the making of jewels. It was a risky business, so jewelers were either very rich or very poor. The production and sale of refined gold was strictly controlled by the Ottoman authorities to prevent the flow of precious metals abroad. The farming of the money mints of Istanbul was often in Jewish hands in the 15th and 16th centuries. In some areas of the empire, e.g., the Barbary States, Yemen, and Iraq, the handicraft of making jewels was a Jewish monopoly until the 19th century and even later. Some branches of food industry that were connected with ritual precepts, e.g., the production of cheese, were in Jewish hands. In many parts of the empire money changing and the farming of government taxes, tolls, and monopolies (*iltizām*) were occupations in which Jews predominated from the 15th century. This was sometimes dangerous, as it aroused popular hostility. These occupations, sometimes connected with the functions of administrators of the treasury (**ṣarrāf bashi*) of the governor of the province and his banker, developed into important banking enterprises which controlled the growing industry in Ottoman cities. The first modern banks were opened in the 19th century. The pasha's banker during the 16th and 17th centuries in Egypt was known by the title Çelebi. He often combined the office of *ṣarrāf bashi* and several other official positions in the financial administration. Some Çelebis were executed. Jews in many cities were active as *sarrafs* (money changers). They were expert in all Ottoman and European currencies, and often were accused of clipping the edges of the coins that passed through their hands or cheating on their weight. Jews lent money to gentiles, but this profession was not as common with Jews in the Ottoman cities as it was in the cities of Christian Europe, because of the possibility of borrowing money from Muslim vakfs at low interest.

Foreign Jewish merchants and their representatives were protected against ill treatment by Ottoman government officials through the stipulations of the capitulations agreements which awarded them the same protection as their Christian compatriots. During the period of Western strength and Ottoman decline, the capitulations were transformed into a system of extraterritorial privilege and immunity.

The populations of some towns in Ereẓ Israel – Jerusalem, Safed, Hebron, and Tiberias – were so poor that they had to rely on financial assistance (*ḥalukkah*) from other towns in the empire and foreign countries. The Jewish communities and congregations throughout the empire supported the poor, but the poorest members could not take part in the public life of their communities because they did not pay taxes.

There were Jews in the Ottoman Empire, especially during the 16th century, who were compelled by the Ottoman authorities to buy flocks of sheep in Anatolia or the Balkans and bring them to Istanbul. Jews from Salonika and other cities had to undertake this activity, and there were Jews that went bankrupt from dealing with flocks. Jews in the empire worked at many crafts, such as tailors, carpenters, pharmacists, bakers, fishermen, mirror makers, glassmakers, printers, bookbinders, actors, dancers, musicians, and other crafts. Shops of Jews were situated either in Jewish neighborhoods or in markets among shops owned by Muslims and Christians. This situation existed in Istanbul, Aleppo, Izmir, Bursa, Jerusalem, and other cities. In Salonika, Jews worked also as porters and fishermen.

In Istanbul Jewish fishermen also sold wines. Many Jews, especially in Egypt and Aleppo during the 16th and 17th centuries, were active in farming port customs and custom houses, while others were *multazims*. From the last decade of the 16th century the Ottoman government changed the tax system, and tax farming was transferred to Muslims. Jews were now gradually reduced to secondary positions, as agents or managers of tax farms. This situation continued in the 17th century onward in cities such as Aleppo and Izmir. In spite of their diminished role, Jews continued in the 18th century to occupy an important position in the Ottoman economy and administration. There were Jews who served as contractors and purveyors for the military. In Egypt the rebellious Mamluk ruler Ali Bey al-Kabīr (ruled 1760–73) imposed heavy fines on the Jewish merchants, which destroyed them financially. It is obvious that many changes occurred in the economic and social structure of Ottoman Jewry in the space of 500 years or more. The rivalry of the powerful Greek and Armenian communities in the capital and the decline of the whole empire and its gradual dismemberment into national states in the Balkans and protectorates in Africa influenced the economic position of the Jews. The weakened economic structure of the empire and the empty government treasury, which was sometimes close to bankruptcy – felt all the more because of the corrupt bureaucracy – imposed heavy burdens on the weak taxpayers. From the 17th century the economic decline of the empire and the involvement of European traders in the international trade in dominions of the Ottoman Empire and their commerce with Western Europe reduced the economic opportunities of the Ottoman Jews. The competition between Jewish and Christian merchants who were supported by European ambassadors and consuls caused many Jews to be forced out of positions as principals in large-scale trade to secondary occupations as agents, brokers, and interpreters. In spite of the Jewish economic decline, in the 18th century Jewish traders living in Ottoman cities continued to trade with Livorno, Holland, England, and Leipzig. Hundreds of Jewish brokers in important commercial cities like Istanbul, Izmir, Aleppo, and Salonika received incomes from British, French, and Dutch merchants. Friction between Jews and non-Jews increased in the 19th century, and one of its results was an increase in blood libels (see above). In spite of the decrease of Jews in the trade of the 19th century, they owned large trading houses and firms in Salonika, Istanbul, Izmir, Aleppo, Egypt, and elsewhere, e.g., in Salonika the firms of the *francos* Alatini, Modiano, Fernandez, and Mizrahi, which traded not only in Macedonia but all over the empire.

Another factor which had a great influence on the economic life in the 18th and 19th centuries was the above-mentioned capitulations. The *francos* who lived particularly in the main cities of the empire became the local Jewish elite as a result of their privileges and political and economic rights. The *reʿāya*, the Ottoman nationals, were in a worse position in matters connected with daily life than the *ḥimāya*, the foreign citizens, or the local owners of *berāts*, as they were deprived of the protection of the European powers. At the end of the 18th century, the Ottomans tried to compete with the foreign consuls by selling *berāts* to the *reʿāya*, both Jews and Christians. These *berāts* conferred the privilege to trade with Europe, together with important legal, fiscal, and commercial privileges and tax exemptions. They enabled non-Muslim *reʿāya* to compete with foreign merchants. The Jews played no significant role in these transactions because of the general decline in their position. In the 19th century the positions of preeminence in international trade, with few exceptions, remained in the hands of the Greeks. These times also witnessed the general decay of Ottoman industry and its "Jewish" branches. A flood of cheap manufactured goods flowed into the Turkish market. The imported textiles competed successfully with local wool, cotton, and silk manufactures. In the beginning of the 20th century, the nationalism of the Young Turk movement, and later the rise of the Republic of *Turkey brought about socio-economic developments which changed the entire economic structure of Ottoman-Turkish Jewry.

THE ORGANIZATION OF JEWISH COMMUNITIES IN THE EMPIRE

Religious and Secular Administration (1453–1520)

The first chief rabbi in Istanbul was Moses *Capsali (1420–50) from the Romaniot population in Byzantium, and there are some traditions about him. According to the 17th century chronicler *Sambari (but no other source) Capsali sat in the sultan's *divan* at the side of the grand mufti and the patriarch. Sambari says that the sultan loved Capsali as his own soul, and describes Capsali as a very modest person. He notes that he was also responsible for collecting taxes from the Jews and delivering them to the sultan's treasury. Sambari's description contains many details that do not confirm what we know about the status of the Jews, especially in regard to the sultanic *divan*. According to the chronicler Elijah Capsali, who wrote his book *Seder Eliyahu Zuta* in 1523, was from Crete; Moses Capsali was the leading rabbi of the Istanbul community and *dayyan* of the Jewish community even before the Ottoman conquest. Mehmed II honored Capsali with royal garments, the privilege of riding a horse, and an escort of Ottoman dignitaries at home. Capsali became a welcome personage in the sultan's court. He went around the communities in Istanbul and collected charity to help the Spanish expellees. He had a sultanic decree which enabled him to confiscate property and have people arrested. He also acted against the young Jewish men who fraternized with the Janissaries. According to the mid-17th century chronicler David Conforte, all the other rabbis in Istanbul were subordinate to Capsali owing to the formal status the sultan had granted him. It seems that Capsali was officially appointed to the office of "the leader rabbi" of the Istanbul community by the Ottoman authorities. After the arrival of the Spanish expellees in the last decade of the 15th century the government abandoned the practice of appointing one religious-judicial leader for all the Jews in Istanbul, and in the last years of his rabbinate the fiscal power was transferred from Capsali to the ***kâhya* and later to other functionaries. It is clear that Capsali found it difficult to impose his authority over the Spanish congregations in the capital because he forced them to follow Istanbul rules and traditions. He was involved in a few disputes with other rabbis. In the 1490s the leaders of some Romaniot congregations sought to ban anyone who taught anything, even Greek philosophy, to the *Karaites. Only after their decision on the ban did they call for Capsali to make it official. He refused and denied the ban, but the ban was forcibly declared later in Capsali's presence. Those who were jealous of him wrote slanderous letters to Joseph *Colon in Italy and stirred up opposition to him. After Capsali's death, the rabbi Elijah *Mizraḥi, a famous Romaniot scholar and the head of the most important academy in Istanbul in that period, and also an expert in ethical and natural sciences, became the leader rabbi of the Romaniots in Istanbul. He was asked by the majority of the congregations in the capital in 1518 to ban the *kâhya* She'altiel and later to annul the ban. Rabbi Mizraḥi was also active before the Ottoman authorities when irregular taxes were demanded from the Jews of Istanbul. It appears that he received a formal confirmation of his authority from the Ottoman authorities, but there is no proof that he presided over the Spanish congregations, even though he was admired by them. He helped them and wrote decisions for them. Capsali tried to impose his authority over the Sephardim, but Mizraḥi decided that they could not be forced to act against the ruling of their rabbis. After Mizraḥi's death in 1526, the Romaniots had their own rabbis. The Sephardi congregations in the capital did not have a single rabbinical authority over all of the Sephardi rabbis. Owing to the existence of various ethnic groups, the Jews in the empire did not have a *ḥakham bashi* until 1835, in contrast to the existence of a Greek patriarch and an Armenian patriarch who were appointed by the sultans and represented the Greek and the Armenian nations in the empire during the entire Ottoman period.

It seems that the function of kâhya was not introduced until the final years of Capsali or after his death. The Ottoman rulers decided to rely on the kâhya and to deal with him in all financial and secular matters related to the Jews of Istanbul, including tax collection. This kâhya *Shealtiel (Salto) was a Spanish Jew, and in 1518, after many complaints of bribery and illegal arbitrary taxes had been lodged against him by the Jews, the community banned him and his sons from holding the position of kâhya or performing any other function involving contact with the Ottoman authorities. He was returned to office on April 29, 1520, by the leaders of the congregations and R. Elijah Mizraḥi. After the death of She'altiel no successor replaced him. During the Ottoman period there existed in Istanbul and other communities other kâhyas dealing with taxes and other matters before the authorities.

Communal Organization during the 16th–19th Centuries

The great scholar R. Joseph Ibn Lev describes the divisions and differences between the congregations of the empire after the arrival of the Spanish and Portuguese refugees as follows: "Even in Salonika, where everyone speaks the native language, when the refugees came each language group founded its own congregation and no one switches from one congregation to the other. Each congregation supports the poor speaking its language, each is inscribed separately in the king's register, and each seems to be a town unto itself" (Responsa, II n. 72). All those coming from a town or a definite region founded a special congregation (*kahal*) for themselves, spoke their own language, and paid taxes separately in accordance with their registration in the governmental registers. In the 1560s R. Moses Almosnino described the Jewish community of Salonika as a "republic." Each congregation had a secular administration run by elected *parnasim* and treasurers, whose primary responsibilities were to supervise the collection of taxes and see to all internal political, administrative, and financial matters. Sometimes the lay leaders in some communities were also granted judicial authority. This executive council was composed of six to 12 members, elected for one to three years at the most. The elite of the congregations – the wealthy and the nobility – aided the lay leaders in the running of public affairs, and it was from this class that the lay leaders were elected. Generally the poor in the communities lacked representation. Every congregation had a religious administration consisting of the *ḥakham* (rabbi) of the the *kahal* (congregation) or *kehillah* (community), who served principally as the *dayyan* of his congregation. Sometimes he also headed it, like Rabbi Joseph *Caro in Safed. Frequently he was called *marbiẓ Torah*, *dayyan*, or *rosh ve-kaẓin*; and he taught and performed various religious functions. In the Musta'rab communities, the head of the community was called *dayyan*. Sometimes the rabbi held all of these positions, sometimes they were divided up. Other officials were the treasurer (*gizbar*), *gabbai* of the synagogue, and tax assessors (*ma'arikhim*). Each congregation also had officials serving as readers and cattle slaughterers; they were paid salaries from the communal funds Each congregation had institutions such as a synagogue, *talmud torah*, yeshivah, and *bet din*, as well as charitable societies such as *Bikur Kholim* – visiting the sick, and extending help to the poor, a burial society (*Hevrat Kbarim, Ḥesed shel Emet*), ransom society (*pidyon shevuyim*), and others. If the members of the congregation were few, then two or three joined together to found educational institutions such as a *talmud torah*. The well-known Great Talmud Torah of Salonika was used jointly by the children of all the congregations in town.

The congregations and the communities based their economic, cultural, and religious life upon *haskamot* and *takkanot* (ordinances, regulations) instituted by their rabbis, scholars, and communal leaders, together with appointed members, e.g., regulations not to transfer membership from one congregation to another; agreements relating to many fields of private and public life, such as the appointment of lay and spiritual leaders and their duties; an agreement that no one may be married without the presence of ten adult male Jews, one of whom shall be the *ḥakham*, and that should anyone marry in any other way the marriage is to be considered void. The best known of the agreed *takkanot* is that relating to the renting of houses: If anyone rented a house or shop from a gentile, then no other Jew could enter that house or shop as long as it was rented to the other Jew, and even if the Jew vacated the rented house or shop, no other Jew was allowed to enter it until the passage of three years from the day it was vacated. These are called *Takkanot ha-Ḥazakah*. There were different regulations about the inheritance of women. Individuals opposing the regulations were placed under a ban and excommunicated. Frequently in medium-sized and large communities the religious leaders met and decided on new regulations as results of new and burdensome realities. Sometimes these regulations dealt with the division of taxes among the congregations. There were many objections to these regulations, and the rabbis dealt with the question of how to enforce them, especially when wealthy persons objected. The Jewish courts of law, *battei din*, had the authority to deal with civil and religious matters, but many Jews also turned to the *bet din* in cases concerning money matters (*dinei mamonot*). The Jewish courts of the empire had to turn to the state authorities to enforce their decisions, for on occasion an offender did not follow their ruling. In the larger communities there also existed higher Jewish courts of law. *Berurei Averot* (*Memunei Averot*) committees existed in a few communities, such as Istanbul, Salonika, Sofia, Bursa, Magnesia, and Safed during the 16th and 17th centuries. Their members dealt independently with religious and moral offenders through the agency of the local *bet din*. In Izmir there was a *berurei ha-kenasot* council which dealt with such problems. In spite of the regulations of many communities forbidding Jews to turn to Muslim courts of law, it was acceptable among the Jews to appeal to these courts. Sometimes the communal leaders and the local *dayyanim* appealed to the Muslim courts of law to enforce their decisions. In the 17th and 18th centuries, in some of the large communities, such as Salonika, Izmir, and Edirne, the congregations chose a local chief rabbi, and sometimes the office of chief rabbinate was shared between two or even three rabbis. In Izmir from the 17th century until the middle of the 19th century there functioned a *dayyan* for *dinei mamonot* and a *dayyan* for *Issur ve-Heter* problems.

DISPUTES BETWEEN CONGREGATIONS AND INSIDE THE COMMUNITIES (15TH–19TH CENTURIES). After the arrival of the expellees to the Ottoman Empire, friction and disputes arose between the congregations, especially between the Romaniots and Spanish and Portuguese refugees. The Spanish refugees regarded themselves as more learned, cultured, and of good descent and wanted to dominate the communities, while the Romaniots and their famous scholars regarded themselves as more important, since they were the permanent and earlier settlers and had admitted the former. An additional cause of friction was the differences in their customs, one of the many being the matter of *sivlonot* (presents sent by a man to his betrothed). In the Romaniot customs this is seen as indicating that *kiddushin* may have taken place; this is not so, however, according to the Sephardi custom (see *Betrothal). On the death of Rabbi Elijah Mizraḥi a conflict occurred between Sephardim and Romaniots about the Jewish custom of chanting elegies on the eve of the Hebrew new moon. The Sephardim has done this even when a new moon fell on a Saturday, and the Romaniots responded that mourning on Saturday was strictly forbidden. The Romaniots published in 1510 the Romaniot *maḥzor* and in 1557 a Pentateuch was published with translations into Spanish and Greek, in Hebrew characters. In the beginning of the 16th century the Romaniots and the Sephardim disputed the Ashkenzi and Romaniot custom of giving the rabbis ordination ("*semikhah*"). There was also a disagreement between the Romaniot and the Iberian Jews over the question of whether it was permitted to eat a ritually slaughtered animal in which there was a *sirkha* or adhesion of the lobes of the lung. During the 16th and 17th centuries many congregations fought against individuals or groups that joined other congregations, or established new ones, and regulations forbidding this act were issued by many congregations and communities. In Istanbul the policy of the congregations in the 16th century permitted the individuals to join other congregations, but not before tax payment time. In many Ottoman Jewish communities instability was a widespread phenomenon. Even the Romaniot community of Ioannina split into two in the second half of the 16th century, and each congregation established two different burial societies. There were many struggles between congregations in Greek and Turkish communities, such as Salonika, Izmir, Cairo, Arta, Ioannina, Patras, Navpaktos (Lepanto), Bursa, and Safed. There were conflicts between congregations over new, wealthy members. Many disputes resulted from the form of tax collection. In the majority of the communities in the 16th–19th centuries the Sephardim were dominant and dictated communal life. On the other hand, there were communities such as Arta and Ioannina where the Romaniots were dominant. Generally the Italian and Sicilian congregations cooperated with the Spanish ones, and in the middle of the 16th century the Spanish prayer book was accepted by a majority of the communities. The Musta'rab congregations in Ereẓ Israel, Syria, and Egypt were autonomous throughout the Ottoman period. During all the Ottoman period there was strife between the rich, middle class, and the poor in the communities and the congregations. Most of these were the result of the unwillingness of the poor and the middle-class members to pay taxes to the Ottoman authorities or to the Jewish community in the amount requested by the community leaders. Such disagreements increased during the 19th century and caused tension in communities such as Istanbul, Izmir, Salonika, Damascus, and others. These tensions often erupted into disputes and quarrels. For instance, in Izmir in 1840–42, 1847, and the 1860s the leadership of the community was in the hands of the rich, many of whom were *francos*. The poor hoped that the communal taxes would be reduced, but on the contrary, the indirect tax paid on the meat "*gabela*" was increased. The document "*Shav'at 'Aniyim*" ("Cry of the Poor"), written by the poor in 1847, and other documents tell the story of these disagreements, and show that all efforts of spiritual leaders, including the local *ḥakham bashi*, Ḥayyim Palagi, to improve the situation of the poor failed. These struggles led to the temporary removal of Rabbi Palagi and a turning of poor people to the missionaries. It was characteristic of the Ottoman authorities and most of the religious communal hierarchy to support the rich, and the oppression of the poor in the community continued for many years. Similar controversies broke out in Salonika in 1872 and in Istanbul during 1880–84. The Ottoman reforms influenced the internal life of the communities and especially diminished the authority of the traditional spiritual leaders. From the 1860s more rabbis joined the poor, and local leadership was transferred to the hands of modern leaders, most of whom did not have personal economic interests involved in leading the community. The flourishing of the Jewish press also influenced this process.

THE ḤAKHAM BASHI. The Armenian and Greek Orthodox communities (millets) in the capital had patriarchs – acknowledged and confirmed by the Ottoman authorities – who supervised all the congregations. Only the Jewish millet had no confirmed rabbis. A total of 347 years had passed since the death of the chief rabbi of Istanbul Moses Capsali. In January 1835 the sultan Mahmud II (1808–39) confirmed R. Abraham ha-Levi as *ḥakham bashi* in Istanbul, a gesture made at the request of the Jewish subjects of the sultan in Istanbul. They had no Christian European powers behind them and were jealous of the honor of official confirmation accorded by the government to the Greek and Armenian patriarchs. This was in fact a turning point in the policy of the Ottoman authorities, which hitherto had not interfered in the internal affairs of the Jewish community and for centuries past had given no official status to its representatives. It was also an Ottoman interest to promote the principle and image of a pluralistic Ottoman society, so that it became a matter of state interest to advance the position of the Jewish community and grant it greater prominence. The new position meant that the *hakham bashi* was now regarded as the civil and religious head of the Jewish community, as well as its official representative to the authorities. The original copies or authentic texts of the *berāt hümayun* (imperial confirmation of appointments; occurring from 1835 onward), which were also granted to chief rabbis in Edirne, Salonika, Izmir, Bursa, Jerusalem, and Damascus, show that the significance and consequences of this policy went beyond mere confirmation of appointments. It contained an official recognition of the Jewish millet. As mentioned above, Abraham ha-Levi became *ḥakham bashi* of Istanbul in 1836. He appeared at the sultan's court in official garb, accompanied by ten of the community notables and thousands of other Jews, swore loyalty to the sultan and the monarchy, and paid his tax. The sultan handed him the *berāt* of his appointment. This *ḥakham bashi*, however, was not suitable for office, and after one and a half years R. Samuel Ḥayyim was appointed in his stead. The latter was an erudite rabbi who headed a yeshivah in Balat (a suburb of Istanbul). At the end of a year of service, he was relieved of office by the government because he was an Austrian national. He remained, however, as a chief *dayyan*. Moses Prisco (1839–41) was elected in his place, being called "the old rabbi" because of his advanced age. *Ḥakham bashis* were also appointed in the provinces of the empire: in Ereẓ Israel, Cairo, Alexandria, Baghdad, Yemen, Libya, Sarajevo, and elsewhere. In fact, the *rav ha-kolel* continued to be regarded by the Jews of Istanbul as their religious and spiritual leader, while the office of the *ḥakham bashi* was seen as an external imposition and as far as the community was concerned it was only ceremonial and representative. In time, this office gained great prestige and importance and came to be held by renowned scholars, such as Jacob Avigdor (1860–63) and Yakir Geron (1863–72) in Istanbul and by 1864, the office of *ḥakham bashi* appears to have completely supplanted in Istanbul the older office of *rav ha-kolel*. In other cities the office of *ḥakham bashi* was held by famous decisors, such as Ḥayyim Palagi from Izmir. Between the years 1863 and 1908/9 the title of the chief rabbi was *kaymakam ḥakham bashi*, and from 1909 the last *ḥakham bashi* in the Ottoman Empire, Ḥayyim Nahoum, again held the title *ḥakham bashi*.

CULTURAL LIFE

The Spiritual Revival in the 16th Century

With the growing influx of refugees and immigrants, the Ottoman Empire became a center of Torah study. The yeshivot of Salonika, Istanbul, Safed, and Jerusalem took the places of the splendid and well-known yeshivot of Castilia. Istanbul, called by scholars "a large city of scholars and scribes," maintained Torah institutions and magnificent yeshivot, such as the yeshivah of Elijah Mizraḥi, where both sacred and secular studies were pursued; the yeshivah of Joseph Ibn Lev, in which great talmudic scholars studied and which was supported financially by Doña Gracia Mendes; the yeshivah of Elijah ha-Levi, the pupil of Elijah Mizraḥi, who headed his teacher's yeshivah; and in the beginning of the 17th century the yeshivot headed by Rabbi Joseph Mitrani (of Trani; "Maharit"), supported by the wealthy philanthropist Abraham ibn Yaish and his sons and by the wealthy Jacob Ancawa (Elnekave). Pupils of Joseph Trani served as rabbis in towns of the empire. Yeshivot also existed in Izmir, Bursa, Angora, Nikopol, Tirya, and those in Adrianople after the expulsion from Spain included the magnificent yeshivah of Joseph Fasi. Salonika became a center of Jewish learning. The poet Samuel *Usque called it "a metropolis of Israel, city of righteousness, loyal town, mother of the Jewish nation like Jerusalem in its time." *Talmud torahs* and yeshivot flourished there whose names were famous throughout the Jewish world and brought scholars together from all parts of the empire, such as the yeshivah of Jacob ibn Ḥabib and his son Levi b. Ḥabib and those of Joseph Taitaẓak, Samuel de Medina, Joseph Ibn Lev (before he went to Istanbul), Isaac *Adarbi, and others. Similarly well known was the Great Talmud Torah of Salonika, which contained many hundreds of pupils whom it also clothed and fed. The heads of the aforementioned yeshivot and their scholars left a ramified responsa literature which served as a foundation for the studies of **posekim* and *dayyanim*, as well as an important, and sometimes the sole, source for the history of their times. With the expulsion from Spain, and even before it, Safed became a great center for immigration of Spanish refugees. The town grew and its economic development brought spiritual growth in its wake. Safed attracted scholars from many countries. It developed into a great center of Torah, Kabbalah, ethics (*musar*), and *piyyut*, becoming an important spiritual center in Ereẓ Israel, as well as for the Diaspora. Important and well-known Yeshivot were founded there, among them the Yeshivah of Jacob Berab; Berab taught a generation of outstanding pupils, among whom were four ordained pupils (see **Semikhah*) who also headed well-known yeshivot: Joseph Caro, the author of the Shulḥan Arukh, Moses Mitrani (of Trani; "Mabit"), Abraham *Shalom, and Israel di *Curiel. Other famous yeshivot were headed by Moses Galante, Elisha Galiko, Yom Tov Zahalon, Samuel de Uzeda, and Solomon Sages. Not only local students but also scholars who came from other regions of the empire studied in their yeshivot. The yeshivot obtained their economic support from the wealthy and from charities in all parts of the empire. (For further information see *Safed.) In Jerusalem there existed before the Ottoman conquest two yeshivot founded by the **nagid* Isaac ha-Cohen Sulal and, after the expulsion, in 1521 one yeshivah was headed by R. David Ibn Shushan who was helped by the kabbalist Abraham ben Eliezer ha-Levi, and the other yeshivah by R. Israel Ashkenazi. Other yeshivot in Jerusalem during the 16th century were headed by R. Levi Ibn Habib, R. Joseph Korkos, and R. Bezalel Ashkenazi. The Sephardi yeshivot taught according to the learning system of "*iyyun*" which was developed in Spain's yeshivot.

Aside from these, yeshivot and places of study in which esoteric lore, *Kabbalah, and the Zohar were the main subjects of study were established in Safed during this period. The students prostrated themselves at the graves of the pious in the fields of Safed and its vicinity. Among its outstanding scholars were Solomon ha-Levi Alkabeẓ, Moses *Cordovero, the heads of the pre-Lurianic Kabbalah and the well-known Isaac Luria Ashkenazi (Ha-Ari), the founder of the Lurianic Kabbalah and teacher of many disciples, among them Ḥayyim *Vital. There were also kabbalists and heads of yeshivot in Safed from North Africa, such as Joseph Magrabi (ha-Ma'aravi), Joseph b. Tabul, Masyud Azulai, Solomon ha-Ma'aravi (Abunaha), and others. The yeshivah of Moses ibn Machir was located at *Ein Zeitim, near Safed. Jerusalem's development after the Ottoman conquest in 1516 was slow compared to that of Safed. The economic situation was unstable, but the heads of the yeshivot and the rabbis of the town strove to prevent the town from being deserted. After the conquest, the spiritual hegemony passed from the Musta'rabs to the Sephardim. Doña Gracia Mendes founded a yeshivah of scholars in Tiberias, most of whom came from Safed. They were maintained by her appropriations and were thus able to devote all their time to Torah study. In addition to her contributions, there was a society in Istanbul for the benefit of the yeshivah. At the end of the 16th century, when Tiberias was abandoned, this yeshivah was also closed.

A major development in the standing of the yeshivot and the study of Torah occurred in Egypt. The Spanish refugees who settled there developed the Torah institutions which had long served the dwellers in Egypt itself, now attracting to them pupils from other places. Among the well-known yeshivot were those of David ibn Abi Zimra (Radbaz), Isaac Berab, Bezalel Ashkenazi, Jacob Castro, and Abraham Monzon.

In the 16th and 17th centuries numerous and renowned sages concentrated in the Ottoman Jewish communities. The broad intellectual class in the 16th century, as described in many sources, was an alert and lively one, and its needs dictated to the rabbis the style, form, and frequently the content of their literary work. This activity produced dozens of halakhic books, especially responsa literature, and primarily works of an exegetic and homiletic nature. Prominent sages such as the rabbis Meir Arama (d. c. 1545), Joseph Taitazak, Solomon le-Bet ha-Levi, Moses Almosnino, and many others prepared numerous anthologies and collections of commentaries. While the literature of the 16th century had a propensity for dealing with philosophical issues, by the end of the century and during the 17th a more central role was claimed by talmudic midrash and legend and their interpretation. The leading codifier of Jewish law was Rabbi Joseph Caro (1488–1575), whose magnum opus, *Beit Yosef*, a codification of all Jewish law, organized as a commentary on the *Arba'ah Turim*, was published in 1535 and the digest of this work, the *Shulḥan Arukh*, was printed for the first time in Venice in 1564–65. The scholars in the 16th century outside Ereẓ Israel devoted themselves mainly to philosophy and the sciences. Kabbalah was limited to a small group in communities such as those of Istanbul, Salonika, Edirne, Bursa, and others. This trend changed in the 17th and 18th centuries as a result of the popularization of the *Zohar* in the Jewish communities and the profound influence of the kabbalists and kabbalistic *minhagim* among the communities of the empire. Between 1750 and 1900 intellectual life existed primarily in the great communities of the empire. In a majority of the small communities only low- ranking rabbis, "*kelei kodesh*," served as ritual slaughterers and cantors, and frequently also as teachers (*melamdim*). In this period 275 scholars in Greece, Turkey, and the Balkans wrote 450 books, the majority in Izmir, Istanbul, and Salonika, and others in Edirne, Rhodes, Bursa, and other communities in Greece, Turkey, and the Balkans. Dozens of books were also written in Egypt, Ereẓ Israel, and Syria. During this period the number of the yeshivot were rapidly reduced and most were in the homes of well-to-do Jews. Most of those yeshivot were small and their students devoted themselves only to Torah learning, and did not learn philosophy and the sciences.

Heterodox Spiritual Trends among Ottoman Jewry

The study of the Lurianic Kabbalah spread during the first half of the 17th century throughout the Ottoman Empire, and among its heterodox outgrowths was the *Shabbatean movement. The persecutions and pogroms in the *Ukraine and *Poland, on the one hand, and a decline in the study of **halakhah* accompanied by the spread of the study of esoteric lore and Kabbalah, on the other, led to the rise of messianic hopes, which were given a strong stimulus with the appearance of *Shabbetai Ẓevi. At the time it was believed that the advent of the messiah and the coming of the redemption would take place in 1666. After his meeting with *Nathan of Gaza in 1665, on his way back to Jerusalem after fulfilling the office of a Jerusalem emissary, Shabbetai Ẓevi proclaimed himself the messiah who would redeem his people on 5 Sivan 5426 (June 18, 1666) and announced his intention to depose the sultan. He traveled from Jerusalem to other communities such as Aleppo and Izmir, and on December 30, 1665, sailed to Istanbul, taking special advantage of the fact that the royal court had then been transferred to Edirne. Nathan became Shabbetai Ẓevi's foremost pupil and adherent and aroused messianic expectations in Jewish communities throughout Europe and the Ottoman Empire. Many Jews made preparations to dispose of their property, rent ships, and travel to the Holy Land. Shabbetai Ẓevi himself was excommunicated in Jerusalem in 1665. In Izmir he appeared with his secretary, Samuel *Primo, and was supported by the majority of the community leaders and Jewish residents. His appearance in Istanbul and his royal behavior aroused the anger of the sultan. Shabbetai Zevi was brought before the council (*divan*) of the Grand Vizier Ahmed Köprülü, who decided to imprison him in Gallipoli, in a comfortable prison, including visitors. In September 1666, Shabbetai was transferred to Edirne, where he was brought again before the *divan* and, in order to save his life, converted to Islam with a group of his followers who imitated him. The descendants of those apostates numbered hundreds of families and formed a separate sect, called *Doenmeh (Turk. "apostate"). Members of the sect lived in Edirne, Istanbul, Salonika, and Izmir. They continued to believe in Shabbetai Ẓevi as the messiah. The appearance of Shabbetai Ẓevi and his companions humiliated the Jews of the empire, whose status had in any case declined in comparison with that of previous times. The movement gave rise to apostasy, disappointment, and despair, undermining the important economic positions held by the Jews. The remaining Shabbateans did not cease their activities. The Shabbatean emissary Abraham Miguel *Cardozo went to Istanbul in order to influence its rabbis to adhere to Shabbateanism. In Izmir, Nehemiah *Ḥayon and his friends were excommunicated. Jacob *Frank, a pseudo-messiah, a late adherent of the Shabbatean movement and founder of the Frankist movement, traveled from Poland to Volhynia and then to Turkey, where he lived in Izmir and Salonika, becoming friendly with the Doenmeh. Not finding Salonika favorable, he returned, however, to Poland. The Shabbateans and their adherents also penetrated into Egypt, Persia, Iraq, *Kurdistan, and North Africa. Various customs were introduced in these places under the influence of this movement, and they added to the prayers in Kurdistan the following words: "As instituted by our messiah, exalted be his majesty." The Shabbetai Ẓevi affair affected the status of rabbinic authority, and both rabbis and lay leaders were impelled to strengthen and consolidate the community's central institutions.

Social and Family Life

The Jewish males carried out extensive religious and social activities in the synagogues. Many well-to-do and middle-class Jews were active in the charity institutions of the community. The Jews spent most of their social life among their Jewish friends, participating in wedding, bar-mitzvah ceremonies, funerals, and memorial gatherings. It was not common to have social relationships with Muslims and Christians; such relations were generally limited to business contacts.

Family life in the communities were influenced by the realities of Ottoman urban life, especially crowded living conditions, poor public sanitation, endemic diseases, and traditional Jewish family norms. In the 16th century the breakup of the Spanish Jewish family, stemming from the expulsion, had a traumatic influence on family life. The main goal of family life among all Jewish groups was to rebuild strong families and to produce many live children and descendants. Every group like the Romaniots, Ashkenazim, Sephardim, and Musta'rabim had special family manners and customs, but the normal behavior of all groups followed the *halakhah* in all Jewish communities. The families were patriarchal at all levels of society. In spite of the fact that some women did earn a livelihood from various professions and crafts, interest-bearing loans or real estate, the majority stayed at home. Even those women who were economically active had the outlook of women in general and found their personal satisfaction in the sphere of the home. At the same time women were cognizant of their ability to protect their rights and to limit any infringement of them. The accepted woman's destiny, which was endorsed by male society, was to find total fulfillment in home and family life. In no community until the 19th century was higher education a part of a woman's life. She freed her husband to go about his business, principally to earn a livelihood. Most women invested their personal funds with close relatives, usually a husband, son, or brother. They seldom left their houses, and when they did, veiled faces and garments covering them from head to toe was the order of the day. Women from all Jewish groups were raised to expect arranged marriage at an early age, generally when 13–16 years old. Even divorcees and widows, especially young ones, hoped to remarry and invested much effort to achieve this. The men also married very young, at around 16–18. There were also cases of child marriage among girls, especially orphans. Polygamy was usual among the Musta'rabim; this phenomenon existed to a small extent in Spanish and Italian society as well. In spite of the legal agreement that the Sephardi husband not take a second wife during the life of his first, the Jewish courts frequently permitted the man to do so, particularly in cases where the couple was childless after 10 years of marriage. In the majority of these cases the Sephardi woman preferred divorce. There were also cases of polygamy among the Romaniots. The Musta'rabic woman was also less afraid of *yibbum*, whereas her Sephardi counterpart generally preferred *ḥalizah*. It was a common phenomenon in communities for a woman to marry her sister's widower. In neither community did divorce carry a stigma; many women demanded divorce on their own initiative.

A woman depended on her family to protect her rights at marriage, and most women knew how to guard their rights and possessions. The families took charge of the young couples, and usually the new couple lived in the first years after marriage with the husband's family. The Jewish courts of law dealt with many cases of abandoned women (*agunot*). Generally the *agunah* was lacking all basic necessities, and the Jewish courts of law made efforts to release the woman from this miserable status, in order to enable her to remarry. The ketubbah of every woman had a few special clauses depending on ethnic origin, such as forbidding polygamy in the Spanish ketubbah, inheritance regulations, such as the Toledo ones in the Spanish ketubbah, the inheritance regulations in the Romaniot ketubbah and the regulations in Ashkenazi marriage contracts. The Musta'rabim also wrote their own inheritance regulations. Jewish society coped with many problems of parenthood and child bearing, because of the prevalence of divorce, widowhood, and the phenomenon of men and women marrying a second or third time. Generally an average-sized Jewish family numbered three children. There was a high rate of miscarriages and stillborn babies. Marriages of cousins were very common. The first marriage was arranged by the family, and most men after divorce or widowhood found new mates. Women also chose to marry again. Sometimes Jews turned in family matters to the Muslim courts of law, especially in order to force divorce, or in matters of inheritance. Jewish boys and girls were usually given traditional and the more common names of heads of households that were found among the Jews of Sephardi and Portuguese origin. Other names were of Romaniot, Italian, Arabic, and Turkish origin. The process of the Europeanization among the Ottoman Jews during the second half of the 19th century had a direct effect on the secularization of Jewish society, so that many French and other European names entered the local nomenclature. Nevertheless, most of the Jewish babies were still given traditional names. Most of the men's names were Hebrew, and approximately 30 percent of the women's names were Hebrew. Jewish society insisted on high standards of personal and public morals and kept the traditional *halakhah* and *minhagim*. A majority of the communities' members behaved according to these obligations. Even so, there were cases of moral transgression, and the communal regulations point out cases of Jews who loved music, festivities, luxury, gambling, and an extravagant life. There were cases of men and women who had intimate relations with Christians and Muslims. The Jews in the cities of the empire had a tendency of their own choice to group together in Jewish quarters, but there were also Jews who dwelt with non-Jews. Generally, Jewish quarters were very crowded. The majority of houses were built of wood and brick, and every century there broke out fires in which hundreds of Jewish houses and their possessions were burned. The well-to-do Jews lived in large houses in the Jewish quarter, and sometimes built palaces among those of the Muslims and Christians, but a majority of the Jewish residents lived in densely populated residential areas. Many buildings had three floors or more. Most houses had an open courtyard in the center and a cellar for storing wine, cheese, wheat, and other foodstuffs. Very poor families lived in only one room.

Ladino Literature

Some books in Judeo-Spanish (or Ladino) written in Hebrew script were published in the cities of the empire soon after the arrival of the expellees. One of the books was the translation of the Pentateuch in Istanbul in 1547 at the press of Eliezer Gershon Soncino. Other famous Ladino works published in Istanbul were an account of the city of Istanbul by Rabbi Moses Almosnino, *Regimiento de la Vida*, which was published in 1564. In spite of the scarcity of such works during the 16th and 17th centuries, a revival of Ladino literature occurred in the 18th century, although a serious decline occurred in the cultural condition of the Jews in the empire. The situation had so deteriorated that a majority could not read the sacred literature. As a consequence books began to be published in the Spanish vernacular spoken by the Jews who came from Spain, the *Ladino. For a long period it was the only language spoken by them, because they never mastered Turkish. Religious literature was printed in Hebrew, however, and the presses in Salonika, Istanbul, and Izmir were renowned for the Hebrew books they published.

The spiritual leaders waged a fierce struggle for the preservation of Judaism. This effort was expressed in the popular anthology *Me-'Am Lo'ez* ("From a Foreign Nation") by R. Jacob b. Meir *Culi (1689–1732), the most eminent Ladino author. Original books on ethics in Ladino, or translations of books from Hebrew to Ladino, became a favorite genre during the 18th and 19th centuries. Published works in Ladino deal with *maḥzorim*, *siddurim*, *kinot*, kabbalistic works, midrashim, ethical works, biblical commentaries written by Sephardi commentators, and a poem for Purim.

Among the published works were Abraham de Toledo's popular Judeo-Spanish poem "La Coplas de Joseph ha-Ẓaddik" (1732), which had some 400 quatrains with its own peculiar melody; "Meshivat Nefesh" (1743) – a translation and commentary by Shabbetai Vitas of the poems of Solomon ibn *Gabirol, and numerous works and translations of historical, scientific, and religious studies, including *Sulkhan Arukh*, and the compositions of the great poet Rabbi Moshe Faro (d. 1776) *Suzikar Peshrevi* and *Shadarban*. During various periods between the middle of the 18th century and the end of the 19th century, pamphlets of folk songs, poems on historical subjects connected with Jewish festivals and on secular subjects, works on Jewish and general history, as well as *Shevilei Olam* ("Paths of the World"), a compilation of wisdom and knowledge, were published. History textbooks were translated from Hebrew into Ladino, the translators preserving the original Hebrew titles. Novels and stories, such as *Ahavat Ẓiyyon* by *Mapu, and works by M. Mendelssohn and others were also translated from Hebrew.

The education of the Jewish population in the Balkan countries and in the Turkish-speaking provinces of the empire (Anatolia) was rooted in newspapers, literary periodicals, and original and translated works published in Ladino. According to the bibliography of Moses Gaon and Avner Levi, over 300 newspapers and magazines were published in that language during a period of 100 years. The publishing of literature and periodicals in Ladino was mainly concentrated in Salonika, Istanbul, and Izmir, the last of which was the cradle of Ladino literature. The first attempts to publish Ladino newspapers in Izmir were made during the middle of the 18th century, but these were short-lived. The first weekly to be published in Izmir in 1842 was called *La Buena Esperanza*, edited by Raphael Uziel, but it ceased to appear after a few issues. In 1846 a second attempt was made by the same editor; this time his publication lasted half a year. In 1874 a new weekly under the same title began to appear and its publication continued for 40 years. Its editor was Aaron Joseph Hazzan. In 1889 a newspaper named *La Nouvelliste*, which remained in existence 30 years, was founded. Another weekly, *El-Messeret*, which exhibited a Turkish nationalistic tendency, began to appear in 1897 in Ladino and Turkish. The continuation of *Me-'Am Lo'ez* by Isaac Magriso (from the end of Exodus) and a translation of Esther appeared in Izmir (1864). In Istanbul from the 19th century most books, pamphlets, and literary magazines were published in Ladino. The most important publisher was Benjamin Raphael b. Joseph, who between 1889 and 1928 produced at least 30 books. Among the many periodicals that appeared in Istanbul the oldest were *Journal Israélite* (1841–60), by Ezekiel Gabbai; *La Luz de Israel* ("The Light of Israel"), by Leon Ḥayyim Castro, published from 1853; *El Tiempo*, whose first editor (1871) was Isaac R. *Camondo and last (from 1889), David *Fresco, the greatest of the Ladino writers. The *Al-Sharkiyah* ("The Eastern") appeared from 1869 in four languages: Ladino, Turkish, Greek, and Bulgarian (all in Rashi script). The following newspapers and weeklies should also be mentioned: *El Nacional* (1871), *El-Telegrafo* (1872), and *El Amigo de la Familia* (1881).

The pioneer of the Ladino press in Salonika was Judah Nehamah (1826–1899), who published in 1865 the first scientific monthly in Ladino, *El Lunar* ("The Month"). It contained articles on history, philosophy, astronomy, law, commerce, and art. It published biographies of Jewish personalities and a translation of a history of the universe (as a serial). *La Epoca* (from 1875) was a periodical devoted to political, commercial, and literary subjects. In 1910 it became a daily and the elite of the Jewish authors in Salonika contributed to it. The newspapers *Selanik* appeared (1869) as an official organ of the Ottoman government in four languages (but in Hebrew characters): Turkish, Greek, Bulgarian, and Ladino. It was issued by the order of Midhat Pasha, called the father of the Revolution of the Young Turks. He was appointed governor of Salonika in 1873. Among the periodicals which appeared in other towns, one that is important as a source for Jewish history is the *Yosef Da'at* ("The Progress") edited by Abraham Danon in Edirne (1888). Many other periodicals and newsletters in Ladino, Greek, Turkish, French, and Italian, which began to appear at the end of the 19th century and later, belong to contemporary history. In 1899 Avram Leyon and Avram Ibrahim Naon edited in Istanbul a new journal, *Ceride-i Lisan*, in Turkish with the purpose of making Turkish a living language among the Jews; however it met with only limited success. In Sofia, *El Amigo del Puevlo* was published in Ladino from 1890 to 1899. Baruch Mitrani published the monthly Hebrew-Ladino *Be-Mishol ha-Keramim* in the 1890s. *La Boz de Israel* was put out in Bulgarian and Ladino by Yehoshua Kalev after 1896. *El Progreso* appeared twice weekly, starting in 1897. *La Verdad* was published by Abraham Tajir from 1898 to 1910. Ladino journals were published also in Jerusalem and Egypt.

POWERFUL JEWS, PHYSICIANS, COUNSELORS, LORDS, AND MEDIATORS IN THE OTTOMAN EMPIRE

Jewish physicians and state councilors were active in the sultan's court throughout the Ottoman period, especially in the 15th and 16th centuries. Among the important ones was Jacob Pasha (Hekim Yakub, the physician to the sultan Murad II and his son Mehmed II). He was granted tax exemptions for himself and his descendants in perpetuity. Jacob converted to Islam at an advanced age and was appointed vizier before his death in the early 1480s. At the same time (c. 1481) the Portuguese physicians Ephraim ben Nissim Ibn Sanchi and his son Abraham also served at the court. During the 16th century the most significant physicians at the court were the members of the *Hamon family, Joseph and his son Moses of Granada (who served the sultans *Beyazid II, *Selim I, and *Suleiman I, the Magnificent) and the grandson and great grandson, Joseph and Isaac Hamon. Joseph *Hamon accompanied Selim I in 1516 to Egypt and Ereẓ Israel during his conquests. Moshe* Hamon brought benefits to Jews in the empire such as his activity to prevent blood libels (see above).

There were also prominent Jewish businessmen and bankers who held focal positions in the financial centers of the empire – the treasury and lease of taxes. During the reign of Suleiman I, Don Joseph Nasi was influential at court. Nasi was a principal spokesman in foreign affairs and exerted himself on behalf of Jews. He was involved in the efforts to free the anusim imprisoned in *Ancona, the Papal state, and to organize a Jewish economic ban on the city. Selim II made him ruler of the island of Naxos and of the other Cyclade islands, and elevated him to the rank of duke. Nasi built a luxurious palace for his family at Belvedere, on the shores of the Bosporus. He helped the poor and supported the Portuguese *anusim* who settled at the time in the Ottoman Empire. He also assisted his mother-in-law, Gracia Mendes, in her philanthropic activities. Don Solomon ibn Yaish, a Crypto-Jew who reached Turkey in 1585, was also close to the sultanate and received the rank of duke of the isle of Mytilene. He helped the poor of Safed and Turkey, and assisted the *Jabez family, printers in Istanbul. R. Moses Almosnino enumerates a list of court Jews in Istanbul who helped him obtain the Writ of Freedem (*mu'afname*) from the sultan for the Jewish community of Salonika: Joseph Nasi, Judah Di Sigura, Abraham Salma, Meir Ibn Sanji, and Joseph Hamon. Other royal physicians at Suleiman's court included Don Gedaliah *Ibn Yahya, Abraham ha-Levi Migas and Moses Bataril. Generally, these court Jews were very wealthy and tried to help their brethren in Istanbul and in other Ottoman Jewish communities by using their political connections. From 1564 Solomon Ashkenazi served as the personal physician of the sultan and was sent by Sultan Selim II to arrange the peace treaty between the Ottoman Empire and Venice in 1573; thanks to his activity, the order of Venice to expel its Jewish residents was rescinded. The female physician Boula Eksati, wife of the Solomon *Ashkenazi, was an expert in pox diseases and healed Sultan Ahmed I (1603–17). Solomon Ashkenazi was the close adviser of the vizier Mehmed Sokolli during the reign of Selim II, and maintained his position during the reign of the sultan Murad III. Three known Jewish women holding the title *kiera (kira) achieved great influence at the courts of the sultans in the 16th century: Strongila (Fatima), Esther *Handal, and Esperanza *Malchi.

Another active Jewish diplomat at the court was Don Solomon Ibn Ya'ish, who had previously been called Alvaro Mendes (1520–1603). He settled in Istanbul in 1580 and served the sultans Murad III (1574–95) and Mehmed III (1595–1603). He became duke of the island of Mytelene (Midilli). With agents throughout Europe, he gained substantial wealth for himself and acquired valuable information about international developments for the Sublime Porte. One of his diplomatic achievements was establishing close diplomatic relations between the Ottoman Empire and England. Another famous person serving at the court of Murad III was the physician Moses Benveniste, who dealt also with diplomacy until he was exiled to Rhodes in 1584. At the end of the 16th century David Passi also served at the court. It seems that he converted and was appointed grand vizier under the name Halil Pasha. At the beginning of the 17th century the palace medical staff had consisted of 41 Jewish physicians, but by the mid-17th the Jewish medical staff was reduced to only four Jews. Still, Jews served at court until the second half of the 18th century and even in the beginning of the 19th. Sultan Ibrahim I (1630–48) sent his Jewish diplomat Samuell Markus to Madrid. Moses ibn Judah Bikhri and his son Judah, born in Amsterdam, were envoys of Turkey in the time of Sultan Mehmed IV (1648–87). The Italian Israel Conegliano (Conian; c. 1650–c. 1717) settled in Istanbul in 1675 and became the physician of Grand Vizier Kara Mustafa Pasha, but was also consulted by Sultan Mehmed IV (1648–87). Despite the economic and political decline of the Jews in the 18th century, the sultans continued to employ persons from the Jewish community as physicians and advisers. The physician Tobias b. Moses *Cohn was the physician of the vizier Mehmet Rami, the grand vizier of Mustafa II (1695–1703), as well as of Ahmed III (1703–30).Tobias retired in 1714; Naphtali b. Mansur was the close adviser of Baltaji Ahmed Pasha. A physician named Benveniste attended the vizier Sivas Pasha; he had great influence upon the policies of the realm. Daniel de *Fonseca, of Portuguese origin (c. 1668–c. 1740), settled in Istanbul in 1702 and served as a physician and diplomat to the French Embassy, and in 1714 became the physician of Ahmed III until 1730. Other Jewish court physicians during the reigns of Mahmud I (1730–54) and

Osman III (1754–57) were Isaac Çelebi, Joseph Rofeh, David Halevi Ashkenazi, and Judah Handali. Eliezer Iskandari was physician to Sinan Pasha, the Egyptian viceroy and one of the grand viziers in the time of the sultan Murad IV (1623–40) and of his son Mehmed IV (1648–87). He was also adviser on Jewish affairs. Judah Baruch served as sarraf bashi to Sultan Mahmud I (1730–54), using his position to dissuade Maria Theresa from her plan to deport all the Jews of Austria.

Meir *Adjiman was appointed banker of the Sublime Porte by Selim III (1789–1807) and had great influence in the government. Adjiman was murdered by the Janissaries and the office was given to his two nephews Baruch and Jacob *Adjiman who were active on behalf of their fellow-Jews. These two were killed by the sultans Selim III and Mustafa IV. The son of one of them, Isaiah *Adjiman, was appointed in their place, but he too was put to death by Mahmud II. The high-ranking *Çelebi* Siman Tov Shaki was one of those who came and went in the royal court. He and Solomon Camondo, of the well-known family, purchased the concession for the sale of gum from the government. Ezekiel Gabbai was the royal banker and manager of the sultan's affairs (*sarrāf bashi*). His grandson, Ezekiel Gabbai, also served in the highest offices during the reign of the sultans Abdul-Aziz and Abdul-Hamid. He brought great benefits to his coreligionists and was the head of the community of Istanbul. There were wealthy and influential Jews not only in the capital city but also in the offices of chancellor of the pasha's exchequer, master of the mint, and the offices of bankers in other countries of the empire. As already stated, a large number of prominent physicians, specialists in different branches of medicine, served at the courts of the sultans, the viziers, and the *valis*. This important office furnished them with a high personal status and also with the ability to exercise influence at the royal court on behalf of Jews throughout the empire. The Jewish physicians wore different clothes from other Jews, and instead of the yellow hat wore a tall pointed scarlet one. Some of them were freed from burdensome taxes. Many Jewish translators served the Ottoman authorities and European ambassadors and consuls, while others served European agencies as diplomats, such as Taragano family members who served Britain as translators and as vice consuls in Çanakkale. Some members of the Picciotto family also served during the 18th and 19th centuries as consuls of certain European states in Aleppo.

REIGN OF ABDUL-HAMID AND THE LAST YEARS OF THE EMPIRE

During the reign of the sultan Abdul-Hamid II (1876–1909) the attitude of the Sublime Porte toward the Jews was positive and there were four Jewish representatives in the first short-lived (1877–78) parliament, the *mejlis mabʿuthān*, in which minority groups also participated. However, the authoritarian regime of the sultan led him to disregard the constitution which he had proclaimed, so that it never became truly effective. Abdul-Hamid attempted to buttress his power by imposing a strongly centralized rule. Free intellectual and national impulses in his empire were hampered. The *Ḥibbat Zion movement, the *Bilu *aliyah*, and Zionist aspirations met with not only local opposition from the Arabs in Ereẓ Israel, but even more with opposition from the Ottoman government in Istanbul. The attempts of Theodor *Herzl to change the attitude of Abdul-Hamid and his viziers were of no avail. *Aliyah* to Ereẓ Israel was severely restricted and could only be maintained due to the corruption of the bureaucracy. In spite of this, many schools in the Ottoman Jewish communities were established by the Alliance Israélite Universelle, which spread secular culture among the students. The majority of the 403 teachers who were trained in Paris between 1868 and 1925 were born in the Ottoman Empire. Seventy percent of the female teachers were Ottoman residents. Many retired teachers who had served the Alliance for decades became notables, journalists, heads of communities, and politicians. Most mass education in the majority of the communities continued to take place in the Alliance schools or in Alliance-run or -influenced *talmudei torah* until the end of World War I. Many Jews adopted the French language as their medium of cultural and intellectual life. During the latter half of the 19th century some *maskilim* acted in the communities, such as Rabbi Abraham Danon from Edirne, who composed and published a number of works in Hebrew. In 1879 he founded the society for the Friends of Enlightenment (Dorshei Haskalah). The society sought to bring to Ottoman Jewry the Enlightenment movement from Western Europe. Among the new *maskilim* in the communities were Salomon Rozanes from Bulgaria, Abraham Galanté from Turkey, and Joseph Nehama from Salonika.

Some members of the Doenmeh sect took an active part in the formation of the ideology of the Ottoman Society of Union and Progress, which was the mother of the constitutional revolution against Abdul-Hamid and his government (1908). It is known that some prominent Jews were also members of the society, e.g., R. Ḥayyim *Bejerano (c. 1846–1931). However, the story that the revolution of 1908 was a "Jewish-Masonic plot" received wide circulation. Originating among various clerics and nationalists, the false tale about the Jewish origin of the revolution was taken up by some British circles and during World War I seized upon by Allied propaganda as a means of discrediting their Turkish enemies. As the Young Turks had been very successful in their propaganda among non-Ottoman Muslims, it seemed a good idea to demonstrate that they themselves were neither Turks nor Muslims. A characteristic statement is found in a book by an English author published in 1917: "… David belongs to the Jewish sect of Dunmehs. Carasso is a Sephardini Jew from Salonika…." Professor Bernard *Lewis says that no doubt Turkish-speaking Ottoman Muslims of Balkan and other origins played a part in the movement. "There seems, however, to be no evidence at all, in the voluminous Turkish literature on the Young Turks, that Jews ever played a part of any significance in their councils, either before, during or after the Revolution.… The Salonika lawyer Carasso … was a minor figure. Javid … was a doenmeh … and not a real Jew; he seems in any case to have been the only member of his community to reach front rank …" (B. Lewis, *The Emergence of Modern Turkey*, 207–8). In any case, later developments in the Republic of Turkey indicate that the attitude of the Young Turks toward the Jews as a nation was not influenced by the part supposedly played by Jews in the origins of the society.

At the end of the 19th century, Ottoman Jewry constituted the fifth largest Jewish community in the world, after those of Russia, Austria-Hungary, the United-States, and Germany. It numbered in 1895, according to the Ottoman census, 184,139 persons, and increased to 256,003 in 1906, before the loss of territories in Macedonia and Thrace in consequence of the Balkan Wars in 1912–13. The great majority of the Jewish population was poor and little educated. They were a single group, but there were controversies between traditionalists and modernists in the communities. Most of the rabbis and scholars made efforts to accept modern trends and to solve social and family problems affected by modernism and secularism. Such a trend can be seen in the responsa literature of the period and in lectures by well-known rabbis. In 1892 the Sephardim celebrated 400 years of settlement in the Ottoman Empire. The Young Turk Revolution and the Constitutional Period that followed the Hamidan absolutism in 1908 and 1909 guaranteed associative rights to Ottoman subjects despite some restrictions. This caused an awakening of the Jewish communities which reorganized their associations and created new ones. These associations included also sports and several Zionist organizations whose activities until World War I focused in particular on the revival of the Hebrew language. Within the community of Istanbul the Zionists tried to act against the *ḥakham bashi* and the Alliance Israélite Universelle. Zionist associations occupied a middle ground between tradition and modernity. During the last two decades of the empire, the handful of Jews who were involved in general state politics, usually at the side of Turkish nationalists, acted on a strictly individual basis. Most of the Jews in the empire, excluding the Jewish community in Ereẓ Israel, remained largely indifferent to any direct political involvement.

Jews served actively in the Ottoman army during the Balkan Wars and during World War I, and they also strove to demonstrate their loyalty to the government by getting young non-Ottoman Jewish volunteers to enlist in the military in order to demonstrate the community's determination to join the war effort. Jewish bankers in and out of the empire and Jewish charitable organizations provided money for wartime expenditure. Following the Ottoman entry into the war on the side of Germany and Austria on November 11, 1914, Jewish subjects of enemy countries were required to close their stores and shops and leave the empire, with some 2,000 colonists from Ereẓ Israel going overland from Jaffa and Tel Aviv to northern Ereẓ Israel and Damascus, while 11,277 went by ship to Alexandria. The Ottoman government allowed Jews to remain as long as they adopted Ottoman citizenship. The government also allowed Jewish foreign educational and charitable institutions operating to continue as long as they were managed by Ottoman Jews. In 1915–16 the Jewish population of Ereẓ Israel suffered starvation, the plague, and other diseases, such as typhus, and cholera. American Jews, via the American ambassador to the Porte, Henry *Morgenthau, and German Jewish organizations sent food and money to the Jewish residents of Ereẓ Israel during these years. Jews throughout the empire suffered, along with other elements of the population from various developments during the war, including deportation of Jewish populations from the war zones of Eastern Anatolia, Thrace, *Gallipoli, and later Ereẓ Israel, But since most Jews lived outside the war zones and were helped by food shipments from American Jews, few Jews died in comparison with other groups of the population.

[Yaacov Geller and Haïm Z'ew Hirschberg / Leah Bornstein-Makovetsky (2nd ed.)]

OTTOMAN JEWRY AND ZIONISM

For generations, Ottoman Jews nurtured deep feelings about the idea of the Return to Zion, which were manifested in Jewish tradition and religious beliefs. By contrast, their attitude toward political Zionism was conditioned by the policy of the Ottoman government. Ottoman Jewry was noted for its loyalty and was in no position to dissent. Thus throughout his negotiations with the Turkish government, Herzl could not expect the assistance of any Ottoman Jew. In fact Moses Halevi, the chief rabbi in Constantinople, warned the chief rabbi in Jerusalem, Jacob Saul Elyashar, not to become involved with a movement to which the sultan objected. Elyashar, determined not to incur the government's displeasure, avoided meeting Herzl.

It was not until after the Young Turk Revolution of July 24, 1908, that the climate of opinion became more favorable. Early in September both Ahmed Riza, a prominent Young Turk leader (later president of the Chamber) and editor of *Meḥveret*, and Tewfik Pasha, the foreign minister, made exceptionally friendly statements about Zionism and were willing to lift former restrictions on Jewish immigration to Palestine. Ḥayyim Nahoum, the chief rabbi of Turkey, confirmed to Victor Jacobson, head of the Zionist Agency in Constantinople, that the new régime viewed Jewish settlement in Palestine with favor, although they would not allow Palestine to become politically autonomous. Jacobson, on his part, took great pains to dispel the notion that Zionism entertained separatist aspirations or ran counter to Ottoman interests. His efforts, as well as those of *Jabotinsky, who assisted him, bore fruit, since there was much latent sentiment for the idea of settlement in the Holy Land; the Jewish community of Salonika in particular proved a tower of strength.

The Salonika Community

There were approximately 80,000 Jews in Salonika, out of a total population of 173,000. Jacob Meir, their chief rabbi (later Sephardi chief rabbi of Palestine), was very sympathetic to Zionism; so was Saadiah Levi, the editor of *L'Epoca*, the local Jewish paper, and Joseph Na'or, the respected mayor of Salonika. But the greatest asset was Emmanuel Carasso, a prominent figure in the Young Turk movement and a deputy for Salonika in the Ottoman parliament. He thought that the leadership of the Committee of Union and Progress (CUP) was not as hostile to Zionism as was generally assumed, although Zionist aims should be made more palatable to it. Of equal importance was the conversion to Zionism of Nissim Matzliah and Nissim Russo, both of whom were deputies to the Ottoman parliament. They were members of the small group that founded the CUP and despite their youth were very influential. Matzliah was secretary of the CUP and later also of the parliament.

Like Carasso, Russo and Matzliah saw no incompatibility between patriotism and interest in Palestine. They were eager to convince Turkish politicians that opposition to Zionism was based on a misconception. In a meeting which took place on December 31, 1908, in the presence of Jacobson and Jabotinsky, they declared that they had decided to join the Zionist Organization and found an Ottoman branch, provided it would disclaim any separatist political aims. They suggested that the CUP should first be won over and, through it, the parliament and consequently also the government. Hilmi Pasha was singled out in particular. As the most influential statesman in the parliament and minister of the interior, he was the "man of the future." Russo was his former secretary and hoped to sway him. Jointly with Matzliah he considered submitting a memorandum to the CUP and the Ministry of the Interior and, in order to keep the public in Istanbul better informed, they thought it absolutely essential that the Zionists publish a paper.

Turkish Support for Zionism

Behor Effendi, who in 1908 was elected senator (the only Jew to attain that eminence), became appreciably friendlier. This was also true of Faradji, who thought that the development of an intellectual center in Palestine was of crucial importance to world Jewry; the absence of antisemitism in Turkey made the idea realizable. This coincided with the proposal made by Carasso early in February 1909 to found an Ottoman Immigration Company for Palestine and Turkey in general.

Russo and Matzliah soon approached a number of prominent CUP leaders, such as Ahmed Riza, Enver Bey, and Talaat Bey, and found them quite sympathetic; the most explicit statement was made by Nâzim Bey, a leading member of the Unionist Central Committee. He would have liked to see six to eight million Jews in Turkey; they were the "most reliable element." He approved of Carasso's plan and was willing to join the board of the proposed Immigration Company, but with regard to Palestine he would allow no more than two to four million Jews to come; settlement in excess of this number would constitute "a danger."

Voltre-Face

Russo and Matzliah had hardly taken stock of the situation when the Young Turks staged their second coup in April 1909, which brought in its wake a radical change in direction. Promises of equality for all Ottoman subjects without distinction of religion and race became invalid and slogans like Freedom and Liberty were discarded. Ottomanism gave way to Turkism, and the dream of a free association of people in a multinational and multi-denominational empire vanished forever. Turkey became a centralized state, and for the non-Turkish nationalities this was a crippling blow.

Attitudes toward Zionism also hardened. In consequence Ottoman-Jewish leaders became reserved, and even Carasso, Matzliah, and Russo remained aloof. David Fresco, the editor of *El Tiempo*, the Judeo-Spanish periodical, with whom Jacobson had planned in 1908 to co-edit a paper, turned against the Zionists and in a series of articles – from December 1910 to February 1911 – accused them of disloyalty to Turkey.

In 1912–14, Turkish policy toward Jewish settlement in Palestine changed markedly and *pari passu* Ottoman Jewry adopted a friendlier tone. But it was not until 1918 that they were able to come out openly in favor of Zionism.

Diplomatic Overtures

Publication of the Balfour Declaration, coupled with the conquest of Jerusalem by the British, made restoration of Palestine to Turkey unlikely. To Talaat Pasha, the grand vizier, the only option that remained open was diplomacy. On January 5, 1918, he met German-Jewish leaders in Berlin and agreed to resuscitate the defunct Ottoman-Israelite Union for Immigration and Settlement in Palestine. Thereafter, he delegated to Emmanuel Carasso, his confidant, the task of negotiating with the German-Jewish leaders on the creation of the Jewish Center in Palestine under Ottoman sovereignty. Carasso considered the plan advantageous to Turkey. It also had a strong personal appeal for him; he had no difficulty in reconciling his duty as a Turkish patriot with that of a nationalist Jew.

Talaat invited the German-Jewish delegation (VJOD), which included the Zionists, to come to Constantinople in order to bring the negotiations to a successful conclusion. Once again, Carasso had to work out the details. Accordingly, the Settlement Company was to be given the right to acquire land, administer concessions, regulate Jewish immigration and settlement, and grant local autonomy to individual settlements, so that in due course, the Jews would become a majority in the country. In Carasso's opinion – and so he had told the grand vizier – the fear that the Jews would ultimately go their own way had little substance. Should Turkey remain weak she would lose Palestine to the Arabs anyhow, whereas Jewish help in making Turkey a viable state was worthy of consideration. Once Turco-Jewish cooperation was established, a relationship of trust was likely to develop, and separatist tendencies would die out.

Nahoum also acted as one of the chief intermediaries between the Turkish government and a German-Jewish delegation. The negotiations proved abortive but indicative of the new spirit that prevailed among Ottoman Jews was Nahoum's statement, made a few years after the war, though under changed conditions:

Jewish aspirations in Turkey center on the restoration of Palestine. This back-to-the-land movement was the most important factor in the awakening of the desire for the repopulation of Palestine; it was proved that the regeneration of Palestine was possible. The Balfour Declaration became the basis for the settlement of the Jewish question, and today the Jews of Turkey do not fail to cooperate with all their might with the rest of the Jews in the intellectual, economic, and commercial restoration of Palestine/Israel.

[Isaiah Friedman (2nd ed.)]

BIBLIOGRAPHY: Rosanes, Togarmah; I.S. Emmanuel, *Histoire des Israélites de Salonique* (1936); A. Galanté, *Documents officiels turcs concernant les Juifs de Turquie* (1931); idem, *Histoire des Juifs d'Istanbul*, 2 vols. (1941–42); J. Nehama, *Histoire des Israélites de Salonique*, 5 vols. (1935–59); B. Lewis, *Notes and Documents from the Turkish Archives* (1952); A. Danon, in: REJ, 40 (1900), 206–30; 41 (1901), 98–117, 250–65; U. Heyd, in: *Oriens*, 6 (1953), 229–313; S. Schechter, *Studies in Judaism* (1938); Z. Werblowsky, *Joseph Karo, Lawyer and Mystic* (1962); M. Franco, *Essai sur l'histoire des Israélites de l'empire Ottoman* (1897); A. Inan, *Aperçu general sur l'histoire économique de l'Empire Turc-Ottoman* (1941); R. Mantran and J. Sauvaget, *Règlements fiscaux ottomans* (1951); Hirschberg, Afrikah; idem, in *Religion in the Middle East*, 1 (1969), 119–225; I. Ben-Zvi, *Erez Yisrael vi-Yshuvah* (1955); M. Benayahu, *Marbiz Torah* (1957); A. Ben-Yaacov, *Yehudei Bavel* (1965); J. Braslawi, in: *Kol Erez Naftali* (1969), 244–57; M.D. Gaon, *Ha-Ittonut be-Ladino* (1965); I.R. Molho, in: *Ozar Yehudei Sefarad*, 2 (1959), 27–40 (Spanish), 31–42 (Heb.); idem, in: *Sinai*, 28 (1951), 296–314; I.R. Molho and A. Amarijlio, in: *Sefunot*, 2 (1958), 26–60; D. Weinryb, in: *Zion*, 2 (1937), 189–215; 3 (1938), 58–83; S. Hazan, *Ha-Ma'alot li-Shelomo…* (1894, repr. 1968); A. Yaari, *Ha-Defus ha-Ivri be-Kushta* (1967); idem, in: *Aresheth*, 1 (1959), 97–222; Yaari, Sheluhei; J.M. Landau, *The Jews In Nineteenth-Century Egypt* (1969); E. Neumark, *Massa el Erez ha-Kedem* (1947); J. Sambari, in: Neubauer, Chronicles, 115–62; M. Azuz, in: A. Elmaleh (ed.), *Hemdat Yisrael* (1946), 157–68; Y. Kafih, in: *Sefunot*, 2 (1958), 246–86; E. Capsali, *Likkutim Shonim mi-Sefer de-Vei Eliyahu* (1869); Conforte, Kore; R.A. Ben-Simon, *Tuv Mizrayim* (1908); E. and Y.Y. Rivlin, in: *Reshumot*, 4 (1926), 77–119; A. Almaliah, *Ha-Rishonim le-Ziyyon* (1970); S. Ettinger, *Toledot Yisrael ba-Et ha Hadashah*, vol. 3 of H.H. Ben-Sasson (ed.), *Toledot Am Yisrael* (1969); D. Ahi-Ya'akov, in: *Gesher*, 15 no. 4 (1969), 78–84; D. Ben-Gurion, *Zikhronot* (1971); U. Heyd, in: *Sefunot*, 5 (1961), 135–49; J.M. Landau, *ibid.*, 417–60; A. Tartakower, *Shivtei Yisrael* (1969), 253–62; N. Leven, *Hamishim Shenot Historyah*, 2 vols. (1912–22; trans. of his: *Cinquante ans d'histoire*, 2 vols., 1911–20); E. Livneh, *Aharon Aharonson, ha-Ish u-Zemanno* (1969); M. Medzini, *Ha-Mediniyyut ha-Ziyyonit* (1934); S. Marcus, in: *Ozar Yehudei Sefarad*, 5 (1962), 84–101; Y. Molho, *ibid.*, 80–94; 6 (1963), 153–5; 8 (1965), 17–32; 9 (1966), 45–58; 10 (1967), 20–37; I.M. Goldman, *The Life and Times of Rabbi Ibn Abi Zimra* (1970). **ADD. BIBLIOGRAPHY:** A. Cohen, *Palestine in the 18th Century* (1973); S.J. Shaw, *History of the Ottoman Empire and Modern Turkey* (1977), index; N. Ülker, *The Rise of Izmir 1688–1740* (1975), index; H. Inalcik, *The Ottoman Empire, the Classical Age 1300–1600* (1973); M. Benayahu, *"Ha-Tenu'ah ha-Shabeta'it be-Yavan,"* in: *Sefunot* 14 (1971–1978); H. Bentov, in: *Sefunot*, 13 (1971–78), 5–102; A. Cohen and B. Lewis, *Population and Revenue in the Towns of Palestine in the Sixteenth Century* (1978); H. Gerber, in: *Zion*, 43(1978), 38–67; J.M. Landau, *Abdul-Hamid's Palestine* (1979); N. Zenner, in: *Pe'amim*, 3 (1979), 45–58; M. Benayahu, in: *Sefunot*, 11 (1971–1977), 267–298; idem, *ibid.*, 12 (1971–1978), 42–51; A. Schochet, in: *Cathedra*, 13 (1979), 6–9, 15, 30–37; A. Ben-Ya'akov, *Yehudei Bavel mi-Sof Tekufat ha-Ge'onim ve-ad Yameino* (1979); M.A. Epstein, *The Ottoman Jewish Communities and Their Role in the Fifteenth and Sixteenth Centuries* (1980); H. Gerber, in: *Sefunot*, 16 (1980), 235–72; Y. Barnai, in: S. Ettinger (ed.), *Toledot ha-Yehudim be-Arzot ha-Islam*, 1 (1981), 73–118; 2 (1986), 183–300; 3, 89–197; H. Gerber, in: JQR n.s. 71 (1981), 100–18; M. Rozen, in: *Pe'amim*, 9 (1981), 112–24; idem, in: *Mi-Kedem u-Mi-Yam* 1 (1981), 101–31. B. Braude and B. Lewis (eds.), *Christians and Jews in the Ottoman Empire*, 1–2 (1982); J.R. Hacker, *ibid* 1 (1982), 117–25; R. Mantran, *ibid.* 1 (1982), 127–40; *P. Dumont, ibid.*, 1 (1982), 209–42; C.V. Findley, *ibid.*, 1 (1982), 344–65; Benayahu, in: M. Stern (ed.), *Umma ve-Toldote'ah* (1983), 281–87; Gerber, in: *Sefunot*, 17 (1983), 104–35; L. Bornstein-Makovetsky, in: *Bar-Ilan*, 20–21 (1983), 242–70; H. Gerber, *Yehudei ha-Imperyah ha-Otmanit ba-Me'ot ha-Shesh-Esre ve-ha-Sheva-Esre, Hevra ve-Kalkalah* (1983); A. Cohen, *Jewish Life Under Islam* (1984), index; S. Schwarzfuchs, in: *Rassegna Mensile di Israel*, 50 (1984), 707–24; A. Shmuelevitz, *The Jews of the Ottoman Empire in the Late Fifteenth and Sixteenth Centuries, Administrative, Economic, Legal and Social Relations as Reflected in the Responsa* (1984); S.W. Baron, *A Social and Religious History of the Jews*, 18: (1983); L. Bornstein-Makovetsky, in: *Hevrah u-Kehillah* (1984), 3–24; B. Lewis, *The Jews of Islam* (1984); J.M. Landau, *Tekinalp, Turkish Patriot 1883–1961* (1984); Y.R. Hacker, in: *Zion*, 49 (1984), 225–63; H. Jacobsohn, in: Z. Ankori (ed.), *Me'az ve-ad Atah* (1984), 67–72; D. Kushner, in: *Pe'amim*, 20 (1984), 37–45; H. Jacobsohn, *Yehudim be-Darkhei ha-Shayarot u-be-Mikhrot ha-Kesef shel Makedonya* (1984); Y. Barnai, in: N. Gross (ed.), *Yehudim be-Kalkalah* (1985), 133–48; H. Gerber, in: *Sefunot*, 18 (1985),133–46; M. Benayahu, in: *Michael*, 9 (1985), 55–146; M. Rozen, *Ha-Kehillah ha-Yehudit bi-Yrushalayim ba-Me'ah ha-Yod Zayin* (1985), index; H. Inalcik, *Studies in Ottoman Social and Economic History* (1985); L. Bornstein-Makovetsky, in: *Michael*, 9(1985), 27–54; J.M. Landau, in: *Ha-Ziyyonut*, 9 (1984), 195–205; A. Galante, *Histoiré des Juifs de Turquie*, 9 Vols (ca. 1985); H. Gerber, in: *Journal of Turkish Studies* 10 (1986), 143–54; Y.R. Hacker, in: *Mehkarim be-Mistikah Yehudit … Sefer Isaiah Tishby* (1986), 507–36; idem, in: *Pe'amim*, 26 (1986), 108–27; L. Bornstein-Makovetsky, in: S.A. Cohen and E. Don-Yehiya (eds.), *Conflict and Consensus in Jewish Political Life* (1986), 15–30; Y.R. Hacker, in: *Zion*, 52 (1987), 25–44; L. Bornstein-Makovetsky, in: Z. Ankori (ed.), *Me-Lisbon le-Saloniki ve-Kushta* (1988), 69–95; E. Bashan, in: JHS, 29 (1988), 53–73; M. Rozen, in: REJ, 147 (1988), 309–52; Barnai, in: S. Almog (ed.), *Antisemitism Through the Ages* (1988), 189–94; L. Bornstein-Makovetsky, in: A. Toaff and S. Schwarzfuchs (eds.), *The Mediterranean and the Jews: Banking, Finance and International Trade* (1989), 75–104; E. Bashan, *ibid.*, 57–73; J.M. Landau (ed.), *Toledot Yehudei Mizrayim ba-Tekufah ha-Otmanit (1517–1914)* (1988); B. Masters, *The Origins of Western Economics and the Dominance in the Middle East* (1988), index; L. Bornstein-Makovetsky, in: *Sefunot*, 19 (1989), 53–122; A. Marcus, *The Middle East on the Eve of Modernity* (1989), index; A. Rodrigue, *French Jews, Turkish Jews, The Alliance Israélite Universelle and the Politics of Jewish Schooling in Turkey, 1860–1927* (1990); L. Bornstein-Makovetsky, in: *Pe'amim*, 45 (1990), 129–46; R. Dalven, *The Jews of Ioannina* (1990); Y.H. Hacker, in: *Zion*, 55 (1990), 27–59; Y. Harel, in: *Pe'amim*. 44 (1990), 110–31; S.J. Shaw, *The Jews of the Ottoman Empire and the Turkish Republic* (1991); L. Bornstein-Makovetsky, in: A. Haim (ed.), *Hevrah u-Kehillah* (1991), 3–24; H. Inalcik, in: C.E. Bosworth et al. (eds.), *The Islamic World from Classical to Modern Times: Essays in Honor of Bernard Lewis* (1991), 513–49; L. Bornstein-Makovetsky, in: A. Rodrigue (ed.), *Ottoman and Turkish Jewry: Community and Leadership* (1992); Barnai, *The Jews in Palestine in the Eighteenth Century* (1992); W.F. Weiker, *Ottomans, Turks and the Jewish Polity, A History of Jews in Turkey* (1992); G. Veinstein, *Salonique, 1850–1918* (1992); A. Levy (ed.), *The Sephardim in the Ottoman Empire* (1992); Y.R. Hacker, in: *Ottoman and Turkish Jewry* (1992), 1–65; R. Kastoryano, in: *Ottoman and Turkish Jews, Community and Leadership* (1992), 253–277; E. Benbassa, *ibid*, 225–52; H. Beinart (ed.), *Moreshet Sepharad* (1992); A.

Meyuhas Ginio (ed.), *Jews, Christians, and Muslims in the Mediterranean World after 1492* (2002), 207–15; B. Braude, *ibid.*, 216–36; J.M. Landau, *Jews, Arabs, Turks* (1993), 11–86; A. Cohen and E. Simon-Pikali, *Yehudim be-Veit ha-Mishpat ha-Muslemi: Ḥevrah ve-Kalkalah ve-Irgun Kehillati ba-Me'ah ha-Shesh Esre* (1993); E. Bashan, in: *Sefunot,* 21(1993), 41–69; A. Levi, in: *Pe'amim,* 55 (1993), 38–56; Z. Zohar, *Masoret u-Temurah* (1993); L. Bornstein-Makovetsky, in: Sh. Trigano (ed.), *Société juive à travers les âges*, 3 (1993), 433–62; M. Rozen, *ibid.*, 298–337; E. Benbassa, *Une diaspora sépharade en transition: Istanbul* XIXe–XXe *siècles* (1993); A. Levy (ed.), *The Jews of the Ottoman Empire* (1994), 1–150, 425–38; S. Spitzer, in: *Asufot,* 8 (1994), 369–386; B. Arbel, *Trading Nations, Jews and Venetians in the Early Modern Period* (1995); L. Bornstein-Makovetsky, in: *Mi-Kedem u-mi-Yam,* 6 (1995), 13–34; E. Benbassa and A. Rodrigue, *The Jews of the Balkans* (1995); D. Quataert, in: D. Quataert and E.J. Zürcher, *Workers and the Working Class in the Ottoman Empire and the Turkish Republic 1839–1950* (1995), 59–74; A. Cohen, *Yehudim be-Veit ha-Mishpat ha-Muslemi: Ḥevrah ve-Kalkalah ve-Irgun Kehilati be-Me'ah ha-Shemoneh Esre* (1996), index; M. Rozen, in: *Yemei Ha-Sahar* (1996), 13–38; S. Deshen and W.P. Zenner (eds.), *Jews Among Muslim Communities in the Pre-Colonial Middle East* (1996); I. Karmi, *The Jewish Community of Istanbul in the 19th Century* (1996); L. Bornstein-Makovetsky, in: *Michael,* 14 (1997), 139–70; idem, in: M. Abitboul et al. (eds.), *Ḥevrah ve-Dat, Yehudei Sefarad le-Aḥar ha-Gerush* (1997), 3–30; M.Z. Benaya, *Moshe Almosnino Ish Saloniki* (1996); N. Greenhaus, *Ha-Misui ba-Kehillah ha-Yehudit be-Izmir ba-Me'ot ha-Sheva-Esre ve-ha-Shemoneh Esre* (1997); Y.R. Hacker, in: *Zion,* 62 (1997), 327–68; J. Frankel, *The Damascus Affair – Ritual Murder, Politics and the Jews in 1840* (1997); M. Rozen. in: *Turcica, 30* (1998), 331–46; M.M. Weinstein, in: *Studies in Bibliography and Booklore,* 20 (1998), 145–76; Y. Harel, in: *Ladinar,* 1 (1998), 190–98; Y. Ben-Naeh, in: *Cathedra,* 92 (1999), 65–106; B. Rivlin (ed), *Pinkas ha-Kehillot – Yavan (1999)*; E. Eldem, *The Ottoman City between East and West* (1999); L. Bornstein-Makovetsky, *Pinkas Beit ha-Din be-Kushta* (1999); E. Bashan, *Mishpaḥat Taragano, Diplomatim Yehudim ba-Dardanelim 1699–1817* (1999); C.B. Stuczynski, in: *Pe'amim,* 84 (2000), 104–24; R. Lamdan, *A Separate People: Jewish Women in Palestine, Syria and Egypt in the 16th Century* (2000); E. Benbassa and A. Rodrigue, *Sephardi Jewry, A History of the Judeo-Spanish Community, 14th–20th Centuries* (2000); G. Nassi (ed.), *Jewish Journalism and Printing Houses in the Ottoman Empire and Modern Turkey* (2001); L. Bornstein-Makovetsky, in: *Pe'amim,* 86–87 (2001), 124–74; B. Özdemir, in: *Turkish-Jewish Encounters* (2001), 107–28; M. Rozen, *A History of the Jewish Community in Istanbul, The Formative Years, 1453–1566* (2002); L. Bornstein-Makovetsky, in: *These Are the Names,* 3 (2002), 21–64; Y. Harel, in: AJS *Review,* 26 (2002), 1–58; M. Rozen (ed.), *The Last Ottoman Century and Beyond: The Jews in Turkey and the Balkans 1808–1945,* 1–2 (2002–5); Y. Harel, *Bi-Sefinot shel Esh la-Ma'arav* (2003); Y. Hacker, *ibid.*, 287–309; Y. Ben-Na'eh, in: *Kehal Israel,* 2 (2004), 341–68; L. Bornstein-Makovetsky, in: *Mi-Mizrah u-mi-Ma'arav* 7 (2004), 117–60; J.M. Landau, *Exploring Ottoman and Turkish History* (2004), 335–72; M. Mazower, *Salonica…Christians, Muslims and Jews 1430–1950* (2004); M. Rozen, in: S. Faroqhi and R. Deguilhem (eds.), *Crafts and Craftsmen in the Middle East* (2005),195–234; Z. Keren, *Kehilat Yehudei Rusçuk, 1788–1878* (2005); I. Friedman, *Germany, Turkey and Zionism, 1897–1918* (1977; 1998^{2}), 142–45, 397–98; E. Benbassa, *A Sephardic Chief Rabbi in Politics, 1892–1923* (1997).

OTWOCK, town and health resort near Warsaw, Poland. It became popular among middle-class Jews from central Poland as a fashionable resort. A ḥasidic dynasty derives its name from this town. There were 2,356 Jews living in Otwock in 1908 (20.9% of the total population), and 5,408 in 1921. The 357 members of the Jewish loan society of Otwock in 1924 comprised 162 artisans, 156 merchants, and 39 members of other professions.

[*Encyclopaedia Judaica* (Germany)]

Holocaust Period

On the outbreak of World War II there were 14,200 Jews in Otwock. In October 1939, one month after the occupation of the town, the Nazis burned all the synagogues there. In the summer of 1940 a few hundred young men were deported to the forced-labor camp at Tyszowce. A closed ghetto was established in January 1941. A year later, 150 young men were deported to the newly opened *Treblinka death camp, where they were among the first victims. In April 1942, 400 Jews were deported to the nearby forced-labor camp in Karczew. The great deportation to the Treblinka death camp began in August 1942. About 7,000 Jews were deported and exterminated in Treblinka, while 3,000 others, who offered passive resistance and hid themselves, were found, and most were killed on the spot. Another 700 Jews who succeeded in fleeing into the surrounding forests were killed by German armed groups searching the woods. The forced-labor camp in Karczew was liquidated on Dec. 1, 1942. After the war about 400 Jews settled in the town, but eventually all of them left Poland. A home for Jewish children and a Jewish sanatorium were active during the first postwar years.

[Stefan Krakowski]

BIBLIOGRAPHY: *Sefer Yizkor – Otwock, Karczew* (Heb. and Yid., 1968); Yad Vashem Archives.

OUAKNIN, MARC-ALAIN (1957–), rabbi, scholar. Born in Paris as one of five siblings, Ouaknin came from a family of both Sephardi and Ashkenazi origin. His father, Jacques Ouaknin, born in Marrakech and himself author of several books on Judaism, was a former chief rabbi of Marseilles, and his mother, Eliane-Sophie, was born in Lille to an Alsatian-Luxembourg Ashkenazi family. A best-selling author of many books on Jewish thought, philosophy and Kabbalah, Ouaknin is an associate professor at Bar-Ilan University in Israel, where he teaches comparative literature. After public school, Ouaknin was trained at the yeshivah of Aix-les-Bains and at Gateshead in England. He started to study medicine in Strasbourg but after two years turned to philosophy at the University of Nanterres Paris X, while simultaneously beginning rabbinical studies at the *Séminaire israélite in Paris. During the 1980s, Ouaknin's encounter with Edmond *Jabes and Emmanuel *Lévinas determined the future of his work. His Ph.D. dissertation, under the direction by Pierre Kaufmann and the guidance of Lévinas and presented in 1986, was partly published in his *The Burnt Book: Reading the Talmud* (French, 1986), gained immediate recognition, and was later translated into German (1990), English (1994), Japanese (1994), Spanish (1999), and Italian (2000). A combination of poetry, mysticism, and phenomenology, his numerous books have reached a large audience. Geared to accessibility, they have introduced the basic main ideas and traditions of Judaism and Kabbalah, taking a modern approach. Among his books are *Lire aux éclats Eloge de la caresse* (1989); *Ouvertures hassidiques* (1990) *Méditations érotiques, essais sur Emmanuel Lévinas* (1992); *Tsimtsoum, Introduction à la méditation hébraïque* (1992); *Bibliothérapie, Lire c'est guérir* (1994); *The Mysteries of the Alphabet: the Origins of Writing* (1999); *The Mysteries of the Kabbalah* (French, 2000; English, 2001); *The Mystery of Numbers* (2004). In addition he published popular books written with Dory Rotnemer about Jewish humor and Jewish names, and also about Jerusalem, where he lives. Translated into many languages, his work has become a subject for academic research in places such as Belgium, Spain, and Italy.

BIBLIOGRAPHY: J. Eladan, *Penseurs juifs de langue française* (1995); J.J. Bailly, "Eros et Infini. Essai sur les écrits de Marc-Alain Ouaknin" (Ph.D. diss., Brussels, 2005); M. Kavka, "Saying Nihilism: A Review of Marc-Alain Ouaknin's *The Burnt Book*," in: Sh. Magid (ed.), *God's Voice from the Void: Old and New Studies in Bratslav Hassidism*, (2002), 217–36; F. Eskenazi & É. Waintrop, *Le Talmud et la République: enquête sur les Juifs français à l'heure des renouveaux religieux* (1991).

[Sylvie Anne Goldberg (2nd ed.)]

OUDTSHOORN, town in the Cape midlands of the Republic of South Africa. For many years Oudtshoorn was the center of the ostrich-feather industry, and Jewish immigrants played an outstanding part in its development. Arriving in the area about 1880, approximately 30 years after the town was founded, Jewish traders mainly from Lithuania mastered the methods of ostrich-farming and helped to develop world-wide markets for the feathers. Among the pioneers and recognized experts in the industry were men like the Rose brothers, and the eldest, Max, who came from Lithuania in 1890, was known as the "ostrich feather king." When the market collapsed shortly before World War I, the Roses fought hard to save the industry from ruin. At the height of the ostrich boom, Oudtshoorn had the largest Jewish population in rural South Africa, numbering 1,500 in 1913. Because of the intense communal and religious life of the Oudtshoorn community, it was sometimes called the Jerusalem of Africa. A Hebrew congregation was formed in 1883; the first synagogue was built in 1888 and another in 1896; one of these is now disused. Other communal institutions, including Zionist and philanthropic societies and a Hebrew day school, were established. The Jewish community produced many professional men and business leaders, and Jews were also prominent in the civic and cultural life of the town, in several cases serving as councilors and mayors. After the decline of the ostrich-feather industry, the Jewish population was considerably reduced. In 1968 they numbered about 300. By the turn of the century the total had fallen below 60. The Oudtshoorn Hebrew Congregation, still active despite its small numbers, celebrated its 120th anniversary in 2004, with Jewish leaders from all over the country participating in the festivities.

BIBLIOGRAPHY: G. Saron and L. Hotz, *Jews in South Africa* (1955), index; L. Feldman, *Oudtshoorn – Yerushalayim d'Afrike* (Yid., 1940); M. Gitlin, *The Vision Amazing* (1950), index; I. Abrahams, *Birth of a Community* (1955).

[Louis Hotz]

OULIF, CHARLES NARCISSE (1794–1867), French lawyer and community leader, born in Metz. Oulif supported the revolution of July 1830 and was a tireless promoter of equality for the Jews. He secured the abolition in the court of Metz of the humiliating Jewish *oath (*more Judaico*) and of the term "Jew" in documents within its jurisdiction. Also in Metz, Oulif established a school for Jewish youths and was among the founders of a society for the encouragement of technical education for Jews. Both institutions served as models for similar ones in other cities.

BIBLIOGRAPHY: AI, 28 (1867), 265–9.

OURY, GERARD (1919–2006), dramatic artist, author, film director. Oury was born in Paris. He is one of the leading directors of comedies in the French film industry and has worked with all the great comedians of France. He began his career as an actor in Paris with the Comédie Française in 1939/40, but had to abandon it upon the Nazi conquest. He spent 1943 to 1945 in Geneva, and only returned to the Comédie Française in 1961. Some of his films have featured Jewish characters or elements. Among his many successful films, many featuring Louis de Funes, are *Le Corniaud* (1964), *La Grande Vadrouille* (1966), *Le Cerveau* (1968), *La Folies des Grandeurs* (1971), *Les Aventures de Rabbi Jacob* (1973), and *L'As des As* (1982).

[Gideon Kouts]

OUZIEL, BEN-ZION MEIR ḤAI (1880–1953), chief rabbi of Israel, *rishon le-Zion*. Ouziel was born in Jerusalem, where his father, Joseph Raphael, was the *av bet din* of the Sephardi community of Jerusalem, as well as president of the community council. At the age of 20 he became a yeshivah teacher and also founded a yeshivah called Maḥazikei Torah for Sephardi young men. In 1911, he was appointed *ḥakham bashi* of Jaffa and the district. Immediately upon his arrival in Jaffa he began to work vigorously to raise the status of the Oriental congregations there. In spirit and ideas he was close to the Ashkenazi rabbi of the Jaffa community, A.I. Kook, and their affinity helped to bring about more harmonious relations than previously existed between the two communities. During World War I he was active as leader and communal worker. His intercession with the Turkish government on behalf of persecuted Jews finally led to his exile to Damascus, but he was permitted to return to Ereẓ Israel, arriving in Jerusalem before the entry of the British army. In 1921 he was appointed chief rabbi of Salonika, accepting this office with the consent of the Jaffa-Tel Aviv community for a period of three years. He returned to become chief rabbi of Tel Aviv in 1923, and in 1939 was appointed chief rabbi of Ereẓ Israel. Ouziel was a member of the temporary committee of Jews in Ereẓ Israel, a member of the Va'ad Le'umi, and a representative at the meeting which founded the Jewish Agency. He appeared before the Mandatory government as a representative of the Jewish community and on missions in its behalf, and impressed all with his dignity and bearing. He was also founder of the yeshivah Sha'ar Zion in Jerusalem. He contributed extensively to newspapers and periodicals on religious, communal, and national topics, as well as Torah novellae and Jewish philosophy.

He was the author of *Mishpetei Ouziel*, responsa (1st ed., 3 vols., 1935–60; 2nd ed., 4 vols., 1947–64); *Sha'arei Ouziel* (1944–46), consisting of *halakhah*, general topics, and a selection of his addresses, letters, and other writings; *Mikhmannei Ouziel* (1939); *Hegyonei Ouziel* (1953–54), and still other works in manuscript. He made "Love, truth, and peace" the motto of his life. This verse (Zechariah 8:19) hung framed above his desk and was inscribed on his notepaper. Two days before his death he dictated his testament. It said, inter alia, "I have kept in the forefront of my thoughts the following aims: to disseminate Torah among students, to love the Torah and its precepts, Ereẓ Israel and its sanctity; I have emphasized love for every man and woman of Israel and for the Jewish people as a whole, love for the Lord God of Israel, the bringing of peace between every man and woman of Israel – in body, in spirit, in speech, and in deed, in thought and in meditation, in intent and in act, at home and in the street, in village and in town; to bring genuine peace into the home of the Jew, into the whole assembly of Israel in all its classes and divisions, and between Israel and its Father in Heaven."

BIBLIOGRAPHY: Tidhar, 2 (1947), 796f.; S. Don-Yaḥya, *Ha-Rav Ben-Ẓiyyon Meir Ḥai Ouziel* (1955); *Or ha-Me'ir, Mukdash le-Yovelo ha-Shivim shel… B.M.Ḥ. Ouziel…* (1950), 1–26 (Heb. pagination).

[Itzhak Goldshlag]

OVADIA, NISSIM J. (1890–1942), chief Sephardi rabbi of Paris. Born in Adrianople, Turkey, the descendant of rabbis, Ovadia was educated at the Alliance Israélite Universelle school and at Yeshiva Bikur Holim. A promising student, he then went to Jerusalem to complete his rabbinical training at the Beit Midrash le-Rabbanim of the Ezra School, from which he was ordained. The Sephardi *bet din* awarded him the *hattarat hora'ah* (see *Semikhah), he then went to Vienna to be assistant rabbi to the Sephardi community. In 1918 he was elected chief rabbi. During the 1920s he attended the University of Vienna and received his Ph.D. in 1927.

An active Zionist, he used the occasion of the World Zionist Congress in Vienna to establish the World Sephardic Foundation, the presidency of which he later assumed. He published a daily and high holiday Sephardi prayerbook with Judeo-Spanish translations.

In 1929 he accepted the call of the Jewish community of Paris and became chief Sephardi rabbi. He brought together the immigrants from Salonica, Constantinople, and Smyrna into one viable community and created a magnificent synagogue in the heart of Paris. Three schools became two, he organized a youth organization, and other committees to meet the needs of the community.

When the Germans invaded in May 1940, he remained in Paris, but by June it became too dangerous for him to stay, so he sought refuge in Orléans. He found a temporary haven in the Collège Saint Croix. On August 30 he crossed the Spanish border and then immigrated to New York via Portugal in March 1941. He sought to replicate his experience in Paris in New York and established the Central Sephardic community of America and became its chief rabbi, but ill health cut short his career. He had a heart attack in May 1942 and another, fatal one, in August.

BIBLIOGRAPHY: J.M. Papo, *Sephardim in Twentieth Century America* (1987).

[Michael Berenbaum (2nd ed.)]

OVCHINSKI, LEVI (d. 1941?), rabbi, scholar, and historian. Born in Daugieliszki (Vilna province), Lithuania, Ovchinski studied at the yeshivah in Lida. After living for a time in Swinciany, in 1897 he was appointed rabbi in Alt-Autz, Courland, and afterward rabbi of Mittau (Jelgava). Rabbi Ovchinski and his two sons-in-law perished during the Holocaust.

Ovchinski wrote several reference works: *Naḥalat Avot* (1894), a biographical lexicon of Jewish scholars who were omitted from or only briefly mentioned in Ḥ.J.D. *Azulai's *Shem ha-Gedolim*, and A. Walden's *Shem ha-Gedolim he-Ḥadash*. In a similar category is Ovchinski's *Hadrat Ẓevi* (1914) containing the biographies of the rabbis Naḥman Idl Margolies and Ẓevi Hirsch Nurock (father of Mordechai *Nurock). His main work was *Toledot ha-Yehudim be-Kurland* (1908, 1911[2]; a Yiddish translation was published in Riga in 1928 entitled *Di Geschikhte fun di Yidn in Letland fun Yor 1561–1923*), the historical section of this book being based principally on R. *Wunderbar's volume on the same subject. The second section dealing with the history of the communities of Latvia and their rabbis is Ovchinski's most important contribution to the historiography of Latvian Jewry, based on and utilizing the minute books of the communities and burial societies, as well as other sources.

BIBLIOGRAPHY: *Yahadut Latvia* (1953), 368–9; M. Bobe, *Perakim be-Toledot Yahadut Latvia* (1965), 205–6.

[Joseph Gar]

OVED, MARGALIT (1937–), dancer, choreographer, singer, composer, and teacher. She was born in the British Protectorate of Aden to a pearl merchant father and a midwife mother. The Yemenite-Jewish traditions and the hundreds of multicultural Adenite songs she absorbed in her childhood played an important role in her work. Oved came to Israel in 1949 with the "Magic Carpet" airlift. She began working with Sara *Levi-Tanai in 1950 as an original member of the Inbal Dance Company, and studied with choreographers Jerome *Robbins and Sophie *Maslow. With astonishing dramatic and vocal resources, gesture mastery, drumming, and charismatic presence, she was Inbal's leading performer for 15 years, including its 1957 world tour.

In 1965, Oved married American-Jewish businessman Mel Marshall, and moved to Los Angeles where she taught Yemenite dance and choreographed at UCLA for 22 years. Oved's innovative approach to modern dance theater used folk traditions as well as other sources of inspiration. She drew from desert imagery (*Landscape*, 1968), Jewish heritage (*David and Goliath*, 1968; *In the Beginning*, 1970), and Western sources (*Cinderella*, 1972; *The Birds*, after Aristophanes, 1986), and the music of Debussy and Liszt. In her work, she often utilized live or recorded multitrack sung-spoken-drummed compositions.

Oved received a travel and teaching grant from the National Endowment for the Arts in the early 1970s. In 1982 her company toured Israel and in 1988 she performed at the Kennedy Center in Washington, D.C., for the 40th anniversary of Israel's statehood. She returned to Inbal as its director in 1994 and in 1996 she performed with her son's critically acclaimed Israeli dance company, the Barak Marshall Dance Company. Oved created over 45 choreographies and Israeli folkdances, and recorded 22 musical compositions. She starred in the first Israeli-produced film, *Hill 24 Doesn't Answer* (1955), and was the subject of the 1968 American film documentary *Gestures of Sand*. Her honors include a 1973 Hadassah Myrtle Wreath Award and the 1998 French ADAMI Award for outstanding performance at the Bagnolet Festival.

BIBLIOGRAPHY: S. Levi-Tanai, "A Personal Testimony," in: *Be-Regel Yeḥefah (Barefooted: Jewish-Yemenite Tradition in Israeli Dance)*, ed. N. Bahat-Ratzon (Tel Aviv, 1999); A. Fuller Snyder, producer/director, *Gestures of Sand*. In association with the Department of Dance and Academic Communications Faculty, University of California, Los Angeles, 196; 15 minutes.

[Karen Goodman (2nd ed.)]

°OVID (43 B.C.E.–17 C.E.), Roman poet. Ovid, offering counsel to young Romans concerning the place and time of their amorous adventures, advises them not to omit the place where the Syrian Jew performs his rite each seventh day (*Ars Amatoria* 1:75). The seventh day, celebrated by the "Palestinian Syrian" (the Jew), "a day not favorable for transacting business," is commended as a suitable time for the beginning of a courtship (*ibid.*, 1:415). Ovid also warns against respect for the "foreign" Sabbath or consideration for the rainy season (*Remedium Amoris* 217 f.).

[Jacob Petroff]

OVITZ, MICHAEL (1946–), U.S. talent agent entertainment executive. Born in the Los Angeles suburb of Encino to a father who was a liquor wholesaler, Ovitz attended Birmingham High School and was elected student body president. While at the University of California, Los Angeles, he became president of Zeta Beta Tau fraternity and worked as a tour guide at Universal Studios. After graduating in 1968, he briefly considered medical school, but went to work instead for the William Morris Agency, starting in the mail room. Ovitz hatched a plan with four other agents to start a new talent agency and in January 1975, they established Creative Artists Agency. Within four years CAA earned $90.2 million per year and had grown to become the third largest firm in Hollywood. CAA continued to grow and diversify its client base over the next two decades, becoming an iconic talent agency known for a team of agents dressed in black Armani suits who worked long hours in an I.M. Pei-designed Beverly Hills headquarters decorated with modern art. In 1995, after brokering the sale of Universal Studios and then refusing a position there, Ovitz accepted the position of president of Disney Studios. However, a short 14 months later Ovitz was fired and given a severance package worth $110 million – a decision which was questioned in a series of shareholder suits and chronicled in James Stewart's book *Disney War* (2005). Since leaving Disney, Ovitz has pursued a series of unsuccessful business ventures including forming Artists Management Group (AMG), a management and film and television production company which he founded in 1998 but was forced to sell three years later.

[Adam Wills (2nd ed.)]

OVRUCH, city in Zhitomir district, Ukraine. The first information on the Jews, in a document of 1629, mentions three families in the town. Until 1750 the community was dependent on the taxation imposed on the community of *Chernobyl. A court ordered that Ovruch be separated from Lithuania and annexed to the province of Volhynia. According to the census of 1765, there were 607 Jews in Ovruch and its environs who paid the poll tax. There were 1,773 Jews in 1847 and 3,445 (46.5% of the total population) in 1897. The end of the 18th century witnessed the spread of Ḥasidism in Ovruch and its environs. Abraham Dov *Baer, a student of Mordecai of Chernobyl, served as *av bet din*. In the second half of the 19th century, two members of the *Shneersohn family served as rabbis.

During the Russian Revolution the Jews of Ovruch were attacked several times. At the end of 1918 the Ukrainian hetman, Kozyz-Zyrko entered the town and in the course of 17 days plundered all the Jewish homes, killing 80 people. With the introduction of Soviet rule the religious and communal life of the Jews was paralyzed. In 1926 there were 3,400 Jews in Ovruch (53% of the total population). In the mid 1930s 26% of the Jewish earners were factory workers; 33%, white collar workers; and 30%, artisans, most of them organized in cooperatives in which they constituted the majority of members. In 1939 the Jews numbered 3,862 (33% of the total population). The town was occupied by the Germans on August 22, 1941; presumably many Jews succeeded to escape. In September 1941 the 1st SS Infantry Regiment murdered the town's Jews as well as those from the environs, according to their report 516 persons in all. In 1957 the Jews numbered there 2,200.

In 1963, on the eve of the High Holidays, the militia broke into privately held services in Ovruch, arresting five Jews; each member attending the services was fined. In the late 1960s the Jewish population was estimated at about 2,000. Most left in the 1990s.

BIBLIOGRAPHY: Committee of Jewish Delegations, *The Pogroms in the Ukraine…* (1927), 134–40; L. Chasanowich, *Der Yidisher Khurbn in Ukraine* (1920), 3–20.

[Yehuda Slutsky / Shmuel Spector (2nd ed.)]

OVSAY, JOSHUA (1883 or 1885–1957), Hebrew literary critic. Born in Russia, he lived in the U.S. from 1918 to 1955, when he immigrated to Israel.

His first publication in Hebrew appeared in *Ha-Meliẓ* and he subsequently contributed essays and articles on literature to the Hebrew (and occasionally the Yiddish) press. Some of his essays on writers and books were collected in *Ma'amarim u-Reshimot* (1947). He edited the writings of Moses Halevy (with Hillel *Bavli) and the literary anthology *Koveẓ Sippurim mi-Mendele ad Bialik* (1942). He also translated Dickens' *Old Curiosity Shop* (1924).

BIBLIOGRAPHY: Waxman, Literature, 5 (1960²), 206f.; Kressel, Leksikon, 1 (1965), 35.

[Getzel Kressel]

OWL, bird belonging to the family Strigidae. Because of the strange appearance of species of the owl, some of their conspecies were called *kippuf*, that is, resembling a *kof* ("ape"). It was also said that "their eyes are directed forward like those of human beings" and that "they have jaws like those of human beings" (Nid. 23a). They were regarded as an evil omen, so that although "all kinds of birds are a good sign in a dream," species of owls are not (Ber. 57b). Most of them utter a hooting cry like a groan, and as they inhabit ruins, they sound as though mourning over the devastation, and hence symbolize in the Bible destruction and desolation. The majority of them are included in the Pentateuch among the birds prohibited as food, and even those not mentioned there are unclean according to the principle that a bird "is unclean if (when perched on a cord stretched for it) it divides its toes evenly, two on each side" (Ḥul. 65a; cf. Ḥul. 3:6). The owl's toes, divided into two in front and two behind, assist it in seizing its prey.

The Bible contains at least 11 names of owls. Of these the *tinshemet, ka'at, kos, yanshuf, shalakh*, and *bat ya'anah* are mentioned in the lists of unclean birds in Leviticus and Deuteronomy. For the biblical names of owls the following identifications have been suggested.

(1) The *tinshemet* (Lev. 11:18; Deut. 14:16; JPS, "horned owl"; AV, "swan") is the barn screech owl (*Tyto alba*), its Hebrew name (which occurs also in Lev. 11:30 as that of an unclean creeping thing, but there refers to the *chameleon) being derived from נשם ("to breathe") on account of its heavy breathing. Because of its odd appearance it was regarded as "the strangest (or "the most repulsive") of birds" (Ḥul. 63a).

(2) The *ka'at* (Lev. 11:18; Deut. 14:17; JPS, AV, "pelican") is mentioned among the birds that inhabit ruined places (Isa. 34:11; Zech. 2:14). Referring to his sighing and emaciated body by reason of his suffering, the psalmist (Ps. 102:6–7) compares himself to "a *ka'at* of the wilderness." Its Hebrew name denotes vomiting (*meki*) in a reference apparently to the fact that, as do other owls, it regurgitates the bones of its prey. In desert regions there occurs a species of owl – the *Athene noctua saharae* owl – that fits in with the biblical descriptions of the *ka'at*.

(3) The *kos* (Lev. 11:17; Deut. 14:16; JPS, AV, "little owl"), that occurs together with *ka'at*, of which it is a conspecies, in Psalms (102:7), is probably the little owl (*Athene noctua glaux*), its Hebrew name being onomatopoeic. It has no "ears," that is, no crest of feathers. Symbolizing, as it did, wisdom to the ancient Greeks because of its large wide-open eyes, it appeared on the coins of Athens.

(4) The *yanshuf* (Lev. 11:17; Deut. 14:16; JPS, AV, "great owl"), depicted by Isaiah (34:11) as inhabiting devastated Edom together with the *ka'at*, has been identified with the long-eared owl (*Asio otus*), its Hebrew name being connected with *neshef* ("night") or with *neshifah* ("hooting"). It is found in winter in the north of Israel.

(5) The *shalakh* (Lev. 11:17; Deut. 14:17; JPS, AV, "cormorant") which, according to the Talmud, "catches fish out of the sea" (Ḥul. 63a), has been identified with the fish owl (*Ketupa zeylonensis*), the only owl in Israel that feeds on fish. It is found near Lake Kinneret.

(6) The *bat ya'anah* (Lev. 11:16; Deut. 14:15; JPS, "ostrich," AV, "owl") is, according to the ancient translations, the *ostrich, which however lives in the open desert and which rarely utters a cry, whereas the *bat ya'anah* is described as inhabiting desolate places (Isa. 34:13) and as emitting a mournful cry (Micah 1:8). For these reasons it has been identified with one of the species of owl that utters a cry when calling to one other (*ya'anah* is apparently derived from *anah* (ענה), "to answer"), this being characteristic of three strains of the species *Bubo bubo*, one of which, the dark desert eagle owl (*Bubo b. ascalaphus*), has been identified with the biblical *bat ya'anah*.

(7) The *tannim* has been identified with the second, light-colored strain of the previous species – with the *Bubo b. desertorum*. It lives in the desert and in ruins and emits a sighing cry, the name *tannim* being derived from *tanah* (תנה; "to weep"). Since it occurs together with the *bat ya'anah* among birds in the above passages, it is difficult to accept the customary modern identification of *tannim* as *jackal.

(8) The *o'aḥ* (JPS, "ferret"; AV, "doleful creature"), mentioned with the *bat ya'anah* as inhabiting ruined places (Isa. 13:21), has been identified with the third strain of the above species – the Palestinian eagle owl (*Bubo b. aharonii*), its name being onomatopoeic. The largest of the owls, it is found in the Jordan Valley, and feeds on hares and rats, reptiles and birds.

(9) The *kippod* (JPS, AV, "bittern") and the *kippoz* (JPS, "arrowsnake," AV, "great owl") are mentioned in the account of the destruction of Edom, where various birds lived and nested (Isa. 34:11, 15). Associated as its name is with the meaning of rolling oneself up into a ball, the *kippod* has been identified with the short-eared owl (*Asio flamneus*) which adopts a rotund posture and lives near swamps and in ruined places, and hence Isaiah (14:23) prophesies that Babylonia would be made into "a possession for the *kippod* and pools of water."

The hedgehog is also called *kippod* or *koppad* in the Mishnah (Shab. 5:4), because it rolls itself up into a ball.

(10) The *lilit* (JPS, "night monster," AV, "screech owl"), which also occurs in Isaiah's prophecy about Edom (34:14), refers to a species of bird (cf. Nid. 24b), the word, connected with *laylah* ("night"), denoting a nocturnal bird, perhaps the tawny owl (*Strix aluco*). In the *aggadah* it is the name of a night-demon (see *Lilith).

The *sa'ir*, mentioned alongside the *lilit*, is apparently also a species of owl. This word is now applied to the smallest of the owls, the *Otus scopus*. Another view holds that it refers to a species of demon (cf. Lev. 17; II Chron. 11:15).

BIBLIOGRAPHY: Lewysohn, Zool, 162ff.; R. Meinertzhagen, *Birds of Arabia* (1954), 318f.; J. Margolin, *Zoologyah*, 2 (1959), 275; F.S. Bodenheimer, *Animal and Man in Bible Lands* (1960), 54, 117f., 128; J. Feliks, *The Animal World of the Bible* (1962), 72–81; M. Dor, *Leksikon Zoologi* (1965), Eng. index.

[Jehuda Feliks]

OWNERSHIP (Heb. בַּעֲלוּת, *ba'alut*). As a proprietary right, ownership is the most important of all rights in property, all other rights being inferior to it. The distinction between ownership and other proprietary rights is apparent not only in matters of civil law but is especially significant in other halakhic matters. Thus, the *etrog* ("citron") and other three species prescribed for the festival of Sukkot must be one's own property and not borrowed or stolen (Sh. Ar., OH 649:1–2). This principle of ownership applies also to the first fruits of one's own field which have to be brought to the Temple and over which the scriptural recital (Deut. 26:1–11) is to be made (Bik. 1:1–2; Git. 47b).

The Talmud indicates that a person is the owner of property if it is in his possession for an unlimited period, or if possession thereof is due to revert to him for an unlimited period after he has temporarily parted with the property in question. At first glance, the distinctive feature of ownership appears to be the fact that a person is free to deal as he pleases with the property he owns, a power not available to the holder of any other proprietary right. It will be seen, however, that this feature is not in itself sufficient to define ownership, since it does not always apply. For instance, an owner must not use his land in a manner that interferes with a neighbor's use of his land (see *Nuisance) nor may he use his property in such manner as to commit an offense. Furthermore, a person who has agreed to encumber or submit to any restraint whatsoever on the use of his land nevertheless remains the owner. A person who lets his property, for instance, even for a long-term period continues to be the owner. It is therefore apparent that the rights of ownership may adhere even to those who are not free to deal as they please with their property. Nor does the suggestion that ownership is characterized by a person's right to sell or alienate his property prove to be sufficiently distinctive. Thus the usufructuary may also transfer his right to another (Maim. Yad, Mekhirah, 23:8) and the borrower or lessee may also do so – with the owner's permission – yet these parties do not become owners of the property to which their rights extend. On the other hand, at the time when the laws of the jubilee year were operative, the owner could not sell his land forever, yet he was its owner. Moreover, sometimes a right in property other than ownership exceeds the owner's rights therein, such as the case of a tenant who holds a 100-year lease.

Possession (Reshut).

The distinctive quality of ownership is closely connected with the concept of *reshut* ("possession"); so much so that the commentators do not always discriminate between the two and sometimes use the term *reshut* to denote ownership. *Reshut* (see also *acquisition) is a person's control over property, established by the existence of three requirements: (1) his ability and (2) intention to use the property (3) at any time he may wish to do so – even if only for a period of limited duration. All three requirements must be satisfied and operate simultaneously for the possession to be effective; hence coins which are in a place that cannot be reached are not in a person's *reshut*, even if they are his own (Tosef. Ma'as. Sh. 1:6). If such place is accessible to him, however, because "the way is open" and caravans pass there, the coins are said to be in his *reshut*, but not otherwise (TJ, Ma'as. Sh. 1:2, 52d). Similarly, chattels which have been stolen are in the *reshut* of the thief, since the latter is able to use the property at his pleasure and the owner is unable to prevent him from doing so or to use the property himself. Land cannot be stolen and is therefore always in possession of its owner, and since it cannot be carried away or hidden the owner can always have it restored to his use through the mediation of the court. He therefore remains free to use the land whenever he pleases, unlike a purported robber. Similarly, an object which is deposited remains in the *reshut* of its owner, not that of the bailee, from whom the owner can demand its return at any time. If, however, the bailee should refuse to return the property and denies the existence of a bailment, he will be deemed a robber and the property will thus be in his *reshut* (BM 7a and Alfasi ad loc.). Property on hire or loan for a fixed period, which the owner may not revoke, is in the *reshut* of the hirer or borrower for the duration of the stated period. In the same way, when a person sells the usufruct of his field, the field will be in the *reshut* of the usufructuary (BB 8:7), since the latter, not the owner, may use the field at his pleasure (Maim. Yad, Mekhirah, 23:7).

For the same reason, an object which is found on premises which are kept or reserved for the owner is in the latter's possession. This is so even if the premises are kept for him because people keep away from there of their own accord and not because of his own ability and power to guard his field (BM 102a); if however he is unable to use a thing which is on his premises, for instance when it is hidden and nobody expects to find it there, it will not be in his *reshut*. Property which is on a person's premises when they are not kept for him will not be in his *reshut*, as it is deemed certain to be lost or taken by others and is therefore not freely at his disposal (see *Acquisition, Modes of).

Ownership and Possession

These are by no means identical concepts. The *amora*, R. Johanan, states that stolen property is in the *reshut* of the thief, but the person robbed remains the owner (BM 7a). The same may be said with regard to hired property. *Reshut* nevertheless appears to be an essential element in the determination of ownership, for, as indicated, a person is held to be the owner if the property is permanently in his possession for an unlimited period – even if it passes out of his *reshut* for a limited period but is due to revert to him permanently (cf. Ran, Ned. 29a). Thus the law that a swarm of bees and doves of a dovecote may be owned has rabbinic authority only – for the sake of keeping the peace (BK 114b; Ḥul. 141b) – as in strict law these cannot be owned because they cannot be permanently kept in a person's *reshut*. Similarly, geese and fowl which have escaped are ownerless because they cannot be restored to the owner's *reshut* (Tos. to Ḥul. 139a). This is also the case in respect of *lost property which the owner has despaired of finding and having restored to his *reshut* (see *Ye'ush*).

Permanent *reshut* is not the only requirement of ownership, however. Ownership may cease when a person makes up his mind that the property is to pass permanently out of his *reshut*, or that it shall not return permanently into his *reshut*, as by way of *ye'ush*, or when he renounces the property (see *Hefker*), or when he conveys it to another. Consequently a deafmute, idiot, or minor, none of whom has legal understanding, cannot lose ownership in any of these ways (BM 22b; Git. 59a). Hence it may be said that the right of ownership is characterized by two basic attributes: a positive one, that the property is in the *reshut* of the claimant for a period of unlimited duration; and a negative one, that such person shall not have resolved to remove the property permanently from his *reshut*.

Ownership of Limited Duration

Despite the general principles outlined above, it is possible for ownership to be limited in point of time. The outstanding example of this is a returnable gift, which, in the opinion of Rava, is a proper gift making the donee the owner as long as the gift is with him (Suk. 41b). The comment of the *rishonim* (Asheri *ibid.* 30; Ritba, Nov. Git. 83a; Kid. 6b) is that such a gift is a complete and full conveyance, and the return of the gift requires a fresh conveyance. Since it is a condition of the gift that it must be returned to the original donor, such a gift in fact only confers title for a limited period (cf. *Keẓot ha-Ḥoshen*, ḤM 241:4). Another example of ownership of limited duration is that cited by R. Isaac of the creditor acquiring a pledge for a debt (BM 82a). In this case it may also be said that this is a complete and full acquisition and the return of the pledge to the debtor requires an assignment thereof by the creditor. The Talmud discusses the question of such an assignment being involved even in the case of hire (Av. Zar. 15a).

The most important example of ownership for a limited period is to be found in the sale of land at the time that the jubilee year was customary, for in the jubilee year land reverted to the vendor. This is also the case when land is sold for any period of limited duration. In this case the acquisition is called *kinyan perot* (i.e., usufruct) in the Babylonian Talmud (Git. 47b) and *kinyan nekhasim* in the Jerusalem Talmud (Git. 4:9, 46b). It is stated in the latter that the purchaser may not dig any wells while the field is in his possession (*Mishneh la-Melekh*, to Maim. Shemittah, 11:1). According to the Babylonian Talmud (*ibid*), *kinyan perot* – before the occurrence of the first jubilee – was like an acquisition of the land itself, since people had not yet been accustomed to the restoration of the land and looked upon a sale as leading to a permanent and irrevocable acquisition. However, in the opinion of Simeon b. Lakish, from the second jubilee onward *kinyan perot* was not like the acquisition of the land itself and the seller remained the owner because at the end of the stipulated period the land would revert permanently to his possession. R. Johanan is of the opinion that *kinyan perot* is like a *kinyan* of the land itself and that the Pentateuch provided for the termination of such ownership in the jubilee year and the restoration thereof to the owner of the land. The dispute also extends to land which is sold for a fixed period. The *halakhah* was decided in accordance with the view of Simeon b. Lakish.

Because of the element of possession in the concept of ownership, it is possible for a person to own only part of a thing, provided that it is possible for such part to be in his separate possession. Thus, it can sometimes happen that one person may own land and another may own the trees on it (BB 37a–b), or one person may own a house and another the top story (BM 117b).

In the State of Israel, the Cooperative Houses Law 5713 – 1952, in keeping with Jewish Law and contrary to the law in force until then, makes provision for the separate ownership of each apartment in a cooperative house.

BIBLIOGRAPHY: Gulak, Yesodei, 1 (1922), 131–4; Herzog, Instit, 1 (1936), 69–75; S. Albeck, in: *Sefer Bar-Ilan*, 7–8 (1970), 85–94. **ADD. BIBLIOGRAPHY:** M. Elon, *Ha-Mishpat ha-Ivri* (1988), 3:1364f., 1383f.; idem, *Jewish Law* (1994), 4:1627, 1647.

[Shalom Albeck]

OXFORD, English university town. The presence of Jews is first recorded in 1141, when they were despoiled by both claimants to the throne during the civil war. The Jewry was in the center of the town (the present St. Aldate's Street). Oxford Jews suffered greatly from the confiscatory tallage imposed in 1210. An ecclesiastical synod of the Province of Canterbury held there (1222) renewed the anti-Jewish regulations of the Fourth *Lateran Council and condemned to death a deacon who had converted to Judaism. In the 13th century Oxford possessed an *archa. The Jewish population was, however, at all times small, probably never exceeding 150. Besides acting as moneylenders, the Jews were notorious as university landlords, which was one reason for the student riot against them in 1244, after which relations with university members were regulated. The wealthiest Oxford Jew of the period was David of Oxford (d. 1244), remarkable details of whose private

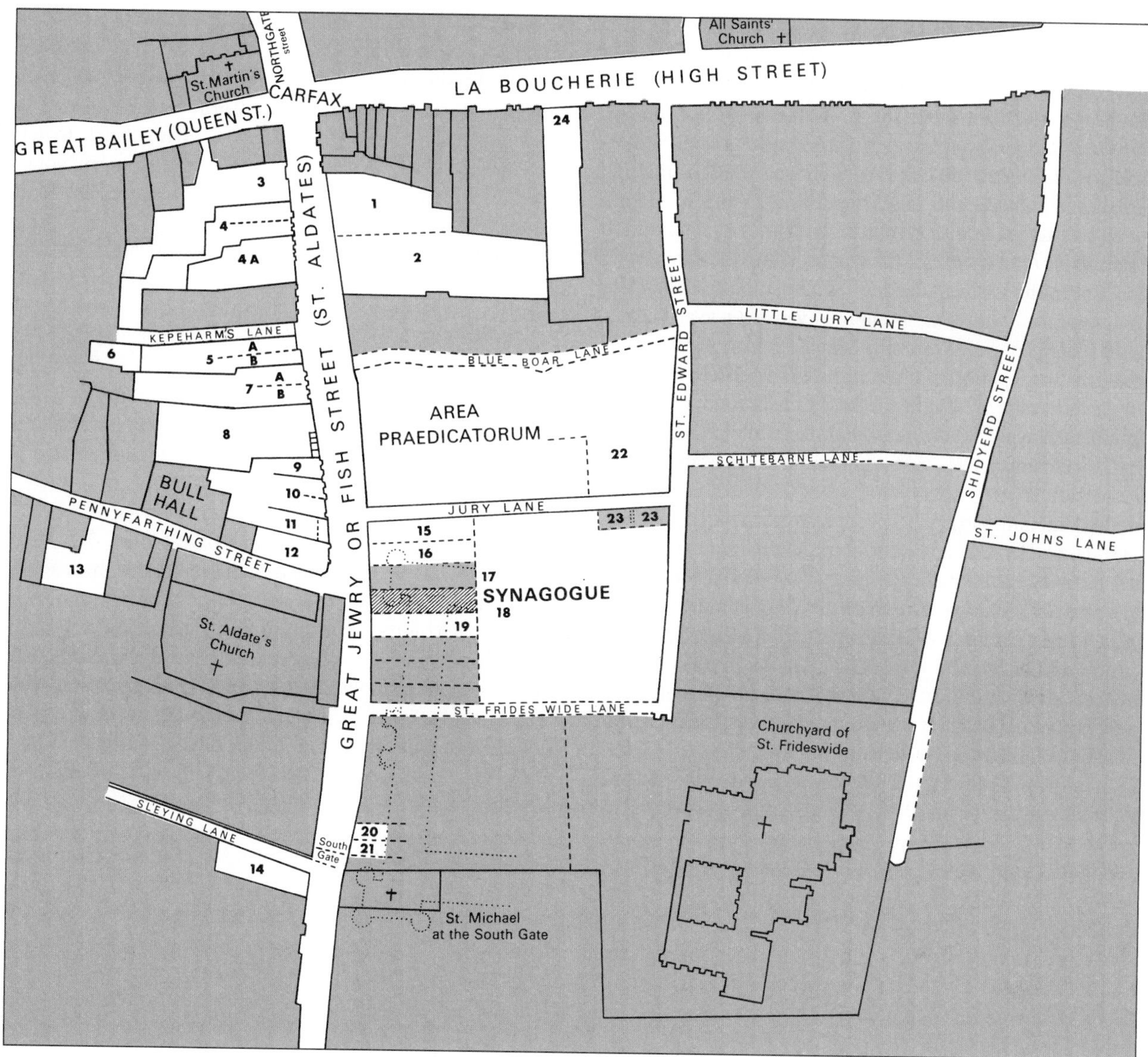

1. Isaac b. Moses; Alberic Convers (Joscepin); Moses b. Isaac; Gildhall 1229.
2. Isaac b. Moses; Alberic Convers; David of Oxford; Domus Conversorum; Lower Gildhall.
3. Jacob b. Mag. Moses ('Jacob's Hall').
4. Moses b. Diaie; Bassena; Ekekin b. Bassena.
5. Moses of Wallingford (?); Bonefey b. Moses; Reyna; Floria la Vedua (a).
6. Chera.
7. (a) Milo b. Deudone (b) Chera [or Vivo].
8. Josce of Colchester; Moses of Oxford; Josce b. Moses; Jacob le Eveskel; Benedict le Eveske; Sarah widow of Benedict; Ducklington's Inn.
9. Samuel of Berkhamsted.
10. father of Pya; Benedict of Caus; Pya.
11. Benedict of Winchester; Vives b. Benedict; Avegay b. Benedict.
12. Meir; Benedict de la Cornere.
13. Lumbard of Cricklade; Moyses Hall.
14. Mildegod; Vives le Lung (Keresy's Place).
15. [Simeon b. Moses?] Aaron Canis.
16. [Mag. Moses b. Simeon?]; Bonamy b. Jacob; Vives of Gloucester; Margalicia.
17. Copin of Worcester; Moses b. Jacob and Issac le Eveske.
18. Moses of Bristol and Deudone; Copin of Worcester; The Synagogue.
19. [Benjamin?]; Copin of Oxford; Mildegod; Jacob Mildegod.
20. Copin of Worcester.
21. Copin of Worcester.
22. David of Oxford; Muriel.
23. Jacob and Cresse ff. Mag. Moses.
24. Jacob and Cresse ff. Mag. Moses.

The medieval Jewry of Oxford and house owners recorded in the town registers. After C. Roth, Jews of Medieval Oxford, 1951.

life are extant. Oxford was the place of residence of R. Yom Tov and R. Moses Yom Tov of London whose son Jacob of Oxford (d. 1276/1277) was a leading member of the community. *Berechiah Natronai ha-Nakdan, author of the *Fox Fables*, is perhaps identical with Benedict le Puncteur of Oxford (c. 1200). In 1268 Oxford Jewry was heavily fined for an alleged outrage on a crucifix and in 1278–79 several Jews were arrested and some executed on charges of clipping the coinage.

From the 17th century onward Jewish-born teachers of Hebrew, mostly converts, found their way to Oxford. Permanent settlement began after the mid-18th century but a community was organized only in 1841. Jews were first admitted to the university in 1854. By the end of the century the undergraduate element was large enough to reinforce the shrinking town community – a student society was established in 1904. Samuel *Alexander became a Fellow of Lincoln College in 1882 and James Joseph *Sylvester professor of geometry in 1883. However, such appointments became frequent only in the second quarter of the 20th century. Several distinguished German Jewish refugees arrived after 1933 and during World War II the community was enormously swollen by evacuees from London. In 1967 the Jewish population was approximately 400, in addition to approximately 200 undergraduates. However regular synagogue services were held only on the High Holidays and in termtime.

In the 16th century Hebrew studies began systematically to be pursued in the university. A regius professorship of Hebrew was established in 1546. Its incumbents included Edward *Pococke (from 1648 to 1691), E.B. Pusey (1828–1882), S.R. *Driver (1883–1914), and Herbert *Danby (1936–1953). The acquisition of the library of David *Oppenheim in 1817 made the Hebrew collection of the *Bodleian Library outstanding. H.M.J. *Loewe was lecturer in Oriental languages (1914–1931). A readership in Jewish studies was established in 1939, its first incumbent being C. *Roth.

Although Oxford was arguably slower than Cambridge in welcoming Jews, in the 20th century a major Jewish presence manifested itself at the university. Between 1910 and 1971 there were 13 Jewish presidents of the Oxford Union Society, the famous debating club, including Philip *Guedalla, Leslie *Hore-Belisha, Jeremy *Isaacs, and Leonard *Stein. Since 1951, there have been at least ten Jewish heads of Oxford colleges, among them Sir Isaiah *Berlin, Sir Zelman *Cowen, A.L. *Goodhart, Lord *Goodman, and H.L.A. *Hart. During World War II, a motion at the Oxford Union Society calling upon Britain to admit more Jewish refugees was reputedly the only one in its history to be passed unanimously. In recent years, Oxford has emerged as a major academic center of Jewish Studies, most notably with the establishment in 1972 of the Oxford Centre for Hebrew and Jewish Studies, founded chiefly by David *Patterson, which is housed in premises on St. Giles in central Oxford and in Yarnton Manor outside of town. It was given considerable funding by the *Wolfson family. The Centre has also facilitated the emergence of Oxford as a notable venue for Yiddish Studies, something almost inconceivable a century or even 50 years earlier.

In the mid-1990s the Jewish population of the town numbered approximately 700. The 2001 British census showed a declared Jewish population of about 500, with approximately another 500 students. Oxford has an Orthodox synagogue and Masorti and Progressive congregations as well as a University Jewish Society.

BIBLIOGRAPHY: C. Roth, *Jews of Medieval Oxford* (1951); idem, in: *Oxford Magazine* (March 7, 1963); idem, in: *Oxoniensia*, 15 (1950), 63–80; idem, in: M. Praz (ed.), *English Miscellany*, 9 (1958), 163–71; Neubauer, in: *Collectanea of the Oxford Historical Society*, 2 (1890), 277–316; Cohen, in: JHSET, 13 (1936), 293–322. **ADD. BIBLIOGRAPHY:** D.W. Lewis, *The Jews of Oxford* (1992); M. Jolles, *A Directory of Distinguished British Jews, 1830–1930* (2002), 145–53; W.D. Rubinstein, *Great Britain*, index; C. Cluse (ed.), *The Jews of Europe in the Middle Ages* (2004).

[Cecil Roth / William D. Rubinstein (2nd ed.)]

OYSHER, MOISHE (1907–1958), **ḥazzan*. Born in Lipkon, Bessarabia, and taken to Canada in 1921, Oysher joined a Yiddish theatrical company, appeared on the Yiddish stage in New York, and led his own company in Buenos Aires, 1932. Returning to New York in 1934, he decided to become a *ḥazzan* like his father and grandfather. He conducted services in New York, and was noted for ḥasidic interpretations of the traditional prayers. He starred in Yiddish films, *The Cantor's Son, Yankel the Blacksmith*, and *Der Vilna Balebesel*, and made numerous recordings.

OYVED, MOYSHE (**Good** (né **Gudak**), **Edward**; 1885–1958), Yiddish writer, artist, sculptor, and gem expert. Oyved was born in Skempe, Poland and came to England in 1903, settling in the East End of London. Working as a watchmaker, he began trading in antique watches and cameo brooches and founded Cameo Corner, a shop for antique jewelry patronized by the fashionable, including the royal family. His first Yiddish book, *Aroys fun Khaos* (1917; *Out of Chaos*, 1918), was followed by *Lebns Lider* ("Life's Songs," 1924); in *Visions and Jewels* (1925), a collection of 124 autobiographical stories and short tales, he wrote about Nahum *Sokolow, Max *Nordau, Sholem *Asch, Jacob *Epstein, and others; the deluxe *The Book of Affinity*, 1935, had original color lithographs by Jacob Epstein. At 60 he began to sculpt, creating works such as "Ram with Candelabra" and "Community of Israel," lamenting the six million Jews who died in the Holocaust. The London Yiddish literary circle that included Kafka's friend Dora Diamant issued *Loshn un Lebn*, 69 (1945) to celebrate his 60th birthday. His papers are at the Central Zionist Archives in Jerusalem.

BIBLIOGRAPHY: LYNL, 6 (1965), 570–1. **ADD. BIBLIOGRAPHY:** Rejzen, Leksikon, 2 (1927), 721–2; L. Prager, *Yiddish Culture in Britain* (1990), 502–3; D. Mazower, *The Ben Uri Story …* (2001), 37–58.

[Charles Samuel Spencer / Leonard Prager (2nd ed.)]

OZ, AMOS (1939–), Israeli writer. Oz was born in Jerusalem, the son of Yehuda Arieh and Fanya Klausner. At the age of 14, after his mother's suicide, he went to live in Kibbutz Ḥuldah, where he finished high school and stayed on as a member for two decades. From 1986 he lived with his family in the southern town of Arad, in the Negev desert. Oz studied Hebrew literature and philosophy at the Hebrew University in Jerusalem.

Oz's first collection, *Arẓot ha-Tan* (*Where the Jackals Howl and Other Stories*, 1981), appeared in 1965, followed a year later by his first novel, *Makom Aḥer* (*Elsewhere, Perhaps*, 1985). The short stories received high praise from critics, and his popularity soared with the publication of his second novel, *Mikhael Sheli* (1968; *My Michael*, 1972). Oz became one of the leading figures in the "New Wave" movement in the 1960s (other prominent writers in this group are Amalia *Kahana-Carmon, A.B. *Yehoshua, and Aharon *Appelfeld) and the most popular author of his generation. From his earliest fiction, his writing has been marked by a unique, recognizable style. The stories are constructed as concentric circles, focusing on a psychological conflict, a psychic drama. That drama, the struggle between the ego and its shadow, is typically the kernel of the story. Around this inner ring the narrative builds a family drama, which is a projection of the tensions within the psychic drama. Wider circles radiating from this dramatic center are society, landscape (the kibbutz and the jackals around it), and politics (the tensions with the Arabs). The outermost sphere is the divine one, manifesting the same contending forces found within the psychic drama. Although the religious element in Oz's work is usually camouflaged, it is one of its most important themes. Tensions between the different psychic forces are reflected in the struggle between the dull, humdrum, secure existence within society's borders and the vibrant, alluring, and destructive experiences that lie beyond those borders. These conflicts are manifest in Oz's subsequent work in the struggle between light and darkness, life and death, God and Satan, mind and body, man and woman, Jews and Arabs, culture and nature. Other collections of stories include *Ad Mavet* (1971; *Unto Death*, 1978), *Har ha-Eẓah ha-Ra'ah* (1976; *The Hill of Evil Council*, 1978). Among Oz's novels are *Menuḥah Nekhonah* (1982; *A Perfect Peace*, 1986), *Kufsah Sheḥorah* (1987; *Black Box*, 1989), *Lada'at Ishah* (1989; *To Know a Woman*, 1991). Typically, Oz's novels and novellas open with a clash between two sworn enemies (be they psychological, societal, or political), then progress toward a reconciliation of those opposites, so that previously antagonistic forces are seen as complementary, needing each other for their very existence. Thus the seemingly binary relations reveal themselves to be dialectical. The idea that the enemy is also one's brother can be found in Oz's early story "Before His Time," and throughout his oeuvre. It underlines the fact that, unlike S.Y. Agnon, A.B. Yehoshua, and many other Israeli authors who were influenced by Freud, Oz is a follower of Carl Gustav Jung. Jung's ideas are reflected in Oz's work in three principal areas. First, in the structure of the psyche: the ego is depicted as a weak and unstable element at the top of a pyramid whose main volume is the collective unconscious, the latter being the reservoir of primordial urges, creativity and supreme intelligence. Second, the major psychic processes portrayed in Oz's fiction are typically Jungian: the "self" is attained only when the protagonist is reconciled with the dark aspects of his personality; the "self" reveals the image of God in human beings; the "treasure hunt" represents the search for "self." Third, Jung's writing, and to a great extent his interpretations of the alchemists' texts, furnished Oz with a huge reservoir of symbols. Oz uses these symbols in conjunction with others taken from different mythological traditions (Christianity, Judaism, Greek mythology). Most of the mythological symbols employed by Oz are in keeping with Jung's interpretation of them. The psychic processes mentioned above, conveyed through typical Jungian symbols, form the core of most of Oz's stories and novels from his earliest writing.

Oz's texts can be read on many levels, which explains why they are popular despite their complex themes. *Black Box* is a case in point. The psychological content of the novel is camouflaged (the protagonists are implicitly characterized as "anima" and "animus" figures, and the novel as a whole is an examination of male-female relations). However, it was the overt social context (the tensions between Ashkenazi and Sephardic Jews, right wingers and leftists, etc.) that drew the attention of both readers and critics. These social aspects were underscored in the theater and film versions of the novel. Thus Oz's work is a unique example of a complex modern literary text that has also great appeal to the general public. Other novels by Oz include *Ha-Maẓav ha-Shelishi* (1991; *Fima*, 1993); *Al Tagidi Laylah* (1994; *Don't Call It Night*, 1996); *Oto ha-Yam* (1998; *The Same Sea*, 2001). Oz's first books were extolled by critics and scholars. Even though certain critics have argued that his later novels lack the creativity and originality of his earlier fiction, Oz's popularity in Israel has not diminished. His autobiographical novel *Sippur al Ahava ve-Ḥoshekh* (2002; *A Tale of Love and Darkness*, 2004) was enthusiastically received by critics and readers alike.

Since the Six-Day War in 1967, Oz has been active in the Israeli peace movement and with groups and organizations that advocate a two-state solution to the Israeli-Palestinian conflict. He has been a spokesman for the *Peace Now movement since its founding in 1977. His numerous essays about Israeli politics and culture were collected in the following books: *Be-Or ha-Tekhelet ha-Azah* (1979; *Under This Blazing Light*, 1996), *Poh va-Sham be-Ereẓ Yisrael* (1982; *In the Land of Israel*, 1984), *Mimordot ha-Levanon* (1988: *The Slopes of Lebanon*, 1990), *Kol ha-Tikvot* ("All Our Hopes," 1998), and *Be'eẓem Yesh Kan Shetei Milḥamot* ("But These are Two Different Wars," 2002). Oz also published books for young readers, including *Sumkhi* (1978; *Soumchi*, 1980) as well as two collections of literary essays: the first, *Shetikat ha-Shamayim* ("The Silence of Heaven," 1993; German translation 1998), discusses the works of S.Y. Agnon; the second is entitled *Matḥilim Sippur* (1996; *Beginning a Story*, 1998).

Oz is one of Israel's most popular novelists. His books have been translated into more than 30 languages. He has won several literary prizes in Israel (among them the Brenner Prize in 1976, the Bialik Prize in 1986, and the Israel Prize in 1998) as well as worldwide. He has been named Officer of Arts and Letters in France and in 1997 was awarded the Knight's Cross of the Legion d'Honneur. In 1992 he received the Frankfurt Peace Prize, in 2004 the Literature Prize of the German daily *Die Welt*, and in summer 2005 the prestigious German Goethe Prize. For detailed information concerning translations into various languages, see the ITHL website at www.ithl.org.il. A bibliography of Amos Oz's works and translations (1965–2002) appeared in 2004.

BIBLIOGRAPHY: N. Gertz, *Amos Oz* (Monograph, 1980); A. Balaban, *Between God and Beast: An Examination of Amos Oz's Prose* (1993); R. Kalman (ed.), *Amos Oz – Bibliography 1984–1996* (1998); G. Shaked, *Ha-Sipporet ha-Ivrit*, 5 (1998), 205–229; A. Komem and I. Ben-Mordechai (eds.), *Sefer Amos Oz* (2000); Y. Mazor, *Somber Lust – The Art of Amos Oz* (2002).

[Avraham Balaban (2nd ed.)]

OẒAR HATORAH, society for the religious education of Jewish youth in the Middle East and North Africa. Oẓar Hatorah was founded in 1945 as a nonprofit organization by Isaac Shalom of New York City, Joseph Shamah of Jerusalem, and Ezra Teubal (d. 1976) of Buenos Aires. Its founders were concerned about a result of the secularization of Jewish national life: Jewish spiritual decline and intellectual impoverishment. They hoped to rectify this by establishing schools, teaching both religious and secular subjects, throughout the Middle East and North Africa. The society, following the receipt of funds from private individuals, local communities, and the *American Jewish Joint Distribution Committee, began its work with an investigation of Jewish communities in Morocco, Algeria, Tripolitania, Cyrenaica, Egypt, Syria, Iraq, and Israel (then Palestine). With the aims of providing good teaching, facilities, food, and medical care, by 1970 Oẓar Hatorah was running 23 schools and a summer camp in Morocco, 41 schools and a summer camp in Iran, two elementary schools in Syria, and an elementary school in Lyons, France, and a total of 13,610 students had been enrolled in its schools.

OZE or **OSE**, a worldwide organization for child care, health, and hygiene among Jews, with headquarters in Paris. Launched in czarist Russia in 1912, its name is an acronym of three Russian words, Obshchestvo Zdravookhraneniya Yevreyev, which mean "Society for the Protection of the Health of the Jews." As the work of OZE, outlawed in Russia in 1919, spread to other countries and continents, the three initials were fitted with new words: Oeuvre de Secour aux Enfants in France; Irgun Sanitari Ivri in Palestine; and Organización para la Salud y Enseñanza in Latin America. Whatever the language, the general meaning of the name and its purpose remained the same. It signified the effort to cure or prevent sickness among Jewish people everywhere, restore and guard the health of children in OSE institutions, combat epidemics, and create living conditions under which neither individual sickness nor widespread diseases could gain new footholds.

The systematic work of OSE, which began in 1912, was interrupted by World War I which called for special relief measures on behalf of the war victims and hundreds of thousands of refugees and deportees from the war-stricken areas. By the end of the war, in 1917, 34 branches of OSE were already in operation in Russia. They maintained 60 dispensaries, 12 hospitals, 125 nurseries, 40 feeding centers for school children, 13 summer camps, four sanatoriums for tuberculosis patients, and other medical and child-care institutions. After the end of the war, branches of OSE spread to the new states such as Poland, Lithuania, Latvia, and Romania, as well as to central and western Europe, where they became very active and built a wide network of medical institutions. At that time, the headquarters of the organization were transferred to Berlin. In Poland, the branches united in 1921 under the Polish name TOZ (Towarzystwo Ochrony Zdrowia) which meant the same as OSE and had the same program of activities. Before the outbreak of World War II, TOZ maintained 368 medical and public health institutions in 72 localities, where 15,443 members carried on the activities of the organization.

In the interval between the two world wars, the OSE in Poland, Romania, Lithuania, and Latvia had under its supervision and guidance hundreds of institutions for all kinds of medical aid and child care. As a result, child mortality among Jews in the countries of eastern Europe was reduced considerably, the favus disease was eradicated, the spread of tuberculosis arrested, and general health and sanitary conditions among Jews improved. The yearly budget of all the institutions amounted to over two million dollars, about 75% acquired from local sources and about 25% from grants from the American Jewish Joint Distribution Committee and from Jewish communities all over the world. The outbreak of World War II and the Nazi Holocaust put an end to the flourishing activities and growth of the OSE. The institutions of OSE were closed, their property confiscated and looted, and their inmates and personnel sent to concentration camps and gas chambers.

After the war, OSE shifted its activities to new countries in North Africa and Latin America and to Israel, where it adjusted its program to the new conditions of life of Jews in these countries. In the postwar years, OSE carried out its relief and rehabilitation work in ten countries of Europe, nine in the western Hemisphere, four in Africa, and in Israel, maintaining 91 medical and child-care institutions with about 85,000 children and adults under their care. The basic program of work there was the protection of mother and child, fighting epidemic diseases, school medicine and hygiene, dissemination of knowledge about preventive medicine and public health, medical research, and scholarships to physicians and nurses for professional specialization and studies. The OSE is accredited with consultative status at the United Nations Economic and Social Council, UNICEF, and the World Health Organization as a nongovernmental organization specializing in public health and child-care work among Jews.

BIBLIOGRAPHY: J. Lestschinsky, *Ose; 40 Years of Activities and Achievements* (1952); *OSE-Rundschau*, 1–8 (1926–33); continued as: *Revue "Ose,"* 9–15 (1934–50); *Folks-gezunt*, 1–15 (1923–38); L. Gurvich, *Twenty Five Years OSE 1912–1937* (1937); L. Wulman, *Fifteen Years of Jewish Health Activities in Poland* (1937); idem, *Between Two Wars* (1941); *American OSE Review*, 1–7 (1942–50); *OSE Mail*, 1–7 (1948–54).

[Leon Wulman]

OZERY (Pol. **Jeziory**, Yid. **Ozhor**), town in Grodno oblast, Belorussian S.S.R. Formerly one of the royal estates where the Magdeburg *Law applied, the town was later the property of Polish nobles. Jews are mentioned in Ozery in 1667 in the *pinkas* of the Lithuanian Council (see Councils of the *Lands), in connection with a "revenge of murder" during an "assembly" in the town. In that century a wooden synagogue, widely known for its beauty, was built. In 1826 a *siddur* – *Tefillat Nehora ha-Shalem* – was printed at the press of Zimel Nochumowicz (of the *Romm family of printers). From 552 in 1847 the Jewish population grew to 1,892 (42.4% of the total population) in 1897, then declined to 867 (49.4%) in 1921. Ozery was known as a place for Torah study, attracting young men from the surrounding district. The main sources of Jewish livelihood were sawmills, lake fishing, tanning and other crafts, and trade. In 1937 about 89% of the 73 shops in the town were owned by Jews. Among the economic associations organized by Ozery Jews were a committee for Jewish crafts, an association of retail traders, a cooperative bank, and a free loan fund (Gemilut Ḥasadim), which had 170 members in 1924. In the mid-1920s an elementary school belonging to the CYSHO (Central Yiddish School Organization) functioned. Zionist activity started at the beginning of the century, and groups supporting the labor parties in Ereẓ Israel were active before World War II; Ozery had a center for training *ḥalutẓim*, and there was also some emigration to Ereẓ Israel. Jews from the town were among the pioneers of Jewish colonization in the Argentine.

Holocaust Period

During World War II, when the Germans occupied Ozery, the Jews were brutally treated: they were conscripted into forced labor and their property confiscated. A ghetto was soon established, enclosed by barbed wire and guarded by Jewish police and Belorussians. A Judenrat was also established. The inmates of the ghetto were taken to work in the forests and tobacco plantations, for a daily wage of one mark, half of which was deducted as "Jewish tax." Jews from nearby towns such as Eisiskes, Vasilishki, Nowy Dwor, and Porechye, were also concentrated in the ghetto of Ozery. On Nov. 11, 1942, all the Jews (1,370 according to a Nazi document) were transferred to the Kelbasin forced-labor camp near Grodno, and a few weeks later all were deported to death camps.

BIBLIOGRAPHY: S. Dubnow (ed.) *Pinkas Medinat Lita* (1925); Institut far Vaysruslendisher Kultur, *Tsaytshrift*, 2–3 (1928), 370; KS, 8 (1931/32), 237; *Grodner Opklangen* (1950), 6.

[Dov Rubin]

OZICK, CYNTHIA (1928–), U.S. writer, best known for literature exploring the opposition between the Jewish and the pagan worlds and the problem of what it means to be a Jew in the U.S. diaspora. Ozick was born in New York to Yiddish-speaking Russian Jewish immigrants and was educated at New York University. She did graduate work in literature at Ohio State University (1949–50), writing her thesis on the later novels of Henry James, an important early aesthetic influence. She later taught a fiction workshop at the Chautauqua Writers' Conference.

Ozick emerged as a gifted short-story writer in the early 1960s, publishing her first full-length novel, *Trust*, in 1966. This ambitious work, praised as both Jamesian and Tolstoyan in its stylistics, has strong mythological tendencies and an allegorical frame. The novel follows an unnamed female narrator's quest for identity amid the confusion of modern American life. Judaism, with its responsibility to the past and future (represented by Enoch, her mother's current husband), provides one option; the spontaneous life of nature (represented by Nick, the mysterious father she has never met but is seeking) provides another option. In Ozick's second and more successful book, *The Pagan Rabbi, and Other Stories* (1971), the title story is a fantasy about a young rabbi's struggle between Pan and Moses, nature and Judaism. The second tale, "Envy; or, Yiddish in America," likewise explores the conflict for the traditional Jew living in a gentile world; the protagonist, Edelshtein, an immigrant Yiddish poet who cannot get translated or published in English, satirically attacks the successful but secular, pantheist Yiddish novelist, Ostrover, a figure based on Isaac Bashevis Singer. Edelshtein reveals Ozick's belief that for Jewish literature to be valuable it must remain focused on Jewish themes and reject assimilation. The central problem and paradox for Ozick is that, as an observant Jew living in the U.S. and writing in English, she cannot escape the belief that all fiction is to some degree idolatrous and all writing in English a betrayal of Judaism. The last story in the collection, "Virility," is a feminist, Jewish tale exposing the falsehood of an assimilated male Jewish writer's claim to be a spokesman of universal values. The celebrated poet Edmund Gate turns out to be a plagiarist, while the true poet is none other than his aged "Tante Rivkah" who has remained true, in poverty and loneliness, to her Jewish origins. Ironically, when Rivkah's final poems are published posthumously under her own name, they no longer receive the glowing reviews they received when published under Gate's name.

Many of Ozick's other works, including *Bloodshed and Three Novellas* (1976) and *The Messiah of Stockholm* (1987), explore the issues and moral dilemmas facing the Jewish writer who, as Harold Bloom has written about Ozick, must struggle to reconcile her need to create fiction and her "fear of making stories into so many idols." *The Messiah of Stockholm* tells the story of Lars Andemening, an orphan of World War II who becomes fixated on the idea that he is the son of Bruno *Schulz, the famous Polish Jewish writer killed by the Nazis. The devastating impact of the Holocaust is a dominant theme in many of Ozick's works, including *Levitation: Five*

Fictions (1982), the novels *The Cannibal Galaxy* (1983) and *The Shawl* (1989). *The Cannibal Galaxy* is the story of Joseph Brill, a young Orthodox Parisian Jew, who survives the war hidden in a priest's library only to unsuccessfully attempt after the war to create a Jewish school that braids the best of Jewish and western traditions. *The Shawl*, arguably Ozick's most powerful and controversial work, combines two short stories. The title story, a work of bare, brutal horror, tells of the murder of Magda, the baby daughter of the assimilationist Jewish Pole, Rosa Lublin; Magda is killed when a Nazi throws her against an electrified fence. The second story, "Rosa," follows the destructive impact of the Shoah on Rosa, who has become "a madwoman and a scavenger" in Miami, writing letters in her best Polish to her dead daughter. While continuing to explore ethical, theological, and philosophical issues, Ozick turned to a lighter tone in her comic novel, *The Puttermesser Papers* (1997), a fantastic, episodic novel reminiscent of 18th-century picaresque tales. The novel follows the magical adventures of Jewish attorney Ruth Puttermesser, from her creation of a female golem who helps her to become mayor of New York to her death and experiences in paradise. Here and elsewhere Ozick combines the realistic and the surrealistic, comedy, tragedy, and philosophy, in order to create beautifully rich texts exploring Jewish life in America. Her 2004 realistic novel *Heir to the Glimmering World* is the story of a teenage orphan working for a German immigrant family headed by a professor who obsessively studies the Karaites, an obscure Jewish sect.

Despite her brilliant use of humor, Cynthia Ozick is a philosophical writer who takes Judaism more seriously than did the first generation of post-World War II Jewish writers in America. In a series of forthright and brilliant essays published in the Jewish press, she has written of the Messiah and the need to find a place for him in the modern city, of Holiness and the Sabbath day, and of the Jewish commitment to history as an answer to present-day idolatries. But she is aware of the tensions and difficulties which such commitment implies, especially for the creative writer ("Holiness and its Discontents," 1972). Her collections of essays, including *Art and Ardor* (1983), *Metaphor and Memory* (1989), *Fame and Folly* (1996), and *Quarrel and Quandary* (2000), explore a variety of topics with insight and thoughtfulness. Ozick does not betray the nostalgia of some older writers for the pieties of the ghetto; her sense of the relevance of the Jewish "myth" is related to a keen awareness of the contemporary western world with its combination of enchantment and squalor. At the same time, she shows a more positive identification with Israel and its fate than is to be found in her older contemporaries among the New York Jewish novelists. This became marked after the Six-Day War of 1967, and even more so after the Yom Kippur War of 1973.

BIBLIOGRAPHY: H. Bloom (ed.), *Cynthia Ozick: Modern Critical Views* (1986); H. Fisch, in: *Haaretz* (Oct. 10, 1973); E. Kauvar, *Cynthia Ozick's Fiction: Tradition and Invention.* (1993).

[Craig Svonkin (2nd ed.)]

OZON, Obóz Zjednoczenia Narodowego (Pol. "Camp of National Unity"), a paramilitary, antisemitic organization created in Poland on Oct. 2, 1937 by Colonel Adam Koc, under the auspices of President Moscicki and the minister of defense, Rydz-Smigly. Its program called for the protection of peasant ownership, the improvement of smallholdings, and the control of population by encouraging peasants to migrate to the cities. By camouflaging its antisemitism with problems of national self-defense, OZON hoped to compete with other rightist Fascist organizations such as ONR and win over the masses. Based on nationalism, Catholicism, and antisemitism, OZON hoped to divert the attention of workers and peasants from the real issues of the day, such as unemployment and poverty. It encouraged disorder and lawlessness, advocated segregation in the universities, and made assaults on Jewish rights. No Jew – not even one who had fought for Poland's independence in *Pilsudski's Legion – was eligible to join OZON. Many arbitrary and even brutal anti-Jewish policies and acts, such as restricting the right of *shehitah*, insisting that "Aryan" principles should prevail in professional organizations, establishing economic boycotts, destroying Jewish property, and encouraging pogroms in *Radom, *Czestochowa, *Brest-Litovsk, and *Vilna, were carried out under the aegis of OZON. In December 1938 Koc, whose totalitarian tendencies were becoming too apparent, was forced to give up his leadership of OZON and was replaced by General Skwarczynski. The antisemitic activities of OZON continued, however, under new leadership, and Skwarczynski asked the Polish *Sejm to take energetic measures to reduce the number of Jews in Poland, for national defense reasons. As a result the Polish government opposed the British mandatory restrictions on the admission of Jews to Palestine and sent a delegation to *Madagascar to study the possibilities of Jewish immigration there. OZON continued its activities until the defeat of Poland in September 1939.

BIBLIOGRAPHY: S. Segal, *The New Poland and the Jews* (1938), 68–75; R.L. Buell, *Poland: Key to Europe* (1939), index; I. Gruenbaum, in: EG, 1 (1953), 113–6; *Wielka Encyklopedia Powszechna*, 8 (1966), 90. **ADD. BIBLIOGRAPHY:** E. Melzer, *No Way Out, The Politics of Polish Jewry 1935–1939* (1997), index; idem, "*Mifleget ha-Shilton OZON ve-haYehudim be-Polin 1937–1939*," in: *Galed* (1978), 397–426.

[Dov Rabin]

OZORKOW, town in Lodz province, Poland. Founded in 1811, the settlement expanded rapidly and was granted urban status in 1816. Its Jewish population grew in size because it was dependent on the development of the textile industry in Lodz. In 1860 there were 1,978 Jews (38% of the total population) and on the eve of the Holocaust in 1939 they numbered about 5,000 (33% of the total population). During the 19th century Jews established workshops for weaving. Jewish tailors were also employed by industrial enterprises in Lodz on a contractual basis. The first democratic elections to the community council were held in 1922 when 12 members were elected representing the Zionist parties, *Mizrachi, *Agudat Israel, *Bund, and *Po'alei Zion-Left. On the eve of World War II Solomon

Winter, the delegate of the Zionists, was president of the community. There was a ramified network of schools in Ozorkow established at the initiative of the Zionists (Yavneh) and Agudat Israel (Yesodei ha-Torah). The public libraries established by the Zionist Organization and Po'alei Zion stimulated cultural activities such as drama circles, evening schools, and the sports societies *Maccabi and Ha-Kokhav (Gwiazda). In addition to the two large synagogues, the Great Synagogue and the Bet ha-Midrash, there were *shtieblach* (ḥasidic houses of prayer). The last rabbi of the community was R. David Behr. The Jews were also represented on the municipal council and their delegates held the position of vice mayor.

[Shimshon Leib Kirshenboim]

Holocaust Period

At the outbreak of World War II there were several battles around Ozorkow, and immediately after occupying the city on Sept. 5, 1939, the Germans seized and shot 24 Jews in the street. The beautiful synagogue and the *bet ha-midrash* were burned and the Jews were forced to demolish the walls. Frequent raids took place for slave labor in addition to the regular supply of labor contingents from the *Judenrat. Toward the end of 1939 many Jewish families were evicted from their homes and the ghetto was gradually established. The liquidation of the community took place during the spring and summer of 1942 in a series of *Aktionen*, the first of which was the selection of 500 Jews who were sent in an unknown direction, probably to the *Chelmno death camp. In April the Germans carried out a public hanging of eight Jews to "punish" the community for the escape of a woman from the ghetto. The largest *Aktion* took place on May 21–23, 1942, when 2,000 Jews were sent to Chelmno and 800 of the able-bodied to the *Lodz ghetto. All children below the age of ten were seized and deported. The final deportation took place on Aug. 21, 1942, when about 1,200 craftsmen and artisans were transferred to the Lodz ghetto. A memorial book, *Ozorkov*, was published in Hebrew in 1967.

[Danuta Dombrowska]

BIBLIOGRAPHY: Dabrowska, in: BŻIH, no. 13–14 (1955). **ADD. BIBLIOGRAPHY:** *Ozorkov*, 1967; S. Lipman, "*In die Lagern arum Poisen*," in: *Bletter fun Payn un umkum*" (1949), 86–87; *Sefer Lentshits* (1953), 178–92.

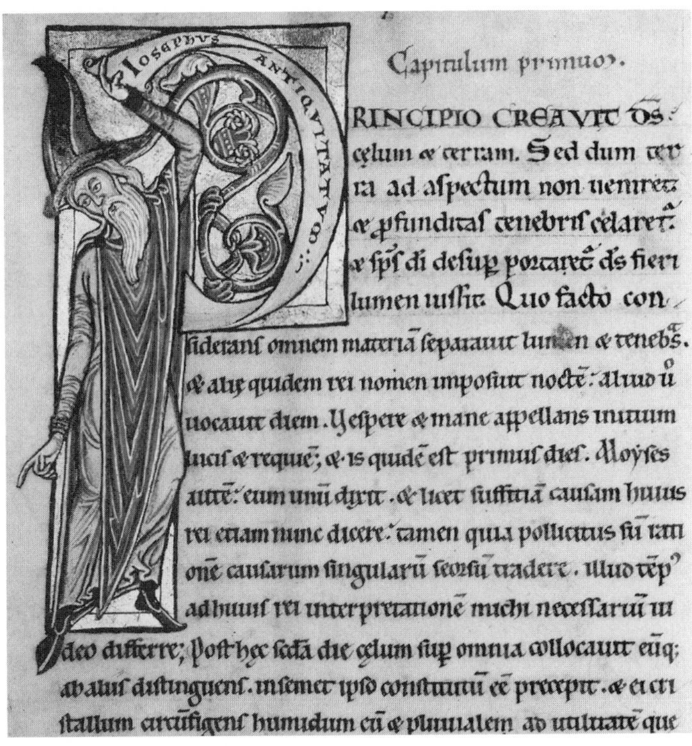

Initial letter "P" of the word Principio *in a Latin manuscript of* The Antiquities of the Jews *by Josephus Flavius, France, 12th century. The figure in the illuminated letter is wearing the medieval Jewish pointed hat. Paris, Bibliothèque Nationale, Cod. Lat. 5047, fol. 2 column 2. Photo Bildarchiv Foto Marbug, Marburg-Lahn.*

PA-PER

PABIANICE (Rus. **Pabyanitse**; Yid. **Pabianits**,), city in Lodz province, central Poland. One of Poland's most ancient towns, Pabianice was officially granted municipal status in the 14th century. The prohibition against Jewish residents, based on a privilege *de non tolerandis Judaeis*, appears to have been abrogated when the town came under Prussian domination. Jews then began to settle in the old city of Pabianice. The growth of the Jewish population was closely tied to the development of the local textile industry, and the spinning mills which were set up under subcontract for the textile factories of Lodz. In 1850 steam-powered machines were introduced into the Jewish-owned factories and large numbers of Jewish workers were employed in them from that time on, although Jews were compelled to compete against Polish workers who sought vigorously to supplant them. In 1913 the Polish workers of one Jewish-owned factory declared a strike because the owner hired four Jewish workers. The number of Jews increased from 27 in 1808 to 5,017 in 1897 (18% of the total population). Because Pabianice was in a battle region during World War I, the activity of the spinning mills was almost entirely interrupted and many Jews left, but they returned immediately after the armistice. In 1921 the Jews numbered 7,230, about 33% of the population. Their relative number, however, decreased so that in 1938 the 8,357 Jews in the town constituted only 16% of the total population. Economic competition between the Poles and Jews led to an encroachment on Jewish enterprises and during the 1930s Jewish poverty became widespread. Many Jews actually suffered from hunger.

The Jews of Pabianice were greatly influenced by *Ḥasidism, the *ẓaddikim* of *Sochaczew, *Radoshits, and *Komarno having lived in the city. One of the rabbis of Pabianice was Mendele Alter, a brother of the Rabbi of Gur. After R. Alter left to become rabbi of Kalish, his position was filled by his son, R. Abraham. The community's synagogue was first built by Jewish workers in 1847. Restored in 1880, it was famous for its frescoes and wooden engravings and the artistic construction of its Ark. Many organizations were active in the community between the world wars. The *Mizrachi organization was founded in 1918, and Revisionists began their activities in 1927. The *Po'alei Agudat Israel and Ẓe'irei Emunei Israel of the community were affiliated with *Agudat Israel. A large school, Or Torah, which also served as a cultural center for adults, was established by Agudat Israel. In 1919 the Zionists organized a Hebrew high school.

[Shimshon Leib Kirshenboim]

Holocaust Period

German forces entered the city on Sept. 8, 1939, and immediately introduced a series of repressive acts against the Jewish population. On Rosh Ha-Shanah the synagogue was destroyed and the building converted into a stable. On the Day of Atonement an intensive campaign of kidnapping was carried out in the streets and in the clandestine places of worship. In November many Jews were brutally evicted from their homes, in order to make room for Germans. At the same time the chairman and three other members of the *Judenrat were arrested and two of them murdered. In February 1940 a ghetto was formed in the old district of the town into which 8,000–9,000 Jews were crowded. Contact with the non-Jewish population was still possible and anyone could leave or enter the ghetto at will. Jewish artisans continued to earn wages, and thus supplement the meager rations allocated by the Germans. However, as a result of internal dissension, several members of the Judenrat, including its chairman, Jehiel Rubinstein, were denounced by a group of Jews, resulting in their arrest and dispatch to concentration camps in Germany where they met their deaths.

In February 1942 the Germans carried out a medical examination of all the Jews in Pabianice of 10 years of age and older. The able-bodied were stamped "A," while the elderly and sick were marked "B." The liquidation of the ghetto took place on May 16, 1942. Some 3,500 Jews in the "A" category and a few children were sent to the *Lodz ghetto. The 150 patients in the hospital were murdered on the spot, 180 tailors were detained in Pabianice to finish the work they had started, while the rest of the Jewish population – the "B" category – were sent to their deaths in the *Chelmno camp. After the liquidation of the ghetto, some 250 Pabianice Jews were employed in the large storehouse located nearby in Dombrowa where the clothing of the murdered Jewish population of western Poland (*Warthegau*) was processed, sorted, and repaired.

A memorial book, *Sefer Pabianice* (1956) was published in Yiddish in Tel Aviv by the society of immigrants from Pabianice.

[Danuta Dombrowska]

BIBLIOGRAPHY: Dąbrowska, in: BZIH, nos. 13–14 (1955); idem (ed.), *Kronika getta lodzkiego*, 1 (1965), passim. **ADD. BIBLIOGRAPHY:** M. Baruch, Pabianice, *Rzgow i wsie okoliczne* (1903); *Sefer Pabianice, Yiskor buch fun der farpainigter Kehille* (1956); *Dzieje Pabianic* (ed. G. Missalowa) (1968).

PABLO DE SANTA MARIA (**el Burguense**; c. 1350–1435), one of the most prominent apostates of Christian Spain, bishop, and theologian. He was born Solomon Halevi, a member of a distinguished Jewish family of *Burgos which had produced several tax farmers and financiers of the Castilian kingdom. In his youth he belonged to the circle of Jewish scholars whose most outstanding members were his relative Don Meir *Alguades, Joseph *Orabuena, and Don Benveniste de la *Cavallería. During the early 1380s he corresponded with R. Isaac b. *Sheshet on questions of ritual law (Responsa Ribash, ch. 187–92) and from this may be deduced his familiarity with *halakhah*. He had some knowledge of Jewish and Arabic philosophy and had read Christian theological works. From a humorous letter written in Hebrew to Meir Alguades in honor of the festival of Purim, it appears that he was in "England" in 1389. Some believe that he was detained there as a Castilian hostage but the more logical assumption is that his stay was connected with a diplomatic mission and that the reference is not to England itself but to Acquitaine, then under English rule.

The circumstances of Pablo's apostasy are obscure: according to Christian tradition he was baptized on July 21, 1390, but from a letter sent him after his conversion by his disciple Joshua *Lorki, also known as Geronimo de Sante Fe, there is reason to assume that he was converted after the outbreak of the riots of 1391 (see *Spain). It is in any case clear that he was already perplexed over questions of faith several years prior to his apostasy. His conversion to Christianity was to a certain extent a protest against the Averroistic views advanced by a considerable number of Jewish intellectuals in Spain. There is no doubt that he was vitally influenced by the apostate *Abner of Burgos, whom he frequently quotes in his own works. His four sons, his daughter, and his three brothers were baptized together with him. At first his wife refused to follow his example, but she accepted baptism a few years later. After his conversion, which left a powerful imprint on Jewish intellectuals, he sent a letter to Joseph Orabuena explaining the reasons that prompted his conversion to Christianity. This letter, which was widely circulated, also reached his disciple Joshua Lorki, who was converted some years later. In a lengthy letter, addressed to Pablo, Lorki asked him the reasons for his decision and expressed fundamental reservations on the messianic role of Jesus. Only the last part of Pablo's reply has been preserved; it includes the idea that it is incumbent upon every Jew to delve into the Bible and the Oral Law so as to discern the messianism of Jesus.

To increase his knowledge of Christian theology, Pablo traveled to Paris, where he studied until 1394 and was ordained a priest. On completing his studies, he settled in Avignon, where he became one of the favorites of Pope *Benedict XIII and one of his staunchest supporters. It was during this period that he began his anti-Jewish activity, when he attempted to induce King John I of Aragon to issue anti-Jewish laws. His ascent in the Catholic hierarchy was rapid: in 1396 he was appointed archdeacon of Trevinno, in 1403 bishop of Cartagena, and from 1415 until his death, he was bishop of Burgos. He also held the position of *canciller mayor* to the king of Castile from 1407.

Pablo left a number of works: the first, *Scrutinium Scripturarum*, was completed in 1432. The first part describes a dialog between the Jew, Saul and the Christian, Paul. The Jew argues against the tenets of Christianity and the Christian refutes all his objections. In the second part, an apostate asks his teacher to elucidate a number of points of Christian dogma which are not sufficiently clear to him. In 1429 Paulus completed the *Aditiones ad postillam Magistri Nicolai Lyra* ("Additions to the Biblical Commentary of *Nicholas de Lyra"). He also wrote a historical poem, *Las Siete edades del Mundo or Edades trovadas*, as well as a work on the history of Spain from antiquity until 1412, *Suma de las crónicas del mundo*. Toward the end of his life, he wrote a book on his origins and genealogy. His brothers held important positions in Castilian society: PEDRO JUÁREZ became governor of Burgos and ALVAR GARCÍA the notary of the royal office. This was also the case with his sons: GONZALO GARCIA DE SANTA MARÍA rose to the rank of bishop; ALONSO OF CARTAGENA succeeded his father as bishop of Burgos and wrote *Defensorium unitatis christianae* in defense of the Conversos; PEDRO DE CARTAGENA became a military commander of the kings of Castile, and ALVAR SÁNCHEZ DE CARTAGENA was a diplomat in the service of the kingdom.

BIBLIOGRAPHY: Baer, Spain, index; I. Abrahams, in: JQR, 12 (1900), 255–63; P.L. Serrano, *Los conversos Pablo de Santa María y Alfonso de Cartagena* (1942); F. Cantera, *La conversión del célebre talmudista Salomón Leví* (1933); idem, *Alvar García de Santa María y su familia de conversos* (1952), index; idem, in: *Homenaje a Millás-Vallicrosa*, 1 (1954), 301–7.

[Joseph Kaplan]

PACHECO, RODRIGO BENJAMIN MENDES (d. 1749), early U.S. merchant. Pacheco, whose place of birth is unknown, went to New York City early in his career and was made freeman of the city in 1712. Increasingly prominent as his mercantile business flourished, Pacheco petitioned the authorities in 1728 with others for the right to purchase land for a Jewish cemetery. He was instrumental in the erection of the Shearith Israel synagogue on Mill Street, in 1729–30. In 1731 Pacheco was appointed colonial agent for the province. Around 1740 he did a brisk business in shipping supplies to the new colony of Georgia, where his contact was the Nunezes family. A more extensive enterprise was carried on there by a competitor, Jacob *Franks, who, unlike Pacheco, was Ashkenazi. In the wake of a bitter legal entanglement over his business affairs, Pacheco settled permanently in London in 1731.

BIBLIOGRAPHY: J.R. Marcus, *Early American Jewry*, 1 (1951), 158; 2 (1953), 293; L. Hershkowitz and I.S. Meyer (eds.), *Lee Max Friedman Collection of American Colonial Correspondence* (1968); M. Stern, *Americans of Jewish Descent* (1960).

[Leo Hershkowitz]

PACHT, ISAAC (1890–1987), U.S. attorney, judge, and community leader. Pacht, who was born in Millie, Austria, was taken to the U.S. while a boy. After his graduation from Brooklyn Law School in 1912, he moved to Los Angeles and in 1913 was admitted to the California bar. Pacht was a practicing attorney except for the periods when he served as judge of the Superior Court (1931–32) and judge of the California District Court of Appeal (1932–35). He was deeply involved in California prison reform and served for a number of years as president of the State Board of Prison Directors (1940–50), under appointment by Governor Culbert Olson. Governor Earl Warren appointed Pacht chairman of the California Commission on Criminal Law and Procedure (1947–49). Extremely active in Los Angeles Jewish affairs, Pacht held posts including chairman (the first) of the United Jewish Welfare Fund (1932–34); president of the Jewish Institute of Religion of Los Angeles; and president of the Los Angeles Jewish Community Council (1949–51). He also served as president or director of the Vista Del Mar Child Care Service for more than 40 years. He was the founding chairman of the Jewish Community Foundation of Los Angeles. Established in 1954, it has evolved into one of the city's largest foundations.

[Max Vorspan]

PACHTER, CHARLES (1942–), Canadian printmaker, painter, illustrator. Charles Pachter was born and raised in Toronto. He studied art history at the University of Toronto (1960–64), and printmaking at the Ontario College of Art. In 1962–63 he studied at the Sorbonne and at the Académie de la Grande Chaumière in Paris. He held his first solo exhibition at the Pollock Gallery in Toronto in 1964. Focusing on printmaking, he completed his M.F.A. at the Cranbrook Academy of Art in Michigan in 1966.

While still a graduate student, Pachter collaborated with Canadian writer Margaret Atwood to create five limited edition handmade books of her poems. Lifelong friends, he and Atwood collaborated again on their master work, *The Journals of Susanna Moodie* (1980). Pachter's early lithographs and silkscreens, which focused on family, identity, and interpersonal relationships, also include a series of powerful expressionistic self-portraits. Fascinated by the relationship of art to national identity – the Canadian flag has remained a continuing theme – Pachter's art has often centered on popular Canadian images, including the Mounties, hockey players, and the moose. In the 1970s, his work incorporated images of Queen Elizabeth II and the moose, leading viewers to question the continuing relevance of the monarchy in a post-colonial Canada. Portraits of prominent Canadians have served as subjects for his art. His mural, *Hockey Knights in Canada*, highlights a Toronto subway station and his stylized life-size sculpture of a moose stands on the University of Toronto campus. An entrepreneur by nature, Pachter played a leadership role in the development of artists' districts in Toronto in the 1970s and 1980s. Pachter's work is represented in public and private collections in Canada and internationally, including the National Library of Canada, Le musée d'art contemporain, Montreal, the Art Gallery of Ontario, Toronto, and the Centre d'Art Présence Van Gogh, Saint Rémy de Provence, France. In 2000, Pachter was made a member of the Order of Canada; in 2002, France named him a Chevalier dans l'Ordre des Arts et des Lettres.

BIBLIOGRAPHY: Welsh-Ovcharov, with introduction by M. Atwood, *Charles Pachter* (1992).

[Joyce Zemans (2nd ed.)]

PACIFICI, ALFONSO (1889–1983), Italian lawyer and thinker. Born in Florence, he came under the influence of Rabbi S.H. *Margulies and became the leader of the group who attempted to revitalize Jewish life in Italy through "integral" Judaism, combining religion, culture, and Zionism. A remarkable orator with a striking appearance and great personal charm, he exercised a considerable influence on a whole generation of Jews in Italy, even those who subsequently disagreed with his increasingly uncompromising orthodoxy. In

1916, he founded (with Dante *Lattes) the weekly *Israel.* He settled in 1934 in Ereẓ Israel, where he continued his activities, mainly for Orthodox educational institutions. His ideas are expressed in such works as *Discorsi sullo Shemà* (1953), *Israel Segullà* (1955), and its semi-autobiographical sequel *Interludio* (1959).

In 1984 a small book was published in Hebrew, "From Florence in Italy to Jerusalem," containing a part of his autobiography and two articles by the editors S. Auerbach and G.B. Sarfatti; in Jerusalem a street was dedicated in his memory, Segullat Israel Street, the title of one of his books; his archive has been transferred to the Central Archives for the History of Jewish People in Jerusalem and an "inventario" of it was published (ed. R. Spiegel) in 2000.

BIBLIOGRAPHY: *Israel* (June 5, 1969); Roth, in: *Menorah Journal*, 47 (1959), 41–49; RMI, 35 (1969), 233f.

[Cecil Roth / Alfredo-Mordechai Rabello (2nd ed.)]

PACIFICI, RICCARDO (1904–c. 1943), Italian rabbi and scholar. Born in Florence and trained there at the Collegio Rabbinico Italiano, Pacifici served as assistant rabbi in Venice in 1928–31. He was the head of the rabbinical seminary (and later rabbi) in Rhodes, and in 1936 was appointed rabbi of Genoa. His published works (1929–36) include monographs on Venetian Jewish history (including a volume on the inscriptions in the Jewish cemetery in the Lido; 1929), historical accounts of the Jews of Rhodes (1933, 1935) and of the Genoese community (1939, 1948), and a selection of sermons and addresses, *Discorsi sulla Torà* (1968). At the height of Nazi and Fascist persecution he published a Midrash anthology. After making great efforts to assist the victims of Nazi terror (DELASEM; Delegazione Assistenza Emigranti Ebrei), he was arrested and deported by the Germans in 1943, his subsequent fate being unknown.

BIBLIOGRAPHY: Milano, Bibliotheca, index; A. Segre, in: R. Pacifici, *Discorsi sulla Torà* (1968), xii–xxxiii; A. Luzzatto, *Riccardo Pacifici* (1967), incl. bibl.

[Alfredo Mordechai Rabello]

PACIFICO, DAVID (invariably called "**Don Pacifico**"; 1784–1854), merchant and diplomat. Born in Gibraltar, Pacifico was a British subject. In 1812 his business activities took him to Lagos, Portugal, where he was appointed Portuguese consul to Morocco (1835–37) and to Greece (1837–42). In 1847 the Greek minister, Coletti, in deference to one of the Rothschilds who happened to be in Athens at the time, prohibited the populace of Athens from burning a wooden effigy of Judas Iscariot on the Friday before Easter as was the yearly custom. Riots broke out and Pacifico was attacked and his house destroyed. Pacifico demanded a sum of 800,000 drachmas (then equivalent to £26,618) as compensation. The Greek government refused to consider his claim and even confiscated Pacifico's real estate. In order to defend his interests as a British subject, the British Admiral Park – upon the instruction of the foreign minister, Lord Palmerston – blockaded the port of Piraeus and captured 200 Greek ships. The Greek government was compelled to pay 120,000 drachmas and £500. Pacifico retired to London, where he died. The incident was important in its time as Palmerston had to defend himself for having supported the lawsuit of a Jew. Palmerston replied that it was not right that because "a man is of Jewish persuasion" he should be outraged. In the British Parliament, Palmerston made a celebrated speech (June 25, 1850) which concluded that all British subjects ought to be able to say, as did citizens of ancient Rome, "*Civis Romanus sum*" ("I am a citizen of Rome"), and thereby receive protection from the British government. Palmerston's resolute assertion of British super-patriotism helped to make him prime minister five years later. The "Don Pacifico" affair was one of the most famous such incidents of mid-Victorian Britain.

BIBLIOGRAPHY: *Hansard Parliamentary Reports* (June 25, 1850), cols. 380–444; M. Molho, in: *Joshua Starr Memorial Volume* (1953). **ADD. BIBLIOGRAPHY:** ODNB online; A.M. Hyamson, "Don Pacifico," in: JHSET, 18 (1953–55), 1–39.

[Simon Marcus / William D. Rubinstein (2nd ed.)]

PACKMAN, JAMES JOSEPH (1907–1969), U.S. newspaperman and public relations executive. Born in Poland, Packman was taken to the U.S. in 1910. His long newspaper career included 20 years on the *Los Angeles Examiner* (1923–43) and the managing editorship of the *Milwaukee Sentinel* (1943–52). In 1958 he became a consultant on political and foreign affairs and newspaper operation, and in 1961 was appointed director of public relations for the Golden Gate National Bank, San Francisco.

PADDAN-ARAM (Heb. פַּדַּן אֲרָם), place mentioned only in Genesis and prominently associated with the lives of the Patriarchs. Paddan-Aram seems to have been either identical with, or included within, the area of Aram-Naharaim and is described by Abraham as "the land of my birth" to which he sent his servant to find a wife for Isaac (24:4, 10; 25:20). It is most frequently mentioned in connection with Jacob's flight from Esau and his residence with his uncle Laban, the brother of Rebekah his mother. All but one of the tribes of Israel originated there (28:2–7; 31:18; 33:18; 35:9, 26; 46:15; 48:7).

Paddan-Aram must have been situated in northern Mesopotamia since it included the city of Haran (28:10; 29:4). The repeated description of Laban as an Aramean (25:20; 28:5; 31:20, 24) would imply an Aramean population speaking the Aramaic language (31:47). In fact, the name is generally accepted as deriving from the Aramaic *paddânâ*, "a field, or plain," and meaning "the Plain of Aram," corresponding to the Hebrew *sedeh Aram* (Hos. 12:13).

BIBLIOGRAPHY: Albright, Stone, 180; B. Maisler, in: *Zion*, 11 (1946), 3.

[Morris M. Schnitzer]

PADEH, BARUCH (1908–2001), Israeli physician. Born in Belorussia, he studied medicine in Prague and graduated in

1927. Padeh immigrated to Palestine, worked as a physician in the kibbutzim of the Jordan Valley, and settled in Degania B. In 1936 he also became regional commander of the *Haganah. In 1938, he went to New York to study hematology and, upon his return in 1940, he resumed his work as a regional physician. In 1947–48 he served as the regional physician of the Southern Front. In 1949 he moved to Tel Hashomer hospital where he became deputy director in 1955. In 1956 he was appointed chief medical officer of the IDF, and in 1971 he became director general of the Ministry of Health. In 1974, he went back to the north of Israel and was director of Poriah hospital. Later he became a family physician in Kaẓrin, in the Golan Heights. Padeh, is remembered as the physician who set the medical standards for the Medical Army Corps as well as the Civil Medical System and Services. He was particularly interested in the development of family practice and community medicine. Padeh was also the founder of the genetic studies of the Israeli population in the 1950s. He received many awards and prizes for his services, and in 1985 he was awarded the Israel Prize in medicine.

[Bracha Rager (2nd ed.)]

PADERBORN, town in N.W. Germany. The earliest documentary source reflecting the presence of Jews in the city of Paderborn dates from 1342; the existence of a stone house belonging to them at this time attests to their wealth. In a dispute between Bishop Herman von Spiegel in 1378 and the city of Paderborn, the bishop referred to "his Jews" who were under his protection. Nevertheless, an organized Jewish community came into being in the city only in 1590. A prayer room was opened in the 17th century. In 1640 seven Jewish families were permitted to live in Paderborn; by 1652 the number had increased to 14 families. The Jews of the city were mentioned among those benefiting from a general letter of protection granted in 1661. They played a leading role in the federation of Jewish communities in the bishopric. Numbers remained fairly constant until the end of the 18th century. By 1764 a synagogue is noted in the city; a cemetery plot was purchased in 1728. In 1778 there were 19 "protected" Jews in the town and in 1803 there were 26, in addition to two communal employees. In the course of the 19th century the community grew from 288 persons in 1840 to 389 in 1913. A new synagogue was built in 1881 (destroyed by the Nazis in 1938). Together with the synagogue, the community also maintained a religious school. After 1938 the prayer room of the Jewish orphanage (consecrated in 1863) was used as the cultural center for the continuously declining community. In 1932 there were still 310 Jews in Paderborn, but in 1939 only 123 remained, the greater part of whom were later deported. In July 1942 the staff and children of the orphanage (founded 1856) were also deported. From the summer of 1939 until March 1943 the town contained a so-called "Jewish Retraining Center" for some 100 people who were forcibly employed by the Nazi authorities in Paderborn. On March 1, 1943, all the inmates of the center were deported to Auschwitz; only 10 survived. After World War II a community was reestablished in Paderborn in 1950, including the districts of Bueren, Hoexter, Lippstadt, *Soest, and Warburg. In 1962 it numbered 55 members. The new synagogue was dedicated in 1959. The Jewish community numbered 35 in 1989 and 85 in 2004. About 70% of the members are immigrants from the former Soviet Union.

[Bernhard Brilling]

Province (formerly Bishopric) of Paderborn

The presence of Jews in the bishopric of Paderborn is first mentioned as early as 1258; in 1281 they were put under the protection of the bishop who intervened actively, following the murder of Jews in Bueren in 1292. Sources remain scanty until the 17th century. In the intervening years, Jewish communities were slowly built in the towns of the bishopric. Jurisdiction over the Jews had passed to the municipalities, which restricted Jewish economic activity to trading in unredeemed pawned articles, gold, and jewels, so as not to compete with local merchants. In the 16th century the Jews of Warburg were permitted to engage in *moneylending and restricted commercial activity, providing it did not interfere with the guilds. In the beginning of the 17th century jurisdiction over the Jews reverted to the bishop. By 1646 there were 67 Jewish families in the bishopric, and by 1677 there were 144. From 1619 the rabbinate for the **Landjudenschaft* of the bishopric was located in Warburg, the largest Jewish community until the emancipation. In 1661 a general letter of protection was addressed by Bishop Ferdinand von Fuerstenberg to the Jewries of Warburg, Paderborn, Beverungen, Peckelsheim, and Borgentreich (among others), granting them liberal privileges. In part as a result of the need to defend themselves against the municipalities and in part due to the need for funds to support a rabbi and maintain a cemetery, a federation of Jewish communities in the bishopric was organized in 1628, responsible directly to the bishop. At the head of the community was an *Obervorgaenger* at whose suggestion the other officials were appointed by the bishop. During 1649–50 the office was filled by Solomon Levi, and in the following year by the Court Jew Behrend *Levi, later accused of embezzlement and removed. Some of his successors in the well-paid position were likewise corrupt, and in 1677 three non-salaried officials took over the duties of the head of the community. A Diet (*Va'ad Gadol*) met once every three years in varying places. During the 18th century the Diet elected the community's elders. Among the duties of the organized community, tax assessment was perhaps the most important; the community was often divided over the inequities of the tax system and the domination of the federation by a few wealthy families. The rabbinate was given a free hand in ritual matters; dues collected through taxation of *se'udot mitzvah* went to the support of Ereẓ Israel.

The economic condition of the Jews in the bishopric steadily improved as restrictions on their economic activity were removed. In 1661 they were granted permission to engage in retail trade in dry goods; permission for peddling was granted in 1687. They became prominent in the import trade in tobacco, as well as the leasing of the salt monopoly. All restrictions were lifted in 1704 and Jews expanded their commercial activity still more, trading in agricultural produce and playing a leading role in establishing Warburg as a grain center. They were among the prominent merchants at the *Leipzig fairs. In 1802 the bishopric was secularized and in 1803 became a province of Prussia. Emancipation, introduced during the Napoleonic invasion, was eclipsed during the reaction that followed and came into its own only toward the end of the century. In the period following the Franco-Prussian War, Jews took an increasingly active part in the economic and social life of the province, as well as coming into prominence in the arts and sciences, a development that came to an end only with the liquidation of Jewish life by the Nazis.

[Bernhard Brilling]

BIBLIOGRAPHY: *Baun wir doch aufs neue das alte Haus – juedisches Schicksal in Paderborn* (1964), incl. bibl.; *Westfalia Judaica*, ed. by B. Brilling, 1 (1967), 119, 213; *Germania Judaica*, 2 pt. 2 (1968), 643f.; *Aus Geschichte und Leben der Juden in Westfalen*, ed. by H. Ch. Meyer (1962), 45–46, 254 (bibl.); M. Kreutzberger, *Katalog*, 1 (1970), 203; B. Altmann, in: JSOS, 3 (1941), 159–88; 5 (1943), 163–86; idem, *Die Juden im ehemaligen Hochstift Paderborn zur Zeit des 17. und 18. Jahrhunderts* (1923), unpublished dissertation, University of Freiburg in Breisgau; M. Grunwald, in: ZGJD, 7 (1937), 112–4. **ADD. BIBLIOGRAPHY:** *Germania Judaica*, vol. 3, 1350–1514 (1987) 1083–84; M. Naarmann, *Die Paderborner Juden 1802–1945. Emanzipation, Integration und Vernichtung. Ein Beitrag zur Geschichter der Juden in Westfalen im 19. und 20. Jahrhundert* (Paderborner historische Forschungen, vol. 1) (1988); G. Birkmann, *Bedenke, vor wem du stehst. 300 Synagogen und ihre Geschichte in Westfalen und Lippe* (1998), 192–95; M. Naarmann, "Von ihren Leuten wohnt hier keiner mehr," in: *Juedische Familien in Paderborn in der Zeit des Nationalsozialismus* (Paderborner historische Forschungen, vol. 7) (1998); D. van Faassen, *Juden im Paderborner Land im 17. und 18. Jahrhundert* (2000). **WEBSITE:** www.jg-paderborn.de.

PADUA, capital of Padua province, N. Italy. In documents dated 1134 and 1182 two or three persons with the surname Judaeus are mentioned, although some scholarly opinion holds that they were not Jews. In 1289 the physician Jacob Bonacosa, a Jew, translated *Averroes' *Colliget*, a medical text. Several loan banks were founded by Jews who came from various parts of Italy, such as Pisa, Roma, Bologna, and Ancona in the 1360s, and in the 1380s and 1390s from Germany and Spain. In 1380 Jewish bankers were responsible for three powerful loan and trading concerns with a capital investment of 20,000 ducats. Taxation imposed by Padua's rulers, the Carraras, was not heavy, and the populace was normally tolerant of the Jews. The community grew rapidly in wealth and social position; there was a synagogue and cemetery. In 1405 Padua became part of the Venetian republic. In 1415 an attempt was made by the Venetian authorities at the request of the Paduan city council to lower the interest rate of Jewish loan bankers to between 12% and 15%. The attempt was opposed vigorously by the Jewish bankers who closed their places of business in retaliation. The strike was backed by students who were deprived of their source of credit. During the first years of Venetian rule Jewish economic progress continued at a rapid pace. Their situation deteriorated, however, in the second quarter of the century. In part due to internal difficulties within the Venetian republic increasing pressure was directed against the economic status and legal position of the Jewish community. In 1420 the authorities imposed a lower rate of interest.

The situation of the loan bankers gradually worsened and they were expelled from the city in 1456. A major role in the expulsion of the bankers was taken by John *Capistrano and his followers. The rest of the community was not expelled, however, and a Jewish loan banker returned to the city by 1468. Jewish moneylending was officially permitted again in 1483. In 1475, when rumors spread about a blood libel at *Trent, the Jews of Padua were set upon by the mob, despite appeals by the senate. Tempers rose again in 1491 when the populace was incited by Bernardino de *Feltre and other Franciscan monks. Influenced by the monks, the town council sought several times to expel the Jews. The opening of the first Monte di *Pietà in 1492 did not adversely affect the economic status of the loan bankers. in 1509, led by Maximilian I of Hapsburg, the Lansquenets descended upon Italy. Jewish property was sacked, first by Austrians and afterward by the returning Venetian soldiers. Two leading bankers, Vita Meshullam and Naphtali Herz Wertheim, were completely ruined and Jewish loans ran to a total of about 15,000 ducats. The development of the community's inner life continued during the 16th century and its legal status was strengthened despite the numerous ways in which Jews were publicly degraded. In 1547 the republic of Venice ordered Jewish banks closed so as not to compete with the local Monte di Pietà. The Jews successfully turned to commerce; there were Jewish proprietors in many of the town shops, especially those dealing in jewelry, cloth, and drapery.

Early in the 16th century the Jews were ordered to live in their own quarter, but they were not completely restricted to a ghetto and some of the wealthier families lived among Christians on the most elegant streets. The idea of establishing a ghetto similar to those in Rome or Venice was decided on between 1581 and 1584 but not actually put into effect until 1601. The district itself centered around a small square where the synagogue was situated. There were five gates to the ghetto, one of which was surmounted by a tablet with an inscription in Latin and Hebrew prohibiting both Jews and Christians from coming near the ghetto's gates at night. Until 1715 Jews were compelled to listen to malevolent anti-Jewish sermons in the churches. Giving in to various pressures, the town council allowed the burning of the Talmud and other Hebrew books in 1556. Nevertheless, Padua remained an important center for Hebrew studies by virtue of its rabbinical academies and the fact that Jews were drawn there from all over Europe to study in its university.

In 1616 the Jewish population of Padua numbered 665, chiefly engaged in the silk industry. The community suffered gravely from a plague, 421 of the 721 Jews dying in 1630–31. In 1688 the community of Padua helped ransom 600 Jews of Belgrade who had been captured and maltreated by the Imperial troops. Hostility toward the Jews grew in the 17th century during the wars waged by Venice against the Turks. Because of rumors that the Jews had given help to Buda (see *Budapest) during the siege by the Austrian and Venetian armies, on Aug. 20, 1684, the populace sacked the ghetto. Loss of life was narrowly prevented by the intervention of the army and the town authorities. As a result of the outbreak, the death penalty was established for causing riots. To commemorate the community's rescue, a day of thanksgiving (the *Purim di-Buda*) was celebrated each year. Another "Purim" was celebrated in 1795 to commemorate the putting out of a fire which might otherwise have destroyed the community. Disturbances occasionally arose because medical students sought to perform autopsies on dead Jews, despite the fact that the Jews paid up to 100 lire annually to the *studium patavinum* in order to prevent this. Incidents connected with this problem occurred in the 16th and 17th centuries until a fixed itinerary for Jewish funerals was worked out by the authorities.

When the French troops entered Padua on April 29, 1797, the Jews were temporarily emancipated; in August the central government decreed that Jews were free to reside wherever they wished. The ghetto was renamed Via Libera ("Liberty Way") and its gates taken down. From 1805 to 1814 Padua was part of Napoleon's kingdom of Italy; R. Isaac Raphael b. Elisha *Finzi took part in the Paris *Sanhedrin convened by the emperor. However, when the Austrians entered Padua in January 1814, the populace attacked the Jews, who were considered friends of the French. Having to appear satisfied with the change of regime, the Jews celebrated the entrance of the Austrians in the German synagogue. After the Treaty of Vienna (in 1815), when Padua again came under Austrian rule, the Jews were allowed to enjoy practically all rights, except that of serving in public office. In 1840 the Jewish population of Padua numbered 910. Full emancipation was obtained only in 1866, when Padua once more became part of the kingdom of Italy. By 1881, the Jewish population had risen to 1,378; thereafter, however, the cultural and social life of the community deteriorated and by 1911 the number had decreased to 881. Because of discrimination affecting all Italian Jewry, the Jews of Padua either left for other Italian centers or emigrated to other countries, among them Ereẓ Israel; by 1938 their number had further declined to 586.

There were three synagogues in Padua. One of German rite, which was opened in 1525, served also as a *bet midrash* for the whole community from 1682. In the same year the Ashkenazi synagogue, or Scuola grande, was inaugurated. In 1892 the Scuola adopted the Italian rite. In 1943 the building was severely damaged by a bomb, and in 1960 its huge ark was taken to the Yad Eliyahu Synagogue in Tel Aviv. The third synagogue, of Sephardi rite, built in 1617 on the initiative of the influential Marini family, was closed down in 1892. In 1958 its ark was taken to Hechal Shelomo in Jerusalem. The synagogue of Italian rite, built in 1548 and completed later in the 16th century, closed down in 1892. It was reopened after World War II and in 1970 was the only synagogue in the city.

Community Life

Until the close of the 18th century the administrators of the Jewish community were chosen according to their country of origin; in 1577 there was a "general assembly" (*capitolo generale*), a "directional council" (*capitolo ristretto*), and three *parnassim* or *memunim*. Internal laws for all aspects of life, social or spiritual, were based on talmudic law until the French conquest. A statute was drawn up by the community in 1815 (revised in 1826 and recognized by Venice in 1828), requiring members to pay taxes proportionate to their incomes. The statute was modified again in 1832, 1841, and 1866, and finally thoroughly revised on the initiative of S.D. Luzzatto. The new regulations took effect from Jan. 27, 1894, and remained in use until replaced by a comprehensive law for all the Jewish communities in 1930. The community maintained relations with Ereẓ Israel, especially through emissaries sent to Jerusalem, Hebron, Safed, and Tiberias. In 1713 a philanthrophic society, the fraternity of Lomedei Torah ve-Shomerei Mitzvah, was founded, whose members paid a relatively high admission fee and made a fixed annual contribution. In return, in case of illness members received medical and surgical assistance, plus a daily allowance for the duration of illness; expenses for funerals and burial were also defrayed by the fraternity. This fraternity was still in existence in 1970, side by side with the brotherhood Malbish Arumim, the "S.D. Luzzatto Cultural Circle," and branches of various Zionist movements.

Of particular importance in the Padua community was academic activity. Jews studied medicine simultaneously with Torah. From 1519 to 1619 about 80 Jews obtained degrees in medicine in Padua, and from 1619 to 1721, 149 Jews graduated as physicians. Numbers of Jews from Germany, Poland, and the Levant also came to study in Padua. Some pressure was exerted by Christian doctors and the ecclesiastical authorities, so that the senate prohibited Jewish doctors from practicing outside the ghetto, but this was not too strictly applied. Jewish medical students were allowed to wear the black beret of their colleagues, rather than the yellow one required of other Jews (see Jewish *Badge). Among those students who distinguished themselves particularly were Moses Abba Delmedigo, physician and philosopher, and Abraham b. Meir de *Balmes of Lecce.

In the field of Hebrew studies, Padua was of particular importance in the second half of the 15th century, under the guidance of Judah *Minz, one of the major rabbinical authorities of that period. Judah was followed by his son, Aaron Minz, and by his brother-in-law, Meir *Katzenellenbogen, whose responsa constitute a vital source for the history of the Jews of that time. Other prominent figures in Padua were Meir b. Ezekiel ibn *Gabbai, Menahem Delmedigo, Jonathan b. *Treves, Raphael b. Joshua Ẓarefati, Jacob b. Moses Levi, Benzion b. Raphael, and Judah b. Moses Fano (16th century); Isaac Ḥayyim *Cantarini, Samuel de *Archivolti, Aryeh and Abraham Cattalani, Judah b. Samuel Cantarini, Solomon and Shabbetai b. Luzzatto, Judah b. Samuel Cantarini, Samuel and Ḥayyim Moses *Cantarini, Solomon and Shabbetai b. Luzzatto, Judah b. Samuel Cantarini Samuel and Ḥayyim Moses *Cantarini, Solomon and Shabbetai b. Isaac Marini, Aaron Romanin, Samuel David b. Jehiel *Ottolengo (17th century); Moses Ḥayyim Luzzatto, Michael Terni, Abraham Shalom, Solomon Nizza, Jacob Raphael Ezekiel *Forti, Solomon Eliezer Ghirondi and Benzion Ghirondi (18th century); Isaac Raphael b. Elisha *Finzi, Israel Conian, Mordecai Samuel b. Benzion Aryeh *Ghirondi, Ephraim Raphael Ghirondi, Leone Osimo, Graziadio Viterbi, Giuseppe *Basevi, Eudi Lolli, Alessandro Zammatto, Filosseno Luzzatto, Giuseppe *Almanzi, Eugenia Gentilomo, Gabriele Trieste, Marco Osimo (19th century); and Gustavo Castelbolognesi, Paolo Nissim, and Dante *Lattes (20th century). Padua had one last touch of splendor in the 19th century with the inauguration of the Istituto Superiore Rabbinico, later known as the Collegio Rabbinico *Italiano, the first rabbinical seminary in Europe to combine secular and traditional Jewish study. The institute was initiated by Isacco Samuel *Reggio, and Lelip Della Torre and S.D. *Luzzatto were among the rectors. The institute itself (transferred to Rome in 1870) exerted a considerable influence on the spiritual life of Italian Jews. From 1962 to 1965 Dante Lattes edited the journal *Rassegna Mensile di Israel* in Padua. Some Hebrew works were printed in Padua.

Printing

In 1563 Meir b. Ezekiel b. Gabbai's *Derekh Emunah* was printed by Lorenzo Pasquato of Padua, with Samuel Boehm serving as proofreader. This was followed by Shem Tov b. Shem Tov's *Derashot ha-Torah* in 1567. A conference of Italian communities convened at Padua in 1585 to consider a new approach to Pope Sixtus v on the question of printing the Talmud, then available only in a censored and emasculated edition. In 1622 Hebrew printing was continued in Padua by Gaspare (later Giulio) Crivellari, who printed Jacob Heilprin's *Naḥalat Ya'akov*, followed in the same year by the printing of *Kinot Eikhah*, printed by Abraham Catalono, and Leon de Modena's Hebrew-Italian dictionary, *Galut Yehudah* (1640–42). In the 19th century Antonio Bianchi printed S.D. Luzzatto's *Isziah* (1885) and other works, between 1834 and 1879. Francesco Sacchetto printed Luzzatto's Pentateuch commentary in 1872.

Modern Period

In 1931 the community of Padua had a Jewish population of 586. In 1941 the interior of the Scuola grande was desecrated by Fascist bands. Between 1943 and 1945 more than 85 Jews, among whom was Rabbi Eugenio Cohen Sacerdoti, were sent to extermination camps. After the war (1948) there were 269 Jews in Padua and their number had declined to 220 by 1970.

BIBLIOGRAPHY: A. Ciscato, *Gli Ebrei in Padua* (1801); Milano, Bibliotheca, index, s.v. *Padova*; Milano, Italia, index; G. Gabrieli, *Italia Judaica* (1924), index; Roth, Italy, index; C. Roth, *Venice* (1930), index; U. Cassuto, *Gli Ebrei a Firenze* (1918), index; J. Pinkerfeld, *Battei Keneset be-Italyah* (1954), index; D. Carpi, "*Ha-Yehudim be-Padova bi-Tekufat ha-Renaissance*" (unpublished doctoral dissertation, Hebrew, Jerusalem, 1967), Fr. summary; idem, in: RMI, 28 (1962), 47–60; 32 (1966), nos. 9–10, 1–306; P.C.I. Zorattini, *ibid.*, 34 (1968), 582–91; A. Modena and E. Morpurgo, *Medici e Chirurgi Ebrei… nell'Università di Padova…* (1967); C. Roth, *Il Purim di Buda* (1934); U. Nahon, *Aronot Kodesh…* (1970); Z. Shazar, *Ha-Tikvah li-Shenat HaTaK* (1970); D.W. Amram, *Makers of Hebrew Books in Italy* (1909), index; Ḥ.D. Friedberg, *Toledot ha-Defus ha-Ivri be-Italyah* (1956^2), 83f.

[Alfredo Mordechai Rabello]

PADWAY, JOSEPH ARTHUR (1891–1947), U.S. labor lawyer and politician. Padway, who was born in Leeds, England, went to Milwaukee in 1905. Admitted to the Wisconsin bar in 1912, he was appointed legal counsel for the Wisconsin State Federation of Labor three years later. He was elected state senator on the Socialist ticket and served in the 1925 session of the legislature. Padway was twice appointed to the Milwaukee civil court bench (1924, 1926). After 1927 he was associated with the Progressive Republicans in Wisconsin. Padway played a major role in shaping Wisconsin labor legislation between 1915 and 1935. Upon his appointment as the first general counsel of the American Federation of Labor, he moved to Washington where he served until his death. In this capacity, he successfully defended the constitutionality of the National Labor Relations (Wagner) Act before the United States Supreme Court.

BIBLIOGRAPHY: L.J. Swichkow and L.P. Gartner, *The History of the Jews of Milwaukee* (1963), 163, 253–4.

[Louis J. Swichkow]

PAGEL, JULIUS LEOPOLD (1851–1912), German physician and medical historian. Pagel was born in Pomerania, and practiced medicine in Berlin and was appointed professor of history of medicine at the University of Berlin. He wrote over 100 books and articles dealing mainly with medical history. These included many medical biographies taken from unpublished manuscripts and a full description of methods of therapy used in the 19th century. He edited *Biographisches Lexikon hervorragender Aerzte des 19. Jahrhunderts* (1901) and coedited with Max Neuburger the *Handbuch der Geschichte der Medizin* (1902–05).

His youngest son, WALTER PAGEL (1898–1983), pursued two careers – he was a pathologist and a famous historian of science. Born in Berlin he was lecturer in pathology and medical history at Heidelberg (1928–33). With the advent of Hitler he left for England where he became pathologist, first at the Central Middlesex County Hospital, London, and from the beginning of World War II, at Clare Hall Hospital, Hertfordshire.

He published books and articles in the fields of pathology, bacteriology, tuberculosis, and allergic phenomena. On medical history, his publications include *Jo. Bapt. van Helmont; Einfuehrung in die philosophische Medizin des Barock* (1930); *The Religious and Philosophical Aspects of Van Helmont's Science and Medicine* (1944); and *William Harvey, Some Neglected Aspects of Medical History* (1944).

BIBLIOGRAPHY: S.R. Kagan, *Jewish Medicine* (1952), 242–3, 556.

[Suessmann Muntner]

PAGIS, DAN (1930–1986), Hebrew poet and scholar. Born in Radautz in Romanian Bukovina, Pagis grew up in Vienna. During World War II he was interned in a concentration camp. In 1946 he arrived in Israel and lived for a while in kibbutz Merḥavyah. Later he worked as a teacher at a regional school in Kiryat Gat and at the same time enrolled at the Hebrew University of Jerusalem. Pagis earned his Ph.D. there and was subsequently appointed professor of medieval Hebrew literature. He published several scholarly works, including *The Secular Poetry and Poetics of Moses Ibn Ezra and His Generation* (1970), *Change and Tradition in Secular Poetry: Spain and Italy* (1976), *Al Sod Ḥatum* ("A Secret Sealed," 1986), and *Poetry Aptly Explained – Studies and Essays on Medieval Hebrew Poetry* (1993).

Together with his academic work, Pagis published eight books of poetry and is considered one of the seminal poets of his generation. The horrors and memories of the Holocaust are a major theme in his work. Other concerns are the unbridled passage of time, scenes from daily life, and the abortive fruits of the scientific revolution. Pagis' poetry exhibits word-play, wit, and sophistication while avoiding pathos and striving for simple expression. His poetry collections include *She'on Ha-Ḥol* ("The Shadow Dial," 1959), *Shehut Meuḥeret* ("Late Leisure," 1964); *Gilgul* ("Transformations," 1970); *Mo'aḥ* ("Brain," 1975); *Milim Nirdafot* ("Double Exposure," 1982); *Shenem Asar Panim* ("Twelve Faces," 1984); *Shirim Aḥaronim* ("Last Poems," 1987). His *Collected Poems* appeared in 1991. Pagis also wrote a book for children ("The Egg that Disguised Itself," 1973) and edited a critical edition of the collected verse of David Vogel. *Selected Poems* in English translation appeared in 1972 and 1992. Various poems have been translated into other languages, and two books appeared in German translation (1990, 1993).

BIBLIOGRAPHY: A. Zehavi, "The Confines of Language and Beyond," in: *Modern Hebrew Literature,* 9:1–2 (1983), 70–78; W. Bargad and S.F. Chyet, in: *Israeli Poetry* (1986), 103–5; A. Dykman, "A Poet in the Eternal City," in: *Compar(a)ison,* 2 (1994), 41–56; S. DeKoven Ezrahi, "Conversations in the Cemetery," in: *Holocaust Remembrance* (1994), 121–33; T. Rübner, "Dan Pagis," in: *Begegnung und Erinnerung* (1995), 103–16.

[Anat Feinberg (2nd ed.)]

°PAGNINI, SANTES (Xanthus Pagninus; 1470–1536), Italian Hebraist and Bible scholar. Born in Lucca, Pagnini entered the Dominican order in 1487 and, under the direction of Savonarola, later studied Hebrew, his teacher being the Spanish convert Clement Abraham. Pagnini became one of the foremost Hebraists of the age and, at the request of Pope Leo X, taught in Rome for many years before settling in Lyons, where from 1524 until death he combated French heterodoxy. His greatest achievement was his *Utriusque instrumenti nova translatio* (Lyons, 1528), of which the Old Testament portion was the first since Jerome to be based directly on the original Hebrew. This Bible, the prefaces to which include two letters from Giovanni Pico della *Mirandola, reputedly took 25 years to prepare; and its notation of the biblical text according to chapter and verse has been retained until the present day. Pagnini's Latin translation inspired the Italian Bible of the Florentine reformer Antonio Brucioli (Venice, 1532) and the later Italian Protestant Bible of Geneva (1562).

Other works by Pagnini were *Institutionum hebraicarum abbreviatio* (Lyons, 1528; Paris, 1556); the authoritative and pioneering *Thesaurus linguae sanctae sire Lexicon hebraicum* (Lyons, 1529); and *Isagogae ad sacras literas, liber unicus. Ejusdem isagogae ad mysticos Sacrae Scripturae sensus, libri decem et octo* (Lyons, 1536). He also wrote a commentary on the Psalms. Pagnini's Bible and Hebrew grammar were widely consulted in the 16th century.

BIBLIOGRAPHY: C. Roth, *Jews in the Renaissance* (1959), 146f.; F. Secret, *Les Kabbalistes chrétiens de la Renaissance* (1964), index; *New Catholic Encyclopedia,* 10 (1967), 862.

[Godfrey Edmund Silverman]

°PAHLAVI, MOHAMMAD REZA SHAH (1919–1980), shah of *Iran. Mohammad Reza Shah, the eldest son of Reza Shah, was born in Teheran in 1919. He completed his primary school in Switzerland and returned to Iran in 1935. In Teheran he graduated from military school in 1938.

Mohammad Reza replaced his father on September 16, 1941, shortly before his 22nd birthday. At that time his country was occupied by Britain and the U.S.S.R., a situation which lasted until several months after the end of the World War II. He increasingly involved himself in governmental affairs, relying mostly on manipulation rather than leadership. In the context of regional turmoil and the Cold War, the shah established himself as an indispensable ally of the West. With this foreign policy, he agreed to grant the State of Israel de facto recognition in March 1950, thus making Iran the second Muslim country after Turkey which recognized Israel de jure.

In 1953 he had severe problems with his prime minister, Mossadeq, and the shah was obliged to leave Iran. After three days of riots and demonstrations in Teheran, mostly organized by the CIA, the shah returned home and began to rule with an iron hand, by creating the State Security and Intelligence Organization known as SAVAK. Gradually all political parties were banned in Iran. In 1963 he decreed a vast daring social, economic, and cultural reform known as the "White Revolution" and thus clashed with Islamic authorities, among them Ayatollah *Khomeini. In December 1971 he held an extravagant celebration of 2,500 years of the Persian monarchy. Soon afterward he invaded three islands in the Persian Gulf and annexed them to Iran. In 1975 he founded a royal, artificially made political party by the name of Rastākhiz and urged all Iranians to join it. In 1976 he replaced the Islamic calendar with an "Imperial" calendar, which began with the foundation of the Persian empire more than 25 centuries earlier. These actions were viewed as anti-Islamic and resulted in religious opposition, and unrest among young liberal and leftist groups in Iran, whose active fight against the shah actually had begun in 1963 and turned to violent armed combat from 1971 on.

The shah's regime suppressed its opponents with the help

of SAVAK. Relying on oil revenues, which increased sharply in late 1973, the shah pursued his gigantic projects of developing Iran as a mighty regional power, while sidestepping democratic arrangements, refusing to allow meaningful civic and political liberties, and remaining unresponsive to public opinion. His socioeconomic changes benefited some classes at the expense of others, creating a gap between the ruling elite and the disaffected populace. Islamic leaders, especially Khomeini and his followers, took advantage of the situation by creating a sociopolitical ideology tied to Islamic principles. They openly called for the overthrow of the shah. The shah's government collapsed following widespread uprisings in 1978–79 and consequently the shah was forced to leave the country (January 16, 1979). Khomeini came back from exile to take over power in Iran (February 1, 1979). Thus an Islamic Republic succeeded the shah's regime.

After leaving Iran, the shah, who was suffering from advanced cancer, began wandering from one country to the next. Finally he was allowed treatment in New York City, which led to the Iranian takeover of the American Embassy in Teheran by "Students of Imam's Line," and the taking hostage of more than 50 Americans for 444 days. Mohammad Reza Shah died in Cairo, Egypt, on July 27, 1980.

Mohammad Reza's reign is considered the Golden Age of the Jewish community in Iran. The friendly relations between Iran and Israel contributed to the good feeling of Iranian Jewry. The amicable close relations with Israel began gradually to grow after the clash between the shah and his prime minister, Mossadeq, when the monarch needed U.S. assistance more than ever. He realized that the weight of the Jewish community in the U.S. might help him work out his socioeconomic plans and his desire to turn Iran into a regional power. Iran requested and received help from Israel in many fields: agriculture, military, intelligence, medicine, among others. The Israeli embassy in Teheran became one of the most active diplomatic institutions in Iran. These relations reached their peak in 1967 when Israel defeated Egypt, Syria, and Jordan in the *Six-Day War. However, a gradual deterioration in relations was felt after the *Yom Kippur War (October 1973) when the shah felt he could do without Israel, and, to some degree, without the U.S. if he would use his astronomic oil revenues. This political miscalculation turned out to be the beginning of the end for him.

According to unofficial statistics, there were between 100,000 to 120,000 Jews in Iran in 1948. About 10% of them were wealthy, more than 50,000 were regarded as poor, and the rest were reported as middle class. From 1948 to 1954, Israel absorbed almost all the poor in several waves of immigration. Iran's economic boom benefited the Jews enormously, especially after the mid-1960s and the gradual realization of the shah's projects related to his White Revolution.

On the eve of the "Islamic Revolution" (1978) there were about 80,000 Jews in Iran, constituting one-quarter of one percent of the general population. Of these Jews, 10% were very rich, the same percentage were poor (aided by the Joint Distribution Committee), and the rest were classified from middle class to wealthy. About 70 of the 4,000 academics teaching at Iran's universities were Jews. Jewish physicians, 600 in number, constituted 6% of all physicians. The 4,000 Jewish students studying in universities made up 4% of the total student population. Never in their history had the Jews of Iran attained such a degree of affluence, education, and professional status as they did in the last decade of the shah's regime. The emergence of the Islamic Republic of Iran completely changed the picture.

BIBLIOGRAPHY: E. Abrahamian, *Iran Between the Two Revolutions* (1982); P. Avery, *Modern Iran* (1965); U. Bialer, "The Iranian Connection in Israel's Foreign Policy," in: *The Middle East Journal*, 39 (Spring 1985), 292–315; R. Graham, *Iran: The Illusion of Power* (1979); F. Halliday, *Iran: Dictatorship and Development* (1979); Sh. Hillel, *Ru'aḥ Qadim* (1985); G. Lenczowski, *Russia and the West in Iran, 1918–1948* (1949); idem, *Iran under the Pahlavis* (1978); A. Netzer, "*Be'ayot ha-Integrazya ha-Tarbutit, ha-Ḥevratit ve-ha-Politit shel Yehudei Iran*," in: *Gesher*, 25:1–2 (1979), 69–83; J. Nimrodi, *Massa Ḥayay*, 2 vols. (2003); Sh. Segev, *Ha-Meshulash ha-Irani* (1981); J. Upton, *The History of Modern Iran: An Interpretation* (1968).

[Amnon Netzer (2nd ed.)]

°**PAHLAVI, REZA SHAH** (1878–1944), shah of Iran. Reza Shah was born to a rather poor family in the village of Ālasht in the province of Māzandarān and died in exile in Johannesburg, South Africa. His father died when Reza was about six months old. Pressed by poverty, his mother took Reza to Teheran where at the age of 15 he joined the Russian-trained Cossack Brigade. His proficiency in handling machine guns elevated him to the rank equivalent to captain in 1912. He participated bravely in many military expeditions and within a few years was promoted to the rank of brigadier general (1918).

In 1921 he headed a British-orchestrated coup and occupied Teheran; soon after he became war minister (Wright, chapter 12). Three years later, he became prime minister (1924). His intrigues and fame caused the deposition of the last Qājār king, Ahmad Shah, and thus in 1925 he was proclaimed shah of Iran by the Parliament (Majles). He chose the pre-Islamic family name of Pahlavi, to show his strong nationalistic leanings towards ancient Iran as well as his intention of keeping his distance from Islam and its influence on Iran and of working to modernize the country (see Banani). These tendencies, to a large extent, also benefited the Jews of Iran.

Though Jews according to the constitution were still regarded as a religious minority with the right to send one Jewish representative to the Majles, their socio-economic situation improved beyond recognition. They were called to serve in the army in which some reached the rank of colonel. More than in previous decades, Jews were eager to leave the ghettos and live whereever they chose. They stopped paying *jizyah* (special non-Muslim poll tax); they were accepted in state schools and colleges. Another important factor concerning the Jews of Iran was their rapid acculturation: they, too, demonstrated nationalistic tendencies, participating on all Iranian national holidays, changing their Jewish names to

Iranian names, and hailing Reza Shah as the Cyrus the Great of their time (Netzer, 1979).

It appeared that Reza Shah's pro-German inclinations had nothing to do with the anti-Jewish policy of Germany. He actually was looking for a strong foreign European protector to neutralize the Iranian long-time "foes," namely Russia and England (Ramazani, pp. 171ff.). Nevertheless, those tendencies created an anti-Jewish atmosphere in many cities in Iran (Netzer, 1986). For this policy, and other geopolitical reasons, his country was occupied by Russia and England (end of August 1941) and in September he lost his throne and was exiled to South Africa. He was replaced by his 22-year-old son, Mohammad Reza Shah (see previous entry).

BIBLIOGRAPHY: E. Abrahamian, *Iran Between the Two Revolutions* (1982); A. Banani, *The Modernization of Iran: 1921–1941* (1961); A. Netzer, "*Anti-Semitism be-Iran, 1925–1950*," in: *Pe'amim*, 29 (1986), 5–31; idem, "*Ba'ayot ha-Integrazya ha-Tarbutit, ha-Ḥevratit ve-ha-Politit shel Yehudei Iran*," in: *Gesher*, 25:1–2 (1979), 69–83; R.K. Ramazani, *The Foreign Policy of Iran: 1500–1941* (1966); D.N. Wilbur, *Iran, Past and Present* (1948); D. Wright, *The English amongst the Persians* (1977).

[Amnon Netzer (2nd ed.)]

PA'IL (Pilevsky), MEIR (1926–), Israeli officer, radical politician, and historian, member of the Eighth and Ninth Knessets. Pa'il was born in Jerusalem and studied at the Taḥkemoni School in Jerusalem, at Beit Ḥinukh in Ḥolon, and at the Balfour Reali Gymnasium in Tel Aviv. He served in the Palmaḥ in 1943–48. In April 1948 he was witness to the massacre performed at Deir Yassin by an IẒL unit, as an observer on behalf of the Haganah. During the War of Independence he served as a deputy commander of a battalion, and as operations officer in the staff of the Negev Brigade. After the War of Independence he served in the IDF as commander of the Central School for Officers, and head of the Department for Fighting Doctrine in the General Staff. He retired from the IDF in 1971 with the rank of colonel.

Pa'il studied general history and Middle Eastern studies at Tel Aviv University, and received a doctorate in history in 1974. His thesis dealt with the growth of the Israeli military system out of the Zionist underground movements before the establishment of the state.

Pa'il joined Mapam in 1948, but left it in 1969 against the background of its decision to run in the elections to the Seventh Knesset in the Alignment list with the *Israel Labor Party. He then became active in the Movement for Peace and Security. In 1973 he was one of the founders of Tekhelet Adom that joined the radical Moked, and was elected to the Eighth Knesset on its list. In 1977 he was one of the founders of Maḥaneh ha-Semol ha-Yisraeli (known as "Sheli") and was elected to the Ninth Knesset on its list. In 1980 he resigned from the Knesset as part of a rotation agreement, and was replaced by Se'adyah Martziano. In the Knesset he served on the Education, Culture, and Sports Committee, and the Immigration and Absorption Committee. He remained in Sheli until the party disintegrated in 1983. After 1984 he became the academic director of the Center for Historical Research of the IDF at Ef'al, in cooperation with the United Kibbutz Movement. He was one of the founders and an active member of the Israeli Council for Israeli-Palestinian Peace, and one of the founders of the Israeli Association for Military History.

He was a prolific writer of books and articles about Israeli's military and political history. Among his numerous works are *Min ha-Haganah li-Ẓeva Haganah* (1979); with Menahem Brinker, *Iyyunim ba-Tarbut ha-Politit be-Yisrael* (1985); *Palmaḥ: Ha-Ko'aḥ ha-Meguyyas shel ha-Haganah* (1995); and *Ha-Mefaked: Manhigut Ẓeva'it be-Darkhei No'am* (2003).

[Susan Hattis Rolef (2nd ed.)]

PAILES, ISAAC (1895–1978), French painter. Born in Russia, Pailes went to Paris at the age of 22. After years of struggle, he achieved success. His original training as a sculptor can be discerned in his work. The subject matter is largely limited to clowns, still lifes, and vistas of France.

PAIVA, JACQUES (d. 1687), London diamond merchant originally from Holland, one of the earliest Jewish settlers in Fort St. George (*Madras). He was authorized by the East India Company in London to travel to Madras in 1684, taking with him "one man-servant, one Christian maid, and one Jewish servant to attend on his wife in his voyage to the port, he paying the charge of their transportation." During his stay in Madras, Paiva was one of the representatives of the "Hebrew" merchants. While on a trip to the diamond mines in Golconda in 1687, he fell dangerously ill and was taken back to Fort St. George, where he died. He was buried in the cemetery at the Memorial Hall in Peddenaipetam, which apparently had been acquired with Paiva's help. His will throws remarkable light on the gem trade between England and India in the 17th century. His widow subsequently lived with Elihu Yale, the governor of Madras after whom Yale University is named.

BIBLIOGRAPHY: W.J. Fischel, in: *Journal of the Economic and Social History of the Orient*, 3 (1960), 78–107, 175–95; C. Roth, *Anglo-Jewish Letters* (1938), 78–81; H.D. Love, *Vestiges of Old Madras*, 4 vols. (1913). **ADD. BIBLIOGRAPHY:** E. Samuel, "Manuel Levy Duarte (1631–1714): An Amsterdam Merchant Jeweller's Trade with London," in: idem, *At the Ends of the Earth: Essays on the History of England and Portugal* (2004), 232–32, index.

[Walter Joseph Fischel]

PAKISTAN, Islamic republic, S. Asia, established-in 1947 after the partition of India. At the beginning of the 20th century, the largest city, Karachi, had about 2,500 Jews engaged as tradesmen, artisans, and civil servants. Their mother tongue was Marathi, indicating their *Bene Israel origin. In 1893 the Jews of Karachi built the Magen Shalom Synagogue (D.S. Sassoon, *Ohel Dawid*, 2 (1932), 576), and in 1936 one of the leaders of the Jewish community, Abraham Reuben, became the first Jewish councilor on the city corporation. The Jews lived primarily in Karachi, but there was a small community served by two synagogues in Peshawar in the northwest frontier province. The following Jewish organizations existed at that time: the Young Men's Jewish Association, founded in 1903, whose aim was to encourage sports as well as religious and social activities of the Bene Israel in Karachi; the Karachi Bene Israel Relief Fund, established to support poor Jews in Karachi; the Karachi Jewish syndicate, formed in 1918, to provide homes to poor Jews at reasonable rents.

The foundation of an Islamic state immediately prior to the establishment of the State of Israel created a rising feeling of insecurity within the Jewish community; this anxiety was later exacerbated by the disturbances and demonstrations directed against the Jews during the Arab-Israel wars in 1948, 1956, 1967, and 1973. A large number of Jews moved from Pakistan to India, which became for some the stepping stone to a further migration to Israel and the United Kingdom. The small community in Peshawar ceased to exist, and the synagogues were closed. By 1968 the total number of Jews in Pakistan had decreased to 250, almost all of whom were concentrated in Karachi, where there was one synagogue, a welfare organization, and a recreational organization. Out of Muslim solidarity with the Arab states and the Palestinians, Pakistan did not establish any ties with Israel and frequently joined in anti-Israel moves in the United Nations and the boycott initiated by the Arab states. Only in 2005 were some steps towards rapprochement made, vociferously condemned by Islamic groups in the capital, Islamabad.

BIBLIOGRAPHY: World Jewish Congress Institute of Jewish Affairs, *Jewish Communities of the World* (1971), 72. **ADD. BIBLIOGRAPHY:** EIS² 8 (1995), 240–4 (incl. bibliography); L. Ziring, *Pakistan at the Crosscurrent of History* (2003).

[Walter Joseph Fischel, Paul Gottlieb, and E. Elias]

PAKS, town in W. central Hungary. Jews first settled there in 1720, and in 1770 numbered 64. Initially they were mainly peddlers and small traders, who paid only a small protection tax to the estate owners. In 1844 a meeting of rabbis was held in Paks which tried unsuccessfully to effect a compromise between the Orthodox and the adherents of Reform. Finally there was a split, and although the community remained Orthodox, a separate status quo ante congregation was established. In 1788, on instructions from Emperor *Joseph II, a Jewish school with German as the language of instruction was founded, changed to Hungarian by the community in 1870. The school was closed down in 1919. The Jewish population numbered 1,129 in 1869, 1,011 in 1900, 891 in 1920, 782 in 1930, and 730 in 1941. Rabbis of the community included Solomon Beer (Solomon Lazar; appointed 1746), Jehiel Ze'ev (1780), Isaac Krishaber (1795), Ezekiel *Banet (1825), and Paul (Feiwel) Horovitz (1844).

After the German occupation (March 19, 1944), a ghetto for 1,000 Jews was set up. These were deported to *Auschwitz on July 4–6. There were 180 Jews living in Paks in 1946, dropping to 20 by 1961.

BIBLIOGRAPHY: *Magyar Zsidó Szemle* (1898), 378ff; (1899), 142ff.

[Baruch Yaron]

PAKULA, ALAN JAY (1928–1998), U.S. director, producer, and screenwriter. The son of a Polish immigrant, Pakula grew up in the Bronx and was a 1948 Yale graduate. Instead of taking over the family printing business, Pakula moved to Hollywood. In the early 1950s, he worked at Warner Brothers, MGM, and Paramount Pictures before collaborating with director Robert Mulligan in 1957 to produce his first film, *Fear Strikes Out*. The two formed Pakula-Mulligan Productions, which produced numerous films from 1957 to 1969. One of their greatest successes was an adaptation of Harper Lee's *To Kill a Mockingbird* (1962), which was nominated for best picture. Other Pakula-Mulligan films were *Love with a Proper Stranger* (1963), *Inside Daisy Clover* (1966), *Up the Down Staircase* (1967), and *The Stalking Moon* (1968). Pakula married actress Hope Lange in 1963, but the two divorced in 1969. Pakula made his directorial debut in 1969 with *The Sterile Cuckoo*. The thriller-suspense movie *Klute* (1971), which Pakula directed and co-produced, was the first of what is known as his "paranoia trilogy." *The Parallax View* (1974) was the second installment, followed by *All the President's Men* (1976), the movie starring Robert Redford and Dustin Hoffman as the *Washington Post* reporters who helped uncover the Watergate scandal. It was the top-grossing film of the year, won four Oscars, and earned Pakula a nomination for best director. In 1982, Pakula directed, wrote, and co-produced *Sophie's Choice*, a film about a Holocaust survivor. Pakula's screenplay was nominated for best adaptation. Pakula's first original screenplay, *See You in the Morning* (1989), about a man who marries a widow with stepchildren, was based on his life; in 1973 Pakula married widow Hannah Cohn Boorstin, who had three children. *The Pelican Brief* (1993) was Pakula's biggest box-office hit. His last film was *The Devil's Own* (1997). Pakula died in a car accident.

[Susannah Howland (2nd ed.)]

PALACHE (Pallache, Palacio, de Palatio, al-Palas, Pallas, Palaggi, Balyash, etc.), family whose name first occurs in Spain as Palyāj. The historian Ibn Dāʾūd relates (in his *Sefer ha-Qabbalah*, ed. by G.D. Cohen (1967), 66, no. 64 Eng. sect.), "R. Moses the Rabbi (one of the *Four Captives) allied himself by marriage with the Ibn Falija (Palyāj) family, which was the greatest of the families of the community of Córdoba, and took from them a wife for his son R. *Ḥanokh." Moses al-Palas (b. c. 1535), an outstanding rabbi and orator, was born in *Marrakesh. He later lived in *Tetuán, where his sermons attracted large audiences, including many former Marranos. When he returned to Marrakesh, he delivered a lengthy discourse on the ethics of the Jewish religion – at the request and in the presence of the Spanish ambassador. This success encouraged him to undertake a journey through the countries inhabited by the descendants of the victims of the Spanish Expulsion in order to preach to them. He visited the Balkans, Turkey, and Palestine and lived in Salonika for a time. He appears to have finally settled in Venice, where he published *Va-Yakhel Moshe* (1597) and *Ho'il Moshe* (1597), which includes homilies, eulogies, and sermons, as well as a biography of the author. R. Isaac Palache was a distinguished rabbi in *Fez in about 1560. He had two sons, Samuel Palache (d. 1616) and Joseph (see below). They and their children held an important place in the economic life of that period and from the beginning of the 17th century became active at the courts of Europe, particularly the Netherlands which maintained relations with Morocco. In Madrid, the Inquisition probably suspected them of inciting the Marranos to leave the country and return to Judaism. To escape prosecution, they took asylum in the house of the French ambassador, and offered their services to King Henry IV; they left Spain a short while later. According to some historians, Samuel was the first Jew to settle in the Netherlands as a declared Jew. He was responsible for obtaining the authorization for his coreligionists to settle. He gathered the first *minyan* in Amsterdam at his home for Day of Atonement prayers in 1596. Palache is also said to have built the first synagogue in that country. According to documents in the Netherlands archives, the right to settle in the country was refused to him, and during the same year, 1608, he was appointed ambassador to The Hague by the Moroccan sultan Mulay Zīdān. In 1610 he successfully negotiated the first treaty of alliance between a Christian state (the Netherlands), and a Muslim state (Morocco). In 1614 he personally assumed the command of a small Moroccan fleet which seized some ships belonging to the king of Spain, with whom Morocco was at war. The Spanish ambassador, who was very influential in London, had him arrested when he was in England. He accused him of piracy; reverberations of his trial were widespread. Once acquitted, he returned to the Netherlands. When he died in The Hague, Palache was given an imposing funeral attended by Prince Maurice of Nassau. Samuel Palache's two sons, Isaac and Jacob-Carlos, also engaged in diplomatic work. The former was entrusted with Dutch interests in Morocco from 1624, and the latter represented the sultan in Copenhagen. Samuel's brother, Joseph Palache (d. after 1638), succeeded him in his diplomatic position. Joseph Palache's five sons held very important offices. One of them, Isaac Palache (d. 1647) was known as "the lame." His variegated career included a mission to the Ottoman sultan (1614–1), important negotiations in Danzig (1618–19), a professorship in Hebrew at the University of Leiden, and missions to Morocco and Algiers in 1624 on behalf of the Dutch. In 1639 he was called upon to redeem the Christian captives who were held by the famous marabout of Tazerwalt. He became involved in a violent conflict with his brothers over succession rights and converted to Christianity. Another son, Moses Palache (d. after 1650), was secretary to his uncle Samuel at the French court, interpreter and secretary to the sultan of Morocco, and the de facto – but not official – foreign minister of four successive Moroccan sovereigns; his name was cited by Manasseh Ben Israel to Oliver Cromwell as an example of the loyalty of the Jews when he sought authorization for them to settle in England. Joshua Palache (d. after 1650) and his son Samuel Palache were merchants of international status and tax farmers of the leading Moroccan port, Safi. David Palache (d. 1649), another of Joseph's sons, was a diplomat. Entrusted with a mission to Louis XIII of France, various accusations were brought against him. His innocence was finally proven and he reassumed his position as Moroccan ambassador to the Netherlands. Abraham Palache (d. after 1630) was a financier in Morocco and diplomat. The descendants of the main branch of the Palache family lived in Amsterdam, where Isaac Palache was elected chief rabbi in 1900. His son Judah Lion *Palache was professor of Semitic languages at the University of Amsterdam and died in an extermination camp during the Holocaust. Another branch lived in Izmir, where Ḥayyim *Palache and his son Abraham Palache were noted rabbis in the 19th century.

BIBLIOGRAPHY: SIHM, ser. 1, index vol. s.v. *Pallache*; H.I. Bloom, *The Economic Activities of the Jews in Amsterdam* (1937, repr. 1969), 75–82; D. Corcos, in: *Zion*, 25 (1960), 122–33; J. Caillé, in: *Hespéris-Tamuda*, 4 (1963), 5–67; Hirschberg, Afrikah, 2 (1965), 228–42.

[David Corcos / Haïm Z'ew Hirschberg]

PALACHE (Palaggi), ḤAYYIM (also called by the acronym *Ḥabif*; 1788–1869), rabbi and *ḥakham bashi*. Born in Izmir (Smyrna), Palache, a member of the distinguished *Palache family, was the grandson on his mother's side of Joseph Raphael *Ḥazzan (author of *Ḥikrei Lev*) and was a disciple of Joseph Gatenio (author of *Beit Yiẓḥak*). He became *av bet din* in 1837. In 1847 he was appointed as *rav sheni* ("second rabbi") with the title *dayyan*, authorized to render judgment alone, and later was awarded the rabbinical title *marbiẓ Torah* (see Abraham Palache, *Ḥelkam ba-Ḥayyim*, 1874). His position as *marbiẓ Torah* is attested by Ḥayyim Palache himself: 'I, the *marbiẓ Torah* of this place, the town of Izmir … and its environs' (*Male Ḥayyim: Ha-Takkanot*, 42, 74), i.e., the neighboring towns of Izmir as well, such as Tiriya, Manissa, and Bergama. In 1855 he was appointed as *rav kolel* ("chief of the rabbis"; *Ḥayyim ba-Yad* (1873), nos. 63, 74, 75). In 1865, at the age of 77, he was appointed *ḥakham bashi* of *Izmir. Because of Palache's advanced age, some of his colleagues took charge of the community and administered it according to their will. At the end of November 1865 the Jews of Izmir elected an administrative committee composed of a president and nine members. At their first meeting the members of the committee invited Palache to appear alone, without his advisers and followers, and compelled him to sign a declaration stating that he would not sign any document without prior authorization by the majority of the members of the committee. Palache signed, but the administrative committee did not function for a long time. At that time the administrators of the community bought the monopoly of the *gabella* (tax) for the sale of wine, alcohol, and salt for the ridiculously low price of 10,000–12,000 francs. When the people complained, they decided to pay 44,000 francs for the monopoly, but when the community demanded an accounting of its financial situation, the officials refused to comply. In order to put an end to this situation, Palache repealed this tax. The entire group of Gabelleros, as well as those interested in leasing monopolies, swore to remove the aged rabbi. Following the argument which broke out in the community, the government ordered the *ḥakham bashi* of Istanbul (Constantinople), Yakir Gueron, to send someone to Izmir to restore order. In December 1866 R. Samuel Danon, secretary of Gueron, was sent. He convinced Gueron that the only solution to these complicated intrigues was to remove Palache and that he himself should be appointed in the former's place. Gueron responded affirmatively to his secretary's report, which was signed by only 60 of Izmir's inhabitants. He requested that the government remove Palache, and the vizier's order of removal was sent to Izmir. Most of the Jewish inhabitants of Izmir, however, so strongly opposed the order that the pasha of Izmir had to consult a higher authority. According to a new order, the pasha was supposed to delay the execution of the vizier's first order, to remove Palache only temporarily, and to appoint Danon in his place. This began a series of requests – for and against Palache – to Gueron. The supporters of Palache eventually succeeded in October 1867 in having him returned to his rabbinic post and recognized as the chief rabbi of the Izmir community. Palache did not exploit his victory for revenge, and he dealt mercifully with the Gabelleros, who asked for his pardon. One of the conditions of his reelection was that immediately on assuming the post, administrative procedures would be instituted (*Nizamnamé du Ḥakham-Hané*). However, Palache's death prevented his fulfilling his promise.

Palache was a prolific writer. Many of his manuscripts were burned and a great number were not published, but 26 works were printed, among them: *Darkhei Ḥayyim* (Izmir, 1821), on *Pirkei Avot*; *Lev Ḥayyim* (vol. 1, Salonika, 1823; vols. 2–3, Izmir, 1874–90), responsa, interpretations, and comments on the Shulḥan Arukh; *Nishmat Kol Ḥai* (2 vols., Salonika, 1832–37), responsa; *Ẓedakah Ḥayyim* (Izmir, 1838); *Ḥikekei Lev* (2 vols., Salonika, 1840–53), homilies and eulogies; *Nefesh Ḥayyim* (1842); *Torah ve-Ḥayyim* (1846); *Kaf ha-Ḥayyim* (1859); *Mo'ed le-Khol Ḥai* (1861); *Ḥayyim ve-Shalom* (2 vols., 1857–72); *Sefer Ḥayyim* (1863); and *Ginzei Ḥayyim* (1871).

ABRAHAM PALACHE (1809–1899), son of Ḥayyim, was also a distinguished rabbinical scholar. Four months after Ḥayyim Palache's death the *ḥakham bashi* of Istanbul appointed Joseph Ḥakim, chief rabbi of Manissa, as *ḥakham bashi* of Izmir. This was done in order to satisfy the demands of the older generation, but Ḥakim was elected by only a small minority. Three quarters of the Jews of Izmir opposed him, and their objections were intensified by his opposition to the teaching of languages in Jewish schools. Many people in Izmir then approached the local ruler, Ishmael Pasha, to appoint Abraham Palache to the post of *ḥakham bashi*, but their request was rejected. Several French, English, and Italian Jews who were in Izmir then turned to their local consuls, asking that a request, signed by 15,000 Izmir Jews, be sent to the sultan demanding, among other things, the appointment of Palache as *ḥakham bashi*. The Italian consul took the necessary steps with his ambassador in Istanbul, as well as with Ishmael Pasha, and succeeded in having the request fulfilled. In August 1869, according to a supreme order, Joseph Ḥakim was removed and the following year, 1870, Palache was appointed as *ḥakham bashi* of the Izmir community and served in this post for almost 30 years. Palache wrote numerous works in Hebrew and one in Ladino: *Shama Avraham* (Salonika, 1850), responsa; *Berakh et Avraham* (Salonika, 1857), homilies; *Shemo-Avraham* (2 vols., 1878–96), ethics and homilies; *Va-Yikra Avraham* (1884); *Va-Yashkem Avraham* (1885), studies in Psalms; *Va-Ya'an Avraham* (1886), responsa; *Avraham Anokhi*, studies on the Torah (1889); *Avraham Ezkor* and *Yemaher Avraham* (1889): *Ve-Avraham Zaken* (1899), homilies: and in Ladino, *Ve-Hokhi'aḥ Avraham* (2 vols., 1853–62).

BIBLIOGRAPHY: M.D. Gaon, *Yehudei ha-Mizraḥ be-Ereẓ Yisrael*, 2 (1938), 560f., I.I. Ḥasida, *Rabbi Ḥayyim Palaggi u-Sefarav* (1968); Y.Y. Kohen, in: *Yad la-Koré*, 9 (1968), 66–68.

[Yaacov Geller]

PALACHE, JUDAH LION (1886–1944), Orientalist and teacher. Palache was born in Amsterdam, a son of Isaac Palache, the *ḥakham* of the Spanish-Portuguese congregation. He studied at the Ets-Ḥayyim rabbinical seminary and at Amsterdam and Leyden universities and was a student of Snouck-Hurgronje. From 1925 he was professor of Bible and Semitic languages at the University of Amsterdam. Though no longer Orthodox, he served as *parnas* of the Spanish-Portuguese congregation and was active in some of its institutions. During World War II Palache was deported to Theresienstadt and later sent to an extermination camp. A great part of a major work he was compiling on Hebrew semantics was lost during the war.

Palache's scholarly interests lay in Judaism and *Islam as well as in comparative Semitic philology. Among Palache's published works are *Het Heiligdom in de voorstelling der semietische volken* (1920); *Inleiding in de Talmoed*, an introduction to the Talmud (Dutch, 1922, 1954[2]; *Introduction to the Talmud*, 1934); *De Hebreeuwsche literatuur...* (with A.S. Levisson and S. Pinkhof, 1935); The *'Ebed-Jahveh enigma in Pseudo-Isaiah* (1934); and posthumously: *Sinai en Paran*, ed., with an introduction by M. Reisel (1959), and *Semantic Notes on the Hebrew Lexicon* (translated from Dutch and ed. by R.J.Z. Werblowsky, 1959).

BIBLIOGRAPHY: M. Reisel, in: J.L. Palache, *Sinai en Paran* (1959), 9–12; R.J.Z. Werblowsky, in: J.L. Palache, *Semantic Notes on the Hebrew Lexicon* (1959), 7–9 (introd.).

PALÁGYI, LAJOS (1866–1933), Hungarian poet. Palágyi, who was born at Óbecse, was a brother of the philosopher Menyhért *Palágyi. Palágyi had a hard struggle against poverty, and in order to be able to devote himself to the writing of poetry earned his living as an instructor at teachers' seminaries and later as a journalist. He was one of the writers who engaged in the struggle which resulted in 1895 in the official recognition of the Jewish religion in Hungary. Palágyi belonged to the group of Hungarian philosophical poets influenced by the German philosopher Schopenhauer. His poems won several prizes, but never enjoyed wide popularity. Several of them deal with Jewish themes, including *Bibliai emlékek* ("Biblical Reminiscences," 1896). He also published *Magányos úton* ("On the Lonely Road," 1893); *Költemények* ("Poems," 1907); the dramatic *A rabszolgák* ("Slaves," 1899); and the epic *Az anyaföld* ("Mother Earth," 1921). He translated Goethe's *Faust* into Hungarian (1909). Palágyi was at first regarded as a socialist poet but he never actually joined the socialist movement since, in his own words, "the sufferings of humanity cannot be cured by institutions. Hearts and brains must be renewed." He turned his back on society and his opposition to socialism grew progressively stronger. Nevertheless in 1920, following the Hungarian revolution, he was expelled from the distinguished Petőfi literary society and deprived of his pension. Eleven years later he published a pamphlet in self-justification, telling the story of his persecution.

BIBLIOGRAPHY: *Magyar Zsidó Lexikon* (1929), 678–9; *Magyar Irodalmi Lexikon*, 2 (1965), 420–1; J. Sporer, *Palágyi Lajos élete és költészete* (1937).

[Baruch Yaron]

PALÁGYI, MENYHÉRT (**Melchior**; 1859–1924), philosopher; brother of the poet Lajos *Palágyi, Palágyi taught at the University of Kolozsvár (Cluj). When Kolozsvár was seized by Romania in 1919, he moved to Germany.

His *Neue Theorie des Raumes und der Zeit* (1901) anticipated Einstein and Minkowski. His works on logic (1902 and 1903) against psychologism were criticized by Husserl. His *Kant und Bolzano* (1902) revived interest in Bolzano. Palágyi also worked in epistemology, aesthetics, and natural philosophy (where he worked out a system of world mechanics). His later work appears in *Ausgewaehlte Werke*, 3 vols. (1924–25).

BIBLIOGRAPHY: Kövesi, in: *Encyclopedia of Philosophy*, 6 (1967), 18–19; Boyce Gibson, in: *Journal of Philosophical Studies*, 3 (1928), 15–28.

[Richard H. Popkin]

PALANGA (Ger. **Polangen**), resort town on the Baltic Sea in Lithuania. Jews were granted privileges of town dwellers in Palanga by the Polish king Sigismund III (1587–1632), and were permitted to own land and to engage in crafts and commerce. These privileges were confirmed by subsequent rulers in 1639 and 1742. There were 398 Jews living in Palanga and the vicinity in 1765. At the beginning of the 1820s, Palanga was included in the Russian province of *Courland. The community numbered 729 in 1850, 925 in 1897 (43% of the total population), 455 in 1923, and approximately 700 in 1939. The production of decorative objects and jewelry made from amber found on the seashore, for which Palanga is famous, was formerly a Jewish industry. Many Jews also earned their livelihood by providing various services for summer vacationers. Between the world wars Jews were active in local government, serving on the city council as mayor or deputy mayor. The deteoriating economy resulting from antisemitism caused many to immigrate to South Africa, the United States, and Palestine. Soon after the outbreak of the German-Soviet war on June 22, 1941, Palanga was occupied by the Germans and all the Jews were concentrated at the bus station. The males aged 13 and above were taken outside the town and murdered in pits they were forced to dig. The women and children were held for a month in the synagogue, and then executed.

BIBLIOGRAPHY: Mark, in: *Lite*, 1 (1951), 1454–74; *Yahadut Lita*, 1 (1959), 45, 54; Gar, in: *Algemeine Entsiklopedie*, 6 (1963), 366, 367, 374. **ADD. BIBLIOGRAPHY:** Dov Levin (ed.), *Pinkas ha-Kehilot – Lithuania* (1996).

[Joseph Gar / Shmuel Spector (2nd ed.)]

PALATINATE (Ger. **Pfalz**), region in W. Germany, also known as Western or Rhenish Palatinate. In the Middle Ages it was the domain of the counts and electors of the Palatinate, who were closely connected with the ruling house of the duchy of Bavaria. The first mention of Jews in the region is as residents of *Speyer in 1084. Communities existed in *Weinheim, *Kaiserslautern, *Heidelberg, and *Landau, all of which suffered during the *Black Death (1348) persecutions. To the indignation of the populace, Elector Rupert I (1329–90) permitted refugees from the massacres perpetrated in *Worms and Speyer to settle in Heidelberg and other nearby localities. Heidelberg eventually emerged as the leading Jewish community, and in 1369 authorities granted it permission to enlarge its cemetery. The nephew of Rupert I, Rupert II (1390–98), and his son Rupert III (1398–1410), king of Germany and Holy Roman Emperor (1400), expelled Jews from the Palatinate. In the course of the 14th and 15th centuries, however, Jews expelled from German cities managed to return and to settle in the villages of the Palatinate. An official inquiry of 1550 revealed the presence of 155 Jewish heads of families. These constituted a *Landjudenschaft, which convened fairly regularly to discuss the problem of tax distribution (which in 1554 was fixed at 1,000 florins annually for a period of six years). Charles Louis (1632–80) introduced taxes on circumcision, burial, and marriage. He also granted the Portuguese and Ashkenazi communities in *Mannheim extraordinary privileges (1660). Mannheim rapidly became the largest Jewish community in the Palatinate, with 63 families in 1697, while Heidelberg had only eight. The increasing Jewish population of the Palatinate, which overflowed into other German states where there were fewer Jews, resulted in the use by Jews of such names as Landau, Weinheim, Mannheim, and Oppenheim, which had their origin in Palatinate localities. The leading Austrian families of *Court Jews, the *Wertheimers and *Oppenheimers, were originally from the Palatinate, as was the *Seligmann-Eichthal family. The electors of the Palatinate employed many Court Jews, purveyors, and military *contractors. One of them, Lemle Moses Reinganum, established a 100,000 florin endowment for Talmud study, the renowned Mannheim *Klaus* (1706), which remained in existence for more than two centuries.

The number of Jews in the Palatinate continued to increase despite a temporary setback caused by the devastations of the wars of conquest (1688–89) of Louis XIV. In 1722 there were 535 registered Jewish families in the Palatinate, 160 of them in Mannheim. The first **Landrabbiner* served in 1706 and the third, David Ullmann (Ulmo), a member of an influential family, was recognized as *Landrabbiner* in 1728 despite his youth. Although the *Landjudenschaft* had opposed his nomination, ignored his authority, and demanded that he be examined by three eminent rabbis, Ullmann nevertheless served with official support until 1762. His successor, Naphtali Hirsch *Katzenellenbogen (d. 1800), was also *Oberrabbiner* (chief rabbi) of the Mannheim *Klaus*. Elector Charles Theodore (1742–99) attempted to restrict the Jewish population of the Palatinate to 300 after a 1743 inquiry revealed the presence of 488 Jewish families and protracted negotiations over the payment of the 45,000 florins tax burden were conducted with the *Landjudenschaft*. All "honorable" professions, that of butcher in particular, were declared open to Jews; and Jews were allowed to open cemeteries. The majority of Palatinate Jews were livestock merchants, peddlers, and dealers in wine, hops, tobacco, and other agricultural products. By 1775 the number of Jewish families was 823; a quarter of them lived in Mannheim.

Under French rule (1792–1814) the Jews enjoyed equality but lost it on the return to Bavaria. In 1818 *Napoleon's "Infamous Decree" (1808) was extended indefinitely in the Palatinate. The struggle for Jewish emancipation was led by Elias Gruenebaum (b. 1807), rabbi of Landau (1836–93), an energetic advocate of Reform Judaism in both liturgy and education. Emancipation was granted only in 1848 and 1851. Anti-Jewish disturbances broke out in the villages of the Palatinate in 1819 (see *Hep! Hep!), the early 1830s, and in 1849.

The Jewish population of Rheinbayern (Rhenish Bavaria), which numbered some 2,000 families in 1821, grew to 13,526 persons in 1833 and to 15,412 in 1840 (2.65% of the total population), after which it began to decline (to 10,108 in 1900 and to 6,487 in 1933). In 1840 the population was distributed among 180 localities, 40 of which had at least 100 Jews. Ingenheim, one of the largest, had 551 Jews (one-third of the total population). By October 1937 there remained 4,300 Jews in 67 localities, only nine of which contained more than 100 persons. Those communities that grew after World War I were Ludwigshafen (1,400 in 1931) and Pirmasens (800 in 1931), both of which were themselves part of developing industrial cities. After 1933 the Jews of the primarily rural communities suffered from a relentless campaign to exclude them from the trade in livestock, wine, tobacco, leather, hops, etc., all of which were traditional Jewish occupations. During the *Kristallnacht* (November 1938) many synagogues of the Palatinate were burned down and hundreds of male Jews were arrested. Jews were also evicted from the villages to the cities and subsequently deported during World War II. In 1970 there were 668 Jews living in the federal state of Rheinland-Pfalz (300 in Neustadt). The Jewish communities in Rheinland-Pfalz numbered 352 in 1989 and 3,078 in 2004. The increase is explained by the immigration of Jews from the former Soviet Union.

BIBLIOGRAPHY: H. Arnold, *Von den Juden in der Pfalz* (1967); H. Schnee, *Die Hoffinanz und der moderne Staat*, 4 (1963), 178–86; M. Stern, *Koenig Ruprecht von der Pfalz in seinen Beziehungen zu den Juden* (1898); L. Loewenstein, *Geschichte der Juden in der Kurpfalz* (1895); R. Herz, *Die Juden in der Pfalz* (1937): B. Rosenthal, in: MGWJ, 79 (1935), 443–50. **ADD. BIBLIOGRAPHY:** R. Bender (ed.), *Pfaelzische Juden und ihre Kultuseinrichtungen* (Suedwestdeutsche Schriften, vol. 5) (1988); H. Arnold, *Juden in der Pfalz. Vom Leben pfaelzischer Juden* (1988²); H. Morweiser, *Pfaelzer Juden und IG-Farben* (1988); *A. Kuby, Juden in der Provinz* (1989²); idem (ed.), *Pfaelzisches Judentum gestern und heute* (1992); P. Karmann (ed.), *Juedisches Leben in der Nordpfalz* (1992); M. Strehlen (ed.), "Ein edler Stein sei sein Baldachin …," in: *Juedische Friedhoefe in Rheinland-Pfalz* (Denkmalpflege in Rheinland-Pfalz) (1996); B. Kukatzki, *Pfaelzisch-juedischer Alltag im Kaiserreich* (1997); idem, *Bibliographie zur Geschichte der Juden in der Suedpfalz* (Landauer Arbeitsberichte und Preprints, vol. 10) (2001).

[Henry Wasserman]

PALDI (Feldman), ISRAEL (1892–1979), Israeli painter. Paldi was born at Berdyansk, Russia, and immigrated to Palestine in 1909. He spent the years 1910–20 in Europe. On his return to Palestine he exhibited in David's Tower in Jerusalem (1923) and was a leader of the Modern Artists in Tel Aviv (1927).

Paldi's work is extremely individual in style. In the 1920s he was an expressionist, and his work was full of stormy color and movement. Later it became simple, restrained, and even naive under the influence of the School of *Paris. In 1942 Paldi did pioneer work in making colored abstract plaster reliefs, using unusual materials such as sand, and in the late 1950s his painting became almost monochrome. Thereafter his work was characterized by an effort to integrate color and form, often by decorative methods.

BIBLIOGRAPHY: Roth, Art, 907–8; H. Gamzo, *Painting and Sculpture in Israel* (1958), 41, plate 43.

[Yona Fischer]

PALENCIA, city in north central Spain in the province of Palencia, Castile. Palencia had an important Jewish community, which is thought to have started as early as the 11th century. However, the earliest available information on Jewish settlement in Palencia dates from 1175, when Alfonso VIII delivered 40 Jews to the bishop of the town and placed them under his jurisdiction (this agreement was reratified in 1351). In 1192 Alfonso VIII exempted all Jews and Moors in the town from the payment of royal taxes, as they were already paying their share of the town's revenues. During the 13th century the population remained at 40 families and the community continued to prosper, as did many of the communities in Castile. In 1295 the Jews participated in the revolt against the king and the destruction of the bishop's palace. At the beginning of the 14th century *Asher b. Jehiel, giving his verdict (Responsa 21, §8) concerning the *eruv* arrangements introduced by R. Jacob b. R. Moses Debalincia (Palencia), decreed that the latter was to retract his instructions because he had misled the public. R. Asher demanded that R. Jacob be considered a "rebellious scholar" and banned from the Jewish community.

The community of Palencia suffered during the civil war between Pedro of Castile and Henry of Trastamara: according to the testimony of R. Samuel Ẓarẓa in his *Mekor Ḥayyim*, Henry claimed a large sum from the community; in R. Samuel's words, "they were in great distress." The community of Palencia was not spared during the persecutions of 1391 and it also had its *Conversos. Palencia and its surrounding region, however, witnessed the appearance of a popular prophet, who at the beginning of the 15th century called for repentance and announced the forthcoming redemption.

In 1480 the Jews and Conversos were separated into distinct quarters. A new quarter was allocated to them on Maria Gutiérrez Street (now Martín Calleja). After the 1492 Expulsion the name of the street was changed to Santa Fé, and a fine was to be imposed on anyone who referred to the street as *judería* (*Jewish Quarter). In 1485 the Jews were ordered to wear a distinctive sign and Christians were forbidden to lodge in Jewish houses, although they could work for them by day. The Jews were called upon to contribute 501, 183 maravedis toward the redemption of the prisoners of Malaga. It is known that during the Expulsion period – as early as May 1492 – a decree was issued to sell the synagogue located on the present-day Street of San Marcos. The proceeds of this sale were given to poor Jews to assist their departure from Palencia. Another synagogue was converted into a hospital in November 1492. There is little information available on the Conversos of Palencia. The prophetic movement of the Maiden Inés was formed in 1500 in the region of Palencia, at *Herrera de Pisuerga. Most of the Jews of Palencia moved to Portugal in 1492.

According to a local tradition the first Jews settled near the church of San Julián, which no longer exists, but was on the right bank of the river Carrión. Until the 15th century the Jews lived in various parts of Palencia. The majority was concentrated in the area of Plaza de León, where the synagogue was located between Manflorido and Regimiento Villarrobedo streets. The *judería vieja* (the old Jewish quarter) in *La Pellejería* was in the area that is now between the streets San Marcos and Cardenal Almaraz. Nothing has remained of the medieval Jewish quarter. In 1480 the Jews had to be in an enclosed quarter, the *judería nueva*, situated in today's Martín Calleja street. It was a narrow street. In 1492 it was renamed Santa Fe street.

BIBLIOGRAPHY: Baer, Spain, index; Baer, *Urkunden*, 2 (1936), index; J. González, *El Reino de Castilla a la época de Alfonso VIII* (1960), 129f., 132; F. Cantera, in: *Sefarad*, 22 (1962), 93ff.; P. León Tello, *Los judíos de Palencia* (1967).

[Haim Beinart / Yom Tov Assis (2nd ed.)]

PALE OF SETTLEMENT (Rus. **Cherta [postoyannoy yevreyskoy] osedlosti**), territory within the borders of czarist Russia wherein the residence of Jews was legally authorized. Limits for the area in which Jewish settlement was permissible in Russia came into being when Russia was confronted with the necessity of adjusting to a Jewish element within its borders, from which Jews had been excluded since the end of the 15th century. These limitations were consonant with the general conception of freedom of movement of persons which then applied. At the time, most of the inhabitants of Russia, not only the serfs but also townsmen and merchants, were deprived of freedom of movement and confined to their places of residence.

After the first partition of Poland in 1772, when masses of Jews living within the former country came under Russian rule, it was decided (1791) to permit the presence of the Jews not only in their former regions of residence, but also in the new areas which had then been annexed from Turkey on the Black Sea shore, in whose rapid colonization the Russian government was interested. On the other hand, Jewish merchants were prohibited from trading in the provinces of inner Russia. These decrees were intended to serve the national and economic interests of the state by preventing competition of the Jewish with Russian merchants and encouraging settlement in the desolate steppes of southern Russia; after a time these formed the provinces of *Kherson, *Dnepropetrovsk (Yekaterinoslav), and Taurida (*Crimea). The Russian government also sought thus to reduce the excess of Jews in the branches of commerce and innkeeping within the territory annexed from Poland. In 1794 the earlier decree was ratified and applied to the regions which had been annexed with the second partition of Poland (1793) also – the provinces of *Minsk, *Volhynia, and *Podolia – as well as to the region to the east of the River Dnieper (the provinces of *Chernigov and *Poltava).

With the third partition of Poland (1795), the law was also applied to the provinces of *Vilna and *Grodno. In 1799 *Courland was added to the Pale of Settlement. In the "Jewish Statute" promulgated in 1804, the province of Astrakhan and the whole of the northern Caucasus were added to the regions open to Jews. In 1812, upon its annexation, *Bessarabia was also included. The "Kingdom of Poland," incorporated into Russia in 1815, which included ten provinces that later became known as the "Vistula Region," was not officially included within the Pale of Settlement, and until 1868 the transit of Jews through it to the Lithuanian and Ukrainian provinces was prohibited by law. In practice, however, the provinces of the Vistula Region were generally included within the Pale of Settlement.

To sum up, it was the intention of the Russian legislators of the reigns of Catherine II and Alexander I to extend the Pale of Settlement beyond the regions acquired from Poland only to those areas where Jews could serve as a colonizing element. However, from the reign of Alexander II the restrictive aspects of the Pale of Settlement became accentuated, for while freedom of movement for non-Jews in Russia increased, in particular after the emancipation of the serfs, the restrictions on the movement of Jews beyond the Pale remained in force, and became explicitly underlined within

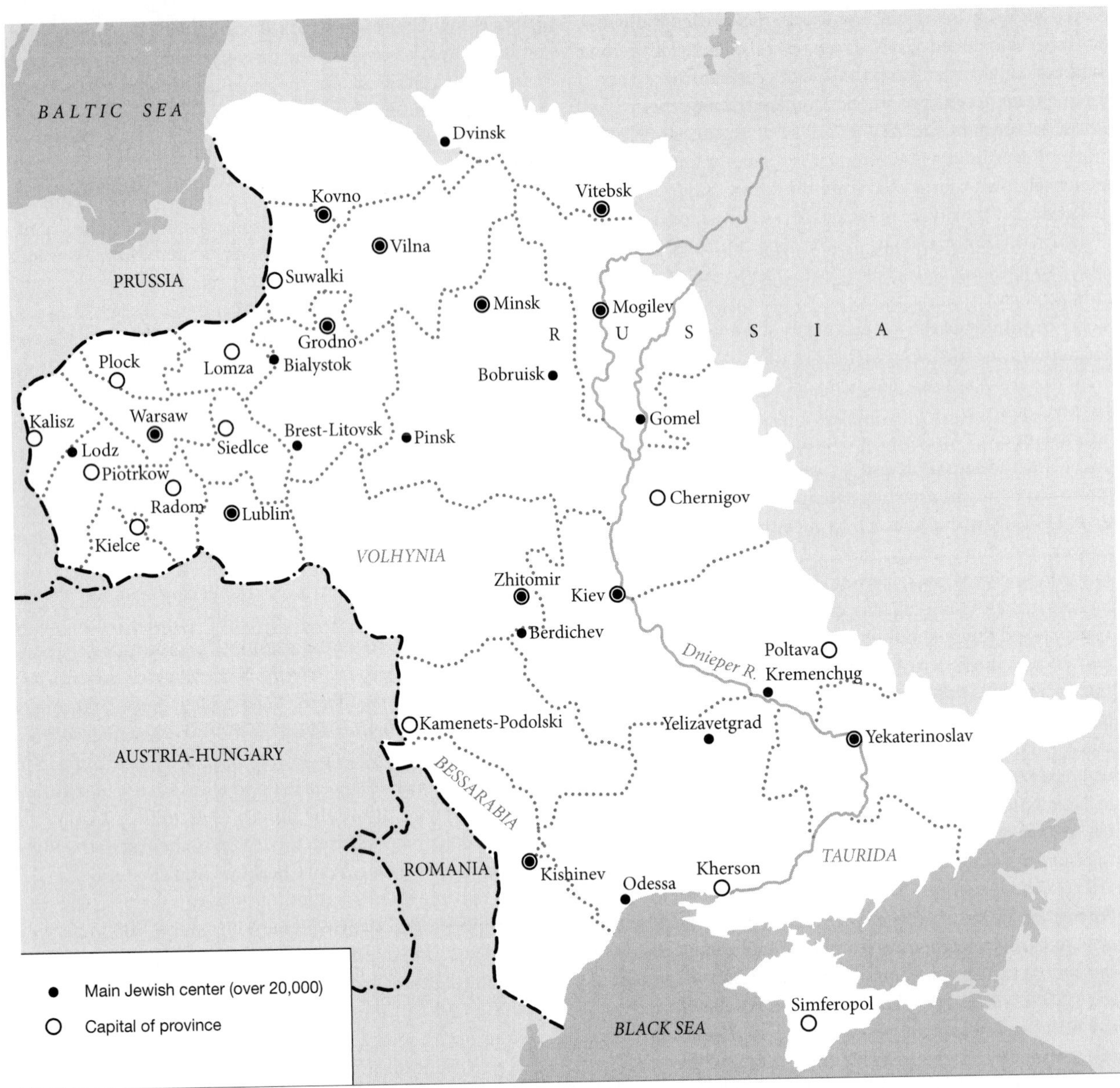

The Pale of Settlement at the end of the 19th century.

the Pale itself. This was accomplished both by anti-Jewish enactments on the part of the government and by the growing impatience of Jewish society and liberal public opinion with these disabilities.

Czar Nicholas I (under whom the term "Pale of Settlement" was coined) removed Courland from the Pale in 1829; however, the rights of the Jews already settled and registered there were maintained. In 1835 the provinces of Astrakhan and the northern Caucasus were excluded from the Pale. In 1843 Nicholas I ordered the expulsion of the Jews from a strip of 50 versts (about 33 mi.) in width extending along the border with Prussia and Austria. Many difficulties were encountered in the application of this law, and in 1858 it was redrafted to apply only to those Jews who would wish to settle in the border zone after that year. A similar law which had applied to the provinces of Russian Poland (where the border zone closed to Jewish residence was 21 versts in width) was abrogated in 1862. In 1827 severe restrictions were imposed on the residence of Jews in Kiev, the largest town in southern Russia, that served as an important commercial center for the surrounding regions which had a dense Jewish population.

Under Alexander II, rights of residence beyond the Pale began to be granted to various classes of the Jewish population: in 1859 to merchants able to pay the registration fees of the First Guild; in 1861 to university graduates, as well as those engaged in medical professions (dentists, male and female nurses, midwives, etc., from 1879); and in 1865 to various craftsmen. The right of residence throughout Russia was also granted to *Cantonists who had remained Jews and to their offspring (the so-called "Nicholas soldiers"). The Jews hoped that these regulations would prove to be the first steps toward the complete abolition of the Pale of Settlement. However, they were disappointed when these alleviations came to a complete halt after 1881, as part of the general reaction in Russia at this period. The "Temporary (*May) Laws" of 1881 prohibited any new settlement by Jews outside towns and townlets in the Pale of Settlement (this law did not apply to the Vistula Region). Jews who had been living in villages before the publication of the decree were authorized to reside in those same villages only. The peasants were granted the right of demanding the expulsion of the Jews who lived among them. These decrees were bound up with intensified administrative pressure, brutality by local authorities, and the systematic acceptance of bribery on the part of the lower administrative ranks. Occasionally, new places were excluded from the Pale of Settlement, such as *Rostov and *Taganrog (1887) and the spa town of *Yalta (1893). During the years 1891–92, thousands of Jewish craftsmen and their families were expelled from *Moscow.

At the beginning of the 20th century political and economic pressure on the Russian government intensified, and in various places alleviations in the "Temporary Laws" occurred. From 1903 some village settlements which had assumed an urban character were given the status of townlets, and the Jews were thus granted the legal right of living in them. Up to the outbreak of World War I some 300 settlements were thus opened for Jewish residence. In 1904 instructions were issued that all the Jews authorized to reside outside the Pale of Settlement could also settle in the rural areas there.

In 1910 the Jewish members of the *Duma, N. *Friedman and L. *Nisselovich, with the support of the Constitutional-Democratic Party, proposed a bill for the abolition of the Pale of Settlement. However, the balance of power in the Duma between the liberals and reactionaries made the proposal of demonstrative value only. The extreme Right retorted with a counter-motion "to expel the Jews from Russia"; the original motion was voted upon in February 1911 and transferred to the commission for personal freedom, where it fell into oblivion and was no longer mentioned in plenary session of the Duma. In August 1915, when many thousands of expelled and refugee Jews from the battle zones streamed into the interior of Russia, the government was compelled to permit the residence of these refugees in the towns of inner Russia, with the exception of St. Petersburg and Moscow; thus the existence of the Pale of Settlement in practice was brought to an end. After the Revolution of February 1917 the provisional government abolished the Pale of Settlement among the rest of the anti-Jewish restrictions.

The Pale covered an area of about 1 million sq. km. (386,100 sq. mi.) from the Baltic Sea to the Black Sea. According to the census of 1897, 4,899,300 Jews lived there, forming 94% of the total Jewish population of Russia and c. 11.6% of the general population of this area. The largest of the other nations living within the area of the Pale were the Ukrainian, Polish, Belorussian, Russian, Lithuanian, Moldavian (mostly in Bessarabia), and German. These (with the exception of the Germans) were essentially concentrated in their own territorial regions, where they formed the majority of the population. The Jews were a minority in every province (from 17.5% in the province of Grodno to 3.8% in the province of Taurida); 82% of the Jews lived in the towns and townlets of the Pale and their concentration in these was prominent: They formed 36.9% of the urban population, and in nine provinces they formed the majority of the urban population (province of Minsk – 58.8%; Grodno – 57.7%; Mogilev – 52.4%; etc.). In the townlets and many small towns all the inhabitants or the overwhelming majority were Jews. The 10 largest communities were *Warsaw (219,149 persons); *Odessa (138,915); *Lodz (98,677); *Vilna (64,000); *Kishinev (50,237); *Minsk (47,562); *Bialystok (41,900); *Berdichev (41,617); Yekaterinoslav (*Dnepropetrovsk; 40,009); *Vitebsk (34,470), and *Kiev 31,800.

It was, however, not only the limitation of their residential area which oppressed the Jews. By force of historical circumstances they were also restricted in their occupations. They were concentrated in commerce (38.6% of the Jews gainfully occupied) and crafts (35.4%); 72.8% of the total of persons engaged in commerce within the Pale of Settlement were Jews, as well as 31.4% of those engaged in crafts. Jewish artisans concentrated in certain branches of crafts (tailoring; shoemaking). Very few had the possibility of engaging in agriculture. The competition among the merchants, shopkeepers, and craftsmen was intense and gave rise to pauperization and the development of a Jewish proletariat which could not be integrated. This situation, together with the incessant anti-Jewish decrees and the waves of pogroms, especially during the years 1881–84 and 1903–06, resulted in a constant stream of Jewish emigration from the Pale of Settlement to Western Europe and the United States. Even this great emigration was, however, insufficient to counterbalance the natural growth of the Jews in the Pale of Settlement.

The language spoken by the Jews in the Pale of Settlement was Yiddish (according to the census of 1897 by 99% of the Jews). Most Jewish children received a Jewish education in the *ḥeder* and the yeshivah. Jewish literature and newspapers in Yiddish, Hebrew, Russian, and Polish circulated in many thousands of copies. The masses of *ḥasidim* were attached to the "courts" of their spiritual leaders in *Lubavich (Chabad), *Stolin, *Talnoye (Talna), *Gora Kalwaria (Gur), *Aleksandrow, etc. More modern movements such as *Ḥibbat Zion and Zionism, the *Bund and the socialist parties were also active in the towns and townlets of the Pale, either openly or illegally underground.

World War I, the disintegration of the Russian Empire, the Revolution, and the civil war in Russia, destroyed the foundations of this Jewish world, which was finally annihilated in the Holocaust. With the perspective of time, assessment of the Pale of Settlement has changed; it is necessary to consider not only its negative aspects but also its positive, unintended results, as forming a framework for an independent Jewry, as the area of settlement of a whole Jewish nation in which generations of Jews developed their own culture, and as the source of the establishment and development of large Jewish centers in America, South Africa, and many other countries, as well as Israel.

BIBLIOGRAPHY: Yu. Hessen, in: YE, 7 (c. 1910), 590–7; J. Bikerman, *Cherta yevreyskoy osedlosti* (1911); Dubnow, Hist Russ, 3 (1920), index; J. Lestschinsky, *Dos Yidishe Folk in Tsifern* (1922), 13–84; B. Dinur, in: *Zion*, 23 (1958), 93–101; I. Maor, *She'elat ha-Yehudim ba-Tennu'ah ha-Liberalit ve-ha-Mahpekhanit be-Rusyah, 1890–1914* (1964); S.W. Baron, *The Russian Jew under Tsars and Soviets* (1964), index; Y. Slutsky, in: *He-Avar*, 13 (1966), 41–58; S. Ettinger, *Toledot Am Yisrael*, 3 (1969), index s.v. *Teḥum ha-Moshav.*

[Yehuda Slutsky]

PALERMO, capital of Sicily. Jews apparently lived there in Roman times. Evidence of their presence is first supplied by Pope *Gregory I. His intervention in 598 with Bishop Victor of Palermo, who had requisitioned the synagogue and hospice, indicates that the community had by then attained some prosperity. The Jews could not resume possession of the buildings since they had been consecrated as churches, but they were indemnified and the religious objects restored to them. During the Muslim period the community was augmented by Jews who had been sold as slaves in Sicily and ransomed by their coreligionists. A description by the 10th-century Muslim geographer Ibn Hawkal mentions the location of the Jewish quarter in Palermo. Documents from the *Genizah* shed light on important events regarding Jewish life under Muslim rule. A rhymed letter written in Hebrew in the 10th or 11th centuries by a Jew of Palermo addressed to a Jewish leader (perhaps the head of the Diaspora in Babylon) gives a moving account of the suffering of the population during an episode of civil war among Muslim factions that led to Byzantine intervention. According to the author, the armies desecrated synagogues. Nevertheless, Sicilian Jews prospered during the Muslim period. They donated money to the Palestine yeshivah, collected money to ransom prisoners, and conducted a lucrative trade between Sicily, North Africa, and Egypt. Like the other Jews in Sicily in this period, those of Palermo had to pay a poll tax (*jizya*) and an impost on real estate (*khârāj*), and in the second half of the 11th century they had to pay a special tax on imported goods, the tenth (*– ushr*). A letter written on the eve of the conquest by the Normans, around 1060, describes the suffering of the people of Palermo. Other letters from this period provide information on the last Muslim ruler of Palermo, Muḥammad Ibn al-Babā al-Andalusī. The latter appointed Zakkār ben Amār as *nagid* over the Jews, and he was also in charge of supplying most of the provisions of the ruler. With the fall of Palermo (1072) the Jews came under the jurisdiction of the Normans, who continued collecting the *jizya* from them, in addition to the impost they paid to the local archbishop in 1089. However, the Jews were recognized as full citizens with the right to own property, excepting Christian slaves, and free to engage in a variety of crafts. A prominent number were fishermen and artisans, and Jews had virtually a monopoly of the silk and dyeing industry. The art of silk weaving was developed in Palermo by Jews brought there as prisoners from Greece by Roger II in 1147; they later settled throughout Italy, leading in this craft for four centuries. In 1211 a tax was collected for the right to practice dyeing by the ecclesiastical curia in Palermo. According to *Benjamin of Tudela, 1,500 Jews (or Jewish families) were living in Palermo around 1172. In 1312 Frederick II of Aragon revoked a former decree that expelled the Jews from the Cassaro situated in the city center and confined them to a special quarter outside the city walls. However, despite repeated attempts to segregate the Jews and relegate them to a separate quarter, the Jews continued to live until the expulsion in the Cassaro, where many Christians also lived. Before 1393 the Jews of Palermo had been allowed to wear a distinguishing *badge much smaller than the size stipulated for the other Sicilian Jews. The Jews of Palermo had to attend missionary sermons. The incitement of fanatical preachers frequently resulted in bloodshed, as in a riot which occurred in Palermo in 1339. In 1393 the Palermo community petitioned King Martin I to prevent the inquisitors from persecuting foreign Jews who came to the city under the pretext of being Christians. It is probable that that petition attests to the arrival in Palermo of refugees from the Iberian Peninsula following the pogroms and forced conversions of 1391. Besides paying taxes levied by the royal administration, the Jews in Palermo sometimes had to contribute funds to rebut libels; in 1437 they paid 150 gold ounces to defray the expenditure of the war against the Kingdom of Naples, and in 1475 they paid 500 gold ounces to silence a false accusation. In 1450 Alfonso confirmed the appointment of Iacob Exarchi, papal commissioner, to investigate matters concerning the Jews of Sicily. He was to look into the religious practices of the Jews, investigate the practice of usury, and ensure the separation of Jews from Christians. In the same year the Jewish communities, headed by the community of Palermo, paid 10,000 florins in return for a royal writ that approved their old privileges. In 1453, following complaints that the Jews of Palermo were forced to pay an unfair portion of the tax burden, the viceroy decreed that they were to pay only one-seventh of the tax burden rather than a quarter. The investigations initiated in 1473 by the inquisitor, the Dominican Salvo de Cassetta, hit the Palermo community particularly hard, accusing it of crimes against the Christian faith, The accusations concerned blasphemy against the Virgin, probably because the Jews were found to possess an anti-Christian polemic compilation, known as *Toledot Yeshu*. Several Jews were found guilty of that crime, and after having been tortured they confessed and were burned. On August 2, 1474, the Jewish community of Palermo paid a fine of 5,000 florins in return for a royal pardon that did not include Jews outside Palermo. However, in the same month Pope Sixtus ordered the archbishop of Palermo to assist Salvo de Cassetta in implementing his commission and proceeding against the Jews of Sicily. The investigations were probably at the root of the anti-Jewish riots that broke out in the summer of 1474 throughout Sicily.

Obadiah *Bertinoro, who spent some months in Palermo in 1487–88, gives a vivid description of the community which he estimated at 850 families, mainly coppersmiths, ironworkers, laborers, and porters, much despised by the Christians because of their ragged clothing. The main synagogue, with its sweet-voiced cantors and its elaborate subsidiary buildings, was the most beautiful he had ever seen.

Twelve *proti* (from the Greek πρῶτοι) or notables assisted by councilors were in charge of the communal administration (see *Sicily). In 1393, by a decree issued by King Martin I, the Giudecca, or Jewish community body of Palermo, was given the function of acting as a court of appeal in legal disputes among the Sicilian Jews. Outstanding among those who contributed to the cultural life of the community were the physician Master Busach; *Moses of Palermo, translator of works from Arabic, who served at court; the poet Saul b. Nafusi of Palermo; the *dayyan* Anatol b. Joseph who spent about ten years in Palermo (1170–80); the poet and physician *Ahitub b. Isaac to whom Solomon b. Abraham *Adret of Barcelona addressed a polemic against the kabbalist Abraham *Abulafia; Joseph *Abenafia, born in Syracuse, physician at the court of Martin I, was the first *dienchelele of the Jewish communities of the realm. However, it is uncertain whether the story of the poet and physician Moses *Remos, who was unjustly sentenced to death and wrote a poem on the eve of his execution in Palermo, has an historical basis. It is possible that the story is connected to the trials held in Palermo in 1474. In 1491 the intervention of the Jews in Palermo prevented Jewish refugees from Provence who had arrived in Sicily from being sold as slaves.

After the decree of expulsion of 1492 was issued, the Jews of Palermo, then numbering about 5,000, were obliged to leave the island. After the expulsion, according to inquisitorial records, about 170 families of converts were living in the city, and according to 16th-century Sicilian historian Tommaso Fazello, there was a multitude of converts who attempted to return to Jewish rites. In June 1511 an auto da fé was conducted in Palermo and 10 New Christians were burned at the stake for the first time in Sicily. Palermo also served as a slave market where Jewish prisoners were sold after Spanish victories in the North African campaigns of 1510 and 1535. When the Jews were temporarily readmitted to the Kingdom of the Two Sicilies, in 1695–1702 and 1740–46, a few presumably came to Palermo. In the early 1920s a *minyan* could be obtained, at the most, composed of Jews from central or eastern Europe who had acquired Italian citizenship. Two of them, Philippsohn and Beretvas, lectured at the faculty of medicine. Most had left Sicily before 1938, when Mussolini's racial laws deprived them of Italian citizenship. On July 22 the allied forces entered Palermo, and subsequently abolished the racial laws. At that time many refugees from the concentration camp of Ferramonti came to Palermo, among them Meir Artom, son of Elia S. Artom of Florence. Meir's letters to his father describe the refugees he encountered, and the fact that the allied forces established a synagogue in Palermo. Though in the early 21st century there were Jews living in Palermo, there was no organized Jewish community in the city.

BIBLIOGRAPHY: C. Roth, *Gleanings* (1969); Milano, Bibliotheca, index. **ADD. BIBLIOGRAPHY:** S.D.Goitein, *A Mediterranean Society*, 1–6; idem, "Sicily and Southern Italy in the Cairo Geniza Documents," in: *Archivio Storico per la Sicilia Orientale*, 67 (1971), 9–33; M. Ben Sasson, *The Jews of Sicily 825–1068* (1991); M. Gil, *In the Kingdom of Ismael*, vol. 1 (1997), 531–89 and index; Simonsohn, *The Jews in Sicily*, 1–6, index; G. Palermo, "New Evidence about the Slaughter of the Jews in Modica, Noto and Elsewhere in Sicily (1474)," in: *Henoch*, 22:2–3 (2000), 247–317; M. Krasner, "La comunità ebraico palermitana nel XV secolo attraverso uno studio sui documenti notaril" (Ph.D. dissertation, Tel Aviv, 2003); N. Zeldes, *The Former Jews of this Kingdom. Sicilian Converts after the Expulsion (1492–1516)* (2003); idem, "Un tragico ritorno: schiavi ebrei in Sicilia dopo la conquista spagnola di Tripoli (1510)," in: *Nuove Effemeridi. Rassegna trimestrale di cultura*, 14:54 (2001), 47–55; N. Bucaria, "Tempio di Palermo non c – era il Sefer Torah. Le lettere di Meir Artom al padre," in: N. Bucaria, M. Luzzati, A. Tarantino (eds.), *Ebrei e Sicilia* (2002), 279–97; H. Bresc, *Arabes de langue, juifs de religion. L'evolution du judaïsme sicilien dans l'environment latin, XIIe–XVe siècles* (2001).

[Sergio Joseph Sierra / Nadia Zeldes (2nd ed.)]

PALESTINE, one of the names of the territory of the southern Levant known as the Land of *Israel and much later as the Holy Land. The name "Palestine" was originally an adjective derived from Heb. פְּלֶשֶׁת, *Peleshet* (Isa 14:29, 31; see also *Prst* or *Plst* in ancient Egyptian and *Pilišti*, *Palaštu* in Assyrian sources). The name is first used geographically in the mid-fifth century B.C.E. by Herodotus in the form of Συρία ἡ Παλαιστίνη, i.e., "the Philistine Syria"; subsequently, the name was shortened and the adjective "Palaistinei" became a proper noun. Philo identifies "Palaistinei" with biblical *Canaan. In talmudic literature Palestine is used as the name of a Roman province, adjoining the provinces of *Finukyah* (Phoenicia) and *Aruvyah* (Arabia; Gen. R. 90: 6). From the fourth century, however, the three provinces into which the Land of Israel was divided were referred to as the "first," "second," and "third Palestine," respectively.

Muslims used the term "Filasṭīn" for the "first Palestine" only, differentiating between it and "Urdunn" (Jordan); but these designations soon fell into disuse, as the Muslims generally referred to provinces by the names of their capital cities. The Crusaders renewed the use of the "three Palestines," the borders of which, however, differed from those of the Roman provinces. After the fall of the Crusader kingdom, Palestine was no longer an official designation, but it was still used in non-Jewish languages as the name of the "Holy Land" on both sides of the Jordan. It was not an administrative unit under the Ottoman Empire, when it was part of the province of Syria. In the disciplines of historical geography and biblical history of the 19th century (e.g., E. Robinson), Palestine was the name commonly used in the western world for the region, with "western" Palestine used in reference to the entire country west of the Jordan River, and "eastern" Palestine to Transjordan (see the maps of the Palestine Exploration Fund published in the early 1880s).

This was the situation until 1922, when the British, who had received the Mandate over Palestine on both sides of the Jordan from the League of Nations, practically restricted the application of the name to the part west of the Jordan, while east of the Jordan and south of the Yarmuk they established the emirate of Transjordan, which in 1946 became a kingdom. In 1948 the State of Israel was established in a large part of western Palestine, its territory demarcated in the *Armistice agreements of 1949 with the neighboring Arab countries. Transjordan annexed the Arab-inhabited part of western Palestine occupied by the Jordanian army and changed its own name to the Hashemite Kingdom of *Jordan, and Egypt retained and administered the *Gaza Strip. Thus, Palestine as a political entity ceased to exist. During the *Six-Day War (1967) the Israel army occupied the whole of the country west of the Jordan (hence the term "West Bank"; referred to also as "Judea and Samaria" or the "occupied" or "administered" territories), which also included the Gaza Strip, as well as the *Sinai Peninsula and the *Golan Heights. However, the latter were never geographically part of the earlier designation of Palestine. The name Palestine is now loosely used in the west to refer to the territories of Area A that are under the autonomous rule of the *Palestinian Authority, even though by 2006 a State of Palestine had not yet been proclaimed. See also *Israel, Land of: Names.

ADD. BIBLIOGRAPHY: M. Noth, "Zur Geschichte des Namens Palästina," in: *Zeitschrift des Deutschen Palaestine-Vereins*, 62 (1939), 125–44; D. Cole, J. Greenfield, and K.M. Kenyon, "What is 'Palestine'?" in: *Biblical Archaeology Review*, 4 (Nov./Dec. 1978), 43–45; for a different view see: D.M. Jacobson, "Palestine and Israel," in: BASOR (1999), 65–74.

[Abraham J. Brawer / Shimon Gibson (2nd ed.)]

PALESTINE, INQUIRY COMMISSIONS, a series of commissions and committees that conducted inquiries into the internal developments, system of government, and political status of Palestine against the background of British and international commitments to assist in the establishment of a National Home for the Jewish people (see *Balfour Declaration). The first of these endeavors, the King-Crane Commission (1919), was appointed by the United States. Four commissions were appointed by the British government during the period of the Mandate, after the outbreaks of Arab violence in 1921, 1929, and 1936. After World War II, a joint Anglo-American Committee was appointed by the British and U.S. governments in 1945, and the UN Special Committee on Palestine (UNSCOP) was appointed by the United Nations in 1947.

King-Crane Commission (1919)

After World War I the United States, Great Britain, and France agreed, on President Wilson's suggestion, to appoint a special committee to visit the regions of the former Ottoman Empire involved in recent agreements, negotiations, and declarations "to acquaint themselves as fully as possible with the shade of opinion there … with the social, racial, and economic conditions … and to form as definite an opinion as the circumstances and the time at your disposal will permit, of the divisions of territory and assignment of mandates." As a result of obstruction by France and the lukewarm attitude of Britain, however, the only members actually appointed were two Americans, H.C. King, president of Oberlin College, Ohio, and C.R. Crane, a Chicago businessman with many connections in the Near East, particularly Turkey.

In their report, presented only to the American Peace Commission (published in a somewhat condensed form in December 1922 and officially published only in 1947), King and Crane recommended the preservation of the unity of Syria, including both Lebanon and Palestine, which should be granted a reasonable measure of local autonomy; and that a Mandate over Syria be entrusted to the United States or, if that seemed impracticable, to Great Britain. The commission further recommended "a serious modification of the extreme Zionist program for Palestine of unlimited immigration of Jews, looking finally to making Palestine distinctly a Jewish State." Policy toward Palestine should be governed by the principle laid down by President Wilson on July 4, 1918: "The settlement of every question on the basis of the free acceptance of that settlement by the people immediately concerned." Since, according to the commission's findings, the non-Jewish population of Palestine – nearly 90% of the whole – were "emphatically against the entire Zionist program," their wishes should be respected.

The commission declared that the Zionist claim "that they have a 'right' to Palestine, based on an occupation of two thousand years ago, can hardly be seriously considered." A further consideration was the fact that, since Palestine was the Holy Land for Jews, Christians, and Muslims alike, the Jews could not be proper guardians of the holy places. The complete Jewish occupation of Palestine "would intensify, with a certainty like fate, the anti-Jewish feeling both in Palestine and in all other portions of the world which look to Palestine as 'the Holy Land.'"

In view of all these considerations, the commission recommended that "Jewish immigration to Palestine should definitely be limited and that the project for making Palestine distinctly a Jewish commonwealth should be given up." The commission's report was never submitted to the Paris Peace Conference, and its recommendations were never acted upon.

Haycraft Commission of Inquiry (1921)

A commission of inquiry into the disturbance of May 1921 (see *Israel, Land of: Historical Survey) was appointed by Sir Herbert *Samuel, then high commissioner for Palestine, "to inquire into the recent disturbances in the town and neighbourhood of Jaffa and to report thereon." It was headed by Sir W. Haycraft, chief justice of Palestine, and its members were H.C. Luke, assistant governor of Jerusalem, and J.N. Stubbs of the Legal Department. The commission found that the immediate reason for the riots (in which 47 Jews and 48 Arabs were killed and 146 Jews and 73 Arabs wounded) was a clash between Jewish Communist and the general Jewish labor movement May Day demonstrations in Jaffa, which served as "a spark igniting explosive material." However, the commission stated that "the racial strife was begun by Arabs," while "the police were, with few exceptions, half-trained and inefficient, in many cases indifferent and in some cases leaders of or participators in violence." The fundamental cause of the disturbances, the commission found, was the Arab feeling of discontent with, and hostility to, the Jews due to political and economic causes and connected with Jewish immigration and with their conception of Zionist policy as derived from Jewish exponents. Much could be done, the commission suggested, to allay hostility between Arabs and Jews if responsible people on both sides would sit together to discuss the questions arising between them in a "reasonable spirit," on the basis that the Arabs should implicitly accept the government's policy on the subject of the Jewish National Home and "that the Zionist leaders should abandon and repudiate all pretensions that go beyond it."

Commission on the Palestine Disturbances of 1929 (The Shaw Commission)

This commission was appointed by the British colonial secretary, Lord Passfield, after the serious disturbances of August 1929, which broke out in connection with the question of Jewish rights at the *Western (Wailing) Wall. In the disturbances 133 Jews were killed and 339 wounded, mainly in Jerusalem and Hebron; Arab casualties, chiefly from police action, were 116 dead and 232 wounded. The commission's terms of reference were "to enquire into the immediate causes which led to the recent outbreak in Palestine and to make recommendations as to the steps necessary to avoid a recurrence." It consisted of Sir Walter Shaw, former chief justice of the Straits Settlements, as chairman, and three members of parliament Sir H. Betterton (Conservative), R.H. Morris (Liberal), and H. Snell (Labour).

Although Prime Minister Ramsay MacDonald stated that matters of major policy were definitely outside its terms of reference, the commission went into Arab political and economic grievances in considerable depth and detail. It found that the outbreak in Jerusalem was from the beginning "an attack by Arabs on Jews" and apportioned "a share in the responsibility" to Al-Hajj Amin *Husseini, the mufti of Jerusalem. In dealing with the causes of the trouble, the commission stated: "There can be no doubt that racial animosity on the part of the Arabs, consequent upon the disappointment of their political and national aspirations and fear for their economic future, was the fundamental cause of the outbreak of August last," and that the Churchill *White Paper of 1922 charged the Palestine government with the primary duty of "holding the balance between the two parties in the country." It considered the policy of the government to be of a dual nature and that it had succeeded in steering a middle course between the conflicting policies proposed by the two parties.

The commission accepted most of the Arab claims and recommended that a new statement of policy should be issued, containing "a definition in clear and positive terms" of the meaning of the passages in the Mandate providing for "the safeguarding of the rights of the non-Jewish communities." It recommended: that immigration policy be reviewed to prevent a repetition of what the commission described as the excessive immigration of 1925 and 1926; that a special inquiry should be undertaken into the prospects of introducing improved methods of cultivation and that a new land policy be introduced, having regard for the natural increase in the present rural population; and that a special commission be appointed to determine rights and claims in connection with the Western Wall.

In a long note of reservations, Harry Snell attributed a greater share in the responsibility for the disturbances to the mufti, blamed the government for not having issued an official denial that the Jews had designs on the Muslim holy places, ascribed the outbreaks mainly to fears and antipathies fostered by the Arab leaders for political needs, and declared that what was needed was not so much a change of policy, as a change of mind on the part of the Arab population.

The British government appointed Sir John Hope-Simpson to report on questions of immigration, land settlement, and development and issued a preliminary statement accepting the substance of the Shaw Commission Report. In reply to trenchant criticism of the report by the Permanent Mandates Commission of the *League of Nations, the government further defended the commission's conclusions. The Hope-Simpson report, which was issued on October 21, 1930, simultaneously with the Passfield *White Paper, stated that: If all the cultivable land in Palestine were divided up among the Arab agricultural population, there would not be enough to provide every family with a decent livelihood; until further development took place and the Arabs adopted better methods of cultivation, "there is no room for a single additional settler, if the standard of life of the fellaheen is to remain at its present level"; and that with thorough development of the country, there would be room "for no less than 20,000 families of settlers from outside."

Palestine Royal Commission (Peel Commission; 1937)

The commission was appointed by the British government on August 7, 1936, with very wide terms of reference.

(1) "To ascertain the underlying causes of the disturbances which broke out in Palestine in the middle of April.

(2) "To inquire into the manner in which the Mandate for Palestine is being implemented in relation to the obligations of the Mandatory towards the Arabs and Jews respectively.

(3) "To ascertain whether, upon a proper construction of the terms of the Mandate, either the Arabs or the Jews have any legitimate grievances upon account of the way in which the Mandate has been, or is being implemented.

(4) "If the Commission is satisfied that any such griev-

ances are well founded, to make recommendation for their removal and for the prevention of their recurrence."

The commission was headed by Earl Peel, a former secretary of state for India, and its members were Sir H.G.M. Rumbold, Sir E.L.L. Hammond, Sir W.M. Carter, Sir H. Morris, and Professor R. Coupland. The commission's report, issued on July 7, was the most thorough study of the problem conducted by any of the inquiry commissions and committees. It started with a comprehensive survey of the history of Palestine and the connection of Jews and Arabs with it, as well as a bird's-eye view of Jewish history in the Diaspora, showing a deep and sympathetic understanding of the Zionist movement and its aims. After a thorough study of British promises to Jews and Arabs during World War I and of the terms of the Mandate, it reached the conclusion that "the primary purpose of the Mandate … is to promote the establishment of the Jewish National Home." The commission found that the Jewish National Home was now a "going concern" and that its establishment had been to the economic advantage of the Arabs as a whole. At the same time, however, "with almost mathematical precision the betterment of the economic situation in Palestine meant the deterioration of the political situation." The underlying causes of the disturbances in 1936 were, therefore, found to be the desire of the Arabs for national independence and their hatred and fear of the establishment of the Jewish National Home, the same causes that had led to the disturbances in the past.

"It is impossible," the commission commented, "to see the National Home and not to wish it well. It has meant so much for the relief of unmerited suffering. It displays so much energy and enterprise and devotion to a common cause. In so far as Britain has helped towards its creation, we would claim, with Lord Balfour, that to that extent, at any rate, Christendom has shown itself not oblivious of all the wrong it has done, but at the same time the difficulties which confront the National Home should not be underestimated, and it must be admitted that the situation in Palestine has reached a deadlock." The solution of the problem of Palestine must be a drastic one. All other recommendations would be but palliatives. "We cannot – in Palestine as it now is – both concede the Arab claim to self-government and secure the establishment of the Jewish National Home," the report declared. "The disease is so deep-rooted that the only hope of a cure lies in a surgical operation." This operation was to be the partitioning of the country and the establishment of separate Jewish and Arab states, while Jerusalem and Bethlehem, with a corridor to the sea at Jaffa, and Nazareth would remain under British Mandate (see *Palestine, Partition; *Israel, State of: Historical Survey, 1880–1948).

Palestine Partition Commission (The Woodhead Commission; 1938)

This commission was appointed on January 4, 1938, to recommend boundaries for the Arab and Jewish areas and the enclaves to be retained permanently or under British Mandate as proposed by the Peel Commission. In effect it reported that Partition was impracticable (see *Palestine, Partition and Partition Plans for a more detailed account).

Anglo-American Committee of Enquiry Regarding the Problems of European Jewry and Palestine (1946)

The terms of reference of the committee, appointed by the governments of the United States and Britain in November 1945, was to examine political, economic, and social conditions in Palestine as they bore upon the problem of Jewish immigration and settlement therein and the wellbeing of the peoples now living therein; to examine the position of the Jews in those countries in Europe where they had been the victims of Nazi and Fascist persecution and to make estimates of those who wished or would be impelled by their conditions to migrate to Palestine or other countries outside Europe; and to make recommendations for *ad interim* handling of these problems, as well as for their permanent solution.

This committee differed from its predecessors in two important respects. First, it represented both Britain and the United States. Of its 12 members, six were British (J.E. Singleton, W.F. Crick, R.H.S. Crossman, F. Leggett, R.E. Manningham-Bullet, and Lord Morrison) and six were Americans (J.C. Hutcheson, F. Aydelotte, F.W. Buxton, B.C. Crum, J.G. *MacDonald, and W. Phillips), with Singleton and Hutcheson as joint chairmen. Secondly, it connected, for the first time, the problem of world Jewry with that of the Jews in Palestine, thereby tacitly admitting that the Jewish problem and the problem of the Jewish National Home must be seen as one. The committee therefore visited Germany, Poland, Czechoslovakia, Austria, Italy, and Greece even before it carried out its investigations in Palestine.

In its unanimous report and recommendations, the committee found that no country other than Palestine was ready to give substantial assistance in finding homes for Jews wishing or impelled to leave Europe, but that Palestine alone could not solve their emigration needs. It therefore recommended that the U.S. and British governments should endeavor to find new places for the *Displaced Persons, in addition to Palestine, and that 100,000 certificates for immigration to Palestine be authorized immediately for the Jewish victims of Nazi and Fascist persecution. Future immigration to Palestine should be regulated according to the Mandate, and the Land Transfers Regulation of 1940 should be annulled and replaced by new ones based on "a policy of freedom in the sale, lease, or use of land, irrespective of race, community, or creed." As for long-term policy, the committee recommended the guiding principle that Palestine should be neither a Jewish state nor an Arab state, and that Jew should not dominate Arab nor Arab dominate Jew. Until the hostility between Jews and Arabs disappeared, the government of Palestine should be continued under the Mandate. In effect, therefore, the committee proposed de facto abrogation of the 1939 *White Paper policy. The British government's rejection of the committee's recommendations (in particular the proposal for the issue of

100,000 certificates), despite President Truman's acceptance of the report, led to a further deterioration in the Palestine situation; consequently, the British government turned the whole problem over to the United Nations, which appointed the UN Special Committee on Palestine (UNSCOP).

United Nations Special Committee on Palestine (UNSCOP; 1947)

The General Assembly of the United Nations, at a special meeting convened in April 1947 at the request of the British government, appointed this committee to prepare a report on Palestine. It consisted of 11 members: representatives of Australia (J.D. Hood), Canada (I.C. Rand), Czechoslovakia (K. Lisicky), Guatemala (J.G. Granados), India (A. Rahman), Iran (N. Entezam), the Netherlands (N.S. Blom), Peru (A. Ulloa), Sweden (E. Sandstrom), Uruguay (E.R. Fabregat), and Yugoslavia (V. Simic), with the Swedish delegate Justice Emil Sandstrom as chairman, and Alberto Ulloa of Peru, vice chairman. Its terms of reference gave the committee "the widest powers to ascertain and record facts, and to investigate all questions and issues relevant to the problems of Palestine." In its report, published on August 31, 1947, it recommended unanimously that the Mandate for Palestine should be terminated at the earliest possible date and that independence should be granted in Palestine at the earliest practical date. The majority, composed of the representatives of Canada, Czechoslovakia, Guatemala, the Netherlands, Peru, Sweden, and Uruguay, proposed the partitioning of Palestine into a Jewish state, an Arab state, and a special international regime for Jerusalem and its environs (see *Palestine, Partition and Partition Plans). The minority, consisting of the representatives of India, Iran, and Yugoslavia, proposed the establishment of a binational federal state. The majority proposals were adopted by a special meeting of the General Assembly on November 29, 1947; 33 member states (including the United States and the U.S.S.R.) voted in favor, 13 against (including all the Arab states) and 10 (including Great Britain) abstained.

For bibliography see *White Papers.

[Daniel Efron]

PALESTINE, PARTITION AND PARTITION PLANS.

The first partition of Palestine took place in 1922, when the British government excluded Transjordan from the area to which the provisions of the *Balfour Declaration would apply. The Zionist Executive reluctantly acquiesced in this decision. The *Revisionist movement, established in 1925, hotly opposed the separation of Transjordan; its basic slogan was "a Jewish state on both sides of the Jordan." The idea of partitioning western Palestine between Jews and Arabs was first broached officially in 1937 by the Palestine Royal Commission (see *Palestine, Inquiry Commissions, Peel Commission) as a method of enabling each nation to exercise sovereignty and achieve its principal national aims in part of the country while maintaining a British foothold centered in Jerusalem. The proposal was at first approved by the British government and accepted in principle, after a vigorous controversy, by the majority of the *yishuv* and the Zionist movement. The British withdrew their support, however, after the Palestine Partition Commission (the Woodhead Commission, see below) had failed to produce a "practicable" partition plan, and instead adopted in 1939 the *White Paper policy, which would ultimately have created an independent Palestinian state with a permanent Arab majority.

The abortive Morrison-Grady scheme of 1946 (see below), which would have left more than two-fifths of the country in British hands and given neither Arabs nor Jews more than limited autonomy, was rejected by both sides, and it was not until Britain put the problem before the United Nations that a new partition plan was evolved. This was done by the UN Special Committee on Palestine (UNSCOP, see below), which recommended the establishment of a Jewish and an Arab state joined in an economic union, with Jerusalem and its environs as a separate international enclave. This proposal was accepted by the Jews and rejected by the Arabs, while the British refused to play any part in implementing it.

The partition of western Palestine was not merely a theoretical proposal, but one of the possibilities inherent in the situation created by two generations of Zionist settlement before and during the British *Mandate. Jewish land purchases, mainly by the *Jewish National Fund, and the establishment of Jewish towns and villages had created areas of contiguous Jewish settlement, with a self-reliant and economically viable community that was prepared and able to defend itself and institutions of self-government based upon the voluntary allegiance of the Jewish population. Without such a *yishuv*, fortified by the moral, political, and financial support of Jews around the world, no decision by any external body could have been implemented. Ultimately, the partition of western Palestine was the result of two forces: the capacity of the *yishuv* to hold its own by force against the attacks of Palestinian Arabs and the surrounding Arab states on the one hand, and the inability of the *yishuv* to gain control of the whole of western Palestine, on the other. The following are the details of the partition plans presented by the various commissions and committees.

Palestine Royal Commission

(See *Palestine, Inquiry Commissions). This commission, often referred to as the Peel Commission, published its report on July 7, 1937. It came to the conclusion that partition was the best solution for both sides. Although this proposal meant neither Jews nor Arabs would get all they wanted, the commission believed that it offered many advantages to both sides. The Arabs would obtain national independence and finally be delivered from fear of ultimate subjection to Jewish rule. By converting the Jewish National Home into a Jewish state, the Jews would not only be free of the fear of Arab rule, but they "will attain the primary objective of Zionism – a Jewish nation, planted in Palestine, giving its nationals the same status in the world as other nations give theirs. They will cease at last to live a 'minority life.' A new sense of confidence and security would replace the existing feeling of fear and suspicion and both Jews and Arabs would obtain the inestimable boon of peace." (See Map: Peel Partition Plan).

The commission therefore proposed that Palestine be divided into

(1) a Jewish state, comprising the whole of Galilee and the Jezreel Valley, most of the Beth-Shean Valley, and the Coastal Plain from Ras el-Nakura (Rosh ha-Nikrah) on the Lebanese border to Be'er Tuviyyah in the south;

(2) an Arab state comprising Transjordan, the hill country of Samaria and Judea, and the Negev;

(3) a British zone under permanent Mandate, consisting of Jerusalem, Bethlehem, and their environs, a corridor to the coast at Jaffa, and Nazareth. British treaties of alliance with the Jewish and the Arab state would guarantee the protection of minorities, facilities for British forces, etc., and the Jewish state would pay a subvention to the Arab state. (For details of proposed boundaries, see *Israel, Land of: Geographical Survey.)

The 20th Zionist Congress (Zurich, Aug. 3–17, 1937) declared that the Peel Commission's scheme was "unacceptable," but empowered the Executive to negotiate with the British government on "precise terms" for the establishment of "a Jewish state," provided that any scheme that might emerge would be submitted for approval to a newly elected Congress.

Palestine Partition Commission

In 1938 the British government appointed the Palestine Partition Commission (generally known as the Woodhead Commission, after its chairman Sir John Woodhead) "to recommend boundaries for the proposed Arab and Jewish areas and the British enclaves that would (a) afford a reasonable prospect of the eventual establishment… of self-supporting Arab and Jewish states; (b) necessitate the inclusion of the fewest possible Arabs and Arab enterprises in the Jewish area and vice versa; and (c) enable the British government to carry out its 'Mandatory responsibilities.'" The commission, whose report was published in October 1938, found that the Peel Commission's scheme (Plan A) was impracticable. One member favored Plan B, which would have excluded Galilee and a small area in the south from the Jewish state as proposed in Plan A; two others preferred Plan C, which provided for small Jewish and Arab states, with Galilee, a Jerusalem enclave, and the Negev under British mandate; and a fourth rejected all three plans. The commission, therefore, was unable to recommend boundaries that would meet its terms of reference, and the British government came to the conclusion that partition was impracticable.

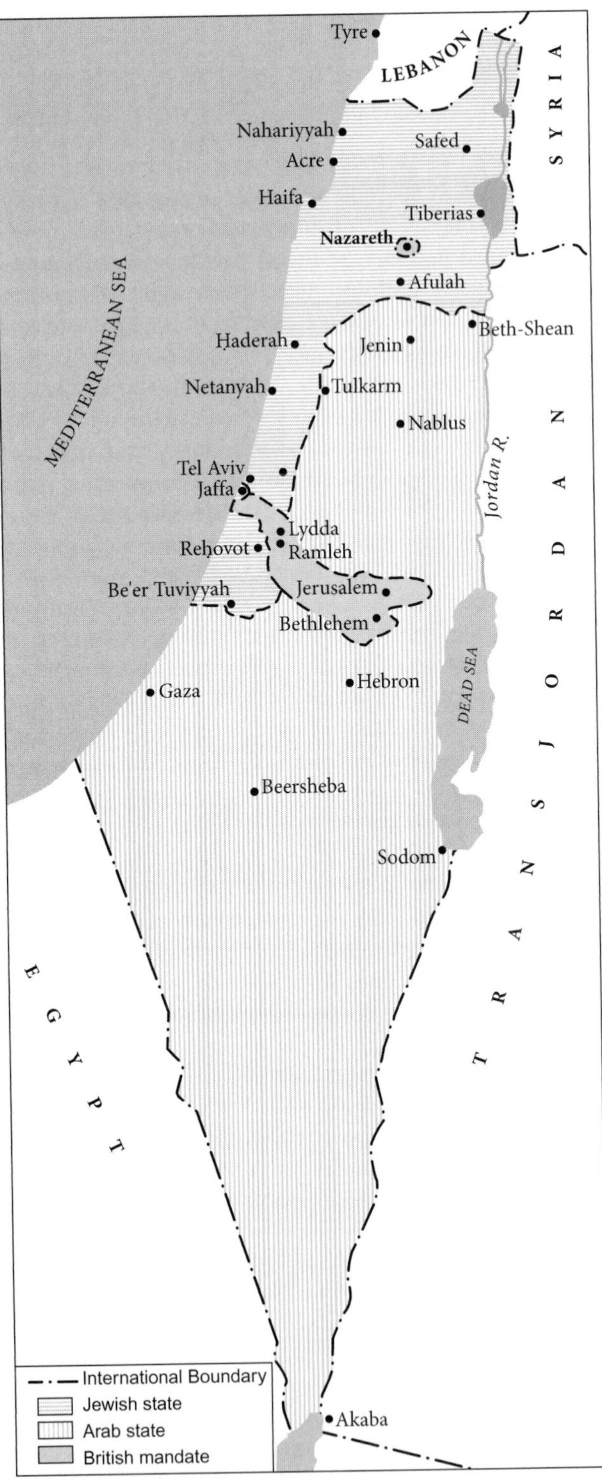

Map 1. The Peel Partition Plan, 1937. After Zev Vilnay, New Israel Atlas, *Jerusalem, 1968.*

The Morrison-Grady Scheme

This was a plan evolved in July 1946 by British and American representatives, headed by Herbert Morrison, then lord president of the council, and T. Grady of the U.S. State Department. It purported to be based on the report of the Anglo-American Committee (see *Palestine, Inquiry Commissions), but actually had little or nothing in common with it. The scheme provided for the division of Palestine into four provinces: an Arab province, consisting of about 40% of the area; a Jewish province, with 17%, and two British provinces – the Jerusalem district and the Negev – covering 43% of the area. A British high commissioner, assisted by a nominated executive council, would head the central government. The Arab and Jewish provinces would have elected legislatures, with executives appointed by the high commissioner from among their members. The powers of these executives would be very limited:

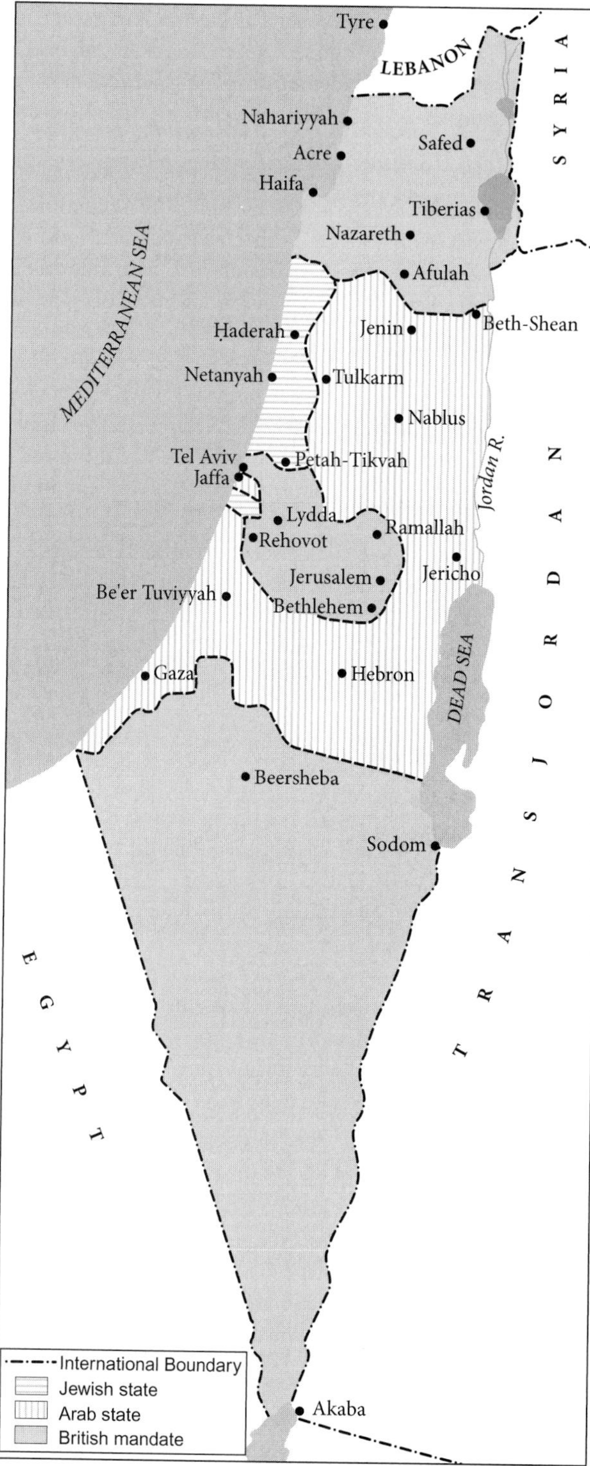

Map 2. "Plan C" examined by the Woodhead Palestine Partition Commission, 1938. After Zev Vilnay, New Israel Atlas, *Jerusalem, 1968.*

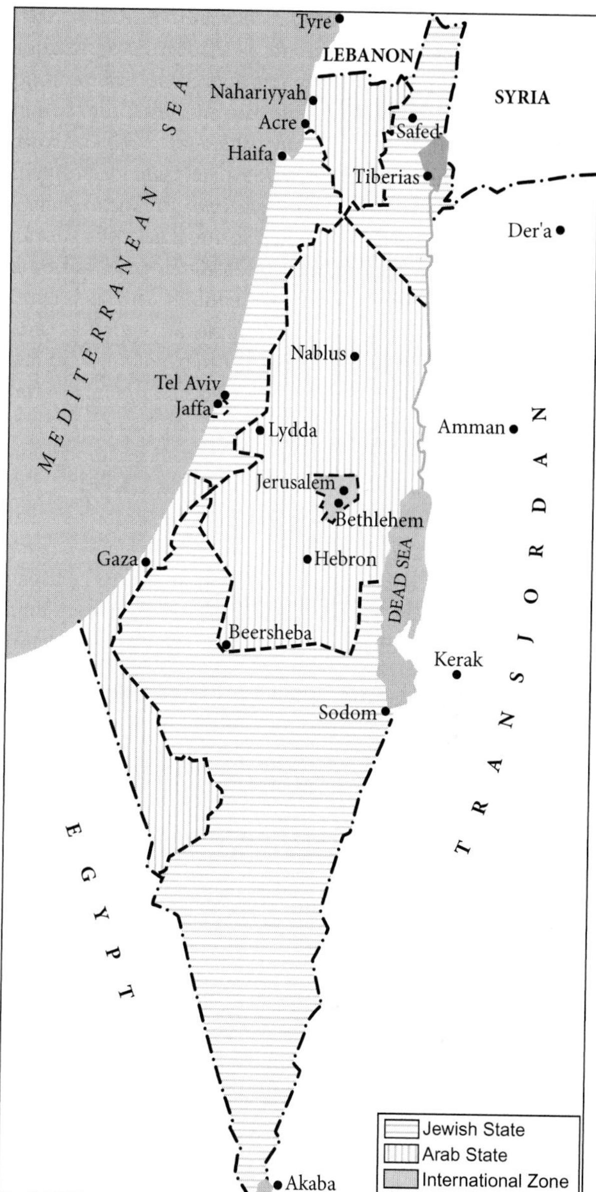

Map 3. The UNSCOP Partition Plan, 1947. After Zev Vilnay, New Israel Atlas, *Jerusalem, 1968.*

defense, foreign relations, and customs and excise would be controlled by the central government, and bills passed by the provincial legislatures would require the high commissioner's assent. The Land Transfer Regulations of the 1939 White Paper would be repealed. The Arab legislature would be free to permit or refuse Jews permission to buy lands in its province, while the Jews would be permitted to buy land in their own area. Final control over immigration would rest with the high commissioner, who would act according to the recommendations of the provincial governments, provided the economic absorptive capacity was not exceeded (see *White Papers). As for the future, the plan left the way open for either partition or for federal unity. The U.S. government declined to accept the plan as a basis for consideration, and it was rejected by the Zionist Congress.

UN Special Committee on Palestine

UNSCOP was appointed by the UN General Assembly in May 1947 after Britain had submitted the Palestine problem to the UN (see *Palestine, Inquiry Commissions). The seven-member majority called for the partition of Palestine into an Arab state, a Jewish state, and a "Special International Regime" for Jerusalem, all three to be linked in an economic union. The minority proposed the establishment of a binational federal state, while the Australian representative abstained.

The majority proposals, with slight territorial modifications, were adopted by a special meeting of the General Assembly on Nov. 19, 1947. The Arab state was to comprise western Galilee, the hill country of Samaria and Judea (excluding Jerusalem), and the Coastal Plain from Isdud (Ashdod) to the Sinai frontier; the Jewish state would include eastern Galilee, the Jezreel Valley, most of the Coastal Plain, and the Negev. Each state was thus to consist of three sections linked at two crossing points. The Jerusalem enclave was to be under UN trusteeship. (See Map: UNSCOP Partition Plan). (For details of proposed boundaries, see *Israel, State of: Frontiers.)

The proposals were accepted by the Jews and rejected by the Arabs, who announced that they would do all in their power to bring about the collapse of the plan, while the British stated that they would do nothing to enforce it. In the end, the United Nations decision was implemented by the *Haganah and the Israel Defense Forces, which repelled attacks against Jewish centers and enabled the *yishuv* to establish the State of Israel, with its legislature, government, and administration in effective control of its territory. The de facto boundaries of the State of Israel, which were determined by the *Armistice agreements concluded in 1949 with Egypt, Lebanon, Jordan, and Syria, were roughly similar to those proposed in the UN resolution, with the addition of western Galilee and a broad corridor from the coast to western Jerusalem. The special international regime for Jerusalem could not be implemented and the city was divided along the cease-fire lines between Israel and Jordan.

The question of partition came to the fore again after the *Six-Day War of June 1967, as a result of which Israel found itself in control of the entire area that had constituted western Palestine. In Israel, some of those (headed by *Ḥerut leaders) who were opposed to any withdrawal from the new cease-fire lines, especially the Palestinian areas, based their attitude on the total negation of any "renewed partition of Ereẓ Israel." The majority of Israel opinion, however, supported the policy of withdrawing from a part of the newly occupied territories in exchange for effective peace treaties with the neighboring Arab states, which would put an end to the Israel-Arab conflict and grant Israel "defensible borders." This policy guided the Israel government in 1970–71 in its negotiations with Egypt and Jordan under the auspices of UN representative Gunnar Jarring, in accordance with the Security Council resolution of Nov. 22, 1967. The issue of withdrawal from territories occupied during the Six-Day War continued to be a divisive issue in Israeli politics in the following decades, though a majority of the Israeli public seemed to become reconciled to the idea despite the ups and downs of the peace process initiated in 1994 with the Oslo Accords.

For bibliography see *White Papers.

[Daniel Efron]

PALESTINE ECONOMIC CORPORATION (now known as PEC **Israel Economic Corporation**), a public company, incorporated in the United States through the merger of two agencies interested in the economic development of Palestine. According to its charter, its principal purpose was "to afford financial aid to commercial, banking, credit, industrial, and agricultural enterprises, cooperative or otherwise, in or relating to Palestine." In 1922 a group of prominent Jews headed by Robert *Szold formed a corporation called Palestine Cooperative Co., Inc. In 1926 another group of non-Zionist American Jews, headed by Bernard *Flexner, formed the Palestine Economic Corporation under the laws of the State of Maine. The purpose was to combine the assets of Palestine Cooperative Company, Inc. and the assets in Palestine of the Reconstruction Committee of the American Jewish *Joint Distribution Committee into a single corporation. Flexner and Szold both had a close personal relationship with Louis D. *Brandeis, and his urgings and inspiration were probably the most important factor leading to the foundation of the company. The initial authorized capital was $3,000,000. The object was to establish an organization to which American Jews might give material aid on a business basis for productive enterprises in Palestine. At first the corporation invested and operated through the Central Bank of Cooperative Institutions in Palestine, Palestine Mortgage and Credit Bank Ltd., Palestine Water Company Ltd., Bayside Land Corporation Ltd., and Loan Bank Ltd.

The Central Bank for Cooperatives was a major factor in financing diversified cooperative institutions and furthering the cooperative movement in Palestine. For many years, it was the only credit institution dealing solely with kibbutzim and cooperative societies introducing tested cooperative principles developed in western Europe. Apart from building low-cost housing and developing large urban areas, the Bayside Land Corporation was responsible for the preparation of a master plan by eminent British town planners for the future development of the city of Haifa, which was subsequently adopted by the Palestine government and is the plan pursuant to which the modern city of Haifa has been developed. The Mortgage and Credit Bank engaged in the construction and financing of houses for workers, both urban and rural. It was instrumental in reducing costs of construction, through competitive bidding, supervision, inspection of building materials and methods, and building houses in large groups. The Loan Bank made loans to artisans, farmers, and small businesses. The Water Company introduced modern American well-boring machinery and greatly contributed to the enlargement of new wells for domestic and agricultural use. The company also engaged in geological, hydrographical, and geophysical investigations of the country and trained early settlers. It participated in the initial capital of the Palestine Electric Company and in the formation of Palestine Potash Ltd., which received the concession for the exploitation of mineral deposits in the Dead Sea. Over the years these activities were expanded, and by 1971 the company had investments in some 50 different corporations engaged in industry, construction, transport, marketing finance, and agriculture in Israel. Its stock was purchased by investors throughout the United States. In 1931 it increased its authorized capital to $10,030,000, and this was subsequently increased to $25,030,000. As of the end of 1970, its capital and surplus was close to $25,000,000 and its stockholders numbered many thousands. The company paid regular dividends from 1933, with the exception of the years of World War II. In 1969 Albert Levinson was president of the corporation, Robert Szold honorary chairman, and Joseph Meyerhoff chairman of the board. In later years, PEC merged with the IDB Corporation, one of the largest in Israel. Its last president was Joseph Ciechanover.

In the 1990s the company was involved in a broad cross-section of Israeli companies engaged in various fields of business, including high tech and communications, manufacturing, building and construction, shipping and consumer products. Among PEC's holdings were the high-tech firms of Scitex Corporation Ltd. and Elron Electronic Industries Ltd.; the cell phone company Cellcom Israel Ltd.; the cable television company that serves the Tel Aviv metropolitan area and two other areas in Israel, Tevel Ltd.; the largest paint factory in Israel, Tambour Ltd.; the canning factory Caniel-Israel Can Company Ltd.; the Property and Building Corporation Ltd.; El-Yam Ships Ltd.; and the Super-Sol Ltd. supermarket chain. PEC is also involved in several venture capital funds and early stage development companies.

[Julius Weiss / Shaked Gilboa (2nd ed.)]

PALESTINE EXPLORATION FUND, a British society for the exploration of the Holy Land, founded in 1865 under the patronage of Queen Victoria; the first president and secretary were, respectively, the Archbishop of York and G. Grove. The society was to be conducted strictly on scientific principles, not subject to any religious dogma. The quarterly statement of the society, first published in 1869, was still appearing in 1971. Between 1911 and 1970, six volumes of an annual were published. After World War I it joined forces with the British School of Archaeology in Jerusalem.

The first activities of the fund included a survey of Jerusalem. It maintained C. *Warren's expedition to Jerusalem, where work was carried out mainly around the enclosure Wall of the Temple. From 1874 to 1882, the fund was engaged in its second large project: the survey of the region west of the Jordan. This work was completed by C.R. *Conder, C.W. *Wilson, and H.H.H. Kitchener and included a 26-sheet map and *Memoirs* (5 vols.). At about the same time, the society supported C.S. *Clermont-Ganneau's researches in Palestine and made a partial survey of Transjordan. In 1890 the fund resumed excavations: at Tell el-Ḥesi, directed by W.M.F. *Petrie and F.J. *Bliss; in Jerusalem, directed by Bliss and Dickie; and in the hills of the Shephelah, directed by Bliss and R.A.S. *Macalister. From 1905 to 1909, it financed Macalister's large excavations at *Gezer and afterward started work at *Beth Shemesh, under the direction of Duncan and Mackenzie. After World War I, the fund took part in the work on the hill of Ophel, directed by Mackenzie, Macalister, and J.W. *Crowfoot, and in the excavations at Samaria, under the direction of Crowfoot. After World War II, it participated in the excavations of K. *Kenyon in Jericho and Jerusalem. In addition to its field work, the Palestine Exploration Fund has published a series of English translations of Oriental sources and the accounts of ancient pilgrims. It has an excellent library and archives at the London headquarters.

[Michael Avi-Yonah]

PALESTINE LIBERATION ORGANIZATION (PLO), Palestinian organization founded in May 1964 at a Palestinian Congress held in East Jerusalem (then under Jordanian rule) following intensive efforts of Ahmad al-Shuqeiri, until then the representative of the Palestinian Arabs in the League of Arab States. The Congress was convened under strict Jordanian control and received the personal congratulations of King *Hussein, who indicated his intention to give full patronage to the newly established organization. The Congress, comprised mainly of senior Palestinian figures from Jordan and the Gaza Strip, approved the "Palestinian [Pan] National Charter" (*al-mīthāq al-qawmī al-filasṭīnī*) and the PLO's organic law, giving decisive powers to its Chairman Shuqeiri, including the appointment of the Executive Committee members.

The foundation of the PLO, which was fully supported by Egyptian President Gamal Abdel *Nasser, and reluctantly acquiesced to by King Hussein of Jordan, was the result of two separate processes: an authentic rise of self-assertion and revolutionary trends among young Palestinian refugees, and inter-Arab circumstances. Attentive to growing frustration and an urge for autonomous action for the liberation of Palestine among Palestinians in the Gaza Strip, already in 1959 Nasser suggested the establishment of a "Palestinian Entity" – a political organization that would represent the Palestinian national cause in the international arena. The Jordanian position reflected concern lest any expression of Palestinian nationalism might arouse separatist tendencies among the Palestinians in the kingdom, who constituted a majority of the population and could threaten the very existence of the Hashemite regime. In the strained relations between Nasser and his arch-rival, Abdel Karim Qassem, then the ruler of Iraq, Nasser's call was challenged by Qassem, who called for establishing a militant Palestinian organization which would operate against Israel from the West Bank and the Gaza Strip.

By the end of 1963 Nasser's prestige as champion of pan-Arabism had reached an impasse following Syria's secession in September 1961 from the union with Egypt (the United Arab Republic) and his entanglement in a costly and unsuccessful military involvement in Yemen. In addition, he came under increasing pressures from Syria's new Bath regime, which urged him to go to war with Israel over the ensuing inauguration of its National Water Carrier exploiting the Jordan River's water to irrigate new areas in the northern Negev.

Nasser perceived these as pressures detrimental to his priorities – unity first, then total war against Israel – and Egypt's security, repeating his rejection of an untimely war against Israel that could end with a disaster for the Arabs. To escape the trap set for him by the Syrian regime, Nasser called for an Arab summit conference in Cairo, which was held in January 1964. The summit, which was meant to preserve Nasser's control of collective Arab action against Israel and his all-Arab leadership, approved a plan of preventing Israel's use of the Jordan River's waters by diverting its tributaries originating in Lebanon and Syria in other directions. In view of Israel's possible military response against the diversion plan, the summit established a Joint Arab Command to supervise military preparations for the imminent war with Israel. The summit also discussed the issue of establishing a Palestinian Entity, but could not reach an agreement on this. Jordan adhered to its objection to the proposed institution on political grounds. Other states, such as Syria and Algeria, wanted a militant organization that would wage a popular armed struggle against Israel, while the Saudis feared it would be merely an Egyptian political instrument which would be used against them. The Arab summit thus refrained from officially approving the establishment of a Palestinian Entity and, instead, instructed Shuqeiri to examine the attitudes among the Palestinians regarding such an idea, without even mentioning the word "entity" in its decisions. Nonetheless, the decision enabled Shuqeiri to embark on a series of visits to Palestinian communities in the Arab states, which indicated their strong support for the idea fostered by Nasser. The enthusiasm with which Shuqeiri was received by Palestinians in Jordan apparently convinced King Hussein that his best choice was to co-opt the Palestinian Entity project rather than resist it.

Although the second Arab summit conference, held in Alexandria in September 1964, approved the establishment of the PLO, the organization remained highly controversial. It was criticized by militant Palestinian organizations, such as Fatah, and Arab regimes alike. In the coming three years the PLO, headed by Shuqeiri, was the subject of much discontent and bitter attacks by almost all the states. Seen as Nasser's protégé, the PLO could not escape its image as an instrument serving Nasser's Arab policies and primarily to legitimize the latter's desire to avoid war with Israel. In addition, though the PLO was meant to be merely a political organization, Shuqeiri constantly pushed the limits initially set for PLO activities in a military direction, if not armed capability. Challenged by Fatah, which began its military operations against Israel in early January 1965, Shuqeiri managed to bring about the establishment of the Palestinian Liberation Army, which comprised three regular brigades deployed in Egypt, Syria, and Iraq (*Ein Jallout*, *Hittin*, and *Qadisiyya*, respectively, named after great historic Muslim victorious battles). However, these brigades were fully subordinated to the military establishment of these states while the PLO maintained only a nominal command. By late 1965, Shuqeiri had become anathema to the Jordanian authorities due to his inexorable efforts to propagate the establishment of Palestinian recruitment centers in Jordan on behalf of the PLO, openly challenging the Jordanian monarch's authority and leading to arrests of PLO activists there. The growing tension between King Hussein and Shuqeiri coincided with the collapse of the summit-generated detente in inter-Arab relations as of late 1965, which led to Nasser's return to his aggressive policies in the inter-Arab arena, especially against the Western-backed monarchies of Saudi Arabia and Jordan. Until the June 1967 War, the Palestinian National Council (PNC – a sort of parliament of the Palestinian people) convened twice more in Gaza. In the meantime, Fatah and other newly established Palestinian guerrilla groups supported by Syria, won some prestige for their warfare against Israel, leading to further marginalization of Shuqeiri and his PLO, who lost even Nasser's interest.

In the aftermath of the 1967 defeat, Shuqeiri became a burden for Nasser as well as to Palestinian military and political activists. At the Khartoum Summit Conference convened in September of that year, Shuqeiri found himself isolated in his effort to pressure the Arab leaders to include a fourth "no" in their resolutions, namely that there should be no compromise of Palestinian national rights, which led to his walkout from the conference. At the same time, the success scored by the Palestinian guerrilla groups in entangling the Arab states in war against Israel and the defeat of the Arab regular armies in this war boosted the prestige of guerrilla warfare, which strengthened demands by Fatah and other guerrilla factions for a substantial representation in the PLO. Shuqeiri resigned in December 1967 and was replaced by Yahya Hamuda, another veteran Palestinian politician, who did not represent the guerrilla groups. The fourth session of the PNC, held in Cairo in July 1968, which approved Shuqeiri's resignation, recognized the success of the guerrilla organizations by including them for the first time and electing their leaders to key positions in the organization, most significant of which was the election of Fatah's leader Yasser *Arafat as the PLO's spokesman. The heavy representation in the PNC and the PLO Executive obtained by the guerrilla groups led, in February 1969, at the fifth council session, to their seizure of full control of the PLO, with majority on the Executive. Yasser Arafat was elected chairman, signifying that the guerrilla groups had taken over the PLO.

Thus the PLO represented the core claim of the new Palestinian generation, which intended to play an active role in determining their people's fate rather than leaving it to the Arab states. The fourth PNC session of July 1968 already represented a watershed in PLO history. It changed from being merely a political representative of the Palestinians to a loose umbrella organization for various Palestinian groups, military and civilian alike, with the guerrilla groups as its hard core, as well as for Palestinian communities all over the world. A major result of the changing nature of the PLO was a persistent and uncompromising claim for exclusive authority to speak in the name of the Palestinian people, sometimes imposed by violence on Palestinian figures under Israeli occupation in the West Bank and Gaza strip who dared broach ideas such as the establishment of a Palestinian state in the occupied territories only, or those conducting talks with the Israeli authorities about the political future of these areas.

The new nature of the PLO now also came to be manifested in ideological terms. At the July 1968 PNC session radical modifications were introduced in the PLO Charter. Unlike the pan-Arab (*qawmī*) character of Shuqeiri's PLO, the new Charter assumed a clear Palestinian national nature, bearing the title "The Palestinian National (*watanī*) Charter." The Charter stated that "the Palestinian Arab people" (being an "inseparable part of the Arab nation") "possesses the legal right to its homeland." The Palestinians were defined as those … "Arab citizens who were living permanently in Palestine until 1947" and their descendants, as well as "Jews who are of Palestinian origin" (1964) – or "who were living permanently in Palestine until the beginning of the invasion" (1968), dated in another resolution of the Council as 1917. Only they "will be considered Palestinians" in the future Palestinian state to be established on the whole territory of Mandatory Palestine. The Charter stipulated that the *Balfour declaration, the mandate, the partition of Palestine, and the establishment of the "Zionist entity" were "null and void"; "the claim of a historical or spiritual tie between Jews and Palestine" was denied, "Judaism… is not a nationality, …the Jews are not one people." "The liberation of Palestine… is a national duty to repulse the Zionist, imperialist invasion… and to purge the Zionist presence from Palestine." "The Palestinian people… through the armed Palestinian revolution, reject any solution that would be a substitute for the complete liberation of Palestine." "Armed struggle is the only way to liberate Palestine" and is defined as "a strategy and not a tactic," and the "Fidā'iyyūn [i.e., guerrillas] and their action form the nucleus of the popular Palestinian war of Liberation." The Charter stated that it could be changed by a two-third majority of the PNC.

The new Charter served as a rallying point among the various factions coalesced in the PLO under Fatah leadership, but also subjected the PLO to much criticism in the Western world, due to its extreme language and determination to eliminate the state of Israel as well as to force most of its citizens to leave historic Palestine. It is against this backdrop that in the following years the PLO's political thinking began gradually changing albeit without actually modifying anything in the Charter until May 1996 (see below). Thus, in 1969 the PLO adopted the idea of establishing a secular democratic Palestinian state in which Muslims, Christians, and Jews would be living in harmony. However, this idea was met with objections by some factions, and failed to attract world public support. In the early 1970s, as the Palestinian national cause began penetrating the world's public consciousness – primarily due to Palestinian international terrorism – the PLO leadership also came under growing pressure in the inter-Arab arena to modify its practical political positions. Hence, following the defeat and expulsion of the Palestinian guerrilla groups from Jordan in 1970–71, President Anwar al-*Sadat of Egypt repeatedly urged the PLO leadership to accept a realistic solution based on the West Bank and Gaza Strip, but to no avail.

In the first two decades following the 1967 war the PLO, now dominated by Fatah, focused its efforts toward achieving two main goals: bringing the Palestinians at large to accept the PLO as their exclusive national movement, and pushing the issue of Palestinian national rights, primarily their right to self-determination, into the international limelight in order to finally obtain Arab and international recognition of the organization as the sole legitimate political representative of the Palestinians. Initially, these efforts focused mainly on the Arab world and did not always suit the interests and considerations guiding the Arab regimes. Nonetheless, the combination of the diminished prestige and legitimacy of leading Arab regimes following the defeat of 1967; strong popular support among leftist and nationalist groups in Arab countries for the "Palestinian resistance"; the ongoing guerrilla warfare against Israel and Israel's massive retaliations; and most of all the participation of Palestinian factions in headline-grabbing international terrorism – all turned out to be decisive elements in a process of growing international awareness of the Palestinian issue and the magnification of the PLO's stature both in the Middle East and worldwide. Hence, the relative Arab success in the 1973 war against Israel, and especially the ensuing skyrocketing oil prices and embargo by the Arab oil producers against the United States and Holland, led most of the international community, including the Western European states, to recognize the Palestinian people's right for self-determination, despite reservations about its political course and violent modes of action. By the mid-1970s the PLO had attained full recognition by the majority of the Palestinians in the Arab states and Diaspora as well as in the occupied West Bank and Gaza Strip. The success of the Palestinian organizations in combining terrorism with diplomacy was indeed unique in the worldwide community of underground and terrorist organizations.

The aftermath of the 1967 war also witnessed an increase in the efforts to build the national institutions and mechanisms of an effective Palestinian national organization. The result was that, from 1969 on, the PLO became increasingly dominated by Fatah, whose members or supporters constituted the majority of the bureaucratic personnel in the PLO institutions and organs.

One of the main lessons learned by the founding fathers of Fatah from the national struggle against Zionism during the Mandate and up to the 1948 Palestinian disaster was the need for a centralized national authority based on social and political institutions. This was necessary in order to ensure maximum capability of mobilization of the constituents of the Palestinian community and compliance with the PLO's decision making. However, in the absence of territorial sovereignty and ability to reach out to the major Palestinian communities in the Arab world, the PLO could hardly impose its full and exclusive authority on all Palestinian factions – some of which represented the interests of Arab regimes. Under these circumstances Fatah had to compromise and accept a loose confederation of independent organizations, each with its own agenda and sources of financial and military resources. The PLO under Arafat thus functioned more as an overall national framework than a practical structure of a "state in the making." The PLO consisted of the main following representing institutions:

(1) The "Palestinian National Council," which functioned as an occasional parliament and consisted of representatives from military organizations (the main constituent), civil trade unions such as workers, writers, engineers, doctors, women, and students, as well as delegates of Palestinian communities of refugees both in the Arab world and the Diaspora. In the absence of regular elections (except in the trade unions), the majority of the Council members, whose number changed from session to session according to internal political compromises, were appointed, not elected. Effectively, the composition of the Council and other Palestinian national bodies was determined by the heads of the military organizations and reflected their relative strengths, even in the case of civil bodies. Being the largest representative body of the Palestinian people, the main function of the Council was to legitimize major decisions and policies shaped by Fatah's leadership, headed by Arafat. With neither the readiness nor ability to introduce changes into the Palestinian National Charter, especially from the mid-1970s, the National Council, through successive decisions – such as the adoption of a "two states solution" and participation in the Madrid process of the 1990s effectively sanctioned the PLO's deviation from strict adherence to the Charter,.

(2) The Executive Committee, functioning as a government with representatives of the main military organizations and several independent members, usually identified with Fatah. The Executive Committee was composed of departments acting as ministries, such as Foreign Affairs, Military, Finance, Propaganda/Information, Education and Culture, and Refugees. Beside the Executive Committee there existed bodies dealing with operations, security and intelligence, research and planning, culture and humanities and publishing institutes responsible for the frequent publications. The PLO established a system of official representatives functioning as embassies and had standing and diverse contacts with international organizations such as the United Nations and its agencies and with left-wing parties and Arab lobbies worldwide. The Executive Committee offered financial aid to families of the fallen and those injured in the course of actions and protest acts. It also ran productive enterprises under Fatah responsibility established for the employment of the families of the fallen. Along the years it developed into a profit-making financial concern (*samed*).

(3) The Central Council, established in 1969 as an emergency body, consisted of 50–60 members of the major military organizations. The necessity for such a body stemmed from the occasional difficulties of convening the PNC and the need for legitimizing the Executive Committee's decisions on important political matters.

The PLO was also most active in setting up a Palestinian educational system, primarily in the refugee camps in Jordan, Lebanon, and Syria, which deepened the bond between the national organization, Palestinian society, and the military groups. The main effort of the Palestinian organizations in the military and political spheres (mobilization and institutionalization) was directed at the inhabitants of the refugee camps, which the PLO wished to turn into ex-territorial bases, or "states within a state," and in fact it succeeded in getting semi-official recognition from the host states for a time (Lebanon, 1969–82; Jordan, 1969–70). The preference for the refugee camps may be attributed to the fact that the majority of the Palestinian leaders were refugees themselves and had drawn much of their legitimization from this common background.

Despite their rhetoric in support of the Palestinian goal of liberating Palestine, however, the Arab states were ambivalent in their practical relations with the PLO due to the contradiction between their *raison d'état* and the Palestinian *raison de la nation*. This problem was acute in politically divided countries, such as Jordan and Lebanon, where large numbers of Palestinians lived. With the growing presence of armed Palestinian groups in these states and repeated Israeli military raids in retaliation for Palestinian terrorist operations across the borders and abroad, the collision between the state and the Palestinian establishment was inevitable, as demonstrated by the elimination of the Palestinian military presence in Jordan in 1970–71 and the failed attempts of the Lebanese army to impose control over Palestinian military activities in 1968–73, which was one of the main reasons for the eruption of the Lebanese civil war (1975–90). Israel's invasion of Lebanon and pressure for the expulsion of PLO headquarters and military units from this country deprived the PLO of its last semi-autonomous territorial base and practically eliminated its military options, giving rise to other strategies of international diplomacy and civil mobilization of the Palestinians in the West Bank and Gaza Strip.

Following the October 1973 War, confronted with Egyptian and Syrian determination to employ diplomacy as a legitimate means to recover their territories occupied by Israel, and induced by the Soviet Union to adopt a "strategy of phases," the PLO resolved, at its 12th PNC meeting held in Cairo in June 1974, to establish a "combatant Palestinian National Authority on any liberated part of Palestine." The decision also reflected the PLO's intensifying competition with Hashemite Jordan over attaining exclusive representation of the occupied West

Bank in the internationally-supervised diplomatic process. Indeed, in November 1973, the Arab summit conference held in Algiers recognized the PLO as "the legitimate representative of the Palestinian people" at the expense of Jordan. Furthermore, in October of the following year the Arab summit conference held in Rabat resolved that the PLO was the "sole legitimate representative of the Palestinian people," effectively excluding Jordan from the Middle East peace process. From an Israeli and American viewpoint, however, the PLO remained inadequate as a partner in the peace process due to its extreme ideology, terrorist attacks on Israeli civilian targets, and its objection to the very existence of Israel, or to UN resolution 242, which established the legal international basis of a peaceful settlement of the Arab-Israeli conflict.

In retrospect, the decision of June 1974 came to be interpreted as the beginning of the PLO's shift toward acceptance of a Palestinian state in the West Bank and Gaza Strip only, alongside Israel. This tendency became clearer in the following years. Thus, in March 1977, the PLO adopted the resolution made by the Arab summit conference in Cairo (October 1976), affirming the inalienable right of the Palestinian people to "establish its independent state on its own national soil." In the late 1970s, PLO leaders were willing to meet non-Zionist "progressive" Israeli figures and then also leftist-Zionists – under the auspices of Communist European governments such as Romania and Hungary.

Although the PLO itself possessed neither military power nor a specific guerrilla apparatus, it was often identified with terrorist activities. This was mainly because of the direct responsibility of Fatah leaders, including Arafat, for such actions and their dominant position within the PLO. The early 1970s witnessed intensified international terrorism against foreign airliners – hijacking, attacks on passengers in terminals, and the taking of hostages – waged by some PLO member organizations, primarily the Popular Front for the Liberation of Palestine (PFLP) and Fatah. Despite the worldwide image of the PLO as a terrorist organization, its participation in international terrorism was marginal and never rose above 5 percent. Nonetheless, the impact of Palestinian terrorism was of far-reaching international dimensions owing to the innovation and novelty displayed in the Palestinian terrorist actions both in the selection of targets and in their execution, making them a model for other terrorist organizations. Furthermore, the support of the Palestinian organizations by the Arab states enabled them to supply various underground and terrorist organizations with weapons, training, documentation, liaison agents, and escape routes. Fatah ceased its involvement in international terrorism in 1974 out of political considerations and a desire for PLO inclusion in the Middle East peace process. However, this type of guerrilla warfare was continued by the PFLP (and, from 1975, only by its dissident group headed by Wadi Haddad) and by other dissident factions such as that of Abu Nidal.

From the outset, the PLO managed to extract funds from the oil monarchies in the Gulf as well as from Palestinians working in those countries. These Arab funds enabled it to build a growing institutional system and bureaucracy and run political, economic, and financial enterprises, social, health, and educational institutions, a diverse press, research centers, and enterprises publishing books and periodicals. In addition, the PLO established diplomatic representation in many world capitals as well as a worldwide information/propaganda network. PLO chairman Arafat was constantly traveling around the Arab and developing world capitals for consultations and conferences (including a November 1974 appearance at the UN General Assembly, at the latter's invitation). In the course of the 1970s the PLO won recognition from an increasing number of states and Arafat came to be received as a head of state. From 1969, and more so from 1974, the PLO became a recipient of "steadfastness" (*ṣumūd*) funds which allowed the organization to distribute them among its followers in the West Bank and Gaza Strip. The Baghdad Arab summit conference of November 1978 allocated for this purpose an annual sum of $100 million (apart from allocations to the PLO itself) for 10 years. This aid was to be jointly distributed to the Palestinian residents of the West Bank and Gaza Strip by Jordan and the PLO. Despite their animosity, a "Jordan-PLO Joint Committee for the Occupied Territories" was established to distribute these funds, and a limited presence of PLO offices and representatives was again permitted. This enabled Fatah to deepen its penetration within the Palestinian population in the occupied territories and build an institutional political infrastructure to support the organization from within.

The Joint Jordan-PLO Committee paved the road to further rapprochement between the two contenders, which took place following the expulsion of the PLO and its military buildup from Lebanon in late August 1982 and the Reagan Plan of September 1. In 1983–85 King Hussein and PLO Chairman Arafat conducted a series of talks with the aim of reaching a formula for joint Jordanian-Palestinian political action in the context of the Middle East peace negotiations and future Jordanian-Palestinian confederation.

The problem of PLO participation in the peace process was indeed a major procedural obstacle for moving from the Israel-Egypt and Israel-Syria military disengagement agreements signed in early 1974 to a comprehensive settlement which was to be discussed within the framework of the Geneva conference. The problem was a result of the PLO's status as the "sole legitimate representative of the Palestinian people," as recognized by the Rabat summit conference in October 1974. However, knowing the Israeli attitude toward the PLO, the Arab regimes had been well aware of the implications of such a decision on the peace process. Moreover, in 1975, following the signing of the Israel-Egypt Interim Agreement in Sinai, Israel received an American commitment that the U.S. government would not have contacts with the PLO as long as the organization did not renounce terrorism, accept resolution 242, and recognize Israel's right to exist. The PLO, however, adamantly objected to making such compromises before being recognized as an equal party in the Arab-

Israeli peacemaking process. It was this deadlock regarding the Palestinian participation in the Geneva conference that led Sadat to his decision to take the initiative and visit Jerusalem. This, however, did not make PLO decision-making any easier. The Israel-Egypt peace negotiations forced the PLO leaders to close ranks with the radical Arab regimes, in order to survive politically. Thus, the PLO joined the "Steadfastness and Confrontation Front" established in Tripoli, Libya, in December 1977 in response to Sadat's visit to Jerusalem. Hussein's pressure on the PLO to accept UN Resolution 242 in the course of their negotiations in 1983–86 failed, as did that of Egypt's President Husni *Mubarak. The main obstacle to a renewed peace process in the 1980s was a formal acceptance by the PLO of Israel's right to exist, renunciation of terrorism in all forms, and a clear commitment to peaceful coexistence with Israel. In the diplomatic code this was formulated as "accepting Resolution 242."

On the PLO's part, there was an additional reason for rejecting Resolution 242: The resolution spoke of the need to resolve the "refugee" problem, without mentioning the Palestinian refugees and certainly not the Palestinian people and its national rights. Suggestions by the U.S. administration to accept the principles of the resolution while registering a reservation concerning Palestinian national rights proved unacceptable to the PLO. Evasive, open-ended remarks – like accepting "all" UN resolutions – were unacceptable to the U.S. and Israel, as were the PLO's pre-condition that it be recognized by the U.S. (once it endorsed Resolution 242), or receive a priori acceptance of its demands for Palestinian statehood and self-determination. The vital issue of accepting the principles of Resolution 242 therefore remained unresolved through most of the 1980s.

Israel's invasion of Lebanon in June 1982 and the siege of Beirut ended in late August, after nine weeks of fighting, in the expulsion of the Palestinian armed forces and bureaucracy. The evacuation of 11,000–14,000 PLO personnel from Beirut was internationally supervised, and tacitly supported by most Arab states, including Saudi Arabia, Syria, and Lebanon. The PLO headquarters and military units moved to Tunisia, while others were accepted in Sudan, Yemen, and South Yemen. With its headquarters in Tunis and military forces dispersed and far from the borders of Israel, the PLO was stripped of its military option, politically weakened, and under threat of demise. In December 1983 Arafat and 4,000 of his men were evacuated from Tripoli – again with international supervision and support. In 1983–86, Arafat succeeded in reinfiltrating some of his apparatus into Lebanon and renewing the military infrastructure by smuggling weapons into the Palestinian camps, especially in the southern parts of the country.

The *Intifada in the West Bank and Gaza Strip, which erupted in late 1987, came as a surprise to the PLO, sending a threatening message viv-à-vis the PLO's authority over the Palestinian people "inside" the homeland. At the 19th PNC session, in November 1988, the PLO proclaimed the establishment of an independent Palestinian state on the basis of UN Resolution 181 (of November 1947, on the partition of Palestine). One month later Arafat publicly renounced terrorism and accepted Resolutions 242 and 338. The decision was taken under pressure from the Palestinian "inside" leadership following a year of Intifada and American pressure conditioning the opening of a political dialogue with the PLO on such steps.

However the dilemma within the PLO still existed as to whether to abandon the armed struggle and cling to the political process or to keep both on the agenda. This dilemma was manifested on several occasions, such as the terrorist action conducted on Israel's coastline in May 1990 by the Palestine Liberation Front (PLF), which Arafat refused to denounce, causing the cessation of the diplomatic dialogue between the PLO and the U.S. Another example was the support shown by Arafat for Iraq during the Gulf crisis in 1991. This position brought on Arafat and the PLO the wrath of the Gulf oil monarchies and a decision to cease all funding by these states to the PLO and the Palestinians in the occupied territories. This led to a financial crisis within the PLO's mainstream Fatah, forcing it to reduce activities such as the publication of newspapers, welfare services, and funding of its supporters in Arab states and the occupied territories. Furthermore, the growing power of *Hamas (the Islamic Resistance Movement) in the occupied territories and its refusal to join the PLO as one of its factions and on Arafat's conditions, all determined the PLO's reluctant acceptance of the American formula for the Madrid conference in late 1991. The PLO had to acquiesce to Israel's conditions for the participation of Palestinian delegates from the occupied territories within the framework of a joint Jordanian-Palestinian delegation. However, during the talks, the Palestinian delegates were constantly and overtly instructed by the PLO.

During the winter-spring of 1993, the PLO and unofficial Israeli delegates began exploring ways in Washington to overcome the deadlocked Israeli-Palestinian talks. The secret talks held in Oslo, Norway, soon amounted to full-fledged official negotiations, representing the PLO's attempt to regain control of the diplomatic process with Israel and keep the American hosts at bay. In August, Arafat informed Israeli Prime Minister Yitzhak Rabin that the PLO was committed to the peace process in the Middle East, reaffirming its recognition of Resolutions 242 and 338. A few weeks later the Declaration of Principles between Israel and the PLO was signed on the White House lawn. The most conspicuous part of the document was the parties' mutual recognition. The PLO was officially recognized by Israel and the U.S. government as the legal representative of the Palestinian people in the peace process and in implementing its resolutions until elections to the *Palestinian Authority (PA) were held. The elections for the PA's council and chairperson were held in January 1996, reaffirming Arafat's unchallenged position, with Fatah members winning a dominant position in the Council. Arafat remained the PLO chairman and at the same time the chairman of the PA.

Although in principle the PLO stands above the PA and the Oslo accords were all signed between Israel and the PLO, in the late 1990s the PLO was increasingly shunted aside by the PA, with the latter occupying the center of Palestinian society and politics. The PLO retained its headquarters in Tunis, with Farouq Qaddoumi as the main figure identified with the organization and its commitment to Palestinian Diaspora communities. In spite of funds funneled by Arafat to refugee camps in Lebanon, the PLO's scope of action and responsibilities were reduced considerably after the establishment of the PA. Arafat's control of PLO-PA funds enabled him to transfer financial aid to Palestinian communities, especially in Lebanon, in violation of the conditions of the donating countries. This was also manifested in the PNC session in April 1996 in Gaza, whose aim was to express support for the peace process and alter the Palestinian National Charter in accordance with Arafat's commitment in his letter to Prime Minister Rabin of September 11, 1993. In this letter Arafat undertook to alter the Palestinian National Charter by nullifying those articles in the Charter that explicitly or implicitly denied Israel's right to exist or called for its destruction. With the changing of governments in Israel in May 1996 and the election of Netanyahu as prime minister, however, Israel demanded an unequivocal decision in this matter, reflecting the weakening of trust between the two parties. In November 1998, in the presence of U.S. President Clinton, Arafat convened the PLO's Central Council and passed the necessary resolution which won Israel's approval.

The eruption of the al-Aqsa Intifada in October 2000 and deterioration of Israeli-Palestinian relations into murderous violence against Israeli citizens and massive military retaliations by Israel against PA headquarters and installations; and the confinement of Arafat in his compound in Ramallah in late 2002, all underscored the importance of Arafat as the living symbol of the Palestinian resistance and continued struggle against Israel.

The death of Arafat in November 2004 and the election of Mahmoud Abbas as the PA's new chairman (in addition to his appointment as PLO chairman) introduced little change in the relations between these two institutions. However, with Abbas at the helm, the PLO lost much of the revolutionary, militant image symbolized by Arafat with his rhetoric and military uniforms. Instead, the new PA leader tried to introduce a clear civilian image and statesmanlike thinking in managing the PA. At the same time, he had to accept Qaddoumi, an ardent opponent of the Oslo process and a symbol of the PLO revolutionary legacy, as chair of the Central Committee of Fatah, the main decision-making body of the mainstream Palestinian movement. All these equations were thrown into confusion with the surprise victory of *Hamas in the PA's parliamentary elections of January 2006. (For Israel's subsequent clashes with Hamas, see *Israel, State of: Historical Survey.)

BIBLIOGRAPHY: H. Cobban, *The Palestinian Liberation Organization: People, Power and Politics*, 1984); M. Shemesh, *The Palestinian Entity 1959–1974, Arab Politics and the PLO* (1988); J.R. Nassar, *The Palestine Liberation Organization: From Armed Struggle to the Declaration of Independence* (1991); B. Rubin, *Revolution Until Victory? The Politics and History of the PLO* (1994).

[Avraham Sela (2nd ed.)]

PALESTINE OFFICE, the name of a Zionist institution whose meaning and function was entirely different before World War I and after it. (1) In 1908 a Palestine office *(Palaestinaamt)* was established in Ereẓ Israel, with its seat in Jaffa, by the executive of the World Zionist Organization. Headed by Arthur *Ruppin, it served under the Ottoman regime as the central agency for Zionist settlement activities, including land purchase and aiding immigration. (2) After World War I the name Palestine Offices was applied to Zionist "consulates" in the Diaspora countries charged with the organization, regulation, and implementation of Jewish immigration to Palestine. The first Palestine Office of this kind was set up in Vienna in 1918. Subordinated from 1921 to the Immigration Department of the Zionist Executive, which functioned under the provisions of the Mandate as the *Jewish Agency for Palestine, the Palestine offices were run in every country by a commission (*Palaestinaamtskommission*) composed of representatives of various Zionist parties, on the basis of parity or according to their strength at the last Zionist Congress, frequently with a preponderance of Labor Zionists and always with a strong representation of pioneering youth movements. The composition and functions of the Palestine offices were governed by the resolutions of Zionist Congresses, particularly the 12th, 13th, and 14th (1921–25).

In the 1920s and 1930s the Palestine Office distributed the immigration "certificates" issued by the Mandatory government to the Jewish Agency; dealt with *hakhsharah* (i.e., agricultural training of *ḥalutzim*); provided information to prospective immigrants; prepared and provided the necessary travel documents; and served as a link to the British consulates and the authorities of the country concerned. In those years Palestine offices existed in most European capitals (the largest being in Warsaw) as well as in exit ports to Palestine (like Trieste) and large provincial towns of some countries with a dense Jewish population (like Poland). After the outbreak of World War II, the Geneva Palestine Office engaged in rescuing Jews from Axis-dominated territories and transferring them to Palestine. In later stages of the war, the offices in Istanbul and Teheran – and after its end, those in Vienna, Munich, Rome, and Marseilles – acquired particular importance in these rescue operations. After World War II the Palestine offices unofficially assisted the "illegal" *immigration to Palestine of refugees and survivors of the Holocaust.

With the establishment of the State of Israel (1948), the jurisdiction and activities of these offices underwent considerable change. They were named offices of the immigration Department of the Jewish Agency and, mostly administered by emissaries from Israel, were charged with nongovernmental functions complementary to those of the consulates of the Israel government, as, e.g., the promotion and organization of Jewish immigration to Israel and particularly the transport of immigrants needing the Jewish Agency's assistance.

BIBLIOGRAPHY: World Zionist Organization *Protocols of the Zionist Congresses*, esp. of the 12th, 13th, and 14th; Zionist Organization, *Executive Report... to the 22nd Zionist Congress* (1946); JL, s.v. *Palestina-Aemter.*

[Aharon Zwergbaum]

PALESTINIAN AUTHORITY (PA, the Palestinian designation being Palestinian National Authority), semi-official, self-governing Palestinian body established in May 1994 in accordance with the Israel-PLO Declaration of Principles (DOP) signed on September 13, 1993 on behalf of the *Palestine Liberation Organization (PLO). On its establishment the PA governed most of the Gaza Strip and the town of Jericho in the Jordan Valley, representing the first step in the implementation of the interim arrangements for Israeli withdrawal ("redeployment") from territories in the West Bank and Gaza Strip. This process was to culminate in "permanent status talks" to begin in May 1996 on all major issues in dispute between the two parties (settlements, Jerusalem, Palestinian refugees, and the final status of the PA and its territory). The DOP agreement stipulated that the transfer of responsibilities to the PA would be completed within five years and would include education and culture, health, social welfare, direct taxation, and tourism. It was also agreed that a Palestinian police force would be established in order to maintain internal security and prevent hostile acts of terror against Israel by the Palestinian population under its authority. Israel would retain overall authority for security and defense regarding all external threats, and particularly the safety of the Israeli settlers.

The Israel-PLO negotiations that led to the establishment of the PA became possible following King Hussein's proclamation, on July 31, 1988, formally relinquishing Jordan's legal and administrative control over the Palestinian territories. After this act, the Palestinian National Council (PNC) unilaterally declared, at its November 1988 meeting in Algiers, the establishment of an independent Palestinian state based on the UN partition resolution of November 1947. On May 17, 1994, Israel and the PLO signed the Cairo Agreement. This elaborated the transfer of authority to the Palestinians as well as the security arrangements between the two sides. Soon after, the PLO officially established the PA. It was the nucleus of a government apparatus, which assumed control of the Gaza Strip (excluding the Israeli settlements) and Jericho. Before the end of June of that same year, Yasser *Arafat arrived in Gaza to chair the PA. The interim agreement (Oslo II), signed on September 28, 1995, between Israel and the PA, set the timetable and modalities for the later stages of the process. In accordance with this agreement, by late December 1995 the IDF had withdrawn from five major towns in the West Bank (out of the six stipulated in the agreement) in preparation for elections to both the Palestinian Council and the office of PA chairman. Withdrawal from the city of Hebron was postponed by Shimon Peres's government as a consequence of terrorist attacks and growing Israeli public resentment of the Oslo process.

The interim agreement divided the West Bank into three jurisdictional zones:

Area A (3 percent of the West Bank territory), including the urban areas, under full Palestinian authority; Area B (27 percent of the West Bank), including a large part of the rural area, under Palestinian authority for all civil matters, including public order, and Israeli authority for security matters; and Area C, the rest, and most of the West Bank, including the settlements, the IDF bases, the Jordan Valley, and the desert area – under full IDF authority, except for personal law. In February 1995 the Higher State Security Court was established in Gaza. One of its first decisions was the abolition of the Israeli legal system (military and civilian) that had existed since the occupation of these territories in 1967. Instead, the previous legal system was applied – the Jordanian law in the West Bank and the British Mandatory law in the Gaza Strip. According to the interim agreement, both legal systems were to be valid in criminal and civil matters only. The agreement, however, left in force Israeli law in all three zones of the West Bank.

The PA held its first meeting on May 26, 1994, with 20 members of the temporary nominated forum (with the absence of its chairman, Yasser Arafat). The lion's share of the PA's bureaucracy initially came from PLO headquarters in Tunis, though it was later complemented and probably outweighed by active local members of Fatah, the mainstream organization, many of whom had spent varying periods in Israeli prisons or in exile. The PA's new bureaucracy doubled the already existing apparatus of teachers and officials (about 20,000), who had been employed by the Israeli civil administration in the West Bank and Gaza. Furthermore, the PA created a huge body of various security and police forces, encompassing 25,000–30,000 men, mostly from previous Palestinian security apparatuses and military units. Within a short time the PA became the largest employer in the territory under its control. Furthermore, Palestinian dependence on external financial aid channeled through the PA gave the latter increased power, which would also be bolstered by its strategy of centralizing the economy.

Within less than two years, by building up official institutions of power, the PA managed to bring to bear policy-making capabilities and enforce order in a society that had never enjoyed self-government. This was mainly apparent in the emergence of numerous security organizations, all subordinated to Chairman Arafat but lacking coordination among them and fighting for power and financial allocations. In November 1994 the PA's security apparatus clashed with Islamist rioters at the Filastin Mosque in Gaza, killing a number of them. The riots were the result of accusations made by the Islamic Jihad that the PA had provided Israeli security apparatuses with intelligence that enabled it to eliminate one of its leaders. Similarly the PA had the upper hand in the clash with Jordan over the appointment to the prestigious position of mufti of Jerusalem. In October 1996 Arafat's security apparatus acted to enforce the appointment of Sheikh ʿIkrameh Sabri to this position and replace the Jordan-appointed Sheikh ʿAbdin.

In addition to establishing its radio and television authority, the PA also established its own print media organs. Apart from the independent daily *al-Quds*, which had been published in Jerusalem since 1968, two other daily newspapers were launched by the PA or at its behest in Ramallah in the West Bank in 1995. *Al-Hayat al-Jadida* ("The New Life") was founded by PA Cabinet member Nabil ʿAmr. The paper has been considered the PA's official organ. The other daily, *al-Ayyam* ("The Days"), was started by Akram Haniyya. In the summer of 1997 the PA also opened a stock exchange in which only companies registered in the PA areas could be listed. In the field of education the PA inherited eight universities and 15 colleges. By the late 1990s these institutes of higher education encompassed 71,000 students and 4,100 faculty members.

On January 20, 1996, the first elections to the Palestine (Legislative) Council (PLC) and PA presidency took place under international supervision. Many participated – approximately 88 percent of eligible voters in Gaza and 70 percent in the West Bank. Palestinian residents of East Jerusalem also participated in the elections, though in a much lower proportion. The Islamic Resistance Movement (*Hamas) officially boycotted the elections. In practice, however, the movement encouraged its adherents to cast their votes in favor of independent candidates – identified as Islamists – winning five seats in the PLC. As expected, the Fatah list – shaped and backed by Yasser Arafat – won 49 of the total 88 seats in the PLC (more than 55 percent). In addition, other independent Fatah candidates were elected, giving the movement 75 percent of the Council's seats.

Political opposition to the PA remained in disarray, having negligible impact, except for Hamas. The opposition, whose leaders and sources of political and financial support were based outside the Palestinian territory, had consisted of three main types and forms: (a) The Ten Front, a loose Syrian-based alignment of militant Palestinian groups, including: the Popular Front for the Liberation of Palestine (PFLP); the Democratic Front for the Liberation of Palestine (DFLP; in March 1999 it was expelled from the Front because of its leader's repeated statements recognizing the State of Israel); the Palestine Liberation Front (PLF); Palestine Popular Struggle Front (PPSF); Popular Front for the Liberation of Palestine-General Command (PFLP-GC), Palestine Revolutionary Communist Party, Fatah al-Intifada (Fatah of the Uprising), al-Sa'iqa, Hamas; and the Islamic Jihad; (b) Individuals like Haidar Abdel Shafi (who resigned his membership in the PLC in 1996) and other Cabinet and Council members, most conspicuous of whom was Abdel Jawad Saleh, former mayor of al-Bireh and PLO Executive member; c) PLO mainstream figures in the Diaspora, such as Faruq al-Qaddoumi, head of the PLO Political Department, who voiced his objections to the Oslo Agreement and its implementation by Arafat. Despite this opposition Qaddoumi not only retained his position but maintained his working relationship with Arafat and was considered the strongest candidate to succeed him as PLO Chairman.

The PA's performance came under growing Israeli public criticism as a result of continued terrorist attacks on Israelis both in the occupied territories and within the Green Line, carried out mainly by Hamas and the Islamic Jihad. The debate in Israel about Arafat's policies turned increasingly toward the view that he had been avoiding decisive measures of repression against Islamist terrorism and its sponsors because he was not interested in putting an end to violence and in fact perceived it as a legitimate means of struggle even in the course of the Oslo process. Arafat was forced to take decisive measures against Hamas and the Islamic Jihad following the suicide bombings of February–March 1996 in Jerusalem, Tel Aviv, and Ashkelon. However, the scope of his measures then was never repeated. In fact, Arafat used the Islamic opposition as an instrument in the face of Israeli delays and procrastination in the peace process, using rapprochement and antagonism vis-à-vis his own opposition in accordance with his needs vis-à-vis Israel. In December 1995, prior to the elections to the PLC slated for January, Arafat's delegates tacitly gave the green light to Hamas's leadership in Cairo to continue its attacks against Israel as long as it did not "embarrass" the PA, namely, did not leave signs that the action had been initiated from PA-controlled areas. Arafat's policy in this respect became a major obstacle in the peace process and a primary arguing point for all the opponents of the Oslo process in Israel. Another argument against the PA was the continued incitement against Israel in the PA's official media and school textbooks, perceived by many Israelis as a clear indication that the PA was not seeking peace and coexistence with Israel. This became apparent during Netanyahu's government (1996–99), which in the Wye Memorandum insisted on reciprocity in the implementation of the provisions of the agreement, making it conditional on putting an end to terrorism and incitement.

The main criticism of the Palestinian militant opposition organizations against the PA leadership revolved around the terms and modalities of the DOP. In this view, Arafat had made excessive concessions to Israel, leaving important issues up in the air, dependent on Israel's good will, such as Jerusalem, the territory to be ceded to the PA, and most of all the right of return for the Palestinian refugees. Criticism against the PA within the Palestinian community, primarily in the West Bank, hinged on the dominant role played by the PLO people arriving from Tunisia and other Arab states after capturing key positions at the expense of local inhabitants. This criticism may have been unjustified given the large number of local Palestinians in the PA's bureaucracy and yet it was and remained a dominant perception among many Palestinians. The international community of donors, which provided the bulk of the PA's budget, expressed similar concerns about the lack of transparency and accountability and the general financial management of the PA.

By 1997 internal criticism of the PA grew vehement, revolving around Arafat's authoritarian rule, the PA's centralized decision-making process, mismanagement of financial allocations, and growing manifestations of corruption, abuse of power, and human rights violations by the security agencies and senior officials of the PA. The campaign of criticism came from within Fatah itself, particularly the younger members of the PLC. This led to the appointment of an investigative committee, whose report to the elected PA Council was submitted in the fall of 1997. The report revealed that $326 million (or 37 percent of the PA's budget) was unaccounted for due to fraud, corruption, and mismanagement. The report also recommended the dismissal of three cabinet members on grounds of corruption. Although the three resigned, Arafat refused to accept their resignations or adopt the report, even though he accepted it in principle. In August 1998, after much procrastination and pressures by the critics, Arafat announced a new cabinet, enlarged by ten new members, leaving the three ministers charged with corruption in place and shifting the three leading critics within the cabinet to posts without portfolios. Though the new cabinet won a vote of confidence in the PLC, 28 members voted against it, of whom 11 were Fatah members. The reshuffle led to the resignation from the cabinet of the minister of agriculture, Abdel Jawad al-Saleh, and the minister of higher education, Hanan Ashrawi.

The foundation of the PA, along with the elections to its Council, finally shifted the center of gravity of Palestinian politics from the Diaspora to the Gaza Strip and West Bank. This centralization came to the fore in Arafat's dual role as chairman of the PLO Executive Committee and PA chairman. This initially drew the criticism of many Palestinians, especially among the West Bank intellectual elite. However, this criticism diminished with the growing use of coercive means by the PA, along with policies of control, containment, and cooption of existing non-government organizations and institutions of higher education.

From the outset, the PA's existence was marked by dependence on external financial sources, due to the urgent need for infrastructure and economic development. To insure the implementation of the Oslo Agreement, in October 1993, the major economic powers (particularly the U.S., Canada, the European Community, and Japan) met under the auspices of the World Bank to devise plans for financial aid to the PA. Pledges made in late 1993 reached $2.4 billion over four years (by late 1997 the total amount of pledges had reached $3.68 billion), of which a total of $1.8 billion was provided in two main forms: long-term projects for infrastructure, industry, and other development purposes; and short-term, stopgap measures such as creating new jobs to curtail unemployment and cover budgetary deficits. The World Bank founded the Holst Fund (named after late Norwegian Foreign Minister Jorgen Holst) to marshal the short-term aid. (This was originally intended to operate until late 1997, but was extended to 1998.) An Ad Hoc Liaison Committee was set up to monitor the disbursement process, while the PLO established PECDAR (the Palestine Economic Council for Development and Reconstruction) as the main vehicle for economic policy. For the first three projects of the World Bank's Emergency Assistance Program (EAP), which were approved in May 1994, donors pledged an immediate $42 million. However, problems arose soon after the funds started flowing to the PA. There were discrepancies in accountability and transparency concerning the way the financial aid was being spent. A number of PA ministries contended for primacy, including the PLO political department headed by Farouq Qaddoumi. Other problems were caused by external economic circumstances such as the Israeli curfews, roadblocks, and closures of Palestinian cities, imposed because of terrorist acts perpetrated by the Islamic opposition movements. The closures had an immediate effect on the Palestinian population's ability to pay their taxes to the PA. Moreover, the PA-Israel economic agreement signed in 1994 in Paris remained mostly unimplemented. All this came against the backdrop of years of uprising (Intifada) and the large-scale expulsion of Palestinians from the Gulf states since 1990, reducing remittances from these Arab countries. Thus, much of the aid flowing to the PA was spent to make good the PLO's deficits. In response the donor nations tended to hold back further sums. In August 1994, the UN appointed Terje Larsen, who had been the initiator of the Oslo academic track negotiations, as the envoy in charge of the disbursement of funds in Gaza. Larsen's plan included a new mechanism for controlling the funds through committees composed of representatives of both the PA and the donor countries. All the committees were to be devoted to key areas, such as the creation of jobs, education, infrastructure, etc. Private Palestinian investors are another source of investment in the PA. They come mainly from Jordan, but there are also some from elsewhere in the Diaspora. In 1993, Padico (Palestinian Development and Investment Company) was founded with a capital of $200 million. This initiative helped build factories and some tourist projects with the financial aid of Palestinians, Jordanian banks, and U.S. and Egyptian companies. Following the interim agreement in September 1995, U.S. Secretary of State Warren Christopher hosted an Ad Hoc Liaison Committee (AHLC) aimed at creating a framework for increased assistance to the PA by the European countries. More specifically, it meant to support projects that addressed infrastructure needs and created employment opportunities for Palestinians. However, prospects for a larger scope of private investment by Palestinians faded because of the PA's centralized economy and the sense of insecurity caused by terrorist attacks and closures. These obstacles to sustained economic development culminated in the virtual halt of the Oslo process after the formation of a right-wing government in Israel headed by Binyamin Netanyahu (May 1996).

The Netanyahu term as prime minister led to significant erosion of PA trust in Israeli intentions regarding the future implementation of the DOP. The Hasmonean Tunnel riots of September 1996 (in which the Palestinians lost 79 people) essentially set the tone for the next two years of Netanyahu's stay in power, despite the agreements the latter signed with Arafat – the Hebron Agreement (January 1997) and the Wye Memorandum (October 1998). While the Hebron Agreement was fully implemented, the Wye Memorandum, which accounted for further Israeli redeployments in order to bring about the final status talks, was only partly implemented. In addition, other issues on the agenda remained long-delayed, such as the release of prisoners from Israeli prisons, opening the "safe passage" from the Gaza Strip to the West Bank, and building a harbor and airport in the Gaza Strip (the latter was finally opened in 1998). At the same time, the economic conditions of the Palestinian population constantly deteriorated due to repeated closures imposed by Israel following terrorist attacks on its civilians inside the "Green Line." The advent of a Labor-led government headed by Ehud *Barak in May 1999 raised Palestinian expectations for rapid progress in the peace-making process. However, the continued delay in implementing further Israeli deployments and fear that Barak was trying to gain time and achieve a settlement with Syria first sowed increasing doubts about the prospects for a breakthrough in the Oslo process.

The combination of growing economic depression and continued diplomatic stalemate aggravated the PA's problem of legitimacy and played a significant role in shaping its political conduct. Arafat's legitimacy problem was clearly manifested by the growing opposition within his own organization, Fatah. It is in this context that from the fall of 1998 Arafat made repeated declarations regarding his intention to proclaim an independent Palestinian state by May 4, 1999 (the deadline for reaching a final status agreement). These declarations, apparently meant to pressure Israel into moving faster in implementing further redeployments in the West Bank, met with widespread international objections and forced Arafat to back down from such a unilateral measure. However, this was another setback for the PA and for Arafat personally, further eroding his standing. In November 1999, 20 academics and members of the PLC – including Fatah members – signed a declaration condemning the peace process as a conspiracy against Palestinian national aspirations and accusing PA leaders of corruption and oppression. Although Arafat was not directly blamed for the stalemate and corruption, this petition was yet another indication of the growing impatience among Palestinians with the PA's performance on both the diplomatic and economic fronts.

In December 1999–January 2000 the PA enjoyed a temporary respite due to the celebration of the new millennium. In the previous years both Israel and the PA had made efforts to prepare for expected waves of pilgrims and tourists, with not much coordination, though each side invested a great deal of financial and administrative effort in these preparations (the number of hotel rooms in Bethlehem was doubled within two years). In March, Arafat hosted Pope *John Paul in his visit to PA-controlled Bethlehem.

In view of the failure of the Camp David summit and subsequent American mediation efforts to bring about an agreed-upon Framework Agreement for Permanent Status, the growing Palestinian frustration culminated in the eruption of the al-Aqsa Intifada in late September 2000. Though the riots began in response to the visit of Ariel *Sharon to the Temple Mount, the continued violence and its encouragement by Arafat pointed to the underlying causes, namely, frustration over the stalemated Oslo process and over the PA's conduct as a governing institution. After the outbreak of the violence dozens of representatives of the multi-factional Intifada leadership met with Arafat and urged him to declare war against corruption. The demand to stop the embezzlement of funds led to the assassination of the head of the PA's broadcasting service, allegedly on grounds of transferring funds to his personal account. The perpetrators, identified with Fatah's armed branch (*tanzim*), were never prosecuted. These events had some effect on the willingness of potential donors to continue providing funds to the PA. Thus, the Arab League refused to transfer millions of dollars in aid to the PA out of fear that top officials would get their hands on the money. Western donors, however, while reducing aid transfers, also changed priorities in aid commitments. Thus, less funds were disbursed for direct budget needs and more was allocated for specific projects and emergency aid.

The continued violence and Israeli reprisals – directed at the PA's offices, security headquarters, police stations, prisons, and, finally, the symbols of authority connected with Arafat himself, brought about a steady and systematic destruction of the PA's capabilities and risked its very existence. Under Sharon's leadership, Israeli policies toward Arafat became more vehemently hostile. The growing terrorist attacks by Palestinians of all factions, with Fatah taking the lead, and unprecedented understanding of Israel's need to fight terrorism following the September 11, 2001, attacks in New York and Washington and the capture of *Karin A*, a boat manned by Palestinian security personnel loaded with arms provided and financed for by Iran, led Israel to intensify its attacks on the PA's symbols of authority. In December the government declared Arafat "irrelevant" after placing him under virtual house arrest at his headquarters in Ramallah and preventing his arrival in Bethlehem for the Christmas Mass at the Church of the Nativity. This was followed by Israeli statements, especially from right-wing politicians, expressing the wish to expel or get rid of Arafat, ostensibly in order to allow an alternative leadership to take over with whom Israel could negotiate. The deterioration of security in Israeli cities due to the increasing wave of suicide bombings culminated in Israel's invasion of PA areas and the "isolation" of Arafat in his office while it raided Palestinian cities, refugee camps, and villages throughout April 2002 in order to destroy the terrorist infrastructure.

Although the Israeli incursion ("Operation Defensive Shield") temporarily shifted international criticism from Arafat to Israel, it brought the PA to its lowest point ever, leaving in its wake tremendous destruction and disarray after four weeks of operations, a heavy Israeli military presence around the cities of the West Bank and continuous Israeli military raids to destroy the Palestinian terrorist infrastructure. Henceforth, Palestinian terrorism was reduced considerably in the West Bank.

[Avraham Sela (2nd ed.)]

From this point on, international pressure, driven mostly by President Bush, who was stunned by Arafat's complicity in the *Karin A* affair with the Iranian "axis of evil," aimed at marginalizing and ultimately removing Arafat from political life. Under the banner of reforming the PA, the United States and eventually the European Union insisted that a position of prime minister be established responsible for reform, chiefly to unify the dozen or so security forces in the PA;, that a technocrat with international experience and reputation be made finance minister; and that all revenue and expenditure, especially the payroll of PA personnel, be under the jurisdiction of the Ministry of Finance. Arafat was known for personally paying security personnel and other public servants; this state of affairs made it difficult if not impossible to ensure that international aid, which accounted for over 60 percent of PA revenue, would not be diverted to terrorism. United States pressure came in the form of inaction; it henceforth hardly criticized Israeli military moves directed against Palestinian terrorism and was only slightly more assertive when Israel began building the security fence in July 2002, mostly in territory within Judea and Samaria. Along with the stick, however, came an important carrot. In a speech in June 2002, President Bush for the first time committed the United States to the establishment of a Palestinian state. According to the roadmap plan based on the speech sanctioned by Russia, the European Union, and Egypt on September 17, 2002, the PA was to begin dismantling Palestinian terrorist organizations in its midst. Israel would then withdraw its forces from areas "A" in the West Bank, paving the way for the establishment, no later than the end of 2003, of an interim internationally recognized Palestinian state. Final status negotiations would then ensue. The plan envisioned a permanent Palestinian state by 2005.

For a leader like Arafat, permanently besieged in the *muqata'a* in Ramallah by Israeli tanks, the thrust of the roadmap was hardly good news; trying to dismantle fighting organizations, most notably the Al-Aqsa Martyr Brigades and *Hamas, could mean civil war, while reform would undermine if not destroy his political base. And all this to achieve an interim state with 42 percent of the territory, when he could have had a permanent state with over 96 percent of the territories in the Camp David summit in July 2000. Already by May 2002, at a conference in Ramallah, major Palestinian civic leaders were calling for a united command of the factions, including Hamas; In Gaza, half-measures to curtail Hamas terrorist attacks had led in September 2002 to the murder of the head of the riot prevention squad, a lieutenant-colonel, by Hamas activists and though the killers were known, local security personnel were not willing to arrest them. Arafat was slowly losing his legendary grip on Palestinian politics. Gaza, where terrorism against settlers and across the Green Line increased between 2002 and 2005 in contrast to its reduction in Judea and Samaria, also became the scene of increasing internal lawlessness expressed in the rising frequency of fights between Hamas and Fatah, inter-Fatah violence and the kidnapping of foreigners and officials. Lawlessness reached its height in July 2004 when Arafat, ostensibly as part of the reform package of uniting the security forces, appointed Musa Arafat, the head of military intelligence loathed by Fatah activists, as director of security in Gaza. Fatah activists in large numbers turned against their leader for the first time with massive violence against security personnel for over two weeks. Musa Arafat faced two assassination attempts and eventually was murdered in a raid on his home in September 2005.

Though powerless to prevent the creation of the new office of prime minister given to Mahmud Abbas in April 2003 and the appointment of Salam Fayyad, a respected economist and former senior official in the World Bank, as minister of finance, Arafat succeeded in preventing both the unification of the security forces and the payment of security personnel in the official payroll, leading Mahmud Abbas to resign in September 2003. Needless to say, Arafat's death in November 2004 left his successor as head of the PLO and PA, Mahmud Abbas, with a difficult legacy.

To enhance his authority without too much loss of legitimacy and to buy time until he could rebuild the PA's security forces, Abbas decided to hold presidential elections first and postpone legislative elections until later . His strategy seemed to be successful when the young guard leader of Fatah, Marwan Barghuti, first decided from an Israeli jail to contest the presidency and then withdrew under public pressure, allowing Abbas to win nearly 80 percent of the vote in the elections of January 9, 2005. After the elections, however, Abbas, a senior bureaucratic official without any "fighting" past, seemed to lose the opportunity to assert his authority; besides forcing some aging and ineffective senior security personnel to retire, Abbas did very little to get security personnel to act. Though they abounded on the payroll (an estimated 50,000 received salaries, they were not willing to restore law and order in Gaza, which after total Israeli withdrawal in the summer of 2005 became the litmus test of the PA's capabilities to govern. To some extent, the results of four rounds of local elections conducted through 2005, in which Hamas affiliated lists did better than those affiliated to Fatah, were an indication of the PA's ability and the leader at its head to improve governance. The crushing blow came in the January 2006 legislative elections, when Hamas won a parliamentary majority that gave it effective control of the PA apparatus. Given this new reality, coupled with the considerable lawlessness in the PA and the novelty of a weak leader at the helm of a political entity in the Middle East, in 2006 the PA's fate, along with the future of Palestinian statehood, remained in question. (For Israel's subsequent clashes with Hamas, see *Israel, State of: Historical Survey.)

[Hillel Frisch (2nd ed.)]

BIBLIOGRAPHY: G.E. Robinson, *Building a Palestinian State, the Unfinished Revolution* (1997); H. Frisch, "The Palestinian Strategic Debate over the Intifada," in: *Terrorism and Political Violence*, 15:2 (Summer 2003), 1–20; A. Jamal, *Media Politics And Democracy In Palestine: Political Culture, Pluralism, and the Palestinian Authority* (2005); H. Frisch, *Countdown to Statehood: Palestinian State Formation in the West Bank and Gaza* (1998); "Jews, Israel and Peace in the Palestinian Authority Textbooks: The New Textbooks for Grade 4 and 9," compiled and translated by Arnon Groiss (2004); B.M. Rubin, Barry and J.C. Rubin, *Yasir Arafat: A Political Biography* (2005); "A Performance-Based Road Map to a Permanent Two-State Solution to the Israeli-Palestinian Conflict," at: www.mideastweb.org/quartetrm3.htm

PALEY, GRACE (1922–), U.S. short story writer and poet as well as cultural and political figure. Born in the Bronx, N.Y., in 1922, daughter of revolutionary Russian Jewish immigrants, Paley became Poet Laureate of Vermont, where she made her home. Her first collection of short stories, *The Little Disturbances of Man: Stories of Women and Men at Love*, was published in 1959. Other publications include *Enormous Changes at the Last Minute* (1974), *Later the same Day* (1985), *Long Walks and Intimate Talks* (1991), *The Collected Stories* (1994), *Just as I Thought* (1998), and *Begin Again: Collected Poems* (2000). Most of her works have been translated into several languages.

Among her many honors, Paley was a Guggenheim Fellow, winner of a National Institute of Art and Letters award, and senior fellow of the National Endowment for the Arts for her lifetime contribution to literature.

A pacifist, feminist, ecologist, secular Jew, and member of the War Resisters' League, Paley was always politically active. Growing up on stories of discrimination, racism, and exile, in an environment of radicalism, she was sensitive to everyone's shortcomings: "Some feminists were sometimes racists, some African Americans were sometimes misogynist, some Jews did sometimes act as though they were in charge of human suffering."

Differences of race, religion, class, gender, and age coexist in her narrative world, and human rights are the crucial question. The fear and inability to acknowledge these differences and accept anyone different from us can cause an "intersection of oppressions." Through her poetics and in her life Paley suggested the best way to find one's own identity was by expressing one's subjectivity while acknowledging differences and welcoming the "other."

Paley also addressed the pain of the historical experiences of different groups – the Holocaust, slavery, dictatorships, and wars – with wit and irony. She described racism as "the most severe inherited illness of the United States." Her humor and her matter-of-factness were among her most Jewish characteristics, clearly evident in her use of a colloquial but precise language, rich in oblique biblical references.

A gender perspective is at the core of Paley's work. Most of her stories are set in a New York populated by women friends, mothers, and their children, shouldering the day-to-day problems of life from the safety of the block. Mothers have also to face the most demanding job: negotiating their personal needs, being daughters themselves, and carrying out their roles as mothers caring for children.

The complexity of her writing comes from mixing techniques, forms, and genres with a wide breadth of subjects. Paley shares with her narrators and characters a "dislike" for plot, "the absolute line between two points," "not for literary reasons," they explain, but because it limits hope: "Everyone, real or invented, deserves the open destiny of life."

BIBLIOGRAPHY: J. Arcane, *Grace Paley's Life Stories. A Literary Biography* (1993); G. Bach and H.H. Blaine, *Conversations with Grace Paley* (1997); N. Batt, *Grace Paley* (1998); N. Isaac, *Grace Paley. A Study of the Short Fiction* (1990); J. Taylor, *Grace Paley. Illuminating the Dark Lives* (1990); Monographic Journals, in: *Delta*, 14 (1982)

[Annalucia Accardo (2nd ed.)]

PALEY, WILLIAM SAMUEL (1901–1990), U.S. radio and television executive. Born in Chicago, Paley joined his father Samuel Paley's cigar manufacturing business, in which he served as vice president from 1922 to 1928. In the course of advertising cigars over the airwaves Paley became impressed with the potential of the radio medium and in 1928 bought a financially unsuccessful chain of 16 eastern U.S. radio stations which he renamed the Columbia Broadcasting System (CBS). Under his direction CBS grew into one of the three giant coast-to-coast radio networks in the United States. After World War II Paley led CBS into the field of television, where it once again established itself as one of the three great national networks. As chairman of the board of CBS from 1946 on, he revolutionized the television industry by taking control of all programming away from the advertising agencies and investing it in the network itself. By the mid-1960s CBS television led both NBC and ABC on all national ratings, and the initial $400,000 investment with which Paley had bought the chain in 1928 was reputedly worth close to $70,000,000.

During World War II he served as deputy chief of the psychological warfare division of the Allied command (SHAEF) in Europe. Paley established the William S. Paley Foundation, Inc., and as president was responsible for the foundation's generous donations to the Weizmann Institute of Science, Reḥovot, as well as to other Israel institutions and funds. In later years Paley concentrated upon improving CBS's Nielsen ratings, the standard measure of the audience share enjoyed by shows. His attention to detail was legendary, and he invested much time and energy in watching the network's shows and suggesting how they might be improved. He was also a trustee and board member of many public institutions and amassed one of the largest known private collections of French post-impressionist art. Paley's autobiography, *As It Happened: A Memoir*, appeared in 1979.

[Rochelle G. Saidel]

PALGRAVE, English family. SIR FRANCIS (1788–1861) was an English historian. The son of a London stockbroker named Meyer Cohen, Palgrave was an infant prodigy and, at the age of eight, made a French translation of *The Battle of the Frogs and the Mice*, a Greek classic attributed to Homer, which was published by his father (1797). When he married a non-Jew in 1823 he became a Christian and adopted his mother-in-law's maiden name. In 1827 he qualified as a barrister, but displayed increasing interest in English history and his plans for the publication of the national records were officially approved. Knighted in 1832, Palgrave became first deputy keeper of the Public Records in 1838, retaining the post until his death. In this capacity he was in effect the chief organizer of the Public Record Office and distinguished himself as the first English historian to make systematic use of medieval records. His two outstanding works were *The Rise and Progress of the English Commonwealth* (1832) and *The History of Normandy and England* (4 vols., 1851–64). Francis Palgrave's four sons also gained renown in various spheres. SIR FRANCIS TURNER (1824–1897) became assistant secretary of education (1855–84). A close friend of the poet Tennyson, he is remembered for his classic anthology, *The Golden Treasury of the Best Songs and Lyrical Poems in the English Language* (1861; revised 1896), which went through dozens of editions. Between 1885 and 1895 F.T. Palgrave was professor of poetry at Oxford. WILLIAM GIFFORD (1826–1888) was born in London and educated at Charterhouse school and Oxford. After serving as an army officer in India, he converted to Catholicism and was for some time a Jesuit missionary in Syria and Arabia. He later renounced Catholicism, briefly changing his name back to "Cohen," and then became a diplomat, ending his career as British minister-resident in Montevideo. He published a *Narrative of a Year's Journey through Central and Eastern Arabia, 1862–1863* (1865). SIR ROBERT HARRY INGLIS (1827–1919), a successful banker, edited *The Economist* (1877–83) and *The Dictionary of Political Economy* (3 vols., 1894–99). He also published his father's collected historical works (1919). The youngest son, SIR REGINALD FRANCIS DOUCE (1829–1904), who was clerk of the House of Commons (1886–1900), edited the *Rules, Orders and Forths of Procedure of the House of Commons* (1886–96), and wrote *The Chairman's Handbook* (1877).

BIBLIOGRAPHY: R.H. Emden, *Jews of Britain* (1943), 77–82: Edwards, in: J.M. Shaftesley (ed.), *Remember the Days. Essays… Presented to Cecil Roth* (1966), 303–22; E. Elath, *Britanniah u-Netiveha le-Hodu* (1971), 164–5. **ADD. BIBLIOGRAPHY:** ODNB online; M. Allan, *Palgrave of Arabia: The Life of William Gifford Palgrave, 1826–1888* (1972); B. Braude, "The Heine-Disraeli Syndrome Among the Palgraves of Victorian England," in: Todd M. Endelman (ed.), *Jewish Apostasy in the Modern World* (1987), 108–41.

PALLENBERG, MAX (1877–1934), Austrian actor. Seen first in his hometown, Vienna, his talent was discovered relatively late by *Max Reinhardt. Pallenberg performed after 1914 at Reinhardt's Deutsches Theater in Berlin. He excelled in roles which gave him the opportunity to develop his enormous "vis comica," nurtured by elements of improvisation in the commedia dell'arte tradition. He was also able to show the depths of tragedy behind comic characters like Molière's Miser, *Molnar's Liliom, *Offenbach's Menelaos, and the Soldier Schweik in the theatrical version of Hašek's novel. A career peak was his role of Mephisto in Goethe's *Faust I* at the Salzburg Festival 1933, directed by Reinhardt. He perished in a plane accident, survived by his actress wife Fritzi *Massary.

BIBLIOGRAPHY: A. Polgar, *Max Pallenberg* (1921).

[Jens Malte Fischer (2nd ed.)]

°**PALLIÈRE, AIMÉ** (1875–1949), French writer and theologian. Born into a devout Catholic family, as an adolescent Pallière intended to take holy orders but instead his spiritual odyssey led him first into the Salvation Army and eventually as the result of a chance visit to the Lyons synagogue on the Day of Atonement – toward Judaism. Although he wished to become a Jew, he was persuaded by the Liberal Italian rabbi, E. *Benamozegh, who became his spiritual mentor, to settle for the status of a Noachide, without full conversion to Judaism. Nevertheless, he lived the life of an ardent and ascetic Jew. Although he recognized only Orthodox Judaism as authentic, Pallière became a spiritual guide to the Paris Liberal (i.e., Reform) synagogue and the French *Reform movement. He was much sought after as a lecturer and was for some time president of the World Union of Jewish Youth. He edited its periodical *Chalom* and also contributed to *Foi et Réveil*. Toward the end of his life, Pallière drew closer to the religion of his birth. Among his published works the best known is the autobiographical *Le Sanctuaire Inconnu* (1926; *The Unknown Sanctuary*, 1928). He also wrote *Bergson et le Judaïsme* (1932); *L'Ame Juive et Dieu* (n.d.); *Le Voile Soulevé* (1936); and some of his sermons were published. In 1914 he edited Benamozegh's *Israël et l' Humanité*.

BIBLIOGRAPHY: E. Fleg, in: A. Pallière, *The Unknown Sanctuary* (1928); *Le Rayon* (Jan. 1950).

[Colette Sirat]

PALM (Heb. תָּמָר, mishnaic Heb. דֶּקֶל), the *Phoenix dactylifera*. In the Bible the word *tamar* refers only to the tree; it refers to the fruit also only in rabbinic literature. According to rabbinic tradition, the "honey" enumerated among the seven species with which Israel is blessed (Deut. 8:8) is the honey of the date. The date palm is tall and straight (Song 7:8–9), and the righteous are compared to its straight trunk and evergreen foliage (Ps. 92: 13). In its shade the prophet Deborah judged the people (Judg. 4:5). Because of the arched appearance of the tree top, it is also called *kippah*, symbolizing the "head" (Isa. 9:13, 19:15). Its long leaves are called the *kappot* of the palm tree and are one of the *four species taken on the feast of Tabernacles (Lev. 23:40). According to the rabbis, the "*kappot of palm*" means the *lulav*, this being the stage when the leaves are close together (*kafut*, Suk. 32a). The tradition of using the closed leaves and not the open ones termed *ḥarut* may originate in the potential danger from the prickly leaflets of the latter, especially during festival processions (cf. Suk. 4:6). The palm needs a hot climate for its fruit to ripen and grows mainly in the valley of Jericho, the lowland of the southern coast, and the plains of the wilderness, so that Rabban Simeon b. Gamaliel asserted that "palms are an indication of valleys" (Pes. 53a). It does grow in the mountains but does not produce edible fruit there, whence the rebuke, "You are a mountain palm" (Sifra, ed. by J.H. Weiss (1862), 68a). It was therefore laid down that first fruits may not be brought from mountain palms (Bik. 1: 3), but only from those growing in Jericho (Tosef. *ibid.* 1:5, cf. Deut. 34:3). Dates were a valuable export (Dem. 2:1), and Pliny refers to the reputation of the Jericho dates and their excellent quality (*Natural History* 13:45). He describes four varieties of dates, which are also mentioned in the Mishnah (Av. Zar. 1:5). In the Bible a number of places are named after the palm: Hazazon Tamar (Gen. 14:7), Ba'al Tamar (Jud. 20:33); Tadmor (Palmyra, I Kings 9:18). Three women were named Tamar: *Judah's daughter-in-law, *David's daughter, and *Absalom's daughter. Its beautiful form was used as a model for sculpture (cf. Jer. 10:5). There were ornaments like *timmorot* ("palm trees") in the Temple (I Kings 6:29; cf. Ez. 40:16, *timmorim*). The *aggadah* compares Isaac and Rebekah (Lev. R. 30: 10), Moses and Aaron (Targ. to Song 2:12), David and the Messiah with the palm tree (PdRE 19). The Hasmoneans took the palm as an emblem of their victory (I Macc. 13:37; II Macc. 14:4), and it appears on their coins. The Romans also engraved the image of captive Judea – *Judea capta* – sitting in mourning beneath the palm. A palm branch symbolizes the victory of the Jew against his accusers (Lev. R. 30:2): "dreaming of palm trees is a sign that one's sins have come to an end"; "dreaming of a *lulav* ["palm branch"] indicates that one is serving God wholeheartedly" (Ber. 57a).

Rabbinic literature contains much information about the growing of palm trees. Among other things, it mentions that there are male and female palms, that it is necessary to pollinate the female from the male blossom in order to obtain fruit, and that this must be done during a limited number of days (cf. Pes. 4:8). It is asserted that "the palm has desire," and in that connection the story is told of a female palm in the vicinity of Tiberias which longed for a palm in Jericho, and only began to yield fruit after being pollinated by it (Gen. R. 41:1). Of its many uses the Midrash (*ibid.*) says: "As no part of the palm has any waste, the dates being eaten, the branches used for *Hallel*, the twigs for covering [booths], the bast for ropes, the leaves for besoms, and the planed boards for ceiling rooms, so are there none worthless in Israel…."

BIBLIOGRAPHY: Loew, Flora, 2 (1924), 306–62; H.N. and A.L. Moldenke, *Plants of the Bible* (1952), index; J. Feliks, *Olam ha-Ẓome'aḥ ha-Mikra'i* (1968[2]), 40–47. **ADD. BIBLIOGRAPHY:** Feliks, Ha-Tzome'aḥ, 49, 171.

[Jehuda Feliks]

PALMA, LA, city in Andalusia, near Córdoba, S.W. Spain. The only information available on a Jewish settlement there dates from the end of the period of Jewish residence in Spain. The town was located on the estate of Don Luis de Puertocarrero, who granted refuge to the *Conversos of Córdoba when they fled to La Palma after the riots of 1473. The small community reached the high point of its history with the arrival of another large group of Conversos who had fled from *Ciudad Real on the outbreak of further anti-Converso riots in 1474. In La Palma the Conversos once again returned to Judaism, calling upon the services of a rabbi who later himself became converted to Christianity (adopting the name Fernando de Trujillo) and who, upon entering the service of the *Inquisition in Ciudad Real in 1483, denounced the whole community by revealing the details of its return to Judaism. In 1485, upon payment of 60 castellanos, its share in the expenses of the war against Granada, the community of La Palma was incorporated into that of *Córdoba.

BIBLIOGRAPHY: Baer, Spain, index; H. Beinart, in: *Zion*, 20 (1957), 13ff.; idem, *Anusim be-Din ha-Inkvizizyah* (1964), index; Suárez Fernández, Documentos, 256.

[Haim Beinart]

PALMAḤ (abbreviation for *peluggot maḥaẓ;* "assault companies"), the permanently mobilized striking force of the *Haganah and later, until its dissolution, part of the Israel Defense Forces (IDF). The Palmaḥ was established by an emergency order of the Haganah's national command on May 19, 1941, when the Axis forces were nearing the approaches to Palestine. In view of the worsening situation, nine assault companies were to be established and placed in a state of readiness: three in northern Galilee, two in central Galilee, three in southern Galilee, and one in the Jerusalem area. They were to consist of volunteers from existing Haganah units prepared to report for active service at 24 hours' notice and serve in any capacity whenever and wherever required. The Palmaḥ was to serve as a national and regional fighting reserve. For purposes of administration and training the companies would be under the orders of the area commander, but for operational purposes, they were to be directly subordinate to the Haganah's high command, which would appoint a commander for each company on a permanent basis. A staff officer was appointed to supervise training and organization through the area commanders.

Yiẓḥak *Sadeh was appointed general staff officer for Palmaḥ affairs and set about establishing the first six companies, which were to be composed entirely of volunteers, in coordination with the area commanders of the Haganah. While it was in the process of formation, the Palmaḥ was called upon to participate in special operations in advance of the Allied invasion of Syria and Lebanon, which were under the command of the Vichy French. On the day before the official establishment of the Palmaḥ, a boat carrying 23 men, with a British liaison officer, sailed in secrecy to sabotage the refineries in Tripoli (Lebanon), but all traces of the detachment were lost. Scores of Arabic-speaking members of the Palmaḥ crossed the frontier dressed as Arabs and carried out intelligence and sabotage work in these countries. The first units of A and B companies participated in the invasion of Syria and Lebanon in June 1941 as saboteurs, guides, scouts, and intelligence men.

Gradually, the number of companies grew to 12, which were combined into battalions and, together, constituted a corps. Sadeh became its commander, with a staff of the type usual in such a force. The commander of the Palmaḥ was directly subordinate to the Haganah chief of staff. The Palmaḥ assumed the character and function of a commando unit and, in addition to the infantry, prepared a special naval force to carry out tasks that would be required in connection with *"illegal" immigration: sabotage and small engagements at sea. It also established the nucleus of an air force disguised as a civilian flying club, in which pilots were trained to fly light planes which were more than once engaged as fighters against enemy forces. The Palmaḥ achieved high standards in physical fitness, field training, and guerilla fighting by day and night. It was the first of the Haganah forces to establish the battalion as a tactical and administrative unit. It developed high-level intelligence, sabotage, and scouting. Special attention was paid to educational activity and ideological guidance. On the principle of training every fighting man according to his ability, more section and platoon commanders were trained than were needed for current operations, on the assumption that in an emergency the Palmaḥ would widen its framework and absorb many recruits.

As the mobilized units of the Haganah until the *War of Independence, the Palmaḥ served, in effect, as a kind of laboratory for experiments in training methods and operational, tactical, and administrative concepts. Although stationed in different parts of the country, it made up a national army not restricted to local self-defense. It was given six main tasks:

(1) to prepare during World War II for guerilla warfare against German and Italian invasion forces if these reached Syria, Lebanon, and Palestine;

(2) to carry out, after the war, the main military operations, on land and sea, against the British Mandatory regime;

(3) to play a central role in halting a possible Arab military invasion;

(4) to punish Arab terrorist units that attacked the Jewish population;

(5) to assume the offensive at the first suitable opportunity;

(6) to establish settlements in strategically and politically important areas. The general staff of the Haganah decided in June 1941 that in the event that the front reached Palestine, the Palmaḥ would operate in strategic areas distant from Jewish centers.

At first the Allies financed part of the maintenance of the Palmaḥ units, but when the danger of foreign invasion passed, they went underground. For lack of a national budget, the fighters maintained themselves by working in settlements, mainly kibbutzim, and in the ports. In 14 days' work per month, they earned their keep for the rest of the month, which was mainly given over to training. No wages were customary in the Palmaḥ: the men received small sums for pocket-money, traveling expenses, and clothes. It fostered a comradeship in arms between officers and men, which stood the test of fire. Discipline was founded on personal conviction. According to a special decision of the staff, the men went into the reserves: privates after two years' service, squad commanders (equivalent to corporal or sergeant) after three years, and platoon commanders after four years.

In 1945, when Yiẓḥak Sadeh was appointed chief of the Haganah general staff, his deputy, Yigal *Allon, was appointed to command the Palmaḥ. In August 1948, when Allon became the commander of the southern front with the rank of *aluf* (brigadier general), his deputy, Uri Brenner, was appointed acting commander of the Palmaḥ, retaining the post until the corps was disbanded in 1948.

In 1947, when the security situation of the *yishuv* was becoming graver, units of the Palmaḥ operated in Upper Galilee, western Galilee, the Jezreel Valley, the Eẓyon Bloc, and the Negev. Others provided covering forces for convoys in hilly regions or Arab-populated areas in Upper Galilee, the road to Jerusalem, and the Negev. In the War of Independence, when the reservists were called up and the Palmaḥ received new recruits, it operated in three brigades: Yiftaḥ, under Shemu'el (Mula) Cohen; Harel, under Yosef Tabenkin; and the Negev, under Naḥum Sarig. The Palmaḥ was an integral part of the Israel Defense Forces and played a major role in all stages of the war, from the defense of isolated settlements and dangerous supply routes in strategic areas to important offensives which liberated parts of the country. Yiftaḥ led Operation Yiftaḥ to liberate Upper Galilee and Safad and repulse invading Syrian and Lebanese forces. At a later stage it fought on the southern front, the Negev, and Sinai. Harel bore the brunt of Operation Harel for the establishment and widening of the Jerusalem corridor, the liberation of the Jerusalem suburbs and Mount Zion, and the breaking through to the Jewish Quarter of the Old City. It was also active in the operations that led to the liberation of the Negev and the occupation of northern Sinai.

At the beginning of August 1948 Allon was appointed commander of the southern front. The question of whether the Palmaḥ should continue to preserve its special character under the command of its own special staff was raised by David *Ben-Gurion, prime minister and minister of defense in the provisional government, and others who argued that all units must be under the direct command of the IDF general staff in all respects. The leaders of the Palmaḥ, on the other hand, believed that the separate framework was necessary in order to enable it to continue to make its own special contribution to the war effort and character of the IDF. The provisional government accepted Ben-Gurion's view and decided on November 7, 1948, to disband the separate staff of the Palmaḥ. In May 1948 the three Palmaḥ brigades were merged with other IDF units.

Many of the leading officers of the IDF rose from service in the Palmaḥ. To mention only the generals, they included, in addition to Yiẓḥak Sadeh and Yigal Allon, three chiefs of staff – Moshe *Dayyan, Yiẓḥak *Rabin, and Haim *Bar-Lev – as well as Yoḥai Bin-Nun, Avraham Eden, David Elazar, Yeshayahu Gavish, Mordecai Hod, Yitzḥak Hofi, Amos Ḥorev, Uzzi Narkis, El'ad Peled, Mattityahu Peled, Ezer Weizman, Ẓvi Zamir, and Raḥavam Ze'evi: This is only one indication of the Palmaḥ's special contribution to the building of the IDF, in addition to its major role in the main operations during the Haganah period and the War of Independence.

BIBLIOGRAPHY: Y. Allon, *Shield of David; The Story of Israel's Armed Forces* (1970); idem, *The Making of Israel's Army* (1970); Y. Bauer, *From Diplomacy to Resistance* (1970); *Sefer ha-Palmaḥ*, ed. by Z. Gilead, 2 vols. (1953); Y. Sadeh, *Mah Ḥiddesh Palmaḥ* (1950); Y. Allon, *Ma'arekhot Palmaḥ* (1966).

[Yigal Allon]

PALM BEACH COUNTY, carved out of Dade County in 1909, was comprised in 2005 of 37 cities and more than 45 miles of shoreline along Florida's Gold Coast. It is one of the two largest of Florida's 67 counties in land area.

The first southern Florida (except Key West) community to host Jews was probably West Palm Beach, where Jews settled by 1893 when the railway that was coming down Florida's east coast arrived there. Russian Jewish immigrants Isidor Cohen, Jake Schneidman, and Julius Frank opened retail stores on Narcissus and Clematis Streets, which were close to the ferry that brought shoppers from Palm Beach. Max Serkin was a produce broker. Of these, only Serkin remained; the others followed the railway to Miami when it was extended there in 1896. The Serkin's daughter, Jeanette, born in 1896, is the first known Jewish child born in the county. By 1912 Max Greenberg left Daytona Beach to open Pioneer Hardware in Lucerne (later Lake Worth). The Joseph Schupler family opened a hat store in West Palm Beach in 1915, joining Joseph Mendel, a cigar manufacturer, the Cohen's Riviera Citrus Packing Company, and Shrebnick clothing for a total of about six Jewish families in the area. The Dickson brothers, a carpenter and a plasterer, settled in 1919. In 1923 the Jewish Cemetery Association was established to purchase lots in Woodlawn Cemetery, and Temple Beth Israel (later named Temple Israel) was founded. Joseph Mendel, serving as mayor of West Palm Beach at the time, was instrumental in forming the congregation, and Max Serkin was the first president. The next year the Jewish Junior League was created for social activity. By 1926 there was a second congregation, Beth El. Jewish merchants continued to settle, among them Myers Luggage and Cy Argintar's Men's Shop, as well as professionals, including dentist Dr. Blicher and lawyer Joe Lesser. Meanwhile on Palm Beach, wealthy Jews Henry Morgenthau, Mortimer Schiff, the Seligmans, Springolds, and Florenz Zeigfield had homes. A major hurricane hit in 1928 and many merchants lost their merchandise. The next year, the land bubble burst. Pioneer Virginia Argintar recalled, "One day I was riding in a limousine; the next, I waited for the bus." Dr. Carl Herman, an avid anti-Zionist, served Temple Israel for 17 years. Kosher boarding houses opened in Palm Beach. Growth was slow at first; as late as 1940, the Jewish population in Palm Beach County was only 1,000.

Harry and Florence Brown from St. Louis were the first Jews to settle in Boca Raton in 1931 at a time when it was still possible to sit in the middle of Old Dixie Highway and play cards! In 1936, Harry's sister, Nettie, arrived with her husband Max Hutkin, a Polish immigrant. They opened Hutkin's Food Market. Max was the founding president of Temple Beth El (1967), the first Jewish congregation in Boca Raton. Today, with a membership of 2,000 families, it is one of the largest Reform congregations in the nation.

In 1932 Sam Schutzer established a Jewish newspaper, *Our Voice*, which he published for 43 years, finally merging with the *Jewish Floridian* in 1975. In 1936 the Persoff family moved to Delray Beach to work in a jewelry store in the "art" colony. Carl Altman formed the Lake Worth Benevolent Association in 1939 to assist Jews in difficulties. During the war years of the 1940s, *seders* and Sabbath services were held for Jewish naval and air personnel in the area. In 1946 Lake Worth Hebrew Association was founded, which became Temple Beth Sholom in 1953. In 1960 when President John Kennedy began to come to Palm Beach, Jewish physician Dr. Rotter was on call. The first co-op was built, inviting "snowbirds" to purchase instead of rent apartments for the season. The Jewish Federation of Palm Beach County started in 1962, the List family donated land for Camp Shalom in West Palm Beach, and Temple Emanu-El was founded in a Palm Beach storefront.

Shopping malls and air-conditioning have changed the shape of local businesses. More recent entrepreneurs include Irwin Levy, Robert Rapaport, and Aaron Schecter, who began developing Century Village in 1967. Century Village attracted large numbers of retired garment workers and teachers, often from New York and other northeastern states. These "cities within cities" provide a wide range of educational, recreational, and entertainment activities. Temple Anshei Sholom was founded in 1971 on land adjacent to Century Village. In the 1970s and 1980s, Kings Point retirement community became successful in Delray Beach and its environs, and numerous golf club communities followed the trend. The "rush" of Jewish settlement accelerated. In and around these communities, more congregations were established. In 1973 the Jewish Community Day School was started by Rabbis Irving Cohen, William H. Shapiro, and Hyman Fishman, with Ann Leibovitz and Carol Roberts, who later served as mayor of West Palm Beach. The next year (1974) the Jewish Community Center of the Palm Beaches was founded. In 1975 the Federation established a branch office in Boca Raton. Four years later the South County Jewish Federation was formed; the campus today sits on 50 acres of land. Rabbi Bruce Warshal was the professional, working with Helene Eichler, and James Baer the founding president. By 1980 the Jewish population was more than 100,000. *Palm Beach Jewish World*, later purchased by Jewish Media Group of Miami, was established by Robert D. Rapaport, who also founded the Jewish Arts Foundation in 1987. That year there were 31 congregations serving 150,000 families.

Of the 1.2 million people who live in Palm Beach County (2005), about 238,000 are Jews, making this the second largest Jewish population in the state (after Broward County). Many have moved north from Miami-Dade County. The Boca Raton (south county) metropolitan area is more than 50% Jewish, with 20 congregations, a JCC on land donated by Richard Siemans and, since 1982, a Jewish day school. Ninety-eight percent of the Jews were born elsewhere in the U.S., most are seniors, and the mayor of Boca Raton since 2001, Steven L. Abrams, is Jewish. Elected to the U.S. Congress in 1996, Robert Wexler of Boca Raton was a senior member of the House International Relations Committee. Serving as chief justice of Florida's Supreme Court was Barbara Pariente of West Palm Beach, only the second woman appointed to the court in 1997. In the West Palm Beach area (north county) there are 29 congregations and 18 Jewish educational institutions, including a 7.5-acre Day School K-8. The Orthodox community is the largest segment with 12 of the congregations. The JCC of Greater

Palm Beaches has two campuses (in West Palm Beach on land donated by Robert Rapaport, and in Boynton), and the Morse Geriatric Center with 280 beds opened in 1983. As the Jewish community grew, so did incidents of antisemitism. This waned as the Jewish organizations established a more solid base. Until today Jews play prominent roles in all areas of the general community, including politics. Continuing growth for the Jewish community is a prediction for the future in Palm Beach County.

[Marcia Jo Zerivitz (2nd ed.)]

°**PALMER, EDWARD HENRY** (1840–1882), English Orientalist. Born in Cambridge and educated at Cambridge University, he took part in the 1867 Sinai Survey Expedition of the Palestine Exploration Fund. In 1869/70 he traveled with Tyrwhitt Drake in the desert of Tih, Edom, Moab, and the Lebanon, and this resulted in a two-volume work, *Desert of the Exodus* (1871), in which he described the discovery of, *inter alia*, the site of Kurnub in the Negev. He was appointed professor of Arabic in 1871. In 1881 he left Cambridge and edited the *Arabic and English Name Lists of the Survey of Western Palestine* (1881) in which his excellent knowledge of Arabic and other Oriental languages served him well. In 1882 he was dispatched on a secret mission to Sinai in connection with British operations in Egypt against Arabi Pasha; he was assassinated there by Bedouin. His works include *Jerusalem: the City of Herod and Saladin*, written jointly with W. Besant (1888).

ADD. BIBLIOGRAPHY: ODNB online.

[Michael Avi-Yonah]

PALMER, LILLI (1914–1986), actress-writer. Born Lillie Marie Peiser to surgeon Dr. Alfred Peiser and actress Rose (née Lissmann) in Posen, East Prussia (now Poland), Palmer was educated at the Ilka Gruening School of Acting in Berlin. She made her first stage appearance in 1932 in *Die Eiserne Jungfrau*. She left Germany after Adolf Hitler rose to power in 1933 and began performing at the Moulin Rouge in Paris. In 1935, Palmer moved to England, where she made her screen debut in *Crime Unlimited* (1935) and appeared in Alfred Hitchcock's *Secret Agent* (1936); she made her London stage debut in *Road to Gadahar* (1938). Palmer met actor Rex Harrison in 1939, and performed with him in the 1940 play *No Time for Comedy*. Palmer and Harrison married in 1943, and had one son, Carey, who became a playwright. They moved to the United States together. Palmer starred in such films as *Cloak and Dagger* (1946) and *Body and Soul* (1947). The couple appeared together on Broadway and in the film *The Four Poster* (1952). Palmer and Harrison returned to England and divorced in 1957. Soon after, she married novelist Carlos Thompson. Her film and television career continued both in America and abroad, which included *The Diary of Anne Frank* (1967) and *The Boys from Brazil* (1978). Toward the end of her life, Palmer wrote her autobiography, *Change Lobsters, and Dance* (1976), which centered on her 17-year relationship with Harrison. She also wrote the novels *Red Raven* (1978), *Time to Embrace* (1980), *Night Music* (1983), and *Face Value* (1986).

[Adam Wills (2nd ed.)]

PALM SPRINGS AND DESERT AREA, California. The area is defined by the Coachella Valley, which stretches from Palm Springs proper east to the city of Coachella. The Jewish Federation which serves the entire community estimated that the Jewish community numbers some 20,000 residents in an overall population of some 350,000. Within the Jewish community some 55% of the population lives year round in the valley, with the rest spending various periods of time in the desert.

Many of the first Jews who came to the desert were somehow connected to Hollywood. Temple Isaiah was the first Jewish institution to be founded some 53 years ago. It later created the Federation. As the general community grew and expanded, so did the Jewish community. Today, the community boasts five synagogues plus two Chabad entities, including Temple Isaiah of Palm Springs, which is multi-denominational; Temple Sinai of Palm Desert, which is Reform; the Desert Synagogue of Palm Springs, which is Modern Orthodox; Congregation Beth Shalom, B. Dunes, which is Conservative, and Har-El, Palm Desert, the Reform Congregation.

There are two Jewish Day Schools, Desert Torah Academy, run by Chabad, and Jewish Community School of the Desert. The Jewish Community Center functions without walls as a committee of the Federation. The community also has a full service Jewish Family Service organization, which specializes in a whole array of services for seniors. The community is very proud of its Holocaust Memorial, located in the Palm Desert municipal park, built at the initiation of two local survivors, Earl Greif and Joseph Brandt. Many National and international Jewish organizations have strong constituent groups in the Palm Springs area, including ADL, AIPAC, JNF, American Friends of Hebrew University, and Technion.

More and more of the newcomers to the Jewish community are working people who came to the desert for professional opportunities. Many inhabitants are retirees who enjoy its wonderful climate and who avoid the heat of the desert by either leaving for the summer months or undertaking their activities in the morning. The Jewish community is growing and active.

[Alan Klugman (2nd ed.)]

PALOMBO, DAVID (1920–1966), Israeli sculptor. He was born in Jerusalem and studied sculpture, restoration, and mosaics under Ze'ev *Ben-Zvi, later teaching at the Bezalel School of Art, Jerusalem. He made his home on Mount Zion, where he founded a studio for the production of mosaics, wrought-iron work, and jewelry. In his small sculpture he moved from simplified representation to total abstraction using a diversity of materials including wood and rough or cut stone. Wrought iron attracted him and his talent was well suited to large-scale works as parts of architectural concepts. His first monumental work was the entrance gate to the *Yad Vashem Memorial in Jerusalem (1961). This embodied a rhythmic composition of welded iron bars and steel electroplatings, a technique which he subsequently repeated. The impact of these works springs from the contrast of simple but expressive elements against the starkness of concrete walls. Palombo worked on other projects, of which the most important, the gates of the Knesset building in Jerusalem (1966), was finished shortly before his death in a road accident on Mount Zion.

BIBLIOGRAPHY: Spencer, in: *Ariel* (Autumn 1967), 58–61, includes plates; B. Tammuz, *Art In Israel* (1966), 153–4.

[Yona Fischer]

PALTI (Heb. פַּלְטִי, a hypocoristicon of a name like פַּלְטִיאֵל, Paltiel; "God is [my] deliverance"), son of Laish from Gallim in Benjamin. Saul's daughter *Michal, who had been given in marriage to *David, was given in marriage to Palti when David incurred Saul's jealousy and had to flee the court to save his life. After Saul's death, *Abner, angered by Saul's son Ish-Bosheth, secretly offered David to win over the men of Israel for him. David, however, refused to even begin negotiations unless he brought Michal to him. It was probably under pressure of the powerful Abner that Ish-Bosheth took Michal away from Palti and returned her to David. It is related that the unhappy Palti followed Michal in tears until Abner ordered him to turn back (II Sam. 3:15–16).

PALTIEL (d. 975), astrologer, physician, and statesman at the court of the *Fatimid caliph al-Muʿizz. Paltiel is referred to in two Hebrew sources. Ahimaaz, his relative, lists him in his genealogy (*Megillat Aḥimaʿaẓ*, ed. B. Klar (1944), 35–45), indicating that in 962, with al-Muʿizz's conquest of the south Italian city of Oria, which was Paltiel's birthplace, the caliph was taken with Paltiel's astrological skills and appointed him as his chief aide. The *Sefer Ḥasidim* of *Judah b. Samuel of Regensburg notes that Paltiel was captured during the conquest of Oria, and that he became the physician of the Fatimid ruler. Ahimaaz describes how during the conquest of *Egypt by the caliph (969), Paltiel was charged with provisioning the army. It appears that Paltiel was *Wāsiṭa* (somewhat lower than vizier). He appears to have served as state secretary, or in some similar position, and in connection with this office he handled matters of military administration. Ahimaaz refers to him by the title *nagid* on three occasions. For this reason, J. *Mann and others presume that he was the first to bear this title in Egypt. However, it has already been shown that his public office had no connection with duties performed for his coreligionists, as was the case with a *nagid* at a later date (S.D. Goitein and M.R. Cohen). M. Ben-Sasson thinks that this story in the Ahimaaz scroll was written under the impression of the existence of the heads of the Jews (*negidim*) in North Africa. The author of the Ahimaaz scroll gives Paltiel the title *nagid*, a title that was relevant in the same period to *Kairouan. He considers Paltiel the first courtier in the Fatimid court, and a leader who worried about the Jewish population.

It seems quite clear to Robert *Bonfil that the story of Paltiel as we find it in *Sefer Ḥasidim* displays more than three consecutive stages of mythologization. But on the other hand it does not seem possible to say exactly how many stages there were, nor to determine exactly when and where they took place.

Other scholars have tried to identify Paltiel with well-known personalities of his generation. M.J. de Goeje (in: ZDMG, 52 (1898), 75–80) stated that Paltiel was none other than al-Jawhar, a well-known Fatimid military leader. Thus, he concluded that Jawhar must have been a Jew. D. Kaufmann and W.J. Fischel sought to identify him with a Jewish convert to Islam, Yaʿqūb *Ibn Killis, the first of the Fatimid viziers of Egypt. A. *Marx maintains the view of de Goeje on the basis of the *Sefer Ḥasidim* reference. It has been established, however, that neither of these identifications is correct. B. *Lewis identified him with Mūsā ibn Eleazar, who was captured during the Fatimid conquest of Oria, and of whom it is known that he became the physician of the caliph al-Muʿizz, and was with him during his conquest of Egypt. A number of Mūsā's medical writings are extant, and he was also a friend of Yaʿqūb ibn Killis. Moshe Gil suggests identifying Paltiel with Faiṣal ben Ṣāliḥ, a Fatimid statesman and military commander. R Bonfil prefers this identification, and thinks that this identification would indeed quite reasonably explain many details that remain obscure in Lewis' hypotheses, but as Gil is well aware, he does find a proper answer to numerous other details. There are opinions of some historians that the story about Paltiel is a legend invented by his family members.

According to the Ahimaaz scroll Paltiel donated large sums for the academy sages and for the mourners of the sanctuary in Jerusalem, for the academy of the *geonim* in Babylon and for the poor and needy of the various communities. He also brought the remains of his parents in caskets to Jerusalem. This scroll also tells that after Paltiel's death, the office of court physician to the Fatimid caliphate was filled for four generations by Paltiel's descendants.

BIBLIOGRAPHY: Marx, in: JQR, 1 (1910/11), 78–85; Mann, Egypt, index; Fischel, Islam, 65–68; Neustadt, in: *Zion*, 4 (1939), 135–43; Hirschberg, *ibid.*, 23–24 (1958/59), 166f.; Hirschberg, Afrikah, 1 (1965), 152–4; Lewis, in: *Bulletin of the School of Oriental and African Studies*, 30 (1967), 177–81. **ADD BIBLIOGRAPHY:** M. Gil, *Ereẓ Yisrael ba-Tekufah ha-Muselemit ha-Rishonah, 634–1099*, 1 (1983), 299–302; R. Bonfil, in: M. Fishbane (ed.), *The Midrashic Imagination – Jewish Exegesis Thought and History* (1993), 228–54; M. Ben-Sasson, *Ẓemiḥat ha-Kehillah ha-Yehudit be-Arẓot ha-Islam, Kayrawan 800–1057* (1996), 39, 355–57; M. Cohen, *Jewish Self-Government in Medieval Egypt* (1980), 5, 12–27; M. Gil, *Jews in Islamic Countries in the Middle Ages* (2004), index.

[Abraham David / Leah Bornstein-Makovetsky (2nd ed.)]

PALTOI BAR ABBAYE, *gaon* of Pumbedita from 842 to 857; father of *Ẓemaḥ Gaon. Paltoi was a powerful, energetic, and strong-minded personality. His appointment heralded a new era of prominence for the gaonate of Pumbedita. His authority was such that the exilarch had to come to his academy in order to convene a public assembly. During his gaonate the ties with the outside communities were strengthened and increased. Paltoi and Ẓemaḥ were the first *geonim* to establish contact with the community of North Africa. A community in Spain sent a request to Paltoi "to write the Talmud and its explanations for them," basing their request on the grounds that "the majority of the people have recourse to digests of the *halakhah* (*hilkhot ketu'ot*) and say 'what need have we for the difficulties of the Talmud?'" Paltoi vigorously protested against this. "They are not acting correctly, and it is forbidden to do this. They thereby cause a decline in the study of the Torah, causing it to be forgotten." His extant responsa, which are to be found in most collections of geonic responsa, as well as being quoted in the works of the *posekim, only represent a minority of those he wrote. New fragments were published by A.N.Z. Roth.

BIBLIOGRAPHY: Abramson, Merkazim, 10, 16; Assaf, Ge'onim, 52f., 171; A.N.Z. Roth, in: *Tarbiz*, 25 (1956), 140–8; M. Margolioth, *ibid.*, 149–53.

[Meir Havazelet]

PALTROW, GWYNETH (1972–), U.S. actress. Paltrow was born in Los Angeles, the daughter of the Tony Award-winning actress Blythe Danner and the film director Bruce Paltrow, who was said to have had generations of rabbis in his family tree. In 1991, Gwyneth quit the University of California to actively pursue a career in acting. She made her film debut with a small part in *Shout* (1991) and then had featured roles in a variety of films before playing the title role of Emma Woodhouse in *Emma* (1996), which led to her being offered the role of Viola in *Shakespeare in Love* (1998). For the latter role, she won an Oscar as best actress.

[Stewart Kampel (2nd ed.)]

PAM, HUGO (1870–1930), U.S. jurist and Zionist leader. Pam, who was born in Chicago, practiced law in that city with his brother Max. In 1911 he was elected to the Cook County Superior Court, on which he served for 20 years. As a judge he developed a special interest in the psychology of criminal behavior, which led him to be chosen vice president of the Illinois Society of Mental Hygiene. He also served for three years as president of the American Institute of Criminal Law and Criminology. Pam became active in organized Jewish life in 1912, when he joined the Federation of American Zionists, of which he was later vice president. He took part in the founding of the *American Jewish Congress in 1916. After World War I, he traveled to Russia and Poland on behalf of *HIAS to survey conditions in the Jewish communities there.

[Aaron Lichtenstein]

PAMIERS, town in the department of Ariège, France. The earliest evidence of the presence of Jews in Pamiers goes back to 1256. They were then under the authority of the abbot of Saint Antonin of Pamiers who, in 1274, protested against the Jews having to pay the royal poll tax and claimed their contributions belonged to him alone. The community appears to have been relatively well established by 1279; in that year a series of internal regulations (concerning the restriction of private expenditures, religious discipline, and mutual assistance) were drawn up and immediately approved by the abbot of Saint Antonin. The text of these regulations, the oldest of their type, has been preserved. The community was administered by two or more trustees and internal taxes were levied. The subsequent abbots of Saint Antonin continued to assure the relatively favorable condition of the Jews. When Saint Antonin became a bishopric, the Jews were still protected from the excesses of the inquisitors (1298). However, the bishop was unsuccessful in his opposition to the expulsion order of 1306. A community was reconstituted between 1315 and 1322. Although Bishop Jacques Fournier ordered a relentless search for volumes of the Talmud so as to have them burnt (see *Talmud, Burning of), he nevertheless protected his Jewish subjects from the persecutions of the Pastoureaux to the extent that many Jews from the rest of the region sought refuge in the town. After the expulsion of 1322, Jews occasionally passed through Pamiers and are thus mentioned in the toll tariffs of 1327 and 1340. A third community was formed after 1359. At the close of the 19th century, a Hebrew seal of a certain Solomon Vidal b. Pourtaya was found and survives as the only material trace of the Jews of Pamiers.

BIBLIOGRAPHY: G. Saige, *Juifs en Languedoc…* (1881), index; Gross, Gal Jud, 438; J. de Lahondes, in: *Annales de Pamiers*, 1 (1882), 38, 86, 144; J. Ourgaud, *Notice historique sur… Pamiers* (1865), 108, 130, 255; J.A. Blanchet, in: REJ, 18 (1889), 139–41; E. Ferran, in: *Bulletin philologique et historique* (1903), 184ff.; J.M. Vidal, *Le Tribunal d'inquisition à Pamiers* (1906), 67, 80; B. Blumenkranz, in: *Archives Juives*, 5 (1968–69), 38ff., 47ff.

[Bernhard Blumenkranz]

PAMPHYLIA, region in the southern part of Asia Minor. According to a Roman decree quoted in I Maccabees (15:16ff.), Pamphylia was among those countries notified by the Roman consul Lucius (142 B.C.E.) of the renewed pact of friendship between the Roman Senate and the Jewish nation under the high priest Simeon. Numerous scholars have deduced from this document that a Jewish community existed in Pamphylia (cf. F.-M. Abel, *Les Livres des Maccabées* (1949), 269) as well as the other districts mentioned in the decree. There is, however, only sparse information on Jewish communities in Pamphylia. There is some information about the Jews in Pamphylia in the city of Side in I Maccabees 15:23 (cf. also a late inscription from the Byzantine period from Side (*Journal of Hellenic Studies*, 28 (1908), 195)), and also mention of Jews in Pamphylia in Philo's *Legatio ad Gaium*, 281, and in Acts 2:10. Josephus makes no mention of such a community, and refers to the area primarily in connection with Herod, who was nearly shipwrecked not far from Pamphylia on his way to Rome in 40 B.C.E. (Ant. 14:377; Wars 1:280).

BIBLIOGRAPHY: Schuerer, Gesch, 3 (1909[4]), 22; Juster, Juifs, 1 (1914), 192.

[Isaiah Gafni]

PAMPLONA (**Pomplona, Pampeluna**), city in northen Spain; capital of the former kingdom of Navarre. Pamplona's Jewish community appears to have been founded during the renewed Christian domination of the peninsula after the Muslim conquest. The earliest information, however, on the Jews in the city dates from the tenth century. In 958 *Ḥisdai ibn Shaprut visited Pamplona on a diplomatic mission to confer with Sancho I, king of León, who had found refuge there. At that time there was already a Jewish quarter in the section of the city known as the Navarrería. Even though there is no extant information, there is no doubt that a Jewish community continued to exist in Pamplona throughout the 11th and 12th centuries. In 1274 anti-Jewish riots occurred, the Jewish quarter was apparently destroyed, and the community's property confiscated. In 1336 the Jewish quarter was rebuilt in the same place. In 1280 the town was ordered to restitute the property and allocate space for the erection of Jewish homes. Nonetheless, only after the suppression of the French *Pastoureaux (1320) was the community able to start rebuilding the quarter. In the 14th century there were around 500 Jews in Pamplona.

Numerous accounts and receipts involving the Jews of Pamplona in the 14th century are extant in the archives of the town. A considerable part of the documents are written in Hebrew and bear the signatures of royal agents, physicians, and merchants who were involved in royal transactions. Among other occupations, the Jews of Pamplona owned vineyards and farms or traded with communities in Navarre, Aragon, and Castile. King Charles II of Navarre (1349–87) even exempted the Jews of Pamplona from the prohibition of bringing grapes into the town, as they were for private use and the taxes from Jews were based on their incomes from wine. As evidenced from the tax accounts, the community possessed considerable means but, nevertheless, was – like the other communities of Navarre – in a state of crisis and decline. Pamplona was the site of the disputation on Dec. 26, 1375, between R. Shem Tov b. Isaac Shaprut and Pedro de Luna, who later became the anti-pope *Benedict XIII. Toward the close of the 14th century R. Ḥayyim *Galipapa, the author of *Emek Refa'im*, was rabbi of Pamplona.

At the beginning of the 15th century there were over 200 Jewish families living in Pamplona; this increase in the Jewish population was probably due to refugees from the persecutions of 1391 which took place in the kingdoms of Aragon and Castile. In 1400 the king gave Isaac Alburji, who was probably a goldsmith in the employ of the court, 345 gold florins from the taxes collected in the community. Other Jews were employed as purveyors to the court. In 1407, however, Charles III ordered the sale of Jewish property, and notables of the community were imprisoned. During 1410–11 a plague ravaged Pamplona and many members of the community were among the victims; the community, however, appears to have recovered. In 1469 Leonor, the daughter of John II – in her function as regent of the kingdom – ordered that a strict watch be kept over the Jews to assure that they only lived in their quarter of town. When the Jews were expelled from Spain in 1492, some of them went to Pamplona. They suffered the same fate as the rest of the community, however, when the Jews of the kingdom of Navarre were expelled in 1498.

The Jewish quarter was in the southeast of the so-called Navarrería district. The *juderiía* was by the city walls in the south and in the east. After the expulsion in 1498 the quarter was renamed *Barrio Nuevo*, which is in today's *calle de la Merced*. The Jewish quarter occupied an area of about 20,000 square meters. In this area there were three different quarters: the first one was the smallest, where there was the *Sinagoga Mayor*. This quarter occupied the area of the square of Santa María la Real and part of Dormitalería street. The second quarter, which was larger, was in what is today *calle de la Merced*. The third quarter was in the area that is covered today by the streets Tejería, San Augustin, and Labrit.

BIBLIOGRAPHY: Baer, Spain, index; Baer, *Urkunden*, 1 (1929), index; M. Kayserling, *Juden in Navarra…* (1861), index; J. Ma. Sanz Artibucilla, in: *Sefarad*, 5 (1945), 339; F. Cantera y Burgos, *Sinagogas españolas* (1955), 263. **ADD. BIBLIOGRAPHY:** F. Juanto Manrique, in: *Ligarzas*, 2 (1970), 77–85; J.J. Martinena Ruiz, *La Pamplona de los burgos y su evolución urbana* (1974), 177–89; J. Carrasco Pérez, in: *Minorités et margineaux en France méridionale et dans la péninsule ibérique (VIIe–XVIIIe siècles)* (1986), 221–63; B.R. Gampel, *The Last Jews on Iberian Soil* (1989).

[Haim Beinart / Yom Tov Assis (2nd ed.)]

PANĂ, SAŞA (originally **Alexander Binder**; 1902–1981), Romanian poet and author. Born in Bucharest, Pană qualified as a physician and, while serving as an army medical officer, achieved a reputation as a writer.

Generally considered the most fanatical propagator of avant-garde literary trends, he was the guiding spirit of the literary review *Unu* (1928–32), Romania's most important avant-garde magazine. Pană's blunt manifesto begins with the words: "Reader, disinfect your brains." His poems are notable for their scorn of literary conformism. He wrote essays and, after World War II, sketches and short stories inspired by army life mainly satirizing the behavior of officers. Pană also wrote some short plays and translations from Paul Eluard and Ilarie *Voronca. Between 1926 and 1968 he published some 30 volumes. In the collection of verse entitled *Pentru libertate* ("For Freedom," 1945) there is a poem about the transportation of Romanian Jews to Transnistria and the crimes committed by the SS. Another volume on the same theme, *Poeme fără imaginaţie* ("Poems without Imagination," 1948) was dedicated "to all the victims of the Nazi brutes… to Benjamin Fordane and Ilarie Voronca…" Pană edited *Uliţa evreească* ("The Jewish Street," 1946), a volume of reproductions of wood carvings by Aurel Mărculescu, and an album by the same author (1967) depicting scenes from life in the Transnistrian camps to which the artists had been transported. In 1969 Pană published an anthology of Romania's avant-garde literature (*Anthologia literaturii românte de avangard*).

BIBLIOGRAPHY: G. Calinescu, *Istoria Literaturii Române…* (1941), 803, 922; L. Cristescu, in: *Contemporanul* (July 2, 1965).

[Dora Litani-Littman]

PANAMA, a republic in Central America. Out of the general population of 2,667,000 (1997), some 7,000 are Jews (1997). The Isthmus of Panama serves as a transit route for merchandise and passengers between South and North America as well as between the Atlantic and the Pacific. Jews and Conversos used those routes; they were present in Panama under camouflage and had a secret place of prayer in "Panama the Old" (a city destroyed by the buccaneer Henry Morgan).

In the Virgin Islands, a hurricane, a tidal wave, and a cholera epidemic during the disastrous year of 1867 sent a wave of Jewish immigrants to Panama. They were joined by Jews from Jamaica and Curaçao. From 1852 "The Hebrew Benevolent Society" had existed in Panama City, and in 1867 the Jews were numerous enough to found, under the leadership of Elias Nunez Martinez, "The Kol Shearith Israel Burial and Charitable Society," and the cornerstone of the Jewish cemetery was laid. From the earliest days the settlement of Spanish-Portuguese Jews was held in high esteem by the population and the authorities.

In 1890 a congregation was formed in the city of Colon, "Kahal Kadosh Yangakob" (The Holy Congregation of Jacob). A synagogue was inaugurated on April 13, 1913.

In Panama City, following Colon's lead, there was a Jewish "Hall of Worship" and a Spanish-Portuguese synagogue was finally inaugurated on March 15, 1935. Under the influence of the majority, consisting of Virgin Island Jews, Reform Judaism was adopted.

The community Kol Shearith Israel established a sisterhood, which was instrumental in 1954 in founding a Jewish day school, Instituto Albert Einstein, which consists of pre-primary, primary, and secondary grades and provides general and Jewish education on high academic standards to a large number of Jewish children. While opposing the formation of a Zionist organization, the community supported the State of Israel. Members of the community became quite prominent in Panamanian life: Joshua Lindo was one of the leaders for the independence of Panama from Colombia; David Henry Brandon founded the fire corps, fire being one of the main causes of disaster in Panama; Herbert de Castro founded the Panama philharmonic orchestra; Edward Maduro wrote the words of the patriotic "March of Panama"; Aida de Castro, known in Panama as the "angel of Dalo Seco," organized the leper colony and worked to eradicate leprosy; Max Shalom Delvalle was president of the republic in 1967; Eric Shalom Delvalle Maduro was president in 1984–85.

After World War I a large Jewish immigration came from Syria and Palestine, evolving into the largest community in Panama, "Shevet Ahim," which followed the strictly Orthodox rite. They also help found a religious Jewish school in 1977 – Academia Hebrea de Panamá.

Ashkenazi Jews, who began to arrive in the 1930s, established the "Beit El" community and synagogue.

Owing to intermarriages, the Kol Shearith Israel congregation diminished considerably.

A small community existed in the American Canal Zone; the city of Balboa was home to its synagogue, which ceased to exist with the closing of the Canal Zone.

With the movement of Jews to the capital city Panamá, the two synagogues in Colon – Agudat Ahim and Kahal Kadosh Yangakob – disbanded, as did the small synagogue in the city of David. A central council acts as a unifying body for the congregations in Panama. WIZO and B'nai B'rith are active.

Whereas most Ashkenazi and Oriental Jews deal mainly in commerce, the Spanish-Portuguese Jewish families continued the Caribbean tradition of plantations, agro-industry, shipping, and banking.

Jews are also active in the political, academic, industrial, and scientific life of Panama, and a significant number of Jews are government ministers, mayors, university rectors, and entrepreneurs.

In the early 21st century there were four synagogues in Panama, three of them Orthodox and one Conservative. Shevet Ahim, the largest communal organization, inaugurated its second synagogue, Ahavat Sion, in 1999, in honor of Rabbi Sion Levy, who had been serving as its spiritual leader for more than half a century. This community has a membership of 700 families, most of them of Aleppan origin, who lead a strictly Orthodox way of life that influences also other sectors. Beit El, the Ashkenazi community, has a membership of 80 families and is led by Rabbi Aaron Layne of Chabad Lubavitch. About 85 percent of the Jewish households keep kosher, and there are a large number of kosher services. Kol Shearith Israel, with about 150 families, is liberal-progressive in its religious outlook. In 2000 it opened the Jewish school Colegio Isaac Rabin.

In the UN Assembly of November 1947, Panama voted in favor of the partition of Palestine and the foundation of two states: Jewish and Arab. Relations with Israel are cordial. Israel maintained an embassy in Panama until 2003; Panama has an embassy in Israel.

BIBLIOGRAPHY: H. de Lima Jesurun, *La Communidad Judía de Panamá* (1977); E.A. Fidanque, *Jews and Panama* (1970); *Kol Shearith Israel – Cien Años* (1977); A. Osorio Osorio, *Judaísmo e inquisición en Panamá Colonial* (1980); idem, *Medio milenio de presencia hebrea en Panama* (2004).

[Mordechai Arbell (2nd ed.)]

PANET, EZEKIEL BEN JOSEPH (1783–1845), Transylvanian rabbi. He was born in Bielitz (Bielsko), Silesia. Under the *Familiants Laws, as the second son of his father, he was forbidden to marry in the country and went to Linsk in Poland. He continued his studies in Linsk until 1807, when he was appointed rabbi of Ostrik in Galicia, and in 1813 became rabbi of Tarcal in Hungary. Panet held the ḥasidic rabbis in high esteem and maintained close contacts with them. While in Tarcal he became particularly intimate with the ḥasidic rabbi Isaac *Taub, the rabbi of Nagykallo. According to the inscription on his tombstone, Panet also engaged in Kabbalah.

After the death of R. Mendel, the rabbi of Alba-Iulia, in 1823, the community asked R. Moses *Sofer to recommend a successor. Panet was one of three candidates recommended by Sofer, and he was elected, serving until his death. From 1754 to 1868 the rabbi of this ancient community was regarded as the chief rabbi of Transylvania, and in fact his seal bore the Latin inscription: *Supperabi Transilvaniae-sigil-Ezechiel Panet.*

The Jewish population of the district was small at the time, and religious life was at a low ebb. Panet acted energetically in bringing about a religious revival. Since there were practically no other rabbis in the province, he supervised the religious life of the whole area, making regular journeys for this purpose to the smallest and most isolated communities. During his period of office the community of Alba-Iulia gradually transferred from the Sephardi rite, which had hitherto prevailed, to the Ashkenazi. Although according to a family tradition Panet left about 18 bound volumes in manuscript, only one of his works was published (posthumously): the responsa *Mareh Yeḥezkel u-She'arei Ẓiyyon* (1875). It is the first volume of responsa of a Transylvanian rabbi, and in addition to its halakhic value is important as a source for the contemporary history of the Jews of Transylvania. Panet also collected funds for the Hungarian *kolel in Ereẓ Israel. Panet's descendants (some of whom spelled their name Paneth) were well-known rabbis in the Orthodox communities of Transylvania and Hungary. A genealogical table of his descendants and where they served as rabbis appears in the work of his descendant Philip Paneth (see bibl.). One of his sons, MENAHEM MENDEL (d. 1884), founded the Dej ḥasidic dynasty.

BIBLIOGRAPHY: "*Toledot Yeḥezkel*," in: H.B. Panet, *Derekh Yivḥar* (1894); M. Eisler, in: IMIT (1901), 241–3; P. Paneth, *Rabbenu Jecheskël* (Eng., 1927); J.J. Cohen, in: *Ha-Ma'yan*, 4 no. 2 (1964), 34–45.

[Yehouda Marton]

PANETH, FRIEDRICH ADOLF (1887–1958), Austrian physical and radioactivity chemist. Paneth, a son of Joseph Paneth, a physiologist who discovered certain histological cells which still bear his name, was born in Vienna. Both his parents were born Jews, but they brought up their children as Protestants. Paneth worked from 1912 to 1917 at the Institute for Radium Research in Vienna, where with the Hungarian chemist George Hevesy he carried out the first use of radioactive tracers to measure physical properties. From 1918 he held professorships successively at the Prague Institute of Technology, and Hamburg, Berlin, Koenigsberg universities. When the Nazis came to power in 1933 he went to London, where he worked first at the Imperial College and then as reader in atomic chemistry in the University of London. In 1939 he was appointed professor of chemistry at Durham University, where he remained for 14 years. During this time he was chairman of the chemistry division of the British Canadian atomic energy team in Montreal (1943–45). In 1947 he was elected a fellow of the Royal Society. On his retirement from Durham in 1953 he returned to Germany as director of the Max Planck Institute for Chemistry at Mainz.

Paneth's prolific output of scientific papers dealt mainly with radioactive tracers, free radicals, and neutron radiation. He developed new methods for the analysis of helium and used them to determine the age and origin of meteorites. His books include *Radio-Elements as Indicators, and Other Selected Topics in Inorganic Chemistry* (1928) and *The Origin of Meteorites* (1940).

BIBLIOGRAPHY: H. Dingle et al. (eds.), *Chemistry and Beyond* (1964); H.J. *Emeléus*, in: Royal Society of London, *Biographical Memoirs*, 6 (1960), 227–46; *Chemiker-Zeitung*, 81 (1957), 618.

[Samuel Aaron Miller]

PANEVEZYS (**Panevezhis**; Lith. **Panevežys**; Rus. **Ponevezh**), city in N. Lithuanian S.S.R. In 1766 the Jewish community numbered 254; in 1847, 1,447 Jews were registered, and in 1897, 6,627 Jews (50% of the total population) lived in Panevezys. An ancient *Karaite community is also known to have existed there. A number of noted rabbis officiated in Panevezys, among them Isaac Jacob *Rabinovich (Itzele Ponevezher), Joseph Sh. *Kahaneman, and Jeroham Leibovich. The Hebrew poet Judah Leib *Gordon served as a teacher in the city from 1853 to 1860. Naphtali *Friedman, a noted advocate, served as delegate from Panevezys to the third *Duma.

In May 1915, during World War I, the Jews of Panevezys were sent along with other Lithuanian Jews to the interior of Russia by the Russian military authorities. Most of them returned after the Russian Revolution. In 1923 there were 6,845 Jews living in Panevezys (35% of the total population), most of them occupied in small trade and crafts and some in larger business enterprises and industry.

The community had an active social and cultural life. Its educational institutions included Hebrew and Yiddish primary schools, two Hebrew secondary schools (one belonging to the Zionist-orientated *Tarbut educational system and the other, for girls, to the religious Yavneh), a Jewish pro-gymnasium, and libraries.

The Panevezys Yeshivah, which had a high reputation, was founded by Liebe Miriam Gavronsky, daughter of K.Z. Wissotszky. When the Jews were expelled during World War I, the yeshivah was first moved to *Ludza in Vitebsk province and then to Mariupol (*Zhdanov) in the Ukraine. After World War I Rabbi Kahaneman founded the great Ohel Yiẓḥak yeshivah in Panevezys with about 200 students. In 1944 the yeshivah was reestablished by Rabbi Kahaneman in *Bene Berak, Israel.

Panevezys was occupied by the Germans in 1941 a few days after the outbreak of the German-Soviet war. A ghetto was established from which Jews were transported and murdered in September 1941. They were buried in 12 mass graves. In 1968 the Jewish cemetery at Panevezys was destroyed.

BIBLIOGRAPHY: *Lite*, 1 (1951), index; 2 (1965), index; *Yahadut Lita*, 1 (1959), index; 3 (1967), 335–7; J. Gar, in: *Algemeyne Entsiklopedie: Yidn*, 6 (1964), index.

[Joseph Gar]

PANIGEL, ELIYAHU MOSHE (1850–1919), Sephardi chief rabbi of Ereẓ Israel. Orphaned in childhood, Panigel was raised by his uncle, the Sephardi chief rabbi of Ereẓ Israel (*rishon le-Zion*), Rabbi Raphael Meir *Panigel. He was sent on fund-raising missions to Algeria by the Misgav la-Dakh Hospital in Jerusalem and to North Africa, Italy, India, the Caucasus and Bokhara, by the Jerusalem community. An outstanding preacher and cantor, he eulogized Herzl in Jerusalem upon his death in 1904. In 1907 he was appointed *ḥakham bashi* (chief rabbi of the Ottoman Empire) and Sephardi chief rabbi of Ereẓ Israel but was forced to resign in 1908. When Jerusalem was captured by the British in 1917, he publicly welcomed General Allenby and the Jewish Legion.

BIBLIOGRAPHY: M.D. Gaon, *Yehudei ha-Mizraḥ be-Ereẓ Yisrael*, 1 (1928), 527–30.

[Geulah Bat Yehuda (Raphael)]

PANIGEL, RAPHAEL MEIR BEN JUDAH (1804–1893), chief rabbi of Jerusalem. Panigel was born in Bulgaria, but when he was three years old his parents, who were well-to-do, emigrated to Ereẓ Israel. In 1828 and in 1863 he went as an emissary of Jerusalem to the countries of North Africa, remaining there on both occasions for several years. In 1845 he went to Italy as an emissary of Hebron. While in Rome he succeeded in making peace between two rival factions in the community. He was also received with great respect at the Vatican by Pope Gregory XVI. In 1866 he supported Ludwig August *Frankl in his endeavor to establish a modern school in Jerusalem. In 1880 he was appointed *rishon le-Zion, and in 1890 the Turkish authorities appointed him *ḥakham bashi* (head of the Jewish community of Ereẓ Israel). He was acceptable to all the communities and esteemed by the authorities. He was the author of *Lev Marpe* (the initials of his name; 1887), talmudic novellae, responsa, and homilies. Some of his novellae were published in the Jerusalem *Me'assef* and in *Torah mi-Ẓiyyon*. His other works have remained in manuscript.

BIBLIOGRAPHY: A.M. Luncz, in: *Yerushalayim*, 4 (1892), 214–5 (Heb. pt.); Frumkin-Rivlin, 3 (1929), 312; M.D. Gaon, *Yehudei ha-Mizraḥ be-Ereẓ Yisrael*, 2 (1937), 533–4; Yaari, Sheluḥei, index, s.v.

[Abraham David]

PANKEN, JACOB (1879–1968), judge and U.S. Socialist leader. Born in the Ukraine, Panken was taken to the United States as a child. He worked in leather factories in New York City and attended school in the evenings. Panken was admitted to the bar in 1905. In 1917, he was elected a judge of New York City's Municipal Court and served until 1928. In 1934 he was appointed a judge of the Domestic Relations Court, a post which he held for 20 years. Panken was attracted to the labor movement from his youth. At the age of 18 he organized a leather goods union and later helped found the Ladies Garment Workers Union (1900). In those days, gangsters had ties with employers as well as with politicians in New York City's East Side. Thus, prominent figures in the socialist movement were the objects of violence. Panken was shot at in 1904 and assaulted by thugs in 1906.

Panken represented U.S. Socialists at a number of international congresses and at the same time maintained an association with Jewish movements. When World War I broke out, he was one of the organizers of the People's Relief Committee to aid the Jews of Eastern Europe. Later, he helped to organize the American branch of *ORT and for many years was its president. He was also president of the *Jewish Daily Forward* from 1917 to 1925. His writings include *Socialism in America* (1931) and *The Child Speaks: The Prevention of Juvenile Delinquency* (1941).

[Charles Reznikoff]

PANN, ABEL (**Abba Pfefferman**; 1883–1963), Israeli painter and draftsman. Pann was born in Kreslawka in the Vitebsk region of White Russia. Although his father Nahum was a rabbi and the head of a yeshivah, he did not object to his son becoming a painter, and even encouraged it. Until he was 20 years old, Pann received an Orthodox Jewish education. His first art teacher was Judah Pan of Vitebsk, who also taught Marc Chagall and Ossip Zadkine. In 1898 Pann began his art studies in the Academy of Fine Arts in Odessa, while at the same time being involved with Zionist activities. The most significant experience in Pann's life was his traveling to Kishinev after the pogroms (1903) as part of delegations that were dispatched to document the horrors.

From 1903 until 1913 he stayed in Paris, learning sketching and painting models at the Académie Julian. In this period Pann gained fame as a caricaturist. Pann arrived in Jerusalem as a part of a world journey. At the invitation of Boris Schatz, director of the Bezalel art academy, he stayed to teach and became deputy director for one year. During World War I Pann, who had returned to Paris to settle his affairs, was forced to remain there until the end of the war. In May 1920 Pann returned to teach at Bezalel; in 1924 he resigned to dedicate himself to biblical painting. Until his last day Pann continued to paint biblical scenes. In the Israeli art world his work was identified as part of the Jewish Art movement that was rejected by the modern Israeli view of the arts in the 1940s and later. In the Jewish world his art was a success. An exhibition of his art at the Israel Museum in 2003 promoted new awareness of the power of his art, especially his biblical paintings.

Pann's artistic style ranged from the humoristic to agony paintings, and then again to beauty and colorful visions. The suffering of the Jews in pogroms again became a part of his artistic creation in the series *The Jug of Tears* (1915–16, Israel Museum, Jerusalem). This series included 50 pastel drawings on cardboard. The series' sketches created the impression of journalistic documentation of the expelled Jews, desolated towns, rapes, and murders.

Pann's attitude toward the biblical scene was influenced by his journeys in Ereẓ Israel. Pann's confrontation with eastern figures, such as the Arabs and the Bedouins, reinforced biblical myth for him and provided a picture of realistic existence relevant to the biblical heroes. The audience for Pann's art, especially the Zionists among them, would identify with those feelings.

BIBLIOGRAPHY: Y. Zalmona, *The Art of Abel Pann: From Montparnasse to the Land of the Bible* (2003); Jerusalem, Mayanot Gallery, *Abel Pann 1883–1963* (1987).

[Ronit Steinberg (2nd ed.)]

PANOFSKY, ERWIN (1892–1968), U.S. art historian. Born in Hanover, Germany, he studied at universities in Berlin, Munich, and Breslau, receiving his Ph.D. from the University of Freiburg in 1914. He taught at the University of Hamburg from 1926 to 1933. After the Nazis achieved power in Germany, Panofsky was dismissed from his position and fled to the U.S. in 1934. Despite this traumatic period, Panofsky never publicly addressed his Jewish identity, and instead promulgated a liberal humanism in his writing about art. His scholarship on Jan van Eyck describes a particular German contribution to art history, perhaps arising from a need for an exile to identify a period in German history unsullied by the Nazis. Beginning in 1935, he was a professor of art history at the Institute for Advanced Studies at Princeton University, at the same time that Albert Einstein taught there. He remained at Princeton for the remainder of his life. He wrote on art from the medieval, Baroque, and Renaissance periods and developed the study of iconology in art history, that is, the manner in which theme, style, and symbol intersect in an image. His differentiation of iconography, that is, the descriptive aspects of a work of art, from iconology, a deeper level of interpretation which involves situating the image in a wider social, institutional, and cultural context, still defines the purview of modern art history. Panofsky is best known for his publications *Studies in Iconology* (1939); *Albrecht Durer* (1943); *Early Netherlandish Painting* (1953), with Dora Panofsky; *Pandora's Box: The Changing Aspects of a Mythical Symbol* (1956); and *Meaning in the Visual Arts* (1957). He also wrote in 1934 a still widely read interpretation of Jan van Eyck's *Arnolfini Wedding*. Panofsky's "Style and Medium in the Moving Pictures" (1937) is regarded as a classic film commentary. He was a member of the American Academy of Arts and Sciences and the British Academy; he received the Haskins Medal of the Medieval Academy of America in 1962.

BIBLIOGRAPHY: D. Kuspit, "Taking Refuge in Humanism: The Troubling Views of Erwin Panofsky," in: *The Forward* (Aug. 2, 1996); C. Landauer, "Erwin Panofsky and the Renascence of the Renaissance," in: *Renaissance Quarterly* (June 1994).

[Nancy Buchwald (2nd ed.)]

PANOV, VALERY (**Valery Matyevich Shulman**; 1938–), Russian/Israeli dancer and choreographer. He was born in Witebsk and changed his name to Panov in 1958. He studied at the Leningrad choreographic school (1951–1957) and also at the Vilnius ballet school (1953–56) as well as at the Moscow choreographic school (1954). In his Russian career Panov was the leading dancer of the Leningrad Maly Theater Ballet (1957–1964) and soloist of the Kirov Ballet (1963–72) from which he was expelled and briefly imprisoned after his application for an exit visa to Israel. In 1974 he left the Soviet Union with his wife, dancer Galina Pavlova, for Israel, where he appeared as guest artist with the *Batsheva and Bat-Dor dance companies (1974–77). Thereafter he was guest choreographer and principal dancer at the German opera ballet and staged ballets in San Francisco, Vienna, Stockholm, Antwerp, and Santiago.

Panov, who was one of the greatest virtuoso dancers in the Soviet Union, received the Lenin Prize in 1969 and the title of Honored Artist of the Russian Federation. He also published an autobiography in 1978.

In 2000 Panov founded in the Israeli city of Ashdod the Panov Theater and ballet school. His troupe of 24 dancers regularly performs ballets staged by him.

BIBLIOGRAPHY: IDB, 2:1068–71.

[Amnon Shiloah (2nd ed.)]

PAP, ARTHUR (1921–1959), philosopher. Born and brought up in Zurich, where his father was a successful businessman, he moved to New York in 1941. He taught at the University of Chicago, where he was greatly influenced by Rudolf Carnap, one of the founders of the Vienna school of Logical Positivism. Pap assumed a teaching position at Yale University in the mid-1950s.

Considered one of the ablest philosophers of his generation, Pap developed a modified, flexible type of logical positivism. The flexible approach that characterized his work is clearly seen in his five books and numerous articles, particularly in *Semantics and Necessary Truth* (1958), which is perhaps the most careful and meticulous inquiry into the notion of necessary proof. His *Elements of Analytic Philosophy* (1949) and *An Introduction to the Philosophy of Science* (1962) reflect his desire to make science philosophically accurate in its formulations and to make philosophy scientific in its approach.

BIBLIOGRAPHY: *New York Times* (Sept. 8, 1959), 35.

PAP, KÁROLY (1897–1945), Hungarian author. Born in Sopron, where his father Miksa *Pollák was the rabbi of the Neolog community, Pap was an officer in the Austro-Hungarian army during World War I and was decorated for bravery. After demobilization, he joined Béla *Kun's October Revolution and became a Hungarian Red Army commander. On the collapse of the revolution he was arrested, reduced to the ranks, and condemned to 18 months' imprisonment. After his release he left the country until 1925. Then, settling in Budapest, he began writing poetry and stories. He soon became known as a short story writer, but wishing to remain independent, he refused to take any employment.

Pap's first novel, *Megszabaditottál a haláltól* ("Thou Hast Delivered Me from Death," 1932), which dealt with a popular

Jewish Messiah in the time of Jesus, was enthusiastically received by liberal and radical writers, notably the great Hungarian author, Zsigmond Móricz, who gave him much encouragement. The character of Jesus and the period in which he lived recur constantly in Pap's writings, not because of any attraction to Christianity but because, in his opinion, this "classical" period of Judaism retained traces of the Divinity, and at the same time presented social contrasts and gave Jews the taste of suffering. His great autobiographical novel, *Azarel* (1937), which portrayed his father's house through the eyes of a child, aroused great indignation among some Jewish readers because of the cruel frankness of its descriptions. In his sensational essay, *Zsidó sebek és bűnök* ("Jewish Wounds and Sins," 1935), Pap made a thorough and candid analysis of his Jewish and non-Jewish social surroundings. He traced the history of the Jews, particularly of Hungarian Jewry, in order to expose conventional lies, especially those concerning emancipation. He found only one solution to the Jewish problem: acceptance of the fate of a national minority. He himself was fanatically attached to all aspects of Jewish life and was uncompromising in his loyalty.

During World War II the Budapest Jewish Theater performed two biblical plays by Pap: *Bathsheba* (1940) and *Moses* (1944). In May 1944 he was sent to a labor camp. From there he refused to escape and was deported to Buchenwald, and is presumed to have died in Bergen-Belsen. Three works which appeared posthumously were *A szűziesség fátylai* ("The Veils of Chastity," 1945), *A hószobor* ("The Snow Statue," 1954) and *B városában történt* ("It Happened in the City B," 2 vols., 1964).

BIBLIOGRAPHY: *Magyar Irodalmi Lexikon*, 2 (1965), 433–4; D. Keresztúry, in: Pap Károly, *A hószobor* (1954), introd.; A. Komlós, in: *Nyugat*, 2 (1935), 41–43.

[Baruch Yaron]

PAPA (c. 300–375), Babylonian *amora*. Papa studied under *Rava (Er. 51a) and Abbaye (Ber. 20a). After the latter's death he founded an academy at *Naresh (near Sura), where he held the post of *resh metivta* (head of the academy) (Ta'an. 9a) for 19 years, until his death. Although some of Rava's former pupils expressed dissatisfaction with Papa's teaching (*ibid.*), his academy was famous for the number of its pupils (Ket. 106a). The extent of Papa's learning is revealed by the number of occasions in which he participated in halakhic disputes. Papa's opinions are frequently the last ones quoted in the talmudic *sugyot*, and often take the form of reconciling and accepting conflicting opinions (Meg. 21b; Ta'an. 29b; Ḥul. 46a). In these cases he prefaces his decision with the word *hilkakh* "therefore." In other cases he uses the expression *shema mina*, "from this we can deduce" (the *halakhah* in a certain matter; Yoma 28b; Yev. 103a).

Papa belonged to a wealthy family and increased his fortune by his own successful business ventures (Pes. 113a). He engaged in the sale of poppy seeds (Git. 73a) and in the expert brewing of date beer (Ber. 44b; Pes. 113a; BM 65a). Rava commented on his wealth by adapting Ecclesiastes 8:14, stating "Happy are the righteous, who prosper in this world" (Hor. 10b). On one occasion Papa had to defend himself against a charge of practicing usury (BM 65a). On another, however, his action in returning some land which he had bought from a man who needed the money was praised as going beyond the strict requirements of the law (Ket. 97a). Papa was renowned for his impartiality in judgment (BM 69a) and his piety (Shab. 118b; Nid. 12b). He also had a deep respect for his fellow scholars (MK 17a) and made a point of visiting the local rabbi of any town he visited (Nid. 33b). He once undertook a self-imposed fast in atonement for speaking unkindly of a scholar (Sanh. 100a), although fasting did not agree with him (Ta'an. 24b). On another occasion, when he heard a particularly wise decision from a student, he offered him his daughter's hand in marriage (Hor. 12b). His deepest affections were reserved for his colleague Huna ben Joshua (Shab. 89a), the friendship dating from their student days (Pes. 111b; Hor. 10b). Huna served as Papa's deputy at Naresh (Ber. 57a; *Sherira Ga'on* 3:3) and was his business partner (Git. 73a). It is related that the two refused to part even for a journey (Yev. 85a).

In the course of his many business travels, Papa collected numerous popular sayings which he often quoted in discussion. Among them are: "If you hear that your neighbor has died, believe it; if you hear that he has become rich, do not believe it" (Git. 30b); "Sow corn for your use that you should not be obliged to purchase it; and strive to acquire landed property" (Yev. 63a). He also suggested advice on family relationships: "If your wife is short bend down to hear her whisper," i.e., always consult her, even if she is less important than you are (BM 59a). Papa's second wife was the daughter of Abba of Sura (Ket. 39b).

The formula to be recited at a *hadran on the completion of the study of a tractate includes the recitation of the names of 10 "sons of Papa." Although all are mentioned in the Talmud, some of them are definitely not the sons of this Papa (e.g., Surḥav and Daru). Among the various reasons that have been given for this recital is that it assists the memory.

BIBLIOGRAPHY: Hyman, Toledot, s.v.; J. Newman, *The Agricultural Life of the Jews in Babylonia* (1932), index s.v. *R. Pappa*; Ḥ. Albeck, *Mavo la-Talmudim* (1969), 417–80. Epstein, *Introduction*, 391–93.

PAPA (Hung, **Pápa**), town in N.W. Hungary. A few families first settled in Papa under the protection of the Esterházy family; by 1714 the first synagogue was built. At that time the tax collector of the city was a Jew. A new synagogue was built in 1743. In 1748 Count F. Esterházy authorized Jews to settle in Papa and organize a community. A Bikkur Ḥolim society was founded in 1770. The first Jewish private school was opened in 1812, and the community school, founded in 1826, had 504 pupils in 1841. In 1899 the first junior high school was founded. The synagogue erected in 1846 was an important step toward the introduction of Reform: Space was left for an organ although none was installed; the *bimah was set in front of the Ark and not in the center of the synagogue. After the religious schism in Hungarian Jewry in 1869 the *Neologists left the community, but returned five years later. During the *Tiszaeszlar blood libel case (1882) anti-Jewish riots broke out in Papa but they were suppressed by the authorities.

The first rabbi of the community was Bernard Isaac, followed by Selig Bettelheim. The Orthodox rabbi Paul (Feiwel) Horwitz initiated the meeting of rabbis in *Paks in 1844. Leopold *Loew (1846–50) was the first rabbi to introduce Reform. Moritz *Klein, rabbi from 1876 to 1880, translated part of *Maimonides' *Guide of the Perplexed* into Hungarian. He was followed by Solomon *Breuer (1880–83). The last rabbi was J. Haberfeld, who perished with his congregation in the Holocaust.

The anti-Jewish laws of 1938–39 caused great hardship in the community, and from 1940 the young Jewish men were sent to forced-labor battalions, at first within Hungary, but later to the Russian front (1942). The Jewish population in Papa increased from 452 in 1787 to 2,645 in 1840 (19.6% of the total population), and 3,550 in 1880 (24.2%). After the beginning of the 20th century a gradual decline began; there were 3,076 Jews in 1910 (15.3%), 2,991 in 1920, 2,613 in 1941 (11%) and 2,565 in 1944. After the German occupation on March 19, 1944, the Jews were confined in a ghetto on May 24 with another 2,800 Jews from nearby villages. All were deported to Auschwitz in the beginning of July. In 1946 there were 470 Jews in the town (2% of the population) and by 1970 the number had fallen to 40.

BIBLIOGRAPHY: J. Barna and F. Csukási, *A magyar zsidó felekezet… iskoláinak monográfiája* (1896); *Zsidó Világkongresszus Magyarországi Képviselete Statisztikai Osztályának Közleményei*, 4 (1947); 8–9 (1948); 13–14 (1949); *Új Élet*, 25 (1970), 1.

[Laszlo Harsanyi]

PAPER-CUTS. Jewish paper-cuts present an interesting branch of traditional folk art which fulfilled a specific part in the life of the community. The subjects of Jewish paper-cuts were connected with customs and ceremonies, and associated with holidays and family life. They were encountered widely among the Jews of Poland and Russia in the 19th century and the early years of the 20th century; Jewish paper-cuts were also known in Germany and probably in Holland; some Italian Jewish parchment *ketubbot* (marriage contracts) of the late 17th, 18th, and 19th centuries were decorated with cut-outs as well as some elaborate *Scrolls of Esther. Paper-cuts are also to be found – with some characteristic style differences – in North Africa and the Middle East. But most information available concerns the East European cut-outs.

The cut-out is basically a pattern cut out of paper, often tinted and mounted on a layer of different color. Sheets of paper were usually folded, with half a design drawn on one side. The folded sheet was then fastened with thin nails to a wooden board and the design cut out with a sharp knife. By unfolding the paper a symmetrical design was obtained. Circular or multilateral designs were folded several times and asymmetrical compositions were cut out separately.

Paper-cuts present a rich variety of forms and motifs with texts drawn from the Holy Scriptures.

Motifs

In the center there is usually the seven-branched *menorah*, the Ten Commandments, or a Torah scroll; at the top they are decorated with a crown, Magen David, or an eagle. They are surrounded by motifs from the animal world and plant life, or geometrical forms. Among the animals the most frequent are lions, deer, eagles, and tigers, which have a symbolic connotation (Avot 5:23). Sometimes bears, camels, and a wide selection of birds are used; mythological figures such as winged gryphons, cherubs, and leviathans; or the old motif of the tree of life; the symbols of the 12 signs of the Zodiac are also frequently used.

Types

MIZRAḤ AND SHIVVITI. The *Mizraḥ* ("East") was the most impressive and intricate form of Jewish paper-cuts hung up in homes and in synagogues on the eastern wall to indicate the direction of prayer (to Jerusalem). The *Mizraḥ* in the synagogue was generally called *Shivviti* according to the saying "*Shivviti Adonai le-Negdi Tamid*" ("I have set the Lord always before me"; Ps. 16:8) which appears mostly on these paper-cuts. Usually rectangular and framed under glass, they were made of white paper, almost always tinted with water colors and inscribed with biblical sayings. These paper-cuts presented artists with vast opportunities to exercise their skill, and are often admired for their delicacy and finesse.

"*Shevuoslekh*" and "*Royselekh*" represent another widely encountered type of paper-cuts, rectangular or circular, used to decorate the windows on Shavuot: "*Shevuosl*" from the name of the holiday; "*Roysele*" from rosette or flower. It was customary on this holiday to decorate the doors with greenery, while these paper-cuts were stuck onto the glass panes of the small windows of Jewish homes. Thus they were smaller than the *Mizraḥ*, made of white paper, seldom colored, and often displayed the short text "*Ḥag ha-Shavuot ha-Zeh*" ("this holiday of Shavuot"). While most of them show the usual motifs, some depict soldiers and cavalrymen, a subject which seems to have excited the imagination of the Talmud students poring over their books. Visible from the street, they must have been familiar to non-Jews as well. "Torah Flags," carried by children at the Simḥat Torah processions, were often decorated with these cuts. At the top of the flag stick, candles were fixed inside apples or potatoes. The motifs of the flags were symbols of the 12 tribes or contained inscriptions suitable for the festival of Simḥat Torah. They were two-sided and made of colored paper.

A "*Kimpetbriv*" or "*Shir-Hamales*" was a kind of amulet put up on the four walls of the birth room to protect the mother and her newborn child against the evil power of the witch *Lilith, who, according to ancient beliefs, snatched the infants away. Texts included "Let the witch perish," "God will destroy devils," etc. The center always featured a psalm beginning with the words *"Shir ha-Ma'alot"* ("A song of degrees"; cf. Ps. 120), from which the amulet took its name. The expression *kimpet* derives from the old Yiddish-German *kindbett* ("childbed"), while *brivl* means "letter" or "note." Others were calendars, to count the days of the Omer; *"Ushpizin"* to hang up in the *sukkah*; *"Mi-she-Nikhnas Adar,"* displayed on the walls of the synagogue during the month of Adar, etc. Paper lanterns whose sides were decorated with cut-outs were lit during open air weddings or on memorial days of great rabbis.

The beginning of the 20th century saw the disappearance of the Jewish paper-cuts and only old people remembered the art of their youth. Many of those preserved were destroyed during World War II and relatively few remain in public or private collections. In the late 20th century Jewish paper-cuts became a popular art form.

The paper-cuts from North Africa and the Middle East were called *Menorah*, because the *menorah*, one or more, always appeared as the central motif. They included many inscriptions, mostly on the arms of the candelabras. The underlayer of these cut-outs was made from thin, colored metal sheets. Two groups stand out. The first group is a counterpart of the *Mizraḥ* and the second includes smaller paper-cuts used as charms. The motifs are the same as in European paper-cuts but they have a specific Oriental style. Very often the *ḥamsa* ("the five-finger hand"), unknown in Europe, appears on these paper-cuts.

Origin

It would be difficult to determine when the first Jewish paper-cuts originated. Information dating from as far back as the 17th and 18th centuries points to the fact that the European Jews of this time were acquainted with this type of art. The fact, however, that Jewish paper-cuts can be traced to Syria, Iraq, and North Africa, and that there is a similarity in the cutting techniques (with a knife) between those of East European Jews, and those of the Chinese, in their ancient folk craft, may indicate that the origin goes back even further.

BIBLIOGRAPHY: B.W. Segel, in: *Globus*, 61 (1892), 235; R. Lilienthal, *święta żydowskie* (1909), 249; J. Reizes, in: *Das Zelt*, 1 (1924), pt. 2; G. Frankel, in: *Lud*, 8 (Pol., 1929); idem, in: Haifa, Museum of Ethnology and Folklore, *Catalog* (Heb. and Eng., 1959); idem, in: JC (Dec. 11, 1964); idem, in: *Polska Sztuka Ludowa*, 3 (1965); idem, in: *Jewish Heritage* (Fall, 1967); M. Narkis, in: *Ofakim*, 2 (1944); F. Landesberger, in: HUCA, 26 (1955), 516; Mayer, Art, index.

[Giza Frankel]

PAPERNA, ABRAHAM BARUCH (d. 1863), Italian Hebrew writer and anthologist. Born in Leghorn where he also served as rabbi, Paperna was primarily interested in modern Hebrew poetry in Italy. His anthology of this poetry, *Kol Ugav* (1846), contains an appendix with biobibliographical data on the poets. He possessed a collection of manuscripts of authors whose works are reproduced in the anthology, as well as of other writers he mentions. He also contributed introductions to several books that were published in Leghorn. One of his pupils was Sabato *Morais. Ḥ.N. *Bialik (*Iggerot*, 3 (1938), 155) was deeply impressed by his anthology.

[Getzel Kressel]

PAPERNA, ABRAHAM JACOB (1840–1919), Hebrew writer and critic. Paperna, who was born in Kapuli, Russia, was brought up in the spirit of the moderate Haskalah which prevailed in his father's house. In 1861 he started publishing articles and poems in *Ha-Meliẓ* and *Ha-Karmel*. He studied in the government rabbinical seminaries of Zhitomir (1863–64) and Vilna (1864–67). At the same time he became acquainted with Russian literature and was particularly influenced by Russian literary criticism. In 1867 he published a collection of articles entitled *Kankan Ḥadash Male Yashan* ("A New Vessel Full of Old [Wine]"), in which he criticized the Hebrew literature of the Haskalah in the realistic manner introduced by Uri *Kovner. Paperna's aim was to give the Hebrew reader elementary concepts in literary theory and to point out the main weaknesses of the Hebrew literature of his day. The latter included dilettantism, exaggerated use of pompous and ornate language, and versification instead of poetry. At the same time he acknowledged the achievements of contemporary Hebrew literature and paid tribute to some of its leading figures. A bitter controversy arose over Paperna's second brochure *Ha-Dramah bi-Khelal ve-ha-Ivrit bi-Ferat* ("Drama in General and Hebrew Drama in Particular," 1868). The brochure opens with an explanation of the basic concepts of poetry and concentrates upon tragedy, bringing examples from Greek and English drama. It then gives an account of the history of Hebrew drama from M.Ḥ. *Luzzatto to A.D. *Lebensohn's *Emet ve-Emunah*. In *Ha-Meliẓ* (1869), Paperna published an essay *Ha-Avot ve-ha-Banim* by S.Y. * Abramovitsh (Mendele Mokher Seforim). This was to be part of a larger article on the development of the novel but the fierce controversy which this essay engendered apparently deterred him from continuing this work. Upon his graduation from the rabbinical seminary in 1867, he was appointed teacher in the government school in Zakroczym, Poland, and in 1869 he moved to Plotsk where he worked as a teacher for some 45 years. During this time he wrote a number of Hebrew-Russian text books. After a lapse of almost 20 years Paperna returned to the field of Hebrew literature, probably under the influence of the national revival among the Jews in Russia. He wrote poems and essays, as well as two booklets, *Siḥot Ḥayyot ve-Ofot* (1892), and *Mishlei ha-Zeman* (1893), which were sharp satires on modern civilization with allusions to the particular situation of the Jews in Russia. His memoirs appeared in the Russian-Jewish anthology *Perezhitaje*. His works were edited by Y. Zmora and published in Tel Aviv in 1952. Together with his contemporaries Uri Kovner and Mendele Mokher Seforim, Paperna raised

Hebrew literary criticism from the level of personal invective directed against the author to systematic analysis guided by principles of literary forms and aesthetic theory.

BIBLIOGRAPHY: Klausner, Sifrut, 4 (1954²), 176–89; I. Averbuch, in: *Orlogin*, 9 (1953), 166–87; A. Sha'anan, *Ha-Sifrut ha-Ivrit ha-Ḥadashah li-Zrameha*, 1 (1962), 262–6; Waxman, Literature, index s.v. *Papirno*. **ADD. BIBLIOGRAPHY:** M. Ungerfeld, "*A.Y. Paperna*" in: *Ha-Po'el ha-Ẓa'ir*, 40 (1969), 20; A. Kinstler, "*Reshit Bikkoret ha-Deramah ba-Sifrut ha-Ivrit: al Paperna*," in: *Molad*, 2 (1969), 379–390; I. Parush, "*Tarbut ha-Bikkoret u-Vikkoret ha-Tarbut: Iyyunim be-Sifro shel Paperna, Kankan Ḥadash Male Yashan*," in: *Meḥkarei Yerushalayim ba-Sifrut Ivrit*, 14 (1993), 197–239.

[Yehdua Slutsky]

PAPI, name of two *amoraim*.

PAPI I, Babylonian *amora* of the fourth century. A disciple of Rava, the greatest *amora* of his time, he became the son-in-law of R. *Isaac Nappaḥa (Ḥul. 110a) and the head of an academy attended, among others, by Rav *Ashi (Ḥul. 77a; 82a; RH 29b) and Mar *Zutra (Suk. 46a). He was apparently a well-to-do landowner, and, after reciting the sanctification of the Sabbath for his family and students, he would repeat the ceremony for the benefit of his tenants who arrived later from the field (RH 29b). Papi was on friendly terms with the exilarch Mar Samuel, at whose home he would sometimes dine (Beẓah 14b). When the exilarch ordered the case of a certain Bar Ḥama who was charged with murder to be investigated, Papi successfully defended the accused, whereupon the latter "kissed his [Papi's] feet and undertook to pay his poll tax for him for the rest of his life" (Sanh. 27a–b).

PAPI II, Palestinian *amora* of the fourth century, somewhat later than the above. His teacher was Joshua of Sikhnin, and his few recorded sayings are for the most part aggadic traditions in the name of his teacher or in the name of R. Levi, whose traditions were chiefly transmitted by Joshua of Sikhnin. Among the statements cited by him is a prediction that the future rebuilt Jerusalem would be three times or even 30 times as large as the old city (BB 75b).

BIBLIOGRAPHY: Hyman, Toledot, s.v.; Ḥ. Albeck, *Mavo la-Talmudim* (1969), 418–19.

[Moses Aberbach]

PAPIERNIKOV, JOSEPH (1897–1993), Yiddish poet. Born in Warsaw, he attended a Russian secondary school. Because of his fine voice and sensitive ear for music, he was accepted as choir boy by Cantor Gershon *Sirota in the Tlomacka Synagogue in Warsaw. At an early age he joined the Left Po'alei Zion party, which supported the development of a modern Yiddish literature, and there he found the first audience for his lyrics. In 1924 he immigrated to Palestine, where he remained except for an extended sojourn in Poland (1929–33). After his first poem was published in 1918, his melodious poetry, with its rich imagery and folklike quality, was welcomed in numerous Yiddish journals in Poland and other countries, and his lyric "*Zol Zayn az Ikh Boy in der Luft Mayne Shleser*" ("I Build my Castles in the Air"), to which he also composed the music, became a popular folk song. Eight collections of Papiernikov's poems were printed before World War II, including *In Zunikn Land* ("In the Sunny Land," 1927) and *Far Mir un far Ale* ("For Me and the Others," 1936) and a volume of his translations of S. Essenin's poetry (1933). A faithful lyric recorder of the hardships of the pioneers in the Jewish homeland, Papiernikov's post-Holocaust poetry, short stories, and memoirs, which were collected in several volumes, have a more elegiac tonality. He was honored with several literary awards, and a volume of tributes to him was published on the 40th anniversary of his settling in Israel: *40 Yor Papiernikov in Erets-Yisroel* (1965).

BIBLIOGRAPHY: Rejzen, Leksikon, 2 (1927), 870–1; M. Ravitch, *Mayn Leksikon*, 1 (1945), 159–61; 3 (1958), 309–12. **ADD. BIBLIOGRAPHY:** NLYL, 7 (1968), 105–7; D. Sadan, *Heymishe Ksovim*, 1 (1972), 133–9; E.S. Goldsmith, in: *Jewish Book Annual*, 47 (1989), 170–81.

[Israel Ch. Biletzky]

PAPO, IZIDOR JOSEF (1913–1996), Yugoslav surgeon. Born in Ljubusko, Papo received his M.D. from the University of Zagreb in 1937 and specialized in surgery at the state hospital in Sarajevo in 1937–41. During World War II he fought from 1941 in the partisan Yugoslav Liberation Army, advancing to the rank of lieutenant-general and heading the Supreme Command's surgical staff. He became a member of the Communist Party in June 1943. From 1947 he was a professor of surgery and in 1948 head of the surgery clinic of the Yugoslav Military Medical Academy and surgeon-in-chief of the Yugoslav army. He settled in Belgrade. After the war he turned to heart, lung, and respiratory system surgery and wrote papers in the field of general and cardiovascular surgery and was co-deviser of the method of reconstruction of the esophagus known as Yudin-Papo. He was also responsible for various innovations in cardiovascular surgery. Papo received the highest Yugoslav and foreign decorations and awards and was made honorary knight commander in the Order of the British Empire and a fellow of the American College of Cardiology as well as of the British Royal College of Surgeons.

[Eugen Werber]

PAPO, SAMUEL SHEMAIAH (1708–after 1774), Italian rabbi. Papo was apparently born in Ragusa where his father, Abraham David Papo, the teacher of David *Pardo, was rabbi. Many of his father's responsa are preserved in the *Shemesh Ẓedakah* of Samson *Morpurgo. In his early youth Papo moved to Ancona and studied in the *bet midrash* of Joseph Lehava (Fiammetta) and, after the latter's death, in that of his son-in-law, Samson Morpurgo. He also studied under Moses Ḥayyim Morpurgo, son of Samson; Jehiel ha-Kohen; and Isaac Costantini. In July 1758, on the recommendation of Costantini, he was granted the title *ḥakham* by the communal council. From 1756 to 1761 he served as *dayyan of the town and signed all the documents of the *bet din*. From 1761 to 1774 his name no longer appears in the records of the sessions of the *bet din*. He may have left Ancona for business reasons or waived his right to participate in the local *bet din* because of disagreements that broke out between him and Isaac Shabbetai Fiano, rabbi and *av bet din*. In 1753 during Ḥ.J.D. *Azulai's first mission to Italy, Papo exerted himself to extend every honor and esteem to Azulai during his stay in Ancona (from Ḥeshvan 24 to Kislev 12). In his diary, the *Ma'gal Tov* (ed. by A. Freimann (1921), 6), Azulai refers to Papo in terms of respect and admiration: "Master of the Talmud," "the luminary," etc. The close ties of friendship thus formed grew stronger with the passage of time, as is testified by a correspondence still in manuscript. Papo endured much suffering and many troubles during his life because of his unswerving integrity. Many halakhic responsa by him are preserved in manuscript, all testifying to his erudition and acumen.

BIBLIOGRAPHY: Roth, in: *Sinai*, 21 (1947), 326; Wilensky, *ibid.*, 25 (1949), 80–81.

[Guiseppe Laras]

PAPP, JOSEPH (Joseph Papirofsky; 1921–1991), U.S. theatrical producer. Born in Brooklyn, New York, Papp served in the U.S. Navy during World War II (1942–46). He founded the non-profit Shakespeare Workshop in 1954 and had the name changed to the Shakespeare Festival in 1960 which he directed until 1991.

Papp's off-Broadway productions include *Hair* (1967), *The Basic Training of Pavlo Hummel* (1971), *Short Eyes* (1974), *A Chorus Line* (1975), *For Colored Girls Who Have Considered Suicide/When the Rainbow is Enuf* (1976), and *Streamers* (1976). Papp's on-Broadway productions include, *Two Gentlemen of Verona* (1971), *Sticks and Bones* (1972), *That Championship Season* (1972), *Much Ado About Nothing* (1972), and *The Pirates of Penzance* (1980). Papp also produced *The Haggadah* (1981) for PBS Television.

He taught (as an adjunct professor) at both Yale University and Columbia University and received numerous awards and commendations including Tony Awards in 1957, 1958, 1972, 1973, 1976 and 1981. Papp also received multiple Drama Desk and Drama Critics Circle Awards. In 1979 he received Canada's Commonwealth Award of Distinguished Service and in 1981 the American Academy and Institute of Arts and Letters Gold Medal Award for Distinguished Service to the Arts. He believed in the theater as a social force as well as entertainment.

[Jonathan Licht]

PAPPENHEIM, BERTHA (1859–1936), social worker and leader of the German Jewish feminist movement. Born in Vienna to a wealthy Orthodox family, Bertha Pappenheim was treated by Josef *Breuer, a colleague of Sigmund *Freud, who regarded her case ("Anna O.") as a major breakthrough in psychoanalysis. She subsequently moved to Frankfurt and became the headmistress of an orphanage in 1895. In 1904 she founded the *Juedischer Frauenbund (and edited its periodical), affiliated to the German women's movement. She visited Galicia, Romania, and Russia, organizing relief work and aid to refugees. Her major efforts were directed against white slavery, prostitution, and illegitimacy. In 1914 she founded an institute at Neu-Isenburg (near Frankfurt) for unwed mothers, prostitutes, and delinquent women, and later for children as well. Bertha Pappenheim directed her organization with a firm hand and led study groups on the ethics of social work at the Frankfurt Lehrhaus. As a strong advocate of modern Jewish social work, she spearheaded the founding of German Jewry's national social welfare organization, the Zentralwohlfarhtsstelle der deutschen Juden, in 1917. A religious Jew, she remained a vigorous opponent of Zionism. She died soon after she was interrogated by the Gestapo. She translated into German the memoirs of (her ancestor) *Glueckel of Hameln (1910, republished: 2005), the *Ẓe'enah u-Re'enah* (1930), and the *Maaseh Buch* (1929), and wrote under the pen name of Paul Berthold.

BIBLIOGRAPHY: D. Edinger (ed.), *Bertha Pappenheim: Leben und Schriften* (1963); idem, in: JSOS, 20 (1958), 180–6. **ADD. BIBLIOGRAPHY:** M. Kaplan, *The Jewish Feminist Movement in Germany* (1979); G. Maierhof, "Bertha Pappenheim," in: *Wegbereiterinnen der modernen Sozialarbeit* (1999), 63–85; M. Brentzel, *Anna O. – Bertha Pappenheim* (2002); M. Brentzel, *Sigmund Freuds Anna O. – Das Leben der Bertha Pappenheim* (2004); G. Maierhof and C. Wenzel, *Ariadne. Forum fuer Frauen-und Geschlectergeschichte. Juedisch-Sein, Frau-Sein, Bund-Sein. Der Juedische Frauenbund 1904–2004*, no. 45/46.

PAPPENHEIM, SOLOMON (1740–1814), Hebrew linguist and poet. Born in Zuelz (Germany), Pappenheim served as a *dayyan* in Breslau until his death. He first became known as a linguist in his three-part *Yeri'ot Shelomo* (1784, 1811, and 1831), a study of synonyms. Although an ardent advocate of the Haskalah, Pappenheim opposed religious reforms and David *Friedlaender's proposal (1812) that education be entrusted to the government.

His contribution to modern Hebrew literature is his small book, *Aggadat Arba Kosot* ("Legend of Four Glasses"; Berlin, 1790 and often reprinted), a work influenced by family tragedies and by *Night Thoughts* by the English poet Edward Young. Pappenheim's book, which begins with sorrow and ends with exultation and faith, is written in poetic prose. The poet, on the one hand, writes in a classical, rationalist vein from the standpoint of the structure and spirit of the work, and he preaches and believes in reason and morality. On the other hand, he is influenced by the sentimentalism that had begun to affect contemporary literature, which cried out against fate and yearned for nature and night. *Aggadat Arba Kosot* is one of the foundations of Hebrew lyricism, and its influence may be seen in the poetry of A.D.B. (Adam ha-Kohen) *Lebensohn and his son, M.J. *Lebensohn.

BIBLIOGRAPHY: H.A. Wolfson, in: *Jewish Studies... Israel Abrahams* (1927), 427–40; F. Delitzsch, *Zur Geschichte der juedischen Poesie* (Leipzig, 1836), 110; Lachower, Sifrut, 1 (1963), 96–99; Klausner, Sifrut, 1 (1952), 254–60; H.G. Shapira, *Toledot ha-Sifrut ha-Ivrit ha-Ḥadashah* (1939), 346–54; Zinberg, Sifrut, 5 (1959), 114–6; Zeitlin, Bibliotheca, index.

[Elieser Kagan]

PAPPUS AND JULIANUS (Lulianus; second century C.E.), patriot brothers, perhaps from Laodicea. According to rabbinic tradition the two brothers, "when the government ordered the Temple to be rebuilt," set up (exchange-?) tables from Acre to Antioch to provide for those who came from the Exile (Gen. R. 64). It is also related that they were captured in Laodicea and condemned to death by *Trajan, the sentence being carried out immediately (Ta'an. 18b; Sifra, Emor, 9:5) or, according to an alternative account (Mekh. SbY to 21:13; Sem. 8:15), only after their judge – either Trajan or Lusius *Quietus, governor of Judea – had himself been killed. Rashi, who identifies Pappus and Julianus with the "Martyrs of Lydda" mentioned in the Talmud, indicated that they sacrificed themselves by claiming to have killed a princess for whose murder the whole of Jewry was held responsible (*Sefer ha-Arukh*, s.v. הרג; Rashi, Ta'an. 18b). Despite attempts to make them appear to transgress the commandments, Pappus and Julianus chose death rather than comply (TJ, Sanh. 3:6, 21b; TJ. Shev, 42:2, 35a). From these various sources it would seem that Trajan gave permission to rebuild the Temple, in commemoration of which a holiday was instituted. Later, after the execution of Pappus and Julianus, which might coincide with the Trajanic persecutions of 117 C.E., the holiday was abolished.

BIBLIOGRAPHY: Lieberman, in: JQR, 36 (1945/46), 243–6; Allon, Toledot, 1 (1958[3]), 260f.; L. Finkelstein, *Akiba* (Eng., 1936), 231–4, 313–6.

[Lea Roth]

PAPPUS BEN JUDAH (end of the first and beginning of the second century C.E.), *tanna* and aggadist. A contemporary of Rabban Gamaliel and R. Joshua (TJ, Ber. 2:9 according to the correct reading of the *Kaftor va-Feraḥ;* cf. L. Ginzberg, *Perushim ve-Ḥiddushim ba-Yerushalmi*, 1 (1941), 410), Pappus was imprisoned with Akiva at the time of the Hadrianic persecutions. Before their imprisonment Pappus had attempted to deter Akiva from continuing to teach his disciples, fearing the spies who were all around them. Thereupon Akiva told him the famous fable of the fox and the fish which illustrated that the Jewish people without Torah would be like fish out of water and would suffer a spiritual death. When Pappus later found himself in prison with Akiva, he said to him: "It is well with thee, Akiva, who hast been imprisoned for studying Torah, but woe to Pappus who has been imprisoned for vain, worldly things" (Ber. 61b). Pappus was distinguished for his pious character, and conducted himself with special stringency. He would lock his wife indoors when he went out so that she would not talk to other people (Git. 90a). This behavior was compared by Meir to a man who when finding a fly in his drink would throw away both fly and drink. Pappus' aggadic interpretation of Genesis 3:23 to the effect that man is equal to the angels was rejected by Akiva (Gen. R. 21:5). A long aggadic discussion between him and Akiva occurs in *Mekhilta Be-Shallaḥ*, 6.

PAPYRI. Papyri mentioning Jews and Judaism have been found in excavations at *Masada (dating to the period of the Jewish War against Rome in the first century C.E.), in caves in the Judean desert at *Qumran and Murabba'at (from the first and second centuries C.E., with the dramatic exception of one document thought to be from the eighth century B.C.E.; see *Dead Sea Scrolls; *Bar Kokhba), and in Egypt. The languages used are Greek, Latin, Aramaic, Hebrew, and Nabatean. Another important discovery was the *Nash papyrus discovered by L.W. Nash and published in 1903. The earliest Jewish papyri from Egypt are written in an Aramaic not greatly different from biblical Aramaic. Such papyri, dating from the late sixth through the fifth centuries B.C.E., have been found at various sites, including *Elephantine, Memphis, and, most recently, Hermopolis Magna. At Elephantine, a Jewish and Samaritan military colony, dating from the seventh or sixth century, provides an important source of papyri from the fifth century, when Egypt was under Persian domination. Most of these papyri are legal documents concerning marriage, divorce, manumission of slaves, loans, business contracts, litigation, and sales or gifts of property. Certain private letters are found on papyri and ostraca. The papyri attest to the existence of a Temple of YHWH, and the celebration of a Feast of Unleavened Bread, though possibly not in the form which is familiar from the Bible; evidence for the observance of the Sabbath is less certain. Geographical and racial considerations made it necessary for the Jews of Elephantine to tolerate and recognize other deities. The Temple was destroyed in 410, but certainly restored a few years later. The colony seems to have survived the change from Persian to Saitic rule, but to have disappeared finally in the course of the fourth century B.C.E. The Greco-Roman material from the Ptolemaic and the two Roman periods (323 B.C.E.–641/2 C.E.) which has been collected in Tcherikover, et al. *CPJ* (1957–60), contains over 500 documents, both papyri and ostraca, concerning Jews from many parts of Egypt, particularly the towns of the Fayum. The criteria taken by the editors for deciding whether a document is "Jewish" are, broadly: the occurrence of specifically Jewish institutions, Jewish names, and places of exclusively Jewish settlement, though the editors state the difficulty of identifying Jewish names, and have accordingly omitted many uncertain cases (ibid., 1 introduction). The papyri, in conjunction with ostraca and inscriptions, give a full picture of the social and economic state of the Jews in towns and villages throughout Egypt. Jews are found negotiating loans, participating in contracts, paying taxes in the same way as the other inhabitants of Egypt, fitting into the existing legal and bureaucratic structure, and even adopting Greek, Roman, and Egyptian names. The papyri provide religious information attesting to the existence of synagogues and the affirmation, at certain times, of the right of Jews to practice their religion. Evidence of the spread of Jewish religious and cultural influence can be seen in some demotic papyri and magical texts, and in the practice, among non-Jews, of adopting names connected with the Sabbath. The reliability of the papyri in points of detail provides valuable historical evidence which can be used to supplement and sometimes correct the evidence of *Philo and *Josephus, who drew their material from the richer and socially superior

Alexandrian Jews. Papyri give evidence, for instance, of the spread of the Jewish Revolt of 115–7 C.E. in Egypt, information which is given by no other source.

BIBLIOGRAPHY: Tcherikover, Corpus; idem, in: *Sefer Magnes* (1938), 199ff. (English summary); idem, *Ha-Yehudim be-Mizrayim ba-Tekufah ha-Hellenistit ha-Romit le-Or ha-Papirologyah* (1963²); idem and F. Heichelheim, in: HTR, 35 (1942), 2544; idem, *Auswaertige Bevoelkerung im Ptolemaeerreich* (1925, 1963²), 100ff.; A.E. Cowley (ed. and tr.), *Aramaic Papyri of the Fifth Century B.C.* (1923); G.R. Driver (ed.), *Aramaic Documents of the Fifth Century B.C.* (1957); E.G. Kraeling, *Brooklyn Museum Aramaic Papyri* (1953); R. Yaron, *Introduction to the Law of the Aramaic Papyri* (1961); H. Cazelles, in: *Syria*, 32 (1955), 75–100 (Fr.); H.I. Bell, *Cults and Creeds in Graeco-Roman Egypt* (1953), 27–33; W.F. Albright, in: JBL, 56 (1937), 145–76 (includes the Nash papyrus Ms.); idem, in: BASOR, no 115 (1949), 10–19 (facs. of Nash papyrus). **ADD. BIBLIOGRAPHY:** K.W. Clark, "The Posture of the Ancient Scribe," in: *Biblical Archaeologist*, 26 (1963), 63–72; B. Porten, "Aramaic Papyri and Parchments: A New Look," in: *Biblical Archaeologist* 42 (1979), 74–104; M. Haran, "Book-scrolls in Israel in Pre-exilic Times," in: *Journal of Jewish Studies*, 33 (1982), 161–73; idem, "Book-scrolls in Eastern and Western Communities from Qumran to High Middle Ages," in: HUCA, 56 (1985), 21–62.

[Alan Keir Bowman]

PAPYRUS. The plant *Cyperus papyrus* grows in the swamps of Israel. It was formerly very widespread in Lower Egypt and in old Egyptian drawings symbolized the region. The use of papyrus was very varied; it was employed for boats, utensils, shoes, and paper, and its soft stalks were also used as food. In the Bible it is called *gomë* (גֹּמֶא) or *eveh* (אֵבֶה), and in the Mishnah *papir* or *neyar*. *Gomë* was used for making the ark of Moses (Ex. 2:3). Boats which sailed beyond the rivers of Ethiopia were made of it (Isa. 18:2). Together with the *reed *(kaneh)* it grew near marshes and swamps, and Isaiah (35:7) prophesied that both would grow in the desert. The Book of Job (8:11–12) notes that papyrus cannot grow without swamp, that it shrivels up in the winter when the grass begins to go green, and that then it is ready for harvesting. The Tosefta speaks of papyrus vessels being more valuable than those made of plaited wicker (Kel. BM 5:15). Papyrus barrels were also made (Kel. 2:5), as well as clothes, "a shirt of papyrus" (Tosef., Kel. BB 5: 2) serving as clothes for the poor (Gen. R. 37:8). The main use of papyrus was in the manufacture of paper, especially in the era of the Mishnah and Talmud. Paper was made from the stalk, which bears the inflorescence, and which was cut into fine strips and stuck together in length and in breadth with glue – the *kolon shel soferim* ("scribes' glue"; Gr. Κὸλλα, glue) which contained leaven and was therefore forbidden on Passover (Pes. 3:1, 42b). The Jerusalem Talmud (Pes. 3:1, 29d) notes that in Alexandria this glue was prepared in large vessels. According to Josephus (Ant., 14:33) there was a place called Papyron near the Jordan. *Gemi* is frequently mentioned in the Mishnah and Talmud as material for the making of baskets, mats, and ropes. It is possible that papyrus (*gomë*) is also included in this name (cf. Rashi to Ex. 2:3), though it seems that it generally also refers to the fibers of other plants. The Bible once mentions *eveh* ships as being light and swift (Job 9:25–26). This word is connected with the Akkadian *apu*, the name of swamp plants used for weaving, including the papyrus.

Nowadays papyrus has almost disappeared from lower Egypt. In Israel it used to grow over the large expanse of the Ḥuleh swamp, where the Arab villagers earned their livelihoods by weaving mats from it. With the draining of these swamps only a few acres of papyrus remain in the local nature reserve. The papyrus is a perennial, growing to a height of up to 15 feet. The triple shaft of the inflorescence is 2½–3½ inches thick at the base and from it the papyrus strips were made. The plant dies in winter, and the stalks rot. The peat in the Ḥuleh is formed from the layers of the rotted plants.

BIBLIOGRAPHY: Loew, Flora, 1 (1926), 558–71; J. Feliks, *Olam ha-Ẓome'aḥ ha-Mikra'i* (1968²), 294–7; H.N. and A.L. Moldenke, *Plants of the Bible* (1952), 318 (index), s.v. **ADD BIBLIOGRAPHY:** Feliks, *Ha-Tzome'aḥ*, 42.

[Jehuda Feliks]

PARABLE, from the Greek παραβολή (lit. "juxtaposition"), the usual Septuagint rendering of Hebrew *mashal* ("comparison," "saying," and "derived meanings"). No distinction is made in biblical usage between parable, allegory, and fable; all are forms of the *mashal* and have the same functions of illustration and instruction. The comparison may be explicit or implied. It may take the form of declarative or interrogative sentences (e.g., Prov. 26:1; 27:4). When developed into a short story, an interpretation or application is usually appended.

The story-parable, often introduced by "like" or "as," is told in terms drawn from ordinary experiences and usually makes one principal point. Some examples are Nathan's parable (II Sam. 12:1–5), and the parables of the Surviving Son (II Sam. 14:5b–7), the Escaped Prisoner (I Kings 20:39–40), the Disappointing Vineyard (Isa. 5:1b–6) and the Farmer's Skill (Isa. 28:24–29). All but the last-named are followed by explicit interpretations. The rhetorical question with which the Book of Jonah ends may suggest that the book was intended as a parable. Ruth, too, may be a parable, with its more subtle point underlined by the appended genealogy.

The allegory-*mashal* is a more artificial narrative having individual features which are independently figurative, so that it becomes a kind of riddle. The one of the Eagles and the Vine (Ezek. 17:3–10) is described as both *ḥidah* ("riddle") and *mashal*. The oracular Laments of the Lioness (ibid. 19:2–9) and the Transplanted Vine (ibid. 19:10–14) and the stories of the Harlot Sisters (ibid. 23:2–21) and the Cooking-Pot (ibid. 24:3b–5) are allegorical. A third type of *mashal* is the fable, where animals or inanimate objects are made to speak and act like men. Judges 9:8–15 and II Kings 14: 9–10 are examples; in each case the moral is made explicit.

A riddle (*ḥidah*) is a kind of parable whose point is deliberately obscured so that greater perception is needed to interpret it; Samson's riddle (Judg. 14:14) is an example. *Mashal* and *ḥidah* are used almost synonymously in Ezekiel 17:2; Habakkuk 2:6; Psalms 49:5 and 78:2; and Proverbs 1:6. Certain proverbs are in effect parable-riddles, e.g., Proverbs 30:15a, 15b–16, 18–19, and 21–31.

Other biblical forms related to the parable type of *mashal* are: prophetic oracles where a metaphor is extended into a lively description, e.g., Isaiah 1:5–6; Hosea 2:2–15; 7:8–9, 11–12; Joel 4:13; and Jeremiah 25:15–29; prophetic oracles proclaimed through symbolic actions, e.g., I Kings 11:29; II Kings 13:15–19, and Isaiah 20:2–6; extended personifications as of Wisdom and Folly in Proverbs 1:20–33; 8:1–36; 9:1–6, 13–18; and revelatory dreams and visions having symbolism which the sequel interprets as allegorical, e.g., Genesis 37:6–11; 40:9–13, 16–19; Zechariah 1:8–11; 2:1–4; and Daniel 2:31–45.

[Robert B.Y. Scott]

IN THE TALMUD AND MIDRASH

The rabbis made extensive use of parables as a definitive method of teaching in the Talmud, and especially in the Midrash. Jesus, in his parables, was employing a well-established rabbinic form of conveying ethical and moral lessons. There are 31 parables in the New Testament, some of which are found in a slightly different version in rabbinical literature (cf. Shab. 153a with Matt. 25:1–12; and TJ, Ber. 2:8, 5c, the parable given by R. Zeira in his funeral oration on the death of R. Avin, the son of R. Ḥiyya, with Matt. 20:1–16), which contains thousands of examples, and a comparison between the parallel parables reveals the greater beauty and detail of the latter. The word *mashal* in rabbinical literature refers nearly always to the parable; only in such phrases as *ha-mashal Omer* or its Aramaic equivalent *matla amra* ("the *mashal* says"; cf. Ex. R. 21:7 and Lev. R. 19:6) and in the phrase *mashal hedyot* ("a folk *mashal*") does it bear the meaning which it does in the Bible of a proverb (see also *Proverbs, Talmudic). The standard formula, however, always introduces a full parable. That the use of parables was a distinct and recognized method of moral instruction is clear from the statements that "fox fables and fuller fables" (see below) were among the attainments of Rabban Johanan b. Zakkai (Suk. 28a; BB 134a), and that R. Meir consistently divided his discourses into three parts, *halakhah*, *aggadah*, and parables (Sanh. 38b). It is in this context that R. Johanan refers to the 300 animal parables of R. Meir (see *Animal Tales).

The rabbis not only used the parable extensively, they also emphasized its great value in opening a door to an understanding of the spirit of the Torah. Both of these aspects are reflected in a passage in the Midrash. Regarding the word *mashal* in Ecclesiastes 12:9 in the sense of parable, "and Koheleth… taught the people knowledge; yea he pondered and set out many *meshalim*," the Midrash ascribes the first use of parables to Solomon. On this the Midrash gives five parables, to illustrate the manner in which the parable aids the understanding of the Bible. R. Naḥman gives two, one of the "thread of Ariadne," which he applies to a palace of many doors, and the other of a man cutting a path through the jungle. R. Yose compares the parable to a handle with which an otherwise unwieldy basket can be carried; R. Shila gives the parable of a jug of boiling water carried by the same method, while R. Ḥanina of a bucket let down to a well of cold and sweet water. The passage concludes: "Let not the parable be lightly esteemed in thine eyes, since by its means one can master the whole of the words of the Torah." Realizing that the parable may not be the most profound or weighty means of instruction, the passage adds that just as one uses a candle, which is almost worthless, to find a precious stone which has been lost, "a parable should not be lightly esteemed in thine eyes, since by means of it a man arrives at the true meaning of the words of the Torah" (Songs R. 1:1, no. 8).

The parable is usually introduced by the phrase, *Mashal; le-mah ha-davar domeh le…* "A parable; to what can this matter be compared to…"), but so characteristic a picture is it of rabbinical teaching that the phrase is often omitted and the parable is introduced merely with the prefix *le* ("to").

The material is so vast that only some of the most salient features and the most striking parables can be given.

King Parables

One of the most frequent motifs is the king (i.e., God), of which there are many permutations.

THE KING AS RULER, WITH MANKIND AS HIS SUBJECTS. This, for instance, is the basis of the parable of R. Johanan b. Zakkai to illustrate the verse "at all times let thy garments be white, and let not thy head lack ointment" (Eccles. 9:8), which he interprets to mean that man should ever be prepared to meet his Maker. It is the parable of a king who announced a forthcoming banquet without stating the time. Those who were prescient dressed for the occasion and waited; those who were foolish went about their ordinary work, confident that they would be informed of the time. Suddenly the summons came. The wise entered properly dressed, while the fools had to come in their soiled garments. The king was pleased with the former, but was angry with the latter (Shab. 153a).

THE KING AS FATHER, WITH ISRAEL AS THE SOMETIMES WAYWARD BUT BELOVED SON. A king left his wife before her child was born and went overseas, remaining there many years. The queen bore a son who grew up. When the king returned she brought the son into his presence. The son looked at a duke, and then at a provincial governor and said successively of them, "This is my father." The king said, "Why do you gaze at them? From them you will have no benefit. You are my son, and I am your father." (PR 21:104). Many of these parables have the same theme as the New Testament parable of the prodigal son.

THE KING AS THE HUSBAND AND ISRAEL AS THE WIFE. To emphasize the honor due to God, the Midrash tells the parable of the king who had a number of children with a *matrona* ("a noble lady" – the term usually used in these parables for the king's consort). She was undutiful to him, and he announced his intention of divorcing her and remarrying. When she discovered the name of the woman whom he intended to marry, she called her children together and told them, hoping that they would intercede with their father because they found her objectionable. When they answered that they did not mind, she said, "I appeal to you in the name of the honor of your father" (Deut. R. 3:11). One of these "family" parables calls for special mention. R. Simeon b. Yoḥai asked R. Eleazar b. Yose ha-Gelili whether his father, a noted aggadist, had ever explained to him the verse: "(and gaze upon Solomon) even upon the crown wherewith his mother hath crowned him" (Song 3:11). Eleazar answered in the affirmative with a parable of a king who had an especially beloved daughter. At first he called her "my daughter," but as his affection for her increased he called her "sister," and finally he used to refer to her as "mother." So Israel is referred to as a daughter (Ps. 45:11), then as a sister (Song 5:2), and then as a mother (reading *le'ummi*; "my nation," in Isa. 51:4 as *le'immi*, "to my mother"). On hearing this explanation, R. Simeon b. Yoḥai arose and kissed him on his head (Ex. R. 52:5). The reason for R. Simeon's enthusiasm is probably to be found in the fact that the rabbis found themselves in a grave theological quandary. If the king of the Song of Songs is the Almighty, how can his mother be referred to, and his parable answered it by explaining that "mother" was but an endearing term for "daughter."

THE KING AND HIS SUBJECTS, OF WHOM ISRAEL IS THE FAVORITE. Thus the Midrash explains the striking difference between the 70 bullocks offered during the first seven days of Sukkot (Num. 29:12–34), which are regarded as expiations for the seventy *nations, and the single bullock offered on the eighth day (v. 36), which represents Israel with the parable of a king who made a banquet for seven days to which all the people were invited. At the conclusion of the seven days he said to his close intimate, "We have now done our duty to all the people; let us both have an intimate meal with whatever comes to hand, a piece of meat, or fish, or even vegetables" (Num. R. 21:24).

So standard is the motif of the king in parables that it is frequently used without any connotation of royalty, and it could be substituted for the word "man" without affecting the parable. Thus the above-mentioned parable of searching for a precious stone with a candle is made to refer to a king. Similarly there is the parable of R. Judah ha-Nasi in which he explained to Antoninus the responsibility shared by body and soul for transgressions – to the effect that a king had a beautiful orchard bearing choice fruit. In order to prevent pilfering of the fruit by the watchmen, he appointed one who was lame, and thus could not climb the tree, and one who was blind, who could not see it. The lame watchman, however, arranged for the blind one to carry him to the fruit. When the theft was discovered each pleaded physical inability to steal the fruit, but the king, realizing how they had acted, placed the blind man on the shoulders of the lame and punished them as one man. "So will the Holy One, blessed be He, replace the soul in the body and punish both for their sins" (Sanh. 91a/b). It is obvious that in this passage the word "king" is a mere literary device.

Animal Parables

Parables taken from the animal world, especially fox fables, are very popular (see *Animal Tales). R. Akiva explained to Pappus b. Judah why he continued to teach Torah at the risk of his life by the parable of the fox who invited the fish to leave the water to avoid being caught in the fishermen's nets. The fish replied that, while in the water it was in its natural element where it might die but might also live, whereas out of its element it would surely die (Ber. 61b). R. Joshua b. Hananiah dissuaded the Jews from breaking out in revolt against the Romans by telling them the parable of the crane which extracted a thorn from the tongue of a lion, and when it asked for its reward, was told that it had been sufficiently rewarded by the lion not closing its jaws on it after it had extracted the thorn (Gen. R. 64:10). The doctrine that later and greater troubles cause the former and lesser ones to be forgotten is illustrated by the parable of the man who, saved from a wolf, told all his friends about his escape. Subsequently avoiding a similar fate from a lion, he made this escape the subject of his story, until he was delivered from the poisonous sting of a snake, and then told the story of that deliverance (Ber. 13a). Many of the fables have their origin or parallel in the fables of other ancient peoples.

It is not certain what are the "parables of *kovesim*" which are mentioned together with fox fables among the accomplishments of Johanan ben Zakkai. It is usually rendered "fables of launderers" ("fullers") and, in fact, the launderer is a well-known figure in Roman comedy. No such parables, however, exist in rabbinic literature.

Parables from Nature

Every phenomenon of nature or of plants is made the subject of parables. The rabbis point out that there is hardly a fruit which is not regarded as a parable of Israel (Ex. R. 36:1), and the most sustained and extensive parables in the Midrash are on the vine, the palm (cf. Num R. 3:1), the cedar, etc. One of the most beautiful in this class is the blessing which R. Isaac of Palestine invoked upon his host R. Naḥman in Babylon when he took leave of him. When Naḥman asked for his blessing, R. Isaac claimed that it was difficult to think of a subject for a blessing, since Naḥman had been blessed with all the blessings of this world, wealth, health, honor, and children, and he continued: "Let me tell you a parable. A man was journeying in the wilderness. He was hungry, thirsty, and weary, and he lighted on a tree which had sweet fruits, pleasant shade, and a stream of water flowing beneath it. He ate of the fruit, drank of the water, and rested under its shade. When about to resume his journey he said, "O Tree, with what shall I bless thee? With the blessing of sweet fruit? Thou already hast it. That thy shade be pleasant? It already is. That water shall flow by thee? It does. May it be God's will that all the shoots taken from thee be like thee," and he proceeded to explain, "May all thy children be like thee" (Ta'an, 5b–6a).

Many of the parables are taken from daily life, and are a rich source for social history. R. Levi gives a parable to explain the verse, "Better the day of death than the day of one's birth" (Eccles. 7:1). It is the parable of two ships sailing in the Mediterranean. One was leaving the harbor and the other coming in. Everyone was happy at the ship which was leaving, while the ship which had completed its journey slipped in without incident. There was an intelligent man there, who said, "I see something topsy-turvy. There is no point in rejoicing at the ship which is leaving, since they know not what conditions she may meet, what seas she may encounter, and what wind she may have to face, whereas all should rejoice for this ship which has successfully completed its voyage" (Ex. R. 48:1). An essentially earthy parable is given to explain the fact that the 70 bullocks sacrificed on the seven days of Sukkot are made up of 13 the first day, decreasing in number by one each day. "It is to teach you the way of the world (*derekh erez*, usually meaning "etiquette," but here obviously to be translated literally). "A man is given hospitality by a friend. On the first day he gives him poultry, on the second meat, on the third fish, on the fourth vegetables. So daily he gives him less luxurious food, until in the end he feeds him on pulse" (Num. R. 21:25). An almost daring example of this type of parable is the one in which R. Huna, in the name of R. Johanan, interprets Exodus 32:11, "thy people that thou hast brought out of the Land of Egypt," as the retort of Moses to God that He was to blame for the idolatrous tendencies of the children of Israel. The parable says: "A wise man opened a cosmetic shop for his son in the street of the harlots. The site played its part, the trade played its part, and the young man – in his prime – played his part. He got into evil ways, and his father came and caught him with a harlot. His father began to shout at him, saying 'I'll kill you!' But a friend who was with him, said to him, 'You have ruined him and yet you shout at him! You disregarded all occupations and taught him only to be a cosmetician. You abandoned all other sites and opened a shop for him only in the street of the harlots.' So said Moses, 'Lord of the Universe, thou didst disregard the whole world and enslaved thy children in Egypt, where they worship lambs, and thus thy children learned from them and made a golden calf'" (Ex. R. 43:7).

[Louis Isaac Rabinowitz]

POST-TALMUDIC PERIOD

Medieval writers also had frequent recourse to *meshalim* (parables, *fables, or *allegories) in their works. Parables and allegories could be for them an instrument for interpreting the Bible or other holy books (like the *remez*, allegorical interpretation of biblical texts), a philosophical way of explaining metaphysical realities, or a rhetorical means on the literary level. Philosophical parables can be found in the *Ḥovot ha-Levavot* of *Baḥya ibn Paquda, in the *Kuzari* of *Judah Halevi (both of whom use the standard formula of the parable of the king, and both of a "king in India," *Ḥovot ha-Levavot* 3:9; *Kuzari* 1:109; cf. also Ḥovot 2:6), or in Maimonides' *Guide of the Perplexed* (see his "Parable of the Royal Palace" in Guide III, 51). In spite of its name, Samuel ha-Nagid's *Ben Mishlei* is more a collection of ethical aphorisms or moral remarks, continuing the biblical book of Proverbs, than a book of parables. Literary parables and fables are particularly frequent in many prose writings, above all in **maqāma* or *maqāma*-like compositions from the classical and the post-classical period. Joseph *Ibn Zabara, Judah *Al-Ḥarizi, *Jacob ben Eleazar, *Kalonymus ben Kalonymus, Vidal Benvenist, *Mattathias, etc., are among the best-known medieval authors of rhymed narratives including parables. Fables are abundant in the *Mishlei Shu'alim* of *Berechiah ha-Nakdan, in the Hebrew versions of the *Calila e Dimna*, and in the *Meshal ha-Kadmoni* by Isaac *Ibn Sahula. While the function of these parables could be in many cases a purely literary one, sometimes they were used as a way of cautiously articulating certain feelings of the members of a minority that could not be freely expressed, or simply with a pedagogic purpose.

In ḥasidic literature the most striking parables are the tales in *Naḥman of Bratzlav's *Sefer Ma'asiyyot*. Parables, most of them popular, and all striking, were especially characteristic of the method of preaching of Jacob *Krantz, the *Maggid* of Dubnow.

[Louis Isaac Rabinowitz / Angel Saenz-Badillos (2nd ed.)]

BIBLIOGRAPHY: O. Eissfeldt, *Der Maschal im Alten Testament* (1913); A. Bentzen, *Introduction to the Old Testament*, 1 (1952²), 167–77; Johnson, in: VT, Supplement, 3 (1955), 162–9; Haran, in: EM, 5 (1968), 548–53 (incl. bibl.). IN TALMUD AND MIDRASH: Ziegler, *Die Koenigsgleichnisse des Midrasch beleuchtet durch die roemische Kaiserzeit* (1903); I.J. Weissberg, *Mishlei Kadmonim* (1950²). For a collection of parables see: Ḥ.N. Bialik and J.H. Rawnitzki, *Sefer ha-Aggadah* (1908–) and C.G. Montefiore and H. Loewe, *A Rabbinic Anthology* (1938), passim. W. Bacher, *Die exegetische Terminologie der juedischen Traditionsliteratur*, 1 (1899), 121f., 2 (1905), 120f.; S. Lieberman, *Greek in Jewish Palestine* (1942), 144–60. **ADD. BIBLIOGRAPHY:** POST-TALMUDIC PERIOD: M.A.L. Beavis, in: CBQ, 52:3 (1990), 473–98; J. Stern, in: *S'vara*, 2:2 (1991), 35–48; Y. David (ed.), *Sippurei Ahavah shel Ya'akov ben Eleazar (1170–1233?)* (Heb., 1992/3); M.M. Epstein, in: *Prooftexts*, 14:3 (1994), 205–31; M. Gómez Aranda, in: *Judaísmo hispano*, 1 (2002), 109–19; Isaac ben Sahula, *Meshal Haqadmoni: Fables from the Distant Past: A Parallel Hebrew-English Text*, ed. and trans. R. Loewe (2004). ḤASIDIC LITERATURE: A. Wineman, in: *Hebrew Studies*, 40 (1999), 191–216.

PARADISE, the English derivative of Παράδειοος, Greek for "garden" in the Eden narrative of Genesis 2:4b–3:24 (see *Garden of Eden). One of the best-known and most widely interpreted pericopes in the Bible, this narrative is at the same time one of the most problematic. While on the surface the narrative unfolds smoothly, its deeper meaning, its composition and literary affinities, and many of its allusions, assumptions, and implications raise questions that are presently insoluble.

CONTENTS OF THE NARRATIVE

The pericope divides naturally into two sections, one relating God's beneficent acts in creating man and placing him in a paradise; the other, man's disobedience and consequent banishment from paradise. The masoretic *parashah* division considers 2:4a ("This is the story of heaven and earth when they were created") the beginning of this narrative, but most scholars today take 4a as the conclusion of the first creation story (1:1–2:4a), the opening verse of which it echoes, and begin the Eden narrative with 2:4b. More ambiguous is the position of 2:25 ("The two of them were naked, the man and his wife, yet they felt no shame"): some, accepting the present chapter division, consider it the climax of the perfect state created by God before man's disobedience; others (including NJPS) see that climax in 2:23–24 and take 2:25 as the introduction, which sets the theme, to the section on the "fall" in which awareness of nakedness and the making of clothing are prominent (3:7, 10–11, 21).

After the Lord God had made earth and heaven, but before the appearance of grasses and shrubbery, God created man out of lumps of soil and breathed life into him (man thus combines both earthly and divine elements). As man's home He created a garden in Eden filled with fruit-bearing trees, including the tree of life and the tree of knowledge of good and bad, which man was prohibited to eat on pain of death. God then created, also out of earth, all the animals and the birds of the sky and brought them to Adam to be named. God then fashioned a woman out of one of Adam's ribs, and Adam found her a fitting helper. The two were naked, but were unashamed of the fact. The serpent convinced the woman that God's threat of death for eating from the tree of knowledge was idle and that in fact its fruit would make the couple like divine beings who know good and bad. The woman and then the man ate some of the forbidden fruit and became aware of their nakedness; they then sewed some fig leaves into loincloths for themselves. Each participant in this act of disobedience was punished by God. The serpent was condemned to a life of crawling on its belly, and of enmity with mankind. The woman was condemned to painful pregnancy and childbirth; further, she would be dominated by her husband. The man was condemned to a life of struggling to eke out a living from the earth. To prevent him from eating from the tree of life, too, and acquiring the attribute of immortality, the Lord banished the man and his wife from the garden and set up *cherubim and "the fiery ever-turning sword" to guard the way to the tree of life.

SPECIFIC PROBLEMS

Many details of the narrative are elusive or troublesome.

The Location of the Garden

The text states that the garden is located "in Eden, in the east" (2:8), and that "a river issues from Eden to water the garden, and it then divides and becomes four branches:... Pishon,... which winds through the whole land of Havilah ... Gihon,... which winds through the whole land of Cush ... the Tigris,... and ... the Euphrates" (2:10–14, NJPS translation). Starting from what is clear, the Tigris and the Euphrates, scholarly opinion has divided into two schools. The first reasons that the two unknown rivers must be great world rivers on the scale of the Tigris and Euphrates; this view is supported by the Gihon's association with Cush, which usually means Nubia in the Bible, from which it is concluded that the Gihon is the Nile. Accordingly the fourth river is thought to be the Indus or the Ganges. These views, and their many variants, would locate the garden at some hypothetical common point of origin of the Tigris, Euphrates, Nile, and Indus or Ganges. The second school reasons that the two unknown rivers must be near the Tigris and the Euphrates. The Gihon's association with Cush presents no problem for this view since the ancient Near East also had another area known as Cush, the land of the Kassites (Akk. *Kaššû/Kuššu-*, Greek *Kossaîoi*) in present-day Luristan, east of the Tigris (cf. also the Mesopotamian associations of Cush in Gen. 10:8–10). This accords well with the Samaritan version's translation of Gihon as *ʾAsqop*, apparently the river Choaspes, modern Kerkha – in Luristan. If, following the apparent order of the biblical text, one then looks further east for the Pishon, the Kar-n in Elam becomes a candidate. However, this school also admits other possibilities, e.g., that the Gihon is the Diyala and Pishon the Kerkha or even the Arabian Wadi er-Rumma (for other aspects of this problem see *Havilah). According to any of these views, since the common meeting point of these rivers in antiquity was, or was believed to be, the Persian Gulf, the latter would be the undivided river mentioned in Genesis 2:10a (but could it ever be referred to as a river?). This would conform with the implication of Genesis 11:2, 9 that the garden was located east of Shinar (probably Sumer) and Babylon. Since Sumerian tradition (the Eden story has many Mesopotamian affinities) located its paradise in Dilmun, somewhere in or along the Persian Gulf, this school seems to be on the right track. Often associated with this school is the explanation of "Eden" (traditionally connected with Heb. *ʿeden* pl. *ʿadanim*, "luxury, delight") as the Sumerian *edin* ("plain"), a term which is often used as a geographic designation for the plain between the Tigris and Euphrates in southern Mesopotamia. However, this does not conform precisely to the text's suggestion that the garden is east of the Mesopotamian plain. Furthermore, the assumption of this view that Genesis 2:10 speaks of four rivers flowing into one, rather than vice versa, is debatable. It is at least equally possible that the single source river is understood to be located at the head of the Tigris and the Euphrates in the north, in which case the identification of Pishon and Gihon remains problematic. The location of Eden and its rivers clearly remains an open question.

The Trees of Life and Knowledge

As elusive as the identification of the rivers of paradise is the meaning of "the tree of knowledge of good and bad" (*ʿeẓ ha-daʿat tov wa-raʿ*; for the syntax cf. *ha-daʿat ʾoti* in Jer. 22:16). Several theories have been proposed over the centuries, but none has won general acceptance.

MORAL DISCERNMENT. This view takes "good and bad" in the moral sense of right and wrong (cf. Isa. 5:20; Amos 5:14;

Micah 3:2) and "knowledge" as the ability to distinguish (cf. II Sam. 19:36; Isa. 7:15) the one from the other. Critics of this view note that the very prohibition presumes that man knows the rightness of obedience and the wrongness of disobedience, and ask how the biblical God can be conceived as wishing to withhold moral discernment from man.

SEXUAL KNOWLEDGE. The main evidence supporting this interpretation is the frequent use of "to know" (not only in Hebrew and other ancient Near Eastern languages) in the sense of "to be intimate with"; it also finds a distinction between homosexual and heterosexual indulgence in the phrase "to know good and bad," ignoring the objective case of the nouns. Another argument for interpreting "knowledge of good and bad" in the Garden of Eden story as "sexual awareness" is the use of "to know good and bad" in contexts which may conceivably refer (actually they are far more embracing) to the sexual urge (Deut. 1:39, before it develops; Manual of Discipline 1:9–11, when it develops; II Sam. 19:36, after it has faded). Indeed, the immediate consequence of eating from the tree is awareness of nakedness, and the first action reported after the expulsion from the garden is Adam's "knowing" Eve (4:1). As regards the latter, however, *we-ha-ʾadam yadaʿ* (instead of *wa-yedaʿ ha-ʾadam*) can indicate the past perfect tense and could be interpreted as "Now the man had known," which suggests that Adam knew his wife before eating from the tree. Further, critics of the sexual awakening theory cite God's declaration to the heavenly court in 3:22 that through this knowledge "man has become like one of us." It is inconceivable that the Bible would attribute sexuality to God; and the answer that the reference here is to human procreation as the counterpart of divine creativity seems forced. Genesis 2:23–24 seems naturally to include sexuality as established already before eating from the tree. Furthermore, eating from this tree was prohibited even before the woman was created.

UNIVERSAL KNOWLEDGE. This view understands "good and bad" as a merism, expressing totality by two extremes (cf. II Sam. 14:17 and 22, where David is said in one verse to resemble an angel [cf. Gen. 3:22] in "understanding [lit. "hearing"] good and bad" and in the other to be as "wise as an angel… in knowing all that is on the earth"; cf. also "good and bad," meaning "anything at all," Gen. 24:50; 31:24, 29; II Sam. 13:22). Against this interpretation it is pointed out that man did not, in fact, gain universal knowledge.

MATURE INTELLIGENCE. This view notes passages where knowledge of good and bad is said to be absent in children (Deut. 1:39; Isa. 7:15; cf. Manual of Discipline 1:9–11), and notes that unconcern with nakedness is typical of early childhood, while shame comes with maturation. Critics argue that Adam's ability to name the animals and God's holding him responsible for disobedience assume something beyond childlike intelligence. These objections, however, may not be decisive, and there may be some significance in the fact that this interpretation was assumed by certain *tannaim* (Gen. R. 15:7; cf. Ber. 40a; Sanh. 70b).

CIVILIZING HUMAN RATIONALITY. This view identifies the knowledge acquired by eating from the tree as the mental capacity which distinguishes man from beast and is the source of civilization. Critics point out that man's assignment "to till the garden and tend it" (2:15) itself constitutes civilized behavior; that the only change reported in the text is awareness of nakedness; and that the arts and crafts of civilization for the most part originate only with Adam's descendants (4:20ff.). However, Adam himself, not only his descendants, became a farmer (3:19, 23), a typically civilized occupation. Becoming aware of nakedness is also a distinguishing mark of civilization and may be only the first of many civilized acts.

The latter point, like this interpretation as a whole, may claim some support in comparative ancient Near Eastern literature. The beginning of the Mesopotamian *Gilgamesh Epic* (Pritchard, Texts, 72–99, 503–7) describes the early life of Gilgamesh's friend Enkidu; he lived with, and in the manner of, wild animals, knowing nothing of civilized ways. His rise to civilization began when a harlot seduced him. After a week of cohabitation Enkidu "now had [wi]sdom, [br]oader understanding," and the harlot described his change as having "become like a god" (*ibid.*, p. 75c, lines 29, 34), much as Adam and Eve became "like divine beings who know good and bad" (Gen. 3:5, 22; if the beginning of the last-quoted line from the Gilgamesh Epic is really to be restored, "Thou art [wi]se," the parallel with Gen. 3:5, 22 would be even more complete; however, a restoration "Thou art [beauti]ful" is also possible; cf. Pritchard, Texts, 77a, line 11). Subsequently the harlot clothed Enkidu and introduced him to human food and drink and other aspects of civilization. Clearly the change in Enkidu was far more than sexual, as some have held. The text stresses Enkidu's resultant alienation from his erstwhile animal companions and his acquisition of human ways. The "wisdom" and "understanding" he gained constitute human intelligence. (A sort of commentary on this passage appears in Dan. 4:29–30, which describes Nebuchadnezzar's life while exiled in terms reminiscent of Enkidu's early life (some literary relationship between the two passages must be presumed), while Dan. 4:13 states explicitly that the change is from a human mind (lit. "*heart") to an animal mind, and verse 31 specifies a loss of "knowledge" (*mandaʿ*).) Some parts of the Enkidu narrative are known to be modeled on creation myths, and the narrative of his civilization may similarly reflect an as yet unknown text about the first man. Be that as it may, this narrative supports the view that the knowledge gained from the tree of knowledge was human rationality (cf. below, for knowledge in the "Myth of Adapa"). However, such comparative literary support cannot be considered an infallible guide to the biblical meaning, since literature often undergoes reinterpretation when transferred from one society to another. Far less problematic, but still not lacking in ambiguity, is the "tree of life." Clearly it confers immortality (3:22, "he might also take from the tree of life and eat, and live forever!"). It is not included in God's prohibition (2:16–17), so it may be that God originally intended Adam to live forever; only after man had disobeyed and obtained the divine prerogative of "knowing good and bad" was this boon revoked (3:19, 22–24). It is not clear whether immortality would have been conferred by eating this tree's fruit once or only by continuous eating. Since Adam had access to the tree before the expulsion, the fact that he had not already gained immortality suggests that the fruit had to be eaten continuously, but the urgency of the expulsion (3:22–24) suggests that a single eating may have sufficed.

The Serpent

The text is at pains to point out the creatureliness of the serpent, describing it as one "of all the wild beasts that the Lord God had made" (3:1, 14); it is distinguished from the other beasts only by its shrewdness (3:1). Its insignificance is underlined in 3:9–19, where God interrogates Adam and Eve, and both respond, while the serpent is not questioned and does not respond. In view of the prominent role played by serpents in ancient Near Eastern religion and mythology this treatment of the serpent amounts to desecration and demythologization, quite possibly intentional. As a result, the source of evil is denied divine or even demonic status: evil is no independent principle in the cosmos, but stems from the behavior and attitudes of God's creatures.

From early times the serpent has been seen as a symbol, whose meaning is widely debated. Some have stressed the serpent's well-known phallic symbolism and fertility associations, taking the narrative to reflect an attitude toward human sexuality, fertility cults, and the like. Others see the serpent as representing man's own shrewdness. Since in ancient Near Eastern mythology the forces of chaos which oppose the forces of creation and cosmos are widely represented as serpents, many see the serpent here, too, as a personification of the forces of chaos. According to this view, disobeying God undermines the cosmic order. Alternatively, the serpent may represent ethical evil in general, a meaning that serpentine mythological motifs are given elsewhere in the Bible (e.g., Isa. 26:21–27:1).

Mythological Features

Certain details of the narrative seem not to conform to "classical" biblical religion, but rather to reflect more primitive notions and premises. The very need to withhold immortality from man bespeaks divine jealousy: God and the divine beings are unwilling to have man acquire both of the distinctive characteristics of divinity, "knowledge of good and bad" and immortality (even if they may be willing to have man acquire immortality alone). The Eden narrative is deeply rooted in ancient Near Eastern and folkloristic traditions. In spite of some adaptation of these traditions to biblical theological tenets, it seems that some of the primitive notions of these traditions resisted adaptation.

LITERARY COMPOSITION

Critics generally hold that the Eden narrative stems from a different source than the preceding creation narrative (Gen. 1:1–2:4a or 4b). Divergent authorship is indicated, according to the documentary hypothesis, by the two narratives' contradictory orders of creation (ch. 1: trees, animals, man and woman; ch 2: man, trees, animals, woman). On the basis of vocabulary and content the first narrative is assigned to the Priestly Document (P), while the second is assigned to the Jehovist, or Yahwist, Document (J; for a contrary view see Cassuto, *Genesis I*, ad loc.).

The Eden pericope in itself appears to combine more than one narrative of the same events. Many doublets in the text point to at least two parallel recensions. The following are some of the doublets which have been suggested: 2:5 and 6 (primordial irrigation), 2:8 and 9 (planting the garden), 2:8 and 15 (placing man in it), 2:23 and 3:20 (naming the woman), 3:7 and 21 (clothing the couple), 3:18b and 19a (man's future food), 3:18a and 17c, d, 19a (man's future occupation), 3:19b and 19c (man's return to the earth), 3:23 and 24 (expulsion from paradise). Other seemingly disjunctive elements are 2:9b (the two trees clumsily seem attached to the verse) and 10–14 (the rivers). On these points there is general agreement, at least in principle. However there is no unanimity at all when it comes to regrouping the variants in order to reconstruct the hypothetical earlier recensions.

LITERARY AND FOLKLORISTIC AFFINITIES

The Eden narrative's affinities with primitive folklore and other biblical and ancient Near Eastern, especially Mesopotamian, compositions are many, yet there is no single piece of ancient literature which resembles the narrative as a whole, either in its details or theological significance.

The primordial absence of produce and standard forms of irrigation resemble the immediately postdiluvian conditions, which presumably duplicate primordial conditions in the Sumerian "Rulers of Lagās" (in: JCS, 21 (1967), 283). The notion of a divine garden, paradigm of fertility, is mentioned elsewhere in the Bible (Gen. 13:10; Isa. 51:3; Ezek. 36:35; Joel 2:3); a fragmentary passage in the Gilgamesh Epic (Pritchard, Texts, p. 89c) and a fuller passage in Ezekiel 28:11–19 speak of its jewel-bearing trees; the Ezekiel passage is a narrative and reflects a different version of the Eden story (cf., also Ezek. 31:5–9, 16–18). Yet another paradise narrative is the Sumerian tale of "Enki and Ninhursag" (Pritchard, Texts, 37–41), which describes the land (or island) of Dilmun, east of Sumer, as a pure, clean, and bright land, where there is neither sickness nor death, and where the animals live in harmony. One episode in the narrative involves the sun-god's watering Dilmun with fresh water brought up from the earth, thus making it fertile. The earth-goddess Ninhursag gives birth to eight plants, which the water-god Enki proceeds to devour. This leads Ninhursag to curse Enki; this nearly causes the latter's death, but ultimately Ninhursag is made to heal him. Aside from the Eden narrative's manifest similarities to these stories, the differences are also significant; most noticeable is the far more natural configuration of the narrative in Genesis 2–3, in contrast to the fantastic or supernatural nature of the other accounts, including Ezekiel's. Placing man in the garden "to till and tend it" faintly echoes the Mesopotamian creation stories according to which man was created to free the gods from laboring to produce their own food (Pritchard, Texts, 68; cf. W.G. Lambert, *Atrahasis* (1969), 42–67; A. Heidel, *The Babylonian Genesis* (1942), 69–71; S.N. Kramer, *The Sumerians* (1963), 149–50). In the Bible this is not seen as the purpose of man's creation – in fact, the creation of man and the placing of him in the garden are separated by several verses; and there is no suggestion at all that God or the other heavenly beings benefit from man's labor. The theme of lost immortality appears briefly near the end of the Gilgamesh Epic. From the bottom of the sea Gilgamesh brought up a plant which contained the power of rejuvenating the aged; he called it "The Man Becomes Young in Old Age," declaring, "I myself shall eat [it], and thus return to the state of my youth" (in Pritchard, Texts, 96). Later, however, Gilgamesh set the plant down while bathing, and a serpent made off with it and subsequently shed its skin (11. 285–9; in 1. 296 the serpent is referred to as "ground-lion"; some take this as simply an epithet of the serpent, but others, following the testimony of Akkadian lexical texts, take "ground-lion" as "chameleon" (which etymologically means "ground-lion")). The belief that snakes, or lizards, regain their youth when they cast their skins is common among primitive peoples (cf., the analogous belief about molting eagles in Isa. 40:31; Ps. 103:51). This is a reflex of the well-known folklore motif of how the serpent cheated man out of immortality, for the significance of which see below. The loss of immortality is treated in great detail in the Akkadian Myth of Adapa (Pritchard, Texts, 101–3). Priest and sage of the city of Eridu, Adapa had been given "wise understanding… to teach the patterns of the land" (A, 3 (this apparently means to teach mankind the patterns of civilization), had been shown "the heart of the heaven and the earth" (B, 57–58)). The god Ea "had given him wisdom, eternal life he had not given him" (A, 4). While he was fishing in the Persian Gulf to supply Ea's temple at Eridu with fish, the south wind swamped Adapa's boat, so Adapa broke its wing with a curse. As Adapa was summoned before the chief god Anu in heaven to account for this behavior, Ea warned him not to eat and drink the bread and water of death that would be presented to him there. However, Anu had been disposed favorably to Adapa by another of Ea's stratagems, so that he in fact desired to supplement Adapa's wisdom by offering him the bread and food of life. Unaware, Adapa refused it, accepting only a garment and some anointing oil Ea had approved; and so he lost (eternal) life. Adapa is to be identified with Oannes, known from other sources to have been the first of approximately seven antediluvian sages who taught humanity civilization, paralleling the culture-founding Cainite genealogy from Adam through Lamech's children (Gen. 4), with Oannes-Adapa occupying the position of Adam. To this some have added the evidence of an Akkadian synonym list which supposedly equates Adapa, written *a-da-ap/b*, with "man" (E.A. Speiser in Pritchard, Texts, 101 n. 1; see also M. Civil (ed.), *Materials for the Sumerian Lexicon*, vol. 12, p. 93 line 20); however it is doubtful that this is Adapa, whose name is not written this way, and the very significance of the equation is uncertain. Not all details of the relationship of the Myth of Adapa to the Eden narrative are clear or necessarily convincing, but some relationship does seem indicated. The contrasts, aside from obviously wide divergence in details and plot, are most profound and characteristic in the area of underlying religious outlook. Although the Myth of Adapa does not make it clear whether Ea simply erred or purposely deceived Adapa, it expresses in either case a resigned acceptance of death as a situation beyond rational human control. The biblical narrative, on the other hand, assumes that death and other forms of misfortune in this world are the earned results of human behavior whose consequences man knew in advance. The theme of man's being cheated out of immortality by the serpent or some other skin-sloughing animal appears in the folklore of several peoples. Another frequently occurring motif is that of the perverted message, wherein God sent to man a message of immortality which the messenger perverted into a message of mortality, thus dooming mankind ever since. At times these two motifs are combined: God's message instructed man to rejuvenate himself by casting off his old skin, but the faithless messenger gave this information to the serpent instead, and told man that his life would end in death. On the basis of these motifs, J.G. Frazer surmised that an earlier version of the Eden narrative related as follows: the garden contained two trees – the tree of life and the tree of death (cf. the food and drink offered Adapa). God sent a message, through the serpent, that man should eat from the tree of life, not the tree of death. The clever serpent, however, reversed the message, leading the human couple to eat from the tree of death (cf. the deception of Adapa), while he himself ate from the tree of life and thus gained immortality (cf. Pritchard, Texts, 96 referred to above).

The material surveyed above leads to the conclusion that the biblical Eden narrative has roots in ancient Near Eastern literature. Yet, as noted above, these parallels are fragmentary, dealing with only a few motifs each, and the discrepancies in detail are often great. How these gaps were bridged cannot be said with certainty, presumably because of ignorance of the process of transmission of ancient Near Eastern literature to the Bible. Quite possibly these stories became known to the biblical authors in proto-Israelite versions which they molded, with creative editorial skill, into a unique narrative with a wholly new meaning.

[Jeffery Howard Tigay]

PARADISE AND HELL IN LATER JEWISH THOUGHT

Paradise and Hell, the places of reward for the righteous and punishment for the wicked after death, are traditionally referred to as the Garden of Eden and *Gehinnom respectively. In the Bible these two names never refer to the abode of souls after death; nevertheless, the idea of a fiery torment for the wicked may have been suggested by Isaiah 66:24. The earliest possible allusion to Gehinnom in the new sense is found in the Apocrypha, in which the general phrase "accursed valley" is used to describe the place where the wicked will be judged and punished (I En. 27:1ff.). The name Gehenna (= Gehinnom) first appears in the New Testament (e.g., Matt. 5:22, 29ff.), as does "Paradise," the abode of the blessed (e.g., Luke 23:43). The word *pardes* ("park," "orchard") occurs in biblical and talmudic sources, but rarely, if ever, in the sense of "heavenly abode." The oldest Jewish source to mention Gan (= Garden of) Eden and Gehinnom is probably a statement of Johanan b. Zakkai at the end of the first century C.E.: "There are two ways before me, one leading to Paradise and the other to Gehinnom" (Ber. 28b). Jewish teaching about a future life was never systematized, and the varied statements in rabbinic literature cannot be combined into a consistent whole. "Days of the Messiah" and "World to Come" are sometimes sharply distinguished, sometimes virtually identified. Some passages indicate that the righteous and wicked will enter Gan Eden and Gehinnom only after the resurrection and last judgment; in others, the departed take their assigned places immediately after death. Other descriptions of future bliss and punishment make no mention of locale.

APOCALYPTIC LITERATURE

The apocalypses frequently mention the punishment of the wicked by fire (I En. 90:26ff.; IV Ezra 7:36; Testament of Abraham (A) 12). In II Enoch 10 the places of reward and punishment are located in the third heaven; usually Hell is underground, as in II Enoch 40:12. Hell is sometimes identified with *Sheol (I En. 22:8ff.). In the Bible, however, Sheol was the abode of all the dead, and it was not a place of retribution. Now it becomes to some extent a place of punishment. The Apocalypses of Baruch and Ezra come closer to the old notion: Sheol is the temporary abode of souls between death and the last judgment (II Bar. 23:5; IV Ezra 4:41); but reward and punishment may begin during this period (II Bar. 36:11). The punishment at the end of time is final, and there is no hope of any further change or repentance (*ibid.* 85:12). The sources also describe the rewards of the righteous; Assumption of Moses 10:10 includes among the satisfactions of the righteous that they will see the wicked suffering in Gehenna.

RABBINIC LITERATURE

Gehinnom and Gan Eden existed even before the world was created (Pes. 54a), Gehinnom at the left hand of God, Gan Eden at His right (Mid. Ps. 90:12).

Gehinnom

So vast is Hell, it may be compared to a pot of which the rest of the universe forms the lid (Pes. 94a). Gehinnom is not only for punishment, but also for purgation. According to Bet Shammai, those whose merits and sins are evenly balanced will be purified in the flames of Gehinnom, and thus rendered fit to enter Gan Eden. Bet *Hillel held that such marginal persons would, by God's mercy, escape the ordeal (Tosef., Sanh. 13:3; RH 16b–17a). A widely held view was that the wicked will be punished in Gehinnom for 12 months only, after which they will be annihilated, to suffer no more. Only a limited group, chiefly those who by word and deed have repudiated their loyalty to the Jewish people and the basic doctrines of Jewish faith, will endure endless torment (Tosef., Sanh. 12:4, 5; RH 17a). However, R. Akiva cited Isaiah 66:23 concerning the 12-month sentence, indicating that even the wicked after having atoned for their sins in purgatory will join the righteous in Gan Eden (Eduy. 10). The severity of Gehinnom was mitigated in rabbinic thought. It was widely believed that all Israel, except for a few arch sinners, would have a share in the world to come, and so could not be unconditionally doomed to Hell (Sanh. 10). Abraham was said to stand at the entrance of Gehinnom and prevent his circumcised descendants from being incarcerated there (Er. 19a; cf. the reference to "Abraham's bosom" in Luke 16:23). Moreover, all the condemned, including gentiles, would have respite from punishment on the Sabbath (Sanh. 65b). The possibility that the reprobates might repent, acknowledge the justness of their punishment, and thus open the way to their redemption is mentioned in several places (Er. loc. cit.; on the sons of Korah, see Ginzberg, Legends, 6 (1928), 103, n. 586). That the piety of a son may mitigate the punishment of a deceased parent is implied in Kiddushin 31b (cf. II Macc. 12:42ff.) and stated explicitly in a post-talmudic story (*Kallah Rabbati*, 2:9, ed. Higger, 202ff.). The special effectiveness of the recital of **Kaddish* for this purpose is mentioned in medieval writings (e.g., Baḥya ben *Asher, Deut. 21:8). Some Palestinian rabbis denied that there is, or will be, a place called Gehinnom. They held that at the final judgment sinners will be destroyed by the unshielded rays of the sun or by a fire issuing from their own bodies (Gen. R. 6:6; 26:6).

Gan Eden

A place is reserved for every Israelite in both Gan Eden and Gehinnom. Before being assigned to their proper abode, the wicked are shown the place they might have occupied in Heaven, and the righteous, the place they might have occupied in Hell (Mid. Ps. 6:6; 31:6). In contrast to passages that depict the righteous sitting at golden tables (Ta'an. 25a) or under elaborate canopies (Ruth 3:4) and participating in lavish banquets (BB 75a), Rav (third century C.E.) declared that in the world to come – Gan Eden is not specifically mentioned – there will be no sensual enjoyment and no transaction of business or competition, but the righteous will sit crowned, enjoying the radiance of the Divine Presence (Ber. 17a). Some 11 persons, mostly biblical figures, entered Paradise alive (Ginzberg, Legends, 5 (1925), 5–96) and legend tells in detail how R. Joshua b. Levi accomplished this feat (Ket. 77b).

MEDIEVAL LITERATURE

A number of post-talmudic writings give longer and more fully elaborated descriptions of Gan Eden and Gehinnom, which are in substantial agreement with the briefer accounts in the Talmud and classic Midrashim. Among these writings are tractate *Gan Eden* and tractate *Gehinnom*, the *Iggeret of R.*

Joshua b. Levi, *Midrash Konen*, and *Otiyyot de-R. Akiva*. They generally picture Heaven and Hell each divided into seven sections; souls are assigned to the several sections in accordance with the level of their merits or the heinousness of their sins. The Jewish accounts of Hell are tame compared to those in medieval Christian literature, as is apparent from Dante's *Divine Comedy*, written in the 14th century. On the other hand, Gan Eden is not pictured as a place of completely static bliss: the Messiah is there awaiting the day of the redemption (according to *Midrash Konen*, suffering for the sins of Israel), and he enlists the help of the righteous souls in urging God to speed the final deliverance (see J.D. Eisenstein, *Oẓar Midrashim*, 1 (1915), 85, 87). In the 13th–14th centuries the poet *Immanuel b. Solomon of Rome wrote the fullest account of Paradise and Hell in Hebrew literature; it is entitled *Tophet and Eden* and is the last section of his *Maḥbarot*. It was possibly suggested by Dante's *Divine Comedy*, but possesses little literary power or religious depth. Its most notable feature is the inclusion of a section in Eden for pious gentiles in accordance with the prevailing Jewish teaching. Moreover, unlike Dante, Immanuel did not mention reprobates in *Tophet* by name. Some medieval philosophers explained earlier references to Paradise and Hell as figures of speech. Heaven meant the joy of communion with God, and Hell meant to be deprived of eternal life (Maim., Yad, Teshuvah 8:1, 5). To Joseph *Albo, Hell is the state of the soul which, having sought only material gratifications in this life, has no means of obtaining satisfaction in the nonmaterial life beyond the grave (*Ikkarim* 4:33). The Kabbalists developed and adapted the relatively simple notions of Gan Eden and Gehinnom to fit into their complex systems, and especially in order to reconcile them with the doctrine of reincarnation (see **Gilgul*).

MODERN PERIOD

Moses *Mendelssohn flatly rejected the idea of Hell as incompatible with the mercy of God (*Gesammelte Schriften*, 3 (1843), 345–7). Modern Jews of all religious viewpoints, including those who vigorously uphold the belief in personal immortality, have generally discarded the idea that Paradise and Hell exist literally. Since these concepts, though once widely accepted, were never regarded as dogmatically binding, the rejection of them has not occasioned any strain, even on Orthodoxy.

[Bernard J. Bamberger]

BIBLIOGRAPHY: J. Frazer, *Folklore in the Old Testament*, 1 (1919), 45–77; Th. C. Vriezen, *Orderzoek naar de paradijs-voorstelling bij de oude Semietische Volken* (1937), incl. bibl.; P. Humbert, *Etudes sur le récit du paradis et de la chute dans la Genèse* (1940), incl. bibl.; U. Cassuto, in: *Studies in Memory of M. Schorr* (1944), 248–58; J.L. McKenzie, in: *Theological Studies*, 15 (1954), 541–72; E.A. Speiser, in: BASOR, 140 (1955), 9–11; idem, in: *Festschrift Johannes Friedrich* (1959), 473–85; R. Gordis, in: JBL, 76 (1957), 123–38; B.S. Childs, *Myth and Reality in the Old Testament* (1962^2), 43–50; N.M. Sarna, *Understanding Genesis* (1966), 23–28; T.H. Gaster, *Myth, Legend and Custom in the Old Testament* (1969), 6–50, 327–71; J.A. Bailey, in: JBL, 89 (1970), 137–50. See also Commentaries to Genesis 2:4–3. IN JEWISH PHILOSOPHY: R.H. Charles, *Eschatology* (1963^2); K. Kohler, *Heaven and Hell in Comparative Religion* (1923); H. Strack and P. Billerbeck, *Kommentar zum Neuen Testament*, 4 (1928), 1016–65.

PARAF, PIERRE (1893–1989), French author, editor and broadcasting executive. Born in Paris, Paraf, a graduate in law, was an officer in the French army during World War I, then took up journalism, and from 1930 until 1939 was literary editor of the Paris daily *La République*. He later worked for the left-wing daily *Combat* and for the monthly *L'Europe*. In 1936 he joined the French radio service and eventually became chief editor of French Radio-Television. After the French military collapse in 1940, he fought with the underground until the liberation in 1944. Paraf showed strong Jewish loyalties in his work and writings. In one of his early books, *Quand Israël Aima* (1929), he expressed his pride in belonging to the Jewish people. With the writer Bernard *Lecache, he founded in 1927 the Ligue internationale contre le Racisme et l'Antisémitisme. He was president of the Mouvement contre le Racisme, l'Antisémitisme et pour la Paix and a member of the executive of the League for the Rights of Man. After World War II he directed the monthly review *Amitié France-Israël* and wrote books on Jewish and Zionist themes. Among them were *Israël dans le monde* (1947) and *L'Etat d'Israël dans le monde* (1960). His other books include *Les cités du bonheur* (1945), *L'Ascension des peuples noirs* (1958), *Les démocraties populaires* (1962), and *Le Racisme dans le monde* (1964).

[Godfrey Edmond Silverman]

PARAGUAY, South American republic; population (est. 2005) 4,960,000, Jewish population 900.

A few isolated Jews came to Paraguay from France, Switzerland, and Italy toward the end of the 19th century and merged with the native population without ever establishing a Jewish community. On the eve of World War I a number of Sephardi Jews immigrated from Palestine. The families Arditi, Cohenca, Levi, Mendelzon, and Varzan formed the first *ḥevra kaddisha* (Alianza Israelita) in 1917 and established the first synagogue with other Sephardim from Turkey and Greece. A second immigration wave in the early 1920s brought Jews from the Ukraine and Poland who founded the Ashkenazi community, Unión Hebraica. Until 1937 Jews immigrated to Paraguay without limitations according to the liberal constitution of 1870. In 1937 restrictions were imposed on the acceptance of refugees and the minister of foreign affairs instructed the consuls in Europe to avoid granting visas to Jews. At the end of the 1930s together with the increase of antisemitism in public opinion, some projects of agricultural colonization of Jews in the department of Concepción and the areas of the Chaco were considered. One of the requisites for this project was the deposit of $1,000 for each adult immigrant. But this project failed as a result of the opposition by the bishop of those areas, Emilio Sosa Gaona, some sections of the army, members of the Parliament, and the agitation provoked by agents of the German Nazi government. As a result, between 1933 and 1945 only some 1,000 Jews from Germany, Austria, and Czechoslovakia were permitted to immigrate to Paraguay. Nevertheless, some Paraguayan consuls in Europe – Paris, Cologne, Warsaw, Lisbon, and Prague – sold thousands of visas and passports to Jewish refugees. Many of them used those documents as stepping stones to Argentina, Brazil, and Uruguay where immigration laws were more severe. Others, who remained in Europe, tried to receive, with the aid of the passports, the status of alien citizens and some of them did succeed in saving their lives.

The Jews in Paraguay lived in the capital Asunción and established the Unión de Israelitas pro Socorro Mutuo. This group built the main synagogue, later located within the premises of the Unión Hebraica. After World War II a last group of immigrants, mostly survivors from the concentration camps, arrived.

In the beginning of the 21st century the Jewish community was estimated at some 300 families or 900 persons. The size of the community is decreasing through immigration to Argentina and Brazil, but there are also occasional immigrants from those countries, especially due to marriage. The intermarriage rate was rising; most of the intermarried couples give their children a Jewish education. There is a continuous trickle of emigrants to Israel, and since 1948 some 480 people made *aliyah*.

Most Paraguayan Jews engage in commerce or industry. There are about 25 Jewish professionals, most of whom studied in Paraguay. The community supports a Jewish school, named "Escuela Integral Estado de Israel," in which Hebrew is taught in addition to the official curriculum, which is attended by more than two thirds of the Jewish children of school age. About 50 Jewish students are enrolled at the university, in addition to others who study abroad. In Paraguay there are some 40,000 Germans or people of German descent, many of whom had openly supported the Nazis before and during World War II. A number of prominent Nazis, among them Dr. J. *Mengele of *Auschwitz, found temporary shelter in Paraguay. There were some short-lived antisemitic decrees in 1936 and some antisemitic incidents prior to the establishment of the strong-arm regime of General Alfredo Stroessner in 1954, which established a dictatorship until 1989. After that time, Jews were not disturbed. Paraguay voted in 1947 for the UN Resolution on the partition of Palestine and has been friendly to Israel ever since. An Israel Embassy was established in 1968. The Consejo Representativeo Israelita del Paraguay represents the Jewish community vis-à-vis the public and authorities. There is also a sports club, a *B'nai B'rith, *Wizo chapter, and a *Ha-No'ar ha-Ẓiyyoni movement. In 1968 another youth organization, Centro Israelita Juvenil, was established.

There were three synagogues: Ashkenazi, Sephardi, and Chabad. In Asunción there is also a Jewish museum with a Holocaust memorial.

BIBLIOGRAPHY: Associación Filantrópica Israelita, Buenos Aires, *Zehn Jahre Aufbauarbeit in Suedamerika* (Ger. and Sp., 1943); A. Monk and J. Isaacson, *Comunidades Judías de Latinoamérica* (1968); J. Shatzky, *Comunidades Judías en Latinoamérica* (1952); J. Beller, *Jews in Latin America* (1969).

[Benjamin (Benno) Varon (Weiser) / Efraim Zadoff (2nd ed.)]

PARAH (Heb. פָּרָה "heifer"), name of the fourth treatise in the Mishnah and the Tosefta in the order of **Tohorot*. This tractate is based upon the pentateuchal law of the burning of the *red heifer as set forth in Numbers 19:1–22.

The tractate is divided into 12 chapters whose subject matter is the proper age for the validity of the heifer and other sacrificial animals; the type of work that invalidates the heifer (3:1, 3, 4); the degree of redness required (2:2, 5); the preparation of the priest prior to the burning of the heifer (3:1, 5, 8); the manner of bringing the spring water (3:3, 4); the procedure of the bringing and burning of the heifer (3:6, 7, 9–11; 4:2, 3); irrelevant intentions at the time of the slaughtering of the heifer (4:1, 3); defilement of those engaged in the preparation and burning of the heifer (4:4); qualifications for vessels containing the purifying waters (5); laws pertaining to work done with the spring water and the procedure of its mingling with the ashes of the heifer (6; 7; 8:1, 2; 9:4); the type and condition of spring water considered fit for the purifying waters (8:8–11; 9:1–3); status of the mixture after defilement (9:5–9); ritual uncleanness of objects coming in contact with the purifying waters or their vessels (10); cases of doubt if the purifying waters were defiled (11:1–2); laws of the hyssop used in the sprinkling of the purifying waters (11:7–9; 12:2, 6); procedure in the sprinkling on the ritually unclean (12:3–5, 11).

It is stated that until the destruction of the Temple no more than nine heifers were actually prepared (3:5), and the names of those who prepared them are given. Of significance is chapter 3 outlining extreme measures instituted by the rabbis to guarantee the ritual purity of the priest who was to burn the heifer. These were enacted as safeguards from certain opposing views of the Sadducees. The tractate includes discussion on some general principles of ritual uncleanness, not directly related to the major theme (8:4–7; 11:4–6; 12:8–10).

The Tosefta *Parah* consists of 12 chapters, which embody and supplement in detail the laws contained in the Mishnah. Noteworthy is the section on laws pertaining to the different standards of ritual purity between a **ḥaver* and an **am-ha-areẓ* (4:12–5:3). It should be noted that while J. Sussmann (1969) adduced considerable evidence for the observance of the laws of ritual purity in Ereẓ Israel throughout the amoraic period, he was unable to bring any direct evidence for the existence or use of the ashes of the red heifer during this period. Similar questions have been raised concerning the practices of the Dead Sea sect (see: J. Neusner, 1987, 146ff.). There is no *Gemara* on the tractate in the Babylonian Talmud nor in the Jerusalem Talmud. Neusner published a translation of the Mishnah (1991) and the Tosefta (2002) of Parah.

BIBLIOGRAPHY: P. Blackman, *Mishnayot*, 6 (Eng., 1955), 401–5; H. Danby, *Mishnah* (Eng., 1933), 697–714; H.L. Strack, *Introduction to the Talmud and Midrash* (1931), 61–62. **ADD. BIBLIOGRAPHY:** Epstein, *The Gaonic Commentary on the Order Toharot*

(Hebr.) (1982); S. Lieberman, *Tosefet Rishonim*, vol. 3 (1939); J. Sussman, *"Babylonian Sugiyot to the Orders of Zera'im and Tohorot"* (Hebrew; Ph.D. Thesis, 1969), 306–16; J. Neusner, *A History of the Mishnaic Laws of Purities* (1974–77), vol. 9–10; idem, *From Mishnah to Scripture* (1984), 59–66; idem, *The Mishnah Before 70* (1987), 143–68; idem, *The Philosophical Mishnah 3* (1989), 63–74; idem, *Purity in Rabbinic Judaism* (1994), 157–69.

[Jacob Kelemer]

PARAH, PERATH (Heb. פָּרָה, פְּרָת), town (Parah) listed among the cities of Benjamin with Avvim and Ophrah (Josh. 18:23). Jeremiah was bidden by the Lord to hide his girdle by the Perath (AV translation: Euphrates); when the girdle was later removed, it was found spoiled, as a prophetic sign (Jer. 13:4, 7). It is now generally assumed that these references are to the ancient settlement at Tell Fāra and to the Wadi Fāra, a deep gorge near Jeremiah's birthplace Anathoth. In Hasmonean times, Bacchides fortified the place (I Macc. 9:50; as Pharathon). The Zealot leader Bar Giora camped at Ain near the river Pheretai in the First Jewish War (Jos., Wars, 4:512). The Wadi Fāra contains many remains of the Byzantine period. Its main source, ʿAyn Fāra (1,135 cu.m. daily), supplied Herodian Jericho with water by means of a rock-cut channel; during the British Mandate this water was pumped to Jerusalem.

BIBLIOGRAPHY: Avi-Yonah, Geog, 36–37, 105; Abel, Geog, 2 (1938), 404.

[Michael Avi-Yonah]

PARAN (Heb. פָּארָן), biblical appellation for the main desert in the eastern Sinai peninsula. Its boundaries can be reconstructed by means of a number of biblical references. In their campaign against Canaan, the kings of Shinar, Ellasar, Elam, and Golim reached El-Paran, "which is by the wilderness" (Gen. 14:6), a place generally identified with Elath on the Red Sea. Moses spoke to Israel "in the Arabah, near Suph [Red Sea?], between Paran and Tophel" (Deut. 1:1). The Red Sea, therefore, was probably the southern extremity of the Paran wilderness. On the other hand, when Ishmael was cast out with Hagar by Abraham, presumably from Beer-Sheba, he dwelt in the wilderness of Paran (Gen. 21:21). The 12 spies of Moses were sent from the wilderness of Paran to Canaan, and returned to "the wilderness of Paran, to Kadesh" (Num. 13:3, 26), which is usually described in the Bible as situated in the wilderness of Zin. Paran, therefore, extended as far north as Kadesh and even the periphery of Beer-Sheba. David went to the wilderness of Paran in his wanderings (I Sam. 25:1) and came into contact with Nabal, "a man in Maon," which is in southern Judah. Thus it also extended to the northeast. The Israelites entered it from the wilderness of Sinai (Num. 10:12), or, more specifically, from Hazeroth. If the identification of Hazeroth with ʿAyn al-Ḥaḍra near Jebel Ḥillāl is correct (rather than with ʿAyn Ḥaḍra in southeastern Sinai, as some have suggested), Paran would be limited to the Tih Desert in the northeastern part of the Sinai Peninsula, which agrees roughly with the story of Hadad, the Edomite pretender, who fled from Midian to Egypt by way of Paran (I Kings 11:18). An element of doubt is created, however, by the juxtaposition of Mt. Paran with Mt. Sinai and Mt. Seir in Deuteronomy 33:2 and Habakkuk 3:3; some interpreters regard this mountain as synonymous with Mt. Sinai, while others look for a separate Mt. Paran at a site called Jebel Fārān, a place mentioned by some travelers, but not located by others. It can perhaps best be defined as the eastern part of the Tih Desert, placed between the desert of Shur near Egypt and the desert of Zin near the Judean Mountains. It is crossed by the eastern confluents of the Brook of Egypt (Wadi al-ʿArīsh).

In later times, the name occurs as that of a tribe (Ptolemy, *Geographia*, 3:5 17), and in the Byzantine period, in the description of the area in which St. Nilus searched for his son, who had been kidnapped by the Saracens (PG, vol. 79, pp. 667ff.).

BIBLIOGRAPHY: Aharoni, Land, index; Glueck, in: AASOR, 15 (1935), 104.

[Michael Avi-Yonah]

PARAPET (Heb. מַעֲקֶה). Ancient roofs were flat and in general use (cf. Josh. 2:6; Judg. 16:27; I Sam. 9:25f; Isa. 22:1; et al.), and the Bible enjoins "when thou buildest a new house, then thou shalt make a parapet for thy roof, that thou bring not blood upon thy house, if any man fall from thence" (Deut. 22:8). The parapet must be not less than 10 handbreadths high and strong enough to keep a person who leans on it from falling (Sif. Deut. 229; Maim. Yad, Roẓe'aḥ 11:3). The law was given a far wider application, however, and made to include the need to remove any object that constitutes a public or a private hazard. Such precautions include fencing or covering a well or a pit (Maim. *ibid.*, 11:4) and not keeping a savage dog or a shaky ladder in one's house (BK 15b). The statement of R. Eleazar (BK 4:9), that "No precaution is adequate [for a vicious ox] save the slaughterer's knife," is based by Abbaye on this same law (BK 46a). For the same reason one who keeps a wild dog or cat in his house is placed under the ban (Ket. 41b). Even if only the owner is endangered and he is willing to take the risk, he is forbidden and forcibly prevented if necessary (Maim. *ibid.*, 4f.).

[Harry Freedman]

PARCZEW, district capital in the province of Lublin, E. Poland. Since it lay on the border of the kingdom of Poland and the Duchy of Lithuania, it served as the seat of the sessions of the Sejm until 1564, a fact which greatly affected the sources of livelihood of the Jews living there. An organized Jewish community existed from the beginning of the 16th century. In 1564, 11 houses were owned by Jews. Between 1563 and 1570 a violent struggle was waged between the Jewish community and the municipal council, which sought to move Jewish merchants and craftsmen from the center of the town to its suburbs. In 1591 a compromise was reached: The Jews were to remain in their former places of residence in exchange for their consent to bear an equal share of obligations imposed on the town, an arrangement ratified by the king in 1623. In 1654 King John II

Casimir authorized the Jews to build houses, to engage in commerce within the boundaries of the town, and to manufacture alcoholic liquor for their own needs. In 1674 among the 331 townsmen who paid the poll tax, 84 were Jews. The town was severely damaged in the Northern War (1700–21), and by 1718 only four Jews remained in Parczew. In the course of time Jews made an important contribution to the development of the town and its economy. In 1762 Jews owned 47 houses. In 1765 there were 303 Jews who paid the poll tax, including nine bakers, six tailors, six hatters, and one locksmith. In the 29 villages in the vicinity 151 Jews paid the poll tax. Between 1790 and 1795 Jews established tanneries in the town. Under Russian rule there were no restrictions against the residence of Jews in Parczew. In 1827 the community numbered 1,079 (37% of the total population), and by 1857 had increased to 1,692 (about 50% of the total). During the second half of the 19th century, Jews earned their livelihood mainly from tailoring, weaving, and carpentry, as well as from the retail trade in agricultural produce. During this period the influence of *Ḥasidism intensified. In 1921 there were 4,005 Jews (51% of the population) in the town. Between the two world wars, branches of the Zionist parties and youth organizations as well as the *Agudat Israel were active in Parczew.

[Arthur Cygielman]

Holocaust Period

On the outbreak of World War II there were 5,000 Jews in Parczew. On Sept. 19, 1942, the Germans began to deport the town's Jewish population to the *Treblinka death camp. During this deportation, as well as those from a number of places in the vicinity, several thousand people fled to the Parczew forest (Lasy Parczewskie). Most of them were shot by German armed units, which searched the woods frequently, but a few hundred managed to establish themselves within the forest in a family camp called Altana. A guerrilla battalion under the command of a Jewish officer, Alexander Skotnicki, operated in the Parczew forest. Its largest detachment was a Jewish guerrilla company commanded by Jechiel Grynszpan. When the Parczew region was liberated (at the end of July 1944), about 150 Jewish partisans and about 200 survivors of the Jewish family camp, which existed thanks to the defense provided by the Jewish partisans, left the forest.

[Stefan Krakowski]

BIBLIOGRAPHY: R. Mahler, *Yidn in Amolikn Poyln in Likht fun Tsifern* (1958), index; Warsaw, Archiwum Główne Akt Dawnych, *Lustracje woj. lubelskiego* (1660), pp. 49, 58; ibid. for. (1762), p. 40; Lodz, Archiwum Państwowe, *Archiwum Kossowskich z Glogowy*, no. V-29/1; W.A.P. Lublin, *Księgi gródzkie lubelskie księgi miasta Parczewa* (= CAHJP, ḤM 7049, 6706); B. Wasiutyński, *Ludność żydowska w Polsce w wiekach XIV i XX* (1930), 34; I. Schiper (ed.), *Dzieje handlu żydowskiego na ziemiach polskich* (1937), index; M. Zakrzewska-Dubasowa, *Parczew w XV–XVIII wieku* (1962), 26, 27, 28, 40, 46–48; T. Brustin-Bernstein, in: *Bleter far Geshikhte*, 3, no. 1–2 (1950), 51–78.

PARDES (Heb. פַּרְדֵּ"ס), in the Middle Ages the word *pardes* was used as a mnemonic for the four types of biblical exegesis, an acronym of *peshat ("the literal meaning"), *remez* ("hint," i.e., veiled allusions such as *gematria, and *notarikon), *derash ("homiletical interpretation"), and *sod* ("mystery," i.e., the esoteric interpretation), the word being made up of the initial letters of these words. For the meaning of the word in mysticism, see *Kabbalah.

PARDES ḤANNAH-KARKUR (Heb. פַּרְדֵּס חַנָּה־כַּרְכּוּר), predominantly rural community in the northern Sharon, Israel, about 4 mi. (7 km.) N.E. of Ḥaderah, created in 1969 through the amalgamation of Pardes Ḥannah and Karkur. Karkur was founded in 1913 by a group of English Jews, "Aḥuzzat London," on land acquired the year before by the Palestine Land Development Company and guarded by members of *Ha-Shomer who remained and worked on the place, together with other Jewish laborers, until the 1920s. In 1919 building began, but a part of the English group arrived only in 1925–26. In 1927 Karkur already numbered 300 inhabitants, and the initially hard conditions improved after abundant groundwater was found. The moshav, based mainly on citrus, had 900 inhabitants in 1948; its population increased to 3,000 in 1952, but has since remained the same. Most inhabitants are from Eastern Europe; others are from Yemen. It is the site of a *dew research station.

Pardes Ḥannah was established in 1929 by the Palestine Jewish Colonization Association for the settlement of veteran farm laborers. In 1939 the moshavah was enlarged to include the neighboring village of Meged founded in 1933. During the 1930s, immigrants from Central Europe joined Pardes Ḥannah, some of whom erected the Tel Shalom quarter. In 1947 a housing project was set up named Neveh Asher, after Selig *Brodetsky. During World War II, the British authorities expropriated Pardes Ḥannah lands to build large military camps which after 1948 became two large *ma'barot (immigrant transit camps), bringing the population from 2,350 inhabitants to over 10,000. When the *ma'barot* were closed down at the end of the 1950s, only some of their inhabitants remained and were transferred to local housing. The population figure then shrank to 7,500 but slowly rose again to 13,400 in 1970. The economy of Pardes Ḥannah-Karkur was based on highly intensive and fully irrigated farming as well as on industry. There were several large schools, including the agricultural high school of the Farmers' Union (*Hitaḥadut ha-Ikkarim) and No'am, the combined yeshivah high school. In the mid-1990s the population of Pardes Hannah-Karkur was approximately 19,400, rising to 28,800 in 2002. The local council's area of jurisdiction extends over 9 sq. mi. (23 sq. km.). Pardes Hannah-Karkur serves as an urban center for the region, its economy now based on services, commerce, industry (wood and building materials, agricultural machinery, and plastics), and agriculture (citrus groves, field crops and fruit orchards). "Pardes Ḥannah," meaning "Hannah's Citrus Grove," commemorates a cousin of Baron Edmond de *Rothschild.

BIBLIOGRAPHY: A. Ever-Hadani (ed.), *Aḥuzzah Alef London-Karkur 1913–1968* (1969), with Eng. summ.

[Efraim Orni / Shaked Gilboa (2nd ed.)]

PARDES, ELIYAHU (1893–1972), chief rabbi of Jerusalem and leader of religious Zionism. Born in Jerusalem, descendant of a long line of Sephardi rabbis, he served as an educator and administrator from 1915 to 1952. He was among the founders of the religious-nationalist group "Al ha-Mishmar" in 1925 and played an active role in the leadership of the Mizrachi Organization. During this period, he also served on the Jerusalem rabbinic court and was sent on several trips as educational emissary to North Africa, Europe and South America. In 1953 he was elected rabbi of Ramat Gan and, from 1961 until his death, he served as chief rabbi of Jerusalem.

He was deeply committed to the Zionist cause, and worked tirelessly to inculcate in the younger generation a love of Israel and concern for settlement, both within Palestine and abroad. He was among the first educators to struggle for the revival of the Hebrew language and its use in daily life. He was a lover of peace, and constantly attempted to unite the various political, religious and ethnic groups within the *Yishuv.* As a rabbinic scholar, he wrote on *halakhah*, ethics and homiletics. A selection of his articles and responsa appeared in 1974.

PARDES, SHMUEL AARON (1887–1956), rabbi. Born in 1887 in Stashov, Poland, he studied in Kensk and then in Ostovsvski, where he was ordained. He then served as rabbi in Zarick, where he established a Torah publication called *Ha-Pardes*, which was suspended during World War I. However, it followed him to Zavyertza, where he had become rabbi after the war, and then to the United States, where he immigrated in 1924. Some of the most respected rabbis in Europe published their commentaries in *Ha-Pardes*. He served as rabbi in Bendin and then as *dayyan* in Chestokova before immigrating to the U.S. He became rabbi of the Montgomery Street Synagogue in New York and then moved to Chicago as rabbi of Bikur Cholim, where in 1927 he reestablished *Ha-Pardes*, which became a quasi-organ of the Agudat Harabbonim. He used the platform of his journal to support men like himself, East European rabbis, and to criticize his more Westernized colleagues of the Rabbinical Council of America. *Ha-Pardes* is among his most enduring contributions.

He wrote "*Pilpul be-Inyan Batla Da'ata Ezel Kol Adam*," in *Sefer Kevod Ḥahamin* (1935), and was editor of Yehuda Leib Graubart's *Ḥavalim be-Ne'imim*, vol. 5 (1939).

BIBLIOGRAPHY: M.D. Sherman, *Orthodox Judaism in America: A Biographical Dictionary and Sourcebook* (1996).

[Michael Berenbaum (2nd ed.)]

PARDESIYYAH (Heb. פַּרְדֵּסִיָּה), Jewish village with municipal council status, in central Israel, about 4 mi. (6 km.) southeast of Netanyah. Founded in 1940, it initially housed a few families of Jewish laborers originating from Yemen who were employed in the citrus groves in the vicinity. The village expanded greatly in the 1950s, as it was in the neighborhood of large *ma'barot* (immigrant camps), part of whose area was included in Pardesiyyah's municipal boundary. The village had 332 inhabitants in 1955, 1,587 in 1961, and 800 in 1970. In the mid-1990s the population was approximately 1,820, and at the end of 2002 it was 5,920 residents, occupying an area of half a square mile (1.3 sq. km.). Income was much higher than the national average. The Lev Hasharon Mental Health Center is located there.

[Efraim Orni / Shaked Gilboa (2nd ed.)]

PARDO, family which apparently originated in Prado del Rey, Castile, and which flourished during the 16th–18th centuries in the Ottoman Empire, Italy, the Netherlands, England, and America. The more celebrated members of the family are dealt with under separate entries.

DAVID (d. 1657), the son of Joseph *Pardo, served as rabbi in Amsterdam. He was born in Salonika and moved to Amsterdam with his father. In 1618 he was appointed rabbi of the Beth Israel congregations. After the three Sephardi congregations had amalgamated into the Talmud Torah congregation (1639), he was appointed one of its four rabbis and trustee of the cemetery. He published an edition in Latin characters of Ẓaddik b. Joseph Formon's Ladino translation of *Ḥovot ha-Levavot* by Baḥya ibn Paquda (Amsterdam, 1610). His son, Josiah, was a disciple and son-in-law of Saul Levi *Morteira. After teaching in the Yesiba de los Pintos of Rotterdam, which was transferred to Amsterdam in 1669, he emigrated to Curaçao (Antilles). From 1674 he was *ḥakham* of the community there and appears to have founded the local yeshivah, Ez Ḥayyim ve-Ohel Ya'akov. In 1683 he left for Jamaica, where he also served as rabbi. David Pardo (d. c. 1717), the rabbi of the Portuguese community of Surinam, was probably his son.

The Pardo family was scattered throughout North America, where they became known as Brown (or Browne; although the actual meaning of Pardo is "grey"). Saul Pardo (d. 1708), known as Saul Brown, was the first *ḥazzan* of the Jewish community of New York. He held this office in the She'erit Israel synagogue until 1682.

BIBLIOGRAPHY: Kayserling, Bibl, index; L. Blau, *Leo Modenas Briefe und Schriftstuecke* (1907), 79ff.; J. Mendes dos Remedios, *Os Judeus Portuguesesem Amsterdam* (1911), 9, 13, 16, 41; J.S. da Silva Rosa, *Geschiedenis der Portugeesche Joden te Amsterdam* (1925), index; C. Roth, *A Life of Menasseh. Ben Israel* (1934), index; H.I. Bloom, *The Economic Activities of Jews of Amsterdam* (1937), index; Brugmans-Frank, 211ff.; H.B. Grinstein, *The Rise of the Jewish Community of New York* (1945), 484, 488; J.R. Marcus, *Early American Jewry*, 1 (1951), 35, and index s.v. *Brown*; Wiznitzer, in: HJ, 20 (1958), 110f., 117f.; Emmanuel, in: AJHSP, 44 (1954–55), 216f., 221, 225 n.; Hershkowitz, *ibid.*, 55 (1965–66), 324ff. and index s.v. *Brown, Browne.*

PARDO, DAVID SAMUEL BEN JACOB (1718–1790), rabbinical author and poet. Born in Venice, he went to Sarajevo for a time as a result of a dispute over an inheritance, and from there to Spalato, in Dalmatia. From approximately 1738 he was a teacher of children, at the same time studying under the local rabbi, Abraham David Papo. Eventually Pardo was appointed rabbi of the town. From 1760 he was rabbi of Sarajevo. From 1776 to 1782 he traveled to Erez Israel, settling in Jerusalem where he served as head of the yeshivah Ḥesed le-Avraham u-Vinyan Shelomo. Pardo was regarded as one of

Jerusalem's great rabbis. Of his many works his series of commentaries and novellae on tannaitic literature are especially original. His first work was *Shoshannim le-David* (Venice, 1752), a commentary on the Mishnah. The somewhat sharp language he employed in the first part in criticizing contemporary scholars gave rise to friction between him and David Corinaldi and Mas'ud Rokeaḥ in Leghorn. But after he mitigated his language in the second part and published an apology, a reconciliation took place.

Pardo's *Ḥasdei David* (Leghorn, 1776–90; Jerusalem, 1890) on the Tosefta is considered the most important commentary on this work (the portion on *Tohorot*, the manuscript of which is in the National Library of Jerusalem, has not been published). He completed the work in Jerusalem on his 68th birthday. Portions of it were published in the Romm Vilna edition of the Talmud with the text of the Tosefta. Similarly, his *Sifrei de-Vei Rav* (Salonika, 1799), which he commenced in 1786 and was published by his son Abraham after his death, is the most important commentary on the *Sifrei*. In it he makes use of commentaries of Hillel b. Eliakim, Solomon ibn Okhana, and Eliezer ibn Nahum, all of which he had in manuscript. Other works he wrote are *Mikhtam le-David* (Salonika, 1772), halakhic decisions and responsa; *Maskil le-David* (Venice, 1761), a supercommentary on Rashi's biblical commentary; *La-Menazze'aḥ le-David* (Salonika, 1765), on those talmudic passages where alternative explanations are given; and *Mizmor le-David* (Leghorn, 1818), notes on the *Perot Ginnosar* of Hezekiah da Silva and Ḥayyim ibn Attar on Shulḥan Arukh, *Even ha-Ezer*. Pardo's liturgical poems and prayers are included in the Sephardi daily and festival prayer books. His arrangement of the *Avodah* for the Day of Atonement, which was adopted in the Sephardi rite, appeared in his *Shifat Revivim* (Leghorn, 1788).

Of his sons, Jacob Pardo became chief rabbi of Ragusa and died in Jerusalem. He was a noted talmudist and well versed in Kabbalah. His chief works were *Kohelet Ya'akov* (Venice, 1784), a commentary on the early prophets; *Appe Zutre (ibid.*, 1797), on *Hilkhot Ishut* of the Shulḥan Arukh *Even ha-Ezer*; and *Minḥat Aharon* (*ibid.*, 1809), which deals mainly with the laws of prayer. A second son, Isaac, was rabbi of Sarajevo, while a third, Abraham, who married the daughter of Ḥ.J.D. *Azulai, became head of the yeshivah Ḥesed le-Avraham u-Vinyan Shelomo after his father-in-law's death. Pardo's disciples included Shabbetai b. Abraham Ventura, who succeeded him as rabbi of Spalato, David Pinto, and Abraham Penso.

BIBLIOGRAPHY: Frumkin-Rivlin, 3 (1929), 95–98; Rosanes, Togarmah, 5 (1938), 117–22, 175–7; M.D. Gaon, *Yehudei ha-Mizraḥ be-Ereẓ Yisrael*, 2 (1938), 539–40; M. Benayahu, *Ḥ.J.D. Azulai* (Heb., 1959), 71–72, 357–60.

[Shlomoh Zalman Havlin]

PARDO, JOSEPH (d. 1619), Italian rabbi and merchant. Pardo was born in Salonika, but went to Venice before 1589, and there he served as rabbi to the Levantine community and also engaged in business. He and Judah Leib *Saraval made themselves responsible for the collection of money from the Jews of Italy for the poor of Ereẓ Israel. He also financed the publication of several books: *Genesis Rabbah* (Venice, 1597–1606) with the commentary *Yefeh To'ar* of Samuel Jaffe Ashkenazi. He was unsuccessful in his plan to publish a number of intended publications, one an edition of the Talmud which was to have been published in Salonika, and another the *Ma'amar Yayin ha-Meshummar* which was later published by Nathan Shapira with his own additions (Venice, 1660). In 1601 Pardo wanted to publish a new commentary on the Pentateuch consisting of literal interpretations culled from the works of the classical commentators. The work of preparing the commentary was given to Leone de *Modena, who, as he states in his introduction to the commentary (which is still in manuscript) succeeded in preparing the sections only on the weekly portions of *Bereshit*, *Pinḥas*, *Mattot*, and *Masei*. He also relates there that Pardo became bankrupt and moved to Amsterdam (probably toward the end of 1608 or the beginning of 1609). From 1609 until his death Pardo served as rabbi of the Beit Ya'akov congregation of Amsterdam. One of the regulations he introduced was that every member was obliged to pay a fixed sum yearly for the communities of Jerusalem and Safed. Two **bakkashot* he composed were published in the *Imrei No'am* (Amsterdam, 1628, pp. 158–9).

His grandson JOSEPH PARDO (d. 1677) was the reader of the Spanish and Portuguese congregation in London; he died in Amsterdam. He was the author of *Shulḥan Tahor*, on *Oraḥ Ḥayyim* and *Yoreh De'ah*, which is written with the maximum of brevity. It was published a number of times, first by his son David Pardo in 1686 in London; in 1689 it was published with a Spanish translation. Apparently it lost its popularity with scholars in the course of time because of its excessive brevity.

BIBLIOGRAPHY: A. Neubauer, in: REJ, 22 (1891), 82–84; J. Blau, *Kitvei ha-Rav Yehudah Aryeh mi-Modena* (1905), 79–81, 127, 139, 190; S. Seeligman, *Bibliographie en Historie... Sepharadim in Amsterdam* (1927), 26–30; I. Solomons, in: JHST, 12 (1928–1931), 88–90; Ch. Tchernowitz, *Toledoth ha-Poskim* 3 (1947), 297–99; I.S. Emmanuel, in: *Sefunot*, 6 (1962), 401–402; I. Sonne, *Kobez al-Jad*, 5 (1950), 215–216.

[Abraham David]

PARDO, MOSES BEN RAPHAEL (d. 1888), rabbi and rabbinical emissary. Pardo was born in Jerusalem. After serving as rabbi in Jerusalem for many years, he left the city in 1870, traveling to North Africa on a mission on behalf of Jerusalem. On his return trip in 1871 he stopped at Alexandria and accepted an offer to serve as the rabbi of the Jewish community there, a post which he retained until his death. Pardo was the author of *Hora'ah de-Veit Din* (Izmir, 1872), on divorce laws; *Shemo Moshe* (*ibid.*, 1874), responsa; and *Ẓedek u-Mishpat* (*ibid.*, 1874), novellae to *Ḥoshen Mishpat*.

BIBLIOGRAPHY: Frumkin-Rivlin, 3 (1929), 312; M.D. Gaon, *Yehudei ha-Mizraḥ be-Ereẓ Yisrael*, 2 (1937), 541f.; J.M. Landau, *Ha-Yehudim be-Miẓrayim* (1967), index.

PARENT AND CHILD.

STATUS OF THE CHILD

In Jewish law, there is no discrimination against a child because of the mere fact that he is born out of lawful wedlock. While the said fact may complicate the question of establishing paternity, once the identity of the father is clearly known there is no distinction in law so far as the parent-child relationship is concerned, between such a child and one born in lawful wedlock. This is also the position with regard to a **mamzer*. On the status of a child with one non-Jewish parent, see below. For further details, see **Yuḥasin*.

PARENTAL RIGHTS

Except as detailed below, the principle in Jewish law is that parents have no legal rights in respect of their children, neither as to their person nor their property (Ket. 46b–47a; Sh. Ar., ḤM 424:7). So far as male children are concerned, the father is entitled to the finds of his son even if the latter is a *gadol* (i.e., beyond the age until which his father is obliged by law to maintain him), provided that the son is dependent on him (lit. "seated at his table"); this is "for the reason of enmity," i.e., in order to avoid the enmity which might arise between father and son if the former, who supports his son without even being obliged to by law, was not even entitled to the finds that come to the son without any effort or investment on his part (BM 12a–b; Sh. Ar., ḤM 270:2 and commentaries). For the same reason the father is entitled to the income of his dependent son (*Rema*, ḤM 270:2). Hence a father who is obliged by law to maintain his son – for example, because he has so undertaken in a divorce agreement – has no claim to the finds or income of the son, and therefore he is entitled to set them off against his liability to maintain him (*Taz*, ḤM 270:2; PDR 3:329). As regards his daughter, the father is entitled to everything mentioned above, even if she is not dependent on him, until she becomes a major (*bogeret*), since until then she remains under his authority. For the same reason, until she reaches her majority, the father will be entitled to her handiwork and to give her in *marriage (Ket. 46a–47a; Yad, Ishut 3:11; see also Avadim 4:2). The mother has none of these rights in respect of her children since in law she has no pecuniary obligations toward them (see below).

PARENTAL OBLIGATIONS

The general rule is that the legal obligations toward their children are imposed on the father alone and not on the mother (*Maggid Mishneh*, Ishut, 21:18).

Maintenance

OBLIGATIONS OF THE FATHER. The father's duty to maintain his son embraces the responsibility of providing for all the child's needs, including his daily care (Yad, Ishut 13:6; Sh. Ar., EH 73:6, 7). The rules concerning the duty of maintenance also apply with regard to the father's duty to educate his son and to teach him Torah, to see that he learns a trade or profession, and to bear all the necessary expenses connected with this (Kid. 29b, 30; Sh. Ar., YD 245:1, 4). Until the son reaches the age of six years (see below), these obligations must be borne by the father even if he has limited means and the son has independent means of his own, e.g., acquired by inheritance (Sh. Ar., EH 71:1). These obligations are imposed on the father by virtue of his paternity, whether or not he is married to the child's mother, and therefore notwithstanding termination of the marriage between the child's parents, by death or divorce, or the fact that the child was born out of wedlock (Resp. Ribash no. 41; Resp. Rosh 17:7; contrary to Ran, on Rif at end of Ket. ch. 5, who is of the opinion that the father's obligation to support his children is linked with his obligation to maintain his wife).

OBLIGATION OF THE MOTHER. The mother has no legal obligation to maintain her children, even if she is able to do so out of her own property or income (*Ba'er Heitev*, EH 71, n. 1). She may only be obliged to do so on the strength of the rules of *ẓedakah* ("charity") if, after providing in full for her own needs, she is able to satisfy the needs of her children when they have no property or income of their own, and the father, being poor, is unable to support them (*Pitḥei Teshuvah*, EH 82 n. 3; PDR 2:3). The position is different, however, if the mother has undertaken to maintain her children, for example in a divorce agreement. In this event, if the mother has the means to support her children at a time when the father is not legally obliged to do so (i.e., because they are above the specified age), she alone will have to maintain them as she is obliged to do by virtue of law (her undertaking); the father's duty in this case is based on the rules of *ẓedakah* only, and since the children have property of their own (the right to be maintained by the mother) they are no longer in need of *ẓedakah* (PDR 3:170; 4:3, 7). On the wife's duty to take care of her children as part of her marital duties toward her husband, see *Husband and Wife.

If the child's mother is not entitled to maintenance from the father – e.g., because the parties are divorced – and the child is in need of her care, so that she can no longer continue to work and support herself, there will be legal grounds for obliging the father to maintain her to a certain extent, including payment of the rental for her dwelling. Because it is in the interests of the child to be with the mother, she must dwell with him, and because the expenses necessary for taking care of the child devolve on the father, he has to bear them within the limits of the remuneration he would otherwise be called upon to pay any other woman for taking care of the child. This would include the cost of the child's dwelling (with the mother) – notwithstanding the fact that the mother is in a position to defray all the said expenses out of her own means (PDR 1:118f.; 2:3, 5f.). After being divorced, the mother may also claim from the child's father any of the said expenses she incurred before she filed her claim for them, since, unlike the case of a married woman, there is no room for considering that she has waived this claim (PDR 1:230, 234; 2:164f.; Resp. Maharsham, pt. 2, no. 236).

THE STANDARD OF MAINTENANCE. Unlike maintenance for a wife (see *Husband and Wife), the standard of maintenance to which children are entitled is determined by their actual needs and not by the financial status of their father (Yad, Ishut 13:6; Sh. Ar., EH 73:6). For this purpose the needs of a child will not be limited to an essential minimum, but they may vary according to whether the child is from a rich or a poor family. Certainly, under the laws of *ẓedakah*, a wealthy father may be made liable to maintain his children as befits them and not merely as absolutely necessary, although in a case where a child has other sources of income, and thus is not in need of *ẓedakah*, he will not be entitled to maintenance (Sh. Ar. EH 82:7; PDR 2:3, 8; 4:3, 7). On the other hand, in determining the essential, minimum attention will be paid to what the father is capable of earning and not merely to his actual income.

ADDITIONAL OBLIGATIONS TOWARD DAUGHTERS. In addition to maintaining his daughter, the father has to see to her marriage to a worthy husband, and, if the need arises, to provide her with a dowry sufficient at least – if his means permit – to cover a year's raiment (Ḥelkat Meḥokek 58, n. 1). Although the father is not legally obliged to give a dowry in accordance with his means, it is a mitzvah for him and he should do so (Ket. 68a; Sh. Ar., EH 58:1 and 71:1, Rema, ad loc. n. 4). On the father's death, and in the absence of a testamentary disposition depriving his daughter of a dowry, his heirs are bound to give the daughter a dowry based on an assessment of what her father would have given her had he been alive; in the absence of data that might form the basis for such assessment, the heirs have to give her one-tenth of the estate for the purpose of her marriage (see *Succession; Ket. 68a; Sh. Ar., EH 113:2, 10).

CHILDREN ENTITLED TO MAINTENANCE UNTIL A CERTAIN AGE. An opinion that a *takkanah* of the *Sanhedrin (i.e., the *Takkanat Usha*) laid down that the father must maintain his children as long as they are minors (sons until the age of 13 and daughters until 12) was not followed, and the *halakhah* was laid down to the effect that the father's legal obligation is only to maintain his children until they reach the age of six full years (Ket. 49b., 65b; Sh. Ar., EH 71:1); above this age the obligation flows merely from the laws of *ẓedakah*, and, insofar as they are applicable (see above), fulfillment of the obligation will be compulsory. Since it concerns a person's own children, the charitable duty is more stringent in this case than it is with ordinary *ẓedakah*, and therefore the father will be required to exert himself to the utmost in order to satisfy his children's needs (Ket. and Sh. Ar. loc. cit.; Yad, Ishut 12:14, 15:21:17, *Maggid Mishneh*; Sh. Ar., YD 251:4). In the course of time it became apparent that the legal position as described above did not adequately protect the interests of children above six years of age, as the father tried to evade his duty. Hence it was ordained in a *takkanah* of the Chief Rabbinate of Palestine (1944) that the father shall be bound to maintain his sons and daughters until they reach the age of 15 years, provided they have no independent means of support (see Freimann, bibl.).

MAINTENANCE OUT OF THE DECEASED'S ESTATE. The father's obligation to maintain his children is imposed on him as father and terminates upon his death without being transmitted to his heirs as a charge on the estate. Hence the minor heirs cannot demand from the others that they should be maintained out of the estate in addition to their normal share of the legacy; the estate will therefore be divided amongst all the heirs, each of them, regardless of age, being given his rightful share (BB 139a; Sh. Ar., ḤM 286:1). The position is different, however, with regard to the maintenance of the daughters of the deceased. Jewish law excludes daughters from succession to their father's estate when he is survived by sons or their descendants (see *Succession), and instead, in such a case, entitles daughters to be maintained out of the estate until their majority or marriage – whichever comes first – to the same extent as they were entitled during their father's lifetime (i.e., in accordance with their needs; Ket. 52b, 53b; Sh. Ar., EH 112:16). This right of the daughter flows from the conditions of her mother's *ketubbah* as her independent right, and therefore she cannot be deprived of it without her own consent, neither by her father's testamentary disposition nor by her mother's waiver of the respective condition of the *ketubbah* in an agreement with the father, and it remains in force notwithstanding the divorce of her parents (Ket. loc. cit., Yad, Ishut 12:2; 19: 10; *Rema*, EH 112:1). If the assets of the estate are not sufficient to satisfy both the daughters' right of maintenance and the heirs' rights of succession (*nekhasim mu'atim*), the daughters' right takes preference (Ket. 108b; Sh. Ar., EH 112:11); even if the assets of the estate should suffice for both (*nekhasim merubbim*) but there is established reason to fear that the sons might squander them and thus endanger the daughters' maintenance, the court will have power to take any steps it may deem fit for the preservation of the daughters' right (*Rema* loc. cit.).

Custody of Children

The law deals here with the determination of a child's abode, taking into account the responsibility of the parents for his physical and spiritual welfare, his raising, and his education. The rule is that the child's own interest is always the paramount consideration and his custody is a matter of a parental duty rather than a right, it being a right of the child vis-à-vis his parents.

DIFFERENT RULES FOR BOYS AND GIRLS. In pursuance of this rule, the halakhic scholars laid down that children below the age of six years must be in the custody of their mother, since at this tender age they are mainly in need of physical care and attention. Above the age of six, boys must be with their father, since at this age they are in need of education and religious instruction, a task imposed by law upon the father, and girls with their mother ("the daughter must always be with her mother"), since they are in need of her instruction in the ways of modesty (Ket. 102b, 103a; Yad, Ishut, 21:17; Sh. Ar., EH 82:7). As these rules are directed at serving the welfare of the child, the court may diverge from them if in a proper case it considers it necessary in the interests of the child, and even order that he be removed from both his parents and be kept in a place where, in the court's opinion, his interests are better served (*Rema*, EH 82:7; *Pitḥei Teshuvah* ad loc., n. 6, in the name of Radbaz). The custody of the child is a matter not of the rights of the parents but of the rights of the child in respect of his parents. The principle of the matter is that the rule establishing the right that the daughter be always with her mother establishes the daughter's right and not the mother's; similarly in the case of the son until the age of six, it is the son's right which is established and not the father's (Resp. Maharashdam, EH 123; see also Resp. Radbaz, no. 123). As Ereẓ Israel is looked upon as the best possible place for bringing up and educating a Jewish child, his removal abroad will generally not be approved, but the court may nevertheless permit this to the mother or father if it is satisfied that in the circumstances it is necessary in the better interests of the child (PDR 1:103–7, 173–8).

RELATION BETWEEN CUSTODY AND DUTY OF MAINTENANCE. The rules concerning the custody of children have no influence on the parental obligation to maintain them. Hence the fact that the children are with their mother in accordance with these rules does not relieve the father from his obligation to maintain them – whether this is based on law or the rules of *ẓedakah* (Sh. Ar., EH 82:7). Moreover, the mother is not obliged to accept the children inasmuch as, on principle, the duty to take care of them is imposed on the father only; should she therefore refuse to take them, she may send them to him and he will not be entitled to reject them (Yad, Ishut 21:18; Sh. Ar., EH 82:8). However, if a boy above the age of six should be with his mother contrary to law, i.e., without the consent of the father or permission of the court, the father will be entitled to refuse to pay for the boy's maintenance for any period he is not with him (ibid).

ACCESS OF THE NON-CUSTODIAN PARENT. The custodian parent has no right to deprive the other of access to their child, nor the child of access to the other parent, since the child is entitled to derive education and care from both his parents and to maintain his natural tie with both of them, so as not to grow up as if orphaned of one of them. For the purpose of realization of this right of the child, it is incumbent on the parents to come to an understanding between themselves, failing which the court will decide the question of access on the basis of the child's interest rather than those of his parents. Since for each of the parents it is a matter of a duty (not of a right) toward their child, they will not be entitled to make performance of the one's obligation dependent upon performance of the other's. Thus the fact that the mother refuses to allow her son to visit his father, or the father to have access to him, in defiance of an agreement or order of the court to this effect, will not entitle the father to withhold the son's maintenance for as long as the mother persists in her attitude; nor will the mother be entitled to refuse the father access to the child because the father withholds the latter's maintenance (PDR 1:113, 118, 158, 176).

CUSTODY IN CASE OF DEATH OF EITHER OR BOTH PARENTS. In this case too the decisive question is the welfare of the child. On the death of either parent, it is presumed to be best served by leaving the child with the surviving parent, while in principle no special right of custody exists in favor of the parents of the deceased. Only when clearly indicated in the interests of the child, having the regard for all the circumstances including the care of teaching him Torah, will the court order otherwise (PDR 1:65–77). On the death of both parents, custody of the child will generally be given to the grandparents on the side of the parent who would have been entitled to custody had both been alive (*Rema*, EH 82:7 and *Ḥelkat Meḥokek* ad loc., n. 11; Resp. Radbaz no. 123).

AGREEMENTS BETWEEN PARENTS CONCERNING THEIR CHILDREN

An agreement between parents as to maintenance or custody of their child will not avail to affect his rights unless proved to be in his best interest, nor will it preclude him, since he is represented by one parent, from claiming their enforcement against the other. The child is not party to an agreement between the parents, and the rule is that "no obligation can be imposed on a person in his absence" (BM 12a; PDR 2:3). Hence the father, in a claim against him by the child for maintenance, will not escape liability on a plea that he is free of such a liability by virtue of an agreement made with the mother in which she took this liability upon herself (PDR 2:171–7; 5:171, 173). The effect, if any, of such agreement is merely that it may possibly give the father the right to recover from the mother any amount he may have to expend on the child's maintenance, but toward the child it is of no effect (PDR 5:171). Similarly, a divorce agreement in which the mother waives the right to custody of her children below the age of six, or the father to custody of his sons above this age, will not preclude the children from claiming through the other parent that the court should disregard the terms of the agreement and decide the matter in their own best interest only, in the light of all the circumstances. For this purpose, the question of whether the change of his abode may detrimentally affect the child's mental well-being will be a weighty consideration (PDR 1:177) and, in a proper case, if the court considers it just to do so, it will also pay due regard to the child's own wishes (*Ḥelkat Meḥokek* 82, n. 10 and *Ba'er Heitev* ad loc., n. 6). The court's approval of such an agreement will not preclude a fresh approach to the court, owing to the fact that the circumstances have later changed, nor an application for the reconsideration of the case with regard to the child's best interests in the light of such a change (Resp. Radbaz no. 123; PDR 4:332–6).

CHILDREN OF PARENTS WHO ARE NOT BOTH JEWISH

Unless both parents are Jewish, the father has no legal standing in relation to the children, neither as regards maintenance nor custody. If the father is Jewish and the mother not, the child will be considered a non-Jew while, halakhically speaking, the non-Jewish father will not be considered his father (see *Yuḥasin). Since the duty of maintenance, like all other paternal duties, is only imposed on the person halakhically recognized as the father – toward his halakhically recognized child – there is therefore no room for the imposition of any recognized legal obligation incumbent on the father of a child qua father, except if he and the mother are both Jewish. A different, and so far apparently unsupported, opinion was expressed by R. Ben Zion Ouziel (*Mishpetei Uziel*, EH no. 4).

IN THE STATE OF ISRAEL

Matters of child maintenance by Jewish parents are governed by Jewish law (s. 3 of the Family Law Amendment (Maintenance) Law, 1959; see also no. 507/61 in PD 16 (1962), 925, 928; no. 426/65, PD 20, pt. 2 (1966), 21). Other matters, including custody – in the case of Jewish parents – are also governed by Jewish law, except as otherwise provided in the Capacity and Guardianship Law, 1962. For their greater part both the above-mentioned laws are based on principles of Jewish law (see Elon, bibl.), and they regulate the legal position of both parents as regards maintenance and custody of their children even where one parent is a non-Jew.

For the social and ethical relationship between parent and child, see *Family; *Parents, Honor of, on patrilineal descent, see *Reform Judaism.

[Ben-Zion (Benno) Schereschewsky]

FURTHER DEVELOPMENTS IN ISRAELI LAW

Custody and Education – Rights and Obligations of Parents

The Capacity and Guardianship Law, 5722 – 1962 (hereinafter – "the Capacity Law" or "the Law") establishes an Israeli civil arrangement which occasionally contradicts certain principles of Jewish law. While the legal principles of Section 25 of the law, dealing with child custody, do to a certain extent resemble the principles of Jewish law, the general principles underlying the arrangement are in fact different. In addition, Section 79 of the law states that a religious court, such as the rabbinical court, that has jurisdiction in matters pertaining to this law, should employ the principles of the Capacity Law. Section 15 of the Capacity Law provides, inter alia, that the biological parents, who are their child's natural guardians, have a right and duty to educate their child. The nature of this right and duty are analyzed by the Israel Supreme Court in the Nagar case (ST 1/81 *Nagar v. Nagar* 38(1) PD 365, 392–398, per Justice Menachem Elon).

Child Maintenance

According to Section 3 of the Family Law Amendment (Maintenance) Law, 5719 – 1959, (hereinafter – "Maintenance Law"), a person responsible for child maintenance is obligated to do so in accordance with the provisions of personal law applying to that individual; thus, in the case of a Jew the principles of Jewish law would apply. The interpretation given by the civil courts to the father's and mother's obligation to provide for their children under Section 3 of the Maintenance Law, in accordance with "the personal law applicable to them," created greater equality between the respective obligations of the father and the mother to provide for their children. While traditional Jewish law, until less than 300 years ago, placed no obligation on the mother to provide financial support for her children, the interpretation of Israel's Supreme Court, which is Israeli, judge-made law, wrought a change in this situation. A number of obligations included in the overall requirement to provide for the maintenance of Jewish children are governed by the laws of charity (*ẓedakah*), both in terms of their source and in terms of the criterion for obligating a parent or parents to pay them. With respect to these obligations, Justice Kister ruled that the father and mother are equally obligated to bear the cost (CA 166/66 *Goldman v. Goldman*, 20 (2) PD 533). In those instances, the mother and the father are obligated to bear the cost of their children's maintenance in light of their respective financial situations. Even if the father is wealthy, his obligation to pay for his children's maintenance does not exempt the mother from her obligation to share equally in the burden of payments for their children's maintenance, if she is wealthy. This interpretation of the principles of Jewish law reflects a modern innovation. Initially, the mother's obligation was broadened, but in a limited manner. Rabbi Meir Posner extended the mother's responsibility to bear the cost of maintenance for her children (see *Beit Meir*, EH 82.5). However, he held that the mother's responsibility to bear the cost of child maintenance if she is wealthy does not apply if the father or his relatives can bear the expense of such maintenance alone. In his opinion, the father and his relatives have a prior responsibility to bear the maintenance costs themselves. Only when the father and his relatives are unable to bear the full cost, or even part of maintenance, does the wealthy mother bear the responsibility in full or in part. Some years after Justice Kister delivered his innovative ruling that, in the aforementioned circumstances, the mother and father share an equal obligation to bear the cost of maintenance, Rabbi Yisraeli ruled in a similar vein in a decision in the Rabbinic Court of Appeals. In his view, child maintenance costs assessed according to the laws of *ẓedakah* are the responsibility of the father and the mother, to be shared equally (File 5733/39, PDR 9 251, p. 263). Another leading judgment in this context was delivered by Israel Supreme Court Justice Elisha Sheinbaum (CA 591/81 *Portugez v Portugez*, 36 (3) PD) 449). Relying inter alia on the novel formulations of Jewish law articulated by Justice Kister and Rav Yisraeli, Justice Sheinbaum ruled that the father and mother share an equal obligation for child maintenance payments determined in accordance with the laws of *ẓedakah*. With regard to the mother's obligation, he made no distinction between a case in which the father is poor and one in which the father is wealthy. In his opinion, both parents' obligations are established in light of their respective economic ability, and in accordance with the minor's needs. From that time on, that principle became the guiding principle in Supreme Court decisions regarding the obligations of Jewish parents for child maintenance costs based on the laws of *ẓedakah*. (See, e.g., CA 74/80 *Notkovich v. Notkovich*, 37(4) PD 197.)

In one area – child maintenance for small children until the age of six – the obligation to pay a certain basic component of maintenance, called "essential needs," is imposed upon the father alone. In this area, Israeli civil courts have ruled in a manner that shows a trend toward reducing the scope of those "essential needs" to the lowest possible minimum, so as to assure greater equality between father and mother in their obligation to bear the costs of child maintenance. At an earlier stage Justice Sheinbaum defined "essential needs" as the basic needs necessary for the child's actual sustenance (see *Portugez*, ibid). Years later, Family Court Judge Yehoshua Gaiffman ruled that the definition of "essential needs" should be restricted so as to engender greater equality between father and mother with respect to child maintenance obligations. According to this approach, the "essential needs" are not the child's various vital needs. Rather, they consist of those basic needs, the satisfaction of which is necessary for his very existence. (FF (Tel Aviv) 31980/96 *Anon. v. Anon.*; FF (Tel Aviv) 82010/96 *Sa'ar v. Hefer*). Nevertheless, the sources of Jewish law do not provide any such definition of "essential needs." In full awareness and intentionally, Israeli civil rulings offer their own interpretation of child maintenance rules in Jewish law. Judge Gaiffman stated, "Jewish law's rules of fairness are a normative framework that must be filled with content, and not a framework incapable of change" (Sa'ar case, ibid). As a result of the limitation of the scope of "essential needs" which are imposed exclusively on the father, the remaining needs, excluded from the category of "essential needs," are governed by the principles of charity, thus creating an equal obligation for both parents.

Israeli legislation also intervened to engender greater equality between Jewish fathers and mothers in the area of child maintenance in Israeli civil courts. In 1981, Section 3A was added to the Family Law Amendment (Maintenance) Law, 5719 – 1959. This section stated that: "(a) The father and mother of a minor are liable for his maintenance. (b) Irrespective of who has charge of the minor, his maintenance is due from his parents in proportion to their respective incomes from any source." The application of this section was supposed to be independent of the rules of the personal law of the parent obliged to pay child maintenance. Where the parent is Jewish, even in cases where the principles of Jewish law stipulate an unequal division of the obligation to pay child maintenance, Section 3A of the law mandates a deviation from these principles so as to create greater equality between the father and mother in the obligation to provide child maintenance. Opinions of both scholars and Supreme Court justices were divided regarding the application of Section 3A to Jews who have their own personal law. There are those who argue that Section 3A does not apply to Jews and other segments of the population who are subject to a specific personal status law, while others disagree. (See the reference to this question in the *Portugez* ruling, ibid).

The Best Interest of the Child

The influence of the views of professional experts in behavioral sciences regarding the concept of "the best interest of the child" is now felt in Israeli rabbinical courts. When parents divorce and fail to reach agreement on child custody, Israeli rabbinical courts were directed by the Israeli Chief Rabbinate to decide custody by requesting expert opinions from psychologists or social workers. These opinions evaluate the best interest of the child in the specific circumstances of the case, making specific and practical recommendations concerning custody that give expression to that interest. (ST 1/60 *Winter v. Be'eri*, 15 PD 1457. This decision, delivered by Dayyan E. Goldsmith, was also printed in Resp. Ezer Mishpat (1994), 28, p. 339). These experts' recommendations are based on prevalent contemporary conceptions, which are the product of analysis of research findings in the behavioral sciences. In addition, the decisions of rabbinical courts reflect the importance ascribed by the rabbinic courts to the stance of the experts in their recommendations to the court (PDR 11, 153). As mentioned, the *dayyanim* operate in accordance with the guidelines issued by Israel's Chief Rabbinate, which instructed them to request an opinion from social welfare officials where divorcing parents have not reached an agreement regarding the custody of the children (see Winter case, above). Dayyan Goldschmidt explained that the halakhic basis for the Chief Rabbinate's directive is the obligation incumbent upon *dayyanim* who decide custody cases to determine what is in the best interest of the child in question – an obligation that stems from the court's role as "the father of orphans" (BK 37a; *Winter* case, ibid).

The social worker's evaluation and recommendation is important because of the great weight assigned by Israel's rabbinic courts to the principle of the best interest of the child when deciding issues of custody. According to Dayyan Goldschmidt, this is the overriding and exclusive principle (the Winter case, ibid; File 5714/226, PDR 1, 145, 157; Appeal 5719/170, PDR 3, 353, 358; Appeal 5740/182, PDR 11, 366, 368–369). A similar view is found in the rulings of other *dayyanim* who ruled that the principle of the best interest of the child is the decisive consideration in matters of child custody. Among these are Rabbi E.Y. Waldenberg (*Resp. Ẓiẓ Eliezer* 17 §50) and *dayyanim* of the Rabbinic Court of Appeals in a panel that included Chief Rabbis Herzog and Ouziel, and Dayyan Shabbetai (Collection of Rulings of the Chief Rabbinate of Eretz Israel, Rabbinical Court of Appeals, vol. 2 (5745 – 1985).

This stance also finds expression in a ruling of Supreme Court Justice Menachem Elon in the *Nir* case (LCA 458/79 *Nir v. Nir*, 35(1) PD 518, 523–524), where he wrote as follows:

> It seems to me that not only is there no substantive difference between the approaches of these two legal systems [i.e., the rabbinical courts and the civil courts], but in fact, I tend to believe that, even from the perspective of the burden of proof,

there is no significant difference between them. In both systems, the principal and general rule is that in each and every case the court is obliged, at its own initiative, to examine the best interest of the child, and it may not rely upon any of the various assumptions, and rule on that basis alone without further examination.

Corporal Punishment

When a parent or teacher resorts to corporal punishment, and claims to have employed that method for educational purposes, a defense plea frequently raised in Israel in the past was that a parent or teacher does not bear either criminal responsibility or responsibility in torts for such an action, since parents and educators are authorized to punish children for the sake of their education and/or for imposing discipline and authority on them, including the imposition of corporal punishment, when such punishment is "reasonable" (Cr. A 7/53 *Rassi v. Attorney General of the State of Israel*, 7 PD, 790, 793–794).

The Supreme Court ruling in the *Anon.* case (CA 4596/98 *Anon. v. State of Israel*, 54(1) PD 145, per Justice Dorit Beinish) reflects a new trend toward the protection of the child from injury at the hands of parents or educators who administer corporal punishment. This ruling displays the influence of studies by experts in the behavioral sciences indicating the unfortunate results of all forms of corporal punishment, even in its "mild" form. Those studies indicate that children who were subjected to "mild" corporal punishment subsequently suffered from psychological problems, whether in childhood or in their adult years. The use of any form of corporal punishment causes damage. Justice Beinish intentionally chose the path of judicial activism. The policy she laid down proscribed all use of corporal punishment for educational purposes. According to her ruling, even "mild" corporal punishment is generally forbidden, and only in exceptional and unusual circumstances is it permitted.

The Supreme Court's ruling in this matter provoked public controversy over the extent to which, if at all, Justice Beinish's stance is at variance with the position of Jewish law on the question of corporal punishment for educational purposes. In this context, it was argued that the Supreme Court's position contradicts the general approach of Jewish law, as expressed in the verse, "He who spares the rod hates his son, but he who loves him disciplines him early" (Prov. 13:24). In fact, legislation was proposed, attempting to cancel the effect of the aforementioned ruling: ("He Who Spares the Rod Hates His Son" (Permission for Educational Punishment) Draft Bill 5760 – 2000, Knesset Proceedings 37 (5760), 10071–10072). However, there were also other views on this matter. Before Justice Beinish's ruling, when addressing the question of the punishment of an older child, Rabbi Jehiel Jakob Weinberg wrote that, under the circumstances, corporal punishment for educational purposes should be opposed, having consideration inter alia for the stance of "the modern pedagogues" (Resp. Seridei Esh, vol 3. no. 95). Furthermore, Rabbi Yitzhak Levi based his own negative view of the use of corporal punishment upon a number of considerations, among them the contemporary, negative view of corporal punishment for educational purposes taken by professional experts – an attitude that also finds expression in Israeli civil law. In view of all the relevant considerations, including his analysis of Jewish law sources, he concluded that such punishment produces results diametrically opposed to the intent of those administering it; it leads to rebellion and hatred, and is liable to cause damage to children. Thus, in his opinion, "we should totally avoid any kind of hitting" (see bibliography, Levi, p. 158). The same view also finds expression in the writings of scholars of Jewish law. Some of them stress that Jewish law's treatment of corporal punishment for educational purposes has established a ramified complex of limitations and restrictions that restrain it and even make it difficult to implement (see bibliography, Shmueli, 374). Similarly, there were those who argued that Justice Beinish's position is not far from the basic position of contemporary Jewish law regarding corporal punishment. Their claim is that the qualified permission granted for corporal punishment constituted isolated exceptions in Jewish law, which was in fact moving toward a clear preference for education by more peaceful and pleasant methods, while stressing the inherent dangers of corporal punishment. In their view, this trend has gained increasing acceptance, especially during the last few decades. Furthermore, it may be assumed that this tendency will become increasingly predominant, in view of the trend towards attributing cardinal importance to the best interest of the child in responsa literature and recent decisions of rabbinic judges. Another factor promoting and reinforcing this process is that many of the *dayyanim* and *posekim* interpret the best interest of the child in light of the opinions of social workers and psychologists who are influenced by the findings of research in the behavioral sciences. This research includes studies that demonstrate the psychological damage caused by corporal punishment for educational purposes (see bibliography, Kaplan, *Ha-Megamah*).

[Yehiel Kaplan (2nd ed.)]

BIBLIOGRAPHY: Gulak, Yesodei, 3 (1922), 66–70; A. Aptowitzer, in: *Ha-Mishpat ha-Ivri*, 2 (1926/27), 9–23; A.H. Freimann, in: *Sinai*, 14 (1943/44), 254–62; ET, 1 (1951[3]), 5–7, 228; 2 (1949), 22f., 378; 4 (1952), 744f.; 6 (1954), 329–32; M. Elon, in: ILR, 3 (1968), 430–2; 4 (1969), 119–26; Elon, *Mafte'aḥ*, 8–11; B. Schereschewsky, *Dinei Mishpaḥah* (1967[2]), 359–94. **ADD. BIBLIOGRAPHY:** M. Elon, *Ha-Mishpat ha-Ivri* (1988) 1:273, 275, 306f, 364, 687f.; II. 994, 1069; idem, *Jewish Law* (1994), I:321, 323, 365f, 440; 2:846f.; 3:1202, 1289; M. Elon and B. Lifshitz, *Mafte'aḥ ha-She'elot ve-ha-Teshuvot shel Ḥakhmei Sefarad u-Ẓefon Afrikah* (legal digest), 1 (1986), 88; B. Lifshitz and E. Shochetman, *Mafte'aḥ ha-She'elot ve-ha-Teshuvot shel Ḥakhmei Ashkenaz, Ẓarefat ve-Italyah* (legal digest) (1997), 59–61; H. Ḥavshush, "*Mezonot Yeladim: Ḥiyyuvei Horim*," in: *Din 'Ivri* (2005); Y.Z. Gilat, *Dinei Mishpaḥa: Yaḥasei Horim vi-Yladim* (2000); Y.S. Kaplan, "The Interpretation of the Concept 'The Best Interest of the Child,'" in: G. Douglas and L. Sebba (eds.), *Children's Rights and Traditional Values*, (1998), 47–85; idem, "*Ha-Megamah ha-Ḥadashah be-Inyan Anishah Gufanit shel Yeladim le-Ẓorkhei Ḥinukh*," in: *Kiryat ha-Mishpat*, 3 (2003), 447; Y. Levi, "*Haka'at Yeladim (Teguvah)*," in: *Teḥumin*, 17 (1997), 157; B. Shmueli, "*Anishah Gufanit shel Yeladim be-Veit Horeihem al pi ha-Mishpat ha-Ivri – Gishot Mesoratiyyot u-Zeramim Moderniyyim*," in: *Pelilim*, 10 (2001/2), 365.

PARENTS, HONOR OF (Heb. כִּבּוּד אָב וָאֵם; lit. "the honoring of father and mother"), the fifth commandment in the *Decalogue. The importance attached by the Bible to this precept is apparent from the fact that the declared reward for its observance is the lengthening of "thy days ... upon the land which the Lord thy God giveth thee" (Ex. 20:12). The rabbis also emphasized that the observer of this commandment would enjoy reward both in this world and in the next (Pe'ah 1:1). Viewing it as a reflection of the godliness in man, they declared that the Bible equated the honor due to parents with that due to God (Ex. 20:12; Prov. 3:9) since "there are three partners in man, the Holy One blessed be He, the father, and the mother." According to the rabbis, when a man honors his father and his mother, God declares, "I ascribe merit to them as though I had dwelt among them and they had honored Me" (Kid. 30b). Further, they stated that since a child intuitively honors his mother more than his father because she is usually kinder to him, the Pentateuch placed the honor of the father before that of the mother (Ex. 20:12). A child, however, fears his father more than his mother, and the Pentateuch accordingly placed the fear of the mother before that of the father (Lev. 19:3; Kid. 30b–31a).

If his parents are in need, the son fulfills the commandment by sustaining them with such items as food, drink, clothing, and blankets, and guides them in old age. Fear of parents is to be expressed in that the son must neither stand nor sit in their usual place, contradict them nor support their opponents in a scholarly dispute (Kid. 31b; Rashi ad loc.). During the first 12 months after his father's death, the son should say, "Thus said my father, my teacher, for whose resting place may I be an atonement." After the initial 12 months, the son says, "His memory be for a blessing, for the life of the world to come" (Kid. 31b). The rabbis differed concerning the monetary expenses to which the son was obliged to go in fulfillment of the fifth commandment. One viewpoint was that the father had to reimburse the son for his actual expenditure, but not for his loss of time. Another opinion was that it was always at the son's personal expense. The *halakhah* declared that the *mitzvah* must be fulfilled at the father's expense, the son, however, being obliged to utilize his own funds when his father was impoverished (Kid. 32a; Sh. Ar., YD 240:5). Receiving great emphasis is the gracious attitude which the son must display in discharging this obligation. It was stated that a son may give his father pheasants as food and yet this act, if performed begrudgingly, will cause the son to lose his portion in the world to come. Yet another may gain the world to come by requesting, in a spirit of kindness and respect, that his father undertake difficult work such as grinding flour in a mill (Kid. 32a; TJ, Kid. 1:7, 61b). A father, however, could renounce the honor due to him and thereby relieve his son of his responsibilities (Kid. 32a). The rabbis held that this commandment had been revealed to the Jews at Marah (Ex. 15:25), before the revelation at Sinai (Sanh. 56b). Individuals, whether Jew or gentile, who excelled in the performance of this precept were praised. The heathen Dama, son of Netina of Ashkelon, refused to awaken his father although he needed the key that was lying under his father's pillow to conclude a transaction which would have brought him a profit of 600,000 gold coins (Kid. 31a). When R. Tarfon's mother wished to climb into bed, he would bend down to let her ascend by stepping upon him. R. Joseph, on hearing his mother's footsteps, would say, "I will arise before the approaching *Shekhinah*" (Kid. 31a–b). Married women were exempted from fulfilling this precept if it conflicted with their husband's wishes (Kid. 30b; Sh. Ar., YD 240:17). A child was obligated to honor his stepfather, stepmother, and eldest brother (Ket. 103a; Sh. Ar., YD 240:21, 22). It is not permitted for a child to transgress a prohibition at his father's request since both father and son are obligated to observe the divine commandments (Yev. 6a).

For legal obligations see *Parent and Child.

BIBLIOGRAPHY: I. Abrahams, *Jewish Life in the Middle Ages* (1932^2), 123f.; H. Loewe and C.G. Montefiore, *A Rabbinic Anthology* (1938, repr. 1960, 1963), cha. 22 and 24.

[Aaron Rothkoff]

PARENZO, 16th–17th-century family of Hebrew printers in Venice. JACOB (d. 1546) had come to Venice from Parenzo, on the Dalmatian coast of Italy, whence the family name, but was probably of German origin. His son MEIR (d. 1575) probably learned the printing trade at the Bomberg press, where he worked together with Cornelio *Adelkind in 1545, and his own productions compare favorably in beauty and elegance with those of his masters. Parenzo worked for some time as a typesetter and corrector at the press owned by Carlo Querini. During 1546–48 he worked on his own, publishing five works, and later an edition of the Mishnah with Bertinoro's commentary for Querini, although from about 1550 his main work was with Alvise *Bragadini. The Parenzos used various *printer's marks: Meir, a seven-branch *menorah*, and a rather daring design with Venus directing arrows at a seven-headed dragon; and his brother, ASHER, a mountain rising from the sea, with a laurel wreath above and a flying eagle at the left. Meir's *colophons abound in editions prepared by him. In 1547 the great French engraver and typecutter Guillaume *Le Bé, and later Jacob of Mantua, produced Hebrew type for him. At Meir's death (1575), his brother Asher took over working for the Venetian printer Giovanni di *Gara, as well as for Bragadini, until 1596. GERSHON BEN MOSES, probably a nephew of Meir and Asher, descendants of Jacob Parenzo, worked for the Venetian printer Giovanni di Gara during 1599–1609 as did his son Moses in 1629.

BIBLIOGRAPHY: Steinschneider, Cat Bod, 2842 (7818); 2984 (8761); Ḥ.D. Friedberg, *Toledot ha-Defus ha-Ivri be-Italyah* (1956^2), 69ff.; A.M. Habermann, in: *Aresheth*, 1 (1959), 61–90; A. Yaari, *Diglei ha-Madpisim ha-Ivriyyim* (1944), nos. 14, 35, 36; idem, in: KS, 30 (1955), 113–7; D.W. Amram, *Makers of Hebrew Books in Italy* (1909), index.

PARḤON, SALOMON BEN ABRAHAM IBN (12th century), lexicographer. Born in Qal'a, Spain, he was a student of Judah *Halevi and Abraham *Ibn Ezra. Parḥon immigrated to

Italy, where in 1160 at Salerno he completed his *Maḥberet he-Arukh*, a biblical lexicon written in Hebrew and his only extant work. On the one hand, the title is reminiscent of Menaḥem b. Jacob ibn *Saruq's dictionary and, on the other, of Nathan b. *Jehiel's. *He-Arukh* comprises the whole of medieval Hebrew lexicography after *Ibn Janaḥ and is, as Parḥon states in his introduction, an epitome of Ibn Janaḥ's *Book of Roots* (*Sefer ha-Shorashim*, 1896). Parḥon also acknowledges the use of excerpts from Ibn Janaḥ's other books and from Judah b. David *Ḥayyuj, the Hebrew translator of Ibn Janaḥ's *Book of Roots*. Ten years after Parḥon's dictionary appeared Judah ibn *Tibbon claimed it was merely a plagiarism of Ibn Janaḥ's lexicon. However, this claim is unjust because in addition to the necessity of taking into consideration the rather liberal medieval attitude toward utilizing the works of others, *Maḥberet he-Arukh* contains original material in its own right. For example, material pertaining to the development of religious ritual, which is of considerable historical interest, and original explanations of biblical passages are found in the work. The introduction to the dictionary comprises a compendium of biblical Hebrew grammar and terminates with a short excursus on medieval Hebrew prosody. Its appendix (appearing immediately after the introduction in S.G. Stern's 1844 edition) is entitled "About biblical matters, as to which one has to dispel one's doubts," and deals with problems of style and syntax following Ibn Janaḥ's *Kitab al-luma'* (*Sefer ha-Rikmah*, 1964). The major importance of *Maḥberet he-Arukh*, however, was that, being written in Hebrew, it transferred to Christian countries the advances in Hebrew philology made under the influence of Arabic linguists in Spain. In his introduction Parḥon asserts this to be one of his aims since he found that in Italy only the *Maḥberet* of Menaḥem ibn Saruq was known. Accordingly, he followed the example of his teacher, Abraham Ibn Ezra, the most important popularizer of Spanish scholarship in Christian lands. The *Maḥberet he-Arukh* became an extremely popular work, not least because of the fluency, lucidity, and purity of Parḥon's Hebrew style, a style befitting a pupil of Abraham Ibn Ezra.

BIBLIOGRAPHY: S.G. Stern (ed.), Salomon ben Abraham ibn Parḥon, *Maḥberet he-Arukh* (1844); W. Bacher, in: J. Winter and A. Wuensche, *Juedische Literatur*, 2 (1897), 190; idem, in: ZAW, 11 (1891), 35–99.

[Yehuda Elitzur]

PARIENTE, Moroccan family of Spanish origin. JACOB (early to mid-16th century) was a leader of the community of Spanish exiles in *Fez, a signatory of its *takkanot*, and a liturgical poet. A tradition holds that he was king of that part of Morocco called the Rif. ABRAHAM (early to mid-16th century) represented the *Safi community before David *Reubeni in Portugal. The wealthy merchant and diplomat SOLOMON (mid-17th century) served as interpreter and negotiator for four English governors in Tangiers and leader of its Jewish community. In additon to extensive commercial negotiations, Pariente also negotiated a peace treaty in which he is suspected of inserting a clause favoring the Moors. In 1662 he apparently supported King Mulay Muhammad b. al-Sharīf, though not his successor Mulay al-*Rashīd. The merchant JACOB (mid-17th century) served as the interpreter for Roland Frejus on his voyages from Marseilles to Morocco in 1666 and 1671. He helped increase the commercial ties between the two countries by means of his friendship with Aaron Carsinet, the Jewish goldsmith and banker of Mulay al-Rashīd. The descendants of JUDAH BEN ABRAHAM (late 18th century) of Rabat founded the Pariente bank in Tangiers, which was important until the mid-20th century. In the early 20th century the philanthropist JOSEPH lived in Tangiers and SAMUEL was a Hebrew scholar and collector of antiquities and manuscripts in Tetuán.

BIBLIOGRAPHY: J.M. Toledano, *Ner ha-Ma'arav* (1911), 78–79; Hirschberg, Afrikah, 2 (1965), 254, 281; idem, in: H.J. Zimmels et al. (eds.), *Essays Presented to Chief Rabbi Israel Brodie…* (1967), 157; I. Laredo, *Memorias de un viejo tangerino* (1935), 180–4; J. Ben-Naim, *Malkhei Rabbanan* (1931), 17, 64; D. Corcos, in: *Sefunot*, 10 (1968), 55ff.

PARIS, capital of *France. In 582, the date of the first documentary evidence of the presence of Jews in Paris, there was already a community owning at least a synagogue, situated in the neighborhood of the present church of St. Julien le Pauvre. The murder of the Jew *Priscus, purveyor to King Chilperic, was avenged by a Christian mob – proof of the good relationship existing between the two religious groups. However, the sixth Council of Paris (614 or 615) decided that Jews who held public office, and their families, must convert to Christianity. When giving the council's decisions the force of law, King Clothaire II ignored the baptism clause, reiterating the ban on Jews holding public office and laying down severe penalties for any breach of this. Although these two documents are proof not only that there were Jews living in Paris but also that their social standing was high, there is no reason to believe that one Solomon, who is mentioned as a toll-collector in Paris in 633, was a Jew or even an apostate. In the tenth and 11th centuries the Jews appear to have lived in the present Rue de la Harpe, between the Rue de la Huchette and Rue Saint Sévérin, and a street later known as the Rue de la Vieille Juiverie which lies between Rue Saint Sévérin and Rue Monsieur le Prince. In the tenth century a synagogue stood at the intersection of these two streets. From 1119 at the latest there was a *Jewish quarter, the *vicus Judaeorum*, situated right in the center of Paris on the Ile de la Cité; its boundaries were the present Rue de la Cité (the central part of which was called Rue des Juifs), the Quai de la Corse, and the Rue de Lutèce. The synagogue, which was 8 meters wide and 31 meters long, was built on the site of the present Marché aux Fleurs; after the expulsion of 1182 it was converted into the St. Madeleine Church. According to Rigord, biographer of Philip Augustus and one of the sources of *Joseph ha-Kohen's *Emek ha-Bakha*, Paris Jews owned about half the land in Paris and the vicinity. They employed many Christian servants, and the objects they took in pledge included even church vessels; jealousy of their prosperity gave rise to the rumor that they used the latter as wine goblets at table.

Far more portentous was the *blood libel which arose against the Jews of *Blois in 1171, appeared simultaneously in a number of other places, and reached the region of Paris. Even though *Louis VII, in answer to the intervention of the leaders of the Paris community, promised to take care that no similar accusation arose in the future and above all that no persecution resulted from it, he was unable to prevent this slander from being deeply engrained in the public mind, even among children. Thus Philip Augustus was told by a playmate when he was only six years old that Jews killed Christian children; according to his biographer, the hatred he conceived at this time was the origin of his expulsion order of 1182. On this occasion, the crown confiscated the houses of the Jews as well as the synagogue and the king gave 24 of them to the drapers of Paris and 18 to the furriers.

Rabbinical questions were addressed to the scholars of Paris from Rome around 1125. About 20 years later the rabbis of Paris took part in a *synod convened by *Solomon b. Meir (Rashbam) and Jacob b. Meir *Tam. In the second half of the 12th century Mattathias Gaon was head of a yeshivah in Paris; his son was the *posek* Jehiel. Among the other scholars of Paris before 1182 were the tosafists Yom Tov and *Ḥayyim b. Hananel ha-Kohen, the commentator Moses, the *posek* Elijah b. Judah, and Jacob b. Simeon, known for his activities in various fields. That the secular sciences were also studied is attested by the 12th-century epitaph (discovered in the 15th century) of one Zour, physician and astrologer. This stone points to the existence of a Jewish cemetery in Rue Pierre Sarrazin, behind Rue de la Harpe.

When the Jews were permitted to return to the kingdom of France in 1198 they settled in Paris in and around the present Rue Ferdinand Duval, which, coincidentally, became the Jewish quarter once again in the modern era. Around the end of the 12th century they lived especially in the present Rue de Moussy, Rue du Renard Saint Merry, Rue de la Tacherie, and on the Petit Pont; they were probably restricted to the Petit Pont in 1294, the date when residence in Jewish quarters became obligatory. However, the number of streets in Paris where Jews actually lived in the Middle Ages, as well as places named after them (Moulin aux Juifs, Ile aux Juifs, Cour de la Juiverie, etc.), was actually much greater; an exhaustive study of the Jewish settlement in Paris with precise dates is still lacking. The first scholarly history of Paris, written by Henri Sauval (1623–1676), barrister in the *parlement* of Paris, contained an important chapter devoted to the Jews (vol. 2, book 10, 508–32). Although permission to publish the *Histoire de Paris* was granted in 1654, it was not in fact published until 1724.

In the reign of *Louis IX, after the denunciations of Nicholas *Donin and Pope Gregory IX's order that Jewish books be examined, the famous *disputation on the Talmud was held in Paris in 1240. The Jewish delegation was led by *Jehiel b. Joseph of Paris. After the condemnation of the Talmud, 24 cart-loads of Jewish books were burned in public in the Place de Grève, now the Place de l'Hôtel de Ville (see *Talmud, Burning of). A Jewish moneylender called Jonathan was accused of desecrating the *Host in 1290, his supposed crime being revealed by various miracles. A commemorative chapel was speedily erected on the site of this alleged desecration (of which not only Jonathan and his family but also the whole Jewish community were accused) and the tale was spread in stories and pictures. It is said that this was the main cause of the expulsion of 1306.

Tax rolls of the Jews of Paris in 1292 and 1296 give a good picture of their economic and social status. One striking fact is that a great many of them originated from the provinces. In spite of the prohibition on the settlement of Jews expelled from England (1290), a number of recent arrivals from that country are listed. As in many other places, the profession of physician figures most prominently among the professions noted. The majority of the rest of the Jews engaged in *moneylending and commerce. In the space of only four years, as witnessed by the amount of the tax imposed on them, the Jews became considerably impoverished. During the same period the composition of the Jewish community, which numbered at least 100 heads of families, changed to a large extent through migration and the number also declined to a marked degree. One of the most illustrious Jewish scholars of medieval France, *Judah b. Isaac, known as Sir Leon of Paris, headed the yeshivah of Paris in the early years of the 13th century. He was succeeded by Jehiel b. Joseph, the Jewish leader at the 1240 disputation. After the wholesale destruction of Jewish books on this occasion until the expulsion of 1306, the yeshivah of Paris produced no more scholars of note.

After the return in 1315 the number of Jews who settled in the city and region of Paris – to judge from their contribution to the enormous fine imposed on the Jews of France a year before the expulsion of 1322 – was little greater than those who had lived there before. However, these few were left untouched by both the *Pastoureaux persecutions and accusations of having poisoned the wells. Relative to this community, the new one formed in Paris from 1359 was quite large. Notables of this period included *Manessier de Vesoul, *procureur-général* and *commissaire* of the Jews of Langue-d'oyl; his associate *Jacob of Pont-Sainte-Maxence; Mattathias b. Joseph, chief rabbi of France and head of the yeshivah (1360–85); and his successor, his son Jonathan, whose authority was contested by one of his father's former pupils, Isaiah b. Abba Mari, also known as Astruc de Savoy. Although Hugues Aubriot, the provost of Paris, took the Jews under his protection, this was to no avail against the murderous attacks and looting in 1380 and 1382 perpetrated by a populace in revolt against the tax burden. King Charles VI relieved the Jews of responsibility for the valuable pledges which had been stolen from them on this occasion and granted them other financial concessions; but the community was unable to recover from those blows, either financially or in number. Not many years later, in 1394, it was further struck by the Denis de *Machaut affair. Machaut, a Jewish convert to Christianity, had disappeared and the Jews were accused of having murdered him or, at the very least, of having imprisoned him until he agreed to return to Judaism. Seven Jewish notables were condemned to death, but their sentence was commuted to a heavy fine allied to imprisonment until Machaut reappeared. This affair was a prelude to the "definitive" expulsion of the Jews from France in 1394.

There is no evidence of Jews in Paris, not even of lone individuals, in the 15th and 16th centuries. In 1611 the physician Elijah of Montalto was called to the court of Marie de Médicis; though he had some contact with Concini, Marshal of Ancre, and his mistress L. Galigaï, there is no reason for supposing that either of these was a Jew. Still less should the old clothes dealers of Paris be taken for secret Jews just because their guild was known as the "synagogue"; in 1652 they murdered a citizen who used this term with reference to them. From the beginning of the 18th century the Jews of *Metz applied to the authorities for permission to enter Paris on their business pursuits; gradually the periods of their stay in the capital increased and were prolonged. At the same time the city saw the arrival of Jews from *Bordeaux (the "Portuguese") and from *Avignon. From 1721 to 1772 a police inspector was given special charge over the Jews, an office which the successive holders used to extort what they could from them in money and goods. After the discontinuation of the office, the trustee of the Jews from 1777 was Jacob Rodrigues *Péreire, a Jew from Bordeaux, who had charge over a group of Spanish and Portuguese Jews, while the German Jews (from Metz, Alsace, and Lorraine) were led by Moses Eliezer Liefman *Calmer, and those from Avignon by Israel Salom. The German Jews lived in the poor quarters of Saint-Martin and Saint-Denis, and those from Bordeaux, *Bayonne, and Avignon inhabited the more luxurious quarters of Saint Germain and Saint André. Large numbers of the Jews eked out a miserable living in peddling and selling secondhand clothes and rags. The more well-to-do were moneylenders, military purveyors (especially of horses), and traded in jewels. There were also some craftsmen among them: jewelers, painters, engravers, designers, and embroiderers. Inns preparing kosher food existed from 1721; these also served as prayer rooms since otherwise services could only be held in private houses – in either case strictly forbidden by the police. From at least 1736 an innkeeper from La Villette allowed his garden to be used for burials; after 1780 the Portuguese community acquired an adjoining plot of land which could officially be used for a cemetery. Soon after the Ashkenazim also acquired a cemetery, in Montrouge. Neither continued in use for very long but both were still in existence in 1971. The first publicly acknowledged synagogue was opened in Rue de Brisemiche in 1788. The number of Jews in Paris just before the Revolution was probably no greater than 500. On Aug. 26, 1789 they presented the Constituent Assembly with a petition asking for the rights of citizens. The Paris commune came to the defense of its Jewish residents, sending a deputation to the assembly to plead for them; full citizenship rights were granted to the Spanish, Portuguese, and Avignon Jews on Jan. 28, 1790.

After the freedom of movement brought about by emancipation, a large influx of Jews arrived in Paris, numbering 2,908 in 1809. These Jews were exempt from the general Jewish disabilities imposed by *Napoleon in 1808. Most of them lived in the present third and fourth *arrondissements*. In 1819, when the Jewish population of Paris had reached between 6,000 and 7,000 persons, the *consistory began to build the first Great Synagogue, in Rue Notre Dame de Nazareth. It stood for no more than 30 years and had barely been rebuilt when, in 1852 (the year of the foundation of the Rothschild Hospital), it became apparent that it was not large enough for a Jewish population which had reached 20,000. General difficulties beset the building of new synagogues (those in Rue de la Victoire and Rue des Tournelles were completed in 1877), but local difficulties led to the transfer of the Rabbinical Seminary of Metz to Paris in 1859. The consistory had established its first primary school in 1819; a second school was added in 1846, and three others between 1864 and 1867. At the same time charitable associations increased; their buildings frequently also served as prayer rooms for immigrant Jews. The capital was the seat of the Central Consistory of France (as well as the Consistory of Paris) and from 1860 of the *Alliance Israélite Universelle. Two Jewish journals serving all France were published in Paris: *L'Univers Israélite* and the *Archives Israélites*. The 30,000 or so Jews who lived in Paris in 1869 constituted about 40% of the Jewish population of France. The great majority originated from Metz, Alsace, Lorraine, and Germany, and there were already a few hundred from Poland. Apart from a very few wealthy capitalists, the great majority of the Jews belonged to the middle economic level. Alongside the peddlers, merchants, and dealers in secondhand goods, the proportion of craftsmen – painters, hat-makers, tailors, and shoemakers – was increasing. Many organizations and societies – the first dating from 1825 – encouraged young Jewish men and women to acquire an aptitude for and pride in manual work. The liberal professions also attracted numerous Jews; the community included an increasing number of professors, lawyers, and physicians.

With the loss of Alsace and Lorraine in 1871, the Jewish population of France numbered only 60,000 persons, almost two-thirds of whom lived in Paris. After 1881 their numbers were augmented by refugees from Poland, Russia, and the Slav provinces of Austria and Romania; this influx led to a noticeable increase in the percentage of manual workers among Parisian Jews. At the same time there was a marked increase in the antisemitic movement, particularly with the foundation of the journal La *Croix in 1883 and the agitation of E.A. *Drumont. The *Dreyfus affair, from 1894, split the intellectuals of Paris into "Dreyfusards" and "anti-Dreyfusards" who frequently clashed on the streets, especially in the Latin Quarter. With the law separating church and state in 1905, the Jewish consistories lost their official status, becoming no more than private religious associations. The growing numbers of Jewish immigrants to Paris resented the heavy hand of a consistory, which was largely under the control of Jews from Alsace and Lorraine, now a minority group.

These immigrants formed the greater part of the 13,000 "foreign" Jews who enlisted in World War I. Especially after 1918, Jews began to arrive from North Africa, Turkey, and the Balkans, and in greatly increased numbers from Eastern Europe. Thus in 1939 there were around 150,000 Jews in Paris (over half the total in France), the overwhelming majority Yiddish-speaking recent immigrants. The Jews lived all over the city but there were large concentrations in the north and east. More than 150 Landsmannschaften composed of immigrants from Eastern Europe and many charitable societies united large numbers of Jews, while at this period the Paris Consistory (which retained the name with its changed function) had no more than 6,000 members. Only one of the 19th-century Jewish primary schools was still in existence in 1939, but a few years earlier the system of Jewish education – which was strictly private in nature – acquired a secondary school and a properly supervised religious education, for which the consistory was responsible, in the synagogues, prayer rooms, and also in a few state high schools. As well as the French Jewish journals, the Yiddish press became increasingly important. Many great Jewish scholars were born and lived in Paris in the modern period. They included the Nobel prizewinners René *Cassin and A. *Lwoff. In the plastic arts Jews played an especially prominent part in the School of *Paris.

[Bernhard Blumenkranz]

Hebrew Printing

The first books containing Hebrew type issued in Paris were printed by A. Gourmont from 1508; and other works were printed during the next half-century. Robert Stephanus produced particularly beautiful Bibles between 1539 and 1556. Hebrew printing was resumed in 1620 by S. Cramoisy. When Louis XIII established a printing press in 1640, it had a Hebrew department of which, however, little use was subsequently made. Under Napoleon I the printer Setier issued some liturgical items. From the middle of the 19th century until the present day the firm of E. Durlacher, the first Jewish printer in Paris, has printed mainly liturgies.

Holocaust Period

On June 14, 1940, the Wehrmacht entered Paris, which was proclaimed an open city. Most Parisians left, including the Jews. However, the population returned in the following weeks. The German-imposed census of Jewish persons and businesses in November 1940 recorded a total of 149,734 Jews (over six years of age), 7,737 Jewish businesses (private), and 3,456 companies considered Jewish. The Jewish population figure was similar to the prewar one, but large numbers of Parisian Jews had preferred to remain in the southern, unoccupied French territory and a sizable number of well-known Jews fled to England and the U.S. (André *Maurois, Georges Gombault, Pierre Lazareff), while some, e.g., René *Cassin and Gaston Palewski, joined General De Gaulle's Free French movement in London. In August 1940 a number of Jewish shops on the Champs Elysées were stoned by French Nazis under German protection. The anti-Jewish measures which followed (see *France, Holocaust Period) first affected the Parisian Jews. Jews were active from the very first in Résistance movements. The march to the Etoile on Nov. 11, 1940, of high school and university students, the first major public manifestation of resistance, included among its organizers Francis Cohen, Suzanne Djian, and Bernard Kirschen (see also *Partisans, Jewish, in General Resistance in France).

The first major roundups of Parisian Jews of foreign nationality took place in 1941: about 5,000 "foreign" Jews were deported on May 14, about 8,000 "foreigners" in August, and about 100 "intellectuals" on December 13. On July 16, 1942, 12,884 Jews were rounded up in Paris (including about 4,000 children). The Parisian Jews represented over half the 85,000 Jews deported from France to extermination camps in the East; most of them were sent to Compiègne or *Drancy and from there to *Auschwitz, while about three convoys, in March 1943, were despatched to *Majdanek and one transport, in May 1944, to Kovno (*Kaunas). During the night of Oct. 2–3, 1941, seven Parisian synagogues were attacked. After an attempt to place the blame on the Jews themselves, it rapidly transpired that the attacks were instigated by the German SD (security police) in Paris (see *Gestapo) and carried out by French Fascists, led by Eugène Deloncle, with explosives supplied by the SD. SS-*Brigadefuehrer* Max Thomas, R.T. *Heydrich's representative to Belgium and France, was then recalled to Berlin, but his Paris subordinate, *Standarten-fuehrer* Helmut Knochen, kept his position and was even promoted.

Several scores of Jews fell in the Paris insurrection in August 1944. Many streets in Paris and the outlying suburbs bear the names of Jewish heroes and martyrs of the Holocaust period and the Memorial to the Unknown Jewish Martyr, a part of the *Centre de Documentation Juive Contemporaire, was erected in 1956 in the heart of Paris.

[Lucien Steinberg]

Contemporary Period

In 1968 Paris and its suburbs contained about 60% of the Jewish population of France. Between 1945 and 1950 the Jewish population of the area grew from 125,000 to 150,000, and in 1968 it was estimated at between 300,000 and 350,000 (about 5% of the total population). In 1950 two-thirds of the Jews were concentrated in about a dozen of the poorer or commercial districts in the east of the city. The social and economic advancement of the second generation of East European immigrants, the influx of North Africans, and the gradual implementation of the urban renewal program caused a considerable change in the once Jewish districts and the dispersal of the Jews throughout other districts of Paris. The greatest change took place in the neighborhoods that in 1956–57 were still inhabited by artisans and small traders of East European origin. By 1968 the inhabitants of these neighborhoods had been replaced by the most impoverished of the North African immigrants. Between 1945 and 1968, the urbanization of the Paris region became accelerated. In 1941 10% of the Jews of Paris resided in the inner suburbs of the city; by 1966 about 20% were living outside the city limits. North African Jews were partly relocated in the large housing developments reserved for repatriated citizens. Between 1957 and 1966 the number of Jewish communities in the Paris region rose from 44 to 148. Like other suburban inhabitants, the Jews were employed mostly in Paris.

Paris is the center of Jewish activities in France, as all the major institutions have their headquarters there. The Paris Consistory, traditionally presided over by a member of the *Rothschild family, officially provides for all religious needs. Approximately 20 synagogues and meeting places for prayer observing Ashkenazi or Sephardi (North African) rites are affiliated with the consistory, which also provides for the religious needs of new communities in the suburbs. This responsibility is shared by traditional Orthodox elements, who, together with the Reform and other independent groups, maintain another 30 or so synagogues. The Orientation and Information Office of the Fonds Social Juif Unifié has advised or assisted over 100,000 refugees from North Africa. It works in close cooperation with government services and social welfare and educational institutions of the community. The numerous educational and cultural activities of various kinds include efforts to draw young people and intellectuals back into the Jewish community. From 1957 the *World Jewish Congress held an annual French-language colloquium of intellectuals. The Centre Universitaire d'Etudes Juives (CUEJ) exists for the purpose of introducing university students to Jewish culture. Paris was one of very few cities in the Diaspora with a full-fledged Israel-type school, conducted by Israel teachers according to the Israel curriculum. It served the relatively large colony of Israelis, as well as some French Jews who aspired to give their children a genuine Hebrew education. Numerous cultural and Zionist associations also present varied programs for the Jewish public each evening. However, only one-third of the Jewish population maintains any relations with community institutions. The *Six-Day War (1967), which drew thousands of Jews into debates and pro-Israel demonstrations, was an opportunity for many of them to reassess their personal attitude toward the Jewish people. During the "students' revolution" of 1968 in nearby Nanterre and in the Sorbonne, young Jews played an outstanding role in the leadership of left-wing activists (see *New Left) and often identified with Arab anti-Israel propaganda extolling the Palestinian organizations, particularly the terrorist Popular Front, as an example of the Third World struggle against imperialism. Eventually, however, when the "revolutionary" wave subsided, it appeared that the bulk of Jewish students in Paris, including many supporters of various New Left groups, remained loyal to Israel and strongly opposed Arab terrorism, although many of them criticized the Israel government for "ignoring the right of the Palestinian people to self-determination." The tension created by the Six-Day War also exacerbated frictions and led to several violent clashes between North African Arabs and Jews in lower middle class and proletarian quarters of Paris. Young Jews began to organize for self-defense against physical attacks, but the clashes ceased mainly through the intervention of the local police.

LATER DEVELOPMENTS. Since the 1970s Paris has undergone important urbanization which has transformed the countryside. One can no longer separate the 20 arrondissements within the confines of the capital which in 2005 contained 2.15 million inhabitants out of the 10.5 million residents of the Parisian (Ile de France) megalopolis. The Greater Paris economic and social conurbation covers 12,000 square kilometers in which, however, the numerous municipalities retain their autonomous administration.

Estimated at 300,000–350,000 persons, the Jewish community of Greater Paris ranks third (after Greater New York and Los Angeles) among the Jewish cities in the Diaspora. Paris and its environs have always attracted migrants and immigrants: it is a cosmopolitan city in which there live together people of every origin, race, color, and creed.

Within this mixture, the Jews constitute a sizable minority in Paris proper (about 6%–8% of the total population) and in several suburban towns. The great wave of immigration of Jews originating from North Africa in 1955–65 changed the ethnic composition of the Jewish community in the Paris area: Sephardi Jews are now the majority, even if, with the exception of Alsace, the Ashkenazi Jews are more numerous than in the other regions of France. Within Paris proper, the formerly typically Jewish neighborhoods have taken on a Sephardi nature. Some of them are on the way to disappearing, while others have been "Judaized." Parisian Jews, however, live in every district in the city. The Jewish population of the Paris region is very mobile, partly due to constant urban renewal. In their new places of residence, they establish new communities, most often with Sephardi majorities.

Moreover, the best known Jewish livelihoods – petty craftsman, small tradesman – have practically disappeared. The Jews are found in every type of occupation and practice in all professions. They play an important role in the Paris intelligentsia.

Community. All of the large Jewish organizations have their offices in Paris. Even if some of them intentionally focus their activities in the provinces, Paris remains the main decision making center of community life. This Jacobinism, a constant of French political life, does not strengthen community unity.

In principle, the main religious organization is the Association consistoriale israélite de Paris (ACIP) comprising the community synagogues of the Paris area. The ACIP, however, is skirted by a number of ultra-Orthodox groupings such as Lubavitch, which form highly visible groups on the Paris scene. The ACIP does not succeed in controlling its synagogues, their *kashrut*, and certain of their public manifestations. At the other end of the scale Liberal and Conservative movements are developing which are modern and open to Jews in search of identity; they play an increasingly significant role in the return to Judaism and in transmitting it among milieux recognized by neither the ultra-Orthodox nor by the Orthodox consistory. The religious sector faces serious competition from the large number of associations offering cultural activities, all types of recreational or even political events. These associations may number a few dozen, a few hundred, or even a few thousand members. Large or small, they are the place for frequent meetings among Jews of all religious, Zionist, secular, and political trends. They are the expression of the broad ideological diversity found among the Jewry of the Paris area.

Finally, one cannot forget those Jews considered "peripheral" by the organized community: they rarely, actually almost never, have any connection to any Jewish organization whatsoever. Parisian cosmopolitanism clearly favors the formation of free unions, mixed marriages, and divorces, most often without a *get*. These Jews are nevertheless Jews, perhaps not according to *halakhah*, but through their affirmation of their attachment to their Jewish identity. They probably constitute the majority of the Jewish population in the Greater Paris region.

Cultural Life. Paris remains the center of the intellectual and cultural life of French Jewry. Conferences, colloquia, exhibitions, and other focal manifestations of Judaism in all its multifacetedness proceed apace. Paris is the home of the largest Jewish library in Europe, that of the Alliance Israélite Universelle; another very important library devoted to Yiddish literature, Bibliothèque MEDEM; and significant archival collections concerning the history of Jews in France. The Centre de Documentation Juive Contemporaine and its Memorial des Martyrs Juifs is one of the leading memorial sites for the Holocaust created after World War II. A new Musée d'Art Juif is under construction. Yet, most research carried out on Judaism, its history, its culture, and Jewish languages is to a large degree integrated within institutes of higher learning. Numerous teams at the Centre National de la Recherche Scientifique deal with research which may be called the "science of Judaism and Jewishness." A dozen Paris universities have departments or courses of study devoted to Hebrew, to other Jewish languages, or more generally to teaching and research related to Judaism and Jewish studies. Paris today is one of the main centers for Jewish intellectual life in the Diaspora.

[Doris Bensimon-Donath]

BIBLIOGRAPHY: Gross, Gal Jud, 496ff.; B. Blumenkranz, *Bibliographie des Juifs en France* (1963), s.v. *L. Kahn* for 10 works and many periodical articles; J. Hillairet, *Evocation du vieux Paris*, 1 (1951), 361f.; idem, *Dictionnaire historique des rues de Paris* (1964²), index; idem, *L'Ile de la Cité* (1969), 34–37; I. Loeb, in: REJ, 1 (1880), 60–71; M. Ginsburger, *ibid.*, 78 (1924), 156ff.; P. Hildenfinger, *Documents sur les Juifs à Paris au XVIIIe siècle* (1913); L. Berman, *Histoire des Juifs de France* (1937), passim; Z. Szajkowski, in: *Yidn in Frankraykh* (1942), passim; idem, *Franco-Judaica* (1962), index; idem, *Analytical Franco-Jewish Gazetteer 1939–1945* (1966), index; R. Anchel, *Les Juifs de France* (1946), passim; U. Issembert-Gannat, *Guide de Judaïsme à Paris* (1964); C. Korenchandler, *Yidn in Paris* (1970); David H. Weinberg, *The Jews in Paris in the 1930s: A Community on Trial* (1977). HOLOCAUST PERIOD: J. Billig, *Le Commissariat Général aux questions Juives*, 3 vols. (1955–60), incl. bibl. index; L. Steinberg, *Les autorités allemandes en France occupée* (1966), incl. bibl. index; C. Lévy and P. Tillard, *Betrayal at the Vel d'Hiv* (1969); Centre de Documentation Juive Contemporaine Bibliothèque, *Catalogue No. 1: La France…* (1964), index; G. Reitlinger, *Final Solution* (1968²), 327–51 and passim; L. Steinberg, *La révolte des Justes* (1970), incl. bibl. 1945–1970: M. Roblin, *Juifs de Paris* (1952); C. Roland, *Du ghetto à l'Occident* (1962).

PARIS, HAILU (1933–), U.S. Orthodox rabbi, Beta Israel. Paris was born in Ethiopia and immigrated to the United States with his widowed mother in 1936. He graduated from the Erna Michael College of Hebraic Studies of Yeshiva University and obtained his master's degree in Jewish education from the Ferkauf Graduate School. In 1965 he was appointed assistant rabbi and subsequently rabbi to Mt. Horeb Congregation in the Bronx, a congregation of black Jews. He also studied at Yeshivat ha-Darom in Israel in 1957–58.

Rabbi Paris was active in the Ha-Ẓa'ad ha-Rishon, an organization set up for the integration of black Jewish youth into the Jewish community, and a member of the Pro-Beta Israel Committee of New York. He spent nearly a year with the Beta Israel community in Ethiopia in 1965–66.

PARIS SCHOOL OF ART (Jewish School of). In the history and criticism of 20th-century painting, "School of Paris" has become a widely used term, generally designating a style that is not necessarily or typically French, but which is followed by a large number of foreign-born artists living in France. It was only in the third decade of the 20th century, however, that this term began to be accepted. Because of the great number of foreign-born artists who had settled permanently in Paris, or who had lived there briefly but been profoundly influenced by French art, it became necessary to refer to most of them as artists of the School of Paris rather than of the French School.

The Jewish School

As many of these foreign artists, especially between 1910 and 1940, happened also to be of eastern European Jewish origin, the term "Jewish School of Paris" was then coined to refer more specifically to a school of painting which gravitated only peripherally around the main schools of modern art of France, such as fauvism, cubism, or surrealism, but which had developed certain features of its own. Some of these features, however, can also be detected in the work of non-Jewish and even French-born painters of the School of Paris, who associated closely with the artists of the so-called "Jewish School." The latter has therefore been more properly called by some critics and art historians the "School of Montparnasse," because it was in this Left Bank neighborhood that many of the artists concerned lived and worked, or congregated in their leisure hours. Nationalist or antisemitic French critics and publicists have often argued that the main trends of 20th-century avant-garde French art were dictated or dominated by foreigners and, more specifically, by Jews, who thus, they claimed, exerted a disruptive influence on French traditions. In fact the influence of Jewish artists, whether French or foreign-born, on the major schools of contemporary French painting has been, on the whole, very modest.

Fauvist School

Among the fauvist painters who began to attract attention in 1905, only Russian-born Sonia *Delaunay-Terk and a group of Hungarian-born painters – Béla *Czobel, Robert Berény (1887–1954), Bertalan Pór (1880–1964), Lajos Tihanyi (1885–1939), Vilmos Perlrott-Csaba (1879–1954), and István Farkas (1887–1944) – were Jews of foreign origin, and these were never leading figures in the fauvist group. Among the French-born fauvists, Léopold Levy (1882–1967) was a painter of great distinction, but he somehow failed to achieve the reputation he deserved. Nevertheless, he exerted a decisive influence on Turkish painting as a teacher for many years at the School of Fine Arts in Istanbul. Between 1910 and 1914, the French fauvist master Matisse was an influential figure in German expressionist painting, mainly through a few German-Jewish artists who had been his pupils in Paris and who subsequently achieved eminence in Germany and Israel. The two most important were Rudolf Levy (1875–1944) and Jakob *Steinhardt.

The Cubists

Among the Paris cubists, Sonia Delaunay-Terk, a convert from fauvism, was slow to gain recognition as an artist of great significance. Her later transition to an idiom of abstract art ensures her place in art history as one of the pioneers of what was subsequently known as op art. Henryk Berlewi (1894–1967), a Pole, was another pioneer of op art. Other Jewish artists who achieved some prominence among the Paris cubists, or as one-time disciples of cubism, are German-born Otto *Freundlich, Polish-born Henri Hayden (1883–1970) and Louis Marcoussis (1883–1941), French-born Henry Valensi (1883–1960) and Marcelle Cahn (1895–1981), and Russian-born Nechama Szmuszkowicz (1895–?), Serge Charchoune (1889–1975), and Jacques Pailes (1895–?). Hungarian-born Alfred Reth (1884–1965) was one of the first painters to formulate the cubist idiom in Paris, though he was never an active member of the cubist group. The French poet and painter Max *Jacob, a close friend of Picasso and the other cubist masters, played an important part as a representative of cubist poetry, but was never a cubist in his painting. Although he was also a member of the group between 1910 and 1914 and was influenced to some extent by its style, Marc *Chagall denied any allegiance to cubism. Without ever being a true cubist, except in his sculpture, Amedeo *Modigliani was closely associated with the Paris cubists. Three Russian-born artists, Chana *Orloff, Ossip *Zadkine, and Jacques *Lipchitz earned worldwide fame as masters of cubist sculpture. Jules *Pascin, a Bulgarian, was a prominent figure in the Paris art world in the heyday of cubism, although he was not a true cubist in his own drawings and paintings. The same can be said of Polish-born Moise *Kisling. Though influenced by his close friend Modigliani and by cubist theory, Kisling was never an orthodox cubist.

The Surrealists

There were no Jewish artists of real significance among the Paris dadaists of 1917 to 1922, although Marcel *Janco (1895–1984) had been a leader in the original Zurich dada group. After 1922, Romanian-born Victor Brauner (1903–1966) and Jacques Herold (1910–1987) slowly came to the fore as representatives of French surrealist paintings. By the time he died, Brauner was generally recognized as one of the major surrealists. Meret Oppenheim (1913–1985), a German, achieved historical importance as the inventor of a number of famous surrealist objects. Kurt Seligmann (1900–1962), a Swiss artist who sank into undeserved neglect, achieved prominence as a surrealist both in Paris and in New York and produced many of the finest surrealist engravings. Romanian-born Grégoire Michonze (1902–1982), a close associate and friend of Max Ernst (d. 1976) and other major surrealists, excelled in dreamworld allegories rather than in surrealism.

Closely allied at one time to the surrealist group, the Paris neoromantics who flourished around 1930 included almost more painters of Jewish origin than any other 20th-century school of French painting, but can scarcely be said to constitute a Jewish School of Paris. These neoromantic painters, widely scattered by Nazism throughout western Europe and the United States, at one time included: from Russia, Eugene Berman (1899–1972) and his brother Leonid (1896–1976), Philippe Hosiasson (1898–1978), and Léon Zack (1892–1980); from Austria, Victor Tischler (1890–1950), Joseph Floch (1896–1977), and Georg Merkel (1881–1976); from Egypt, Josiah Victor Ades (1893–?); from Poland, Jacques Zucker (1900–1981); and from the United States, Maurice Grosser (1905–1986). The Jewish School of Paris or School of Montparnasse thus appears to have developed as a somewhat marginal phenomenon that was never too closely associated with any of the major movements of contemporary French art, but was influenced by most of these movements in turn. Around 1910, large numbers of foreign-born painters began to choose the cafés of the Boulevard Montparnasse, especially the Café du Dôme, as their leisure-time headquarters. Until 1914, these foreign artists included a considerable number of Germans, among whom the sculptor Wilhelm Lehmbruck subsequently proved to be one of the most important. His many Jewish friends, who met him regularly at the Café du Dôme, included Jules Pascin, Otto Freundlich, Rudolf Levy, Georges Kars (1880–1945), and Eugen von Kahler (1882–1911), the last two from Czechoslovakia. Of the many gifted Paris painters who have not yet been granted the recognition they deserved, Kars is certainly one of the finest; under the influence of Cézanne and of cubist theory rather than cubist style, he achieved, especially in his drawings, a rare synthesis of romantic feeling and classical form. Eugen von Kahler is now remembered mainly as a promising participant in some of the early activities of the Munich Blaue Reiter (Blue Rider) School, in which he associated with Klee and Kandinski.

Montparnasse and La Ruche

During World War I and the years that immediately followed it, social and political upheavals in eastern Europe, especially in Russia, Poland, Romania, and Hungary, brought about a great increase in the numbers of refugee artists who became permanent or semipermanent residents of Paris. Many of these artists were Jews, refugees from persecution or from other limitations, such as a lack of interested collectors, in their native country. Some American Jewish artists, such as Abraham *Rattner, also went to live in Paris and began to associate, in Montparnasse, with French or other foreign-born artists. Even before 1914, many of these foreign-born Jewish artists had been living in a couple of ramshackle old studio buildings located in the tangle of narrow streets that extended behind Montparnasse railway station, especially in the studios of La Ruche, where Chagall had lived before 1914, and of the Cité Falguière, where Modigliani lived at one time. Russian-born Chaim *Soutine remains a legendary representative of this earlier period of the Jewish School of Paris and of the whole history of Montparnasse as an art colony. Montparnasse's almost slum-like little ghettos of more or less improvised studios, however, were also occupied at one time or another by a number of non-Jewish artists, such as the cubist master Fernand Léger, so that they never constituted purely Jewish enclaves in the Left Bank art world. The painter Jacques *Chapiro published a nostalgic and somewhat romanticized historical record of La Ruche and its inmates, among whom the Polish-born sculptor Léon Indenbaum (1890–1981) stands out as an artist who deserves to be more widely known.

The major representatives of the so-called Jewish School of Paris would now appear to be Pinkus Krémègne (1890–1981), Michel Kikoine (1892–1968), *Mané-Katz (1894–1962), Balgley (1891–1934), Adolphe Milich (1891–1944), Adolf Feder (1887–1943), Isaac Dobrinsky (1891–1973), Maurice Blond (1899–1974), Abraham Mintchine (1898–1931), Joseph Pressmane (1904–1967), Zygmund Landau (1898–1962), Zygmund Schreter (1896–1977), David Seifert (1896–1980), Marc Sterling (1898–1976), Charles Tcherniawsky (1900–1976), and Isaac Antscher (1899–1992). Most of them were born in Russia, Poland, or other former provinces of the czarist empire, including Lithuania and Bessarabia. To these names should be added those of a number of former Paris residents on whose subsequent work the School of Montparnasse left a lasting mark, and who later achieved distinction elsewhere, such as Max Band (1900–1974) in the U.S. and Josef Iser (1881–1963) in Romania. The Jewish School of Paris is distinguished, in general, by its expressionist insistence on communicating emotion or mood rather than formal relationships or effects of light and color. Nevertheless, many of its members, especially Mané-Katz, Kikoine, and Feder, are noted for their effects of color and texture. The more typical painters of the school tended to rely heavily on impasto effects obtained by using a heavily loaded brush or palette knife in such a way as to create the impression that they actually drew with their pigment or even modeled it, as a sculptor might, in low relief. Several Jewish painters of the School of Montparnasse, including some of those already mentioned, refrained from allowing themselves the kind of exuberance or sensuality that characterizes, above all, the still life and landscape painting of Mané-Katz, Feder, and Kikoine. Thus Leopold Gottlieb (1883–1934), a much younger brother of the famous 19th-century Polish painter Maurycy *Gottlieb, stood out as a representative of an almost classical pictorial refinement, always avoiding effects of color or texture that might appear over-rich. The Russian-born painter Joseph Lubitch (1896–1990) likewise remains, in a minor key, a belated disciple of French impressionism, often delighting in effects that recall Whistler. Another Russian, Arbit Blatas (1908–1999), tempers the neo-primitive violence of fauvism by handling its style in an elegiac, intimate, and almost neoromantic mood.

Victims of Nazism

In 1940 the Nazi occupation of Paris decimated the city's Jewish population. Among the more prominent artists who died as victims of Nazi extermination camps were Otto Freundlich, Henri (Chaim) Epstein, Adolf Feder, Tobias Haber (1906–1943), Abram Weinbaum (1890–1943), Alice Hoherman (1902–1943), Abrami Mordkin (1874–1943), Georges Ascher (1884–1943), Jacques Gotko (1900–1943), Samuel Granovsky (1889–1942), David Goychmann (1900–1942), David Michael Krever (1904–1941), Jacob Macznik (1905–1944), Ephraim Mandelbaum (1884–1942), Leon Weissberg (1893–1943), Lajos Tihanyi, and Istvan Farkas. These martyred artists were gifted with such outstanding and diverse talents that it would now be as unfair to try to force them all into a Jewish school as it was, under the Nazi regime, to deny them their human rights because they were Jews. One who deserves particular mention is the Russian-born sculptor Moyshe Kogan (1879–1942). Before migrating from Germany to Paris, he had already distinguished himself in Munich as the only sculptor of the Blue Rider Group.

After World War II

After 1945, the School of Paris soon began again to attract many foreign-born Jewish painters and sculptors, though now mainly from the U.S., Israel, French North Africa, and, of course, from among the eastern European survivors of the Holocaust. The Algerian-born abstract painter Jean *Atlan soon achieved prominence as a recognized master of postwar French painting. In the same school of non-geometrical and more lyrical abstract painting, Philippe Hosiasson and Léon Zack, both former neoromantics, also came to be recognized as masters. Romanian-born Robert Helman (1910–1990) and Turkish-born Albert Bitran (1931–) also came to the fore after 1950, each with a distinctive idiom of non-geometrical abstraction. Russian-born Alexander Garbell (1903–1970), a master of elegant brush work and of subtle color harmonies and textures, experimented for a while with an abstract idiom but soon returned to a style of revised post-impressionism better suited to his temperament. Of the small group of abstract painters hailing from Hungary, the most outstanding in the late sixties was Zsigmund Kolozsvari, known professionally as Kolos-Vari (1889–1983). Alfred Aberdam (1894–1963), who was born in Austrian Galicia, began to attract attention in Paris only after 1945. A painter of unusual refinement, he revealed in his mature work a surprising affinity with some Italian mannerist and baroque masters of the later Renaissance, though he expressed himself in a pictorial idiom that seems to have derived from the neoromantic painters of the 1930s.

As public interest in modern art grew after World War II, artists all over the world found themselves free to cater to a much wider variety of tastes than formerly, and after 1945 French painting and that of the School of Paris came to be characterized by an ever increasing diversity of styles. There is even less justification to use the term "Jewish School" for this later generation of Jewish painters than between the two world wars. Polish-born Marek Halter (1932–), for instance, might well be classed among the new realists, although his work reveals a far greater refinement of draftsmanship and painterly discretion than that of Bernard Buffet. A native Parisian, Jacques Winsberg (1929–) also attracted attention as a new realist or "misérabiliste," concerning himself, like Buffet, mainly with effects of pathos. Another Frenchman, Gabriel Zendel (1906–1980), on the other hand, brought new life to the moribund idiom of cubism by exploiting it with a more varied sense of color and of texture. Though born in Russia, Chapoval (1912–1953) was educated in France and, as an early representative of French tachisme or lyrical and nongeometrical abstraction, immediately achieved considerable prominence. Polish-born Georges Goldkorn (1907–1961), Felicia Pacanowska (1907–?), and Abram Krol (1884–?) came to the fore mainly as outstanding graphic artists, Goldkorn and Pacanowska in the field of etching, Krol in woodcuts. Krol, a gifted French poet as well as an artist, became well known among bibliophiles all over the world as a remarkable creator of beautiful books. German-born Johnny Friedlaender (1912–1992) likewise earned an international reputation as a virtuoso of rare technical brilliance, especially in his color etchings.

In addition to Jean Atlan, Algeria gave Paris three other painters of note. Smadja, after studying with the cubist master Fernand Léger, developed a lyrical, non-geometric abstract style of his own. The expressionist Corsia (1915–1985) succeeded in infusing a truly Mediterranean sensuality and sense of color into an idiom inherited from Van Gogh. A Mediterranean sense of color and light is also typical of Assus, a belated post-impressionist. Two Moroccan artists worthy of mention are André Elbaz, whose North African Jewish themes are handled in an expressionist idiom previously used mainly for eastern European Jewish subjects, and Hasdai Elmosnino, who was profoundly influenced by French painting before emigrating to a new home in Canada. Among other painters of North African origin is Tunisian-born Jules Lellouche (1903–1965), a post-impressionist who was often haunted by nostalgic memories of classical Venetian painting. Among Polish-born survivors of the Holocaust who distinguished themselves as painters in Paris after 1945, Maryan (1927–1977), who eventually moved to New York, proved to be a worthy heir to the great tradition of eastern European Jewish visionary fantasy that first obtained international recognition in the early works of Chagall, Issachar Ryback, and Yankel Adler. But Maryan's art is disturbed by macabre memories, transmuted into a peculiarly sardonic and bitter kind of clowning.

Traditionalists and Individualists

In addition to all the artists who have been named, a number of other Jewish painters, several of them French-born, distinguished themselves in Paris in the 20th century, but in the traditional schools of strictly French art rather than in any of its more experimental innovations. Several other Jewish artists, moreover, attracted attention at various times as individualists whose work fails to fit into any of the categories of contemporary criticism. Russian-born Eugéne Zak (1884–1926), for example, achieved a curious synthesis of mildly cubist stylization and almost Pre-Raphaelite idealism that is perhaps unique. Frenel (1898–1980), who was born in Ereẓ Israel as Frenkel, is a somewhat mystical or romantic painter of Jewish themes whose work expresses little of the anguish and turbulence of Mané-Katz and other eastern European Paris painters who have handled similar themes. In this respect, Frenel belongs rather with Balgley and with Polish-born J.D. Kirszenbaum (1900–1954), an artist whose work likewise escapes classification under any of the usual headings of contemporary painting. Arthur Kolnick (1890–?) is notable for his tender and poetic paintings of traditional types and scenes recalled from the ḥasidic communities of his native Galicia. Emma Stern (1878–1967), who fled to Paris from Nazi Germany, began painting late in life. With her scenes of a happy childhood in small towns in the Saarland, she was soon acclaimed as a new Grandma Moses. When Simon Segal (1898–1970) left Russia for Berlin, he was profoundly influenced by German expressionism; but in France he developed a style of his own in which a new kind of realism suggests a mysterious affinity with Permeke and the Flemish expressionists. Finally, in the late 1960s, the American-born painter and sculptor Zev, originally named Dan Harris (1914–1986), injected an element of "Alice in Wonderland" nonsense into traditional surrealist fantasy, which he thus enriched with some novel, individual, and technically refined sculpture. It would probably be correct to say that most of the Jewish painters of the School of Paris settled in the French capital in order to escape from more traditional or Orthodox Jewish backgrounds, especially in eastern Europe, as much as from the limitations imposed on them by persecution or by their status as Jews. In their work as artists, as well as in their lives as members of the Paris bohemian community, most of these artists were cultural assimilationists, though many of them were also haunted from time to time by nostalgic memories of the life from which they had chosen to escape. In the work of Soutine, for instance, there are practically no direct memories of his Russian-Jewish background. In the works of most other painters of the so-called Jewish School of Paris, such memories appear only occasionally, and generally in an idealized and almost idyllic form; they then seem to express nostalgia for the past, or even guilt feelings about having abandoned it. Following the great commercial success of Chagall's Jewish themes, some of these artists reverted to similar themes, handled with great pathos or nostalgic humor, in what can only be regarded as deliberate exploitation of a new fashion for such memories of a vanished world.

BIBLIOGRAPHY: Edouard Roditi Archives, Leo Baeck Institute, New York; W. George, in: Roth, Art, 639–718.

[Edouard Roditi]

PARIUM (or **Parion**; Turk. **Kemer**), ancient city on the Asian side of the Dardanelles. It was the first settlement point for the Jews in the region of *Canakkale during the Roman era. The earliest literary evidence about the Parium Jews, from 48 B.C.E., contains a decree by Julius Gaius, Roman consul, which indicates that Jewish rights and privileges were granted to enable them to maintain their customs in the face of local hostility, including the right of assembly, feasts in accordance with their tradition, and monetary contributions for common meals and holy festivals. From the decree, it can be surmised that there was a synagogue in Parium. There is no further information about the Parium Jews. Nonetheless, the fact that Teucer of Cyzius, author of *Historia Judaica*, lived in a city close to Parium in the middle of the first century B.C.E., points to a Jewish presence in this region.

BIBLIOGRAPHY: J. Flavius, Ant., 213–16; Strabo, *Geography,* 13:1, 1; *Handbook for Travelers in Constantinople, Brusa, and the Troad* (1893), 135; P.R. Trebilco, *Jewish Communities in Asia Minor* (1994), 13; A. Galanté, *Histoire des Juifs d'Anatolie,* 4 (1987), 224.

[M. Mustafa Kulu (2nd ed.)]

PARIZ UN VIENE, 16th-century Yiddish epic. Until the recent discovery of a complete copy of the Verona 1594 edition, whose preface mentions Elia Levita (Elye Bokher/Bachur) apparently as the author's mentor, the poem was conventionally attributed to Levita. That attribution thus now seems at least complicated (for it might well be an elaborately ironic subterfuge – certainly not unthinkable for Levita) if not altogether untenable. *Pariz un Viene* nonetheless clearly derives from and participates in the same north Italian Renaissance cultural milieu in which Levita wrote his *Bove-Bukh*, and like that text, this one is also an adaptation of an Italian romance into Yiddish (717 *ottava rima* stanzas in 10 cantos). Here, however – unlike Levita's masterfully entertaining but hardly intellectually ambitious *Bove-Bukh* – the Yiddish version utterly transforms its source into a veritable masterpiece of Renaissance or quasi-Humanist poetic narrative, directly influenced, for instance, by Ariosto's *Orlando furioso.* The conventional plot of the vassal's son who must prove himself before being granted the princess as his bride is transformed from hackneyed cliché into a complexly layered and dramatically progressing, politically serious, and delightfully humorous *tour de force*.

BIBLIOGRAPHY: Ch. Shmeruk, *Prokim fun der Yidisher Literatur-Geshikhte* (1988), 97–120; A.M. Babbi, in: *Quaderni di Lingue e Letterature* (Verona), 11 (1986), 393–97; V. Marchetti et al. (eds.), *Elia Bahur Levita, Paris un Viene, Francesco Dalle Donne, Verona 1594* (1988; facsimile Verona 1594]; Ch. Shmeruk, *Pariz un Vyenah: Mahadurah bi-Kortit be-Tseruf Mavo, He'arot ve-Nispaḥim* (1996); A. Schulz, *Die Zeichen des Körpers und der Liebe: 'Paris und Vienna' in der jiddischen Fassung des Elia Levita* (2000); J.C. Frakes (ed.), *Early Yiddish Texts: 1100–1750* (2004), 393–414; J. Baumgarten, *Introduction to Old Yiddish Literature* (2005), 186–206.

[Jerold C. Frakes (2nd ed.)]

PARKER, DOROTHY (1893–1967), U.S. poet and author. Daughter of a Jewish father and a Scottish mother, she began her career by writing reviews for *Vogue* and *Vanity Fair* (who found her reviews too harsh) and then for *The New Yorker.* Her first book of verse, *Enough Rope* (1926), was a best seller, and was followed by two others, all three later being collected in *Not So Deep As a Well* (1936). She also became known as a short story writer, her prizewinning tale, "Big Blonde" (1929), being generally considered her best. Collected short stories appeared in *Laments for the Living* (1930), *After Such Pleasures* (1933), and *Here Lies* (1939); in 1944 a collection of her prose and verse appeared as *The Portable Dorothy Parker,* with an introduction by W. Somerset Maugham. Dorothy Parker was witty, sardonic, elegant, and often profound. She also wrote Hollywood screenplays, and a drama in which she collaborated with Arnaud d'Usseau, *Ladies of the Corridor* (1953), was successfully staged in New York.

BIBLIOGRAPHY: J. Keats, *You Might as Well Live* (1970); N.W. Yates, *American Humorist* (1964), 262–73; S.J. Kunitz, *Twentieth Century Authors, first supplement* (1955); Paris Review, *Writers at Work* (1958), 69–82.

[Sol Liptzin]

PARKER, JOHN (1875–1952), British author of reference works on the theater. Born Jacob Solomons in New York, Parker was the son of a Polish Jewish father who died young. His Jewish mother, who came from Cardiff, moved to London in the 1880s. After a career in journalism, he became London manager of the *New York Dramatic News* from 1903 to 1921 and in 1912 began the annual reference work for which he became well known, *Who's Who in the Theatre* (which was preceded by a similar work he edited from 1908, *The Green Room Book*). He changed his name to "John Parker" in 1917. Parker continued to edit this work through 11 editions over the next 40 years almost single-handedly. He insisted on absolute accuracy, never allowing actors to falsify their ages, as was common. He was also a successful shipping agent and a talented illustrator.

BIBLIOGRAPHY: ODNB online.

[William D. Rubinstein (2nd ed.)]

PARKER, SARAH JESSICA (1965–), U.S. actress. Born in Nelsonville, Ohio, Parker made her first television appearance at age eight in *The Little Match Girl.* Her parents divorced when she was young; her mother, Barbra, who is Jewish, married Paul Forste. Parker, her two brothers, and sister joined her stepfather's four children in one large family. At nine Parker was cast in the Broadway production of *The Innocents*, prompting the family to move to New Jersey. She was then cast in *The Sound of Music* along with four siblings and then got the lead in *Annie* on Broadway. What followed was a succession of television and movie roles. She appeared in *The Sunshine Boys, Miami Rhapsody*, and *The First Wives Club.* But her role as the sex columnist Carrie Bradshaw on the hit television series *Sex and the City* transformed her career. Parker played the central character, one of four single friends in New York. The series catalogued their romances, and Parker won numerous best actress awards. Because of her far-out clothing on the show, she also became a fashion icon whose photographs later adorned the covers of major fashion magazines. Despite the racy material, the show, which ran for six years, appeared in syndication around the world with the steamy material and dialogue toned down. Parker is married to the actor Matthew Broderick, who also had a Jewish mother and a non-Jewish father. The couple married in a civil ceremony in a historic synagogue in New York that is no longer used as a house of worship. Parker has done a number of shows of a Jewish cultural nature. She was host of the Hebrew version of *Sesame Street* called *Shalom Sesame*, read Jewish folk tales on National Public Radio, and narrated a documentary on Ḥasidim.

[Stewart Kampel (2nd ed.)]

°**PARKES, JAMES WILLIAM** (1896–1981), English theologian and historian. Educated in Guernsey and at Oxford, Parkes, a member of the Church of England, was ordained as an Anglican priest in 1926 and from 1928 to 1934 was study secretary of the International Student Service in Geneva. Actively aware of the antisemitism prevalent in the Central and Eastern European universities, he wrote his earliest book, *The Jew and His Neighbour* (1930, 1938[2]). He then embarked on what was planned as a comprehensive history of antisemitism, the chief responsibility for which he saw in the policy of the Christian Church (*The Conflict of the Church and the Synagogue*, 1934; *The Jew in the Medieval Community*, 1938). He wrote a long series of other works on antisemitism, the origins of Christianity, the history of Palestine, etc., in all of which he demonstrated a strong sympathy with the Jewish people and appreciation of Judaism as a religious system. Parkes collaborated with many Jewish organizations and was president of the Jewish Historical Society of England (1949–51). His important private library on Jewish history and Jewish-Gentile relations, which he collected at his home in Barley (near Cambridge) and was incorporated in 1956 as a center for the study of relations between the Jewish and non-Jewish worlds, was given by Parkes to the University of Southampton, where the university established a research fellowship for the study of the relations of Jewish and non-Jewish communities. In 1967 Parkes published *Arabs and Jews in the Middle East – A Tragedy of Errors*. Parkes' autobiography, *Voyage of Discoveries*, appeared in 1969. James Parkes was one of the most sincere, outspoken, and influential Christian philo-semites of 20th century Britain.

ADD. BIBLIOGRAPHY: ODNB online.

[Cecil Roth]

PARLAMENTSKLUB, JUEDISCHER, Jewish caucus active in the Austrian House of Deputies (*Reichsrat*) during the legislative period 1907–11, the first Austrian parliament elected by equal ballot. It consisted of the deputies of the Jewish national parties of Galicia and Bukovina, not including Jews of other parties. Three of its members, Adolf *Stand, Heinrich Gabel, and Arthur *Mahler, were elected in Galicia, where a number of Jewish deputies also were elected as Poles. The fourth member and chairman Benno Straucher came from Bukovina. The Jewish caucus issued a declaration demanding national autonomy for the Jews as well as a democratic and sound social policy in general. Straucher became a forceful speaker for the rights of Austrian Jews. Despite its small membership the Jewish caucus became a political factor in parliament, although it was frequently paralyzed by the antagonism of the Polish caucus (*Polenklub*). In 1911 only Straucher of all the initial members was reelected. A Jewish caucus existed also in the provincial diet (*Landtag*) of Bukovina.

BIBLIOGRAPHY: A. Boehm, *Die zionistische Bewegung*, 1 (1935), 344.

[Hugo Knoepfmacher]

PARMA, city in N. Italy, capital of the province and former duchy of the same name. Jews are mentioned in Parma around the middle of the 14th century when the town was ruled by the Visconti dukes of Mantua. When the *Black Death was raging in 1348, the Jews were accused of poisoning wells and fountains, and some were put to death. Under the Visconti, Jewish moneylenders were able to carry on business in Parma. In 1440 Elias, physician and lecturer at the medical school of Pavia, was appointed physician to the duke of Parma; among other physicians who practiced there were Giacobb, who may be identical with Giacobbe who treated Duke Erede I of Este in 1467, and Abraham, son of Moses of Prato (1480).

Under the rule of the Sforza, about the middle of the 15th century, the Jews enjoyed the protection of the dukes against oppression by the municipal authorities. The Franciscan Bernardino da *Feltre instigated the expulsion of some Jewish women who had given dancing lessons to aristocratic women in Parma. In 1488 Bernardino succeeded in having a Christian loan-bank (**Monte di Pietà*) established there; the Jewish loan-bankers began to leave the town, taking refuge in Piacenza and the smaller centers of the duchy. Following the bull "cum nimis absurdum" issued by Pope *Paul IV in July 1555, Jews were no longer permitted to carry on their moneylending activities or to reside in Parma. Under Paul's successor, Pius IV, the

Jews were permitted in 1562 to open loan-banks in 16 smaller centers in the duchy of Parma and Piacenza (at Colorno, Roccabianca, Soragna, Borgo San Donnino (now Fidenza), Busseto, San Secondo Parmense, and Sissa). The concession, valid for a duration of 12 years, was later renewed for eight centers only; these included the first five mentioned above. Renewals were granted every 12 years, the last dating from 1669. The loan-banks were a necessity for the predominantly agricultural population. The Jews were accorded political equality on July 12, 1803 by the French commissaire Moreau de Saint-Méry, but this was rescinded in 1816 by the archduchess Marie Louise. Jews were now beginning to resettle in Parma itself. Publication of a *Rivista Israelitica* was begun in Parma in 1845, but lasted only for three years. Emancipation followed the inclusion of Parma in the Kingdom of Sardinia. In 1866 the renewed community of Parma drew up its constitution and arranged for the building of a synagogue. Rabbis of Parma include Donato Camerini (1866–1921), editor of a prayer book according to the Italian rite (Parma, 1912). The community numbered 510 in 1840, and 684 in 1881, declining to 415 in 1911.

[Alfredo Mordechai Rabello]

In 1931 there were 232 Jews in the community of Parma. During the Holocaust at least 12 were sent to extermination camps. After the war the community had a membership of 86, which declined to 60 by 1969.

[Sergio Della Pergola]

Palatina Library

The Palatina Library in Parma contains one of the richest collections of Hebrew manuscripts and incunabula in the world, among them many valuable illuminated manuscripts. Included in the collection are early Bible codices, and it is especially rich in liturgical manuscripts. Important manuscripts of Midrashim and rabbinical works include the commentaries of Menahem b. Solomon *Meiri. In 1816 Marie-Louise, Napoleon's wife, bought the G.B. de' *Rossi collection of more than 1,500 manuscripts. In 1846 the library acquired over 100 Hebrew manuscripts from the collection of M.B. *Foa of Reggio Emilia. The codices are amply described by G.B. de' Rossi in his *Manuscripti codices Hebraici bibliothecae* (3 vols., 1803); the 55 manuscripts later acquired by de' Rossi were described by M. Steinschneider in: HB, 6–7 (1863–64); 12 (1872); 14 (1874) and by P. *Perreau (*Catologo dei Codici ebraici de… non descritti dal de' Rossi*, 1880). G. Tamani described the library's illuminated manuscripts (in: *La Bibliofilia*, 70 (1968), 39–139).

[Alfredo Mordechai Rabello]

BIBLIOGRAPHY: Roth, Italy, index; Milano, Italia, index; V. Rovè, *L'Educatore Israelita*, 18 (1870); A. Orvieto, in: *Il Vessillo Israelitico*, 43 (1895), 323–7, 357–60; E. Loevinson, in: RMI, 7 (1932), 350–8; G. Bachi, *ibid.*, 12 (1938), 204–5; 28 (1962), 37 (statistics); P. Colbi, *ibid.*, 29 (1963), 438–45; E. Urbach, in: MGWJ, 80 (1936), 275–81; M.A. Szulwas, *Ḥayyei ha-Yehudim be-Italyah…* (1955), index. PALATINA LIBRARY: Zunz, Gesch, 240; G. Gabrieli, *Manoscritti…* (1930); idem, in: RMI, 7 (1932–33), 167–75; E. Loevinson, *ibid.*, 477–92; U. Cassuto, *I Manoscritti Palatini ebraici della Biblioteca apostolica Vaticana…* (1935); G. Tamani, *Studii nell Oriente e le Bibbie* (1967), 201–26.

PARNAKH, VALENTIN YAKOVLEVICH (1891–1948?), Russian poet and choreographer. Parnakh was born in Taganrog and educated in St. Petersburg and Paris. His earliest poems, written under the influence of his friend O. *Mandelshtam, were published in the Acmeist literary journal *Giperborey* ("The Hyperborean") in 1913. On the recommendation of A. Blok, V. Meyerhold accepted Parnakh's poetry for publication in his art journal *Lyubov k trem apelsinam* ("The Love for the Three Oranges," 3, 1914), to which Parnakh later contributed also essays on the dance. In 1914, he traveled through the Middle East. His first collection of verse, *Samum* ("The Simoom," 1919), includes several pieces ("To the Palms of Palestine," "The Psalm," "Zechariah, Ch. 11," etc.) inspired by his visit to Ereẓ Israel. During World War I, Parnakh lived in France, England, and Italy, returning to Russia in 1917. His choreographic talent was acknowledged by S. *Eisenstein, who in 1921 invited him to teach modern dance in the Proletkult Drama Workshop. Between 1919 and 1932, Parnakh made several extended trips to France, where he published four collections of experimental poetry in Russian, two scholarly monographs in French (*L'Inquisition*, 1930; *Histoire de la danse*, 1932), and numerous essays and translations (in *Nouvelle Littéraires, Bifur, Europe, La Courte Paille*, and other periodicals of the French avant-garde). Parnakh's essay "In the Russian World of Letters" (*The Menorah Journal*, 3, 1926) for the first time introduced such Russian-Jewish writers as M. *Gershenzon, O. Mandelshtam, B. *Pasternak, and B. *Lapin to the American-Jewish reader. Parnakh's greatest literary achievement was his annotated anthology of the Jewish poets who were victims of the Spanish and Portuguese Inquisitions (*Ispanskiye i portugalskiya poety, zhertvy inkvizitsii*, 1934), published after almost two decades of research. The book contained numerous biographical articles as well as records of trials and autos-da-fé. Its appearance in Moscow on the eve of the Stalinist purges and the Holocaust of European Jewry became a poignant literary event which deeply influenced such poets as Akhmatova and Mandelshtam.

Nothing is known about Parnakh's subsequent life and literary activity, except that his translation of Agrippa d'Aubigné, the French Huguenot poet, was published in 1949 in Moscow. His other works include: *Le quai* (1919); *Karabkaetsya akrobat* (with the author's portrait by P. Picasso) (1922); *Slovosdvig. Mot dynamo* (poems in Russian and French) (1920); *Vstuplenie k tantsam* (1925).

BIBLIOGRAPHY: G. Struve, *Russkaya literatura v izgnanii* (1956), 161–2; *The Prose of Osip Mandelstam* (1967), 47–48, 199; S. Eisenstein, *Izbr. proizv.*, 1 (1964), 267, 639; A. Blok, *Zapisnye knizhki* (1965), 207, 559; N. Berberova, *The Italics Are Mine* (1969), 569.

[Omri Ronen]

PARNAS (Heb. פַּרְנָס; "leader"; also called *rosh*), head of the community. The *parnas* was usually elected, sometimes for life but more customarily for a definite term of one year or three years. In larger communities in the later Middle Ages and early modern times, there were several *parnasim* who led the community in rotation, each for one month; they were then called *parnas ha-ḥodesh* ("the *parnas* of the month"; this system is described in detail in the *takkanot* of Cracow for 1595). The leaders of the territorial autonomy structure also used this title, which was later attached to partial, functional leadership, when a distinction was made between the *parnas ha-kahal* ("of the community"), *parnas ha-galil* ("of the province"), *parnas ha-shuk* ("of the market"), the *parnasim* of the guilds and the like. In modern times the title Parnas is employed for the president of a community or a congregation (in the Spanish and Portuguese congregation of London he is called Parnas – Presidente).

BIBLIOGRAPHY: Baron, Community, 3 (1942), index s.v. *Parnasim*.

[Natan Efrati]

PARNAS, ḤAYYIM NAḤMAN (d. 1854), Lithuanian scholar. Parnas was born in Dubnov. After the death of his first wife, Parnas remarried and settled in Vilna. It was his practice to study wrapped in *tallit* and *tefillin* until mid-afternoon each day in his father-in-law's *bet ha-midrash* and to continue studying for the rest of the day at home. By means of his extraordinary diligence he achieved a mastery of both *halakhah* and Kabbalah. He delivered daily discourses on Isaac *Alfasi and the commentary on him by Nissim b. Reuben *Gerondi before the leading figures of the community in the *bet ha-midrash*. In 1850 he established a yeshivah in Vilna. In his prayers he followed the ritual of the "Ari" (Isaac *Luria), and every Sabbath, before the reading of the Law, when the congregation was going over the weekly portion, he studied the Zohar on it.

Parnas took an active interest in communal affairs and was himself widely esteemed. For many years he administered the distribution of Vilna's philanthropic funds, including those for indigent Jews residing in Ereẓ Israel. His approbations appear in a number of contemporary works. The last section of the *Sha'agat Aryeh* printed in the Slavuta edition (1833) contains some novellae of Parnas which display talmudic erudition. He concerned himself with the needs of the community as a whole and of the individuals in it, and because of his grasp of worldly matters many turned to him for advice on their problems.

BIBLIOGRAPHY: S.J. Fuenn, *Kiryah Ne'emanah* (1915), 257; Ḥ.N. Maggid-Steinschneider, *Ir Vilna* (1900), 63, 185; H. Brawermann, *Anshei Shem* (1892), 36a.

[Samuel Abba Horodezky]

PARNAS, YAKUB KAROL (1884–1942?), Polish biochemist. Born in Tarnopol, Galicia, Parnas worked at the University of Strasbourg (1914–16), and then directed a physiology institute at Warsaw University. From 1921 he was professor of medical chemistry at Lvov. In 1942, although he had left the Jewish faith, he fled to Russia, where he died. His main work was on biochemistry of muscle and biological synthesis of ammonia. Among his books was *Chemja fizjologiczna z szczegolnem uwzględnieniem fizjologji zwierzęcej* ("Physiological Chemistry with Special Reference to Animal Physiology," 1922) and together with F. Czapek he edited *Monographien aus dem Gesamtgebiet der Physiologie der Pflanzen und der Tiere* (1914).

PARNIS, MOLLIE (1903?–1992), U.S. fashion designer and philanthropist. Parnis was the eldest of five children of Abraham and Sara Parnis, immigrants from Austria. Her first design was prompted by a date with her future husband, Leon Livingston, who took her to a football game and suggested that she change for dancing that evening. Parnis redesigned her only dress. They married in 1930 and opened their own dress business, Parnis-Livingston, in 1933; Parnis was the designer and Livingston handled the business details. Their enterprise flourished into a multimillion dollar business and the wives of several U.S. presidents wore their creations. Parnis continued the business following her husband's death in 1962; she was known for creating tasteful, classic designs from good fabrics. Parnis, a lover of art and literature, invited actors, politicians, writers, and journalists to her home on Park Avenue, which came to be known as Mollie Parnis' salon. A philanthropist, she created the Mollie Parnis Livingston Foundation of New York, which helped create parks in rundown areas of New York City. She sponsored a similar prize in Jerusalem. Parnis set up an award for newspaper, magazine, and television journalists under the age of 35 in memory of her only son, Robert Livingston, who died in 1979. Parnis retired from the dress business in 1984 but continued with the Mollie Parnis Livingston Foundation of New York until her death.

[Sara Alpern (2nd ed.)]

PARODY, HEBREW.

Parody in Early Hebrew Literature

Parody is the use of a recognizable literary form as a vehicle to ridicule or mock something or someone. The writer takes a well-known, serious work as his model and invests it with new and amusing contents, at times in order to deride the original or its author, at others to express his views and criticisms of contemporary political and social issues. This technique is used in order to grasp the attention of the reader who will easily recognize the parodied text. Parody, though it uses different forms, is in fact a literary genre in its own right and one of the keenest weapons of satire. In Hebrew literature, parody is an ancient genre. Although mockery for its own sake is not among the things allowed a Jew, the mockery of idolatry is permitted (Meg. 25b) and, by inference, the mocking of anything morally or legally defective. Evidence of this concealed form of derision is found already in the Bible: "Elijah mocked them [the prophets of the Baal]) and said: Cry aloud; for he is a god; either he is musing, or he is gone aside, or he is on a journey, or peradventure he sleepeth, and must be awaked" (I Kings 18:27) and, incidentally, in various places in the Talmud and the Midrash. It is not always possible to identify the source which is being imitated; however, the meter and rhythm of the work make it almost certain that it is a parody on something.

Well known among the fables of Simeon Bar-Kappara, many of which are parodies, is the riddle Bar-Kappara puts in the mouth of the son-in-law of Judah ha-Nasi, Ben-Elasah, who was rich but ignorant and did not participate in the learned conversation of the wise men gathered in Judah's house. The riddle had two objects: first, to mock the rich ignoramus, and secondly, to criticize Judah himself for leading the people with a "high hand." Judah immediately realized that Bar-Kappara was behind his son-in-law's riddle and was angry with the true author. The "riddle" was in fact a parody on the fables of Solomon or of Ben-Sira and is one of the gems of early Hebrew satire:

The netherworld looked down from heaven
Turbulence at the sides of her house
Scaring all winged creatures
The young men saw me and hid themselves
And the aged rose up and stood;
He who flees shall say: Alas, alas!
And he who is trapped is trapped by his own sin (TJ, MK 3:1).

Generally it may be said that the use of such allegoric or heroic language for mundane trivia should be considered parody, even if it is difficult to identify its source. An unusual homily in the Talmud itself should also be regarded as a kind of parody in talmudic *pilpul* style: "Where is Haman [of the Book of Esther] mentioned in the Torah? It is written, Hast thou eaten of the tree, whereof I commanded thee that thou shouldest not eat?" (Gen. 3:11). It cannot be assumed that anyone would have thought that that question which Adam was asked hinted even faintly at Haman in the Book of Esther. The novelty consists not only in the fact that the Hebrew letters of "Haman" and *Ha-Min* are identical but also in the juxtaposition of the evil Haman and the "tree" on which he was hanged. This witticism is in fact an imitation of more serious homilies, sometimes hair-splitting in their attempts to make a point, which were common in the Babylonian academies, and thus displays one of the most obvious characteristics of parody.

Parody Since the 12th Century

Hebrew parody as an established literary form is post-talmudic, dating for the most part from the 12th century. It first appeared in Spain, then in Provence and Italy, from where it passed to the literary centers of the Netherlands, Germany, and eastern Europe. Among the secular poems of the Spanish and Italian poets are many excellent parodies on diverse subjects. The poem *Al ha-Zevuvim* ("On Flies") by Abraham *Ibn Ezra, who was one of the cleverest satirists of Hebrew poetry, is clearly an imitation of an epic. It begins with witty rhymes and pretentious language:

To whom shall I flee for help from my oppression?
Whom shall I implore against the devastation of the flies?
Which will not give me respite
With all their power they oppress me like enemies
And flutter over my eyes and eyelids,
Reciting passionate love songs in my ears;
I venture to eat my meal alone
And they partake of it like wolves,
And even drink out of my glass of wine as though
I had invited them like lovers or friends.

By using such thundering sentences when speaking merely of tiny flies, Ibn Ezra forcefully achieves the amusing effect of parody. The satiric poetry of Todros *Abulafia (Toledo, second half of the 13th century), or of Solomon *Bonafed (Kingdom of Aragon, first half of the 15th century), in particular against other poets or against personal enemies, also often has a parodic nature. Also the rhymed prose work by *Santob (Shem Tov) de Carrion, *The Debate between the Pen and the Scissors*, can be considered as a political allegory in the form of parody.

The *Ma'ariv le-Furim*, written by *Menahem b. Aaron (who lived in 14th-century Toledo), is an amusing parody on the *piyyut Leil Shimmurim Hu Zeh ha-Laylah* ("This is the Night of Vigil"), by *Meir b. Isaac, included in the *Ma'ariv* prayer for the first day of Passover. This parody was unaccountably included in a serious edition of the festival prayers and *piyyutim*. With light and boisterous rhymes the author of the parody includes all creation in the joy of Purim:

On this night all creatures get drunk
To remember the law established on Purim
And damned be the man who lifts his hands
To drink abominable water.

and so on, in similar style. Apart from its relevance to Purim, this parody is apparently also a protest against the abundance of *piyyutim* composed by the *paytanim* of that period, many of which have been included in the prayer book, and especially in the prayer books for holidays.

The poems by Joseph *Ibn Zabara (who lived in 12th-century Spain) on the subjects of doctors and women, specify in a typically medical jargon all the remedies for the fever and other illnesses. They are obviously caricatures of Hippocrates' "collections." One of the masters of Hebrew satire and parody was the Spanish poet Judah *Al-Ḥarizi. His amusing book of *maqāmāt, Taḥkemoni*, is written in the spirit of the Arab poet Abu Muhammad al-Qasem Al-Ḥarīrī (1054–1122), whose book of *maqāmāt* Al-Ḥarizi translated into Hebrew. The *Taḥkemoni* abounds in droll parodies on contemporary personalities and on customs which Al-Ḥarizi found amusing. For example, he ridicules the ceremony of **kapparot* on the eve of the Day of Atonement by relating the words of a cock, who for fear of being killed had escaped to the roof of the synagogue. The style of the cock's speech is biblical, although there is a suggestion too of the style of the contemporary preachers whom Al-Ḥarizi mocks in other places. The book also contains a parody on the commandment for phylacteries at the end of Gate 5 (Segal 453), on bloody combats in Gate 7 (Segal 466), and on a bombastic host in Gate 34 (Segal 580), etc.

Another of the early Hebrew parodists was *Judah b. Isaac ibn Shabbetai, born in Toledo or Burgos in the 13th century. He was the author of *Minḥat Yehudah Sone ha-Nashim* ("The Tribute of Judah the Misogynist"), a satire on bachelors and women-haters in the style of the Bible and of medieval stories. He also wrote *Milḥemet ha-Ḥokhmah ve-ha-Osher* ("The War of Wisdom and Wealth," 1214) and *Divrei ha-Alah ve-ha-Niddui* ("The Words of the Curse and the Ban," date unknown).

A parody of a different kind is *Iggeret Al Tehi ka-Avotekha* ("Be not as your fathers"), written by Isaac Efodi (Profiat *Duran) in the 15th century to his friend Bonat Bongiorno, who had apostatized. Written in the mild language of the pastoral epistles of Christian preachers, Duran equivocally advises his friend "to remain in the Christian faith." By pretending to prove the mistakes of the Jews, as it were, he actually mocks Christianity and its preachers and, by inference, the apostates. The name of the parody and its flattering style misled many into thinking that this really was an epistle of the Church, until they came to the end and its conclusions.

KALONYMUS B. KALONYMUS. While the poets of the Golden Age in Spain wrote in biblical Hebrew, they employed Arabic meters. The contents of their poetry, especially the secular, was also influenced by contemporary poetry in general and by Arabic poetry in particular. Their parodies, too, were mostly imitations of contemporary literature (e.g., epic poems, love songs, and medical treatises). Gradually satire ceased to be the concern only of poets, rhetoricians, and rhymists, and scholars began to take a casual interest in it. Parody in talmudic style was welcomed on those days when jesting was allowed, the days which "Jews ordained, and took upon them, and upon their seed, and upon all such as joined themselves unto them, so as it should not fail, that they would keep these two days according to the writing thereof, and according to the appointed time thereof, every year" (Esth. 9:27).

The father of parody in the style of the Talmud was Kalonymus b. Kalonymus, who was born in 1286 and lived in Italy from 1318, and who was one of the outstanding physicians of his time. Besides his profound knowledge of Torah and rabbinic literature, he mastered several languages and translated a selection of medical and philosophical books from Arabic into Latin at the request of the Italian King Robert, a lover of art and literature. His translations served as a bridge between the knowledge of East and West. His most famous work is *Massekhet Purim*, "Tractate Purim," written in the language and form of a talmudic tractate. Its four chapters contain a humorous debate regarding food, drink, and drunkenness on Purim. At the end of the tractate the author says that it was his intention

> to gladden people on Purim and the reader will not lose but [will gain] like him who reads a book of medicine and of matters that benefit the body and do not harm the soul, because I, Kalonymus, invented this essay, the mishnah and the gemara and I call to witness R. Shakran ("Liar") and his brother R. Kazvan ("Deceiver"), who are mentioned at the end of the tractate.

A literary masterpiece in style, presentation, and contents, *Massekhet Purim* serves as more than a mere jest, for much can be learned from it regarding the life, customs, and food, etc., of the 13th-century Italian Jews. Among the Purim customs which Kalonymus mentions are: horse riding in the streets of the town, waving pine branches, and dancing around a rag puppet which symbolized the figure of Haman. *Massekhet Purim* also specifies 24 Italian dishes, popular among the Jews, some of which are otherwise unknown. The 24 dishes represent the 24 "contributions to the priests" donated by the people at the time of the Temple in Jerusalem and the 24 books of the Bible.

Although other works by the same author met with no opposition, Kalonymus' *Massekhet Purim* was frowned upon by extremist rabbis who considered a parody in talmudic style to be a sacrilege. They banned reading the book and even condemned it to be burned. Samuel ben Abraham *Aboab, in his *Devar Shemu'el*, wrote:

> He who reads that book called *Massekhet Purim* will be grieved for by all God-fearing people, who saw, and straight away were amazed, how the author dared print it and felt no remorse – hopefully the book will be put away and will become like something which has been lost, so that it shall not be seen and shall not be found…"

It therefore became rare and passed from hand to hand in manuscript. In the 19th century it was printed anonymously by various publishers, sometimes supplemented by other facetious Purim parodies of a later date. Jonah Wilheimer, who published it in Vienna in 1871, relates in his preface that he copied it from an old manuscript found in a collection of books (including some formerly belonging to Jacob *Emden) which he bought from an Amsterdam bookseller. He writes:

> I hereunder publish *Megillat Setarim* and *Massekhet Purim* without inquiring into who wrote these books or whose spirit collected them, but rather hailing this delightful treasure, because the author(s) have made a jest to cheer the readers with their sweet language in the style of the authors of the Talmud, and so as not to withhold what is good from its rightful owners, I publish them.

Massekhet Purim served as a blueprint for other imitations of talmudic tractates and also of liturgical literature in all its forms; prayers, *seliḥot*, lamentations for the Ninth of Av, and especially the Passover *Haggadah*. Steinschneider lists three Purim tractates in his list of 31 parodies and hundreds of other comic works, and Davidson mentions a further 21 in his list of 500 parodies in Hebrew and other languages (see bibliography). In a list of Hebrew manuscripts in Offenbach, Germany, a *Massekhet Purim* with Latin translation is mentioned, but it was apparently never printed. One *Massekhet Purim*, together with other Purim parodies collected from the large anonymous Purim literature, appeared in 1844, published by Solomon b. Ephraim Bloch, at the "Royal Court Press" in Hanover, where Jews had lived since the 13th century. A novel feature of this edition is its illustrations – one of a drunkard in the shade of trees in the innyard, and one of four people, including a woman, in festive fancy dress.

Most of the later editions of *Massekhet Purim* are followed by *Megillat Setarim*, which consists of three chapters. It begins in the style of *Pirkei Avot*:

> Ḥavakbuk received instruction (in drinking) from Karmi, who handed it down to Noah, and Noah to Lot and Lot to Joseph's brothers (apparently by virtue of the "cup" found in Benjamin's sack, Gen. 44:12), and Joseph's brothers to Nabal the Carmelite (who was "very drunken," I Sam. 25:36), and Nabal the Carmelite to Ben Hadad (king of Aram in Ahab's time, of whom it is said, who "was drinking himself drunk," I Kings 20:16), and Ben Hadad to Belshazzar (who "drank wine before the thousand," Dan 5:1), and Belshazzar to Ahasuerus (thanks to whose feast blessed with "royal wine in abundance" the festival of Purim came about), and Ahasuerus to Rabbi Bibi (according to Shab. 80b, a certain Rabbi Bibi "got drunk," as a result of which he became a central figure in *Megillat Setarim*).

The characters of Ḥavakbuk ha-Navi and Karmi figure in *Sefer Ḥavakbuk ha-Navi*, which was appended to a number of editions of *Massekhet Purim*, beginning with the Venice edition of 1551. It is a parody in a pure and precise biblical style (of the books of the prophets) in praise of wine on Purim. The modification of the prophet's name from "Ḥavakkuk" to "Ḥavakbuk" ("he embraced the bottle") is the sort of humorous pun which recurs throughout the parody. All personal and place names are derived from the Bible, and with a change of meaning, are made to recall wine and everything connected with it:

Karmi (a biblical first name, here meaning a vineyard); Boẓrah (the town Basra; here it alludes to the vintage); Be'eri (a biblical first name, here meaning a water well); Ha-Tiroshta (appellation of Nehemiah, "because he was allowed to drink the king's wine"; here the allusion is to *tirosh*, new wine); *kos* ("glass"); *enav* ("grape"); and *bakbuk* ("bottle"). In the parody, Karmi, king of Israel from Boẓrah and Be'eri contend for the kingship. The prophet Ḥavakbuk brings the word of God to the waverers between Karmi and Be'eri. Influenced by Ḥavakbuk's powerful words, the people forsake Be'eri and "return to Karmi with all their heart," after the prophecy was fulfilled that "at midnight God directed a very strong east wind and dried up the sea, the rivers and lakes and destroyed the canals and wells." The parody ends with a sentence based on Deuteronomy 34:10; "And there hath not arisen a prophet since in the house of Karmi, like unto Ḥavakbuk in all the signs and wonders, which he wrought in the sight of Israel."

Both *Megillat Setarim* and *Sefer Ḥavakbuk ha-Navi* were erroneously attributed to Kalonymus b. Kalonymus since they were appended to most editions of his *Massekhet Purim*. Other writers, Lavi ha-Levi (known also as Leon de Blautes (de Valentibus)) and Elijah Baḥur *Levita, were also credited with their authorship. Neubauer and Davidson, however, established that the actual author of these parodies was *Levi b. Gershom.

MASSEKHET HANUKKAH. Ḥanukkah, like Purim, is a festival of celebration and games, but very little entertaining literature has been written for it. What there is consists mainly of songs, riddles, and witticisms concerning food and drink, in particular various local Ḥanukkah dishes, all of which symbolize historical events connected with Ḥanukkah. Although the Scroll of Antiochus, which relates the Jewish victory in Hasmonean times and the miracle of Ḥanukkah, is an imitation of the style of the Book of Esther, it is in no way a parody. There are, however, three special Ḥanukkah "tractates," modeled on the *Massekhet Purim* and concentrating especially on the secular aspects of the festival – the food and entertainment. The first, the author of which is unknown, was found in manuscript in the collection of David *Franco-Mendes and published, with an introduction by A.Z. Ben-Yishai in *Aresheth*, 3 (1964), 173–92. It is written as a profound talmudic discussion on the essence of the festival, its joys, and its "laws." It details the quantity of the special Ḥanukkah delicacies a Jew must eat "until he is nauseated" or until "he breathes his last." There are actual descriptions of local color, for which no other source is extant, obviously written by a person who was observant of his environment. It tells of the pastimes current among the well-to-do, cultured Jews of that day, which goes far to explain the reprimands of the great rabbis of the 18th century, Jacob Emden, Moses Ḥagiz, and Ẓevi Hirsch Kaidonover among them, who in their writings admonished their contemporaries "who spend their days going to the theaters and circuses, in dancing, card-playing, and even hunting." Another Ḥanukkah tractate, by Joshua Calinari, appeared in Venice, and later in Salonika, while the third, by Jacob Segre, remained in manuscript.

PARODIES AGAINST CATHOLICS, APOSTATES, AND FALSE MESSIAHS. The opposition to the false Messiah, Shabbetai Ẓevi, and to his movement in the 17th and 18th centuries, produced an extensive polemical literature in Hebrew, both in poetry and in prose. The Italian poets, Jacob and Emanuel Frances, published a book of satiric poems called *Ẓevi Mudaḥ*, directed at him. The parody *Haggadah le-Tishah be-Av* is also attributed to the two brothers. (The Ninth of Av was chosen for the recital of the "*Haggadah*" parody because Shabbetai Ẓevi "abolished" the fast on that day and turned it into a feast.) Two versions of this parody, preserved in manuscript, were published by A.M. Habermann, in *Kobez al Jad* 13, pt. 2 (1940), 185–206. Using the framework of the Passover *Haggadah*, including instructions for the various *seder* customs connecting the different sections, the author unleashes his sarcasm and contempt, curses and abuse upon the false messiah. For example, his version of *Dayyeinu* ("It would have been enough"):

> Had he made himself false Messiah
> And not abolished the fast of the Fourth,
> It would have been enough.
> Had he abolished the Fast of the Fourth and not abolished the fast of the Fifth,
> It would have been enough.
> Had he abolished the Fast of the Fifth and not turned it into a regular feast,
> It would have been enough.
> Had he turned it into a regular feast and not eaten and distributed forbidden fats,
> It would have been enough.
> Had he eaten and distributed forbidden fats and not desecrated

the Sabbath,
It would have been enough.
Had he desecrated the Sabbath and not uttered the Ineffable Name,
It would have been enough.
Had he uttered the Ineffable Name and not permitted murder,
It would have been enough.
Had he permitted murder and not apostatized,
It would have been enough.
Had he apostatized and not desecrated the name of God in public, to the hazard of all the Jews of the Diaspora,
It would have been enough.

In the defensive war against incitement or coercion of Jews to convert (mainly on the part of the Catholics), and against the false messiah Shabbetai Ẓevi, satiric parodies came to be written which were circulated in manuscript for fear of the authorities, and which were preserved in various archives. Some of these parodies were printed only hundreds of years later, in countries enjoying a free press. One of the bitterest of those directed against the Catholics is *Pilpul al Zeman, Zemannim, Zemanneihem* by Jonah ha-Kohen Rafa, which was printed in London in 1908, some 226 years after the author's death, from a manuscript in the Montefiore collection. It is a derisive imitation of Jewish ritual style, in the manner of the Passover *Haggadah*, and of the *Avodah* (the Temple service of the Day of Atonement). The descriptions of the Christian *carnival, of gluttony and drunkenness, and of other gratifications of the flesh, point at the debauchery of the Catholic priests of those days, which was far removed from the holy and ascetic life preached by the Church. The author's sharp, unrestrained pen, and his insight into contemporary church and monastery life, highlight the suffering and distress of the Jewish community confronted with religious incitement or coercion.

The Early Haskalah

One of the fathers of Hebrew parody of the Haskalah was Judah Leib *Ben Ze'ev, one of the early *maskilim* and Hebrew philologists. His *Meliẓah le-Furim*, based on the prayers of the Day of Atonement, is a paeon of praise to wine and utter abandon. The uncurbed Purim joy, permitted according to the *halakhah*, served as a cover for the freedom of drinking and gluttony. At the same time the *Meliẓah* also utilized sacred prayers to convey profane ideas, without which no work by a *maskil* of that generation was complete. Parodies of a different kind are Ben Ze'ev's erotic poems, which were never published, but passed from hand to hand like secret pamphlets. One of the poems, *Derekh Gever be-Almah* (a play on the word *almah*; the title can mean "The Way of a Certain Man" or "The Way of a Man with a Maiden"), is a precise description of sexual intercourse, in a garbled combination of fractions of biblical verses. Through this erotic parody Ben Ze'ev wanted to prove that classical Hebrew could express not only holy and exalted ideas, but even intimate, earthy matters.

Not only the Bible and the Talmud served as a framework for amusing parodies at times of festivity, but the Zohar also was used. One of the parodies of the Zohar is *Zohar Ḥadash le-Furim*, whose author was the Polish writer Tobias *Feder. *Zohar Ḥadash* was published in *Oẓar ha-Sifrut*, 3 (1887–90). Even the names of chapters are borrowed from the Zohar. In a language comprehensible only to those familiar with the original, it deals with the festivity of Purim and the purpose of drinking, utilizing biblical verses in a display of homiletics and a pseudo-mysticism. Like the amusing names of the *tannaim* in Kalonymus' *Massekhet Purim*, in the *Zohar Ḥadash* there are also names alluding to Purim dishes and to inebriating drinks.

Another Hebrew philologist, Ẓevi Hirsch Sommerhausen, who lived in Holland and Belgium, was the author of one of the best Hebrew parodies which has retained its popularity, *Haggadah le-Leil Shikkorim*, a parody of the traditional Passover *Haggadah*. It is reminiscent of the classical wine-songs in the Hebrew poetry of Spain and in the poetry of the other peoples – the Greek Anacreon and the Persian Omar Khayyam. Sommerhausen's *Haggadah* begins with these Anacreonic rhymes:

Drink and eat, eat and drink,
Dissipate every heart-ache
Eat and drink, drink and eat
Till you don't know black from white.

At the end is a German poem by the author (in Hebrew letters) in praise of wine, even specifying particular types.

Another booklet of this period "including all the intoxication rules of Purim" is *Even Shetiyyah* (1861). The name originally refers to the foundation rock in the Temple, but may also be translated "drinking stone." The rules which the anonymous author gives include those "forbidding water on Purim":

> (a) it is forbidden to touch, carry, or look at a vessel which contains water or is used for water; (b) he who finds water in his house on Purim should cover it with earth, and he who has a well in his yard should invalidate it with three partitions; (c) laundrymen and all who work with water are forbidden to join the congregation on Purim; (d) it is forbidden to walk on the river bank on Purim; (e) it is forbidden to sail a boat on the river; (f) it is forbidden to drink wine mixed with water on Purim, even if it was mixed before the feast; (g) it is forbidden to walk outside in the rain; (h) it is forbidden to lick salt on Purim, and similar prohibitions.

PARODIES DIRECTED AGAINST ḤASIDISM AND EXTREME ORTHODOXY. There was hardly a poet or author among the early *maskilim* who did not, on some occasion, attempt to write parody, principally as a weapon of derision against his "ideological" adversaries. In particular they mocked Ḥasidism, its customs, and its way of life. Joseph *Perl was a Ḥasid in his youth but, after his stay at the centers of the Haskalah, he became a fanatical adversary of Ḥasidism and a militant *maskil*. He wrote classical parodies directed against ḥasidic literature, in particular the *Shivḥei ha-Besht*, and the stories of *Naḥman of Bratslav. These allegorical stories, which are today considered gems of Hebrew literature, were, at the time of their publication, derided by the linguistically pedantic *maskilim* for their confused language and strange contents. So successful were the parodies that they deceived many innocent Ḥasidim into thinking that they had really been written by ḥasidic authors. In *Megalleh Temirin* ("Revealer of Secrets," 1819), written in the form of 151 epistles which the "obscurantist" Jews were supposed to have exchanged, Perl gives a biased caricature of Ḥasidism in Volhynia and Galicia, and of the *ẓaddikim* whom he despised, and whom he describes as swindlers and avaricious men. It is written in a corrupt Hebrew, spiced with Yiddish idioms and Slavic expressions. His second book, *Boḥen Ẓaddik* (1838), also in the form of letters, is a continuation and explanation of the first. Another satirical work aimed at the Ḥasidim of Galicia is *Ha-Ẓofeh le-Veit Yisrael* (1858) by Isaac *Erter, written in biblical language and in the spirit of Haskalah.

Some of the parodies against Ḥasidism were written in Yiddish poetry and prose. A very popular parody in its time was *Tsvey Khasidimlekh* by N. Goldberg, modeled on *Heine's *Die Grenadiere.*

It tells of two Ḥasidim traveling to the *ẓaddik* Israel of Ruzhin to celebrate the feast of Sukkot and "to listen to his talk with the Divine Guests (*ushpizin*)." On the way, they hear of the rabbi's arrest and imprisonment, together with others suspected of plotting rebellion. The dialogue between the two Ḥasidim is modeled directly on that of Heine's grenadiers, who return from Russian captivity, and while on their way hear of the defeat of Napoleon and his imprisonment. The two Ḥasidim are deeply shaken when they hear of the rabbi's arrest, and the more sentimental of them begs his friend (like Napoleon's grenadier) that if he die of chagrin, he be buried at the rabbi's town, Ruzhin, and covered with its earth. In one hand of the deceased, who is to wear a *tallit* and *tefillin*, they should place a *shofar* and in the other a bottle of brandy. When the rabbi is released and treads on the Ḥasid's tomb, the latter will arise, blow a prolonged blast, and drink to the health of the rabbi.

Another parody directed against Ḥasidism and popular in its time was *Dos Lid fun'm Kugil* (1863), on the model of *Schiller's poem *The Bell.* It was written by Abraham *Gottlober, a popular and prolific Hebrew and Yiddish author who published many such satiric works both in poetry and in prose, mainly against Ḥasidism, in the spirit of the Haskalah.

Sefer ha-Kundas (1824) is a witty parody in the style and form of the Shulḥan Arukh. The book is divided into paragraphs, and the paragraphs into sections, which determine, in a style typical of the Shulḥan Arukh, how the true prankster must behave in order to justify his title. It is a satire on the strict way of life, which robbed young children of the joy of living by prematurely imposing ritualistic duties upon them. In many cases they rebelled against the severe restrictions by complete licentiousness. The author also wanted to prove how common this type of prankster was among the youth of good families in Vilna. There are differences of opinion as to the identity of the author of *Sefer ha-Kundas.* It is often ascribed to Aaron of Berdichev, whose exact identity is unknown, but according to Zinberg and others, it was Abraham Isaac, the son of Rabbi Ḥayyim Landa, a learned young man who was familiar with the teaching of the *maskilim.* Pressed by the hostile environment, Landa was compelled to divorce his wife. In order to avenge himself on his former father-in-law and on the leaders of the Vilna community, he wrote *Sefer ha-Kundas*, relating "the prankster's deed, ruses and actions and his doings from the beginning of the year to its end." *Kundas* (perhaps related to the Polish word *kondys* – a farmer's dog, lacking manners) is a common appellation in the Yiddish of eastern European Jews for a mischievous, prankish boy, or a social outcast who uses vulgar and obscene language, affronting the dignitaries and appearing wherever there is a crowd. The dignitaries of Vilna considered *Sefer ha-Kundas* to be a dangerous pamphlet and banned it soon after its publication, burning all available copies so that it should not be circulated. Only individual copies survived, one of which was published 88 years later by the student of Jewish folklore David *Maggid in 1913, with an introduction by the publisher about the parody and its author.

In recent generations, remote from the controversies of the Haskalah, evaluation of the works written in the heat of the polemics of that time have changed, and literary critics now regard *Sefer ha-Kundas* as a "gay sunbeam peeping through the dark clouds of seriousness" of the Haskalah period (see S. Niger, *Bleter far Geshikhte fun der Yidisher Literatur,* 1954). According to this view, this was the first book in the Hebrew literature of the 19th century, which was amusing for its own sake and without any polemical or didactic aim. This seems also to have been the view of Ḥ.N. *Bialik, who, in writing a children's poem describing a merry, mischievous boy, admitted to having been influenced by the 19th-century *Sefer ha-Kundas.*

Isaac Dov *Levinsohn was one of the early Russian *maskilim.* He was the author of several parodies, including *Divrei Ẓaddikim*, similar to Joseph Perl's *Megalleh Temirin*, concerning *ẓaddikim* and Ḥasidim, and *Oto ve-et Beno*, a tractate in talmudic style, protesting against unfair trade practices, etc. Judah Leib *Gordon, the greatest Hebrew poet of the late Haskalah, who successfully tried his hand at all literary forms, also attempted parody, especially in his *Shirim le-Et Meẓo.* It includes *maqāmāt*, epigrams, and a long and witty parodic poem in Aramaic called *Be-Niggun Akdamot.* Gordon derides the conduct of the provincial Jewish tradesmen in the 1800s who came on business to St. Petersburg, where no one knew them, "with the aim of making great profits and stuffing their bellies with delicious food and other delights." With all his reservation toward Yiddish, Gordon tried his hand at writing poems in that language collected in a volume with the Hebrew title of *Siḥat Ḥullin.* The majority of the poems are humorous imitations of naive folktales, which may be considered parodies. One of them, *Eliyahu ha-Navi min ha-Nahar Ridevka* ("The Prophet Elijah of the river Ridevka"), is the story of a pretty shopkeeper, the wife of a yeshivah student, who suddenly becomes rich thanks to "the prophet Elijah" who enters through the window while her good-for-nothing husband studies Torah at the *bet ha-midrash* until late at night. The "Elijah" is a gentile lover who is a public official and who bestows many presents upon the pretty shopkeeper in return for her favors. This is a parody on those Jewish folktales which attribute any obscure success in the life of the individual to miraculous events and to the "appearance of Elijah." The Haskalah orientation of this parody and of similar poems is obvious.

The jesters (*badḥanim), whose job it was to entertain the bride and bridegroom on their wedding day, composed many entertaining parodies in Yiddish, interspersed with Hebrew words and phrases. Most have been forgotten, while some have been preserved in Jewish folklore, though the sources which inspired the jesters are not always identifiable.

Modern Times

PARODY AS A SOCIALIST WEAPON. With the development of political movements in the late 19th and early 20th centuries, the war against religious Orthodoxy and the "obscurantists" slackened and new battles broke out in Jewish society on nationalistic and socialistic issues. The *maskilim* began to employ satirical parody as a weapon against unfair trade, widespread ignorance, and the miserable social position of religious personnel, particularly of teachers and yeshivah students. Themes from the life of Jewish society which did not receive adequate treatment in journalism or in serious literature were reflected gaily in an exaggerated and biased light in satire. These satires were modeled on the common liturgy which was well known to all Jews in those days, and were thus intelligible even to people not used to reading belles letters for their own sake. Not only "professional" authors but also adroit dabblers in writing engaged in such parody. Many of the writers are anonymous and it is almost impossible to identify them, despite the effort of literary scholars to decipher and identify some of their pen names. But even as anonymous amateurs these writers make a substantial contribution to the knowledge of Jewish social life in various periods; these descriptions cannot be ignored in the study of all classes of Jewish life, at differing times and in diverse countries. The language of this "unofficial" literature also contributed in its own way to the development and crystallization of modern Hebrew.

Massekhet Aniyyut ("A Tractate on Poverty," 1878), by Isaac Meir Dick, considered the "father of the Yiddish folktale," is one of the most successful parodies in Hebrew literature. It severely criticizes the poor social and economic conditions of Lithuanian Jews at that time. It also contains autobiographical elements: in those years the school where Dick taught was closed down, and a state school was opened in its stead to which Dick could not adjust, and he thus remained jobless. Sachs published the parody, unknown to its author, and it made a great impression, reflecting as it did the reality of Jewish society at the time.

The parody *Kiẓẓur Shulḥan Arukh li-Melammedim u-le-Morim* by Joseph *Brill of Minsk, whose pen name was Iyov, printed in *Oẓar ha-Sifrut*, 3 (1889), also belongs to the class of "socialistic" parodies. An outstanding parodist, he described in a lively, biting, and comical fashion the miserable position in Jewish society of "the educators of the generation" – the *melammedim* of the old system and the teachers of the new.

Even with the change in the contents and purpose of parodies, traditional books of worship, such as the festival prayers and in particular the Passover *Haggadah*, continued to serve as a model for topical parodies. The authors directed their satire against local affairs, such as profiteering, exploitation of the poor, cultural emptiness, excessive materialism, and similar negative phenomena. When the aim of the parody was to protest against the decrees and restrictions of unjust authorities, the disguise of stories and prayers was used in order to circumvent censorship. The *Mah Nishtanah* questions of the *Haggadah* and the recurring answer "We were the slaves of..." would be given new topical contents each year. The same was done to the chorus of the song *Ḥad Gadya*. In addition to parodies on traditional liturgical literature, parodies on popular contemporary works, Jewish and gentile, eventually came to be written.

The following parodies are of a salient socialistic orientation: *Seder Haggadah li-Melammedim* (1882), with a commentary by Levi Reuben Zimlin, a teacher in Odessa, imitates the Passover *Haggadah* "imbued with moral lessons for *melammedim* and for landlords who inspire them with awe for a loaf of bread that does not satiate." The book contains recommendations by Gottlober, Lilienblum, and others. *Seder Haggadah le-Ḥoveshei Beit ha-Midrash* ("Haggadah of Bet Midrash Students," 1899), by Elijah Ḥayyim Zayantshik, describes the miserable state of students ("he will divide the food he eats into two shares, so that one remains for the morrow, because a miracle does not occur every day, and the second share is the *afikoman*, because after that there is nothing to eat or drink but water"), and bitterly criticizes the treasurers, supervisors, and landlords who neglect the students. *Massekhet Soḥarim* ("Traders' Tractate," 1900) by Abraham Shelomo Melamed (1862–1951), a Hebrew teacher in Feodosia, in the Crimean Peninsula, is a parody in the style of the Mishnah and Gemara and a bitter satire on the various tradesmen ("wheat tradesmen, wood tradesmen, contractors and shopkeepers") who engaged in unfair trade, profiteering, international bankruptcy, and arson in order to collect the insurance money. *Massekhet Shetarot* ("Bills' Tractate," 1894) by "*La-Saifa ve-la-Safra*" (pen name of Abraham Abba Rokovsky, born in Poland, who translated many books from various languages into Hebrew, including Alroy by Disraeli), is also a parody in talmudic style "depicting the world of trade, its customs, stratagems and wicked impulses" (from the publisher's introduction to the book).

HEBREW PARODY IN THE U.S. At the time of the large-scale immigration to the U.S. from Russia and other eastern European countries during the late 19th century, the newcomers were able to give vent to their feelings through parody. They had immigrated to the new country to seek their fortune and discovered only chaos in Jewish life. Far from the old *bet ha-midrash* tradition, many of the Jews in the U.S. had largely abandoned Jewish tradition, and satire was a convenient genre for adroit writers to express their anger and bitterness at this development. Abraham Kotlier, born near Kovno, immigrated to the United States in 1880 and lived in Cleveland as a bookseller for over 50 years, before moving in his old age to Ereẓ Israel. His first parody, *Massekhet Derekh Ereẓ ha-Ḥadashah* ("Tractate on the Way of Life of the New Country"), was a devastating attack on Jewish immigrants living in the U.S., their faults and vices, and on the Jewish administrators and "Reform" leaders who corrupted Jewish life. It was first published serially in the Yiddish weekly *Folks Fraynd*, and later on its own in St. Petersburg (1893). It also appeared in Warsaw in 1898 together with *Maḥzor Katan – Hagaddah le-Fesaḥ*, a volume of *piyyutim* and a *Haggadah* "according to the American custom." A third edition was published in Tel Aviv in 1927.

Gershon *Rosenzweig, born in Russian Poland, was a teacher who went to the U.S. in 1888. He contributed to the Hebrew and Yiddish press, specializing mainly in parodies and aphorisms. He also edited and published some of the Hebrew periodicals: *Ha-Ivri* (1892–1902), *Kadimah* (1899), and *Ha-Devorah* (1912). In a series of "tractates" first published in *Ha-Ivri* and then in the collection *Talmud Yanka'i*, Rosenzweig satirizes U.S. Jewish life. According to Rosenzweig, Columbus refused to have the country he discovered called after him, and it was therefore called "America," deriving from the Aramaic *Amma-Reika* ("an empty people"). There is hardly an aspect of Jewish life in America that Rosenzweig does not touch upon. He pours out his protest against the low standards of education, the neglect of the younger generation, and the Reform rabbis. He attacks the fact that most synagogues are mortgaged, that ignorance among Jews was becoming even more widespread; he criticizes the prevalence of card games, and touches also on the inferior state of Jewish writers, and the mediocre Yiddish press which fed its readers on "cheap sensations and trash." In *Massekhet Okẓin* ("Tractate Sarcasm") Rosenzweig treats the subject of plagiarisms, which were then very common. In yet another tractate, *Massekhet Maḥaloket mi-Talmud Ẓivoni* ("Tractate Discord, from the Colored Talmud"), Rosenzweig discusses the quarrels between Portuguese Jews and German Jews in Philadelphia.

During the period of "prohibition" in the United States Gershon Kiss published *Massekhet Prohibishon* (1929), in which he depicted humorously, in talmudic style, the many and diverse maneuvers carried out in order to circumvent the laws of prohibition, as well as all the mishaps occurring due to the consumption of noxious drinks. Here is an excerpt from one of the chapters:

> Mishnah. How does one hide the drinks? One hides them in the walls and under the floor, in pits, ditches and caves, in toilets, bathrooms, and any place out of reach of the city guardians. Gemara. The rabbis have taught: The pious men of olden days used to hide the drinks in the walls and under the floor and in pits, bushes, and caves, but pious men of recent times have decided once and for all that there is no hope of storing them, so they immediately store them in their stomachs.

Ephraim *Deinard, born in Russian Latvia, was a scholar, traveler, and bookseller who lived in the U.S. for many years. He published several satires in parodic form, including one called *Sefer ha-Kundas* ("The Book of the Prankster," 1900), and *Sefer ha-Ployderzakh* ("The Chatterbox"), a caricature of contemporary Jewish newspapers in America. The title page describes it as "a general gazette for everyone, and the attentive reader will merit life in this world, and I am positive he will not have to read any other gazette."

HEBREW PARODY IN COMMUNIST RUSSIA. During the early years in post-1917 Russia, when Judaism, the Zionist movement, and Hebrew culture generally were the subjects of persecution, many bitter satirical parodies were written attacking the oppressive regime and its supporters. In particular, the "Yevsektsia," the department of the Communist Party responsible for the liquidation of Jewish communities and institutions and the suppression of the various Jewish parties, and especially the Zionist ones, came under protest. As these parodies could not appear in print they passed from hand to hand as "underground literature." They were modeled on well-known prayers and folksongs in Hebrew, Yiddish, and Russian. One of the most successful parodies on the Bolshevik regime was *Massekhet Admonim min-Talmud Bolshevi* ("Tractate of the Reds from the Bolshevik Talmud"), signed by Avshalom Bar-Deroma, the pen name of A.S. Melamed (see above). It was brought out of Russia by the author in the early 1920s, and was published in Tel Aviv in 1923.

PARODY IN MODERN EREẒ ISRAEL. Jewish settlement in Ereẓ Israel, from the second half of the 19th century onward, gave rise to many varied social conflicts which were reflected in mostly verbal satire, such as new words sung to old and familiar tunes. During the period of Turkish rule hardly any satires had been written due to the despotism of the regime. Those which were circulated treated only of internal affairs of the Jewish *yishuv*. One of the major conflicts within the *yishuv* before World War I was the struggle for the place of Hebrew as the language of the people. When the Hilfsverein founded the Technion in Haifa, it declared its intention of having German as the language of instruction. The protagonists of Hebrew carried their struggle to the press and published, among other items, a parody in talmudic style, *Massekhet Bava Tekhnikah* (1910), by Kadish Yehudah Leib *Silman. Silman was a teacher and journalist, born in Russia, who wrote and edited textbooks, and published various humorous works. Another "internal" parody, an anonymous satire against the plague of anniversary celebrations prevalent in the *yishuv* among the communal workers and writers of the time, was called *Ha-Yabbelet* ("The Ulcer," 1914).

Under the semi-democratic rule of the British Mandate in Ereẓ Israel between 1918 and 1948, there was a greater degree of freedom of criticism, and political satire against the regime was allowed to develop. During the 29 years of the Mandate many humorous and satirical papers appeared, most of them of one issue only, usually for holidays and festivals, especially Purim. A political parody which had a great impact was *Haggadah shel ha-Bayit ha-Le'ummi* ("*Haggadah* of the National Home") by "Afarkeset," a regular columnist in the daily *Haaretz*. It appeared for Passover 1930, when a British commission was visiting the country to investigate the bloody riots of the Arabs a year earlier and the slaughter of the Jews of Hebron and other towns. It begins with *Mah Nishtannah*:

> How does the present rule [the British] differ from the former [Turkish] rule? Under the former regime we settled to the west of the Jordan as well as to its east, while this regime has completely closed the land of Gad and of Reuben to us. Under the former regime we bought lands and received *kushans* [sales certificates], while this regime hinders the buying of new lands and invalidates old *kushans*. Under the former regime there were no riots, while under this one they have occurred four times. Under the former regime we were residents enjoying the protection of consuls, while under this regime we are all citizens and we lack protection and defense.

The following chant appears in the same parody, based on the *Dayyeinu* of the Passover *Haggadah*:

> What a long line of kindnesses has John Bull bestowed on us: Had he given us the Balfour Declaration and not appended a second part that contradicts the first – it would have been enough. Had he appended a second part that contradicts the first and not given us an alien police force – it would have been enough. Had he given us an alien police force and not ignored Arab incitement – it would have been enough. Had he ignored Arab incitement and not distributed high positions to the inciters – it would have been enough. Had he distributed high positions to the inciters and not negotiated with them regarding the future of the country – it would have been enough. Had he negotiated with the inciters and not sent us a commission to investigate sabotage – it would have been enough. Had he sent us a commission to investigate sabotage and it had not interviewed various land specialists – it would have been enough. Had it interviewed various land specialists and not drawn conclusions and not closed the country to Jewish immigration – it would have been more than enough.

Under the British Mandate theatrical troupes were also established, a large part of whose program consisted in satires against the regime, only some of which have appeared in print. The unique life during the Mandate and the contrasts between the three elements in the population – Jews, Arabs, and British – is reflected to some extent in *Palestine Parodies* (Eng., 1930). Tel Aviv, the largest town in Ereẓ Israel, became the subject of a special parodic *Haggadah* on its 25th anniversary. Its author did not spare the eminent status of "the first Hebrew town," and severely criticized the leaders of the town for their many words and few actions. The citizens, too, came under fire for their lack of social etiquette, and the confusion of foreign languages rivaling Hebrew. Nor was the British regime spared.

The life of the State of Israel, its new parliament, austerity at home, and international adventures all gave rise to an improvised satirical literature, much of it concentrated in the Friday and holiday supplements of the daily press. It featured too in the entertainment programs of the radio. The Talmud, which was studied in the secondary schools as well as in the many yeshivot, continued to be a popular model on which to build parodies. In *Massekhet Yamim Tovim* ("Tractate of Holidays," 1959), M.Y. Bar-On, a journalist and translator, wittily criticized the faults of the state and of the different strata of its society, alluding to various public scandals.

PARODIES OF WRITERS ON WRITERS. Hebrew parody through the ages was mostly of the sort which used easily recognizable literary forms as a vehicle for social, religious, or political themes. Such were, of course, the works of Kalonymus b. Kalonymus, Ben Ze'ev, Sommerhausen, and the extensive Purim literature, all intended mainly for entertainment. However, there were also examples of the type of parody designed to deride the very work or literary form which it emulates. Among these were the writings of Joseph Perl against the early books of Ḥasidism, mocking not only the ḥasidic movement but also its literature, with its entangled style, faulty syntax, and confused presentation. This was the start of parodies of "writers on writers." Some of the work of Joseph Brill (see above) also belongs to this category.

Brill's "*Midrash Soferim*" ("Midrash of Writers," in: *Ha-Shaḥar*, 10; 1880–81) is a witty satire directed against various literary types. Of contemporary newspaper editors he writes: "There are three who eat and do not labor – a son-in-law supported by his father-in-law, a soldier on guard and a boorish editor." He lashes out at "the scholars and historians who peck like hens, and who prefer one grain of barley on the mound of an ancient hill, already rotten and mouldy, to all the precious stones and jewels glittering in the valley of the present."

Well-known Hebrew authors and poets of the 20th century, among them Frischmann, Bialik, Tchernichowsky, Shneour, Berkowitz, Shlonsky, and Hameiri, occasionally wrote parodies on other writers and on literary works, some of them simply for amusement and entertainment, others for genuine criticism. They appeared mostly under pen names, scattered in newspapers, appearing for festivals, especially Purim, in Russia, Poland, the U.S., and Israel. The Hebrew stage, which became firmly established towards the middle of the 20th century, and especially the smaller entertainment theaters, produced many topical satires which, however, seldom appeared in print. Some well-known Yiddish authors also wrote occasional parodies, mostly anonymously or under a pen name. Joseph *Tunkel was a prominent Yiddish humorist and parodist. A regular columnist of Yiddish papers in Poland, he published special collections of parodies, including *Mitn Kop Arop* (1931), *Di Royte Hagode* (1917), *Di Bolshevistishe Hagode* (1918), and some on writers and on literature: *Der Krumer Shpigl* (1911), and *Kataves* (1923). Small theatrical troupes in Yiddish, in countries where Yiddish was spoken and Yiddish newspapers appeared, also owed much of their popularity to topical parodies.

BIBLIOGRAPHY: I. Davidson, *Parody in Jewish Literature* (1907), incl. list of 500 parodies; J. Chotzner, *Humour and Irony of the Bible* (1883); idem, *Hebrew Satire* (1911); N.S. Leibowitz, *Ha-Shome'a Yiẓḥak; Mivḥar ha-Ḥiddud ve-ha-Hittul* (1907); M. Steinschneider, *Gesammelte Schriften*, 1 (1925), 196–214; idem, in: MGWJ, 46 (1902); 47 (1903); 48 (1904); Zinberg, Sifrut, passim; Waxman, Literature, 2 (1960), 603ff., and passim; W. Jerrold and R.M. Leonard (eds.), *Century of Parody and Imitation* (1963); J. Kabakoff, *Ḥalutzei ha-Sifrut ha-Ivrit ba-Amerikah* (1967), 211–66. **ADD. BIBLIOGRAPHY:** A. Sh. Melamed, *Masekhet Soḥarim* (1899 or 1900); C. Colahan, in: *Sefarad*, 39:1 (1979), 87–107; 39:2, 265–308; T. Fishman, in: *Prooftexts*, 8, 1 (1988), 89–111.

[Aharon Zeev Ben-Yishai]

PAROKHET AND KAPPORET (Torah Ark curtain and valance). The Torah Ark curtain is a screen hanging over the Torah Ark which serves as a partition between the Ark and the prayer hall. The Hebrew term *parokhet* is based on its identification with the curtain, *parokhet*, which separated the holy section of the Tabernacle and the Temple from the Holy of Holies (Ex. 26:31–35; 40:21). This identification is based on the concept of the synagogue as a "lesser sanctuary" (Ezek. 11:16). According to the available literary and visual sources, the curtain became a fixture in Ashkenazi and Italian synagogues during the Middle Ages. We have no information about the existence of Torah Ark curtains in communities outside Europe until the 20th century. According to the literary and visual material from Spain, it seems that the outer curtain was not customary in Spanish communities. On the other hand, they did apparently use an inner curtain, as evidenced by the presence of an inner curtain in all Sephardi Diaspora communities. In Italy all arks have inner curtains, whereas an outer curtain is present only in some communities – perhaps out of reluctance to hide the ornate doors. Since the curtain serves as a cover for the Ark, its position within the hierarchy of ceremonial objects is that of a "secondary" ceremonial object. Only when the need arises to use it as a covering for the *bimah*, that is, as the cloth on which the Torah itself is rested, does it become a primary ceremonial object, requiring *genizah*.

Like other ceremonial objects in the synagogue, the Torah Ark curtain is usually donated by individual members of the congregation, frequently to commemorate life-cycle events. This has engendered the custom of embroidering the name of the donor and the occasion of the donation directly on the curtain or on an attached piece of cloth. In the 20th century, dedicatory plaques of beaten silver appeared in Iraq.

The traditional design of the Torah Ark curtain varies from community to community. In most, the curtain was made of a choice fabric according to the local cultural conception. In most communities a luxurious fabric, which had previously been in the family's possession, was used, and a common practice was specifically to use a costly piece of woman's clothing. The typical curtain in Iraq was made from the *izar*, the upper veil worn by a woman when she leaves her house. Torah Ark curtains in the communities of Iran and Afghanistan were principally made of *suzani* embroidered sheets, and in Iran a tradition also developed of using paisley-printed cotton material with Hebrew inscriptions.

Yemeni Torah Ark curtains were designed, as were covers for the *tevah* and for Torah scroll cases, in the form of a large sheet in the center surrounded by a broad patchwork frame with a chessboard pattern. In the Sephardi communities of the Ottoman Empire it became customary to make Torah Ark curtains from silk velvet with gold embroidery, or from women's dresses, also of silk-embroidered velvet. In such cases the different parts of the dress were disassembled and re-sewn in order to create a rectangle.

It appears that neither in the eastern communities nor in the Sephardi Diaspora did this custom arouse opposition on the part of the rabbis. European rabbis, however, differed regarding the fashioning of Torah Ark curtains from used material, especially from clothing in general and from women's clothing in particular. The circumstances under which pieces of clothing were used generally involved vows taken by women in times of stress, or used elegant clothing purchased for reuse of the cloth. Rabbinical objections to the practice abound in the responsa literature, where we find repeated questions on this subject. Those objecting to the reuse of fabrics relied on the law that the Temple utensils must be made of new material, which was not previously used (Men. 22a). The more permissive rabbis, who were willing to take popular feeling into consideration, cited midrashic commentaries on the episode of the copper mirrors donated by the women of Israel for the Tabernacle (*Midrash Tanhḥuma, Pekudei* 9). According to this interpretation, it is permitted to use a piece of clothing, provided its form is changed.

Alongside curtains of costly materials, European communities began to use embroidered Torah Ark curtains. In Italy, a center of the art of embroidery, many communities traditionally embroidered curtains using the Florentine stitch technique, which is particularly conducive to the execution of detailed and precise patterns. Community women used it to embroider a variety of Jewish motifs, including biblical themes, such as the Giving of the Torah, and scenes from calendar and life-cycle events.

An entirely different embroidery tradition developed in the communities of central and western Europe, where there were professional embroiderers who specialized in gold embroidery on a silk velvet background. The most outstanding motif of the 18th-century Torah ark curtain in these communities is that of a pair of columns, topped by a pair of lions flanking a Torah crown. Between the two columns is an ornate sewn or embroidered rectangular sheet. This motif dates back to the earlier architectonic motif of an actual gate, above which is the verse that identifies it as the gateway to heaven: "This is the gateway to the Lord – the righteous shall enter through it" (Ps. 118:20). Underlying the depiction of this motif on Torah Ark curtains is the identification of the Torah Ark with the "gateway to heaven." Originally found in Italy, the motif spread eastward to Turkey, northward to Bohemia and Moravia, and westward to Germany.

The Torah Ark valance (Heb. *kapporet*) is a short curtain hung on the Torah Ark, above the curtain (*parokhet*). This ceremonial object, which first appeared in eastern Europe at the end of the 17th century, evolved in connection with the identification of the Torah Ark in the synagogue with the *Ark of the Covenant, and of the upper part with the *kapporet* on the Ark of the Covenant in the Tabernacle (Ex. 25:21). Accordingly, it was customary in eastern Europe to inscribe the verse "He made a cover of pure gold" (Ex. 37:6) on the upper part of the Ark. The identification then came to be applied to the short curtain hung over the upper part of the Ark to conceal the rod on which the main curtain (the *parokhet*) was mounted. Indeed, we find the verse "Place the cover (*kapporet*) upon the Ark of the Covenant" (Ex. 26:34) embroidered on early Torah Ark valances. As part of the synagogue furnishings, the valance was probably introduced under the influence of 17th-century interior decoration in Europe, where such valances were integral parts of curtains in general. Further influence of the cultural environment is evident in the scalloped lower edge of the valance.

The identification of the valance hung on the Torah Ark with the gold cover on the Ark of the Covenant is also evident in the motifs used in its decoration. Thus, most early valances employ the motif of a pair of cherubim flanking a Torah Crown, as per the biblical description of two golden cherubs with outspread wings mounted on the ends of the cover (Ex. 37:7–9). The depiction of the cherubim as a pair of eagles, lions, or griffons is based on the traditional interpretation of the creatures figuring in Ezekiel's Vision of the Chariot (Ezek. 1:5; 10:14–15). Another characteristic motif of the valance is the Tabernacle utensils embroidered on the scalloped edges. The Ark of the Covenant is embroidered on the central scallop below the Torah crown; the showbread table and the seven-branched candelabra are generally embroidered on matching scallops on either side of the central one, as are the golden altar and sacrificial altar on another pair of matching scallops. Later an additional motif, the motif of "*three* crowns" (Pirkei Avot 4:13) appeared in the upper part of the Torah Ark valance.

The Torah Ark valance spread from eastern Europe to central and western Europe (but not to the Italian communities), and by the beginning of the 18th century it had already become common. In most instances, valances were donated separately from the Torah Ark curtain. During the 18th century, a workshop in Prague specialized in the embroidery of Torah Ark valances. A unique feature of the Prague valances is the addition of a pair of freestanding wings attached to the upper part of the Torah Ark on either side of the valance. These wings were fashioned from rigid materials and covered with an embroidered cloth. German valances are more varied than those from Prague, displaying a richer vocabulary of iconographic motifs.

In eastern Europe, where Torah Arks typically show greater iconographic variety, the motifs on the valance disappeared in the course of the 18th century, most of the valances known from this area being made of patterned fabrics without embroidered motifs or inscriptions. In contrast, in central and western Europe, velvet valances with motifs and dedicatory inscriptions in rich gold embroidery continued to be fashioned up to the 20th century. The existence of valances in distant communities at the beginning of the 20th century, and even in our time, is evidence of the influence of the European valances.

BIBLIOGRAPHY: D. Cassuto, "A Venetian *Parokhet* and its Design Origins," in: *Jewish Art*, 14 (1988), 35–43; J. Gutmann, "An Eighteenth-Century Prague Jewish Workshop of Kapporot," *Visible Religion*, 6 (1988), 180–90; F. Landsberger, "Old-Time Torah Curtains," in: J. Gutmann (ed.), *Beauty in Holiness, Studies in Jewish Customs and Ceremonial Art* (1970), 125–63; V.B. Mann, "Jewish-Muslim Acculturation in the Ottoman Empire: The Evidence of Ceremonial Art," in: A. Levy (ed.), *The Jews of the Ottoman Empire* (1994); B.Yaniv, "The Origin of 'The Two-Column Motif' in European Parokhot," in: *Jewish Art*, 15 (1989), 26–43; idem, "The Cherubim on Torah Ark Valances," in: *Assaph*, 4 (1999), 155–70.

[Bracha Yaniv (2nd ed.)]

°PARROT, ANDRÉ (1901–1980), French archaeologist. He directed the French excavations at Tello and Larsa in Iraq from 1931 to 1933 and at *Mari in Syria (1933–64). He was curator in chief of the French national museums from 1946 and professor at the Ecole du Louvre and the Protestant Theology Faculty of Paris (both institutions from 1936). His contributions in the field of Near Eastern archaeology are highlighted by his excavations of the palace of Mari. His recovery of more than 20,000 tablets of the Mari royal archives, composed mainly during the reign of Zimrilim (18th century B.C.E.), immeasurably increased the historical understanding of Western Asia, especially as regards the Patriarchal Age.

His contributions on Mari include *Une Bille Perdue* (1945); an assortment of studies appearing in *Syria*, a French quarterly on Oriental art and archaeology, and the series *Archives Royales de Mari* (vols. 1–9, 1950–60), and *Mission archéologique de Mari* (3 vols., 1956–67), all scholarly publications which he helped edit. He wrote voluminously on ancient Near Eastern history, literature, architecture, philology, and similar subjects. Many of his semipopular works, marked by clarity, humor, and enthusiasm, are concerned with the problems of the biblical past and its Oriental background.

[Zev Garber]

PARTISANS. Jewish partisans composed part of the resistance movement and the guerrilla war in Europe against Nazi Germany during World War II. The first nuclei of partisans were composed of individuals or groups that were forced to flee from the Nazis and their collaborators; soldiers who were thrown into areas that were occupied by the enemy; and prisoners of war who escaped from camps. Their natural bases were the forests and swamps of eastern *Poland, Lithuania, Belorussia, and the Ukraine, the mountainous areas of the Alps, *Yugoslavia, *Slovakia, and *Greece. While the parti-

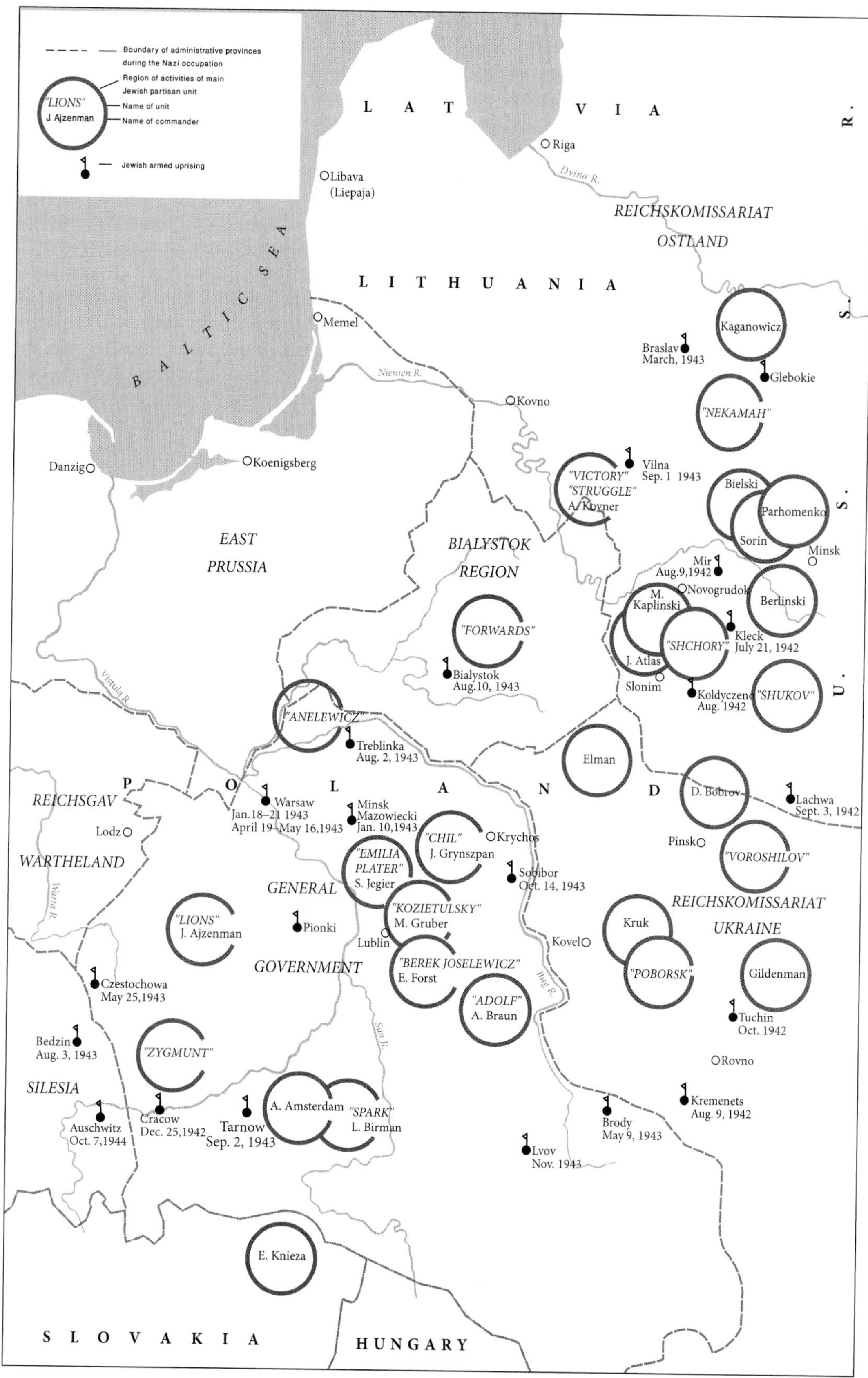

Major Jewish partisan units and armed uprisings, 1941–44.

san movement as a whole became a substantial force in the military and political battles of World War II, the motivations, organizational forms, and development of the Jewish partisan movement was basically different. Unlike the non-Jews in occupied areas, the Jews were condemned by the Nazis to total extermination. As a result of this situation, two unique aspects of the movement stand out: Jews joined the partisan struggle as a path of revenge on the murderous enemy; they also wished to combine partisan fighting with attempts to save themselves and other Jews.

Jews participated in the partisan movement throughout occupied Europe – from Briansk east of the U.S.S.R. to *France, *Italy, *Yugoslavia, and *Greece. It is impossible to arrive at exact numbers of Jews in partisan units, but it is possible to conjecture that tens of thousands of Jews fought in the partisan struggle as a whole. Some fought as Jews in Jewish units; others fought as Jews in mixed units. An indeterminate number of Jews fought while passing as non-Jews. The number of Jews who actually fought, however, was only a tiny proportion of the European Jews who wished to participate in and had access to the partisans, but were prevented from doing so for a number of reasons. One should distinguish between subjective obstacles to their participation, which resulted from the nature of the condition of Jewish life in eastern Europe, and difficulties that resulted from their objective situation and attitude of the non-Jewish environment.

The Jews were a classically urban element. Existence in dense forest, in the wilds of nature, was alien to them. In addition, the traditionally strong family ties that held them together also held them back from leaving their homes. The youth, who were the prime candidates for escape into the forests, were sometimes the only source of support of the family under conditions of a bitter struggle for physical survival and uncertainty about the future. Moreover, the consolidation of Jews or other groups in the forests was conditional upon basic factors. A central condition for the establishment of any partisan force was contacts with the inhabitants of the surrounding area. The partisans were in need of safe places of refuge in the event of emergency, loyal sources of intelligence, and the supply of food, horses, etc. All these things could be obtained from villagers who lived near the partisan camps. The villagers would provide the necessary services either out of fear or because they believed that cooperation would be to their benefit in the future. However, the Polish, Lithuanian, Belorussian, and Ukrainian countryside was hostile toward Jews. The villagers, with the exception of those few who remained loyal to Jews under the most difficult conditions, not only refused to aid the Jews in establishing themselves in the forests, but often turned Jews over to the Germans or murdered Jews who managed to reach the forests and looted their property.

The chances of being accepted into a partisan unit were conditional upon physical strength, military experience, and the possession of arms, except in a handful of Jewish units that served as family camps with the double purpose of hiding and fighting. The sources of arms were those left by retreating armies and passed into the hands of the movements through the underground, or they were private property. Such arms were not given to Jews, who were thus forced to acquire weapons from the enemy by clandestine purchase, robbery, or acquisition in battle. By these means, it was possible to acquire only the most minimal store of weapons.

The partisan movement itself was not free of antisemitism. The extreme right-wing factions of the Polish underground viewed the Jews as "bandits" prowling around the forests. They took arms away from the Jews and even murdered many of them. They did not believe that Jews were actually going to fight. The leftist groups took a less hostile stand toward the Jews. In Lithuania, Belorussia, and the Ukraine, antisemitism was somewhat restrained after permanent contact had been established between the partisan areas and the Soviet high command; but the Soviet command did not approve of the existence of separate Jewish partisan units and obligated the Jews to integrate into the multinational partisan frameworks.

The very act of leaving the ghetto for the forests was bound up with many obstacles and difficulties. The Jewish population in central Poland was far from the areas of dense forest. The attempts by the Jewish Fighting Organization in *Warsaw, *Częstochowa, and Zaglębie to establish contact with Polish underground organizations and to smuggle groups of Jewish fighters into the forests most often ended in failure; the fighters were captured or murdered before they could reach their destination, or early in their stay in the forest. In the large ghettos in *Warsaw, *Vilna, and *Bialystok, a sharp dispute took place among the members of the Jewish Fighting Organization over which path to choose: resistance inside the ghetto or escape to the forests and carrying on the struggle within the ranks of the partisan movement. In Warsaw it was finally decided to concentrate all forces for resistance within the ghetto; the division between the ZOB and the ZZL was over whether there should be an escape plan as part of the battle plan itself, or whether the uprising was indeed a last stand. In Vilna and Bialystok a two-pronged method was arrived at, i.e., after the uprising in the ghetto the surviving fighters turned to the forests.

The most important obstacle that prevented the mass escape of the Jews to the forests was a chronological factor. The expansion and strengthening of the partisan movement began only during 1943. By then most of the Jews in Europe had already been deported to and murdered in Nazi death camps. Although the Jews had in many cases been the first to pave the way in the forests, these pioneer partisans had only limited chances of absorbing large groups of people and maintaining their existence for a longer period.

In western Europe the obstacles were of a different nature, for there the Germans succeeded in deceiving the Jews by well conceived tactics. The resistance movement mostly took the form of an urban underground, which was not to the benefit of the Jews.

However, despite all the obstacles and stumbling blocks, tens of thousands of Jews reached the ranks of the partisan movement. Many Jews fought as individuals (sometimes hiding their Jewish identity) in mixed partisan units, while others belonged to separate Jewish units or groups of Jews united in larger partisan frameworks. Many Jewish partisans rose to commanding ranks and were among the parachutists sent by the Soviet High Command to organize and command partisan camps in large areas. A number received medals for their leadership, and their names and feats of heroism became legendary.

Among the Jewish groups were some that had organized earlier in the Jewish Fighters' Organizations in the ghettos (the *Fareinikte Partizaner Organizatsie* [FPO] in Vilna, the organizations in Bialystok, the remnants of the Jewish Fighting Organization after the Warsaw ghetto uprising). They were equipped and trained during their stay in the ghetto, and their later struggle in the forests was but a logical continuation of the path they had chosen. There were also groups and camps of Jews, mostly from small townlets, who had escaped in whole families or individually during the deportations or from a camp. Together with the youth who were engaged in actual fighting were Jewish family camps in the forests. These camps absorbed women and children, the aged and sick, and a small number of fighters who protected them and provided for their indispensable needs. Most of the time these family camps existed under the aegis of Jewish fighting units or large partisan battalions whose commanders demonstrated a humane attitude and sensitivity toward Jews.

Many Jewish fighters tried to combine their war against the enemy with extending aid to the surviving Jews who were still hiding in the ghettos, and with taking revenge against people who were known to have murdered Jews or betrayed them to the Germans. In many cases, Jewish units that established themselves in the forests became the focal point for uniting prisoners of war and members of other nationalities and constituted the beginning of a powerful partisan center. There were about 15,000–20,000 Jewish partisans in the area under the control of the Soviet command. A large partisan concentration existed in the forests of Rudnik around Vilna. Groups of fighters from the FPO reached this area in September 1943 and formed the fighting Jewish Brigade, which consisted of four battalions, under the command of Abba *Kovner. Earlier, a group of fighters, under the command of Josef Glazman, had left the ghetto and merged with an existing Jewish group to form the fighting group Nekamah ("Revenge") in the forests of Navocz. The commander of the unit, which was later disbanded, was B. Boyarski. Members of the *Kovno ghetto underground also reached the forests of Rudnik. These partisans crystallized into a Jewish bloc in the "Lithuanian Brigade," which consisted mostly of Jews.

During 1943 those in the forests surrounding Bialystok were practically all Jews. A group of young women active in the underground in the city helped to supply them. Women were often more fluent and unaccented in the native languages and, unlike men, they were not circumcised. It was easier for them to pass as non-Jews. Surrounding *Slonim in the forests of Lipiczansk were a number of Jewish units and Jewish family camps. The most famous of these units was that under the command of Jehezkiel *Atlas, who cooperated with the Pobeda ("Victory") unit. Atlas' company gained much experience in battle. In the forests of Lipiczansk, an area of western Belorussia, the group under the command of Hirsch Kaplinski, which numbered more than 100 people – most of them from the town of *Zhetil (*Dyatlovo) – was also active. In central Belorussia, in the forest area of Naliwki, was a large camp of Jewish fighters. In the autumn of 1943 its membership reached more than 1,000, some of whom were fighters and the rest members of the family camp. This camp functioned under the leadership of the Bielski brothers and was composed of simple people from the tiny townlets in the area. Later on, the camp was divided into a fighting company named after *Ordzhonikidze and a family camp named after Kalinin.

In the swamplands of Polesie, Jews were active in general units and separate Jewish ones. The Jewish units were formed by the escapees from the townlets. In a small townlet in the center of Polesie, *Lachva, about 600 Jews revolted and fled in the direction of the forests. Only about 120 of the youth succeeded in reaching the forests, with one rifle and one revolver among them. In Volhynia, Jews were among the first fighters in the forests. The emissary Konishtschook, who arrived from the Minsk area to organize partisan action in Volhynia, united Jewish youth from the neighboring townlet. The most daring military offensives were those of the unit commanded by M. Gildenman, which was a branch of Suborov's forces.

An important chapter in the annals of the partisan movement was contributed by the Jews of *Minsk. The Jews who organized the underground in the Minsk ghetto were among the key organizers of the partisan movement in Soviet territory. There were also a number of Jews in many Soviet brigades. Many Jews were in positions of command and in the ranks of the fighters in the Kovpak camp. Jewish survivors from the *Skalat ghetto joined this camp during its march over the Carpathians and established the 7th Jewish Brigade of the Kovpak camp.

Within the boundaries of the Polish Generalgouvernement, Jewish units were active in cooperation with the leftist People's Army. Most of these units were active in the *Lublin and *Kielce areas. Many individual Jews filtered through to the units of the military underground of the Polish government-in-exile in London, but this organization did not encourage the escape of Jews into the forests, and its extremists even pursued and murdered Jews.

About 2,000 Jews fought in the ranks of Tito's partisan movement, and a number of Jewish groups even existed independently for a period of time. Moshe Pijade was one of Tito's first and closest collaborators. In September 1943 a group containing a few hundred fighters and a substantial number of nurses formed the Jewish "Rab Battalion" within the Italian concentration camp on the Adriatic island by that name.

They joined the partisans as a well-organized unit, but later dispersed and fought in various units. According to official figures, 250 Jews fought with general partisan units in Bulgaria. In Italy as well Jews were scattered among the Italian fighters. Eugenio Caló from Pisa was the founder of a partisan unit in the Val di Piana, and among its members was Emmanuele Artom. Another Italian Jew, Giulio Bolaffi, from Turin, founded and commanded the "4th Alpine Battalion" that was active in the area of the Vale d'Suza in Piedmont.

Jews were among the founders of the partisan movement in Slovakia. The beginnings of this movement were in 1942, but the partisan struggle in Slovakia became a full-scale war in the summer of 1944 with the national Slovak rebellion. Members of many national groups fought in this uprising, including about 2,500 Jews. Two Jewish labor camps – Sered and Novaky – were in the area liberated by the partisans and organized Jewish units, and the inmates of these camps joined the rebellion. At the height of the uprising, four parachutists from Palestine reached Slovakia; two of them remained in Slovakia and the other two passed into Hungary. The two who remained in Slovakia fell into the hands of the Nazis on their way to the last center of the rebels in Banska Bystrica; both were shot in November 1944. After the rebellion was suppressed in October 1944, the partisans retreated to the mountains. There were 2,000 Jews (out of a total of 15,000) in the ranks of the Slovak partisan movement after the uprising.

The participation of Jews in the French Resistance was substantial; constituting only about 1% of the total population of France, at one stage Jews composed about 15–20% of the Resistance. It is necessary to distinguish between Jews who joined general organizations and units of the Resistance and those who formed independent Jewish units.

In contrast to the situation in several eastern European countries, Judaism was not an obstacle to acceptance of candidates into the ranks of the French Resistance. Nonetheless, most Jewish fighters preferred to suppress the fact of their origin, either for security reasons or because they felt their identity as Frenchmen more important than their identity as Jews.

The role of Jews both in the ranks of the Resistance and in positions of leadership and command was outstanding. Among the six men who founded the organization called Libération were three Jews. At the time of the liberation of France, there were at least three Jews among the 16 members of the National Committee, the highest institution of the underground. Jean-Pierre Lévy was the founder of the Franc Tireurs. The commander of the Franc Tireurs et Partisans Français (FTP) in the Paris region in 1942–43 was "Colonel Gilles" (the underground name of Joseph Epstein of Warsaw). The leader of the FTP in Toulouse, who fell during the uprising toward the end of the fight for the liberation, was "Captain Philippe" (Ze'ev Gustman). The French underground hero, Jacques Bingen, whose name was commemorated on a stamp bearing his image, left France in 1940, joined De Gaulle's forces, and was returned to France in 1943 as the head of the Free French delegation in the northern region.

Among the independent Jewish groups, a distinction should be drawn between Jewish Communists from eastern Europe and Jewish groups that united on the basis of national and religious motives. The groups of Jewish Communists, opposing the party line of alliance with Hitler (until June 22, 1941), formed a number of commando units that operated in Paris in 1942–43. These groups of the FTP, and, in the south, groups of the Jewish Organization for Resistance and Mutual Aid, engaged in daring and efficient actions, such as the execution of Nazi officers and collaborators, mining railroad tracks, and raids on enemy arms' depots.

A distinct nationalist Jewish character was the sign of a movement whose nucleus was composed of members of the Jewish Scouts, Zionist youth movements, and members of the *He-Ḥalutz from Holland who had reached France. The movement of Jewish Scouts at first engaged in welfare activities and "passive resistance." It aided in the evacuation of Jewish children from Paris to provincial towns, forging documents, and smuggling Jews over borders, but eventually it did not content itself with these activities and, together with the Armée Juive, established the Organization Juive de Combat (OJC).

Robert Gamzon established the Jewish Maquis. This unit entered into action with the landing of the Allies on French shores, attacking the retreating German forces and capturing an armed German train. Other groups of the OJC, whose headquarters were in Toulouse, were established in Paris, Lyons, Grenoble, Marseilles, Chombron, Nice, and other cities. The OJC testified to carrying out 1,925 actions, including 750 instances of sabotaging trains, destroying 32 factories that worked for the enemy, and blowing up 25 bridges. It also executed 152 militiamen, traitors, and secret agents (including General Phillipo, a German spy). In 175 actions against the Germans, it killed 1,085 of the enemy's men. In addition, as a result of the organization's activities, the German army lost seven planes (blown up on the ground), 286 trucks, and more than 2,000,000 liters of gasoline. Groups of the OJC also participated in the battles for the liberation of Marseilles and Grenoble.

At the end of the war, the Zionist partisans were among the first to plan and organize the "illegal" immigration to bring the remnants of the Holocaust out of eastern Europe and over the borders to Palestine. On their way to Palestine, the Jewish partisans organized a unique group known as "Partisans, Soldiers, Pioneers" (PḤḤ). An organization of partisans and ghetto fighters exists in Israel, and in 1970 it began to expand into a worldwide Jewish organization.

BIBLIOGRAPHY: Y. Suhl (ed.), *They Fought Back* (1968); J. Robinson, *And the Crooked Shall be Made Straight* (1965), 213–26 and index; *European Resistance Movements 1939–1945*, 1 (1960), 2 (1964), passim; *Sefer Milḥamot ha-Getta'ot* (1954^2 = *The Fighting Ghettos*, partial trans. by M. Barkai, 1962); M. Kahanovich, in: *Yad Vashem Studies*, 1 (1957), 153–67; A.Z. Bar-On, ibid. (1960), 167–89; J. Ariel, ibid., 6 (1967), 221–50; H. Michel, ibid., 7 (1968), 1–16; *Sefer ha-Partizanim ha-Yehudim*, 2 vols. (1958); A. Lidowski, *Ba-Ye'arot* (1946); R. Korchak, *Lehavot ba-Efer* (1956); A.Z. Bar-On and D. Levin, *Toledoteha shel Maḥteret* (1962); K. Nir, *Shevilim be-Ma'gal ha-Esh* (1967); B.

West, *Hem Hayu Rabbim* (1968); Y. Yelinek, in: *Yalkut Moreshet*, 1, no. 1 (1963), 47–67 (Eng. summ.); H. Smolar, *Yidn in Gele Lates* (1952[2]); D. Knout, *Contribution à l'histoire de la résistance juive en France, 1940–1944* (1967). **WEBSITE:** www.jewishpartisans.org.

[Israel Gutman]

PARTNERSHIP.

Formation

The earliest form of commercial partnership in Jewish law was partnership in property, or joint ownership. Craftsmen or tradesmen who wished to form a partnership were required to place money in a common bag and lift it or execute some other recognized form of *kinyan* for movables (Ket. 10:4; Yad, Sheluḥin 4:1). The need for executing a *kinyan* precluded an agreement concerning a future matter (Maim., ibid. 4:2), since there can be no *acquisition of a thing that is not yet in existence. In later times this difficulty was overcome when the *halakhot* concerning the need for acquisition formalities were interpreted as having reference only to the formation of the partnership and not to matters in continuation thereof (Maharik Resp. no. 20).

From the tenth century onward, new developments became acknowledged with regard to the manner of forming a partnership. Thus the German and French scholars recognized formation of a partnership by mere agreement between the contracting parties (*Ha-Ittur*, vol. 1, s.v. *Shittuf*; *Mordekhai* BK 176; Resp.Rosh no. 89:13). A second development was recognition of each partner as the agent of his other partners (*Haggahot Maimuniyyot*, Gezelah 17:3 n. 4), which offered the possibility of partnership formed solely by verbal agreement (see *Agency, Law of). A further development, that of recognizing each partner as the hireling of his other partners (*Hassagot Rabad*, Sheluḥin, 4:2), facilitated partnership agreement with reference also to further activities. The drawback of partnership by way of agency or hire is that each partner has the power to dissolve the partnership at any time. Another method was formation of a partnership by personal undertaking, each partner taking a solemn oath to perform certain acts on behalf of the partnership (Ribash Resp. no. 71).

Partnership formation by agreement alone was most prevalent from the 16th to the 19th centuries, particularly in the communities of the Spanish exiles, in reliance on the principle of accepted trade *customs (e.g., *kinyan sitomta*: see BM 74a and codes). It was on the basis of a trade custom that formation of a partnership through verbal agreement alone was recognized, even by the mere recital of the single word "*beinenu*" (*Rosh Mashbir*, ḤM no. 31; *Kerem Shelomo*, Ribbit, 8) or by implication (*Shemesh Ẓedakah*, ḤM 35). Texts of the standard partnership deeds developed over the years indicate that, in general, formation of the partnership agreement rested on a number of elements, mainly *kinyan sudar* (acquisition by the kerchief), personal undertaking, and hire (see, e.g., *Darkhei No'am*, ḤM, 54). In this way it was possible to form a partnership with a minimum of formalities, valid also in respect of future activities, and not retractable from prior to expiry of the specified period (see *Contract).

It may be noted that the fraternal heirs are deemed to be partners until the inheritance is divided among them (see *Succession).

Distribution of Profits and Losses

In the earliest discussions of partnership in Jewish law, the question of distribution of profits was treated in cases of an unequal capital investment by the individual partners (Ket. 10:4). In the first *halakhot* two conflicting opinions were expressed: in the Mishnah, distribution in proportion to the amount invested; in the Tosefta, equal distribution of the partnership profits. In the Talmud, application of the mishnaic *halakhah* was limited to cases of capital gain or those in which it was impossible to make a physical division (TJ, BK 4:1, and Ket. 10:4; Ket. 93). Talmudic sources reflect no hard and fast rule concerning the distribution of profit deriving from commercial activity. For a long period of time, from the geonic period until the 19th century, these *halakhot* were applied by the scholars in both fashions discussed above. In centers of Jewish life where there was a great deal of activity in commerce and the crafts, the tendency was to decide in favor of an equal distribution of profits in all cases; in centers where there were many loan transactions the tendency was to decide in favor of a distribution pro rata to investment. Thus in the 12th and 13th centuries the principle of an equal distribution was followed in Spain, whereas the German and French scholars took the view that, in general, the gain, whenever divisible, should be shared in proportion to the investment of each partner.

In general, profit earned by a partner in an unlawful manner, for example, through theft, has not been considered as belonging to the partnership (*Ha-Ittur*, vol. 1, s.v. *Shittuf*; *Siftei Kohen*, ḤM, 176 n. 27). A contrary ruling with regard to partnership gains from theft was laid down in Germany and France in the 14th century, as an outcome of the persecution of the Jews (*Haggahot Maimuniyyot*, Sheluḥin 5:9 no. 4; see also *Contract, on the attitude of Jewish law to illegal contracts). From the 17th century onward the application of this *halakhah* came to be confined to cases of necessity on account of danger (*Siftei Kohen*, loc. cit.), or those in which an act, although illegal, falls within the scope of the partnership business (*Arukh ha-Shulḥan*, ḤM 176:60).

A tax waiver in favor of one partner benefits the whole partnership, except when a waiver is granted at the taxing authority's own initiative (ḤM 178:1). A condition that all profits shall belong to the partnership has been interpreted in accordance with the *ejusdem generis* rule, so as to exclude therefrom all unusual or unforeseeable profits (Rosh, Resp. no. 89:15). A partner who salvages part of the partnership assets from a robbery does so for the benefit of the partnership in the absence of his prior stipulation to the contrary (BK 116b and codes). The partners may not deal in goods whose use is prohibited, for example, for reasons of ritual impurity (Maim. Yad, Sheluḥin 5:10).

Until the end of the 12th century, any loss attributable to a partner's personal fault had to be borne by the partner himself, on the principle that an agent is liable for the consequences of a departure from his mandate (Yad, Sheluḥin 5:2; see also *Agency). From the 13th century onward, the general trend has been toward collective partnership responsibility for a loss occasioned by one of its members. At first it was laid down that the partnership bear such a loss as if the member's liability were that of *bailee for reward; later it was ruled that a partner be regarded as a gratuitous bailee for this purpose; and later still that the partnership bear the loss occasioned by a member even if it was the result of his own negligence (Mordecai BB 538). The partner himself must bear any loss occasioned through his own acquiescence or active participation (Mabit, Resp. vol. 2, pt. 2, no. 158).

Each partner is responsible as a surety for the undertakings made by his other partners in respect of a partnership matter (Yad, Malveh 25:9). This liability is secondary, however, as is usual in simple *suretyship in Jewish law, and effective only upon default of the principal debtor (*Sefer ha-Terumot*, 44). According to another opinion, one partner is a surety for the other only when he has expressly subjected his person and assets as a surety for the undertaking, in which event he becomes the principal debtor (Rosh, Resp. no. 89:3).

Powers and Duties of the Partners

The rule is that a partner may not deviate from the regular course of activities of the partnership, and his powers, if not defined by agreement, are governed by trade custom (*Ha-Ittur*, vol. 1, s.v. *Shittuf*; Yad, Sheluḥin 5:1; Rosh. Resp. no. 89:14). When the intention of the partners cannot be ascertained, a number of activities have been recorded as constituting deviation from the partnership. In the course of time the early partnership *halakhot* came to be interpreted in favor of wider powers for the individual partner. Thus, with regard to the rule that a partner might not transact partnership business away from the place of the partnership (Yad, loc. cit.), it was decided that the restriction did not apply to a market place situated in the same area (*Netivot ha-Mishpat, Mishpat ha-Kohanim* 176 n. 35) nor to the case in which one partner provided the other partners with suitable indemnities against possible loss (*Arukh ha-Shulḥan* ḤM 176:46–47).

The question of whether a partnership member has power to execute credit transactions was already disputed in geonic times. One approach tended to recognize the power of a partner to sell on credit in all cases, because it was considered that he was bound to be careful about securing the repayment of money in which he had a personal stake (*Sha'arei Ẓedek*, 4:8, 4). A second approach denied a partner the power to sell on credit unless this accorded with a custom followed by all local traders (Rif., Resp. no. 191) and, by way of compromise, it was laid down that it sufficed if the custom was followed by a majority of local traders (Rosh. Resp. no. 89:14). It was also laid down that a partner is exempted from liability if an overall profit results from all his transactions (*Ḥokhmat Shelomo* ḤM 176:10).

A partner may not introduce outsiders into the partnership activities as partners (Yad, Sheluḥin 5:2), but may employ them on his own behalf and at his own responsibility (Rashdam, ḤM, 190). It was ruled that a member of a partnership might not engage in private transactions (ibid.), but this was later permitted when the same kind of merchandise as the partnership dealt in was involved (*Matteh Yosef* vol. 1 ḤM no. 9) or in association with an outsider (*Sma*, ḤM 176 n. 32). Partnership merchandise may not be sold before the appointed season for its sale (Git. 31b and codes).

In general, a partnership member is not entitled to remuneration for his services (Reshakh, Resp. pt. 1 no. 139), but some of the *posekim* allowed this in the case of unusually onerous services (*She'ilat Yavez* no. 6; *Simḥat Yom Tov* no. 23). Similarly, a partner is not entitled to a refund of the amount expended on his subsistence while on partnership business (ḤM 176:45), except for extraordinary expenses (*Taz*, ad loc.). A partner who is unable to participate in the partnership activities on account of illness, or for some other personal reason, is not entitled to share in the profits earned by the partnership during his absence and must also defray his medical expenses, etc., out of his own pocket, unless local custom decrees otherwise (BB 144b and codes). If partnership property is later found in the possession of one of the partners, his possession will not avail against any of the other partners (Alfasi, BB 1; see *Ḥazakah*). Each partner may compel the other to engage in the partnership activities and also to invest additional amounts therein (*Netivot ha-Mishpat, Mishpat ha-Urim*, ḤM 176:32).

The act of a partner may be validated by subsequent ratification, which may also be implied from the silence of the remaining partners (Maharik, Resp. no. 24). Far-reaching powers are afforded a partnership member through application of the principle that an act may be "for the benefit of the partnership." In the opinion of a number of scholars, a partner may deviate from the customary framework of the partnership activities when he considers this to be necessary in the interests of the partnership, provided that the terms of the partnership agreement expressly permit him to trade in all kinds of merchandise, and that there is no radical departure from the customary partnership practices (Resp. Maharashdam, ḤM 166; *Ne'eman Shemu'el* no. 100). One partner may oblige another who is suspected of an irregularity with regard to a partnership matter to deliver an oath in accordance with a rabbinical enactment (Shevu. 7:8). For this reason it was originally forbidden for a Jew to take a gentile as a partner, as the latter was likely to make an idolatrous reference in swearing his oath, but this is permissible now because of "their belief in the Maker of heaven and earth" (Ran on Rif, Git. 5).

Representation of the Partnership by One of its Members

In talmudic law the principle was established that only when all the partners are in the same town can they be represented by the partner who is plaintiff in an action, this even without their express power of attorney (Ket. 94a and codes). From the 13th century onward, the following guiding rules came to be laid down: one partner represents the others when there is an equal division of profits between them; partners who have not been joined as plaintiffs may not thereafter renew the action in their own names unless they plead new issues; one partner represents the others only when he makes a claim against the defendant and not a waiver in his favor (*Shitah Mekubbeẓet*, Ket. 94). Other scholars expressed opinions in favor of the reverse situation, i.e., that one partner represents the others only if there is no denial of liability on the defendant's part and there is no dispute between them (Maharit, Resp., vol. 2 ḤM no. 16); the plaintiff partner represents the remaining partners once the latter have knowledge of the suit, even if they are not all present in the same town (Resp. Solomon b. Isaac ha-Levi, ḤM no. 41); the partner who is on the scene may sue in all cases, but may not recover the shares of his absent partners (*Piskei ha-Rosh*, Ket. 10:12); the absent partners have the right to sue in their own names if they do so immediately after their return to the town in question, but lose this right after a certain period of delay (*Mikhtam le-David*, ḤM no. 31; *Edut bi-Yhosef* vol. 2 no. 38). The partners may each plead in turn, or empower one of them to represent all (Maharam of Rothenburg, Resp., ed. Prague, nos. 332, 333). A partner has authority to collect debts owing to the partnership in terms of a bond of indebtedness of which he is the holder (Rashba, Resp. vol. 1, no. 1137). One partner generally does not represent the remaining partners as defendant in an action unless empowered by them to do so (*Mordekhai*, Ket. 239). The defendant does, however, represent his absent partners if he is in possession of the subject matter of the claim (Tur, ḤM 176:31). See also *Agency; *Practice and Procedure.

Dissolution of Partnership

The activities of a partnership formed for an unspecified period of duration may be terminated at any time at the instance of any of its members, except if this is sought when it is not the season for the sale of its merchandise, and provided there are no outstanding partnership debts for which all partners are liable. A partnership formed for a specified period may not – according to the majority of the *posekim* – be dissolved before the stipulated date (Yad, Sheluḥin 4:4). The existence of a partnership is also terminated when its capital has been exhausted, its defined tasks completed, and on the death of any of its members. Improper conduct on the part of a member – such as theft – does not, in the opinion of the majority of the *posekim*, serve to terminate the partnership. On dissolution of a partnership, division of its monies – if in the same currency – may be made by the partner in possession thereof, and this need not necessarily be done before the court. Division of the partnership assets must be made before three persons, who need only be knowledgeable in the matter (Yad, Sheluḥin 5:9).

Iska ("In Commendam" Transactions)

Freedom to contract a partnership is limited to some extent in the case where one party provides the capital and the other the work. In order to avoid a situation in which the party furnishing the capital ultimately receives an increment on his investment which is in the nature of interest, there was evolved a form of transaction known as *iska*, i.e., "business," in which half of the furnished capital constitutes a loan to the "businessman," or active partner, and the other half is held by him in the form of a deposit (BM 104b and codes). The parties to an *iska* are free to stipulate as they please, provided that they observe the principle that the "businessman" must enjoy some greater benefit than the "capitalist," by way of remuneration for his services (BM 5:4). It would seem that the profits from the loan part of the capital belong to the businessman, and the profit from the deposit part, after deduction of the former's remuneration, belong to the capitalist. Unless otherwise agreed upon, the businessman is to receive wages as a regular worker if he devotes himself entirely to the affairs of the business, and if not, he may be paid a token amount. Another possibility, if nothing is stipulated, is that the businessman receives two-thirds of the profits, and bears one-third of the losses (Yad, Sheluḥin 6:3) or, according to another opinion, one-half of the losses (*Hassagot Rabad* thereto). The businessman's liability in respect of the loan half of the capital is absolute, whereas his liability in respect of the deposit half is that of a gratuitous bailee (Yad, Sheluḥin 6:2), or, according to another opinion, that of a bailee for reward (*Hassagot Rabad, ibid.*).

According to one school, an *iska* is constituted whenever the partnership arrangement involves an active as well as an inactive partner, and it makes no difference whether the inactive partner alone or both of them contribute the capital (Yad, Sheluḥin, 6:1); according to another school, there is no *iska* unless the distinction between an investing but inactive and an active but noninvesting partner is clearly maintained in the partnership arrangement (*Beit Yosef*, YD 177). The capital-investing partner takes no share in the profits of a prohibited *iska* (*Piskei ha-Rosh*, BM 8:7).

That an *iska* is essentially a legal device designed to avoid the prohibition against *usury may be seen from the fact that a nominal remuneration may be agreed upon for the active partner, and from the rule that the latter may not distinguish between the loan and the deposit parts but must put to work the whole amount of the capital invested (Yad, Sheluḥin 7:4). In most respects the law of *iska* follows the law of partnership, but the following basic differences may be noted: the "businessman," unlike a partner in a regular partnership, may retract from the contract at any time, as in the case of a worker (Tur ḤM 176:28), and he must receive remuneration for his services (*Mishpat Ẓedek*, vol. 2, no. 16, et al.).

Joint Ownership

As already indicated, the *halakhot* of partnership developed mainly from the law of joint ownership. Characteristic of this is the power of each part-owner to compel the others to carry out the usual and required activities with regard to the common property – such as the construction of a gate to the premises – or to refrain from any unusual use of the property, such as keeping an animal on the premises; similarly, each part-owner may bring about a dissolution of the partnership by compelling a partition of the common property, provided that thereupon each share still fits the original description of the property and, in the case of immovable property, that it is possible to erect a partition against exposure to the sight of neighbors. If the common property does not allow for proper subdivision, the interested partner may offer to sell his share to the remaining partners or to purchase their shares from them; if the matter cannot be settled in this manner, the property must be sold, or let to a third party, or an arrangement must be made for its joint use by the partners, simultaneously or successively, all in terms of detailed rules on the subject (BB 1–3, and codes).

A Legal Persona

A cooperative body in modern legal systems is an entity with rights and obligations quite apart from those of its component members (see G. Procaccia, Ha-Ta'agid Mahuto... vi-Yẓirato (1965), p. 39). According to the law of the State of Israel, a registered partnership is a legal persona, capable of suing and being sued (The Partnerships Ordinance, 1930, sec. 61 (1)). However, this approach is foreign to Jewish law, the *halakhah* recognizing man alone – whether individually or in cooperation with others – as the subject-matter of the law, so that it does not accord an association a separate personality (see Gulak, Yesodei (1922), 50). It is for this reason that the word "partners" rather than "partnership" is the more commonly employed halakhic term. Thus a suit brought by the partners against one of their number, e.g., arising out of fraud (see **Ona'ah*), is not the suit of the partnership but of its individual members (Yad, Sheluḥin, 5:6; Sh. Ar. ḤM 176:4). Nevertheless, even though the partnership as such does not have the status of an independent legal persona, the moment a person is recognized as a partnership member his rights and obligations change and no longer correspond to those attaching to the individual or to an agent. Thus one partner represents his fellow partners vis-à-vis third parties, and unlike an agent, renders them bound by the consequences of his acts in certain circumstances, even without having been appointed as their representative (Yad, Sheluḥin, 3:3). Similarly, if jointly owned property is later found in the possession of one of the co-owners, the latter's possession will not be recognized, despite the rule that the onus of proof is on the person seeking to recover from the neighbor (BB 4a and codes); subsequent ratification of a fellow partner's acts amounting to deviation from the customary partnership activities suffices to absolve the latter from liability for such deviation – according to some of the *posekim* even if they are only passed over in silence without protest (*Shenei ha-Me'orot ha-Gedolim* no. 26). Thus the special standing which the law affords a partner to some extent lends a partnership the coloring of a legal persona.

In the State of Israel

The laws of partnership are governed by the above-mentioned mandatory partnership ordinance, which is based on the British Partnership Act, 1890, but differs from it mainly in that it necessitates registration of a partnership to which it lends the character of a legal persona (sec. 61 (1)). Still unclear is the position as regards the standing of an unregistered partnership (PD 15:1246; Pesakim Meḥoziyyim, 56:362). Case law shows that the *halakhah* is sometimes quoted with regards to problems left unresolved within the framework of the Partnership Ordinance (e.g., on the questions of dissolution of partnership (PD 21:576) and the share of each of the spouses in the profits and losses deriving from their common enterprise (Pesakim Meḥoziyyim, 23:418)). In cases where the parties agree to submit their dispute to a rabbinical court, the issue will be decided in accordance with Jewish law (see PDR 2:376, 5:310).

[Shmuel Dov Revital]

Partnership of Members of a Professional Association

The laws of partnership in Jewish Law have also been used by members of a professional association. The Tosefta states that "the wool workers and the dyers are allowed to say: 'We will all be partners in any business that comes to the city'" (Tosef., BM 11, 24). In such a case, unlike the normal manner of creating partnership detailed above, the partnership is created pursuant to an internal regulation of a particular professional association. This method of forming a partnership is similar to other internal regulations mentioned in the Tosefta regarding an arrangement for mutual insurance among members of the association of donkey drivers and sailors. In Jewish Law, the laws of partnership also influence various aspects of the public law, especially in tax law; see *Taxation.

Further Developments in the State of Israel

Another case in which the civil court had recourse to the rules of partnership in Jewish law concerned the division of a partnership's assets equally among three brothers. The court considered the question of whether the parts should be distributed to the parties by way of lottery, or whether one of two partners should be given the priority in choosing a particular part of the partnership property for sentimental reasons. The court cited the Jewish Law principle, "when brothers or partners divide the field, and all of the shares are equal, and there is no good or bad location, the division is made exclusively by measurement. However, if one of the partners says: 'Give me my share on this side so that it will be close to my field and become like one big field,' his request is accepted and the others are compelled to oblige, for to refuse such a request is conduct suitable for Sodom" (Yad, Shekhenim 12, 1; Sh. Ar, ḤM 174:1; see *Law and Morality). Accordingly, the Court ruled that when one of the partners has a preference for a particular part because he cultivated and cared it for years, that preference should be taken into consideration – at least to the same extent that the financial interest of one of the partners should to be taken into consideration, such as the fact that the field under consideration is adjoining to his field (ḤM (Tel Aviv) 309/59 *Re The Partnership of the Litvinsky Brothers*, 18 PDM 65 *per* Judge Lamm).

Since 1975, matters of partnership are regulated in the Partnership Ordinance [New Version], 5735 – 1975.

Regarding partnership of spouses in spousal assets see *Matrimonial Property.

[Menachem Elon (2nd ed.)]

BIBLIOGRAPHY: J.S. Zuri, *Mishpat ha-Talmud*, 4 (1921), 55–59; 5 (1921), 154–6; idem, *Arikhat ha-Mishpat ha-Ivri… Ḥok Ḥevrat ha-Shutafut* (1940); Gulak, Yesodei, 1 (1922), 135–7; 2 (1922), 192–8; Gulak, Oẓar, 147f., 217–23; E.E. Hildesheimer, *Das juedische Gesellschaftsrecht…* (1930); Herzog, Instit, 1 (1936), 213–23; 2 (1939), 155–66; Elon, Mafte'aḥ, 321–41. **ADD. BIBLIOGRAPHY:** M. Elon, *Ha-Mishpat ha-Ivri* (1988), 1:373, 559ff., 562, 586, 599, 603, 605, 626, 653, 663, 703, 745ff., 747, 755, 764, 765ff.; 2:1102, 1110ff., 1233; 3:1345, 1364.; idem, *Jewish Law* (1994), 1:451; 2:680 ff., 683, 722, 741, 746, 749, 774, 808, 819, 867, 919 ff., 921, 931, 941, 942 ff.; 3:1325, 1335 ff., 1477, 1606, 1627 ff.; M. Elon and B. Lifshitz, *Mafte'aḥ ha-She'elot ve-ha-Teshuvot shel Ḥakhmei Sefarad u-Ẓefon Afrikah* (legal digest) (1986), 486–501; B. Lifshitz and E. Shochetman, *Mafte'aḥ ha-She'elot ve-ha-Teshuvot shel Ḥakhmei Ashkenaz, Ẓarefat ve-Italyah* (legal digest) (1997), 326–39; *Enẓiklopedyah Talmudit*, s.v. *"Gud o Iggud,"* 5:233 ff.; s.v. *"Ḥalukat Shutafut,"* 15:409 ff.; S. Revital, *"Pesikat Batei-Din Rabaniyyim be-Inyanei Shutafim,"* 13–14, in: *Dinei Yisrael* (1986), 91.

PARTOS, OEDOEN (1909–1976), Israeli composer. Partos studied the violin and viola, and composition (with Zoltán Kodály) at the academy in his native Budapest. In 1924 he became first violinist of the Lucerne orchestra, then appeared as soloist in Hungary and Germany, and from 1936 to 1938 taught violin and composition at the conservatory in Baku. In 1938 he went to Palestine and joined the Palestine (later Israel Philharmonic) Orchestra as first viola player until 1950. He also became active as teacher and composer and in 1953 was appointed director of the Israel (later Rubin) Conservatory and Academy of Music in Tel Aviv. In the same year he received the Israel Prize for his symphonic fantasia *En Gev.*

Partos' interest in Near Eastern musical subjects and techniques had already been aroused during his stay in Baku. In Palestine he was confronted with the added musical traditions of the Oriental Sephardi and Yemenite Jews, toward which he was drawn by Bracha *Zefira, for whose recitals he prepared several imaginative settings of such tunes.

His works include *Shir Tehillah*, concerto for viola and orchestra (1945); *Yizkor,* for viola and string orchestra (1946), also in versions for violin or viola or cello and piano, based on an East Ashkenazi synagogal chant and commemorating the Holocaust; *En Gev,* symphonic fantasia (1951), on the motive E-G-B (Israel Prize, 1953); *String Quartet No. 2 – Tehillim* (1960); *Ḥezyonot*, for flute, piano, and string orchestra (1957), also performed as a ballet *The Mythical Hunter*; a quintet for flute and strings (1958); a violin concerto (concluded 1958); *Nebulae* for woodwind quintet (1967); *Metamorphoses*, for piano (1971); *Three Fantasies*, for two violins in 31-tone system (1972); and *Music for Chamber Orchestra* (1973), and several cantatas and choral works, some of which were published as *Shirei Makhelah* (1953), including the well-known *Ein Addir ka-Adonai*, based on a Sephardi melody. His last works include *Metamorphoses*, for piano (1971); *Three Fantasies*, for two violins in 31-tone system (1972); and *Music for Chamber Orchestra* (1973).

BIBLIOGRAPHY: P.E. Gradenwitz, *Music and Musicians in Israel* (1959), 73–78, 152–3; *Who Is Who in ACUM* (1965), 63; I. Shalita *Enẓiklopedyah le-Musikah* (1950²), cols. 750–2.

[Bathja Bayer]

PARTRIDGE (Heb. חָגְלָה, *ḥoglah*), bird. Two species of the partridge are found in Israel, the see-see partridge (*Ammoperdix heyi*) and the chukar partridge (*Alectoris graeca*). The latter is called *ḥajel* in Arabic, which is the *ḥoglah* mentioned as the name of one of Zelophehad's daughters (Num. 26:33) and as the place-name Beth-Hoglah (Josh. 15:6). These two species of partridge, which are kosher birds, are extensively hunted because of their delicious meat. They belong to the family of pheasants, like the *pheasant and the *quail, which are both included in the Talmud among four species of game birds, the best of which is stated to be the שְׂכְלִי (*shikhli*), apparently the chukar partridge, and the least tasty the quail (Yoma 75b). The two species of partridge mentioned above are distinguished by the intensive cries of the male during the breeding season, so that the biblical name קוֹרֵא (*kore*, "calling") is appropriate for both of them, although it is applied nowadays only to the see-see partridge. This bird is found in large flocks in the Judean Desert and the Negev. In the breeding season the partridges separate into pairs, and the female lays between five and 14 eggs in a nest. Sometimes two females lay eggs in the same nest, in which case one gains the upper hand and drives the other away; however her small body is unable to keep such a large number of eggs warm, so that eventually the embryos die. It was to this that the proverb referred when speaking of one who robs another of his possessions without ultimately deriving any benefit: "As the partridge that broodeth over young which she hath not brought forth, so is he that getteth riches, and not by right; in the midst of his days he shall leave them" (Jer. 17:11). A similar phenomenon occurs sometimes in the chukar partridge's nest. These two species of partridge feed on seeds and on insects which they hunt, a circumstance referred to in David's question when he asked Saul why he was hunting him "as the partridge hunts" (the flea; I Sam. 26:20). In the Mishnah (Ḥul. 12:2) the *kore* is mentioned as a kosher bird, the male of which also sits on the eggs, as is indeed done by the partridge. Some (Rashi and others) identified the *kore* with the cuckoo, but this identification is incorrect and was rejected already by the *tosafot* (to Ḥul. 63a s.v. *neẓ*).

BIBLIOGRAPHY: J. Feliks, *Animal World of the Bible* (1962), 56f. **ADD. BIBLIOGRAPHY:** Feliks, Ha-Ẓome'aḥ, 276.

[Jehuda Feliks]

PARVAIM (Heb. פַּרְוַיִם), the region from which Solomon is said to have obtained gold for the ornamentation of his Temple (II Chron. 3:6). The word may possibly derive from the Sanskrit *pûrva*, "eastern." Some scholars identify Parvaim with Sāq al-Farwayn near Mt. Shammar in northwest Arabia; others, with Farwa in southern Arabia.

BIBLIOGRAPHY: S.J. Simons, *Geographical and Topographical Texts of the Old Testament* (1959), 346, n. 869.

PARVEH (Heb. פַּרְוֶה Yid.), term applied to foods which cannot be classified as milk or meat, and which may therefore be eaten with either without infringing the *dietary laws. Fish, vegetables, and eggs are included in this category. *Parveh* utensils are kept apart from meat or milk vessels.

The origin of the word is problematic. It may be derived from the Hebrew root ערב ("mixed"). The Mishnah refers to *bet ha-parvah* (spelled Heb. פַּרְוָה), a courtyard, to which the high priest was taken for ritual immersion, distinguished by being neither holy nor profane (Yoma 3:3). In the *Gemara* the word, used in a derogatory sense to indicate a bird which it is forbidden to eat, was derived from the name of a wicked magician (Ḥul. 62b). It has also been posited that *parveh* originates from the Latin *parvus* ("small"). The Yiddish word *pare* ("steam") has also been suggested. Finally, there is a theory that the word is of Slavonic origin ("a pair"): the Czech *párové*, for instance, denotes an item that may have a dual purpose.

BIBLIOGRAPHY: JC (Jan. 17, 24, 31; Feb. 7; March 7, 27, 1964).

PARZEN, HERBERT (1896–1985), U.S. rabbi, author, editor. Born in Ozorkow, Poland, he came to the United States in 1909, earning his B.A. at the University of Michigan in 1919 and then entering the Jewish Theological Seminary, where he was ordained in 1926. He also earned an M.H.L. from the seminary that year and an M.A. from Columbia University. The seminary awarded him an honorary doctorate in 1972.

He began his rabbinate at Temple Aaron in St. Paul (1926–28) and then at Temple Ahavai Shalom in Portland, Oregon, where he brought new leadership to a declining congregation and also was president of the Portland Chapter of the Zionist Organization of America (1939–41). During World War II he moved to the East Coast to serve as rabbi of Temple Israel in Freeport (1942–44), and then as chaplain in the House of Detention for Women in New York City (1945–79). He also served as program director of the United Synagogue of America, New York City (1952–55); executive director of the Jewish Reconstructionist Foundation, New York City (1955–58); assistant director of information for the Jewish Agency for Israel, New York City (1958–60); and then at the Herzl Institute, New York City, where he was research associate and lecturer on Jewish history and literature (1970–83).

He was a contributor on the early history of Zionism in America to the American Jewish Historical Society and Theodor Herzl Foundation (1958).

He wrote *Herzl Speaks His Mind* (1960) and was the editor of *Essays on the History of Zionism*, Volumes 3–4 (Herzl Press, 1961–71). He also wrote *A Short History of Zionism*, (1962), *Architects of Conservative Judaism* (1964), and *The Hebrew University, 1925–1935* (1974.)

He also translated from the Yiddish *A Diary of the Lodz Ghetto* by Sholom Frank and worked as the associate editor of *Conservative Judaism* (1952–55) and editor of *United Synagogue Review* (1953–55) and *Rabbinical Assembly Bulletin* (1954–56).

BIBLIOGRAPHY: P.S. Nadell, *Conservative Judaism in America: A Biographical Dictionary and Sourcebook* (1988)

[Michael Berenbaum (2nd ed.)]

°**PASCAL, BLAISE** (1623–1662), French religious philosopher, writer, and scientist. Pascal, an ardent Christian, was a member of the austere Catholic group known as the Jansenists. He is famous for his *Pensées sur la religion* (1670), fragments intended to form part of an *Apologie de la religion chrétienne*. An authoritative modern edition is that published in 1908–14 by the Jewish scholar Léon *Brunschvicg. In the *Pensées*, Pascal sought to convince the unbeliever of the existence of God and the superiority of the Christian religion by showing that only through God and Jesus could man surmount the misery of the human condition and understand the mystery of his own dual nature. His proofs and arguments include the biblical prophecies and the survival and role of the Jewish people. He studied the Bible closely and found himself drawn to talmudic and midrashic literature in order to penetrate the deeper message of the prophecies. He quoted the Midrash, the Talmud, and Maimonides, though he had only secondhand access to the sources through the medieval *Pugio Fidei* of the Spanish Dominican, Raymond *Martini.

Meditation on the Bible led Pascal to ponder the role of the Jewish people. Just as he saw the Hebrew prophets as the harbingers of Christianity, so he saw Israel as a symbolic forerunner of the Messiah, its survival bearing witness to the divine scheme of salvation. Thus Israel was both glorious and lowly: glorious as God's elect, lowly because of its rejection of Jesus. But Pascal did not content himself with this traditional Christian view of the Jewish people. He delved deeper and was impressed by the loyalty of the Jews to their religion. He admired Jewish law for its strictness, its perfection, and its durability. He also noted the unique bond of brotherhood which links Jews. He marveled even more at a phenomenon "without precedent or equal in the world": that Jews love deeply, unreservedly, to the point of martyrdom, the book in which their leader, Moses, chastised them for their ingratitude to God, predicting their downfall and dispersal among the nations. This loyalty to religion, against their own "honor," exists, in Pascal's view, only among the Jews.

While Pascal admired the faithfulness and obstinate survival of the Jews, he rejected the "excessive formalism" of Jewish law, and condemned the Jews for their lack of spirituality and for their blindness to Christian truth; but equally, he condemned "unspiritual" Christians. Ardently desiring a purified spiritual religion for Jews and Christians alike, Pascal wrote: "The Messiah, according to unspiritual Jews, must be a great temporal prince. Christ, according to unspiritual Christians, came to exempt us from loving God… Neither view represents Christianity or Judaism. True Jews and true Christians have always waited for a Messiah who would make them love God, and, through this love alone, triumph over their enemies."

BIBLIOGRAPHY: J. Mesnard, *Pascal, his Life and Works* (1952); M.V. Hay, *The Prejudices of Pascal...* (1962); Lovsky, in: *Cahiers Sioniens*, 5 (1951), 355–66; L. Goldmann, *Le Dieu Caché* (1955); C. Lehrmann, *L'Elément juif dans la littérature française*, 1 (1960^2), 120–5.

[Lionel Cohen]

PASCANI, town in Jassy province in Moldavia, N.E. Romania. The town may have been founded by Jews, since in 1859, ten years after its foundation, 86 Jews and only five Christians lived there. The ground for the synagogue, the Jewish cemetery (opened in 1870), and the ritual bath (founded in 1872) was granted by the owner of the estate on which the town was established. The locality began to develop after 1879, when the railway from Jassy to Cernauti (Chernovtsy) and Lemberg was built. Pascani was also a railway junction for Bucharest. In 1899 there were 1,862 Jews (14.7% of the total population) in Pascani, six religious schools (*ḥadarim*), and four synagogues; by the eve of World War I the latter had increased to five. In 1900 a modern primary school was opened by the community at the suggestion of a Christian pharmacist who donated money for this purpose. A second school was opened in 1911 with the aid of the *Jewish Colonization Association. During the Peasants' Revolt of 1907 a Jew was killed and many Jewish houses were plundered. Between 1880 and 1913 proposals were made for changing the status of the town to a city, but these were rejected by parliament on the ground that the situation of the Jews might thereby be improved. By 1910 the Jewish population had decreased to 1,543. Pascani was a ḥasidic center in Romania, as the *ẓaddik* M.L. Friedman, son of I. Friedman (of the *Ruzhin dynasty), the rabbi of Buhusi, lived there.

In World War II most Pascani Jews were deported to Bostosam and some to Roman. In 1947 the Jewish population numbered 870, decreasing to 500 in 1950. In 1969 only about 20 Jewish families had remained. There was one synagogue.

BIBLIOGRAPHY: PK Romanyah, 195–7; E. Schwarzfeld, *Impopularea, reîmpopularea și întemeierea tîrgurilor și tîrgutoarelor în Moldova* (1914), 40, 41, 98; V. Tufescu, *Tirgdșoarele din Moldova și importanța lor economícă* (1942), 93, 94, 114, 116, 124, 129, 138.

[Theodor Lavi]

PASCHELES, WOLF (Ze'ev; 1814–1857), author, publisher, and bookseller. Born in Prague, Pascheles published – while in his teens – *Deutsche Gebete fuer Frauen* (1828) of which several editions appeared under various titles. With the money earned on the first edition, he opened the first Jewish bookstore in Prague.

He wrote a biography of Solomon *Heine together with one of the Viennese merchant Herrmann Tedesco (1845). In 1857 he edited and published E. Bondi's *Mikhtevei Sefat Kodesh*, a Hebrew chrestomathy (including biographies of famous Jews) with interlinear German translation. Pascheles' greatest successes were his collections of legends and biographies, medieval and modern, under the title *Sippurim* (1846/47) which went through many editions. Among the contributors were I.M. *Jost, Solomon Kohn, R.J. Fuerstenthal, and S.J. *Kaempf. A popular edition was published (1888, 1909^3) by his son-in-law Jacob Brandeis. Adaptations of the *Sippurim* were prepared by S. Schmitz (1921, 1926) and H. Pollitzer (*Die goldene Gasse*, 1937) as well as a selection and translation into English by C. Field (*Jewish Legends...*, n.d.). Pascheles' miniature Pentateuch, with German translation by H. *Arnheim, and his *Illustrierter israelitischer Volkskalender*, which appeared from 1860 to 1935, was also popular. He also published a popular series called *Juedische Universal-Bibliothek*, which included works on Jewish history, biographies, and contemporary events. After Pascheles' death these were edited by his son Jacob and his son-in-law, J. Brandeis, who continued the book-selling and publishing firm (catalogs appeared 1879–94).

BIBLIOGRAPHY: Society for the History of Czechoslovak Jews, New York, *Jews of Czechoslovakia*, 1 (1968), 341, 533.

PASCIN, JULES (1885–1930), painter. Pascin was born in Viddin, Bulgaria, the son of a Sephardi grain merchant, Marcus Pincus. In 1891 the family settled in Bucharest. After leaving high school, Pascin traveled, taking courses at several art academies. On his return, his clever drawings earned him a contract with the Munich satirical weekly *Simplicissimus*. He changed his name to Pascin. In 1905 he went to Paris and there became a celebrated figure on the Left Bank. During World War I he left for the United States and became a U.S. citizen. In 1920 he returned to Paris and, in spite of a life of dissipation, produced about 500 oils as well as drawings, prints, colors, and a few small sculptures. Suffering from incurable cirrhosis of the liver, he committed suicide by hanging himself in his studio, leaving bizarre instructions for a Jewish funeral.

His acute draftsmanship can be seen in his *Simplicissimus* cartoons and in his humorous and often savage illustrations of books, among them an edition of Heinrich Heine's *Die Memoiren des Herrn von Schnabelewopski*. This draftsmanship was the basis of all his compositions and some critics claimed that his oils were only "drawings heightened by paint." His paintings have a quasi-surrealist quality. Pascin also made prints using a sharp needle directly on copper (similar to drawing) for preserving impressions of travel, suburban scenes, and café life. Though most of his work depicts women singly or in groups, he was also a keen observer of many milieus and he drew or painted children at play, circus artists, and nightclub scenes. He was fascinated by figures from folklore and the Bible including the Prodigal Son, Salome, and Bathsheba.

BIBLIOGRAPHY: A. Werner, *Pascin* (Eng., 1962); G. Diehl, *Pascin* (Fr., 1968).

[Alfred Werner]

PASHHUR (Heb. פַּשְׁחוּר), son of Immer, priest and chief officer in the Temple during the last years of the kingdom of Judah (Jer. 20:1–6). Pashhur was deputy to the high priest and responsible for the maintenance of order in the Temple.

In the narrative of Jeremiah 20:1–6 it is related that he beat Jeremiah and put him in the stocks as a punishment for his harsh prophecy against Judah and Jerusalem (Jer. 19:15). Jeremiah responded by declaring "The Lord does not call your name Pashhur, but Terror (Heb. *magor*) on every side." One interpretation of this play on words derives the name Pashhur from the Aramaic root *pwš* ("to rest") and the Aramaic word *seḥor* ("round about"), i.e., where formerly there was peace and quiet, there will now be terror all about. Jeremiah prophesied that Pashhur would be taken into exile and would die in a foreign land: "And you, Pashhur, and all who dwell in your house, shall go into captivity, to Babylon you shall go; and there you shall die, and there you shall be buried…" (Jer. 20:6).

BIBLIOGRAPHY: de Vaux, Anc Isr, 378–9; Waechter, in: ZAW, 74 (1962), 57–62.

[Josef Segal]

PASMANIK, DANIEL (1869–1930), Zionist writer and leader. Born in Gadyach, Ukraine, Pasmanik studied medicine in Switzerland and Bulgaria and from 1899 served as an instructor in medicine at Geneva University. He joined the Zionist Movement in 1900 and became one of its leading publicists and theoreticians. In 1905, upon his return to Russia, he joined the editorial board of the monthly *Yevreyskaya Zhizn* and later of the weekly *Razsvet*. He advocated the evolutionary concept of Zionism, practical work in Ereẓ Israel, and active Zionist participation in Diaspora life (see *Helsingfors Program). Pasmanik's articles appeared in Russian, Yiddish, German, Hebrew, Polish, and Croat periodicals; several were published in pamphlet and book form. An entire Zionist generation was educated largely on Pasmanik's writings. He also contributed articles to *Die *Welt*, to the non-Zionist *Yevreyskiy Mir*, and to the *Yevreyskaya Entsiklopediya*. In 1905 (January–October) he published pseudonymously, in *Yevreyskaya Zhizn*, a much-discussed, largely autobiographical novel, "*Istoriya odnogo yevreyskago intelligenta*" ("The Story of a Jewish Intellectual"). He was also among the first theoreticians of *Po'alei Zion, with his *Teorie un Praktike fun Poalei Zionizmus* (1906). During the civil war in Russia (1917–21), Pasmanik sided with the counterrevolutionary White armies of generals Denikin and Wrangel, who were responsible for innumerable anti-Jewish pogroms. In 1919 he emigrated to Paris, where in 1920–22 he was coeditor of the Russian émigré paper *Obshcheye Delo*. Association with these circles estranged Pasmanik from the Zionist movement.

Pasmanik's main writings include: *Kritika "teoriy" Bunda* ("A Critique of the 'Theories' of the Bund," 1906); *Sudby yevreyskago naroda: problemy yevreyskoy obshchestvennosti* ("The Destiny of the Jewish Nation…," 1917); and *Russkaya revolyutsiya i yevreystvo: bolshevizm i iudaizm* ("Jewry and the Russian Revolution…," 1923). His study *Stranstvuyushchiy Izrail: psikhologiya yevreystva v razseyanii* ("The Wandering Jew: The Psychology of Diaspora Jewry," 1910) was also published in German (1911) and Yiddish (1918). Pasmanik's last book, *Qu'est-ce que le judaïsme?* was published in 1930. Several studies on medical topics appeared in specialized German and French publications.

[Joseph B. Schechtman]

PASSAIC-CLIFTON, twin cities 12 mi. E. of New York City in N.E. New Jersey; total population of Passaic, 67,500 (2000), total population of Clifton, 79,026 (2000), combined Jewish population estimated at 10,500 (2000). Passaic is bordered on three sides by Clifton and their Jewish population is normally considered as a single unit. No systematic demographic study has been taken of the area since 1949, but it seems apparent that in the period 1950–70 the Jewish population of Passaic decreased considerably, although Jewish businesses continued to be located there, and that Clifton's Jewish population has developed since 1945 at Passaic's expense.

Passaic was founded by Dutch settlers in the late 17th century, but until the 1860s was little more than a transportation hub. In 1859, however, the advent of waterpower there led to its transformation into an industrial city. Incorporated as a village in 1869, Passaic, three years later, achieved the status of city. Up until the 1860s, however, it had no Jewish residents. Significantly, the first sustained industrial enterprise at Passaic was a mill owned by a Jewish man. Jacob Basch & Co. opened in 1862, and eventually it was joined by additional woolen and worsted establishments; by 1910 Passaic's well-known worsted mills employed nearly 43% of all its industrial employees. Unfortunately, when the woolen industry abandoned the city after World War II, its earlier prosperity was severely undermined. Inasmuch as the textile industry traditionally attracted cheap labor, Passaic became a haven for European immigrants. By 1910 just over half of the city's 54,773 people were foreign born; an estimated 3,500 were Jewish, although the great preponderance was Slavic. During the first decade of the 20th century, moreover, Passaic became overcrowded, leading newcomers to make their residences beyond its borders in Acquackanonk Township, which in 1917 was incorporated as Clifton, as well as in the towns of Garfield and Wallington, which are also adjacent to the city. As a result of the textile industry's demise, the offspring of Passaic's white population began to move away, their places being filled by nonwhite minorities.

While Jacob Basch, the mill owner, was the city's original Jewish settler, a onetime itinerant peddler named Moses Simon undertook to organize its Jewish community. Although the Simon family supposedly had settled near Passaic in 1870, communal activity did not begin until 1885, by which time the pattern of immigration had shifted. Passaic's Jewish population was originally largely occupied in small retail businesses that serviced the ethnic neighborhoods. By 1900, however, members of the community were also involved in legal and financial affairs as well. A sociological survey conducted in 1937 reported that 43% of the gainfully employed Jews in Passaic were engaged in commercial trade, 22% in manufacturing, and 12% in professional services; a more recent study, made in 1949, found 40% in trade, 30% in the professions, and only 12% in manufacturing.

Almost from its inception, members of the Jewish community also participated in civic life as well, a tradition that began with Jacob Basch's son Henry, who took an active interest in municipal affairs beginning in the 1880s. As early as 1892 Jews gained minor elective offices, such as election judge; in 1904 Joseph Spitz was elected as a council representative from his ward, and in 1919 Abram Preiskel, in being elected to the board of commissioners, became the first Jew to win a city-wide political contest. Passaic's first Jewish mayor, Morris Pashman, was elected in 1951; in 1967 Bernard D. Pinck was elected mayor, and he was succeeded by Gerald Goldman in 1971. Clifton's first Jewish councilman, Fred Friend, was elected in 1931, and in 1962 Ira Schoem was elected as that city's first Jewish mayor. In both cities members of the Jewish community have long been active in the deliberations of the respective boards of education.

[Michael H. Ebner]

Passaic's first Jewish congregation, B'nai Jacob (Orthodox), was founded in 1889; by 1911 it had been joined by six others, all Orthodox. More Orthodox congregations were established after World War I, and eventually some have been rebuilt in the newer sections of the city. Passaic's Conservative synagogue, Temple Emanuel (1923), quickly became the city's leading congregation. About 1938 the Ahavas Israel was founded and grew substantially to become the second largest Conservative congregation and Hebrew school. There were about 18 congregations at that time. The Clifton Jewish Center (1943, Conservative) and Beth Sholom Reform Temple (1959) were established to serve the population which had shifted to the suburbs of Passaic from the early 1940s. The Jewish Community Council of Passaic-Clifton (organized in 1933), now the Jewish Federation of Greater Clifton-Passaic, administers the United Jewish Appeal and coordinates all community bodies, which include the Passaic-Clifton YM-YWHA, and The Daughters of Miriam, as well as a variety of other fraternal and service groups such as Jewish Family Service and Holocaust Resource Center. The Hillel Academy (1945), an Orthodox day school, offers intensive Jewish education. The Passaic-Clifton Board of Rabbis (founded in 1953) directs the Va'ad Ha-Kohol, which supervises *kashrut* in the community. A unique institution is the Passaic United Hebrew Burial Association (*ḥevra kaddisha*) which built the Jewish Memorial Chapel in 1949. It is one of two such nonprofit institutions in the United States and is owned and administered by the Jewish community.

[Edwin N. Soslow]

About 1960 the Jewish population was declining; the Orthodox were getting older and fewer and the Conservatives were moving to nearby more suburban locations. During the late 1970s a committee was formed to attract more Jews into the community (partially to "shore-up" real estate values). They put ads in the Jewish press which attracted Orthodox Jews from areas in New York City. In 1983, the construction of an *eruv* in Clifton-Passaic attracted many Orthodox Jews to the community. A significant resettlement of Russian Jews took place in the 1980s.

In the early 21st century the Conservative Jewish population was aging and diminishing and the Orthodox group was more vibrant, growing larger both from within and from outside. They were founding and building their own institutions. One ultra-Orthodox group has a school built for girls (in 1995, Yeshiva K'tana) and one for boys at a different location. The other Orthodox group erected a new Hillel school building to accommodate 800 boys and girls from preschool to the 8th grade. The *mikveh* was built in the middle 1980s. Thirteen major synagogues were operating in the early 21st century as well as many small congregations that meet in houses.

[Edward W. Schey, Robert Moskowitz, Jacqueline Klein, and Jane Mandelbaum (2nd ed.)]

BIBLIOGRAPHY: *Jewish Roots: A History of the Jewish Community of Passaic and Environs* (1959); S.M. Robinson, in: S.M. Robinson and J. Starr (eds.), *Jewish Population Studies* (1943), 22–36; B.B. Seligman, *Jewish Population of Passaic, New Jersey, 1949: A Demographic Study* (1951).

PASSAU, city in Bavaria, Germany. Jews are mentioned in an early tenth-century local customs regulation (Raffelsteten). Documentary evidence for their presence in the city of Passau, however, dates only from 1210, when Bishop Mangold compensated the Jews of the city after they had been robbed. In 1206 they were released from paying customs and taxes in return for their aid in helping the bishop collect his tithes. They earned their livelihood in moneylending. A *Judenstrasse* is first mentioned in 1328, a synagogue in 1314, and a cemetery in 1418. (Before 1418 Jews were buried in Regensburg.) The Black *Death persecutions of 1349 caused considerable loss to the community, but Jews were again resident in Passau in 1390. In March 1478 a petty thief "confessed" to having stolen and sold the Host to Jews. On being tortured, 10 Jews confessed to having stabbed the Host and caused its blood to flow. All (including the witness) were sentenced to death. Concomitantly approximately 40 Jews accepted Christianity while the rest were expelled; the synagogue and Jewish homes were demolished. A church erected on the site became the object of pilgrimages. Small numbers of Jews were permitted to reside in Passau in later centuries. The Jewish settlement reached 73 in 1910; 48 in 1932; and 40 in 1933, and was affiliated with the Straubing community. In 1968 there were 13 Jews recorded as residents of Passau.

BIBLIOGRAPHY: *Germania Judaica*, 1 (1963), 266–7; 2 (1968), 647–8; M. Stern, in: *Jeschurun*, 15 (1928), 541–60, 647–76; W.M. Schmid, in: ZGJD, 1 (1929), 119–35; PK, Germanyah; M. Pfamholz, in: *Festschrift fuer Lorenz Spindler (196?)*; J.R. Marcus, *Jew in the Medieval World* (1965), 155–8.

PASSI, DAVID (16th century), Turkish statesman. Passi was born in Portugal a Marrano, lived for a time in Venice, and then settled as a Jew in Constantinople. French, English, Venetian, and Neapolitan envoys all highly appreciated his services, which were largely toward forming an Anglo-Turkish alliance against Spain. The sultan is reported to have said that he had slaves like the grand vizier in abundance, but none like Passi. According to a report of 1585, he was invested with the Duchy of Naxos, like Joseph *Nasi before him. He worked, generally, in close cooperation with the physician Moses *Benveniste. In 1589 these two were responsible for the schemes for currency reform, and when the janissaries subsequently attacked the divan, Passi was wounded. In 1591, as a result of a defamatory letter which he wrote to the chancellor of Poland about the grand vizier Sinan Pasha, he was put in chains and exiled to Rhodes; he returned after Sinan's death shortly thereafter, but played no further part in public life.

BIBLIOGRAPHY: C. Roth, *The House of Nasi: The Duke of Naxos* (1948), 204–12; *Times Literary Supplement* (July 6, 1922); Wolf, in: JHSET, 11 (1924–27), 26–28, 63–64, 85ff.

[Cecil Roth]

PASSOVER (Heb. פֶּסַח, Pesah), a spring festival, beginning on the 15th day of Nisan, lasting seven days in Israel and eight in the Diaspora. It commemorates the Exodus from Egypt. The first and seventh days (the first two and last two in the Diaspora) are *yom tov* (a "festival" on which work is prohibited), and the other days *ḥol ha-mo'ed* ("intermediate days" on which work is permitted).

Names and History

The biblical names for the festival are: *ḥag ha-Pesaḥ* ("the feast of the Passover," Ex. 34:25), so called because God "passed over" (or "protected") the houses of the children of Israel (Ex. 12:23), and *ḥag ha-Maẓẓot* ("the feast of Unleavened Bread"; Ex. 23:15; Lev. 23:6; Deut. 16:16). Pesaḥ is the paschal lamb, offered as a sacrifice on the eve of the feast (14th Nisan) in Temple times; it was eaten in family groups after having been roasted whole (Ex. 12:1–28, 43–49; Deut. 16:1–8). A person who was unable (because of ritual impurity or great distance from the Sanctuary) to keep the "first Passover" could keep it a month later – *Pesaḥ Sheni* ("the Second Passover," also called "Minor Passover," Num. 9:1–14).

According to tradition, the Passover rites were divinely ordained as a permanent reminder of God's deliverance of His people from Egyptian bondage. The critical view points to two distinct festivals in the Bible; the feast of unleavened bread, a pastoral feast, and the Passover, an agricultural feast (see below).

In the Book of Joshua (5:10–11), it is said that the Israelites led by Joshua kept the feast at Gilgal. The Book of Kings relates that Passover was kept with special solemnity in King Josiah's reign in the seventh century B.C.E.: "The king commanded all the people, saying: 'Keep the Passover unto the Lord your God, as it is written in this book of the covenant. For there was not kept such a Passover from the days of the judges that judged Israel, nor in all the days of the kings of Israel, nor of the kings of Judah; but in the eighteenth year of King Josiah was this Passover kept to the Lord in Jerusalem'" (II Kings 23:21–23).

As far as can be ascertained, the Passover festival was kept throughout the period of the Second Temple. Josephus records contemporary Passover celebrations in which he estimates that the participants who gathered in Jerusalem to perform the sacrifice in the year 65 C.E., were "not less than three millions" (Jos., Wars, 2:280). The Talmud (Pes. 64b) similarly records: "King Agrippa once wished to take a census of the hosts of Israel. He said to the high priest, 'Cast your eyes on the Passover offerings.' He took a kidney from each, and 600,000 pairs of kidneys were found there, twice as many as those who departed from Egypt, excluding those who were unclean and those who were on a distant journey; and there was not a single paschal lamb for which more than ten people had not registered; and they called it: 'The Passover of the dense throngs.'" Allowing for hyperbole, the account of immense crowds assembled to offer the paschal lamb cannot be too far from historical reality.

The Samaritans considered all the biblical rules regarding the sacrifice of the lamb in Egypt (Ex. 12) to be applicable for all time. The practice, as recorded in the Mishnah (Pes. 9:5), is that only *Pesaḥ Miẓrayim* ("Passover of Egypt") required the setting aside of the lamb four days before the festival, the sprinkling of the blood on lintel and doorposts, and that the lamb be eaten in "haste." The Mishnah (Pes. 10:5) explains the commands of the lamb sacrifice and the eating of **matzah* ("unleavened bread") and *maror* ("bitter herbs") as follows: the lamb is offered because God "passed over" (*pasaḥ*); the unleavened bread is eaten because God redeemed the Israelites from Egypt (Ex. 12:39); and the bitter herbs, because the Egyptians embittered their lives (Ex. 1:14).

With the destruction of the Temple, the offering of the paschal lamb came to an end, although it is possible that for a time the sacrifice was continued in modified form in some circles (Guttman, in: HUCA, 38 (1967), 137–48). The other rites and ceremonies of the Passover festival continued as before. The Samaritans, however, still sacrifice the paschal lamb in a special ceremony on Mt. Gerizim near Shechem. The Last Supper, mentioned in the New Testament (Mark 14, Matt. 26, Luke 22), may be the *seder* meal. Early Christians observed Easter on Passover and Roman Christians on the Sunday after Passover. Later the *blood libel against Jews was frequently connected with the Passover festival.

The Seder

The special home ceremony on the first night of Passover, the *seder* ("order"; pl. *sedarim*), is based on the injunction to parents to inform their children of the deliverance from Egypt: "And thou shalt tell thy son in that day, saying: It is because of that which the Lord did for me when I came forth out of Egypt" (Ex. 13:8). The Mishnah (Pes. 10:4) gives a formula of four questions (see **Mah Nishtannah* which are asked by the child and to which the father replies "according to the son's intelligence." During the Middle Ages a special order of service for the *seder* was adapted with a formal reply to the questions (culled from various rabbinic sources), and with supplementary material such as table hymns and jingles calculated to appeal to children. These are recorded in the Passover *Haggadah. The Mishnah (Pes. 10:1) rules that even the poorest man in Israel must not eat on the first night of Passover unless he reclines. In mishnaic times, free men would normally recline at meals, and on this night all must demonstrate that they are free. In the Middle Ages, in many communities the custom of reclining at meals during the year was abandoned, but it became a duty to recline at the *seder*. During the *seder*, one must partake of four cups (*arba kosot*) of wine (Pes. 10:1). These were interpreted symbolically as corresponding to the four expressions of redemption in the Book of Exodus (6:6–7), or the four cups mentioned in the Book of Genesis (40:11–13) in connection with the dream of the chief butler (TJ, Pes. 10:1, 37c).

On the *seder* table are the following items: three (in some rites two) cakes of *maẓẓot* placed one on top of the other; a roasted egg and shankbone or other bone (as reminders of the paschal lamb and the festival offering in Temple times); a dish of salt water (for "dipping" and as a symbol of the Israelites' tears); *maror* such as lettuce (or horseradish) for "dipping"; and *ḥaroset ("clay"), a paste made from almonds, apples, and wine (Pes. 10:3) for the purpose of sweetening the bitter herbs, and as a symbol of the mortar the Israelites used when building under the lash of their taskmasters.

The *seder* follows this standard order:

(1) *kaddesh* ("sanctification"): the festival is introduced by the *Kiddush* benediction in which God is praised for giving the festivals to Israel;

(2) *reḥaẓ* ("wash"): the hands are washed in accordance with the ancient practice of ritual purification before partaking of anything dipped in liquid;

(3) *karpas* ("greens"): the parsley is dipped in salt water;

(4) *yaḥaẓ* ("division"): the middle *matzah* is broken in two and one half is hidden. This latter portion is known as the *afikoman* ("the after-meal") and is eaten at the end of the meal, as a reminder of the paschal lamb which was eaten at the end so that its taste would remain in the mouth. It is customary for children to look for the *afikoman*, a prize being given to the successful finder;

(5) *maggid* ("recitation"): the *Haggadah* is recited;

(6) *raḥzaḥ* ("washing"): the ritual washing of the hands before breaking bread;

(7) *moẓi* ("bringing forth"): Grace before Meals is recited: "Blessed art Thou… who bringest forth *[ha-moẓi]* bread…";

(8) *matzah*: pieces of the top *matzah* and the broken middle one are eaten;

(9) *maror*: the bitter herbs are dipped in the *ḥaroset* and eaten;

(10) *korekh* ("binding"): a sandwich is made of pieces of the bottom *matzah* and bitter herbs and eaten. This is a reminder of Hillel's practice in Temple times, based on the verse: "They shall eat it [the paschal lamb] with unleavened bread and bitter herbs" (Num. 9:11);

(11) *shulḥan arukh* ("prepared table"): the festive meal is eaten;

(12) *ẓafun* ("hidden"): the *afikoman* is found and eaten;

(13) *barekh* ("blessing"): Grace after Meals is recited;

(14) *Hallel* ("psalms of praise"): Psalms 115–8 are recited. It was customary in Temple times to recite these psalms at the time of the offering of the paschal lamb (Pes. 5:7);

(15) *nirẓah* ("acceptance").

It is customary to have on the *seder* table a full cup of wine known as "*Elijah's cup." Reflections on past deliverance awaken hope for the final redemption, and Elijah, being the herald of the Messiah (Mal. 3:23), is welcomed; toward the end of the *seder*, the front door of the house is opened to demonstrate that this is a "night of watching" (Ex. 12:42) on which Israel knows no fear. In the Diaspora the *seder* is repeated on the second night. On the second night of Passover the counting of the *omer* is begun. The laws of Passover in the Talmud occur in the talmudic tractate *Pesaḥim*. In the United States several additional prayers have been suggested by different groups. These include a prayer on behalf of the Holocaust victims, one for Russian Jewry, and a prayer of thanksgiving for the State of Israel, usually combined with a fifth cup of wine.

The Laws and Customs of Passover

No *ḥameẓ* ("leaven") is to be found in the house or owned during Passover (Ex. 12:15, 19). On the night before the festival, the house is thoroughly searched for *ḥameẓ* (Pes. 1:1). All leaven found in the house is gathered together in one place and burned on the following day before noon (see *Bedikat Ḥameẓ* (*Ḥameẓ*, Sale of).

According to rabbinic authorities, the obligation to eat *matzah* applies only to the first night (Pes. 120a); it is customary, therefore, to prepare special *matzot*, the wheat of which has been under observation from the time of reaping or grinding (*matzah shemurah*), for it. During the remainder of the festival, though leaven may not be eaten, there is no obligation to eat *matzah*. Some rabbinic authorities were opposed to the use of *matzot* baked by machine.

Utensils in which leaven has been cooked, baked, or boiled must be specially treated before they can be used on Passover. The method is to immerse them in a caldron of boiling water, or, if they are utensils used on a fire, to heat them in a fire until they glow. However, not all vessels can be treated so. Unlike other forbidden food which becomes neutralized and may be eaten if mixed in 60 times its bulk, on Passover, the smallest admixture of *ḥameẓ* is enough to render a dish forbidden (see *Dietary Laws).

On the first day of Passover in the synagogue, a special prayer for dew (*tal*) is recited and the phrase *morid ha-geshem* is not said. On the Sabbath of Passover, the *Song of Songs* is read in the synagogue (Ashkenazi rite). Full *Hallel* is recited on the first day (two days in the Diaspora) and half-*Hallel* the rest of the festival. On the last day *Hazkarat Neshamot* is recited. When the liturgy refers to the festival, it does so as "the period of our freedom." *Ḥerut* ("freedom"), is, in fact, the dominant note of Passover.

[Louis Jacobs]

Critical View

The feast of Passover consists of two parts: The Passover ceremony and the Feast of Unleavened Bread. Originally both parts existed separately; but at the beginning of the Exile they were combined.

Passover was originally not a pilgrimage feast, but a domestic ceremony consisting of the slaughtering and eating of the paschal animal. This animal – according to Exodus 12:21 (J) a sheep or goat; according to Deuteronomy 16:2, either a sheep or a bovine animal; according to Exodus 12:5 (P; cf. II Chron. 35:7), a year-old lamb or kid – was killed; in accordance with later texts (Ex. 12:6; Lev. 23:5; Num. 9:3–5; 28:16 (33:3); Josh. 5:10: Ezek. 45:21; Ezra 6:19; II Chron. 35:1) – on the 14th of the first month (i.e., the 14th of Nisan, March/April), "between the evenings" (Ex. 12:6b; Lev. 23:5; Num. 9:3, 5, 11; 28:4, 8), i.e., at the setting of the sun. The early texts, Exodus 23:15 and 34:18, however, place the Festival of Unleavened Bread in "the season of the *ḥodesh* of Abib, since it was at the *ḥodesh* of Abib that you went free from Egypt," and Deuteronomy 16:1ff. places the slaughtering of the Passover sacrifice in "the *ḥodesh* of Abib, seeing that it was in this *ḥodesh* of Abib that you went free from Egypt at night…, so that you may remember the day you went free from Egypt"; and it has been argued that the last cited passage in particular makes poor sense unless *ḥodesh* designates not a 30-day period ("month") but a single day, i.e., the New Moon. (Both senses of *ḥodesh* are well attested; which is intended in this case can be confirmed only from the context.) The rite of touching the lintel and the doorposts of the house (formerly the tent) with blood from the paschal animal was connected with the slaughter (Ex. 12:7, 13 [P], 22 [J]). The flesh of the animal was boiled, according to Deuteronomy 16:7; but later – by II Chronicles 35:13a – this was interpreted in light of the P (Ex. 12:8–9) to mean broiling (cf. LXX, Deut. 16:7), and this is the rabbinic *halakhah* (Pes. 5:10). The flesh was then eaten with unleavened bread and bitter herbs (Ex. 12:8b; cf. Deut. 16:3a), during the night (Ex. 12:8a), in a community meal, in which the whole family or a combination of families (Ex. 12:4), but no uncircumcised persons (Ex. 12:48b; cf. 12:44–45, 48a [P]), took part. No flesh was allowed to remain until the next day (Deut. 16:4b).

Nothing is found in the Bible about the original meaning of the Passover rite. There is no clue in the name "Passover" (Heb. *pesaḥ*) because its etymology is uncertain. The assumption that the Passover was originally a sacrifice of the firstborn (G. Beer and others) is incorrect (1) because, according to Exodus 22:28–29 and Leviticus 22:27, the firstborn of the sheep, ox, and goat was to be offered on the eighth day, (2) because according to PC (Ex. 12:5), the Passover animal had to be a year old, and (3) because the regulations about the firstborn in Exodus 34:19, 20a and 13:11–13 are connected with the eating of *matzot* (Ex. [34:18]; 13:3–10), but not with the Passover (Ex. [34:25]; 12:24–27a; Kutsch, Segal).

Originally the Passover was celebrated by transient breeders of sheep and goats, later by the Israelites, to secure protection for their flocks prior to leaving the desert winter pasture for cultivated regions (Rost). The rite of the blood (see above) as well as the regulation, which was later still in force (Ex. 12:46b; cf. Num. 9:12), whereby no bone of the Passover animal was to be broken, had an apotropaic significance. The oldest literary record in Exodus 12:21 (J) already presupposes the Passover. Hence the old nomadic custom is "historicized" by being connected with the main event in the Israelite salvation history, the Exodus. The reason for this connection was, from a traditional-historical standpoint, the situation of departure which belonged also to the Passover. Moreover, the rite of the blood made it possible to connect the Passover with the story of the killing of the Egyptian firstborn (Ex. 12:23), which was also inserted into the tradition of the Exodus as the reason why the Pharaoh let the Israelites go (Ex. 11:4aβ–8; Kutsch). This "historicization" has determined the character of the Passover: it became the feast commemorating the Exodus (cf. Ex. 12:11–14α [P]; Deut. 16:1, 3). Originally, the Passover was celebrated among the families (Ex. 12:21 [J]) in tents; after the territorial occupation, in houses. After the cultic centralization of King Josiah, the celebration of the Passover was transferred to the central Sanctuary in Jerusalem (Deut. 16:2, 7; II Kings 23:21–23). The requirement that the slaughtering, preparing, and eating of the paschal animals was to take place in the forecourts of the Temple was maintained after the Exile (II Chron. 30:1–5; 35:13–14; Jub. 49:16, 20). Later, because of the large numbers of participants, the paschal animal was killed at the Temple place, but boiled and eaten in the houses of Jerusalem (e.g., Pes. 5:10; 7:12). The transfer of the Passover feast to the Temple entailed the end of the rite of blood; the blood of the paschal animals was, like other sacrificial blood, now poured on the base of the altar (II Chron. 30:16; 35:11).

The reason for the institution of a second Passover on the 14th day of the second month (Num. 9:10–12 [Ps]), which is wrongly ascribed in II Chronicles 30 to King Hezekiah of Judah, is not a difference in calendar between Judah and Northern Israel (cf. S. Talmon, in: VT, 8 (1958), 48–74) but the possibility that a Jew might be prevented from taking part in the feast on the 14th day of the first month because of uncleanness or a distant journey.

Feast of the Unleavened Bread

Unlike the Passover, the seven-day Feast of Unleavened Bread, which was celebrated in the month of Abib (Ex. 13:4; 23:15; 34:18), is probably taken over from the Canaanites. The main custom of the feast is the eating of unleavened bread or *matzot* (e.g., Ex. 23: 15; 34:18). The required pilgrimage (Ex. 23:14–15, 17; 34:23; Deut. 16:16), originally to a local sanctuary, later – after the cult centralization of Josiah – to Jerusalem, is secondary to the eating of *matzot*.

Originally the feast extended over a week beginning not on the day following the Paschal night, but on a "morrow after the Sabbath." The counting of the seven weeks until the "Feast of Weeks" (Pentecost; Lev. 23:11, 15–16) was also to begin on the "morrow after the Sabbath." In Deuteronomy 16:9 it is described as the day on which the Israelites "first put the sickle to the standing grain" and the grain harvest is begun. Because of its proximity to the traditional date of the Exodus, the *matzot* feast was also connected with the Exodus and thus "historicized" (e.g., Ex. 12:29–34, 37–39 [J]; cf. 12:15–20; 23:15; 34:18 [P]; Deut. 16:3b). A yearly celebration of the march through the Jordan (according to Josh. 3–4) on the Feast of Unleavened Bread (Kraus, Soggin) cannot be derived from the late text Joshua 5:10–12; and the thesis that therefore the *matzot* feast was celebrated in older times as an "election feast" in Gilgal (Wildberger) is contradictory to the fact that the Exodus was also remembered in the celebration of the Passover. Until shortly before the Exile (Deut. 16:7b), the participants in the celebration of the Passover returned home after the celebration at the Temple (the instructions about the *matzot* feast in Deut. 16:3aβ, 3b, 4a, 8 and 16 are a secondary enlargement [Horst]; even then the Passover and *matzot* feasts (as pilgrimages) were still celebrated separately. To fix a common date for the Jews in Babylonia the *matzot* feast after 587 B.C.E. was given a fixed date, the 15th to 21st of the first month, and thus connected with the Passover (first mentioned Ezek. 45:21; Lev. 23:5,6; Num. 28:16, 17; Josh. 5:10, 11; Ezra 6:19, 22; II Chron. [30:15, 13 21–22] 35: 17a, 17b; cf. also the Passover papyrus from Elephantine).

Passover in the New Testament

The combined Passover – *matzot* Feast is also presupposed in the New Testament. The name here refers (a) to the celebration of the Passover (Matt. 26:18; Mark 14:1; Heb. 11:28); (b) to the whole feast (Matt. 26:2; Luke 2:41; 22:1; Acts 12:4; especially in John 2:13, 23, et al.; for this name "[feast of] unleavened bread" [Mark 14:1, 12; Luke 22:1, 7; Acts. 12:3; 20:6] is also used), and (c) as in the Old Testament (e.g., Ex. 12: 21), to the Passover lamb (Mark 14:12, 14, 16; Luke 22:8, 15; John 18–28; II Cor. 5:7). The connection of the death of Jesus with the Passover is important. According to the synoptic gospels, Jesus was crucified on the 15th day of Nisan, the first day of the feast; they understand the last supper of Jesus as a Passover meal, during which the salvational meaning of Jesus' death is disclosed (Mark 14:22, 24). The gospel of John, on the other hand, dates the death of Jesus to the 14th of Nisan (John 19:14; cf. 18: 28), to the hour of the Passover slaughtering (cf. John 19:14, 31; Mark 15:33–34, 37; cf. Pes. 5:1; Jos. Wars, 6:423), and the meal to the night of the 13th of Nisan. This does not have calendaric (Jaubert), but theological reasons. Unlike the synoptic gospels, John interprets Jesus as the Passover lamb (John 1:29; 19:36; cf. e.g., otherwise I Cor. 5:7; I Pet. 1:19; Rev. 5:6).

[Ernst Kutsch]

Passover Cookery

Leaven, grain (except in the form of *matzot* and *matzah* meal), and pulses are forbidden in some rites during the Passover week. Ashkenazim also refrain from eating rice. The ceremonial food placed on the *seder* table varies little from community to community, although the ingredients in the *ḥaroset* change in different localities. The basic recipe of honey, wine, nuts, fruit, and spices is however common to all.

Although *matzah*-meal dumplings (*kleys, kneydlekh*) are considered a typical Passover dish, Ashkenazi ultra-Orthodox Jews do not eat them, in case they should ferment slightly; the same applies to the *maẓẓah*-and-chocolate layer cake, popular in Israel among all communities at Passover. Lithuanian Jews, even the ultra-Orthodox, eat a fermented beet soup called *risel borsht*. Other Ashkenazim also eat borsht and *khreyn*, a condiment prepared from grated horseradish which is colored with beet juice. Sephardim and North Africans have lamb as the main course at the *seder* meal, and serve stuffed lamb intestines during the week. Among the North Africans, white truffles are considered a Passover delicacy. Sephardim generally do not cook with *matzah* meal but use *matzah* with eggs and in meat dishes. All communities adapt year-round recipes to Passover, substituting in dishes such as pancakes potato flour and or *matzah* meal for flour. Ashkenazi desserts include: cinnamon balls, *teyglekh* (honey cakes), *plava* cake (a sponge cake in which ground almonds replace the flour), coconut cakes, and candies containing carrots, cinnamon, or ginger. Sephardim eat a sponge cake called *bisquitte pané d'Espagne*, and the North Africans, cakes of honey, almonds, and cinnamon, as well as French-style doughnuts (*beignets*) made with *matzah* meal. Among Moroccan Jews a feast is held at the end of Passover called *Maimuna.

Women and Passover Observance

Over the centuries the connection between Jewish women and Passover was largely expressed through their roles in cleaning the homes to meet the stringencies of the holiday and preparing the special *seder* meals. Although women such as Yocheved, mother of Moses; Miriam, Moses's sister and guardian; Pharaoh's daughter, who saved and adopted Moses; and Shifra and Puah, the midwives who risked their lives to save Hebrew infant boys, played important roles in the biblical accounts of the Passover epic, their stories were largely glossed over in the Passover *Haggadah*, the ritual narration of the Exodus from Egypt. However, during the last quarter of the 20th century, particularly in North America, women have taken a broader role in Passover observances, reclaiming Jewish women heroes from history and, together with Jewish men, reconfiguring the *Haggadah* and *seder* experience to be more reflective of women's central contributions to Jewish history and Judaism.

The Passover *seder* provided a framework of expression for many liberation movements during the 1960s and 1970s. Just as African slaves in the United States had sung spirituals such as "Go Down Moses," identifying with the Hebrew slaves in Egypt, in the late 20th century a panoply of groups utilized the format of the *Haggadah* to tell their own stories. The *seder* structure became a vehicle for expressing the yearning for liberation, from the oppression of Egypt to racism, war, gulags, and sexism. Black-Jewish Freedom Seders, a part of the civil rights movement in the United States, gave way to Save Soviet Jewry Freedom Seders in the 1980s. Passover *sedarim* that stressed themes of women's liberation began with a small group of women in 1975. By 2005, thousands of women celebrated feminist *sedarim* annually in synagogues and Jewish community centers around the world, as events separate and apart from their personal *sedarim* with family and friends.

The first feminist *seder* was organized by novelist Esther M. Broner, Marcia Freedman, and Nomi Nimrod in Haifa in 1975. Inspired by this experience, Broner and Nimrod wrote *The Women's Haggadah*, first used in New York and Haifa in 1976. Subsequently a version of this work was published in **Lilith*, the Jewish feminist magazine, making it more widely accessible. *The Women's Haggadah* follows the order of the traditional *seder* but alters the elements to insert the lives of biblical and rabbinic women into the story, to invoke past and current oppression of women, and to enhance the spiritual journey of self-discovery. For example, the list of ten plagues includes violence against women. Subsequently, women throughout the United States organized similar *sedarim*, often composing their own text.

By the 1980s, the Conservative, Reform, and Reconstructionist movements published new *Haggadot*, which made various changes to include women, at least in the English translations. For instance, in the Conservative movement's *Haggadah, Feast of Freedom*, the passage about the four sons is rendered as the "four children," although the Hebrew is not changed. In midrashic sections of the *Haggadah*, alternate rabbinic texts describing the righteousness of Jewish women are included, and in the English translation of the narrative the genders are alternated. The commentary also cites the roles of important women in the story of the Exodus.

Another ritual innovation that began in the same era and became widespread in the United States in the 1990s was to place a cup in honor of Miriam the Prophet on the *seder* table alongside the cup of Elijah. This cup was filled with water, recalling the Midrash that the Israelites had fresh well water during their wanderings in the wilderness thanks to Miriam. Finally, in addition to their traditional activities preparing for the festival, in recent decades women more frequently conduct or co-conduct the *seder* in their own homes. As women have become cantors and rabbis, they often lead public *sedarim*, as well.

See also **Haggadot*, Passover: Feminist Haggadot.

[Rela M. Geffen (2nd ed.)]

In Art

While the Haggadah, by its presence and use, dominates the *seder* table, other manifestations of the artistic impulse are by no means lacking. The table itself is a center of attraction as an object around which to gather and feast. The most important item on the Passover table is the *seder* plate, or a basket. A special Passover plate (*ke'arah*) is mentioned in mishnaic times and throughout history, but no indication of its actual decoration is known in early times. Illuminated medieval *Haggadot* illustrate a large round plate on the table in Ashkenazi ones, and a wicker basket in some Sephardi and Italian manuscripts. A custom of placing the basket on a child's head when reciting **Ha Laḥma* was illustrated in the Barcelona Haggadah (British Museum, Add. Ms. 14761).

Extant *seder* plates from the time of the Renaissance and onward were made of practically every material: wood, copper, brass, pewter, porcelain, faience, stoneware, and plastics. Many of the old simple plates are of pewter because it shines like silver when well kept, cleaned, and polished, and also lends itself easily to engraving. The motif most usually found on these pewter plates is the paschal lamb; another favorite is a five-or six-pointed star in the center. Plates are frequently adorned with scenes from the Passover story: the *seder* meal, the rabbis at Bene-Berak, the four sons, the story of the **Ḥad Gadya*, or the order of the *seder* ceremony. Hebrew inscriptions are another typical and popular decorative scheme. The favorite, usually in the center, consists of the *Kiddush*, or an important citation from the *Haggadah* such as the *Ha Laḥma*. There is often a well-loved psalm or the grace after meals.

The earliest ceramic plates for Passover were probably made in Spain. In the ceramic group, the most important plates were made in the 16th century of majolica in Italian workshops, some by Isaac Cohen Modon. Fourteen such plates are known and were all executed in dark brown, decorated with colored pictures illustrating Passover rituals and figures. There are also blue Delft plates for Passover use inscribed "*Pesaḥdic*" or "*Yontefdic*." An interesting type of *seder* plate is the three-tiered open one, on which the three *matzot* are placed. This type was probably invented in the 18th century, in order to overcome the problem of the *matzot* covering the decorated plate, and the different items placed on top of the *matzot*. Many of these plates, executed in eastern Europe, were made of silver frame and glass tiers. They are round or square, with decorated tops, some with decorative receptacles for the five items. A traditional modern *seder* plate of the same type was made by Ludwig Wolpert of contemporary materials – a silver frame supporting three glass partitions in which the three ceremonial *maẓẓot* are clearly visible. The *maror, ḥaroset*, roast egg, and shankbone, in glass dishes, rest on top of the upper partition.

In addition to the *seder* plate there are wine cups for *Kiddush*, a special cup for the prophet Elijah, and others for drinking the ritual four cups of wine. The most splendid of all cups is reserved for the prophet Elijah. The favorite theme on these vessels is the return of Zion. One features the Messiah entering Jerusalem on a donkey, led by Elijah blowing a ram's horn, while David is playing his harp.

The *seder* has inspired other ceremonial objects of particular artistic quality: a cloth to cover the *maẓẓot*; a towel for drying of the hands after washing; a pillow for the father to lean against; and a white robe for him to wear.

[Abram Kanof]

BIBLIOGRAPHY: P. Goodman, *The Passover Anthology* (1961), incl. bibl.; I. Levy, *A Guide to Passover* (1958); M.M. Kasher, *Haggadah Shelemah* (1967[3]); J.B. Segal, *The Hebrew Passover* (1963); Schauss, *Guide of Jewish Holy Days* (1966[4]), 38–85; T. Gaster, *Passover: Its History and Traditions* (1949); S.J. Zevin, *Ha-Mo'adim ba-Halakhah* (1963[10]), 215–91. CRITICAL VIEW: F. Horst, *Das Privilegrecht Jahres…* (1930), 81ff.; L. Rost, in: ZDPV, 66 (1943), 205–16; J. Jeremias, in: *Theologisches Woerterbuch zum Neuen Testament*, 5 (1954), 895–903; A. Jaubert, *La date de la Cène* (1957); E. Auerbach, in: VT, 8 (1958), 1–18; E. Kutsch, in: *Zeitschrift fuer Theologie und Kirche*, 55 (1958), 1–35; H. Haag, in: *Dictionnaire de la Bible, Suppléments*, 6 (1960), 1120–49; H. Wildberger, *Jahwes Eigentumsvolk* (1960); H.-J. Kraus, *Gottesdienst in Israel…* (19622); J.A. Soggin, in: VT Supplement, 15 (1966), 263–77; P. Grelot, in: VT, 17 (1967), 201–7; A.B. Ehrlich, *Randglossen zur hebraeischen Bibel*, 1 (1968), 312–3. IN THE ARTS: Mayer, Art, index. **ADD. BIBLIOGRAPHY:** E.M. Broner with N. Nimrod, *The Telling* (1993); T.R. Cohen, *The Journey Continues: The Ma'yan Passover Haggadah* (2002); S.C. Anisfeld, T. Mohr, and C. Spector (eds.), *The Women's Passover Companion* (2003); idem, *The Women's Seder Sourcebook* (2003); R.A. Rabbinowicz, (ed.), *Passover Haggadah: The Feast of Freedom* (1982).

PASSOVER, ALEXANDER (1840–1910), Russian jurist. The son of an army surgeon, Passover was born in Uman, Ukraine, and graduated from Moscow University in 1861. He was denied a professorship because of his refusal to renounce Judaism, and became a prosecutor's secretary at the Moscow District Court. Passover was admitted to the Odessa bar in 1871 and after the Odessa pogrom of that year was one of several Jewish lawyers who represented the victims in court proceedings against the perpetrators. From 1874 he practiced in St. Petersburg, where he founded a seminary for law students and where he acquired a reputation as an outstanding jurist and an authority on Russian and foreign law. His advice on civil-law matters was sought by public bodies and his interpretations of judicial rulings in Russian legal journals were sometimes adopted by the Supreme Court. For some years, he sat on the board of the St. Petersburg Bar Association, but resigned in 1889 when the board gave the Ministry of Justice statistics on Jews in the legal profession.

Passover was an active figure in the Jewish community and initiated research projects on the economic situation of the Jews in Russia. He bequeathed his large library, containing a huge amount of anti-Jewish literature, to the St. Petersburg Academy of Sciences.

BIBLIOGRAPHY: S. Ginsburg, *Amolike Peterburg* (1944), 101–10; *Russian Jewry 1860–1917* (1966), index.

[David Bar-Rav-Hay]

PASSOVER, SECOND (Heb. פֶּסַח שֵׁנִי, *Pesaḥ Sheni*), According to the Bible (Num. 9:6–13) every person unable to offer the *Passover sacrifice on the 14th of Nisan because of ritual defilement or because of unavoidable absence from Jerusalem was bound to observe the Passover ritual for one day, one month later, on the 14th of Iyyar. The only biblical reference to the actual observance of the Second Passover is to the time of *Hezekiah, and occurs in II Chronicles 30:1–27. Since the date of the Second Passover falls during the mourning period of the counting of the *Omer and only four days before *Lag ba-Omer, no special ritual is now observed except the omission of the *Taḥanun in the liturgy. Some people eat unleavened bread on Second Passover, as a symbolic remembrance.

PASSOW, AARON HARRY (1920–1996), U.S. educator. Passow's major efforts focused on curriculum appraisal, particularly in programs for the gifted and for the socially disadvantaged. Born in Liberty, New York, he studied at the New York State College for Teachers at Albany, and at Teachers College, Columbia University. He later taught at both universities, and became a professor at the latter. He directed the Talented Youth Project at Columbia (1954–65), which studied programs for the gifted in various parts of the United States. In 1965 he became chairman of the Teachers College Committee on Urban Education and directed a comprehensive study of the Washington, D.C., public schools (1966–67), a major analysis of problems facing public education in an urban depressed area. He served as chair of the Department of Curriculum and Teaching at Columbia's Teachers College (1968–77) and director of the college's Educational Institutes and Programs division (1975–80). He was also president of the World Council on Gifted and Talented Children.

When Passow retired from teaching in 1991, his friends and colleagues at Columbia's Teachers College established the A. Harry Passow Scholarship, which is awarded to the doctoral student with the outstanding certification exam/paper in the Department of Curriculum and Teaching. In addition, the World Council for Gifted and Talented Children grants the A. Harry Passow Leadership Award to an individual who has international stature as a leader in gifted education and has significantly influenced policy and practices in the field.

Passow published *Planning for Talented Youth* (1955); *Secondary Education for All: The English Approach* (1961); *Developing a Curriculum for Modern Living* (1957); *Education of the Gifted* (1958); *Education in Depressed Areas* (1963); together with others, *Education of the Disadvantaged* (1967); *Urban Education in the 1970s* (1971); *Secondary Education Reform* (1976); and *State Policies Regarding Education of the Gifted* (1993).

[Abraham J. Tannenbaum / Ruth Beloff (2nd ed.)]

PASTA (Negri), GUIDITTA (1798–1865), Italian soprano singer. Pasta was born in Saronno, Lombardy, and entered the Milan conservatory at the age of 15 to study under Asiolo, later studying in Paris. Her stage debut in Brescia (1815), and early performances in London (1817, in Cimarosa's *Penelope* and other parts), met with so little favor that she retired to Italy for a further period of study with Scappa. Her "second debut" in Venice (1819) revealed her as a much-matured singer, and her successes steadily mounted, until in Paris in 1821 her gifts as a vivid, gripping powerful actress-singer were the focus of sensational acclaim. From then Pasta was the *Prima donna* of Europe; and although her singing was found imperfect in technique and liable to "off-nights," the two-and-a-half octave range and peculiarly expressive timbre of her voice excited the imaginations of Bellini and Donizetti, both of whom created masterpieces for her (Donizetti's *Anna Bolena*, Milan, 1830; Bellini's *La Sonnambula*, Milan, March 1831; and *Norma*, Milan, December 1831). Pasta has been called "the Callas of her day." She sang regularly in London, Paris, and St. Petersburg until 1837, but thereafter her stage appearances became less frequent, although in 1840, on the offer of a huge fee, she sang for a season in St. Petersburg. Her last London appearances (1850) proved distressing to admirers in that her voice showed signs of exhaustion; critics nevertheless remarked that her acting powers were undiminished. She died at Blevio, near Lake Como.

[Max Loppert]

PASTERNAK, BORIS LEONIDOVICH (1890–1960), Soviet Russian poet and novelist. A son of the painter Leonid *Pasternak, the younger Pasternak ultimately became one of the very few Soviet writers whose work is essentially Christian in spirit. Born and educated in Moscow, he also studied at the University of Marburg, Germany. He is chiefly remembered as one of the truly great Russian poets of all time, his exquisitely polished verse being highly intellectual, erudite, and occasionally obscure. His prose, too, is essentially poetic in nature, emphasizing language, structure, and style. Among Pasternak's favorite subjects are the wholesomeness of nature, the artificiality of man-made ideas, and the futility of ideologies. A recurrent theme is the irrelevance of politics to human happiness, and the inability of truly sensitive and intelligent men to choose sides at times of political upheaval because unquestioning allegiance to any political grouping requires renunciation of one's intellectual and ethical independence and a willingness to condone violence perpetrated in the name of a noble cause. Pasternak's verse collections include *Poverkh baryerov* ("Over the Barriers," 1917, 1931[2]), *Sestra moya – zhizn* ("My Sister – Life," 1922), *Devyatsot pyaty god* ("The Year 1905," 1927), and *Vtoroye rozhdeniye* ("Second Birth," 1932). After World War II he published a number of outstanding translations of world classics, mainly drama.

Pasternak's abhorrence of violence and consequent flight from political realities in search of individual happiness forms the leitmotif of his most famous work, the novel *Doctor Zhivago*, which was smuggled out of the U.S.S.R. and first published in Italy in 1957 (Eng. tr., 1958). The event became a major political, as well as literary, sensation. In 1958 Pasternak was awarded the Nobel Prize for Literature, but the political storm in the U.S.S.R., during which it was suggested that he be expelled from the country, forced him to decline the award. After his death, he was halfheartedly reinstated into the pantheon of Soviet poetry, and some of his verse was reprinted. *Doctor Zhivago*, however, continued to be banned. The novel reveals Pasternak's total estrangement from Judaism and his faith in the superiority of Christianity. The best Soviet appreciation of Pasternak was written by Andrei Sinyavsky (see Yuli *Daniel).

BIBLIOGRAPHY: P.S.R. Payne, *The Three Worlds of Boris Pasternak* (1962), incl. bibl.; G. Ruge, *Pasternak: a Pictorial Biography* (1959); G.R.A. Conquest, *The Pasternak Affair; Courage of a Genius; a Documentary Report* (1962); J. Stora, in: *Cahiers du Monde Russe et Soviétique* (July–Dec., 1968), 353–64.

[Maurice Friedberg]

PASTERNAK, JOSEPH (1901–1991), U.S. film producer. Pasternak, who was born in Szilagy-Somlyo, Hungary, immigrated to the United States in 1921, and two years later began working in films. By the end of the 1920s he was a producer for Universal Pictures in Central Europe. From 1936 he produced more than 100 films in the United States, always light comedy musicals. These include *Three Smart Girls* (Oscar nomination for Best Picture, 1936) with Deanna Durbin – the first of 10 films she made for Pasternak, including *100 Men and a Girl* (Oscar nomination for Best Picture, 1937) and *It Started with Eve* (1941); movies that starred Mario Lanza; *Destry Rides Again*, with Marlene Dietrich (1939); *Anchors Aweigh*, with Frank Sinatra and Gene Kelly (Oscar nomination for Best Picture, 1945); *In the Good Old Summertime*, with Judy Garland (1949); *The Merry Widow*, with Lana Turner (1952); *Love Me or Leave Me*, with Doris Day and James Cagney (1955); *Ten Thousand Bedrooms*, with Dean Martin (1957); *Ask Any Girl*, with Shirley Maclaine (1959); *Please Don't Eat the Daisies*, with Doris Day (1960); *Where the Boys Are*, with George Hamilton (1960); *The Courtship of Eddie's Father*, with Glenn Ford (1963); *Girl Happy* (1965) and *Spinout*, with Elvis Presley (1966); *Penelope*, with Natalie Wood (1966); and *The Sweet Ride*, with Jacqueline Bisset (1968).

Pasternak wrote an autobiography, *Easy the Hard Way* (1956), and a cookbook, *Cooking with Love and Paprika* (1966).

[Ruth Beloff (2nd ed.)]

PASTERNAK, LEONID OSIPOVICH (1862–1945), Russian artist. Born in Odessa, Pasternak studied medicine in Moscow, but in 1883 went to Munich to enroll at the Academy of Art. Returning to Odessa, he did a full year's military service, then met and married the pianist Rosa Kaufmann. In 1888 his first large canvas, *Letter from Home*, was bought by the Tretyakov Gallery, Moscow. The Pasternaks moved to Moscow, where he opened a school of painting, edited a periodical, *The Artist*, and for some years taught at the Moscow School of Painting, Sculpture, and Architecture. He was a close friend of Leo Tolstoy, whom he often portrayed. His illustrations for Tolstoy's *Resurrection* were exhibited at the Paris World Exhibition, 1900. In 1921 Pasternak, with his wife, went to Paris, and in 1938 immigrated to England, spending his last years in Oxford. Pasternak was at his best not as an oil painter but as a draftsman, whose portrait studies superbly catch the sitter's character. He painted portraits of outstanding Zionists, among them *Bialik, *Sokolow, *Tchernichowsky, and *Weizmann. In 1924 he visited Palestine, where he made drawings and watercolors of the countryside. He was the father of the poet and novelist Boris *Pasternak.

BIBLIOGRAPHY: Russell, in: *Studio*, 161 (1961), 98–101; Bialik, in: *Saturday Review* (April 4, 1959), 18–21.

[Alfred Werner]

PASTOUREAUX ("Shepherds"), the name given to the participants in two popular Crusades in France called against the Muslims in Spain. The first movement emerged in Picardy in 1251, inspired by a leader who called himself the "ruler of Hungary." Claiming to have had a vision in which the Virgin Mary ordered him to take up the cross, he rapidly gathered 30,000 adherents, mainly young men and women, who marched toward the south. This group of Pastoureaux did not attack the Jews until they arrived in Bourges: there they broke into synagogues, destroyed books, and robbed the Jews. At Bordeaux they were turned back by the seneschal of Gascony and dispersed.

A similar movement arose in the southwest in 1320. Jewish chroniclers (Solomon *Ibn Verga, Joseph *ha-Kohen, and Samuel *Usque) telescoped these two movements by attributing to the second the beginnings of the first. This time the religious aim of waging war against the Muslims in Spain was accompanied by a social revolt against the rich and the higher clergy. Thus, the civil and religious authorities swiftly intervened against the crusaders, and *Philip V the Tall and Pope *John XXII called on them to protect the Jews. In fact, the Pastoureaux turned first against the Jews, intending to use their riches to purchase weapons; they also put to death those Jews who refused to accept baptism. The anti-Jewish persecutions first began in *Agen or Agenais, *Bordeaux or Bourdeilles, *Gascony and Bigorre, Mont-de-Marsan and Condom, Auch, Rabastens, Gaillac, *Albi, Lezat, and especially Verdun-sur-Garonne and *Castelsarrasin, where several hundreds of Jews were killed or committed suicide. The events at *Toulouse were reported by an eyewitness, the German Jew Baruch, who was employed as a teacher by the local Jewish community. The viscount of Toulouse, who had been informed of the massacre perpetrated by the Pastoureaux in Castelsarrasin and the neighboring localities between June 10 and 12, set out at the head of an armed detachment in order to check their advance. He returned with 24 cartloads of Pastoureaux, intending to imprison them in a castle of the town, but the populace came to their assistance and released them. At once they invaded the Jewish quarter, looting the houses and putting to death anyone who refused baptism. When they marched toward *Carcassone, extremely severe repressive measures were taken against them. A number succeeded in reaching Aragon, where they persecuted the Jews anew, particularly in *Montclus. King James II of *Aragon ordered the suppression of the Pastoureaux, and on this occasion many of them were slaughtered.

According to Jewish chroniclers, 120 communities suffered at the hands of the Pastoureaux, and this appears to be an accurate estimate. Baruch also relates that although the pope called upon the authorities to protect the Jews, the Inquisition would not allow those who had been forcibly baptized to return to Judaism.

BIBLIOGRAPHY: C. de Vic and J.J. Vaissete, *Histoire générale de Languedoc...* (1730), passim; S. Grayzel, in: HJ, 17 (1955), 89–120; J. Duvernoy (ed.), *Registre d'inquisition de Jacques Fournier, évêque de Pamiers* (1965).

[Bernhard Blumenkranz]

PAT, JACOB (1890–1966), Jewish labor leader, teacher, author, and journalist. Pat was born in *Bialystok into a working-class family, was an outstanding student in the *Musar yeshivot, and joined the Zionist socialist circles of his native town on the eve of the 1905 revolution. He was a member of the *Zionist-Socialist Workers' Party and from 1917 of the *United Jewish Socialist Workers' Party. In 1920 he joined the Bund and at first adhered to its left wing. He began his pedagogic career as a Hebrew teacher and was later headmaster of several schools, as well as an active proponent of Yiddish culture. After World War I he acted as secretary of the Democratic Jewish Community of Bialystok. From 1921 to 1939 he lived in Warsaw. He served as secretary of the center of the Yiddish school network (CYSHO; 1921–29). He was a recognized spokesman of the Bund and in 1929 he became a member of the editorial board of its daily organ *Folkstsaytung*. Pat was also a member of the Jewish community council of Warsaw. On the eve of World War II he arrived in the United States as a member of the Bund delegation, and remained there. He was a member of the body representing the Polish Bund in the U.S. until its dissolution (1947), but his main activity was within the *Jewish Labor Committee, of which he was the general secretary until 1963. Though formerly an outspoken anti-Zionist, Pat headed the new trend in the Bund which called for a change in the attitude toward the Jewish state in Palestine, even before its establishment. He was an ardent orator and a versatile lecturer. He began to write Hebrew novels in 1905, later changing to Yiddish, and he was a prolific author and publicist who dealt with a wide range of subjects. In the United States Pat was co-editor of the monthly *Zukunft*. His writings include *Bundistn* 1–2 (1926–29) and *Ashes and Fire* (1947).

BIBLIOGRAPHY: I.S. Hertz (ed.), *Doyres Bundistn*, 3 (1968), 61–65.

[Moshe Mishkinsky]

PATAI, JÓZSEF (1882–1953), Hungarian and Hebrew poet, translator, and editor. Patai, who was born in Gyöngyöspata, taught at a Budapest municipal high school (1908–19).

He published a Hebrew verse collection, *Sha'ashu'ei Alumim* ("The Pleasures of Youth," 1902), and two anthologies of Hungarian poetry *Babilon vizein* ("By the Waters of Babylon," 1906) and *Sulamit látod a lángot?* ("Shulamit, Do You See the Flame?" 1919). A selection of his poems also appeared in English (1920). He published Hungarian versions of the Hebrew poetry of many eras, his translations eventually appearing in five volumes entitled *Héber költők* ("Hebrew Poets," 1910–12;

1921²). Three of his most important works were his volume of early recollections, *A középső kapu* ("The Middle Gate," 1927); *A föltámadó Szentföld* ("The Holy Land Restored," 1926), on his first visit to Palestine; and his biography of Theodor *Herzl (1931; *Star over Jordan*, 1946).

Patai also distinguished himself as editor of the Zionist monthly *Mult és Jövő*, which he founded in 1912 and edited for 27 years. By publishing good translations of major Jewish writers from many countries, he imbued Hungarian Jewish intellectuals with an appreciation for Jewish literature, art, and thought. Patai also combated the anti-Zionists, he and some associates founding the Magyar Zsidók Pro Palestina Szövetsége ("League of Hungarian Jews for Palestine"), and organizing annual pilgrimages to Ereẓ Israel.

In 1938 Patai emigrated to Palestine. At first he lived in Jerusalem but later settled in Givatayim. His subsequent publications include the three-volume selection of his writings *Mivḥar Kitvei Yosef Patai* (1943); and a volume based on his lectures at the Hebrew University (*Mi-Sefunei ha-Shirah*, 1939). His son, Raphael *Patai translated two of his works into English: *The Middle Gate: A Hungarian Jewish Boyhood* (1994) and *Souls and Secrets: Hasidic Stories* (1995).

His wife, EDITH (Ehrenfeld) PATAI (1889–1976), author and lyric poet, wrote works of Jewish and Zionist inspiration, notably *Engem is hiv a föld* ("The Land Calls Me Too," 1927) and a novel, *Szent szomjúság* ("Sacred Thirst," 1936). His sons were the folklore authority Raphael Patai, and Shaul Patai (1918–), professor of chemistry at the Hebrew University of Jerusalem.

BIBLIOGRAPHY: *Magyar Irodalmi Lexikon*, 2 (1965), 448–9; I. Pap, *Patai Edith, a költő* (1936).

[Baruch Yaron]

PATAI, RAPHAEL (1910–1996), anthropologist, biblical scholar, and editor. A son of József *Patai, he was born in Budapest, Hungary. In 1933 he settled in Palestine, where he was awarded the first Ph.D. degree of the Hebrew University in 1936. Returning to Budapest for a brief period, he was ordained at the rabbinical seminary. In 1938 Patai became an instructor in Hebrew at the Hebrew University. In 1942–43 he served as academic secretary of the Haifa Technion. In 1944 Patai founded the Palestine Institute of Folklore and Ethnology in Jerusalem and served as its director of research until 1948. In 1945 he launched and edited the journal of the institute, *Edoth (Communities); a Quarterly of Folklore and Ethnology*. In 1949 he began editing a series of books for the institute entitled *Studies in Folklore and Ethnology* (5 vols.) and another series *Social Studies* (2 vols.).

In 1947 he went to the U.S. and in 1948–57 was professor of anthropology at Dropsie College. From 1966 to 1976 he was professor of anthropology at Fairleigh Dickinson University, Rutherford, New Jersey. During 1956–68 Patai served as president of the American Friends of Tel Aviv University in New York. In 1956 he became director of research of the Herzl Institute, New York, and from 1957 also editor of the Herzl Press.

His main contribution to scholarship resides in two fields – the culture of the ancient Hebrews and Jews and that of the modern Middle East including Israel.

He published several hundred articles and more than two dozen books, among them: *Ha-Mayim* (A Study in Palestinology and Palestinian Folklore, 1936); *Ha-Sappanut ha-Ivrit* ("Jewish Seafaring in Ancient Times,, 1938); *Man and Earth in Hebrew Custom, Belief and Legend* (2 vols., 1942–43); *Madda ha-Adam* ("An Introduction to Anthropology," 2 vols., 1947–48); *Man and Temple in Ancient Jewish Myth and Ritual* (1947, 1967²); *Israel Between East and West* (1953, 1970²); *Sex and Family in the Bible and the Middle East* (1959); *Golden River to Golden Road: Society, Culture and Change in the Middle East* (1962, 1967, 1969, 1971); *Hebrew Myths* (with Robert Graves, 1964); and *The Hebrew Goddess* (1967). Subsequent works include: *The Arab Mind* (1973); *The Jewish Mind* (1977); *The Vanished Worlds of Jewry* (1980); *The Seed of Abraham: Jews and Arabs in Contact and Conflict* (1986); *Between Budapest and Jerusalem* (1992); *The Jewish Alchemists: A History and Source Book* (1994); and *The Jews of Hungary* (1995).

Patai also edited a number of important publications, such as: *The Republic of Syria* (2 vols., 1956); *The Republic of Lebanon* (2 vols., 1956); *The Kingdom of Jordan* (1956⁸); *Herzl Year Book* (1958-65); *The Complete Diaries of Theodor Herzl* (5 vols., 1960); *Studies in Biblical and Jewish Folklore* (with Francis Lee Utley and Dov Noy, 1960); *Women in the Modern World* (1967); and *Encyclopedia of Zionism and Israel* (2 vols., 1971).

[Tovia Preschel/Rohan Saxena (2nd ed.)]

PATERSON, city in N.E. New Jersey. Jews first settled in Paterson in the early 1840s. In 1904 there were 1,250 Jews in the city, and the Jewish population increased to about 35,000 in the late 1940s. However, by 1960 the number declined to 15,000. By 2000, the Jewish population of Paterson declined to less than 1,000 – with approximately 30,000 Jews living in the surrounding communities of Wayne, Fair Lawn, Franklin Lakes, Wyckoff, Oakland, Pompton Lakes, Glen Rock, and Ridgewood. Jewish settlers of the 1840s came from Germany, Bohemia, and Hungary. They were primarily tailors and merchants. In 1847 a group of them organized Congregation B'nai Jeshurun, becoming the first Jewish congregation in New Jersey. In the late 1870s Congregation B'nai Jeshurun gradually changed from a traditional Orthodox synagogue to a more liberal Reform congregation. An Orthodox group was to maintain a daily minyan on a lower level through their years in Paterson. In 1894 a new large, impressive synagogue was built on the corner of Broadway and Straight Street due to the generosity of Nathan *Barnert, a Jewish philanthropist, who served as mayor of Paterson from 1883 to 1886 and was re-elected in 1889. A bronze statue at the Paterson City Hall Plaza was dedicated in his honor in 1925. Barnert, who also served two terms as alderman in the 1870s, was later to establish the Miriam Barnert Hebrew Free School, the Nathan and Miriam Barnert Hospital and the Barnert Home for Orphans and the Aged.

In 1886 the Russian and Polish Jews who had migrated to Paterson in the early 1880s did not wish to affiliate with Congregation B'nai Jeshurun because of this synagogue's trend toward Reform Judaism. They organized their own congregation, Congregation B'nai Israel. Another large and impressive synagogue was built on Godwin Street, becoming known as the Big Shul. Romanian Jews established Ahavath Joseph Congregation, known as the Little Shul, a block away on Godwin Street in the early 1900s. The Lubavitch founded the United Brotherhood Anshai Lodz or Polish Shul on Fair Street in the early 1900s. In 1907 a Conservative synagogue, Congregation Emanuel, was dedicated on Van Houten Street, moving to Broadway and East 33rd Street in 1929. Congregation Ohav Sholom, another Orthodox shul, was founded about 1915. The Water Street Shul was organized and built on the North West side of the Passaic River. Paterson also maintained a *mikveh* on Paterson Street. Even with this growth in Jewish life, there was growing antagonism towards Jews and other "new immigrants" at this time. Newspaper editorials clearly indicated that undesirable Europeans were those from southern and Eastern Europe, including the Jews then beginning to arrive from Russia and Poland. These Jewish immigrants, who had fled the Russian pogroms, especially those in the Polish textile centers of Lodz and Bialystok in 1905 and 1906, were attracted to the "Silk City" of Paterson. A sampling of Russian Jews in Paterson reported by the U.S. Immigration Commission in 1911 indicated that more than 91% had worked in textile mills prior to coming to the United States. Gradually the new Jewish immigrants moved into a troubled silk industry. New and improved machinery had made it possible for employers to replace skilled, expensive English, German, and Irish labor with less skilled and cheaper Jewish, Italian, and other "new immigrant" labor, creating antisemitic feeling in the city. The exposure of Jewish workers to radical ideas, labor organizations, and strikes in Europe helped to continue Paterson's long tradition of labor troubles. Close to 5,000 Jews worked in the silk industry in 1913. When a bitter strike erupted that year, the Jewish textile workers joined other ethnic workers to fight against the four-loom system, the fine system, and the blacklist. As labor difficulties continued even after the strike, many silk manufacturers moved their factories to Pennsylvania coal-mining towns and to the South. Many Jews acquired machinery during the 1920s and opened small shops often with only one or two employees. During the 1920s, as many as 90% of the silk-manufacturing shops in Paterson were operated by Polish Jews. Competition was intense, and few shops prospered. By the end of World War II the silk industry in Paterson had virtually disappeared, while the city's other important sources of employment and economic activity, in addition to manufacturing, retail, and wholesale establishments, began a period of stagnation.

After 1940, the city's suburbs, Clifton to the south, Fair Lawn to the east, and Wayne to the west, grew substantially, as did their Jewish populations. The number of Jewish congregations in Paterson declined after 1945. In 2005, the last remaining synagogue in Paterson – Temple Emanuel – was preparing to move to Franklin Lakes, the present home of Barnert Temple-Congregation B'nai Jeshurun. The only Jewish presence remaining in Paterson would be the yeshiva on Park Avenue and the Jewish Federation Apartments.

Distinguished Jewish residents, or former residents of Paterson, include United States Senator Frank *Lautenberg, who served in the Senate from 1982 to 2000 and was elected to a fourth term in 2002; father-and-son poets Louis and Allen *Ginsberg; former Democratic Congressman Charles S. Joelson, who served as a judge of the Superior Court of New Jersey; Jacob Fabian, theater mogul in the 1920s whose generous philanthropy made it possible to build the magnificent and historic Temple Emanuel sanctuary; and Henry and Joe Taub, founders of Automatic Data Processing (ADP). Henry Taub was the president of the American Jewish Joint Distribution Committee.

Passaic County Jewish Organizational Life

Yavneh Academy was founded in 1942 as the Paterson Yavneh Yeshiva. It started with six children in its kindergarten. In 1954, it erected a school in Paterson and later moved to Paramus in 1981. A Workmen's Circle Children's school, also called the "Shula," opened in Paterson in 1921. The Gerrard Berman Day School: Solomon Schechter of North Jersey opened in Pompton Lakes in 1985 and moved to its current Oakland location in 1993. In 1906 a small group of young women who met regularly at the Barnert Hebrew Free School came together to form the YWHA. In 1914 the YMHA was incorporated and five years later it moved to Orpheus Hall on Broadway. In 1976 the YM-YWHA of North Jersey opened in Wayne to serve the cultural, social, educational, health, and physical recreation needs of the suburban Passaic County Jewish community. In the 1970s Wayne became a major hub of Jewish life for suburban Passaic. It had three synagogues – Congregation Shomrei Torah, Temple Beth Tikvah, and the Chabad Center of Passaic County. The Jewish Federation of North Jersey was evolved from the Jewish Community Council of Paterson, founded in 1933 to coordinate the work of various organizations in their local and national fund-raising campaigns. In 2004, the Federation merged with the UJA Federation of Bergen County & North Hudson to form the UJA Federation of Northern New Jersey. In 1944 the Jewish Social Service Bureau of Paterson was formed to oversee the welfare of homeless Jewish children. This agency was later to become Jewish Family and Children's Service. Daughters of Miriam Home for Orphans and the Aged first opened in 1921 in Paterson as an orphanage and elderly shelter. In 1926 it moved to its current location in Clifton and became strictly a nursing home in the 1950s.

[Alan J.Grossman (2nd ed.)]

BIBLIOGRAPHY: Jewish Historical Society of North Jersey, *Our Paterson Jewish Heritage* (1987); W.N. Jamison, *Religion in New Jersey* (1964); R.J. Vecoli, *People of New Jersey* (1965); U.S. Immigration Commission, *Immigrants in Industries*, Pt. 5: Silk Goods… (1911); W. Nelson and C.A. Shriner, *History of Paterson and Its Environs*, 3 vols. (1920); J. Haberman, *Jews in New Jersey* (Ms. Rutgers University); M.W. Garber, "Silk Industry of Paterson New Jersey" (1968; unpublished Ph.D. dissertation, Rutgers University); J. Nathans, "The World of the Jewish Historical Society of North Jersey," unpublished address (2002).

PATHROS (Heb. פַּתְרוֹס), region mentioned five times in the Bible (Isa. 11:11; Jer. 44:1, 15; Ezek. 29:14; 30:14), either in connection with *Miẓrayim or with a city of Lower Egypt (Nof = Memphis or *Zoan = Tanis). The name is derived, like the Greek Παθουρης, Φαθωρης (LXX, Jer. 51:1, 15; Ezek. 29:14; 30:14), from the Egyptian expression *pa to resy* ("the Southern Land"), i.e., Upper Egypt. In the Bible, Pathros is named as a region where Jewish communities existed, both before and after the fall of Jerusalem in 587. According to Ezekiel 29:14, Pathros is considered the original home of the Egyptians.

BIBLIOGRAPHY: A. Erman, in: ZAW, 10 (1890), 118–9; G. Steindorf, in: *Beitraege zur Assyriologie und semitischer Sprachwissenschaft*, 1 (1890), 344.

[Alan Richard Schulman]

PATINKIN, DON (Dan) (1922–1995), Israel economist and educator. He was born in Chicago and after teaching at the University of Chicago (1947–48) and at the University of Illinois (1948–49), he settled in Israel in 1949 and began teaching at the Hebrew University in Jerusalem (full professor, 1957). In 1956 he became director of research at the Falk Institute for Economic Research in Israel. From 1982 to 1986 he was rector of the Hebrew University of Jerusalem and its president 1988–89. Patinkin's principal fields of interest were the theory of money, monetary influences on an economy, and the general economic development of the State of Israel. He wrote *Keynesian Economics and the Quantity Theory* (1954), *Money, Interest and Prices* (1956, 1965[2]), *The Israel Economy: The First Decade* (1959), and *On the Nature of the Monetary Mechanism* (1967). In 1970 he was awarded the Israel Prize in economics.

PATINKIN, MANDY (1952–), U.S. actor and singer. Born in Chicago, Patinkin attended the Julliard School of Drama and then performed in regional theater before appearing in New York in Shakespeare Festival productions. He rose to prominence with his Tony Award-winning portrayal of Che Guevara in the musical *Evita* (1980) and later starred in Stephen Sondheim's musical *Sunday in the Park with George* (Tony nomination, 1984). Other Broadway roles include *The Shadow Box* (1977); *The Secret Garden* (1991); *Falsettos* (1992); *Mandy Patinkin in Concert: Mamaloshen* (1998); *The Wild Party* (Tony nomination, 2000); and *Celebrating Sondheim* (2002).

In 1995 he joined the cast of the television series *Chicago Hope* and won an Emmy Award for Best Actor in a Dramatic Role. He starred in the TV movies *Sunday in the Park with George* (1986), *Broken Glass* (1996), *The Hunchback* (1997), and *Strange Justice* (1999), and was a regular on the TV series *Dead Like Me* (2003–4).

Patinkin has appeared in films including *The Big Fix* (1978), *Night of the Juggler* (1980), *Ragtime* (1981), *Daniel* (1983), *Yentl* (1983), *Maxie* (1985), *The Princess Bride* (1987), *Alien Nation* (1988), *The House on Carroll Street* (1988), *Dick Tracy* (1990), *True Colors* (1991), *Impromptu* (1991), *The Doctor* (1991), *The Music of Chance* (1993), and *Lulu on the Bridge* (1998).

His mother wrote two cookbooks: *Grandma Doralee Patinkin's Jewish Family Cookbook* (1997) and *Grandma Doralee Patinkin's Jewish Holiday Cookbook* (1999).

[Jonathan Licht / Ruth Beloff (2nd ed.)]

PATKIN, MAX ("The Clown Prince of Baseball"; 1920–1999), U.S. baseball player and entertainer, known for his goofy antics as a rubber-necked, double-jointed comic genius in a career that spanned 50 years. Born in Philadelphia, Patkin was a minor league pitcher before an arm injury curtailed his career. Patkin then joined the Navy during World War II, and began clowning around in lopsided games while in the service. One day while stationed in Hawaii in 1944, Joe DiMaggio homered off Patkin, and in mock anger, Patkin threw his glove down and chased DiMaggio around the bases, much to the delight of the fans. Thus a career in show business was born. Patkin, successor to Al *Schacht as the second Clown Prince of Baseball, was hired as a comic coach by Bill Veeck, owner of the Cleveland Indians and later the St. Louis Browns, to boost the attendance of his teams. Patkin also began performing his celebrated slapstick and pantomime routines at minor league games across the U.S., Canada, Puerto Rico, and Mexico. With his rubbery face transformed into dozens of shapes, an oversize nose, a 6′3″ rail-thin body inside an oversized uniform – Veeck said that Patkin was put together by someone who couldn't read the instructions very well – a question mark on the back of his uniform in place of a number, and a ballcap that he wore sideways, Patkin was tailor-made for clowning. He became even more famous after he starred as himself in the movie classic *Bull Durham* (1988). Patkin estimated that he performed more than 4,000 times – never missing a game between 1946 and 1993 – and played to as many as 75,000 fans in Cleveland and as few as four in Great Falls, Montana, on the night Neil Armstrong stepped onto the moon. Patkin retired from clowning on August 19, 1995, and his trademark uniform and cap were donated to the Baseball Hall of Fame. Patkin published his autobiography, *The Clown Prince of Baseball*, in 1994.

[Elli Wohlgelernter (2nd ed.)]

PATRAS, port city in N. Peloponnesus, Greece. There were Jews living in Patras in ancient times, as can be assumed from the Hebrew inscriptions found in the local church of St. Anastasius; *Benjamin of Tudela reported the presence of 50 Jews there in the 12th century. Under Byzantine rule the Jews owned land and farms. When the Venetians conquered the town in

1532, they took Jewish prisoners whom they sold as slaves in Italy. Sailors from Naples and Sicily, who attacked Patras in 1595, plundered and murdered Jews. Already in the 16th century there were four synagogues in the city, one Ashkenazi and three Sephardi (two were Sicilian and one was of Iberian origin). Many noted scholars lived there: Moses Alashkar (d. after 1535), author of responsa; Shem Tov b. Jacob Melammed, author of *Keter Shem Tov* and *Ma'amar Mordechai;* David Vital, author of *Mikhtam le-David* and *Keter Torah*; Jacob ha-Levi (d. 1636), author of responsa; Meir Melammed, author of *Mishpetei Ẓedek*; and others. Mordecai Ẓevi, father of false messiah Shabbetai Ẓevi, is noted as originating in Patras before moving to Izmir. In the 17th century, during the Turko-Venetian War, when the Venetians captured the city in 1647, the Jews fled the town. Many fell into slavery and were redeemed by the Jewish communities of Italy and Amsterdam. However, a small number of Jews returned to Patras. In the fighting in 1684, Jews fled the city and many reached Larissa. Others fell into slavery and were redeemed by the Jewish communities of Salonika, Italy, and western Europe. Returning in 1715 when Turkish rule was re-established, Jewish merchants integrated into local trade, and with the development of the port they traded with Venice, and Holland. Jewish silk merchants from Patras traveled as far as Persia for their purchases. In the Russian-Turkish War of 1770, the Greek-Orthodox persecuted the Jews, but in the fighting the Ottoman Turkish soldiers barely distinguished between the Jews and the Greek-Orthodox, and almost destroyed the Jewish community. In 1809, the Jews were a small fraction of the population, but nonetheless had an important role in local commerce. The Jewish community ceased to exist at the time of the Greek Revolution (1821–29). The 17 families that were left in the city at the end of the Ottoman Period had fled to Larissa, Chalkis, and Corfu at the onset of the fighting and disturbances. When the Greek government was formed in 1832, Patras became a center for the Jews, attracting them from Zakynthos, Arta, Preveza, and mainly Corfu. In the Greek-Turkish War of 1881, the community temporarily disbanded and fled, but soon returned to the city. At the end of the 19th century, the Greek historian Thomopoulos accused the Jews of dishonesty in their profession as moneylenders and accused them of being responsible for plagues. In 1902, the community consisted of some 15–20 poor families of peddlers. In 1905 the Jewish community was officially recognized by the Greek government. In 1923 there were 40 to 50 Jews living in the town, most of them merchants or commission agents. In late 1943–early 1944, 242 Jews fled from the town in order to escape the Nazis; others were deported when, on March 28, 1944, the Germans apprehended 12 families who had not managed to hide. The city itself, as well as the region, was a place for hiding Jews fleeing from arrest by the Germans in Salonika and Athens. Several Jews from Patras joined the partisans. Vito Belleli was executed by the Germans after being caught as a partisan. In 1946, there were 122 Jews in the city; most were dependent on financial help from the Joint Distribution Committee. In 1948 there were 150 Jews in Patras, by 1958 their number had dwindled to 37, and 19 Jews were registered in 1967. Most of the Jews left for Athens, Israel, and the United States. By the late 1970s, only five families remained in the city. The synagogue was destroyed in 1980, and the remnants of its interior were eventually displayed in the Jewish Museum in Athens.

BIBLIOGRAPHY: J. Starr, *Jews in the Byzantine Empire* (1939), 229; idem, *Romania* (1949), 73–76; J. Nehama, *In Memoriam*, ed. by M. Molho, 2 (1949), 57, 164; M. Molho and J. Nehama, *Sho'at Yehudei Yavan* (1965), index. **ADD. BIBLIOGRAPHY:** B. Rivlin and L. Bornstein-Makovetsky, "Patras," in: *Pinkas Kehillot Yavan* (1999), 310–18.

[Simon Marcus / Yitzchak Kerem (2nd ed.)]

PATRIA, ship bearing "illegal" Jewish immigrants to Palestine which sank in Haifa Bay. Early in November 1940, the steamers *Milos* and *Pacific*, together carrying 1,771 Jewish refugees from Central Europe, arrived in Haifa (see: *Immigration, "Illegal"). The passengers were transferred on board the 12,000-ton French liner, *Patria*, which had been chartered by the British, to be deported to the island of *Mauritius, by order of the British Mandatory government in accordance with the Defense Regulations (Entry Prohibition; 1940). They were not to be permitted entry to Palestine at any time. On the morning of November 25, when the transshipment of the passengers of the *Atlantic* – another ship with about 1,800 "illegal" immigrants – was in progress and some 130 of them were already on the *Patria*, the ship blew up and sank within 15 minutes inside Haifa Bay with a loss of life of about 260 persons; the number of bodies finally recovered was 209. This disaster was caused by the ignition of explosives brought aboard in an attempt to sabotage the engines and thus prevent the deportation. The survivors of the *Patria* were permitted to remain in Palestine and were interned for some time at the detention camp at *Athlit. They were released by groups in the course of 1941. However, the remaining passengers of the *Atlantic*, about 1,600 persons, mostly from Austria, Czechoslovakia, and Poland, were deported to Mauritius and interned there until August 1945.

BIBLIOGRAPHY: M.M. Mardov, *Strictly Illegal* (1964) 56–83; B. Ḥabas, *Gate Breakers* (1963), 126–49; G.E. Steiner, *Patria* (Heb., 1964); Yad Vashem, *Ha-Sho'ah ve-ha-Gevurah be-Aspaklaryah shel ha-Ittonut ha-Ivrit*, 2 (1966), 11842–884.

[Aharon Zwergbaum]

PATRIARCHS, THE, the founding fathers of the people of Israel, *Abraham, *Isaac, and *Jacob.

History and Use of the Term

IV Maccabees 7:19 refers to "our patriarchs, Abraham, Isaac, and Jacob," but the same work (16:25) also speaks of, "Abraham and Isaac and Jacob and all the patriarchs." (The New Testament applies the term to Abraham (Heb. 7:4), to the 12 sons of Jacob, and to David (Acts 7:8–9 and 2:29).) However, the rabbinic restriction of the designation to Abraham, Isaac, and Jacob (Ber. 16b) follows the biblical Hebrew pattern which frequently features this triad and never extends it to include others.

The development of the concept may be traced through the *Genesis narratives (28:13; 32:9) to its first usage in Exodus 2:24. The Hebrew term *ha-avot* in its absolute form, meaning "the [three] fathers," par excellence, is never used in the Hebrew Bible, only the possessive suffixed form, either in conjunction with the three names (Deut. 1:8; 6:10; 9:5; 29:12; 30:20; I Chron. 29:18. Not quite analogous is the usage in Ex. 3:6, 15, 16; 4:5), or alone in unambiguous reference to the Divine promises (Deut. 1:21, 35 and passim 26 times; Ex. 13:5, 11; Num. 14:23; Josh. 1:6; 5:6; 21:41; Judg. 2:1; Jer. 11:5; 32:22; Ezek. 20:42; 47:14). In fact, mention of the patriarchs in the Bible is predominantly in this connection.

The Chronological Background

The joint lifetimes of the three patriarchs cover a period of just over 300 years (Gen. 21:5; 25:26; 47:28). However, in the absence of external synchronistic controls, their place within the framework of history was formerly sought relative to the date of the Exodus and the duration of the Egyptian slavery. But given that both of these are now thought by most scholars not to be historical events, it is more productive to examine the individual tales of the patriarchs to determine when each might have been written and for what purpose. (For current thinking on the historicity of the Patriarchal Period see *Genesis, *History, Beginning.) In general, the patriarchs and their activities are reflections of life in later Israel projected backward into ancient times.

The Mesopotamian Background

One of the peculiarities of the patriarchal narratives is the consistent association with *Mesopotamia. The family originated in Ur (Gen. 11:28; 15:7; Neh. 9:7; cf. Josh. 24:2–3), then moved to Haran in the north (Gen. 11:31). Abraham found a wife for Isaac there (24:4ff.) and Jacob fled there from Esau's wrath (28:2, 10). He spent a good part of his adult life there and all the tribes except Benjamin originated in that area. This association ends abruptly with Jacob.

The Onomasticon

The patriarchs are descended from Shem son of Noah through the line of Eber (Gen. 10:21–32; 11:10–32). Of 38 names connected with the family, 27 never recur in the Bible. A large number conform to the onomastic patterns common to the Western Semites during the first half of the second millennium B.C.E. and later. Of special interest is the identity of the personal names, Peleg (10:25; 11:16–19), Serug (11:20–23), Nahor (11:22–27; 24:10), and Terah (11:24–32), with place names in the vicinity of *Haran, mentioned as early as the *Mari and Kultepe texts. Haran shows a high degree of aramaization in the eighth to seventh centuries (Dion., CANE II, 1284), reflected in the importance of this area and its Aramean connections in Genesis.

Patriarchal Society

Given that the patriarchal narratives were composed over centuries, they vary in their depictions of the patriarchs in society. Sometimes the patriarchs are shown as ass-nomads (Gen. 12:16; 22:3, 5), constantly on the move, primarily raisers of sheep and cattle (12:16; et al.), and, as such, restricted in the scope of their wanderings (33:13). Other traditions refer to large numbers of camels (Gen. 12:16; 24:10). They are tent-dwellers (12:8, et al.), but their travels take place between great urban centers into which they rarely venture. These peregrinations are confined to sites in the sparsely populated central hill country and the Negev, viz., Shechem, Beth-El, Hebron, Beer-Sheba, Gerar, and, in the case of Jacob, also central Gilead. Some traditions picture the patriarchs in the first stages of agriculture (26:12; cf. 37:7). Grave traditions associate them with the cave of Machpelah in Hebron (49:29–30; 50:13). There are also traditions of the patriarchs as warriors. Abram the noble warrior in Genesis 14 (Muffs) commands a professional fighting force, which successfully defeats an international invading army. Jacob boasts of having taken land from the Amorites with his sword and bow (Gen. 48:22).

Sometimes the contacts of the patriarchs with their neighbors are peaceful. They make pacts with them (14:13; 21:22–32; 26:28–31) and purchase land from them (23:2–30; 33:19). In another account, though (Genesis 34), Jacob's family wipes out a city of *Hivites. The closeness of the patriarchs with the Arameans mirrors periods of Aramean-Hebrew cooperation during the monarchy (cf. Gen. 32:44–54 with II Kings 16:5). Social institutions unattested in the Torah outside of the patriarchal narratives are paralleled elsewhere in ancient Near Eastern sources. Concubinage in cases of childlessness (16:2; 30:2) is well attested (15:2–4) and transference of the birthright (25:29–34; 27:1–29, contrast Deut. 21:15ff.) is also found.

The Religion of the Patriarchs

The Bible represents the patriarchs etiologically as religious figures. Circumcision is traced back to Abraham (Gen. 17:9–27), who also founds religious sites at Shechem (Gen. 12:6), Hebron (Gen. 13:18), and Moriah (Gen. 22:14). He also recognizes the sanctity of (Jeru)salem (Gen. 14:18–20). The vision of Jacob and his vow (Genesis 28) serve as the foundation legend for Jeroboam's temple at Bethel (I Kings 13:26ff.). The tradition of Joshua 24:2 mentions the idolatry of Abraham's forebears (cf. Gen. 31:19, 30, 32; 35:2–4), which inspired the later accounts of Abraham the idol smasher wholly absent from Genesis. The appellation, "the God of my [your/his] father" has earlier and later parallels. The possessive suffix is used in reference to each and all of the patriarchs (Gen. 26:24; 28:13; 31:42; 32:10; 46:1, 3; 50:17; Ex. 3:6), but is never employed by or to Abraham in respect of Terah.

The patriarchal narratives are extraordinary in the depiction of experiences in direct variance with the moral and religious ideas and cultic norms found in the legal sections of the Torah. Abraham married his paternal half-sister (Gen. 20:12; contrast Lev. 18:9, 11); Jacob was simultaneously married to two sisters (contrast Lev. 18:18); Abraham planted a sacred tree (Gen. 21:33; contrast Deut. 16:21); Jacob set up sacred stone pillars (Gen. 28:18, 22; 31:13, 45–52; 35:14; contrast Ex. 23:24); there are no festivals; and the fathers build altars, never using existing ones, and they offer sacrifices without priest or temple (Gen. 12:7–8; 13:4, 18; 22:9, 13; 26:25; 31:54; 30:20; 35:1, 3, 7; 46:1).

The patriarchal accounts are distinguished by the employment of numerous divine names, several of them unique (see Names of *God): *El Elyon* (Gen. 14:18, 22), *El Ro'i* (16:13), *El Olam* (21:33), *El Beth-El* (31:13; 35:7), *El Elohei Yisrael* (33:19–20), and, most frequent of all, *El Shaddai* (17:1; 28:3; 35:11; 43:14; 48:3; Ex. 6:3). In addition, one finds *Paḥad Yiẓḥak* (Gen. 31–42; cf. 31:53) and *Abbir Ya'akov* (49:24). It should be pointed out that the *El* element is a widespread Semitic word for God and occurs as a component in theophoric names beyond the Canaanite sphere. In the patriarchal narratives it always appears as a generalized name which becomes personalized only in combination with an identifying element. For these reasons, it is unlikely to be identical with the proper name El, designating the head of the Canaanite pantheon. It is significant that Genesis, unlike the rest of the Bible, contains no reference either to Baal or to fertility cults.

[Nahum M. Sarna / S. David Sperling (2nd ed.)]

Patriarchs and Matriarchs in the *Aggadah*

Only Abraham, Isaac, and Jacob may be designated as the patriarchs, and *Sarah, *Rebekah, *Rachel, and *Leah, the matriarchs (Ber. 16b; Sem. 1:14). Sarah conceived on Rosh Ha-Shanah (Ber. 29a). The patriarchs were born and died in Tishri (R. Eliezer) or Nisan (R. Joshua, RH 11a) except for Isaac, who was born on Passover. They were indeed the "Fathers of the world" (Shek. 8a). Although they eventually begot children they were originally sterile (Yev. 64b). The matriarchs were also at first barren because the Almighty longed for their prayers (Song R. 2:14, no. 8). The merit and faith of the patriarchs were great. The Almighty rebuked Moses by contrasting his lack of faith with their unwavering faith (Sanh. 111a). They were the first to make the Almighty known to man (Men. 53a), and they instituted the daily services (Ber. 26b). All three patriarchs were on an equal spiritual level (Gen. R. 1:15). Yet in a sense Jacob was the choicest of the patriarchs: Abraham and Isaac both begot wicked sons – Ishmael and Esau, respectively – whereas all Jacob's sons were loyal to God ("his bed was complete"; Lev. R. 36:5; Zohar, Gen. 119b). The three patriarchs were tested in many ways, including by famine, so that their descendants would be worthy of receiving the Torah (Midrash Sam. 28:2). Neither the *yeẓer ha-ra* (the "evil inclination" – hypostasized) nor the Angel of Death had mastery over them, and in death they were not touched by worms; they were given a foretaste of the bliss of the hereafter here on earth (BB 17a). They constituted the divine chariot of Ezekiel's vision (Gen. R. 47:6). God turned their meditations into the key that opened the road to freedom for their descendants (Gen. R. 70:6), and it was for the sake of the patriarchs and matriarchs that He liberated the Israelites from Egypt (RH 11a).

The virtue of the patriarchs stood their descendants in good stead; and it was for their sake that God hastened their redemption (RH 11a; see also *Zekhut Avot*). When the Israelites sinned with the golden calf, Moses prayed for forgiveness on their behalf, but only when he recalled the patriarchs were they forgiven (Shab. 30a; Deut. R. 3:11).

There are differences of opinion whether "Merit of the Fathers" (*zekhut avot*) would always operate in favor of their descendants. One view is that it would continue forever (Lev. R. 36:6), while another held that it would come to an end, and that it had even ceased already (*ibid.*); another view boldly declared that labor was more precious than the "Merit of the Fathers" (Gen. R. 74:12). Mamre-Hebron was called Kiriath-Arba ("the City of Four"; Gen. 35:27) because four couples were buried there: Adam and Eve; Abraham and Sarah; Isaac and Rebecca; and Jacob and Leah (Eruv. 53a).

[Harry Freedman]

See also *Pentateuch: The Traditional View.

BIBLIOGRAPHY: Albright, Stone, 200–72; Alt, Kl Schr, 1 (1953), 1–78; F.M.T. Boehl, *Opera Minora* (1953), 26–49; Cross, in: HTR, 55 (1962), 225–59; Gibson, in JSS, 7 (1962), 44–62; C.H. Gordon, *The Ancient Near East* (1945), 113–33; idem, in: BA, 3 (1940), 1–12; Haran, in: *Sefer D. Ben-Gurion* (1964), 40–70; idem, in: *Annual of the Swedish Theological Institute*, 4 (1965), 30–55; J.M. Holt, *The Patriarchs of Israel* (1964); Kaufmann Y., Toledot, 2 (1960), 1–32; Rowley, in: BJRL, 32 (1949), 44–79; N.M. Sarna, *Understanding Genesis* (1966), 81–231; Segal, in: JQR, 52 (1961/62), 41–68; de Vaux, in: RB, 53 (1946), 321–46; 55 (1948), 321–47; 56 (1949), 7–36; G.E. Wright, *Biblical Archaeology* (1962), 36–52; Yeivin, in: RSO, 38 (1963), 277–302. PATRIARCHS AND MATRIARCHS IN THE AGGADAH: Ginzberg, Legends, index; B. Mazar (ed.), *World History of the Jewish People*, 2 (1970). **ADD. BIBLIOGRAPHY:** Y. Muffs, in: JJS, 33 (1982), 81–107; See also bibliography to *Genesis; *History: Beginnings.

PATRIARCHS, TESTAMENTS OF THE TWELVE, an early Jewish pseudepigraphic work, giving the last words of the 12 sons of Jacob to their descendants who assembled before their deaths. Although there are Christian passages in the book, with clear hints at salvation through Jesus and in some versions even a reference to Paul (Test. Patr., Ben. 11), which led some scholars to believe that the Testaments are a Christian work, the opinion of most scholars today is that the Testaments are Jewish and that the Christian passages are later interpolations.

The book has been preserved in Slavonic, Armenian, and Greek versions, the last being the original and not a translation from Hebrew or Aramaic. The book seems to have been written before Paul, because he apparently quotes (I Thess. 2:16) the present Testament of Levi (6:11). It is likely that all the 12 Testaments, with the probable exception of the Testament of Asher in which hatred of sinners and even their killing is preached (in contrast to the other Testaments where compassion to enemies is recommended), were written by one Jewish author, but even this difference can be explained by the different sources of this Testament. The individual Testaments contain mostly aggadic descriptions of incidents in the lives of the sons of Jacob, especially Joseph, profound ethical teachings, and eschatological prophecies as in apocalyptical literature.

It is unlikely that the Greek work is based on a single Hebrew or Aramaic pseudepigraphon no longer extant, but on the other hand it is certain that the Testaments derive from Jewish Palestinian literature and thought. The Greek book is a product of a final stage of rich literary output of pseudepigraphic testaments of the individual sons of Jacob. One source was the Aramaic Testament of *Levi and another a Hebrew Testament of *Naphtali, one fragment of which has been found among the *Dead Sea Scrolls. Another Testament of Naphtali is preserved in medieval Hebrew translation, most probably from the Greek, and shows literary affinity to the Testament of Naphtali in the actual book and the same ethical approach as the Testaments of the Twelve Patriarchs. It is clear, however, that this Testament of Naphtali is not one of its sources, though it is close to them in content and approach. The material about the wars of Jacob and his sons, included in the Book of Jubilees, in the actual Testament of Judah, and in Hebrew medieval narrative (see *Midrash Va-Yissa'u), points to the conclusion that there existed an ancient Hebrew (or Aramaic) Testament of Judah, which contained descriptions of these wars of the sons of Jacob, and it was used both by the author of the Book of Jubilees and the present Greek Testament of Judah. It is unknown if there were also other Hebrew or Aramaic Testaments of the sons of Jacob, which could have served as direct or indirect sources of the Testaments; the Jewish Palestinian material could have reached the author by other channels. There is also a Greek influence, both ethical and literary, in the Testaments of the Patriarchs.

It is important to note that the known sources of the Testaments have a connection with the Dead Sea Scrolls; not only have fragments of the Aramaic Testament of Levi (which is quoted in the Damascus Document) and a fragment of the Hebrew Testament of Levi and fragments of the Book of Jubilees been found in Qumran, but also the doctrines propagated in the Testaments are close to the doctrines of the Dead Sea sect and the author often refers to prophecies of *Enoch, ideas in the Book of Enoch being close to those of the Dead Sea sect. Like the literature of the Dead Sea sect, the Testaments of the Patriarchs show a strong dualistic tendency, both moral and spiritual, and the ethics both of the Dead Sea Scrolls and the Testaments are based on it (see Manual of Discipline 3, 25 and Test. Patr., Reu. 2:3). In the Scrolls and in the Testaments the demonic leader of the evil spirits is named Belial. The main difference is that while in the Dead Sea sect the dualism is sharper – humanity being divided between the Sons of Light and Sons of Darkness and their lots preordained –in the Testaments of the Patriarchs the doctrine of predestination is absent and the struggle between good and evil has to be fought by man himself. This is also the opinion of the Testament of Asher, although it is nearer to the Dead Sea sect than the other Testaments because it too preaches hatred against sinners, while the other Testaments differ from the sect in their humanistic approach. These affinities and differences between the Testaments and the Dead Sea sect can be explained by the suggestion that the author of the Testaments was a member of a movement in Judaism of which the Dead Sea sect was a part. It is very probable that his spiritual, and possible also literary, tradition originated in a fusion between that of the Dead Sea sect and similar groups and the Pharisaic outlook. Thus, for instance, the Testaments mention the belief in the resurrection of the dead, while the sectarian documents speak only about an afterlife of the soul. The extremely humanistic approach of the Testaments (with the exception of that of Asher) is a development from the precept of nonviolence toward the wicked world outside and temporary obedience to it, an idea known from the Scrolls; in the Testaments, nonviolence and the humility of spirit in the face of the wicked is unconditional and linked with compassion, and all hatred is eliminated. The love of God and fellow men, central doctrines of the Testaments, are found in rabbinic literature. The two precepts are combined and united in the Testaments of the Patriarchs, in the teachings of Jesus, and in the Jewish source of the early Christian Didache (the Jewish "Two Ways"). A similar fusion of elements from the Dead Sea sect and doctrines found in rabbinic sources and a similar ethical approach as in the Testaments (and the Jewish source of the Didache) is typical of Jesus' message. There is even an important parallel to Jesus' beatitudes and woes (Math. 5, 3–12, Luke 6, 20–26) in the Testament of Judah (ch. 25). Thus, the Testaments of the Patriarchs, though originally written in Greek, are one of the most important sources for the understanding of Jesus' message. In the context of the history of Jewish thought, they are one of the most sublime documents of Jewish ethics in antiquity.

The eschatology of the Testaments is often obscured by Christian interpolations which destroy the original context and meaning. Even so, it is clear that the messianic belief of the author was similar to that of the Dead Sea sect and of the Book of Jubilees and similar ideas must have already appeared in the sources of the Testaments: Levi and Judah are exalted and preference is given to Levi above Judah, the priesthood being more important than the monarchy; in the Testament of Naphtali, Levi is compared to the sun and Judah to the moon. Like the Dead Sea sect, the author of the Testaments looked forward to two eschatological figures: a levitic high priest and a king from Judah; these are the Messiahs from Aaron and from Israel of the Dead Sea sect.

The Testaments of the Patriarchs were translated from a Greek manuscript by Robert Grosseteste bishop of Lincoln, into Latin (c. 1175–1253; this version was translated into English by A. Gilby in 1581). The argument of the supremacy of the priesthood of Levi, the sun, over Judah, the moon, was used and developed in favor of the papacy against the power of the emperor and Dante, an adherent of monarchy, denounced this ideology in *De Monarchia* 3:4–5.

BIBLIOGRAPHY: EDITORS AND TRANSLATIONS: R.H. Charles (ed.), *The Greek Versions of the Testaments of the Twelve Patriarchs* (1908, repr. 1960); M. de Jonge (ed.), *Testamenta XII Patriarcharum* (1964); R.H. Charles, *The Testaments of the Twelve Patriarchs Translated from the Editor's Greek Text* (1908); M.E. Stone, *The Testament of Levi, A First Study of the Armenian Mss.* (1969). BIBLIOGRAPHY: M. de Jonge, *The Testaments of the Twelve Patriarchs* (1953); R. Eppel, *Le Piétisme juif dans les Testaments des douze Patriarches* (1930); A.S. van des Woude, *Die messianischen Vorstellungen der Gemeinde von Qumrân* (1957), esp. ch. 2; J. Becker, *Untersuchungen zur Entstehungsgeschichte der Testamente der zwoelf Patriarchen* (1970); M. Braun, *History and Romance in Graeco - Oriental Literature* (1938), 44ff.; C. Burchard, J. Jervell, and J. Thomas, *Studien zu Testamenten der zwoelf Patriarchen* (1969); M. Philonenko, *Les Interpolations Chrétiennes des Testaments des douze Patriarches et les Manuscrits de Qoumran* (1960); A. Dupont-Sommer, in: *Semitica*, 4 (1951–52), 33–53; J. Liver, in: HTR, 52 (1959), 149–85; F.M. Braun, in: RB, 67 (1960), 516–69; D. Flusser, *Jesus* (Eng., 1969), 76–82; idem, in: HTR, 61 (1968), 107–27; idem, in: A.J. Toynbee (ed.), *The Crucible of Christianity* (1969), 227.

[David Flusser]

PATRICOF, ALAN (1934–), U.S. financier. Born in New York, Patricof, son of a stockbroker, earned a bachelor's degree from Ohio State University in 1955 and a master's from Columbia Business School in 1958. From 1960 to 1968 he was assistant vice president and then vice president of Central National Corporation, a private, family investment management organization. While at Central National, he became a founder and chairman of the board of *New York* magazine, which later acquired the *Village Voice* of New York and started *New West* magazine. He also participated in the founding of the Datascope Corporation and LIN Broadcasting Corporation. He founded Patricof Company Ventures in 1969. Later he founded a separate investment banking company specializing in entrepreneurial companies. An international arm, Apax Partners, was founded in 1977 and had eight offices in Europe. His firm managed $1.5 billion invested in more than 130 companies. He had an early stake in Apple Computer and helped finance a company that became the second-largest recycler of automobile batteries. Patricof emerged as a major fundraiser for Bill Clinton's presidential elections and for later Democratic candidates. He was a member of the Council on Foreign Relations and was active in a number of philanthropic causes, from hospitals to education.

[Stewart Kampel (2nd ed.)]

PATT, GIDEON (1933–), Israeli politician, member of the Seventh to Thirteenth Knessets. Born in Jerusalem, Patt received a national religious education and did his military service in the IDF in the *Naḥal. In 1953–55 he was personal assistant to MK Joseph Sapir of the *General Zionists when he served as minister of transportation. In 1956 he traveled with his family to the United States, where he attended New York University, graduating in economics and international finance. During his stay in New York he served as director of the National Youth Department of the Zionist Organization of America and was a member of the joint ZOA-Hadassah Youth Commission.

Returning to Israel with his family right after the Six-Day War in 1967, Patt served as bureau chief of Joseph Sapir, who was now minister without portfolio in the National Unity Government headed by Levi *Eshkol. He was elected to the Seventh Knesset in December 1969 on the Gaḥal list, and served as chairman of the Liberal Party Economic Council. In the government formed by Menaḥem *Begin in June 1977 he was appointed minister of construction and housing. In January 1979, he replaced Yigael *Hurwitz as minister of commerce, industry, and tourism. In that capacity he headed a committee that examined ways of increasing tourism to Eilat. In Begin's second government, formed in August 1981, he was appointed minister of industry and trade. In the National Unity Government of 1984–88 he served as minister of science and development, and in the governments of 1988–92 as minister of tourism. Patt was one of the members of the Liberal section in the Likud who objected to Yitzhak *Modai's leadership of the Liberals, which finally led Modai to leave the Likud in March 1990. Patt was not reelected to the Fourteenth Knesset in 1996. In 1997 he was appointed president of Israel Bonds in the United States by Prime Minister Binyamin *Netanyahu and Minister of Finance Dan *Meridor. He served in this position until 2002. In 2001 he was the first to cross the one-billion-dollar line in the raising of funds for the Bonds. In 2005 Patt unsuccessfully contested the post of chairman of the Jewish Agency in the World Likud Council.

[Susan Hattis Rolef (2nd ed.)]

PATTERSON, DAVID (1922–), English scholar. Patterson, who was born in Liverpool, was appointed lecturer in post-Biblical Hebrew at the University of Oxford in 1956. He has also taught Hebrew literature at Cornell University, New York. He served as general editor of the Modern Hebrew Literature series, published by the Cornell University Press and the East and West Library. Probably his most important role was as the founder and first president (1972–94) of the Oxford Center for Postgraduate Hebrew Studies. A fellow of both the American Jewish Academy of Arts and Sciences and the Society of Humanities, Cornell University since 1983, he was awarded the National Brotherhood Award of the Conference of Christians and Jews in the U.S. in 1978. Patterson received the Stiller Prize in Jewish literature. As literary historian, Patterson applied modern critical theories and standards to the major and minor Hebrew novels, short stories, and dramas of the early phases of modern Hebrew belles lettres. His primary interest was with the intrinsic aesthetic qualities of these compositions. His translation of Moshe *Shamir's novel *Melekh Basar va-Dam*, published as *King of Flesh and Blood* (1958), and the English renditions that illustrate and substantiate his conclusions in his *Abraham Mapu, Creator of the Modern Hebrew Novel* (1964) and *Hebrew Novel in Czarist Russia* (1964), convey the subtleties and flavor of the originals. A collection of his articles on Hebrew literature, *A Phoenix in Fetters*, appeared in 1989.

[Avraham Holtz / Rohan Saxena]

°**PATTERSON, JOHN HENRY** (1867–1947), British soldier and author; commanding officer of the Zion Mule Corps and the *Jewish Legion. Born in Dublin, Ireland, into a Protestant family, Patterson's education included the study of the Bible. He was employed as an engineer in the construction of bridges in the British colonies of East Africa, and he described some of his experiences there in his books, *The Man-eaters of Tsavo* (1907) and *In the Grip of the Nyika* (1909). In the Boer War he commanded the 33rd Battalion of the Imperial Yeomanry and in 1915 he was appointed commander of the Zion Mule Corps. With the rank of lieutenant-colonel, he went through the entire Gallipoli campaign with Joseph *Trumpeldor and the Jewish volunteers from Ereẓ Israel. From that time he became an ardent supporter of the Zionist idea. When the Gallipoli campaign ended and the unit broke up, Patterson associated himself with Vladimir *Jabotinsky's efforts in London for the formation of a Jewish Legion which would fight with the British for the liberation of Palestine from Turkish rule. With this objective in mind he wrote his book, *With the Zionists in Gallipoli* (1916). When the first battalion of the Jewish Legion was created in Britain, Patterson became its commander with the rank of colonel and accompanied it to the battle front of Samaria and the Jordan Valley, remaining in command until a year after World War I. He described this experience in his book, *With the Judeans in the Palestine Campaign* (1922). From then on Patterson became attached to the Zionist Movement and maintained particularly close relations with Jabotinsky. In 1939 he violently condemned the *White Paper policy of Malcolm MacDonald in the press, defining it as a betrayal. In 1940 he participated in Jabotinsky's campaign in the United States for the formation of a Jewish army to fight the Nazis.

BIBLIOGRAPHY: V. Jabotinsky, *Story of the Jewish Legion* (1946), index; R.N. Salaman, *Palestine Reclaimed* (1920), index. **ADD. BIBLIOGRAPHY:** J.B. Schechtman, *The Jabotinsky Story: Rebel and Statesman* (1956).

[Yehuda Slutsky]

PAUKER (née **Rabinsohn), ANA** (1890–1960), Romanian Communist leader and cabinet minister. Born into a religious family in Bucharest, she received a traditional Jewish education and became a Hebrew teacher at an elementary school run by the Jewish community. Influenced by her future husband, MARCEL PAUKER (1896–1938), one of the founders of the Romanian Communist Party, she joined the party, which shortly thereafter became illegal. She was imprisoned from 1936 to 1941, and on her release – as the part of an exchange of prisoners – she went to the Soviet Union, returning in 1944 with the Russian forces. During World War II she participated in the Soviet military effort to combat Nazi Germany, organizing a Romanian military division from the Romanian POWs in the Soviet Union to fight against the Antonescu regime and its Hitlerite allies.

After World War II Pauker was the organizer of the Romanian Democratic Front and became minister of foreign affairs in 1947. She also held the posts of secretary of the party central committee and first deputy prime minister in the cabinet of Petre Groza. In 1945 she turned down the post of secretary general of the Party and recommended Gheorghe Gheorghiu-Dej in her place. In 1952, as a result of a move to give a more Romanian character to the party, she was expelled from it, deprived of all her posts, and put under house arrest for several years. Among the charges against her was the accusation that she favored mass emigration to Israel between 1948 and 1951, but this charge was not substantiated. She was also accused of having been both a right winger and a left winger. Long before her death Ana Pauker severed any ties she may have had with the Jewish community, although many of her own close relatives were among the first Romanian settlers in the State of Israel. Nonetheless, she was described by people who knew her well as having continued to show a certain respect for some of the fundamental Jewish traditions, which she knew from her parents' home.

Her husband, Marcel Pauker, whom she divorced, was accused of various "deviations" from the Comintern line, called to Moscow, arrested, condemned to death, and executed.

BIBLIOGRAPHY: *New York Times* (June 15, 1960), 41. **ADD. BIBLIOGRAPHY:** R. Levy, *Ana Pauker, The Rise and Fall of a Jewish Communist* (2001).

[Isac Bercovici / Paul Schveiger (2nd ed.)]

°**PAUL I** (1754–1801), emperor of Russia, son of Catherine II and Peter III; ascended the throne in 1796. His decrees concerning the Jews testify that he acted tolerantly toward them. The dispute between Christians and Jews in *Kaunas (Kovno) which continued for decades, was settled by the decree that the Jews be allowed to remain in the city and that no obstacles be placed in their way in following their trades and handicrafts. Paul I also opposed the expulsion of the Jews from *Kamenets-Podolski and *Kiev.

During the discussion, at the end of the 18th century, between the *Courland authorities and the Senate which took an extremely negative stand toward the Jews, Paul I asked Baron Heiking to handle the problem. On Heiking's advice, the privilege of citizenship to the Jews of Courland was granted on March 14, 1799, and thus also municipal rights. The czar opposed G.R. *Derzhavin's advice to question the validity of the oath of the Jews before the courts. In addition, Paul I took a stand in the struggle between the *Ḥasidim and **Mitnaggedim* by liberating the head of the former, *Zalman Shneur of Lyady, and he rejected all *blood libel accusations leveled against the Jews.

Paul's policy toward the Jews was at first a continuation of Catherine's policy to develop craftsmanship and trade, but in the few years of his reign Paul made numerous concessions to the aristocracy which resulted in the imposition of many restrictions upon the Jews. Paul I was murdered in 1801 before he had time to examine the proposals of Senator Derzhavin's report, containing 88 slanders against the Jews, but they were taken up by his successor, Czar *Alexander I, who made them the foundation of his Jewish legislation.

BIBLIOGRAPHY: I. Gessen, *Yevrei v Rossii*, 1 (1916), 201–7; Dubnow, Hist Russ, 1 (1916), 321–34: R. Mahler, *Divrei Yemei Yisrael – Dorot Aḥaronim*, 3 (1955), 116–29.

°**PAUL IV** (1476–1559), pope from 1555; born **Giovanni Pietro Caraffa**. Even before his election he was a leading spirit in the Counter-Reformation and staunch enemy of all forms of heresy. Because of this, he was extremely hostile to the Jews, as shown by his zeal as head of the *Inquisition from 1542. Scarcely had he been elected pope than he bore down upon the Jews in the Papal States with implacable ruthlessness. He was mainly responsible for the burning of the Talmud in 1553. In his Bull *Cum nimis absurdum* of July 14, 1555, he decreed that in every town the Jews were to gather together in one street or one quarter, which was to be locked at night (the ghetto), and all synagogues except one were to close. Jews were to sell all their houses and landed property, confine themselves to trading in second-hand clothing and rags, and avoid all contact with Christians. They were forbidden to employ Christian wet nurses or domestic servants, and were ordered to wear the Jewish *badge on their clothes. He directed his hatred in particular against the Marranos of *Ancona, who had been invited there by previous popes in order to develop trade between Ancona and Turkey. Paul IV had some hundred of the Marranos of Ancona thrown into prison; 50 were sentenced by the tribunal of the Inquisition and 25 of these were burned at the stake. Paul IV may he considered the instigator of one of the most wretched periods in the history of the Jews in Italy – the period of the ghettos, which dragged on for three centuries.

BIBLIOGRAPHY: Milano, Italia, index s.v. *Paolo IV*; idem, *Ghetto di Roma* (1964), index s.v. *Paolo IV*; Roth, Italy, index; J. Sonne, *Mi Paolo ha-Revi'i ad Pius ha-Ḥamishi...* (1954).

[Attilio Milano]

°**PAUL VI** (1897–1978), pope from 1963. Born **Giovanni Battista Montini** in Concesio, near Brescia, he was ordained in 1920. In 1922 he joined the Vatican Secretariat of State and in 1937 was appointed surrogate to the secretary of state, Cardinal Pacelli (later Pope Pius XII). He was in daily contact with *Pius XII until 1954 and thus was a primary source of evidence for the latter's conduct during the war and his attitude toward the Jews. Montini was appointed prosecretary of state in 1952, archbishop of Milan in 1954, and became a cardinal in 1958. The second Vatican Council, convoked by his predecessor, *John XXIII, was brought to a conclusion by Paul VI (see *Church Councils). According to reliable sources, his personal intervention led to the approval of the *Nostra Aetate* declaration on the attitude of the Church to the non-Christian religions by those bishops who had been reluctant to give the declaration their approval even in its modified form. Paul VI promulgated the declaration in 1965. The pontificate of Paul VI is noted for the extensive trips undertaken by the pontiff. During his first major journey, a pilgrimage to the Holy Land (January 4 to 6, 1964), he spent 12 hours in Israel, but avoided the use of the word "Israel" in all the addresses he made on this occasion. While his attitude toward the State of Israel was reserved, it appeared to have modified after the 1967 *Six-Day War. In 1969 the pope officially received for the first time Israel's foreign minister, Abba *Eban. On the other hand, Paul's sermons were not always in line with the council's declaration, especially his reference to the part played by the Jews in the death of Jesus in his sermon on Palm Sunday in 1965, which seemed to indicate a reversal to pre-council theological attitudes.

BIBLIOGRAPHY: G. Schwaiger, *Geschichte der Paepste im 20. Jahrhundert* (1968); M. Serafian, *The Pilgrim* (1964); X. Rynne, *Second Session* (1964), *Third Session* (1965), *Fourth Session* (1966).

[Willehad Paul Eckert]

PAUL, GABRIEL HOWARD (**Gabe**; 1910–1998), U.S. baseball executive. Born in Rochester, New York, Paul began his 64-year association with baseball with the Rochester Red Wings of the AA International League as a shoeshine boy in the clubhouse at the age of ten. The next year he was promoted to bat boy, and at 16 was hired as publicity and ticket manager for the team. He also served as Rochester correspondent for *The Sporting News*. Paul became traveling secretary for the Cincinnati Reds in 1936, and was promoted to assistant general manager after returning from two-year military service during World War II. Paul was named vice president and general manager of the Reds on September 27, 1951, a post he held until 1960. He rebuilt the team by restructuring its minor leagues and scouting and signing Latin American and black players. In 1956 the Reds set a National League record for most home runs with 221, and Paul was named Executive of the Year. He served as general manager for the new franchise in Houston for six months, and then served as general manager of the Cleveland Indians from 1961 to 1973, during which time he co-owned the team from 1962 to 1966. After selling his interest in the Indians, Paul became part of the Cleveland-based syndicate of George Steinbrenner that purchased the New York Yankees from CBS on January 3, 1973. Paul was installed as Yankee president in April 1974, and was the architect of the 1977–78 championship teams. He returned to Cleveland as president of the Indians in 1978 and retired in 1984. He was responsible for changing the minor league draft system from drawing numbers out of a hat to drafting in reverse order of finish in the standings; led the fight to split each major league into two divisions; pushed through the free agent drafting of players; supported the designated hitter; and put through the rule change that required fielders to bring their gloves off the field after each half-inning.

[Elli Wohlgelernter (2nd ed.)]

PAULI, JOHANNES (c. 1455–c. 1535), German friar and humorist. Born in Pfeddersheim, Alsace, Pauli abandoned Judaism in his youth and entered the Franciscan order. From 1479 he taught in various church institutions and became a popular preacher. A chance meeting with the Christian Hebraist Conrad *Pellicanus in 1496 led "Paul Feddersheimer" (as the former called Pauli) to promise Pellicanus the gift of some Hebrew manuscripts bequeathed to him by his father. These texts (of Isaiah, Ezekiel, and the Minor Prophets) were duly dispatched from Mainz.

Pauli is remembered for one major work, *Schimpf und Ernst* (Thann, 1522), a collection of 693 jests and moral anecdotes drawn from ancient and medieval sources and from oral tradition. Some 60 editions of this work were printed before 1700. Although he mocked at human failings, Pauli invariably gave an ethical point to his graphic stories, which partly inspired the Elizabethan era's *Hundred Merry Tales*, a source much read and exploited by William *Shakespeare.

BIBLIOGRAPHY: H. Oesterley, in: Johannes Pauli, *Schimpf und Ernst* (1866), 1–12; B. Riggenbach (ed.), *Das Chronikon des Konrad Pellikan* (1877); H. Oesterley, in: ADB, 25 (1887), 261–2 (incl. bibl.); J. Bolte, *Schimpf und Ernst*, 2 vols. (1923); C. Roth, *Jewish Contribution to Civilization* (1956), 80, 84; F. Secret, *Les Kabbalistes chrétiens de la Renaissance* (1964), 142. **ADD. BIBLIOGRAPHY:** R.G. Warnock (ed.), *Die Predigten Johannes Paulis* (1970); A.E. Pearsall, *Johannes Pauli (1450–1520) on the Church and Clergy* (1994).

[Godfrey Edmond Silverman]

PAULI, WOLFGANG (1900–1958), Swiss physicist and Nobel laureate born in Vienna. His father was a physician born in Prague, who changed the family name from Pascheles to Pauli, and his mother, a writer, was born in Vienna. He was educated at the Doebling Gymnasium and received his doctorate in physics from the Ludwig-Maximilian University of Munich supervised by Arnold Sommerfeld (1921). After working for a year with Max Born at the University of Goettingen and a further year with Niels Bohr in Copenhagen, he was a lecturer in physics at the University of Hamburg (1923–28). In 1928 he was appointed professor of theoretical physics at the Federal Institute of Technology, Zurich (1928–40). In 1940 he held a German passport which classified him as 75% Jewish even though it was not stamped "Jewish." The Nazi threat and his failure to obtain Swiss naturalization at the time led him to move to Princeton University (1940–46). Further difficulties concerning his status at his former university were resolved following his receipt of the Nobel Prize and he returned to Zurich for the rest of his career. He served as head of the mathematics and physics section (1950–52). Pauli was one of the most influential theoretical physicists of the 20th century. He showed a precocious command of mathematics and physics while a schoolboy, and his life-long interest in quantum mechanics began at university. Early on he recognized the importance of particle spin in exploring the structure of the atom. He formulated the exclusion principle which states that no two fermions (defined as the elementary particles other than bosons) can have identical quantum numbers. This principle has profound implications for understanding the composition of the periodic table and cosmological issues. He was awarded the 1945 Nobel Prize in physics for this contribution which he was unable to receive personally because of political difficulties over his travel documents from the U.S. Later he predicted the existence of the neutrino, the elusive particle that accounts for the loss of energy in beta decay. He also elucidated the basis of the Zeeman effect whereby the spectral line is split into two or more components when the light source is placed in a magnetic field. This finding facilitated the adaptation of this observation to nuclear physics and astronomy. His work on spinors and the Pauli master equation also had important applications for studying particle spin. His other honors included foreign membership in the Royal Society of London (1953). Pauli was less successful as a teacher because his analytical, non-didactic style was often difficult to follow, and he could be abrasive in scientific discourse and criticism.

Towards the end of his life Pauli became dissatisfied with science and his thoughts and writing incorporated much of his longstanding discourse with Carl Jung which had started for therapeutic reasons. He expressed no specific monotheistic belief but incorporated Jewish mysticism into his general mystical philosophy.

[Michael Denman (2nd ed.)]

PAUL OF TARSUS (d. c. 65 C.E.), the "Apostle to the Gentiles." The sources for Paul's life and doctrines are in the New Testament – in the Acts of the Apostles and in the seven Pauline epistles known to be genuine (which are the oldest part of the New Testament). The Epistle to the Hebrews does not even pretend to be written by Paul, the three so-called Pastoral Epistles (the two Epistles to Timothy and the Epistle to Titus) are pseudepigrapha, and there are doubts about the authorship of the Epistle to the Ephesians, the Epistle to the Colossians, and the second Epistle to the Thessalonians.

His Life

Paul was a Jew, born during the first years of the common era. His original name was Saul, and he was a native of Tarsus in Cilicia and possessed Roman citizenship, but according to Jerome (De Viris Illustribus, ch. 5), his family originated from Giscala (Gush Ḥalav) in Galilee. This may explain his adherence to the Pharisaic form of Judaism (Acts 26:5) and his studies in Jerusalem, where, according to Acts 22:3, he was a pupil of Rabban *Gamaliel the Elder; however, neither his Jewish nor his Greek learning was extensive or deep. Initially, he was a fanatical persecutor of the Christians and, according to the account in the New Testament, he was sent to Damascus on the authority of the high priest in order to arrest any Christians that he found there and bring them to Jerusalem for trial; on the way he had a vision of *Jesus, and he converted to Christianity and was baptized in Damascus.

He made three missionary journeys, converting gentiles to Christianity and founding Christian communities. He visited, among other places, Cyprus, Asia Minor, and Antioch; he went to Greece and stayed for a long time in Corinth, and later spent two years in Ephesus in Asia Minor. It was from Greece that he set out for Jerusalem, together with delegates from the churches of Asia and Greece, carrying contributions that had been collected to relieve the poverty of the mother Church of Jerusalem.

Paul was not the first to preach Christianity to gentiles, but he was the most important of these missionaries. The first followers of Jesus formed a group within Judaism, and gentile Christians became a serious problem for the mother Church. Finally, it adopted the position that the Mosaic Law was not to be imposed upon them (Acts 15) and permitted Paul's mission to the gentiles (Gal. 2:6–9). But not only did Paul refuse to restrict his activities to gentiles, he also strongly opposed the observance of all Jewish practices in his gentile Christian communities. The complexity of the situation became evident during Paul's last visit to Jerusalem. He had in his previous missionary activities already been persecuted by gentiles as well as by Jews, who were well aware of his teachings. So it began to be said in Jerusalem that he was teaching "the Jews who are among the gentiles to forsake Moses, telling them not to circumcise their children or observe the customs" (Acts 21:21). Although the leaders in Jerusalem succeeded in appeasing the local community, Jews from Asia instigated violent riots against Paul when he visited the Temple. In the end, he was rescued by Roman soldiers, who put him under protective arrest; he spent two years in detention in Caesarea and was then sent for a decision on his case to Rome, where he passed a further two years in custody. According to a well-established tradition, he was slain there during the Neronian persecution of Christians.

His Attitude toward the Jewish Law

Although Paul's assertion that "no human being will be justified by the works of the law" (Rom. 3:20) can be understood in a broader theological and philosophical sense, what he was chiefly opposing was the Law of the Jews. Paul's concept that Christ's death abolished Mosaic Law cannot be explained as a new development of the eschatological idea which sometimes occurs in later rabbinic sources, namely that in the world to come the commandments will no longer be valid; of this idea there is no trace in his teachings.

Paul's attitude toward Jewish Law is extreme and cannot be explained as stemming only from his theology of the Cross. For him the old Mosaic covenant was "a dispensation of death, carved in letters on stone… a dispensation of condemnation… [which]… fadeth away," in comparison with the new covenant, which is the "dispensation of the Spirit" (II Cor. 3:6–11). "For the law brings wrath, but where there is no law there is no transgression" (Rom. 4:15), and "all who rely on works of the law are under a curse" (Gal. 3:10–14).

Sometimes Paul's argument against the commandments of Judaism comes close to a rationalistic, liberal approach. Thus he says: "Eat whatever is sold in the meat market without raising any question on the ground of conscience, for the earth is the Lord's and everything in it" (I Cor. 10:23–26). But Paul's argumentation often goes beyond a purely liberal attitude and is not based solely on christological grounds. For him, there is no essential difference between the days of the week and the different kinds of food.

It seems clear from all his assertions that Paul's conversion meant for him liberation from the yoke of Jewish Law. The new covenant of Christianity was freedom from the law.

Paul could not say in so many words that Jewish Law had also ceased to have validity for Jews converted to Christianity, not only because he maintained that he who accepts the validity of the law and transgresses it is condemned, and because he did not want to shame the "weak brethren," but also because it was obviously unwise to provoke the wrath of the mother Church in Jerusalem. He thought, moreover, that "everyone should remain in the state in which he was called" (I Cor. 7:17–20). Although, for the purpose of winning over Jews to Christianity, he tended to "become as a Jew" (I Cor. 19–21), to the Jews themselves it seemed that he was unwilling to fulfill the commandments of the law in his private life.

Paul's numerous expressions of his attitude toward the law could not be fully accepted by later Christianity, since they imply opposition to all religious legal obligations; but, although he was not the only early Christian who, by abrogation of the Jewish *halakhah*, paved the way for the separation of Christianity from Judaism, his arguments against the Jewish way of life had a very strong impact upon the development of gentile Christianity. As the Apostle to the Gentiles and an opponent of the Jewish religious way of life, he aroused opposition from all groups of Jewish Christians, who were united in their polemics against him.

In contrast to Paul's hostile attitude toward the law, he always – with the exception of an anti-Jewish passage in his earliest letter (I Thess. 2:14–16) – showed a positive attitude toward the Jews themselves. He was certain that the election of Israel was not abrogated and that, after the gentiles had accepted the new faith, Israel would also become Christian, and so "all Israel will be saved" (Rom. 9–11).

BIBLIOGRAPHY: W. Wrede, *Paulus* (Ger., 1905, Eng., 1908); A. Schweitzer, *Paul and his Interpreters* (1912); K. Barth, *Der Roemerbrief* (1929); W.L. Knox, *St. Paul* (1932); J. Klausner, *From Jesus to Paul* (1943); H.J. Schoeps, *Theologie und Geschichte des Judenchristentums* (1949); idem, *Paul, the Theology of the Apostle in the Light of Jewish Religious History* (1961); idem, *Das Judenchristentum* (1964); M. Buber, *Zwei Glaubensweisen* (1950); L. Baeck, in: JJS, 3 (1952), 93–110; A.D. Nock, *St. Paul* (1955); W.D. Davies, *Paul and the Rabbinic Judaism* (1955^2); A. Schweitzer, *The Mysticism of Paul the Apostle* (1956); S. Sandmel, *The Genius of Paul* (1958); G. Strecker, *Das Judenchristentum in den Pseudoklementinen* (1958); D. Flusser, in: *Scripta Hierosolymitana*, 4 (1958), 215–66; S. Pines, *The Jewish Christians of the Early Centuries of Christianity According to a New Source* (1966); G. Bornkamm, *Paulus* (1969); S. Ben-Chorin, *Paulus* (Ger., 1970). **ADD. BIBLIOGRAPHY:** J. Murphy O'Connor, *Paul: A Critical Life* (1998).

[David Flusser]

PAULY, ROSA (née **Rose Pollak**, 1894–1975), soprano singer. Pauly was born in Eperjes, Hungary, and studied in Vienna with Rosa Papier-Paumgartner. After she made her debut in a minor role in *Martha* at Hamburg (1918), she appeared with opera companies in Cologne (singing the title role in the German premiere of Janáček's *Káta Kabanová* in 1922); at the Krolloper, Berlin, as Leonore, Donna Anna, Senta, Carmen, and Maria in Krenek's *Der Diktator* (1927–31); and at the Staatsoper, Vienna (1931–38). A dramatic soprano of great theatrical power, she was particularly noted for her interpretation of the title role in *Elektra* in which she made her American debut at a concert performance with the New York Philharmonic Orchestra (March 1937), and in which she sang under Beecham at Covent Garden (1938). After guest appearances in the United States, Canada, and South America in 1941, Pauly moved to Israel where she taught singing. She made few recordings, among them Strauss' *Elektra*.

ADD. BIBLIOGRAPHY: Grove online.

[Max Loppert / Israela Stein (2nd ed.)]

°**PAUSANIUS** (second century C.E.), author of the travel book "A Circuit of Greece" in Greek. He includes customs and historical data as well as an actual guide to sights. In his treatment of the area around Olympia he describes the Jordan's course, and in his book on Arcadia he speaks of the tomb of Queen *Helena of Adiabene in Jerusalem; elsewhere he mentions various peculiarities of Palestine.

PAVEL, OTA (**Otto Popper**; 1930–1973), Czech author, fiction writer, and journalist. Pavel was born in Prague into a mixed Czech-Jewish family. His father and two brothers were deported to the Theresienstadt concentration camp. Pavel worked as a miner and later as an editor at sports magazines, where he published many articles. His stories and novels, which move between reality and fiction, touched both sports and his own experience. These include *Dukla among the Skyscrapers* (1964); *A Box Full of Champagne* (1967); and *The Cup from the Lord* (1971). Later he published collections of autobiographical stories, such as *Death of the Beautiful Deer* (1971), which recounts in a humorous way the life of his family in the Protectorate of Bohemia and Moravia, and *How I Came to Know Fish* (1974) from the post-war era. A key figure in most of his stories is his assimilated Jewish father, Leo, who is portrayed – as is the whole family – with understanding and tolerance. His collected works (seven volumes), including many unknown or yet unpublished stories, appeared in the Czech Republic until 2002. Karel Kachyňa's films *Death of the Beautiful Deer* and *The Golden Eels* and the TV movie *Carps for Wehrmacht* are based on Pavel's stories. Some of his works were translated into English, German, and Hebrew.

BIBLIOGRAPHY: A. Mikulášek, *Literatura s hvězdou Davidovou*, vol. 1 (1998); O. Pavel, *Jak šel táta Afrikou* (1994) with preface by Arnošt Lustig on Pavel's relation to Judaism; V. Pavlová, *Vzpomínky na Otu Pavla* (1993); *Slovník českých spisovatelů* (2000).

[Milos Pojar (2nd ed.)]

°**PAVELIĆ, ANTE** (1889–1959), Nazi-appointed ruler of Croatia during World War II. Born in Mostar (Herzegovina), Pavelić was an obscure Zagreb lawyer who came into prominence in 1929, when he founded the extreme right-wing Croatian separatists, Ustaše. In 1934, from his place of exile in Italy, he organized the assassination in Marseilles of King Alexander I of Yugoslavia (who was killed together with French Foreign Minister Louis Barthou) during the king's state visit to France (October 1934). After the German invasion of Yugoslavia in April 1941, the Germans and Italians appointed him "Poglavnik" (leader) of the Independent State of Croatia. He created a fascist-racialist regime, repressing all opposition and instituting ruthless persecution of the Serbs and other minorities living in Croatia, particularly Jews, through arbitrary arrests, deportations, killing of thousands of innocent people, the destruction of Orthodox Serb churches, forcible conversions of Serbs to Catholicism, and exile with plunder of property. Pavelić was a fierce antisemite, and together with his aides Eugen Kvaternik and his minister of the interior, Andrija Artuković (extradited from the United States to Yugoslavia in 1986 and sentenced to death), he was instrumental in murdering about 35,000 Jews and several times that number of Poles. Under his regime, these Jewish victims were not sent to Poland, but were murdered in local concentration camps. Under Pavelić's aegis, a Croatian Muslim division was formed in Bosnia and was visited by the Jerusalem Mufti, Hajj Amin al-Husseini. After the Axis' defeat, Pavelić found his way to Argentina, via Austria and Italy. He lived under assumed names and died two years after an assassination attempt in Spain.

See *Yugoslavia, Holocaust Period; *Zagreb

[Zvi Loker]

PAVIA, city in N. Italy. In 750 the Jew Lullo took part in a religious *disputation in Pavia with the Christian Peter of Pisa. In the ninth century a Jewish scholar named Moses, whose name is associated with the diffusion of mystical lore in Europe, left *Oria to settle in Pavia; his relationship to the 11th century R. Moses of *Pavia is obscure. In 1225 the Jews were expelled from Lombardy, including Pavia. In 1389 Jewish loan-bankers reappeared in the city. They were so violently attacked in the sermons of Bernardino da *Feltre between 1480 and 1494 that the inhabitants demanded their expulsion. However, Duke Giangaleazzo Sforza refused to comply. Popular agitation for the exclusion of the Jews nevertheless continued. When Pavia was besieged by the French in 1527 its inhabitants solemnly vowed that if they surmounted the catastrophe they would "cleanse" the town of Jews. However, the efforts of the numerous delegations later dispatched to the authorities in Milan to obtain their agreement came to nothing.

The physician *Elijah b. Shabbetai taught medicine at the University of Pavia at the beginning of the 15th century – the only authenticated case of a Jewish university teacher in Europe at this period. A chair of Hebrew was established at the end of the 15th century and was renewed in 1521, the first incumbent being the erudite apostate Paolo *Riccio. The duchy of Milan came under Spanish rule in 1535, and the Jews in Pavia obtained short residence permits for a time. In 1558 only seven Jewish families remained in Pavia, and they left during the series of expulsions between 1565 and 1597 which drove all Jews from the duchy of Milan.

BIBLIOGRAPHY: Invernizzi, in: *Bollettino della Società pavese di storia patria*, 5 (1905), 191–240, 281–319; Roth, Italy, index; Milano, Italia, index; Milano, Bibliotheca, index; Roth, Dark Ages, index.

[Attilio Milano]

PAVLOGRAD, city in Dnepropetrovsk district, Ukraine. Jews began to settle in Pavlograd shortly after its establishment in 1780. In 1803 there were 167 Jews, 21 of them merchants. During the 19th century Pavlograd became an important center for the grain and flour industry, which helped to support a considerable increase in the Jewish population. There were 979 Jews registered in the community in 1847, increasing to 4,382 (27.8% of the total) in 1897. Pavlograd had a *talmud torah* and a few private Jewish schools. The 1926 census showed 3,921 Jews (20.9% of the total population), with the number dropping by 1939 to 2,510 (7.5% of the total population). In the Soviet period there was a Yiddish school, and a Jewish kolkhoz. The Germans occupied Pavlograd on October 10, 1941. They concentrated the local Jews and those from the environs in a labor camp within the territory of the Soviet army base. Between November 1941 and January 1942 they murdered most of the Jews in pits near the village of Mavrino. The remainder were killed in June 1942. According to Soviet reports 3,700 people, local residents and from the environs, were murdered, most of them Jews. After the war Jews returned to Pavlograd and in 1970 there were about 1,000 Jews there. Most left in 1990s.

[Yehuda Slutsky / Shmuel Spector (2nd ed.)]

PAVOLOCH, townlet in Zhitomir district, Ukraine. A Jewish community is first known to have existed in the townlet at the beginning of the 17th century. In 1736 the *Haidamacks carried out a pogrom in Pavoloch, massacring 35 Jews and engaging in plunder. In 1753 three local Jews, including the rabbi, were involved in a *blood libel, known as the Zhitomir Trial. They were executed, and all the town's Jews were obliged to pay a high fine. Records of 1765 show 1,041 Jews as paying the poll tax in Pavoloch and its vicinity. Jews numbered 2,113 in 1847, and in 1897 the number rose to 3,391 (42% of the total population). During the Civil War the townlet declined and most of its inhabitants left. Jewish residents numbered 1,837 (88.2% of the population) in 1926, dropping to 639 by 1939. The Germans entered the town in late July 1941. They found 156 Jews and murdered them. The others probably managed to escape. There is no information on Jews living in Pavoloch after World War II.

[Yehuda Slutsky / Shmuel Spector (2nd ed.)]

°**PAWLIKOWSKI, JÓZEF** (c. 1768–1829), Polish nobleman, Jacobin, publicist, and lawyer. During the period of the Great Sejm (1788–92) Pawlikowski discussed Jewish problems in anonymous pamphlets. The pamphlet "About the Polish subjects" (1788) sharply critcizes Jewish innkeepers for making the peasants drink heavily; his study *Myśli Polityczne o Polsce* (Political Thoughts of Poland, 1789) insists on barring Jews from leasing taverns but formulates an extremely liberal reform program of the social and political laws for the benefit of the Jews. Pawlikowski was the only representative of the Polish Enlightenment who accorded equal importance to social emancipation of the peasants, townsmen, and Jews. In contradistinction to others he did not consider the Jews to be exploiters as a whole, but saw them as an oppressed and largely poor people. He felt that it was unrealistic to direct the majority of the Jews toward agriculture. Espousing the necessity of complete tolerance and the granting of all urban rights to the Jews, he stated that the introduction of these changes was subject to the Jews gaining a secular education. He therefore proposed the transfer of the Jewish schools to the National Education Commission, adding that "one cannot demolish anything belonging to their religion"; he also warned, "let us not act like the old Spaniards." In 1826 Pawlikowski was imprisoned in Warsaw and died there.

BIBLIOGRAPHY: B. Leśnodorscy, *Polscy jakobini* (1958); E. Rostworowski, *Legendy i fakty XVIII w.* (1963); *Bibel*, 1 (1968), 312–3.

[Jacob Goldberg]

PAZ, DUARTE DE (d. c. 1542), representative in Rome of Portuguese Marranos. Of Marrano descent, Duarte began a career in diplomacy as the Portuguese military attaché for North Africa. He won the confidence of King John III, who knighted him in 1532 and sent him on a secret mission. Instead he went to Rome to enlist the Curia's intercession for the Marranos. He had a cool and cunning style and plied the cardinals and Pope Clement VII with money made available for this purpose by the Marranos. His initial success was the issuance on Oct. 17, 1532 of a papal decree abrogating the bull *Cum ad nihil magis* of 1531, which had introduced the Inquisition into Portugal. His second success, on April 7, 1533, was the issuance of a bull pardoning the Marranos for "lapses" into Judaism on the ground that their forced conversions were not valid (see *Inquisition, *Portugal). Continuing his activities under Pope Paul III (1534–49), Duarte achieved another success on Oct. 2, 1535, when a papal bull extended the civil rights of Marranos, resulting in the immediate release of 1,800 Marranos from Portuguese dungeons. By this time King John had taken furious notice of Duarte's insubordinate activities and ordered him stripped of commission and honor. In January 1536 Duarte was attacked by masked men, stabbed 14 times, and left for dead on the road. Because of concealed armor he was wearing and the subsequent careful nursing by the pope's doctors, he recovered and accused King John of having ordered his assassination. John denied the accusation, and in any event, since Duarte was no longer in a position to defend his constituents effectively, he proceeded to bring his affairs to a close. When the Marranos questioned Duarte accusingly about a missing 4,000 ducats, enraged, he turned completely against them and denounced both them and their new representative, Diogo Antonio, in many courts in Europe. While on a visit to *Ferrara he was taken by surprise and imprisoned. On his release, he openly espoused Judaism and migrated to Turkey, where, shortly before his death, he reportedly became a Muslim.

BIBLIOGRAPHY: Baron, Social, index; M.A. Cohen (trans.), *Usque's Consolation for the Tribulations of Israel* (1965), 1–9; Graetz, Hist, 4 (1894), 512–20; Roth, Marranos, index.

PE (Heb. פֵּא; ף ,פ), the 17th letter of the Hebrew alphabet; its numerical value is 80. In the Proto-Sinaitic inscriptions this letter seems to be represented by the drawing of either a mouth *(peh)* or corner *(pê'āh)* ‹, ‹. In the 11th and 10th centuries B.C.E., its form was 𐤐 (which presumably was the prototype of Greek (Γ) → and Latin (P). The later West-Semitic variants are Hebrew ︎ノ (Samaritan ࠐ), Phoenician 𐤐 and Aramaic ︎ך → פ in the medial and ך in final positions. The latter forms are the ancestors of the Jewish (modern Heb.) פ and ף From the Nabatean ︎ף (final) → ف (medial) developed the Arabic ف (the single diacritic mark distinguishes it from ق which developed from the *qaf*). See *Alphabet, Hebrew.

[Joseph Naveh]

PEACE (Heb. שָׁלוֹם, *shalom*).

In the Bible

The verb *shalem* (so both the perfect, Gen. 15:16, and the participle, Gen. 33:18) in the *qal* means "to be whole, complete, or sound."

"PEACE." The range of nuances is rather wide. That the iniquity of the Amorites has not yet become *shalem* (Gen. 15:16) means that it is not yet complete. That Jacob arrived *shalem* in the city of Shechem (Gen. 33:18) means that he arrived there safe. To be *shalem* with somebody means to be loyal to him (Gen. 34:21; I Kings 8:61; 11:4; etc.), and one's *sholem* (Ps. 7:5) is one's ally. Although recent translations show a great improvement in this regard, the noun *shalom* is still interpreted to mean "peace" more often than is warranted. It, of course, very frequently means health and/or well-being: Genesis 29:6 (twice); 37:14 (twice); 43:28. In this sense, *shalom* is frequently equivalent to a sentence, "It is well," and *le* may be added to express the English "with"; *shalom* is used alone in this way in II Samuel 18:28, and with *le* in II Samuel 18:29, 32. In Genesis 43:23 and Judges 19:20, "It is well with you" is equivalent to "Don't worry about that," referring in the second case to a roof under which to spend the night (the last clause in verse 18). That the antithesis in Isaiah 45:7 is not between "peace" and "evil," but between prosperity (*shalom*) and adversity (*ra'*), has happily long been the dominant view (cf. *shalom, ṭov, yeshu'ah*, Isa. 52:7). It needs to be noted, however, that not "peace" but safety is the meaning of *shalom* in Leviticus 26:6 (cf. verses 25bb–26: within the land, they shall dwell secure – with never a savage beast or an invader – but only because the enemy will be kept out by dint of successful warfare); Jeremiah 12:12; Zechariah 8:10; and elsewhere. In the above-cited verse Isaiah 52:7, *shalom* stands in synonymous parallelism with *ṭov* in the sense of physical good; it likewise shares with *ṭov* the sense of moral good. Thus *ṭov* has the former meaning in Psalm 34:13 and the latter one in verse 15 – where it is paralleled by *shalom*. Translate:

(13) Is there anyone among you who desires life, is eager for longevity and to experience well-being (*ṭov*)? (14) Then guard your tongue against evil and your lips against speaking deceit. (15) Shun evil and do good (*ṭov*); seek and pursue integrity/equity (*shalom*). For the interpretation of Psalm 37:37b, it makes no difference whether or not one reads in 37a *shemor ṭov u-re'eh yosher*, "practice probity and cultivate equity" (in light of verse 3 where, conversely, *shekhon erez* is to be emended to *shemor ẓedek* (*ẓedeq*), "practice righteousness," in light of the preceding "do good" and the following "cultivate honesty" as well as the *shemor* of this verse): 37b must in any case be translated "for there is a happy future for the man of integrity." Similarly, in Zechariah 8:16, in which the second *'emet* is obviously an erroneous repetition of the first, the sense is: "Speak the truth to each other, and judge equitably (lit. judge judgment of equity [*shalom*]) in your gates." And again in verse 19: "… The Fast of the Fourth Month, and the Fast of the Fifth Month, and the Fast of the Seventh Month, and the Fast of the Tenth Month shall become [occasions of] rejoicing and gladness and happy seasons for the House of Judah – only love truth and equity [*shalom*]." (Alluding to this verse, Esth. 9:30 characterizes Queen Esther's ordinance for the observation of the new holidays – the Purim of the provinces and the Purim of Shushan – as "an ordinance of equity and truth.") The parallelism alone would not suffice to tip the balance in favor of this meaning of *shalom* in Psalm 72:3, 7, for in Isaiah 60:17 the context precludes any interpretation of *shalom/ẓedaqah* other than "prosperity/success" (see *Righteousness). In Psalm 72:3, however, the context points once again to "equity." The prosperity of the country (in contrast to that of the king) is actually treated only in one corrupt verse near the end (verse 16). Finally, Y. Muffs has pointed out that, in light of the Akkadian idiom *šalmeš atalluku* (*maḥar* x), *be-shalom u-ve-mishor halakh itti*, Malachi 2:6, means "he served me with integrity and equity" (more idiomatically, "loyally and conscientiously" – H.L. Ginsberg). Even apart from the Akkadian evidence, the sense of Malachi 2:6 is clear from the foregoing and from the context: Levi, the ancestor of the priestly caste, saved the masses (*rabbim*), or laity by his conscientiousness in making *torah* rulings, from committing ritual offenses; his unworthy descendants, by being lax in this regard, often out of partiality, make the masses (*rabbim*), or laity, stumble by their rulings (*torah*).

PEACE AND THE LIKE. Of course *shalom* does mean "peace" too. But first it must be pointed out that it often approaches this meaning without quite reaching it. YHWH's *berit* (covenant) of *shalom* with Phinehas (Num. 25:12) and with Zion (Isa. 54:10) were, for pity's sake, neither peace treaties terminating previous wars nor nonaggression pacts to refrain from starting new ones. They were solemn – actually unilateral – promises of divine grace. So too the *priestly blessing (Num. 6:24–26), after wishing YHWH's blessing, protection, friendliness, favor, and benignity, ends not, bathetically, with "and may He grant you peace" but, appropriately, "and may He extend grace (*shalom*) to you." In Jeremiah 16:5, YHWH's grace (*shalom*) is explicated as "kindness (*ḥesed*) and mercy (*raḥamim*)"; and in light of that passage it is probable that a *vav* has been lost at the end of Num. 6:24–26 before the initial *vav* of verse 27, so that *shelomo*, is to be read "His grace." In line with this is the phrase "intentions of *shalom*" for "gracious kind, intentions" (on the part of YHWH) in Jeremiah 29:11. A step closer to mere "peace" is "friendship" (or "alliance"), which sense *shalom* has in Judges 4:17: "there was *shalom* between King Jabin of Hazor and the family of Heber the Kenite," so that Jabin's general Sisera, fleeing from the Israelites, believed that he would find safety in the tent of Heber. So, too, one's *shalom*-men are one's friends or allies; Jeremiah 20:10; 38:22; Obadiah 7. Finally, *shalom* obviously means precisely "peace" in I Kings 2:5; Psalm 120:7; Ecclesiastes 3:8; Job 15:21, in which passage it stands in antithesis to war or marauding; but the cases in which this sense can be attributed to the word in good conscience are a small proportion of the total number of its occurrences. Thus it is not true that in Deuteronomy 20:10 the Torah required Israel to invite its adversary "to settle the dispute amicably" "before the commencement of hostilities." The Israelite army has already been mobilized, verse 2a, and has already marched up to an enemy city (not necessarily the first), verse 10a, and it now invites the city not "to settle the dispute amicably" but to surrender on ignominious terms in order to avoid a worse fate (verses 10–17). *Shalom* here means not peace but submission, and the verb *hishlim* definitely means not "to make peace" but "to submit," not only in Deuteronomy 20:12 but also in Joshua 10:1, 4; 11:19; II Samuel 10:19; I Chronicles 19:19; and presumably also I Kings 22:45; Proverbs 16:7. *Isaiah's vision of an age where there would be no more war between nations, Isaiah 4:2–4 (Micah 4:1ff.), is unparalleled. It should not, however, be confused with pacifism. The reason for his opposition to alliances is explained in the Book of *Isaiah. It does not mean that he believed that self-defense was wrong. On the contrary, he predicts that in a penitent Judah those charged with defense (so long as defense, despite 2:2–4, remains necessary) will be endowed with charismatic valor (Isa. 28:6).

[Harold Louis Ginsberg]

In the Talmud

With the possible exception of *justice, peace is the most exalted ideal of the rabbis of the Talmud. No words of praise are too exaggerated to emphasize the importance of this ideal. On the statement of Rabban Simeon b. Gamaliel, "By three things the world is preserved, by truth, by judgment, and by peace" (Avot 1:18), the Talmud declares that they are in effect one, since "if judgment is executed, truth is vindicated, and peace prevails" (TJ, Ta'an. 4:2, 68a). The rabbis interpret Hosea 4:17 to teach that "even if Israel is tied to idols, leave him, as long as peace prevails within it" (Gen. R. 38:6). The role of the scholars is to increase peace in the world (Ber. 64a), and it is to bring the rule of peace that Elijah will come (Eduy. 8:7). There is not a blessing or prayer in the liturgy, the *Amidah*, the *Kaddish*, the Priestly Blessing, and the Grace after Meals, which does not conclude with the prayer for peace (Lev. R. 9:9). "*Shalom*" is the standard greeting among Jews both on meeting and on saying farewell, so that the phrase for greeting and for answering the greeting is "to enquire of the peace of" and to "answer the peace of" (Ber. 2:1, 4b). *Shalom* is one of the names of God (Shab. 10b; Lev. R. 9:9). "The Holy One, blessed be He, found no vessel more worthy of retaining a blessing within it than peace" (Uk. 3:12).

It is permitted to deviate from the strict line of truth in order to establish peace (Yev. 65b), and the Talmud declares with regard to Numbers 5:23, "if in order to establish peace between husband and wife the Name of God, which was written in holiness, may be blotted out, how much more so to bring about peace for the world as a whole" (TJ, Sot. 1:4, 16d). It will be seen that the ideal of peace encompasses the whole gamut of human relationship, between man and his fellowman, and between nation and nation, bringing about the ideal of universal peace.

*Aaron is regarded as the prototype of the ideal of peace (Avot 1:12; cf. Yoma 71b), and in the parallel passage in *Avot de-Rabbi Nathan* (12, p. 48) there is a loving and detailed account of the manner in which he used to devote himself to the bringing about of his ideal. In this Aaron stands in contrast to his brother Moses, who exemplifies the ideal of justice. Aaron's assent to the demand of the people to fashion the golden calf is contrasted with Moses' demands as the rival claims of the ideals of peace and justice when they clash, and the one can be achieved only at the price of the denial of the other, Moses maintaining, "Let justice pierce the mountain" (cf. "*Fiat Justitia, Ruat Coelum*"), whereas Aaron maintained the love and pursuit of peace at all cost. In a similar vein is the homily of Rabban Johanan b. Zakkai on the injunction that no iron tool was to be used in the building of the altar, which had to be made of "whole stones" ("*avanim shelemot*" interpreted as "stones which bring peace" Deut. 27:5–6; cf. Ex. 20:22). "Is it not an a fortiori argument? If the stones of the altar which can neither see nor hear nor speak, but because they bring peace between Israel and their Father in Heaven, the Holy One, blessed be He said, 'thou shalt lift up no iron tool upon them'; how much more so he who brings about peace between man and his fellow, between husband and wife, between city and city, between nation and nation, between government and government, and between family and family" (Mekh., Ba-Ḥodesh, 11). Abbaye's favorite maxim was "man should always strive to increase peace with his brother, his relations, with every other man, even with the heathen in the market place, in order that he be beloved on high and well-liked on earth, and acceptable to his fellowman" (Ber. 17a; SER 26), and there is a whole series of enactments and adjustments of the law made "in the interest of peace" (*mi-penei darkhei shalom*).

Nevertheless, Judaism is not uncompromisingly pacifist in its outlook. It sees universal peace as an ideal which will be achieved only in the messianic age, and Maimonides concludes his famous Code with the declaration that in that era there will be "neither famine nor war, neither jealousy nor strife." Judaism believes that war is sometimes morally justified and divides war into "the war of *mitzvah*," "the obligatory war" (*milḥemet ḥovah*; the war of the two are sometimes identified), and the optional war (cf. Maim. Yad, Melakhim 5–7; see *Mitzvah*). Nevertheless, the whole weight of the ethics of the rabbis recoiled from the glorification of war. This attitude is strikingly expressed in a Mishnah (Shab. 6:4) which lays it down that a man may not go out wearing his arms on the Sabbath, and "if he did so he is obligated to bring a sin-offering." In answer to the opposite opinion that they can be regarded as adornments, the rabbis indignantly retorted, "they are nought but a reproach, as it is written, 'and they shall beat their swords into plowshares and their spears into pruning-hooks, Nation shall not lift up sword against nation, neither shall they learn war any more'" (Isa. 2:4).

[Louis Isaac Rabinowitz]

In Post-Talmudic Jewish Thought

The medieval Jewish thinkers discuss peace under the two headings of world peace and of the avoidance of internal strife and contention in the Jewish community. Jews in the Middle Ages had no voice in international affairs. World peace in the here and now was for them a purely academic question. Their discussions of it, consequently, are in a messianic context. Saadiah (*Emunot ve-Deot* 7:10) points to the continuing wars among nations, including wars of religion, to demonstrate that the prophetic vision of peace on earth can only apply to the messianic age. Maimonides (Yad, Melakhim 12:5) similarly considers the establishment of peace for all mankind to be an accomplishment of the Messiah. David Kimḥi (to Isa. 2:4) states that the nations will bring their disputes to the Messiah for arbitration. He will decide so wisely and justly that war between nations will be purposeless. It has frequently been pointed out that in medieval illustrated *Haggadot* the wicked son is depicted as a warrior, the wise son as a peace-loving sage.

Joseph Albo (*Sefer ha-Ikkarim* 4:51) defines peace as the harmony of opposites. There is no virtue in one extreme predominating over another, but only in the harmony between the irascible and the patient, the niggardly and the extravagant, and so on. Peace of mind means the attainment of harmony among the different parts of the soul. Isaac Arama (*Akedat Yiẓḥak*, 74) holds that the conventional view of peace as a mere negation of strife fails to do justice to the richness of the concept. Peace is a positive thing, the essential means by which men of differing temperaments and opinions can work together for the common good. Pearls of individual virtue would be dim in isolation if not for the string of peace that binds them together and so increases their luster. That is why peace is a name of God, for it is He who gives unity to the whole of creation.

[Louis Jacobs]

Medieval Jewish thinkers suggested three fundamental concepts regarding the way to make an end to war and to bring about a state of peace. According to the first, this can be done by reforming man qua man – that is, by changing the consciousness of the individual. Putting an end to war involves subduing those internal impulses and motives that impel people to violence. Peace will come about as a consequence of the perfection – either intellectual or psychological – of humankind. Maimonides, for instance, viewed the prophetic vision of peace as a natural and necessary outgrowth of the dominion of the intellect over man's destructive impulses. For him, violence and war, the inflicting of harm by people on one another, have their source in irrationality and ignorance. However, the apprehension of truth – "knowledge of God" – displaces man's awareness from his attachment to illusory goods and interests, and completely eliminates the irrational factors that give rise to mutual conflict between individuals, groups, and nations (Guide 3:11: Laws of Kings, 12:1). Similarly, Abraham bar Hiyya describes the peace foretold by the prophets as the consequence of a radical change in human consciousness. However, it is in the realm of interpersonal relations that this transformation is to take place. Man's destructive impulses are to be overcome not by intellect, but by the sense of intimacy and mutual identification that will grow among people once they have all chosen to adopt the same path. The projected utopian peace will be expressed and embodied in the universal effectiveness of the commandment to "love thy neighbor as thyself" (*Hegyon ha-Nefesh*, ed. G. Wigoder, p. 150).

According to a second concept, peace will come about by reconstructing the international framework – that is, by creating a new world order, either through law and justice or through domination and force. The image of world peace described by several medieval commentators and thinkers took the form of a judicial arrangement between the rival nations, a kind of an international court that would mediate their quarrels and conflicts. This vision speaks not of a human society that has risen above all striving; it speaks, rather, of a procedure for conflict resolution presided over by a supreme, utopian judge whose authority and righteousness are accepted by all. For instance, for David *Kimḥi (Commentary on Micah, 4, 3) and Isaac *Arama (*Akedat Yiẓḥak*, gate 46, 133b), the prophetic tiding "and he shall judge between the nations" (Isa. 2:4; Micah 4:3), does not refer to the kingship of God but to the sages of Jerusalem or to the messiah. They therefore granted the judicial institution universal authority. Other thinkers, however, interpreted the envisioned international structure as a kind of Pax Judaica, a single, central government in Zion to which all people would be subject. These portrayals, of a destined universal domination of the people of Israel or the king-messiah rest upon biblical or midrashic sources, but they also reflect contemporary historical reality: living out the present in submission, subject to the gentile powers, thinkers like *Saadiah Gaon (*Doctrines and Beliefs*, 8, 8) and *Albo anticipate a complete reverse.

Finally, according to a third concept, peace will be achieved by an internal reformation of society – that is, by a change in the socio-political order. Peace will come about as a result of either the annulment or the improvement of existing political structures. Isaac *Abrabanel foresaw a universal theocracy, the kingship of God on earth. Ultimate peace would involve the disappearance of national and political boundaries and the abrogation of political structures through the unification of all humanity in the light of monotheistic faith – that is to say, through the religious perfection of humanity (Commentary to Isa. 2;4, Commentary to Micah 4). Isaac Arama, however, discusses peace and war in relation to the law of the state, the present operative political and judicial order. Unlike the conceptions described above, in which peace was portrayed primarily from a utopian point of view, Arama looks at this issue in light of actual, contemporary historical reality as well. "For if the social order and law (*nimmus*) are defective and distant from the natural truth [...] quarrel and strife cannot but break out amongst them" (*Akedat Yiẓḥak*, 46). It is thus the task of the lawgiver to ordain a social order that will educe such motives, both on the part of the ruler and on the part of his subjects.

[Aviezer Ravitzky (2nd ed.)]

In Modern Jewish Thought

Modern Jewish thought, without any denominational differences, except possibly on the question of religious toleration, is unanimous on the great value of peace. Morris Joseph (*Judaism as Creed and Life* (1903), 456–7) is typical of the whole modern trend when he writes that only the peace-loving Jew is a true follower of the prophets, that the greatest sacrifices should be made to avoid war, that a Jew cannot consistently belong to a war party, and that the Jew's religion, history, and mission all pledge him to a policy of peace, as a citizen as well as an individual. A.I. Kook, commenting on the ruling that the office of the priest "anointed for war" (Deut. 20:2–4) is not a hereditary one, remarks that the idea of a hereditary position is to express permanence in human affairs. However, peace is the only state deserving of permanence. Consequently, there can be no question of a hereditary appointment for a functionary connected with warfare, but only for one who operates in times of peace (Zevin: *Le-Or ha-Halakhah* (1946), 27–28). The Reform *Union Prayer Book* contains this prayer: "Grant us peace, Thy most precious gift, O Thou eternal source of peace, and enable Israel to be its messenger unto the peoples of the earth. Bless our country that it may ever be a stronghold of peace, and its advocate in the council of nations."

[Louis Jacobs]

BIBLIOGRAPHY: IN THE BIBLE: Koehler-Baumgartner, 973–4; Y. Muffs, *Studies in the Aramaic Legal Papyri from Elephantine* (1969), 203–4. IN TALMUD: G.F. Moore, *Judaism*, 2 (1927), 195–7; J.S. Kornfeld, *Judaism and International Peace* (193ff.); A. Cronbach, in: CCARY, 46 (1936), 198–221; M. Wald, *Jewish Teaching on Peace* (1944); L.I. Rabinowitz, in: JQR, 58 (1967/68), 148 no. 20. **ADD. BIBLIOGRAPHY:** A. Ravitzky, "Peace," in: A.A. Cohen and P. Mendes-Flohr (eds.), *Contemporary Jewish Religious Thought* (1987), 685–702.

PEACE MOVEMENTS, RELIGIOUS. Within Israel since the Six-Day War of 1967, Orthodox Judaism has politically largely become associated with an uncompromising stance concerning issues of territory and the Arab-Israel conflict. This has become an integral part of the ideologies and policies expressed by the *National Religious Party and *Gush Emunim. Over the years, however, a number of small, religious peace movements have been founded in an attempt to promote an alternative message based, also, on recourse to religious and theological sources.

Oz ve-Shalom ("Strength and Peace") was founded in the 1970s by religious intellectuals as a religious response to Gush Emunim. The movement called for territorial compromise and for ending control over millions of Palestinians. It had only a minor influence on the religious population, and most of its impact was on the general Israeli public.

In the wake of the Lebanon War of 1982, the Netivot Shalom ("Paths of Peace") Movement was founded as an umbrella organization consisting of members of Oz ve-Shalom and of members of *yeshivot hesder* (yeshivah studies combined with army service).

Netivot Shalom was headed by rabbis such as Aaron *Lichtenstein and Yehudah Amital, and by religious intellectuals such as Uriel Simon and Aviezer *Ravitzky. Its members called for withdrawal from the territories in exchange for peace and emphasized humanistic values in light of religious sources.

In 1988, a moderate religious political party, Meimad, was founded under the leadership of Rabbi Amital. This party failed to obtain the minimum number of votes necessary for a seat in the Knesset, and this was seen as a clear indication of the limited religious support for a moderate stance on the question of the territories. Meimad was reformed early in 1993 as an ideological and educational organization to lend support to the renewed peace process of the Rabin government, and later became an independent political party which then joined the Labor Party to form "One Israel." Following the Labor victory in the 1999 elections, Meimad's representative, Rabbi Michael *Melchior, served as a minister in Ehud Barak's government.

In 1992, the Committee of Rabbis for Human Rights was formed and obtained some prominence in its support of Palestinian human rights. Unlike the other religious peace organizations, the Rabbis for Human Rights was composed of rabbis from all the major religious streams – Orthodox, Conservative, and Reform.

BIBLIOGRAPHY: *You Must Not Remain Indifferent* (1988); D. Newman, in: *L'eylah*, 31 (1991), 4–10; T. Hermann & D. Newman, in: C. Liebman (ed.), *Religious and Secular: Conflict and Accommodation between Jews in Israel* (1992), 151–172. **ADD. BIBLIOGRAPHY:** *Torah, Zionism, Peace: A Collection of Essays* (Heb., 1982); "Oz V'Shalom: A

Moment Interview," in: *Moment*, 117 (1986), 25–30, 44–46; Y. Landau (ed.), *Religious Zionism: Challenges and Choices* (1986); *Violence and the Value of Life in Jewish Tradition* (1987).

[David Newman]

PEACE NOW (*Shalom Akhshav* – Israeli peace movement). Shalom Akhshav was launched in July 1977 with a letter signed by 300 men, all of them reserve officers in the Israel Defense Force, to Prime Minister Menaḥem Begin, appealing to him to return the territories in the West Bank and Gaza conquered in the Six-Day War, in the interests of peace, and making their slogan "Better Peace (*shalom*) than the wholeness (*shlemut*) of the Land of Israel."

The movement was characterized by the fact that it was completely independent of any political party or grouping, and by the decorous manner in which it conducted its propaganda. That it responded to a widespread popular demand was evidenced by the fact that its first mass demonstration, held on April 1, 1978, in Malkhei Israel Square in Tel Aviv, was attended by numbers variously estimated at between 20,000 and 30,000. After a demonstration outside the residence of the prime minister on March 30, on his return from the United States, and also on April 21, they were received by the prime minister. Two days later, 350 professors and university lecturers issued a proclamation in support of them, to which a similar number added their names in August, and on April 26 over 3,000 lined the road from Sha'ar Hagai to Jerusalem when Begin passed it on his way to Tel Aviv. A number of similar demonstrations took place subsequently on various occasions.

Peace Now enthusiastically acclaimed the Camp David Agreement in September 1978. In subsequent months they protested vigorously against every step by the government which they felt impeded the implementation of the Peace Treaty, and autonomy on the West Bank, such as the proposal to "thicken" the existing settlements there or to establish new ones.

Peace Now was also in the forefront of the protest movement against the Lebanon War and was the major organizer of the mass rally in Tel Aviv in September 1982 after the Sabra and Shatilla massacre. Throughout the 1980s and 1990s it continued to press for withdrawal to Israel's pre-1967 borders and the establishment of a Palestinian state. The collapse of the Camp David summit in 2000 despite Prime Minister Ehud Barak's far-reaching concessions paralyzed the movement for a time, but it again became vocal in 2002. The main support of the Peace Now movement came from the middle classes and liberal and intellectual circles.

[Louis Isaac Rabinowitz]

PEACH (Heb. פֶּרְסֵק or אֲפַרְסֵק, mishnaic), the tree and the fruit of the *Persica vulgaris* (*Prunus persica*). This tree was first grown in Ereẓ Israel during the Greco-Roman era, hence its name *afarsek*, i.e., "Persian apple" in the Mishnah (Gr. μῆλον περσικόν). Characteristic of the peach are the red fibers extending from a deeply grooved kernel. The Mishnah accordingly lays it down that peaches become liable for tithing "after they begin to show red veins" (Ma'as, 1:2). Under suitable conditions, peaches can grow to a substantial size, and the *aggadah* states that it happened that a single peach became large enough to provide more than a meal for a man and his ass (TJ, Pe'ah 7:4, 20a). The Mishnah states that the peach used to be grafted onto the almond (as it is today) and forbids the practice since it constitutes *kilayim* ("*mixed species"; Kil. 1:4). On the other hand, the statement (TJ, Kil. 27a according to the reading of the Mussafia in his additions to the *Arukh*) that the grafting of a walnut tree on a peach produces the fruit *karyah-persikah* ("Persian walnuts"), a sort of crossbreed between the walnut and the peach, belongs to agricultural folklore.

The name *nucipersica* ("Persian nut") occurs on an inscription discovered in a Roman villa and this name entered into the botanical literature of the Middle Ages for a species of peach with a skin as smooth as that of the outer husk of the walnut. It is certain that these two unrelated species cannot be grafted and no hybrid can be produced from them. After the ruin of Jewish agriculture in Ereẓ Israel at the end of the talmudic era, peach plantations all but disappeared. During recent years, however, they have been planted in large numbers and are found in abundance.

BIBLIOGRAPHY: Loew, Flora, 3 (1924), 159–63; J. Feliks, *Kilei Zera'im ve-Harkavah* (1967), 101–3. **ADD. BIBLIOGRAPHY:** Feliks, Ha-Ẓome'aḥ, 30.

[Jehuda Feliks]

PEACOCK, bird called ταως in Greek and *tavvas* in the Mishnah. The peacock (*Pavo cristatus*) is a ritually clean bird (see *Dietary Laws) belonging to the pheasant family. In mishnaic times some wealthy people in Ereẓ Israel bred the peacock as an ornamental bird and even ate it on occasion, its head in particular being regarded as a great delicacy (Shab. 130a). According to the Tosefta (Kil. 1:8), "chicken, peacock, and pheasant, although resembling one another, are each heterogeneous with the other." A poetic comment on the peacock's beauty is given in the Midrash (Tanḥ. B., Lev. 33; cf. Gen. R. 7:4): "Although the peacock comes from a drop of white matter, it has 365 different colors, as many as the days in a year." The peacock originates from India, from where, it is suggested, Alexander the Great imported it into Europe. The *tukkiyyim* conveyed to Solomon in ships of Tarshish (I Kings 10:22; II Chron. 9:21) are most probably to be identified with peacocks, called in Tamil *togai, tokai*, an identification found also in ancient translations. In modern Hebrew *tukki* is mistakenly used to denote a parrot.

BIBLIOGRAPHY: Lewysohn, Zool, 189f., no. 241; F.S. Bodenheimer, *Animal and Man in Bible Lands* (1960), 121, 125; J. Feliks, *Kilei Zera'im ve-Harkavah* (1967), 118f., 129–32; idem, *Animal World of the Bible* (1962), 60.

[Jehuda Feliks]

PE'AH (Heb. פֵּאָה; "corner"), name of the second treatise of the Mishnah, in the order of *Zera'im*. Despite its name, this tractate deals with the laws of all the different dues to the poor, namely: *pe'ah, leket* ("gleaning of grapes"), *peret* ("fallen grapes"), *ma'aser ani* ("poor man's tithe") which are enjoined in Leviticus 19:9, 10, and Deuteronomy 24:19; 14:28, 29.

The tractate is divided into eight chapters whose contents are: required amount and size of field to which the law of *pe'ah* applies (1:1, 2; 3:6); the type of field and agricultural produce from which *pe'ah* may be given (1:4, 5; 3:4); modes of division in a field (2:1–4; 3:1, 2); procedure in giving *pe'ah* (4:1–5); type of gleanings which constitute *leket* (4:10, 11; 5:1, 2); type of harvest, position of leftover sheaves and amount of sheaves that require the giving of *shikhḥah* (5:7, 8; 6:2–11; 7:1, 2); laws of *peret* and *olelot* (7:3–7); laws of *ma'aser ani* (8:2, 5–7); obligation of consecrated land to the Temple in connection with dues to the poor (1:6; 4:6–9; 7:8). Thus 1–4:9 deals with the laws of *pe'ah*; 4:10–5:6 with *leket*; 5:7–7:2 with *shikhḥah*; 7:3 with *peret*; 7:4–7, 8 with *olelot*; 8, especially from Mishnah 5 onward, with *ma'aser ani* and charity. A number of topics unrelated to the immediate subject of the tractate are included: enumeration of *mitzvot* having no fixed measure (1:1); legal transactions involving small amounts of land (3:6, 7); laws of renunciation of ownership (1:6; 6:1). The first of these has been included (with variant readings) in the prayer book as part of the morning introductory prayers.

The Tosefta has four chapters, which, besides complementing and interpreting the Mishnah, include several interpretations and emendations based on the Talmud (Tosef., 1:6; 2:2; see Epstein, Tanna'im, 252). The Tosefta also contains some aggadic passages, such as "The Almighty combines a good intention with an action, but an evil intention the Almighty does not combine with an action" (1:4). In the last chapter, in which charity is highly praised, it is stated that charity and deeds of lovingkindness equal all the *mitzvot* in the Torah (4:19), that he who shuts his eyes to charity is like one who practices idolatry (4:20). There is no *Gemara* on the tractate in the Babylonian Talmud but there is in the Jerusalem Talmud, which includes much aggadic literature.

BIBLIOGRAPHY: H.L. Strack, *Introduction to the Talmud and Midrash* (1931), 29–30; P. Blackman (ed. and tr.), *Mishnayot*, 1 (1951); J.D. Herzog (ed. and tr.), *Mishnayot*, 2 (1947).

[Jacob Kelemer]

PEAR (Heb. אַגָּס, mishnaic), *Pyrus communis*. Although it is first mentioned in rabbinic literature this does not necessarily mean that the pear was not grown in Ereẓ Israel in biblical times. A member of the same genus, the Syrian pear *Pyrus syriaca* (mishnaic Heb. *ḥizrar*), grows wild in Ereẓ Israel in Upper Galilee (Kil. 1:4). The same Mishnah mentions a variety of pear called *krostomlin* which is regarded as belonging to the same species. The reference is to the pear called by Pliny (*Natural History*, 15:53) *crustumina*. It seems that during the time of the Mishnah they began to grow this excellent species in Ereẓ Israel, hence its Roman name. In modern Israel the Arabs used to grow small local pears, but excellent large species have been introduced by the Jews, and today pears are found in abundance.

BIBLIOGRAPHY: Loew, Flora, 3 (1924), 235–40; J. Feliks, *Kilei Zera'im ve-Harkavah* (1967), 93–95. **ADD. BIBLIOGRAPHY:** Feliks, Ha-Tzome'aḥ, 18.

[Jehuda Feliks]

PEARL, DANIEL (1963–2002), U.S. journalist. Born in Princeton, N.J., Pearl grew up in Encino, Calif., where his father was a professor at the University of California in Los Angeles. Pearl, who had dual American-Israeli citizenship, earned a bachelor's degree in communications from Stanford University and had several newspaper jobs before joining the Atlanta bureau of *The Wall Street Journal* in 1990. He moved to the Washington bureau in 1993 and three years later to the *Journal's* London bureau as Middle East correspondent. In 2000, Pearl became the newspaper's South Asia bureau chief. While investigating the case of Richard Reid, who was convicted of carrying a bomb in his shoe on an airline, Pearl was kidnapped by a militant group in Pakistan calling itself the National Movement for the Restoration of Pakistani Sovereignty. The group said Pearl was a spy and sent the United States a range of demands, including the freeing of all Pakistani terror detainees and the release of a halted U.S. shipment of F-16 fighter jets to the Pakistani government. The press deliberately kept word of his Israeli parents out of the story to protect one of their own. Threatening to kill Pearl, the group released photographs of Pearl handcuffed with a gun at his head and holding up a newspaper. There was no response to pleas from Pearl's editor, and from his wife, who was pregnant with their first child. Six days later, Pearl was killed and the kidnappers later severed his head. Pearl's body was found five months later in a grave near Karachi. In February 2003, a videotape titled *The Slaughter of the Spy-Journalist, the Jew Daniel Pearl* was released. It shows his murder and records Pearl saying "I am a Jew and my father was a Jew." Then his throat was cut. The video made its way to the Pakistani government and the U.S. government, and eventually it leaked onto the Internet through a Jihadist site. On the video, Pearl described his Jewish upbringing and his family's involvement with the creation of the State of Israel. Four Islamic men were later convicted and sentenced to death for the kidnapping and murder. The prosecution relied on technical evidence provided by the Federal Bureau of Investigation, which traced e-mails to the defendants.

A collection of Pearl's writings, *At Home in the World: Collected Writings from the Wall Street Journal*, was published in 2002. The following year, Mariane Pearl, the widow, and Sarah Crichton, published *A Mighty Heart*, and Ruth and Judea Pearl, Daniel's parents, published *I Am Jewish: Personal Reflections Inspired by the Last Words of Daniel Pearl* in 2004. The family and friends also established the Daniel Pearl Foundation to continue his mission and to address the root causes of the tragedy in the spirit, style, and principles that shaped Pearl's work and character.

[Stewart Kampel (2nd ed.)]

PEARLMAN, MOSHE (1911–1986), author and journalist. Pearlman was born in London where he graduated from the

London School of Economics. During World War II he served in the British army in North Africa and Greece, attaining the rank of major. Concurrent with his army service and after it, he was involved in the organization of "illegal" immigration, Aliyah Bet. Pearlman was at kibbutz Ein Ḥarod for the year in 1936 and returned to the country as an immigrant in 1948. In the War of Independence he was in charge of the Israel army press liaison unit and served as the army's chief spokesman. He remained head of the Press Unit until 1952 and during the same time period was the organizer and first director of the Government Press Office. From 1952 to 1956 he was the director of the Israel Broadcasting Service, Kol Yisrael. He was sent as an ambassador on a special mission to Zaire (then the Belgian Congo) in 1960 and in 1967 served as special assistant to Defense Minister Moshe Dayan during the period of the Six-Day War. His first book, *Collective Adventure*, described his year on a kibbutz; among his other works are *In the Footsteps of Moses, In the Footsteps of the Prophets*, and *The Capture and Trial of Adolf Eichmann*. He also worked as a collaborator with public figures, for example, with David Ben-Gurion on *Ben-Gurion Looks Back*, and with Teddy Kollek on *Jerusalem: A History of 40 Centuries*.

PEARLSTEIN, PHILIP (1924–), U.S. painter, printmaker, watercolorist, and draftsman. Although the human figure stands at the center of Pearlstein's art he professes lack of interest in the psychological aspects of his models, preferring instead to focus on color, light, and composition. Working from life, Pearlstein most commonly paints nude studio models in harsh lighting with a precise, smooth brushstroke.

Born in Pittsburgh, Pennsylvania, Pearlstein's interest in art manifested itself when he was a child. Indeed, he was awarded first and third prize in *Scholastic Magazine*'s National High School Art Exhibition. After completing one year of study at the Carnegie Institute of Technology (now called Carnegie Mellon University), he was drafted into the army. While enlisted Pearlstein made documentary sketches and watercolors of training scenes and the life of the soldier, thinking that upon his return to the United States he would become an illustrator. Instead, following the war he renewed his studies at Carnegie Tech, graduating in 1949 with a B.F.A. With a degree in hand he moved to New York and enjoyed his first work as a professional artist as a catalog illustrator. In 1955 he earned an M.A. from New York University in art history, writing his thesis on Francis Picabia. Around this time Pearlstein showed his expressionistic, heavily impastoed landscape paintings at his first one-person show at the Tanager Gallery. In the early 1960s he began to focus on studio models, first painting figures in an expressionist manner akin to his landscapes and then, starting in 1963, painting in a more straightforward fashion on an increasingly larger scale. Typical of Pearlstein's work is *Two Female Models Sitting and Lying on a Navajo Rug* (1972, Des Moines Art Center, Iowa), which shows a pair of unidealized, unemotional females lounging on a brightly patterned rug. The sitting female's head is cropped and the reclining figure's body is contorted, allowing the artist to explore the complicated pose, which he paints from a high vantage point. In his oversized canvases, Pearlstein privileges accessories – such as rugs, mirrors, chairs, and other furniture, often with decorative upholstery – as highly as the humans he depicts.

In the 1970s Pearlstein reintroduced watercolors to his repertoire. Pearlstein's watercolors, as his paintings, are factual, dispassionately rendered, representational works that eschew symbolism and narrative. Watercolors of nude studio models preoccupied the artist from this period forward, as have sepia washes of both landscapes and nudes.

Through the years Pearlstein's teaching helped him to refine his own art, first at the Pratt Institute (1959–63) and then at Brooklyn College (1963–87). While he is best known for his monumental nudes, Pearlstein also made portraits, including a 1979 *Time* magazine cover of Henry Kissinger. Pearlstein wrote about his art technique and philosophy in several articles.

BIBLIOGRAPHY: J. Viola, *The Painting and Teaching of Philip Pearlstein* (1982); R. Bowman, *Philip Pearlstein: The Complete Paintings* (1983); J. Perreault, *Philip Pearlstein: Drawings and Watercolors* (1988); R. Storr, *Philip Pearlstein: Since 1983* (2002).

[Samantha Baskind (2nd ed.)]

PEARLSTINE, NORMAN (1942–), U.S. journalist. Born in Philadelphia, PA., Pearlstine was educated at Haverford College, where he earned his undergraduate degree, and the University of Pennsylvania Law School. Pearlstine had a long and varied career in journalism. From 1967 to 1992, he was with Dow Jones & Company, except for a two-year period, from 1978 to 1980, when he was an executive editor at *Forbes* magazine. He was a reporter for *The Wall Street Journal* in Dallas, Detroit, and Los Angeles from 1967 to 1973, when he was named the paper's Tokyo bureau chief. He was named the first managing editor of *The Asian Wall Street Journal* in Hong Kong in March 1976. He returned to the *Journal* in the spring of 1980 as national news editor. In 1982 he was named editor and publisher of *The Wall Street Journal* in Brussels. He was appointed managing editor of *The Wall Street Journal* in September 1983 and became executive editor, one of the most influential positions in American journalism, in June 1991. He helped widen the boundaries of business journalism, from Wall Street and Main Street to Madison Avenue, Hollywood economics, the legal community, and beyond. He resigned from Dow Jones, the parent company, in June 1992. At the *Journal*, he oversaw the paper's expansion from one section to three, transformed the paper into a high-profile publication, and helped create the Asian and European editions. Just before leaving the organization, he helped create the personal finance magazine *SmartMoney* for Dow Jones and the Hearst Corporation. In April 1993 Pearlstine became general partner of Friday (his wife was Nancy Friday, an author) Holdings LP, a multimedia investment company. Pearlstine, a member of the Bar Association of the District of Columbia and the American Bar Association, in 1995 became editor in chief of Time Inc., the world's largest magazine publisher. In that post, he oversaw the editorial content of Time Inc.'s magazines, including *Time, Life, Fortune, Sports Illustrated, People, In Style,* and *Entertainment Weekly,* among others. In addition, he had overall business responsibilities for Time Inc.'s new media, international, and television activities. In 2005, Pearlstine turned over his responsibilities at Time Inc., to John Huey, who had worked together with him for 17 of his last 25 years, starting at the *Journal.* At the time, two of every three American adults read at least one of Time Inc.'s 155 magazines each month.

[Stewart Kampel (2nd ed.)]

PECAR, SAMUEL (1922–2000), writer. He was born in Colonia López, an agricultural colony of JCA in Entre Rios (Argentina). In 1930 his family moved to San Fernando, in the outskirts of Buenos Aires. Between 1951 and his *aliyah* in 1962 he participated in the literary section of *Nueva Sion*, the organ of the Zionist Socialist party Mapam in Argentina, and in 1957–58 also in the Jewish daily in Spanish, *Amanecer.* At that time he published three books that humorously criticized Jewish community life in Argentina: *Cuentos de Kleinville* ("Stories of Smallville," 1954), *La generacion olvidada* ("The Forgotten Generation," 1958); *Los rebeldes y los perplejos. Cuentos casi serios* ("The Rebels and the Perplexed. Almost Serious Stories," 1959). These works made him one of the most representative authors acknowledged by the Argentina Jewish community.

In Israel he worked in the Latin American Department of the Histadrut, where he specialized in agrarian cooperativism on which he published *Manual del Cooperativismo Agrario en Israel* (1964) and *Manual de Contabilidad de Cooperativas Agropecuarias* (1981). In 1969–87 he was a high school teacher in development areas in the Negev.

Samuel Pecar continued his literary work in Spanish, describing his experience in Israel: *La edad distinta: confesiones de un inmigrante en Israel* ("The Different Age: Confessions of a New Immigrant in Israel," 1970), *El hombre que hizo retroceder el tiempo* ("The Man Who Turned Back the Time," 1984) and *Yo soy mi alquimia* ("I Am My Alchemy," 1992), written with much irony. His mature literary texts expressed Pecar's understanding of the utopian components of Zionism in Israel, manifested in two of his novels: *El segundo génesis de Janán Saridor* (Mexico, 1994) and *La última profecía* (Buenos Aires, 2001), which appeared posthumously. Thematically and ideologically, these works transcend the limits of the experience of Latin American immigrants, narrating the human existential dimension and the general epic of a new life in Israel.

Pecar founded in 1985 the Association of Israeli Writers in Spanish (AIELC), over which he presided until his death. He affiliated AIELC to the International Association of Jewish Writers in Spanish and Portuguese and achieved the professional recognition of the Spanish-speaking *olim* by the Federation of Associations of Israeli Writers. Under the auspices of this federation he co-edited, with Itzhak Gun, the anthology *Mi-Sham Le-Kan: Soferim Yisra'elim Kotevim Sefaradit* ("From There to Here, Israeli Authors Write in Spanish," 1994), with works of 41 writers. A collection of his works, including unpublished texts, appeared in Argentina after his death: *La Ultima Profecia y Otros Textos. Del Schelem Aleijem argentino al Premio Presidente de Israel por su obra en hebreo* (Buenos Aires, 2001). Pecar received the President of Israel Literature Award.

[Leonardo Senkman (2nd ed.)]

PECHERSKY, ALEXANDER (1919–), Jewish lieutenant in the Soviet army who organized and successfully led the revolt in the Nazi death camp of *Sobibor. The uprising was a heroic chapter in the history of anti-Nazi resistance and led to the survival of some 50 inmates of Sobibor .

Born in Kremenchung, he moved as a child to Rostov-on-Don. Pechersky was trained as a musician before he was drafted into the Soviet army when German forces invaded Soviet Russia in the summer of 1941. In October 1941 he was captured by the Germans and imprisoned. He contracted typhoid but managed to conceal it from his captors, to avoid certain death. In May 1942, he managed to escape. He was caught again and sent to Borishov. An examination revealed that he was circumcised – Jewish. He was sent to the SS Sheroka Street camp in Minsk and then, in September 1943, when the Minsk ghetto was destroyed, he was sent to Sobibor. He arrived along with 79 other Soviet POWs. He alone was selected to work on construction. The remainder were gassed on arrival. There, together with six other Jews, he immediately started to prepare a detailed plan for a revolt, which was executed on October 14, 1943. Pechersky's men attacked the German officers, killing ten of them. With the weapons taken from the dead officers the prisoners killed or wounded 38 Ukrainian guards. Of the 600 camp inmates, about half escaped, but many of them were killed in the surrounding minefields or as a result of the large-scale manhunt organized by the Germans and by Polish fascists. Shortly afterward, the camp was dismantled. Pechersky and a group of his comrades succeeded in escaping and reaching the Soviet partisans. Later he rejoined the Soviet army and was seriously wounded in August 1944. He was demobilized and returned to his hometown. He was a major witness at the 1963 trial of 11 Ukrainian guards who had served at Sobibor.

BIBLIOGRAPHY: Y. Suhl (ed.), *They Fought Back (1967),* 7–50; Ainsztein, in: JSOS, 28 (1966), 19–24; idem, in: *Jewish Observer and Middle East Review* (April 23, 1965), 14–22; Lev, in: *Sovetish Heymland,* 2 (1964), 78–93; V. Tomin and A. Sinelnikov, *Vozvrashcheniye nezhelatel'no* (1964). **ADD. BIBLIOGRAPHY:** Y. Arad, *Belzec, Sobibor, Treblinka: Operation Reinhard Camps* (1987).

[Yosef Guri]

°PÉCHI, SIMON (c. 1567–c. 1639), Hungarian statesman, poet, and author, leader of the Judaizing "Sabbatarian" sect. Born in Transylvania, Péchi was at first employed as tutor of A. Eössy's children; Eössy, the founder of the sect, introduced him to the court of Prince Stephen Báthory. As emissary of

Báthory, Péchi set out on his political travels to Romania and Turkey and even reached Italy and Africa. There he probably acquired a knowledge of Hebrew. From 1613 he was chancellor of Transylvania under the rule of Prince Gabriel Bethlen. In 1621 he was imprisoned for reasons which are unknown but was subsequently set free. During the reign of Prince George Rákóczy, his position was so strong that he was even authorized to propagate his views in public.

In a description of the usages of the sect it is reported that in addition to the observance of the Sabbath, the wives of the members of this sect adopted the Jewish dietary laws. At the height of the sect's success about 20,000 Transylvanian Hungarians of the "Székely" tribe were among its members (1635). After a brief period and a change of political circumstances, a law was passed in Transylvania which rendered the members of the sect liable to the death penalty and confiscation of their property if they did not return to Christianity within one year. Péchi remained steadfast in his beliefs until 1638 but finally converted to Calvinism. Although death penalties were not applied, the property of the members of the sect was seized.

Péchi was a talented poet and author, and according to the opinion of S. *Kohn, historian of Hungarian Jewry and researcher on the "Sabbatarians," his works are of exceptional value. Péchi's translations from Psalms and the Jewish prayer book are of special importance, being the first in this area.

BIBLIOGRAPHY: Á. Szilády (ed.), *Péchi Simon Psalteriuma* (1913); S. Kohn, *A szombatosok* (1889); M. Guttmann and S. Harmos, *Péchi Simon szombatos imádságos könyve* (1914).

[Baruch Yaron]

PECHINA (Arabic **Bajjana**), village located N. of *Almeria on the S. coast of Spain. Until 922, when it was incorporated into Andalusia by ʿAbd al-Raḥmān III, Pechina was a separate state under Umayyad protection. During its period of independence (ninth–tenth centuries), Pechina was a prosperous, busy seaport which was settled by Arabs from the *Yemen. The Jews also shared in its prosperity, and for the most part were merchants. When *Saadiah Gaon addressed the important Jewish communities of southern Spain, Pechina was included among them in his letter (Abraham ibn Daud, *Sefer ha-Qabbalah – The Book of Tradition*, ed. by G.D. Cohen (1967), 79; see also index). Even in the late tenth century, as the town declined, a large and important Jewish community existed there. Its leader, Samuel ha-Kohen b. Josiah of Fez, Morocco, was a learned scholar who corresponded with *Sherira Gaon and supported *Ḥanokh b. Moses in his struggle against *Joseph ibn Abitur who also visited Pechina for the religious authority in Cordoba. Samuel's leadership virtually marks the final greatness of the Pechina community, most of whose members moved to developing Almeria in the tenth century. Pechina is considered by some scholars to be identical with the Spanish town of Calsena.

BIBLIOGRAPHY: E. Lévi-Provençal, *La Péninsule Ibérique au Moyen-Age* (1938), 47–50; Ashtor, Korot, 1 (1966²), 207–10.

PECS (Hung. **Pécs**; Ger. **Fuenfkirchen**), town in S. Hungary. The celebrated Turkish traveler Evlia Cselebi found Jews there (1663). During the conversionary activities of the Catholic Church at the end of the 17th century, following the end of the Turkish conquest, the Jews were expelled from the city; the city council then solemnly pledged (1692) that no Jews would set foot in Pecs again. It was not until 1788 that Jews were again permitted to settle there. Among the first to arrive was the Engel family who were among the leaders of the Jewish community for over a century. An organized community was formed in Pecs in 1840, but it already had a cemetery in 1827. The first synagogue was built in 1843 and the second in 1869; the latter, which was declared to be an architectural monument, still exists. Rabbis of Pecs were Israel Loew (officiated 1842–57); Alexander *Kohut, author of *Arukh ha-Shalem* (1872–80); A. Perls (1889–1914), one of the most notable Jewish preachers in Hungary; and Z. Wallenstein (1923–44). The Jewish population numbered 72 in 1840, 385 in 1850, 4,126 in 1910, 4,030 in 1930 and 3,486 in 1941. Up to World War I the Jews in Pecs were prosperous and included several industrialists as well as merchants, contractors, wage earners, and artisans. After the enactment of the anti-Jewish laws in Hungary of 1938 and 1939, many who were thus deprived of their livelihood turned to crafts. The Jews in Pecs assisted refugees from Germany both from their own resources and with the aid of the "Wanderfuersorge." A number of Jewish doctors who had served in the Polish army arrived in Pecs after the German occupation (on March 19, 1944) and were also helped by the community. In May of that year the Jews in Pecs were concentrated into ghettos and at the end of June were sent to Auschwitz under conditions of extreme cruelty.

After the war 414 Jewish survivors returned. In 1945 the community was reorganized, and in 1971 numbered approximately 500. By the turn of the century the population had dropped to around 300 mostly elderly Jews.

BIBLIOGRAPHY: A. Scheiber, in: MHJ, 8 (1965), 80; J. Schweitzer, *A pécsi izraelita hitközség története* (1966); idem, in: *Guttenberg Jahrbuch* (1966).

[Joseph Schweitzer]

PEDDLING, the retail sale of wares or trade services and the buying up of agricultural and village produce by an itinerant seller, craftsman, or buyer who made relatively short trips, usually recurrent, to the places where his clients or employers lived. From the Middle Ages it was an important source of livelihood for Jews in many countries. In the Muslim Near East many Jews were engaged either in peddling their crafts, as shown by the evidence of the ninth-century Karaite Benjamin al-*Nahawendi, or in peddling wares, e.g., in 12th-century Egypt, as revealed in the responsa of *Maimonides. Peddling wares and crafts remained the source of income for many Jews up to the 20th century. It is difficult to determine to what extent the traders buying from and selling to feudal lords in 11th-century Western Europe could be considered as peddlers. With the predominance of *moneylending there from the 12th century onward, the Jews ceased to engage in peddling until the 15th century; a new situation then obtained, a combination of general economic trends, the tendency of Jews expelled from cities to settle in nearby villages and estates, and the movement of Jews from the west eastward. Expulsions and the development of an economy based on great landed estates created similar conditions for peddling in Bohemia. Jews were permitted to settle on these estates, the express condition of this settlement being the "*Versilbern*," i.e., their obligation to purchase at a fixed price, the total agricultural produce of the estate. The Jewish leaseholder would pass on the produce to customers through Jewish peddlers, who also sold spices, tobacco, textiles, and manufactured utensils – again supplied to them by the leaseholder – to the peasants. The leaseholder often maintained a warehouse and processing plant and concentrated on wholesale commerce. The peddler was thus dependent, economically, legally, and socially, on the wholesaler from whom he received and offered wares on credit. By means of this system *Court Jews, who were often military contractors as well, were able to tap the economy of the country at its roots to supply immense amounts of grain, fodder, and livestock for the army. The Jewish peddler was a fixture of Bohemian rural life until well into the 19th century, when his role as intermediary in the purchase of agricultural produce declined: He sold hardware, haberdashery, sewing articles, and trinkets, and bought the peasants' by-products: feathers, furs, and hides. Poorer peddlers also bought old clothes, rags, bones, and junk. The peddler lived amicably among his Christian neighbors, to whom he was identical in dialect, dress, and manners. Generally a strict observer of the dietary laws, he adopted a special diet of eggs, cheese, onions, and bread on his Sunday until Friday peddling excursions. The hard lot of the peddler was depicted by L. *Kompert in several stories, especially "*Der Dorfgeher*," the name by which the peddler was generally known. Many Bohemian and Moravian communities were founded by peddlers, a prominent example being that of *Carlsbad. There were communities in the south of Bohemia and Moravia, such as *Kolodeje, which consisted mainly of peddlers doing business in upper and lower Austria, where Jews were not permitted to settle.

In Germany, following the expulsions of the 15th and 16th centuries, many Jews settled in villages and on estates of the gentry where they gradually adapted themselves to peddling from house to house (known in German as *hausieren*), becoming to a certain degree the itinerant middlemen between estates and villages on the one hand and towns on the other. The large estate (*Gut*) looked for intermediaries to bring its increasing amount of produce to the townspeople free of the limitations imposed by town and guilds. The activity of the Jewish peddlers was viewed with suspicion and animosity by feudal circles and townsfolk, who were wary of the changes the proliferation of peddlers was making in the relationship between the town and its surroundings. Legislation was enacted against the peddlers in several German principalities. From the second half of the 17th century the situation was exacerbated by the continuous emigration of Jews from Poland to Germany, many of whom turned to peddling. The traveling peddler was sometimes identified with wandering Jewish beggars (*Betteljuden*), as well as with vagabonds in general; smuggling also came naturally to be associated with their mobility, in particular near borders. Frequently *Schutzjuden employed their unlicensed brethren as peddlers, thereby offering them legal protection and security. Thus, in Luebeck (1658) the first of a continuous series of complaints lodged against Jewish *Hausierer* accused them of buying up precious metals, probably for reminting by the *Schutzjuden* *mintmasters. When the Jews were compelled to leave Luebeck in 1699, they settled in nearby Moisling, but complaints against the activity of Jewish peddlers in the city of Luebeck continued to be made up to the mid-19th century.

In Prussia it was objected in 1672 that Jewish peddlers "are not ashamed to go around buying and selling on holy Sunday, going to villages and entering the public houses offering their wares" (S. Stern, *Der Preussische Staat und die Juden*, I Akten, p. 29). Innumerable laws prohibiting all forms of *hausieren* were passed in many German principalities and towns. Measures taken against peddling in 1819 were one cause for thousands of Jews to emigrate from Bavaria to the U.S. Similar laws against peddling were enacted in Baden, Hesse, and Wuerttemberg. In these states emancipation was made conditional on the Jews abandoning peddling. The rapid development of 19th-century Germany gradually made the peddler's role obsolete, though he persisted in agricultural or remote regions. In the main, *Alsace-Lorraine was similar to Germany, and from there peddlers penetrated into those parts of France prohibited to Jews. The rural peddler, who was found mainly in southern Germany in the middle and late 19th century, generally lived amicably among his Christian neighbors. A staunch upholder of Orthodoxy, he often had special cooking utensils, inscribed "*kasher*," reserved for his use in the local inns.

In the variegated Jewish economic life of Poland-Lithuania, various forms of peddling were common, including market hawkers and rural peddlers engaged in buying and selling; women were often found among them. In Lvov there was even a guild of Jewish street vendors. However, major cities passed laws prohibiting peddling, which was blamed for unbusinesslike practices and regarded as endangering the livelihood of Christians. Established Jewish traders, too, often opposed the competition of the mobile peddlers. In the *Pale of Settlement of Czarist Russia peddling was an important means of livelihood up to 1917, particularly in the eastern part of the region. A rapidly growing population in the townlets and expulsion from the villages led many to take up peddling. Numerous Jewish craftsmen left their homes on Sunday, worked all week in villages, and returned home on Friday; because of this they were known as *Wochers*. More important than the peddler who brought wares to sell was the one who bought up agricultural produce, in particular goods (like flax and hemp) which could be supplied to industrial centers at home or exported to Germany. In the large cities there were also many Jewish hawkers. Peddling could not, of course, survive in a Communist economy, but in Poland and the Baltic states it continued up to the Holocaust.

Jewish rural peddlers, immigrants from Alsace-Lorraine and the Rhineland, began to appear in England toward the middle of the 18th century, becoming common in most of southern England in the late 18th and early 19th century. The poet Robert Southey stated in 1807: "You meet Jew peddlers everywhere, traveling with boxes of haberdashery at their backs, cuckoo-clocks, sealing wax… miserable prints of King and Queen… even the Nativity and Crucifixion." Some Jews were also street vendors in London and other large cities. The influx of East European Jews in the 1880s caused a sudden resurgence in street vending in London and other major cities. Penniless immigrants, immediately off the boat, began hawking wares bought on credit; in 1906, 600 of *Glasgow's 6,000 Jews were engaged in peddling and the percentage in *Edinburgh was even higher. Street vending was the springboard to other commercial occupations; the father of Simon *Marks, founder of Marks and Spencer's, proudly exhibited the cart from which he conducted his first business. After World War II the life of the East End, and including that of the Jewish street vendor, was depicted in the writings of H. Pinter, A. Wesker, W. Mankowitz, and Bernard Kops. The latter portrays this vanishing world in his play *The Hamlet of Stepney Green.*

In the Netherlands peddling and street vending received a fresh impetus with the arrival of Ashkenazim in the early 20th century. In 1921 31.6% of Amsterdam's 6,500 peddlers were Jews. The situation was identical in Belgium where there were about 1,600 Jewish market vendors in 1937, primarily in Brussels.

NORTH AMERICA. The vast areas of North America made peddling important generally until about the middle of the 19th century. Sephardi peddlers appeared as early as 1655. Of licenses granted to peddlers in Pennsylvania, one out of 18 was to a Jew in 1771, five out of 49 in 1772, and four out of 27 in 1773. Trade in calico, cutlery, snuff, and similar goods was often conducted by barter in return for skins and furs. Peddlers frequently traded with Indians, who learned to respect the peaceful and peculiar Jewish peddler with his strange dietary laws: some Cherokees named one "the eggeater." The wares of the peddler, those he sold and those he purchased for sale, were generally handled by a wealthy wholesale trader with sufficient capital, like David *Franks, Joseph Simon, or the *Gratz family. Business was conducted through frontier entrepôts where furs and skins were exchanged for cash and additional negotiable goods. Occupational hazards were financial failure and murder on the highway.

In the second and third decades of the 19th century mass emigration of Jews from southern Germany and Prussian Poland brought many of them to peddling in the United States. They dealt mainly in consumer goods, haberdashery, trinkets, and jewelry. Carrying a pack sometimes weighing around 100 lb., the peddler served the farmers' stores and sold to him at his home. About one-half of all Jewish peddlers in the period 1820–80 arrived in this immigration wave, settling predominantly in the west, beyond the Appalachians in the Middle West, and after 1865 in the Far West. Many new colonists knew German, which helped the German-Jewish peddler. In order to operate properly in these newly developed areas, the peddler needed a store to replenish his supplies, but here the functions were complementary, unlike in Europe where they were fiercely competitive. An enterprising peddler, often the first in the vicinity, opened a store to supply fellow peddlers, thus moving up economically and socially. After settling, peddlers became the nucleus of a community. The Jewish population of Cincinnati grew from a handful in 1818 to 3,300 in 1850, a large percentage of whom were peddlers, future peddlers, and former peddlers. Immediately after the 1849 gold rush Jewish peddlers arrived to ply the mines, and communities were soon founded in San Francisco and Sacramento, the supply center for the mining area. One such man was Levi *Strauss, manufacturer of the original blue jeans; many others founded stores. The Jewish peddler was present throughout the far west: the *Goldwater department stores of Arizona were founded by a peddler: Meyer *Guggenheim began his meteoric career as a peddler in the west. The *Seligman family of New York were peddlers from Baiersdorf, Bavaria. Other successful peddlers were Adam *Gimbel, Moses and Caesar *Cone, and Nathan *Straus.

The Chicago Jewish community leader Abraham Kohn (d. 1871) described in his diary his way of life on becoming a peddler within a week of his arrival from Bavaria: "Leading such a life that none of us is able to observe the smallest commandment. Thousands of peddlers wander about America: young, strong men, they waste their strength by carrying heavy loads in the summer's heat; they lose their health in the icy cold of winter. And thus forget completely their Creator. They no longer put on the phylacteries; they pray neither on working day nor on the Sabbath. In truth, they have given up their religion for the pack which is on their backs" (AJA, 3 (1951) p. 99). He found consolation in the many acquaintances from Bavaria he encountered in his rise to financial success – within two years he owned a store in Chicago. The turnover in the profession was rapid; the average peddling term being between one and five years and the average age 18–25. Unlike in Europe, where peddling was a traditional continuous occupation, in the U.S. the individual Jew used peddling as a short-term step to more stable commercial ventures. After amassing some capital he tended to enter into a partnership with a compatriot, being especially inclined to enter the clothing trade and open a shop. Country peddling became obsolete with the growth of retail trade. The mail-order business, developed especially by Julius *Rosenwald's Sears-Roebuck Co., struck hard.

Jewish vendors appeared in strength on American streets with the mass emigration from Eastern Europe in the late 19th and early 20th centuries. The Lower East Side of New York witnessed the emergence of open air markets and pushcart traders and peddlers offering every conceivable type of merchandise. The situation in Chicago was similar. In 1890–93 a census conducted in New York among 23,801 Jewish families revealed that peddling was the second most common occupation (after *tailoring), with 2,440 full-time peddlers. Their ranks were swelled in times of economic crisis and unemployment. The great number of peddlers at any one given moment barely suggested the multitudes who had passed through this apprenticeship. A vivid picture of the East Side peddler was given by Harry *Golden and other Jewish authors.

BIBLIOGRAPHY: Bohemia: R. Kestenberg-Gladstein, in: *Zion*, 12 (1947), 49–65, 160–185; idem, *Neuere Geschichte der Juden in den boehmischen Laendern* (1969), 96ff., 350f.; S.H. Lieben, in: *Afike Jehuda Festschrift* (1930) 39ff.; O. Donath, *Boehmische Dorfjuden* (1926); I. Ziegler, *Dokumente zur Geschichte der Juden in Karlsbad* (1913). Germany: M. Grunwald, *Hamburg's deutsche Juden his zur Aufloesung der Dreigemeinden* (1904), 23, 57, 60, 150; F. Nienhaus, *Die Juden im ehemaligen Herzogtum Cleve* (1914), 24–28; A. Mueller, *Geschichte der Juden in Nuernberg* (1968), 61, 105ff., 123ff.; S. Stern, *Der Preussische Staat und die Juden*, 1 (1962), Akten, no. 2, 23, 27, 28, 144, 156, 165, 213, 377, 419, 441, 455; 2 (1962), Akten no. 187, 201, 549, 551, 553, 602, 609, 611, 660; A. Kapp, in: ZGJD, 6 (1935), 45–47; H. Schwab, *Jewish Rural Communities in Germany* (1956); E. Baasch, in: *Vierteljahreshefte fuer Sozial-und Wirtschaftspolitik*, 16 (1922), 370–98; D.A. Winter, *Geschichte der juedischen Gemeinde in Moisling/Luebeck* (1968), 1–85; S. Schwarz, *Die Juden in Bayern* (1963), 125, 195–205; H. Gonsiorowski, *Die Berufe der Juden Hamburgs* (1927), 39f., 48ff., 65f., 74–77; L. Kahn, *Geschichte der Juden in Sulzburg* (1969); C. Rixen, *Geschichte und Organisation der Juden im ehemaligen Stift Muenster* (1906), 52–57; A. Taenzer, *Die Geschichte der Juden in Jebenhausen und Goeppingen* (1927), 102–43; A. Welder-Steinberg, *Geschichte der Juden in der Schweiz* (1966); M. Aschkewitz, *Zur Geschichte der Juden in Westpreussen* (1967), 85ff., 95f.; T. Oelsner, in: JSOS, 4 (1942), 241–68, 349–98; B. Brilling, *Geschichte der Juden in Breslau* (1960), 22f.; F. Kynass, *Der Jude im deutschen Volkslied* (1934), 84f., 90f., 135–8; A. Blum, *Die wirtschaftliche Lage der juedischen Landbevoelkerung im Grossherzogtum Baden* (1901), 31f. Austria: D. Herzog, *B'nai B'rith Mitteilungen fuer Oesterreich*, 33 (1933), 341–6; L. Moses, *Geschichte der Juden in Niederoesterreich* (1935), 91ff.; G. Wolf, in: *Neuzeit*, 27 (1887), 87f. Poland: R. Mahler, *Toledot ha-Yehudim be-Polin* (1946), s.v. index *Rokhelim*; S. Dubnow (ed.), *Pinkas ha-Medinah* (1925), 60, 70, 258f. W.H. Glicksman, *In the Mirror of Literature* (1966), 170ff., 189ff., 192, 198; J. Jacobson, in: MGWJ, 64 (1920), 222ff.; L. Shelomowitch, in: *Yidishe Ekonomik*, 3 (1939), 194–209; I. Schiper (ed.) *Dzieje handlu żydowskiego na ziemiach polskich* (1937). The Low Countries: K. Liberman, in: *Yidishe Ekonomik*, 2 (1938), 250–65; S. Kleerekoper, in: *Studia Rosenthaliana*, 1 (1967), 73ff.; H. Bloom, *Economic Activity of the Jews of Amsterdam* (1937), index. France: Z. Szajkowski, *Poverty and Social Welfare among French Jews (1800–1880)* (1954), 30f.; idem, *The Economic Status of the Jews in Alsace, Metz, and Lorraine (1648–1789)* (1954), 62ff.; idem, *Franco-Judaica* (1962), index; idem, in: JSOS, 8 (1946), 307f. England: A.M. Jacob, in: JHSET, 17 (1953), 63–72; J. Rumney, *ibid.*, 13 (1936), 336ff.; V.D. Lipman, *Social History of the Jews in England, 1850–1950* (1954), 28–32; L.P. Gartner, *The Jewish Immigrant in England, 1870–1914* (1960), index; C. Roth, *Essays and Portraits in Anglo-Jewish History* (1962), 130–9; A. Rubens, in: JHSET, 19 (1960). U.S.; M. Whiteman, in: JQR, 53 (1963), 306–21; idem in: *Studies and Essays in Honor of A.A. Neuman* (1962), 503–15; F.S. Fierman, in: *Password*, 8 (1963), 43–55; O. Handlin, *Adventure in Freedom* (1954), index; R. Glanz, *The Jew in Old American Folklore* (1961), 122–46; idem, in: JSOS, 7 (1945), 119–36; idem, *The Jews of California* (1960); W.J. Parish, in: *New Mexico Historical Review*, 35 (1960), 1–29; M. Freund, *Jewish Merchants in Colonial America* (1939); S. Stern, in: E.E. Hirschler (ed.), *Jews from Germany in the United States* (1955), 36–39; H.L. Golden, *Forgotten Pioneer* (1963); M. Rischin, *The Promised City* (1962), index; A. Schoener (ed.), *Portal to America: The Lower East Side 1870–1925* (1967); AJA, 8 (1956), 87–89; 19 (1967), 6–8; A.V. Goodman, *ibid.*, 3 (1951), 81–111; W.L. Provol, *ibid.*, 16 (1964), 26–34; L.M. Friedman, in: AJHSP, 44 (1955/56), 1–7; AJHSP, 38 (1948/49), 22ff.; 40 (1950/51), 59ff., 327; 53 (1963/64), 271; 54 (1964/65), 488–90; 56 (1966/67), 296–300; L. Berg, in: *Commentary* (July 1965), 63–67; J.R. Marcus (ed.), *Memoirs of American Jews*, 3 vols. (1955).

[Henry Wasserman]

°**PEDERSEN, JOHANNES** (1883–1951), Danish Semitist, religious historian, and biblical scholar. He studied Semitic philology under Frants Buhl, the reviser of Gesenius' *Lexicon*. From 1916 to 1921 Pedersen was a lecturer on the Old Testament, and from 1921 to 1950 professor of Semitic philology, at Copenhagen University. Among his works on Semitic philology are a Hebrew grammar (*Hebraeisk Grammatik*, 1926), a treatise of fundamental importance on the Keret (Kirta) text (COS I, 333–43) from Ras Shamra (*Die Krt-Legende*, 1941), and a translation and commentary on the Phoenician language Karatepe texts (in: *Acta Orientalia*, 21 (1950–53), 35–56). He also published a number of treatises on Islam in Danish. Of singular importance are Pedersen's achievements in biblical research. In 1920 he published the first volume of *Israel* (*Israel: Its Life and Culture*, Eng. tr., 1926), in which he endeavors to describe Israelite thinking and social life in terms of the mentality and behavior of a primitive civilization, thus making an attempt to extricate himself from the preconceived theological and philosophic notions that have influenced the interpretation of the old Israelite texts since Hellenistic times. In the second volume, published in 1934 (Eng. tr., 1940), Pedersen traces the development of Israelite civilization from the period of Judges until the Exile. The foundation of the religious development was the spontaneous experience of a cooperation between the divine forces and man himself; with David, purposefulness took the place of spontaneity in the relation to God, and the deity was looked upon as the strong will of personality. The preaching of the prophets emphasized the overwhelming greatness of God and the inferiority of man, thus preparing the way for Judaism's ideas of God and man. From the point of view of social development, the contact with the Canaanite way of life and urbanization resulted in a crisis in the ancient pattern of life.

In *Israel* and in his articles "Die Auffassung vom Alten Testament" (in: ZAW, 49 (1931), 161–81) and "Passahfest und Passahlegende" (*ibid.*, 52 (1934), 161–76), Pedersen condemned Higher Criticism's distinction of sources in the Pentateuch. He does not deny that there are discernible layers in the Pentateuch, yet he maintains that these cannot be distinguished and dated: "All sources are both pre-Exilic and post-Exilic." In 1931 Pedersen published *Scepticisme israélite*, a study of Ecclesiastes, and in Festschriften to Mowinckel (1955, pp. 62–72) and Rowley (1955, pp. 238–46), he shed light on the problems behind Genesis 2–3, with the help of late Jewish texts and old Oriental myths, especially the Adapa myth written in Akkadian (COS I, 449).

BIBLIOGRAPHY: Two festschriften published in honor of Pedersen's 60th and 70th birthdays: *Mélanges d'histoire des religions... J. Pedersen*, 1–3 (1944–47); *Studia Orientalia Joanni Pedersen* (1953). **ADD. BIBLIOGRAPHY:** H. Ringgren, in: DBI, 2:254–55.

[Eduard Nielson]

PEEL COMMISSION, name commonly used for the Royal Commission on Palestine under the chairmanship of Earl Peel, appointed by the British government on August 7, 1936, to study the underlying causes of the Arab riots. In July 1937 the commission presented its report recommending the partitioning of Palestine into a Jewish state, an Arab state, and a British mandatory enclave, but its recommendations were not implemented.

PEERCE, JAN (originally **Jacob Pincus Perelmuth**; 1904–1984), U.S. operatic tenor. Born in New York he first studied medicine, and began his musical career as a dance band violinist and occasional singer. In 1933 he obtained a long-term engagement as a singer at Radio City Music Hall, New York. Toscanini heard him and chose him to sing with the NBC Symphony Orchestra in 1938. After his operatic debut in Philadelphia and a recital in New York, he was cast by the Metropolitan Opera in 1941 to sing the leading tenor role in *La Traviata*. Peerce was acclaimed for his colorful quality, his sensitive interpretations, and a temperament suited both to the Italian and German lieder. Retaining his interest in Jewish life, he appeared in cantorial recitals, and made recordings of cantorial works and Jewish folksongs. He toured widely in America and Europe, London and West Germany, toured the U.S.S.R. under U.S. State Department auspices in 1956 (again in 1963), and sang in Israel many times.

BIBLIOGRAPHY: Biancolli, in: *Opera News*, 30 (Jan. 29, 1966), 26.

[Claude Abravanel]

°**PÉGUY, CHARLES-PIERRE** (1873–1914), French Catholic poet, editor, and essayist. Born in Orleans, Péguy studied at the Ecole Normale Supérieure in Paris, where he came under the influence of Henri *Bergson. Politically a radical, he puzzled men of both the left and the right with his unique fusion of socialism and Catholicism. His abiding sympathy for the Jewish people is to be seen in his activities, his writings, and his circle of friends. From 1893, he helped to rally student support for the retrial of *Dreyfus, for socialism, and for the defense of the republic. In 1900 he launched his celebrated *Cahiers de la Quinzaine*, which popularized the works of many Jewish authors, including André *Spire, Edmond *Fleg, André *Suarès, and the English novelist Israel *Zangwill. Jewish subscribers played a major part in keeping the journal alive. Péguy's bookshop near the Sorbonne became a rendezvous for liberal writers and intellectuals. A man of stern convictions, Péguy cherished four great spiritual traditions: Hebrew, Greek, Christian, and French. He believed that, while the Catholics had read for only two centuries and the Protestants since Calvin, Israel – the "eternally anguished people" – had read for 2,000 years. He adhered to the Catholic view that the Old Testament prefigured the New, but regarded the Jewish people as "the only race to have given prophets... to be of the race of prophets." Thus, Péguy considered his friend, Bernard *Lazare, though an atheist, "a prophet of Israel," because of his quest for justice. For Péguy, Israel's vocation was to remain faithful to itself and pursue its historic mission of prophecy, and he hinted that Israel's divine mission had not ended with the Christian revelation. In *Notre jeunesse* (1910), Péguy criticized the reactionary turncoat Daniel *Halévy, who had once been his friend. *Notre Patrie* (1905), *Portrait de Bernard Lazare* (1928), and *L'Argent* (1913) reflect other aspects of his philo-Semitism. Péguy's thought seems to have been influenced by Jewish messianism. This is particularly apparent in his poem, *Le Mystère de la Charité de Jeanne d'Arc* (1910 and many subsequent editions), in which Joan, fighting for both the soul and the homesteads of France, becomes the symbol of mankind's struggle for temporal salvation and his "eternal need for spiritual salvation." Péguy died in action on the Marne at the beginning of World War I.

BIBLIOGRAPHY: A. Salomon, *In Praise of Enlightenment* (1963), 375–86; A. Suarès, *Péguy* (Fr., 1915); D. Halévy, *Charles Péguy et les Cahiers de la Quinzaine* (1918); Rabi, in: *Esprit*, 32 no. 8–9 (1964), 331–42; Prajs, in: *Cahiers Paul Claudel*, no. 7 (1968), 387–404.

[Jacqueline Kahanoff]

PEIERLS, SIR RUDOLF ERNST (1907–1995), British physicist. Peierls, who was born in Berlin, held an appointment at the Federal Institute of Technology in Zurich from 1929 to 1932. In 1933 he went to England and pursued research at Manchester University for four years. He became professor of applied mathematics at Birmingham University and worked on the atomic energy project there from 1940 to 1943. In the latter year he went to the U.S. and was for three years one of the leading scientists on the Manhattan Project at the Los Alamos Laboratory. In 1946 he returned to Birmingham, where he remained until 1963, when he was appointed professor of physics at Oxford. He was elected a Fellow of the Royal Society in 1945 and was knighted in 1968.

From the outset of his academic life, Peierls was deeply involved in the development of atomic energy. At Birmingham at the outbreak of World War II, he and Otto *Frisch considered the theoretical questions involved in chain reaction and concluded that the energy liberated by a five-kilogram bomb would be equivalent to several thousand tons of dynamite. In a short paper, which also outlined a possible thermal diffusion method for the separation of uranium 235 and suggested how the bomb could be detonated, they were the first in the world to enunciate the practical possibility of the atom bomb with scientific precision. The Peierls-Frisch paper was one of the factors that influenced the British government to begin an atomic energy program prior to the Manhattan Project. Peierls' publications included: *Quantum Theory of Solids* (1955), *Laws of Nature* (1955), *Surprises in Theoretical Physics* (1979), and the autobiographical *Bird of Passage* (1985).

Sir Rudolph's son, RONALD FRANK PEIERLS (1935–), was also a physicist. Born in Manchester, he went to the United States and had posts at the Institute for Advanced Study at Princeton, NJ, and Cornell University before being appointed to the physics division at Brookhaven National Laboratory, Long Island, NY, in 1966. His main interest was the nature and properties of interactions between elementary particles.

[Julian Louis Meltzer]

PEIPER, TADEUSZ (1891–1969), Polish poet, playwright, and literary theorist. Born in Cracow, Peiper spent the years 1914–20 in Spain, returning to Poland in 1921, when he organized the Awangarda Cracow group of poets whose leading theorist he then became. During the years 1922–23 and 1926–27 Peiper edited the group's official periodical *Zwrotnica*. Believing that human progress depends on man's conquest of nature, he called for artistic glorification of the machine, technology, and invention as weapons in this struggle. Peiper also maintained that the poet's task was creative and utilitarian and that his duty was to write about organized human society in order to improve it. Although he did not succeed in founding a school, Peiper made a valuable contribution to Polish literature between the world wars. After the Nazi invasion, he fled to Moscow, where he contributed to the weekly *Wolna Polska* and to *Nowe Horyzonty*, returning to Warsaw after the defeat of Nazi Germany.

His works include verse collections such as *A* (1924), *Żywe linie* ("Living Lines," 1924), and *Poematy* (1935); *Nowe usta* ("The New Mouth," 1925), a lecture on poetry; *Tędy* ("This Way," 1930), collected articles, essays, and sketches; plays such as *Skoro go nie ma* ("Since He is Not Here," 1933); and the novel *Krzysztof Kolumb, odkrywca* ("Christopher Columbus the Discoverer," 1949).

BIBLIOGRAPHY: *Słownik współczesnych pisarzy polskich*, 2 (1964), 639–42.

[Stanislaw Wygodzki]

PEIXOTTO, U.S. family of Sephardi origin. DANIEL LEVI MADURO PEIXOTTO (1800–1843), a physician, was born in Amsterdam, and was taken to New York in 1807 by his father MOSES LEVI MADURO PEIXOTTO (1767–1828), a merchant who served as *ḥazzan* of New York's Congregation Shearith Israel from 1820 until his death. Daniel Peixotto graduated from Columbia College in 1816 and became a leading physician in New York City, serving as editor of the *New York Medical and Physical Journal* and as a founder of the New York Academy of Medicine. He was an active Jacksonian Democrat and a leader and intellectual mentor of the Jewish community. From 1835 until 1841 he was a professor at the newly founded medical school of Willoughby University near Cleveland, Ohio, a forerunner of the Case-Western Reserve University Medical School.

His son, BENJAMIN FRANKLIN PEIXOTTO (1834–1890), was a lawyer, diplomat, and Jewish communal leader. Born in New York City, he was brought by his family to Cleveland, then back to New York, later resettling in Cleveland during 1847–66. There he became a clothing merchant, and also frequently wrote editorials for the daily *Cleveland Plain Dealer*. Peixotto was a founder and president of the Mercantile Library Association and Lyceum, and a follower of Democratic Senator Stephen A. Douglas of Illinois, under whose guidance he studied law. A trustee and founder of the Sunday School at Congregation Tifereth Israel (now The Temple), he served as Grand Sar (president) of *B'nai B'rith during 1863–64 and was the prime mover for its Jewish Orphan Asylum (now Bellefaire) established in Cleveland in 1869. In 1866 Peixotto moved to New York to practice law, then transferred to San Francisco in 1869.

Early in 1870, moved by the Romanian persecution of Jews, Peixotto succeeded in becoming the first U.S. consul in Bucharest, appointed by President Grant through the intervention of the *Seligmans. His financial needs in the unpaid position, as well as political support, were provided, not always reliably, by a group of wealthy U.S. Jews, along with the B'nai B'rith, the *Board of Delegates of American Israelites, and prominent French and English Jews led by Sir Francis *Goldsmid. In Bucharest Peixotto pressed vigorously for Jewish emancipation, to which Romanian Jews were legally entitled by the Treaty of Paris of 1856, and also took the initiative in founding Jewish schools, cultural societies, and Romanian B'nai B'rith, as part of his plan to modernize Jewish life in that country. Although he accomplished little toward emancipation, his well-publicized presence inhibited new antisemitic legislation and avoided or mitigated several pogroms. His unofficial inquiry in the summer of 1872 about the possibility of large-scale Romanian Jewish immigration to the U.S. was loudly endorsed by that regime, but scandalized most of Peixotto's backers and was rejected by them as a policy. Although much embarrassed, he continued to endorse emigration privately while serving in Bucharest until 1876. From 1877 to 1885 Peixotto was U.S. consul in Lyons, and then lived in New York City, engaging in law, Republican politics, and Jewish communal affairs until his death.

His son was GEORGE DA MADURO PEIXOTTO (1859–1937), a painter. Born in Cleveland, he received his art education in Dresden during his father's service in Romania. He became a notable portrait painter, executing portraits from life of Cardinal Manning, President McKinley, Chief Justice Waite, and John Hay, among others. His *Grandchildren of Mark Hopkins* won wide praise, and his *Family Group* was exhibited at the Paris Salon in 1893. Peixotto's portrait of Sir Moses *Montefiore at the latter's centenary in 1884 hung in the Corcoran Gallery, and his painting of Julius *Bien hangs in the National Museum, Washington, D.C. Murals by him decorated the New Amsterdam Theater and the Criterion Club in New York City.

BIBLIOGRAPHY: J.L. Blau and S.W. Baron, *Jews of the United States 1790–1840*, 2 (1964), 437–9, 469–75, 597–601; M.U. Schappes, *Documentary History of the Jews in the United States* (1951²), 611; D. de Sola Pool, *Portraits Etched in Stone* (1952), 428–32; L.P. Gartner, in: AJHSQ, 58 (1968/69), 25–117; AJYB, 6 (1904/05), 163; I.J. Benjamin, *Three Years in America 1859–1862*, 1 (1956), 51–52; *New York Times* (Oct. 13, 1937).

[Lloyd P. Gartner]

PEIXOTTO, JESSICA BLANCHE (1864–1941), U.S. professor of economics. Granddaughter of Dr. Daniel Levy Maduro *Peixotto and daughter of Raphael Peixotto and Myrtilla Jessica Davis Peixotto, Jessica Peixotto was born in New York City but educated in San Francisco. After graduating from Girls' High School in 1880, she studied privately at home for a decade but in 1891 decided to enroll as a special student at the University of California, Berkeley against her father's wishes. After received her B.A. in 1894, she continued graduate studies in political science and in 1900 became the second woman to receive a Ph.D. from Berkeley. Her dissertation, *The French Revolution and Modern French Socialism*, was published in 1901.

In 1904, Jessica Peixotto was invited to teach at Berkeley as a lecturer in sociology, although her field was social economics. In 1907, she became assistant professor of economics, and in 1918, she was promoted to full professor of social economics; she was the first woman to achieve that rank at the University of California and also the first woman to head a department. She established and chaired the Heller Committee for Research in Social Economics and initiated a special program within the economics department that eventually resulted in the creation of a professional school of social work at Berkeley.

In addition to her thesis, Peixotto published several books and numerous reports, articles, and course syllabi in periodicals. Among her most important works are *Getting and Spending at the Professional Standard of Living: A Study of the Costs of Living on Academic Life* (1927) and *Cost of Living Studies, II: How Workers Spend a Living Wage* (1929). A festschrift, *Essays in Social Economics in Honor of Jessica Blanche Peixotto* (1935), published at the time of her retirement from Berkeley, pays tribute to her life and work.

Jessica Peixotto was also actively involved in public service. She was a member of the Berkeley Commission of Public Charities (1910–13) and then the California State Board of Charities and Corrections (1912–24), chairing the Committee on Children and the Committee on Research. During World War I, she worked in Washington as the executive officer of the child welfare department of the Women's Committee of the Council of National Defense and then as head of the council's child conservation section. In 1928, she was elected vice president of the American Economic Association. She later served on the Consumers' Advisory Board of the National Recovery Administration (1933). Peixotto received honorary law doctorates from Mills College (1935) and the University of California (1926).

BIBLIOGRAPHY: J.R. Baskin, "Peixotto, Jessica Blanche," in: *Jewish Women in America*, 2:1040–41; H.R. Hatfield. "Jessica Blanche Peixotto," in: *Essays in Social Economics in Honor of Jessica Blanche Peixotto* (1935), 5–14, 361–63; "Economics at Cal: At the Cutting Edge for 100 Years," in: *The Econ Exchange*, vol. 5, no. 1 (Spring 2002), 1–5.

[Harriet Pass Freidenreich (2nd ed.)]

PEIXOTTO, JUDITH SALZEDO (1823–81), U.S. teacher and principal. Granddaughter of Moses Levi Maduro *Peixotto and daughter of Dr. Daniel Levy Maduro Peixotto and Rachel Seixas Peisotto, Judith Peixotto lived all her life in New York City. After their father's death in 1843, she and her younger sisters Zipporah and Sara Naar were among the earliest Jewish women to be hired as teachers in New York City. Judith Peixotto taught at the Ward School No. 10 for Girls on James Street in the Fourth Ward from 1847 to 1850. The first Jewish principal in the New York City public schools, she directed the James Street Female Evening School for learners over 12 from 1849 to 1850 and then served for several years as one of three principals of the elementary school. After her 1852 marriage to David Solis Hays, a well known pharmacist, Judith Peixotto Hays gave up teaching and raised a large family of eight children.

BIBLIOGRAPHY: A. Ben-Ur, "Peixotto, Judith," in: *Jewish Women in America*, 2:1041–42. Elfrida D. Cowen. "Judith Salzedo Peixotto," AJHS 26 (1918), 249–50.

[Harriet Pass Freidenreich (2nd ed.)]

PEKAH (Heb. פֶּקַח; "He [God] has opened [His eyes]," i.e., given heed), son of Remaliah, king of Israel from 735 to 732 B.C.E. (II Kings 15:27–32). In the inscriptions of Tiglath-Pileser III, his name appears in the form *Pa-qa-ḥa*. It is stated that Pekah was the *shalish* (apparently, "army commander") of high rank of Pekahiah son of Menahem and that he conspired against his royal master in Samaria with the aid of "fifty men of the Gileadites and… slew him, and reigned in his stead" (II Kings 15:25). The statement in the Bible that Pekah reigned for 20 years (II Kings 15:27) can hardly be accepted as it stands, since he was killed by *Hoshea son of Elah (II Kings 15:30) in 732 B.C.E. at the very latest, while *Menahem son of Gadi is still mentioned in Tiglath-Pileser III's inscriptions as king of Samaria in 738 (or 743, at the earliest). For this reason, some scholars think that Pekah reigned in Gilead (cf. II Kings 15:25) for a certain period overlapping the reigns of the kings in Samaria, and seized the throne in Samaria only in 736, most probably with the aid of *Rezin, king of Aram. From both the biblical sources and the Assyrian documents it is clear that the military and political alliance of Pekah and Rezin operated against Judah, on the one hand, and against Assyria, on the other. The stronger partner in the alliance was Rezin (cf. Isa. 7:2), whose help Pekah evidently needed against rivals to his throne. According to II Kings 15:37, Pekah and Rezin first attacked Judah in the reign of Jotham and continued the war into the reign of Ahaz (II Kings 16; II Chron. 28). In the opinion of most commentators the occasion for the war was an attempt by Aram and Israel to force Ahaz to join an anti-Assyrian alliance led by Aram-Damascus and supported by Egypt. The armies of Aram and Israel invaded Judah (II Chron. 28:5–15) and laid siege to Jerusalem (II Kings 16:5; Isa. 7:2). The allies intended to contract the kingdom of Judah's territory to the advantage of the kingdom of Israel, to depose the Davidic dynasty, and to install as king in Jerusalem a certain "son of Tabeel," possibly a Transjordanian and an ancestor of the *Tobiads. But the course of events was completely changed by the appearance of Tiglath-Pileser III in southern Syria and Palestine. In 734 B.C.E. the Assyrian armies undertook an expedition against Philistia, along the Phoenician coast, and it is possible that during his campaign Tiglath-Pileser III detached the coastal region (the Dor district and the Sharon region) from the kingdom of Israel. In 733 B.C.E. the Assyrian army besieged Damascus, at the same time conquering northern Transjordan, Gilead, and Galilee and deporting the population of these areas to Assyria (II Kings 15:29). Tiglath-Pileser III himself mentions, in his Annals, the capture of (Ramoth) Gilead and cities in Galilee and the deportation of their populations. In the following year (732 B.C.E.) the Assyrian armies apparently invaded the hill country of Ephraim and threatened to capture the capital, Samaria. According to the biblical narrative, Hoshea son of Elah then conspired against Pekah and usurped the throne (II Kings 15:30). Pekah's policy, in contrast to that of Menahem and his son Pekahiah, apparently showed allegiance to Assyria, had grave consequences for the kingdom of Israel, and marked the beginning of the process which culminated in the fall of Samaria about a decade later. The most fertile areas of the kingdom were conquered by the Assyrians and turned into the Assyrian provinces of *Gilead, *Megiddo, and *Dor (cf. Isa. 8:23).

BIBLIOGRAPHY: Bright, Hist, 254–60; Albright, in: BASOR, 140 (1955), 34–35; J. Cook, in: VT, 14 (1964), 121–35; Oded, in: *Tarbiz*, 38 (1968/69), 205ff.; Mazar, in: IEJ, 7 (1957), 137–45; Tadmor, in: H.H. Ben-Sasson (ed.), *Toledot Am Yisrael bi-Ymei Kedem* (1969), 134–5.

[Bustanay Oded]

PEKAHIAH (Heb. פְּקַחְיָה; "YHWH has opened [the eyes]"), the son of *Menahem; ruled Israel in Samaria for two years (c. 737/6–735/4 B.C.E.) during the reign of Uzziah, son of Amaziah, over Judah (II Kings 15:22–24). The Bible provides no information about Pekahiah's acts or about the condition of the northern kingdom in his day, apart from the formulaic comment, "He did what was evil in the sight of the Lord…" (II Kings 15:24). It may be presumed that Pekahiah continued the policy of his father, Menahem, and displayed his loyalty to Assyria. In the second year of his reign he fell victim to a conspiracy led by his army commander *Pekah, son of Remaliah, who killed him with the support of 50 Gileadites and took his place on the throne (II Kings 15:25).

BIBLIOGRAPHY: Bright, Hist, 254.

[Bustanay Oded]

PEKARSKY, MAURICE BERNARD (1905–1962), Hillel director. Born in Jedwavne, Poland, Pekarsky came to the United States with his family and settled in Grand Rapids, Michigan. He attended the University of Michigan, received his B.A. cum laude in 1930, and went on to study at the University of California and then at the University of Iowa with famed social psychologist and close friend Kurt *Lewin. He was ordained at the Jewish Institute of Religion and then joined the Hillel Foundations, where he remained for the rest of his life. He directed the Hillel Foundation at Cornell (1933–37) and Northwestern (1937–40), and then moved to the University of Chicago from 1940 onward, taking five years off in 1950 to move to Jerusalem, where he established the Hillel program at The Hebrew University. Within Hillel, he was responsible for the establishment of the National Hillel Summer Institute, which he guided, and also headed its department of leadership training. He could have been national director but felt most at home on the campus, most at ease with students. Abram Sachar, who recruited him for Hillel, said of Pekarsky, "His was no negative faith. He was serenely positive in his relationship to a living God.… [He] had an inner fire that warmed without burning, that glowed without searing, and legions of students carried that brightness away with them from his presence."

His medium of expression was the spoken word. He was a teacher, not a writer, and he was keenly aware that the printed word is frozen into finality. His written work consists largely of incomplete notes for speeches, which he continually reworked in the search for greater coherence and clarity of expression. Pekarsky's lectures and class notes were published by Hillel in tribute to his work and his mind. He tried to synthesize faith and reason; to unite the world of the East and the West. A firmly committed believer, he was more interested in psychology than theology.

Alfred *Jospe, his friend and colleague, summed up his legacy. "He gave all those he encountered an awareness of the importance of the dialectical method in the education process.… If you asked him a question, you did not get an answer, but a reformulated question," deeper, more profound, more insistent than the one that was asked. He was as eager to learn as to teach – eager to learn so he might teach.

Jospe said that "under his leadership the Hillel Foundation at the University of Chicago became a unique intellectual and cultural center for the entire campus community, a forum for the study and discussion of vital issues of moral and social significance. He attracted some of the great minds on the faculty of the University of Chicago to Hillel" not only to speak but to learn. It was a tradition that empowered his successors and served as an example to others.

BIBLIOGRAPHY: Alfred Jospe (ed.), *The Legacy of Maurice Pekarsky* (1965).

[Raphael Jospe (2nd ed.)]

PEKELIS, ALEXANDER HAIM (1902–1946), jurist and communal worker. Born in Odessa, Russia, Pekelis studied at various European universities. In 1932 he was appointed lecturer in jurisprudence at the University of Florence but the local Fascist party had him removed. He became professor of jurisprudence at the University of Rome in 1935 where he founded and edited a review, *Il Massimario Della Corte Toscana*. Pekelis left Italy following the enactment of the antisemitic laws in 1938 and settled in Paris where he practiced law. Just before the Nazi occupation of France in June 1940, Pekelis went with his wife and five children to Lisbon and in 1941 emigrated to the United States. He lectured at the New School for Social research in New York City and at the same time studied at the Columbia University Law School, where he was editor in chief of the *Columbia Law Review*. In 1945, he became chief consultant to the Commission on Law and Social Action of the American Jewish Congress, a post he held until his death in an airplane accident at Shannon, Ireland, while returning from an international Zionist conference as a representative of the Labor Zionist movement.

Pekelis made an important contribution to the struggle against antisemitism with the formulation of a bold new program for the American Jewish Congress entitled "Full Equality in a Free Society – A Program for Jewish Action." He drafted the bill, enacted two years after his death, which ultimately eliminated the numerus clausus in the medical schools of New York state. Pekelis contributed many articles urging a "jurisprudence of welfare," the submission of "private governments" to constitutional requirements, the establishment of a "Human Rights Agency" by the United Nations and an annual "Supreme Court Yearbook" which would critically examine that court's decisions. Many of his proposals were subsequently adopted.

BIBLIOGRAPHY: M.R. Konvitz, ed., *Law and Social Action: Selected Essays of Alexander H. Pekelis* (1950).

[Will Maslow]

PEKERIS, CHAIM LEIB (1908–1993), mathematician. Born in Alytus, Lithuania, Pekeris immigrated to the United States in his late teens. He did research at the Massachusetts Institute of Technology from 1936 to 1940, and from 1941 to 1946 headed the mathematics-physics group in the war research division at Columbia University. After two years at the Institute for Advanced Study at Princeton, he went to Israel in 1948, to establish the department of applied mathematics at the Weizmann Institute of Science. Under his direction, an eight-year gravimetrical and seismic mapping survey of the country was undertaken, and methods of prospecting were developed which laid the basis for Israel's petroleum-boring programs.

Pekeris' own main interests were the internal constitution of the earth, including the study of the origin and nature of earthquakes, theoretical seismology, the calculation of ocean tides, and the way fluids flow through pipes and around obstacles.

[Julian Louis Meltzer]

Pekeris' work has gained for him a number of distinguished honors outside Israel. In 1971 he was elected foreign and honorary member of the American Academy of Arts and Sciences. In 1974 he was awarded the Vetlesen Prize – also known as the Nobel Prize of the earth sciences – and in 1980 was the recipient of the coveted Gold Medal of the Royal Astronomical Society, previous members of which include Einstein and Eddington. Also in 1980 he was awarded the Israel Prize for the exact sciences.

PEKERMAN, JOSÉ NESTOR (1949–), Argentinean soccer player, coach, and teacher of young players. Born in Villa Domínguez, Entre Ríos, he played for the Argentinos Juniors (1970–1974) and in the Colombian league, where he finished his career as a player. He was coach of the minor league teams of Colo-Colo in Chile and the Argentinos Juniors. He gained fame when, after having been chosen as coach of the Argentinean youth team, he won the world championships in Qatar (1995), Malaysia (1997), and Argentina (2001). In 2003 he turned down an offer to coach the Argentinean national team but did accept this post in September 2004 after the death of Marcelo Bielsa.

Pekerman is known for his professionalism, modesty, and leadership.

[Alejandro Dubesarsky (2nd ed.)]

PEKI'IN (Heb. פְּקִיעִין), village in Upper Galilee; noted for its tradition of continuous Jewish settlement throughout the ages. Peki'in can possibly be identified with Baca (Jos., Wars 3:39), the town which marked the boundary between the Upper and Lower Galilee. Fragments of reliefs with Jewish symbols are found dispersed in the village, dating from the late Roman period. According to the *Pesikta de-Rav Kahana*, Beqa' was the place where R. *Simeon b. Yoḥai and his son R. Eleazar lived in a cave for 13 years during the Hadrianic persecution of Jews which followed the Bar Kokhba War (132–35). In the *Midrash Kohelet Rabbah* (10:11), which is the main source of the story, the place is called Peki'in. During their stay in the cave they lived from the fruits of an old mulberry tree. Above the cave stood a giant carob tree and a spring was located below it. Votive gifts and oil lamps were placed in the crevice of the cave by Jews and non-Jews alike. Additional places of importance in the village included the marked grave of the talmudic scholar R. *Abba Oshayah of Tiria, which was located near the spring of Ein Tiria to the west of Peki'in and surrounded by large and hallowed trees, referred to by the Jews of the village as the "groves." Also located there was the tomb of R. Yose of Peki'in, which is mentioned in the Zohar and other sources. The antiquity, mystery, and wonder surrounding the Jews of Peki'in were added to by the presence of Jewish fellaheen in this outlying corner of Upper Galilee and their claim of being the last group of Jews who were never exiled. Their features, their clothing, their language, and their Arabic village life until the second third of the 20th century all added to the character of the village.

The Jews of Peki'in are first mentioned in the travel book of R. Moses *Basola (1522). He refers to them as "*fallaḥim*" ("workers of the land") and to the village by its Arabic name, "Bukayyʿa." Responsa of the Safed rabbis of the 16th century dealing with *mitzvot* to be fulfilled only in the Land (of Israel) – the priestly tithes, the levitical tithes, and the Sabbatical Year, all of which concern Jewish farm workers in Galilee – also testify to the existence of Jewish agriculture in Bukayyʿa. The Jews of the village were also engaged in the breeding of silkworms. Sixteenth-century Turkish tax registers from the Istanbul archives, which mention the number of taxable Jewish families in ten Galilee villages during the years 1525–73, include 33 to 45 Jewish families in Bukayyʿa. From time to time groups of Jews engaged in commerce and the leasing and tilling of lands; other groups engaged in the study of Torah and the Zohar "under the carob tree of R. Simeon b. Yoḥai." Peki'in was also a summer resort for urban Jews, especially for those from Tiberias. The Jews of the towns sought refuge there when plagues broke out. In 1602 R. Joseph *Trani of Safed visited Peki'in to instruct the local Jews, who were cultivating mulberries for silkworms.

The name Peki'in again appears during the 18th century. In 1742, the kabbalist R. Ḥayyim *Attar, who during the same year had emigrated to Ereẓ Israel with his disciples, lived there for about two months. After the severe earthquakes of 1759, many of the victims from Safed fled there. The rabbis of Safed also established a yeshivah for some time in the village. The refugees included the son of Rabbi Jacob of Vilna, who was from the group led by R. *Judah he-Ḥasid, which had emigrated to Ereẓ Israel. R. Joseph Sofer, author of *Edut bi-Yhosef*, lived and died in Peki'in. R. Reuben Satanov, author of *Ahavat Ẓiyyon*, also lived and studied the Zohar there. In 1783 some members of the ḥasidic *aliyah* from Russia and Poland established themselves there after leaving Safed and Jerusalem.

In 1820 only 20 families of Jews were left in Peki'in; their number rose to 50 (totalling 300 persons) in 1832 – mainly Sephardim. In 1856, 50 Jews remained in Peki'in and, in 1900, 11 families of farmers (93 persons). During the riots of 1929, the Jews of Peki'in were compelled to abandon their village out of fear of the Arab gangs. Upon their return to the village, they were occasionally compelled to seek work in the Jewish settlements. After the riots of 1936–39, only one family returned to the village. In 1948 Peki'in's population included 800 Druze, 242 Christians, 68 Muslims, and one Jewish family, Zeynati (from the old inhabitants). In 1948 Peki'in was incorporated into Israel; part of the Arab inhabitants left, and Jews – new immigrants – were settled there. The ancient synagogue and the cemetery were renovated with the assistance of I. *Ben-Zvi and are considered historical sites. The traditional tombs of R. Oshayah of Tiria and R. Yose of Peki'in were also repaired. In 1955, the moshav Peki'in ha-Ḥadashah ("New Peki'in") was established above Ein Tiria. The new settlers arrived from Spanish and French Morocco, from Tangier, Fez, and Marrakesh. In 1968, "Old" Peki'in had 2,070 inhabitants, about three-quarters Druze and the rest Christian Arabs, mostly of the Greek Orthodox denomination. In the mid-1990s the population of Peki'in ha-Ḥadashah stood at approximately 210, increasing to 290 in 2002. In the synagogue of Peki'in (built in 1873) and on the walls of some of the houses of the village are incorporated fragments of reliefs, showing Jewish symbols such as the seven-branched candlestick (*menorah*), the *shofar* and *lulav*, the vine, etc. These remains prove the existence of a synagogue in the village during the talmudic period.

BIBLIOGRAPHY: J. Braslavski (Braslavi), *Le-Ḥeker Arẓenu* (1954), index; idem, in: BJPES, 3 (1935/36), 24–29; idem, in: *Ma'aravo shel-Galil ve-Ḥof ha-Galil* (1965), 137ff.; B. Lewis, *Notes and Documents from the Turkish Archives* (1952), 9, 20–21; Goodenough, Symbols, 218–9, 572–3; I. Ben-Zvi, *She'ar Yashuv* (1965), index. **ADD. BIBLIOGRAPHY:** Z. Ilan, *Ancient Synagogues in Israel* (1991), 54–55; Y. Tsafrir, L. Di Segni and J. Green, *Tabula Imperii Romani. Iudaea – Palaestina. Maps and Gazetteer* (1994), 73, s.v. "Baca, Beca."

[Michael Avi-Yonah and Joseph Braslavi (Braslavski)]

PEKING (Beijing), capital of China. In the second half of the 13th century Marco Polo reported the presence of Jews in Beijing among the followers of the Mongol emperor Kublai Khan. The Scottish traveler, John Bell, who visited Beijing in 1720–21, found a few Jews, supposedly descendants of these early arrivals. This remnant disappeared and no Jews settled in Beijing until modern times. During World War II there were about 100 Jews of various nationalities (or stateless) in Beijing, mostly European refugees. All of them left the Chinese capital after the war.

BIBLIOGRAPHY: I. Cohen, *Journal of a Jewish Traveller* (1925), 189–94.

[Rudolf Loewenthal]

PEKOD (Heb. פְּקוֹד), *Aramean tribe that once inhabited the eastern bank of the Lower Tigris, and is identified with the Puqudu mentioned in Assyrian texts beginning with the time of Tiglath-Pileser III. The Pekod tribe was organized and put under the jurisdiction of the governor of Arrapha. However, the tribe participated in many revolts and was subsequently deported. Many individuals of this tribe are known from the sources. In the Bible, Pekod is mentioned in Jeremiah's prophecy against Babylon (Jer. 50:21) in a wordplay: *pqd*, "to punish." The Babylonian king is called to go up against well-known enemies (see *Chaldea), such as the tribe of Pekod, which was practically unconquerable, and thus exhaust himself and bring upon himself punishment and doom. Ezekiel 23:23 mentions Pekod as a typical representative of the Babylonian "mobile" administration. The verse speaks of peoples sent to conquered territories to fill various posts or as settler-deportees. Pekod (like similar tribes) could act as a police force or fill other posts.

BIBLIOGRAPHY: E. Forrer, *Die Provinzeinteilung des assyrischen Reiches* (1920), 96, 98ff.; Luckenbill, Records, index; J. Bright, *Jeremiah* (1965), 359; J.A. Brinkman, *A Political History of Post-Kassite Babylonia* (1968), index. For further bibl. see *Aram, Arameans.

[Pinhas Artzi]

PELICAN, one of the largest of water birds. Three species of the pelican (genus *Pelecanus*) are occasionally seen in Israel in the nature preserve that was formerly part of the Ḥuleh swamps, as well as in fish ponds. The pelican may be the שַׂקְנַאי (*saknai*) mentioned in the Talmud (Ḥul. 63a) as a bird that was eaten in some places but not in others since there were doubts as to its *kashrut*. Its Hebrew name is derived from the pouch (*sak*) under its lower bill jaw used for storing the fish it catches. The Septuagint identifies the pelican with the קָאַת (*ka'at*; Lev. 11:18; Isa. 34:11; et al.), which was apparently the view, too, of an *amora* (Ḥul. loc. cit.), who identified the *ka'at* with the *kik* (Ḥul. loc. cit with the reading of the Arukh) said to be found in the neighborhood of seas and to be very fatty (Shab. 21a). But the identification of *ka'at* with the pelican, a waterfowl, is improbable, since it is mentioned in the Bible as a bird that inhabits the desert and ruins, and is a species of *owl. This identification has, however, passed into modern Hebrew.

BIBLIOGRAPHY: Lewysohn, Zool, 184f., 368; F.S. Bodenheimer, *Animal and Man in Bible Lands* (1960), 64; M. Dor, *Leksikon Zo'ologi* (1965), 343.

[Jehuda Feliks]

PELLA or **PAḤAL**, ancient city situated east of the Jordan River, 8 mi. (c. 13 km.) South-east of Beth-Shean. The present name of the site is Khirbet Faḥil. The first mention of it occurs in the Egyptian Execration texts, dating to the late 19th century B.C.E. as Pi-ḥi-lim. It is mentioned as well in almost all Egyptian sources relating to Canaan, appearing in the list of Canaanite cities of Thutmosis III as *Phr*; in Anastasi Papyri (3 and 4) as a center for the manufacture of chariots; in the Beth-Shean stele of Seti I as a place which revolted against Egypt and besieged Rehob, and was subsequently subdued in one day by the first regiment of the Amon brigade; and in the list of Ramses II. From El-Amarna letter 148, it appears that Hazor and Tyre contended for possession of *Piḥili*, whose prince at that time was Motbaal. A large "migdol" type temple has recently been uncovered at the site. After 1300 B.C.E. the place is not mentioned in extant sources; however, Late Bronze and Iron Age pottery was found there. It revived in the Hellenistic period, when it was known as Pella, after the Macedonian capital. A legendary account by Stephen of Byzantium (Eth. 103–4) has the city being founded by Alexander the Great (332/331 B.C.E.). The city was captured by Antiochus III in 218 B.C.E. (Polybius 5:70, 12) and later by Alexander Yannai, who destroyed it (Jos., Ant., 13:397). Pompey restored it and incorporated it into the Decapolis league. Prior to Jerusalem's siege by Titus, its Christian community moved to Pella. Some Christians, including the author Aristion of Pella, remained there afterward. In Byzantine times it was the seat of a bishop. The hot baths located there (Ḥamta di Paḥal) are mentioned in the Jerusalem Talmud (Shev. 6:1, 36c). In 635/636 Muslim Arabs defeated the Byzantine forces near Pella and took the city, which continued to exist for some time (as Fiḥl) with a mixed Greek and Arab population.

The site was investigated in the 19th century by the travelers C. Irby and J. Mangles in 1818, and subsequently by the explorer E. Robinson in 1852. Excavations of the site were undertaken in 1958 by N. Richardson and R.W. Funk, in 1967 by R.H. Smith, and since 1979 and into the 1990s by R.H. Smith, A.W. McNicoll, and J.B. Hennessey. The earliest remains date from the Neolithic period, while its rapid decline took place in late Umayyad times. The rich finds, both in architecture and tomb deposits as well as small finds, indicate that Pella was a prosperous town from the Hellenistic to the Umayyad periods. Hellenistic and Byzantine civic buildings, a theater or odeon, and three churches have been uncovered.

BIBLIOGRAPHY: G. Schumacher, *Pella* (Eng., 1888); D.C. Steuernagel, *Der 'Adschlūn* (1925), 398ff.; J. Richmond, in: PEFQS, 166 (1934), 18ff.; Funk and Richardson, in: BA, 21 (1958), 82ff.; H. Seyrig, in: *Syria*, 36 (1959), 68ff.; Press, Ereẓ, s.v. **ADD. BIBLIOGRAPHY:** J. Basil Hennessy et al., "Pella," in: *Archaeology of Jordan*, vol. 2 (1989), 406–41; R.H. Smith, "Excavations at Pella of the Decapolis, 1979–1985," in: *National Geographic Research*, 1 (1987), 478–89.

[Michael Avi-Yonah / Shimon Gibson (2nd ed.)]

PELLEG (Pollak), FRANK (1910–1968), Israeli musician. Born in Prague, Pelleg conducted at the Prague Opera before going to Palestine in 1936. There he initiated chamber music concerts at the Tel Aviv Museum. After the War of Independence Pelleg headed the Music Department of the Ministry of Education (1948–52). In 1951 he moved to Haifa, where he managed the affairs of the Haifa Philharmonic Orchestra and was its musical adviser. He also served the Haifa Theatre in the same capacity. A well-known pianist and harpsichordist, Pelleg traveled widely and was noted for his interpretation of Bach.

He lectured at the Tel Aviv Museum and at the Samuel Rubin Israel Academy of Music, Tel Aviv University, at the Technion and at the University of Haifa. He composed for the piano and for chamber orchestras, and wrote vocal music and also incidental music for the theater. Pelleg wrote a number of works on music, among them *Da et ha-Muzikah* (1946) and *Kelei ha-Neginah* (1965).

[Yemima Gottlieb]

°**PELLICANUS (Pellikan), CONRAD (Kursiner, Kuers(ch)ner**, also known as **Pellicanus Rubeaquensis**; 1478–1556), German *Hebraist and Bible scholar. Born in Rouffach, Alsace, Pellicanus entered the Franciscan order in 1493. He first obtained Hebrew manuscripts of the Prophets from the convert Johannes *Pauli, an eminent Rhenish preacher, and it was the laborious study of these manuscripts which determined his subsequent scholarly career. In Tuebingen he met Johann *Reuchlin, and on his encouragement began copying Hebrew texts; later he learned Aramaic and translated books on grammar and Kabbalah. One of the pioneer Christian Hebraists of Northern Europe, Pellicanus was the first Christian to publish a Hebrew grammar, *De modo legendi et intelligendi Hebraeum* (Strasbourg, 1504), a forerunner of Reuchlin's *De rudimentis Hebraicis*. After teaching Bible in Basle (1502–07) and Rouffach (1508–11), he became a wandering scholar for some years. He visited the library of *Trithemius in Sponheim, met Jacques Lefèvre d'Etaples in Paris, and copied and acquired Hebrew books. In 1519 he became Guardian in his order's monastery in Basle, where he again met his old friend and pupil, Sebastian *Muenster. By publishing *Luther's writings in 1520, Pellicanus contributed decisively to the Reformation in Basle. This, however, led to a conflict with the order, and he was deposed from his Guardianship (1523). Pellicanus was then appointed professor of theology at Basle University, but in 1526 he accepted a call from the Swiss reformer Huldreich (Ulrich) Zwingli, an old friend and colleague, to become professor of Hebrew at Zurich. By then he had married, and formally embraced Protestantism.

Pellicanus was a prominent collaborator in the Zwinglian Bible translations into German; he published a voluminous *Commentaria Bibliorum* (Zurich, 1532–39), which reveals his wide reading in the Christian Kabbalah. He translated many rabbinic works, including *Genesis Rabbah* and commentaries on the Pentateuch by Abraham Ibn Ezra and Baḥya b. Asher, as well as part of Guillaume *Postel's version of the Zohar on Genesis. He also copied Gerard *Veltwyck's *Shevilei Tohu* and Postel's kabbalistic treatise on the Candelabrum (*Or Nerot ha-Menorah*), both of which he translated into Latin. These have been preserved in manuscript in Zurich.

BIBLIOGRAPHY: M. Adam, *Vitae germanorum theologorum* (Frankfurt, 1653[2]), 262–99; E. Silberstein, *Conrad Pellicanus; ein Beitrag zur Geschichte des Studiums der hebraeischen Sprache in der ersten Haelfte des XVI. Jahrhunderts* (1900); F. Secret, *Le Zôhar chez les kabbalistes chrétiens de la Renaissance* (1964[2]), index; idem, in: *Bibliothèque d'Humanisme et Renaissance*, 22 (1960), 389ff.; idem, *Les kabbalistes chrétiens de la Renaissance* (1964), index; idem, *G. Postel (1510–1581) et son Interprétation du Candélabre de Moyse en hébreu, latin, italien et français* (1966), introd. and 33ff.; Baron, Social[2], 13 (1969), 164, 166, 169, 394–5; G.E. Weil, *Élie Lévita, Humaniste et Massorète (1469–1549)* (1963), 10–25, 248–54. **ADD. BIBLIOGRAPHY:** B. Riggenbach (ed.), *Das Chronikon des Konrad Pellikan* (1877/1980) (autobiography, in Latin); Ch. Zuercher, *Konrad Pellikans Wirken in Zuerich…* (1975) (with bibliography).

[Godfrey Edmond Silverman / Aya Elyada (2nd ed.)]

PELTIN, SAMUEL HIRSH (1831–1896), Polish author. Peltin settled in Warsaw in 1855, and established there in 1865 the Polish weekly **Izraelita*. In this journal, which he edited until his death, he wrote articles on religion, ethics, and Jewish history, and defended the Jewish cause against antisemitic attacks. He also wrote a number of tales of Jewish life, and translated the works of Leopold *Kompert and other writers. In his youth he compiled a Polish textbook, especially designed for Jewish children. He left many works in manuscript, including a book on Jewish history entitled "Historia Zydow." Peltin was active in the Reform Temple in Warsaw and attempted to give a Polish rather than a German orientation to the service and the sermon, and invest it with the character suited to an enlightened Polish Jewish intellectual.

BIBLIOGRAPHY: N. Sokolow (ed.), *Sefer Zikkaron* (1889), 91; J. Shatzky, *Di Geshikhte fun Yidn in Varshe*, 3 (1953), 165–71.

PELTZ, ISAC (1899–1980), Romanian novelist. Born in Bucharest, Peltz first wrote essays, prose poems, sketches, and stories, which appeared in several volumes between 1916 and 1924. His prizewinning first novel, *Viața cu haz și fără a numitului Stan* ("The Humorous and Not-So Humorous Life of Stan," 1929) heralded the career of one of the most prolific and highly praised writers in Romanian literature. For the first time, Jewish ghetto life with all its color and its drama was given artistic form in Romanian literature. Peltz's novels told the full story of the Jewish slums. Painting immense frescoes of the people of the ghetto – artisans, tradesmen, peddlers, unsuccessful poets and writers, prostitutes, tramps, and beggars – he showed partiality for the poverty-stricken.

Outstanding among the novels of this type are *Calea Văcărești* (1934) and *Foc in Hanul cu Tei* ("Fire at the Linden Inn," 1935), which were republished several times. A dramatic adaptation of the former was staged in 1942. Other pre-World War II novels include *Horoscop* (1932) and *Nopțile Domnișoarei Mili* ("The Nights of Miss Mili," 1937). Peltz described the horrors of the Nazi period and the sufferings of the Jews in the novel *Israel însîngerat* ("Bleeding Israel," 1946). His postwar novel *Maz și lumea lui* ("Max and his World," 1957), conforming to the norms of the Stalinist period, was a satire directed against the Romanian Jewish bourgeoisie. His other works include *De-a viața și de-a moartea* ("Playing Life and Death," 1942), *Inimi sbuciumat* ("Anguished Souls," 1962), short stories, and *Cum i-am cunoscut* ("How I Knew Them," 1964).

BIBLIOGRAPHY: G. Călinescu, *Istoria Literaturii Romîne…* (1941), 708–10; E. Lovinescu, *Memorii*, vol. 3, 40–42; C. Baltazar, *Scritor și Om* (1946), 107–12; Șerbu, in: *Viața Romînească* (1957), no. 7; V. Rapeanu, *Foc în Hanul cu Tei* (1961), introd.; V. Ardeleanu, *Calea Văcărești* (1966), introd.

[Abraham Feller]

PEMBER, PHOEBE YATES (1823–1913), hospital superintendent during the American Civil War and author of a highly regarded memoir. Pember was born in Charleston, South Carolina, to the well-to-do Jacob Clavius Levy and Fanny Yates, the fourth of seven children. Widowed in 1861 when her husband, Thoman Pember, died of tuberculosis, she arrived in Richmond, Virginia, where her acquaintance with the wife of Secretary of War Randolph led to an offer to serve as superintendent or chief matron of one of the five "divisions" of Chimborazo Hospital, the largest in the world at the time and fated to treat 76,000 patients during the war. Each division consisted of around 30 wards housing 40–60 patients and another 20 or so Sibley tents for convalescents. Pember took up her duties in December 1862 and remained at her post until the collapse of the Confederacy in April 1865, walking through near-empty wards as "every man who could crawl had tried to escape a Northern prison."

Pember's memoir, *A Southern Woman's Story* (1879), tells of hospital life at a time when twice as many patients were dying of disease as were being killed in battle, neither the etiology of disease nor the principles of hygiene were understood, and the only surgical procedure known to physicians was amputation. In this environment, facing chronic shortages of food, medicine, and equipment and fighting off raiders of the medicinal whiskey barrel and hordes of rats consuming the flesh of the dying, Pember acted with energy and determination, heroically bringing what little relief she could to the stricken. Sometimes humorous, often harrowing, and never sparing in its criticism of incompetence, Pember's memoir throws light on the lives and deaths of ordinary people caught in a murderous war and giving "the last full measure" of themselves. After the war Pember traveled widely in Europe and the United States. She died in Pittsburgh.

BIBLIOGRAPHY: B.I. Wiley, Introduction to Phoebe Yates Pember, *A Southern Woman's Story* (1959), with private correspondence appended; "History of Chimborazo Hospital, CSA," in: *Southern Historical Society Papers*, 36 (1908; reprinted 1991), 86–94.

[Fred Skolnik (2nd ed.)]

PENAL LAW.

Principles of Legality

Under talmudic law, no act is a criminal offense and punishable as such unless laid down in express terms in the Bible (the Written Law). For this purpose, it is not sufficient that there should be a provision imposing a specified penalty in respect of any given act (*onesh*) – e.g., the murderer shall be killed (Num. 35:16–21), or the adulterers shall be killed (Lev. 20:10) – so long as the commission of the act has not first distinctly been prohibited (*azharah*) – e.g., you shall not murder (Ex. 20:13; Deut. 5:17), or you shall not commit adultery (ibid.). Where such prohibition is lacking, even the availability of a penal provision will not warrant the imposition of the penalty provided (Zev. 106a–b, et al.); the penal provision is a *nuda lex*, which may be interpreted as a threat of *divine punishment, in respect of which no prior prohibition is required (Mak. 13b).

All biblical injunctions are either positive (*mitzvot aseh*) or negative (*mitzvot lo ta'aseh*), i.e., either to do or to abstain from doing a certain thing. Any negative injunction qualifies as prohibition for the purposes of penal legislation (Maim. Comm. to Mishnah, Mak. 3:1). But no prohibition may he inferred, *e contrario*, from any positive injunction (Tem. 4a). The prohibitory provision is required not only for capital offenses (Sanh. 54a–b), but also for offenses punishable by *flogging (Mak. 4b; Ket. 46a), and even for offenses punishable by *fines (Sifra, *Kedoshim*, 2, 1). A prohibition may not be inferred, either by analogy or by any other form of logical deduction; from the prohibition on intercourse, for instance, with the daughter of one's father or of one's mother (Lev. 18:9), the prohibition on intercourse with one's full sister could not be inferred, but had to be stated expressly (Lev. 18:11).

Similarly, the penal provision must be explicit as applying to an offense constituted of certain factual elements, and may not be extended to cover other offenses, whether by way of analogy or by way of other logical deductions. Thus, for instance, malicious witnesses who commit *perjury by testifying that an innocent man has committed a capital offense are to be executed only if the accused has not yet been executed himself: for it is written, "you shall do to him as he schemed to do to his fellow" (Deut. 19:19), and not as has been done already to his fellow, and the latter may not be inferred, *a fortiori*, from the former (Mak. 5b). The reason underlying this seemingly hairsplitting precaution has been said to be that, if the punishment laid down by law were the right and proper one for the lesser crime or the lesser evil, it could not be the right and proper punishment for the graver one (Maharsha to Sanh. 64b), and the Divine Legislator having seen fit to penalize the lesser offense, no human legislator should presume to improve on or rectify His action, least of all by human logic (*Korban Aharon, Middot Aharon*, 2:13). This strict legality already gave rise to practical difficulties in talmudic times. "Not in order to contravene the law, but in order to make fences around the law" (Sanh. 46a; Yev. 90b; Yad, Sanh. 24:4), were the courts empowered to impose punishments even where the principle of legality could not be observed (see *Extraordinary Remedies). Such extralegal sanctions were imposed not only at the discretion of the courts, but also by virtue of express penal legislation (see **Takkanot*).

Parties to Offenses

As a general rule, only the actual perpetrator of an offense is criminally responsible in Jewish law. Thus no responsibility attaches to procurers, counselors, inciters, and other such offenders who cause the offense to be committed by some other person (except, of course, where the incitement as such constitutes the offense, as, e.g., incitement to idolatry: Deut. 13:7–11).

PRINCIPALS AND AGENTS. Even when a person hires another to commit a crime, criminal responsibility attaches only to the agent who actually commits it, and not to the principal who made him commit it (Kid. 42b–43a; BK 51a, 79a; BM 8a, 10b; et al.). Where the commission of the offense entails some enjoyment, as the consumption of prohibited food or consummation of prohibited intercourse, it is clear that he who has the enjoyment pays the penalty (Kid. 43a); but even where the agent derives no enjoyment at all from the commission of the offense, it is he who is responsible, because as a person endowed with free will he has to obey God rather than men (Kid. 42b). There are several exceptions to this rule: first, where the agent is not capable of criminal responsibility, whether because he is a minor, or insane, or otherwise exempt from responsibility, his principal is responsible (BM 10b; *Rema*, ḤM 182:1, 348:8); or, where the actual perpetrator is an innocent agent, that is, ignorant of the fact that it is an offense he commits (Tos. to Kid. 42b s.v. *amai*; Tos. to BK 79a s.v. *natnu*; *Mordekhai*, BM 1, 237; and cf. Redak, II Sam. 12:9). Further exceptions apply to particular offenses and are derived from biblical exegesis, such as stealing trust money (Ex. 22:6), slaughtering and stealing oxen or sheep (Ex. 21:37), or trespass on sacred things (Lev. 5:15) – for all of which the principal and not the agent is criminally responsible (Kid. 42b–43a). However, the blameworthiness of the procurer did not escape the talmudic jurists: everybody agrees that he is liable to some punishment, lesser (*dina zuta*) or greater (*dina rabba*; Kid. 43a), and the view generally taken is that he will be visited with divine punishment (Kid. 43a; Yad, Roẓe'aḥ 2:2–3). The matter is very distinctly put apropos the biblical injunction that, where a woman committed bestiality, both she and the beast should be killed (Lev. 20:16): "The woman has sinned, but what sin did the beast commit? But because it caused mischief, it must be stoned – and if a beast which does not know any difference between good and evil is stoned because of the mischief it caused, a fortiori must a man who caused another to commit a capital offense be taken by God from this world" (Sifra, Kedoshim, 10:5). Maimonides goes even further, allowing not only for divine punishment but also for human capital punishment, whether by the king by virtue of his royal prerogative (see *Extraordinary Remedies), or by the court in exercise of its emergency powers, wherever circumstances of time and place so require (Yad, Roẓe'aḥ 2:4); and indeed capital punishment was actually imposed on a father who had ordered his son to commit homicide (Ribash, Resp. no. 251). But short of capital punishment, courts are at any rate admonished to administer "very hard floggings" and impose severe imprisonment for long periods, so as to deter and threaten potential criminals that they may not think they can commit with impunity their crimes by the hands of others (Yad, Roẓe'aḥ 5). See also *Agency, Law of.

JOINT OFFENDERS. As a general rule, a criminal offense is committed by a single person acting alone, and not by two or more acting together (Sifra, Va-Yikra, 7; Shab. 92b). Thus, where an offense is committed by joint offenders, all are liable only if the offense could not have been committed otherwise than by all of them together; if the offense could have been committed by any one (or more) of them, they are all entitled to the benefit of the doubt that none of them did actually complete the offense (Yad, Shab. 1:15–16). Where, therefore, a man is beaten to death by several people, none of them would be criminally liable (Sanh. 78a); but where the death was clearly caused by the last stroke, the man who struck last would be guilty of murder (Yad, Roẓe'aḥ 4:6–7). It might be otherwise where death could not have ensued unless by the combined action of all attackers together: in such a case they would all be liable (Rashba, Nov., BK 53b). Like accessories before and at the offense, so are accessories after the fact free from responsibility for the offense – except, again, in the case of incitement to idolatry, where the protection of the offender is made an offense (Deut. 13:9).

Attempts and Inchoate Offenses

From the foregoing it is already apparent that, as a rule, no offense is committed unless it is completed: he who completes the offense is guilty; he who commits only part of the offense, or does not achieve the criminal result, is not guilty (Sifra, Va-Yikra, 7, 9; Shab. 92b–93a). No criminal intent, however far-reaching, suffices to render any act punishable which is not the completed offense defined by law (Kid. 39b; Ḥcyŏ 142a). In exceptional cases, however, the attempt as such constitutes the completed offenses, e.g., malicious perjury (Deut. 19:16), where the false witnesses are liable only if the result intended by them had not yet been achieved (Mak. 1:6). But, again, the potential turpitude of the attempt to commit an offense has not escaped juridical notice: he who raises a hand against another, even without striking him, is not only wicked, but should (according at least to one great scholar) have his hand cut off, if he is prone to strike frequently (Sanh. 58b and Rashi). Extralegal punishments have indeed been inflicted time and again on attempts, especially of murder (e.g., Maharam of Rothenburg, Resp., ed. Prague, no. 383; and cf. *Darkhei Moshe*, ḤM 421, n.7).

Criminal Responsibility

No person is criminally responsible for any act unless he did that act willfully (Av. Zar. 54a; BK 28b; Yad, Yesodei ha-Torah 5:4; Sanh. 20:2). Willfulness is excluded by duress (**ones*), a concept much wider in Jewish than in other systems of law. For the purpose of penal law, it can be roughly divided into five categories:

(1) coercion;

(2) threats of death, including governmental decrees threatening criminal prosecution;

(3) torture;

(4) *force majeure*, including sickness and other happenings beyond one's control; and

(5) mistakes of fact and unconsciousness.

As distinguished from duress for the purposes of civil law, generally no duress is recognized in criminal law which flows from any monetary cause, as, e.g., the necessity to save any property from perdition (*Beit Yosef*; ḤM 388; *Rema*, ḤM 388:2).

DURESS BY COERCION. The coercion by violence of a married woman to commit *adultery (nowadays known as rape) exempts her from any criminal responsibility (Deut. 22:26). No such coercion is recognized in regard to the male adulterer, because he cannot physiologically be raped (Yev. 53b). Where the woman is in an isolated spot ("in the open country": Deut. 22:25), or otherwise incapable of summoning help, she will be presumed to have been coerced against her will (Naḥmanides ad loc.; Sif. Deut. 243), even where she could have resisted by striking back, but failed to do so in the belief she was not allowed to, she is deemed to have been raped (Naḥmanides, *ibid.*). It is irrelevant that, after having been forced to submit, she eventually acquiesced: it is the duress of human urges and human nature that then compels her to surrender (Yad, Issurei Bi'ah 1:9).

DURESS BY THREATS. There are three grave offenses of which it is said that a man must let himself be killed rather than commit any of them, namely, idolatry, adultery or *incest (*gillui arayot*), and *homicide (Sanh. 74a; Yad, Yesodei ha-Torah 5:2; Sh. Ar., YD 157:1). This rule has sometimes been wrongly interpreted as excluding the defense of duress by threats of death in the case of any of these offenses; as a matter of law, however, where the rule is disobeyed and any such offense is committed in order to escape death, the offender is not criminally responsible, however reprehensible he may be morally or religiously (Yad, *ibid.* 4). It is irrevocably presumed that where a man acts under threat of immediate death and in order to save his life, any criminal intent in respect of that act is excluded or superseded, and he cannot be criminally responsible for it.

In the Middle Ages, the threat of prosecution and death became a very effective inducement to denounce Judaism and outwardly embrace another religion. So long as a man did only what was really required to save his life, the transgression was recognized as being committed under duress; as soon as he did anything not so required, it was deemed to be done willfully, however strong the initial duress may have been (*Rema*, YD 124:9; Ribash, Resp. nos. 4, 11, 12).

DURESS BY TORTURE. Duress by torture is closely related to the two foregoing categories; on the one hand, it entails physical force, and the sheer force applied may be sufficient to deprive the victim of his free will; on the other hand, it entails threats of death, or of ever more torture to come until death may ensue, and hence any criminal intent will be replaced or superseded by the wish to have the torture terminated (cf. Ket. 33b for an instance of torture to compel to idolatry).

DURESS BY FORCE MAJEURE. Duress by force majeure as an instance of duress is well illustrated by the case of a man who fell ill, and his doctors prescribed for his cure the consumption of prohibited food: while partaking of such food is a criminal offense, the patient will not be liable to punishment, as his intent was not criminal but medical (Yad, *ibid.* 6). It is, however, made clear that this defense would not hold good for all offenses: thus, a man cannot be heard to say that, for medical reasons and in order to save his life, he had to commit adultery (Yad, *ibid.* 9) or even a lesser indecency (Sanh. 75a). Other unforeseen circumstances which may make a man act unlawfully, contrary to his real intentions, are, e.g., attacks by wild beasts (cf. BM 7:9), or accidents such as fire (BM 47b, 49b) and other like dangers: the defense of duress in these cases is closely related to that of self-defense or self-help (see below). It is noteworthy that in English and Israeli law, the commission of an offense in order to avoid grievous harm or injury which could not otherwise be avoided is excused by reason of "necessity" (Sec. 18, Criminal Code Ordinance, 1936).

DURESS BY MISTAKE OR UNCONSCIOUSNESS. A lesser form of duress is the "duress of sleep" (cf. Ber. 4b): a man who has fallen asleep is not criminally (as distinguished from civilly; BK 2:6) responsible for anything he did while asleep, for the reason that he acted without any criminal (or other) intent. The same applies to acts of automatism or anything done in a state of unconsciousness, however induced. Jewish law – again, as distinguished from other systems of law – includes within this category, as a species of duress, also the common mistake of fact: it is regarded as the "duress of the heart" (Shev. 26a) if a man acts under a misapprehension of relevant facts, and any criminal intent may be excluded by such other intent as is warranted by the facts mistakenly believed to exist. If a man acts under such factual misapprehension, it is as if he acted outside the physical world as it really exists, hence the analogy with sleep and unconsciousness. Similarly, the forgetfulness of old age may constitute duress (Ber. 8b).

THE DEAF AND DUMB, LUNATICS, INFANTS, AND THE BLIND. Apart from these forms of duress, which are applicable to all persons, there are special categories of persons who are wholly exempt from criminal responsibility for reason of the duress inherent in their infirmity or deficiency, namely, the deaf and dumb, the insane, and infants – all regarded in law as devoid of reason (Yev. 99b; Ḥag. 2b; Git. 23a; et al). Persons who are both deaf and dumb (Ter. 1:2) are equated with infants for all purposes of the law (cf. Tur, ḤM 235:19), and the law exempting infants from criminal responsibility is derived from scriptural exegesis (Mekh. Mishpatim 4; Sanh. 52b, 54a, 68b). It is not quite settled at what age infancy ends for purposes of criminal law: there are dicta to the effect that divine punishment is not imposed for sins committed before the age of 20 (TJ, Bik. 2:1, 64c: TJ, Sanh. 11:7, 30b; Shab. 89b; Tanh. Koraḥ 6), and it is said that where Heaven exempts from punishment, men ought not to punish (cf. Sanh. 82b); on the other hand, with the age of 13 for the male and 12 for the female, the age of reason is reached (Nid. 45b; Yad, Ishut 2:1, 10), and there would no longer be any rational cause for exemption from responsibility. Some scholars hold that, while human beings are criminally responsible as from the age of 13 and 12, respectively, no capital punishment would be imposed until they reached the age of 20. However that may be, we find exhortations to punish infants by flogging, even below the age of reason, not because of their responsibility, but only in order to deter them from further crime (Yad, Genevah 1:10). As far as sexual crimes are concerned, an infant girl is deemed to be so easily tempted as to deprive her of any willfulness (Yev. 33b, 61b; TJ, Sot. 1:2, 16c).

The insane is a person whose mind is permanently deranged (Yad, Edut 9:9). Monomaniacs who "go around alone at nights, stay overnight in cemeteries, tear their clothes, and lose everything they are given" (Ḥag. 3b; Tosef., Ter. 1:3), as well as idiots who are so retarded as to be unable to differentiate between contradictory matters (Yad, *ibid.* 10; ḤM 35:10), are presumed to be insane. They are not criminally responsible for any of their acts (BK 87a; cf. Git. 22b), and it is – in contradistinction to modern systems of law – irrelevant whether any causal connection can be established between the disease and the offense: once insanity is shown, criminal responsibility is excluded. Persons who suffer from transient attacks of insanity, such as epileptics, are criminally responsible only for acts committed during lucid intervals (cf. Yad, *ibid.* 9; ḤM 35:9). Apart from being devoid of reason, the insane are also devoid of will – hence any sexual offense committed by an insane woman is deemed to have been committed unwillfully (*Mishneh la-Melekh*, Ishut 11:8).

Opinions were divided among talmudic jurists in regard to the criminal responsibility of the blind (BK 86b; Tosef., Mak. 2:9), but the rule eventually evolved that blindness does not affect such responsibility any more than the obligation to obey all the laws; but a blind person who kills inadvertently is exempt from exile to a *city of refuge, because his act is near to duress (Yad, Roẓe'aḥ 6:14). The blind man differs from the deaf and dumb in that he freely expresses himself, while with the latter one never knows whether he is in possession of his mental and volitive faculties or not, and Jewish law does not recognize any presumption of sanity.

INTOXICATION. Self-induced intoxication as such is not regarded as duress sufficient to exempt from criminal responsibility for acts committed while drunk (Tosef., Ter. 3:1), except where the intoxication amounts to the "drunkenness of Lot" (Gen. 19:33–35), that is to say, to virtual unconsciousness (Er. 65a).

IGNORANCE OF LAW. Talmudic law differs from most (if not all) other systems of law also in one further respect: namely, that ignorance of law is a good defense to any criminal charge. Not only is nobody punishable for an offense committed bona fide, i.e., in the mistaken belief that his act was lawful, but it is incumbent upon the prosecution to show that the accused was, immediately before the commission of the offense, expressly warned by two competent witnesses that it would be unlawful for him to commit it, and that if he committed it he would be liable to that specific penalty provided for it by law (Sanh. 8b; et al.; and see *Evidence, *Practice and Procedure). It is this antecedent warning that enables the court to distinguish between the intentional (*mezid*) and the unintentional (*shogeg*) offender (Yad, Sanhedrin 12:2 and Issurei Bi'ah 1:3), the latter category comprising not only those acting "with a claim of right" in ignorance of the law, but also those who by accident or misadventure achieved any criminal result without intending it (Yad, Roẓe'aḥ 6:1–9), or who achieved any result (however criminal) different from the criminal result they intended to achieve (ibid. 4:1). Within the category of unintentional offenders, a distinction is made between those nearer to duress and those nearer to criminality: the former acted without negligence, and their conduct was in no way blameworthy; the latter acted recklessly and in disregard of common standards of behavior (the most striking example is the man who maintained that it was perfectly lawful to kill). While neither is, as a matter of law, criminally responsible, the one nearer to criminality may not be entitled to resort to cities of refuge (Yad, ibid. 6:10) and is liable to be flogged and imprisoned for purposes of deterrence (Yad, ibid. 2:5 and Sanh. 24:4). Previous warning of illegality was held to be unnecessary where the nature of the offense or its planning rendered the warning impracticable, such as in cases of perjury (Ket. 32a) or burglary at night (Sanh. 72b), or where it was redundant, as in the case of the *rebellious elder (Sanh. 88b) or of recidivists (Sanh. 81b; and cf. Maim. Yad, Sanhedrin 18, 5). Some scholars held the warning unnecessary also where the offender was a man learned in the law (Sanh. 8b).

SELF-DEFENSE AND RESCUE. Another important cause of exemption from criminal responsibility is the right and duty of defense against unlawful attack and of protection from danger; where any person (including an infant) pursues another with the manifest intent to kill him, everybody is under a duty to rescue the victim, even by killing the pursuer (Sanh. 8: 7; Yad, Roẓe'aḥ 1:6). This general rule has been extended to cover the killing of an embryo endangering the life of the mother (Yad, ibid. 9; and see *Abortion) and the killing of a rapist caught before completion of his offense, if he could not otherwise be induced to desist (Yad, ibid. 10). It would be as unlawful to kill the pursuer where the victim could be rescued by some other means (though even then the killer would not be guilty of murder (Yad, ibid. 13)), as it would be unlawful not to kill the pursuer if the victim could not otherwise be rescued (Yad, ibid. 14–16). Thus the nature of this defense is not just duress; here the criminal intent is superseded by the intent to fulfill a legal duty, and hence the defense is one of justification.

JUSTIFICATION. In the more technical sense of the term, justification exempts from criminal responsibility the following three categories of persons: officers of the court who kill or injure any person (or property) in the course of performing their official duties (cf. Mak. 3:14; Yad, Sanhedrin 16:12); any person lawfully engaged in the execution of convicts (Lev. 24:16; Deut. 13:10, 17:7, 21:21, 22:21, 24); and any person who acts upon the advice or instruction of the court as to what is the law (Sifra, Va-Yikra, 7, 1–2; Hor. 2b, 3b).

[Haim Hermann Cohn]

Forms of Punishment: Biblical Law; Extra-Legal Punishment; "The King's Law"

The strict laws of evidence in Jewish criminal law, which, in order to convict, inter alia require that the transgressor be admonished by two competent witnesses before committing the transgression, pose great difficulties for a system of criminal justice that is intended to prevent criminal behavior. For the purposes of maintaining public order and of dealing with criminal behavior, two additional tracks of judgment and punishment exist. The first track is "punishment not prescribed in the law" – the granting of broad discretionary authority to a court of law to prescribe punishment in accordance with the exigencies of the time (regarding the implementation of that authority in the post-Talmudic era, see entry *Capital Punishment). The second track is "the King's Law" – a legal system parallel to that of Torah Law, which complements biblical law with judgment and punishment in cases in which punishment and execution in accordance with biblical law are impossible.

These two tracks grant considerable discretionary authority to the courts, both with regard to prescribing punishment in specific instances and with regard to the enactment of general regulations in criminal law. One important distinction between these two systems and the criminal system in accordance with biblical law is that, when biblical law prescribes a specific punishment for a particular transgression, the courts are not permitted to deviate from the prescribed punishment (Yad, Sanh., 14:1–3). In the system of extra-legal punishment and in the King's law, on the other hand, the judges are not hampered by any such restriction. For a comprehensive discussion on the various systems of judgment and punishment, and on the punishment policy of Jewish law, see entry *Punishment.

Ignorance of the Law

We explained above that the purpose of admonition is to inform the transgressor of the law, hence the conclusion that ignorance of the law may serve as a defense in Jewish law. In light of the distinction cited above between biblical law and the alternative punitive systems, some scholars explained the requirement of admonition in biblical law, in which the purpose of punishment is not necessarily the betterment of society, not as a vehicle for informing the transgressor of the law, but rather as part of the requirement that the transgression, *as a religious transgression*, must constitute an act of contempt and defiance of God's commandments. On the other hand, in the framework of punishment by virtue of the King's law, which is a Jewish law system of punishment designed for the *betterment of society*, as practiced *de facto* in Jewish communities at various times, no admonition was required. Moreover, in relation to various offenses, we find that ignorance of the law does not render a criminal act unintentional for all intents and purposes. For example, a murderer who did not know that murder is forbidden does not flee to a city of refuge; rather, his offense is considered "close to intentional" (Yad, Roẓe'aḥ 6:10). A woman who commits the sin of adultery becomes forbidden to her husband, even if she did not know that her actions were against the law (Resp. Maharik, no. 137). Against this background, there were those who differentiated between ignorance of the law with regard to commandments between God and man, which are considered as unintentional for all intents and purposes, and ignorance of the law when there is also a component of transgression against other individuals, in which ignorance of the law does not transform the offense into a normal unintentional transgression.

Factual Errors – Reasonable Error and Unreasonable Error

In addition to the above distinction within the category of ignorance of the law between an offense that is "close to intentional" and one that is "close to coerced," we should note a similar distinction within the category of ignorance of the facts. Jewish law distinguishes between factual errors that are considered reasonable, in which the individual ignorant of the facts is considered to be "coerced," and factual errors containing a component of negligence. In other words, had the individual checked his facts before committing the act, he would have discovered the true situation, and the error would have been avoided. In such a case, the individual committing the error is considered an unintentional transgressor (*shogeg*) and is therefore required to bring a sin-offering (Yad, Shegagot 5:6). With regard to murder, when the fatal act was committed as the result of a reasonable error regarding the facts, i.e., in a case in which we cannot hold the killer responsible in any way for his ignorance of the facts, he is considered as one who was coerced (*anus*), and will not even be required to flee to a city of refuge (see *City of Refuge). Conversely, when the unintentional act is the result of negligence, the perpetrator is required to flee to a city of refuge (Tosef., Makkot, 2:2). Regarding murder, even in cases of ignorance of the facts, there exists an additional category termed "an unintentional act close to an intentional one" (*shogeg karov le-mezid*), in which the killer was indeed ignorant of the facts, but he committed a dangerous act that was obviously potentially lethal, in which case he may not flee to a city of refuge (Mak. 8a; TJ, Mak. 2, d; Meiri, Nov., Mak. 7b).

The Theoretical Justification for Killing a "Pursuer" (*rodef*) in Self-Defense

Amongst the authorities in Jewish law, we find a diversity of justifications for the lack of criminal responsibility of an individual who killed in self-defense, or in defense of another individual. One approach sees the fundamental justification in the very act of saving the intended victim, on the basis that the rescuer was commanded to save the victim, as all Jews are commanded to rescue others (Yad, Roẓe'aḥ 1:6). According to another approach, while the assailant's intention to do harm is indeed a necessary condition to justify killing him, the essential justification is in fact that the would-be murderer intends to commit a capital offense, and killing him before he commits the offense prevents him from actually committing it (Rashi, to Sanh. 73a). The difference between the two approaches is liable to manifest itself in a situation in which, for example, the pursuer himself is in mortal danger, e.g., if a building collapsed on him on the Sabbath. According to the first approach, the offender is no longer a threat to others, and we are therefore obligated to violate the Sabbath in order to save his life, as we would save the life of any individual. According to the second approach, on the other hand, the would-be attacker, in attempting to murder another human being, falls within the category of one whose life is not to be saved, and we may therefore not violate the Sabbath in order to save him (Rashi, *Sanhedrin* 72b). Another case in which an operative distinction between the two approaches could possibly arise is when the attacker is not punishable by law, e.g., if he is a minor or was himself coerced into attacking his fellow under threat of death. If the justification for killing the pursuer is to save the victim, the fact that the pursuer is not punishable is irrelevant; on the other hand, if the justification is that we wish to prevent the wrongdoer from committing an offense, it would not, apparently, be permissible to kill a pursuer who is not punishable by law (regarding this point, some legal authorities have differentiated between the *prohibition*, which applies equally to every human being, and the *punishment*, which apparently does not apply to every individual in every case; therefore, any pursuer, even if he is not punishable, intends to violate the prohibition, and he may therefore be killed). It seems that we must justify the permission to kill a potential pursuer by a *combination of both principles*: the need to save the victim, and the fact that the act of pursuit involves an offense punishable by death, as certain halakhic authorities have indeed maintained (Meiri, *Bet ha-Beḥirah, Sanhedrin* (Sofer edition), p. 266).

Self-Defense from Injury

Among halakhic authorities post-dating Maimonides, we find a discussion of the permission to inflict injury upon an individual who attacks and strikes another, even when there is no mortal danger. From the biblical verse, "Then thou shalt cut off her hand, thine eye shall have no pity" (Deut. 25:12), the Sages understood that a person whose life is being threatened by a pursuer must be saved, even by mortally injuring the pursuer (*Sifri*, Deut. 293, Yad, Roẓe'aḥ 7–9). Rabbenu Asher extends this principle to any case in which one individual strikes another; even if there is no mortal danger, any other individual is permitted to strike the assailant, if there is no other way to stop him (*Piske ha-Rosh* on BK, 3:13; see also Maharshal, *Yam shel Shelomo*, on BK 3:9). Rabbenu Asher's justification for this is in order to prevent the offender from committing the sin of striking another person (for the various justifications, see above).

Regarding the extent of striking that is permitted, the authorities ruled that the injury to the assailant should be minimal, and if it is possible to physically distance the assailant from his victim without striking him, that is what should be done. Physical violence beyond the extent that is necessary would be grounds for a legal suit by the assailant against the rescuer (*Mordekhai*, BK, 38; Rabbenu Asher, *ibid.*; *Terumat ha-Deshen, Pesakim u-Khetavim*, 208; Sh. Ar., ḤM, 421:13). A discussion of this matter can be found in the decision of the Supreme Court of the State of Israel in the *Afanjar* case (CA 89/78 *Afanjar* v. *State of Israel*, PD 33(3)141). The Court was called upon to decide the question of whether the defense of necessity could be invoked by the appellant, who had acted violently towards plainclothes police officers who broke into his apartment in the middle of the night. The appellant claimed that he did not know that the intruders were police officers, and that he thought that he was protecting himself and others in the apartment with him from bodily harm and humiliation. After an extensive discussion of the sources cited above, the Court (per Justice Menachem Elon) acquitted the appellant, stating that the principle of self-defense entitled him to act as he did, since his purpose was to prevent harm or injury to his own person and those of his friends (ibid., 157–158; for an extensive discussion of the ruling, see *Assault).

Application of Jewish Criminal Law in the Israeli Legal System

Justice Elon's reliance on Jewish law as a source for the interpretation of Israeli criminal law sparked a debate in the Supreme Court. The then President of the Court, J. Sussmann, while agreeing with Justice Elon's conclusion, wrote that "we cannot draw on Jewish law to help solve this problem. To be sure, Jewish law is a valuable cultural asset of our people, from which the legislator and the courts can both draw much inspiration. However, we are dealing with a specific directive in the realm of criminal law, which arose from a different source and has nothing in common with Jewish sources. I would be so bold as to question whether the application of Jewish criminal law would really be acceptable to the Israeli public. For example, would the majority of the Israeli public be prepared, in the year 1979, to execute an adulterous woman by stoning her, in accordance with Jewish law, or to execute the daughter of a priest by burning?" (p. 160 of the *Afanjar* decision, see above).

The answer to Justice Sussmann's question is that Jewish criminal law, as set out in the Torah, prescribes many death penalties for transgressions that no one would dream of punishing by death today. However, we must point out that even in Jewish law, *actual execution* of a capital sentence was considered a rare and extraordinary occurrence, to the point that capital punishment was almost never carried out (for an extensive discussion, see entry *Capital Punishment). As stated above, over the years the system of punishment in Jewish criminal law developed and adapted for its own use various means of dealing with the phenomena of criminal behavior, within the framework of the judicial autonomy that was granted to various Jewish communities. This development will be a subject for study and discussion in the context of applying the principles of Jewish law to the criminal system of Israeli law.

In the *Afanjar* case, the Court said as follows:

> As we have seen, the principle of protecting others involves concepts rooted in public policy and in a social and moral view of the duty to come to the aid of another person who is in danger of bodily injury … this is the view reflected in the sources of Jewish law, where the rule, "Do not stand idly by the blood of your fellow" constitutes a fundamental principle of Judaism. In my opinion, fundamental concepts founded on moral attitudes and cultural values should be interpreted in light of the moral and cultural heritage of Judaism.… In light of the Law and Administration Ordinance (Amendment) Law (no. 14), 1972, which abolished the interpretational subordination of the Criminal Code Ordinance to the laws of England, and in light of the Penal Law, 5737 – 1977, in which section 4 of the Criminal Code Ordinance, prescribing subordination, was repealed, we are certainly obliged to provide our own independent and original interpretation, in accordance with the specific circumstances of each and every case, of fundamental principles such as the one that is before us (p. 155).

On specific criminal offenses in Jewish law, see, *inter alia*, *Homicide, *Rape, *Theft and Robbery, and *Bribery. On particular punishment, see, *inter alia*, *Capital Punishment, *Divine Punishment, *Flogging, *Fines, *Imprisonment, *Ḥerem.

[Menachem Elon (2nd ed.)]

BIBLIOGRAPHY: ET, 1 (1951), 162–72, 193–5, 303–5, 321–4; 11 (1965), 291–314; J.D. Michaelis, *Mosaisches Recht*, 6 vols. (1770–75); M. Duschak, *Das mosaisch-talmudische Strafrecht* (1869); H.B. Fassel, *Ve-Shaftu ve-Hiẓẓilu: Das mosaisch-rabbinische Strafgesetz und strafrectliche Gerichts-Verfahren* (1870); S. Mayer, *Geschichte der Strafrechte* (1876); B. Berger, *Criminal Code of the Jews* (1880); S. Mendelsohn, *Criminal Jurisprudence of the Ancient Hebrews* (1891; repr. 1968); G. Foerster, *Das mosaische Strafrecht in seiner geschichtlichen Entwicklung* (1900); H. Vogelstein, in: MGWJ, 48 (1904), 513–33; J. Steinberg, in: *Zeitschrift fuer vergleichende Rechtswissenschaft*, 25 (1911), 140–97; I.S. Zuri, *Mishpat ha-Talmud*, 1 (1921); 6 (1921); S. Assaf, *Ha-Onshin Aḥarei Ḥatimat ha-Talmud* (1922); H. Cohen, in: *Jeschurun*, 9 (1922), 272–99; V. Aptowitzer, in: JQR, 15 (1924/25), 55–118; idem, in: HUCA, 3 (1926), 117–55; J. Manen, in: HHY, 10 (1926), 200–8; L. Kantor, *Beitraege zur Lehre von der strafrechtlichen Schuld im Talmud* (1926); M. Higger, *Intention in Talmudic Law* (1927); P. Dykan, *Dinei Onshin*, 1 (1938; 1955[2]); 2 (1947; 1962[2]); 3 (1953); idem, in: *Sinai*, 60 (1966), 51–62; H.E. Goldin, *Hebrew Criminal Law and Procedure* (1952); J. Ginzberg, *Mishpatim le-Yisrael* (1956); M. Minkowitz, *Ha-Maḥashavah ha-Pelilit ba-Mishpat ha-Talmudi u-va-Mishpat ha-Mekubbal ha-Angli* (1961); D. Daube, *Collaboration with Tyranny in Rabbinic Law* (1965); M. Elon, in: ILR, 3 (1968), 94–97; Elon, Mafte'aḥ s.v. *Onshin, Dinei*. **ADD. BIBLIOGRAPHY:** M. Elon, *Ha-Mishpat ha-Ivri* (1988), 1:65, 226, 297, 312, 421–25, 496, 815f; 2:992; 3:1464; idem, *Jewish Law* (1994), 1:73, 255, 353, 373; 2:515–19, 604, 998; 3:1200; 4:1739; idem, *Jewish Law: Cases and Materials* (1999), 213–62; M. Elon and B. Lifshitz, *Mafte'aḥ ha-She'elot ve-ha-Teshuvot shel Ḥakhmei Sefarad u-Ẓefon Afrikah* (Legal Digest) (1986), 2:329–45; B. Lifshitz and E. Shochetman, *Mafte'aḥ ha-She'elot ve-ha-Teshuvot shel Ḥakhmei Ashkenaz, Ẓarefat ve-Italyah* (Legal Digest) (1997), 228–36; A. Dassberg, "*Ha-Hatra'ah, Mekor ha-Din, ve-Taamo*," in: *Teḥumin*, 12 (5751 – 1991), 307–26; A. Enker, *Hekhre'aḥ ve-Ẓorekh be-Dinei Onshin* (1977) 151–63; idem, "*Yesodot be-Mishpat ha-Pelili ha-Ivri*," in: *Mishpatim*, 24 (1994–1995), 177–206; idem, "*Ta'anat i-Yedi'at ha-Din be-Mishpat ha-Pelili Ha-Ivri*," in: *Mishpatim*, 25 (1995), 87–128; idem, "The Rationale of Self-Defense in Jewish Law," in: *Pelilim*, 2 (1991), 55–91; A. Kirschenbaum, "*Mekomah shel ha-Anishah be-Mishpat ha-Pelili ha-Ivri*," in: *Iyyunei Mishpat*, 12 (1988), 253–73; S. Albeck, *Yesodot ha-Averah be-Dinei ha-Talmud* (1997), 100–40; M. Drori, "The Concept of "Shegagah in Jewish Law: Mistake of Law and Mistake of Fact," in: *Shenaton ha-Mishpat ha-Ivri*, 1 (1974), 72–97.

PENINNAH (Heb. פְּנִנָּה; possibly "coral"), second wife of *Elkanah (I Sam. 1:1–2). Peninnah had sons and daughters, while *Hannah, Elkanah's first wife, was barren (1:2). In I Samuel 1, which deals with Samuel's birth, Peninnah plays a secondary role. She seems to have been her husband's less favored wife (cf. 1:5) and is portrayed as a rather unkind woman who made life difficult for Hannah, her rival (1:6–7).

In the *Aggadah*

The *aggadah* elaborates on the manner in which Peninnah taunted Hannah on account of her childlessness. Every morning she would mockingly ask whether Hannah had washed her sons' faces, and in the afternoon would sarcastically enquire when she expected them home from school (PR 43, 181b). According to one tradition, this cruelty had a righteous intent; Peninnah hoped thereby that she would encourage Hannah to pray for children (BB 18a; Mid. Ḥag. to Gen. 22:1). She was nevertheless ultimately punished. Two of her children died whenever Hannah gave birth; and she thus witnessed the death of eight of her ten children. The last two were spared solely as a result of Hannah's intercession with the Almighty on her behalf (PR, *ibid.*, 182a).

BIBLIOGRAPHY: IN THE AGGADAH: Ginzberg, Legends, 4 (1913), 58, 60; 6 (1928), 216–8, 220; I. Ḥasida, *Ishei ha-Tanakh* (1964), 363f.

PENN, ALEXANDER (1906–1972), Hebrew poet. Born in Nizhne-Kolymsk, Russia, he came under the influence of Mayakovski, Yesenin, and *Pasternak, and wrote poetry in Russian. In 1927 he settled in Palestine where he founded, together with Nathan Axelrod, the first film studio. In 1929, encouraged by A. *Shlonsky, he began to publish his poems which were mostly lyrical, inspired by the Israel landscape. He was also, however, a pioneer of the topical political *chanson*. His poems were published in *Ketuvim*, *Moznayim*, *Davar*, and *Turim*. According to his own testimony, 1934 was a turning point in his literary work, when he cut down on his lyrical poetry and devoted himself increasingly to poems of political and social message, which he published mainly in the Marxist press. From 1947 he served as editor of the literary and art supplement of the Communist daily, *Kol ha-Am*. A selection from his poetry was published in Russian translation in the Soviet Union (1965), the collection of translations from modern Hebrew poetry published in Russian in the Soviet Union. After the 1967 Six-Day War, Penn left Maki, the Israel Communist Party, because of its "nationalistic regression." A collection of his poems (*Beli Gag*), including an introduction by Uzi Shavit, was published in 1985. The poems and songs written by Penn were edited and published in two volumes in 2005.

BIBLIOGRAPHY: G. Kressel, Leksikon, 2 (1967), 643–5. **ADD. BIBLIOGRAPHY:** Y. Saaroni, *Penn u-Fanav; Deyukan u-Sevivato*, in: *Siman Keriah*, 2 (1973), 295–308; Y. Besser, "*Shirah shel Mamashut Kefulah*," in: *Yedioth Aharonoth* (November 18, 1977); P. Ginosar, "*Shiro ha-Ivri ha-Rishon shel A. Penn*," in: *Hadaor*, 56:33 (1977), 547; H. Halperin, *Yesodot Statiyyim ve-Dinamiyyim bi-Yẓirot Alexander Penn ve-Gilguleihem* (1986); idem, *Shalekhet Kokhavim: Alexander Penn – Ḥayyav vi-Yẓirato ad 1940* (1989); S. Yaniv, "*Le-Gilgulah shel Tavnit Dzenerit* (*Yesenin, Shlonksy, Penn*)," in: *Alei Siaḥ*, 27–28 (1990), 41–49; H. Alon, "*Ha-Ḥavayah ha-Nashit be-Shirav shel A. Penn*," in: *Iton 77*, 278 (2003), 14–16.

[Getzel Kressel]

PENN, ARTHUR (1922–), U.S. director, screenwriter, and producer. Born in Philadelphia, Penn spent most of his childhood in New York and New Hampshire with his mother. In high school, he returned to his hometown and began studying his father's watchmaking profession after graduating. His entertainment career began in 1943 when he enlisted in the Army and started performing in a theater troupe. Toward the end of the war, he decided to study acting at Black Mountain College in North Carolina and the Italian universities of Perugia and Florence. In 1948, he started working for the new NBC TV. At NBC, he wrote television plays and directed episodes of Goodyear Television Playhouse and Philco Playhouse, including William Gibson's *The Miracle Worker* for television (1956).

In 1958 Penn directed *The Miracle Worker* on Broadway, winning the Tony award, and also made his film debut directing *The Left-Handed Gun*. Penn returned to *The Miracle Worker* in 1962, directing the film version, which earned him a best director Oscar nomination. *Bonnie and Clyde* (1967) also earned Penn a best director nomination. Penn co-wrote *Alice's Restaurant* in 1969, based on Arlo Guthrie's recording, which earned him another best director nomination. *Little Big Man* (1970) was a commercial success. Penn later produced and directed *Penn & Teller Get Killed* (1989). In the 1990s, he directed two made-for-TV movies: *The Portrait* (1993) and *Inside* (1996). Other Penn films are *The Chase* (1965) with Robert Redford, *Night Moves* (1973), *The Missouri Breaks* (1976) with Marlon Brando, *Four Friends* (1981), *Target* (1985), and *Dead of Winter* (1987). Penn also turned to television, directing episodes and consulting on the show *100 Center Street* (2001). Penn's brother is the renowned photographer Irving *Penn.

[Susannah Howland (2nd ed.)]

PENN, IRVING (1917–), U.S. photographer. Born in Plainfield, N.J., Penn studied at the Philadelphia Museum School of Industrial Art, graduating in 1938. He is best known for his "aristocratic" fashion photography, but he is also a master of portraiture and still life. Originally a painter, Penn began working for *Vogue* magazine in 1943 and became one of America's most successful fashion photographers. His work was known for his cool, refined, and glamorously stylized images. Penn used plain backgrounds and natural light and was adept at capturing the essence of his sitter's personality. He photographed many of the world's most famous people and traveled worldwide to capture other human subjects. Many times his photographs were so ahead of their time that they came to be appreciated as important works years after their creation. A famous series of posed female nudes, from the normal to the plump, were shot in 1949–50 but were not seen until a few were exhibited in 1980. In 2002, 53 of them appeared in a solo exhibition at the Metropolitan Museum of Art in New York. By posing his subjects against a simple gray or white backdrop, to form a starkly acute corner, Penn was able to bring a sense of drama to his portraits, driving the viewer's focus onto the person and what the person's expression revealed. These subjects included Martha Graham, Marcel Duchamp, Georgia O'Keeffe, W.H. Auden, Igor Stravinsky, and Marlene Dietrich. Penn started his own studio in 1953. His photographs are always posed or arranged. He also photographed still-life objects, including found objects, with great detail, clarity, and unusual arrangements, and his work is part of every major museum photography collection. His favorite model, Swedish-born Lisa Fonssagrives (1911–1992), a world-famous dancer, fashion designer, photographer, and sculptor, was also his wife.

[Stewart Kampel (2nd ed.)]

PENN, JACK (1909–1996), South African plastic surgeon. Penn was born in Cape Town and studied at the University of Witwatersrand. He was appointed professor of plastic maxillo-facial surgery at the University of Witwatersrand, Johannesburg in 1944. During World War II he commanded the Brenthurst Military Hospital for Plastic Surgery in Johannesburg; as consultant to the Union Defence Force, he held the rank of brigadier.

In 1950 he resigned his professorship and opened a private clinic, which he also named Brenthurst Clinic. He was regarded as one of the world's leading plastic surgeons.

During the Israeli War of Independence and subsequently during the Sinai Campaign, the Six-Day War in 1967, and the Yom Kippur War of 1973 he brought a plastic surgery unit to Israel.

Penn was also a talented sculptor, and his sculptures include those of Ben-Gurion, Dayan, Smuts, Herzog, etc., and full-sized statues of the first white and first black registered nurses in S. Africa. After World War II he was invited by the Johannesburg government to treat the victims of the Hiroshima and Nagasaki atomic bombs, and initiated reconstructive surgery in Rhodesia, Mozambique, French Equatorial Africa, and Taiwan.

In 1980, Penn was appointed to the new President's Council by South African Prime Minister R.P.W. Botha.

His publications include *Brenthurst Papers, Letters to My Son* (1974), his autobiography *The Right to Look Human* (1974; 2nd ed., 1976), and *A Sense of Responsibility* (1978).

[Louis Isaac Rabinowitz]

PENN, SEAN (1960–), U.S. actor. Born in Burbank, California, Penn is the middle son of Catholic actress Eileen Ryan and Jewish actor/director Leo Penn, who was blacklisted during the McCarthy era for refusing to testify and later established himself as a director on shows such as *Columbo* and *Diagnosis: Murder*. A Santa Monica native, he spent his leisure time surfing, playing tennis, and watching movies. At 16, he began directing and starring in Super-8 films with his brother Chris. He graduated from Santa Monica High School in 1978 and worked as a technician and assistant to Pat Hingle at the Los Angeles Group Repertory Theater, studied acting with Peggy Feury at the Loft Studio, and had a few minor television roles. Leo Penn asked director Kenneth C. Gilbert to cast his son in a *Barnaby Jones* episode in 1979, which led to a part in the Broadway show *Heartland* (1981), another favor from a family friend. While the play only lasted three weeks, the experience convinced Penn to try out for *Taps* (1981), which in turn led to his break-out performance as Jeff Spicoli in *Fast Times at Ridgemont High* (1982). Penn married the pop star Madonna in 1985. They starred together in *Shanghai Surprise* (1986), a film that was critically panned. A drunken driving conviction while filming *Colors* (1988) led to a 60-day sentence in the Los Angeles County Jail, which he served out on weekends so as to not interfere with the production schedule. Penn divorced Madonna in 1989, the same year he earned praise for his portrayal of a conflicted and angry GI in the film *Casualties of War*. In 1991, Penn wrote and directed his first feature film, *The Indian Runner*, which was followed by *The Crossing Guard* (1995) and *11'09'01 – September 11* (2002). Highly praised performances in *Carlito's Way* (1993) and *Dead Man Walking* (1995) helped pave the way for his best actor win at the Cannes Film Festival for *She's So Lovely* (1997). Penn won both an Oscar and another Golden Globe for his role in *Mystic River* (2003). In 2005, Penn went on assignment to Iran to report for the *San Francisco Chronicle*.

[Adam Wills (2nd ed.)]

PENNSYLVANIA, one of the 13 original states of the U.S.; general population 12,283,000 (2001), Jewish population 282,000 (est.), 2.3% of the total. Pennsylvania has nearly 30 cities and towns numbering over 100 Jews each, nine of which have over 1,000. (Some of these communities include geographically larger areas than in earlier decades.) About 88% of the Jews live in either greater Philadelphia or Pittsburgh. Approximately 197 congregations existed in Pennsylvania in 2002. More than a dozen colleges offered majors in Jewish studies, and many more offered minors and courses. Jewish educational institutions included Gratz College, the Reconstructionist Rabbinical College, and the University of Pennsylvania's Center for Advanced Judaic Studies in *Philadelphia as well as Judaic Studies program at many of the major colleges.

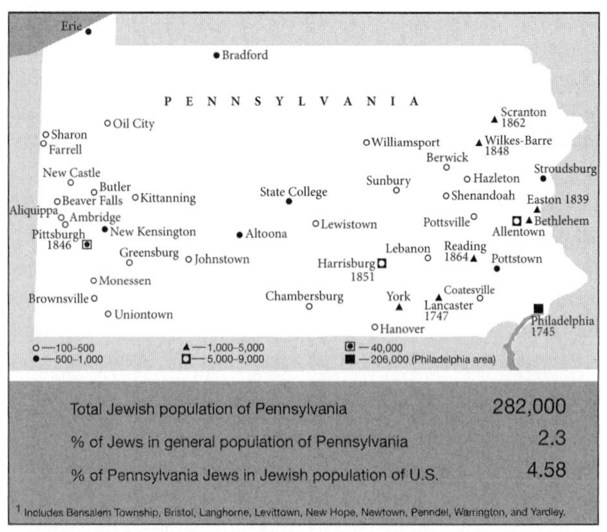

Jewish communities in Pennsylvania and dates of establishment. Population figures for 2001.

Following the first permanent European settlement in Pennsylvania in 1643, the colony passed through Dutch (1655) and English (1664) rule until 1681, when William Penn acquired the territory. By 1656 New Amsterdam Jews traded along the Delaware River on Pennsylvania's eastern border, and by 1681 several Jews probably settled in the southeastern area. While most of these Jews were of Spanish-Portuguese origin, during the 18th century many came from Central Europe. Isaac Miranda (d. 1732) of Tuscany, a prominent Philadelphia landowner and public official, was the first Jew to settle in *Lancaster, where he died a convert to Christianity. His son George traded with the Shawnee Indians along the Allegheny River. By 1747 – when ten Jewish families lived in Lancaster – a cemetery was purchased by Isaac Nunez Ricus (Henriques) and Joseph *Simon, the leading merchant who had a trading outpost at Fort Pitt (later Pittsburgh). An early Jewish resident of Lancaster, Isaac Cohen, was Pennsylvania's first physician.

Jews settled at an early date in the port of Philadelphia, where many of them, such as the traders David *Franks and Nathan *Levy, engaged in shipping by the 1750s. Michael *Gratz arrived in 1759 from London and joined the mercantile enterprises of his brother Barnard. Franks, Levy, Andrew Levy, and Joseph Simon speculated in western land, suffering damages from Indian raids. Franks, Barnard Gratz, and Aaron *Levy were among the purchasers of land from the Illinois Indians in 1773. Levy became a landowner in nearly every county and founded Aaronsburg, which he named for himself, in 1786. Another early Jewish settlement was at Easton, north of Philadelphia on the Delaware. The merchant Myer Hart de Shira (Texeira) was among its founders, and by 1750 11 Jewish families lived there. Some lived in Reading from 1753 and in York from 1758. By the end of the American Revolution (1783), in which Jews played military and financial roles, about 800 Jews lived in the state. They enjoyed political rights, except that of membership in the General Assembly, although before the revolution David Franks (1748) and Benjamin *Cohen (1755) sat in that body. Rebecca Gratz founded the Hebrew Sunday School Society (1838) and other organizations in Philadelphia.

There were many areas of the state in which few Jews lived until numbers of German Jews arrived after 1825. Jews arrived in Pittsburgh, Reading, Pottsville, and Wilkes-Barre during the 1830s, in Harrisburg, *Scranton, Erie, and Allentown during the 1840s, in Honesdale from 1849, and in Hazelton, Altoona, and Uniontown during the 1860s. In some of these areas, real communities did not emerge for decades. In Lancaster, where Jews had lived during the colonial and early federal eras, a new community was not re-established until the latter part of the 19th century. In Harrisburg, the first congregation formed in 1853. In Hazelton, a traditional synagogue opened in 1893, and a second Reform congregation in 1906. Women played a leading role in organizing social welfare and educational organizations.

There were only nine congregations in Pennsylvania in 1856, which grew by 1877 to 26 for approximately 17,000 Jews. Daughters of Israel, the first national Jewish women's organization, was founded in Pittsburgh in 1872. Between 1889 and 1910 over 100,000 East European Jews immigrated to the state, so that by 1917 there were 320,000 Jews. New Jewish communities arose in Bethlehem, Greensburg, Johnstown, McKeesport, Mt. Carmel, New Kensington, Shamokin, Sharon, Sunbury, and Washington during the 1880s, and in Braddock and West Chester during the next decade. By 1927 there were 405,000 Jews, the number growing moderately thereafter. In 1970, the estimated Jewish population of the state was 444,000, after which it declined. Most Jews settled in large cities, but many settled in the state's numerous mining and industrial towns. Though many began as blue-collar workers, most established themselves as merchants, serving immigrant industrial workers.

Several demographic and occupational trends influenced Jewish communities. As early as the 1920s, children raised in smaller towns tended to move to cities with larger Jewish populations. Particularly after World War II, both boys and girls were encouraged to pursue higher education and often did not return to the small family businesses. The children of merchants relocated to larger cities and to other regions of the country. Thus many smaller towns included only one or two generations of a family. Braddock, an extreme example, a mill town near Pittsburgh, was estimated to have 1,350 Jews in 1942 and 250 in 1975. Hazelton, estimated to have 1,700 Jews in 1942, had 900 in 1974, and 300 in 2004. In Johnstown, where the estimated Jewish population declined from 1,350 in 1942 to 980 in 1974, had 275 in 2004, three congregations had merged into one by 1976. The Jewish populations of these towns continued to decline.

Medium-sized communities such as Allentown and Harrisburg, with more diverse economic possibilities, often grew or were stable in the decades following 1950. Although some cities, such as Scranton, declined in Jewish population, other communities expanded. Harrisburg opened a Jewish Community Center in 1958 and a home for the aged in 1977. These medium-sized communities were usually large enough to sustain a variety of congregations, a day school, and a Jewish community center.

In addition, from the mid-1950s Jews tended to move from the large cities to developing suburbs. Thus, many Jews left Philadelphia for the western, northeastern, and northwestern suburbs of the city. On the other hand, Pittsburgh, second in size and importance to Philadelphia, was suburbanized very little.

Some small towns with Jewish communities founded by Jewish workers and merchants and their families became part of growing suburban or exurban communities. Coatesville, a declining community about 40 miles (64 km) from Philadelphia (estimated Jewish population 305 in 1975), by the 1980s had a shrinking Conservative congregation, Beth Israel, founded in 1916. In 1994 they relocated to Uwchland (about 10 miles or 16 km away) in an exurban area, growing significantly as a result. The small Chester County Jewish federation and three other suburban county federations became regions of the Jewish Federation of Greater Philadelphia by the early 1990s. In a small town in Delaware County, Beth Israel of Media, a formerly Orthodox congregation founded in 1929, was in decline when it joined the Reconstructionist movement in 1972. With new leadership, the congregation grew as suburban Philadelphia expanded, opening a new building in 1997 in Media.

A final demographic trend was the movement of Jews from the northeastern states to the Sunbelt, particularly California and Florida. Pennsylvania Jewish population declined significantly after 1970, despite significant immigration from the Soviet Union and its successor states.

By the 1990s 30 colleges offered courses in Jewish studies. In 1994, 29,000 Jewish students were estimated to be studying in Pennsylvania colleges. By 2005, many colleges had active Hillels or Jewish student centers, among them the University of Pennsylvania, Pennsylvania State University, Dickinson, Lehigh, Muhlenberg, Bucknell, Temple, and the University of Pittsburgh and Carnegie-Mellon University, which shared a joint Hillel.

Jewish communal life centralized during the 20th century, and Jewish welfare federations were organized in Allentown (1948), Altoona (1920), Butler (1938), Easton (1939), Erie (1946), Harrisburg (1933), Johnstown (1938), Lancaster (1928), Levittown (1956), New Castle and Norristown (1936), Philadelphia (1901), Pittsburgh (1912), Pottsville (1935), Reading (1935), Scranton (1945), Sharon (1940), Uniontown (1939), Wilkes-Barre (1935), and York (1928). Most federations in communities with fewer than 1,000 Jews were no longer functioning in 2004. Jewish federations in the largest cities joined to create a representative office in Harrisburg, the Pennsylvania Jewish Coalition, in 1981. In 2005, Jewish newspapers were published in Philadelphia and Pittsburgh.

Pennsylvania played a major role in Jewish camping in the 20th century. Camp Emma Farm opened near Pittsburgh in 1908, eventually becoming Camp Emma Kaufman, affiliated with the local Jewish Community Center. Jewish summer camps under a wide range of religious and community sponsorship operated in northeast Pennsylvania in the Poconos. Many were established in the decade and a half after World War II, including Camp Ramah (Conservative), B'nai B'rith Perlman camp, Camp Harlam (Reform), and camps serving Jewish community centers in New Jersey and New York as well as Pennsylvania. At the Habonim (Labor Zionist) movement's Camp Galil in Bucks County, explosives were hidden in 1947 before being smuggled to the Haganah in Palestine.

A number of Jews with Pennsylvania backgrounds achieved national or international prominence. Binyamin Netanyahu (later prime minister of Israel) and his brother Yonatan (killed in the Israeli raid at Entebbe in 1976) both attended Cheltenham High School outside Philadelphia while their father was teaching in the U.S. Both Sandy Eisenberg Sasso, the first woman Reconstructionist rabbi, and Amy Eilberg, the first woman Conservative rabbi, were from the Philadelphia area.

Jews in Pennsylvania have held high federal, state, and local offices. Representatives in the U.S. Congress have included: Lewis Charles Levin (1845–51), Henry M. Phillips (1857–59), Myer Strouse (1863–67), Benjamin Golder (1925–33), Henry Ellenbogen (1933–38), Leon Sacks (1937–43), Samuel A. Weiss (1941–46), Earl Chudoff (1949–58), Herman Toll (1959–67) Marc Lincoln Marks (1977–1983), Joshua Eilberg (1967–79), Marjorie Margolies-Mezvinzky (1993–95), Jon Fox (1995–99), and Allyson Y. Schwartz (2005–). Milton *Shapp served as governor from 1971 to 1979. During this time he campaigned for the Democratic nomination for president (1976.) Edward Rendell, former mayor of Philadelphia and former national chair of the Democratic Party, became governor in 2003. Jews served in the state cabinet from the 1920s. Alice Liveright was secretary of welfare from 1931 to 1935. Michael Masch, a former Philadelphia budget director, was appointed in 2003 as secretary of budget and administration, the state's chief operating officer. Arlen Specter was U.S. Senator from 1981, eventually chairing the Judiciary committee. In 1996, Specter briefly campaigned for the Republican nomination for president. Horace Stern, a State Supreme Court justice from 1936, was chief justice from 1952 to 1956. Sandra Shultz Newman was the first woman elected to that court (1995–). Norma Levy Shapiro was the first woman appointed to the U.S. Third District Court in 1978, serving until 1998. Sophie Masloff was mayor of Pittsburgh from 1988 to 1991. Herbert Fineman, Democrat from Philadelphia, served as speaker of the state House of Representatives from 1969 to 73 and in 1975–77. Robert C. Jubelirer, a Republican from Altoona, was president pro tempore of the state senate from 1985 to 1992 and 1994– .

The estimated Jewish population (2004) of the following communities (including suburbs or surrounding areas) was Philadelphia – 206,000; Pittsburgh – 42,200; Lehigh Valley (including Allentown) – 8,500; Harrisburg – 7,000; Scranton – 3,100; Wilkes-Barre – 3,000; Lancaster – 3,000; Reading – 2,200; York – 1,800; Erie – 850; State College – 700; Pottstown – 650; Stroudsburg, 600; Altoona – 575; Wayne County (including Honesdale) – 500; Lebanon – 350; Hazleton – 300; Sharon – 300; Johnstown – 275; Butler – 250; Williamsport – 225; New Castle – 200; Sunbury (including Shamokin) – 200.

BIBLIOGRAPHY: J.R. Marcus, *Early American Jewry* (1955), 3–164. **ADD. BIBLIOGRAPHY:** AJYB (1918–2004), passim; H.S. Linfield, *Statistics of Jews and Jewish Organizations* (1939); J. Feldman, *The Jewish Experience in Western Pennsylvania: A History: 1775–1945* (1986); D. Ashton, *Jewish Life in Pennsylvania* (1998); M. Coleman, *The Jews of Harrisburg: An Informal History by a Native Son* (ca. 1978); J.F. Miller, *Voices of Hazelton: A Century of Jewish Life* (1993); E. Morawska, *Insecure Prosperity: Small Town Jews in Industrial America 1890–1940* (1996); R. Perlman, *From Shtetl to Milltown: Litvaks, Hungarians, and Galitzianers in Western Pennsylvania 1875–1925* (2001); J. Trachtenberg, *Consider the Years; The Story of the Jewish Community of Easton, 1752–1942* (1944); L. Winograd, *The Horse Died at Windber: A History of Johnstown's Jews of Pennsylvania* (1988); D. Brener, *Lancaster's Gates of Heaven: Portals to the Past: The 19th Century Jewish Community of Lancaster, Pennsylvania and Congregation Shaarai Shomayim, 1856–1976.* (1976); M. Levin, *The Jews of Wilkes-Barre, 1845–1995: 150 Years in the Wyoming Valley* (1999).

[Edward L. Greenstein / Robert P. Tabak (2nd ed.)]

PENSO DE LA VEGA, JOSEPH (1650–1692), *Marrano writer and merchant. Joseph was born in Amsterdam. His father Isaac Penso Felix, a native of Espejo, Spain, had been imprisoned by the *Inquisition in Spain, and supposedly vowed to embrace Judaism openly within a year of his release. When freed he fled with his family to Antwerp and then to Amsterdam, and formally returned to Judaism at Middleburg. A charitable man, Isaac was said to have distributed 80,000 guldens as tithes from his profits.

Joseph Penso spent a short period in Leghorn, but lived mainly in Amsterdam, where he was a member of several literary academies and produced many and varied works. Besides funeral orations, wedding verses, and similar occasional pieces, he claimed to have written more than 200 epistles to different European statesmen. One of his earliest efforts was a Hebrew drama, *Asirei ha-Tikvah* (Amsterdam, 1673), an allegorical depiction of the victory of the will over the passions.

His Spanish books, all published in Amsterdam, include the *Triunfos del Aguila* (1683), on the relief of Vienna by John Sobieski; *Retrato de la Prudencia* (1690), which eulogized William of Orange when he became king of England; a collection of *Discursos académicos, morales, retóricos y sagrados* (1685), which he delivered at the Academia de los Floridos in Amsterdam; and *Rumbos Peligrosos* (1684), containing three short novels. These works, particularly the last named, enjoyed considerable vogue, but suffer the defects of the period: excessive display of erudition, digressions, and baroque floridness. One of his outstanding works is *Confusión de Confusiones* (1688), the first book to treat the workings of the stock exchange. It is still considered one of the best descriptions of dealings in stocks and shares. In the form of four dialogues between a "fastidious philosopher," a "prudent merchant," and an "erudite stockholder," Penso explains what stocks are, how they are bought and sold, the use of options, speculative maneuvers, and so on, and describes the operations of the Dutch trading companies. In spite of its serious subject, the work is enlivened by whimsical explanations of the origins of this kind of dealing and ironic descriptions of the bourse, of Amsterdam's coffee houses, and of the life of stock traders. Selections of it were translated into English by H. Kellenbenz and published under the same title in 1957.

BIBLIOGRAPHY: Roth, Marranos, 336–7; M.B. Amzalak, *Joseph de la Vega e o seu livro Confusión de Confusiones* (1925); idem, *As Operações de Bolsa segundo Joseph de la Vega* (1926); idem, *Trois précurseurs Portugais* (193–?); J. Caro Baroja, *Los Judios en la España moderna y contemporánea*, 2 (1962), 157–9.

[Kenneth R. Scholberg]

PENTATEUCH.

This article is arranged according to the following outline:

INTRODUCTION

Definition

The first five books of the Hebrew Bible are known as the Torah, the Five Books of Moses, and also as the Pentateuch, from the Greek *pentateuchos*, meaning five scrolls. Traditional Judaism refers to it as the *ḥummash*, another form of the number five. The original Pentateuch is written in Hebrew, with each book bearing an ancient Hebrew title derived from its incipit: *Bereshit*, *Shemot*, *va-Yikra*, *Be-Midbar*, and *Devarim*. The Septuagint translators gave the texts the Greek names of Genesis, Exodos, Leviticon, Arithmoi, and Deuteronomion, which in turn influenced the more commonly used names of Latin derivation: Genesis, Exodus, Leviticus, Numbers, and Deuteronomy.

Outline

Although many older individual literary narratives are extant from Mesopotamia and Egypt, the Pentateuch is a unique literary creation in two ways. First, it combines prose, poetry, and law in developing its story-line. Second, it begins with a description of the creation of the universe and ends with the death of Moses. Thus, unlike myths of gods and heroes, or lists of kings and the lengths of their reigns, the stories of the Torah are arranged chronologically to detail the development and movement of a people over time. As such, it is the first history-writing on earth.

The book of Genesis describes creation, the destruction via the flood, and the subsequent re-population of the world. It explores the theme of relations between the God YHWH and humanity in the world that the deity has created. God makes a covenant with all humankind through its common ancestor Noah, promising the security of the cosmos. Then the focus narrows to the family of the patriarchs, Abraham, Isaac, and Jacob, with whom God makes a second covenant promising protection, prosperity, progeny, and property. Originally from Mesopotamia, they settle in Canaan, and then make their way to Egypt, where their descendants, the Israelites, are enslaved. In Exodus, YHWH makes himself known in the world beyond the Israelites through a series of miracles, introduced by their leader Moses, that both demonstrate this God's control of the forces of nature and succeed in pressuring the Egyptians to release the Israelites from bondage. YHWH then makes a third covenant with Israel, the text of which is the Ten Commandments, during a revelation at Mount Sinai, also known as Horeb. YHWH also gives laws by which they are instructed to live, and YHWH gives instructions for building a Tabernacle, which will be the location of future revelations and will house the ark, containing the tablets of the covenant. Leviticus then is different in that it contains few stories but provides more laws regarding the moral and ritual behavior of the people, from commandments about holidays, sacrifices, and purity to the commandment to love one's fellow human beings as oneself. Numbers details their journey in the wilderness for 40 years with the ultimate goal of moving back to Canaan and claiming it as their own land, to be known as Israel. In Deuteronomy Moses addresses the Israelites in a speech in which he reviews their history and exhorts them to keep their covenant with God. The book, and the Torah, end as Moses concludes his farewell address and dies within sight of the promised land.

Special Place in the Hebrew Bible, Judaism, and Biblical Scholarship

The Torah has a singular status in relation to the rest of the Hebrew Bible. First, the events it narrates are central to and assumed by the remaining biblical books. Second, many other biblical books refer to it or allude to passages in it. The Torah also holds a special place in Jewish tradition because of the significance of the events it describes and because of the law contained in it that became normative within Judaism. This special status has continued in modern biblical scholarship in that the questions raised concerning its history and authorship form the foundation for the historical development of the field.

CONTENTS AND STRUCTURE

The story detailed in the Torah can be divided into six major parts:

1. The primeval history (Genesis 1–11)
2. The patriarchs (Genesis 12–50)

3. The Exodus from Egypt (Exodus 1:1–15:21; interim: 15:22–16:36)

4. Sinai/Horeb covenant and laws (Exodus 17–40; Leviticus)

5. The journey (Numbers)

6. Moses' farewell (Deuteronomy)

These parts are not entirely discrete: for example, Exodus 15:22–16:36 fit neither the Egypt nor the Sinai sections, but rather describe events of the journey between the two settings. Additionally, it is possible to place Numbers 1–10 in the Sinai/Horeb section, since it describes preparations at the mountain for the upcoming journey, or to connect Exodus 16–18 to the Exodus section since it precedes the arrival at Sinai. However, such variations are minor and do not undermine the basic division of the Pentateuch into six major parts.

The Primeval History

The primeval history provides etiologies for the state of the world and how it came to be that way. It sets up literary themes and historical backgrounds that demonstrate the worldview of the Israelite authors who produced it. It also provides basic descriptions of YHWH; who God is, how and why God acts, and the power God has to create and act upon his creation. This power is always present in the background of Pentateuchal narrative, and it occasionally moves into the foreground, manifesting itself in extraordinary acts of God in human history.

The Torah begins with the creation of the universe and everything in it. Upon completion, God rests, seeing that the creation is "very good." That is: the initial state of creation is pictured as positive. The story of the Garden of Eden sets a major theme for the remainder of the Primeval History, one that endures really throughout the Hebrew Bible: the development of the relationship between God and humanity. God creates humans to tend the garden and commands obedience. The humans disobey. The basic conflict established between God's commandments and humanity's disobedience is a fundamental theme in the remainder of the biblical narrative, and it raises issues of God's justice and the divine ability and propensity for punishment, but it also demonstrates God's compassion, mercy, and forgiveness. The knowledge of good and bad acquired in the Garden of Eden comes at the price of labor, pain, a hostile environment, and mortality. Adam and Eve are exiled from the garden. The competition between their children for God's favor is followed by the murder of Abel by Cain. Over the generations, the essential goodness of creation becomes corrupted by humanity to the point that "YHWH saw that human bad was great in the earth" (Gen. 6:5) and the deity decides to wipe out all life on earth as a result. He plans to repopulate the earth from the descendants of Noah, the most righteous man in his generation. God's great flood devastates the earth, after which God covenants with Noah never again to dismantle the creation via the waters that surround the habitable earth. This is the first of three covenants that frame the Pentateuch's history, and the sign of this covenant is the rainbow in the sky.

But the corruption of humans and their fundamental disobedience continue. The conflicts between men are illustrated in the story of Noah and his son Ham, and conflicts with God result in the dispersion of humans from Babylon (also called "Babel") and their separation from one another by the birth of different languages.

The Patriarchs

The focus narrows considerably in this next section. The man who is to become the patriarch of Israel and other nations, Abraham, is introduced. Favored with a revelation from YHWH, Abraham is instructed to migrate from Mesopotamia to Canaan. There God makes a covenant that promises Abraham protection, offspring, land, and wealth. The sign of the covenant is circumcision. Implied is the demand on Abraham's part for loyalty and complete obedience to YHWH. The basic theme of divine commandment and human obedience is further explored as Abraham, willing to sacrifice his son Isaac at God's command, passes the deity's test, but other members of his extended family who are not obedient to God's word, such as Lot's wife, are punished for it.

YHWH renews the covenant with Isaac, and then with Jacob. Jacob is a complicated, fairly well-developed character. His name means "supplanter," and it is his brother Esau whom he supplants as he buys Esau's birthright and then tricks his father Isaac into bestowing the blessing of the preeminent son on him rather than on Esau. Jacob is deceived in turn by his father-in-law Laban, and then by Jacob's own sons in the disappearance of his favorite son, Joseph. He himself ceases to be the deceiver after wrestling with "a man" whom Jacob understands to have been God himself as he exclaims, "I have seen God face to face." As a result of the encounter, Jacob's name is changed to Israel, which the biblical author takes to mean "struggles with God," explaining "for you have struggled with God and with men and you have prevailed." This new moniker reflects Jacob's own struggles with God, but it also points to the future clashes of Jacob's descendants, the children of Israel, with their God.

After Jacob, all future covenant renewals will be made between God and the children of Israel, the Israelites as a whole. Also, the portrayal of Jacob in the text changes; after he is named "Israel," Jacob slowly becomes a more passive character, a stark contrast to the protagonist he had been from the time of his birth.

The narratives of the patriarchs end with the story of Joseph's rise to power in Egypt and the migration of Israel/Jacob and the family to Egypt. They are the heirs of a covenant promising them nationhood, a land, and a relationship with YHWH, and their return to Canaan is foreshadowed by Joseph's request to have his bones preserved and brought back with the Israelites for re-burial in Canaan.

The Exodus

The descendants of Jacob are slaves in Egypt, and YHWH remembers the covenant with them and acts to free them. The

Exodus is not simply a story of liberation from slavery, however. There are three interdependent themes that play out in this story and through the remainder of the Torah's narrative. First is the forging of a nation out of the descendants of Jacob, the "children of Israel." As they move from slavery to freedom, they will receive the laws that bind them together as a nation and that also bind them in a covenant with their God. The second theme is the revelation of this God beyond the Israelites to the entire world. YHWH successfully challenges the greatest nation on earth, Egypt, overwhelming it with a series of miraculous events – including ten plagues and the parting of the Red Sea – that culminate in the liberation of their Israelite slaves. In so doing, God makes Himself known to the entire world, demonstrating His mastery over all of the forces of nature and thereby over all of the Egyptian gods. The third theme focuses on the person of Moses, the man chosen to represent YHWH to Pharaoh and to the Israelites. Moses is pictured as a reluctant hero, a man who does not wholly belong to either the heavenly or the earthly realms and is tragically doomed to try to reconcile the two. He encounters YHWH at a burning bush and is given a mission he does not want, despite the enormous power YHWH has granted to him over the forces of nature. Moses returns to Egypt to free his people, a rebellious and unhappy community of slaves who complain to him and about him. Yet Moses defends them to YHWH when God loses patience with their rebelliousness. The struggles between God and humans reach a peak during the forty-year period of wandering in the desert, begun in the book of Exodus but detailed further in Numbers.

Sinai/Horeb Covenant and Laws

These three themes introduced in the Exodus story are continued and further interwoven in this, the largest unit of the Torah. After liberation from Egypt, the Israelites are brought to Sinai/Horeb, where YHWH speaks aloud to all of them from inside a fire on the mountain, detailing their responsibilities in the maintenance of the covenant relationship God has forged with them. Up to this point, YHWH has dictated only the terms of the covenant pertaining to divine commitment to humans. The covenant with the patriarchs in Genesis had been specific only with reference to YHWH's promises to the descendants of Abraham, Isaac, and Jacob. During the revelation at Sinai, YHWH specifies and thereby limits the human responsibilities and obligations required in return for the divine promises.

The Decalogue forms the basis of this third major covenant of the Torah, the Israelite covenant (also known as the Mosaic covenant or the Sinai covenant). YHWH roots it in the historical act of salvation of the Israelites from slavery, and details the specific ritual and ethical injunctions by which the Israelites are to live. The first four commandments are ritual ones; that is, they pertain to the relations between humans and God. The last six are ethical laws; they pertain to relations between humans and their fellow human beings. Thus the two basic themes of the book of Genesis, relations between God and humans, and relations among humans on earth, are formally engaged.

The Ten Commandments in Exodus 20 are followed by the Covenant Code, a corpus of law in Exodus 21–23. The entire book of Leviticus further elaborates the details of these and other laws pertaining to the two categories, ritual and ethical, apparent in the Ten Commandments. Ritual laws are concerned with priests, purity, sacrifice, holidays, dietary rules, and apostasy. Pervading much of the ritual law is a concept of distinction: between pure and impure, holy and secular, permitted and forbidden. Ethical laws govern behavior among humans and include economic laws, laws of sexual relations, rules of courts and justice, injuries, and general issues of how one should treat one's fellow human being.

In the Torah, the concept of covenant binds the legal and narrative texts together. *Law is always given within a context of history.* The laws are backgrounded by YHWH's historical act of salvation from slavery, the covenants that God has kept with their forefathers, and future promises of the Israelites' well-being in the land that God will give them.

In this section, the ark, the Tabernacle, the priesthood, and the Sabbath are all associated with knowledge of YHWH, and the book of Exodus culminates in the Tabernacle's consecration. All are tangible ways by which the Israelites will be aware of the presence of YHWH, and all are signs that they have been chosen to be YHWH's people, and YHWH will be their God. The keeping of the Sabbath is the sign of the Israelite covenant. The priesthood is bestowed upon Aaron, Moses' Levite brother, and upon Aaron's male descendants.

The narrative further explores Moses' role as prophet, caught between the world of God and the world of humans. Moses' role is to represent the people to YHWH, and YHWH to the people, receiving the full impact of the complaints of each about the other. This peaks in the golden calf story, in which Moses successfully pleads with God not to destroy the rebellious nation but then himself unleashes his anger and punishment on them.

The Journey

The themes of the Exodus culminate in this fifth section, the journey from Sinai/Horeb to the promised land. In a series of seemingly unrelated episodes, the themes of nationhood, the revelation of YHWH, and the character of Moses are further developed and serve to unify the individual stories contained in the book of Numbers. A major concern for the journey is the purity of the camp; the nation among whom YHWH dwells must be a holy one. And YHWH does dwell in the camp. God's closeness to the people is demonstrated on a daily basis, as they are led personally by YHWH via a pillar of cloud by day, a pillar of fire by night. When they are hungry, their God feeds them with the miraculous appearance of manna. When they complain about the manna, their God brings them quail. When they are thirsty, their God makes water come from a rock. And yet, despite this extreme closeness – or perhaps, as a result of it – the humans' rebelliousness reaches its zenith.

Moses declares himself unable to bear the burden of the entire nation alone, and YHWH extends prophetic ability to others. But Moses' singular, albeit lonely and difficult, prophetic status is confirmed by YHWH Himself in the story of Miriam's leprosy, in which Miriam and Aaron challenge Moses saying, "Hasn't God spoken through us too?!" And the people, too, convey Moses' singular status when they reject him as leader in the story of the scouts who bring back a mixed report of the promised land. Fear of the residents of the land prompt the Israelites to try to replace Moses with a new leader and return to Egypt. YHWH threatens to destroy them and start over with Moses' own descendants. Moses reminds YHWH of his own declaration of mercy and compassion, and once again the impossibility of standing between humans and God is illustrated in the figure of Moses. As a result of their fear and rebelliousness, YHWH condemns the generation of former slaves to die in the wilderness as they travel for 40 years. Their children, born in freedom, will be the ones to take possession of the land.

As a result, Korah, Dathan, and Abiram accuse Moses and Aaron of failing to bring them to the land, and they charge Moses specifically with raising himself above the people, who are all holy. YHWH eliminates the rebels with fire and earthquake, and confirms the special holiness of the Levites, and especially of Aaron, by causing Aaron's rod to blossom. The rod is to be saved in the tabernacle "as a sign to rebels." Moses, however, takes the rod and strikes it against a rock to bring water for the continually complaining and rebellious Israelites. As a result, in the greatest tragedy of the Torah, Moses unwittingly aligns himself with the rebellious human community, and is condemned to die along with them without setting foot in the promised land.

The themes of rebellious humans and Moses' special status continue in the remaining stories in the book of Numbers. The book ends with a confirmation that the older generation has died out and with accounts relating to the acquisition of land east of the Jordan River and distribution of the land that the next generation will possess on the other side of that river.

Moses' Farewell

The book of Deuteronomy presents a speech by Moses to the people as they stand on the plains of Moab, east of the Jordan River, preparing to enter the promised land. Moses summarizes the events from Exodus through Numbers, dwelling particularly on the history of his and the people's experience in the journey from slavery to freedom. He also gives them another corpus of laws (Deut. 12–26).

Moses' speech centers on the theme of covenant, warning the people of their tendency to rebellion, and reminding them that success in their new land depends on their fulfillment of the covenant forged with YHWH at Sinai. In other words, the people have a choice, and a fundamental role in how their destiny as a nation will play out. They can choose to abide by the terms of the covenant and thereby ensure their well-being and longevity in the land, or they can choose to reject their covenantal obligations, in which case they will bear the responsibility for their national destruction. Moses details the blessings that will flow from YHWH to the people for keeping the covenant, and the curses entailed in breaking it.

Moses writes "this *torah*" in a book and gives it to the Levites, who are to keep it beside the ark and read it publicly. Then he designates Joshua as his successor, and he blesses the people. He climbs a mountain overlooking the promised land, sees it, and dies.

Thus the Pentateuch ends with a summary of the preceding sections and a recapitulation of the major themes. The emphasis throughout the prose, poetry, and law of Deuteronomy is on the theme of covenant, which serves to bind and unify all of the previous themes pertaining to the relations between God and humans.

THE AUTHORS

Jews traditionally viewed the Torah as a unified document, revealed by God to Moses. The Torah itself does not say this; but Deuteronomy 31:9, 24–26 report that Moses writes "this *torah*" on a scroll, and this was taken to mean that the full Pentateuch had been recorded by Moses. The account of the first time that the Torah of Moses was read publicly also was taken to mean that, on the death of Moses, the whole of the Pentateuch was complete, having been divinely revealed (Ezra 3:2; 7:6; Neh. 1:7–9; 8:1, 14; 9:14; 10:30; 13:1). Rabbinic commentators through the centuries noted problems in the text that raised questions about Mosaic authorship, but through interpretation and elaboration they sought to reconcile the contradictions, reacting strongly against those who denied the unity of the Five Books. As a fundamental principle of Jewish faith, Maimonides stated that "the whole of the Torah found in our hands this day is the Torah that was handed down by Moses and that is all of divine origin" (commentary to Sanh. 10 (11):1).

From the 11th to the 21st centuries, however, scholars have been expressing doubts about Mosaic authorship. At present, except for Orthodox Jews and fundamentalist Christians who believe in Mosaic authorship as a matter of faith, no scholar on earth holds that Moses – or any one person – was the recorder of the Torah. This is not an issue of divine versus human composition. It has nothing to do with whether the Torah was dictated, revealed, or inspired by God. It rather concerns the persons who wrote it down: who they were, and when they lived. Scholars still debate the number of authors and when they wrote the texts, but the evidence rules out a single author. What made the evidence so compelling was the convergence of numerous independent lines of evidence, several of which remain unchallenged.

Doublets and Terminology

These began with the convergence of two lines of evidence: doublets and terminology. Doublets are two variations of a story: the Torah has two accounts of creation (Gen. 1:1–2:3 and 2:4–24), two accounts of the covenant with Abraham (Genesis 15 and 17), and two accounts of Moses getting water from a rock at Meriba (Exodus 17 and Numbers 20). It is possible for doublets to occur in a single-author work, but the number of doublets in the Torah is so large that it indicates a more complex compositional history. There are more than 15 in Genesis alone, besides creation and the Abrahamic covenant. They include:

The Genealogy from Adam. Gen. 4:1–2, 17–26; and 5:1–28, 30–32

The flood. Gen. 6:5–8; 7:1–5, 7, 10, 12, 16b–20, 22–23; 8:2b–3a, 6, 8–12, 13b, 20–22; and 6:9–22; 7:8–9, 11, 13–16a, 21, 24; 8:1–2a, 3b–5, 7, 13a, 14–19; 9:1–17

Abraham's move from Mesopotamia to Canaan. Gen. 12:1–4a; and 12:4b–5

Abraham tells a king that his wife is his sister. Gen. 12:10–20; and 20:1–18; and 26:6–14 (this is a triplet)

Abraham and Lot part. Gen. 13:5, 7–11a, 12b–14; and 13:6, 11b–12a

Hagar and Ishmael. Gen. 16:1–2, 4–14; and 16:3, 5–16; and 21:8–19 (a triplet)

The prophecy that Isaac will be born. Gen. 17:16–19; and 18:10–14

The naming of Beer Sheba. Gen. 21:22–31; and 26:15–33

Jacob and Esau, and Jacob's move to Mesopotamia. Gen. 26:34–35; 27:46; 28:1–9; and 27:1–45; 28:10

Jacob at Beth-El. Gen. 28:10, 11a, 13–16, 19; and 28:11b–12, 17–18, 20–22; and 35:9–15 (a triplet)

Jacob's children. Gen. 29:32–35; 30:1–24; 35:16–20; and Gen. 35:23–26

The change of Jacob's name to Israel. Gen. 32:25–33; and 35:9–10

Joseph is taken to Egypt. Gen. 37:2b, 3b, 5–11, 19–20, 23, 25b–27, 28b, 31–35; 39:1; and 37:3a, 4,12–18, 21–22, 24, 25a, 28a, 29–30

It is not just that the number of doublets is large. It was observed that when each pair of doublet stories is separated, one of the stories refers to the deity as God (Hebrew *El* or *Elohim*) while the other refers to the deity by the proper name YHWH. Moreover, it was observed that this distinction continues in the Torah up to the moment that God reveals this proper name to Moses (Ex. 3:13–15), and then it stops. This was evidence that there were at least two sources that had been used in the Torah, one that said that God's proper name was not known until the generation of Moses, and one that pictured the divine name as known from the early generations of humans. Works describing this phenomenon often speak of the sources as having "different names of God," but that is not correct. Any work of literature or history might use different names for the same person. The phenomenon here is much stronger. It is that different works had different ideas of when God made the divine name YHWH known to humankind.

These source texts came to be known by the symbols E (for the text that referred to God as Elohim until Moses) and J (for the text that referred to God by the name YHWH, which was spelled *Jahwe* by the German scholars who first outlined this). Additionally, a third source was identified that followed the same pattern as E, stating definitively that God's name was not known until the time of Moses (Ex. 6:3). This source came to be known as P (the Priestly source). And a fourth source was observed to underlie the book of Deuteronomy. It is written in an entirely different, easily identifiable character and vocabulary. It contains doublets of the first four books as well as contradictions of detail. This source is known as D.

In addition, it has recently been recognized that the J source never uses the word God (Elohim) in narration. Persons in J use it in speech, but the narrator never once uses the word. This reinforces the evidence concerning the divine name with notable consistency. Specifically: the words El, Elohim, and YHWH occur over 2,000 times in the Torah, and the number of exceptions (where the wrong term occurs in a source) is only three.

The convergence of the two lines of evidence – doublets and the divine name – are reinforced by other terms, phrases, and names that occur only in particular sources but not in others. For example, we can cite the following:

(a) The phrase "gathered to his people" occurs only in P (11 times) and never in the other sources. Likewise the phrase "and he [or they] fell on his face" (eight times), the phrase "be fruitful and multiply" (12 times), the term "to expire" (*gw'* – 11 times), and the word "congregation" (Hebrew *'edâ* – more than 100 times) occur exclusively in P. Conversely, there are words used throughout the other sources of the Torah that *never* occur in P, such as: *rhm* (mercy/merciful); *hnn* (grace/gracious); *swb* (repent/repentance); and *hsd* (faithfulness).

(b) Meanwhile, the term "to know" as a euphemism for having sexual intercourse occurs only in J (five times) and never in the other sources. Likewise the name Sheol (six times) and the term "to suffer" (Hebrew *'sb* – seven times) occur exclusively in J.

(c) The name of the mountain where Moses leads Israel is named Sinai in J and P (20 times), but it is Horeb or "the Mountain of God" in E and D (14 times).

There are at least 25 of these characteristic terms, occurring over 500 times in the Torah. This is far too many to be just the result of clever scholars arranging their source identifications so that the right words will always show up in the right verses. Thus the evidence of doublets and different terminology converge towards a common explanation.

Narrative Flow

The source identifications are confirmed by another body of evidence: continuity of texts. It is possible to divide the sources with all of the doublets separated, with the divine name occurring consistently within the source texts, and with the characteristic terms and phrases likewise falling consistently in their sources – and then one can read the sources as complete, continuous texts, The P text flows as a continuous narrative, regularly picking up where it left off once the intervening J and E material are removed. The combined text of J and E likewise flows with hardly a gap when intervening material is removed (see below). One can read each of these texts as a nearly complete work. For example, when the J and P flood stories are separated, each flows as a continuous story without gaps, repetitions, or contradictions. Likewise, P's story of Korah's rebellion against Moses flows as a complete story when separated from J's story, also complete, of Dathan's and Abiram's rebellion. Either can be read as a continuous story (J = Num.16:1b–2a, 12–14, 25–26, 27b–32a, 33–34. P = 1a, 2b–11, 15–24, 27a, 32b, 35), and the two clauses that merge the stories and thus break the flow (Num. 16:24, 27) are editorial additions (confirmed by the fact that they do not occur in the Septuagint). The stories of Hagar and Ishmael (J = Gen. 16:1–2, 4–14. P = 16:3, 15–16), Jacob and Esau (J = Gen. 25:21–34; 27:1–45; 28:10. P = 26:34–35; 27:46; 28:1–9), the Red Sea (J = Ex. 13:21–22; 14:5a, 6a, 9a, 10b, 13–14, 19b, 20b, 21b, 24, 25b, 27b, 30–31. P = 14:1–4, 8, 9b, 10a, 10c, 15–18, 21a, 21c, 22–23, 26–27a, 28–29), and the spies (J = Num. 13:17–20, 22–24, 27–31, 33; 14:1b, 4, 11–25, 39–45. P = 13:1–16, 21, 25–26, 32; 14:1a, 2–3, 5–10, 26–29), are all further examples of intertwined J and P texts, that when separated yield complete and continuous independent narratives. Sometimes, P narratives only make sense in light of earlier P stories. For example, the P account of the heresy at Peor (Num. 25:6–19 (English 25:6–26:1a)) appears to begin *in medias res*, with the Israelite man and Midianite woman acting in the sight of Moses and the people, who "were weeping at the entrance of the tent of meeting." The weeping is unexplained unless the intervening J and E material is removed. Then we find that, five chapters earlier, the previous P story, the death of Aaron, ends with the people weeping for Aaron in its last verse (20:29). Thus the narrative flow of the P text appears to be consistent and intact.

Relationships of the Sources to Each Other and to History

J AND E. The J and E sources both contain historical referents that lie in the period during which the country was divided into the two kingdoms of Israel and Judah. The historical referents of J disproportionately relate to Judah, and those of E relate to Israel. Thus they had to have both been written during the divided monarchy, before the destruction of Israel by Assyria: between 922 and 722 B.C.E. These distinct historical connections both (1) support the identification of the sources and (2) point to the historical setting in which each was written. Neither source demonstrates awareness of either the fall of Israel or the dispersion of the northern tribes. J's reference to Esau/Edom breaking Israel's yoke from its neck (Gen. 27:40) probably places its composition after Hadad's rebellion against Solomon, or perhaps after Edom's full independence from Judah during the reign of the Judean king Jehoram (849–842 B.C.E.). The E text offers no similar clues to narrow its dates of composition further within the period of the divided monarchy.

The elements of J indicating a Judean provenance are as follows:

In J, Abraham resides in Hebron/Mamre (Gen. 13:18; 18:1). Hebron was the capital of Judah, and the home city of Zadok, the Judean high priest of David and Solomon.

Shechem was the capital of the northern kingdom of Israel, built by Jeroboam I, the king who had rebelled against Judah. The J account of Israel's acquisition of Shechem is derogatory, involving the taking of Dinah by Shechem and the massacre of the city by Simeon and Levi (Genesis 34).

The J birth accounts of the eponymous ancestors of the tribes include only Reuben, Simeon, Levi, and Judah (Gen. 29:32–35). Among these tribes, only Judah existed with a territorial identity in the era of the monarchy. The J text includes the story of Reuben's taking Jacob's concubine, and the story of Simeon's and Levi's massacre of Shechem. As confirmed in Jacob's deathbed blessing in Genesis 49, a poetic text included in J, these acts result in the preeminence passing to the fourth son: Judah.

In the J story of Joseph, Judah is the brother who saves Joseph from the other brothers' plans to kill him (Gen. 37:26–27; 42:22), and it is Judah who promises Jacob that Benjamin will survive the journey to Egypt (Gen. 43:8–9).

The author of J is the only author to include a lengthy story from the life of Judah (Genesis 38), culminating in the birth of Peres, the eponymous ancestor of the clan from which the Judean royal family was traced.

In the J story of Num. 17–20, 22–24, Moses sends scouts ahead to the promised land, and they see only Judah; they miss all the other tribes of Israel. The favorable spy in this story is Caleb; the Calebite territory was located in Judah and included Hebron.

Judah bordered Edom, which Israel did not, and J includes a lengthy account of the birth, youthful relations, and break between Jacob and Esau, the ancestor of the Edomites. These stories reflect the kinship and historical relations with Edom on several points. J also includes the list of the kings of Edom (Genesis 36).

The religious iconography in J also corresponds to the situation in Judah. The ark, located in Judah, figures prominently in J stories but is never mentioned in E. J includes a description of the ark's movements in the wilderness (Num. 10:33–36), and J associates the presence of the ark with military success (Num. 14:41–44). The J Decalogue only prohibits the making of molten gods (Ex. 34:17), a prohibition which denounces the golden calves of northern Israel, which were molten, without denigrating the golden cherubs of the Temple in Judah, which were wooden and gold-plated. In J, cherubs are depicted as guarding the path to the tree of life, consistent with the cherub iconography of Judah. Cherubs are never mentioned in E.

The elements of E that indicate a northern, Israelite provenance are as follows:

In E, Jacob struggles with God and etiologically names the site of this event Peni-El (Gen. 32:31). The Israelite city of Peni-El was built by Jeroboam I, the founding monarch of the northern Israelite kingdom (I Kings 12:25).

E has an account of Joseph's deathbed wish to be buried in his homeland and an account of the Israelites taking his remains during the exodus. The traditional site of Joseph's grave was at the city of Shechem, which was also built by Jeroboam and served at one point as the capital of Israel (I Kings 12:25).

In contrast to the J story of Simeon's and Levi's massacre of the inhabitants of Shechem, in E the territory around the city of Shechem is acquired by peaceful purchase (Gen. 33:18–19).

The E birth accounts of the eponymous ancestors of the tribes include all of the tribes of Israel: Dan, Naphtali, Gad, Asher, Issachar, Zebulon, Ephraim, Manasseh, and Benjamin (Gen. 30:5–24a; 35:16b–19), but they do not include Judah.

In E, the birthright goes to Joseph, creating the northern tribes of Ephraim and Manasseh. Also, Ephraim is favored over Manasseh in E (Gen. 48:13–20), corresponding to the historical preeminence of Ephraim, Jeroboam's tribe (and the term "Ephraim" is frequently used in the Hebrew Bible as an alternate name for the northern kingdom of Israel). The term for the additional portion thus awarded to Joseph is the unusual *sekem* (Shechem; 48:22), a pun on the name of the Israelite capital city, which was located in the hills of Ephraim.

In the E Joseph story, Reuben rather than Judah is the brother who saves Joseph from the other brothers' plans to kill him (Gen. 37:21–22), and it is Reuben rather than Judah who promises Jacob that Benjamin will survive the journey to Egypt (Gen. 42:37).

In E's depiction of the Israelites' slavery in Egypt, the Egyptian taskmasters are identified as "officers of the corvee" (*sarê missîm*; Ex. 1:11). The northern Israelite tribes' hostility to the Solomonic policy of *missîm* was an explicit ground for their secession, which, according to the report of I Kings, was initiated by the stoning of Rehoboam's officer of the *missîm* (I Kings 12:18).

The heroic role of Joshua is developed in E but not in J. Joshua is identified as being of northern Israelite origins, of the tribe of Ephraim. Not only does E show definite signs of northern provenance, but there are elements of E that coincide particularly with the interests of the Levites of northern Israel who were of the priestly group from Shiloh. Specifically:

Only E includes the story of the golden calf heresy, led by Aaron. The Shiloh Levites' high priest Abiathar had been expelled from the Jerusalem priestly hierarchy by Solomon, his prerogatives thus passing to an Aaronid high priest (Zadok). According to I Kings, the Shiloh prophet Ahijah had initially supported the kingship of Jeroboam but later rejected it when the new king established golden calves at Bethel and Dan. The E golden calf story thus merges and denigrates the two symbols of the exclusion of the Shiloh Levites, Aaron and the golden calf, while praising the Levites who violently purge the people of the heresy.

Like the golden calf story, the E story of Aaron's and Miriam's criticism of Moses over Moses' Cushite wife (Numbers 12) also denigrates Aaron, who is reprimanded directly by God. This story explicitly declares Moses' revelation to be superior to Aaron's, and, like the golden calf story, portrays Aaron addressing Moses submissively as "my lord."

The iconography of E likewise corresponds to the situation in Israel, and especially to the concerns of the Shiloh Levites. For example, the Tabernacle is originally associated with the northern Israelite religious center at Shiloh. E includes a description of the Tabernacle's establishment in relation to the camp in the wilderness, emphasizing its importance for revelation (Num. 10:33–36), but the Tabernacle is never mentioned in J. As opposed to J's prohibition of making molten gods, which attacks only the northern golden calves, E forbids the making of any "gods of silver and gods of gold" (Exod 20:23), thus applying to both the Israelite golden calves and the Judean golden cherubs. And in the E story of the golden calf, Moses smashes the tablets of the Decalogue, and there is no E account of a second set of tablets being made. This casts aspersions on the ark in Judah, which would thus either be empty or contain inauthentic tablets.

Both J and E relate a story of the establishment of Bethel (Gen. 28:10–22); and both kingdoms, Judah and Israel, had claims and interests in Bethel.

In addition to the interests of the Shiloh Levite priests detailed above, another sign that E derives from priestly origins is the fact that it includes a lengthy law code, the Covenant Code (Exodus 21–23). All other legal texts in the Hebrew Bible are found in priestly sources (D, P, and Ezekiel). J, however, lacks the law codes that are characteristic of priestly texts, and J shows no other manifest signs of composition in priestly circles.

Thus there is strong cumulative evidence for the origins of E and J in the northern and southern kingdoms, respectively.

RJE. The J and E texts were combined in an editorial process that sought to unify the two narrative strands into one flowing narrative, and this combined JE text, when separated from P, does form a complete and nearly continuous narrative. The extent to which the Redactor of J and E, known as RJE, was successful is measured by the fact that there is still debate over where and how to separate the two texts. When E and J are separated, neither flows continuously without gaps. This indicates that the Redactor of J and E was willing to cut some material to make the two sets of stories fit together more readily. For example, while the J source begins with the Garden of Eden (Genesis 2–3), the E text has no primeval history at all. The first E narrative is found in Gen. 20:1–18, a story about Abraham and Sarah at Gerar, deceiving King Abimelech into thinking that Sarah is Abraham's sister. The very beginning of the original E source is missing, and it is impossible to know whether it ever contained a creation story or an account of the flood, or whether it began with Abraham's movement to Canaan. The Redactor of JE chose to begin the combined narrative with J's version of all of these events.

The most likely time frame for the unification of J and E would have been shortly after the destruction of the northern Israelite kingdom in 722 B.C.E. They were definitely combined prior to the composition of the Priestly source, as P's account follows the chronology and events of the combined J and E. The parallels of characters, events, and order between P and JE are so close as to indicate that J and E were edited together and then were known to and followed by the composer(s) of P.

P. The Priestly source follows the combined JE in its contents and order: creation, flood, Abraham's migration to Canaan, Abraham's parting from Lot, the Abrahamic covenant, Ishmael's birth by Hagar, divine destruction of the cities, birth of Isaac, Isaac's marriage to Rebekah, death of Abraham, Jacob's parting from Esau, Jacob's children, Jacob's being renamed Israel, Joseph in Egypt, Jacob in Egypt, enslavement in Egypt, the plagues, the exodus, the Red Sea, water from a rock in the wilderness, manna, revelation at Sinai, law code at Sinai, the scouts, rebellions in the wilderness, Peor, the death of Moses. Where P's narrative does not match JE, the differences can be explained in terms of consistent concerns of P. Certain themes and characteristics of the JE narratives are completely missing from the P source. In JE, encounters between God and humans take place regularly, including such blatant anthropomorphisms as God's walking in the garden of Eden (J), making Adam's and Eve's clothes (J), closing Noah's ark (J), smelling Noah's sacrifice (J), wrestling with Jacob (E), standing on the rock at Meribah (E), and being seen by Moses at Sinai/Horeb (J and E). Such anthropomorphisms are absent from P. There are no angels in P, no dreams conveying divine meaning; in fact, the word "prophet" appears only once in P (Exod 7:1), and there it is used figuratively. P takes great pains to emphasize that the only legitimate communication between God and humans takes place through *priests*. And it is not through just any priest. It must be an Aaronid priest, at the Tabernacle, according to the proper rituals as described in the P legal sections. For example, in P's flood story, one pair of each kind of animal is brought into the ark (Gen. 6:19; 7:8, 9, 15); but in the J version, seven pairs of clean and one pair of unclean animals are brought (Gen. 7:2, 3). J has extra clean (sacrificial) animals because at the end of J's story Noah offers a sacrifice. There is no sacrifice in any P story until Aaron is inaugurated as High Priest, hence no extra animals on the ark for sacrifices in the P version. Similarly, P leaves out the sacrificial animals in its account of the Abrahamic covenant (Genesis 17), and P leaves out the story of the near sacrifice of Isaac completely. And, above all, P leaves out the stories of the golden calf and of Moses' Cushite wife, both of which denigrate Aaron.

The Priestly text is replete with technical information missing from JE, such as ages, dates, measurements, numbers, and precise instructions. P is particularly concerned with ritual and other matters pertaining to priests. Contrary to J, E, and D, in P only descendants of Aaron are priests, while all other Levites are designated as lower-level clergy. P also adds two major autumn holidays (Lev. 16:29–34; 23:23–32; Num. 29:1–11) to the standard list of three seasonal holidays contained in the other texts. P's perspective on the history of ancient Israel is often more concerned with justifying the sacral institutions of the Jerusalemite priesthood than with representing history for its own sake. For example, the creation in Genesis 1 justifies the institution of the Sabbath; the covenant with Abraham establishes the rite of circumcision (Gen. 17); and P's description of the events at Sinai center on the building of the sanctuary (Ex. 25ff.). The Tabernacle is of central importance to P, mentioned over 200 times. It is mentioned three times in E, and never in J or D; (for more on the Tabernacle, see below).

In P, the description of the flood is dramatic, a cosmic event in which "all the fountains of the great deep were split open, and the apertures of the skies were opened." After 150 days, the ark comes to rest on the mountains of Ararat, the precise date is given, and after months of recession of the water, God commands Noah to exit. Noah sends out a raven to determine that the earth has dried, and he and his family exit the ark with the animals. The event takes one year. J's version of the flood, however, begins with YHWH's being "grieved to His heart" over the state of humans. YHWH instructs Noah to come into an ark, and YHWH closes the ark for him. It rains forty days and forty nights. At the end, Noah sends out a dove three times to determine that the earth has dried. Then he builds an altar to YHWH and makes a sacrifice, "and YHWH smelled the pleasant smell." Anthropomorphisms of the deity are characteristic of J and completely lacking in P. The dates and measurements are important to P, much less so to J. J's language is simple; P's dramatic.

As with J and E, the most compelling types of evidence for dating the P text are its historical referents, linguistic classification, and references in and to other biblical books. All of these point solidly to a pre-exilic date, likely during the reign of King Hezekiah of Judah (715–687 B.C.E.).

In addition to the Tabernacle, the ark, tablets, cherubs, Urim and Thummim, other historical referents in P demonstrate the pre-exilic interests of the author. P alone among the four source works of the Torah calls for hierarchical divisions among the clergy. This is a pervasive concern in P legal sections and in P narrative. P insists that only Levites descended from Aaron are priests, and all other Levites are second-level clergy, and specific tasks for each group are assigned. According to the report in 2 Chronicles, Hezekiah was the king who established these divisions and assigned these tasks (II Chron. 31:2). Ezekiel's prediction of the priestly divisions had led 19th century scholars to place the authorship of P after Ezekiel, but Ezekiel distinguishes not the descendants of Aaron, but only the Zadokite Aaronids from other Levites. Furthermore, there is no evidence that the author(s) of P accepted Ezekiel's visions as legally authoritative. On the contrary, the P model of the tabernacle (see below) is structurally incompatible with Ezekiel's vision of the Temple. In any case, new linguistic evidence indicates that P was composed prior to Ezekiel (see below).

P's exclusion of non-Aaronid Levites from the priesthood and concern with the house of Aaron is reflected also in the source's treatment of Aaron himself in the Exodus stories. P places Aaron alongside Moses from the beginning in Exodus, identifies Aaron as Moses' older brother (Ex. 6:20; Num. 26:59). Neither JE nor D identify Aaron (or Miriam) as Moses' sibling at all. E refers to Aaron as Moses' "Levite brother" (Ex. 4:14), which, if anything, indicates that they are not siblings in this source. (Why say "Levite" at all if they are siblings?) P provides for Aaron's consecration and for the consecration of his sons to the priesthood, depicts the Aaronid succession, including the death of his eldest two sons, his own death, his replacement by his third son Eliezer, and the eternal promise of priesthood through Eliezer's son Phinehas. J, E, and D instead understand *all* Levites to be priests. The other biblical work that clearly identifies only Aaronids as priests is the Chronicler's work; and the books of Chronicles praise Hezekiah as foremost among the kings of Israel and Judah. Only one other king compares with Hezekiah, according to Chronicles, and that is Solomon. Solomon is the first to give the Aaronid priests their exclusive hold on the Jerusalem priesthood, with the banishment of Abiathar. Thus, the biblical books that hold the same view of the priesthood as P focus on the two kings who formalized P's priestly distinctions: Solomon and Hezekiah. Since P had to have been written long after Solomon's time, the reign of Hezekiah is the provenance that appears to be reflected in the Priestly source.

P's demand for centralization of sacrifice further points to the reign of Hezekiah. According to both the books of Kings and Chronicles, Hezekiah was the king who initiated centralization. His centralization of worship at the Temple in Jerusalem placed all sacrifice under the auspices of the Aaronid priesthood. The D source also calls for centralization, but scholars almost unanimously recognize D as a product of the reign of Josiah (see below).

Later books refer to the P text, further demonstrating that P is pre-exilic. There are allusions to passages in P in the books of Jeremiah and Ezekiel. The familiarity of the book of Jeremiah, dating from the late 7th/early 6th centuries, with the P source is evident by its negative use of P material. Jeremiah reverses P's language and takes an opposite point of view in what are visibly deliberate plays upon P's characteristic language. For example, Jeremiah says: "I looked at the earth, and here it was unformed and void, and to the heavens, and their light was gone" (Jer. 4:23). This is a clear reversal of Gen. 1:1–3 (P). In addition, the character of the texts in Ezekiel that are similar to P appear to depend on P, rather than the other way around. For example, Ezekiel 5–6, a genre known as a "covenant lawsuit," depends on the covenant text in Lev 26:3, 15. Ezekiel's review of the Exodus in Ezekiel 20 also is based on the story in the P version in Exodus 6 (compare Ezek. 20:28 and Ex. 6:8; Ezek. 20:5 and Ex. 6:3; Ezek. 20:33–34 and Ex. 6:6; Ezek. 20:8 and Lev. 26:21; Ezek. 20:13,16, 24 and Lev. 26:43). The allusions to P in Ezekiel accord with the other evidence for pre-exilic composition of P.

As noted above, P's account follows the chronology and events of the combined JE so closely that it indicates that the composer of P was familiar with the RJE text. This further fits with the evidence of P having been composed during the time of Hezekiah, whose reign in Judah covered the years following the fall of Israel. The combination of J and E resulted in a narrative in Judah that was derogatory toward Aaron, identifying him as the maker of the golden calf, and unacceptable to Jerusalem's Aaronid priests on various other grounds as well. P's tie with the Aaronid priesthood explains the motivation for composing P under the reign of Hezekiah, as an alternative to JE. In virtually every P story it is possible to identify components that reflect an overall design of composition of P as an alternative to JE. P follows the order of JE, but promotes Aaron, denigrates Moses (e.g., for striking the rock at Meribah), leaves out the stories of the golden calf and Aaron's criticism of Moses' wife, eliminates anthropomorphisms of the deity, dreams, angels, and all references to prophets (except Aaron), depicting the Aaronid priesthood as the only legitimate channel to the deity. P eliminates all references to repentance and divine mercy, making sacrifice the sole method of atonement and forgiveness, and further eliminates all depictions of sacrifice prior to the consecration of Aaron and the Tabernacle; the Aaronid priesthood is the only divinely sanctioned authority to conduct sacrifices. Thus the differences between the P versions and the JE versions of stories are not only observable but, in nearly every case, explainable. P's addition of Joshua alongside Caleb in the scouts story can be similarly explained: JE establishes the merit of Joshua to be Moses' successor by his disassociation from the golden calf incident. P does not include the golden calf incident, since it denigrates Aaron, and so it establishes Joshua's merit by adding him to the scouts episode.

D. As with the other sources, D has its own character, distinctive vocabulary and phraseology, and it sometimes duplicates and sometimes contradicts stories and laws found in JE and P. Its first 30 chapters are the farewell speech of Moses. The remaining four chapters contain the last acts of Moses and include two songs that he gives the people that picture their future. At the book's center is a law code (Deuteronomy 12–26). Chapters 1–11 and 27–30 frame the law code as an introduction and powerful conclusion.

There are signs that the law code (called Dtn) is very old, with at least parts of it deriving from the period before the first kings of Israel. For example, the laws of war in Deuteronomy 20–21 reflect the pre-monarchic period of general conscription, when the Israelite tribes were summoned to battle. The rise of the monarchy led to the replacement of the tribal musters by professional armies. Laws giving authority and legal jurisdiction to the Levites indicate composition by Levites. The law code and the chapters that frame it include signs of which Levite group produced the work. The fact that Aaron is largely ignored and negatively cast in Deuteronomy excludes the Aaronid priests as possible authors of this work. Diametrically opposed to the Aaronid view of Israel's priesthood that is found in P, Deuteronomy does not distinguish between descendants of Aaron and other Levites. D is negative with regard to Aaron, mentioning him only to report his death and to identify him as the maker of the golden calf. D also refers to the Cushite wife episode, which likewise was unfavorable to Aaron. Conversely, Moses is the favored hero of the D text, sympathetically portrayed as the great leader speaking words of wisdom to the Israelites as they are about to enter the promised land. The law code in Deuteronomy also never refers to the ark, the cherubs, or any other religious implements that were housed in the Jerusalem Temple, or to the office of the High Priest. Still, D demands centralization of worship, which excludes the Levites of the various high places outside of Jerusalem as its authors. The most likely provenance of this work is therefore among the Levites of Shiloh, the pre-Jerusalem center of Israelite religion, or their successors, the same group that produced the E source.

The frame and final form of Deuteronomy have long been recognized to be connected in some essential way with the reign of King Josiah in Judah (640–609 B.C.E.). Among the last acts of Moses, Moses is said to have written the "scroll of the *torah*," which is to be placed by the ark for future reference. The book of Joshua refers to the existence of this scroll three times (1:8; 8:31, 34; 23:6). Then the scroll is not mentioned again until it is reported to have been brought out from the temple by the priest Hilkiah and read to King Josiah (II Kings 22:8). Josiah then implemented a series of religious reforms, aimed at centralizing worship at the Temple in Jerusalem, as Hezekiah had done before him. The components of the Josianic reform conform to the requirements of the Deuteronomic law code (Deuteronomy 12–26). Although P also demands centralization, in the description of Josiah's reform there is the explicit connection to Moses' scroll. Additionally, as part of his reform Josiah destroys the golden calf altar of Jeroboam at Bethel. II Kings 23 describes this act in the same terms used in Deuteronomy for Moses' destruction of the golden calf of Aaron. Josiah's treatment of the Asherah of Jerusalem and other altars also reflects specific commands of the D law code. Further, there are numerous parallels of wording and action between the characterization of Moses in Deuteronomy and of Josiah in II Kings: The words "none arose like…" are applied only to Moses and Josiah (Deut. 34:10 and II Kings 23:25); both grind a golden calf – or its altar – "thin as dust," in both cases at a wadi (Deut. 9:21 and II Kings 23:6; cf. also II Kings 23:12 and Deut. 12:3); and Moses instructs the people to "Love YHWH your God with all your heart and with all your soul and with all your might" (Deut. 6:5), and Josiah is described as "a king who returned to YHWH with all his heart and with all his soul and with all his might" (II Kings 23:25), an expression that occurs nowhere in the Hebrew Bible but these two passages. There are numerous other parallels (cf. Deut. 17:8–13 and II Kings 22:13; Deut. 17:11, 20 and II Kings 22:2; Deut. 31:11 and II Kings 23:2).

Thus the bulk of Deuteronomy was composed and compiled during the 7th century B.C.E. Still, portions of Deuteronomy show signs of having been composed after the destruction and exile of Judah in 587 B.C.E., and added to the Josianic edition in a subsequent second edition: Deut. 4:25–31; 8:19–20; 28:36–37, 63–68; 29:21–27; 30:1–10, 14–20. Each of these passages is identified as an exilic addition by a combination of several factors: terminology, theme, grammar, syntax, literary structure, and comparative data. All refer to the themes of apostasy, destruction, exile, and dispersion. Their wording and themes match with demonstrably exilic portions of the books of Kings, such as I Kings 9:6–9; and II Kings 21:8–15. Deuteronomy is thus a complex combination of texts that reflect composition and editing that fits with several historical periods.

J, E, P, and D are the largest recognized sources of the Pentateuch, though there are smaller sources. Four poems especially stand out as originally independent works which are probably the oldest sections of the Torah. They are the Blessing of Jacob (Genesis 49), the Song of the Sea (Exodus 15), the Song of Moses (Deuteronomy 32), and the Blessing of Moses (Deuteronomy 33).

R. The final editor, responsible for assembling the Torah from these sources is known as the Redactor, or R. His work had to have taken place after the Babylonian exile in order for him to have had all of the sources available to him. The separate stages of the editing of D (the law code, the Josianic edition, and the exilic edition) would have to have been completed by his time. The combination of JEP and D required little more than moving the accounts of the promotion of Joshua and the death of Moses to the end of Deuteronomy. The portions of the Torah that are traceable to him favor the Aaronid priesthood as does P; and, in his organization of the text, he favored P, indicating his connection with the same group that had produced P centuries earlier. The relationship between R and P is further confirmed by the presence of passages that are similar to P, but which are supplemental and which appear to originate in a later period, specifically the time of the Second Temple. For example, Numbers 15:1–31 and Numbers 29–30 share substantial terminology and interests with the Priestly source, but these passages also duplicate much information that is already given in P (cf. Leviticus 1–7). A striking difference between these R passages and the P texts with which they overlap, however, is that the P texts constantly emphasize the required presence of the Tabernacle (see above), but the R passages never mention the Tabernacle. This is consistent with a Second Temple period date for R. The Tabernacle is associated only with the First Temple in biblical and rabbinic passages. P, coming from the First Temple period, mentions the Tabernacle more than any other subject. R never mentions it at all. R therefore appears to derive from the days of the Second Temple, a time when priests could no longer insist on the presence of the Tabernacle for sacrifice.

The books of Ezra and Nehemiah report that Ezra read the Torah publicly in Jerusalem in this period (5th century B.C.E.). That appears to have been the complete Torah, because the accounts in the books of Ezra and Nehemiah refer to passages from all of the main sources: J, E, P, and D. Ezra himself or someone from his circle is likely to have been the Redactor (R) of the Torah. Ezra is identified as a scribe, as one who was particularly concerned with the Torah, as an Aaronid priest (which fits with the sympathy with and similarity to P), and as the first person known to possess a scroll of the complete Torah (see Ezra 7:6, 10, 14).

Observable Signs of Editing. There are observable editorial devices employed by R, such as epanalepsis, reconciling phrases, framing devices, and supplemental passages.

Epanalepsis, or resumptive repetition, is an editorial device in which a line is repeated following an insertion of one text into the body of another. For example, in Ex. 6:12 Moses says, "How will Pharaoh listen to me, when I am uncircumcised of lips?" The narrative is then interrupted by a partial genealogy that culminates in Aaron's family. Then a transitional summary of what had been said prior to the interruption leads to the repetition in v. 30 of Moses saying "I am uncircumcised of lips, and how will Pharaoh listen to me?" The epanalepsis in this case has the character of an editor's mechanism for inserting a text into a pre-existing account and then returning to the flow of the story.

Due to the nature of the different source texts with their diverse interests and often blatant contradictions of detail, it was necessary for the Redactor occasionally to insert reconciling phrases to soften the resulting inconsistencies. These phrases are superfluous to the narrative, serving only to reconcile such inconsistencies. For example, in J and E, Jacob's travels from Haran to Canaan have him first arriving in Shechem, then returning to Bethel, where God had appeared to him years earlier. The P account pictures him coming from Paddan Aram directly to Bethel. His arrival at Bethel in P begins, "And God appeared to Jacob when he was coming from Paddan Aram" (Gen. 35:9), which conflicts with the preceding J and E texts that state that Jacob had already returned and dwelled in the land. R therefore added a reconciling phrase to these J and E accounts of Jacob's prior arrival at Shechem, stating, "which was in the land of Canaan when he was coming from Paddan Aram" (33:18b). The Redactor also added the word "again" to the P verse (35:9), rendering the P report of the divine appearance at Bethel an additional theophany to that of E.

The Redactor used three literary frames to unite the originally separate source texts into a sensible chronological flow. The first of these was the Book of Generations, which begins "This is the Book of Generations of humans" (Gen. 5:1) and was cut by the Redactor and arranged through Genesis at key points to delineate the genealogies from Adam to Jacob (Gen. 5:1–28, 30–32; 7:6; 9:28–29; 11:10–26, 32). In Exodus, R used the P version of the plagues that YHWH inflicted on the Egyptians to frame the J, E, and P stories of the plagues, the Exodus, and the crossing of the Red Sea. In the P source, each of the plagues on the Egyptians is followed by "But Pharaoh's heart was strengthened, and he did not listen to them, as YHWH had spoken" (Ex. 7:13, 22; 8:15; 9:12). R inserted similar phrases following plagues in the JE stories as well (Ex. 8:11b; 9:35; 10:20, 27) to give unity to the entire section. The third framing device is derived from the "List of Stations," an originally independent text, now located in Numbers 33. This is the series of chronological-geographical notices of the stations of Israel's journey from Egypt to the border of Canaan. Rather than a summary of all of the places mentioned in the stories up to that point, this list was originally an independent document like the Book of Generations, which the Redactor used as a framework for the wilderness stories. He distributed the pieces of the list of the people's journeys through the text, setting each of his stories in its appropriate place, thus giving continuity to the books of Exodus (starting in chapter 12), Leviticus, and Numbers.

Each of the three texts from which the editorial frames are constructed has the character of P material. The plagues text is itself part of the Priestly source, and the other two resemble P in language and content, indicating that the Redactor of the final Torah favored P. For example, the Book of Generations refers to God as Elohim, not YHWH, and states that humans are created in God's image, as does P. The Priestly plagues narrative forms the governing structure for much of the book of Exodus, and the itinerary and language reflected in the List of Stations accords with the Priestly narrative as well.

Contradictions. There are contradictions within the Torah that are almost all explained when the sources are separated. For example, there is a contradiction of whether Joseph is sold by Midianites or by Ishmaelites (Gen. 37:25–36; 39:1), but the Ishmaelites are in J, and the Midianites are in E. There is a contradiction as to whether Moses' father-in-law is named Reuel or Jethro (Ex. 2:16–18; 3:1; 4:18; 18:1); or whether the mountain of God is Sinai or Horeb. And these too fall into J and E, respectively. There are numerous other contradictions of detail between P and JE. In the Priestly creation story (Genesis 1) God creates plants, then animals, then man and woman; but in the J creation account the order is man, then plants, then animals, then woman. In Gen 6:3, God limits the lifespan of humans to 120 years (J); but P reports many people living longer than this (Gen. 9:29; 11:10–23, 32). Benjamin's birthplace is Bethlehem in Gen. 35:16–19 (E), but it is Paddan Aram in 35:23–26 (P). In Numbers 11 (E) the people are tired of eating only manna, and so they are fed birds; but in Exodus 16 (P) it is reported that they had been getting birds along with the manna from the beginning. In J's version of the scouts story, Caleb alone stands against the spies who give a discouraging report of the promised land (Num. 13:30; 14:24), but in P's account, it is both Caleb and Joshua (14:6–9, 38). When the Israelites are seduced by foreign women at Peor, in J they are Moabite women (Num. 25:1), but in P they are Midianite

(25:6; 31:1–16). Traditional explanations of each of these contradictions individually have never been able to account for the fact that the reconciliation of the contradictions works within the source lines that are determined on the basis of other evidence as well.

Linguistic Evidence. Especially since the 1970s, scholars working on linguistic analyses of Hebrew have made it possible to trace the stages in the development of Hebrew prose to which the source texts each belong (Milgrom 1970; Polzin 1976; Rendsburg 1980; Zevit 1982; and Hurvitz 1967, 1972, 1974, 1995). J and E belong to the earliest stages of Biblical Hebrew. P and D represent a later stage than J and E, but still a stage closer to J and E than to the Late Biblical Hebrew of post-exilic texts. Biblical scholarship had commonly regarded Ezekiel as a basis for P, but the linguistic evidence has now established the priority of P. Hurvitz (1982) who found that P is written in an earlier stage of Hebrew than the book of Ezekiel, which is exilic. This powerful linguistic evidence is consistent with the evidence of the historical referents of each source, and it accords also with the evidence of identifiable relationships among the sources. The consistency of the linguistic evidence with the hypothesis is now one of the strongest bodies of evidence. It has rarely been mentioned by opponents of the hypothesis and has thus far received no serious challenge.

Thus the Torah was composed by a number of different authors. Their originally separate works were combined in several editorial steps into a continuous, unified work. This process, from the composition of the earliest works to the final redactions, took approximately six centuries (from the 11th to the 5th century B.C.E.). This picture of the formation of the Torah from source documents is known as the documentary hypothesis.

Some of the arguments against the hypothesis include:

(1) *No other works in the ancient world were composed in this complex way.* The hypothesis was said to picture the Torah as a "crazy patchwork" of texts, and critics of the hypothesis said that no ancient works were composed this way. This was not a strong argument in itself since it did not entertain the possibility that the Torah's formation was unique. And, in any case, the argument was incorrect, as a number of works have in fact been shown to have been composed in this way, with examples coming from the *Epic of Gilgamesh*, Qumran, the Septuagint, the Samaritan Pentateuch and Tatian's *Diatesseron*.

(2) *The literary design of the Torah has too much unity to have been composed in this way.* This argument is based on structures of biblical texts, claiming that the design of large sections of the text is such that it rules out the combined composition that the hypothesis pictures. For example, chiasms were identified in the flood story and elsewhere that the hypothesis pictured as composite texts. In every case, however, the chiasms were found to be incorrectly or even artificially constructed.

(3) *Doublets were a known feature of ancient Near Eastern literature, not a mark of multiple sources.* This assertion is false. Since there was no long prose in the ancient Near East prior to these texts, they cannot have come out of any known tradition of double stories in prose literature or history. And in ancient Near Eastern poetry, the work that shows this sort of formation is the *Epic of Gilgamesh*, and this epic has been shown to have been composed from sources in the manner of the Torah.

(4) *The hypothesis is circular.* It is argued that biblical scholars have manipulated the passages to put all of the right terminology in the right places – and then claimed that the terminology is proof of the hypothesis. For example, the scholars divide the sources according to the occurrences of the name of God and then claim that the distinction in the divine name in the texts proves that they are distinct sources. However, those who make this argument have never taken account of the fact that all of these lines of evidence converge – thousands of occurrences of the words YHWH and Elohim, hundreds more occurrences of other characteristic terms, Hebrew that corresponds to the fitting periods, contradictions that are resolved, signs of editing that come at the junctures between sources – and that no scholar is capable of manipulating so many elements to work out.

(5) *Alternative models.* There are many variations on what the sources were and how they came to be connected. For example, supplementary hypotheses are based on the idea that some texts were never independent sources but rather were composed as expansions of other texts. Although critical scholars tend to agree on the identification of the P and D texts, the last few decades have seen a great deal of debate on the identification of J and E as separate sources. In particular, some doubt the existence of E as a source independent of J. Proponents of this view tend to greatly reduce the amount of material attributed to E, and the E narratives that remain are viewed as deliberate corrective supplements to J. The evidence for separate J and E texts as originally identified in the documentary hypothesis remains more compelling. There are five main types of evidence that demonstrate the separate existence of J and E: doublets, contradictions, terminology, consistent characteristics, and narrative continuity.

In another model, P is divided into two "schools" of authors: the Priestly School and the Holiness School. The narrative and legal texts are divided between these schools. At present, this new model has been proposed but not tested. The biggest objections to be evaluated are that it starts on an unproven premise (that Numbers 28–29 is P yet differs from other texts that are identified with P) and that it breaks up the continuity of P. The narrative flow is one of the stronger arguments for the documentary hypothesis, but the H-versus-P model breaks this flow frequently without any explanation.

Those who oppose the hypothesis – both from the traditional side and from the more radical side – have never responded to the evidence of the continuity of the sources, the linguistic evidence, or the convergence of the several lines of evidence.

HISTORY OF SCHOLARSHIP

Questions about the unity of the Pentateuch and its Mosaic authorship go back at least to the third century C.E. In the 11th century Isaac Ibn Yashush said that the list of Kings of Edom (Genesis 36) must have been written long after Moses. In the 12th century, Ibn Ezra listed passages in the Torah that each seemed to go against authorship by Moses, but he just cautiously wrote in his commentary: "And if you understand, then you will recognize the truth." In the 14th century, Bonfils wrote about Ibn Ezra's passages, "This is evidence that this verse was written in the Torah later, and Moses did not write it." Christian scholars raised questions in those centuries as well. In the 17th century, Hobbes, Spinoza, and Isaac de la Peyrere all argued that the Torah could not have been written by Moses or any one person.

In the 18th century, H.B. Witter, J. Astruc, and J.G. Eichhorn each independently discovered the existence of more than one source in the Torah. They noted the convergence of the doublets with the divine name associated with each story. Eichhorn used the signs J and E for the two sources they found. Even after they divided the stories between the two sources, however, doublets continued to exist in the E texts. And these doublets contained striking differences in character, language, and content. One group of stories that referred to the deity as Elohim was particularly interested in priestly matters, so it came to be known as P. J, E, and P were found to flow through the first four books of the Pentateuch. The book of Deuteronomy, however, is written in an entirely different character and vocabulary. It contains doublets of sections from the first four books, as well as contradictions of detail. Deuteronomy came to be recognized as an independent fourth source, known as D. The date of D was the first to be established in biblical scholarship, based on the work of W.M.L. de Wette (1805). De Wette found that the laws of Deuteronomy specifically reflected details of King Josiah's reforms, as described in II Kings.

In 1943, M. Noth showed that the biblical books of Deuteronomy through II Kings were a continuous work. Pointing to such evidence as similarity of language, continuity of themes, and narrative flow, Noth showed that this was not a loose collection of writings but rather a thoughtfully arranged work drawing from a variety of sources. The Deuteronomistic History (Dtr.), as it came to be known, tells a continuous story of the history of the people of Israel in their land. The book of Deuteronomy was constructed so that its covenant would stand as the foundation of the history, characterizing the fate of the nation as dependent on how well they kept the commandments of Deuteronomy. The history of the kings of Israel in the books of Kings, as opposed to the history in the books of Chronicles, is constructed to culminate in the reign and reform of Josiah, the only king who receives a completely positive rating ("good in the eyes of YHWH") by the historian. The history is written with the same terms and phrases as the book of Deuteronomy. The construction of this history from Moses to Josiah is further made manifest by changes in major themes that occur after the Josiah narratives: the concern with centralization of sacrifice and the comparison of the Judean kings to David both cease after the Josiah pericope. It was thus first demonstrated by F. Cross and his students that the original, Josianic edition of the history (Dtr.1) was updated and expanded in an exilic edition (Dtr2).

The date of P has remained an extremely controversial issue of the documentary hypothesis. Reuss argued that the prophets do not quote or refer to P and that therefore the law was later than the prophets. Graf took this argument further, defending the thesis that the composition of extensive priestly laws and rituals could only be a late development, reflecting the hierocratic rule of the Second Temple period. Further consolidating and developing the arguments put forward by Graf, J. Wellhausen defended a post-exilic date for P along the following lines: First, he claimed that P *assumed* the centralization of sacrifice, as proper worship and ritual can occur exclusively at the Tabernacle in the Priestly text. Wellhausen reasoned that in the period prior to Josiah's reform, cultic activities were conducted everywhere, and people who were not priests served in the various temples and high places. Josiah abolished the outlying cultic places and established the Temple in Jerusalem as the only place in which worship of YHWH could take place, and where only priests descended from Aaron could officiate. The priests who served in the high places and provincial temples came to be secondary cultic officials over time, and these were the "Levites" of P. Wellhausen pointed out that Ezekiel had predicted that in the future, only descendants of Zadok (David's Aaronid priest) would be considered legitimate (Ezek. 44:15–16). In P, only Aaronids are priests. Wellhausen concluded that P was written in the days of the Second Temple, when the Aaronid priests came to power, having taken Ezekiel's prophecy as their inspiration. Wellhausen claimed that the high priest described in P is a reflection of the head of the religious community in the Second Temple period.

Second, Wellhausen argued that the numerous sacred institutions in P demonstrate the power of the priests during the Second Temple period. This is the reason for the large number of sacrifices and gifts to the priesthood which are not mentioned in earlier literature, such as the daily and festival offerings (Num. 28–29); sin and guilt offerings (Lev. 4–5); tithe for the Levites (Num. 18:21–24); etc. Similarly, the laws of purity and impurity characteristic of P (e.g., Num. 19; Lev. 11, 12, 13–15, 21–22) result from the intensification of the hierocracy of the Second Temple period. Wellhausen also noted the increasing number of religious institutions in P that do not depend on living in the land, such as the Sabbath and circumcision, which, in effect, became the distinguishing markers of the Jews in exile. Additionally, the holiday of Yom Kippur (Lev. 23:17ff.; 23:23–32; Num. 29:1–11), which has no connection with the agricultural life of the people, appears in P as an expression of the supreme spirituality of Second Temple Judaism and the sense of sin inherent in a post-exilic community.

Lastly, Graf and Wellhausen argued that the Tabernacle, described in detail in P (Ex. 25–30; 35–40; Num. 1–4; 7–8), is a fictional creation of the Jerusalem priesthood of the Second Temple period and is only a reflection of the Jerusalem Temple. According to Graf and Wellhausen, the Tabernacle never existed; it was a fiction produced by a Second Temple author who wanted to establish a law code that was in the interests of the Temple priests of that time. The Priestly Tabernacle was thus a literary and legal fiction created by the post-exilic author(s) of P to support the rebuilt Temple and the reestablished priesthood in Jerusalem of their day.

Starting with the work of Y. Kaufmann, recent scholarship is increasingly demonstrating that it is impossible to explain the development of P against the background of the Second Temple period. The main premises of Reuss, Graf, and Wellhausen were mistaken. Prophets *do* quote P (cf. Jer. 4:23 and Gen. 1:1–3; Jer. 3:16 and P's expression "Be fruitful and multiply," as well as P's emphasis on the ark; Jer 7:22 and Lev 7:37f; Ezek 5:7 and Lev 26:3, 15; Ezek. 5:10 and Lev. 26:29; Ezek. 5:17 and Lev. 26:22, 25; Ezek. 20:28 and Ex. 6:8; Ezek. 6:3b–6a and Lev. 26:30, 31a; Ezek. 22:26 and Lev. 10:10). P does not *assume* centralized religion; it *demands* it (Lev. 17:3–4), reckoning bloodguilt to anyone who offers a sacrifice at a place other than the Tabernacle, with the punishment of being cut off from the rest of one's people. And the Priestly source emphasizes the ark, the tablets, the cherubs, and the Urim and Thummim in connection with the Tabernacle—all items described as having existed in the First Temple, but missing from the Second Temple. It does not make sense that the Tabernacle and its implements would figure so prominently in a text written after their destruction. Research on the Tabernacle by F. Cross, M. Haran, R. Friedman, and M. Homan argues that the Tabernacle was real, not a Second Temple fiction, and that it was pre-exilic. The linguistic evidence developed by Hurvitz and others (see above) confirms that P is in fact composed in the Classical Biblical Hebrew of the pre-exilic period.

Critical scholarship originated among European Protestant scholars and was perceived to be threatening to Jewish traditional beliefs and even, in some cases, to be antisemitic. Wellhausen's scholarship did indeed have an antisemitic (and anti-Catholic) component. Wellhausen openly expressed his hostility to the legal (i.e., Jewish) and priestly (i.e., Catholic) portions of the Torah. In his introduction he stated that when he learned of Graf's hypothesis that the law was a late addition to the original spiritual religion of the prophets, he was ready to accept it "almost before I heard his reasons." But, despite this original opposition to the new scholarship regarding the authors of the Torah, Jewish scholars came to accept and even champion this research. This was due both to the weight of the evidence for the hypothesis and the improving relations between Jewish and Christian scholars in the late 20th and early 21st centuries. Notable in this respect were (1) the development of biblical studies in Israeli universities, starting especially with Yehezkel Kaufmann in Jerusalem, and (2) the rise of a generation of American Jewish biblical scholars who were trained by Christian scholars at Johns Hopkins, Harvard, and Yale universities. The new scholarship came to be taught at the non-orthodox rabbinical schools as well and appears in the commentaries used in Conservative, Reform, and Reconstructionist synagogues. Even a small number of Orthodox scholars have acknowledged it or come to terms with some portion of it in ways that they judge to be reconcilable with tradition.

LAWS

The Ten Commandments

According to the book of Exodus, God gives the commandments to the Israelites on Mt. Sinai/Horeb following the exodus from Egypt. Deuteronomy emphasizes that the covenant established on Sinai/Horeb is based on the revelation of the Ten Commandments (Hebrew *aseret ha-debarim*, "the ten words," or "the ten things," Exod 34:28; Deut 10:4). Unlike other sets of biblical laws that emphasize the role of Moses as a mediator (cf. Exodus 19; Ex. 20:22; 34:32; Lev. 17:1; Deut. 6:1), the Ten Commandments are attributed directly to the deity, speaking aloud from the sky (Ex. 20:1) in the first person (Ex. 2, 3, 5, 6; Deut. 5:6, 7, 9, 10). The Ten Commandments thus have a central place within the Torah; they are presented as the direct address of the deity, identified as a complete and separate covenant, and given a special name to distinguish them from other biblical laws. They continue to be of central importance to other biblical traditions as well: for example, they are reflected in the prophets (Hos 4:1; Jer 7:9) and the psalms (Psalms 50; 81).

There are three versions of the Ten Commandments that appear in the Torah: Exodus 20, which was an independent source, then later elaborated upon by the Redactor; the J version is in Exodus 34:14–28; and the D version in Deuteronomy 5. Although there are important differences among the versions in their language, content, and emphases, all of the Pentateuchal sources demonstrate the centrality of the law in the covenant between God and Israel that is forged at Sinai/Horeb.

In the 1950s, three scholars (E. Bickermann, G. Mendenhall, and K. Baltzer) independently recognized a formal similarity between the Israelite covenant and international legal documents of the ancient Near East. This contribution has aided immensely in understanding the covenant not only as religious, ethical, and ritual prescriptions for the Israelites, but as a legally binding contract between God and Israel as separate parties. The ancient Near Eastern treaty documents, with which the Sinai covenant bears striking parallels, were dictated by regional kings known as suzerains to the local city kings, their vassals, who were subject to them. The treaties formalized relations between the two parties, dictating precisely what was required of the vassal in order to sustain peaceful relations with its suzerain. They regularly included a specific group of formal elements:

1. The suzerain's introduction of himself by name.
2. An historical prologue, detailing the history of the re-

lations between the parties; specifically, something that the suzerain had done for the vassal. The intention here was to demonstrate that the vassal was somehow in the suzerain's debt.

3. The prime stipulation of the treaty, which was that the vassal was to be loyal to this suzerain and have allegiance to no other.

4. Secondary stipulations, including the amount and type of tribute owed to the suzerain by the vassal, the obligation of the vassal to appear at the suzerain's court when summoned, and the necessity of the vassal to supply troops for the suzerain's military defense.

The Sinai covenant, especially in Exodus 20, contains the same key elements:

1. Introduction: I am YHWH your God

2. Historical prologue: who brought you out from the land of Egypt, from a house of slaves

3. Prime stipulation: you shall have no other gods

4. Secondary stipulations: you shall not make a statue; you shall not bring up the name of YHWH your God for a falsehood; remember the Sabbath; honor your father and your mother; etc.

Other similarities between the ancient Near Eastern suzerainty treaties and the Ten Commandments have been noted as well. Suzerainty treaties included an oath sworn by the vassal pledging allegiance to the suzerain and to the requirements of the treaty; cf. Ex. 24:3, 7, in which the Israelites pledge their obedience. Ancient Near Eastern treaties included a provision for the treaty document, requiring that it be deposited in a sacred place; cf. Ex. 25:16, 21; 40:20, in which the covenant text is deposited in the ark in the Tabernacle. Additionally, treaties were usually sealed with a feast shared between the two parties, preceded by a sacrifice. Blood from the sacrifice was sprinkled symbolically on both parties, representing death for the one who breaks the oath thus taken. Exodus 24 describes a feast shared by God and the elders of Israel, in which the blood of the sacrifice is sprinkled on the people, and on the altar that represents the deity. Lastly, treaties ended with a list of curses and blessings cited as sanctions relative to the observance of the treaties; cf. Deuteronomy 27–28.

Despite sharing a common form, style, and language with ancient Near Eastern suzerainty treaties, key elements of the Decalogue demonstrate the uniqueness of biblical Israel against its ancient Near Eastern background. First, there is the tradition that these laws came from God rather than any human ruler; in fact, the nation's suzerain is a deity, rather than a human overlord. That the laws of interaction among the human community and between the Israelites and their deity are embedded within the context of history is also unique. All of the laws in the Pentateuch are understood only within the context of Israelite history. Further, the implications of presenting YHWH as the suzerain to whom the Israelites owe their exclusive allegiance are that other deities are categorically eliminated from worship by ancient Israel. Some scholars see the origin of monotheism here, others monolatry. In either case, the religious prohibition of other gods in Israel is effected by the appropriation of politico-legal terminology.

Aniconism is another unique feature of biblical religion presented in the Ten Commandments. Whereas all contemporary cultures employed cultic representations as a means of communicating with the deity, the second commandment forbade the Israelites from doing so. Likewise, the institution of the Sabbath as a mandatory day of rest has no equivalent in the ancient world. Scholars have attempted to determine the origins of the concept and etymology of the term. The Torah itself offers two theological explanations (Ex. 20:11 and Deut. 5:10–12) for what appears to have originally been a social and humanitarian precept; for example, Ex. 16:22–30 presupposes the practice before the laws are even given. The fourth commandment seems to recall and reinforce a traditional observance.

The Ten Commandments in Exodus 20 and Deuteronomy 5 relate to two principal types of concerns: ethical and ritual. The first four commandments refer specifically to how Israel is to relate to its deity, detailing the ritual prescriptions against the worship of other gods, idolatry, invoking the holy name of YHWH in a false oath, and violating the Sabbath (which in Ex. 20:8–11 is given an explicitly religious explication, recalling God's creation of the universe; but cf. Deut. 5:12–15). The last six commandments (honoring one's parents, prohibitions against murder, adultery, theft, giving false testimony, and coveting) are ethical prescriptions which address the issue of harmonious social relations within the Israelite community. Notably, the J Decalogue in Exodus 34 is concerned solely with ritual matters.

Other Laws

In addition to the Ten Commandments, the Torah contains hundreds of supplemental laws concerning both ethical and ritual matters. By tradition, there are 613. They can be found scattered through the sources but are especially concentrated in the Priestly text (in particular the book of Leviticus) and in Deuteronomy. In addition, scholars speak of three distinct law codes set within the Pentateuchal sources: the Covenant Code embedded in the E source (Exodus 21–23), the Law Code of Deuteronomy (Deuteronomy 12–26), and the Holiness Code within the P text (Leviticus 17–26). The latter two of the three of the Codes end with lists of blessings and curses to be enacted depending on the obedience or disobedience of the Israelites to the Code. Twice the Torah instructs: "You shall not add onto it, and you shall not subtract from it." (Deut. 4:2; 13:1)

Just as in the Decalogue, laws in the rest of the Torah deal with both ethical and ritual matters. Ethical laws, detailing proper relations among humans within the Israelite community, include both civil and criminal matters. Civil matters frequently overlap with ritual law (see below). Criminal legislation is characterized to a large extent by the principle of justice: punishment should suit the crime. The famous case of "eye for an eye" stands on its own in the Covenant Code (Ex.

21:23–25). P elaborates it in Lev 21:23–25 and applies it principally to cases of murder and bodily injury (Lev. 24:19–21) but also invokes it in the case of restitution for the property of another (Lev. 24:18). Deuteronomy connects it with civil and criminal legislation, as in the law of the false witness (Deut. 19:19–21). It appears to be meant as a principle of justice, not as a literal action to be performed, because it includes "burn for a burn" in a case where there is no burning (Ex. 21:22–25).

Ritual laws, pertaining to the proper conduct of the Israelites toward the deity, are also found among the several legal sources of the Pentateuch, with some notable differences in the laws between the sources. For example, dietary laws detail the foods that are fit for sacrifice in Deut. 14:3–21 and Leviticus 11, and sacrificial offerings and tithes to the priesthood appear in Lev. 7:28–34 and Deut. 18:3; in Num. 15:18–21 and Deut. 18:4; in Lev. 23:9–20 and Deut. 26:1–10; and one should note especially the differences between Num. 18:21–32 and Deut. 14:22–29; 26:12–15.

However, the distinction between ethical and ritual laws that seems clear in the Decalogue breaks down somewhat in the other legal texts of the Pentateuch. The Covenant Code begins by listing social/ethical laws in Exodus 21 and the first part of 22 and then intersperses ritual legislation (Ex. 22:21, 29–31; 23:13ff.). The P laws (including H) usually keep ritual law separate but also sometimes intersperse ethical and ritual laws. Notably, Leviticus 19, which is a centerpiece of the commandments concerning holiness, mixes laws about justice, sexual practices, consulting the dead, mixing plant species, mixing animal species, caring for the blind and deaf, respecting parents, and respecting the Sabbath. In a notable merger of the ethical and the ritual, it prohibits the blending of plants that are separate in nature, and it commands the Israelites to leave gleanings and corners of their fields for the poor and oppressed. It condemns idolatry, but it commands Israelites to be kind to aliens, who may be idolators. And near its midpoint it includes the ultimate expression of ethical law: "Love your neighbor as yourself."

Meanwhile, the religious laws in Deuteronomy, many of which overlap with P legislation, are formulated from a more communal/social perspective. For example, sacrifice in Deuteronomy is not performed for its "pleasing odor" to the deity or for "food of God" (cf. Lev. 1:9, 13, 17; 21:6, 8, 17, 21); the emphasis instead is on offerings consumed by the offerer in the sanctuary and shared with the poor, the Levite, the alien resident, the orphan, and the widow. D is generally more concerned with secular matters (e.g., the judiciary: Deut. 16:18–20; 17:8–13; the monarchy: 17:14ff.; the military: Deuteronomy 20; family and inheritance: 21:18–23; 22:13–29; 24:1–4; 25:5–9; loans and debts: 15:1–18; 24:10–13) than P, omitting altogether certain cultic institutions and offenses punishable by death in P (e.g., D has no warning against blasphemy, an extremely serious sin discussed in the Covenant Code (Ex. 22:27) and in P (Lev. 24:15–16; Num. 30)).

The overlap between ethical and ritual spheres of activity in both D and P is due to the primacy of the concept of holiness. The need for obedience to even the most secular of ethical laws is based ultimately in Israel's responsibility to attain and maintain a status of holiness in order for the deity to remain within the community. It should be noted that there are differences between P (including H) and D in their conception of the attainment of holiness. In P holiness is a status toward which the people are enjoined to strive (Lev. 11:44, 45; 19:2; 20:26) and is contingent upon physical proximity to the divine presence and the preservation of the divine presence within the community by means of obedience to the Priestly laws and the proper performance of ritual. In D holiness is a result of God's choice of Israel and devolves automatically upon every Israelite, who consequently must not profane it by defilement (cf. Deut. 7:6; 14:2, 21 in which the people are called "holy" in the present tense; cf. the related P passages in which only God is called holy in the present, not the people: Lev. 11:41, 45; 19:2; 20:26 (D. Wright, 1992; M. Weinfeld 1972)). However, in both cases the ethical is grounded in the ritual, and the two are often indistinguishable within the legislation.

Laws pertaining to the Sabbath provide a good example of this. In P it is a requirement to observe the Sabbath day because God created the world in six days and rested on the seventh. In effect, in resting on the seventh day the community reenacts the culmination of creation. Deuteronomy and the Covenant Code supply a different reason for the Sabbath: the Israelite must rest on the Sabbath to provide a respite for himself, his family, his community, and his servants (Deut. 5:14; Ex. 23:12). In this way, the Sabbath is given an ethical rationale. D further supplies a religious motivation for keeping the Sabbath, one derived not from creation, but rather from the Exodus (Deut. 5:15).

Both sources also contain laws concerning the Sabbatical year. However, Leviticus 25 highlights the need for the land to rest, while Deuteronomy 28 makes no mention of not working the land, emphasizing instead the release of debts. Similarly, the cities of refuge in P serve as sacred, Levitical cities. The manslayer is required to live there until the death of the high priest, which results in the ritual expiation of the manslayer's bloodguilt. In D they serve the purpose of protecting the manslayer from the blood avenger (Deut. 19:6), and no set period of time is prescribed for habitation there.

There are numerous other differences and contradictions between the laws of D and P. For example, Deut. 14:21 prohibits only Israelites from eating anything that has died a natural death, commanding them to give it to the stranger or sell it to a foreigner. On the other hand, Lev. 17:15 states that "any living being, whether a citizen or an alien, who will eat carcass or a torn animal shall wash his clothes and shall wash with water and will be impure until evening and then will be pure."

Laws pertaining to festivals differ among the sources as well. The laws of Passover are identical in P (Ex. 12:1–14) and the Covenant Code; in both sources the Passover sacrifice is of sheep, and the ceremony is performed in the house, centering on the sprinkling of the blood on the lintel and doorposts. D details instead a public sacrifice of both sheep and cattle, with no mention of any domestic ceremony (Deut. 16:1–8). In the case of the autumn festival (known in later Judaism, though not in the Torah, as Rosh Ha-Shanah) and Yom Kippur, however, P is unique. No other source contains any mention of these holidays, while P details laws and ordinances pertaining to them.

HISTORICITY

Story and History in Genesis

For the later periods of Israelite history, we often have outside information from other ancient Near Eastern texts or from archaeological material that can confirm or disconfirm the historical information we draw from the Bible. Because we do not have this for the time period in which Genesis is set (the beginning of time through most of the second millennium B.C.E.), many scholars will say that there is no history in the book of Genesis. This is simply not the case. There is much historical information that can be gleaned from the stories of Noah's family, Abraham, and the sibling rivalry of Isaac's sons, for example. They are valued literature, *and* they contain information that is useful to the historian.

There are two ways in which story and history intersect in the book of Genesis. The first is in the idea of historical memory. An example of this is the story of Abraham's migration from Mesopotamia to the promised land. Although it is doubtful that we will ever find evidence for the existence of a historical Abraham, we do know from other sources that there were great migrations of people from Mesopotamia to the area of Canaan in the Late Bronze Age (second millennium B.C.E.). It is conceivable that, generations later, the authors who wrote the stories about the southwesterly movement of Abraham's family had a historical memory of their ancestry deriving from Mesopotamia. In fact, through Genesis the Israelite authors make no secret of the cultural debt they owe to Mesopotamia; the story of the Tower of Babel, for example, names the city of Babylon (Babel) as the center from which people originally spread throughout the world.

The second way we can gain historical information from the book of Genesis is to view some of the stories as analogies of later historical situations. That is, if we understand them in terms of when they were written, we learn more about the historical context of the authors (early to mid-first millennium B.C.E.) than about the earlier period in which they are set. The authors use the stories to explain their present circumstances, to explain the world in which they lived and how it was configured.

Other stories in Genesis also reflect the authors' historical contexts, and especially the relationship between Israel and her neighbors. In the story of the destruction of Sodom and Gomorrah (Genesis 19), Abraham's nephew Lot and his family are warned to escape. They are instructed not to look back, but Lot's wife disobeys and turns into a pillar of salt. Lot and his daughters hide in the hills, thinking they are the sole survivors on earth. The daughters, believing that the responsibility for re-populating the earth lies with them, devise a plan to inebriate their father and take turns sleeping with him so that they might each conceive a child. Their plan works, and the end of this bizarre story is that the daughters name their sons "Moab" and "Ben-ammi." The author explains that these are the ancestors of the Moabites and Ammonites – nations neighboring Israel in the first millennium B.C.E. Rather than a side-note for the sake of gratuitous sex and incest, this narrative is an explanation by the author of his or her own historical context: the story acknowledges the Israelites' kinship with the Moabites and Ammonites but casts aspersions on their ancestry by linking their eponymous ancestors' births to incest.

The story of Jacob and Esau is the best example of authors formulating a story to explain their contemporary historical circumstances. Rebekah's twin sons begin fighting in the womb, and when she seeks an oracular explanation she is told, "Two nations are in your womb, and two peoples will be dispersed from inside you, and one people will be mightier than the other people, and the older the younger will serve." The delphic subtlety of this oracle is easily overlooked. In biblical Hebrew, the subject may either precede or follow the verb, so the matter of who will serve whom here is left open.

Esau is born first, meriting him both the birthright (inheritance) and the preeminent blessing of his father Isaac. But he sells his birthright to Jacob for a pot of red lentil stew, earning himself the nickname "Edom" (red). When it comes time for Isaac to die, he commands Esau to hunt game and prepare a feast, after which he will bless Esau. Rebekah overhears, disguises Jacob so as to deceive her blind husband, and prepares a feast for Jacob to bring before Esau returns. Thinking that Jacob is Esau, Isaac blesses Jacob with abundance and tells Jacob that he will be his brother's superior. When Esau returns, the deception is discovered, but Isaac can neither change the blessing he has already granted nor offer Esau a blessing of similar status. The best he can offer in Esau's blessing is that Esau will one day "break his yoke from your neck."

The analogy with the author's own historical moment is transparent: Rebekah is told that her twins are "two nations," and Esau's nickname is Edom. Jacob will later have his name changed to Israel. This is the story of the struggle between the nations of Israel and Edom. Under King David in the 10th century B.C.E., Israel defeated the older kingdom of Edom and dominated it for over a century, becoming larger and more prosperous. Edom finally broke Israel's yoke from its neck in the mid-ninth century B.C.E. Some time later, this history became an integral part of the stories of Israel's forefathers Isaac and Jacob, which both foreshadow and justify the historical events of the author's world.

The Exodus

The story of the Exodus, God's physical salvation of the Israelites from slavery, is the foundational event for Israelite nationhood and for Jewish history. Yet recent scholarship casts doubt on the historicity of this central event. Because the events were recorded so long after they occurred, and because we lack direct archaeological and extra-biblical textual evidence that the Exodus happened in the way the Torah describes it, many mainstream scholars would deny that an Exodus occurred at all. The lack of Egyptian records for any of the events described in the biblical story is compounded by the absence of any archaeological evidence for a mass movement of people out of Egypt to Canaan, who spent 40 years in the Sinai wilderness along the way. There is, however, a great deal of circumstantial evidence from Egyptian textual and archaeological sources in support of parts of the biblical narrative. The Bible itself also yields historical memories and other clues to the veracity of the basic Exodus story.

In Exod. 2:10, Moses is named by the Egyptian princess: "And she called his name Moses, and she said, 'Because I drew him from the water.'" The author is here offering a Hebrew etymology for Moses' name – from the mouth of an Egyptian princess. Given the unlikelihood that the princess would know Hebrew, much less give the child a Hebrew name, this would seem to be an argument against the story's historicity. However, unlike the story's author, modern scholars are aware that the name is not Hebrew but Egyptian: from an Egyptian word meaning "is born," as in the name Rameses, meaning "Ra (the sun god) bore him." The fact that Moses has an Egyptian name, and that this is unknown to the author of the text who supplied him with a Hebrew etymology, actually argues for the ancient tradition of a leader named Moses, long before the story was written in the form we have it. Additionally, the fact that Moses and other Israelite leaders such as Phinehas and Hophni bear Egyptian names is evidence that some Israelite ancestors did live for a time in Egypt.

Historians place the exodus in the early 13th century B.C.E. Although there is no Egyptian evidence for an exodus of Israelite slaves at this time, there were Semitic slaves working there from centuries earlier, and there was in fact a Semitic dynasty originating in Canaan, that took over and ruled Egypt from the mid-16th century to the 14th. Some historians have suggested that the expulsion of these Semitic rulers, the Hyksos, forms the background for the exodus story. In 1308, Seti I took back Egypt for the Egyptians and kicked out the Hyksos. This would accord with the reference to a new pharoah who did not know Joseph (Ex. 1:8); Semitic rulers of Egypt might have been more generous to fellow Semites living there than the new Egyptian rulers would be toward Semites who still lived in Egypt after the expulsion of the Hyksos.

The Israelite slaves are described as building store-cities for Pharaoh called Pithom and Rameses (Ex. 1:11). According to Egyptian records, Rameses II (1279–1212) commissioned the building of a new capital called "Pi-Rameses" on the eastern delta, which is where Jacob's family settles and their descendants remain until the time of the Exodus (Gen. 46:28–34; 47:1–10; Ex. 8:18; 9:26).

Other Egyptian records state that there were officials who were designated to distribute grain rations to the 'Apiru who were transporting stones to the great pylon of Rameses. The term 'Apiru, known from Ugaritic, Hittite, and Mesopotamian records as well as Egyptian ones, seems to have designated outlaws or refugees who lived in bands outside of organized society and functioned as an unskilled labor force in Egypt. Scholars debate the etymology of the term as well as its proper pronunciation (it could be rendered Hapiru or Habiru). Its similarity to the term "Hebrew" (*'ibri*) is intriguing.

Other Egyptian records have similar indirect bearing on details of the Exodus story. One record indicates that Pharaoh Seti I had built a tight network of strongholds along the coast of the northern Sinai, and some scholars have suggested that this might be the "Way of the Philistines" referred to in Ex. 13:17, a route that the Israelites avoid taking (albeit for a different reason in the story). Papyri Anastasi provide reports of Egyptian frontier officials stationed in the border zone between Egypt and Sinai, revealing tight Egyptian control over the eastern frontier at the end of the 13th century. Neither Egyptians nor foreigners could enter or leave without a special permit. The papyri also record the entry of many foreigners, such as an entire tribe from Edom, seeking food during times of drought. The Elephantine Stele, a monument dating from 1180 B.C.E. found on the island of Elephantine, describes an Egyptian faction rebelling against the pharaoh. They had bribed some Asiatics (Semites) who were in Egypt to aid in their rebellion, paying them in silver, gold, and copper (cf. Ex. 3:21–22; 11:2; 12:35–6). The pharaoh foiled the plot and drove the Asiatics out of Egypt.

To this may be added elements of Israelite religion and culture that reflect some sort of acquaintance with Egypt. The dimensions of the biblical Tent of Meeting and its courtyard correspond to those of the battle tent of Rameses II. Whatever the explanation of this correspondence, it suggests minimally some kind of experience with Egyptian culture.

Beyond the evidence from Egypt is the application of historical method to the Bible itself. The historian asks about a report: What is the likelihood that someone fabricated it? Who had an interest in fabricating it? In the case of the Egyptian bondage and exodus, one asks why Israel would have made up a story of being descended from slaves. One would be more skeptical if they had told a story of being descended from gods or kings or heroes. Similarly, there is the extreme unlikelihood of Israel fabricating the report of Moses' father-in-law being a Midianite priest. Why would anyone make that up?

The element of the story that frequently generates the most skepticism is the census, claiming tremendous numbers of Israelites in the wilderness (600,000 males). The numbers are unlikely. Some try to reduce them by taking the word for thousand (Hebrew *'elep*) to mean rather "clan." But the sums of the tribes listed in the text add up if the word means thousands, and they do not if it means "clans" – rendering this understanding impossible. It is better to recognize that the census numbers are not historical, but at the same time to recognize that this has nothing to do with whether the exodus was historical.

Thus there is no *direct* evidence for the story described in the book of Exodus. It is not necessary, nonetheless, to dismiss the entire account as fictional. The task of the modern historian is to examine the cumulative value of different types of evidence to reconstruct history. Details of the biblical story should be examined against extra-biblical evidence and weighed accordingly. While it is unlikely that the Exodus occurred in the way the Torah describes, there is a substantial amount of evidence that suggests the origin of at least some Israelites in Egypt.

The Tabernacle

The Tabernacle (*miskan*; also known as the "Tent of Meeting," *'ohel mo'ed*; and the "tent of testimony" *miskan ha'edut*) is the central concern of the Priestly narrative and laws. Key events in the P story are set at the Tabernacle, and entire chapters are devoted to the record of the Tabernacle's construction and contents. In a revelation at Sinai, Moses is instructed to build the Tabernacle (Exodus 26), and once it is constructed and consecrated (Exodus 40) it becomes the place of communication between God and Moses for the remainder of Moses' life. The Priestly legal sections require the presence of the Tabernacle for the fulfillment of numerous laws and especially for sacrifice, which according to P can be performed only at the Tabernacle (Lev. 1:3, 5; 3:2, 8, 13; 4:5–7, 14–18; 6:9, 19, 23; 14:11; 16:1–34; 17:1–9; Num. 5:17; 6:10; 19:4). The P legal sections emphasize repeatedly that execution of these laws at the Tabernacle is the rule *forever* (Ex. 27:21; 28:43; 30:21; Lev. 3:17; 6:11; 10:9; 16:29, 34; 17:7; 24:3, 8; Num. 18:23; 19:10).

As mentioned above, a crucial element of the Graf-Wellhausen model for a postexilic date for P was the idea that the Tabernacle never really existed but was rather a fiction, invented by the Priestly author as a means to write laws applying to the Second Temple. However, the sheer detail of the Tabernacle's description – its construction, the fabrics, wood, and precious metals involved – suggests otherwise. There is no comparably detailed description of anything else in the Priestly work, nor is there any justification for going into such intricate detail in a work of pure fiction. Furthermore, evidence collected by scholars since the beginning of the 20th century also undermines the arguments for the Tabernacle as fictional. Parallel institutions of tent shrines in the Semitic world, from ancient Phoenician to modern Islamic examples, have been described (see Cross 1961: 217–19, and references; and 1973, p. 72). Of particular interest is the pre-Islamic *qubbah*, a small, portable red-leather tent. The biblical Tabernacle is likewise protected by a red-leather covering (Exod 26:14).

Cross (1961) argued that the Priestly description of the Tabernacle refers to the tent that David erected to house the ark in Jerusalem (II Sam. 6:17 = I Chron. 16:1). Haran (1965) argued that it is the Tabernacle of Shiloh, which the Priestly writers believed to have been carried there from Sinai. There are passages that depict the place of worship at Shiloh as a tent. The structure is also called a house (*byt*) in Judg. 18:31; I Sam. 1:24, and a temple (*hykl*) in I Sam. 1:9; 3:3. It is called the Tent of Meeting in I Sam 2:22b, but some have argued that this half verse is a gloss, since its language is so similar to the P passage in Ex. 38:8 but is embedded in a context that is not Priestly, and it does not appear in the Greek or 4QSam[a]. However, Ps. 78:60 agrees with this identification of the Shiloh structure, referring to it as a tent, and the P source in Josh. 18:1; 19:51 also speaks of a tent at Shiloh. It is possible to reconcile these accounts by postulating a sanctuary building at Shiloh that housed the Tabernacle.

The book of Chronicles consistently locates the Tabernacle in the Temple of Solomon (I Chron. 16:33 (MT); 23:32; 2 Chron. 24:6; 29:5–7), and the book of Lamentations speaks of the destruction of the Tabernacle along with the Temple (Lam. 2:6–7). This idea of locating the Tabernacle inside the Temple has been questioned due to the lateness of Chronicles as a source, and the assumption that Chronicles simply follows the P conception of the Tabernacle. However, writing in the period of the Second Temple, which did not contain the Tabernacle, it would not have served the Chronicler to develop P's perspective that sacrifice and other ritual practices can be performed nowhere other than at the Tabernacle. Furthermore, there is evidence that references to the Tabernacle in Chronicles were based on the Chronicler's preexilic source. Halpern (1981) has demonstrated that a substantial number of terms, phrases, and concerns in the Chronicler's history are found consistently through the accounts of the kings of Judah, ceasing completely after the reign of Hezekiah. This suggests that the Chronicler used a source text that recounted the history of the Judean monarchy down to the time of Hezekiah. The Tabernacle is one more item that is treated frequently and with importance down to the time of Hezekiah and then is not mentioned thereafter.

Adding further evidence to the idea that the Tabernacle existed and was housed inside Solomon's Temple, R.E. Friedman (1980) has approached the matter of the Tabernacle's historicity from the perspective of the measurements given for its construction. If the frames overlap with each other, conforming to the description of the materials in Exodus 26, the Tabernacle was 10 cubits high, 20 cubits long, and 8 cubits wide on its exterior. These dimensions correspond to the size of the space under the wings of the cherubs in the holy of holies in Solomon's Temple (I Kings 6:20; II Chron. 3:8). Additionally, a temple discovered at Arad shares the same dimensions (Aharoni 1973).

Thus the Tabernacle may have stood under the wings of the cherubs in the Solomonic Temple, or it may have been stored elsewhere in the Temple while the corresponding space under the cherubs' wings symbolized its presence. This would accord with the report in I Kings 8:4 (= II Chron. 5:5) that the Tabernacle was brought to the Temple at the time of Solomon's dedication, and with the other reports of the Tabernacle's presence in the Temple in the books of Chronicles, Lamentations, and Psalms. Psalm 61:5, for example, states "I shall abide in your tent forever, I shall trust in the covert of your wings." A rabbinic source likewise understands the Tabernacle to be stored inside the first Jerusalem Temple.

The evidence for the existence of the Tabernacle in the First Temple in Jerusalem, coming from this variety of archaeological, biblical, and rabbinic sources, both contributes to our knowledge of history and bolsters the case for the pre-exilic composition of P.

CENTRAL VALUES

Despite the variety of the Torah's sources and the great number and diversity of its laws, the Torah has remarkable unity. People have read and studied it meaningfully as a whole for millennia without being aware of its having been constructed from multiple sources. Even today, those who are aware of the Torah's literary history are able to read the final product and appreciate its unity as a work. This is due to several factors, which all derive from central values of the Torah:

History

Containing the world's earliest history-writing, the Torah tells its stories in chronological sequence. Each episode fits into a logical progression of events so that it is told against the background of everything that has come before it. This gives it a natural sense and unity that it would not have if it were merely a book of collected stories. This may seem obvious to us today, but no work before the Torah's sources had ever done this.

Monotheism

The Torah's account is grounded in its monotheism, thus connecting all its stories to its single focal point: the relationship between one God and the human community. Israel's was the first enduring monotheism, and the Torah is the work that established this concept at the heart of the religion of Israel and promoted it in Christianity and Islam. Scholars differ as to the point in history at which Israel became properly monotheistic, and as to which of the Torah's sources are properly monotheistic – as opposed to monolatry, which is the worship of one God while not denying that other gods exist. There can be little doubt that P and D are fully grounded in a belief in only one God. The creation and flood stories P depict a single deity in control of all the forces of the universe. Both P and D expect there to be only one place of sacrifice and worship, which is arguably the most compatible of all laws with monotheism: one God, one sanctuary, one altar. Deuteronomy declares as explicitly as any monotheistic statement in the Bible: "*He* is God. There is no other outside of Him" (4:35, 39). And it goes on to say in one of the most famous lines in the Torah and in Judaism ever since: "YHWH is one" (6:4). Some take this to mean merely "YHWH alone," but "alone" is an exceedingly rare meaning of biblical Hebrew *'ehad*. Even in one of the oldest layers of Deuteronomy, the Song of Moses asserts: "there is no god with me" (32:39). In J and E and in some of the earliest poetry there is more room for scholarly disagreement, since J refers to the *benei elohim* (Gen. 6:1–4), and the Song of the Sea asks "Who is like you among the gods?" (Ex. 15:11). Some take the first commandment of the Decalogue to be monolatry rather than monotheism because it says "You shall not have other gods before my face [or: in my presence]" (Ex. 20:3), seemingly not denying the existence of other gods. However, one must be cautious in this judgment because the issue may be linguistic rather than theological. It is difficult to construct a commandment to be monotheistic without referring to the divine beings who are being denied. In any case, by the conclusion of the Torah, the full work is manifestly monotheistic, with that doctrine coming to dominate the passages that may or may not have originally been monotheistic themselves. And this has both the religious value of establishing that doctrine and the structural value of binding the Torah into unity.

Covenant

The three covenants provide a structure in which all the laws and stories can fit and be understood. The Noahic covenant guarantees the security of the cosmos. The Abrahamic covenant promises that Abraham's descendants will have the land, independence (their own kings), and that YHWH will be their God. The Sinai (or Israelite, or Mosaic) covenant provides for security and well-being in the land. Every law can be understood as one of the covenant's requirements. Every story can be interpreted in terms of one or more of the covenants. Israel's salvation from Egypt is understood as fulfilling the promises of the Abrahamic covenant. Israel's rebellions in the wilderness can be understood as issues of compliance with the terms of the Sinai covenant. This contributes to the coherence and connection of all the Torah's components to one another.

All the Families of the Earth

The Torah is remarkable in that it establishes its concern in its first chapters as being the wellbeing of the earth. The ancient Israelite authors chose to begin their story not with Abraham or the exodus or Sinai, but rather with the birth of the earth and the skies above it. The authors set the story of their people in the context of God's relations with all humankind. The first 11 chapters are a story of the obstacles to that relationship. Then the deity turns to a single man, Abraham, and establishes a special relationship with him, and God tells him what the end result of this is to be: blessing for all the families of the earth. These are among God's first words to Abraham, God's first words to Isaac, and God's first words to Jacob. Each Israelite is commanded to love his or her neighbors as oneself. In case there would be any misunderstanding, they are commanded repeatedly to care for the alien (*ger*) as for themselves. The first occurrence of the word *torah* in the Torah is the command: "There shall be one *torah* for the citizen and for the alien" (Ex. 12:49). Despite hostilities from Esau's descendants the Edomites, Israelites are forbidden to abhor an Edomite. Despite everything that the Egyptians have done, Israelites are forbidden to abhor an Egyptian. The Torah thus ends with the people of Israel poised at the border of the promised land, with the choice to bring blessing or curse to themselves and the opportunity to bring blessing on all the nations and families of the earth.

With these four values – and sheer literary skill – the Redactors of the Torah constructed a logical, unified, and, above all, meaningful work of prose and poetry, law and history, that became the foundation and heart of the Jewish religion and the Jewish people ever after.

CANONIZATION

The earliest concept of a "Book of the Torah" as a sacred scripture is found at Josiah's reform, and refers to the book of Deuteronomy (II Kings 22–23, and see above). The addition of the redacted works of Genesis through Numbers was accomplished by the mid-5th century B.C.E., when the Pentateuch was recognized by the postexilic community as the "Book of the Torah of Moses" (Neh. 8:1–2). The "Book of the Torah" introduced by Ezra (Ezra 7) already contained passages from Leviticus (cf. Neh. 8:14, 15, 18b with Lev. 23:39ff) and Numbers (cf. Neh. 13:1–2 with Deut. 23:4–5). Thus, after Genesis through Numbers was added to Deuteronomy, the term "Torah" acquired a broader application, referring to the entire Pentateuch. Though the canonization of the full Tanakh took place many centuries later, the text, status, and authority of the Torah was established at this relatively early stage; that is, in the biblical world itself.

[Richard Elliott Friedman and Shawna Dolansky Overton (2nd ed.)]

THE TRADITIONAL VIEW

The traditional view of the Pentateuch is in the most striking and most extreme contrast to the critical theories adumbrated above. Whereas the critical theory depends upon the assumption that the Pentateuch (in particular) is a composite work consisting of different documents, composed at different times and edited into a composite whole, the traditional view is fundamentally based upon the belief that the whole of the Pentateuch, the *Torah proper, is a unitary document, divinely revealed, and entirely written by Moses, with the exception of the last eight verses of Deuteronomy, which record the death of Moses and, according to one opinion, were written by Joshua (BB 15a; according to the other they were written by Moses at the dictation of God "with tears" (*dema*), but Elijah Gaon of Vilna renders the word "mixed up"). In other words, on the death of Moses the whole of the Pentateuch was complete, having been divinely revealed. Nor can any rigid doctrine be laid down as to the exact manner of communication of this revelation. Only human terms can be employed to convey the fact of revelation; that is the wider meaning of the well-known phrase, "the Torah speaks in human language" (*dibberah torah ki-leshon benei adam*) and this, the only method available, is obviously inadequate to convey the mystery of *mattan torah* ("the giving of the Torah"), of the confrontation of Moses with God. The almost radical explanation of Ibn Ezra (in Ex. 20:2) as to the differences between the two versions of the Decalogue (Ex. 20 and Deut. 5), in which he maintains that the variations in wording and spelling are unimportant, is as an acceptable doctrine as the talmudic explanation of the alternative openings of the fifth commandment by saying: *zakhor ve-shamor be-dibbur eḥad ne'emru* ("remember [the Sabbath day] and keep [the Sabbath day] were uttered simultaneously"). All that can be said with certainty is that, as explicitly stated in Numbers 12:6–8, the manner of the divine communication to Moses differed from that to any other prophet, whereas the other prophets received their messages while their normal cognitive faculties were in a state of suspense, Moses alone received that communication while in full possession of all his normal cognitive faculties, "mouth to mouth, even apparently and not in dark speeches" (Num. 12:8), or, even more explicitly: "And the Lord spoke unto Moses face to face as a man speaketh to his friend" (Ex. 33:11). "Mouth to mouth" and "face to face" illustrate the inevitable anthropomorphism involved in using human terms to convey the mystery of divine communication. The unitary belief is clearly expressed by Maimonides. His formulation of the eighth of the 13 Principles (commentary to Sanh. 10 (11): 1; for the complete text see JQR, 19 (1907), 53f.) is: "That the Torah has been revealed from heaven: This implies our belief that the whole of the Torah found in our hands this day is the Torah that was handed down by Moses and that it is all of divine origin. By this I mean that the whole of the Torah came to him from before God in a manner which is metaphorically called 'speaking'; but the real nature of the communication is unknown to everybody except to Moses to whom it came. In handing down the Torah, Moses was like a scribe writing from dictation the whole of it, its chronicles, its narratives, and its precepts." In his code Maimonides defines the person who denies the Torah as he "who says even of one verse or of one word that it is not of divine origin, or that Moses wrote it on his authority" (Yad, Teshuvah 3:8 based on Sanh. 99a). It is stated more succinctly in the prayer book formulation of the eighth of the 13 Principles of Faith of Maimonides: "I believe with a perfect faith that the whole Torah now in our possession is the same that was given to Moses our teacher."

Traditional Judaism rejected not only the Higher Criticism, i.e., the documentary theory, but also the Lower Criticism – textual criticism. With the sole exception of insignificant plene and defective spelling, the masoretic text is regarded as the only authoritative and authorized text of the Pentateuch. Insofar as textual criticism is concerned, one is on solid ground in maintaining the accuracy of the masoretic texts. The Sif. Deut. 356 states that "three scrolls were found in the Temple… In one of them they found written… in the other two they found written… the sages discarded the reading of the one and adopted that of the two: and ultimately one approved text was deposited in the Temple archives" (MK 3:4; Kelim 15:6), and a special group of readers, who were paid from the Temple funds, checked the text from time to time (TJ, Shek. 4:3, 48a). With loving care and sacred devotion the subsequent generations of scribes jealously guarded every letter of the text. Detailed regulations were laid down in order to ensure that the copying of the scrolls should be free from human error (see *Sefer Torah). There has been nothing like it in the history of literature or religion, and in this respect the masoretic text stands indisputably in a class by itself. It could not under any circumstances be expected that those who did not accept the supreme sanctity of the revealed word of the Torah, whether they were Alexandrian Jews who had come under the influence of Greek philosophy, or the sects of the

Dead Sea who rejected the *halakhah* of the Pharisees, should have the same approach of *noli me tangere* with regard to the handing down of every letter of the Torah. To them there was no harm in adding, diminishing, or amending for the sake of greater clarity or preconceived theological doctrines. In addition, the texts found in the Dead Sea Scrolls, which are a thousand years earlier than the textus receptus of Ben *Asher of 975, substantially confirm the accuracy of the present text and can be said on the whole to have demolished the ingenious emendations of two centuries of textual critics. One is therefore justified in regarding the traditional text as the most exact and authoritative. As Lieberman comments, "the sacred text of the Bible was handled by Jews, whose general reverence and awe in religious matters need not be stressed." To the sphere of the establishment of the correct text belongs the system of *keri* and *ketiv* (words written in one way but read in another), *tikkunei soferim, dates on certain letters, and special signs (for this, see Lieberman in bibl.).

With regard to the *tikkunei soferim*, Lieberman comes to the conclusion, after a close examination of the relevant sources, that they represent a later stage than that of the *keri* and the *ketiv*. This latter system modified the reading without altering the text, whereas the *tikkunei soferim* actually changed letters but only in order to remove indelicate, gross anthropomorphic, and unworthy expressions from the text, and their number is minute. It has been suggested that the very fact of the difference between the *keri* and the *ketiv* is evidence of the authenticity of the text, which was regarded as so inviolable that instead of being altered to remove difficulties, the emendations were, so to speak, relegated to the margin. The rabbis had a profound and extensive knowledge of every word, jot, and tittle of the Bible. The statement of the Talmud (Kid. 30a) that the *soferim* were so called because they counted (*soferim*) every letter of the Torah (and the passage proceeds to give the statistical results of that counting) expresses only the mechanical aspect of their intense preoccupation with the sacred text. Every word, every expression, and every deviation from the norm was made the subject of profound study. That study, however, went far beyond linguistic research; the Pentateuch was the textbook from which the whole corpus of *halakhah* had to be derived. They were therefore perfectly and acutely aware of the contradictions, real and apparent, in the text. But they resolved those contradictions by a complicated, but largely logical system of interpretations (see *Hermeneutics). Nor were differences in style unnoticed by them. The Midrash (Deut. R. 1:1) has a beautiful passage on the "healing which comes to the tongue" of the person who occupies himself with Torah, which is directly based on the unique style of Deuteronomy.

The justification on scientific and scholarly grounds of the theory of the unitary nature of the Pentateuch maintained by traditional Judaism is not nearly as satisfactory as that of the textual criticism of the text. Generally speaking, traditional scholars have not faced up to the challenge of the Documentary Hypothesis, and instead of accepting its challenge and answering it, have taken refuge in theological dogmatism. Almost the only attempt to face up to its challenge was that of David *Hoffmann in his brilliant *Die Wichtigsten Instanzen gegen die Graf-Wellhausensche Hypothese* and his biblical commentaries. He not only attempts to demolish the critical theory, but maintains, on grounds of scholarship, the doctrine of the unity of the Pentateuch. Other and more popular attempts, for example those of J.H. Hertz (see bibl.), constitute special pleading and suffer from the fact that they tend to create the false impression that the growing number of scholars who call into question the validity of the Wellhausen theory and its followers – such as J. Robertson (*The Early Religion of Israel*), J. Orr (*The Problem of the Old Testament*), W.L. Baxter (*Sanctuary and Sacrifice*), Y. Kaufmann (*Toledot ha-Emunah ha-Yisre'elit*, 1937), and U. Cassuto (*The Documentary Hypothesis*, 1961; *Commentary on the Book of Genesis*, 1961–64; *A Commentary on the Book of Exodus*, 1967) – ipso facto maintain the traditional view of the unity of the Pentateuch, an assumption which is at variance with the facts.

On the other hand, the documentary theory, or at least the evidence that the Pentateuch is not a unitary document, has been so convincing to many Orthodox scholars that various attempts have been made to adopt a syncretistic view which combines an acceptance of this theory with that of the implications which derive from the belief in the unitary nature of the Pentateuch, upon which traditional Judaism is based. The most determined exponent is L. Jacobs, who quotes approvingly the following statement of J. Abelson: "The correct perspective of the matter seems to be as follows: the modern criticism of the Bible on the one hand, and faith in Judaism on the other hand, can be regarded as two distinct compartments. For criticism, even at its best, is speculative and tentative, something always liable to be modified or proved wrong and having to be replaced by something else. It is an intellectual exercise, subject to all the doubts and guesses which are inseparable from such exercises. But our accredited truths of Judaism have their foundations more deeply and strongly laid than all this. And our faith in them not only need be uninjured by our faith in criticism, but need not be affected by the latter at all. The two are quite consistent and can be held simultaneously." An even more striking attempt at such a syncretism which makes possible a complete acceptance of the critical theory with a somewhat mystic view of the belief in the unitary theory has been made by a strictly Orthodox modern scholar, M. Breuer (see bibl.).

[Louis Isaac Rabinowitz]

ADD. BIBLIOGRAPHY: Y. Aharoni, "The Solomonic Temple, the Tabernacle, and the Arad Sanctuary," in: H.A. Hoffman, Jr. (ed.), *Orient und Occident, Cyrus Gordon Festschrift* (1973); K. Baltzer, *The Covenant Formulary* (1971); F.M. Cross, *Canaanite Myth and Hebrew Epic* (1973); idem, "The Priestly Tabernacle," in: BA, 10 (1947), 45–68; idem, "The Priestly Tabernacle," in: *Biblical Archaeology Review*, 1 (1961): 201–28; idem and D.N. Freedman, *Studies in Ancient Yahwistic Poetry* (1975²); S.R. Driver, *Introduction to the Literature of the Old Testament* (1891⁹); O. Eissfeldt, *The Old Testament: An Introduction*. tr. P. Ackroyd (1965); D.N. Freedman, *Divine Commitment and Hu-*

man Obligation (1997); R.E. Friedman, *Who Wrote the Bible?* (1987); idem, *The Hidden Book in the Bible* (1998); idem, *The Exile and Biblical Narrative* (1981); idem (ed.), *The Poet and the Historian* (1984); idem, "The Tabernacle in the Temple," in: BA, 43 (1980); idem, "Pentateuch," in: D.N. Freedman (ed.), *The Anchor Bible Dictionary* (1992); B. Halpern, *The Emergence of Israel in Canaan* (1983); idem, "Sacred History and Ideology: Chronicles' Thematic Structure – Indications of an Earlier Source," in: R.E. Friedman (ed.), *The Creation of Sacred Literature* (1981), 35–54; M. Haran, "The Priestly Image of the Tabernacle," in: HUCA, 36 (1965), 191–226; idem, "Behind the Scenes of History: Determining the Date of the Priestly Source," in: JBA, 100 (1981), 321–33; A. Hurvitz, "The Evidence of Language in Dating the Priestly Code," in: *Revue Biblique*, 81 (1974), 24–56; idem, *A Linguistic Study of the Relationship Between the Priestly Source and the Book of Ezekiel* (1982); A.W. Jenks, *The Elohist and North Israelite Traditions* (1977); A.S. Kapelrud, "The Date of the Priestly Code," in: *Annual of the Swedish Theological Institute*, 3 (1964), 58–64; Y. Kaufmann, *The Religion of Israel*, tr. and ed. Moshe Greenberg (1960; Heb. ed., 1937); J. Levenson, "Who Inserted the Book of the Torah?" in: *Harvard Theological Review*, 68 (1975), 203–33; B. Levine, "Late Language in the Priestly Source: Some Literary and Historical Observations," in: *Proceedings of the Eighth World Congress of Jewish Studies* (1983), 69–82; S. McEvenue, *The Narrative Style of the Priestly Writer* (1971); G.E. Mendenhall, *Law and Covenant in Israel and the Ancient Near East* (1955); J. Milgrom, *Cult and Conscience* (1976); idem, *Studies in Levitical Terminology* (1970); idem, "Priestly Terminology and the Political and Social Structure of Pre-Monarchic Israel," in: JQR, 69 (1978), 65–81; S. Mowinckel, *Erwagungen zur Pentateuch Quellenfrage* (1964); M. Noth, *A History of Pentateuchal Traditions* (1972; Ger. ed., 1948); M. Paran, "Literary Features of the Priestly Code: Stylistic Patterns, Idioms and Structures" (Heb.; Ph.D. diss., Hebrew University, 1983); R. Polzin, *Late Biblical Hebrew: Toward an Historical Typology of Biblical Hebrew Prose* (1976); G. Von Rad, *The Problem of the Hexateuch* (1966); G. Rendsburg, "Late Biblical Hebrew and the Date of P," in: *Journal of the Ancient Near East Society*, 12 (1980):, 65–80; R. Rendtorff, *Das uberlieferungsgeschichtliche Problem des Pentateuch* (Beihefte zur Zeitschrift fur die alttestamentliche Wissenschaft 147) (1977); J.H. Tigay (ed.), *Empirical Models for Biblical Criticism* (1985); J. Van Seters, *In Search of History* (1983); M. Weinfeld, "The Covenant of Grant in the Old Testament and in the Ancient Near East," in: JAOS, 90 (1970), 184–203; idem, *Deuteronomy and the Deuteronomic School* (1972); J. Wellhausen, *Prolegomena zur Geschichte Israels* (1885; repr. 1973; Ger. ed., 1883); W.M.L. De Wette, *Dissertatio critica qua a prioribus Deuteronomium Pentateuchi libris diversam, alius cuiusdam recentioris auctoris opus esse monostratur* (1805; repr. in *Opuscula Theologica* (1830)); D.P. Wright, *The Disposal of Impurity: Elimination Rites in the Bible and in Hittite and Mesopotamian Literature* (1987); G.E. Wright (ed.), "The Lawsuit of God: A Form-Critical Study of Deuteronomy 32," in: B. Anderson and W. Harrelson (eds.), *Israel's Prophetic Heritage* (1962); Z. Zevit, "Converging Lines of Evidence Bearing on the Date of P," in: *Zeitschrift fuer die alttestamentliche Wissenschaft*, 94 (1982), 502–9; idem, "The Priestly Redaction and Interpretation of the Plague Narrative in Exodus," in: JQR, 66 (1975), 193–211.

PENTATEUCH, SAMARITAN, Hebrew text of the Pentateuch used by the *Samaritans. The first copy of the Samaritan Pentateuch to reach the hands of Western Bible scholars was that obtained in Damascus by Pietro della Valle in 1616. Subsequent travelers brought to Europe other copies of the Samaritan Pentateuch, Targum, and other Samaritan literature. The interest created among Bible scholars was considerable, and for a long time hopes were high that at last an older version or recension of the Hebrew Bible than that of the Masoretic Text had been recovered. The first edition of the Samaritan Pentateuch to be printed was that in the Paris Polyglot Bible of 1629–45 and the London Polyglot of 1657. These earliest editions and the improved one of Blayney (Oxford, 1790), based on several manuscripts, proved inadequate for the purpose of precise textual criticism. The edition of A.F. von Gall (Geissen, 1918, repr. 1966), based on a large number of manuscripts, made the task of careful textual study much easier. From the Polyglot editions until the time of W. *Gesenius (see below), there grew up a lively debate about the relative merits of the Samaritan Pentateuch and the Masoretic Text. Several attempts to draw conclusions from detailed comparative analysis of the two versions were made, but it was the monumental examination of them by Gesenius in 1815 (*De pentateuchi samaritani origine, indole et auctoritate commentatio philologico-critica*) that produced the most lasting effect. From then, and for a century thereafter, his verdict that the Masoretic Text was superior and prior held sway. Gesenius listed and analyzed the roughly 6,000 textual differences in terms of eight categories or classes:

(1) grammatical revision by the Samaritan;

(2) glosses and explanations introduced into the text;

(3) emendation of words;

(4) additional or corrected readings supplied from parallel passages;

(5) larger additions and interpolations;

(6) emendation of place names;

(7) adjustment of forms of expression to the northern (Samaritan) dialect of Hebrew; and

(8) a special category, which included emendation of the verb (sing. or plur.) occurring with the Divine Name, removal of anthropomorphisms and anthropopathisms, etc.

In addition he regarded the Samaritan orthography (especially the gutturals) as inadequate and due mainly to scribal carelessness.

[John Macdonald]

The dictum of Gesenius holds true in its main points to this day. The text of the Samaritan Pentateuch always presents the *lectio facilio* against the more archaic and difficult forms of the Masoretic Text. Even a seemingly early form like *ʾatti* is in reality a late Aramaism. The Samaritan pronunciation of their Pentateuch, which is a sacred and zealously guarded tradition of the sect, shows clear affinity to the language of the Qumran Scrolls:

(1) The above-mentioned personal pronoun *ʾatti*, which is the equivalent of *ʾat* in the Masoretic Text, is *ʾatti* also in the Scrolls;

(2) The masoretic suffixes *-kem, -tem* are *-kemmah, -temmah* in the Scrolls. In the Samaritan Pentateuch they are spelled in the masoretic way but always pronounced like the longer forms found in the Scrolls;

(3) The stress in the Samaritan pronunciations is penultimate (not ultimate like that denoted by the Tiberian tradition), which causes *sewa*-vowels of Masoretic Text to become full vowels like in the text of the Scrolls, e.g., Sedom (MT) = Shadem (Samaritan) = Sodom (Scrolls). From all this it can be concluded that the text of the Samaritan Pentateuch in its present form presents a later stage of development than the Masoretic Text. Its peculiarities do not reflect a special Ephraimitic dialect but represent the common Hebrew prevalent in Palestine between about the second century B.C.E. and the third century C.E.

[Ayala Loewenstamm]

The best-known difference of substance is the additional text regarded by the Samaritans as the tenth command of the Decalogue. After Exodus 20:14 [17] (and Deut. 5:18) the Samaritan Pentateuch has a lengthy addition which consists in the main of Deuteronomy 27:2, 3 (part), 4–7, and 11:30. This, it is generally agreed, is a deliberate Samaritan interpolation designed to provide support for their claim that Gerizim is "the chosen place." Connected with this is the Samaritan Pentateuch variant בחר (*baḥar*) against the Masoretic Text's יבחר *(yivḥar)*, which occurs in all the relevant passages in Deuteronomy 12:5ff. – the claim being that Shechem had been chosen as the place of the Lord's sanctuary. On the other hand, R.H. Pfeiffer (in bibl., 102) represented the viewpoint of many students of Samaritanism when he cited the probability of a Judean attempt to minimize biblical support for the Samaritan claim for the priority and legitimacy of their temple on Gerizim. He also asserted that in their scrupulous regard for the sacred text the Samaritans left anti-Samaritan (pre-schism) additions untouched. "With utter disregard for geographical reality, the gloss in Deuteronomy 11:30 removes Gerizim and Ebal from the vicinity of Shechem (still attested in the reference to the terebinth of Moreh) to the Jordan Valley at Gilgal, near Jericho (cf. 27:12, 'when you have crossed over the Jordan'); similarly in Joshua 8:30–35 the altar was built on Gerizim [sic!] while the Israelites were still encamped at Gilgal." His explanation is that "The early account of the origin of the cult at Shechem (Deut. 11:29; 27:11–26) was thus first given a Deuteronomistic interpretation (in 11:26–28, 31–32; 27:7–10); then the scene was removed to Gilgal and connected with the famous stones there (27:1–4, 8), and finally, after the Samaritan schism, 'Gerizim' was changed to 'Ebal' in Deuteronomy 27:4 (where the Samaritan Pentateuch still reads 'Gerizim') and in Joshua 8:30." This assessment of a problematic Samaritan Pentateuch passage is supported by several scholars (e.g., O. Eissfeldt, in bibl.), who agree that both Judeans and Samaritans were forced to take defensive measures in order to maintain the supremacy of their rival claims. Another problem concerns the fact that the Septuagint often agrees with the Samaritan Pentateuch against the Masoretic Text. Some examples of this agreement are: Genesis 4:8, "Cain said to his brother Abel, 'Come, Let us go out into the field'"(the Masoretic Text lacks Cain's words); Genesis 47:21, "As for the people, he made slaves of them" (MT "As… he removed them to the cities"); in Exodus 12:40 the 430 years of the Israelite sojourn in Egypt include their sojourn in Canaan as well (SP-LXX add "and their fathers"). However, in most cases the Samaritan text agrees with the Masoretic against the Septuagint, as shown by B.K. Walthe. The following example of agreement between the Samaritan Pentateuch and the Septuagint introduces a type of the former's variant from the Masoretic Text that was used by Samaritan exegetes and theologians in later times as proof texts for their distinctive credal statements. Deuteronomy 32:35 contains the words "against the day [ליום] of vengeance and recompense" in contrast to the Masoretic Text's "vengeance is mine [לי] and recompense," in a difference comprising a masoretic omission or Samaritan addition of two Hebrew letters. This "proof text" is used for the Samaritan belief in the Day of Vengeance and Recompense after the Resurrection. An example of this sort of Samaritan Pentateuch variant is Genesis 3:19 (against MT); the latter reads "and to dust you shall return," while the former has "and to your dust Thou shalt return," a difference of one Hebrew letter (*kaf*). This variant is a "proof text" for the Samaritan teaching about the Resurrection. (The principal SP variants are included in BH in the *apparatus criticus.*)

Dating

Most authorities agree that the Samaritan Pentateuch, with its approximately 2,000 agreements with the Septuagint against the Masoretic Text, existed in the third century B.C.E., and it is likely that the old or proto-Palestinian text-type came to exist in three recensions, a Judean and a Samaritan soon after the time of Ezra (or a little earlier), and a Greek (LXX) in the third century. Pfeiffer (in bibl., 101) expresses a widely held view of the dating of the Samaritan Pentateuch when he writes: "We may infer… that the Samaritan community adopted the Pentateuch as its Bible soon after its canonization about 400 B.C.…" The Masoretic and Samaritan texts (in spite of their variants) were recensions of the final edition of the Pentateuch, as also the Septuagint. Evidence that the Samaritan Pentateuch existed in B.C.E. times is provided from another source. Among the Qumran discoveries from 1947 onward the text of some fragments of biblical manuscripts clearly resembles the Samaritan text-type. Here are some Samaritan-Qumran agreements occurring in the Book of Exodus: to the Divine Command in 7:16–18 the Samaritan text adds its execution by Moses and Aaron; the Qumran text has the latter statement. In 7:29 the Qumran text has the start of the Samaritan text's expansion. Similar textual traits are found in 8:19; 9:5; 9:19; and 11:2. The Samaritan and the Qumran text add "and he smote them" in 17:13. The omission of 29:21 and 30:1–10 is a feature of both texts. However, the Qumran fragment texts sometimes agree with the Samaritan, sometimes with the Septuagint against the Samaritan, and sometimes with the Masoretic against either or both the Samaritan and the Septuagint.

Manuscripts

The best-known copy of the Samaritan Pentateuch is the so-called "Abish'a (אבישע) Scroll," for which the Samaritans, since medieval times, have claimed a very ancient origin. The oldest part of this text was edited in 1959 by Pérez Castro. According to the colophon of the scroll itself the text was written by Abisha son of Phinehas, the great-grandson of Moses, in the 13th year after the Israelite conquest of Canaan. However, it is generally agreed that the scroll cannot have been written before the 12th century C.E. A fine scroll written in 1227 C.E. is a model exemplar of the best copies known. Written in gold letters, the scroll (roll) is wound around rollers of silver and has three parallel columns setting out the Hebrew, Aramaic (Targum), and Arabic versions in the one Samaritan script. The best-known manuscripts otherwise are not in roll form, but in book form, written on vellum or paper. There are no indications of vowel signs, but the text is divided into sentences and the whole into 964 paragraphs (Kiẓẓim = קצים; in other codices they number 966).

Script

On paleographic grounds, according to J. Purvis's investigation (1968), "the ancestry of the Samaritan script is to be traced ultimately to the cursive paleo-Hebrew of the sixth century B.C.E., although the direct percentage is the paleo-Hebrew of the late Hasmonean period" (in bibl., 36). There is no general accord about this, for there is a lack of evidence for the paleo-Hebrew script used in Samaria (or, for religious purposes, by the Samaritans) before the earliest-known Samaritan epigraphic materials, so that a complete history of the Samaritan script going back before Hasmonean times is not available. The Samaritan script, which is known in both uncial and cursive form, must have been in use at the time when Ezra introduced the "square" (אשורי) script for the Judean Bible. The Samaritan alphabet is the only descendant of the early Hebrew script which is still in use.

Versions

There seems to have once existed a Greek translation of the Samaritan Pentateuch (see Glaue and Rahlfs, in bibl.). Known as the *Samareitikon*, it was written after the Septuagint, by which it was influenced, but before Origen who refers to it. Its place of origin is unknown. A copy of the Samaritan Aramaic Targum was acquired for the first time by Pietro della Valle, along with the Hebrew text, in 1616. The Samaritans believe it to have been composed by Markah, i.e., in the fourth century C.E. According to J. Nutt (in bibl.), the Samaritans of his day believed it to have been the work of Nethanel (נתנאל; first century B.C.E.), but as there was a high priest of that name in the fourth century C.E., local tradition has probably confused the identification. The text is unsatisfactory in many respects, particularly in the orthography, and there are too few complete copies available for collation. The edition of Peterman-Vollers (1872) is the only complete one which is based on a number of manuscripts. The Aramaic of the Targum is similar to that of Markah's *Memar* and of the *Defter* (fourth century C.E.) of the Liturgy, and is undoubtedly Palestinian in type. The translation is literal and therefore comparable to the Targum of *Onkelos. The Arabic translation was made probably in the 13th century by Abu Said or (if he was only the reviser, as some think) by *Abu al-Ḥasan of Tyre in the 11th century (A.E. Cowley, in bibl., xxiv). This translation exists in several manuscripts. It is a fairly literal translation of the Hebrew (not the Targum), and some scholars have seen in it possible dependence on *Saadiah, but this is uncertain. The chief evaluation of the available texts was made by P. Kahle (in bibl., and subsequent articles) and L. Goldberg (in bibl.).

See also *Samaritan Language and Literature.

[John Macdonald]

BIBLIOGRAPHY: J.H. Peterman and C. Vollers, *Pentateuchus Samaritanus* (1872–91); J. Nutt, *Fragments of a Samaritan Targum* (1874); P. Kahle, *Die arabischen Bibelübersetzungen* (1904), x–xiii; A.E. Cowley, *The Samaritan Liturgy* (1909), xxiii–xxiv; P. Glaue and A. Rahlfs, *Fragmente einer griechischen Übersetzung des samaritanischen Pentateuchs* (1911); A.F. von Gall, *Der hebräische Pentateuch der Samaritaner* (1914–18, 19633); Ch. Heller, *The Samaritan Pentateuch, an Adaptation of the Massoretic Text* (1923); L. Goldberg, *Das samaritanisch Pentateuchtargum* (1935); R.H. Pfeiffer, *Introduction to the Old Testament* (1948), 101–2; P. Kahle, in: *Studia Orientalia Ioanni Pedersen* (1953), 188–92; O. Eissfeldt, *The Old Testament, an Introduction* (1965), 694–5, 782; J. Purvis, *The Samaritan Pentateuch and the Origin of the Samaritan Sect* (1968); R. Macuch, *Grammatik des samaritanischen Hebräisch* (1969); Ẓ. Ben-Ḥayyim, *Ivrit ve-Aramit Nosaḥ Shomron*, 1 (1957), xxvii–xxviii. **ADD. BIBLIOGRAPHY:** B. Waltke, in: ABD, 5:932–40; A. Tal, *The Samaritan Pentateuch edited according to MS 6 (C) of the Shekhem Synagogue* (1994).

PENUEL (or **Peniel**; Heb. פְּנִיאֵל, פְּנוּאֵל), fortified city near the ford of the river Jabbok, where Jacob fought with the angel of the Lord and received the appellation Israel (Gen. 32:31). It appears with Succoth (with which it is also connected in the story of Jacob) as a city in Transjordan which refused to give food to Gideon and his men in their pursuit of the Midianites (Judg. 8:8); returning victorious, Gideon destroyed the tower of Penuel and slew the men of the city (Judg. 8:17). According to the last biblical reference to the place, it was built by Jeroboam I, king of Israel, after he built Shechem, apparently to be used as a capital for his lands beyond the Jordan (I Kings 12:25). Shishak captured Penuel in his campaign in the fifth year of Rehoboam, together with neighboring Succoth and Mahanaim (no. 53 on his list of conquered towns). It is now usually identified with the eastern mound of Tulūl al-Dhahab on the southern side of a bend in the Jabbok; the pottery on the site extends from the Late Bronze to the Byzantine periods. Some scholars suggest that both mounds of Tulūl al-Dhahab mark the site of Penuel, while others identify the western mound, on the northern side of the Jabbok, with *Mahanaim.

BIBLIOGRAPHY: Albright, in: BASOR, 35 (1929), 12–13; Glueck, in: AASOR, 18–19 (1939), 232–4; de Vaux, in: RB, 47 (1938), 411–3; Press, Ereẓ, s.v.; Abel, Geog, 2 (1938), 406; Aharoni, Land, index.

[Michael Avi-Yonah]

PENUELI (formerly **Pineles**), **SHEMUEL YESHAYAHU** (1904–1965), Hebrew critic and teacher. Born in Galicia, he taught at the Hebrew Teachers' Seminary in Vilna and settled in Ereẓ Israel in 1935. For 11 years he was the principal of the school at Nahalal, and later became the principal of the Givat ha-Sheloshah Teachers' Seminary. In 1954 he was appointed lecturer in literature at Tel Aviv University, subsequently becoming head of the department.

He published articles on literature and education. The literary critic's task, according to Penueli, is to uncover the author's subconscious as it is revealed in his works. Therefore, Penueli relied heavily on psychological theories, especially on Freud. His books on Hebrew literature include: *Demuyyot be-Sifrutenu ha-Ḥadasha* (1946); *Ḥayyim Hazaz* (1954); *Yeẓirato shel S.Y. Agnon* (1960); *Safrut ki-Feshutah* (1963); *Massah al ha-Yafeh she-be-Ommanut ha-Sifrut* (1965); *Brenner u-Gnessin ba-Sippur ha-Ivri shel Reshit ha-Me'ah ha-Esrim* (1965). He also co-edited the English anthology *Hebrew Short Stories*, 2 vols. (1965).

BIBLIOGRAPHY: G. Kressel, Leksikon, 2 (1967), 645.

[Getzel Kressel]

PENZANCE, seaport in S.W. England. Jews trading with the fleet settled here in the mid-18th century and a small community was formed. In 1807 a synagogue was built in New Street, under the auspices of the merchant and distiller Lemon Hart (1768–1845), subsequently warden of the Great Synagogue in London. The most notable person in the intellectual life of the community was Solomon Ezekiel (1781–1867), who organized the "Penzance Hebrew Society for Promoting the Diffusion of Religious Knowledge" and carried on a vigorous running polemic against local conversionists. Toward the end of the 19th century, the community decayed. The synagogue was sold in 1906. In the early 21st century, the only organized Jewish community in Cornwall was in Truro.

BIBLIOGRAPHY: C. Roth, in: JC, Supplement (May and June 1933); idem, *Rise of Provincial Jewry* (1950).

[Cecil Roth]

PENZIAS, ARNO ALLAN (1933–), U.S. physicist, Nobel Prize laureate. Born in Munich, Penzias left Germany in 1939, when he and his younger brother were placed on the *Kindertransport* by his parents, who were able to obtain visas to the United States. The family reunited in England and left for America shortly thereafter. Penzias attended New York City public schools, and received his doctorate in physics from Columbia University. Most of his professional career (1961–95) was spent at the Bell Telephone Laboratories. He performed research in radio astronomy and telecommunications and became vice president of its world famous research organization. As a scientist he is best known for his 1965 discovery, with Robert W. Wilson, of "background" radiation from the far reaches of space, supporting the "Big Bang" theory of the creation of the universe, work for which he and Wilson shared the 1978 Nobel Prize in physics. The author of two books on the societal impact of information technology, Penzias made significant contributions to our understanding of the chemistry of interstellar space, especially the complex molecules thought to underlie the origin of life. Subsequently moving to California, he advised and encouraged new hi-tech companies.

[Bracher Rager (2nd ed.)]

PE'OT (Heb. פֵּאוֹת; lit. "corners"), sidelocks grown in accordance with the prohibition of the Torah that "Ye shall not round the corners of your heads" (Lev. 19:27). The Talmud has interpreted this to mean that it is forbidden to "level the growth of hair on the temple from the back of the ears to the forehead" (Mak. 20b). The hair in this area may not be completely removed even with depilatory powder, scissors, or an electric shaver which may be used in shaving the face (see *Beard and Shaving). Although a negative precept, women are exempt from leaving *pe'ot* since the parallel prohibition against "marring the corners of the beard" (Lev. 19:27; Kid. 1:7; Kid. 35b) obviously does not extend to women. According to Maimonides a minimum of 40 hairs must be left for *pe'ot* (Yad, Avodat Kokhavim, 12:6). However, the Shulḥan Arukh (YD 181:9) rules in accordance with Rashi (Mak. 20a) that hair must be allowed to grow in front of the ears until it reaches the upper cheekbones (zygomatic arch). However, the maximum length of *pe'ot* has been determined by the custom of a particular time and place rather than by *halakhah*. The kabbalistic writings of Isaac *Luria attribute great significance to *pe'ot* because the numerical value (see *Gematria) of *pe'ah*, 86, is the same as the numerical value of *Elohim* (i.e., God). It has become customary for Ḥasidim and Orthodox Yemenites to leave *pe'ot*, either short ones which are curled behind the ears or long ones hanging down at the sides of the head.

PEPPER (Heb. פִּלְפֵּל, *pilpel*), the fruit of the perennial creeping plant *Piper nigrum*, which grows in India and in the neighboring tropical regions. The Hebrew name, like its English one, is derived from the Sanskrit *pippali*. Probably it was first brought to Ereẓ Israel after the expeditions of Alexander the Great. R. Johanan notes that in former times pepper was not yet available for spicing roast meat and *roquet* was used instead (Er. 28b). Pepper was an expensive spice and sometimes the seeds of bitter vetch were used as a substitute (Eccles. R. 6:1). In the time of the Mishnah and the Talmud, people were very fond of pepper and attempts may have been made to cultivate it. The *aggadah* states that the emperor Hadrian challenged Joshua b. Hananiah to the effect that despite the Land of Israel's virtues it lacked some things, such as pepper, and in reply Joshua brought him pepper from Niẓḥana (seemingly a locality in Upper Galilee) in order to prove "that the Land of Israel lacks nothing" (Eccles. R. 2:8, no. 2; see also *Cinnamon). R. Meir uses the same phrase about pepper and adds that it is subject to the law of *orlah just like other local trees (Ber. 36b). In addition to its use as a spice, pepper was also used to dispel halitosis and a woman was permitted to go out on the Sabbath with a peppercorn in her mouth (Shab. 6:5). A proverb had it that "Better one peppercorn than a basket full of gourds" (Meg. 7a). The term *pilpul (Avot 6:6; Tem. 16a) is connected with *pilpel* and from it is derived the verb *palpel*, to show sharpwittedness in learning. In the Middle Ages, pepper was a medium of exchange and was called "black money." A species resembling pepper is *pilpela arikhta*, long pepper (Pes. 42b), extracted from the bunches of unripe fruit of the species *Piper longum*. In Israel today the name *pilpel* is applied to the decorative tree *Schinus molle* and also to paprika, both of which originate in America and were unknown to the ancients.

BIBLIOGRAPHY: Krauss, Tal Arch, 1 (1910), 118 f.; Loew, Flora, 3 (1924), 49–62. **ADD. BIBLIOGRAPHY:** Feliks, Ha-Tzome'aḥ, 125.

[Jehuda Feliks]

PEPPER, JOSEPH (1904–?), British meteorologist. Born in London, Pepper began work at the Meteorological Office, then under the supervision of the Air Ministry, in 1932. During the 1930s and World War II, he served as a meteorologist and weather forecaster in the Royal Air Force and Royal Navy in various parts of the world, including the Atlantic Ocean, Cyprus, and Singapore. He published research on the winds of the North Atlantic Ocean and, while engaged in various other tasks, began writing a work on climatic conditions in various parts of the world, together with an analysis of information gathered during the 1940s and the early 1950s on the Antarctic region. One result of this work was his book, *The Meteorology of the Falkland Islands and Dependencies 1944–1950* (1954). Before his retirement from government service Pepper prepared a comprehensive work on the rules of forecasting. He subsequently taught at the Central London Polytechnic.

[Dov Ashbel]

PERAHIA, MURRAY (1947–), U.S. pianist and conductor. Born in New York City into a Sephardi family, Perahia began studying piano in 1952 with Jeanette Haien. In 1966, he entered Mannes College, New York, where he studied composition and conducting. He continued his piano studies with Balsam, and later with Horszowski. He had collaborated in chamber music with such outstanding musicians as Casals and members of the Budapest Quartet before his debut with the New York Philharmonic Orchestra (1972). Later that year he gained international fame as prizewinner at the Leeds International Piano Competition. His memorable London debut in a recital revealed him to be a pianist of rare sensitivity and intelligence. Perahia appeared as soloist with the leading orchestras and conductors. From 1981 until 1989, he was artistic co-director of the Aldeburgh Festival, where he previously collaborated with Benjamin Britten and Peter Pears. In 1992 a hand injury compelled him to withdraw from public performances. In 1994 he returned to the stage as a soloist. At the core of his repertoire are works by Mozart, Chopin, Schumann, Brahms, and Bach. He reestablished the Haendel suites and many of the Scarlatti sonatas as a rewarding repertory for pianists. Perahia has won numerous music awards – among them the Avery Fisher Prize (1975). He is an honorary fellow of the Royal College of Music and the Royal Academy of Music.

ADD. BIBLIOGRAPHY: Grove online; *Baker's Biographical Dictionary* (1997).

[Max Loppert / Naama Ramot (2nd ed.)]

PERAḤYAH, AARON BEN ḤAYYIM ABRAHAM HA-KOHEN (1627?–1697), rabbi and halakhic authority of *Salonika. Peraḥyah was born in Salonika and studied there under Asher b. Ardut ha-Kohen, Ḥasdai ha-Kohen *Peraḥyah, and *Ḥayyim Shabbetai. In 1689 he succeeded Elijah *Covo as chief rabbi of Salonika. He was regarded as an important *posek* among Salonika rabbis.

His works are: *Paraḥ Matteh Aharon* (2 parts, Amsterdam, 1703), responsa which reflect the contemporary condition of Turkish Jewry in general and of Salonikan Jewry in particular; *Pirḥei Kehunnah (ibid.*, 1709), novellae to the tractates *Bava Kamma, Bava Meẓia, Ketubbot, Gittin, Avodah Zarah*, and *Kiddushin*; *Bigdei Kehunnah* (Saloniki, 1753), eulogies and homilies; and *Zikhron Devarim* (*ibid.*, 1758), source references for the *Arba'ah Turim* of *Jacob b. Asher. In his *Paraḥ Matteh Aharon* he mentions another work, on *Alfasi, of which nothing is known.

BIBLIOGRAPHY: Michael, Or, 136–7; M. Molho, *Essai d'une Monographie sur la Famille Perahia à Thessaloniki* (1938), 33–44; I.S. Emmanuel, *Maẓẓevot Saloniki*, 2 (1968), 491–4.

[Abraham David]

PERAḤYAH, ḤASDAI BEN SAMUEL HA-KOHEN (?1605–1678), rabbi and halakhist. Peraḥyah belonged to a well-known family in Salonika. He was one of the outstanding disciples of *Ḥayyim Shabbetai. In 1647 he was appointed one of the *dayyanim* of the old Italian community of the city. In 1671, after the death of Menahem Shullam, he was appointed chief rabbi there, and served, apparently, until his death.

Peraḥyah left behind homilies, novellae, and responsa. His collected responsa, *Torat Ḥesed*, were published in Salonika in 1722, and others appear in the works of his associates and disciples. Among his pupils were Daniel Gerasi, Jacob di Boton, and his kinsman, Aaron ha-Kohen *Peraḥyah.

BIBLIOGRAPHY: M. Molho, *Essai d'une Monographie sur la Famille Perahia à Thessaloniki* (1938), 27–33; I.S. Emmanuel, *Maẓẓevot Saloniki*, 1 (1963), 403–6, no. 908.

[Abraham David]

PERAḤYAH BEN NISSIM (13th century), talmudist. No biographical details are known of him. In a document dated 1240 he is mentioned as being in Fostat, Egypt. In 1247 he wrote a commentary on the *halakhot* of Isaac *Alfasi and a manuscript of it in the tractate *Shabbat*, written in 1304, is preserved in the Bodleian Library.

Extracts from the work are cited in the novellae on Maimonides' *Mishneh Torah*, which are published at the beginning of the *Ma'aseh Roke'aḥ* of Mas'ud Roke'ah, and additional fragments were published by Assaf in *Kirjath Sepher*. Many of the quotations from Maimonides given by M.L. Sachs in his *Ḥiddushei ha-Rambam la-Talmud* (1963) were taken from this work. A section of the work on chapters five and six was published at the end of the *Siyya'ta di-Shemayya* (1970).

BIBLIOGRAPHY: S. Assaf, in: *Sinai*, 16 (1940), 106; idem, in: KS, 23 (1946–47), 233–5; Z. Benedict, in: KS, 28 (1952/53), 211–3; Mann, Egypt, 1 (1920), 248 n. 1, 2 (1922), 297 no. 1.

[Shlomoh Zalman Havlin]

PEREC, GEORGES (1936–1982), French author. Grandson of Isaac Leib *Peretz's nephew David, Georges Perec lost his father in the defense of France in 1940 and his mother in the deportation from *Drancy (February 1943). For the major part of the Nazi occupation of France, Perec was hidden in a Catholic boarding school at Villard-de-Lans (Isere) and after the Liberation he was brought up in Paris by his paternal aunt and her husband, a trader in fine pearls. Perec's early orphanage marked him deeply, and lies near the root of his highly defended but engagingly unpretentious literary personality. He was educated in Paris and at Etampes, where his philosophy teacher, Jean Duvignaud, encouraged him in his early decision to become a writer. Perec dropped out of a history degree at the Sorbonne and constructed his own "university" through reading, through friendships (notably with a group of Yugoslav artists and thinkers), and through La Ligne générale (1958–60), a cultural movement aiming to renew Marxism from within. Perec did two years' military service in a parachute regiment (1958–59), then worked briefly in market research before spending a year at Sfax, in Tunisia. From 1961 until 1978 Perec was employed as a research librarian in a neurophysiological laboratory.

Many of Perec's early writings have been lost. Every one of his published works is an exercise in a different style. *Les Choses. Une histoire des années soixante* (Prix Renaudot, 1965; transl. as *Things, A Story of the Sixties*, 1990), is an ironical portrait of a generation bewildered by the arrival of prosperity, written in a deceptively simple language intentionally echoing the style of Flaubert's *Sentimental Education;* it made Perec famous as the "sociologist" of his own generation. Perec's following works were not in the same vein and were less widely read until the 1980s. *Quel Petit Vélo a guidon chromé au fond de la cour?* (1966) is a mock epic. *Un homme qui dort* (1967; transl. as *A Man Asleep*, 1990) is a second-person narrative of adolescent depression in which the technique of collage is used almost invisibly (a film version was made by Perec and Bernard Queysanne in 1974), and *La Disparition* (1968) is a murder mystery novel written under the constraint of a lipogram on e. Perec became well known in Germany for a series of radio plays: *Die Maschine* (1968, with Eugen Helmle), *L'Augmentation* (1969), *Tagstimmen* (1971, with Eugen Helmle and Philippe Drogoz), etc. He also performed remarkable "alphabetic exercises" as a member of Ou Li Po (the "Workshop for Potential Literature" founded by Raymond Queneau) including palindromes, univocalics, and heterogrammatic poetry (*Alphabets*, 1976).

Perec's incessant formal innovations accompany a lifelong concern with autobiography. *La Boutique obscure* (1973) is a record of his dreams; *Espèces d'espaces* (1974) is a personal reflection on his relationship to spatiality; *Je me souviens* (1978; stage adaptation by Sami Frey, 1988) a record of "shared" memories. *W ou le souvenir d'enfance* (1975, incorporating earlier texts, transl. as *W or The Memory of Childhood*, 1988) is Perec's most direct approach to self-description and self-analysis, conducted by unusual means. It consists of two apparently unrelated texts printed in alternating chapters, which converge on a common image, that of the concentration camp. Its deceptive design is to make the reader share some of the inextinguishable anguish and guilt of a childhood survivor of the Holocaust.

La Vie mode d'emploi (Prix Medicis, 1978; transl. as *Life, A User's Manual*, 1987) is Perec's masterpiece, "the last great event in the history of the novel" (Italo Calvino). It describes the contents of a block of flats at a frozen moment of time – June 23, 1975, towards eight in the evening – together with the life-histories of the characters and the objects (and even the cats) caught in the novelist-painter's artfully calculated frame. Its success allowed Perec to live thereafter as a full-time writer. He pursued two projects related to the understanding of his own Jewish background: a "genealogical saga" of his family (unfinished), and a television essay on Ellis Island, as a kind of "alternative autobiography" (with Robert Bober, 1979–80). He also produced a film, published a novella about a forged painting representing many other paintings, each of which refer in some way to *Life, A User's Manual* (*Un Cabinet d'Amateur*, 1979), and continued to provide crosswords for the weekly magazine *Le Point*. After 1978, Perec also traveled widely, to Poland, America, Italy, and Australia, where he spent one month as writer in residence at the University of Queensland. He died, leaving many works incomplete. His unfinished "literary thriller" *53 Jours* (*53 Days*) was published in 1989. Other works that have appeared in translation are *Ellis Island*, *A Void* (a novel written without the letter "e"), and *Three by Perec*.

Perec's standing in French and world literature has not ceased to grow since 1982, as the originality and underlying coherence of his extremely diverse output comes into clearer focus.

BIBLIOGRAPHY: Benabou, "Georges Perec et la judeité," in: *Cahiers Georges Perec 1* (1985); C. Burgelin, *Georges Perec* (1988). **ADD. BIBLIOGRAPHY:** D. Bellos, *Georges Peres. A Life in Words* (1993).

[David Bellos]

PEREFERKOVICH, NEHEMIAH (1871–1940), Russian Orientalist and philologist. Born in Stavropol, Caucasus, son of a *Cantonist soldier, he studied Oriental languages at the University of St. Petersburg. Beginning in 1893 he published essays, critical articles, and studies in *Voskhod* and other Russian-Jewish and Russian newspapers, under his own name or under the pseudonyms Al-Gavvas or Vostochnik.

He also wrote on Jewish history and literature for Russian encyclopedias and for the *Yevreyskaya Entsiklopediya*, of which he was an editor. His principal scientific work was a translation of the Mishnah, the Tosefta, the *Mekhilta, Sifra*, and the tractate *Berakhot* of the Babylonian Talmud into Russian (8 vols., 1898–1912), a popular work which was widely used by Jews and Christians alike. He also wrote popular books in Russian on the problems of Judaism, the Talmud, and the Shulḥan Arukh, as well as a textbook on Jewish history and religion for Jewish pupils attending Russian secondary schools. After the Revolution he settled in Riga, where he taught in local secondary and high schools and contributed articles to the Jewish and Hebrew press on public issues. He dedicated himself to research on the Yiddish language, and wrote a dictionary of Hebrew words and expressions in Yiddish (*Hebraizmen in Yidish*, 1929, 1931[2]).

BIBLIOGRAPHY: Rejzen, Leksikon, 2 (1927), 944–6; LNYL, 7 (1968), 200–1.

[Yehuda Slutsky]

PEREIRA DE PAIVA, MOSES (17th century), Sephardi communal leader in Amsterdam. In 1686 he was head of a delegation to the Jewish community of *Cochin (India), sent to collect data on its history and way of life. He was warmly received by the leaders of the "white" Jewish community and his visit led to a close contact between the Jews of Amsterdam and Cochin, which lasted until Dutch rule over Malabar ended in 1795. On his return, he published *Notisias dos Judeos de Cochim* (Amsterdam, 1687), a comprehensive report on the origin, economic situation, traditions, and communal organizations of the "white" Jews, naming all the householders and particularly mentioning David Rahabi. He also deals with the "black" Jews, whom he calls the Malabar Jews, though according to him they are Jews only by religion and not by race.

BIBLIOGRAPHY: M. Pereira de Paiva, *Notisias dos Judeos de Cochim*, ed. by M.B. Amzalak (1923), introd.; *Souvenir Volume of Cochin Synagogue…* (Cochin, 1968), 31–50; Steinscheider, Cat Bod, 2723.

[Walter Joseph Fischel]

PÉREIRE, ÉMILE (Jacob; 1800–1875) and **ISAAC** (1806–1880), French economists, bankers, and journalists. The Péreire brothers were the grandsons of Jacob Rodrigues *Péreire. Born and educated in Bordeaux, both became prominent disciples of Claude Henri de Rouvroy, Comte de St. Simon, and his socioeconomic system. After the dispersion of the St. Simonians, the Péreires turned to political and economic writing, and during the 1830s their articles in *Le Globe, Le Temps, and Le Journal des Débats* attracted much attention. Emile's emphasis on railway development led James de *Rothschild to finance the Chemin de Fer du Nord and half a dozen other railway lines. In 1848 the Péreires gave up their cooperation with the Rothschilds and joined the *Foulds. Four years later, together with the Foulds and many other leading French financiers and politicians, they formed the Credit Mobilier, France's first modern investment bank. After spectacular initial successes the bank's fortunes sank with the Second Empire, and it was liquidated in 1867. Both Péreires were members of the French parliament and active in Jewish affairs.

In 1832 Emile edited the St. Simonian *Globe* and, from 1832 to 1835, *Le National*, the organ of the republican party. A boulevard in Paris was named after him. Isaac wrote *Leçons sur l'industrie et les finances* (1832), *Le rôle de la Banque de France* (1864), *Principe de la constitution des banques* (1865), and *La question réligieuse* (1878). In the late 1870s Isaac published his own paper, *La Liberté*, in which he advanced his political and industrial views. Isaac's son EUGENE (1831–1908), a civil engineer, railway administrator, and banker, was a member of the Chamber of Deputies and active in Jewish affairs. He inherited his grandfather's interest in the education of deaf-mutes.

BIBLIOGRAPHY: C.H. Castille, *Les Frères Péreire* (1861); M. Aycard, *Histoire du Crédit Mobilier* (1867); B. Mehrens, *Die Entstehung und Entwicklung der grossen franzoesischen Kreditinstitute* (1911); P.H. Emden, *Money Powers of Europe* (1938), index; H. Spiel, *Fanny von Arnstein, oder Die Emanzipation* (1962).

[Joachim O. Ronall]

PÉREIRE (Pereira), JACOB RODRIGUES (1715–1780), French educator of deaf-mutes and communal leader. Péreire was born into a Marrano family in Berlanga, Spain. After his father's death, Péreire was taken by his mother to France, and they returned to Judaism. Péreire's studies in anatomy and physiology helped him in his work as the first French educator of congenital deaf-mutes. He taught deaf-mutes to communicate by articulating sounds and lip-reading rather than by the use of signs. He strove to educate pupils, regardless of their social class, to the maximum level of ability in relation to their probable future. His achievements brought him great distinction and a grant by King Louis XV. Other educators were inspired by Péreire's work to efforts along similar lines, the best known of them being Edouard Séguin, a pioneer in the education of deaf-mutes. Péreire also gained distinction in other fields. A mathematical invention won him an annual pension and in 1753 his proposals for increasing the speed of sailing vessels received honorable mention. Péreire was active in Jewish life. In 1749 he became the voluntary counselor of the Sephardi community in Paris, and in 1761 was appointed officially to the position. Péreire himself wrote little, but his thought, as transmitted by Séguin, has received recognition in the educational writings of the 20th century. His works comprise a study of the articulation and vocabulary of a Tahitian native (1772) and *Observations sur les Sourds et Muets*, published by the Académie Royale des Sciences in 1778. His grandsons were Emile and Isaac *Péreire.

BIBLIOGRAPHY: W. Boyd, *From Locke to Montessori* (1914), 36–41; J. Fynne, *Montessori and her Inspirers* (1924), 13–62; E. Séguin, *Jacob Rodrigues Péreire…* (Fr., 1847); F. Hément, *Jacob Rodrigues Péreire…* (Fr., 1875); F. Manuel Alves, *Os judeus no distrito de Braganca* (1925), xcviii–civ; La Rochelle, in: REJ, 4 (1882), 150ff.; L. Kahn, *Les Juifs à Paris* (1889), 52, 54, 58–59.

[William W. Brickman]

PEREK SHIRAH (Heb. פֶּרֶק שִׁירָה; "chapter of song"), a short, anonymous tract containing a collection of hymnic sayings in praise of the creator placed in the mouths of His creatures. All creation, except man, is represented – the natural and supernatural orders, inanimate nature, the heavens and all their hosts, the world of plants, and the world of animals – each according to its kind. Together the hymns comprise a kind of cosmic song of praise by the whole of creation. They are set in a prose midrashic framework imparting a firm literary structure to a collection that in itself lacks textual continuity. Most of the "hymns" are in fact biblical verses, the greater part of them citations from Psalms. At the end of *Perek Shirah* there are pseudepigraphic additions, apparently of a later date, praising the one who says *Perek Shirah*. The connection between many of these texts and the creature uttering the praise in each hymn is not clear. The anthropomorphism of creation in the composition, at first sight totally foreign to the spirit of Judaism, has, from the first references in literature until the most recent, given rise to violent opposition and accusations of forgery. Consequently there have been various attempts, some apologetic, to deny the work's apparent simplicity in favor of a philosophical-allegorical, talmudic-didactic, or kabbalistic-mystical interpretation.

The text has been preserved in several manuscripts, including *genizah* fragments, the earliest dating from about the tenth century. The versions differ considerably in content and arrangement, and classification of the manuscripts reveals the existence of three distinct traditions: Oriental, Sephardi, and Ashkenazi. The first printed edition, with a commentary by Moses b. Joseph de *Trani (printed as an appendix to his *Beit ha-Elohim*; Venice, 1576), was followed by dozens of corrupt editions, generally accompanied by commentaries.

Perek Shirah is first mentioned in a polemical work of *Salmon b. Jeroham, a Jerusalem Karaite of the first half of the tenth century. References to it can be found in European sources at the end of the 12th century, and from the 13th century onward various interpretations are known, mainly kabbalistic. It would seem that from the outset *Perek Shirah* was intended as a liturgical text, as also seems apparent from the pseudepigraphic mystical additions. In the early Ashkenazi manuscripts it was included in *maḥzorim* and collections of special prayers in close proximity to prayers issuing from circles of *Ḥasidei Ashkenaz. The spread of the later custom of reciting *Perek Shirah* as a prayer and its inclusion in printed *siddurim* was mainly due to the influence of the Safed kabbalists.

Talmudic and midrashic sources contain hymns on the creation usually based on homiletic expansions of metaphorical descriptions and personifications of the created world in the Bible. The explicitly homiletic background of some of the hymns in *Perek Shirah* indicates a possible connection between the rest and tannaitic and amoraic homiletics, and suggests a hymnal index to well-known, but mostly unpreserved, homiletics. The origin of this work, the period of its composition, and its significance may be deduced from literary parallels. A tannaitic source in the tractate *Ḥagigah* of the Jerusalem (Ḥag. 2:1, 77a–b) and Babylonian Talmud (Ḥag. 12a–14b), on hymns of nature associated with apocalyptic visions and with the teaching of *ma'aseh bereshit*, serves as a key to *Perek Shirah*'s close spiritual relationship with this literature. Parallels to it can be found in apocalyptic literature, in mystic layers in talmudic literature, in Jewish mystical prayers surviving in fourth-century Greek Christian compositions, in *Heikhalot* literature, and in *Merkabah mysticism. The affinity of *Perek Shirah* with *Heikhalot* literature, which abounds in hymns, can be noted in the explicitly mystic introduction to the seven crowings of the cock – the only non-hymnal text in the collection – and the striking resemblance between the language of the additions and that of **Shi'ur Komah* and other examples of this literature. In *Seder Rabbah de-Bereshit*, a *Heikhalot* tract, in conjunction with the description of *ma'aseh bereshit*, there is a clear parallel to *Perek Shirah's* praise of creation and to the structure of its hymns. The concept reflected in this source is based on a belief in the existence of angelic archetypes of created beings who mediate between God and His creation, and express their role through singing hymns. As the first interpretations of *Perek Shirah* also bear witness to its mystic character and angelologic significance, it would appear to be an apocalyptic chapter of *Heikhalot* literature.

Some parallels to *Perek Shirah* exist outside Hebrew literature: the Testament of Adam (preserved in Syriac, Greek, and in later translations), which contains horaries of praise by the whole of creation framed in an apocalyptic angelologic vision similar to that in *Seder Rabbah de-Bereshit*, the Greek *Physiologus* of the second century, which reveals structural and formal parallels to *Perek Shirah*; and Islamic oral traditions (*Ḥadīth*) and *Ikhwān al-Ṣafāʾ* ("Sincere Brethren"), writings on the praise of created beings.

BIBLIOGRAPHY: M. Steinschneider, in: HB, 13 (1875), 103–6; Ginzberg, Legends, 1 (1909), 42–46; 5 (1925), 60–62; Scholem, Mysticism, 62: M. Beit-Arié, *"Perek Shirah,"* critical ed., 2 vols. (Ph.D. thesis, Hebrew University of Jerusalem, 1966). **ADD. BIBLIOGRAPHY:** J.M. Baumgarten, in: RQ, 36 (1978), 575–78.

[Malachi Beit-Arie]

PERELMAN, CHAIM (1912–1984), Belgian philosopher. Perelman, who was born in Warsaw, Poland, became professor of logic and metaphysics at the Université Libre in Brussels in 1944. He was also dean of the faculty of philosophy and letters and director of the Ecoles des Sciences de l'Education. Many of his early writings dealt with mathematical logic. In later years he was especially concerned with the concept of justice and with forms of discursive reasoning other than deductive reasoning.

A full statement of his theory of argument is presented in the two-volume *Traité de l'Argumentation* (1958), published jointly with Mme. L. Olbrechts-Tyteca. Some of his other major works are *De l'Arbitraire dans la Connaissance* (1933), *De la Justice* (1945), *Justice et Raison* (1963), and *Rhétorique et Philosophie* (1952). He published numerous articles in philosophical journals. Perelman was secretary-general of the Fédération Internationale des Sociétés de Philosophie, president of the Société Belge de Philosophie and of the Société Belge de Logique et Philosophie des Sciences. He was a member of the board of governors of the Hebrew University, and the secretary-general of the Belgian Friends of the Hebrew University. *Justice, Law and Argument* (essays) and *The Realm of Rhetoric* appeared in English translation in 1980.

[Myriam M. Malinovich]

PERELMAN, RONALD OWEN (1943–), U.S. financier. To many people, Perelman symbolized the corporate-raider rogue of the 1980s, a highly visible and aggressive businessman who achieved power and immense wealth by buying and selling companies. His strategy usually involved the issuance of "junk bonds," high-yield, high-risk instruments often likely to default. His private life – his extravagant homes, multiple marriages, and a bitter child-custody case – was sometimes as high-profile and controversial as his professional deeds. At the same time, Perelman, a devout Jew, contributed millions to Jewish-related causes, including the Ronald O. Perelman Institute for Judaic Studies, endowed in 1995 at Princeton University in New Jersey.

Perelman began his career in Philadelphia, where he was raised. In 1966, after earning an undergraduate degree at the University of Pennsylvania and an M.B.A. at the University's Wharton School of Business, he went to work for his father, Raymond Perelman, the owner of a sheet-metal business. When he was 35, he moved to New York to strike out on his own. In 1979, with the aid of a $1.7 million loan from his first wife, a Philadelphia heiress, he purchased 40 per cent of Cohen Hatfield Industries, a jewelry store operator. He stripped the company of its non-performing assets and within a short time had the leverage to acquire MacAndrews & Forbes, a holding company, for $45.7 million. He sold its cyclical textile business, but kept its two biggest generators of cash, a licorice-extract business and a chocolate company, selling the latter in 1986 for $45 million. By issuing millions of dollars in junk bonds, Perelman was also able to buy a series of diverse companies, including Consolidated Cigars, Movie Labs, Technicolor, Video Corp. and Pantry Pride. In 1986, he completed one of the decade's most bitterly contested takeovers, acquiring 83% of Revlon, the venerable cosmetics and fragrance giant founded by Charles H. *Revson in 1923. Revlon, once dominant in the beauty business, had been struggling for years and Perelman saw an opportunity to get it at a price lower than its potential. Opposed by Revlon's board, he fought a long and contentious court battle and was able to win the company in a $1.8 billion leveraged buyout, becoming chairman. Reversing the decline of the fading but well-known firm proved daunting. Already beset by thinning margins, increasing competition, a loss of department store business, and an ill-fated plunge into health care products, Revlon had accumulated close to $1 billion in debt, which Perelman assumed when he took over. A publicly owned firm when Perelman acquired it, Revlon went private in 1987, remaining so until 1996, when it was again listed on the New York Stock Exchange. That did not keep it from falling even deeper into debt and Perelman was forced to use hundreds of millions of dollars of his own money to keep Revlon afloat. His personal fortune, once estimated at $6.5 billion, had fallen to half that figure by 2004, when Revlon's debt load was approaching $2 billion. At the same time, the company – which had not recorded a profit since 1997 – was embarking on a program aimed at halving its debt in two years.

[Mort Sheinman (2nd ed.)]

PERELMAN, SIDNEY JOSEPH (1904–1979), U.S. humorist. Perelman was born in Brooklyn, but grew up in Providence, Rhode Island, and studied at Brown University, where he edited a humorous magazine. He began his professional career in 1925 as a contributor to the humor magazines *Judge* and *College Humor* and began to write for the movies in 1930. From 1934 he published amusing or satirical pieces in the *New Yorker*, to which he contributed steadily for more than 30 years.

Perelman's versatility as a humorist extended to the theater. Among his better known comedies are *One Touch of Venus* (1943), written in collaboration with Ogden Nash, and *The Beauty Part* (1963). His work for the movies included scripts for the *Marx Brothers, and his screenplay for the movie *Around the World in Eighty Days* won him the New York Critics' Award as the Best Screen Writer of 1956. He also wrote three amusing travel books: *Westward Ha!* (1948), *The Swiss Family Perelman* (1950), and *Eastward Ha!* (1977). Other works include *Dawn Ginsbergh's Revenge* (1929); *Strictly from Hunger* (1937); *Look Who's Talking* (1940); *Crazy Like a Fox* (1944); *The Best of S.J. Perelman* (1947); *Listen to the Mocking Bird* (1949); *The Road to Miltown; or, Under the Spreading Atrophy* (1957); *The Rising Gorge* (1961); *Chicken Inspector No. 23* (1966); *Baby, It's Cold Inside* (1970); *Vinegar Puss* (1975); *The Last Laugh* (1981); and *That Old Gang O'Mine: The Early and Essential S.J. Perelman* (1984).

The bulk of Perelman's work was made up of the relatively brief *New Yorker* pieces. A continuous sparkle of fantastic wit animates his writing, whether it be burlesque, parody, or satire. Perelman exploited all the possibilities of the English language for comic effects, especially through the devices of pun and anticlimax. With mingled compassion and mockery, he pointed up the weakness and folly of the individual as a puppet and victim of 20th-century society and its mass media. In a 1975 interview with the *Philadelphia Inquirer*, Perelman commented on the demise of the light satiric essay as well as the tempering of his own comic tone in his later years: "It is not easy to satirize the absurd when the absurd has become official."

BIBLIOGRAPHY: N.W. Yates, *American Humorist* (1964), 331–50; Paris Review, *Writers at Work*, second series (1963), 241–56; S.J. Kunitz, *Twentieth Century Authors*, first supplement (1955), incl. bibl. **ADD. BIBLIOGRAPHY:** T. Teicholz (ed.), *Conversations with S.J. Perelman* (1995).

[Israel J. Kapstein / Robert L. DelBane (2nd ed.)]

PERELMANN, JEROHMAN JUDAH LEIB BEN SOLOMON ZALMAN (1835–1896), Lithuanian talmudist known as Ha-Gadol mi-Minsk ("the great scholar of Minsk"). Perelmann was born in Brest-Litovsk (Brisk), and in his youth he studied in Kovno at the yeshivah of Israel *Lipkin of Salant, where he was renowned as the "Brisk prodigy." In 1865 he was appointed rabbi of Seltso, in 1875 of Pruzhany, and in 1883 of Minsk, where he served until his death. He was one of the rabbis who supported the Ḥovevei Zion movement. His responsum about this matter was published in *Sinai* (6 (1940), 210–21). His *Or Gadol* (1924), consisting of responsa and studies mostly on *Even ha-Ezer,* together with a small portion on *Oraḥ Ḥayyim* and *Yoreh De'ah,* was published by his son Isaiah together with notes, glosses, and novellae. His *Or Gadol ve-Yitron ha-Or,* notes and novellae on the Mishnah, was published in the Romm Vilna edition of the Mishnah.

BIBLIOGRAPHY: B. Eisenstadt, *Rabbanei Minsk* (1898), 34, 62f.; D. Katz, *Tenu'at ha-Musar,* 2 (1959), 449–52; *Yahadut Lita,* 1 (1960), index; 3 (1967), 80f.; Habermann, in; *Aresheth*, 3 (1961), 135.

[Samuel Abba Horodezky]

PEREMYSHLYANY (Pol. **Przemyslany**), town in Lvov district, Ukraine. Peremyshlyany was part of Poland until the partition of 1772 when it was annexed by Austria. Regained by independent Poland in 1919, it belonged to the province of Tarnopol. In 1945 it was incorporated into Soviet Ukraine. The Jewish community was already active during the period of the *Council of the Four Lands and became particularly famous during the 18th and 19th centuries because of its dynasty of ḥasidic leaders. These included R. Aaron Leib of Peremyshlyany (d. in Ereẓ Israel, 1773) who was the son of R. Meir of Peremyshlyany, known as "the First" or "the Great"; both were disciples of *Israel b. Eliezer Ba'al Shem Tov. The son of R. Aaron Leib was R. Meir of *Peremyshlyany, one of the most outstanding personalities among the *ẓaddikim* of Galicia. The town expanded during the 19th century. In 1865 the combined population was about 2,200 and by 1921 there were 4,093 inhabitants, including 2,051 Jews. In the 1933 elections to the Jewish community council a Zionist delegate was elected president. The interest-free loan fund and the orphanage were among the most active welfare institutions. As a result of antisemitic agitation, a bomb was thrown into the *bet ha-midrash* in 1935.

[Shimshon Leib Kirshenboim]

Holocaust Period

The number of Jews had grown to nearly 6,000 in 1941 with the influx of refugees from the vicinity and from western Poland. The German forces arrived on July 1, 1941. Three days later they burned down the main synagogue and pushed a number of Jews into the flames. In the fall of 1941 kidnappings for labor camps in Kurowice and Jaktorow began. About 500 Jewish men were taken on Oct. 5, 1941, to Brzezina forest and murdered. In May 1942 a Gestapo official removed the inmates of the Jewish hospital and killed them. Other acts of terror continued at the end of July and in September until the end of 1942. Most of the victims were sent to *Belzec extermination camp. In August 1942 a ghetto was set up, to include Jews from *Glinyany and Swirz as well. On May 23, 1943, the ghetto was wiped out and the city declared **judenrein*.

After the war the Jewish community was not renewed in Peremyshlyany. A number of Jews who came out of the forests or from hiding, along with a number of returnees from the Soviet Union, came to their native town, but most emigrated either to Israel via Poland or to other countries abroad. In the late 1960s there were about five Jewish families in the town.

[Aharon Weiss]

PEREMYSHLYANY, MEIR BEN AARON LEIB OF (1780?–1850), ḥasidic *ẓaddik*. He was the grandson of R. Meir of Peremyshlyany, a disciple of *Israel b. Eliezer Ba'al Shem Tov (the Besht), who, according to a later ḥasidic tradition, assisted the Ba'al Shem Tov in his struggle against the *Frankists. R. Meir, who was born in Peremyshlyany, Galicia, was a disciple of Mordecai of Kremenets. In 1813, the year of his father's death, he became rabbi in Peremyshlyany and leader of the ḥasidic community there. As a result of a slander against him, he was compelled to leave for Lipkany, Bessarabia, where he held rabbinical office. This episode is mentioned by his Ḥasidim and in a document of the Austrian authorities of 1827. Meir lived in Lipkany for three years and became involved in a dispute with the Ḥasidim of Abraham Joshua *Heschel of Apta (Opatow). To this may be added the testimony of Abraham (Dov) Baer *Gottlober according to which Meir was always accustomed to live in the border towns, and that he changed his place of residence several times. From Lipkany he returned to Peremyshlyany and in 1843 he moved to Nikolayev, where he lived for the last seven years of his life.

In 1826 Joseph *Perl applied to the Austrian authorities for permission to reprint the *Sefer Vikku'aḥ* (of Israel *Loebl, 1798). At the end of this volume was a list of ḥasidic leaders, among whom was the name of Meir of Shebsh. Perl changed the name to Meir Shebseir, in accordance with the reading in a manuscript. The Austrian censorship wrongly identified Meir Shebseir with Meir of Peremyshlyany and as a result ordered an enquiry as to whether he and the other ḥasidic rabbis were in opposition to the government, encouraging their followers to disobey the law, but the results of the investigation were negative. In 1839 the police of Lvov submitted to the government an indictment against "miracle-workers," which contained, among others, the name of Meir of Peremyshlyany. The government ordered an investigation, the results of which are unknown.

Meir was on friendly terms with Israel of *Ruzhin, whom he assisted in crossing the border when the latter was persecuted by the authorities, and Solomon b. Judah Aaron *Kluger of Brody, who eulogized Meir upon his death. In *Megalleh Temirin* by Joseph Perl some of Meir's actions are described with derision, e.g., that he engaged in the healing of the sick and childless women. Meir was accustomed to spend his money freely among the poor, as related by both his Ḥasidim and a *maskil*, Dr. Solomon Rubin, opposed to Ḥasidism. He was known for his strange behavior, which his Ḥasidim interpreted as being merely external and his opponents as insanity. He gained popularity as a *ẓaddik* and had many followers. Reports of the miracles which he performed were at first circulated orally and later in print.

Meir made no original contribution to ḥasidic doctrine, nor did he write any halakhic or homiletical works. After his death, however, his followers collected his teachings which were included in various works or handed down from hearsay; among them the following three works in Yiddish: *Ma'aseh Nora me-ha-Ẓaddik... R. Meir mi-Peremyshlani, Eyn Emese Mayse fun R. Meir' mi-Peremyshlany*, and *Shivḥei R. Meir*.

They were collected and published in *Divrei Me'ir* (1909), *Or ha-Me'ir* (1926), and *Margenita de-Rabbi Meir* (ed. Margalioth, 1926). A *Seder Hakkafot* ("Order of the *Hakkafot* [for Simḥat Torah]," 1891) which he composed was also published.

BIBLIOGRAPHY: I. Layfer, *Tiferet Maharam* (1958[2]); I. Berger, *Eser Atarot* (1910), 37–56; M.H. Brawer, *Zikhronot Av u-Veno* (1966), 15–16; M. Ben-Yeḥezkel, *Sefer ha-Ma'asiyyot*, 1 (1968[3]), 108–13; 2 (1968[3]), 301–3; 4 (1968[3]), 85–87; 5 (1968[3]), 420–4; 6 (1968[3]), 269–72; A.B. Gottlober, *Zikhronot mi-Ymei Neuray*, in: *Ha-Boker Or*, 5 (1880), 310; 6 (1881), 162, 168–9, 289; Horodezky, Ḥasidut, index; R. Mahler, *Ha-Ḥasidut ve-ha-Haskalah* (1961), index; Ch. Shmeruk, in: *Zion*, 21 (1956), 94.

[Zeev Gries]

PERES (Persky), SHIMON (1923–), Israeli statesman, chairman of the Israel Labor Party 1977–92, 1995–97, and 2003–05, member of the Knesset since the Fourth Knesset; prime minister of Israel 1984–86 and 1995–96. Born in Vishneva, in Belorussia, Peres immigrated with his family to Palestine in 1934. He attended the Ge'ulah School in Tel Aviv and the Agricultural School at Ben-Shemen. In 1940 he was one of the founders of kibbutz Alummot, and served as secretary of Tenu'at ha-No'ar ha-Oved ve-ha-Lomed youth movement. Peres started to work with David *Ben-Gurion and Levi *Eshkol in the *Haganah command in 1947, and continued to serve them after the establishment of the state. In 1949 he was appointed head of the Ministry of Defense mission to the U.S., which was engaged in purchasing military equipment. In 1950 he was appointed temporary head of the naval services in the IDF. In 1952 he was appointed deputy director general of the Ministry of Defense and the following year director general. In 1955, after it became known that President Gamal Abdel Nasser of Egypt had signed a major arms deal with Czechoslovakia, Peres helped forge close ties with France, which also viewed Nasser as an enemy. In 1959 he was assigned the task of setting up the nuclear reactor in Dimonah. He also played a major role in rehabilitating Israel's arms industries, and advanced the development of the Israel Aircraft Industry (IAI).

Peres was first elected to the Fourth Knesset in 1959 on the Mapai list, and was appointed deputy minister of defense – a position he held until 1965. In that year he left Mapai; together with Ben-Gurion, Moshe *Dayan, and others, he was one of the founders of the *Rafi party, and was appointed its secretary general. When Prime Minister Golda *Meir established her government after the elections to the Seventh Knesset, Peres was first appointed minister without portfolio responsible for the economic development of the occupied territories, but in December 1969 was promoted to minister of immigrant absorption. The following year he was appointed minister of communications. In 1974 he served as minister of information in the short-lived government formed by Meir. After Meir's resignation he failed in his first contest against Yitzhak *Rabin for the Labor Party leadership. In the government formed by Rabin in 1974 he served as minister of defense. As minister of defense he played a major role in reorganizing the IDF in the aftermath of the Yom Kippur War. In this period he was considered more hawkish than Rabin, and actually gave in to the newly founded *Gush Emunim, permitting the permanent settlement of Elon Moreh. On February 23, 1977, Peres once again lost in a contest for the Labor Party leadership, but following Rabin's resignation, on April 7, 1977, became party chairman. Under his leadership the Labor-Mapam Alignment suffered a bitter defeat in the elections to the Ninth Knesset in 1977, and for the first time since the establishment of the state the *Ḥerut movement, within the framework of the Likud, gained power. In opposition Peres acted to strengthen the ties of the Labor Party abroad, especially within the framework of the Socialist International, and in 1978 was elected as one of this organization's vice presidents. Peres led the Alignment in opposition until 1984. As a result of the draw in the results of the elections to the Eleventh Knesset in 1984, a National Unity Government was established with the Likud, based on parity, and a rotation in the premiership. Under the coalition agreement Peres served as prime minister in the years 1984–86, while Likud leader Yitzhak *Shamir served as vice premier and minister for foreign affairs. In the years 1986–88 the two leaders switched positions. In April 1987 Peres concluded the London Agreement with King Hussein of Jordan, which dealt with the convening of a Middle East peace conference, but the agreement was not approved by the inner cabinet in which the Alignment and the Likud were equally represented, and at the end of 1987 the first Intifada broke out. In the National Unity Government formed by Shamir in 1988, after the elections to the Twelfth Knesset, Peres was appointed minister of finance. In March 1990, following the stalemate in the peace process, Peres decided to bring down the government in a vote on a motion of no confidence, but after the government fell, in what Rabin was later to term the "rotten trick," he failed to form an alternative government, and in June 1990 Shamir established a narrow government without Labor.

Following Peres' failure to establish a government, Rabin announced that he would once again contest the Labor Party leadership, and on February 19, 1992, won the leadership contest, and replaced Peres as leader of the Labor Party. In the elections to the Thirteenth Knesset held later that year, Rabin led the Labor Party to its first clear-cut victory since the 1973 elections, and in the government that he formed Peres was appointed vice premier and minister for foreign affairs. In cooperation with Rabin Peres approved the Oslo Process initiated by his deputy Yossi *Beilin, which led to Israel's recognition of the PLO and the signing of the Declaration of Principles on September 13, 1993. Together with Rabin and PLO chairman Yasser Arafat, he received the Nobel Prize for Peace on December 10, 1994. Following Rabin's assassination on November 4, 1995, Peres was appointed prime minister and minister of defense. In the first direct election of the prime minister held simultaneously with the elections to the Fourteenth Knesset in 1996, Peres was defeated by Binyamin *Netanyahu by a very small margin. In 1996, following the elections, he established the Peres Center for Peace, designed to further the implementation of the peace agreements by means of social and economic cooperation.

In June 1997, Peres was replaced by Ehud *Barak as chairman of the Labor Party. Following Barak's victory over Netanyahu in the direct election of the prime minister held simultaneously with the elections to the Fifteenth Knesset in 1999, Peres was appointed minister for regional cooperation, but was largely ignored by Barak in his political moves. In 2000, following the resignation of Ezer *Weizman from the presidency, Peres was a candidate for the position, but lost to the Likud's Moshe *Katzav. Following Barak's defeat by Ariel *Sharon in the next direct election of the prime minister, held in February 2001, Sharon invited the Labor Party to join his government, and Peres, who once again served as acting chairman of the party, was offered the post of deputy prime minister and minister for foreign affairs. However, Labor left the government in November 2002, and Amram Mitzna was elected chairman of the Labor Party. Peres continued to serve in the Sixteenth Knesset in opposition, and after Mitzna's resignation from the leadership of the party, once again became acting chairman of the party. In January 2005, after all of Sharon's coalition partners left the government, Labor once again joined the government, and Peres was appointed vice premier and minister for regional cooperation. In 2005, Amir *Peretz scored an upset victory over Peres for the Labor Party chairmanship and Peres switched allegiance to support Prime Minister Ariel Sharon, who established a new party, Kadimah.

Among his numerous writings are *From These Men: Seven Portraits* (1979); *The New Middle East* (1994); *Battling for Peace: Memoirs*, edited by David Landau (1995); and *The Imaginary Voyage: With Theodor Herzl in Israel* (1999).

BIBLIOGRAPHY: Y. Livni, *Ha-Mahapekhah, Ha-Mada'im ve-ha-Ḥazon ha-Ḥevrati: Al Utopia Re'alit, Siḥah bi-Shnayim, Shimon Peres ve-Yiẓhak Livni* (1984); M. Golan, *The Road to Peace: A Biography of Shimon Peres* (1989); M. Keren, *Professionals Against Populism: The Peres Government and Democracy* (1995); O. Azulai-Datz, *Ha-Ish she-Lo Yada le-Naẓe'aḥ: Shimon Peres be-Malkodet Sisyphus* (1996); Y. Kotler, *Ha-Zarzir ve-ha-Orev: Ariel Sharon ve-Shimon Peres Kemot Shehem* (2002); H. Misgav, *Lo Otto ha-Yam: Siḥot im Shimon Peres* (2004).

[Susan Hattis Rolef (2nd ed.)]

PERETZ, ABRAHAM (1771–1833), one of the first maskilim in Russia and a leader of the Jewish community. Son of the rabbi of Lubartow, Peretz married the daughter of wealthy Joshua *Zeitlin of Shklov. He was a fellow-student of J.L. *Nevakhovich, and at the end of the 18th century he settled in St. Petersburg, where he became the protégé of Prince Potëmkin. He made his fortune in commerce and shipbuilding and earned the title of commercial adviser from Czar Paul I. Making connections with the Russian upper classes, he was on familiar terms with Minister Speranski. Peretz maintained contact with the Berlin *maskilim* and was among the subscribers of *Ha-Me'assef*. He also took part in the work of the Committee for the Drafting of Jewish Legislation (1802), presenting various memoranda to the committee. He assisted Jewish *shtadlanim* who came to the capital and encouraged Nevakhovich to write his Russian pamphlet *Vopl dshcheri yudeyskoy*. He lost his fortune as a result of unsuccessful contracts with the army during the Napoleonic invasion of Russia (1812). In 1813 he divorced his wife, converting to Christianity along with his son Gregory (Hirsch), and married a German woman.

Peretz's son GREGORY (1788–1855) received his early education in the house of his grandfather Joshua Zeitlin. In 1803 he rejoined his father in St. Petersburg and received an important position in government administration. From 1820 to 1822 he was a member of a secret society which sought to introduce reforms into the Russian government. Among other projects he also conceived of the establishment of a "Society for the Liberation of the Jews Dispersed in Russia, and even in Europe, and their Settlement in Crimea, or even in the Orient, as a Unified Nation." After the revolt of the *Decembrists (1825) he was imprisoned and banished to northern Russia. Twenty years later (1845) he received authorization to leave for Odessa. Of Abraham's other sons, mention should be made of ALEXANDER, a mining engineer who played an important role in the industrial development of the Ural Mountains. Another son, YEGOR, was a member of the National Council; his diary (publ. 1927) contains important material on the discussions of the Jewish problem in the council during the early 1800s. A great-grandson of Gregory, VLADIMIR (1870–1936), was a historian of Russian and Ukrainian literature and theater and a member of the Russian Academy of Sciences. Together with his brother LEV, Peretz wrote a monograph entitled *Dekabrist Grigori Abramovich Peretz* (1926).

BIBLIOGRAPHY: S.L. Zitron, *Shtadlonim* (Yid., 1927), 53–67; S. Ginsburg, *Meshumodim in Tsarishn Rusland*, 9 (1946), 34–53.

[Yehuda Slutsky]

PERETZ, AMIR (1952–), Israeli politician, chairman of the New Histadrut and the Israel Labor Party, member of the Knesset since the Twelfth Knesset. Peretz was born in Bozar in Morocco, and immigrated with his family to Israel in 1956. The family settled in the development town of *Sederot that was established in 1955. His parents both worked for kibbutz-owned industries. He was educated at Beit Ḥinukh in Sha'ar ha-Negev, and at the high school in Sederot. Peretz had hoped for a career in the IDF, but after he crushed his leg in training, and a prolonged rehabilitation period, was forced to leave active military service with the rank of captain. After leaving the IDF Peretz joined the *Israel Labor Party, and unlike most of the young local leaders of Oriental origin (such as Moshe *Katzav of Kiryat Malakhi, David Magen of Kiryat Gat, and Meir *Sheetrit of Yavneh), was also an active member of the Israeli peace movement.

Peretz was elected head of the local council of Sederot in 1983. As head of the local council he acted to extract industries to his town, to change the nature of the relationship between Sederot and the neighboring kibbutzim, and to build a new community center. He resigned his position after being elected to the Twelfth Knesset on the Labor Alignment list, because the Labor Party advocated that Knesset members should not serve simultaneously in other public positions, except secretary general of the Histadrut. After entering the Knesset Peretz soon joined a group of young Laborites that included Haim *Ramon, Yossi *Beilin, and Avraham *Burg, who represented themselves as the future leadership of the Israel Labor Party. He was at first a member of the prestigious Knesset Foreign Affairs and Security Committee, but after the Labor Party went into opposition in March 1990, handed his seat over to a more senior member, while joining the State Control Committee and Labor and Welfare Committee. In the Thirteenth Knesset he was chairman of the Labor and Welfare Committee. In 1994 he ran in primaries in the Labor Party as candidate for secretary general of the Histadrut – a position he had always dreamed of holding – in order to introduce major reforms to save the ailing trade union federation from disintegration, but lost to Haim Haberfeld. When Ramon decided to run on an independent list against Haberfeld, Peretz joined him, and when at the end of 1995, after the assassination of Yitzhak *Rabin, Ramon returned to serve in the government under Shimon *Peres, Peretz became acting chairman of the New Histadrut, a position he continued to hold until elected chairman of the party in 2005. Prior to the elections to the Fifteenth Knesset, in March 1999, being disappointed with the leadership of Ehud *Barak, Peretz and two additional members of the Labor parliamentary group broke away to form a new party called Am Eḥad, that claimed to represent the workers and old age pensioners. Am Eḥad, headed by Peretz, gained two seats in the Fifteenth Knesset and three in the Sixteenth. Am Eḥad joined the government formed by Ariel *Sharon in March 2001, but left it in March 2002. In the beginning of 2005 Peretz and another member of Am Eḥad rejoined the Labor Party. In the meantime, as chairman of the New Histadrut Peretz declared numerous general strikes over the issues of the erosion of welfare benefits and wages and the government's policy of privatization.

Peretz defeated Shimon Peres in the 2005 elections for the Labor Party chairmanship, following which he resigned as Histadrut chairman. In the 2006 general elections the Labor Party received 19 seats and Peretz became minister of defense in the government formed by Ehud *Olmert of Kadimah.

[Susan Hattis Rolef (2nd ed.)]

PERETZ, ISAAC LEIB (Yitskhok Leybush; 1852–1915), Yiddish and Hebrew author. Peretz was one of the three classic Yiddish writers – with S.Y. *Abramovitsh and *Sholem Aleichem – and the founder of Yiddish modernism. In the first decade of the 20th century he was at the center of an active literary circle in Warsaw. His closest friend was Jacob (Yankev) *Dineson, and he was a mentor to many other leading authors such as Sholem *Asch, H.D. *Nomberg, S. *An-ski, A. *Reisen, and Y.Y. *Trunk. He began writing in Hebrew but is more often remembered for his Yiddish fiction.

Peretz was born in Zamość, Poland, a relatively modern town known for its opposition to the ḥasidim. According to his memoirs, however, one of his early teachers may have been secretly ḥasidic. At about the age of 13, Peretz studied for a short time at yeshivot in Zamość and the nearby town of Sheversin. He was especially enthusiastic about his readings of Maimonides, whose *Mishneh Torah* influenced his concise Hebrew style. After Peretz gained access to a large private library, he avidly read Polish, Russian, German, and French books. The writings of Heinrich *Heine and Ludwig Börne had a lasting impact on Peretz's literary tastes. For secular learning he hoped to study at a gymnasium or at the rabbinical institute in Zhitomir, but his mother opposed these plans, and he did not receive a systematic education. While the middle-class family was traditional, his father's business travels brought him into broader contact with the outside world. When Peretz was about 19 he married Sarah, the daughter of Gabriel Judah Lichtenfeld, a respected Hebrew author. Peretz seems to have had more in common with his father-in-law than with his bride, whom he divorced a few years later. The two progeny of this marriage were Lucian, born in about 1874, and a book of Hebrew poems published together with Lichtenfeld in 1877.

Peretz lived in Warsaw in 1876, where he met Hebrew authors and started publishing Hebrew poems in *Ha-Shaḥar*, before returning to Zamość. It is significant that the poem "*Nagniel*," printed in A.B. Gottlober's *Ha-Boker Or* ("The Morning Light," 1876), alludes to Y.L. Gordon's poetry and criticizes the outmoded style of Hebrew *meliẓah*. (Even 20 years later, in a long article published in *Ha-Ẓefirah* – "*Ma haya Gordon, Balshan o Meshorer?*" ("What was Gordon, a Linguist or a Poet?") – Peretz continued to attack the neobiblical style of the Hebrew *maskilim*). Lichtenfeld and Peretz jointly published *Sippurim be-Shir ve-Shirim Shonim* ("Stories in Verse and Various Poems," 1877), a poetry collection that received little notice, though Peretz *Smolenskin and Reuven Asher *Braudes praised it. In spite of their initialing most of the poems separately or together, it is not always easy to determine the nature of their collaboration; the volume was signed by "Shenei Ba'alei Assufot" ("Two Compilers (or Authors, or Wise Men))," alluding both to Ecclesiastes 12:11 with A. Ibn Ezra's commentary and to a talmudic usage. The longer poems attributed to Peretz show both Heine's influence and Peretz's narrative inclinations. Joseph *Klausner and Samuel *Niger are among the few 20th century critics who recognized the importance of

Peretz's early poems, such as "*Ḥayei Mishorer Ivri*" ("The Life of a Hebrew Poet") and "*Ḥannah – Shir Sipuri*" ("Hannah – A Narrative Poem"). The first, while followed by the initials of both Peretz and Lichtenfeld, appears to be as much based on Peretz's biography as was his later Yiddish ballad "*Monish*." The second, initialed by Peretz alone, uses lyrical six-line stanzas (with the rhyme scheme ababcc) to tell a melodramatic tale. Later in life Peretz was embarrassed by having published *Sippurim be-Shir ve-Shirim Shonim*, because he doubted its value and perhaps also because some poems – probably by Lichtenfeld – lampoon ḥasidic rebbes.

Peretz remarried in 1878, with Helena Ringelbaum, and worked as a lawyer in Zamość for the next decade. He again lived in Warsaw in 1886–87 and published Hebrew fiction and poetry in leading publications such as *Ha-Yom*, *Ha-Ẓefira*, and *Ha-'Asif*. After losing his right to practice law in 1888, Peretz became more active in Yiddish publishing and moved to Warsaw permanently. From 1891 until the end of his life, Peretz worked as a record-keeper for the Jewish Community of Warsaw.

Not until 1886 did he publish his first prose work. As Samuel Niger showed, Peretz's early Hebrew fiction is remarkable for its clear language, extensive use of monologue and dialogue, and probing of psychological states. Several of the earliest stories have enduring value and anticipate his mature work. "*Ha-Kaddish*" ("The Kaddish," 1886) and "*Heẓiẓ ve-Nifga*," ("Looked and Was Injured" (referring to the dangers of mystical practices), 1886), set in a small-town synagogue and yeshivah, evoke the traditional world of study and prayer. Peretz's language is effective because he avoids the outmoded rhetoric of maskilic *meliẓah*. One character in "*Heẓiẓ ve-Nifga*" even comments on the weakness of the neobiblical style of authors who wrote in *Bikkurei ha-Itim*. Peretz consciously moved away from the supposedly "pure" language of Haskalah Hebrew writers, who used "bits of verses mixed with complete biblical verses," instead of striving to capture "the language of human beings" ("*Heẓiẓ ve-Nifga*," section 4).

In 1888 Peretz responded to Sholem Aleichem's call for contributions to his new anthology *Di Yudishe Folksbibliotek* ("The Jewish Popular Library"), sending him the ballad "*Monish*." In a letter dated June 17, 1888, Peretz expresses his literary program: "I write for myself, for my own pleasure; and if I sometimes remember the reader, he is from the higher class in society, a person who has read and studied in a living language." (In this context, "a living language" seems to refer primarily to Polish and Russian.). Despite his claim that he writes for himself, Peretz's letters often mention his social goals. He was enraged when Sholem Aleichem (like the editors of *Ha-Ẓefirah*) made editorial revisions of "*Monish*" without consulting him. Nevertheless, he sent several stories to him for inclusion in the subsequent volume of *Di Yudishe Folksbibliotek* (1889). Among these earliest Yiddish stories, "*Der Khelmer Melamed*" ("The Teacher from Chelm") is a comic folktale about trying to eradicate the evil impulse (*der yetser hore*) but finding that this threatens population growth; "*Yankl Pesimist*" ("Jacob the Pessimist") and "*Venus un Shulamis*," based on conversations between yeshivah boys, illustrate Peretz's lively use of dialogue.

While "*Monish*" was well received and Peretz continued writing Yiddish poetry, his major original contribution was in prose. In addition to his many stories, Peretz wrote countless literary, cultural, and political essays for newspapers and journals. His first Yiddish book was *Bakante bilder* ("Familiar Scenes," 1890), edited by Jacob Dineson. It includes three stories, two of which use the avant-garde technique of internal monologue. Both "*Der Meshulekh*" ("The Messenger") and "*Der Meshugener Batlen*" ("The Mad Talmudist") are centered in the minds of the main characters. Peretz probes their psychological states *in extremis*, as the messenger freezes to death and the talmudist torments himself over his desires and unstable identity. Unlike many early Yiddish writers who wrote about Jewish types, Peretz tried to represent unique individuals with their psychological aberrations.

In 1890 Peretz joined a group making a statistical survey that was financed by the philanthropist Ivan (Jan) *Bloch. Peretz visited many small towns and villages in the province of Tomaszow, collecting not only statistical data about the Jewish population (which were never published) but also raw material for his literary works. Peretz's impressions of this expedition are reflected in sketches entitled *Bilder fun a Provints-Rayze* ("Pictures from a Provincial Journey," 1891), in which he describes the poverty and pettiness of life in Southeastern Poland. Back in Warsaw, Peretz plunged into various social and cultural activities.

His first book of Hebrew prose was a short collection of two stories: *Ha-Illemet; Manginot ha-Zeman* ("The Mute; Melodies of the Age," 1892). These Hebrew stories show Peretz's unusual ability to empathize with the experiences of women. *Ha-Illemet*, in particular, follows the tormented life of a mute woman who loves a local boy. After she is married off to an older man against her wishes, she drifts toward madness. The story anticipates one of the most haunting 20th century Yiddish/Hebrew stories, Yakov Steinberg's "*Di Blinde*" / "*Ha-Iveret*" ("The Blind Woman," 1912). Like two of the stories in his *Bakante Bilder* (1890), those of his first volume of Hebrew fiction probe deeply into individual psychology. Whereas the Yiddish stories use first-person internal monologue, the Hebrew stories use third-person narrative to enter the consciousness of women.

Following Sholem Aleichem's example, Peretz edited three volumes of Yiddish anthologies called *Di Yudishe Bibliotek* ("The Jewish Library," 1891–95). Assisted by David Pinsky, he also edited numerous issues of *Yontev Bletlekh* ("Holiday Papers," 1895–96), filling them with his own poems, stories, and essays under various pseudonyms. Peretz's *Yontev Bletlekh* were sufficiently popular and anti-traditional that they elicited hostile responses from Orthodox circles. He also edited a Hebrew collection called *Ha-Ḥeẓ* ("The Arrow, 1894), which includes the important story "*Mishnat Ḥasidim*" ("Teachings of the Ḥasidim"). His collection *Literatur un Lebn*

("Literature and Life," 1894) features two classic Yiddish stories that were widely read by workers in the socialist movement. *"Bontshe Shvayg"* ("Bontshe the Silent") uses narrative irony to question the passive acceptance of poverty and misfortune; *"Dos Shtrayml"* ("The Fur Hat") is narrated by a skeptical hatmaker who pretends to believe that the *shtrayml* he creates has vast power. Both stories implicitly criticize religious tradition and authority.

In the 1890s, Peretz published extensively in both Hebrew and Yiddish. Like his Yiddish fiction in *Bakante Bilder*, his Hebrew stories showed his interest in psychology. In addition, the stories *"Leil Zeva'ah"* ("A Night of Torment") and *"Be-Ma'on Kayiẓ"* ("In a Summer House"), published in 1893, use dialogue extensively and effectively. Peretz's attraction to folklore is suggested by *"Ha-Maḥshavah ve-ha-Kinnor"* ("The Thought and the Harp," 1894), subtitled "an Arabic legend"; but it was sometimes read as a political allegory, as does other short fiction in Yiddish and Hebrew, such as *"In Gemoyzekhts"* ("In the Muck," 1893), *"Mayselekh fun Dul-Hoyz"* ("Stories from the Madhouse," 1895) and *"Be-Agaf ha-Meshuga'im"* ("In the Insane Asylum," 1896). In 1890, 1892, and 1895–97 – after the Hebrew journal *Ha-Ẓefirah* became a daily – Peretz published dozens of stories, articles, and poems in that paper. Of particular interest is *"Eshet Ḥaver"* ("A Friendly Wife" / "The Wife of a Friend," 1890), which enters the mind of an impoverished woman. When she reproaches her talmudist husband for doing nothing to obtain provisions for the Sabbath and Passover, he angrily berates her for disturbing his study, leaving her to contemplate suicide. Peretz recycled this Hebrew text as the Yiddish story *"A Kas fun a Yidene"* ("A Woman's Anger", 1893). Another recurrent technique is Peretz's use of first-person narrators, personae who often create the impression of telling their stories orally. Among these narrators is Yoḥanan the Teacher (in a sequence of stories called *"Sippurei Yoḥanan ha-Melammed"* – or, in Yiddish, *"Yokhanan Melameds Mayselekh,"* 1897), whose tales were later incorporated into Peretz's volume of neo-ḥasidic tales.

Between 1893 and 1899 Peretz was involved in socialist circles, and some Yiddish stories such as *"Di Toyte Shtot"* ("The Dead City," 1895) present a harsh picture of poverty in the shtetl. *"Ha-Isha Marat Ḥannah (Ẓeror Mikhtavim)"* ("The Woman Mrs. Hannah (A Bundle of Letters)," 1896) graphically shows how – because of the inheritance laws in Czarist Russia – a helpless widow is prevented from inheriting her husband's estate by a ruthless brother-in-law. *"Veberlibe"* ("Weaver Love," 1897) uses the epistolary form to describe the sufferings of a poor weaver. In 1899, because of a lecture he gave to striking workers, Peretz was arrested and served three months in prison. While imprisoned he told the tale *"Oyb Nisht Nokh Hekher"* ("If Not Higher," 1900) to his friend and cellmate Mordecai *Spector. According to one of Peretz's letters, Spector was so impressed by the story that he threatened that, if Peretz did not write it down, he would request to be moved to a different cell (YIVO *Bleter*, 28 (1946), 198).

Some of Peretz's best stories were neo-ḥasidic. The Hebrew story *"Ha-Mekubbalim"* ("Kabbalists," 1891; Yiddish version, *"Mekubolim,"* 1894) is the earliest of the stories that were later included in the genre and volume called *Khasidish* ("Ḥasidic"). Instead of praising the rebbe in the manner of *Shivehei ha-BeShT*, however, *"Ha-Mekubalim"* uses irony to show his inadequacy. With *"Mishnat Ḥasidim"* ("Teachings of the Ḥasidim," 1894; Yiddish version, 1902), Peretz begins to move away from social satire and toward the recreation of traditional materials. This story is brilliantly told in the voice of a disciple of the rebbe, echoing the writings of Nathan Sternharz of Nemirov. To enhance the neo-ḥasidic effect, Peretz introduces a persona, "Ha-Yatom mi-Nemirov," ("The Orphan from Nemirov"), who signs this story, the subsequent *"Dem Rebns Tsibek"* ("The Rebbe's Pipe," 1895), and *"Der Feter Shakhne un di Mume Yakhne"* ("Uncle Shakhne and Aunt Yakhne," 1895). Two masterpieces in Peretz's neo-ḥasidic corpus are the aforementioned *"Oyb Nisht Nokh Hekher"* and *"Tsvishn Tsvey Berg"* ("Between Two Mountains"), both published in 1900. These texts revolve around the long-standing tension between the *ḥasidim* and the *mitnaggedim*, which Peretz often represents more broadly as the opposition between emotion and intellect. In *"Oyb Nisht Nokh Hekher,"* a skeptical Litvak – a Jew from Lithuania, the center of talmudic study – becomes a disciple of an inspirational rebbe upon seeing his kindness and good deeds. In *"Tsvishn Tsvey Berg,"* narrated by a ḥasidic disciple, the two mountains that come together are the Rebbe of Biale and the Rabbi of Brisk. Moving beyond the Enlightenment tradition of anti-ḥasidic satire, Peretz balances the narrator's adulation of his ḥasidic leader with his portrait of an adversarial rabbi. The naïve superstitions expressed by the ḥasidic narrator, moreover, suggest a layer of authorial irony that also counteracts the narrator's enthusiastic but unquestioning endorsement of the ḥasidic world.

An interesting twist is Peretz's allusion to Rabbi *Naḥman of Bratslav in his series of *"Reb Nakhmanke's Mayselekh"* ("Rabbi Nachman's Tales," 1903–4). Although Peretz wrote to Israel Zinberg that he was never a ḥasid and had only once met a ḥasidic leader, the Bialer Rebbe, he used the ḥasidic tradition effectively in his neo-ḥasidic stories. Instead of simply relying on Western literary forms, Peretz sought inspiration from within the Judaic tradition. At the Czernowitz Yiddish conference in 1908, he therefore stated that "Reb Naḥman with his seven beggars" was the first Jewish *folks-dikhter*, and that in ḥasidic tales lie the origins of Yiddish literature. Peretz's return to ḥasidic tales influenced Martin *Buber in his retellings of the stories by Naḥman of Bratslav (1905–6) and about the Ba`al Shem Tov (1907).

Peretz became increasingly interested in Jewish folklore and ethnography in 1900–1, when his commitment to a kind of cultural nationalism took the place of his former socialist ideology. As part of his neo-romantic return to the "folk," Peretz continued to add to his neo-ḥasidic stories and began work on the *Folkstimlekhe Geshikhtn* ("Folk Tales," 1904–15). Elements of irony and satire remain, as in the stunning tale

"*Dray Matones*" ("Three Gifts," 1904), but Peretz also includes straightforward recreations of Yiddish folktales. *Folkstimlekhe Geshikhtn* was a popular success and was favorably received in literary circles.

Dialogue always played an important role in Peretz's fiction, and this may have led to his secondary career as a dramatist. He wrote one-act and full-length plays and was actively involved in performances by amateur and professional troupes. He gave lectures on theater in an effort to educate the audience and raise the artistic level. A letter from Dineson reveals that Peretz even dreamed of founding a serious Yiddish theater in the United States. In 1903 Peretz published the Hebrew drama *Ḥurban Beit Ẓaddik* ("The Ruin of the Ẓaddik's House"). This was the first version of the later Yiddish play *Di Goldene Keyt* ("The Golden Chain," 1909) about the conflict of generations. The plot revolves around a ḥasidic rebbe's determination to prolong the Sabbath, and thus, by force of will, liberate the world from pettiness and anguish. Besides *Di Goldene Keyt* and several realistic one-act plays in Hebrew and in Yiddish, he published two major Yiddish dramas: *Bay Nakht afn Altn Mark* ("At Night in the Old Market," 1907) and *In Polish af der Keyt* ("Chained in the Vestibule," 1908–9). The former is a symbolic drama in verse in which the author attempts to unfurl all of Polish Jewish history. Deeply pessimistic, the play has prompted much discussion, has been variously interpreted, and has been criticized both for its absence of plot and for its ambiguity.

One of Peretz's important, though unfinished, literary works is *Mayne Zikhroynes* ("My Memoirs," 1913–14), the main source for his biography until 1870. (Another biographical source that intimately describes his later years is R. Peretz-Laks' *Arum Peretzn*.) In the last years of his life, Peretz was active in the cultural life of Polish Jews. Their sufferings in the early years of the First World War greatly depressed him. Peretz, who had always assiduously followed his literary pursuits, worked almost up to the last moment. He died of a heart attack at home, having just written the phrase, "*Shtiler, shtiler, er vil danken…*" ("Quieter, quieter, he wants to thank …"). Peretz's funeral, purportedly attended by 100,000 people in Warsaw, demonstrated his popularity.

Peretz's originality as a Hebrew stylist has received too little recognition, in part because Hebraists have tended to dismiss him as a Yiddishist. Moreover, derivative Hebrew authors like his contemporary David *Frischmann were unable to appreciate his contribution. H.N. *Bialik added to the problem by claiming that "*nusaḥ* Mendele" (the Hebrew style of S.Y. Abramovitsh) was the only true path for modern Hebrew literature. Even before "*nusaḥ* Mendele" came into being (with Abramovitsh's short fiction from 1886 to 1896), there was another axis of Hebrew writing that ran from ḥasidic and anti-ḥasidic authors (especially Naḥman of Bratslav, Nathan Sternharz, and Joseph Perl) to Peretz. Their uniqueness lay in the ability to create the illusion of a lively, vernacular Hebrew by ignoring the maskilic norms of *meliẓah*, and they achieved unusual vitality by using a style that sounds as if it has been translated from Yiddish.

Peretz laid the foundations of both Yiddish modernism and a new Hebrew style. He excelled in the genre of short fiction, and in compressed form he conveyed psychological depth. Around 1900 the center of gravity in his fiction shifted from social satire to a remaking of traditional forms in Judaic literature. He achieved the greatest artistic success where he was able to suspend his works "between two mountains": the *ḥasidim* and the *mitnaggedim*, emotion and intellect, or tradition and innovation.

In Peretz's lifetime, the best edition of his Yiddish works was *Ale verk* ("Complete Works," 10 vols., 1909–13). A more complete edition is *Ale verk fun I.L. Peretz*, 18 vols. (1925–6), followed by an additional volume, *Briv un redes* ("Letters and Speeches," ed. N. Meisel). Also useful, because it provides the original publication date of each text, is *Ale verk*, edited by S. Niger, 11 vols. (1947–8). Peretz's Hebrew work was collected in *Ketavim* ("Writings," 4 parts, 1899–1901) and, more comprehensively, in *Kitvei I.L. Peretz* ("Writings of I.L. Peretz," 10 vols., 1922–7); currently the most accessible edition is *Kol kitvei I.L. Peretz* ("The Complete Works of I.L. Peretz," ed. S. Meltzer, 1961–2). Friedlander (1974) reprinted some of the Hebrew verse that was not included in Peretz's collected works. A.R. Malachi lists many other Hebrew works that were excluded from the editions of Peretz's works, in YIVO *Bleter*, 28 (1946), 157–64. Translations of Peretz's fiction and memoirs may be found in many anthologies, including *Selected Stories*, ed. I. Howe and E. Greenberg (1974), *The I.L. Peretz Reader*, ed. R. Wisse (1990), and *Classic Yiddish Stories*, ed. K. Frieden (2004).

BIBLIOGRAPHY: N. Meisel, *Y.L. Peretz, Zayn Lebn un Shafn* (1945); idem, *Yitshok Leybush Peretz un Zayn Dor Shrayber* (1951); S. Niger, *Y.L. Peretz* (1952); idem, in: *Tekufah*, 30–31 (1946), 439–502; S. Meltzer (ed.), *Y.L. Peretz ve-Yeẓirato*, Book 2: *Al Y.L. Peretz: Divrei Soferim Ivrim* (1961). **ADD. BIBLIOGRAPHY:** Ber Borokhov, in: *Y.L. Peretz: a Zamlbukh tzu Zayn Ondenkn* (1915); S.L. Tsitron, *Dray Literarishe Doyres*, vol. 1 (1920); J. Klausner, *Yoẓerim u-Vonim*, vol. 2 (1929); R. Peretz-Laks, *Arum Peretzn* (1935); Y.Y. Trunk, *Poyln*, vol. 5: *Peretz* (1949); A.R. Malachi, in: YIVO *Bleter*, 34 (1950), 221–30, 236 (1952), 355–61; Y.D. Berkovitsh, *Ha-Rishonim ki-Venei Adam* (1953–54); Kh. Shmeruk, *Peretzs Yiesh-Vizie* (1971); Y. Friedlander, *Bein Ḥavayah le-Ḥavayah: Massot al Yeẓirato ha-Ivrit shel Y.L. Peretz* (1974); D.C. Jacobson, *Modern Midrash* (1987); R. Wisse, *I.L. Peretz and the Making of Modern Jewish Culture* (1991); K. Frieden, *Classic Yiddish Fiction* (1995).

[Yehuda Arye Klausner / Ken Frieden (2nd ed.)]

PEREYASLAV-KHMELNITSKI (formerly **Pereyaslav**), city in Kiev district, Ukraine. A Jewish community is known to have existed in the city as early as 1620. It is also known that Jews in Pereyaslav-Khmelnitski suffered greatly during the *Chmielnicki insurrection. In 1654, on the occasion of the union of the Ukraine and Russia, Czar Alexis Mikhailovich maintained the limitation of Jewish rights of 1620. From that time until 1800, no information on Jews in Pereyaslav is available. In 1897, the city listed 5,754 Jews (40% of the total population). Pereyaslav suffered heavily from the Zielony bands; a pogrom in July 1919, which lasted four days, caused the death of 20 Jews and considerable damage to the community. The number of Jews in 1926 was 3,590 (27% of the population), dropping by 1939 to 937 persons (11.3% of the total population). At the beginning of the Soviet regime there were eight *battei-midrash*, six *shoḥatim* and 26 kosher butchers in the city. The town was occupied by the Germans on September 17, 1941, and soon the Jews who remained were murdered by them. Pereyaslav was the birthplace of *Shalom Aleichem; his house was reconstructed in the local museum, and his books and theatrical posters are displayed, some of them in Hebrew.

BIBLIOGRAPHY: J. Slutsky, in: *He-Avar*, 9 (1962), 18; I.Z. Diskin, *ibid.*, 14 (1967), 220–8; E. Tcherikower, *Di Ukrainer Pogromen in 1919* (1965), index.

[Shmuel Spector (2nd ed.)]

PEREZ (Heb. פֶּרֶץ; "he who breaches," "bursts forth"), one of the twins born to *Judah by *Tamar; father of Hezron and Hamul and ancestor of King David. He is said to have received his name on account of the sudden and unexpected priority of his birth to that of his twin brother Zerah, who was the first to put out a hand from their mother's womb (Gen. 38:27–29). The story of Perez' birth may well reflect a lost chapter in the tribal history of Judah when the older clan of Zerah lost its preeminence to the more vigorous Perezites. The Perezites are listed as an important clan in the census taken by Moses in the wilderness (Num. 26:20–21). One of them served as the first monthly chief of all the captains of David's army in the annual roster of military duty (I Chron. 27:3). Descendants of the Perezites were among the lay leaders who lived in Jerusalem after the return from the Babylonian Exile (Neh. 11:4–6). They are said to have numbered 468 "men of substance." The high station of the clan in Judah may be measured by the blessing that the men of Beth-Lehem bestowed on Boaz: "May your house be like the house of Perez whom Tamar bore to Judah" (Ruth 4:12). King David was descended from Perez through Boaz (4:18–22).

In the *Aggadah*

Perez, together with his brother Zerah, inherited Judah's characteristic valor and piety (Gen. R. 85:9). An indication of his virtue is seen in the fact that David's genealogy (Ruth 4:18–22) begins with his name (Zohar II 104a). The *plene* spelling of the word *toledot* ("generations") in that name is to signify that the Messiah, too, would claim descent from him (Ex. R. 30:3).

BIBLIOGRAPHY: IN THE AGGADAH: Ginzberg, Legends, index; I. Ḥasida, *Ishei ha-Tanakh* (1964), 370.

PEREZ, JUDAH BEN JOSEPH (first half of 18th century), rabbi in Venice and Amsterdam. Perez was the author of (1) *Seder Keri'ei Mo'ed* (Venice, 1706), a kabbalistic ritual text for the festivals; (2) *Peraḥ Levanon* (Berlin, 1712), commentaries and homilies on the Torah (together with homilies by Isaac Cavallero taken from *Naḥal Eitan*); (3) *Sha'arei Raḥamim* (Venice, 1710), kabbalistic liturgies compiled from various works; (4) *Aseret ha-Devarim* (Amsterdam, 1737), containing a commentary on Exodus 19–20, poetical paraphrases in Aramaic and Arabic, and hymns in honor of *Simeon b. Yoḥai; and (5) *Fundamento Solido* (Amsterdam, 1729), a compendium of the Jewish religion in Spanish. Perez also edited *Divrei Yosef* (Venice, 1715), responsa of Joseph b. Mordecai ha-Kohen of Jerusalem.

In the Nehemiah *Ḥayon controversy he was also suspected of being a Shabbatean, since he was Ḥayon's scribe for some time and possibly also his disciple. He accompanied Ḥayon on his journey to Berlin. One of Abraham Michael *Cardoso's pamphlets *Megalleh Amukkot minni Ḥoshekh*, was erroneously attributed to Perez.

BIBLIOGRAPHY: Fuerst, Bibliotheca, 3 (1863), 77–78; Steinschneider, Cat Bod, 1366; Kayserling, Bibl, 88; I. Sonne, in: *Kobez al Jad*, 2 (1937), 193.

°**PEREZ BAYER, FRANCISCO** (1711–1794), Spanish ecclesiastic and Orientalist; professor of Hebrew successively in Valencia and Salamanca. Francisco Perez Bayer was the most distinguished Spanish Hebraist of his day. He was the first person to study accurately the important historical inscriptions in the El Transito synagogue of Toledo (*De Toletano Hebraeorum Templo*, 1752 Ms.). His works on ancient Hebrew coinage (*De Numis hebraeo-samaritanis*, 1781), though later corrected in many details, laid the basis for the serious study of Jewish numismatics.

BIBLIOGRAPHY: L.J. Gascía, *Pérez Bayer y Salamanca* (1918); F. Mateu y Llopis, in: *Sefarad*, 11 (1951), 37ff.

[Cecil Roth]

PEREZ BEN ELIJAH OF CORBEIL (variously referred to as **RaF**, **MaHaRaF**, **MaRaF**, **M**orenu **ha**-**R**av Perez; d. c. 1295), one of the most eminent tosafists of the 13th century. Perez was known as "Head of the French yeshivot," apparently an official title. On his mother's side he was connected with the *Kimḥi family of Provence. His teachers were *Samuel of Evreux, *Jehiel of Paris, and *Isaac of Corbeil. His brother, Joseph of Tours, was also a well-known scholar. Perez lived in Corbeil, but toward the end of his life moved elsewhere (see *Teshuvot Ḥakhmei Provence* (1967), 92). He became acquainted with *Meir b. Baruch of Rothenburg during a visit to Germany and apparently the two studied together for some time. The comments (both written and oral) and glosses of Perez on the customs of Meir contributed to their spread in France and Provence. Some of these notes were collected by one of his pupils, and a small portion published as glosses to the *Tashbeẓ* (Cremona, 1556) of Samson b. Zadok, a pupil of Meir who collected the customs of his teacher. Perez did the same with the *Sefer Mitzvot Katan (SeMaK)* of his teacher, Isaac of Corbeil, and his glosses to it, which were more extensive and preserved in a much better state, were published in all editions of the *SeMaK* from the first 1510 edition of Constantinople onward. Better and more complete versions than those published are extant in various manuscripts. The divergence of the published work from the original is evident from the many differences in the manuscripts. Perez's glosses to the *SeMaK* differ from those to the *Tashbez*, since they constitute an actual book written with the express purpose of improving his master's work (even though the form in which we have it has passed through other hands) and his own name is mentioned in the body of the work. The work on *Tashbez* constitutes merely glosses on the text.

Perez's chief claim to fame in the history of rabbinic literature rests on the fact that he was one of the first to edit collections of *tosafot* to the Talmud, and that he was a prolific tosafist in his own right. However, it should be noted that many of the *tosafot* attributed to him are basically extracts from his lectures, noted down by the "pupils of Rabbenu Perez," whom Menahem ha-*Meiri extolled as illuminating and sustaining the Talmud in France. Perez's *tosafot* achieved considerable popularity, their study being widespread in Spain and Italy as early as the middle of the 14th century.

Notwithstanding his popularity, however, most of his *tosafot* are found either in manuscript or in the works of others, only a few having been published, those to *Bava Kamma* (Leghorn, 1819) and to single folios of other tractates (e.g., *Pesaḥim*, until page nine in the *Gemara Shelemah*, 1, 1960). There are many varying manuscripts of his commentary on *Bava Kamma*, apparently reflecting the editing of different pupils. In sum, it may be said fairly definitely that most of what has survived in the name of Perez is the work of his pupils, based to a very large extent upon his words. Of Perez's pupils, the most well known is *Mordecai b. Hillel. Most of them, however, including the compiler of the *Issur ve-Hetter*, attributed to *Jeroham b. Meshullam, are not known by name. Perez is cited hundreds of times in the Orḥot Ḥayyim of *Aaron b. Jacob ha-Kohen of Lunel, in the related work, the *Kol Bo*, and in the anonymous *Sefer ha-Neyar*, and he is often quoted by his pupil *Ḥayyim b. Samuel b. David in his *Ẓeror ha-Ḥayyim*. A list of the standard *tosafot* that were edited in the *bet midrash* of Perez is to be found in Urbach's work (see bibliography).

BIBLIOGRAPHY: Landauer, in: ZHB, 22 (1919) 27–31; Urbach, Tosafot, index; Ḥayyim b. Samuel of Tudela, *Ẓeror ha-Ḥayyim*, ed. by S. Haggai-Yerushalmi (1966), 3–7 (introd.); I. Ta-Shema, in: *Sinai*, 64 (1969), 254–7.

[Israel Moses Ta-Shma]

PEREZ BEN MOSES OF BRODY (18th century), rabbi and preacher. Before moving to Brody, Perez studied with Rabbi Israel, *av bet din* in Lokachi, and with R. Baruch Kahana in Ferrara. In 1769 he published *Sefer Beit Perez* (Zolkiew), a homiletic work on the holidays and other religious events of the year. In addition to the classical sources, the author relies on the Zohar, *Eleazar b. Judah of Worms' *Ma'aseh Roke'aḥ*, and on *Samuel b. Meir in ascertaining both the literal and hidden and mystical meanings of the Torah. He preached with success throughout Poland and Lithuania where many communities sought him as rabbi and preacher. His second work, *Shevaḥ u-Tehillah le-Ereẓ Yisrael* (Metz, 1772), only four pages in length, deals with the holiness of the land of Israel.

BIBLIOGRAPHY: Bruell, Jahrbuecher, 4 (1879), 96.

PERGAMENT, MOSES (1893–1977), composer and music critic. Born in Helsinki, Finland, Pergament studied the violin in St. Petersburg (and served as violinist for four years in the Helsinki Philharmonic Society) and at the Stern Conservatory, Berlin. He settled in Stockholm, where he worked as music critic on the *Svenska Dagbladet* and on the *Aftontidningen*. He also worked as a part-time choral and orchestral conductor. In almost all of his compositions he used motifs traceable to Jewish biblical cantillation and to folk songs of eastern European Jewry. Notable among his works are: *Rapsodia ebraica* for orchestra (1935), written as a reaction to the massacres of the Jewish people under the Nazis; the choral symphony *Den judiska Sangen* ("The Jewish Song," 1944); the radio opera *Eli* (1959); *Dibbuk*, a fantasy for violin and orchestra (1935); *Swedish Rhapsody* for orchestra (1940); the ballet *Krelantems och Eldeling*, Intermezzo for flute and strings (1973), and more than 100 songs. Among his writings are *Svenska tonsättare* (1943); *Vandring med fru musica* (1943); *Ny vandring med fru musica* (1944); and *Jenny Lind* (1945).

BIBLIOGRAPHY: Grove online; Larsson, "Moses Pergament and 'The Jewish Song,'" in: *Kungl. musikaliska akademien årsskrift* (1979), 28–40.

[Israela Stein (2nd ed.)]

PERGAMENT, OSIP YAKOVLEVICH (1868–1909), Russian lawyer, writer, and civic leader. In 1894 he qualified as a lawyer and appeared in many important political cases. He also wrote on Bessarabian civil and commercial law. Pergament played an active part in the social life of Odessa and was a member of the municipal council. He was elected to the Second and Third Dumas, in which he took part in debates of both a political and scientific nature, as well as arguing against Jewish persecution. He wrote *Yevreyskiy vopros i narodnaya svoboda* ("The Jewish Problem and National Liberty," 1906), and *Yevreyskiy vopros i obnovleniye Rossii* ("The Jewish Problem and the Renewal of Russia," 1908).

BIBLIOGRAPHY: S. Streich, in: YE, 12 (c. 1910), 372–3.

PERGAMUM, ancient city (and kingdom) near the N.W. coast of Asia Minor (now Bergama, Turkey). Independent from the early third century B.C.E., Pergamum thrived primarily during the early Roman advances eastward in the first half of the second century. Following the death of the last king of Pergamum, Attalus III Philometor (133 B.C.E.), the district came under direct Roman influence as part of the province of Asia. Josephus records a "decree of the people of Pergamum" pertaining to relations with the Jewish nation (Ant., 14:247–55). The document, probably written during the reign of John Hyrcanus I (c. 113–112), refers to a decree of the Roman senate renewing its alliance with the Jews. Of particular interest are its concluding assurances of friendship between Pergamum and Hyrcanus, "remembering that in the time of Abraham, who was the father of all Hebrews, our ancestors were their friends, as we find in the public records." A similar claim, describing the common ancestry of the Jews and

Spartans, is recorded elsewhere (cf. Jos., Ant., 12:226; I Macc. 12:21; cf. II Macc. 5:9), and these should be understood as an accepted mode of Greek diplomatic correspondence. Relations between Judea and Pergamum are further cited by Josephus during the reign of Herod the Great, who included the city among those to which generous donations and gifts were offered (Wars, 1:425). By the first century B.C.E. a Jewish community existed in Pergamum, as Cicero refers to the confiscation of funds in Pergamum intended for the Temple in Jerusalem (*Pro Flacco* 28:68).

BIBLIOGRAPHY: Schuerer, Gesch, 3 (1909[4]), 13, 112 n. 45; idem, Hist, 322 n. 30; M. Stern, *Ha-Te'udot le-Mered ha-Ḥashmona'im* (1965), 151–3, 162–5; A. Schalit, *Koenig Herodes* (1969), 834 (index), s.v. *Pergamon.*

[Isaiah Gafni]

PERGOLA, RAPHAEL DELLA (1876–1923), Italian rabbi. Della Pergola studied at Florence and for seven years served as rabbi of Gorizia. In 1910 he was appointed head of the Jewish community of Alexandria, Egypt, retaining this post until shortly before his death which occurred in Florence. He was also of great help to the refugees from Ereẓ Israel who went to Egypt during World War I. One of the leading Zionists in Alexandria, in 1918, when the cornerstone of the Hebrew University was laid in Jerusalem, Della Pergola was invited by Weizmann to participate in the ceremony.

BIBLIOGRAPHY: Politi, in: *Israel* (Aug. 28, 1923), 1; B. Taragan, *Les communautés israélites d'Alexandrie* (1932), 58–60; idem, *Le-Korot ha-Kehillah ha-Yehudit be-Alexandriyyah* (1947), 108–10.

PERI (Pflaum), HIRAM (Heinz; 1900–1962), Romance and Renaissance scholar. Born in Berlin, Peri's doctoral dissertation, published in 1926, was devoted to the Jewish Renaissance philosopher Leone Ebreo (Judah *Abrabanel). In 1925 he immigrated to Palestine and in 1927 became assistant librarian at the Jewish National and University Library, Jerusalem. From 1928 Peri lectured on Romance languages and literature and on the history of Renaissance literature at the Hebrew University (from 1948 as professor).

Peri's scholarly interests extended to a wide range of subjects. He wrote many articles on the history of the theater, on Ladino grammar and poetry, on the relations between Church and Synagogue and religious disputations in the Middle Ages. He edited and annotated the Hebrew edition of Burkhardt's classic *Kultur der Renaissance in Italien*, with a supplement of his own (*Tarbut ha-Renaissance be-Eiropah*; 1949, 1953), and served as an editor and contributor in his field with the *Encyclopedia Hebraica.* A volume of studies was published in his memory (*Romanica et Occidentalia*, ed. by M. Lazar (1963), and contains a bibliography of works by Peri, see pp. 17–22).

BIBLIOGRAPHY: G. Scholem and M. Lazar, *Al Professor Ḥiram Peri* (1964).

PERI, YA'AKOV (1944–), former head of the Shabak (Israel's General Security Service) and afterwards chairman of Bank Hamizrachi. Peri was born in Tel Aviv and grew up in Netanyah. After his military service he studied the history of Ereẓ Israel and the Middle East at Tel Aviv University and The Hebrew University of Jerusalem. In 1966 he joined the Shabak as field worker in the Arab Department. In 1987 he was nominated deputy head of the organization and in 1988 took over as head. This was the period of the first Intifada and later of the Oslo accords, developments that forced him to make organizational changes in order to improve flexibility in dealing with the new problems. In 1994 he went on leave to study management, marketing, and economics at Harvard University. In 1995 he retired from the Shabak and joined the business sector as president and CEO of Cellcom, a new cellular phone company. In 2003, after eight years as head of the company, he left Cellcom and was named chairman of Bank Mizrachi. In addition, he was the chairman of the board of Lipman Electronic Engineering and a member of the board of Magal Security Systems. Peri was also the prime minister's coordinator for prisoners of war and missing soldiers.

[Shaked Gilboa (2nd ed.)]

PERI EẒ-ḤAYYIM (Heb. פְּרִי עֵץ־חַיִּים; "fruit of the tree of life"), Hebrew periodical devoted to halakhic responsa and published in Amsterdam from 1691 to 1807. *Peri Eẓ Ḥayyim*, a forerunner of Hebrew periodical literature, was issued by the well-known yeshivah Eẓ Ḥayyim founded in 1616. In the 18th century the yeshivah became the largest and most important Torah center not only of Sephardi Jewry but of Ashkenazi Jewry as well. Accordingly, halakhic queries addressed to the yeshivah's outstanding talmudists reflect the entire spectrum of Jewish life in the 17th and 18th centuries and all aspects of *halakhah.* Decisions or advice were requested on such matter as inheritance laws, civil claims, social conflicts, shipping merchandise, piracy, the slave trade, the value of coinage and its fluctuations, Jewish housing difficulties in Holland, *agunot*, and marriages between those of greatly differing ages. Most of the decisions are dated and signed by the rabbis who gave them. The responsa indicate that, in the main, Dutch Jewry lived completely within the religious tradition, even though some of the inquirers, particularly among the women, no longer knew Hebrew. Halakhic inquiries came predominantly from Holland and its colonies, with some coming from the Mediterranean littoral and elsewhere. There are letters that reveal their writers to have been Marranos, whose problems are also clarified in these responsa. Although almost all the responsa are on halakhic matters, occasionally information about and reactions to other things are also recorded. Thus, there are praises for the art of printing and for science, accounts of the history of the Spanish Jews in Amsterdam, and the Hebrew poet David *Franco-Mendes' history of the yeshivah Eẓ Ḥayyim and of *Peri Eẓ-Ḥayyim.* Only a few copies of each responsa were published and as a result a complete set is no longer extant. Of the 952 responsa, 948 have been preserved and these are housed in different libraries throughout the world (e.g., the Ets Ḥayyim library in Amsterdam, the Rosenthal collection of the Amsterdam University

Library, the National Library in Jerusalem, and the library of J.L. Maimon in Jerusalem). In 1936 Max Hirsch Menko published, with an introduction and indexes, a German synopsis of all the extant responsa.

BIBLIOGRAPHY: Y. Raphael, *Rishonim va-Aḥaronim* (1957), 323–7; Y. Toury, in: *Benjamin De Vries Memorial Volume* (1968), 319–20.

[Getzel Kressel]

PERIZZITES (Heb. פְּרִזִּי), pre-Israelite inhabitants of Palestine, who lived in the neighborhood of Shechem (Gen. 13:7; 34:30; Josh. 17:15; Judg. 1:4, 5), in particular in Bezek (Khirbat Ibzīq, northeast of Shechem). The Perizzites are listed among the traditional group of six (sometimes five or seven) pre-Israelite peoples of the Promised Land (Ex. 3:8, 17; Deut. 7:1; Josh. 3:10, et al.) but, unlike the others, are not included among the descendants of Canaan (Gen. 10:15–17).

The origin of the term Perizzite is still unknown. Some scholars have surmised a connection with the word *perazot*, "unwalled towns or suburbs"; others, on the basis of the element *brz* in their name, that is found in the (Sumerian) Akkadian *parzi(llu)* and the West Semitic *barzel*, meaning "iron," suggest that the Perizzites were migrating metalworkers. Others, basing themselves on the fact that *Pire/izzi* is attested as the name of an envoy sent by King Tushratta of Hurri-Mitanni to Egypt, identify the Perizzites as an Anatolian ethnic group who reached Canaan, perhaps as migrating workers or slaves, as part of the political agreement between the Hittites and Egypt during the 18th Dynasty. The sources are the *El-Amarna tablets nos. 27, 28, and 29. On no. 27 there is a hieratic Egyptian note: *Pirasi*. Other forms of the same personal name in Egyptian transliterations are *Pirisija, Pirisim*, names of slaves. There is also the Nuzi-Hurrian personal name *Pirzu*. These occurrences of the name support the tentative conclusion that the Perizzites, who, in the Bible, are indeed separated from Canaanites, are of Anatolian-Hurrian origin.

BIBLIOGRAPHY: W.F. Albright, in: JPOS, 2 (1922), 110–39; idem, *Vocalization of the Egyptian Syllable Orthography* (1934), 43; H.L. Ginsberg and B. Maisler (Mazar), in: JPOS, 14 (1934), 234–67; I.J. Gelb et al., *Nuzi Personal Names* (1943), 115; Alt, Kl Schr, 3 (1959), 38; W. Held, *Beziehungen Aegyptens mit Vorderasien* (1962), 378, nos. 17–18; P. Welten, in: ZDPV, 81 (1965), 138.

[Pinhas Artzi and Irene Grumach]

PERJURY. Witnesses are guilty of perjury if it is proved, by the evidence of at least two other competent and consistent witnesses, that they had not been present at the time and at the place where they had testified to have been when the event in issue had happened (Mak. 1:4). Such false witnesses are known as *edim zomemim* (lit. conspiring witnesses). It is not sufficient that anything to which those witnesses had testified is contradicted by new witnesses, to the effect that what they had testified was untrue (as for "contradictions," see *Witness): such contradictions are only the starting point of the evidence required to convict those witnesses of perjury (Maim., Yad, Edut 18:4), namely, that they could not possibly have witnessed the facts to which they had testified (*ibid.* 18:2). Even though the evidence of the first set of witnesses had been accepted by the court as truthful, it is the evidence of the latter set of witnesses, testifying to the "alibi" of the first, that is to be accepted as conclusive (Mak. 5b; Yad, Edut 18:3) irrespective of the actual number of witnesses in each set. The latter set of witnesses must testify in the presence of the first set. Should this not be possible, e.g., if the first set are dead, this constitutes a "contradiction" and both testimonies will be discarded (cf. Yad, Edut 18:5). Where no evidence of perjury in the technical sense was available, but the evidence had conclusively been contradicted (e.g., where the murdered man appeared in court alive), the court would inflict disciplinary lashes (*Makkat Mardut* – see *Flogging; Yad, Edut 18:6; *Sha'arei Ẓedek* 4:7, 24 and 45; Rosh, resp., 58:4; et al.).

The punishment for perjury is laid down in the Bible: "You shall do to him as he schemed to do his fellow… Nor must you show pity: life for life, eye for eye, tooth for tooth, hand for hand, foot for foot" (Deut. 19:19–21). The Sadducees interpreted this law literally: the false witness would not forfeit his life, unless and until the man against whom he had testified had been executed; but the Pharisean interpretation, which is the source of the law as it was eventually established, was that the witness must be made to suffer what he had schemed to do, but not what he had actually caused to occur, to his fellow (Sif. Deut. 190; Mak. 1:6) – so that the biblical law was held to be applicable only where a man had been sentenced on the strength of false testimony, but before he was executed; the witnesses who had testified against him were then formally tried and convicted of perjury (Yad, Edut 20:2). This was a highly improbable contingency, as there was hardly an interval between sentence and execution (see *Practice and Procedure). The enunciation of this rule is followed in the Talmud by the objection that it could not be right to take the life of the witness when the life of the person he had schemed to kill had not in fact been taken; or, if the Bible really required that to be the law, then a fortiori must the life of the witness be taken after that person had been executed: if a man is liable to die because of having intended to kill, surely he must be liable to die if he had actually killed. The objection was dismissed in reliance on the rule (see *Penal Law) that no criminal offense can be created by analogy or logical deduction (Mak. 5b; and cf. Sanh. 74a and 76a; et al.).

Later commentators theorized that God's presence in the court (cf. Deut. 19:17) would sufficiently enlighten the minds of the judges to detect the falsehood of the testimony in time, before execution, for it is written, "do not bring death on the righteous and innocent, for I will not acquit the wrongdoer" (Ex. 23:7). It follows that the offense of perjury can have been committed only where the accused had not yet been executed, for a man who was executed must have been rightly convicted (Naḥmanides, commentary, Deut. 19:19).

The rule was, however, limited to capital cases only. Perjured witnesses were given the same non-capital punishments as had already been inflicted on those against whom they had testified (Yad, Edut 20:2), and where the defendant in a civil case had paid the judgment debt, the amount so paid was recovered from the witnesses (Tur, ḤM 38:2). Where the sanction imposed on the strength of their testimony could not be imposed on them (e.g., where an alleged manslayer had been banished to a *city of refuge, or where a priest had been suspended from office), they would be flogged (Yad, Edut 20:8–9; Tur, ḤM 38:3). To be convicted of perjury, no previous warning had to be given to false witnesses (Ket. 33a; Yad, Edut 18:4; Tur, ḤM 38:9). No single witness could be convicted of perjury: the conviction had always to be in respect of both (or all) the witnesses who had testified falsely together (Mak. 1:7); and when once one false witness had alone been convicted, it was said that innocent blood had been shed (Mak. 5b). As perjured witnesses are disqualified from being admitted as a witness in future, all convictions of perjury must be given wide publicity (Sanh. 89a; Maim., Yad, Edut 18:7), to fulfill the biblical command that "all others will hear and be afraid" (Deut. 19:20).

BIBLIOGRAPHY: D. Hoffmann, in MWJ, 5 (1878), 1–14; O. Baehr, *Das Gesetz ueber falsche Zeugen nach Bibel und Talmud* (1882); J. Horovitz, in: *Festschrift… David Hoffmann* (1914), 139–61; idem, *Untersuchungen zur rabbinischen Lehre von den falschen Zeugen* (1914); J.S. Zuri, *Mishpat ha-Talmud*, 7 (1921), 46; Gulak, Yesodei, 4 (1922), 161–3; ET, 8 (1957), 609–23; L. Finkelstein, *The Pharisees*, 1 (1962[3]), 142–4; 2 (1962[3]), 696–8; Z. Dor, in: *Sefer ha-Shanah Bar-Ilan*, 2 (1964), 107–24; P. Daykan, in: *Sinai*, 56 (1964/65), 295–302; S. Schmida, *"Li-Ve'ayat Edei Sheker"* (Diss., 1965). **ADD. BIBLIOGRAPHY:** M. Elon, *Ha-Mishpat ha-Ivri* (1988), 1:331f.; idem, *Jewish Law* (1994), 1:397f.

[Haim Hermann Cohn]

PERL, JOSEPH (1773–1839), author of significant satirical works and leading figure in the Galician *Haskalah. Perl was born in Tarnopol, where he spent most of his life. In his youth he was attracted to Ḥasidism and acquired knowledge of the movement's way of life and literature. Under the influence of the *maskilim*, especially those of Brody in Galicia, Perl joined the Haskalah movement as early as the beginning of the 19th century. Perl was very active in Jewish education and public life. In 1813 he established in Tarnopol the first modern Jewish school in Galicia, whose curriculum, in the spirit of moderate Haskalah, included both general and Jewish studies. He supported and directed the school throughout his life. He sought to modernize the Jewish community of Tarnopol by attempting to enlist the aid first of the Russian government and then, after 1815, of the Austrian government. Perhaps most conspicuous was his vigorous fight against the ḥasidic movement, which had spread throughout Volhynia and Podolia as well as Galicia. Perl's literary activity began around 1814. In 1814–16, Perl published calendars which contain both scientific information and excerpts from talmudic literature in the vein of the *maskilim*. The entire body of his work has never been published, and some of his works are at present in the process of publication for the first time. Those of Perl's works in manuscript stored in his valuable library in Tarnopol were probably, for the most part, destroyed during the Holocaust; vestiges of this collection are preserved in the National Library in Jerusalem. During his lifetime some of Perl's works were circulated in manuscript, while others were published years after they had been presented to the censor for approval, e.g., *Boḥen Ẓaddik* ("The Test of the Righteous"), which was written in 1825 and published in 1838.

Perl signed his principal satirical works with the pseudonym Obadiah b. Pethahiah, which often prevented the reading public from identifying him as the author. Until recently Perl was known only as a Hebrew writer, but he wrote a polemic against Ḥasidism in German, and was also the author of works in Yiddish. His principal satirical work, *Megalleh Temirin* ("The Revealer of Secrets"; Vienna, 1819), was written in a parallel Yiddish version, which was first published only in 1937 by YIVO in Vilna. Periodical stories in the manner of Naḥman of Bratslav's *Sippurei Ma'asiyyot* were published in both their Hebrew and Yiddish versions in 1969 by the Israel Academy for Sciences and Humanities in Jerusalem. It is also known that he adapted a Yiddish version of a historical novel, *Antigonus*, and apparently translated Fielding's *Tom Jones* into Yiddish, probably from a German version.

Although Perl made an important contribution to the creation of Yiddish fiction during the first half of the 19th century he did not advocate the use of this language. Like other Haskalah authors his aim in employing Yiddish was practical – to propagate Haskalah ideas among the Yiddish-speaking masses. Yet none of Perl's Yiddish works, which in spite of his intention show an original and idiomatic use of language, appeared during his lifetime.

Both in his public activities and in his writings Perl fought Ḥasidism because he believed their doctrines and leaders to be obstacles to the modernization of Jewish life. By means of denunciatory and hostile notes and memoranda (recently discovered and published) sent incessantly to the officials, he encouraged the Austrian authorities in Galicia to intervene against the Ḥasidim. In the literary sphere he battled against the movement by means of propaganda, parody, and satire. Characteristic is his German manuscript, *Ueber das Wesen der Sekte Chassidim* (1816), in which he condemned the ḥasidic movement, its practices and beliefs, on the grounds that they jeopardized the welfare of the state and misled a multitude of innocent believers. Addressing both gentile and Jewish readers he denigrates Ḥasidism by creating a hostile, often distorted anthology of quotations lifted out of context from the ḥasidic sources. Perl wrote stories in the manner of Naḥman of Bratslav, in fact, pretending that they had been discovered after the rabbi's death by one of his Ḥasidim. Thus he published a supplement, as it were, to Naḥman's incompleted *Ma'aseh me-Avedat Bat Melekh*, claiming it to have been in the possession of a Ḥasid who was close to the rabbi toward the end of his life. Similarly, Perl wrote another story, *Ma'aseh me-Avedat Ben Melekh*, in Hebrew and Yiddish. These stories use the style and some themes and motifs of R. Naḥman only to further the Haskalah aim of criticizing and eventually eradicating Ḥasidism.

Perl's principal work, *Megalleh Temirin*, shows the influence of 18th-century satirical stories written in the form of letters, which achieved great popularity in France and Germany (especially Montesquieu's *Persian Letters* and Wieland's satirical writings). Perl integrated the structure of the secular European satirical letter not only with the style, language, and ideas of the ḥasidic letter, but with its typographical form as well. An imitation of the ḥasidic story, *Megalleh Temirin* is made up of 151 letters, a preface, and an epilogue.

The story's main character, Obadiah b. Pethahiah, who is possessed of magical powers, presents himself as a fervent Ḥasid who had miraculously obtained these letters. Here the denunciations of Ḥasidism contained in Perl's German manuscript reappear amplified by many annotations attached to the correspondence. The annotations interpret the views and facts mentioned in the letters, and they also serve as a medium for Obadiah's ironic commentary. The letters reveal a number of plots, the principal one being the search for the German "book" (Buch) which endangers Ḥasidism and undermines the authority of its leaders by revealing their innermost secrets. Therefore it must be obtained at any cost and destroyed, and revenge taken on its author. The hunt for the "book," which is actually Perl's own German manuscript, yields several subplots based on intrigues and schemes set within ḥasidic life. The search, resembling a comedy of errors, ends in complete failure. Other aspects of the plot reveal the machinations of the Ḥasidim in their struggle for influence and material gain. In Perl's satire, the ḥasidic leaders do not stop short of employing stratagems of bribery, deceit, blackmail, and intimidation against their rivals, whether rabbis or *maskilim*. In spite of his intention to demean Ḥasidism, its philosophy and practices, a number of descriptions escape Perl's satiric control, communicating vitality, naturalness, and humor. The Hebrew in which these letters are written contains Yiddishisms lending flexibility and expressiveness to the speech of the Ḥasidim. Like many *maskilim* Perl considered this ḥasidic Hebrew a ludicrous language, offensive to the Haskalah ideal of a "pure" Hebrew language written in biblical style and according to grammatical rules. In spite of these feelings Perl's ḥasidic Hebrew conveys great liveliness.

Boḥen Ẓaddik, (Prague, 1838), a sequel to *Megalleh Temirin*, consists of two sections, the first, a discussion of readers' reactions to *Megalleh Temirin*, and the second, a series of letters. Obadiah b. Pethahiah reappears in this work as a man who possesses a magical device – a board on which people's conversations are secretly recorded. The board, however, can be erased only by an absolutely honest man, and the search for this ideal person brings Obadiah into contact with the diverse elements composing Jewish society, each of whose weaknesses and follies is mercilessly exposed. Thus the number of subjects coming in for satirical treatment is increased to include not only Ḥasidim, but rabbis, traders, artisans, and even *maskilim*, all of whom are found defective, each in his own way. At the end of these wanderings the honest man is discovered, paradoxically, as a Jewish pious farmer in a remote village in southern Russia, which is governed in an almost utopian fashion by Jewish farmers. Taking to heart all that he learned from his travels, Obadiah turns his back on Ḥasidism and preaches in a pathetic manner to his people.

Perl also wrote letters published in Hebrew periodicals in Austria: Of special importance are his letters protesting against the collection of funds in the name of R. *Meir Ba'al ha-Nes. Ironically, there is an unpublished letter in which a Ḥasid jests at the foibles of the contributors to the periodical *Kerem Ḥemed*, who pursue honor and empty phrases and whose spiritual horizons are narrow. Perl's satire, employed to promote the aims of the Haskalah, is of interest today primarily because of its literary merit and authenticity, qualities that have outlived the author's immediate intentions. An English translation entitled *Joseph Perl's Revealer of Secrets: The First Hebrew novel*, with an introduction by Dov Taylor, was published in 1997. Avraham Rubinstein edited and wrote an introduction to Perl's *Ueber das Wesen der Sekte Chassidim* (1977).

BIBLIOGRAPHY: N. Gordon, in: HUCA (1904), 235–42; I. Davidson, *Parody in Hebrew Literature* (1907), 61–74; Klausner, Sifrut, 2 (1937), 278–314; I. Weinles, in: *Yosef Perls Yidishe Ksovim* (1937), 7–70; R. Mahler, *Ha-Ḥasidut ve-ha-Haskalah* (1961), 155–208; Ch. Shmeruk, in: *Zion*, 21 (1957), 94–99; S. Werses, in: *Tarbiz*, 32 (1962/63), 396–401; idem, in: *Hasifrut*, 1 (1968–69), 206–27; idem and Ch. Shmeruk (eds.), *Yosef Perl, Ma'asiyyot ve-Iggerot* (1969), 11–86, Eng. summary: A. Rubinstein, in: KS, 37 (1961/62); 38 (1962/63). **ADD. BIBLIOGRAPHY:** S. Werses, "*Ginzei Y. Perl bi-Yerushalayim ve-Gilgulehem*," in: *Ha-Universitah*, 19:1 (1974), 38–52; Z. Carpenter, "Yosef Perl et la Haskalah; une approche historique et littéraire," in: *Ẓafon*, 22–23 (1995), 51–65; M. Caplan, "Science Fiction in the Age of Jewish Enlightenment," in: *Prooftexts*, 19:1 (1999), 93–100; Ch. Shmeruk, "*Devarim ke-Havayatam u-Devarim she-ba-Dimyon be* 'Megalleh Temirin'," in: *Ha-Keriah la-Navi* (1999), 144–55; J. Dauber, "Some Notes on Hebraisms in the Yiddish '*Megalle Temirin*'," in: *Zutot*, 1 (2001), 180–85; N.B. Sinkoff, "The 'Maskil,' the Convert and the 'Agunah': J. Perl as a Historian of Jewish Divorce Law," in: *AJS Review*, 27:2 (2003), 281–99.

[Samuel Werses]

PERL, MARTIN LEWIS (1927–), U.S. physicist and Nobel laureate. Perl was born in Brooklyn, New York City, and graduated early from Madison High School (1943), his education boosted by strong parental encouragement, prodigious reading and a great interest in working with tools, wood, chemicals and Erector (construction) sets. He gained his B.S. in chemical engineering at the Polytechnic Institute of Brooklyn (now Polytechnic University) (1948), a course interrupted by World War II service in the U.S. Merchant Marine and Army. He worked for the General Electric Company before pursuing his now definitive career choice of physics at Columbia University (1950) where he completed his thesis under the supervision of I.I. Rabi (1955). He was a member of the physics department of the University of Michigan (1955–63), where he became professor, before moving to Stanford University's Linear Accelerator Center (1963) and where he has been professor of physics since 1970. His first 10 years of experimental research was in the complicated field of strong interactions of elementary particles such as the pion and proton. His basic interest in fundamental problems in physics led him to study the relation between the electron and the muon, which have many similar properties, although the muon is much heavier. Speculating that there might be heavier members of the electron-muon family, his theoretical and practical skills led to the discovery of the tau lepton, for which he received the Nobel Prize in physics (1995) and the Wolf Prize for physics (1982). His work thus extended the electron-muon to the electron-muon-tau family of which no heavier members have yet been found. His subsequent research centers on the relation between electrons, muons, and tau particles and on the search for elementary particles with a fraction of the electric charge of the electron. Perl's other research interests are in optical and electronic devices and liquid drop technology. Perl has always been a strong supporter of Israel and Jewish life in the U.S. He practices Reconstructionist Judaism.

[Michael Denman (2nd ed.)]

PERLA, JEROHAM FISCHEL BEN ARYEH ẒEVI (1846–1934), scholar and commentator. Born in Warsaw, Perla at the age of 15 went to study under Joshua Leib Diskin in Lomza, and when Diskin left Lomza he became the pupil of Ḥayyim *Soloveichik of Brest-Litovsk. Perla was invited by many communities, including those of Cracow and Lublin to accept the position of communal rabbi. Believing that the burdens of office would interrupt his study, however, he refused all the calls extended to him and devoted himself entirely to study, supported by his wife, who kept a shop in Warsaw. Perla spent 40 years on his remarkable three-volume commentary on Saadiah's *Sefer ha-Mitzvot*, which he completed in 1917. With the appearance of this extensive and brilliant work Perla's reputation spread, reaching Ereẓ Israel long before he himself arrived there, and due to it he entered into correspondence with Ḥayyim *Sonnenfeld. They became close friends after Perla's arrival in Jerusalem in 1924, but otherwise Perla shunned people in order to spend his whole time studying. It is said that in his house there was a chest containing many manuscripts, including a commentary on Eliezer b. Nathan's *Raban*, equal in length to Perla's commentary on the *Sefer ha-Mitzvot*. Perla began to publish a commentary on *Kaftor va-Feraḥ* of Estori ha-Parḥi called *Pirḥei Ẓiyyon*, but only the first five chapters appeared (1966). The manuscript of the remainder was taken back to Europe by Perla's son and was lost in the Holocaust. Perla died in Jerusalem.

BIBLIOGRAPHY: J. Gelis, *Mi-Gedolei Yerushalayim* (1967), 233–8; Saadiah Gaon, *Sefer ha-Mitzvot...im Be'ur...Yehudah Yeruḥam Perla* (1962), preface.

[Anthony Lincoln Lavine]

PERLBACH, MAX (1848–1921), German historian. Born in Danzig, Perlbach worked as a librarian at the following institutions of higher learning: Koenigsberg (1872–76), Greifswald (1876–83), and Halle (1883–1903), and was then appointed to direct the Royal Library at Berlin. His scientific work dealt mainly with the history of the provinces of East and West Prussia during the Middle Ages.

The works he wrote or edited include *Ueber die Ergebnisse der Lemberger Handschrift fuer die aeltere Chronik von Oliva* (1871); *Preussische Regesten bis zum Ausgang des 13. Jahrhunderts* (1876); *Simon Grunaus preussische Chronik* (1876); *Quellen-Beiträge zur Geschichte der Stadt Koenigsberg im Mittelalter* (1878); *Preussisch-polnische Studien zur Geschichte des Mittelalters* (1886); and *Prussia Scholastica: Die Ost-und Westpreussen auf den mittelalterlichen Universitaeten* (1896). Perlbach also edited some Polish medieval sources for the *Monumenta Germaniae Historica* (1888, 1893).

[George Schwab]

PERLBERG, ABRAHAM NATHAN (1889–1934), Hebrew author and educator. Born in Kolno, Poland, Perlberg studied at the Lomzhe yeshivah. After moving to Warsaw, he gave private lessons to the children of wealthy *maskilim*, including Aaron *Zeitlin. After immigrating to the United States in 1913, Perlberg taught at the Bet Hasefer Haleumi (National Hebrew School for Girls) in Brooklyn and Manhattan, becoming principal of the Manhattan branch of that school in 1920. Those schools taught *Ivrit be-Ivrit* (Hebrew in Hebrew), with an emphasis on Modern Hebrew literature and conversation. They were aimed at girls because the nationalist movement made the education of Jewish women an essential part of its program.

Perlberg taught at the Mizrachi Bet Hamidrash L'morim (Hebrew Teachers' Seminary), which later became part of Yeshivat Isaac Elhanan and Yeshivah University, from 1917 until his death. Many of his students went on to become leading rabbis and scholars, including Solomon Feffer, Morris Goodblatt, Robert *Gordis, Hyman Grinstein, Isaac *Klein, Hayim Leaf, and Frank Zimmerman.

The town of Ra'ananah was founded in Palestine by a group of American Jews in 1922. According to an oral tradition, Perlberg suggested the name for the town.

Perlberg published widely in Hebrew journals for adults and children, including *Hadoar, Haaretz, Ha-Toren, Nir, Aviv*, and *Ha-Do'ar La-Noar*, and was the assistant editor of *Ha-Toren* and one of the editors of *Aviv*. He wrote poems, songs, and plays for children as well as articles about education and pedagogy. Many of his writings were collected posthumously in *Kitvei A.N. Perlberg* (1939).

[David Golinkin (2nd ed.)]

PERLE, JOSHUA (**Yehoshua**; 1888–1943), Yiddish novelist. Born in Radom, Poland, Perle spent most of his life in Warsaw. Initially influenced by Sholem *Asch's romantic literary style, Perle later, under the influence of Maxim Gorky, adopted a grittier, more naturalistic mode of writing. His outstanding achievement is the autobiographical novel *Yidn fun a Gants Yor* ("Ordinary Jews," 1935), based on his own impoverished childhood and complicated family. Well received by the critics and widely read, it garnered several prestigious prizes. Perle was prolific, writing novels, short stories, literary sketches, criticism, and articles that appeared in Warsaw Yiddish publications and literary journals. He wrote naturalistic descriptions of the petit bourgeois, big city types, office workers, officials, and the impoverished masses. He was also a friend and mentor to younger Yiddish writers, and his home on Orla Street became a literary salon. Perle continued writing and was active in literary circles into World War II. On Simḥat Torah, October 21, 1943, he was sent to Birkenau and vanished without a trace. His son also perished, his wife having committed suicide before the war. Perle's stories and articles from the Warsaw Ghetto years were found after the war in the hidden archives of Emanuel *Ringelblum and several were later published.

BIBLIOGRAPHY: Rejzen, Leksikon, 2 (1927), 936–9; M. Ravitch, *Mayn Leksikon* (1945), 168–70; Finkelstein, intro. in: J. Perle, *Yidn fun a Gants Yor* (1951).

[S. Kumove (2nd ed.)]

PERLE, RICHARD NORMAN (1941–), U.S. foreign policy thinker and entrepreneur. Born in New York City and raised in Los Angeles, Perle was educated at the University of Southern California (B.A., 1964), London School of Economics, and Princeton University (M.A., 1967). Perle went to Washington, D.C., in 1969 to work on a campaign in support of President Nixon's antiballistic missile program. After its success, he joined the staff of U.S. senator Henry M. Jackson from 1969 to 1980, specializing in foreign policy and arms control issues. Perle was largely responsible for Jackson's amendment watering down the SALT I arms control treaty. He also drafted the Jackson-Vanik Amendment, which tied Soviet trade status with the United States to the Soviet Union's willingness to allow Jewish emigration to Israel. While working for Jackson in the Senate, Perle was discovered by the FBI to have passed classified national security information to the Israeli embassy; he was "reprimanded" by Jackson but never prosecuted.

From 1981 to 1987 Perle was assistant secretary of defense for international security policy in the Reagan administration, where he was largely responsible for opposing arms control initiatives and weakening existing arms control treaties. Perle maintained close ties to the Likud Party in Israel and was a policy advisor to former prime minister Binyamin Netanyahu. From 1987 to 2004 he was a member of the Defense Policy Board at the Pentagon, and was chairman from 2001 to 2003. He belongs to several right-wing think tanks/lobbying groups and he was a founder of the Project for the New American Century (PNAC), and an author of its famous 2000 report calling for American world military and economic supremacy, whose recommendations have been the foundation of American foreign policy in the second Bush administration (many members of PNAC were appointed to important positions in the government in 2001). Perle was a signatory of a letter sent to President Clinton in 1998 calling for a U.S. war against Iraq, and is regarded as a chief promoter of that war. He was among the strongest supporters in Washington of Ahmad Chalabi, the exiled Iraqi who was found to be the source of much of the false information used to promote public support for the war in 2002 and 2003. Perle has also advocated military attacks on Syria, Iran, and North Korea.

Perle's private business activities frequently prompted accusations of unethical behavior. In 2003 he was criticized because of his directorship of a firm that sells eavesdropping software and his involvement in a venture capital fund formed to invest in businesses "that are of value to homeland security and defense," for which he reportedly solicited Saudi investment, at the same time that he was advocating the Iraq war as a member of the Defense Policy Board. In 2004 Perle was implicated in the looting of Hollinger International, Inc., a media company that owned several large newspapers, of $400 million by its chairman, Conrad Black, and his deputy, David *Radler. Perle was a member of Hollinger's executive committee along with Black and Radler, and has been accused of "breach[ing] his fiduciary duties" while accepting $5.4 million in compensation and bonuses, and while the company made large investments at Perle's direction, most of which were lost.

[Drew Silver (2nd ed.)]

PERLES, family of scholars and writers. JOSEPH PERLES (1835–1894), born in Baja, Hungary, studied at the Breslau Jewish Theological Seminary and at the University of Breslau. He served as preacher of the Bruedergemeinde of Posen (Poznan) during 1862–71, and then as rabbi of the Jewish community of Munich, rejecting offers to succeed A. *Geiger in Berlin and to lecture at the newly founded *Landesrabbinerschule in Budapest. Perles, a faithful and outstanding pupil of the Breslau seminary, was among its first graduates, and his interests extended over a wide area of Jewish scholarship. Ancient versions of the Bible was one of his fields; his dissertation was on the Syriac version, *Meletemata Peschitthoniana* (1859), and he edited his father-in-law's (S.B. Schefftel) *Be'urei Onkelos* (1888). His work in medieval literature and Bible exegesis was extensive. Perles' main scholarly contribution was to Hebrew and Aramaic lexicography and philology, to which he devoted such studies as *Zur rabbinischen Sprach-und Sagenkunde* (1873), which sheds light on the aggadic sources of the *Thousand and One Nights; Beitraege zur Geschichte der hebraeischen und aramaeischen Studien* (1884); and *Beitraege zur rabbinischen Sprach-und Alterthumskunde* (1893). Perles' sons were MAX (1867–1894), a noted oculist, and FELIX (1874–1933), rabbi and scholar. Felix was drawn into the Zionist movement in Vienna and in 1899 he became rabbi at Koenigsberg. Like his father, Felix Perles had wide scholarly interests: Bible criticism, Hebrew and Aramaic lexicography, apocryphal and pseudepigraphical literature, medieval Hebrew poetry, liturgy, Jewish dialects, and abbreviations. His best-known works are his critique of W. Bousset's *Religion des Judentums im neutestamentlichen Zeitalter* (1903), and the collection of essays, *Juedische Skizzen* (1912, 1920^2). Joseph Perles' wife, ROSALIE (1839–1932), was a writer and journalist for a number of German-Jewish papers and periodicals. She wrote a preface to a volume of her husband's sermons – edited by their son Felix (1896) – and published some lectures. Her *Aphorismen* appeared posthumously in 1932.

BIBLIOGRAPHY: JOSEPH PERLES: W. Bacher, in: JQR, 7 (1894/95), 1–23 (where an almost complete bibliography is given in the footnotes). FELIX PERLES: Hedwig Perles, in: MGWJ, 81 (1937), 369–92 (bibliography, reprinted).

PERLES (Perls), ISAAC MOSES (1784–1854), Hungarian rabbi. Born in Brod, Moravia, Perles studied under Meshullam Eger in Pressburg and with Joseph b. Phinehas, rabbi of Posen. He served as rabbi in several Hungarian communities: Kojetin (from 1813), Holics (1820), Eisenstadt (1822), and Bonyhad (1841). During his last years difficulties arose between him and his community. They were in the main connected with reforms in the life of the community which Perles, despite his generally liberal approach, refused to countenance. Matters reached such a stage that he was denounced to the government as "interfering with order and authority, hating light and progress," or as "robbing and wronging his congregants, making demands upon them, and taking by force… in excess of that to which he was entitled." The government, knowing that the charges were baseless, ignored them, but as a result of the dispute Perles left Bonyhad and returned to Brod, where he died after a few months. After his death his grandson Abraham Ẓevi published his work *Beit Ne'eman* (1907), including responsa of great interest and prefaced by Perles' biography. His son Meir (1811–1893) was born in Brod. Although a profound talmudic scholar, he did not join the Orthodox camp. He served as rabbi in Carei (Mare) from 1834. In *Beit Ne'eman* there is a letter to him from Moses *Sofer dated 1834.

BIBLIOGRAPHY: ZHB, 12 (1908), 68–70; P.Z. Schwartz, *Shem ha-Gedolim me-Ereẓ Hagar*, 1 (1914), 51a; 2 (1914), 2b; N. Ben-Menaḥem, *Mi-Sifrut Yisrael be-Ungaryah* (1958), 170, no. 91.

[Naphtali Ben-Menahem]

PERLES, MOSES MEIR BEN ELEAZAR (1666–1739), rabbi and author. Perles was born in Prague. About 1708 he was in Frankfurt, Amsterdam, and Rotterdam, and in his work *Megillat Sefer*, he tells of the troubles which befell him in the winter of 1708, while he was in an isolated village outside Vienna: on the Sabbath of *Zakhor* and Purim he had neither *Sefer Torah* nor Scroll of Esther, and he vowed to compile a commentary on the latter if he were delivered. He reached Vienna, where he lived in the house of Samson *Wertheimer, acting as his secretary. Wertheimer supported him after he returned to Prague. Perles kept his vow and compiled his commentary entitled *Megillat Sefer* (Prague, 1710), which is based mainly on Rashi's commentary to Esther. In his introduction he also mentions his other works, which have remained in manuscript: *Penei Ḥammah* on the *aggadot* of the Talmud; *Or Olam*, sermons for the festivals; *Kiryat Arba*, sermons on the biblical portions read on the four special *Sabbaths before Passover; and *Me'ir Netivot* (which according to one view is identical with *Or Olam*). He died in Prague.

His sons included Aaron, who published the *Seder ha-Nikkur* of the *Sefer ha-Ittur* with the commentary *Tohorat Aharon* (Offenbach, 1725) containing extracts from the works of the *posekim* and the laws of porging in German, and Moses, who compiled *Mishmeret ha-Bayit* (Prague, 1739), containing in 10 *mishmarot* ("vigils"), sermons and ethical admonitions.

BIBLIOGRAPHY: Steinschneider, Cat Bod, 725, 1981; Neubauer, Cat, 792; S. Hock and D. Kaufmann, *Die Familien Prags* (1892), 280–1.

[Yehoshua Horowitz]

PERLHEFTER, ISSACHAR BEHR BEN JUDAH MOSES (d. after 1701), Bohemian rabbi. Born in Prague, a member of the *Eybeschuetz family, he married Bella, the daughter of Jacob Perlhefter of Prague, whose family name he adopted. They moved to Vienna, but after the expulsion of its Jews in 1670, he went to Altdorf where he taught Hebrew to Johann *Wagenseil who was a professor there. Perlhefter's wife, a highly cultured woman, taught Wagenseil's daughter dancing and music. Perlhefter was next appointed rabbi of Mantua where his father had previously served. After six years Perlhefter was forced to leave, as a result of a dispute over Mordecai of Eisenstadt, a follower of *Shabbetai Ẓevi whom Perlhefter at first supported, but subsequently exposed when his deceptions became known. Perlhefter later returned to his native city where he was appointed *dayyan* and scribe, a position formerly held by his grandfather. Perlhefter was the author of *Ohel Yissakhar* on the laws of *sheḥitah*, with a Judeo-German translation (Wilhermsdorf, 1670); *Ma'aseh Ḥoshen u-Ketoret* (Prague, 1686), an excerpt from Abraham b. David *Portaleone's *Shiltei ha-Gibborim* (Mantua, 1619) on archaeology: and *Ba'er Heitev* (Prague, 1699) on the *Targum Jonathan* to the Pentateuch.

BIBLIOGRAPHY: D. Kaufmann, *"Die letzte Vertreibung der Juden aus Wien und Niederoesterreich,"* in: *Jahresbericht der Landes-Rabbinerschule in Budapest 1887–88* (1889), 201f.

[Louis Isaac Rabinowitz]

PERLMAN, ALFRED EDWARD (1902–1983), U.S. railroad executive and first Jewish president of a major American railway system. Perlman was born in St. Paul, Minnesota, and spent his early career working with the engineering and administrative departments of major United States railroad corporations. From 1952 to 1954 he was president of the New York Central System and in 1965 he became president and chief administrative officer of the Pennsylvania–New York Central Transportation Company, which went bankrupt in 1970. Some of the major contributions that Perlman's management team made to the railway include creating a smaller, more productive workforce; improving services, such as tightening the freight schedules; extending strategic sidings to minimize train delays; strengthening and replacing bridges and structures; installing VHF radio communication systems; expanding intermodal facilities and services; and implementing total management and cost control systems.

Among Perlman's many public offices in the United States and abroad were those of an adviser to the Korean (1949) and Israeli (1950) railroad systems. He was chairman of the Eastern Railroads Presidents' Conference, a member of most professional organizations connected with railroading, and a contributor to professional publications.

BIBLIOGRAPHY: Perlman's 16-page *Western Pacific Railroad: The Feather River Route* was published in 1975. **ADD. BIBLIOGRAPHY:** J. Daughen and P. Binzen, *The Wreck of the Penn Central* (1999).

[Joachim O. Ronall / Ruth Beloff (2nd ed.)]

PERLMAN, HELEN HARRIS (1905–2004), U.S. social work educator. Perlman, who was born in St. Paul, Minnesota, received a B.A. in English literature from the University of Minnesota in 1926. She worked for family and child guidance agencies in Chicago and New York (1927 to 1940). In 1940 she became a lecturer and a student supervisor at the School of Social Work of Columbia University. During this period, she often gave lectures on the treatment of social and emotional problems in people's daily lives, speaking at the New York School of Social Work and other schools and conferences throughout the U.S. In 1943 she received her master's degree in social work from Columbia.

In 1945 she was appointed professor of social work at the University of Chicago's School of Social Administration. She was best known for her contributions to the theory of social casework and to training for social work practice.

In the 1950s she integrated her clinical experience and her studies with experts in the Freudian and Rankian schools of thought and developed the "Chicago School" of social service practice. Her work, together with later work by other colleagues, established the Chicago School's problem-solving approach, an influential approach that is still used in practice today.

For many years Perlman served on the editorial board of the *Journal of American Orthopsychiatry*. She also served on the editorial board of *Social Work*, the major publication of the National Association of Social Workers (NASW), as well as on the curriculum development committee of the Council on Social Work Education (CSWE). The council named her a Pioneer of Social Work Education.

Her widely read book *Social Casework: A Problem Solving Process* (1957; 1958²) has been translated into more than 10 languages. Her other publications include *So You Want to Be a Social Worker* (1962), *Persona* (1968), *Relationship* (1979), *Looking Back to See Ahead* (1989), and *The Dancing Clock & Other Childhood Memories* (1989).

[Joseph Neipris / Ruth Beloff (2nd ed.)]

PERLMAN, ITZHAK (1945–), Israeli violinist. Perlman studied at the Tel Aviv Academy of Music with Rivka Goldgart. A child prodigy, he gave a solo violin recital at age 10 and appeared on American television in 1958. He later studied at Juilliard with Delay and Galamian, aided by a scholarship from the America-Israel Cultural Foundation. He made his Carnegie Hall debut in 1963. Winning the Leventritt Competition (1964) launched his international career, through which he has become known as one of the world's leading musicians. Perlman is noted for the warmth and beauty of his tone, brilliant technique, a genuine humanity and joie de vivre. In 1965, he performed eight concerts throughout Israel, which culminated in a performance of Tchaikovsky pieces in Tel Aviv for which he received a 15-minute ovation. He played as a soloist in the Israel Philharmonic concerts in Warsaw and Budapest (1987, representing its first performances in Eastern Bloc countries) and the orchestra's first visits to the Soviet Union (1990), China, and India (1994). He regularly returns to Israel. In chamber music he has often been heard with such colleagues as *Zukerman, *Ashkenazy, and Argerich. From 1997 Perlman developed a new role as director/soloist and appeared with the English Chamber Orchestra, the Chicago Symphony, and other noted orchestras. His vast repertoire encompasses all the standard violin works as well as klezmer and contemporary music. Several composers wrote works for him and his recordings regularly appear on the best-seller charts and have won 15 Grammy Awards. Among them are the Bach solo sonatas and partitas, the Paganini *Caprices*, and much of the virtuoso repertory. He performed the violin solos in Steven *Spielberg's Academy Award-winning film *Schindler's List*. Perlman made a habit of encouraging young talent and over the years held a variety of teaching posts, including close involvement, alongside wife, Toby, in the Perlman Music Program for Young People, beginning in 1998. Among his many awards are the Medal of Liberty (1986), in appreciation of his outstanding contribution to American life and achievements, the Royal Philharmonic Society's gold medal (1996), and the National Medal of Arts (2000). The Harvard, Yale, and Hebrew universities are among the many institutions to have awarded him honorary degrees. He is an honorary citizen of Tel Aviv. Stricken with polio at age four, he has also been an advocate for the rights of the disabled. His daughter, pianist Navah Perlman, has performed to critical acclaim in major concert venues throughout North America, Europe, and Asia.

BIBLIOGRAPHY: Grove online; Baker's Biographical Dictionary (1997); C.H. Behrman, *Fiddler to the World: The Inspiring Life of Itzhak Perlman* (1992).

[Naama Ramot (2nd ed.)]

PERLMAN, JACOB (1898–1967), U.S. economist. Perlman was born in Bialystok, Poland, and was taken to the United States in 1912. After a brief period of teaching at the University of North Dakota he entered government service, and during the 1930s worked with the Bureau of Labor Statistics and the Social Security Administration. In 1949 he became a technical expert for the United Nations and was sent as economic adviser to the governments of Colombia, Greece, Bolivia, and the Philippines. From 1956 to 1965 he was head of the Office of Economic and Manpower Studies of the National Science Foundation. In addition to his work for governmental and international institutions, Perlman also taught at various universities in the United States and abroad. He specialized in development economics and particularly in the study of the economic effects of science and technology. Perlman died while on a visit to Israel.

BIBLIOGRAPHY: *New York Times* (April 10, 1968), 43.

[Joachim O. Ronall]

PERLMAN, SAMUEL (1887–1958), editor and translator. Born in Minsk, Perlman settled in Ereẓ Israel in 1914. During World War I he was among those exiled to Alexandria; there he directed a school for refugee children. On his return he became an editor of *Haaretz. He again left for abroad, and, in Berlin, was one of the editors of *Haolam. Later, together with *Jabotinsky, he founded the Ha-Sefer publishing house; the two were also the joint editors of the first modern Hebrew atlas (1926). Between 1926 and 1932, Perlman was a teacher and the director of the Boston *Hebrew Teachers' College. Returning to Ereẓ Israel in 1932, he became active in the publishing field, joining Devir in 1944. While he wrote articles on literary subjects, he engaged primarily in translation; Perlman's major work was the translation into Hebrew of Heine's prose works. He also translated works by Herzl and Strindberg.

BIBLIOGRAPHY: Kressel, Leksikon, 2 (1967), 679.

[Getzel Kressel]

PERLMAN, SELIG (1888–1959), U.S. labor economist. Born in Bialystok, Poland, Perlman immigrated to the United States in 1908. After a brief period in New York, he became interested in the work of the *Bund. While studying at the University of Wisconsin, he investigated the Lawrence strike for the United States Commission on Industrial Relations (1914–15). From 1918 he taught economics at the University of Wisconsin at Madison.

Perlman's main field was the social development of the American, British, and Russian labor movements. He modified his early Marxist socialism as being too theoretical in its approach to social and economic problems and turned his attention to the labor movement and trade unionism. These he regarded as indispensable to a stable industrial society because of their tendency to strengthen labor's bargaining position and their regard for private property. Perlman was active in secular Jewish affairs, especially in the American Jewish Labor Movement. He developed a special relationship with the garment industry unions. In his later years, he showed interest in Zionism and the State of Israel. His best-known book is *A Theory of the Labor Movement* (1928). He was a contributor to the *History of Labor in the United States* (1918–52).

BIBLIOGRAPHY: Witte, in: *Industrial and Labor Relations Review*, 13 (1960), 335ff.

[Mark Perlman]

PERLMANN, MOSHE (1905–2001), U.S. scholar in Oriental studies. Born in Odessa, Russia, Perlmann studied in Odessa, Jerusalem, and London. He lived in Palestine from 1924 to 1937 and studied Arabic and Islam at the Hebrew University. He received a Ph.D. in Islamic history from the University of London. He moved to the United States in 1940 and held positions in several U.S. universities, while maintaining a steady output of articles and studies in Oriental history, literature, and thought. Perlmann taught at the New School for Social Research (1945–52) and Dropsie College (1948–55). From 1955 to 1961 he held the position of lecturer in Israeli studies at Harvard. In 1961 he became a professor of Arabic at the University of California in Los Angeles until his retirement in 1973.

One of Perlmann's earliest projects was a compilation of all the references in the Talmud to health or medicine. This collection was published in 1926 as *Midrash ha-Refu'ah*. Perlmann translated Carl Brockelman's *History of the Islamic Peoples* (1947). His own writings include studies of early Arab manuscripts, and *Chapters of Arab-Jewish Diplomacy, 1918–22* (1944), a collection of printed materials that deal with early attempts at rapprochement. He also published letters written by Leo *Levanda to J.L. *Gordon, with an introduction in which he discusses these two literary figures and the relationship between them (in: *American Academy for Jewish Research, Proceedings* (1967), 139–85).

He also wrote *Gesammelte Schriften: islamische und juedisch-islamische Studien* (with M. Schreiner, 1983). He translated and edited *Shaykh Damanhuri on the Churches of Cairo, 1739* (1975) and edited *The History of Al-Tabari: The Ancient Kingdoms* (1987).

PERLMUTTER, ABRAHAM ẒEVI (1844?–1926), rabbi in Poland. At the age of 18 he was nominated as rabbi in a townlet, later officiating in Leczyca, Raciaz, and other communities. Although descended from *mitnaggedim*, he sought the company of Polish *ẓaddikim* and was particularly close to the *ẓaddik* of Gostynin, Jehiel Meir *Lifschits ("Ba'al ha-Tehillim") from whom he received the authorization to study languages to assist him in his public activities. In 1886 he was appointed rabbi in *Radom, where he participated in many community activities. He was awarded a silver medal after the coronation of Czar *Nicholas II in 1894. Perlmutter was active in improving the condition of Jewish soldiers stationed in the barracks in Radom and established a *kasher* kitchen there. He was also instrumental in abolishing a severe decree against Jewish peddlers. In 1909 he was appointed rabbi in Warsaw, a position he held until his death. In 1917 he was coopted to the provisional state council of Poland, which had been organized under the German occupation. In 1919 he was elected to the first Polish parliament (Sejm) as representative of *Agudat Israel for the Warsaw district. As the doyen of the Jewish representatives he was the first to present his party's declaration on the claims of Orthodox Jews in parliament. Even in his eighties Perlmutter continued to pursue his communal activities and he participated in the Polish and world conventions of Agudat Israel.

[Yitzchak Arad]

PERLMUTTER, IZSÁK (1866–1952), Hungarian painter. Born in Budapest, Perlmutter painted large pictorial studies; *Village in the Morning Sun* won the Hungarian government gold medal in 1905. Later he concentrated on interpreting the life of the peasants in Hungary. The Uffizi Gallery of Florence commissioned his self-portrait in 1926. He left a collection of his work to the Jewish Museum of Budapest.

PERLOV, YITSKHOK (Isaac Perlow; 1911–1980), Yiddish poet, novelist, and editor. Born in Biała Podlaska, until the end of World War I he lived in Minsk, then in Warsaw and in the Soviet Union (1940–46). In 1947 he sailed to Ereẓ Israel on the *Exodus* but was returned to Germany by the British, an experience he described in *Ekzodus 1947* ("Exodus 1947," 1948) and *Di Mentshn fun Eksodus 47* ("The People of Exodus 47," 1949). In 1949 he emigrated to Israel, and in 1961 to New York. He began his literary career in 1928 with poems in the *Literarishe Bleter* and then published widely in the Yiddish press in Poland, Germany, Israel, and the United States. His works, some of which appeared under pseudonyms such as A. Bril, Y.B. Avromarin, Itshe Matlies, and P. Itzkhakov, include the poems *Frunza Verda* (1932), *Untergang* ("Doom," 1935), *Undzer Like-Khame* ("Our Solar Eclipse," 1947), *Undzer Regnboygn* ("Our Rainbow," 1948) and the novels *Blondzhende Kayafn* ("Straying Comedians," 1936); *Der Tsurikgekumener* ("The Returnee," 1952), *In Eygenem Land* ("In One's Own Land," 1952), *Matilda Lebt* ("Matilda Is Alive," 1954), *Dzebelye* (1955); *Flora Ingber* (1959) and *Mayne Zibn Gute Yor* ("My Seven Good Years," 1959). In addition, two novels, *Di Kenign fun di Zumpn* ("The Queen of the Swamps") and *Der Elnter Dor* ("The Lonely Generation") appeared in the New York daily *Forverts*. Perlov wrote many dramatic works, of which *Goldene Zangen* ("Golden Stalks," 1938), *Abi Men Zet Zikh* ("Only to See Each Other," 1939), and *Blinde Pasazhirn* ("Stowaways," 1939) were performed in Poland prior to World War II. In 1959 he published his Yiddish translation of Boris Pasternak's *Dr. Zhivago*. His collected works, edited by R. Ariel, appeared in Tel Aviv (1954).

BIBLIOGRAPHY: LNYL, 7 (1968), 185–6.

[Yekhiel Szeintuch / Tamar Lewinsky (2nd ed.)]

PERLSTEIN, MEYER A. (1902–1969), U.S. pediatrician and educator. Perlstein, who was born in Chicago, practiced medicine there from 1929. A specialist in cerebral palsy and other children's neurological diseases, Perlstein was chief of the children's neurology clinic at Cook County Hospital, director of the Cerebral Palsy project at Michael Reese Hospital, and chairman of the medical advisory board of the Therapeutic Day Nursery and of the Illinois Children's Hospital School. Perlstein taught pediatrics at Northwestern University and at the postgraduate school of Cook County Hospital. A founder (1949) and president (1954) of the American Academy for Cerebral Palsy, Perlstein was a consultant and medical advisory board member of many organizations for the benefit of those affected by neurological diseases. He wrote many articles for professional journals and produced movies on medical subjects. In addition he was active on the American Physicians Fellowship Committee of the Israel Medical Association.

PERLZWEIG, MAURICE L. (1895–1985), Reform rabbi and official of the World Jewish Congress. Born in Poland, the son of a cantor who moved to London, Perlzweig was educated in England, where he was founder and chairman of the University Labor Federation of Great Britain and (from 1933) president of the World Union of Jewish Students and deputy member of the Executive of the Jewish Agency. He also officiated at the Liberal Synagogue in London. A founding member of the World Jewish Congress and the first chairman of its British section, in 1942 Perlzweig was nominated head of the World Jewish Congress Department of International Affairs in New York and represented it at the Economic and Social Council of the United Nations and subsidiary bodies. He attended numerous international conferences and meetings as a spokesman of Jewish interests and causes and drafted many documents submitted to the United Nations, particularly the Commission of Human Rights and Sub-Commission on Prevention of Discrimination, on crucial problems of Jewish communities around the world. While working for the World Jewish Congress, Perlzweig had an influence in securing a commitment by the Allies to hold the *Nuremberg Trials of Nazi war criminals.

[Natan Lerner]

PERLZWEIG, WILLIAM ALEXANDRE (1891–1952), U.S. biochemist. Born in Ostrog, Russia, Perlzweig was taken to the U.S. in 1906. He worked at the Rockefeller Institute for Medical Research. In 1917 he served in the U.S. Army Sanitary Corps. From 1930 he was professor of biochemistry and nutrition at the Duke University Medical School, Durham, North Carolina. He contributed a great number of papers in the field of vitamins and clinical chemistry.

°**PERNERSTORFER, ENGELBERT** (1850–1918), leader of the Austrian Social Democratic Party. Pernerstorfer's attitude toward the Jewish question and antisemitism was peculiarly ambivalent: this was in part to blame for the failure of the Austrian Social Democrats to come to grips with the Jewish question in his time. Pernerstorfer was a school friend of Victor *Adler and godfather at the baptism of the then seven-year-old Friedrich *Adler. He started his public career as editor of Georg von *Schoenerer's periodical, but parted with him in 1883 because of the latter's virulent antisemitism. Although he was considered by his contemporaries to have antisemitic inclinations, Pernerstorfer vigorously opposed political antisemitism. His positive attitude toward Zionism stemmed from his general conception of nationality and his opposition to the cosmopolitanism professed by his Jewish colleagues in the Social Democratic leadership, among them Robert Danneberg; Pernerstorfer averred that the left wing of the party was all Jewish. In 1916 he published an article in Martin Buber's monthly *Der *Jude*, in which he favored national autonomy for East European Jewry, and stated that the Central Powers would profit from a Jewish national home in Palestine. National Socialist propaganda later portrayed Pernerstorfer as a full-scale antisemite.

BIBLIOGRAPHY: E. Silberner, *Sozialisten zur Judenfrage* (1962), 237–40, bibl. 344–7; idem, in: HJ, 13 (1951), 122–3, 129–33; 15 (1953), 15; A. Gerlach, *Der Einfluss der Juden in der oesterreichischen Sozialdemokratie* (1939, national-socialistic); J. Braunthal, *Victor und Friedrich Adler* (1965), index; idem, *In Search for the Millennium* (1945); *Neue Oesterreichische Biographie*, 2 (1925), 97–116.

[Meir Lamed]

PERPIGNAN, city in S. France, near the Spanish border. Formerly the capital of the counts of *Roussillon, in 1172 it passed to the kings of Aragon. The earliest mention of Jews in Perpignan dates from 1185; they are said to have owned real estate around this time. Toward the middle of the 13th century, King James I of Aragon offered the Jews of Perpignan land to settle which they would own in freehold. Endeavoring to attract Jews from France, he granted those of Perpignan a number of privileges and exempted them from the payment of various indirect taxes and tolls (1269). Autonomy in civil law was also granted. In 1271 the annual tax of the community amounted to 15,000 sólidos in Barcelona currency. Noteworthy among the scholars of Perpignan were R. Menahem b. Solomon *Meiri and R. Abraham *Bedersi, pupil of Joseph *Ezobi. In response to R. Abraham's petition (1274), the king granted the community a privilege to protect them against the threats of *informers. He renewed it in 1275, also forbidding the clergy to expel the Jews or summon them before the Church tribunal. At that time the community leadership consisted of 20 to 28 counselors who were appointed for life. Infante John authorized them to convene and issue regulations, appoint procurators and other communal officials, to enforce obedience to the regulations within the community, and to punish offenders.

Some members of the community engaged in maritime commerce (in partnership with Jewish merchants of *Barcelona, *Seville, and other places); others were local merchants; an appreciable number practiced moneylending (including several of the community's trustees). Most important of the crafts was the textile industry, but there were also several silversmiths during the 14th century.

When the Kingdom of *Majorca was created after the death of James I and the seat of the monarchy established in Perpignan, the government began to oppress the local Jewish community. From the close of the century, a series of decrees were issued which sought to restrict relations between Jews and Christians; the Jews were ordered to wear special dress (1314). Restrictive decrees issued for the Kingdom of Majorca were also applied in Perpignan. A poll tax was imposed and around 1317 the king of Majorca seized the promissory notes of the Jews. There is no doubt that living conditions in Perpignan were influenced by the presence of the royal court in the town and the Jews were particularly conscious of the severity of the crown's persecution of the Jews of the kingdom. During the *Pastoureaux persecutions (1320), copies of the Talmud found in the town were burnt. Conditions improved during the reign of Pedro IV. In 1347 he appointed his physician Maestre Crescas as a trustee of the community so as to prevent any inequalities in the financial and tax administration.

At the time of the *Black Death (1348–49) several of the community's notables converted in order to escape persecution. In 1363 Perpignan contributed toward the levy of 10,000 livres in Barcelona currency imposed to further the war against Castile. When the vessel containing the Host was stolen from a church and pledged with a Jew, the infante ordered the bailiff to conduct an inquiry in order to prevent an attack on the Jewish quarter (1367). On June 29, 1370, anti-Jewish riots broke out in Perpignan and the king appointed a procurator to investigate the damage.

During the 1360s and 1370s, Perpignan became renowned as a center of astronomers. The astronomical tables prepared by Jacob b. David Yom Tov were translated into Catalan there in 1361. In 1372 Crescas David was made physician to the king and a year later Bonet Maimon of Perpignan was appointed to the same office. The rabbis of this period included Samuel Carcossa, who was invited to Barcelona for debates with the rabbis of Aragon and Catalonia. In 1372 the king authorized the Jews of Perpignan to travel to France on business, and in 1377 protection was also granted to Jews who came to trade in Roussillon and Cerdagne from the exterior. In 1383 Pedro gave the community of Perpignan a privilege which prohibited apostates from entering the Jewish quarter in order to engage in disputes on religious questions. He also granted it permission to try informers. Anti-Jewish riots broke out on Aug. 17, 1391. During their course the Jews were given refuge in the fortress, while the inhabitants looted Jewish property. When representatives of the town demanded the conversion of the Jews, the king replied that forced conversion was prohibited. He nevertheless forbade the Jews to leave Perpignan, where refugees from other parts of Catalonia had also arrived. On September 22 John I ordered the bailiff to draw up a list of property to which there were no heirs, especially that of Jews who had been martyred. On December 19 he ordered the Jews who were in the fortress to return to their homes and decreed that they were not to be molested or forced to accept baptism. The Jews of Perpignan undertook not to leave the country and in practice continued to live in the fortress until 1394.

Although the community was declining, at the beginning of the 14th century there were still 200–250 families living there, but it had lost its importance and most of the members were poor. In 1408 King Martin ratified the administrative arrangements for the election of trustees. Christians were forbidden to interfere in the affairs of the community and extensive rights were given to the trustees. In 1412 Pope *Benedict XIII wrote to the community of Perpignan on the subject of the propagation of Christianity among the Jews, writing his instructions in Hebrew so as to leave no doubt about his intentions. The community was called upon to send two delegates to a disputation to be held in *Tortosa. At that time, Vicente *Ferrer visited the town, preaching to the Jews there. Ferdinand I prohibited the building of a new synagogue or the repair of the existing ones in 1415; he also forbade the Jews to practice medicine and pharmacy or to employ Christians in their service.

The Papal *Inquisition was active in Perpignan at the close of the 14th century. In 1346 a *Converso, Johanan David, a butcher by trade, was condemned to the stake. Many others were condemned during the 1420s and 1440s. After the Spanish Inquisition had been set up, 22 Conversos were sent to the stake in 1485. The French Army led by Louis XI and Charles VIII invaded Roussillon in 1462 and conquered Perpignan in 1475. Following the edict of expulsion from Spain (1492), a number of Jews sought refuge in Perpignan, then under Charles VIII of France; but an expulsion decree was issued against the Jews of the town in September 1493. The remnants of the large community, 39 families, sailed from Marseilles to Naples and from there to Constantinople.

At the beginning of the 20th century, there were several Jewish families living in Perpignan.

BIBLIOGRAPHY: R.W. Emery, *Jews of Perpignan in the Thirteenth Century* (1959), includes documents: 134–95; Baer, Spain, index; Baer, Studien, 142f.; Baer, Urkunden, 1 (1929), index; I. Loeb, in: REJ, 14 (1887), 55ff.; P. Vidal, *ibid.*, 15 (1887), 19–55; 16 (1888), 1–23, 170–203; J. Miret i Sans, *Itinerari de Jaume I "El Conqueridor"* (1918); J.E. Martínez Fernando, in: *Analecta Sacra Tarraconensia*, 26 (1953), 94–95; A. López de Meneses, in: *Sefarad*, 14 (1954), 108, 275, 283, 285; J.M. Millás Vallicrosa, *ibid.*, 19 (1959), 365ff.; F. Vendrell de Millás, *ibid.*, 20 (1962), 331f.; A. Pons, in: *Hispania*, 79 (1960), 209ff.

[Haim Beinart]

°PERREAU, PIETRO (1827–1911), Italian philosemitic priest and Orientalist. Perreau was born in Piacenza. In 1860 he was appointed deputy librarian of the Palatina library of *Parma (in charge of the de *Rossi collection) and in 1876 he became its director. In his *Guida Storica Antica e Monumentale della Città di Parma* (1887), Perreau describes the acquisition of Hebrew manuscripts by the Palatina library, and in his *Catalogo dei codici ebraici…* (1880) he covers the manuscripts which were not described by de Rossi. *Steinschneider published Perreau's descriptions of Hebrew manuscripts (Parma in: HB, 7–8 (1864–65); 10 (1870); 12 (1872); and in Jeshurun, 6 (1868)).

Perreau published an edition of *Immanuel of Rome's commentary to the Psalms (1879–82), Esther (1880), and Lamentations (1881). He also published various studies on biblical books such as Song of Songs (*La cantica di Solomone…* 1882); on Jewish communities in Italy (in: *Vessillo israelitico*, 27 (1879); *Corriere Israelitico*, 25, 26 (1886–8); and *Educazione e Cultura degl'Israeliti in Italia nel Medio Evo*, (1885)); and on Jews in England in the 11th and 12th centuries (in: *Corriere Israelitico*, 25, 1887). Perreau wrote a lexicon of Hebrew abbreviations, *Oceano dello Abbreviature…* (1883).

BIBLIOGRAPHY: M. Steinschneider, in: HB, 21 (1881/82), 103; idem, in: *Aresheth*, 4 (1966), 123–4 (Heb. tr. by Y. Eldad); Milano, Bibliotheca, index.

[Alfredo Mordechai Rabello]

°PERROT, JEAN (1920–), French prehistorian. He studied in France and later in Palestine. In 1950 when Kol Zion la-Golah (overseas broadcasts from Jerusalem) was established, he headed the French department. Perrot was research director at the Centre National de la Recherche Scientifique and from 1951 was head of the French archaeological mission to Israel. He excavated the remains of Chalcolithic culture at Tell Abu Matar in Beersheba (1952–60), Mesolithic and Natufian remains at Einan (1956–62), Neve Ur (1966), and Munḥata (1962–67), a Chalcolithic cemetery at Azor, and various sites in the western Negev. He participated in the excavations of Tell al-Fāriʿa, Hazor, and Khirbat Minim. He published a series of excavation reports and studies on the early art and history of Ereẓ Israel. His work was directed toward the study of the evolution of civilizations from the fifth millennium onward that led to the rise of the great river valley cultures. He later extended his work to Iran and Turkey.

[Michael Avi-Yonah]

PERRY, FRANK (1930–1995), U.S. director, producer, writer. A Manhattan native, Perry began his entertainment career as a teenager working as a parking lot attendant for the Westport Country Playhouse in Connecticut. Eventually, he produced plays at the Playhouse. After serving in the Korean War, Perry made his directorial debut in 1962 with *David and Lisa*. Nominated for two Academy Awards, including best director, the script was adapted from the Theodore Isaac Rubin novel by his wife, Eleanor, with whom he collaborated on many films until they separated in the 1970. *Ladybug Ladybug* (1963) marked Perry's debut as both director and producer. In 1968, Perry directed and produced *The Swimmer*, based on the John Cheever story. The following year he directed and produced *Trilogy* (1969), written by Truman Capote. One of Perry's best-known works is *Diary of a Mad Housewife* (1970), which his wife adapted from Sue *Kaufman's novel. A character study of a dysfunctional family, it was a topic Perry revisited in an adaptation of Joan Didion's *Play It as It Lays* (1972). Perry directed and co-wrote *Mommie Dearest* (1981) about Joan Crawford's dysfunctional life, starring Faye Dunaway and based on Crawford's daughter's tell-all. Perry also made a number of television films, including *The Thanksgiving Visitor* (1967), *Dummy* (1979), *Skag* (1980), and *J.F.K.: A One-Man Show* (1984). Other Perry films are *Last Summer* (1969), *Doc* (1971), *Man on a Swing* (1974), *Rancho Deluxe* (1975), *Monsignor* (1982), *Compromising Positions* (1985), and *Hello Again* (1987). Perry's final film, *On the Bridge* (1992), was a documentary about his own battle with prostrate cancer. He died from the disease in 1995.

[Susannah Howland (2nd ed.)]

PERSIA (Heb. פָּרַס, *Paras*), empire whose home coincided roughly with that of the province of Fars in modern Iran. Its inhabitants, calling themselves Persians, are first mentioned in Assyrian records of approximately 640 B.C.E. According to these records, the king of "Parsuwash" acknowledged the

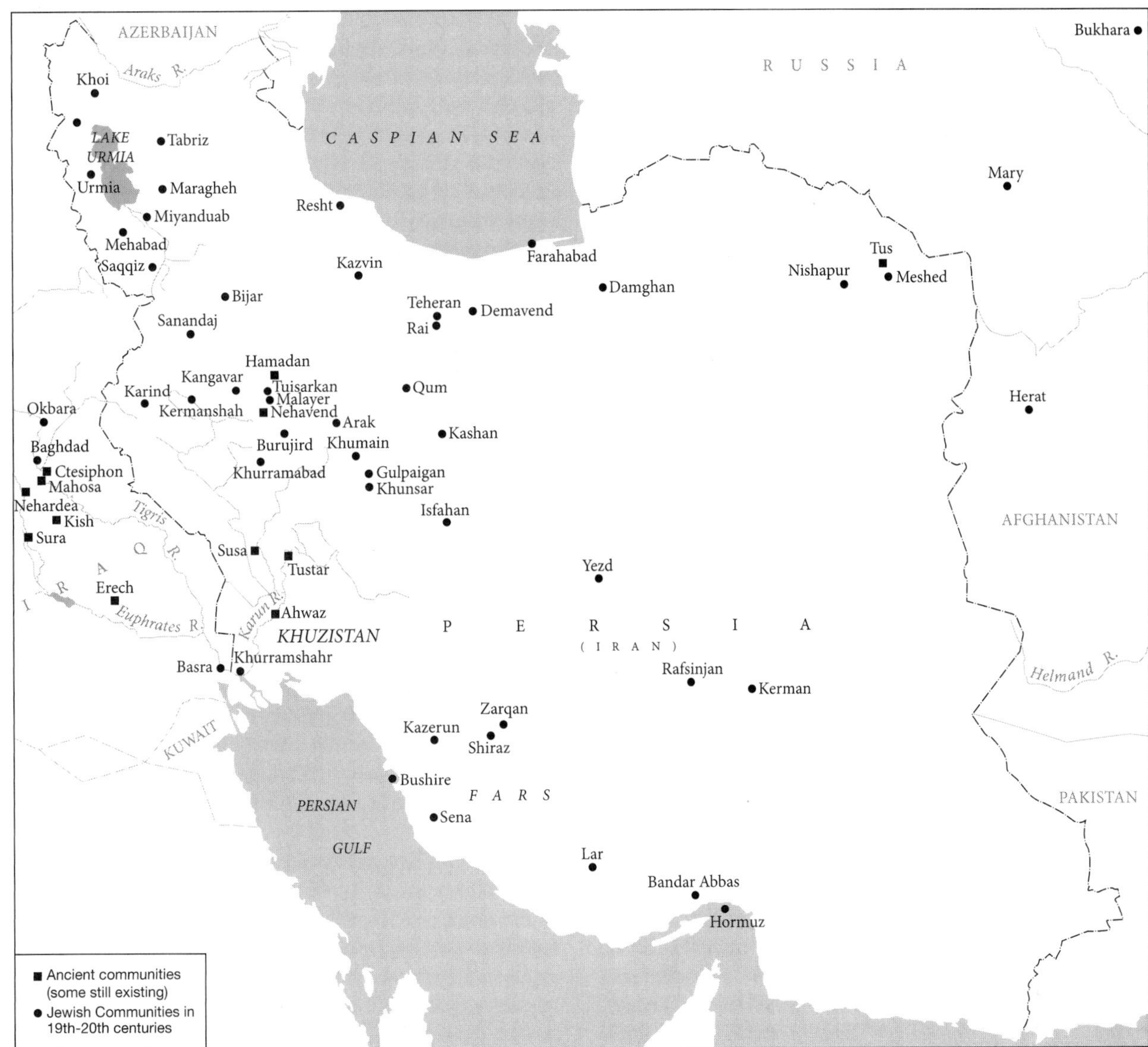

Jewish communities in Persia.

suzerainty of the Assyrian king Ashurbanipal. According to the Persian tradition followed by Herodotus, the Persians had submitted to the *Medes in the second quarter of the seventh century. Several central terms of political life, such as the word for king and even the name Pārsa, appear to show Median peculiarities. On the other hand, the Persians came under the cultural influence of *Elam, and it was in the Elamite language that accounts were kept in the Persian treasury at Persepolis, in the Persian homeland, as late as 459 B.C.E. The Persians' dependence on the Medes was terminated by *Cyrus II who rebelled against the last of the Median kings, Astyages. Astyages marched against him, but the Median army revolted and handed over their king to Cyrus in 550. Plundering Ecbatana (now Hamadan), the Median capital, Cyrus became ruler of Media. According to official Persian tradition, he was a maternal grandson of Astyages and was supported by Median nobles. To the outside world, his seizure of the Median crown looked like a mere change of dynasty. Media, which in alliance with *Babylon had destroyed the Assyrian Empire in 612, was a great power, whereas the Persians had been unknown before Cyrus. Therefore, foreigners (e.g., Herodotus) continued to speak of "Medians" when meaning "Persians." In Daniel 8:3 the two-horned ram is a symbol of Media and Persia.

Cyrus went on to conquer the Lydian kingdom of Croesus in 547, and the Babylonian Empire of *Nabonidus in 539. His son *Cambyses II (525) added Egypt to the Persian dominions, which now extended from the Nile to the Syr-Darya (Jaxartes) and the Indus. The death of Cambyses (522) was followed by a civil war, won by *Darius I, a distant relation of Cambyses. Direct descendants of Darius I ruled the empire for six generations after him. *Darius III, from another branch of the same family, lost the empire to Alexander the Great. Kings from Cyrus to Darius III were:

Cyrus 559–530 B.C.E.
Cambyses 530–522
Darius I 522–486
Xerxes I 486–465
Artaxerxes I 465–424
Xerxes II 424–423
Darius II 423–404
Artaxerxes II 404–359
Artaxerxes III 359–338
Arses 338–336
Darius III 336–330

The paramount fact in the history of the Achaemenids was the failure of Darius I in 490 and Xerxes I in 480–479 to conquer Greece. The Athenians and their allies wrested the Aegean coast of Asia Minor and the Aegean Islands from the Persians during 479–469, and also supported the Egyptian revolt in 459–454. The Peloponnesian War between Athens and Sparta (432–404) allowed Persia to recoup its territorial losses, but economically and culturally the Greeks remained preeminent. Greek silver, and in the fourth century its imitation, was the money used in the Persian Empire; Greek merchandise, as illustrated by finds of Greek vases, dominated the foreign commerce of Persia; and Greek mercenaries became an essential part of Persian armies. For the first time in history, the monarchical, hierarchical, and priestly "East" faced the republican, egalitarian, and secular "West," and the Persian bowman following his king was always outdone by the Greek infantryman ready to die in obedience to the law of his city.

The king ruled "by the favor of Ahuramazda," the supreme god, and his power of life and death was unlimited. Nevertheless, once fixed in a certain prescribed form, his decisions could not be revoked by him, "according to the law of the Medes and the Persians" (Dan. 6:9). In practice, the king consulted his counselors (Ezra 7:14; cf. Esth. 1:13; Jonah 3:6), and could not afford to offend the Persian nobility. He could execute a wicked judge, and with his skin upholster the judge's seat, but it was a son or another relative of the judge who would be appointed to judge from the same bench (Herodotus 5:25). Though the high officials, the royal guard, and the standing army were recruited from among Persians and Medes, non-Iranians could occupy high posts. Of the 23 high royal officers (*ustarbar*) who are mentioned in the *Murashu documents, only eight have Iranian names. Though the Achaemenian king stressed that he was a "Persian, son of a Persian, Aryan of Aryan lineage," the Persians were not "nationalists." "Nationalism" in the ancient Near East meant belonging to a city (e.g., Babylon, Jerusalem) and its deities. The Persians were tribesmen; their grandees were not citizens, or even inhabitants of a city, but lived on their estates. Being aristocrats, they did not need to be "nationalists," and used the talents of their subjects freely and easily.

Cyrus and his heirs, following the Assyrian practice, used Aramaic as the language of administration throughout the Persian Empire. As the Persian kings and their grandees were illiterate, the written language of administration was of no concern to them. Even in the ritual, the written language was Aramaic (R.A. Bowman, *Aramaic Ritual Texts from Persepolis*, 1970). The interpreters were on hand to translate the Persian orders into Elamite or Aramaic and to read aloud in Persian, an Indo-European language, the documents written in Aramaic or Elamite. The Persian script, borrowed indirectly from the Babylonians, was also cuneiform and as such inconvenient for writing on papyrus or leather. It seems to have been used only for monumental inscriptions engraved on stone or on metal.

The empire was divided into enormous administrative units known as satrapies. The satrapy "Beyond the River" (Abar-Nahara, e.g., Ezra 5:3), to which Judah belonged, extended from the *Euphrates to the Mediterranean. The satrap was the head of the administration, commander of the troops, and supreme judge and tax collector of his satrapy. Each satrapy had to pay a fixed tribute to the king, in cash and/or kind. The provinces within the satrapies had to maintain the troops, the administration of the satrapy, and the viceroy. Nehemiah, governor of the miniscule province of Judah, had to feed over 150 men daily (Neh. 5:17). There were various taxes (Ezra 4:13; 7:24), and taxation was heavy (Neh. 5:4). In addition, there was the baksheesh (Mal. 1:8). The satrap was virtually omnipotent in his satrapy, as the story of the temple of *Elephantine shows, but he had to consult his advisers and it was prudent to submit controversial questions to the king (Ezra 5:6). However, the dimensions of the satrapy made local self-administration necessary, and Nehemiah in his quarrel with the neighbors of Jerusalem does not appeal to the satrap of Abar-Nahara ("trans-Euphrates"), but mobilizes the Jewish militia (Neh. 4:7ff.). Self-administration extended to private law, and the scribes drafting private contracts made the Aramaic common law prevalent throughout the Persian Empire.

In Ezekiel 27:10 and 38:5, the name "Persia" is probably a corruption. Deutero-Isaiah expected that Cyrus would rebuild Jerusalem (44:28; 45:1). Having conquered Babylonia, Cyrus reversed the Babylonian policy and returned captive gods and their worshipers to their homes. However, by taking care of *Marduk in Babylon and of "the God who is in Jerusalem" (Ezra 1:3), Cyrus became the legitimate successor of the kings of Babylon and of the kings of the House of David. After the restoration of the Temple and Darius I and until the revolt against Rome in 66 C.E., the priests of Jerusalem offered a sacrifice daily for the welfare of the heathen overlord of Zion. Written in the first half of the fourth century B.C.E., the work of the Chronicler (Chronicles, Ezra-Nehemiah) expresses this recognition of alien domination: the Temple was restored "by command of the God of Israel and by order of Cyrus and Darius and Artaxerxes, king of Persia" (Ezra 6:14). However, Jerusalem was an insignificant town in an enormous empire, and if the Persian kings took the trouble to humor the God of Jerusalem, they did it rather for the sake of the Babylonian and Persian Jewry. Knowledge of the latter is almost nil. The story of *Susanna in the Apocrypha reflects Jewish self-government in Babylonia. The story of *Tobit illustrates the family life, faith, and also the superstitions of Persian Jews. However, the society which produced *Zerubbabel, *Ezra, and *Nehemiah was not that of Tobit and Susanna.

Again, almost nothing is known about contacts between the Persians and the Jews. Yet Gadal-Yama (Gadal-YHWH, Gedaliah), who in 422 was called upon to serve as a cuirassier to the royal army in a campaign at Erech (Uruk) and was the beneficiary of a fief, must have had Iranian comrades. One source indicates that a Persian magus was on friendly terms with a servant of the Lord in Elephantine (E.G. Kraeling, *Brooklyn Museum Aramaic Papyri* (1953), 4:24, 175). Because so little is known about the Iranian religions in Achaemenian Persia, it is difficult to determine the nature and extent of their influence on the Jews in the Persian period. The Jews preserved a favorable memory of the Persian kings, as their rule brought them two centuries of peace. By favoring the clergy, the Persian king laid the foundation for the later role of the high priests. For the first and last time, Jerusalem and the whole Diaspora, from the Indus to the Nile, remained under the sway of the same overlords. From Babylonia, Zerubbabel, Ezra, and Nehemiah came to the aid of Jerusalem. The Jews at Elephantine could ask Jerusalem for assistance. When, after the death of *Alexander, the unity of the political world of which the Jews were a part was destroyed, the religious and spiritual link that had been forged between Jerusalem and the Diaspora under the Achaemenids remained, and it has persisted for 23 centuries.

[Elias J. Bickerman]

Pre-Islamic Persia

Traditions and legends connect the origin of the Jewish Diaspora in Persia with various events in Israel's ancient history, the starting points being regarded as the deportation of the Israelites in the time of Tiglath-Pileser III (d. 727 B.C.E.) from Samaria to the "cities of Media and Persia," the forced migration in the time of Sargon II of Assyria (d. 705) and of his son Sennacherib (681), or the destruction of the Temple by Nebuchadnezzar (d. 586). When the famous "Cyrus Declaration" (538 B.C.E.) allowed those Jews who were living as exiles on the "rivers of Babylon" to return to their homeland, Judea, and to rebuild their national life, some of them, who had established themselves economically and socially in their new surroundings, preferred to remain on Babylonian-Persian soil. These remaining exiles can be regarded as the nucleus of the permanent Jewish settlements which gradually expanded from the chief centers in Babylon to the interior provinces and cities of Persia, Ecbatana, Susa, and other places. The emergent group of Jewish colonies spread, in the words of the Book of Esther, "over all the provinces of the king… scattered among all peoples of the Persian Empire."

Favored by the tolerant attitude of the rulers toward their Jewish subjects, such dignitaries as Zerubbabel, Ezra, Nehemiah, Daniel, Mordecai, and Esther emerged from these settlements and were able to play a leading role at the royal Persian court. The gratitude of the Jews toward the Persian Achaemenid rulers found expression in subsequent generations in a mishnaic injunction that a picture of Susa, the capital of the Persian kings, should be affixed on the eastern gate of the Temple to remind the Jews of their deliverance and the tolerance of the Achaemenids (Mid. 1:3b; Men. 98a). The overthrow of the Achaemenid dynasty resulting from Alexander the Great's conquest of Persia and the rule of the Seleucids over the eastern parts of Alexander's empire does not seem to have hindered the existence and expansion of Jewish settlements in Persia.

Under the Parthian dynasty (249 B.C.E.–226 C.E.) the size and influence of well-organized Jewish communities beyond the Euphrates and Tigris was acknowledged in contemporary literature. Philo, in his *Embassy to Gaius* (245), mentions the "large number of Jews in every city" in the trans-Euphratian Diaspora. Josephus refers to Jews in Babylonia, Media, and other distant provinces, and stresses that "Jews beyond the Euphrates are an immense multitude and not estimated by numbers." Apocryphal literature, in particular the Book of the Maccabees, alludes to the existence of Jews in "the cities of Persia and Media"; and the anonymous author of the *Sibylline Oracles* refers to Jews "in every country and every sea." The New Testament makes special mention of Jewish pilgrims coming to Jerusalem from the eastern Diaspora, from Elymais, Susa, and other territories. The Book of Tobit refers to Jews in Media, in particular to the city of Rhages. The Mishnah mentions a R. Nahum of Media (Naz. 5:4; BB 5:2) and talmudic sources contain a reference to an epistle sent by Rabban Gamaliel "to our brethren in the exile of Babylon, Media, and other remote provinces" (Sanh. 11a).

Under the Sassanid dynasty (226–642) the Jewish Diaspora in Persia had grown considerably; it also increased with the voluntary movements of Jews from the Roman provinces into Persia, as well as through the forced migration of Jews from territories adjacent to Persia. According to the Armenian historian, Moses of Chorene, in 364 C.E. Shapur II (309–379) transferred a great number of Jews, some say 7,000, to the interior of Persia. The Babylonian Talmud, a product of Babylonian Jewry in the Sassanid period, though concentrating mainly on Jewish life within the boundaries of Babylon, affords glimpses into the geographical diffusion of Jewish settlements beyond the Euphrates and Tigris, and apart from the dense Jewish population in such cities as *Sura, *Pumbedita, *Nehardea, *Mahosa, *Nisibis, *Naresh, *Ctesiphon (Be-Ardashir), there were Jewish settlements remote from Babylonian centers, in the interior provinces of the Sassanid Empire, in Media, *Elam, Khuzistan, Susiana, in such cities as Hulvan, *Nehavend, *Hamadan (Ecbatana), Be Lapat (Gundashapur), *Ahwaz (Khurramshahr), *Susa, and Tustar, and up to the Persian Gulf. The spread of Jewish settlements throughout the Sassanid realm is also indicated by the express reference to them in the inscription of Karter, one of the leaders of the Mazdaan priesthood in the period following Shahpur I.

The First Six Centuries under the Caliphate (642–1258)

LEGAL STATUS. The battle at Nehavend in 642 which signaled the defeat of the Sassanid army by the invading Arab Muslims terminated the national and political independence which Persia had enjoyed for nearly 12 centuries, from the time of Cyrus the Great until Yazdegerd III. The changes resulting from the Muslim Arab conquest of Persia affected the whole structure of the Persian Empire in its political, religious, cultural, and linguistic aspects. Politically, Persia ceased to be an independent entity, being incorporated as a province into the great Arab-Islamic empire. The development of Persia was henceforth controlled and shaped to a large degree by the political authorities, the *Umayyad and *Abbasid caliphs of *Damascus and *Baghdad respectively, and the viceroys appointed by them. Increasingly Arabic words infiltrated the Persian language, written from then on in Arabic script. The Islamic conquest replaced Zoroastrianism with *Islam as the state religion. These changes had a profound impact on the many religious minorities within Persia and in particular on the Jewish settlements within the Babylonian-Persian Diaspora, affecting first their legal and political status. The attitude of Islam toward the non-Muslims living within an Islamic realm was regulated by a contract which deprived the **dhimmis* of social and political equality, making them in effect "second-class" citizens. At various periods in history this led to the enactment of discriminatory measures which were embodied in the so-called "Covenant of *Omar."

THE CRADLE OF JEWISH SECTARIANISM. The religious and social fermentation affecting the Persian population in the early centuries of Islamic rule also touched Jewish life, giving rise to Jewish sectarian movements, freethinkers, heretics, and pseudo-messianic claimants. The first recorded sectarian movement initiated by a Persian Jew was connected with the name of *Abu ʿĪsā, a tailor who lived in the time of the Umayyad caliph ʿAbd al-Malik ibn Marwān (d. 705). Greatly influenced by the heterodox tendencies manifest within the Islamic environment, he proclaimed himself a messiah, acknowledged Moses, Jesus, and Muhammad as true prophets, advocated fundamental changes in the Jewish calendar, Jewish ritual, and prayer, aimed at a reform of and a revolt against rabbinic Judaism. He seems to have gained a considerable following among the Jews of Isfahan and other places. His adherents were described as a community of simpleminded, uneducated Jews: "barbarian, ill-bred peoples, destitute of intellect and knowledge." Abu ʿĪsā's messianic claims and political ambitions brought him into open conflict with the Islamic authorities and he is said to have been killed in a battle with the troops of the caliph. After his death his movement continued under his disciple *Yudghan of Hamadan, who broke even more radically with the *halakhah*. His adherents, known as Isunians or Isfahanians, are said to have been eagerly awaiting the return of their mahdi, Abu ʿĪsā, in Isfahan until the tenth century. A certain Mushka of Qum created another movement proclaiming Muhammad as a true prophet, and calling on his adherents to wage a "holy war." In the remote region of *Khurasan in the ninth century, a Jew from the city of Balkh, known as *Ḥiwi al-Balkhi, arose among the scattered Jewish communities. Hiwi's heretical teachings are known mainly through the 200 answers which *Saadiah Gaon wrote in refutation of his beliefs.

The greatest schism in Oriental Jewry in these early centuries was the rise of the *Karaite movement founded by *Anan b. David in the eighth century; some of its most distinguished leaders hailed from Persia, such as Benjamin b. Moses *Nahāwendī, Daniel b. Moses al-Qūmisi, and others. The Karaite scholar and traveler Jacob al-*Kirkisānī (tenth century) depicts the spread and distribution of Karaite communities over many Persian provinces and cities, such as Isfahan, Tustar, Jibāl, Khurasan, Fars, etc. Due to Saadiah Gaon's intervention and the activities of subsequent *geonim* and exilarchs, rabbinic-talmudic Judaism asserted its influence on the Persian communities, though Karaite communities continued to exist in many Persian cities well into the 16th century.

RELATIONSHIP BETWEEN CENTER AND PERIPHERY. The backbone of the communal organization of Babylonian Persian Jewry was the *exilarch, the *resh galuta*, appointed by the Islamic authorities, who was responsible for the collection and prompt delivery of the annual poll tax levied on every male. He and the *gaon* of the talmudic academies in Babylonia were the recognized authorities for the widely scattered Jewish Diaspora in the East. The relationship between the Babylonian authorities, the center, and Persia, the periphery, expressed itself in subsequent centuries in a twofold way, financially and culturally. The Persian communities were expected to send financial support to Babylonia for the maintenance of the talmudic academies of Sura and Pumbedita. Available sources refer to the annual contributions made by Nehavend, Fars, Hulvan, and other communities, but also indicate that some Persian communities refused or were delinquent in sending their contributions, which sometimes led to the despatch of special envoys from Babylonia to collect the revenue through the intervention of the Islamic authorities. The tenth-century chronicle of *Nathan b. Isaac ha-Kohen ha-Bavli, and a parallel version in **Seder Olam Zuta*, recount a dispute between *Kohen Zedek b. Joseph, the head of the academy in Pumbedita, and the exilarch *Ukba over the jurisdiction over the Jews of Khurasan.

The Babylonian authorities made their influence felt on the Persian communities by controlling their education and by exercising their prerogative of appointing judges, *dayyanim*, and rabbis for the Persian communities. The chief rabbi of Isfahan, in the time of *Benjamin of Tudela, was Sar Shalom and the spiritual leader of *Samarkand Obadiah ha-Nasi, both appointed by the Babylonian *gaon*. As the 12th-century "*Iggeret*" of Gaon *Samuel b. Ali indicates, vigorous efforts were made to foster talmudic education in the Persian communities culminating in the establishment of a yeshivah in Hamadan, which together with Isfahan seemed to have been the cultural center of the Persian Diaspora at this period. According to the *Iggeret*, the Babylonian *gaon* sent his own son-in-law, *Zechariah b. Barachel, and later dispatched a distinguished student of his, Jacob b. Eli, to Hamadan to deal with halakhic questions and advise the community. There is mention also that a young rabbinical student, David of Hamadan, arrived in Baghdad with a letter of recommendation from the *pakid*, the trustee of the Hamadan yeshivah. It is noteworthy that part of the correspondence preserved between Baghdad and Hamadan was written in Persian.

ECONOMIC ACTIVITIES OF THE JEWS. The position as *dhimmī* within Islamic society allowed the Jews complete freedom in the pursuit of economic opportunities. Scanty though the data are, a thorough examination of the available Muslim and Hebrew sources indicates that Persian Jews were engaged in many branches of artisanship and handicraft, as weavers, dyers, gold and silversmiths, and also as merchants and shopkeepers, jewelers, wine manufacturers, and dealers in drugs, spices, and antiquities. Due to the imposition of heavy land taxes, their share in agriculture declined to a great extent. When Baghdad became the capital of the Abbasid caliphate (762), a fundamental change occurred in the economic stratification of Babylonian-Persian Jewry. With the ever-increasing urbanization of the Islamic east and the development of trade and commerce on an international scale, a wealthy class of Jewish merchants emerged in the leading centers of the Diaspora, such as Baghdad, Ahwaz, *Isfahan, and *Shiraz.

From the tenth century on, Jewish merchants began to participate in banking and moneylending and to play a leading role as financial experts and bankers (see *Banking) in the service of the caliphs and their viziers. Known as *Jahābidha* ("court bankers"), they carried out major financial transactions such as the administration of deposits, remittance of funds from place to place through the medium of *suftaja* ("letter of credit") – widely used instrument of the prevailing credit economy – and by supplying huge loans for the caliph, his viziers, his court, and his army. Jewish court bankers were also to be found at the courts of the Buyids, the Ghaznavids, and the Seljuk sultans. In the time of Sultan Mahmud (997–1030) of the Ghaznavid dynasty, the Jew Isaac, a resident of Ghazni, was in the sultan's service and was entrusted with the administration of his lead mines in Balkh in Khurasan. Numerous Court Jews also served the Seljuk sultans. Their celebrated vizier, Niẓām al-Mulk (d. 1192), though in his Persian work, *Siyāsat Nameh*, he emphatically rejected the employment of *dhimmī* in governmental service, at the same time maintained close and friendly associations with Jewish officeholders, tax-farmers, bankers, and money experts who had been called upon to assist him. Many of the wealthy Jewish merchants were subjected to extortion, confiscation, and torture at various intervals, causing a wave of emigration to other parts of the Islamic world. Notable among those Persian Jews who emigrated in the 11th century were the two Jewish merchants from Tustar known as the Banu Sahl al-Tustari, who rose to great influence and position in the service of the Fatimid caliphs in *Egypt.

THE GEOGRAPHICAL SETTING. The status of **dhimmī* allowed the Jews complete freedom of movement and settlement within the Islamic realm. During the first six centuries of Islamic rule over Persia, the Jewish Diaspora experienced an unprecedented expansion and remarkable geographical diffusion into all the provinces of Persia and the eastern lands of the caliphate. Muslim geographers and historians, rabbinic and geonic sources, and the account of *Benjamin of Tudela and other 12th-century travelers make it possible to discern the major areas of Jewish settlement. Jewish colonies were established in all the interior provinces of Persia. These settlements seemed to have served as a springboard for further expansion into the easternmost provinces of Khurasan and *Transoxiana and even China. Jewish communities are recorded in *Nishapur, *Balkh Ghazni, Kabul, Seistan (Sistan), *Merv, Samarkand, Khiva, *Bukhara, and other regions. No clear picture emerges of the numerical strength of the Jewish Diaspora in Persia in this period. Some Persian and Arab geographers of the tenth century make comparative statements showing the relative strengths of some non-Muslim groups in various Persian provinces. Thus, the tenth-century Arab geographer, al-Muqaddasī, in comparing the various non-Muslim minorities stated, "in the province of Jibāl Jews are more numerous than Christians; in the province of Khuzistan Christians are few and Jews not numerous; while in the province of Fars the Zoroastrians are more numerous than the Jews and there are only a few Christians."

Concrete figures appear for the first time in the 12th century thanks to the travels of Benjamin of Tudela and *Pethahiah of Regensburg. According to Benjamin's account, 30,000 Jews lived in *Hamadan; 15,000 in *Isfahan; 10,000 in *Shiraz; 25,000 in *ʿAmadiya; 4,000 in Tabaristan; 7,000 in Susa; 4,000 in Hulvan; 80,000 in Ghazni; 50,000 in Samarkand; and in the region of the Persian Gulf, 500 in Kish and 5,000 in Qatif. There is no doubt that all these figures are unreliable and exaggerated, arrived at by hearsay alone. This far-flung Diaspora in Persia and Khurasan was not just an agglomeration of immigrants without guidance and leadership; it was dependent, culturally and religiously, on the official Jewish authorities in Baghdad, the exilarchs and the *gaon*, who controlled and guided them throughout this period. Benjamin of Tudela emphasizes that the Jewish leadership in Babylonia had considerable authority over all the Jewish communities under the caliph and stresses the extent of their jurisdiction "over all the Jewish communities in Mesopotamia, Shinear, Media, Elam, Khurasan, Persia, Saba, Armenia, over the mountains of Ararat, Caucasus, Georgia, unto the borders of Tibet and *India." Similarly, Pethahiah of Regensburg speaks of the power of the *gaon* "in all the lands of Assyria, Damascus, in the cities of Persia and Media, in Babylon." The extent and scope of the Jewish Diaspora in Persia must have been well known to the Persian authorities, as illustrated in the appearance of pseudo-

Messiah David *Alroy in ʿAmadiya in the time of the Seljuk sultan Sanjar (d. 1156). Realizing that the messianic movement might encroach on his authority, the sultan, according to the report of Benjamin of Tudela, threatened to eliminate "all the Jews in all the parts of the Persian Empire" unless the movement was stopped.

Under the Il-Khan Dynasty (1258–1336)

The invasion of Persia by Hulagu Khan, culminating in the conquest of Baghdad and the overthrow of the Abbasid caliphate in 1258, also brought about a fundamental change in the situation of the Jews in the Persian Diaspora. Under Hulagu and some of his successors of the newly established Il-Khan dynasty, the concept of the *dhimma* ("the protected people") and the division between "believers" and "nonbelievers" were abolished, and all the various religions put on equal footing. Thus Persian Jews were afforded a unique opportunity to participate actively in the affairs of the state and in the time of Arghun Khan (1284–91), a Jew by the name of *Saʿd al-Dawla al-Safī ibn Hibatallah achieved an unexpected and spectacular rise to power and influence. Under subsequent Il-Khan rulers another Persian Jew, Faḍl Allah ibn Abi al-Khayribn Ali al-Hamadhānī, had a similarly meteoric rise and fall. The cultural climate which had enabled these two Jews to achieve power in the economic and political sphere also led to the genesis and growth of *Judeo-Persian literature.

Under the Safawid Dynasty (1502–1736)

The fate of the Jews in Persia and Babylonia under Tamerlane (d. 1405), the greatest world conqueror Asia has produced after Genghis Khan, is shrouded in obscurity. It must be assumed that in the wake of the devastating campaigns which spread destruction and annihilation over all the lands of western Asia, the Jews did not escape the atrocities which Tamerlane and his army committed everywhere. The Jewish settlements were undoubtedly reduced and decimated through warfare, the intolerance of the authorities, and the fanaticism of the masses. But that the Jewish settlements in Persia, although weakened and reduced in numbers, survived these troubled centuries became evident with the emergence of a new dynasty, the Safawids. Under this dynasty the Jews once again appear on the scene, and according to European travelers of that period they were living in "all the cities of Persia" and were estimated at about 30,000.

The founders of the Safawid dynasty put the country on entirely new political and religious bases. They introduced Shiʿism as the state religion and established a hierarchy of clergy with almost unlimited power and influence in every sphere of life. The concept of the "ritual uncleanliness" of nonbelievers, the principal cornerstone of their interconfessional relationship, made the life of the Jews in Persia a sequence of suffering and persecution. Under no other Persian dynasty was the hatred of the Jews more intense. They experienced a temporary improvement under Shah *Abbas I (d. 1629) who introduced reforms in order to weaken the theocratic basis of the state and free Persia from the fetters of its all-too-powerful Shiʿa clergy, and to break the political, economic, and cultural isolation of the country.

Realizing that the most urgent requirement for Persia was increased population and economic ties with the outside world, Shah Abbas fundamentally changed the policy of the state toward non-Muslims and foreigners. Far from being antagonistic, as were his predecessors, toward Europeans and nonbelievers, he encouraged the immigration of foreigners – merchants, settlers, and artisans – from neighboring countries such as Armenia, Georgia, Turkey, and also from Europe. By granting freedom of religion and special privileges and facilities to all who were prepared to come to his territory, he was able to succeed. This liberal and tolerant attitude made Persia at that time the meeting place of European envoys, emissaries, diplomats, merchant-adventurers, and missionaries – all eager to obtain commercial, political, or religious concessions and privileges. Never before in the history of Persia's relationship with the outside world were the economic and political ties between Persia and Europe closer.

For the Jews of Persia, the second part of the 17th century was a time of great suffering and persecutions. The conception of the ritual uncleanliness of the Persian Jew, which led to the introduction of a special headgear enforced on all Jews in Persia and to a crusade against Hebrew books, culminated under Shah *Abbas II (1642–66) in the forced conversion of all the Jews in Persia, a catastrophe which brought them to the very brink of destruction. This persecution, a tragic parallel to the Inquisition of Spain, was regarded as more cruel than that of the time of Ahasuerus and Haman. European sources as well as the Judeo-Persian chronicles of *Babai ibn Lutf and Babai ibn Farḥad describe in great detail the sufferings of the Jews during the time of Shah Abbas II. They show how in Isfahan, the capital, and in other communities the Jews were compelled to abandon their religion, how their synagogues were closed and they were led to the mosque, where they had to proclaim a public confession of Muslim faith. After their forced conversion, they were called new Muslims; they were then, of course, freed from the payment of the poll tax and from the wearing of a special headgear or badge. Despite all the measures on the part of the Shiʿa clergy to supervise the Islamization of the Jews, most of them adhered tenaciously and heroically in secret to their religion and began to live a dual life as secret Jews, repeating the phenomenon of *Marranos in an Islamic version. The double life of these forcibly converted Jews did not escape the attention of the Persian authorities, and led finally to an edict issued in 1661 allowing the Jews to return openly to their religion.

When J. Fryer visited Persia a decade later (1672–81), he found the Jews "congregated on their Sabbaths, new moons, and feast days in synagogues without disturbance." Under the successors of Shah Abbas II, Shah Suleiman (d. 1694) and Shah Husein (d. 1722), the persecution and oppression of the Jews were, however, renewed, and it was only with the rise of a new and remarkable ruler, *Nadir Shah (1736–47), that the Jews of Persia were saved from complete annihilation.

COMMUNAL AND RELIGIOUS LIFE. The establishment of Persia as a national state under the Safawid dynasty had far-reaching repercussions on Jewish community life in Persia. During the Abbasid period, the exilarch or the *gaon*, from his central seat in Baghdad, exerted supreme authority in all religious and cultural matters over all the Jewish communities in the far-flung Diaspora of Asia, including Persia, which then formed a part of the Eastern caliphate. With the rise of the Safawids, the official bonds which the Persian Jewish communities might still have maintained formally with Jewish authorities outside the borders of the country were completely severed. The official representative of the Jews in Persia, the chief rabbi of Isfahan, was no longer appointed by the *gaon* of Baghdad as in preceding centuries, nor were Persian Jews expected or willing to support the Jewish academies in Baghdad. Persian Jews ceased to be responsible to any central Jewish leadership and their communal life was put on a purely territorial basis.

Due to their geographical proximity to the central government and their numerical strength the Jews of Isfahan, the new capital of the Safawid dynasty, assumed the religious and cultural leadership and functioned as representatives and spokesmen for all Persian Jewry. At the head of the community of Isfahan was a *nasi*, who was assisted by the rabbi, mullah, or *dayyan*. The *nasi*, who was highly respected, was responsible for the prompt payment of taxes to the local authorities. If the taxes were not paid in due time or in the due amount requested, he could be dismissed by the authorities or even imprisoned. On the other hand, if the authorities were satisfied, the *nasi* would receive a sign of distinction and honor. It seems that in the time of the Safawids there existed in Isfahan, as part of the general administration, a special divan which regulated the financial affairs of the non-Muslims and examined petitions of protest, grievances, requests, or complaints from the Jews against officials of the administration. At the head of the divans stood a high official appointed by the grand vizier, sometimes assisted by a Jewish apostate who acted as adviser or spy for the authorities.

The frequent mention of a "Jewish quarter" indicates the geographical separation of the Jews from the Christian and Muslim population. The Jewish quarter housed the residences of the Jewish population, their synagogues, and schools, the *mikveh*, and other religious institutions. In the time of the Safawids Isfahan had at least three synagogues, while *Kashan is said to have had ten; it can be assumed that at least one synagogue existed in every Jewish settlement in Persia. The religious life of the Jews in Safawid Persia was established on a rigid, rabbinical, traditional basis. There were also some Karaite communities, especially in Kazerun. A typical feature in the religious life of the Persian Jew at this, and indeed at all times, was the custom of making pilgrimages to some of the Jewish "holy places" in Persia, in particular to the mausoleum of Mordecai and Esther in Hamadan, to the tomb of the prophet Daniel in Susa, and to the burial places of other biblical heroes believed to be interred on Persian soil. At this period another "holy place" came into prominence, the alleged visiting place of Serah bat Asher in the vicinity of Isfahan at Pir Bakrān.

Despite the territorial limitation, the Jews of Persia had contacts with the outside Jewish world, particularly with Ereẓ Israel through "messengers from Zion" who toured the Jewish communities in that period, fostering the love for Zion and collecting funds for the charitable institutions in the Holy Land. Among these early *sheliḥim* were R. Moses *Alshekh (c. 1593) from Safed, Baruch Gad of *Jerusalem, and above all, R. Yahuda Amram Divan (d. 1752) who repeatedly visited the Jewish communities in Persia. The messianic movement of *Shabbetai Ẓevi made an impact on Persian Jewry. It was in this period that the Jews began to migrate to territories outside the border of Persia to neighboring regions such as *Afghanistan, Turkestan, Samarkand, and Bukhara in the east, and to Kurdistan, the Caucasus, and Egypt in the west. Persian Jews also moved to India; most famous of them was *Sarmad, the Jew of Kashan, who became a fakir and a Sufi dervish.

Under the Kajar Dynasty (1794–1925)

The political and religious foundations of the Kajar dynasty which ruled over Persia were essentially a continuation of those of the Safawid dynasty. The Shiʿite concept of the ritual uncleanliness of the nonbelievers prevailed, with the related attitude of the Persian authorities toward their non-Muslim minorities, Christians and Jews alike. The intolerant attitude toward the Jews led to innumerable legal and political restrictions which made their daily life, throughout the 19th century, an uninterrupted sequence of persecution, oppression, and discrimination. The reports of many European missionaries and travelers to Persia describe the tragic fate of the Jews in Persia during the Kajar dynasty. Whole Jewish communities, as well as many individual Jews, were forcibly converted to Islam in many provinces of the Persian Empire, a movement which reached its peak in the forced conversion of the whole Jewish community in *Meshed in 1839 under Muhammad Shah (1834–48).

Even during the reign of Nasr-ed-Din Shah (1848–96), who realized the necessity for thorough reform of the whole Persian administration and social structure, persecution of the Jews continued, coupled with legal and social discriminations of the severest nature, including the enforcement of a special Jewish badge and Jewish headgear. The entire community was held responsible for crimes and misdemeanors committed by its individual members; the oath of a Jew was not accepted in a court of justice; and a Jew who converted to Islam could claim to be the sole inheritor of family property, to the exclusion of all relatives who had not changed their religion.

The Jewish minority in Persia had been left entirely to itself and no outside organization, Jewish or other, had taken any interest in its fate. Contact with the Jewish world at large, and particularly with the Jews in Ereẓ Israel, was occasionally maintained through the *sheliḥim* sent on behalf of the communities of Hebron, Tiberias, Safed, and Jerusalem, to the remote Jewish communities in Persia, Bukhara, and Afghanistan. In the middle of the 19th century four brothers of one Jewish family were the busiest and most popular physicians in the city of *Teheran. One of them, Hak Nazar, was for some time court physician of Muhammad Shah. They had, however, just as little influence on the actual political situation of their coreligionists as did the European physicians subsequently appointed by Nasr-ed-Din and his successors, among whom figured most prominently the Austrian physician, J.E. *Polak. In the second half of the 19th century the Persian Jews acquired a powerful ally in their struggle for justice and emancipation – Western European Jewry.

THE INTERVENTION OF WESTERN JEWRY. Reports on the plight of Persian Jews moved the *Board of Deputies of British Jews and later the *Anglo-Jewish Association under Sir Moses *Montefiore and the *Alliance Israélite Universelle under Adolphe *Crémieux to action, urging intervention by the British and French ministers in Teheran. When news of a terrible persecution of Jews in Hamadan reached London in 1865, Sir Moses Montefiore decided to leave for Persia and to obtain from the shah an edict of safety for the persecuted Persian Jews. However, he was dissuaded by the British Foreign Office, who stated that "the journey would be perilous even to a younger man and could be undertaken by him at the risk of his life." In addition to their political plight, the Jews of Persia experienced new hardship through the outbreak of a famine in 1871, which the leaders of European Jewry tried to alleviate through a relief fund. The Jewish leaders in Paris and London were again on the point of considering sending a Jewish delegation to Persia when the news reached them in 1873 that Nasr-ed-Din Shah, anxious to appear as a tolerant and progressive monarch, had embarked on a visit to Europe. Seizing their opportunity, the leaders of the Alliance Israélite Universelle and the Anglo-Jewish Association organized a movement intended to impress the shah with the importance and influence of European Jewry, to stress their equality and emancipation in all European countries and their unanimous desire to see an improvement in the condition of their coreligionists in Persia.

In every European capital through which the shah planned to travel, committees of the most influential Jews were organized to present him personally with petitions calling for the improvement of the Persian Jews' situation. This was carried out in Berlin on May 4, 1873, in Amsterdam on June 10, in Brussels on June 17, in London on June 24, in Paris on July 12, in Vienna on August 6, and in Constantinople on August 20. In London the shah had a meeting with *Disraeli and also received Sir Moses Montefiore in private audience in Buckingham Palace. In all these petitions the spirit of Cyrus the Great was recalled and the grievances of the Jews in Persia were listed. The highlight of these activities was the memorable interview in Paris between the shah and Adolphe Crémieux and his associates on July 12, 1873. Apparently impressed by the strength and unity of European Jewry, the shah promised to make the protection of his Jewish subjects his own and his grand vizier's special responsibility, to establish a special court of justice for the Jews, and above all to help in the establishment of Jewish schools in Persia as suggested by the European representatives. In order to encourage and strengthen the persecuted Persian Jews, the text of the petitions submitted to the shah in the various capitals of Europe, together with the reply of the shah and his minister, were translated into Hebrew and published as a booklet called *Mishlo'aḥ Manot* (1874), which was distributed among the Jewish communities in Persia. Despite all the well-meaning promises of the shah, the central government in Persia failed to prevent new outbreaks of hostilities against the Jews. There was, therefore, enough reason to intervene again and to remind Nasr-ed-Din during his last journey to Europe of his previous promises and assurances. On July 4, 1889, a deputation of British Jewry, led by Sir Albert Sassoon, had an interview with the shah in Buckingham Palace. The members of the deputation included Lord Rothschild, Sir J. Goldsmid, and Sebag Montefiore. The demand for the establishment of Jewish schools in Persia was again the central issue.

Under Shah Muzaffar-ed-Din (1896–1907) a definite improvement in the destiny of Persian Jews took place in connection with the constitutional movement, which had far-reaching consequences for all religious groups in Persia. Persian Jews took an active part in this constitutional movement, receiving official thanks for their efforts from the first parliament of Persia in 1906, although neither the Jews, the Armenian Christians, nor the Zoroastrian minority were yet permitted to send their own deputy to parliament and had to agree to be represented by a Muslim deputy. For Persian Jews the constitutional movement meant a step forward toward their emancipation and equality. The dualism in legislation between the religious laws, the shariʿa, and the civil law, was abolished, as were the discriminatory and humiliating medieval restrictions against the Jews. Unfortunately for the country, three months after parliament convened Shah Muzaffar-ed-Din died, and under the new ruler, Shah Muhammad Ali (1907–09), the constitutional movement quickly disappointed the high hopes placed in it by the liberal elements among the Muslims and the Jews in Persia.

At this stage the Persian Jews were assisted in their struggle for survival by the intervention of the U.S. diplomatic representative in the country. Reference to Persian Jews appeared in U.S. diplomatic correspondence in 1918, in connection with the relief activities of the *American Jewish Joint Distribution Committee. The State Department, as well as U.S. diplomatic representatives abroad, helped the committee in distributing funds, food, and other necessities to the starving Jews everywhere. This intervention also continued in the period after World War I, through the U.S. representative in Persia from 1921 to 1924, namely the minister plenipotentiary, Joseph Saul *Kornfeld, a former rabbi. The dissolution of the Persian parliament; the deposition of Shah Muhammad Ali by the National Assembly; the reconvening of a second parliament in 1909 by Ahmed Shah (1909–25); the great financial crisis which brought the American experts, M. Shuster and A.C. Millspaugh, to Persia; the steady changes in the cabinet and the government; and the encroachment of Russia in the north and Great Britain in the south – all this contributed to a state of unrest and danger, so that at the outbreak of World War I, Persia stood at the very brink of disintegration.

THE ESTABLISHMENT OF JEWISH SCHOOLS IN PERSIA. For the Persian Jews the rule of Muzaffar-ed-Din was a turning point, since at this period the first Jewish schools of the Alliance Israélite Universelle were established in Persia. The idea of Jewish schools in Persia, conceived in 1866, became in 1873 the central issue in the discussions between the Jewish authorities in Europe and the Persian government; in 1889 it was still a matter of discussion alone, but finally, after ten years, it was realized. In 1898 the first school of the Alliance Israélite Universelle was opened in Teheran, followed by similar schools in Hamadan in 1900, in Isfahan in 1901, in Shiraz and Sena in 1903, and in *Kermanshah in 1904. As two main dangers threatening Jewish survival in Persia during the 19th century were Christian missionary activities and the *Bahai movement, the Jewish schools of the Alliance played an important role in the struggle for spiritual survival. The educational facilities available to Persian Jews were considerably strengthened and augmented from 1944, not only through the activities of the American Jewish Joint Distribution Committee and the establishment of vocational training schools and workshops under the auspices of the *ORT, but also by a new educational movement sponsored by a group of prominent U.S. and European philanthropists and generously supported by the Joint. This movement, known as "Oẓar ha-Torah" or "Gandj Danesh," which aimed at strengthening traditional Judaism and Hebrew education among the Jewish communities in *Morocco, Persia, and elsewhere, succeeded in establishing, in close cooperation with the Alliance Israélite Universelle, new schools, teacher training seminars, summer camps, and other educational facilities. Under the leadership of its first director, Rabbi I.M. Levi, Oẓar ha-Torah instilled a new religious spirit into the younger generation.

ALIYAH TO THE HOLY LAND. The 19th century was also characterized by a mass immigration of Persian-speaking Jews from Persia and neighboring countries to Ereẓ Israel. Almost parallel with the *Ḥibbat Zion movement in Russia, but probably without any direct contact with it, a great number of Persian-speaking Jews set out for the Holy Land. They came from Teheran and Shiraz, from Hamadan, *Yezd, and Isfahan, from Kashan and Meshed, from *Herat and Kabul, from Bukhara and Samarkand. The awakening of Persian Jews in the 20th century was also expressed in a Zionist movement which spread throughout most of the Jewish communities in Persia. This renaissance found literary expression in the establishment of a Judeo-Persian and Hebrew press in Teheran, which printed the first Persian textbook of modern Hebrew. This was followed by a history of the Zionist movement, written in Persian in Hebrew characters (1920) by Aziz b. Jonah Naim, and a Hebrew translation of Herzl's *Der Judenstaat* and his biography by A. Bein. This circle also published a Jewish newspaper in Persian, *Ha-Ge'ullah*, and another called *Ha-Hayyim*, which became the mouthpiece of the Jewish renaissance movement founded by Shmuel Haim who functioned as Jewish representative in the Majles in 1923–26. Some of Bialik's poems were translated into Persian by Aziz b. Jonah Naim and published in these periodicals.

Under the Pahlavi Dynasty (1925–1979)

The political and social conditions of Persian Jews were fundamentally changed with the ascent to the throne of Riza Khān Pahlavi and the establishment of the new Pahlavi dynasty in 1925. In 1921, Riza Khān Pahlavi took Teheran; in 1923 he became prime minister; and on Oct. 31, 1925 the parliament in Teheran deposed the last Kajar ruler and entrusted Riza Khān with the provisional government. On Dec. 15, 1925, he was crowned shah of Persia and became the founder of the new Pahlavi dynasty. Bent on secularization and Westernization of his country, Riza Shah, and after him his son Muhammad Riza, carried out far-reaching reforms affecting the social, cultural, and political structure of the country. By breaking the power of the Shiʿa clergy, which for centuries had stood in the way of progress, by freeing the country from the fetters of fanatical and intolerant circles, and by eliminating the Shiʿa concept of the ritual uncleanliness of the nonbelievers – once the basic foundation of the state attitude toward non-Muslims – the shah laid the foundations for a revival which had most beneficial effects on the Jewish sector of the population. No other country except *Turkey went through so fundamental a change in so short a time as Persia (or, as it has since been called, *Iran) under the new dynasty. This change brought about the political emancipation of the Jews in Persia, for which they, assisted by Western European Jewry, had struggled in the latter half of the 19th century. When World War II broke out, with the subsequent political upheavals and the deposition of Riza Khān Pahlavi, the whole process of the Jewish regeneration in Iran was in jeopardy. Yet under Riza Shah's successor, Muhammad Riza, a very favorable climate was provided for the continuous improvement of Jewish life in Persia.

For the modern period, see *Iran.

[Walter Joseph Fischel]

BIBLIOGRAPHY: PRE-ISLAMIC PERIOD: J. Obermeyer, *Die Landschaft Babylonien* (1929); Neusner, Babylonia (incl. bibl). MUSLIM PERIOD; W.J. Fischel, *Jews in the Economic and Political Life of Medieval Islam* (1937, 1969²); idem, in: *Tarbiz*, 6 (1935), 523–6; idem, in: *Zion*, 1 (1935), 49–74; 2 (1937), 273–93; idem, in HJ, 7 (1945), 29–50; 8 (1946), 66–77; idem, in: *Alexander Marx Jubilee Volume* (1950), 203–30; idem, in: JSOS, 12 (1950), 119–60; idem, in: HTR, 45 (1952), 3–45; idem, in: *Ha-Kinnus ha-Olami le-Madda'ei ha-Yahadut 1947* (1952), 477–86; idem, in: *Joshua Starr Memorial Volume* (1953), 111–28; idem, in: PAAJR, 22 (1953), 1–21; idem, in: L. Finkelstein (ed.), *The Jews* (1960³), 1149–90; idem, in: JAOS, 85 (1865), 148–53. 19th–20th CENTURIES: H. Levy, *Tarikh Yahud Iran*, 3 vols. (1956–60); A. Ben-Jacob, *Yehudei Bavel* (1965); I. Ben-Zvi, *Meḥkarim u-Mekorot*

(1967), 285–410. **ADD. BIBLIOGRAPHY:** M. Gil, *Tustaries, Family and Sect* (1981); V.B. Moreen, *Iranian Jewry's Hour of Peril and Heroism* (1987); V.B. Moreen, *Iranian Jewry during the Afghan Invasion* (1990); A. Netzer, *"Redifot u-Shemadot be-Toledot Yehudei Iran ba-Me'ah ha-17,"* in: *Pe'amim* 6 (1980), 32–6; idem, *"Aliyat Yehudei Paras ve-Hityashevutam be-Ereẓ-Yisrael,"* in: *Miqqedem u-Miyyam* (1981); idem, *"Kivrot Ester u-Mordekhai ba-Ir Hamadan she-ba-Iran,"* in: *Am ve-Areẓ* (1984), 177–84; idem, *"Tekufot u-Shelavim be-Maẓav ha-Yehudim ve-ha-Pe'ilut ha-Ẓiyyonit be-Iran,"* in: *Yahadut Zemanenu*, vol. 1 (1983), 139–62; idem, *"Anti-Shemiyut be-Iran, 1925–1950,"* in: *Pe'amim*, 29 (1986), 5–31; idem, "Jewish Education in Iran," in: H.S. Himmelfarb and S. Dellapergola (eds.), *Jewish Education Worldwide* (1989), 447–61; idem, *"Korot Anusei Mashhad lefi Ya'akov Dilmanian,"* in: *Pe'amim*, 42 (1990), 127–156.

PERSITZ, ALEXANDRE (1910–1975), French architect. Born in Moscow, Persitz was taken to France as a child. After World War II, most of which he spent in Nazi concentration camps, he collaborated with Auguste Perret, in rebuilding Le Havre port. After 1947, together with his partner A.G. Héaume, he opened a practice in Paris. They designed the Sephardi community's synagogue; Don Isaac Abrabanel (1960) and Persitz collaborated with Georges Goldberg in designing the Memorial to the Unknown Jewish Martyr (1956). He was chief editor of *Architecture d'aujourd'hui* (1949–65) and wrote many articles on contemporary architecture, particularly synagogues.

PERSITZ, SHOSHANAH (1893–1969), Israeli publisher and politician. Born in Kiev, the daughter of Hillel *Zlatopolski the banker and Zionist leader, she was educated at the universities of Moscow and Paris. From 1909 she was a leading figure in the Hebrew language movement Tarbut in Russia. In 1917, together with her husband, she established the Omanut publishing house in Moscow and in 1920, in Frankfurt. When she settled in Palestine in 1925, Persitz brought her press with her and headed it until her death. For many years Omanut Press was the main publisher of Hebrew educational material and books for youth. From 1926 to 1935 Persitz was a councillor of the Tel Aviv Municipality and director of its education department. From 1949 to 1961 she was a member of the *Knesset, representing the *General Zionists, and served as chairman of the Knesset's education committee. In 1968 she was awarded the Israel Prize in education.

[Benjamin Jaffe]

°**PERSIUS** (34–62 C.E.), Roman satirist. Persius gives a vivid picture of a Jewish Sabbath or festival celebration in Rome, which he calls "Herod's day" (presumably another name for one of the Jewish holidays, though some regard it as referring to the celebration of Herod's birthday): "The lamps on the greasy windows garlanded with violets emit thick smoke, the tail of a tunny fish swims in the red dish, and the white jug overflows with wine; you silently move your lips and turn pale at the Sabbath of the circumcised" (*Satire* 5). Persius also refers to Sabbath (or Ḥanukkah?) observance in the home of a Jew or a convert to Judaism. His allusion to turning pale at the Sabbath of the circumcised probably indicates that he, like *Martial and so many other Romans, had confused the Sabbath with a fast day. Persius' satire reflects the view of the educated Romans on what they considered the superstitious cult of the Jews.

[Jacob Petroff]

PERSKI, JOEL DOV BAER (1816–1871), Hebrew author and translator. Perski, who was born in Volozhin, made major contributions to the field of translation into Hebrew. One is *Kevod Melakhim* (Koenigsberg, 1851–53), a translation of *Telemaque* by Fénelon with Perski's own notes. The work probably interested him on account of its didactic content, since Telemachus is aided in his travels by the wise comments and interpretations of Minerva, who in the form of a mentor gives him lessons on the proper conduct of life and especially on the duties of a king and the principles of sound government. Another work is *Ḥayyei Asaf* (1858) on the life of Aesop, including morally instructive incidents from his life. The work concludes with the translations of some 35 of Aesop's fables. Perski also wrote a commentary, *Heikhal Ra'anan* and *Shemen Ra'anan*, on the *Yalkut Shimoni* on Genesis (1864); and *Battei Kehunnah*, a commentary on the *Midrash Rabbah* to Genesis and Exodus (1871). He died in Vilna.

BIBLIOGRAPHY: *Yahadut Lita*, 3 (1967), 177.

PERSKY, DANIEL (1887–1962), Hebraist, educator, and journalist. Born in Minsk, Persky settled in the United States in 1906 and devoted all his efforts to the Hebraist movement in that country. From 1921 until his death, with the exception of six years in Europe and in Ereẓ Israel (1927–33), he taught at the Herzliah Hebrew Teachers' College in New York. For many years he published an article in each issue of the Hebrew weekly, *Hadoar*, which enjoyed great popularity. His books are largely drawn from these articles, many of them dealing with Hebrew language and syntax. They include *Ha-Medabber Ivrit* (1921; *Spoken Hebrew*, 1921): *Ivri Anokhi* (1948); *Dabberu Ivrit* (1950; *Lashon Nekiyyah* 1962); *Matamim le-Ḥag* (1939); *Zemannim Tovim* (1944); *Kol ha-Mo'ed* (1957); *Le-Elef Yedidim* (1935); and *Ẓeḥok me-Ereẓ Yisrael* (1951).

Persky edited several children's magazines, including *Eden* (1924–25) and *Hadoar la-No'ar* (1934–46). He published posthumously works of several of his colleagues, including I. Beaber and Solomon Rabinowitz, translated the constitution of the United States into Hebrew, and wrote in Yiddish. For English translations see Goell, Bibliography, 35, 74, 89.

A leading figure in Hebrew-speaking circles in the U.S., he carried on a voluminous correspondence with Hebrew writers all over the world and through friends gave many of them financial assistance. His visiting card bore the legend "I am a slave of Hebrew forever."

BIBLIOGRAPHY: MacDonald, in: *The New Yorker* (Nov. 28, 1959), 57–105; Waxman, Literature, 4 (1960), 1081–82; Glenn, in: JBA, 20 (1962/63), 73–75; Kressel, Leksikon, 2 (1967), 692f.

[Eisig Silberschlag]

PERSOFF, NEHEMIAH (1920–), U.S. actor. Born in Jerusalem, Persoff was taken to New York in 1929. He joined the Actors Studio and in 1947 appeared on Broadway in *Galileo*. His other Broadway appearances include *Monserrat* (1949), *Richard III* (1949), *Peter Pan* (1950), *King Lear* (1951), *Peer Gynt* (1951), *Camino Real* (1953), *Reclining Figure* (1954), *Mademoiselle Colombe* (1954), *Tiger at the Gates* (1955), and *Only in America* (1959). His later stage work in California included *Two, I'm Not Rappaport,* and his biographical one-man show *Nehemiah Persoff's Sholem Aleichem*.

He had roles in such films as *A Double Life* (1948), *On the Waterfront* (1954), *The Harder They Fall* (1956), *The Wrong Man* (1956), *Green Mansions* (1958), *Al Capone* (1959), *Some Like It Hot* (1959), *The Big Show* (1961), *The Comancheros* (1961), *The Greatest Story Ever Told* (1964), *Panic in the City* (1968), *Yentl* (1983), *Twins* (1988); and he was the voice of Papa Mousekewitz in the animated adventure film *An American Tail* (1986) and its three sequels (1991, 1999, 2000).

In addition to his appearance in episodes of dozens of television shows, Persoff figured in the cast of such series as *The Untouchables* (1961–63), *High Hopes* (1978), and *This Is the Life* (1983). His many TV movies include *The Dangerous Days of Kiowa Jones* (1966), *Cutter's Trail* (1970), *Michael O'Hara the Fourth* (1972), *Eric* (1975), *Killing Stone* (1978), *FDR: The Last Year* (1980), *Sadat* (1983), and *The Big Knife* (1988).

Persoff turned to painting in 1985, studying sketching in Los Angeles. Specializing in watercolor, he has had many of his works exhibited in California.

[Ruth Beloff (2nd ed.)]

PERSOV, SHMUEL (1890–1950), Soviet Yiddish writer. After having been active in the Jewish Labor *Bund during the Revolution of 1905, he emigrated from Russia to the United States at the age of 16. His literary career began in 1909 with articles in the New York radical periodical *Fraye Arbeter Shtime*. He returned to Russia after the 1917 Revolution filled with enthusiasm for the new regime. He worked in a Moscow cooperative and wrote articles on economics for Russian journals as well as literary sketches and short stories in Yiddish. He helped to found the Yiddish section of the Moscow Association of Proletarian Writers. His short story "Sherblekh" ("Derelicts," 1922) anticipated the method of socialist realism. His volume *Kornbroyt* ("Rye Bread," 1928) dealt with the conflict between adherents and saboteurs of the revolutionary regime. He revealed the psychological difficulties encountered by small Jewish tradesmen in their attempt to adjust to the new Communist reality. He wrote mainly in the genre of documentary stories, portraying various types of Soviet Jews, most notably colonists in the Crimea and Birobidzhan, builders of the Moscow metro, and heroes of World War II. In the late 1940s, during the arrests of activists of the *Jewish Anti-Fascist Committee, he was accused of writing anti-Soviet articles and was executed on November 23, 1950, almost two years before the execution (August 12, 1952) of the committee's leadership, including David Bergelson, Itsik Fefer, David Hofstein, Peretz Markish, and Leyb Kvitko.

BIBLIOGRAPHY: Rejzen, Leksikon, 2 (1927), 941ff. **ADD. BIBLIOGRAPHY:** G. Kostyrchenko, *Tainaia politika Stalina* (2001), index.

[Sol Liptzin / Gennady Estraikh (2nd ed.)]

PERTH, capital of Western Australia, founded in 1829. The first Jew arrived in the same year, but up to the 1880s only a few Jews lived in Perth. The Perth Hebrew Congregation was founded in 1892 and the synagogue opened in 1897, but the community of Fremantle, the port of Perth some nine miles (14 km.) distant, was established earlier. Most of the Jewish settlers came from Eastern Europe both before and after World War I, but a number also arrived from Palestine. A Liberal (Reform) congregation Temple David, was formed in 1952. In 1970 the Jewish community, which numbered about 3,300, was the third largest in Australia. In recent decades Perth's Jewish community has expanded considerably. According to the optional religious question asked in the 2001 Australian census, 4,871 declared Jews lived in Perth; the actual number was probably more than 6,000. Many were recent migrants from South Africa, for whom Perth was the nearest community in an English-speaking democracy. Perth's Orthodox synagogue, the Perth Hebrew Congregation, was led by a number of rabbis who were prominent spokesmen for the community, including David Isaac Freedman (1874–1939), Louis Rubin-Sacks (1910–1983), and Shalom Coleman (1918–). There was an Orthodox day school, Korsunski-Carmel College, established in 1959. David Mossenson's *Hebrew, Israelite, Jew: The History of the Jews of Western Australia* (Perth, 1990) gives a full account of the community's evolution.

BIBLIOGRAPHY: D.J. Benjamin, in: *Australian Jewish Historical Society Journal*, 2 (1946), 293–329; *ibid.*, 3 (1949), 434–6. **ADD. BIBLIOGRAPHY:** H.L. Rubinstein, *Jews in Australia I*, index; W.D. Rubinstein, Australia II, index; D. Mossenson, *The Perth Hebrew Congregation, 1892–2002* (2003).

[Israel Porush / William D. Rubinstein (2nd ed.)]

PERU, republic in South America; general population (2005) 27,000,000, Jewish population (2004) 2,600.

Colonial Period

The discovery of Peru and its mineral potential attracted a large number of *Crypto-Jews known as "Portuguese," who disregarded the restrictions on the immigration of *New Christians and arrived in the capital *Lima which was founded by Francisco Pizarro in 1535. On February 7, 1569, Philip II, king of Spain, issued the decree that ordered the establishment of the Inquisition in Lima, which started the persecution of Crypto-Jews and descendants of Jews. Until 1595 the number of victims was very small, and the Crypto-Jews were able to prosper, especially in commerce of import and export. The first auto da fé in Lima was carried out on December 17, 1595, with ten "Judaizers," four of whom were freed, but one, Francisco Rodríguez, who was burned alive. On December 10, 1600, 14

Crypto-Jews were punished, and on March 13, 1605, another 16. After that date the frequency and numbers declined. This was due to the general declaration of pardon for "Judaizers" declared in 1601 that consequently attracted a large number of New Christians, many of them Crypto-Jews, who attained important status in the economic life of the Spanish colony. Thus the sensational trials against Crypto-Jews were generally directed against the rich and wealthy, with the Holy Office confiscating their properties after their condemnation. This was the case of Antonio Cordero – local representative of a merchant from Sevilla – who was denounced by a local trader for not being prepared to sell to him on Saturday and for refusing to eat pork. The case was investigated secretly with torture, and later led to the great auto da fé of January 23, 1639, in which 70 persons were accused as Judaizers. The most famous among them was Francisco Maldonado de Silva, who during the 12 years that he spent in prison remained loyal to the Jewish faith and also converted two Catholic prisoners to Judaism. All the rest were members of what the Spanish authorities called "The Great Conspiracy" Crypto-Jewish congregation in Lima. The last victim of this congregation was Manuel Enríquez, burnt at the stake in 1664, together with the effigy of doña Murcia de Luna who died under torture. This display of severity was accompanied by the menace of total expulsion in 1646 which was evaded through the payment of the tremendous sum of 200 thousand ducats; this was the final episode of many years of offenses against Crypto-Jews. According to unsubstantiated sources there were 6,000 Crypto-Jews in Peru.

The last victims accused as "Judaizers" were Ana de Castro, on December 23, 1736, and Juan Antonio Pereira on November 11, 1737. The final activity of the Inquisition in Lima was recorded in 1806. By that time persons recognized as Crypto-Jews had disappeared.

One of the famous Crypto-Jewish families in colonial times was the "León Pinelo" family whose name was adopted by the Jewish school in Lima in 1946.

Contemporary Period

EARLY IMMIGRATION, 19th CENTURY. There are no archival records on the early immigration of Jews to Peru in the Republican period, yet their presence can be traced through the search in directories of social clubs of foreign residents or in the advertisements of Jewish business firms that started to appear in the newspapers and in the commercial directories from the middle of the 19th century. In 1852, in the daily *El Comercio,* the photographer Jacobo Stein and Co., a Polish Jew from New York, with "a daguerreotype at the disposal of the beauties of Lima," advertised his services. Other advertisements publicized the confectionery Phailes and Blanc (1853) and the tobacco shop José Cohen and Brothers (1855). The director of the English Club was E. Bergman (1857) and several German Jews were members of the Club Germania from 1863. Other Jewish names, such as Alsop, Isaac, Villiers, and Michael appear in the 1864 directory of the Sociedad de Carreras (Professionals Association) that later became the Jockey Club of Peru. These names are the evidence of the presence of Jewish professionals and merchants in Peru, many of whom were born in Alsace Lorraine and other places in Germany and France, escaping from Europe following the failure of the 1848 revolution, as a result of the economic and political crises and of antisemitism. Other Jews arrived from England and the United States, representing construction companies, railways, and other industries that traded with Peru. In 1875 there were around 300 Jews in Lima, 55% of them were Germans, 15% French, 10% English, 10% Russians, and 20% others. They were industrialists, bankers, diamond dealers, jewelers, engineers, merchants, and professionals. Among them were representatives of the famous French firms of Rothschild (first exchange and stock agents), Dreyfus (jeweler and guano dealer), and others.

THE CEMETERY. In 1868 10 Jews fell victim to the yellow fever epidemic that caused the deaths of 6,000 Peruvians. The Jews were buried in the old Britannic Cemetery of Callao (Protestant). In total, 25 Jews were buried in the Britannic Cemetery between 1861 and 1871. The need to bury Jewish dead and to assist their widows and orphans motivated the Jewish residents in Lima to establish a beneficiary association. In April 1869 they created a provisional directory called Sociedad de Beneficencia Israelita (Jewish Beneficiary Association), presided over by Jacobo Herzberg and Miguel Badt. This association was officially founded in July 1, 1873, under the presidency of Natazzius Hurwitz, with deputies Paul Ascher and Jacobo Brillman. In March 1875 they laid the cornerstone for the Jewish cemetery of Baquíjano (Campo Santo Israelita de Baquíjano), in the same ground occupied today by the Jewish cemetery of Bellavista. The land was bought from Enrique Meiggs, and the license was obtained by two American Jewish engineers who worked with him in the railway company through their diplomatic legation.

DECLINE. The Jewish population, however, started to decrease, and by 1898 only 43 Jews remained in Peru. Jewish immigration was discontinued owing to the economic consequences of Peru's defeat in the war with Chile in 1879. In addition, almost all the Jewish immigrants were men, and the majority married non-Jewish Peruvian women, thus losing the Jewish tradition in their homes and among their descendants. Towards the end of the 19th century there was hardly any Jewish activity in Lima, and only elderly persons preserved their Jewish identity.

IQUITOS. At the same time that European Jews settled in the coast city of Lima, about 1870 a different wave of Jewish immigrants reached the Peruvian jungles. These were young Jewish men, arriving from the Brazilian cities Manaos and Belém (State of Pará), who had come originally from Tangier (Morocco) and were sailing to explore the Amazon River. They settled in the city of *Iquitos, especially during the rubber boom. Later, penetrating along the Amazon River, they opened new routes in the jungle. It is estimated that 200 Jews arrived in Iquitos during those years. In 1895 they purchased a plot of land in the General Cemetery of Iquitos in which they buried their dead. In 1909 they founded the Sociedad de Beneficencia Israelita de Iquitos (Jewish Beneficiary Association of Iquitos) with 38 members. Among the most frequent names are Benzaquén, Alexander, Cohen, Edery, Toledano, Bendayán, Abensur, etc. The 1912 crisis and the fall of rubber prices caused a large movement of emigration, and very few Jews, married to local women, remained in Iquitos. By 1949 there were only 17 of the original Jewish immigrants. Today there is a small community composed of their descendants, who convene to celebrate Friday nights and the Holy Days. Some of them made *aliyah* and settled in Israel. (For the contemporary history of this community see *Iquitos.)

SECOND MIGRATORY WAVE, 20TH CENTURY. Sephardi immigration to Peru started around the beginning of the 20th century with the arrival of Jews from Turkey (108 from Istanbul, Smyrna, and Edirne), a few from Greece (12 from Salonica), Morocco (eight from Tangier), and Egypt (six from Cairo). Among them were the Calvo, Levi, Sarfaty, Alalú, Varón and Alcabés families. They joined the Sociedad de Beneficencia Israelita that was founded by the German Jews, but in November 1920 they established their own institution. This Sephardi communal organization, the Sociedad de Beneficencia Israelita Sefaradí, was constituted officially on November 24, 1925, and on September 17, 1933, it inaugurated its synagogue and social premises at the same location it still occupies in the early 21st century.

Ashkenazi Jews started to immigrate to Peru around 1912, coming principally from Romania (55%) and Poland (25%), and the rest from Russia (10%), Hungary (5%), and other European countries. Among them were the Eidelman, Gans, Vainstein, Gleiser, and Waisman families. They settled in the neighborhood of Chirimoyo and, on June 11, 1923, founded the Unión Israelita del Perú that was officially recognized on November 16, 1929. After moving among rented places they purchased a plot in 1933, inaugurating their synagogue and social premises on July 29, 1934.

German-speaking Jewish refugees arrived in Peru between 1933 and 1939 from Germany (70%), Austria (25%), and other countries. In 1935 they revived the old Sociedad de Beneficencia Israelita that received a new legal status as the Sociedad de Beneficencia Israelita de 1870. They inaugurated their own building on September 24, 1948.

The majority of the Jews, Sephardim and Ashkenazim, dedicated themselves to peddling, traveling in the provinces to buy and sell merchandise, introducing the use of credit that was little known at the time. Many of them settled in the different provinces of Peru, particularly near the important intersections of highways and railways or near the port cities Callao, Huancayo, Trujillo, Arequipa, Piura, Lambayeque, and Ica. German Jews who were musicians, professionals, or scientists tended to settle in Lima, where they could work in their profession. Some of them, however, went to the provincial towns, where it was easier to validate their European title and exercise their profession as doctors, pharmacists, engineers, and professors. It is estimated that in 1947 there were 2,800 Jews in Lima and 1,200 in the provinces.

Towards the end of the 1950s the Jewish families left the provinces and concentrated in Lima, in order to provide Jewish education to their children in the León Pinelo School (founded in 1946) and to facilitate their studies in the universities of the capital. Moreover, in Lima they could find a Jewish social framework in which they could meet a potential mate. By the end of the 1960s practically no Jews were left in the provinces of Peru.

INSTITUTIONAL DEVELOPMENT. The Zionist Federation was founded in 1925 by Ashkenazim and Sephardim, and its first president was Sassone Sarfaty. In 1935 the Comité de Protección al Immigrante Israelita (Comité for the Defense of the Jewish Immigrant) was founded, being affiliated to HICEM, the JDC, and later to HIAS and ICA. The committee took care of the legal and illegal immigrants, obtained visas for them, sought employment for them, helped establish their relatives, sent money and packages to Europe. It also provided services to immigrants in transit to other countries, maintained a Home for Immigrants (1939–41) and Spanish courses. After the war it took care of the remittances of war reparations from Germany.

In 1940 WIZO was created (headed by Teresa Topf), in 1944 OSE-ORT (headed by Max Heller), in 1949 the Pioneer Women Organization (headed by Charna Goldemberg). From 1941 there was a permanent Campaign for the War Victims, in which several members of WIZO, OSE, the British Red Cross, and other groups of women from the three congregations were active. In 1945 the JTA (Jewish Telegraphic Agency) was established.

The growing influence of antisemitism throughout the world, including in Peru, and the news on the atrocities committed by the Nazis against the Jews motivated the decision of the Jews of Lima to form an association for common civil objectives. On February 4, 1942, they founded the "Directory of the Jewish Community of Peru," headed by Max Heller, Jacobo Franco, and Leopoldo Weil, that on June 20, 1944, was registered as the Asociación de Sociedades Israelitas del Perú (Association of the Jewish Organizations of Peru). Also merged under this umbrella organization were all the activities of the cemetery that had been conducted since 1940 by one *ḥevra kaddisha*. Created during the same year was also the Bikur Cholim society and the Hogar de Ancianos (old age home).

The umbrella organization changed its name in 1975 to Asociación Judía del Perú, under which it still functions. During the war years, the main tasks of this representative organ were concentrated on the external front in the struggle against antisemitic manifestations that occasionally appeared in the press and in Peruvian public life. Likewise they collected products and money which they sent to Europe to assist Jewish survivors, and they took care of the few Jewish families that were able to immigrate to Peru.

During the Holocaust period, immigration to Peru was affected by the official negative policy towards the admission of non-white and non-Christian immigrants. Despite the sympathy expressed by the Peruvian representative in the Evian Conference towards the Jewish refugees, the Ministry of Foreign Affairs prohibited its consuls in Europe from issuing visas to Jews. This discriminatory policy was the main reason that between 1933 and 1943, when Peru broke relations with Germany, legal Jewish immigration numbered only around 500 persons.

In June 27, 1945 the Comité Peruano Pro Palestina Hebrea (Peruvian Committee in Favor of a Jewish Palestine) was established, headed by the president of the Senate, José Gálvez Barrenechea, with distinguished members, such as Luis Valcárcel, Gerardo Klingue, Manuel Beltroy, and César Miró. The committee's mission was to disseminate among intellectuals, journalists, and politicians the idea of the Jewish people's need to obtain its own state and to gain the sympathy of the Peruvian people in this cause. This led to Peru's vote in favor of the Partition of Palestine in the UN Assembly of November 29, 1947. The main Jewish activists who supported this task were Marcos Roitman, Marcos Perelman, Walter Neisser, and Isaac Wecselman.

In recognition of his Zionist activities, Marcos Roitman was nominated in 1951 as the honorary consul of Israel in Peru, inaugurating the consulate in 1953. In 1956 diplomatic relations between Israel and Peru were raised to the level of legations and in 1958 to that of embassies, with Tuvia Arazi as the first ambassador of Israel in Peru.

On the internal front the Jewish community was active in creating youth movements, a home for golden agers, assistance to the needy, a social club, synagogues, a cemetery, and in particular to provide Jewish education. In 1934 a Peruvian branch of Maccabi was opened, followed in 1936 by the Sephardi youth movement Hashachar and in 1942 by Hashomer of the German Jews. In 1938 Betar was founded and in 1943 all the youth movements (except Betar) were merged in the Asociación Juvenil Israelita – AJI (Association of Young Jews) that identified itself with the Zionist movement and in 1947 was affiliated to Ha-No'ar ha-Ẓiyyoni. In 1962 the German Jews established the apolitical group Kineret. A Communist youth movement, Juventud judía vanguardista-comunista (Jewish Youth of Communist Avant-Garde) was founded in 1945 but existed only for two years.

In March 1945 the Comité Pro Colegio Hebreo (Committee for a Jewish School) was founded, headed by Israel Brodsky, who inaugurated the Leon Pinelo School on April 24, 1946. (On the history of the school, see *Lima.) Since 1954 the school has been located in the same building, educating the great majority (over 90%) of the Jewish population from kindergarten to high school.

LATER DEMOGRAPHIC AND INSTITUTIONAL DEVELOPMENT. The demographic and economic experience of the Peruvian Jews resembles the expansion and contraction of an accordion, but, arriving at the limits of their possible contraction, they risk facing extinction (see table below). Starting with a small group of very poor individual Jews who immigrated in the 1910s, they grew into a prosperous community in the 1950s and 1960s. Later, however, started a process of decrease and decline that brought them to a crossroad at which they had to choose between the reorganization of the community and its adaptation to the actual economic and demographic reality, or the continuity of the institutional inertia, that might lead to the loss of attraction of communal frameworks, especially the synagogues and the prestigious Jewish Leon Pinelo school.

Peru – Documented Jewish Population, 1875–2004

Year	No. of Jews	Places	Total in Peru
1875	300 / 50	Lima / Iquitos	350
1898	43 / 200	Lima / Iquitos	243
1917			300
1930			1,000
1933			1,500
1939			2,500
1947	2,800 / 1,200	Lima / Provinces	4,000
1968	5,300 / 150	Lima / Provinces	5,450
1988	3,200	Lima	3,200
2000	2,700	Lima	2,700
2004	2,600	Lima	2,600

The 1960s were a period of generational change in which the Jews of the second generation, most of whom were born and educated in Peru, assumed the leadership of the community. Communal prosperity continued, relations with Israel were strengthened, Keren Hayesod increased its campaigns, more people went on *aliyah* to Israel, and the Jewish school attracted more than 80% of the Jewish children in Lima with *sheliḥim* (emissaries) from Israel acting as director and teachers.

Hebraica (the social club) appointed a director of activities from abroad, and three new rabbis were nominated for the three congregations. While the communities in the provinces were disappearing, the community in Lima was growing until it reached 5,500 persons.

In the 1970s, however, the contraction of the Jewish community began, both economically and demographically, due to the military coup d'état of General Velasco (1968–80) that affected the land owners (agrarian reform), industry (industrial community), and real estate (law of renting). The national economic crisis, the politicization of the universities with strikes and decline in level of quality scared the young Jews who started to emigrate in order to study abroad, particularly in Israel and the United States. The number of mixed marriages increased, and there appeared the first manifestations of open antisemitism through an anti-Zionist attitude and support of the Palestinians. At the same time there was an increase in delinquency and insecurity that motivated the beginning of emigration of Jewish families who made *aliyah* or sought other destinations on the American continent. The Jewish population fell to 4,500 in the late 1970s.

The 1980s were a period of communal weakening, with a growing emigration that resulted from the economic crisis caused by the external debt, the delinquency, the kidnappings, the terrorism of the underground guerrillas Sendero Luminoso ("Shining Path") and the Movimiento Revolucionario Tupac Amarú – MRTA (Revolutionary Movement Tupac Amaru), all of which generated pessimistic future expectations. The birth rate of the Jews declined and, combined with the above-mentioned factors, the school population, which in 1976 comprised 1,024 pupils fell to 540 in 1990. The Jewish institutions suffered from economic impoverishment. The proliferation of children of mixed marriages started the debate on "who is a Jew." At the end of the 1980s the number of Jews was reduced to 3,200.

In the 1990s the communal decline became evident. The country's economic deterioration continued, and unemployment and Jewish poverty grew in the community. The dictatorship of Fujimori, in its second administration, created tension, fear, and confusion. *Aliyah* decreased because of the problems in Israel and the feeling of marginalization of the immigrants from Latin America with respect to the Russians. Mixed marriages increased, as did emigration to the United States. The number of pupils in the Jewish school was reduced to 430. After 18 years, towards the end of this decade the annual trip to Israel of the school children was suspended due to economic reasons, as well as to the security situation in Israel. There was a constant decline of Jewish donors. At the same time there started a religious revival in certain sectors of middle-aged Jews; a rabbi of Chabad joined the Peruvian Jewish community, being supported by part of the few disposable donations, particularly of the Ashkenazi Unión Israelita. The number of Jews fell to 2,700.

While the religious revival is a general phenomenon in the world, in the case of Peru it coincides with the repetition of a well-known historical situation, in which Jews who feel instability and uncertainty in the future come closer to religion in search of refuge and answers.

In the 2000s, in an atmosphere of a certain national optimism for the recuperation of democracy that followed the election of President Alejandro Toledo, there emerged the demand for an urgent regeneration of the community in order to reorganize its large patrimony that contains superfluous services.

Over the years the Jews who were born and educated in Peru started to occupy important places in the professions, art, business, and finances of the country, and more recently in its political life. Within the Jewish community, the highest rank was achieved by the engineer Eduardo Bigio, who was president of the Committee of Human Relations of the Jewish community, from its foundation in the 1970s until his *aliyah* in 2001. Bigio was also president of the Committee of the Third World in the World Jewish Congress, having worked for more than 40 years in the defense of Jewish causes in the public life of Peru. In the sphere of national politics, the highest level was achieved by Efraim Goldemberg, as minister of foreign affairs and later minister of economy, under the administrations of Alberto Fujimori; the second vice president David Waisman, under the administration of Alejandro Toledo; and the Member of Congress Jacques Rodrich. The fact that Eliane Karp, the wife of President Toledo, is a Jew who had lived in Israel is also significant for the Jewish community.

CURRENT PROBLEMS. The Jews of Peru, like other communities who share similar characteristics, are confronting problems and tensions both on the level of each individual family and on that of the whole community. Each family has to find the balance between the cost of communal affiliation and the benefits it expects to receive (from the school, clubs, social assistance, etc.). It is evident that discontinuity of affiliation may lead to assimilation in the present generation or in that of their children. A second problem concerns the confrontation between the expectations of a universal and international English-speaking education and an education that gives priority to the Jewish dimensions. The preference for non-Jewish schools endangers the subsistence of the community, which is incapable of maintaining a Jewish school for a small number of students. A third problem is the capacity of the Jewish community to organize itself, in view of the demographic decline and the deterioration of the average family income. The cost of maintenance of Jewish institutions, with their administration and professional leadership, is becoming very steep. Communal services are often based on the donations of a few philanthropists, so that they depend on the good will and economic situation of individual persons more than on their capacity to institutionally balance their costs. The last and most serious problem is the "elitization" that results from the division of the Jews according to their economic capacities. While the economic burden of maintaining the unity and homogeneity of the community is becoming very heavy, particularly among families who are less devoted to Jewish solidarity, the economic elite becomes more preoccupied with its economic well-being, weakening the communal spirit. This leads to a polarization of the community, a situation in which only the rich can enjoy the expensive services and the impoverished families drop out.

BIBLIOGRAPHY: N. Lorch, *Ha-Nahar ha-Lohesh* (1969); Asociación Filantrópica Israelita, Buenos Aires, *Zehn Jahre Aufbauarbeit in Suedamerika* (Ger. and Span., 1943); Sociedad de Beneficencia Israelita de 1870, *25 Jahre Hilfsverein deutschsprechenden Juden* (1960); J. Shatzky, *Yidishe Yishuvim in Latayn Amerike* (1952), 175–80; A. Monk and J. Isaacson, *Comunidades Judías de Latino-américa* (1968), 109–12; J. Toribio Medina, *Historia de la Inquisicion de Lima*, 2 vols. (19562); M.A. Cohen, in: *The Jewish Experience in Colonial Latin America* (1971), introd. **ADD. BIBLIOGRAPHY:** L. Trahtemberg, *La Inmigración Judía al Perú 1848–1948* (1987); idem, *Los Judíos de Lima y de las Provincias del Perú* (1989); idem, *Participación del Perú en la Partición de Palestina* (1991).

[Leon Trahtemberg (2nd ed.)]

PERUGIA, city in Umbria, central Italy. The Perugian statute of 1279, decreeing the expulsion of the Jews from the town, is proof that a Jewish settlement had previously been in existence in Perugia. It seems, however, that this measure was never put into effect and in succeeding years there was an active Jewish group in Perugia, mostly engaged in moneylending. The artist Matteo di Ser Cambio, who acted as "procurator" of the Jews of Perugia in 1414, illuminated a Hebrew manuscript there about this time. The creation of the *Monti di Pietá (1462), in conjunction with violent anti-Jewish preaching by the Franciscans, had dire consequences for the Jews in Perugia, and they were banished in 1485. Though later readmitted to the town, they were banished again in 1569 by the bull *Hebraeorum Gens* of *Pius v. Under *Sixtus v (1587) they returned temporarily, but in 1593 were banished finally by *Clement viii. A few Jews graduated in medicine in the University of Perugia between 1547 and 1551, including David *de'Pomis. In the 1920s and 1930s many foreigners (including some from Ereẓ Israel) studied there, receiving moral support in the home of Bernard Dessau, the professor of physics and a father of wireless telegraphy, and his wife, the artist Emma Dessau. There is again a handful of Jews living in Perugia, affiliated to the community of Rome, and services are held irregularly.

BIBLIOGRAPHY: A. Fabretti, *Sulla condizione degli ebrei in Perugia dal xiii al xvii secolo* (1891); Scalvanti, in: *Annali della Facoltá di Giurisprudenza… di Perugia*, 8 (1910), 93–125; RMI, 25 (1959), 151ff.; Roth, Italy, index; Milano, Italia, index; Luzzatto, in: *Vessillo Israelitico*, 45 (1897), 81ff.; Momigliano, *ibid.*, 65 (1918), 384–7; Narkiss, in: KS, 23 (1968), 285–360.

[Ariel Toaff]

PERUTZ, LEO (1884–1957), Austrian novelist. Perutz, the son of a Prague industrialist, lived in Vienna as a freelance writer after World War i, in which he served as an officer. After the *Anschluss* in 1938 he immigrated to Ereẓ Israel. In his vivid historical novels Perutz displays the visionary power and technical skill of the born storyteller.

His works, which have a fantastic and eerie quality, include one about Hernando Cortez, *Die dritte Kugel* (1915); *Zwischen neun und neun* (1918; *From Nine to Nine*, 1927), set in Prague; the prizewinning *Der Marques de Bolibar* (1920; *The Marquis de Bolivar*, 1926); *Der Meister des juengsten Tages* (1923; *The Master of the Day of Judgment*, 1929); *Turlupin* (1924), on Richelieu and his age; *Wohin rollst du, Aepfelchen?* (1928; *Where Will You Fall?*, 1930), set in postwar Vienna and Soviet Russia; and *Der schwedische Reiter* (1936). The last novel published during the author's lifetime, *Nachts unter der steinernen Bruecke* (1953), evokes the Prague of Rudolf ii; *Der Judas des Leonardo*, set in the Milan of Ludovico Sforza, appeared in 1959. Perutz' short stories were collected in *Der Kosak und die Nachtigall* (1927) and *Herr, erbarme dich meiner* (1930). His plays such as *Die Reise nach Pressburg* (1930) and *Morgen ist Feiertag* (1936) were less successful.

[Harry Zohn]

PERUTZ, MAX FERDINAND (1914–2002), British biochemist and Nobel laureate. Perutz was born in Vienna and went to Cambridge in 1936. In 1947 he became head of a unit of molecular biology, and in 1962 chairman of the Medical Research Council Laboratory of Molecular Biology. In 1937 he started the study of the structure of crystalline proteins by X-ray diffraction. After 30 years this enabled a complete analysis to be made of the positions of all the 2,600 atoms in the myoglobin molecule and the 10,000 atoms in the molecule of hemoglobin, the component of blood which carries oxygen to the body cells. In 1962 Perutz shared the Nobel Prize for chemistry for "research into the structure of globular proteins." Perutz contributed to scientific periodicals, mainly in the above field. He wrote *Proteins and Nucleic Acids: Structure and Function* (1962). He was elected a fellow of the Royal Society and member of several national academies of science, and was the recipient of other awards.

BIBLIOGRAPHY: *Le Prix Nobel en 1962* (1963).

[Samuel Aaron Miller]

PERVOMAISK, city in Odessa district, Ukraine. It was formed in 1920 by the amalgamation of three neighboring localities; Bogopol, the most ancient of them (Podolia), Olviopol, and the village of Golta, in the Kherson oblast. In 1799 there were 253 Jews in the first two localities. (In 1847 there were about 1,400 Jews in Bogopol.) The number of Jews in the three communities was 8,636 (40.8% of the total population) in 1897. Most of them (about 6,000, or 82% of the population) lived in Bogopol. There were pogroms on April 17–18, 1881, and on October 22, 1905; Jews were wounded and much property looted. In December 1919, when the soldiers of *Denikin retreated before the Red Army, they engaged in bloodshed and rioting. There were 9,896 Jews (31%) in Pervomaisk in 1926, dropping to 6,087 (18.5% of the total population) by 1939. There were two Jewish kolkhozes and children attended two Yiddish schools, one of them with high school classes. The Germans captured the town on August 2, 1941. The Golta part of the town was annexed to Romanian Transnistria, and the other two parts remained under German occupation. Hundreds of Jews were murdered in Bogopol, and on September 17, 1941 a ghetto was established. In October some 120 were killed, and in December 3,600 were murdered at the Fray-Leben kolkhoz. In February–March 1942, 1,600 Romanian Jews were executed. In the Olviopol part Jews were concentrated in the clubhouse and burned alive. In late 1942 Jews from the Golta ghetto (Romanian part) were sent to the Bogdanovka and Akmechetka, and most of them perished there. All together 5,469 people were murdered, most of them Jews. According to the 1959 census, Jews numbered about 2,200 (5% of the population). Most left in the 1990s.

BIBLIOGRAPHY: *Reshummot*, 3 (1923), 435–7.

[Yehuda Slutsky / Shmuel Spector (2nd ed.)]

ABBREVIATIONS

GENERAL ABBREVIATIONS

This list contains abbreviations used in the Encyclopaedia (apart from the standard ones, such as geographical abbreviations, points of compass, etc.). For names of organizations, institutions, etc., in abbreviation, see Index. For bibliographical abbreviations of books and authors in Rabbinical literature, see following lists.

*	Cross reference; i.e., an article is to be found under the word(s) immediately following the asterisk (*).
°	Before the title of an entry, indicates a non-Jew (post-biblical times).
‡	Indicates reconstructed forms.
>	The word following this sign is derived from the preceding one.
<	The word preceding this sign is derived from the following one.

ad loc.	*ad locum*, "at the place"; used in quotations of commentaries.
A.H.	*Anno Hegirae*, "in the year of Hegira," i.e., according to the Muslim calendar.
Akk.	Addadian.
A.M.	*anno mundi*, "in the year (from the creation) of the world."
anon.	anonymous.
Ar.	Arabic.
Aram.	Aramaic.
Ass.	Assyrian.
b.	born; *ben, bar.*
Bab.	Babylonian.
B.C.E.	Before Common Era (= B.C.).
bibl.	bibliography.
Bul.	Bulgarian.
c., ca.	Circa.
C.E.	Common Era (= A.D.).
cf.	*confer*, "compare."
ch., chs.	chapter, chapters.
comp.	compiler, compiled by.
Cz.	Czech.
D	according to the documentary theory, the Deuteronomy document.
d.	died.
Dan.	Danish.
diss., dissert,	dissertation, thesis.
Du.	Dutch.
E.	according to the documentary theory, the Elohist document (i.e., using Elohim as the name of God) of the first five (or six) books of the Bible.
ed.	editor, edited, edition.
eds.	editors.
e.g.	*exempli gratia*, "for example."
Eng.	English.
et al.	*et alibi*, "and elsewhere"; or *et alii*, "and others"; "others."
f., ff.	and following page(s).
fig.	figure.
fl.	flourished.
fol., fols	folio(s).
Fr.	French.
Ger.	German.
Gr.	Greek.
Heb.	Hebrew.
Hg., Hung	Hungarian.
ibid	*Ibidem*, "in the same place."
incl. bibl.	includes bibliography.
introd.	introduction.
It.	Italian.
J	according to the documentary theory, the Jahwist document (i.e., using YHWH as the name of God) of the first five (or six) books of the Bible.
Lat.	Latin.
lit.	literally.
Lith.	Lithuanian.
loc. cit.	*loco citato*, "in the [already] cited place."
Ms., Mss.	Manuscript(s).
n.	note.
n.d.	no date (of publication).
no., nos	number(s).
Nov.	Novellae (Heb. *Ḥiddushim*).
n.p.	place of publication unknown.
op. cit.	*opere citato*, "in the previously mentioned work."
P.	according to the documentary theory, the Priestly document of the first five (or six) books of the Bible.
p., pp.	page(s).
Pers.	Persian.
pl., pls.	plate(s).
Pol.	Polish.
Port.	Potuguese.
pt., pts.	part(s).
publ.	published.
R.	Rabbi or Rav (before names); in Midrash (after an abbreviation) – *Rabbah.*
r.	recto, the first side of a manuscript page.
Resp.	Responsa (Latin "answers," Hebrew *She'elot u-Teshuvot* or *Teshuvot)*, collections of rabbinic decisions.
rev.	revised.

Rom. Romanian.
Rus(s). Russian.

Slov. Slovak.
Sp. Spanish.
s.v. *sub verbo, sub voce*, "under the (key) word."
Sum Sumerian.
summ. Summary.
suppl. supplement.

Swed. Swedish.

tr., trans(l). translator, translated, translation.
Turk. Turkish.

Ukr. Ukrainian.

v., vv. *verso*. The second side of a manuscript page; also verse(s).

Yid. Yiddish.

ABBREVIATIONS USED IN RABBINICAL LITERATURE

Adderet Eliyahu, Karaite treatise by Elijah b. Moses *Bashyazi.
Admat Kodesh, Resp. by Nissim Ḥayyim Moses b. Joseph |Mizraḥi.
Aguddah, Sefer ha-, Nov. by *Alexander Suslin ha-Kohen.
Ahavat Ḥesed, compilation by *Israel Meir ha-Kohen.
Aliyyot de-Rabbenu Yonah, Nov. by *Jonah b. Avraham Gerondi.
Arukh ha-Shulḥan, codification by Jehiel Michel *Epstein.
Asayin (= positive precepts), subdivision of: (1) *Maimonides, *Sefer ha-Mitzvot;* (2) *Moses b. Jacob of Coucy, *Semag.*
Asefat Dinim, subdivision of *Sedei Ḥemed* by Ḥayyim Hezekiah *Medini, an encyclopaedia of precepts and responsa.
Asheri = *Asher b. Jehiel.
Aeret Ḥakhamim, by Baruch *Frankel-Teomim; pt, 1: Resp. to Sh. Ar.; pt2: Nov. to Talmud.
Ateret Zahav, subdivision of the *Levush*, a codification by Mordecai b. Abraham (Levush) *Jaffe; *Ateret Zahav* parallels Tur. YD.
Ateret Ẓevi, Comm. To Sh. Ar. by Ẓevi Hirsch b. Azriel.
Avir Ya'akov, Resp. by Jacob Avigdor.
Avkat Rokhel, Resp. by Joseph b. Ephraim *Caro.
Avnei Millu'im, Comm. to Sh. Ar., EH, by *Aryeh Loeb b. Joseph ha-Kohen.
Avnei Nezer, Resp. on Sh. Ar. by Abraham b. Ze'ev Nahum Bornstein of *Sochaczew.
Avodat Massa, Compilation of Tax Law by Yoasha Abraham Judah.
Azei ha-Levanon, Resp. by Judah Leib *Zirelson.

Ba'al ha-Tanya – *Shneur Zalman of Lyady.
Ba'ei Ḥayyei, Resp. by Ḥayyim b. Israel *Benveniste.
Ba'er Heitev, Comm. To Sh. Ar. The parts on OḤ and EH are by Judah b. Simeon *Ashkenazi, the parts on YD AND ḤM by *Zechariah Mendel b. Aryeh Leib. Printed in most editions of Sh. Ar.
Baḥ = Joel *Sirkes.
Baḥ, usual abbreviation for *Bayit Ḥadash*, a commentary on Tur by Joel *Sirkes; printed in most editions of Tur.
Bayit Ḥadash, see *Baḥ*.
Berab = Jacob Berab, also called Ri Berav.
Bedek ha-Bayit, by Joseph b. Ephraim *Caro, additions to his *Beit Yosef* (a comm. to Tur). Printed sometimes inside *Beit Yosef*, in smaller type. Appears in most editions of Tur.
Be'er ha-Golah, Commentary to Sh. Ar. By Moses b. Naphtali Hirsch *Rivkes; printed in most editions of Sh. Ar.
Be'er Mayim, Resp. by Raphael b. Abraham Manasseh Jacob.
Be'er Mayim Ḥayyim, Resp. by Samuel b. Ḥayyim *Vital.
Be'er Yiẓḥak, Resp. by Isaac Elhanan *Spector.
Beit ha-Beḥirah, Comm. to Talmud by Menahem b. Solomon *Meiri.
Beit Me'ir, Nov. on Sh. Ar. by Meir b. Judah Leib Posner.
Beit Shelomo, Resp. by Solomon b. Aaron Ḥason (the younger).
Beit Shemu'el, Comm. to Sh. Ar., EH, by *Samuel b. Uri Shraga Phoebus.
Beit Ya'akov, by Jacob b. Jacob Moses *Lorberbaum; pt.1: Nov. to Ket.; pt.2: Comm. to EH.
Beit Yisrael, collective name for the commentaries *Derishah, Perishah*, and *Be'urim* by Joshua b. Alexander ha-Kohen *Falk. See under the names of the commentaries.
Beit Yiẓḥak, Resp. by Isaac *Schmelkes.
Beit Yosef: (1) Comm. on Tur by Joseph b. Ephraim *Caro; printed in most editions of Tur; (2) Resp. by the same.
Ben Yehudah, Resp. by Abraham b. Judah Litsch (ליטש) Rosenbaum.
Bertinoro, Standard commentary to Mishnah by Obadiah *Bertinoro. Printed in most editions of the Mishnah.
[Be'urei] Ha-Gra, Comm. to Bible, Talmud, and Sh. Ar. By *Elijah b. Solomon Zalmon (Gaon of Vilna); printed in major editions of the mentioned works.
Be'urim, Glosses to Isserles *Darkhei Moshe* (a comm. on Tur) by Joshua b. Alexander ha-Kohen *Falk; printed in many editions of Tur.
Binyamin Ze'ev, Resp. by *Benjamin Ze'ev b. Mattathias of Arta.
Birkei Yosef, Nov. by Ḥayyim Joseph David *Azulai.
Ha-Buẓ ve-ha-Argaman, subdivision of the *Levush* (a codification by Mordecai b. Abraham (Levush) *Jaffe); *Ha-Buẓ ve-ha-Argaman* parallels Tur, EH.

Comm. = Commentary

Da'at Kohen, Resp. by Abraham Isaac ha-Kohen. *Kook.
Darkhei Moshe, Comm. on Tur Moses b. Israel *Isserles; printed in most editions of Tur.
Darkhei No'am, Resp. by *Mordecai b. Judah ha-Levi.
Darkhei Teshuvah, Nov. by Ẓevi *Shapiro; printed in the major editions of Sh. Ar.
De'ah ve-Haskel, Resp. by Obadiah Hadaya (see *Yaskil Avdi)*.

Derashot Ran, Sermons by *Nissim b. Reuben Gerondi.
Derekh Ḥayyim, Comm. to *Avot* by *Judah Loew (Lob., Liwa) b. Bezalel (Maharal) of Prague.
Derishah, by Joshua b. Alexander ha-Kohen *Falk; additions to his *Perishah* (comm. on Tur); printed in many editions of Tur.
Derushei ha-Ẓelaḥ, Sermons, by Ezekiel b. Judah Halevi *Landau.
Devar Avraham, Resp. by Abraham *Shapira.
Devar Shemu'el, Resp. by Samuel *Aboab.
Devar Yehoshu'a, Resp. by Joshua Menahem b. Isaac Aryeh Ehrenberg.
Dikdukei Soferim, variae lections of the talmudic text by Raphael Nathan*Rabbinowicz.
Divrei Emet, Resp. by Isaac Bekhor David.
Divrei Ge'onim, Digest of responsa by Ḥayyim Aryeh b. Jeḥiel Ẓevi *Kahana.
Divrei Ḥamudot, Comm. on *Piskei ha-Rosh* by Yom Tov Lipmann b. Nathan ha-Levi *Heller; printed in major editions of the Talmud.
Divrei Ḥayyim several works by Ḥayyim *Halberstamm; if quoted alone refers to his Responsa.
Divrei Malkhi'el, Resp. by Malchiel Tenebaum.
Divrei Rivot, Resp. by Isaac b. Samuel *Adarbi.
Divrei Shemu'el, Resp. by Samuel Raphael Arditi.

Edut be-Ya'akov, Resp. by Jacob b. Abraham *Boton.
Edut bi-Yhosef, Resp. by Joseph b. Isaac *Almosnino.
Ein Ya'akov, Digest of talmudic *aggadot* by Jacob (Ibn) *Habib.
Ein Yiẓḥak, Resp. by Isaac Elhanan *Spector.
Ephraim of Lentshitz = Solomon *Luntschitz.
Erekh Leḥem, Nov. and glosses to Sh. Ar. by Jacob b. Abraham *Castro.
Eshkol, Sefer ha-, Digest of *halakhot* by *Abraham b. Isaac of Narbonne.
Et Sofer, Treatise on Law Court documents by Abraham b. Mordecai *Ankawa, in the 2nd vol. of his Resp. *Kerem Ḥamar.*
Etan ha-Ezraḥi, Resp. by Abraham b. Israel Jehiel (Shrenzl) *Rapaport.
Even ha-Ezel, Nov. to Maimonides' *Yad Ḥazakah* by Isser Zalman *Meltzer.
Even ha-Ezer, also called *Raban* of *Ẓafenat Pa'ne'aḥ,* rabbinical work with varied contents by *Eliezer b. Nathan of Mainz; not identical with the subdivision of Tur, Shulḥan Arukh, etc.
Ezrat Yehudah, Resp. by *Isaar Judah b. Nechemiah of Brisk.

Gan Eden, Karaite treatise by *Aaron b. Elijah of Nicomedia.
Gersonides = *Levi b. Gershom, also called Leo Hebraecus, or Ralbag.
Ginnat Veradim, Resp. by *Abraham b. Mordecai ha-Levi.

Haggahot, another name for *Rema.*
Haggahot Asheri, glosses to *Piskei ha-Rosh* by *Israel of Krems; printed in most Talmud editions.
Haggahot Maimuniyyot, Comm,. to Maimonides' Yad Ḥazakah by *Meir ha-Kohen; printed in most eds. of Yad.
Haggahot Mordekhai, glosses to *Mordekhai* by Samuel *Schlettstadt; printed in most editions of the Talmud after *Mordekhai.*
Haggahot ha-Rashash on Tosafot, annotations of Samuel *Strashun on the Tosafot (printed in major editions of the Talmud).
Ha-Gra = *Elijah b. Solomon Zalman (Gaon of Vilna).
Ha-Gra, Commentaries on Bible, Talmud, and Sh. Ar. respectively, by *Elijah b. Solomon Zalman (Gaon of Vilna); printed in major editions of the mentioned works.
Hai Gaon, Comm. = his comm. on Mishnah.
Ḥakham Ẓevi, Resp. by Ẓevi Hirsch b. Jacob *Ashkenazi.
Halakhot = Rif, *Halakhot.* Compilation and abstract of the Talmud by Isaac b. Jacob ha-Kohen *Alfasi; printed in most editions of the Talmud.
Halakhot Gedolot, compilation of *halakhot* from the Geonic period, arranged acc. to the Talmud. Here cited acc. to ed. Warsaw (1874). Author probably *Simeon Kayyara of Basra.
Halakhot Pesukot le-Rav Yehudai Ga'on compilation of *halakhot.*
Halakhot Pesukot min ha-Ge'onim, compilation of *halakhot* from the geonic period by different authors.
Ḥananel, Comm. to Talmud by *Hananel b. Ḥushi'el; printed in some editions of the Talmud.
Harei Besamim, Resp. by Aryeh Leib b. Isaac *Horowitz.
Ḥassidim, Sefer, Ethical maxims by *Judah b. Samuel he-Ḥasid.
Hassagot Rabad on Rif, Glosses on Rif, *Halakhot,* by *Abraham b. David of Posquières.
Hassagot Rabad [on Yad], Glosses on Maimonides, *Yad Ḥazakah,* by *Abraham b. David of Posquières.
Hassagot Ramban, Glosses by Naḥmanides on Maimonides' *Sefer ha-Mitzvot;* usually printed together with *Sefer ha-Mitzvot.*
Ḥatam Sofer = Moses *Sofer.
Ḥavvot Ya'ir, Resp. and varia by Jair Ḥayyim *Bacharach
Ḥayyim Or Zaru'a = *Ḥayyim (Eliezer) b. Isaac.
Ḥazon Ish = Abraham Isaiah *Karelitz.
Ḥazon Ish, Nov. by Abraham Isaiah *Karelitz
Ḥedvat Ya'akov, Resp. by Aryeh Judah Jacob b. David Dov Meisels (article under his father's name).
Heikhal Yiẓḥak, Resp. by Isaac ha-Levi *Herzog.
Ḥelkat Meḥokek, Comm. to Sh. Ar., by Moses b. Isaac Judah *Lima.
Ḥelkat Ya'akov, Resp. by Mordecai Jacob Breisch.
Ḥemdah Genuzah, , Resp. from the geonic period by different authors.
Ḥemdat Shelomo, Resp. by Solomon Zalman *Lipschitz.
Ḥida = Ḥayyim Joseph David *Azulai.
Ḥiddushei Halakhot ve-Aggadot, Nov. by Samuel Eliezer b. Judah ha-Levi *Edels.
Ḥikekei Lev, Resp. by Ḥayyim *Palaggi.
Ḥikrei Lev, Nov. to Sh. Ar. by Joseph Raphael b. Ḥayyim Joseph Ḥazzan (see article *Ḥazzan Family).
Hil. = Hilkhot … (e.g. *Hilkhot Shabbat).*
Ḥinnukh, Sefer ha-, List and explanation of precepts attributed (probably erroneously) to Aaron ha-Levi of Barcelona (see article **Ha-Ḥinnukh*).
Ḥok Ya'akov, Comm. to Hil. Pesaḥ in Sh. Ar., OḤ, by Jacob b. Joseph *Reicher.
Ḥokhmat Sehlomo (1), Glosses to Talmud, *Rashi* and Tosafot by Solomon b. Jehiel "Maharshal") *Luria; printed in many editions of the Talmud.
Ḥokhmat Sehlomo (2), Glosses and Nov. to Sh. Ar. by Solomon b. Judah Aaron *Kluger printed in many editions of Sh. Ar.
Ḥur, subdivision of the *Levush,* a codification by Mordecai b. Abraham (Levush) *Jaffe; *Hur* (or *Levush ha-Hur)* parallels Tur, OḤ, 242–697.
Ḥut ha-Meshullash, fourth part of the *Tashbeẓ* (Resp.), by Simeon b. Zemaḥ *Duran.

Ibn Ezra, Comm. to the Bible by Abraham *Ibn Ezra; printed in the major editions of the Bible *("Mikra'ot Gedolot").*
Imrei Yosher, Resp. by Meir b. Aaron Judah *Arik.
Ir Shushan, Subdivision of the *Levush,* a codification by Mordecai b. Abraham (Levush) *Jaffe; *Ir Shushan* parallels Tur, ḤM.
Israel of Bruna = Israel b. Ḥayyim *Bruna.
Ittur. Treatise on precepts by *Isaac b. Abba Mari of Marseilles.

Jacob Be Rab = *Be Rab.
Jacob b. Jacob Moses of Lissa = Jacob b. Jacob Moses *Lorberbaum.
Judah B. Simeon = Judah b. Simeon *Ashkenazi.
Judah Minz = Judah b. Eliezer ha-Levi *Minz.

Kappei Aharon, Resp. by Aaron Azriel.
Kehillat Ya'akov, Talmudic methodology, definitions etc. by Israel Jacob b. Yom Tov *Algazi.
Kelei Ḥemdah, Nov. and *pilpulim* by Meir Dan *Plotzki of Ostrova, arranged acc. to the Torah.
Keli Yakar, Annotations to the Torah by Solomon *Luntschitz.
Keneh Ḥokhmah, Sermons by Judah Loeb *Pochwitzer.
Keneset ha-Gedolah, Digest of *halakhot* by Ḥayyim b. Israel *Benveniste; subdivided into annotations to *Beit Yosef* and annotations to Tur.
Keneset Yisrael, Resp. by Ezekiel b. Abraham Katzenellenbogen (see article *Katzenellenbogen Family).
Kerem Ḥamar, Resp. and varia by Abraham b. Mordecai *Ankawa.
Kerem Shelmo. Resp. by Solomon b. Joseph *Amarillo.
Keritut, [Sefer], Methodology of the Talmud by *Samson b. Isaac of Chinon.
Kesef ha-Kedoshim, Comm. to Sh. Ar., ḤM, by Abraham *Wahrmann; printed in major editions of Sh. Ar.
Kesef Mishneh, Comm. to Maimonides, *Yad Ḥazakah,* by Joseph b. Ephraim *Caro; printed in most editions of *Yad Ḥazakah.*
Kez̤ot ha-Ḥoshen, Comm. to Sh. Ar., ḤM, by *Aryeh Loeb b. Joseph ha-Kohen; printed in major editions of Sh. Ar.
Kol Bo [*Sefer*], Anonymous collection of ritual rules; also called *Sefer ha-Likkutim.*
Kol Mevasser, Resp. by Meshullam *Rath.
Korban Aharon, Comm. to *Sifra* by Aaron b. Abraham *Ibn Ḥayyim; pt. 1 is called: *Middot Aharon.*
Korban Edah, Comm. to Jer. Talmud by David *Fraenkel; with additions: *Shiyyurei Korban;* printed in most editions of Jer. Talmud.
Kunteres ha-Kelalim, subdivision of *Sedei Ḥemed,* an encyclopaedia of precepts and responsa by Ḥayyim Hezekiah *Medini.
Kunteres ha-Semikhah, a treatise by *Levi b. Ḥabib; printed at the end of his responsa.
Kunteres Tikkun Olam, part of *Mispat Shalom* (Nov. by Shalom Mordecai b. Moses *Schwadron).

Lavin (negative precepts), subdivision of: (1) *Maimonides, *Sefer ha-Mitzvot;* (2) *Moses b. Jacob of Coucy, *Semag.*
Leḥem Mishneh, Comm. to Maimonides, *Yad Ḥazakah,* by Abraham [Ḥiyya] b. Moses *Boton; printed in most editions of *Yad Ḥazakah.*
Leḥem Rav, Resp. by Abraham [Ḥiyya] b. Moses *Boton.
Leket Yosher, Resp and varia by Israel b. Pethahiah *Isserlein, collected by *Joseph (Joselein) b. Moses.
Leo Hebraeus = *Levi b. Gershom, also called Ralbag or Gersonides.
Levush = Mordecai b. Abraham *Jaffe.
Levush [Malkhut], Codification by Mordecai b. Abraham (Levush) *Jaffe, with subdivisions: [*Levush ha-] Tekhelet* (parallels Tur OḤ 1–241); [*Levush ha-] Ḥur* (parallels Tur OḤ 242–697); [*Levush] Ateret Zahav* (parallels Tur YD); [*Levush ha-Buz̤ ve-ha-Argaman* (parallels Tur EH); [*Levush] Ir Shushan* (parallels Tur ḤM); under the name *Levush* the author wrote also other works.
Li-Leshonot ha-Rambam, fifth part (nos. 1374–1700) of Resp. by *David b. Solomon ibn Abi Zimra (Radbaz).
Likkutim, Sefer ha-, another name for [*Sefer] Kol Bo.*

Ma'adanei Yom Tov, Comm. on *Piskei ha-Rosh* by Yom Tov Lipmann b. Nathan ha-Levi *Heller; printed in many editions of the Talmud.
Mabit = Moses b. Joseph *Trani.
Magen Avot, Comm. to *Avot* by Simeon b. Z̤emaḥ *Duran.
Magen Avraham, Comm. to Sh. Ar., OḤ, by Abraham Abele b. Ḥayyim ha-Levi *Gombiner; printed in many editions of Sh. Ar., OḤ.
Maggid Mishneh, Comm. to Maimonides, *Yad Ḥazakah,* by *Vidal Yom Tov of Tolosa; printed in most editions of the *Yad Ḥazakah.*
Maḥaneh Efrayim, Resp. and Nov., arranged acc. to Maimonides' *Yad Ḥazakah* , by Ephraim b. Aaron *Navon.
Maharai = Israel b. Pethahiah *Isserlein.
Maharal of Prague = *Judah Loew (Lob, Liwa), b. Bezalel.
Maharalbaḥ = *Levi b. Ḥabib.
Maharam Alashkar = Moses b. Isaac *Alashkar.
Maharam Alshekh = Moses b. Ḥayyim *Alashekh.
Maharam Mintz = Moses *Mintz.
Maharam of Lublin = *Meir b. Gedaliah of Lublin.
Maharam of Padua = Meir *Katzenellenbogen.
Maharam of Rothenburg = *Meir b. Baruch of Rothenburg.
Maharam Shik = Moses b. Joseph Schick.
Maharash Engel = Samuel b. Ze'ev Wolf Engel.
Maharashdam = Samuel b. Moses *Medina.
Maharḥash = Ḥayyim (ben) Shabbetai.
Mahari Basan = Jehiel b. Ḥayyim Basan.
Mahari b. Lev = Joseph ibn Lev.
Mahari'az = Jekuthiel Asher Zalman Ensil Zusmir.
Maharibal = *Joseph ibn Lev.
Mahariḥ = Jacob (Israel) *Ḥagiz.
Maharik = Joseph b. Solomon *Colon.
Maharikash = Jacob b. Abraham *Castro.
Maharil = Jacob b. Moses *Moellin.
Maharimat = Joseph b. Moses di Trani (not identical with the Maharit).
Maharit = Joseph b. Moses *Trani.
Maharitaz̤ = Yom Tov b. Akiva Z̤ahalon. (See article *Z̤ahalon Family).
Maharsha = Samuel Eliezer b. Judah ha-Levi *Edels.
Maharshag = Simeon b. Judah Gruenfeld.
Maharshak = Samson b. Isaac of Chinon.
Maharshakh = *Solomon b. Abraham.
Maharshal = Solomon b. Jeḥiel *Luria.
Mahasham = Shalom Mordecai b. Moses *Sschwadron.
Maharyu = Jacob b. Judah *Weil.
Maḥazeh Avraham, Resp. by Abraham Nebagen v. Meir ha-Levi Steinberg.
Maḥazik Berakhah, Nov. by Ḥayyim Joseph David *Azulai.

*Maimonides = Moses b. Maimon, or Rambam.
*Malbim = Meir Loeb b. Jehiel Michael.
Malbim = Malbim's comm. to the Bible; printed in the major editions.
Malbushei Yom Tov, Nov. on *Levush,* OḤ, by Yom Tov Lipmann b. Nathan ha-Levi *Heller.
Mappah, another name for *Rema.*
Mareh ha-Panim, Comm. to Jer. Talmud by Moses b. Simeon *Margolies; printed in most editions of Jer. Talmud.
Margaliyyot ha-Yam, Nov. by Reuben *Margoliot.
Masat Binyamin, Resp. by Benjamin Aaron b. Abraham *Slonik
Mashbir, Ha- = *Joseph Samuel b. Isaac Rodi.
Massa Ḥayyim, Tax *halakhot* by Ḥayyim *Palaggi, with the subdivisions *Missim ve-Arnomiyyot* and *Torat ha-Minhagot.*
Massa Melekh, Compilation of Tax Law by Joseph b. Isaac *Ibn Ezra with concluding part *Ne'ilat She'arim.*
Matteh Asher, Resp. by Asher b. Emanuel Shalem.
Matteh Shimon, Digest of Resp. and Nov. to Tur and *Beit Yosef,* ḤM, by Mordecai Simeon b. Solomon.
Matteh Yosef, Resp. by Joseph b. Moses ha-Levi Nazir (see article under his father's name).
Mayim Amukkim, Resp. by Elijah b. Abraham *Mizraḥi.
Mayim Ḥayyim, Resp. by Ḥayyim b. Dov Beresh Rapaport.
Mayim Rabbim, , Resp. by Raphael *Meldola.
Me-Emek ha-Bakha, , Resp. by Simeon b. Jekuthiel Ephrati.
Me'irat Einayim, usual abbreviation: *Sma* (from: *Sefer Me'irat Einayim*); comm. to Sh. Ar. By Joshua b. Alexander ha-Kohen *Falk; printed in most editions of the Sh. Ar.
Melammed le-Ho'il, Resp. by David Ẓevi *Hoffmann.
Meisharim, [*Sefer*], Rabbinical treatise by *Jeroham b. Meshullam.
Meshiv Davar, Resp. by Naphtali Ẓevi Judah *Berlin.
Mi-Gei ha-Haregah, Resp. by Simeon b. Jekuthiel Ephrati.
Mi-Ma'amakim, Resp. by Ephraim Oshry.
Middot Aharon, first part of *Korban Aharon,* a comm. to *Sifra* by Aaron b. Abraham *Ibn Ḥayyim.
Migdal Oz, Comm. to Maimonides, *Yad Ḥazakah,* by *Ibn Gaon Shem Tov b. Abraham; printed in most editions of the *Yad Ḥazakah.*
Mikhtam le-David, Resp. by David Samuel b. Jacob *Pardo.
Mikkaḥ ve-ha-Mimkar, Sefer ha-, Rabbinical treatise by *Hai Gaon.
Milḥamot ha-Shem, Glosses to Rif, *Halakhot,* by *Naḥmanides.
Minḥat Ḥinnukh, Comm. to *Sefer ha-Ḥinnukh,* by Joseph b. Moses *Babad.
Minḥat Yizḥak, Resp. by Isaac Jacob b. Joseph Judah Weiss.
Misgeret ha-Shulḥan, Comm. to Sh. Ar., ḤM, by Benjamin Ze'ev Wolf b. Shabbetai; printed in most editions of Sh. Ar.
Mishkenot ha-Ro'im, Halakhot in alphabetical order by Uzziel Alshekh.
Mishnah Berurah, Comm. to Sh. Ar., OḤ, by *Israel Meir ha-Kohen.
Mishneh le-Melekh, Comm. to Maimonides, *Yad Ḥazakah,* by Judah *Rosanes; printed in most editions of *Yad Ḥazakah.*
Mishpat ha-Kohanim, Nov. to Sh. Ar., ḤM, by Jacob Moses *Lorberbaum, part of his *Netivot ha-Mishpat;* printed in major editions of Sh. Ar.
Mishpat Kohen, Resp. by Abraham Isaac ha-Kohen *Kook.
Mishpat Shalom, Nov. by Shalom Mordecai b. Moses *Schwadron; contains: *Kunteres Tikkun Olam.*
Mishpat u-Ẓedakah be-Ya'akov, Resp. by Jacob b. Reuben *Ibn Ẓur.
Mishpat ha-Urim, Comm. to Sh. Ar., ḤM by Jacob b. Jacob Moses *Lorberbaum, part of his *Netivot ha-Mishpat;* printed in major editons of Sh. Ar.
Mishpat Ẓedek, Resp. by *Melammed Meir b. Shem Tov.
Mishpatim Yesharim, Resp. by Raphael b. Mordecai *Berdugo.
Mishpetei Shemu'el, Resp. by Samuel b. Moses *Kalai (Kal'i).
Mishpetei ha-Tanna'im, Kunteres, Nov on *Levush,* OḤ by Yom Tov Lipmann b. Nathan ha-Levi *Heller.
Mishpetei Uzzi'el (Uziel), Resp. by Ben-Zion Meir Hai *Ouziel.
Missim ve-Arnoniyyot, Tax *halakhot* by Ḥayyim *Palaggi, a subdivision of his work *Massa Ḥayyim* on the same subject.
Mitzvot, Sefer ha-, Elucidation of precepts by *Maimonides; subdivided into *Lavin* (negative precepts) and *Asayin* (positive precepts).
Mitzvot Gadol, Sefer, Elucidation of precepts by *Moses b. Jacob of Coucy, subdivided into *Lavin* (negative precepts) and *Asayin* (positive precepts); the usual abbreviation is *Semag.*
Mitzvot Katan, Sefer, Elucidation of precepts by *Isaac b. Joseph of Corbeil; the usual, abbreviation is *Semak.*
Mo'adim u-Zemannim, Rabbinical treatises by Moses Sternbuch.
Modigliano, Joseph Samuel = *Joseph Samuel b. Isaac, Rodi (Ha-Mashbir).
Mordekhai (Mordecai), halakhic compilation by *Mordecai b. Hillel; printed in most editions of the Talmud after the texts.
Moses b. Maimon = *Maimonides, also called Rambam.
Moses b. Naḥman = Naḥmanides, also called Ramban.
Muram = Isaiah Menahem b. Isaac (from: Morenu R. Mendel).

Naḥal Yizḥak, Comm. on Sh. Ar., ḤM, by Isaac Elhanan *Spector.
Naḥalah li-Yhoshu'a, Resp. by Joshua Ẓunẓin.
Naḥalat Shivah, collection of legal forms by *Samuel b. David Moses ha-Levi.
*Naḥmanides = Moses b. Naḥman, also called Ramban.
Naẓiv = Naphtali Ẓevi Judah *Berlin.
Ne'eman Shemu'el, Resp. by Samuel Isaac *Modigilano.
Ne'ilat She'arim, concluding part of *Massa Melekh* (a work on Tax Law) by Joseph b. Isaac *Ibn Ezra, containing an exposition of customary law and subdivided into *Minhagei Issur* and *Minhagei Mamon.*
Ner Ma'aravi, Resp. by Jacob b. Malka.
Netivot ha-Mishpat, by Jacob b. Jacob Moses *Lorberbaum; subdivided into *Mishpat ha-Kohanim,* Nov. to Sh. Ar., ḤM, and *Mishpat ha-Urim,* a comm. on the same; printed in major editions of Sh. Ar.
Netivot Olam, Saying of the Sages by *Judah Loew (Lob, Liwa) b. Bezalel.
Nimmukei Menaḥem of Merseburg, Tax *halakhot* by the same, printed at the end of Resp. Maharyu.
Nimmukei Yosef, Comm. to Rif. *Halakhot,* by Joseph *Ḥabib (Ḥabiba); printed in many editions of the Talmud.
Noda bi-Yhudah, Resp. by Ezekiel b. Judah ha-Levi *Landau; there is a first collection *(Mahadura Kamma)* and a second collection *(Mahadura Tinyana).*
Nov. = Novellae, Ḥiddushim.

Ohel Moshe (1), Notes to Talmud, *Midrash Rabbah,* Yad, *Sifrei* and to several Resp., by Eleazar *Horowitz.

Ohel Moshe (2), Resp. by Moses Jonah Zweig.
Oholei Tam. Resp. by *Tam ibn Yaḥya Jacob b. David; printed in the rabbinical collection *Tummat Yesharim.*
Oholei Ya'akov, Resp. by Jacob de *Castro.
Or ha-Me'ir Resp by Judah Meir b. Jacob Samson Shapiro.
Or Same'aḥ, Comm. to Maimonides, *Yad Ḥazakah,* by *Meir Simḥah ha-Kohen of Dvinsk; printed in many editions of the *Yad Ḥazakah.*
Or Zaru'a [the father] = *Isaac b. Moses of Vienna.
Or Zaru'a [the son] = *Ḥayyim (Eliezer) b. Isaac.
Or Zaru'a, Nov. by *Isaac b. Moses of Vienna.
Orah, Sefer ha-, Compilation of ritual precepts by *Rashi.
Oraḥ la-Ẓaddik, Resp. by Abraham Ḥayyim Rodrigues.
Oẓar ha-Posekim, Digest of Responsa.

Paḥad Yiẓḥak, Rabbinical encyclopaedia by Isaac *Lampronti.
Panim Me'irot, Resp. by Meir b. Isaac *Eisenstadt.
Parashat Mordekhai, Resp. by Mordecai b. Abraham Naphtali *Banet.
Pe'at ha-Sadeh la-Dinim and Pe'at ha-Sadeh la-Kelalim, subdivisions of the *Sedei Ḥemed,* an encyclopaedia of precepts and responsa, by Ḥayyim Hezekaih *Medini.
Penei Moshe (1), Resp. by Moses *Benveniste.
Penei Moshe (2), Comm. to Jer. Talmud by Moses b. Simeon *Margolies; printed in most editions of the Jer. Talmud.
Penei Moshe (3), Comm. on the aggadic passages of 18 treatises of the Bab. and Jer. Talmud, by Moses b. Isaiah Katz.
Penei Yehoshu'a, Nov. by Jacob Joshua b. Ẓevi Hirsch *Falk.
Peri Ḥadash, Comm. on Sh. Ar. By Hezekiah da *Silva.
Perishah, Comm. on Tur by Joshua b. Alexander ha-Kohen *Falk; printed in major edition of Tur; forms together with *Derishah* and *Be'urim* (by the same author) the *Beit Yisrael.*
Pesakim u-Khetavim, 2nd part of the *Terumat ha-Deshen* by Israel b. Pethahiah *Isserlein' also called *Piskei Maharai.*
Pilpula Ḥarifta, Comm. to *Piskei ha-Rosh, Seder Nezikin,* by Yom Tov Lipmann b. Nathan ha-Levi *Heller; printed in major editions of the Talmud.
Piskei Maharai, see *Terumat ha-Deshen,* 2nd part; also called *Pesakim u-Khetavim.*
Piskei ha-Rosh, a compilation of *halakhot,* arranged on the Talmud, by *Asher b. Jehiel (Rosh); printed in major Talmud editions.
Pitḥei Teshuvah, Comm. to Sh. Ar. by Abraham Hirsch b. Jacob *Eisenstadt; printed in major editions of the Sh. Ar.

Rabad = *Abraham b. David of Posquières (Rabad III.).
Raban = *Eliezer b. Nathan of Mainz.
Raban, also called *Ẓafenat Pa'ne'aḥ* or *Even ha-Ezer,* see under the last name.
Rabi Abad = *Abraham b. Isaac of Narbonne.
Radad = David Dov. b. Aryeh Judah Jacob *Meisels.
Radam = Dov Berush b. Isaac Meisels.
Radbaz = *David b Solomon ibn Abi Ziumra.
Radbaz, Comm. to Maimonides, *Yad Ḥazakah,* by *David b. Solomon ibn Abi Zimra.
Ralbag = *Levi b. Gershom, also called Gersonides, or Leo Hebraeus.
Ralbag, Bible comm. by *Levi b. Gershon.
Rama [da Fano] = Menaḥem Azariah *Fano.
Ramah = Meir b. Todros [ha-Levi] *Abulafia.
Ramam = *Menaham of Merseburg.
Rambam = *Maimonides; real name: Moses b. Maimon.
Ramban = *Naḥmanides; real name Moses b. Naḥman.
Ramban, Comm. to Torah by *Naḥmanides; printed in major editions. ("Mikra'ot Gedolot").
Ran = *Nissim b. Reuben Gerondi.
Ran of Rif, Comm. on Rif, *Halakhot,* by Nissim b. Reuben Gerondi.
Ranaḥ = *Elijah b. Ḥayyim.
Rash = *Samson b. Abraham of Sens.
Rash, Comm. to Mishnah, by *Samson b. Abraham of Sens; printed in major Talmud editions.
Rashash = Samuel *Strashun.
Rashba = Solomon b. Abraham *Adret.
Rashba, Resp., see also; *Sefer Teshuvot ha-Rashba ha-Meyuḥasot le-ha-Ramban,* by Solomon b. Abraham *Adret.
Rashbad = Samuel b. David.
Rashbam = *Samuel b. Meir.
Rashbam = Comm. on Bible and Talmud by *Samuel b. Meir; printed in major editions of Bible and most editions of Talmud.
Rashbash = Solomon b. Simeon *Duran.
*Rashi = Solomon b. Isaac of Troyes.
Rashi, Comm. on Bible and Talmud by *Rashi; printed in almost all Bible and Talmud editions.
Raviah = Eliezer b. Joel ha-Levi.
Redak = David *Kimḥi.
Redak, Comm. to Bible by David *Kimḥi.
Redakh = *David b. Ḥayyim ha-Kohen of Corfu.
Re'em = Elijah b. Abraham *Mizraḥi.
Rema = Moses b. Israel *Isserles.
Rema, Glosses to Sh. Ar. by Moses b. Israel *Isserles; printed in almost all editions of the Sh. Ar. inside the text in Rashi type; also called *Mappah* or *Haggahot.*
Remek = Moses Kimḥi.
Remakh = Moses ha-Kohen mi-Lunel.
Reshakh = *Solomon b. Abraham; also called Maharshakh.
Resp. = Responsa, *She'elot u-Teshuvot.*
Ri Berav = *Berab.
Ri Escapa = Joseph b. Saul *Escapa.
Ri Migash = Joseph b. Meir ha-Levi *Ibn Migash.
Riba = Isaac b. Asher ha-Levi; Riba II (Riba ha-Baḥur) = his grandson with the same name.
Ribam = Isaac b. Mordecai (or: Isaac b. Meir).
Ribash = *Isaac b. Sheshet Perfet (or: Barfat).
Rid= *Isaiah b. Mali di Trani the Elder.
Ridbaz = Jacob David b. Ze'ev *Willowski.
Rif = Isaac b. Jacob ha-Kohen *Alfasi.
Rif, *Halakhot,* Compilation and abstract of the Talmud by Isaac b. Jacob ha-Kohen *Alfasi.
Ritba = Yom Tov b. Abraham *Ishbili.
Riẓbam = Isaac b. Mordecai.
Rosh = *Asher b. Jehiel, also called Asheri.
Rosh Mashbir, Resp. by *Joseph Samuel b. Isaac, Rodi.

Sedei Ḥemed, Encyclopaedia of precepts and responsa by Ḥayyim Ḥezekiah *Medini; subdivisions: *Asefat Dinim, Kunteres ha-Kelalim, Pe'at ha-Sadeh la-Dinim, Pe'at ha-Sadeh la-Kelalim.*
Semag, Usual abbreviation of *Sefer Mitzvot Gadol,* elucidation of precepts by *Moses b. Jacob of Coucy; subdivided into *Lavin* (negative precepts) *Asayin* (positive precepts).
Semak, Usual abbreviation of *Sefer Mitzvot Katan,* elucidation of precepts by *Isaac b. Joseph of Corbeil.

Sh. Ar. = *Shulḥan Arukh,* code by Joseph b. Ephraim *Caro.

Sha'ar Mishpat, Comm. to Sh. Ar., ḤM. By Israel Isser b. Ze'ev Wolf.

Sha'arei Shevu'ot, Treatise on the law of oaths by *David b. Saadiah; usually printed together with Rif, *Halakhot;* also called: *She'arim of R. Alfasi.*

Sha'arei Teshuvah, Collection of resp. from Geonic period, by different authors.

Sha'arei Uzzi'el, Rabbinical treatise by Ben-Zion Meir Ha *Ouziel.

Sha'arei Ẓedek, Collection of resp. from Geonic period, by different authors.

Shadal [or Shedal] = Samuel David *Luzzatto.

Shai la-Moreh, Resp. by Shabbetai Jonah.

Shakh, Usual abbreviation of *Siftei Kohen,* a comm. to Sh. Ar., YD and ḤM by *Shabbetai b. Meir ha-Kohen; printed in most editions of Sh. Ar.

Sha'ot-de-Rabbanan, Resp. by *Solomon b. Judah ha-Kohen.

She'arim of R. Alfasi see *Sha'arei Shevu'ot.*

Shedal, see Shadal.

She'elot u-Teshuvot ha-Ge'onim, Collection of resp. by different authors.

She'erit Yisrael, Resp. by Israel Ze'ev Mintzberg.

She'erit Yosef, Resp. by *Joseph b. Mordecai Gershon ha-Kohen.

She'ilat Yaveẓ, Resp. by Jacob *Emden (Yaveẓ).

She'iltot, Compilation arranged acc. to the Torah by *Aḥa (Aḥai) of Shabḥa.

Shem Aryeh, Resp. by Aryeh Leib *Lipschutz.

Shemesh Ẓedakah, Resp. by Samson *Morpurgo.

Shenei ha-Me'orot ha-Gedolim, Resp. by Elijah *Covo.

Shetarot, Sefer ha-, Collection of legal forms by *Judah b. Barzillai al-Bargeloni.

Shevut Ya'akov, Resp. by Jacob b. Joseph Reicher.

Shibbolei ha-Leket Compilation on ritual by Zedekiah b. Avraham *Anav.

Shiltei Gibborim, Comm. to Rif, *Halakhot,* by *Joshua Boaz b. Simeon; printed in major editions of the Talmud.

Shittah Mekubbeẓet, Compilation of talmudical commentaries by Bezalel *Ashkenazi.

Shivat Ẓiyyon, Resp. by Samuel b. Ezekiel *Landau.

Shiyyurei Korban, by David *Fraenkel; additions to his comm. to Jer. Talmud *Korban Edah;* both printed in most editions of Jer. Talmud.

Sho'el u-Meshiv, Resp. by Joseph Saul ha-Levi *Nathanson.

Sh[ulḥan] Ar[ukh] [of Ba'al ha-Tanyal], Code by *Shneur Zalman of Lyady; not identical with the code by Joseph Caro.

Siftei Kohen, Comm. to Sh. Ar., YD and ḤM by *Shabbetai b. Meir ha-Kohen; printed in most editions of Sh. Ar.; usual abbreviation: *Shakh.*

Simḥat Yom Tov, Resp. by Tom Tov b. Jacob *Algazi.

Simlah Ḥadashah, Treatise on *Sheḥitah* by Alexander Sender b. Ephraim Zalman *Schor; see also *Tevu'ot Shor.*

Simeon b. Ẓemaḥ = Simeon b. Ẓemaḥ *Duran.

Sma, Comm. to Sh. Ar. by Joshua b. Alexander ha-Kohen *Falk; the full title is: *Sefer Me'irat Einayim;* printed in most editions of Sh. Ar.

Solomon b. Isaac ha-Levi = Solomon b. Isaac *Levy.

Solomon b. Isaac of Troyes = *Rashi.

Tal Orot, Rabbinical work with various contents, by Joseph ibn Gioia.

Tam, Rabbenu = *Tam Jacob b. Meir.

Tashbaẓ = Samson b. Zadok.

Tashbeẓ = Simeon b. Zemaḥ *Duran, sometimes also abbreviation for Samson b. Zadok, usually known as Tashbaẓ.

Tashbeẓ [Sefer ha-], Resp. by Simeon b. Ẓemaḥ *Duran; the fourth part of this work is called: *Ḥut ha-Meshullash.*

Taz, Usual abbreviation of *Turei Zahav,* comm., to Sh. Ar. by *David b. Samnuel ha-Levi; printed in most editions of Sh. Ar.

(Ha)-Tekhelet, subdivision of the *Levush* (a codification by Mordecai b. Abraham (Levush) *Jaffe); *Ha-Tekhelet* parallels Tur, OḤ 1-241.

Terumat ha-Deshen, by Israel b. Pethahiah *Isserlein; subdivided into a part containing responsa, and a second part called *Pesakim u-Khetavim* or *Piskei Maharai.*

Terumot, Sefer ha-, Compilation of *halakhot* by Samuel b. Isaac *Sardi.

Teshuvot Ba'alei ha-Tosafot, Collection of responsa by the Tosafists.

Teshjvot Ge'onei Mizraḥ u-Ma'aav, Collection of responsa.

Teshuvot ha-Geonim, Collection of responsa from Geonic period.

Teshuvot Ḥakhmei Provinzyah, Collection of responsa by different Provencal authors.

Teshuvot Ḥakhmei Ẓarefat ve-Loter, Collection of responsa by different French authors.

Teshuvot Maimuniyyot, Resp. pertaining to Maimonides' *Yad Ḥazakah;* printed in major editions of this work after the text; authorship uncertain.

Tevu'ot Shor, by Alexander Sender b. Ephraim Zalman *Schor, a comm. to his *Simlah Ḥadashah,* a work on *Sheḥitah.*

Tiferet Ẓevi, Resp. by Ẓevi Hirsch of the "AHW" Communities (Altona, Hamburg, Wandsbeck).

Tiktin, Judah b. Simeon = Judah b. Simeon *Ashkenazi.

Toledot Adam ve-Ḥavvah, Codification by *Jeroham b. Meshullam.

Torat Emet, Resp. by Aaron b. Joseph *Sasson.

Torat Ḥayyim, , Resp. by Ḥayyim (ben) Shabbetai.

Torat ha-Minhagot, subdivision of the *Massa Ḥayyim* (a work on tax law) by Ḥayyim *Palaggi, containing an exposition of customary law.

Tosafot Rid, Explanations to the Talmud and decisions by *Isaiah b. Mali di Trani the Elder.

Tosefot Yom Tov, comm. to Mishnah by Yom Tov Lipmann b. Nathan ha-Levi *Heller; printed in most editions of the Mishnah.

Tummim, subdivision of the comm. to Sh. Ar., ḤM, *Urim ve-Tummim* by Jonathan *Eybeschuetz; printed in the major editions of Sh. Ar.

Tur, usual abbreviation for the *Arba'ah Turim* of *Jacob b. Asher.

Turei Zahav, Comm. to Sh. Ar. by *David b. Samuel ha-Levi; printed in most editions of Sh. Ar.; usual abbreviation: *Taz.*

Urim, subdivision of the following.

Urim ve-Tummim, Comm. to Sh. Ar., ḤM, by Jonathan *Eybeschuetz; printed in the major editions of Sh. Ar.; subdivided in places into *Urim* and *Tummim.*

Vikku'aḥ Mayim Ḥayyim, Polemics against Isserles and Caro by Ḥayyim b. Bezalel.

Yad Malakhi, Methodological treatise by *Malachi b. Jacob ha-Kohen.

Yad Ramah, Nov. by Meir b. Todros [ha-Levi] *Abulafia.
Yakhin u-Vo'az, Resp. by Ẓemaḥ b. Solomon *Duran.
Yam ha-Gadol, Resp. by Jacob Moses *Toledano.
Yam shel Shelomo, Compilation arranged acc. to Talmud by Solomon b. Jehiel (Maharshal) *Luria.
Yashar, Sefer ha-, by *Tam, Jacob b. Meir (Rabbenu Tam); 1st pt.: Resp.; 2nd pt.: Nov.
Yaskil Avdi, Resp. by Obadiah Hadaya (printed together with his Resp. *De'ah ve-Haskel).*
Yaveẓ = Jacob *Emden.
Yehudah Ya'aleh, Resp. by Judah b. Israel *Aszod.
Yekar Tiferet, Comm. to Maimonides' *Yad Ḥazakah,*by David b. Solomon ibn Zimra, printed in most editions of *Yad Ḥazakah.*
Yere'im [*ha-Shalem*], [*Sefer*], Treatise on precepts by *Eliezer b. Samuel of Metz.
Yeshu'ot Ya'akov, Resp. by Jacob Meshullam b. Mordecai Ze'ev *Ornstein.
Yiẓhak Rei'aḥ, Resp. by Isaac b. Samuel Abendanan (see article *Abendanam Family).
Ẓafenat Pa'ne'aḥ (1), also called *Raban* or *Even ha-Ezer,* see under the last name.
Ẓafenat Pa'ne'aḥ (2), Resp. by Joseph *Rozin.
Zayit Ra'anan, Resp. by Moses Judah Leib b. Benjamin Auerbach.
Ẓeidah la-Derekh, Codification by *Menahem b. Aaron ibn Zerah.
Ẓedakah u-Mishpat, Resp. by Ẓedakah b. Saadiah Huẓin.
Zekan Aharon, Resp. by Elijah b. Benjamin ha-Levi.
Zekher Ẓaddik, Sermons by Eliezer *Katzenellenbogen.
Ẓemaḥ Ẓedek (1) Resp. by Menaham Mendel Shneersohn (see under *Shneersohn Family).
Zera Avraham, Resp. by Abraham b. David *Yiẓḥaki.
Zera Emet Resp. by *Ishmael b. Abaham Isaac ha-Kohen.
Ẓevi la-Ẓaddik, Resp. by Ẓevi Elimelech b. David Shapira.
Zikhron Yehudah, Resp. by *Judah b. Asher
Zikhron Yosef, Resp. by Joseph b. Menahem *Steinhardt.
Zikhronot, Sefer ha-, Sermons on several precepts by Samuel *Aboab.
Zikkaron la-Rishonim . . ., by Albert (Abraham Elijah) *Harkavy; contains in vol. 1 pt. 4 (1887) a collection of Geonic responsa.
Ẓiẓ Eliezer, Resp. by Eliezer Judah b. Jacob Gedaliah Waldenberg.

BIBLIOGRAPHICAL ABBREVIATIONS

Bibliographies in English and other languages have been extensively updated, with English translations cited where available. In order to help the reader, the language of books or articles is given where not obvious from titles of books or names of periodicals. Titles of books and periodicals in languages with alphabets other than Latin, are given in transliteration, even where there is a title page in English. Titles of articles in periodicals are not given. Names of Hebrew and Yiddish periodicals well known in English-speaking countries or in Israel under their masthead in Latin characters are given in this form, even when contrary to transliteration rules. Names of authors writing in languages with non-Latin alphabets are given in their Latin alphabet form wherever known; otherwise the names are transliterated. Initials are generally not given for authors of articles in periodicals, except to avoid confusion. Non-abbreviated book titles and names of periodicals are printed in *italics*. Abbreviations are given in the list below.

AASOR	*Annual of the American School of Oriental Research* (1919ff.).
AB	*Analecta Biblica* (1952ff.).
Abel, Géog	F.-M. Abel, *Géographie de la Palestine,* 2 vols. (1933-38).
ABR	*Australian Biblical Review* (1951ff.).
Abr.	Philo, *De Abrahamo.*
Abrahams, Companion	I. Abrahams, *Companion to the Authorised Daily Prayer Book* (rev. ed. 1922).
Abramson, Merkazim	S. Abramson, *Ba-Merkazim u-va-Tefuẓot bi-Tekufat ha-Ge'onim* (1965).
Acts	Acts of the Apostles (New Testament).
ACUM	*Who is who in ACUM* [*Aguddat Kompozitorim u-Meḥabbrim*].
ADAJ	*Annual of the Department of Antiquities, Jordan* (1951ff.).
Adam	Adam and Eve (Pseudepigrapha).
ADB	*Allgemeine Deutsche Biographie,* 56 vols. (1875–1912).
Add. Esth.	The Addition to Esther (Apocrypha).
Adler, Prat Mus	1. Adler, *La pratique musicale savante dans quelques communautés juives en Europe au XVIIe et XVIIIe siècles,* 2 vols. (1966).
Adler-Davis	H.M. Adler and A. Davis (ed. and tr.), *Service of the Synagogue, a New Edition of the Festival Prayers with an English Translation in Prose and Verse,* 6 vols. (1905–06).
Aet.	Philo, *De Aeternitate Mundi.*
AFO	*Archiv fuer Orientforschung* (first two volumes under the name *Archiv fuer Keilschriftforschung)* (1923ff.).
Ag. Ber	*Aggadat Bereshit* (ed. Buber, 1902*).*
Agr.	Philo, *De Agricultura.*
Ag. Sam.	*Aggadat Samuel.*
Ag. Song	*Aggadat Shir ha-Shirim* (Schechter ed., 1896).
Aharoni, Ereẓ	Y. Aharoni, *Ereẓ Yisrael bi-Tekufat ha-Mikra: Geografyah Historit* (1962).
Aharoni, Land	Y. Aharoni, *Land of the Bible* (1966).

Ahikar	Ahikar (Pseudepigrapha).
AI	*Archives Israélites de France* (1840–1936).
AJA	*American Jewish Archives* (1948ff.).
AJHSP	*American Jewish Historical Society – Publications* (after vol. 50 = AJHSQ).
AJHSQ	*American Jewish Historical* (Society) *Quarterly* (before vol. 50 =AJHSP).
AJSLL	*American Journal of Semitic Languages and Literature* (1884–95 under the title *Hebraica,* since 1942 JNES).
AJYB	*American Jewish Year Book* (1899ff.).
AKM	Abhandlungen fuer die Kunde des Morgenlandes (series).
Albright, Arch	W.F. Albright, *Archaeology of Palestine* (rev. ed. 1960).
Albright, Arch Bib	W.F. Albright, *Archaeology of Palestine and the Bible* (1935³).
Albright, Arch Rel	W.F. Albright, *Archaeology and the Religion of Israel* (1953³).
Albright, Stone	W.F. Albright, *From the Stone Age to Christianity* (1957²).
Alon, Meḥkarim	G. Alon, *Meḥkarim be-Toledot Yisrael bi-Ymei Bayit Sheni u-vi-Tekufat ha-Mishnah ve-ha Talmud,* 2 vols. (1957–58).
Alon, Toledot	G. Alon, *Toledot ha-Yehudim be-Ereẓ Yisrael bi-Tekufat ha-Mishnah ve-ha-Talmud,* I (1958³), (1961²).
ALOR	Alter Orient (series).
Alt, Kl Schr	A. Alt, *Kleine Schriften zur Geschichte des Volkes Israel,* 3 vols. (1953–59).
Alt, Landnahme	A. Alt, *Landnahme der Israeliten in Palaestina* (1925); also in Alt, Kl Schr, 1 (1953), 89–125.
Ant.	Josephus, *Jewish Antiquities* (Loeb Classics ed.).
AO	*Acta Orientalia* (1922ff.).
AOR	*Analecta Orientalia* (1931ff.).
AOS	American Oriental Series.
Apion	Josephus, *Against Apion* (Loeb Classics ed.).
Aq.	Aquila's Greek translation of the Bible.
Ar.	*Arakhin* (talmudic tractate).
Artist.	Letter of Aristeas (Pseudepigrapha).
ARN¹	*Avot de-Rabbi Nathan,* version (1) ed. Schechter, 1887.
ARN²	*Avot de-Rabbi Nathan,* version (2) ed. Schechter, 1945².
Aronius, Regesten	I. Aronius, *Regesten zur Geschichte der Juden im fraenkischen und deutschen Reiche bis zum Jahre 1273* (1902).
ARW	*Archiv fuer Religionswissenschaft* (1898–1941/42).
AS	*Assyrological Studies* (1931ff.).
Ashtor, Korot	E. Ashtor (Strauss), *Korot ha-Yehudim bi-Sefarad ha-Muslemit,* 1(1966²), 2(1966).
Ashtor, Toledot	E. Ashtor (Strauss), *Toledot ha-Yehudim be-Miẓrayim ve-Suryah Taḥat Shilton ha-Mamlukim,* 3 vols. (1944–70).
Assaf, Ge'onim	S. Assaf, *Tekufat ha-Ge'onim ve-Sifrutah* (1955).
Assaf, Mekorot	S. Assaf, *Mekorot le-Toledot ha-Ḥinnukh be-Yisrael,* 4 vols. (1925–43).
Ass. Mos.	Assumption of Moses (Pseudepigrapha).
ATA	Alttestamentliche Abhandlungen (series).
ATANT	Abhandlungen zur Theologie des Alten und Neuen Testaments (series).
AUJW	*Allgemeine unabhaengige juedische Wochenzeitung* (till 1966 = AWJD).
AV	Authorized Version of the Bible.
Avad.	*Avadim* (post-talmudic tractate).
Avi-Yonah, Geog	M. Avi-Yonah, *Geografyah Historit shel Ereẓ Yisrael* (1962³).
Avi-Yonah, Land	M. Avi-Yonah, *The Holy Land from the Persian to the Arab conquest (536 B.C. to A.D. 640)* (1960).
Avot	*Avot* (talmudic tractate).
Av. Zar.	*Avodah Zarah* (talmudic tractate).
AWJD	*Allgemeine Wochenzeitung der Juden in Deutschland* (since 1967 = AUJW).
AZDJ	*Allgemeine Zeitung des Judentums.*
Azulai	Ḥ.Y.D. Azulai, *Shem ha-Gedolim,* ed. by I.E. Benjacob, 2 pts. (1852) (and other editions).
BA	*Biblical Archaeologist* (1938ff.).
Bacher, Bab Amor	W. Bacher, *Agada der babylonischen Amoraeer* (1913²).
Bacher, Pal Amor	W. Bacher, *Agada der palaestinensischen Amoraeer* (Heb. ed. *Aggadat Amora'ei Ereẓ Yisrael),* 2 vols. (1892–99).
Bacher, Tann	W. Bacher, *Agada der Tannaiten* (Heb. ed. *Aggadot ha-Tanna'im,* vol. 1, pt. 1 and 2 (1903); vol. 2 (1890).
Bacher, Trad	W. Bacher, *Tradition und Tradenten in den Schulen Palaestinas und Babyloniens* (1914).
Baer, Spain	Yitzhak (Fritz) Baer, *History of the Jews in Christian Spain,* 2 vols. (1961–66).
Baer, Studien	Yitzhak (Fritz) Baer, *Studien zur Geschichte der Juden im Koenigreich Aragonien waehrend des 13. und 14. Jahrhunderts* (1913).
Baer, Toledot	Yitzhak (Fritz) Baer, *Toledot ha-Yehudim bi-Sefarad ha-Noẓerit mi-Teḥillatan shel ha-Kehillot ad ha-Gerush,* 2 vols. (1959²).
Baer, Urkunden	Yitzhak (Fritz) Baer, *Die Juden im christlichen Spanien,* 2 vols. (1929–36).
Baer S., Seder	S.I. Baer, *Seder Avodat Yisrael* (1868 and reprints).
BAIU	*Bulletin de l'Alliance Israélite Universelle* (1861–1913).
Baker, Biog Dict	*Baker's Biographical Dictionary of Musicians,* revised by N. Slonimsky (1958⁵; with Supplement 1965).
I Bar.	I Baruch (Apocrypha).
II Bar.	II Baruch (Pseudepigrapha).
III Bar.	III Baruch (Pseudepigrapha).
BAR	*Biblical Archaeology Review.*
Baron, Community	S.W. Baron, *The Jewish Community, its History and Structure to the American Revolution,* 3 vols. (1942).

Baron, Social — S.W. Baron, *Social and Religious History of the Jews*, 3 vols. (1937); enlarged, 1-2(1952^{2}), 3-14 (1957–69).

Barthélemy-Milik — D. Barthélemy and J.T. Milik, *Dead Sea Scrolls: Discoveries in the Judean Desert*, vol. 1 *Qumram Cave* I (1955).

BASOR — *Bulletin of the American School of Oriental Research.*

Bauer-Leander — H. Bauer and P. Leander, *Grammatik des Biblisch-Aramaeischen* (1927; repr. 1962).

BB — (1) *Bava Batra* (talmudic tractate). (2) *Biblische Beitraege* (1943ff.).

BBB — Bonner biblische Beitraege (series).

BBLA — *Beitraege zur biblischen Landes- und Altertumskunde* (until 1949–ZDPV).

BBSAJ — *Bulletin*, British School of Archaeology, Jerusalem (1922–25; after 1927 included in PEFQS).

BDASI — *Alon* (since 1948) or *Hadashot Arkheʾologiyyot* (since 1961), bulletin of the Department of Antiquities of the State of Israel.

Begrich, Chronologie — J. Begrich, *Chronologie der Koenige von Israel und Juda* (1929).

Bek. — *Bekhorot* (talmudic tractate).

Bel — Bel and the Dragon (Apocrypha).

Benjacob, Oẓar — I.E. Benjacob, *Oẓar ha-Sefarim* (1880; repr. 1956).

Ben Sira — see Ecclus.

Ben-Yehuda, Millon — E. Ben-Yedhuda, *Millon ha-Lashon ha-Ivrit*, 16 vols (1908–59; repr. in 8 vols., 1959).

Benzinger, Archaeologie — I. Benzinger, *Hebraeische Archaeologie* (1927^{3}).

Ben Zvi, Eretz Israel — I. Ben-Zvi, *Eretz Israel under Ottoman Rule* (1960; offprint from L. Finkelstein (ed.), *The Jews, their History, Culture and Religion* (vol. 1).

Ben Zvi, Ereẓ Israel — I. Ben-Zvi, *Ereẓ Israel bi-Ymei ha-Shilton ha-Ottomani (1955).*

Ber. — *Berakhot* (talmudic tractate).

Beẓah — *Beẓah* (talmudic tractate).

BIES — Bulletin of the Israel Exploration Society, see below BJPES.

Bik. — *Bikkurim* (talmudic tractate).

BJCE — Bibliography of Jewish Communities in Europe, catalog at General Archives for the History of the Jewish People, Jerusalem.

BJPES — Bulletin of the Jewish Palestine Exploration Society – English name of the Hebrew periodical known as:
1. *Yediʿot ha-Ḥevrah ha-Ivrit la-Ḥakirat Ereẓ Yisrael va-Attikoteha* (1933–1954);
2. *Yediʿot ha-Ḥevrah la-Ḥakirat Ereẓ Yisrael va-Attikoteha* (1954–1962);
3. *Yediʿot ba-Ḥakirat Ereẓ Yisrael va-Attikoteha* (1962ff.).

BJRL — *Bulletin of the John Rylands Library* (1914ff.).

BK — *Bava Kamma* (talmudic tractate).

BLBI — *Bulletin of the Leo Baeck Institute* (1957ff.).

BM — (1) *Bava Meẓia* (talmudic tractate). (2) *Beit Mikra* (1955/56ff.). (3) British Museum.

BO — *Bibbia e Oriente* (1959ff.).

Bondy-Dworský — G. Bondy and F. Dworský, *Regesten zur Geschichte der Juden in Boehmen, Maehren und Schlesien von 906 bis 1620*, 2 vols. (1906).

BOR — *Bibliotheca Orientalis* (1943ff.).

Borée, Ortsnamen — W. Borée *Die alten Ortsnamen Palaestinas* (1930).

Bousset, Religion — W. Bousset, *Die Religion des Judentums im neutestamentlichen Zeitalter* (1906^{2}).

Bousset-Gressmann — W. Bousset, *Die Religion des Judentums im spaethellenistischen Zeitalter* (1966^{3}).

BR — *Biblical Review* (1916–25).

BRCI — *Bulletin of the Research Council of Israel* (1951/52–1954/55; then divided).

BRE — *Biblical Research* (1956ff.).

BRF — *Bulletin of the Rabinowitz Fund for the Exploration of Ancient Synagogues* (1949ff.).

Briggs, Psalms — Ch. A. and E.G. Briggs, *Critical and Exegetical Commentary on the Book of Psalms*, 2 vols. (ICC, 1906–07).

Bright, Hist — J. Bright, *A History of Israel* (1959).

Brockelmann, Arab Lit — K. Brockelmann, *Geschichte der arabischen Literatur*, 2 vols. 1898–1902), supplement, 3 vols. (1937–42).

Bruell, Jahrbuecher — *Jahrbuecher fuer juedische Geschichte und Litteratur*, ed. by N. Bruell, Frankfurt (1874–90).

Brugmans-Frank — H. Brugmans and A. Frank (eds.), *Geschiedenis der Joden in Nederland* (1940).

BTS — *Bible et Terre Sainte* (1958ff.).

Bull, Index — S. Bull, *Index to Biographies of Contemporary Composers* (1964).

BW — *Biblical World* (1882–1920).

BWANT — *Beitraege zur Wissenschaft vom Alten und Neuen Testament* (1926ff.).

BZ — *Biblische Zeitschrift* (1903ff.).

BZAW — *Beihefte zur Zeitschrift fuer die alttestamentliche Wissenschaft*, supplement to ZAW (1896ff.).

BŻIH — *Biuletyn Zydowskiego Instytutu Historycznego* (1950ff.).

CAB — *Cahiers d'archéologie biblique* (1953ff.).

CAD — *The* [*Chicago*] *Assyrian Dictionary* (1956ff.).

CAH — *Cambridge Ancient History*, 12 vols. (1923–39)

CAH^{2} — *Cambridge Ancient History*, second edition, 14 vols. (1962–2005).

Calwer, Lexikon — *Calwer, Bibellexikon.*

Cant. — Canticles, usually given as Song (= Song of Songs).

Cantera-Millás, Inscripciones — F. Cantera and J.M. Millás, *Las Inscripciones Hebraicas de España* (1956).
CBQ — *Catholic Biblical Quarterly* (1939ff.).
CCARY — Central Conference of American Rabbis, *Yearbook* (1890/91ff.).
CD — *Damascus Document* from the Cairo *Genizah* (published by S. Schechter, *Fragments of a Zadokite Work*, 1910).
Charles, Apocrypha — R.H. Charles, *Apocrypha and Pseudepigrapha . . .*, 2 vols. (1913; repr. 1963–66).
Cher. — Philo, *De Cherubim.*
I (or II) Chron. — Chronicles, book I and II (Bible).
CIG — *Corpus Inscriptionum Graecarum.*
CIJ — *Corpus Inscriptionum Judaicarum,* 2 vols. (1936–52).
CIL — *Corpus Inscriptionum Latinarum.*
CIS — *Corpus Inscriptionum Semiticarum* (1881ff.).
C.J. — Codex Justinianus.
Clermont-Ganneau, Arch — Ch. Clermont-Ganneau, *Archaeological Researches in Palestine,* 2 vols. (1896–99).
CNFI — *Christian News from Israel* (1949ff.).
Cod. Just. — Codex Justinianus.
Cod. Theod. — Codex Theodosinanus.
Col. — Epistle to the Colosssians (New Testament).
Conder, Survey — Palestine Exploration Fund, *Survey of Eastern Palestine*, vol. 1, pt. I (1889) = C.R. Conder, *Memoirs of the . . . Survey.*
Conder-Kitchener — Palestine Exploration Fund, *Survey of Western Palestine*, vol. 1, pts. 1-3 (1881–83) = C.R. Conder and H.H. Kitchener, *Memoirs.*
Conf. — Philo, *De Confusione Linguarum.*
Conforte, Kore — D. Conforte, *Kore ha-Dorot* (1842^2).
Cong. — Philo, *De Congressu Quaerendae Eruditionis Gratia.*
Cont. — Philo, *De Vita Contemplativa.*
I (or II) Cor. — Epistles to the Corinthians (New Testament).
Cowley, Aramic — A. Cowley, *Aramaic Papyri of the Fifth Century B.C.* (1923).
Colwey, Cat — A.E. Cowley, *A Concise Catalogue of the Hebrew Printed Books in the Bodleian Library* (1929).
CRB — *Cahiers de la Revue Biblique* (1964ff.).
Crowfoot-Kenyon — J.W. Crowfoot, K.M. Kenyon and E.L. Sukenik, *Buildings of Samaria* (1942).
C.T. — Codex Theodosianus.

DAB — *Dictionary of American Biography* (1928–58).
Daiches, Jews — S. Daiches, *Jews in Babylonia* (1910).
Dalman, Arbeit — G. Dalman, *Arbeit und Sitte in Palaestina,* 7 vols.in 8 (1928–42 repr. 1964).
Dan — Daniel (Bible).
Davidson, Oẓar — I. Davidson, *Oẓar ha-Shirah ve-ha-Piyyut,* 4 vols. (1924–33); Supplement in: HUCA, 12–13 (1937/38), 715–823.
DB — J. Hastings, *Dictionary of the Bible,* 4 vols. (1963^2).
DBI — F.G. Vigoureaux et al. (eds.), *Dictionnaire de la Bible,* 5 vols. in 10 (1912); Supplement, 8 vols. (1928–66)
Decal. — Philo, *De Decalogo.*
Dem. — *Demai* (talmudic tractate).
DER — *Derekh Ereẓ Rabbah* (post-talmudic tractate).
Derenbourg, Hist — J. Derenbourg *Essai sur l'histoire et la géographie de la Palestine* (1867).
Det. — Philo, *Quod deterius potiori insidiari solet.*
Deus — Philo, *Quod Deus immutabilis sit.*
Deut. — Deuteronomy (Bible).
Deut. R. — *Deuteronomy Rabbah.*
DEZ — *Derekh Ereẓ Zuta* (post-talmudic tractate).
DHGE — *Dictionnaire d'histoire et de géographie ecclésiastiques,* ed. by A. Baudrillart et al., 17 vols (1912–68).
Dik. Sof — *Dikdukei Soferim,* variae lections of the talmudic text by Raphael Nathan Rabbinovitz (16 vols., 1867–97).
Dinur, Golah — B. Dinur (Dinaburg), *Yisrael ba-Golah,* 2 vols. in 7 (1959–68) = vols. 5 and 6 of his *Toledot Yisrael,* second series.
Dinur, Haganah — B. Dinur (ed.), *Sefer Toledot ha-Haganah* (1954ff.).
Diringer, Iscr — D. Diringer, *Iscrizioni antico-ebraiche palestinesi* (1934).
Discoveries — *Discoveries in the Judean Desert* (1955ff.).
DNB — *Dictionary of National Biography,* 66 vols. (1921–222) with Supplements.
Dubnow, Divrei — S. Dubnow, *Divrei Yemei Am Olam,* 11 vols (1923–38 and further editions).
Dubnow, Ḥasidut — S. Dubnow, *Toledot ha-Ḥasidut* (1960^2).
Dubnow, Hist — S. Dubnow, *History of the Jews* (1967).
Dubnow, Hist Russ — S. Dubnow, *History of the Jews in Russia and Poland,* 3 vols. (1916 20).
Dubnow, Outline — S. Dubnow, *An Outline of Jewish History,* 3 vols. (1925–29).
Dubnow, Weltgesch — S. Dubnow, *Weltgeschichte des juedischen Volkes* 10 vols. (1925–29).
Dukes, Poesie — L. Dukes, *Zur Kenntnis der neuhebraeischen religioesen Poesie* (1842).
Dunlop, Khazars — D. H. Dunlop, *History of the Jewish Khazars* (1954).

EA — El Amarna Letters (edited by J.A. Knudtzon), *Die El-Amarna Tafel,* 2 vols. (1907 14).
EB — *Encyclopaedia Britannica.*
EBI — *Estudios biblicos* (1941ff.).
EBIB — T.K. Cheyne and J.S. Black, *Encyclopaedia Biblica,* 4 vols. (1899–1903).
Ebr. — Philo, *De Ebrietate.*
Eccles. — Ecclesiastes (Bible).
Eccles. R. — *Ecclesiastes Rabbah.*
Ecclus. — Ecclesiasticus or Wisdom of Ben Sira (or Sirach; Apocrypha).
Eduy. — *Eduyyot* (mishanic tractate).

EG — *Enziklopedyah shel Galuyyot* (1953ff.).
EH — *Even ha-Ezer.*
EHA — *Enziklopedyah la-Ḥafirot Arkheologiyyot be-Ereẓ Yisrael,* 2 vols. (1970).
EI — *Enzyklopaedie des Islams,* 4 vols. (1905–14). Supplement vol. (1938).
EIS — *Encyclopaedia of Islam,* 4 vols. (1913–36; repr. 1954–68).
EIS² — *Encyclopaedia of Islam, second edition (1960–2000).*
Eisenstein, Dinim — J.D. Eisenstein, *Oẓar Dinim u-Minhagim* (1917; several reprints).
Eisenstein, Yisrael — J.D. Eisenstein, *Oẓar Yisrael* (10 vols, 1907–13; repr. with several additions 1951).
EIV — *Enẓiklopedyah Ivrit* (1949ff.).
EJ — *Encyclopaedia Judaica* (German, A-L only), 10 vols. (1928–34).
EJC — *Enciclopedia Judaica Castellana,* 10 vols. (1948–51).
Elbogen, Century — I Elbogen, *A Century of Jewish Life* (1960²).
Elbogen, Gottesdienst — I Elbogen, *Der juedische Gottesdienst ...* (1931³, repr. 1962).
Elon, Mafte'aḥ — M. Elon (ed.), *Mafte'aḥ ha-She'elot ve-ha-Teshuvot ha-Rosh* (1965).
EM — *Enẓiklopedyah Mikra'it* (1950ff.).
I (or II) En. — I and II Enoch (Pseudepigrapha).
EncRel — *Encyclopedia of Religion,* 15 vols. (1987, 2005²).
Eph. — Epistle to the Ephesians (New Testament).
Ephros, Cant — G. Ephros, *Cantorial Anthology,* 5 vols. (1929–57).
Ep. Jer. — Epistle of Jeremy (Apocrypha).
Epstein, Amora'im — J N. Epstein, *Mevo'ot le-Sifrut ha-Amora'im* (1962).
Epstein, Marriage — L M. Epstein, *Marriage Laws in the Bible and the Talmud* (1942).
Epstein, Mishnah — J. N. Epstein, *Mavo le-Nusaḥ ha-Mishnah,* 2 vols. (1964²).
Epstein, Tanna'im — J. N. Epstein, *Mavo le-Sifruth ha-Tanna'im.* (1947).
ER — *Ecumenical Review.*
Er. — *Eruvin* (talmudic tractate).
ERE — *Encyclopaedia of Religion and Ethics,* 13 vols. (1908–26); reprinted.
ErIsr — *Eretz-Israel,* Israel Exploration Society.
I Esd. — I Esdras (Apocrypha) (= III Ezra).
II Esd. — II Esdras (Apocrypha) (= IV Ezra).
ESE — *Ephemeris fuer semitische Epigraphik,* ed. by M. Lidzbarski.
ESN — *Encyclopaedia Sefaradica Neerlandica,* 2 pts. (1949).
ESS — *Encyclopaedia of the Social Sciences,* 15 vols. (1930–35); reprinted in 8 vols. (1948–49).
Esth. — Esther (Bible).
Est. R. — *Esther Rabbah.*
ET — *Enẓiklopedyah Talmudit* (1947ff.).
Eusebius, Onom. — E. Klostermann (ed.), *Das Onomastikon* (1904), Greek with Hieronymus' Latin translation.
Ex. — Exodus (Bible).
Ex. R. — *Exodus Rabbah.*
Exs — Philo, *De Exsecrationibus.*
EẒD — *Enẓiklopeday shel ha-Ẓiyyonut ha-Datit* (1951ff.).
Ezek. — Ezekiel (Bible).
Ezra — Ezra (Bible).
III Ezra — III Ezra (Pseudepigrapha).
IV Ezra — IV Ezra (Pseudepigrapha).

Feliks, Ha-Ẓome'aḥ — *J. Feliks, Ha-Ẓome'aḥ ve-ha-Ḥai ba-Mishnah* (1983).
Finkelstein, Middle Ages — L. Finkelstein, *Jewish Self-Government in the Middle Ages* (1924).
Fischel, Islam — W.J. Fischel, *Jews in the Economic and Political Life of Mediaeval Islam* (1937; reprint with introduction "The Court Jew in the Islamic World," 1969).
FJW — *Fuehrer durch die juedische Gemeindeverwaltung und Wohlfahrtspflege in Deutschland* (1927/28).
Frankel, Mevo — Z. Frankel, *Mevo ha-Yerushalmi* (1870; reprint 1967).
Frankel, Mishnah — Z. Frankel, *Darkhei ha-Mishnah* (1959²; reprint 1959²).
Frazer, Folk-Lore — J.G. Frazer, *Folk-Lore in the Old Testament,* 3 vols. (1918–19).
Frey, Corpus — J.-B. Frey, *Corpus Inscriptionum Iudaicarum,* 2 vols. (1936–52).
Friedmann, Lebensbilder — A. Friedmann, *Lebensbilder beruehmter Kantoren,* 3 vols. (1918–27).
FRLT — *Forschungen zur Religion und Literatur des Alten und Neuen Testaments* (series) (1950ff.).
Frumkin-Rivlin — A.L. Frumkin and E. Rivlin, *Toledot Ḥakhmei Yerushalayim,* 3 vols. (1928–30), Supplement vol. (1930).
Fuenn, Keneset — S.J. Fuenn, *Keneset Yisrael,* 4 vols. (1887–90).
Fuerst, Bibliotheca — J. Fuerst, *Bibliotheca Judaica,* 2 vols. (1863; repr. 1960).
Fuerst, Karaeertum — J. Fuerst, *Geschichte des Karaeertums,* 3 vols. (1862–69).
Fug. — Philo, *De Fuga et Inventione.*

Gal. — Epistle to the Galatians (New Testament).
Galling, Reallexikon — K. Galling, *Biblisches Reallexikon* (1937).
Gardiner, Onomastica — A.H. Gardiner, *Ancient Egyptian Onomastica,* 3 vols. (1947).
Geiger, Mikra — A. Geiger, *Ha-Mikra ve-Targumav,* tr. by J.L. Baruch (1949).
Geiger, Urschrift — A. Geiger, *Urschrift und Uebersetzungen der Bibel* 1928²).
Gen. — Genesis (Bible).
Gen. R. — *Genesis Rabbah.*
Ger. — *Gerim* (post-talmudic tractate).
Germ Jud — M. Brann, I. Elbogen, A. Freimann, and H. Tykocinski (eds.), *Germania Judaica,* vol. 1 (1917; repr. 1934 and 1963); vol. 2, in 2 pts. (1917–68), ed. by Z. Avneri.

GHAT	*Goettinger Handkommentar zum Alten Testament* (1917–22).
Ghirondi-Neppi	M.S. Ghirondi and G.H. Neppi, *Toledot Gedolei Yisrael u-Ge'onei Italyah ... u-Ve'urim al Sefer Zekher Ẓaddikim li-Verakhah . . .*(1853), index in ZHB, 17 (1914), 171–83.
Gig.	Philo, *De Gigantibus.*
Ginzberg, Legends	L. Ginzberg, *Legends of the Jews,* 7 vols. (1909–38; and many reprints).
Git.	*Gittin* (talmudic tractate).
Glueck, Explorations	N. Glueck, *Explorations in Eastern Palestine,* 2 vols. (1951).
Goell, Bibliography	Y. Goell, *Bibliography of Modern Hebrew Literature in English Translation* (1968).
Goodenough, Symbols	E.R. Goodenough, *Jewish Symbols in the Greco-Roman Period,* 13 vols. (1953–68).
Gordon, Textbook	C.H. Gordon, *Ugaritic Textbook* (1965; repr. 1967).
Graetz, Gesch	H. Graetz, *Geschichte der Juden* (last edition 1874–1908).
Graetz, Hist	H. Graetz, *History of the Jews,* 6 vols. (1891–1902).
Graetz, Psalmen	H. Graetz, *Kritischer Commentar zu den Psalmen,* 2 vols. in 1 (1882–83).
Graetz, Rabbinowitz	H. Graetz, *Divrei Yemei Yisrael,* tr. by S.P. Rabbinowitz. (1928 1929[2]).
Gray, Names	G.B. Gray, *Studies in Hebrew Proper Names* (1896).
Gressmann, Bilder	H. Gressmann, *Altorientalische Bilder zum Alten Testament* (1927[2]).
Gressmann, Texte	H. Gressmann, *Altorientalische Texte zum Alten Testament* (1926[2]).
Gross, Gal Jud	H. Gross, *Gallia Judaica* (1897; repr. with add. 1969).
Grove, Dict	*Grove's Dictionary of Music and Musicians,* ed. by E. Blum 9 vols. (1954[5]) and suppl. (1961[5]).
Guedemann, Gesch Erz	M. Guedemann, *Geschichte des Erziehungswesens und der Cultur der abendlaendischen Juden,* 3 vols. (1880–88).
Guedemann, Quellenschr	M. Guedemann, *Quellenschriften zur Geschichte des Unterrichts und der Erziehung bei den deutschen Juden* (1873, 1891).
Guide	Maimonides, *Guide of the Perplexed.*
Gulak, Oẓar	A. Gulak, *Oẓar ha-Shetarot ha-Nehugim be-Yisrael* (1926).
Gulak, Yesodei	A. Gulak, *Yesodei ha-Mishpat ha-Ivri, Seder Dinei Mamonot be-Yisrael, al pi Mekorot ha-Talmud ve-ha-Posekim,* 4 vols. (1922; repr. 1967).
Guttmann, Mafte'aḥ	M. Guttmann, *Mafte'aḥ ha-Talmud,* 3 vols. (1906–30).
Guttmann, Philosophies	J. Guttmann, *Philosophies of Judaism* (1964).
Hab.	*Habakkuk* (Bible).
Ḥag.	*Ḥagigah* (talmudic tractate).
Haggai	*Haggai* (Bible).
Ḥal.	*Ḥallah* (talmudic tractate).
Halevy, Dorot	I. Halevy, *Dorot ha-Rishonim,* 6 vols. (1897–1939).
Halpern, Pinkas	I. Halpern (Halperin), *Pinkas Va'ad Arba Araẓot* (1945).
Hananel-Eškenazi	A. Hananel and Eškenazi (eds.), *Fontes Hebraici ad res oeconomicas socialesque terrarum balcanicarum saeculo XVI pertinentes,* 2 vols, (1958–60; in Bulgarian).
HB	*Hebraeische Bibliographie* (1858–82).
Heb.	Epistle to the Hebrews (New Testament).
Heilprin, Dorot	J. Heilprin (Heilperin), *Seder ha-Dorot,* 3 vols. (1882; repr. 1956).
Her.	Philo, *Quis Rerum Divinarum Heres.*
Hertz, Prayer	J.H. Hertz (ed.), *Authorised Daily Prayer Book* (rev. ed. 1948; repr. 1963).
Herzog, Instit	I. Herzog, *The Main Institutions of Jewish Law,* 2 vols. (1936–39; repr. 1967).
Herzog-Hauck	J.J. Herzog and A. Hauch (eds.), *Real-encyklopaedie fuer protestantische Theologie* (1896–1913[3]).
HḤY	*Ha-Ẓofeh le-Ḥokhmat Yisrael* (first four volumes under the title *Ha-Ẓofeh me-Ereẓ Hagar)* (1910/11–13).
Hirschberg, Afrikah	H.Z. Hirschberg, *Toledot ha-Yehudim be-Afrikah ha-Zofonit,* 2 vols. (1965).
HJ	*Historia Judaica* (1938–61).
HL	*Das Heilige Land* (1857ff.)
ḤM	*Ḥoshen Mishpat.*
Hommel, Ueberliefer.	F. Hommel, *Die altisraelitische Ueberlieferung in inschriftlicher Beleuchtung* (1897).
Hor.	*Horayot* (talmudic tractate).
Horodezky, Ḥasidut	S.A. Horodezky, *Ha-Ḥasidut ve-ha-Ḥasidim,* 4 vols. (1923).
Horowitz, Ereẓ Yis	I.W. Horowitz, *Ereẓ Yisrael u-Shekhenoteha* (1923).
Hos.	Hosea (Bible).
HTR	*Harvard Theological Review* (1908ff.).
HUCA	*Hebrew Union College Annual* (1904; 1924ff.)
Ḥul.	*Ḥullin* (talmudic tractate).
Husik, Philosophy	I. Husik, *History of Medieval Jewish Philosophy* (1932[2]).
Hyman, Toledot	A. Hyman, *Toledot Tanna'im ve-Amora'im* (1910; repr. 1964).
Ibn Daud, Tradition	Abraham Ibn Daud, *Sefer ha-Qabbalah – The Book of Tradition,* ed. and tr. By G.D. Cohen (1967).
ICC	International Critical Commentary on the Holy Scriptures of the Old and New Testaments (series, 1908ff.).
IDB	*Interpreter's Dictionary of the Bible,* 4 vols. (1962).
Idelsohn, Litugy	A. Z. Idelsohn, *Jewish Liturgy and its Development* (1932; paperback repr. 1967)
Idelsohn, Melodien	A. Z. Idelsohn, *Hebraeisch-orientalischer Melodienschatz,* 10 vols. (1914 32).
Idelsohn, Music	A. Z. Idelsohn, *Jewish Music in its Historical Development* (1929; paperback repr. 1967).

IEJ	*Israel Exploration Journal* (1950ff.).
IESS	*International Encyclopedia of the Social Sciences* (various eds.).
IG	*Inscriptiones Graecae,* ed. by the Prussian Academy.
IGYB	*Israel Government Year Book* (1949/50ff.).
ILR	*Israel Law Review* (1966ff.).
IMIT	*Izraelita Magyar Irodalmi Társulat Évkönyv* (1895 1948).
IMT	International Military Tribunal.
INB	*Israel Numismatic Bulletin* (1962–63).
INJ	*Israel Numismatic Journal* (1963ff.).
Ios	Philo, *De Iosepho.*
Isa.	Isaiah (Bible).
ITHL	Institute for the Translation of Hebrew Literature.
IZBG	*Internationale Zeitschriftenschau fuer Bibelwissenschaft und Grenzgebiete* (1951ff.).
JA	*Journal asiatique* (1822ff.).
James	Epistle of James (New Testament).
JAOS	*Journal of the American Oriental Society* (c. 1850ff.)
Jastrow, Dict	M. Jastrow, *Dictionary of the Targumim, the Talmud Babli and Yerushalmi, and the Midrashic literature,* 2 vols. (1886 1902 and reprints).
JBA	*Jewish Book Annual* (19242ff.).
JBL	*Journal of Biblical Literature* (1881ff.).
JBR	*Journal of Bible and Religion* (1933ff.).
JC	*Jewish Chronicle* (1841ff.).
JCS	*Journal of Cuneiform Studies* (1947ff.).
JE	*Jewish Encyclopedia,* 12 vols. (1901–05 several reprints).
Jer.	Jeremiah (Bible).
Jeremias, Alte Test	A. Jeremias, *Das Alte Testament im Lichte des alten Orients* 1930^4).
JGGJČ	*Jahrbuch der Gesellschaft fuer Geschichte der Juden in der Čechoslovakischen Republik* (1929–38).
JHSEM	Jewish Historical Society of England, *Miscellanies* (1925ff.).
JHSET	Jewish Historical Society of England, *Transactions* (1893ff.).
JJGL	*Jahrbuch fuer juedische Geschichte und Literatur* (Berlin) (1898–1938).
JJLG	*Jahrbuch der juedische-literarischen Gesellschaft* (Frankfurt) (1903–32).
JJS	*Journal of Jewish Studies* (1948ff.).
JJSO	*Jewish Journal of Sociology* (1959ff.).
JJV	*Jahrbuch fuer juedische Volkskunde* (1898–1924).
JL	*Juedisches Lexikon,* 5 vols. (1927–30).
JMES	*Journal of the Middle East Society* (1947ff.).
JNES	*Journal of Near Eastern Studies* (continuation of AJSLL) (1942ff.).
J.N.U.L.	Jewish National and University Library.
Job	Job (Bible).
Joel	Joel (Bible).
John	Gospel according to John (New Testament).
I, II and III John	Epistles of John (New Testament).
Jos., Ant	Josephus, *Jewish Antiquities* (Loeb Classics ed.).
Jos. Apion	Josephus, *Against Apion* (Loeb Classics ed.).
Jos., index	*Josephus Works,* Loeb Classics ed., index of names.
Jos., Life	Josephus, *Life* (ed. Loeb Classics).
Jos, Wars	Josephus, *The Jewish Wars* (Loeb Classics ed.).
Josh.	Joshua (Bible).
JPESB	Jewish Palestine Exploration Society Bulletin, see BJPES.
JPESJ	Jewish Palestine Exploration Society Journal – Eng. Title of the Hebrew periodical *Kovez ha-Ḥevrah ha-Ivrit la-Ḥakirat Erez Yisrael va-Attikoteha.*
JPOS	*Journal of the Palestine Oriental Society* (1920–48).
JPS	Jewish Publication Society of America, *The Torah* (1962, 1967^2); *The Holy Scriptures* (1917).
JQR	*Jewish Quarterly Review* (1889ff.).
JR	*Journal of Religion* (1921ff.).
JRAS	*Journal of the Royal Asiatic Society* (1838ff.).
JHR	*Journal of Religious History* (1960/61ff.).
JSOS	*Jewish Social Studies* (1939ff.).
JSS	*Journal of Semitic Studies* (1956ff.).
JTS	*Journal of Theological Studies* (1900ff.).
JTSA	Jewish Theological Seminary of America (also abbreviated as JTS).
Jub.	Jubilees (Pseudepigrapha).
Judg.	Judges (Bible).
Judith	Book of Judith (Apocrypha).
Juster, Juifs	J. Juster, *Les Juifs dans l'Empire Romain,* 2 vols. (1914).
JYB	*Jewish Year Book* (1896ff.).
JZWL	*Juedische Zeitschift fuer Wissenschaft und Leben* (1862–75).
Kal.	*Kallah* (post-talmudic tractate).
Kal. R.	*Kallah Rabbati* (post-talmudic tractate).
Katz, England	*The Jews in the History of England, 1485-1850 (1994).*
Kaufmann, Schriften	D. Kaufmann, *Gesammelte Schriften,* 3 vols. (1908 15).
Kaufmann Y., Religion	Y. Kaufmann, *The Religion of Israel* (1960), abridged tr. of his *Toledot.*
Kaufmann Y., Toledot	Y. Kaufmann, *Toledot ha-Emunah ha-Yisre'elit,* 4 vols. (1937 57).
KAWJ	*Korrespondenzblatt des Vereins zur Gruendung und Erhaltung der Akademie fuer die Wissenschaft des Judentums* (1920 30).
Kayserling, Bibl	M. Kayserling, *Biblioteca Española-Portugueza-Judaica* (1880; repr. 1961).
Kelim	*Kelim* (mishnaic tractate).
Ker.	*Keritot* (talmudic tractate).
Ket.	*Ketubbot* (talmudic tractate).

Kid.	*Kiddushim* (talmudic tractate).
Kil.	*Kilayim* (talmudic tractate).
Kin.	*Kinnim* (mishnaic tractate).
Kisch, Germany	G. Kisch, *Jews in Medieval Germany* (1949).
Kittel, Gesch	R. Kittel, *Geschichte des Volkes Israel,* 3 vols. (1922–28).
Klausner, Bayit Sheni	J. Klausner, *Historyah shel ha-Bayit ha-Sheni,* 5 vols. (1950/512).
Klausner, Sifrut	J. Klausner, *Historyah shel haSifrut ha-Ivrit ha-Ḥadashah,* 6 vols. (1952–582).
Klein, corpus	S. Klein (ed.), *Juedisch-palaestinisches Corpus Inscriptionum* (1920).
Koehler-Baumgartner	L. Koehler and W. Baumgartner, *Lexicon in Veteris Testamenti libros* (1953).
Kohut, Arukh	H.J.A. Kohut (ed.), *Sefer he-Arukh ha-Shalem,* by Nathan b. Jehiel of Rome, 8 vols. (1876–92; Supplement by S. Krauss et al., 1936; repr. 1955).
Krauss, Tal Arch	S. Krauss, *Talmudische Archaeologie,* 3 vols. (1910–12; repr. 1966).
Kressel, Leksikon	G. Kressel, *Leksikon ha-Sifrut ha-Ivrit ba-Dorot ha-Aḥaronim,* 2 vols. (1965–67).
KS	*Kirjath Sepher* (1923/4ff.).
Kut.	*Kuttim* (post-talmudic tractate).
LA	Studium Biblicum Franciscanum, *Liber Annuus* (1951ff.).
L.A.	Philo, *Legum allegoriae.*
Lachower, Sifrut	F. Lachower, *Toledot ha-Sifrut ha-Ivrit ha-Ḥadashah,* 4 vols. (1947–48; several reprints).
Lam.	Lamentations (Bible).
Lam. R.	*Lamentations Rabbah.*
Landshuth, Ammudei	L. Landshuth, *Ammudei ha-Avodah* (1857–62; repr. with index, 1965).
Legat.	Philo, *De Legatione ad Caium.*
Lehmann, Nova Bibl	R.P. Lehmann, *Nova Bibliotheca Anglo-Judaica* (1961).
Lev.	Leviticus (Bible).
Lev. R.	*Leviticus Rabbah.*
Levy, Antologia	I. Levy, *Antologia de liturgia judeo-española* (1965ff.).
Levy J., Chald Targ	J. Levy, *Chaldaeisches Woerterbuch ueber die Targumim,* 2 vols. (1967–68; repr. 1959).
Levy J., Nuehebr Tal	J. Levy, *Neuhebraeisches und chaldaeisches Woerterbuch ueber die Talmudim . . .,* 4 vols. (1875–89; repr. 1963).
Lewin, Oẓar	Lewin, *Oẓar ha-Ge'onim,* 12 vols. (1928–43).
Lewysohn, Zool	L. Lewysohn, *Zoologie des Talmuds* (1858).
Lidzbarski, Handbuch	M. Lidzbarski, *Handbuch der nordsemitischen Epigraphik,* 2 vols (1898).
Life	Josephus, *Life* (Loeb Classis ed.).
LNYL	*Leksikon fun der Nayer Yidisher Literatur* (1956ff.).
Loew, Flora	I. Loew, *Die Flora der Juden,* 4 vols. (1924 34; repr. 1967).
LSI	*Laws of the State of Israel* (1948ff.).
Luckenbill, Records	D.D. Luckenbill, *Ancient Records of Assyria and Babylonia,* 2 vols. (1926).
Luke	Gospel according to Luke (New Testament)
LXX	Septuagint (Greek translation of the Bible).
Ma'as.	*Ma'aserot* (talmudic tractate).
Ma'as. Sh.	*Ma'ase Sheni* (talmudic tractate).
I, II, III, and IVMacc.	Maccabees, I, II, III (Apocrypha), IV (Pseudepigrapha).
Maimonides, Guide	Maimonides, *Guide of the Perplexed.*
Maim., Yad	Maimonides, *Mishneh Torah (Yad Ḥazakah).*
Maisler, Untersuchungen	B. Maisler (Mazar), *Untersuchungen zur alten Geschichte und Ethnographie Syriens und Palaestinas,* 1 (1930).
Mak.	*Makkot* (talmudic tractate).
Makhsh.	*Makhshrin* (mishnaic tractate).
Mal.	Malachi (Bible).
Mann, Egypt	J. Mann, *Jews in Egypt in Palestine under the Fatimid Caliphs,* 2 vols. (1920–22).
Mann, Texts	J. Mann, *Texts and Studies,* 2 vols (1931–35).
Mansi	G.D. Mansi, *Sacrorum Conciliorum nova et amplissima collectio,* 53 vols. in 60 (1901–27; repr. 1960).
Margalioth, Gedolei	M. Margalioth, *Enẓiklopedyah le-Toledot Gedolei Yisrael,* 4 vols. (1946–50).
Margalioth, Ḥakhmei	M. Margalioth, *Enẓiklopedyah le-Ḥakhmei ha-Talmud ve-ha-Ge'onim,* 2 vols. (1945).
Margalioth, Cat	G. Margalioth, *Catalogue of the Hebrew and Samaritan Manuscripts in the British Museum,* 4 vols. (1899–1935).
Mark	Gospel according to Mark (New Testament).
Mart. Isa.	Martyrdom of Isaiah (Pseudepigrapha).
Mas.	Masorah.
Matt.	Gospel according to Matthew (New Testament).
Mayer, Art	L.A. Mayer, *Bibliography of Jewish Art* (1967).
MB	*Wochenzeitung* (formerly *Mitteilungsblatt*) *des Irgun Olej Merkas Europa* (1933ff.).
MEAH	*Miscelánea de estudios drabes y hebraicos* (1952ff.).
Meg.	Megillah (talmudic tractate).
Meg. Ta'an.	*Megillat Ta'anit* (in HUCA, 8 9 (1931–32), 318–51).
Me'il	*Me'ilah* (mishnaic tractate).
MEJ	*Middle East Journal* (1947ff.).
Mehk.	*Mekhilta de-R. Ishmael.*
Mekh. SbY	*Mekhilta de-R. Simeon bar Yoḥai.*
Men.	*Menaḥot* (talmudic tractate).
MER	*Middle East Record* (1960ff.).
Meyer, Gesch	E. Meyer, *Geschichte des Alterums,* 5 vols. in 9 (1925–58).
Meyer, Ursp	E. Meyer, *Urspring und Anfaenge des Christentums* (1921).
Mez.	*Mezuzah* (post-talmudic tractate).
MGADJ	*Mitteilungen des Gesamtarchivs der deutschen Juden* (1909–12).
MGG	*Die Musik in Geschichte und Gegenwart,* 14 vols. (1949–68).

MGG² *Die Musik in Geschichte und Gegenwart, 2nd edition (1994)*
MGH *Monumenta Germaniae Historica* (1826ff.).
MGJV *Mitteilungen der Gesellschaft fuer juedische Volkskunde* (1898–1929); title varies, see also JJV.
MGWJ *Monatsschrift fuer Geschichte und Wissenschaft des Judentums* (1851–1939).
MHJ *Monumenta Hungariae Judaica,* 11 vols. (1903–67).
Michael, Or H.Ḥ. Michael, *Or ha-Ḥayyim: Ḥakhmei Yisrael ve-Sifreihem,* ed. by S.Z. Ḥ. Halberstam and N. Ben-Menahem (1965²).
Mid. *Middot* (mishnaic tractate).
Mid. Ag. *Midrash Aggadah.*
Mid. Hag. *Midrash ha-Gadol.*
Mid. Job. *Midrash Job.*
Mid. Jonah *Midrash Jonah.*
Mid. Lek. Tov *Midrash Lekaḥ Tov.*
Mid. Prov. *Midrash Proverbs.*
Mid. Ps. *Midrash Tehillim* (Eng tr. *The Midrash on Psalms* (JPS, 1959).
Mid. Sam. *Midrash Samuel.*
Mid. Song *Midrash Shir ha-Shirim.*
Mid. Tan. *Midrash Tanna'im* on Deuteronomy.
Miége, Maroc J.L. Miège, *Le Maroc et l'Europe,* 3 vols. (1961 62).
Mig. Philo, *De Migratione Abrahami.*
Mik. *Mikva'ot* (mishnaic tractate).
Milano, Bibliotheca A. Milano, *Bibliotheca Historica Italo-Judaica* (1954); supplement for 1954–63 (1964); supplement for 1964–66 in RMI, 32 (1966).
Milano, Italia A. Milano, *Storia degli Ebrei in Italia* (1963).
MIO *Mitteilungen des Instituts fuer Orientforschung* 1953ff.).
Mish. Mishnah.
MJ *Le Monde Juif* (1946ff.).
MJC see Neubauer, Chronicles.
MK *Mo'ed Katan* (talmudic tractate).
MNDPV *Mitteilungen und Nachrichten des deutschen Palaestinavereins* (1895–1912).
Mortara, Indice M. Mortara, *Indice Alfabetico dei Rabbini e Scrittori Israeliti ... in Italia ...* (1886).
Mos Philo, *De Vita Mosis.*
Moscati, Epig S, Moscati, *Epigrafia ebraica antica* 1935–1950 (1951).
MT Masoretic Text of the Bible.
Mueller, Musiker [E.H. Mueller], *Deutisches Musiker-Lexikon* (1929)
Munk, Mélanges S. Munk, *Mélanges de philosophie juive et arabe* (1859; repr. 1955).
Mut. Philo, *De Mutatione Nominum.*
MWJ *Magazin fuer die Wissenshaft des Judentums* (18745 93).

Nah. Nahum (Bible).
Naz. *Nazir* (talmudic tractate).
NDB *Neue Deutsche Biographie* (1953ff.).
Ned. *Nedarim* (talmudic tractate).
Neg. *Nega'im* (mishnaic tractate).
Neh. Nehemiah (Bible).
NG² *New Grove Dictionary of Music and Musicians* (2001).
Nuebauer, Cat A. Neubauer, *Catalogue of the Hebrew Manuscripts in the Bodleian Library ...,* 2 vols. (1886–1906).
Neubauer, Chronicles A. Neubauer, *Mediaeval Jewish Chronicles,* 2 vols. (Heb., 1887–95; repr. 1965), Eng. title of *Seder ha-Ḥakhamim ve-Korot ha-Yamim.*
Neubauer, Géogr A. Neubauer, *La géographie du Talmud* (1868).
Neuman, Spain A.A. Neuman, *The Jews in Spain, their Social, Political, and Cultural Life During the Middle Ages,* 2 vols. (1942).
Neusner, Babylonia J. Neusner, *History of the Jews in Babylonia,* 5 vols. 1965–70), 2nd revised printing 1969ff.).
Nid. *Niddah* (talmudic tractate).
Noah Fragment of Book of Noah (Pseudepigrapha).
Noth, Hist Isr M. Noth, *History of Israel* (1958).
Noth, Personennamen M. Noth, *Die israelitischen Personennamen. ...* (1928).
Noth, Ueberlief M. Noth, *Ueberlieferungsgeschichte des Pentateuchs* (1949).
Noth, Welt M. Noth, *Die Welt des Alten Testaments* (1957³).
Nowack, Lehrbuch W. Nowack, *Lehrbuch der hebraeischen Archaeologie,* 2 vols (1894).
NT New Testament.
Num. Numbers (Bible).
Num R. *Numbers Rabbah.*

Obad. Obadiah (Bible).
ODNB online *Oxford Dictionary of National Biography.*
OḤ *Oraḥ Ḥayyim.*
Oho. *Oholot* (mishnaic tractate).
Olmstead H.T. Olmstead, *History of Palestine and Syria* (1931; repr. 1965).
OLZ *Orientalistische Literaturzeitung* (1898ff.)
Onom. Eusebius, *Onomasticon.*
Op. Philo, *De Opificio Mundi.*
OPD *Osef Piskei Din shel ha-Rabbanut ha-Rashit le-Ereẓ Yisrael, Bet ha-Din ha-Gadol le-Irurim* (1950).
Or. *Orlah* (talmudic tractate).
Or. Sibyll. Sibylline Oracles (Pseudepigrapha).
OS *L'Orient Syrien* (1956ff.)
OTS *Oudtestamentische Studien* (1942ff.).

PAAJR *Proceedings of the American Academy for Jewish Research* (1930ff.)
Pap 4QSᵉ A papyrus exemplar of IQS.
Par. *Parah* (mishnaic tractate).
Pauly-Wissowa A.F. Pauly, *Realencyklopaedie der klassichen Alertumswissenschaft,* ed. by G. Wissowa et al. (1864ff.)

PD	*Piskei Din shel Bet ha-Mishpat ha-Elyon le-Yisrael* (1948ff.)
PDR	*Piskei Din shel Battei ha-Din ha-Rabbaniyyim be-Yisrael.*
PdRE	*Pirkei de-R. Eliezer* (Eng. tr. 1916. (1965²).
PdRK	*Pesikta de-Rav Kahana.*
Pe'ah	*Pe'ah* (talmudic tractate).
Peake, Commentary	A.J. Peake (ed.), *Commentary on the Bible* (1919; rev. 1962).
Pedersen, Israel	J. Pedersen, *Israel, Its Life and Culture,* 4 vols. in 2 (1926–40).
PEFQS	*Palestine Exploration Fund Quarterly Statement* (1869–1937; since 1938–PEQ).
PEQ	*Palestine Exploration Quarterly* (until 1937 PEFQS; after 1927 includes BBSAJ).
Perles, Beitaege	J. Perles, *Beitraege zur rabbinischen Sprach- und Alterthumskunde* (1893).
Pes.	*Pesaḥim* (talmudic tractate).
Pesh.	Peshitta (Syriac translation of the Bible).
Pesher Hab.	Commentary to Habakkuk from Qumran; see 1Qp Hab.
I and II Pet.	Epistles of Peter (New Testament).
Pfeiffer, Introd	R.H. Pfeiffer, *Introduction to the Old Testament* (1948).
PG	J.P. Migne (ed.), *Patrologia Graeca,* 161 vols. (1866–86).
Phil.	Epistle to the Philippians (New Testament).
Philem.	Epistle to the Philemon (New Testament).
PIASH	*Proceedings of the Israel Academy of Sciences and Humanities* (1963/7ff.).
PJB	*Palaestinajahrbuch des deutschen evangelischen Institutes fuer Altertumswissenschaft,* Jerusalem (1905–1933).
PK	*Pinkas ha-Kehillot,* encyclopedia of Jewish communities, published in over 30 volumes by Yad Vashem from 1970 and arranged by countries, regions and localities. For 3-vol. English edition see Spector, *Jewish Life.*
PL	J.P. Migne (ed.), *Patrologia Latina* 221 vols. (1844–64).
Plant	Philo, *De Plantatione.*
PO	R. Graffin and F. Nau (eds.), *Patrologia Orientalis* (1903ff.)
Pool, Prayer	D. de Sola Pool, *Traditional Prayer Book for Sabbath and Festivals* (1960).
Post	Philo, *De Posteritate Caini.*
PR	*Pesikta Rabbati.*
Praem.	Philo, *De Praemiis et Poenis.*
Prawer, Ẓalbanim	J. Prawer, *Toledot Mamlekhet ha-Ẓalbanim be-Ereẓ Yisrael,* 2 vols. (1963).
Press, Ereẓ	I. Press, *Ereẓ-Yisrael, Enẓiklopedyah Topografit-Historit,* 4 vols. (1951–55).
Pritchard, Pictures	J.B. Pritchard (ed.), *Ancient Near East in Pictures* (1954, 1970).
Pritchard, Texts	J.B. Pritchard (ed.), *Ancient Near East Texts* ... (1970³).
Pr. Man.	Prayer of Manasses (Apocrypha).
Prob.	Philo, *Quod Omnis Probus Liber Sit.*
Prov.	Proverbs (Bible).
PS	*Palestinsky Sbornik* (Russ. (1881 1916, 1954ff).
Ps.	Psalms (Bible).
PSBA	*Proceedings of the Society of Biblical Archaeology* (1878–1918).
Ps. of Sol	Psalms of Solomon (Pseudepigrapha).
IQ Apoc	The *Genesis Apocryphon* from Qumran, cave one, ed. by N. Avigad and Y. Yadin (1956).
6QD	*Damascus Document* or *Sefer Berit Dammesk* from Qumran, cave six, ed. by M. Baillet, in RB, 63 (1956), 513–23 (see also CD).
QDAP	*Quarterly of the Department of Antiquities in Palestine* (1932ff.).
4QDeut. 32	Manuscript of Deuteronomy 32 from Qumran, cave four (ed. by P.W. Skehan, in BASOR, 136 (1954), 12–15).
4QEx[a]	Exodus manuscript in Jewish script from Qumran, cave four.
4QEx[α]	Exodus manuscript in Paleo-Hebrew script from Qumran, cave four (partially ed. by P.W. Skehan, in JBL, 74 (1955), 182–7).
4QFlor	*Florilegium,* a miscellany from Qumran, cave four (ed. by J.M. Allegro, in JBL, 75 (1956), 176–77 and 77 (1958), 350–54).).
QGJD	*Quellen zur Geschichte der Juden in Deutschland* 1888–98).
IQH	*Thanksgiving Psalms* of *Hodayot* from Qumran, cave one (ed. by E.L. Sukenik and N. Avigad, *Oẓar ha-Megillot ha-Genuzot* (1954).
IQIs[a]	Scroll of Isaiah from Qumran, cave one (ed. by N. Burrows et al., *Dead Sea Scrolls* ..., 1 (1950).
IQIs[b]	Scroll of Isaiah from Qumran, cave one (ed. E.L. Sukenik and N. Avigad, *Oẓar ha-Megillot ha-Genuzot* (1954).
IQM	The *War Scroll* or *Serekh ha-Milḥamah* (ed. by E.L. Sukenik and N. Avigad, *Oẓar ha-Megillot ha-Genuzot* (1954).
4QpNah	Commentary on Nahum from Qumran, cave four (partially ed. by J.M. Allegro, in JBL, 75 (1956), 89–95).
IQphyl	Phylacteries *(tefillin)* from Qumran, cave one (ed. by Y. Yadin, in *Eretz Israel,* 9 (1969), 60–85).
4Q Prayer of Nabonidus	A document from Qumran, cave four, belonging to a lost Daniel literature (ed. by J.T. Milik, in RB, 63 (1956), 407–15).
IQS	*Manual of Discipline* or *Serekh ha-Yaḥad* from Qumran, cave one (ed. by M. Burrows et al., *Dead Sea Scrolls* ..., 2, pt. 2 (1951).

IQS[a]	The *Rule of the Congregation or Serekh ha-Edah* from Qumran, cave one (ed. by Burrows et al., *Dead Sea Scrolls* ..., 1 (1950), under the abbreviation IQ28a).
IQS[b]	*Blessings* or *Divrei Berakhot* from Qumran, cave one (ed. by Burrows et al., *Dead Sea Scrolls* ..., 1 (1950), under the abbreviation IQ28b).
4QSam[a]	Manuscript of I and II Samuel from Qumran, cave four (partially ed. by F.M. Cross, in BASOR, 132 (1953), 15–26).
4QSam[b]	Manuscript of I and II Samuel from Qumran, cave four (partially ed. by F.M. Cross, in JBL, 74 (1955), 147–72).
4QTestimonia	Sheet of Testimony from Qumran, cave four (ed. by J.M. Allegro, in JBL, 75 (1956), 174–87).).
4QT.Levi	*Testament of Levi* from Qumran, cave four (partially ed. by J.T. Milik, in RB, 62 (1955), 398–406).
Rabinovitz, Dik Sof	See Dik Sof.
RB	*Revue biblique* (1892ff.)
RBI	*Recherches bibliques* (1954ff.)
RCB	*Revista de cultura biblica* (São Paulo) (1957ff.)
Régné, Cat	J. Régné, *Catalogue des actes . . . des rois d'Aragon, concernant les Juifs* (1213–1327), in: REJ, vols. 60 70, 73, 75–78 (1910–24).
Reinach, Textes	T. Reinach, *Textes d'auteurs Grecs et Romains relatifs au Judaïsme* (1895; repr. 1963).
REJ	*Revue des études juives* (1880ff.).
Rejzen, Leksikon	Z. Rejzen, *Leksikon fun der Yidisher Literature,* 4 vols. (1927–29).
Renan, Ecrivains	A. Neubauer and E. Renan, *Les écrivains juifs français* ... (1893).
Renan, Rabbins	A. Neubauer and E. Renan, *Les rabbins français* (1877).
RES	*Revue des étude sémitiques et Babyloniaca* (1934–45).
Rev.	Revelation (New Testament).
RGG^3	*Die Religion in Geschichte und Gegenwart,* 7 vols. ($1957–65^3$).
RH	*Rosh Ha-Shanah* (talmudic tractate).
RHJE	*Revue de l'histoire juive en Egypte* (1947ff.).
RHMH	*Revue d'histoire de la médecine hébraïque* (1948ff.).
RHPR	*Revue d'histoire et de philosophie religieuses* (1921ff.).
RHR	*Revue d'histoire des religions* (1880ff.).
RI	*Rivista Israelitica* (1904–12).
Riemann-Einstein	*Hugo Riemanns Musiklexikon,* ed. by A. Einstein (1929^{11}).
Riemann-Gurlitt	*Hugo Riemanns Musiklexikon,* ed. by W. Gurlitt ($1959–67^{12}$), Personenteil.
Rigg-Jenkinson, Exchequer	J.M. Rigg, H. Jenkinson and H.G. Richardson (eds.), *Calendar of the Pleas Rolls of the Exchequer of the Jews,* 4 vols. (1905–1970); cf. in each instance also J.M. Rigg (ed.), *Select Pleas* ... (1902).
RMI	*Rassegna Mensile di Israel* (1925ff.).
Rom.	Epistle to the Romans (New Testament).
Rosanes, Togarmah	S.A. Rosanes, *Divrei Yemei Yisrael be-Togarmah,* 6 vols. (1907–45), and in 3 vols. ($1930–38^2$).
Rosenbloom, Biogr Dict	J.R. Rosenbloom, *Biographical Dictionary of Early American Jews* (1960).
Roth, Art	C. Roth, *Jewish Art* (1961).
Roth, Dark Ages	C. Roth (ed.), *World History of the Jewish People,* second series, vol. 2, *Dark Ages* (1966).
Roth, England	C. Roth, *History of the Jews in England* (1964^3).
Roth, Italy	C. Roth, *History of the Jews in Italy* (1946).
Roth, Mag Bibl	C. Roth, *Magna Bibliotheca Anglo-Judaica* (1937).
Roth, Marranos	C. Roth, *History of the Marranos* (2nd rev. ed 1959; reprint 1966).
Rowley, Old Test	H.H. Rowley, *Old Testament and Modern Study* (1951; repr. 1961).
RS	*Revue sémitiques d'épigraphie et d'histoire ancienne* (1893/94ff.).
RSO	*Rivista degli studi orientali* (1907ff.).
RSV	Revised Standard Version of the Bible.
Rubinstein, Australia I	*H.L. Rubinstein, The Jews in Australia, A Thematic History, Vol. I (1991).*
Rubinstein, Australia II	*W.D. Rubinstein, The Jews in Australia, A Thematic History, Vol. II (1991).*
Ruth	Ruth (Bible).
Ruth R.	*Ruth Rabbah.*
RV	Revised Version of the Bible.
Sac.	Philo, *De Sacrificiis Abelis et Caini.*
Salfeld, Martyrol	S. Salfeld, *Martyrologium des Nuernberger Memorbuches* (1898).
I and II Sam.	Samuel, book I and II (Bible).
Sanh.	*Sanhedrin* (talmudic tractate).
SBA	Society of Biblical Archaeology.
SBB	*Studies in Bibliography and Booklore* (1953ff.).
SBE	*Semana Biblica Española.*
SBT	*Studies in Biblical Theology* (1951ff.).
SBU	*Svenkst Bibliskt Uppslogsvesk,* 2 vols. ($1962–63^2$).
Schirmann, Italyah	J.Ḥ. Schirmann, *Ha-Shirah ha-Ivrit be-Italyah* (1934).
Schirmann, Sefarad	J.Ḥ. Schirmann, *Ha-Shirah ha-Ivrit bi-Sefarad u-vi-Provence,* 2 vols. (1954–56).
Scholem, Mysticism	G. Scholem, *Major Trends in Jewish Mysticism* (rev. ed. 1946; paperback ed. with additional bibliography 1961).
Scholem, Shabbetai Ẓevi	G. Scholem, *Shabbetai Ẓevi ve-ha-Tenu'ah ha-Shabbeta'it bi-Ymei Ḥayyav,* 2 vols. (1967).
Schrader, Keilinschr	E. Schrader, *Keilinschriften und das Alte Testament* (1903^3).
Schuerer, Gesch	E. Schuerer, *Geschichte des juedischen Volkes im Zeitalter Jesu Christi,* 3 vols. and index-vol. ($1901–11^4$).

Abbreviation	Meaning
Schuerer, Hist	E. Schuerer, *History of the Jewish People in the Time of Jesus*, ed. by N.N. Glatzer, abridged paperback edition (1961).
Set. T.	*Sefer Torah* (post-talmudic tractate).
Sem.	*Semaḥot* (post-talmudic tractate).
Sendrey, Music	A. Sendrey, *Bibliography of Jewish Music* (1951).
SER	*Seder Eliyahu Rabbah.*
SEZ	*Seder Eliyahu Zuta.*
Shab	*Shabbat* (talmudic tractate).
Sh. Ar.	J. Caro Shulḥan Arukh. OḤ – *Oraḥ Ḥayyim* YD – *Yoreh De'ah* EH – *Even ha-Ezer* ḤM – *Ḥoshen Mishpat.*
Shek.	*Shekalim* (talmudic tractate).
Shev.	*Shevi'it* (talmudic tractate).
Shevu.	*Shevu'ot* (talmudic tractate).
Shunami, Bibl	S. Shunami, *Bibliography of Jewish Bibliographies* (1965^{2}).
Sif.	*Sifrei Deuteronomy.*
Sif. Num.	*Sifrei Numbers.*
Sifra	*Sifra* on Leviticus.
Sif. Zut.	*Sifrei Zuta.*
SIHM	Sources inédites de l'histoire du Maroc (series).
Silverman, Prayer	M. Silverman (ed.), *Sabbath and Festival Prayer Book* (1946).
Singer, Prayer	S. Singer *Authorised Daily Prayer Book* (1943^{17}).
Sob.	Philo, *De Sobrietate.*
Sof.	*Soferim* (post-talmudic tractate).
Som.	Philo, *De Somniis.*
Song	Song of Songs (Bible).
Song. Ch.	Song of the Three Children (Apocrypha).
Song R.	*Song of Songs Rabbah.*
SOR	*Seder Olam Rabbah.*
Sot.	*Sotah* (talmudic tractate).
SOZ	*Seder Olam Zuta.*
Spec.	Philo, *De Specialibus Legibus.*
Spector, Jewish Life	*S. Spector (ed.), Encyclopedia of Jewish Life Before and After the Holocaust (2001).*
Steinschneider, Arab lit	M. Steinschneider, *Die arabische Literatur der Juden* (1902).
Steinschneider, Cat Bod	M. Steinschneider, *Catalogus Librorum Hebraeorum in Bibliotheca Bodleiana*, 3 vols. (1852–60; reprints 1931 and 1964).
Steinschneider, Hanbuch	M. Steinschneider, *Bibliographisches Handbuch ueber die . . . Literatur fuer hebraeische Sprachkunde* (1859; repr. with additions 1937).
Steinschneider, Uebersetzungen	M. Steinschneider, *Die hebraeischen Uebersetzungen des Mittelalters* (1893).
Stern, Americans	M.H. Stern, *Americans of Jewish Descent* (1960).
van Straalen, Cat	S. van Straalen, *Catalogue of Hebrew Books in the British Museum Acquired During the Years 1868–1892* (1894).
Suárez Fernández, Docmentos	L. Suárez Fernández, *Documentos acerca de la expulsion de los Judios de España* (1964).
Suk.	*Sukkah* (talmudic tractate).
Sus.	Susanna (Apocrypha).
SY	*Sefer Yeẓirah.*
Sym.	Symmachus' Greek translation of the Bible.
SZNG	*Studien zur neueren Geschichte.*
Ta'an.	*Ta'anit* (talmudic tractate).
Tam.	*Tamid* (mishnaic tractate).
Tanḥ.	*Tanḥuma.*
Tanḥ. B.	*Tanḥuma.* Buber ed (1885).
Targ. Jon	Targum Jonathan (Aramaic version of the Prophets).
Targ. Onk.	Targum Onkelos (Aramaic version of the Pentateuch).
Targ. Yer.	Targum Yerushalmi.
TB	Babylonian Talmud or Talmud Bavli.
Tcherikover, Corpus	V. Tcherikover, A. Fuks, and M. Stern, *Corpus Papyrorum Judaicorum*, 3 vols. (1957–60).
Tef.	*Tefillin* (post-talmudic tractate).
Tem.	*Temurah* (mishnaic tractate).
Ter.	*Terumah* (talmudic tractate).
Test. Patr.	Testament of the Twelve Patriarchs (Pseudepigrapha). Ash. – Asher Ben. – Benjamin Dan – Dan Gad – Gad Iss. – Issachar Joseph – Joseph Judah – Judah Levi – Levi Naph. – Naphtali Reu. – Reuben Sim. – Simeon Zeb. – Zebulun.
I and II	Epistle to the Thessalonians (New Testament).
Thieme-Becker	U. Thieme and F. Becker (eds.), *Allgemeines Lexikon der bildenden Kuenstler von der Antike bis zur Gegenwart*, 37 vols. (1907–50).
Tidhar	D. Tidhar (ed.), *Enẓiklopedyah la-Ḥalutẓei ha-Yishuv u-Vonav* (1947ff.).
I and II Timothy	Epistles to Timothy (New Testament).
Tit.	Epistle to Titus (New Testament).
TJ	Jerusalem Talmud or Talmud Yerushalmi.
Tob.	Tobit (Apocrypha).
Toh.	*Tohorot* (mishnaic tractate).
Torczyner, Bundeslade	H. Torczyner, *Die Bundeslade und die Anfaenge der Religion Israels* (1930^{3}).
Tos.	*Tosafot.*
Tosef.	Tosefta.
Tristram, Nat Hist	H.B. Tristram, *Natural History of the Bible* (1877^{5}).
Tristram, Survey	Palestine Exploration Fund, *Survey of Western Palestine*, vol. 4 (1884) = *Fauna and Flora* by H.B. Tristram.
TS	*Terra Santa* (1943ff.).

TSBA	*Transactions of the Society of Biblical Archaeology* (1872–93).
TY	*Tevul Yom* (mishnaic tractate).
UBSB	United Bible Society, *Bulletin.*
UJE	*Universal Jewish Encyclopedia*, 10 vols. (1939–43).
Uk.	*Ukẓin* (mishnaic tractate).
Urbach, Tosafot	E.E. Urbach, *Ba'alei ha-Tosafot* (1957²).
de Vaux, Anc Isr	R. de Vaux, *Ancient Israel: its Life and Institutions* (1961; paperback 1965).
de Vaux, Instit	R. de Vaux, *Institutions de l'Ancien Testament,* 2 vols. (1958 60).
Virt.	Philo, *De Virtutibus.*
Vogelstein, Chronology	M. Volgelstein, *Biblical Chronology (1944).*
Vogelstein-Rieger	H. Vogelstein and P. Rieger, *Geschichte der Juden in Rom,* 2 vols. (1895–96).
VT	*Vetus Testamentum* (1951ff.).
VTS	*Vetus Testamentum* Supplements (1953ff.).
Vulg.	Vulgate (Latin translation of the Bible).
Wars	Josephus, *The Jewish Wars.*
Watzinger, Denkmaeler	K. Watzinger, *Denkmaeler Palaestinas,* 2 vols. (1933–35).
Waxman, Literature	M. Waxman, *History of Jewish Literature,* 5 vols. (1960²).
Weiss, Dor	I.H. Weiss, *Dor, Dor ve-Doreshav,* 5 vols. (1904⁴).
Wellhausen, Proleg	J. Wellhausen, *Prolegomena zur Geschichte Israels* (1927⁶).
WI	*Die Welt des Islams* (1913ff.).
Winniger, Biog	S. Wininger, *Grosse juedische National-Biographie ...,* 7 vols. (1925–36).
Wisd.	Wisdom of Solomon (Apocrypha)
WLB	*Wiener Library Bulletin* (1958ff.).
Wolf, Bibliotheca	J.C. Wolf, *Bibliotheca Hebraea*, 4 vols. (1715–33).
Wright, Bible	G.E. Wright, *Westminster Historical Atlas to the Bible* (1945).
Wright, Atlas	G.E. Wright, *The Bible and the Ancient Near East* (1961).
WWWJ	*Who's Who in the World Jewry* (New York, 1955, 1965²).
WZJT	*Wissenschaftliche Zeitschrift fuer juedische Theologie* (1835–37).
WZKM	*Wiener Zeitschrift fuer die Kunde des Morgenlandes* (1887ff.).
Yaari, Sheluḥei	A. Yaari, *Sheluḥei Ereẓ Yisrael* (1951).
Yad	Maimonides, *Mishneh Torah (Yad Ḥazakah).*
Yad	*Yadayim* (mishnaic tractate).
Yal.	*Yalkut Shimoni.*
Yal. Mak.	*Yalkut Makhiri.*
Yal. Reub.	*Yalkut Reubeni.*
YD	*Yoreh De'ah.*
YE	*Yevreyskaya Entsiklopediya,* 14 vols. (c. 1910).
Yev.	*Yevamot* (talmudic tractate).
YIVOA	*YIVO Annual of Jewish Social Studies* (1946ff.).
YLBI	*Year Book of the Leo Baeck Institute* (1956ff.).
YMḤEY	See BJPES.
YMḤSI	*Yedi'ot ha-Makhon le-Ḥeker ha-Shirah ha-Ivrit* (1935/36ff.).
YMMY	*Yedi'ot ha-Makhon le-Madda'ei ha-Yahadut* (1924/25ff.).
Yoma	*Yoma* (talmudic tractate).
ZA	*Zeitschrift fuer Assyriologie* (1886/87ff.).
Zav.	*Zavim* (mishnaic tractate).
ZAW	*Zeitschrift fuer die alttestamentliche Wissenschaft und die Kunde des nachbiblishchen Judentums* (1881ff.).
ZAWB	*Beihefte* (supplements) to ZAW.
ZDMG	*Zeitschrift der Deutschen Morgenlaendischen Gesellschaft* (1846ff.).
ZDPV	*Zeitschrift des Deutschen Palaestina-Vereins* (1878–1949; from 1949 = BBLA).
Zech.	Zechariah (Bible).
Zedner, Cat	J. Zedner, *Catalogue of Hebrew Books in the Library of the British Museum* (1867; repr. 1964).
Zeitlin, Bibliotheca	W. Zeitlin, *Bibliotheca Hebraica Post-Mendelssohniana* (1891–95).
Zeph.	Zephaniah (Bible).
Zev.	*Zevaḥim* (talmudic tractate).
ZGGJT	*Zeitschrift der Gesellschaft fuer die Geschichte der Juden in der Tschechoslowakei* (1930–38).
ZGJD	*Zeitschrift fuer die Geschichte der Juden in Deutschland* (1887–92).
ZHB	*Zeitschrift fuer hebraeische Bibliographie* (1896–1920).
Zinberg, Sifrut	I. Zinberg, *Toledot Sifrut Yisrael,* 6 vols. (1955–60).
Ẓiẓ.	*Ẓiẓit* (post-talmudic tractate).
ZNW	*Zeitschrift fuer die neutestamentliche Wissenschaft* (1901ff.).
ZS	*Zeitschrift fuer Semitistik und verwandte Gebiete* (1922ff.).
Zunz, Gesch	L. Zunz, *Zur Geschichte und Literatur* (1845).
Zunz, Gesch	L. Zunz, *Literaturgeschichte der synagogalen Poesie* (1865; Supplement, 1867; repr. 1966).
Zunz, Poesie	L. Zunz, *Synogogale Posie des Mittelalters,* ed. by Freimann (1920²; repr. 1967).
Zunz, Ritus	L. Zunz, *Ritus des synagogalen Gottesdienstes* (1859; repr. 1967).
Zunz, Schr	L. Zunz, *Gesammelte Schriften,* 3 vols. (1875–76).
Zunz, Vortraege	L. Zunz, *Gottesdienstliche vortraege der Juden ...* 1892²; repr. 1966).
Zunz-Albeck, Derashot	L. Zunz, *Ha-Derashot be-Yisrael*, Heb. Tr. of Zunz Vortraege by H. Albeck (1954²).

TRANSLITERATION RULES

HEBREW AND SEMITIC LANGUAGES:

	General	*Scientific*
א	not transliterated[1]	ʾ
בּ	b	b
ב	v	v, ḇ
גּ	g	g
ג		ḡ
דּ	d	d
ד		ḏ
ה	h	h
ו	v – when not a vowel	w
ז	z	z
ח	ḥ	ḥ
ט	t	ṭ, t
י	y – when vowel and at end of words – i	y
כּ	k	k
כ, ך	kh	kh, ḵ
ל	l	ḻ
מ, ם	m	m
נ, ן	n	n
ס	s	s
ע	not transliterated[1]	ʿ
פּ	p	p
פ, ף	f	p, f, ph
צ, ץ	ẓ	ṣ, ẓ
ק	k	q, k
ר	r	r
שׁ	sh[2]	š
שׂ	s	ś, s
תּ	t	t
ת		ṯ
ג׳	dzh, J	ğ
ז׳	zh, J	ž
צ׳	ch	č
◌ָ		å, o, ő (short) â, ā (long)
◌ַ	a	a
◌ֲ		a, ^{a}
◌ֵ		e, ẹ, ē
◌ֶ	e	æ, ä, ę
◌ֱ		œ, ĕ, ^{e}
◌ְ	only *sheva na* is transliterated	ə, ĕ, e; only *sheva na* transliterated
◌ִ ◌ִי	i	i
◌ֹ וֹ	o	o, o, o
◌ֻ וּ	u	u, ŭ û, ū
◌ֵי	ei; biblical e	
‡		reconstructed forms of words

1. The letters א and ע are not transliterated.
   An apostrophe (') between vowels indicates that they do not form a diphthong and are to be pronounced separately.
2. *Dagesh ḥazak* (forte) is indicated by doubling of the letter, except for the letter שׁ.
3. Names. Biblical names and biblical place names are rendered according to the Bible translation of the Jewish Publication Society of America. Post-biblical Hebrew names are transliterated; contemporary names are transliterated or rendered as used by the person. Place names are transliterated or rendered by the accepted spelling. Names and some words with an accepted English form are usually not transliterated.

YIDDISH

א	not transliterated
אַ	a
אָ	o
ב	b
בֿ	v
ג	g
ד	d
ה	h
ו, וּ	u
וו	v
וי	oy
ז	z
זש	zh
ח	kh
ט	t
טש	tsh, ch
י	(consonant) y (vowel) i
יִ	i
יי	ey
ײַ	ay
כּ	k
כ, ך	kh
ל	l
מ, ם	m
נ, ן	n
ס	s
ע	e
פּ	p
פֿ, ף	f
צ, ץ	ts
ק	k
ר	r
שׁ	sh
שׂ	s
תּ	t
ת	s

1. Yiddish transliteration rendered according to U. Weinreich's Modern *English-Yiddish Yiddish-English* Dictionary.
2. Hebrew words in Yiddish are usually transliterated according to standard Yiddish pronunciation, e.g., חזנות = *khazones*.

LADINO

Ladino and Judeo-Spanish words written in Hebrew characters are transliterated phonetically, following the General Rules of Hebrew transliteration (see above) whenever the accepted spelling in Latin characters could not be ascertained.

ARABIC

ا ء	a[1]	ض	ḍ
ب	b	ط	ṭ
ت	t	ظ	ẓ
ث	th	ع	c
ج	j	غ	gh
ح	ḥ	ف	f
خ	kh	ق	q
د	d	ك	k
ذ	dh	ل	l
ر	r	م	m
ز	z	ن	n
س	s	ه	h
ش	sh	و	w
ص	ṣ	ي	y
ـَ	a	ـَا ى	ā
ـِ	i	ـِي	ī
ـُ	u	ـُو	ū
ـَو	aw	ـِيّ	iyy[2]
ـَي	ay	ـُوّ	uww[2]

1. not indicated when initial
2. see note (f)

a) The EJ follows the *Columbia Lippincott Gazetteer* and the *Times Atlas* in transliteration of Arabic place names. Sites that appear in neither are transliterated according to the table above, and subject to the following notes.

b) The EJ follows the *Columbia Encyclopedia* in transliteration of Arabic names. Personal names that do not therein appear are transliterated according to the table above and subject to the following notes (e.g., Ali rather than ʿAlī, Suleiman rather than Sulayman).

c) The EJ follows the *Webster's Third International Dictionary, Unabridged* in transliteration of Arabic terms that have been integrated into the English language.

d) The term "Abu" will thus appear, usually in disregard of inflection.

e) Nunnation (end vowels, *tanwīn*) are dropped in transliteration.

f) Gemination (*tashdīd*) is indicated by the doubling of the geminated letter, unless an end letter, in which case the gemination is dropped.

g) The definitive article *al-* will always be thus transliterated, unless subject to one of the modifying notes (e.g., El-Arish rather than al-ʿArīsh; modification according to note (a)).

h) The Arabic transliteration disregards the Sun Letters (the antero-palatals (*al-Ḥurūf al-Shamsiyya*).

i) The *tā-marbūṭa* (o) is omitted in transliteration, unless in construct-stage (e.g., *Khirba* but *Khirbat Mishmish*).

These modifying notes may lead to various inconsistencies in the Arabic transliteration, but this policy has deliberately been adopted to gain smoother reading of Arabic terms and names.

GREEK

Ancient Greek	*Modern Greek*	*Greek Letters*
a	a	*Α; α; ᾳ*
b	v	*Β; β*
g	gh; g	*Γ; γ*
d	dh	*Δ; δ*
e	e	*Ε; ε*
z	z	*Ζ; ζ*
e; e	i	*Η; η; ῃ*
th	th	*Θ; θ*
i	i	*Ι; ι*
k	k; ky	*Κ; κ*
l	l	*Λ; λ*
m	m	*Μ; μ*
n	n	*Ν; ν*
x	x	*Ξ; ξ*
o	o	*Ο; ο*
p	p	*Π; π*
r; rh	r	*Ρ; ρ; ῥ*
s	s	*Σ; σ; ς*
t	t	*Τ; τ*
u; y	i	*Υ; υ*
ph	f	*Φ; φ*
ch	kh	*Χ; χ*
ps	ps	*Ψ; ψ*
o; ō	o	*Ω; ω; ῳ*
ai	e	*αι*
ei	i	*ει*
oi	i	*οι*
ui	i	*υι*
ou	ou	*ου*
eu	ev	*ευ*
eu; ēu	iv	*ηυ*
–	j	*τζ*
nt	d; nd	*ντ*
mp	b; mb	*μπ*
ngk	g	*γκ*
ng	ng	*νγ*
h	–	‘
–	–	’
w	–	*ϝ*

RUSSIAN

А	A
Б	B
В	V
Г	G
Д	D
Е	E, Ye[1]
Ё	Yo, O[2]
Ж	Zh
З	Z
И	I
Й	Y[3]
К	K
Л	L
М	M
Н	N
О	O
П	P
Р	R
С	S
Т	T
У	U
Ф	F
Х	Kh
Ц	Ts
Ч	Ch
Ш	Sh
Щ	Shch
Ъ	omitted; see note [1]
Ы	Y
Ь	omitted; see note [1]
Э	E
Ю	Yu
Я	Ya

1. Ye at the beginning of a word; after all vowels except ***Ы***; and after **Ъ** and **Ь**.
2. O after ***Ч***, ***Ш*** and ***Щ***.
3. Omitted after ***Ы***, and in names of people after ***И***.

A. Many first names have an accepted English or quasi-English form which has been preferred to transliteration.
B. Place names have been given according to the *Columbia Lippincott Gazeteer*.
C. Pre-revolutionary spelling has been ignored.
D. Other languages using the Cyrillic alphabet (e.g., Bulgarian, Ukrainian), inasmuch as they appear, have been phonetically transliterated in conformity with the principles of this table.

GLOSSARY

Asterisked terms have separate entries in the Encyclopaedia.

Actions Committee, early name of the Zionist General Council, the supreme institution of the World Zionist Organization in the interim between Congresses. The Zionist Executive's name was then the "Small Actions Committee."

*****Adar**, twelfth month of the Jewish religious year, sixth of the civil, approximating to February–March.

*****Aggadah**, name given to those sections of Talmud and Midrash containing homiletic expositions of the Bible, stories, legends, folklore, anecdotes, or maxims. In contradistinction to **halakhah*.

*****Agunah**, woman unable to remarry according to Jewish law, because of desertion by her husband or inability to accept presumption of death.

*****Aharonim**, later rabbinic authorities. In contradistinction to **rishonim* ("early ones").

Ahavah, liturgical poem inserted in the second benediction of the morning prayer (**Ahavah Rabbah*) of the festivals and/or special Sabbaths.

Aktion (Ger.), operation involving the mass assembly, deportation, and murder of Jews by the Nazis during the *Holocaust.

*****Aliyah**, (1) being called to Reading of the Law in synagogue; (2) immigration to Ereẓ Israel; (3) one of the waves of immigration to Ereẓ Israel from the early 1880s.

*****Amidah**, main prayer recited at all services; also known as *Shemoneh Esreh* and *Tefillah*.

*****Amora** (pl. **amoraim**), title given to the Jewish scholars in Ereẓ Israel and Babylonia in the third to sixth centuries who were responsible for the **Gemara*.

Aravah, the *willow; one of the *Four Species used on *Sukkot ("festival of Tabernacles") together with the **etrog, hadas*, and **lulav*.

*****Arvit**, evening prayer.

Asarah be-Tevet, fast on the 10th of Tevet commemorating the commencement of the siege of Jerusalem by Nebuchadnezzar.

Asefat ha-Nivḥarim, representative assembly elected by Jews in Palestine during the period of the British Mandate (1920–48).

*****Ashkenaz**, name applied generally in medieval rabbinical literature to Germany.

*****Ashkenazi** (pl. **Ashkenazim**), German or West-, Central-, or East-European Jew(s), as contrasted with *Sephardi(m).

*****Av**, fifth month of the Jewish religious year, eleventh of the civil, approximating to July–August.

*****Av bet din**, vice president of the supreme court (*bet din ha-gadol*) in Jerusalem during the Second Temple period; later, title given to communal rabbis as heads of the religious courts (see **bet din*).

*****Badḥan**, jester, particularly at traditional Jewish weddings in Eastern Europe.

*****Bakkashah** (Heb. "supplication"), type of petitionary prayer, mainly recited in the Sephardi rite on Rosh Ha-Shanah and the Day of Atonement.

Bar, "son of . . . "; frequently appearing in personal names.

*****Baraita** (pl. **beraitot**), statement of **tanna* not found in *Mishnah.

*****Bar mitzvah**, ceremony marking the initiation of a boy at the age of 13 into the Jewish religious community.

Ben, "son of . . . ", frequently appearing in personal names.

Berakhah (pl. **berakhot**), *benediction, blessing; formula of praise and thanksgiving.

*****Bet din** (pl. **battei din**), rabbinic court of law.

*****Bet ha-midrash**, school for higher rabbinic learning; often attached to or serving as a synagogue.

*****Bilu**, first modern movement for pioneering and agricultural settlement in Ereẓ Israel, founded in 1882 at Kharkov, Russia.

*****Bund**, Jewish socialist party founded in Vilna in 1897, supporting Jewish national rights; Yiddishist, and anti-Zionist.

Cohen (pl. **Cohanim**), see Kohen.

*****Conservative Judaism**, trend in Judaism developed in the United States in the 20th century which, while opposing extreme changes in traditional observances, permits certain modifications of *halakhah* in response to the changing needs of the Jewish people.

*****Consistory** (Fr. *consistoire*), governing body of a Jewish communal district in France and certain other countries.

*****Converso(s)**, term applied in Spain and Portugal to converted Jew(s), and sometimes more loosely to their descendants.

*****Crypto-Jew**, term applied to a person who although observing outwardly Christianity (or some other religion) was at heart a Jew and maintained Jewish observances as far as possible (see Converso; Marrano; Neofiti; New Christian; Jadīd al-Islām).

*****Dayyan**, member of rabbinic court.

Decisor, equivalent to the Hebrew *posek* (pl. **posekim*), the rabbi who gives the decision (*halakhah*) in Jewish law or practice.

*****Devekut**, "devotion"; attachment or adhesion to God; communion with God.

*****Diaspora**, Jews living in the "dispersion" outside Ereẓ Israel; area of Jewish settlement outside Ereẓ Israel.

Din, a law (both secular and religious), legal decision, or lawsuit.

Divan, diwan, collection of poems, especially in Hebrew, Arabic, or Persian.

Dunam, unit of land area (1,000 sq. m., c. ¼ acre), used in Israel.

Einsatzgruppen, mobile units of Nazi S.S. and S.D.; in U.S.S.R. and Serbia, mobile killing units.

*****Ein-Sof**, "without end"; "the infinite"; hidden, impersonal aspect of God; also used as a Divine Name.

*****Elul**, sixth month of the Jewish religious calendar, 12th of the civil, precedes the High Holiday season in the fall.

Endloesung, see *Final Solution.

*****Ereẓ Israel**, Land of Israel; Palestine.

*****Eruv**, technical term for rabbinical provision permitting the alleviation of certain restrictions.

*****Etrog**, citron; one of the *Four Species used on *Sukkot together with the **lulav, hadas*, and *aravah*.

Even ha-Ezer, see Shulḥan Arukh.

*****Exilarch**, lay head of Jewish community in Babylonia (see also *resh galuta*), and elsewhere.

*****Final Solution** (Ger. *Endloesung*), in Nazi terminology, the Nazi-planned mass murder and total annihilation of the Jews.

*****Gabbai**, official of a Jewish congregation; originally a charity collector.

*****Galut**, "exile"; the condition of the Jewish people in dispersion.

*__Gaon__ (pl. **geonim**), head of academy in post-talmudic period, especially in Babylonia.

Gaonate, office of *gaon.

*__Gemara__, traditions, discussions, and rulings of the **amoraim*, commenting on and supplementing the *Mishnah, and forming part of the Babylonian and Palestinian Talmuds (see Talmud).

*__Gematria__, interpretation of Hebrew word according to the numerical value of its letters.

General Government, territory in Poland administered by a German civilian governor-general with headquarters in Cracow after the German occupation in World War II.

*__Genizah__, depository for sacred books. The best known was discovered in the synagogue of Fostat (old Cairo).

Get, bill of *divorce.

*__Ge'ullah__, hymn inserted after the **Shema* into the benediction of the morning prayer of the festivals and special Sabbaths.

*__Gilgul__, metempsychosis; transmigration of souls.

*__Golem__, automaton, especially in human form, created by magical means and endowed with life.

*__Ḥabad__, initials of *ḥokhmah, binah, da'at*: "wisdom, understanding, knowledge"; ḥasidic movement founded in Belorussia by *Shneur Zalman of Lyady.

Hadas, *myrtle; one of the *Four Species used on Sukkot together with the **etrog*, **lulav*, and *aravah*.

*__Haftarah__ (pl. **haftarot**), designation of the portion from the prophetical books of the Bible recited after the synagogue reading from the Pentateuch on Sabbaths and holidays.

*__Haganah__, clandestine Jewish organization for armed self-defense in Ereẓ Israel under the British Mandate, which eventually evolved into a people's militia and became the basis for the Israel army.

*__Haggadah__, ritual recited in the home on *Passover eve at seder table.

Haham, title of chief rabbi of the Spanish and Portuguese congregations in London, England.

*__Hakham__, title of rabbi of *Sephardi congregation.

*__Hakham bashi__, title in the 15th century and modern times of the chief rabbi in the Ottoman Empire, residing in Constantinople (Istanbul), also applied to principal rabbis in provincial towns.

Hakhsharah ("preparation"), organized training in the Diaspora of pioneers for agricultural settlement in Ereẓ Israel.

*__Halakhah__ (pl. **halakhot**), an accepted decision in rabbinic law. Also refers to those parts of the *Talmud concerned with legal matters. In contradistinction to **aggadah*.

Ḥaliẓah, biblically prescribed ceremony (Deut. 25:9–10) performed when a man refuses to marry his brother's childless widow, enabling her to remarry.

*__Hallel__, term referring to Psalms 113-18 in liturgical use.

*__Ḥalukkah__, system of financing the maintenance of Jewish communities in the holy cities of Ereẓ Israel by collections made abroad, mainly in the pre-Zionist era (see *kolel*).

Ḥalutz (pl. **ḥalutzim**), pioneer, especially in agriculture, in Ereẓ Israel.

Ḥalutziyyut, pioneering.

*__Ḥanukkah__, eight-day celebration commemorating the victory of *Judah Maccabee over the Syrian king *Antiochus Epiphanes and the subsequent rededication of the Temple.

Ḥasid, adherent of *Ḥasidism.

*__Ḥasidei Ashkenaz__, medieval pietist movement among the Jews of Germany.

*__Ḥasidism__, (1) religious revivalist movement of popular mysticism among Jews of Germany in the Middle Ages; (2) religious movement founded by *Israel ben Eliezer Ba'al Shem Tov in the first half of the 18th century.

*__Haskalah__, "enlightenment"; movement for spreading modern European culture among Jews c. 1750–1880. See *maskil*.

*__Havdalah__, ceremony marking the end of Sabbath or festival.

*__Ḥazzan__, precentor who intones the liturgy and leads the prayers in synagogue; in earlier times a synagogue official.

*__Ḥeder__ (lit. "room"), school for teaching children Jewish religious observance.

Heikhalot, "palaces"; tradition in Jewish mysticism centering on mystical journeys through the heavenly spheres and palaces to the Divine Chariot (see Merkabah).

*__Ḥerem__, excommunication, imposed by rabbinical authorities for purposes of religious and/or communal discipline; originally, in biblical times, that which is separated from common use either because it was an abomination or because it was consecrated to God.

Ḥeshvan, see Marḥeshvan.

*__Ḥevra kaddisha__, title applied to charitable confraternity (**ḥevrah*), now generally limited to associations for burial of the dead.

*__Ḥibbat Zion__, see Ḥovevei Zion.

*__Histadrut__ (abbr. For Heb. **Ha-Histadrut ha-Kelalit shel ha-Ovedim ha-Ivriyyim be-Ereẓ Israel**). Ereẓ Israel Jewish Labor Federation, founded in 1920; subsequently renamed Histadrut ha-Ovedim be-Ereẓ Israel.

*__Holocaust__, the organized mass persecution and annihilation of European Jewry by the Nazis (1933–1945).

*__Hoshana Rabba__, the seventh day of *Sukkot on which special observances are held.

Ḥoshen Mishpat, see Shulḥan Arukh.

Ḥovevei Zion, federation of *Ḥibbat Zion, early (pre-*Herzl) Zionist movement in Russia.

Illui, outstanding scholar or genius, especially a young prodigy in talmudic learning.

*__Iyyar__, second month of the Jewish religious year, eighth of the civil, approximating to April-May.

I.Ẓ.L. (initials of Heb. *__Irgun Ẓeva'i Le'ummi__; "National Military Organization"), underground Jewish organization in Ereẓ Israel founded in 1931, which engaged from 1937 in retaliatory acts against Arab attacks and later against the British mandatory authorities.

*__Jadīd al-Islām__ (Ar.), a person practicing the Jewish religion in secret although outwardly observing Islām.

*__Jewish Legion__, Jewish units in British army during World War I.

*__Jihād__ (Ar.), in Muslim religious law, holy war waged against infidels.

*__Judenrat__ (Ger. "Jewish council"), council set up in Jewish communities and ghettos under the Nazis to execute their instructions.

*__Judenrein__ (Ger. "clean of Jews"), in Nazi terminology the condition of a locality from which all Jews had been eliminated.

*__Kabbalah__, the Jewish mystical tradition:

Kabbala iyyunit, speculative Kabbalah;

Kabbala ma'asit, practical Kabbalah;

Kabbala nevu'it, prophetic Kabbalah.

Kabbalist, student of Kabbalah.

*__Kaddish__, liturgical doxology.

Kahal, Jewish congregation; among Ashkenazim, *kehillah*.

***Kalām** (Ar.), science of Muslim theology; adherents of the Kalām are called *mutakallimūn.*

***Karaite**, member of a Jewish sect originating in the eighth century which rejected rabbinic (*Rabbanite) Judaism and claimed to accept only Scripture as authoritative.

***Kasher**, ritually permissible food.

Kashrut, Jewish *dietary laws.

***Kavvanah**, "intention"; term denoting the spiritual concentration accompanying prayer and the performance of ritual or of a commandment.

***Kedushah**, main addition to the third blessing in the reader's repetition of the *Amidah* in which the public responds to the precentor's introduction.

Kefar, village; first part of name of many settlements in Israel.

Kehillah, congregation; see *kahal.*

Kelippah (pl. **kelippot**), "husk(s)"; mystical term denoting force(s) of evil.

***Keneset Yisrael**, comprehensive communal organization of the Jews in Palestine during the British Mandate.

Keri, variants in the masoretic (*masorah) text of the Bible between the spelling (*ketiv*) and its pronunciation (*keri*).

***Kerovah** (collective plural (corrupted) from **kerovez̦**), poem(s) incorporated into the **Amidah.*

Ketiv, see *keri.*

***Ketubbah**, marriage contract, stipulating husband's obligations to wife.

Kevuz̦ah, small commune of pioneers constituting an agricultural settlement in Erez̦ Israel (evolved later into *kibbutz).

***Kibbutz** (pl. **kibbutzim**), larger-size commune constituting a settlement in Erez̦ Israel based mainly on agriculture but engaging also in industry.

***Kiddush**, prayer of sanctification, recited over wine or bread on eve of Sabbaths and festivals.

***Kiddush ha-Shem**, term connoting martyrdom or act of strict integrity in support of Judaic principles.

***Kinah** (pl. **kinot**), lamentation dirge(s) for the Ninth of Av and other fast days.

***Kislev**, ninth month of the Jewish religious year, third of the civil, approximating to November-December.

Klaus, name given in Central and Eastern Europe to an institution, usually with synagogue attached, where *Talmud was studied perpetually by adults; applied by Ḥasidim to their synagogue ("*kloyz*").

***Knesset**, parliament of the State of Israel.

K(c)ohen (pl. **K(c)ohanim**), Jew(s) of priestly (Aaronide) descent.

***Kolel**, (1) community in Erez̦ Israel of persons from a particular country or locality, often supported by their fellow countrymen in the Diaspora; (2) institution for higher Torah study.

Kosher, see *kasher.*

***Kristallnacht** (Ger. "crystal night," meaning "night of broken glass"), organized destruction of synagogues, Jewish houses, and shops, accompanied by mass arrests of Jews, which took place in Germany and Austria under the Nazis on the night of Nov. 9–10, 1938.

***Lag ba-Omer**, 33rd (Heb. **lag**) day of the **Omer* period falling on the 18th of *Iyyar; a semi-holiday.

Leḥi (abbr. For Heb. ***Loḥamei Ḥerut Israel**, "Fighters for the Freedom of Israel"), radically anti-British armed underground organization in Palestine, founded in 1940 by dissidents from *I.Z.L.

Levir, husband's brother.

***Levirate marriage** (Heb. *yibbum*), marriage of childless widow (*yevamah*) by brother (*yavam*) of the deceased husband (in accordance with Deut. 25:5); release from such an obligation is effected through *ḥaliz̦ah.*

LHY, see Leḥi.

***Lulav**, palm branch; one of the *Four Species used on *Sukkot together with the **etrog, hadas*, and *aravah.*

***Ma'aravot**, hymns inserted into the evening prayer of the three festivals, Passover, Shavuot, and Sukkot.

Ma'ariv, evening prayer; also called **arvit.*

***Ma'barah**, transition camp; temporary settlement for newcomers in Israel during the period of mass immigration following 1948.

***Maftir**, reader of the concluding portion of the Pentateuchal section on Sabbaths and holidays in synagogue; reader of the portion of the prophetical books of the Bible (**haftarah*).

***Maggid**, popular preacher.

***Maḥzor** (pl. **maḥzorim**), festival prayer book.

***Mamzer**, bastard; according to Jewish law, the offspring of an incestuous relationship.

***Mandate, Palestine**, responsibility for the administration of Palestine conferred on Britain by the League of Nations in 1922; mandatory government: the British administration of Palestine.

***Maqāma** (Ar. pl. **maqamāt**), poetic form (rhymed prose) which, in its classical arrangement, has rigid rules of form and content.

***Marḥeshvan**, popularly called Ḥeshvan; eighth month of the Jewish religious year, second of the civil, approximating to October–November.

***Marrano(s)**, descendant(s) of Jew(s) in Spain and Portugal whose ancestors had been converted to Christianity under pressure but who secretly observed Jewish rituals.

Maskil (pl. **maskilim**), adherent of *Haskalah ("Enlightenment") movement.

***Masorah**, body of traditions regarding the correct spelling, writing, and reading of the Hebrew Bible.

Masorete, scholar of the masoretic tradition.

Masoretic, in accordance with the masorah.

Meliz̦ah, in Middle Ages, elegant style; modern usage, florid style using biblical or talmudic phraseology.

Mellah, *Jewish quarter in North African towns.

***Menorah**, candelabrum; seven-branched oil lamp used in the Tabernacle and Temple; also eight-branched candelabrum used on *Ḥanukkah.

Me'orah, hymn inserted into the first benediction of the morning prayer (*Yoz̦er ha-Me'orot*).

***Merkabah**, *merkavah*, "chariot"; mystical discipline associated with Ezekiel's vision of the Divine Throne-Chariot (Ezek. 1).

Meshullaḥ, emissary sent to conduct propaganda or raise funds for rabbinical academies or charitable institutions.

***Mezuzah** (pl. **mezuzot**), parchment scroll with selected Torah verses placed in container and affixed to gates and doorposts of houses occupied by Jews.

***Midrash**, method of interpreting Scripture to elucidate legal points (*Midrash Halakhah*) or to bring out lessons by stories or homiletics (*Midrash Aggadah*). Also the name for a collection of such rabbinic interpretations.

***Mikveh**, ritual bath.

***Minhag** (pl. **minhagim**), ritual custom(s); synagogal rite(s); especially of a specific sector of Jewry.

***Minḥah**, afternoon prayer; originally meal offering in Temple.

*Minyan, group of ten male adult Jews, the minimum required for communal prayer.
*Mishnah, earliest codification of Jewish Oral Law.
Mishnah (pl. mishnayot), subdivision of tractates of the Mishnah.
Mitnagged (pl. *Mitnaggedim), originally, opponents of *Ḥasidism in Eastern Europe.
*Mitzvah, biblical or rabbinic injunction; applied also to good or charitable deeds.
Mohel, official performing circumcisions.
*Moshav, smallholders' cooperative agricultural settlement in Israel, see moshav ovedim.
Moshavah, earliest type of Jewish village in modern Ereẓ Israel in which farming is conducted on individual farms mostly on privately owned land.
Moshav ovedim ("workers' moshav"), agricultural village in Israel whose inhabitants possess individual homes and holdings but cooperate in the purchase of equipment, sale of produce, mutual aid, etc.
*Moshav shittufi ("collective moshav"), agricultural village in Israel whose members possess individual homesteads but where the agriculture and economy are conducted as a collective unit.
Mostegab (Ar.), poem with biblical verse at beginning of each stanza.
*Muqaddam (Ar., pl. muqaddamūn), "leader," "head of the community."
*Musaf, additional service on Sabbath and festivals; originally the additional sacrifice offered in the Temple.
Musar, traditional ethical literature.
*Musar movement, ethical movement developing in the latter part of the 19th century among Orthodox Jewish groups in Lithuania; founded by R. Israel *Lipkin (Salanter).
*Nagid (pl. negidim), title applied in Muslim (and some Christian) countries in the Middle Ages to a leader recognized by the state as head of the Jewish community.
Nakdan (pl. nakdanim), "punctuator"; scholar of the 9th to 14th centuries who provided biblical manuscripts with masoretic apparatus, vowels, and accents.
*Nasi (pl. nesi'im), talmudic term for president of the Sanhedrin, who was also the spiritual head and later, political representative of the Jewish people; from second century a descendant of Hillel recognized by the Roman authorities as patriarch of the Jews. Now applied to the president of the State of Israel.
*Negev, the southern, mostly arid, area of Israel.
*Ne'ilah, concluding service on the *Day of Atonement.
Neofiti, term applied in southern Italy to converts to Christianity from Judaism and their descendants who were suspected of maintaining secret allegiance to Judaism.
*Neology; Neolog; Neologism, trend of *Reform Judaism in Hungary forming separate congregations after 1868.
*Nevelah (lit. "carcass"), meat forbidden by the *dietary laws on account of the absence of, or defect in, the act of *sheḥitah* (ritual slaughter).
*New Christians, term applied especially in Spain and Portugal to converts from Judaism (and from Islam) and their descendants; "Half New Christian" designated a person one of whose parents was of full Jewish blood.
*Niddah ("menstruous woman"), woman during the period of menstruation.
*Nisan, first month of the Jewish religious year, seventh of the civil, approximating to March-April.
Niẓoẓot, "sparks"; mystical term for sparks of the holy light imprisoned in all matter.
Nosaḥ (nusaḥ) "version"; (1) textual variant; (2) term applied to distinguish the various prayer rites, e.g., *nosaḥ Ashkenaz*; (3) the accepted tradition of synagogue melody.
*Notarikon, method of abbreviating Hebrew works or phrases by acronym.
Novella(e) (Heb. *ḥiddush (im)*), commentary on talmudic and later rabbinic subjects that derives new facts or principles from the implications of the text.
*Nuremberg Laws, Nazi laws excluding Jews from German citizenship, and imposing other restrictions.
Ofan, hymns inserted into a passage of the morning prayer.
*Omer, first sheaf cut during the barley harvest, offered in the Temple on the second day of Passover.
Omer, Counting of (Heb. *Sefirat ha-Omer*), 49 days counted from the day on which the *omer* was first offered in the Temple (according to the rabbis the 16th of Nisan, i.e., the second day of Passover) until the festival of Shavuot; now a period of semi-mourning.
Oraḥ Ḥayyim, see Shulḥan Arukh.
*Orthodoxy (Orthodox Judaism), modern term for the strictly traditional sector of Jewry.
*Pale of Settlement, 25 provinces of czarist Russia where Jews were permitted permanent residence.
*Palmaḥ (abbr. for Heb. *peluggot maḥaẓ*; "shock companies"), striking arm of the *Haganah.
*Pardes, medieval biblical exegesis giving the literal, allegorical, homiletical, and esoteric interpretations.
*Parnas, chief synagogue functionary, originally vested with both religious and administrative functions; subsequently an elected lay leader.
Partition plan(s), proposals for dividing Ereẓ Israel into autonomous areas.
Paytan, composer of *piyyut* (liturgical poetry).
*Peel Commission, British Royal Commission appointed by the British government in 1936 to inquire into the Palestine problem and make recommendations for its solution.
Pesaḥ, *Passover.
*Pilpul, in talmudic and rabbinic literature, a sharp dialectic used particularly by talmudists in Poland from the 16th century.
*Pinkas, community register or minute-book.
*Piyyut, (pl. piyyutim), Hebrew liturgical poetry.
*Pizmon, poem with refrain.
Posek (pl. *posekim), decisor; codifier or rabbinic scholar who pronounces decisions in disputes and on questions of Jewish law.
*Prosbul, legal method of overcoming the cancelation of debts with the advent of the *sabbatical year.
*Purim, festival held on Adar 14 or 15 in commemoration of the delivery of the Jews of Persia in the time of *Esther.
Rabban, honorific title higher than that of rabbi, applied to heads of the *Sanhedrin in mishnaic times.
*Rabbanite, adherent of rabbinic Judaism. In contradistinction to *Karaite.
Reb, rebbe, Yiddish form for rabbi, applied generally to a teacher or ḥasidic rabbi.
*Reconstructionism, trend in Jewish thought originating in the United States.
*Reform Judaism, trend in Judaism advocating modification of *Orthodoxy in conformity with the exigencies of contemporary life and thought.

Resh galuta, lay head of Babylonian Jewry (see exilarch).

Responsum (pl. ***responsa**), written opinion (*teshuvah*) given to question (*she'elah*) on aspects of Jewish law by qualified authorities; pl. collection of such queries and opinions in book form (*she'elot u-teshuvot*).

***Rishonim**, older rabbinical authorities. Distinguished from later authorities (**aḥaronim*).

***Rishon le-Zion**, title given to Sephardi chief rabbi of Ereẓ Israel.

***Rosh Ha-Shanah**, two-day holiday (one day in biblical and early mishnaic times) at the beginning of the month of *Tishri (September–October), traditionally the New Year.

Rosh Hodesh, *New Moon, marking the beginning of the Hebrew month.

Rosh Yeshivah, see *Yeshivah.

***R.S.H.A.** (initials of Ger. *Reichssicherheitshauptamt*: "Reich Security Main Office"), the central security department of the German Reich, formed in 1939, and combining the security police (Gestapo and Kripo) and the S.D.

***Sanhedrin**, the assembly of ordained scholars which functioned both as a supreme court and as a legislature before 70 C.E. In modern times the name was given to the body of representative Jews convoked by Napoleon in 1807.

***Savora** (pl. **savoraim**), name given to the Babylonian scholars of the period between the **amoraim* and the **geonim*, approximately 500–700 C.E.

S.D. (initials of Ger. *Sicherheitsdienst*: "security service"), security service of the *S.S. formed in 1932 as the sole intelligence organization of the Nazi party.

Seder, ceremony observed in the Jewish home on the first night of Passover (outside Ereẓ Israel first two nights), when the *Haggadah is recited.

***Sefer Torah**, manuscript scroll of the Pentateuch for public reading in synagogue.

***Sefirot, the ten**, the ten "Numbers"; mystical term denoting the ten spheres or emanations through which the Divine manifests itself; elements of the world; dimensions, primordial numbers.

Selektion (Ger.), (1) in ghettos and other Jewish settlements, the drawing up by Nazis of lists of deportees; (2) separation of incoming victims to concentration camps into two categories – those destined for immediate killing and those to be sent for forced labor.

Seliḥah (pl. ***seliḥot**), penitential prayer.

***Semikhah**, ordination conferring the title "rabbi" and permission to give decisions in matters of ritual and law.

Sephardi (pl. ***Sephardim**), Jew(s) of Spain and Portugal and their descendants, wherever resident, as contrasted with *Ashkenazi(m).

Shabbatean, adherent of the pseudo-messiah *Shabbetai Ẓevi (17th century).

Shaddai, name of God found frequently in the Bible and commonly translated "Almighty."

***Shaḥarit**, morning service.

Shali'aḥ (pl. **sheliḥim**), in Jewish law, messenger, agent; in modern times, an emissary from Ereẓ Israel to Jewish communities or organizations abroad for the purpose of fund-raising, organizing pioneer immigrants, education, etc.

Shalmonit, poetic meter introduced by the liturgical poet *Solomon ha-Bavli.

***Shammash**, synagogue beadle.

***Shavuot**, Pentecost; Festival of Weeks; second of the three annual pilgrim festivals, commemorating the receiving of the Torah at Mt. Sinai.

***Sheḥitah**, ritual slaughtering of animals.

***Shekhinah**, Divine Presence.

Shelishit, poem with three-line stanzas.

***Sheluḥei Ereẓ Israel** (or **shadarim**), emissaries from Ereẓ Israel.

***Shema** ([Yisrael]; "hear… [O Israel]," Deut. 6:4), Judaism's confession of faith, proclaiming the absolute unity of God.

Shemini Aẓeret, final festal day (in the Diaspora, final two days) at the conclusion of *Sukkot.

Shemittah, *Sabbatical year.

Sheniyyah, poem with two-line stanzas.

***Shephelah**, southern part of the coastal plain of Ereẓ Israel.

***Shevat**, eleventh month of the Jewish religious year, fifth of the civil, approximating to January–February.

***Shi'ur Komah**, Hebrew mystical work (c. eighth century) containing a physical description of God's dimensions; term denoting enormous spacial measurement used in speculations concerning the body of the **Shekhinah*.

Shivah, the "seven days" of *mourning following burial of a relative.

***Shofar**, horn of the ram (or any other ritually clean animal excepting the cow) sounded for the memorial blowing on *Rosh Ha-Shanah, and other occasions.

Shoḥet, person qualified to perform **sheḥitah*.

Shomer, *Ha-Shomer, organization of Jewish workers in Ereẓ Israel founded in 1909 to defend Jewish settlements.

***Shtadlan**, Jewish representative or negotiator with access to dignitaries of state, active at royal courts, etc.

***Shtetl**, Jewish small-town community in Eastern Europe.

***Shulḥan Arukh**, Joseph *Caro's code of Jewish law in four parts:
Oraḥ Ḥayyim, laws relating to prayers, Sabbath, festivals, and fasts;
Yoreh De'ah, dietary laws, etc;
Even ha-Ezer, laws dealing with women, marriage, etc;
Ḥoshen Mishpat, civil, criminal law, court procedure, etc.

Siddur, among Ashkenazim, the volume containing the daily prayers (in distinction to the **maḥzor* containing those for the festivals).

***Simḥat Torah**, holiday marking the completion in the synagogue of the annual cycle of reading the Pentateuch; in Ereẓ Israel observed on Shemini Aẓeret (outside Ereẓ Israel on the following day).

***Sinai Campaign**, brief campaign in October–November 1956 when Israel army reacted to Egyptian terrorist attacks and blockade by occupying the Sinai peninsula.

Sitra aḥra, "the other side" (of God); left side; the demoniac and satanic powers.

***Sivan**, third month of the Jewish religious year, ninth of the civil, approximating to May–June.

***Six-Day War**, rapid war in June 1967 when Israel reacted to Arab threats and blockade by defeating the Egyptian, Jordanian, and Syrian armies.

***S.S.** (initials of Ger. *Schutzstaffel*: "protection detachment"), Nazi formation established in 1925 which later became the "elite" organization of the Nazi Party and carried out central tasks in the "Final Solution."

***Status quo ante** community, community in Hungary retaining the status it had held before the convention of the General Jewish Congress there in 1868 and the resultant split in Hungarian Jewry.

***Sukkah**, booth or tabernacle erected for *Sukkot when, for seven days, religious Jews "dwell" or at least eat in the *sukkah* (Lev. 23:42).

***Sukkot**, festival of Tabernacles; last of the three pilgrim festivals, beginning on the 15th of Tishri.

Sūra (Ar.), chapter of the Koran.

Ta'anit Esther (Fast of *Esther), fast on the 13th of Adar, the day preceding Purim.

Takkanah (pl. ***takkanot**), regulation supplementing the law of the Torah; regulations governing the internal life of communities and congregations.

***Tallit (gadol)**, four-cornered prayer shawl with fringes (*ẓiẓit*) at each corner.

***Tallit katan**, garment with fringes (*ẓiẓit*) appended, worn by observant male Jews under their outer garments.

***Talmud**, "teaching"; compendium of discussion on the Mishnah by generations of scholars and jurists in many academies over a period of several centuries. The Jerusalem (or Palestinian) Talmud mainly contains the discussions of the Palestinian sages. The Babylonian Talmud incorporates the parallel discussion in the Babylonian academies.

Talmud torah, term generally applied to Jewish religious (and ultimately to talmudic) study; also to traditional Jewish religious public schools.

***Tammuz**, fourth month of the Jewish religious year, tenth of the civil, approximating to June-July.

Tanna (pl. ***tannaim**), rabbinic teacher of mishnaic period.

***Targum**, Aramaic translation of the Bible.

***Tefillin**, phylacteries, small leather cases containing passages from Scripture and affixed on the forehead and arm by male Jews during the recital of morning prayers.

Tell (Ar. "mound," "hillock"), ancient mound in the Middle East composed of remains of successive settlements.

***Terefah**, food that is not **kasher*, owing to a defect on the animal.

***Territorialism**, 20th century movement supporting the creation of an autonomous territory for Jewish mass-settlement outside Ereẓ Israel.

***Tevet**, tenth month of the Jewish religious year, fourth of the civil, approximating to December–January.

Tikkun ("restitution," "reintegration"), (1) order of service for certain occasions, mostly recited at night; (2) mystical term denoting restoration of the right order and true unity after the spiritual "catastrophe" which occurred in the cosmos.

Tishah be-Av, Ninth of *Av, fast day commemorating the destruction of the First and Second Temples.

***Tishri**, seventh month of the Jewish religious year, first of the civil, approximating to September–October.

Tokheḥah, reproof sections of the Pentateuch (Lev. 26 and Deut. 28); poem of reproof.

***Torah**, Pentateuch or the Pentateuchal scroll for reading in synagogue; entire body of traditional Jewish teaching and literature.

Tosafist, talmudic glossator, mainly French (12–14th centuries), bringing additions to the commentary by *Rashi.

***Tosafot**, glosses supplied by tosafist.

***Tosefta**, a collection of teachings and traditions of the *tannaim*, closely related to the Mishnah.

Tradent, person who hands down a talmudic statement on the name of his teacher or other earlier authority.

***Tu bi-Shevat**, the 15th day of Shevat, the New Year for Trees; date marking a dividing line for fruit tithing; in modern Israel celebrated as arbor day.

***Uganda Scheme**, plan suggested by the British government in 1903 to establish an autonomous Jewish settlement area in East Africa.

***Va'ad Le'ummi**, national council of the Jewish community in Ereẓ Israel during the period of the British *Mandate.

***Wannsee Conference**, Nazi conference held on Jan. 20, 1942, at which the planned annihilation of European Jewry was endorsed.

Waqf (Ar.), (1) a Muslim charitable pious foundation; (2) state lands and other property passed to the Muslim community for public welfare.

***War of Independence**, war of 1947–49 when the Jews of Israel fought off Arab invading armies and ensured the establishment of the new State.

***White Paper(s)**, report(s) issued by British government, frequently statements of policy, as issued in connection with Palestine during the *Mandate period.

***Wissenschaft des Judentums** (Ger. "Science of Judaism"), movement in Europe beginning in the 19th century for scientific study of Jewish history, religion, and literature.

***Yad Vashem**, Israel official authority for commemorating the *Holocaust in the Nazi era and Jewish resistance and heroism at that time.

Yeshivah (pl. ***yeshivot**), Jewish traditional academy devoted primarily to study of rabbinic literature; *rosh yeshivah*, head of the yeshivah.

YHWH, the letters of the holy name of God, the Tetragrammaton.

Yibbum, see levirate marriage.

Yiḥud, "union"; mystical term for intention which causes the union of God with the **Shekhinah*.

Yishuv, settlement; more specifically, the Jewish community of Ereẓ Israel in the pre-State period. The pre-Zionist community is generally designated the "old yishuv" and the community evolving from 1880, the "new yishuv."

Yom Kippur, Yom ha-Kippurim, *Day of Atonement, solemn fast day observed on the 10th of Tishri.

Yoreh De'ah, see Shulḥan Arukh.

Yoẓer, hymns inserted in the first benediction (*Yoẓer Or*) of the morning **Shema*.

***Ẓaddik**, person outstanding for his faith and piety; especially a ḥasidic rabbi or leader.

Ẓimẓum, "contraction"; mystical term denoting the process whereby God withdraws or contracts within Himself so leaving a primordial vacuum in which creation can take place; primordial exile or self-limitation of God.

***Zionist Commission (1918)**, commission appointed in 1918 by the British government to advise the British military authorities in Palestine on the implementation of the *Balfour Declaration.

Ẓyyonei Zion, the organized opposition to Herzl in connection with the *Uganda Scheme.

***Ẓiẓit**, fringes attached to the **tallit* and **tallit katan*.

***Zohar**, mystical commentary on the Pentateuch; main textbook of *Kabbalah.

Zulat, hymn inserted after the **Shema* in the morning service.

ISBN-13: 978-0-02-865943-5
ISBN-10: 0-02-865943-0